dev.	development
dwt	dead weight tonnage
ECU	European Currency Unit
EEC/EC/EU	European Union
EMS	European Monetary System
est	estimated
°F	degrees Fahrenheit
ft	feet
g	grams
GDP	Gross Domestic Product
GNP	Gross National Product
HEP	hyd[illegible]
in	in[illegible]
kg	ki[illegible]
km	ki[illegible]
km^2	sq[illegible]
kw	ki[illegible]
kwh	ki[illegible]
LNG	liquefied natural gas
m	million/meters
[illegible]	miles
[illegible]	Non-Governmental Organization
[illegible]	Newly Industrialized Country
[illegible]	personal computer
[illegible]	square
[illegible]	television
[illegible]	videocassette recorder

RESOURCES

Electricity generation: total per year in kilowatt hours (kwh), and total available capacity (kw)

Oil production: barrels per day (b/d); total oil reserves in billion barrels (bbl)

Estimated livestock resources

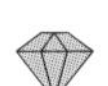
Main mineral resources

Fish catch per year

ENVIRONMENT

Protected land as percentage of total land area

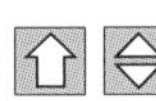
Trend indicators: increase/no variation/decrease in the importance of environmental issues as a national concern

SIGNATORY TO THE FOLLOWING TREATIES

International Tropical Timber Agreement (ITTA) *Geneva, 1983*

Convention on the International Trade in Endangered Species of Wild Fauna and Flora (CITES) *Washington, DC, 1973*

United Nations Convention on the Law of the Sea (UNCLOS) *Montego Bay, Jamaica, 1982*

Protocol on Substances that Deplete the Ozone Layer (Montreal Protocol) *Montreal, 1987*

MEDIA

Media censorship assessment

Main national newspapers

Television stations: state-owned/independent

Radio stations: state-owned/independent

Satellite TV availability

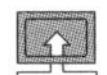
Cable TV availability

CRIME

Total prison population (where available)

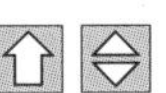
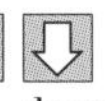
Crime trend indicators: increase/no variation/decrease over previous year

EDUCATION

Literacy rate (percentage of total population)

HEALTH

Doctor/population ratio

Major causes of death

WEALTH

Sample blue collar/managerial wage rates (in local currency)

MAP SYMBOLS AND LETTERING

ADMINISTRATION

International border
Disputed border (*de facto*)
Disputed border (territorial claim)
Undefined border
Cease-fire line
Internal administrative border

COMMUNICATIONS

International airport
Expressway/Highway
Major road
Secondary road
Unsurfaced road, track
Railroad
Canal
Tunnel
Mountain pass

HYDROGRAPHY

Major river
Minor river
Seasonal river
Lake
Seasonal lake
Wetland
Salt lake
Salt pan
Waterfall
Dam/reservoir

OTHER SYMBOLS

▲ Highest point in country
▲ High point
Site of interest (mentioned in text)

LETTERING

ECUADOR	Country name
DUBLIN	Capital city
San Francisco Dover	Cities and towns (type is graded according to population size and map scale)
QUEBEC	Administrative division
LANGUEDOC	Regional name
HIMALAYAS *Lake Baikal* *Congo* *Mt Fiji* *Baffin Bay* *SULU SEA*	Physical and hydrographic features

The Dorling Kindersley

World Reference Atlas

THE DORLING KINDERSLEY

WORLD REFERENCE ATLAS

DORLING KINDERSLEY
London New York Stuttgart

A Dorling Kindersley Book

Managing Editor
Ian Castello-Cortes

Managing Art Editor
Philip Lord

Project Editors
Catherine Day, Jo Edwards, Jane Oliver

Project Designers
Martin Biddulph, Scott David, Karen Gregory

Editors
Debra Clapson, Alastair Dougall,
Ailsa Heritage, Susan Turner
Chris Whitwell, Elizabeth Wyse

Designers
Yahya El-Droubie,
Rhonda Fisher, Nicola Liddiard

Project Cartographers
John Plumer, Julie Turner
James Mills-Hicks
Caroline Bowie, Ruth Duxbury

Cartographers
James Anderson, Roger Bullen, Tony Chambers,
Clare Ellam, Julia Lunn, Michael Martin,
Peter Winfield, Claudine Zante, Jan Clark

Additional Editorial Assistance
Caroline Lucas
Crispian Martin St. Valery
Laura Porter
Sally Wood, Nicholas Kynaston

Additional Design Assistance
Paul Bayliss, Carol Ann Davis,
Adam Dobney, Kenny Laurenson

Picture Research
Sarah Moule

Readers
Jane Bruton, Reg Grant, Ann Kramer, Lesley Riley

Index Gazetteer
Jayne Parsons, Margaret Hynes, Barbara Nash, Janet Smy

Editorial Direction
Andrew Heritage, Louise Cavanagh

Art Director
Chez Picthall

Production
Hilary Stephens

Published in the United States by Dorling Kindersley Publishing, Inc.,
95 Madison Avenue, New York, New York 10016

Library of Congress Cataloging-in-Publication Data
Dorling Kindersley Publishing, Inc.
The Dorling Kindersley World Reference Atlas.-1st American ed..
1994
p. cm
Includes index/gazetteer
Contents: World chronology - The nations of the world - Global issues
ISBN: 1-56458-651-0
1. Atlases. I. Title. II. Title: World Reference Atlas
G1021.D63 1994<G&M>
912--dc20
94-19376
CIP
MAP

Reproduction by Colourscan (Singapore) and Face Creative Services (London)
Text film output by Lyledale T/A Elements (London)
Printed and bound by New Interlitho (Italy)

Foreword

THIS ATLAS is presented to the public in the full knowledge that the world is in a state of continual flux. Political fashions and personalities come and go, while the ebb and flow of peoples and ideas across the face of the planet create constant shifts in the cultural landscape. All the material assembled for this Atlas has been researched from the most up-to-date and authoritative sources; our team of consultants and contributors, designers, editors and cartographers have endeavored not only to explain the meaning of this material, to place it in a useful and clear context, but also to present it in a way that has a lasting value and relevance, regardless of the turmoil of daily events. The Atlas is thus intended not so much as a "snapshot" of the state of the world today, but rather a detailed portrait in which the underlying features and characteristics of its subject are brought to life.

The publishers would like to thank the many consultants and contributors whose diligence, perseverance and attention to detail made this book possible.

General Consultants

Anthony Goldstone, Senior Editor Asia-Pacific, *The Economist* Intelligence Unit, London
Professor Jack Spence, Director of Studies, The Royal Institute of International Affairs, London

Regional Consultants

Asia
Anthony Goldstone, London

Africa
James Hammill, Lecturer in African Politics, University of Leicester
Kaye Whiteman, Editor-in-Chief, *West Africa Magazine*, London

Russia and CIS
Martin McCauley, Senior Lecturer, School of Slavonic and East European Studies, University of London

Central and South America
Nick Caistor, Producer, Latin American Section, BBC World Service

USA
Michael Elliot, Diplomatic Editor, *Newsweek*, Washington, DC

Europe
John Ardagh, London
Rory Clarke, Senior Editor Europe, *The Economist* Intelligence Unit, London
Charles Powell, Centre for European Studies, St Antony's College, Oxford

Middle East
John Whelan, Ex Editor-in-Chief, *Middle East Economic Digest*

Pacific
Jim Boutilier, Professor in History, Royal Roads Military College, Victoria, Canada

Caribbean
Canute James, *The Financial Times*, Kingston, Jamaica

Contributors

Janice Bell, School of Slavonic and East European Studies, University of London
Gerry Bourke, Asia Correspondent, *The Guardian*, Islamabad
Vincent Cable, Director, International Economics Programme
P K Clark, MA, Former Chief Map Research Officer, UK Ministry of Defence
Ken Davies, Senior Editor, *The Economist* Intelligence Unit, London
Roger Dunn, Analyst, Control Risks Group, London
Aidan Foster-Carter, Senior Lecturer in Sociology, University of Leeds
Professor Murray Forsyth, Centre for Federal Studies, University of Leicester
Natasha Franklin, School of Slavonic and East European Studies, London
Adam Hannestad, *Blomberg Business News*, Copenhagen
Peter Holden, *The Economist* Research Department, London
Tim Jones, Knight Ritter, Brussels
Angella Johnstone, Home Affairs Correspondent, *The Guardian*, London
Oliver Keserü, International Chamber of Commerce, Paris
Robert Macdonald, *The Economist* Intelligence Unit
William Mader, Former Europe Bureau Chief, *Time* magazine, Washington DC
Professor Brian Matthews, Institute of Commonwealth Studies, London
Nick Middleton, Oriel College, Oxford
Professor Mya Maung, Department of Finance, Boston College
Judith Nordby, Leeds University
Simon Orme, London
Professor Richard Overy, Department of History, King's College, London
Steve Percy, East Asia Service, BBC World Service
Douglas Rimmer, Honorary Senior Research Fellow, Centre for West African Studies, University of Birmingham
Donna Rispoli, Linacre College, Oxford
Ian Rodger, *The Financial Times*, Zürich
The Royal Institute of International Affairs, London
Struan Simpson, St. James Research, London
Julie Smith, Brasenose College, Oxford
Elizabeth Spencer, London
Michiel Van Kuyen, Erasmus University, Rotterdam
Steven Whitefield, Pembroke College, Oxford
Georgina Wilde, Regional Director, Asia-Pacific, *The Economist* Intelligence Unit, London
H P Willmott, Visiting Professor, Dept. of Military Strategy & Operations, The National War College, Washington, DC
Andrew Wilson, Sydney Sussex College, Cambridge
Tom Wingfield, *Reuters*, Bangkok
The World Conservation Monitoring Centre, Cambridge
Database research:
CIRCA Research and Reference Information Limited, Cambridge, UK
Roger East, Rosemary Payne, John Coggins, Tanya Joseph, Stephen Lewis, Frances Nicholson, Jolyon Pontin, Darren Sagar, Farzana Shaikh

CONTENTS

OVERSEAS TERRITORIES & DEPENDENCIES

3
GLOBAL ISSUES

4
INDEX ~ GAZETTEER

HOW THE ATLAS WORKS

THIS ATLAS is divided into the four main sections detailed below. Each section has four main elements: maps, charts, icons and text. The opposite page explains how each of these is used in the book. The central section of the book is the Nations of the World, which includes detailed mapping and encyclopedic information for every one of the world's 191 countries as defined by the UN.

The political reference map of the world includes an inset map of the world's time zones

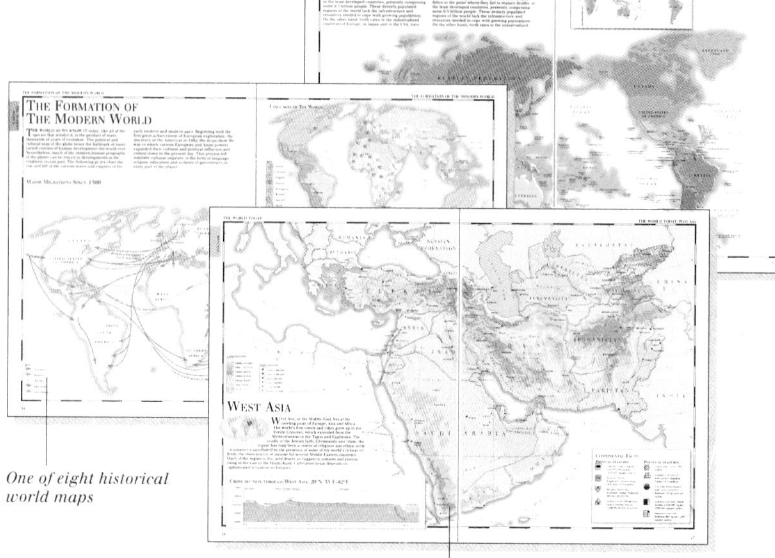

One of eight historical world maps

The eight continental and regional maps provide a detailed overview of the physical and political geography of each part of the world

1 THE WORLD TODAY: Ten double-page spreads examine the world and its continents. Regional maps highlight major physical features, with additional data about the continent's physical and political geography listed in the fact box. Introductory texts offer a concise view of each continent – its physical geography, people and resources, while illuminating cross-sections offer a different perspective.

A further eight double-page spreads are devoted to The Formation of the Modern World, which surveys world history over the last 500 years focusing on key dates and periods, starting with The Age of Discovery: 1492.

2 THE NATIONS OF THE WORLD: 580 pages of information broken down on a nation-by-nation basis, and listed alphabetically. For a detailed explanation of how this section works, refer to opposite page.

National coverage is presented across one, two, three or four double-page spreads

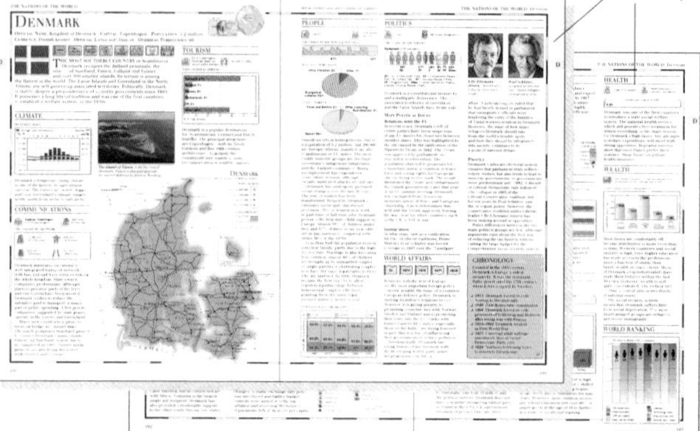

3 GLOBAL ISSUES: 18 pages of double-page spreads which examine major issues in the modern world, presented thematically on a global map supplemented by regional examples, diagrams, text and captions.

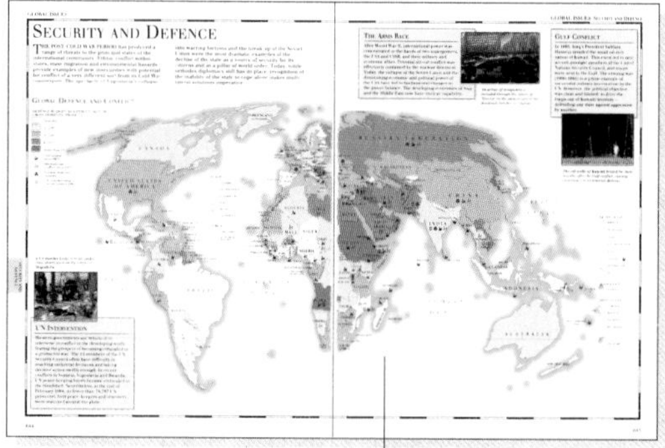

One of the nine Global Issues double-page spreads, which combines a world map with diagrams, illustrations and informative text

4 INDEX – GAZETTEER: 77 pages of index list all the names shown on the national maps. Cross-references are made to alternative place name forms and spellings. This section also includes a listing of international organizations.

THE NATIONS OF THE WORLD

THE NATIONS OF THE WORLD is the largest section in the Atlas. Countries are arranged alphabetically for ease of reference. Each nation is mapped, has an introductory Country Profile Reference Panel and is analyzed under 18 consistent subject headings. See following pages for a complete listing.

The Atlas is designed so that every country entry is structured in the same way. The title headings are always arranged in the same sequence and all the information is comparable from one country to another.

This makes it very easy to find exactly what you want to read about in a particular country section. It also makes comparisons between countries much easier.

In addition to the explanations and definitions provided overleaf, both endpapers carry a detailed key to the icons, map symbols and abbreviations used in this section of the Atlas.

BUSINESS AND LAND USE MAPS

The world's 70 largest countries are also provided with business and land use maps to reflect the more complex nature of their economies. These give an instant idea of where major business sectors are located and the nature of the nation's agriculture.

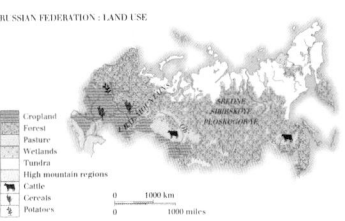

NATIONAL FLAGS

The national flag of each country is shown in color and in its correct geometric proportions.

LOCATOR MAPS

The locator maps are always found next to the country name. They provide both a world and regional location for each country.

COUNTRY MAPS

Each country is mapped in considerable detail. The maps show the national boundaries and neighboring countries, the major physical features, main road and rail infrastructure and population and administrative centers. A key provides a breakdown of land height (in feet and meters) and of populated places.

REGIONAL MAPS

Regional maps are featured for 13 of the world's leading countries. The regions or cities are chosen to reflect national differences or because they are of particular economic importance. Each map has a full explanatory text.

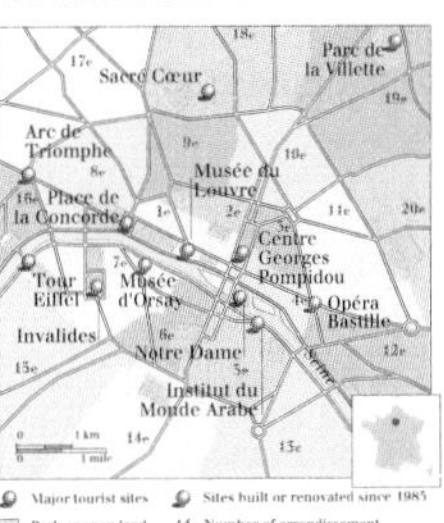

CHARTS

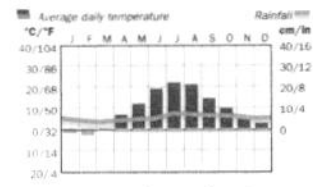

Charts are used to show each country's climate, social makeup and the economy. All countries have a standard set of charts.

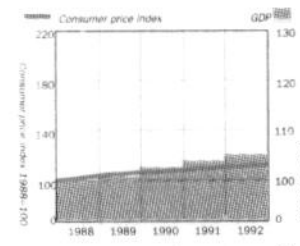

The top 70 countries have additional charts. This chart, for example, provides a guide to the country's economic performance.

This sort of chart can be found in the Defense, Education and Health sections. It shows how much major countries spend on each, as a proportion of Gross National Product.

ICONS

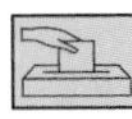

Icons are a key feature of the book. The design of the icon gives an indication of the information being represented.

Icons are of three types. The icons appearing under the title give a ready reference to the political, economic and social status of the country.

Icons under section headings appear for all countries.

Grouped icons are mostly found in the world's top 70 countries.

Trend icons show whether the trend of their subject matter is increasing, decreasing or level.

TEXT

The text in the Atlas is intended to be highly accessible so that essential information can always be found quickly.

The larger countries are presented across more pages and thus have more text, reflecting their greater complexity. Longer text entries have, however, been broken down by introducing sub-headings to guide the reader to the subject of interest.

The text for larger countries has more detailed profiles of political and economic systems and reports on cities and/or regions of special interest.

Key to Charts and Icons

Icons and trend indicators vary. Not all variations are shown in the key below, but where they do occur the symbols have been "stacked."

COUNTRY PROFILE REFERENCE PANEL

These icons are colored yellow when the information is applicable.

Date of independence, or date current borders set.

Democratic system of election in use.

Convertible national currency.

International aid status: donor/receiver/neither.

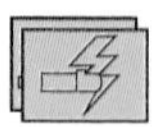

Net energy importer/exporter.

Compulsory military service.

Death penalty not in use.

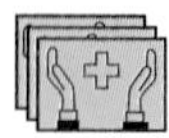

Welfare provision: full social security/ health benefits only/ unemployment benefits only.

CLIMATE

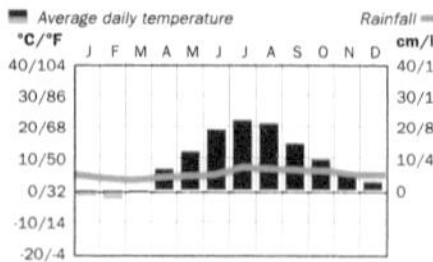

Statistics are given for the the national capital. They represent maximum summer and minimum winter averages.

COMMUNICATIONS

The country's principal international airport with annual passenger numbers.

Total size of national merchant or cargo fleet.

THE TRANSPORTATION NETWORK

National communications infrastructure given in miles and kilometers.

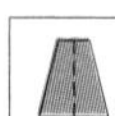

Extent of national road network

Extent of expressways or major national highways

Extent of commercial railroad network

Extent of inland waterways navigable by commercial craft

TOURISM

Number of visitors per year, including business travelers.

Indicators showing trend in recent visitor numbers (up/level/down).

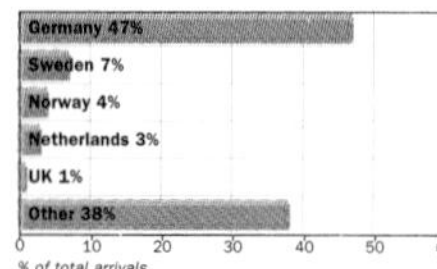

The state of each nation's tourism is explained, with reasons given when there is no significant tourist industry. The chart shows the percentage of total visitors by country of origin.

PEOPLE

Main languages spoken, in descending order of importance.

Population density. This is an average over the whole country.

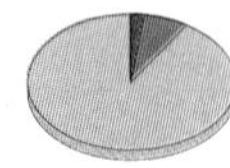

The pie chart proportions show the religious affiliations of those who profess a belief.

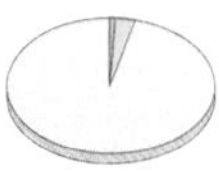

This pie chart illustrates the ethnic origin of the country's population.

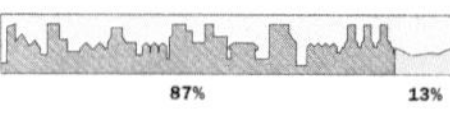

This graph represents the proportion of the population living in urban areas (gray) and rural areas (green).

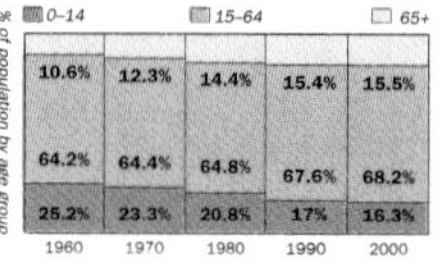

This chart shows the breakdown of the population by age groupings over a 40-year period, providing an interesting insight into the nation's demography.

POLITICS

Date of next election. Where the situation is not clear, "uncertain" is used.

Name of head of state. In many cases this is a nominal position and does not indicate that this is the nation's most powerful person.

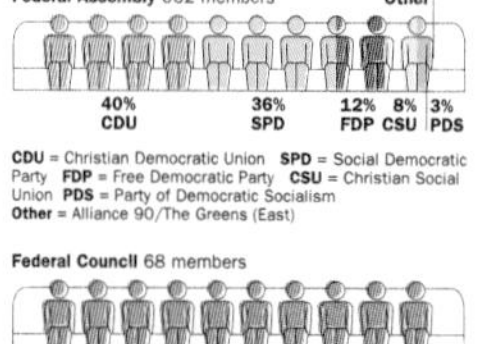

A graphic representation of the political makeup of the nation's government, based on each party's showing at the last election. Where there are two houses, the most important elected body is shown first.

WORLD AFFAIRS

Abbreviations in the flag symbols indicate a nation's membership of international organizations. United Nations and World Bank membership is assumed. Gray flags signify no additional membership of international organizations. The main issues that dominate each nation's politics are outlined in the text.

AID

The amount of net international aid donations or receipts is given in US$. Undisclosed military aid is not included.

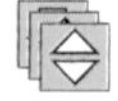

Symbols indicate whether aid payments or receipts are rising, level or declining.

DEFENSE

The defense budget, the nation's annual expenditure (in US$) on arms and military personnel.

Symbols indicate if the trend in defense spending is rising, level or declining.

0 Defense spending as % GDP 40
2%

Spending on arms is shown as a proportion of Gross Domestic Product (GDP). The general state of the country's defenses and the status of the military is discussed in the text.

THE ARMED FORCES

Icons represent the main branches of the national armed forces.

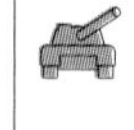

Army: equipment and personnel

Navy: equipment and personnel

Air force: equipment and personnel

Nuclear capability: armaments

ECONOMICS

Gross National Product (GNP) – the total value of goods and services produced by a country.

Average exchange rate against the US$ over the last year. Some currencies are too volatile for a useful figure to be given.

❑ World GNP Ranking	24th
❑ GNP per Capita	$24,388
❑ Balance of Payments	$2.2bn
❑ Inflation	5.6%
❑ Unemployment	10.6%

The score cards are intended to give a broad picture of the country's economy. Gross National Product (GNP) includes income from investments and businesses held abroad. Balance of payments is the difference between a country's payments to and receipts from abroad.

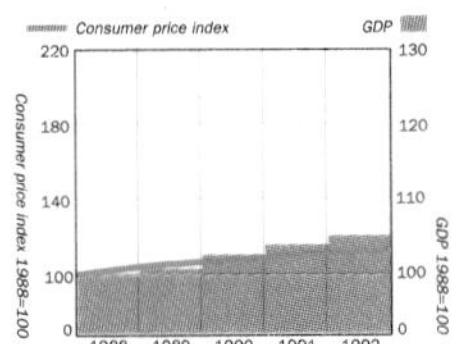

This graph shows year-on-year variations in GDP and consumer prices.

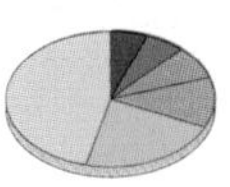

This pie chart gives a broad picture of the nation's principal import trading partners.

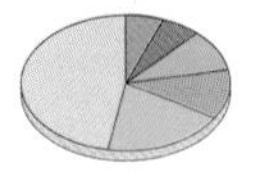

This pie chart gives a broad picture of the nation's principal export trading partners.

RESOURCES

Electricity generation is expressed in kilowatt hours (kwh) per year, and total available capacity (kw).

Oil produced in barrels per day (b/d). Refining capacity, oil reserves and other fossil fuels are given where applicable.

Estimated livestock resources.

Main mineral reserves are listed in descending order of economic importance.

Fish catch per year (where appropriate).

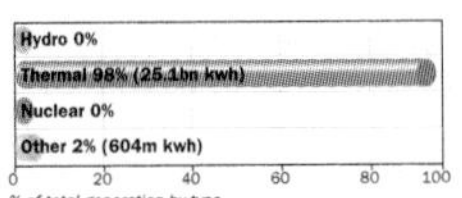

Percentages of the different energy sources used for the generation of electricity are represented graphically. An account of the nation's resource base is given in the text.

ENVIRONMENT

Percentage of land that is protected or conserved by law. Protection is often only theoretical.

Symbols indicate a trend in the importance of environmental issues as a national concern.

ENVIRONMENTAL TREATIES

National signatory to international environmental treaties.

ITTA: timber

CITES: endangered species

UNCLOS: marine dumping

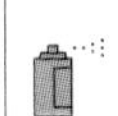

Montreal Protocol: CFC emissions

MEDIA

An assessment of political censorship in national media.

PUBLISHING AND BROADCAST MEDIA

National broadcast and print media, by size and ownership.

Main national newspapers

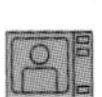

Television stations: state-owned/independent

Radio: state-owned/ independent

Satellite TV availability

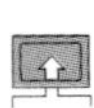

Cable TV availability

CRIME

Prison population statistics (where available).

Symbols show general trend in crime figures.

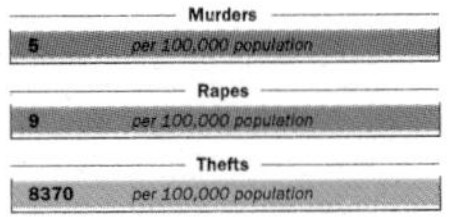

This section records official crime figures only. Reported statisitics are normally lower than the actual figures.

CHRONOLOGY

Beginning at a significant date in the recent history of the nation, the outline chronology continues through to the present day.

EDUCATION

Literacy icon. A person who is able to read and write a short statement about his or her every-day life is defined by UNESCO as literate. Literacy percentages are given for each country.

0 Education spending as % GNP 25
7.6%

The state's total budget for education is shown as a proportion of its Gross National Product (GNP).

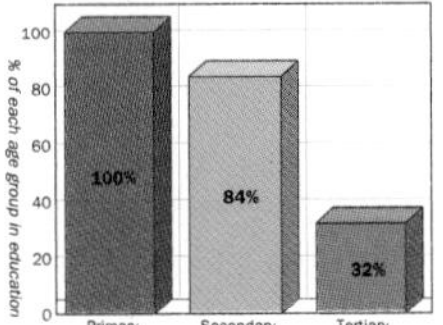

This graph shows the percentages of each age group in education. Primary is up to age 11; secondary is age 11–16/18; tertiary is further education, beyond high school level.

HEALTH

Ratio of doctors per head of population is given as a national average.

Major causes of death are listed.

0 Health spending as % GNP 25
0.5%

Health spending is shown as a proportion of the Gross National Product (GNP).

WEALTH

This section highlights wealth disparities by contrasting sample blue-collar and managerial salaries. Earnings are shown in local currency.

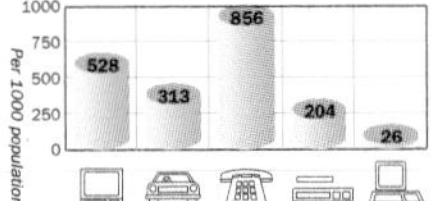

This graph shows the comparative ownership of consumer goods. Figures may reflect access to, rather than ability to purchase, high-value consumer durables.

WORLD RANKING

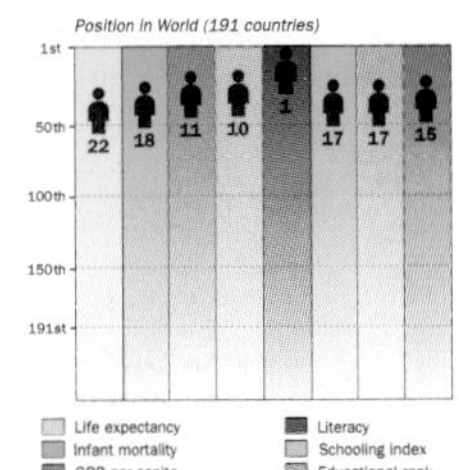

The World Ranking is based on the UN Human Development Index. Expert consultants have advised on various indicators, covering a range of financial, medical, educational and social fields.

1

The World Today

The Political World

The Physical World

• North America • South America • Europe • Africa
• West Asia • North Asia • South Asia
• Australasia & Oceania

The Formation of the Modern World

• The World in 1492 • The Age of Discovery 1492-1648
• The Age of Expansion 1648-1789
• The Age of Revolution 1789-1830
• The Age of Empire 1830-1914
• The Age of Global War 1914-1945
• The Modern Age 1945-1994

THE POLITICAL WORLD

IN TODAY'S RAPIDLY EVOLVING WORLD, a political perspective on international boundaries is more important than ever before. The world currently comprises 191 independent states – more than at any previous time – and 58 dependencies. Antarctica is the only land area on the earth's surface which is not part of and does not belong to any one country.

A massive transformation has taken place since 1950, when the world comprised only 82 countries. In the decades following World War II, many states came into being as they achieved independence from their former colonial rulers. Most recently, the breakup of the Soviet Union in 1991 swelled the ranks of independent states. Generally, a worldwide trend towards fragmentation has been seen as nationalist aims have come to the fore. Civil wars are currently being waged in many parts of the world, including Yugoslavia, Angola, Rwanda, Liberia, Indonesia, Afghanistan and Yemen. Within the former Soviet Union itself instability continues, notably in the fighting between Azerbaijan and Armenia over Nagorno Karabakh and in the conflict within Georgia.

The Russian Federation is the world's largest state; Vatican City is the smallest. In 1993, Eritrea became the most recent addition to the world map.

THE WORLD POLITICAL MAP

Time Zones

The World is divided into 24 time zones, which are measured in relation to 12 noon Greenwich Mean Time (GMT), on the Greenwich Meridian (0°). The time zones do not follow a regular pattern, but are adapted to regional administrative boundaries.

The world's 24 time zones. *Numbers on the map indicate the number of hours that must be added or subtracted, as appropriate, in that time zone to reach* GMT. *Thus, East Coast USA (+5) is 5 hours behind* GMT.

The Physical World

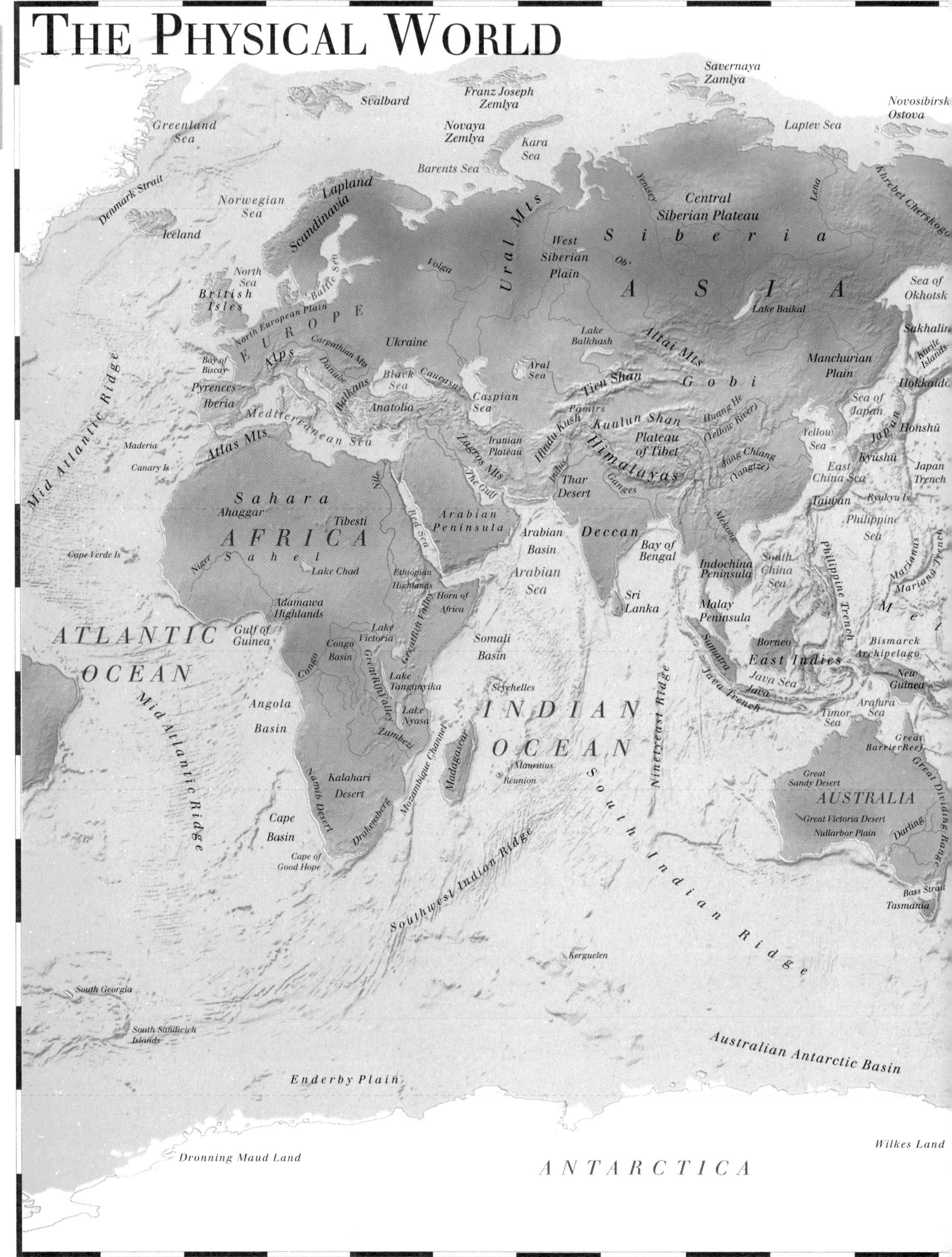

Savernaya Zamlya
Franz Joseph Zemlya
Svalbard
Novosibirsk Ostova
Greenland Sea
Novaya Zemlya
Kara Sea
Laptev Sea
Barents Sea
Denmark Strait
Lapland
Norwegian Sea
Scandinavia
Ural Mts
Yenisey
Central Siberian Plateau
Lena
Iceland
Khrebet Cherskogo
West Siberian Plain
Siberia
Volga
Ob'
North Sea
Baltic Sea
British Isles
ASIA
Sea of Okhotsk
North European Plain
EUROPE
Lake Baikal
Lake Balkhash
Sakhalin
Carpathian Mts
Ukraine
Altai Mts
Kurile Islands
Bay of Biscay
Alps
Danube
Aral Sea
Manchurian Plain
Black Sea
Caucasus
Tien Shan
Gobi
Hokkaido
Pyrenees
Iberia
Balkans
Caspian Sea
Pamirs
Sea of Japan
Mid Atlantic Ridge
Mediterranean Sea
Anatolia
Huang He (Yellow River)
Kunlun Shan
Honshū
Madeira
Atlas Mts
Iranian Plateau
Hindu Kush
Plateau of Tibet
Yellow Sea
Japan
Zagros Mts
Himalayas
Chang Chiang (Yangtze)
Kyūshū
Canary Is
Indus
Japan Trench
East China Sea
Nile
The Gulf
Thar Desert
Ganges
Sahara
Ryukyu Is
Ahaggar
Taiwan
Tibesti
Red Sea
Arabian Peninsula
Philippine Sea
AFRICA
Arabian Basin
Deccan
Mekong
Cape Verde Is
Sahel
Bay of Bengal
Niger
Philippine Trench
Marianas
Mariana Trench
Lake Chad
Ethiopian Highlands
Arabian Sea
Indochina Peninsula
South China Sea
Horn of Africa
Adamawa Highlands
Sri Lanka
Malay Peninsula
Lake Victoria
Great Rift Valley
ATLANTIC OCEAN
Gulf of Guinea
Somali Basin
Bismarck Archipelago
Congo Basin
Borneo
Sumatra
East Indies
Congo
Lake Tanganyika
New Guinea
Seychelles
Java Sea
Java
Ninetyeast Ridge
Java Trench
Angola Basin
Lake Nyasa
INDIAN OCEAN
Arafura Sea
Timor Sea
Zambezi
Madagascar
Great Barrier Reef
Mozambique Channel
Mauritius
Reunion
Great Sandy Desert
Namib Desert
Kalahari Desert
Great Dividing Range
AUSTRALIA
Drakensberg
Great Victoria Desert
Cape Basin
Nullarbor Plain
Darling
Cape of Good Hope
Southwest Indian Ridge
South Indian Ridge
Bass Strait
Tasmania
Kerguelen
South Georgia
South Sandwich Islands
Australian Antarctic Basin
Enderby Plain
Wilkes Land
Dronning Maud Land
ANTARCTICA

ARCTIC OCEAN
Limit of permanent pack ice
Ellesmere Island
Queen Elizbeth Islands
Greenland
Greenland Sea
Siberian Sea
Chukchi Sea
Beaufort Sea
Baffin Bay
Baffin Island
Bering Strait
Brooks Range
Yukon
Mackenzie
Great Bear Lake
Great Slave Lake
Arctic Circle
Iceland
Bering Sea
Aleutian Basin
Aleutian Islands
Aleutian Trench
Gulf of Alaska
Coast Mountains
Rocky Mountains
Canadian Shield
Hudson Bay
Ungava Peninsula
Labrador Sea
Lake Winnipeg
Mid Atlantic Ridge
Vancouver I
NORTH AMERICA
Coast Ranges
Great Plains
Missouri
Great Lakes
Appalachian Mountains
Grand Bank
Emperor Seamount Chain
Mendocino Fracture Zone
Mississippi
North America Basin
ATLANTIC OCEAN
Azores
Baja California
Murray Fracture Zone
Hawaiian Islands
Gulf of Mexico
Tropic of Cancer
Yucatán Peninsula
West Indies
Greater Antilles
Sierra Madre
Caribbean Sea
Lesser Antilles
Guatemala Trench
Mid Pacific Mountains
PACIFIC OCEAN
Polynesia
Micronesia
Melanesia
Guiana Highlands
Equator
Gilbert Is
Line Islands
Phoenix Is
Galapagos Islands
Amazon
Amazon Basin
Andes
SOUTH AMERICA
Brazilian Basin
Fiji
Tonga
Tonga Trench
Cook Is
Tuamotu Islands
East Pacific Ridge
Peru Basin
Peru
Mato Grosso
Brazilian Highlands
Tropic of Capricorn
Chile Trench
Paraná
Kermadec Trench
Southwest Pacific Basin
Pampas
Tasman Sea
North Island
New Zealand
Patagonia
Tristan da Cunha
Argentine Basin
Mid Atlantic Ridge
Campbell Plateau
Falkland Is
Tierra del Fuego
South Georgia
Cape Horn
Drake Passage
Antarctic Peninsula
Antarctic Circle
Bellinghausen Sea
Weddell Sea
Ross Sea
Byrd Land
Ronne Ice Shelf
ANTARCTICA
Ross Ice Shelf

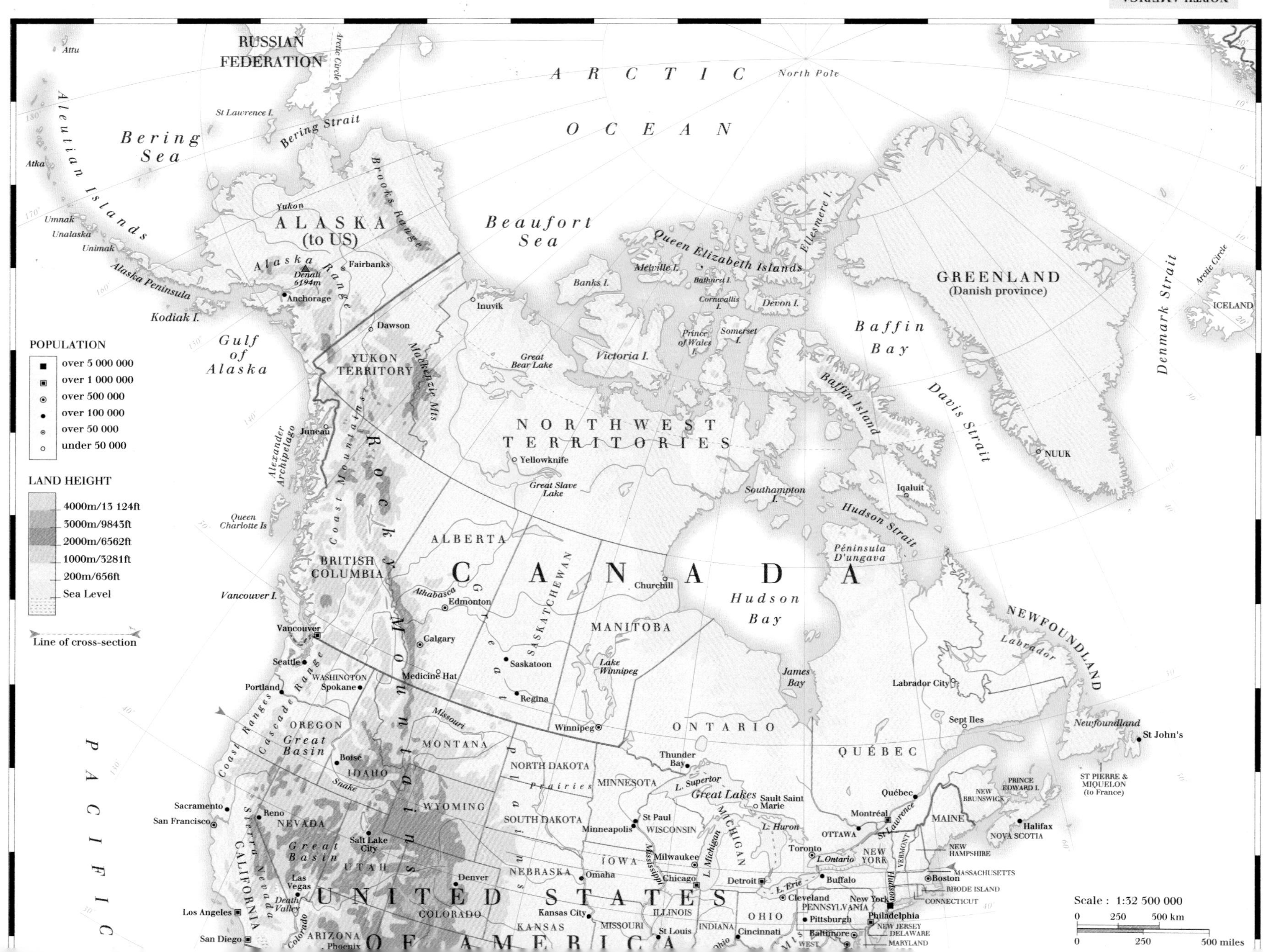
Scale : 1:32 500 000
0 250 500 km
0 250 500 miles
POPULATION
over 5 000 000
over 1 000 000
over 500 000
over 100 000
over 50 000
under 50 000
LAND HEIGHT
4000m/13 124ft
3000m/9843ft
2000m/6562ft
1000m/3281ft
200m/656ft
Sea Level
Line of cross-section
ARCTIC OCEAN
North Pole
Arctic Circle
Denmark Strait
ICELAND
GREENLAND
(Danish province)
NUUK
Davis Strait
Baffin Bay
Baffin Island
Ellesmere I.
Queen Elizabeth Islands
Devon I.
Somerset I.
Cornwallis I.
Bathurst I.
Melville I.
Prince of Wales I.
Banks I.
Victoria I.
Southampton I.
Beaufort Sea
Iqaluit
Hudson Strait
Péninsula D'ungava
Hudson Bay
James Bay
CANADA
NORTHWEST TERRITORIES
YUKON TERRITORY
BRITISH COLUMBIA
ALBERTA
SASKATCHEWAN
MANITOBA
ONTARIO
QUÉBEC
NEWFOUNDLAND
Labrador
Newfoundland
St John's
ST PIERRE & MIQUELON
(to France)
PRINCE EDWARD I.
NEW BRUNSWICK
NOVA SCOTIA
Halifax
Labrador City
Sept Iles
Québec
Montréal
St Lawrence
OTTAWA
Toronto
L. Ontario
L. Erie
L. Huron
L. Superior
L. Michigan
Great Lakes
Sault Saint Marie
Thunder Bay
Great Bear Lake
Great Slave Lake
Yellowknife
Inuvik
Churchill
Lake Winnipeg
Winnipeg
Regina
Saskatoon
Edmonton
Calgary
Medicine Hat
Athabasca
Dawson
Mackenzie Mts
Coast Mountains
Rocky Mountains
Great Plains
Prairies
Vancouver
Vancouver I.
Queen Charlotte Is
Alexander Archipelago
Juneau
ALASKA
(to US)
Brooks Range
Alaska Range
Fairbanks
Denali 6194m
Anchorage
Yukon
Gulf of Alaska
Kodiak I.
Alaska Peninsula
Aleutian Islands
Unimak
Unalaska
Umnak
Atka
Attu
Bering Sea
Bering Strait
St Lawrence I.
RUSSIAN FEDERATION
UNITED STATES OF AMERICA
MAINE
NEW HAMPSHIRE
VERMONT
MASSACHUSETTS
RHODE ISLAND
CONNECTICUT
NEW YORK
NEW JERSEY
DELAWARE
MARYLAND
PENNSYLVANIA
OHIO
MICHIGAN
INDIANA
ILLINOIS
WISCONSIN
MINNESOTA
IOWA
MISSOURI
NORTH DAKOTA
SOUTH DAKOTA
NEBRASKA
KANSAS
MONTANA
WYOMING
COLORADO
IDAHO
UTAH
WASHINGTON
OREGON
NEVADA
ARIZONA
CALIFORNIA
Boston
Hudson
New York
Philadelphia
Baltimore
Pittsburgh
Buffalo
Cleveland
Detroit
Cincinnati
Chicago
Milwaukee
St Louis
Mississippi
Missouri
Ohio
St Paul
Minneapolis
Omaha
Kansas City
Denver
Salt Lake City
Boise
Snake
Spokane
Seattle
Portland
Cascade Range
Great Basin
Sierra Nevada
Coast Ranges
Reno
Las Vegas
Death Valley
Colorado
Phoenix
Sacramento
San Francisco
Los Angeles
San Diego
PACIFIC

NORTH AMERICA

NORTH AMERICA'S climate is as varied as its topography: much of Canada is snowbound or clothed in forest, its sparse population congregating along the US border. Along the continent's western flank are the spectacular Rocky Mountains. Along the east lie the older, wooded Appalachians. Between these are the Great Plains – grazed by herds of livestock or sown with cereals. These plains were once home to tribes of native Americans, supplanted by incoming white settlers. US population and industry are concentrated in the temperate northeast, while the hotter south and drier west are rural and thinly populated. North America is rich in minerals and oil. Mexico is the world's largest Spanish-speaking nation. The Caribbean and Central America contain some 30 countries and numerous small islands. The climate is tropical and prone to storms, the landscape mountainous and volcanic.

CROSS-SECTION THROUGH NORTH AMERICA: 43°N, 126°W–65°W

CONTINENTAL FACTS

PHYSICAL FEATURES

- LARGEST LAKE: Lake Superior, Canada/ USA 32,140 square miles (83,270 sq km)
- LONGEST RIVER: Mississippi-Missouri, USA 3,740 miles (6,019 km)
- HIGHEST POINT: Denali (formerly Mt. McKinley), Alaska, USA 20,322 ft (6,194 m)
- LOWEST POINT: Death Valley, California, USA 282 ft (86 m) below sea level

POLITICAL FEATURES

- TOTAL POPULATION: 435.9 million
- LARGEST CITY WITH POPULATION: Mexico City, Mexico 20.2 million
- COUNTRY WITH HIGHEST POPULATION DENSITY: Barbados 1,549 people per square mile
- LARGEST COUNTRY: Canada 3,851,817 square miles (9,976,139 sq km)
- SMALLEST COUNTRY: Grenada 131 square miles (340 sq km)

SOUTH AMERICA

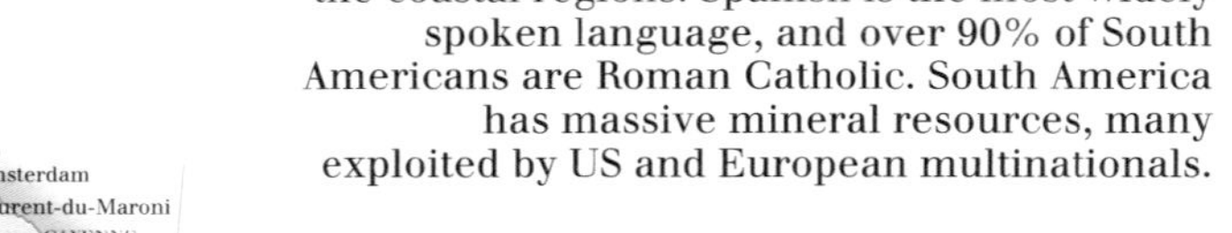

THE WORLD'S fourth largest continent includes one of its most important resources – the Amazonian rainforest. It is a major source of oxygen and includes half of all known living species, while the Amazon – the world's second longest river – contains one-fifth of the world's fresh water. The Andes mountain chain reaches down South America's western flank, sheltering the prairies of the Gran Chaco, the Pampas and the wastes of the far south. Most South Americans are *mestizo* – of mixed European and Amerindian descent and live in the coastal regions. Spanish is the most widely spoken language, and over 90% of South Americans are Roman Catholic. South America has massive mineral resources, many exploited by US and European multinationals.

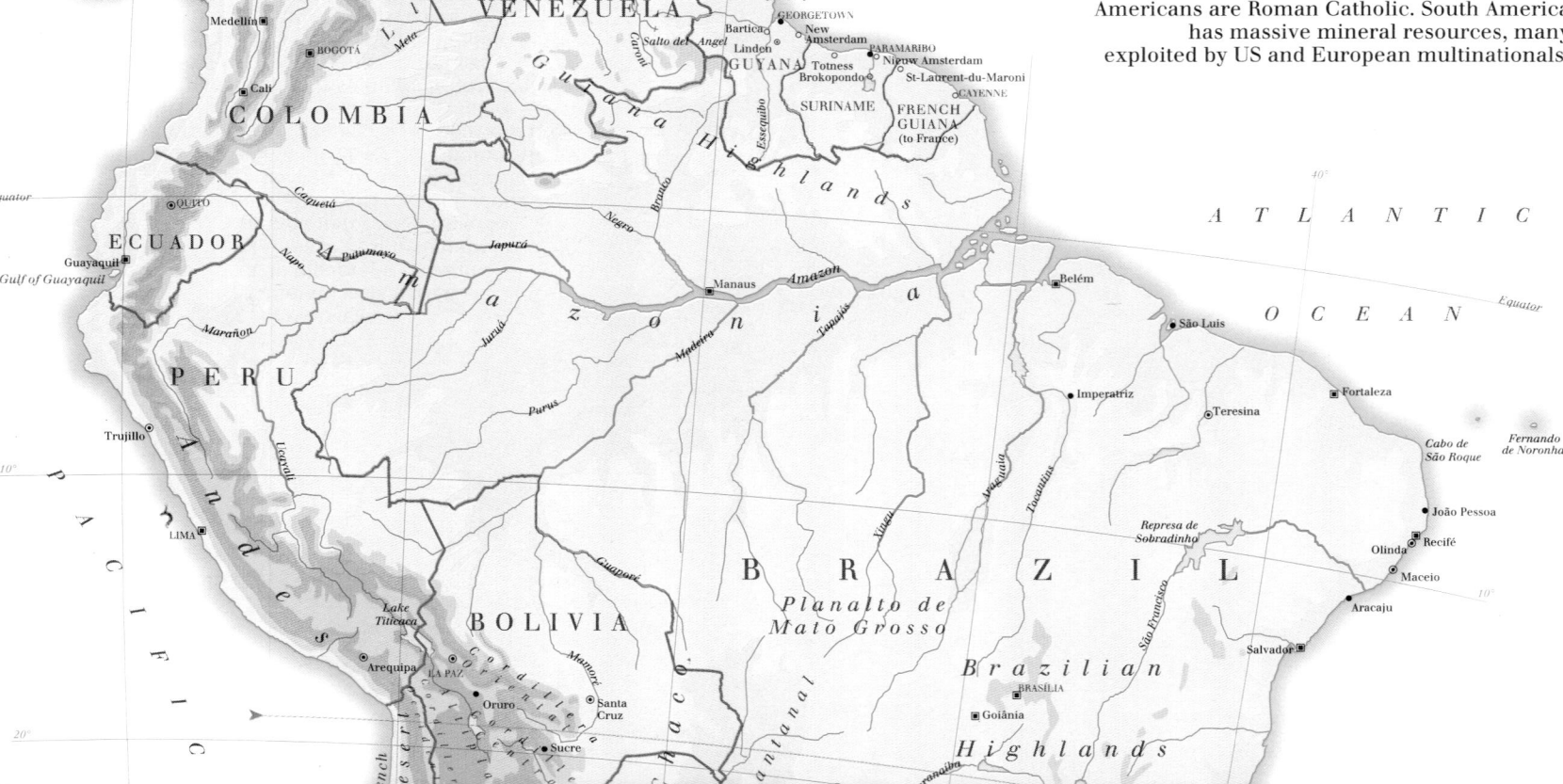

Caribbean Sea
ARUBA (to Neth.)
NETHERLANDS ANTILLES (to Neth.)
Lesser Antilles
TRINIDAD & TOBAGO
PANAMA
Barranquilla
Maracaibo
Lago de Maracaibo
Valencia
CARACAS
Turmero
Montería
Magdalena
Cauca
Cucuta
Medellín
BOGOTÁ
Cali
COLOMBIA
VENEZUELA
Llanos
Orinoco
Apure
Arauca
Meta
Caroni
Salto del Angel
Guiana Highlands
Morawhanna
Charity
GEORGETOWN
Bartica
Linden
New Amsterdam
GUYANA
Totness
Brokopondo
PARAMARIBO
Nieuw Amsterdam
St-Laurent-du-Maroni
CAYENNE
SURINAME
FRENCH GUIANA (to France)
Essequibo
Branco
Negro
Equator
QUITO
ECUADOR
Guayaquil
Gulf of Guayaquil
Caquetá
Putumayo
Napo
Japurá
Amazonia
Manaus
Amazon
Marañon
Juruá
Purus
Madeira
Tapajós
PERU
Trujillo
LIMA
Ucayali
Andes
PACIFIC
Lake Titicaca
Arequipa
LA PAZ
Oruro
Sucre
BOLIVIA
Cordillera Oriental
Cordillera Central
Altiplano
Mamoré
Santa Cruz
Guaporé
Chaco
Pantanal
ATLANTIC OCEAN
Belém
São Luis
Imperatriz
Teresina
Fortaleza
Cabo de São Roque
Fernando de Noronha
João Pessoa
Recifé
Olinda
Maceio
Aracaju
Salvador
Represa de Sobradinho
São Francisco
Tocantins
Araguaia
Xingu
BRAZIL
Planalto de Mato Grosso
Brazilian Highlands
BRASÍLIA
Goiânia
80°
70°
60°
40°
10°
20°

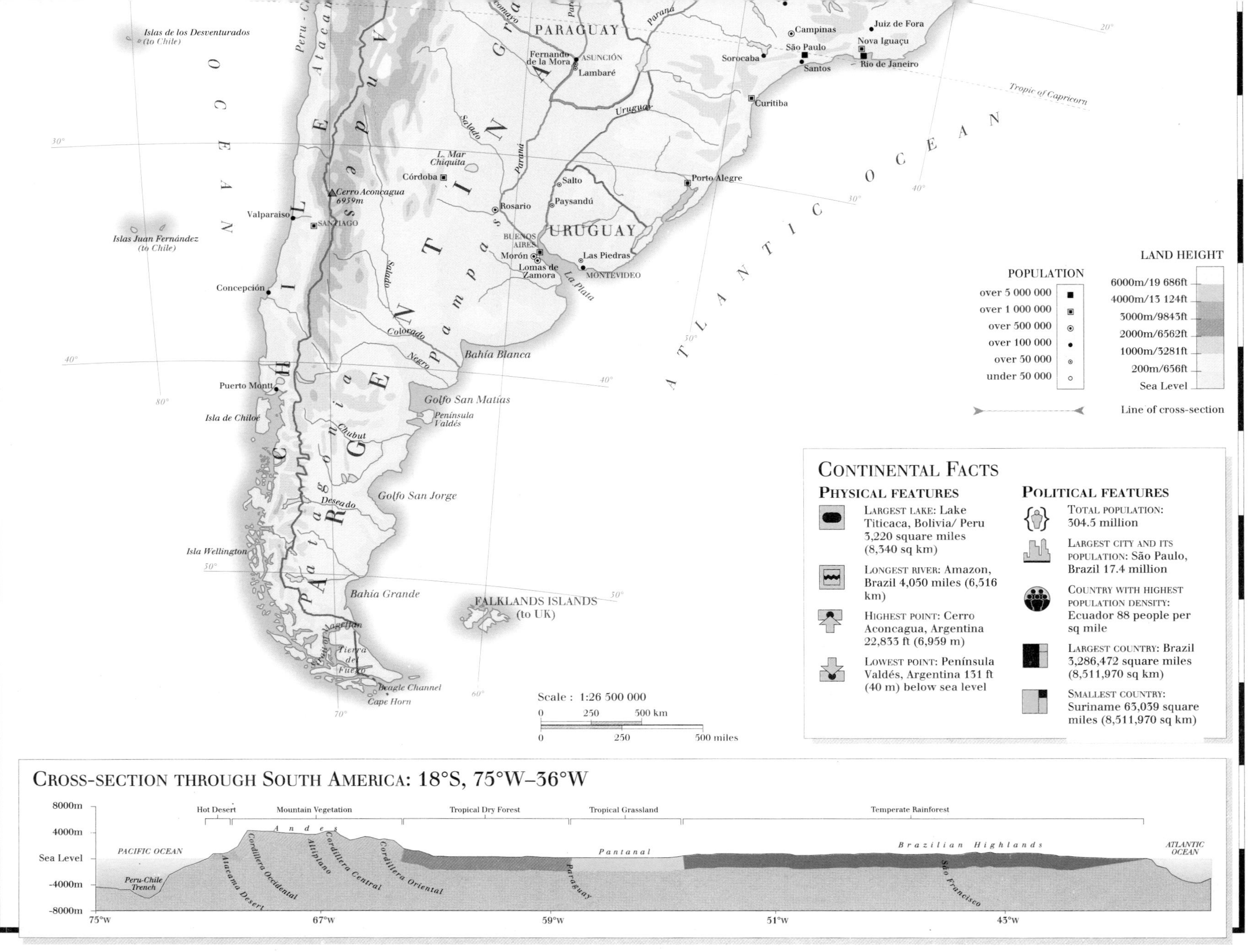
Islas de los Desventurados (to Chile)
Islas Juan Fernández (to Chile)
OCEAN
PARAGUAY
Fernando de la Mora
ASUNCIÓN
Lambaré
Campinas
Juiz de Fora
Nova Iguaçu
São Paulo
Sorocaba
Santos
Rio de Janeiro
Tropic of Capricorn
Curitiba
Uruguay
Paraná
Salado
L. Mar Chiquita
Córdoba
Cerro Aconcagua 6959m
Valparaiso
SANTIAGO
Rosario
Salto
Paysandú
Porto Alegre
URUGUAY
BUENOS AIRES
Morón
Lomas de Zamora
Las Piedras
MONTEVIDEO
La Plata
Concepción
Andes
Pampas
ARGENTINA
CHILE
Patagonia
Colorado
Negro
Bahía Blanca
Puerto Montt
Isla de Chiloé
Golfo San Matías
Península Valdés
Chubut
Golfo San Jorge
Deseado
Isla Wellington
Bahía Grande
FALKLANDS ISLANDS (to UK)
Tierra del Fuego
Beagle Channel
Cape Horn
ATLANTIC OCEAN
Scale : 1:26 500 000
0 250 500 km
0 250 500 miles
POPULATION
over 5 000 000
over 1 000 000
over 500 000
over 100 000
over 50 000
under 50 000
LAND HEIGHT
6000m/19 686ft
4000m/13 124ft
3000m/9843ft
2000m/6562ft
1000m/3281ft
200m/656ft
Sea Level
Line of cross-section
CONTINENTAL FACTS
PHYSICAL FEATURES
LARGEST LAKE: Lake Titicaca, Bolivia/ Peru 3,220 square miles (8,340 sq km)
LONGEST RIVER: Amazon, Brazil 4,050 miles (6,516 km)
HIGHEST POINT: Cerro Aconcagua, Argentina 22,833 ft (6,959 m)
LOWEST POINT: Península Valdés, Argentina 131 ft (40 m) below sea level
POLITICAL FEATURES
TOTAL POPULATION: 304.5 million
LARGEST CITY AND ITS POPULATION: São Paulo, Brazil 17.4 million
COUNTRY WITH HIGHEST POPULATION DENSITY: Ecuador 88 people per sq mile
LARGEST COUNTRY: Brazil 3,286,472 square miles (8,511,970 sq km)
SMALLEST COUNTRY: Suriname 63,039 square miles (8,511,970 sq km)
CROSS-SECTION THROUGH SOUTH AMERICA: 18°S, 75°W–36°W
8000m
4000m
Sea Level
-4000m
-8000m
Hot Desert
Mountain Vegetation
Tropical Dry Forest
Tropical Grassland
Temperate Rainforest
PACIFIC OCEAN
Peru-Chile Trench
Atacama Desert
Cordillera Occidental
Altiplano
Andes
Cordillera Central
Cordillera Oriental
Pantanal
Paraguay
Brazilian Highlands
São Francisco
ATLANTIC OCEAN
75°W
67°W
59°W
51°W
43°W

EUROPE

THE SMALLEST CONTINENT AFTER AUSTRALIA, Europe has a wide variety of climates and landscapes. The tundra of the far north gives way to a cool, wet, heavily forested region. The North European Plain is well drained, fertile and rich in oil, coal and natural gas. The shores of the Mediterranean are generally warm, dry and hilly, ideal for cultivating olives, citrus fruits and grapes. A great curve of mountain ranges, including the Pyrenees, Alps and Carpathians, divides north from south. To the east, the rolling plains of European Russia and Ukraine, clothed in coniferous forests or plowed for wheat, run up to the Ural Mountains. Europeans are mainly Christian – Catholic or Protestant – and speak a variety of languages, most of which spring from Latin (Romance), Germanic or Slavic roots.

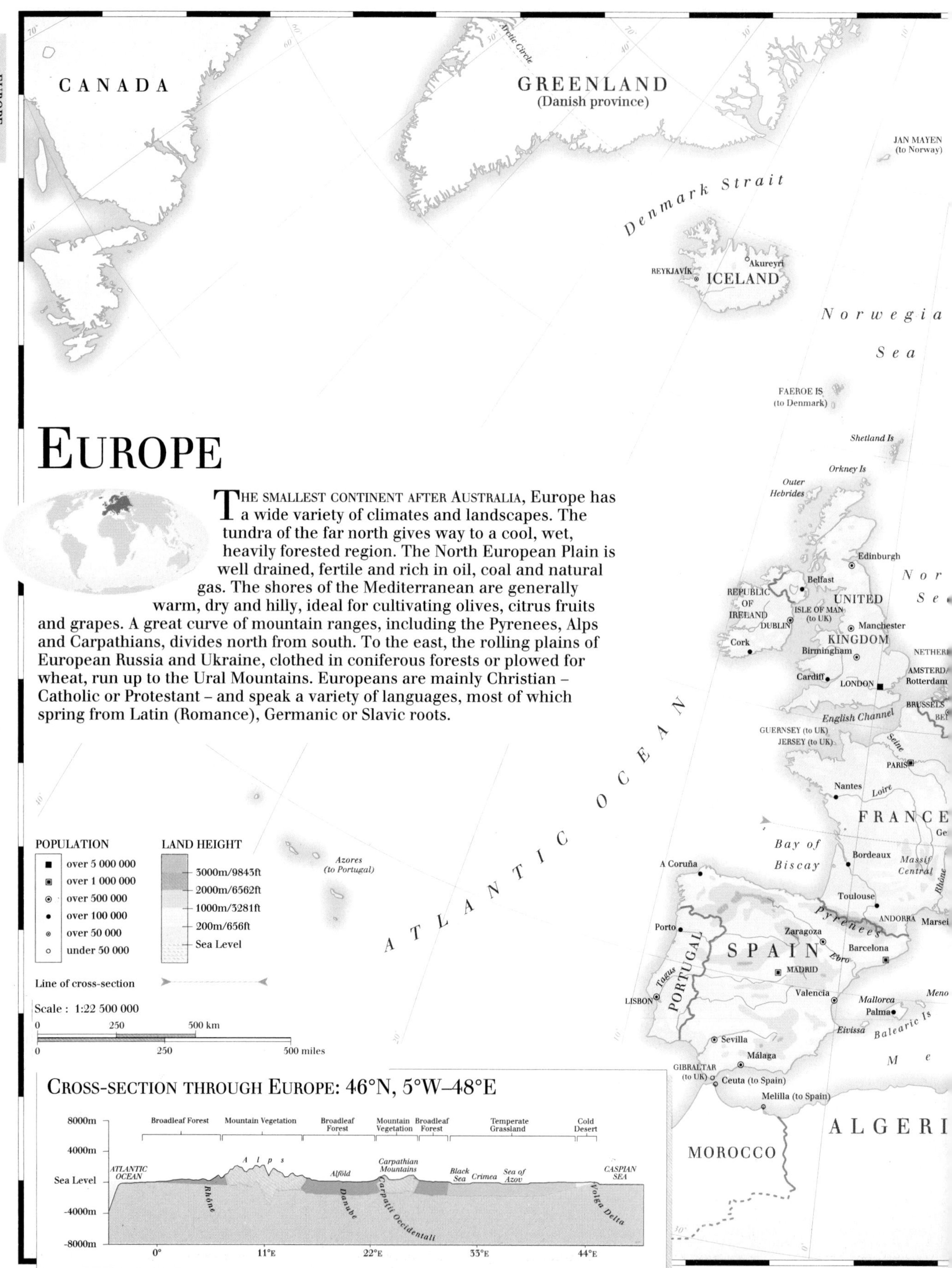

CONTINENTAL FACTS
PHYSICAL FEATURES
LARGEST LAKE: Ladoga, European Russia 7,100 square miles (18,390 sq km)
LONGEST RIVER: Volga, European Russia 2,290 miles (3,688 km)
HIGHEST POINT: El' brus, Caucasus Mts, European Russia 18,510 ft (5,642 m)
LOWEST POINT: Volga Delta, Caspian Sea, European Russia 92 ft (28 m) below sea level
POLITICAL FEATURES
TOTAL POPULATION: 692.13 million
COUNTRY WITH HIGHEST POPULATION DENSITY: Monaco 39,681 people per sq mile
LARGEST CITY AND ITS POPULATION: Moscow, European Russia 8.8 million
LARGEST COUNTRY: European Russia 1,527,341 square miles (3,955,818 sq km)
SMALLEST COUNTRY: Vatican City, Italy 0.17 square miles (0.44 sq km)
SVALBARD (to Norway)
Novaya Zemlya
Karskoye More
Barents Sea
Arctic Circle
Pechora
Murmansk
Tromsø
Arkhangel'sk
Severnaya Dvina
Kemi
NORWAY
SWEDEN
Gulf of Bothnia
Vaasa
FINLAND
Onezhskoye Ozero
Ladozhskoye Ozero
Trondheim
Tampere
Turku
HELSINKI
St Petersburg
RUSSIAN FEDERATION
EUROPEAN RUSSIA
European Plain
Yaroslavl'
Kazan'
Nizhniy Novgorod
Ufa
Ural
Orenburg
Samara
Uppsala
Åland
OSLO
Örebro
STOCKHOLM
Vänern
Vättern
TALLINN
Tartu
ESTONIA
MOSCOW
Kristiansand
Göteborg
Gotland
Baltic Sea
RIGA
LATVIA
Šiauliai
Daugavpils
LITHUANIA
Orsha
Tula
Volga
Saratov
KAZAKHSTAN
DENMARK
Malmö
COPENHAGEN
KALININGRAD (to Russian Fed.)
VILNIUS
MINSK
Voronezh
Gdańsk
North European Plain
BELORUSSIA
Homyel'
Don
Volgograd
Astrakhan'
Volga Delta
Hamburg
Elbe
BERLIN
Wisla
WARSAW
Łódź
Kharkiv
KIEV
Dnieper
Donets'k
Rostov-na-Donu
GERMANY
POLAND
UKRAINE
Dnipropetrovs'k
Caspian Sea
Frankfurt am Main
PRAGUE
Kraków
CZECH REPUBLIC
SLOVAKIA
Dniester
Carpathian Mts
MOLDOVA
CHIŞINĂU
Sea of Azov
Krasnodar
Makhachkala
Danube
Strasbourg
München
VIENNA
BRATISLAVA
Miskolc
Iaşi
Odesa
Crimea
Caucasus
El'brus 5642m
BUDAPEST
Salzburg
AUSTRIA
HUNGARY
Alföld
Carpaţii Occidentali
ROMANIA
Braşov
GEORGIA
TBILISI
AZERBAIJAN
ARMENIA
AZERB.
LJUBLJANA
SLOVENIA
ZAGREB
CROATIA
Timişoara
Novi Sad
BUCHAREST
Black Sea
Trabzon
Milano
Po
BELGRADE
Varna
ITALY
SAN MARINO
BOSNIA & HERZEGOVINA
SARAJEVO
YUGOSLAVIA
BULGARIA
SOFIA
MONACO
Split
Podgorica
Plovdiv
Istanbul
ANKARA
Irmak
IRAN
Appennino
Adriatic Sea
SKOPJE
MACEDONIA
Bursa
TURKEY
ROME
TIRANA
Thessaloníki
VATICAN CITY
ALBANIA
Gaziantep
Napoli
Lárisa
İzmir
Konya
Adana
Tyrrhenian Sea
GREECE
SYRIA
IRAQ
Sardinia
ATHENS
Cágliari
Pátra
Aegean Sea
Palermo
Ionian Sea
NICOSIA
Sicily
LEBANON
CYPRUS
Iráklеio
MALTA
Crete
ISRAEL
Mediterranean Sea
TUNISIA
LIBYA
EGYPT

FRANCE
PORTUGAL
SPAIN
ITALY
GREECE
TURKEY
SYRIA
LEBANON
ISRAEL
JORDAN
CYPRUS
MALTA
SAUDI ARABIA
YEMEN
ATLANTIC OCEAN
Black Sea
Mediterranean Sea
Red Sea
Gulf of Aden
INDIAN OCEAN
Gulf of Guinea
ATLANTIC
MOROCCO
Atlas Mts
ALGERIA
TUNISIA
LIBYA
EGYPT
SUDAN
ERITREA
DJIBOUTI
ETHIOPIA
SOMALIA
KENYA
UGANDA
RWANDA
BURUNDI
TANZANIA
ZAIRE
CONGO
GABON
EQUATORIAL GUINEA
CAMEROON
CENTRAL AFRICAN REPUBLIC
CHAD
NIGER
NIGERIA
BENIN
TOGO
GHANA
BURKINA
IVORY COAST
LIBERIA
SIERRA LEONE
GUINEA
GUINEA-BISSAU
GAMBIA
SENEGAL
MALI
MAURITANIA
WESTERN SAHARA (Occupied by Morocco)
SAO TOME & PRINCIPE
SEYCHELLES
Islas Canarias (to Spain)
ASCENSION (to St Helena)
GIBRALTAR (to UK)
Ceuta (to Spain)
Melilla (to Spain)
Sahara
Ahaggar
Aozou Strip
Nubian Desert
Sudd
Ethiopian Highlands
Horn of Africa
Adamawa Highlands
Great Rift Valley
Nile
Blue Nile
White Nile
Niger
Congo (Zaire)
L. Chad
L. Victoria
L. Tanganyika
Lake Volta
Buḥeirat Nâṣir
Lac'Assal
Tropic of Cancer
Equator
Kilimanjaro 5895m
Tanger
RABAT
Casablanca
Fez
Oran
ALGIERS
Constantine
TUNIS
Sfax
TRIPOLI
Banghāzī
Marrakech
Laâyoune
Sabhā
Alexandria
CAIRO
Aswân
Port Sudan
KHARTOUM
El Obeid
ASMARA
DJIBOUTI
Hargeysa
Dirē Dawa
ADDIS ABABA
MOGADISHU
Kismaayo
Juba
Nouâdhibou
NOUAKCHOTT
DAKAR
BANJUL
BISSAU
CONAKRY
FREETOWN
MONROVIA
BAMAKO
OUAGADOUGOU
NIAMEY
Agadez
Kano
ABUJA
N'DJAMENA
Abéché
YAMOUSSOUKRO
Abidjan
ACCRA
LOMÉ
PORTO-NOVO
Ibadan
Lagos
Port Harcourt
Douala
YAOUNDÉ
MALABO
Bata
Príncipe
SÃO TOMÉ
LIBREVILLE
BANGUI
Kisangani
Kananga
Mbuji-Mayi
Pointe-Noire
CABINDA (to Angola)
BRAZZAVILLE
KINSHASA
LUANDA
KAMPALA
Mbale
Kisumu
NAIROBI
KIGALI
BUJUMBURA
Mwanza
DODOMA
Mombasa
Zanzibar
Dar es Salaam
VICTORIA

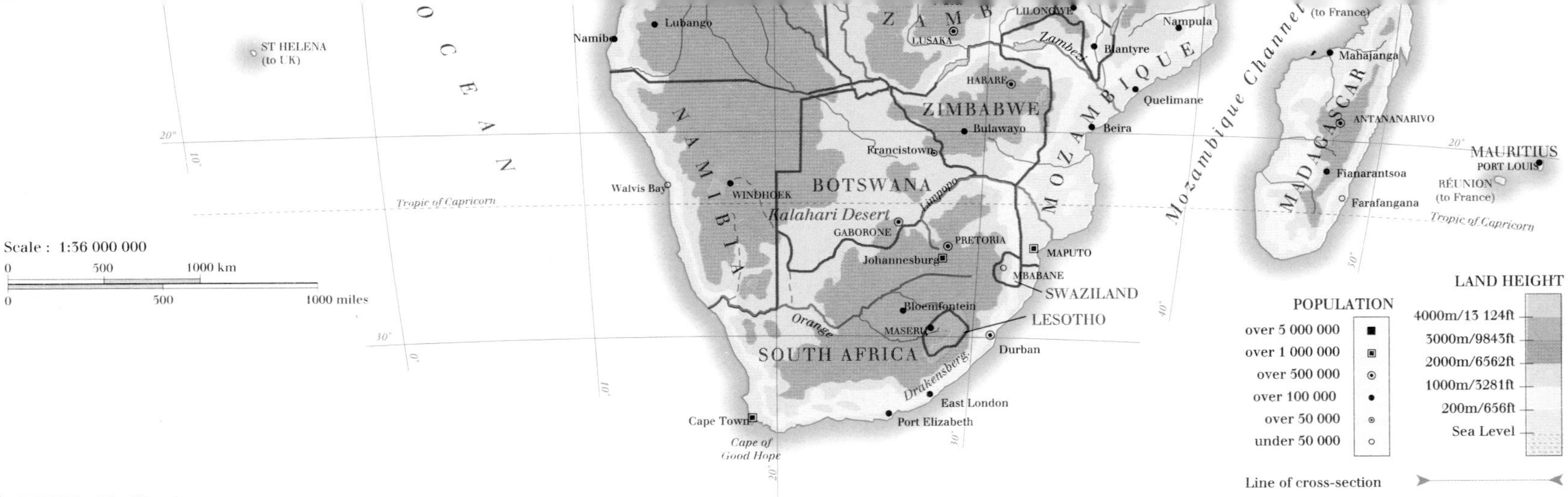

ST HELENA (to UK)
OCEAN
Tropic of Capricorn
Scale : 1:36 000 000
0 500 1000 km
0 500 1000 miles
Namibe
Lubango
Walvis Bay
WINDHOEK
NAMIBIA
BOTSWANA
Kalahari Desert
GABORONE
Francistown
ZAMBIA
LUSAKA
LILONGWE
Zambezi
Blantyre
Nampula
Quelimane
Beira
HARARE
ZIMBABWE
Bulawayo
MOZAMBIQUE
Mozambique Channel
Limpopo
PRETORIA
Johannesburg
MAPUTO
MBABANE
SWAZILAND
LESOTHO
MASERU
Bloemfontein
Orange
SOUTH AFRICA
Durban
Drakensberg
East London
Port Elizabeth
Cape Town
Cape of Good Hope
(to France)
Mahajanga
MADAGASCAR
ANTANANARIVO
Fianarantsoa
Farafangana
MAURITIUS
PORT LOUIS
RÉUNION (to France)
POPULATION
over 5 000 000
over 1 000 000
over 500 000
over 100 000
over 50 000
under 50 000
LAND HEIGHT
4000m/13 124ft
3000m/9843ft
2000m/6562ft
1000m/3281ft
200m/656ft
Sea Level
Line of cross-section

AFRICA

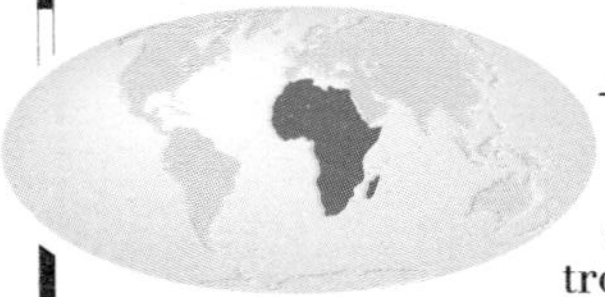

AFRICA IS THE SECOND LARGEST CONTINENT after Asia. It is dominated by the Sahara in the north and the Great Rift Valley in the east. The Mediterranean climate of the extreme north and south enables cultivation of grapes and other fruit. A belt of tropical rainforest lies along the Equator, and Africa's great tropical grasslands provide grazing for herds of wild animals and domestic livestock. A narrow strip of Egypt is watered by the world's longest river, the Nile, which sustained prehistoric communities. The center and south of the continent are rich in minerals. Almost one-tenth of the world's population lives in Africa – a wide variety of peoples with their own distinctive languages and cultures. Although Islam and Christianity are widespread, many Africans adhere to their own local customs and religious beliefs.

CONTINENTAL FACTS

PHYSICAL FEATURES

LARGEST LAKE: Lake Victoria 26,560 square miles (68,880 sq km)

LONGEST RIVER: Nile, Uganda/ Sudan/ Egypt 4,160 miles (6,695 km)

HIGHEST POINT: Kilimanjaro, Tanzania 19,341 ft (5,895 m)

LOWEST POINT: Lac' Assal, Djibouti 512 ft (156 m) below sea level

POLITICAL FEATURES

TOTAL POPULATION: 681.7 million

LARGEST CITY AND POPULATION: Cairo, Egypt, 9 million

COUNTRY WITH HIGHEST POPULATION DENSITY: Mauritius 1,380 people per sq mile

LARGEST COUNTRY: Sudan 967,493 square miles (2,505,810 sq km)

SMALLEST COUNTRY: Seychelles 108 square miles (280 sq km)

CROSS-SECTION THROUGH AFRICA 7°N, 15°W–55°E

4000m
8000m
Sea Level
-4000m
-8000m
14°W
0°
14°E
28°E
42°E
Tropical Rainforest
Tropical Dry Forest
Tropical Rainforest
Tropical Dry Forest
Mountain Vegetation
Tropical Dry Forest
Tropical Grassland
Wetlands
Tropical Grassland
Mountain Vegetation
Tropical Grassland
Hot Desert
ATLANTIC OCEAN
Lake Volta
Niger
Adamawa Highlands
Sudd
Nile
Ethiopian Highlands
Great Rift Valley
Horn of Africa
INDIAN OCEAN

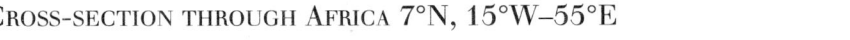

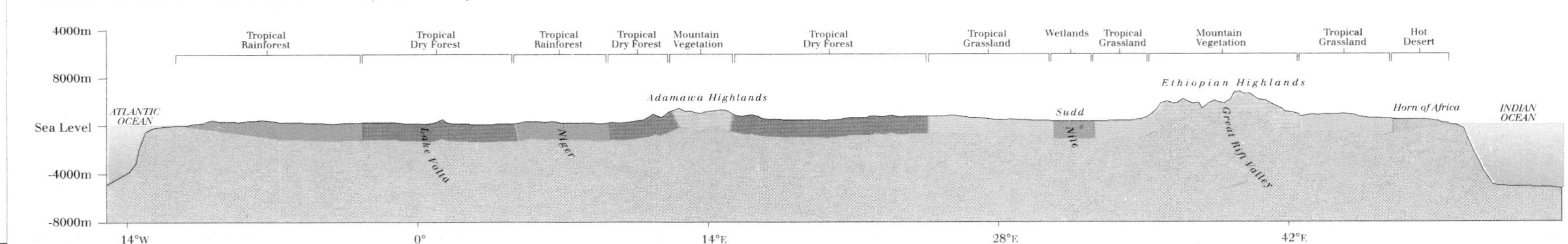

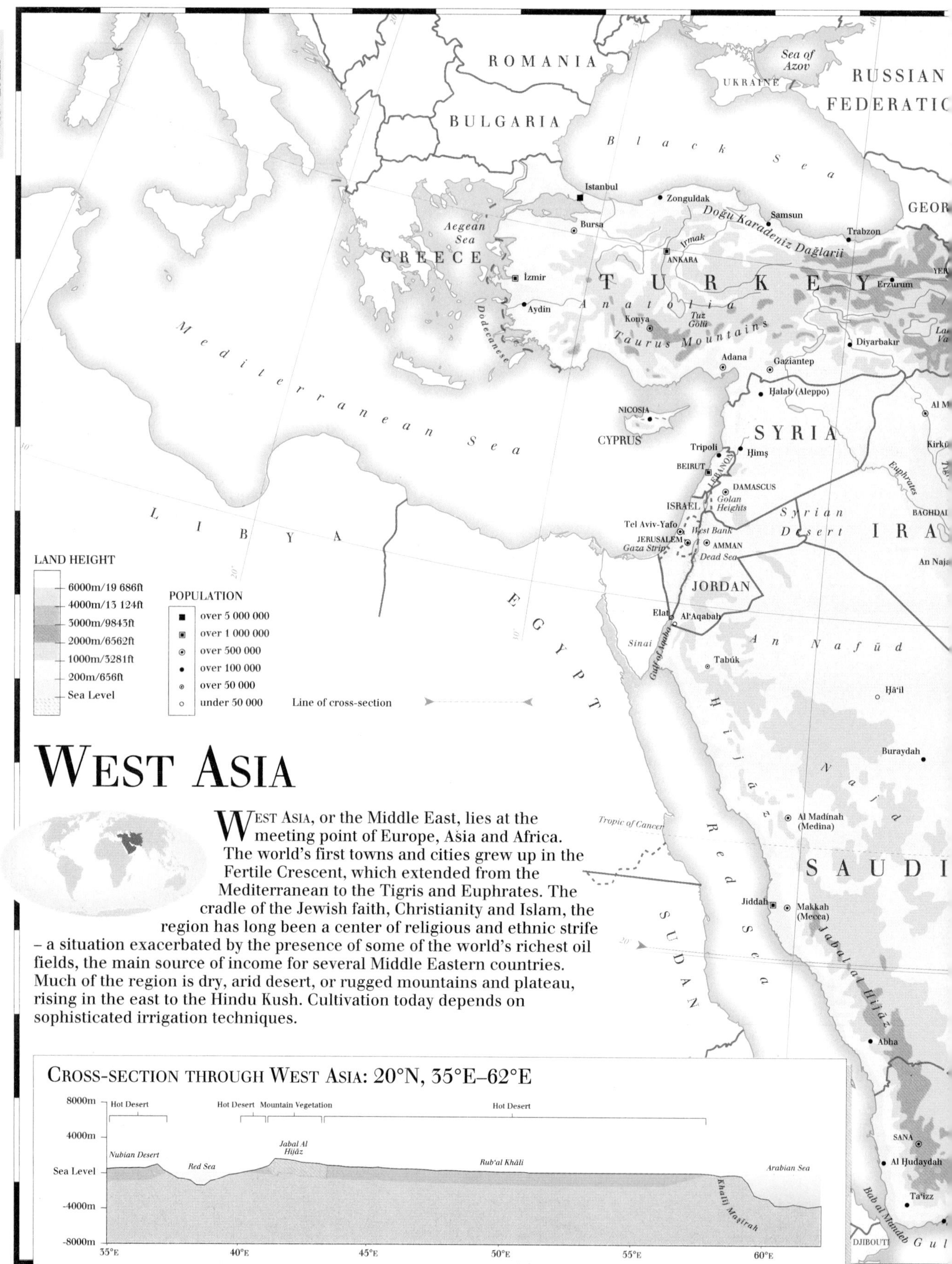

WEST ASIA

West Asia, or the Middle East, lies at the meeting point of Europe, Asia and Africa. The world's first towns and cities grew up in the Fertile Crescent, which extended from the Mediterranean to the Tigris and Euphrates. The cradle of the Jewish faith, Christianity and Islam, the region has long been a center of religious and ethnic strife – a situation exacerbated by the presence of some of the world's richest oil fields, the main source of income for several Middle Eastern countries. Much of the region is dry, arid desert, or rugged mountains and plateau, rising in the east to the Hindu Kush. Cultivation today depends on sophisticated irrigation techniques.

CROSS-SECTION THROUGH WEST ASIA: 20°N, 35°E–62°E

KAZAKHSTAN
Aral Sea
Caspian Sea
UZBEKISTAN
Kyzyl Kum
Ozero Aydarkul'
TASHKENT
Dashkhovuz
Urgench
KYRGYZSTAN
BISHKEK
Karakol
Ozero Issyk-Kul'
Kirghiz Range
Naryn
Tien Shan
Namangan
Osh
Khudzhand
CHINA
Karakumy
Samarkand
TAJIKISTAN
DUSHANBE
Pamirs
AZERBAIJAN
BAKU
Gäncä
Krasnovodsk
Nebitdag
TURKMENISTAN
Chardzhev
Amu
Karshi
Kulyab
Khorog
Kurgan-Tyube
Länkäran
Khrebet Kopetdag
ASHGABAT
Mary
Karakoram Range
Indus
K2 8611m
Tabrīz
Rasht
Mazār-e-Sharīf
Baghlān
Gorgān
Reshteh-ye Kuhhā ye Alborz
Mashhad
Hindu Kush
TEHRĀN
Jalālābād
Peshāwar
ISLĀMĀBĀD
KĀBUL
Rāwalpindi
Hamadān
Qom
Herāt
Dasht-e-Kavīr
AFGHANISTAN
Gujrānwāla
Bākhtarān
Lahore
Chenab
IRAN
Faisalābād
Esfahān
Plateau of Iran
Kandahār
Hāmūn-e Şāberī
Multān
Zagros Mountains
Helmand
Ahvāz
Quetta
Başrah
Ābādān
Kermān
Zāhedān
Indus
Thar Desert
Shīrāz
KUWAIT
KUWAIT CITY
Sukkur
PAKISTAN
INDIA
Persian Gulf
Bandar-e 'Abbās
Strait of Hormuz
Hyderābād
BAHRAIN
MANAMA
Karāchi
Tropic of Cancer
DOHA
Dubai
Sharjah
RIYADH
Al Hufūf
QATAR
Gulf of Oman
ABU DHABI
Şuḩār
Arabian Sea
Ḩaraḑ
MUSCAT
UNITED ARAB EMIRATES
Ar Rustāq
Nazwá
ARABIA
Şūr
Scale : 1:17 500 000
0
250
500 km
0
250
500 miles
Rub 'al Khāli
Khalīj Maşīrah
OMAN
Şalālah
INDIAN OCEAN
YEMEN
Hadhramaut
Al Mukallā
Socotra (to Yemen)
Aden
Continental Facts
Physical features
Largest lake: Caspian Sea 143,205 square miles (371,000 sq km)
Longest river: Euphrates, Syria/ Iraq 1,750 miles (2,815 km)
Highest point: K2, Kashmir, India/ Pakistan 28,252 ft (8,611 m)
Lowest point: Dead Sea, Israel/Jordan 1,286 ft (392 m) below sea level
Political features
Total population: 390.5 million
Largest city and its population: Istanbul, Turkey 6.5 million
Country with highest population density: Bahrain 1,872 people per sq mile
Largest country: Saudi Arabia 830,001 square miles (2,149,690 sq km)
Smallest country: Bahrain 263 square miles (680 sq km)

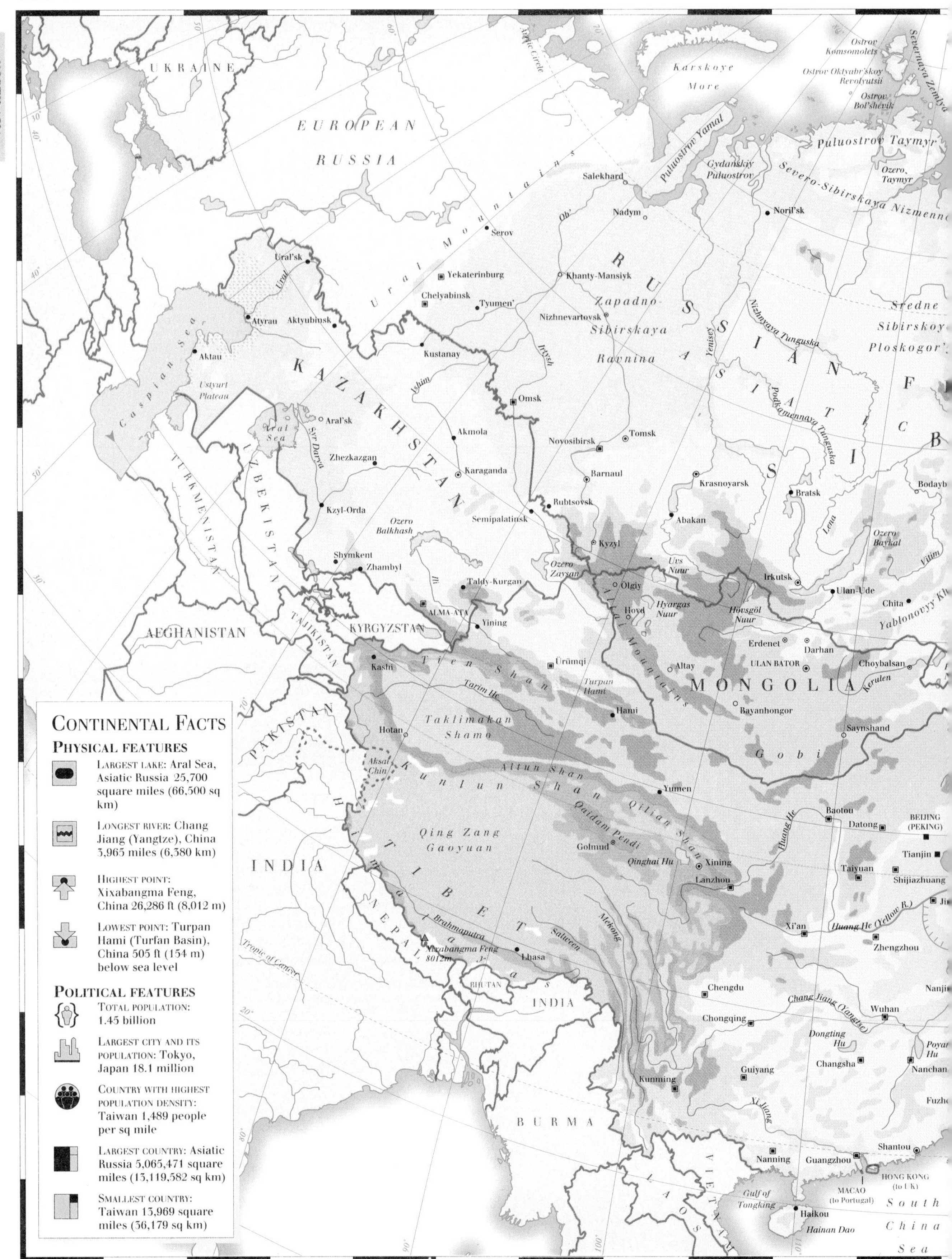

CONTINENTAL FACTS

PHYSICAL FEATURES

LARGEST LAKE: Aral Sea, Asiatic Russia 25,700 square miles (66,500 sq km)

LONGEST RIVER: Chang Jiang (Yangtze), China 3,965 miles (6,380 km)

HIGHEST POINT: Xixabangma Feng, China 26,286 ft (8,012 m)

LOWEST POINT: Turpan Hami (Turfan Basin), China 505 ft (154 m) below sea level

POLITICAL FEATURES

TOTAL POPULATION: 1.45 billion

LARGEST CITY AND ITS POPULATION: Tokyo, Japan 18.1 million

COUNTRY WITH HIGHEST POPULATION DENSITY: Taiwan 1,489 people per sq mile

LARGEST COUNTRY: Asiatic Russia 5,065,471 square miles (13,119,582 sq km)

SMALLEST COUNTRY: Taiwan 13,969 square miles (36,179 sq km)

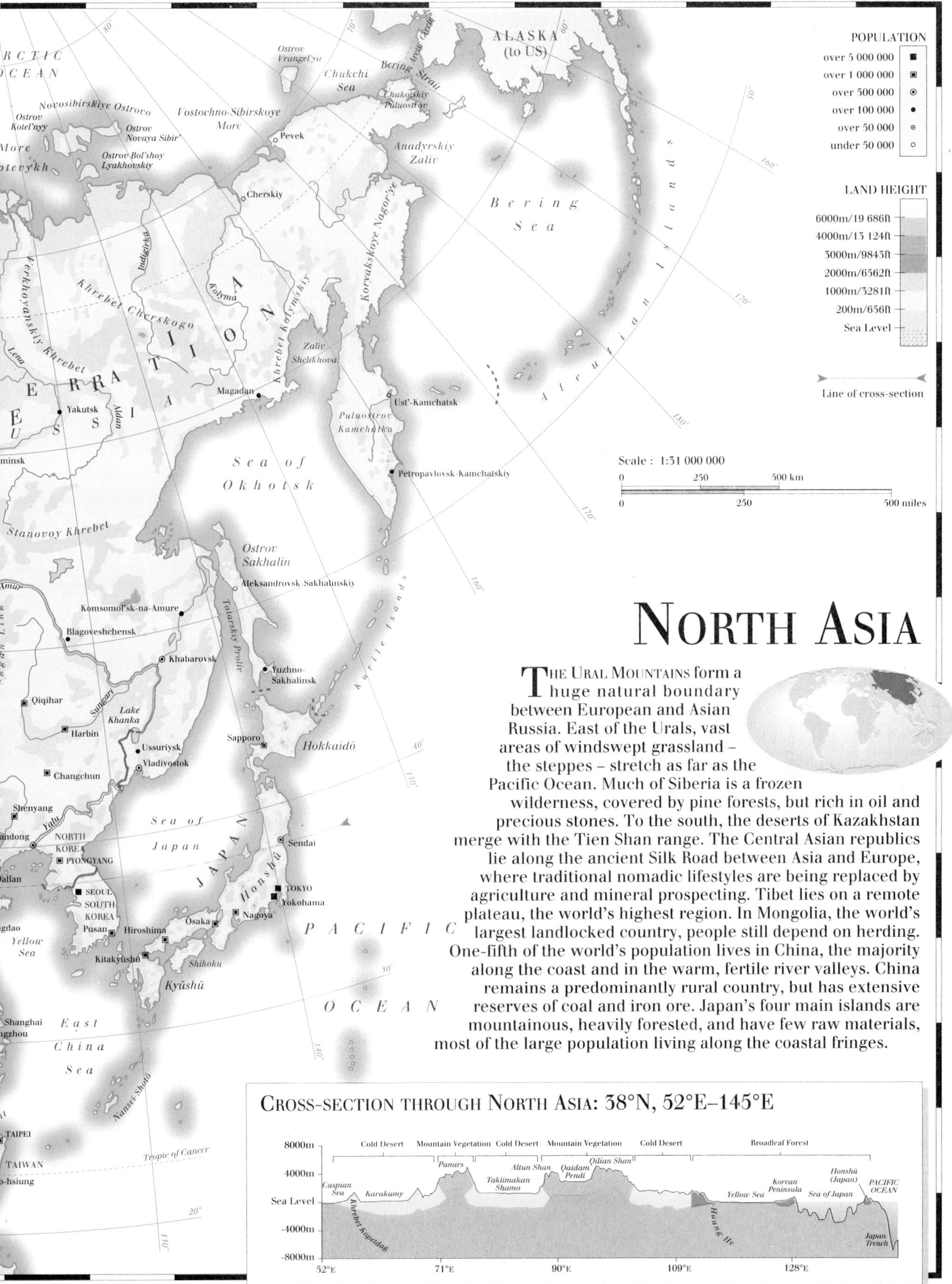

NORTH ASIA

THE URAL MOUNTAINS form a huge natural boundary between European and Asian Russia. East of the Urals, vast areas of windswept grassland – the steppes – stretch as far as the Pacific Ocean. Much of Siberia is a frozen wilderness, covered by pine forests, but rich in oil and precious stones. To the south, the deserts of Kazakhstan merge with the Tien Shan range. The Central Asian republics lie along the ancient Silk Road between Asia and Europe, where traditional nomadic lifestyles are being replaced by agriculture and mineral prospecting. Tibet lies on a remote plateau, the world's highest region. In Mongolia, the world's largest landlocked country, people still depend on herding. One-fifth of the world's population lives in China, the majority along the coast and in the warm, fertile river valleys. China remains a predominantly rural country, but has extensive reserves of coal and iron ore. Japan's four main islands are mountainous, heavily forested, and have few raw materials, most of the large population living along the coastal fringes.

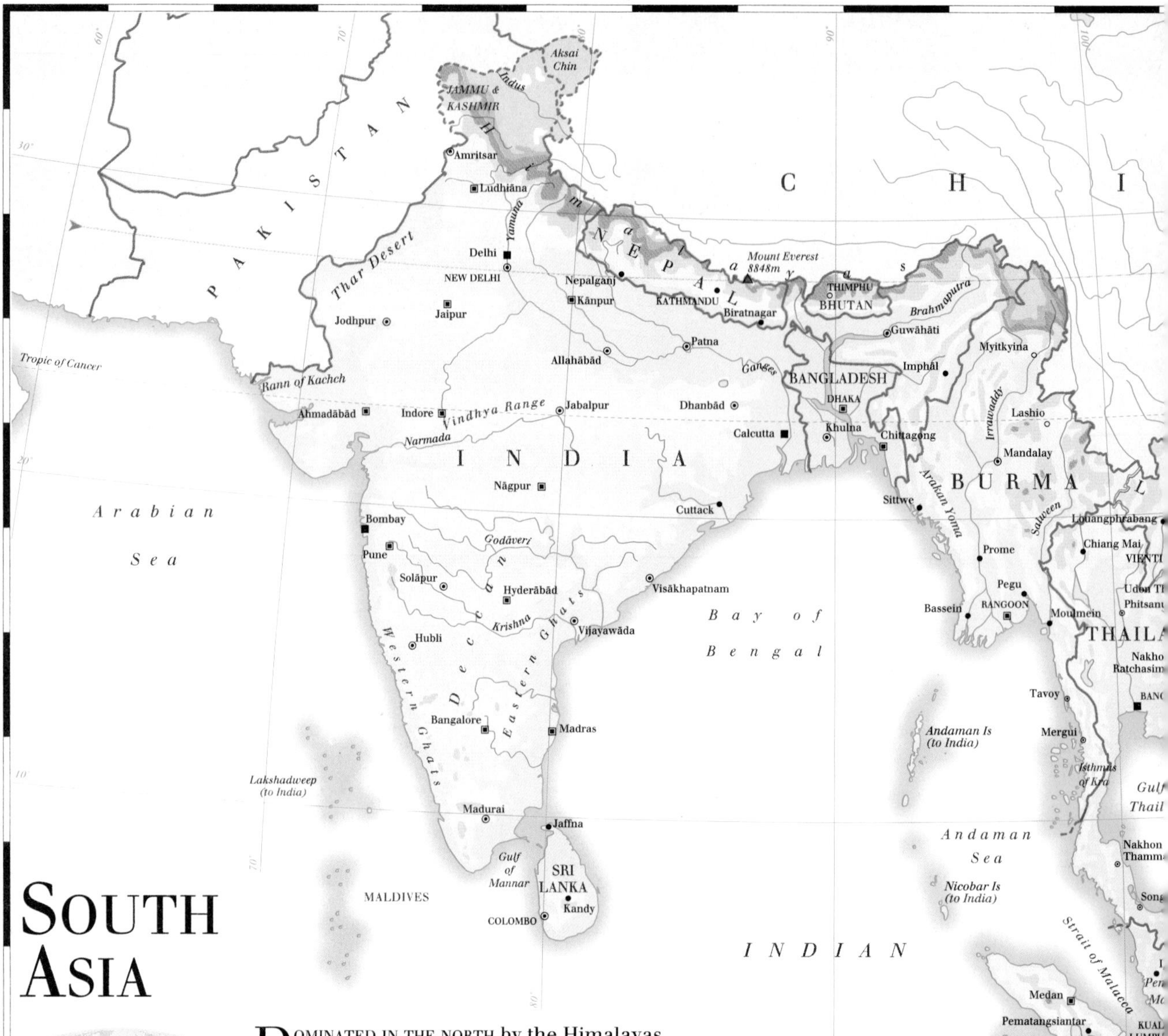

SOUTH ASIA

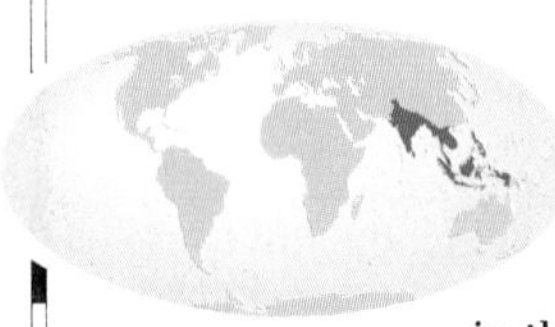

DOMINATED IN THE NORTH by the Himalayas, the highest mountain range in the world, India is isolated from the rest of Asia, forming a densely populated subcontinent. Its climate and topography range from the mountains of Kashmir in the north to coral beaches in the south. It is the birthplace of Hinduism, Buddhism and Sikhism. Much of mainland Southeast Asia is mountainous and forested, the people living in the river valleys and fertile coastal plains. Tropical rainforests, rich in species, cover much of the region. Indonesia forms a huge arc of some 13,000 volcanic islands. The Philippines, the region's only Christian country, comprises over 7,000 mountainous islands.

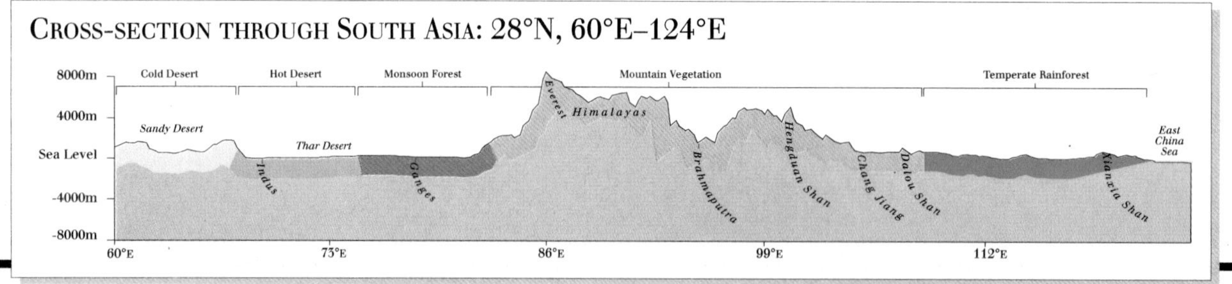

CROSS-SECTION THROUGH SOUTH ASIA: 28°N, 60°E–124°E

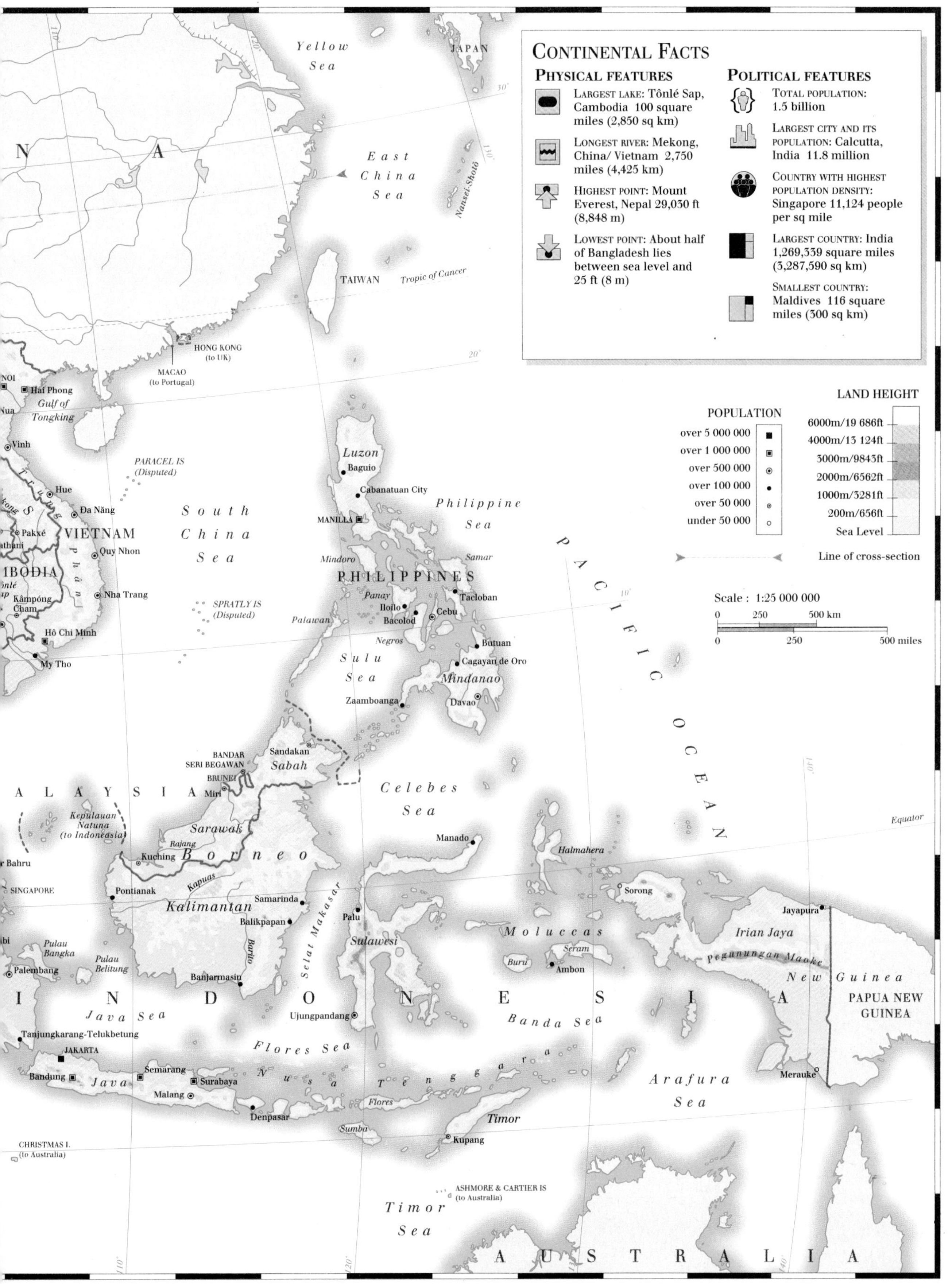
CONTINENTAL FACTS
PHYSICAL FEATURES
LARGEST LAKE: Tônlé Sap, Cambodia 100 square miles (2,850 sq km)
LONGEST RIVER: Mekong, China/ Vietnam 2,750 miles (4,425 km)
HIGHEST POINT: Mount Everest, Nepal 29,030 ft (8,848 m)
LOWEST POINT: About half of Bangladesh lies between sea level and 25 ft (8 m)
POLITICAL FEATURES
TOTAL POPULATION: 1.5 billion
LARGEST CITY AND ITS POPULATION: Calcutta, India 11.8 million
COUNTRY WITH HIGHEST POPULATION DENSITY: Singapore 11,124 people per sq mile
LARGEST COUNTRY: India 1,269,339 square miles (3,287,590 sq km)
SMALLEST COUNTRY: Maldives 116 square miles (300 sq km)
POPULATION
over 5 000 000
over 1 000 000
over 500 000
over 100 000
over 50 000
under 50 000
LAND HEIGHT
6000m/19 686ft
4000m/13 124ft
3000m/9843ft
2000m/6562ft
1000m/3281ft
200m/656ft
Sea Level
Line of cross-section
Scale : 1:25 000 000
0 250 500 km
0 250 500 miles
Yellow Sea
JAPAN
East China Sea
Nansei-Shotō
TAIWAN
Tropic of Cancer
HONG KONG (to UK)
MACAO (to Portugal)
Hai Phong
Gulf of Tongking
Vinh
PARACEL IS (Disputed)
Hue
Đa Năng
Pakxé
VIETNAM
Quy Nhon
Nha Trang
Hô Chi Minh
My Tho
South China Sea
SPRATLY IS (Disputed)
Luzon
Baguio
Cabanatuan City
MANILLA
Philippine Sea
Mindoro
Samar
PHILIPPINES
Panay
Iloilo
Bacolod
Cebu
Tacloban
Palawan
Negros
Butuan
Sulu Sea
Cagayan de Oro
Mindanao
Zaamboanga
Davao
PACIFIC OCEAN
Sandakan
Sabah
BANDAR SERI BEGAWAN
BRUNEI
Miri
Celebes Sea
MALAYSIA
Kepulauan Natuna (to Indonesia)
Sarawak
Rajang
Kuching
Borneo
Manado
Halmahera
Equator
SINGAPORE
Pontianak
Kapuas
Kalimantan
Samarinda
Balikpapan
Selat Makasar
Palu
Sorong
Jayapura
Sulawesi
Moluccas
Irian Jaya
Seram
Buru
Ambon
Pegunungan Maoke
Pulau Bangka
Pulau Belitung
Barito
Palembang
Banjarmasin
New Guinea
PAPUA NEW GUINEA
INDONESIA
Java Sea
Ujungpandang
Banda Sea
Tanjungkarang-Telukbetung
JAKARTA
Flores Sea
Semarang
Bandung
Java
Surabaya
Malang
Nusa Tenggara
Merauke
Arafura Sea
Flores
Denpasar
Sumba
Timor
Kupang
CHRISTMAS I. (to Australia)
ASHMORE & CARTIER IS (to Australia)
Timor Sea
AUSTRALIA

Tropic of Cancer
TAIWAN
South China Sea
Philippine Sea
PHILIPPINES
Sulu Sea
MALAYSIA
BRUNEI
Celebes Sea
Equator
INDONESIA
Banda Sea
Timor Sea
Arafura Sea
ASHMORE & CARTIER ISLANDS (to Australia)
INDIAN OCEAN
NORTHERN MARIANA ISLANDS (to US)
Saipan
GUAM (to US)
PACIFIC
WAKE I. (to US)
MARSHALL ISLANDS
Ratak Chain
Ralik Chain
Majuro
MICRONESIA
Yap
KOROR
Babelthuap
PALAU (to US)
Chuuk Is
Pohnpei
KOLONIA
Kosrae
Gilbert Islands
BAIRIKI
Tarawa
NAURU
TUVALU
Nanumea
Nukufetau
FONGAFALE
Nukulaelae
MELANESIA
Bismarck Archipelago
Bismarck Sea
Rabaul
New Britain
Bougainville
Mt Wilhelm 4509m
PAPUA NEW GUINEA
New Guinea
PORT MORESBY
Solomon Sea
Torres Strait
SOLOMON ISLANDS
Santa Isabel
Malaita
Guadalcanal
HONIARA
Santa Cruz Is
San Cristobal
Rennell
VANUATU
Espiritu Santo
Malekula
PORT-VILA
Éfaté
NEW CALEDONIA (to France)
Îles Loyauté
New Caledonia
NOUMÉA
Vanua Levu
Viti Levu
SUVA
FIJI
Coral Sea
CORAL SEA ISLANDS (to Australia)
Great Barrier Reef
Gulf of Carpentaria
Darwin
Cairns
Townsville
MacKay
Rockhampton
Broome
Great Sandy Desert
NORTHERN TERRITORY
QUEENSLAND
AUSTRALIA
Great Dividing Range
Alice Springs
Simpson Desert
Musgrave Ranges
Gibson Desert
Lake Eyre
Grey Range
Darling
WESTERN AUSTRALIA
Great Victoria Desert
SOUTH AUSTRALIA
Lake Torrens
NEW SOUTH WALES
Brisbane
Gold Coast
Toowoomba
Newcastle
Sydney
Wollongong
CANBERRA
AUSTRALIAN CAPITAL TERRITORY
Murray
Adelaide
VICTORIA
Bendigo
Melbourne
Geelong
Great Australian Bight
Port Lincoln
Geraldton
Kalgoorlie
Perth
Esperance
Bunbury
Albany
Tropic of Capricorn
Bass Strait
Launceston
TASMANIA
Hobart
Tasman Sea
NORFOLK ISLAND (to Australia)
Lord Howe I. (to Australia)
Ball's Pyramid (to Australia)
NEW ZEALAND
Auckland
Hamilton
WELLINGTON
Christchurch
Dunedin
Bounty Islands (to NZ)
Antipodes Islands (to NZ)
Auckland Islands (to NZ)
LAND HEIGHT
3000m/9843ft
2000m/6562ft
1000m/3281ft
200m/656ft
Sea Level
POPULATION
over 5 000 000
over 1 000 000
over 500 000
over 100 000
over 50 000
under 50 000
Scale : 1:40 000 000
0
500
1000 km
0
500
1000 miles

AUSTRALASIA & OCEANIA

OCEANIA EMBRACES THE WORLD'S smallest continent, Australia, large island groups such as New Zealand, Papua New Guinea and Fiji, and the myriad volcanic and coral islands scattered across the Pacific Ocean, consisting of three main groups, Micronesia, Melanesia and Polynesia. Australia, flat and dry, is sparsely populated, most people living along the coastal lowlands, especially in the southeast. The continent's first settlers, the Aboriginal peoples, retain some of their original lands in the interior, but later European and Asian settlers form most of the population. Owing to its isolation from other continents, Australia's flora and fauna have evolved many unique species. The continent is rich in minerals, such as gold, uranium and iron ore, which are the basis of Australia's prosperity. Mountainous Papua New Guinea is covered in tropical rainforest; New Zealand is temperate, rugged and volcanic in the north. The peoples of Oceania colonized the Pacific by AD 1500, and the many insular farming and fishing communities have developed distinctive cultures, the Maoris of New Zealand being among the most notable.

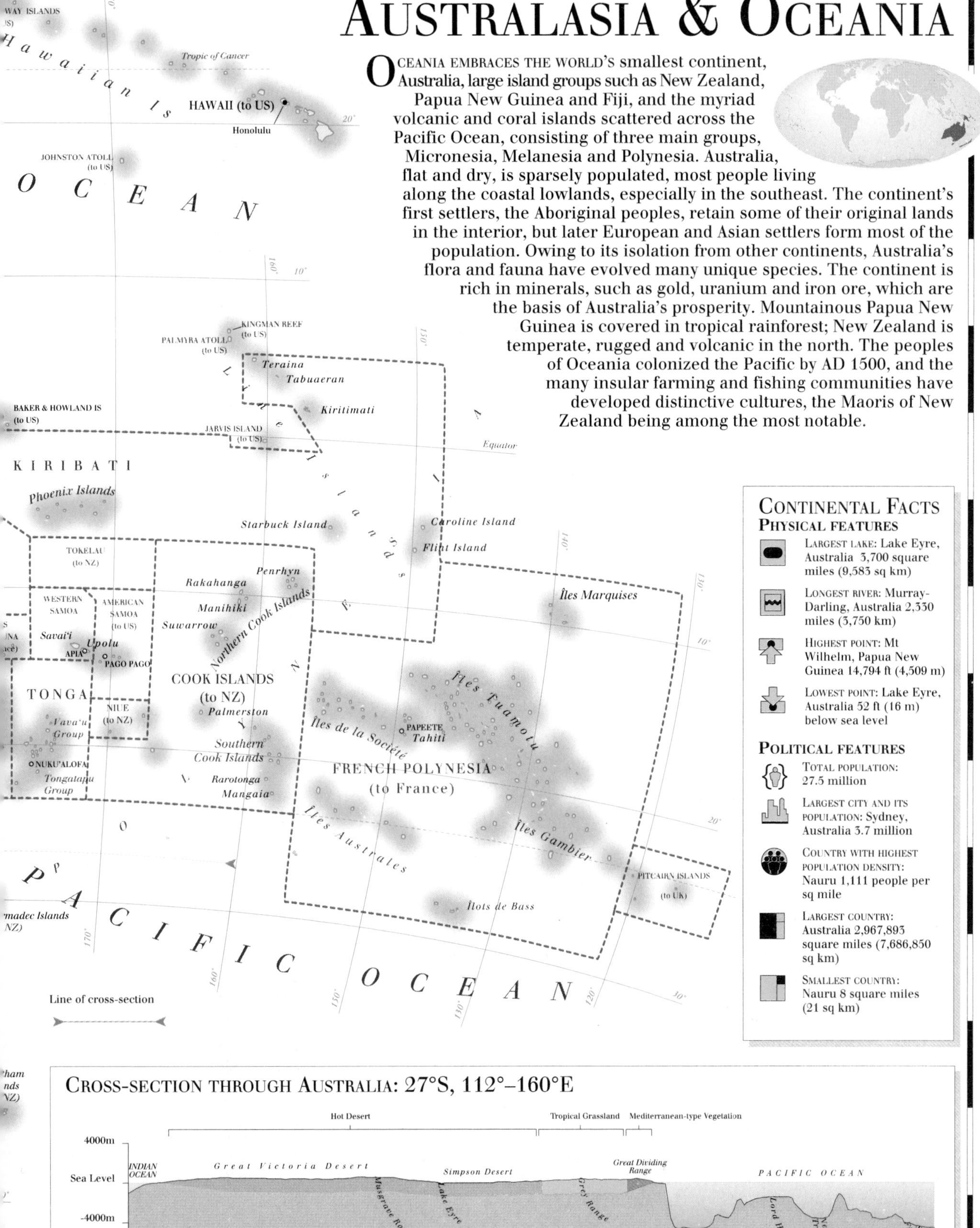

CONTINENTAL FACTS

PHYSICAL FEATURES

- LARGEST LAKE: Lake Eyre, Australia 3,700 square miles (9,583 sq km)
- LONGEST RIVER: Murray-Darling, Australia 2,330 miles (3,750 km)
- HIGHEST POINT: Mt Wilhelm, Papua New Guinea 14,794 ft (4,509 m)
- LOWEST POINT: Lake Eyre, Australia 52 ft (16 m) below sea level

POLITICAL FEATURES

- TOTAL POPULATION: 27.5 million
- LARGEST CITY AND ITS POPULATION: Sydney, Australia 3.7 million
- COUNTRY WITH HIGHEST POPULATION DENSITY: Nauru 1,111 people per sq mile
- LARGEST COUNTRY: Australia 2,967,893 square miles (7,686,850 sq km)
- SMALLEST COUNTRY: Nauru 8 square miles (21 sq km)

The Formation of The Modern World

THE WORLD AS WE KNOW IT today, like all of the species that inhabit it, is the product of many thousands of years of evolution. The political and cultural map of the globe bears the hallmark of many varied courses of human development the world over. Nevertheless, much of the modern human geography of the planet can be traced to developments in the relatively recent past. The following pages chart the rise and fall of the various states and empires of the early modern and modern ages. Beginning with the first great achievement of European exploration, the discovery of the Americas in 1492, the maps show the way in which various European and Asian powers expanded their cultural and political influence and control down to the present day. This process left indelible cultural imprints in the form of language, religion, education and systems of government on every part of the planet.

Major Migrations Since 1500

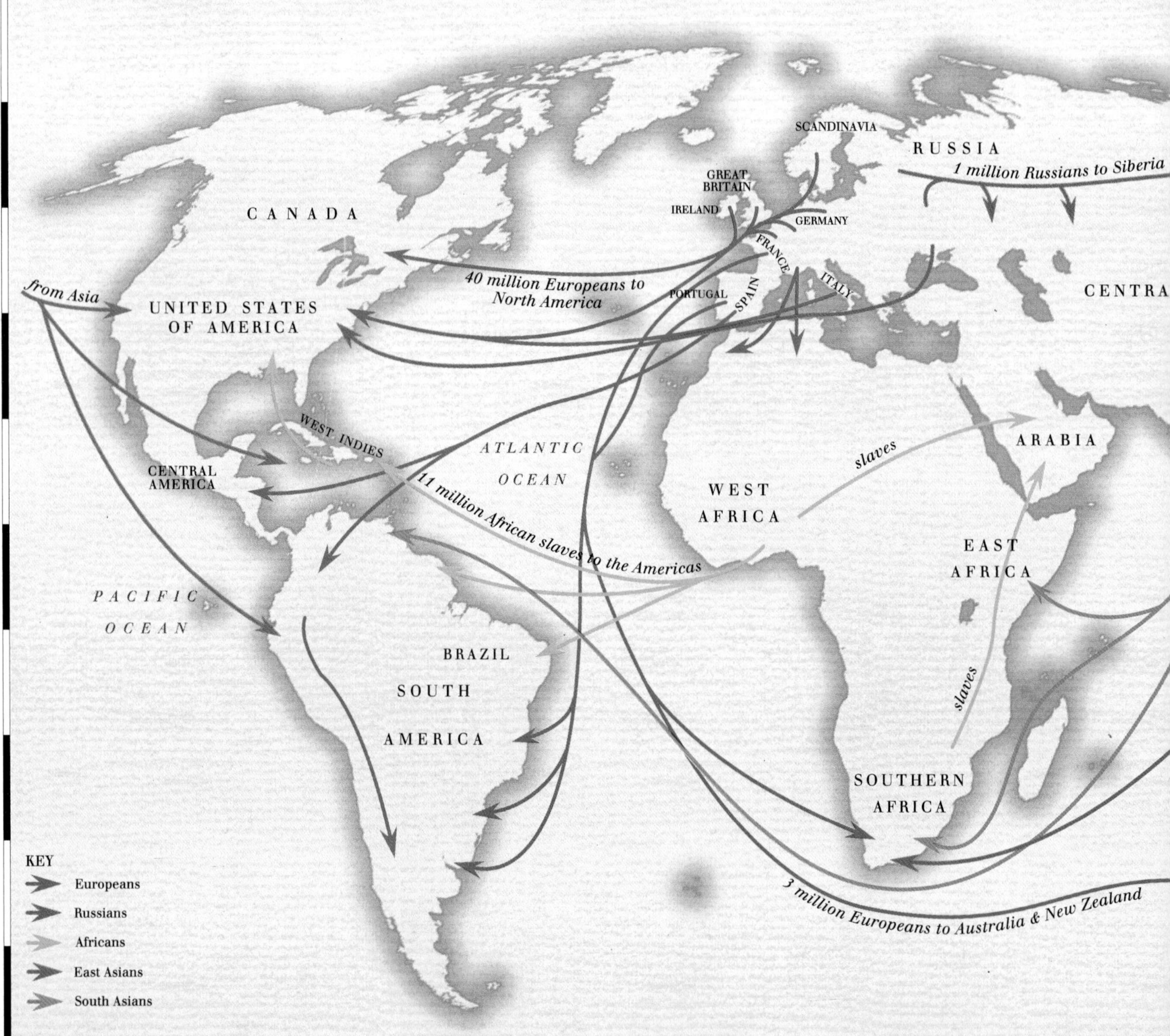

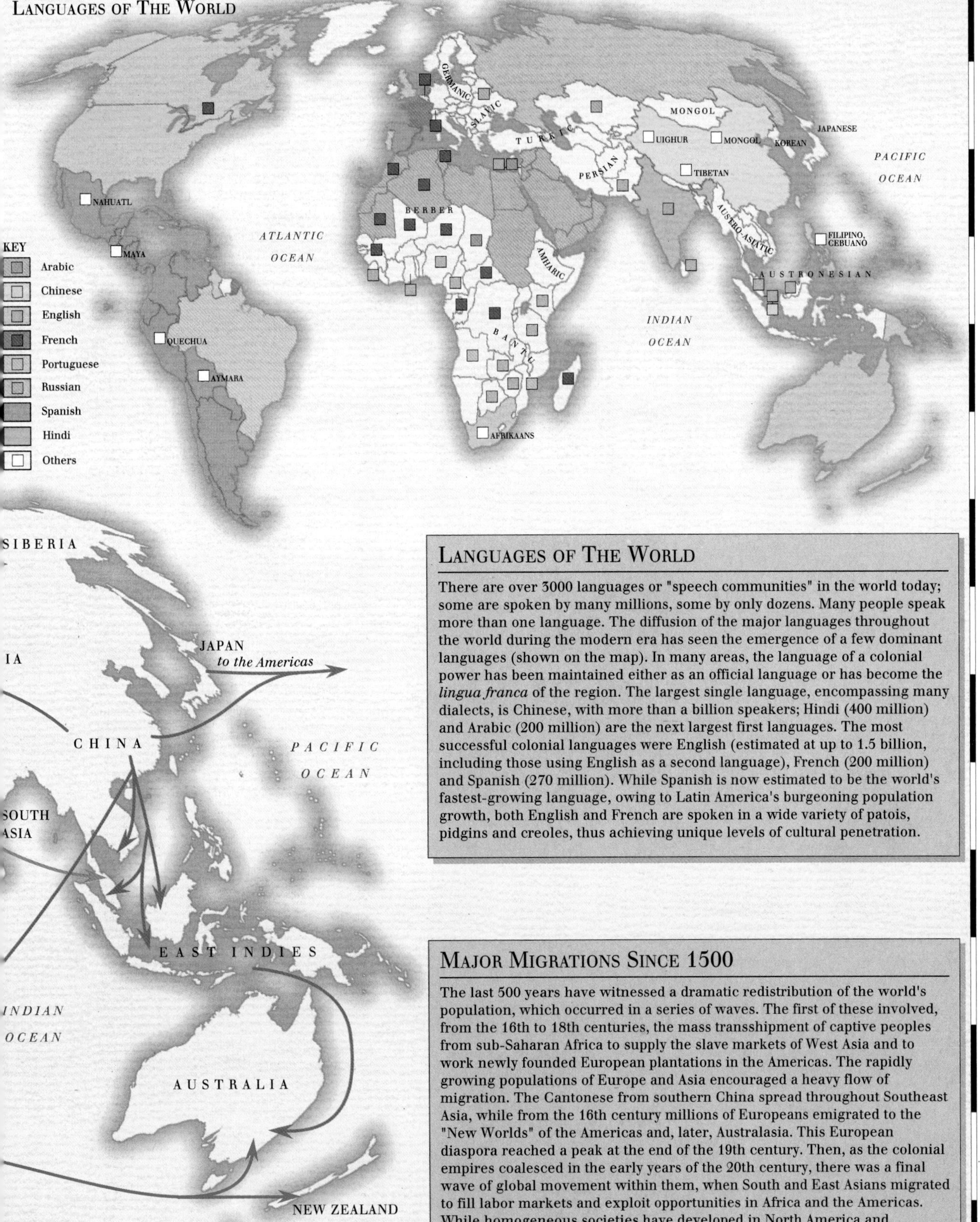

Languages of The World

There are over 3000 languages or "speech communities" in the world today; some are spoken by many millions, some by only dozens. Many people speak more than one language. The diffusion of the major languages throughout the world during the modern era has seen the emergence of a few dominant languages (shown on the map). In many areas, the language of a colonial power has been maintained either as an official language or has become the *lingua franca* of the region. The largest single language, encompassing many dialects, is Chinese, with more than a billion speakers; Hindi (400 million) and Arabic (200 million) are the next largest first languages. The most successful colonial languages were English (estimated at up to 1.5 billion, including those using English as a second language), French (200 million) and Spanish (270 million). While Spanish is now estimated to be the world's fastest-growing language, owing to Latin America's burgeoning population growth, both English and French are spoken in a wide variety of patois, pidgins and creoles, thus achieving unique levels of cultural penetration.

Major Migrations Since 1500

The last 500 years have witnessed a dramatic redistribution of the world's population, which occurred in a series of waves. The first of these involved, from the 16th to 18th centuries, the mass transshipment of captive peoples from sub-Saharan Africa to supply the slave markets of West Asia and to work newly founded European plantations in the Americas. The rapidly growing populations of Europe and Asia encouraged a heavy flow of migration. The Cantonese from southern China spread throughout Southeast Asia, while from the 16th century millions of Europeans emigrated to the "New Worlds" of the Americas and, later, Australasia. This European diaspora reached a peak at the end of the 19th century. Then, as the colonial empires coalesced in the early years of the 20th century, there was a final wave of global movement within them, when South and East Asians migrated to fill labor markets and exploit opportunities in Africa and the Americas. While homogeneous societies have developed in North America and Australia, many diverse ethnic communities remain elsewhere in the world.

THE WORLD IN 1492

WHEN CHRISTOPHER COLUMBUS sailed west from Europe, seeking a quicker route to Asia, he launched a process of discovery that was eventually to bring the disparate regions of the world into closer contact, to form the global map we know today. The largest political entity in the world at that time was the Chinese Ming Empire. Culturally, the Islamic faith had forged a bond of religious unity which extended in a broad swath from Southeast Asia to the Atlantic coast of North Africa. Europe was a mêlée of rival monarchies; sub-Saharan Africa a patchwork of trading kingdoms; the Americas, a separate world of rich tribal cultures, with empires established only in Central America and the central Andes.

GLOBAL STATES AND TERRITORIES

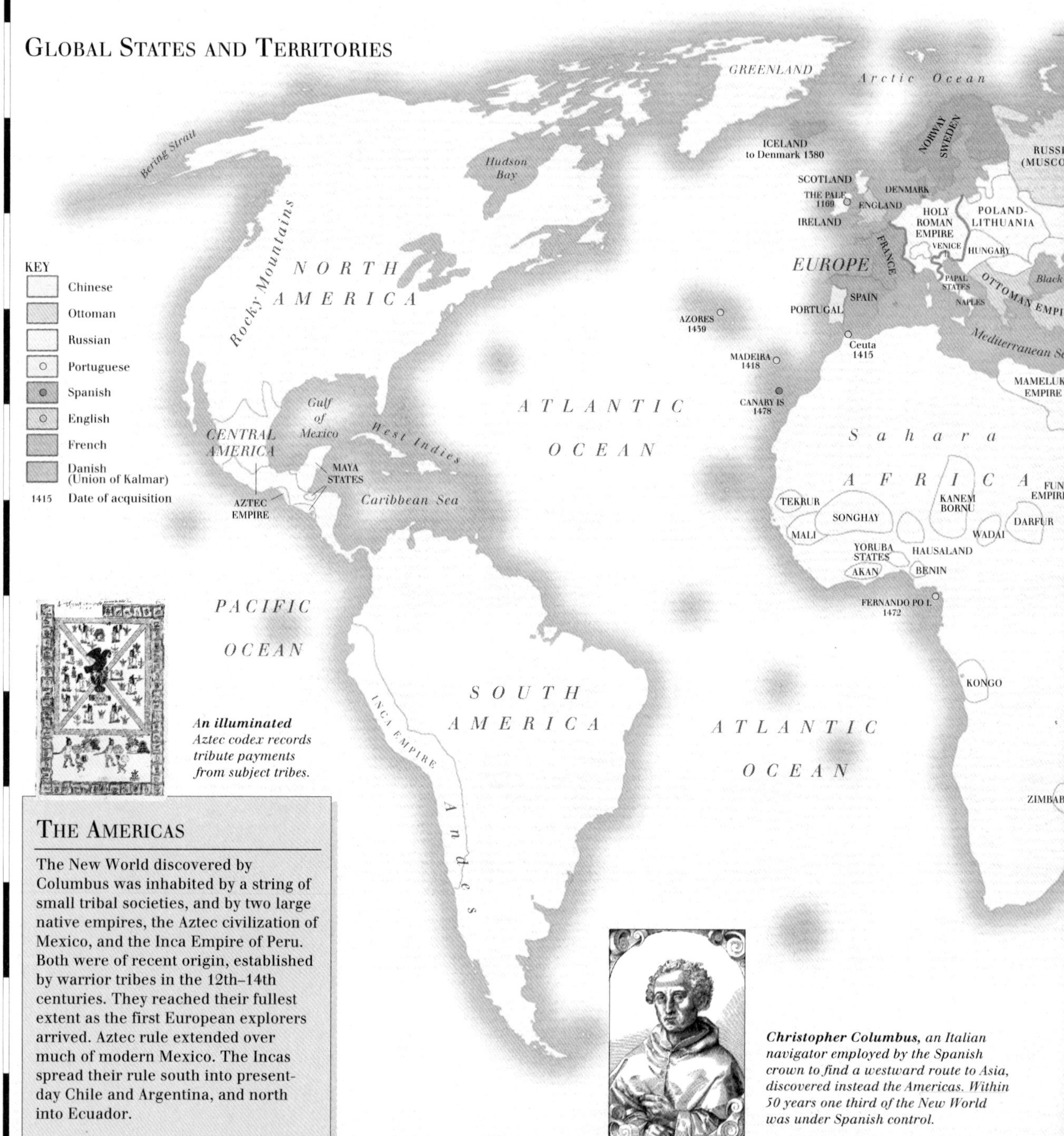

An illuminated Aztec codex records tribute payments from subject tribes.

Christopher Columbus, an Italian navigator employed by the Spanish crown to find a westward route to Asia, discovered instead the Americas. Within 50 years one third of the New World was under Spanish control.

THE AMERICAS

The New World discovered by Columbus was inhabited by a string of small tribal societies, and by two large native empires, the Aztec civilization of Mexico, and the Inca Empire of Peru. Both were of recent origin, established by warrior tribes in the 12th–14th centuries. They reached their fullest extent as the first European explorers arrived. Aztec rule extended over much of modern Mexico. The Incas spread their rule south into present-day Chile and Argentina, and north into Ecuador.

Europe

Although Christian Europe later transformed the exploration and settlement of the world, the Europe from which Columbus sailed was an unstable, violent continent, threatened by invaders from Asia to the east, and from the Ottoman Empire to the south. Civil wars and dynastic conflict resulted in shifting frontiers and small, militarily weak states. Only France, united by the late 15th century, Spain, a single monarchy from the 1490s, Portugal and England were close to their modern forms.

The Portuguese caravel, *buoyant, sturdy and lateen-rigged, was an ideal ocean-going vessel.*

East Asia

The most powerful state in the world in 1492 was Ming China. Set up in 1386 after the collapse of Mongol power, the Ming dynasty ruled an area from Manchuria in the north to the borders of Vietnam in the south. Based on a traditional structure of bureaucratic control, the Ming emperors controlled their vast empire from Peking (Beijing), from where they launched punitive wars against the Mongols and Japanese pirates along the coast. Chinese culture and trade spread throughout East and Southeast Asia, and Chinese navigators reached the Red Sea and the East African coast.

Chinese junks *plied the China seas, and traded as far as the East Indies, Ceylon and East Africa.*

Oceania

The ethnic, political and religious map of Southeast Asia was largely in place by the late 15th century. The largest state was the vast Srivijayan Hindu-Buddhist Empire, which spanned the East Indian archipelago. Muslim traders were already incorporating this rich region into an Indian Ocean trading empire. Farther east, the scattered island groups of the Pacific were being successively colonized by waves of Melanesian colonists.

The outrigger canoe *was the vehicle of Pacific colonization.*

Arab dhows *built a trading network around the Indian Ocean.*

Middle East and Africa

After centuries of invasion from the Christian West and Asian nomadic empires, the Middle Eastern world stabilized around a revival of the Ottoman Empire. Vassal states extended across North Africa to Morocco, which linked the trading kingdoms of sub-Saharan Africa with the markets of Asia. The great cities of the Middle East surpassed those of Europe in wealth and learning.

The magnetic compass, *in use since the 13th century, was a primary navigational tool for the first ocean-going explorers, although early compasses were not always reliable, and ships often went astray. Accurate navigation only came later with the invention of the chronometer.*

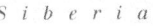

THE AGE OF DISCOVERY: 1492-1648

THE FIRST STATE to take advantage of the new age of exploration was Spain. By the middle of the 16th century, under the Emperor Charles V, Spain was established as the foremost European colonial power, and one of the richest and most powerful kingdoms in Europe. Spanish rule was extended over the whole of Central America, much of South America, Florida and the Caribbean; in Asia, Spanish rule was established in the Philippines. Spain led the way in establishing European settler colonies overseas. By the middle of the 17th century, British, Dutch and French colonists began to challenge Spanish dominance in the Americas and East Asia, while pirates around the world plundered Spain's wealthy merchant convoys.

GLOBAL STATES AND TERRITORIES

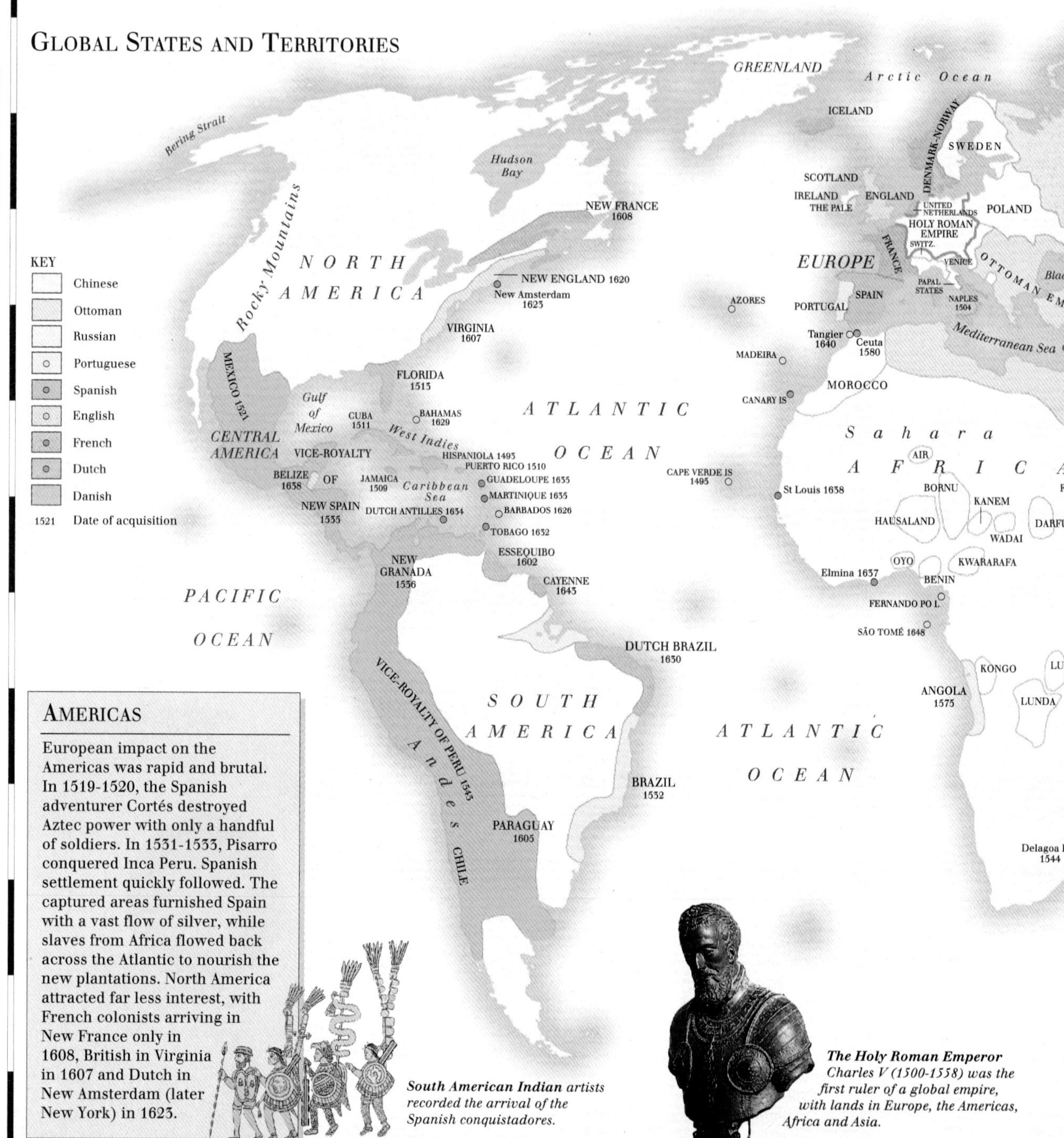

AMERICAS

European impact on the Americas was rapid and brutal. In 1519-1520, the Spanish adventurer Cortés destroyed Aztec power with only a handful of soldiers. In 1531-1533, Pisarro conquered Inca Peru. Spanish settlement quickly followed. The captured areas furnished Spain with a vast flow of silver, while slaves from Africa flowed back across the Atlantic to nourish the new plantations. North America attracted far less interest, with French colonists arriving in New France only in 1608, British in Virginia in 1607 and Dutch in New Amsterdam (later New York) in 1623.

***South American Indian** artists recorded the arrival of the Spanish conquistadores.*

***The Holy Roman Emperor** Charles V (1500-1558) was the first ruler of a global empire, with lands in Europe, the Americas, Africa and Asia.*

EUROPE

For more than a century after Martin Luther inspired the Protestant Reformation in the 1520s, Europe was torn by religious wars. Scandinavia, England and Scotland adopted the new church, but elsewhere bitter civil conflicts led to the prolonged warfare and persecution known as the Thirty Years' War. This ended in 1648; it destroyed wide areas of Central Europe and decimated the German population, but resulted in a religious settlement which carried down to the 20th century. The Dutch Republic and northern Germany became Protestant while southern Germany, Poland and southwest Europe remained Catholic.

***Printing**, using movable type, was a key development in the dissemination of ideas, knowledge and commerce in early modern Europe.*

ASIA

In 1480, the small principality of Muscovy (Moscow) threw off Mongol control, and proceeded to expand Muscovite power over the whole of the area from the Arctic Ocean to the Caspian Sea. In the 1550s, the conquest of Kazan brought Russian power to the Urals, and over the next century it spread across Siberia reaching the Pacific coast by 1649. Much of the area remained uninhabited, but to the south this new empire jostled uneasily with a string of Central Asian Muslim khanates, and with the newly established Manchurian Ch'ing dynasty, which wrested control of China from the Ming in 1644.

***European navigators** and surveyors produced accurate maps and charts of their voyages.*

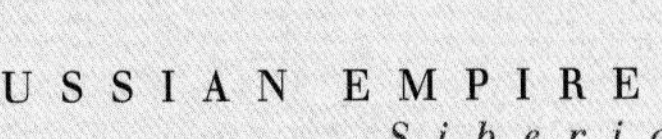

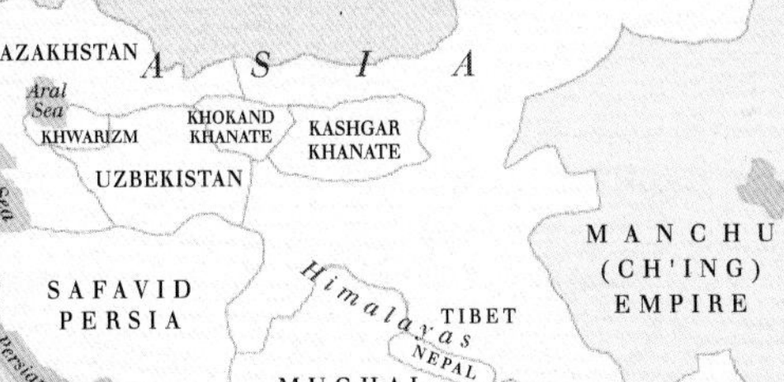

***The Indian Mughal** ruler Shahjahan (1592-1648), builder of the Taj Mahal.*

SOUTH ASIA AND OCEANIA

The Portuguese and the Spanish were the first European powers to open trade with the powerful Asian states of Mughal India and Ch'ing China, the Spanish opening trans-Pacific routes between Central America, the Philippines and China. But the establishment of the Dutch and British East India companies in the early 17th century announced the advent of two new maritime powers.

***West African** trading kingdoms produced artefacts such as this bronze Portuguese soldier from Benin.*

AFRICA AND THE MIDDLE EAST

While Europe was divided by the Reformation, Islam experienced a remarkable resurgence in the 16th century. The revival of the Ottoman Empire brought Islamic rule over much of southeast Europe. Islam spread along trade routes to sub-Saharan Africa. In east Africa, it spread south along the coast. Further east, Muslim rulers established new imperial states in Persia (Iran) and India.

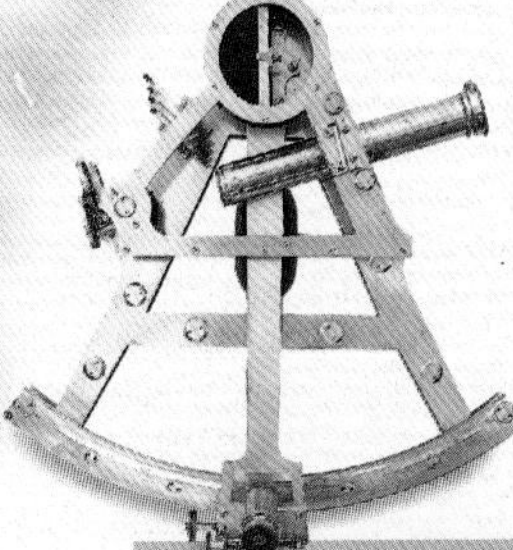

***The sextant** allowed navigators to take accurate measurements of heavenly bodies in relation to the horizon, thus allowing latitude to be calculated correctly. Early sextants had to be hand-held and were often used on shore rather than on board ship.*

The Age of Expansion: 1648-1789

THE YEARS FROM the middle of the 17th century to the end of the 18th century saw a massive consolidation of European discovery and exploration, which took the form of colonial settlement and political expansion. This period also witnessed the beginning of a sharp rise in European population and in its economic strength, accompanied by rapid developments in the arts and sciences. All these factors powered European expansion – a process that would bring European culture to every part of the globe, gradually filling in the world map, and bringing it into often fatal contact with less robust indigenous cultures. By the last quarter of the 18th century, with Europe poised on the brink of political turmoil, only Africa and Australasia remained largely unmolested by European attentions.

Global States and Territories

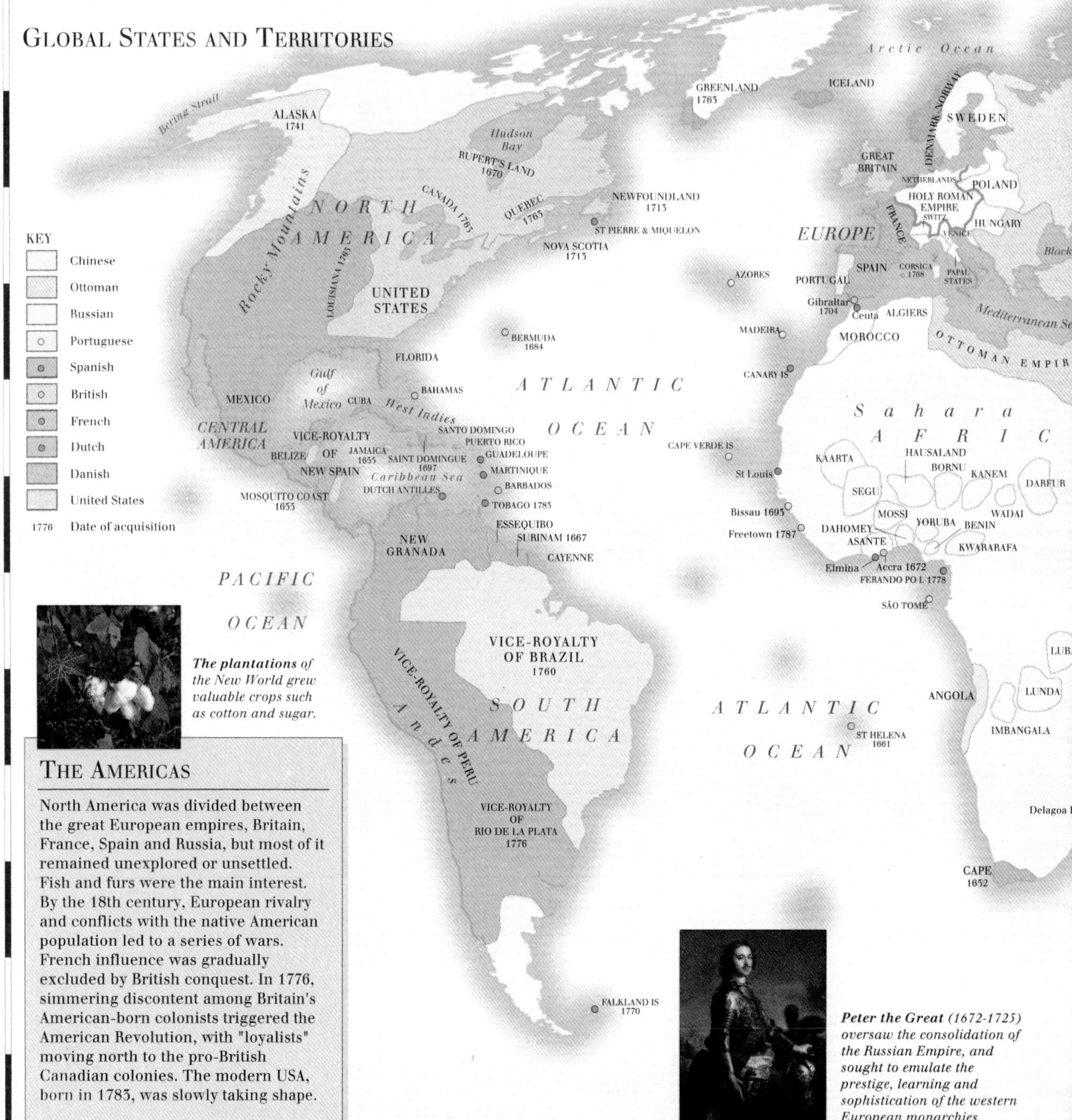

***The plantations** of the New World grew valuable crops such as cotton and sugar.*

The Americas

North America was divided between the great European empires, Britain, France, Spain and Russia, but most of it remained unexplored or unsettled. Fish and furs were the main interest. By the 18th century, European rivalry and conflicts with the native American population led to a series of wars. French influence was gradually excluded by British conquest. In 1776, simmering discontent among Britain's American-born colonists triggered the American Revolution, with "loyalists" moving north to the pro-British Canadian colonies. The modern USA, born in 1783, was slowly taking shape.

***Peter the Great** (1672-1725) oversaw the consolidation of the Russian Empire, and sought to emulate the prestige, learning and sophistication of the western European monarchies.*

EUROPE

After the crisis of the Thirty Years' War, Europe began to develop a more settled state system as successful dynastic houses imposed more centralized rule. The Habsburgs acquired control over Hungary and much of Central Europe. Russia's frontiers pushed into Poland and Ukraine. The French Bourbon monarchy became the most powerful in Europe. Its material wealth and culture made it a rival to the older empires of Asia. French became the common language of educated Europeans and French philosophy led to the intellectual "enlightenment."

Isaac Newton *(1642-1727), the leading scientist of Europe's Age of Reason.*

ASIA

The Ch'ing Dynasty forged the shape of modern China. By 1658 the whole of southern China was under Manchu control. Formosa (Taiwan) was occupied in 1683, outer Mongolia in 1697. A protectorate was established over Tibet in 1751. Over the course of this expansion, the population of China trebled and the economy boomed through trade in tea, porcelain and silk with Russia and the West. Manchu China was powerful enough to resist incursions by the European empires, avoiding the fate of the crumbling Mughal Empire in India, where Britain and France competed for trade and territory.

Dutch and British *East Indiamen carried the vast European trade with Asia.*

Maori New Zealand *was one of the few indigenous cultures to remain untouched by European contact until the 19th century.*

OCEANIA

Southeast Asia and Oceania was an area of small, warring kingdoms, increasingly prey to the ambitions of European traders, first Spanish and Portuguese, then Dutch and British. Yet, by the late 18th century, there was still little formal colonization. Though first discovered by Tasman in 1692, most of Australasia was still unexplored and unsettled, except for a number of small penal colonies set up by the British in New South Wales (1788) and Tasmania (1804).

African slavers *marched their human cargo from the interior to the coast for transshipment.*

AFRICA

During the 17th and 18th centuries Africa was regarded by the rest of the world as a source of two things: gold and slaves. Some 13.5 million slaves were shipped in the 1700s, from the west coast and from Portuguese Angola. African dealers sold to European middlemen, who in turn sold on the surviving slaves. In northern and northeastern Africa, Arab slavers traded with the Ottoman Empire. But the rest of Africa remained isolated from the outside world.

Harrison's chronometer, *invented in 1762, allowed navigators to measure time accurately, and thus calculate longitude correctly. This greatly reduced the risk of shipwreck and heralded the beginning of accurate mapping of the world.*

The Age of Revolution: 1789-1830

In 1789 ROYAL POWER was shattered by the French Revolution. The collapse of the most powerful monarchy in Europe reverberated worldwide. The revolutions in France and America ushered in the idea of the modern nation state, and of popular representative government. Revolutionary outbreaks occurred elsewhere in Europe, and overseas colonies in Latin America won their independence. At the same time, an industrial revolution was taking place in Europe, transforming the old trading economy into a manufacturing base which would require a global supply of raw materials and a global market to fuel it. The revolutionary years thus marked the beginning of the modern political and economic world order.

Global States and Territories

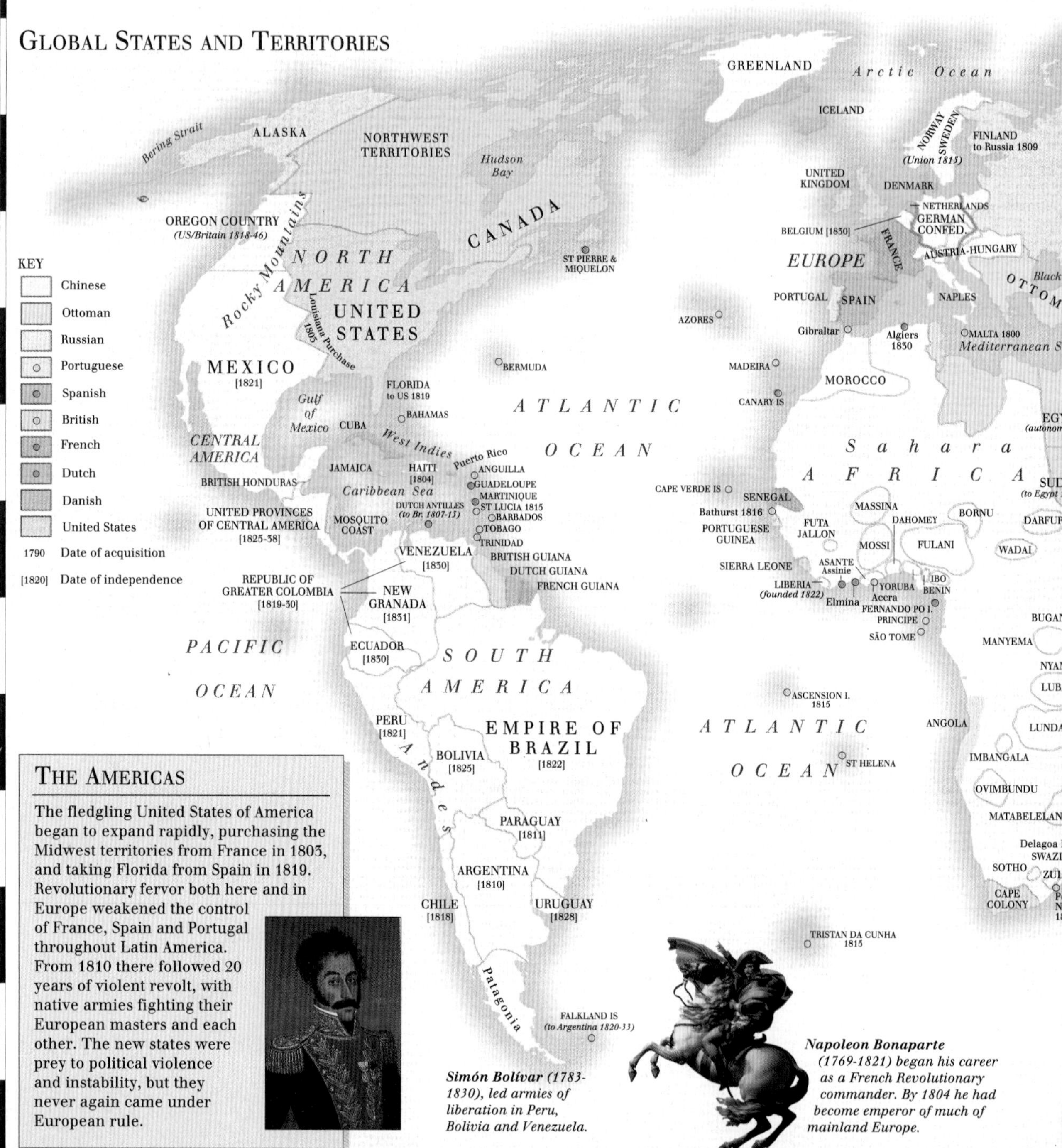

The Americas

The fledgling United States of America began to expand rapidly, purchasing the Midwest territories from France in 1803, and taking Florida from Spain in 1819. Revolutionary fervor both here and in Europe weakened the control of France, Spain and Portugal throughout Latin America. From 1810 there followed 20 years of violent revolt, with native armies fighting their European masters and each other. The new states were prey to political violence and instability, but they never again came under European rule.

Simón Bolívar (1783-1830), led armies of liberation in Peru, Bolivia and Venezuela.

Napoleon Bonaparte (1769-1821) began his career as a French Revolutionary commander. By 1804 he had become emperor of much of mainland Europe.

EUROPE

Under the Revolutionary general, Napoleon Bonaparte, France conquered a large part of Europe and destroyed the old feudal order. Napoleon helped to shape the new nation states that emerged in 19th-century Europe – Belgium, Italy and Germany. He gave much of Europe its modern legal code and systems of education and local government.

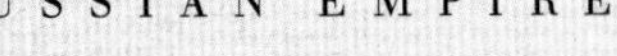

***Steam-powered engines** transformed the European industrial economy.*

ASIA

The principal colonial power in Asia was Russia, whose consolidation of its empire in northern and central Asia continued throughout the 19th century. But now the Dutch began to extend their control of the East Indies, while a bitter struggle between the British and the French was conducted in and around the Indian Ocean. France was gradually forced to concede many of its footholds in India, where the British East India Company rapidly extended its interests by a mixture of diplomacy and military force. But the elusive key to Asia's largest markets remained the slumbering giant of Ch'ing China, whose Manchu rulers, like those of Japan, remained unimpressed by European overtures.

***The spices of the East Indies,** such as pepper, were among the most highly valued traded commodities from Asia.*

***James Cook** (1728-1779) charted much of the Pacific between 1768 and 1779.*

OCEANIA

Although Portuguese and Dutch explorers had confirmed the existence of Australasia in the 16th and 17th centuries, it was not until the voyages of Captain Cook in the 1770s that the geography of the Pacific was established, and the fertile eastern coast of Australia was explored and charted. Over the next 30 years, coastal settlements were established; by 1829, Britain had brought the whole continent under the British flag.

***The first European** migrants to Africa settled in Cape Colony.*

AFRICA

The northern regions of Africa were part of the vast Islamic Ottoman Empire; from here Islam spread south to West Africa and the Horn of Africa. Holy wars (or *jihads*) late in the 18th and early 19th centuries completed the conversion to Islam of much of Saharan and sub-Saharan Africa. In the south, large tribal kingdoms flourished, in the Congo basin, Zimbabwe and southern Africa.

***The development** during the European industrial revolution of mechanized manufacturing plant and machinery, such as power looms, gave Europe effective control of a booming global trade in raw materials and mass-manufactured commodities.*

The Age of Empire: 1830-1914

THE NINETEENTH CENTURY was dominated by the spread of modern industry and transportation, and the expansion of European trade and influence worldwide. Industry made Europe rich and powerful; its capital cities were monuments to the self-confidence of the new European age. Railroads and steamships revolutionized communications, bringing a stream of industrial goods, technical know-how, and European settlers across America, Africa and Asia. Modern industry and weapons brought Europe to the summit of global influence. In these developments lay the origins of the division of the world into rich and poor regions; a developed, prosperous north, an under-developed, dependent south.

Global States and Territories

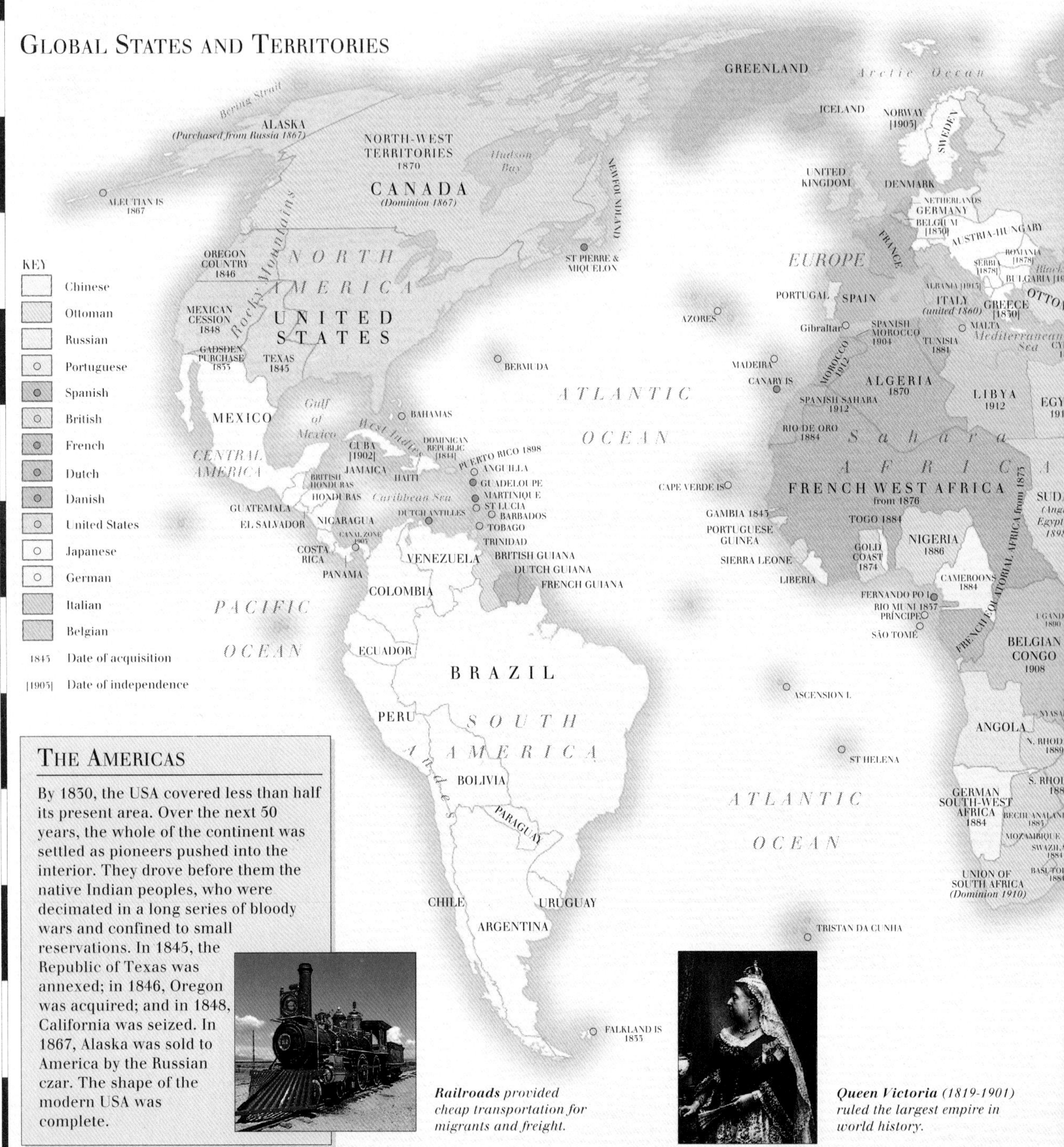

The Americas

By 1830, the USA covered less than half its present area. Over the next 50 years, the whole of the continent was settled as pioneers pushed into the interior. They drove before them the native Indian peoples, who were decimated in a long series of bloody wars and confined to small reservations. In 1845, the Republic of Texas was annexed; in 1846, Oregon was acquired; and in 1848, California was seized. In 1867, Alaska was sold to America by the Russian czar. The shape of the modern USA was complete.

***Railroads** provided cheap transportation for migrants and freight.*

***Queen Victoria** (1819-1901) ruled the largest empire in world history.*

EUROPE

In the 19th century, Europe was transformed into an industrial economy. In the new industrial cities, pressure developed for liberal reforms and parliamentary politics. Nationalists created new states in Germany, Italy, Greece, Serbia and Belgium. While the modern map of Europe gradually began to take shape, European imperialists brought still further areas of the world under their control.

Sailing ships *carried most oceanic trade until 1900.*

ASIA

Building on colonial interests that stretched back into the 18th century, Britain and France transformed the political world of South Asia. Britain extended its rule in India and, in 1885, Burma was brought under British control. The Vietnamese and Chinese Empires were pressured by Europeans anxious to trade and to spread Christianity: the Ch'ing Empire conceded areas of influence; the Vietnamese Empire resisted and was brought by force under French domination. By the 1890s the whole of southern Asia except for Siam was dominated by Europe, which created the modern state structure of the region.

The Japanese emperor *Mutsuhito (1852-1912) opened Japan to Western trade and influence.*

The colonization *of Australia and New Zealand was based on sheep farming.*

OCEANIA

During the 19th century, Australia and New Zealand remained closely tied to the British homeland. British settlers came to farm and later to prospect for gold and other valuable minerals. In 1840, New Zealand came under British rule and the native Maoris were forced off the land. Not until 1872 was the continent of Australia traversed, and not until 1901 was a single state, the Commonwealth of Australia, proclaimed.

Quinine *– the cure for malaria.*

New medicines *made the colonization of Africa possible.*

AFRICA

The political structure of independent Africa was torn up by encroaching European empires. As native societies reacted violently to European intrusion, so European military and political power was increased to secure European interests. In 1884, in Berlin, the European powers divided Africa between them. The "Partition of Africa" established many states' modern frontiers.

The European *imperial powers maintained control of their often far-flung colonies by military superiority. Native forces were rarely a match for the large, highly trained armies, powerful navies and technically advanced weaponry which the Europeans had at their disposal.*

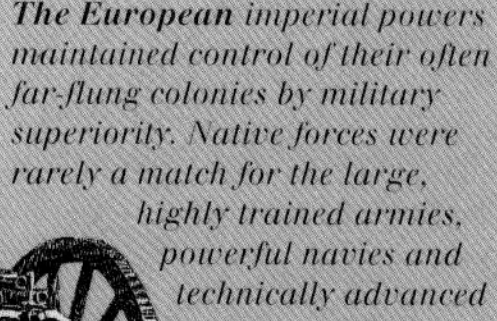

The first machine *gun, invented by Gatling in 1862.*

The Age of Global War: 1914-1945

IN 1914, IMPERIAL AND MILITARY rivalry in Europe provoked the first of two world wars, the largest and most destructive wars in human history. At the end of the first war, in 1918, the old international order was dead. The Russian Empire collapsed in revolution and was transformed by a communist minority into the Soviet Union. The German, Habsburg and Ottoman Empires were dismembered. A fragile peace ensued but the old equilibrium was gone. The rise of strident nationalism in Germany, Japan and Italy destroyed the peace once again in 1939. The second war cost the lives of 50 million people and ravaged Europe and Asia. At its end, in 1945, the USA and the Soviet Union had emerged as the new superpowers.

Global States and Territories

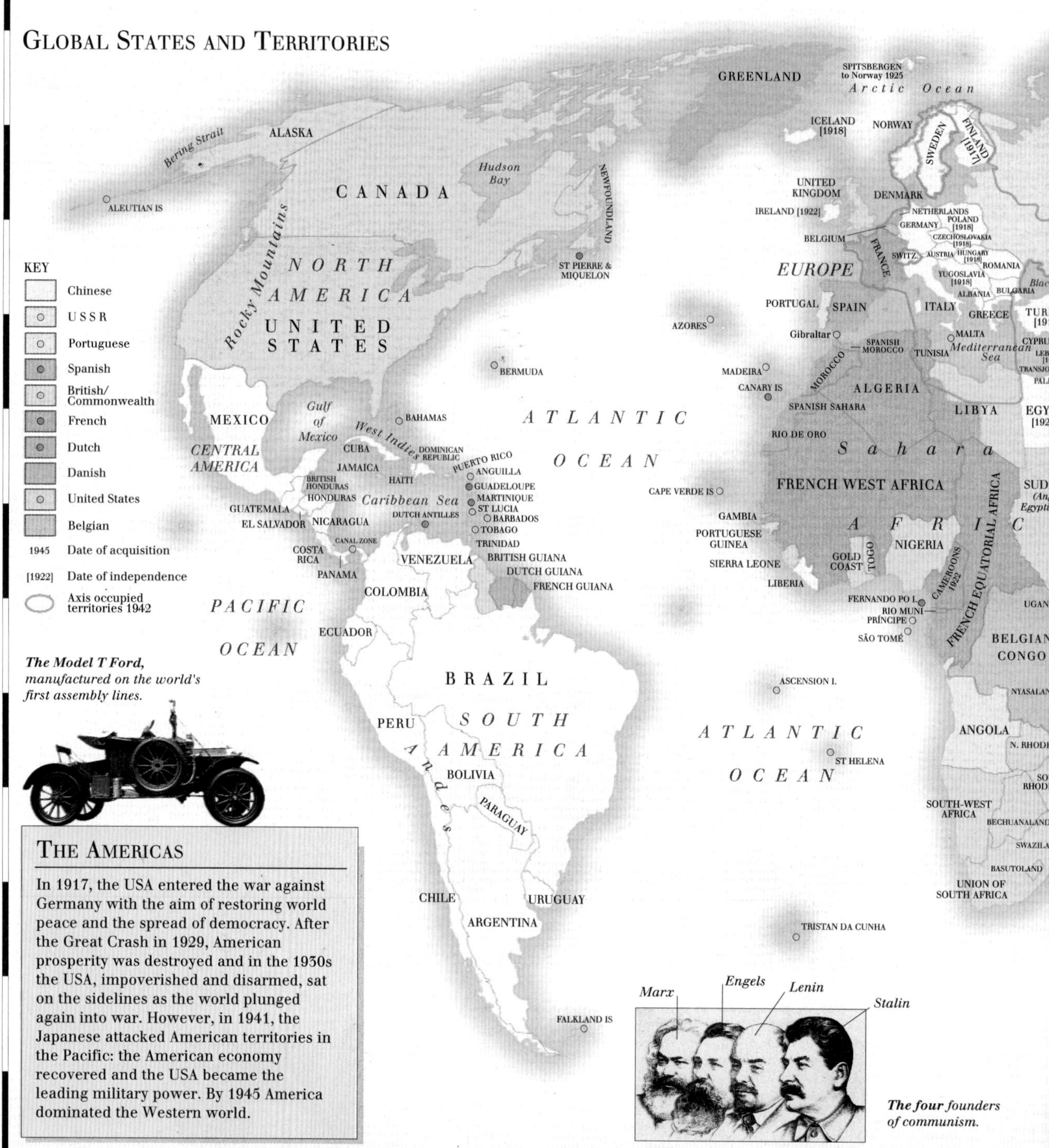

The Model T Ford, manufactured on the world's first assembly lines.

The Americas

In 1917, the USA entered the war against Germany with the aim of restoring world peace and the spread of democracy. After the Great Crash in 1929, American prosperity was destroyed and in the 1930s the USA, impoverished and disarmed, sat on the sidelines as the world plunged again into war. However, in 1941, the Japanese attacked American territories in the Pacific: the American economy recovered and the USA became the leading military power. By 1945 America dominated the Western world.

The four founders of communism.

Europe

Both world wars had their origins in Europe. In 1914 Britain, France and Russia combined to defeat Germany, with US help. In 1918 new nation states were established in Eastern Europe. But, by 1939, revived German nationalism started a second world war; much of Western Europe came under a German "New Order" until the Soviet Union, Britain and the USA developed sufficient military strength to reconquer Europe and defeat Germany.

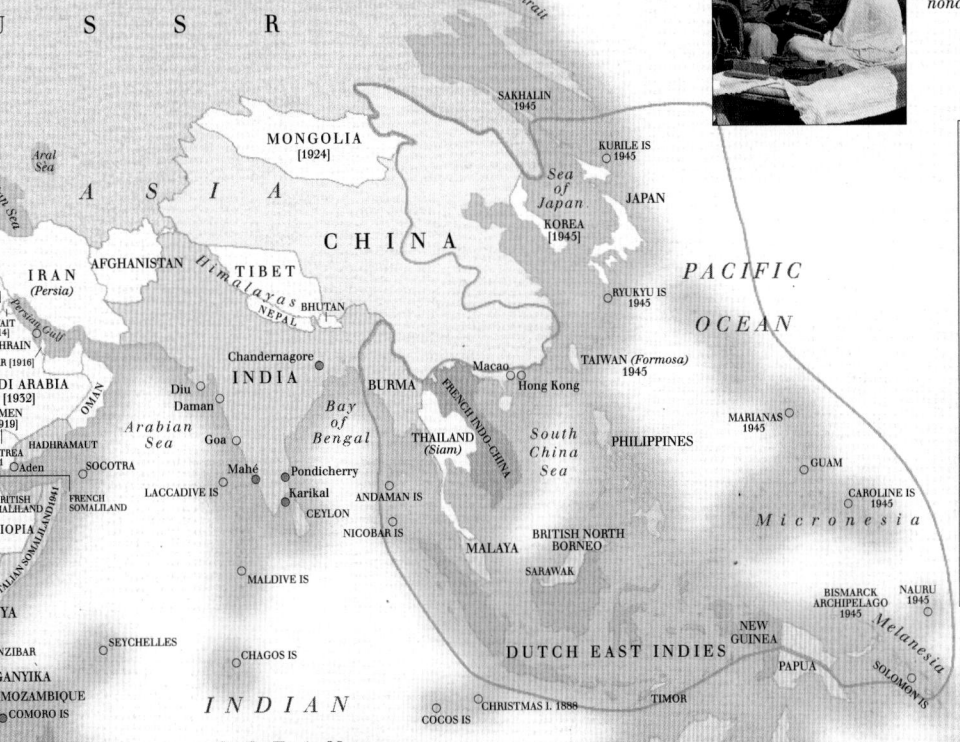

World War II *was decided by mechanical and industrial superiority.*

Asia

The collapse of the Chinese Empire in 1911, followed in 1917 by the disappearance of the Russian Empire, produced instability across Asia. Full-scale war broke out between Japan and China in 1937, with Japan trying to conquer China. The Soviet Union was the victim of German aggression from 1941. Both Japan and Germany were held at bay by communist forces, which eventually succeeded in imposing stable politics on Asia. By 1945, the Soviet Union had reconquered its lost territories and dominated Eastern Europe. In China, communist armies filled the vacuum left by the Japanese defeat.

Mahatma Gandhi *(1869-1948) led India to independence through peaceful noncooperation and protest.*

U S S R

Bering Strait

SAKHALIN 1945

MONGOLIA [1924]

KURILE IS 1945

Aral Sea

A S I A

Sea of Japan

JAPAN

CHINA

KOREA [1945]

IRAN (Persia)

AFGHANISTAN

Himalayas

TIBET

BHUTAN

NEPAL

PACIFIC OCEAN

RYUKYU IS 1945

KUWAIT [1914]

BAHRAIN

Persian Gulf

AUDI ARABIA [1932]

YEMEN [1919]

OMAN

Chandernagore

INDIA

Diu

Daman

Arabian Sea

Goa

Bay of Bengal

BURMA

Macao

Hong Kong

TAIWAN (Formosa) 1945

FRENCH INDO-CHINA

THAILAND (Siam)

South China Sea

PHILIPPINES

MARIANAS 1945

HADHRAMAUT

ERITREA

Aden

SOCOTRA

Mahé

Pondicherry

Karikal

LACCADIVE IS

ANDAMAN IS

CEYLON

NICOBAR IS

GUAM

CAROLINE IS 1945

Micronesia

BRITISH SOMALILAND

FRENCH SOMALILAND

ITALIAN SOMALILAND 1941

THIOPIA

MALAYA

BRITISH NORTH BORNEO

SARAWAK

MALDIVE IS

ENYA

BISMARCK ARCHIPELAGO 1945

NAURU 1945

Melanesia

NEW GUINEA

PAPUA

SOLOMON IS

ZANZIBAR

SEYCHELLES

CHAGOS IS

DUTCH EAST INDIES

NGANYIKA

MOZAMBIQUE

COMORO IS

INDIAN OCEAN

COCOS IS

CHRISTMAS I. 1888

TIMOR

MADAGASCAR

MAURITIUS

RÉUNION

NEW CALEDONIA

AUSTRALIA (Dominion 1926)

LORD HOWE I.

NEW ZEALAND

CHATHAM IS

TASMANIA

AUCKLAND IS

MACQUARIE IS

Oceania

For the only time in its history, Australia was faced with the very real prospect of invasion. In World War II, Japanese armies reached the island of New Guinea, and bombed towns in northern Australia. Japanese submarines attacked Sydney Harbour. The Battle of the Coral Sea, in May 1942, saved Australia, but it took almost three years to clear Japanese forces from the South Pacific, where they hung on grimly to the rich oil and mineral resources they had captured.

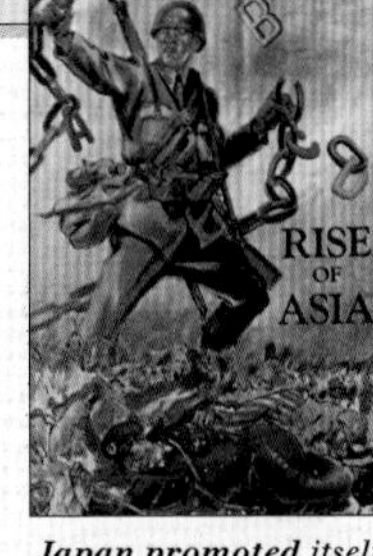

Japan promoted *itself as the liberator of Asia from the chains of European colonialism.*

Haile Selassie *(1892-1975), ruler of Ethiopia, the only independent empire in Africa.*

Middle East

In 1918, the Turkish Empire disappeared after 400 years of Ottoman rule. The modern map of North Africa and the Middle East was carved out of its ruins by the victors of World War I. After World War II, the foundation was laid for a new state of Israel, following the genocide of Europe's Jews by Nazi Germany. This led to conflict between native Arabs and Jewish immigrants.

The conquest *of the air was the most important technological achievement of the period. It added a devastating dimension to warfare, in the form of bombing, while transforming civil transportation.*

A German Zeppelin *airship of the 1930s.*

THE MODERN AGE: 1945-1994

THE WARTIME ALLIANCE between the USA and the Soviet Union turned sour in efforts to reconstruct Europe and the Far East. The world became divided into two hostile camps; liberal-capitalism on the one hand, communism on the other. The two sides fought a "Cold War," each trying to contain and subvert the other. The main conflicts of the war occurred over small issues – Korea (1950-1953), Cuba (1962), Vietnam (1954-1975). Larger wars were avoided because of the nuclear deterrent. With the crumbling of communist power in Russia and Eastern Europe, the stalemate of the Cold War was replaced by a less stable international order, dominated by economic uncertainty and revived nationalism.

GLOBAL STATES AND TERRITORIES

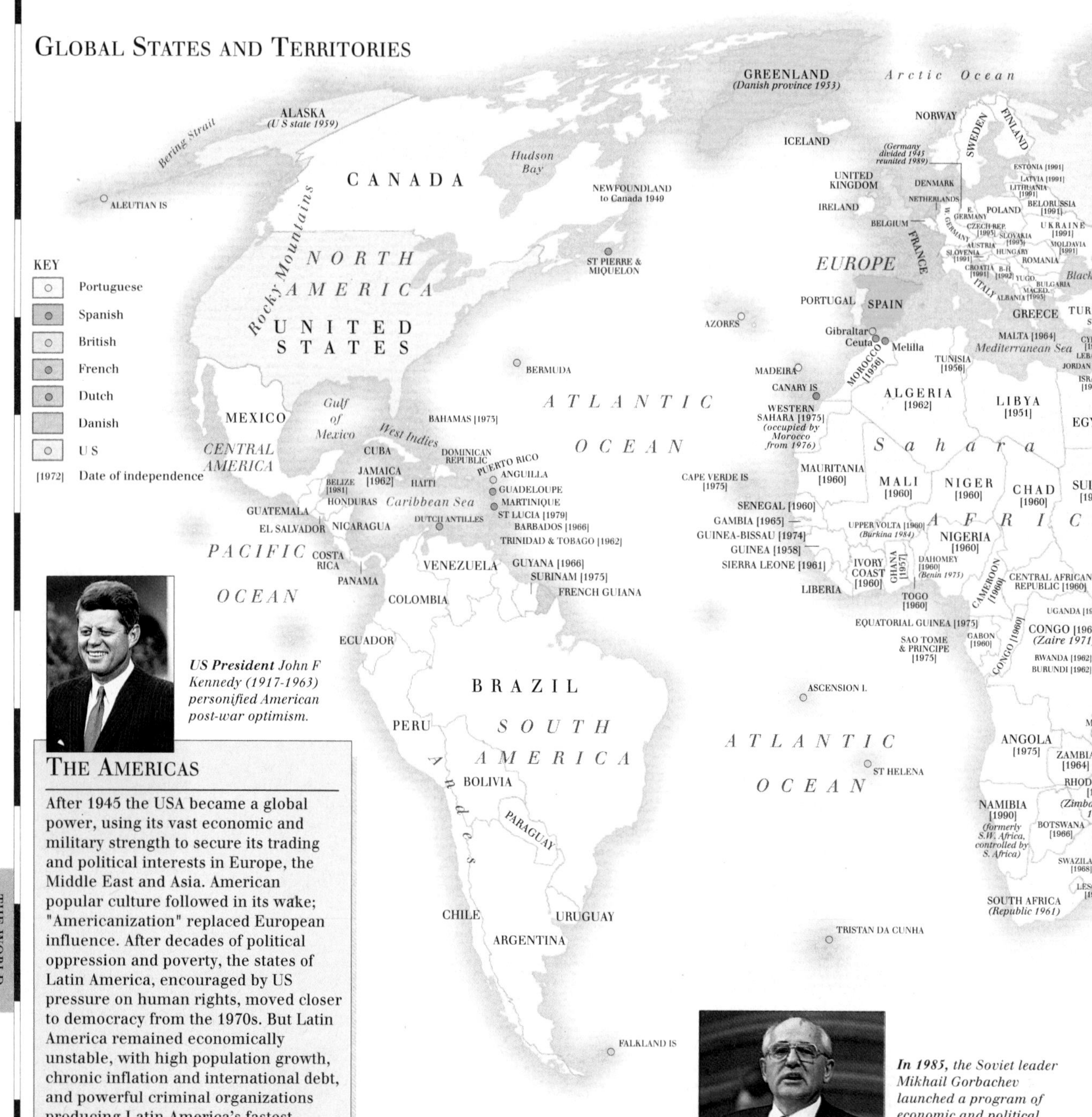

US President John F Kennedy (1917-1963) personified American post-war optimism.

THE AMERICAS

After 1945 the USA became a global power, using its vast economic and military strength to secure its trading and political interests in Europe, the Middle East and Asia. American popular culture followed in its wake; "Americanization" replaced European influence. After decades of political oppression and poverty, the states of Latin America, encouraged by US pressure on human rights, moved closer to democracy from the 1970s. But Latin America remained economically unstable, with high population growth, chronic inflation and international debt, and powerful criminal organizations producing Latin America's fastest growing export, drugs.

In 1985, the Soviet leader Mikhail Gorbachev launched a program of economic and political reforms, which brought Soviet communism to an end.

***The Berlin Wall**, symbol of the Cold War division of Europe, was demolished in 1989.*

EUROPE

In 1945, Europe lay in ruins, but during the next 30 years, Western Europe experienced a long economic boom, restoring widespread prosperity and political stability. It progressed toward economic and political unity under the EC. In Eastern Europe development was overshadowed by Soviet communism until its collapse. As democracies many new nations now face an uncertain future.

ASIA

In southern Asia, popular nationalist movements came to power in India, Burma, Malaya and Indonesia; in China and Indochina, power passed to native communist movements whose roots went back to the 1920s. After 1949, China under Mao Zedong became, with its vast population and large military forces, a second communist superpower. But the success story of modern Asia has been Japan. Defeated in 1945, its economy and cities laid waste by bombing, Japan began a program of economic rebuilding with American aid. By the 1980s, Japan had emerged as one of the world's largest manufacturing economies.

***Chinese communism,** based on the mobilization of peasants and workers, has nevertheless recognized the need for economic reforms.*

RUSSIAN FEDERATION

Bering Strait

KAZAKHSTAN [1991]
Aral Sea
ASIA
MONGOLIA
UZBEKISTAN [1991]
KYRGYZSTAN [1991]
TURKMENISTAN [1991]
TAJIKISTAN [1991]
CHINA
N. KOREA [1953]
Sea of Japan
JAPAN
SOUTH KOREA
IRAN
AFGHANISTAN
Himalayas
TIBET (to China 1950)
BHUTAN
NEPAL
PAKISTAN [1947]
Persian Gulf
RYUKYU IS (to Japan)
BAHRAIN [1971]
QATAR
UNITED ARAB EMIRATES (formed 1971)
SAUDI ARABIA
OMAN
ERITREA [1993]
NORTH YEMEN [1967]
SOUTH YEMEN
(Yemen united 1990)
DJIBOUTI [1977]
ETHIOPIA
SOMALIA [1960]
BANGLADESH [1971] (formerly E. Pakistan)
INDIA [1947]
Arabian Sea
Bay of Bengal
BURMA [1948]
Macao
NORTH VIETNAM [1954]
Hong Kong
LAOS [1954]
(Vietnam united 1976)
TAIWAN [1949]
THAILAND
South China Sea
PHILIPPINES [1946]
PACIFIC OCEAN
MARIANAS
GUAM
SOCOTRA (to S. Yemen)
LACCADIVE IS (to India)
ANDAMAN IS (to India)
CAMBODIA [1954]
SOUTH VIETNAM [1954]
NICOBAR IS (to India)
CEYLON [1948] (Sri Lanka 1972)
MALDIVE IS [1965]
MALAYA [1957]
BRUNEI [1984]
MALAYSIA (formed 1963)
SINGAPORE [1965]
MICRONESIA [1991]
KENYA [1963]
SEYCHELLES [1976]
CHAGOS IS
INDONESIA [1949]
BISMARCK ARCHIPELAGO (to P N G)
NAURU [1968]
PAPUA NEW GUINEA [1975]
Melanesia
SOLOMON IS [1978]
TANZANIA [1964]
COMOROS [1975]
MOZAMBIQUE
INDIAN OCEAN
COCOS IS (to Australia)
CHRISTMAS I. (to Australia)
E. TIMOR (to Indonesia)
MADAGASCAR [1960]
RÉUNION
MAURITIUS [1968]
NEW CALEDONIA
AUSTRALIA
LORD HOWE I. (to Australia)
NEW ZEALAND
CHATHAM IS (to N Z)
AUCKLAND IS (to N Z)
MACQUARIE IS (to Australia)

***A treaty** banning the testing of nuclear bombs in the Pacific was signed in 1986.*

OCEANIA

The post-war economies of Japan, USA and Australia had by the 1990s created a new industrial and trading network around the Pacific Rim. Cheap labor and low overheads drew younger states – South Korea, Taiwan, Singapore, Indonesia – into the system and much of the world's manufacturing is now concentrated there, creating a consequent shift in the balance of the global economy.

***Gamal Abdel Nasser** (1918-1970) of Egypt, galvanized the Arab states to resist the West.*

AFRICA AND THE MIDDLE EAST

The colonial powers, weakened by war, faced an irresistible wave of demands for self-determination. Between 1958 and 1975, 41 African countries gained independence, leaving only South Africa in white hands until 1994. In North Africa and throughout the Middle East, a new form of anti-imperialism emerged in the 1970s in the form of Islamic fundamentalism.

***From the 1950s** to the 1970s, superpower rivalry focused on space exploration. The Soviets put the first man in space in 1961, and the Americans landed on the moon in 1969. Since then, both manned and unmanned missions have become almost everyday events.*

2

The Nations of the World

The Nations of the World

• Afghanistan ~ Zimbabwe

Overseas Territories & Dependencies

AFGHANISTAN

ASIA

Turkmenistan Uzb. Tajikistan China AFGHANISTAN Iran Pakistan

Asia

OFFICIAL NAME: Islamic State of Afghanistan **CAPITAL:** Kābul
POPULATION: 16.5 million **CURRENCY:** Afghani **OFFICIAL LANGUAGES:** Persian and Pashtu

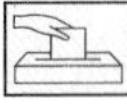

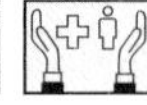

LANDLOCKED IN southwestern Asia, Afghanistan is surrounded by Iran, Pakistan, China, Tajikistan and Turkmenistan. Approximately three-quarters of its territory is inaccessible terrain. Afghanistan effectively has no government, other than a fragile power-sharing arrangement between *mujahideen* leaders, whose factions have been fighting each other since the departure of Soviet invasion forces in 1989. Agriculture is the main economic activity, but less than two-thirds of farmland is cultivated. Since the April 1992 handover of power to the *mujahideen*, women have returned to wearing veils in public.

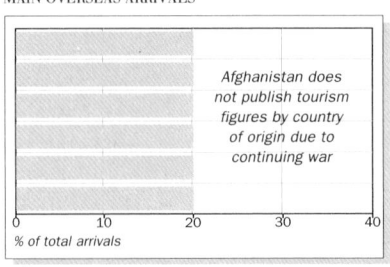

The Band-i-Amir River, *in the Hindu Kush. Afghanistan is mountainous and arid. Many Afghans are nomadic sheep farmers.*

CLIMATE

WEATHER CHART

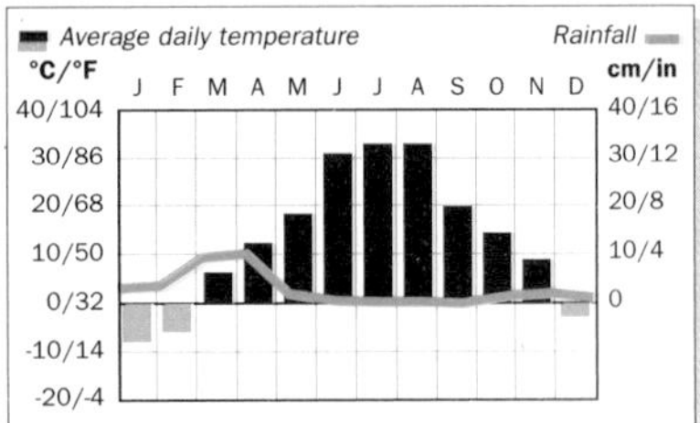

Afghanistan has a harsh continental climate and the severity of winter is accentuated by high altitudes. It has the widest temperature range in the world with lows of –58°F and highs of 127°F.

COMMUNICATIONS

Kābul International

Has no fleet

THE TRANSPORTATION NETWORK

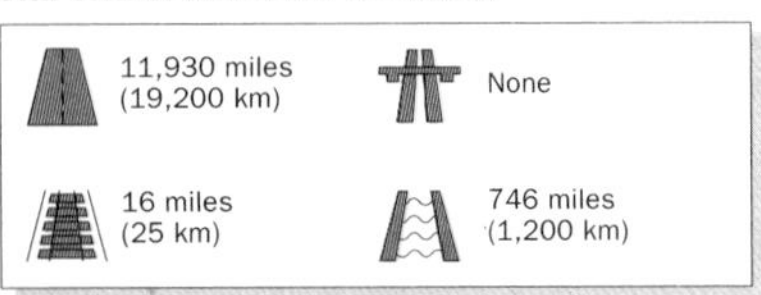

The repair and reconstruction of war-damaged roads and the provision of basic facilities to allow air traffic to function safely are the present priorities. Road rebuilding is usually carried out by local communities. However, neighboring Pakistan has undertaken to rebuild a number of key routes, including the Kābul–Torkam link, which will benefit its own trade with central Asia.

Obtaining and securing key supply routes is a crucial factor in intra-*mujahideen* feuding. The *Hezb-i-Islami* has recently increased its stranglehold on the main eastern artery out of Kābul, and is also seeking to control the Salang Highway, the northern route out of the capital. Much of Afghanistan's outlying territory is sown with land mines.

TOURISM

War zone. Very few tourists

No increase in past year

MAIN OVERSEAS ARRIVALS

Afghanistan does not publish tourism figures by country of origin due to continuing war

0 10 20 30 40

% of total arrivals

Afghanistan is a war zone. There are virtually no visitors apart from occasional UN and aid agency personnel, and journalists. Few hotels or restaurants are open in Kābul. Travel is extremely dangerous due to mines and bandit activity. *Air Ariana*, the Afghan national airline, no longer flies from Kābul, but instead from Dushanbe in neighboring Tajikistan.

The lack of a formal economy means that Afghanistan gets few visits from businessmen, and any expatriates who were previously in Kābul have left.

PEOPLE

Persian, Pashtu, Dari, Uzbek, Turkmen

67 people per sq. mile

THE URBAN/RURAL POPULATION SPLIT

18% **82%**

RELIGIOUS PERSUASION

ETHNIC MAKEUP

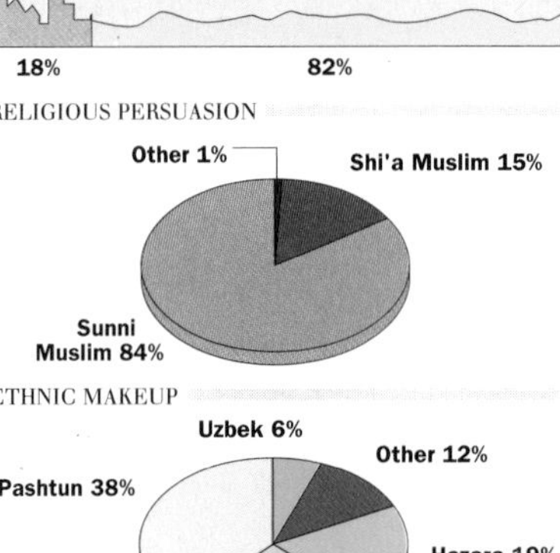

The Pashtuns are the largest ethnic group and the traditional rulers of Afghanistan, making up 38% of the population; the main minorities are Tajiks, Hazaras and Uzbeks. It is these ethnic divisions which have largely, though not exclusively, determined the intra-*mujahideen* feuding that has plagued the country since April 1992. Assaults on Kābul by the *Hezb-i-Islami* group represent an attempt by the Pashtuns to retake control of the capital, which is now under the precarious control of a Tajik–Uzbek alliance. The *Hezb-i-Islami* group's main rivals are the predominantly Tajik *Jamiat-i-Islami*.

Some two million of the country's population were killed as a result of the 1979–1989 war, which followed invasion by the Soviet Union. As many again were maimed. A further six million were forced to flee to neighboring Pakistan and Iran; most have not yet been able to return. Women in Afghanistan have few rights in what is rapidly becoming a male-dominated Islamic fundamentalist society. They are officially discouraged from working and are largely confined to the home.

POPULATION AGE BREAKDOWN

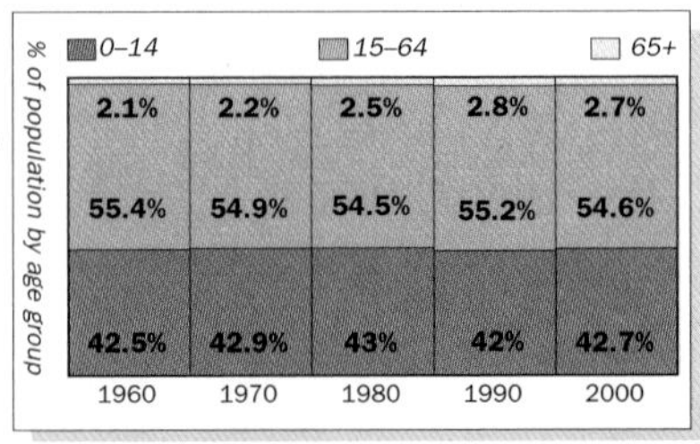

POLITICS

 Uncertain

 President Burhanuddin Rabbani

THE STATE OF THE PARTIES

House of Representatives 234 members

Following the downfall of Najibullah's regime in April 1992, both houses were dissolved and an interim *mujahideen* legislature formed

Senate 192 members

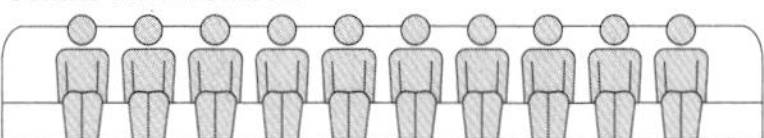

Afghanistan is now technically ruled by a multiparty *mujahideen* cabinet, under the authority of the prime minister.

MAIN POLITICAL ISSUES

Elections
According to the March 7, 1993 Islamabad peace accord, elections were to be held by the end of the year. However, they are still awaited as the civil war continues.

Control of Kābul
Kābul is presently in the hands of the *Jamiat-i-Islami.* Afghanistan's nominal prime minister and leader of the *Hezb-i-Islami,* Golboddin Hekmatyar, is still unable to enter the capital.

PROFILE

The political system has all but collapsed in Afghanistan. All the key players have their own private armies and make their influence felt militarily. The country has been under the control of rival *mujahideen* factions since April 1992, when President Najibullah, who had held power since the withdrawal of Soviet forces in 1989, stepped down.

The main *mujahideen* leaders met in Islamabad in March 1993 and agreed on a basis for government of the country until elections could be held and a constitution formulated. However, two of the most powerful warlords, Rashid Dostam and Ahmad Shah Massoud, the defense minister, were not included in the power-sharing arrangement. President Rabbani, leader of the *Jamiat-i-Islami,* was confirmed as president and Golboddin Hekmatyar, head of the rival *Hezb-i-Islami,* became prime minister.

There is little chance that this government will be able to function viably under present conditions. Even convening the cabinet is problematic, and takes place, at the prime minister's insistence, in a fortified base at Charasaib, south of Kābul.

Burhanuddin Rabbani, *president since 1992.*

Prime Minister Hekmatyar, *the Pashtun leader.*

WORLD AFFAIRS

At the end of 1992, 60,000 refugees, who opposed the neo-communist government in Dushanbe, fled from southern Tajikistan into Afghanistan. Northern Afghanistan faces cross-border bombardments by CIS forces based in Tajikistan. An estimated 3,500 CIS troops are stationed there in an attempt to stem the flow of weapons and militants from Afghanistan to Islamic groups in Tajikistan. Relations with Pakistan, which has attempted to broker peace, are important. It has pledged to provide overland transit facilities for fruit exports to India, and also to consider the provision of port facilities for landlocked Afghanistan.

CHRONOLOGY

The foundations of an Afghan state of Pashtun peoples were laid in the mid-18th century, when Durrani Ahmad Shah became paramount chief of the Abdali Pashtun peoples.

- ❑ **1838–1842** First Anglo-Afghan war. Britain fails in attempt to install Shah Shura on throne.
- ❑ **1878** Second British invasion of Afghan territory.
- ❑ **1879** Under Treaty of Gandmak signed with Amir Yaqub Ali Khan, various Afghan areas annexed by Britain. Yaqub Ali Khan later exiled. New treaty signed with Amir Abdul Rahman, establishing the Durand line, a contentious boundary between Afghanistan and Pakistan.
- ❑ **1919** Declaration of Afghan independence as an autonomous state backed at Paris Peace Conference. Britain briefly declares war on Afghanistan.

A

CHRONOLOGY *continued*

- **1921** Treaty of friendship with Russia signed.
- **1933** Muhammed Zahir Shar in power.
- **1936** Mutual trade agreement signed with USSR.
- **1950** Pakistan closes its border with Afghanistan.
- **1953** Mohammed Daud Khan prime minister. Links with USSR developed.
- **1963** Daud resigns after king rejects his proposals for democratic reforms.
- **1965** Elections held, but monarchy still retains power. Marxist Party of Afghanistan (PDPA) formed and banned. PDPA splits into the *Parcham* and *Khalq* factions.
- **1973** Daud mounts a successful coup, abolishes monarchy and declares republic. *Mujahideen* rebellion begins. Thousands of refugees flee into Pakistan.
- **1978** Opposition to Daud from PDPA culminates in *Saur* revolution. Revolutionary Council under Mohammad Taraki takes power. Daud assassinated.
- **1979** Taraki ousted. Hafizullah Amin takes power. Amin killed in December coup backed by USSR. 80,000 Soviet Army troops invade Afghanistan. Worldwide protests. *Mujahideen* rebellion stepped up into full-scale guerrilla war, with US backing.
- **1980** Babrak Karmal, leader of *Parcham* PDPA, flown in by USSR from Eastern Europe and installed as head of Marxist regime. Fighting escalates.
- **1986** Najibullah replaces Karmal as General Secretary of the Party.
- **1989** Soviet Army withdraws. *Mujahideen* control limited to rural areas. Najibullah remains in power.
- **1991** Russia and USA stop arms supplies to competing factions.
- **1992** Najibullah hands over power to *mujahideen* factions. Pakistan stops supplying arms to its *mujahideen* groups.
- **1993** Civil war continues.

AID

$521m (receipts)

The trend is up

The main official aid is emergency humanitarian assistance from the UN. Saudi Arabia, Iran and Pakistan have promised modest grants. Large-scale funding for reconstruction is conditional on the restoration of peace. Individual *mujahideen* factions receive aid from Islamic states, Muslim organizations and wealthy benefactors.

DEFENSE

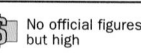

No official figures, but high

Increasing due to war

0 *Defense spending as % GDP* 40

Very high spending by all mujahideen groups

AFGHAN ARMED FORCES

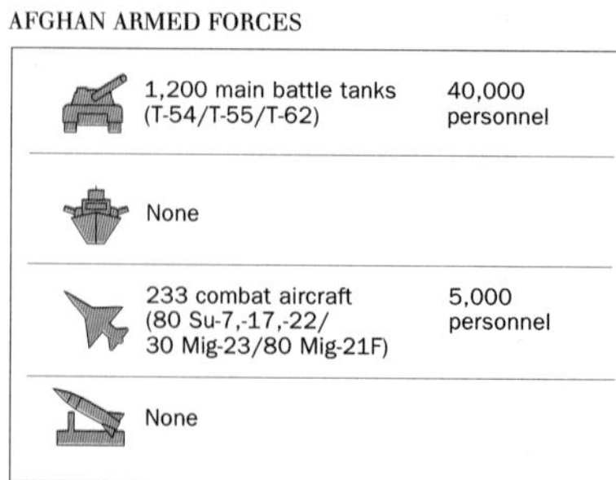

1,200 main battle tanks (T-54/T-55/T-62)
40,000 personnel
None
233 combat aircraft (80 Su-7,-17,-22/ 30 Mig-23/80 Mig-21F)
5,000 personnel
None

In 1991, the US–Russian agreement to suspend military supplies to the Afghan groups marked the end of the superpowers' active involvement in Afghanistan. The Kābul communists, in particular, had been almost totally dependent on Moscow for arms, even after the Soviet withdrawal in 1989. In practice, Afghanistan has no formal defense arrangements. Ahmad Shah Massoud, who holds much of Kābul, is the current defense minister. He controls the *Jamiat-i-Islami,* a leading Tajik *mujahideen* grouping. They have enough ex-Soviet arms stockpiled to last several years. Weapons dumps in no-man's-land on the border with Pakistan supply Golboddin Hekmatyar, the nominal prime minister.

Afghanistan still has around 300–400 of the 1,000 *Stinger* missiles given by the USA to the *mujahideen* in the 1980s. The USA, worried that they may be used against civilian airliners, is offering $100,000 each to buy them back. To date, none have been returned.

ECONOMICS

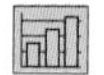
$2.7bn (est)

1,689.76 afghanis

SCORE CARD

- World GNP Ranking........................130th
- GNP per Capita $164
- Balance of Payments................–$143.3m
- Inflation ....*The formal economy*
- Unemployment.......................*has collapsed*

EXPORTS

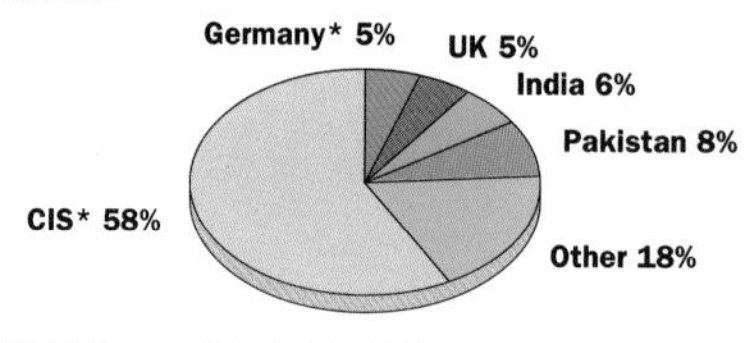

IMPORTS

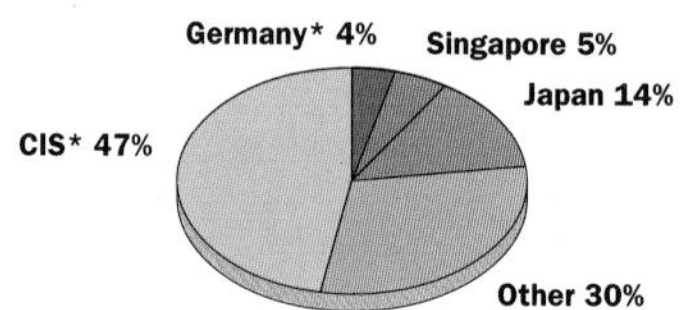

Strengths
Very few, apart from illicit opium trade. Agriculture, still the largest sector, accounted for 45% of GDP in 1986–1987.

Weaknesses
The economy has collapsed. No end to factional fighting in sight. Damage to agriculture, with domino effect on industry. Inaccessible terrain and severed communications links.

Profile
Following ten years of war between the Soviet-backed Kābul government and *mujahideen* rebels, and subsequent *mujahideen* in-fighting, Afghanistan is one of the poorest and least developed countries in the world. It is estimated that $4 billion is needed to rebuild the country and that 80% of its infrastructure has been destroyed. Agricultural activity has fallen back from pre-1979 levels; the Soviets' "scorched earth" policy laid to waste large areas and much of the rural population fled to the cities. Many farmers are now turning back to opium production. Afghanistan is regarded by the UN as the world's largest opium producer. However, most profits are made by Pakistani middlemen.

ECONOMIC PERFORMANCE INDICATOR

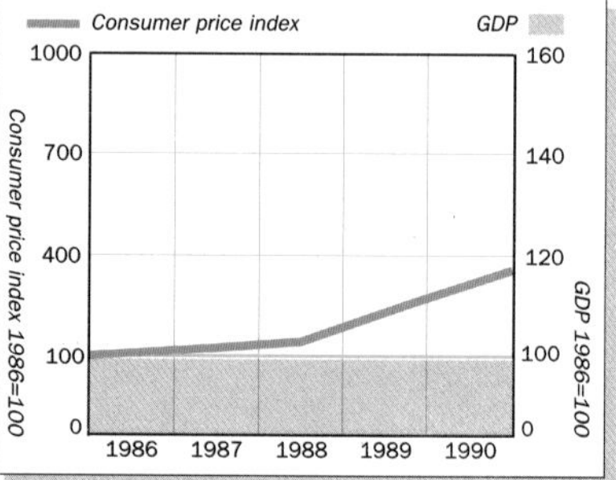

A mujahideen *guerrilla,* *a member of just one of the many factions vying for power in Afghanistan, guards a pass east of Kābul.*

A

RESOURCES

1.1bn kwh (capacity 494,000 kw)

Not an oil producer and has no refineries

12.5m sheep, 1.6m cattle, 1.3m asses, 400,000 horses

Natural gas, salt, coal, copper, lapis lazuli, barytes, talc

ELECTRICITY GENERATION

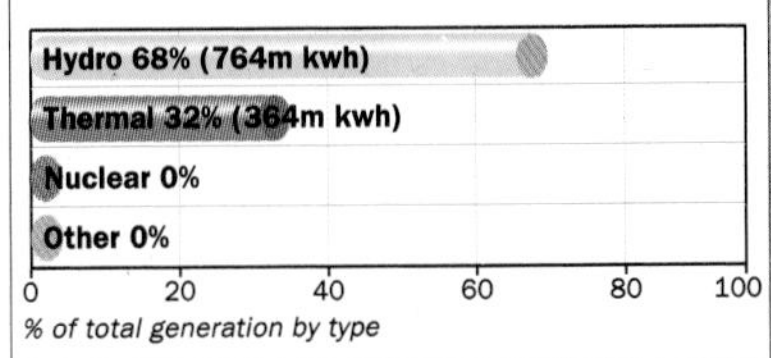

Natural gas and coal are Afghanistan's most important strategic resources. Restoring the power generation system, which has suffered widespread deterioration and destruction, is a government priority. The construction of dams on the Kunar and Laghman rivers is being considered. Coal production has fallen from pre-war levels and mines are also in urgent need of rehabilitation. Western technology is needed to rebuild the gas industry.

AFGHANISTAN : LAND USE

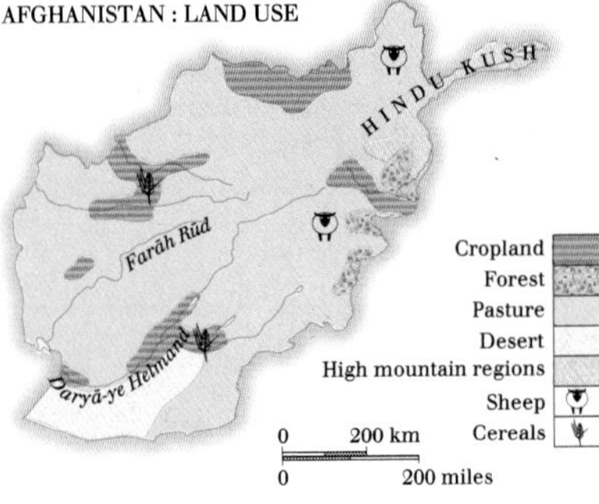

ENVIRONMENT

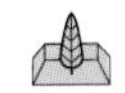

0.3% (0.2% partially protected)

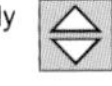

Civil war prevents any initiatives

ENVIRONMENTAL TREATIES

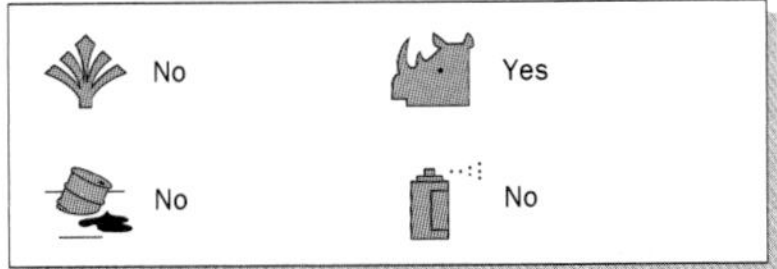

Environmental priorities are low, given Afghanistan's anarchic civil war conditions. However, the country's relative lack of industry, even in Kābul, means that industrial pollution is minimal. The biggest problem facing Afghanistan is land mines – over ten million have been laid – and the UN estimates it will take 100 years to make the country safe for civilians.

MEDIA

Information is regulated by individual factions in the areas which they control

PUBLISHING AND BROADCAST MEDIA

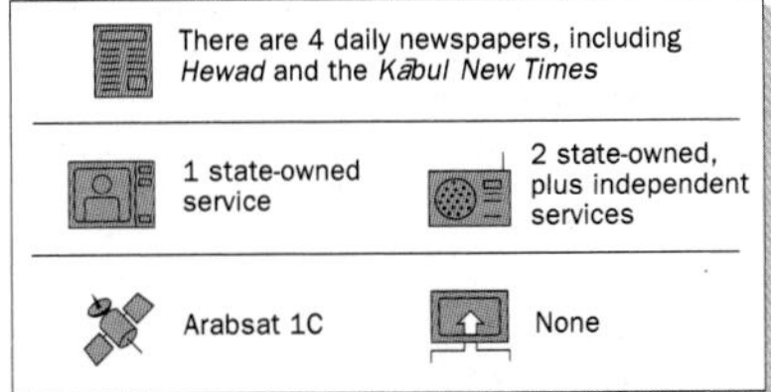

There are 4 daily newspapers, including *Hewad* and the *Kābul New Times*
1 state-owned service
2 state-owned, plus independent services
Arabsat 1C
None

Most of the *mujahideen* factions run their own newspapers and radio stations, which follow the party line and denigrate rivals. The BBC, which broadcasts in Pashtu and Dari, is more popular than Radio Free Afghanistan, especially for its soap operas. These convey information on issues such as health care and the disposal of land mines.

CRIME

Afghanistan does not publish prison figures

Levels of all crimes remain very high

CRIME RATES

No statistics for murders, rapes and thefts are published due to the war situation

Fear of looting in Kābul is stifling economic activity. Banditry operates in most parts of Afghanistan. Herāt, ruled by Amir Ishmail Khan, is an exception – not even the Amir needs a bodyguard.

EDUCATION

29%

0 *Education spending as % GNP* 25

1.8%

THE EDUCATION SYSTEM

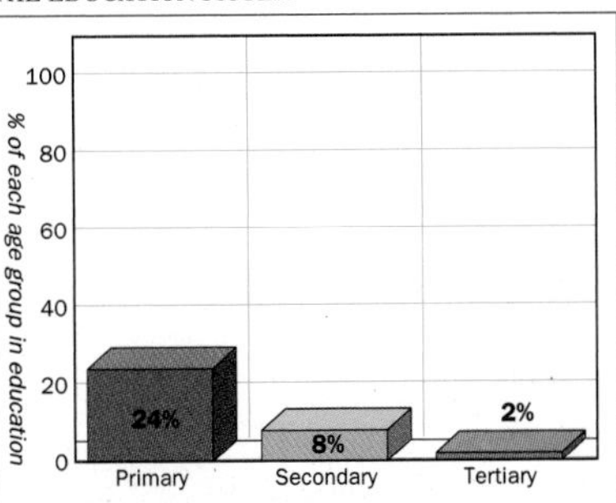

The education system has been destroyed by the war, and as a result illiteracy rates are high. However, some schools have responded to a mid-1993 government directive and reopened. Kābul University has been closed since the fall of the Najibullah regime.

HEALTH

1 per 5,148 people

Infectious, parasitic, respiratory and digestive diseases

0 *Health spending as % GNP* 25

3%

The health service has collapsed completely and almost all medical professionals have left the country. Infant and maternal mortality rates are among the highest in the world, and life expectancy the lowest, at 42 years. Parasitic diseases and infections are a particular problem. The UN has organized a well-water chlorination program, following an outbreak of cholera in Kābul. The admission of women to hospitals is strongly discouraged under increasingly prevalent Islamic laws of modesty.

WEALTH

Faction leaders and arms dealers are the wealthiest groups

CONSUMER GOODS OWNERSHIP

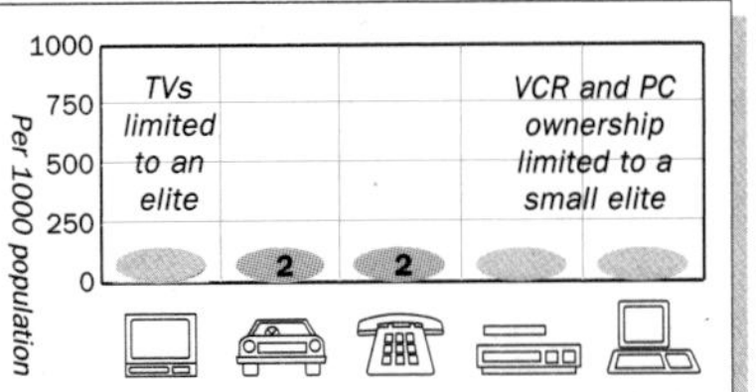

The vast majority of Afghans live in conditions of extreme poverty. The country does not have the resources to feed its people at present – a situation likely to be exacerbated by the return of refugees from neighboring Pakistan and Iran – and is likely to be heavily dependent on outside assistance for its rehabilitation. However, a number of *mujahideen* leaders have accumulated personal fortunes during the war. These derive in part from the substantial foreign aid that was once available and, in some cases, from the trafficking of opium.

WORLD RANKING

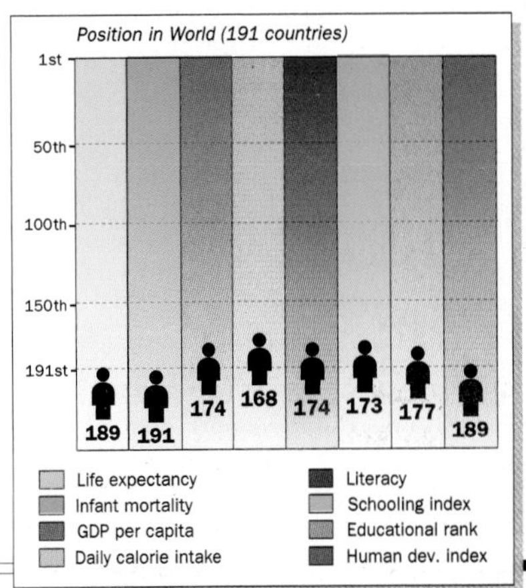

A

ALBANIA

EUROPE
Europe
Yugo. ALBANIA Maced. Italy Greece

OFFICIAL NAME: Republic of Albania **CAPITAL:** Tirana
POPULATION: 3.3 million **CURRENCY:** New Lek **OFFICIAL LANGUAGE:** Albanian

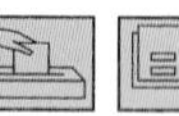

LYING AT THE southeastern end of the Adriatic Sea, opposite the heel of Italy, Albania is a mountainous country vulnerable to earthquakes. It achieved *de facto* independence from Turkey in 1913 and became a one-party communist state in 1944. Albania held its first multiparty elections in 1991. Its return to the international community has been delayed by its support for the ethnic Albanian insurrection in the Kosovo region of Serbia.

CLIMATE

WEATHER CHART

Average daily temperature — *Rainfall*
°C/°F — cm/in
J F M A M J J A S O N D
40/104, 30/86, 20/68, 10/50, 0/32, -10/14, -20/4 — 40/16, 30/12, 20/8, 10/4, 0

The coastal climate is Mediterranean, but rather wet in winter. Heavy rain or snow falls in winter in the mountains.

COMMUNICATIONS

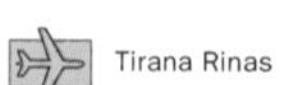
Tirana Rinas

20 ships
85,500 dwt

THE TRANSPORTATION NETWORK

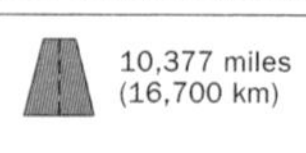
10,377 miles (16,700 km)

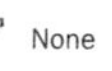
None

425 miles (684 km)

28 miles (43 km)

Albania has Europe's least developed transportation network and lowest ratio of cars to population. Private cars were first allowed in 1991. The horse and cart is the main means of transport.

TOURISM

Albania receives fewer than 100,000 visitors a year

Tourism has grown since 1991

MAIN OVERSEAS ARRIVALS

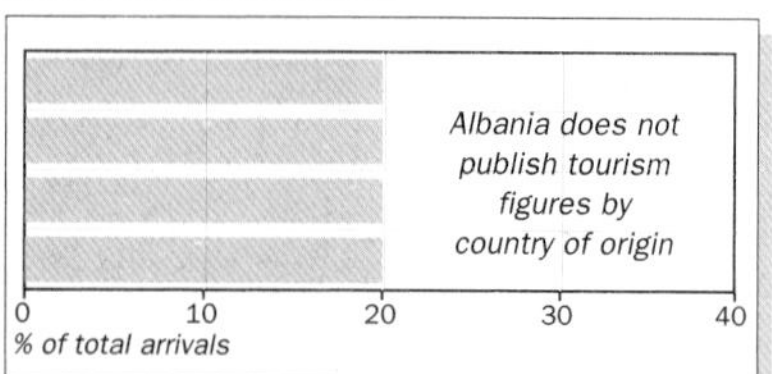

Tourism during the communist era was limited to small organized groups. The government has now begun to exploit Albania's scenic beauty.

PEOPLE

Albanian, Greek

287 people per sq. mile

THE URBAN/RURAL POPULATION SPLIT

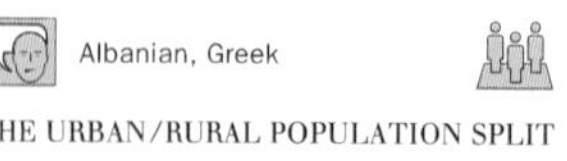

RELIGIOUS PERSUASION

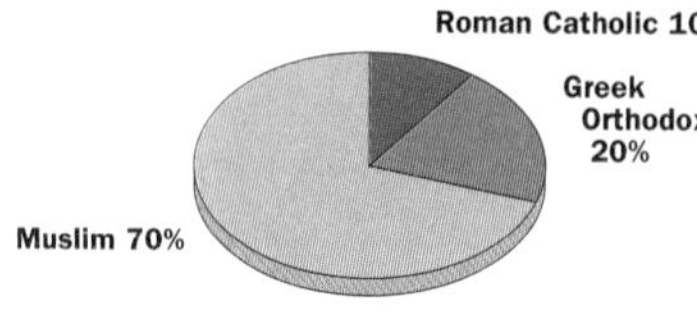

Official statistics admitted the existence of ethnic minorities in Albania only in 1989. The Greek minority strongly contests these statistics, which state that 98% of the population are Albanian. Located mainly in the south and identifying with Athens rather than Tirana, the Greeks claim to make up 10% of the population. They suffer considerable discrimination. Many have sought refuge in northern Greece, but tensions between the two states have also led to a number of these refugees being sent back to Albania.

Under communism, Albania was the only officially atheist state in the world. Many Albanians maintained their beliefs in private – 70% are Muslim. Religious worship is now permitted and mosques have reopened. Society is traditional and male-dominated. The extended family remains strong.

City of a thousand windows. *Berat was preserved as a museum city while a new town was built further down the valley.*

POLITICS

1996

President Sali Berisha

THE STATE OF THE PARTIES

People's Assembly 140 members

66% DPA — **27% SPA** — **5% SDP** — **2% Other**

DPA = Democratic Party of Albania **SPA** = Socialist Party of Albania **SDP** = Social Democratic Party
Other = Union for Human Rights, Albanian Republican Party

Albania was dominated for more than 40 years by communist ruler Enver Hoxha, who died in 1985. At first, it seemed to resist the tide of change that swept through Eastern Europe in 1989. However, by 1990, it became apparent that an upheaval in the one-party communist state could be delayed but not resisted. An increase in popular demonstrations gave reformers within the Party the upper hand and hardliners were forced to concede changes. A mass exodus of Albanians toward the end of 1991 finally persuaded Ramiz Alia, Enver Hoxha's successor, to call multiparty elections. These were held in 1992 and resulted in victory for the center-right DPA-led coalition. The Greek minority was forbidden to field candidates. The main issue in politics is the creation of a Western-style liberal economic state.

WORLD AFFAIRS

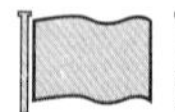

The conflict in the region of Kosovo in Serbia dominates foreign policy. Rich in minerals and 90% ethnically Albanian, Kosovo was an autonomous republic in former Yugoslavia. In 1989, it was forcibly integrated into Serbia. Persecution of Albanians by Serbs has increased tension in the region. Tirana is now suspected of supporting armed resistance groups in Kosovo.

AID

$190m (receipts)

Aid receipts have risen since 1991

The West replaced the Soviet Union as the main source of aid to Albania after 1991. Initially, most was humanitarian food aid. The largest proportion came from Italy, which wished to prevent a potential flood of economic migrants to its shores. Aid is now directed at infrastructure modernization projects.

DEFENSE

 $103.2m

Down 36% in 1991

Officer ranks were reestablished in the Albanian armed forces in 1991. The ability of the under-resourced army to defend Albania's borders has been questioned. Albanians perform 18 months of mandatory military service.

ECONOMICS

 $4.1bn

109.81 new lekë

SCORE CARD

- ❑ WORLD GNP RANKING........................115th
- ❑ GNP PER CAPITA $1,250
- ❑ BALANCE OF PAYMENTS................$-113.9m
- ❑ INFLATION.....................................35.5%
- ❑ UNEMPLOYMENT................................9.1%

STRENGTHS

Europe's highest growth rate in 1993. Growth in agricultural output. Oil and gas reserves.

WEAKNESSES

Rudimentary infrastructure. Low level of technical skills. Regional instability has discouraged foreign investment.

EXPORTS

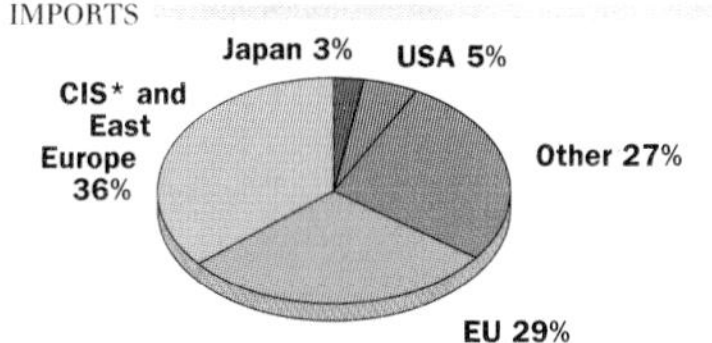

IMPORTS

Japan 3%
USA 5%
CIS* and East Europe 36%
Other 27%
EU 29%

ALBANIA

Total Area : 28 750 sq. km (11 100 sq. miles)

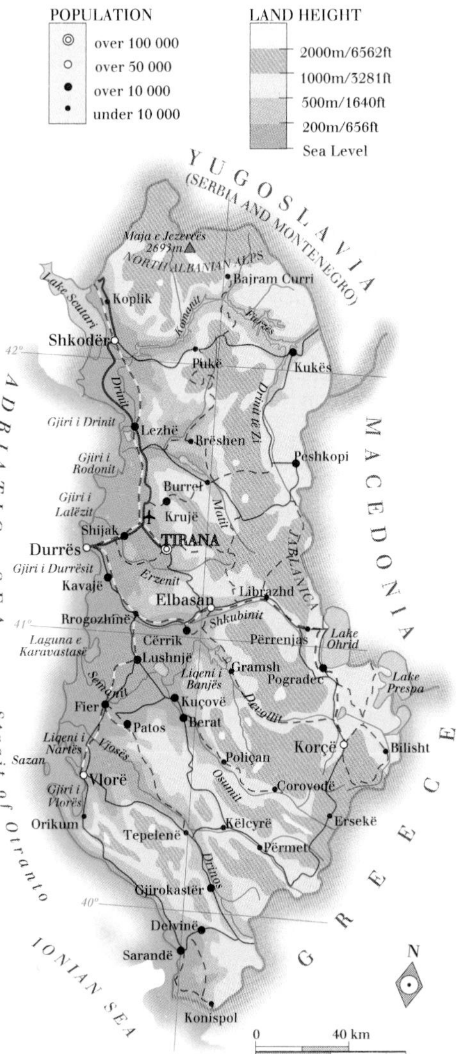

RESOURCES

 4.1bn kwh (capacity 780,000 kw)

 25,700 b/d (reserves 165,000,000 bbl)

 5m poultry, 1.5m sheep, 1.2m goats

Chromium, oil, coal, natural gas, copper, nickel

Albania needs major capital investment to develop its minerals and to create a modern electricity supply system.

ENVIRONMENT

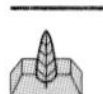 1.6% (0.8% partially protected)

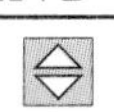 There is no money for environmental protection measures

Industry, which is underdeveloped, has little impact on the environment. Due to years of shortages in the economy, most materials are recycled.

MEDIA

 Since the fall of communism there has been no official censorship

PUBLISHING AND BROADCAST MEDIA

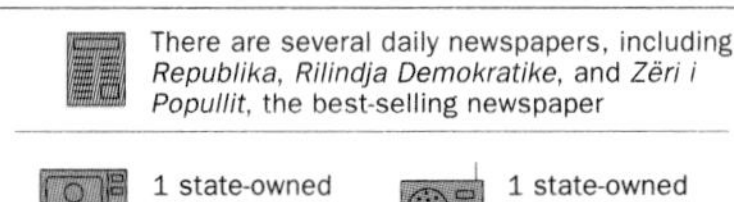

There are several daily newspapers, including *Republika*, *Rilindja Demokratike*, and *Zëri i Popullit*, the best-selling newspaper

1 state-owned service

1 state-owned service

The leading paper, *Zëri i Popullit*, is run by the SPA. Journalists opposing the government can suffer intimidation.

CRIME

 1,640 prisoners

 Crime levels are rising sharply

Most crimes are on the increase; tourists in Tirana are targets for mugging. Cannabis is widely grown.

CHRONOLOGY

Albania gained independence for the first time in its history in 1913.

- ❑ **1924–1939** Ahmet Zogu, crowned King Zog in 1928, in power.
- ❑ **1939–1943** Occupied by Italy.
- ❑ **1944** Communist state; led by Enver Hoxha until 1985.
- ❑ **1948–1961** Pro-Soviet period.
- ❑ **1961–1978** Pro-Chinese period.
- ❑ **1981** Prime minister, Mehmet Shehu, shot dead.
- ❑ **1991** Democratic multiparty state.

EDUCATION

 85%

The system is derived from the Soviet, Chinese and Italian models. Albania has four universities.

HEALTH

 1 per 574 people

 Heart, respiratory and digestive diseases, cancer

The health service is rudimentary and dependent on Western aid for most drugs and medical supplies.

WEALTH

 Demand for imported luxury goods has increased

CONSUMER GOODS OWNERSHIP

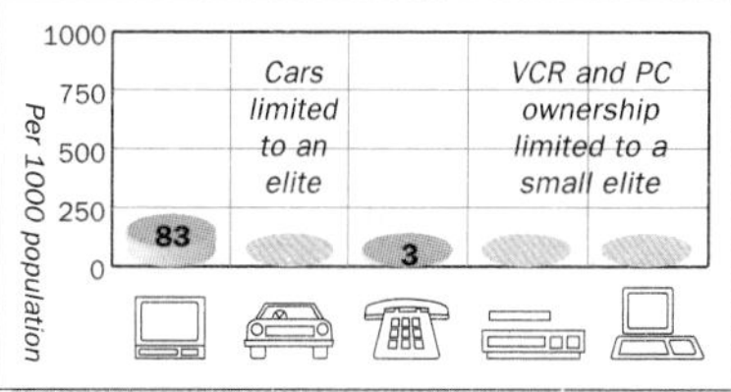

Wealth is limited to a small, slowly expanding group of private-sector entrepreneurs.

WORLD RANKING

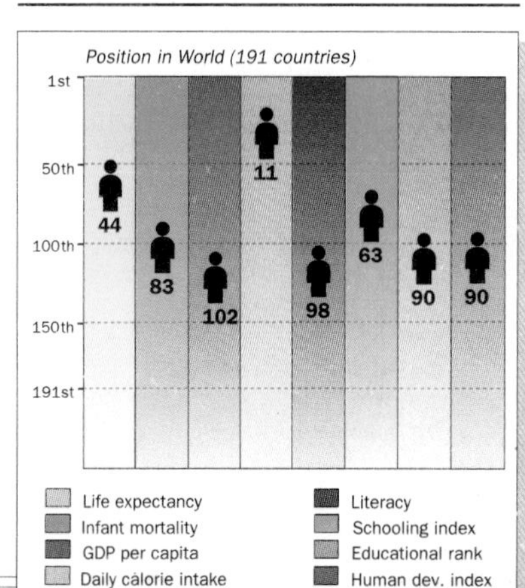

A

ALGERIA

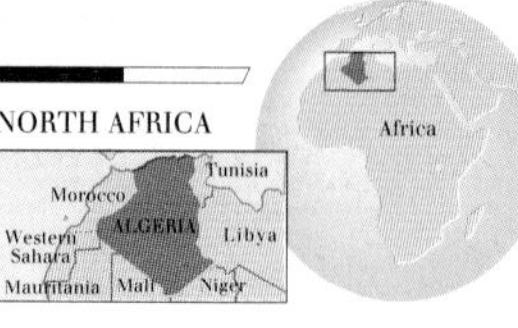

OFFICIAL NAME: Democratic and Popular Republic of Algeria **CAPITAL:** Algiers
POPULATION: 26.4 million **CURRENCY:** Algerian dinar **OFFICIAL LANGUAGE:** Arabic

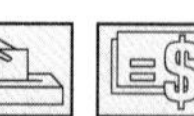

AFRICA'S SECOND LARGEST COUNTRY, Algeria shares borders with Morocco, Mauritania, Mali, Niger, Libya and Tunisia. Algeria won independence from France in 1962. Today, the military-dominated government faces a severe challenge from Islamic fundamentalists. A founder-member of OPEC, Algeria has significant oil and gas reserves. The country also has one of the youngest populations, and highest birthrates, in North Africa.

CLIMATE

WEATHER CHART

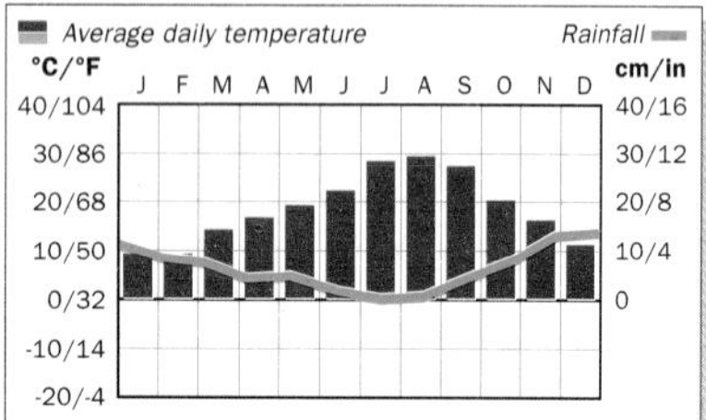

Coastal areas have a warm, temperate climate. The area to the south of the Atlas Mountains is hot desert.

COMMUNICATIONS

Houari Boumedienne, Algiers 3.68m passengers

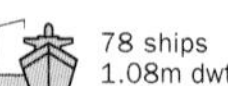
78 ships 1.08m dwt

THE TRANSPORTATION NETWORK

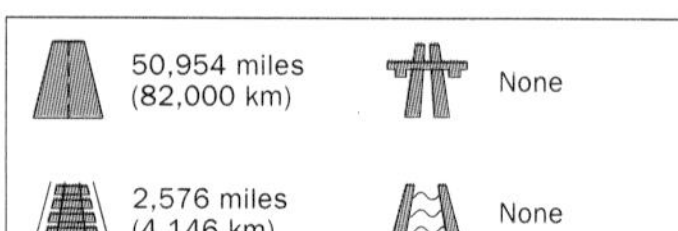

There are five international airports. Rail is the quickest way to travel between the main urban centers.

TOURISM

1.14m visitors

Down 6% in 1990

MAIN OVERSEAS ARRIVALS

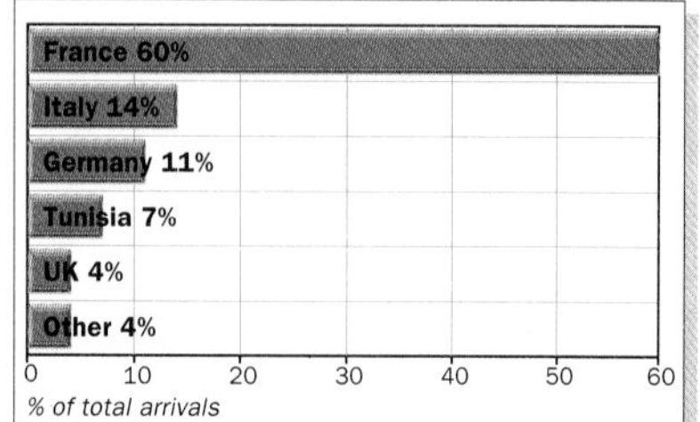

Algeria's once-popular desert safaris are now rare. Tourists are a target for militant Islamic groups.

PEOPLE

Arabic, Berber (Kabyle, Shawia, Tamashek), French

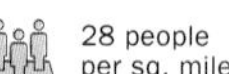

THE URBAN/RURAL POPULATION SPLIT

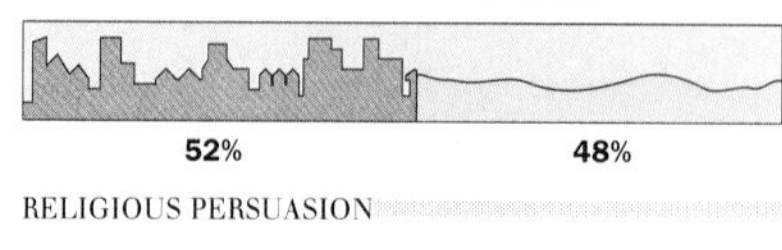

RELIGIOUS PERSUASION

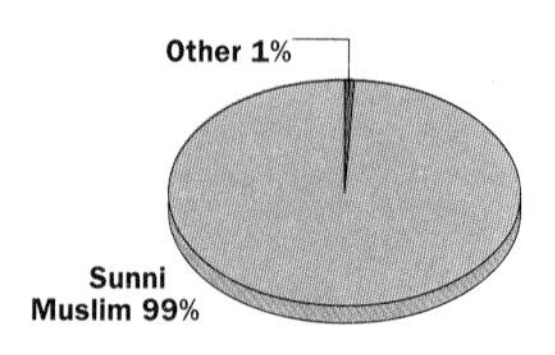

ETHNIC MAKEUP

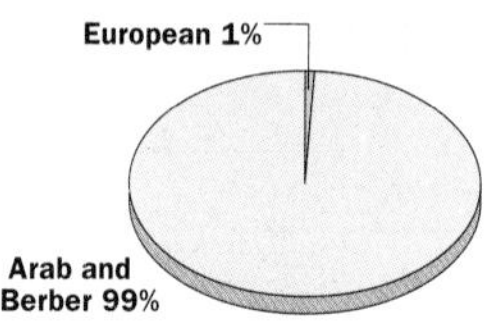

Algeria's population is predominantly Arab, under 30 years of age and urban; about 20% are Berber. More than 85% speak Arabic, the official language, and 99% are Sunni Muslim. Of the million or so French who settled in Algeria before independence, only about 6,000 remain. Most Berbers consider the mountainous Kabylia region their homeland. If the struggle between Islamic fundamentalists and the government intensifies, Kabylia may seek independence. As in the rest of North Africa, the mosque is an important provider of social and medical services.

POPULATION AGE BREAKDOWN

% of population by age group

	1960	1970	1980	1990	2000
65+	3.9%	4.1%	3.9%	3.6%	3.3%
15–64	52.4%	47.5%	49.6%	52.8%	57.4%
0–14	43.7%	48.4%	46.5%	43.6%	39.3%

POLITICS

THE STATE OF THE PARTIES

National People's Assembly 430 members

The National People's Assembly was dissolved in 1992, following the first round of elections

Algeria is currently ruled by the military under a state of emergency. Elections have been promised in 1996.

MAIN POLITICAL ISSUES

Islamic fundamentalism

Nearly 3,000 Algerians have died in the past two years from political violence. The country's new *mujahideen* (holy warriors) are engaged in what they see as a second war of liberation, under the leadership of the Islamic Salvation Front (FIS). They wish to establish a theocracy along Iranian lines. The FIS has had considerable success at the polls. In the 1991 general election it took 188 of the 228 seats contested. However, the army declared a state of emergency and scrapped the second round of voting, in order to stop the FIS from taking power.

The market economy

In 1988, President Bendjedid's administration decided to embark on a series of market reforms, designed to introduce competition into Algeria's large state-run economy. The policy was encouraged by the World Bank and the IMF and included tough austerity measures. The suggestion that the policy showed how Algeria was falling under US and Western influence partly accounted for Islamic fundamentalists' strong showing in the 1991 polls. Since the army takeover in 1991, the policy has been put on hold.

PROFILE

Until 1988, Algeria was a regime in the Soviet model. With the collapse of the Soviet Union, Algeria's aging ruling elite adopted IMF privatization policies. The process was vigorously opposed by Islamic fundamentalists. An army clampdown in 1991 prevented the fundamentalists from taking power, but, apart from vague promises of elections, the future looks unclear. The fundamentalists have established a parallel organization to the state's, based on the mosque. In practice they control most areas outside Algiers.

WORLD AFFAIRS

Algeria's struggle for independence from France lasted from 1954 until 1962. Throughout the 1960s and 1970s, Algeria's success in rejecting a colonial power made it a champion for the developing world. It had a leading voice within the UN, the Arab League and the Organization for African Unity. However, relations with the West remained essentially stable. Algeria was increasingly seen by the diplomatic community as a useful bridge between the West and Iran.

In 1981, Algerian diplomats helped to secure the release of American hostages held in Tehran during the last days of US President Carter's term of office. Algeria also attempted to act in a mediating role during the 1980–1988 Iran–Iraq War.

Algeria's influence overseas has diminished as the country has become increasingly unstable politically. Throughout the 1990s, the government has been under severe pressure from the Islamic fundamentalist FIS. A victory for the FIS in Algeria would greatly encourage Islamic militants in neighboring Morocco and Tunisia, and further undermine Egypt's embattled government.

European governments are also concerned that an FIS takeover could trigger a wave of refugees seeking entry into France, Spain and Italy.

AID

$310m (receipts)
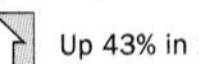
Up 43% in 1991

As a major oil producer, Algeria receives only small quantities of aid. During the 1980s, its economy became dependent on Eastern European manufactures, which were swapped for oil. The collapse of this trade in the 1990s led Algeria to turn to the West for loans. Oil revenues encouraged the West to offer export credits. The IMF provided loans to help Algeria to meet payments on its massive $127-billion debt on condition that the government move toward a market-oriented economy. However, these sources are now threatened by Algeria's growing political instability.

Saharan town, showing the wide range of Algeria's scenery, from lush, irrigated gardens near water sources to barren sand dunes beyond. 80% of Algeria is desert.

ALGERIA

Total Area :
2 381 740 sq. km
(919 590 sq. miles)

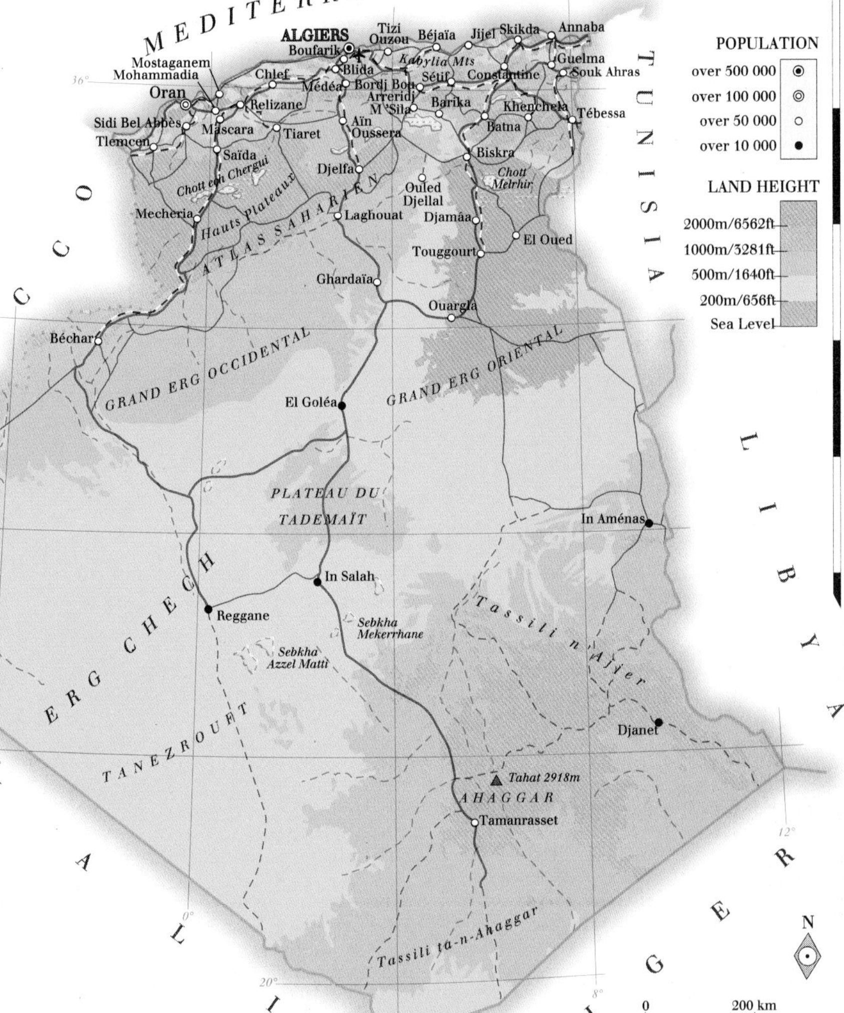

***Former president Bendjedid Chadli,** head of state from 1979 to 1992.*

***Muhammad Boudiaf,** head of state, assassinated in 1992.*

A

CHRONOLOGY

The conquest of Algeria by France began in 1830. By 1900, French settlers occupied most of the best land. In 1954, war was declared on the colonial administration by the National Liberation Front (FLN).

- **1962** Cease-fire reached, followed by declaration of independence and founding of Algerian republic.
- **1965** Military junta topples government of Ahmed Ben Bella. Revolutionary council set up, under Col. Boumedienne.
- **1966** Judiciary "Algerianized." Tribunals try "economic crimes."
- **1971** Oil industry nationalized. Boumedienne continues with land reform, a national health service and "socialist" management.
- **1976** National Charter establishes a socialist state.
- **1978** Col. Boumedienne dies of natural causes.
- **1979** Bendjedid Chadli sworn in as president.
- **1980** Ben Bella released after 15 years' detention. Agreement signed with France, whereby latter gives incentives for return home of 800,000 Algerian immigrants.
- **1981** Algeria helps to negotiate release of American hostages from the US embassy in Teheran, Iran.
- **1985** The two most popular Kabyle (Berber) singers are given 3-year jail sentences for opposing regime.
- **1987** Government introduces limited liberalization by giving private enterprise more freedom. Algeria signs cooperation agreement with Soviet Union.
- **1988** Violence directed at ruling party. State of emergency. Algeria negotiates release of Kuwaiti hostages held on aircraft by Shi'a gunmen. The hijackers escape unpunished.
- **1989** Constitutional reforms, which diminish power of FLN. New political parties are founded, including the Islamic Salvation Front (FIS). The Arab Maghreb Union is established by the leaders of Algeria, Libya, Morocco and Tunisia.
- **1990** Political exiles permitted to return home. FIS wins municipal elections.
- **1991** FIS leaders Abassi Madani and Ali Belhadj arrested. FIS wins large majority in National Assembly.
- **1992** Bendjedid overthrown by military. Second round of elections scrapped. President Boudiaf assassinated. Succeeded by Ali Kafi. FIS leaders Abassi Madani and Ali Belhadj given 12 years in jail.
- **1994** Political violence led by Armed Islamic Group.

DEFENSE

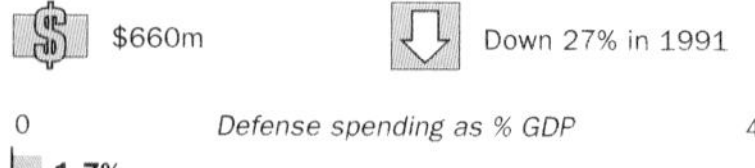

The National Liberation Army (NLA), equipped with Soviet weapons, is the dominant power in politics. There are fears that parts of the army will forge an alliance with Muslim militants. The extreme rebel Armed Islamic Group, which has split from the FIS, is led by former army officers.

ALGERIAN ARMED FORCES

Tanks	960 main battle tanks (330 T-54,-55/ 330 T-62/300 T-72)	120,000 personnel
Navy	2 submarines, 3 frigates, 14 surface vessels and 9 patrol boats	7,000 personnel
Aircraft	242 combat aircraft (30 MiG-17/10 Su-24/ 17 MiG-23BN,-23MF)	12,000 personnel
Missiles	None	

ECONOMICS

$43.2bn 23.82 dinars

SCORE CARD

- WORLD GNP RANKING 43rd
- GNP PER CAPITA $1,640
- BALANCE OF PAYMENTS $1.6bn
- INFLATION 32%
- UNEMPLOYMENT 25%

EXPORTS

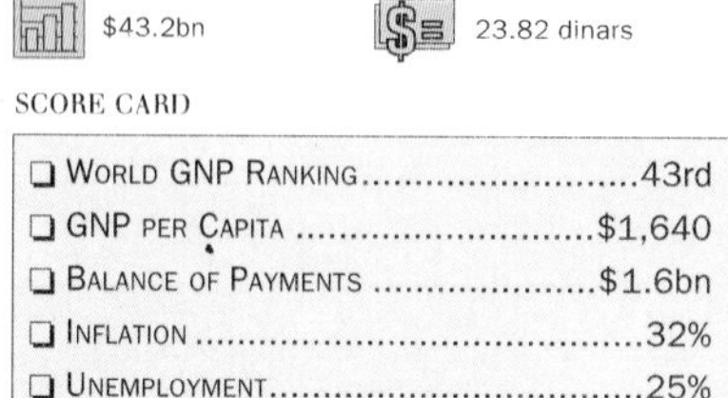

IMPORTS

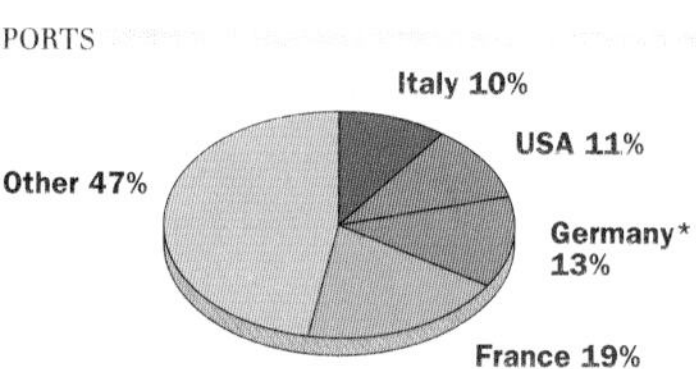

ECONOMIC PERFORMANCE INDICATOR

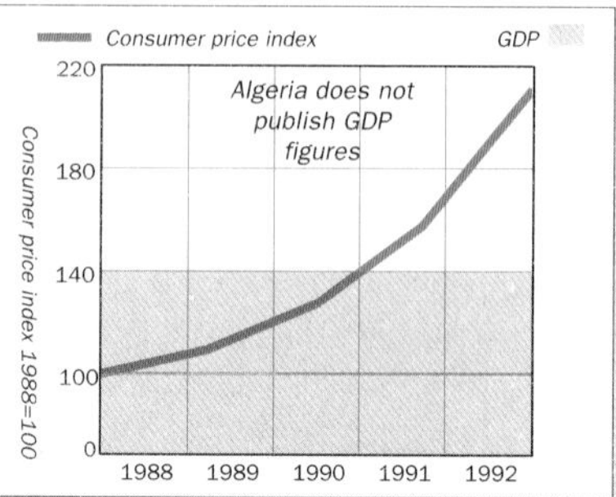

STRENGTHS

Oil and gas. Recent collaboration with Western oil companies should lead to improvements in productivity. Natural gas is supplied to Europe.

WEAKNESSES

Oil revenues yet to recover from the 1986 collapse in world prices. Political turmoil threatens many new projects and has led to an exodus of European and other expatriate workers important to the economy. Lack of skilled labor coupled with high unemployment. Limited agriculture. Shortages of basic foodstuffs. A thriving black market.

PROFILE

Under the pro-Soviet National Liberation Front, the Algerian economy was dominated by centralized socialist planning. In the late 1980s, the economic collapse of the Soviet Union led to a change in policy, and Algeria began moving toward a market economy. However, these reforms were frozen following the military takeover in 1991. The army still favors a centrally planned economy and, as a result, the state still retains control of the vast majority of the economy's most productive sectors.

Only in the oil industry has private investment been encouraged. A number of Western oil companies have signed exploration contracts with Algiers since it has accepted more competitive production-sharing agreements. However, Western investment levels are likely to remain small as long as the political situation is unstable. Algeria is now importing more than half its grain, and long food lines are routine in the capital.

ALGERIA : MAJOR BUSINESSES

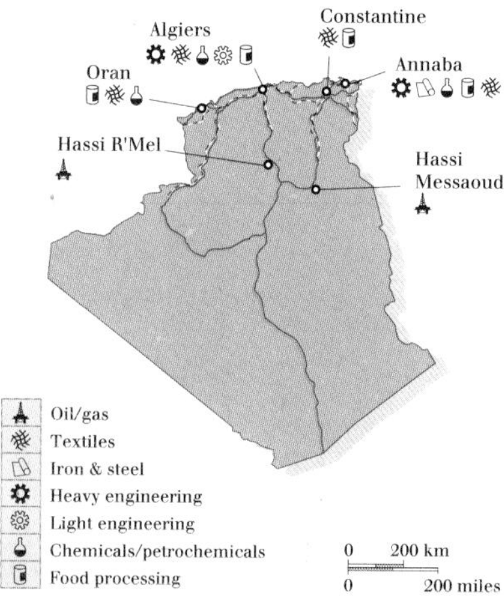

RESOURCES

15.9bn kwh (capacity 4.66m kw)

782,700 b/d (reserves 9,200,000,000 bbl)

12.5m sheep, 3.6m goats, 1.4m cattle, 300,000 asses

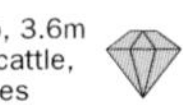

Oil, natural gas, iron, phosphates, lead, zinc, silver, copper, tungsten

ELECTRICITY GENERATION

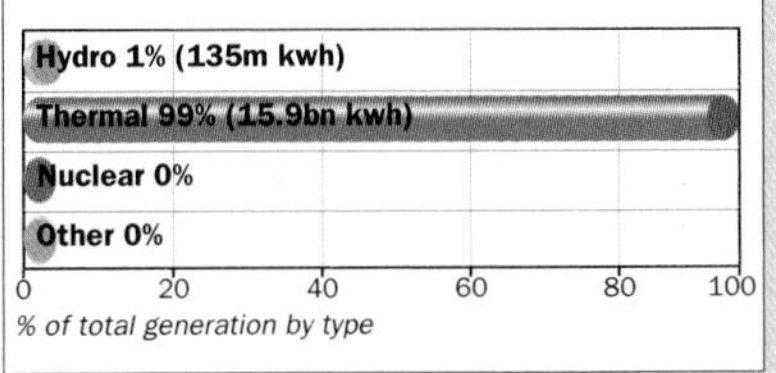

Crude oil and natural gas, Algeria's main resources, were first produced in the 1950s. Algeria also has diverse minerals, including iron ore, zinc, silver, copper ore and phosphates. In the 1960s and 1970s, Algeria sought to become a manufacturing country, with investments in building materials, refined products and steel; none of these sectors is competitive in world markets. Although agriculture employs one-quarter of Algeria's work force, its importance to the economy is diminishing. State forests cover some 2% of Algeria's land. Most are brushwood, but some areas include cork oak trees, Aleppo pine, evergreen oak and cedar. Algeria has a large fishing fleet. Sardines, anchovies, tuna and shellfish are the major species caught commercially.

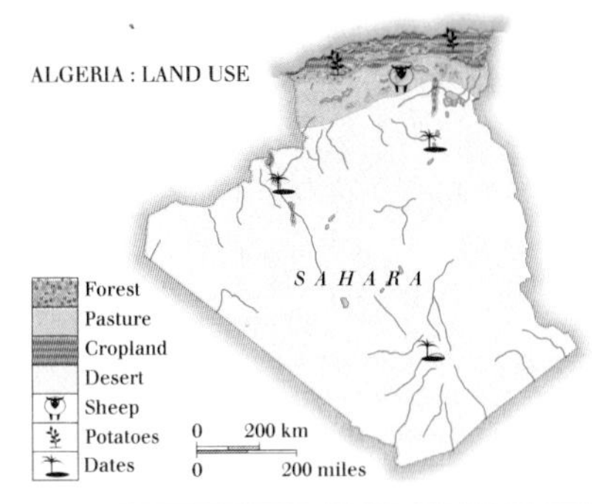

ENVIRONMENT

5% (0.1% partially protected)

Desertification due to pressure on land

ENVIRONMENTAL TREATIES

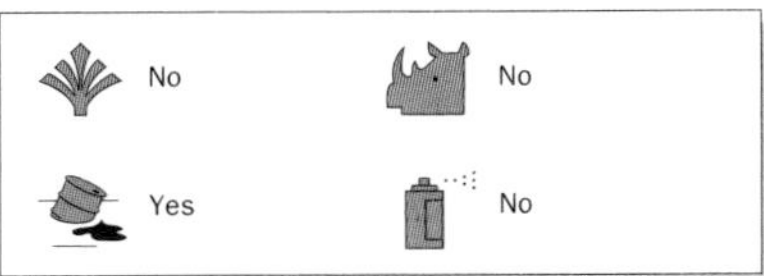

Since most of Algeria is desert or semi-desert, over 90% of the population is forced to live on the remaining 20% of land. The desert is moving northward. Vegetation has been stripped for use as firewood and animal fodder, leaving fragile soils exposed which then require expensive specialized care to conserve them. Water purification techniques are below standard and rivers are being increasingly contaminated by untreated sewage, industrial effluent and wastes from petroleum refining.

MEDIA

The media is under government control

PUBLISHING AND BROADCAST MEDIA

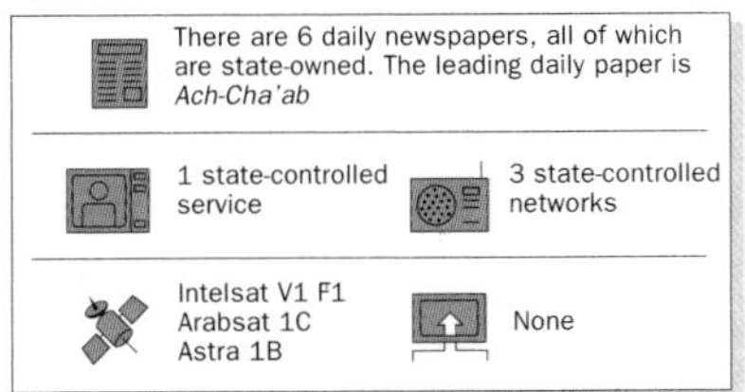

There are 6 daily newspapers, all of which are state-owned. The leading daily paper is Ach-Cha'ab
1 state-controlled service
3 state-controlled networks
Intelsat V1 F1
Arabsat 1C
Astra 1B
None

Newspapers, TV and radio are state-controlled and permit no criticism of government actions. TV is broadcast in Arabic, French and Kabyle (Berber), but Algeria has only about 1.6 million TVs. The six daily newspapers have a combined circulation of 1.4 million. However, distribution is limited outside the main cities.

CRIME

Algeria does not publish prison figures

Crime levels rising sharply

CRIME RATES

Algeria does not publish official statistics for murders, rapes or thefts

Political violence kills about 15 Algerians every day. Foreigners, Jews and Christians are singled out by the radical Armed Islamic Group, many of whom are teenagers. Human rights activists allege that pro-government death squads roam the cities and rural areas seeking out suspected Islamic militants and their relatives.

EDUCATION

57%

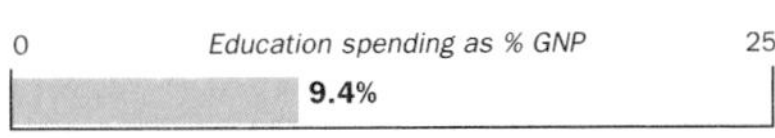

THE EDUCATION SYSTEM

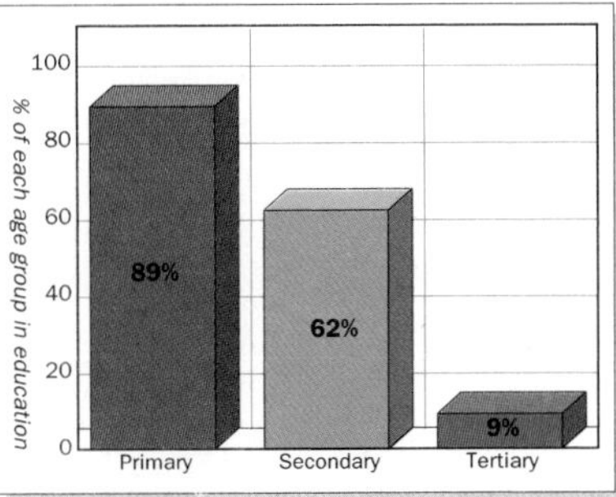

Over three-quarters of the school-age population receive a formal education. The literacy rate is 57%. Since 1973, the curriculum has been Arabized and the teaching of French has diminished. Ten universities and seven polytechnics provide higher education to some 175,000 students.

HEALTH

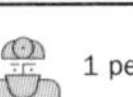

1 per 1,199 people

Respiratory, heart and cerebrovascular diseases, malaria

0	*Health spending as % GNP*	25
1.2%		

Primary health care is rudimentary outside main cities. The infant mortality rate is 5.5%, comfortably below the North African average of 7.3%. Life expectancy is just above the average for the region, at 66 for men and 68 for women.

WEALTH

Waiter, 2,282 dinars per month; doctor, 5,802 dinars per month

CONSUMER GOODS OWNERSHIP

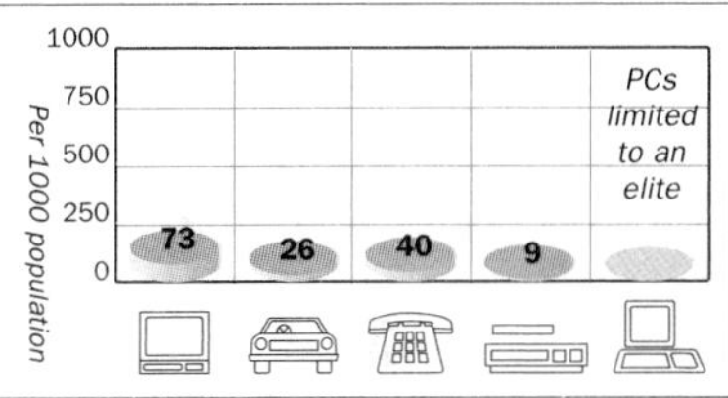

There is great disparity in wealth between the political elite and the rest of the population. Those connected to the military are the wealthiest group. Most Algerians have had to contend with soaring prices for basic necessities.

WORLD RANKING

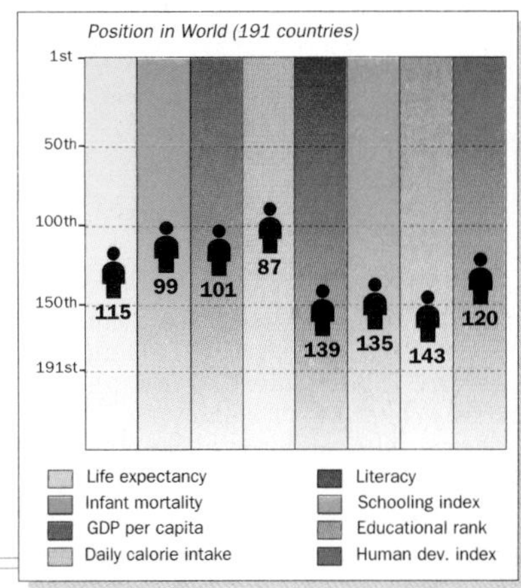

A

ANDORRA

OFFICIAL NAME: Principality of Andorra **CAPITAL:** Andorra la Vella

POPULATION: 58,000 **CURRENCY:** French franc and Spanish peseta **OFFICIAL LANGUAGE:** Catalan

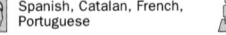

EUROPE
Europe
France
ANDORRA
Spain

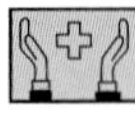

A TINY, LANDLOCKED principality between France and Spain, Andorra lies high in the eastern Pyrenees. From the 13th century, French and Spanish co-princes (today the President of France and the Bishop of Urgel) have governed Andorra. In December 1993, the principality held its first full elections. Andorra's spectacular scenery, alpine climate and duty-free shopping have made tourism, especially skiing, its main source of income.

PEOPLE

Spanish, Catalan, French, Portuguese

287 people per sq. mile

THE URBAN/RURAL POPULATION SPLIT

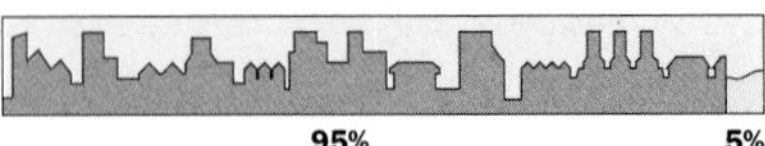

RELIGIOUS PERSUASION

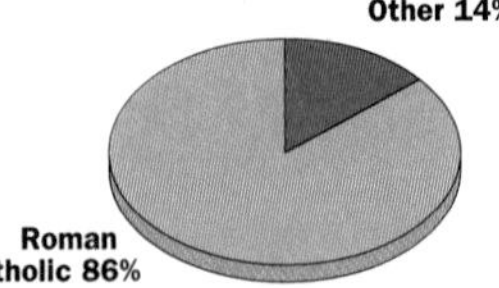

Immigration is strictly monitored and restricted by quota to French and Spanish nationals intending to work in Andorra. Divorce is illegal.

Andorra's outstanding mountain scenery attracts 500,000 skiers a year.

TOURISM

12m visitors

Up 20% between 1990 and 1992

MAIN OVERSEAS ARRIVALS

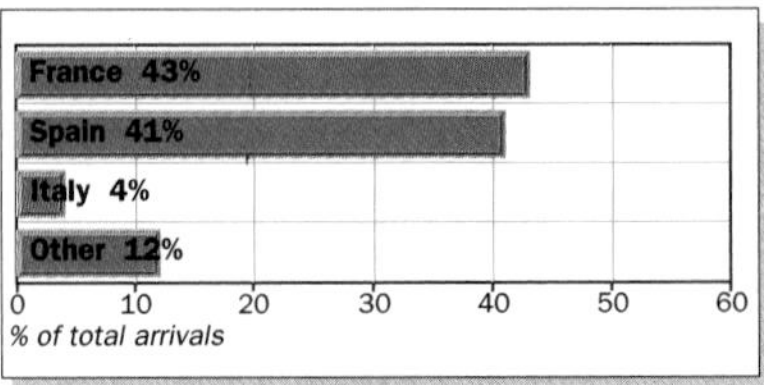

Most tourists visit Andorra to ski or shop. However, the traditional trade from day-trippers from France and Spain, coming to shop in the many tax-free designer-label boutiques is threatened by EU regulations seeking to end Andorra's beneficial tax laws. Five ski resorts receive over 500,000 visitors a year. In summer they cater to mountain hikers; Andorra's wild-flowers attract many, but there is also much for the bird-watcher to see. Hunting wild boar is popular and the goat-like chamois can be hunted under special license.

POLITICS

1997

Co-Princes François Mitterrand and Joan Martí Alanis

THE STATE OF THE PARTIES

General Council of the Valleys 28 members

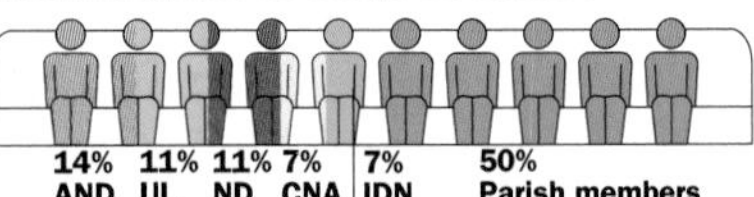

AND = National Democratic Grouping **UL** = Liberal Union
ND = New Democracy **CNA** = National Andorran Coalition
IDN = New Democratic Initiative

14 members are elected on a national list and 14 are elected in 7 dual-member parishes

Until recently, Andorra was a semi-feudal state. But in March 1993 a referendum approved democratic measures which legalized political parties and the right to strike, and altered relations with the co-princes. Following elections in December 1993, an AND-led coalition government was formed.

CLIMATE

WEATHER CHART

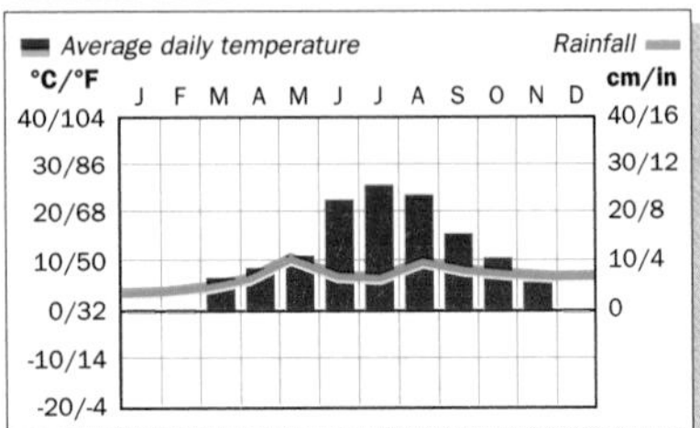

Spring is cool and wet; summers are dry and warm. Snowfalls in December and January lay the ground for good skiing up to March. Andorra's climate supports an abundance of wildflowers.

COMMUNICATIONS

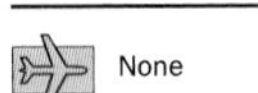

None

Has no fleet

THE TRANSPORTATION NETWORK

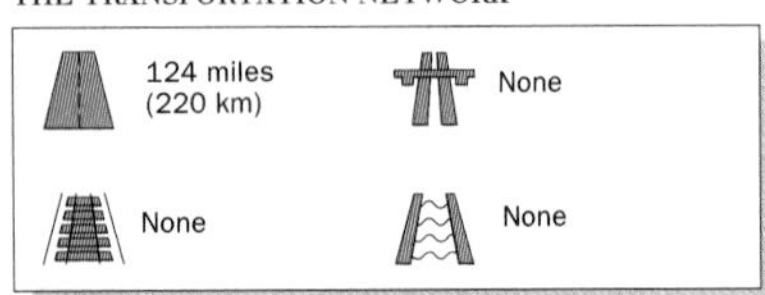

The road from France to Spain climbs to 8,872 feet through one of the most dramatic mountain passes in Europe. During the summer months, the sheer number of day-trippers often brings traffic to a standstill around Andorra la Vella.

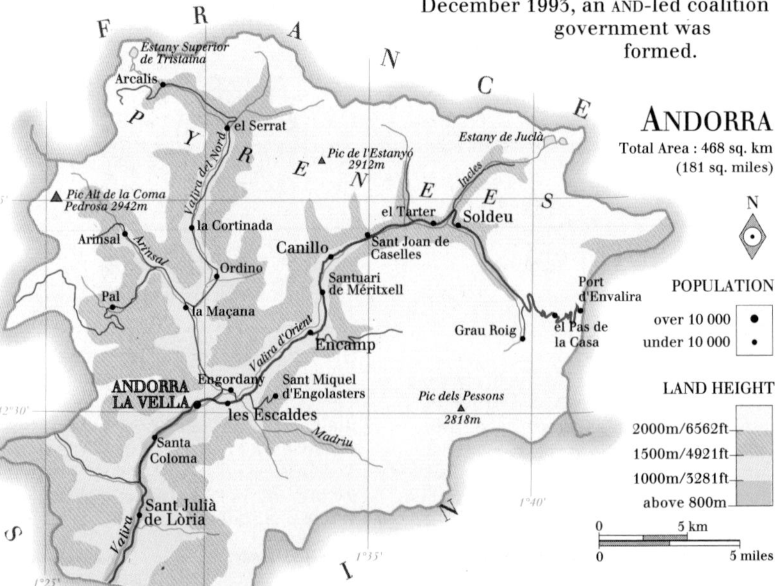

WORLD AFFAIRS

Andorra's limited membership in world bodies reflects its ambiguous status; it is still not recognized by Japan. The main concern is the future of free trade with Spain, following the advent of the EU internal market.

AID

Andorra has no aid receipts or donations

Not applicable

The principality of Andorra neither receives nor provides aid, and has no plans to do so.

DEFENSE

Andorra has no defense budget

Not applicable

Andorra has no defense budget; protection is provided by France and Spain. The French intervention of 1933 was the last military action on Andorran soil.

ECONOMICS

$895m

5.90 francs
142.93 pesetas

SCORE CARD

- ❑ WORLD GNP RANKING........................158th
- ❑ GNP PER CAPITA..........................$15,430
- ❑ BALANCE OF PAYMENTS......Included in Spanish total
- ❑ INFLATION...............................Not applicable
- ❑ UNEMPLOYMENT...................................0%

STRENGTHS
Tourism, the basis of the economy. Strict banking secrecy laws make Andorra an important tax haven; low consumer taxes have also encouraged a healthy luxury retail sector. Farming: cereals, potatoes and tobacco are the major products.

WEAKNESSES
France and Spain effectively decide economic policy. There is a dependence on imported food and raw materials.

EXPORTS

IMPORTS

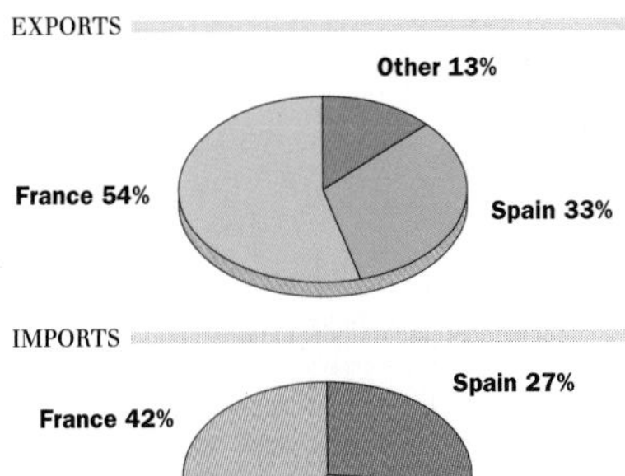

RESOURCES

115m kwh

Not an oil producer and has no refineries

5,600 sheep, 1,700 cattle

None

Water is a major resource, hydropower providing most domestic energy needs. However, Andorra has to import twice as much electricity as it produces, and there are plans to increase capacity. A third of the country is designated forest.

ENVIRONMENT

None

Desire for larger tourist revenues conflicts with nature conservation

Twelve million tourists a year have had an inevitably adverse impact over time on a country of 52,000 people. Concern is growing, at the moment chiefly among NGOs, about the scarring of Andorra's alpine landscape by hotel and ski developments, as well as about the future of its unique mountain flora. Hunting, notably of the Pyrenean chamois and the wild boar, is still a significant tourist attraction. However, restrictions are gradually being introduced to preserve certain animal species.

MEDIA

No political censorship since 1993

PUBLISHING AND BROADCAST MEDIA

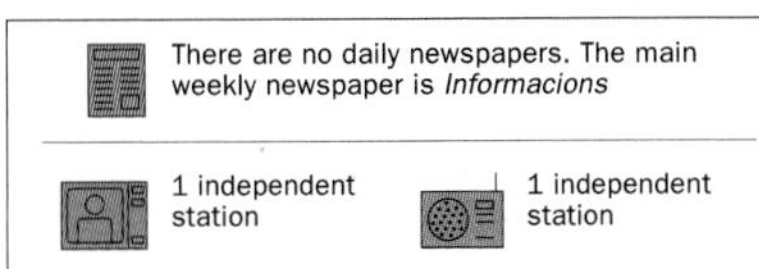
There are no daily newspapers. The main weekly newspaper is *Informacions*

1 independent station

1 independent station

Andorra receives most Spanish and French TV broadcasts. A private television company in Spain broadcasts one hour a day of programs designed specifically for Andorra.

CRIME

Andorra does not publish prison figures

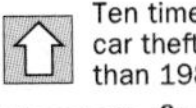
Ten times more car theft in 1990 than 1987

Tourists are natural targets for thieves, most of whom are not Andorran. Thefts of expensive cars for resale in France and Spain are on the increase.

Andorra has two criminal courts – the *Tribunals de Corts*.

EDUCATION

99%

There are 18 schools in Andorra, most of which teach in Spanish and French. Instruction in Catalan is available, but only in the primary schools and one secondary school.

CHRONOLOGY

Since 1278, Andorra has been autonomous, ruled by French and Spanish co-princes.

- ❑ **1933** Andorran revolt against extension of the franchise put down by French.
- ❑ **1970** Women get the vote.
- ❑ **1982** First constitution enshrines popular sovereignty.
- ❑ **1983** General Council votes in favor of income tax.
- ❑ **1984** Government resigns over attempt to introduce indirect taxes.
- ❑ **1991** EC Customs Union comes into effect.
- ❑ **1992** Political demonstrations demanding constitutional reform. Government resigns.
- ❑ **1993** Referendum approves new constitution. Democratic elections.

HEALTH

1 per 467 people

Heart and cerebrovascular diseases

Andorra has one public and one private hospital. Hot springs at les Escaldes are popular with rheumatism sufferers.

WEALTH

Experienced waiter, 170,000 pesetas per month; primary school teacher, 220,000 pesetas per month

CONSUMER GOODS OWNERSHIP

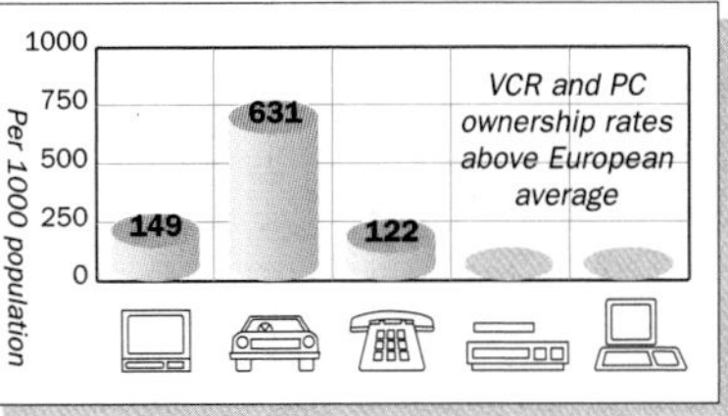

Hotel owners are the wealthiest group in Andorran society; many choose to live across the border in Spain.

WORLD RANKING

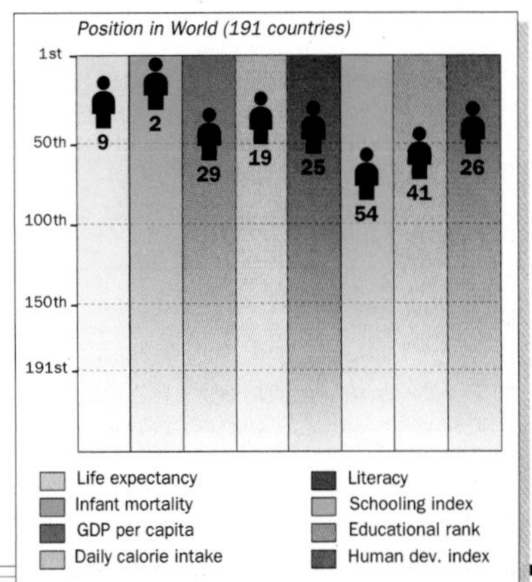

ANGOLA

SOUTHERN AFRICA

Congo Zaire ANGOLA Zambia Namibia Africa

OFFICIAL NAME: People's Republic of Angola **CAPITAL:** Luanda
POPULATION: 9.9 million **CURRENCY:** New kwanza **OFFICIAL LANGUAGE:** Portuguese

An OIL-RICH COUNTRY in southwest Africa, Angola has been in a state of almost permanent civil war since 1975 when the colonial power, Portugal, left. For many years it was a key Cold War frontier in Africa, with the West supporting UNITA against the Soviet-backed MPLA. Elections in 1992 confirmed the MPLA in power. In 1993, UNITA decided to resume the war.

Angola's capital, Luanda. Founded in 1575 by the Portuguese, it became a transshipment point for slaves en route to Brazil.

CLIMATE

WEATHER CHART

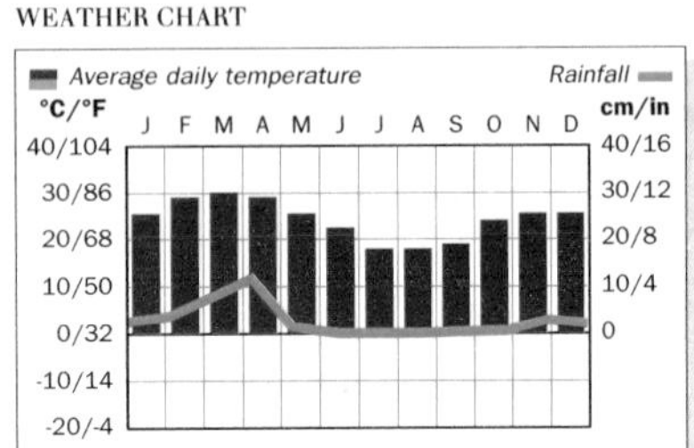

The climate varies from temperate to tropical. Rainfall decreases from north to south. The Benguela Current makes the coast unusually cool and dry.

COMMUNICATIONS

Luanda International 1.33m passengers

29 ships 112,500 dwt

THE TRANSPORTATION NETWORK

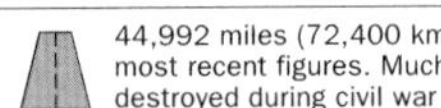

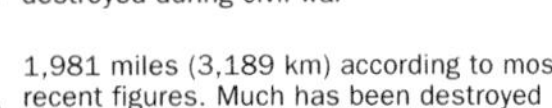

44,992 miles (72,400 km) according to most recent figures. Much has been destroyed during civil war

1,981 miles (3,189 km) according to most recent figures. Much has been destroyed during civil war

The war has destroyed Angola's transportation infrastructure. This has contributed to mass starvation, as relief supplies are unable to reach affected areas. Air travel is the safest means of transportation, although still risky due to UNITA's use of advanced ground-to-air missiles. The war has led to a collapse in port traffic: Namibe handled 6 million tons in 1973, but just 171,000 tons by 1985. The resumption of war in 1993 halted a $340-million road and bridge repair program.

TOURISM

Angola is a war zone. There are no tourists

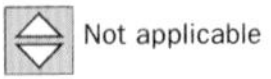

Not applicable

Most overseas visitors are Western journalists, or employees of the big oil multinationals in Cabinda. Angola, a disease-ridden war zone, where up to 500,000 people have died since October 1992, attracts no tourists.

PEOPLE

Portuguese, Umbundu, Kimbundu, Kongo

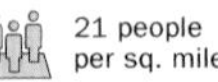

21 people per sq. mile

THE URBAN/RURAL POPULATION SPLIT

28% 72%

ETHNIC MAKEUP

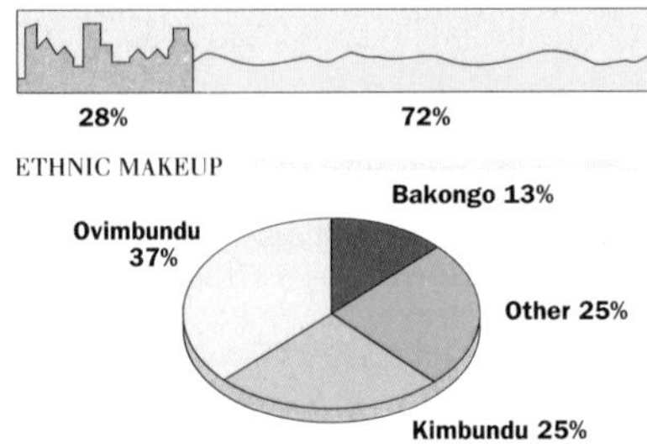

Ethnic tensions in Angola are few. UNITA has cast itself as the sole representative of the Ovimbundu in order to attack the mainly urban-based and largely Kimbundu MPLA. Religion has undergone a revival since the 1980s as the MPLA has now abandoned its Marxist philosophy. For most Angolans life is simply a day-to-day battle for survival.

POLITICS

1996

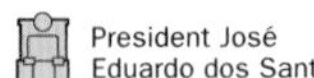

President José Eduardo dos Santos

THE STATE OF THE PARTIES

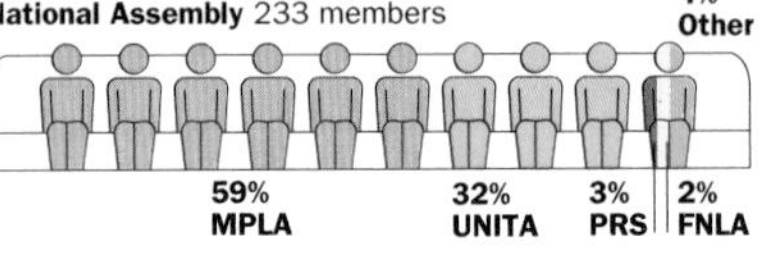

MPLA = People's Movement for the Liberation of Angola **UNITA** = National Union for the Total Independence of Angola **PRS** = Social Renewal Party **FNLA** = National Front for the Liberation of Angola **Other** = Democratic Liberal Party

Angola is dominated by two main groups, the MPLA and UNITA. In 1991, the MPLA, in power since 1975, decided to abandon Marxist one-party rule and embraced market capitalism. In 1992, democratic elections were held. These were unexpectedly lost by Jonas Savimbi's UNITA, which decided to reopen the civil war. Questions were raised about the fairness of the elections, but the EU, UN and other observers thought they broadly represented voters' wishes. Numerous peace efforts culminated in a failed conference in Lusaka, Zambia, in 1994.

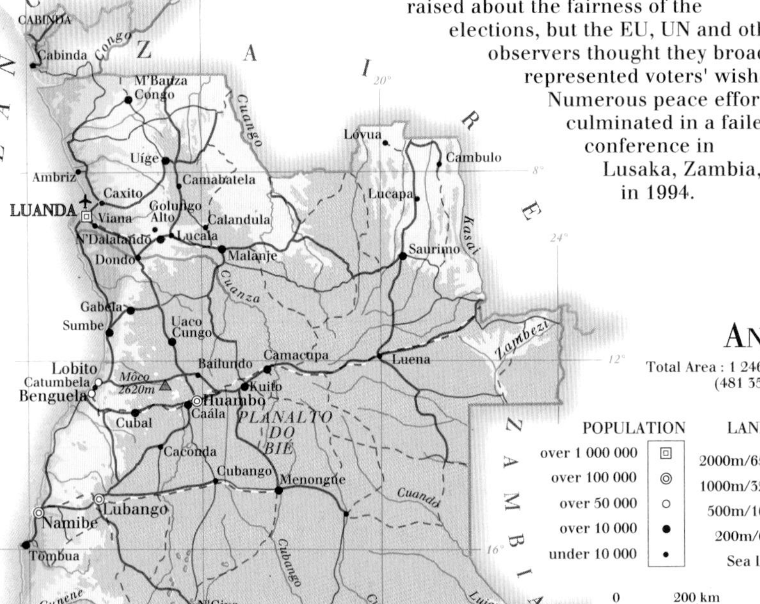

A

WORLD AFFAIRS

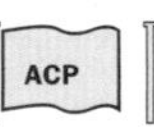

Angola was one of the key Cold War frontiers in Africa, with Soviet advisers and Cuban troops supporting the MPLA, and South Africa and the USA backing UNITA forces. In 1991, the USA, USSR and Portugal brokered a peace agreement under a UN mandate. UNITA forces did not disarm as agreed and were in a stronger position when they resumed the civil war after losing the elections in 1992. MPLA forces, however, with access to the $3.5 billion-a-year oil revenues, began rearming in 1993.

AID

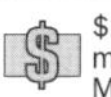
$250m, excluding military aid to both MPLA and UNITA

Up 10% in 1993

In the 1980s, the Soviet Union was the main donor, with over $4 billion in military aid to the MPLA government. At least three million Angolans are dependent on the most basic form of aid – food. Distribution in conditions of war is the major problem. Portugal, the EU and Brazil are the major donors.

DEFENSE

Precise figures n/av, but largest proportion of budget

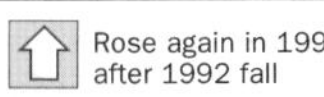
Rose again in 1993, after 1992 fall

In the 1980s conflict with South African-backed UNITA, the Cuban units proved most effective within the 100,000-strong MPLA army. The MPLA army was hastily re-formed in 1993 in response to the resumption of war by UNITA. Oil wealth allows the MPLA access to the world arms market. Brazil is a major supplier, particularly of missiles.

ECONOMICS

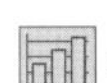
$6.2bn

6,611.20 new kwanza

SCORE CARD

❑ WORLD GNP RANKING	103rd
❑ GNP PER CAPITA	$625
❑ BALANCE OF PAYMENTS	$-511m
❑ INFLATION	92.2%
❑ UNEMPLOYMENT	18.9%

STRENGTHS

Oil sector, which is currently protected from the worst effects of war, earns Angola $3.5 billion a year. Some of the richest mineral deposits in Africa.

WEAKNESSES

Civil war. The oil sector remains a key UNITA war target. Lack of skilled labor.

EXPORTS

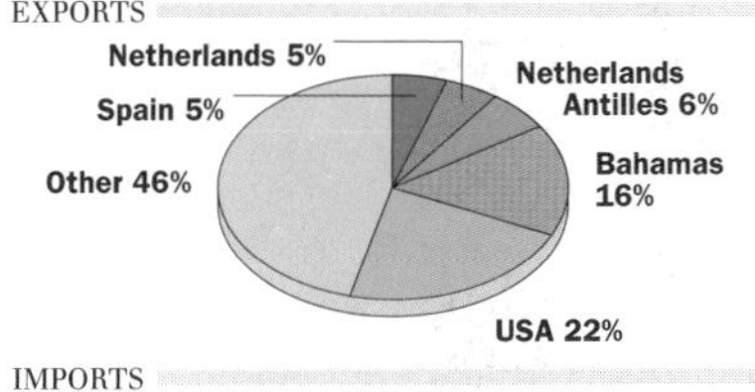

IMPORTS

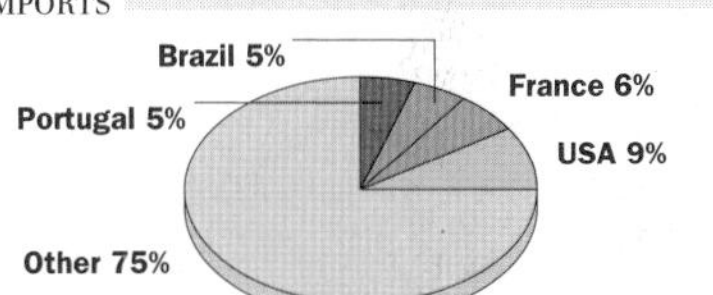

RESOURCES

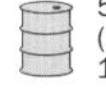
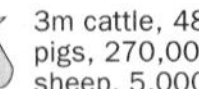

1.8bn kwh (capacity 620,000 kw)

535,300 b/d (reserves 1,500,000,000 bbl)

3m cattle, 485,000 pigs, 270,000 sheep, 5,000 asses

Oil, diamonds, iron, copper, lead, zinc, gold, manganese

Cabinda is the main oil-producing region. Angola has some of the richest alluvial diamond deposits in the world.

ENVIRONMENT

2% (1% partially protected)

War makes any ecological initiatives impossible

The 1990 drought threatened three million Angolans with famine. Other ecological issues do not feature at all.

MEDIA

The constitution recognizes freedom of speech. Minor criticisms are tolerated in practice

PUBLISHING AND BROADCAST MEDIA

There is 1 daily newspaper, *O Jornal de Angola*

1 state-owned service

1 state-owned, also independent services

The *Voice of the Black Cockerel*, UNITA's powerful propaganda radio station in the south, covers most of Angola.

CRIME

Most prisoners are simply killed

Dramatic increase due to war

Murder, theft, corruption and diamond smuggling are commonplace in war-torn Angola. All areas outside main cities are effectively controlled by armed gangs. Both the MPLA and UNITA have poor human rights records.

EDUCATION

42%

The system has all but collapsed in most areas, although the university in Luanda still functions.

CHRONOLOGY

The Portuguese first established forts along the coast of present day Angola in 1482.

- ❑ **1956** Marxist MPLA founded.
- ❑ **1961** FNLA begins intense guerrilla liberation struggle.
- ❑ **1975** Independence from Portugal. Civil war between Soviet and Cuban-backed MPLA and US and South African-backed UNITA.
- ❑ **1979** José Eduardo dos Santos (MPLA) becomes president.
- ❑ **1991** UN-brokered peace.
- ❑ **1992** Elections won by MPLA.
- ❑ **1993** UNITA reopens civil war.

HEALTH

1 per 13,489 people

Malaria, diarrheal and respiratory diseases, severe malnutrition

The system is in a state of collapse, unable to cope with the three million at risk of famine and the estimated 10,000 war wounded a day. Angola has the highest infant mortality rate and the greatest number of amputees (caused by exploding mines) in the world.

WEALTH

Formal employment has effectively collapsed in Angola

CONSUMER GOODS OWNERSHIP

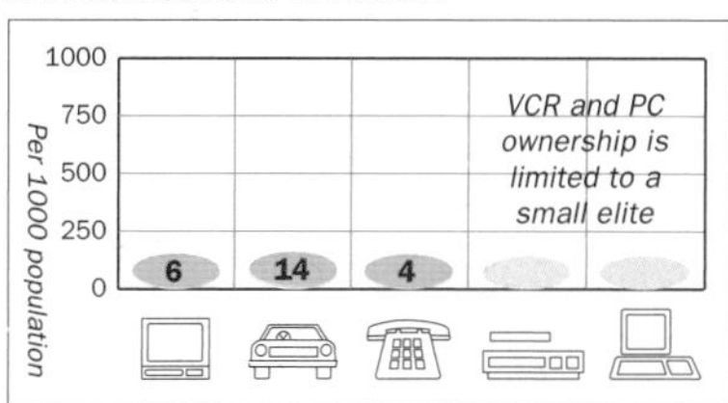

Higher-ranking state officials enjoy luxuries, such as private MPLA shops and access to cars. Much of the rest of the population is struggling to survive.

WORLD RANKING

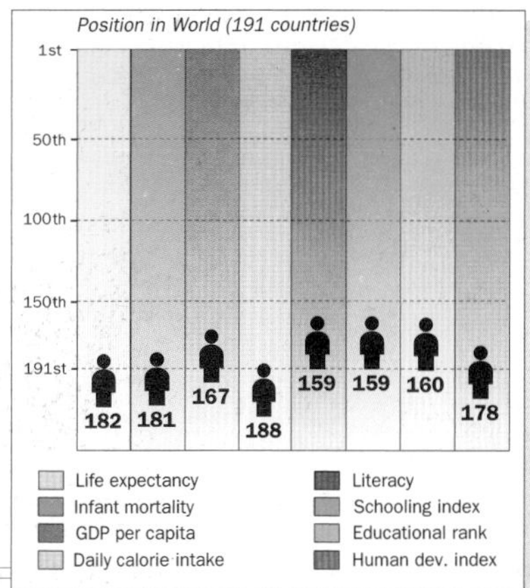

A

ANTARCTICA

OFFICIAL NAME: Antarctica **CAPITAL:** *None*
POPULATION: 4,000 **CURRENCY:** *None* **OFFICIAL LANGUAGE:** *None*

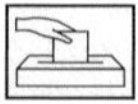

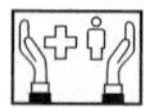

THE FIFTH-LARGEST CONTINENT, Antarctica is almost entirely covered by ice over 1 mile thick. The area sustains a varied wildlife, including seals, whales and penguins. The Antarctic Treaty, which came into force in 1961, provides for international governance of Antarctica. To gain Consultative status, countries have to set up an active program of scientific research in the continent. Several countries support the proposal that Antarctica should become a world park and a sanctuary for whales.

CLIMATE

WEATHER CHART

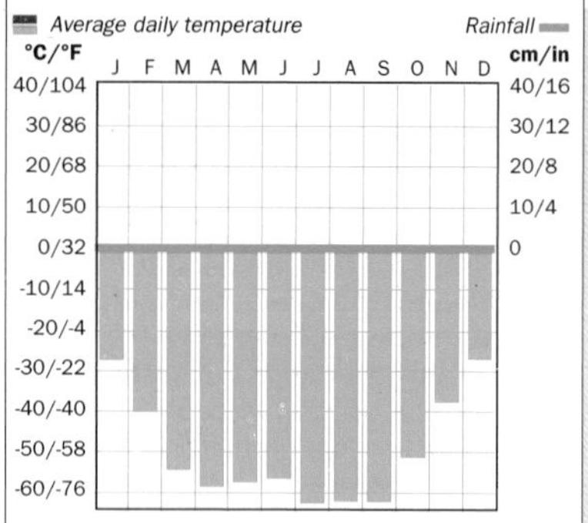

Antarctica is the windiest as well as the coldest continent. Powerful winds create a narrow storm belt around the continent, which brings cloud, fog and severe blizzards. Icebergs, which tend to be slab-shaped, barricade more than 90% of the coastline. Antarctica contains over 80% of the world's fresh water in the form of ice. The blood of polar fish contains anti-freeze agents.

COMMUNICATIONS

 Airstrips to some stations

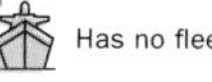 Has no fleet

Ships are the main mode of transportation to Antarctica. They are also used for marine research projects. Air traffic from Chile is growing, and France and the UK are building new airstrips. Most planes have to be equipped with skis.

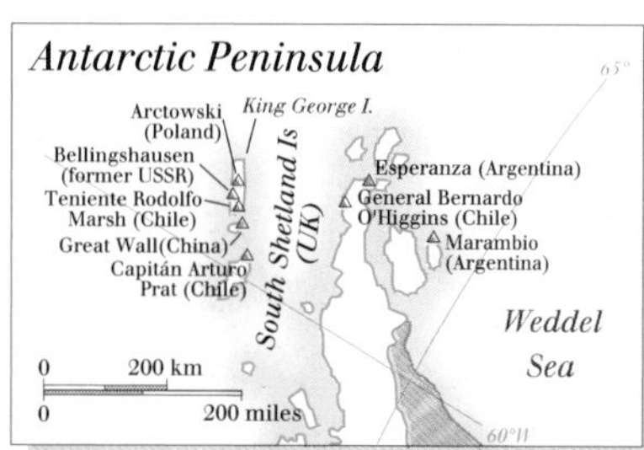

TOURISM

 3,000 visitors

Small increase from year to year

Tourism is mainly by cruise ship to the Antarctic Peninsula, Ross Sea and the sub-Antarctic islands. In 1983, the Chileans began flights to King George Island, where an 80-bed hotel has been built. Main attractions are the wildlife, skiing and visits to scientific stations and historic huts. The growth of tourism has disrupted scientific programs and official regulation of tourism is now essential.

PEOPLE

 English, Spanish, French, Norwegian, Chinese, Polish, Russian, German, Japanese

 0 people per sq. mile

ETHNIC MAKEUP

Antarctica has a transient population of Americans, English, French, Norwegians, Argentinians, Chileans, Chinese, Russians, Poles and Japanese. Most are involved in research. Few stay more than two years

Antarctica has no indigenous population. The people who live in the continent are scientists and logistical staff working at the 40 permanent, and as many as 100 temporary, research stations. Most stations are too far apart for direct contact between different nationalities. A few Chilean settler families reside on King George Island.

ANTARCTICA

Total Area : 13 900 000 sq. km (5 366 790 sq. miles)

Neumayer Channel, Antarctica, Many states are pressing for the whole of Antarctica to be protected as an international park.

POLITICS

 Not applicable

 Consultative Parties to Antarctic Treaty

THE STATE OF THE PARTIES

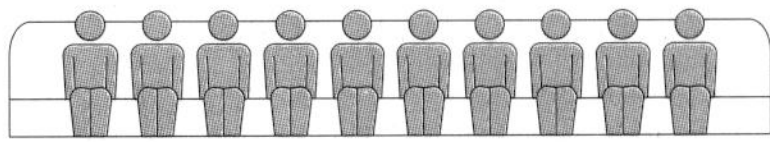

The Antarctic Treaty of 1959 was signed by 12 nations and acceded to by 29. Consultative meetings are held annually to discuss scientific, environmental and political matters

There are 26 signatories to the Antarctic Treaty and 14 nations with observer status. There are territorial claims by Australia, France, New Zealand and Norway, and overlapping claims in the Antarctic Peninsula by Argentina, Chile and the UK. Other states do not recognize these claims. Of main concern is the adoption of a protocol to ban mining. Most member states have agreed to this. Further protection of the environment is proposed by monitoring all scientific activities, and prosecuting any country whose research would lead to detrimental global change.

WORLD AFFAIRS

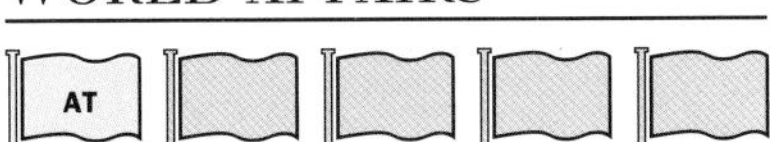

Rivalries exist between nations wishing to preserve Antarctica as a world park and those pursuing territorial claims.

AID

 Each country's research is government-funded

 Subject to individual government budgets

Scientific programs in the Antarctic are almost entirely funded by government agencies in the home countries. Some funding is sometimes provided by scientific institutions and universities.

DEFENSE

 No defense force

 Not applicable

Under the Antarctic Treaty, Antarctica can only be used for peaceful purposes. Any military personnel present perform purely scientific or logistical roles.

ECONOMICS

 Not applicable

 Antarctica has no currency

Research is government-funded and therefore subject to cuts. The exploitation of marine stocks provides no income to Antarctica.

RESOURCES

 Each station has its own generator

 Not an oil producer and has no refineries

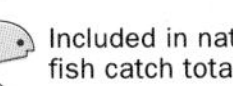 Included in national fish catch totals

 Minerals

The Antarctic's main resources are its marine stocks, including fin-fish, squids, krill, seals and whales. In 1989, France and Australia joined environmental groups in demanding a ban on potential mineral activities, and campaigning for Antarctica to be declared a world park. Chile and Argentina, in particular, see this as a threat to possible territorial claims. Use of alternative energy sources to fossil fuels are being encouraged, such as solar power and wind generators.

ENVIRONMENT

 0.02%

 1994 Antarctic whale sanctuary established

Antarctica is one of the last great wildernesses on Earth. Its layer of ice, over 13,000 ft. thick in places, has taken thousands of years to form. Its ecosystem is so fragile that even a footprint will leave its mark for years. Several species are unique to the continent, including King penguins. A major ecological concern in Antarctica is overfishing, particularly of krill, cod and squid. Also of concern is the depletion of the ozone layer over Antarctica which may have adverse effects of phytoplankton, the foundation of the food chain for marine life. In 1994, the IWC agreed to a French proposal to create an Antarctic whale sanctuary. Together with the Indian Ocean sanctuary, this will protect the feeding grounds of 90% of the world's whales.

MEDIA

 There are no daily newspapers produced in Antarctica. Any papers are brought in from the home countries

A few bases publish newsletters for local distribution. Local radio stations are found at some of the larger bases.

CRIME

 There are no prisons in Antarctica

 Crime is negligible

Crime is negligible. Each person in Antarctica is subject to his own national laws. Occasional petty theft from stations is linked to visits from tourists.

CHRONOLOGY

The Russian explorer Thaddeus von Bellinghausen was the first to sight Antarctica, in 1820. The South Pole was first reached by the Norwegian Roald Amundsen in December 1911.

- ❑ **1912** UK team of five, led by Scott, find they have been beaten to the Pole. All perish on return journey.
- ❑ **1957–1958** International Geophysical Year. Aims to explore Antarctic region scientifically.
- ❑ **1959** Antarctic Treaty signed by 12 countries. Territorial claims frozen. Area to be used only for peaceful purposes.
- ❑ **1978** Convention for the Conservation of Antarctic Seals. Limits number of seals killed.

EDUCATION

 100%

Schoolhouses exist on the Chilean base, Villa Las Estrellas, and the Argentinian base, Esperanza. Teaching is based on the relevant national system. Some researchers' studies contribute to higher degrees.

Antarctic-based research has resulted in a number of scientific breakthroughs, including the discovery of ozone depletion.

HEALTH

 1 medical officer per station

 Deaths are extremely rare in Antarctica

There is no central health system. Each station has its own medical officer who treats mostly minor complaints. Disease is rare, because all personnel are medically screened. The problems usually associated with polar conditions, such as frostbite and snow blindness, are very rare. Serious illness cannot be treated locally, and patients have to be evacuated.

WEALTH

 Most Antarctic researchers draw salaries equivalent to their earnings at home

Wealth disparities reflect the different levels of funding received by each national base. The US bases are the best-funded. Most stations have a TV and VCR. Telephone systems only operate within stations. PCs are supplied for scientific research. There are no cars.

WORLD RANKING

The UN Human Development Index conditions are not applicable to Antarctica

A

ANTIGUA & BARBUDA

CARIBBEAN

North America

Puerto Rico · Redonda I. · ANTIGUA & BARBUDA

OFFICIAL NAME: Antigua and Barbuda **CAPITAL:** St. John's

POPULATION: 64,000 **CURRENCY:** East Caribbean dollar **OFFICIAL LANGUAGE:** English

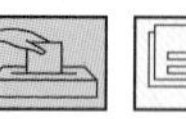

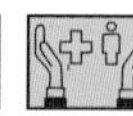

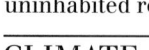

LOCATED BETWEEN the Atlantic and the Caribbean, Antigua, one of the Leeward Islands, was in turn a Spanish, French and British colony. British influence is still strong, and most clearly revealed in the Antiguans' passion for cricket. Antigua has two remote dependencies: Barbuda, 30 miles to the northeast, sporting a magnificent beach; and Redonda, 25 miles southwest, an uninhabited rock with its own king.

CLIMATE

WEATHER CHART

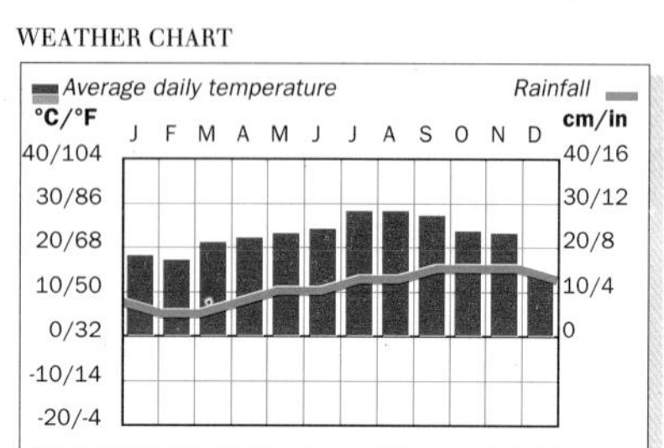

Antigua is less humid than other Caribbean islands. Year-round trade winds moderate the heat.

COMMUNICATIONS

V C Bird International, St. John's
727,292 passengers

310 ships
1.21m dwt

THE TRANSPORTATION NETWORK

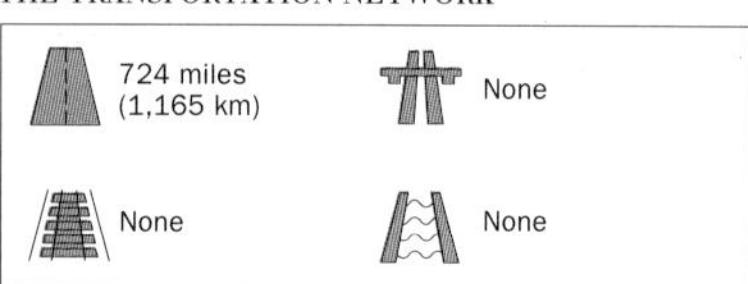

Encouraging tourism lies behind two recent projects: the improvement of the international airport and an extended pier at St. John's to take cruise ships.

TOURISM

209,902 visitors

Up 7% in 1992

MAIN OVERSEAS ARRIVALS

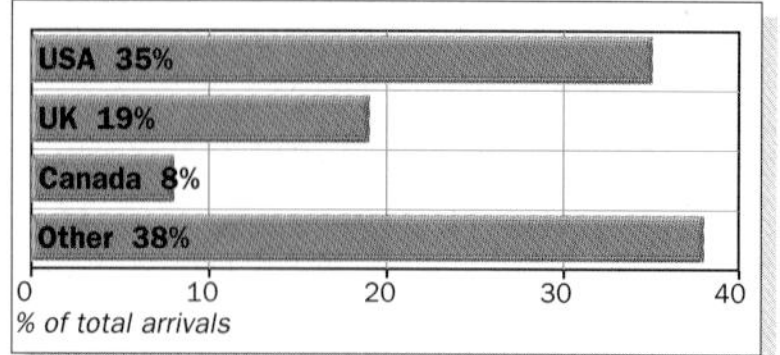

Antigua is increasingly popular with US cruise-ship tourists and the yachting rich who attend the annual Sailing Week. The 18th-century Nelson's Dockyard at St. John's is a major attraction.

PEOPLE

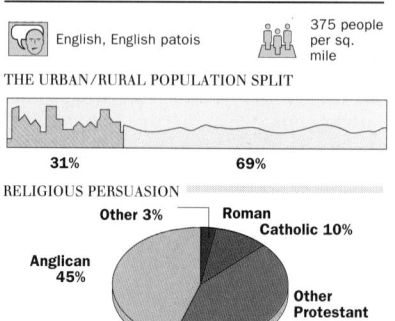

English, English patois

375 people per sq. mile

THE URBAN/RURAL POPULATION SPLIT

31% 69%

RELIGIOUS PERSUASION

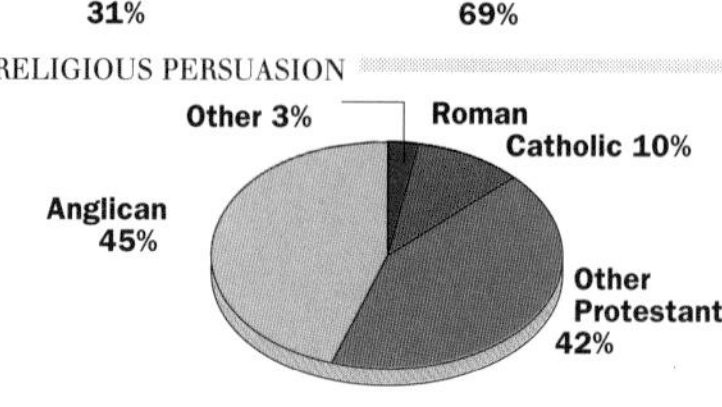

Most of Antigua's population is descended from Africans brought over between the 16th and 19th centuries. There are, in addition, a few Europeans and South Asians. Racial tensions are few. Life is based around the extended family. Since the 1960s, the status of women has risen as a result of their greater access to education, and many are now entering the legal, financial and medical professions. Unemployment is low and wealth disparities are small.

POLITICS

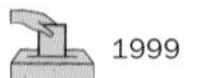

THE STATE OF THE PARTIES

House of Representatives 17 members

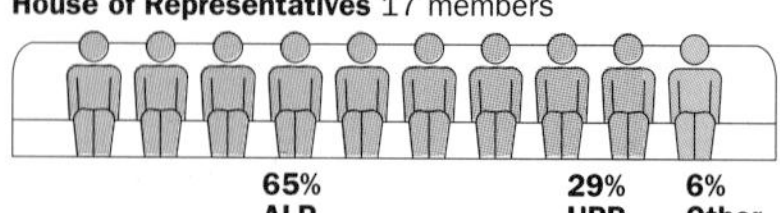

ALP = Antigua Labour Party **UPP** = United Progressive Party
BPM = Barbuda People's Movement

Senate 17 members

11 members chosen by the prime minister, 4 by the leader of the opposition, 1 by the governor-general and 1 by the Barbuda Council

Antigua's multiparty democracy has been dominated for the past 30 years by the Bird family. Vere Bird Sr., prime minister and ALP leader, indicated his intention of retiring in 1993. His two sons, Vere Jr. and Lester, were arguing over the succession, but Vere Jr. was banned from office after being accused of involvement in gun-running. Lester Bird, therefore, took over on his father's retirement in December 1993. He went on to win the general elections in March the following year.

ANTIGUA & BARBUDA

Total Area : 440 sq. km (170 sq. miles)

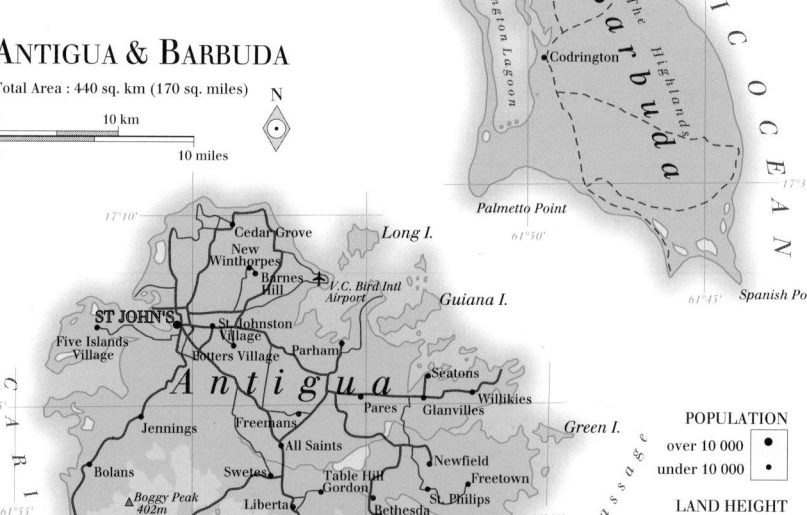

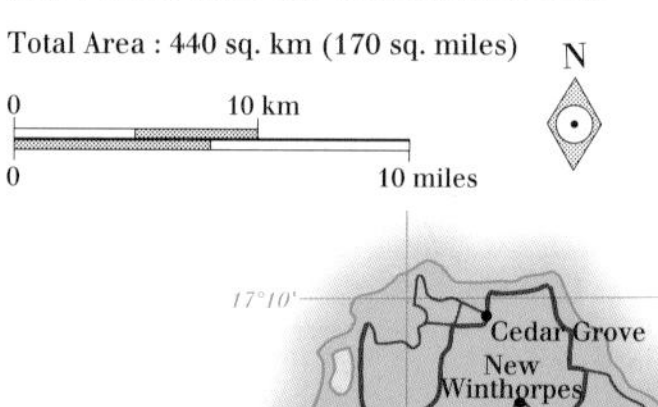

WORLD AFFAIRS

NAM

Antigua backs US policy in the Caribbean, supporting both the US invasion of Grenada in 1983 and economic sanctions against Cuba.

AID

 $7m (receipts)

 Up 75% in 1991

Donors, which include the USA, UK and France, have expressed concern that project development aid may have been misused by the Bird regime. The EU gives aid under the Lomé Convention.

DEFENSE

 $1.4m

 Slight increase in 1992

The USA and UK are the main suppliers of equipment and training to the small army and coastguard. The army is not involved in politics. Two military bases on Antigua are leased to the USA.

ECONOMICS

 $355m

 2.70 East Caribbean dollars

SCORE CARD

- ❑ WORLD GNP RANKING....................169th
- ❑ GNP PER CAPITA........................$5,550
- ❑ BALANCE OF PAYMENTS................$-59.5m
- ❑ INFLATION....................................7.7%
- ❑ UNEMPLOYMENT..............................5%

STRENGTHS

Tourism is a growing business. The extension of the pier at St. John's will encourage more cruise-ship trade. Sailing Week has proved a great success, attracting world-class competition every April.

WEAKNESSES

Very little diversification makes Antigua vulnerable to downturns in the world tourism market.

EXPORTS

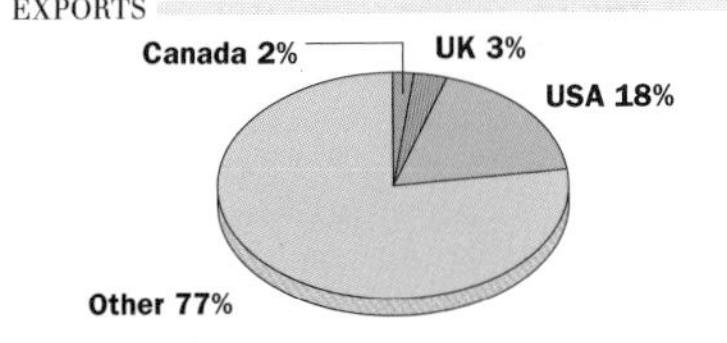

IMPORTS

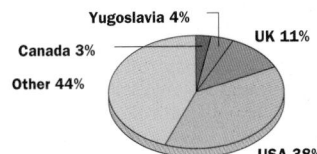

Yugoslavia 4%
UK 11%
Canada 3%
Other 44%
USA 38%

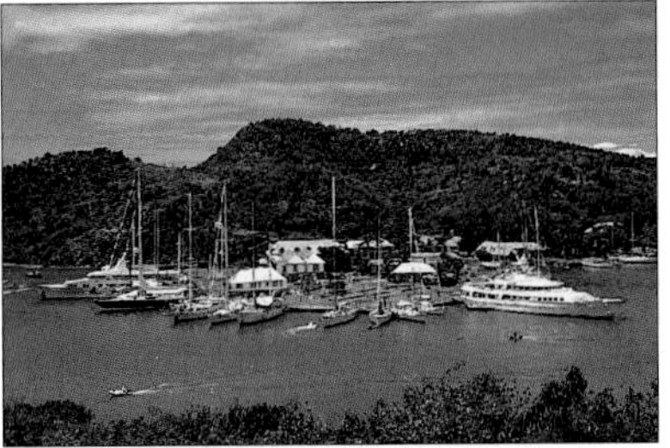

Nelson's Dockyard. *Luxury yachts fitted with 20th-century, state-of-the-art gadgetry contrast with the 18th-century St. John's harbor.*

RESOURCES

 95m kwh (capacity 30,000 kw)

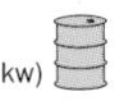 Not an oil producer and has no refineries

 18,000 cattle, 13,000 sheep, 13,000 goats

 None

Antigua has no strategic or commodity resources and has to import almost all its energy requirements.

ENVIRONMENT

 9%

 Continuing state failure to control hotel development

Uncontrolled sewage disposal from beachfront hotels causes problems. In the 1990 McKinnon Swamp incident, untreated hotel effluent killed valuable inshore fish stocks. Antigua's mangrove systems are also threatened by hotel developments.

MEDIA

 Laws forbid political interference with the media, but the opposition press still faces suppression

PUBLISHING AND BROADCAST MEDIA

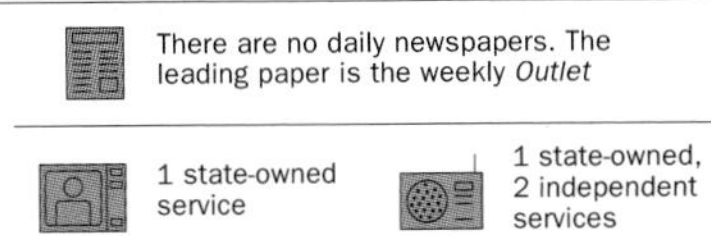

There are no daily newspapers. The leading paper is the weekly *Outlet*
1 state-owned service
1 state-owned, 2 independent services

There are no independent newspapers in Antigua and Barbuda. Three of the weekly newspapers are published by political parties; the fourth is funded by the government.

CRIME

 Antigua and Barbuda does not publish prison figures

 There are no particularly dangerous areas on the islands

Murder is rare on Antigua and Barbuda. Rape, armed robbery and burglary are the main local concerns.

EDUCATION

 90%

Education is based on the British selective 11-plus system. Students go on to the University of the West Indies, or to study in the UK and the USA.

CHRONOLOGY

In 1667, Antigua became a British colony. Barbuda, formerly owned by the British Codrington family, was annexed in 1860.

- ❑ **1941** USA builds military bases.
- ❑ **1951** Universal adult suffrage introduced.
- ❑ **1972** Sugar industry, unable to compete with neighboring states, closed down.
- ❑ **1981** Independence from Britain; opposed by Barbudan secessionist movement.
- ❑ **1983** Supports US invasion of Grenada.
- ❑ **1990** Vere Bird Jr. banned for life from government office.

HEALTH

 1 per 1,606 people

 Heart and respiratory diseases, cancer

By Caribbean standards, Antigua and Barbuda's health system is extremely efficient, with easy access to the state-run clinics and hospitals.

WEALTH

 Minimum wage, 4 East Caribbean dollars per hour

CONSUMER GOODS OWNERSHIP

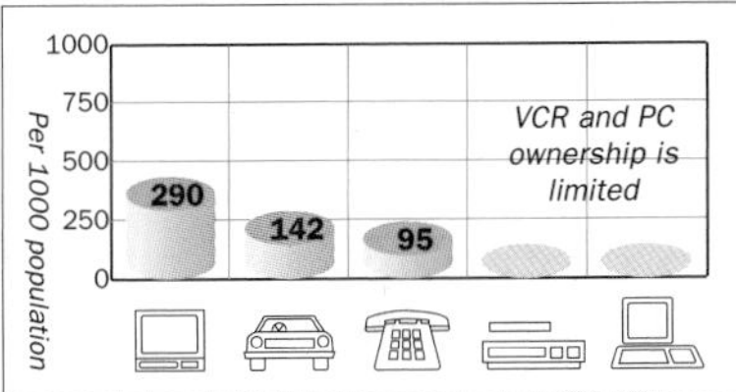

Antigua is fairly socially mobile. Wealthier Antiguans are involved in the tourist industry; Japanese cars, BMWs and satellite dishes are their favored status symbols.

WORLD RANKING

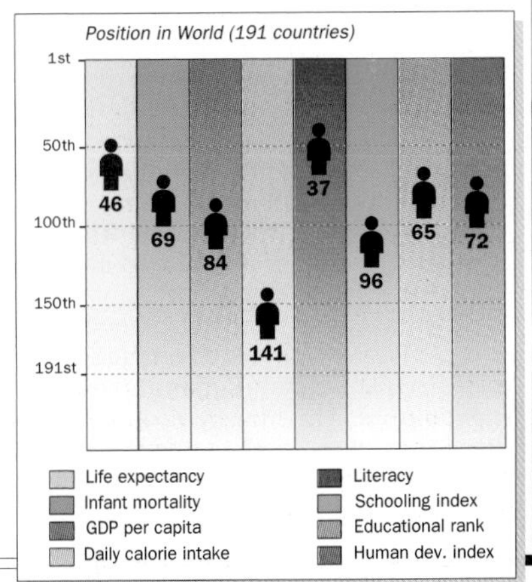

A

ARGENTINA

OFFICIAL NAME: Argentine Republic **CAPITAL:** Buenos Aires
POPULATION: 33.1 million **CURRENCY:** Argentine peso **OFFICIAL LANGUAGE:** Spanish

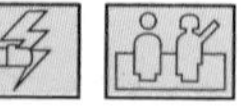

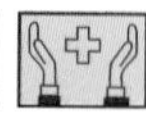

OCCUPYING MOST OF THE SOUTHERN half of South America, Argentina extends 2,145 miles from Bolivia to Cape Horn. The Andes Mountains in the west run north–south, forming a natural border with Chile. To the east they slope down to the fertile central pampas, the region known as Entre Ríos. Agriculture – especially beef, wheat and fruit – and energy resources are Argentina's main sources of wealth. Politics in Argentina in the past have been characterized by periods of military rule. In 1983, however, Argentina returned to multiparty democracy.

***Herding cattle** in the northeast, near Corrientes. Beef, Argentina's first source of wealth, remains a major export.*

CLIMATE

WEATHER CHART

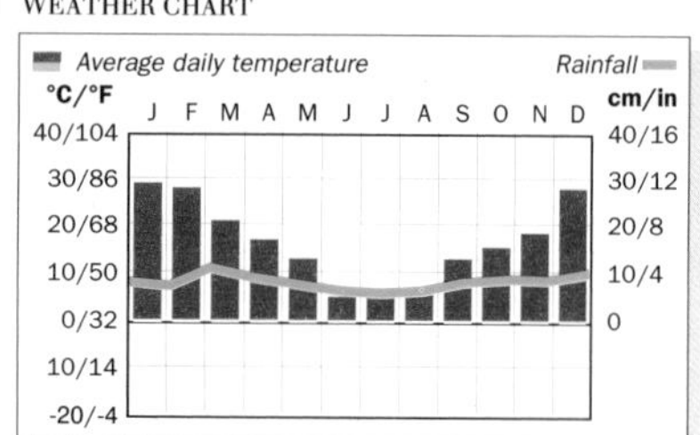

The northeast is near-tropical. The Andes are semi-arid in the north and snowy in the south. The western lowlands are desert, while the pampas have a mild climate with heavy summer rains.

COMMUNICATIONS

Eezeiza Intl, Buenos Aires 2.6m passengers

68 ships 1.01m dwt

THE TRANSPORTATION NETWORK

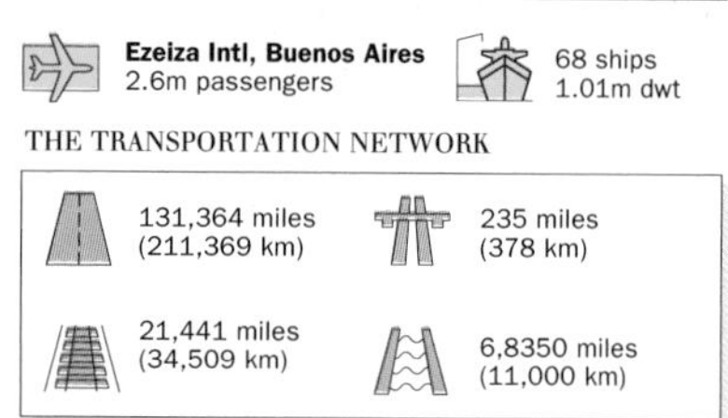

The government plans to privatize as much of the transportation network as possible. The state airline, *Aerolíneas Argentinas*, has been successfully sold off to the Spanish national carrier, *Iberia*. Argentina's antiquated railroad system will be harder to sell, even in the proposed regional sections, which will end the notion of a national railroad. In 1993, virtually the whole system was temporarily closed down, threatening 20,000 jobs.

Private investment is also being sought for new toll roads and for a massive plan to link Buenos Aires to Uruguay and Brazil with a tunnel under the River Plate. Road deaths remain a major problem; Argentina has one of the worst fatality rates in the world.

TOURISM

3.03m visitors

Up 6% in 1992

MAIN OVERSEAS ARRIVALS

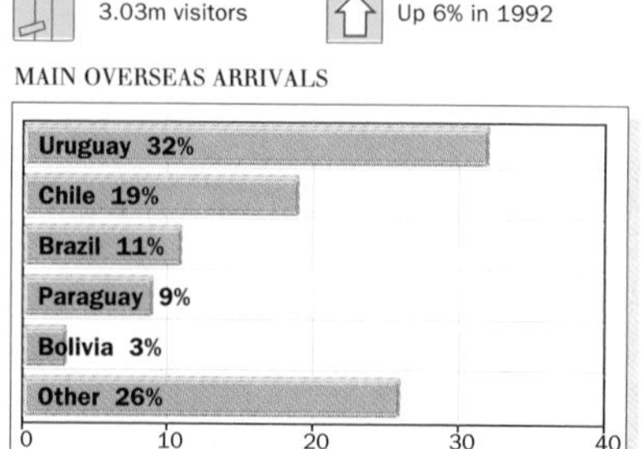

Although tourism is a significant export earner, Argentina is still on the fringe of the world tourism market – 80% of foreign visitors come from adjoining countries, attracted mainly by Buenos Aires' city life and the ski resorts. The resort of Mar del Plata on the coast and the ski area in the Córdoba highlands have become mass tourism destinations. Wealthy Argentinians, however, are abandoning these in favor of foreign trips. The many privatization plans include the very popular state-run casinos.

PEOPLE

Spanish, Italian, Amerindian languages

31 people per sq. mile

THE URBAN/RURAL POPULATION SPLIT

86% 14%

RELIGIOUS PERSUASION

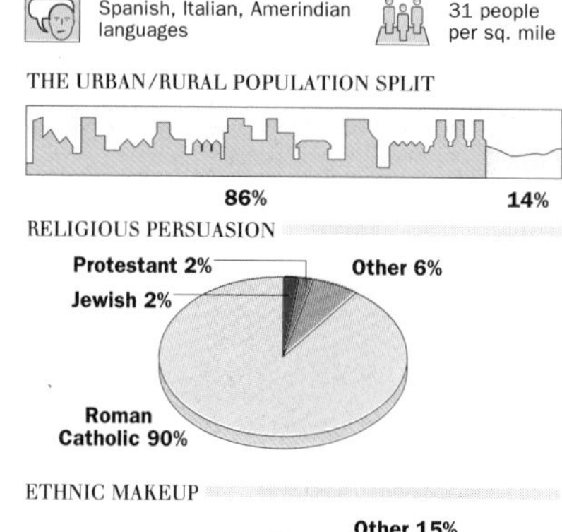

POPULATION AGE BREAKDOWN

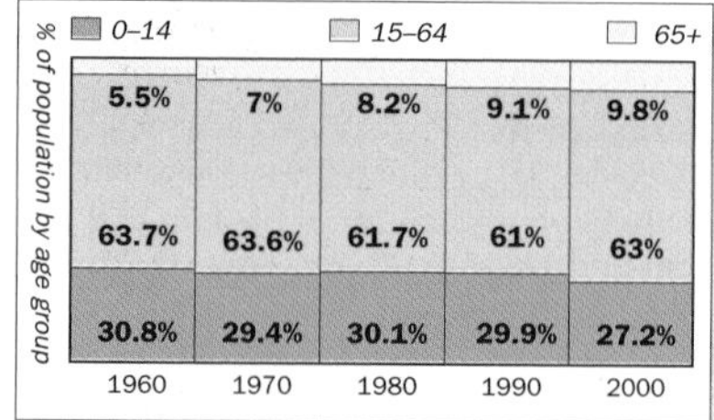

The large proportion of Argentinians of European descent are from recent 20th-century migrations; over one-third are of Italian origin. Indigenous peoples are now a minority, living mainly in Andean regions or in the *Gran Chaco*. Over 85% of Argentinians are urban dwellers, with 40% living in the capital, Buenos Aires. In general, there is little ethnic tension. Bolivian and Paraguayan immigrants remain the poorest groups.

Catholicism and the extended family remain strong in Argentina and social and religious reunions are common. The family also forms the backbone of many successful businesses.

Women have a higher profile than in most Latin American states. Argentinian women were enfranchised before their French counterparts received the vote. Today, many enter professional fields and rise to positions of influence in service businesses such as the media. The exception is politics. Eva Perón, who inspired the musical *Evita*, did help to push women into a more active political role in the 1940s and 1950s, but this trend was reversed under military rule.

POLITICS

Lower House 1995
Upper House 1995

President Carlos Saúl Menem

Argentina is a multiparty democracy; the president is head of state.

MAIN POLITICAL ISSUES

Maintaining economic stability
Carlos Menem's radical privatization policies and his vigorous cutting back of the state sector succeeded in reducing inflation from a high of over 7,000% to 18% by 1992. A new currency, the peso, introduced in 1992, has maintained parity with the dollar. The central aim of policy now is to maintain growth, keeping a tight rein on inflation, and encouraging foreign investment.

Carlos Menem's reelection
Until 1993, Argentina's constitution prevented presidents from standing for consecutive terms. President Menem called an election in 1994 to allow him to change the constitution so that he could stand again. The issue sharply divided the electorate. Menem's supporters wished to secure his free-market policies. His opponents feared Menem could turn into a second Perón, running a *de facto* civilian dictatorship.

The role of the military
Following the military's fall from power in 1983, officers were tried during Alfonsín's administration for the murder of thousands of "suspects." Carlos Menem decided to pardon the officers, but the issue continues to generate controversy. Many remain suspicious of the military's political power. behind the scenes.

THE STATE OF THE PARTIES

Chamber of Deputies 257 members

2% US

50% PJ | 32% UCR | 16% Other

PJ = Justicialist Party (Peronists) **UCR** = Radical Civic Union
US = Socialist Union **MPN** = Neuquen Popular Movement
Other = Democratic Progression Party, Movement for Dignity and Independence, Union of the Democratic Centre, Republican Power

Senate 48 members

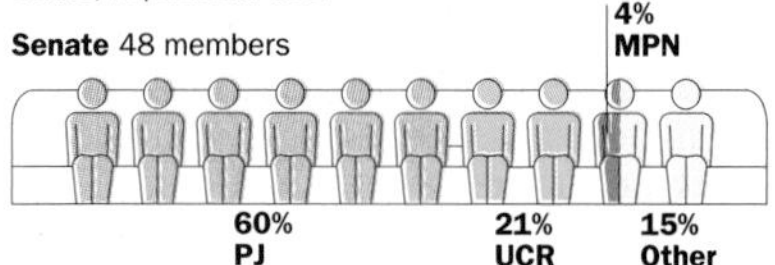

PROFILE

The Peronists have been the dominant civilian political force in Argentina since the 1940s. The party was founded on mass working-class and left-wing intellectual support. It has often been in disagreement with the military, which in practice represents the right and which mounted coups in 1955, 1966 and 1976. The UCR tends to stay in opposition, except when the electorate wishes to register a protest vote, as in 1983. Carlos Menem won elections in 1989 on a populist, left-wing platform. However, he switched tack quickly, steering the Peronists toward right-wing, free-market policies, and in the process gained the support of conservatives.

Carlos Menem, Justicialist Party (Peronist) leader; president since 1989.

Domingo Cavallo, finance minister and architect of radical privatization.

WORLD AFFAIRS

Mercsr | GATT | RG | LAES

Argentina's claim to the Falkland Islands (known in Latin America as the Islas Malvinas) remains at the top of its foreign policy agenda. Following the failure to take the islands from the UK by military action in 1982–1983, the claim is now being pursued through diplomatic channels. Relations between the two states, however, have improved to the point where Argentinian and British troops are serving side-by-side in UN operations in Cyprus.

Argentina is keen to move closer to the USA, which had traditionally been treated with suspicion by the Peronists. The main reason for the change in policy is Argentina's move away, under the Menem administration, from state-run businesses to American-style free-market economics, and the need to attract US investment. Trade relations with Brazil, Uruguay and Paraguay are also being pursued vigorously. The four states are aiming to achieve a tariff-free common market by 1995.

Argentina is actively promoting itself as a member of the "first world." Making its forces available to the UN is part of this strategy, as is the current suggestion of a South Atlantic Defense Alliance with South Africa.

A

AID

 Minimal receipts

 No change from year to year

Receipts, other than restructured loan arrangements with international bodies, are negligible. IMF loans from the 1980s are now regularly serviced.

CHRONOLOGY

The Spanish first established settlements in the Andean foothills in 1543. The indigenous Indians, who had stopped any Inca advance into their territory, also prevented the Spaniards from settling in the east until the 1590s.

- ❑ **1816** United Provinces of Río de la Plata declare independence; 70 years of civil war follow between central government unitarists and provincial federalists.
- ❑ **1835–1852** Dictatorship of Juan Manuel Rosas.
- ❑ **1853** Federal system set up.
- ❑ **1857** Europeans start settling the pampas; six million by 1930. Most land is held by an oligarchy of 200 families.
- ❑ **1877** First refrigerated ship starts frozen beef trade to Europe.
- ❑ **1878–1883** War against the Pampas Indians almost exterminates them.
- ❑ **1916** Hipólito Yrigoyen wins first democratic presidential elections.
- ❑ **1930** Military coup upsets republican constitution.
- ❑ **1943** New military coup. Juan Perón organizes trade unions.
- ❑ **1946** General Juan Perón elected president, with backing of the military and organized labor.
- ❑ **1952** Eva Perón, wife of Juan Perón and charismatic champion of workers' welfare, dies of leukemia.
- ❑ **1955** Military coup ousts Perón. Inflation, strikes, unemployment.
- ❑ **1973** Perón returns from exile in Madrid and is reelected president.
- ❑ **1974** Perón dies; succeeded by his third wife "Isabelita," who is unable to control either left-wing Peronist or urban guerrilla violence.
- ❑ **1976** Military junta under General Videla seizes power. Political parties are banned. Brutal repression of Dirty War sees "disappearance" of over 10,000 "left-wing suspects."
- ❑ **1981** General Galtieri president.
- ❑ **1982** Galtieri orders invasion of Falkland Islands. UK retakes them.
- ❑ **1983** Pro-human rights candidate Raúl Alfonsín (UCR) becomes president in free multiparty elections. Hyperinflation.
- ❑ **1989** Carlos Menem (Peronist) wins presidency.

DEFENSE

$2.1bn

Up 3% in 1993

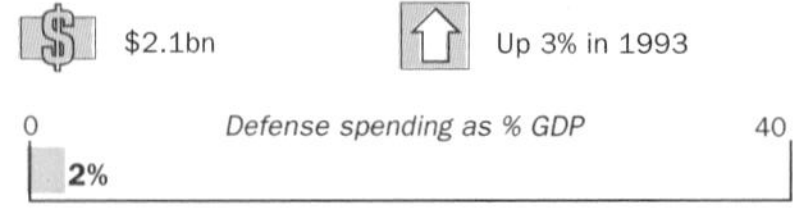

ARGENTINIAN ARMED FORCES

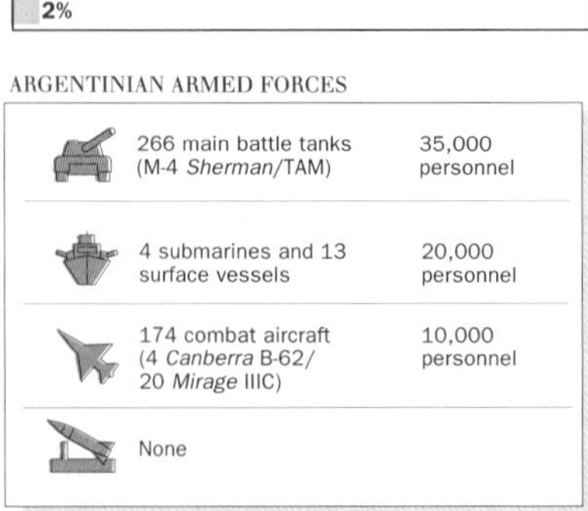

266 main battle tanks (M-4 Sherman/TAM)
35,000 personnel
4 submarines and 13 surface vessels
20,000 personnel
174 combat aircraft (4 Canberra B-62/ 20 Mirage IIIC)
10,000 personnel
None

Despite the military's fall from power in 1983, its influence remains strong; Carlos Menem has felt obliged to grant amnesties to officers found guilty of human rights abuses during the military dictatorship.

Argentina has a well-developed arms industry, much of it built up with Israeli assistance. France was a major source of weapons – the role of *Mirage* fighters and *Exocet* missiles was well publicized during the Falklands war. Recently, the air force has been buying US fighter aircraft. Argentina, despite having signed the Nuclear Non-Proliferation Treaty, is suspected of being close to achieving an independent nuclear capability.

ECONOMICS

 $224.5bn

 1.00 Argentine pesos

SCORE CARD

- ❑ WORLD GNP RANKING 18th
- ❑ GNP PER CAPITA $6,800
- ❑ BALANCE OF PAYMENTS .... $–8.5bn
- ❑ INFLATION 18%
- ❑ UNEMPLOYMENT 7.3%

EXPORTS

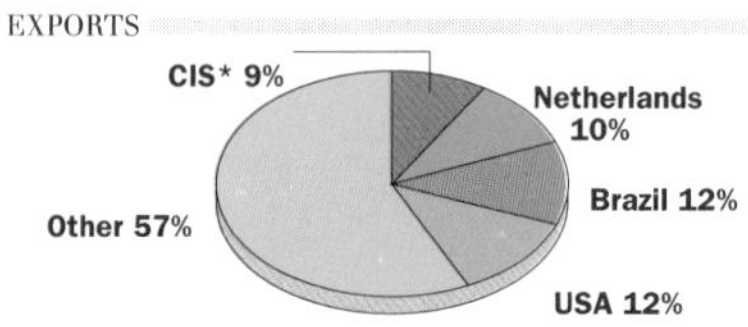

IMPORTS

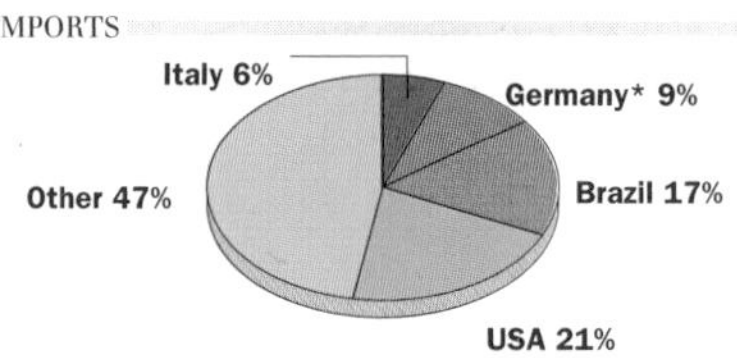

STRENGTHS

Argentina manages an export surplus in most years. A rich and varied agricultural base, powerful agribusiness (mainly beef, wheat, fruit and wine), a wealth of energy resources and a skilled labor force are major strengths. The Menem government's economic reforms, in particular currency stabilization and the reduction in inflation, are starting to make Argentina more attractive to overseas investors.

WEAKNESSES

The recent history of hyperinflation still casts doubts over the longevity of low inflation. Despite Menem's successes in privatizing state-owned industries, many major businesses are still under highly inefficient central control. A long history of political instability remains a deterrent to some investors.

ECONOMIC PERFORMANCE INDICATOR

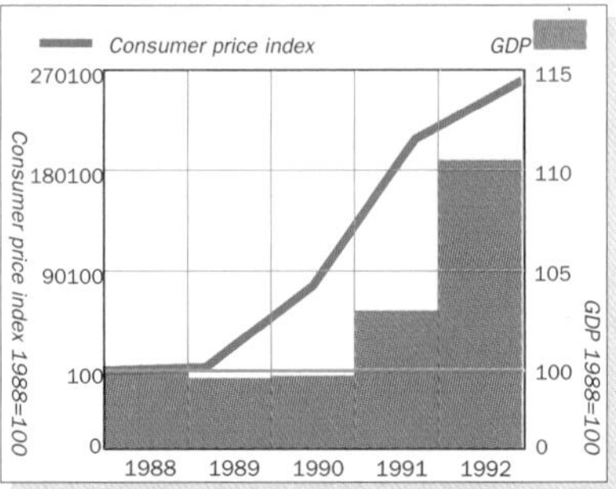

PROFILE

Hyperinflation during the 1980s made economic planning in Argentina impossible. The Menem government was the first to tackle the problem head-on, by imposing wage freezes, refusing to print money to finance deficits and introducing a new stable currency, the peso. Inflation has since dropped dramatically. The Menem administration is now reversing Perón's major legacy, nationalization.

ARGENTINA : MAJOR BUSINESSES

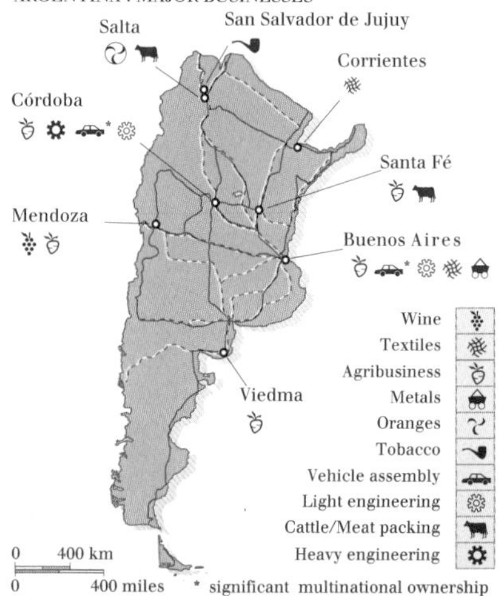

RESOURCES

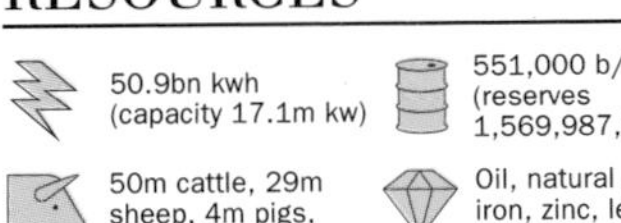

ELECTRICITY GENERATION

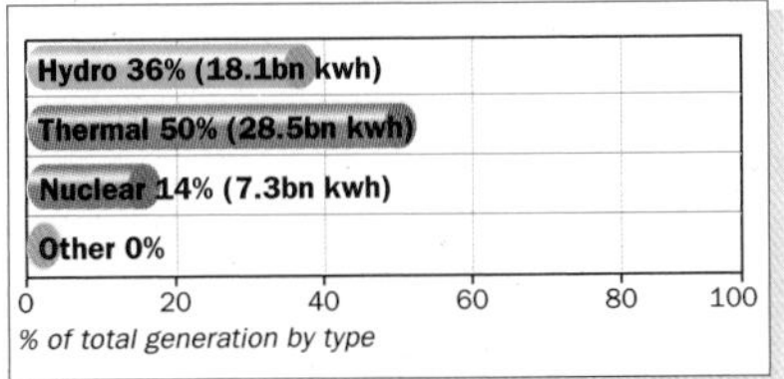

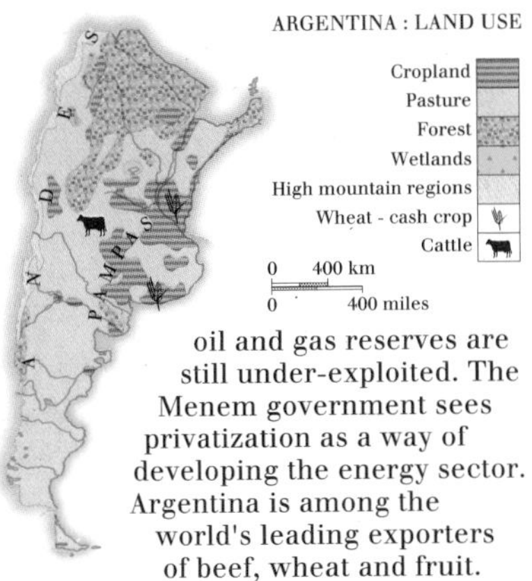

Only one-third of Argentina has been properly surveyed for oil and other mineral resources. Important known oil and gas reserves are still under-exploited. The Menem government sees privatization as a way of developing the energy sector. Argentina is among the world's leading exporters of beef, wheat and fruit.

ENVIRONMENT

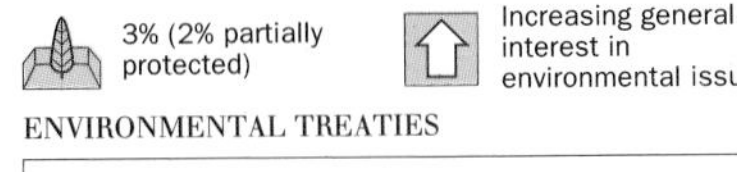

ENVIRONMENTAL TREATIES

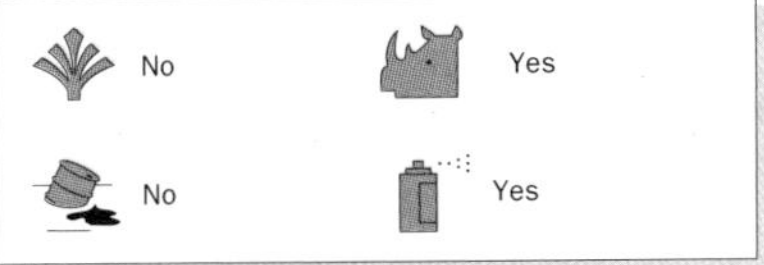

Nuclear power was encouraged by the military, which covered up leaks and accidents from the two main plants – Atocha I and II. Otherwise, the main concerns are the extreme pollution of rivers in Buenos Aires, the 50% depletion of the ozone layer in southern regions and the illegal export of rare birds, particularly from the north.

Environmental issues are of increasing interest to the electorate, but have yet to make a political impact. In 1993, however, residents in Tierra del Fuego succeeded in diverting an oil pipeline to save a colony of penguins.

MEDIA

Freedom guaranteed by the constitution, but media subject to government pressure in practice

PUBLISHING AND BROADCAST MEDIA

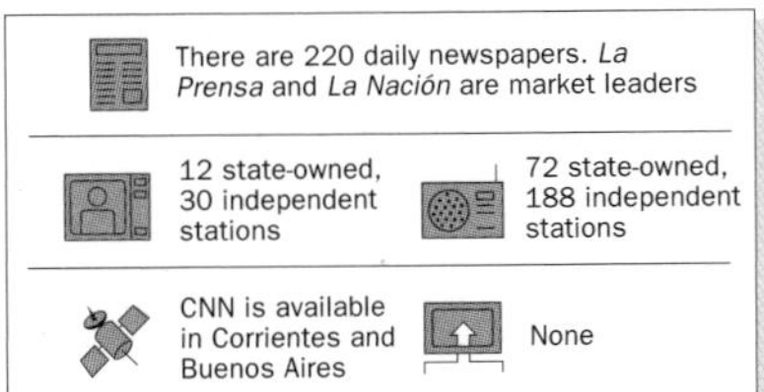

There are 220 daily newspapers. *La Prensa* and *La Nación* are market leaders
12 state-owned,
30 independent
stations
72 state-owned,
188 independent
stations
CNN is available
in Corrientes and
Buenos Aires
None

The press in Argentina was only truly free under the UCR (1983–1989). Many journalists were killed in the late 1970s for expressing their political beliefs. The Menem administration is once again applying pressure on the media, withdrawing state advertising from newspapers critical of its policies.

CRIME

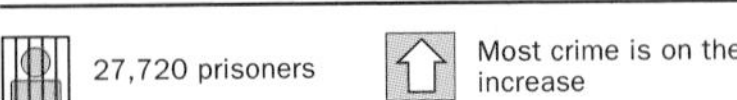

CRIME RATES

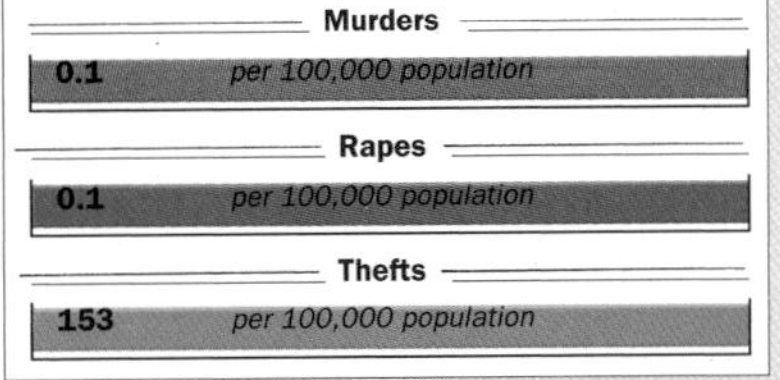

Buenos Aires remains one of the safest cities in Latin America, apart from the shantytown areas, where crime is rising. Drug-money laundering is also a growing problem. The army has still not recovered respect following the human rights abuses of the 1970s.

EDUCATION

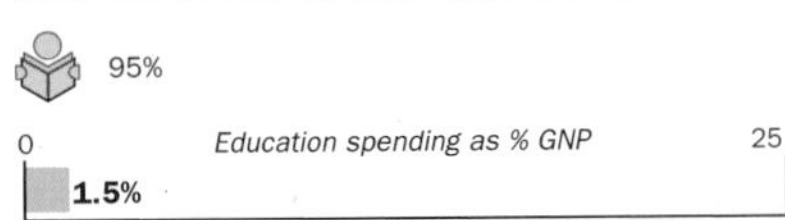

THE EDUCATION SYSTEM

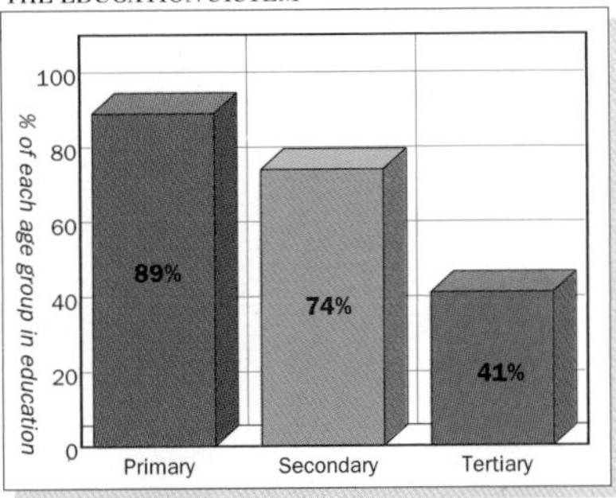

Schooling is effectively a mix of the French and US systems. Schools in the interior have the highest drop-out rate. Argentina has a strong tertiary sector, with most students attending free state universities.

HEALTH

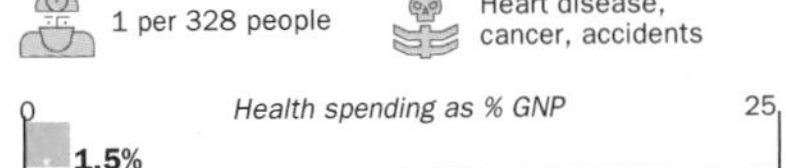

Health care in Argentina is nationwide and Argentina has proportionately more doctors than the USA. Doctors charge, but most Argentinians are covered by insurance policies. High-tech equipment is concentrated in private Buenos Aires hospitals. The recent Worker's Health Plan system was introduced by the Menem administration and designed to improve care for the poor.

WEALTH

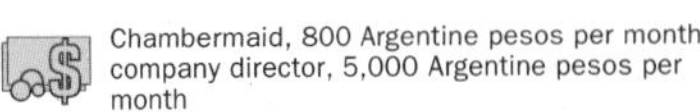

Chambermaid, 800 Argentine pesos per month;
company director, 5,000 Argentine pesos per
month

CONSUMER GOODS OWNERSHIP

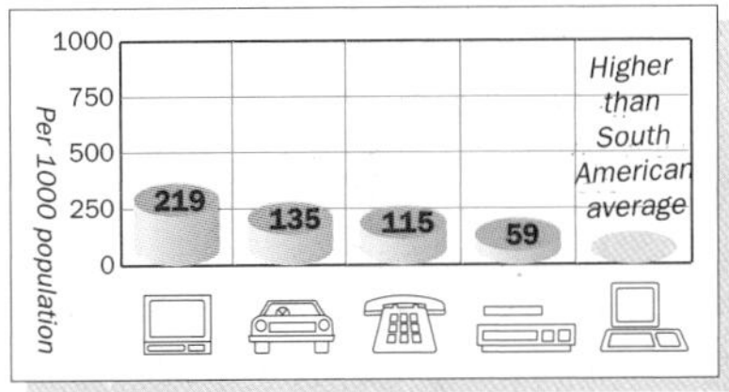

Considerable social mobility can still be achieved in Argentina. The wealthy travel in private jets to their *estancias* (country estates), vacation in Europe and the USA, and play polo and rugby. Argentina is a major market for designer labels – Rolex watches, BMW cars and Italian fashion are particularly favored. Middle-income groups travel to resorts such as Punta del Este in Uruguay or Copacabana in Brazil, and enjoy the European lifestyle of Buenos Aires, which boasts a world-class opera house. The standard of living of the underclass, most of whom are from poor rural interior provinces and trying to find work in Buenos Aires, has been falling since Menem took power.

WORLD RANKING

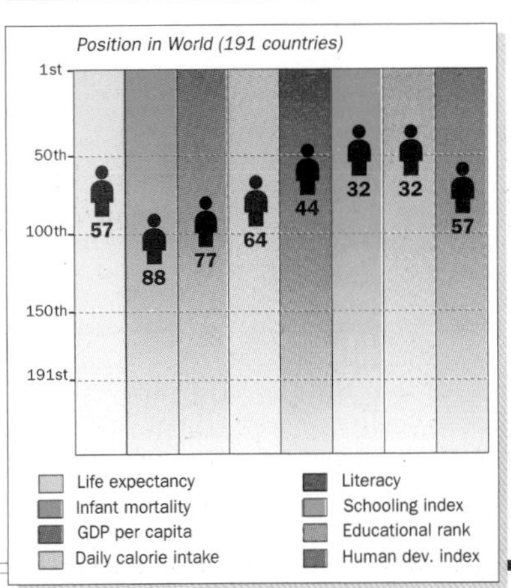

ARMENIA

OFFICIAL NAME: Republic of Armenia **CAPITAL:** Yerevan
POPULATION: 3.5 million **CURRENCY:** Dram **OFFICIAL LANGUAGE:** Armenian

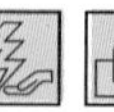

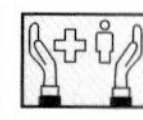

LANDLOCKED IN THE Caucasus Mountains, Armenia is the smallest of the former USSR's republics and was the first to adopt Christianity as its state religion. It is bordered by Muslim states to the south, east and west. Eager to develop links with the CIS, Armenia has kept to a path of radical economic reform including privatization. War with Azerbaijan over the enclave of Nagorno Karabakh has dominated national life since 1988.

__Landscape near Yerevan.__ Armenia's very dry climate results in expanses of semi-desert. Its famous vineyards flourish in sheltered areas.

CLIMATE

WEATHER CHART

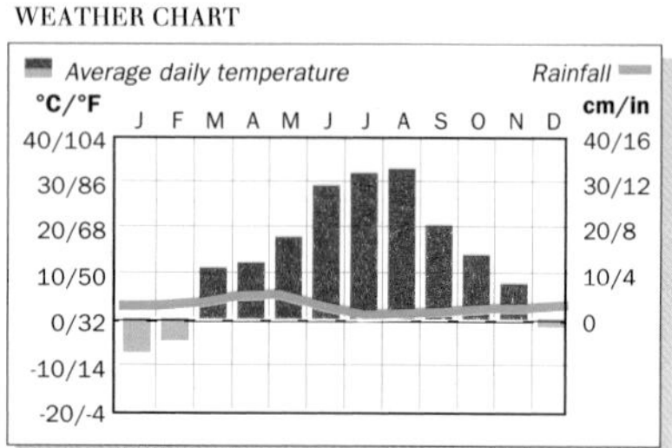

Armenia has a continental climate, with little rainfall in the lowlands. Winters can be very cold.

PEOPLE

Armenian, Russian

306 people per sq. mile

THE URBAN/RURAL POPULATION SPLIT

68% 32%

ETHNIC MAKEUP

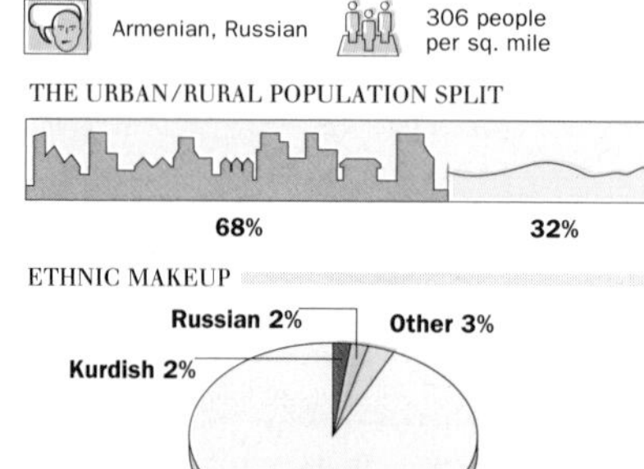

Minority nationalities are well-integrated in the Armenian population. Very strong contacts are maintained with the large number of Armenian emigrants, estimated at some nine million in the USA, France and Syria. 100,000 Armenians who lived in Azerbaijan have been forced to return home since the outbreak of war.

POLITICS

Uncertain

President Levon Ter-Petrosyan

THE STATE OF THE PARTIES

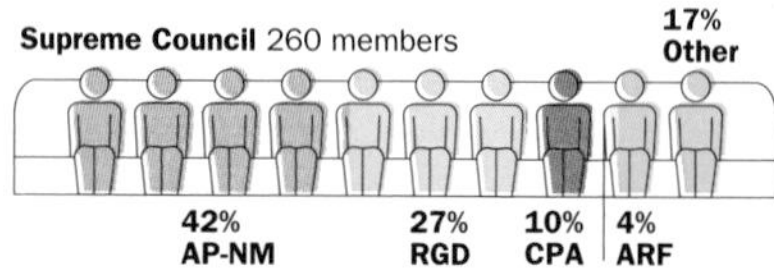

AP-NM = Armenian Pan-National Movement **RGD** = Republican Group of Deputies **CPA** = Communist Party of Armenia **ARF** = Armenian Revolutionary Federation

Armenia has been a multiparty democracy since 1991. The president's party, the AP-NM, has had problems passing legislation against the seven parliamentary opposition parties, but has managed to maintain a path of radical economic reform. The post of prime minister is currently occupied by Bagratyan, a young radical economist. A referendum on a new constitution was due to be held in 1994 to decide whether Armenia should be a presidential or parliamentary republic. The war with Azerbaijan, over the issue of whether the Armenian enclave of Nagorno Karabakh inside Azerbaijan should become part of Armenia, dominates politics. Some nationalist-oriented opposition parties, including the ARF, advocate recognition of an independent Nagorno Karabakh.

COMMUNICATIONS

Yerevan Intl

Has no fleet

THE TRANSPORTATION NETWORK

Public transportation has been badly hit by war-induced fuel crisis. The main road to Georgia is cut because it crosses Azerbaijani territory. The vital Aras Bridge to Iran reopened in 1992.

TOURISM

Very few, due to war with Azerbaijan

Similar levels from year to year

MAIN OVERSEAS ARRIVALS

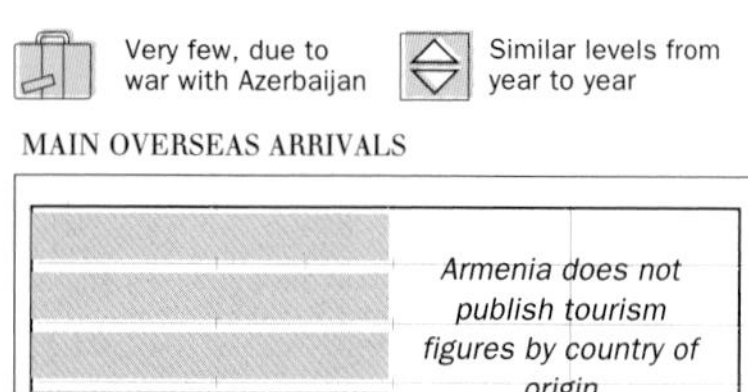

War has discouraged visitors. Ancient churches and the cellar vaults of the cognac-producing regions are Armenia's main attractions.

WORLD AFFAIRS

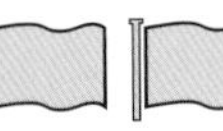

The war with Azerbaijan dominates the agenda. Efforts to improve traditionally sour relations with Turkey have failed, following Armenia's military successes in Nagorno Karabakh. Relations with Iran have cooled as Azerbaijan has developed closer ties with Tehran. Moscow is less supportive of Armenia since Azerbaijan rejoined the CIS.

AID

No figures available as most aid is *ad hoc*

The trend in receipts is up

Most funds have come from Armenians living abroad. Armenia is seeking aid from the EU to restart the Medzamor nuclear power plant, closed since 1989.

DEFENSE

$147.1m

Dramatic increase due to escalation of war with Azerbaijan

The success of the armed forces in the war with Azerbaijan has increased their political profile and their independence from civilian control. In 1993, peace overtures to the Azeris by Armenia's President Ter-Petrosyan were ignored by the army, which mounted a further offensive into Nagorno Karabakh.

ECONOMICS

$7.2bn

370 dram

SCORE CARD

- ❑ WORLD GNP RANKING 92nd
- ❑ GNP PER CAPITA $2,100
- ❑ BALANCE OF PAYMENTS.......................$-8m
- ❑ INFLATION 100.3%
- ❑ UNEMPLOYMENT...............................7.5%

STRENGTHS
Strong ties with Armenian emigrants. Major deposits of rare metals, as yet unexploited. Well-developed machine-building and manufacturing – includes textiles and bottling of mineral water.

WEAKNESSES
Dependent on imported energy, raw materials and semi-finished goods. Gas pipeline through Azerbaijani-controlled region of Georgia often sabotaged.

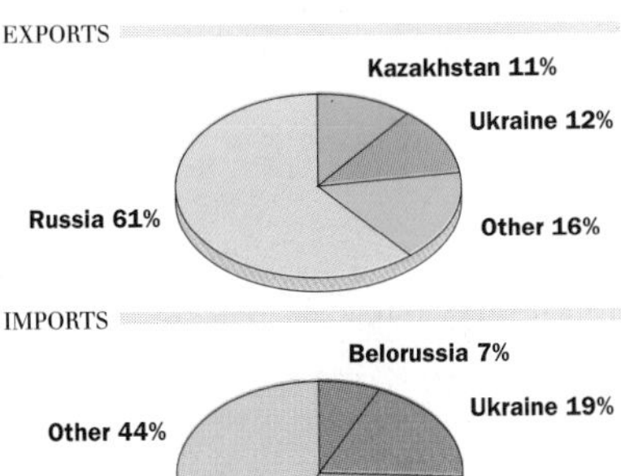

RESOURCES

9.5bn kwh

Minimal oil production

6.7m poultry, 686,500 sheep, 428,900 cattle

Coal, oil, natural gas, rare metals

Armenia has negligible energy resources, but viable deposits of rare metals have been found. Arable land is scarce, producing mainly vegetables and grapes. Abundant sources of mineral water have given rise to a large bottling industry.

ENVIRONMENT

7.4%

War: all environmental measures on hold

The Medzamor nuclear power station was declared unsafe after the 1988 earthquake. It may be reactivated due to the energy crisis, despite opposition from environmental groups. HEP generation near Lake Sevan has seriously reduced the lake's water level.

MEDIA

Criticism of the government is not tolerated in practice

PUBLISHING AND BROADCAST MEDIA

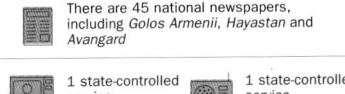

There are 45 national newspapers, including *Golos Armenii, Hayastan* and *Avangard*

1 state-controlled service

1 state-controlled service

There are many independent journals and newspapers, but government control of the paper industry gives it an effective censorship weapon.

CRIME

Armenia does not publish prison figures

Crime levels reasonably stable

Armenia's legal system survived within the Soviet system. Crime levels are lower than those of other ex-Soviet states. Amnesty International gives Armenia a clean bill of health.

EDUCATION

Highest literacy rate of the ex-Soviet republics

The education system, previously conforming to that of the USSR, now emphasizes Armenian history and culture. 14% of the population have received higher education.

CHRONOLOGY

Armenia lost its autonomy in the 14th century. In 1639, Turkey took the west and Persia the east; Persia ceded its part to Russia in 1828.

- ❑ **1877–1878** Massacre of Armenians during Russo-Turkish War.
- ❑ **1915** Ottomans force 1.75 million Turkish Armenians into desert exile; most die.
- ❑ **1917–1918** Russian Armenia's brief anti-Bolshevik alliance with Georgia and Azerbaijan.
- ❑ **1920** Independence. Turkish attack; Bolsheviks counter-invade.
- ❑ **1922** Becomes a Soviet republic.
- ❑ **1988** Earthquake kills 25,000.
- ❑ **1990** Declares Nagorno Karabakh (in Azerbaijan) part of Armenia.
- ❑ **1991** Independence from USSR.

HEALTH

1 per 233 people

Circulatory diseases, cancer, accidents, violence

Hospitals are suffering from the erratic electricity supply, while the breakdown in sewerage and other services has led to a rise in hepatitis and tuberculosis.

WEALTH

Around 70% of the Armenian population live in poverty, as defined by the UN

CONSUMER GOODS OWNERSHIP

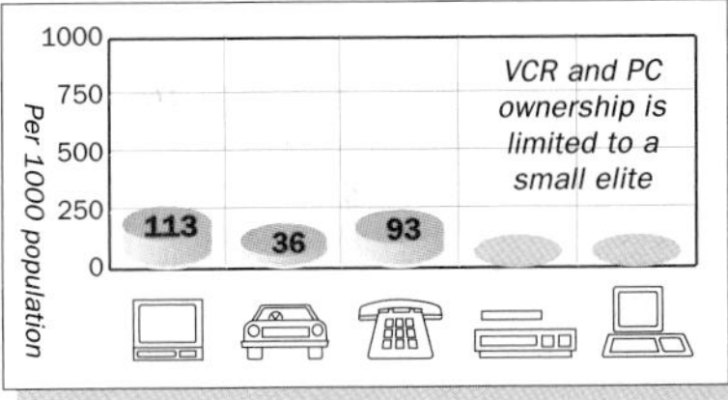

The richest Armenians are those living in the USA and France. The many refugees from Baku are the poorest.

WORLD RANKING

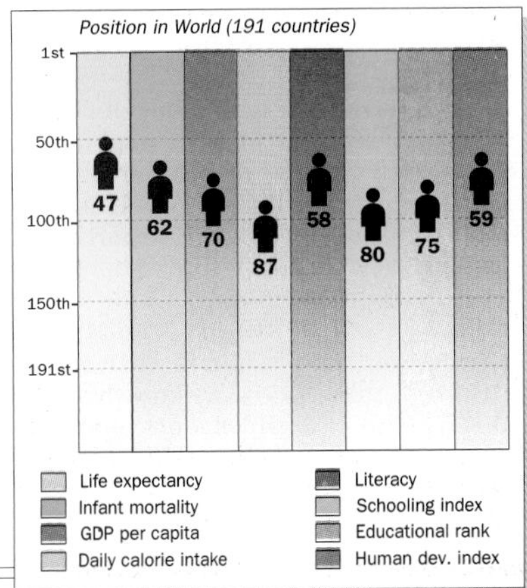

A

AUSTRALIA

AUSTRALASIA
Indonesia
Papua New Guinea
AUSTRALIA
New Zealand
Asia
Pacific Ocean
Australia

OFFICIAL NAME: Commonwealth of Australia **CAPITAL:** Canberra
POPULATION: 17.6 million **CURRENCY:** Australian dollar **OFFICIAL LANGUAGE:** English **OVERSEAS TERRITORIES:** 6

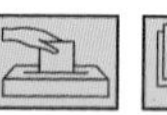

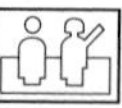

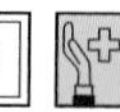

THE WORLD'S SIXTH-LARGEST COUNTRY, Australia is an island continent located between the Indian and Pacific oceans. Its six states and the Northern Territory have a variety of landscapes, including tropical rainforests, the deserts of the arid "red center," snow-capped mountains, rolling tracts of pastoral land and magnificent beaches. Famous natural features include Uluru (Ayers Rock) and the Great Barrier Reef. Most Australians live on the coast. All the state capitals, with the exception of Canberra, are coastal cities. The strip down the length of the eastern seaboard is the country's richest and most populous area. In 2000, Sydney will host the millennium Olympics.

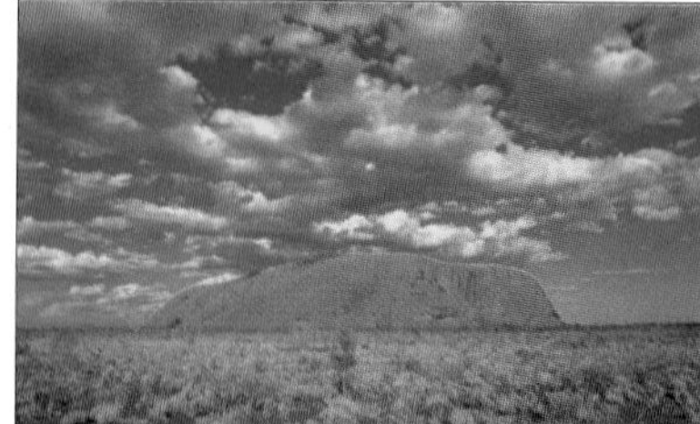

Uluru (Ayers Rock), Northern Territory. *The renaming of Ayers Rock reflects growing Aboriginal influence in Australia.*

CLIMATE

WEATHER CHART

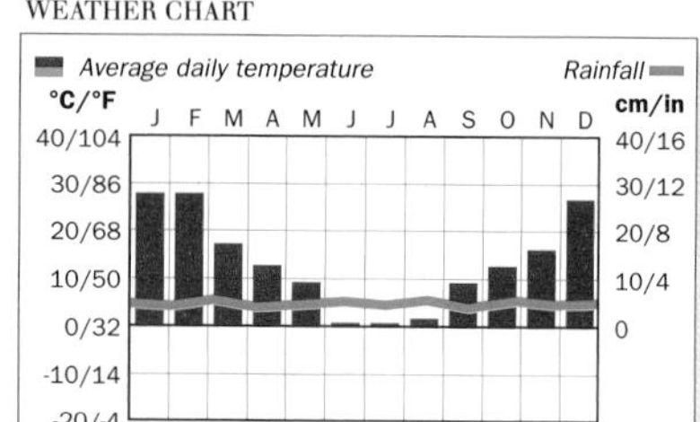

The interior, west and south are arid or semi-arid and very hot in the summer; central desert temperatures can reach 120°F. The north, around Darwin and Cape York Peninsula, is hot all year and humid during the summer monsoon. Only the east and southeast within 250 miles of the coast and the southwest around Perth are temperate. It is in these areas that most Australians live.

COMMUNICATIONS

Kingsford Smith, Sydney 11.23m passengers

125 ships 3.56m dwt

THE TRANSPORTATION NETWORK

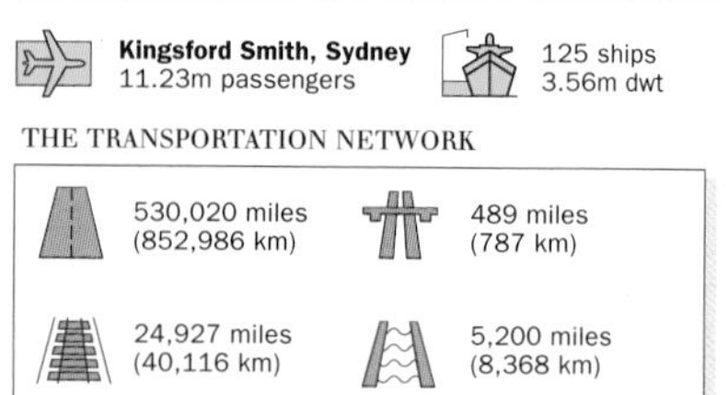

Air transportation is well developed and vital to Australia's sparsely populated center and west. Sydney suffers from air congestion; a third runway is being added to Kingsford Smith Airport and Sydney West airport is due to open in 1998. A high-speed train linking Sydney, Canberra and Melbourne is under discussion. Most freight in Australia travels in massive trucks known as "road trains." Improvements in urban transportation are a priority, particularly in Sydney, in the build-up to the 2000 Olympic Games.

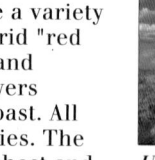

TOURISM

2.6m visitors

Up 10% in 1992

MAIN OVERSEAS ARRIVALS

Origin	% of total arrivals
Japan	24%
Asia (excluding Japan)	19%
New Zealand	17%
UK and Ireland	11%
USA	10%
Other	19%

0 10 20 30 40
% of total arrivals

Growth, while still strong, is slowing from the phenomenal boom seen in the mid-1980s, when tourist arrivals rose by almost 200% in five years. One result of this is that the rush to invest has left many hotels, especially those at the luxury end of the market, struggling in the 1990s.

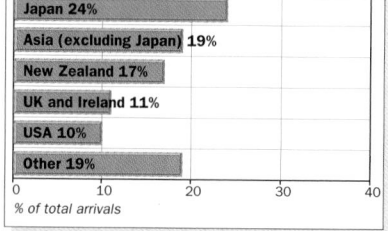

Tourism is now Australia's largest single foreign-exchange earner, accounting for 10% of the total. Faster, cheaper air travel and highly successful government marketing campaigns draw tourists in increasing numbers, especially from Asia, which has been the focus of Australia's strategy to develop tourism's rich potential. The Japanese are now the largest single group of visitors, although many also come from Europe, North America and New Zealand. While Japanese tourists stay a shorter time – on average eight nights – they tend to spend more than other nationalities.

The country's attractions include wildlife, swimming and surfing off Pacific and Indian Ocean beaches, skin-diving along the Great Barrier Reef and skiing in the Australian Alps. Aboriginal culture and the town of Alice Springs are among the outback's attractions. The far north has tropical resorts; the northwest, pearl-fishing. The vineyards of the south and southeast attract many visitors, as do the cultural life of Melbourne and Sydney and the arts festivals held in the state capitals. Sydney's hosting of the Olympic Games in 2000 will give the city a massive economic boost.

INDIAN OCEAN
Bonaparte Archipelago
Derby
Broome
Port Hedland
GREAT SANDY DESERT
Onslow
Hamersley Range
Newman
Lake Disappointment
Paraburdoo
WESTERN AUSTRALIA
GIBSON DESERT
Lake Macleod
Carnarvon
Shark Bay
Dirk Hartog Island
Meekatharra
Lake Carnegie
Mount Magnet
Geraldton
Moora
Kalgoorlie
Perth
Fremantle
Northam
Merredin
Norseman
Rockingham
Bunbury
Collie
Wagin
Bridgetown
Esperance
Ravensthorpe
Cape Leeuwin
Manjimup
Albany

AUSTRALIA

Total Area : 7 686 850 sq. km (2 967 893 sq. miles)

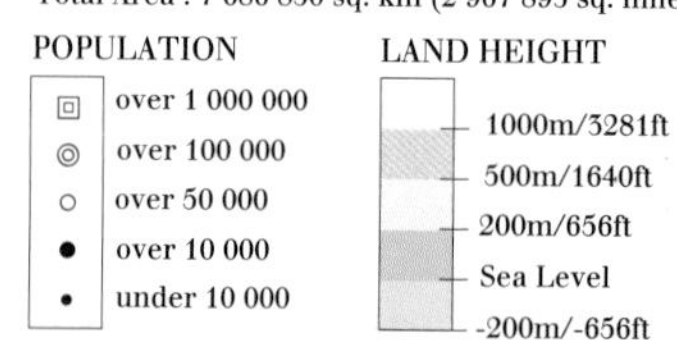

PEOPLE

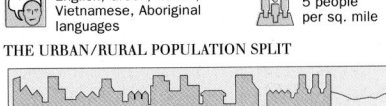

English, Greek, Italian, Vietnamese, Aboriginal languages

5 people per sq. mile

THE URBAN/RURAL POPULATION SPLIT

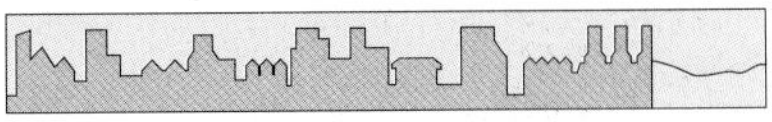

85% 15%

The first settlers arrived in Australia almost 100,000 years ago. Their modern descendants, the Aborigines, today make up less than 1% of the population. European settlement began in 1788 and was dominated by British and Irish immigrants – some of whom were convicts – until the gold rushes of the 1850s. Immigrants of other nationalities – including many Chinese – arrived to prospect for gold, then settled in the cities, especially Melbourne and Sydney. When the new federal government was installed in 1901, one of its first acts was to prevent further Chinese immigration. The act set forth the "White Australia" policy, which conditioned attitudes toward immigration for almost 70 years.

A massive immigration drive after World War II brought many more British settlers to Australia in the 1950s. Further government initiatives to "populate or perish" led to the arrival of large numbers of Italians and Greeks.

From the late 1960s, the "White Australia" policy was progressively wound down. It was officially ended during the 1972–1975 Whitlam administration. Ever since, up to 50% of immigrants each year have come from Asia, transforming Australia from an almost exclusively European enclave into a multicultural society, in which immigrant groups are encouraged to maintain connections with their own cultures and languages.

Aborigines are the exception in an otherwise integrated society. Numbering around 250,000, they remain marginalized economically and socially and still face considerable discrimination. Until the mid-1960s, they were not considered Australian citizens and were denied the vote, full social benefits and inclusion in the census. Aboriginal land had been occupied by settlers on the basis that it was *terra nullius* that belonged to no-one. Since the 1970s, Aborigines have made an increasingly organized stand over land rights and abuse of their civil rights. Government attempts to address the land rights issue initially failed in the face of opposition by powerful mining companies and several state governments. However, the 1992 "Mabo Judgment," rescinding the concept of *terra nullius*, may pave the way to a settlement of Aborigines' grievances.

During the 1950s and 1960s, Catholic–Protestant differences were a strong enough force to cause a rift in the Australian Labor Party (ALP). However, a subsequent policy encouraging mixed denomination schooling, coupled with a decline in religious observance, has largely neutralized the issue.

RELIGIOUS PERSUASION

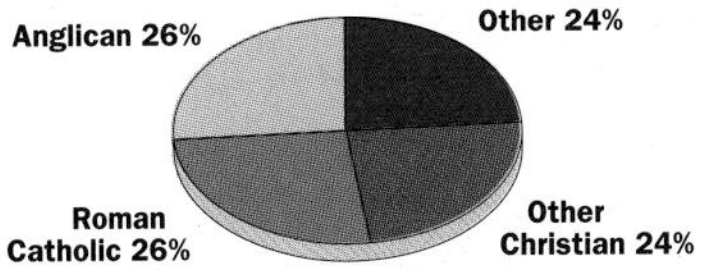

Anglican 26%
Other 24%
Roman Catholic 26%
Other Christian 24%

ETHNIC MAKEUP

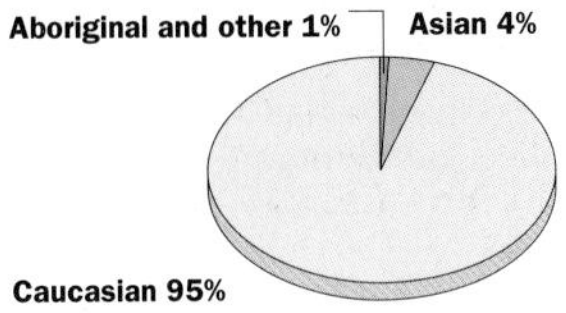

Aboriginal and other 1%
Asian 4%
Caucasian 95%

POPULATION AGE BREAKDOWN

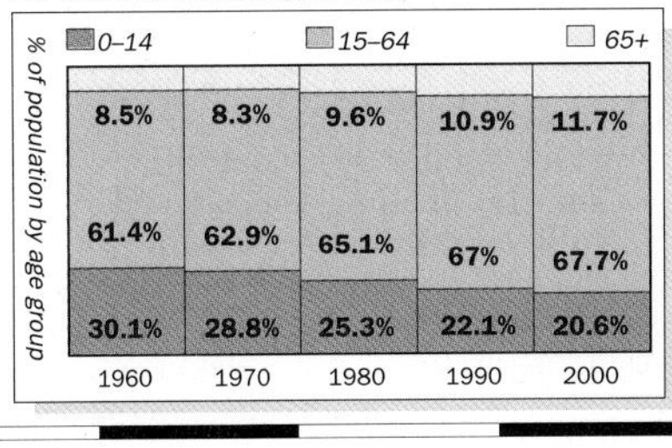

% of population by age group

	1960	1970	1980	1990	2000
65+	8.5%	8.3%	9.6%	10.9%	11.7%
15–64	61.4%	62.9%	65.1%	67%	67.7%
0–14	30.1%	28.8%	25.3%	22.1%	20.6%

A

CHRONOLOGY

Dutch, Portuguese, French and – decisively – British incursions throughout the 17th and 18th centuries signaled the end of 40,000 years of Aboriginal occupancy. Governor Arthur Phillip raised the Union Jack at Sydney Cove on January 26, 1788.

- ❑ **1901** Inauguration of the Commonwealth of Australia.
- ❑ **1915** At the outbreak of World War I, Australian government calls for volunteers for Australian Imperial Force (AIF).
- ❑ **1915** Australian troops suffer heavy casualties at Gallipoli.
- ❑ **1929** Industrial upheaval and financial collapse: "The Great Depression."
- ❑ **1939** Prime Minister Menzies announces Australia will follow Britain into war with Germany.
- ❑ **1941** John Curtin becomes prime minister.
- ❑ **1942** Fall of Singapore to Japanese army. Japanese invasion of Australia seems imminent. Curtin turns to USA for help.
- ❑ **1950** Australian troops committed to UN–US Korean War against North Korean communists.
- ❑ **1962** Menzies government commits Australian aid to war in Vietnam.
- ❑ **1966** Australia adopts decimal currency.
- ❑ **1972** Election of Gough Whitlam government. Aid to South Vietnam ceases.
- ❑ **1975** Whitlam government dismissed by Governor-General Sir John Kerr. Malcolm Fraser forms Liberal–National Party coalition government.
- ❑ **1983** Fraser government defeated. Bob Hawke, having become leader of the Labor Party on the eve of the election, becomes prime minister.
- ❑ **1985** Corporate boom followed by deepening recession, termed "the recession we had to have" by Treasurer Paul Keating.
- ❑ **1992** Paul Keating defeats Hawke in vote to become prime minister. He announces "Turning toward Asia" policy and places republican debate at top of political agenda. Australian High Court's "Mabo Judgment" on Aboriginal land title rescinds concept of *terra nullius*.
- ❑ **1993** March: against most predictions, Keating ALP government reelected. Prime Minister Keating visits UK and outlines republican timetable to Queen Elizabeth II.

POLITICS

 1996  HM Queen Elizabeth II

THE STATE OF THE PARTIES

House of Representatives 148 members

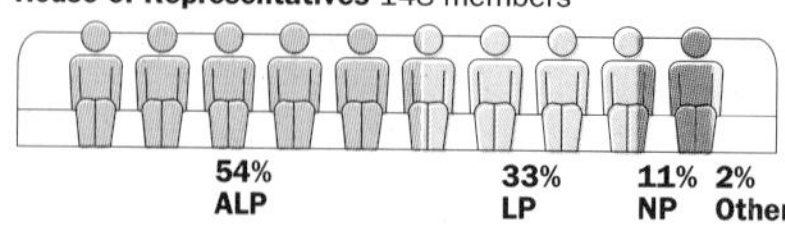

ALP = Australian Labor Party **LP** = Liberal Party
NP = National Party **AD** Australian Democrats
Other = Western Australia Green Party

Senate 82 members

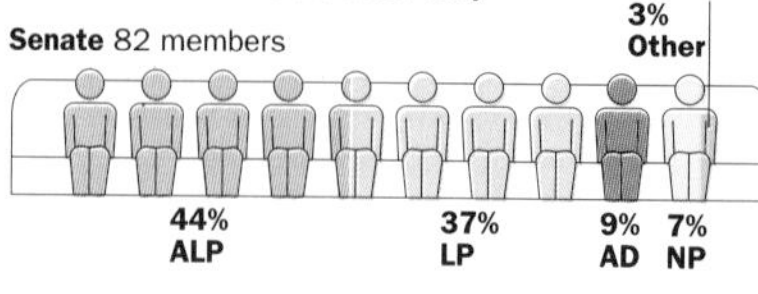

Australia is a parliamentary democracy based on the British model. There are six state governments; all but one (Queensland) are bicameral. The Northern Territory became self-governing in 1978.

Main Political Issues

Aboriginal rights

In 1992, in what became known as the "Mabo Judgement," the High Court decided in favor of Eddie Mabo of Murray Island in the Torres Strait, who had claimed title to land his family had occupied before white settlement. The judgment could have a considerable impact on mining and agricultural interests. Western Australia is fighting the judgment. Prime Minister Keating has suggested a compromise, offering Aborigines compensation for land used by mining companies, as well as an unspecified "social justice package." Australians generally support the judgment, hoping that it will bury the conscience-pricking question of Aboriginal land rights.

Unemployment

Running at over 10%, unemployment was expected to be the issue that would sink Prime Minister Keating's ALP government in the 1993 election. A skillful campaign helped to bring the ALP back to power. For most Australians, however, unemployment remains a central concern. Now that the economy is showing signs of emerging from recession, there are hopes that the unemployment figures will begin to fall. Much new investment, however, is in high-tech, low-labor industries and commentators fear that unemployment will remain at around 10% for a number of years.

The Republic

Despite international press coverage, the republican issue is not of major importance to most Australians. The government is currently downplaying the debate in order to avoid inflaming monarchist groups. A government-appointed consultative group explored the limits of the proposed republican constitution; many had hoped that a reconciliation with Aborigines would be included. However, the group recommended a simple replacement of the British monarch as head of state with an elected president. The Keating administration is hoping that the successful bid to hold the 2000 Olympics in Sydney and the republican issue will help to win it a fourth term in 1996.

Vineyards in South Australia. *Wine-making has been one of Australia's greatest agricultural success stories in recent years.*

PROFILE

The Labor (ALP), Liberal and National parties have dominated Australian politics since 1945. The Liberal and National parties are to the right of the political spectrum and work together in coalition. They broadly represent big business and agricultural interests. The ALP has managed to remain in power by attracting former traditional coalition supporters by, for example, adopting free-market policies. This has also brought a blurring of the differences between parties. However, policies that clearly distinguish the ALP from its opponents, such as its stance on the republican issue, could help it to win again in 1996.

Labor leader and Prime Minister *Paul Keating, won the election of 1993.*

Alexander Downer, *became opposition leader in 1994.*

Brian Howe, *deputy prime minister and minister for housing.*

WORLD AFFAIRS

Australia's international focus has shifted from Europe and the USA toward Asia. Geopolitically it is in an ambiguous position. Having lost its place as a major trading partner for the UK when the latter joined the EEC, Australia has found that it is still regarded as a European outsider by the Asian nations with which it wishes to foster closer links. Australia has taken practical steps to redefine its role. It was the main backer of the 1989 Asia Pacific Economic Cooperation forum (APEC), an attempt to create a multilateral regional trading bloc, similar to the EU and NAFTA. After a faltering start, APEC began to get results. It was the first group to have China, Taiwan and Hong Kong sitting around the same table. The USA was a strong supporter, seeing APEC as a means of promoting free-market economics in Asia. Japan gave APEC its backing and now sees no conflict in belonging to APEC and leading ASEAN, the other key economic grouping. Australia's ambition is for APEC to become the leading association in the region.

Relations with the USA are tense on questions of trade. Australia objects to subsidized US wheat undercutting its own in Asia, particularly in the key Chinese market. It now sees the EU and USA as its main competitors in booming Southeast Asian economies.

However, Australia still supports the West on security issues. Against much public opposition, it sent troops to the 1991 Gulf War. Its commitment to the Pacific region also remains strong. The end of the Cold War, however, has meant that this is now expressed in terms of development aid rather than defense arrangements.

Within the Pacific region, fishing is a major issue. There have been a number of minor skirmishes with Indonesian and Japanese long-line fishing boats. Australia objects to this form of fishing, as it kills large numbers of dolphins, and employs anti-submarine patrols to regulate the industry.

AID

 $1,384m donations | Up 1% in 1993

Australia spends 0.36% of its GNP on aid programs. Most is spent in the Asia–Pacific region. Particular areas of focus are non-governmental organizations and HIV/AIDS programs. By far the greatest recipient, with $335 million, is Papua New Guinea, where Australian companies such as Broken Hill Proprietary have major mining operations.

DEFENSE

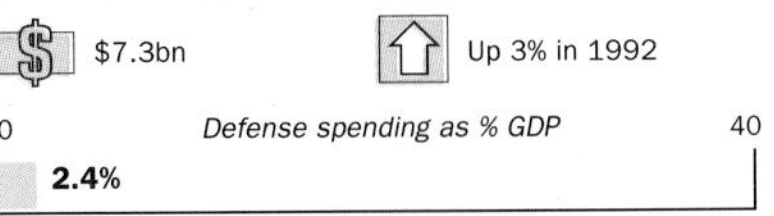

Strategic ties with the USA remain an important element of defense policy. Australia has defense arrangements with the Philippines, Brunei and Thailand, among others. Expenditure is designed to keep Australia self-reliant in defense and to encourage the participation of industry.

AUSTRALIAN ARMED FORCES

103 main battle tanks (103 *Leopard* 1A3)	30,300 personnel
5 submarines, 8 frigates, 3 destroyers and 19 patrol boats	15,300 personnel
157 combat aircraft (22 F-111C/ 52 F-18A,-18B)	22,300 personnel
None	

ECONOMICS

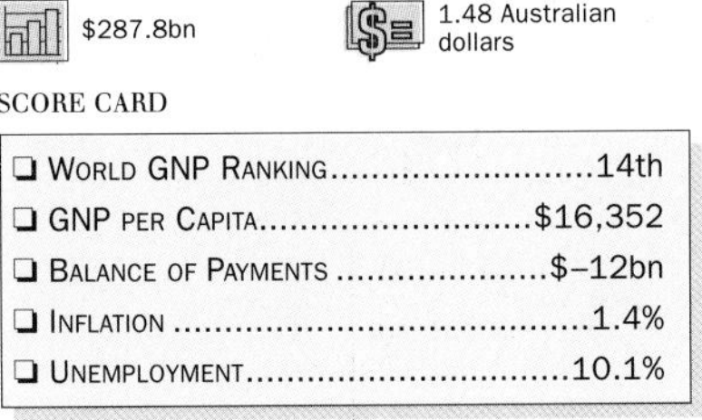
$287.8bn | 1.48 Australian dollars

SCORE CARD

❑ WORLD GNP RANKING	14th
❑ GNP PER CAPITA	$16,352
❑ BALANCE OF PAYMENTS	$–12bn
❑ INFLATION	1.4%
❑ UNEMPLOYMENT	10.1%

ECONOMIC PERFORMANCE INDICATOR

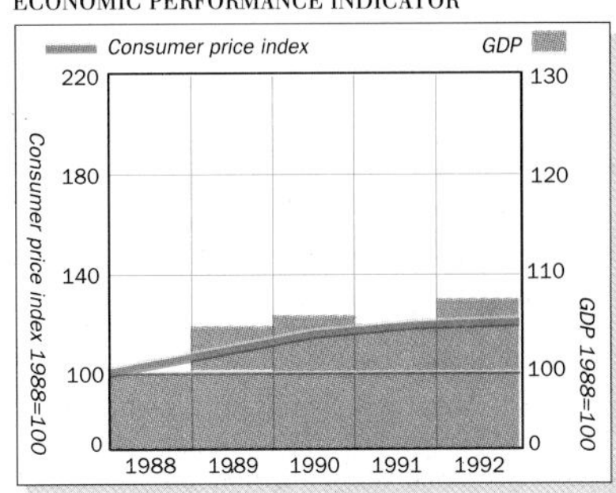

EXPORTS

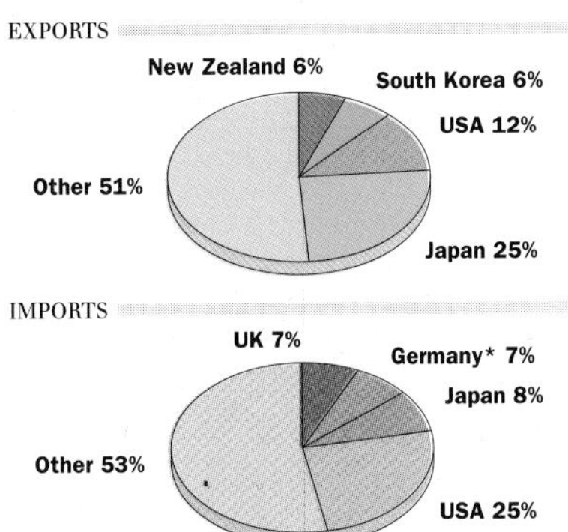

STRENGTHS

Efficient agricultural and mining industries. Vast mineral deposits. Highly profitable tourist industry with huge untapped potential. Successful investor in booming Southeast Asian economies, such as Vietnam.

WEAKNESSES

May suffer from EU and NAFTA protectionist policies. Political instability in some export markets in Southeast Asia could dent exports. Competition from Asian economies with lower wage rates and poorer working conditions. Balance of payments deficit. Unemployment likely to remain high.

PROFILE

Australia's companies are concentrating on the growing Asian market. From accounting for 25% of exports in 1960, Asia now accounts for 60% of Australia's trade. Japan remains its most important trading partner.

In order to compete in Asia, Australia's economy has been undergoing massive structural adjustment. The ALP government has slowly been removing the tariffs that made Australia one of the most heavily protected economies within the OECD. Higher unemployment and the collapse of many businesses accompanied the change. In 1994, however, strong growth was seen.

AUSTRALIA : MAJOR BUSINESSES

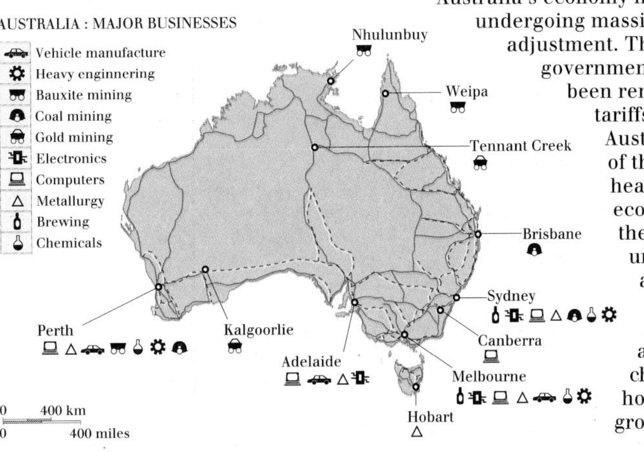

A

RESOURCES

151bn kwh (capacity 33.9m kw)

533,100 b/d (reserves 1,767,900,000 bbl)

165m sheep, 22.4m cattle, 2.7m pigs

Coal, iron, bauxite, zinc, lead, copper, nickel, opals, gold

ELECTRICITY GENERATION

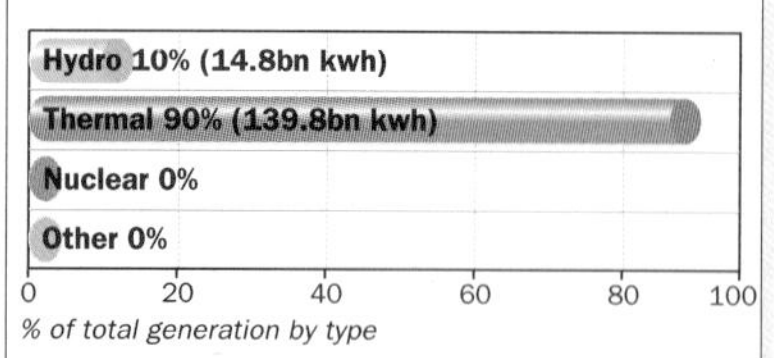

Australia has one of the world's most important mining industries. It is a world leader in exports of coal, iron ore, gold, bauxite and copper. Minerals account for 9.4% of Australia's GDP and 53% of all its merchandise export earnings. Since the first discoveries of coal in 1798, mineral production in Australia has risen every year. From 1982 to 1992 it doubled. Even further growth is expected in the late 1990s. Eighty major new mining projects are already planned, worth some $33 billion. Minerals' share of the total economy will continue to grow into the next century. The industry has benefited from Australia's location. Most increases in production go to the booming economies of Southeast Asia.

While minerals underpin much of Australia's wealth, there is growing concern about the environmental cost of extraction. The "Mabo Judgment" of 1992 could also restrict the industry's operations. Many mining companies are concerned that Aborigines could lay claim to land holding valuable minerals. In 1993, Comalco threatened to halt expansion plans worth over $1 billion if Aboriginal claims over its bauxite leases were upheld. While the state sided with Comalco, a proper legal framework for the industry in the light of the "Mabo Judgment" has yet to be established.

AUSTRALIA : LAND USE

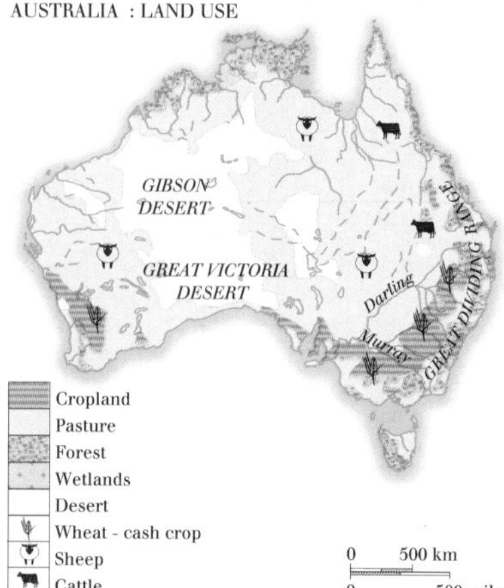

Green Island, on the Great Barrier Reef Marine Park in the far north of Queensland. The reef stretches 1,240 miles down the coast.

ENVIRONMENT

6% (2% partially protected)

Environmental issues are a priority

ENVIRONMENTAL TREATIES

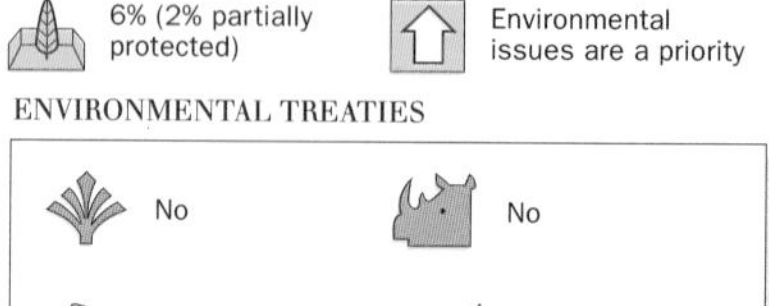

Australia's voters are among the most environmentally conscious in the industrialized world. "Green" issues are dominated by the Australian Conservation Foundation (ACF) and the more radical Greenpeace. The ACF has concentrated on developing links with industry in cooperative conservation programs. Its endorsement of the ALP in 1993 helped to keep the party in power. The ACF has also been behind stricter laws to protect endangered species. Its major success, however, has been in persuading the government to adopt a nationwide policy making environmental concerns a key part of any planning decision.

MEDIA

The press is free from government control

PUBLISHING AND BROADCAST MEDIA

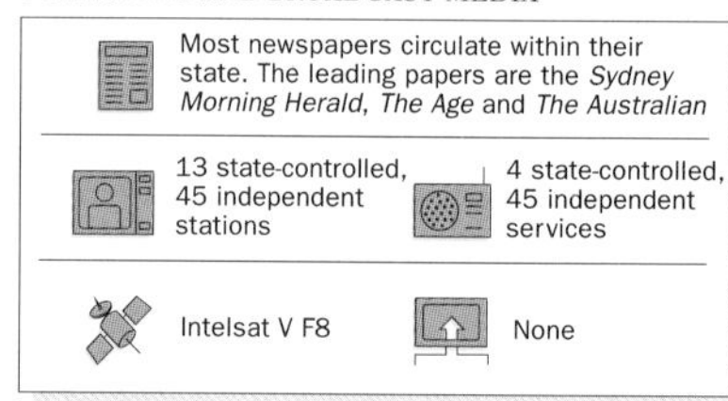

The Australian press is firmly in the grip of "press barons" such as Rupert Murdoch, Kerry Packer and Conrad Black. In 1992, the ALP decided to begin deregulating media industries by auctioning satellite pay-TV. Public-sector broadcasting remains dominated by the politically neutral Australian Broadcasting Corporation (ABC), which receives complaints about its coverage from both main parties.

CRIME

12,557 prisoners

Significant increase in all types of crime

CRIME RATES

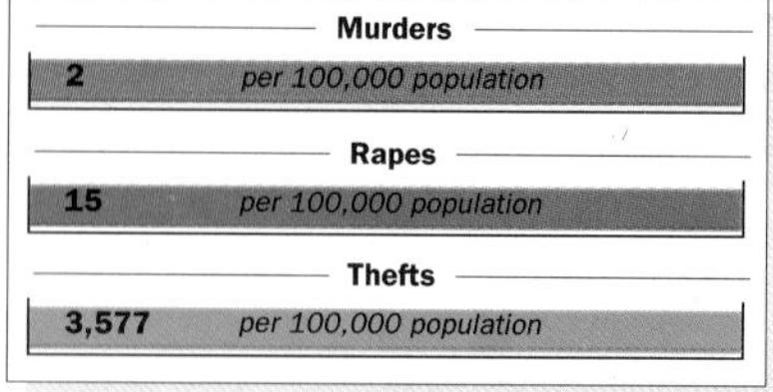

Crime in Australia is on the rise. In the 1980s, the number of recorded crimes rose by about 70%. Most crimes are committed in towns and cities.

Each state has its own police force and court system. Federal courts deal with disputes between states. The High Court and Family Court both have national jurisdiction. Since the 1970s, the legal system has been placing greater emphasis on the rights of the individual. The deaths of a number of Aborigines in custody have, however, led to calls for their greater protection.

Rising drug-related offenses is a major concern. Australia is active in drug control throughout Southeast Asia.

EDUCATION

100%

0 Education spending as % GNP 25

3.8%

THE EDUCATION SYSTEM

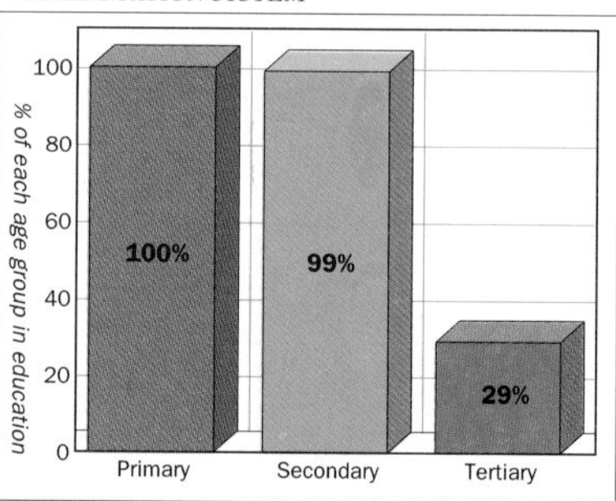

Education in Australia is a state responsibility except in Canberra, where it is funded by the federal government. State education departments run the government schools and set the policies for educational practice and standards for all schools. Non-government schools, run by religious and other groups, exist in all states. Special provision is made for inaccessible outback areas. Schooling is compulsory from age 5–6 to age 15–16 in all states. Universities are independent of state control and are funded by the federal government. In 1990, education accounted for over 13% of government expenditure.

REGIONS

SYDNEY

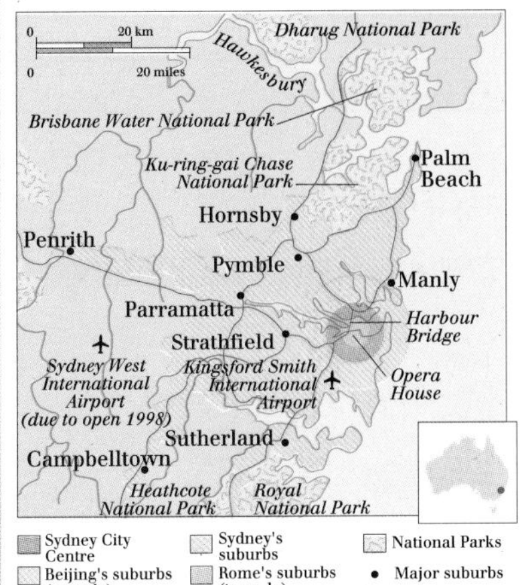

SYDNEY IS Australia's largest and most famous city. Its success in winning the bid to host the 2000 Olympics will further raise its global profile. Since 1932, it has had one of the world's most recognizable structures – the Harbour Bridge, which spans Sydney's stunning harbor. In 1973, its new Opera House also became an instantly recognizable landmark. Sydney has the world's largest suburban area, a conurbation so vast that the city is twice as large as Beijing and six times the size of Rome.

As Australia changes its focus toward Asia, Sydney will gain in importance as one of the key cities of the Pacific Rim.

QUEENSLAND

THE CLOSEST Australian state to the booming economies of Southeast Asia, Queensland's economy has been expanding. In recent years it has experienced a net migration from the southern states. Tourism has been a major beneficiary of closer links with Japan. Cairns in particular has seen rapid growth as the gateway to the Great Barrier Reef. Stretching for over 1,240 mi. along the Queensland coast, it is the largest marine park in the world. Composed mostly of coral polyps, it is also the largest living organism on earth. Clear waters, sponges, algae and 1,500 species of fish make the reef a superb snorkelling and diving location.

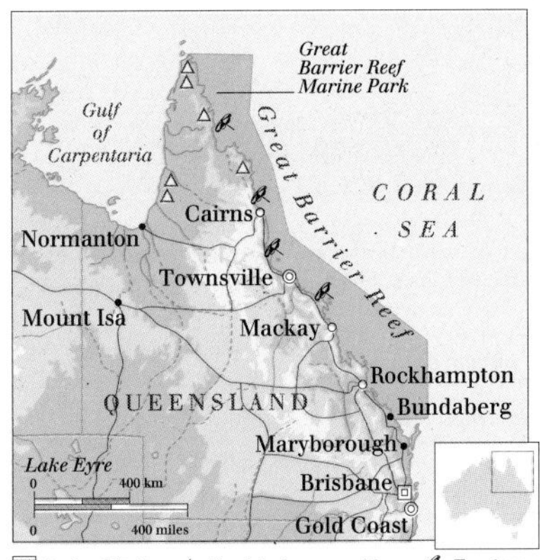

WESTERN AUSTRALIA

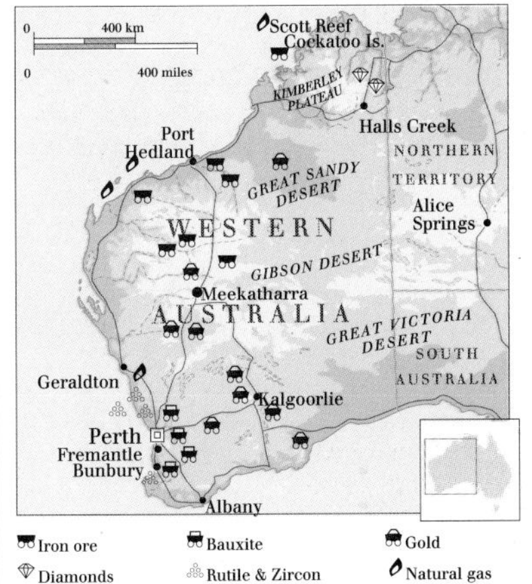

OCCUPYING one-third of the Australian continent, and with a greater land area than Western Europe, Western Australia exports twice as much per capita as the national average. Its main economic strength is its mineral resources. The state produces 11% of the world's iron ore, 60% of Australia's gold, and is a major supplier of bauxite to the West. The northwest shelf includes one of the world's major deposits of natural gas and the largest known diamond deposits, accounting for one-third of global production.

Perth is the state capital. Australia's most isolated city, it is 2,500 miles from the eastern seaboard; it is quicker and cheaper to fly to Hong Kong from Perth than to Sydney. With a population of just over one million, Perth is Australia's fourth largest city. The success of minerals industries has also made it the fastest-growing. The booming economy has brought high-rise steel and glass office blocks, which have transformed the Perth skyline.

HEALTH

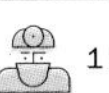 1 per 426 people

 Heart, cerebrovascular and respiratory diseases, cancer

Health spending as % GNP (scale 0–25): 2.9%

Australia's extensive public health service has standards as high as any in the world. Hospital waiting lists are short. Outback areas are served by the efficient Royal Flying Doctor Service. While vigilance continues in the areas of hygiene, nutrition and general living standards, Australian health authorities have targeted Aboriginal health, heart disease, injury prevention, personal fitness and the prevention of cancer – particularly lung, cervical, breast and skin cancer – as current priorities. Life expectancy is 79 years for women and 73 for men.

WEALTH

 Industrial worker, 20,000–23,000 Australian dollars; industrial project engineer, 45,000–50,000 Australian dollars

CONSUMER GOODS OWNERSHIP

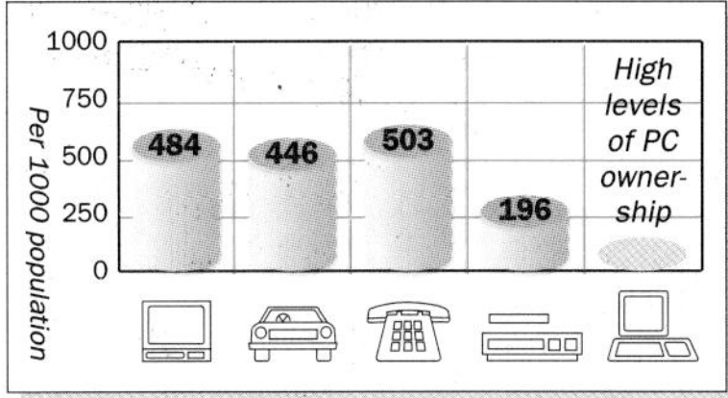

Australians enjoy reasonable equality of wealth. A large proportion of families own two cars and have relatively high disposable incomes. A benign climate helps most to live comfortably. However, high unemployment during the 1990s' recession has widened the gap between rich and poor, and Australia has slipped down the world standard of living list in recent years. The incidence of homelessness, critical poverty and child neglect due to poverty have increased slightly.

WORLD RANKING

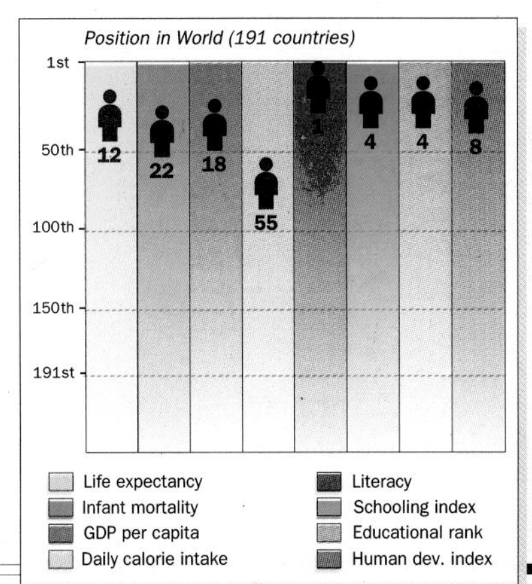

See also OVERSEAS TERRITORIES *p 616*

A

AUSTRIA

OFFICIAL NAME: Republic of Austria **CAPITAL:** Vienna
POPULATION: 7.8 million **CURRENCY:** Austrian schilling **OFFICIAL LANGUAGE:** German

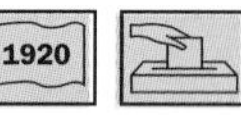

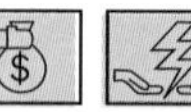

LYING IN THE HEART of Europe, Austria is dominated by the European Alps in the west of the country, while fertile plains make up its eastern half. Created in 1920, after the collapse of the Habsburg Empire, Austria was absorbed into Hitler's Germany in 1938. It gained independence again in 1955 after the departure of the last Soviet troops from the Allied Occupation Force. Austria's economy encompasses successful high-tech sectors, a tourist industry which attracts the wealthier end of the market and a strong agricultural base. In 1995, Austria joined the EU.

CLIMATE

WEATHER CHART

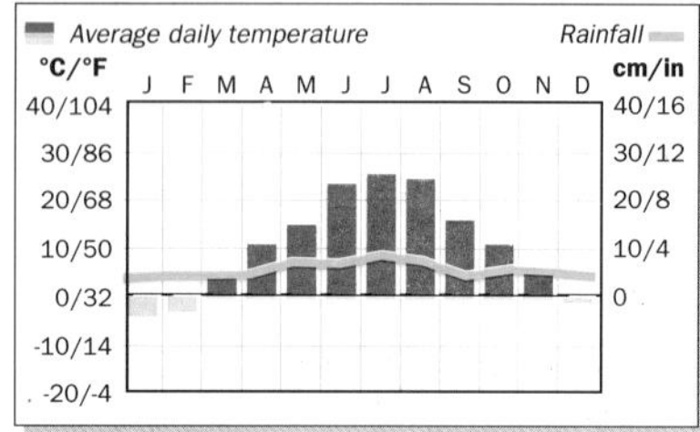

Austria has a temperate continental climate. Alpine areas experience colder temperatures and higher precipitation.

The Tirol is situated in the heart of Austria's Alps. It is the most mountainous region of all and attracts both winter and summer visitors.

COMMUNICATIONS

Wien–Schwechat, Vienna 5.5m passengers

26 ships 208,500 dwt

THE TRANSPORTATION NETWORK

66,894 miles (107,651 km)

899 miles (1,447 km)

3,495 miles (5,624 km)

277 miles (446 km)

Austria's central geographical position has encouraged the development of a sophisticated communications and transportation network.

TOURISM

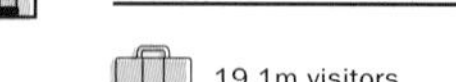

MAIN OVERSEAS ARRIVALS

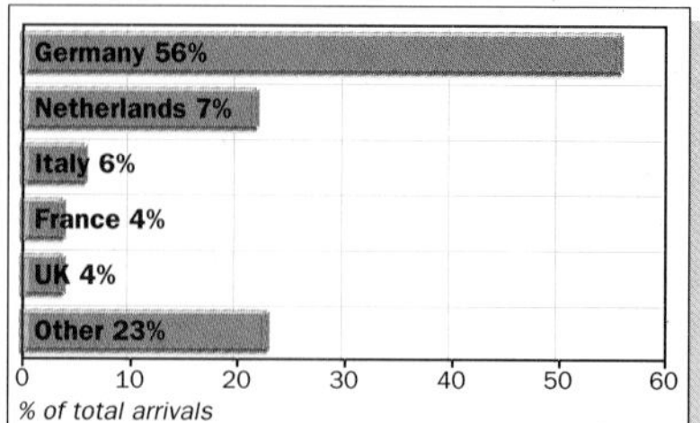

The earnings of the Austrian tourist industry amount to more than 14% of GDP. The well-developed Alpine skiing and winter sports resorts account for almost one-third of the country's total tourist earnings. Many resorts, such as St. Anton and Kitzbühel, cater to the top end of the market. In the summer season, which peaks in July and August, tourists visit the scenic Tirol and the lakes around Bad Ischl. Vienna and Salzburg, the country's second city, are major attractions. The latter is internationally famous for its summer music festival and as the birthplace of Mozart.

AUSTRIA

Total Area : 83 850 sq. km (32 375 sq. miles)

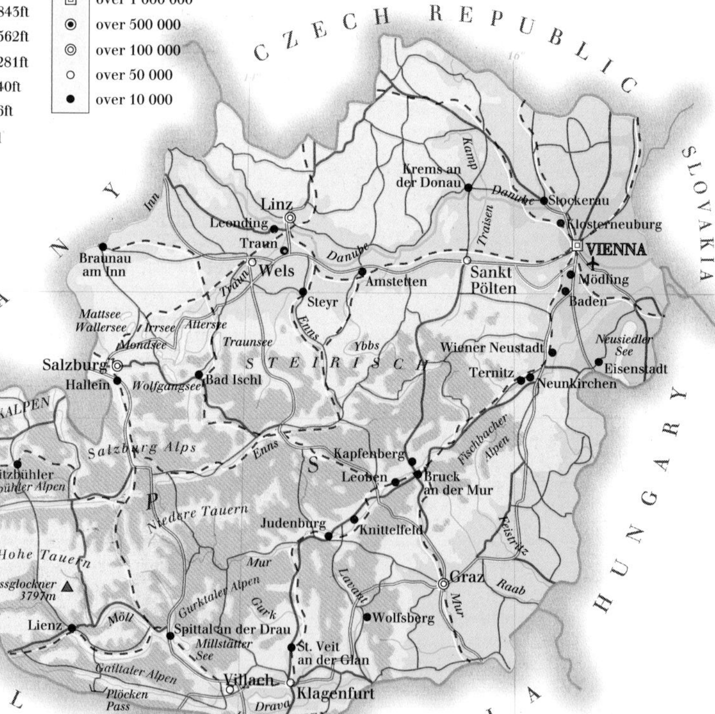

PEOPLE

German, Croatian, Slovene

243 people per sq. mile

THE URBAN/RURAL POPULATION SPLIT

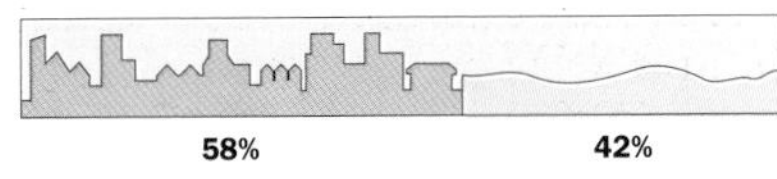

RELIGIOUS PERSUASION

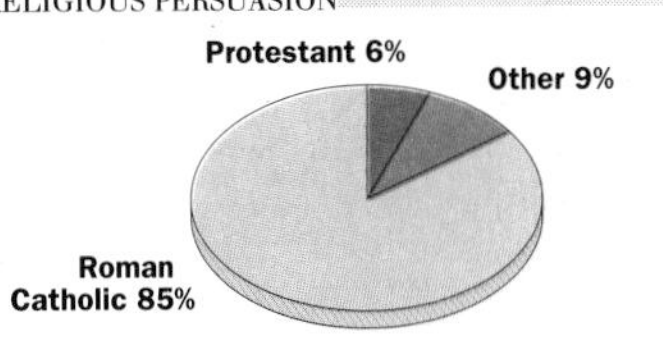

ETHNIC MAKEUP

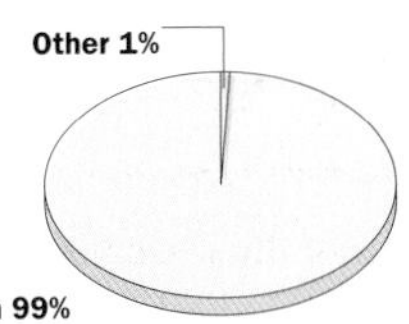

Austrian society is homogeneous. Almost 99% of Austrians are German speakers. However, Austrians like to consider themselves ethnically distinct from Germans. There are few minorities; a small number of ethnic Slovenes, Croats and Hungarians live in the south and east. These minorities have been supplemented by large numbers of immigrants from Eastern Europe and refugees from the conflict in former Yugoslavia. The result has been a perceptible increase in ethnic tension, particularly as the downturn in the economy has led some Austrians to claim that immigrants are taking jobs from the local population.

The nuclear family is the norm in Austria. It is common for both parents to work. While sexual equality is enshrined in the constitution, in practice society is still strongly patriarchal. Compared with the rest of Europe, few women enter politics.

Young Austrians tend to live in their parental home until they marry. This partly reflects the long time taken to complete university degrees, and the fact that students do not receive maintenance grants. Austrians marry at a younger age than the European average. Nominally a Catholic country, Austria has a less conservative society than some German states.

POPULATION AGE BREAKDOWN

% of population by age group

	1960	1970	1980	1990	2000
65+	12%	14.1%	15.4%	15%	15.7%
15–64	65.9%	61.6%	64.2%	67.7%	67.6%
0–14	22.1%	24.3%	20.4%	17.3%	16.7%

POLITICS

1998

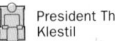

President Thomas Klestil

THE STATE OF THE PARTIES

National Council 183 members

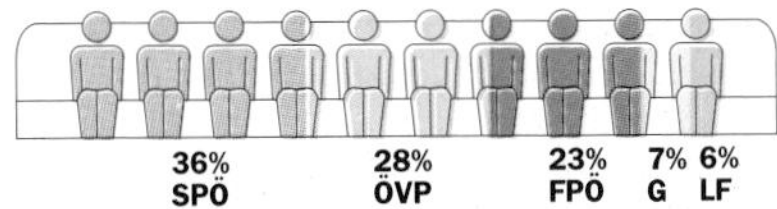

SPÖ = Social Democratic Party of Austria **ÖVP** = Austrian People's Party **FPÖ** = Freedom Party of Austria **G** = Greens **LF** = Liberal Forum

Federal Council 64 members

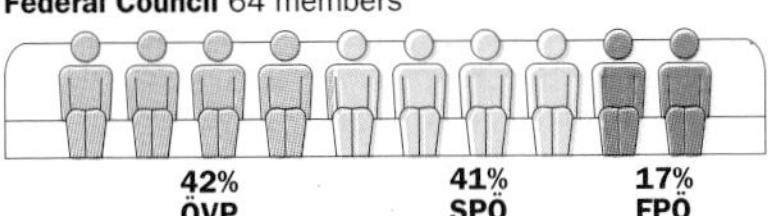

Austria is a federal, multiparty democracy. The chancellor (premier) holds real executive power.

Main Political Issues

Entry into the EU

Austria's population was divided over its entry into the EU. Although Austrians are likely to reap benefits, such as lower food prices and greater consumer choice, there were fears that joining the EU may result in a loss of national identity and independence. The agricultural and environmentalist lobbies had expressed doubts about joining – likely reforms to the EU agricultural policy could endanger the livelihood of up to half of Austria's farmers. Environmentalists feared the increase in trucks carrying heavy goods and transit traffic that will accompany membership. Despite these reservations, the country voted in favor of joining the EU in a referendum held in June 1994.

Economic decline

The economy has become a major issue in recent years. After stability in the 1970s and 1980s, industry has been exposed to the recession in the neighboring countries of Eastern Europe and Germany. As a result, export orders have fallen and unemployment has increased. In particular, the traditional methods of protectionism and subsidies have failed to work and this has been followed by growing social and political tension.

Profile

A coalition headed by the SPÖ, with the ÖVP as the junior partner, has governed Austria since the 1950s. The left-of-center consensus is beginning to show signs of strain as the ÖVP is losing many of its working class voters to the right-wing FPÖ. The main reason is the decline in the economy and the perception that immigrant labor is taking jobs from Austrians. The FPÖ's anti-EU stance had also attracted support. Local government is run by the nine provincial assemblies. Vienna is dominated by the SPÖ. The FPÖ has control of the province of Carinthia.

Dr. Thomas Klestil, *the ÖVP candidate, became Austria's president in 1992.*

Franz Vranitzky. *Elected chancellor in 1992, he leads an SPÖ-ÖVP coalition.*

WORLD AFFAIRS

While Austria wants to be seen as independent of German influence, it cannot avoid the fact that Germany is its main trading partner and the most powerful state in the region. Relations with Germany are therefore Austria's major concern. However, there is a conscious policy to create a diplomatic distance from Berlin. Austria is eager to maintain its direct line to Washington. The fact that Austria supplies much of the US army's small arms helps to cement this relationship.

Keeping a distance from Germany will probably mean that now Austria has joined the EU it will align itself with the Scandinavian countries. It will also support the East European states' early entry into the EU. Austria has been exploiting its geo-political position to increase its influence in the region, and remains an important trading partner of many ex-COMECON states. Austria's constitution bans its forces from serving abroad. It has criticized the failure by the UN and EU to stop the conflict in former Yugoslavia.

AID

$548m (donations)

Small reduction in 1993

Austria is a major donor of aid to Eastern Europe. Much aid is aimed at stemming a large influx of economic refugees from the former communist states. Aid donations to the former Yugoslavia are likely to increase once peace is achieved. Austria was a major exporter to the region and will be seeking a key role in reconstruction.

A

CHRONOLOGY

Austria came under the control of the Habsburgs in 1273. In 1867, the Dual Monarchy of Austria-Hungary was formed under Habsburg rule. Defeat in World War I led to the abdication of the last Habsburg emperor, Charles, in 1918.

- ❑ **1920** Republic of Austria formed after breakup of Habsburg Empire.
- ❑ **1934** Chancellor Dollfuss dismisses parliament and starts imprisoning Social Democrats, Communists and National Socialist Party (NAZI) members. NAZIs attempt coup.
- ❑ **1938** The Anschluss – Austria forcibly incorporated into Germany.
- ❑ **1945** End of German rule. Austria occupied by Russian, British, US and French forces. Provisional government under Karl Renner, veteran of World War I peace negotiations. Elections result in People's Party (ÖVP) and Social Democratic Party (SPÖ) coalition, remains in power for most of the post-war period.
- ❑ **1950** Attempted coup by Communist Party fails. Marshall aid helps economic recovery. USSR resists calls from France, USA and UK for independent Austria.
- ❑ **1955** Soviet troops finally withdrawn. USSR recognizes Austria as a sovereign state.
- ❑ **1971** First single-party government formed by ÖVP under Federal Chancellor Bruno Kreisky. Although a minority administration, the ÖVP's political strength grows throughout the 1970s.
- ❑ **1983** Socialists and the Freedom Party (FPÖ) form a coalition government.
- ❑ **1986** Dr. Kurt Waldheim, former UN secretary-general, elected president, despite war crimes allegations. Franz Vranitsky, Federal Chancellor. Nationalist Jörg Haider succeeds more moderate Norbert Steger as FPÖ leader. SPÖ pulls out of government due to FPÖ's swing to right. Elections produce stalemate. Return to "grand coalition" between SPÖ and ÖVP.
- ❑ **1990** ÖVP loses 17 seats in parliamentary elections.
- ❑ **1992** Thomas Klestil (ÖVP) elected president, replacing controversial Kurt Waldheim. Elections confirm some traditional ÖVP supporters defecting to FPÖ.
- ❑ **1993** FPÖ splits into two. Breakaway Liberal Forum takes over 5 FPÖ seats. Liberal Forum voices opposition to FPÖ's nationalism.

DEFENSE

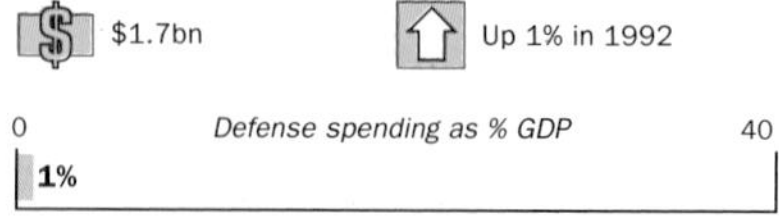

Under the terms of the 1955 State Treaty, which granted Austria its full independence, the country has taken a neutral stance. Despite the small size of its own defense forces, Austria's arms industry is thriving and provides most of the hardware needed to maintain the army. It also exports arms to the USA.

AUSTRIAN ARMED FORCES

Army	159 main battle tanks (159 M–60A3)	46,000 personnel
Navy	None	
Air force	54 combat aircraft (30 SAAB 105 Oe/ 24 J–350e)	6,000 personnel
Missiles	None	

ECONOMICS

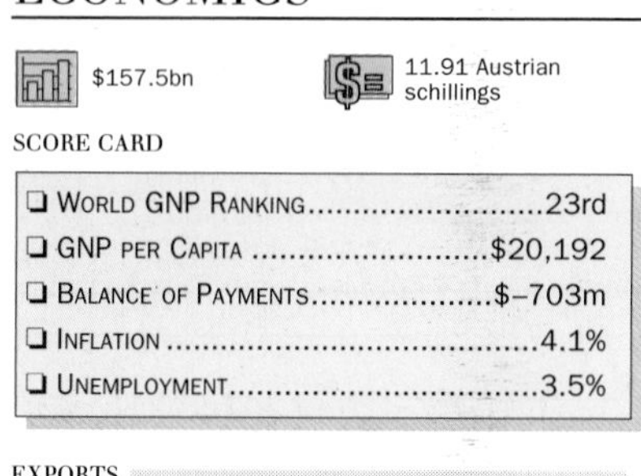

SCORE CARD

- ❑ WORLD GNP RANKING........................23rd
- ❑ GNP PER CAPITA $20,192
- ❑ BALANCE OF PAYMENTS..................$–703m
- ❑ INFLATION 4.1%
- ❑ UNEMPLOYMENT...............................3.5%

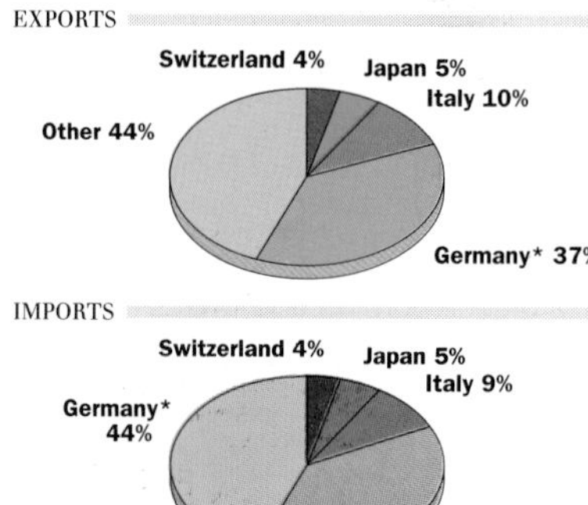

ECONOMIC PERFORMANCE INDICATOR

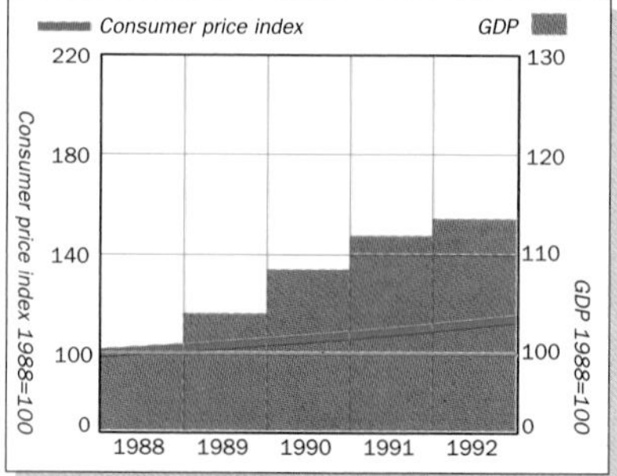

STRENGTHS
Large manufacturing base. Strong chemical and petrochemical industries. Electrical engineering sector, textiles and wood processing industries. Highly skilled labor force. Tourism an important foreign currency earner.

WEAKNESSES
Lacks natural resources. Reliant on imported raw materials, particularly oil and gas. High levels of subsidies to state-owned industry. Weak and overregulated banking system.

PROFILE
Austria's industrial and high-tech sector is highly developed and contributes around 25% to GDP. Some services, notably tourism, are highly sophisticated and profitable. However, the Austrian economy suffers from a weak banking sector. This is partly due to the high level of state subsidies to industry, which has in turn meant that there has been little demand for flexible private finance.

The banking system is likely to suffer the stiffest competition now that Austria has joined the EU. Austrian banks have begun to merge in preparation for the challenge. There will, however, be benefits from EU membership. Prices for many products, particularly food and books, will fall. The Austrian labor market will see an influx of immigrant labor more willing to accept flexible working arrangements and lower wages. There will probably be an increase in foreign investment, as more multinationals locate their headquarters for East European operations in Austria.

AUSTRIA : MAJOR BUSINESSES

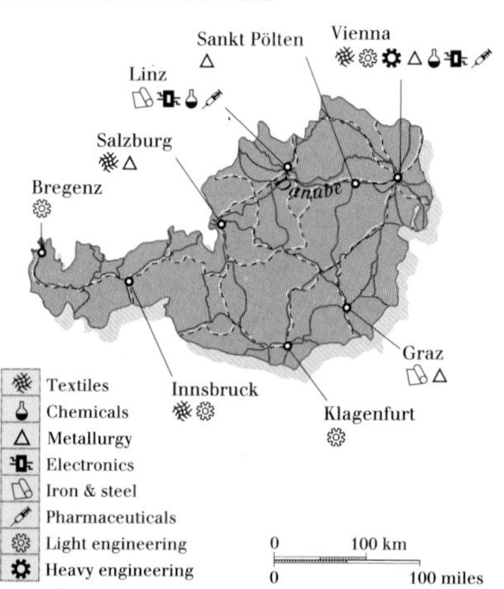

RESOURCES

50bn kwh (capacity 16.8m kw)

24,800 b/d (reserves 93,200,000 bbl)

13.1m chickens, 3.7m pigs, 2.6m cattle

Iron, coal, magnesite, zinc, lead

ELECTRICITY GENERATION

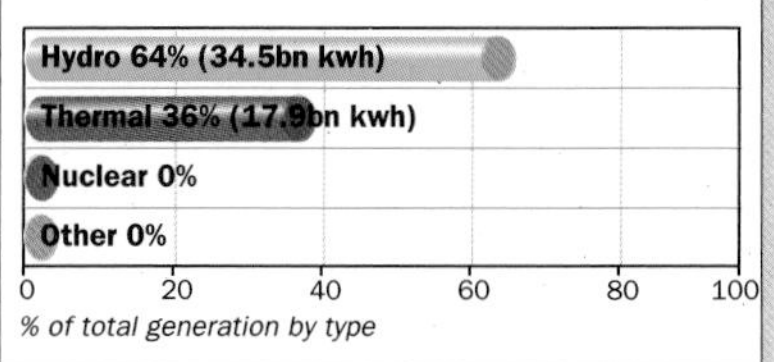

Austria has few resources. It lacks significant oil, coal and gas deposits and has to import over $2.7 billion worth of energy every year. Russia remains one of Austria's main energy suppliers. Gas is provided via pipelines running through the Czech and Slovak republics. Oil is imported up the Danube. Russia and Germany are the major suppliers of iron ore and raw steel for Austria's industry.

AUSTRIA : LAND USE

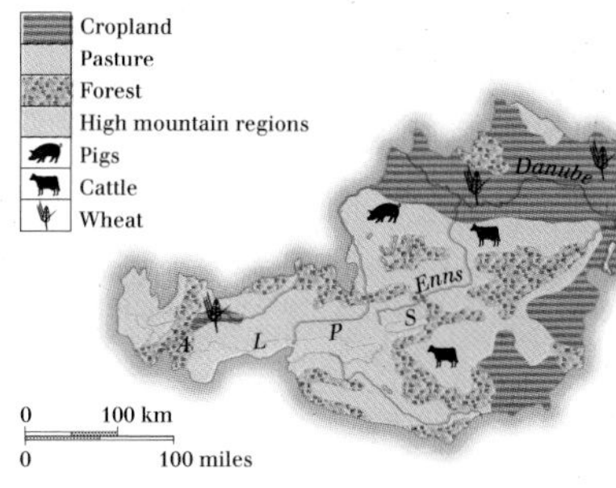

CRIME

5,862 prisoners

Up 8% in 1990

CRIME RATES

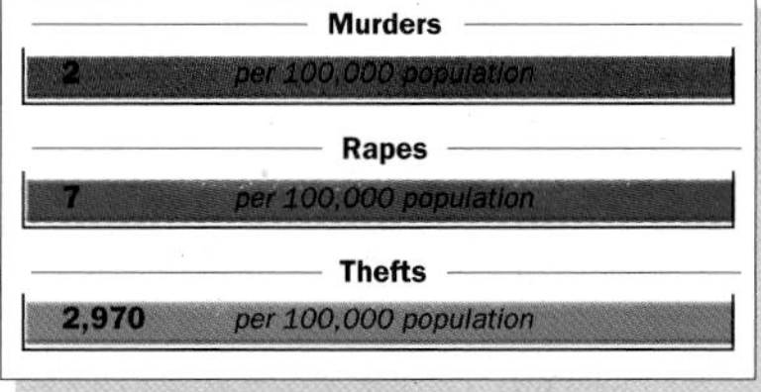

Austria's crime rate is below the European average. However, the number of burglaries is rising. The arrival of the Russian mafia in Vienna has led to an increase in money laundering.

ENVIRONMENT

25% partially protected

Environment is an increasingly important issue

ENVIRONMENTAL TREATIES

No

No

Yes

No

Environmental awareness is high. Domestic waste has to be separated for recycling; heavy fines exist for those who fail to observe the regulations. Car emissions are less controlled, however. Few Austrian cars have catalytic converters and most do not use lead-free gasoline. The safety of nuclear reactors in Slovakia is a major concern.

MEDIA

Media is, for the most part, independent of the government. It is relatively conservative

PUBLISHING AND BROADCAST MEDIA

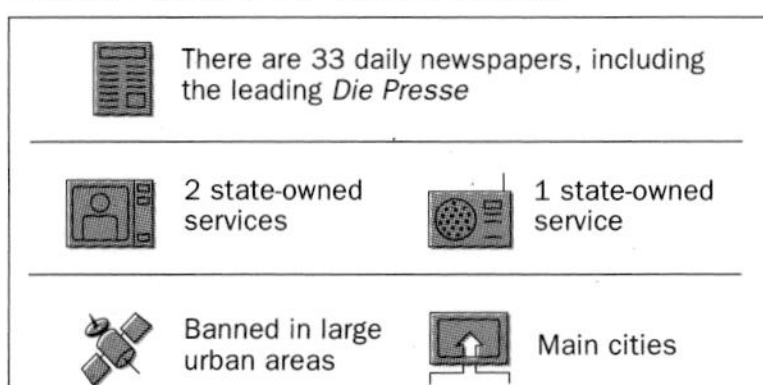

There are 33 daily newspapers, including the leading *Die Presse*
2 state-owned services
1 state-owned service
Banned in large urban areas
Main cities

TV and radio are more tightly controlled than the press. They are controlled by *Österreichischer Rundfunk* (ÖRF), under a politically-appointed director. Cable TV is carefully licensed by ÖRF, to prevent it from taking viewers away from existing stations. Satellite dishes are banned in main cities. Some unlicensed radio stations broadcast from neighboring states.

EDUCATION

99%

0 — Education spending as % GNP — 25

5.5%

THE EDUCATION SYSTEM

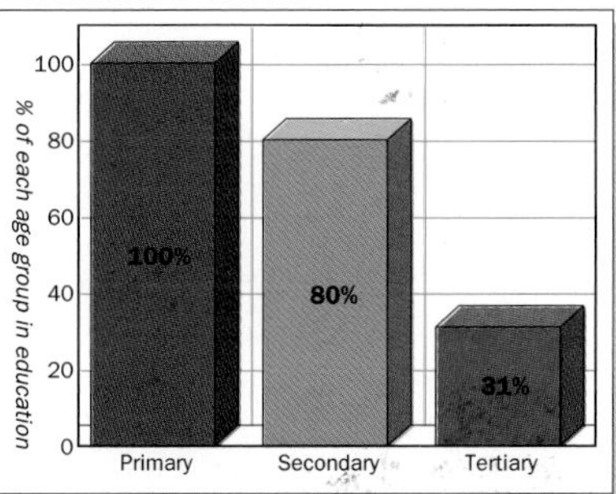

Children are sent to one of two types of school according to their ability. Those in a *Gymnasium* (11–18) are entitled to enter college, children in a *Hauptschule* (11–15) are not. The universities are oversubscribed, with students taking six years or more to finish their basic degrees.

HEALTH

1 per 366 people

Heart and cerebrovascular diseases, cancer

0 — Health spending as % GNP — 25

5%

Austria has relatively high levels of spending on health. The state's ability to continue to maintain the current level of service is being questioned. Many patients choose to use the expanding private health sector to avoid waiting lists for operations.

WEALTH

Agricultural worker, 78 Austrian schillings per hour; doctor, 33,279 Austrian schillings per month

CONSUMER GOODS OWNERSHIP

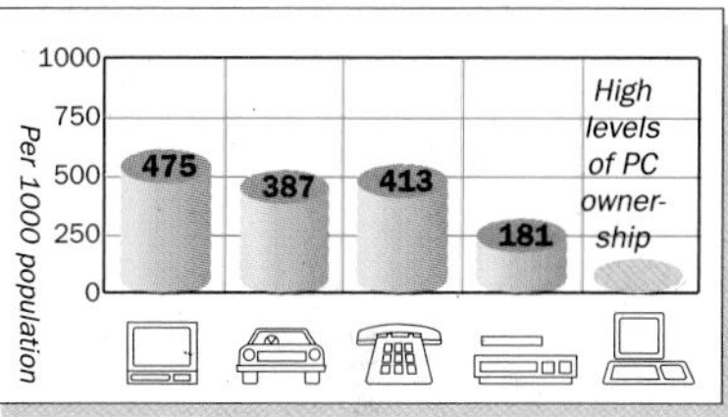

Despite having had a centrist government for most of the last four decades, Austria has retained its traditional social divisions. Inherited wealth is still respected above earned wealth, and social mobility is rather less than in neighboring Germany. Austrians have the highest savings rate of any country in the OECD. Limited amounts are invested in stocks and shares, government bonds or property. Austria's financial markets are restrictive. Strict rules govern the amount of speculation permitted on the Vienna stock exchange and also limit gains and losses to 5% of the amount invested. Government bonds offer low rates of interest and the property market is weak. Viennese tend to rent rather than buy their apartments. The poorest group are the refugees from the conflict in the former Yugoslavia.

WORLD RANKING

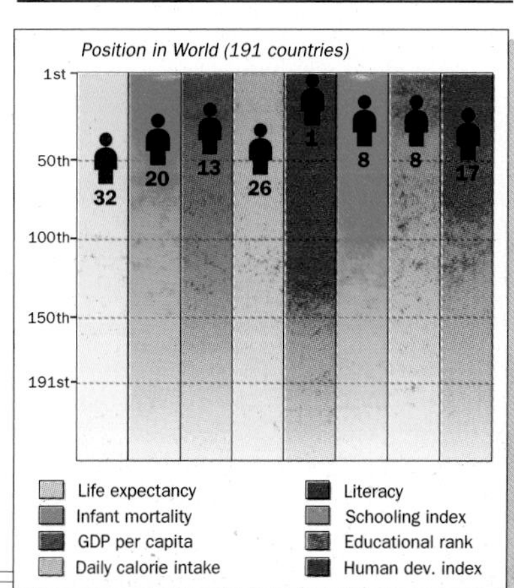

A

AZERBAIJAN

OFFICIAL NAME: Republic of Azerbaijan **CAPITAL:** Baku
POPULATION: 7.3 million **CURRENCY:** Manat **OFFICIAL LANGUAGE:** Azerbaijani

ASIA
Georgia
Russian Fed.
AZERBAIJAN
Armenia
Iran
Asia

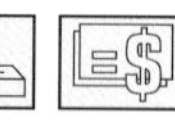

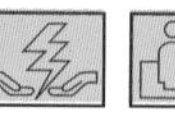
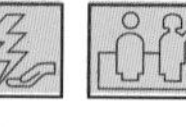
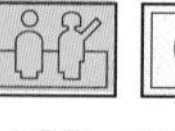
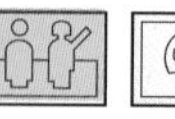

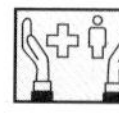

SITUATED ON THE WESTERN COAST of the Caspian Sea, Azerbaijan was the first Soviet republic to declare independence, in 1991. The issue of the disputed enclave of Nagorno Karabakh, which Armenia seeks to annex, led to full-scale war in 1993 and has since dominated all other concerns in Azeri life. The war and an estimated 500,000 refugees have added to the problems of Azerbaijan's troubled economy. Its oil wealth, however, gives it long-term potential.

Landscape typical of the Lesser Caucasus *Mountains near Qazax in the extreme northwest of Azerbaijan.*

CLIMATE

WEATHER CHART

Average daily temperature — Rainfall

°C/°F: 40/104, 30/86, 20/68, 10/50, 0/32, -10/14, -20/4

J F M A M J J A S O N D

cm/in: 40/16, 30/12, 20/8, 10/4, 0

Bitterly cold Azeri winters have become a life-or-death issue for the thousands of war refugees.

COMMUNICATIONS

THE TRANSPORTATION NETWORK

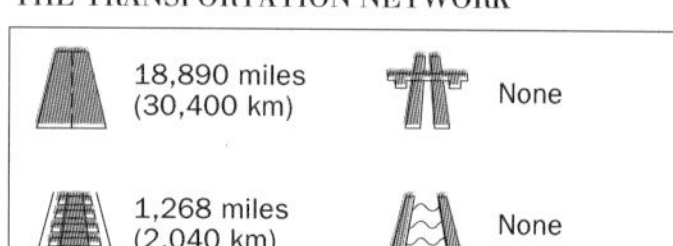

Improving links with Iran and Turkey to the south, rather than with Moscow, is the focus of transportation spending.

TOURISM

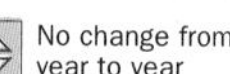

MAIN OVERSEAS ARRIVALS

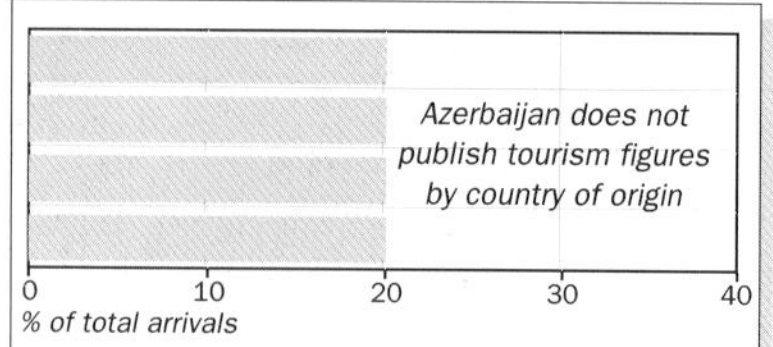

Because of the war over Nagorno Karabakh, and strong anti-Western feelings (Azerbaijan interprets the West as taking the Armenian side in the conflict), there is only a tiny trickle of visitors, most of them on business.

PEOPLE

Azerbaijani, Russian — 212 people per sq. mile

THE URBAN/RURAL POPULATION SPLIT

53% — 47%

ETHNIC MAKEUP

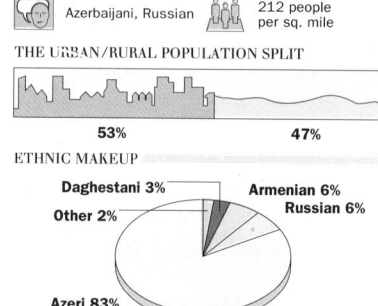

Daghestani 3%, Other 2%, Armenian 6%, Russian 6%, Azeri 83%

At the last census, held in 1989, Azeris made up 83% of the population. Today the proportion is even greater – thousands of Armenians, Jews and Russians have left as a result of rising nationalism among Azeris. Racial hostility against those that remain is increasing. Women, once prominent within the ruling party, have lost their position in political life, and their general status is also declining. The once-effective social security system has collapsed.

POLITICS

Uncertain — President Heydar Aliev

THE STATE OF THE PARTIES

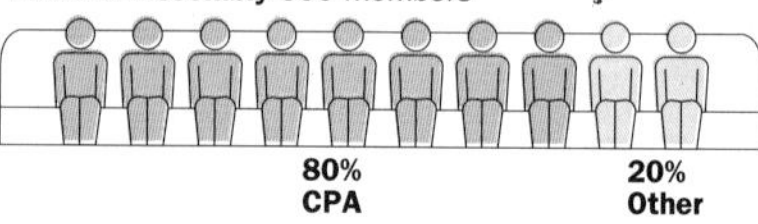

CPA = Communist Party of Azerbaijan **Other** = Popular Front of Azerbaijan (PFA), National Independence Party, Musvat Party, Dozkurt Party

The 1988 decision by Nagorno Karabakh's Armenian-dominated council to unite the enclave with the Armenian republic brought to a head decades of ethnic tension between Armenians and Azeris. Armenian separatists were soon engaged in an escalating war in which thousands were killed and hundreds of thousands made homeless. In 1993, Armenian troops invaded to aid the separatists; over 20% of Azerbaijan's territory is now under Armenian control.

AZERBAIJAN

Total Area : 86 600 sq. km (33 436 sq. miles)

POPULATION
- over 1 000 000
- over 100 000
- over 50 000
- over 10 000
- under 10 000

LAND HEIGHT
- 4000m/13 124ft
- 3000m/9843ft
- 2000m/6562ft
- 1000m/3281ft
- 500m/1640ft
- 200m/656ft
- Sea Level

WORLD AFFAIRS

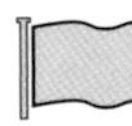
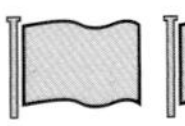

Russia's withdrawal of troops in 1993 ended the chances of a CIS-brokered settlement of the war with Armenia. Armenia, ignoring threats from Iran (which has an Azeri minority of 165 million), has since gained the upper hand. Azeri forces have received some help from Afghan *mujahideen.*

AID

 Mostly military. No figures published  Military aid is rising

Azerbaijan has been receiving covert military aid from Iran and Turkey, both vying for influence in Baku.

DEFENSE

 $1.6bn 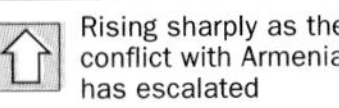 Rising sharply as the conflict with Armenia has escalated

The 30,000-strong Azeri army has performed badly in the war with Armenia. Russia withdrew the last of its 62,000 troops in 1993.

ECONOMICS

 $12.1bn  Manat. Not convertible

SCORE CARD

- ❑ World GNP Ranking..........................70th
- ❑ GNP per Capita $1,660
- ❑ Balance of Payments $499m
- ❑ Inflation...............................1,350% (est)
- ❑ Unemployment.....*No figures, but well over 50%*

Strengths
Oil and natural gas have considerable potential; a $7-billion oil deal has now been struck. The wine industry is efficient by regional standards.

Weaknesses
Years of antiquated practices in the oil industry are reflected in poor production efficiency. The war in Nagorno Karabakh remains an enormous drain on state resources.

EXPORTS

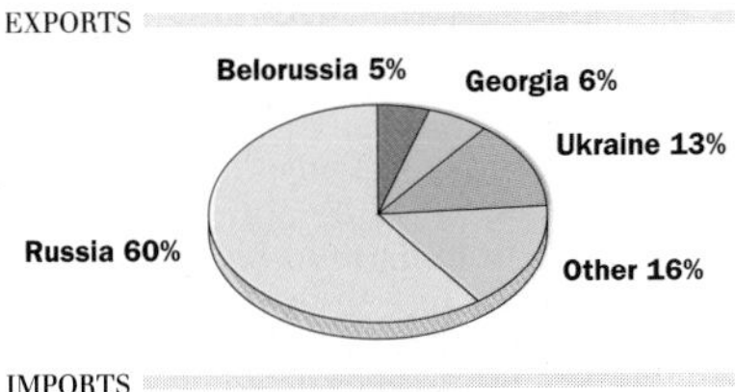

IMPORTS

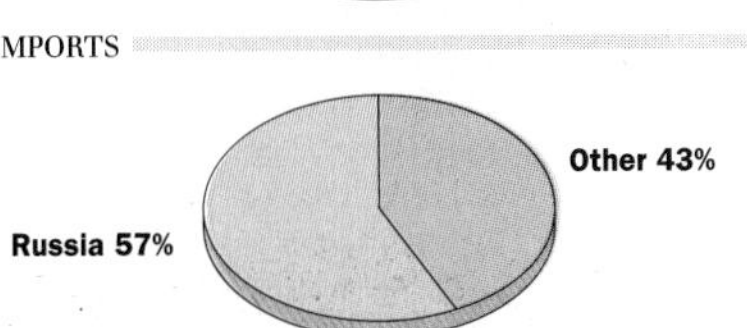

RESOURCES

 Azerbaijan does not publish energy statistics  240,000 b/d (reserves 1,300,000,000 bbl)

 5.3m sheep and goats, 1.9m cattle  Iron, bauxite, copper, lead, zinc, limestone, salt, oil, gas

The USSR did little to modernize Azerbaijan's oil fields, preferring to concentrate on Siberia; Azeri oil production fell from 8% of the USSR's total in 1965 to 0.6% by 1988. Major Western investment is now needed.

ENVIRONMENT

 2.1%  Environmental issues are not yet receiving state attention

Under the Soviet regime there was relatively unchecked oil pollution of the Caspian Sea and an overuse of pesticides in agriculture. Azeris are now far more conscious of the need to protect their environment.

MEDIA

 No press coverage critical of the government is tolerated

PUBLISHING AND BROADCAST MEDIA

 There are 151 newspapers published, including 133 in Azerbaijani

 1 state-controlled service 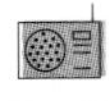 1 state-controlled service

The return of the communists has ended the brief period of press freedom. All comment is now censored.

CRIME

 Azerbaijan does not publish prison figures  Still relatively low, but rising

The judicial system returned to political control in 1993. Levels of crime outside Nagorno Karabakh are relatively low. Within the enclave, however, there are frequent reports of human rights abuses by members of the armed forces.

EDUCATION

 Over 90%

The return of the communists has ended the Democrats' Western-influenced education policy, particularly in the teaching of history, economics and politics. Baku, the main university, has an international reputation for Oriental studies.

HEALTH

 1 per 257 people  Heart, cerebrovascular and respiratory diseases, cancer

The already basic health system in Azerbaijan effectively collapsed as a result of shortages caused by the war.

CHRONOLOGY

Under consecutive Persian, Ottoman and Russian influence, Azerbaijan, one of the world's major oil producers in 1900, was established as an independent state in 1917.

- ❑ **1920** Soviet Red Army invades. Soviet republic established.
- ❑ **1922** Incorporated in Transcaucasian Soviet Federative Socialist Republic (TSFSR).
- ❑ **1930** Forced collectivization of agriculture. Peasant uprisings.
- ❑ **1936** TSFSR disbanded. Azerbaijan a full union republic (ASSR).
- ❑ **1945** Failed attempt to annex Azeri region of Iran.
- ❑ **1985** President Gorbachev makes tackling corruption in CPA a priority.
- ❑ 1988 Nagorno Karabakh council requests unification with Armenia. Outbreaks of ethnic violence.
- ❑ **1990** Nagorno Karabakh tries to secede. Riots in Baku. PFA takes control. Soviet troops move in.
- ❑ **1991** Independence from Moscow.
- ❑ **1993** Internal ethnic conflict over enclave of Nagorno Karabakh escalates into war with Armenia.

WEALTH

 The majority of Azeris live close to the poverty line

CONSUMER GOODS OWNERSHIP

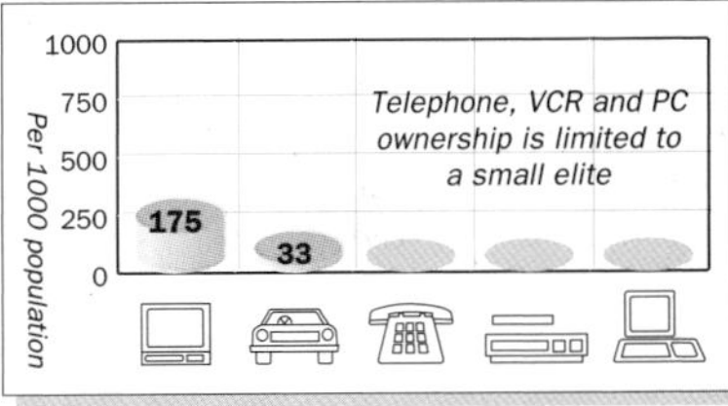

The old Communist Party executives, once more in control of the state economy, are the wealthiest group.

WORLD RANKING

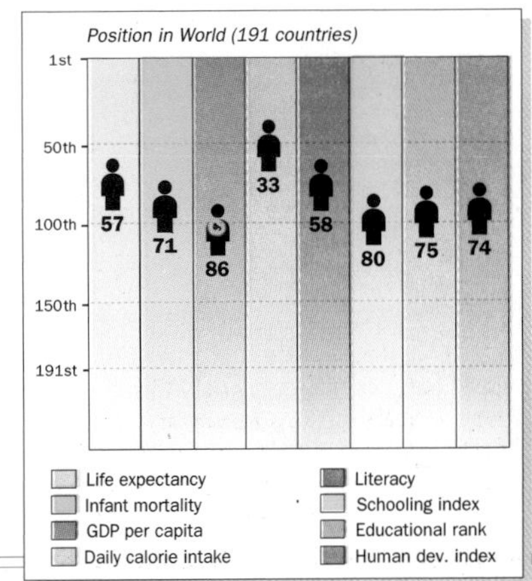

B

BAHAMAS

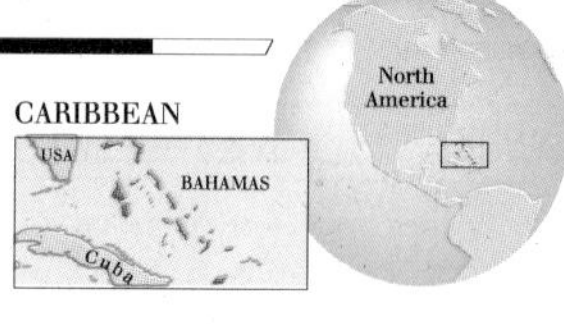

OFFICIAL NAME: The Commonwealth of the Bahamas **CAPITAL:** Nassau
POPULATION: 300,000 **CURRENCY:** Bahamian dollar **OFFICIAL LANGUAGE:** English

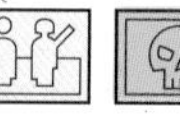

LOCATED OFF THE FLORIDA COAST in the western Atlantic, the Bahamas comprise an archipelago of some 700 islands and 2,400 cays, of which 30 are inhabited. One of the first transatlantic tourist destinations, the Bahamas today is also a major offshore financial center. It has one of the world's largest open-registry fleets, but only 0.2% of the total tonnage is owned by Bahamian nationals.

CLIMATE

WEATHER CHART

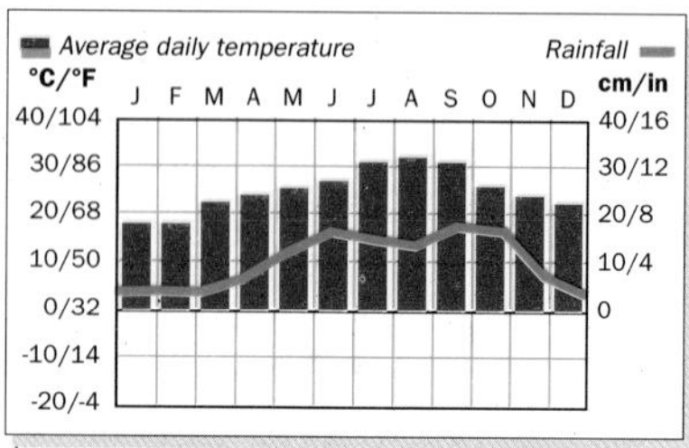

The whole of the Bahamas chain has a typically subtropical climate with consistently mild winters. Hurricanes may occur from July to December.

COMMUNICATIONS

Freeport International
1.23m passengers

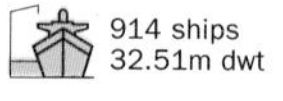

914 ships
32.51m dwt

THE TRANSPORTATION NETWORK

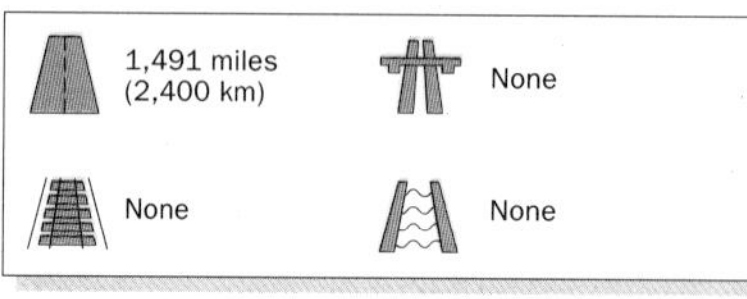

Getting around 700 islands spread over 100,386 sq. miles is a major problem. There are plans to increase the number of ferry and seaplane services.

TOURISM

Up 1% in 1990

MAIN OVERSEAS ARRIVALS

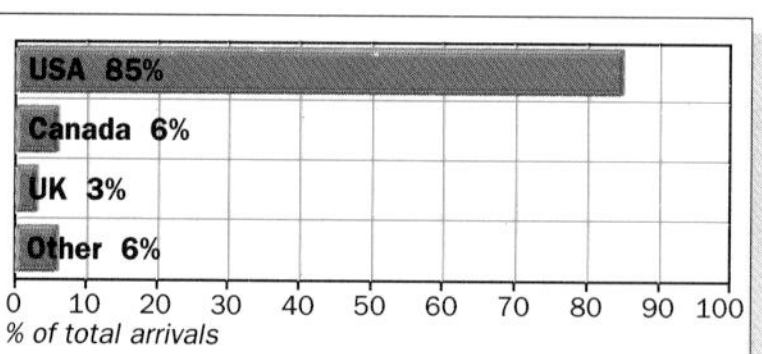

The casinos and beaches are major attractions. Charters from the USA, which arrive in the afternoon, allowing visitors to play the casinos and return home the next morning, are increasingly popular. The Bahamas is also one of the Caribbean's major cruise-ship centers.

PEOPLE

English, English Creole, French Creole

47 people per sq. mile

THE URBAN/RURAL POPULATION SPLIT

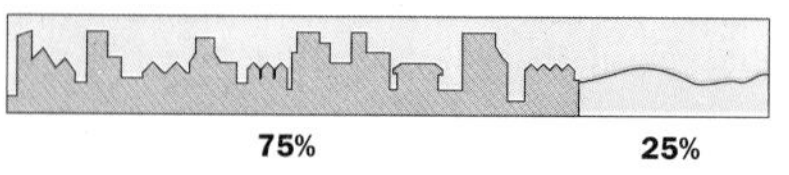

75% 25%

RELIGIOUS PERSUASION

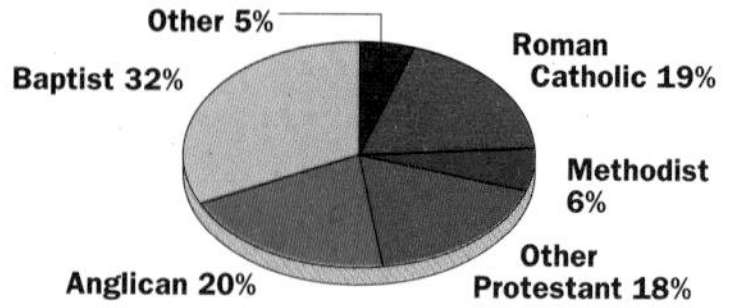

Other 5%
Roman Catholic 19%
Baptist 32%
Methodist 6%
Other Protestant 18%
Anglican 20%

Africans first came to the Bahamas as slaves in the 16th century; their descendants now constitute most of the population. The nuclear family is the norm, although absentee fathers are fairly common, especially in outlying fishing communities. More women are going into the professional sector.

POLITICS

1997

HM Queen Elizabeth II

THE STATE OF THE PARTIES

House of Assembly 49 members

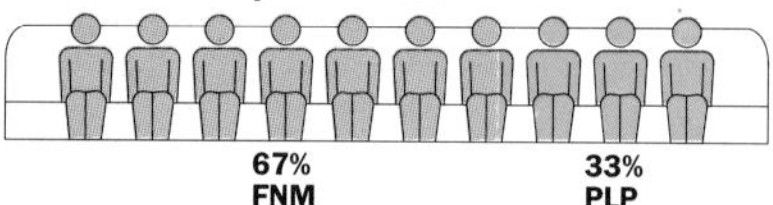

67% FNM
33% PLP

FNM = Free National Movement **PLP** = Progressive Liberal Party

Senate 16 members

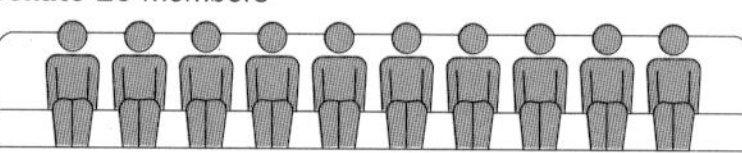

9 members chosen by the prime minister, 4 by the leader of the opposition and 3 by the prime minister after consultation with the leader of the opposition.

The 1992 election defeat of Lynden Pindling, the result of increasing numbers of allegations of narcotics corruption against senior government members, ended a period of 25 years of continuous rule by his PLP. Pindling was instrumental in steering the Bahamas to independence, ending the domination of the white elite "Bay Street Boys" in Bahamian politics and bringing blacks into the political process for the first time. The new administration, under Hubert Ingraham, has concentrated on tightening up ministerial accountability in government. However, investigations into the Pindling administration will probably take several years to complete.

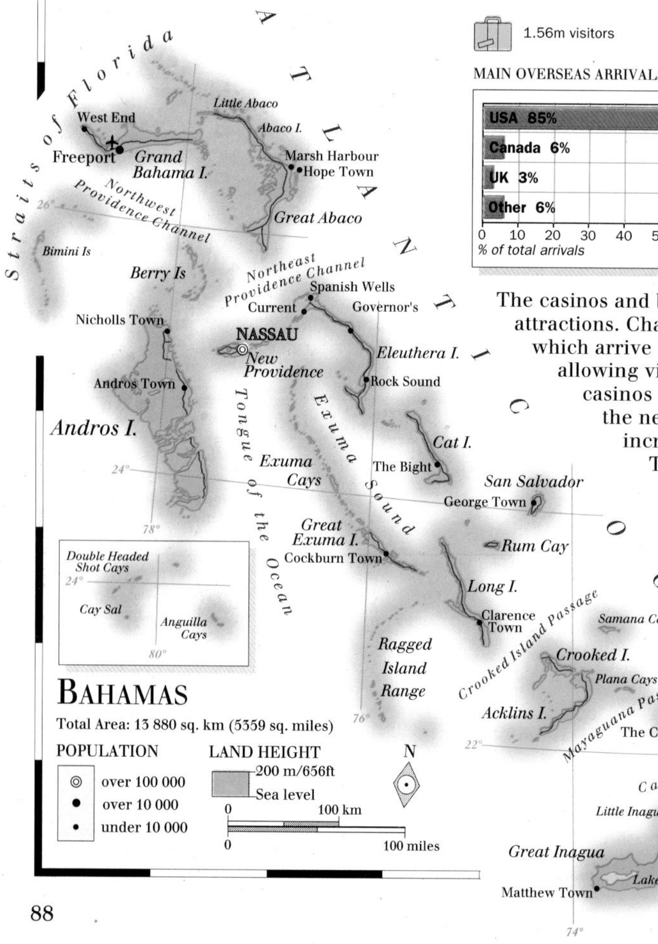

BAHAMAS

Total Area: 13 880 sq. km (5359 sq. miles)

POPULATION
over 100 000
over 10 000
under 10 000

LAND HEIGHT
200 m/656ft
Sea level

0 100 km
0 100 miles

WORLD AFFAIRS

Comm | Caricom | NAM | OAS | CDB

Dealing with Haitian refugees and repairing relations with the USA, following the narcotics scandals of the 1980s, in which several government ministers were allegedly implicated, are the main issues.

AID

 $3m (receipts)

 No change in 1991

One of the healthiest economies in the Caribbean, the Bahamas receives negligible aid. The USA is the principal donor, mainly providing soft loans.

DEFENSE

 $66.96m (including police spending)

 Up 5% in 1992

The UK is the main trainer of and supplier for the 900-strong defense force and coastguard. Intercepting narcotics smugglers and Haitian refugees are the main activities.

ECONOMICS

 $3bn

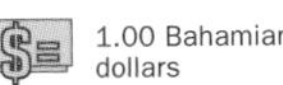 1.00 Bahamian dollars

SCORE CARD

❑ World GNP Ranking	124st
❑ GNP per Capita	$10,000
❑ Balance of Payments	$-113m
❑ Inflation	6.1%
❑ Unemployment	11.7%

Strengths

A major international financial services sector, including banking and insurance, which has benefited from political uncertainty in Hong Kong. Tourism and ship registration are also major businesses.

Weaknesses

Growing competition in financial services from the Cayman Islands and Bermuda.

EXPORTS

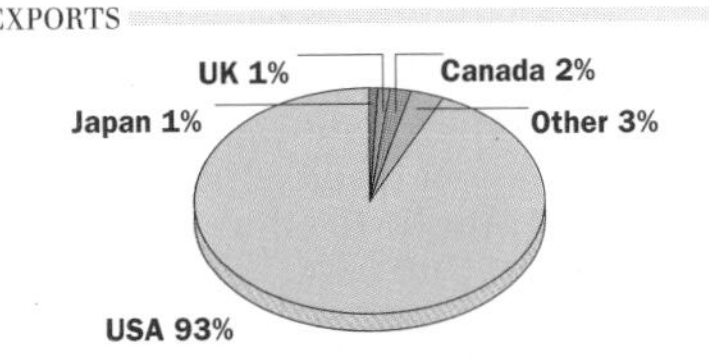

IMPORTS

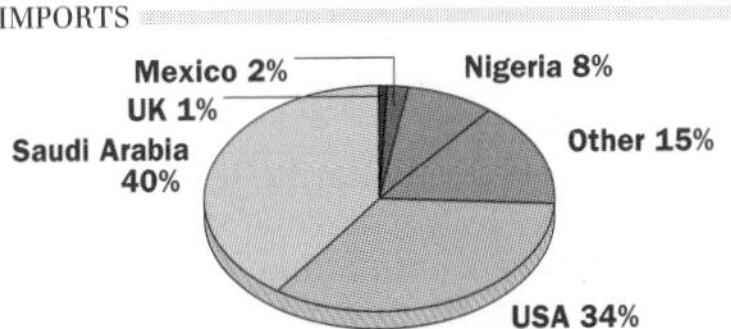

***Archetypal island paradise.** Its natural beauty draws six tourists per inhabitant to visit the Bahamas every year.*

RESOURCES

 950m kwh (capacity 400,000 kw)

 Not an oil producer and has no refineries

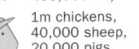

1m chickens, 40,000 sheep, 20,000 pigs

Salt, aragonite

The Bahamas has no strategic resources and all its energy requirements have to be imported.

ENVIRONMENT

 9%

 Plans to increase numbers of protected sites

As in other Caribbean states, hotel overdevelopment is a major cause for concern. Environmental groups have also pointed out the potential for accidents posed by the Bahamas' enormous oil storage depots.

MEDIA

 No restrictions on political reporting

PUBLISHING AND BROADCAST MEDIA

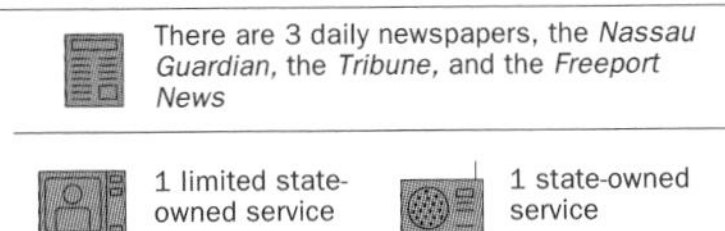

There are 3 daily newspapers, the *Nassau Guardian*, the *Tribune*, and the *Freeport News*

1 limited state-owned service

1 state-owned service

The state-owned TV channel faces very stiff competition from Florida-based US broadcasters.

CRIME

 3,789 prisoners

 Up 8% in 1990

The Bahamas was a key transshipment point for US-bound Colombian cocaine during the 1980s. Today, drug-related crimes such as muggings in tourist resorts and contract killings by competing gangs are increasing.

EDUCATION

 95%

Education follows the standard pattern of other Caribbean states, with a British 11-plus selective system. Students go on to the University of the West Indies.

CHRONOLOGY

Once an English pirate base, the Bahamas, which gained its first parliament in 1729, became a formal British colony in 1783.

- ❑ **1920–1933** US prohibition laws turn the Bahamas into a prosperous bootlegging center.
- ❑ **1959** Introduction of male suffrage.
- ❑ **1962** Women gain the vote.
- ❑ **1973** Independence.
- ❑ **1976** The Bahamas becomes flag of convenience for merchant fleets.
- ❑ **1983** Narcotics smuggling scandals involving Bahamian government.

HEALTH

 1 per 809 people

Heart diseases, cancer, nutritional disorders, accidents

The Bahamian health service combines state and private systems. Access to care in the outlying islands is difficult, relying on unscheduled inter-island or privately owned boats.

WEALTH

 Hotel cook, 13,000 Bahamian dollars per year; professional nurse, 15,000-27,500 Bahamian dollars per year

CONSUMER GOODS OWNERSHIP

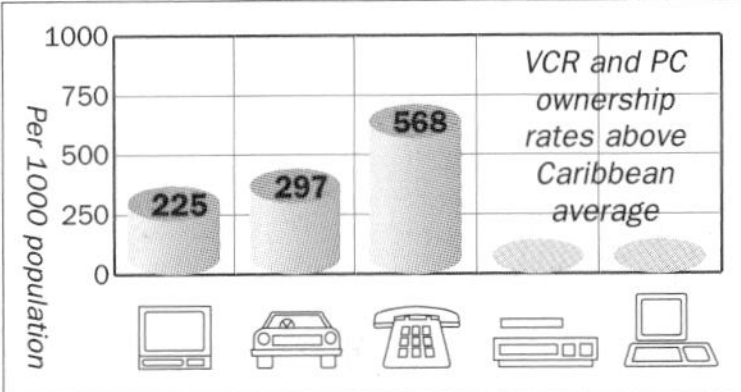

There are marked wealth disparities between urban professionals working in the financial sector and poor fishermen from the outlying islands. Haitian refugees, who have no legal status, are the poorest group.

WORLD RANKING

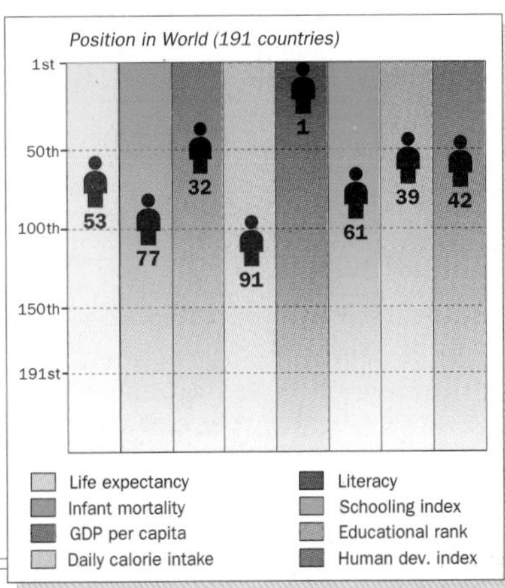

B

BAHRAIN

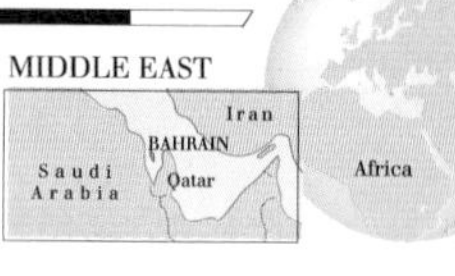

OFFICIAL NAME: State of Bahrain **CAPITAL:** Manama
POPULATION: 500,000 **CURRENCY:** Bahrain dinar **OFFICIAL LANGUAGE:** Arabic

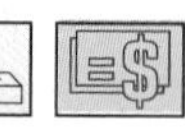

BAHRAIN IS AN ARCHIPELAGO of 33 islands between the Qatar Peninsula and the Saudi Arabian mainland. Only three of the islands are inhabited. Bahrain Island is connected to Saudi Arabia's eastern province by a four-lane causeway that opened in 1986. Bahrain was the first Gulf emirate to export oil; its reserves are now almost depleted. Services such as offshore banking, insurance and tourism are major employment sectors for skilled Bahrainis.

POLITICS

 Not applicable

 Amir Sheikh Isa bin Sulman Al-Khalifa

THE STATE OF THE PARTIES

Bahrain is an absolute monarchy, ruled by the Amir through an appointed cabinet

The Al-Khalifa family has dominated Bahraini politics since 1783. Politics are effectively autocratic and political dissent is not tolerated. Bahrain is one of the few Gulf states with political prisoners. Opponents of the regime – usually Shi'a fundamentalists – are frequently exiled and have their passports canceled. Iran has sought to encourage fundamentalists in Bahrain by distributing cassettes of Iranian mullahs' sermons preaching revolution. Radio broadcasts from Tehran also reach Bahrain. While there is considerable Shi'a discontent at their low social status, there are few channels by which this can be expressed or organized.

The current Amir, Sheikh Isa bin Sulman Al-Khalifa, is a liberal in terms of economic policy, encouraging private enterprise. Politically, he is wary of introducing democracy. An attempt at representative government in 1973 was suspended in 1975 because it provoked instability. The fear that democracy will be used by fundamentalists to gain power, as in Algeria, makes any real liberalization of politics unlikely.

CLIMATE

WEATHER CHART

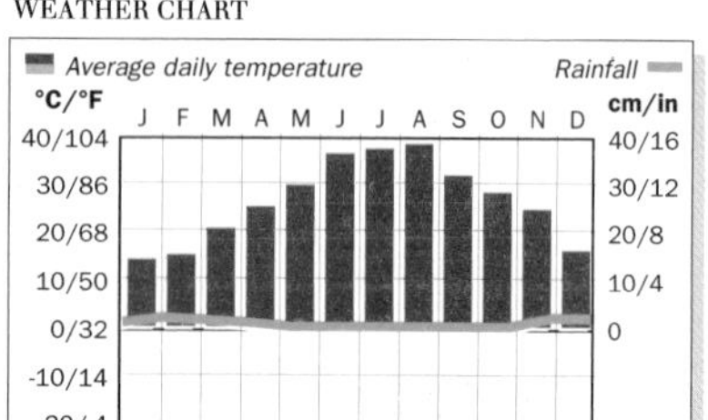

Temperatures soar to 105°F from June to September. Between December and March the weather is pleasantly warm.

PEOPLE

 Arabic

 1,873 people per sq. mile

THE URBAN/RURAL POPULATION SPLIT

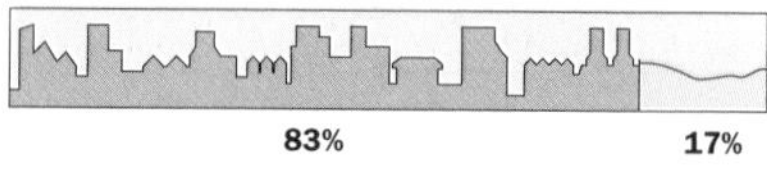

ETHNIC MAKEUP

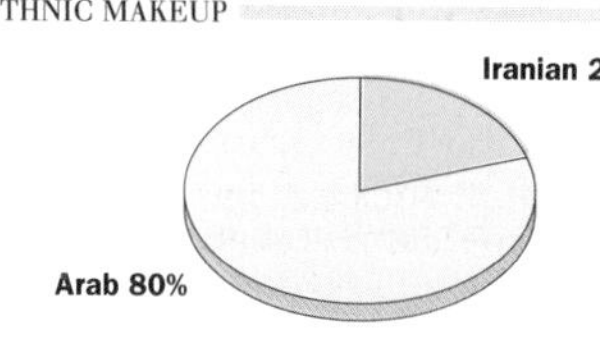

The key division in Bahrain is between Sunni and Shi'a Muslims, 30% and 70% of the country respectively. The ruling class is Sunni and they hold the best jobs in business and the bureaucracy. Shi'a Muslims tend to do menial work and have a lower standard of living. Tension between the two groups can spill over into violence, particularly during religious festivals.

Bahrain has a smaller expatriate population than many other Arab countries. The ruling Al-Khalifa family has responded to declining oil reserves by diversifying the economy to provide service industry jobs for Bahrainis.

Bahrain is the most "liberal" of the Gulf states. Women have access to education and professional jobs and are not obliged to wear veils. Arranged marriages remain common.

The Grand Mosque, Manama. It is the largest building in Bahrain and can accommodate 7,000 people.

COMMUNICATIONS

 **Bahrain International, Muharraq** 1.87m passengers

15 ships 158,700 dwt

THE TRANSPORTATION NETWORK

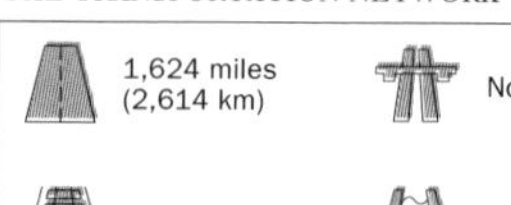 1,624 miles (2,614 km)

None

None

None

Saudi Arabia paid for the 15-mile-long causeway linking it with Bahrain; the four-lane road was completed in 1986.

TOURISM

 1.4m visitors

 Tourist levels have risen since 1991

MAIN OVERSEAS ARRIVALS

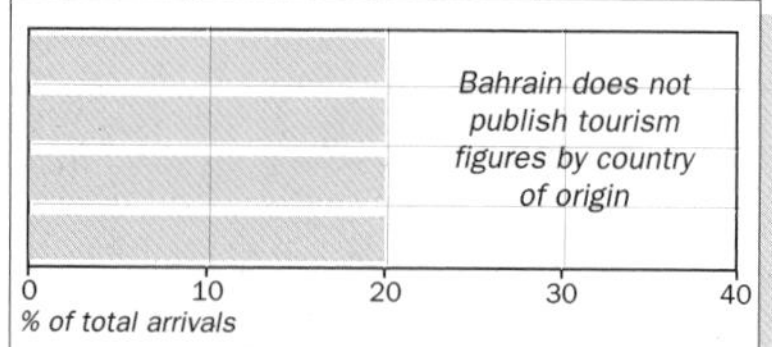

Bahrain's "liberal" lifestyle is reflected in Manama's bars and nightlife. Since the causeway opened in 1986, there has been a boom in weekend tourists from Saudi Arabia and other Gulf states. Bahrain is a business convention center.

WORLD AFFAIRS

ESCWA

Bahrain holds to a staunchly independent line in foreign policy. It maintains good relations with the USA, the main guarantor of its security, yet has also called for relations with Iraq to be restored. Despite objecting to Bahrain's liberal social attitudes, Saudi Arabia finds the Al-Khalifas useful allies against Gulf fundamentalists.

AID

 $101m (receipts)

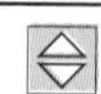 Little change from year to year

Bahrain receives moderate levels of aid, but takes the lion's share of the offshore oil field shared with Saudi Arabia, effectively a subsidy from the latter.

DEFENSE

$236.8m

Up 7% in 1992

The 6,150-strong **defense force** includes a small but well-equipped air force. Bahrain has traditionally maintained close relations with the USA. US airbases on Bahrain were used in the 1990-1991 Gulf War. The small navy must stretch its resources to patrol the 33-island archipelago.

ECONOMICS

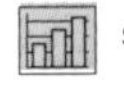

$3.1bn

0.38 Bahrain dinars

SCORE CARD

- ❑ WORLD GNP RANKING........................118th
- ❑ GNP PER CAPITA $6,200
- ❑ BALANCE OF PAYMENTS................$-738.3m
- ❑ INFLATION 2%
- ❑ UNEMPLOYMENT....................................8%

EXPORTS

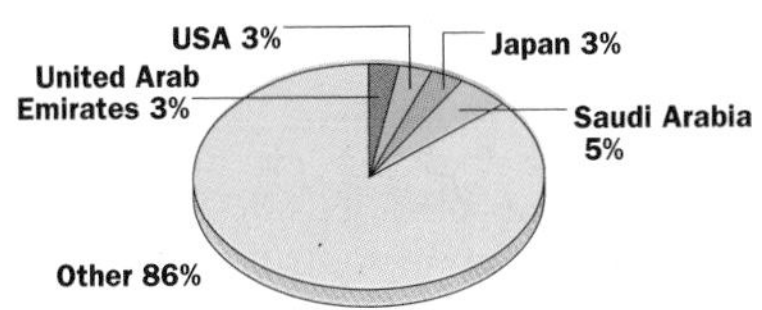

IMPORTS

Japan 6%
USA 7%
Saudi Arabia 42%
UK 11%
Other 34%

STRENGTHS

Oil. Arab world's major offshore banking sector. Lack of restrictions encourages inward investment. Tourism.

WEAKNESSES

Depleted oil reserves and insufficient diversification could lead to future drop in currently high living standards. High levels of government borrowing.

RESOURCES

3.5bn kwh (capacity 1.04m kw)

38,200 b/d (reserves 69,584,000 bbl)

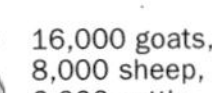

16,000 goats, 8,000 sheep, 6,000 cattle

Oil, natural gas

Bahrain remains dependent on its oil and gas production. Production of crude oil declined however, from 65,000 (b/d) in the 1970s to 38,200 b/d in 1994. Reserves will probably run out by 2010. Because oil has declined, gas has assumed greater importance. Most is used to supply local industries, particularly the aluminum plant established in 1972.

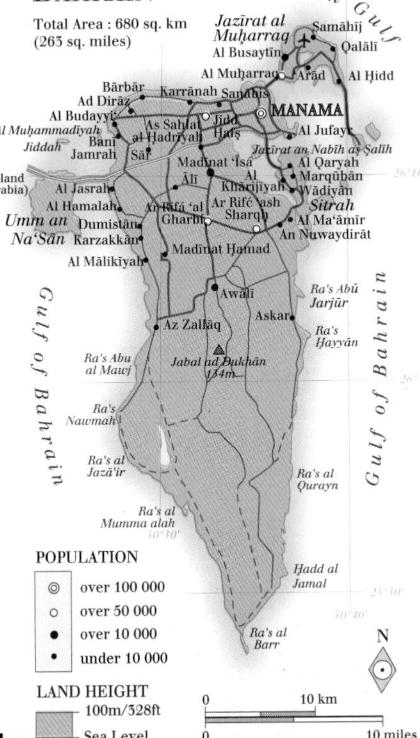

ENVIRONMENT

None

Environmental issues not a priority

Local marine life, particularly the dugong, is vulnerable to upstream oil pollution from the Gulf.

MEDIA

The information ministry is relatively liberal. However, the press is still semi-controlled

PUBLISHING AND BROADCAST MEDIA

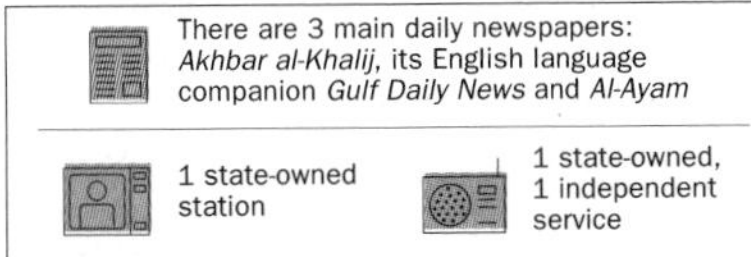

There are 3 main daily newspapers: *Akhbar al-Khalij*, its English language companion *Gulf Daily News* and *Al-Ayam*

1 state-owned station

1 state-owned, 1 independent service

Bahrain has the most liberal information policy in the Gulf. CNN and BBC satellite TV are freely available.

CRIME

Bahrain does not publish prison figures

Down 57% in 1990

Crime is minimal and theft and muggings rare. Suspected political dissidents are monitored by the police.

CHRONOLOGY

Bahrain has been ruled since 1783 by the Al-Khalifa family.

- ❑ **1971** Independence from Britain.
- ❑ **1981** Founder-member of GCC. December: abortive coup backed by Iran. Bahrain gives backing to Iraq in Iran–Iraq war.
- ❑ **1991** Bahrain backs UN in expelling Iraq from Kuwait.
- ❑ **1992** Bahrain calls for Iraq to be admitted to the GCC.

EDUCATION

77%

Female literacy rates are well above the Gulf average. Lack of funding has held up plans for a university.

HEALTH

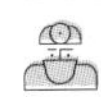

1 per 713 people

Circulatory diseases, perinatal deaths, injury, poisonings

The health service is extensive and run to world-class standards. Bahraini nationals receive free treatment. Some go abroad for advanced care.

WEALTH

Agricultural worker, 196 dinars per month; oil engineer, 698 dinars per month

CONSUMER GOODS OWNERSHIP

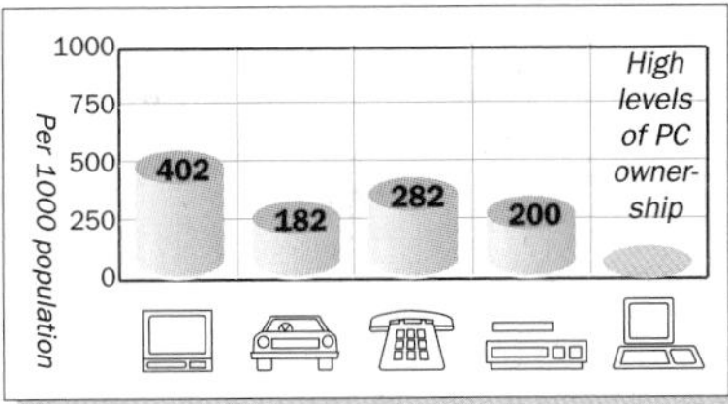

Beneficiaries of the Amir's extensive patronage are the wealthiest group. Shi'a Muslims are the poorest.

WORLD RANKING

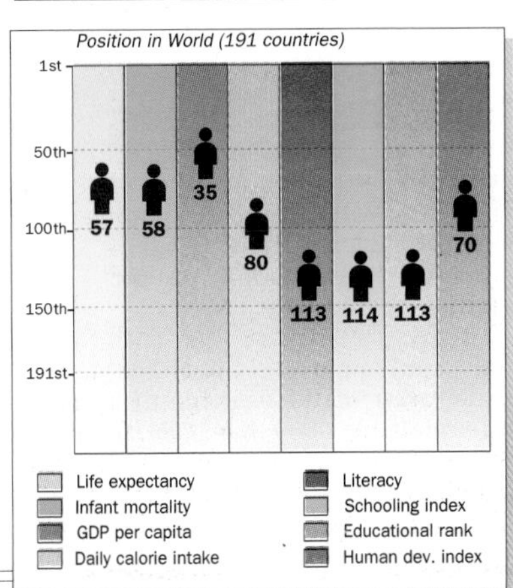

BANGLADESH

SOUTH ASIA

BANGLADESH India Burma Asia

OFFICIAL NAME: People's Republic of Bangladesh **CAPITAL:** Dhaka
POPULATION: 119.3 million **CURRENCY:** Taka **OFFICIAL LANGUAGE:** Bengali

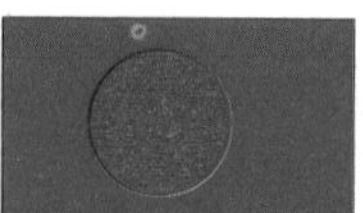

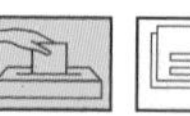

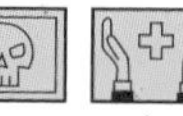

BANGLADESH LIES AT the north of the Bay of Bengal and shares borders with India and Myanmar. Most of the country is composed of fertile alluvial plains; the north and northeast is mountainous, as is the Chittagong region. Since its secession from Pakistan in 1971, Bangladesh has had a troubled history of political instability, with periods of emergency rule. Effective democracy was restored in 1991. Bangladesh's major economic sectors are jute production, textiles and agriculture. Its climate can wreak havoc – in 1991, a massive cyclone killed more than 140,000 people.

CLIMATE

WEATHER CHART

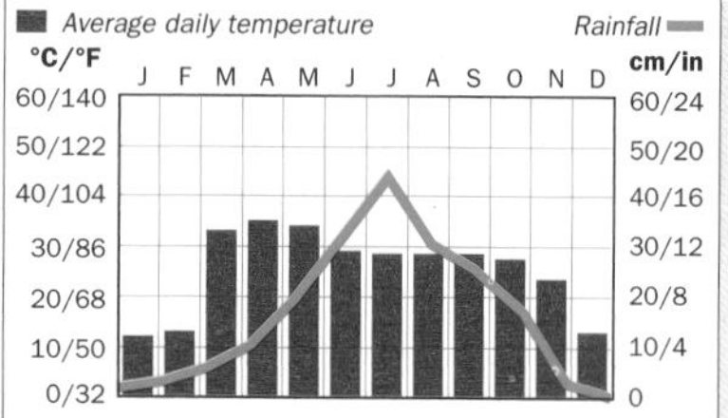

During the monsoon, the water level normally rises 20 feet above sea level, flooding two-thirds of the country. The floods are made much worse when the Ganges, Jamuna and Meghna rivers, which converge in a huge delta in Bangladesh, are swollen by the melting of the Himalayan snows, and heavy rain, in India. Cyclones regularly build up in the Bay of Bengal, with sometimes devastating effects on the flat coastal region.

COMMUNICATIONS

Zia International, Dhaka
1.19m passengers

172 ships
532,600 dwt

THE TRANSPORTATION NETWORK

3,877 miles (6,240 km)

None

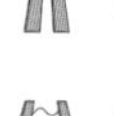
1,735 miles (2,792 km)

5,228 miles (8,433 km)

Most transportation in Bangladesh is by water, although the government is now concentrating on developing road and rail links. A major bridge is currently being built across the Jamuna River, which bisects Bangladesh from north to south. The $500-million project has suffered numerous delays and is now due to be completed in 1996. Bangladesh's two major ports, Mungla and Chittagong, are being upgraded to take advanced container ships.

Begum Khaleda Zia, prime minister since February 1991.

Gen. Ershad, president from 1983 to 1990.

TOURISM

110,475 visitors

Down 2% in 1992

MAIN OVERSEAS ARRIVALS

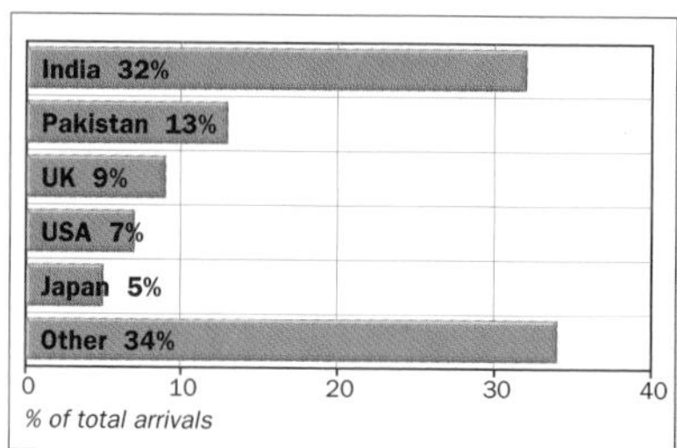

Tourist earnings and numbers have been falling since the mid-1980s. Most visitors are Indian businessmen or Bangladeshis who live overseas, returning to see their relatives. The mogul architecture in Dhaka and the Pala dynasty (7th–10th centuries) city of Sonargaon are major attractions.

Traders on the Meghna River, which flows into the Padma. Bangladesh's flood-plains are among the most fertile in the world.

PEOPLE

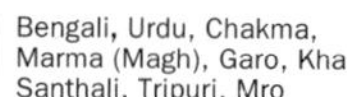
Bengali, Urdu, Chakma, Marma (Magh), Garo, Khasi, Santhali, Tripuri, Mro

1,953 people per sq. mile

THE URBAN/RURAL POPULATION SPLIT

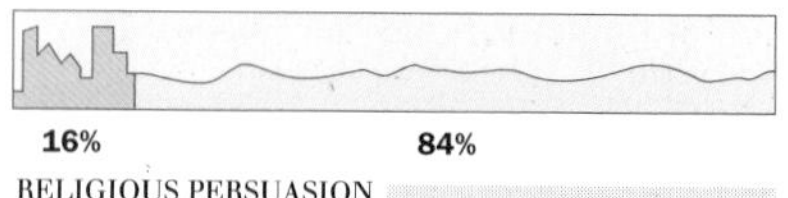

RELIGIOUS PERSUASION

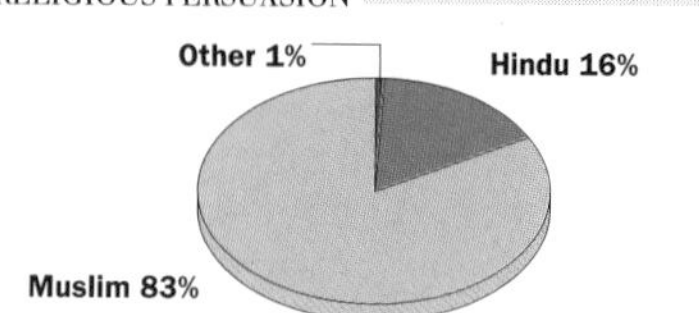

ETHNIC MAKEUP

Other 2%

Bengali 98%

Bangladesh is one of the most densely populated countries in the world, despite the fact that 84% of the population are rural dwellers. As in India, there is considerable Muslim–Hindu tension; the destruction of the Ayodhya Mosque in northern India in 1992 incited violence in Bangladesh.

The only genuinely ethnic-based conflict occurs in the Chittagong Hill Tracts in the southeast, where 12 tribes – mostly Buddhists – demanding autonomy have been waging a low-level guerrilla war since 1974. The south of the country is also having to cope with an influx of refugees fleeing neighboring Myanmar.

Although about 55% of Bangladeshis, rural and urban, still live below the poverty line, there has been an improvement in living standards over the past decade.

The textile trade, by providing an independent income, has been one factor in the growing emancipation of Bangladeshi women. They are now included in official employment statistics and are the main customers of the most successful rural bank. Women lead both the government and opposition.

POPULATION AGE BREAKDOWN

% of population by age group	1960	1970	1980	1990	2000
65+	3.7%	3.5%	3.4%	2.9%	3%
15–64	55.4%	51.1%	50.4%	53.2%	58.2%
0–14	40.9%	45.4%	46.2%	43.9%	38.8%

B

POLITICS

1996

President Abdur Rahman Biswas

THE STATE OF THE PARTIES

National Assembly 330 members

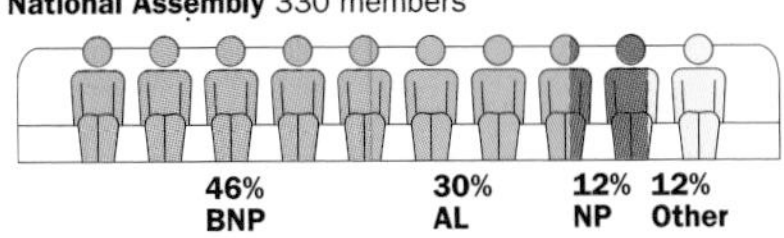

46% BNP | 30% AL | 12% NP | 12% Other

BNP = Bangladesh National Party **AL** = Awami League
NP = National Party **Other** = Islamic Party of Bangladesh, Bangladesh Communist Party

Bangladesh returned to multiparty democracy in 1991, following a period of military rule.

MAIN POLITICAL ISSUES

The state sector
Bangladesh is coming under increasing pressure from multilateral lending institutions, which account for the vast majority of the country's capital inflows, to cut costs in the state sector. Simultaneously, state sector workers are demanding wage increases in line with inflation.

The Chittagong Hill Tracts insurgency
Buddhist Mongol groups have been waging a low-level guerrilla war since 1974, when their demands for partial autonomy and restrictions on Bengali settlers in the region were rebuffed. State policy seems to be to contain rather than eradicate the conflict.

Golam Azam
Golam Azam, leader of the Islamic Party, has been in custody since 1990, accused of atrocities and siding with Pakistan during the war of independence. Hindu groups in Bangladesh are pushing for a dramatic trial; any moves to try him risk inflaming Muslim passions.

PROFILE

Between 1975 and 1990 the military was in power in Bangladesh. The overthrow of President Ershad in 1990 led to a return to multiparty politics; the army remains poised, however, to intervene in the event of a breakdown in law and order. Bangladesh's first woman prime minister, Begum Khaleda Zia, head of the ruling BNP, was elected in February 1991. A change from a presidential to a prime-ministerial system of government followed. Intense factionalism within the Awami League – which steered Bangladesh to independence in 1971 – weakens its ability to challenge the BNP.

BANGLADESH

Total Area : 143 998 sq. km (55 598 sq. miles)

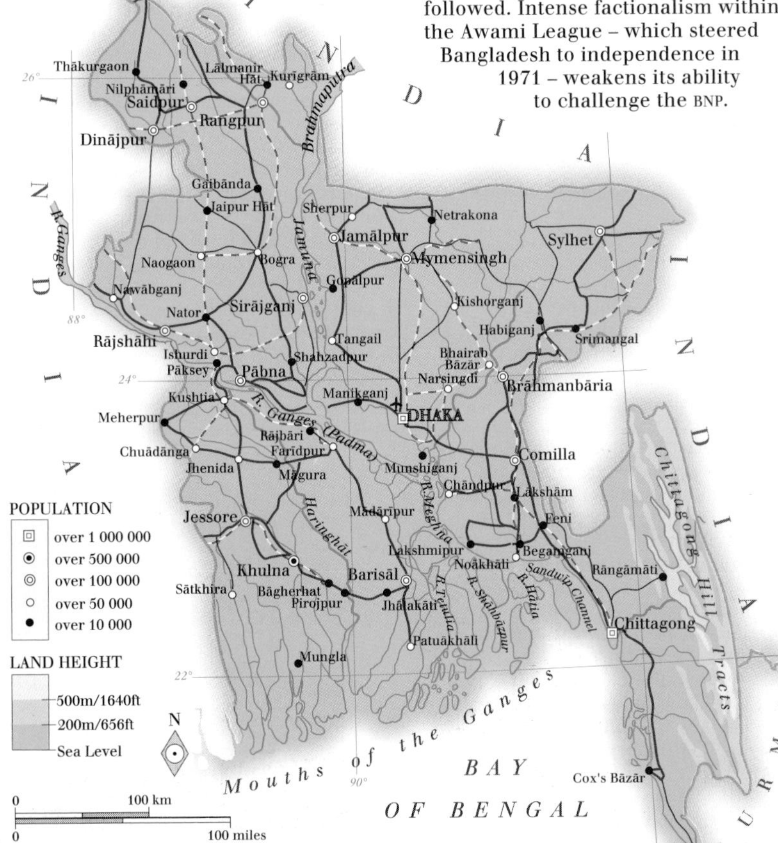

WORLD AFFAIRS

Bangladesh concentrates mostly on maintaining good relations with the West, the main source of essential aid. Relations with Pakistan have slowly been improving since the low point of 1971. Pakistan finally agreed in 1991 to repatriate the 250,000 pro-Pakistani Bihari Muslims languishing in Bangladeshi refugee camps since 1971. Relations with India are strained. The effects of the Indian construction of the Farakka Dam across the Ganges have deprived Bangladeshi farmers of water for irrigation. The failure of Delhi to curb guerrilla groups operating out of India into the Chittagong region has also soured relations.

AID

$1.6bn (receipts)

Down 20% in 1991

Aid disbursements to Bangladesh each year are over 1,000 times greater than the annual value of foreign investment in the country. Aid also finances more than 90% of state capital spending. The Bangladesh Development Aid Consortium meets annually to discuss aid spending under the auspices of the World Bank. One result of the level of aid is that Bangladesh has fallen into one of the traps of an aid-dependent economy: the large middle class has a vested interest in perpetuating a system that provides its members with lucrative contracts and access to external resources.

CHRONOLOGY

British rule in India began in Bengal (now Bangladesh), when Robert Clive, army head of the East India Company, defeated the ruler of Bengal at Plassey in 1765.

- **1905** Muslims persuade British rulers to partition state of Bengal, to create a Muslim-dominated East Bengal.
- **1906** Muslim League established in Dhaka.
- **1912** Partition of 1905 reversed.
- **1947** British withdrawal from India. Partition plans establish a largely Muslim state of East (present-day Bangladesh) and West Pakistan, separated by 992 miles of Indian, and largely Hindu, territory. The capital of the new, bisected state is established at Islamabad in West Pakistan.
- **1949** Awami League founded to campaign for autonomy from West Pakistan.

CHRONOLOGY *continued*

- **1968** General Yahya Khan heads government in Islamabad.
- **1970** Elections give Awami League, under Sheikh Mujibur Rahman, clear majority. Rioting and guerrilla warfare following Yahya Khan's refusal to convene assembly. The year ends with the worst recorded storms in Bangladesh's history – between 200,000 and 500,000 dead.
- **1971** Civil War, as Sheikh Mujibur and Awami League declare unilateral independence. Ten million Bangladeshis flee to India. Pakistani troops defeated in 12 days by *Mukhti Bahini* – the Bengal Liberation Army.
- **1972** Sheikh Mujibur prime minister. Nationalization program for the utilities and tea, jute and textiles industries introduced. Bangladesh achieves international recognition and joins Commonwealth. Pakistan withdraws in protest.
- **1974** Severe floods damage rice crop; famine and inflation exacerbate rising discontent.
- **1975** Sheikh Mujibur assassinated. Military coups end with General Zia Rahman taking power. Institution of single-party state.
- **1976** Banning of trade union federations.
- **1977** General Zia assumes presidency. Islam adopted as first principle of the constitution.
- **1981** General Zia assassinated.
- **1982** General Ershad takes over.
- **1983** Democratic elections restored by Ershad; marred by government intimidation and violence. Ershad assumes presidency.
- **1986** Elections, again affected by intimidation and violence. Awami League and BNP fail to unseat Ershad.
- **1987** Proposed bill to allow military personnel to run for parliament causes anti-government strikes and demonstrations, supported by trade unionists and student groups. Thousands detained; Ershad announces state of emergency.
- **1988** Islam becomes constitutional state religion.
- **1990** Ershad resigns following renewed campaign of demonstrations and strikes. Bangladeshis working in Kuwait suffer significant loss of earnings as a result of Gulf War.
- **1991** Elections won by BNP, headed by Begum Khaleda Zia, who becomes prime minister. Ershad imprisoned. Role of the president reduced to that of titular head of state.

DEFENSE

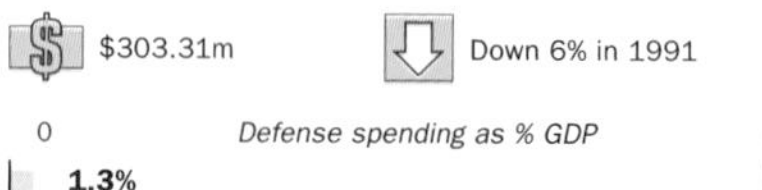

The military, which dominated politics between 1975 and 1990, continues to wield considerable influence behind the scenes. The defense budget accounts for 7.5% of state spending (1.3% of GDP). The army, at 93,000 personnel, is relatively small. China is the major source of weapons.

BANGLADESHI ARMED FORCES

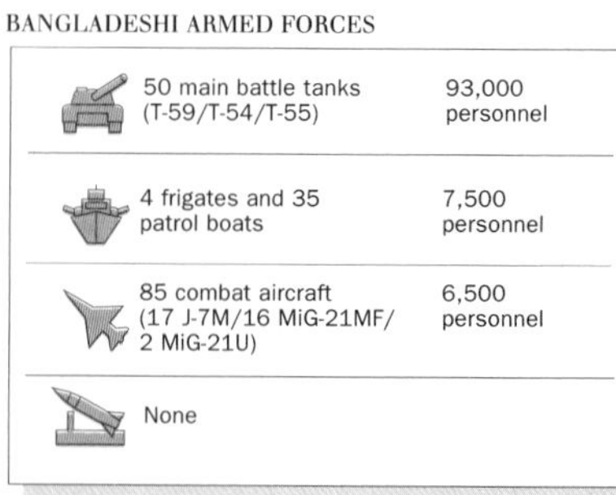

50 main battle tanks (T-59/T-54/T-55)	93,000 personnel
4 frigates and 35 patrol boats	7,500 personnel
85 combat aircraft (17 J-7M/16 MiG-21MF/ 2 MiG-21U)	6,500 personnel
None	

ECONOMICS

$23.4bn   39.00 taka

SCORE CARD

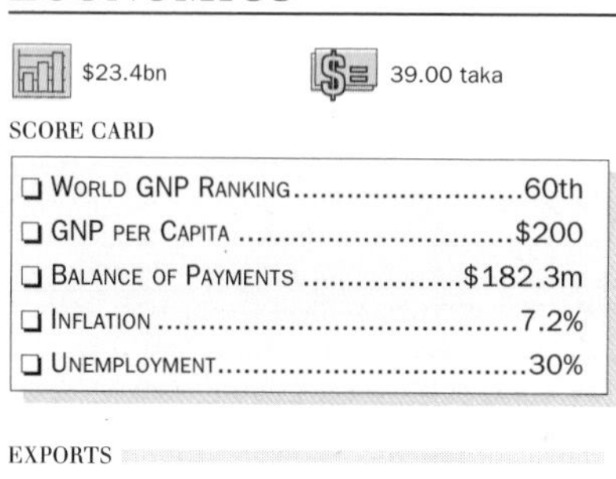

World GNP Ranking	60th
GNP per Capita	$200
Balance of Payments	$182.3m
Inflation	7.2%
Unemployment	30%

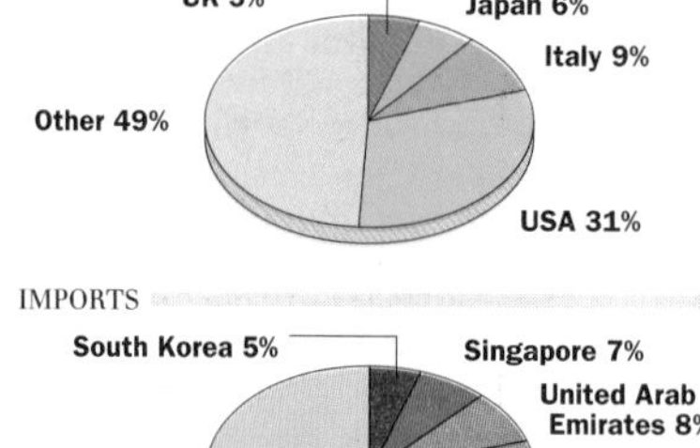

Strengths

Jute is the major industry: Bangladesh accounts for 80% of world jute fiber exports. Low wages ensure a competitive and expanding textile industry, which constitutes one-third of the small manufacturing sector.

Weaknesses

The agricultural sector, which employs 68% of Bangladeshis, is vulnerable to the violent and unpredictable climate.

Profile

Government ministers like to portray Bangladesh as an emerging NIC, but its economy is still overwhelmingly dependent on agriculture and large aid inflows. Agriculture, which provides the major export, jute, is productive: Bangladesh's soils, fed by the Ganges, Jamuna and Meghna rivers, are highly fertile. However, the effects of the weather can be devastating, frequently destroying a whole year's crop. Agricultural wages are among the lowest in the world.

ECONOMIC PERFORMANCE INDICATOR

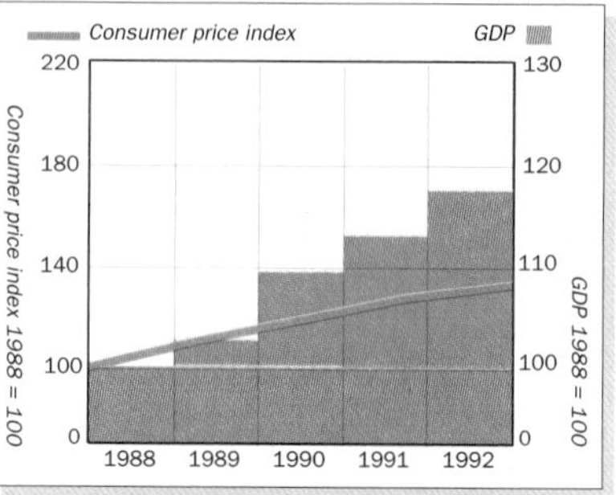

The state sector, which owns large, inefficient and massively loss-making companies (such as the Bangladesh Jute Mills Corporation), is in trouble. The World Bank, which channels most aid into the country, wishes to see loss-making concerns cut their work forces or close down.

Textiles and garments are perhaps the healthiest sectors. Economic zones (Export Processing Zones) with special concessions have attracted foreign investment, and have helped to promote a small indigenous electronics industry. Bangladesh receives generous textile import quotas from the EU and NAFTA, but its economy is so weak that it fails to reach them.

BANGLADESH : MAJOR BUSINESSES

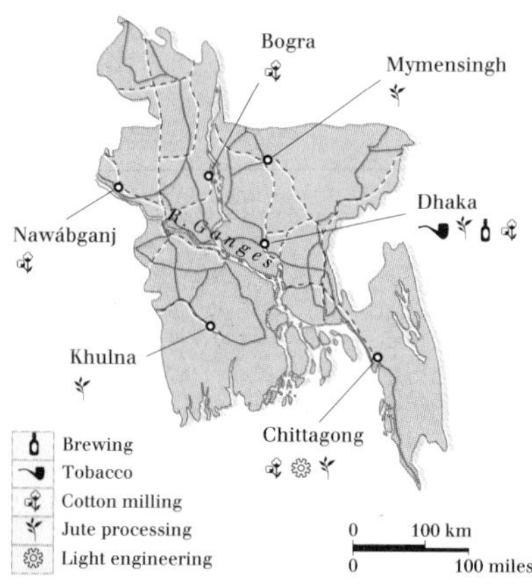

B

RESOURCES

8bn kwh (capacity 2.52m kw)

Not an oil producer; refines 31,200 b/cd

23.2m cattle, 1.2m sheep, 45,000 horses

Salt, oil, natural gas, limestone

Bangladesh is the world's major jute producer, accounting for 80% of world jute fiber exports and about 50%of world jute-manufactured exports. Natural gas from the Bay of Bengal, exploited by the state-owned Bangladesh Oil, Gas and Minerals Corporation, came into use in 1988; production had increased to 6.5 billion cubic yards by 1991. Reserves are estimated at 200 years.

ELECTRICITY GENERATION

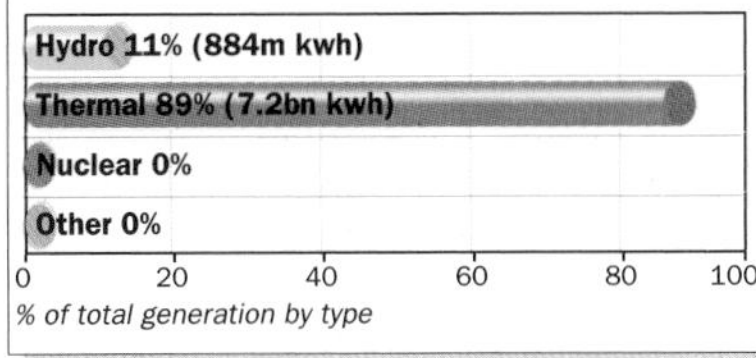

BANGLADESH : LAND USE

R. Jamuna
R. Ganges
Mouths of the Ganges
Cropland
Wetlands
Forest
Rice
Jute - cash crop
0 100 km
0 100 miles

ENVIRONMENT

0.7% partially protected

Protection measures being incorporated into donor programs

Bangladesh's climate, which results in huge death tolls and frequently destroys a whole season's crops, dwarfs all other environmental problems. Bangladesh is too poor to finance environmental initiatives.

ENVIRONMENTAL TREATIES

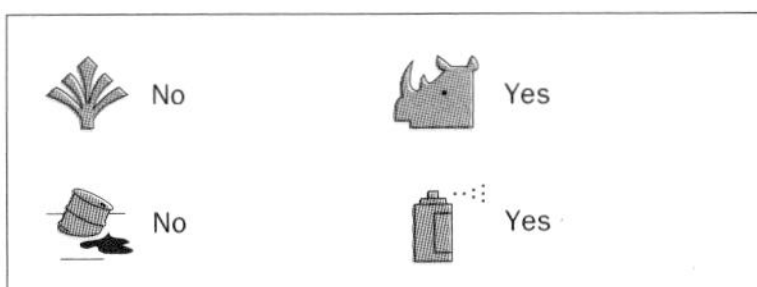

MEDIA

After many years of censorship, political intervention in the media was greatly reduced in 1990

PUBLISHING AND BROADCAST MEDIA

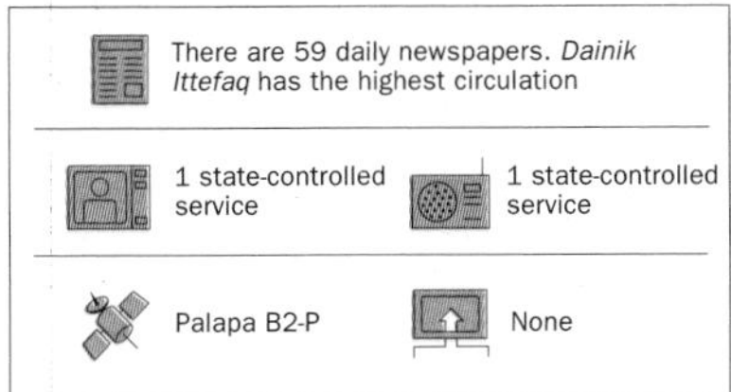

There are 59 daily newspapers. *Dainik Ittefaq* has the highest circulation
1 state-controlled service
1 state-controlled service
None

Since the fall of President Ershad at the end of 1990, the press has enjoyed almost total political independence. Of the daily newspapers, the 11 English-language titles tend to appeal primarily to the urban elite. Among political weeklies, the most respected is called *Holiday* (the owners bought it as a travel magazine and decided not to change the name). Over 70% of TV programs are produced locally; about one-third are in black and white.

CRIME

31,192 prisoners

Up 6% in 1990

CRIME RATES

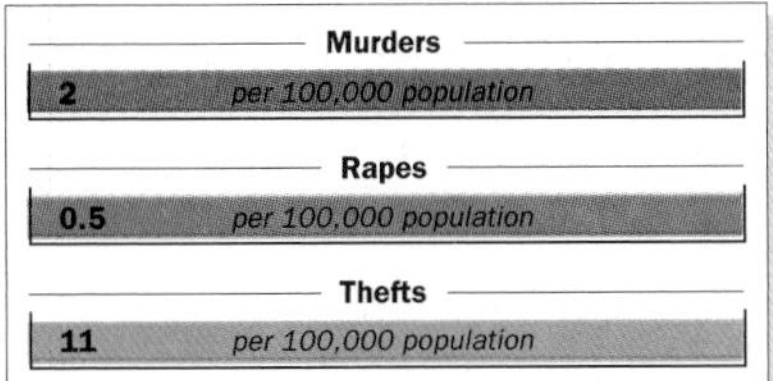

Rising levels of political and religious violence led the new government of 1991 to introduce a controversial anti-terrorism law, which offered swift (and many thought careless) justice with heavy penalties, including death. The Special Powers Act, which was used by Ershad to detain political opponents, is still in force. Deaths in Bangladeshi prisons are common and the army's human rights record, especially that of the paramilitary Bangladesh Rifles in the Chittagong Hills, has also been questioned by Amnesty International.

EDUCATION

35%

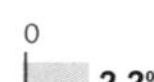

THE EDUCATION SYSTEM

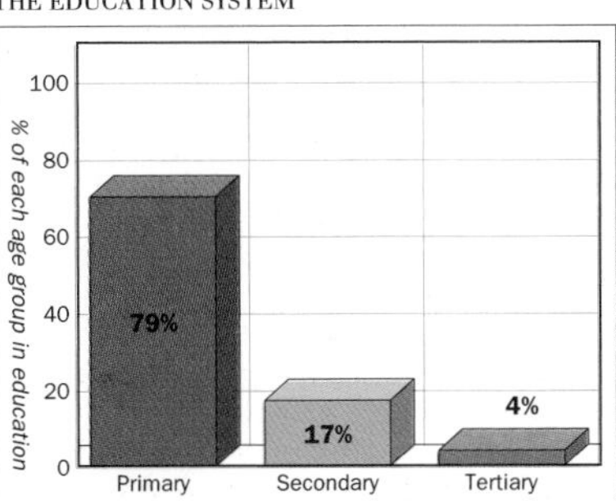

Education in almost all sectors of Bangladeshi society is poorly addressed, with the resultant low literacy figure. The seven universities, with an enrollment of just 50,000, are often forced to close due to political violence on campus.

HEALTH

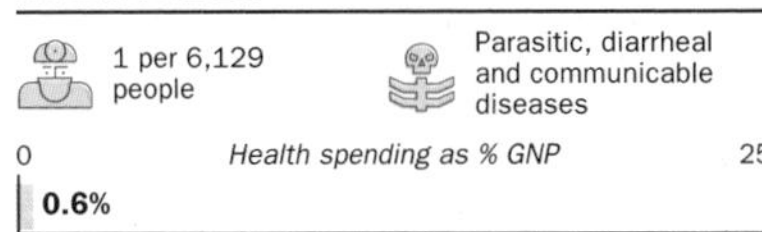

Although primary health care in rural areas has improved over the last decade, Bangladesh's health problems remain severe and are exacerbated by a shortage of medical staff and facilities. The priority given to birth control programs has helped to reduce the population growth rate by 23% over the last 15 years, from 2.6% to 2% a year.

WEALTH

Machine cloth weaver, 950 taka per month; natural gas engineer, 2,850 taka per month

CONSUMER GOODS OWNERSHIP

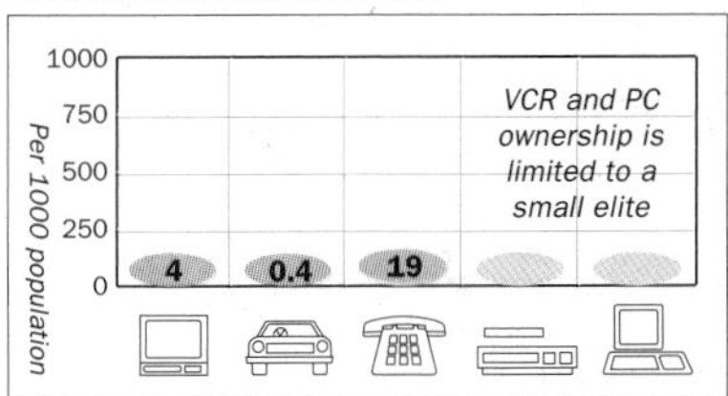

Average incomes are very low, but wealth disparities are not quite as marked as in India or Pakistan. State officials tend to be among the wealthiest.

WORLD RANKING

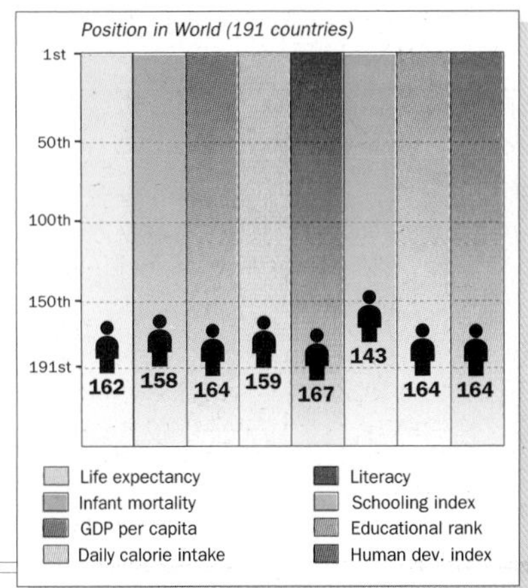

B

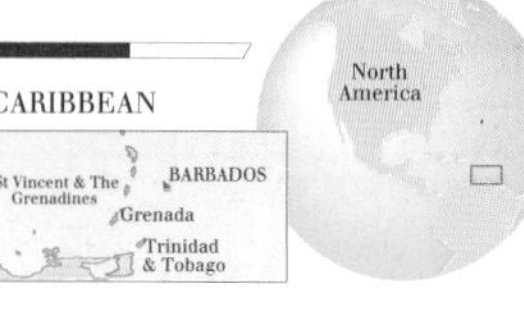

BARBADOS

OFFICIAL NAME: Barbados **CAPITAL:** Bridgetown
CURRENCY: Barbados dollar **POPULATION:** 300,000 **OFFICIAL LANGUAGE:** English

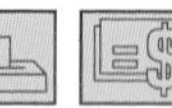

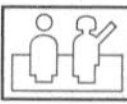

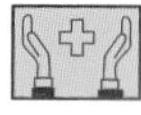

SITUATED TO THE NORTHEAST of Trinidad, Barbados is the most easterly of the West Indian Windward Islands. In the 16th century, the Portuguese became the first Europeans to reach the island, inhabited by Arawak Native Americans. However, Barbados was not colonized until the 1620s, when British settlers arrived. Popularly referred to by its neighbors as "little England," Barbados still retains a strong British influence.

CLIMATE

WEATHER CHART

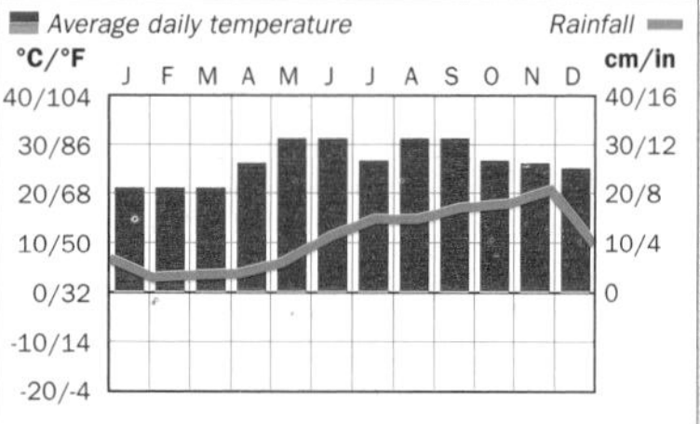

Barbados has a moderate tropical climate and is sunnier and drier than its more mountainous Caribbean neighbors. Hurricanes may occur in the rainy season.

TOURISM

394,222 visitors

Down 6% in 1991

MAIN OVERSEAS ARRIVALS

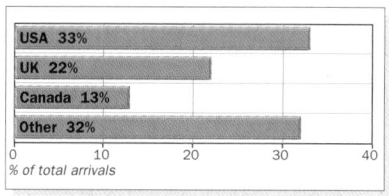

	% of total arrivals
USA	33%
UK	22%
Canada	13%
Other	32%

The airport runway has been improved in an effort to encourage tourists. Visitors come mainly from North America and Europe. Cruise-ship traffic is on the increase.

COMMUNICATIONS

Grantley Adams International, Bridgetown
1.21m passengers

3 ships
79,900 dwt

THE TRANSPORTATION NETWORK

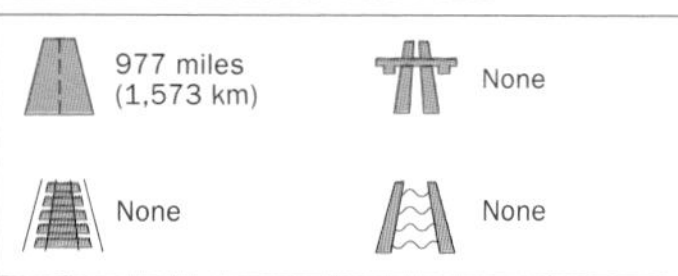

Recent major construction projects have included the resurfacing of the runway at the international airport and the expansion of piers at Bridgetown's port. Upgrading the island's dense road network is a priority. Bus routes cover most of the island.

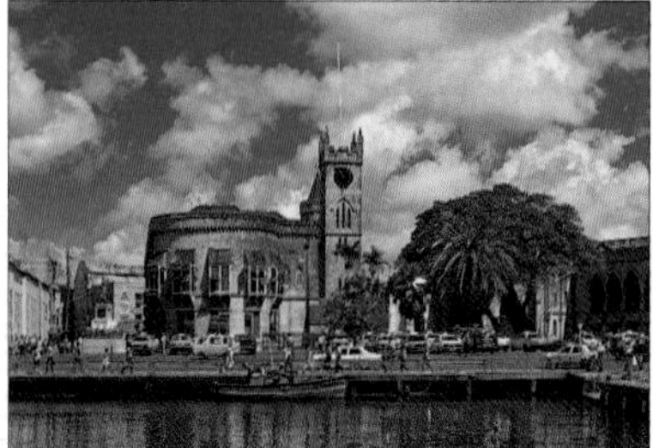

House of Assembly, Trafalgar Square, Bridgetown. *Barbados's parliament, the third oldest in the Commonwealth, dates from 1639.*

PEOPLE

Bajan (Barbadian English), English

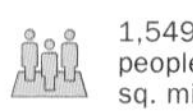
1,549 people per sq. mile

THE URBAN/RURAL POPULATION SPLIT

45% 55%

RELIGIOUS PERSUASION

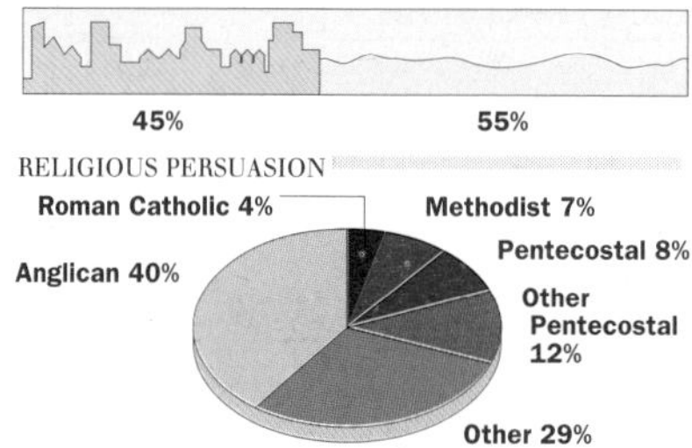

Most Bajans are the descendants of African slaves brought to the island between the 16th and 19th centuries; there are also small groups of South Asians and of Europeans, mainly expatriate Britons, many of whom retire here. There is some latent tension between the white community, which controls most of the economy, and the majority black population, although this rarely spills over into violence. Increasing social mobility has allowed many black Bajans to move into the professional sector and the civil service. Bajans enjoy a higher standard of living than most other Caribbeans.

POLITICS

1999

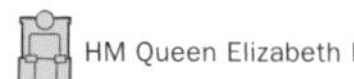
HM Queen Elizabeth II

THE STATE OF THE PARTIES

House of Assembly 28 members

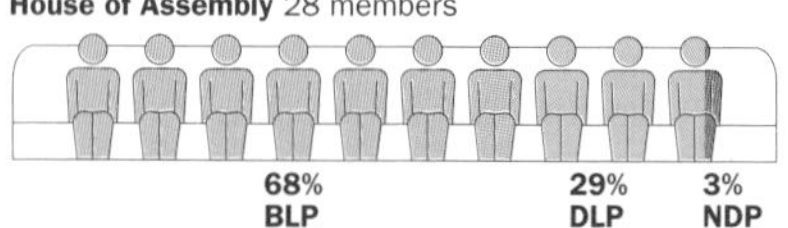

68% BLP **29% DLP** **3% NDP**

BLP = Barbados Labour Party **DLP** = Democratic Labour Party **NDP** = National Democratic Party

Senate 21 members

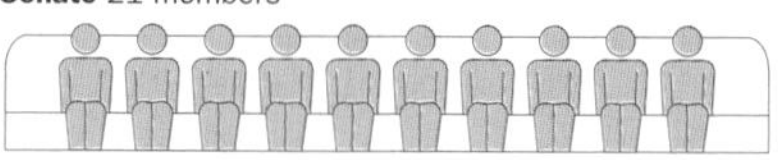

12 members chosen by the prime minister, 2 by the leader of the opposition and 7 by the governor-general

Barbados is a multiparty democracy. The main power brokers are a primarily European, affluent elite, who finance the parties and exert an indirect influence on government policy. The BLP swept to power in the 1994 elections. The main political issue is the handling of the economy. Owen Arthur, BLP leader and prime minister, indicated that his priorities are ensuring economic growth and international competitiveness.

WORLD AFFAIRS

Barbados is a strong supporter of US policy in the region, and was a staging post for the 1983 invasion of Grenada.

AID

$4m (receipts)

Up 33% in 1991

Barbados receives the bulk of its aid from the USA, EU and UK, mainly in the form of development project loans and balance of payments support.

DEFENSE

$10.6m

Up 14% in 1990

The 1,000-strong Barbadian army and the constabulary benefit from financial support and training from the US and the UK governments, which also supply equipment. The country is the headquarters of the Regional Security System, established in 1982 by the Windward and Leeward Islands, a body which acts as a multinational security force for its members.

ECONOMICS

$1.7bn

2.01 Barbados dollars

SCORE CARD

- ❑ WORLD GNP RANKING 142nd
- ❑ GNP PER CAPITA $5,700
- ❑ BALANCE OF PAYMENTS .... $–29.9m
- ❑ INFLATION 5.5%
- ❑ UNEMPLOYMENT 17.1%

STRENGTHS

Well-developed tourism based on climate and accessibility. Sugar industries. Information processing and financial services are important new growth sectors.

WEAKNESSES

Narrow economic base, vulnerable to downturns in tourism, failures of sugar harvest and the threatened liberalization of the sugar market. Relatively high manufacturing costs.

EXPORTS

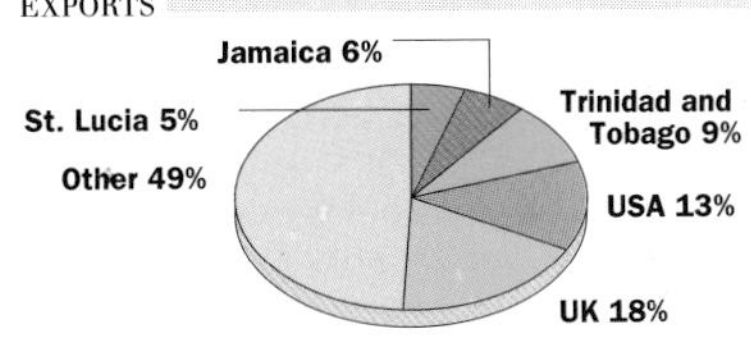

IMPORTS

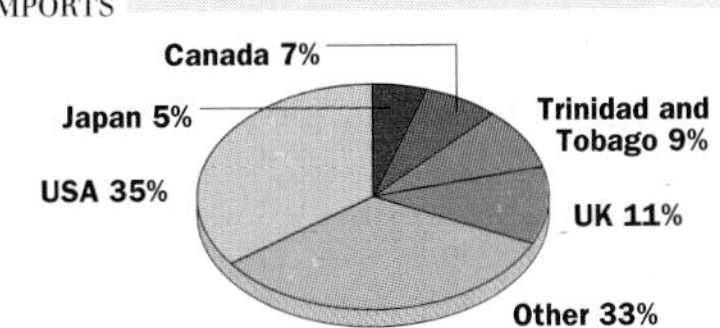

BARBADOS

Total Area : 430 sq. km (166 sq. miles)

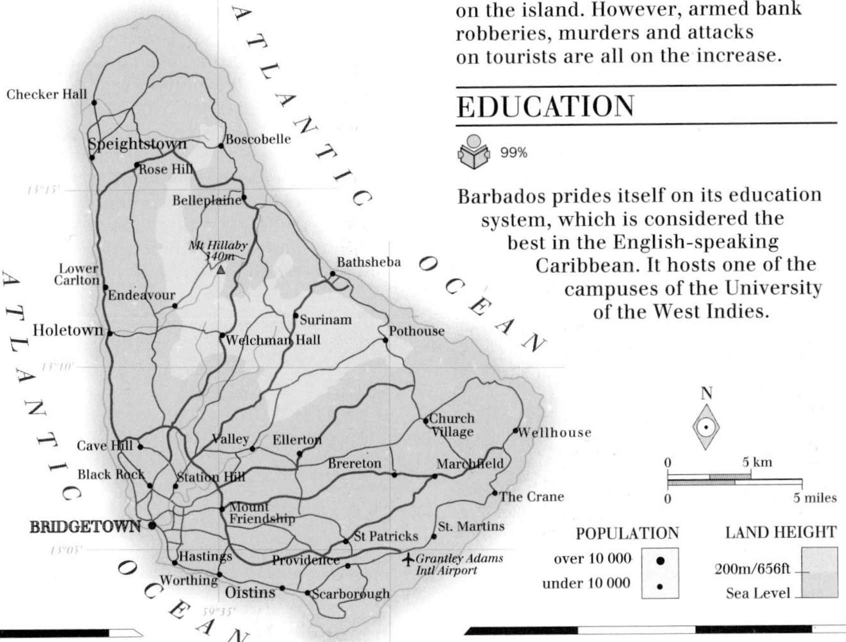

RESOURCES

468m kwh (capacity 140,000 kw)

1246 b/d (reserves 5,892,000 bbl)

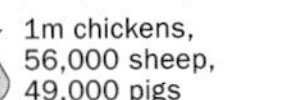

1m chickens, 56,000 sheep, 49,000 pigs

Oil, natural gas

Barbados has few strategic resources. The domestic petroleum industry provides about one-third of the country's energy requirements.

ENVIRONMENT

1%

The only mangrove swamp on Barbados is still unprotected

Oil slicks created by waste dumped from passing ships are polluting the encircling reef and adversely affecting the life cycle of the flying fish, Barbados's main fish stock.

MEDIA

Freedom of expression guaranteed by the constitution. Defamation law restrictive to investigative journalism

PUBLISHING AND BROADCAST MEDIA

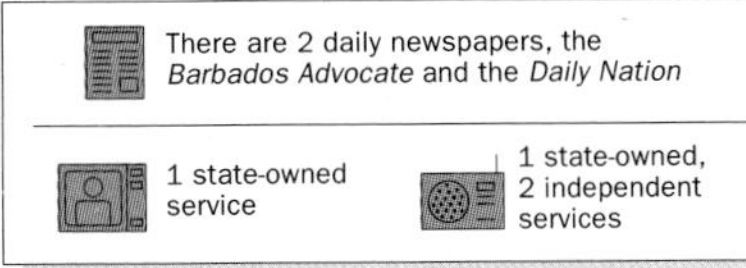

There are 2 daily newspapers, the *Barbados Advocate* and the *Daily Nation*

1 state-owned service

1 state-owned, 2 independent services

There is no political interference in the media in Barbados. The two daily newspapers are privately owned, as are two of the radio stations.

CRIME

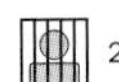

260 prisoners

Up 6% in 1990

Compared with other Caribbean islands, Barbados still has a low crime rate. There are no "no-go" areas on the island. However, armed bank robberies, murders and attacks on tourists are all on the increase.

EDUCATION

99%

Barbados prides itself on its education system, which is considered the best in the English-speaking Caribbean. It hosts one of the campuses of the University of the West Indies.

CHRONOLOGY

Colonized by the British in 1627, Barbados grew rich in the 18th century from sugar produced using slave labor.

- ❑ **1951** Universal adult suffrage introduced.
- ❑ **1961** Full internal self-government. The DLP, led by Errol Barrow, comes to power.
- ❑ **1966** Full independence from Britain.
- ❑ **1983** Supports and provides a base for the US invasion of Grenada.

HEALTH

1 per 1,167 people

Heart and digestive diseases, cancer

The health system is based on subsidized government-run clinics and hospitals, supplemented by more expensive private clinics and private doctors. Facilities are within easy reach of all Bajans.

WEALTH

Plantation field worker, 4 Barbados dollars per hour; oil refinery foreman, 564 Barbados dollars per week (minimum)

CONSUMER GOODS OWNERSHIP

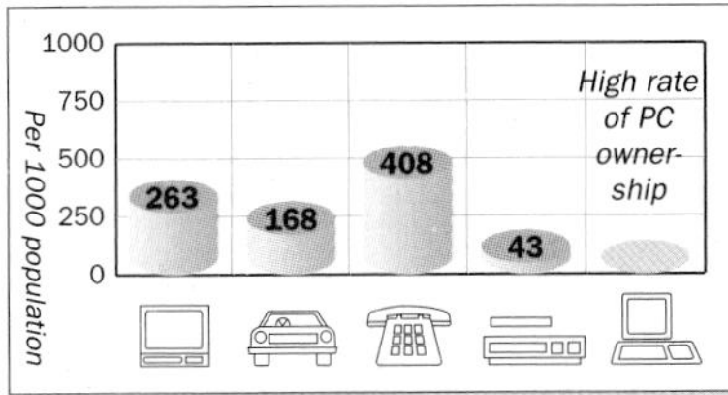

There is a significant disparity between most Bajans and a small affluent group, mostly of European origin, which owns and controls business and industry. Among the latter, status symbols include yachts and exclusive club membership.

WORLD RANKING

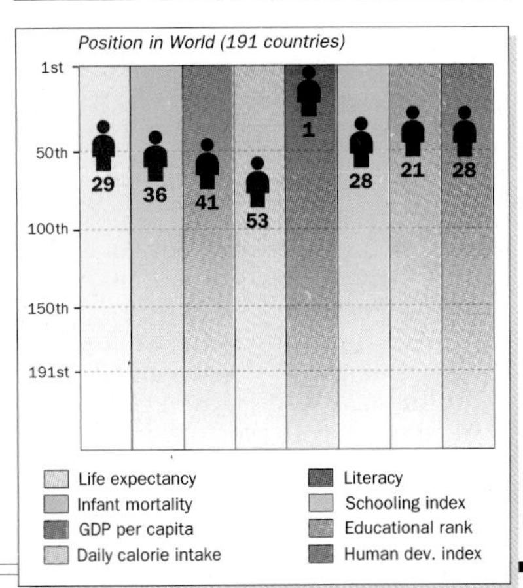

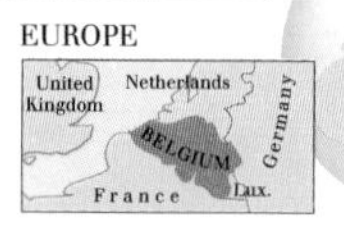

BELGIUM

OFFICIAL NAME: Kingdom of Belgium **CAPITAL:** Brussels
POPULATION: 10 million **CURRENCY:** Belgian franc **OFFICIAL LANGUAGES:** Dutch, French and German

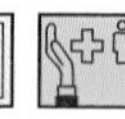

LOCATED BETWEEN GERMANY, France and the Netherlands, Belgium has a short coastline on the North Sea. The south includes the forested Ardennes region; the north is dissected by canals. Belgium has been fought over many times in its history. It was occupied by Germany in both World Wars. Long–standing tensions have existed between the majority Flemish and minority French-speakers since the 1830s. These are now being defused by Belgium's move to a federal political structure and the national consensus on the benefits of EU membership.

CLIMATE

WEATHER CHART

Belgium has a typical maritime climate and is influenced by the Gulf Stream. Temperatures are mild with heavy cloud cover and much rain. The west coast climate can be disrupted by widely fluctuating weather conditions, caused by cyclonic disturbances. Summers tend to be short.

COMMUNICATIONS

THE TRANSPORTATION NETWORK

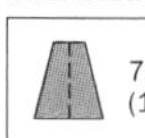

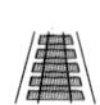

Belgium can be crossed within four hours by car or train, and access to Germany, the Netherlands and beyond is easy. Belgium's highway network is extensive and so well lit that, along with the Great Wall of China, it is the most distinctive sight from orbit. Although the railroad system has been reduced since 1970, it is still one of the world's densest networks. The opening of the Channel Tunnel will improve Brussels' link with London and Paris. Once the TGV line is opened in 1997, it will be possible to reach London in 2 hours and 10 minutes and Paris in 3 hours. Antwerp, an old Hanseatic city, is Europe's second-largest port.

TOURISM

MAIN OVERSEAS ARRIVALS

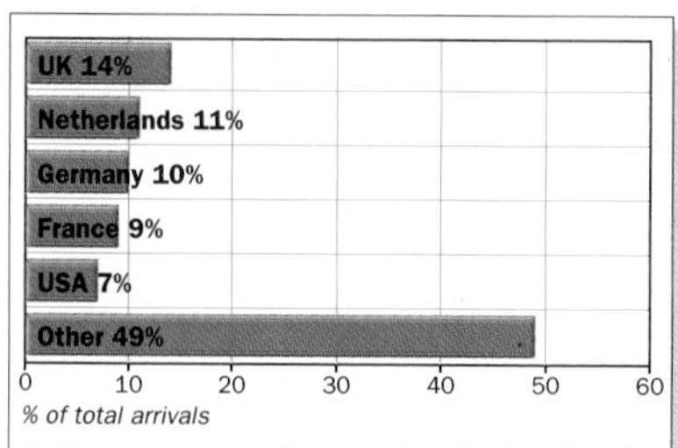

Belgium's main attractions are its historic cities and its museums of Flemish art. Bruges, the capital of west Flanders, is often called the "Venice of the North." With unspoiled Renaissance architecture and a complex canal system, it has become a favorite destination for British weekend visitors and Japanese honeymooners. In Brussels the famous "Grand Place," a cluster of Gothic, Renaissance and Baroque buildings in a cobbled square, survived bombing during World War II. Much of the rest of the old city center, however, was destroyed. Belgium has 15 resorts on its 38-mile coastline, with a single tramline running its entire length. Forests in the Ardennes to the south attract hikers.

Ardennes, southeast Belgium, *is famous for its lakes, forests and cuisine. Rivers, like the Meuse and Semois, dissect the countryside.*

PEOPLE

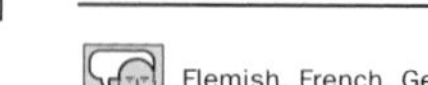

THE URBAN/RURAL POPULATION SPLIT

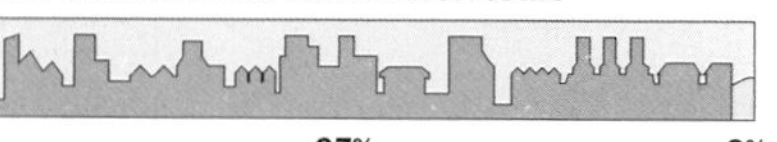

RELIGIOUS PERSUASION

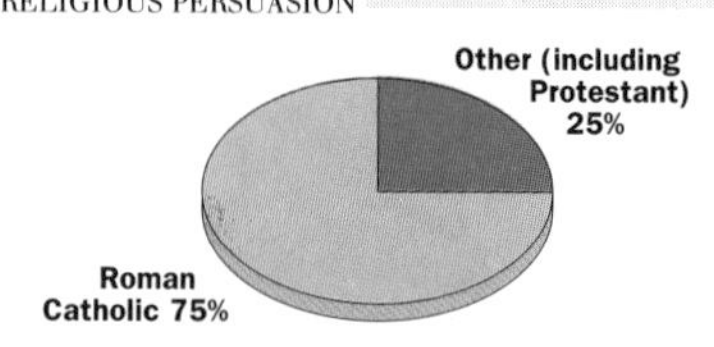

ETHNIC MAKEUP

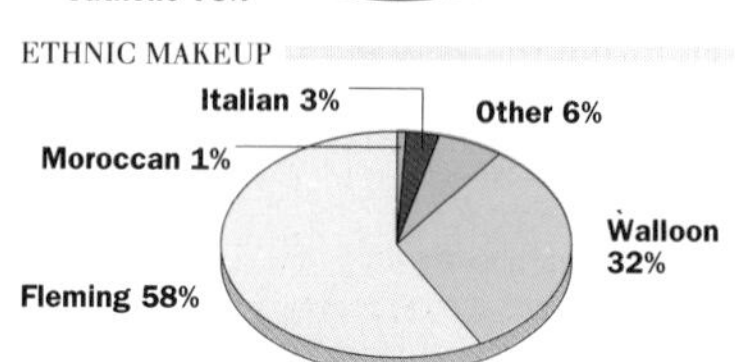

Belgian history has been marked by the divisions between its Flemish and French-speaking communities. Flemish speakers, who are a majority, are concentrated in Flanders. Wallonia is French-speaking and Brussels is 85% francophone. French-speakers were in the ascendancy for many years, as they controlled the profitable coal and steel industries in Wallonia. Their greater economic wealth was reinforced by a constitution that gave them political control. Tensions between French-speakers and Flemings occasionally erupted into violence. However, in the past two decades, the position of the two communities has been reversed. Wallonia's industries have declined and Flanders is now the wealthier region. In order to contain tensions, in 1980 Belgium began to change from being the most centralist to the most federal state in Europe; both communities now have their own governments and control most of their own affairs.

Belgium has a sizable immigrant population. Women gained the vote in 1948. They earn, on average, 25% less than their male counterparts.

POPULATION AGE BREAKDOWN

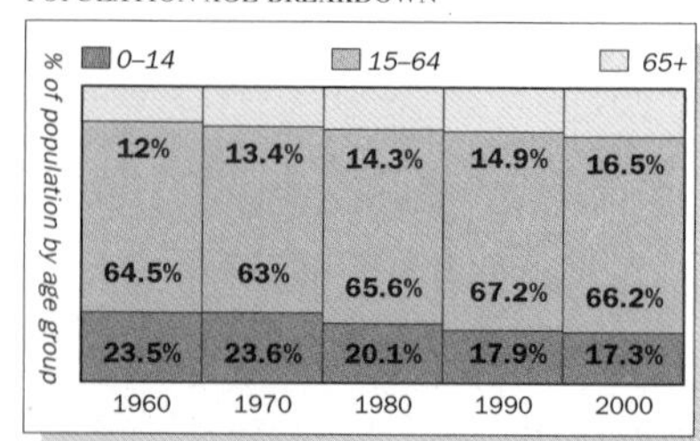

B

BELGIUM

Total Area : 33 100 sq. km (12 780 sq. miles)

POPULATION

- over 1 000 000
- over 100 000
- over 50 000
- over 10 000

LAND HEIGHT

- 500m/1640ft
- 200m/656ft
- Sea Level

0 — 40 km

0 — 40 miles

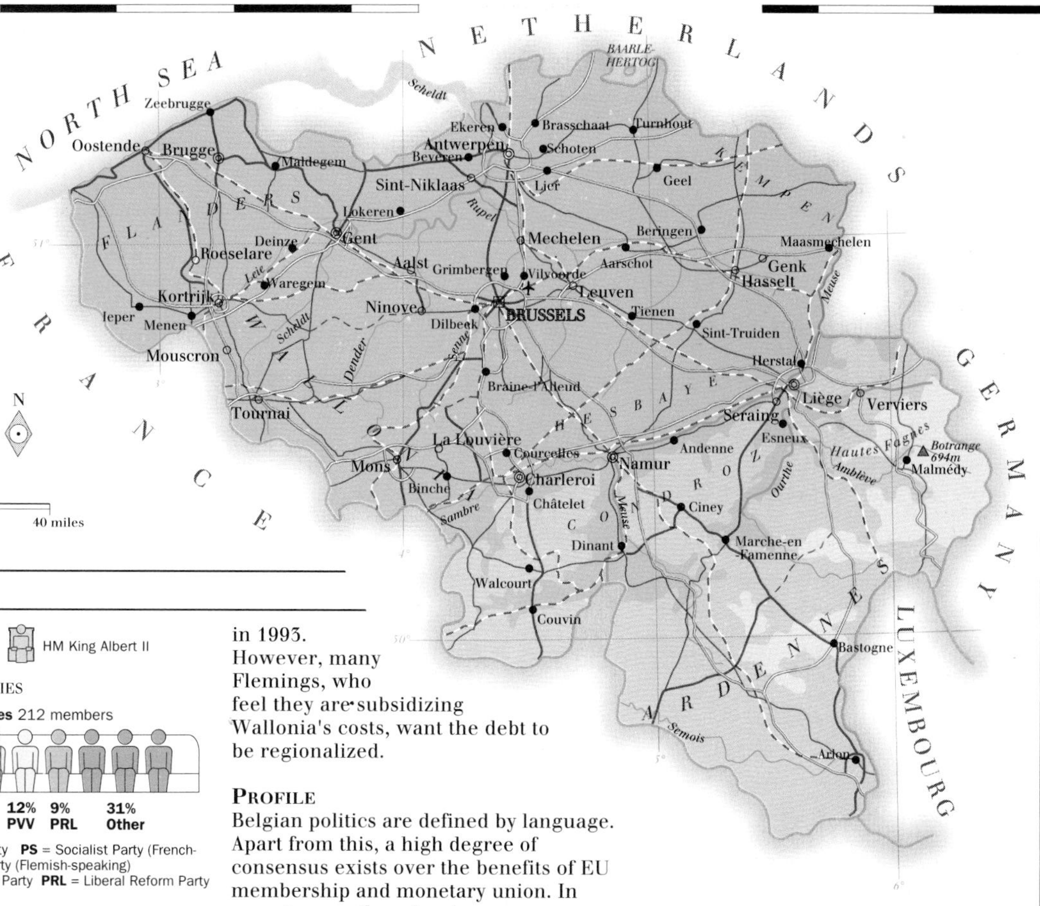

POLITICS

1995 — HM King Albert II

THE STATE OF THE PARTIES

Chamber of Representatives 212 members

18%	17%	13%	12%	9%	31%
CVP	PS	SP	PVV	PRL	Other

CVP = Christian People's Party **PS** = Socialist Party (French-speaking) **SP** = Socialist Party (Flemish-speaking) **PVV** = Freedom and Progress Party **PRL** = Liberal Reform Party

Senate 182 members

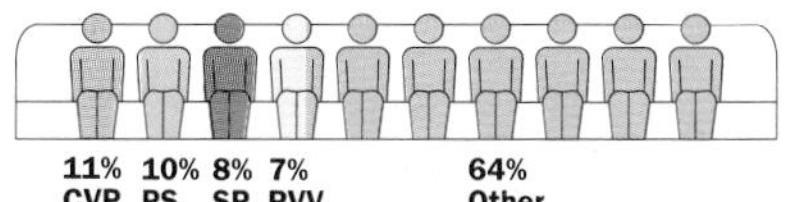

11%	10%	8%	7%	64%
CVP	PS	SP	PVV	Other

106 members are directly elected, 50 elected by provincial councils and 25 co-opted by the elected members and the heir to the throne

Until 1970, Belgium was a unitary state. Tensions between language groups led to four waves of federalist reforms from 1980, which culminated in the St. Michel Accords of 1993, confirming the state as a federal monarchy.

MAIN POLITICAL ISSUES

Language

Tensions between the two language groups are receding. However, the divisions remain strong. Each community has its own Socialist Party (the PS in Wallonia, the SP in Flanders) and the Christian Democrats are split into the francophone PSC and Flemish CVP. Under the premiership of Jean-Luc Dehaene the four parties have worked in an uneasy coalition.

Debt

Belgium's debt is now greater than its national income. The question of how to deal with it dominates and defines most political debate. Dehaene pushed through unpopular tax-raising budgets in 1993. However, many Flemings, who feel they are subsidizing Wallonia's costs, want the debt to be regionalized.

PROFILE

Belgian politics are defined by language. Apart from this, a high degree of consensus exists over the benefits of EU membership and monetary union. In recent years, there has been an increase in support for the racist *Vlaams Blok*, which objects to Belgium's Turkish and Moroccan minorities. *Vlaams Blok* captured 25% of Antwerp's vote in 1991.

The current government is a left-of-center coalition, composed of the Socialist and Christian Democrat parties from the Flemish and French-speaking communities. Although the coalition has a majority in parliament, it had difficulty in securing the necessary two-thirds majority for the constitutional reform enacted in the St. Michel Accords. These gave the three regional governments, Flanders, Wallonia and Brussels, significant powers under a federal government. Most of the population sees this as the best system to cope with the country's diversities.

King Baudouin *died in 1993. He was succeeded by King Albert II.*

Jean-Luc Dehaene, *premier and leader of the Christian People's Party (CVP).*

WORLD AFFAIRS

Belgium's key concern is its leading role in the EU. An enthusiastic supporter of economic and monetary union, during its EU presidency in 1993 it tried to accelerate the Maastricht process by setting the ground rules for a future European Central Bank. The EU is also seen as an anchor for its own federalist structure; many fear that without it Belgium could split into two.

Belgium often contributes troops to UN operations. Belgian soldiers have served in Bosnia and Somalia. The Belgian community in Rwanda had to be evacuated in 1994 after ten Belgian UN troops were murdered during ethnic violence.

AID

$831m (donations)

Down 7% in 1991

In 1993, overseas aid accounted for about 0.7% of budgetary spending. Between 1987 and 1993, most of the aid program was spent on education and agricultural projects in Africa. The former colonies of Burundi and Rwanda were the major beneficiaries.

B

CHRONOLOGY

Formerly ruled by the French dukes of Burgundy, Belgium became a Habsburg possession in 1477. It passed to the Austrian Habsburgs in 1700. Napoleon ended Austrian rule of the Low Countries in 1797.

- ❑ **1814–1815** Congress of Vienna; European powers decide to merge Belgium with the Netherlands under King William I of Orange.
- ❑ **1830** Revolt against Dutch. Provisional government declares independence.
- ❑ **1831** European powers place Leopold Saxe Coburg as King.
- ❑ **1865** Leopold II crowned King.
- ❑ **1885** After agreement by European powers, King Leopold given Congo basin as colony.
- ❑ **1908** King Leopold allows brutality in Congo basin. Parliament takes over control of its administration.
- ❑ **1914** German armies invade. Leopold II declares war on Germany. Germans occupy Belgium until 1918.
- ❑ **1921** Belgo–Luxembourg Economic Union formed. Luxembourg locks its currency to the Belgian franc.
- ❑ **1932** Flemish language accorded equal official status with French.
- ❑ **1936** Belgium declares neutrality.
- ❑ **1940** King Leopold III capitulates to Hitler. Belgium occupied until 1944.
- ❑ **1948** Forms customs union with Luxembourg and the Netherlands (BENELUX).
- ❑ **1950** King wins referendum but rumors over his collaboration in World War II persist. Abdicates in favor of his son, Baudouin.
- ❑ **1957** Signs Treaty of Rome with France, Germany, Italy, the Netherlands and Luxembourg.
- ❑ **1958** Treaty of Rome members form the EEC.
- ❑ **1992** Culmination of reforms transforming Belgium into federal state. Greater powers for regions and city governments.
- ❑ **1992** Christian-Democrat–Socialist government led by Jean-Luc Dehaene takes over federal government.
- ❑ **1993** Death of King Baudouin. Succeeded by Albert II. Belgian EU presidency advances moves toward monetary union agreed upon at Maastricht in 1992.
- ❑ **1994** French-speaking Socialist Party, dominant in Wallonia, racked by political scandal after allegations of corruption and murder. Wallonia's premier, Guy Spittaels, and federal deputy premier, Guy Coeme, resign.

DEFENSE

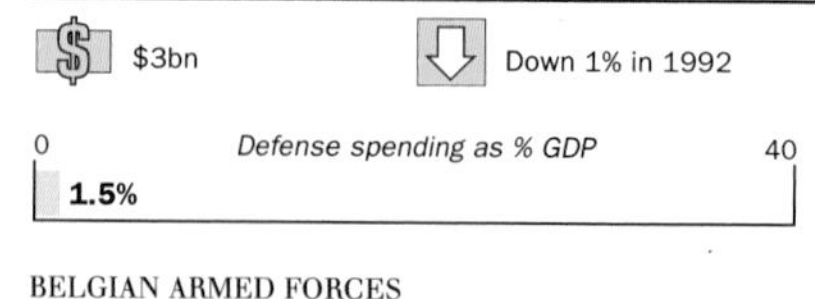

BELGIAN ARMED FORCES

359 main battle tanks (334 *Leopard* 1/25 M–41)	54,000 personnel
4 frigates	4,400 personnel
122 combat aircraft (F-16A,-16B)	17,300 personnel
None	

Belgium spends less on defense than the NATO average and over the next decade the defense budget will fall further. In 1994, as part of Belgium's program to reduce government debt, all three military services were targeted for cuts. The government abolished conscription and cut troop levels from 75,000 to 40,000. The defense budget of around $4.5 billion was frozen for five years.

Spending on paratroopers and planes used for transportation has increased, however. The aim is to allow Belgian forces to fulfill their role in NATO's new rapid reaction forces. It will also make Belgian forces more useful to the UN's worldwide operations.

ECONOMICS

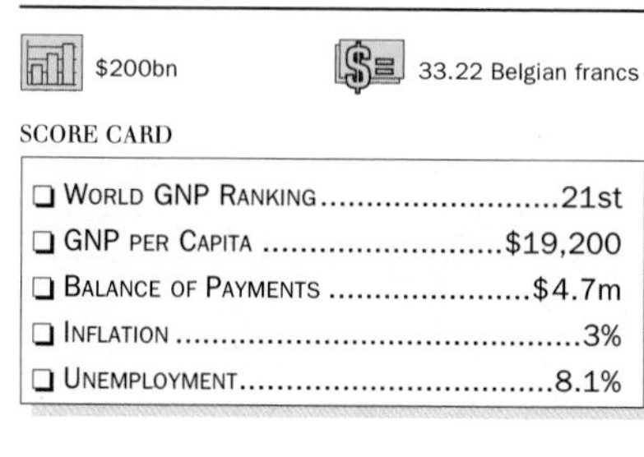

SCORE CARD

- ❑ World GNP Ranking......................21st
- ❑ GNP per Capita......................$19,200
- ❑ Balance of Payments......................$4.7m
- ❑ Inflation......................3%
- ❑ Unemployment......................8.1%

EXPORTS

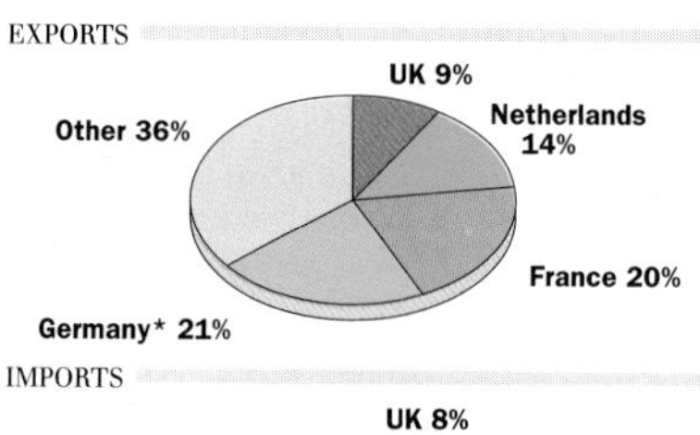

IMPORTS

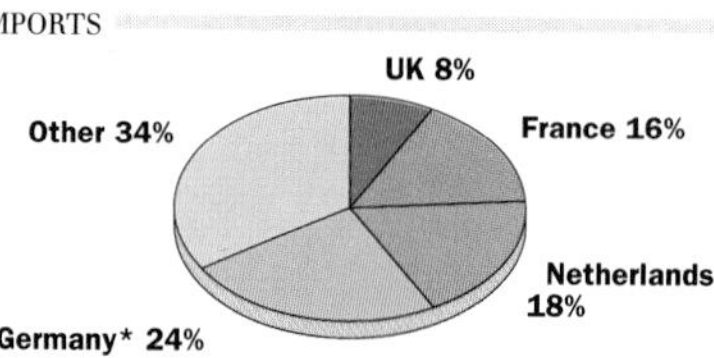

ECONOMIC PERFORMANCE INDICATOR

Consumer price index / GDP

Consumer price index 1988=100: 0, 100, 140, 180, 220

GDP 1988=100: 0, 100, 110, 120, 130

1988 1989 1990 1991 1992

Strengths

One of world's most efficient producers of metal products and textiles. Flanders is a world leader in new high-tech industries. Successful chemicals industry. Highly educated and motivated multilingual work force: estimates suggest productivity is 20% above that of Germany. Location makes Belgium an attractive location for US multinationals. Good sea outlets and access to Rhine inland waterway from Antwerp and Ghent.

Weaknesses

Highest public debt in the EU at 122% of GDP; costs 10% of public income per year to service. Rising unemployment. Large numbers of workers retire early, resulting in high state pension bill. Larger bureaucracy than European average.

Profile

The Belgian economy went into recession with the rest of Europe in the early 1990s. Falling tax revenues coincided with rising unemployment, particularly in Wallonia, and a larger social security bill. In 1993, the Dehaene government introduced a scheme that encouraged work-sharing as a way of combating unemployment. Belgium aims to meet the criteria for European Monetary Union (EMU) by 1996.

BELGIUM : MAJOR BUSINESSES

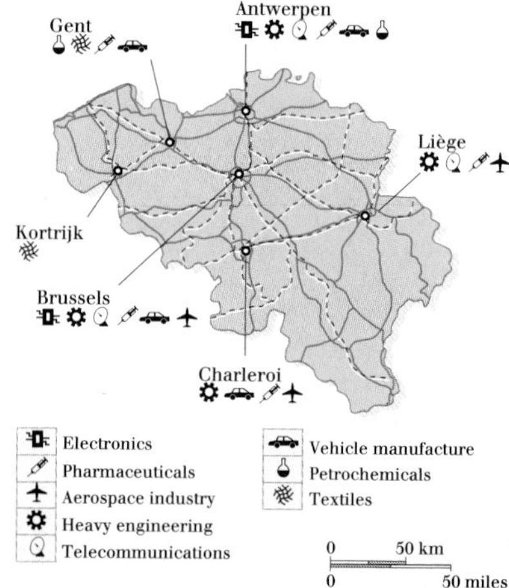

B

RESOURCES

70.2bn kwh (capacity 14.14m kw)

Not an oil producer; refines 607,000 b/cd

30.7m chickens, 6.4m pigs, 3m cattle

Coal, natural gas, shale, marble, sandstone, dolomite

ELECTRICITY GENERATION

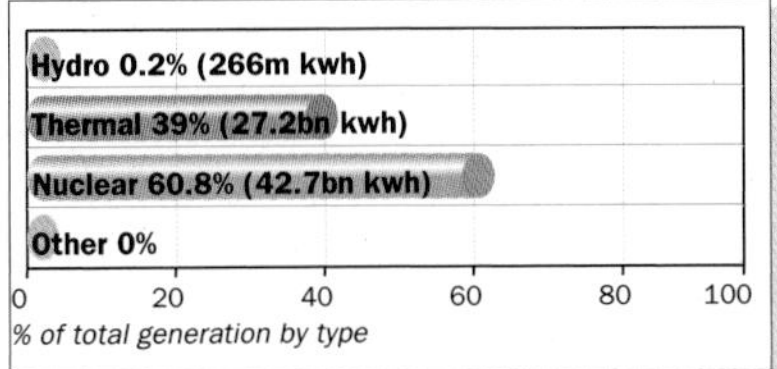

Belgium has few natural resources and depends largely on the export of goods and services. The once-rich coal mines of Wallonia are almost depleted. There is some deciduous and conifer forestry in the Ardennes region.

BELGIUM : LAND USE

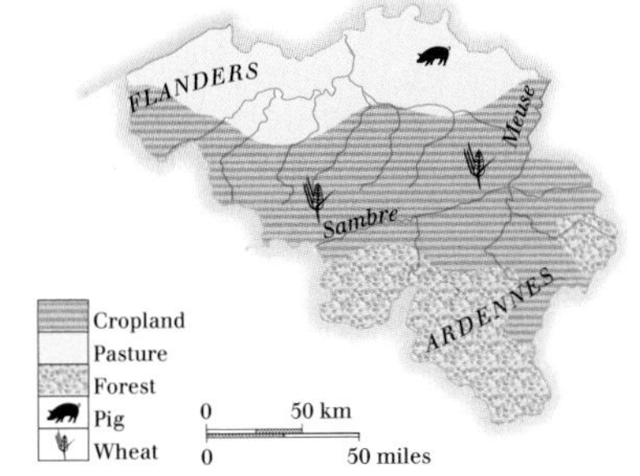

ENVIRONMENT

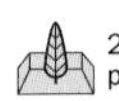

2% partially protected

Government may introduce a green tax to help environment

ENVIRONMENTAL TREATIES

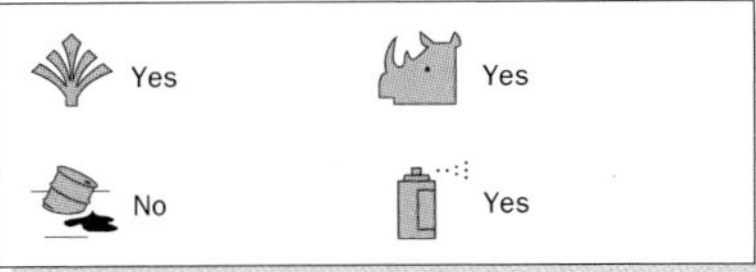

The regional government of Flanders is concerned about the pollution of its groundwater supplies through acid rain, heavy metals, fertilizers and pesticides. It is operating an environmental management plan to meet prescribed standards. Wallonia has initiated strict laws to prevent the illegal dumping of waste, and is also governing air quality and emissions. The population's growing awareness of environmental issues is reflected in the rise of the Green Party.

MEDIA

Censorship is banned under the constitution. All types of media tend to be divided by language

PUBLISHING AND BROADCAST MEDIA

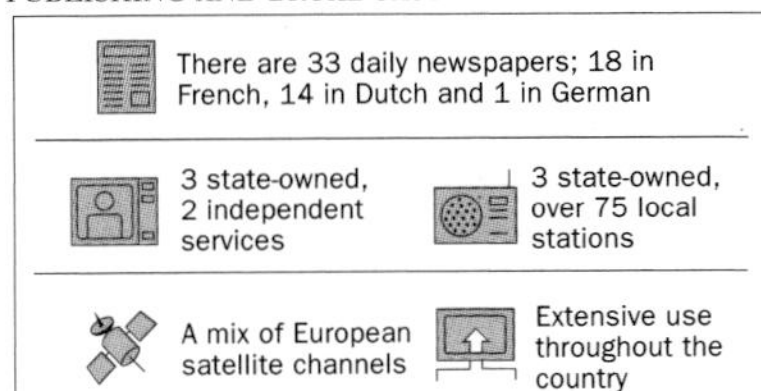

There are 33 daily newspapers; 18 in French, 14 in Dutch and 1 in German
3 state-owned, 2 independent services
3 state-owned, over 75 local stations
A mix of European satellite channels
Extensive use throughout the country

Newspapers tend to be regional and divided by language. Circulation is low, with the most widely read newspaper having a circulation of just 300,000. Over 80% of Belgians have cable TV, receiving as many as 30 channels from all over Europe. Commercial TV only began in 1989, with the Flemish *Station VTM* showing imported English-language programs and game shows.

CRIME

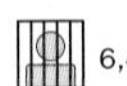

6,450 prisoners

Up 5% in 1990

CRIME RATES

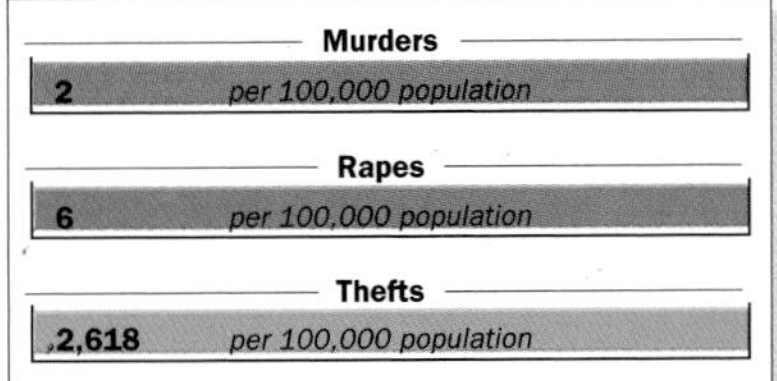

Belgium's crime level is low compared with surrounding countries, though car theft has become more common. The majority of convicted offenses are for minor assaults and theft.

EDUCATION

100%

0 *Education spending as % GNP* 25

4.9%

THE EDUCATION SYSTEM

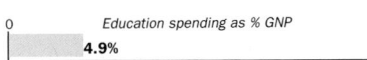

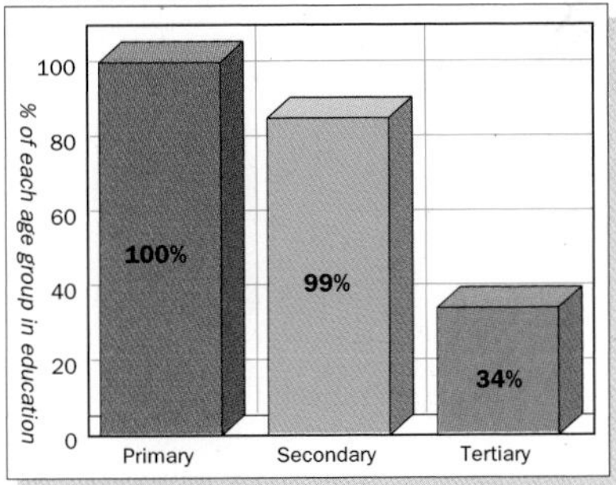

In 1959, parents were given the choice between secular and religious schooling. Since 1989, the system has been administered by the governments of the two main language groups. Education in Flanders is in Dutch; Wallonia teaches in French. All universities are split by language.

HEALTH

1 per 309 people

Heart and respiratory diseases, cancer, accidents

0 *Health spending as % GNP* 25

0.9%

The quality of health care in Belgium is among the best in the world. Belgium is a world leader in fertility treatment and heart and lung transplants. Treatment is not free, but Belgians hold insurance enabling them to claim back up to 75% of their costs. Car accidents are second only to heart disease as a cause of death; in 1990 car accidents resulted in 62,000 cases of personal injury. In 1993, there were 1,600 registered AIDS patients.

WEALTH

Baker, 305 Belgian francs per hour; bank employee, 43,009 Belgian francs per month

CONSUMER GOODS OWNERSHIP

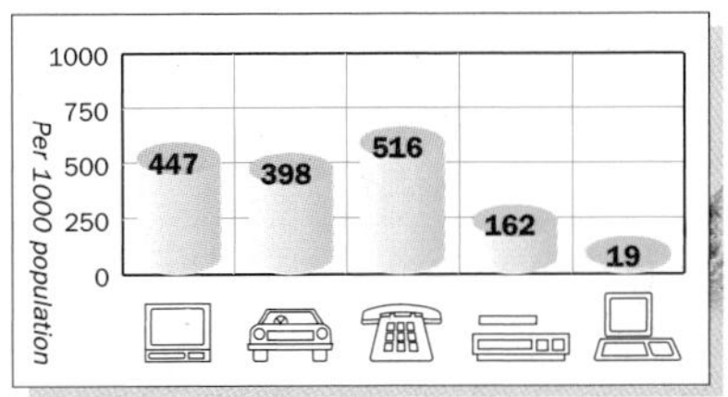

Despite high levels of state debt and the weakening of its traditional industries, Belgium remains one of the richest countries in Europe. GDP per head, at $16,351, is lower than Germany, but higher than the UK or Italy. The figure, however, masks considerable regional differences. Flanders, where most high-tech businesses are located, has an unemployment rate of 6%. In Wallonia it is 11%; 25% of under 25-year-olds in Wallonia are unemployed. The presence of highly paid EU and international bank employees has made Brussels a distinctly wealthy city. In contrast to the state, Belgians are great personal savers. In 1993, they saved, on average, 20% of their income.

WORLD RANKING

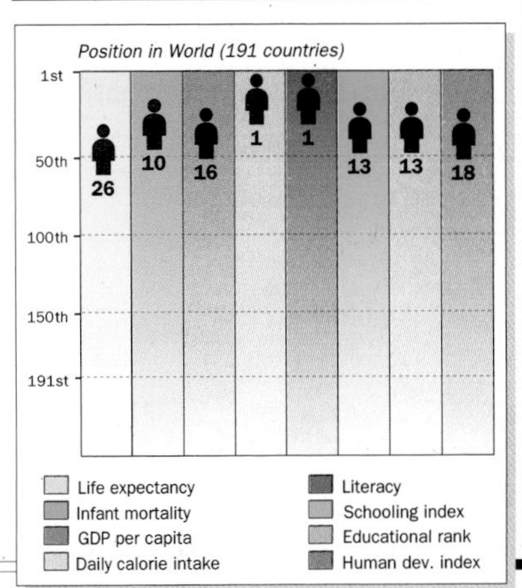

B

BELIZE

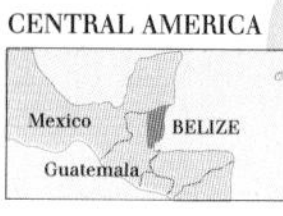

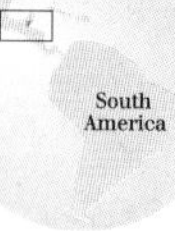

OFFICIAL NAME: Belize **CAPITAL:** Belmopan
POPULATION: 194,000 **CURRENCY:** Belizean dollar **OFFICIAL LANGUAGE:** English

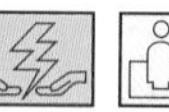

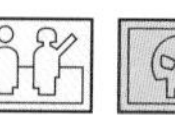

FORMERLY CALLED BRITISH HONDURAS, Belize was the last Central American country to gain its independence, in 1981. It lies on the eastern shore of the Yucatan peninsula and shares a border with Mexico along the River Hondo. Belize is Central America's least populous country, and almost one-half of its land area is still forested. Its swampy coastal plains are protected from flooding by the world's second largest barrier reef.

Small fish market in Belize City. More than 500 tons of Caribbean spiny lobster, the main inshore species, are caught every year.

CLIMATE

WEATHER CHART

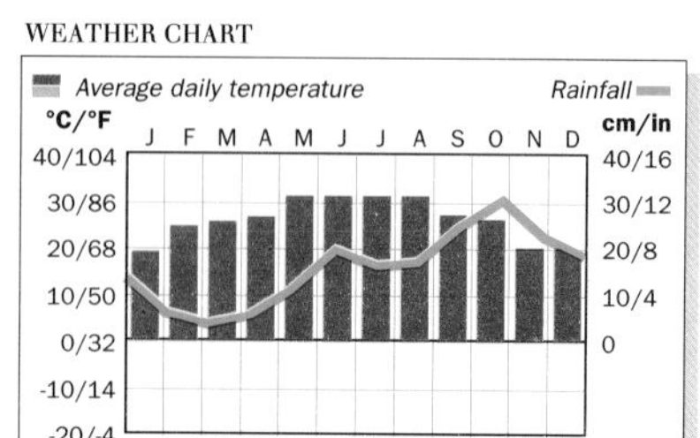

Conditions are hot and humid throughout the year. Coastal regions are affected by hurricanes.

COMMUNICATIONS

Philip S. W. Goldson, Belize City
272,000 passengers

27 ships
48,300 dwt

THE TRANSPORTATION NETWORK

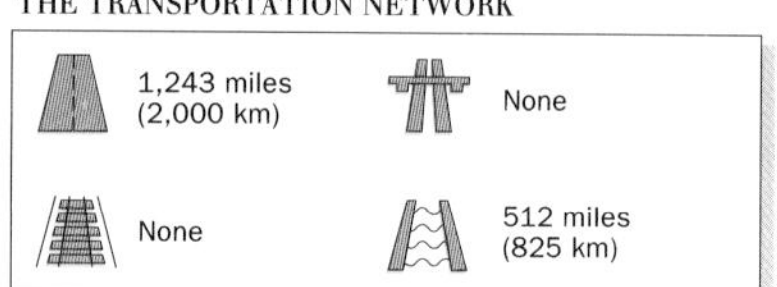

Rising prosperity has led to an increase in road traffic, although traffic lights have yet to be installed. Work to increase the passenger capacity of the airport at Belize City was completed in 1981.

TOURISM

221,826 visitors

Up 1% in 1990

MAIN OVERSEAS ARRIVALS

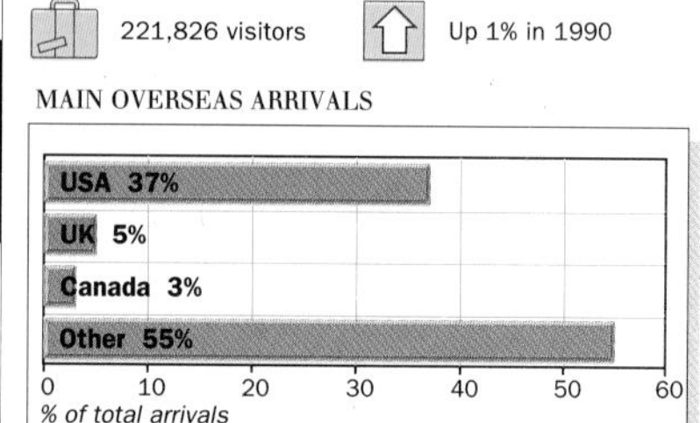

Governments before 1983 sought to limit tourism. However, ecotourism is now encouraged.

PEOPLE

English Creole, Spanish, English, Maya, Garifuna (Carib)

23 people per sq. mile

THE URBAN/RURAL POPULATION SPLIT

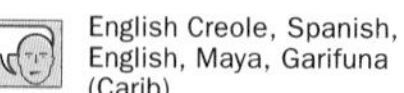

ETHNIC MAKEUP

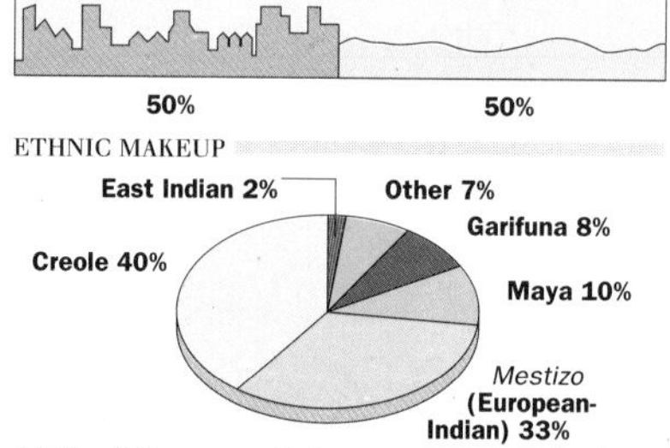

40% of the population can trace their roots back to Africans brought over in the 17th century; the rest is composed of Maya groups, black Caribs (Garifuna), and immigrants from Mexico, the Middle East and India. Belize has a few self-contained communities of Swiss-descended Mennonites.

POLITICS

House of Representatives 28 members

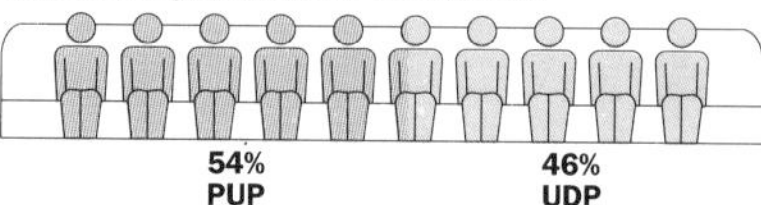

PUP = People's United Party **UDP** = United Democratic Party

Senate 8 members

The members of the Senate are appointed by the governor-general

The desire for independence dominated politics until the 1980s. It was the PUP, under George Price, that negotiated independence from the British in 1981. During the 1984–1989 UDP administration, the maintenance of a pro-US line and fears of communism in the region were the main concerns. The PUP won power back from the UDP in 1989 and today the state of the economy is the key issue. In the absence of any major ideological or policy distinctions between the PUP and UDP, which are both centrist, elections are fought mostly on candidates' records and personalities.

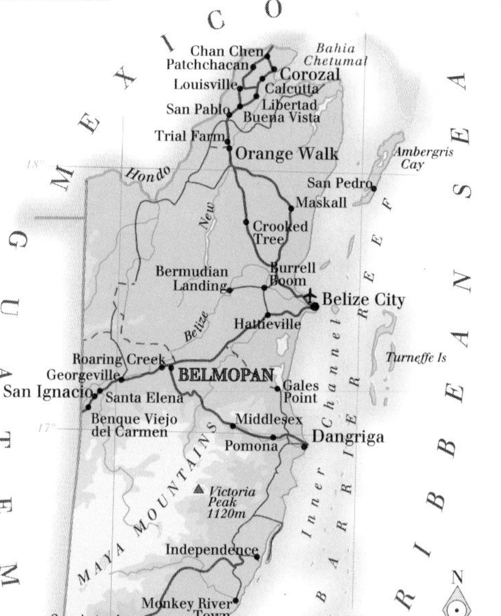

BELIZE

Total Area : 22 960 sq. km (8865 sq. miles)

POPULATION
● over 10 000
● under 10 000

LAND HEIGHT
1000m/3281ft
500m/1640ft
200m/656ft
Sea Level

0 50 km
0 50 miles

B

WORLD AFFAIRS

At the end of 1993, Guatemala officially recognized Belize as an independent state, thus ending a long period of uncertainty and fear of invasion.

AID

 $28m (receipts)  Up 33% in 1991

Belize is one of the highest per capita recipients of US aid; since the staunchly pro-US UDP administration, Belize has been seen as a useful anti-communist buttress in the region.

DEFENSE

 $9.68m  Down 3% in 1990

The 555-strong Belize Defense Force includes two female platoons and is trained by the UK, the USA and Canada. As a result of Guatemala dropping its territorial claim, Britain withdrew its military garrison in 1994.

ECONOMICS

 $373m 

SCORE CARD

❑ WORLD GNP RANKING	163rd
❑ GNP PER CAPITA	$1,970
❑ BALANCE OF PAYMENTS	$-49.1m
❑ INFLATION	2.4%
❑ UNEMPLOYMENT	12%

STRENGTHS
Sugar, textile manufacture, citrus fruits, bananas and cocoa. Small foreign debt, 90% of which is held by multilateral institutions on favorable concessionary terms.

WEAKNESSES
Heavy reliance on imports of processed foods. The economy's small size makes Belize vulnerable to even slight changes in external trading conditions.

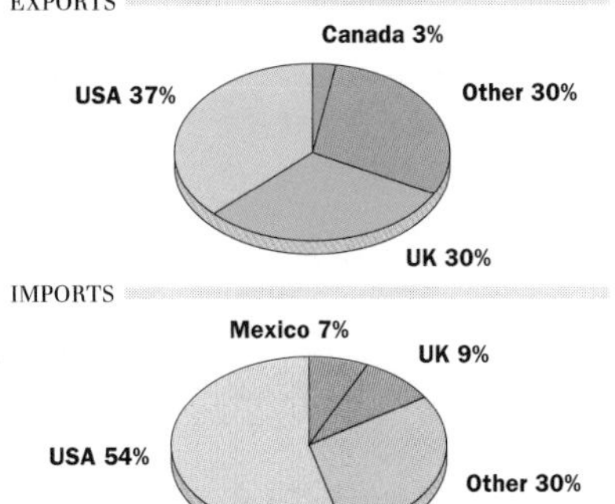

RESOURCES

 105m kwh (capacity 20,000 kw)  Not an oil producer and has no refineries

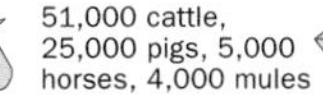

Exploration for oil and gas, largely by US companies, is currently under way in the Corozal basin region.

ENVIRONMENT

 5% partially protected 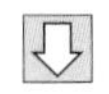 Little protection for unique ecosystems

Belize's low population density, relative poverty and lack of industry have kept its dense tropical forests intact. It is still home to many endangered wild animals, including jaguars, tapirs and rare tropical birds.

MEDIA

 Journalists have occasionally been detained for criticizing the government

PUBLISHING AND BROADCAST MEDIA

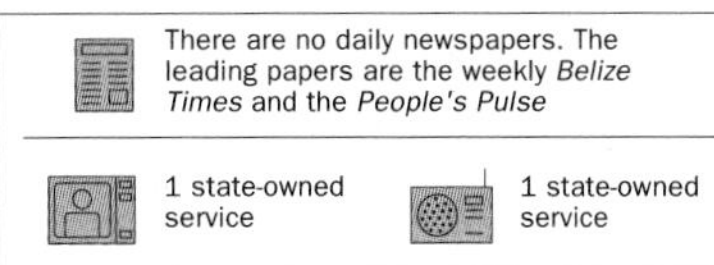

There are no daily newspapers. The leading papers are the weekly *Belize Times* and the *People's Pulse*
1 state-owned service
1 state-owned service

Belize has not suffered the degree of press interference experienced in neighboring states, but the government remains sensitive to even minor criticisms. In 1989, the PUP, newly returned to power, fulfilled its manifesto commitment by establishing a broadcasting corporation modeled on the British BBC, and by revoking the restrictive law of criminal libel. *Amandala* is the most politically independent newspaper, as well as the best for sports coverage.

CRIME

 89 prisoners 

Belize was one of Latin America's major exporters of marijuana to the USA until the US Drug Enforcement Agency destroyed the plantations. It is now an increasingly important transshipment point for Colombian cocaine to the USA. The result is that narcotics-related crime in Belize City has risen sharply since the 1980s.

EDUCATION

 93%

Belize's schools are administered by its three main religious denominations: Roman Catholics, Anglicans, and Methodists. University College of Belize maintains close links with the University of Michigan.

CHRONOLOGY

Originally part of the Maya heartland, between 1798 and 1981 Belize was effectively a British colony.

- ❑ **1919** Demands for more political rights by black Belizeans returning from World War I.
- ❑ **1936** New constitution with limited franchise.
- ❑ **1950** PUP formed. Voting age for women reduced from 30 to 21.
- ❑ **1954** Full adult suffrage.
- ❑ **1972** Guatemala threatens invasion. Britain sends troops.
- ❑ **1980** UN passes unopposed – except by Guatemala – resolution calling for independence.
- ❑ **1981** Full independence.

HEALTH

 1 per 1,956 people 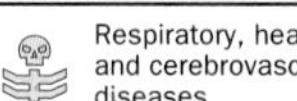

Around 75% of Belizeans have access to government health services, which include seven hospitals and numerous mobile clinics. Sanitation and water supplies are being improved; 62% of homes in Belmopan now have both.

WEALTH

 Skilled laborer, 700 Belizean dollars per month; general manager, 4,600 Belizean dollars per month

CONSUMER GOODS OWNERSHIP

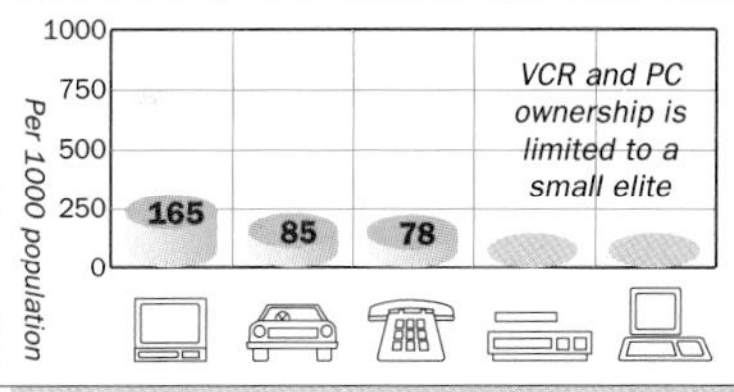

Wealth is more evenly distributed than in the rest of Central America. The drug trade is still a source of wealth.

WORLD RANKING

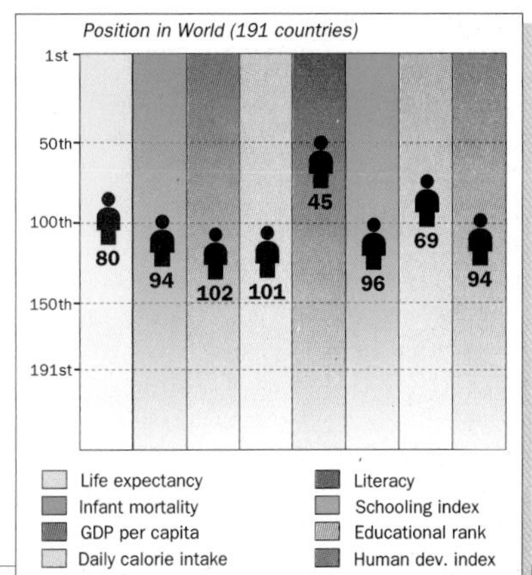

BELORUSSIA (BELARUS)

OFFICIAL NAME: Republic of Belarus **CAPITAL:** Minsk
POPULATION: 10.3 million **CURRENCY:** Belorussian rouble **OFFICIAL LANGUAGE:** Belorussian

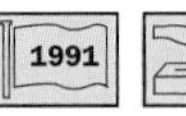

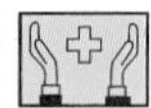

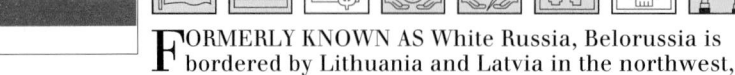

FORMERLY KNOWN AS White Russia, Belorussia is bordered by Lithuania and Latvia in the northwest, Ukraine in the south, and Poland and Russia in the west and east. The landlocked country, which reluctantly became independent of Moscow in 1991, has few resources other than agriculture. The 1986 Chernobyl nuclear disaster in neighboring Ukraine has had many profound and lasting effects on the environment. The health of Belorussians has suffered severely and many areas are still contaminated.

CLIMATE

WEATHER CHART

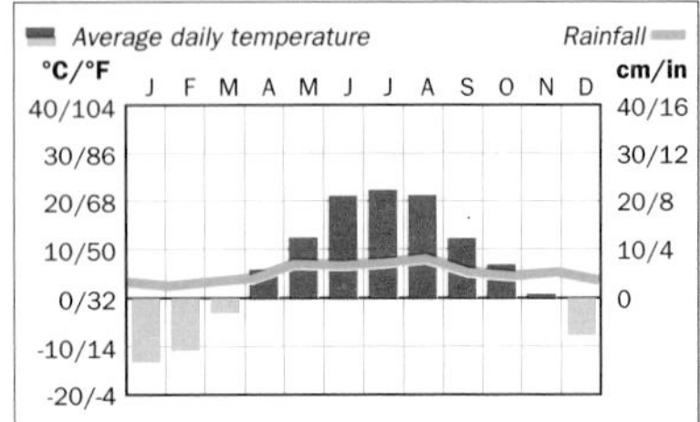

Belorussia has a continental climate. Temperatures in winter drop well below freezing, while in summer they can get fairly high.

Much of southern Belorussia is marshy and sparsely populated. It includes the vast Pripet Marshes and the Dnieper lowlands.

COMMUNICATIONS

Minsk International

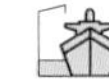

Has no fleet

THE TRANSPORTATION NETWORK

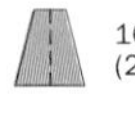

165,036 miles (265,600 km)

None

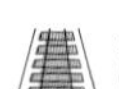

3,474 miles (5,590 km)

Extensive canal and river systems

Belorussia has no direct access to the sea, but is close to the Baltic ports. Railroads are good.

TOURISM

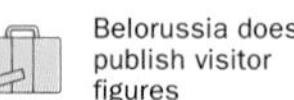

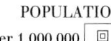

Belorussia does not publish visitor figures

No significant change from year to year

MAIN OVERSEAS ARRIVALS

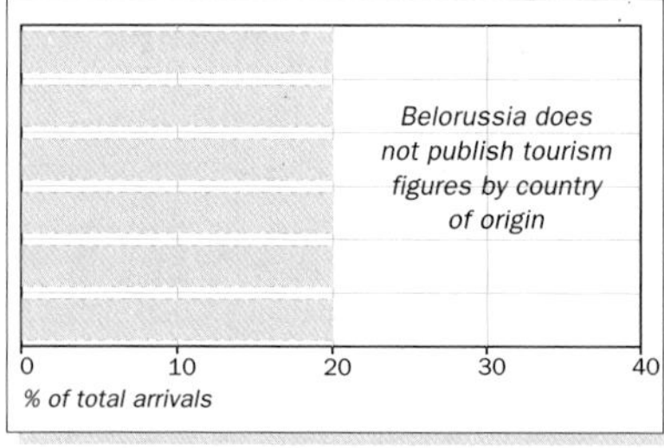

Belorussia has fewer tourists than its Slav and Baltic neighbors. Many of its historic buildings were destroyed during World War II. Minsk was completely flattened and is now characterized by Stalinist architecture and high-rise buildings. There are few assets on which to build a tourist industry.

BELORUSSIA

Total Area : 207 600 sq. km (80 154 sq. miles)

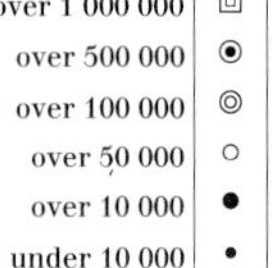

LAND HEIGHT

200m/656ft

100m/328ft

0 50 km

0 50 miles

PEOPLE

Belorussian, Russian

127 people per sq. mile

THE URBAN/RURAL POPULATION SPLIT

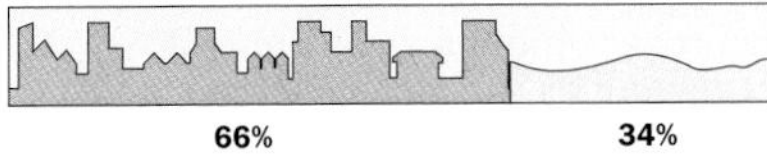

RELIGIOUS PERSUASION

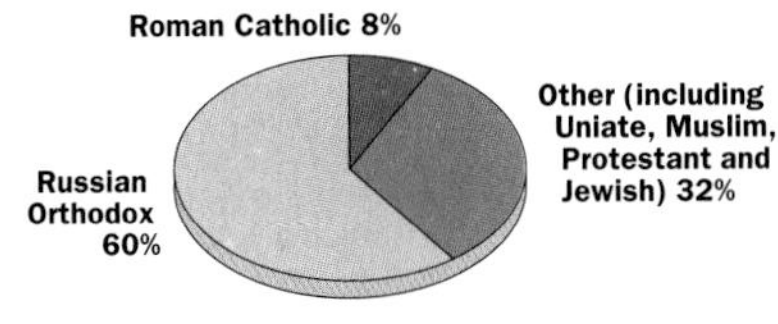

ETHNIC MAKEUP

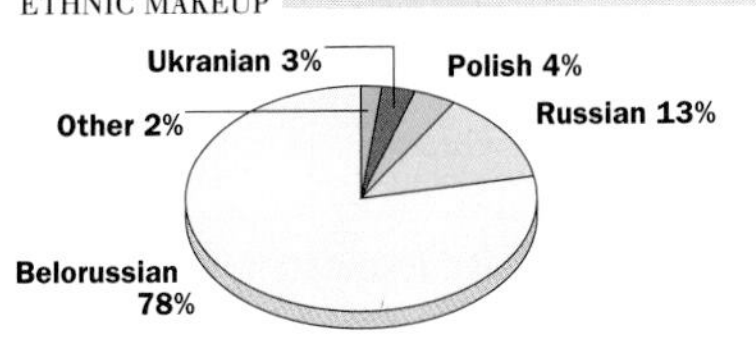

Since only 2% of the population is non-Slav there is little ethnic tension. According to a law passed in September 1992, the entire population has an automatic right to Belorussian citizenship. Only 11% of the population, most of whom live in the countryside, are fluent in Belorussian. Attempts by Chairman Shushkevich to boost the popularity of the official language proved unsuccessful.

POPULATION AGE BREAKDOWN

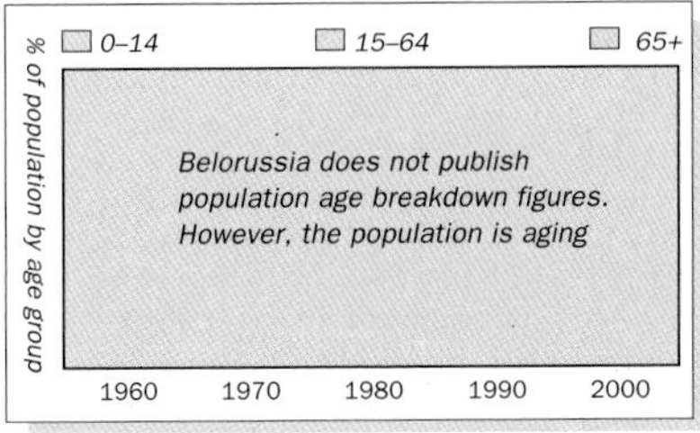

POLITICS

1994

President Aleksandr Lukashenka

THE STATE OF THE PARTIES

Supreme Soviet 360 members

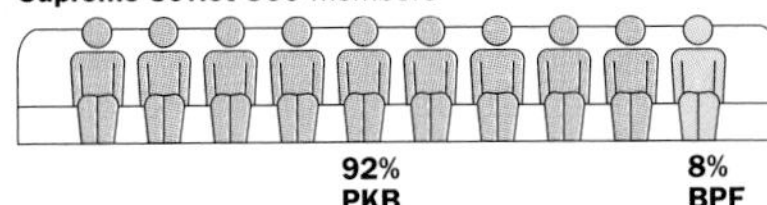

PKB = Communist Party of Belorussia **BPF** = Belorussian Popular Front. Under the 1994 constitution, the Supreme Soviet is to be replaced by a new 260-member assembly

Under the 1994 constitution, Belorussia is a multiparty democracy headed by a directly elected president.

MAIN POLITICAL ISSUES

Relationship with Russia
Belorussia's relationship with Russia is the key political issue. Mechislau Grib, the new parliamentary chairman, is strongly pro-Russian. Under his leadership, Belorussia has agreed to a monetary union that effectively gives Moscow control of Belorussia's economic policy. In return, Russia will take on Belorussia's $1.5 billion debt. Belorussia also hopes for Russian economic support.

The environment
The 1986 Chernobyl nuclear disaster continues to cast a shadow over life in Belorussia. The devastating effects of the accident are still being revealed in higher incidences of leukemia and cancer. Much of Belorussia's land and farm produce is still tainted with fallout radiation. The clean-up operation is slow and laborious and will take decades. It is a major drain on state finances. In 1993, 17% of government spending was set aside for this purpose.

PROFILE
Following independence in 1991, Belorussia was the slowest of the ex-Soviet states to implement political reform. The current parliament was elected in 1990 and is therefore predominantly composed of communist deputies. The pro-democracy Belorussian Popular Front has only 8% of the seats. Much of the real power lies in the hands of the prime minister, the conservative Vyacheslau Kebich. However, with the replacement in 1993 of the moderate Shushkevich by the conservative Mechislau Grib as parliamentary chairman, the reformers now have even less influence than in 1991. The current broad trend is a return to pre-independence politics.

The policy of seeking a closer rapprochement with Russia reflects this. Monetary union in 1993 could well lead to Belorussia eventually joining a unitary Russian state. Much depends on events in Moscow. The leadership in Belorussia is banking on the reformers there losing ground to the conservatives, who are more likely to provide Belorussia with economic aid.

Vyacheslau Kebich, conservative prime minister of the Council of Ministers.

Chairman Stanislau Shushkevich, ousted in a no-confidence vote in 1993.

WORLD AFFAIRS

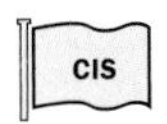

Relations with Russia are paramount. Numerous bilateral agreements have been signed since 1991. These ties are being strengthened now that the pro-Russian communist, Mechislav Grib, has become parliamentary chairman. However, relations could sour if the reformers in Moscow gain power. Many in Russia are opposed to closer links with Belorussia, believing it represents a drain on Moscow's resources for little strategic gain.

The good relations with the West developed by ex-Chairman Shushkevich have cooled. However, Belorussia retains its Most Favored Nation (MFN) trading status with the USA.

AID

Receipts undisclosed

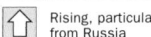

Rising, particularly from Russia

In 1993, the World Bank and IMF granted Belorussia its first loans, on condition that the government carries out economic reforms. Under this package, $98 million was promised by the IMF and $120 million by the World Bank. The anti-reform stance of the current administration makes it unlikely that Belorussia will receive the full package.

The EU has extended some credits to Belorussia to assist in the conversion of the defense industry to non-military production. Belorussia still requires aid to combat the effects of radiation pollution in the wake of the Chernobyl nuclear accident of 1986. Some help is being provided through the Western-sponsored Know-How Fund.

CHRONOLOGY

After forming part of medieval Kievan Rus, Belorussia experienced rule by three of its neighbors – Poland, Lithuania and Russia – before incorporation into the USSR.

- **1917** Nationalists and socialists try to gain autonomy within Russia.
- **1918** Belorussian Bolsheviks stage coup. Independence as Belorussian Soviet Socialist Republic.
- **1919** Invaded by Poland.
- **1920** Minsk retaken by Red Army. Eastern Belorussia reestablished as Soviet Socialist Republic (BSSR).
- **1921** Treaty of Riga – western Belorussia incorporated into Poland. New Economic Policy applied.
- **1922** BSSR merges with Russian Federation to form USSR.
- **1929** Stalin implements collectivization of agriculture.

⇨

B

CHRONOLOGY *continued*

- **1939** Western Belorussia reincorporated into USSR when Soviet Red Army invades Poland.
- **1941–1944** Belorussia under German occupation during World War II .
- **1945** Belorussia a founding member of the UN along with Ukraine and USSR.
- **1965** KT Mazurau, leader of Communist Party of Belorussia (PKB), becomes first deputy chairperson of USSR's Council of Ministers.
- **1986** April: accident at Chernobyl nuclear power plant. Belorussia affected by 70% of plant's radioactive fallout. December: Belorussian intellectuals petition Soviet leader Mikhail Gorbachev over dangers of "linguistic extinction" of Belorussian language.
- **1988** Archaeologist Zianon Pazniak reveals evidence of mass executions (over 300,000) by Soviet military between 1937 and 1941 in Kurapaty woods near Minsk. Popular outrage fuels formation of nationalist Belorussian Popular Front (BPF), with Pazniak as president. PKB authorities crush demonstration.
- **1989** Belorussian adopted as republic's official language.
- **1990** PKB prevents BPF participating in March elections to Supreme Soviet. BPF members join other opposition groups in Belorussian Democratic Bloc (BDB). BDB wins 25% of seats. July: CPB bows to opposition pressure and issues Declaration of the State Sovereignty of BSSR.
- **1991** March: 83% vote in referendum to preserve union with USSR. April: strikes against PKB and its economic policies. August: independence declared. Republic of Belarus adopted as official name. Stanislau Shushkevich elected chairman of Supreme Soviet. December: Belorussia, Russia and Ukraine establish CIS.
- **1992** Supreme Soviet announces Soviet nuclear weapons must be cleared from Belorussia by 1999. Help promised from USA.
- **1993** January: national army comes into existence. Ratification of START-1 and nuclear non-proliferation treaties by Belorussian parliament.
- **1994** Shushkevich ousted from post as chairman of Supreme Soviet. Replaced by pro-Russian former communist, Mechislau Grib. Monetary union (re-entry into rouble zone) agreed with Russia.

DEFENSE

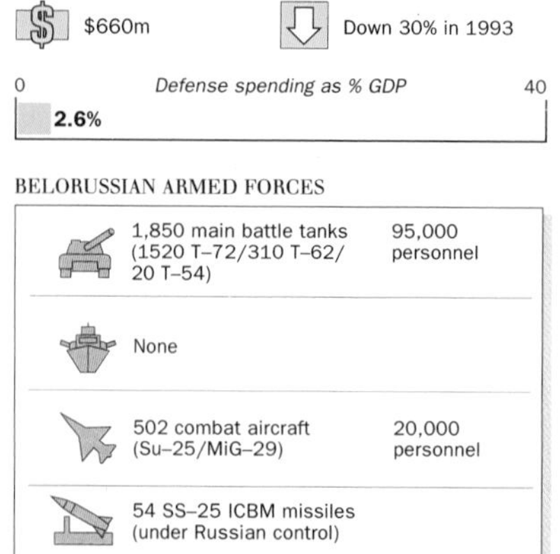

$660m
Down 30% in 1993
0
Defense spending as % GDP
40
2.6%
BELORUSSIAN ARMED FORCES
1,850 main battle tanks (1520 T–72/310 T–62/ 20 T–54)
95,000 personnel
None
502 combat aircraft (Su–25/MiG–29)
20,000 personnel
54 SS–25 ICBM missiles (under Russian control)

Under ex-Chairman Shushkevich, Belorussia was committed to a policy of neutrality. By mid-1993 all tactical nuclear weapons were removed and Belorussia announced its aim of removing its strategic nuclear weapons by 1995. Shushkevich also refused to sign the CIS Collective Security Pact, believing an independent army was essential to Belorussia's sovereignty.

Under Grib, stronger military ties with Moscow are being established and Belorussia is now bearing some of the costs of Russian troops stationed on its territory. However, Belorussia's large defense industry is hoping that the arrangement will mean an increase in orders from Russia.

ECONOMICS

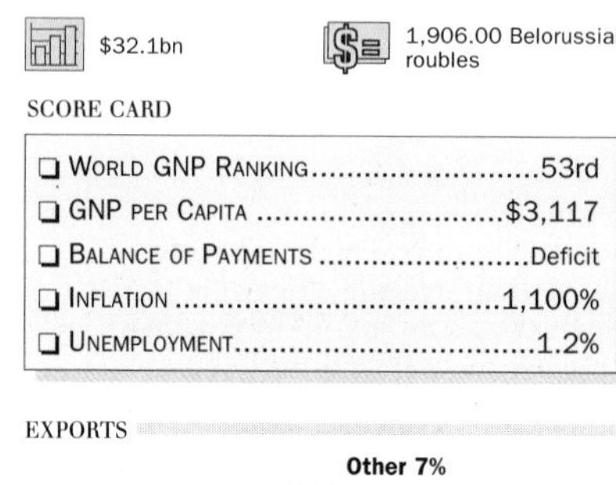

SCORE CARD

- World GNP Ranking 53rd
- GNP per Capita $3,117
- Balance of Payments ......Deficit
- Inflation 1,100%
- Unemployment 1.2%

EXPORTS

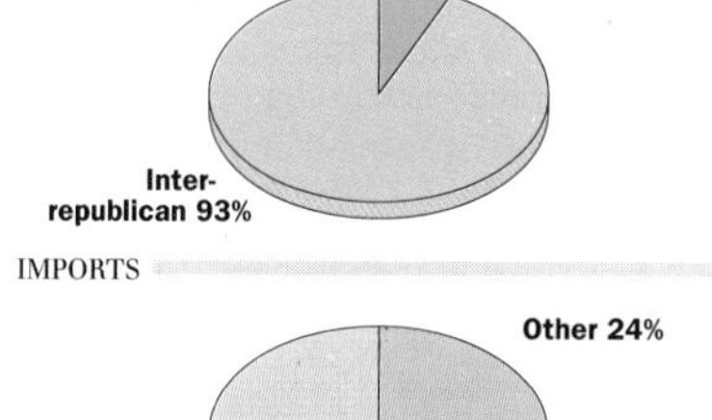

IMPORTS

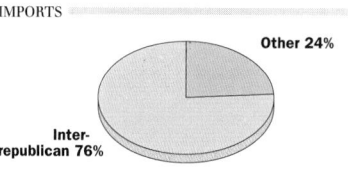

Other 24%
Inter-republican 76%

ECONOMIC PERFORMANCE INDICATOR

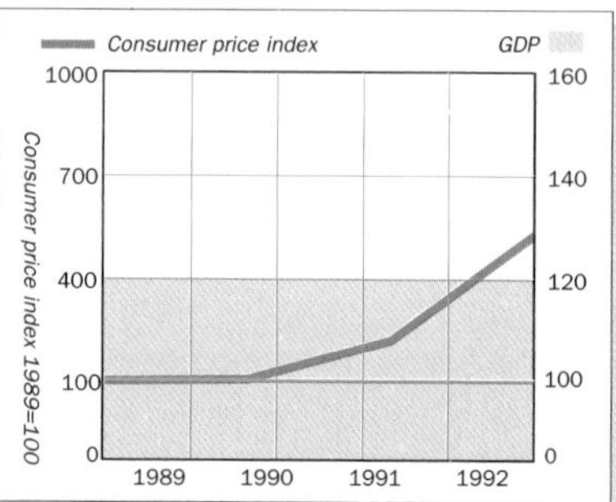

Strengths

Low unemployment rate: just over 1% of labor force (approximately 50,000). Better economic prospects than other CIS states. Monetary union with Russia aids currency stability. Potential of forestry and agriculture.

Weaknesses

Decision not to pursue economic reform will keep increasingly inefficient industries in business. Few natural resources. Dependence on Russia for energy. Clean-up costs of Chernobyl drain government finances.

Profile

Following independence, Belorussia adopted a slower pace of economic reform than the other ex-Soviet states. Chairman Shushkevich was thwarted in his attempts to move more quickly to a market economy by the largely conservative parliament. Grib's accession to its chairmanship has frozen moves toward privatization. He wishes to see a return to the Soviet-style direction of all economic enterprises from the center. Traditional industries will continue to receive heavy subsidies. The small, pro-reform opposition fears the failure to reform will leave Belorussia impoverished.

BELORUSSIA : MAJOR BUSINESSES

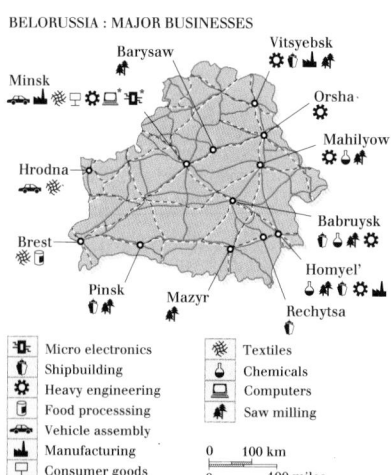

Vitsyebsk, Barysaw, Minsk, Orsha, Mahilyow, Hrodna, Babruysk, Brest, Homyel', Pinsk, Mazyr, Rechytsa

Micro electronics · Shipbuilding · Heavy engineering · Food processing · Vehicle assembly · Manufacturing · Consumer goods · Textiles · Chemicals · Computers · Saw milling

0 100 km
0 100 miles

* significant multinational ownership

RESOURCES

37.6bn kwh (capacity 8.03m kw)

Produces very small quantities of oil

6.4m cattle, 4.7m pigs, 380,000 sheep

Natural gas, coal, rock salts

ELECTRICITY GENERATION

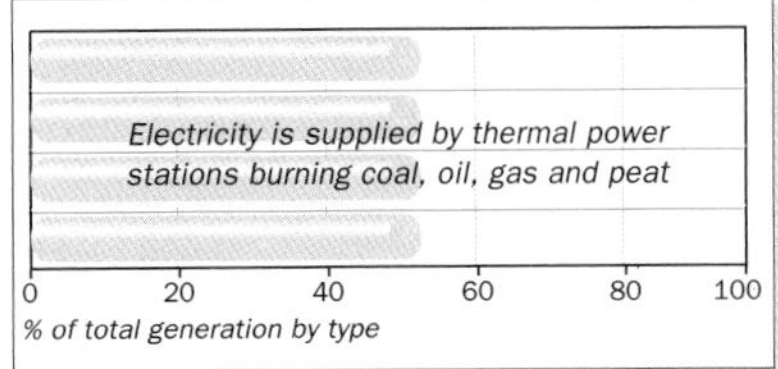

Belorussia has no significant strategic resources and is heavily dependent on the Russian Federation for fuel and energy supplies. Small quantities of oil and natural gas exist close to the Polish border.

BELORUSSIA : LAND USE

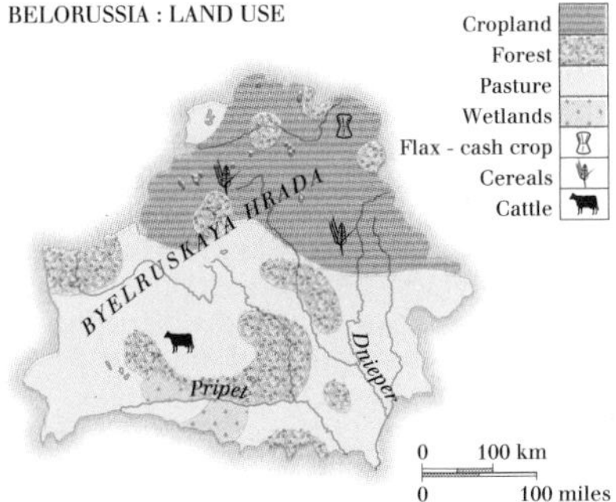

ENVIRONMENT

1.1%

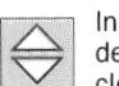

Inadequate funds to deal with Chernobyl clean-up

ENVIRONMENTAL TREATIES

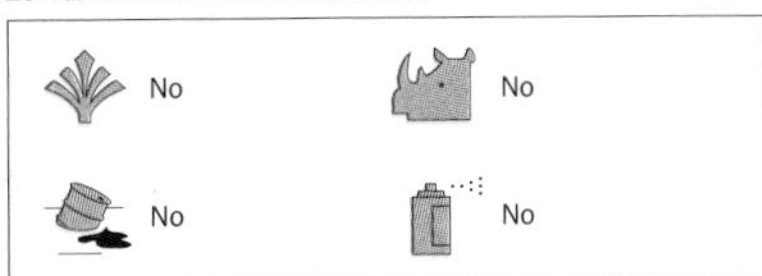

In 1986 a massive leak from Ukraine's Chernobyl nuclear reactor sent a huge cloud of radiation into Belorussia. 70% of the fallout fell on 40% of the country, including the capital Minsk; 2.3 million people were immediately affected. The government at the time kept the leak secret. Farmland, forests and water were all contaminated, including underwater streams feeding rivers in eastern Poland.

Cases of leukemia and cancer are continuing to increase. Some areas in the fallout zone are still being farmed. Unscrupulous dealers are suspected of selling meat meant for destruction. A clean-up program is under way, swallowing 17% of government finances each year. Belorussia is seeking substantial Western aid to cope with the problem.

MEDIA

High level of state censorship

PUBLISHING AND BROADCAST MEDIA

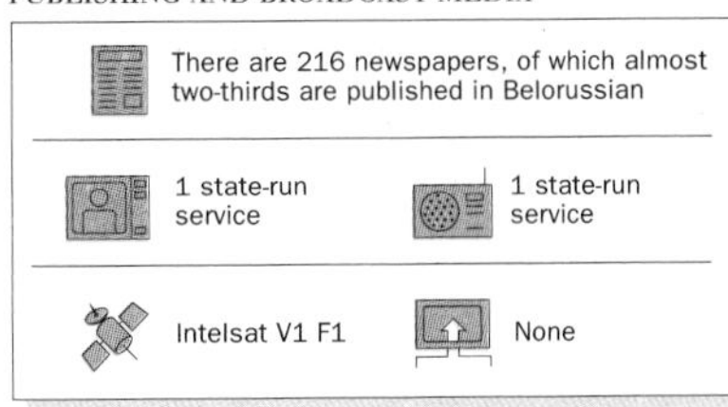

There are 216 newspapers, of which almost two-thirds are published in Belorussian
1 state-run service
1 state-run service
Intelsat V1 F1
None

The media is under central government control and are largely dependent on state subsidies. The one independent TV station was closed down in 1992.

CRIME

Belorussia does not publish prison figures

Rising

CRIME RATES

The rates of all categories of crime have increased since independence

As elsewhere in the former Soviet Union, economic hardship (although unemployment stands at only just over 1%) and a general breakdown in law and order have resulted in a significant rise in crime. The murder rate increased by nearly 50% and muggings by nearly 60% in the first half of 1993. Belorussia has become a transshipment point for illegal drugs destined for Western Europe, while locally produced opium supplies the internal market.

EDUCATION

100%

Education spending as % GNP (0–25): 7.9%

THE EDUCATION SYSTEM

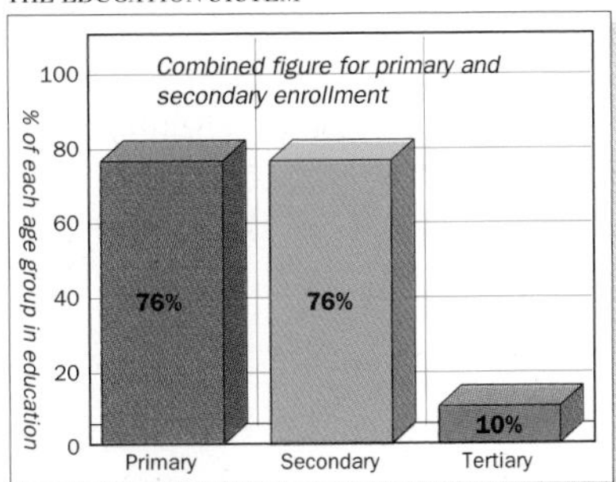

Russian remains the main language of instruction in both secondary and higher education establishments, despite attempts by Shushkevich to promote Belorussian. University education is of a fairly high standard.

HEALTH

1 per 246 people

Circulatory diseases, cancer, accidents, violence

Health spending as % GNP (0–25): Insufficient to cope with abonormal circumstances

Belorussia's good health service has been placed under enormous strain as a result of the Chernobyl nuclear disaster. The number of cancer and leukemia cases is currently 10,000 above the previous annual average. More wards and specialist units have had to be built. Under the Know-How Fund, many Belorussian doctors are being trained in the latest bone-marrow techniques in Europe and the USA.

WEALTH

Inflation is eroding the value of most salaries

CONSUMER GOODS OWNERSHIP

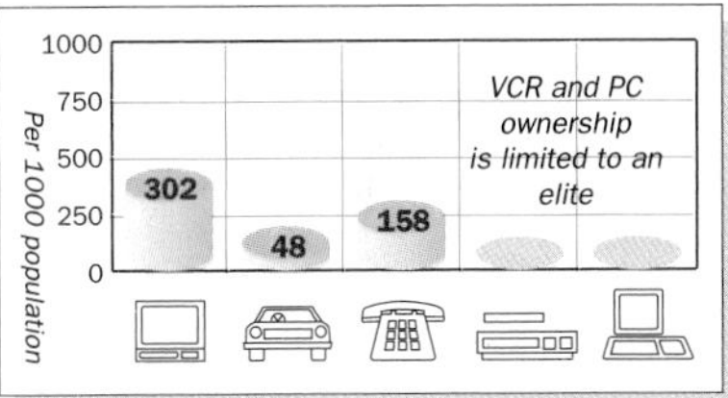

The deteriorating economic situation has resulted in an overall drop in living standards. High inflation has particularly affected people on fixed incomes. Wealth is concentrated in the hands of a small, communist elite which has been opposed to any market mechanisms. Now that they have the upper hand in parliament, they will strengthen their grip on the state's resources. Belorussia is unlikely to see the expansion of entrepreneurial activity to be found in Poland or Russia. However, the state's commitment to low unemployment will mean that the extreme social deprivation to be found in other ex-USSR states should be avoided.

WORLD RANKING

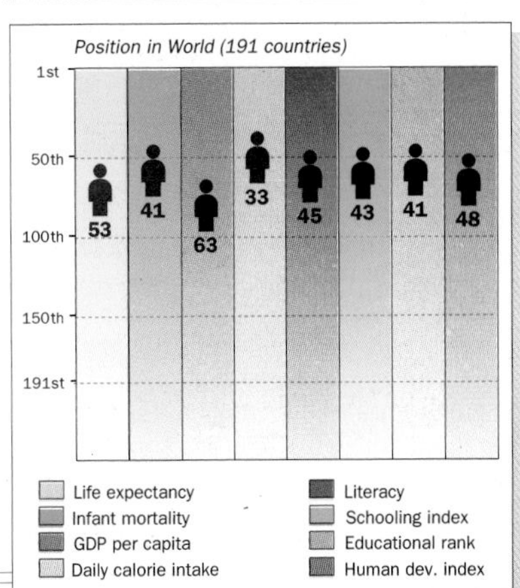

WEST AFRICA

Burkina · Togo · Nigeria · BENIN · Africa

B

BENIN

OFFICIAL NAME: Republic of Benin **CAPITAL:** Porto-Novo
POPULATION: 4.9 million **CURRENCY:** CFA franc **OFFICIAL LANGUAGE:** French

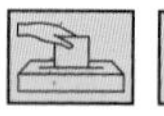

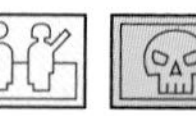

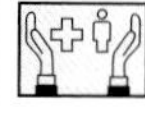

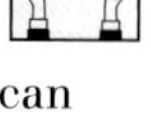

BENIN STRETCHES NORTH from the West African coast, with a 62-mile shoreline on the Bight of Benin. Formerly the kingdom of Dahomey, Benin became a French protectorate and then a part of colonial French West Africa. It achieved independence in 1960. In 1990, Benin became one of the pioneers of African multiparty politics, ending 17 years of one-party Marxist–Leninist rule. Benin's economy is based on a well-diversified agricultural sector.

CLIMATE

WEATHER CHART

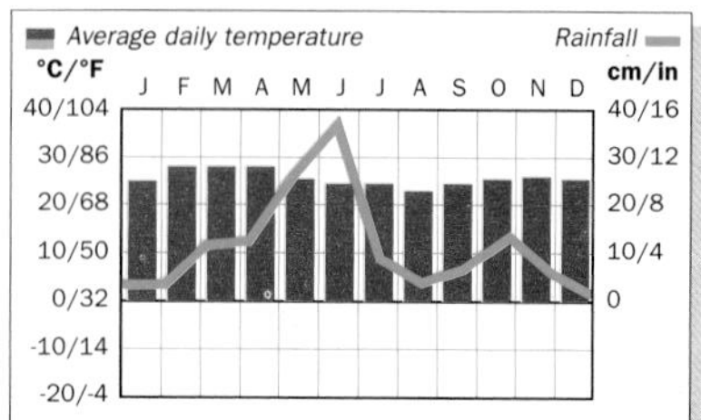

There are two rainy seasons. The hot, dusty *harmattan* wind characterizes the December to February dry season.

COMMUNICATIONS

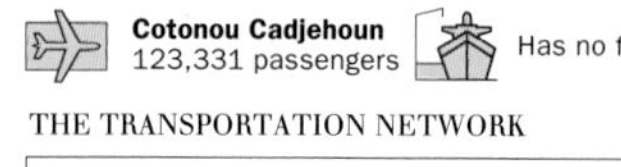

THE TRANSPORTATION NETWORK

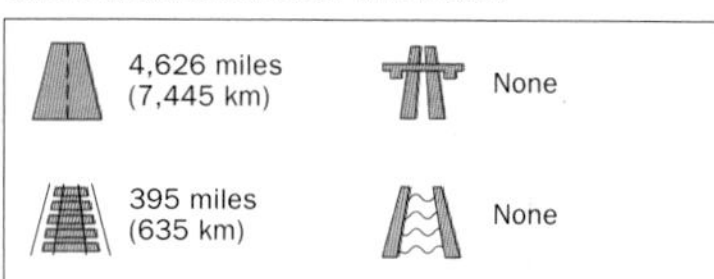

The joint Benin–Niger railroad runs only as far as Parakou. Air travel through Cotonou is increasing rapidly.

TOURISM

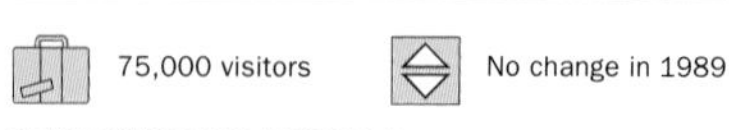

MAIN OVERSEAS ARRIVALS

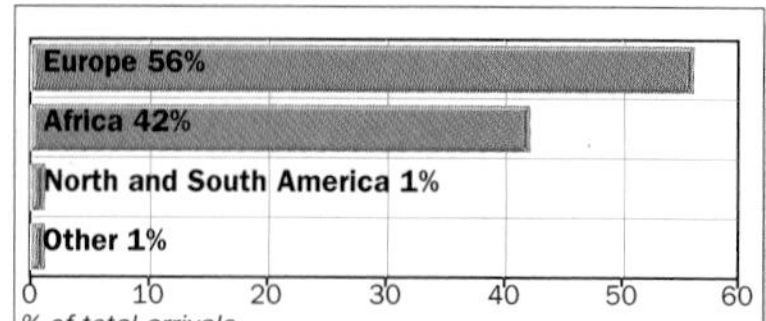

Tourism is not well-developed, although there are plans to develop package tourism. There is some safari tourism in the north, particularly in the Atakora Mountains. Benin is popular as a weekend break for visitors to Nigeria.

PEOPLE

THE URBAN/RURAL POPULATION SPLIT

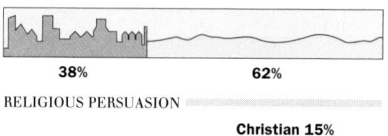

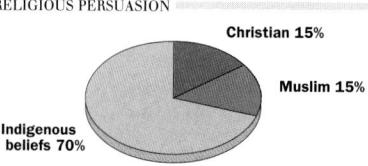

38% 62%

RELIGIOUS PERSUASION

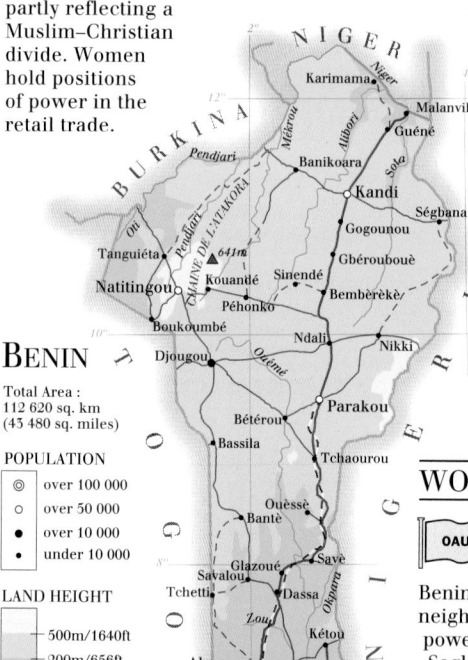

Christian 15%
Muslim 15%
Indigenous beliefs 70%

Benin is politically dominated by the southern Fon people. There is some north–south tension, partly because the south is more developed, and partly reflecting a Muslim–Christian divide. Women hold positions of power in the retail trade.

BENIN

Total Area :
112 620 sq. km
(43 480 sq. miles)

POPULATION

over 100 000
over 50 000
over 10 000
under 10 000

LAND HEIGHT

500m/1640ft
200m/656ft
Sea Level

0 100 km
0 100 miles

POLITICS

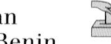

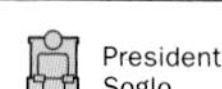

THE STATE OF THE PARTIES

National Assembly 64 members

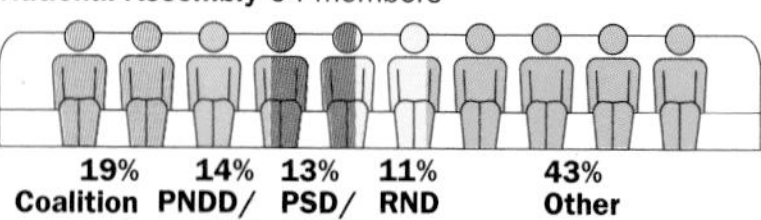

Coalition (composed of: UDFP = Democratic Union of the Forces of Progress, MDPS = Movement for Democracy and Social Progress, ULD = Union for Liberty and Development) **PNDD** = National Party for Democracy and Development **PRD** = Party of Democratic Renewal **PSD** = Social Democratic Party **UNSP** = National Union for Solidarity and Progress **RND** = National Rally for Democracy

Benin has been at the forefront of African democratization. This process began at the National Conference of 1990, when General Kerekou agreed to hold multiparty elections after years of military one-party rule. Following elections in 1991, Kerekou became the first of the African one-party leaders to hand over power peacefully. Nicéphore Soglo, a former official of the World Bank and nephew of General Soglo, who ruled from 1965 to 1967, took over the presidency. The former ruling party failed to gain any seats in the new parliament. The main political parties in Benin are regionally based and depend on the leadership of individuals influential in local communities. Soglo does not have an automatic majority in parliament, but depends on an alliance with Houngbedji, an arch-opponent. As Soglo moves towards the 1996 elections, indications are that the struggle will be tough. The main political issue is the effect on the economy of Soglo's World Bank-style deregulation. To date, the reforms he has introduced have failed to reduce the economic hardships of the late 1980s.

WORLD AFFAIRS

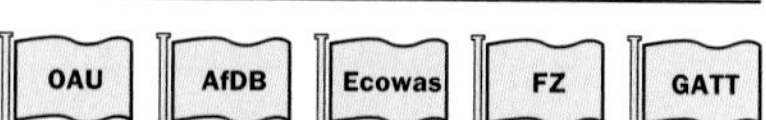

Benin is largely dominated by its giant neighbor, Nigeria, by far the most powerful state in the region. President Soglo was recently chairman of ECOWAS and supports regional integration with neighboring countries. Continuing good relations with France, the main source of aid, is critical.

AID

 $256m (receipts)  Down 6% in 1991

Benin's poverty is such that the maintenance of aid is at the top of the political agenda. France, the main protector of Benin's independence since 1960, is the major aid donor. Other donors include the World Bank and IMF, the EU, Germany, Belgium, the Netherlands, Spain and the USA. Almost all development finance comes from aid, and some has been used to finance debt-servicing. There is the usual problem of finding suitable projects, although Benin has a large, well-educated (if top-heavy) civil service, making implementation easier than in many parts of Africa.

DEFENSE

 $25.71m 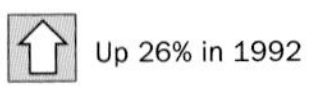 Up 26% in 1992

The 3,800-strong army is actively involved in the attempt to curb smuggling on the border with Nigeria. In 1989, the army was employed internally against rioters.

ECONOMICS

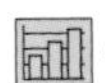 $2.1bn  295.23 CFA francs

SCORE CARD

- World GNP Ranking........137th
- GNP per Capita........$430
- Balance of Payments........$-107m
- Inflation........1%
- Unemployment....Widespread underemployment

Strengths
Agriculture-based economy, with good product diversification. President Soglo's World Bank expertise. New-found political stability.

Weaknesses
Combined problems of smuggling and overvalued CFA make it almost impossible to estimate income. Top-heavy civil service due to return of civil servants from other AOF countries.

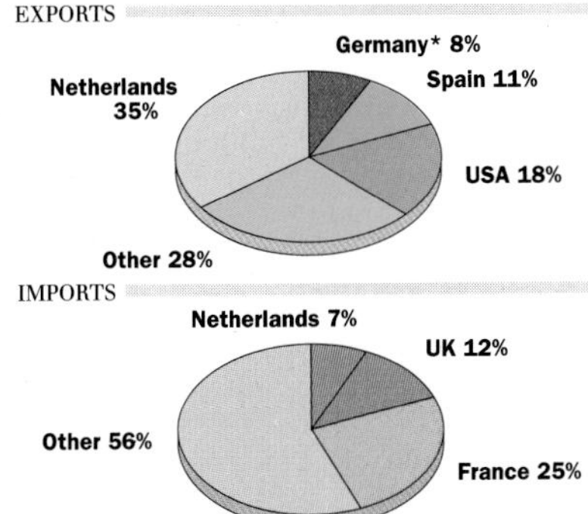

Flat landscape near Cotonou, *characteristic of Benin's coastal region. Numerous lagoons lie behind its short, 62-mile coastline.*

RESOURCES

 5m kwh (capacity 15,000 kw) 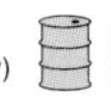 Reserves of 19,900,000 bbl

 932,000 cattle, 890,000 sheep, 680,000 pigs — Oil, limestone, marble, gold

Since 1988 most electricity – which previously had to be imported from Ghana – is generated by the Nangbeto Dam on the River Mono.

ENVIRONMENT

 7%  New, environmentally aware rural development ministry

Desertification in the north is the major problem. Benin has been used in the past as a dumping ground for toxic waste.

MEDIA

 Although freedom of expression is guaranteed under the constitution, the press is quick to defend its rights

PUBLISHING AND BROADCAST MEDIA

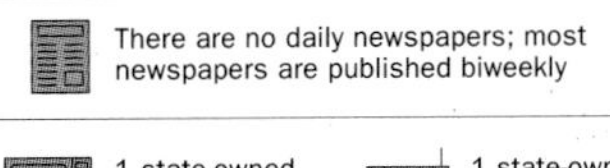

There are no daily newspapers; most newspapers are published biweekly
1 state-owned service
1 state-owned service

The newly independent press faces economic difficulties. The biweekly *La Gazette du Golfe* has failed in its attempt to build a regional market.

CRIME

 Benin does not publish prison figures 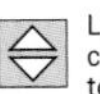 Little significant change from year to year

Benin is relatively free of serious crime, though armed robbery is an increasing problem. There is also a very high level of smuggling, especially along the border with Nigeria.

EDUCATION

 23%

More is spent on education than on defense, and this is reinforced by Benin's active intellectual community, the "Latin Quarter of Africa." The university at Abomey-Calavi is rated highly in medicine and law.

CHRONOLOGY

In 1625 the Fon, indigenous slave traders, founded the kingdom of Dahomey. Dahomey in turn conquered the neighboring kingdoms of Dan, Allada and the coast around Porto Novo.

- **1857** The French establish trading post at Grand-Popo.
- **1889** French attempts to hinder slave trade lead to war with King Behanzin. Behanzin defeated.
- **1892** French protectorate.
- **1904** Dahomey ruled as part of French West Africa.
- **1960** Independence.
- **1975** Renamed Benin.
- **1989** Marxism–Leninism abandoned as official ideology.

HEALTH

 1 per 16,025 people  Communicable and diarrheal diseases, malaria

Outside major towns, health services are scarce. Benin trains many doctors, but more of them work in France than in Benin.

WEALTH

 Railway ticket clerk, 35,000 CFA francs per month; oil industry engineer, 323,000 CFA francs per month

CONSUMER GOODS OWNERSHIP

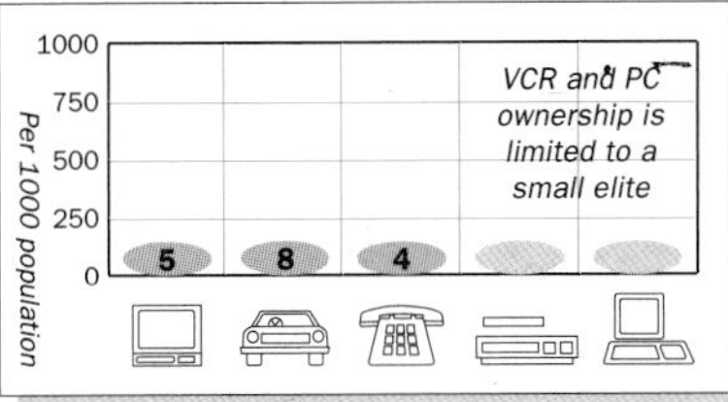

Substantial differences in wealth reflect the strongly hierarchical nature of society, especially in the south. French cars are considered status symbols.

WORLD RANKING

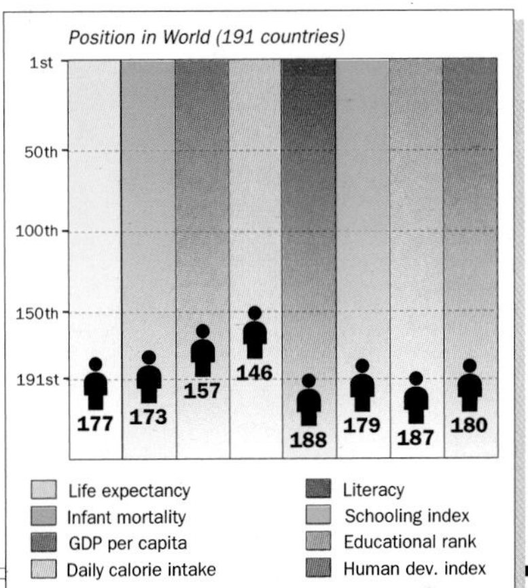

B

BHUTAN

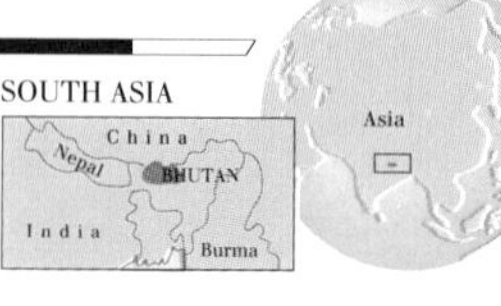

OFFICIAL NAME: Kingdom of Bhutan **CAPITAL:** Thimpu
POPULATION: 1.6 million **CURRENCY:** Ngultrum **OFFICIAL LANGUAGE:** Dzongkha

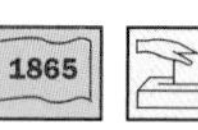

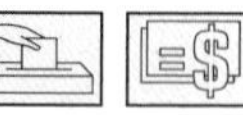

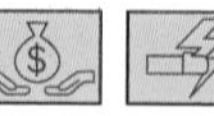

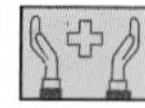

PERCHED IN THE HIMALAYAS between India and China, Bhutan is 70% forested. The land rises from the low, tropical southern strip, through the fertile central valleys, to the high Himalayas inhabited by semi-nomadic yak herders. A formal Buddhist state where power is shared by the king and government, Bhutan began modernizing in the 1960s, but has chosen to do so gradually and remains largely closed to the outside world.

CLIMATE

WEATHER CHART

Average daily temperature — Rainfall
°C/°F: 40/104, 30/86, 20/68, 10/50, 0/32, -10/14, -20/-4
J F M A M J J A S O N D
cm/in: 40/16, 30/12, 20/8, 10/4, 0

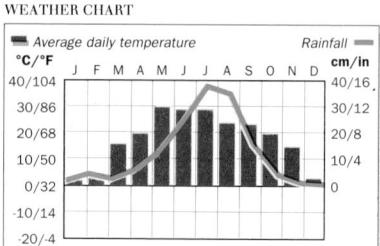

The south is tropical, the north alpine, cold and harsh. The central valleys are warmer in the east than in the west. The summer monsoon affects all parts.

COMMUNICATIONS

Paro International
19,939 passengers

Has no fleet

THE TRANSPORTATION NETWORK

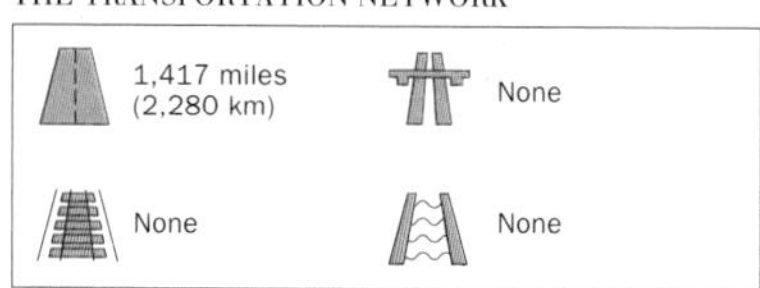

The main surfaced road runs east-west across central Bhutan. Two others run south into India. Only the national airline, Druk Air, flies into Bhutan.

TOURISM

1,480 visitors

Up 4% in 1990

MAIN OVERSEAS ARRIVALS

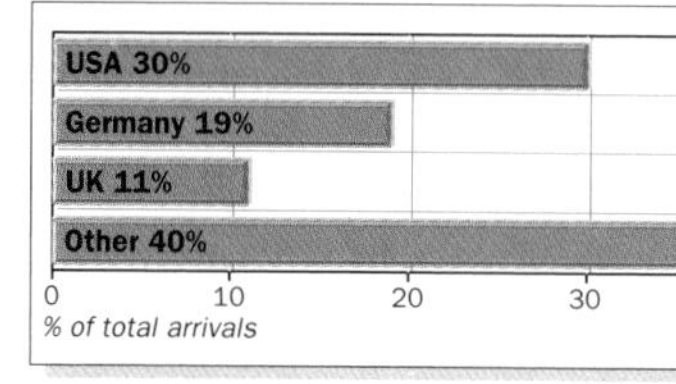

The government's policy of allowing tourism to expand only very slowly aims to protect Bhutan's cultural values and natural environment. Most monasteries are closed to foreigners. First steps to privatize the industry were taken in 1991.

***Less than 10% of Bhutan is arable**, but its fertility allows almost any crop to grow. The diversity of wild plant species inspired its old name: Southern Valleys of the Medicinal Herbs.*

PEOPLE

Dzongkha, Nepali, Assamese

83 people per sq. mile

THE URBAN/RURAL POPULATION SPLIT

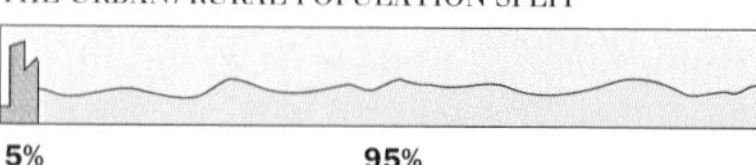

5% 95%

RELIGIOUS PERSUASION

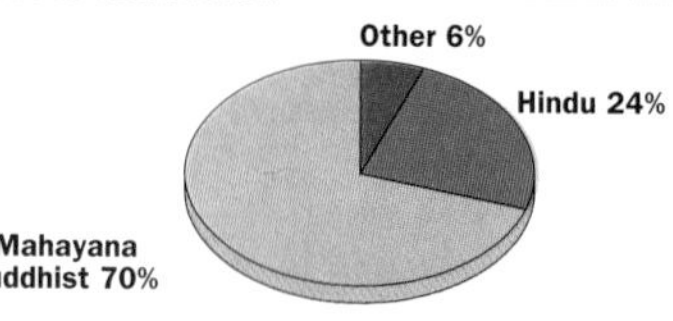

The majority of the population, the Drukpa peoples, originated in Tibet and are devoutly Buddhist. Twenty-five per cent are Hindu Nepalese who settled in the south from 1910 to 1950. Bhutan has 20 languages. Dzongkha, the language of western Bhutan, native to just 16% of the people, was made the official language in 1988 and Nepali was banned. Many southerners have been deported as illegal immigrants, creating fierce ethnic tension.

POLITICS

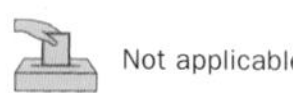

Not applicable

HM *Druk Gyalpo (Dragon King)* Jigme Singye Wangchuck

THE STATE OF THE PARTIES

Bhutan is an absolute monarchy, ruled by the King together with the Council of Ministers, the National Assembly and the head of Bhutan's Buddhist monks

The present King is following his father's plans to modernize Bhutan. Until 1961, the country was run on feudal lines and closed to the outside world. The Drukpa-dominated government's policy of instilling a new sense of national identity has alienated the ethnic Nepalese in the south. It has also led directly to the foundation of the Bhutan People's Party. Banned in Bhutan, it has its headquarters in Kathmandu, Nepal.

BHUTAN

Total Area :
47 000 sq. km (18 147 sq. miles)

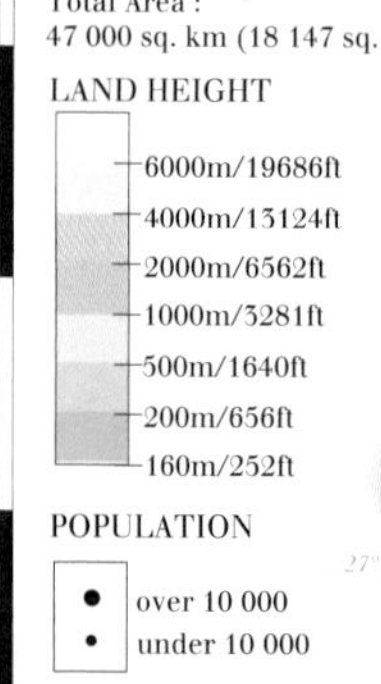

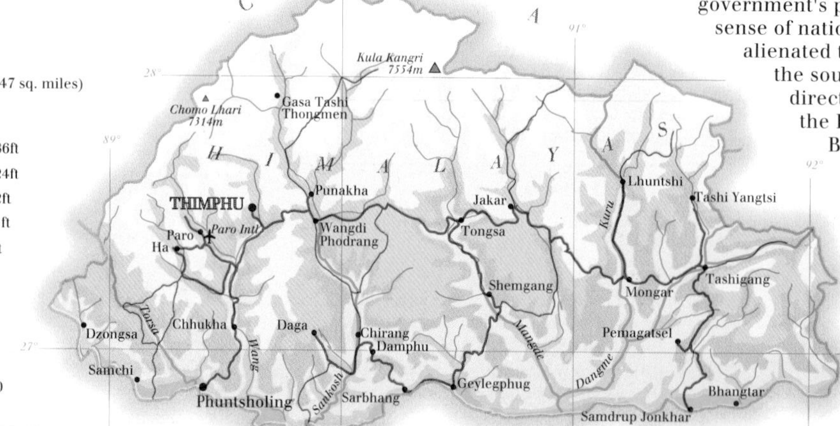

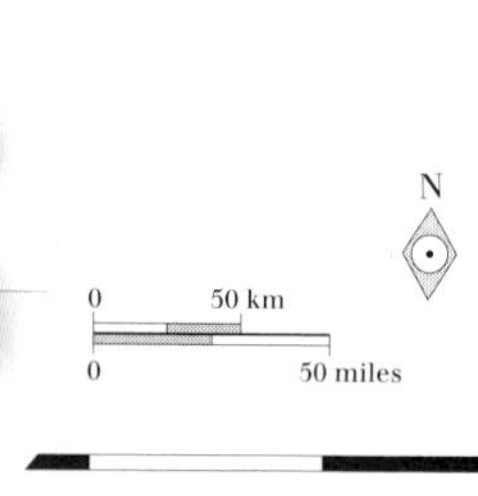

WORLD AFFAIRS

Bhutan's closest relations are with India. It also maintains cordial links with China, and negotiations to settle the China–Bhutan border have been progressing since 1984. Relations with Nepal are cool due to the Bhutan government's policy of sidelining its own ethnic Nepalese population.

AID

 $64m (receipts)

 Up 33% in 1991

Bhutan relies on foreign aid for about half of its annual budget. The largest single donor is India.

DEFENSE

 Small army; India effectively guarantees security

 Little change

Bhutan's 5,000-strong army, under the King's command, is trained by Indian military instructors. India provides *de facto* protection and would act to defend Bhutan against attack.

ECONOMICS

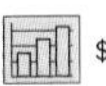 $260m

 31.39 ngultrum

SCORE CARD

❑ WORLD GNP RANKING	172nd
❑ GNP PER CAPITA	$163
❑ BALANCE OF PAYMENTS	$9.4m
❑ INFLATION	8.6%
❑ UNEMPLOYMENT	Low rate

STRENGTHS

New development of cash crops for Asian markets (cardamom, apples, oranges, apricots). Hardwoods in south, especially teak, but exploitation so far tightly controlled. Large hydroelectric potential.

WEAKNESSES

Dependence on Indian workers for many public sector jobs from road-building to teaching. 90% of population dependent on agriculture. Just 6% of land cultivated – expansion difficult because of steep mountain slopes. Very little industry. Few mineral resources.

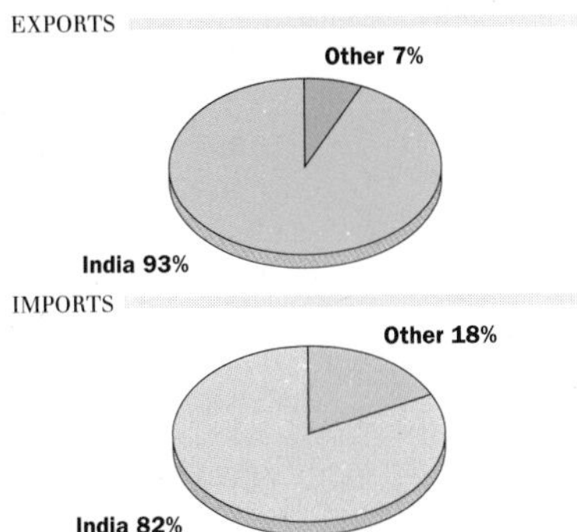

RESOURCES

 1.6bn kwh (capacity 350,000 kw)

 Not an oil producer and has no refineries

2,000 pigs, 1,000 cattle, 1,000 horses

Talc, gypsum, coal, limestone, slate, dolomite

Bhutan's forests remain largely intact and logging is severely controlled. Hydroelectric potential is considerable, but few dams have been built. Power is sold to India from the Chhukha Dam, bringing in substantial foreign earnings.

ENVIRONMENT

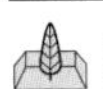 19% (18% partially protected)

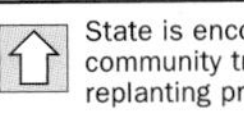 State is encouraging community tree-replanting projects

Bhutan's forests stabilize the steep mountainsides and supply 97% of all fuel needs. Road-building, which began in the 1960s, is the biggest cause of deforestation, which has led to topsoil erosion. The high northern pastures are at risk from over grazing by yaks. Traditional Buddhist values instilling respect for nature and forbidding the killing of animals are still observed.

MEDIA

 All media are controlled by the government

PUBLISHING AND BROADCAST MEDIA

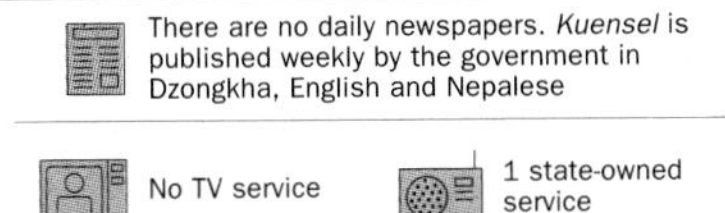

There are no daily newspapers. Kuensel is published weekly by the government in Dzongkha, English and Nepalese
No TV service
1 state-owned service

Bhutan has never had a TV service. TV is banned on the grounds that it would dilute Bhutanese values.

CRIME

 Bhutan does not publish prison figures

 Little variation from year to year

There is little violent crime and levels of theft are low. In 1991, *Driglam namzha*, an ancient code of conduct including the requirement to wear traditional dress, was revived, with fines or imprisonment for non-compliance.

EDUCATION

 38%

Education is free, but not compulsory – 5% of children attend secondary school. Teaching is in English and Dzongkha. There are no universities.

CHRONOLOGY

The Drukpa, originally from Tibet, united Bhutan in 1656. It lost the Duars Strip to British India in 1865.

- ❑ **1907** Monarchy established.
- ❑ **1953** National Assembly set up with some curbs on royal power.
- ❑ **1960** Breaks relations with China after Chinese annexation of Tibet.
- ❑ **1964** First surfaced road finished.
- ❑ **1968** King forms first cabinet.
- ❑ **1971** Joins UN.
- ❑ **1978** New links with China.
- ❑ **1990** Southern Bhutanese start violent campaign for minority rights. Modest privatization plans.

HEALTH

 1 per 9,700 people

 Diarrheal, respiratory diseases, tuberculosis malaria, infant deaths

Free clinics, and Thimpu's hospital, provide basic health care. Progress is being made in child immunization, and monks have recently been persuaded to teach hygiene. Infant mortality is high, at 13.3% of live births. Bhutanese, Tibetan and Chinese traditional medicines are widely practiced.

WEALTH

 Over 80% of people farm their own plots of land and herd cattle and yaks. Most live a subsistence existence

CONSUMER GOODS OWNERSHIP

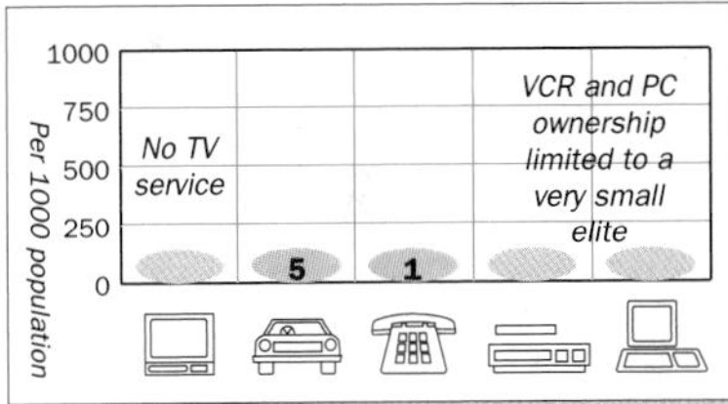

Most people are poor, but starvation is unknown. There is a small middle class of public employees and shop-owners.

WORLD RANKING

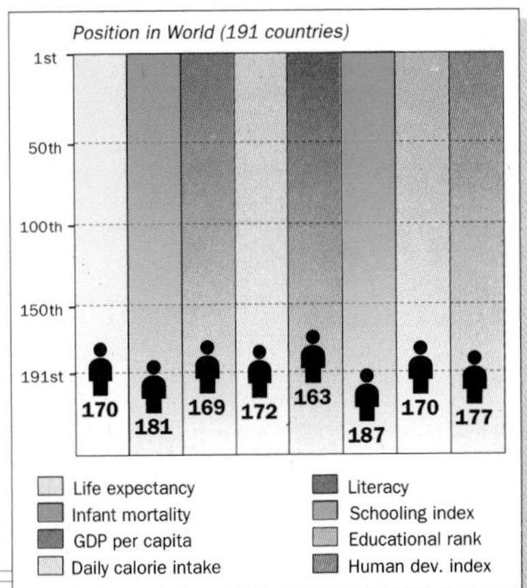

BOLIVIA

OFFICIAL NAME: Republic of Bolivia **CAPITAL:** La Paz
POPULATION: 7.4 million **CURRENCY:** Boliviano **OFFICIAL LANGUAGES:** Spanish, Quechua, and Aymara

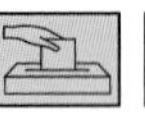

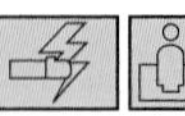

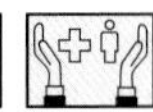

BOLIVIA LIES LANDLOCKED high in central South America. Over half of the population lives on the *altiplano*, the windswept plateau 11,484 ft. above sea level that sits between two ranges of the Andes Mountains. La Paz is the highest capital city in the world. Bolivia also has the world's highest golf course and ski run. The lowland regions in the east are tropical, sparsely populated and underdeveloped, although Santa Cruz, the main city, is growing fast. Bolivia remains one of the poorest nations in South America.

TOURISM

194,000 visitors

Up 16% in 1989

MAIN OVERSEAS ARRIVALS

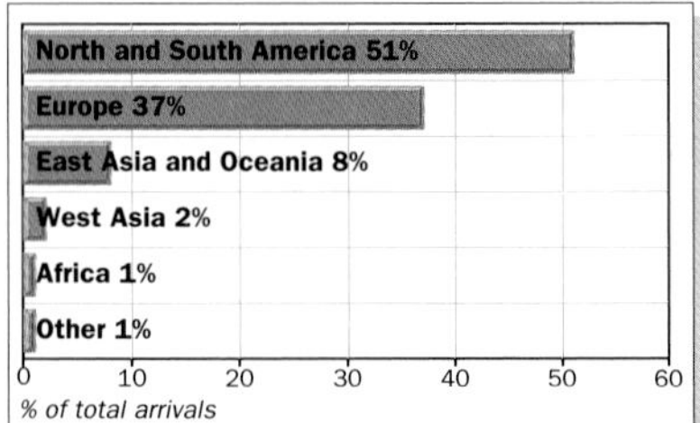

Foreign tourists are attracted mostly by the traditional festivals (especially the carnival in February or March), the variety of Bolivia's scenery, and its Spanish colonial architecture. Major attractions include the Silver Mountain at Potosí, and Lake Titicaca, the highest navigable lake in the world, covering an area of 3,463 sq mi. Recent political stability has encouraged some growth in tourism. The industry's potential is limited, however, by Bolivia's isolation, the rugged, inaccessible terrain and the limited infrastructure.

CLIMATE

WEATHER CHART

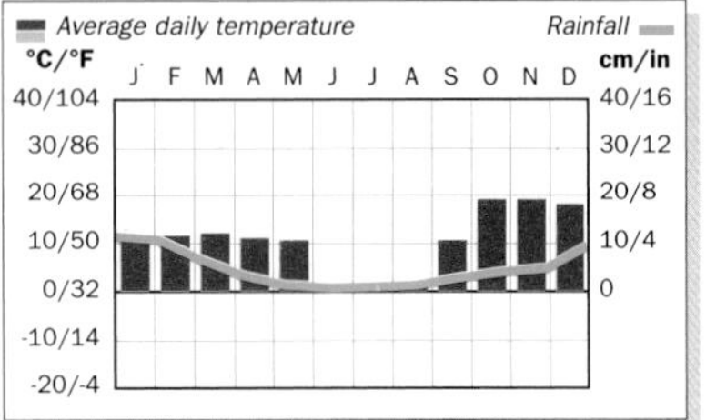

The Andean *altiplano* has an extreme tropical highland climate with frosts at night in winter. Annual rainfall in the west is only 10 in. The hot eastern lowlands receive most rain in summer.

Copacabana on the shores of Lake Titicaca. It lies on a large headland owned by Bolivia on the Peruvian side of the lake.

COMMUNICATIONS

El Alto, La Paz

1 ship
15,800 dwt

THE TRANSPORTATION NETWORK

25,356 miles (40,897 km)

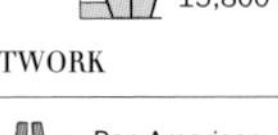
Pan-American Highway

2,264 miles (3,652 km)

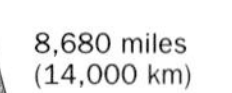
8,680 miles (14,000 km)

Landlocked Bolivia is badly connected. Obtaining port facilities on the Pacific coast and developing a Pacific–Atlantic railroad system, linking Bolivia with both seaboards, are major long-term aims.

***Potato harvest** on the* altiplano.
The government is encouraging migration to the more fertile lands in the east.

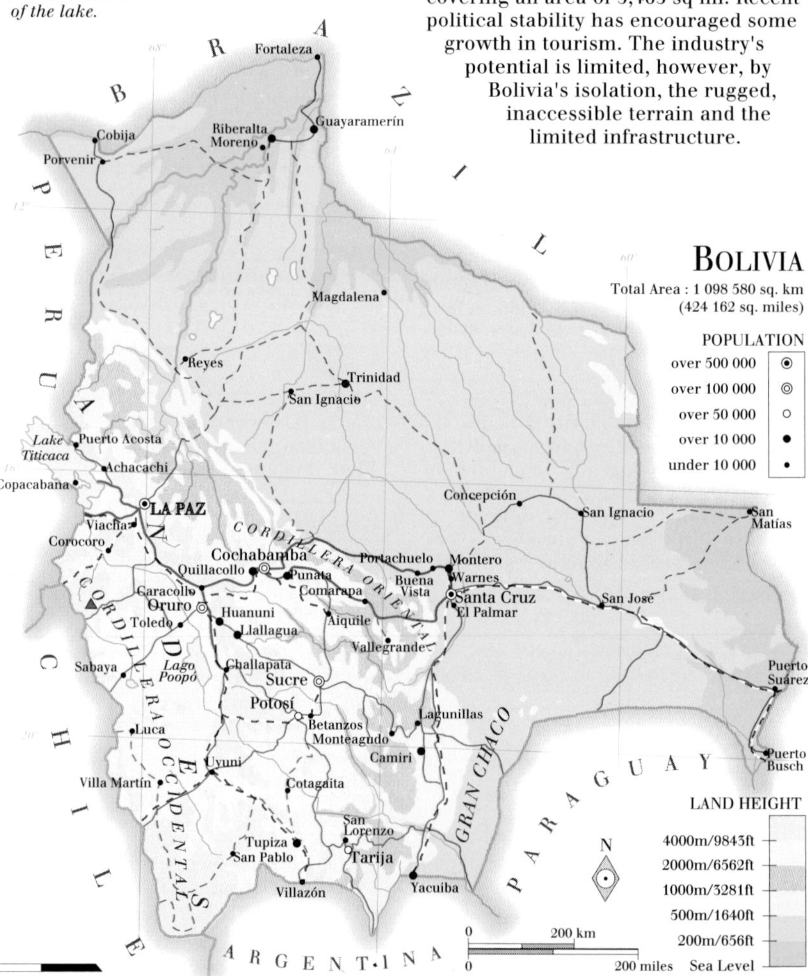

PEOPLE

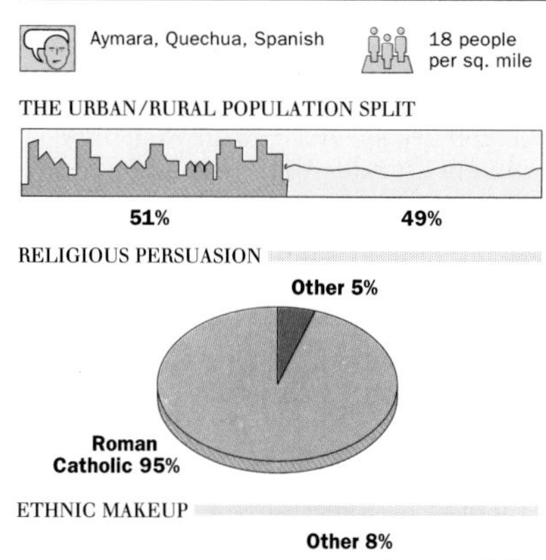

ETHNIC MAKEUP

Other 8%
Quechua 30%
European 10%
Aymara 25%
Mixed 27%

Two-thirds of Bolivia's population are indigenous, yet these groups suffer discrimination at most levels of society. The Aymara and Quechua lead an almost parallel existence and do not take part in the political process or the formal economy, which remain under the control of a few wealthy city families who established their position during Spanish colonial rule. Most Bolivians are poor and many are subsistence farmers or miners. In recent years, the state has been encouraging people to settle in the Santa Cruz region. In addition to Bolivians from the *altiplano*, Asians, South Africans and a few Mennonite communities have migrated there.

Family life tends to be close-knit; Roman Catholic influence and extended family ties among indigenous groups remain strong. Women have low status in Bolivia, particularly in Aymara and Quechua communities.

POPULATION AGE BREAKDOWN

% of population by age group

	1960	1970	1980	1990	2000
65+	3.2%	3.3%	3.4%	3.6%	4.2%
15–64	53.9%	53.8%	53.4%	55%	57.7%
0–14	42.9%	42.9%	43.2%	41.4%	38.1%

WORLD AFFAIRS

Bolivia's main foreign policy concern is its attempt to negotiate an outlet to the Pacific with Peru and Chile. Relations with the USA are complicated. The USA is Bolivia's main source of aid, a key part of the national economy. Aid payments have, however, been made conditional on Bolivia taking measures to destroy the cocaine producing and trafficking industry, itself a major buttress of the Bolivian economy. The result to date has been a balancing act. Military attacks on the cocaine barons have kept US aid flowing, yet Bolivia remains the world's second largest producer of refined cocaine.

Bolivia is strengthening its regional links, particularly with Argentina and Brazil. It is a strong supporter of the idea of a South American common market. As one of the most isolated and poorest economies in South America, it would be the major beneficiary of a tariff-free zone in the Andean region.

Left-wing *MIR* ***leader*** *and president until 1993, Jaime Paz Zamora.*

President Gonzalo Sánchez *de Lozada, MNR leader, took power in 1993.*

POLITICS

Lower House 1997
Upper House 1997

President Gonzalo Sánchez de Lozada

THE STATE OF THE PARTIES

Chamber of Deputies 130 members

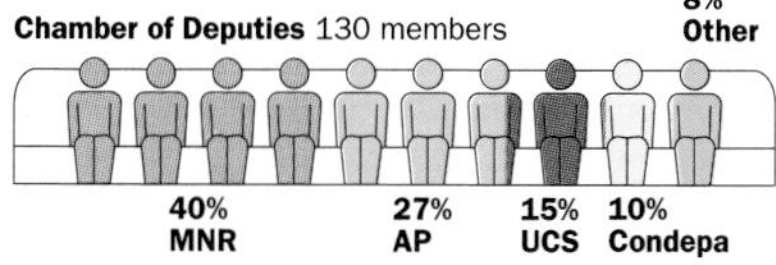

MNR = National Revolutionary Movement **AP** = Patriotic Accord (composed of: ADN = Democratic Nationalist Action, MIR = Movement of the Revolutionary Left) **UCS** = Civic Solidarity Union **Condepa** = Conscience of the Fatherland

Senate 27 members

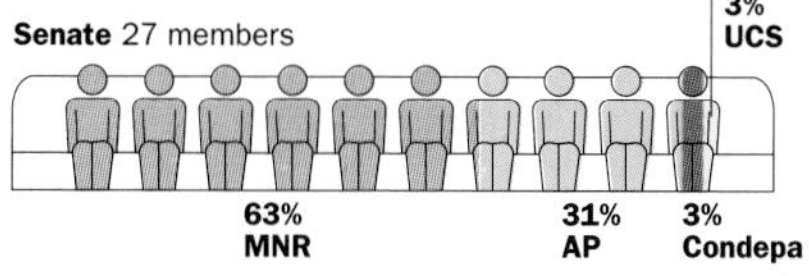

Bolivia is a multiparty democracy.

Main Political Issues

Privatization

Sánchez de Lozada's government is continuing the privatization and free-market economic policies of its predecessors, including the sale of 150 state-owned companies, and the privatization of the mining industry through joint ventures.

Cocaine

Cocaine barons are highly influential in Bolivia, the world's second largest exporter (after Colombia) of refined cocaine. The government is trying to trim the drug barons' power by encouraging new cash crops to replace coca, but with limited success. Cocaine has become a significant, though illegal, foreign exchange earner for Bolivia.

Profile

Between independence from Spain in 1825 and the early 1980s, Bolivia experienced, on average, more than one armed coup a year. The cycle ended in 1982 when, unable to control a general strike, the military agreed to return power to a national congress. Full elections were delayed until 1985.

Behind the scenes, the military and the cocaine barons continue to enjoy influence. The latter, whose profits underpin the whole economy, are frequently implicated in political corruption scandals. They are also the main backers of Max Fernández, the leader of the populist Civic Solidarity Union (UCS), who almost won the presidential elections in June 1993. The pattern of politics remains one of similar parties competing for power in unstable coalitions. The miners' union, the COB, is no longer a political force and will be weakened further by the privatization of the mines.

The congressional elections of 1993 brought the right-wing MNR to power, replacing a left-wing coalition. Policies have changed little, however, and prospects for Bolivia's poor and underemployed remain bleak.

CHRONOLOGY

The Aymara civilization was conquered by the Incas in the late 1400s. Fifty years later, the Incas were defeated by the *conquistadores* and Upper Peru, as it became, was governed by Spain from Lima.

- **1545** Cerro Rico, the Silver Mountain, discovered at Potosí. Provides Spain with vast wealth.
- **1776** Upper Peru becomes part of Viceroyalty of Río de la Plata centered on Buenos Aires.
- **1809** Simón Bolívar inspires first revolutionary uprisings in Latin America at Chuquisaca (Sucre), La Paz and Cochabamba, but they fail.
- **1824** Spaniards suffer final defeat by Bolívar's general, José de Sucre.
- **1825** Independence.
- **1836–1839** Union with Peru fails under presidency of Andrés de Santa Cruz. Internal disorder ensues as wealthy local *caudillos* vie for power.

⇨

B

CHRONOLOGY *continued*

- **1864–1871** Mariano Melgarejo's ruthless rule. Three Indian revolts at seizure of ancestral lands.
- **1879–1883** War of the Pacific. Peru helps Bolivia against Chile, which had invaded nitrate-rich Atacama province. Chile wins. Bolivia is left landlocked.
- **1880–1930** Period of stable Liberal–Conservative governments. Exports from revived mining industry bring prosperity.
- **1903** Rubber-rich Acre province ceded to Brazil after conflict.
- **1914** Republican Party founded.
- **1920** Indian rebellion.
- **1923** Miners bloodily suppressed.
- **1932–1935** Chaco War with Paraguay. Bolivia loses three-quarters of Chaco. Rise of radicalism and labor movement.
- **1951** Víctor Paz Estenssoro of NMR elected president. Military coup.
- **1952** Revolution. Paz Estenssoro and NMR brought back. Land reforms improve Indians' status. Education reforms, universal suffrage, nationalization of tin mines.
- **1964** Military takes over in coup.
- **1967** Che Guevara killed while trying to mobilize Bolivian workers.
- **1969–1979** Military regimes rule with increasing severity. 1979 coup fails. Interim civilian rule.
- **1980** Indecisive elections. Military takes over again.
- **1982** President-elect Dr. Siles Zuazo finally heads leftist civilian MIR government. Inflation 24,000%.
- **1985** Paz Estenssoro's MNR wins elections. Austerity measures. Annual inflation down to 20%.
- **1986** Tin market collapses. 21,000 miners laid off.
- **1988** Anti-narcotics body set up.
- **1989** MIR take power in close-run elections. President Paz Zamora makes pact with 1970s dictator Gen. Hugo Bánzer, head of ADN.
- **1990** 1.6m hectares of rainforest recognized as Indian territory.
- **1992** Strikes halt plans to privatize mining industry.
- **1993** MNR voted back to power.

AID

$473m (receipts)

Large amounts of aid come from the USA, but depend on Bolivia making efforts to eradicate coca farms. Smaller amounts are provided by West European countries. Particularly impoverished rural areas receive project aid from Western NGOs, charities and religious organizations. Corruption and inefficiency, however, hinder the implementation of many projects.

DEFENSE

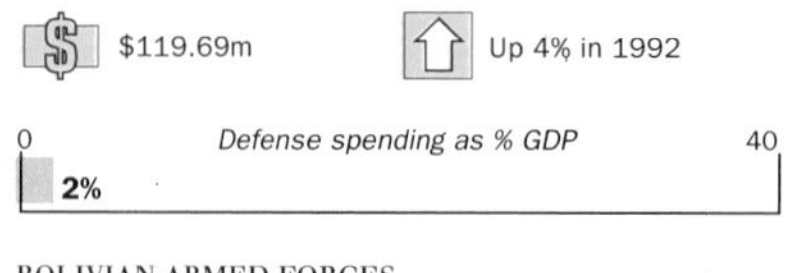

BOLIVIAN ARMED FORCES

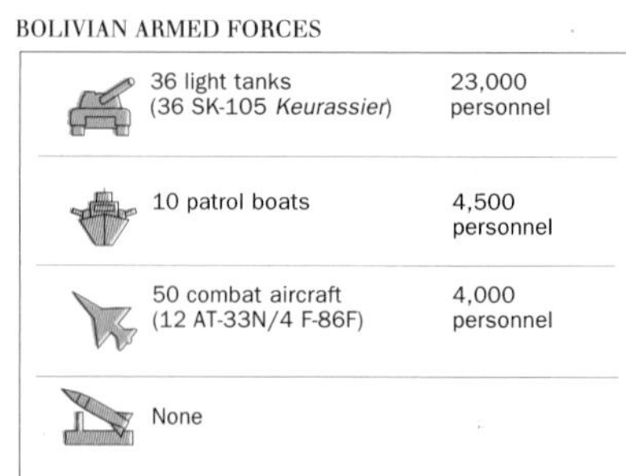

36 light tanks
(36 SK-105 *Keurassier*)
23,000
personnel
10 patrol boats
4,500
personnel
50 combat aircraft
(12 AT-33N/4 F-86F)
4,000
personnel
None

The military has not actively interfered in politics for over a decade – a record for Bolivia. The army is the main focus of defense spending, with weaponry bought almost entirely from the USA. The Bolivian navy consists mainly of gunboats on Lake Titicaca, which borders Peru, and on the Pilcomayo River. The army has worked with US forces against the cocaine business, although many US advisers have suggested that by-passing the Bolivian armed forces would make the operation more effective. The main, but unrealizable, ambition of the military is to recapture territory that would allow Bolivia access to the Pacific. Military service lasts for one year.

ECONOMICS

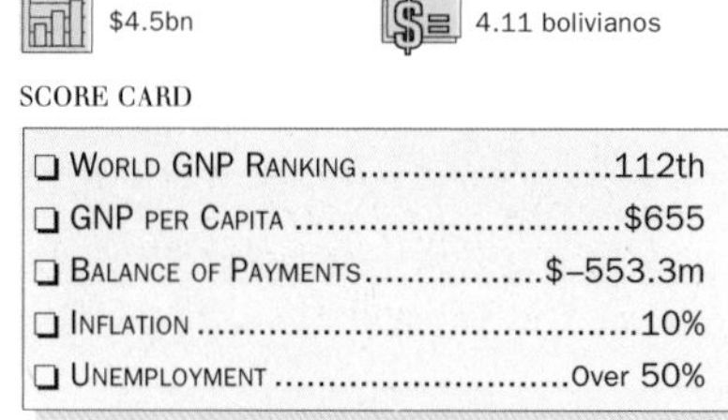

SCORE CARD

World GNP Ranking	112th
GNP per Capita	$655
Balance of Payments	$-553.3m
Inflation	10%
Unemployment	Over 50%

EXPORTS

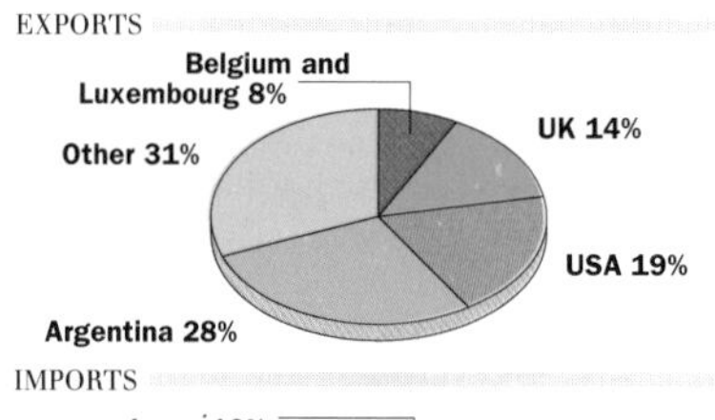

IMPORTS

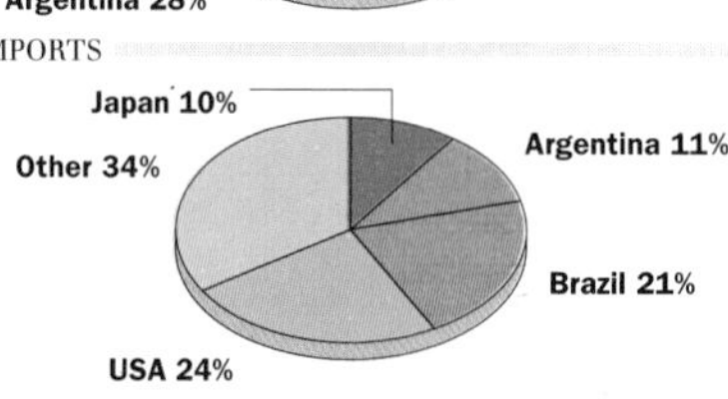

Strengths

Mineral riches: gold, silver, zinc and tin. Newly discovered oil and natural gas deposits.

Weaknesses

Bolivia's extreme poverty has created political instability. Although inflation has been reduced to around 10% annually, a history of hyperinflation – a severe problem until the late 1980s – still deters investors.

Profile

Traditionally, the state has used earnings from the public-owned mining sector to control the economy. Since 1985, however, successive governments have sold off state-owned companies and encouraged joint ventures and private investment in an attempt not only to modernize mining and other state sectors, but also to bring inflation under control and curb foreign debt. Bolivia's medium-term economic prospects have been boosted by the recent discovery of oil and gas fields, which should add a useful foreign exchange earner to the economy. However, there is little prospect of developing a significant industrial base. Overseas investors remain deterred by Bolivia's political instability, the social problems of extreme poverty, and the influence of cocaine barons.

ECONOMIC PERFORMANCE INDICATOR

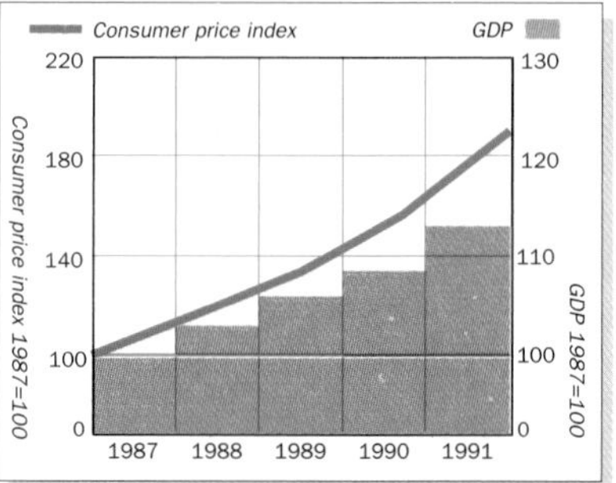

BOLIVIA : MAJOR BUSINESSES

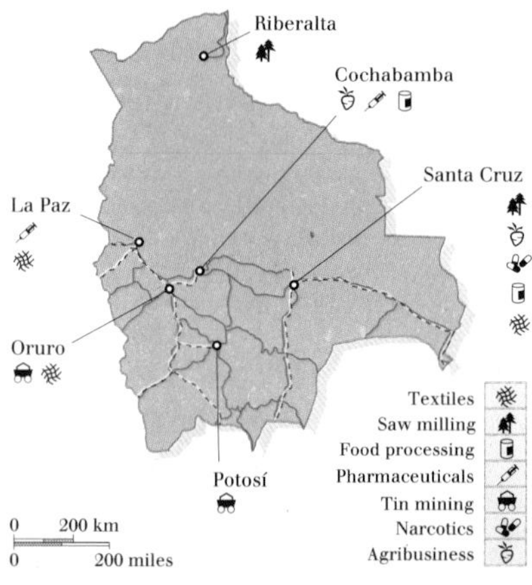

RESOURCES

1.9bn kwh (capacity 740,000 kw)

21,300 b/d (reserves 112,136,000 bbl)

12m sheep, 5m cattle, 2m pigs, 630,000 asses

Tin, natural gas, oil, zinc, tungsten, gold, antimony, silver, lead

ELECTRICITY GENERATION

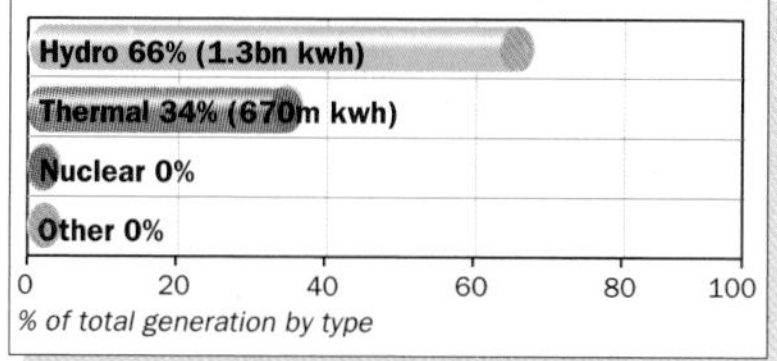

Bolivia is the world's largest tin producer. The government is eager to allow foreign companies to prospect for more oil, and to increase sales of natural gas to Brazil and Argentina.

BOLIVIA : LAND USE

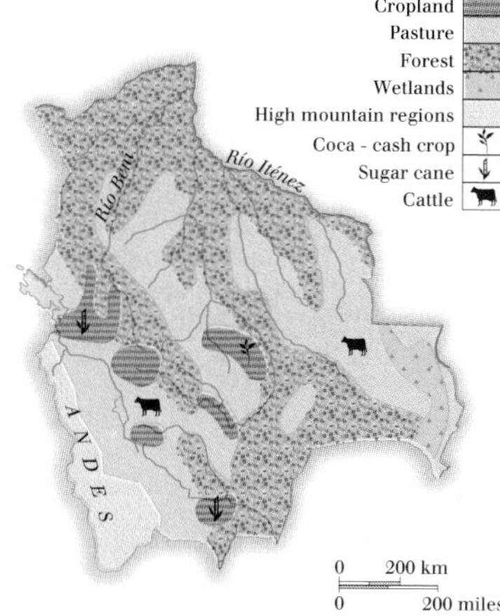

ENVIRONMENT

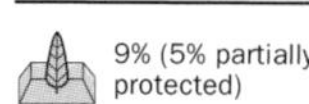

9% (5% partially protected)

No effective controls on exports of rare species

ENVIRONMENTAL TREATIES

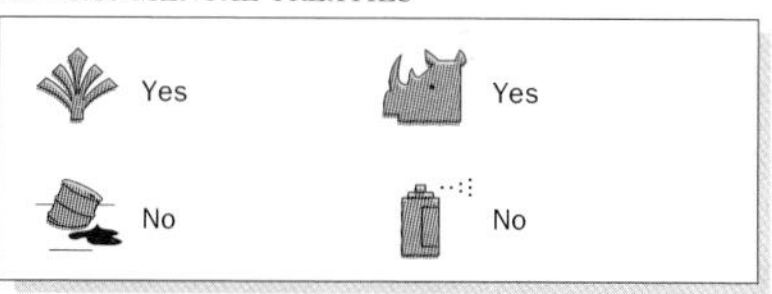

Deforestation is Bolivia's major ecological problem. Land clearances are occurring at the record rate of 200,000 hectares a year. This is one of the world's highest annual depletion rates. Much of the cleared land is turned over to cattle ranching or the growing of coca. The overuse of pesticides and fertilizers in the coca business is also a concern. The industry is effectively uncontrolled and rivers in Amazonia have high pollution levels.

Pollution problems are compounded by waste chemicals used in minerals industries. Mercury, used in the extraction of silver, has been found in dangerous quantities in river systems.

MEDIA

Little formal censorship, but local journalists rarely comment on the drug business for fear of reprisals

PUBLISHING AND BROADCAST MEDIA

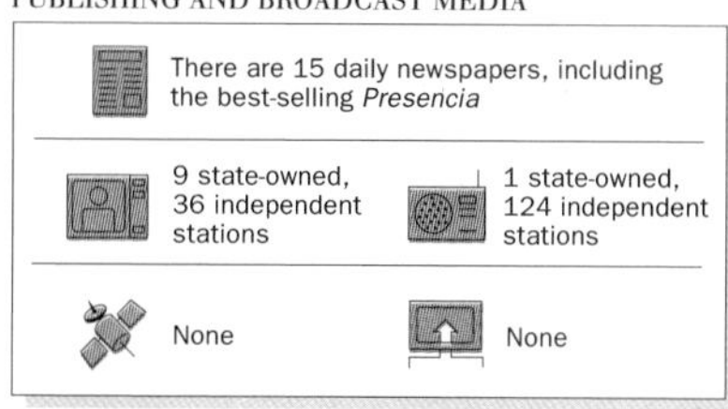

There are 15 daily newspapers, including the best-selling *Presencia*
9 state-owned, 36 independent stations
1 state-owned, 124 independent stations
None
None

Bolivia has the largest number of TV stations in South America. Political parties and cocaine barons frequently exert pressure on the media.

CRIME

Bolivia does not publish prison figures

Crime is rising in drug-trafficking centers

CRIME RATES

General crime levels are relatively low in urban areas. Bolivians are concerned about the increase in violence associated with the drug trade

Violent crime is centered on the drug-trafficking towns in the eastern lowlands, particularly Santa Cruz. However, the main cities are much safer for tourists, and have lower crime rates than cities in neighboring Peru, for example. The Bolivian police and army have a reputation for mistreating poor farmers and miners.

EDUCATION

63%

Education spending as % GNP (0–25): 2.3%

THE EDUCATION SYSTEM

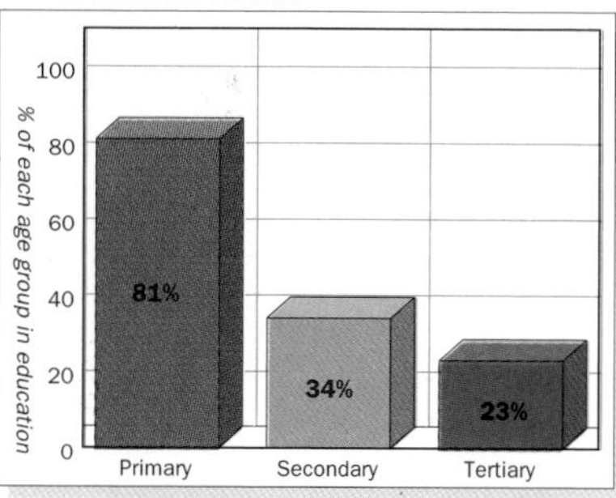

Education is based on a combination of the French and US systems. Although the majority of the population speaks indigenous languages, most teaching is in Spanish. Bolivia has one of the lowest literacy rates on the continent. Only the 51% of the population who live in towns receive schooling.

HEALTH

1 per 2,100 people

Influenza, tuberculosis, other communicable diseases, malaria

Health spending as % GNP (0–25): 0.4%

Bolivia has one of the lowest numbers of doctors per capita in Latin America. Only half the children under one year old are immunized, and diseases that are preventable by vaccination are a major cause of death. Approximately half of the population of Bolivia has safe drinking water. Rural areas are barely served in terms of medical care.

WEALTH

Miner, 695 bolivianos per month; aircraft engine mechanic, 3,086 bolivianos per month

CONSUMER GOODS OWNERSHIP

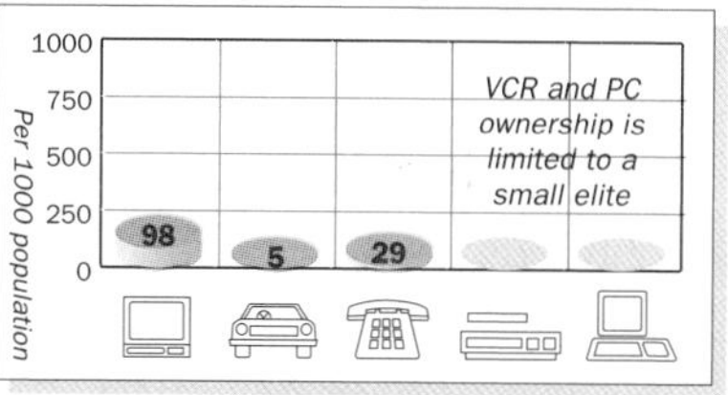

There is little social mobility in Bolivia; the main routes for advancement are the armed forces or the cocaine business. Generally, the indigenous peoples who form the rural poor are the worst off. The Andean highlands are extremely poor; economic growth is concentrated in the fertile, tropical eastern lowlands, where the population density is lowest.

The small number of wealthy Bolivian vacation in Brazil or Miami. German luxury goods, and Mercedes cars in particular, are popular among Bolivians and the small German immigrant population. A recent reduction in tariff barriers has resulted in an increase in the import and sale of electronic goods.

WORLD RANKING

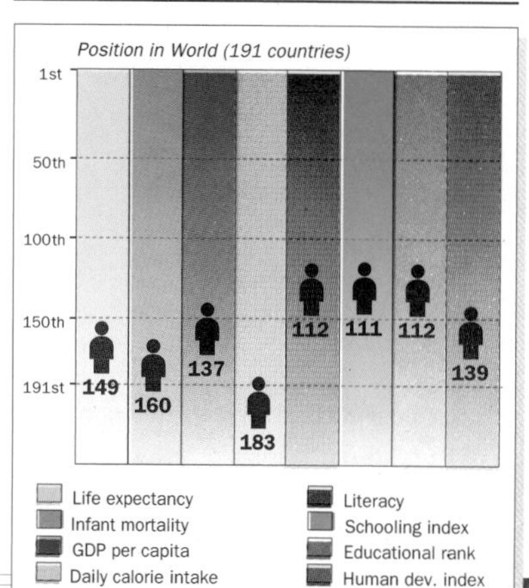

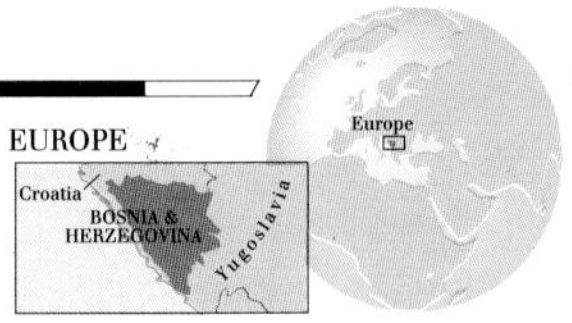

B

Bosnia & Herzegovina

Official Name: The Republic of Bosnia and Herzegovina **Capital:** Sarajevo
Population: 4.2 million **Currency:** Bosnian dinar **Official Language:** Serbo-Croatian

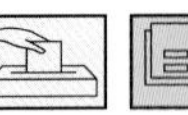
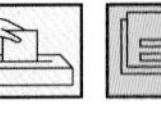

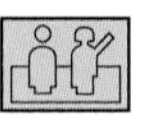

A MOUNTAINOUS COUNTRY with a few miles of coast on the Adriatic Sea, Bosnia is bordered by Croatia, Serbia and Montenegro. Between 1943 and 1990, the Yugoslavian regime largely prevented conflict between Muslims, Croats and Serbs by allowing cultural freedom. Since April 1992, however, the three main ethnic populations of the dissolved Yugoslavia have fought over Bosnia. Tens of thousands have died and many historic cities have been destroyed.

CLIMATE

WEATHER CHART

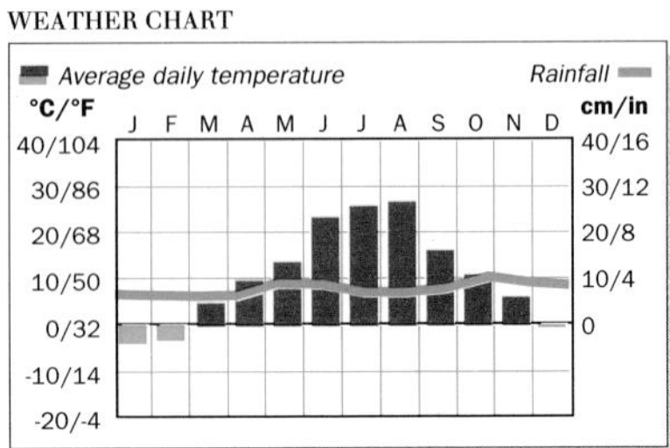

Bosnia has a continental climate with warm summers and bitterly cold winters, often with snow.

COMMUNICATIONS

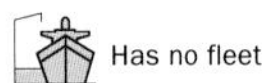

THE TRANSPORTATION NETWORK

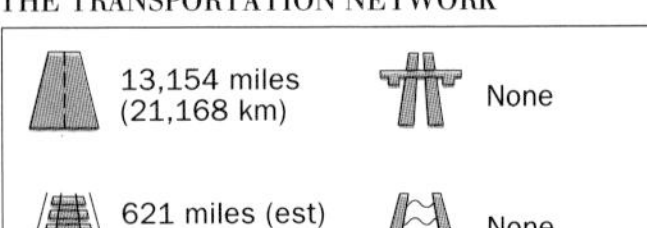

War has severely damaged the communications network, resulting in wrecked bridges, roads and railroads. The capital, Sarajevo, was formerly the focus of all national and international communications networks.

TOURISM

None

No tourism likely until peace settlement

MAIN OVERSEAS ARRIVALS

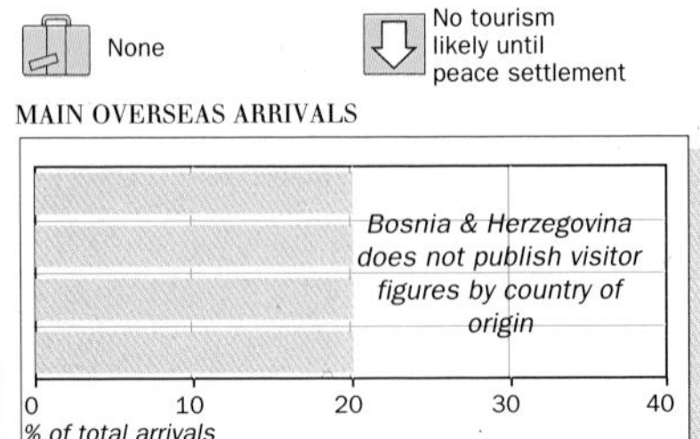

Despite having hosted the 1984 Winter Olympics, Bosnia has not developed the infrastructure for a tourist industry.

PEOPLE

Serbo-Croatian

212 people per sq. mile

THE URBAN/RURAL POPULATION SPLIT

36% 64%

RELIGIOUS PERSUASION

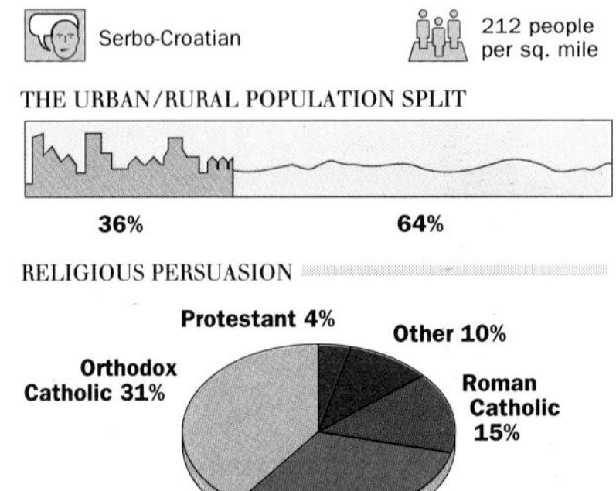

Before the war, the population was 44% ethnic Bosnian (mostly Muslim), 31% Serb, 17% Croat and 8% originally from other parts of former Yugoslavia. Intermarriage was common and ethnic violence rare. Society was largely secular and materialistic. In the aftermath of secession, cultural differences became a basis for dividing society in order to lay claim to other ethnic groups' wealth.

POLITICS

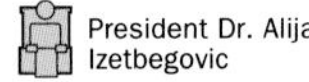

THE STATE OF THE PARTIES

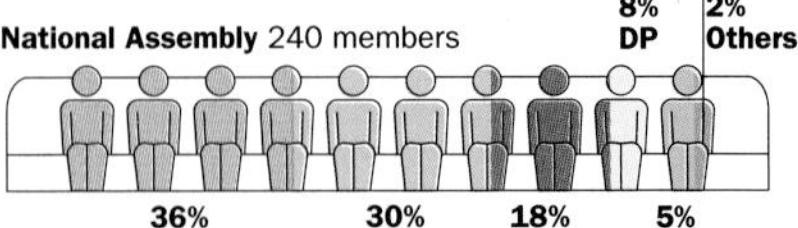

PDA = Party of Democratic Action **SDP** = Serbian Democratic Party **CDU–BH** = Croatian Democratic Union of Bosnia and Herzegovina **DP** = Socialist Democratic Party **ARF** = Alliance of Reform Forces

The Serbian and Croatian parties have withdrawn from the National Assembly since the outbreak of civil war

The electoral defeat of the Yugoslavian Communist Party in 1990 resulted in a coalition of the Muslim PDA, the Serbian SDP and the Croatian CDU–BH. Disputes soon broke out between Serbs and Croats. Backed by the Serb-dominated Yugoslav People's Army, Bosnian Serb territories declared autonomy and allegiance to Serbia. The PDA and CDU–BH then declared Bosnia a sovereign state. Civil war broke out between the three groups in 1992. The Serbs, led by Radovan Karadzic, are the strongest force, and have received most international blame. In 1993, an uneasy truce was reached between the SDP and CDU–BH. Conflict between the PDA and SDP continues. In 1994, the UN tried to contain the fighting by declaring key Muslim towns "safe areas" and by sponsoring peace talks.

Bosnia & Herzegovina

Total Area : 51 130 sq. km (19 741 sq. miles)

POPULATION
- over 100 000
- over 50 000
- over 10 000
- under 10 000

LAND HEIGHT
- 2000m/6562ft
- 1000m/3281ft
- 500m/1640ft
- 200m/656ft
- Sea Level

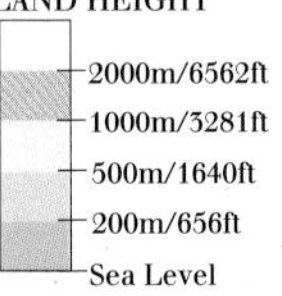

B

WORLD AFFAIRS

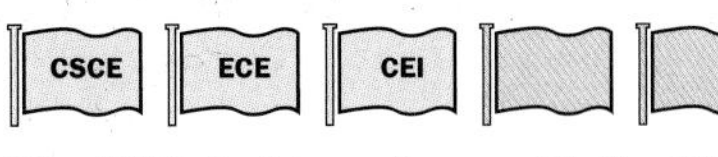

The UN failed to end war with the 1992 Vance-Owen plan for three autonomous communities. NATO threats of air strikes and Russian diplomatic pressure on the Serbs may be the best hope for peace.

AID

 $696m (receipts) in first six months of 1994

 Likely to need increasing amounts of aid

Humanitarian aid has been crucial to the survival of many Bosnians, with the UN playing a vital role in distributing relief. Its Inter-Agency Appeal raised $696 million in the first half of 1994, mainly for Bosnian Muslim refugees, but also for those in Serbia, Montenegro, Macedonia and Croatia.

DEFENSE

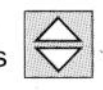 Almost all state spending is on arms

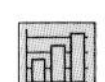 No likely change until peace

It has been estimated that the Muslim government controls 60,000 lightly armed troops and 120,000 reservists. The "Serbian Republic of Bosnia" has 80,000 troops, backed by heavy weapons, and the Croats have 50,000.

ECONOMICS

 $4bn (pre-war)

751.22 Bosnian dinars

SCORE CARD

- ❑ WORLD GNP RANKING........................116th
- ❑ GNP PER CAPITA..........................*The formal*
- ❑ BALANCE OF PAYMENTS..............*economy now*
- ❑ INFLATION.............................*operates under*
- ❑ UNEMPLOYMENT.......................*war conditions*

STRENGTHS

Before 1991, Bosnia was home to five of former Yugoslavia's largest companies. Retail outlets were mostly privately operated and there was a sizable small-business sector. Rising unemployment was the one economic problem. The country has the potential to become a thriving market economy, with a solid manufacturing base.

WEAKNESSES

Enormous foreign investment is needed to repair war damage to infrastructure and the industrial sector.

EXPORTS/IMPORTS

Bosnia & Herzegovina has no significant exports. Most imports are in the form of UN aid and arms from the international market. Oil imports are probably from the Middle East.

RESOURCES

 Output down by 85% owing to war

 Not an oil producer

 11.5m poultry, 1.4m sheep, 884,000 cattle, 608,000 pigs

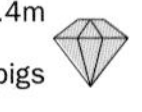 Coal, lignite, iron, bauxite, cement

Bosnia's land is not well suited to agriculture, but has mineral deposits, forests and hydroelectric potential.

ENVIRONMENT

 None owing to war

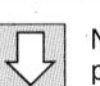 No initiatives possible

Apart from war damage, Bosnia faces the effects of industrial pollution incurred during the communist regime.

MEDIA

 Censorship imposed due to war

PUBLISHING AND BROADCAST MEDIA

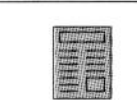 There are two daily newspapers. *Oslobodjenje (Liberation)* has appeared every day since the start of the war

 3 state-run, some independent services

 3 state-run, some independent services

Between secession and war, Bosnia had an independent press with no censorship. The Muslim government has since engaged US p.r. firms to shape media coverage of the war.

CRIME

 Bosnia does not publish prison figures

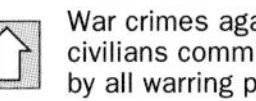

All sides in the civil war have been implicated in human rights abuses, in particular the "ethnic cleansing" of towns and villages, whereby entire populations are forced to evacuate their homes to avoid murder, rape and torture. Army officers have been accused of exploiting their power by running mafia-style operations.

EDUCATION

 93%

Formerly obligatory for eight years, education at all levels has been disrupted or suspended by the war.

***The Muslim town of Mostar.** Its 16th-century bridge at a strategic river crossing and much of the old town have been destroyed by war.*

CHRONOLOGY

Following the defeat in 1943 of the Nazi-backed Croat Ustasa regime by communist partisans led by Tito, Bosnia Herzegovina became one of Yugoslavia's six republics.

- ❑ **1990** Nationalists defeat communists in multiparty elections. PDA leader Dr. Alija Izetbegovic is president.
- ❑ **1991** Serbs declare "Autonomous regions." Parliament announces republican sovereignty.
- ❑ **1992** EC and USA recognize Bosnia. Serbs announce "Serbian Republic." Civil war between Muslims, Croats and Serbs begins. UN sends troops to guard aid convoys.
- ❑ **1994** NATO threat of air strikes on Serbs attacking UN "safe areas."

HEALTH

 War has led to an exodus of doctors

 Cholera and diphtheria epidemics, violence, deaths from war-stress

War has placed an enormous strain on an underfunded service. Thousands have died for lack of basic treatment.

WEALTH

 Most salaries have been eroded by hyperinflation. By 1993, one million people had been displaced by the war and one million had fled Bosnia

CONSUMER GOODS OWNERSHIP

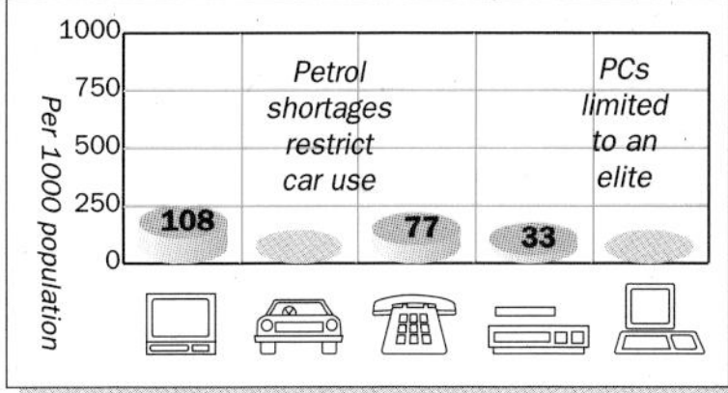

The only people currently acquiring wealth in Bosnia are those involved in profiteering and extortion.

WORLD RANKING

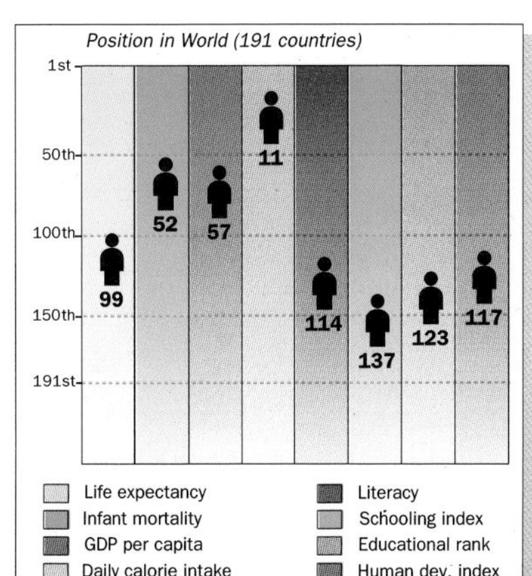

B

BOTSWANA

SOUTHERN AFRICA

Africa

Namibia Zimbabwe BOTSWANA S. Africa

OFFICIAL NAME: Republic of Botswana **CAPITAL:** Gaborone
POPULATION: 1.3 million **CURRENCY:** Pula **OFFICIAL LANGUAGE:** English

ARID AND LANDLOCKED, Botswana's central plateau separates the populous eastern grasslands from the Kalahari Desert and swamps of the Okavango Delta in the west. Botswana is a multiparty democracy, but the Botswana Democratic Party has won every election since independence. Diamonds provide Botswana with a prosperous economy, but rain is an even more precious resource, honored in the name of the currency, *pula*.

***The Okavango Delta.** Plans to draw water from it for irrigation were shelved in 1991 in the interests of wildlife conservation.*

CLIMATE

WEATHER CHART

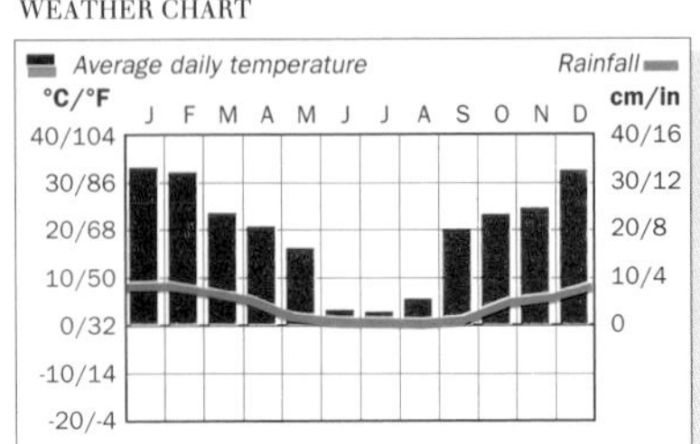

Botswana's subtropical climate is dry and prone to drought. Rainfall declines from 25 in. in the north to under 4 in. in the Kalahari Desert in the west.

COMMUNICATIONS

Sir Seretse Khama Intl, Gaborone
168,000 passengers

Has no fleet

THE TRANSPORTATION NETWORK

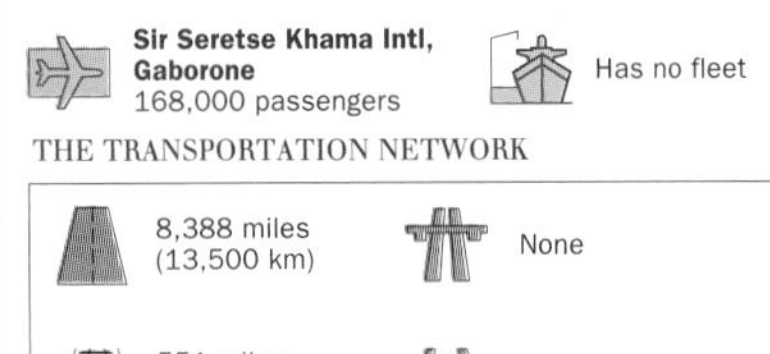

The opening of the trans-Kalahari road to Namibia in 1994 means that Botswana is no longer dependent on South African ports. Upgrading existing road and rail networks is now a priority.

TOURISM

844,295 visitors

Up 22% in 1990

MAIN OVERSEAS ARRIVALS

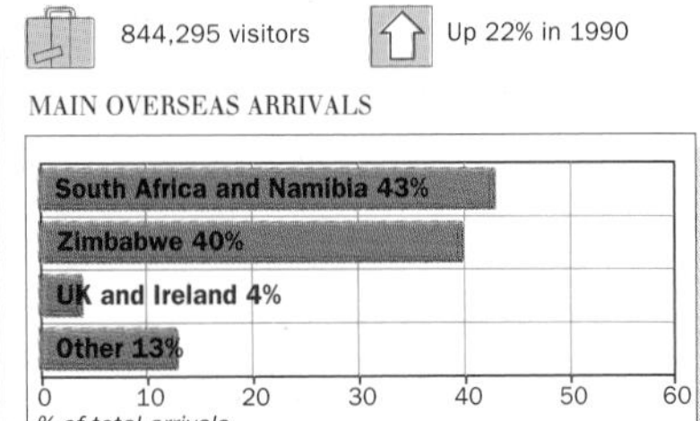

Tourism is aimed at wealthy wildlife enthusiasts and focuses on safaris, especially to the Okavango Delta.

PEOPLE

Tswana, English, Shona, San, Khoikhoi, Ndebele

5 people per sq. mile

THE URBAN/RURAL POPULATION SPLIT

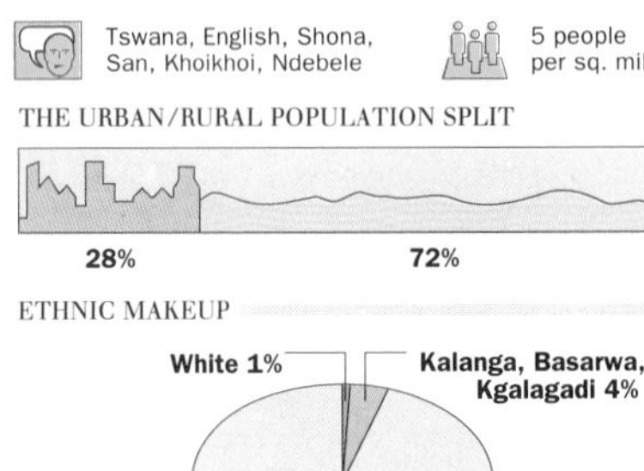

ETHNIC MAKEUP

White 1%
Kalanga, Basarwa, Kgalagadi 4%
Tswana 95%

Botswana's stability reflects its ethnic homogeneity and the continuing importance of traditional forms of authority, notably the village *kgotla*, or parliament. The Tswana make up 95% of the population, with the Bamangwato forming the largest Tswana group. Botswana's first inhabitants, the San, or Kalahari Bushmen, have been marginalized. Whites dominate the professional sector.

POLITICS

1999

President Ketumile Joni Masire

THE STATE OF THE PARTIES

National Assembly 40 members

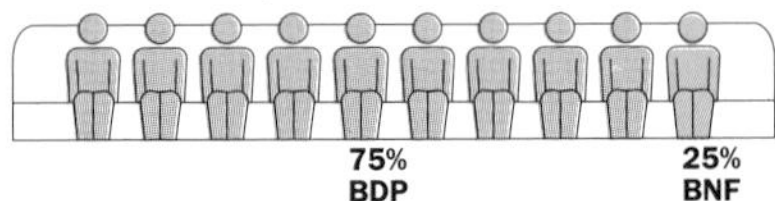

BDP = Botswana Democratic Party **BNF** = Botswana National Front

House of Chiefs 15 members

Comprises the chiefs of the 8 principal tribes, 4 sub-chiefs and 3 members elected by the other members of the House

Formally a multiparty democracy, Botswana has been ruled by a single elected party, the BDP, since independence. In 1991, opposition parties, led by the BNF, formed the Botswana People's Progressive Front (BPPF) to fight the next elections. Economic problems and a string of corruption scandals led to a decline in support for the BDP at elections in 1994. The opposition BPPF increased its seats in the National Assembly from 3 to 13.

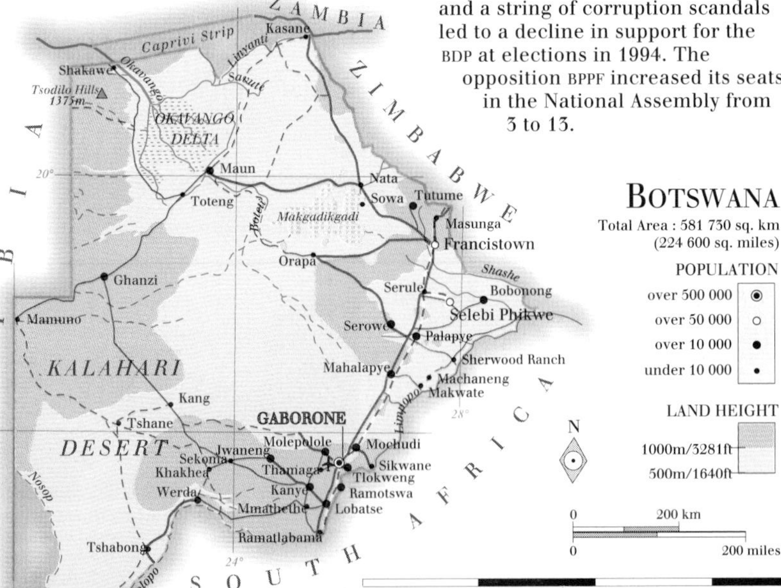

B

WORLD AFFAIRS

Having been at the receiving end of South African destabilization during the 1980s, Botswana's main concern is the republic's progress to democracy and the possible spillover effects of any breakdown in the process. Potential South African domination of the SADC is another fear. Relations with the UK and USA are important internationally.

AID

 $135m (receipts) 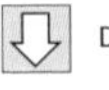 Down 9% in 1991

Botswana's political and economic record has made it a favored aid recipient, notably from the EU, UK, USA and World Bank. Environmental projects aiming to balance wildlife needs with rural development are the priority; 90% of EU aid is environment linked. Transportation also receives aid.

DEFENSE

 $130.9m  Up 19% in 1990

The Botswana Defense Force budget has increased steadily since 1987. This reflects concern over South Africa and ties between army chiefs and the BDP.

ECONOMICS

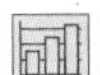 $3.6bn  2.54 pula

SCORE CARD

- ❑ WORLD GNP RANKING........................119th
- ❑ GNP PER CAPITA $2,769
- ❑ BALANCE OF PAYMENTS $47.4m
- ❑ INFLATION 15%
- ❑ UNEMPLOYMENT..................................25%

STRENGTHS

Diamonds: transformed Botswana from subsistence to middle-income economy in 25 years; world's third-largest producer. High economic growth, averaging 11.3% a year in 1980s. Prudent economic management. Large financial reserves. Copper, nickel, beef.

WEAKNESSES

Overdependence on diamonds (80% of export earnings; 50% of GNP). Weak agriculture and industry. Small population, water shortages and drought add to diversification problems. Adverse impact of beef industry on environment. High transportation costs to coast.

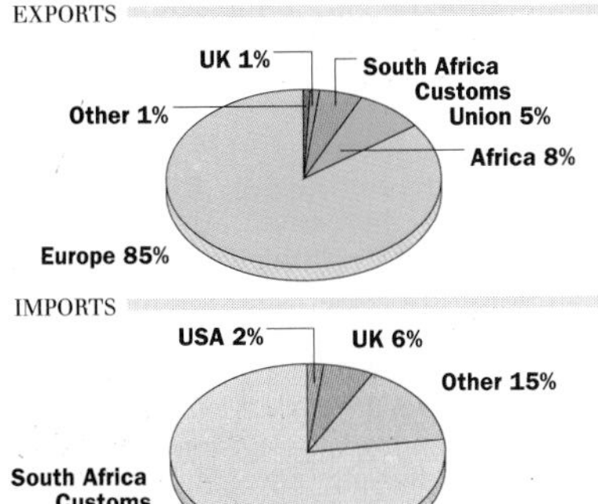

RESOURCES

Energy derived from fuelwood and coal  Not an oil producer and has no refineries

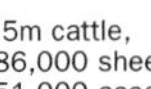 2.5m cattle, 286,000 sheep, 151,000 asses

Diamonds, copper, coal, nickel, soda ash

Diamonds are mined by the 50% state-owned Debswana. Large coal deposits are the basis of power grid expansion. Water is Botswana's scarcest resource.

ENVIRONMENT

 17% (2% partially protected)  National Conservation Strategy regarded among world's best

Botswana is trying to reduce conflict between rural development and the environment by helping communities to earn a living from wildlife protection.

MEDIA

 There is no overt censorship

PUBLISHING AND BROADCAST MEDIA

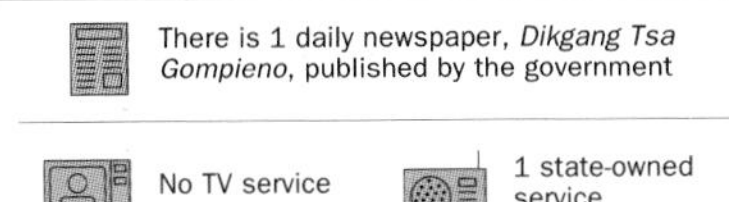

There is 1 daily newspaper, *Dikgang Tsa Gompieno*, published by the government
No TV service
1 state-owned service

The government bias of the one daily paper and radio is offset in the many weekly and other journals. The 20,000 TVs receive South African stations.

CRIME

 Botswana does not publish prison figures  Rising slowly

Crime levels are generally low. Official corruption, diamond smuggling and robbery are the main concerns. Human rights are generally respected.

EDUCATION

 74%

Education is not compulsory. Primary education is free. Enrollment drops from 90% to under 40% at secondary level. Adult literacy projects are well funded.

CHRONOLOGY

From 1600, Tswana migrations slowly displaced San people. In 1895, at local request, the UK set up the Bechuanaland Protectorate to pre-empt annexation by South Africa.

- ❑ **1965** BDP wins first general election, led by Sir Seretse Khama, and then all subsequent general elections.
- ❑ **1966** Independence; Khama president until his death.
- ❑ **1980** Vice-President Quett (later Ketumile) Masire president.
- ❑ **1985–1986** South African raids.
- ❑ **1991** Opposition parties form BPPF to jointly contest 1994 elections.
- ❑ **1992** Strikes. Corruption scandals. Vice President Mmusi resigns.
- ❑ **1993** Scandals continue; more resignations of senior BDP figures.

HEALTH

 1 per 7,185 people  Tuberculosis, heart diseases, pneumonia

The emphasis is on expanding primary health care services. The drought early warning system includes a national nutritional surveillance program.

WEALTH

 80% of the population live in rural areas and those with cattle are better off

CONSUMER GOODS OWNERSHIP

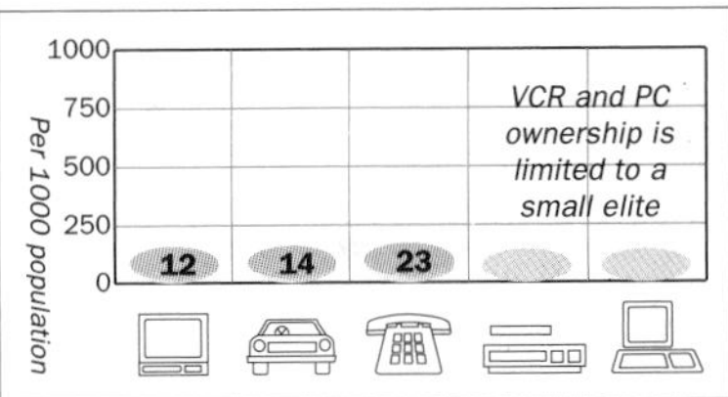

At $2,769, GNP per capita is among Africa's highest, but most people are poor. Wealth belongs to the urban elite.

WORLD RANKING

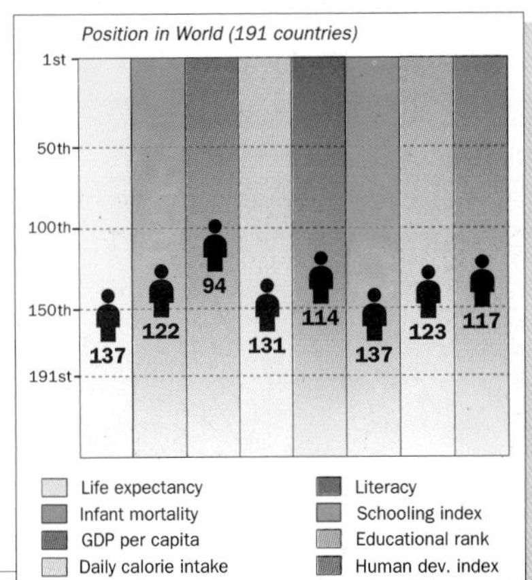

BRAZIL

OFFICIAL NAME: Federative Republic of Brazil **CAPITAL:** Brasília
POPULATION: 153.2 million **CURRENCY:** Real **OFFICIAL LANGUAGE:** Portuguese

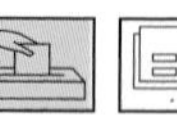

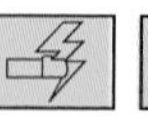

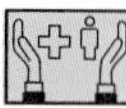

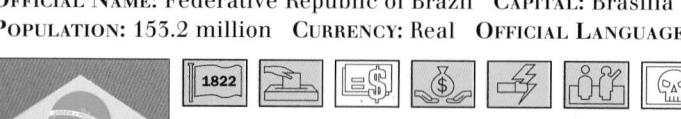

THE LARGEST COUNTRY in South America, Brazil became independent of Portugal in 1822. Today, it is renowned as the site of the world's largest tropical rainforest, the threat to which led the UN's first international environmental conference to be held in Rio de Janeiro in 1992. Covering one-third of Brazil's total land area, the rainforest grows around the massive Amazon River and its delta. Apart from the basin of the River Plate to the south, the country consists of highlands. The mountainous north is part forested and part desert. Brazil is the world's leading coffee producer and also has rich reserves of gold, diamonds, oil and iron ore. Cattle ranching is an expanding industry. The city of São Paulo is the world's second biggest conurbation, with 17 million inhabitants.

BRAZIL

Total Area : 8 511 970 sq. km (3 286 472 sq. miles)

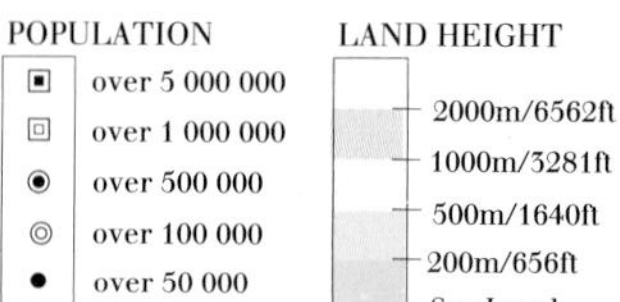

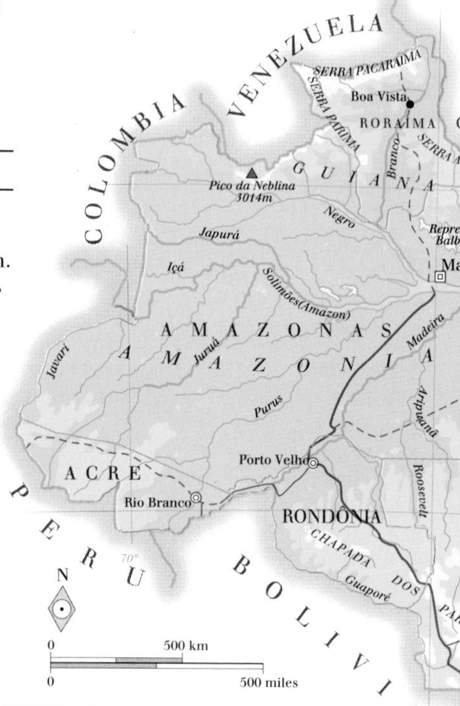

CLIMATE

WEATHER CHART

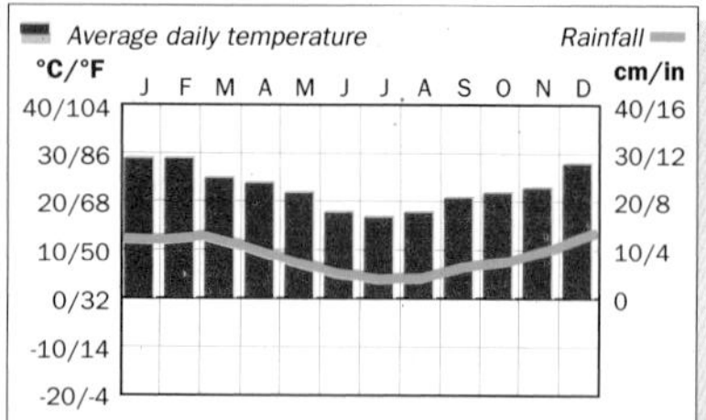

Brazil's share of the Amazon basin, occupying half of the country, has a model equatorial climate. The 59–78 in. of rain are spread throughout the year, although some periods are wetter than others according to region. Temperatures are high, with almost no seasonal variation, but hardly ever rise above 100°F.

The Brazilian plateau, which occupies most of the rest of the country, has far greater temperature ranges. Rain falls mainly between October and April. However, the northeast, the least productive region of Brazil, is very dry and in recent years has been suffering from severe drought. The southern states have hot summers and cool winters, when frost may occur.

COMMUNICATIONS

Guarulhos Intl, São Paulo 5.78m passengers

277 ships 8.5m dwt

THE TRANSPORTATION NETWORK

1.04m miles (1.67m km)

Trans-Amazonian Highway 3,100 miles (5,000 km)

18,680 miles (30,129 km)

31,000 miles (50,000 km)

A vast road network is being built to link the main centers of Brazil. The antiquated railroads are increasingly unreliable. São Paulo's subway is being extended to cope with the city's rapidly expanding population.

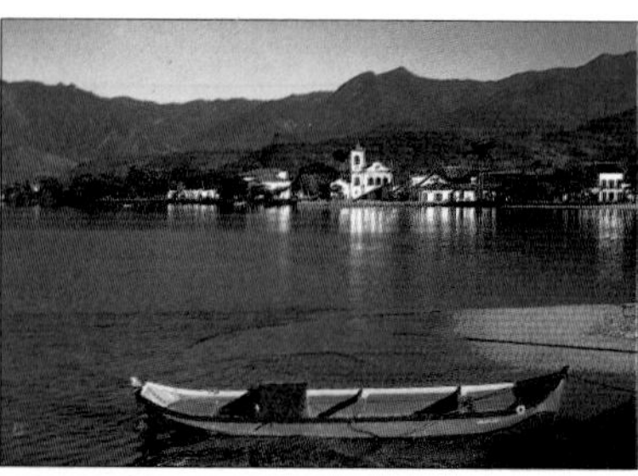

Parati, in Rio state, was one of Brazil's major gold-exporting ports in the 17th century. Its colonial architecture is well preserved.

TOURISM

1.08m visitors

Down 23% in 1990

MAIN OVERSEAS ARRIVALS

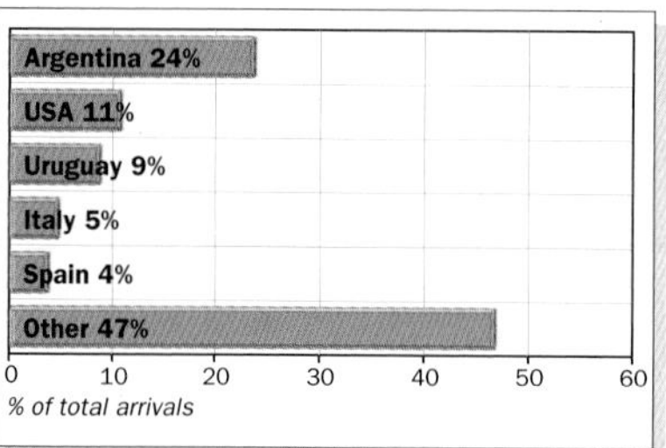

Its 1,240 miles of Atlantic beaches, the folklore and music of the northeast coast and the annual *Mardi Gras* carnival in Rio de Janeiro, are Brazil's major attractions. However, the increasingly affluent and international audience now controls the carnival. The largely Afro-Brazilian residents of Rio's *favelas*, or shantytowns, can no longer afford to take part in the parades that originated in their culture.

Brazil has targeted ecotourism as a major growth area. Foreign investment in tourist facilities in Amazonia is being encouraged by the government. But Brazilians show little interest in ecotourism, prefering to visit Amazonia for the duty-free shopping zone in Manaus.

Brazil is still a relatively cheap destination for European and American tourists. Despite this, visitor numbers are declining, falling from 0.5% to 0.1% of the world market since 1970. Many visitors have been put off by the negative publicity generated by the conditions in the shantytowns and by Brazil's past human rights record.

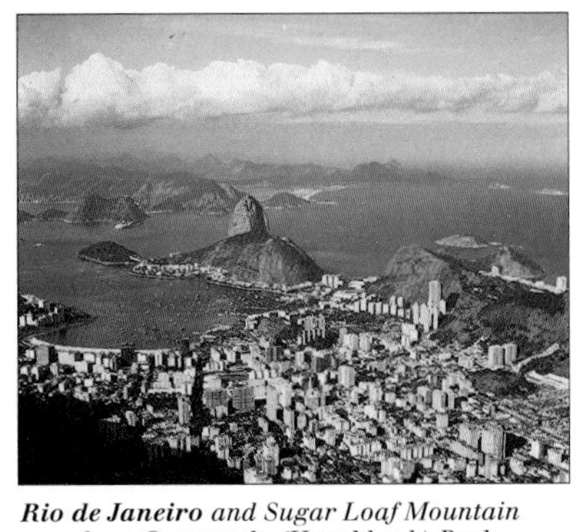

Rio de Janeiro and Sugar Loaf Mountain seen from Corcovado (Hunchback) Peak. With a population of 11 million, the Rio conurbation is Brazil's largest after São Paulo.

PEOPLE

Portuguese, German, Italian, Spanish, Polish, Japanese, Amerindian languages

47 people per sq. mile

THE URBAN/RURAL POPULATION SPLIT

75% | 25%

RELIGIOUS PERSUASION

Other 10%

Roman Catholic 90%

ETHNIC MAKEUP

Black 6%

Mixed 38%

Other (including Portuguese, Italian, German and Amerindian) 56%

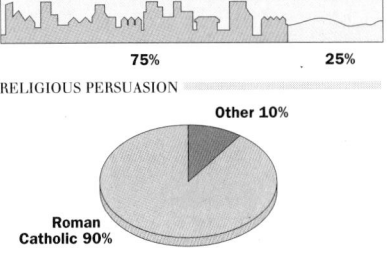

POPULATION AGE BREAKDOWN

% of population by age group

Age group	1960	1970	1980	1990	2000
65+	2.9%	3.4%	4%	4.7%	5.6%
15–64	53.5%	54.3%	58.3%	60.6%	65.3%
0–14	43.6%	42.3%	37.7%	34.7%	29.1%

Brazil's population is highly diverse. It includes indigenous Indian groups who have had little contact with the outside world, as well as the descendants of both its Portuguese colonizers and the Africans brought to work the sugar plantations in the 17th century. More recent immigrant groups include both Italians and Japanese.

Amerindians suffer prejudice from most other peoples in Brazil. Since 1900, 87 Amerindian groups have become extinct as a result of disease, starvation or the forceful taking of their land by miners, settlers and loggers. The Amerindian population today is estimated at just 220,000. Migrants from the poor northeast suffer considerable discrimination in Brazil's larger cities.

Brazil is a profoundly Catholic country with a traditional emphasis on the family. In the urban areas, however, family structures are under pressure. Migrants from the northeast often leave their families behind.

Women in Brazil have had the vote since 1934, but are still discriminated against in jobs and politics. A ministry for women has been established with the aim of defending and promoting their interests.

CHRONOLOGY

The first Portuguese, Pedro Alvares Cabral, arrived in Brazil in 1500. By the time Spain took control of the region in 1580, it was a thriving colony drawing its wealth from sugar plantations in the northeast, worked by imported Africans, or Amerindians captured from further and further inland.

- **1637–1654** Dutch control sugar-growing areas.
- **1763** Rio becomes capital.
- **1788** *Inconfidência* rebellion, led by Tiradentes, fails.
- **1807** French invade Portugal. King João VI flees to Brazil with British naval escort. In return, Brazil's ports opened to foreign trade.
- **1821** King returns to Portugal. Son Pedro made regent of Brazil.
- **1822** Pedro declares independence and is made Emperor of Brazil.
- **1828** Brazil loses Uruguay.
- **1831** Military revolt after war with Argentina (1825–1828). Emperor abdicates. Five-year-old son succeeds him as Pedro II.
- **1835–1845** Rio Grande secedes.
- **1865–1870** Brazil wins war of Triple Alliance with Argentina and Uruguay against Paraguay.
- **1888** Pedro II abolishes slavery; landowners and military turn against him.
- **1889** First Republic established. Emperor goes into exile in Paris. Increasing prosperity as result of international demand for coffee.
- **1891** Federal constitution established.
- **1914–1918** World War I hits coffee exports.
- **1920s** Working class and intellectual movements call for end to oligarchical rule.
- **1930** Coffee prices collapse. Revolt led by Dr. Getúlio Vargas, the "Father of the Poor," who becomes president. Fast industrial growth.
- **1937** Vargas's position as benevolent dictator formalized in "New State," based on fascist model.

B

CHRONOLOGY *continued*

- **1942** Declares war on Germany.
- **1945** Vargas forced out by military.
- **1951** Vargas reelected as leader of Labor Party.
- **1954** US oppose Vargas's socialist policies, including plans to double minimum wage. The right, backed by the military, demand his resignation. Commits suicide.
- **1956–1960** President Juscelino Kubitschek, backed by Brazilian Workers' Party (PTB), attracts foreign investment for new industries, especially from USA.
- **1960–1961** Conservative Jânio da Silva Quadros president. Tries to break dependence on US trade.
- **1961** Brasília, built in three years, becomes new capital. PTB leader, João Goulart, elected president.
- **1961–1964** President's powers briefly curtailed as right wing reacts to presidential policies.
- **1964** Bloodless military coup under army chief Gen. Castelo Branco.
- **1965** Branco assumes dictatorship. Bans existing political parties, but creates two official new ones. He is followed by a succession of military rulers. Fast-track economic development, the Brazilian Miracle, is counterbalanced by ruthless suppression of left-wing activists.
- **1974** World oil crisis marks end of economic boom. Brazil's foreign debt now largest in world.
- **1979** More political parties allowed.
- **1980** Huge migrations into Rondônia state begin.
- **1985** Civilian Senator Tancredo Neves wins presidential elections as candidate of new liberal alliance, but dies before taking office. Illiterate adults get the vote.
- **1987** Gold found on Yanomani lands in Roraima state; illegal diggers rush in by the thousand.
- **1988** New constitution promises massive social spending but fails to address land reform. Chico Mendes, rubber-tappers' union leader and environmentalist, murdered.
- **1989** Brazil's first environmental protection plan "Our Nature" drawn up. Inflation reaches 1,000% a year. First fully democratic presidential elections won by Fernando Collor de Mello of new PRN.
- **1990** Sweeping economic measures. New currency.
- **1991** Finance minister resigns at failure of economic reforms.
- **1992** Earth Summit held in Rio. Collor de Mello resigns and is impeached for corruption.
- **1993** Demarcation of Indian lands is supposed to be complete, but is far from being so.

POLITICS

 Lower House 1998
Upper House 1998

 President Fernando Henrique Cardoso

THE STATE OF THE PARTIES

Chamber of Deputies 517 members

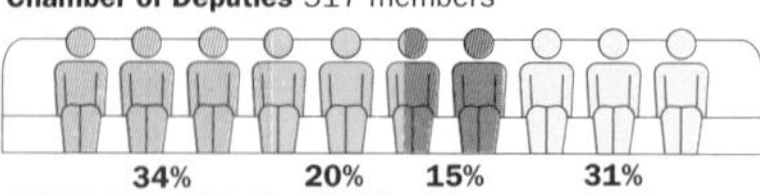

34%	20%	15%	31%
PSDB–PFL–PTB–PL	PMDB	PT	Other

PSDB–PFL–PTB–PL = Brazilian Social Democratic Party/Liberal Front Party/Brazilian Labour Party/Liberal Party
PMDB = Brazilian Democratic Movement Party
PT = Workers' Party

Federal Senate 81 members

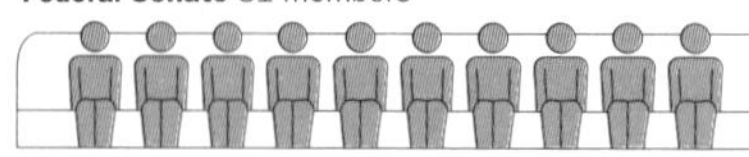

3 members are elected by each of the 26 states and the Federal District

Brazil is a democratic federal republic with 27 regional parliaments and a national congress. In 1993, Brazilians voted to retain directly elected presidents.

Main Political Issues

Controlling inflation

The military regime's difficulties with the economy were the main reason for its withdrawal from politics in 1988. Tackling hyperinflation, which is currently running at over 40% a month, remains the main concern of the civilian government.

Redrafting the constitution

The 1988 constitution, detailing promises for a better future, has proved to be unworkable in practice. The state cannot afford its social security, health and pension commitments. The proliferation of local governments, designed to check federal power, has led to a duplication of functions and is very expensive. The aim now is to develop a shorter and clearer constitution. Reformists want provisions to curb tax evasion and to allow greater foreign investment in state-owned enterprises such as oil. Many also want to see changes in the electoral system in order to curb the increasing involvement of small parties in government.

Eradicating corruption

Former President Collor de Mello's 1992 impeachment for fraud underlines the depth of the problem of corruption in Brazil. Many are now demanding an end to parliamentary immunity: under the current system, elected officials cannot be prosecuted unless they have been suspended from office by a two-thirds vote.

Profile

Brazil's young democracy is characterized by a weak party system, centered around personalities rather than parties. Parties do not have set ideological programs, but tend to form *ad hoc* coalitions to get legislation through congress. The preponderance of small parties adds to the problems.

Politics have been further rocked by recent corruption scandals. Itamar Franco, who became president after Collor de Mello had been impeached for alleged fraud, was himself under investigation in 1993.

The dissatisfaction with the center-right has been a boost to the left. However, a victory for the left, led by the influential Luís da Silva – who came second to Collor de Mello in the 1989 presidential elections – could provoke another military intervention. This was a factor limiting the left's popular support in the approach to the 1994 elections; Brazilians do not want a return to military rule.

The military, in power between 1964 and 1985, was responsible for human rights abuses, particularly against Amazon Indians. Its economic mismanagement left Brazil with a legacy of huge debts and inefficient state industries.

President Fernando Cardoso, *who took office in January 1995.*

Luís Ignacio da Silva, "Lula," *leader of the left-wing Workers' Party.*

Former president Itamar Franco, *whose government introduced the* real.

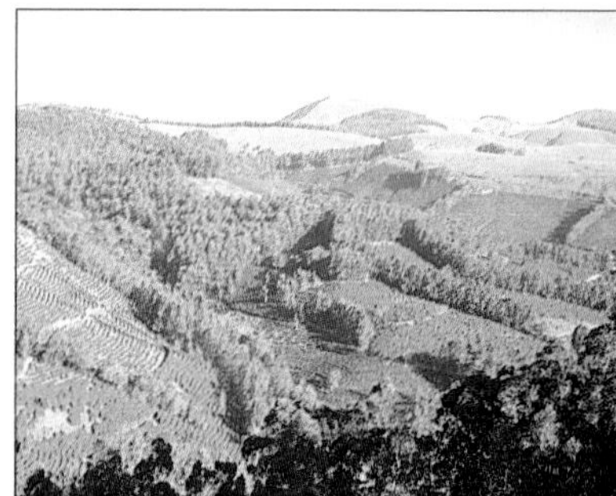

Coffee plantation, *São Paulo state. Coffee was introduced into Brazil in the early 18th century. It is declining in importance and now accounts for less than 4% of export revenues.*

B

WORLD AFFAIRS

Brazil's main foreign policy concern is the formation of MERCOSUR, a common market with Argentina, Paraguay and Uruguay, which will create an additional market of over 40 million for Brazil's relatively efficient producers. A successful outcome to negotiations with Chile and Peru for a Pacific port outlet would further boost Brazil's exports.

Beyond Latin America, relations with the USA and Japan, Brazil's main creditors, are critical. Rescheduling debt, much of it incurred during the military regime, is essential to curb Brazil's inflation problem.

The 1992 Rio Earth Summit was a major boost to Brazil's international image. However, cases of continuing exploitation of Amazon Indian groups have recently come to light.

AID

189m (receipts)

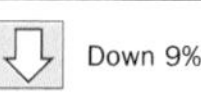
Down 9% in 1993

Brazil's main aid donors are the USA and the EU. Along with official aid, much help comes from NGOs, mainly for environmental and housing projects. Large aid donations were promised by the states attending the Rio Summit in 1992; little has materialized.

DEFENSE

$2.1bn

Down 8% in 1992

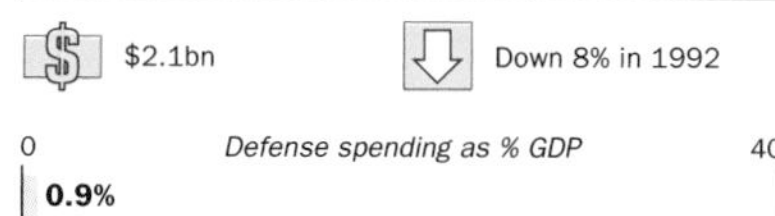

BRAZILIAN ARMED FORCES

520 light tanks (150 M-3/80 X-1A)	196,000 personnel
5 submarines, 19 surface vessels and 30 patrol boats	50,000 personnel
307 combat aircraft (14 F-103E/4 F-103D)	50,700 personnel
None	

Although it withdrew from direct participation in government in 1985, Brazil's military remains a powerful force in national political life. In 1989, it played a behind-the-scenes role in ensuring Collor de Mello's election. It controls the far north for national security reasons. Brazil has a large arms industry. Exports to Iraq, a major market, were hit by a UN embargo in 1991 following the Gulf War. Plans to develop nuclear weapons have now been abandoned by the military.

ECONOMICS

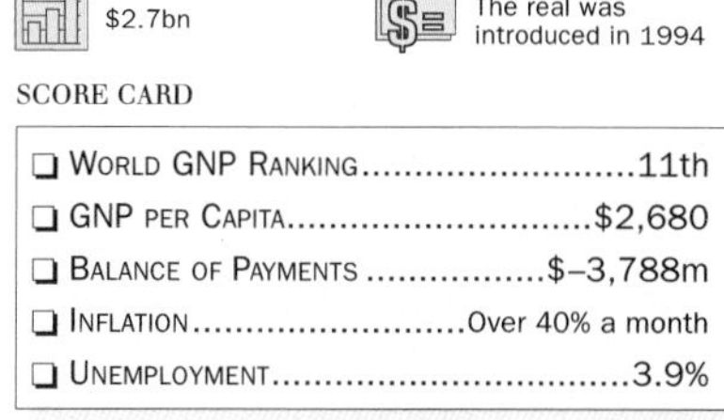

$2.7bn

The real was introduced in 1994

SCORE CARD

❑ WORLD GNP RANKING	11th
❑ GNP PER CAPITA	$2,680
❑ BALANCE OF PAYMENTS	$-3,788m
❑ INFLATION	Over 40% a month
❑ UNEMPLOYMENT	3.9%

EXPORTS

IMPORTS

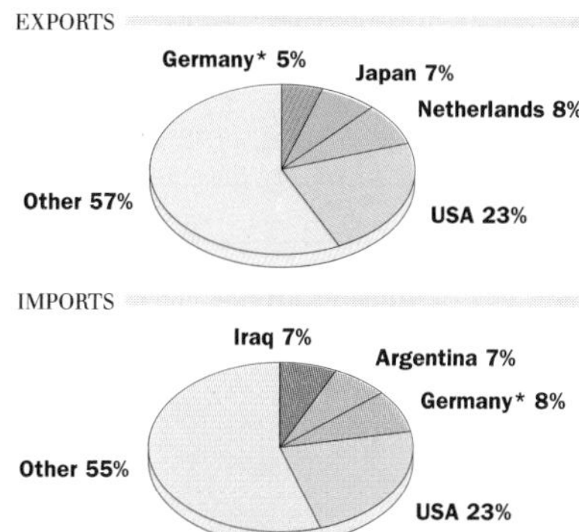

STRENGTHS
Local industry is well developed, making Brazil dominant in the region. Immense natural resources: the world's largest producer of coffee and soybeans and one of the largest sugar and orange juice exporters. Large deposits of gold, silver and iron. One of world's most important steel producers.

WEAKNESSES
Hyperinflation – currently over 40% a month. Corruption among politicians and officials, as well as in business, has created mistrust and an unwillingness by overseas investors to make long-term commitments. Lack of any coherent economic planning in the early 1990s.

PROFILE
Brazil has one of the world's major economies, but also one of the hardest to manage. During the 1960s and 1970s, GDP expanded by an average of 11% a year. The economy underwent major diversification and industrialization, and today Brazil is a significant producer of cars and computers. However, profligate spending during this period left Brazil saddled with a huge debt burden of over $116 billion, which dominated economic affairs in the 1980s.

Although economic reform, initiated by the Collor de Mello administration in 1990, has enabled Brazil to reschedule its debts, the country still faces major problems. The most important is inflation, which was running at over 40% a month in 1994. Inflation is also aggravating wealth disparities between rich and poor – already the greatest in the world. Despite its vast natural and economic resources, Brazil still has 32 million of its people living below the poverty line and has not begun to tackle the problem of homeless street children in Rio, São Paulo and other large cities.

Before his impeachment, President Collor announced a sweeping privatization program as the first step in economic reform. For it to succeed, Brazil needs to attract high levels of foreign investment, but the country's political and economic instability frightens off many companies. Corruption scandals add to the lack of trust among potential investors and intensify the feeling of many that Brazil is only paying lip service to change.

The private sector is highly efficient and has succeeded in working around Brazil's bureaucracy. The array of regulations aimed at protecting Brazil's workers, for example, have led many employers to invest in machinery instead, with resulting increases in productivity.

In sharp contrast to its regulation of industry, the state has imposed few controls on the loggers and gold prospectors in Amazonia.

ECONOMIC PERFORMANCE INDICATOR

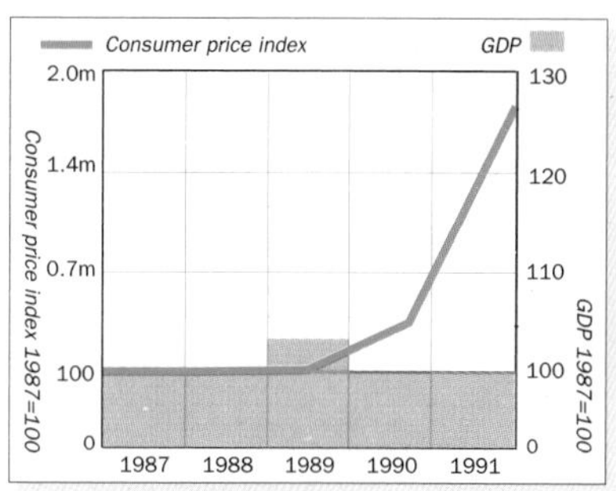

BRAZIL: MAJOR BUSINESSES

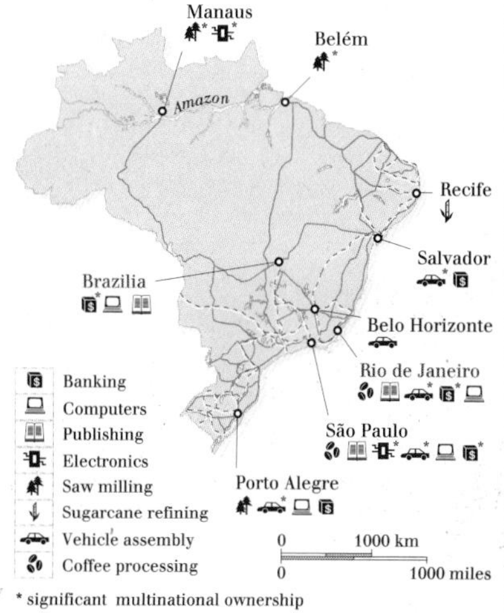

RESOURCES

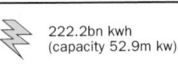

222.2bn kwh (capacity 52.9m kw)

625,700 b/d (reserves 3,030,000,000 bbl)

186.8m cattle, 31.7m pigs, 20.5m sheep

Iron, manganese, coal, bauxite, nickel, oil, tin, silver, diamonds, gold

ELECTRICITY GENERATION

Hydro 93% (207.2bn kwh)

Thermal 6% (12.7bn kwh)

Nuclear 1% (2.2bn kwh)

Other 0%

0 20 40 60 80 100

% of total generation by type

Under the military, Brazil had big ambitions for nuclear power, and commissioned several power stations from former West Germany. Energy from these has been more expensive than expected. Hydropower has been more successful, accounting for 90% of electricity generation. A 1,364-mile pipeline from the Bolivian gas fields to Brazil's industrial south has been proposed, but Brazil is unable to finance the multi-billion dollar project from public funds; its constitution prevents private ownership of energy assets. Ethanol is being made from sugar in an attempt to reduce gasoline imports. Within the agricultural sector, Brazil is the world's largest producer of both coffee and soybeans.

Equatorial vegetation near Manaus *in the center of Amazonas state. The brown waters of the Rio Solimões and the black waters of the Rio Negro meet near Manaus.*

ENVIRONMENT

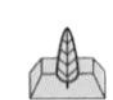

3% (1% partially protected)

Use of alcohol fuels for cars is reducing urban pollution

ENVIRONMENTAL TREATIES

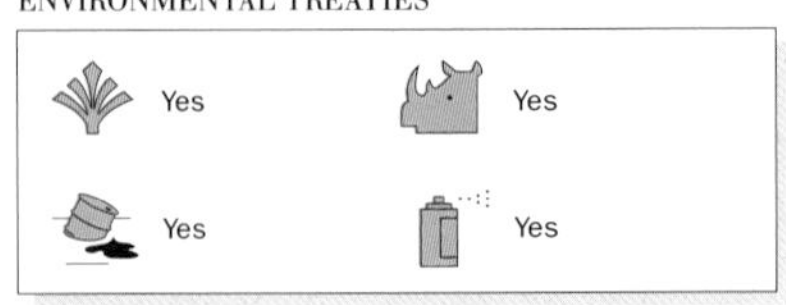

In 1992, the UN held its first Earth Summit in Rio, partly to highlight the destruction of the Amazon rainforest.

The Amazon rainforest contains an estimated 90% of all of the world's plants and animals and is the most complex ecosystem known. However, the demands of agriculture are leading to its destruction at a rate of 1.5 sq. mi. per hour, or 13,514 sq. mi. per year. As a result of such massive clearances, usually for conversion to cattle pasture, vital genetic diversity is being lost.

Brazil faces other environmental problems. Open-cast bauxite mining is polluting rivers and threatening the livelihoods of indigenous Amerindians. In the cities, widespread industrial pollution and untreated sewage are major problems.

MEDIA

Officially there has been freedom from censorship since the military withdrew from politics in 1985

PUBLISHING AND BROADCAST MEDIA

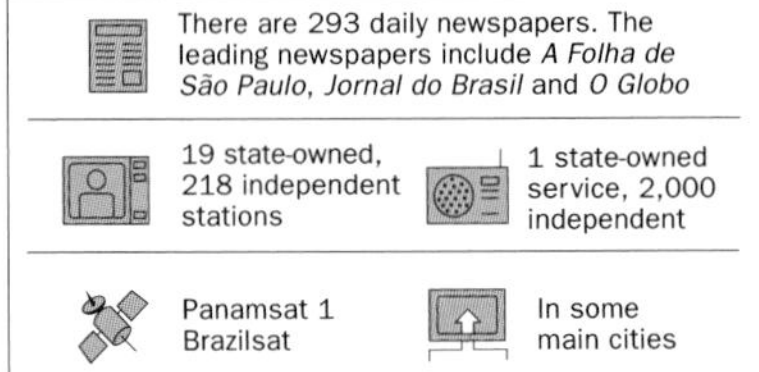

There are 293 daily newspapers. The leading newspapers include A Folha de São Paulo, Jornal do Brasil and O Globo
19 state-owned, 218 independent stations
1 state-owned service, 2,000 independent
Panamsat 1 Brazilsat
In some main cities

Although there is now no official censorship, TV and radio operating licenses are awarded as political favors and state advertising is so extensive it cannot fail to influence editorial policy. Media ownership is also highly concentrated. The *Globo* group, Brazil's only nationwide broadcasting company, was able to exclude the left from news reports and debates during the 1989 presidential elections, thus securing the victory of Collor de Mello.

CRIME

87,053 prisoners

The rate is sharply up. More street children are being murdered

CRIME RATES

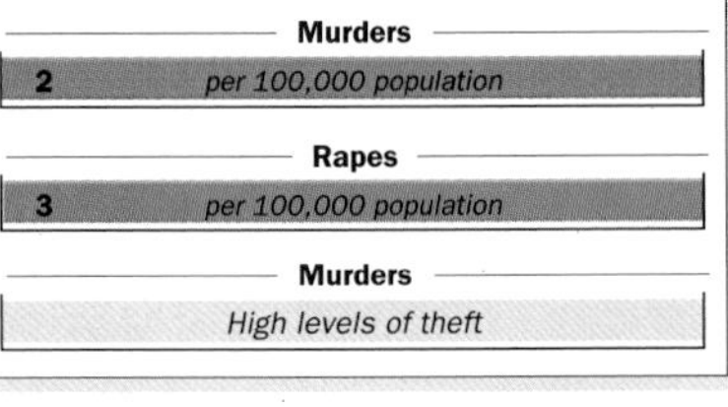

Urban life in Brazil can be violent. The incidence of armed robbery and drug-related crime is rising. Human rights abuses by the police are frequently reported. Death squads, uncontrolled by the government, target street children in particular, especially in Rio, São Paulo and Recife. Since 1985, the rate of street child murders has been rising. However, international condemnation of the crimes has led to action in some areas.

In the countryside, violent land disputes are common. Landless workers are repeatedly displaced and indigenous peoples driven from land to which the government has, in theory, guaranteed their rights. In Roraima state, the discovery of large gold deposits has led to the homelands of Brazil's largest tribe, the Yanomani, being invaded by thousands of gun-toting prospectors, called *garimpeiros*. The government halted their activities during the 1992 Earth Summit in Rio.

EDUCATION

80%

0 *Education spending as % GNP* 25

3.7%

THE EDUCATION SYSTEM

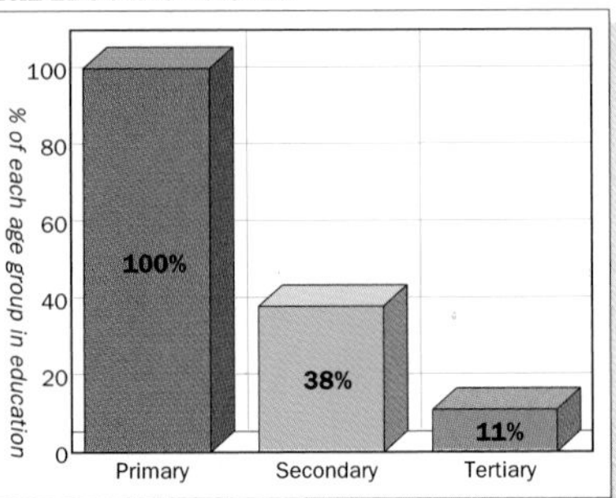

Education follows the French system with a *bachillerato* (*baccalauréat*) at the end of secondary schooling. State schools enjoyed a good reputation until the 1950s, but have declined since then. Most middle-class parents now send their children to private schools. The wealthy send theirs to Switzerland or France. Millions of the poor receive little education – especially those living in the northeast and Amazonia, and the urban poor. Brazil's three million street children have no schooling at all. Public degree courses work on credits, as in the USA. Of Brazil's 95 universities, 55 are administered by the state. São Paulo University is the most prestigious.

REGIONS

NORDESTE

***Cattle ranchers** in Paré state, where land reform is a major political issue.*

NORDESTE, the northeast of Brazil, comprises nine states and is the country's most traditional region, but also its most backward. It was settled by the Portuguese, who brought Africans to work the sugar plantations. In the region's interior, the land is still divided into large ranches owned by a few families. This situation, and several years of drought that have made the land even more barren, have led to the emigration of millions of subsistence farmers to the more prosperous cities of the south, where they encounter great prejudice. The big landowners still hold a great deal of political power nationally, being heavily represented in the Congress, where they regularly obstruct attempts at land reform.

PANTANAL

THE PANTANAL, situated in the center-west of Brazil, bordering Paraguay and Bolivia, is the largest area of wetlands in the world. Flooded for seven months a year, it has some of the most diverse wildlife on the continent, with many thousands of species of birds, caymans (a type of alligator) and many varieties of snake. The inhabitants, or *pantaneros*, are indigenous groups who have adapted their way of life, which includes raising cattle and horses, to the regular flooding. The Pantanal is a great attraction for tourists and scientists who study wildlife behavior. As with many regions in Brazil, it is now coming under pressure from cattle ranchers and those who want to turn the area over to agriculture. However, its special climatic conditions act as a protection from any massive exploitation of its resources.

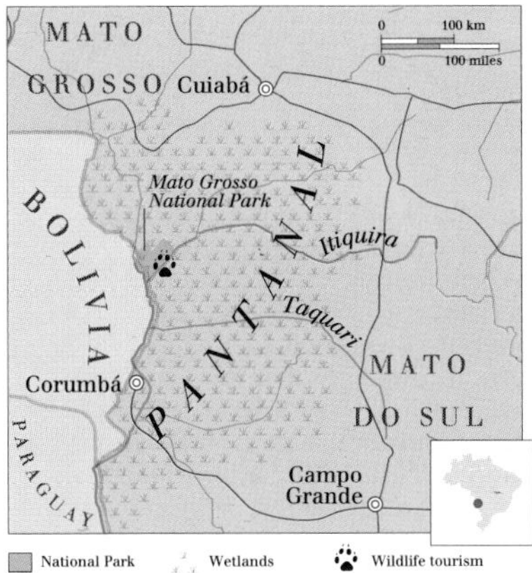

ESTADO DE SÃO PAULO

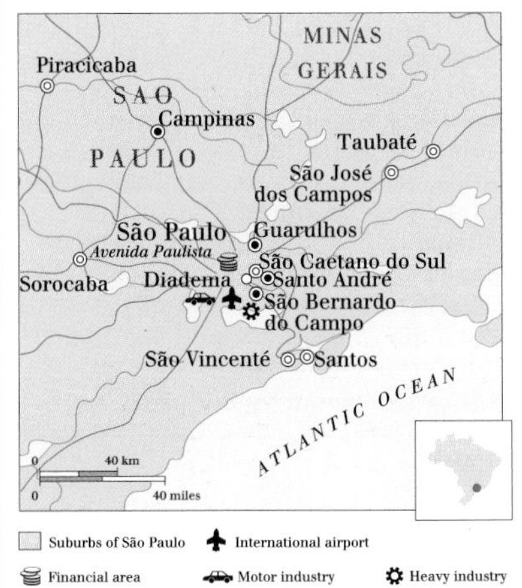

SÃO PAULO STATE, with almost 34 million inhabitants, is among the world's 20 most powerful economies. At its center lies the city of São Paulo, which has over 10 million inhabitants and is the fastest growing city on the continent. Its population is mixed, and includes the *nordestinos* who have come in search of work, and a large Italo-Brazilian community who first helped the city to industrialize. The city is also home to almost two million Japanese descendants, the largest Japanese community outside Japan. The area of Avenida Paulista, once the home of coffee barons and São Paulo's wealthy citizens, is now Brazil's largest financial center. The urban area around São Paulo is the nucleus of Brazilian heavy industry, particularly the car and large-scale engineering industries. On the coast of São Paulo state is Brazil's largest port, Santos, which exports most of the country's coffee, as well as machinery and other heavy goods.

HEALTH

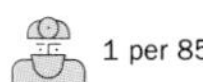
1 per 852 people

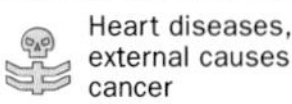
Heart diseases, external causes, cancer

0 *Health spending as % GNP* 25
1.7%

The public health system is limited. Less than 20% of hospitals are state-run and private care is very expensive. The World Bank has criticized the under-financing of preventive health care. On average, only 15% of the health budget is allocated to child health, immunization and other preventive programs. Reported malaria cases tripled between 1980 and 1990; 90% are in Amazonia, mainly in settler towns. Leprosy and parasitic skin infections are also becoming more common, again often affecting settlers.

WEALTH

Due to the high inflation rate, salaries have to be reviewed every month

CONSUMER GOODS OWNERSHIP

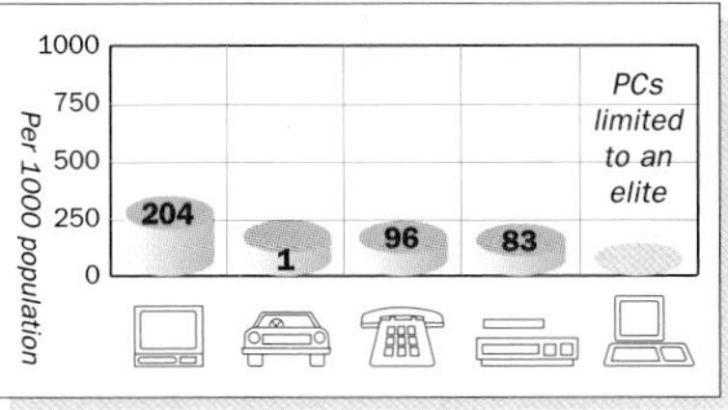

Brazil's large wealth disparities have been growing during the last decade. Relatively low levels of unemployment conceal large-scale underemployment, and the UN classifies over 50% of the population as suffering from poverty. The large number of poor rural migrants to the cities live in the *favelas*, or shantytowns. *Favelas* are now also appearing in the countryside. The wealthy like to drive European cars, vacation in Paris or ski in Switzerland, where most keep their money to avoid interference in their accounts by the government.

WORLD RANKING

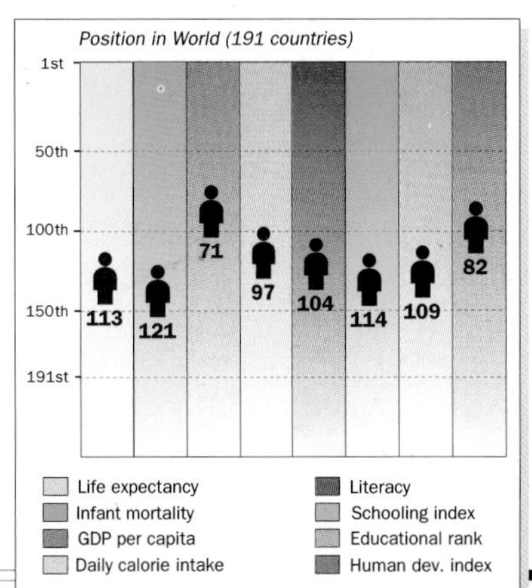

BRUNEI

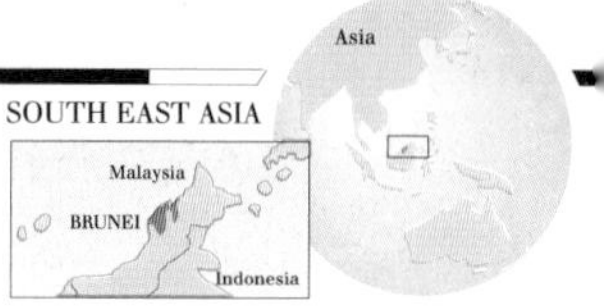

B

OFFICIAL NAME: The Sultanate of Brunei **CAPITAL:** Bandar Seri Begawan
CURRENCY: Brunei dollar **POPULATION:** 300,000 **OFFICIAL LANGUAGE:** Malay

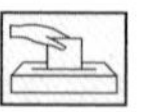

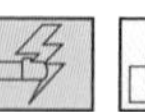

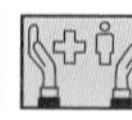

LYING ON THE NORTHWESTERN coast of the island of Borneo, Brunei is divided in two by a strip of the surrounding Malaysian state of Sarawak. The interior is mostly rainforest. Independent from the UK since 1984, Brunei is ruled by decree of the Sultan. It is undergoing increasing Islamization. Oil and gas reserves have brought one of the world's highest standards of living.

CLIMATE

WEATHER CHART

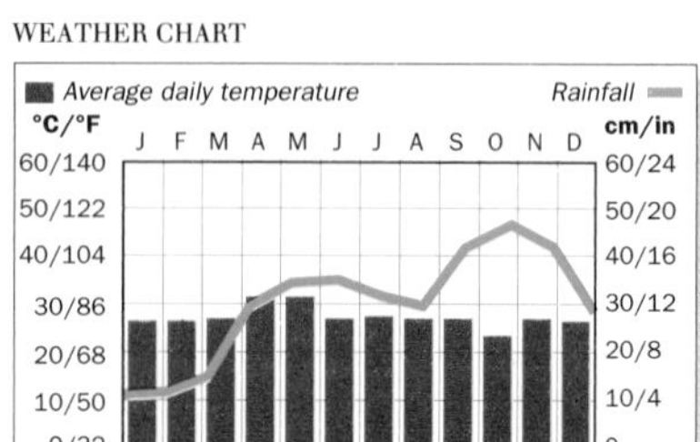

Just 298 miles north of the equator, Brunei has a six-month rainy season with extremely high humidity.

COMMUNICATIONS

Brunei International, Bandar Seri Begawan 10 ships 342,700 dwt

THE TRANSPORTATION NETWORK

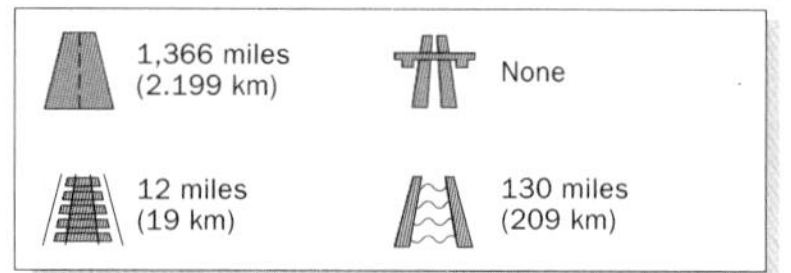

Interest-free loans for civil servants, subsidized gasoline and limited public transportation account for the high rates of car ownership.

TOURISM

305,522 visitors Up 57% in 1992

MAIN OVERSEAS ARRIVALS

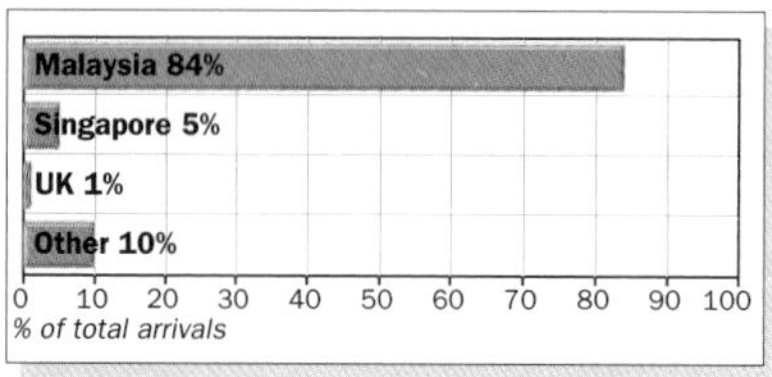

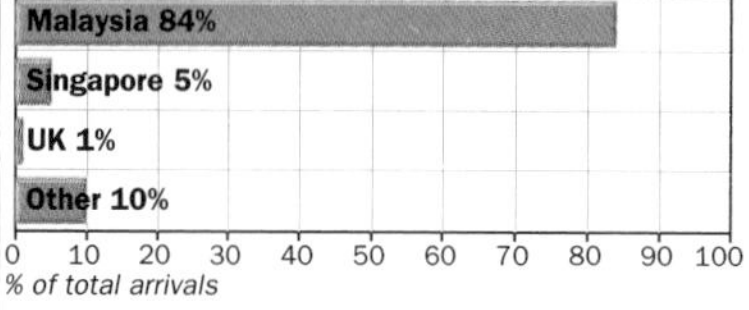

Although eager to protect Bruneians from Western influence, the government wants to develop quality tourism as part of its diversification program. Promoted as the "Gateway to Borneo," Brunei's rainforests could be developed for ecotourism. A former attraction was the Churchill Museum, founded by the late Sultan. This has now been superseded by the Museum of Royal Regalia.

PEOPLE

Malay, English, Chinese

91 people per sq. mile

THE URBAN/RURAL POPULATION SPLIT

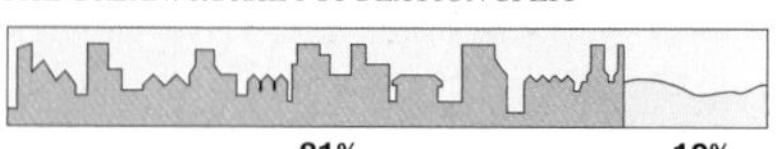

ETHNIC MAKEUP

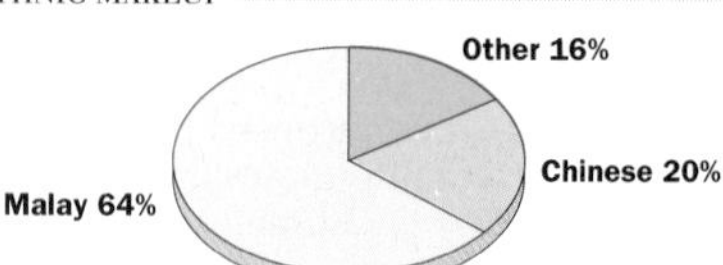

Malays benefit from positive discrimination; many in the Chinese community are either stateless or hold British protected person passports. Among indigenous groups, the Murut and Dusuns are favored over the Ibans. Women, less restricted than in some Muslim states, are obliged to wear headscarves but not the veil. Many hold influential posts in the civil service.

POLITICS

Not applicable

HM Sultan Haji Hassannal Bolkiah Mu'izzadin Waddaulah

THE STATE OF THE PARTIES

Council of Cabinet Ministers

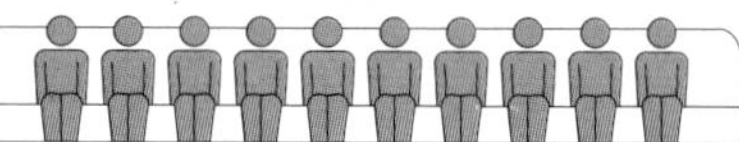

Brunei is an absolute monarchy. The Council of Cabinet Ministers is chosen by the Sultan. Political parties were banned in 1988

Since a failed rebellion in 1962, a state of emergency has been in force and the Sultan has ruled by decree. Hopes for democracy were dashed when political parties were banned in 1988. In 1990, "Malay Muslim Monarchy" was introduced, promoting Islamic values, as the state ideology. This further alienated the large Chinese and expatriate communities. Power is closely tied to the royal family. Two of the Sultan's brothers hold the finance and foreign affairs portfolios; the Sultan himself looks after defense.

WORLD AFFAIRS

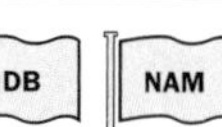

Brunei claims part of the Spratly Islands. Political exiles opposed to the government and based in Malaysia are a main concern. Relations with Britain, the ex-colonial power, are good.

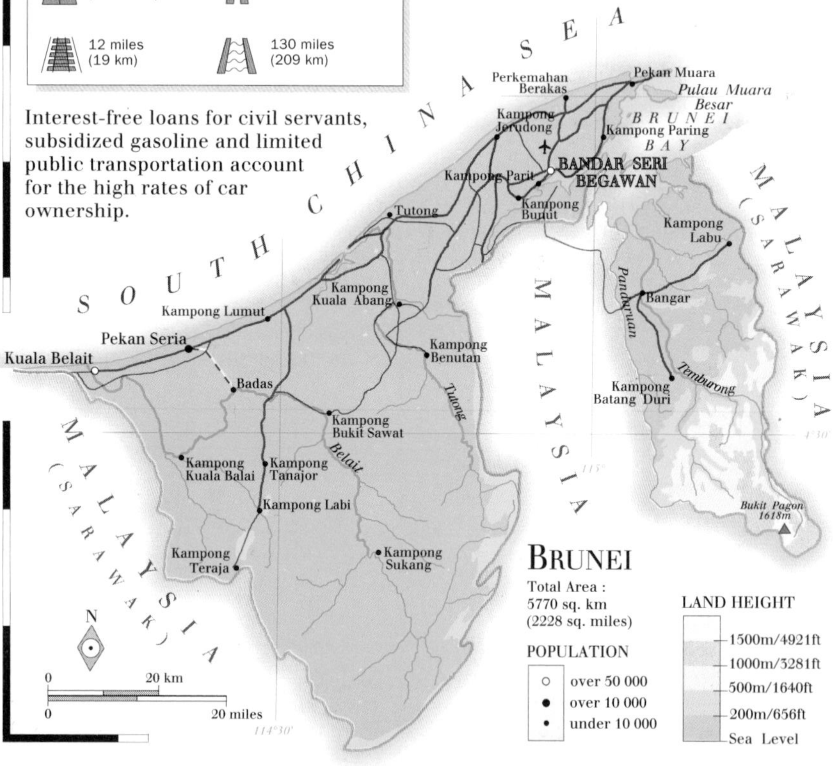

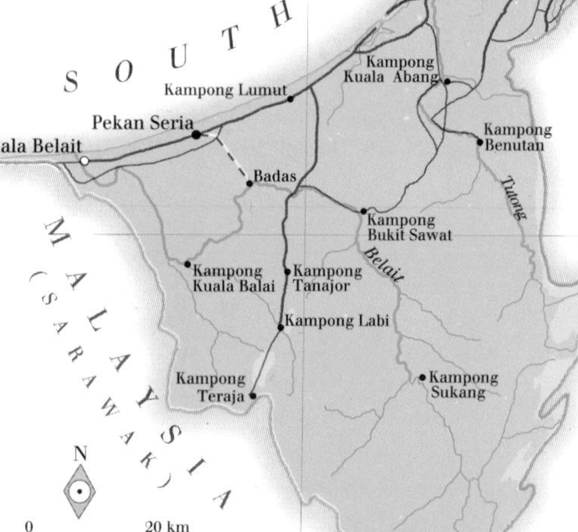

BRUNEI

Total Area : 5770 sq. km (2228 sq. miles)

POPULATION
- over 50 000
- over 10 000
- under 10 000

LAND HEIGHT
1500m/4921ft
1000m/3281ft
500m/1640ft
200m/656ft
Sea Level

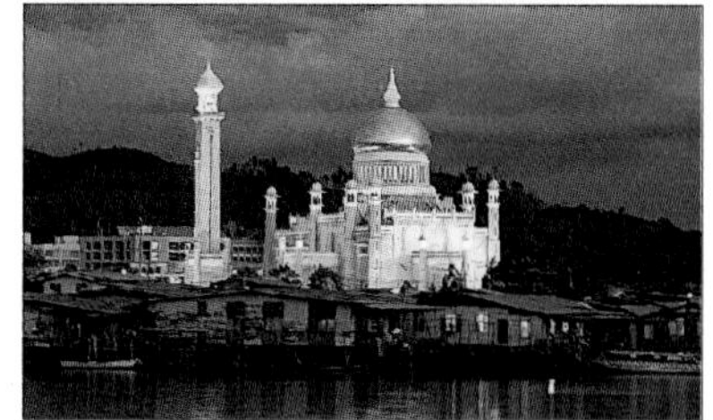

***The magnificent Omar Ali Saifuddin** mosque is surrounded by an artificial lagoon.*

AID

 *Ad hoc* handouts of around $150,000

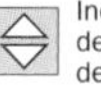 Increase or decrease depends on Sultan's decision

Aid spending is largely *ad hoc*. It has included donations to the Contras in Nicaragua, the Bosnian Muslims and the homeless of New York.

DEFENSE

 $233m

 Up 21% in 1988

As well as being head of the 4,500-strong armed forces, the Sultan has a personal bodyguard of 2,000 UK-trained Gurkhas. The UK and Singapore are close defense allies.

ECONOMICS

 $9bn (est)

 1.64 Brunei dollars

SCORE CARD

- ❑ WORLD GNP RANKING 83rd
- ❑ GNP PER CAPITA $30,000
- ❑ BALANCE OF PAYMENTS $1.1bn
- ❑ INFLATION ....–5.1%
- ❑ UNEMPLOYMENT 6%

STRENGTHS

Known oil reserves for 25 years; gas for 40 years. Earnings from massive overseas investments, mainly in the USA and Europe, now exceed oil and gas revenues.

WEAKNESSES

Single-product economy. Failure of diversification programs could lead to problems in the future.

EXPORTS

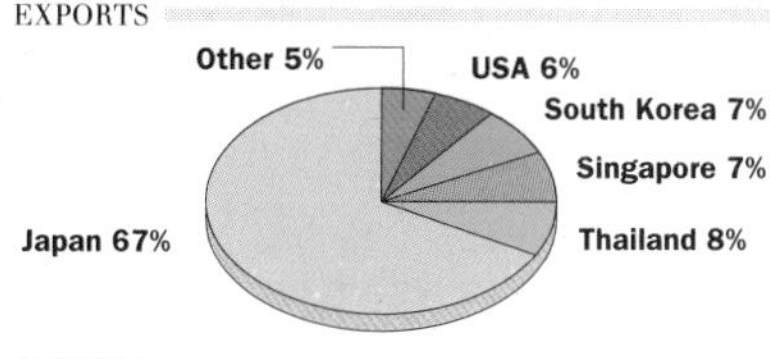

IMPORTS

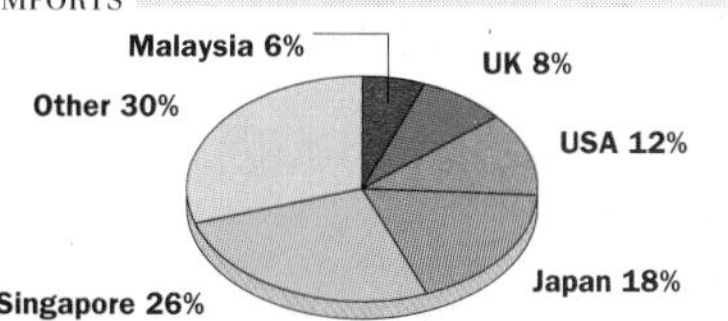

RESOURCES

 1.2bn kwh (capacity 380,000 kw)

 165,400 b/d (reserves 1,350,000,000 bbl)

 25,000 pigs, 10,000 buffaloes

Oil, natural gas

Oil and gas are the major resources, accounting for 0.5% and 9% of world production respectively. Energy policy now focuses on regulating output in order to conserve stocks.

ENVIRONMENT

 14% (5% partially protected)

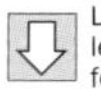 Little impetus behind legislation to protect forests

The Forest Strategic Plan aims to protect Brunei's forests (which account for 80% of its land area), but has yet to make specific areas of responsibility clear. The result is that rainforest is still under threat. Brunei's mangrove swamps, the largest in Borneo, remain unprotected.

MEDIA

 Extensive censorship, including foreign papers. Pictures deemed obscene or blasphemous by Religious Affairs Ministry are blacked out

PUBLISHING AND BROADCAST MEDIA

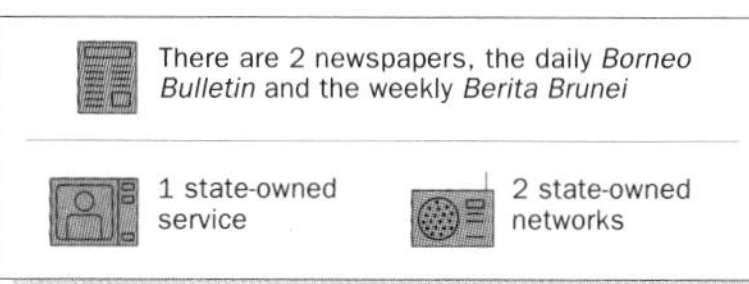

There are 2 newspapers, the daily *Borneo Bulletin* and the weekly *Berita Brunei*

1 state-owned service

2 state-owned networks

The state effectively controls all media. Brunei TV has recently increased its religious programming.

CRIME

 Brunei does not publish prison figures

 Theft up 191% between 1985 and 1990

Crime levels are low. Most crime involves petty theft or is linked to alcohol and drugs (both banned). A stolen car often makes TV news headlines. The state of emergency gives the government the power to detain without charge or trial for indefinitely renewable two-year periods.

EDUCATION

 85%

Free schooling is available to all the population, with the exception of stateless Chinese, who do not qualify. The University of Brunei Darussalam is undergoing Islamization.

HEALTH

 1 per 1,456 people

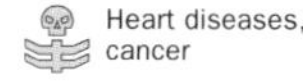 Heart diseases, cancer

The health service is free, although for major surgery Bruneians tend to travel to Singapore.

CHRONOLOGY

Under British control since 1841, Brunei became a formal British Protectorate in 1888.

- ❑ **1929** Oil extraction begins.
- ❑ **1941–1945** Occupied by Japan.
- ❑ **1959** First constitution enshrines Islam as state religion. Internal self-government.
- ❑ **1962** Pro-democracy rebellion crushed with help of British Gurkhas. State of emergency announced: Sultan rules by decree.
- ❑ **1984** Independence from Britain. Brunei joins ASEAN.
- ❑ **1990** Ideology of Malay Muslim Monarchy introduced.
- ❑ **1991** Imports of alcohol banned.
- ❑ **1992** Joins Non-Aligned Movement.

WEALTH

 Average manufacturing wage, 3.5 Brunei dollars per hour

CONSUMER GOODS OWNERSHIP

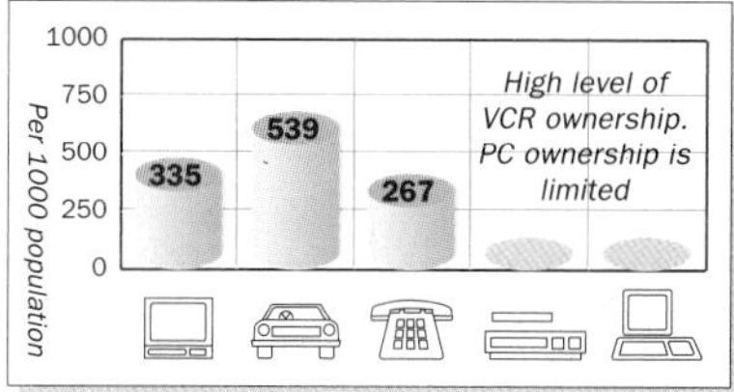

The wealthy in Brunei are those close to the Sultan, the world's richest man, according to *Forbes* magazine. A high standard of living keeps discontent to a minimum. Promotion within the civil service and universal education allow some social mobility among Malays. Bruneians are major consumers of high-tech hi-fi and video equipment, brand-name watches and Western designer clothes. Telephone lines, however, are difficult to install.

WORLD RANKING

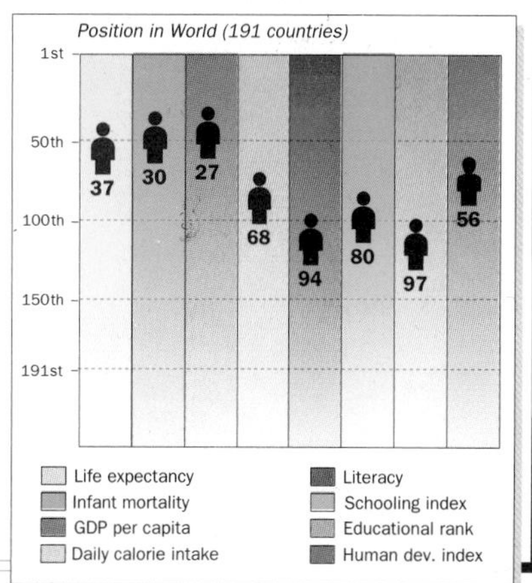

B

BULGARIA

OFFICIAL NAME: Republic of Bulgaria **CAPITAL:** Sofia
POPULATION: 9 million **CURRENCY:** Lev **OFFICIAL LANGUAGE:** Bulgarian

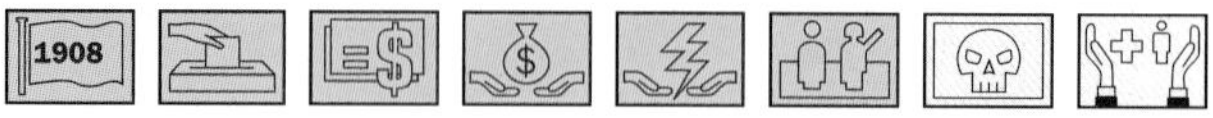

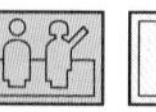

LOCATED IN SOUTHEASTERN EUROPE, Bulgaria is a mainly mountainous country. The River Danube forms the northern border, while the popular resorts on the Black Sea lie to the east. The most populated areas are around Sofia in the west, Plovdiv in the southeast, and along the Danube plain. Bulgaria was ruled by the Turks from 1396 until 1878. It became an independent kingdom in 1908, and was under communist rule from 1947 to 1989, the last 35 of those years under the leadership of Todor Zhivkov. The 1990s brought political instability as the country moved toward democracy.

***Rila Monastery** in the Rila Mountains. It is famous for its 1,200 National Revival Period frescoes dating from the mid-19th century.*

CLIMATE

WEATHER CHART

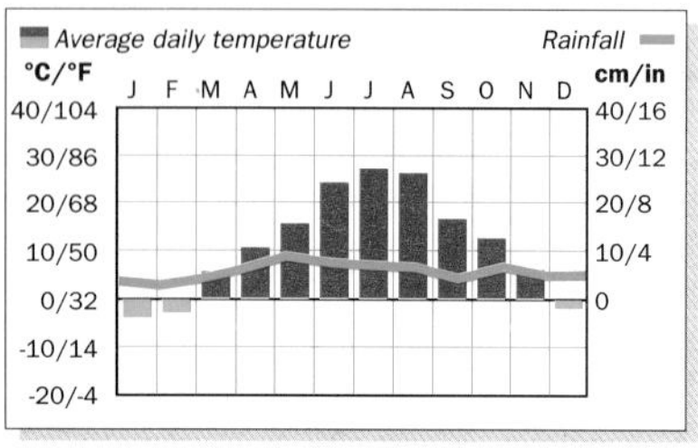

Average daily temperature — Rainfall

°C/°F — J F M A M J J A S O N D — cm/in

40/104, 30/86, 20/68, 10/50, 0/32, -10/14, -20/-4 — 40/16, 30/12, 20/8, 10/4, 0

The central valley and the lowlands have warm summers and cold, snowy winters, but hot or cold winds from Russia can bring spells of more extreme weather. The hotter summers on the Black Sea coast have encouraged the growth of tourist resorts. Snow may lie on the high mountain peaks until June.

COMMUNICATIONS

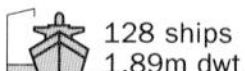

THE TRANSPORTATION NETWORK

22,899 miles (36,934 km)

165 miles (266 km)

2,665 miles (4,299 km)

291 miles (470 km)

The railroads are an integral part of the freight transport system, but have become unsafe through lack of investment. North–south routes were intentionally left undeveloped under the Warsaw Pact. Ferries are used for most traffic across the Danube – in 1989 there was only one bridge. Urban transportation is also lacking. Construction of a subway for Sofia began in 1979. The first section has yet to be completed.

TOURISM

MAIN OVERSEAS ARRIVALS

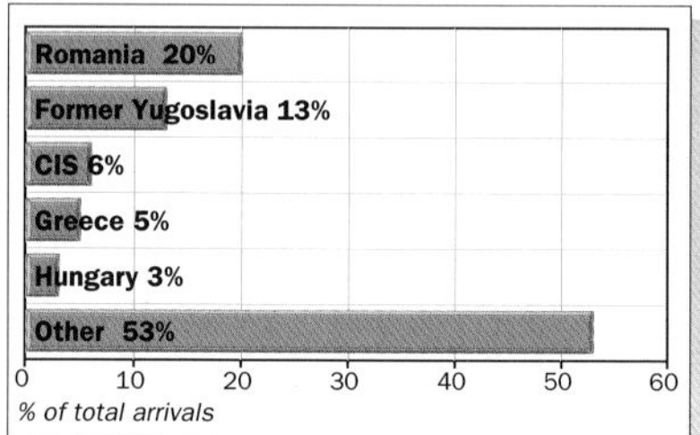

Under communism, Bulgaria's tourist industry catered to the East European mass market, which accounted for about two-thirds of visitors. In 1993, tourism showed unprecedented growth as the country found new popularity with Western visitors, attracted by low prices for sea-and-sun package vacations. Bulgaria is privatizing the industry, hoping to attract more upscale tourism by emphasizing its heritage.

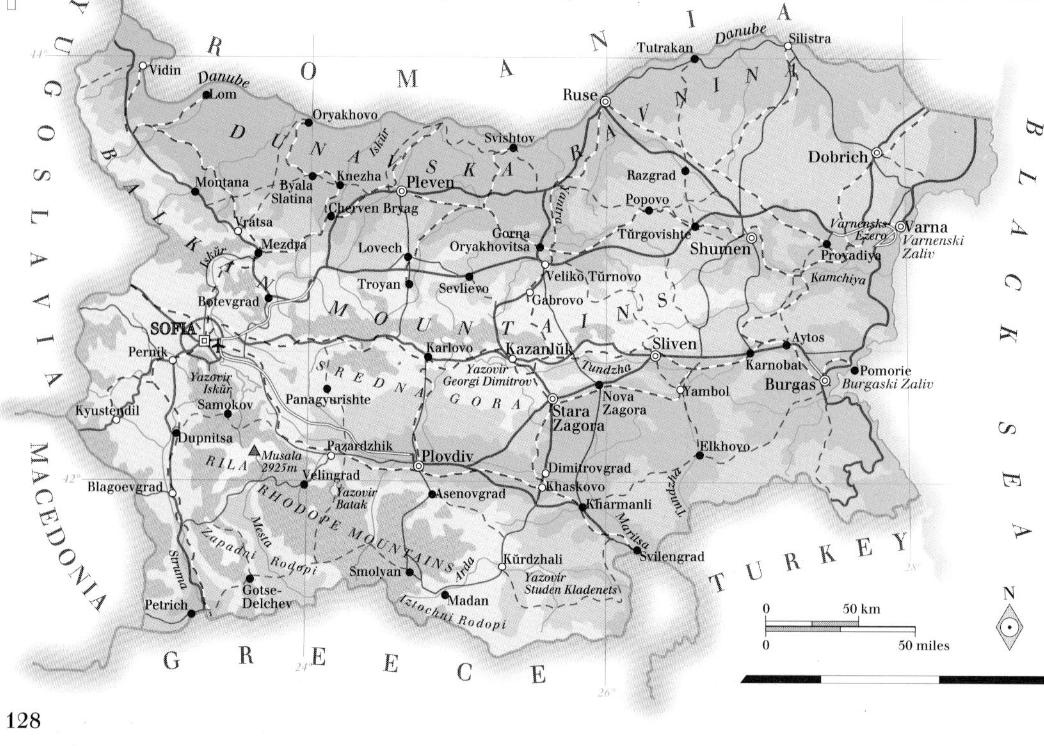

BULGARIA

Total Area : 110 910 sq. km (42 822 sq. miles)

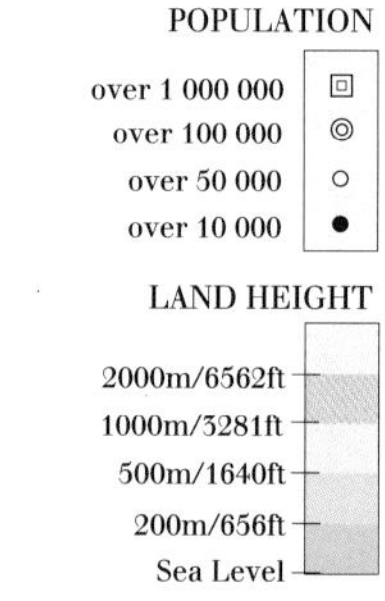

POPULATION

over 1 000 000
over 100 000
over 50 000
over 10 000

LAND HEIGHT

2000m/6562ft
1000m/3281ft
500m/1640ft
200m/656ft
Sea Level

0 — 50 km

0 — 50 miles

B

PEOPLE

Bulgarian, Turkish, Macedonian, Romany, Armenian, Russian

210 people per sq. mile

THE URBAN/RURAL POPULATION SPLIT

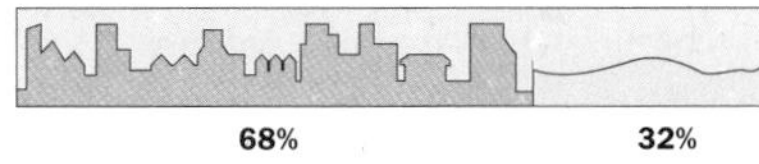

RELIGIOUS PERSUASION

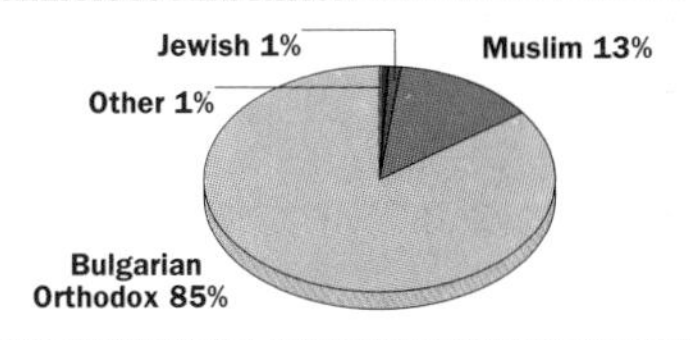

ETHNIC MAKEUP

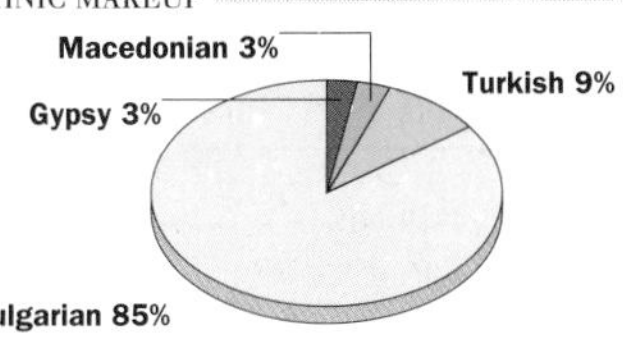

The government has sought to assimilate separate ethnic groups, thereby suppressing cultural identities. During the 1970s, Bulgarian Muslims, or *Pomaks*, had been forced to change Muslim names to Bulgarian ones. Bulgarian Turks were targeted in the 1980s. Despite the granting of linguistic and religious freedom in 1989, there was a mass exodus of ethnic Turks, when 300,000, or 40%, left for Turkey. Their farming skills have traditionally made an important contribution to the agricultural sector. Recent privatization programs left many Turks landless and provoked new emigration. The Turkish party, the MRF, which once held the balance of power in parliament, saw it seats reduced considerably following the 1994 elections. The Gypsy minority has no protection and suffers from discrimination at all levels. Women, particularly Turks, have equal rights in theory but rarely in practice.

POPULATION AGE BREAKDOWN

% of population by age group

	1960	1970	1980	1990	2000
65+	7.5%	9.6%	11.9%	13%	15.6%
15–64	66.4%	67.6%	66%	66.6%	65.3%
0–14	26.1%	22.8%	22.1%	20.4%	19.1%

WORLD AFFAIRS

Although maintaining good relations with Turkey is as important now as it was under communism, Bulgaria's new aims are to raise its profile in international organizations and gain greater trading access to the EU. Bulgaria has sent peacekeepers to Cambodia and has been conscientious in adhering to UN sanctions against former Yugoslavia, despite the costs of lost trade. Trade with former Soviet countries continues to supply important raw materials and spare parts.

AID

$192.8m

Down 49% in 1992

Aid, mainly from the IMF, World Bank, EU and EBRD, is granted mostly for infrastructure works. In 1993, IMF agreements were suspended because of a growing budget deficit. The absence of a modern banking and financial services industry hinders development. Western donors have agreed to reduce commercial bank debt by one-half.

POLITICS

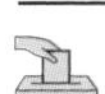

1998

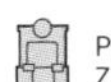

President Zhelyu Zhelev

THE STATE OF THE PARTIES

National Assembly 240 members

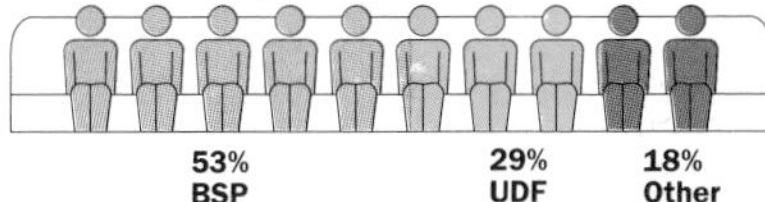

BSP = Bulgarian Socialist Party **UDF** = Union of Democratic Forces **Other** = Popular Union, Movement for Rights and Freedoms, Bulgarian Business Block

Bulgaria is a multiparty democracy.

MAIN POLITICAL ISSUES

Socialists return to power

Bulgaria has suffered from a succession of weak governments, each brought down by no-confidence votes, since its transition to democracy in 1990. In October 1992 the UDF, a broad anti-communist alliance, fell from office and was replaced by a non-party government led by an academic, Lyuben Berov, and supported by BSP (Bulgarian Socialist Party) votes. An early general election in December 1994 returned the BSP to to power with an outright majority in parliament. Its leader Zhan Videnov became prime minister.

Political trials

After several years' delay, former communist officials are being prosecuted for abuses under the former regime. Ex-autocrat Todor Zhivkov has been sentenced to seven years' imprisonment, pending appeal. Parliament has decided to block access to the State Security archives temporarily. Even the suggestion of collaboration was sufficient to force the resignation of the UDF chair; open files would be much too destabilizing.

PROFILE

In practice, Bulgaria is still in a period of transition to a full democracy. The BSP, mostly former communists, are back in power and are resisting political and economic change. The result is one of the slowest privatization programs in Eastern Europe; the old communist web of patronage and influence is still in place. The MRF, which represents the Turks, has been willing to collaborate with their former oppressors, as this has allowed them to reverse laws restricting the Turkish community.

***Zhelyu Zhelev**, a founding-member of the UDF, and president since 1990.*

***Lyuben Berov**, head of the non-party government in office from 1992 to 1994.*

CHRONOLOGY

Bulgaria was part of the Ottoman Empire for five centuries until its independence in 1908. Under King Ferdinand, it took sides with Germany during World War I, and subsequently lost valuable territory to Greece and Serbia. Under King Boris, Bulgaria once again sided with Germany in World War II.

- ❑ **1943** King Boris dies.
- ❑ **1944** Allies fire bomb Sofia. Soviet Army invades. Anti fascist Fatherland Front coalition(FF), including Agrarian Party and Bulgarian Communist Party (BCP), takes power in bloodless coup. Kimon Georgiev prime minister.
- ❑ **1946** September: referendum abolishes monarchy. Republic proclaimed. October: Grand National Assembly elections result in BCP majority. Communist leader Georgi Dmitrov prime minister.
- ❑ **1947** Dmitrov discredits Agrarian leader Nikola Petkov. Petkov arrested and sentenced to death. Dmitrov government receives international recognition. Soviet-style constitution adopted; Bulgaria becomes a one-party state. Country renamed the People's Republic of Bulgaria. Nationalization of the economy begins.

CHRONOLOGY *continued*

- **1949** Dmitrov dies, succeeded as prime minister by Vasil Kolarov.
- **1950** Kolarov dies and is replaced by Vulko Chervenkov. He begins purge of BCP and collectivization.
- **1953** Stalin dies and the power of "Little Stalin," as Chervenkov is called, begins to wane.
- **1954** Chervenkov yields power to Todor Zhivkov. Zhivkov sets out to make Bulgaria an inseparable part of the Soviet Union.
- **1955–1960** Zhivkov exonerates victims of Chervenkov's purges.
- **1962** Zhivkov defeats former ally Anton Yugov in battle for ideological leadership of the BCP.
- **1965** Plot to overthrow Zhivkov discovered by Soviet agents.
- **1968** Bulgarian troops aid Soviet army in invasion of Czechoslovakia.
- **1971** New constitution. Zhivkov becomes president of the State Council and resigns as premier.
- **1978** Purge of the BCP: 30,000 members expelled.
- **1984** Turkish minority forced to take Slavic names. Islamic rights banned; worldwide protests.
- **1989** June–August: exodus of 300,000 Bulgarian Turks. November: Zhivkov ousted as BCP leader and head of state. Replaced by Petur Mladenov. November: mass demonstation in Sofia for democratic reform. December: Union of Democratic Forces (UDF) formed.
- **1990** Economic collapse – food and fuel shortages. January: National Assembly votes to divest BCP of its constitutional right to be leading political party. Zhivkov arrested. April: BCP changes name to Bulgarian Socialist Party (BSP). June: election produces no overall result. August: Zhelyu Zhelev, UDF leader, becomes president. BSP in government. Country renamed the Republic of Bulgaria; communist symbols (grain sheaves and red star) removed from national flag.
- **1991** February: price controls abolished; steep price rises. July: new constitution adopted. October: UDF wins elections.
- **1992** Continued political and social unrest. October: UDF loses vote of confidence and resigns. December: the Movement for Rights and Freedoms (MRF) forms government. Lyuben Berov prime minister.
- **1993** Ambitious program to privatize economy begins. Berov survives no-confidence vote tabled by UDF.
- **1994** Zhivkov begins prison sentence for corruption and human rights abuses.

DEFENSE

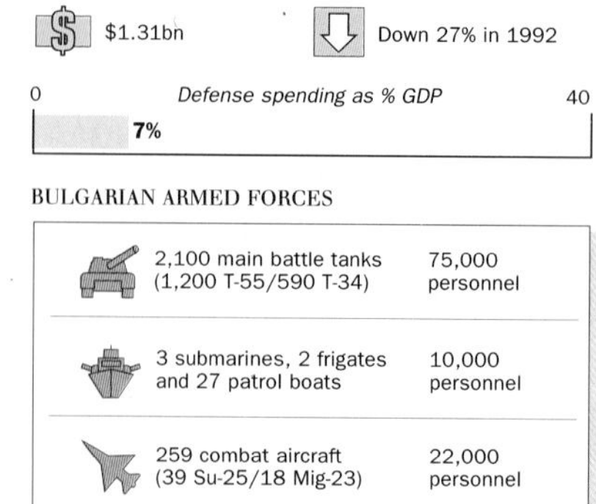

$1.31bn
Down 27% in 1992
0
Defense spending as % GDP
40
7%
BULGARIAN ARMED FORCES
2,100 main battle tanks (1,200 T-55/590 T-34)
75,000 personnel
3 submarines, 2 frigates and 27 patrol boats
10,000 personnel
259 combat aircraft (39 Su-25/18 Mig-23)
22,000 personnel
None

Economic difficulties have forced Bulgaria to trim its defense spending. Moves to reorganize the army have caused serious disaffection in officer ranks. The government's defense priority is to ensure that Bulgaria can maintain national security without its old Soviet backing. It is therefore seeking new alliances. If the conflict in former Yugoslavia were to spread south, Bulgaria would probably join an anti-Serbian alliance. It also needs to decide whether to reduce or expand the large arms industry of the communist era. Its main products were missiles, sub-machine guns, Kalashnikov rifles, ammunition and electronic equipment.

ECONOMICS

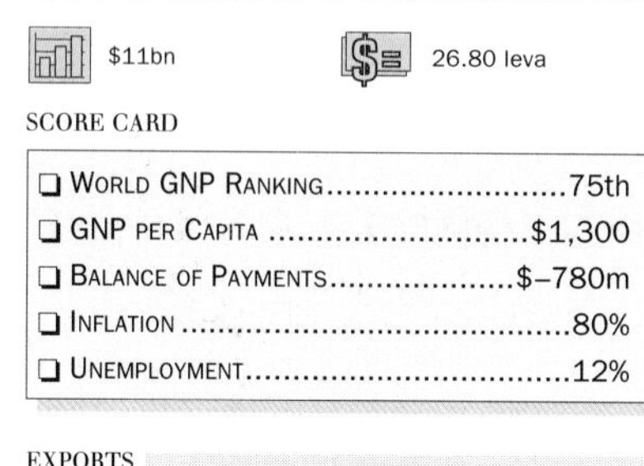

EXPORTS

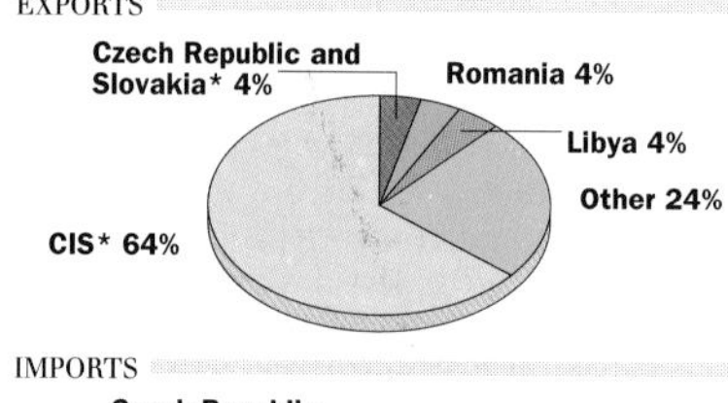

IMPORTS

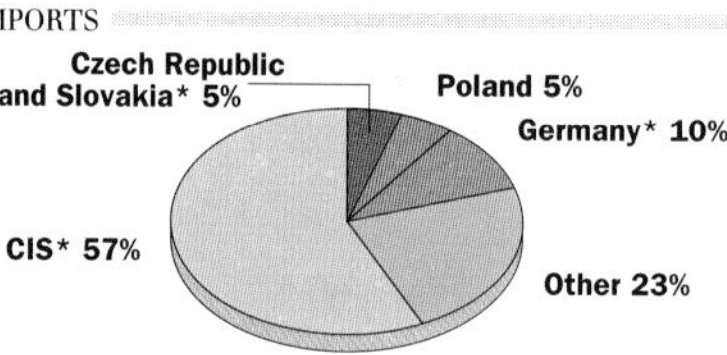

Strengths

Coal and natural gas. Good agricultural production, especially grapes for well-developed wine industry, and tobacco. Strong expertise in computer software.

Weaknesses

Outdated equipment and outstanding debt throughout industry. Dependence on Russia for machinery and spare parts for existing factories. Location prevents easy access to rest of Europe.

Profile

Restructuring the economy is linked to privatization – a process that has been delayed for political and technical reasons. In 1980, joint ventures were allowed. This permitted the party elite to transfer valuable assets to companies that they or their families owned. In 1992, new legislation allowed foreign

ECONOMIC PERFORMANCE INDICATOR

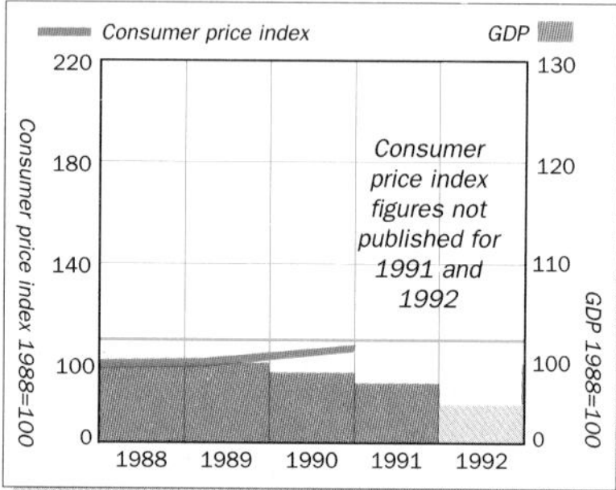

firms to own companies outright. Investment is still negligible. Trade has shifted toward the EU, which by 1992 accounted for a third of foreign trade. The former Soviet Union's share fell from 75% of all foreign trade in 1989 to just over 25% in 1992. Considerable potential exists for trade with Russia and Ukraine. Bulgaria specialized in producing information technology for the COMECON countries; it is now seeks expansion into Western markets.

BULGARIA : MAJOR BUSINESSES

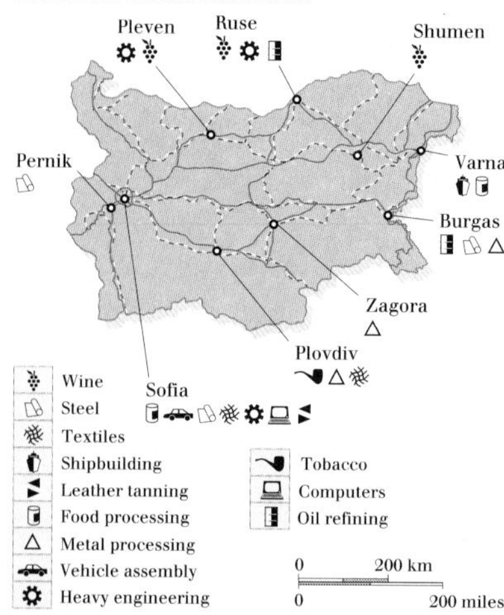

B

RESOURCES

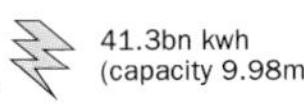

41.3bn kwh (capacity 9.98m kw)

Reserves of 15,000,000 bbl; refines 300,000 b/cd

8.6m sheep, 4.1m pigs, 1.6m cattle, 329,000 asses

Coal, iron, copper, lead, zinc, oil, natural gas

ELECTRICITY GENERATION

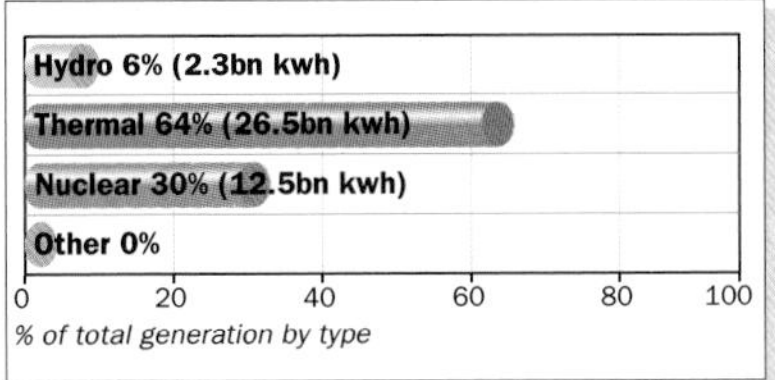

Bulgaria has modest oil reserves and somewhat larger ones of coal and natural gas, but still has to import about 70% of its primary energy needs, much of it from the former Soviet Union. Unreliability of supplies in the past led to frequent winter power cuts. These have largely disappeared as decreased production in heavy industry and improved domestic supply from nuclear sources have lowered import demand. Bulgaria is partly reliant on nuclear power. Two of the four reactors at Kozloduy were upgraded after criticisms over safety measures, and a new plant is being planned. The first generator at the Chaira Dam came into service in 1993 to boost hydroelectric supplies. Bulgaria must decide how many of its 14 coal mines to close – ten are unprofitable.

BULGARIA : LAND USE

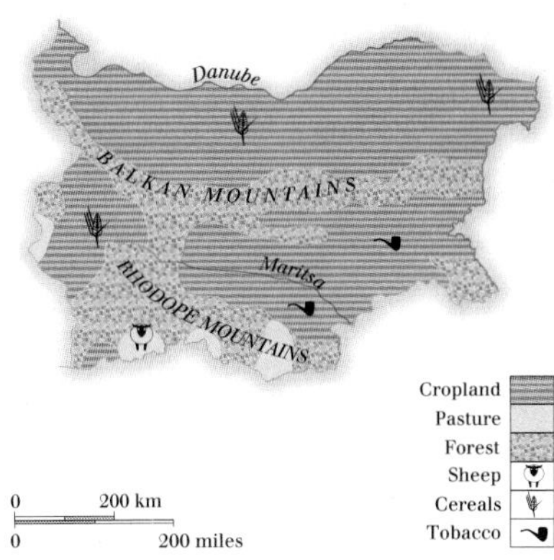

ENVIRONMENT

2%

Several grassroots environmental pressure groups

ENVIRONMENTAL TREATIES

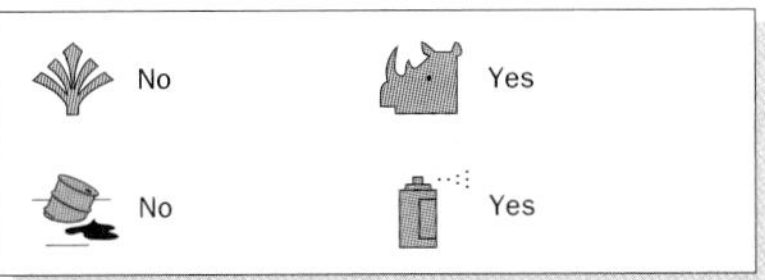

Serious environmental degradation in the 1980s resulted from the state's unwillingness to enforce existing environmental laws, and led to the foundation of the party *Ecoglasnost* in 1989. It has been active in circulating information on pollution, health and nuclear waste dump locations and in bringing polluters to court. Bulgaria's main environmental problems are deforestation and air pollution. The spontaneous formation of regional environmental pressure groups indicates the severity of pollution problems.

MEDIA

Nominally free press since 1989

PUBLISHING AND BROADCAST MEDIA

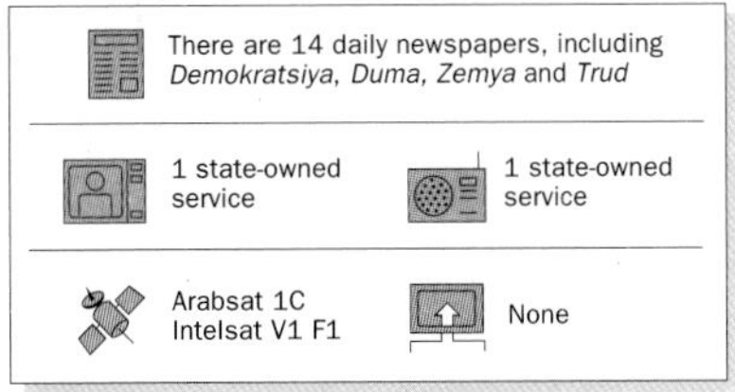

There are 14 daily newspapers, including *Demokratsiya, Duma, Zemya* and *Trud*
1 state-owned service
1 state-owned service
Arabsat 1C Intelsat V1 F1
None

The media was liberalized in 1989 and presently a wide range of dailies are published. No paper is completely independent, as each is linked to some party or interest. The *Bulgarian Business News* and *24 Chasa* are among the most influential, owned by a former communist entrepreneur and supported by the First Private Bank.

CRIME

9,000 prisoners

Rising

CRIME RATES

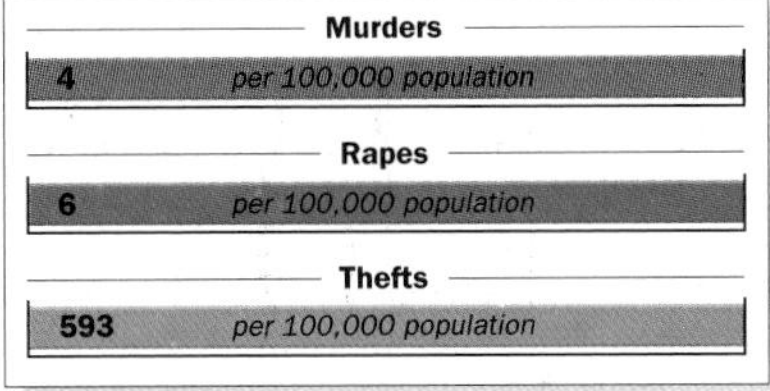

Murders
4 per 100,000 population
Rapes
6 per 100,000 population
Thefts
593 per 100,000 population

Police have been attempting to combat the increase in robberies and muggings. Tourists in the major vacation resorts are targets for muggers. In Sofia, the rise in organized crime is of growing concern. Violations of the Turkish minority's human rights are now a sensitive political issue.

EDUCATION

96%

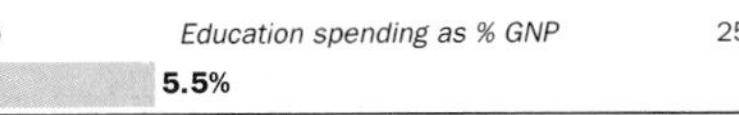

THE EDUCATION SYSTEM

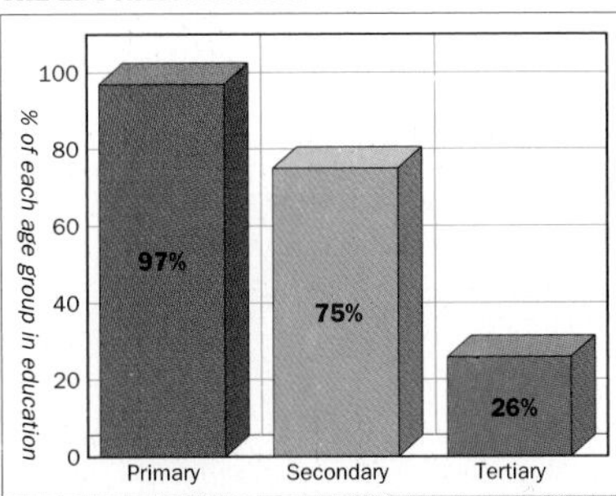

Bulgaria is changing its educational system from a Soviet-inspired to a European-style model. Teaching standards are lowest in the rural and Turkish communities.

HEALTH

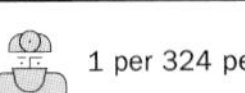

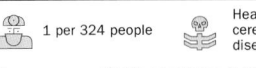

1 per 324 people

Heart and cerebrovascular diseases, cancer

0 Health spending as % GNP 25

Spending cuts have reduced health budget

Although hospital facilities have kept pace with population growth, the emigration of many doctors and nurses has lowered the standard of care. Shortages of medicines are widespread.

WEALTH

Disparities in wealth are considerable

CONSUMER GOODS OWNERSHIP

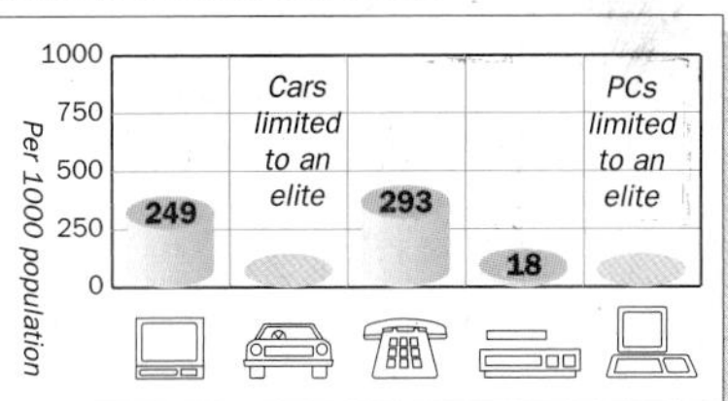

The former Communist Party elite is still the richest group; Turks and Gypsies are the poorest.

WORLD RANKING

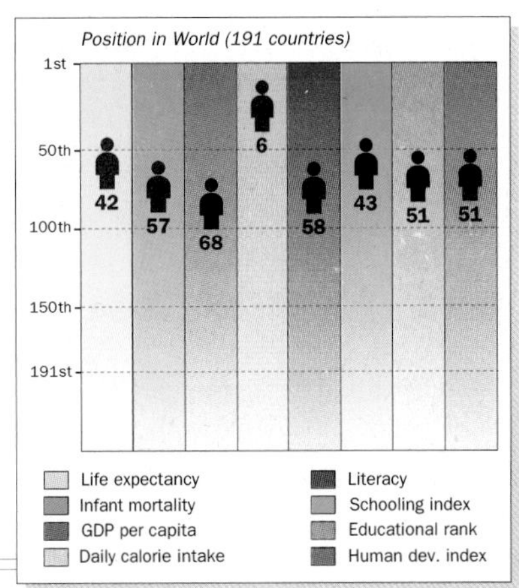

BURKINA

OFFICIAL NAME: Burkina **CAPITAL:** Ouagadougou
POPULATION: 9.5 million **CURRENCY:** CFA franc **OFFICIAL LANGUAGE:** French

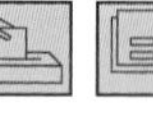

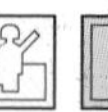

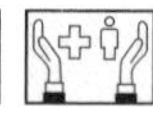

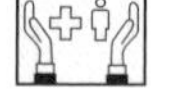

LANDLOCKED IN WEST AFRICA, Burkina (formerly Upper Volta) gained independence from France in 1960. The majority of Burkina lies in the arid fringe of the Sahara known as the Sahel. Ruled by military dictators for much of its post-independence history, Burkina became a multiparty state in 1991. However, much power still rests with President Blaise Compaoré. Burkina's economy remains largely based on agriculture.

CLIMATE

WEATHER CHART

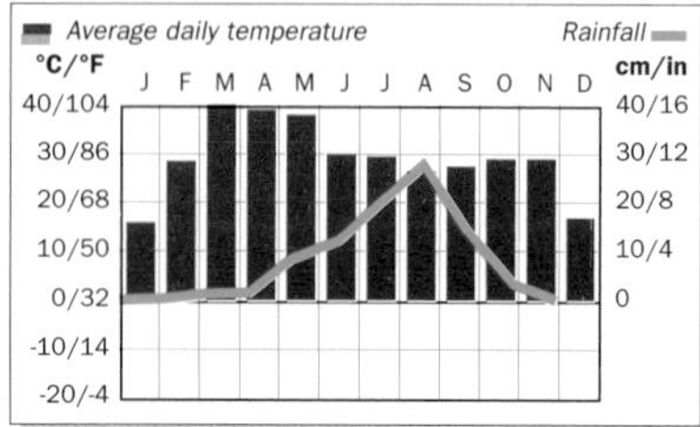

The tropical climate comprises two seasons – unreliable rains from June to October, and a long dry season.

COMMUNICATIONS

Ouagadougou Intl 186,673 passengers

Has no fleet

THE TRANSPORTATION NETWORK

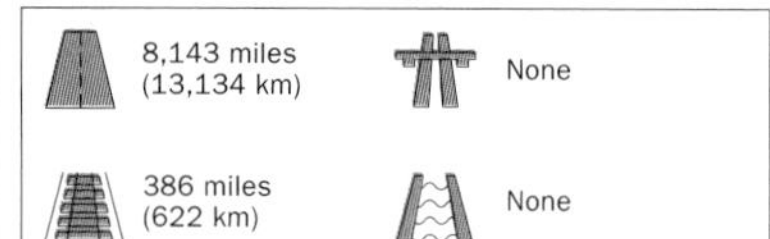

The railroad to the port of Abidjan in the Ivory Coast provides the main commercial route to the sea. Roads through Benin, Togo and Ghana provide alternative access.

TOURISM

106,144 visitors

Up 4% in 1991

MAIN OVERSEAS ARRIVALS

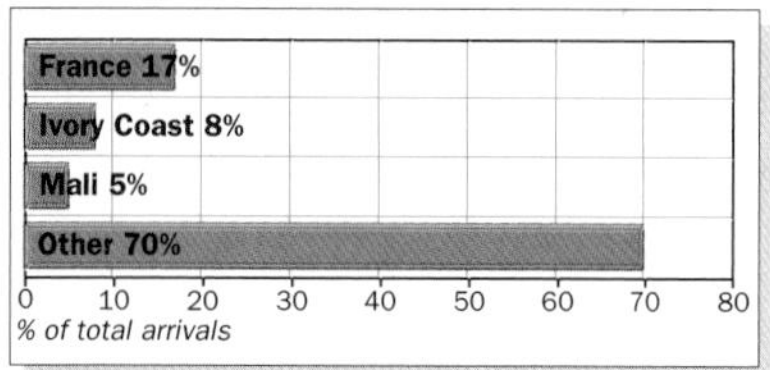

Some potential exists for safari tourism and the cities offer an attractive mix of colonial and African architecture. Big game hunting is allowed in some areas.

PEOPLE

Mossi, Fulani, French, Tuareg, Dyula, Songhai

85 people per sq. mile

THE URBAN/RURAL POPULATION SPLIT

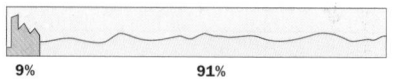

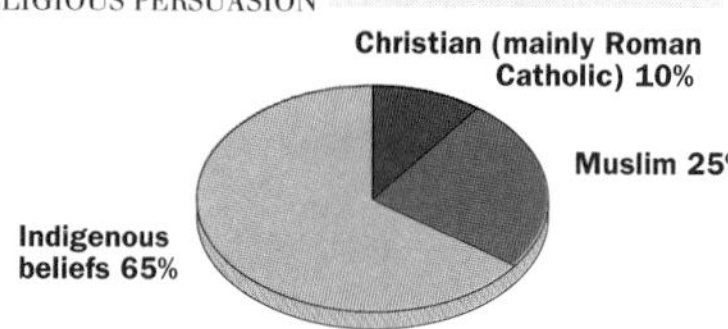

RELIGIOUS PERSUASION

Christian (mainly Roman Catholic) 10%
Muslim 25%
Indigenous beliefs 65%

No ethnic group is dominant in Burkina, although the Mossi people who live in the area of their old empire around Ouagadougou have always played an important role in government. Burkina's first president, Maurice Yameogo, and the present leader, Blaise Compaoré, are both Mossi. The people from the west are much more ethnically mixed.

The extended family is important and reaches from the villages into the towns and cities. Extreme poverty has led to a strong sense of egalitarianism within society. The lack of women in public life belies their real power and influence, particularly within the traditional framework of the extended family. However, most women are still denied access to education and senior professional positions.

Camel ploughing. *Burkina's poor soils and frequent droughts lead many young men to emigrate seasonally in search of work.*

POLITICS

1997

President Blaise Compaoré

THE STATE OF THE PARTIES

Assembly of Popular Deputies 107 members

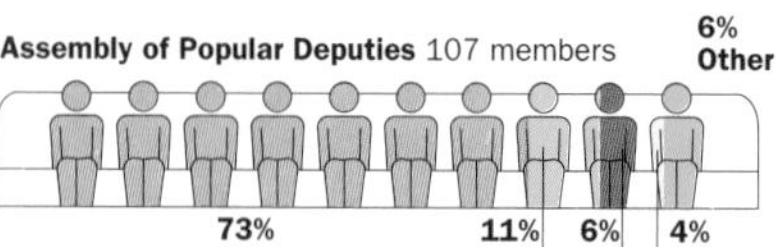

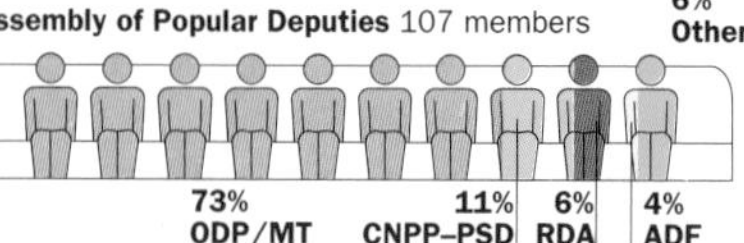

OPT/MT = Organization for Popular Democracy/Labor Movement **CNPP–PSD** = National Convention of Progressive Patriots – Social Democratic Party **RDA** = African Democratic Assembly **ADF** = Alliance for Democracy and Federation

A multiparty democracy in theory, Burkina is still dominated in practice by the former military dictator, Blaise Compaoré. He has been in power since the assassination in 1987 of Capt. Thomas Sankara, Compaoré's former leader. Several of Compaoré's close military colleagues have since been murdered as well.

Compaoré's grip on power in Burkina appears to be solid. In the National Assembly, the ODP/MT alliance offers total support. Most opposition leaders are still living in exile and real opposition within Burkina remains underground. Compaoré's military background also gives him the support of the army. While the military no longer holds ministerial posts – a measure which helps Burkina maintain its democratic image – it remains influential behind the scenes.

There are signs, however, that a small group within the ODP/MT will push for greater democracy once Compaoré retires from office.

WORLD AFFAIRS

FZ

Burkina's landlocked position means good relations with countries to the south are a major foreign policy concern. However, Compaoré's relationship with other ECOWAS states is deteriorating over the war in Liberia.

AID

$409m (receipts)

Up 22% in 1991

External aid, mostly from France and the EU, is important to Burkina's economy. The large number of NGOs has caused organizational problems; there is often difficulty in finding suitable projects for all the prospective donors.

B

BURKINA

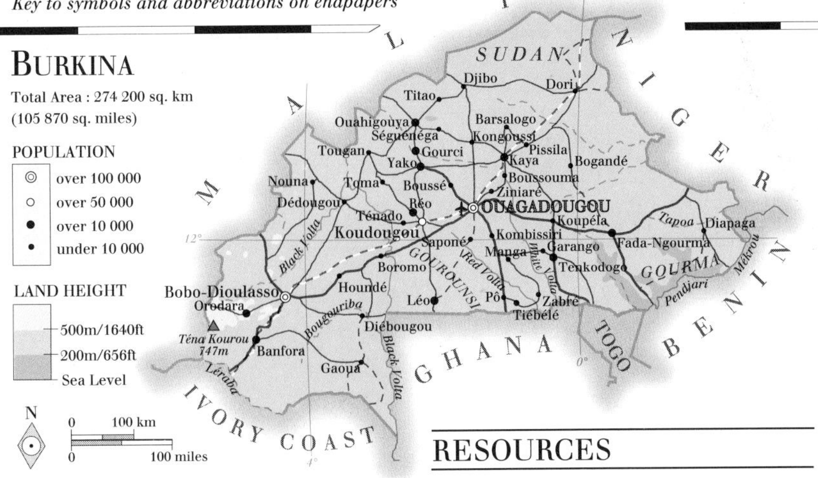

DEFENSE

 $108.1m  Up 41% in 1991

The army's main role has been maintaining internal security. Burkina is reliant on France for most equipment and training.

ECONOMICS

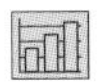 $2.9bn  276.26 CFA francs

SCORE CARD

- ❑ WORLD GNP RANKING........................126th
- ❑ GNP PER CAPITA $305
- ❑ BALANCE OF PAYMENTS...................$–167m
- ❑ INFLATION 4.6%
- ❑ UNEMPLOYMENT.................................16%

STRENGTHS

Significant remittances from plantation workers in Ghana and the Ivory Coast – $100 million a year between 1980 and 1985. Low debt burden. Ability to attract foreign aid. Cotton growing. Gold is now leading non-agricultural export.

WEAKNESSES

Landlocked. Few economically viable natural resources. Prone to drought. Despite the benefits of foreign earnings, seasonal emigration has meant a decline in rural productivity.

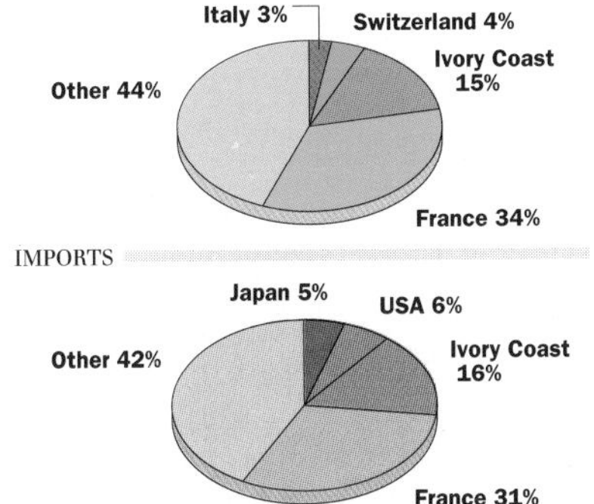

RESOURCES

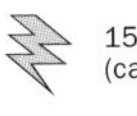 155m kwh (capacity 59,000 kw) Not an oil producer and has no refineries

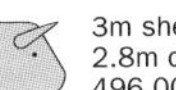 3m sheep, 2.8m cattle, 496,000 pigs Gold, antimony, marble, manganese, silver, zinc

Burkina has considerable mineral wealth, including large manganese and silver deposits. However, the only metal ore being exploited is gold. Three dams to produce hydroelectric power will reduce dependence on thermal energy.

ENVIRONMENT

 10% (8% partially protected)  Droughts of 1973 and 1983 have aggravated desertification

Like other countries on the southern rim of the Sahara, desertification is the major ecological issue. The rate of tree cutting for fuel is on the increase.

MEDIA

 In spite of press freedom guarantees in the 1991 constitution, political censorship still exists in practice

PUBLISHING AND BROADCAST MEDIA

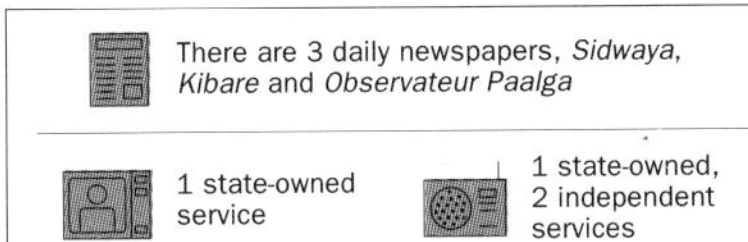

Limited press freedom since 1991 has seen the growth of a number of small independent newspapers funded by opposition parties.

CRIME

 Burkina does not publish prison figures  General crime levels are rising

Crime levels have traditionally been low. However, the urbanization of society and the increase in political violence have increased levels.

EDUCATION

 18%

Education is based on the French system. Recently, practical subjects have received more emphasis.

CHRONOLOGY

Ruled by Mossi kings from the 16th century, Burkina became an outpost of the French Empire in the late 19th century. It was renamed Upper Volta at independence in 1960.

- ❑ **1966** Military coup led by Lt.-Col. Sangoulé Lamizana.
- ❑ **1980** Lamizana ousted, Col. Saye Zerbo becomes president.
- ❑ **1982** Capt. Thomas Sankara takes power. People's Salvation Council (PSC) begins radical reforms.
- ❑ **1984** Renamed Burkina.
- ❑ **1987** PSC reforms cause dissent. Sankara assassinated, Capt. Blaise Compaoré takes power.
- ❑ **1991** New constitution. Compaoré elected president.
- ❑ **1992** Youssouf Ouédraogo made premier as ODP/MT win elections.

HEALTH

 1 per 29,914 people  Malaria, diarrheal and respiratory diseases

The focus of Burkina's health spending is on primary health care and vaccination.

WEALTH

 Shop assistant, 30,250 CFA francs per month; dentist, 100,000 CFA francs per month

CONSUMER GOODS OWNERSHIP

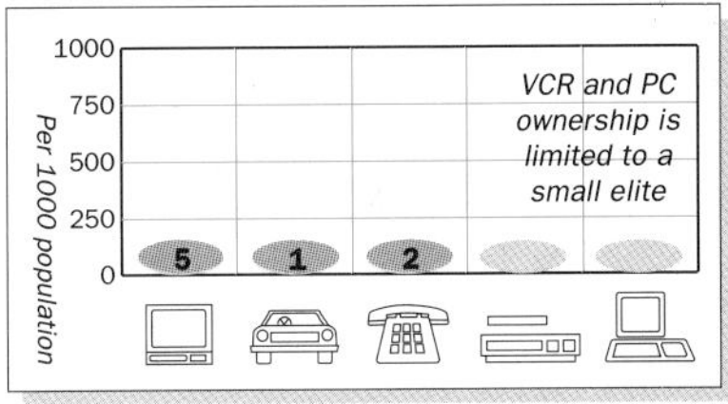

Burkina is a country of extreme, almost universal poverty. Displays of wealth are rare.

WORLD RANKING

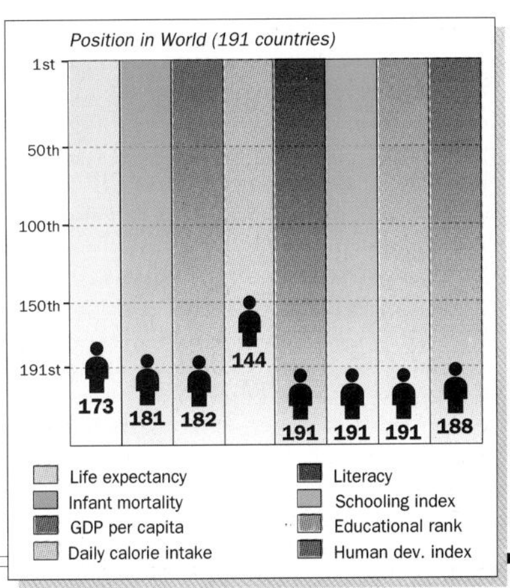

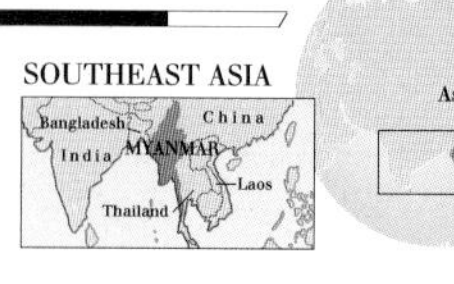

BURMA (MYANMAR)

OFFICIAL NAME: Union of Myanmar **CAPITAL:** Rangoon (Yangon)
POPULATION: 42.5 million **CURRENCY:** Kyat **OFFICIAL LANGUAGE:** Burmese (Myanmar)

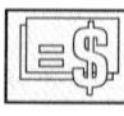

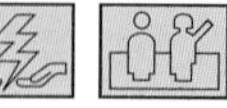

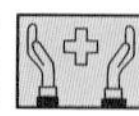

FORMING THE EASTERN shores of the Bay of Bengal and the Andaman Sea in Southeast Asia, Myanmar is mountainous in the north, while the once-forested, fertile Irrawaddy basin occupies most of the country. Myanmar gained independence from British colonial control in 1948 and has recently suffered widespread political repression and ethnic conflict. In 1990, the National League for Democracy (NLD) gained a majority in free elections but was prevented from taking power by the military. Rich in natural resources, which include fisheries and teak forests, Myanmar's economy remains mostly agricultural.

***Transporting timber** on the Irrawaddy River near Mandalay. Burma once had the world's largest reserves of teak.*

CLIMATE

WEATHER CHART

Average daily temperature — Rainfall

°C/°F: 60/140, 50/122, 40/104, 30/86, 20/68, 10/50, 0/32

cm/in: 60/24, 50/20, 40/16, 30/12, 20/8, 10/4, 0

J F M A M J J A S O N D

The tropical climate has three seasons: the wet season, when rainfall in the Irrawaddy delta and Tenasserim peninsula can reach 195 in; summer, when northern Burma experiences 122°F and 100% humidity; and winter, when it is rarely cooler than 59°F except in the northern mountains.

COMMUNICATIONS

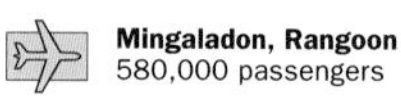

Mingaladon, Rangoon
580,000 passengers

72 ships
1.33m dwt

THE TRANSPORTATION NETWORK

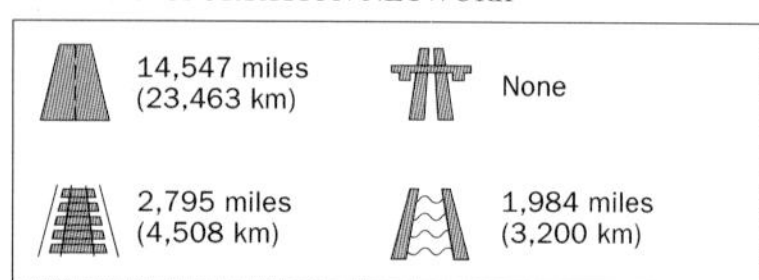

Most current construction projects are linked to the booming China–Burma border trade, the majority of which was legalized in 1989. Old bridges and roads (including the famous Burma, Ledo and Silk Roads, all key routes into China) are being renewed and new ones built with Chinese aid which will make it easier to distribute key products, including opium. However, the motives for their construction are military as well as commercial. The state has recently relaxed its monopoly of transportation: since 1988, private bus companies have had licenses to operate. Air and rail routes, remain under government control.

TOURISM

5,044 visitors

Down 77% in 1989

MAIN OVERSEAS ARRIVALS

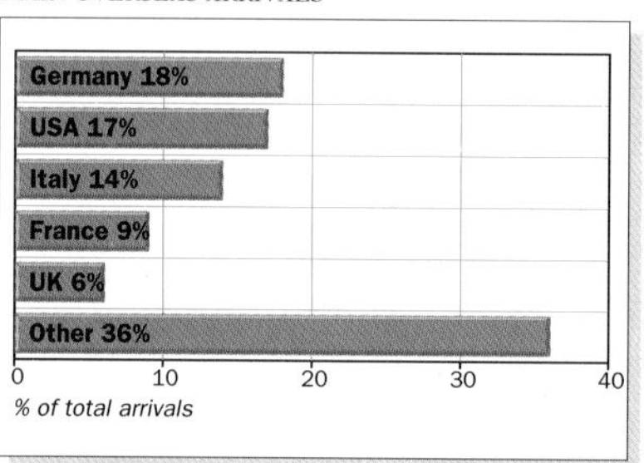

From 1962 until 1988, tourists were limited to one-week stays. Burma has recently adopted an open-door policy, designed to attract foreign exchange. Old hotels are now being renovated and new ones built in joint ventures with private companies. Much of the finance comes from Japan, Singapore, South Korea and Hong Kong. China is also helping to build an international airport at Mandalay. Since 1990, the junta has been face-lifting historic monuments and relocating "unsightly" villages away from temples at Pagan, Mandalay, Sagaing and Amarapura.

PEOPLE

Burmese, Karen, Shan, Chin, Kachin, Mon, Palaung, Wa

161 people per sq. mile

THE URBAN/RURAL POPULATION SPLIT

25% 75%

RELIGIOUS PERSUASION

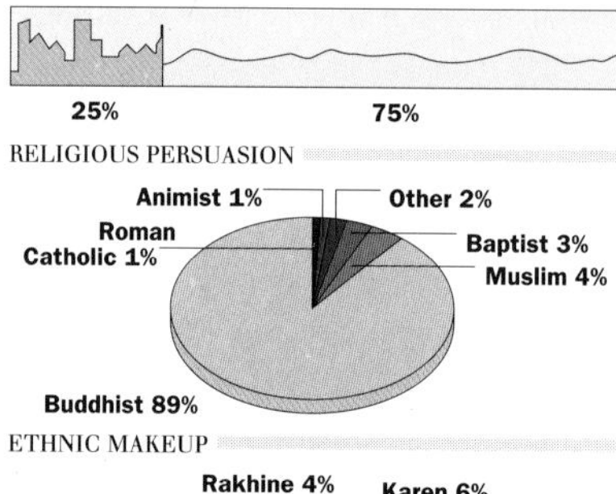

ETHNIC MAKEUP

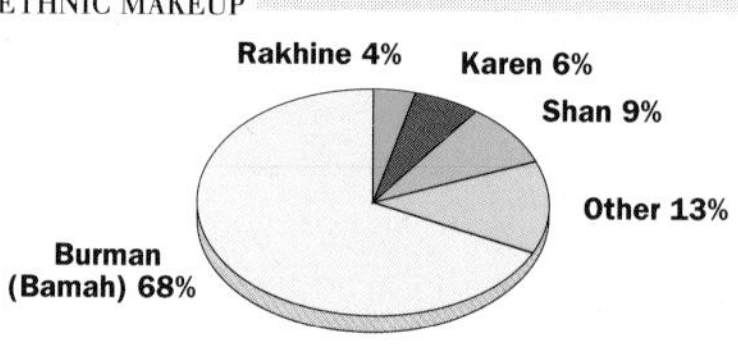

Burma suffers from considerable ethnic tension between the Burman majority and the smaller ethnic groups. At independence, the Shans, Karens, Kachins, Mons, Karennis and Chins all demanded their own states within a federation but were refused by the central government. All groups have kept their demands alive with low-level guerrilla activity against the state; in 1988 they united in a common cause against the military dictatorship, but several groups have recently signed peace treaties with the government.

A savage history, mainly of Burman repression of smaller groups, still plays a large part in the mistrust felt by the minorities for the Burman. Each group maintains a distinct cultural identity. While the Burman claim racial purity, in fact many of them are of mixed blood, or ethnically Chinese.

Family life in Burma is still based around the extended family. Women have a prominent role, with access to education. Many run or own businesses in their own right. However, top jobs in government are still held almost exclusively by men.

POPULATION AGE BREAKDOWN

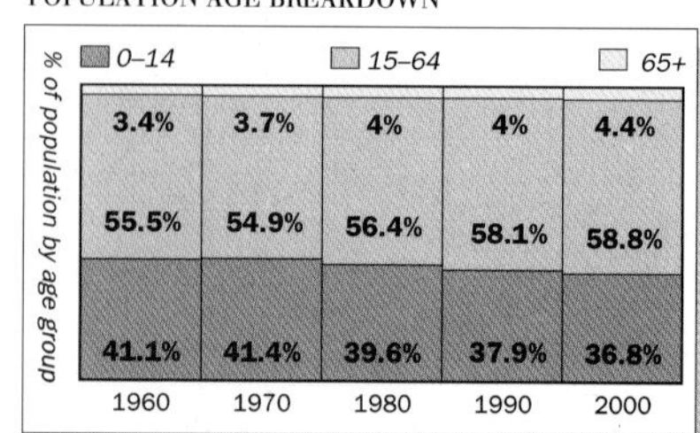

B

POLITICS

Uncertain | General Than Shwe

THE STATE OF THE PARTIES

Constituent Assembly 485 Members

The National League for Democracy (NLD) won 81% of seats in the Assembly in elections in 1990. However, they were prevented from taking power by the State Law and Order Restoration Council (SLORC)

Burma has been ruled by the military-backed SLORC dictatorship since 1988.

MAIN POLITICAL ISSUES

Restoring democracy
The military rules Burma with little regard to human rights. Opposition is not tolerated and torture and killings are commonplace. Ethnic rebel groups (with 30,000 armed members) have allied with democrats to oppose the regime. The focal point of opposition is Aung San Suu Kyi, kept under house arrest but effectively protected by the publicity she has generated in the West.

Refugees
Dislocated by the policies of the military regime, around one million refugees are stranded along Burma's borders with Bangladesh, Thailand, China and India.

PROFILE

Demands for a return to democracy culminated in the student-led political uprisings of 1987–1988. The military seized power in September 1988, ostensibly to maintain order until multiparty elections could be held. Instead, the State Law and Order Restoration Council (SLORC) was formed and all state bodies were abolished. Elections were held in 1990 and won by the NLD. However, the SLORC failed to relinquish power and pro-democracy opposition was brutally crushed. Ethnic rebel forces and opposition groups united to form the parallel Democratic Alliance of Burma government in Manerplaw.

Aung San Suu Kyi, figurehead of the pro-democracy movement.

General Ne Win, Burma's leader 1964–1988

BURMA (MYANMAR)

Total Area : 676 550 sq. km (261 200 sq. miles)

0 — 200 km
0 — 200 miles

POPULATION
over 1 000 000
over 500 000
over 100 000
over 50 000
over 10 000
under 10 000

LAND HEIGHT
4000m/13 124ft
2000m/6562ft
1000m/3281ft
500m/1640ft
200m/656ft
Sea Level

WORLD AFFAIRS

Burma's key relationship is with China. The latter has consistently backed the SLORC military regime and is a major supplier of weapons to the 350,000-strong Burmese army. The relationship is symbiotic, allowing China access to the Indian Ocean and giving it great influence over a regime partly dependent on its support. Burma's neighbors regard the arrangement as one which is seriously destabilizing the whole Asia–Pacific region.

Western governments have been active in the UN and EU in condemning the human rights abuses of the regime, and in 1991 Aung San Suu Kyi received the Nobel Peace Prize for her resistance. In practice, however, they maintain an ambiguous relationship with the SLORC regime. Economic ties are growing stronger, particularly between the SLORC-owned state enterprises and Western multinationals. The latter are well represented in the increasingly profitable Burmese offshore oil and gas drilling industries.

CHRONOLOGY

From the 11th century, Burma's many ethnic groups came under the rule of three Tibeto-Burman dynasties, interspersed with periods of rule by the Mongols and the Mon. The Third Dynasty came into conflict with the British in India, sparking the Anglo-Burmese Wars of 1824, 1852 and 1885.

- **1886** Burma becomes a province of British India.
- **1906** Young Men's Buddhist Association founded to maintain cultural identity under British colonial influence.
- **1930–1931** Economic depression and slump in rice prices provokes uprising led by monk Saya San.
- **1937** Separation from India.
- **1942** Japan invades, receiving help from Burmese Independence Army (BIA) under "Thirty Comrades" previously trained in Japan.
- **1945** BIA swaps sides and, supported by Anti-Fascist People's Freedom League (AFPFL) led by Aung San, helps Allies reoccupy country.
- **1947** UK agrees to Burmese independence. Aung San wins elections, but is assassinated.

B

CHRONOLOGY *continued*

- **1948** Independence under new prime minister, U Nu, who initiates socialist policies. Revolts by ethnic separatists and communists, notably Karen liberation struggle.
- **1958** Ruling AFPFL splits in two. Shan liberation struggle begins.
- **1960** U Nu's faction wins elections.
- **1961** Kachin rebellion begins.
- **1962** Military coup led by Gen. Ne Win. "New Order" policy of "Buddhist Socialism" – isolation from outside world. Mining and other industries nationalized. Free trade prohibited.
- **1964** Ne Win makes Socialist Program Party sole legal party.
- **1976** Social unrest. Attempted military coup. 40% of country now held by ethnic liberation groups.
- **1982** Non-indigenous people barred from public office.
- **1987** UN labels Burma a "least-developed nation." Ne Win accepts need to review economic policy.
- **1988** Student riots. Ne Win resigns. Martial law. More riots; 3,000–4,000 dead. Students and monks take control of many towns. NLD founded to form an alternative government by ex-premier U Nu, Aung San Suu Kyi, daughter of Gen. Aung San, and others. Gen. Saw Maung leads military coup. Students flee cities. SLORC takes power. National Democratic Front of ethnic resistance groups forms Democratic Alliance of Burma to include 11 more groups.
- **1989** Army arrests NLD leaders and steps up anti-rebel activity.
- **1990** Elections permitted. NLD wins 81% of seats. SLORC, however, remains in power. More NLD leaders arrested.
- **1991** Aung San Suu Kyi, under house arrest, awarded Nobel Peace Prize. NLD expells her as result of SLORC pressure. Many parties deregistered.
- **1992** Gen. Than Shwe takes over as SLORC leader.

AID

Undisclosed military and soft loan receipts from China

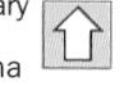
On the increase, mostly from China

In 1988, Western nations, the World Bank and certain UN agencies such as the UNDP halted bilateral aid. The UN has, however, continued funding some development projects through its Drug Control Program and the World Health Organization. The largest bilateral donor is now China, which in 1990 struck an arms deal worth $1.4 billion and recently agreed to a 50 million yuan interest-free loan.

DEFENSE

$1.3bn
Up 19% between 1990 and 1992
0
Defense spending as % GDP
40
4.8%
BURMESE ARMED FORCES
56 main battle tanks (26 Comet/30 Ch T-69II)
350,000 personnel
60 patrol boats (1 Yan Taing Aung/ 1 Yan Gyi Aung)
13,500 personnel
37 combat aircraft (10 F-7/2 FT-7/15 PC-7)
9,000 personnel
None

The SLORC has steadily obtained modern weapons and military technology from around the world, primarily from China, but also from France, Germany, Sweden and former Yugoslavia. In the five years from 1988 to 1993, the army expanded by 20% to 350,000 men.

Since 1988, the army has waged dry-season campaigns against minority groups every year except 1993. It has successfully put down most Mon and Karen insurgent campaigns and has destroyed their bases in southeastern Burma. Its 1989 assault on Muslim minorities in the Arakan region of western Burma resulted in 300,000 seeking refuge in Bangladesh.

ECONOMICS

$37.7bn

6.41 kyats

SCORE CARD

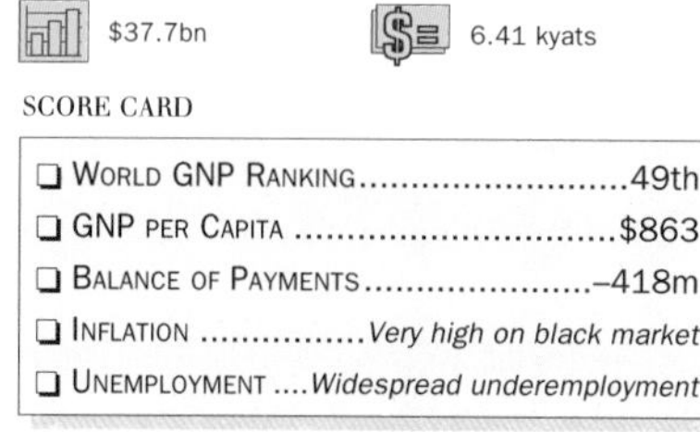

World GNP Ranking 49th
GNP per Capita $863
Balance of Payments .... –418m
Inflation .... Very high on black market
Unemployment .... Widespread underemployment

EXPORTS

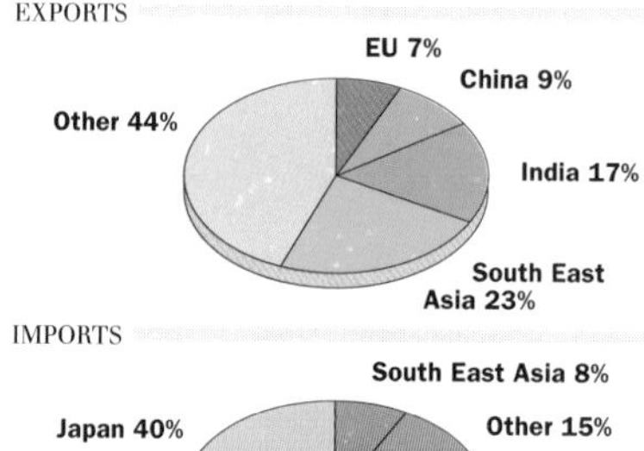

IMPORTS

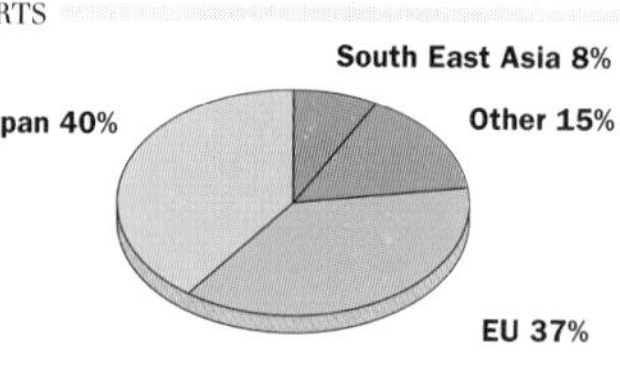

ECONOMIC PERFORMANCE INDICATOR

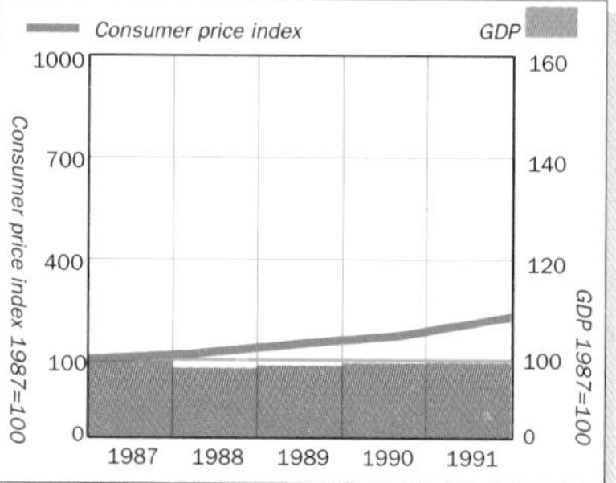

Since 1989, the SLORC's open-door market-economy policy has brought a flood of foreign investment in oil and gas (by Western companies) and forestry, tourism and mining (by Asian companies). The recent boom in trade with China has turned less-developed Upper Burma into a thriving business center full of Chinese goods and foreign visitors. The junta is concentrating on developing the northeastern border states – the area which produces 200 tons of heroin a year, 60% of the world total. Few plans exist for the manufacturing sector, however, and an almost total dependence on imports will continue.

Strengths

Very rich in natural resources: fertile soil, rich fisheries, timber including diminishing teak reserves, gems, offshore natural gas and oil.

Weaknesses

Shortage of skilled labor, managers and technicians. Rudimentary financial systems and institutions. Nationwide black market. Huge external debt. Dependence on imported manufactures.

Profile

Burma's economy is agriculture-based and functions mainly on a cash and barter system. Its key industries are controlled by 20 military-run state enterprises. Every aspect of economic life is permeated by a black market, on which prices are rocketing – a reaction to official price controls.

MYANMAR : MAJOR BUSINESSES

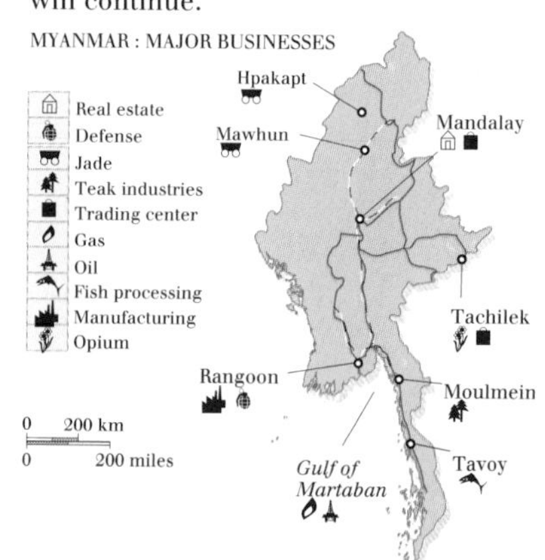

RESOURCES

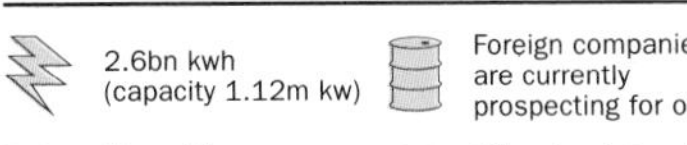

ELECTRICITY GENERATION

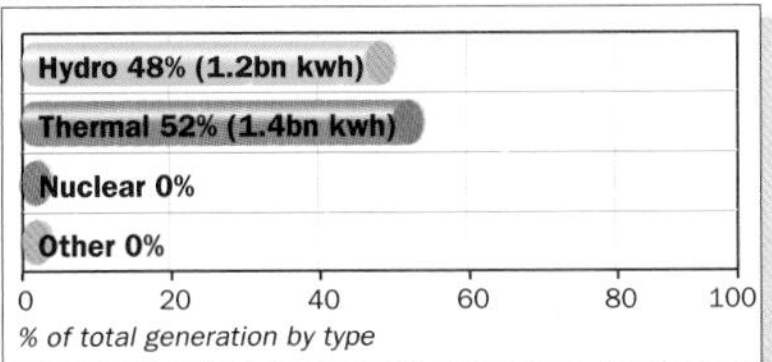

Burma is the world's largest teak exporter. It is also a producer of pearls, rubies and other gems. Foreign capital is funding exploration for natural gas and oil in the Tenasserim peninsula. However, Burma suffers from energy shortages.

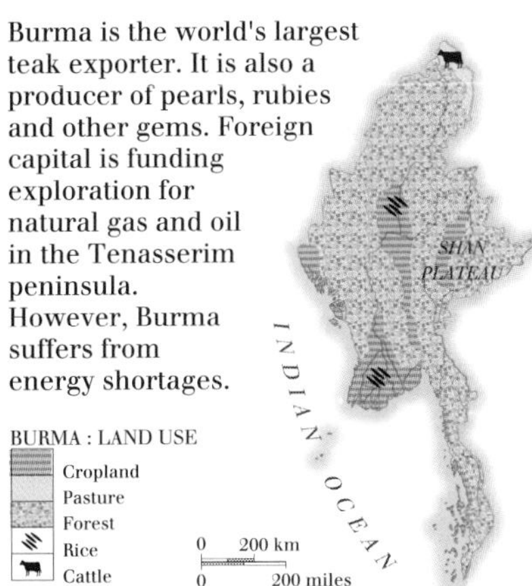

ENVIRONMENT

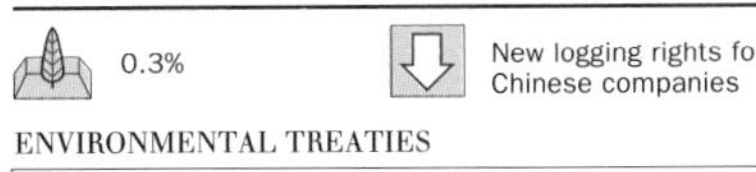

ENVIRONMENTAL TREATIES

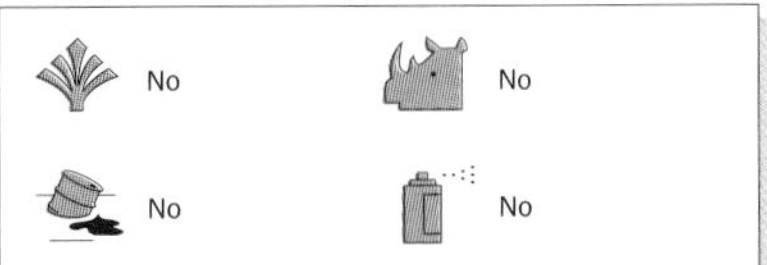

Deforestation is a major problem and has increased since the 1988 coup. Chinese companies have been given unrestricted logging concessions.

MEDIA

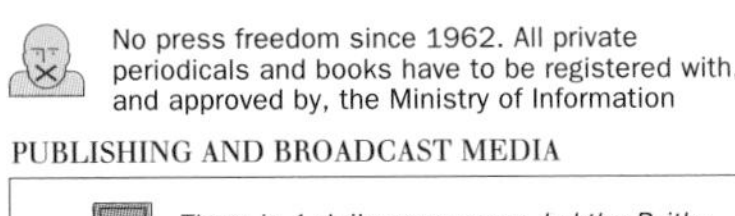

PUBLISHING AND BROADCAST MEDIA

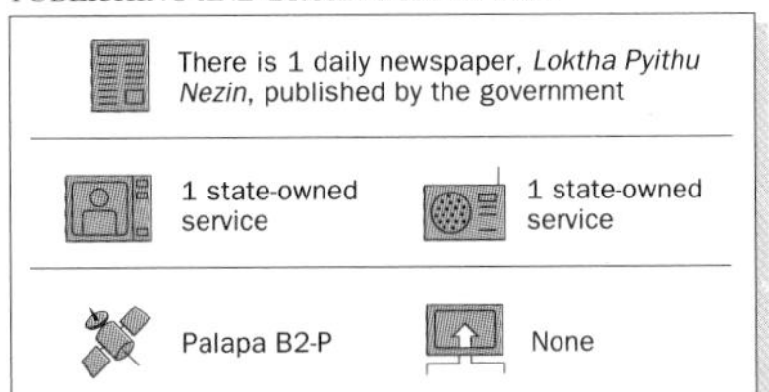

There is 1 daily newspaper, *Loktha Pyithu Nezin*, published by the government
1 state-owned service
1 state-owned service
Palapa B2-P
None

Political dissent of any kind is a criminal offense. An underground pro-democracy press produces anti-government material.

CRIME

CRIME RATES

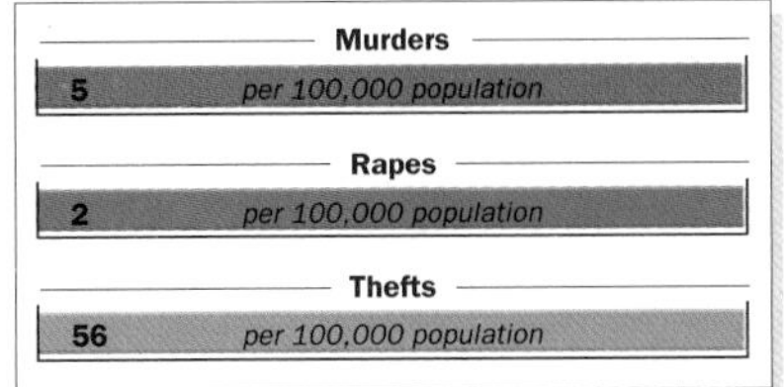

Murders
5 per 100,000 population
Rapes
2 per 100,000 population
Thefts
56 per 100,000 population

Levels of robbery, murder, bribery, corruption, embezzlement and black marketeering are high, compared to similar totalitarian regimes. The state is guilty of illegal activity. The UN reports regularly on human rights abuses against civilians, and the murder of innocent civilians including children, women, Buddhist monks, students, minorities and political dissidents.

There is a nominal civilian judicial system in Burma, but in practice all judges and lawyers are appointed by the junta and all legal functions executed by the SLORC. The most common charge is that of sedition against the state or the army under the 1975 "Law to Protect the State from Destructionists." Among the SLORC's frequent arbitrary "notices" is the Order 2/88 prohibiting assemblies of more than five persons. Most detainees have no legal rights of representation and are either jailed, used as forced labor or put under house arrest without public trial. Amnesty International is banned.

EDUCATION

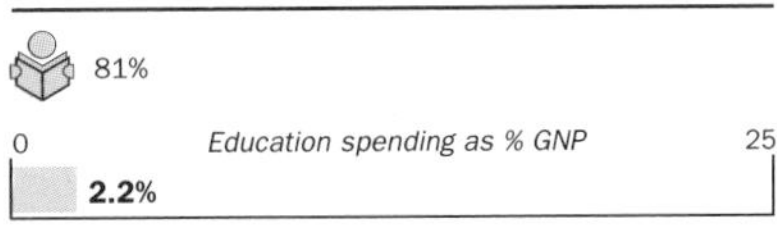

THE EDUCATION SYSTEM

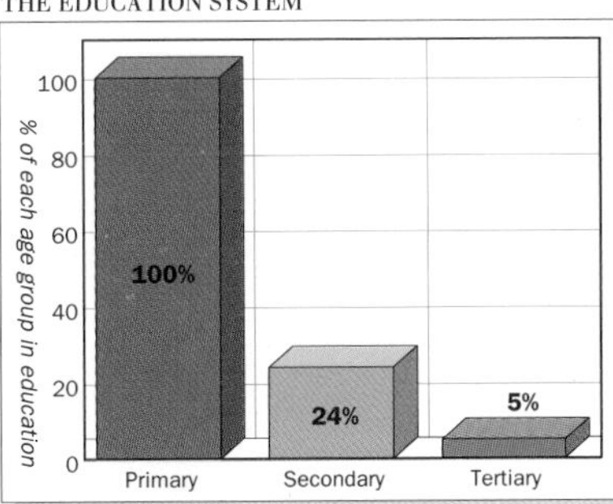

The education system provides ten years of schooling. There are two universities, three medical schools and one technical institute. There is a general shortage of qualified teachers. Most foreign teachers, doctors and engineers have left or are in jail.

HEALTH

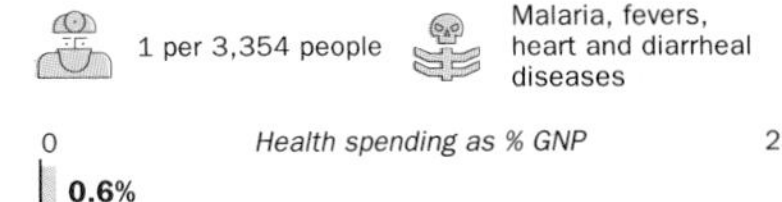

Leprosy, although it affects relatively few people compared with other diseases, has a higher prevalence in Burma than in the rest of Asia. There has been an increase in the incidence of malaria in the last few years. The growing number of AIDS cases is largely due to migrant prostitution across the Thai–Burmese border.

WEALTH

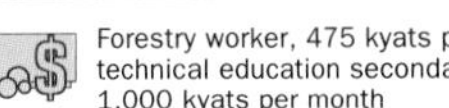

Forestry worker, 475 kyats per month; technical education secondary teacher, 1,000 kyats per month

CONSUMER GOODS OWNERSHIP

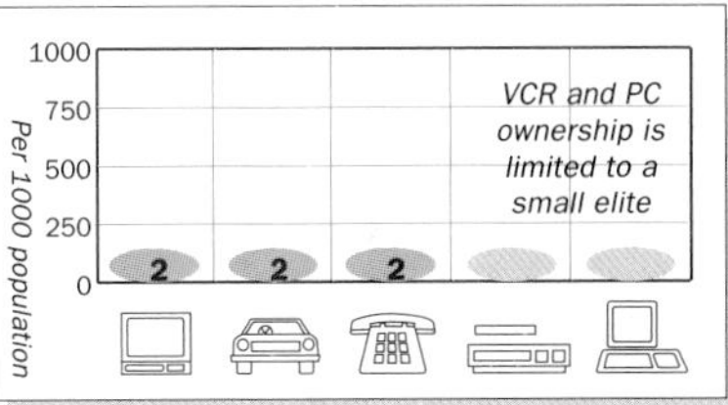

The state monopoly of the production and distribution of goods by rationing under General Ne Win's administration led to an increase in corruption and the rise of a nationwide black market, with huge disparities between official and unofficial prices. Only the military elite and their supporters could afford to live well. The situation has not changed significantly since 1988. Giant military enterprises grouped under a Defense Services holding company, whose capital amounts to 10% of GDP, now reap wealth and distribute privileges for a minority. Nevertheless, traditional social and economic mobility still exist. Climbing the socio-economic ladder is mainly a matter of loyalty to the military. Dissidents forced out of their jobs and hill tribes are the poorest groups.

WORLD RANKING

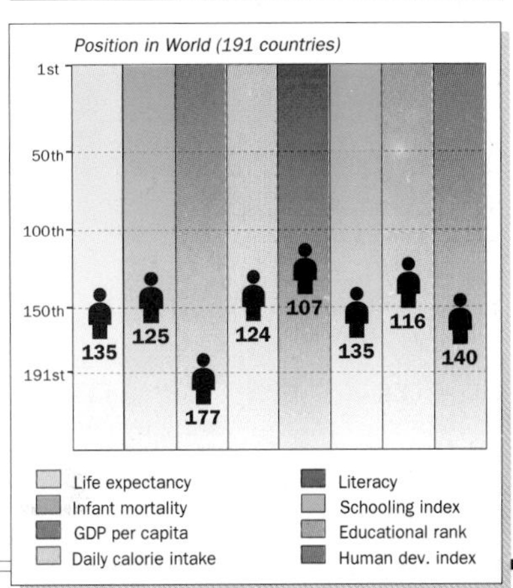

BURUNDI

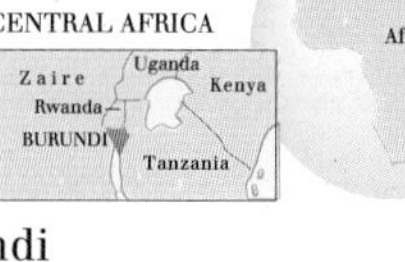

B

OFFICIAL NAME: Republic of Burundi **CAPITAL:** Bujumbura
POPULATION: 5.8 million **CURRENCY:** Burundi franc **OFFICIAL LANGUAGE:** French and Kirundi

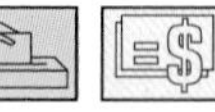

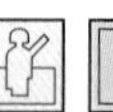

LANDLOCKED BURUNDI lies just south of the equator on the Nile–Congo watershed. Lake Tanganyika forms part of its border with Zaire. Ethnic tension between the Hutu majority and the dominant Tutsi minority remains the main factor in politics. In October 1993, this spilled over into violence as the Tutsi-dominated army mounted a coup that resulted in the assassination of the country's first-ever Hutu president.

Pig farming and fish ponds. The majority of Burundi's population depends on subsistence farming.

CLIMATE

WEATHER CHART

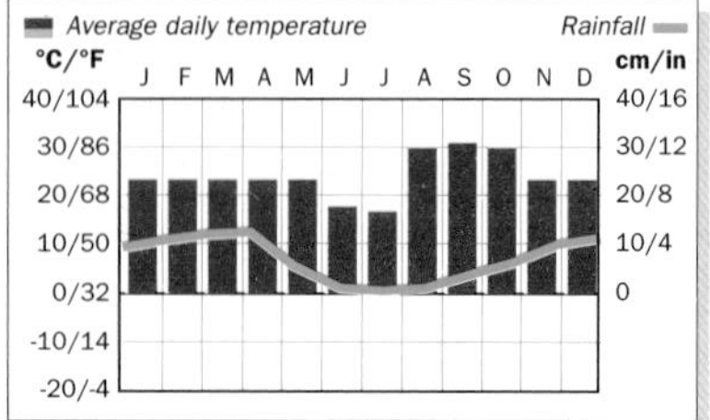

Burundi is temperate with high humidity, much cloud and frequent heavy rain. The highlands have frost.

COMMUNICATIONS

Bujumbura International 70,000 passengers

Has no fleet

THE TRANSPORTATION NETWORK

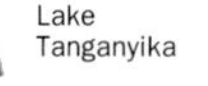

The dense road network has been rehabilitated. There are plans to build a railroad linking Burundi with Rwanda, Uganda and Tanzania.

TOURISM

109,418 visitors

Up 34% in 1990

MAIN OVERSEAS ARRIVALS

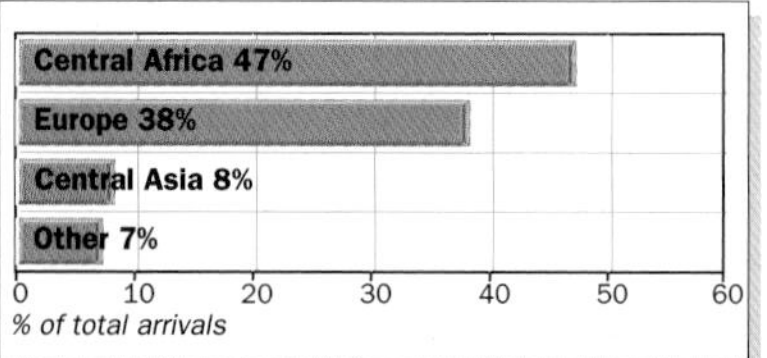

A lack of basic infrastructure and violent ethnic strife deter tourists. The industry has limited potential as Burundi lacks its neighbors' spectacular scenery and big game parks.

PEOPLE

Kirundi, French, Swahili

513 people per sq. mile

THE URBAN/RURAL POPULATION SPLIT

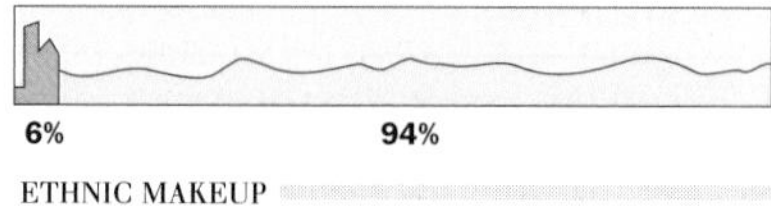

ETHNIC MAKEUP

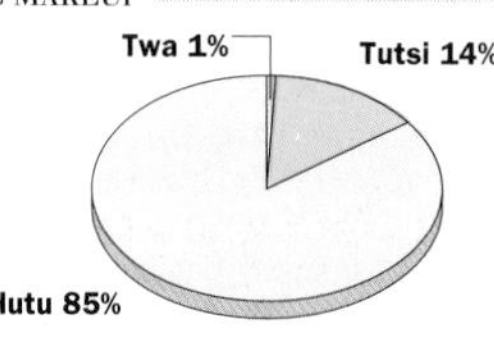

Burundi's history has been marked by violent ethnic conflict between the majority Hutu and the Tutsi, who control the army. Large-scale massacres have occurred repeatedly over the past two decades. Over 120,000 people, mostly Hutu, have been killed in ethnic conflict since October 1992. The Twa pygmies do not suffer similar repression. Most Burundians are subsistence farmers. The capacity of women to work determines their marriageability. 78% of Burundians are Roman Catholic.

POLITICS

1998

Interim president Synvestre Ntibantunganya

THE STATE OF THE PARTIES

National Assembly 81 members

FRODEBU = Front for Democracy in Burundi
UPRONA = Union for National Progress

Politics in Burundi remain sharply divided along ethnic lines, with the minority Tutsi seeking to control the majority Hutu population.

From 1966, the Tutsi UPRONA was the only legal party. Tutsi dominated the civil service, judiciary and the army. The army engaged in occasional mass slaughter of Hutu. In 1990, President Buyoya, a Tutsi, called for greater unity between the two groups, leading to hopes that Hutu could be brought into the political process. His report was approved by referendum and opposition parties were legalized. Burundi's first free presidential elections were held in June 1993. They were won by Melchior Ndadaye, a Hutu and leader of FRODEBU. Tutsi fears of Hutu dominance led to a coup in October and the assassination of Ndadaye. Thousands of Hutu were killed by the army; 150,000 fled into Rwanda and Zaire. In 1994, Burundi's new president and the Rwandan president died when their aircraft was shot down in Rwanda as they were returning from ethnic peace talks.

BURUNDI

Total Area : 27 830 sq. km (10 750 sq. miles)

LAND HEIGHT

- 2000m/6562ft
- 1000m/3281ft
- 500m/1640ft

POPULATION

- over 100 000
- over 50 000
- over 10 000
- under 10 000

WORLD AFFAIRS

In 1994, Burundi asked for UN military intervention to prevent further ethnic violence; the request was declined.

AID

 $253m (receipts)

 Food aid rising sharply to meet risk of famine

The crisis of 1993–1994 led one million Burundians to flee their homes and miss two planting seasons. In 1994, 970,000 were dependent on UN food aid.

DEFENSE

 $32.05m

 Up 1% in 1988

The army is run by Tutsi. In line with the political changes taking place in Burundi, President Ndadaye proposed bringing Hutu into officer ranks. Tutsi resistance to this move was a major factor behind the October 1993 coup. The army has threatened to become a Tutsi militia.

ECONOMICS

 $1.1bn

 247.94 Burundi francs

SCORE CARD

- ❑ WORLD GNP RANKING........................155th
- ❑ GNP PER CAPITA..............................$189
- ❑ BALANCE OF PAYMENTS.....................$-75m
- ❑ INFLATION..4.7%
- ❑ UNEMPLOYMENT....Widespread underemployment

STRENGTHS

Small quantities of gold and tungsten. Potential of massive nickel reserves and oil in Lake Tanganyika.

WEAKNESSES

Failure of democratic process to stem ethnic strife. Overwhelmingly agricultural economy (91% of labor force) under pressure from high birth rate. Little prospect of political stability.

EXPORTS

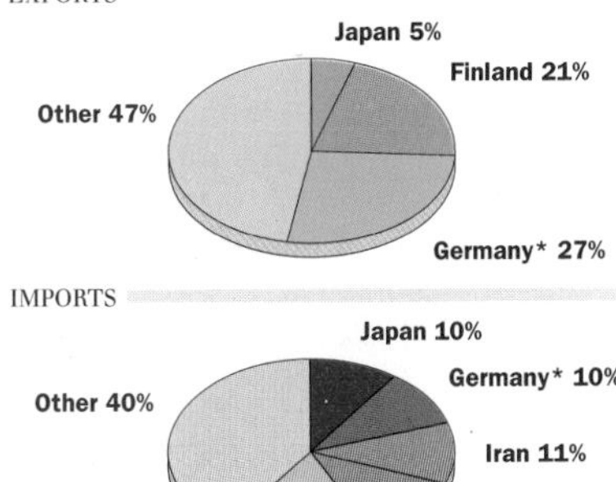

RESOURCES

 106m kwh (capacity 43,000 kw)

 Not an oil producer and has no refineries

420,000 cattle, 400,000 sheep, 84,000 pigs

 Gold, tungsten, nickel, vanadium, oil

Burundi has around 5% of the world's nickel reserves. Extraction, however, is not economically viable. There are also deposits of gold and vanadium. Surveys in the 1980s detected oil reserves below Lake Tanganyika but production has yet to begin. Burundi imports gasoline from Iran and electricity from Zaire. However, once the HEP plants at Mugera and Rwegura are operational, they will meet most domestic electricity requirements.

ENVIRONMENT

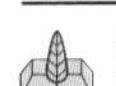 3% partially protected

 Serious deforestation and soil impoverishment

Only 2% of Burundi is forest and even this is now under pressure from one of Africa's highest birth rates. Burundi suffers from the problems associated with deforestation, particularly soil erosion. Some soils are also being exhausted from overuse. Several tree planting programs have been introduced. UNESCO is also running ecological education initiatives at village level aimed at women farmers.

MEDIA

 The media is state-controlled. General thaw in censorship since 1992 constitution in theory. Media has been regularly liberalized

PUBLISHING AND BROADCAST MEDIA

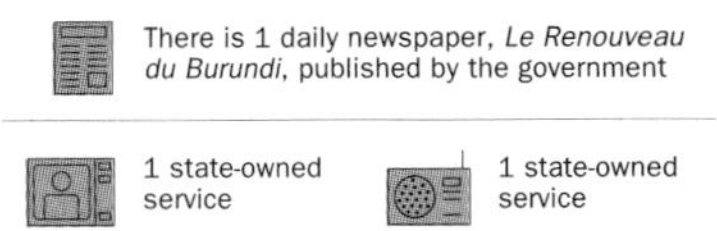

There is 1 daily newspaper, *Le Renouveau du Burundi*, published by the government
1 state-owned service
1 state-owned service

Le Renouveau du Burundi and the Roman Catholic *Burundi Chrétien* are the most influential newspapers. Color TV transmission began in 1985.

CRIME

 Burundi does not publish prison figures

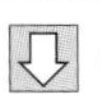 Down 53% in 1990

Burundi has an appalling human rights record. There have been frequent massacres of Hutu by the Tutsi-dominated army. The worst pogroms occurred in 1972, 1988, 1993 and 1994.

EDUCATION

 50%

Primary schooling begins at seven years of age and is compulsory, though further schooling is not. There are 76 primary school children per teacher. The one university is located in the capital.

CHRONOLOGY

From the 16th century, Burundi (formerly Urundi) was ruled by the minority Tutsi with the majority Hutu as their serfs. Merged with Rwanda, Burundi was controlled by Germany from 1884 and by Belgium from 1919.

- ❑ **1946** UN trust territory.
- ❑ **1959** Split from Rwanda.
- ❑ **1961** UN-supervised elections won by Tutsi UPRONA party.
- ❑ **1962** Independence.
- ❑ **1966** Army coup. Monarchy overthrown; becomes a republic.
- ❑ **1972** 150,000 Hutu massacred by Tutsi.
- ❑ **1988** 20,000 Hutu massacred.
- ❑ **1993** June: first free presidential elections. October, army coup; President Ndadaye assassinated.

HEALTH

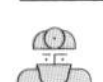 1 per 18,365 people

 Communicable infections, parasitic diseases

2.1 million people have no access to health services. Only 7% of women use contraception; on average, women have seven children. 38% of the population have access to safe drinking water.

WEALTH

 Bus conductor, 63 Burundi francs per hour; bank accountant, 1,100 Burundi francs per hour

CONSUMER GOODS OWNERSHIP

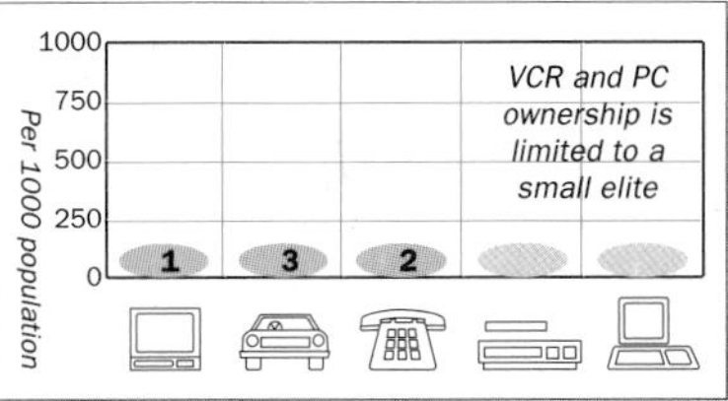

Wealth is concentrated within the Tutsi political and business elite. Most Burundians live a subsistence existence.

WORLD RANKING

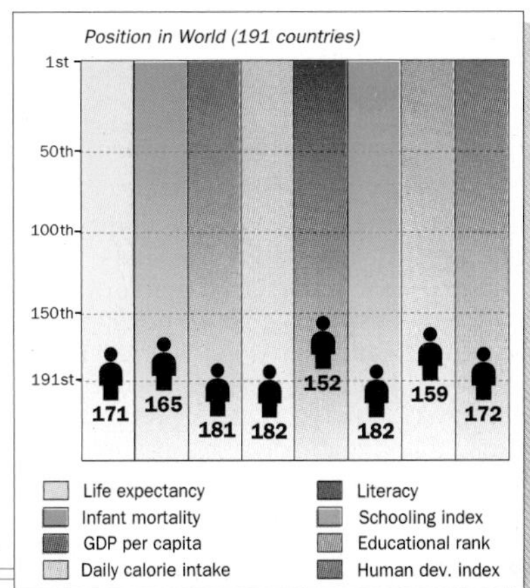

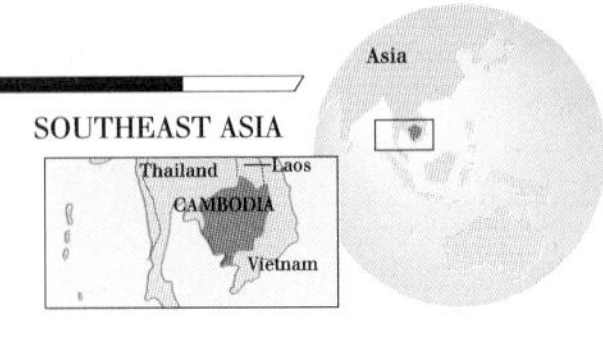

CAMBODIA

OFFICIAL NAME: State of Cambodia **CAPITAL:** Phnom Penh
POPULATION: 8.8 million **CURRENCY:** Riel **OFFICIAL LANGUAGE:** Khmer

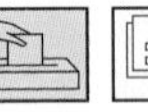

LOCATED IN THE INDOCHINESE PENINSULA in Southeast Asia, Cambodia has a coastline on the Gulf of Thailand and shares borders with Thailand, Laos and Vietnam. Its main topographical feature is the Tônlé Sap, or Great Lake, which drains into the Mekong River. Over three-quarters of Cambodia is forested, with mangroves lining the coast. Rice is the principal crop. Cambodia has emerged from two decades of civil war and invasion from Vietnam. The UN's biggest-ever peacekeeping operation resulted in free elections in 1993.

CLIMATE

WEATHER CHART

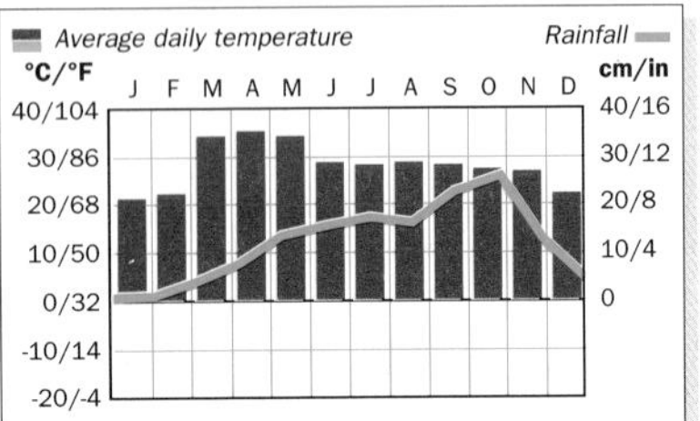

Cambodia has a more varied climate than neighboring Vietnam. Low-lying regions have moderate rainfall and the most consistent yearly temperatures. The wettest areas are the hillsides facing the Gulf of Thailand. The dry season lasts from December to April and is characterized by high temperatures and an average of eight hours of sunshine a day. During the rainy season, Cambodia experiences high humidity and sultry heat. From May to September, winds are southeasterly, while from October to April they are north or northeasterly.

COMMUNICATIONS

 Pochentong, Phnom Penh

 1 ship, 1,500 dwt

THE TRANSPORTATION NETWORK

8,296 miles (13,351 km)

 None

342 miles (550 km))

2,299 miles (3,700 km)

The civil war led to a near-collapse of Cambodia's road and railroad system. Some parts of the network are still subject to attack by Khmer Rouge bandits. International aid is now being used to rehabilitate key routes, such as Highways 3 and 5, and to rebuild the Chroy Changba Bridge out of Phnom Penh. The bicycle and rickshaw are the main forms of urban transportation.

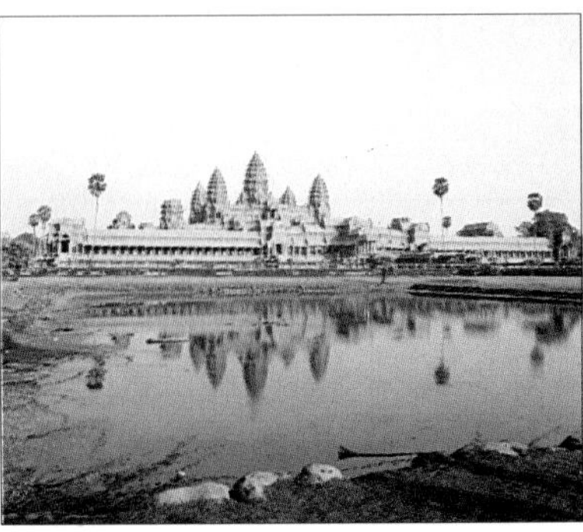

Angkor Wat stands in the ruins of the ancient city of Angkor, once the capital of the Khmer empire. It is now one of Cambodia's leading tourist attractions.

TOURISM

 10,000 (est)

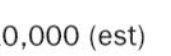

 Significant increase since 1990

MAIN OVERSEAS ARRIVALS

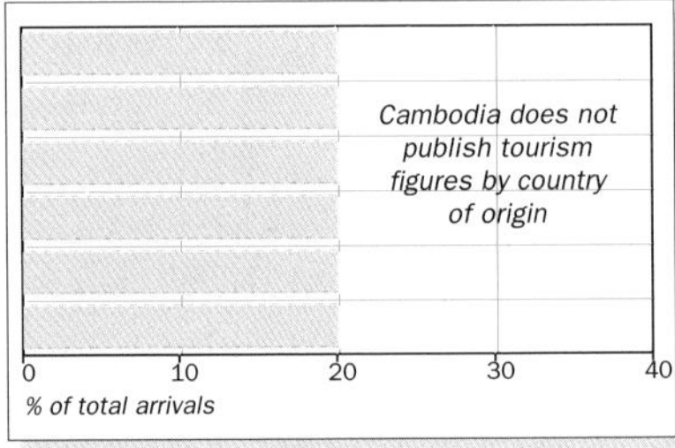

Cambodia, the center of the Khmer empire between 800 and 1400 AD, has some of the most impressive temples in Southeast Asia. The most famous is the extraordinary site at Angkor Wat, near Siĕmréab. During the war it was controlled by the Khmer Rouge, who threatened any visitors with attack. Visitors are now allowed in small numbers; 3,000 visited the site in 1993.

Once basic infrastructure is in place and the political situation has stabilized, Cambodia has considerable tourism potential. It currently attracts adventurous, independent travelers. Tourists are occasionally kidnapped.

PEOPLE

Khmer, French, Chinese, Vietnamese, Cham

 117 people per sq. mile

THE URBAN/RURAL POPULATION SPLIT

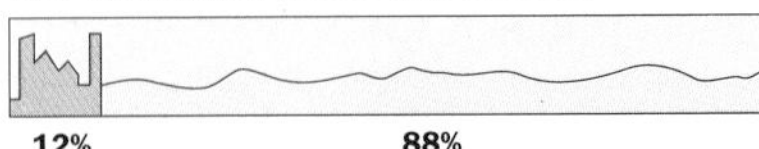

RELIGIOUS PERSUASION

Other 5%

Theravada Buddhism 95%

ETHNIC MAKEUP

Vietnamese 1%

Chinese 4%

Other 1%

Khmer 94%

Cambodian society underwent one of the 20th century's most horrific programs of social transformation between 1975 and 1979 under Pol Pot's Khmer Rouge regime. Over one million Cambodians, or one in eight, died from warfare, starvation, overwork or execution. Half a million more went into exile in Thailand. The Pol Pot regime's reforms led to the scrapping of money, possessions and hierarchy. Only peasants, soldiers of the revolution and some industrial workers were allowed to retain their pre-revolution status. Boys and girls of 13 and 14 were taken from their homes, indoctrinated in the tenets of revolution, and allowed to kill those perceived to be guilty of bourgeois crimes. Violence at all levels was sanctioned in the name of revolution.

Pol Pot's regime ended with the Vietnamese invasion of 1979. Most professionals who had survived emigrated. The effects of revolution and subsequent civil war are still felt and are reflected in the world's highest rate of orphans and widows.

POPULATION AGE BREAKDOWN

% of population by age group

	1960	1970	1980	1990	2000
65+	2.7%	2.8%	2.5%	2.9%	3.5%
15–64	54.8%	54%	64.6%	62.2%	57.9%
0–14	42.5%	43.2%	32.9%	34.9%	38.6%

POLITICS

Uncertain

President Prince Norodom Sihanouk

THE STATE OF THE PARTIES

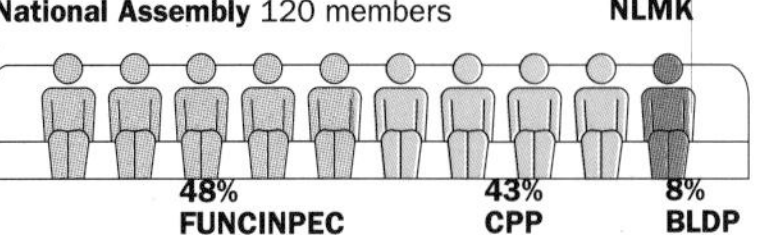

FUNCINPEC = United National Front for an Independent, Neutral, Peaceful and Cooperative Cambodia **CPP** = Cambodian People's Party **BLDP** = Buddhist Liberal Democratic Party **NLMK** = National Liberation Movement of Kampuchea

Cambodia held free multiparty elections under UN supervision in 1993.

MAIN POLITICAL ISSUES

Fledgling democracy
The UN's Cambodia operation, the biggest in the organization's history, introduced a degree of stability to Cambodia's political system. Some 22,000 troops provided the conditions for free elections held in 1993. Whether or not competing political factions can be contained within the newly established democratic framework remains the key political question.

The Khmer Rouge
The Khmer Rouge decided not to take part in the elections of 1993, resuming instead the armed struggle in areas of central and western Cambodia. The group is demanding membership in a government of national reconciliation, but is unwilling to see its troops merged with a national army.

PROFILE

In 1975, the US-installed government was overthrown by the Marxist Khmer Rouge under Pol Pot. Pol Pot was in turn overthrown, following the Vietnamese invasion in 1979. The invasion united Cambodia's three main factions – the Khmer Rouge, FUNCINPEC and the Khmer Peoples' National Liberation Front (KPNLF) – in common cause against the Vietnamese. The coalition was recognized by the UN as the government of Democratic Kampuchea. Vietnam's decision to leave in 1989 led to peace talks in Paris and the signing of the October 1991 Paris Accords. The Paris Accords mandated the UN's UNTAC operation to steer the country to free democratic elections. The task involved imposing the ceasefire agreed, repatriating 370,000 refugees and overseeing the election campaign. Following FUNCINPEC's victory in the elections, Prince Sihanouk proposed a coalition government of national reconciliation. The Khmer Rouge refused to join, as they wanted a greater part in the government than their election results warranted. In 1994 they continued armed resistance.

***Saloth Sar,** who assumed the name Pol Pot, still leads the Khmer Rouge.*

***Prince Norodom Sihanouk.** He abdicated kingship to enter politics in 1955.*

WORLD AFFAIRS

During the years of civil war that followed the Vietnamese invasion, the Phnom Penh government suffered the same isolation that was imposed on Vietnam. Recognized by few countries outside the Soviet bloc, it became an international pariah. The resistance movement that included the Khmer Rouge was allotted Cambodia's seat at the UN and gained the backing of an anti-Soviet, anti-Vietnamese alliance that included the USA and China.

Cambodia's new constitution talks of making the country once again a non-aligned "island of peace." While China and Thailand have disavowed their former support for the Khmer Rouge, the Thai military still provides arms, personnel and sanctuary for its troops, and China has supported King Sihanouk's call to bring the Khmer Rouge into the ruling coalition. By contrast, the USA has threatened to withdraw aid to the government if the Khmer Rouge is allowed to join the coalition. The government has to date been reluctant to fuel the historic animosity that exists with Vietnam.

AID

$62m (receipts)

Up 48% in 1991

Aid is the single most important part of the Cambodian economy. It provides around 70% of government revenues. The coalition government has benefited from large aid commitments from a Japanese-led consortium. However, disbursing aid is difficult.

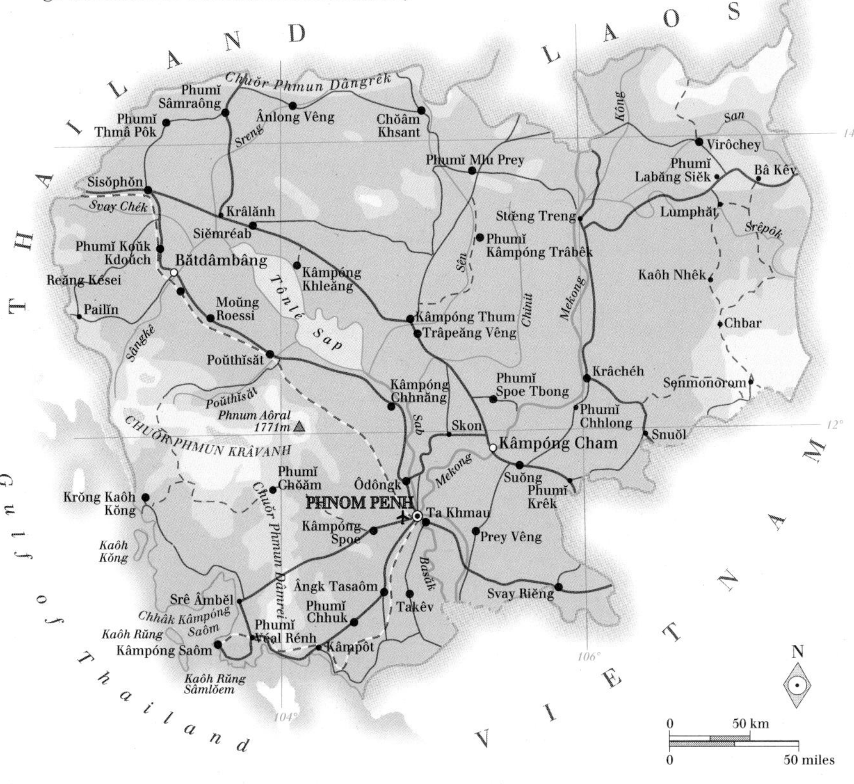

CAMBODIA

Total Area : 181 040 sq. km (69 000 sq. miles)

POPULATION

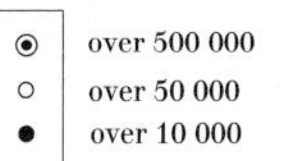

LAND HEIGHT

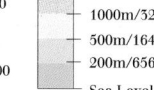

1000m/3281ft
500m/1640ft
200m/656ft
Sea Level

CHRONOLOGY

A former French protectorate, Cambodia gained independence in 1953 as a constitutional monarchy with Norodom Sihanouk as king.

- ❑ **1955** Sihanouk abdicates to pursue political career.
- ❑ **1970** Right-wing coup led by Prime Minister Lon Nol deposes Sihanouk. Exiled Sihanouk forms Royal Government of National Union of Cambodia (GRUNC), backed by formerly hostile communist Khmer Rouge. Lon Nol proclaims Khmer Republic.
- ❑ **1974** GRUNC forces capture Phnom Penh. Prince Sihanouk head of state, Khmer Rouge assumes power. Hundreds of thousands die during radical social program.
- ❑ **1976** Country renamed Democratic Kampuchea. Elections. Sihanouk resigns; GRUNC dissolved. Khieu Samphan head of state; Pol Pot prime minister.
- ❑ **1977** Regime called the Communist Party of Kampuchea (CPK), led by Pol Pot.
- ❑ **1978** Vietnam invades, supported by Cambodian communists opposed to Pol Pot.
- ❑ **1979** Vietnamese capture Phnom Penh. CPK ousted by Kampuchean People's Revolutionary Party (KPRP), led by Pen Sovan. Khmer Rouge starts guerrilla war. Pol Pot held responsible for three million deaths and sentenced to death in absence. Vietnamese and DK (mostly Khmer Rouge) forces begin conflict on Thai border.
- ❑ **1980** Heng Samrin KPRP leader.
- ❑ **1982** Government-in-exile formed, including Khmer Rouge and Khmer People's National Liberation Front, headed by Prince Sihanouk; recognized by UN.
- ❑ **1988** Vietnam announces troop withdrawals. Khmer Rouge offensive. Khmer Rouge refuses to take part in peace talks.
- ❑ **1989** Vietnamese troops withdraw. Khmer Rouge forces make gains.
- ❑ **1990** UN Security Council approves plan for UN-monitored ceasefire and elections. Cambodian factions form Supreme National Council (SNC) but no agreement reached.
- ❑ **1991** SNC agree on elections. Factions sign accord. Sihanouk head of State of Cambodia. Khmer Rouge officials flee after attacks.
- ❑ **1992** Clashes between Cambodian troops and Khmer Rouge. UN ceasefire repeatedly violated.
- ❑ **1993** UN-supervised elections go ahead. UN peace operation leaves.
- ❑ **1994** Khmer Rouge refuses to join peace process.

DEFENSE

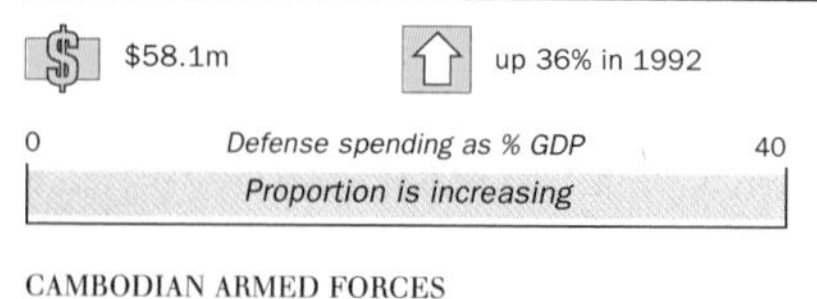

CAMBODIAN ARMED FORCES

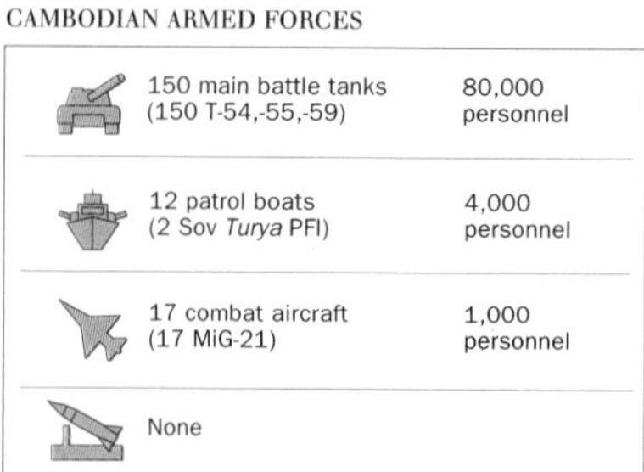

150 main battle tanks (150 T-54,-55,-59)
80,000 personnel
12 patrol boats (2 Sov *Turya* PFI)
4,000 personnel
17 combat aircraft (17 MiG-21)
1,000 personnel
None

The current government's defense priority is unifying the command structures of the three armies of the main coalition partners. This is essential to contain the continuing Khmer Rouge struggle. The Khmer Rouge have so far rejected the terms of a "national reconciliation" advanced by the government.

Despite the fact that the coalition's three armies (the Cambodian People's Armed Forces; FUNCINPEC's Armée Nationale Sihanoukiste; and the KPNLF's Khmer People's National Liberation Armed Forces) number over 150,000 men, they are meeting strong resistance from the Khmer Rouge's estimated 10,000 troops. After some initial victories, the government's forces suffered a series of defeats at the hands of the Khmer Rouge in the west of the country in mid-1994. This partly reflects low morale among coalition forces who are poorly paid and have suffered heavily from disease.

ECONOMICS

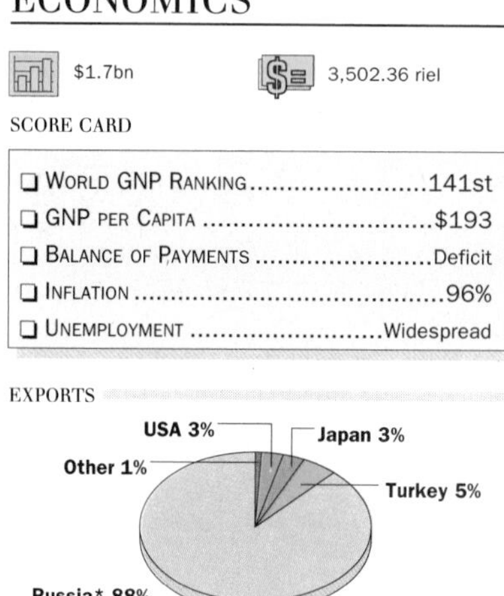

IMPORTS

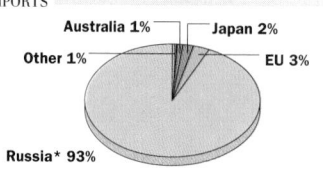

Australia 1% · Japan 2% · Other 1% · EU 3% · Russia* 93%

ECONOMIC PERFORMANCE INDICATOR

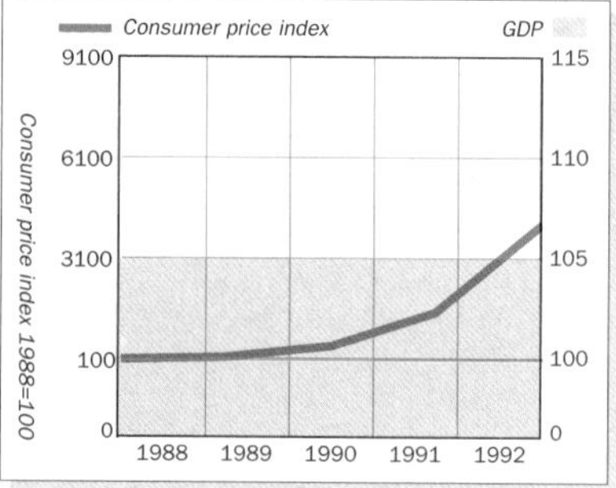

Strengths

Currently very few, as economy is still recovering from civil war. Considerable future potential. Given the right conditions, Cambodia could achieve self-sufficiency in rice. Gems, especially sapphires. Possible offshore oil wealth. Timber trade to Thailand.

Weaknesses

Tiny tax base makes economic reform hard to implement. Dependence on overseas aid; corruption at most levels of government limits its effectiveness. Loss of skilled workers as result of Khmer Rouge anti-bourgeois atrocities in the 1970s.

Profile

Cambodia's economy was devastated during the Pol Pot years. The Vietnamese attempted some reconstruction based on central planning, then switched to policies encouraging the private sector. The presence of the UN encouraged some limited development.

CAMBODIA : MAJOR BUSINESSES

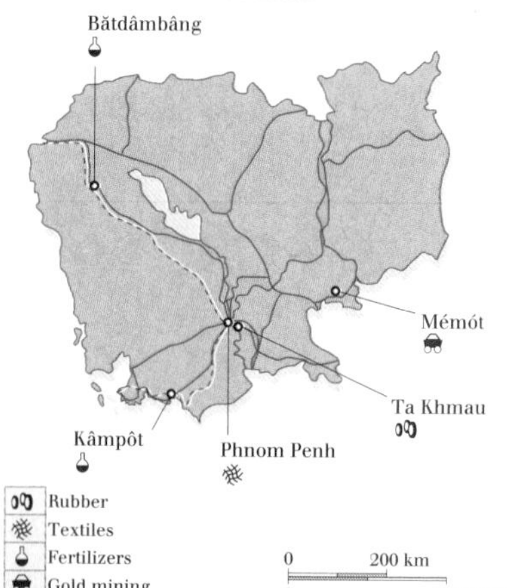

RESOURCES

70m kwh (capacity 35,000 kw)

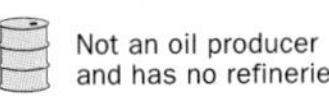

Not an oil producer and has no refineries

2.1m cattle, 1.6m pigs, 750,000 buffaloes

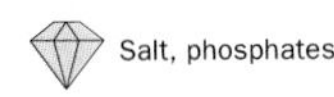

Salt, phosphates

Tropical rainforest timber, particularly teak and rosewood, is Cambodia's most important resource. Most forests are located in the north and west.

ELECTRICITY GENERATION

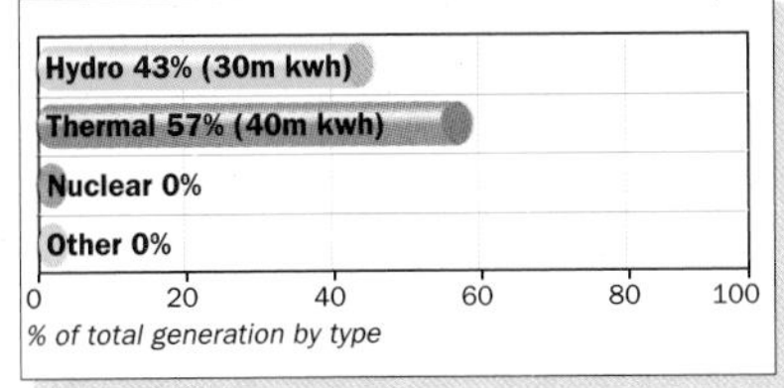

CAMBODIA : LAND USE

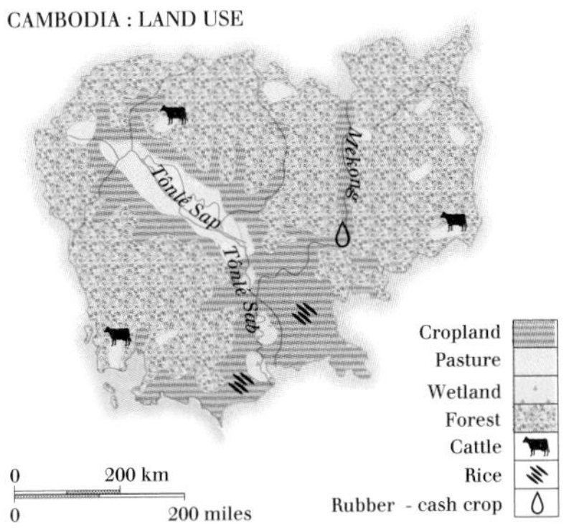

ENVIRONMENT

ENVIRONMENTAL TREATIES

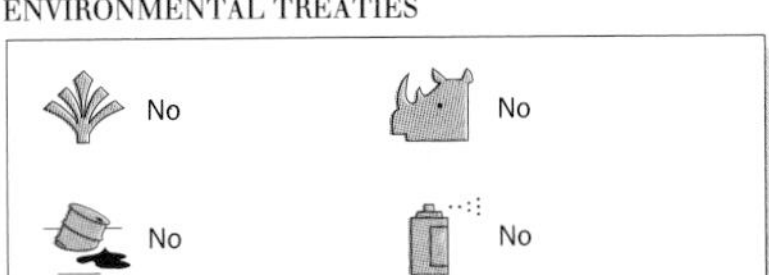

Deforestation is one of the most serious problems facing Cambodia. Timber, one of the country's most valuable assets, was sold in huge quantities by all Cambodian factions to finance their war efforts. According to the UN, in 1992 alone, more than 617,500 acres of forest were cleared. This provided over 1.3 million cubic yards of timber. A moratorium on logging was declared at the end of 1992, but was largely ignored. In many parts of the country logging is impossible to police; at current rates, estimates suggest that what remains of Cambodia's forests will be cut down by the year 2000. The environmental consequences – topsoil erosion and increased risk of flooding – are enormous and will hold back Cambodia's reconstruction.

MEDIA

There are plans to impose censorship

Since the UN-sponsored elections, the press has flourished in Cambodia. Over 40 Khmer-language papers are now on sale. Criticism of the government, over issues such as corruption, is voiced openly. However, the coalition is planning new censorship laws.

PUBLISHING AND BROADCAST MEDIA

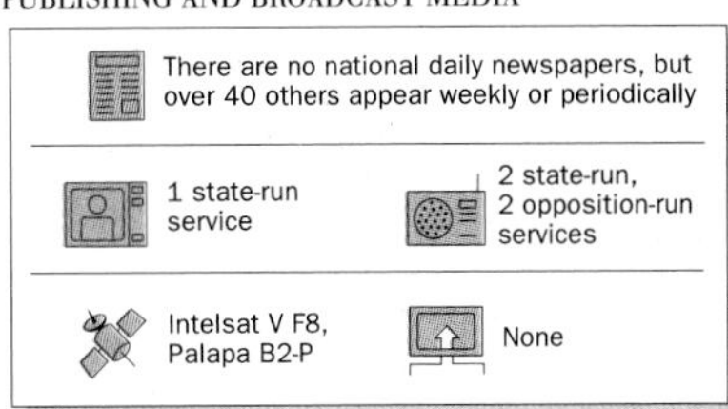

There are no national daily newspapers, but over 40 others appear weekly or periodically
1 state-run service
2 state-run, 2 opposition-run services
Intelsat V F8, Palapa B2-P
None

CRIME

Cambodia does not publish prison figures

Civilian crime rates are now fairly stable

CRIME RATES

Violence is increasing as more areas come under renewed attack by the Khmer Rouge

The UN-sponsored peace process and the successful elections in 1993 led to a dramatic drop in crime in Cambodia. Many areas are experiencing the first period of stability in two decades.

The exceptions are areas controlled by the Khmer Rouge, mostly in the west of the country. The regions around Pailĭn and Bătdâmbâng are particularly dangerous. Khmer Rouge guerrillas carry out frequent terror missions against villages. Police stations are particular targets. An estimated 40,000 civilians were displaced by the Khmer Rouge's May 1994 onslaughts. Western aid agencies have removed their personnel from Bătdâmbâng and Banthey Meanchey. The lack of adequate policing has also led to a rise in banditry in these regions.

EDUCATION

35%

0 — *Education spending as % GNP* — 25

Sufficient to send 80% of children to primary school

THE EDUCATION SYSTEM

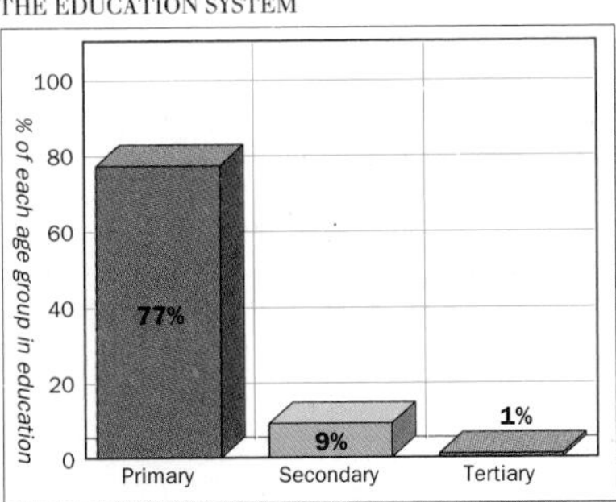

Only 5,000 of Cambodia's 20,000 teachers survived the Pol Pot period. The Vietnamese-installed government trained or retrained about 40,000.

HEALTH

1 per 27,000 people

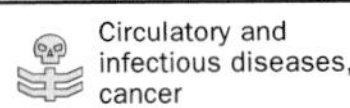

Circulatory and infectious diseases, cancer

0 — *Health spending as % GNP* — 25

Insufficient to provide comprehensive primary care

The Cambodian health system was effectively destroyed by the Khmer's period in power. Only 50 doctors survived the Pol Pot period. In the immediate aftermath of the Vietnamese invasion, Cambodia's health indicators were among the worst in the world. Over 25% of babies were dying before their first birthday.

Conditions have since improved. However, infant mortality remains high and malaria and cholera are endemic.

WEALTH

Most Cambodians live a subistence existence

CONSUMER GOODS OWNERSHIP

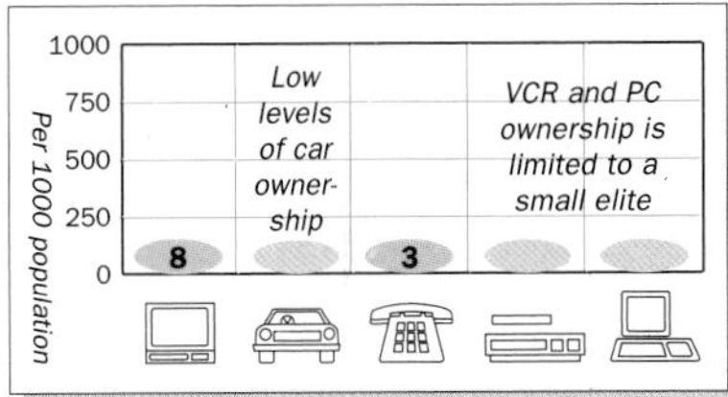

The opening up of the country's economy has led to an influx of capital. The benefits of new investment, however, are limited to those in power.

WORLD RANKING

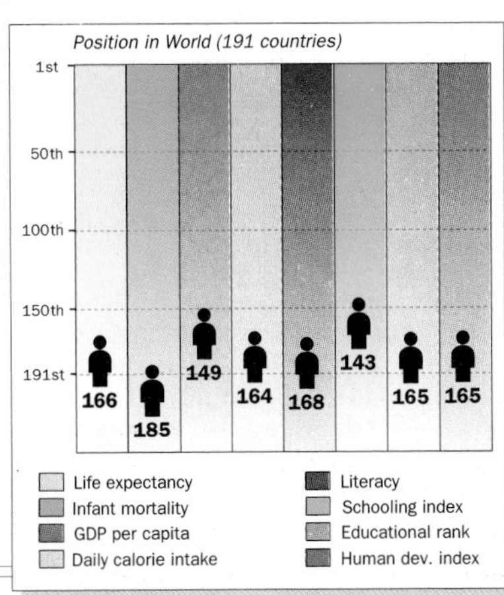

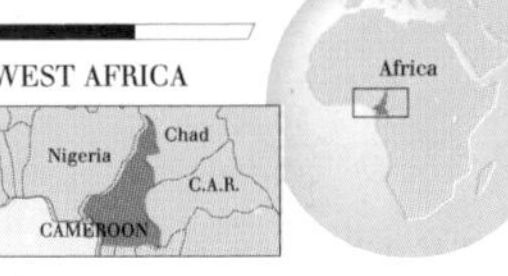

CAMEROON

OFFICIAL NAME: Republic of Cameroon **CAPITAL:** Yaoundé
POPULATION: 12.2 million **CURRENCY:** CFA franc **OFFICIAL LANGUAGES:** French and English

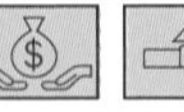

LOCATED ON THE CENTRAL WEST AFRICAN coast, over half of Cameroon is forested, with equatorial rainforest to the south, and evergreen forest and wooded savanna north of the Sanaga River. Most cities are located in the south, although there are densely populated areas around Mount Cameroon, a dormant volcano. For 30 years Cameroon was effectively a one-party state. Democratic elections in 1992 returned the former ruling party to power.

Savanna landscape below Mindif Pic in Cameroon's far north. From here, the land slopes down to the hot, arid Lake Chad basin.

CLIMATE

WEATHER CHART

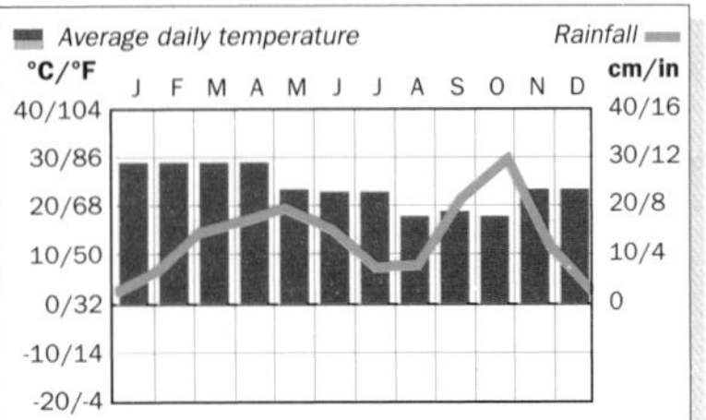

Climate varies from the equatorial south with 195 in. of rain a year to the drought-beset Sahel of the far north.

COMMUNICATIONS

 **Douala International** 436,000 passengers

 2 ships 33,500 dwt

THE TRANSPORTATION NETWORK

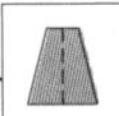 32,444 miles (52,214 km)

 Trans-African Highway

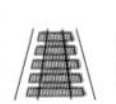 684 miles (1,104 km)

 1,296 miles (2,090 km)

Major projects are the east–west Trans-African Highway and realigning the Douala–Nkongsamba railway.

TOURISM

 100,000 visitors

 Up 15% in 1990

MAIN OVERSEAS ARRIVALS

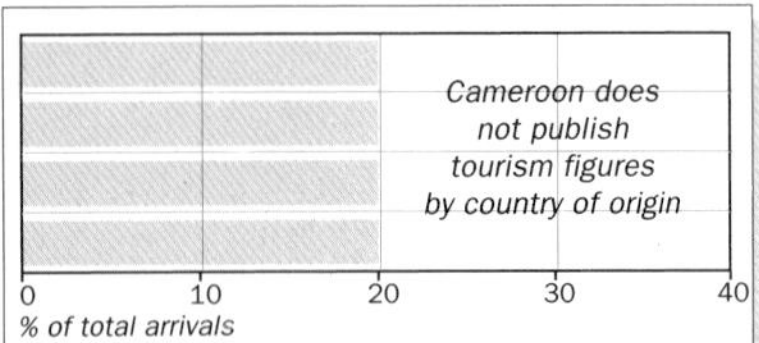

In 1989, the first tourism minister was appointed to boost the still small industry. Some package tours visit the northern game parks. A new airport near Yaoundé will replace the present one. Beaches near Kribi have a few hotels.

PEOPLE

Fang, Bulu, Yaundé, Duala, Mbum, Fulani, Pidgin English, French, English

65 people per sq. mile

THE URBAN/RURAL POPULATION SPLIT

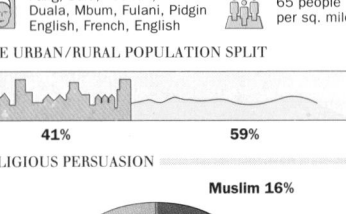

41% 59%

RELIGIOUS PERSUASION

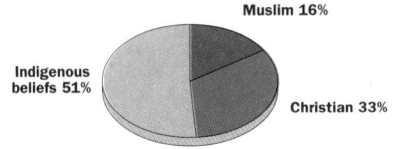

Muslim 16%
Indigenous beliefs 51%
Christian 33%

Cameroon is ethnically diverse – there are 230 groups although no single group is dominant. The largest is the Bamileke of the center southwest, but this group has never held political power. When President Ahidjo, a northern Fulani, retired, he was replaced by Paul Biya of the southeastern Bulu-Beti group. The north–south hostility which affects many other West African states is also present in Cameroon, albeit diminished by the great diversity of peoples. There is tension between competing groups of the south. There are sizeable groups of French-speaking and English-speaking peoples.

POLITICS

 1997

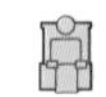 President Paul Biya

THE STATE OF THE PARTIES

National Assembly 180 members

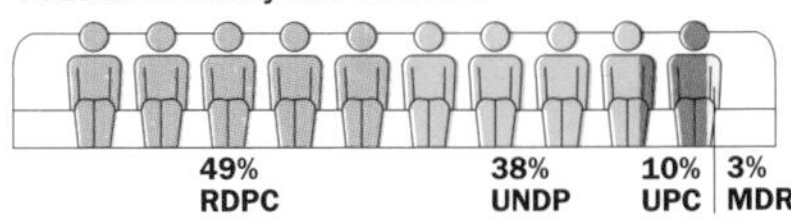

RDPC = Cameroon People's Democratic Movement
UNDP = National Union for Democracy and Progress
UPC = Union of Peoples of Cameroon
MDR = Movement for the Defense of the Republic

Despite ruthless use of the security forces during demonstrations for change in 1990, multiparty elections were held in 1992. They were won by the ruling RDPC. The following presidential elections were won by Paul Biya, although the results have been disputed; the Social Democratic Front (SDF) of John Fru Ndi claims to have defeated Biya. Despite being the most important opposition group, the SDF boycotted the parliamentary elections.

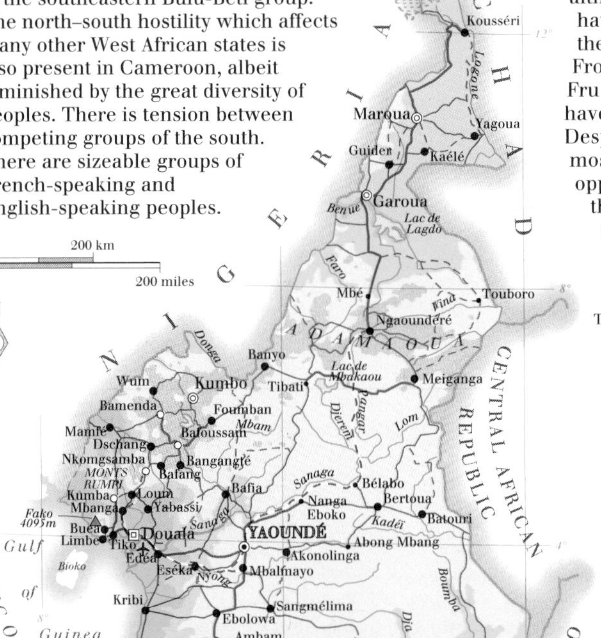

CAMEROON
Total Area : 475 440 sq. km (183 570 sq. miles)

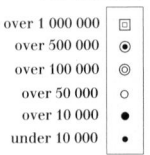

POPULATION
over 1 000 000
over 500 000
over 100 000
over 50 000
over 10 000
under 10 000

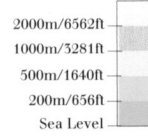

LAND HEIGHT
2000m/6562ft
1000m/3281ft
500m/1640ft
200m/656ft
Sea Level

C

WORLD AFFAIRS

OAU | ECA | GATT | FZ | NAM

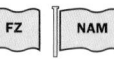

Cameroon's most important relationship is with France, which gives considerable support. Restoring democratic credentials, damaged in the presidential elections, is also a priority. Cameroon has to balance relations carefully between mainly French-owned and US-owned oil companies.

AID

 $501m (receipts)  Up 16% in 1991

France is by far the most important donor, having twice paid Cameroon's back debts to the IMF to avoid blacklisting. However, IMF aid is now virtually frozen because of Cameroon's poor economic performance. Cameroon can no longer afford any of its development projects.

DEFENSE

 $190.9m  Up 34% in 1990

The military has been an active force in supporting the regime and maintaining order in the face of democratic protests since before independence. The 6,600-man army is equipped mainly from France. There is a 4,000-man gendarmerie and Cameroon still has a strong political police, the CENER.

ECONOMICS

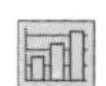 $9.8bn  295.23 CFA francs

SCORE CARD

- ❑ World GNP Ranking.........................79th
- ❑ GNP per Capita $805
- ❑ Balance of Payments ....$–792m
- ❑ Inflation ....–2.2%
- ❑ Unemployment....Widespread underemployment

Strengths

Moderate oil reserves. Very diversified agricultural economy (timber, cocoa, coffee, rubber) and food self-sufficiency preserved through oil boom. Historical liberalism. Private sector in relatively good state. 95% of electricity is HEP.

Weaknesses

Massive fuel smuggling from Nigeria affects refinery profits. Inflated civil service. Growing national debt due to failure to adjust to fall in oil revenues.

EXPORTS

IMPORTS

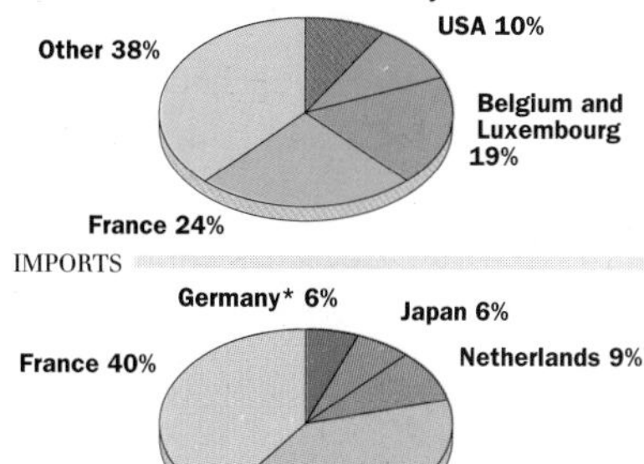

RESOURCES

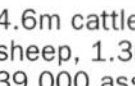

2.7bn kwh (capacity 627,000 kw)

140,400 b/d (reserves 400,000,000 bbl)

4.6m cattle, 3.2m sheep, 1.3m pigs, 39,000 asses

Oil, tin, limestone, natural gas, bauxite, iron, uranium, gold

New oil discoveries may bolster declining extraction rates. In spite of large bauxite deposits, much is imported for the Edea smelter, which takes 50% of national electricity output.

ENVIRONMENT

 4% (2% partially protected)  Environmental forests ministry ineffective

Conservation groups and official nature reserves are attempting to curb commercial timber felling. National parks are celebrated for their flora.

MEDIA

 Press censorship eased in 1990, but it is still fairly severe

PUBLISHING AND BROADCAST MEDIA

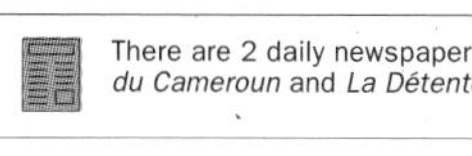

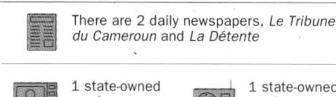

There are 2 daily newspapers, *Le Tribune du Cameroun* and *La Détente*

 1 state-owned service

1 state-owned service

Press censorship has been more severe in the French-speaking areas than in the English-speaking areas. Journalists are still wary of challenging authority.

CRIME

 Cameroon does not publish prison figures. No figures published, but the trend is up

Armed robbery and burglary in Douala and Yaoundé are rising fast. The CENER political police are known to use torture.

EDUCATION

 54%

The French-speaking majority has failed in its attempt to take over the bilingual system. In 1991, two new single-language universities were created.

CHRONOLOGY

One of the great trading emporia of West Africa, Cameroon was divided between the French and British in 1919, after 30 years of German rule.

- ❑ **1955** Revolt; French kill 10,000.
- ❑ **1960** French sector independent.
- ❑ **1961** British southern sector votes to join Cameroon; northern joins Nigeria. Federal system set up. Lasts 11 years – centralized 1972.
- ❑ **1966** One-party state.
- ❑ **1982** Ahidjo dies. Paul Biya succeeds as president.
- ❑ **1983–1984** Coup attempts. Heavy casualties; 50 plotters executed.
- ❑ **1990** Demonstrations and strikes; declaration of multiparty state.
- ❑ **1991** Annexes nine Nigerian villages.
- ❑ **1992** Multiparty elections.

HEALTH

 1 per 13,237 people

Malaria, diarrheal and respiratory diseases

The sharp fall in government provision and financing means that more people are using the private health sector or traditional practitioners.

WEALTH

 Wealth disparities are marked

CONSUMER GOODS OWNERSHIP

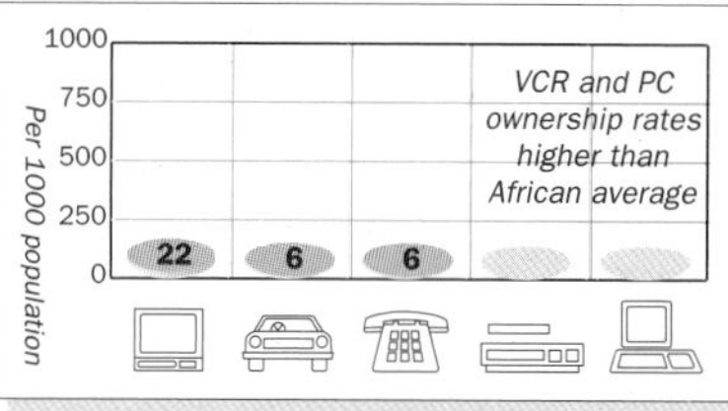

The biggest African importer of French champagne in the oil boom, Cameroon still has a small but very wealthy sector.

WORLD RANKING

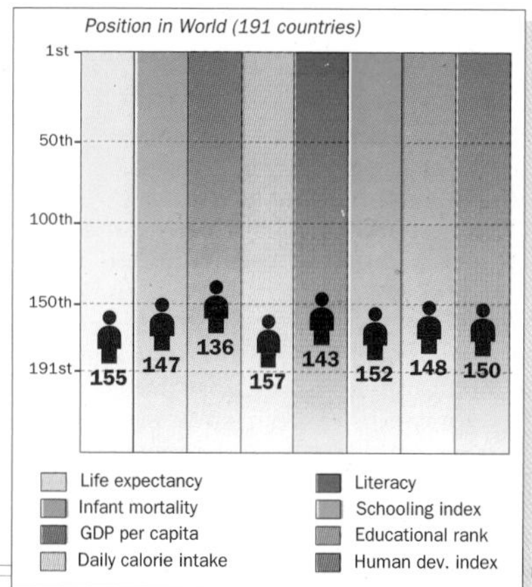

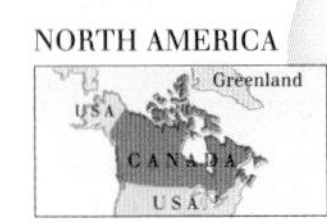

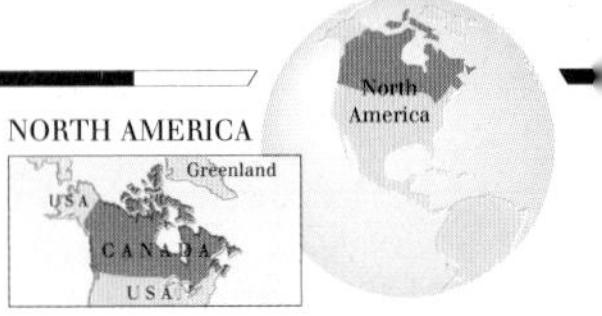

CANADA

OFFICIAL NAME: Canada **CAPITAL:** Ottawa **POPULATION:** 28.2 million
CURRENCY: Canadian dollar **OFFICIAL LANGUAGES:** English, French

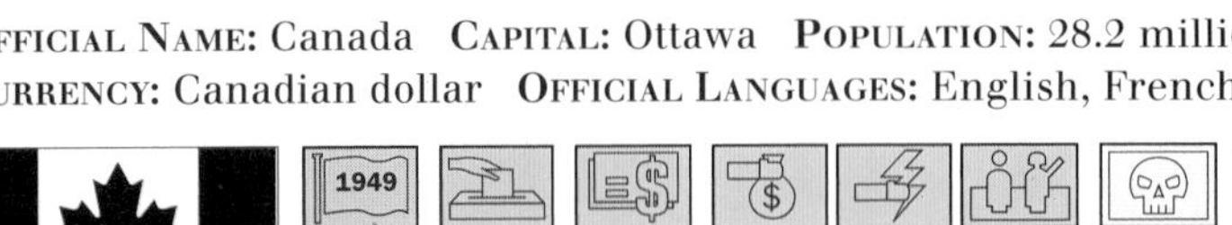

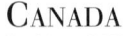

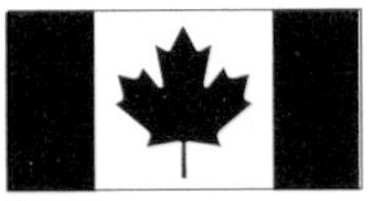

STRETCHING FROM CAPE COLOMBIA on Ellesmere Island in the north to Middle Island in Lake Erie in the south, Canada is the world's second largest country. It stretches across five time zones and is divided into ten provinces and two territories. The interior lowlands around Hudson Bay make up 80% of Canada's land area and include the vast Canadian Shield. West of the shield, the plains of Saskatchewan and Manitoba include vast prairie lands. The St. Lawrence River and Great Lakes lowlands are the most populous areas. Canada's main rivers – the St. Lawrence, Yukon, Mackenzie and Fraser – are among the world's 40 largest. In recent years, the continued political relationship of French-speaking Québec with the rest of the country has been the key constitutional issue.

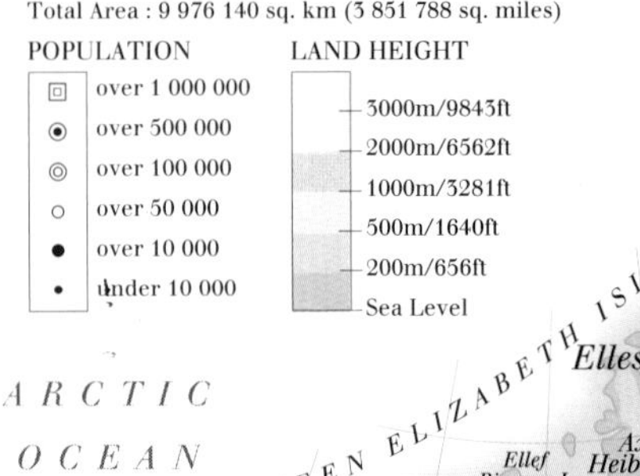

CLIMATE

WEATHER CHART

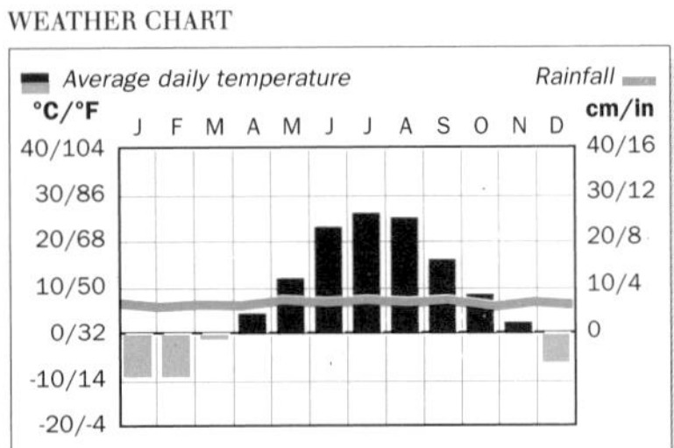

Canada's climate ranges from polar and sub-polar in the north, to cool in the south. Winters in the interior are colder and longer than on the coast, with temperatures well below freezing and deep snow; summers are hotter. The Pacific Coast around Vancouver has the warmest winters; temperatures rarely fall below zero.

COMMUNICATIONS

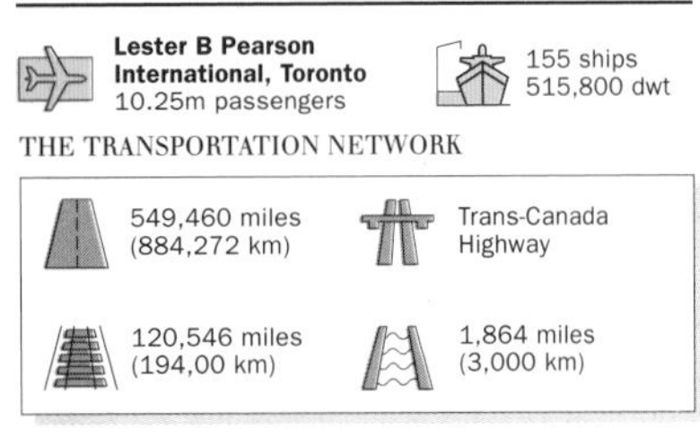

Due to Canada's size the emergence of a national economy has depended on the development of an efficient system of transportation. The Trans-Canada Highway and two trans-continental rail systems are the focus of road and rail networks that reach into the far north. Air services are well-developed and expanding. However, easy access to the cheap water transportation of the Great Lakes–Saint Lawrence Seaway system has helped Ontario and Québec retain their dominance of the economy.

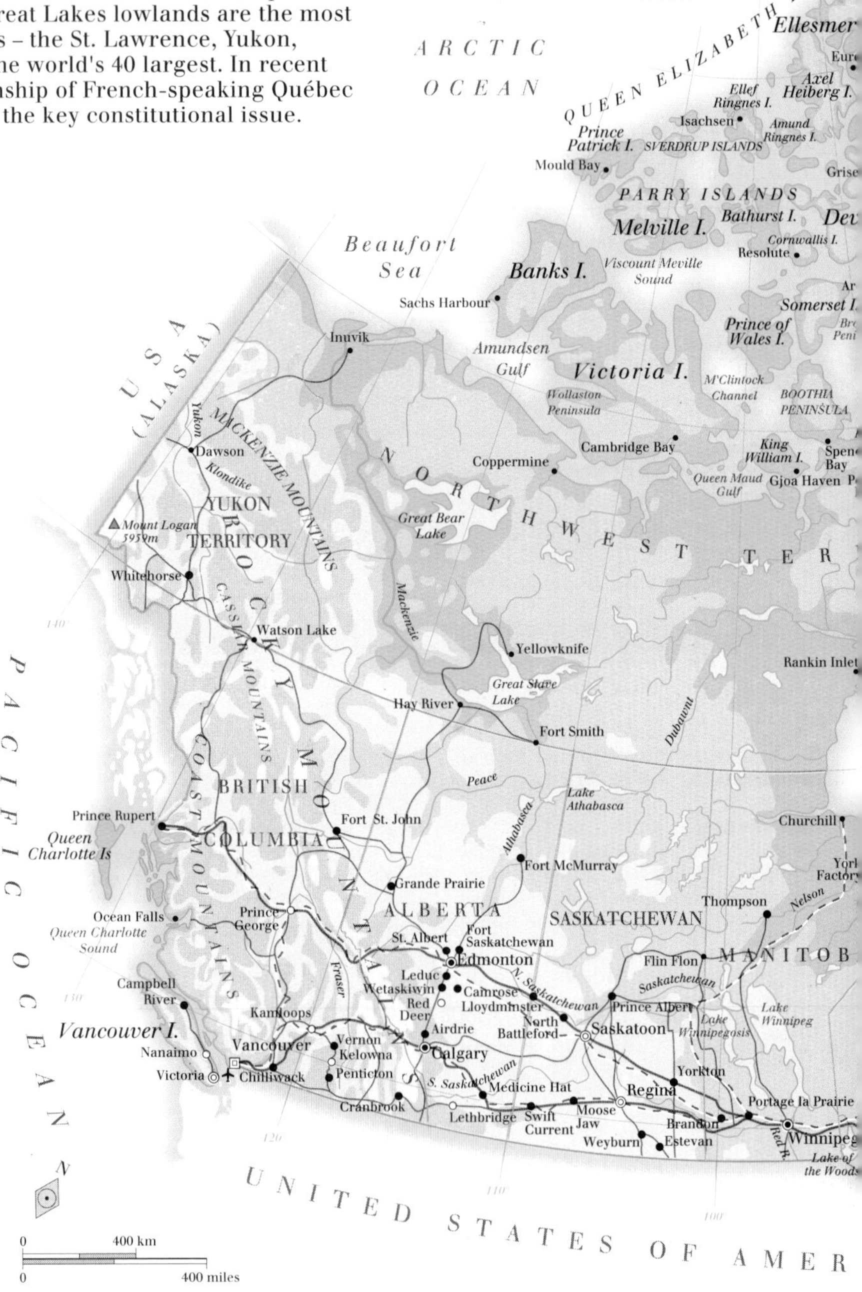

TOURISM

 15m visitors

 Up 1% in 1990

MAIN OVERSEAS ARRIVALS

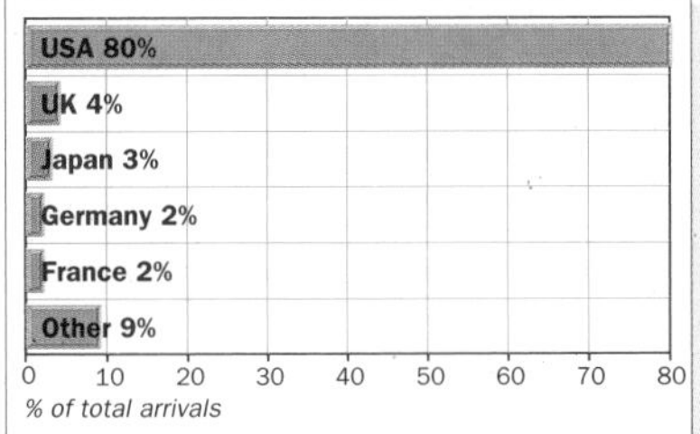

The majority of tourists still come from the USA, despite efforts to attract more European visitors with campaigns emphasizing Canada's unpolluted natural beauty. An increasing number of tourists are Japanese, many on visits to *Anne of Green Gables'* Prince Edward Island home.

PEOPLE

 English, French, Chinese, Italian, German, Ukrainian, Portuguese, Inuktitut, Cree

8 people per sq. mile

THE URBAN/RURAL POPULATION SPLIT

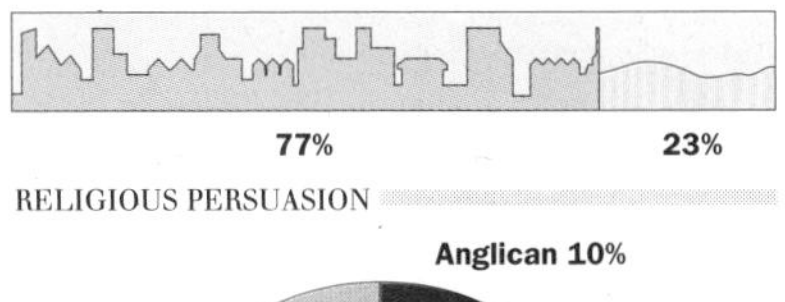

RELIGIOUS PERSUASION

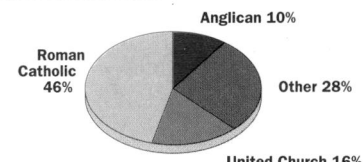

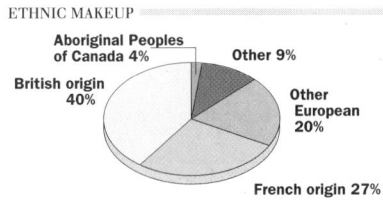

Roman Catholic 46%
Anglican 10%
Other 28%
United Church 16%

ETHNIC MAKEUP

Aboriginal Peoples of Canada 4%
Other 9%
British origin 40%
Other European 20%
French origin 27%

Relations between French-speaking Québécois and the English-speaking majority in Canada have been the dominant ethnic issue of the past 25 years. The Québécois feel distinct from the rest of Canada; their wish to preserve their culture and language from further anglicization has been reflected in the growth of secessionism. Support for pro-separatist parties has increased in the 1990s, mainly because of the failure of the provinces to deal with Québec's demand to be recognized as a "distinct society." However, any referendum on the issue is still likely to produce a "no" vote, as it did in 1980 – ending the violent separatism that had characterized the 1970s.

A dude ranch in British Columbia. Many tourists are attracted by Canada's wide choice of outdoor pursuits.

POPULATION AGE BREAKDOWN

% of population by age group	1960	1970	1980	1990	2000
65+	7.5%	7.9%	9.5%	11.4%	12.7%
15–64	58.9%	61.9%	67.5%	67.7%	68.6%
0–14	33.6%	30.2%	23%	20.9%	18.7%

More than 65% of the population still lives in the 5% of Canada taken up by the Great Lakes–St. Lawrence lowlands. However, Canada's ethnic mix has changed significantly in the past 20 years due to a move from a restrictive immigration policy to one which welcomes those with money or skills. Significant numbers of Asians have moved to Canada. The government promotes a policy that encourages each group to maintain its own culture. Canada is now officially a "Community of communities."

Canada has a long tradition of state welfare more akin to Scandinavia than the USA. Unemployment compensation and health care, supported by high taxes, are still generous, despite recent cutbacks. The government has sought to end inequalities. Measures include "pay-equity" laws which aim to make pay rates for jobs done mainly by women – like receptionists – equivalent to similar jobs for men. Women are well represented at most levels of business and government.

Aboriginal Peoples of Canada account for around 4% of the population. There are some 50,000 Innuit, 213,000 Métis (French-Indian) and 800,000 Canadians of native Indian descent. Around 43,000 live in the north, in the Northwest and Yukon Territories. In 1992, the Innuit successfully settled their longstanding land claim with the Canadian government, paving the way for other indigenous groups. In 1999, the Innuit Nunavut area will become a territory, and the first part of Canada to be governed by Aboriginal Peoples of Canada in modern history.

C

CHRONOLOGY

Peopled for centuries by indigenous Innuits and Indians, Canada began to experience extensive European settlement following the landing of the English expedition led by John Cabot in 1497 and the French landing of Jacques Cartier in 1534.

- ❑ **1754–1763** French and Indian War between Britain and France. France forced to relinquish St. Lawrence and Québec settlements to Britain.
- ❑ **1774** Act of Québec recognizes Roman Catholicism, French language, culture and traditions.
- ❑ **1775–1783** American War of Independence. Canada becomes refuge for loyalists to British Crown.
- ❑ **1846** Oregon Treaty confirms present borders with USA.
- ❑ **1885** Transcontinental railroad completed.
- ❑ **1897** Klondike gold rush begins.
- ❑ **1914–1918** Canadian troops fight in World War I.
- ❑ **1926** Commonwealth Conference. Principle of equal status with London in deciding foreign policy accepted.
- ❑ **1930s** Canada experiences economic depression.
- ❑ **1936** Reciprocity Treaty with the USA lays foundations for increased economic links.
- ❑ **1939–1945** Canadian troops fight in World War II.
- ❑ **1949** Founder-member of NATO. Newfoundland joins Federation.
- ❑ **1951** Canadian troops fight in Korean War.
- ❑ **1968** Liberal Party under Pierre Trudeau in power. Québec Party (PQ) formed to demand complete separation from federal government.
- ❑ **1970s** Québec secessionist movement grows, accompanied by terrorist bombings and murders.
- ❑ **1976** PQ wins Québec elections.
- ❑ **1976** French made official language in Québec.
- ❑ **1980** Separation of Québec rejected in referendum. Pierre Trudeau prime minister again.
- ❑ **1982** UK transfers all powers relating to Canada in British law.
- ❑ **1984** Trudeau resigns. Elections won by Brian Mulroney and Conservatives.
- ❑ **1987** Meech Lake Accord.
- ❑ **1989** Canadian–USA Free Trade Agreement (NAFTA).
- ❑ **1992** Charlottetown Agreement rejected in referendum. Canada, Mexico and USA finalize terms for NAFTA.
- ❑ **1994** NAFTA takes effect.

POLITICS

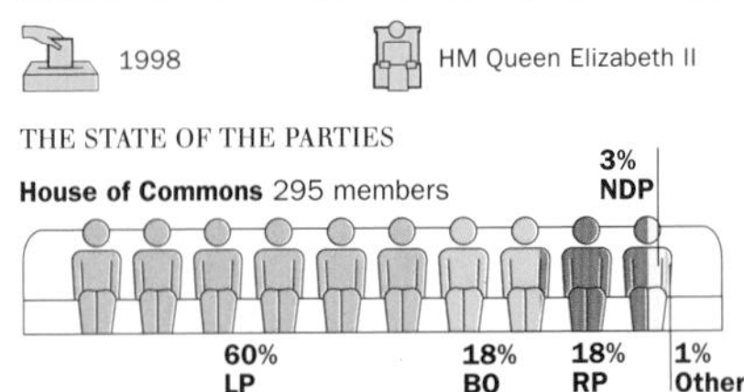

LP = Liberal Party BQ = Québec Bloc RP = Reform Party NDP = New Democratic Party PCP = Progressive Conservative Party

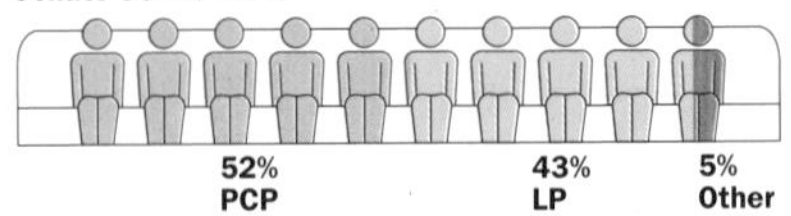

The Senate's members are nominated

Canada is a federal multiparty democracy.

Main Political Issues

The unity of the state
Canada has been struggling to find a place for Francophone Québec and its separatist tendencies almost since the foundation of the state. The issue rose to prominence again in 1976 when the separatist Québec Party (PQ) won power in the 1976 Québec provincial elections. The PQ at first advocated independence then economic association. However, its proposals were rejected in a referendum in 1980 by 59.5% to 40.5%. In 1990, a constitutional agreement, the Meech Lake Accord, recognized Québec as a distinct society within the Canadian Federation. The Accord also granted additional powers to other federal states. However, it was not ratified, as Newfoundland objected to its provisions. In 1992, another proposal, the Charlottetown Agreement, was put to referendum. This recognized Québec as a distinct society and granted the province a guaranteed 25% of seats in the National Assembly. This was turned down both in Québec and at the national level. Opinion polls suggest that a majority of Canadians have lately lost enthusiasm for too much federalism. In 1993, Mr. Robert Bourassa, the then Québec premier, declared that Québec's aspirations could best be met without cutting all ties with Ottawa.

NAFTA
The proposed North American Free Trade Agreement (NAFTA) dominated the Canadian elections of 1988. Many are still opposed to the agreement. There are fears that Canadian workers may suffer from competition from Mexico. Tensions between Canadian and US trade unions have also risen as Canadian workers have been forced to accept more flexible US working practices. Many sectors of business, particularly grains, oilseeds, textiles, oil and gas and engineering services, have benefited from NAFTA.

Niagara Falls is situated between Lakes Erie and Ontario on the Canada–US border. Horseshoe Falls, in Canada, is 49 m high and 790 m across.

Profile

Until recently, Canadian politics were dominated by three main parties. The PCP and LP had few ideological differences. The NDP advocated greater government intervention. Only the PCP and LP had held office. The NDP gained influence when voters registered a mid-term protest.

Major political changes were seen in 1993. Brian Mulroney, the leader of the PCP, resigned in the wake of economic recession, the unpopularity of a new sales tax and the failure of the Charlottetown Agreement. He was replaced by Kim Campbell as PCP leader. However, in elections in October 1993, nine years of PCP rule were brought to an end by a landslide LP victory. The PCP held onto only 2 of its 157 seats while the NDP managed to hold 8 out of 44 seats. The change represented a rejection of mainstream politics by the electorate who voted in favor of parties representing strong regional interests.

***Kim Campbell**, Canada's first woman premier.*

***Brian Mulroney** resigned as PCP leader in 1992.*

***Robert Bourassa**, premier of Québec until 1994.*

WORLD AFFAIRS

Canada's most important relationship is with the USA, its main trading partner. There are tensions in the relationship, however. Canada has not managed to reach agreement on restricting pollution from US border plants, which have been responsible for much of the acid rain affecting Canada's forests. A US–Canadian commission recommended a $5 billion program, but did not suggest sources of funding. Minor maritime waters disputes exist with the USA over stretches of the Northwest Passage; the USA recognizes Canadian claims over the islands, but not the waters. A dispute with France over the boundary of waters around St. Pierre et Miquelon, the French-controlled islands off Newfoundland's coast, was settled in 1993. Until 1993, Canada's trade with Mexico was just 1.6% of that with the USA. However, as trade increases under NAFTA, so too will relations become more important.

AID

$2.6bn (donations)

Up 5% in 1990

Canada's aid budget has been one of the first areas of government spending to be earmarked for cuts. While most Canadians support aid – Canada gives twice as much per capita as the USA – the issue is not politicized to the point where cuts have been reversed.

First to suffer have been the large number of NGOs which the Canadian International Development Agency (CIDA) supports. The regional focus of aid has shifted from traditional areas, such as francophone West Africa, to Southeast Asia. This reflects the growing importance of Canada's Asian minority trade links; Pacific trade is now 65% greater than trade across the Atlantic. Aid now aims to provide specific skills, rather than funding for large-scale development projects.

DEFENSE

$10.4bn

Down 10% in 1992

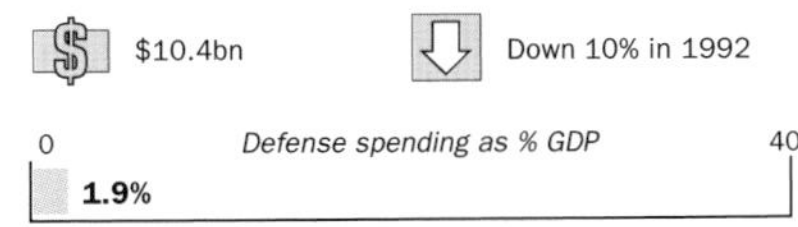

CANADIAN ARMED FORCES

	114 main battle tanks (*Leopard* C–1)	22,000 personnel
	14 frigates, 3 submarines, 4 destroyers and 12 patrol boats	17,000 personnel
	198 combat aircraft (CF–18/CF–5)	22,400 personnel
	None	

Canada cooperates with the USA in the defense of North America. However, in response to the end of the Cold War in Europe, Canada withdrew its forces stationed there in 1992. As in other NATO states, defense spending has been cut significantly. Even so, many Canadians would like to see it cut even further. The focus of defense planning is now the creation of rapid reaction forces. In 1993 and 1994, Canadian troops were deployed in UN peace-keeping operations in Somalia and in the former Yugoslavia.

ECONOMICS

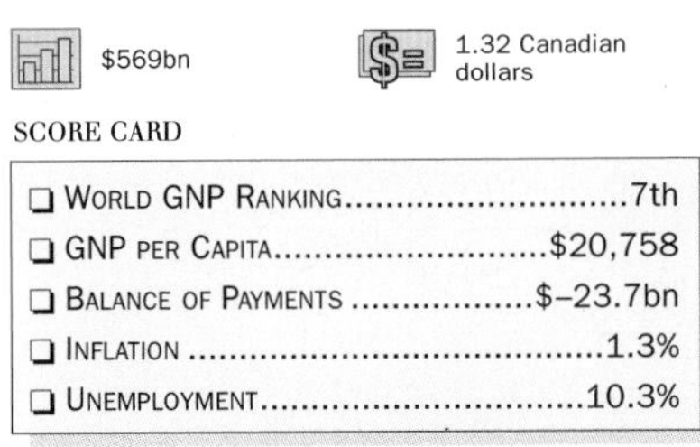

$569bn

1.32 Canadian dollars

SCORE CARD

❑ WORLD GNP RANKING	7th
❑ GNP PER CAPITA	$20,758
❑ BALANCE OF PAYMENTS	$-23.7bn
❑ INFLATION	1.3%
❑ UNEMPLOYMENT	10.3%

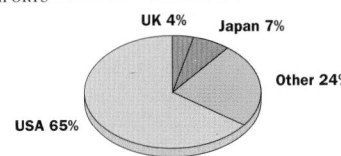

EXPORTS

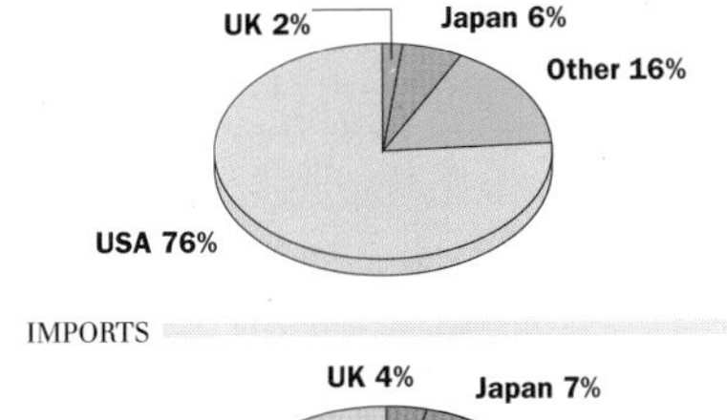

IMPORTS

STRENGTHS

A broad and rich resource base. Provides exports, raw materials for manufacturing sector and massive cheap energy, notably HEP; large oil and gas reserves. Agriculture and forestry contribute 3% of GDP; mining 4%. Successful manufacturing sector contributes 17% of GDP; notably forestry products, transportation equipment, and chemicals. Free access to huge US and Mexican markets through NAFTA.

WEAKNESSES

Increasingly uncompetitive; higher taxes, more regulations, lower productivity relative to most competitors. Political uncertainty over future of Federation dents business confidence. High federal and provincial budget deficits; slow recovery from early 1990s recession.

ECONOMIC PERFORMANCE INDICATOR

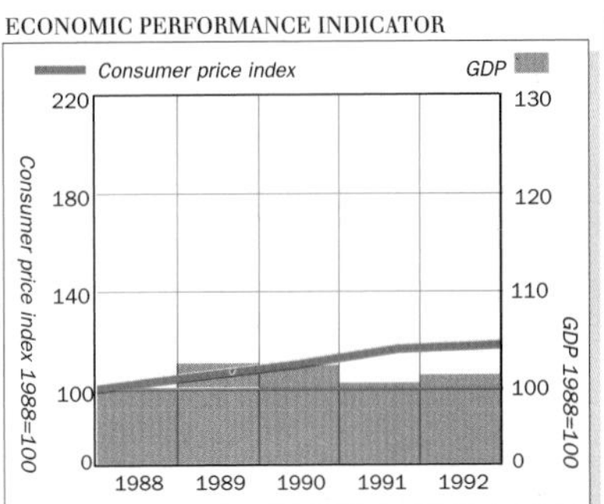

PROFILE

Canada's enormous resource base has delivered one of the OECD's highest standards of living since 1945. After the mid-1980s, however, its manufactured exports faced increasing competition, while prices for its primary exports fell. From 1980–1988, real growth averaged 3.5% a year. After 1989 it stagnated, while budget deficits rose – forcing restructuring at both the federal and provincial levels. Many of Canada's welfare programs were cut back; the defense budget was sharply reduced. The end result was a sharp drop in inflation from 4% to 1.3%, the lowest in the G7, and a resumption of growth after 1993. Another motivation for the changes was Canada's membership in NAFTA. Its firms have had to become more competitive to maintain exports. Most have been successful, but better productivity and a shift to high-tech have left unemployment at around 10%.

CANADA : MAJOR BUSINESSES

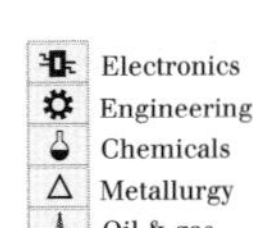

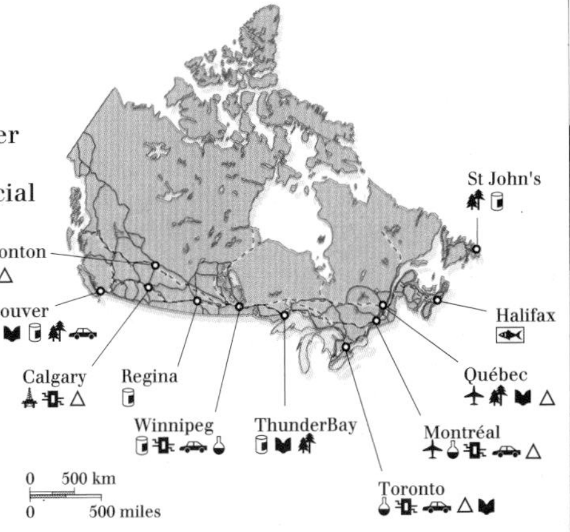

C

RESOURCES

482bn kwh (capacity 104.14 m kw)

1.6m b/d (reserves 5,291,630,000 bbl)

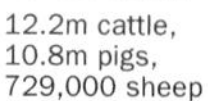
12.2m cattle, 10.8m pigs, 729,000 sheep

Zinc, uranium, asbestos, nickel, potash, gypsum

ELECTRICITY GENERATION

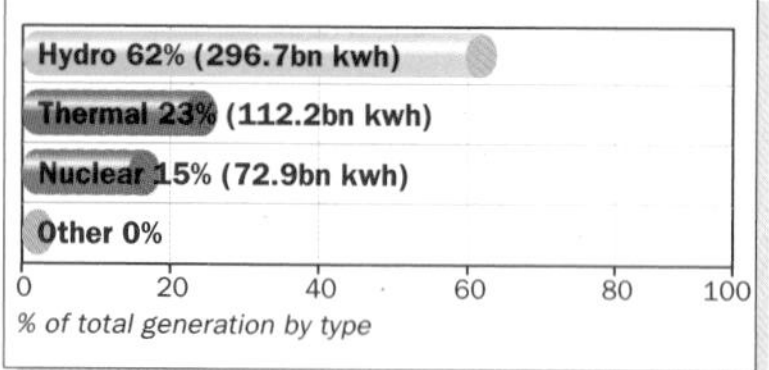

Canada is a country of enormous natural resources. It is the world's largest exporter of forest products and a top exporter of fish, furs and wheat. Minerals have played a key role in Canada's transformation into an urban–industrial economy. Alberta, British Columbia, Québec and Saskatchewan are the principal mining regions. Ontario and the Northwest (NWT) and Yukon Territories are also significant producers. Canada is the world's largest producer of zinc and uranium; the second largest of nickel, asbestos, potash and gypsum. Oil and gas are exploited in Alberta, off the Atlantic coast and in the NWT – huge additional reserves are thought to exist in the high Arctic. Most exports go to the USA. Canada is also one of the world's top hydroelectricity producers.

CANADA : LAND USE

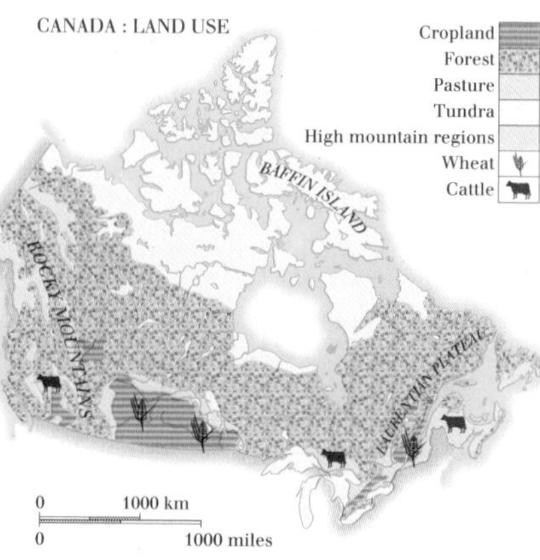

ENVIRONMENT

5% (2% partially protected)

State policies framed with sustainable development in mind

ENVIRONMENTAL TREATIES

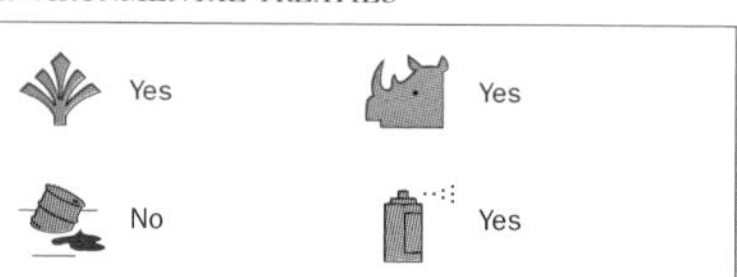

With a population of 28.2 million living in the world's second largest country, Canada does not suffer from the environmental pressures of more populated states. It is justly renowned for vast tracts of wild countryside untroubled by industrial pollution or pollution caused by intensive farming methods.

Canadians have tighter pollution controls than the neighboring USA. However, Canada's rate of carbon-dioxide emissions is higher, at 4.1 tons per person per year, than the Soviet Union's (3.4), Japan's (2.1) or France's (1.7). Per capita production of hazardous waste is also higher than the European average. Environmental measures are now concentrating on bringing both measures up to the world's highest standards.

A particular concern to Canadians has been damage to the ozone layer caused by CFCs. Canada followed the US lead in 1978 by banning the use of CFCs for aerosols. In 1987, Montreal was the site of the international agreement to cut CFC use by half by the year 2000.

MEDIA

No political censorship

PUBLISHING AND BROADCAST MEDIA

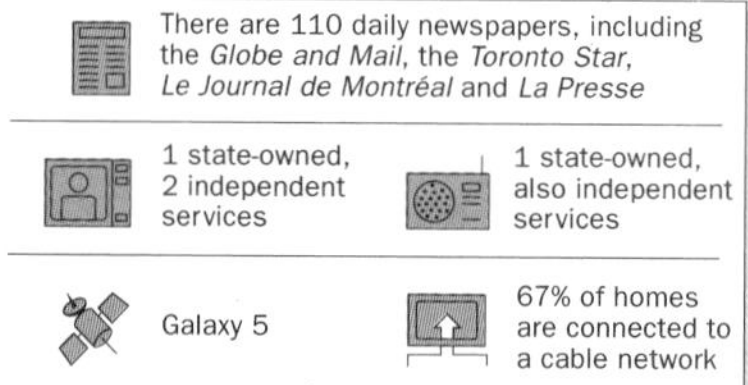

There are 110 daily newspapers, including the *Globe and Mail*, the *Toronto Star*, *Le Journal de Montréal* and *La Presse*
1 state-owned, 2 independent services
1 state-owned, also independent services
Galaxy 5
67% of homes are connected to a cable network

Two of the three national TV networks are run by the Canadian Broadcasting Corporation (CBC), one channel in English, the other in French. Canadian TV is renowned for its news and sports coverage. Over three-quarters of the country can receive broadcasts from the USA. Most cities now have cable TV, which usually offers at least one multilingual or ethnic channel. *La Presse* is the leading French-language daily.

***Fall in the tundra** in northern Canada. Trees such as the black spruce are subject to the effects of acid rain originating in the USA's northern industrial states.*

CRIME

31,302 prisoners

No significant change

CRIME RATES

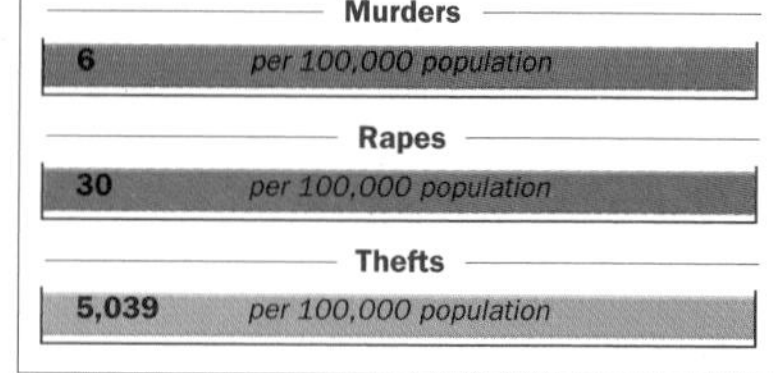

Murders
6
per 100,000 population
Rapes
30
per 100,000 population
Thefts
5,039
per 100,000 population

Crime rates in Canada are much lower than in the USA. Canadians ascribe this to their far tighter gun control laws. In 1993, the regulations were made even stricter. Another factor has been the careful efforts to maintain the inner cities as crime-free zones. The ghetto problems of US inner cities have largely been avoided. However, Canada does have a rising drug problem. Youth crime is also growing, with over 22% of federal charges being laid against youths between the ages of 12 and 17. in 1991. However only 0.04% of youth charges were murder-related.

EDUCATION

99%

0 Education spending as % GNP 25

7%

THE EDUCATION SYSTEM

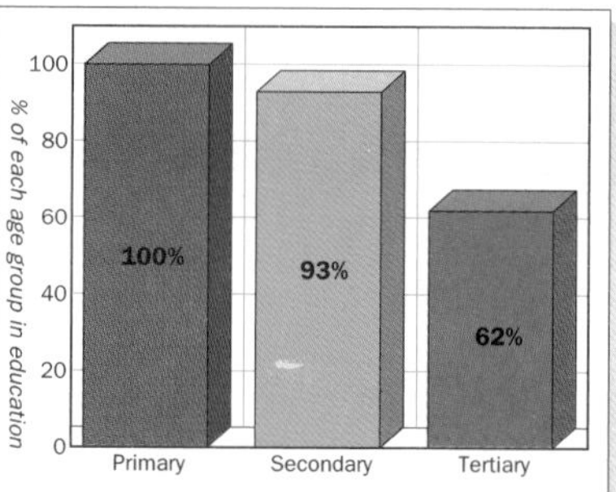

Education policy is a responsibility of the provinces. The period of free compulsory school attendance varies, but is a minimum of nine years. The prime medium of instruction is English in all provinces except francophone Québec. However, in several other provinces, French-speaking students are entitled to be taught in French.

Canada has 69 universities and 203 other higher education institutions. Over 75% of secondary level students go on to some form of higher education – the highest proportion in the industrialized world. The emphasis placed on education is also reflected in the fact that Canada's total education expenditure as a percentage of GDP also tops the league at over 7%.

REGIONS

QUÉBEC

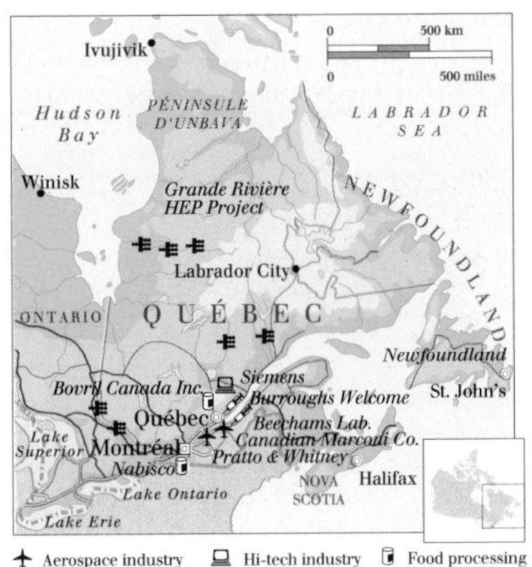

Aerospace industry · Hi-tech industry · Food processing · Hydro-electric power · Pharmaceuticals

ALMOST ALL 6.9 MILLION Québécois live in the south of the province; 50% in Greater Montreal. The northern forests generate 20% of the world's pulp and paper. Québec is also the world's fourth largest hydro-power producer. Secession has long been an issue for the francophone majority. However, support for separatist parties in the early 1990s reflected discontent with traditional parties as much as a wish to go it alone. Separation could be costly, notably in jobs. 90% of exports go to the USA and the rest of Canada. To keep these NAFTA markets, Québec would have to embrace free trade. Presently, it is highly protectionist.

TORONTO

TORONTO is Canada's largest, fastest-growing and most polyglot city. As the destination for 50% of immigrants and most of Canada's internal migrants, it is expected to almost double in size to five million by 2000. One in six housing-starts in Canada during the late 1980s were in Toronto. Like Ontario as a whole, it has a broad industrial base and excellent public services. Toronto is also the country's leading financial and services center – a role it took from Montreal during the secession fears of the late 1970s. Like Montreal, it was hit hard by recession in the early 1990s. Unemployment rose and the city government had to impose unpopular budget cuts.

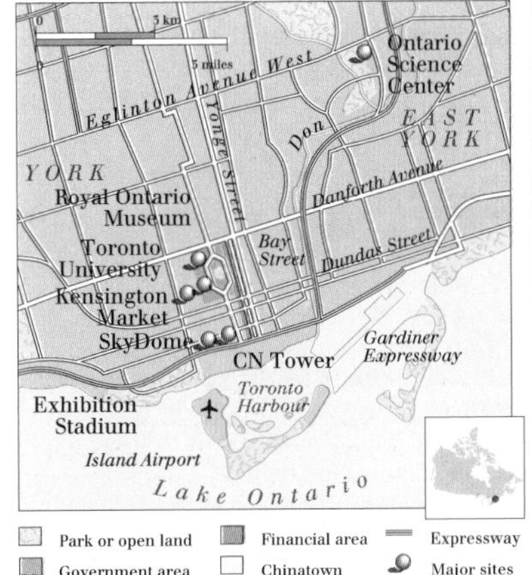

Park or open land · Financial area · Expressway · Government area · Chinatown · Major sites

NORTHWEST TERRITORIES

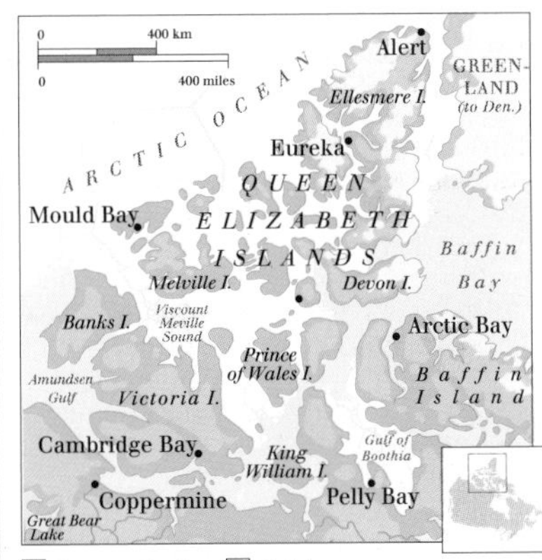

Permanent ice sheet · Pack ice

THE NORTHWEST TERRITORIES cover 1.3 million sq. miles, or one-third of Canada. However, their population is tiny – just 57,650 people. Over 60% are of indigenous descent, mostly Innuit, but also Dene and Métis Indians. The incomer minority work mainly in the mining industry, which has grown rapidly since the discovery of gold in the 1930s. Zinc is the top export, but oil and gas and many other minerals are extracted. There are growing concerns about the effects of mining on the NWT's environment, but the main casualties have been the Innuit. They have largely given up their nomadic, hunting lifestyle and today are Canada's most marginalized and poorest people. However, the 1992 settlement of Innuit land claims in the high Arctic holds out hope of a better future. They have won title to 135,135 sq. mi. of land and now have a say in how it is developed. In 1999, the area will become the self-governing Nunavut Territory, making the Innuit the first of the Aboriginal Peoples of Canada to gain self-determination.

HEALTH

1 per 452 people

Heart and respiratory diseases, cancer, accidents

Health spending as % GNP (scale 0–25): 8.6%

Canada's state health service, funded by a national insurance plan, covers the whole population. However, about 25% use private health facilities. The government is under pressure to cut the budget deficit while facing a higher health bill. Rising costs are the result of an aging population and more expensive treatments. Surveys show, though, that most Canadians want to retain the present system.

WEALTH

Similar wage levels to the USA

CONSUMER GOODS OWNERSHIP

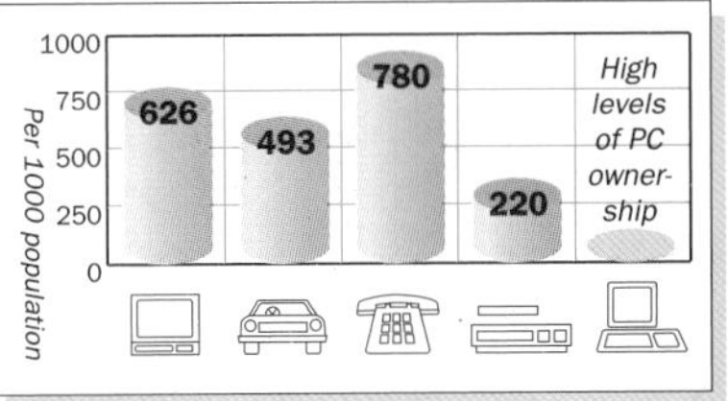

Despite the strains caused by recession during the early 1990s – including a rise in unemployment to 11% – life for most Canadians remains very good. The UN ranks Canada as one of the best countries in the world in which to live. In its 1993 overall assessment of human development indicators, like income, education and life expectancy, Canada came in second behind Japan.

However, disadvantaged groups do exist, particularly among Aboriginal Peoples of Canada. Unemployment, poor housing and mortality rates for Indians and Innuits are well above those for other Canadians; the Innuit suicide rate is three times higher. Those who live on reserves are the poorest group.

WORLD RANKING

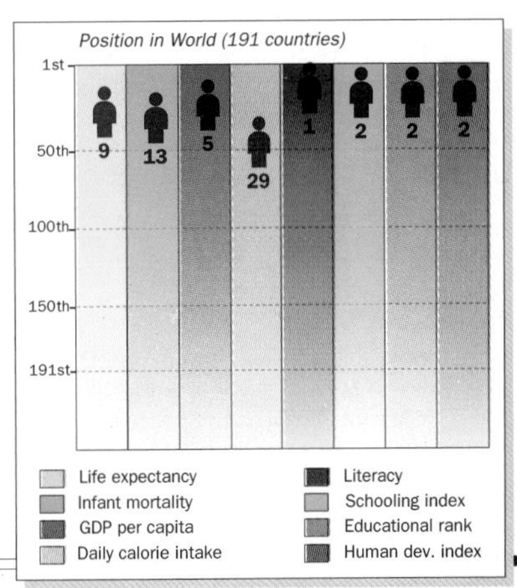

C

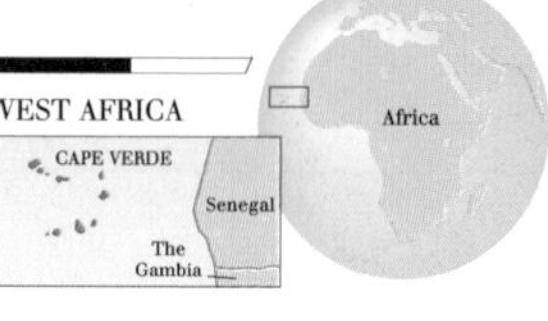

CAPE VERDE

OFFICIAL NAME: Republic of Cape Verde **CAPITAL:** Cidade de Praia
POPULATION: 400,000 **CURRENCY:** Cape Verde escudo **OFFICIAL LANGUAGE:** Portuguese

C

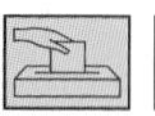

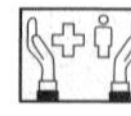

THE CAPE VERDE ARCHIPELAGO off the west coast of Africa became independent of its colonial ruler, Portugal, in 1975. Following a period of single-party socialist rule, Cape Verde held its first multiparty elections in 1991. Most of the islands are mountainous and volcanic; the low-lying islands of Sal, Boa Vista and Maio have agricultural potential, although they are prone to debilitating droughts. Around 50% of the population lives on São Tiago.

CLIMATE

WEATHER CHART

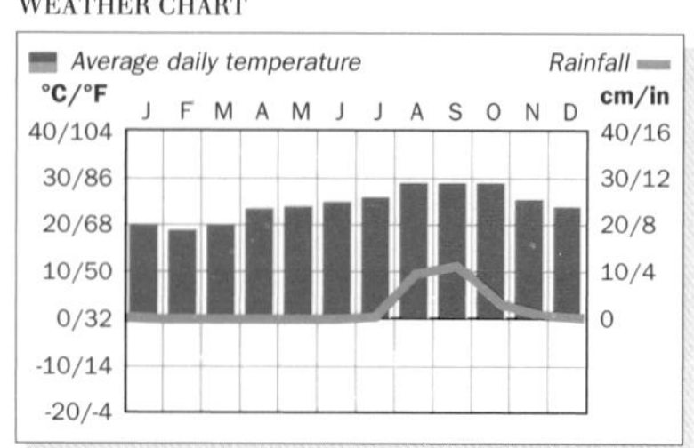

Cape Verde has a very dry climate, subject to droughts that sometimes last for years at a time.

COMMUNICATIONS

Amílcar Cabral, Sal Island 156,000 passengers

17 ships 25,900 dwt

THE TRANSPORTATION NETWORK

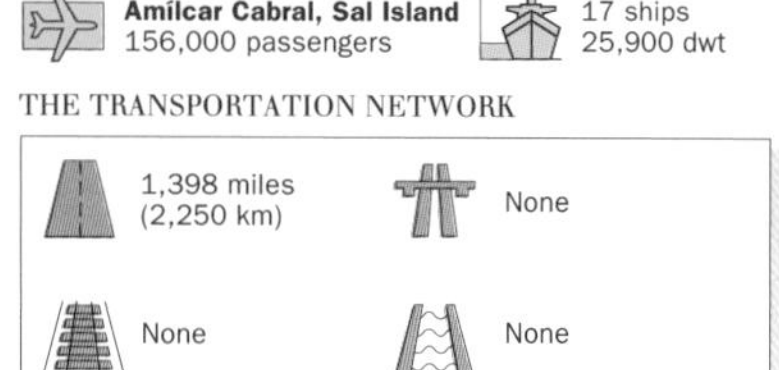

Cape Verde has a strategic position on international sea and air routes, which it is beginning to exploit.

TOURISM

156,000 visitors

Down 5% in 1991

MAIN OVERSEAS ARRIVALS

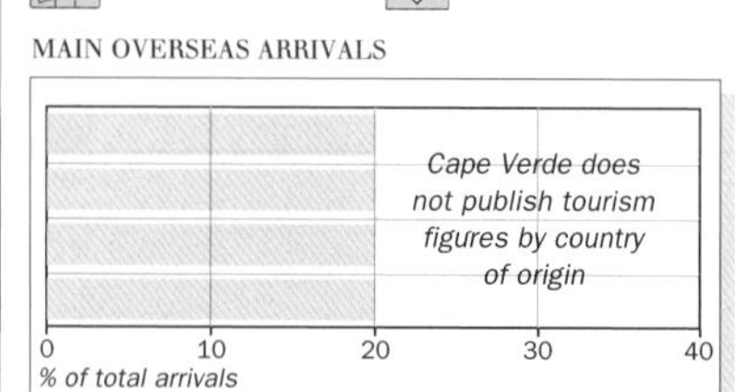

Tourism has not been a government priority and is on a modest scale. The islands of São Tiago, Santo Antão, Fogo and Brava have tourist potential, offering a combination of mountain scenery and extensive beaches.

PEOPLE

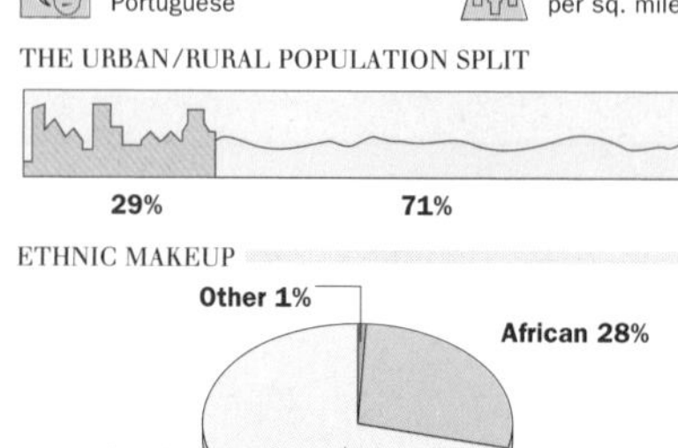

The majority of the population is Portuguese-African *mestiço*; the remainder is largely African, descended either from slaves or from more recent immigrants from the mainland. The Creolization of the culture has led to a relative lack of ethnic tension, although there is some bad feeling between islands. African traditions of the extended family and the Catholic Church have helped to ensure the vitality of family life. Women's role in public affairs is not prominent, in part due to the conservative Catholic influence.

POLITICS

1996

President António Mascarenhas Monteiro

THE STATE OF THE PARTIES

National People's Assembly 79 members

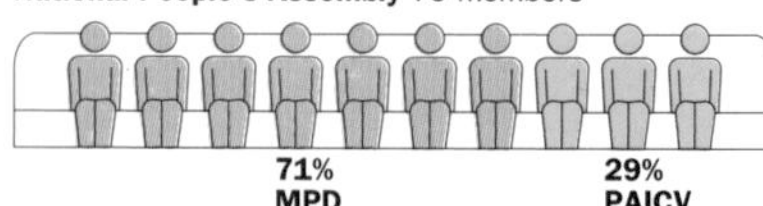

MPD = Movement for Democracy
PAICV = African Party for the Independence of Cape Verde

Cape Verde experienced a peaceful transition to multiparty politics in 1991, when elections brought the MPD to power. Although there had previously been a decade of single-party rule under the PAICV, it had in fact operated a liberal system in which opposition and dissent were tolerated. The large number of Cape Verdeans living abroad, who had remained in contact with the islands, helped to smooth the process as democracy was already widely understood and favored.

The main issue for the government now, apart from preserving the present political consensus, is that of economic survival, particularly in periods of drought. An ideological debate continues over the extent of the successes and failures of the PAICV's period of rule.

WORLD AFFAIRS

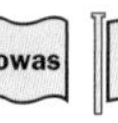

AfDB

Cape Verde aims to diversify its international contacts in order to secure aid, while maintaining good relations with Portugal (this former colonial power is not a major donor.) Within the region, Cape Verde seeks to restore normal relations with Guinea-Bissau, after withdrawing from a proposed union in 1980, and is developing contacts with other mainland nations, such as Senegal.

AID

$79m (receipts)

Fairly constant from year to year

The most important donor is the EU, which has provided substantial food aid in the wake of recent droughts, as well as funding aid programs. The World Bank is also a major source, as are the Netherlands, Sweden, Germany, France and Italy. Aid donations finance almost all development in Cape Verde, which is one of the least industrialized countries in the world.

DEFENSE

$3.5m

Fairly constant from year to year

After independence, small armed forces were established, consisting of a 1,000-strong army, a navy of 200 and an air force of 100. These forces have never been called upon to play a political role; their main duties are to curb smuggling and to protect territorial waters against illegal fishing.

ECONOMICS

$353m

74.01 Cape Verde escudos

SCORE CARD

❑ World GNP Ranking	170th
❑ GNP per Capita	$890
❑ Balance of Payments	$–40.46m
❑ Inflation	14.3%
❑ Unemployment	25%

Strengths

Strategic geographical position, off the westernmost tip of Africa, close to the mid-Atlantic where Africa is nearest to Latin America. This has military and economic advantages, including shipping maintenance and air travel. Low debt servicing costs.

Weaknesses

Permanent threat of drought and problem of water supply, despite desalination plants. Lack of agricultural land and dependency on food aid. Difficulties of communications between islands.

EXPORTS

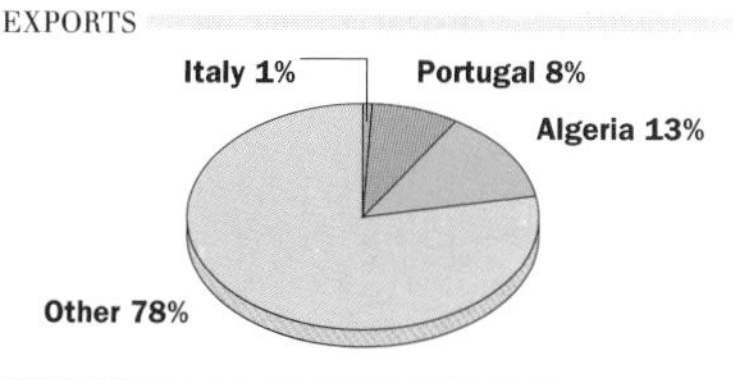

IMPORTS

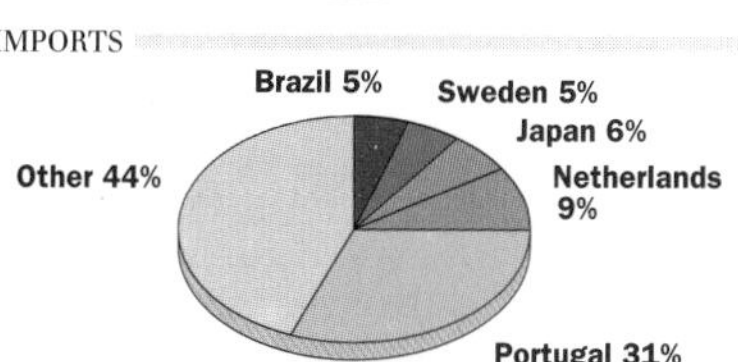

Portuguese colonial-style architecture *on Fogo, one of the larger islands. The volcano in its center is the highest point in Cape Verde.*

RESOURCES

36m kwh (capacity 7,000 kw)

Not an oil producer and has no refineries

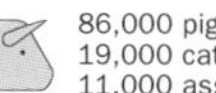

86,000 pigs, 19,000 cattle, 11,000 asses

Salt, pozzolana

Cape Verde has no known strategic resources. With no oil and no possibility of hydroelectric power, it depends on imported petroleum for energy. However, experimental projects have been carried out to investigate the potential of windmills, wave power and biogas.

ENVIRONMENT

None

Introduction of reforestation programs

Cape Verde has recently suffered several years of persistent drought, which has affected food production and reduced livestock herds. It is a very active member of CILSS, which struggles against drought in the Sahel region. One initiative has involved reforestation, undertaken in an attempt to encourage rainfall.

MEDIA

Since multiparty politics, virtually no censorship

PUBLISHING AND BROADCAST MEDIA

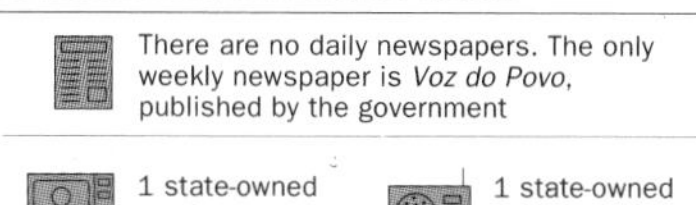

There are no daily newspapers. The only weekly newspaper is *Voz do Povo*, published by the government

1 state-owned service

1 state-owned service

The press is to some extent limited for economic reasons, as it was under single-party rule. An experimental TV station was forced to close in the late 1980s, but French assistance has allowed both TV and radio to start broadcasting again.

CRIME

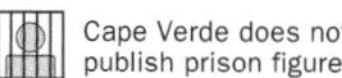

Cape Verde does not publish prison figures

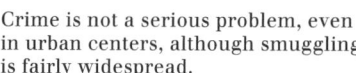

Little change from year to year

Crime is not a serious problem, even in urban centers, although smuggling is fairly widespread.

CHRONOLOGY

Cape Verde was a Portuguese colony from 1462 until 1975, and was ruled jointly with Guinea-Bissau.

- ❑ **1961** Joint struggle for liberation of Cape Verde and Guinea-Bissau (then Portuguese Guinea) begins.
- ❑ **1974** Guinea-Bissau independent.
- ❑ **1975** Independence, but with view to union with Guinea-Bissau.
- ❑ **1981** New constitution formalizes final split from Guinea-Bissau.
- ❑ **1990** Multiparty politics legalized.

EDUCATION

66%

Upon independence, education became a priority after years of neglect. 80% of children now attend primary school.

HEALTH

1 per 7,660 people

Diarrheal, cerebrovascular and respiratory diseases

Health care has improved since the colonial period, yet there are still only 50 doctors in the whole archipelago.

WEALTH

Most Cape Verdeans lead a subsistence existence

CONSUMER GOODS OWNERSHIP

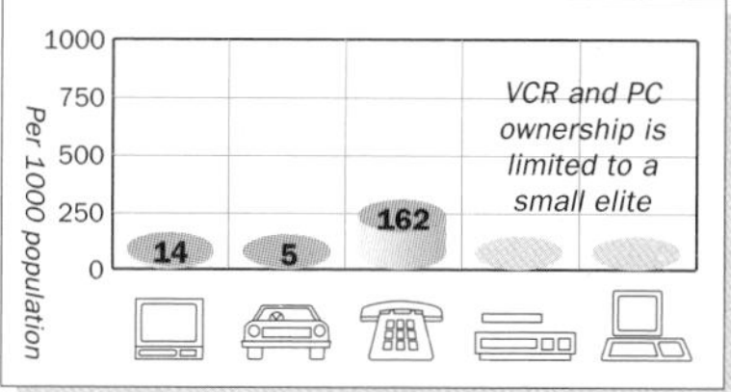

Compared with the 90% of the population in primary production, the small business class in Praia is well-off.

WORLD RANKING

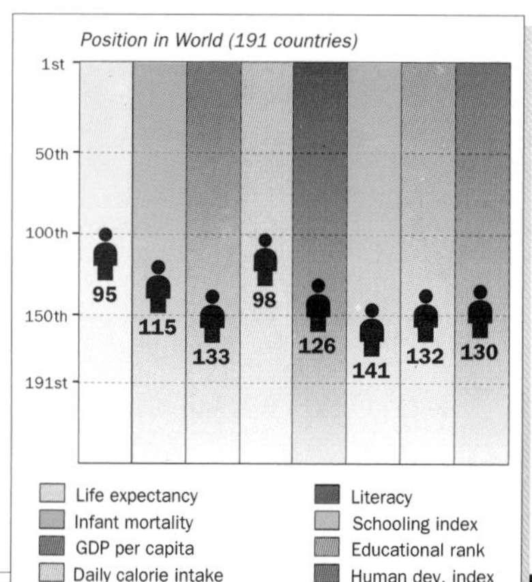

CENTRAL AFRICAN REPUBLIC

CENTRAL AFRICA
Chad
Sudan
Cameroon
CENTRAL AFRICAN REPUBLIC
Zaire

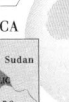

OFFICIAL NAME: Central African Republic **CAPITAL:** Bangui
POPULATION: 3.2 million **CURRENCY:** CFA franc **OFFICIAL LANGUAGE:** French

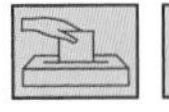

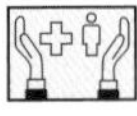

LANDLOCKED AT THE WESTERN end of the Sahel, the Central African Republic (CAR) is a low plateau stretching north from one of Africa's great rivers, the Ubangi, which forms its border with Zaire. Most of the population lives in the equatorial, rainforested south. The arid north sustains less than 2% of the population. Emperor Bokassa's 14-year rule from 1965 to 1979 was followed by military dictatorship. Democracy was restored in 1993.

CLIMATE

WEATHER CHART

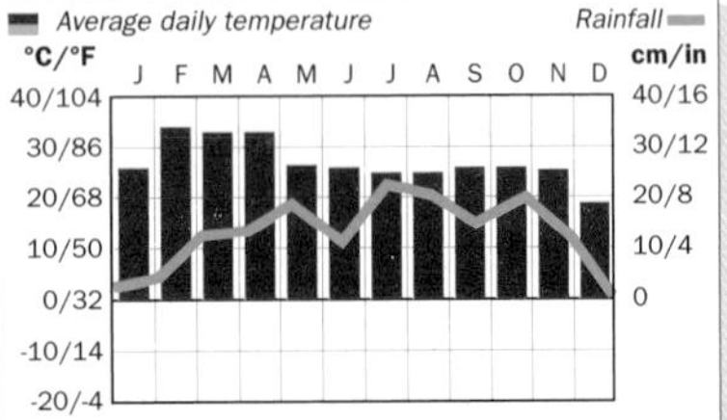

The south is equatorial, the north has a savanna-type climate, and the far north lies within the Sahel.

COMMUNICATIONS

Mpoko, Bangui

Has no fleet

THE TRANSPORTATION NETWORK

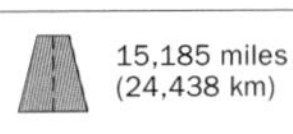

15,185 miles (24,438 km)

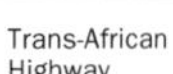

Trans-African Highway

None

496 miles (800 km)

The CAR's limited transportation system is highly dependent on the river link to Brazzaville, Congo, and by rail from there to Pointe-Noire and Zaire's ports.

TOURISM

6,000 visitors

No change in 1992

MAIN OVERSEAS ARRIVALS

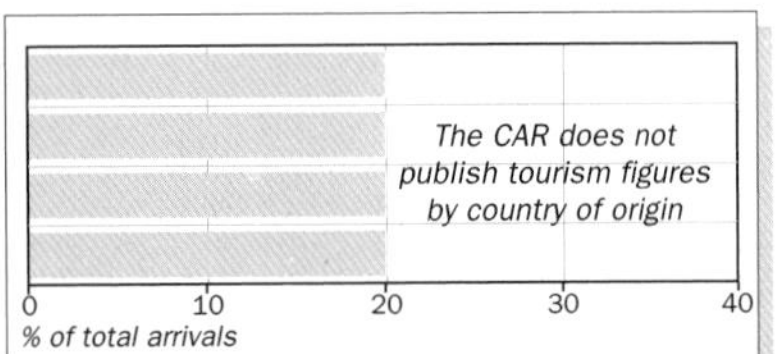

Tourist promotion is small-scale, but since 1979 there has been a modest increase in national park safaris. Plans for a new runway in Bangui will permit air charters, chiefly from France.

PEOPLE

Sango, Banda, Gbaya, French

13 people per sq. mile

THE URBAN/RURAL POPULATION SPLIT

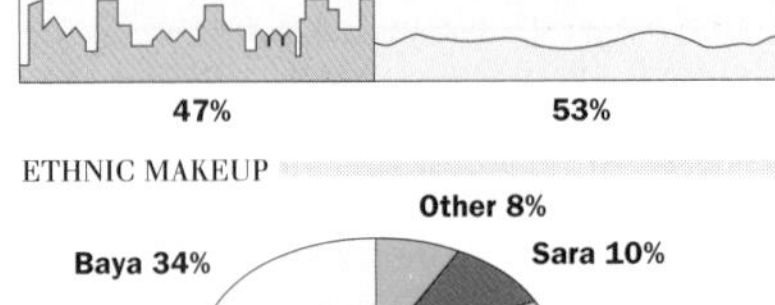

ETHNIC MAKEUP

Other 8%
Sara 10%
Baya 34%
Mandjia 21%
Banda 27%

Although the Baya and the Banda are the largest ethnic groups, the *lingua franca* is Sango. This is spoken by the southern riverine minorities, who provided the political leaders from independence (Presidents Dacko and Kolingba and Emperor Bokassa), until President Patasse, who comes from the interior. Resentment against the river peoples occasionally flares up, but ethnic diversity minimizes polarization. Women, as in other non-Muslim African countries, have considerable power. Elizabeth Domitien was prime minister from 1975–1976 and Ruth Rolland ran for president in 1993.

WORLD AFFAIRS

NAM

Apart from keeping up the momentum of its improving political image in international life, the CAR is anxious to continue good relations with France, whose financial help will be needed for some time, and with Cameroon and Congo – its main outlets to the sea. Otherwise, containing any spillover from the civil war in Chad and insulating itself from the problems in Sudan and Zaire are priorities.

AID

$174m (receipts)

Down 29% in 1991

Almost all development projects are funded from external aid. France, as the former colonial power, provides two-thirds of the total. The EU (notably Belgium, Italy and Germany), Japan and, since 1989, the USA and Israel are major donors. Help from the IMF and World Bank, although currently in a "pause," is probable given the CAR's bankruptcy.

DEFENSE

$21.98m

Up 18% in 1988

The 6,200-strong armed forces (3,500 army and 2,700 gendarmerie) are the subject of major spending and are very well equipped, mostly with French hardware. The French also provide important economic military aid and officers to fill key posts. The French base at Bouar, closed under Bokassa, has been reopened.

POLITICS

Uncertain

President Ange-Félix Patasse

THE STATE OF THE PARTIES

National Assembly 85 members

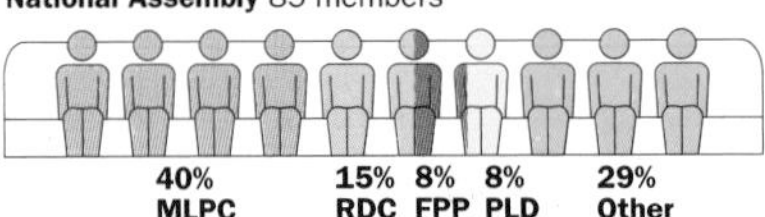

MLPC = Central African People's Liberation Party
RDC = Central African Democratic Rally **FPP** = Patriotic Front for Progress (part of the CFD = Consultative Group of Democratic Forces) **PLD** = Liberal Democratic Party

Economic and Regional Council

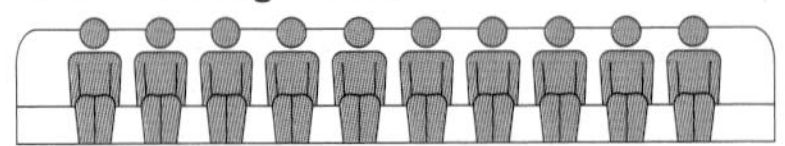

One half of the members are chosen by the president and the other half are elected by the National Assembly

The return to democratic elections in 1993 after Gen. Kolingba's single-party rule brought in Ange-Félix Patasse as president. He was Bokassa's prime minister in the 1970s, but was jailed for dissent and subsequently went into exile in Paris. His party, the MLPC, is the most important in the new parliament but can govern only in coalition with others, notably the CFD grouping led by Abel Goumba, a veteran opposition figure. Balancing coalitions can be a problem in the CAR – it was the confusion of alliances in Dacko's government which led to Kolingba's coup in 1981. Grave economic problems, which have left civil servants unpaid, are the major political concern.

CENTRAL AFRICAN REPUBLIC

POPULATION

Total Area : 622 980 sq. km (240 530 sq. miles)

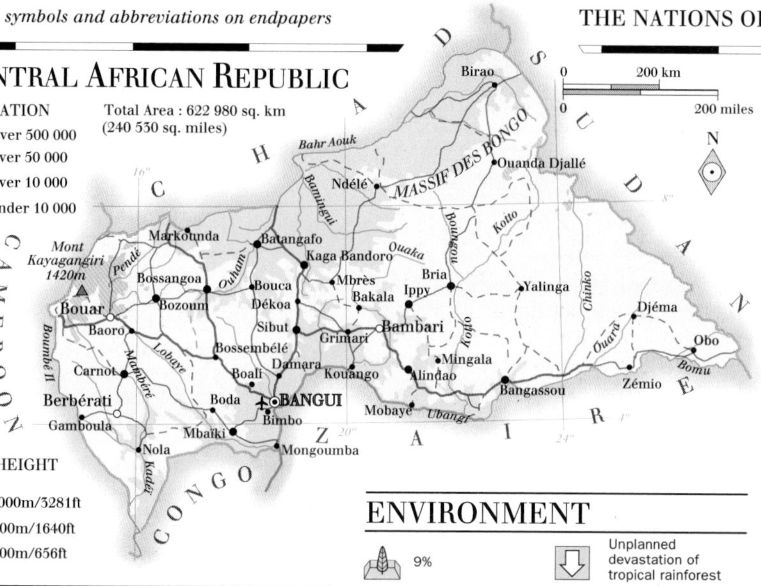

- over 500 000
- over 50 000
- over 10 000
- under 10 000

LAND HEIGHT

- 1000m/3281ft
- 500m/1640ft
- 200m/656ft

CHRONOLOGY

The French established the colony of Ubangi-Shari in 1905 and gave it autonomy as the CAR in 1958.

- 1960 Independence under David Dacko; sets up one-party state.
- 1965 Coup by Jean-Bédel Bokassa.
- 1976 Sets up empire. In 1977, one-quarter of GDP spent on coronation.
- 1979 French help reinstate Dacko.
- 1981 Gen. Kolingba ousts Dacko.
- 1990 Major pro-democracy riots.
- 1993 First multiparty elections.

ECONOMICS

$1.3bn | 295.23 CFA francs

SCORE CARD

- WORLD GNP RANKING........................148th
- GNP PER CAPITA..............................$405
- BALANCE OF PAYMENTS..................$–47.7m
- INFLATION.......................................6.1%
- UNEMPLOYMENT....Widespread underemployment

STRENGTHS

Self-sufficiency in food. Some diversity of export earnings (iron, cotton, timber, diamonds, coffee). Transit zone in central Africa. Trans-African Highway and waterways.

WEAKNESSES

Landlocked. Poor infrastructure. Not enough trained people to run economy.

EXPORTS

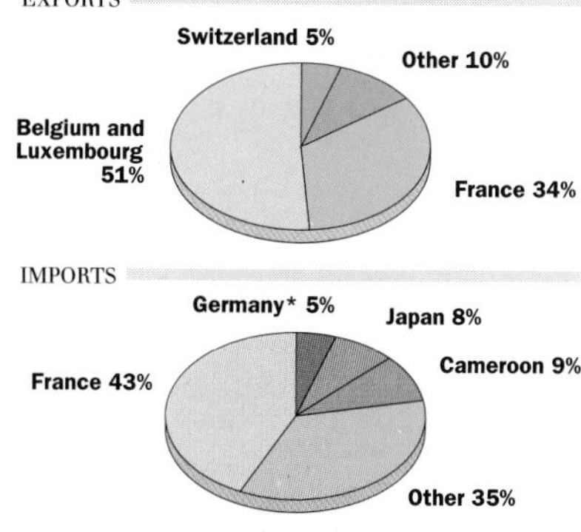

RESOURCES

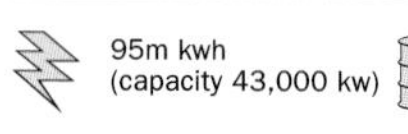

95m kwh (capacity 43,000 kw)

Not an oil producer and has no refineries

2.5m cattle, 397,000 pigs, 130,000 sheep

Diamonds, gold, uranium

Cotton is one of the few major exports, but mineral resources are of potential importance.

ENVIRONMENT

9%

Unplanned devastation of tropical rainforest

There has been an attempt to impose a conservationist forest policy. Hunting of elephants was banned only in 1985; numbers fell from 80,000 in the mid-1970s to 13,000 in 1987.

MEDIA

Although an opposition press has developed, censorship can still be imposed

PUBLISHING AND BROADCAST MEDIA

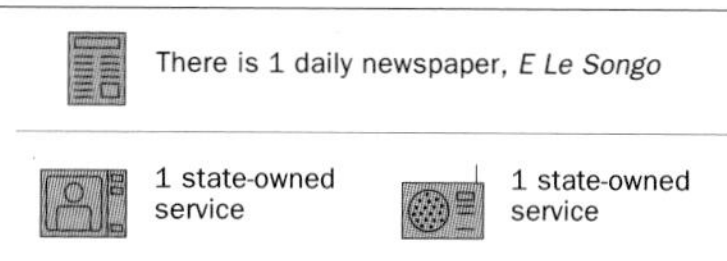

An opposition press has developed with multiparty politics, but is inhibited by lack of resources and journalists. The Catholic Church maintained some independent media under Bokassa.

CRIME

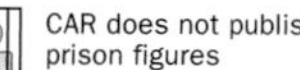

CAR does not publish prison figures

Down 48% in 1989

Human rights abuses have decreased drastically since the excesses of the Bokassa years. The level of criminality is low and increasing urban robbery is regarded as the chief problem. The Muslims form too small a minority to influence the French-style legal system.

Baskets of cotton, Meme village. Cotton is one of the Central African Republic's most significant export crops.

EDUCATION

38%

Schooling, on the French model, is compulsory but in practice is only received by 59% of 6–14-year-olds.

HEALTH

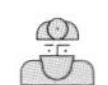

1 per 16,788 people

Communicable and parasitic diseases, malnutrition

Colonial neglect and post-colonial maladministration have resulted in a poorly developed health system.

WEALTH

Bricklayer, 35,000 CFA francs per month; physiotherapist, 82,000 CFA francs per month

CONSUMER GOODS OWNERSHIP

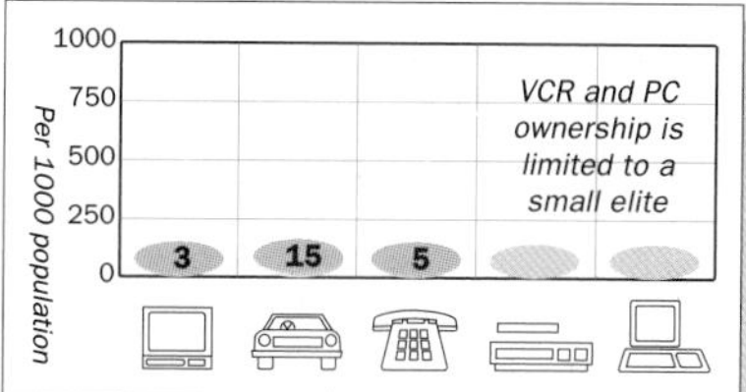

For the political-military elite, which only arose after colonial days, Paris is the choice destination and style leader.

WORLD RANKING

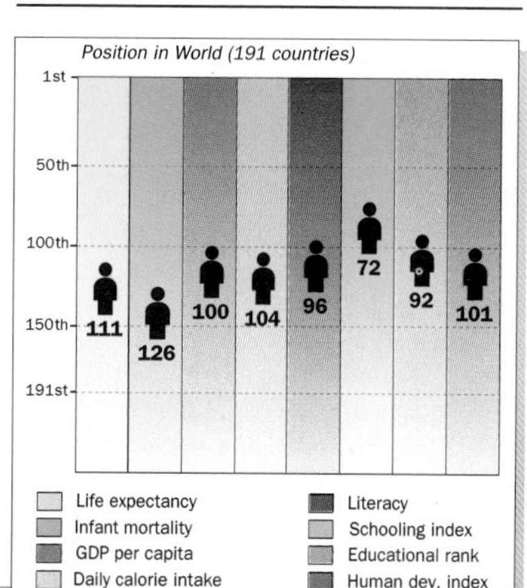

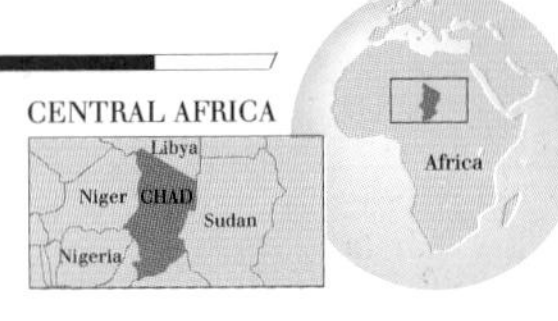

CHAD

OFFICIAL NAME: Republic of Chad **CAPITAL:** N'Djamena **POPULATION:** 5.8 million
CURRENCY: CFA franc **OFFICIAL LANGUAGE:** French

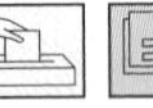

LANDLOCKED IN north central Africa, Chad has had a turbulent history since independence from France in 1960. Intermittent periods of civil war involving French and Libyan troops followed a military coup in 1975. In 1990, a transitional government was established to oversee the change to multiparty politics. Chad remains one of the poorest countries in Africa. The tropical, cotton-producing south is the most populous region. The north is semi-arid desert.

CLIMATE

WEATHER CHART

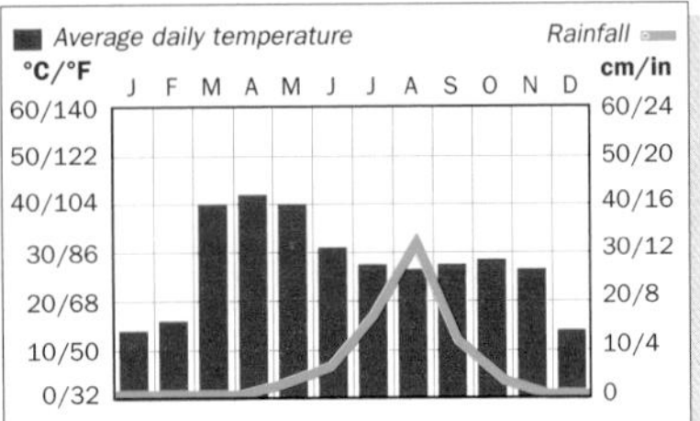

There are three distinct zones: the tropical south, the central semi-arid Sahelian belt and the desert north.

COMMUNICATIONS

N'Djamena International 7,760 passengers

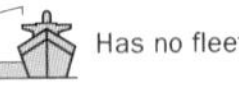
Has no fleet

THE TRANSPORTATION NETWORK

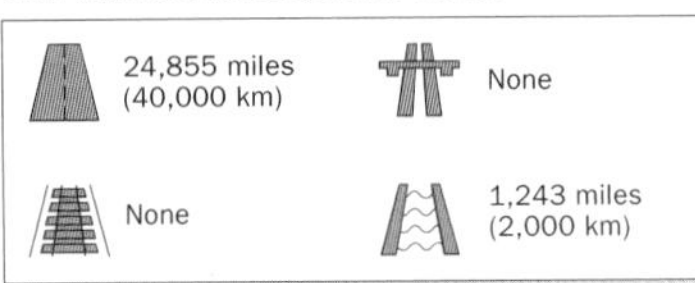

Chad has a limited transportation infrastructure. The nearest rail links are in Nigeria and Cameroon.

TOURISM

29,000 visitors

Tourism has failed to grow since the civil war ended

MAIN OVERSEAS ARRIVALS

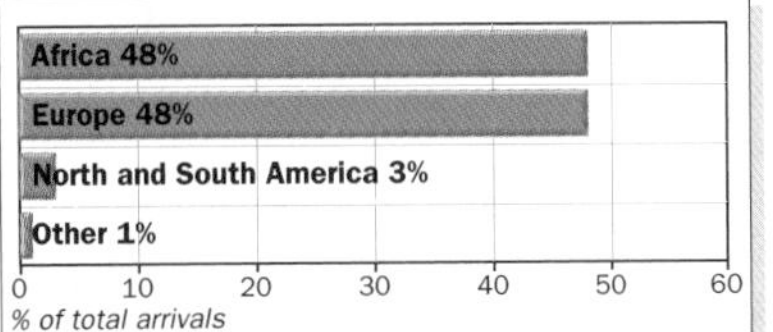

Tourism is now virtually non-existent. The national parks and game reserves are the main potential attractions. The prehistoric rockpainting of the Tibesti plateau and the Muslim cities of central Chad attract the adventurous.

Watering hole at Oum Hadjer, *a village on the Batha watercourse in central Chad, 90 miles east of Ati.*

PEOPLE

French, Sara, Arabic, Maba

10 people per sq. mile

THE URBAN/RURAL POPULATION SPLIT

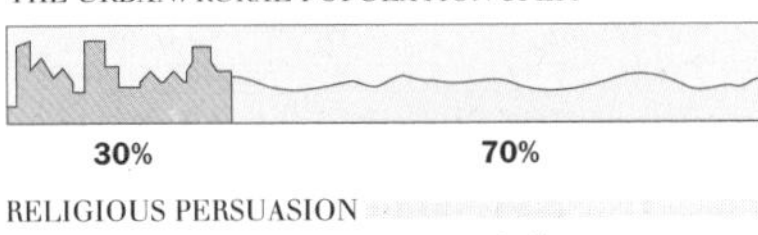

RELIGIOUS PERSUASION

Indigenous beliefs 23%
Muslim 44%
Christian 33%

About half the population, mainly the Sara-speaking and related peoples, is concentrated in the south in one-fifth of the national territory. Most of the rest are located in the central sultanates. The northern third of Chad has a population of 100,000 people, mainly nomadic Muslim Toubeu.

POLITICS

1994 President Idriss Deby

THE STATE OF THE PARTIES

Higher Transitional Council 57 members

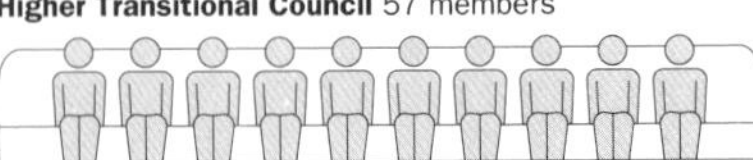

Multiparty elections were scheduled for 1994

Following an invasion from Sudan, where he had been in exile since a previous coup attempt, Idriss Deby overthrew President Hissène Habré in 1990. He promised to bring multiparty politics to Chad, and legalized political parties in 1992, the first time they had been allowed since the early 1960s. However, the transitional process has been subject to delays. Continuing instability has prevented progress on the drawing up of the constitution and the holding of presidential and parliamentary elections. Some opponents question whether President Deby and his backers, the Zaghawa tribesmen, want to give up power at all. France has been intervening to support the fragile government. Meanwhile, the issue of economic recovery has been put on hold.

CHAD

Total Area : 1 284 000 sq. km (495 752 sq. miles)

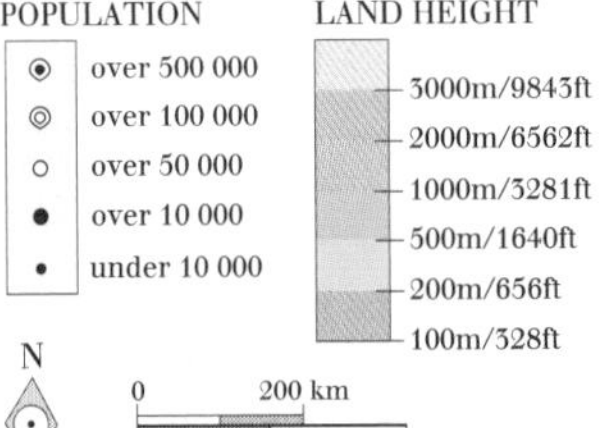

WORLD AFFAIRS

Chad has to balance relations with France and Libya, both of whom have been important influences.

AID

 $262m (receipts)  Down 14% in 1991

France is by far the major donor. Other sources include Libya, the EU, USA, IMF, and Arab funds, especially OPEC. Without assistance to cover civil servants' pay over recent years, the administration would have collapsed.

DEFENSE

 $57.99m 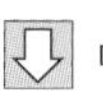 Down 26% in 1989

Upon seizing power, Deby swelled the existing army to 50,000 with irregulars from Darfur in Sudan. The policy has now been reversed and Chad plans to reduce its army to 25,000. France provides military aid.

ECONOMICS

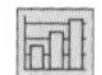 $1.3bn  295.23 CFA francs

SCORE CARD

- World GNP Ranking........149th
- GNP per Capita........$180
- Balance of Payments........$-91.7m
- Inflation........2.2%
- Unemployment....Widespread underemployment

Strengths
Revenues from recent discovery of large oil deposits could transform Chad's poor financial position. Cotton industry; potential for other agriculture in south. Strategic trading location in heart of Africa.

Weaknesses
Development hampered by lack of transportation infrastructure. Frequent droughts.

EXPORTS

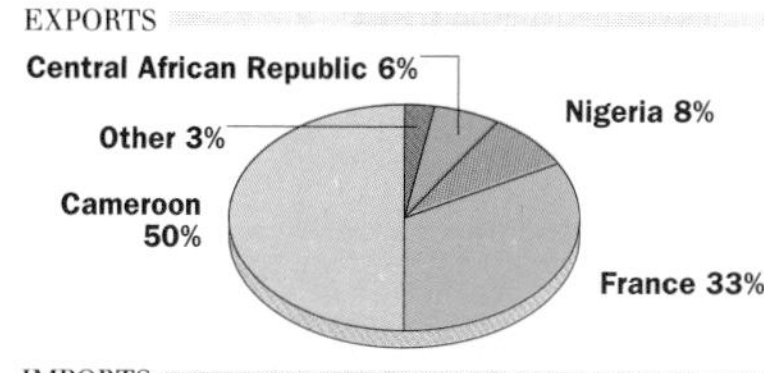

IMPORTS

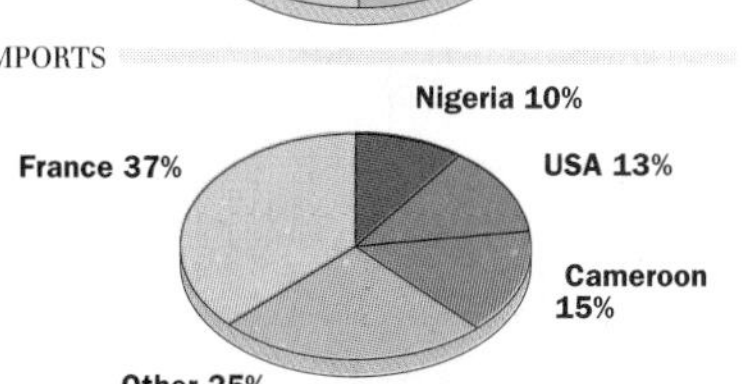

RESOURCES

 82m kwh (capacity 31,000 kw)

 Not an oil producer and has no refineries

4.2m cattle, 1.9m sheep, 239,000 asses

Natron, uranium oil, kaolin

A consortium of ESSO, Shell and ELF has discovered large oil reserves in the south, mostly near Doba, which could make Chad a major African producer. Natron, found north of Lake Chad, is the only mineral currently exploited. Uranium exists in the Aozou strip.

ENVIRONMENT

 0.3% Extensive destruction of habitats due to civil war

The worst single environmental crisis Chad has had to face in recent years was the drought of 1985, which coincided with intensified fighting in the civil war. Most recent governments have not regarded the preservation of the environment as a political priority. Chad has yet to establish an environmental protection ministry.

MEDIA

 The government claims to support press freedom, but interference in editorial decisions has been reported

PUBLISHING AND BROADCAST MEDIA

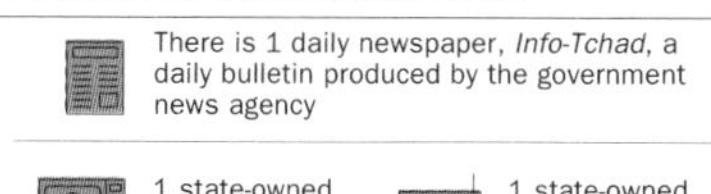

There is 1 daily newspaper, Info-Tchad, a daily bulletin produced by the government news agency
1 state-owned service
1 state-owned service

Since Deby came to power, the press has opened up and a number of outspoken independent publications have appeared. The best known is the weekly *N'Djamena-Hebdo*, produced by Saleh Kebzabo, a well-known journalist who was briefly a member of the transitional government.

CRIME

 Chad does not publish prison figures  Crime is rising

Armed robbery and vandalism are problems, as well as traditional crime such as smuggling. In N'Djamena and the south, the activities of a bandit group known as *les enturbannés*, "the turbanned ones," from President Deby's army, are widely feared.

EDUCATION

 30%

Education is based on the French model, although there are Koranic schools in the north. Recently, World Bank aid has been directed at primary schooling. The literacy rate is among the lowest in Africa.

CHRONOLOGY

Chad gradually came under Arab domination. The French overthrew the last Arab ruler in 1900.

- **1960** Independence. N'Garta Tombalbaye's one-party state.
- **1966** Northern-based rebels start Libyan-backed insurgency.
- **1973** Libyans invade Aozou strip.
- **1975** Coup. Gen. Malloum comes to power; receives French support.
- **1979–1982** Civil war between Christian south and Muslim north.
- **1980** Goukouni Weddeye in power.
- **1982** Hissène Habré (northerner) defeats Goukouni. France transfers military support to Habré.
- **1987** Libyans pushed out of Chad.
- **1990** Idriss Deby invades from exile in Sudan; defeats Habré.

HEALTH

 1 per 47,640 people  Diarrheal, parasitic and communicable diseases

There are only nine city hospitals. Of the 285 smaller health centers, half are run by religious groups or charities.

WEALTH

 Butcher, 17,571 CFA francs per month; central government official, 76,487 CFA francs per month

CONSUMER GOODS OWNERSHIP

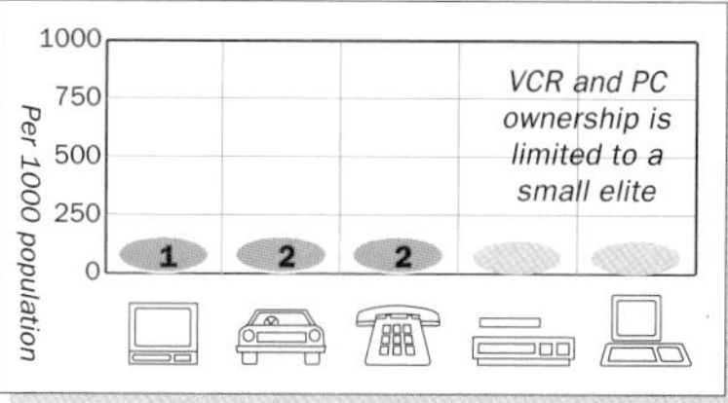

Poverty is almost universal; the middle class is very small. Individuals have been known to achieve wealth – Habré looted the treasury when he left power.

WORLD RANKING

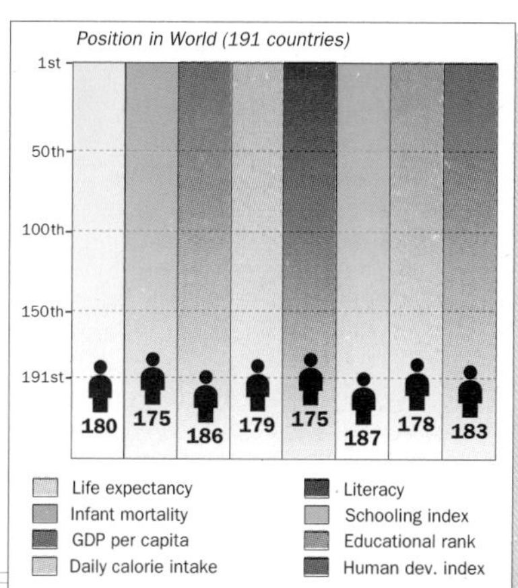

CHILE

OFFICIAL NAME: Republic of Chile **CAPITAL:** Santiago
POPULATION: 13.6 million **CURRENCY:** Chilean peso **OFFICIAL LANGUAGE:** Spanish

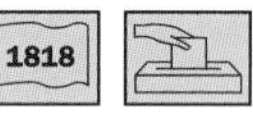

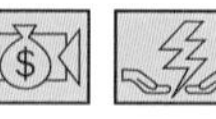

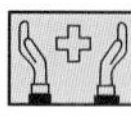

CHILE EXTENDS IN A NARROW RIBBON 2,697 miles down the Pacific coast of South America. The plains of the central pampa lie between a coastal range and the Andes; most of the population lives in the fertile heartland around Santiago. Glaciers are a prominent feature of the southern Andes, as are fjords, lakes and deep sea channels. In 1989, Chile returned to elected civilian rule, following a popular rejection of the Pinochet dictatorship. Now the world's largest copper producer, Chile is enjoying economic growth which has averaged 5% a year.

General Pinochet, *a dictatorial president rejected by popular referendum in 1988.*

President Eduardo Frei. *He took office following elections in 1993.*

CLIMATE

WEATHER CHART

Average daily temperature — Rainfall

°C/°F: 40/104, 30/86, 20/68, 10/50, 0/32, -10/14, -20/-4

J F M A M J J A S O N D

cm/in: 40/16, 30/12, 20/8, 10/4, 0

Chile has an immensely varied climate. The north, which includes the world's driest desert, the Atacama, is frequently cloudy and cool for its latitude. The central regions have an almost Mediterranean climate, with changeable winters and hot, dry summers. The higher reaches of the Andes have a typically alpine climate, with glaciers and year-round snow. The south is the wettest region.

COMMUNICATIONS

Comodoro Arturo Merino Benítez, Santiago
1.95m passengers

THE TRANSPORTATION NETWORK

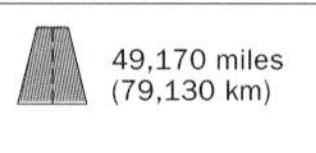

5,086 miles (8,185 km)

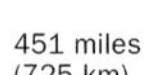

Chile's'unusual shape – 2,697 miles long and nowhere more than 112 miles wide – makes air travel indispensable. Internal air routes are well developed; some, including flights to the Juan Fernández Islands, are served by air taxis. The Pan-American Highway is Chile's only arterial road, crossing the Peruvian border and running down, via the capital of Santiago, to Puerto Montt. Santiago is notorious in Latin America for its severe congestion. It has one of the highest taxi and bus densities in the world.

TOURISM

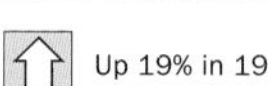

MAIN OVERSEAS ARRIVALS

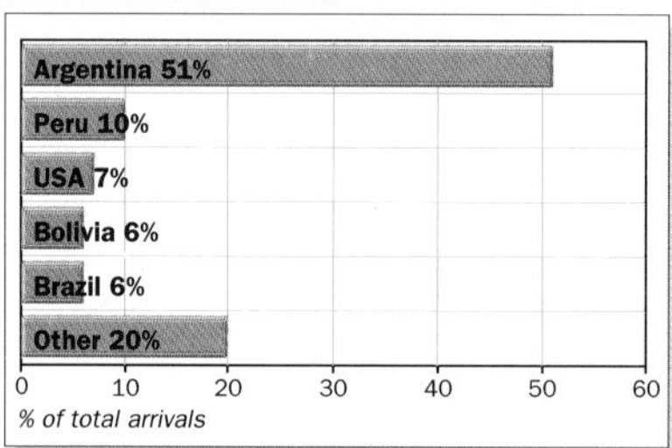

The Pinochet years saw a dramatic decline in tourists from the USA and Western Europe. The number of visitors from neighboring Latin American states remained fairly constant; South Americans with a closer knowledge of Chile's political culture were aware that much of the violence was state-directed and aimed at Chileans, not tourists. Since 1988, tourists have returned and Chile has been making more of its stunning Andean scenery, its immensely long coastline and a number of exceptional sites, including Chuquicamata, the world's largest copper mine, the Elqui Valley wine-growing region, and the spectacular glaciers and fjords of southern Chile. Easter Island in the Pacific is another major attraction.

Peaks in the Paine range, southern Chile. *Fjords, glaciers and a myriad of islands typify Chile's very wet, wild and stormy south.*

PEOPLE

THE URBAN/RURAL POPULATION SPLIT

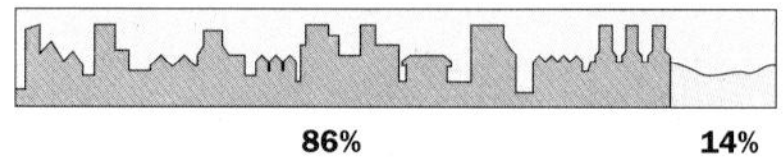

RELIGIOUS PERSUASION

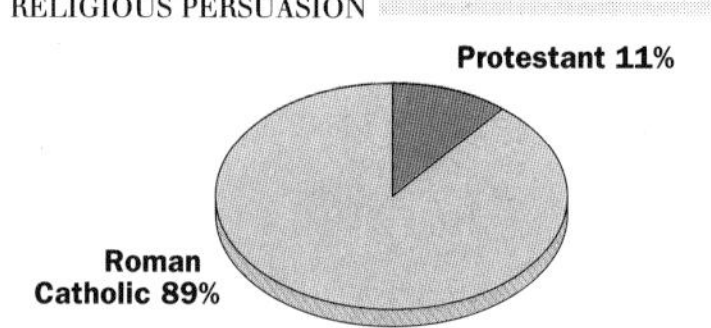

ETHNIC MAKEUP

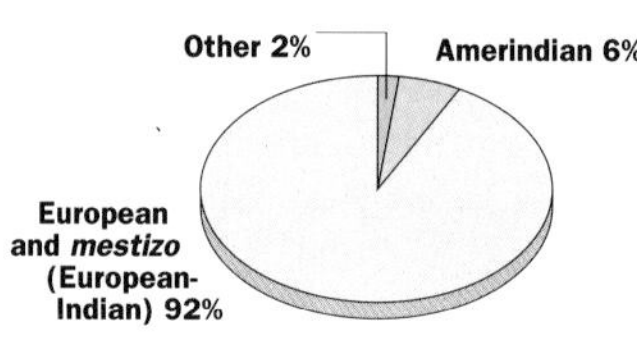

Chile is highly urbanized, with 86% of the population living in towns. Most people are of mixed Spanish-Indian descent. The estimated 800,000 Mapuche Indians live almost exclusively in the south. Santiago is home to one-third of the population. Large slum areas known as *callampas*, or mushrooms, have grown up around Santiago, and water and air pollution are major problems. Many Chileans, especially those in small enterprises, live on subsistence wages. Over 25% of working women are employed in domestic service.

POPULATION AGE BREAKDOWN

% of population by age group

	1950	1960	1970	1980	1990
65+	4.3%	4.7%	5.1%	5.6%	6%
15–64	58.9%	55.9%	55.8%	61%	63.4%
0–14	36.8%	39.4%	39.1%	33.4%	30.6%

POLITICS

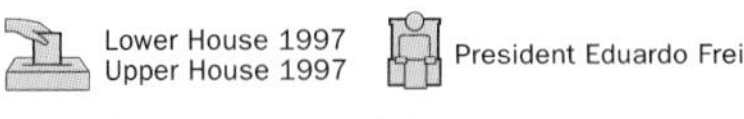

THE STATE OF THE PARTIES

Chamber of Deputies 120 members

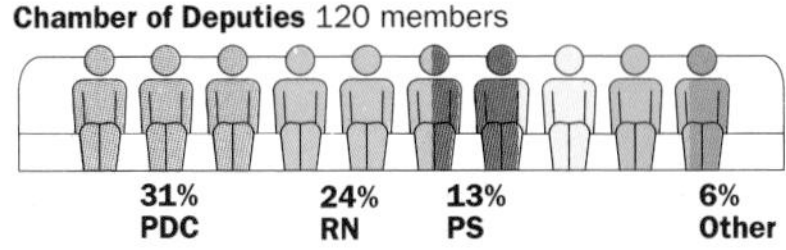

PDC = Christian Democratic Party **RN** = National Renewal
PS = Socialist Party of Chile **PPD** = Party for Democracy
UDI = Independent Democratic Union **Other** = Radical Party

Senate 46 members

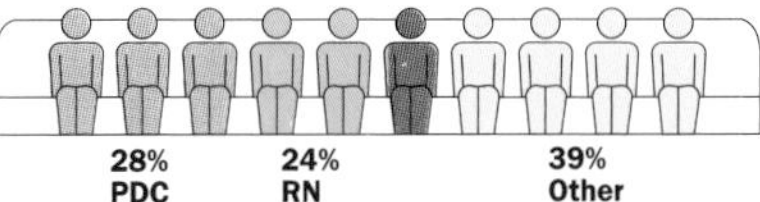

38 members elected and 8 chosen by the outgoing government and the Supreme Court

After 12 years of military rule under Pinochet, Chile returned to multiparty democracy in 1989.

MAIN POLITICAL ISSUES

Human rights abuse trials

The 1989–1993 Aylwin administration resisted popular pressure to try known members of the death squads which operated during the Pinochet regime. It argued that 1988 marked a time for national reconciliation, but knew that the army, still headed by Pinochet, would not tolerate any human rights trials.

Poverty

Opposition groups point out that the promised "trickle down" effect of Pinochet's Chicago School economic policies has not reached Chile's poor. Many believe that the present Frei administration cannot both deliver improved conditions for the poor and maintain Pinochet's economic policies.

PROFILE

In 1988, Chile voted for political change, effectively rejecting the system instituted by the military dictator, Pinochet, and for a return to Chile's once-strong democratic traditions.

Pinochet seized power in a chaotic situation. The socialist Allende government had been attempting the wholesale nationalization of the Chilean economy. Allende's nationalization of the largely US-owned copper mines led the CIA – which had a specific budget to overthrow the democratically-elected Allende – to back the Pinochet coup.

In 1973, the military stormed the presidential palace; it is now accepted that Allende committed suicide during the attack. Subsequently, thousands of Chileans were killed by the military, an estimated 3,000 people "disappeared" and 80,000 political prisoners were taken.

Pinochet's politics – largely based on a notion of the nation-state modeled on Franco's Spain – replaced democratic traditions and conflict. His economic policy reversed Allende's, and was one of the first experiments in the free-market Chicago School of monetarism which was later to be influential in the West, particularly in the UK under Margaret Thatcher.

Although opposition to the regime was brutally suppressed by DINA, the secret police, it also had considerable support – particularly among Chile's business and middle classes, which prospered. Opposition came from the Church – an embarrassment to Pinochet, who saw himself as a champion of Catholicism – and the urban poor.

In 1988, Pinochet, seeking popular legitimacy, held a plebiscite which, given the military's control over the country, he expected to win. Contrary to his expectations, the vote turned not on his economic record but on whether Chile wished to continue living under a military dictatorship. On a turnout of 93%, 55% voted for democracy and 43% for the *status quo*. Pinochet stepped down, but remained head of the army. Patricio Aylwin won the presidential elections held in 1989.

During Aylwin's presidency, Chilean politics became more stable, in part the result of a cross-party consensus on economic policy. The economy continued to grow and social measures, which marginally increased protection for workers, gave Aylwin the support of the trade unions.

In elections at the end of 1993, Eduardo Frei of the PDC was elected president. He has pledged to continue the economic and social policies of his predecessor, and is governing a broad coalition of center-left parties. The armed forces, however, remain strong in politics; they, not the president, appoint their own chief.

CHRONOLOGY

The Spanish first attempted the conquest of Chile against the fierce indigenous Araucanian people in 1535. Santiago was founded in 1541. Chile was subject to Spanish rule until independence in 1818.

- **1817–1818** Bernardo O'Higgins leads the republican Army of the Andes in victories against royalist forces at the battles of Chacabuco and Maipú.
- **1879–1883** War of the Pacific with Bolivia and Peru. Chile gains valuable nitrate regions.

CHRONOLOGY *continued*

- **1891–1924** Parliamentary republic ends with growing political chaos.
- **1936–1946** Communist, Radical and Socialist parties form influential Popular Front coalition.
- **1943** Chile backs USA in World War II.
- **1946–1964** Right-wing Chilean presidents follow US McCarthy policy and marginalize the left.
- **1964–1970** Social reforms of PDC government alienate the right.
- **1970** Salvador Allende elected. Rapid Marxist reforms bring economic chaos.
- **1973** Allende dies in military coup. Brutal dictatorship of Gen. Pinochet. Economy prospers.
- **1988** Referendum votes "no" to Pinochet continuing as president.
- **1989** Democracy peacefully restored; Pinochet steps down after Aylwin election victory.
- **1990** Mapuche set up council to fight for recognition of land titles granted by Allende government.

WORLD AFFAIRS

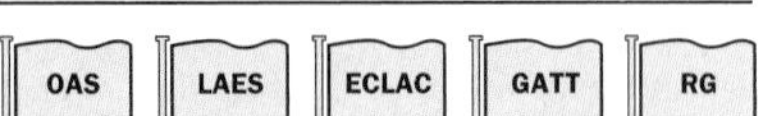

Chile's most important relationship remains with its main trading partner, the USA, which supplies 95% of materials for the critical copper industry. The relationship has not always been easy. Under Allende, the USA actively worked against the government, fearing that the spread of socialism would jeopardize its investments in Chile and the rest of Latin America. Pinochet's human rights record eventually became an embarrassment to the Reagan administration, which qualified its backing for him. Present relations are good; the Frei government concurs with US economic and regional policy in Latin America.

Chile's territorial dispute with Argentina over islands in the Beagle Channel, which almost led to war in 1978, was finally settled in 1984 with Vatican mediation. Chile was awarded 12 islands including Picton, Nueva and Lennox. International arbitration is still deciding ownership of the Laguna del Desierto region. Border disputes also continue with Bolivia and Peru.

AID

 $120m (receipts)  Up 18% in 1991

The majority of aid is in the form of debts rescheduled by the World Bank at the instigation of the USA.

DEFENSE

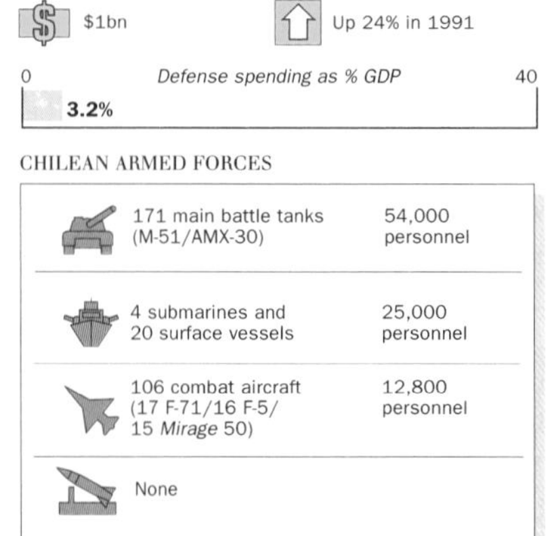

CHILEAN ARMED FORCES

171 main battle tanks (M-51/AMX-30)	54,000 personnel
4 submarines and 20 surface vessels	25,000 personnel
106 combat aircraft (17 F-71/16 F-5/ 15 *Mirage* 50)	12,800 personnel
None	

The military, and in particular the army, enjoyed preferential treatment under Pinochet. Its success in taking power in 1973 was a reflection of its cohesive command structure rather than of any right-wing ideological conviction. Pinochet exercised enormous influence in his position as commander-in-chief, but during his period in office worked with civilian rather than military advisers. The army retains considerable passive influence; the recent Aylwin government decided not to press human rights charges over atrocities committed during the Pinochet years. Much of its equipment is supplied by Chile's own CARDOENS munitions factories.

ECONOMICS

$39.3bn — 428.50 Chilean pesos

SCORE CARD

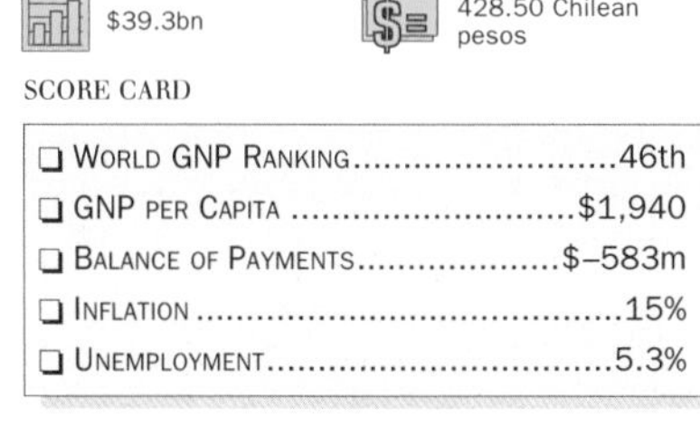

- World GNP Ranking 46th
- GNP per Capita $1,940
- Balance of Payments ....$-583m
- Inflation 15%
- Unemployment 5.3%

EXPORTS

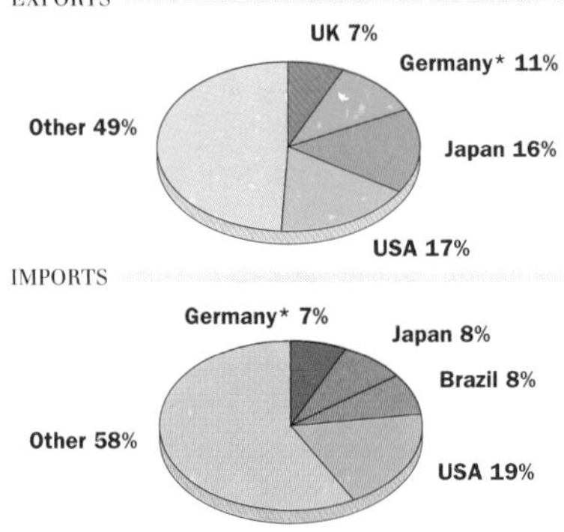

ECONOMIC PERFORMANCE INDICATOR

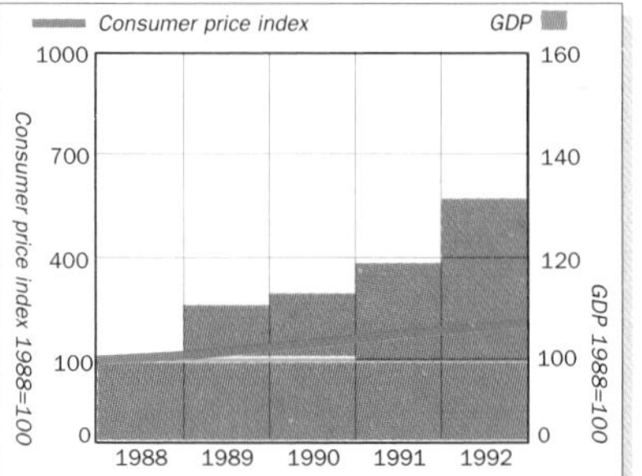

Strengths
The world's biggest copper producer. Political stability and free market policies of the Aylwin government led to a massive inflow of investment, which has kept the economy growing at 5% a year since 1991. Continuing sell-off of the state sector – ruthlessly cut by Pinochet to leave it small and efficient – will attract further investment.

Weaknesses
Dependence on the USA as its largest single trading partner makes Chile vulnerable to changes in US trade policy. Copper revenues are vulnerable to shifts in world market prices.

Profile
Chile's economy has been a battleground for competing ideologies. Under Allende, socialist policies brought huge corporations into the state sector. The Pinochet dictatorship which overthrew him introduced radical monetarist policies. Drastic cutting of the state sector and the selling-off of state enterprises at below market value led to large profits for investors and speculators. Tough economic measures, irrespective of the social consequences, reduced Chile's inflation rate from 400% to 15%.

The Aylwin and Frei governments have continued the market-led approach to the economy with some success. In particular, exports are continuing to rise, helping to finance the capital goods imports which are vital to the modernization of Chile's industrial sector.

CHILE : MAJOR BUSINESSES

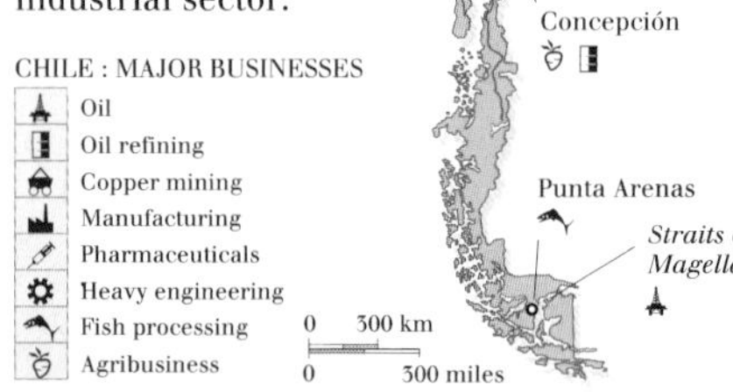

RESOURCES

18.4bn kwh (capacity 4.1m kw)

14,700 b/d (reserves 300,000,000 bbl)

6.6m sheep, 3.3m cattle, 1.4m pigs, 500,000 horses

Copper, gold, silver, iron, molybdenum, iodine

ELECTRICITY GENERATION

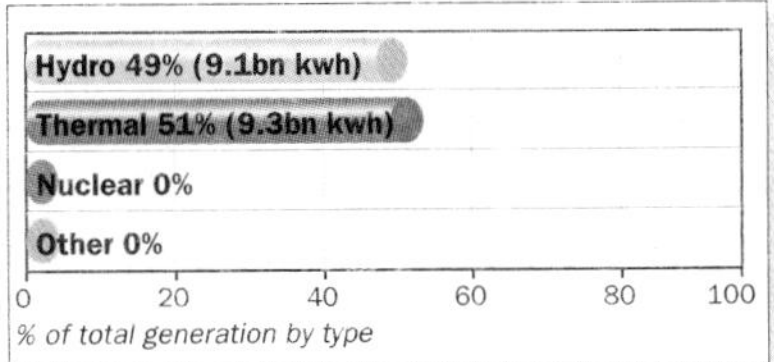

Chile is the world's most important copper producer. The state-owned industry was established in 1968 as a joint venture with US companies, but was fully nationalized under Allende. It accounts for 35% of Chile's GNP. New investments in gold mining will bring Chile into the world's top ten producers. It also leads the world in fishmeal production and has a flourishing wine industry.

CHILE : LAND USE

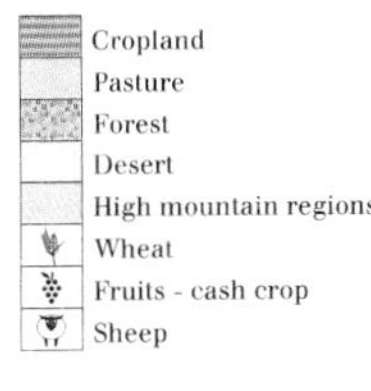

ENVIRONMENT

18% (7% partially protected)

Felling of endangered *araucaria* pines recently banned

ENVIRONMENTAL TREATIES

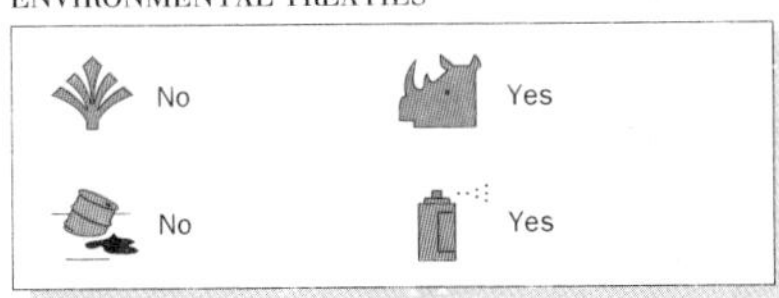

Environmental concerns do not rank highly on the political agenda. Pinochet's constitution enshrined the right to live in a pollution-free environment, but bad smogs still cover Santiago, due in part to diesel fumes from the city's 14,500 buses. The chief concern is logging in the south by Japanese and other foreign companies. The huge growth of the salmon industry, which fences off sea lakes, is resulting in dolphins losing their natural habitats.

MEDIA

Many of the army's powers over the press imposed during the Pinochet regime have yet to be repealed

PUBLISHING AND BROADCAST MEDIA

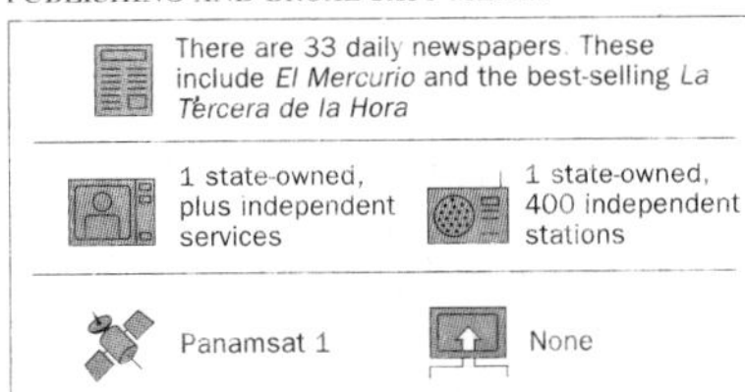

There are 33 daily newspapers. These include *El Mercurio* and the best-selling *La Tercera de la Hora*
1 state-owned, plus independent services
1 state-owned, 400 independent stations
Panamsat 1
None

The media was brutally controlled by Pinochet; journalists "disappeared" in the early years of the regime. It is now relatively free, but journalists can still be tried under military justice for slander or abuse of the armed forces.

CRIME

2,176 prisoners

Up 2% in 1990

CRIME RATES

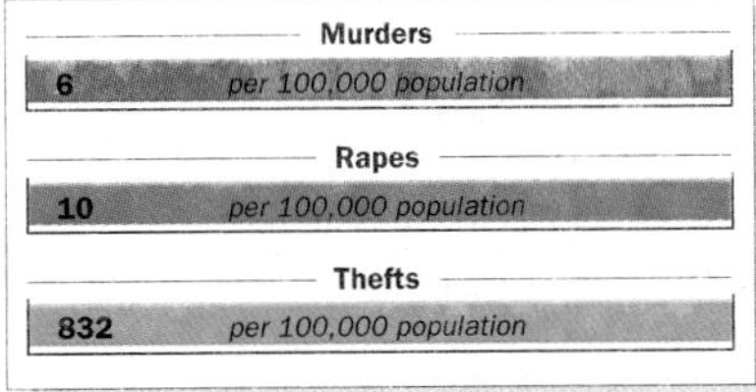

The judiciary is still not independent and is not pursuing the human rights cases from the Pinochet regime, in spite of the discovery in 1991 of the mass graves of victims of the DINA (secret police). Mapuche leaders were among those who "disappeared."

EDUCATION

93%

0 — Education spending as % GNP — 25

3.6%

THE EDUCATION SYSTEM

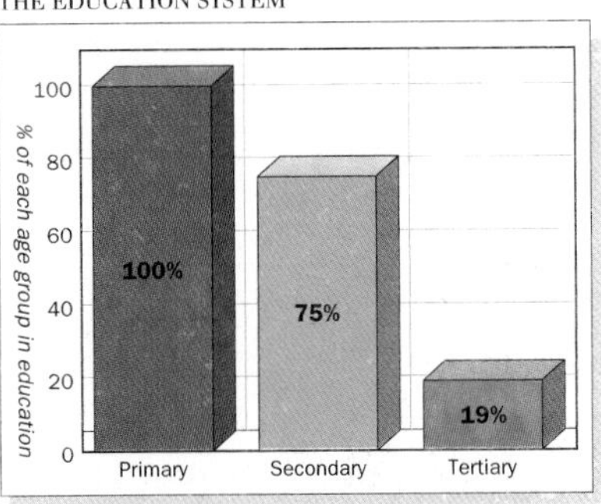

Recent years have seen many new private universities operating for profit and offering vocational courses. Environmental issues and human rights now appear on school curricula.

HEALTH

1 per 2,383 people

Heart diseases, cancer (notably of the stomach), accidents

0 — Health spending as % GNP — 25

2%

The public health service covers 80% of the population, but medical personnel are mostly concentrated in urban areas. Pollution in Santiago is so bad that it is noticeably affecting its inhabitants' health.

WEALTH

Live-in maid, 80,000 Chilean pesos per month; company secretary, 1m Chilean pesos per month

CONSUMER GOODS OWNERSHIP

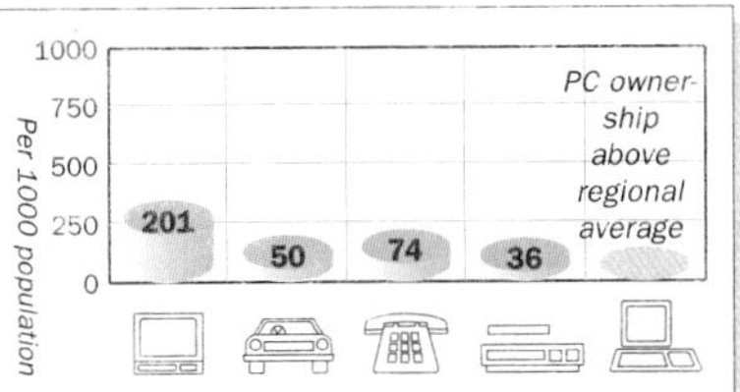

Chile's traditionally large middle class did well under Pinochet and the economic policies of the Chicago School. The wealthiest sections benefited considerably from the sale of state assets at 40% to 50% of their true market value. Five years into the regime, wealth had become highly concentrated, with just nine economic conglomerates controlling the assets of the top 250 businesses, 82% of banking and 64% of all financial loans. The regime's artificially high domestic interest rates enabled those with access to international finance to earn an estimated $800 million between 1977 and 1980, simply by borrowing abroad and lending at home. These groups have retained their position.

The poor, by contrast, are 15% worse off than in 1970, with an estimated four million living just above the UN poverty line and one million below it.

WORLD RANKING

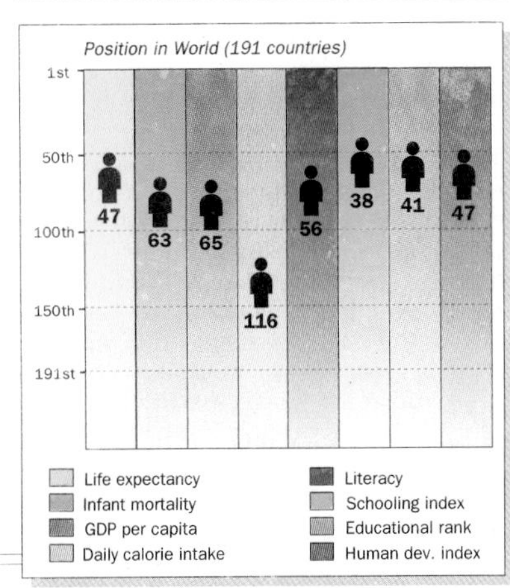

C

CHINA

OFFICIAL NAME: People's Republic of China **CAPITAL:** Beijing
POPULATION: 1.2 billion **CURRENCY:** Yuan **OFFICIAL LANGUAGE:** Mandarin

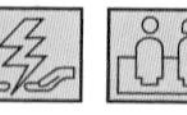

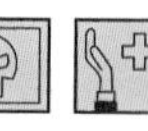
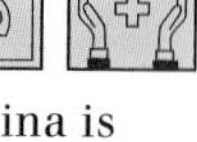

COVERING A VAST AREA of eastern Asia, China is bordered by 14 countries; to the east it has a long Pacific coastline. Two-thirds of China is uplands. The southwestern mountains include the Tibetan Plateau. In the northwest, the Tien Shan Mountains separate the Tarim and Dzungarian basins. The low-lying east is home to two-thirds of the population. From the founding of the Communist People's Republic in 1949, until his death in 1976, China was dominated by Mao Zedong. Under Mao, China became an industrial and nuclear power, but also experienced the disasters of the 1950s Great Leap Forward and the 1960s Cultural Revolution. Today, China is rapidly moving toward a market-oriented economy. However, as the 1989 Tiananmen Square massacre tragically underlined, political reform is not on the agenda of China's aging leadership.

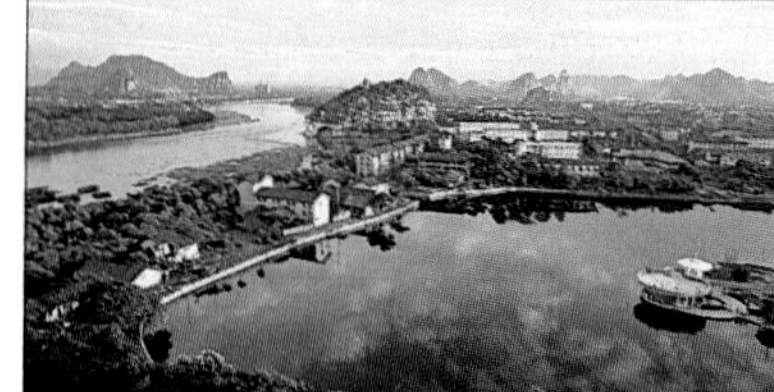

***Li River, Guangxi,** China's most beautiful region. Its spectacular scenery has encouraged large-scale tourist development.*

CLIMATE

WEATHER CHART

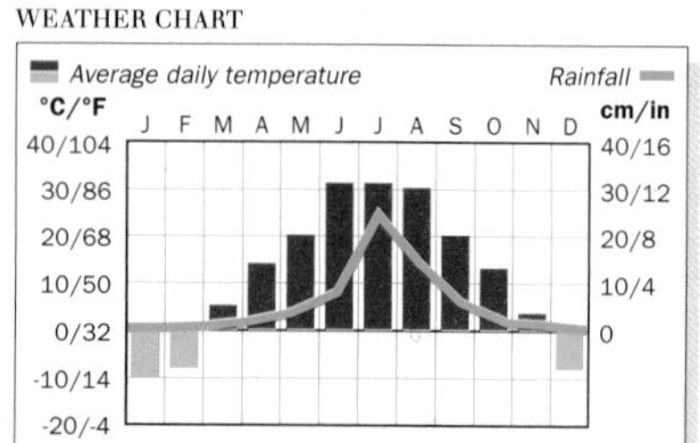

China is divided into two main climatic regions. The north and west are semi-arid or arid, with extreme temperature variations. The south and southeast are warmer and more humid, with year-round rainfall.

Winter temperatures vary with latitude and are warmest on the sub-tropical southeast coast, where they average about 60°F. Summer temperatures are more uniform, rising above 70°F throughout China. On the southeast coast, the July average is about 86°F. In the north and west, temperate summers contrast with harsh winters. In northern Manchuria, rivers freeze for five months and temperatures can fall to –13°F. In the deserts of Xinjiang province, temperatures range from –12°F in winter to 90°F in summer.

Summer and autumn are China's wettest seasons. Only the south and east have wet winters. The winter monsoon, which brings cold, dry air from Siberia, affects the rest of China. Moisture-laden winds from the Pacific during the summer monsoon bring rains to most of the country.

Droughts and floods are frequent. The 1960–1962 drought contributed to the famine which killed millions during the Great Leap Forward.

TOURISM

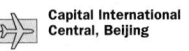

4m visitors

Up 20% in 1990

MAIN OVERSEAS ARRIVALS

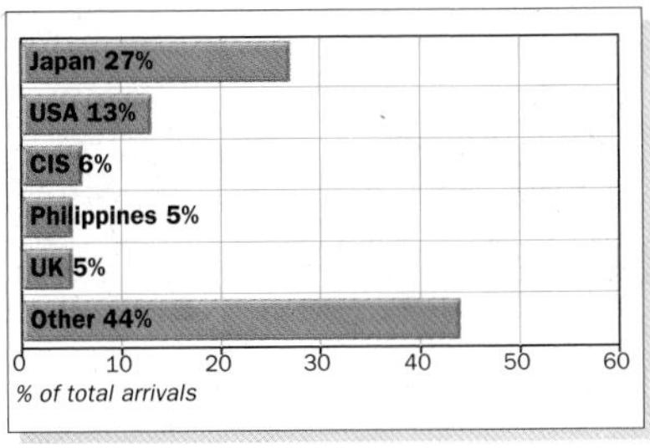

	% of total arrivals
Japan	27%
USA	13%
CIS	6%
Philippines	5%
UK	5%
Other	44%

Most visitors to China are overseas Chinese or business travelers, but an increasing number of tourists are also coming. The easing of restrictions since the 1980s has led to the rapid growth of all kinds of tourism, from luxury tours to backpacking. Most of China is now open to visitors. The Great Wall, the Forbidden City in Beijing and the terracotta warriors at Xi'an remain among the top attractions. The Chinese government has also begun to open up Tibet to tourists. Hong Kong is a major entry point for many visitors.

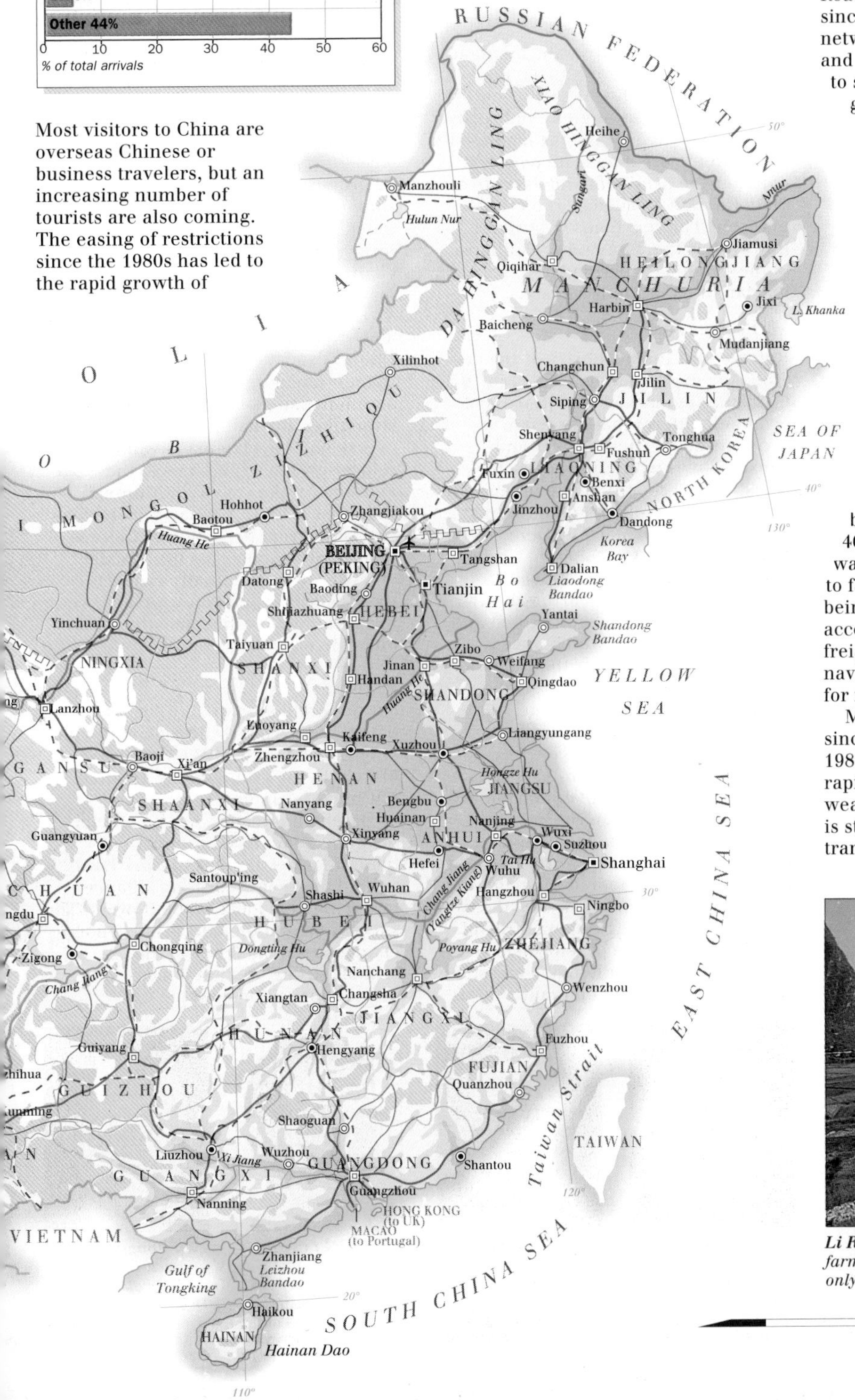

COMMUNICATIONS

Capital International Central, Beijing

1,577 ships 20.41 m dwt

THE TRANSPORTATION NETWORK

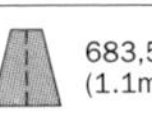

683,507 miles (1.1m km))

None

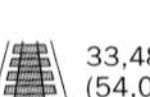

33,480 miles (54,000 km)

68,226 miles (109,800 km)

Roads and rail have been extended since 1949 to provide a basic national network. The aim now is to modernize and expand the transportation system to support the push for economic growth. Additions to the railroad system – all provinces but Tibet are connected to the system – have been concentrated in the west. However, the railroads, especially in the east, are still badly congested. The priority is to develop new lines, and to double-track and electrify the main routes from Beijing to Shanghai and Guangzhou, and between Zhejiang and Hunan provinces. In 1992, a rail link with Kazakhstan was reopened.

The leading ports, including Shanghai and Tianjin, are being steadily improved and the congestion problems of the 1980s have eased. Hong Kong has the best natural harbor and handles 40% of China's exports. The inland waterway system, which was allowed to fall into a state of disrepair, is now being upgraded. Water transport now accounts for about 33% of internal freight traffic. The Chang Jiang is navigable by ships of over 1,000 tons for more than 600 miles from the coast.

Many small airlines have sprung up since the state monopoly ended in 1988. Air transportation is growing rapidly, like private car ownership, as wealth increases. However, the bicycle is still the ubiquitous mode of personal transportation in China.

***Li River valley**, irrigation helps Chinese farmers feed 20% of the world's people, using only 7% of the world's farmland.*

C

PEOPLE

Mandarin, Wu, Cantonese, Hsiang, Min, Hakka, Kan

313 people per sq. mile

THE URBAN/RURAL POPULATION SPLIT

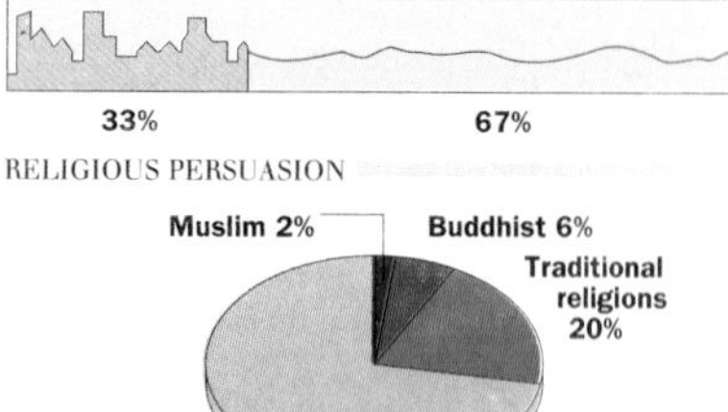

ETHNIC MAKEUP

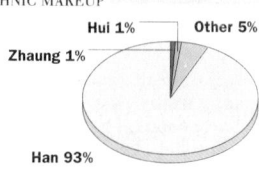

Hui 1%
Other 5%
Zhaung 1%
Han 93%

About 93% of China's population of nearly 1.2 billion are Han Chinese. The remaining 92 million belong to one of 55 minority nationalities, or recognized ethnic groups. The minorities have disproportionate political significance because many, like the Mongolians, Tibetans, or Muslim Uygurs in Xinjiang, live in strategic border areas.

The policy of resettling Han Chinese in remote regions is deeply resented and has led to uprisings in Xinjiang and Tibet, all ruthlessly suppressed. Han Chinese are now a majority in Xinjiang and Nei Mongol Zizhiqu. Tibet, however, is gaining international support for its call for true autonomy.

The government has relaxed family planning controls for minorities, after some small groups were brought near to extinction by the one-child policy adopted in 1979. Most Han Chinese still face strict controls. Even so, the population will top 1.3 billion by 2000.

Chinese society is patriarchal in practice and several generations tend to live together. However, economic change is putting pressure on family life and breaking down the social controls of the Mao era. Divorce and unemployment are rising; materialism has replaced the puritanism of the past. A resurgence of religious belief is another response to the uncertainties of life in today's China.

POPULATION AGE BREAKDOWN

% of population by age group

	1960	1970	1980	1990	2000
65+	4.8%	4.3%	4.7%	5.8%	7%
15–64	56.3%	56%	59.8%	67.7%	66.4%
0–14	38.9%	39.7%	35.5%	26.5%	26.6%

POLITICS

1998

President Jiang Zemin

THE STATE OF THE PARTIES

National People's Congress 2,938 members

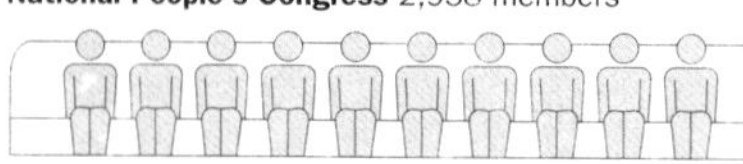

The members of the National People's Congress are elected by the provinces, municipalities and autonomous regions under the government, and by the armed forces. The Communist Party of China (CCP) has effective political control

China is a single-party state, dominated by the Communist Party (CCP), the world's largest political party. The National People's Congress, indirectly elected every five years, is theoretically the supreme organ of state power. It appoints the president and executive State Council, headed by the prime minister. The real focus of power, however, is the 22-member Politburo of the CCP and, in particular, its Standing Committee of six.

MAIN POLITICAL ISSUES

Reform and the authority of the CCP
Since the death of Mao Zedong in 1976, China has embarked on a process of economic reform that has led to divisions between reformers and conservatives within the CCP. Both sides want to secure the dominance of the party and avoid political reform. The reformers, headed by Deng Xiaoping, China's paramount leader, believe only a fast-track move to a "socialist market economy" will save the CCP. They look to South Korea and Taiwan as countries which have achieved high growth without political reform. The conservatives recognize the need for economic change, but want it to be slow and controlled by the center.

The pro-democracy protests of 1989, culminating in the Tiananmen Square massacre, enabled the conservatives under premier Li Peng to gain the upper hand for a while. Several leading reformers were demoted. Deng moved to restore the balance between the two groups. The growing unpopularity of Li Peng and the rise of reformers such as Vice-Premier Zhu Rongji suggest the reformers are again dominant.

Nanjing Donglu (Nanking Road), in central Shanghai, is one of China's most famous shopping streets. With a population of nearly eight million, Shanghai is China's largest city.

Economic reform does, however, pose a real threat to the CCP's authority. The 22 provinces, particularly those in the southeast, are acting increasingly independently of Beijing. At a popular level, party authority is being challenged by growing rural discontent over widening wealth differentials.

The succession
China's leaders are predominantly in their late 80s, so their succession is an immediate issue. Deng has tried to strengthen the hand of the reformers, overseeing the election of younger reform-oriented members to the Politburo at the CCP's 14th National Congress in 1992. China's new leaders will come from here. But, as there is no formal structure for the transfer of power, who eventually comes to the fore will depend on which of the gerontocracy dies first and on the outcome of complex power brokering.

PROFILE

Politics are dominated by the last of the "Immortals" who took part with Mao Zedong in the 1934–1935 Long March. Deng Xiaoping, the architect of China's economic reforms and its paramount leader, has no official post. He is the most prominent of the Immortals, but has to work hard behind the scenes forming alliances to promote his ideas and followers. The succession and the effects of economic change are a challenge to the 52-million-strong CCP, but it faces no real opposition as yet.

***Deng Xiaoping,** China's paramount leader, although he holds no official post.*

***Jiang Zemin,** CCP leader and China's president since Deng resigned the post.*

***Premier Li Peng,** urging economic reform, but keeping conservative values.*

***Zhu Rongji,** vice-premier, reformer and a protégé of Deng Xiaoping.*

C

WORLD AFFAIRS

The push for economic modernization is a key determinant of China's foreign policy. Investment, technology and trade, rather than ideology, now tend to condition its relationships. The other, often interlinked factor, is China's desire to secure regional stability.

China has moved quickly to establish diplomatic links with the states of the former Soviet Union, and vigorous trade is developing across China's northern border. On the Korean peninsula, China has acted to restrain North Korea while deepening ties with Seoul. Relations with Vietnam have been normalized and links with Japan are growing, despite China's suspicions about Tokyo's intentions toward ASEAN. Toward Taiwan, China is currently pursuing a "one country, two systems" approach as a basis for reunification.

Relations with the West are still overcast by the 1989 Tiananmen Square massacre. Relations with the USA, a major export market, are particularly tense. Beijing resents the need to have China's Most Favored Nation (MFN) status confirmed each year by Washington and considers unacceptable US attempts to link MFN to progress on human rights. Relations with the UK are dominated by Hong Kong, and have been strained by London's plans to increase democracy in the colony before handing it back to China in 1997.

AID

 $2.2bn (receipts)

 Up 2% in 1991

Aid was an important part of Chinese diplomacy in the 1970s. Most went to Africa, but other communist and South-east Asian states were also recipients. Outgoing aid has almost dried up since the late 1970s, as the economic reform process has turned China itself into a major aid recipient. Japan is the biggest bilateral donor to China, but the potential of the Chinese market means most developed states provide aid. A significant proportion of aid funding is used to finance high-tech imports. The 1989 Tiananmen Square massacre led to a temporary suspension of aid disbursements by the West.

DEFENSE

 $6.8bn

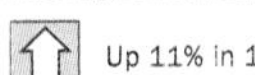 Up 11% in 1992

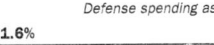

Defense spending as % GDP (0–40): 1.6%

CHINESE ARMED FORCES

8,000 main battle tanks (T-54/T-59/T-69)	2.3m personnel
46 submarines, 37 frigates, 17 destroyers and 860 patrol boats	260,000 personnel
 4,970 combat aircraft (500 Q-5/400 J-5/3000 J-6,-B,-D,-E/500 J-7)	470,000 personnel
ICBM (2 CSS-4/6 CSS-3) IRBM (60 CSS-2) SSBN (12 CSS-N-3)	

China's armed services are grouped in the People's Liberation Army (PLA). It has about three million troops – one-third conscripts, two-thirds in the army. The PLA has close links with the CCP. From 1967, when it restored order after the chaos of the Cultural Revolution, to 1989, when it fired on civilians in Tiananmen Square, the PLA has been used to ensure the party's dominance. It is still used to suppress dissent in Tibet, but elements within the military are thought to want a less political role. The army, in particular, is modernizing, reducing numbers and improving training. China has a large weapons industry, including nuclear weapons, and is a significant arms exporter.

ECONOMICS

 $433bn

 5.76 yuan

SCORE CARD

- ❑ World GNP Ranking.........10th
- ❑ GNP per Capita.........$361
- ❑ Balance of Payments.........$6.4bn
- ❑ Inflation.........5.8%
- ❑ Unemployment ...Widespread underemployment

Strengths

A domestic market of 1.2 billion. Self-sufficiency in food. Mineral reserves. Increasingly diversified industrial sector. Economic reforms which led to growth averaging 10% a year in 1980s, rapid rise in exports. Low wage costs.

ECONOMIC PERFORMANCE INDICATOR

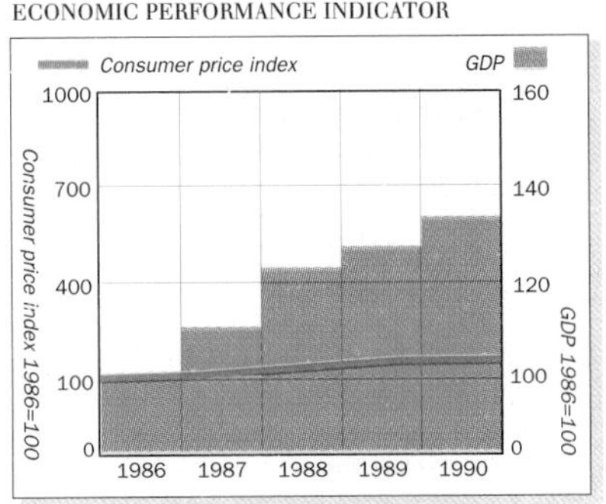

EXPORTS

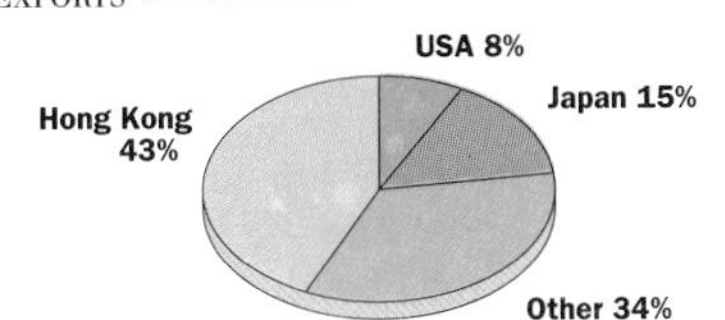

IMPORTS

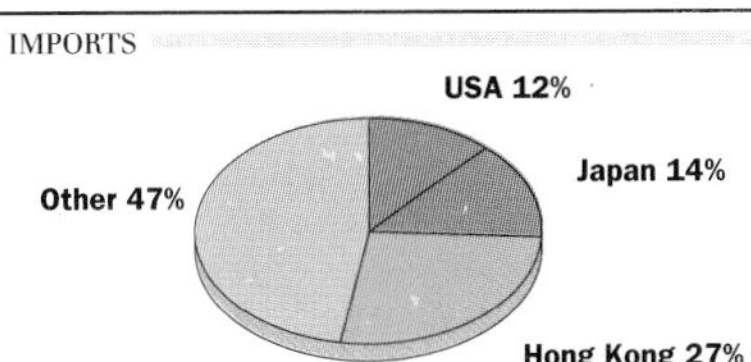

Weaknesses

Population growth and unemployment. Unevenly distributed resources. Poor transportation system. Political reluctance to reform areas such as price control, investment allocation, state industries.

CHINA : MAJOR BUSINESSES

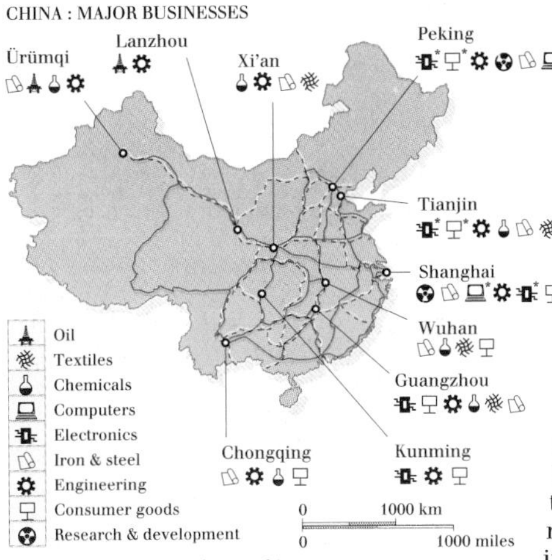

* significant multinational ownership

Profile

China's shift from a centrally planned to a market-oriented economy has steamed ahead since the 1980s, notably in the south, where liberalization has gone furthest. However, growth had to be curbed twice in the 1980s and also in 1992 because of high inflation. China is in danger of remaining in this stop-go cycle unless reforms are extended to reduce price controls and subsidies. At a national level, this would be politically difficult, exacerbating problems in the poorer north and west. In the south, however, some provinces are using the greater autonomy brought by reform to implement changes, including decontrol of rice prices.

REGIONS

BEIJING

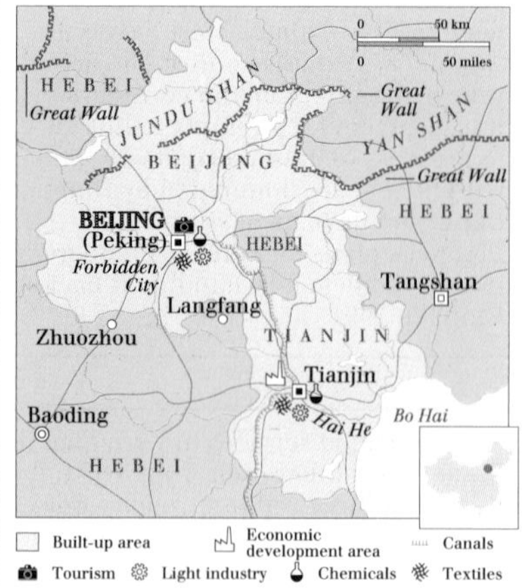

WITH A COMBINED population of almost 19 million, the cities of Beijing and Tianjin have the status of provinces. Beijing is China's capital and the focus of politics. Together with its port of Tianjin, 87 miles away, it also forms a powerful industrial and commercial nexus which has attracted much foreign investment since 1980.

Both cities are leading producers of textiles, chemicals and light industrial goods. Beijing is also China's top tourist destination. Almost two million visitors a year come to see the old imperial capital and its Forbidden City.

In 1992, Beijing attracted over $18 billion in foreign investment, mainly into high-tech and specialized manufacturing industries. Foreign companies like its improved infrastructure and living conditions, and its educated and relatively affluent workforce. However, frequent power cuts and rising land and labor costs are starting to lessen its attractiveness.

Tianjin, and especially its economic development area (TEDA), are benefiting. Costs are lower and city officials are less constrained than their Beijing counterparts by the watchful eye of central government. Tianjin is rapidly developing into China's leading gateway city. It has the country's largest container port and its largest air cargo center.

THE SOUTHEAST

THE SOUTHEASTERN COAST, especially Guangdong province, is the exemplar of modern market-oriented China. It was in Guangdong, and neighboring Fujian province, that the first Special Economic Zones were set up in 1980 to attract foreign investors. The target was the 30 million overseas Chinese, particularly those living in Hong Kong and Taiwan, who have their ancestral home in the two provinces.

Hong Kong and, to a lesser extent, Taiwan, have been responsible for over half of all recent foreign investment into China. Most has been concentrated in Guangdong – notably the Pearl River delta to the south – which has become a center of export-oriented light industry.

Growth has been spectacular and income levels in Guangdong are now ten times the national average. The province has many millionaires and its residents have quickly acquired the consumerist aspirations of their Hong Kong counterparts.

China's paramount leader, Deng Xiaoping, has set Guangdong the target of becoming Asia's largest industrial region within 20 years. However, explosive growth has also brought problems which threaten to undermine future development. Prime among these are rising wage and land costs, and escalating housing and power shortages. They are forcing out many of the low-cost industries that formed the basis of Guangdong's early growth and are deterring high-tech companies.

SHANGHAI

SHANGHAI AND ITS SATELLITE cities in Jiangsu and Zhejiang provinces form China's economic heartland.

Shanghai, a city-state of 12.5 million, is China's largest and most densely populated urban area. It was a focus of foreign settlement in the 19th century and of revolutionary activity in the 20th. In 1921, the Chinese Communist Party was founded there, and it was the base for the 1960s Cultural Revolution.

Despite relative stagnation after 1949, Shanghai remains China's foremost industrial and commercial city, and its leading financial center and port. With important political friends such as Vice-Premier Zhu Rongji and CCP Secretary-General Jiang Zemin, both former mayors, to promote its interests, it is beginning to undergo a revival which could restore it to its status as one of Asia's greatest cities.

Shanghai is popular with foreign firms – they like its workers, who are China's best educated and most highly skilled. Overcrowding in the city center means, however, that most future investment is likely to take place in Shanghai's new development area, across the Chang Jiang estuary.

Jiangsu and Zhejiang provinces are also gearing up for a major investment drive. In 1992, foreign investment approvals for the two totaled nearly $13 billion (those for Guangdong are $18 billion). However, Jiangsu already has a larger industrial output than any other province. And, notwithstanding Guangdong's recent growth, it is still the country's leading producer of light industrial goods. Its capital, Nanjing, is benefiting from rising costs and infrastructure problems in the southeast, as are Shanghai's other satellite cities – Nantong, Ningbo, Hangzhou and Suzhou. The Chang Jiang delta is expected to become the major focus for foreign investors.

REGIONS

THE NORTHEAST

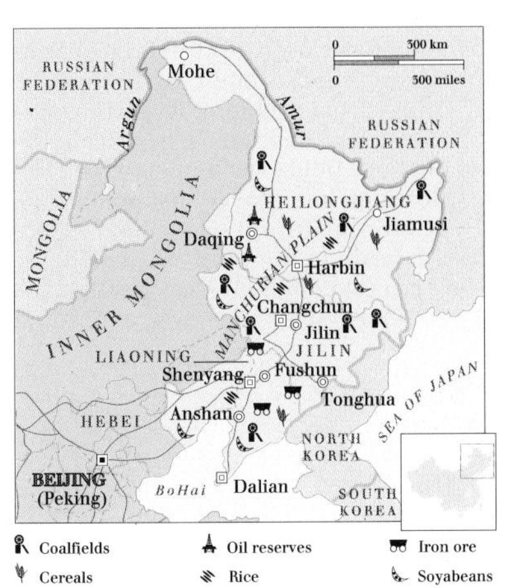

CALLED "DONGBEI" by the Chinese, the northeast is a vast region of 300,000 sq. mi. It was once the territory of the Manchus, founders of China's last dynasty. Today, it comprises Liaoning, Jilin and Heilongjiang provinces.

Except for Liaoning, the region is quite sparsely populated, mainly by the descendants of recent migrants. The fertile Manchurian plain makes the northeast a leading producer of grains and soybeans. It also has rich mineral resources. Heilongjiang has China's largest oilfield, in Daqing. Large coal and iron ore reserves have helped to make Liaoning China's second largest producer of heavy industrial goods.

Growth in the northeast lagged behind most of China during the 1980s, due mainly to the dominance of state industry. However, there are signs of change, notably in Liaoning and Jilin, where the non-state sector has more than doubled since 1992. Growth is encouraged by the region's strategic location. Trade across the northern border with Russia is expanding rapidly. Liaoning borders the Korean peninsula. South Korean firms are beginning to invest heavily, primarily in the port of Dalian. Proximity has also helped to make Dalian the preferred target of Japanese investment in China. By 1993, 125 Japanese companies were operating in the city.

CENTRAL CHINA

THIS REGION focuses on the inland provinces of Henan, Hubei, Hunan and Sichuan. It also includes Anhui and Jiangxi provinces to the east, and Shaanxi and Shanxi to the west.

Traversed by the Chang Jiang and Huang He rivers, central China is the country's agricultural heartland. Henan, Hubei, Hunan and Sichuan are the leading producers of rice and wheat. Minerals, including coal, oil and tungsten, are also important to the region,

Sichuan is China's most populous province, with 10% of the population. Under the leadership of Zhao Ziyang, later China's premier, Sichuan was the testing ground in the late 1970s for the shift from communal to individual farm production, which marked the start of the present era of reform. It has also had success in developing rural enterprises to absorb surplus farm labor. Around 25% of the population is now employed by these.

Sichuan and most other central provinces have a significant industrial base, but have not benefited as much as was hoped from China's "open door" foreign investment policy. This partly reflects their distance from the country's economic hub on the eastern seaboard. The government is now pushing the development of Hubei's capital, Wuhan, as the gateway to central China. A center of industry since the 19th century, Wuhan is the major inland port on the Chang Yiang.

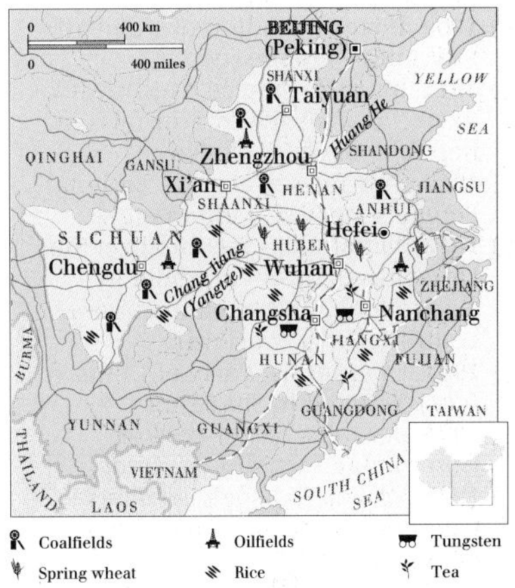

TIBET

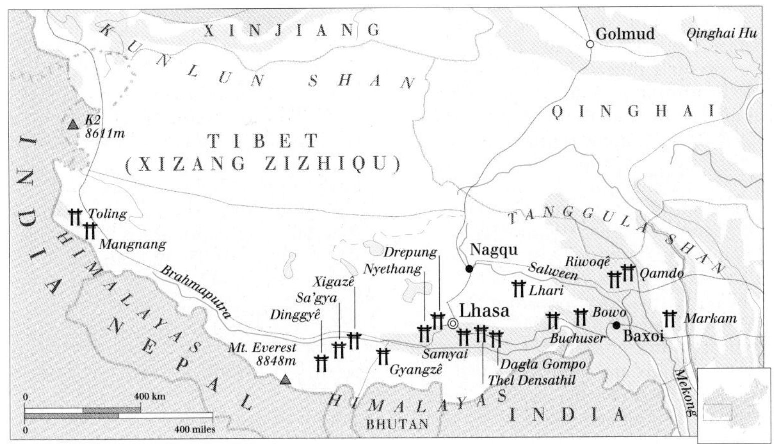

VAST, HIGH AND MOUNTAINOUS, Tibet has features in common with the other provinces and regions of western China – Xinjiang, Qinghai, Gansu, Ningxia and Nei Mongol Zizhiqu. All are sparsely populated, with ethnic minorities making up a significant percentage of their population. Tibet has China's lowest population density. Despite strongly resented Han Chinese immigration, Tibetans are still just in a majority.

Another common feature is opposition to Beijing's centralist policies. Although part of the Manchu empire from the 18th century until 1911, Tibet exercised full control over most of its affairs under the rule of the Dalai Lama, spiritual head of Tibetan Buddhism. In 1950, China invaded Tibet, and ruthlessly crushed the 1959 independence uprising. The Dalai Lama fled to India and established a government in exile. In 1965, Tibet was made a region of China. Opponents of Chinese rule were imprisoned or executed. Clashes between nationalists and Chinese troops in 1987 led to a renewed clampdown on Tibetans.

CHRONOLOGY

China has the world's oldest continuous civilization. Its recorded history begins 4,000 years ago with the Shang dynasty, founded in the north in 1766 BC. Succeeding dynasties expanded China's boundaries; it reached its greatest territorial extent under the Manchu (Qing) dynasty in the 18th century. Chinese isolationism frustrated Europe's attempts to expand into the empire until the 19th century, when China had fallen behind the industrializing West. For the previous 3,000 years, it had been one of the world's most advanced nations.

- **1839–1860** Opium Wars with Britain. China defeated; forced to open ports to foreigners.
- **1850–1873** Internal rebellions against Manchu empire.
- **1895** Defeat by Japan in war over Korean peninsula.
- **1900** Boxer Rebellion to expel all foreigners suppressed.
- **1911** Manchu empire overthrown by nationalists led by Sun Yat-sen. Republic of China declared.
- **1912** Sun Yat-sen creates National People's Party (Guomindang).
- **1916** Nationalists factionalize. Sun Yat-sen sets up government in Guangdong. Rest of China under control of rival warlords.
- **1921** Communist Party of China (CCP) founded in Shanghai.
- **1923** CCP joins Soviet-backed Guomindang to fight warlords.
- **1925** Chiang Kai-shek becomes Guomindang leader upon death of Sun Yat-sen.
- **1927** Chiang turns on CCP. CCP leaders, including Mao Zedong, escape to rural south.
- **1930–1934** Mao formulates strategy of peasant-led revolution.
- **1931** Japan invades Manchuria.
- **1934** Chiang forces CCP out of its southern bases. Start of 7,500-mile Long March.
- **1935** Long March ends in Yanan, Shaanxi province. Mao becomes CCP leader.
- **1936** Chiang agrees to joint offensive with CCP against Japan.
- **1937–1945** War against Japan; CCP Red Army in north, Guomindang in south. Japan defeated.
- **1945–1949** War between Red Army and Guomindang. US-backed Guomindang retreats to Taiwan.
- **1949** October 1: Mao proclaims People's Republic of China.
- **1950** Invasion of Tibet. Mutual assistance treaty with USSR.
- **1950–1958** Land reform; culminates in setting up of communes. First five-year plan (1953-1958) fails.

RESOURCES

618bn kwh (capacity 98.6m kw)

2.8m b/d (reserves 24,000,000,000 bbl)

349.2m pigs, 110.6m sheep, 74.8m cattle

Coal, natural gas, salt, iron, molybdenum, titanium, tungsten

ELECTRICITY GENERATION

	% of total generation
Hydro	18% (110.5bn kwh)
Thermal	82% (507.5bn kwh)
Nuclear	0%
Other	0%

0 20 40 60 80 100

% of total generation by type

China has commercial deposits of most minerals and probably the world's largest reserves of about 17, including molybdenum, titanium and tungsten, in which it dominates the world market.

China is the world's largest coal producer, with an output of over 1.1 billion tons a year, used mainly for power generation. Reserves are estimated at around 800 billion tons, primarily in the Shaanxi and Sichuan basins.

Power generation is lagging well behind demand and China could become an energy importer, despite plans to develop other energy sources. China's first two nuclear plants opened in the early 1990s. The world's largest hydropower station, known as the "Three Gorges" scheme, is being built at Santoup'ing on the Chang Jiang. The scheme has raised controversy over its proposed benefits and costs.

Oil is also a problem. Exports, once a top foreign exchange earner, are falling as onshore fields are depleted. Offshore exploration has proved disappointing. Hopes for the future now center on the Tarim basin in the far west, which Western oil companies say could have Middle East-sized reserves.

CHINA : LAND USE

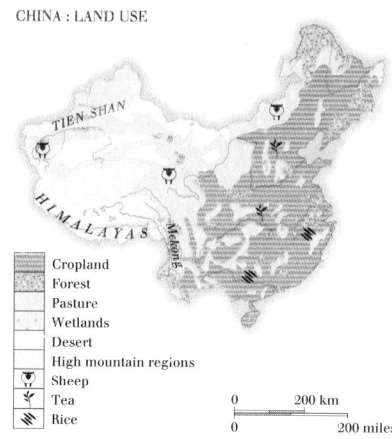

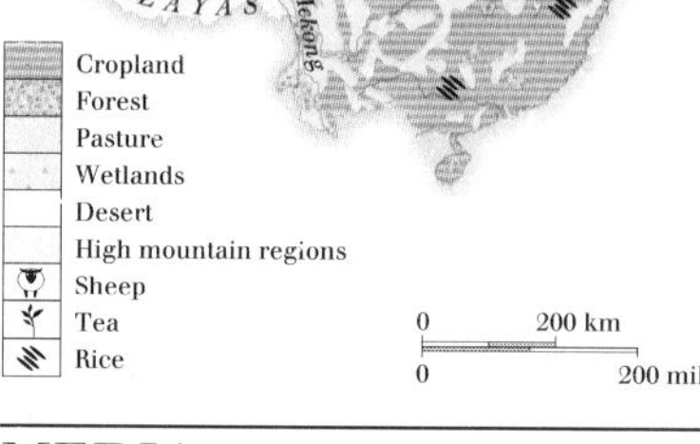

ENVIRONMENT

3% partially protected

Economic growth has precedence over ecological concerns

ENVIRONMENTAL TREATIES

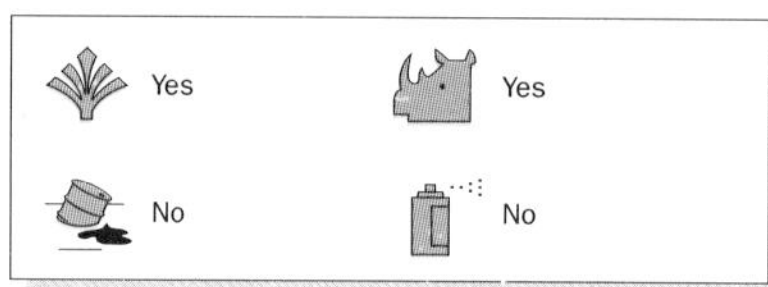

Due to its climate and geology, natural disasters are quite frequent in China. However, their impact is often made worse by human actions. Poor building standards helped push the death toll in the 1976 Tangshan earthquake to over 500,000. The economic policies of the 1950s turned drought into a famine, which is estimated to have killed up to 100 million between 1959 and 1961.

Economic growth is the priority of China's leaders, who tend to view Western pressure for environmental controls with suspicion. As a result, industrial pollution and environmental degradation, already widespread, are increasing. However, the environment appears to be a growing concern among educated Chinese. In 1992, they campaigned, albeit unsuccessfully, to stop the Three Gorges hydroelectric project which will lead to large-scale loss of wildlife habitats and could increase the risk of earthquakes.

MEDIA

The government still attempts to enforce tight censorship, often by withdrawal of licenses

PUBLISHING AND BROADCAST MEDIA

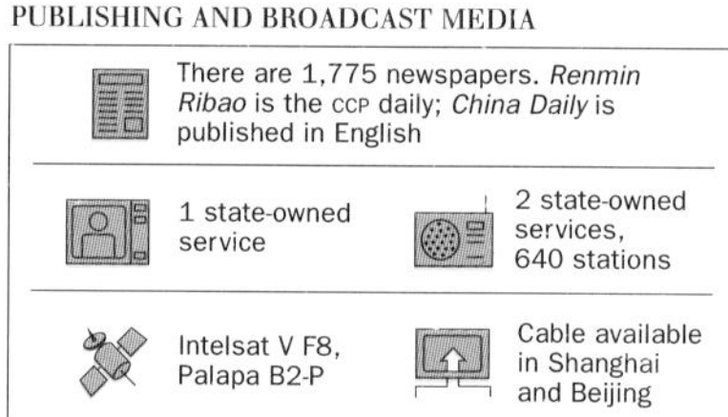

For China's leaders, one less welcome result of a more open, market-oriented economy has been people's increasing access to non-official sources of information. TV ownership is rising with living standards. Many sets, especially in the populous south and east, are tuned to Hong Kong stations. The growing number of satellite-dish owners have an even wider choice.

These changes have undermined but not ended censorship. Recent efforts to control satellite-dish ownership have had limited success, but the printed media remain on a tight rein. Papers considered undesirable have their licenses removed in periodic clean-ups. Millions still buy, but few now read, the CCP-owned *Renmin Ribao* (People's Daily), with its editorials defending revolutionary purity.

CHRONOLOGY *continued*

- 1958 Great Leap Forward to boost production fails; contributes to millions of deaths during 1959–1961 famine. Mao resigns as CCP chairman; succeeded by Lui Saoqi.
- 1960 Sino-Soviet split.
- 1961–1965 More pragmatic economic approach led by Lui and Deng Xiaoping.
- 1966 Cultural Revolution initiated by Mao to restore his supreme power. Youthful Red Guards encouraged to attack all authority. Revolutionary Committee formed, including Mao's wife Jiang Qing. Mao rules with Military Commission under Lin Biao and State Council under premier Zhou Enlai.
- 1967 Army intervenes to restore some order amid countrywide chaos. Lui and Deng purged from party.
- 1969 Mao regains chairmanship of CCP. Lin Biao designated his successor, but quickly comes under attack from Mao.
- 1971 Lin dies in plane crash.
- 1972 US President Nixon visits. More open foreign policy initiated by Zhou Enlai, a moderating force during Cultural Revolution.
- 1973 Jiang Qing, Zhang Chunquio and other "Gang of Four" members elected to Politburo. Deng Xiaoping rehabilitated as vice-premier.
- 1976 January: death of Zhou Enlai. April: mass demonstration of support for Zhou and moderates. Mao strips Deng of posts, confirms Hua Guo Feng as new premier. September: Mao dies. October: "Gang of Four" arrested.
- 1977 Deng regains party posts, begins to extend his power base.
- 1978 Decade of reform and economic modernization launched. Open-door policy to foreign investment; farmers allowed to farm for profit.
- 1980 Deng emerges as China's paramount leader. Economic reform gathers pace; but hopes for political change suppressed.
- 1983–1984 Conservative elderly leaders attempt to slow pace of economic reform under Deng. Several subsequently forced to step down from Politburo.
- 1984 Industrial reforms announced; less successful than earlier agricultural changes.
- 1989 Demonstrations in Tiananmen Square, demanding greater openness in government. Crushed by Army; between 1,000 and 5,000 dead. Beijing under martial law.
- 1992 Trials of pro-democracy activists continue. Plans for socialist market economy accelerated.

CRIME

1.3m prisoners

Up 10% in 1990

CRIME RATES

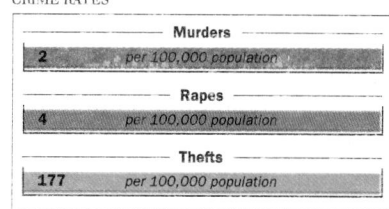

Murders	2 per 100,000 population
Rapes	4 per 100,000 population
Thefts	177 per 100,000 population

China's legal system is a mix of custom and statute, and has a local reputation for arbitrariness. Economic reform and the breakdown of former social controls have been paralleled by a rise in corruption and violent crime. Many new economic crimes have been made capital offenses, but with little effect.

China has a poor human rights record and still holds thousands of political prisoners. The 1989 massacre in Tiananmen Square brought human rights to the fore in China's relations with the USA and EU. Detainees are now occasionally being released. The Red Cross is negotiating with China to allow access to political prisoners.

EDUCATION

73%

Education spending as % GNP (0–25): 2.4%

THE EDUCATION SYSTEM

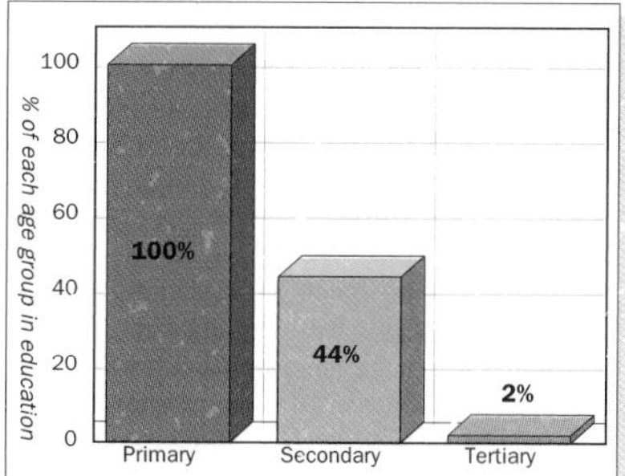

Despite the expansion of education since 1949, illiteracy and semi-literacy are still quite widespread. This is due partly to the Cultural Revolution which left a generation with little education; it also reflects lower rural attendance and attitudes to women. In 1990, 38% of women and 16% of men were illiterate. To raise skill levels, the government has set a target of nine years of education for all. School attendance fell when fees were introduced in the 1980s, but is now nearing 90%. Higher education, which is also fee-paying, attracts only 2% of 20–24 year-olds. Today, however, selection is based on academic rather than political criteria.

HEALTH

1 per 1,077 people

Cardiovascular and diarrheal diseases, cancer, tuberculosis

Health spending as % GNP (0–25): 1.3%

Health care is one of China's successes. Combining traditional and Western medicine, it is based on an extensive primary care network – including paramedic "barefoot doctors" – which extends to the remotest regions. Life expectancy is now on a par with many richer nations, at an average of 70 years. However, economic reform could reduce access. Fees are rising and fewer people are covered by the free care that goes with state employment.

WEALTH

Garment cutter, 215 yuan per month; doctor, 216 yuan per month

CONSUMER GOODS OWNERSHIP

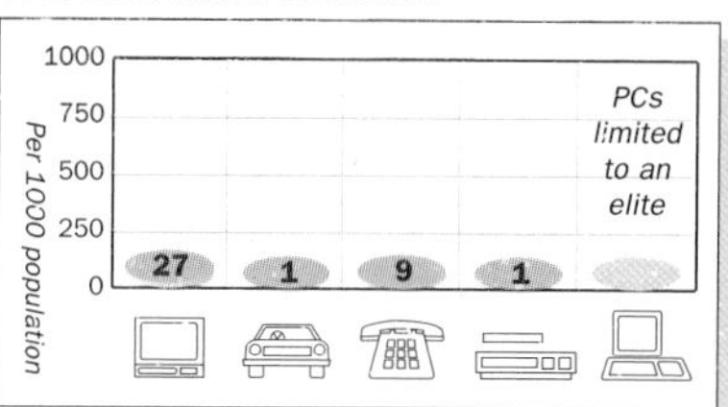

Economic change has led to improved living standards, seen in the growing demand for consumer goods, but also widening wealth disparities. The burgeoning small-business class and employees of companies with foreign investment have benefited most. They mainly live in the east, especially the southeast, which is home to a number of millionaires. The main losers are the 150 million "surplus" agricultural workers, many of whom have migrated to the cities in search of jobs. The majority of Chinese are still farmers. They initially benefited from reform, but their living standards are now threatened by rising production costs.

WORLD RANKING

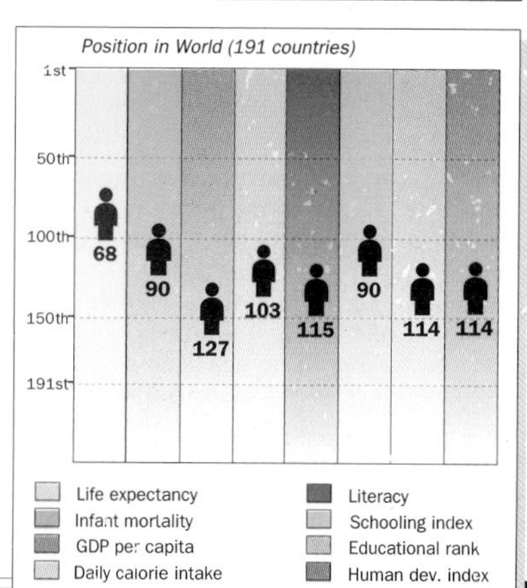

COLOMBIA

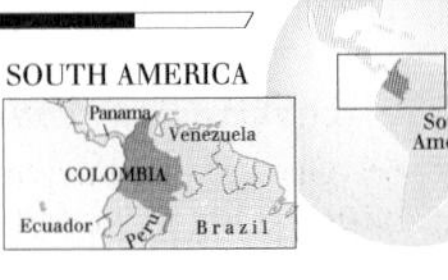

OFFICIAL NAME: Republic of Colombia **CAPITAL:** Bogotá
POPULATION: 33.4 million **CURRENCY:** Colombian peso **OFFICIAL LANGUAGE:** Spanish

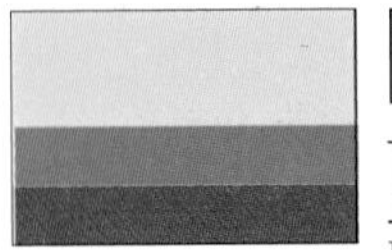

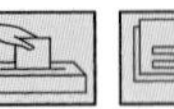
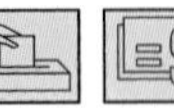

LYING IN NORTHWEST SOUTH AMERICA, Colombia has coastlines on both the Caribbean and the Pacific. The east of the country is densely forested and sparsely populated, and separated from the western coastal plains by the Andes Mountains. The Andes divide into three ranges (*cordilleras*) in Colombia. The eastern range is divided from the two western ranges by the densely populated Magdalena River valley. The Colombian lowlands are very wet, hot and fertile, supporting two harvests and allowing many crops to be planted at any time of year. A multiparty democracy since 1957, Colombia is noted for its coffee, emeralds and gold.

CLIMATE

WEATHER CHART

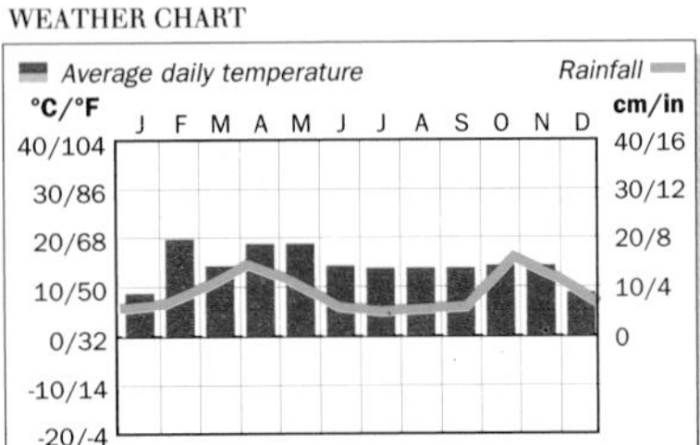

Most of Colombia is wet and the hot Pacific coastal areas receive up to 195 in. of rain a year. The Caribbean coast is a little drier. The Andes have three climatic regions: the *tierra caliente* (hot lowlands), *tierra templada* (temperate uplands) and *tierra fría* (cold highlands). A feature of the last is year-round spring-like conditions such as those found in Bogotá. The equatorial east has two wet seasons.

COMMUNICATIONS

Eldorado, Bogotá
4.66m passengers

48 ships
385,300 dwt

THE TRANSPORTATION NETWORK

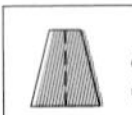
80,267 miles (129,177 km)

Caribbean Trunk Highway

1,572 miles (2,532 km)

8,886 miles (14,300km)

Roads in the north are in reasonable condition. Those in the south and east tend to be rutted and badly affected by the frequent rains. Colombia's antiquated railroad system, which currently has few fast intercity services, is due to be privatized.

Rivers are an important means of transportation; the Magdalena, Orinoco, Atrato and Amazon river systems are all extensively navigable. Plans exist to connect Colombia to the Pan-American Highway.

TOURISM

812,796 visitors

Up 11% in 1990

MAIN OVERSEAS ARRIVALS

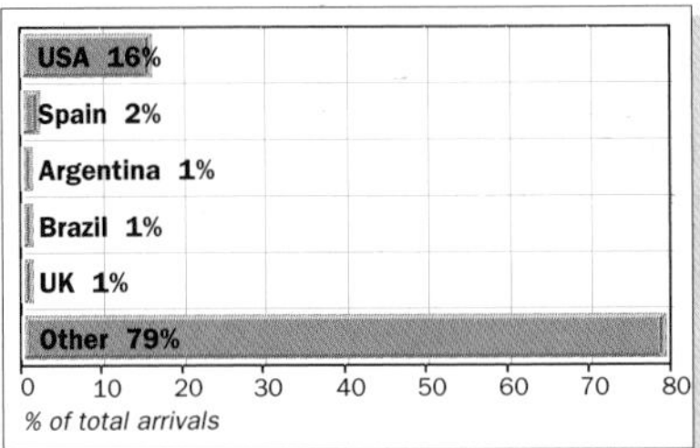

Tourism in Colombia is largely limited to the beaches of the Caribbean coast. Cartagena, Barranquilla and Santa Marta are the main resorts. Cartagena has also been developed as a major Latin American conference center.

Expansion of the tourist business has been limited by Colombia's political instability and the prevalence of narcotics-related crime. The well-publicized activities of drug cartels in Medellín and Cali, and instances of kidnappings in Bogotá, are major deterrents.

Limited infrastructure makes many regions of Colombia, particularly Amazonia to the east of the Andes, almost inaccessible. The Atlantic coast is also barely exploited.

Simón Bolívar and Cristóbal Colón, twin peaks with a height of over 19,030 feet in the heart of the Colombian Andes.

PEOPLE

Spanish, Amerindian languages, English Creole

75 people per sq. mile

THE URBAN/RURAL POPULATION SPLIT

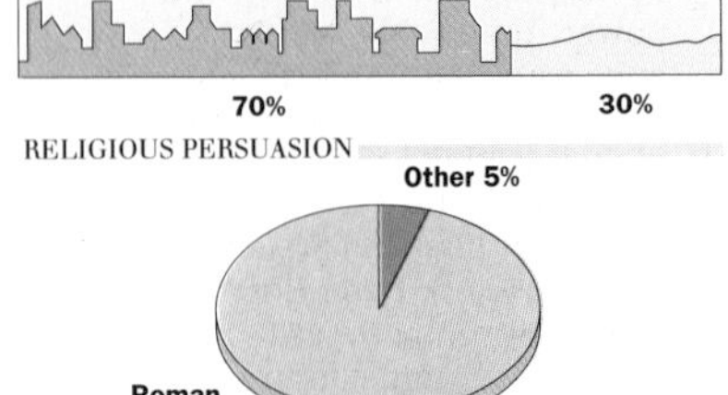

ETHNIC MAKEUP

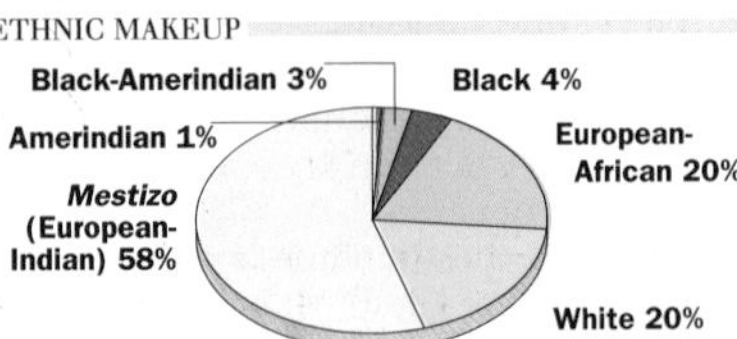

The majority of Colombians are people of mixed blood. An estimated 450,000 indigenous Amerindians are largely concentrated in the southwest and Amazonia, although some communities are scattered throughout the country. A small black population lives along both coasts, and especially in Chocó, Colombia's poorest region. Blacks are the most underrepresented group.

Some progress has been made in giving Amerindians a greater political voice. In 1991, constitutional reforms reserved two seats in the Senate for indigenous representatives, and Amerindian pressure groups are increasingly active. However, harassment by landowners and drug-traffickers in Amazonia continues. Very few investigations into suspected human rights violations against Amerindians have led to prosecutions.

Women in Colombia have a higher profile than in much of the rest of Latin America. Many are prominent in the professional sector, though few reach the top in politics. The traditional extended Catholic family is the norm in Colombia. Regional identity is strong.

POPULATION AGE BREAKDOWN

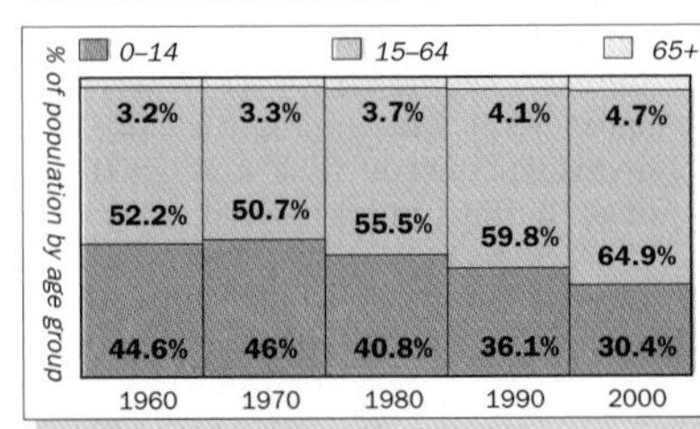

POLITICS

 Lower House 1998
Upper House 1998

 President Ernesto Samper Pizano

Colombia is a presidential democracy. Presidents may not serve two consecutive terms.

MAIN POLITICAL ISSUES

Guerrillas and drug cartels
Guerrilla activity is a major problem in Colombia, causing instability which makes many regions ungovernable. In 1991, the Gaviria administration persuaded two of Colombia's four main guerrilla groups to accept an amnesty. The Armed Revolutionary Force of Colombia (FARC) – communist guerrillas who turned down the plan – are now the main problem.

Gaviria also declared war on the drug cartels of Medellín and Cali. In 1991, Pablo Escobar, leader of the Medellín cartel and one of the country's most powerful men, was captured. He was shot dead by police after escaping from jail. The issue now is whether to keep up the war or try to reach a political compromise with the drug barons.

THE STATE OF THE PARTIES

House of Representatives 163 members

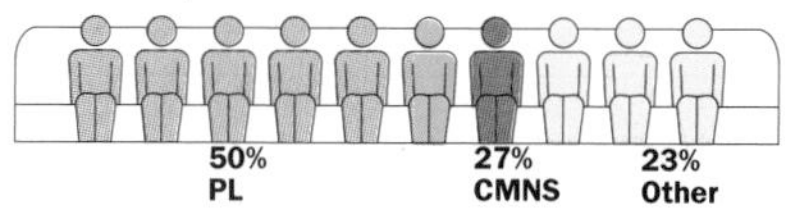

PL = Liberal Party **CMNS** = Conservative Movement of the National Salvation Party **NDF** = New Democratic Force **ADM–19** = Democratic Alliance

Senate 102 members

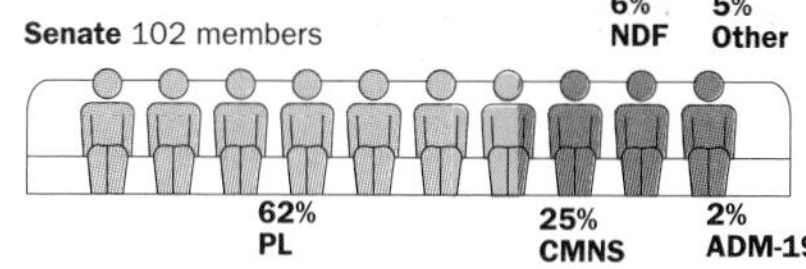

The economy
President Ernesto Samper, on entering office in 1994, pledged to moderate the free market policies of the previous administration and to target subsidies at depressed sectors, such as agriculture.

PROFILE

The Conservatives (PSC) and the Liberals (PL), have shared power in Colombia for the past 40 years. Both have large numbers of followers. However, guerrilla groups, all with different ideologies, and drug cartels continue to disrupt the political process. A new generation of Liberal politicians have been looking to the USA for funds in their attempts to make Colombia more stable.

Carlos Angel César Gaviria Trujillo, *president from 1990 to 1994*

Pablo Escobar, *cocaine king and leader of the Medellín cartel until 1993.*

WORLD AFFAIRS

 AG
 OAS
 CG
 ECLAC GATT

Colombia's most important foreign relations are with the USA, the major market for its exports and also its main source of aid. However, the relationship is not without its difficulties. The USA has intervened directly to attack the drug business in Colombia, making this a condition of aid. Colombia, however, disagrees with many US tactics and has refused US demands that drug traffickers be extradited for trial in the USA.

Relations with neighboring states are fairly stable. A border dispute with Venezuela, Colombia's traditional enemy, is yet to be resolved, but the issue is unlikely to lead to conflict. In 1991, Nicaragua accepted Colombia's sovereignty over the San Andrés and Providencia islands.

AID

 $123m (receipts)

 Up 40% in 1991

Apart from US military aid to help fight the drug cartels, Colombia's aid receipts are mostly spent on education. Improving primary education in rural areas is a priority.

CHRONOLOGY

In 1525, Spain began the conquest of Colombia, which became its chief source of gold.

- ❑ **1819** Simón Bolívar defeats Spanish at Boyacá. Republic of Gran Colombia formed with Venezuela, Ecuador and Panama.
- ❑ **1830** Venezuela and Ecuador split away during revolts and civil wars.
- ❑ **1849** Conservative and Liberal parties established, the former with centralist and the latter with federalist tendencies.
- ❑ **1861–1886** Liberals hold monopoly on power.
- ❑ **1886–1930** Conservative rule.

⇨

CHRONOLOGY *continued*

- ❑ **1899–1903** Liberal "War of 1,000 Days" revolt fails. 120,000 die.
- ❑ **1903** Panama secedes, but is not recognized by Colombia until 1921.
- ❑ **1930** Liberal President Olaya Herrera elected by coalition in first peaceful change of power.
- ❑ **1946** Conservatives take over.
- ❑ **1948** Shooting of Liberal mayor of Bogotá and riot known as *El Bogotazo* sparks civil war, *La Violencia* until 1957; 300,000 killed.
- ❑ **1953–1957** Military dictatorship of Rojas Pinilla.
- ❑ **1958** Conservatives and Liberals agree to alternate government in a National Front until 1974. Other parties banned.
- ❑ **1965** Left-wing guerrilla National Liberation Army and Maoist Popular Liberation Army founded.
- ❑ **1966** Pro-Soviet FARC guerrilla group formed.
- ❑ **1968** Constitutional reform allows new parties, but two-party parity continues. Guerrilla groups proliferate from now on.
- ❑ **1971** M-19 emerges as armed left-wing guerrilla group.
- ❑ **1984** Minister of Justice assassinated for attempting to enforce anti-drug campaign.
- ❑ **1985** M-19 guerrillas blast their way into Ministry of Justice; 11 judges and 90 others killed. Patriotic Union (UP) party formed.
- ❑ **1986** Liberal Virgilio Barco Vargas wins presidential elections, thus ending power-sharing. UP wins 10 seats in parliament. Right-wing paramilitary start murder campaign against UP politicians. Violence by both left-wing groups and death squads run by drug cartels continues.
- ❑ **1989** M-19 reaches peace agreement with government, including the granting of a full pardon. Becomes legal party.
- ❑ **1990** UP and Liberal presidential candidates murdered during general and presidential elections. Liberal César Gaviria elected on anti-drug platform.
- ❑ **1991** New constitution legalizes divorce and prohibits extradition of Colombian nationals. Indigenous peoples' democratic rights guaranteed, but territorial claims not addressed.
- ❑ **1992** Six armed anti-terrorism units set up to combat rising violence.
- ❑ **1992** Medellín drug cartel leader, Pablo Escobar, captured. Escapes.
- ❑ **1993** Pablo Escobar dies in shoot-out with police.

DEFENSE

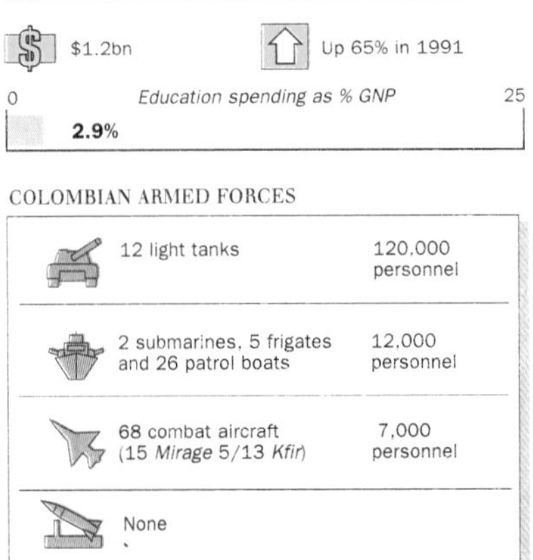
$1.2bn
Up 65% in 1991
0
Education spending as % GNP
25
2.9%
COLOMBIAN ARMED FORCES
12 light tanks
120,000 personnel
2 submarines, 5 frigates and 26 patrol boats
12,000 personnel
68 combat aircraft (15 Mirage 5/13 Kfir)
7,000 personnel
None

The Colombian military is powerful but remains a background force, leaving the politicians to run the country. Its main concern is combating the guerrilla groups and drug barons in Amazonia. The power of drug money has, however, led to some corruption in army ranks and dented the effectiveness of campaigns. Drug barons have their own armed forces, which are often better equipped than the state's.

Colombia participates in the joint Latin American Defense Force. The largest proportion of defense spending goes to the army. Most arms are bought from the USA, although France supplies the Colombian Air Force.

ECONOMICS

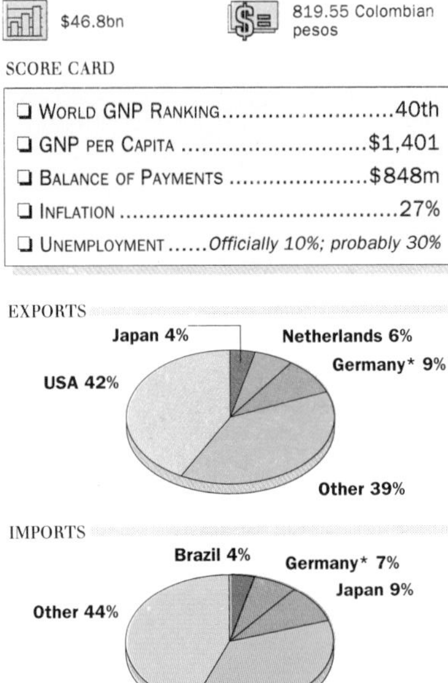

$46.8bn

819.55 Colombian pesos

SCORE CARD

❑ World GNP Ranking	40th
❑ GNP per Capita	$1,401
❑ Balance of Payments	$848m
❑ Inflation	27%
❑ Unemployment	Officially 10%; probably 30%

EXPORTS
Japan 4%
Netherlands 6%
Germany* 9%
USA 42%
Other 39%
IMPORTS
Brazil 4%
Germany* 7%
Japan 9%
Other 44%
USA 36%

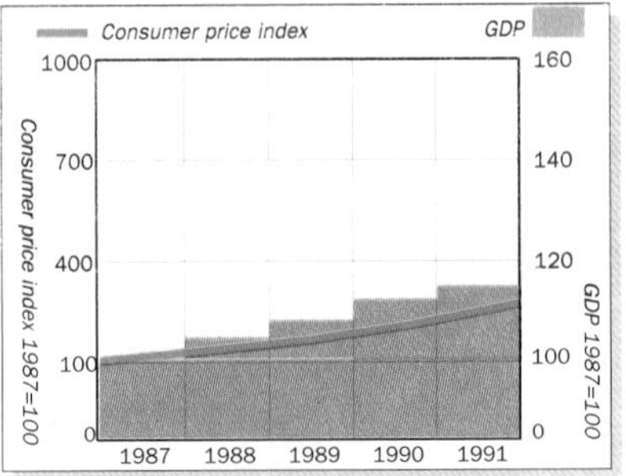
ECONOMIC PERFORMANCE INDICATOR
Consumer price index
GDP
1000
700
400
100
0
160
140
120
100
0
Consumer price index 1987=100
GDP 1987=100
1987
1988
1989
1990
1991

Colombia has a successful private export sector. A program of privatization is reducing the state's involvement further; the railroads, telephone company and banks are all being sold off.

Regional disparities remain marked. Most wealth is centered in the Bogotá, Medellín and Cali regions. Rural areas are largely underdeveloped. The main obstacle to growth is the instability caused by the drug business. Given stability and investment, Colombia's potential for growth is considerable.

Strengths

Substantial oil and coal deposits plus well-developed hydroelectric power makes Colombia almost self-sufficient in energy. Healthy and diversified export sector – especially coffee and coal. Light manufacturer. Worldwide market for cocaine still growing.

Weaknesses

Drug-related violence and corruption discourages foreign investors. Industries serving local markets uncompetitive, due to decades of protection. High unemployment rate – officially 10% but, in reality, probably nearer 30%.

Profile

Of all the Latin American economies, Colombia's is probably the closest to the US model. The state has traditionally played a relatively minor role and

COLOMBIA : MAJOR BUSINESSES

Pulp and paper
Narcotics
Steel
Chemicals
Vehicle assembly
Food processing
Textiles
Oil

Barranquilla
Medellín
Bogotá
Cali
Ibagué
Orito

0 200 km
0 200 miles

* significant multinational ownership

RESOURCES

36,000m kwh (capacity 9.41m kw)

435,800 b/d (reserves 1,935,200 bbl)

24.6m cattle, 2.7m sheep, 2.6m pigs, 2m horses

Oil, natural gas, coal, nickel, emeralds, gold

ELECTRICITY GENERATION

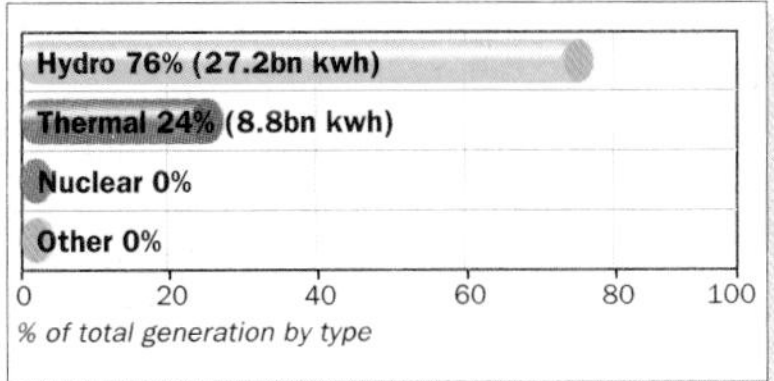

Recent discoveries have made Colombia self-sufficient in oil. Coal surpluses are exported mainly to the UK and USA. Gold reserves are significant. Colombia also produces 60% of the world's emeralds.

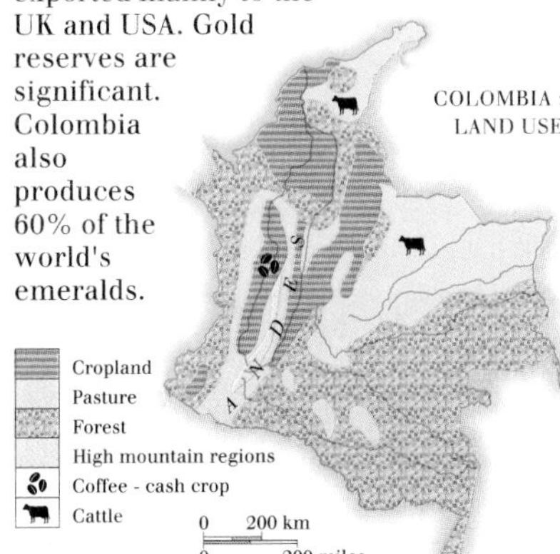

ENVIRONMENT

Rising pollution levels in the Magdalena River

ENVIRONMENTAL TREATIES

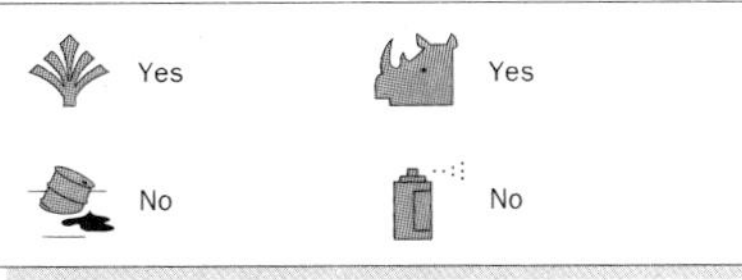

Cattle ranching, logging and coca growing have caused extensive soil degradation and loss of bird habitat.

MEDIA

In theory the press is free, but in practice there is some political censorship. Journalists tend to avoid criticizing drug cartels

PUBLISHING AND BROADCAST MEDIA

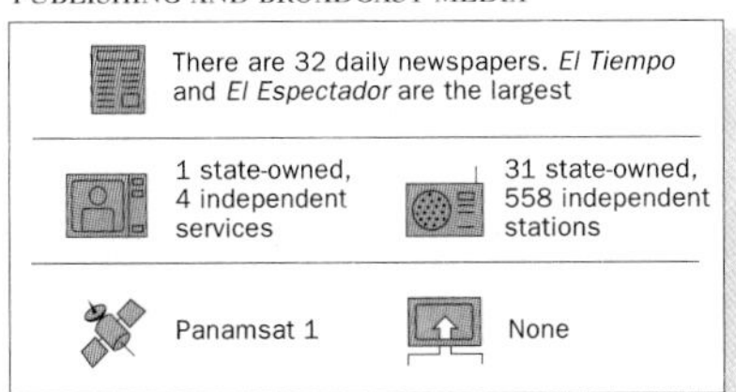

There are 32 daily newspapers. El Tiempo and El Espectador are the largest
1 state-owned, 4 independent services
31 state-owned, 558 independent stations
Panamsat 1
None

The independent press is small. The main papers are owned by corporations whose interests they promote.

CRIME

32,549 prisoners

Very high levels, but falling due to recent guerrilla amnesties

CRIME RATES

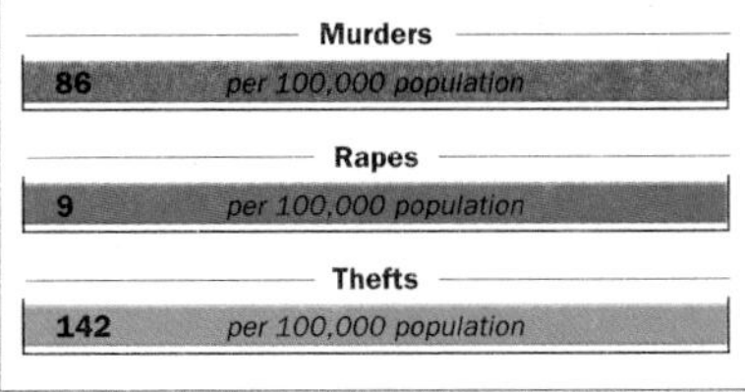

Colombia is the most violent society in Latin America and one of the most violent in the world. Its judicial police reported 28,237 murders in 1992. Homicide is the main cause of death among young men in cities; overall it is the most common cause of death after cancer. Most of the violence is drug-related and Cali and Medellín are the most dangerous cities. The frequency of urban armed robbery makes residents extremely security conscious. Wealthier Colombians employ several security guards.

The army and police have used intimidation and torture in the fight against both guerrillas and drug traffickers, but have themselves also been accused of participating in the trade. A relatively new phenomenon is that of "social cleansing," the murder of street children and beggars by organized armed gangs. Some gangs in Bogotá are funded by local businesses.

Colombia's extensive gem deposits attract large numbers of illegal miners and smugglers. Around 15,000 were estimated to be active in the Boyacá area in 1993.

EDUCATION

87%

0 Education spending as % GNP 25

2.9%

THE EDUCATION SYSTEM

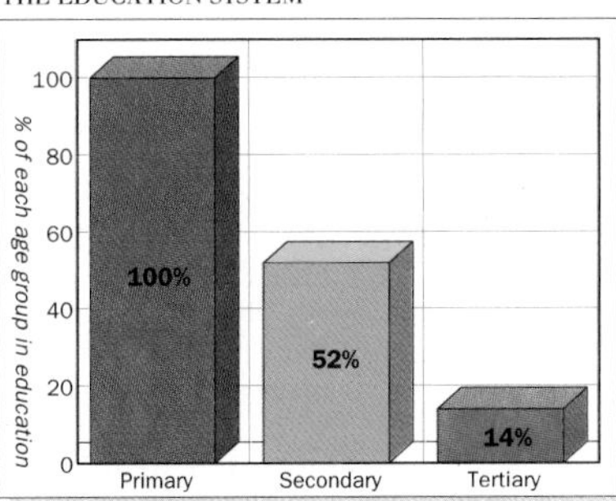

Colombia's education system is a mixture of the French and US models, with a *baccalauréat* exam at the end of secondary schooling. Educational provision in rural areas is uneven and increasing numbers of schools are being closed. The public universities (the main ones are in Bogotá, Medellín and Cali) are occasionally disrupted by political strikes and violence.

HEALTH

1 per 1,102 people

Cancer, murder, heart disease, accidents

0 Health spending as % GNP 25

0.6%

Only 16% of Colombians benefit from any social security system, rather fewer than in most neighboring states. Rural areas have little health provision, as most doctors work in the larger cities. A polio vaccination campaign has largely eradicated the virus, except in coastal regions.

WEALTH

School teacher, 150,000 pesos per month; Senior engineer, 500,000 pesos per month

CONSUMER GOODS OWNERSHIP

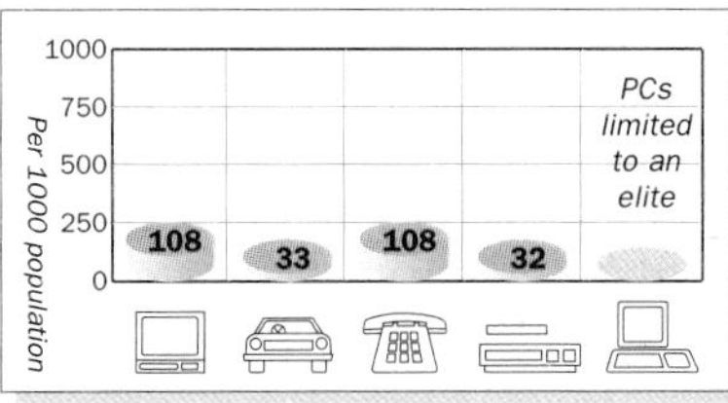

There is little social mobility in Colombia; the historically wealthy Spanish families still dominate political and business life. The rich favor BMWs or jeeps, weekend in Miami or Colombia's Caribbean islands, shop in Paris and Rome, and go to the USA for medical treatment. Their children are educated overseas. The rural poor are mostly landless. The inhabitants of the shantytowns of Cali, Barranquilla, Cartagena and Buenaventura are the poorest groups in Colombian society.

WORLD RANKING

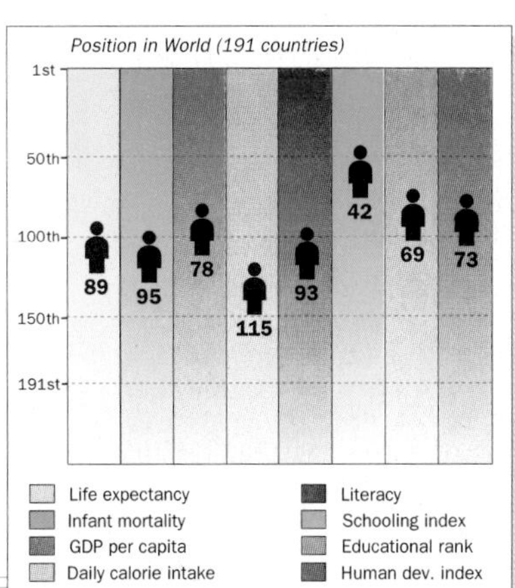

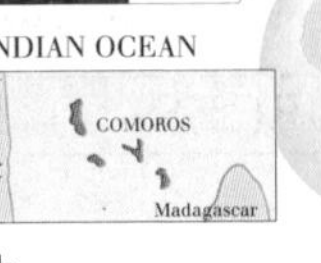

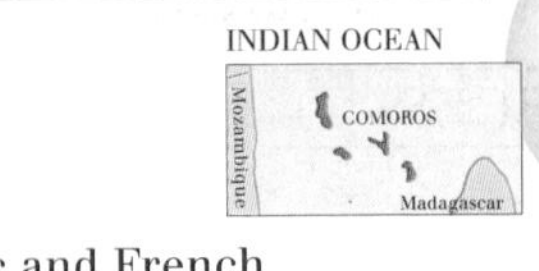

COMOROS

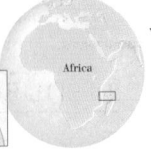

OFFICIAL NAME: Federal Islamic Republic of the Comoros **CAPITAL:** Moroni
POPULATION: 600,000 **CURRENCY:** Comoros franc **OFFICIAL LANGUAGES:** Arabic and French

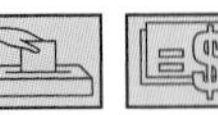

THE REPUBLIC OF the Comoros lies between Mozambique and Madagascar and consists of three main islands and a number of islets. The region is poor, with most of the population engaged in subsistence farming. In 1975 the Comoros, with the exception of the island of Mayotte, became independent of France. Since then instability has plagued the political process, and there have been several coups and counter-coups.

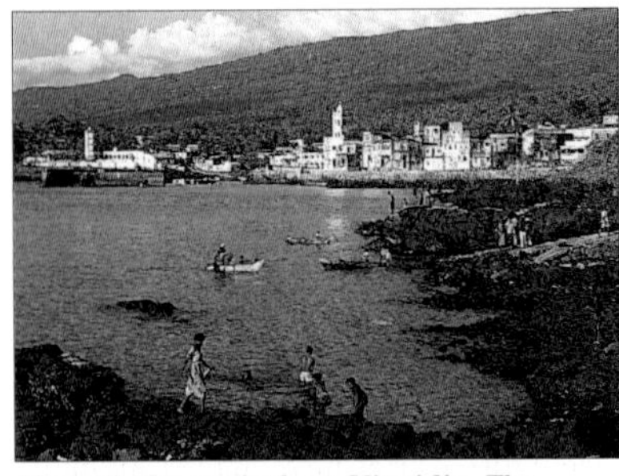

Moroni, the capital, on Njazidja. The Comoros Islands are highly fertile, heavily forested, and often ringed by coral reefs.

CLIMATE

WEATHER CHART

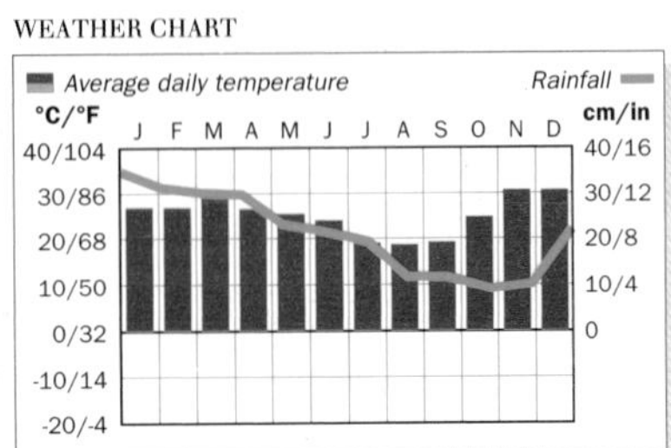

The islands are tropical; hot and humid on the coasts and cooler higher up, notably on Mount Kartala.

COMMUNICATIONS

 **Moroni-Hahaya, Njazidja**

3 ships 2,300 dwt

THE TRANSPORTATION NETWORK

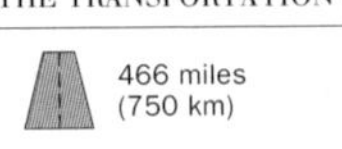

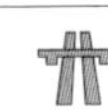

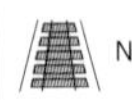

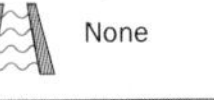

Recent projects have included development of the port at Moroni and upgrading the international airport.

TOURISM

8,000 visitors

No significant change from year to year

MAIN OVERSEAS ARRIVALS

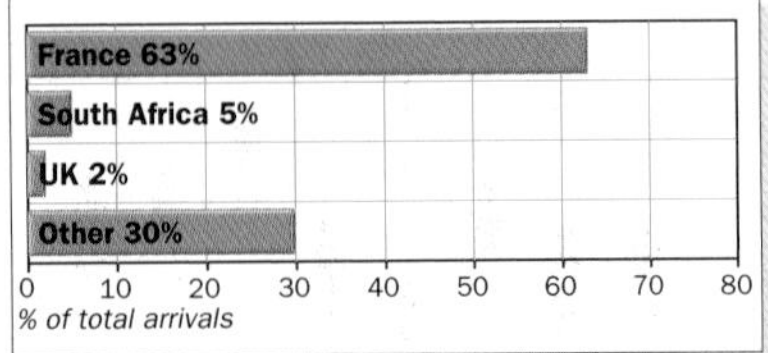

In 1988, Sun International of South Africa joined a major project to build four hotels designed to attract 12,000 visitors a year from South Africa, France and Italy. Mauritius and the Seychelles provide tough competition.

PEOPLE

 Arabic, Comoran, French

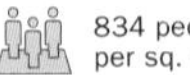 834 people per sq. mile

THE URBAN/RURAL POPULATION SPLIT

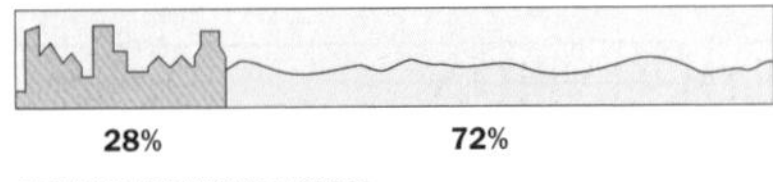

RELIGIOUS PERSUASION

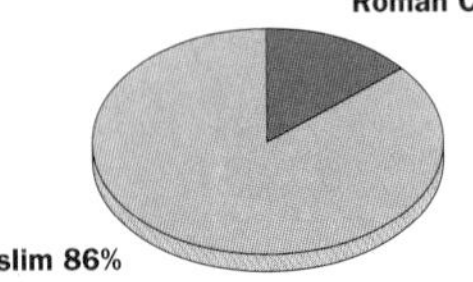

The Comoros have absorbed a diverse population of Polynesians, Africans, Indonesians, Persians and Arabs over its history; in addition, there have also been Portuguese, Dutch, French and Indian immigrants. However, some sections of the community have retained their individual character; Mwali and Mayotte are still primarily African. Ethnic tension is rare, partly due to the unifying force of the predominant religion, Islam.

POLITICS

 1997

 Saïd Mohamed Djohar

THE STATE OF THE PARTIES

Federal Assembly 42 members

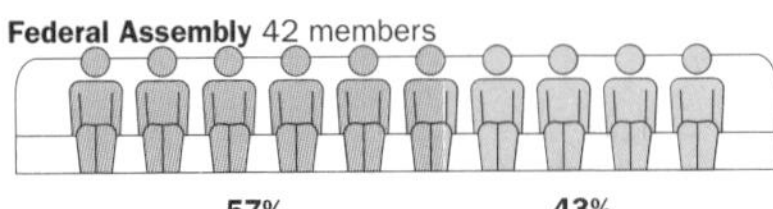

57% **RDR** **43%** **UNDC**

RDR = Union for Democracy and Renovation
UNDC = National Union for Democratic Comoros

Senate 15 members

Five members chosen from each island by an electoral college

The Comoros have begun a transition from one-party rule to a democratic system, although the precise form is still to be established.

In 1989, President Djohar came to power. He committed himself to working toward a new constitution, but political instability has continued. In 1990, 1991 and 1992, for example, there were three more attempted coups. These difficulties have had an adverse effect on the economy. There have been calls for the presidential guard, involved in some of the coups, to be brought under constitutional control.

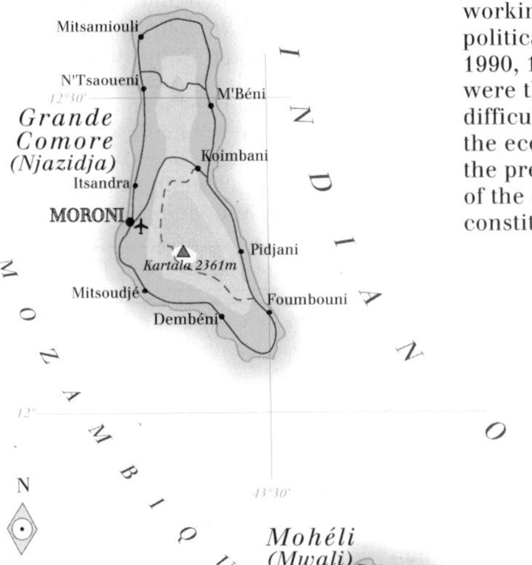

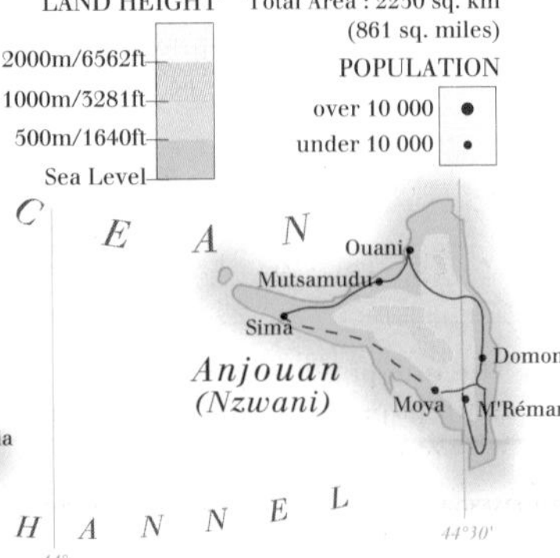

WORLD AFFAIRS

The Comoros have a close relationship with France,their main benefactor. More recently, an economic link has been developed with South Africa, which used the islands for sanctions-busting purposes. In 1985, the Comoros became the fourth member of the Indian Ocean Commission (IOC), with the Seychelles, Mauritius and Madagascar.

AID

$43m (receipts)

Little change from year to year

Foreign aid, mainly from France, accounts for over 40% of GDP, but even so has been insufficient to install the infrastructure necessary for economic development. Because of its Islamic links, the Comoros benefit from some Arab aid, as well as some from the EU, the World Bank and OPEC.

DEFENSE

$3.1m

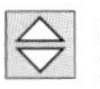
Little change from year to year

The influence of the military is small beyond the presidential guard, financed by France and South Africa, which has been involved in coups.

ECONOMICS

$262m

276.26 Comoros francs

SCORE CARD

- ❑ WORLD GNP RANKING........................171st
- ❑ GNP PER CAPITA $440
- ❑ BALANCE OF PAYMENTS..................$-14.1m
- ❑ INFLATION 2.5%
- ❑ UNEMPLOYMENT.................................16%

STRENGTHS

Vanilla, ylang-ylang and cloves are the main cash crops. Tourism is a potential growth area.

WEAKNESSES

Agriculture is underdeveloped; most production is at a subsistence level using traditional techniques. Over 50% of food requirements are imported. Lack of basic infrastructure, especially electricity and transportation.

EXPORTS

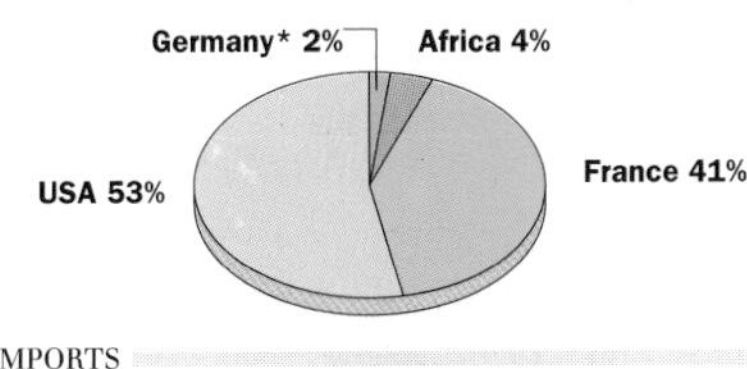

IMPORTS

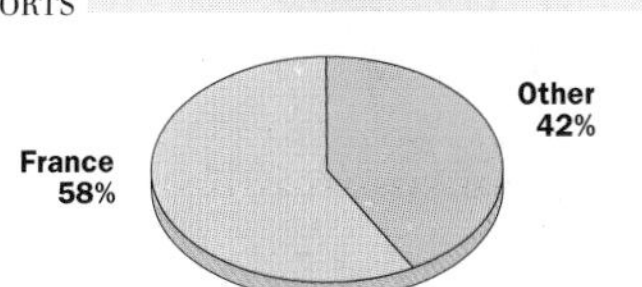

RESOURCES

16m kwh (capacity 5,000 kw)

Not an oil producer and has no refineries

47,000 cattle, 13,000 sheep, 4,000 asses

None

The Comoros have no strategic resources. An HEP plant is under construction on Nzwani, but there is no prospect of moving away from imports for fuel requirements.

ENVIRONMENT

None

The Comoros are too poor for any major initiatives

The environment is not a major priority in the Comoros; natural disasters, such as the volcanic eruption in 1977 which left 20,000 homeless, are of more immediate concern. The government is promoting tourism and recognizes the long-term commercial value of imposing environmental controls on new developments.

MEDIA

The press had little political independence after the 1990 coup attempt, but since then, the situation has slowly been improving

PUBLISHING AND BROADCAST MEDIA

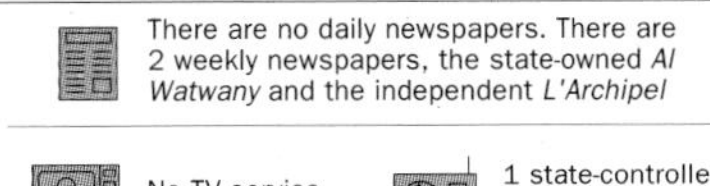

There are no daily newspapers. There are 2 weekly newspapers, the state-owned *Al Watwany* and the independent *L'Archipel*
No TV service
1 state-controlled service

There is currently a shift toward liberalization. The French government has announced that it will fund the establishment of a TV station.

CRIME

The Comoros do not publish prison figures

The general trend is up

Although the judiciary can arbitrate where the government is accused of malpractice, some members of opposition groups have been arrested and imprisoned on political grounds.

EDUCATION

48%

The education system does not extend beyond secondary level. Schools are equipped to teach only basic literacy, hygiene and agricultural techniques. Pupil-teacher ratios are high.

CHRONOLOGY

The Comoros was ruled by matrilineally inherited sultanates until shortly before becoming a French protectorate in 1886.

- ❑ **1912** Proclaimed a French colony.
- ❑ **1961** Internal self-government.
- ❑ **1975** July: Independence. Mayotte votes to remain French. August: President Abdallah overthrown in coup.
- ❑ **1978** Mercenaries led by Bob Denard restore Abdallah to power.
- ❑ **1989** Abdallah assassinated. Saïd Mohamend Djohar named interim president.
- ❑ **1990** Djohar elected president.
- ❑ **1992** September: Pro-Abdallah coup is put down. November: First multiparty elections are chaotic and boycotted by UDZIMA and UNDC.

HEALTH

1 per 12,237 people

Malaria, infectious intestinal and bacterial diseases

Health care is rudimentary; loans have been used to construct two maternity clinics and renovate 30 health centers.

WEALTH

Virtually the whole population live close to the poverty line

CONSUMER GOODS OWNERSHIP

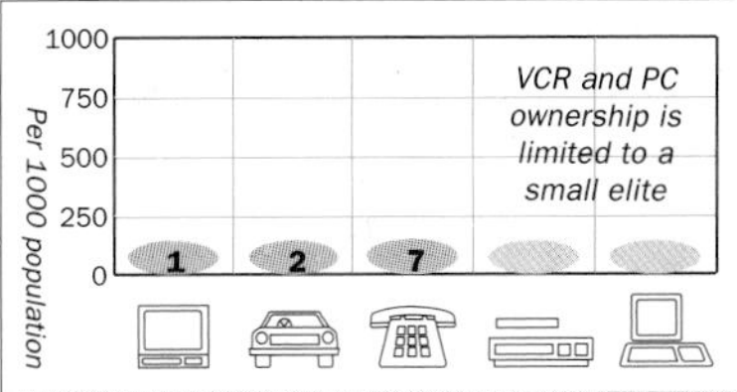

Wealth is concentrated among the political and business elite; most of the population live at subsistence level.

WORLD RANKING

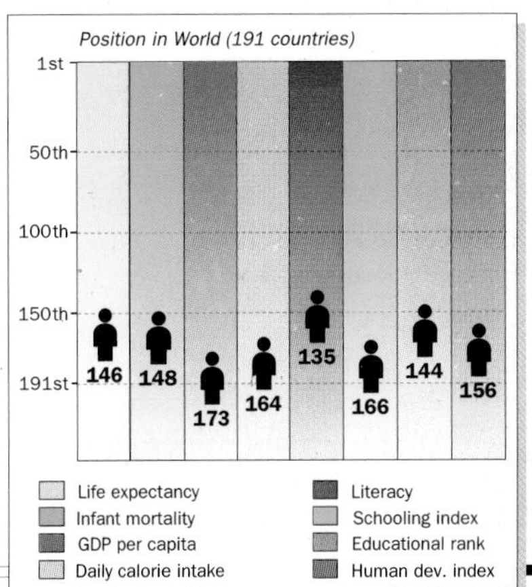

CONGO

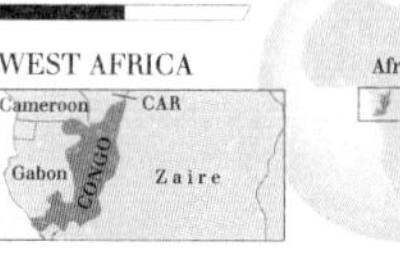

OFFICIAL NAME: The Republic of the Congo **CAPITAL:** Brazzaville
POPULATION: 2.4 million **CURRENCY:** CFA franc **OFFICIAL LANGUAGE:** French

C

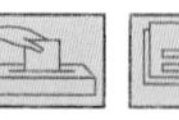

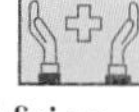

STRADDLING THE EQUATOR in west central Africa, the area now covered by the Congo was first inhabited by Bantu-speaking peoples in the 15th century. In the 1880s it became a French colony, achieving independence in 1960. Rich in oil reserves, the Congo is now emerging from two decades of Marxist-Leninist rule.

CLIMATE

WEATHER CHART

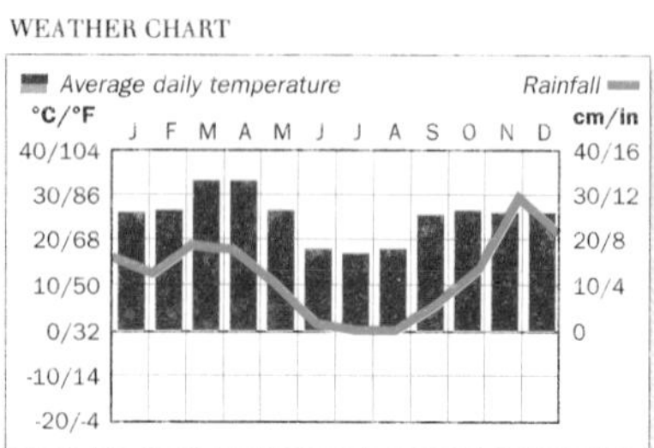

In most years there are two wet seasons and two dry seasons. Rainfall is heaviest in the coastal regions south of the equator.

COMMUNICATIONS

Brazzaville International Has no fleet

THE TRANSPORTATION NETWORK

5,226 miles (8,410 km)	None
498 miles (801 km)	2,725 miles (4,385 km)

The Congo aims to maintain its entrepôt position linking the Central African Republic, Chad and Cameroon with the Atlantic coast. The Congo Ocean Railway runs from Brazzaville to the major port of Pointe-Noire.

TOURISM

39,000 visitors Little change from year to year

MAIN OVERSEAS ARRIVALS

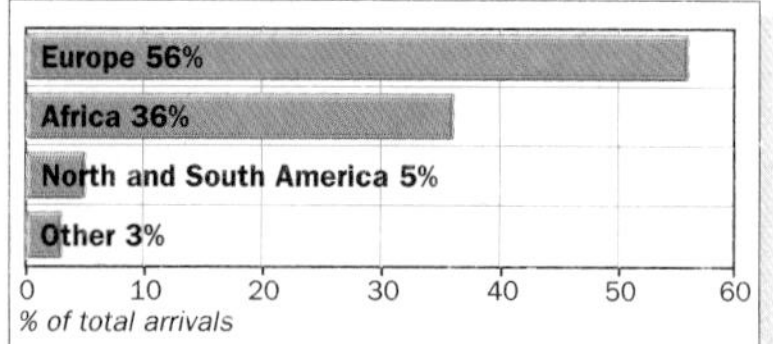

The Marxist-Leninist regime did not seek to develop tourism, and visitors, mostly on safaris and business-related trips, are still rare.

The Loufoulakari Falls, near Brazzaville. Swamps and mangroves border many of the rivers in the Congo's northern region.

PEOPLE

Kongo, Teke, Lingala, French 18 people per sq. mile

THE URBAN/RURAL POPULATION SPLIT

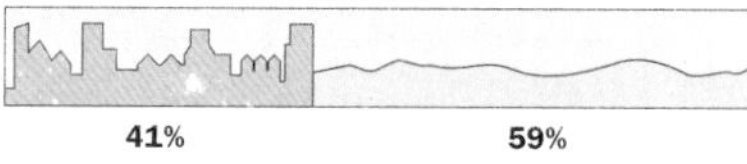

41% 59%

ETHNIC MAKEUP

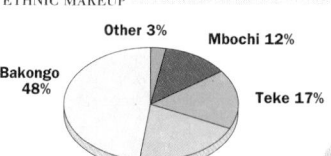

Other 3%
Mbochi 12%
Bakongo 48%
Teke 17%
Sangha 20%

The Congo is one of the most tribally conscious countries in Africa. The main tensions are between the Bakongo, who live in the north, and the Mbochi, concentrated in the more prosperous south. Since the 1950s, women have achieved considerable emancipation.

POLITICS

Lower House 1998
Upper House 1998
President Pascal Lissouba

THE STATE OF THE PARTIES

National Assembly 125 members

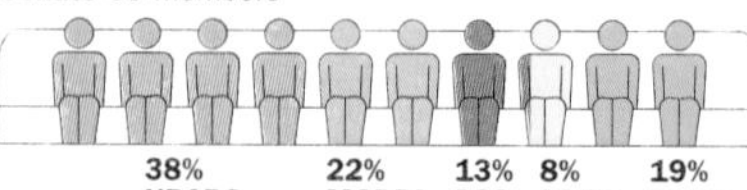

38% UPADS **22% MCDDI** **12% CLP** **8% RDPS** **20% Other**

UPADS = Pan-African Union for Social Democracy **MCDDI** = Congolese Movement for Democracy and Integral Development **CLP** = Congolese Labor Party **RDPS** = Rally for Democratic and Social Progress **RDD** = Rally for Democracy and Development

Senate 60 members

38% UPADS **22% MCDDI** **13% RDD** **8% RDPS** **19% Other**

In 1990, the Congo renounced Marxism. A multiparty constitution was introduced, and legislative and presidential elections were held in 1992. Parties were deadlocked and, in June 1993, President Lissouba called new elections. The results were disputed, but Lissouba's UPADS party won rerun elections.

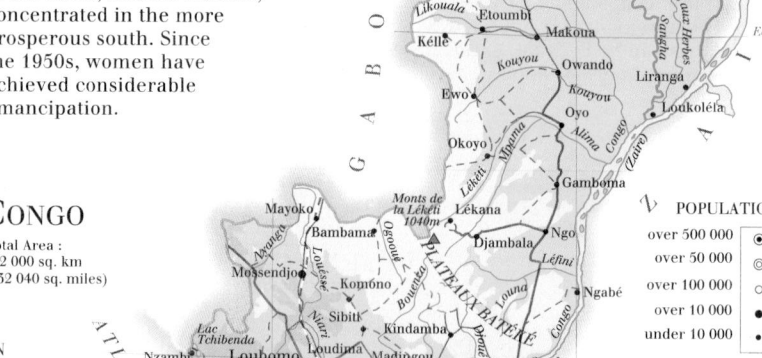

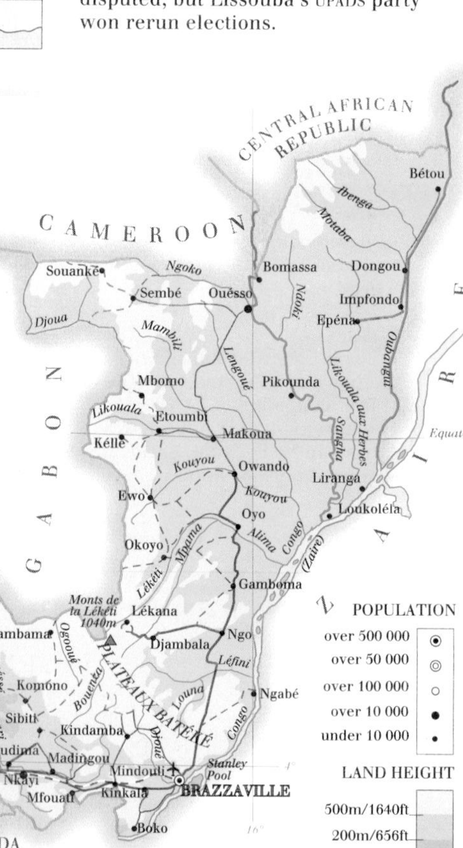

C

WORLD AFFAIRS

Carefully balancing its relations with France and the USA is a priority. Both wish to gain control of the oil industry.

The Congo is eager to maintain the ties developed during the 1970s and 1980s with what was then the communist world. Relations with Eastern Europe, the former Soviet Union, Cuba and particularly China remain strong.

AID

 $133m (receipts)

 Down 38% in 1991

Before 1990, the USSR, Cuba and China were the major donors. Most aid now comes from France. High levels of 1970s debt mean that, despite its oil, the Congo remains dependent on aid.

DEFENSE

 $100.5m

 Fairly stable from year to year

The army backed democratization in 1991, but made sure that its own relatively large numbers (10,000) and budgets were maintained. Although small, the air force is well equipped, with 20 MiG-17s and 12 MiG-21s.

ECONOMICS

 $2.6bn

 276.26 CFA francs

SCORE CARD

- ❑ WORLD GNP RANKING........................133rd
- ❑ GNP PER CAPITA $1,010
- ❑ BALANCE OF PAYMENTS....................$-210m
- ❑ INFLATION ....-5%
- ❑ UNEMPLOYMENT....Widespread underemployment

STRENGTHS

Oil has increased in importance, now providing 90% of export revenues compared with 5% in 1970. Significant timber supplies. Skilled and well-trained workforce helps sustain substantial industrial base in the capital and Pointe-Noire.

WEAKNESSES

$4 billion debt by the late 1980s. Top-heavy bureaucracy inherited from Marxist years. Over-dependence on oil.

EXPORTS

IMPORTS

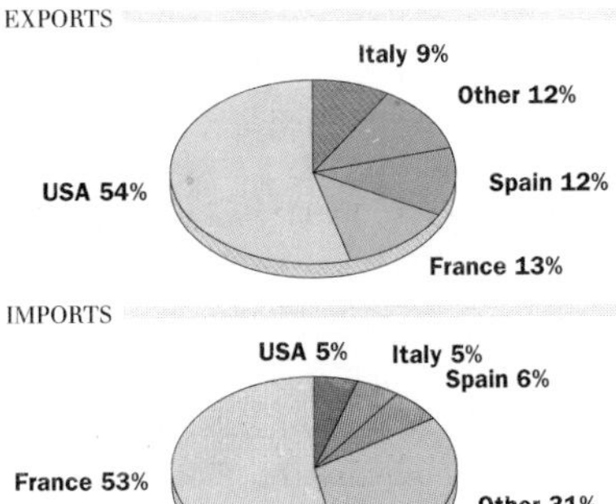

RESOURCES

 398m kwh (capacity 149,000 kw)

 185,100 b/d (reserves 830,000,000 bbl)

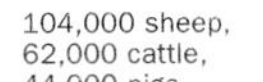 104,000 sheep, 62,000 cattle, 44,000 pigs

Oil, natural gas, bauxite, iron

Oil is by far the Congo's most important resource. Natural gas reserves have yet to be exploited; the oil industry currently flares excess gas. Bauxite and iron ore reserves are not large enough to be profitably mined and phosphate production was abandoned in 1977. Chinese aid has helped build two hydroelectric dams, on the Bouenza and Djoué rivers. A third is currently being built on the Léfini at Imboulou.

ENVIRONMENT

 4% partially protected

 Still no effective controls on deforestation

There is increasing concern about the uncontrolled exploitation of tropical timber. The Congo has also been used in the past as a dumping ground for dangerous toxic waste from the West.

MEDIA

 In theory all censorship restrictions have been lifted. However, occasional acts of censorship and press intimidation are still reported

PUBLISHING AND BROADCAST MEDIA

 There are 2 daily newspapers, *Mweti* and *Aujourd'hui*

 1 state-owned service

 1 state-owned service

During the Second World War, *Radio Brazzaville* was a vital organ of De Gaulle's Free French. Satellite links mean *Canal France Internationale* TV will soon be available.

CRIME

 The Congo does not publish prison figures

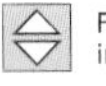 Fairly constant in last 5 years

Armed robbery and smuggling are the major problems. The state's human rights record has improved since the Marxist-Leninist secret police years.

EDUCATION

 57%

Originally pioneered by French Catholic missions, schools are still subject to inspection from Paris.

CHRONOLOGY

The kingdoms of Teke and Loango were incorporated as the Middle Congo (part of French Equatorial Africa) between 1880 and 1883.

- ❑ **1960** Independence. Former priest Fulbert Youlou president.
- ❑ **1964** Marxist-Leninist National Revolution Movement (MNR) becomes only legal party.
- ❑ **1977** President Ngoumbi assassinated. Martial law declared; Yhompi-Opango head of state.
- ❑ **1979** Col. Denis Sassou-Nguesso president.
- ❑ **1990** Return to multiparty democracy.
- ❑ **1992** Elections. Pascal Lissouba (former geneticist) president.
- ❑ **1993** In elections, Lissouba's UPADS party gains majority.

HEALTH

 1 per 4,334 people

 Diarrheal, parasitic and respiratory diseases, malaria

The health service, established by French military doctors at the turn of the century, is considered effective.

WEALTH

 Wage rates among the Congo's middle class are higher than in most African countries

CONSUMER GOODS OWNERSHIP

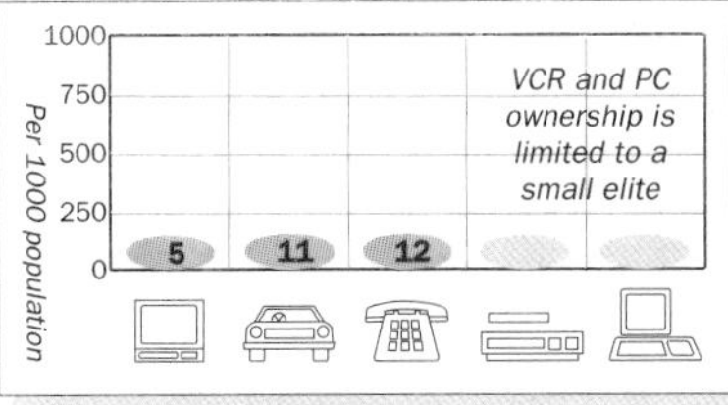

Oil has sustained an active and confident middle class. French label products are seen as status symbols.

WORLD RANKING

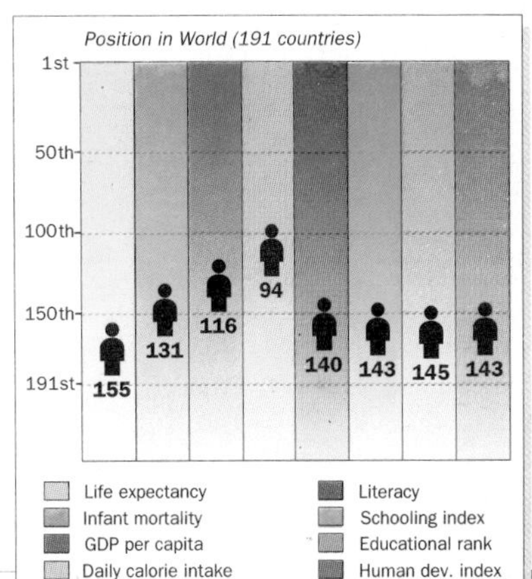

Costa Rica

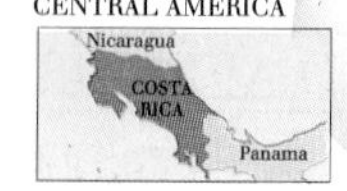

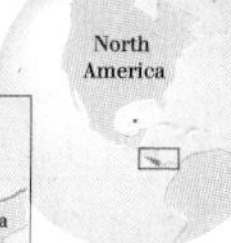

Official Name: The Republic of Costa Rica **Capital:** San José
Population: 3.2 million **Currency:** Costa Rican colón **Official Language:** Spanish

C

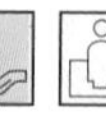

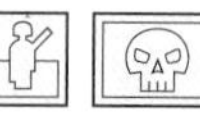

Located in Central America between Nicaragua and Panama, Costa Rica gained independence from Spain in 1821. From 1948 until the end of the 1980s, it was the most developed welfare state in Central America. Costa Rica is a multiparty democracy gradually moving toward a two-party system. Coffee and bananas are the major exports. Its constitution is the only one in the world to forbid national armies; its own was abolished in 1949.

CLIMATE

WEATHER CHART

Average daily temperature
Rainfall
°C/°F
cm/in
J F M A M J J A S O N D
40/104 30/86 20/68 10/50 0/32 -10/14 -20/4
40/16 30/12 20/8 10/4 0

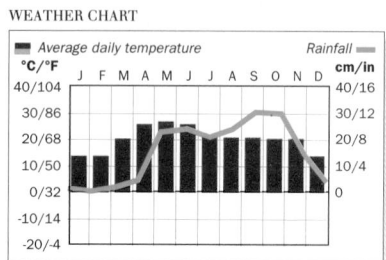

The Atlantic coast has heavy rainfall, while the Pacific coast is much drier. The central uplands are temperate.

COMMUNICATIONS

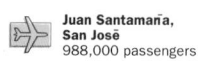

Juan Santamaría, San José
988,000 passengers

4 ships
2,700 dwt

THE TRANSPORTATION NETWORK

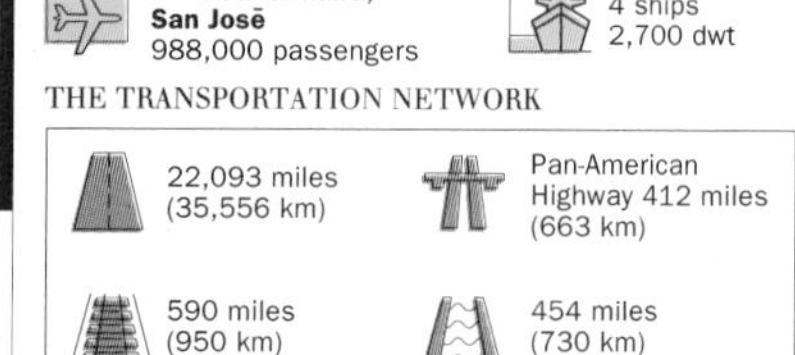

The government is reviving the "Jungle Train" railroad line for tourists. The rest of the network has closed.

TOURISM

988,000 visitors

MAIN OVERSEAS ARRIVALS

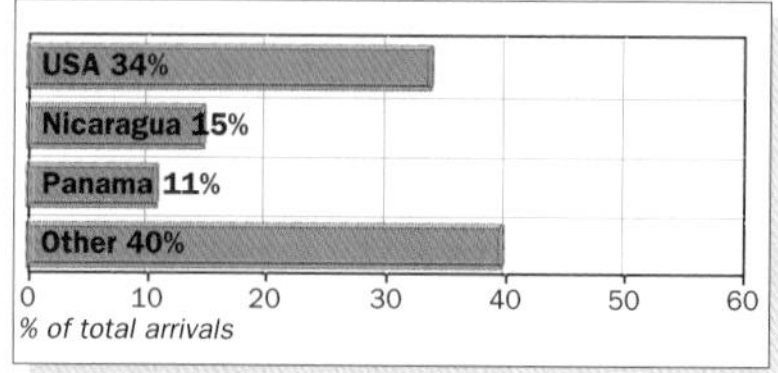

Well-organized government promotions and a reputation for being the only violence-free country in Central America have helped to increase tourist numbers considerably in recent years. Costa Rica attracts many bird-watchers.

PEOPLE

Spanish, English Creole, Bribri, Cabecar

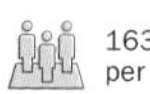

163 people per sq. mile

THE URBAN/RURAL POPULATION SPLIT

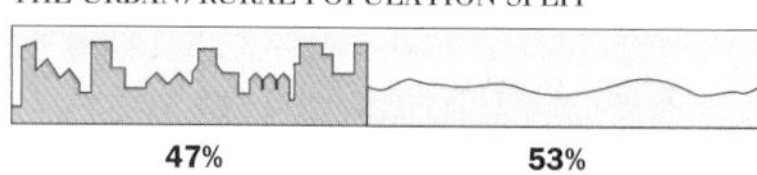

RELIGIOUS PERSUASION

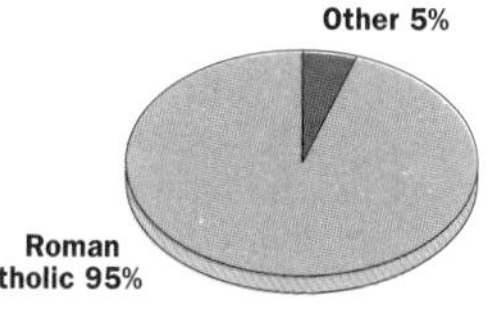

The majority of the population is *mestizo*, of Spanish origin. One-third of people in the Puerto Limón area are black and often English-speaking. There are only about 5,000 indigenous Indians.

POLITICS

THE STATE OF THE PARTIES

Legislative Assembly 57 members

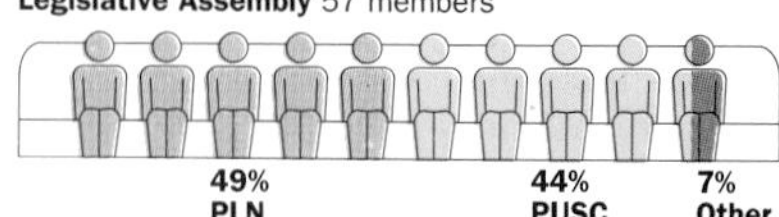

PLN = National Liberation Party **PUSC** = Social Christian Unity Party **Other** = General Union Party, Popular Front, Farmers of Cartaginesa Action

Employees of Costa Rica's extensive bureaucracy tend to belong to one of the two main parties – the PUSC or the PLN. This strengthens the parties' grip on power. Former president Luis Alberto Monge of the PLN, the Calderón family which supports the PUSC, and the major banana and coffee families are powerful behind the scenes, forming coalitions and shaping policies. The USA exercises a very powerful influence on politics. The PLN held power from 1982 until 1990, when Rafael Calderón was elected president. The general elections saw five parties, including the Communist Party, almost disappear from the political scene, and confirmed Costa Rica's movement toward a PUSC-PLN two-party state. These two parties competed, on the basis of similar economic policies, in the 1994 elections which were won by President José María Figueres of the PLN.

WORLD AFFAIRS

Costa Rica has always emphasized its neutrality in foreign affairs, but it has very strong ties with the USA. The protection of export prices for coffee and bananas is a major concern. Costa Rica has long-term aspirations to join NAFTA.

NICARAGUA
CARIBBEAN SEA
PACIFIC OCEAN
PANAMA
La Cruz
Los Chiles
San Juan
Upala
San Rafael
Liberia
Bagaces
Tilarán
Filadelfia
Tempisque
Cañas
Puerto Viejo
Santa Cruz
Quesada
Nicoya
Juntas
Guápiles
Guácimo
Hojancha
Zarcero
San Ramón
Siquirres
Matina
Carmona
Alajuela
Heredia
Puntarenas
SAN JOSÉ
Limón
Paquera
Orotina
Turrialba
Península de Nicoya
Cartago
Paraíso
San Marcos
Jacó
Santa María
Parrita
Bribri
Cerro Chirripó Grande 3819m
Quepos
San Isidro
CORDILLERA DE TALAMANCA
Buenos Aires
Cortés
Palmar
Golfito
San Vito
Neily
Península de Osa
Isla del Coco
0 5 km
0 5 miles
N

Costa Rica

Total Area : 51 100 sq. km (19 730 sq. miles)

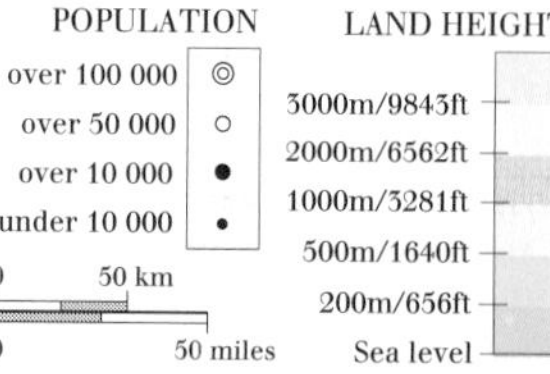

Pineapple plantation near Buenos Aires, *crossed by Pan-American Highway which runs for 411 miles through Costa Rica.*

AID

 $173m (receipts)  Down 24% in 1991

Costa Rica received $150 million in aid a year throughout the 1980s, principally from the USA. However, this was sharply reduced in 1990 after the signing of peace agreements in the region's war-torn countries. The USA sees Costa Rica as a useful base against potential left-wing insurgencies in neighboring El Salvador, Guatemala and Nicaragua.

DEFENSE

 No armed forces; security forces exist  Not applicable

The last period of violence was the 1948 civil war, from which Costa Rica emerged as a neutral, demilitarized modern state. The 7,500-strong National Guard, together with an anti-terrorist battalion of 750 men, are the only security forces, and have little political influence. Spending on security is the lowest in the region. Costa Rica's defense goal is to maintain a neutral line by keeping out of any Central American conflicts.

ECONOMICS

 $6.3bn  147.30 colones

SCORE CARD

- ❑ WORLD GNP RANKING........................101st
- ❑ GNP PER CAPITA............................$1,969
- ❑ BALANCE OF PAYMENTS....................$-432m
- ❑ INFLATION....................................29.3%
- ❑ UNEMPLOYMENT................................5.5%

EXPORTS

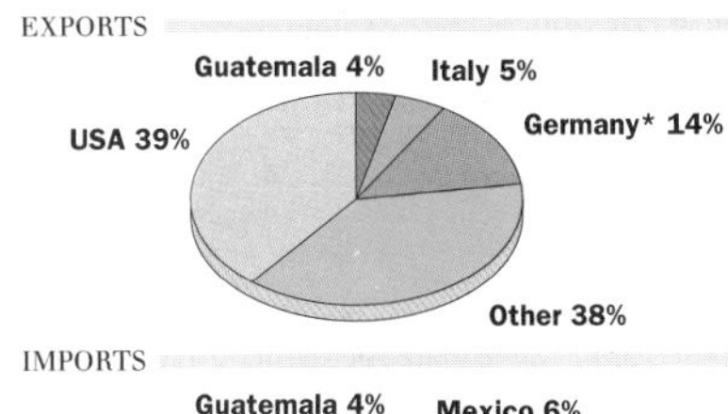

IMPORTS

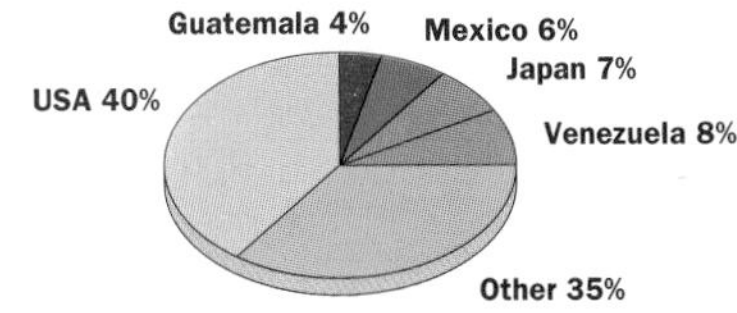

STRENGTHS
Traditional coffee industry still creates largest export revenues. Tourism continuing to grow because of political stability. Government privatization program has lowered costs and encouraged competition.

WEAKNESSES
Main exports of coffee, beef and especially bananas have been hit by falling international prices. Drop of 15% in banana exports due to EU quotas on non-Caribbean bananas. Dependent on imported oil. National economy too small to provide rapid growth; need for regional economic integration.

RESOURCES

 3.6bn kwh (capacity 933,000 kw)  Not an oil producer; refines 15,000 b/cd

 1.7m cattle, 223,000 pigs, 114,000 horses — Bauxite, gold, silver, manganese, mercury

Costa Rica has large bauxite deposits at Boruca – aluminum smelting is an important industry. Small quantities of gold, silver, manganese and mercury are also mined. Self-sufficiency in energy is being pursued through the development of hydroelectric power. Forests cover 34% of the country.

ENVIRONMENT

 12% (3% partially protected)  Monteverde Cloud Forest is an example of a well-run reserve

The remaining rainforests are slowly being cut down to make way for commercial agriculture. The government, however, is beginning to protect land by designating national parks. Ecotourism is being encouraged, as is the sensitive exploitation of natural resources.

MEDIA

 Journalists are supposed to join *Colegio*, a state-run trade union, effectively run by the government

PUBLISHING AND BROADCAST MEDIA

There are 4 daily newspapers, *La Nación, La República, La Prensa Libre* and *Extra*

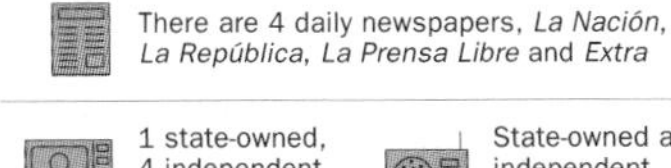

There are four private TV stations providing round-the-clock programming direct from the USA.

CRIME

 Costa Rica does not publish prison figures  Up 3% in 1990

Costa Rica is the least violent Central American country. Crime is mostly petty theft, although there is concern over increasing drug-trafficking. Its human rights record is better than that of neighboring states. The police show some hostility toward refugees, mostly from Nicaragua and El Salvador.

CHRONOLOGY

Costa Rica, ruled since the 16th century by Spain, gained independence in 1821.

- ❑ **1948** Disputed elections lead to civil war; ended by Social Democratic Party (later known as the PLN) forming provisional government under José Ferrer.
- ❑ **1949** Ferrer abolishes army.
- ❑ **1987** Central American Peace Plan initiated by President Arias.

EDUCATION

 93%

Schooling is based on the French system. The regional University of Central America is based in Costa Rica.

HEALTH

 1 per 1,205 people  Heart disease, stomach cancer, perinatal deaths

The public health system is one of the most developed in Latin America. The private system is noted as a regional center for plastic surgery.

WEALTH

 Agricultural worker, 16,661 colones per month; construction worker, 23,319 colones per month

CONSUMER GOODS OWNERSHIP

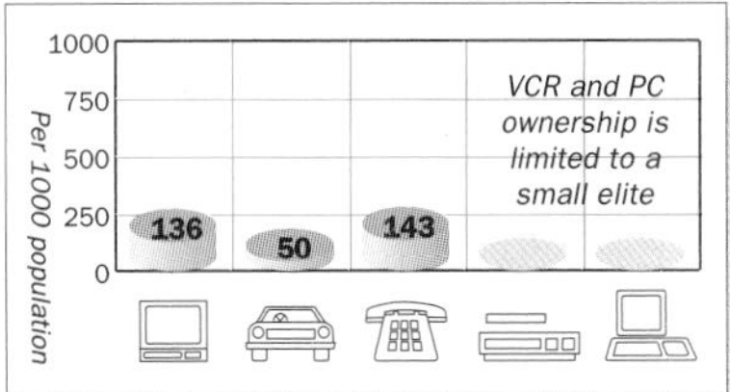

The plantation-owning families are the wealthiest group; the blacks on the Caribbean coast are the poorest.

WORLD RANKING

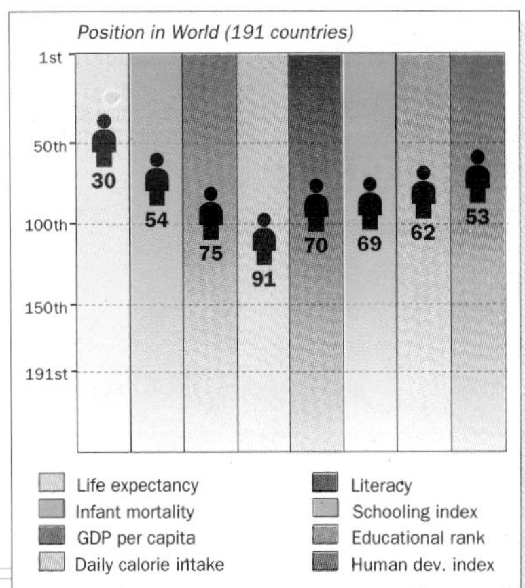

C

CROATIA

OFFICIAL NAME: Republic of Croatia **CAPITAL:** Zagreb
POPULATION: 4.8 million **CURRENCY:** Kuna **OFFICIAL LANGUAGE:** Croatian

EUROPE
Europe
Hungary
Slovenia
CROATIA
Bosnia & Herzegovina
Yugoslavia

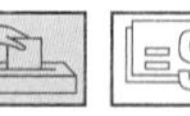

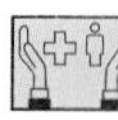

LOCATED TO THE SOUTH OF Slovenia and west of Serbia, Croatia includes the historic regions of Istra, Dalmatia and Slavonia. Croatia's Adriatic coastline is vitally important for tourism and shipping, which have been major contributors to the economy. Since the dissolution of the Federal Republic of Yugoslavia in 1990-1991, Croatia has been involved in warfare in Bosnia and Herzegovina and in defending its own territory. One-third of Croatia is held by Serbian troops.

CLIMATE

WEATHER CHART

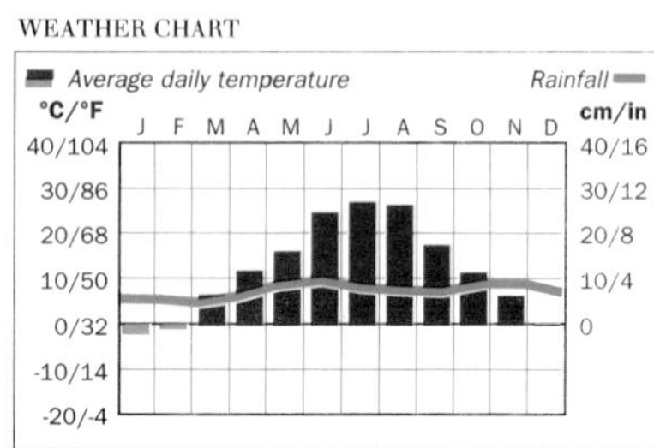

Northern Croatia has a temperate continental climate. Its Adriatic coast has a Mediterranean climate.

COMMUNICATIONS

Pleso International, Zagreb

85 ships
184,000 dwt

THE TRANSPORTATION NETWORK

17,012 miles (27,378 km)

188 miles (302 km)

1,507 miles (2,425 km)

Islands are linked to the mainland by ferries

Communications in Serb-dominated Krajina and Slavonia were badly affected by fighting in 1991–1992. In 1993, Croats regained control of the Maslenica Bridge, a vital link between northern Croatia and Dalmatia.

TOURISM

630,000 visitors in 1991

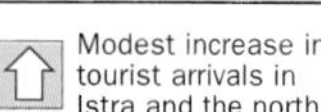
Modest increase in tourist arrivals in Istra and the north

MAIN OVERSEAS ARRIVALS

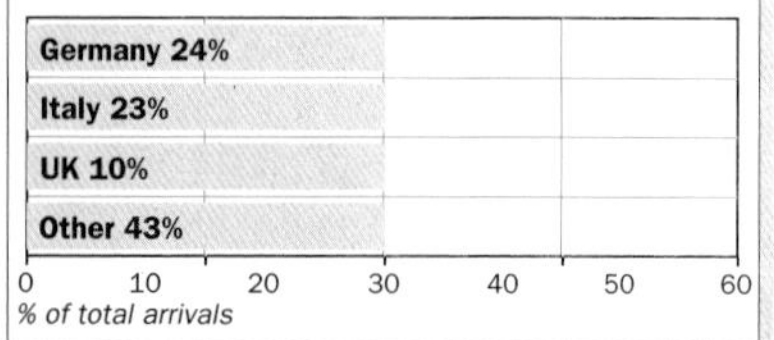

Croatia's seaside resorts, particularly in northern Istra, are leading a modest recovery of the tourist industry.

PEOPLE

Croatian

210 people per sq. mile

THE URBAN/RURAL POPULATION SPLIT

51%

49%

RELIGIOUS PERSUASION

Slavic Muslim 1%
Others 10%
Protestant 1%
Orthodox Catholic 11%
Roman Catholic 77%

Croats make up 80% of the population, Serbs 12%. In 1990 the Serbs, alienated by Croatian nationalism, pressed for autonomy in the areas where they formed a majority, notably Krajina, Baranja, Western Srem and Slavonia. Independence brought the Serb-dominated federal army (JNA) into Croatia, in defense of the Serbs. Conflict erupted in 1992, particularly in Slavonia in eastern Croatia. The 1993 UN-brokered ceasefire led the JNA to withdraw, but the peace was broken by a Croat attack on Serb-held Krajina in late 1993.

POLITICS

1996

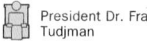

President Dr. Franjo Tudjman

THE STATE OF THE PARTIES

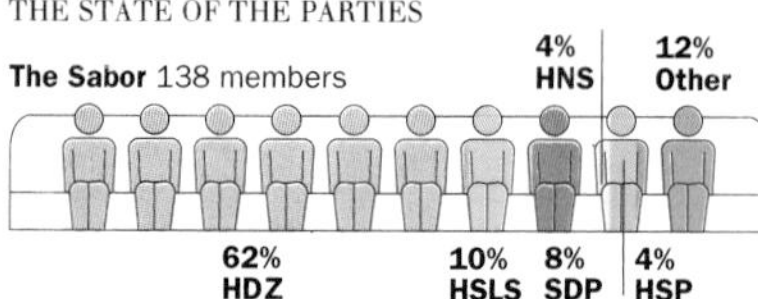

HDZ = Christian Democratic Union **HSLS** = Croatian Social Liberal Party **SDP** = Party of Democratic Change **HNS** = Croatian National Party **HSP** = Croatian Party of Rights **Others** = Croatian Peasant Party, Serbian National Party, Independents, Regional Parties

With the breakup of former Yugoslavia, the Croatian independence movement was led by the right-wing Croatian Democratic Union (HDZ) under Franjo Tudjman. Multiparty elections in 1992 consolidated the HDZ's hold on power. It gained a majority in parliament and Tudjman was elected president. The main political issues remain the status of Serb-held territory in Croatia, and the status of Croats in Bosnia. The agreement to form a Croat and Muslim federation in Bosnia signifies a major policy change by Serbia, with the emphasis now on a political, rather than a military, approach. The HDZ has also begun to address the issue of autonomy for Serbs in Croatia. In early 1994, the Russians were attempting to arrange a ceasefire between Croatian armed forces and the Serbian stronghold of Kradjina.

WORLD AFFAIRS

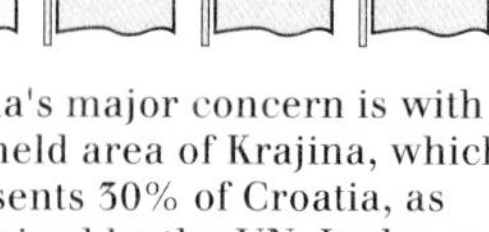

Croatia's major concern is with the Serb-held area of Krajina, which represents 30% of Croatia, as recognized by the UN. It also contains key infrastructural links between Zagreb and Dalmatia. The HDZ and the EU have stated that any peace agreement on the former Yugoslavia must include a satisfactory settlement of the Krajina problem.

The creation in March 1994 of a binational Muslim-Croat federation in Bosnia was widely recognized as a major foreign policy success for President Franjo Tudjman.

AID

$500m (est)

Aid levels have increased

Croatia has been a major target of UNHCR and bilateral humanitarian aid. It has an estimated 526,000 refugees from Bosnia and Serb-held areas in Croatia. The main UNHCR warehouses are in Zagreb, Split and Rijeka.

DEFENSE

Government spends one-third of budget on defense

Defense spending rose by 30% in 1992

Croatia has about 95,000 army, 4,000 navy and 4,000 air force personnel. In addition, the Croat Defense Association (HOS) has about 10,000 armed men in Bosnia. The army tried unsuccessfully to recapture Serb-held Krajina in September 1993. The air force is suspected of breaking the UN-imposed "No-Fly" zone in Bosnia.

ECONOMICS

8.3bn

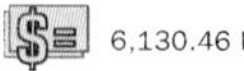 6,130.46 kuna

SCORE CARD

❑ WORLD GNP RANKING	88th
❑ GNP PER CAPITA	$1,789
❑ BALANCE OF PAYMENTS	$-536m
❑ INFLATION	122.6%
❑ UNEMPLOYMENT	17%

STRENGTHS

Tourism recovering in safe areas. Exports to the West growing. Economy well placed to expand in peacetime.

WEAKNESSES

Economic reform held up by outdated infrastructure. Costs of repairing war damage. Refugees an economic strain.

EXPORTS/IMPORTS

Before the conflict, Croatia's main trading partners were the former Yugoslavian republics, Italy and Germany

***Dubrovnik, Dalmatia.** This historic city on the Adriatic coast was shelled and besieged by the Yugoslav federal army in 1991.*

RESOURCES

 8,531bn kwh

 Oil production affected by loss of some fields to Serbia

17.1m poultry, 1.6m pigs, 829,000 cattle

 Coal, bauxite, iron, oil, china clay, natural gas

Croatia generates half its energy needs from thermal and half from hydroelectric sources. It has few minerals, although it does have oil and gas fields. The rich fishing grounds of the Adriatic are a major resource.

ENVIRONMENT

 6%

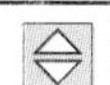 Environmental issues not yet a priority following war

Croatia was the first Yugoslav republic to create reserves in order to protect endangered and unique wetlands.

MEDIA

 The government has extended its influence over the media. The HDZ effectively controls *Hina*, the national news agency

PUBLISHING AND BROADCAST MEDIA

 There are 9 daily newspapers, published locally, including *Vercenji List* in Zagreb and *Slobodna Dalmacija* in Split

 1 state-controlled service

 1 state-controlled service

Inconsistencies in the official media line in war reporting led to enforced guidelines for presenting information.

CRIME

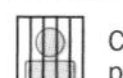 Croatia does not publish prison figures

 Crime has risen since Independence

The Croat militia in Bosnia, the HOS, is suspected of involvement in "ethnic cleansing." The UN has accused all sides in Bosnia of human rights abuses.

CHRONOLOGY

In 1089, Croatia became a vassal of Hungary and then the Habsburgs.

- ❑ **1918-1941** Part of Yugoslavia. Growing Serb-Croat resentment.
- ❑ **1941-1945** Germans install Croat Fascist state. Many Serbs killed.
- ❑ **1945-1991** Croatia a constituent republic in the Yugoslav federation. Nationalism suppressed by state.
- ❑ **1990** HDZ wins republic elections and calls for Croat independence.

EDUCATION

 93%

Croatia has a well-developed education system. It has four universities, at Zagreb, Rijeka, Osijek and Split.

HEALTH

 1 per 436 people

 Cerebrovascular and heart diseases, cancer

Most Croats are covered by a health insurance plan. However, coping with refugees and war casualties poses an extra strain on already scarce funds.

WEALTH

 Standards of living are falling under the government's austerity program

CONSUMER GOODS OWNERSHIP

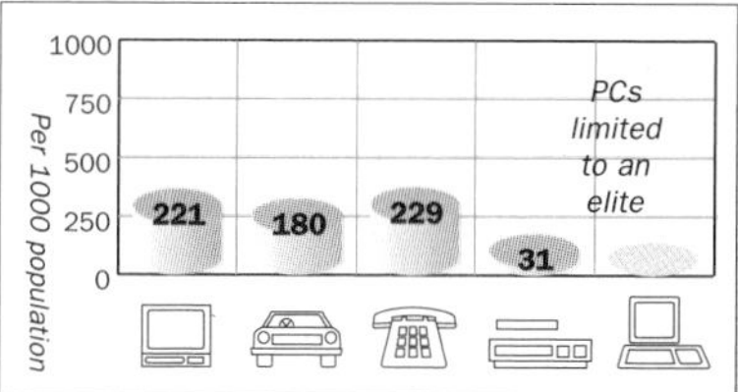

The net monthly wage in Croatia is equal to $149. Many Croatians are finding it difficult to meet basic needs.

WORLD RANKING

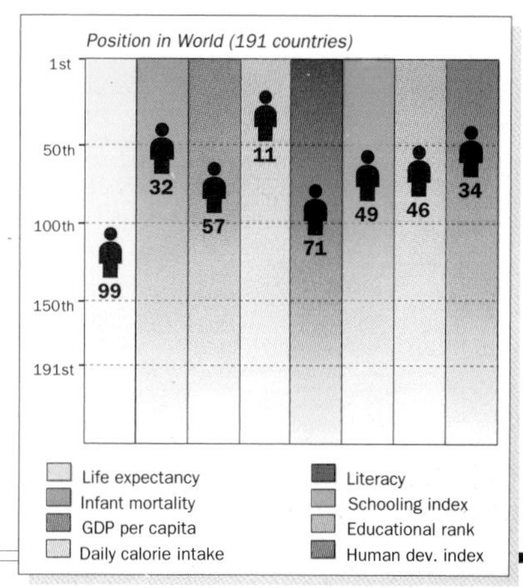

CROATIA

Total Area : 56 540 sq. km (21 830 sq. miles)

LAND HEIGHT: 1000m/3281ft; 500m/1640ft; 200m/656ft; Sea Level

POPULATION: over 500 000; over 100 000; over 50 000; over 10 000; under 10 000

0 50 km / 0 50 miles

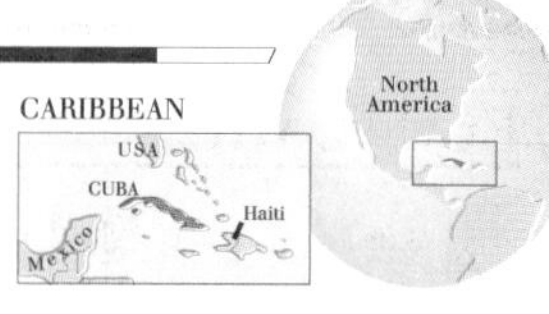

CUBA

OFFICIAL NAME: Republic of Cuba **CAPITAL:** Havana
POPULATION: 10.8 million **CURRENCY:** Cuban peso **OFFICIAL LANGUAGE:** Spanish

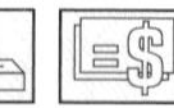

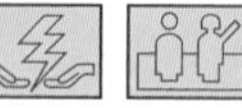

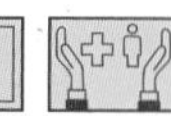

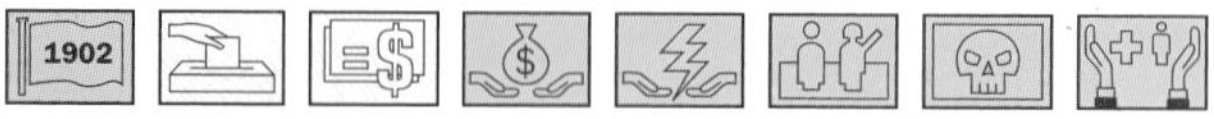

THE CARIBBEAN'S LARGEST ISLAND, Cuba has widely cultivated lowlands, which fall between three mountainous areas. The fertile soil of the lowlands supports the sugar cane, rice and coffee plantations. Sugar, the country's major export, is suffering from depressed world prices. A former Spanish colony, Cuba is the only communist state in the Caribbean. Since the collapse of communism in the Soviet Union, the USA sees Cuba as less of a threat, in marked contrast to 1962, when the Soviet nuclear missiles on the island brought the two superpowers close to war. Cuba is still subject to US sanctions against trade, making it difficult to afford oil imports.

Valle de Viñales, Pinar del Río province. *Cuba's undulating countryside is ideal for growing sugar, the main export crop.*

CLIMATE

WEATHER CHART

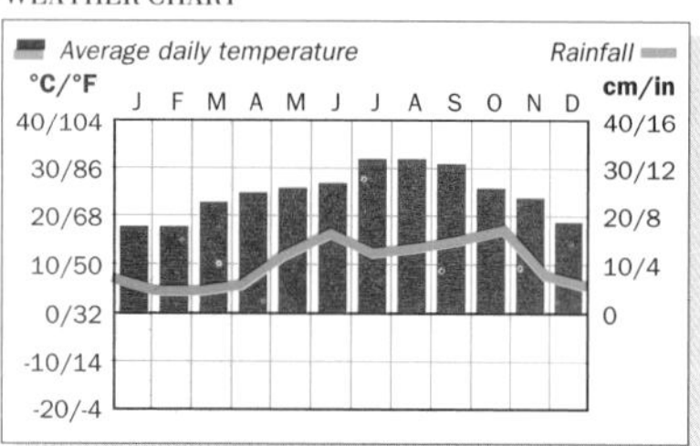

Cuba's subtropical climate is hot all year round and very hot in the summer. Rainfall is heaviest in the mountains, which receive up to 98 inches a year. Generally, the north is wetter than the south; the Guantánamo area receives only 8 inches of rainfall annually. In winter, the west is sometimes affected by cold air from the USA, but only for a day or two at a time.

COMMUNICATIONS

José Martí, Havana
1.2m passengers

85 ships
711,300 dwt

THE TRANSPORTATION NETWORK

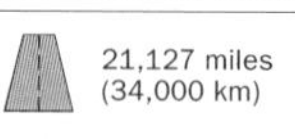

21,127 miles (34,000 km)

357 miles (575 km)

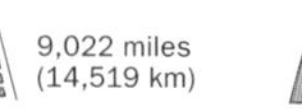

9,022 miles (14,519 km)

149 miles (240 km)

Public transportation has been very cheap in Cuba, although fuel shortages have made it increasingly erratic and unreliable. Cubans rely mostly on traditional black bicycles, which are imported by the thousand from China. Havana owes much of its charm to the number of 40-year-old Chevrolets and Oldsmobiles still being driven around. Although this is another result of sanctions, it keeps the many inventive local spare-parts workshops in business.

TOURISM

424,041 visitors

Up 25% in 1991

MAIN OVERSEAS ARRIVALS

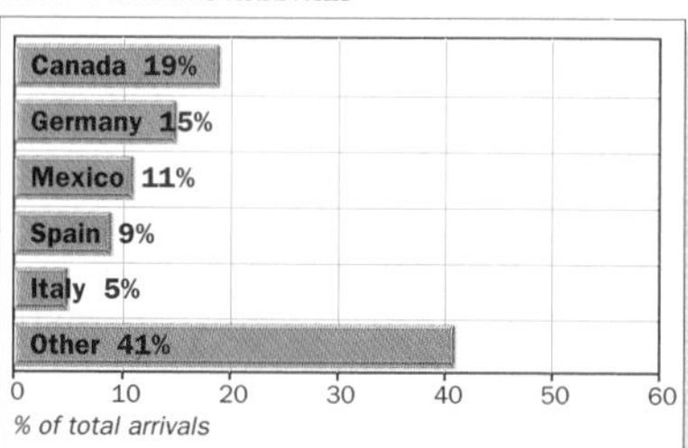

Cuba, once a playground for wealthy Americans, reduced tourism after 1959 as being unfit for a socialist society. Recently the policy has changed. Although most tourist arrivals are from Canada, Germany, Mexico and Spain, some are Americans going via these destinations to skirt the US trade embargo – the Cuban authorities do not stamp US passport holders. About 2,000 affluent Latin American "health-tourists" visit Cuba annually for low-cost, advanced surgery, or to stay at sanatoria.

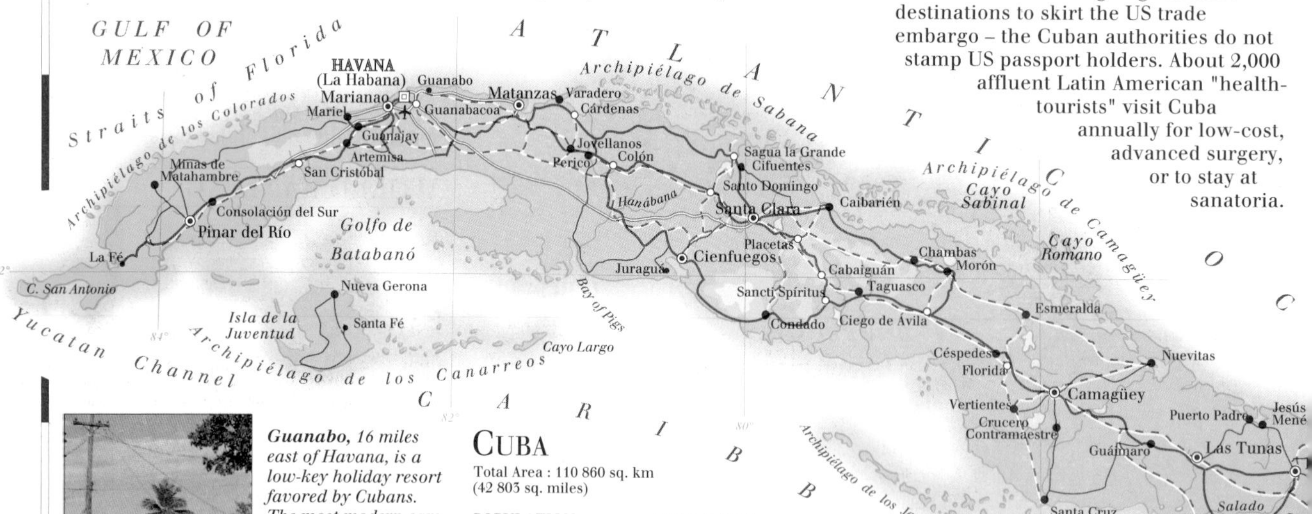

Guanabo, 16 miles east of Havana, is a low-key holiday resort favored by Cubans. The most modern cars in Cuba are imported, along with computers, in exchange for sugar in a special trading deal with Japan.

CUBA

Total Area : 110 860 sq. km (42 803 sq. miles)

POPULATION
- over 1 000 000
- over 500 000
- over 100 000
- over 50 000
- over 10 000
- under 10 000

LAND HEIGHT
- 1000m/3281ft
- 500m/1640ft
- 200m/656ft
- Sea Level

0 50 km
0 50 miles

C

PEOPLE

Spanish

251 people per sq. mile

THE URBAN/RURAL POPULATION SPLIT

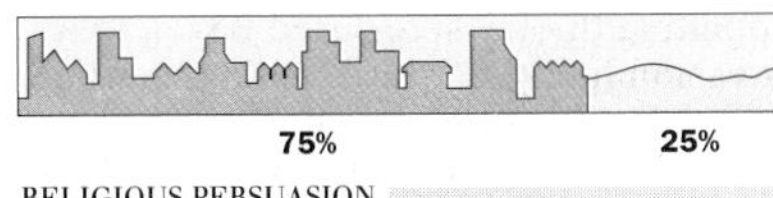

RELIGIOUS PERSUASION

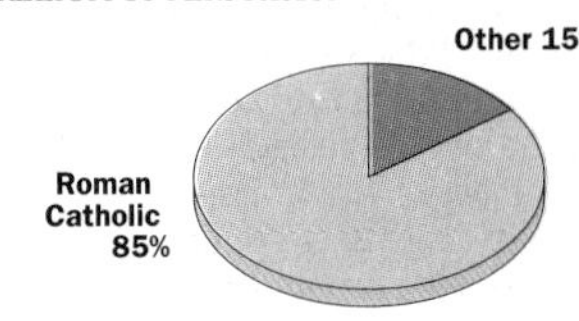

ETHNIC MAKEUP

Chinese 1%
Black 11%
European African 51%
White 37%

Ethnic tension in Cuba is minimal. About 70% of Cubans are of Spanish descent, mainly from the settlers who began arriving in Cuba in the 16th century, but also from the more recent influx of exiles from Franco's Spain. The black population is descended from the slaves and migrants from Cuba's neighboring states, in particular Jamaica.

Living standards in Cuba have fallen dramatically since the collapse of the Eastern European communist bloc, previously its main trading partner. In 1991, further rationing was introduced for most basic foodstuffs; yet in Havana, exotic goods are easily available in the many exclusive dollar stores.

An increasing number of women are playing prominent roles in politics, the military and professional fields. Child-care facilities are freely available and there is a law requiring men to share equally in housework and child-rearing if a wife is working in "social production;" the state, however, does not check how well this law is observed.

POPULATION AGE BREAKDOWN

% of population by age group

	1960	1970	1980	1990	2000
65+	5%	6.1%	7.6%	8.5%	9.4%
15–64	60.8%	56.9%	60.7%	68.8%	67.2%
0–14	34.2%	37%	31.7%	22.7%	23.4%

WORLD AFFAIRS

Since the 1962 stand-off, when Cuba accepted Russian missiles targeted at US cities, Cuba has been considered a danger by the USA and has been subject to diplomatic isolation from countries which support US policies in the Caribbean. The end of aid from Moscow after 1991, following the collapse of the USSR, made conditions in Cuba increasingly difficult. The USA increased pressure on the Castro administration by tightening the rules of the trade embargo, including an effective ban on ships docking in the USA which had been in a Cuban port. Cuba has mustered support in the UN, as well as EU backing, for a lifting of the US embargo, but without effect. The USA has vetoed any UN debate, and will not abandon its stand until Cuba adopts a multiparty democracy.

Iran and the Russian Federation now take most of Cuba's sugar, in exchange for badly needed oil supplies. Iran is now one of Cuba's few supporters worldwide. Trade between the two countries has grown as the Moscow alliance declines in importance.

POLITICS

1998

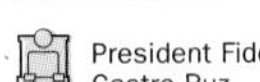
President Fidel Castro Ruz

THE STATE OF THE PARTIES

National Assembly of People's Power 589 members

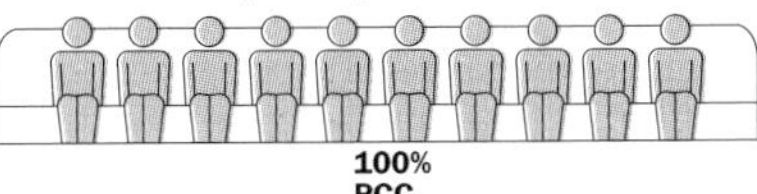

PCC = Cuban Communist Party

Fidel Castro has led Cuba since 1959 and was the founder of the one-party communist system, formalized in the 1976 constitution.

MAIN POLITICAL ISSUES

The succession
Castro has stated his wish to retire from the Council of State when his current term ends in 1998. Contenders for the leadership include his brother Raúl, current defense minister, Roberto Robaina, the foreign minister, and economic guru Carlos Lage. Castro, who has said that the Communist Party must be invigorated with younger minds, is thought to favor Robaina.

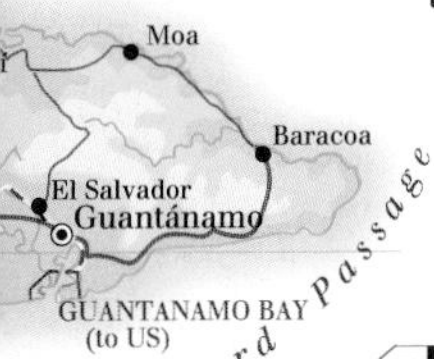

The economy
Cuba chose not to go down the capitalist route when its main patron and supplier, the former USSR, ended aid in 1991. The socialist economy remains in place, although it is increasingly short of supplies and subject to the disabling effects of the US trade embargo.

PROFILE
Cuban politics have always been dominated by the perceived US threat. The party has reacted to the collapse of the USSR by strengthening its dominance, as illustrated by the 1992 imposition of death sentences on several Cuban dissidents. While the USA has tightened economic sanctions as the surest way to end Castro's rule, Castro has increased his powers. Constitutional changes in 1992 gave the president the right to declare a state of emergency and to take full command of the military.

***Raúl Castro**, brother of Fidel and the Minister of Defense.*

***Fidel Castro**, Cuba's leader since 1959. The USA is anxious to oust his regime.*

AID

$42m (receipts)

Up 45% in 1991

Cuba claims to receive no aid, but does receive donations from Spain. Sweden used to be an important donor, but withheld aid payments in 1993 in response to human rights violations by the Castro regime.

CHRONOLOGY

Originally inhabited by the Arawak people, Cuba was claimed by Columbus for Spain in 1492. Development of the sugar industry from the 18th century, using imported slave labor, made Cuba the world's third largest producer by 1860.

- **1868** End of the slave trade.
- **1868–1878** *El Grito de Yara* begins Ten Years' War for independence from Spain.
- **1879–1880** *La Guerra Chiquita.*
- **1895** Second war of independence. Thousands die in Spanish concentration camps.
- **1898** USA declares war on Spain in support of Cuban rebels.
- **1899** USA takes Cuba and installs military interim government.
- **1901** USA is granted intervention rights and military bases, including Guantánamo Bay naval base.

⇨

CHRONOLOGY *continued*

- **1902** Tomás Estrada Palma takes over as first Cuban president. USA leaves Cuba, but intervenes in 1906–1909 and 1919–1924.
- **1909** Liberal presidency of José Miguel Gómez. Economy prospers; US investment in tourism, gambling and sugar.
- **1925–1933** Dictatorship of President Gerardo Machado.
- **1933** Years of guerrilla activity end in revolution. Sergeant Fulgencio Batista takes over and leads military dictatorship.
- **1955** Fidel Castro exiled after two years' imprisonment for subversion.
- **1956–1958** Castro returns to lead a guerrilla war in the Sierra Maestra.
- **1959** Batista flees. Castro takes over; his brother, Raúl, is deputy, Che Guevara third in rank. Wholesale nationalizations; Cuba reorganized on Soviet model.
- **1961** USA breaks off relations. US-backed, anti-Castro Cubans attempt invasion at Bay of Pigs. Fail. Cuba declares itself Marxist-Leninist.
- **1962** US economic and political blockade. Missile crisis in May. Khrushchev agrees to defend Cuba on October 14. US spy planes see nuclear missile on site on October 22. Kennedy orders seizure of weapons on Soviet ships in "quarantine zone." USA prepares for war on October 28. Khrushchev orders return of weapons; November 20. USA lifts "quarantine."
- **1965** Che Guevara resigns to pursue foreign liberation wars. One-party state formalized.
- **1972** Cuba joins COMECON.
- **1976** New socialist constitution. Cuban troops in Angola until 1991.
- **1977** Sends troops to Ethiopia.
- **1980** 125,000 Cubans, including "undesirables" (criminals or people with learning disabilities) flee to USA.
- **1982** USA tightens sanctions and bans flights and tourism to Cuba.
- **1983** US invasion of Grenada. Cuba involved in clashes with US forces.
- **1984** Agreement with USA on Cuban emigration and repatriation of "undesirables" is short-lived.
- **1986** Many government changes, but Soviet-style *glasnost* rejected.
- **1987** Cubans riot in US jails at new repatriation accord.
- **1988** UN's second veto of US attempt to accuse Cuba of human rights violations. Diplomatic relations established with EC.
- **1989** Senior military men executed for arms and drug smuggling.
- **1991** Preferential trade agreement with USSR ends. Severe rationing.
- **1992** USA tightens blockade.
- **1993** All ex-Soviet military leave.

DEFENSE

$1.2bn
Down 15% in 1991
0
Defense spending as % GDP
40
4.5%
CUBAN ARMED FORCES
1,700 main battle tanks (T-54/T-55/T-62)
145,000 personnel
3 submarines, 3 frigates and 28 patrol boats
12,000 personnel
162 combat aircraft (146 MiG); also 200+ SAM launchers
7,000 personnel
None

From 1959 to the 1980s, Cuba's efficient military was one of the achievements of the revolution. Under Castro's brother, Raúl, it succeeded in repelling the US-sponsored Bay of Pigs invasion in 1961. It later took action in Africa in the 1970s, preventing South Africa from taking control of Angola, and Somalia from occupying the Ogaden region. Today, with communist regimes collapsed around the world, it has lost much of its prestige. Russia is still the main supplier of arms and spares, but now has to be paid in increasingly scarce hard currency. In an effort to save money, compulsory military service has been cut from three years to two.

ECONOMICS

$20.9bn   0.76 Cuban pesos

SCORE CARD

- WORLD GNP RANKING..........................64th
- GNP PER CAPITA $1,935
- BALANCE OF PAYMENTS ....In deficit
- INFLATION..High
- UNEMPLOYMENT.................................6%

EXPORTS

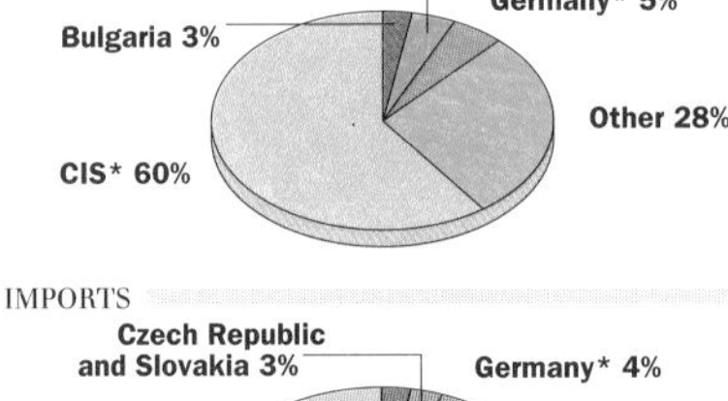

IMPORTS

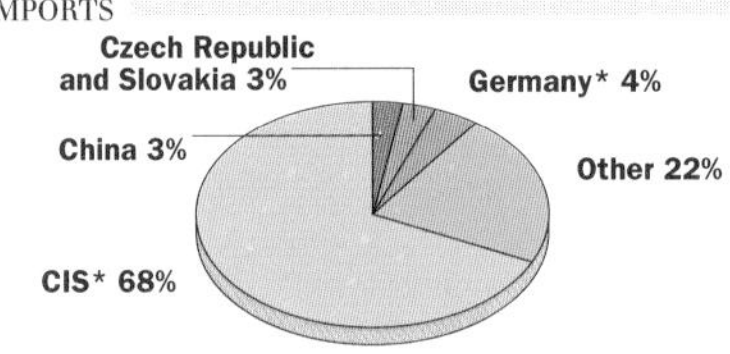

ECONOMIC PERFORMANCE INDICATOR

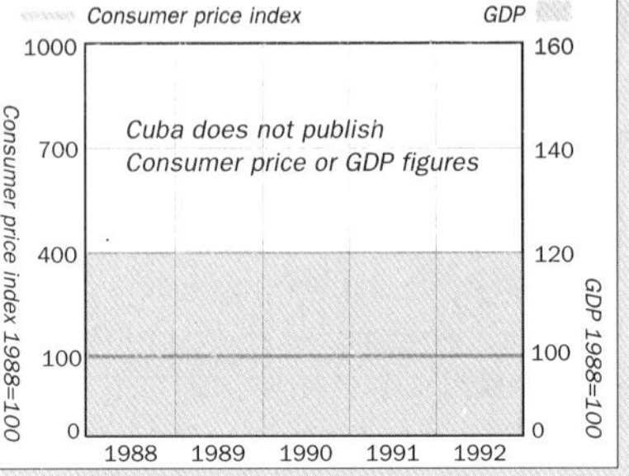

STRENGTHS

A relatively broad base compared with other Caribbean states. Sugar is the main product, followed by nickel, citrus fruits, tobacco and, increasingly, tourism.

WEAKNESSES

US trade embargo robs Cuba of a major market and investment capital; Cuba was once second only to Venezuela in US overseas investment in Latin America. Non-convertible currency is an increasing liability as Russia demands payment for oil in dollars. Loss of ex-communist states as trading partners.

PROFILE

Since 1959, the nationalized economy has oscillated between concentration on sugar and attempts at industrialization. Following a brief experiment in market liberalization, the Castro regime went back to total state control in 1986 – although some moves toward a free market were made in 1993. Since then, the economy has been in recession and is suffering from an acute shortage of fuel, spare parts for the sugar industry and chemicals. Foreign capital is increasingly hard to come by, although Castro is beginning to allow some foreign investment in hotels and tourism. The government is also selling its first oil concessions to foreign companies. The USA is now relying on the regime to collapse with the economy. It is, therefore, unlikely to lift its trade embargo unless Cubans adopt a multiparty democracy and reject Castro.

CUBA : MAJOR BUSINESSES

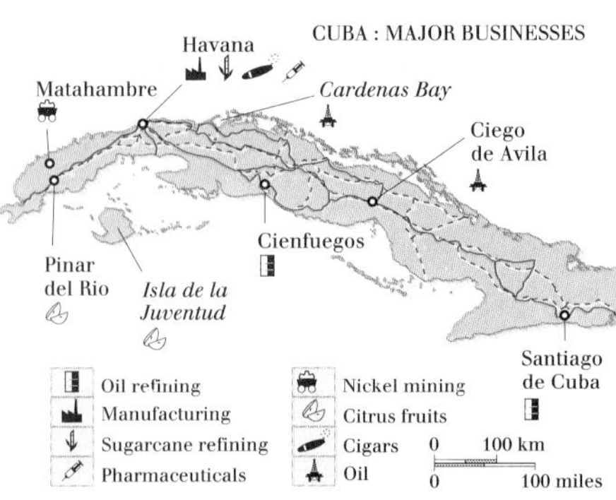

RESOURCES

16.2bn kwh (capacity 4m kw)

15,000 b/d (reserves 100,000,000 bbl)

4.9m cattle, 1.9m pigs, 630,000 horses

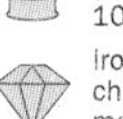
Iron, nickel, cobalt, chromite, gold, manganese, oil

Cuba's major resource is its sugar. Production is the fifth largest in the world and helps to determine international prices. The island also has the world's fourth largest nickel deposits, but lack of investment capital means they are under-exploited and inefficiently worked. Energy policy is aimed at encouraging foreign companies, through profit-sharing agreements, to exploit Cuba's known oil reserves. A Russian-built nuclear reactor was due to be completed in 1995.

ELECTRICITY GENERATION

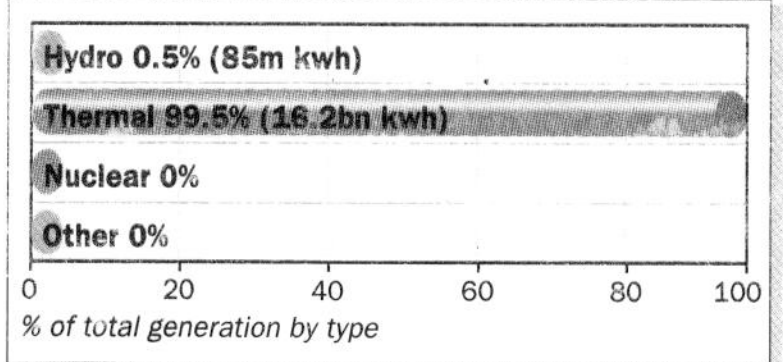

ENVIRONMENT

6% (2% partially protected)

Deforestation rate remains lowest in Latin America

ENVIRONMENTAL TREATIES

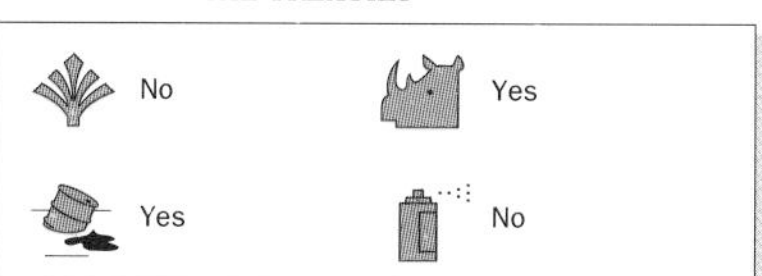

Before the revolution, Cuba had no environmental protection laws at all. At that time, only 14% of its forest cover remained, but a strong drive to replant has raised the tree cover level to 18%. There is concern about a nuclear reactor under construction at Juraguá.

MEDIA

Government censorship; demand for more outspoken media is growing

PUBLISHING AND BROADCAST MEDIA

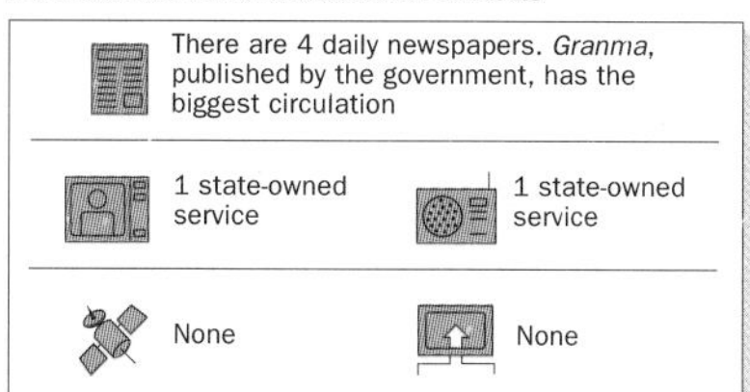

There are 4 daily newspapers. Granma, published by the government, has the biggest circulation
1 state-owned service
1 state-owned service
None
None

The Cuban media is state controlled. Two Florida-based stations, *Radio Martí* and *TV Martí*, financed by the US government, make anti-Castro broadcasts.

CRIME

Cuba does not publish prison figures

Crime is rising

CRIME RATES

Cuba does not publish official statistics for murders, rapes or thefts

Cuba has a low crime rate. Murders are rare and there are few unsafe areas on the island. Political dissent, however, is not tolerated and human rights abuses by the military and police are frequently reported. Occasionally Cuba opens its jails. Petty criminals often flee to the USA as refugees. The Revolutionary Summary Tribunal deals with serious political crimes, as defined by the communist constitution.

EDUCATION

94%

Education spending as % GNP (0–25): 6.6%

THE EDUCATION SYSTEM

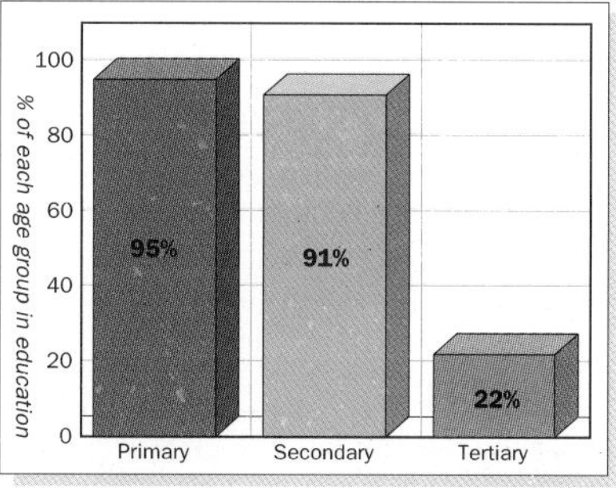

Education in Cuba combines academic with manual work, in line with Marxist-Leninist principles. The high priority given to education under Castro, which is reflected in the high literacy rate, is now being promoted to attract foreign investment in high-tech industries, particularly biotechnology.

HEALTH

1 per 333 people

Heart disease, cancer, nutritional disorders

Health spending as % GNP (0–25): 3%

Life expectancy in Cuba is 76 years, the highest in Latin America, which is a reflection of its efficient, countrywide health service. The US blockade has led to shortages of hospital equipment and raw materials for drugs. The latter are normally supplied by Havana's sizeable pharmaceuticals industry. Cuba's advanced eye surgery techniques attract patients from overseas.

WEALTH

Factory worker, 220 Cuban pesos per month; engineer, 300 Cuban pesos per month

CONSUMER GOODS OWNERSHIP

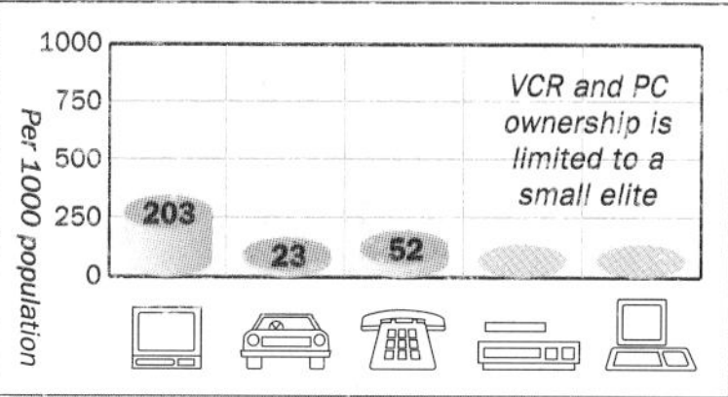

Under Batista, Cuba had huge wealth disparities, and was a playground for the rich. The 1959 revolution succeeded in reducing these, partly by taking over all businesses, from oil companies to barbershops, and partly by prescribing not only minimum but also maximum wages. Economic regulations have varied since then; for a brief period in 1985, different wage rates were allowed in an attempt to provide incentives for hard workers, but this decision was reversed in 1986. In the same year, a purge of old party hands on the grounds of corruption revealed the relatively high standard of living enjoyed by a few government officials. Generally, however, wealth is fairly evenly distributed.

WORLD RANKING

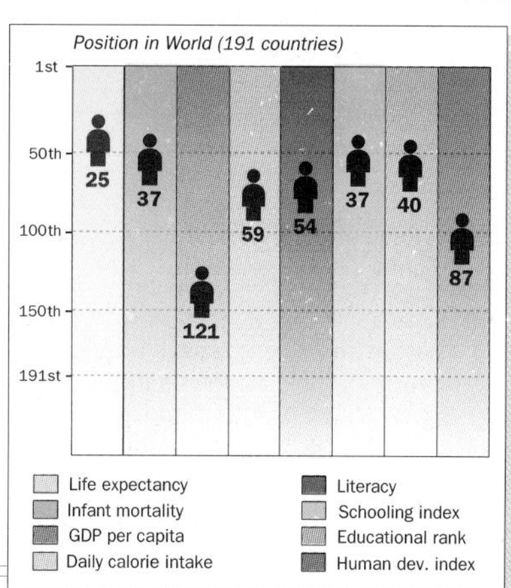

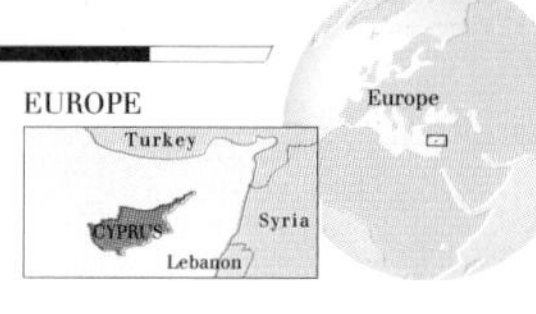

CYPRUS

OFFICIAL NAME: Republic of Cyprus **CAPITAL:** Nicosia **POPULATION:** 708,000
CURRENCY: Cyprus pound (Turkish lira) **OFFICIAL LANGUAGES:** Greek (Turkish)

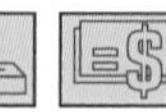

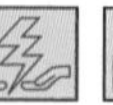
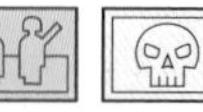
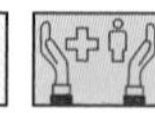

THE ISLAND OF CYPRUS, which rises from a central plateau to a high point at Mount Olympus, lies south of Turkey in the eastern Mediterranean. Cyprus was partitioned in 1974, following an invasion by Turkish troops. The south of the island is the Greek Cypriot Republic of Cyprus (Cyprus); the self-proclaimed Turkish Republic of Northern Cyprus (TRNC) is recognized only by Turkey.

CLIMATE

WEATHER CHART

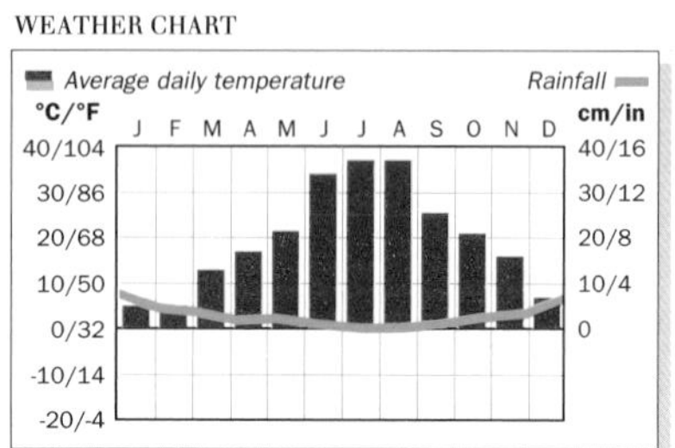

The climate is typically Mediterranean: summers are hot and dry and winters mild, though there is mountain snow.

COMMUNICATIONS

Larnaka 2.48m passengers

1,384 ships 35.55m dwt

THE TRANSPORTATION NETWORK

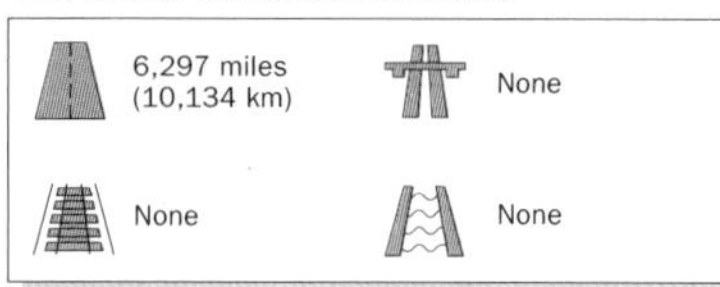

Travel between the two zones is impeded. The south regards the airport in Ercan as an illegal point of entry.

TOURISM

 1.56m visitors  Up 13% in 1990

MAIN OVERSEAS ARRIVALS

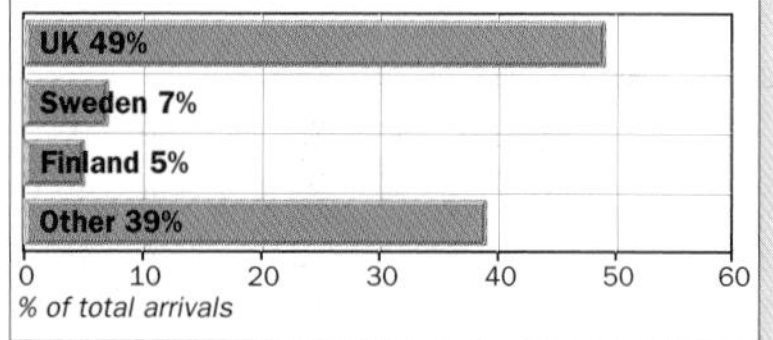

Tourism in southern Cyprus expanded rapidly during the 1980s, as new resorts were built replacing those lost to the north. Tourism in the north is now growing. The Akamas Peninsula is being promoted for ecotourists, who can stay in restored village houses.

PEOPLE

 Greek, Turkish

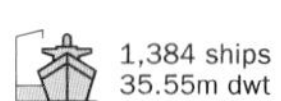

THE URBAN/RURAL POPULATION SPLIT

53% 47%

ETHNIC MAKEUP

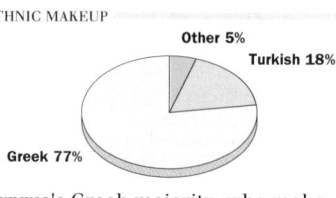

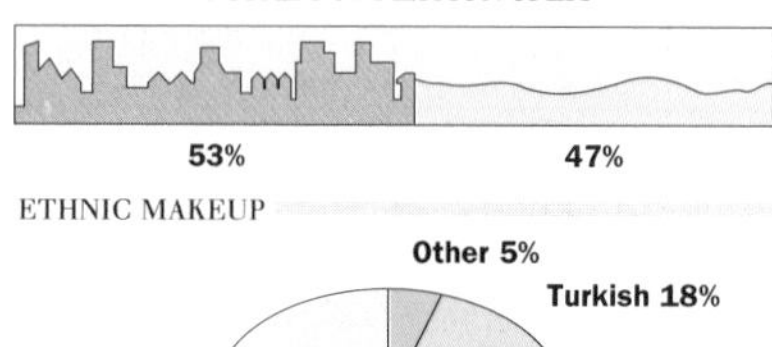

Cyprus's Greek majority, who make up 77% of the population, are Christian. The 18% Turkish minority are Muslims. Some are the descendants of Turks who settled on the island from the 16th century, under the rule of the Ottoman Empire. Turkish Cypriots have been isolated following the 1974 partitioning; since when they have officially been recognized only by Turkey, which has resettled thousands of mainland Turks on the island. Both communities have suffered great upheavals: in 1974, 180,000 Greek Cypriots were forced to flee to the south, while 100,000 Turkish Cypriots fled in the other direction. Wage levels are on average four times higher in the south, where Eastern European contract labor is brought in to staff the hotel industry. Unemployment levels in the north, meanwhile, are rising.

***The 2nd-century theater** at the ruined city of Curium, 9 miles west of Limassol. Curium was a flourishing Mycenaean colony before 1100 BC.*

POLITICS

1996 (Cyprus) 1995 (TRNC)

President Glavkos Klerides (Cyprus) President Rauf Denktaş (TRNC)

THE STATE OF THE PARTIES

House of Representatives (Cyprus) 56 members

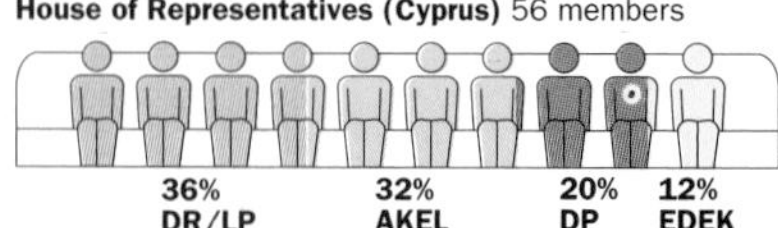

DR/LP = Democratic Rally/Liberal Party **AKEL** = Progressive Party of the Working People (Communist Party) **DP** = Democratic Party **EDEK** = Cyprus National Democratic Union (Socialist Party)

Legislative Assembly (TRNC) 50 members

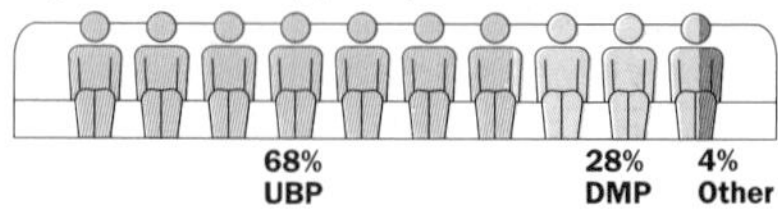

UBP = National Unity Party **DMP** = Democratic Struggle Party (composed of: CTP = Republican Turkish Party, TKP = Communal Liberation Party, YDP = New Dawn Party)

The UN-backed proposal of a two-zoned federation for Cyprus is supported by both the Greek and Turkish governments, eager to solve the dispute. Under this plan, each community would have its own territory but share a number of government functions and ministries. TRNC president Rauf Denktaş, aware of the Greek Cypriots' suppression of the Turks prior to 1974, is unwilling to accept a plan that does not ensure full sovereignty and political equality for Turks. Greek Cypriots , in turn, fear the plan would lead to domination of their affairs by the small Turkish minority, who would be able to veto all government decisions.

WORLD AFFAIRS

The permanent presence since 1974 of 2,000 UN troops manning the "Green Line" – only the Middle East and Kashmir have longer-standing peace-keeping forces – is estimated to cost in excess of $100 million a year. Cyprus's 1990 application for EU membership is a source of contention.

AID

 $34m (receipts)  No change in 1991

Cyprus receives aid from the international agencies, as well as the EU and countries such as the UK. The TRNC is dependent on aid from Turkey of more than $60 million a year.

C

CYPRUS

Total Area : 9251 sq. km (3572 sq. miles)

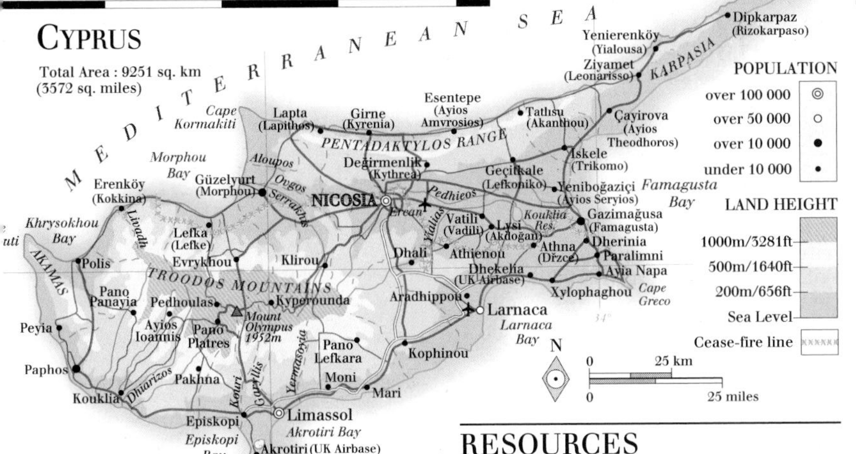

DEFENSE

 $284.5m

 Down 6% in 1991

In addition to UN forces, there are Greek Cypriot, Turkish Cypriot, Greek and Turkish troops posted along the buffer zone that divides the island. Both the 8,000-strong Greek Cypriot and 4,000-strong Turkish Cypriot armies rely heavily on conscripts.

ECONOMICS

 $6.1bn

 0.52 Cyprus pounds 14,922.00 Turkish liras

SCORE CARD

- ❑ WORLD GNP RANKING........................104th
- ❑ GNP PER CAPITA $8,615
- ❑ BALANCE OF PAYMENTS $241.7m
- ❑ INFLATION 6%
- ❑ UNEMPLOYMENT...................................3%

STRENGTHS

Tourism, the basis of the economy. Manufacturing sector and provision of services to Middle Eastern countries.

WEAKNESSES

Tourism damaged by effects of Gulf War. Economic stagnation and lack of foreign investment in TRNC. Collapse of Asil Nadir's manufacturing empire – employer of 12% of Turkish Cypriots.

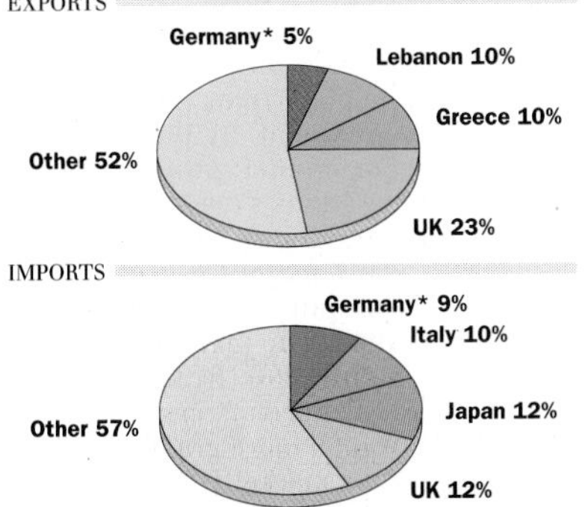

RESOURCES

 1.98m kwh (capacity 471,000 kw)

 Not an oil producer; refines 18,600 b/cd

300,000 sheep, 284,000 pigs, 46,000 cattle

Asbestos, gypsum, iron, bentonite, copper

Cyprus has continued to supply electricity to the TRNC, although it has not been paid for. An oil refinery has been built in a project involving the Greek Cypriot government, BP, Mobil and a local company.

ENVIRONMENT

 0.2% partially protected

 Increasing environmental awareness

The protection of the 60 sq. mile Akamas Peninsula from the threat of development by landholders, including the Orthodox Church, is a major project. This new national park is home to an unusual variety of plant and bird life, and contains the bay where the rare green turtle breeds.

MEDIA

 Freedom of speech is guaranteed in both Cyprus and the TRNC

PUBLISHING AND BROADCAST MEDIA

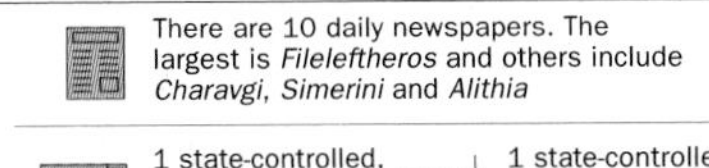
There are 10 daily newspapers. The largest is *Fileleftheros* and others include *Charavgi, Simerini* and *Alithia*

1 state-controlled, 1 independent service

1 state-controlled, 9 independent stations

Cyprus's press is lively and tends to be highly politicized. The radio and TV services for British troops based in Cyprus are also popular.

CRIME

 219 prisoners

 Down 1% in 1990

Crime is not a major problem in Cyprus or the TRNC, where the population is generally law-abiding. Ethnic tensions are largely kept in check by the division of the island. There have been isolated cases of Palestinian-linked terrorism.

CHRONOLOGY

Cyprus came, in turn, under the domination of Egypt, Greece, the Byzantines, the Ottomans and Britain.

- ❑ **1960** Independence from Britain.
- ❑ **1963** Following constitutional violation by Greeks, Turkish Cypriots abandon parliament.
- ❑ **1974** President Makarios overthrown in coup supported by Greek military junta. Turkey invades. Partition.

EDUCATION

 94%

Education is free and compulsory up to the age of 12 (15 in the TRNC). Many Greek Cypriots go to college abroad.

HEALTH

 1 per 484 people

 Heart disease, accidents, cancer

Health care is more advanced in the south; sophisticated surgery is carried out at Nicosia General Hospital.

WEALTH

 Wages in the south are 4 times those in the north

CONSUMER GOODS OWNERSHIP

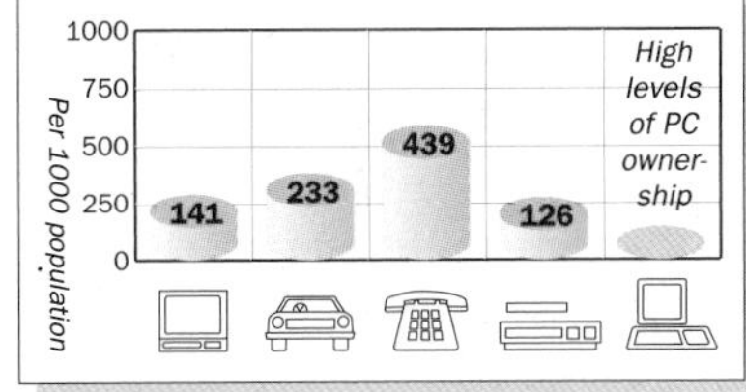

Income per capita in the south is higher than in mainland Greece, and is comparable to that of Spain.

WORLD RANKING

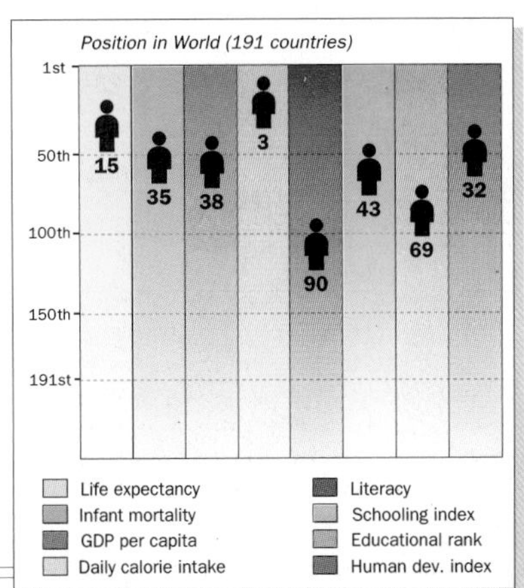

CZECH REPUBLIC

OFFICIAL NAME: Czech Republic **CAPITAL:** Prague
POPULATION: 10.3 million **CURRENCY:** Czech koruna **OFFICIAL LANGUAGE:** Czech

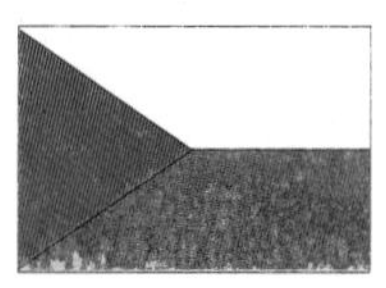

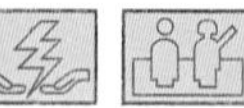

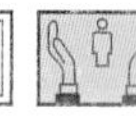

LANDLOCKED IN Eastern Europe, the Czech Republic comprises the territories of Bohemia and Moravia and was formerly part of Czechoslovakia. In 1989, Czechoslovakia's "Velvet Revolution" led to the fall of the communist regime. Free elections followed in 1990. In 1993, the Czech Republic and Slovakia peacefully dissolved their federal union to become two independent states.

CLIMATE

WEATHER CHART

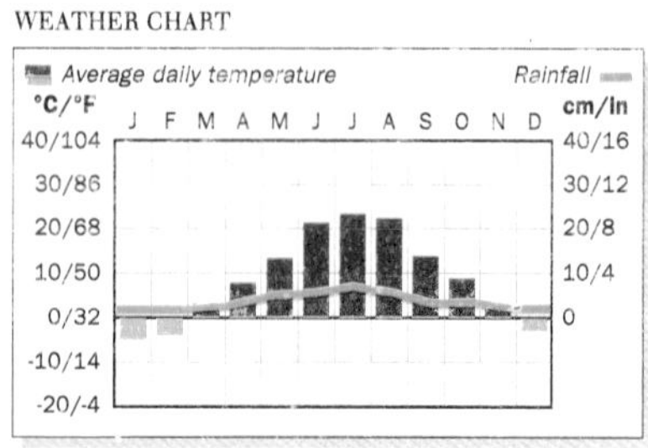

The Czech climate is more moderate than that of Slovakia, though easterly winds bring low temperatures in winter.

COMMUNICATIONS

THE TRANSPORTATION NETWORK

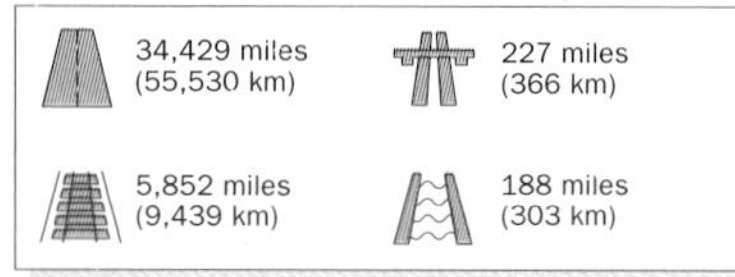

New rail links and highways to Germany are planned. Customs barriers have been installed on the Slovakian border.

TOURISM

MAIN OVERSEAS ARRIVALS

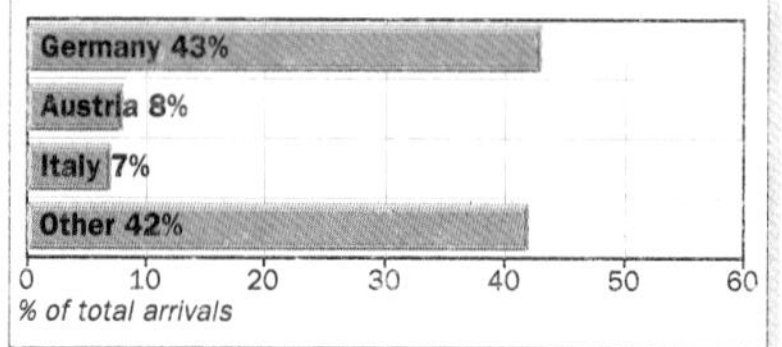

Revenues from the expansion of tourism have kept the Czech economy flush with hard currency. In 1992, 50 million tourists and day-trippers visited the country, the majority of them Germans, bringing in around $1.2 billion. Prague, which rivals Paris as the most beautiful capital in Europe, is visited by most tourists. Skiing and spa towns are the other main attractions.

CZECH REPUBLIC

Total Area : 78 370 sq. km (30 260 sq. miles)

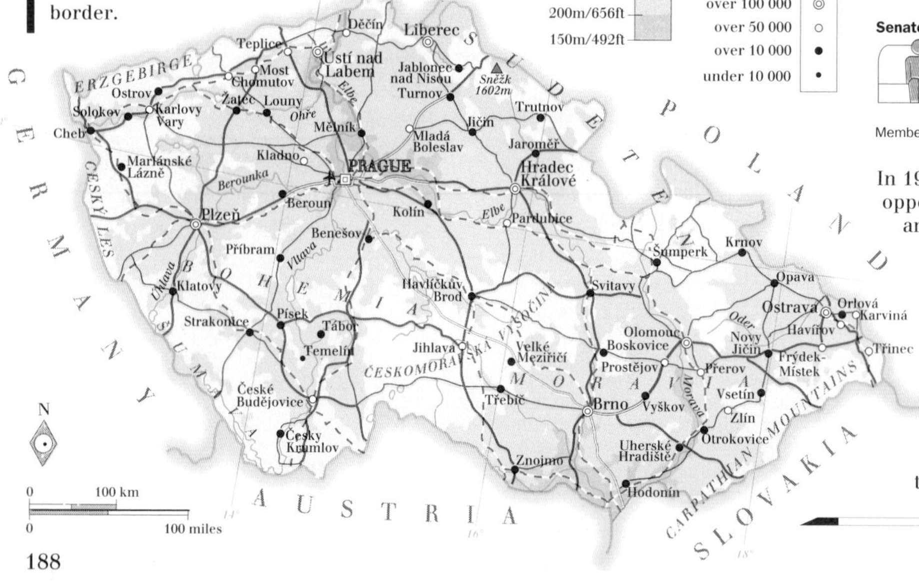

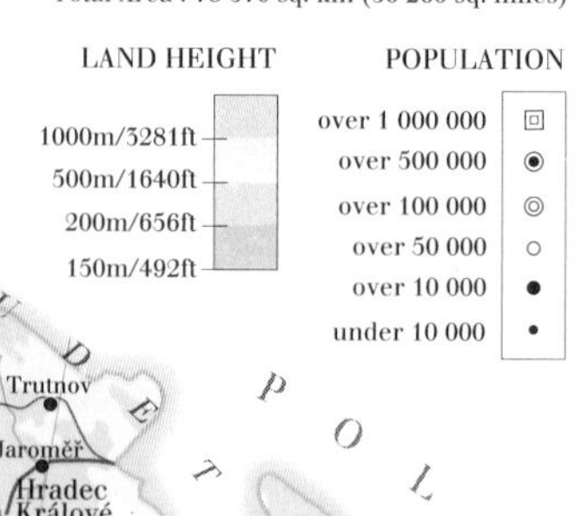

PEOPLE

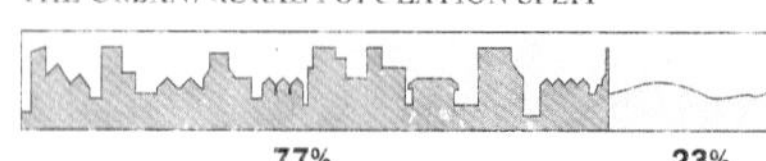

THE URBAN/RURAL POPULATION SPLIT

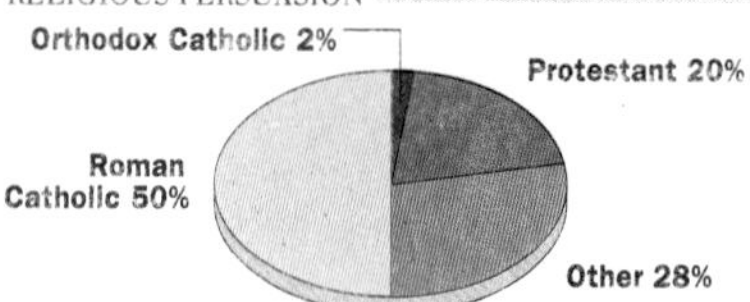

RELIGIOUS PERSUASION

Orthodox Catholic 2%
Protestant 20%
Roman Catholic 50%
Other 28%

Czechs make up 85% and Moravians 14% of the population. The 300,000 Slovaks left in the country after partition now form the largest ethnic minority. Ethnic tensions are minimal, but there is some resentment against Romanian immigrants. A new commercial elite is emerging alongside ex-communist entrepreneurs. Divorce rates are high.

POLITICS

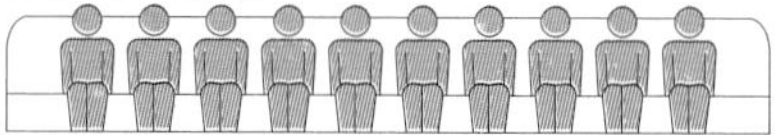

THE STATE OF THE PARTIES

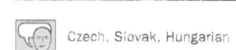

Chamber of Deputies 200 members

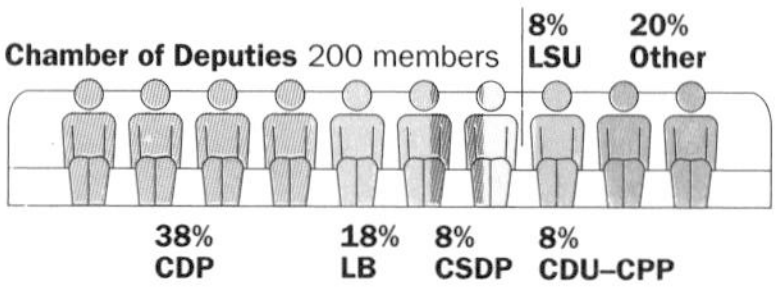

8% LSU, 20% Other, 38% CDP, 18% LB, 8% CSDP, 8% CDU–CPP

CDP = Civic Democratic Party **LB** = Left Bloc
CSDP = Czechoslovak Social Democratic Party
LSU = Liberal Social Union **CDU–CPP** = Christian Democratic Union – Czechoslovak People's Party **Other** = Association for the Republic – Czechoslovak Republican Party, Civic Democratic Alliance, Movement for Autonomous Democracy – Society for Moravia and Silesia

Senate 81 members

Members are elected for 6 years by universal adult suffrage

In 1990, the Civic Forum coalition of opposition groups won free elections and dissident playwright Václav Havel became president. By 1991, the Civic Forum had splintered and Václav Klaus's CDP emerged as the dominant party. Klaus was a major force behind the split from Slovakia in 1993. The main division in politics now is between the radical privatizers and those who want a more gradual transition to a market-led economy.

C

WORLD AFFAIRS

CE | CSCE | GATT | V4 | EBRD

Good relations with Germany are a priority. However, the issue of property restitution for Germans ejected from the republic in 1945 is a source of friction. Germany has implied that the matter must be resolved before it will back Czech membership in the EU. The Czech Republic has downgraded relations with its V4 neighbors.

AID

 The Czech Republic is an aid recipient

 Aid donations are increasing steadily

Aid, mainly from the IMF and the EU, is crucial for modernizing infrastructure such as telecommunications.

DEFENSE

 $804m (est)

 Spending is decreasing as cuts are implemented

The split with Slovakia left an army too large and expensive for the new Czech state. In 1994, plans to cut the military by 20,000 were approved. Professional soldiers with a communist past will be the first to go. The Czech Republic has a strong armaments and explosives industry. It is now seeking markets beyond the former Warsaw Pact.

ECONOMICS

25.7bn (est)

29.96 Czech koruny

SCORE CARD

- ❑ WORLD GNP RANKING..........59th
- ❑ GNP PER CAPITA..........$2,495
- ❑ BALANCE OF PAYMENTS..........$500m (est)
- ❑ INFLATION..........17%
- ❑ UNEMPLOYMENT..........2.6%

STRENGTHS

Skilled industrial labor force. Good industrial base. Speed of privatization of state industries. Attractive to German investors, including Volkswagen. Draw of Prague as tourist center.

WEAKNESSES

Lack of diversification in sectors likely to attract overseas investment. Some reluctance to face costs of restructuring. Rising unemployment.

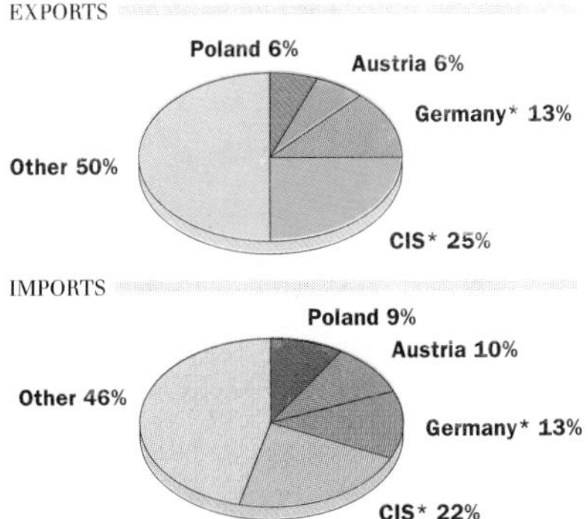

RESOURCES

 Nuclear power generates 29% of electricity output

 Not available

 4.9m cattle, 7m pigs, 1m sheep

 Copper, lead, zinc, coal

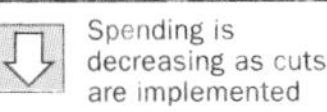

Copper, lead, zinc and coal are the chief resources. The government is aiming to phase out the worst-polluting coal-fired power stations. A 2,000-MW Soviet-designed nuclear power station is due to open in Temelin in the late 1990s.

ENVIRONMENT

 6%

 Public awareness of environmental problems is rising

High pollution levels from the power, chemical and cement industries are the main environmental problem.

MEDIA

 No official censorship

PUBLISHING AND BROADCAST MEDIA

There are 9 daily newspapers. *Mladá Fronta Dnes* has the largest circulation

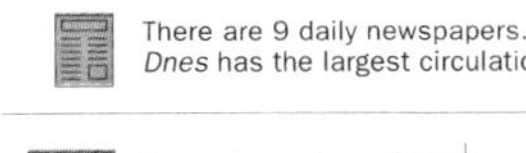

2 state-owned services

Several networks

Since the fall of communism, the Czech media has grown rapidly. Political debates are well covered in the press.

CRIME

 8,002 prisoners

 The crime rate has tripled since 1989

The republic is a major transit point for Turkish drugs destined for Germany. Drug trading, not possession, is illegal.

EDUCATION

 99%

Schooling has reverted to the pre-1945 system. Charles University in Prague was founded in the 13th century.

HEALTH

 1 per 270 people

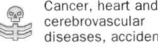

Cancer, heart and cerebrovascular diseases, accidents

In the worst polluted towns, infant mortality reached levels found in the developing world. Wealthy Czechs travel to Germany for complex operations.

The Vltava River in Prague. Over 50 million tourists, mainly from Europe and the USA, now visit Prague each year.

CHRONOLOGY

Following the collapse of the Austro-Hungarian Empire in 1918, the Republic of Czechoslovakia was established.

- ❑ **1968** "Prague Spring." Invasion by Warsaw Pact countries.
- ❑ **1989** Beginning of the "Velvet Revolution." Demonstrations in main cities. Majority of non-communists in parliament.
- ❑ **1990** Free legislative elections.
- ❑ **1993** Split into the Czech Republic and Slovakia.

WEALTH

 Entrepreneurs in the private sector have rapidly acquired wealth

CONSUMER GOODS OWNERSHIP

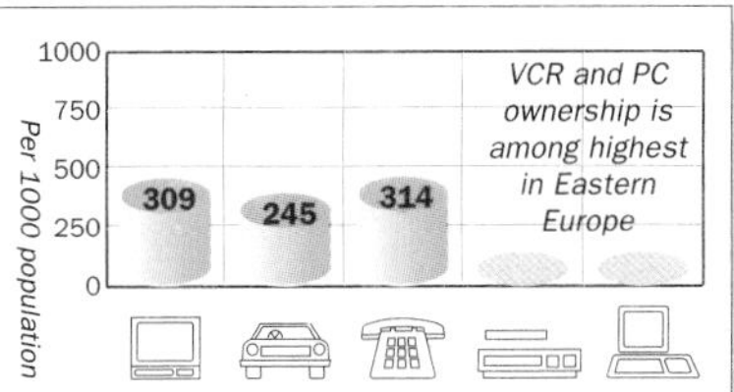

A new entrepreneurial class has emerged since 1989. Almost all Czechs have shares in privatized enterprises.

WORLD RANKING

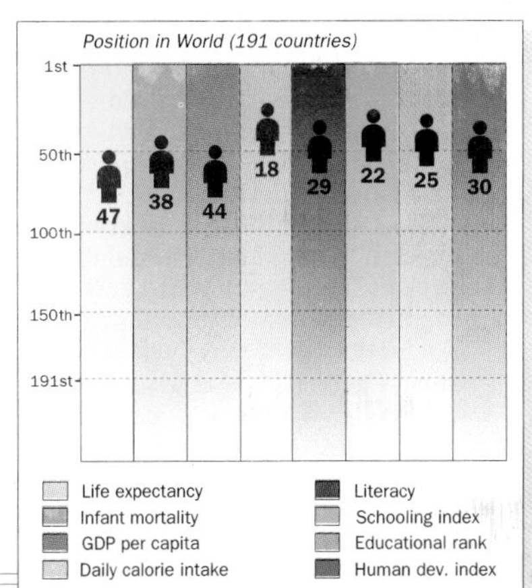

DENMARK

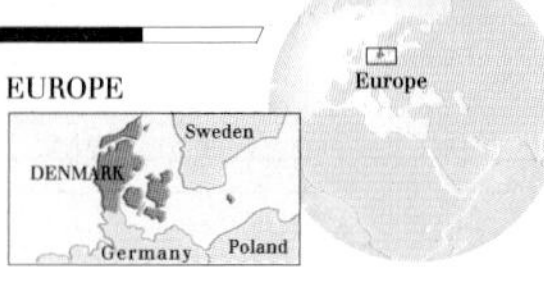

OFFICIAL NAME: Kingdom of Denmark **CAPITAL:** Copenhagen **POPULATION:** 5.2 million
CURRENCY: Danish kroner **OFFICIAL LANGUAGE:** Danish **OVERSEAS TERRITORIES:** 2

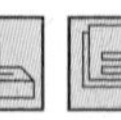
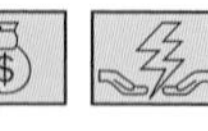

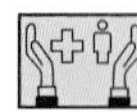

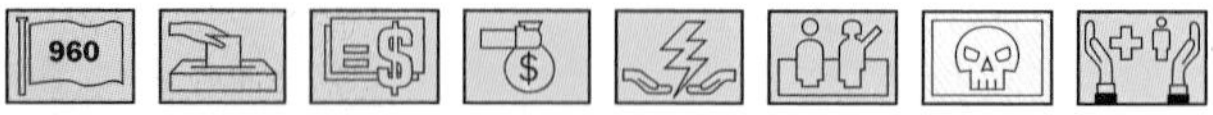

THE MOST SOUTHERLY COUNTRY in Scandinavia, Denmark occupies the Jutland Peninsula, the islands of Sjælland, Fyn, Lolland and Falster, and over 400 smaller islands. Its terrain is among the flattest in the world. The Faroe Islands and Greenland in the North Atlantic are self-governing associated territories. Politically, Denmark is stable, despite a preponderance of minority governments since 1945. It has a long tradition of liberalism and was one of the first countries to establish a welfare system, in the 1930s.

CLIMATE

WEATHER CHART

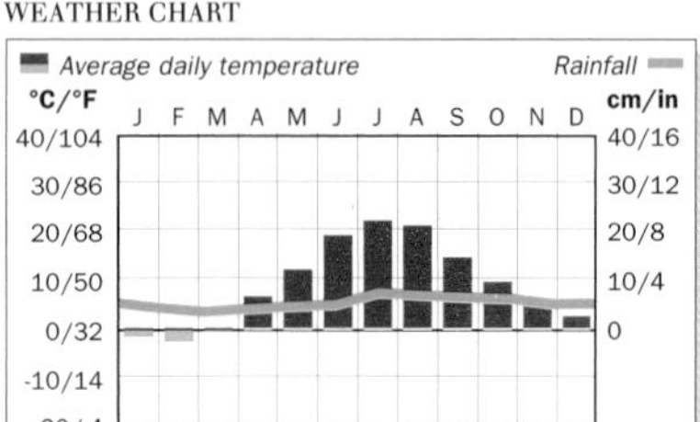

Denmark's temperate, damp climate is one of the keys to its agricultural success. The Faroes are windy, foggy and cool. Greenland's climate ranges north–south from arctic to sub-arctic.

The island of Fyn, like the rest of Denmark, is flat and depends on coastal defenses to prevent flooding by the sea.

TOURISM

51.4 m overnights. Denmark does not record visitor numbers

Up 13% in 1992

MAIN OVERSEAS ARRIVALS

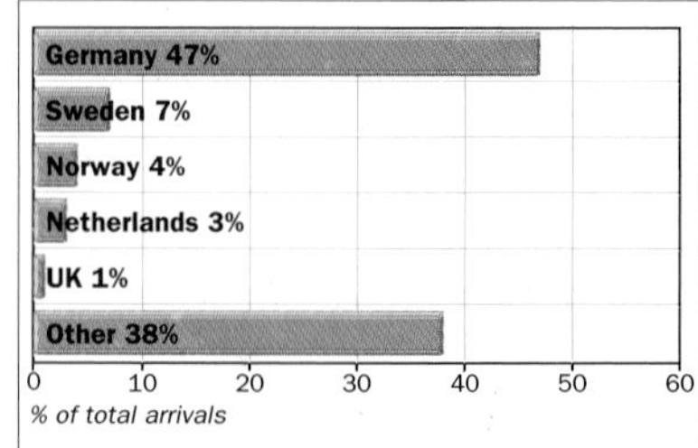

Denmark is a popular destination for Scandinavian, German and Dutch tourists. The principal attractions are Copenhagen – with its Tivoli Gardens and fine 18th-century architecture – as well as Legoland, the countryside and seaside resorts. Greenland attracts wildlife tourists.

COMMUNICATIONS

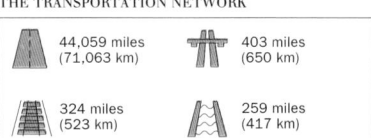

Kastrup, Copenhagen
9.27m passengers

499 ships
6.74m dwt

THE TRANSPORTATION NETWORK

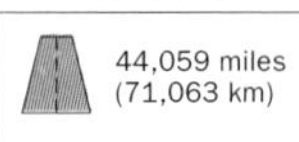
44,059 miles (71,063 km)

403 miles (650 km)

324 miles (523 km)

259 miles (417 km)

Denmark maintains an extensive, well-integrated transportation network, with bus, rail and ferry services linking the whole kingdom. State-owned companies predominate, although plans to privatize parts of the ferry and rail systems have been discussed. Denmark wants to reduce subsidies paid to transportation, a major part of public spending. A few private companies, supported by state grants, operate in the Faroes and Greenland.

Major new construction projects focus on bridge and tunnel links. The much-postponed Storebælt project to connect Denmark's main islands, Fyn and Sjælland, is due to be completed in 1995. Tunnel and bridge projects are also being discussed with Sweden and Germany.

DENMARK

Total Area : 43 070 sq. km (16 629 sq. miles)

POPULATION: over 1 000 000; over 100 000; over 10 000; under 10 000

LAND HEIGHT: 175m/574ft; Sea Level

Ferry link

D

PEOPLE

 Danish

 306 people per sq. mile

THE URBAN/RURAL POPULATION SPLIT

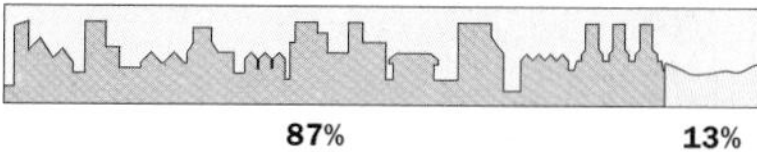

RELIGIOUS PERSUASION

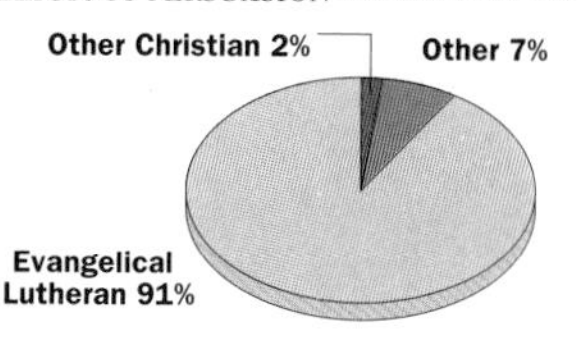

ETHNIC MAKEUP

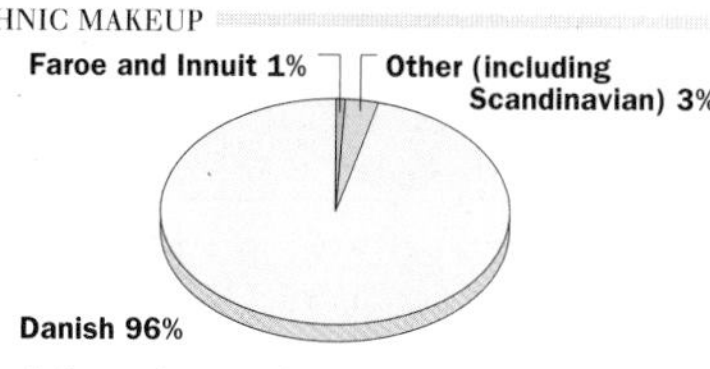

Danish society is homogeneous. Out of a population of 5.2 million, just 200,000 are foreign citizens, mainly from other Scandinavian or EU states. The biggest minority groups are the Innuit, Greenland's indigenous inhabitants, and the Turkish community. Rising unemployment has brought about some ethnic tension, although racially motivated attacks are still rare.

Denmark has undergone profound social changes over the last 20 years. The role of women has been transformed. Helped by Denmark's extensive social and educational provision, 76% of women now work in part-time or full-time jobs. Denmark provides the best state child-support in Europe. Almost 50% of children under two, and 67% of three-to six-year-olds are in day-care centers, compared with under 30% in the 1970s.

Less than half the population lives in a nuclear family, partly due to the high divorce rate. Marriage is also becoming less common; almost 40% of children are brought up by unmarried couples or single parents. Cohabitating couples now have the same legal rights as those who are married. In 1990, Denmark became the first country to allow registered partnerships between homosexual couples, effectively granting them the same legal married status as heterosexuals.

POPULATION AGE BREAKDOWN

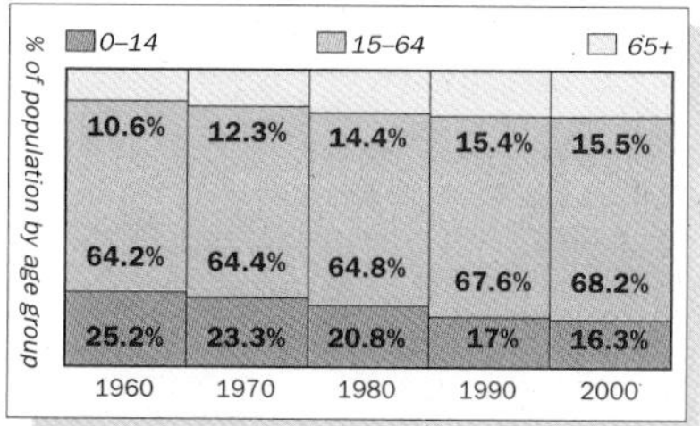

POLITICS

 1998

HM Queen Margrethe II

THE STATE OF THE PARTIES

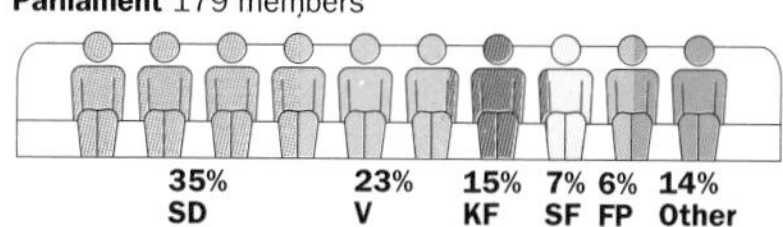

SD = Social Democratic Party **V** = Liberal Party **KF** = Conservative People's Party **SF** = Socialist People's Party **FP** = Progress Party **Other** = Radical Liberals, Unity List, Center Democrats, Christian People's Party

Denmark is a constitutional monarchy and a multiparty democracy. The associated territories of Greenland and the Faroe Islands have home rule.

MAIN POLITICAL ISSUES

Relations with the EU

In recent years, Denmark's left-of-center parties have been suspicious of any EU moves for closer ties between member states. This was highlighted by the stir caused by the ratification of the Maastricht Treaty in 1992. The treaty was approved by parliament but rejected in a referendum. The public objected to proposals for a monetary union, a common defense force and voting rights for European citizens living in Denmark. The result threatened the Treaty and embarrassed the government. Later that year, at an EU summit meeting, Denmark was exempted from clauses on monetary union, defense and European citizenship. A new referendum was held in 1993 and the Treaty approved, leaving the way clear for other countries, such as the UK, to ratify it.

Immigration

In what many saw as a vindication for Danish liberal traditions, Prime Minister Poul Schlüter was forced to resign in 1993 over the "Tamilgate" affair. A judicial investigation ruled that he had falsely denied in parliament that immigration officials were hindering the entry of the families of Tamil workers residing in Denmark. However, the issue of how many refugees Denmark should take from the world's trouble spots, and how they should be integrated into society, continues to be a point of national debate.

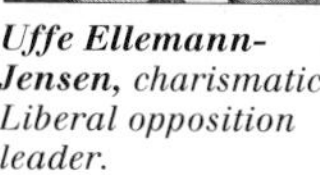

Uffe Ellemann-Jensen, charismatic Liberal opposition leader.

Poul Schlüter, resigned as premier over Tamil refugees immigration issue.

PROFILE

Denmark's intricate electoral system ensures that parliament truly reflects voters' wishes, but also tends to lead to minority governments. SD governments were predominant until 1982. A decade of Conservative-Liberal rule under Prime Minister Poul Schlüter followed. In 1993 the SD regained power, at the head of a center-left coalition. Although the coalition lost ground in the 1994 elections, it looked set to continue to form the government.

Policy differences between the two main political groups are minimal, although arguments exist about the best way of reducing the tax burden without cutting the large budget for the comprehensive Danish social security system.

WORLD AFFAIRS

Relations with the rest of Europe are the most important foreign policy concern, notably the issue of a common European defence policy. Denmark is limiting its defence relations to NATO. However, it is giving priority to promoting economic ties with Norway, Sweden and Finland and is promoting their entry into the EU. Links with former Eastern Bloc states, especially those on the Baltic, are being fostered. In part, this is a way of influencing their governments to reduce pollution.

Internationally, Denmark has a long history of involvement with the developing world, particularly aid programs in Africa.

CHRONOLOGY

Founded in the 10th century, Denmark is Europe's oldest monarchy. It was the dominant Baltic power until the 17th century, when it was eclipsed by Sweden.

- **1815** Denmark forced to cede Norway to Swedish rule.
- **1849** First democratic constitution.
- **1864** Denmark forced to cede provinces of Schleswig and Holstein after losing war with Prussia.
- **1914–1918** Denmark neutral in World War I.
- **1915** Universal adult suffrage introduced. Rise of Social Democratic Party (SD).
- **1920** Northern Schleswig votes to return to Danish rule.

D

CHRONOLOGY *continued*

- **1929** First full SD government takes power under Thorvald Stauning.
- **1930s** Implementation of advanced social welfare legislation and other liberal reforms under SD.
- **1939** Outbreak of World War II; Denmark reaffirms neutrality.
- **1940** Nazi occupation. National coalition government formed.
- **1943** Danish Resistance successes lead Nazis to take full control.
- **1944** Iceland declares independence from Denmark.
- **1945** Denmark recognizes Icelandic independence. After defeat of Nazi Germany, SD leads post-war coalition governments.
- **1948** Faroe Islands granted home rule.
- **1949** Founder-member of NATO.
- **1952** Founder-member of Nordic Council.
- **1953** Constitution reformed; single-chamber, proportionately elected parliament created.
- **1959** Denmark joins the European Free Trade Association (EFTA).
- **1972** Margrethe II becomes Denmark's first queen for nearly 600 years. Vote to join EC.
- **1973** Denmark joins EC.
- **1979** Greenland granted home rule.
- **1975–1982** SD Anker Jorgensen heads series of coalitions; elections in 1977, 1979 and 1981. Final coalition collapses over economic policy differences.
- **1982** Poul Schlüter first Conservative prime minister since 1894.
- **1992** Maastricht Treaty on European Union rejected in referendum.
- **1993** Schlüter resigns over "Tamilgate" scandal. Center-left government led by Poul Nyrup Rasmussen. Danish voters ratify revised Maastricht Treaty. Result greeted with demonstrations.

AID

$1.2bn (donations)

Up 2% in 1991

In GNP terms, Denmark is one of the world's leading aid donors, contributing an average 1% of its national income. It supports both economic and social development projects and policy reforms. Aid is an important political issue; the current debate is over its use as a tool to promote democracy.

Denmark provides aid to Asia and Latin America, but its closest ties are with Africa. Tanzania is the largest single aid recipient. Denmark has also provided considerable support to the other South African SADC states.

DEFENSE

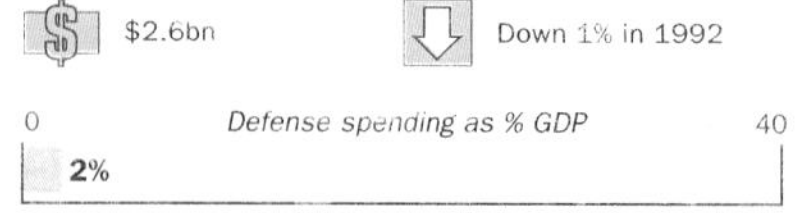

Denmark was neutral until 1945. Apart from its NATO commitments, defense has a low priority. Spending accounts for 2% of GDP. Its troops have joined UN forces on peacekeeping duties in former Yugoslavia. 10,000 army troops are conscripts. Denmark does not have plans to join the WEU forces.

DANISH ARMED FORCES

499 main battle tanks (230 *Leopard* 1A3,4/ 216 *Centurion*/53 M 41)	17,300 personnel
3 frigates, 5 submarines and 33 patrol boats	4,900 personnel
106 combat aircraft (F-16A,-B/F35 *Draken*)	7,000 personnel
None	

ECONOMICS

$122bn

6.79 Danish kroner

SCORE CARD

- WORLD GNP RANKING........................26th
- GNP PER CAPITA.........................$24,388
- BALANCE OF PAYMENTS....................$4.6bn
- INFLATION.......................................2.1%
- UNEMPLOYMENT................................9.5%

EXPORTS

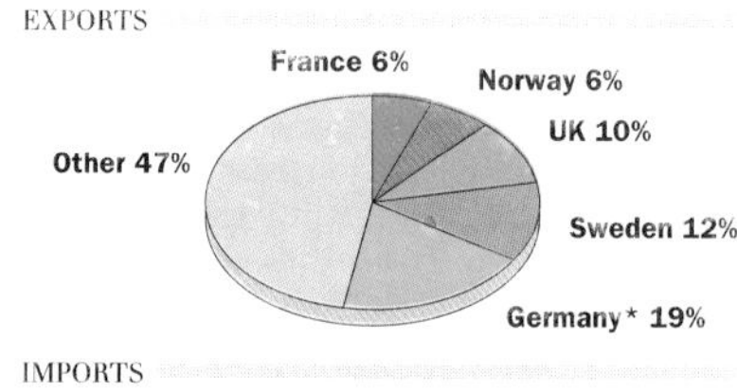

IMPORTS

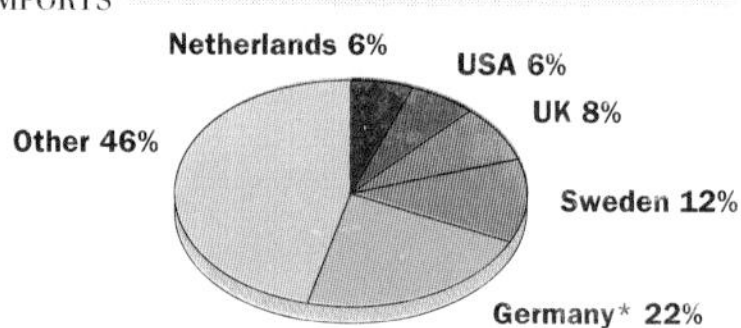

STRENGTHS

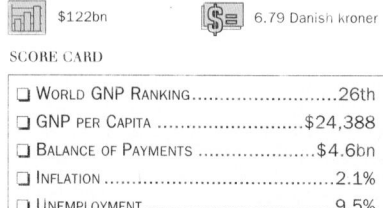

Successful high-tech, high-profit manufacturing industries. Low inflation and moderate budget deficit. Large gas and oil reserves. Skilled population. Large balance of payments surplus.

WEAKNESSES

Rising budget deficit and heavy tax burden. High unemployment, currently around 11%. Low GDP growth; 1.3% in 1992. Frequent minority governments.

PROFILE

Denmark's mix of a large state sector and a private sector has been successful. At $24,388, GNP per capita is one of the highest among the OECD countries.

During the 1980s, the advent of a minority conservative government and the prospect of the wider European market led to a number of major policy changes. A stable exchange rate policy was introduced and tighter budget controls were aimed at reducing inflation and reversing the balance of payments deficit. Real GNP per capita grew by 2.1% a year from 1981 to 1991. The balance of payments went into surplus and inflation was cut to 2%. Denmark refused to join the EMU, but was one of the few countries able to meet the convergence criteria.

After 1991, the recession in Europe led to slower growth. Denmark is expected to weather the recession better than many of its EU neighbors, but high unemployment is a problem. The government wants to impose budgetary constraint and tax cuts to restore growth. However, any attempts to reduce generous welfare provisions will meet with strong opposition.

ECONOMIC PERFORMANCE INDICATOR

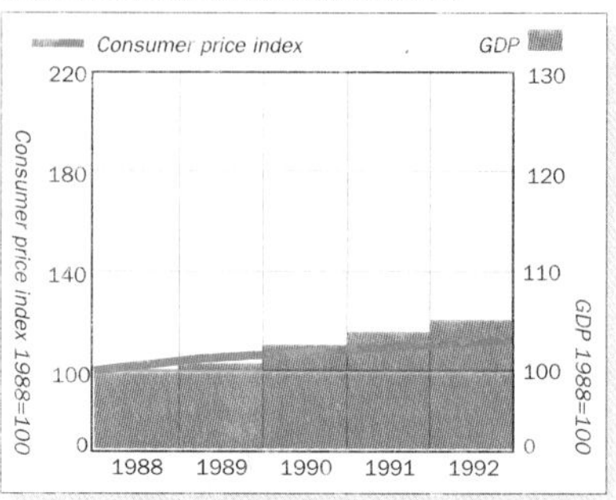

DENMARK : MAJOR BUSINESSES

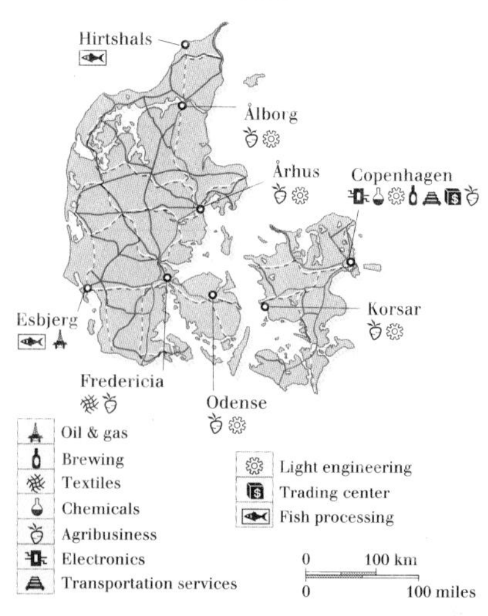

RESOURCES

25.7bn kwh (capacity 9.13m kw)

156,900 b/d (reserves 729,618,000 bbl)

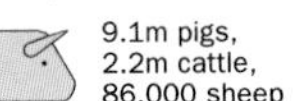
9.1m pigs, 2.2m cattle, 86,000 sheep

Natural gas, oil

ELECTRICITY GENERATION

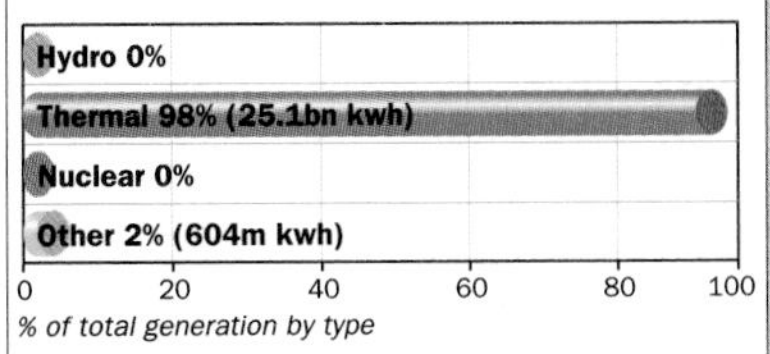

Although a net oil exporter since 1993, Denmark is still an overall importer of energy. The expansion of North Sea oil and gas output should balance import and export costs by 1997. Agriculture is highly efficient.

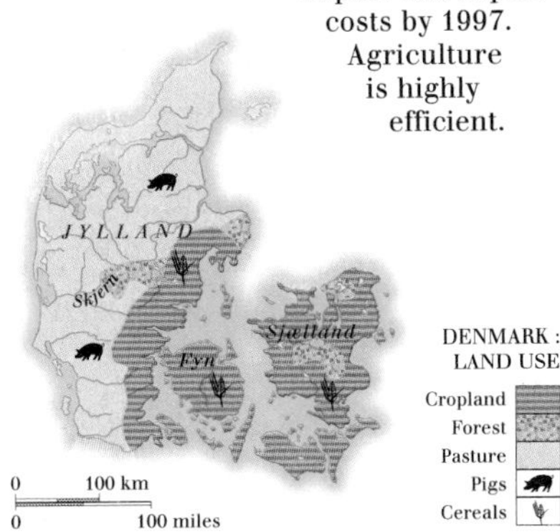

ENVIRONMENT

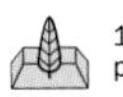
10% (9% partially protected)

Very strict laws in Greenland to protect polar ecosystems

ENVIRONMENTAL TREATIES

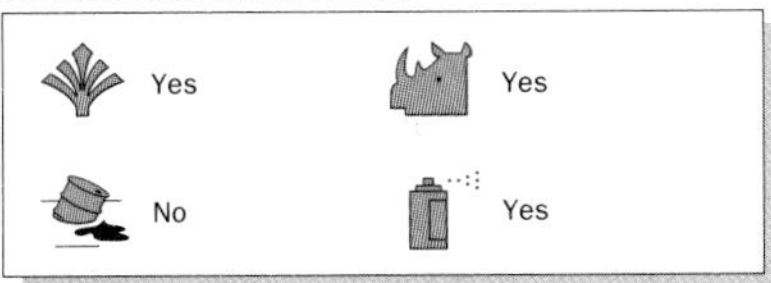

The environment is of popular and governmental concern. Denmark's regulations, including those aimed at reducing ozone-destroying emissions and water pollution, are probably the strictest in Europe. Fears that they may be eroded has been a key element in Danish ambivalence toward the EU. In 1993, Denmark was successful in persuading the EU to locate the Environmental Agency in Copenhagen. It hopes to extend its own standards to the rest of Europe.

MEDIA

Media censorship is forbidden by the constitution

PUBLISHING AND BROADCAST MEDIA

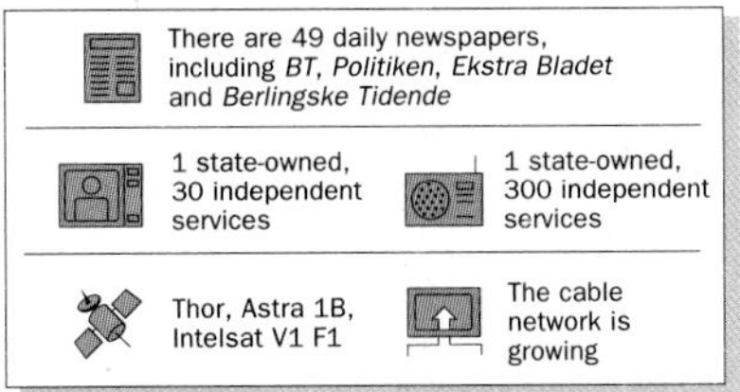

The media has a long history of political independence, and objectivity is prized. Most of the press has a political viewpoint, but expression of this is largely limited to editorials. The tone of both TV and the press is serious; Denmark does not have a scandal-mongering tabloid press as found in the USA, UK and Germany. Invasion of privacy laws are strict.

CRIME

3469 prisoners

Down 2% in 1990

CRIME RATES

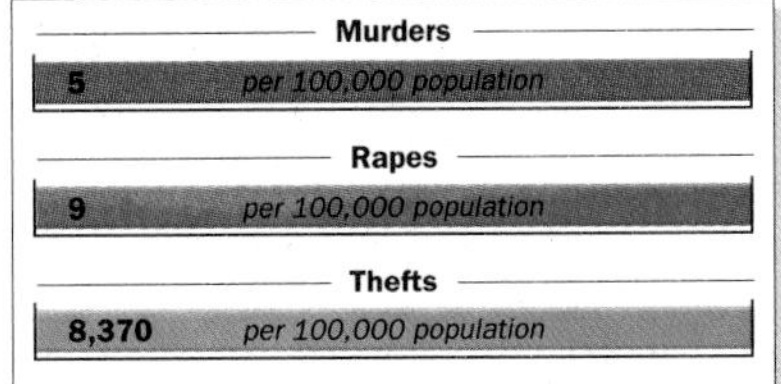

The main concern is that mafia-style organized crime could be imported from Eastern Europe. Computer hacking and drug-trafficking are also problems.

EDUCATION

100%

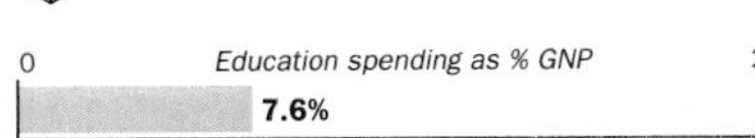

THE EDUCATION SYSTEM

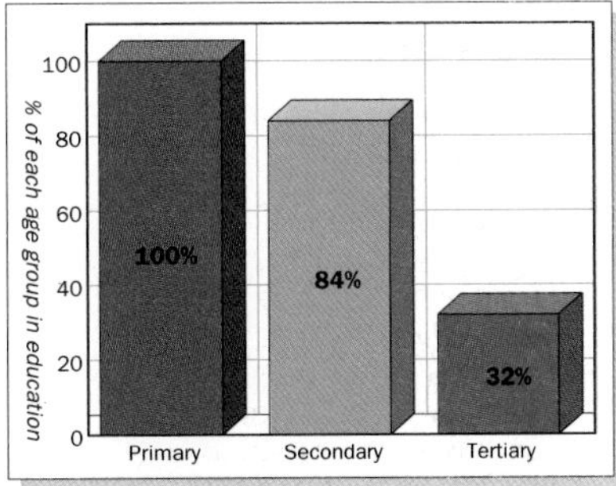

The average educational level is high, partly reflecting the need for a skilled work force. Formal schooling begins at age seven and is mandatory for nine years. However, most children receive pre-school education and over 90% of pupils go on at age 16 to further academic or vocational training.

HEALTH

1 per 375 people

Heart diseases, cancer, accidents

0 *Health spending as % GNP* 25

0.5%

Denmark was one of the first countries to introduce a state social welfare system. The national health service, which still provides free treatment for almost everything, is the main reason for Denmark's high taxes. Any attempts to reduce expenditure will meet with strong opposition. Repeated surveys show that most Danes prefer their system to those based on private health insurance.

WEALTH

Dairy product processor, 120 Danish kroner per hour; airline pilot, 27,671 Danish kroner per month

CONSUMER GOODS OWNERSHIP

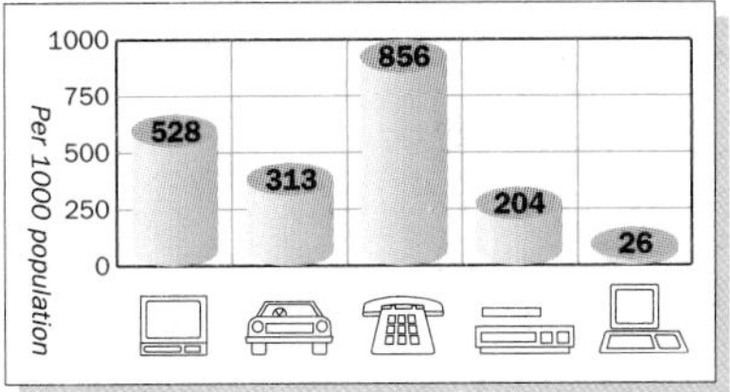

Most Danes are comfortably off. Income distribution is more even than in many Western countries and social mobility is high. Free higher education has made access to the professional sector more a question of ability than family wealth or connections. Many of Denmark's top industrialists have made their fortunes within the last 30 years. However, wealth is still quite concentrated. The richest 10% of Danes control almost two-thirds of national assets.

Because of the social security system, Denmark suffers little from social deprivation. The most disadvantaged groups are refugees and recent immigrants.

WORLD RANKING

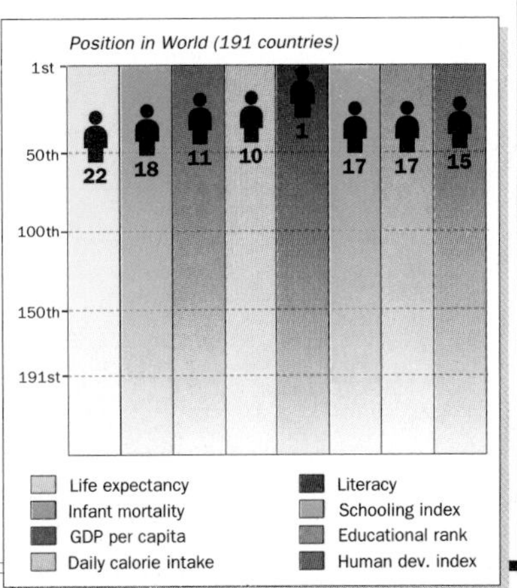

D

DJIBOUTI

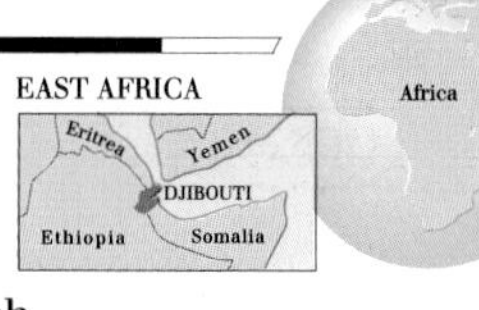

OFFICIAL NAME: Republic of Djibouti **CAPITAL:** Djibouti
POPULATION: 500,000 **CURRENCY:** Djibouti franc **OFFICIAL LANGUAGES:** Arabic and French

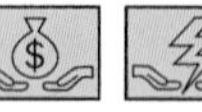

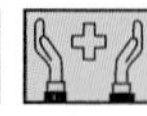

A CITY-STATE with a desert hinterland, Djibouti lies in northeast Africa on the strait joining the Red Sea and the Indian Ocean. Formerly the French Territory of the Afars and Issas, Djibouti became independent in 1977. Its economy relies on its port, the railroad to Addis Ababa, and French aid. A guerrilla war erupted in 1991 as a result of tension between the country's two major ethnic groups – the Issas in the south and the Afars in the north.

CLIMATE

WEATHER CHART

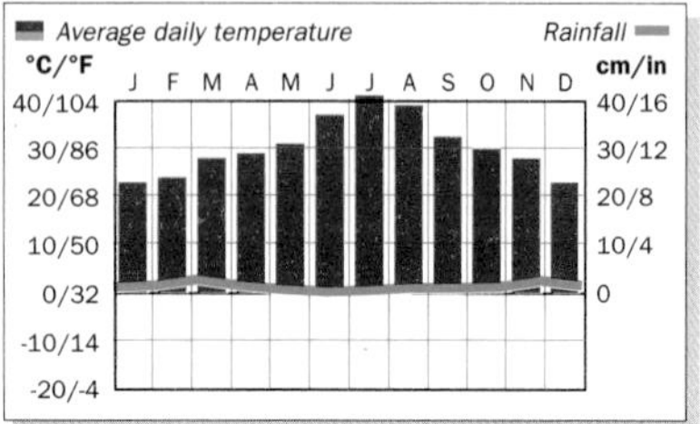

Despite extremely low rainfall, the monsoon season is characterized by very humid conditions. Even locals find the June to August heat unbearable.

COMMUNICATIONS

Ambouli Intl, Djibouti — 2 ships 2,300 dwt

THE TRANSPORTATION NETWORK

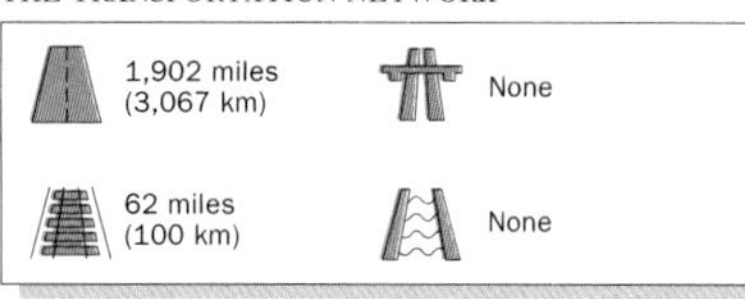

The key to Djibouti's livelihood is its port, created by the French in the 19th century and now a modern container facility. The railroad to Addis Ababa is one of Ethiopia's key links to the sea.

TOURISM

47,000 visitors

Tourism has declined since the start of the guerrilla war

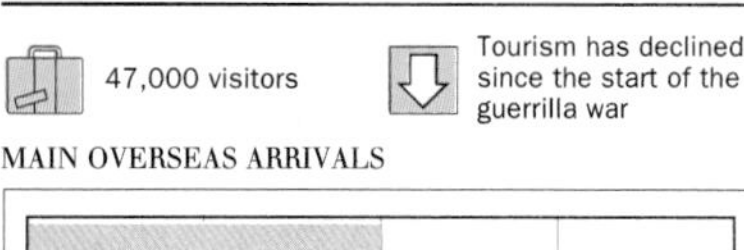

MAIN OVERSEAS ARRIVALS

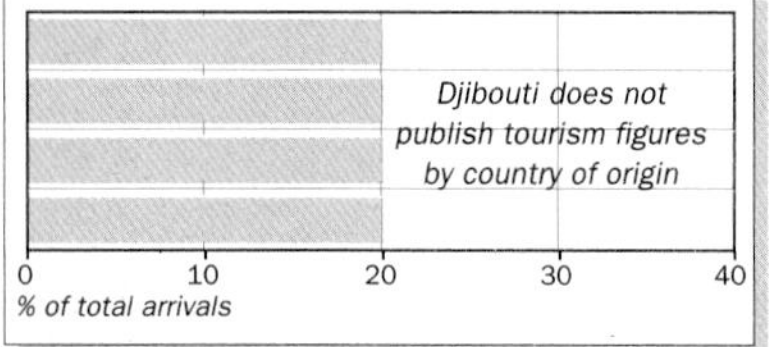

Most visitors are passing through on their way to Ethiopia, or coming to see relatives working in the port.

Nomadic Djiboutian village, *close to Balho near the Ethiopian border.*

PEOPLE

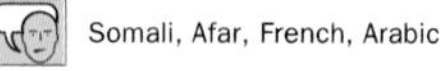

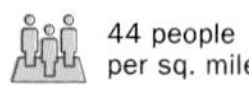

THE URBAN/RURAL POPULATION SPLIT

81% 19%

ETHNIC MAKEUP

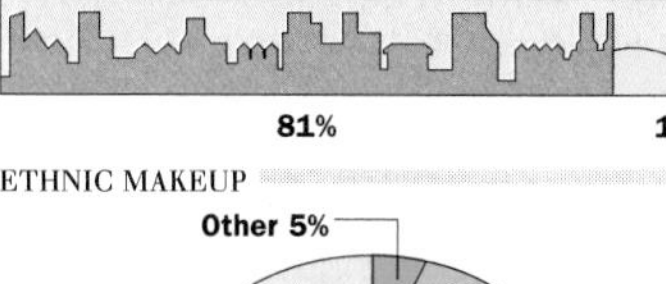

The two main tribes are the Afars and Issas; tension between these groups developed into a guerrilla war in 1991. The population was swelled in 1992 by 20,000 Somali refugees. The rural people are mostly nomadic.

POLITICS

1997 — President Hassan Gouled Aptidon

THE STATE OF THE PARTIES

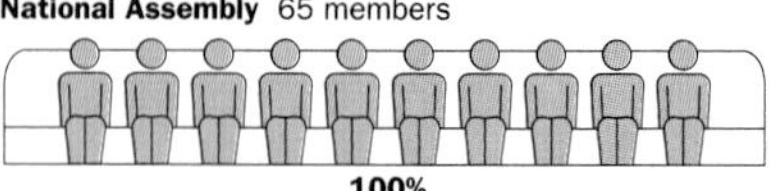

RPP = People's Progress Party

Since independence, politics have been dominated by President Aptidon, an Issa, and a carefully chosen group of Issa and Afar politicians. Behind the scenes, French backing is essential to the ruling group. Afar fears of Issa domination erupted in 1991, when the Afar guerrilla group FRUD took control of much of the country against a background of similar ethnic conflicts in neighboring states. The French intervened militarily to keep Aptidon in power, but forced him to hold elections in 1992. These were won by the RPP, on a turnout of only 49%. The expected parliamentary reforms did not follow, to the displeasure of the French. The country remains divided between RPP-controlled and FRUD-controlled areas.

DJIBOUTI

Total Area : 23 200 sq. km (8958 sq. miles)

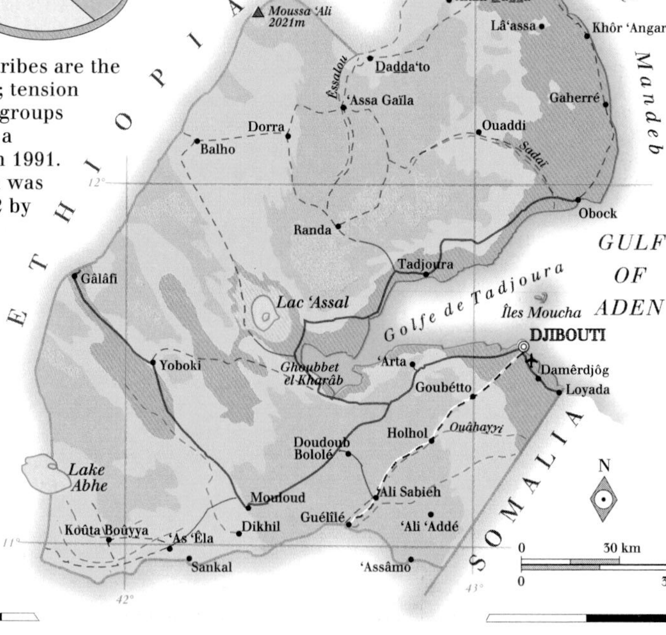

POPULATION

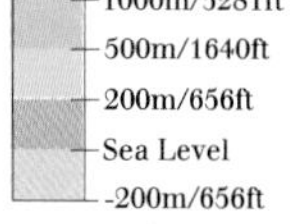

LAND HEIGHT

1000m/3281ft
500m/1640ft
200m/656ft
Sea Level
-200m/656ft

WORLD AFFAIRS

Relations with France, which wants to see faster moves to reform, have soured. Djibouti, Ethiopia and Eritrea all wish to contain Afar militancy; the ethnic group crosses national borders and has demanded its own state.

AID

 $120m (receipts)

 French defense-related aid has increased

France is the major donor, effectively financing one-third of government expenditure. Djibouti has also received aid from Saudi Arabia and Kuwait.

DEFENSE

 Estimated to be 50% of government expenditure in 1992

 Large increase in 1992 to finance anti-FRUD operations

Djibouti's armed forces were increased five-fold in 1992 to an estimated 12,000 personnel, mostly army, to counteract FRUD guerrilla activity. There is a 3,800-strong French garrison.

ECONOMICS

 $480m

 177.76 Djibouti francs

SCORE CARD

- ❑ WORLD GNP RANKING 162nd
- ❑ GNP PER CAPITA $960
- ❑ BALANCE OF PAYMENTS..................$–43.8m
- ❑ INFLATION 3.2%
- ❑ UNEMPLOYMENT.................................40%

STRENGTHS

Free port in key Red Sea location; made large profits from 1991 Gulf War and from 1992 US and UN intervention in Somalia. Development as container transshipment port continuing.

WEAKNESSES

Dependence on French aid and garrison. Civil war has delayed planned Saudi investment. Other ports on Red Sea now providing stiff competition.

EXPORTS

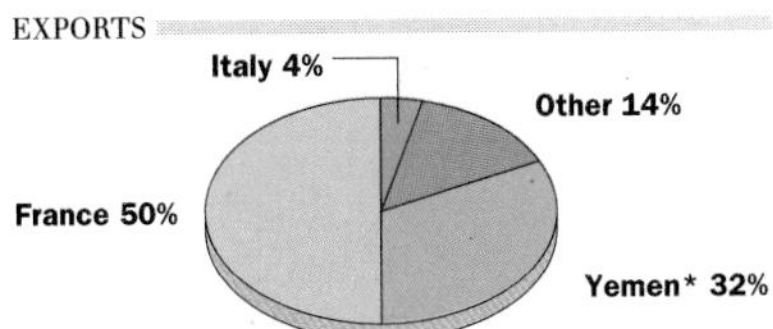

IMPORTS

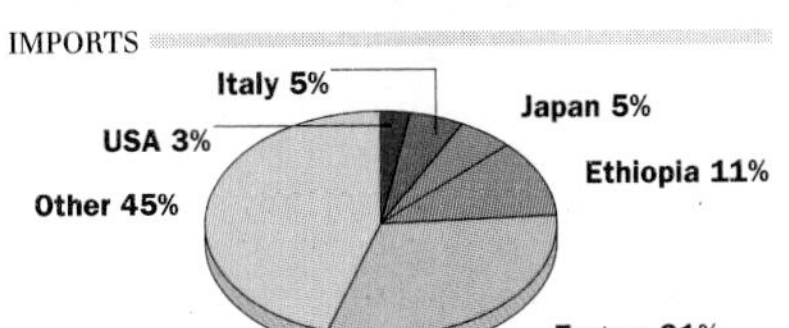

RESOURCES

 175m kwh (capacity 38,000 kw)

 Not an oil producer and has no refineries

415,000 sheep, 72,000 cattle, 58,000 camels

Gypsum, mica, amethyst, sulfur

The few mineral resources are scarcely exploited. Geothermal energy is being developed and natural gas has recently been found. The war has delayed attempts to develop underground water supplies for agriculture.

ENVIRONMENT

 0.4%

Minimal industry presents no ecological threat

The concentration of business around Djibouti port means the inland desert areas are not threatened. Ecological issues are not a national concern.

MEDIA

 The press was freed from restrictions in 1992, but with little effect; most is still state-owned

PUBLISHING AND BROADCAST MEDIA

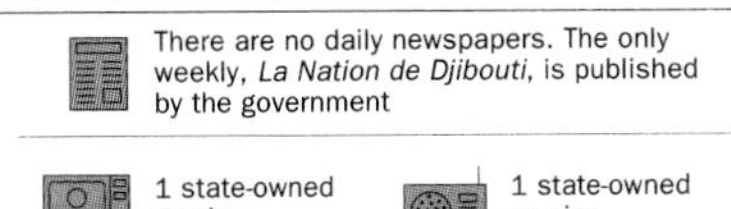

There are no daily newspapers. The only weekly, *La Nation de Djibouti*, is published by the government
1 state-owned service
1 state-owned service

Djibouti is a member of the Arab Satellite Communications Organization. It has two earth stations for radio, TV and telecommunications.

CRIME

 Djibouti does not publish prison figures

 Crime has risen dramatically in northern areas

Crime is difficult to define in a guerrilla war. The government has accused FRUD of atrocities, but its own human rights record has been criticized by Amnesty International. Livestock smuggling across the Red Sea is a problem.

EDUCATION

 48%

Schooling is mostly in French, although there has been a growing emphasis on Islamic teaching, particularly as Saudi Arabia has declared an interest in providing aid for education. Djibouti does not provide university education.

HEALTH

 1 per 5,604 people

 Respiratory and heart diseases

AIDS is a growing problem in Djibouti port, with its large prostitute population. Estimates suggested 3,500 HIV-positive cases in 1992, as against government figures of 1,600. Small French-financed hospitals cater to the urban elite.

CHRONOLOGY

Formerly the Islamic state of Adal, the French made Djibouti the capital of French Somaliland in 1896.

- ❑ **1917** Railroad from Addis Ababa reaches Djibouti's port.
- ❑ **1946** Given French Overseas Territory status.
- ❑ **1977** Independence. Hassan Gouled Aptidon president.
- ❑ **1981** One-party state declared.
- ❑ **1989** Violence erupts between Afar and Issa groups.
- ❑ **1991** FRUD opposition formed. Launches armed insurrection.

WEALTH

 Minimum wage, 15,860 Djibouti francs per month; senior manager (not expatriate), 700,000 Djibouti francs per month

CONSUMER GOODS OWNERSHIP

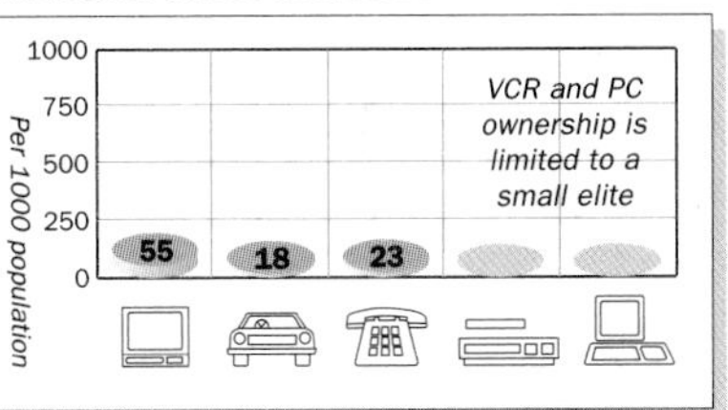

As in many African states, wealth is concentrated among those closest to government. Djiboutians working in the port also do well, although much port labor is expatriate. The war has had little effect on port life, as it is almost completely isolated from the rest of the country. The nomads of the interior are the poorest group.

Trade in the mild narcotic *qat*, grown in Ethiopia and shipped through Djibouti, is highly lucrative. The state is now taking its share of the profits, granting export licenses to only a few favored traders. In Djibouti, as in Yemen and Somalia, *qat* chewing is an age-old, and expensive, social ritual.

WORLD RANKING

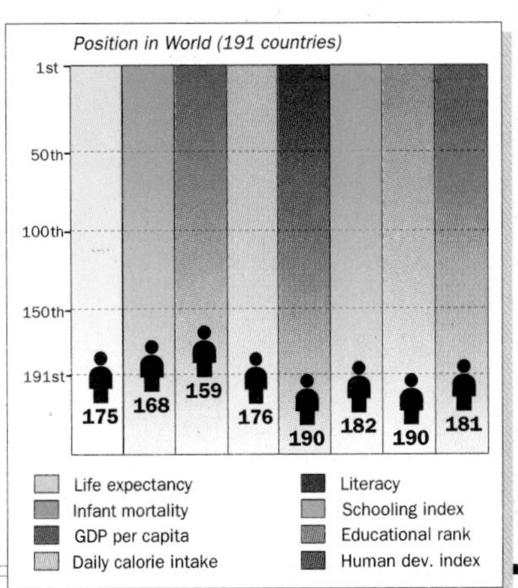

DOMINICA

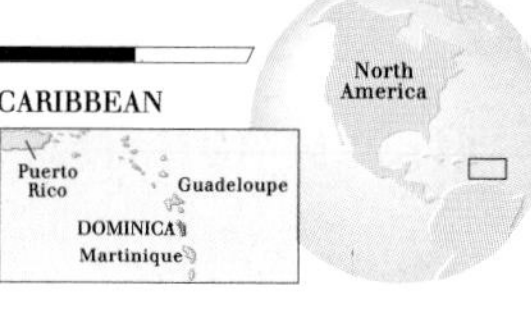

OFFICIAL NAME: Commonwealth of Dominica **CAPITAL:** Roseau
POPULATION: 83,000 **CURRENCY:** East Caribbean dollar **OFFICIAL LANGUAGE:** English

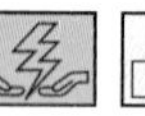

DOMINICA IS RENOWNED as the Caribbean island that resisted European colonization until the 18th century, when it was controlled first by the French, then, from 1759, by the British. Known as the "Nature Island" due to its spectacular, lush and abundant flora and fauna, which are protected by extensive national parks, Dominica is the most mountainous of the Lesser Antilles. Located between Guadeloupe and Martinique in the West Indian Windward Islands group, its volcanic origin has given it very fertile soils and the second largest boiling lake in the world.

CLIMATE

WEATHER CHART

Average daily temperature / Rainfall
°C/°F — cm/in
J F M A M J J A S O N D
40/104, 30/86, 20/68, 10/50, 0/32, -10/14, -20/4 — 40/16, 30/12, 20/8, 10/4, 0

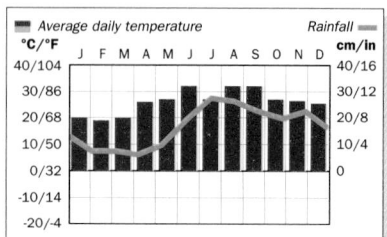

Part of the Windward Islands group in the eastern Caribbean, Dominica is subject to constant trade winds. The rainy season is in the summer, and tropical depressions and hurricanes are likely between June and November. Short, thundery showers in the late afternoon and evening are common all year round.

COMMUNICATIONS

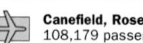

Canefield, Roseau 108,179 passengers — 2 ships 1,600 dwt

THE TRANSPORTATION NETWORK

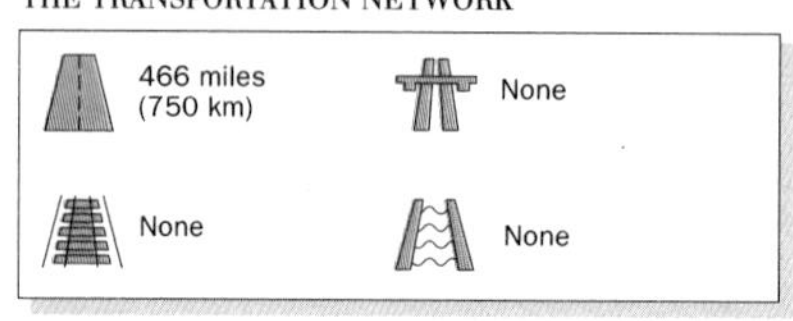

The two airports can take only small propeller aircraft. Improving the road system is now a priority.

TOURISM

55,211 visitors

MAIN OVERSEAS ARRIVALS

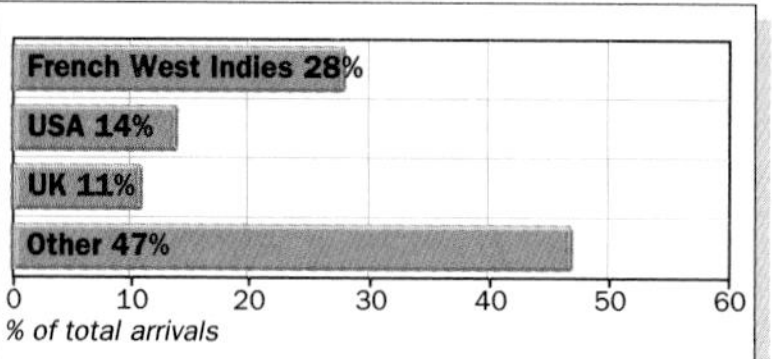

The lack of an airport able to take commercial jetliners (visitors arrive on connecting flights from Barbados or Antigua) has made Dominica less accessible to mass-market tourism than its neighbors. Ecotourism is growing, with visitors coming to view the national parks with their rare indigenous birds, hot springs and sulfur pools.

PEOPLE

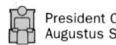

French Creole, English — 344 people per sq. mile

THE URBAN/RURAL POPULATION SPLIT

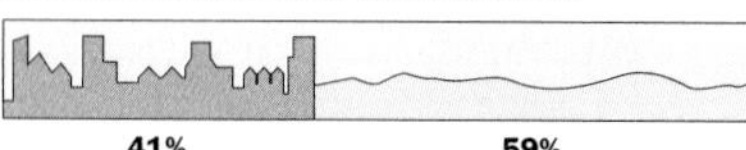

41% 59%

RELIGIOUS PERSUASION

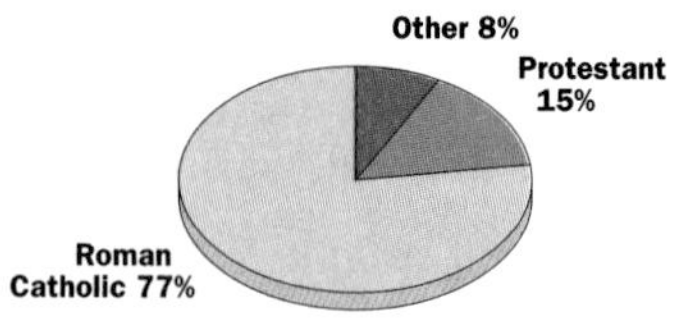

The majority of Dominicans are descendants of Africans brought over to work the banana plantations.

Family life is based on the extended family and in rural areas is often matriarchal.

POLITICS

1995 — President Clarence Augustus Seignoret

THE STATE OF THE PARTIES

49% DFP 27% DUWP 24% LPD

DFP = Dominica Freedom Party DUWP = Dominica United Workers' Party LPD = Labour Party of Dominica

Dominica's electoral system is based on the British model. Politicians tend to come from the professional classes – usually young lawyers and doctors. Occasionally the larger farmers, who provide most party funding, run for office. The DFP, led by Dame Eugenia Charles, has held power since 1980. The dominant political issue is the proposal that Dominica join with the three other islands of the Windwards to form a political and economic union, leading to a single state. The government broadly supports the proposal, but any change will be subject to a referendum.

WORLD AFFAIRS

A disagreement with Latin American states over banana exports to the EU is the dominant issue. Dominica wishes to maintain its preferential market share and has threatened to leave the Organization of American States.

Guadeloupe Passage
Pennville
Clifton
Guillet
Vieille Case
Thibaud
Belmanier
Bense
Calibishie
Larieu
Portsmouth
Prince Rupert Bay
Dos D'Ane
Glanvillia
Wesley
ATLANTIC OCEAN
CARIBBEAN SEA
Melville Hall
Morne Diablotins 1447m
NORTHERN FOREST RESERVE
Dublanc
Marigot
Bataka
Salibia
Colihaut
Coulibistri
Gaulette
Morne Raquette
Salisbury
Layou
Castle Bruce
St Joseph
Good Hope
Saint Sauveur
Mahaut
Petite Soufrière
Rosalie
Massacre
Morne Trois Pitons
Morne Aux Frégates
Canefield Airport
Roger
Laudat
La Plaine
Trafalgar
ROSEAU
Charlotte Ville
Boetica
Giraudel
Bellevue
Délices
Loubiere
Chopin
Pichelin
Pointe Michel
Petite Savane
Fond St. Jean
Soufrière
Tête Morne
Berekua
Scotts Head Village
Martinique Passage
N

DOMINICA

Total Area : 750 sq. km (290 sq. miles)

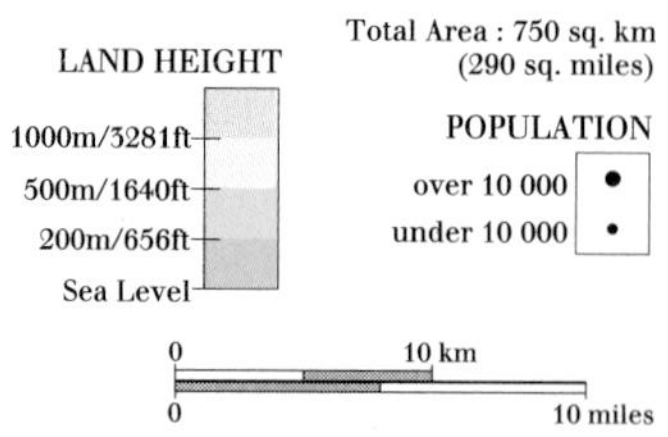

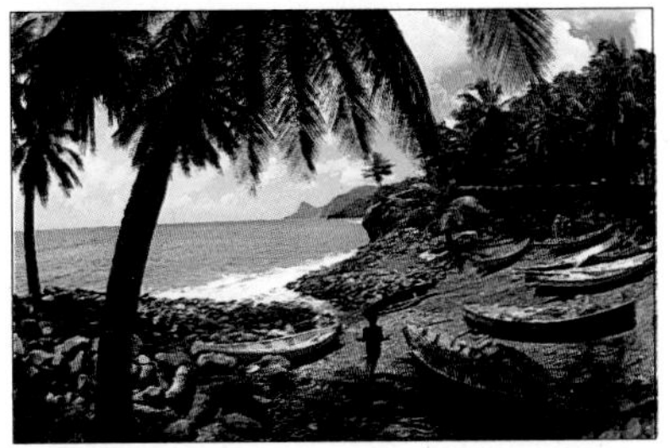

Inshore fishing boats, which mostly supply the domestic market, on a typical Dominican beach.

AID

 $15m (receipts)

 A favored recipient of aid in the region

The generous US aid of the 1980s was a response to Dominica's support for American foreign policy in the region. The EU and UK are also major donors.

DEFENSE

 Dominican Defense Force officially disbanded in 1981

 Not applicable

Dominica has no armed forces, but it does participate in the US-sponsored Regional Security System.

ECONOMICS

 $181m

 2.70 East Caribbean dollars

SCORE CARD

❑ WORLD GNP RANKING	181st
❑ GNP PER CAPITA	$2,200
❑ BALANCE OF PAYMENTS	$-26.3m
❑ INFLATION	6.1%
❑ UNEMPLOYMENT	10%

STRENGTHS

Bananas have been a useful foreign currency earner, though this sector is now threatened.

WEAKNESSES

Dependence on preferential access to US and EU markets for its banana crop (70% of export earnings) highlighted by US moves to deregulate the banana trade. Dominica cannot compete with cheaper Latin American fruit.

EXPORTS

IMPORTS

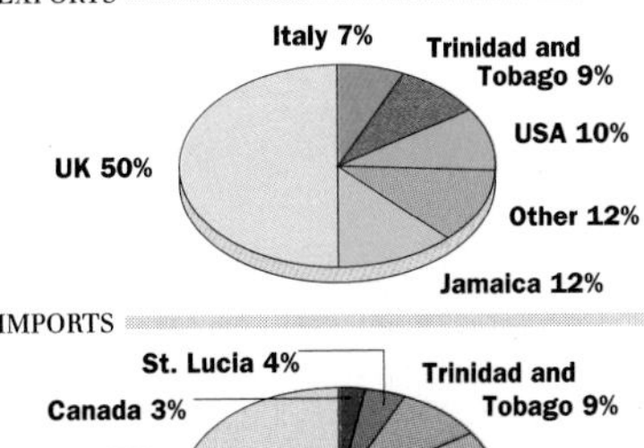

RESOURCES

 30m kwh (capacity 8,000 kw)

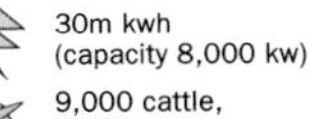 9,000 cattle, 7,000 sheep, 5,000 pigs

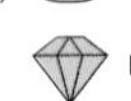 Not an oil producer and has no refineries

None

Dominica has no natural resources and has to import almost all its energy. The development of hydroelectric power at Morne Trois Pitons has been proposed.

ENVIRONMENT

 9%

 Hydropower plans threaten Morne Trois Pitons National Park

The expansion of both agriculture and timber harvesting is threatening Dominica's rainforest; already there is more land under cultivation than planned by the government. Tourism does not currently pose a threat, but this could change if the government succeeds in raising funds to expand the airports to take jets. Two species of parrot – the *Amazonia imperialis* and the Red Necked – are threatened, despite conservation orders. Turtles living on coral reefs off the island will soon be protected.

MEDIA

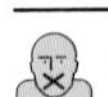 No government restrictions

PUBLISHING AND BROADCAST MEDIA

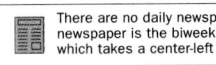

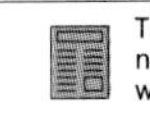 There are no daily newspapers. The dominant newspaper is the biweekly *New Chronicle*, which takes a center-left editorial stance

 No TV service

 1 state-owned station

Local franchises, offering cable TV with selected US networks, serve one-third of the island. Broadcasts from other Caribbean states can also be received. Dominica has one cinema.

CRIME

 Dominica does not publish prison figures

 Up 62% between 1983 and 1986

Dominica has a lower crime rate than most of its Caribbean neighbors. Burglary and armed robbery are the major concerns; murders are rare. Justice is based on British common law and administered by the Eastern Caribbean Supreme Court, which is based in St. Lucia.

EDUCATION

 94%

Education is based on the British system, and retains the selective 11-plus exam for entrance to high school. Students go on to the University of the West Indies or, increasingly, to colleges in the USA and the UK.

CHRONOLOGY

Colonized first by the French, Dominica came under British control in 1759.

- ❑ **1951** Universal suffrage.
- ❑ **1975** Morne Trois Pitons National Park established.
- ❑ **1978** Independence from UK. Patrick John first prime minister.
- ❑ **1980** Eugenia Charles, the Caribbean's first woman prime minister, elected.
- ❑ **1981** Two coup attempts, backed by Patrick John, foiled.
- ❑ **1991** First meeting with Grenada, St. Lucia, and St. Vincent and the Grenadines on constitution for political union.

D

HEALTH

 1 per 2,623 people

 Heart and respiratory diseases, cancer

There are 44 health centers, but difficult communications hamper emergency hospital access for people living in the interior.

WEALTH

 Agricultural field hand, 2 East Caribbean dollars per hour; office manager, 9 East Caribbean dollars per hour

CONSUMER GOODS OWNERSHIP

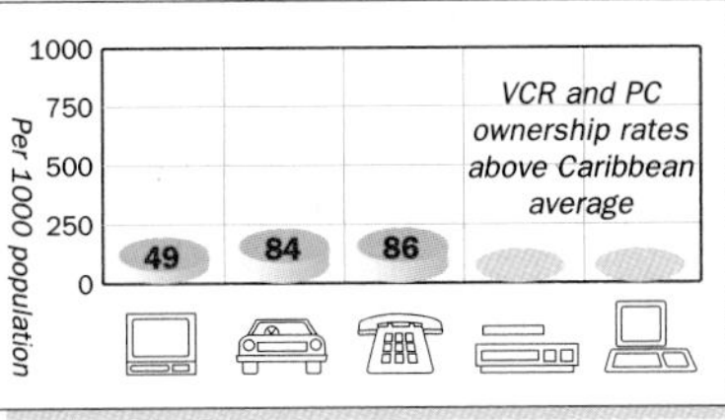

Wealth disparities are not as marked as on the larger Caribbean islands. Dominica now has access to US cable shopping networks. New Japanese cars are particularly favored.

WORLD RANKING

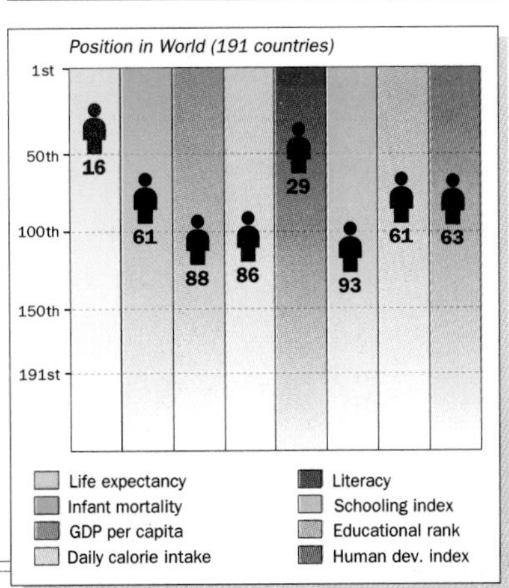

DOMINICAN REPUBLIC

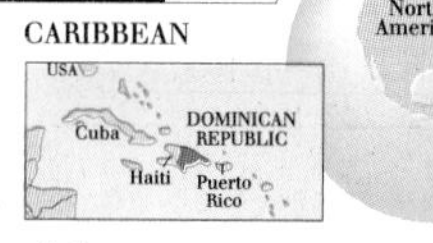

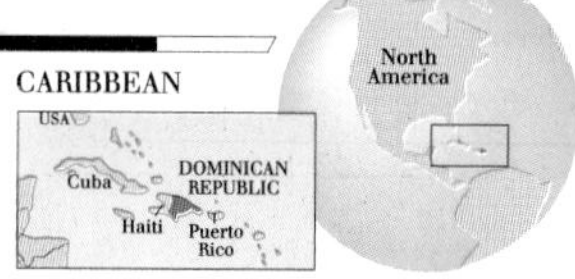

OFFICIAL NAME: Dominican Republic **CAPITAL:** Santo Domingo
POPULATION: 7.5 million **CURRENCY:** Dominican Republic peso **OFFICIAL LANGUAGE:** Spanish

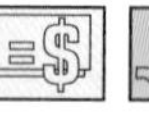

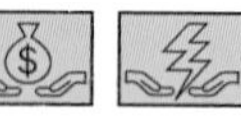

THE LARGEST TOURIST DESTINATION in the Caribbean, greatly favored by Germans and Italians, the Dominican Republic lies 600 miles southeast of Florida. Once ruled by Spain, it occupies the eastern two-thirds of the island of Hispaniola and boasts both the highest point (Pico Duarte, 10,417 ft.) and the lowest point (Lake Enriquillo, 144 ft. below sea level) in the West Indies. Frequent coups and a strong US influence mark its recent history.

View south from Pico Duarte along the fertile banks of the Río Yaque del Norte.

CLIMATE

WEATHER CHART

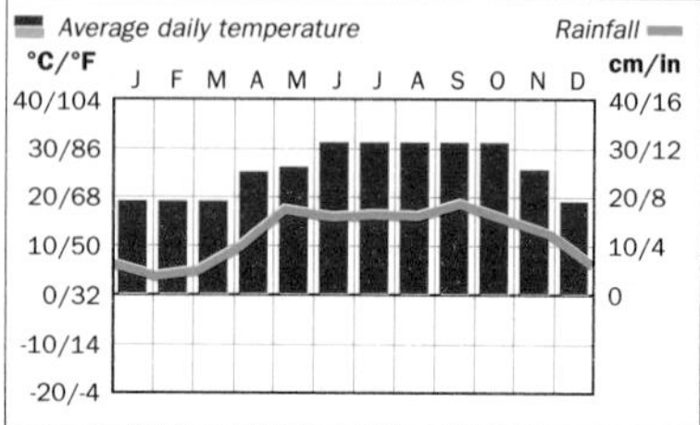

The trade winds blow all year round, providing relief from the tropical heat. The hurricane season runs from June until November.

COMMUNICATIONS

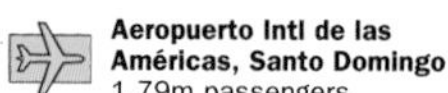

THE TRANSPORTATION NETWORK

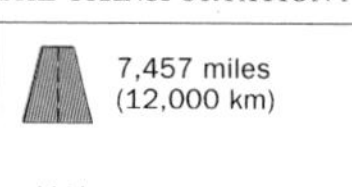

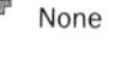

Transportation is mainly by road; railroads are used to transport sugar cane and ores. Improvements to Santo Domingo's airport, aimed at increasing tourism, were completed in 1992.

TOURISM

1.53m visitors

Up 10% in 1990

MAIN OVERSEAS ARRIVALS

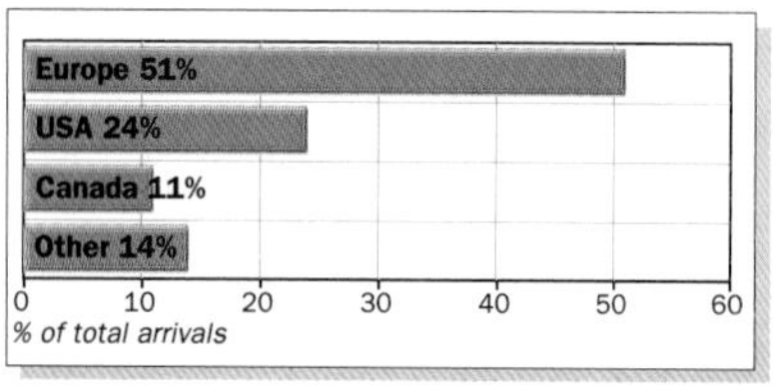

Origin	% of total arrivals
Europe	51%
USA	24%
Canada	11%
Other	14%

The Dominican Republic has good beaches and a hotel capacity of 30,000 rooms, the highest in the Caribbean.

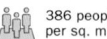

PEOPLE

THE URBAN/RURAL POPULATION SPLIT

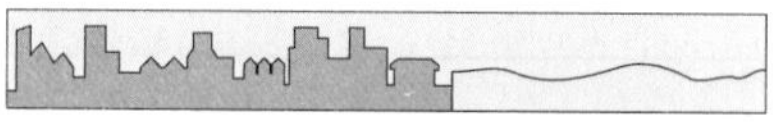

60% 40%

RELIGIOUS PERSUASION

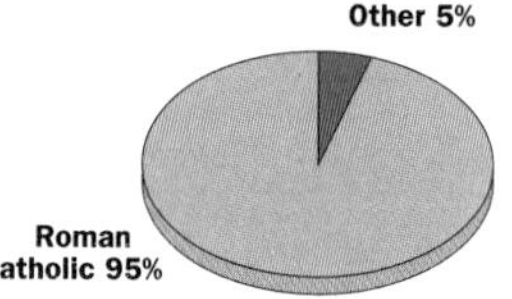

The white population, primarily the descendants of Spanish settlers, still owns most of the land. The mixed race majority – about 73% – controls much of the republic's commerce, and forms the bulk of the professional middle classes. Blacks, the descendants of Africans, are mainly small-scale farmers and often the victims of latent racism, especially in business. Women in the black community work the farms; in the white and mixed-race communities women are starting to appear in the professional sector.

POLITICS

President Sr. Joaquín Balaguer Ricardo

THE STATE OF THE PARTIES

Chamber of Deputies 120 members

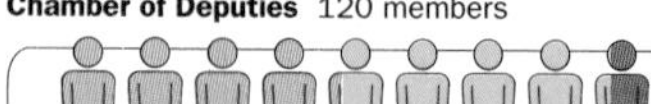

PRSC = Christian Socialist Reform Party **PLD** = Dominican Liberation Party Other = Dominican Revolutionary Party, Independent Revolutionary Party

Senate 30 members

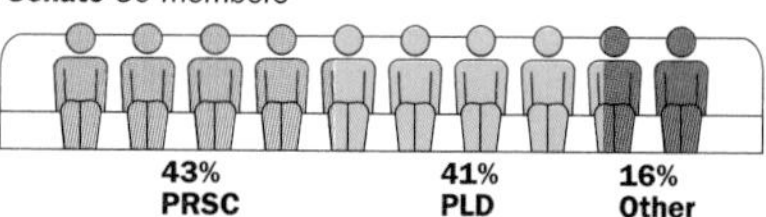

Affluent white landowners and the military hold power behind the scenes; the landowners fund the major political parties, while the military makes clear its support for preferred candidates. There is little political choice between the main parties; all are center-right. Two octogenarians continue to dominate politics – Balaguer of the PRSC and Bosch of the PLD. Cutbacks in government spending are causing popular disaffection.

DOMINICAN REPUBLIC

Total Area : 48 730 sq. km (18 815 sq. miles)

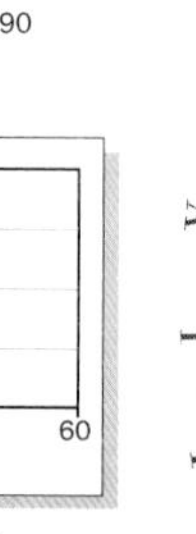

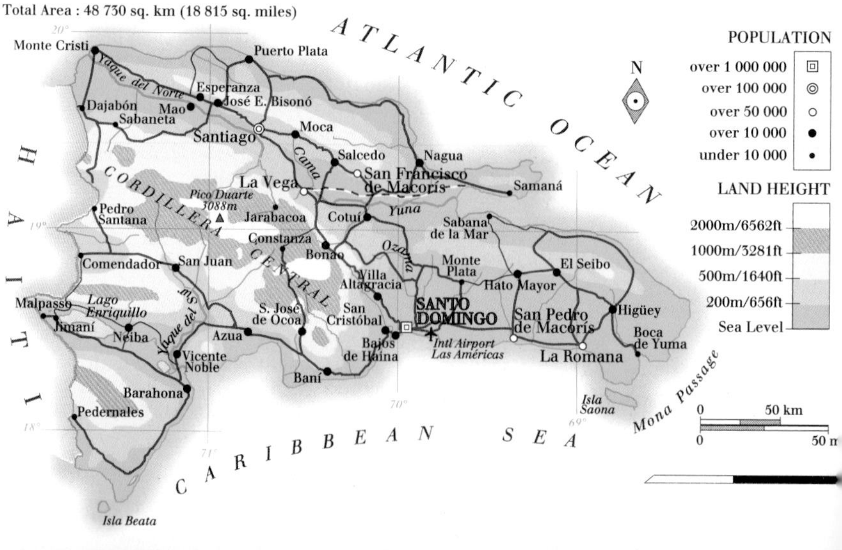

WORLD AFFAIRS

The Dominican Republic's main concerns are whether to join Caribbean or Central and South American economic organizations. It has uneasy relations with its neighbor, Haiti.

AID

 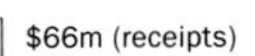 $66m (receipts)

 Down 34% in 1991

Substantial foreign aid is received from the USA and, more recently, from the EU.

DEFENSE

  $35m

 Up 4% in 1991

The 25,000-strong military, apart from its interest in domestic politics, concentrates on preventing illegal immigration from Haiti. The main equipment supplier is the USA.

ECONOMICS

 $7.5bn

 12.48 Dominican Republic pesos

SCORE CARD

❑ WORLD GNP RANKING	90th
❑ GNP PER CAPITA	$1,000
❑ BALANCE OF PAYMENTS	$-58.4m
❑ INFLATION	4.6%
❑ UNEMPLOYMENT	30%

STRENGTHS

Dramatic growth in tourism in recent years. Mining – mainly of nickel and gold – and sugar are major sectors. Tobacco – most is sold to the USA. Large hidden economy based on transshipment of narcotics to the USA.

WEAKNESSES

Major sectors severely affected by current low world prices and cutbacks in US import quotas. Failure to diversify, and loan repayments, are long-term problems.

EXPORTS

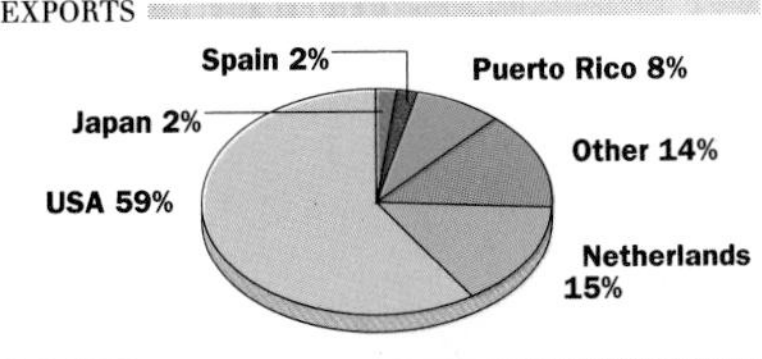

IMPORTS

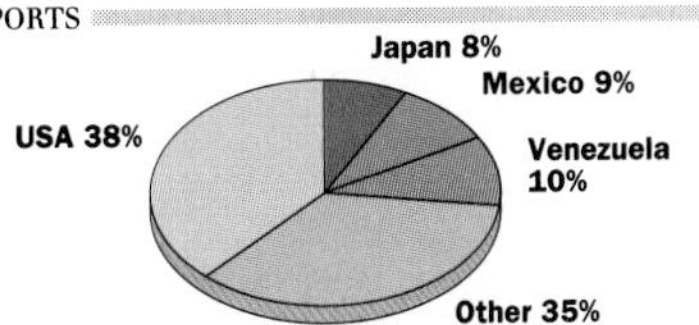

RESOURCES

5.3bn kwh (capacity 1.45m kw)

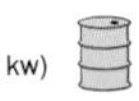 Not an oil producer; refines 15,000 b/cd

21,800 tons

Ferro-nickel, gold, silver

The government is investing $450 million in two new dams to produce HEP as power cuts are almost a daily occurrence. Attempts at oil prospecting have not been successful. Under the terms of the San José Agreement, almost 2 million tons of oil is bought annually from Venezuela and Mexico at preferential terms (20% of the cost is converted into loans).

ENVIRONMENT

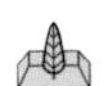 20% (10% partially protected)

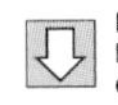 Inadequate legislation has not halted deforestation

The government is lax about enforcing existing laws protecting diminishing forests. Legislation is often conflicting: a 1931 hunting law effectively nullifies recent wildlife protection measures.

MEDIA

 No overt censorship laws, though many instances of newspapers caving in to state pressure

PUBLISHING AND BROADCAST MEDIA

 There are 12 daily newspapers, including *Listín Diario, Ultima Hora* and *El Nacional*

 1 state-owned, 6 independent stations

 10 state-owned, 140 independent stations

Both Mexican and US TV broadcasts can be received easily in the Dominican Republic.

CRIME

 Dominican Republic does not publish prison figures

 Rape down 70% between 1985 and 1988

Recent increases in violent crime are mainly the result of drug traffickers fighting for territory. The USA has accused government officials of complicity in the narcotics trade.

EDUCATION

 83%

Most schools operate a curriculum aimed at preparing pupils for higher education in the USA. However, wealthier Dominicans send their children to universities in Spain.

HEALTH

 1 per 937 people

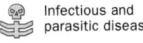

 Infectious and parasitic diseases

Wealthy Dominicans fly to Cuba rather than Florida for medical treatment. The poor rely on a rudimentary public service.

CHRONOLOGY

The 1697 Franco-Spanish partition of Hispaniola left Spain with the eastern two-thirds of the island, today the Dominican Republic.

- ❑ **1865** Independence from Spain.
- ❑ **1930-1961** Gen. Molina dictator.
- ❑ **1962** Bosch Gaviño president.
- ❑ **1965** Civil war; US intervention.
- ❑ **1966-1978** Balaguer president.
- ❑ **1978-1982** Guzmán president; commits suicide in 1982.
- ❑ **1982-1986** Blanco president.
- ❑ **1986** Balaguer reelected president.
- ❑ **1992** Opposition to Columbus celebrations brutally crushed.

WEALTH

 Clothing worker, 333 Dominican Republic pesos per month; oil refinery worker, 2,594 Dominican Republic pesos per month

CONSUMER GOODS OWNERSHIP

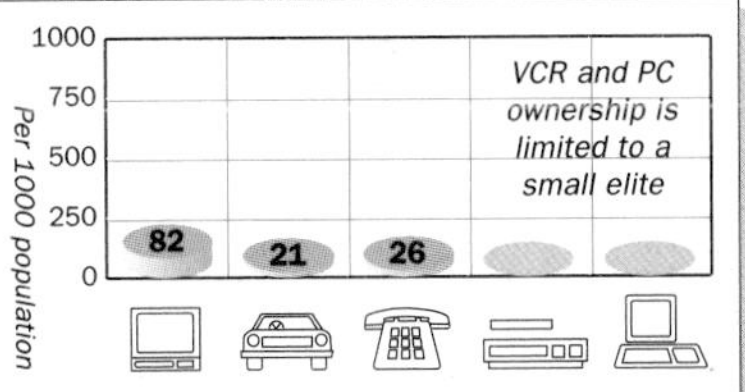

There are great disparities between rich and poor. Generations of governments have promised to close the gap, with few results. The most socially mobile group in the last 20 years has been of mixed race, and has come to dominate the expanding professional sector. Black Dominicans remain at the bottom of the social ladder, accounting for the major portion of small farmers. The old Spanish families are still the wealthiest, retaining their grip on the valuable estates; their younger members spend weekends at Puerto Plata, or on shopping trips to Miami.

WORLD RANKING

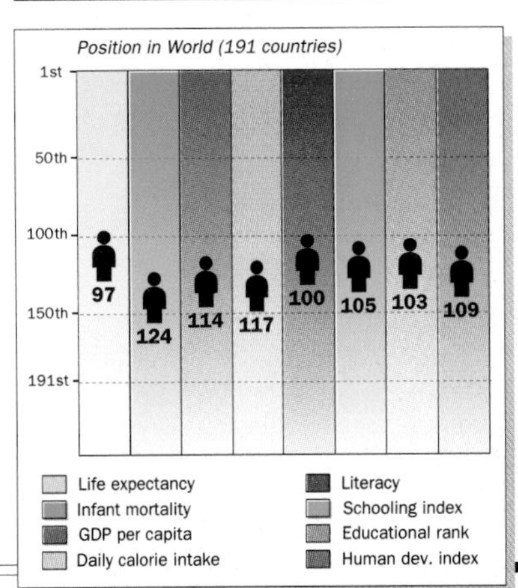

SOUTH AMERICA
Columbia
ECUADOR
Peru
South America

ECUADOR

OFFICIAL NAME: Republic of Ecuador **CAPITAL:** Quito
POPULATION: 11.1 million **CURRENCY:** Sucre **OFFICIAL LANGUAGE:** Spanish

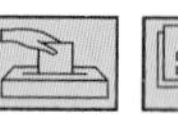

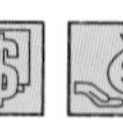

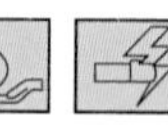

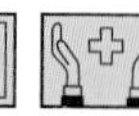

ONCE PART OF the Inca heartland, Ecuador lies on the western coast of South America. It was ruled by Spain from 1533, when the last Inca emperor was executed, until its independence in 1830. Most Ecuadorians live either in the lowland Costa region or in the Andean Sierra. The Amazonian Indians are now successfully pressing for their land rights to be recognized. Oil deposits have boosted the economy in recent years.

CLIMATE

WEATHER CHART

Average daily temperature — Rainfall
°C/°F J F M A M J J A S O N D cm/in
40/104 40/16
30/86 30/12
20/68 20/8
10/50 10/4
0/32 0
-10/14
-20/4

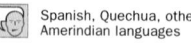

Climate varies from hot equatorial in the Amazon forests, to dry heat in the south and "perpetual spring" in Quito.

COMMUNICATIONS

Mariscal Sucre, Quito 1.71m passengers

55 ships 480,600 dwt

THE TRANSPORTATION NETWORK

23,386 miles (37,636 km)

Pan-American Highway

598 miles (965 km)

930 miles (1,500 km)

Ecuador's extensive road network and antiquated rail system suffer from regular flooding.

TOURISM

306,000 visitors

Down 12% in 1989

MAIN OVERSEAS ARRIVALS

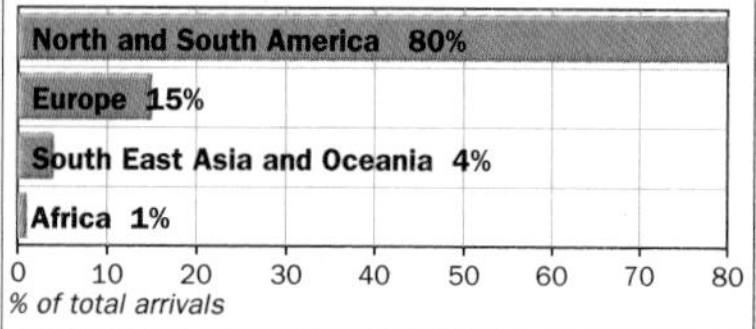

Tourism is well developed. Quito, once the capital of the Inca Empire, is having its Spanish imperial buildings, including 86 churches, restored. Access to the Galápagos is restricted to 40,000 visitors a year.

PEOPLE

Spanish, Quechua, other Amerindian languages

88 people per sq. mile

THE URBAN/RURAL POPULATION SPLIT

56% 44%

RELIGIOUS PERSUASION

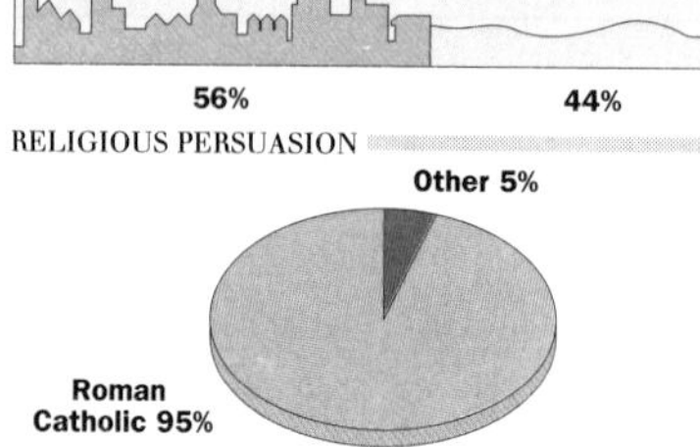

Over half of the population is of Indian-Spanish extraction (*mestizo*). The Indians, who make up about 25% of the population, are currently pressing for Ecuador to be described as a pluri-national state, where different communities of Indians are recognized as distinct nationalities. Their case has been backed by the Catholic Church. The result is a strong and largely unified Indian movement.

POLITICS

1996

President Sixto Durán Ballén

THE STATE OF THE PARTIES

National Congress 77 members

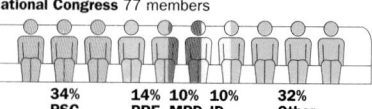

34% PSC **14% PRE** **10% MPD** **10% ID** **32% Other**

PSC = Social Christian Party **PRE** = Ecuadorian Republican Party **MPD** = Popular Democratic Movement **ID** = Democratic Left **Other** = Ecuadorian Conservative Party, Popular Democratic Party, United Republican Party

After years of social democracy, Ecuador followed the rest of Latin America in 1992 and voted for a right-wing, privatizing government dedicated to tackling inflation, which until 1993 had hovered at around 50% for over a decade. The major parties are fairly evenly balanced in terms of political power, and coalition arrangements on specific items of policy are common. The military still has considerable political influence as well as large shareholdings in business.

WORLD AFFAIRS

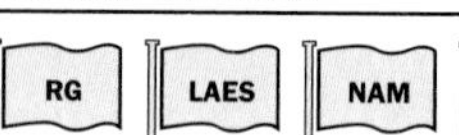

Keeping preferential access to the US and EU markets for bananas is a major concern. Ecuador is developing free-trade agreements with its neighbors.

ECUADOR

Total Area : 283 560 sq. km (109 483 sq. miles)

POPULATION
over 1 000 000
over 500 000
over 100 000
over 50 000
over 10 000
under 10 000

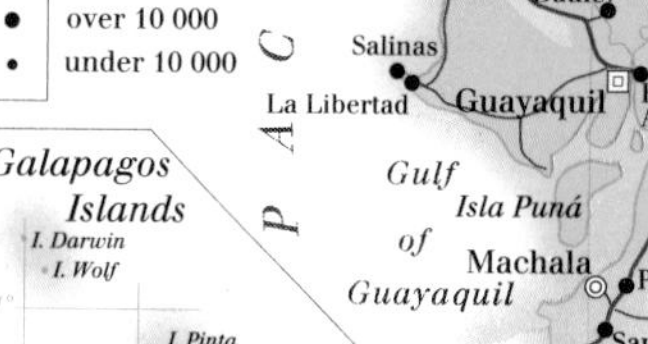

Quito is the highest capital in the world after La Paz in Bolivia. It lies in an Andean valley, lined by 30 volcanoes.

AID

 $220m (receipts)

 Up 42% in 1991

Aid is mostly from the USA and EU, and is essential in tackling Ecuador's $3.2-billion debt. The Galápagos receive generous grants from UNESCO.

DEFENSE

 $260.92m

 Up 41% in 1991

The 58,000-strong military is trained by the USA. Drug gangs are the major concern. Since a brief period of military rule in the mid-1970s, the army has not been directly involved in politics.

ECONOMICS

 $12bn

 1,900.78 sucres

SCORE CARD

❑ WORLD GNP RANKING	71st
❑ GNP PER CAPITA	$1,010
❑ BALANCE OF PAYMENT	$-6m
❑ INFLATION	60.2%
❑ UNEMPLOYMENT	7.9%

STRENGTHS
Net oil exporter. World's biggest banana producer. Fishing industry. Hopes for Andean free-trade accords.

WEAKNESSES
Agricultural land has relatively low productivity. Banana crop vulnerable to new EU import regimes.

EXPORTS

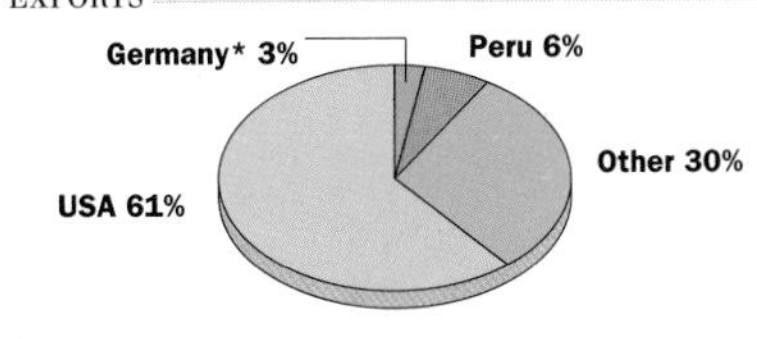

IMPORTS

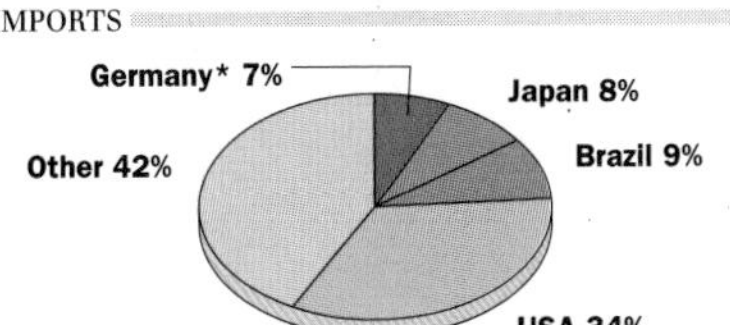

RESOURCES

 6.3bn kwh (capacity 1.66m kw)

 312,600 b/d (reserves 1,599,793 bbl)

 4.2m cattle, 4.2m pigs, 1.3m sheep, 460,000 horses

 Oil, natural gas, gold, silver, copper, zinc

The government is encouraging faster oil exploration and higher output. Ecuador left OPEC in 1992. Over-fishing is threatening mackerel and squid stocks.

ENVIRONMENT

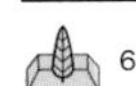 6%

 Area of arid land has increased by 32% in 25 years

The invasion of oil drillers to new areas of Amazonia could spell the end of the Waorani nomads, who have to date successfully avoided all contact with outsiders. In the offshore territory of the Galápagos Islands, the growth in legal and illegal tourism has upset the islands' delicate ecosystems; the land iguana has become sterile and black coral is being stolen in quantity for souvenirs.

MEDIA

 Freedom of speech is guaranteed

PUBLISHING AND BROADCAST MEDIA

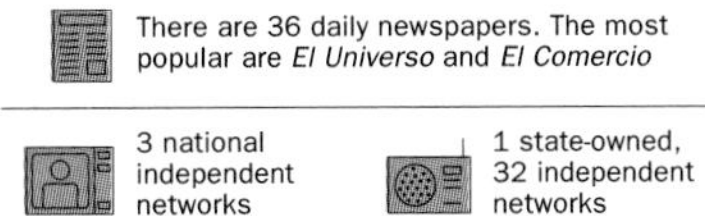

There are 36 daily newspapers. The most popular are *El Universo* and *El Comercio*

3 national independent networks

1 state-owned, 32 independent networks

Ecuador's press is largely independent and free of censorship. It is highly regionalized, based either in the Quito region, or around Guayaquil on the coast. The latter is also a center for commercial radio stations.

CRIME

 Ecuador does not publish prison figures

 Up 1% in 1986

Unlike its neighbors, Ecuador has not suffered from instability caused by left-wing guerrilla action. Minor groups, such as *Alfaro Vive, ¡Carajo!*, have joined the legal political process. Ecuador is classified by the USA as a "transit country" for drugs, and received $6.2 million in anti-drug aid in 1992. Several aircraft have also been donated to help combat trafficking.

EDUCATION

 86%

Around 25% of Ecuadorians – a total of 300,000 students – receive higher education at 16 universities. In schools, teaching is often in Indian languages. Programs have been launched to combat the relatively high levels of adult illiteracy in the countryside.

CHRONOLOGY

Alternating republican and military governments ruled Ecuador from independence in 1830 to 1978.

- ❑ **1941** War as Peru invades part of mineral-rich El Oro Province; Rio Protocol awards it to Peru in 1942.
- ❑ **1948–1960** Prosperity from bananas.
- ❑ **1972** Oil production starts.
- ❑ **1979** Return to democracy.
- ❑ **1983** Economic crisis grows: oil prices fall; floods destroy railway.
- ❑ **1987** President Febres kidnapped briefly by army in protest at his "Andean Thatcherism" experiment.
- ❑ **1990** Indians demand land reform.
- ❑ **1992** Indians granted title to 1 million hectares in Amazonia.

HEALTH

 1 per 939 people

 Intestinal infectious diseases, pneumonia, accidents, murders

Health-care services are now being brought to poor urban districts, but are still unavailable in many rural areas. Between 1987 and 1990, 469 outpatient centers opened. Malaria and stomach cancer are significant health problems.

WEALTH

 Junior company executive, 400,000 sucres per month; chauffeur, 200,000 sucres per month

CONSUMER GOODS OWNERSHIP

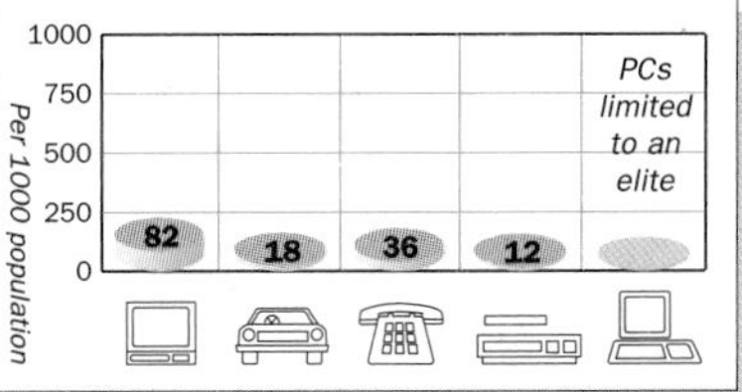

During the 1980s, income per capita dropped by 7.5%. An estimated 60% of the population live in poverty.

WORLD RANKING

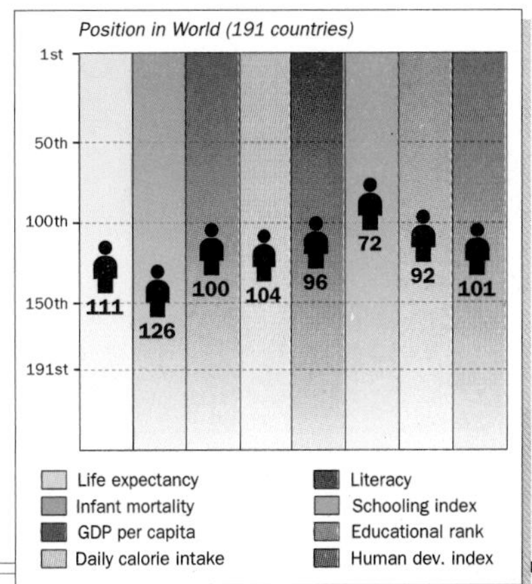

E

EGYPT

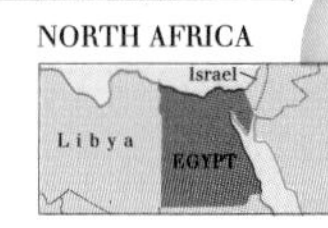
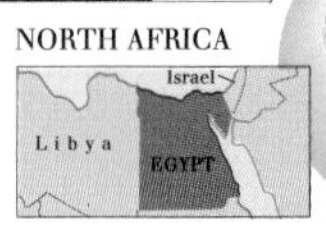

OFFICIAL NAME: Arab Republic of Egypt **CAPITAL:** Cairo
POPULATION: 54.8 million **CURRENCY:** Egyptian pound **OFFICIAL LANGUAGE:** Arabic

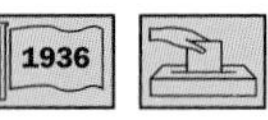

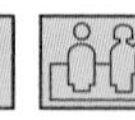

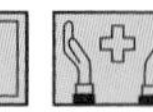

OCCUPYING THE NORTHEAST CORNER of Africa, Egypt is bissected by the highly fertile Nile valley which separates its arid western desert from the smaller semi-arid eastern desert. Egypt's 1979 peace treaty with Israel brought security, the return of the Sinai and large injections of US aid. Its essentially pro-Western military-backed regime is now being challenged by an increasingly influential Islamic fundamentalist movement.

18th-Dynasty Temple of Queen Hatshepsut, dating from the Middle Kingdom, c 1480 BC. It is at Deir el-Bahri on the west bank of the Nile opposite Thebes, Egypt's capital at the time.

CLIMATE

WEATHER CHART

Average daily temperature — Rainfall
°C/°F — cm/in
J F M A M J J A S O N D
40/104, 30/86, 20/68, 10/50, 0/32, -10/14, -20/-4
40/16, 30/12, 20/8, 10/4, 0

Summers are very hot, especially in the south, but winters are cooler. The only significant rain falls in winter along the Mediterranean coast.

COMMUNICATIONS

Cairo International
5.62m passengers

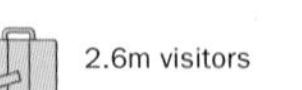
205 ships
1.55m dwt

THE TRANSPORTATION NETWORK

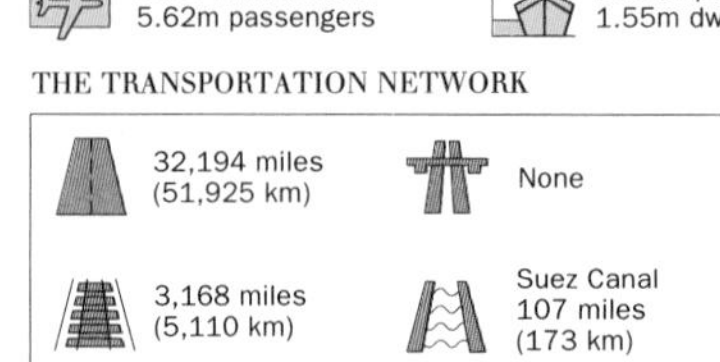

Egypt's cities are linked by adequate roads, but railroads are the main transportation arteries. The Suez Canal is a vital international shipping lane. Cairo's subway opened in 1987.

TOURISM

2.6m visitors

Down 19% in 1993 following terrorist attacks on tourists

MAIN OVERSEAS ARRIVALS

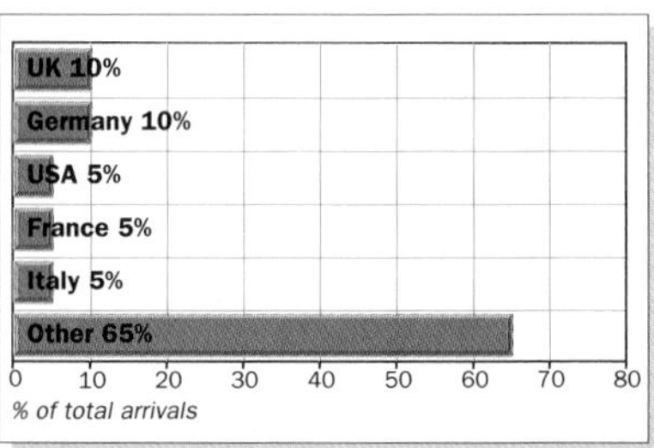

Egypt's wealth of antiquities from its ancient civilizations have made it a key tourist destination since the 1880s. Today, it also offers Nile cruises and some of the world's best scuba diving, notably at the coral reefs near Hurghada on the Red Sea.

In the 1990s, however, the industry went into sharp decline. Islamic fundamentalists began attacking Western tourists. Their aim was to pressure the government into moving the state more toward Islam. The result has been a sharp decline in the number of visitors, from 3.2 million in 1992 to 2.6 million in 1993, and a major dent in foreign exchange earnings. The business convention trade has been particularly affected.

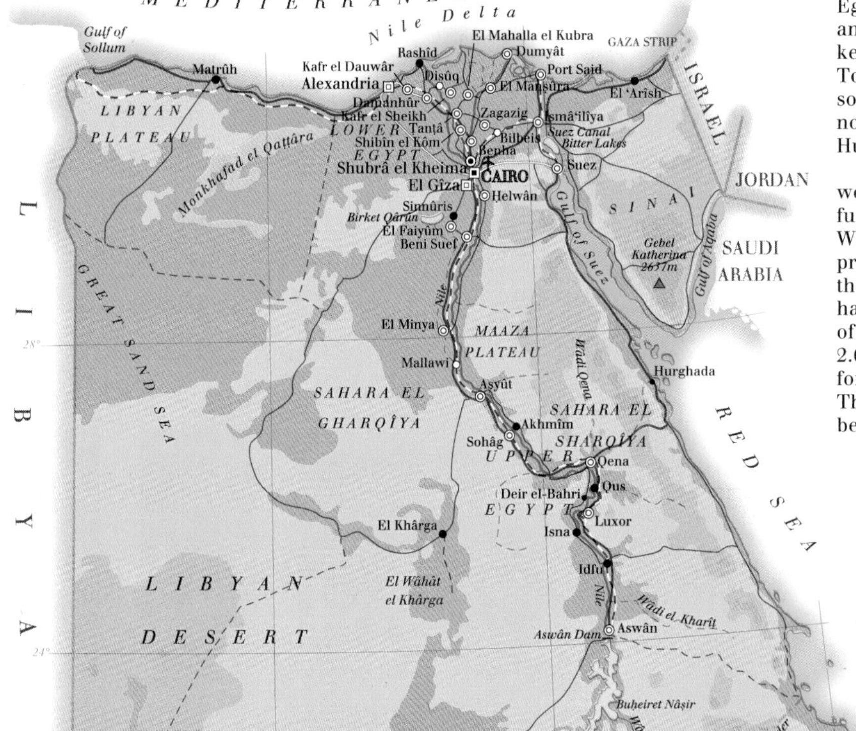

PEOPLE

 Arabic, French, English, Berber

 137 people per sq. mile

THE URBAN/RURAL POPULATION SPLIT

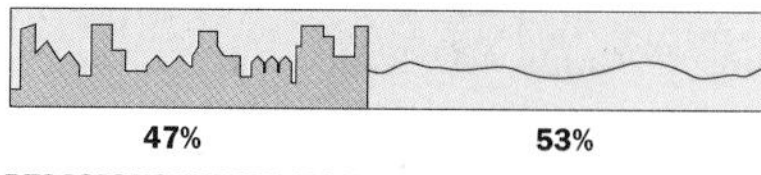

RELIGIOUS PERSUASION

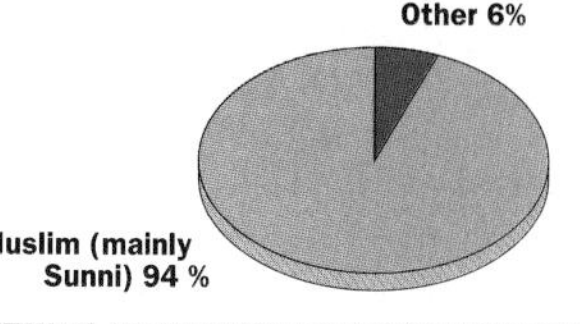

ETHNIC MAKEUP

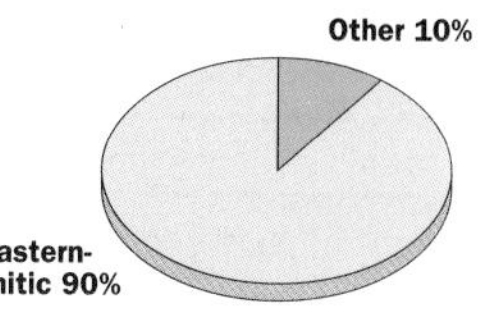

Egypt has a long tradition of ethnic and religious tolerance. Most Egyptians speak Arabic, although many also have French or English as a second language. There are Berber-speaking communities in the western oases. Small colonies of Greeks and Armenians live in the larger towns. Islam is the dominant religion, followed by Coptic Christianity. Although many Jews left Egypt after the creation of Israel in 1948, a small Jewish community remains in Cairo.

Cairo is Africa's most populous city, and Egypt's high birth rate is a key social concern. Aware of the demands this puts on the country's resources, economy and social services, in 1985 the government set up the National Population Council, which made birth control readily available. Since then, the birth rate has dropped by 10%, but Egypt's population is still growing at a rate that will see it double in 30 years. The growing influence of Islamic fundamentalists, who are opposed to contraception, could cause the rate to accelerate.

Egyptian women have traditionally been among the most liberated in the Arab world, playing a full part in the education system, politics and the economy. The steady rise of Islamic fundamentalism, however, threatens their position, particularly in rural areas.

POPULATION AGE BREAKDOWN

% of population by age group

	1960	1970	1980	1990	2000
65+	3.3%	4.3%	4%	3.9%	4.4%
15–64	54.2%	54.3%	56.5%	56.7%	61%
0–14	42.5%	41.4%	39.5%	39.4%	34.6%

POLITICS

 1995

 President Muhammad Hosni Mubarak

THE STATE OF THE PARTIES

People's Assembly 454 members

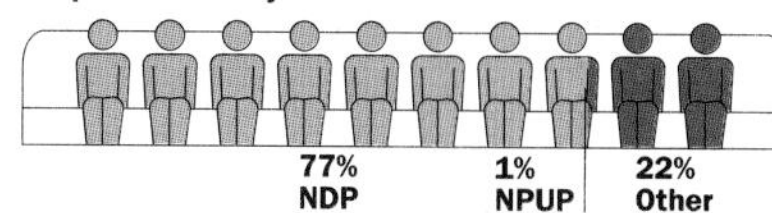

NDP = National Democratic Party
NPUP = National Progressive Unionist Party

Egypt is a multiparty system in theory. In practice, the ruling NDP, backed by the military, runs a one-party state.

MAIN POLITICAL ISSUES

Islamic fundamentalism

The NDP government is engaged in a struggle against Islamic terrorist groups who are seeking to turn Egypt into a Muslim theocracy along Iranian lines. Extremists have committed numerous acts of violence, including attacks on police and tourists. The fundamentalist message, with promises of improved conditions, has proved attractive to both urban and rural poor. The mosques are also growing in prestige as they increasingly provide education and health services that parallel the state's. The NDP's response has been to introduce severe measures to counter the terrorist threat, while allowing religious organizations to pursue their social programs. As long as the NDP retains the support of the army, its position is unlikely to be seriously threatened.

The state of emergency

The ruling NDP party has enforced a national state of emergency since the assassination of President Sadat by Islamic terrorists in 1981. It continues to resist demands for democratic and electoral reforms. As a result, the main conservative and socialist opposition parties boycotted the elections in 1990. An influential strand of liberal opinion in Egypt claims the ban on religion-based political parties fuels violent protest. There have also been calls for reports of human rights abuses to be investigated.

***Hosni Mubarak,** president since the assassination of Anwar Sadat in 1981.*

***Dr. Atif Sidki,** prime minister and minister for international co-operation since 1986.*

PROFILE

Egypt has been politically stable since World War II. Since the death of President Nasser in 1970, it has had just four presidents. Although Anwar Sadat was assassinated in 1981, he was immediately replaced by a man in the same mold, President Hosni Mubarak, who has been in power ever since. The NDP retains a tight grip on the political process through its use of the state of emergency. It has close links with the military (both Sadat and Mubarak were fighter pilots) and with Egypt's massive bureaucracy.

Under Nasser, Egypt promoted Arab socialism, influenced by the Soviet model. Since Sadat, the economy has been liberalized and private enterprise encouraged. However, no parallel liberalization has occurred in politics – one reason for the growing success of Islamic fundamentalists.

WORLD AFFAIRS

Following the 1979 peace treaty with Israel, Egypt has developed closer relations with the USA. Its political and military support for the US-led reaction to Iraq's invasion of Kuwait in 1990 was critical to the success of Operation Desert Storm in 1991. By having the backing of the most powerful state in the region, the Gulf states were able to avoid the charge that they were simply acting at the bidding of the USA. Egypt received considerable economic reward from Saudi Arabia for its participation.

Relations with Iran are tense. Iran actively supports the Islamic groups operating against the NDP government, and characterizes Egypt as a corrupt state under US influence. Egypt is concerned that the international boycott and air exclusion zones imposed on Iraq are simply allowing Iran to extend its power in the Middle East.

Egypt's diplomatic service is the Arab world's largest and many Egyptians serve on international bodies. UN Secretary General Boutros Boutros Ghali is an ex-Minister of State for Egypt. Cairo hosts the headquarters of the Arab League.

AID

 $4.6bn (receipts)

 Falling since massive Saudi injection of aid in 1991

Since the Camp David peace accords of 1978, Egypt has received massive levels of US military aid; the aim was for Egypt to achieve parity with Israel in aid receipts. By 1991, this had almost been achieved.

CHRONOLOGY

Egypt's centuries-old Ottoman occupation ended in 1914 when the country came under British rule. It became fully independent in 1936. Army officers led by Lt.-Col. Nasser seized power.

- **1953** Political parties dissolved, monarchy abolished. Republic proclaimed with General Neguib as president.
- **1954** UK agrees to withdraw troops from Suez Canal in 1956. Nasser deposes Neguib to become president.
- **1956** Suez crisis. British troops withdraw from Canal. UK and USA refuse to help finance Aswân Dam. Nasser orders nationalization of Suez Canal Company to raise revenue for the dam. Israeli, British and French forces invade, but withdraw after pressure from UN and USA.
- **1957** Suez Canal reopens after UN salvage fleet clears blockade.
- **1958** Egypt merges with Syria as United Arab Republic.
- **1960** Soviets begin work on the Aswân Dam.
- **1961** Syria breaks away from union with Egypt.
- **1967** Six Day War with Israel results in loss of Sinai.
- **1970** Nasser dies of heart attack. Succeeded by Anwar Sadat.
- **1971** Readopts the name Egypt. Islam becomes state religion.
- **1972** Soviet military advisors dismissed from Egypt.
- **1974–1975** USA brokers partial Israeli withdrawal from Sinai.
- **1977** Sadat visits Jerusalem for first-ever meeting with Israeli prime minister.
- **1978** Camp David accords brokered by US President Carter, signed by Egypt and Israel.
- **1979** Egypt and Israel sign peace treaty. Egypt is shunned by most Arab states.
- **1981** Sadat assassinated by Islamic extremists. Succeeded by Hosni Mubarak.
- **1982** Last Israeli troops leave Sinai.
- **1986** President Mubarak meets Israeli Prime Minister Shimon Peres to discuss Middle East peace.
- **1989** Saudi Arabia's King Fahd visits Cairo, symbolizing Egypt's rehabilitation in Arab world.
- **1989** After 12-year rift, Egypt and Syria resume diplomatic relations.
- **1990** Egypt participates in UN operation to liberate Kuwait.
- **1991** Damascus declaration provides for a defense pact among Egypt, Syria and Gulf cooperation countries against Iraq.

DEFENSE

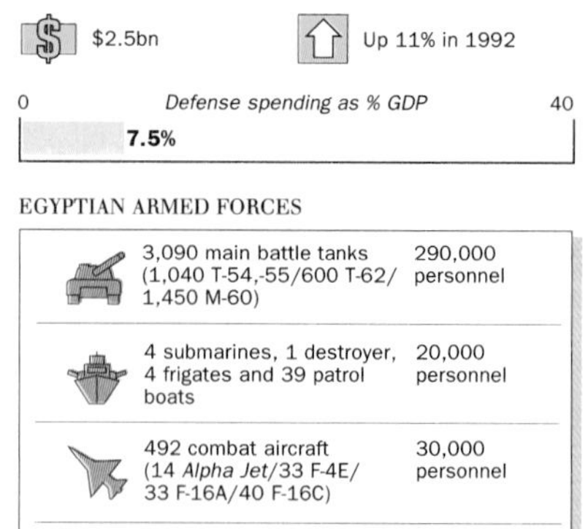

$2.5bn
Up 11% in 1992
0
Defense spending as % GDP
40
7.5%
EGYPTIAN ARMED FORCES
3,090 main battle tanks (1,040 T-54,-55/600 T-62/ 1,450 M-60)
290,000 personnel
4 submarines, 1 destroyer, 4 frigates and 39 patrol boats
20,000 personnel
492 combat aircraft (14 Alpha Jet/33 F-4E/ 33 F-16A/40 F-16C)
30,000 personnel
None

Egypt's armed forces, the largest in the Arab world, are battle-hardened from successive wars with Israel and from participation in Operation Desert Storm to liberate Kuwait in 1991. Over 500,000 reservists augment the regular troops.

After the 1978 Camp David accords with Israel, Egypt stopped buying Soviet weapons and aircraft in favor of Western suppliers. Cooperation with the USA has reaped dividends in the form of more sophisticated defense equipment and improved training. Egypt has a small-arms industry and sells light weapons, notably a version of the AK-47 assault rifle, to other developing countries.

ECONOMICS

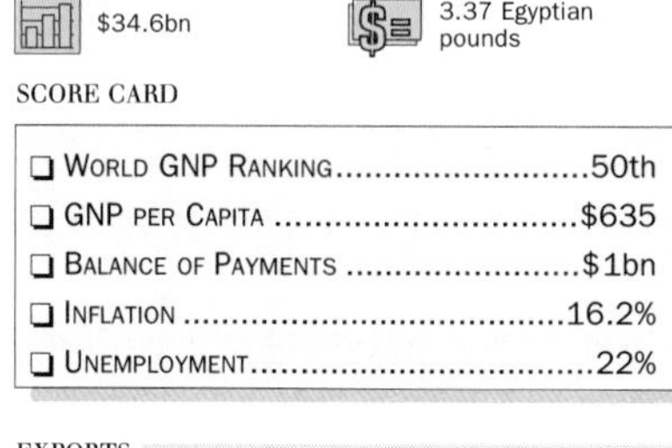

SCORE CARD	
World GNP Ranking	50th
GNP per Capita	$635
Balance of Payments	$1bn
Inflation	16.2%
Unemployment	22%

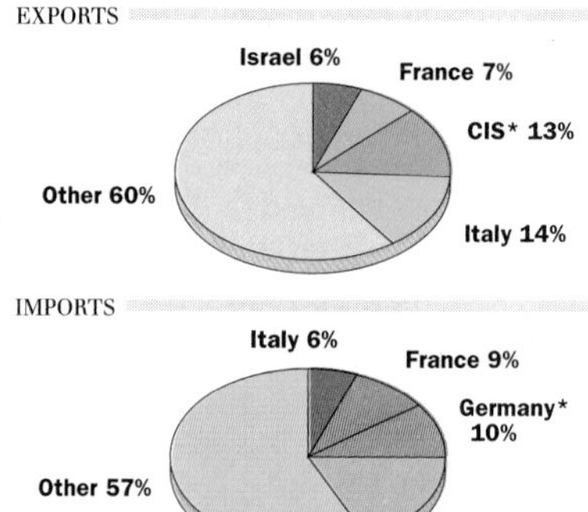

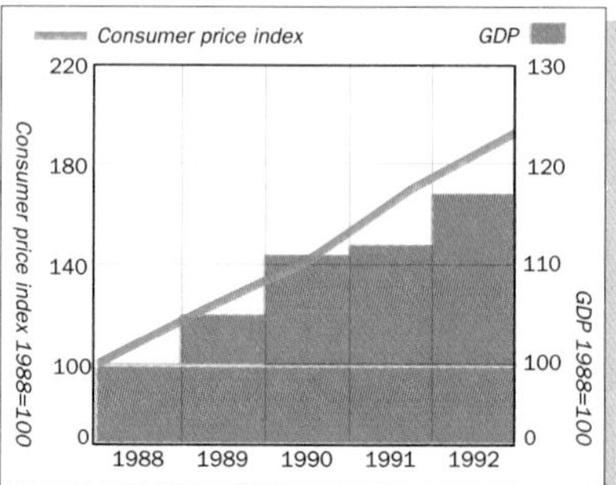

Strengths

Oil and gas revenues. Tourist industry. Remittances from Egyptians working overseas. Suez Canal tolls. Agricultural produce, especially cotton. Light industry and manufacturing.

Weaknesses

Reduction in remittances from Egyptians working overseas due to recession in Gulf states. Dependence on imported technology. High birth rate.

Profile

Under President Nasser, Egypt followed an economic policy inspired by the Soviet model. Rigid and highly centralized, it gave Egypt one of the largest public sectors of all developing countries. Economic restrictions were first relaxed in 1974. President Sadat's open-door policy allowed joint ventures with foreign partners for the first time, although the business classes were the only ones to profit. Most Egyptians suffered from new austerity measures.

Under President Mubarak, economic reform has quickened and policies are more sensitive to the high levels of unemployment and poverty. Priorities now are to reduce import dependence by encouraging manufacturing, and to sustain economic growth to keep up with the increase in population.

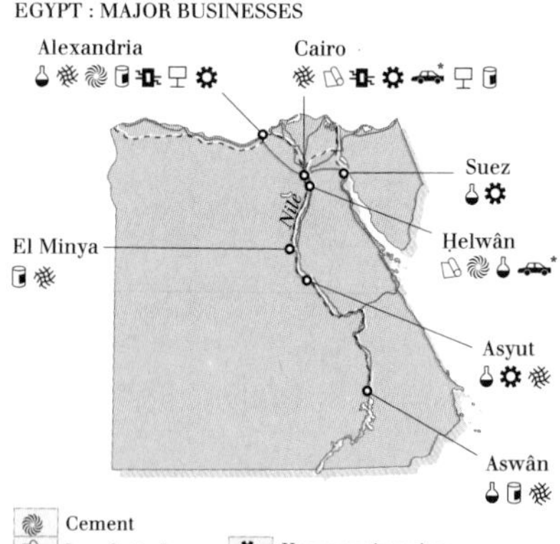

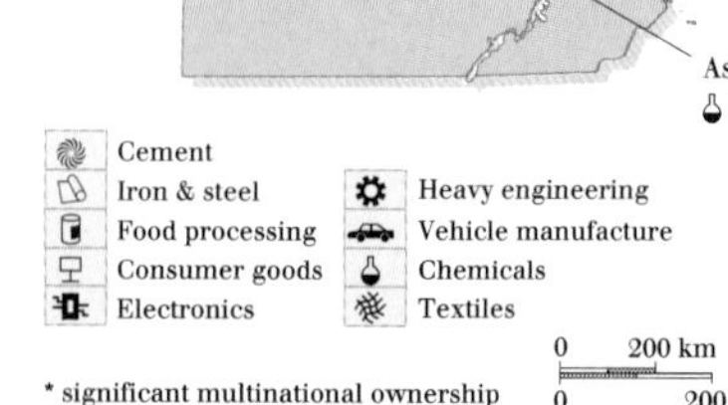

* significant multinational ownership

RESOURCES

39.5bn kwh (capacity 11.7m kw)

880,900 b/d (reserves 6,200,000,000 bbl)

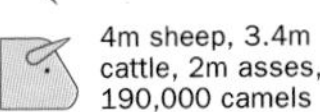

4m sheep, 3.4m cattle, 2m asses, 190,000 camels

Natural gas, oil, phosphates, manganese, uranium

ELECTRICITY GENERATION

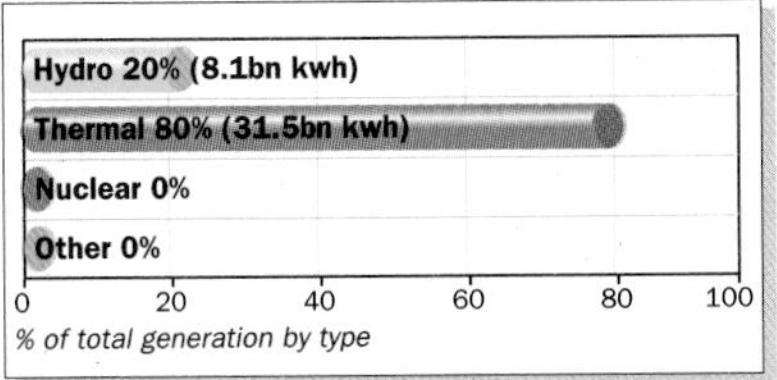

Oil and gas are Egypt's most valuable resources. Most of Egypt's oil comes from the western desert, the Red Sea, Sinai and Upper Egypt. Oil multinationals are involved in new explorations, but Egypt is not as profitable a source as more competitive oil-rich countries, such as Algeria and Yemen. 55% of Egypt's oil production is consumed locally.

Most electricity in Egypt is derived from hydroelectric power and coal rather than oil. The massive Aswân Dam provides the bulk of hydroelectricity. Begun in 1960 and completed ten years later, the dam has a generating capacity of 10 billion kwh. By 1974, revenue from the dam had covered construction costs.

EGYPT : LAND USE

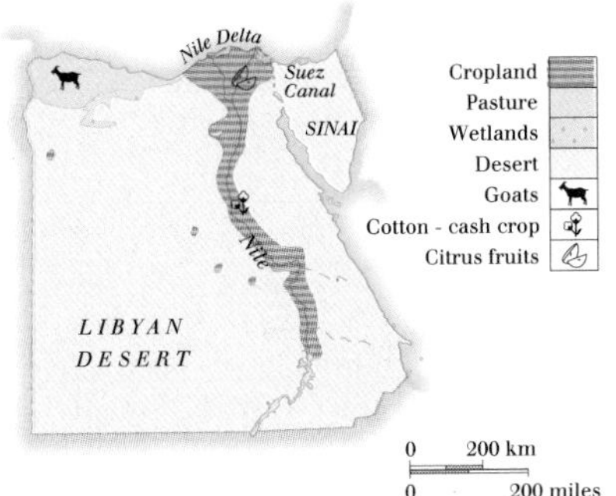

ENVIRONMENT

0.8% (0.7% partially protected)

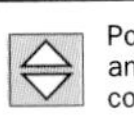

Population control and water are prime concerns

ENVIRONMENTAL TREATIES

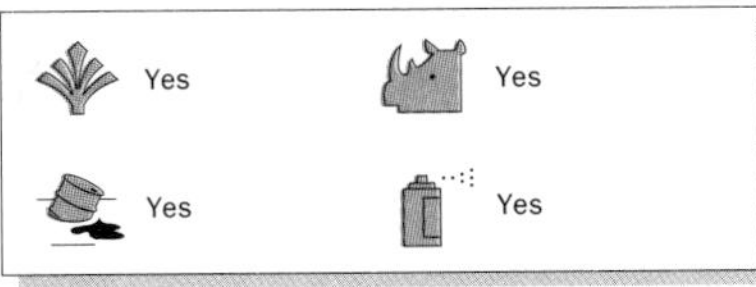

Most of Egypt suffers from a chronic lack of water. The Nile is the only perennial source and is increasingly saline due to the Aswân Dam. The main cities suffer from heavy industrial pollution, and environmental controls are minimal. In Cairo, the recent completion of a sewerage system has improved sanitary conditions.

MEDIA

Free press in theory, but government restrictions in practice

Long regarded as a center of liberal Arab journalism, Egypt is increasingly under siege from Islamic political dogma. Even the leading liberal newspaper *Al Ahram* has altered its coverage. More TV airtime is now given to Islamic sermons and less to secular or Western opinions.

CRIME

Egypt does not publish prison figures

Up 11% in 1990

CRIME RATES

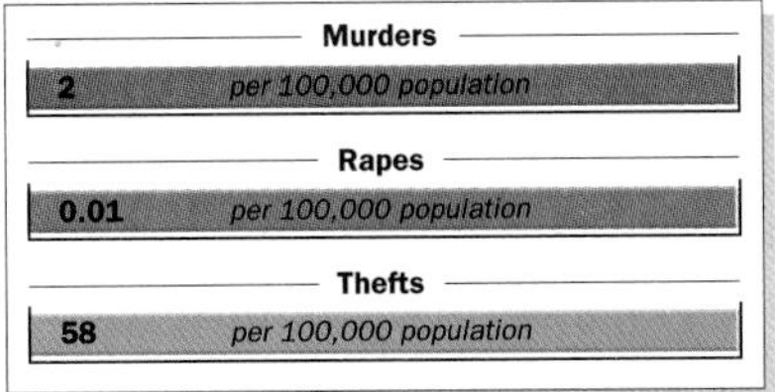

Terrorist attacks have tarnished Egypt's reputation as a law-abiding country; street crime and muggings were previously rare. Inter-community violence – particularly attacks by Muslims on Christians and *vice versa* – has recently become more common. Islamic fundamentalist extremists have also been attacking Western tourists as part of their campaign against the government. Under the state of emergency, the Egyptian police have considerable powers, and there have been reports of human rights abuses.

EDUCATION

48%

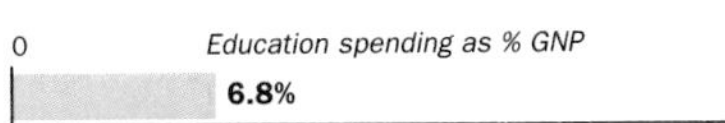

THE EDUCATION SYSTEM

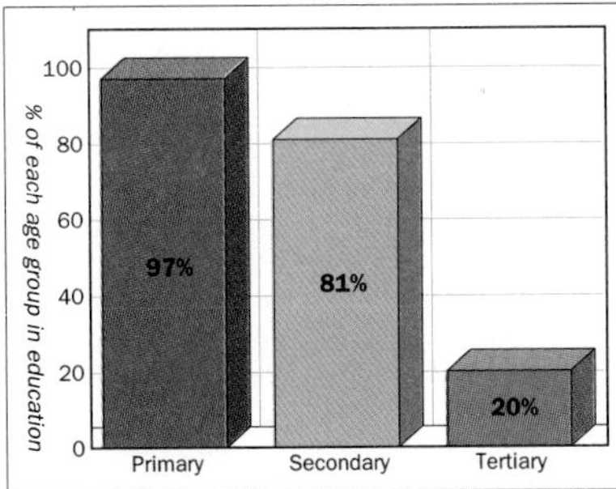

Education is free. Most Egyptians attend primary school to the age of 11, but few complete secondary education, even though it is in theory compulsory until 15 years of age. The literacy rate is 62% for men and 34% for women. Egypt has 13 universities.

PUBLISHING AND BROADCAST MEDIA

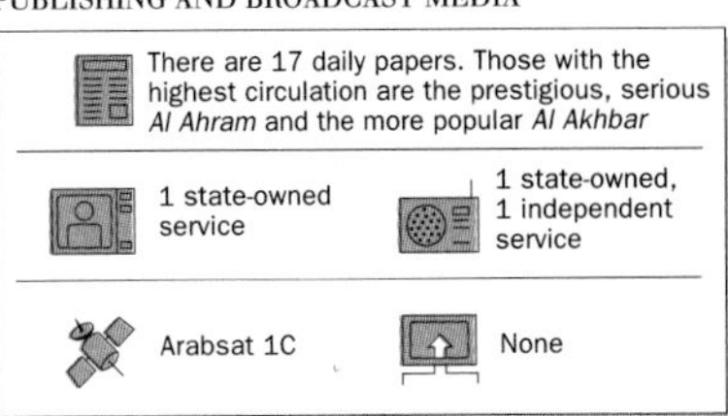

There are 17 daily papers. Those with the highest circulation are the prestigious, serious *Al Ahram* and the more popular *Al Akhbar*
1 state-owned service
1 state-owned, 1 independent service
Arabsat 1C
None

HEALTH

1 per 5,092 people

Digestive, respiratory and heart diseases, perinatal deaths

0 *Health spending as % GNP* 25

1.1%

Health care is rudimentary – there is only one hospital bed for every 500 people. Patient–doctor ratios are among the lowest in the Arab world. Islamic medical centers based on the mosque organization are spreading and replacing the state system.

WEALTH

Wealth heavily concentrated in Cairo

CONSUMER GOODS OWNERSHIP

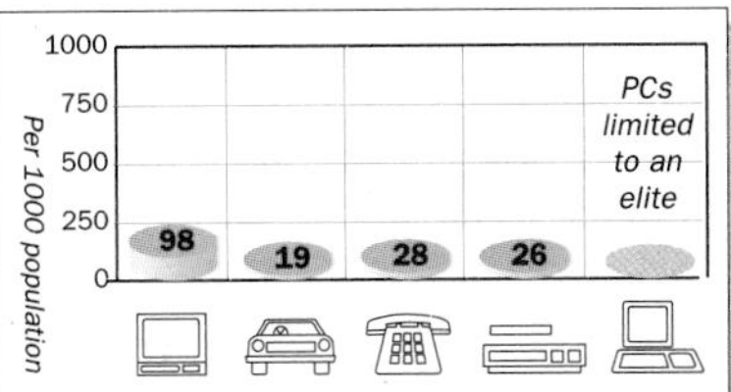

Wealth disparities are highly marked in Egypt. The largely urban Coptic Christian community is the group with the highest standard of living. Most Egyptians are subsistence farmers. The return of many unemployed workers from the Gulf states has further depressed conditions in the countryside.

WORLD RANKING

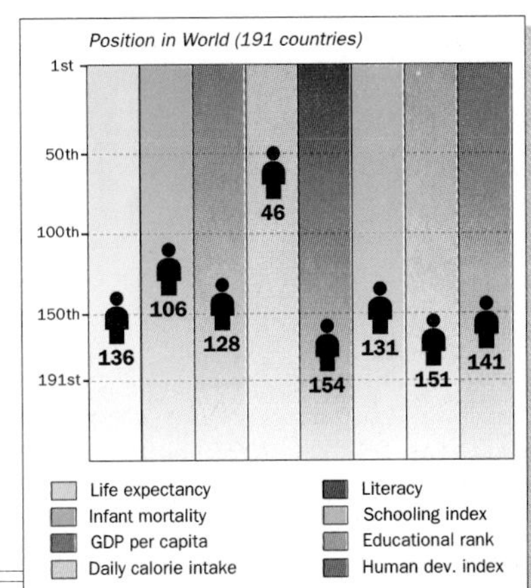

E

El Salvador

Official Name: Republic of El Salvador **Capital:** San Salvador
Population: 5.4 million **Currency:** Colón **Official Language:** Spanish

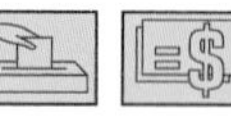

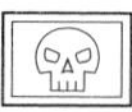

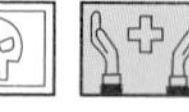

The smallest and most densely populated Central American republic, El Salvador won full independence in 1856. Located on the Pacific coast, it lies within a seismic zone. Between 1979 and 1991, El Salvador was ravaged by a civil war between US-backed right-wing governments and left-wing FMLN guerrillas. Since the UN-brokered peace agreement, the country has been concentrating on rebuilding its shattered economy.

View over the capital, San Salvador. *It lies in a depression in the southern and higher of El Salvador's two mountain ranges, which is punctuated by more than 20 volcanoes.*

CLIMATE

WEATHER CHART

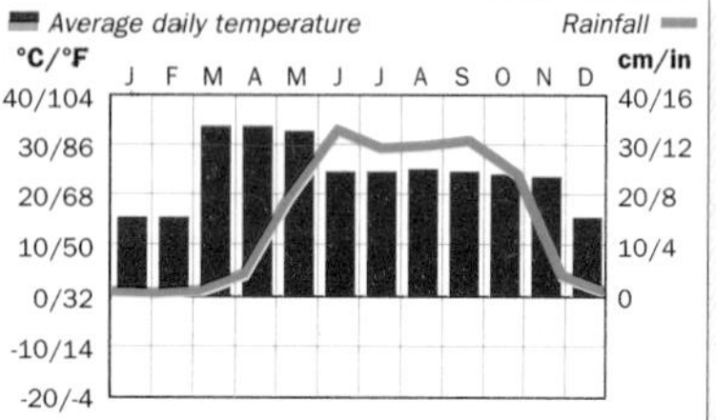

The tropical coastal *tierra caliente* is very hot, with seasonal rains, but the hills are cooler at night. The higher *tierra templada* is drier and also cooler.

COMMUNICATIONS

Cuscatlan, San Salvador 537,961 passengers

Has no fleet

THE TRANSPORTATION NETWORK

7,764 miles (12,495 km)

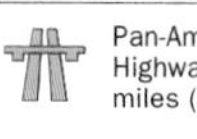

Pan-American Highway 190 miles (306 km)

374 miles (602 km)

Rio Lempa

Infrastructure was badly affected by the civil war. Roads and bridges, natural FMLN targets, are gradually being repaired.

TOURISM

314,482 visitors

MAIN OVERSEAS ARRIVALS

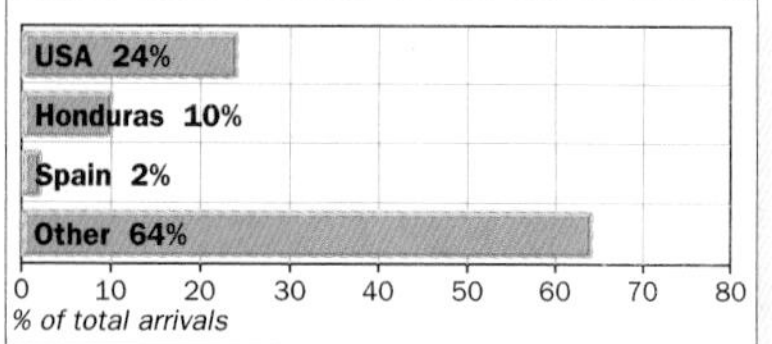

The civil war effectively ended tourism. Peace has brought a few visitors back to the unspoiled beach resorts of El Salvador's Costa del Sol.

PEOPLE

Spanish

653 people per sq. mile

THE URBAN/RURAL POPULATION SPLIT

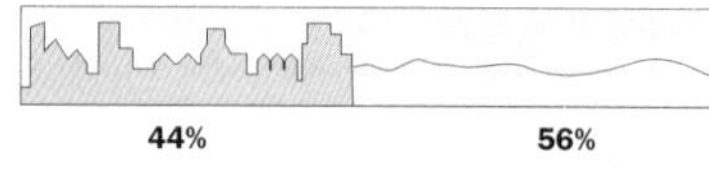

RELIGIOUS PERSUASION

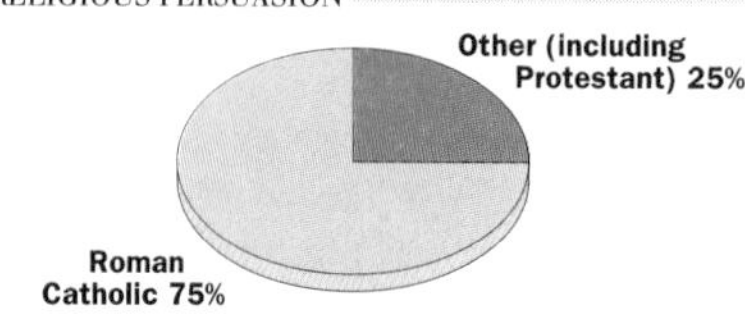

Salvadoreans are largely a mestizo people with few ethnic tensions. The civil war was fought over economic disparities, which still exist.

POLITICS

1997

President Alfredo Félix Christiani Burkard

THE STATE OF THE PARTIES

Legislative Assembly 84 members

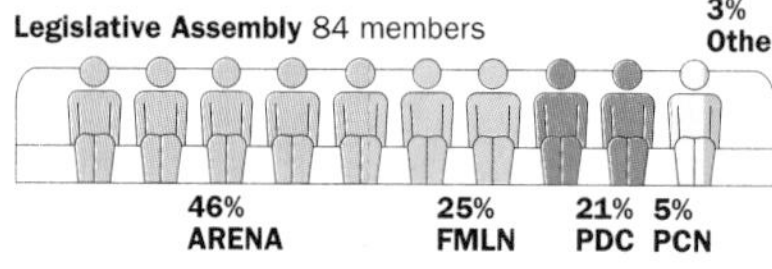

ARENA = National Republican Alliance **FMLN** = Farabundo Martí Liberation Front **PDC** = Christian Democratic Party **PCN** = National Conciliation Party **Other** = Democratic Convergence, National United Movement

El Salvador has traditionally been dominated by two main parties, the centrist PDC and right-wing ARENA. The latter represents the interests of the 14 main coffee-growing families. However, in the 1994 elections, the left-wing FMLN, whose guerrillas at one time controlled one-third of El Salvadorean territory, won 25% of the vote. The elections marked the return of the left and center-left to the formal political system for the first time in 60 years. Apart from the huge task of rebuilding the shattered economy, the major problem is resettling the estimated 500,000 war refugees.

WORLD AFFAIRS

During the 1980s, El Salvador was renowned internationally for abuses of human rights by military death squads, allegedly controlled by ex-ARENA leader, Roberto D'Aubuisson. El Salvador's attempt to defend its record at the UN failed.

Today, conditions have improved and El Salvador is talking of integration with its neighbors, reflecting US policy on the region. Dependence on US aid means that the US ambassador remains one of the most influential figures in El Salvador's external and internal affairs.

AID

$290m (receipts)

Down 17% in 1991

The USA has long been the main aid donor. During the civil war, around 75% of aid was spent on arms for fighting FMLN guerrilla forces. The focus is now to secure peace and achieve national reconciliation by funding rebuilding and refugee resettlement programs. The World Bank and Inter-American Development Fund have also directed hundreds of millions of dollars into El Salvador.

DEFENSE

$145m

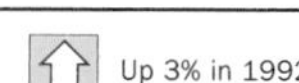

Between 1979 and 1991, the military fought an unrestricted war against the FMLN. Human rights were effectively suspended and governments that opposed the military overthrown. Its main backers were the USA, which supplied over $1 billion worth of arms, and Israel. The peace treaty includes plans to reduce the size of the army and establish a civilian police force.

ECONOMICS

$6.4bn  8.68 colones

SCORE CARD

❑ WORLD GNP RANKING	99th
❑ GNP PER CAPITA	$1,185
❑ BALANCE OF PAYMENTS	$-195m
❑ INFLATION	11.9%
❑ UNEMPLOYMENT	7.5%

STRENGTHS

Very few. El Salvador requires massive injections of aid to survive.

WEAKNESSES

Civil war caused $2 billion worth of damage. Over-dependence on coffee, which accounts for 90% of exports. Rural areas desperately poor, with rising numbers of landless rural poor.

EXPORTS

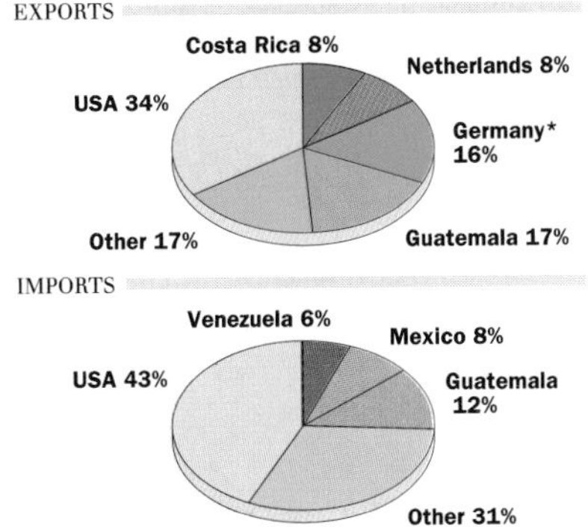

RESOURCES

 2.3bn kwh (capacity 740,000 kw)

 Not an oil producer; refines 15,100 b/cd

1m cattle, 450,000 pigs, 93,000 horses

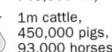

Salt, limestone, gypsum

El Salvador has no significant resources. The restoration of electric service is a priority.

ENVIRONMENT

 1% (0.2% partially protected)

 20,235 hectares set aside for conservation

Most of the rainforest has been cut down for agriculture, leading to topsoil erosion and desertification. Pesticide poisoning of land is a major problem.

MEDIA

 Total censorship by the military during the civil war. The 4 independent TV stations have one owner

PUBLISHING AND BROADCAST MEDIA

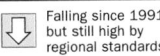

There are 5 daily newspapers. *La Prensa Gráfica* has the highest circulation

2 state-owned, 4 independent stations

1 state-owned, 75 independent stations

Many opposition journalists were murdered during the civil war. The FMLN is now able to publish its views.

CRIME

 El Salvador does not publish prison figures

Falling since 1991, but still high by regional standards

The legal system was largely bypassed by the military during the civil war. It operated the paramilitary death squads responsible for over 50,000 murders. Political violence is still relatively high. The peace terms of 1991 called for an overhaul of the politically appointed legal system.

EDUCATION

 73%

Education is based on the US system. Provision is limited in rural areas. During the civil war, state universities were closed and occupied by the military. The government, however, encouraged the establishment of private universities, now increasingly popular among the middle classes.

CHRONOLOGY

El Salvador was Spanish until 1821. Part of the United Provinces of Central America from 1823-1839, it became independent in 1856.

- ❑ **1932** Army crushes popular insurrection led by Farabundo Martí.
- ❑ **1944–1979** Army effectively rules through PCN.
- ❑ **1979** Reformist officers overthrow PCN government. Fail to curb rising army-backed political violence.
- ❑ **1981** Left-wing Farabundo Martí National Liberation Movement (FMLN) launches civil war.
- ❑ **1991** UN-brokered peace. FMLN recognized as a political party.
- ❑ **1992** Peace achieved.

E

HEALTH

 1 per 2,641 people

 Accidents, violence, circulatory diseases, infections

Health spending almost halved during the civil war. Only the military hospitals are now adequately supplied.

WEALTH

 Machine assembler, 1,772 colones per month; insurance agent, 6,510 colones per month

CONSUMER GOODS OWNERSHIP

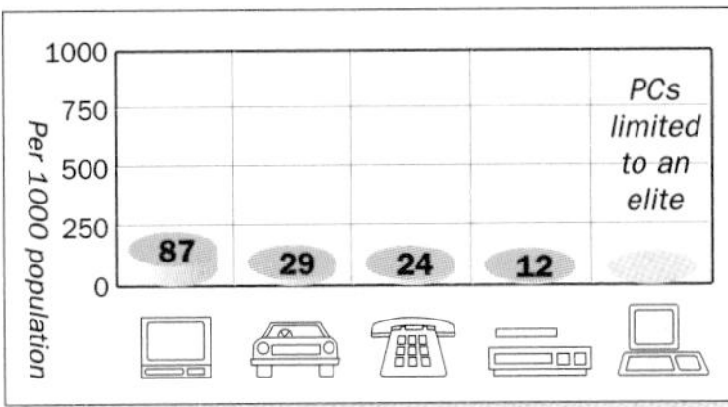

El Salvador has considerable wealth disparities, with 20% owning 70% of national wealth. The rich favor bullet-proof cars and tend to own second homes in Los Angeles or Miami.

WORLD RANKING

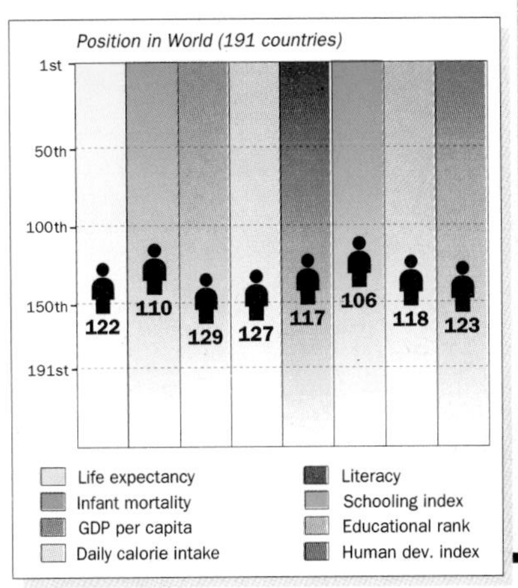

WEST AFRICA

Africa

Cameroon

EQUATORIAL GUINEA

Congo

Gabon

EQUATORIAL GUINEA

OFFICIAL NAME: Republic of Equatorial Guinea **CAPITAL:** Malabo
POPULATION: 400,000 **CURRENCY:** CFA franc **OFFICIAL LANGUAGE:** Spanish

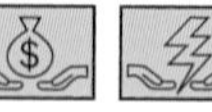

COMPRISING FIVE ISLANDS and the territory of Río Muni on the west coast of Africa, Equatorial Guinea lies just north of the equator. Mangrove swamps border the mainland coast. The republic gained its independence in 1968 after 190 years of Spanish rule. Multiparty politics were accepted in 1991, but observers questioned the fairness of parliamentary elections in 1993.

Bioko, formerly Fernando Po. Although the volcanic land is very fertile, cocoa production fell by 90% during the Macías years.

CLIMATE

WEATHER CHART

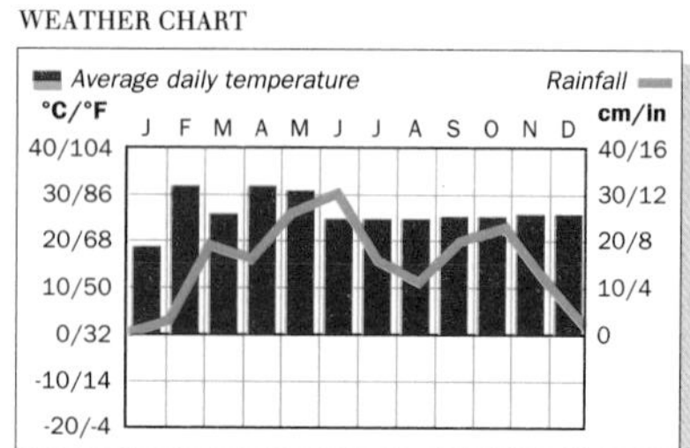

The island of Bioko is extremely wet and humid, with an annual rainfall of 78 inches, while the mainland is only marginally drier and cooler.

COMMUNICATIONS

 **Malabo**

2 ships
6,700 dwt

THE TRANSPORTATION NETWORK

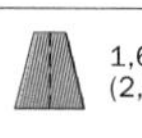 1,633 miles (2,628 km)

 None

None

 None

Apart from once- or twice-weekly *Iberia* flights, all airlinks are through neighboring countries. The Chinese financed the Ncue-Mongomo Highway project in the 1980s.

TOURISM

 A few independent visitors

 Numbers are unlikely to increase

MAIN OVERSEAS ARRIVALS

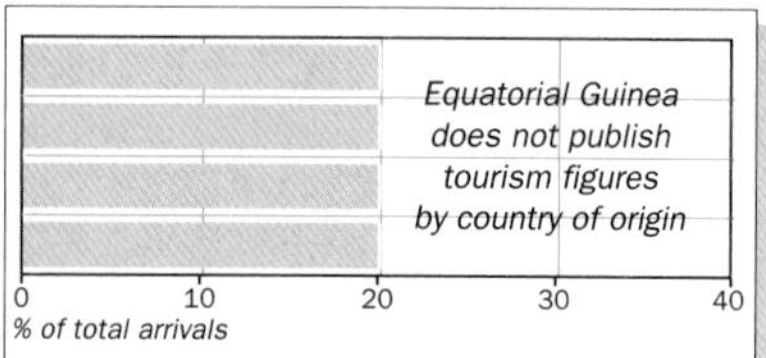

Equatorial Guinea is still very much a destination for the adventurous independent tourist only, despite the potential attraction of Malabo's spectacular scenery and beaches.

PEOPLE

 Spanish, Fang, Bubi

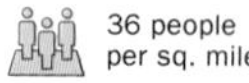 36 people per sq. mile

THE URBAN/RURAL POPULATION SPLIT

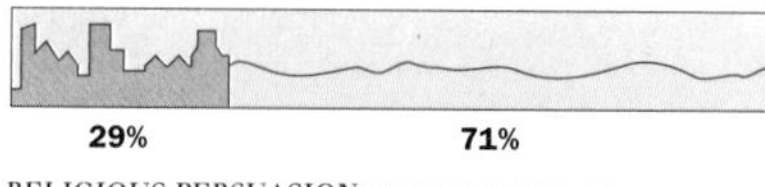

RELIGIOUS PERSUASION

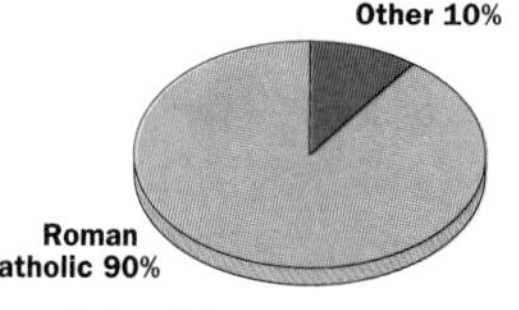

The mainland has a majority of Fang, a people who also inhabit Cameroon and northern Gabon. Bioko is populated by a majority of Bubi and a minority of Creoles, known as *Fernandinos*. The Macías dictatorship consolidated the power of the Fang, especially the Mongomo clan, from which both Macías and his successor Obiang come. The extended family is strong and maintained its solidarity despite disruptive social pressure during the Macías dictatorship.

EQUATORIAL GUINEA

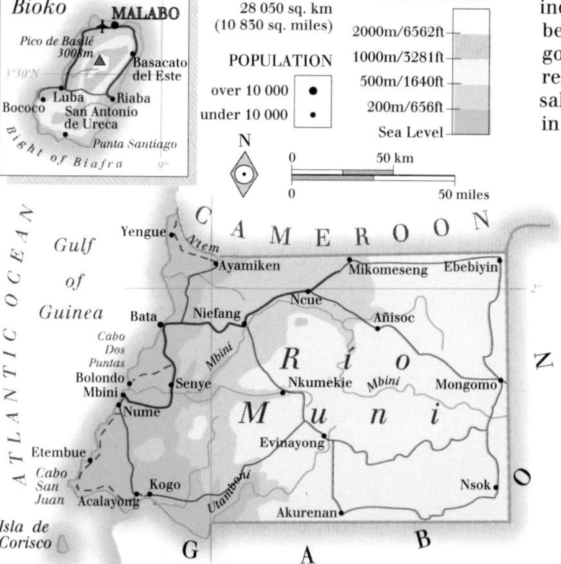

POLITICS

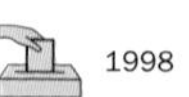 1998

President Brig.-Gen. Teodoro Obiang Nguema Mbasogo

THE STATE OF THE PARTIES

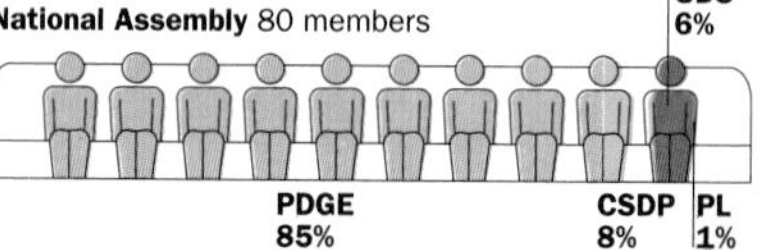

PDGE = Democratic Party of Equatorial Guinea
CSDP = People's Social Democratic Convention
UDS = Social Democratic Union **PL** = Liberal Party

Despite officially being a multiparty state since 1991, some of the several exiled political parties have not yet found it safe to return – opposition leaders who publicize themselves tend to be arrested. The ruling PDGE was set up in 1987 by Teodoro Obiang Nguema Mbasogo, nephew of the dictator Francisco Macías Nguema, whom he overthrew in 1979. It replaced Macías' even more notional party, the National Workers' Party (PUNT), which in 1970 had forced a merger of the parties existing before independence. The PDGE benefits from heavy government patronage, receiving 3% of the salaries of all earners in the country.

The movement towards multiparty politics – which was initiated in 1988 following the first elections for 20 years – has been marked by instability. This appears likely to continue following the controversy surrounding the fairness of elections at the end of 1993. Local observers believe that the country may be vulnerable to a coup.

WORLD AFFAIRS

OAU

AfDB

After a period of extreme isolation under the Macías dictatorship, Equatorial Guinea is seeking to rebuild links, especially its relationship with Spain, traditionally a haven for political dissenters. In 1989, Madrid was the base used by exiled opposition groups forming a coalition to press for democracy. Joining the Franc Zone in 1988 did not bring the expected benefits. Spain is suspicious of French commercial ambitions in the country.

AID

 $174m (receipts)

 Up 71% in 1991

Equatorial Guinea is underdeveloped and aid is vital to get such projects as there are off the ground. Planning and implementation, however, have proved difficult due to the lack of skilled labor, inefficiencies and instances of corruption.

The EU, especially France, Italy and Spain, the World Bank, IMF and Arab funds are all important sources of aid. The Chinese have also provided project aid to Equatorial Guinea.

DEFENSE

 Equatorial Guinea does not release budget figures

 Not applicable

The main concern for the 1,300-man military and paramilitary force is internal security. Morocco has provided a 360-strong presidential guard since the early 1980s to guarantee Obiang's security. Nigeria, Cameroon and Gabon have interests in maintaining the autonomy of the Malabo and Río Muni regions.

RESOURCES

 18m kwh (capacity 5,000 kw)

 Reserves of 3,600,000 bbl

 35,000 sheep, 5,000 pigs, 5,000 cattle

 Oil, natural gas

Offshore and mainland oil and gas reserves have yet to be fully exploited, but companies such as ELF, BP and AGIP are drilling. Bata is served by a 3.2 MW hydropower station built by the Chinese in 1983.

ENVIRONMENT

 None

 Government has no environmental protection expertise

The government has failed to take any serious measures to stop timber companies depleting the rainforest.

MEDIA

 Censorship is liable to be arbitrarily and suddenly imposed

PUBLISHING AND BROADCAST MEDIA

 There is no regular daily press. The formerly daily newspaper *Poto Poto* now appears irregularly

 1 state-owned service

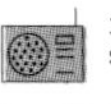 1 state-owned service

There has been very little sign of press liberalization, despite the adoption of multiparty politics. Political parties produce a few tracts and broadsheets.

CRIME

 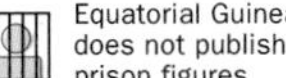 Equatorial Guinea does not publish prison figures

 No measurable change from year to year

Levels of recorded crime are relatively low, although much does not get reported. Many human rights abuses still occur.

CHRONOLOGY

Equatorial Guinea remained a backwater of Spanish colonialism until development began after 1959.

- ❑ **1968** Independence. President Macías launches reign of terror. Puts own family in all top jobs.
- ❑ **1972** Attempt to stop mass exodus: people forbidden to leave country.
- ❑ **1979** Coup puts nephew in power with Spanish approval.
- ❑ **1991** Multiparty constitution.

E

EDUCATION

 50%

Education declined in the Macías years, when attendance rates fell from 90% to 55%. It has now been declared the State's first priority.

HEALTH

 1 per 61,000 people

 Diarrheal and respiratory diseases, malaria

Life expectancy has risen from 37 years in 1960 to 47 in 1990. Restoring basic health care is a priority.

WEALTH

 Most of the population leads a subsistence existence; a minority has formal employment

CONSUMER GOODS OWNERSHIP

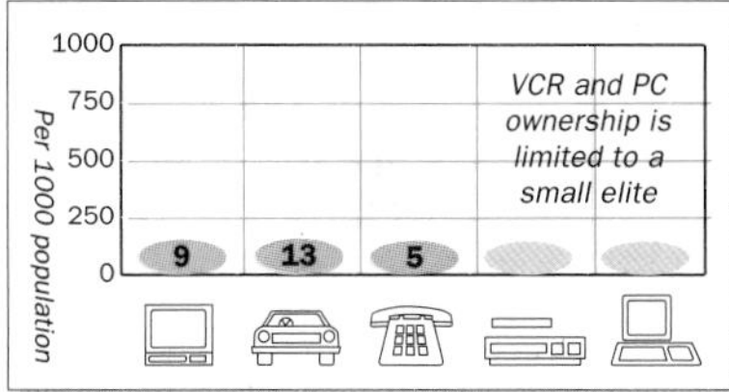

What wealth there is tends to be concentrated in the ruling clan. There is also a relic of Spanish plutocracy.

WORLD RANKING

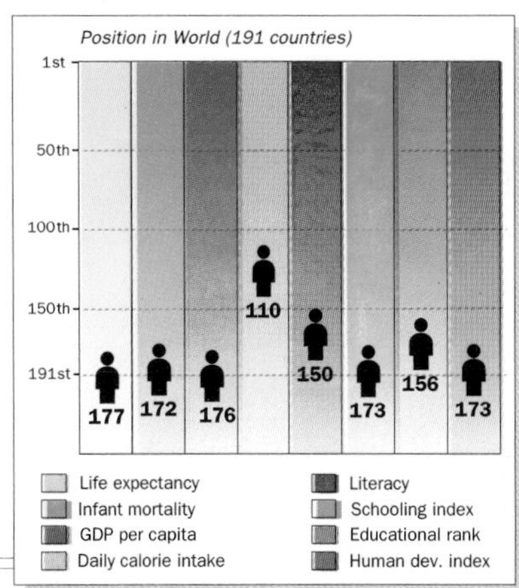

ECONOMICS

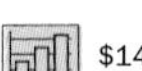 $149m

 295.23 CFA francs

SCORE CARD

- ❑ WORLD GNP RANKING........................183rd
- ❑ GNP PER CAPITA $380
- ❑ BALANCE OF PAYMENTS $4.5m
- ❑ INFLATION ....–0.3%
- ❑ UNEMPLOYMENT ....Little formal employment

STRENGTHS

Fertile soils. Large tropical timber reserves. Cocoa and coffee. Large area of territorial waters, with potential for fisheries. Oil and natural gas reserves yet to be fully exploited.

WEAKNESSES

Lasting effects of economic regression under the Macías dictatorship. Maladministration and ideological attacks on the educated have restricted growth; during the Macías period cocoa production slumped by 90%. Lack of a coherent, trained administration. Continuing problems with communications.

EXPORTS

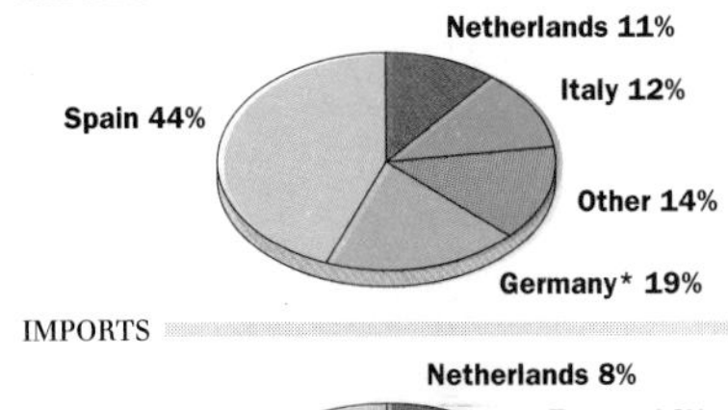

IMPORTS

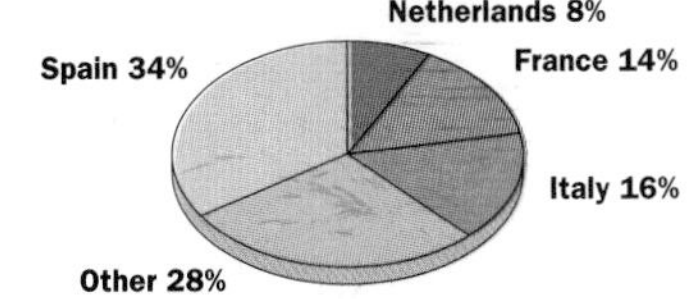

ERITREA

OFFICIAL NAME: State of Eritrea **CAPITAL:** Asmara
POPULATION: 3.5 million **CURRENCY:** Egyptian pound **OFFICIAL LANGUAGES:** Tigrinya and Arabic

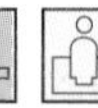

LYING ON THE SHORES of the Red Sea, Eritrea's landscape is dominated by rugged mountains, bush and the Danakil Desert. The country effectively seceded from Ethiopia in 1991, after a 30-year war for independence that left much of its infrastructure in ruins. A failure of the harvest in 1993 compounded the new state's problems, placing 400,000 at risk of famine. The transitional government is due to hold multiparty democratic elections in 1997.

CLIMATE

WEATHER CHART

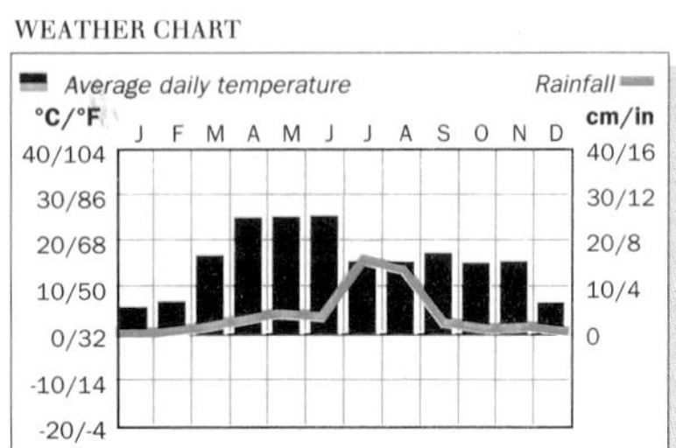

Eritrea's harvest is dependent on rainfall in September. Droughts from July onward are common.

COMMUNICATIONS

 **Yohannes IV, Asmara**  Has no fleet

THE TRANSPORTATION NETWORK

Road network undergoing repair		None	
Railroad not operating currently		None	

All transportation systems require huge investment. Eritrea will benefit as a transit point for landlocked neighbors.

TOURISM

Visitors limited to aid workers and businesspeople

Government is encouraging the tourist sector

MAIN OVERSEAS ARRIVALS

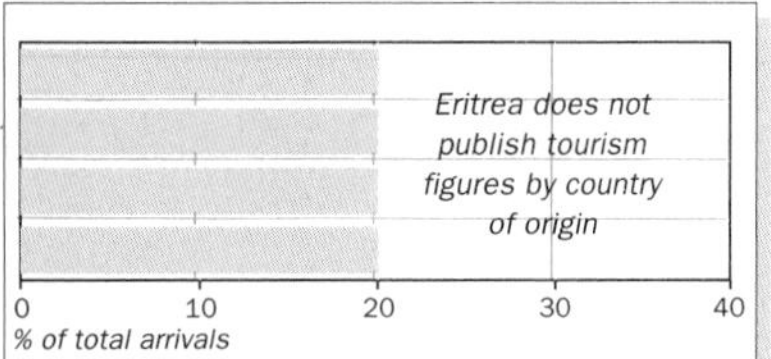

There is very little tourism; most visitors are aid workers or on business. Planners are eager to develop coastal resorts for the regional Arab market. However, the task of clearing mines out of beaches will take several years.

PEOPLE

Tigrinya, Tigre, Afar, Arabic, Bilen, Kunama, Nara, Saho, Hadareb

73 people per sq. mile

THE URBAN/RURAL POPULATION SPLIT

20% 80%

RELIGIOUS PERSUASION

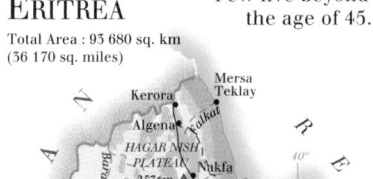

Other (including Animist) 10%
Christian 45%
Muslim 45%

Tigrinya-speakers form the largest of Eritrea's nine main ethnic groups. A strong sense of nationhood has been forged by the 30-year war against Ethiopia. Women played an important role in the war. From 1973, 30,000 fought alongside men, some in positions of command. Their claim to equal rights is likely to be enshrined in the new constitution. Over 80% of the people are subsistence farmers. Few live beyond the age of 45.

ERITREA

Total Area : 93 680 sq. km (36 170 sq. miles)

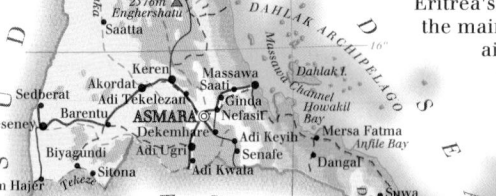

LAND HEIGHT
2000m/6562ft
1000m/3281ft
500m/1640ft
200m/656ft
Sea Level
-200m/-656ft

POPULATION
over 100 000
over 50 000
over 10 000
under 10 000

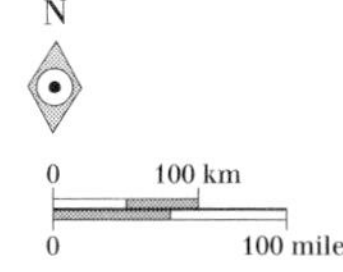

POLITICS

1997 Interim President Issaias Afwerki

THE STATE OF THE PARTIES

Provisional Government of Eritrea

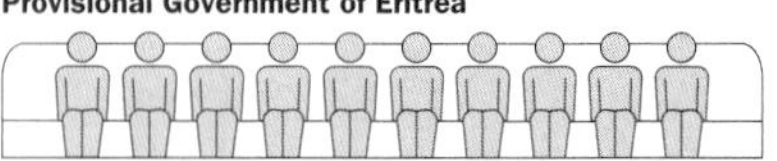

The transitional government will be in place until 1997

Eritrea became a region of Ethiopia as a result of European power politics. Formerly an Italian colony, it came under British mandate in 1941. In 1952, Britain handed the region to Addis Ababa. The long struggle for independence began in the same year. The Eritrean People's Liberation Front (EPLF) finally drove out Ethiopian troops in 1991. A referendum held in May 1993 resulted in 99.8% of voters on a 98.2% turnout voting "yes" to independence.

The country is currently being run by a core of EPLF leaders who conducted the military campaign. Led by Issaias Afwerki, they plan to dissolve the EPLF and to hold multiparty elections in 1997. A new constitution is planned that will forbid parties based on religious or ethnic affiliations. Issaias, a Christian, has also been careful to include Muslims in his transitional cabinet.

WORLD AFFAIRS

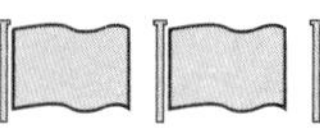

Eritrea's secession was significant for African politics. It marked the first major redrawing of the national borders established by Africa's colonizers. The OAU fears that other African secessionist movements will be encouraged by Eritrea's success. For Eritrea, however, the main concern is attracting Western aid for reconstruction. Relations with Ethiopia's new government, which also fought the Mengistu regime, are good. The EPLF has promised landlocked Ethiopia access to the ports of Assab and Massawa.

AID

 $147m

 Rising; mostly emergency food aid

Eritrea's economy is almost entirely aid-dependent. Food aid, on which 75% of the population survive, is the most pressing need. The failure of the harvest in 1993, which placed 400,000 at risk of starvation, led to the UN pledging a further 225,000 tons of food. Western donors have been less generous with aid for the $2-billion reconstruction costs. Compared with Somalia, Eritrea's aid receipts are tiny.

DEFENSE

 Army unpaid at present

 Demobilization of troops after independence

The 100,000-strong army (30,000 of whom are women) is currently being demobilized. As with the rest of the people, troops are being reintegrated into the national economy on "food for work" schemes. In return for repairing the damage wrought by war on the environment and to the infrastructure, they receive basic rations.

ECONOMICS

 $393m (est)

 3.37 Egyptian pounds

SCORE CARD

- ❑ WORLD GNP RANKING........165th
- ❑ GNP PER CAPITA........$120
- ❑ BALANCE OF PAYMENTS........Deficit
- ❑ INFLATION........12%
- ❑ UNEMPLOYMENT....Widespread underemployment

STRENGTHS

Strategically important position on Red Sea. Potential for a mining industry and for foreign earnings from possible oil exports. Government commitment to reducing dependence on food aid. Potential for tourism on Red Sea.

WEAKNESSES

Lack of basic information and equipment. Coherent economic policy still being formulated. Not an aid priority for Western donors. Legacy of disruption and destruction from civil war. Port of Massawa heavily bombed. Most of population living at subsistence level. Susceptibility to drought and famine. Expense of repatriating and supporting the 750,000 who fled abroad as refugees and now wish to return.

EXPORTS/IMPORTS

Eritrea does not yet publish export or import figures

RESOURCES

 Electricity supply is prone to surges

 Not an oil producer; oil refinery at Assab

 Livestock includes sheep, goats, cattle and camels

 Copper, potash, gold, iron, silver, zinc, oil, silica, granite, marble

Eritrea has substantial copper reserves, and lesser ones of silver, zinc and gold. High-quality silica, granite and marble deposits could be exploited. Onshore and offshore oil deposits are believed to exist. Concessionary exploration deals with Western companies have yet to be established.

ENVIRONMENT

 None at present

 New government conscious of conservation needs

Deforestation and soil erosion are major problems. The Ethiopian army uprooted trees to destroy the cover they provided for Eritrean soldiers. Since 1991, 22 million seedlings have been grown in a replanting project. The Red Sea coast is a conservation priority.

MEDIA

 Most of the media is controlled by the government

PUBLISHING AND BROADCAST MEDIA

 *New Eritrea*, owned by the EPLF, is published every 3 days in Tigrinya and Arabic

 1 state-controlled service

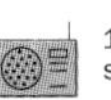 1 state-controlled service

The media is largely controlled by the EPLF who run both the radio and TV services. Independent newspapers are not encouraged.

CRIME

 Eritrea does not publish prison figures

 Crime levels remain low

Crime has not been a problem since independence. The judiciary and police answer to the EPLF. There are a number of political prisoners.

EDUCATION

 20%

Very few schools functioned during the war. There is one university. In an attempt to reduce potential ethnic tension, all children above the age of 11 are being taught in English.

HEALTH

 1 per 48,000 people

 Malaria, potential risk of famine

The risk of famine overrides normal health concerns. Eritreans built their own hospitals during the war with Ethiopia. Health provision is basic.

***Seasonal river beds** carry rain from the Ethiopian highlands into Eritrea, providing essential irrigation for agriculture.*

E

CHRONOLOGY

British military rule replaced Italian colonial authority in 1941.

- ❑ **1952** Eritrea incorporated in Ethiopia.
- ❑ **1961** EPLF begins armed struggle.
- ❑ **1987** EPLF refuses offer of autonomy; fighting intensifies.
- ❑ **1991** EPLF takes control of Asmara. New EPRDF government in Addis Ababa effectively agrees to Eritrean secession.

WEALTH

 Demobilized soldier in Asmara, $325 per month; the 1 million refugees who fled to neighboring countries are destitute

CONSUMER GOODS OWNERSHIP

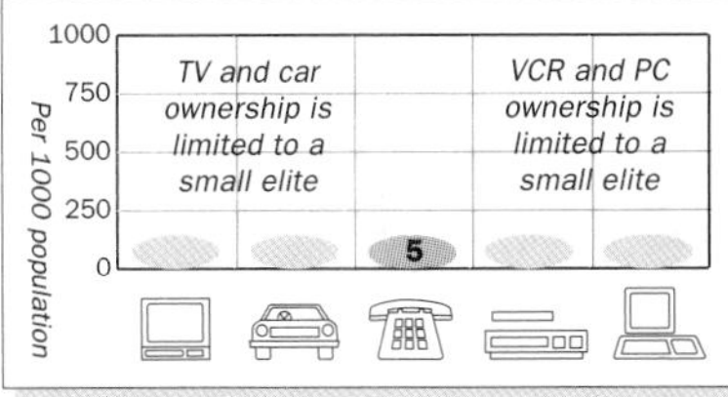

Over 80% of people are subsistence farmers. A few of the 150,000 refugees who fled to Arab and Western countries have built up some personal savings.

WORLD RANKING

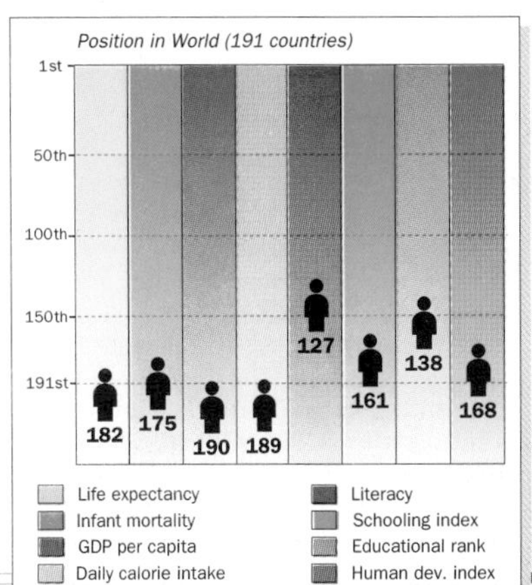

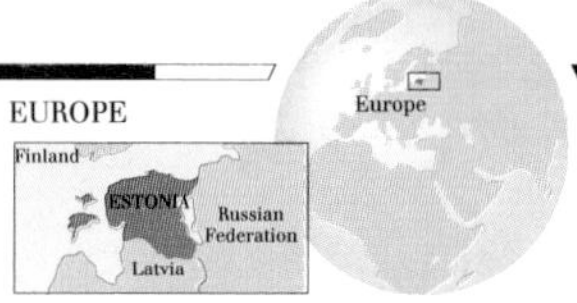

ESTONIA

EUROPE

OFFICIAL NAME: Republic of Estonia **CAPITAL:** Tallinn
POPULATION: 1.6 million **CURRENCY:** Kroon **OFFICIAL LANGUAGE:** Estonian

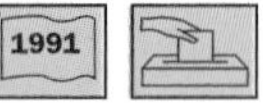
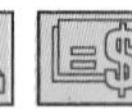

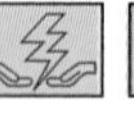

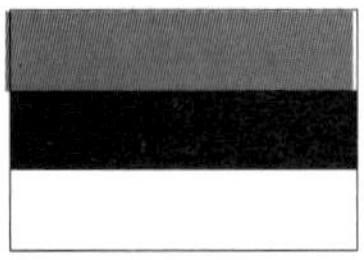

TRADITIONALLY the most Western-oriented of the Baltic states, Estonia is bordered by Latvia and the Russian Federation. Its terrain is flat, boggy and partly wooded, and includes more than 1,500 islands. Estonia formally regained its independence as a multiparty democracy in 1991. In contrast to the peoples of Latvia and Lithuania, the other Baltic states, Estonians are Finno-Ugric and their language is similar to Finnish.

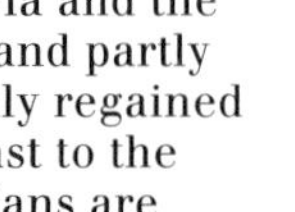

CLIMATE

WEATHER CHART

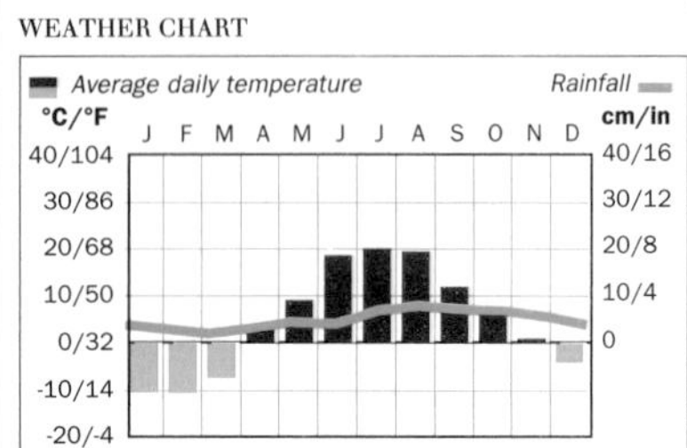

Estonia's coastal location gives it wet springs and cool summers. Winters are cold – even the Baltic freezes.

COMMUNICATIONS

Tallinn Ulemiste

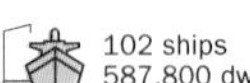
102 ships
587,800 dwt

THE TRANSPORTATION NETWORK

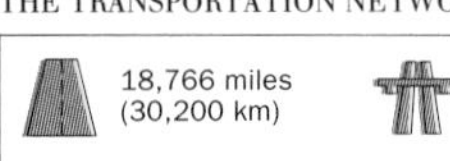

The transportation system is in need of modernization. Tallinn Airport is currently being upgraded.

TOURISM

277,000 visitors

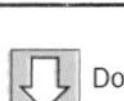
Down 29% in 1992

MAIN OVERSEAS ARRIVALS

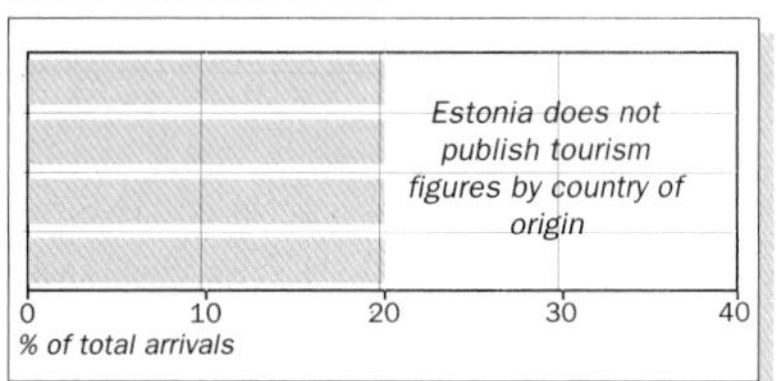

Estonia is a popular destination for Scandinavians, particularly Finns. Tallinn's medieval center is a major attraction. The capital is also an important Baltic yachting center, with many summer regattas.

PEOPLE

Estonian, Russian

91 people per sq. mile

THE URBAN/RURAL POPULATION SPLIT

ETHNIC MAKEUP

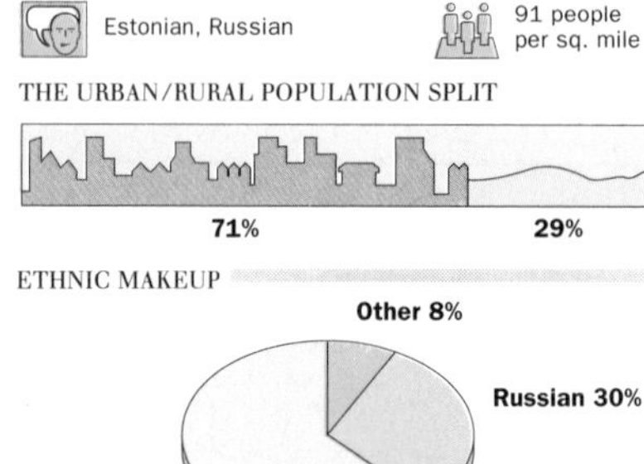

Under Moscow's rule, Estonia underwent a process of enforced Sovietization. The immigration of a large Russian work force, many attracted by Estonia's higher living standards, reduced the proportion of Estonians from 90% to 62% of the population. Since 1991, Estonians have been reasserting their dominance. Non-Estonian Russian speakers are finding it harder to get jobs, and several thousand have left. Estonians are predominantly Lutheran. Families are small; divorce rates are high.

POLITICS

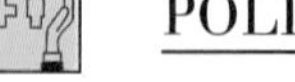

1996

President Lennart Meri

THE STATE OF THE PARTIES

Parliament (Riigikogu) 101 members

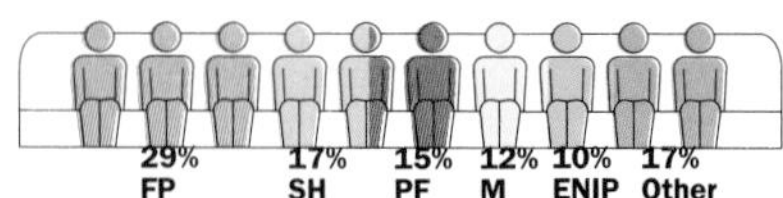

FP = Fatherland Party **SH** = Secure Home **PF** = Popular Front **M** = Moderates **ENIP** = Estonian National Independence Party **Other** = Estonian Citizens, Independent Royalists

Since 1992, Estonian politics have been dominated by a coalition led by the conservative, nationalist FP. President Meri and Prime Minister Maart Laar are both FP members. Other ministers come from the Moderates alliance and the ENIP. The proliferation of parties and factions within parliament makes it hard to pass legislation. The status of Russians is a major issue. A 1993 proposal to classify all non-ethnic Estonians as foreigners was passed in parliament, but vetoed at the last minute by the president under international pressure. The coalition government remains committed to market-led economic reform and is privatizing former Soviet enterprises.

ESTONIA

Total Area : 45 125 sq. km (17 423 sq. miles)

LAND HEIGHT

200m/565ft

Sea Level

POPULATION

over 500 000
over 100 000
over 50 000
over 10 000
under 10 000

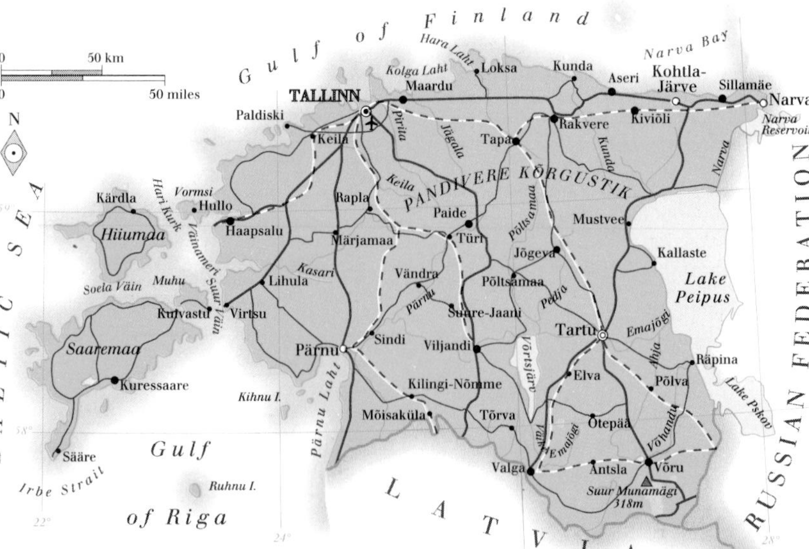

WORLD AFFAIRS

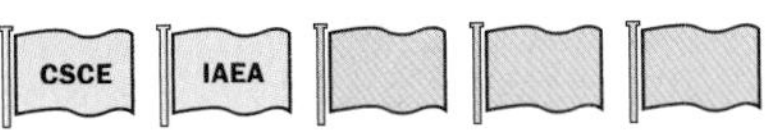

Estonia wants to secure the return of territories ceded to Russia in the Soviet period. It is eager to obtain greater access to EU markets and to develop its links with Germany. Relations with Finland are particularly good. The government has been criticized by the international community for its treatment of the ethnic Russian minority; the prospect of a Russian intervention is Estonia's main fear.

AID

 Estonia does not publish aid receipts  Probably rising

Finland, Sweden, Germany, the EU and the IMF are major sources of aid, which is spent on infrastructure projects.

DEFENSE

 Army set up; navy and air force planned  Increasing

Building up the military is a priority. The withdrawal of the 8000 Russian troops from Estonian territory was completed in 1994. Estonia is seeking to develop a closer relationship with NATO under the Partnership of Peace program.

ECONOMICS

 $6.1bn  13.14 kroons

SCORE CARD

❑ WORLD GNP RANKING	105th
❑ GNP PER CAPITA	$3,820
❑ BALANCE OF PAYMENTS	$113m
❑ INFLATION	32%
❑ UNEMPLOYMENT	1%

STRENGTHS

Oil shale and phosphorite reserves. Light industrial sector. Own stable currency, the kroon. Reduced dependence on Russia. Growing links with Finland and Germany.

WEAKNESSES

Antiquated industrial infrastructure in urgent need of investment. Poor raw materials base. Dependence on imported energy supplies.

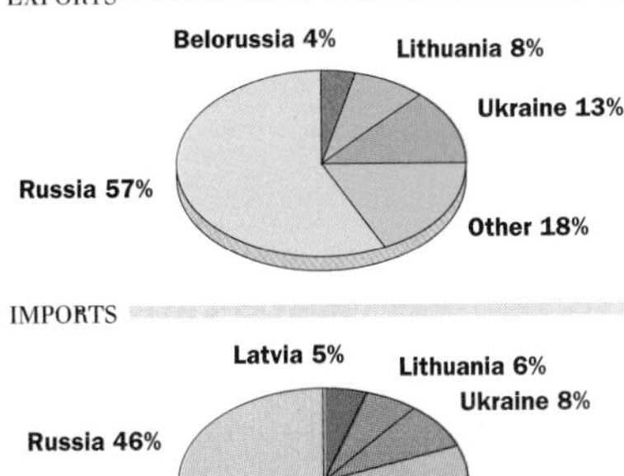

RESOURCES

 Oil shale used to generate electricity  Oil figures not published

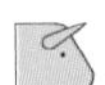 6.8m poultry, 1.1m pigs, 806,000 cattle  Oil shale, phosphorite

The chief resources are oil shale and phosphorite. The latter is processed to make phosphates for agricultural use.

ENVIRONMENT

 None at present, but plans exist 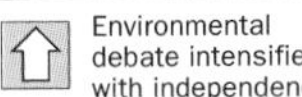

Environmental issues are prominent. Protests against Soviet plans to expand phosphorite mining in the northeast, the most polluted area, were part of the late 1980s independence movement.

MEDIA

 Little censorship for Estonians; Russian access to the media is decreasing

PUBLISHING AND BROADCAST MEDIA

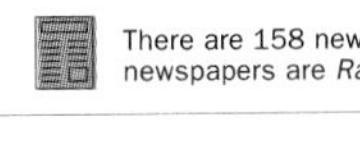

There are 158 newspapers. The main daily newspapers are Rahva Hääl and Päevaleht

 1 state-owned service  1 state-owned service

The media are mostly pro-government. The number of Russian-language programs is declining. Estonians have been able to receive Finnish satellite TV for some years.

CRIME

 Estonia does not publish prison figures 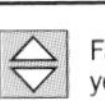 Fairly constant from year to year

Robbery and drugs are the main crime problems. Generally, however, crime levels are still relatively low.

EDUCATION

 Figures not published, but among highest of ex-Soviet republics

Education is becoming increasingly Westernized. Six higher-education establishments have 26,000 students.

HEALTH

 1 per 217 people  Circulatory diseases, cancer, accidents, violence

The health system, improved since the collapse of communism, is better than those of most former Soviet republics.

The Russian Orthodox convent of Pühtitsa at Kuremäe in Estonia's marshy north. Most of the population is Evangelical Lutheran.

E

CHRONOLOGY

After first Swedish and then Russian rule, Estonia enjoyed a brief period of independence from 1921 until its incorporation into the Soviet Union in 1940.

- ❑ **1945–1953** Sovietization; cultural repression, deportations.
- ❑ **1986–1989** Growing independence movement, helped by *glasnost*.
- ❑ **1990** Unilateral declaration of independence.
- ❑ **1991** Independence recognized by Russia.
- ❑ **1992** Multiparty elections.

WEALTH

 Traders are the wealthiest group

CONSUMER GOODS OWNERSHIP

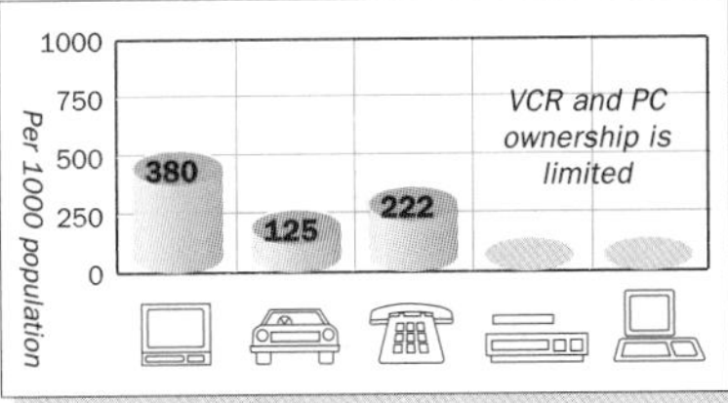

Growing Western economic ties have maintained Estonia's traditionally high standard of living.

WORLD RANKING

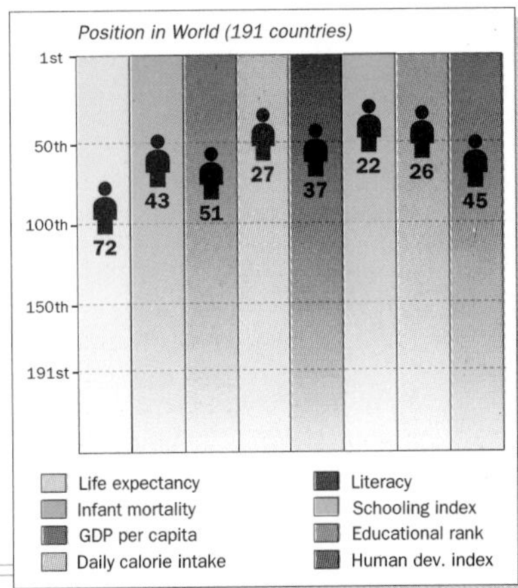

ETHIOPIA

EAST AFRICA

OFFICIAL NAME:

POPULATION: 53 million **CURRENCY:** Ethiopian birr **OFFICIAL LANGUAGE:** Amharic

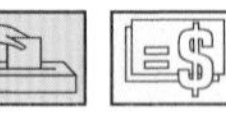

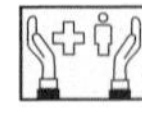

LOCATED IN NORTHEAST AFRICA, Ethiopia reverted to its historical landlocked status in 1993, when Eritrea, its coastal province on the Red Sea, regained its independence. Ethiopia is mountainous except for the desert lowlands in the northeast and southeast and is subject to devastating droughts and famines. Soil erosion due to deforestation is a further burden. Civil war began in the 1960s and ended in 1991 with the defeat of the military dictatorship that had ruled since 1974. Since then, a transitional government has been taking steps to establish a free-market, multiparty democracy which would give Ethiopia's ethnic groups proper representation. Farming reforms and good rains have cut Ethiopia's need for food aid in half.

CLIMATE

WEATHER CHART

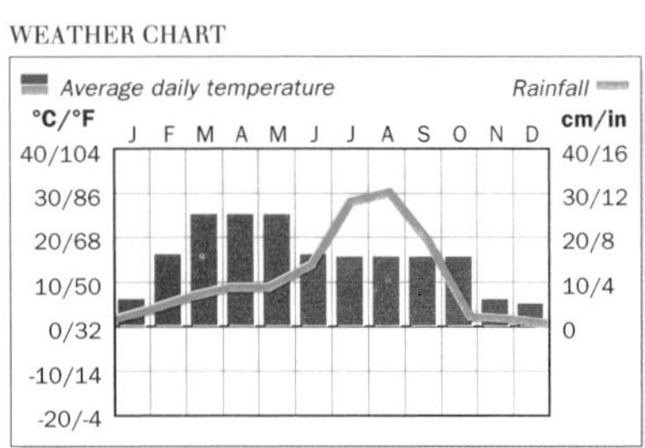

In general, the climate is moderate, except in the lowlands of the Danakil Desert and the Ogaden, which are hot all year round and can suffer severe drought. The highlands are warm, with night frost and snowfalls in the mountains. The single rainy season in the west brings twice as much rain as the two wet seasons in the east. During these cloudy periods, thunderstorms occur almost daily.

COMMUNICATIONS

Bole Intl, Addis Ababa
480,000 passengers

20 ships
87,000 dwt

THE TRANSPORTATION NETWORK

24,534 miles (39,482 km)

Trans-East Africa Highway

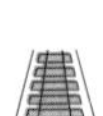
423 miles (681 km)

None

A single railroad links Addis Ababa with Djibouti and the only all-weather roads are those between main business centers. Repairing war damage is a priority, with efforts concentrated on the roads through Eritrea to the Red Sea ports of Assab and Massawa. As ownership of motor vehicles of any kind is rare, pack donkeys and donkey carts are widely used, especially in the highlands.

TOURISM

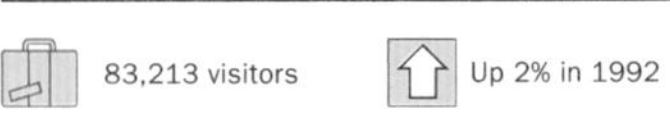

MAIN OVERSEAS ARRIVALS

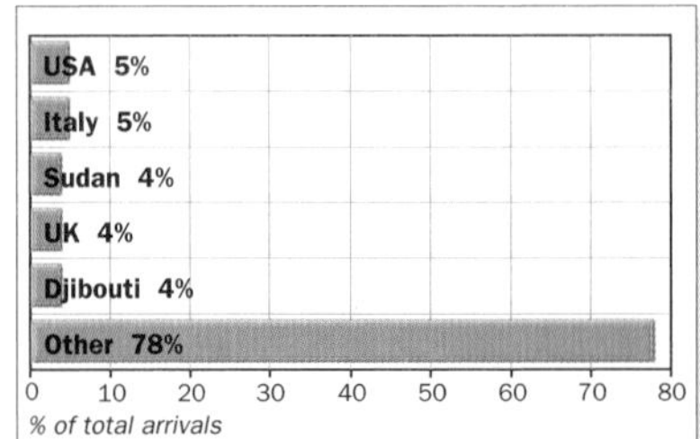

Tourism has always been on a small scale, although since 1991 there has been a moderate increase in the number of visitors. In 1994, the need for permits to travel within the country was abolished. Several new hotels are being built. Most tourists go to Ethiopia on expensive organized tours; Lake Gonder, with its spectacular scenery, is a popular destination. Ethiopia's ancient forts, churches and cities, such as Ãksum, the royal capital of the first Ethiopian kingdom, are now accessible. Some safari tours operate to the five national parks.

***Lalibela, 75 miles northwest of Desē** in Ethiopia's central highlands. An important pilgrimage center, it is famous for its ten 12th-century Christian churches.*

PEOPLE

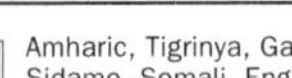

THE URBAN/RURAL POPULATION SPLIT

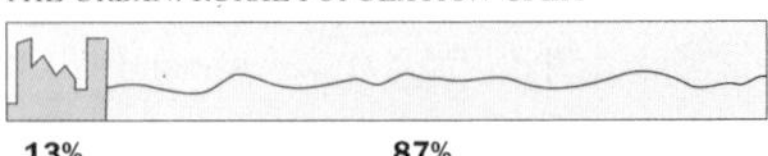

RELIGIOUS PERSUASION

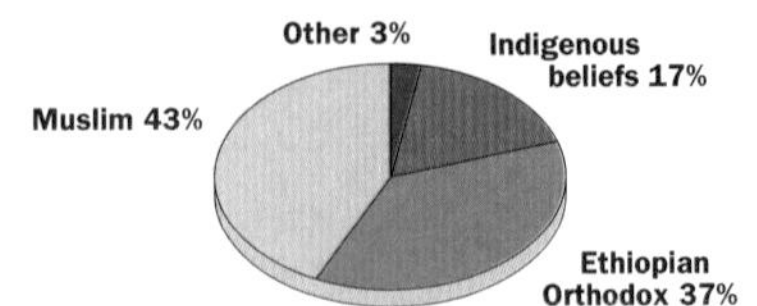

ETHNIC MAKEUP

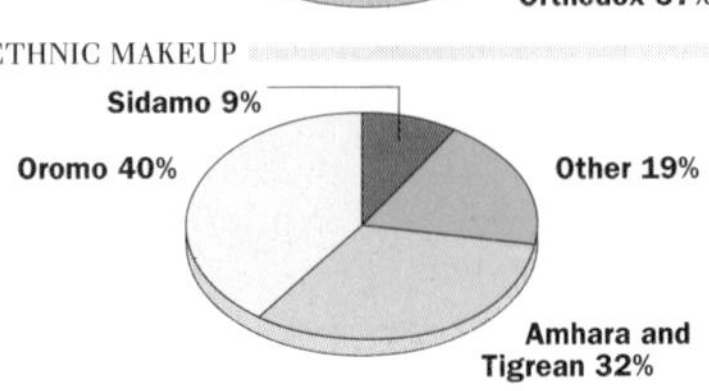

There are 76 nationalities in Ethiopia and 286 languages. Oromos form the largest group, followed by Amharas and Tigreans.

Civil war was sparked by fighting between different ethnic groups, but they later united in opposition to the Mengistu regime's centralist policies. Ethnic tensions are still near the surface, in spite of the new federal structure, and there have been reports of boundary disputes in several regions. The Oromos withdrew from the Tigrean-dominated government in 1992. Opposition to the transitional government has also been voiced by disaffected Amharas, who had held the reins of power for the last century, and by the Orthodox Church. Amnesty International has also expressed concern about the arrest of Amharan leaders.

No discrimination is shown toward minorities. Most of the small Jewish population was evacuated to Israel in 1991. The participation of women in rural organizations is increasing, reflecting the key role women played in the war.

POPULATION AGE BREAKDOWN

% of population by age group

	1960	1970	1980	1990	2000
65+	2.5%	2.5%	2.6%	2.9%	2.8%
15–64	53%	53%	52.9%	51.3%	50.6%
0–14	44.5%	44.5%	44.5%	45.8%	46.6%

ETHIOPIA

Total Area :
1 128 221 sq. km
(435 605 sq. miles)

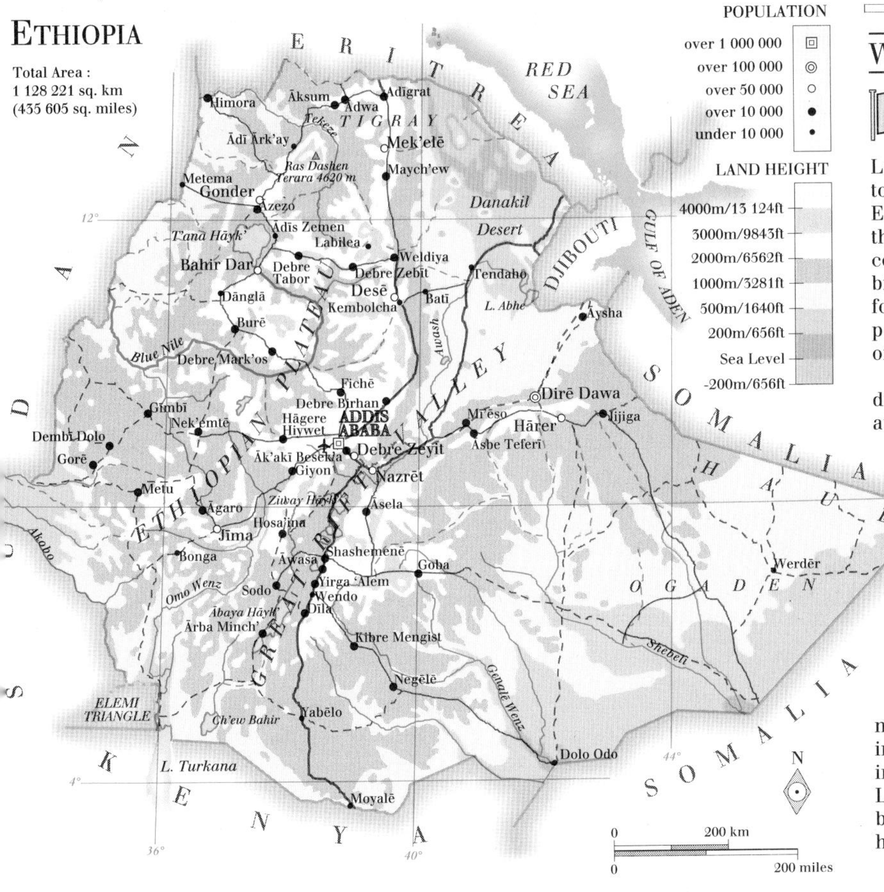

WORLD AFFAIRS

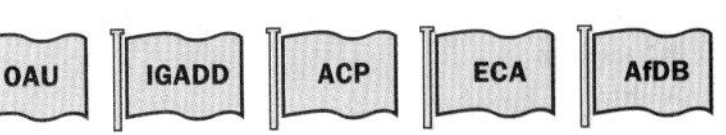

Landlocked Ethiopia is anxious to maintain cordial relations with Eritrea, in order to retain access to the Red Sea. These have been partly cemented in a number of recent bilateral accords, which allow for the harmonization of economic policy and the free movement of peoples.

Ethiopia has been active in regional diplomacy. It has made numerous attempts at brokering peace in Somalia. President Zenawi has played a key role by hosting several Somali reconciliation conferences in Addis Ababa.

During the Mengistu regime, Ethiopia's liberation movements supported dissidents in neighboring Sudan and Somalia. However, the transitional government now has an official policy of not interfering in its neighbors' affairs, in order to reduce regional tensions. Links with the USA, the main bilateral aid donor, and Israel have been strengthened.

E

POLITICS

1994

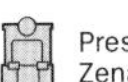

President Meles Zenawi

THE STATE OF THE PARTIES

Council of Representatives 84 members

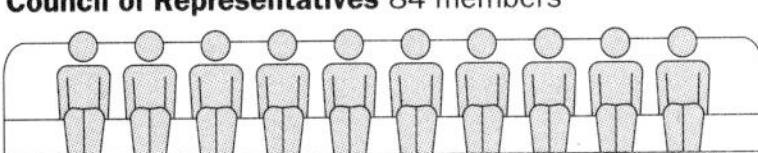

A transitional government is in place. Constitutional elections were to be held in 1994, with legislative elections to follow

Since the collapse of the military dictatorship of Mengistu Haile Mariam in 1991, Ethiopia has been ruled by a transitional government.

MAIN POLITICAL ISSUE

Ethnic representation

The transitional government plans to establish Ethiopia as a democratic ethnic federation of autonomous regions, representing different ethnic groups. Electoral constituencies will each have 100,000 voters, and parliamentary candidates must speak the language of the area they represent. Former members of Mengistu's communist-inspired Workers' Party of Ethiopia are barred from taking part.

PROFILE

The current government was set up in 1991 by the Ethiopian People's Revolutionary Democratic Front (EPRDF), the strongest of the liberation groups that fought Mengistu's Marxist regime and the one chiefly responsible for winning the civil war. The presidency is held by Meles Zenawi, leader of the Tigrean People's Liberation Front, the largest group within the EPRDF. There is growing opposition to the dominance of Tigreans by the Oromos and Amharas, the next largest groups – particularly since January 1994, when the government granted itself a second extension to its caretaker period in office. The regions are largely administered by members of the clan-dominated local liberation movements, which helped to overthrow the Mengistu regime.

***President Meles Zenawi**, leader of the EPRDF, which ousted the Mengistu regime.*

***Mengistu Haile Mariam**, who ran Ethiopia on Soviet lines from 1977–1991.*

CHRONOLOGY

After repelling a devastating Muslim invasion in 1523, Ethiopia developed as an isolated empire until Egyptian and Sudanese incursions in the 1850s led to its renewed political power under Emperor Theodor. His successor, Menelik II, doubled the empire southward and eastward.

- **1896** Italian invasion of Tigre defeated. Europeans recognize Ethiopia's independence.
- **1913** Menelik II dies.
- **1916** His son, Lij Iyasu, deposed for his conversion to Islam and proposed alliance with Turkey. Menelik's daughter, Zauditu, becomes empress with Ras Tafari as regent.
- **1923** Joins League of Nations.
- **1930** Zauditu dies. Ras Tafari crowned Emperor Haile Selassie.
- **1936** Italians occupy Ethiopia. Europe fails to react.
- **1941** Allies oust Italians and restore Haile Selassie, who sets up a constitution, parliament and cabinet, but retains personal power and the feudal system.
- **1952** Eritrea, formerly ruled first by the Italians then by the British, federated to Ethiopia.

⇨

E

CHRONOLOGY *continued*

- **1962** Unitary state created; Eritrea fully absorbed.
- **1972-1974** Famine kills 200,000.
- **1974** Strikes and army mutinies at Haile Selassie's autocratic rule and country's economic decline. The Dergue (Military Committee) stages coup.
- **1975** Becomes socialist state. Nationalizations, worker co-operatives and health reforms.
- **1977** Col. Mengistu Haile Mariam takes over. Somali invasion of the Ogaden defeated with Soviet and Cuban help.
- **1978–1979** Thousands of political opponents killed or imprisoned.
- **1984** Workers' Party of Ethiopia (WPE) set up on Soviet model. Live Aid concert raises funds to relieve famine caused by war and 3 years' drought. One million die.
- **1986** Eritrean rebels now control the whole northeastern coast.
- **1987** People's Democratic Republic of Ethiopia declared with Mengistu as president. New serious drought.
- **1988** Eritrean and Tigrean People's Liberation Fronts (EPLF and TPLF) begin new offensives. Mengistu's budget is for "Everything to the War Front." Ethiopia agrees not to interfere in Somali factional fighting and resumes diplomatic relations severed in 1977.
- **1989** Military coup attempt fails. TPLF in control of most of Tigre. TPLF and Ethiopian People's Democratic Movement form alliance – the EPRDF.
- **1990** WPE renamed Ethiopian Democratic Unity Party and opened to non-Marxists. Moves toward market economy begin. Distribution of food aid for victims of new famine hampered by both government and rebel forces.
- **1991** Mengistu flees country in face of big advances by EPRDF and EPLF. EPRDF enters Addis Ababa and sets up provisional government, dividing country into 14 semi-autonomous regions and promising representation for all ethnic groups. However, fighting continues between the mainly Tigrean EPRDF troops and various opposing groups. EPLF enters Asmara, the Eritrean capital, and sets up government.
- **1992** Regional elections – malpractice by all sides and boycotts by opposition groups. EPRDF gets 90% of votes. Fighting in southeast stops aid delivery to 600,000 Somali refugees who arrived in 1991–1992.
- **1993** Eritrean independence recognized.

AID

$1.1bn (receipts)

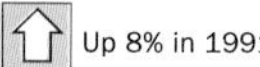

Up 8% in 1991

The World Food Program and the EU are the largest sources of assistance, while the USA has taken over from Italy and the former Soviet Union as the major bilateral donor. Aid per capita is low by regional standards.

However, long-term development assistance and balance of payments support look set to continue their recent growth. Aid is now playing an increasingly important part in the economy. The emphasis is shifting from food aid toward credit for infrastructure development.

DEFENSE

$1.31bn

Up 42% in 1990

Defense spending as % GDP: 21.4% (scale 0–40)

Ethiopia has no formal military alliances. A key issue is improving government control of the many ethnic and clan-based militias. Plans exist to create a national army representing all ethnic groups. Much of the Mengistu regime's $6-billion arms debt to the former USSR is unpaid.

ETHIOPIAN ARMED FORCES

350 main battle tanks (T-54/T-55/T-62)	100,000 (est)
Has no navy	None
38 combat aircraft (20 MiG-21MF)/ 18 MiG-23 BN)	Included under army
None	

ECONOMICS

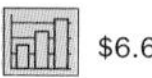

$6.6bn

4.92 Ethiopian birr

SCORE CARD

- World GNP Ranking..........97th
- GNP per Capita..........$125
- Balance of Payments..........$41m
- Inflation..........7.7%
- Unemployment....Widespread underemployment

EXPORTS

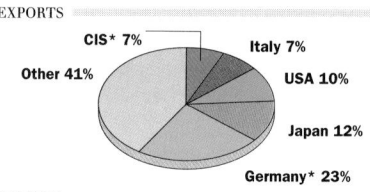

CIS* 7%
Italy 7%
Other 41%
USA 10%
Japan 12%
Germany* 23%

IMPORTS

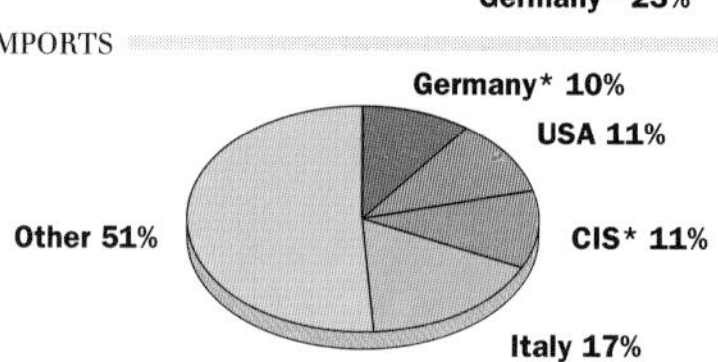

ECONOMIC PERFORMANCE INDICATOR

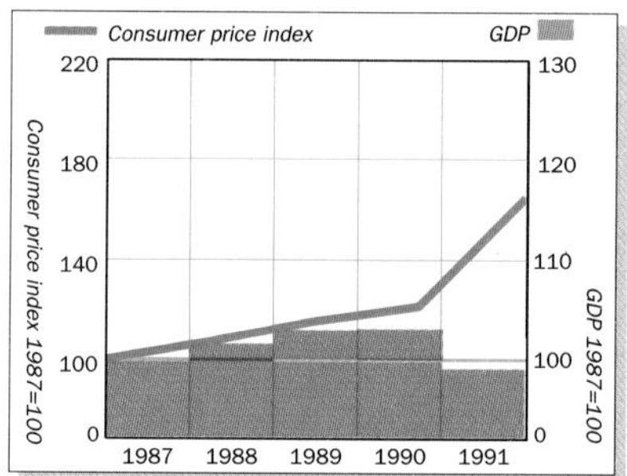

Profile

Since the end of the civil war, Ethiopia has begun moving toward a market economy by encouraging foreign investment and reforming land tenure. Economic decline was reversed in 1993 as agricultural and industrial output grew. The latter was fueled by the purchase of parts and raw materials funded by foreign aid. Ethiopia is the world's second-poorest nation.

Strengths

Peace and greater flows of economic aid. Dismantling of total state control. Coffee production.

Weaknesses

Overwhelming dependence on agriculture – engages 75% of population, accounts for 80% of exports. Periodic serious droughts. War-damaged infrastructure. Massive displacement of population by war and drought. Small industrial base. Lack of skilled workers. Legacy of Mengistu regime's disastrous experiment in a centrally planned economy.

ETHIOPIA : MAJOR BUSINESSES

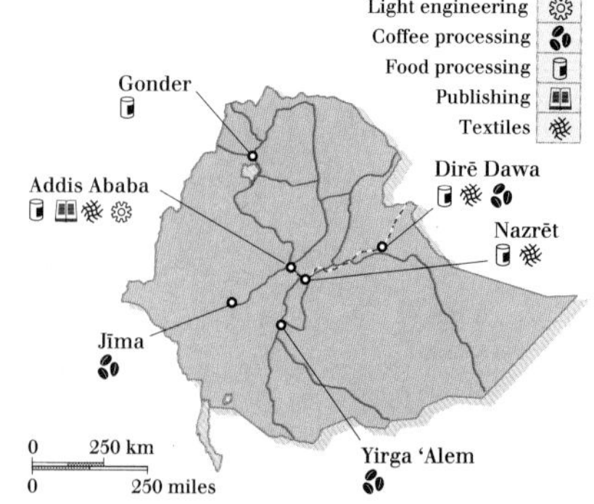

RESOURCES

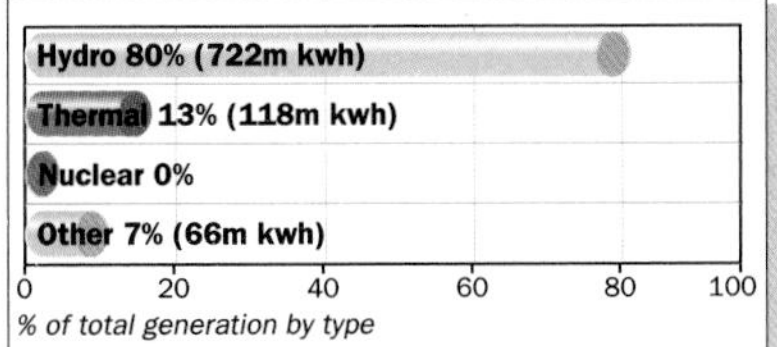

ELECTRICITY GENERATION

Hydro 80% (722m kwh)
Thermal 13% (118m kwh)
Nuclear 0%
Other 7% (66m kwh)
0 20 40 60 80 100
% of total generation by type

Manpower and financial constraints have prevented a systematic survey of mineral resources. Mining presently contributes less than 1% of GDP. Ethiopia has great potential for hydroelectric power, which, in the long run, could offset a domestic reliance on firewood and also slow massive deforestation and soil erosion. Current exploration for oil and gas has revealed reserves in the Ogaden, but exploitation has not begun. When Eritrea seceded in 1993, Ethiopia lost other substantial oil reserves and many oil concessions.

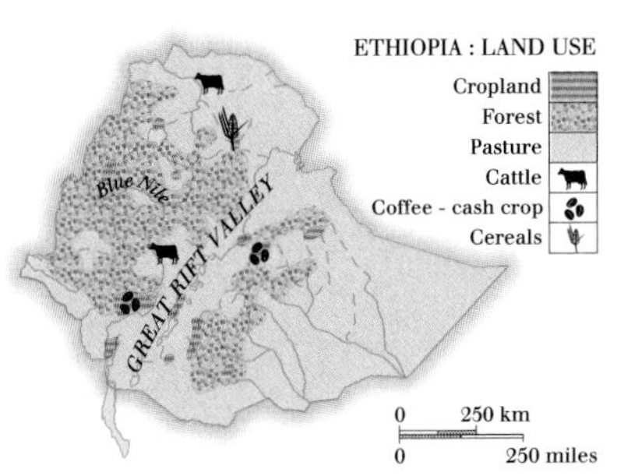

ENVIRONMENT

Soil erosion due to deforestation is the biggest problem

ENVIRONMENTAL TREATIES

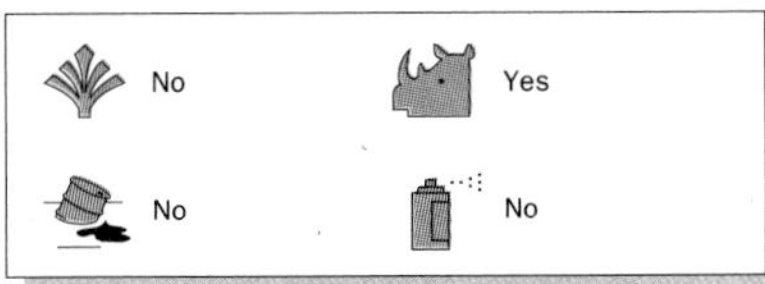

Deforestation for firewood and the resultant rapid soil erosion, particularly in the highlands, are serious problems. Forest cover has fallen from 40% in 1900 to only 2% today. Shortage of wood means that dung is increasingly being used for fuel. Its fertilizer value is put at $123 million a year, enough to increase annual grain harvests by up to 1.5 million tons. Local projects include terracing hillsides to prevent soil and water runoff – 22,320 miles of terraces were built in Tigray in 1992.

MEDIA

There is now considerable freedom of expression compared with the blanket censorship of the Mengistu years

The government remains uneasy about the post-Mengistu independent press, which has become prolific and critical. Legal action has been taken to silence several publications. A recent proliferation of pornographic magazines has also resulted in closures and government clamp-downs.

PUBLISHING AND BROADCAST MEDIA

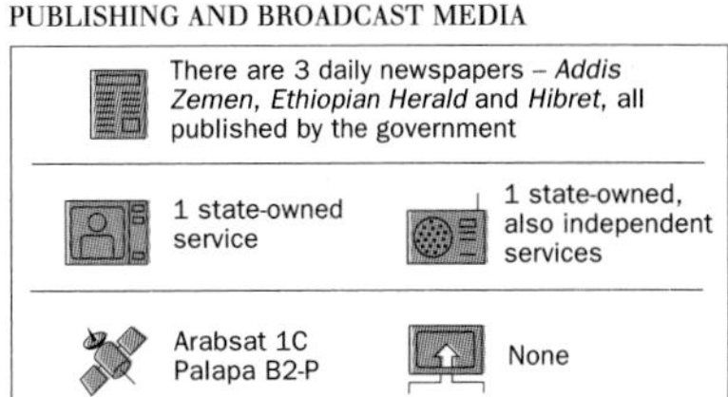

There are 3 daily newspapers – *Addis Zemen, Ethiopian Herald* and *Hibret*, all published by the government
1 state-owned service
1 state-owned, also independent services
Arabsat 1C Palapa B2-P
None

CRIME

13,585 prisoners

Down 2% in 1988

CRIME RATES

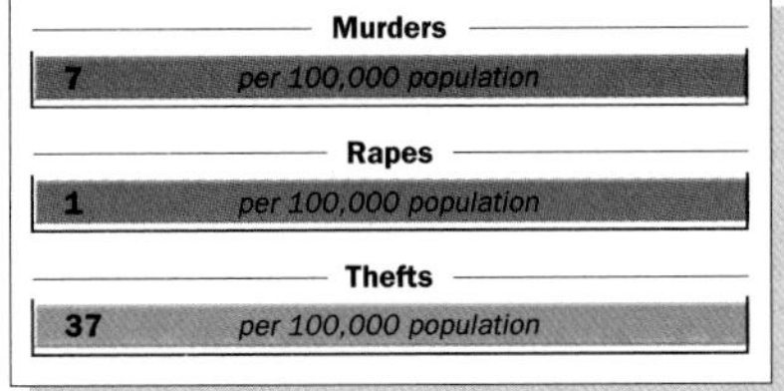

A number of human rights abuses by the transitional government have been documented by the independent Ethiopian Human Rights Council. These include detention without trial, "disappearances" and extra-judicial killings. There is some concern over indiscipline among EPRDF forces, who provide a *de facto* police force in many regions. In many rural areas traditional clan justice has replaced the state system.

EDUCATION

71%

0 *Education spending as % GNP* 25
4.4%

THE EDUCATION SYSTEM

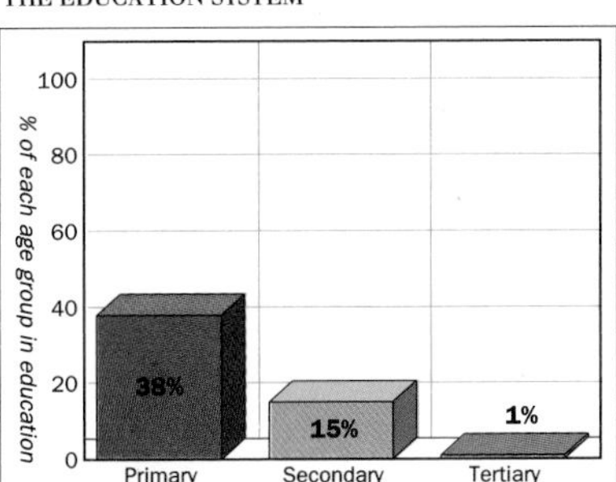

The education system was severely disrupted during the civil war. Addis Ababa University has been a center of political activity, usually anti-EPRDF, and is subject to periodic closures and the dismissal of its leading academics.

HEALTH

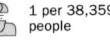

1 per 38,359 people

Diarrheal and respiratory diseases, tuberculosis, malaria

0 *Health spending as % GNP* 25
1.2%

Only about half of the population lives within 7 miles of a health unit. Hospital building, distribution of resources to rural areas, outpatient visits and referrals are all very slow. Skin and eye diseases are common. Church hospitals are of a reasonably high standard.

WEALTH

Most Ethiopians lead a subsistence existence

CONSUMER GOODS OWNERSHIP

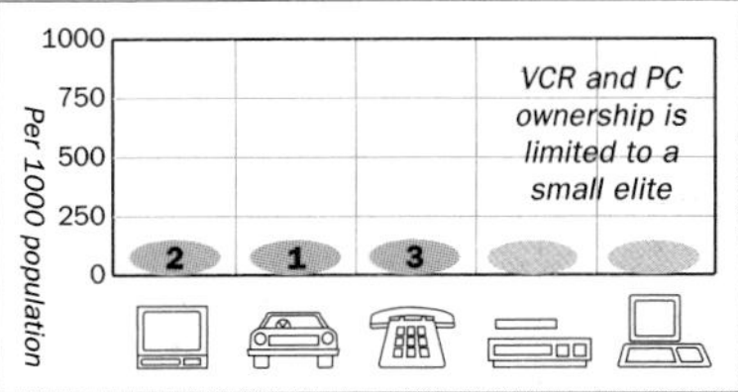

There is very little wealth in Ethiopia. The central plateau is historically the richest region. Average incomes fell by 8.5% in 1991, while prices rose by 25%. Corruption among public employees is rising again, due to pressures on incomes. Ethiopian culture places more value on maintaining traditional social structures than on individual ambition.

WORLD RANKING

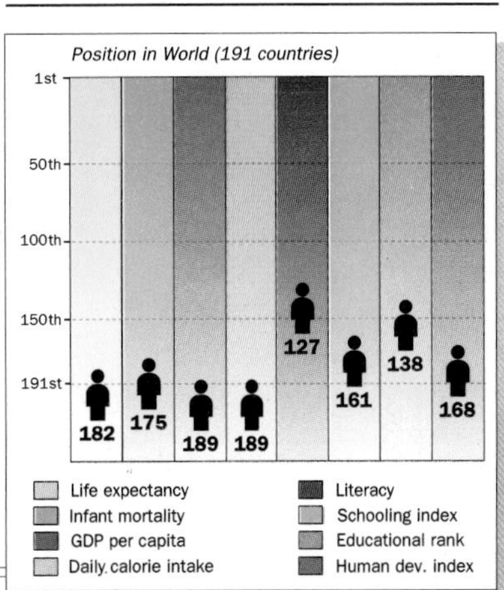

E

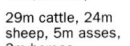

FIJI

OFFICIAL NAME: Republic of Fiji **CAPITAL:** Suva
POPULATION: 700,000 **CURRENCY:** Fiji dollar **OFFICIAL LANGUAGE:** English

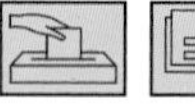

FIJI IS A VOLCANIC ARCHIPELAGO in the southern Pacific Ocean, comprising two large islands and 880 smaller islets. From 1874 to 1970, Fiji was a British colony. The British introduced Indian workers to the islands, and by 1946 their descendants, the Indo-Fijians, outnumbered the Native Fijian population. In 1987, Native Fijians overthrew the democratically elected government. After the coups, thousands of Indo-Fijians left the country.

CLIMATE

WEATHER CHART

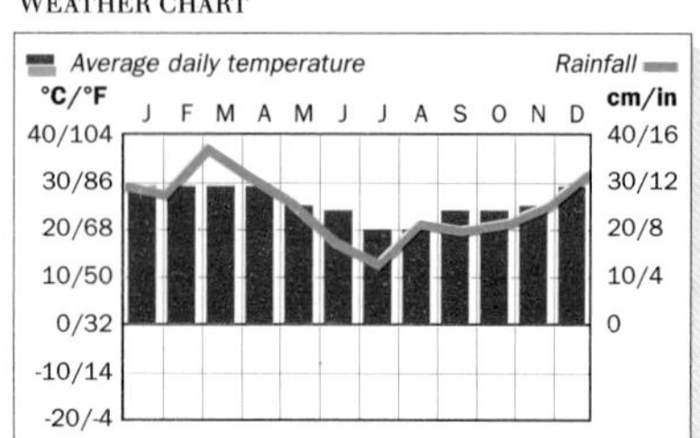

The eastern sides of the main islands are wettest, having more than twice the annual rainfall of the western flanks. Fiji lies in a cyclone path.

COMMUNICATIONS

Nadi International 785,000 passengers

25 ships 62,900 dwt

THE TRANSPORTATION NETWORK

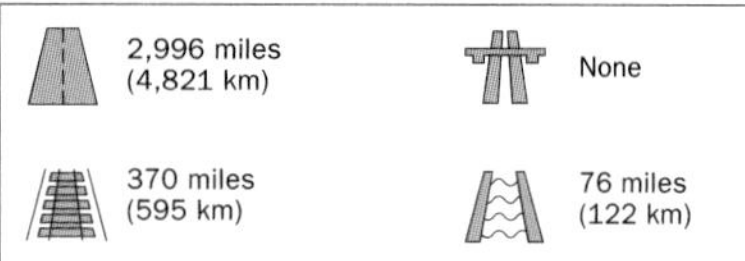

On the axis of Australian–US West Coast air routes, Fiji is well served by international flights. It is promoting an increase in Pacific shipping routes.

TOURISM

278,534 visitors

Up 7% in 1992

MAIN OVERSEAS ARRIVALS

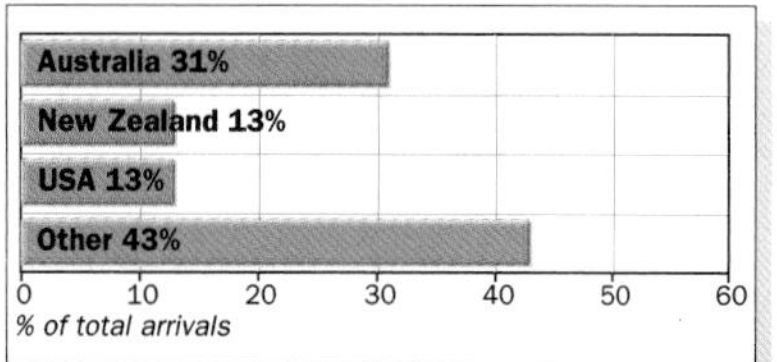

Tourists – mainly from Australia, New Zealand and the US West Coast – are returning, after a 76% drop in numbers following the 1987 coups.

PEOPLE

Fijian, English, Hindi, Urdu, Tamil, Telugu

114 people per sq. mile

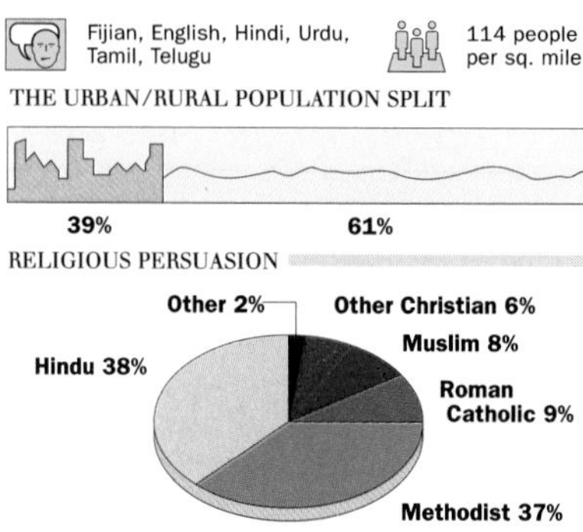

The exodus of Indo-Fijians after the 1987 coups left Native Fijians in the majority for the first time since 1946. There are tensions between urban and rural Native Fijians. Women, who head 12% of households, are lobbying for more rights. They cannot obtain loans without a husband's or father's consent, while children born of marriages to non-Fijian men are denied full citizenship.

POLITICS

1999

President Ratu Sir Kamisese Mara

THE STATE OF THE PARTIES

House of Representatives 70 members

7% FA | 4% Other

44% SVT | 29% NFP | 10% FLP | 6% GVP

SVT = Fijian Political Party **NFP** = National Federation Party **FLP** = Fiji Labour Party **FA** = Fijian Association **GVP** = General Voters' Party **Other** = All Nationals Congress

Senate 34 members

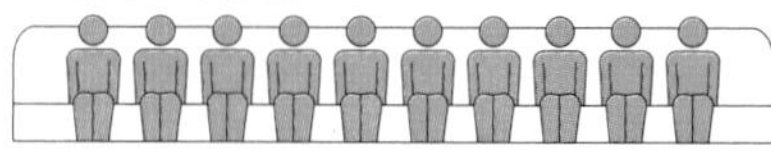

24 members are chosen by the Great Council of Chiefs, 9 by the president and 1 by the Rotuma Island Council

The 1987 coups were justified as defending the land rights of Native Fijians. In practice, they were a move by Native Fijian chiefs to secure their power, which was being threatened both by the growing Indo-Fijian urban class, and by the increasingly Westernized younger Native Fijians. The 1990 constitution, enshrining Native Fijian supremacy, makes any future Indo-Fijian challenge to the current *status quo* unlikely.

SOUTH PACIFIC
Pacific Ocean
Tuvalu
Wallis & Fortuna
Vanuatu
New Caledonia
FIJI
Tonga

FIJI

Total Area : 18 270 sq. km (7054 sq. miles)

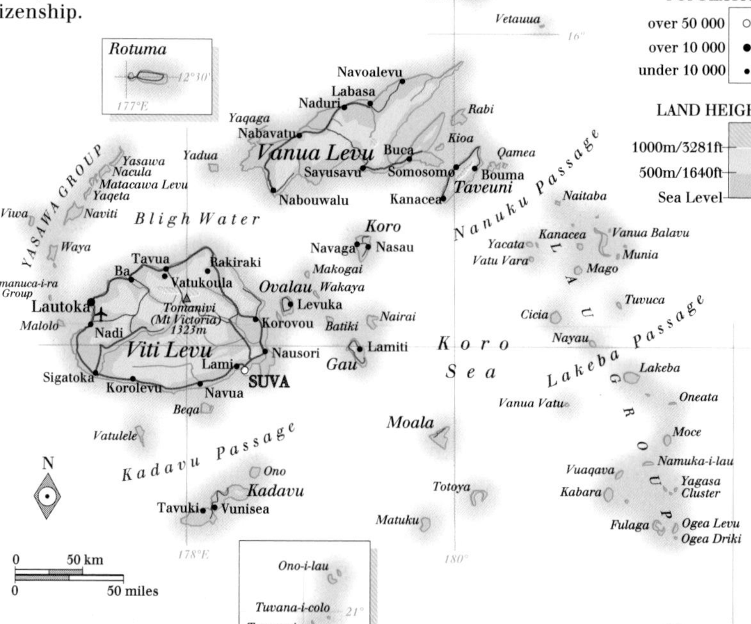

WORLD AFFAIRS

Fiji is still working to repair its international reputation following the coups of 1987, the subsequent discriminatory constitution and its expulsion from the Commonwealth.

AID

 $45m (receipts)

 Fairly stable in recent years

Fiji is one of the world's highest per capita aid recipients. Australia, Japan and the EU are the main donors.

DEFENSE

 $27m

 Up 4% in 1991

Of the 5,000-strong, almost entirely Native-Fijian military, 1,200 are assigned to UN duties and have served in Lebanon and Afghanistan.

ECONOMICS

 $1.5bn

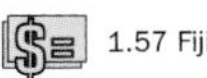 1.57 Fiji dollars

SCORE CARD

❑ WORLD GNP RANKING	146th
❑ GNP PER CAPITA	$1,770
❑ BALANCE OF PAYMENTS	$46m
❑ INFLATION	5.6%
❑ UNEMPLOYMENT	5.9%

STRENGTHS

Relatively well-diversified economy, with a growing tourist industry. Location on Pacific air routes an impetus to tourism; the many regional and international organizations located in Suva also bring benefits.

WEAKNESSES

Privileged access to key world markets now threatened by the new GATT arrangements. Major exports – sugar, copra and gold – subject to large fluctuations in world prices.

EXPORTS

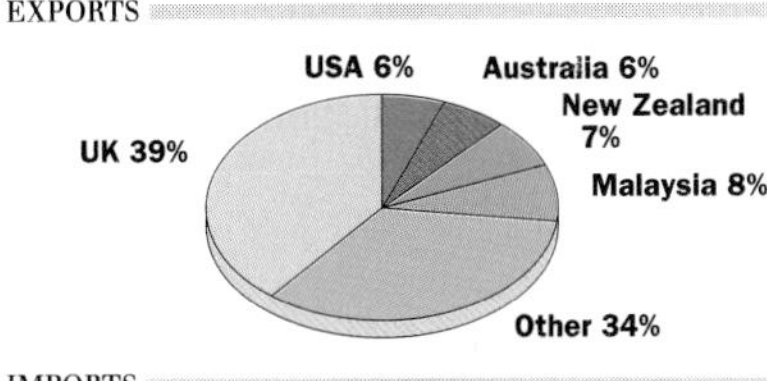

IMPORTS

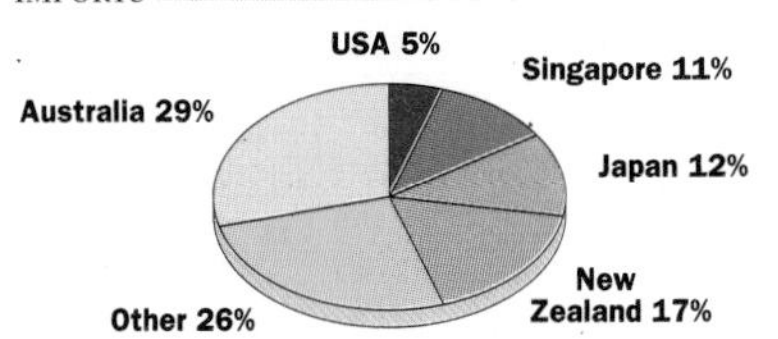

Cane field on the west side of Viti Levu, between Nadi and Lautoka. Sugar accounts for about one-third of Fiji's exports.

RESOURCES

 435m kwh (capacity 200,000 kw)

 Not an oil producer and has no refineries

32,800 tons

Gold, silver

The varied terrain allows diversified agriculture. There are minerals and hydroelectric potential, which is partly developed in the Monasavu project.

ENVIRONMENT

 0.3%

 Overuse of fertilizers

The government is environmentally aware; Fiji is downwind of France's Pacific nuclear test sites. Tourism is damaging the coral reefs.

MEDIA

 Under newly introduced restrictions, no aspersions may be cast on the Fijian leadership

PUBLISHING AND BROADCAST MEDIA

 There are 2 English-language dailies, the *Fiji Times* and the *Fiji Sun*. *Nai Lalakai* and *Shanti Dut* are the Fijian and Indian weeklies

 1 state-owned service

 5 state-controlled, 2 independent stations

Newspapers and videotapes are the major source of information on the islands. Radios keep the many Fijians who are away from home in touch with news from their villages.

CRIME

 859 men 19 women

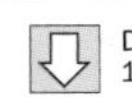 Down 3% between 1985 and 1990

Theft and alcohol-related violence top the crime list. Fiji also has one of the world's highest *crime passionel* rates.

EDUCATION

 87%

Education, originally modeled on the British system, is now mostly run by local committees and is increasingly racially segregated. Attendance, although high, is not compulsory.

CHRONOLOGY

The British decision to import Indian sugar workers between 1879 and 1916, many of whom settled, dramatically changed Fijian society.

- ❑ **1970** Independence from Britain.
- ❑ **1972–1987** Alliance Party maintains Native and Indo-Fijian balance.
- ❑ **1987** Indo-Fijian majority coalition wins power. Two coups led by Maj.-Gen. Rabuka secure minority Native Fijian supremacy. Fiji ejected from Commonwealth.
- ❑ **1989** Mass Indo-Fijian emigration.
- ❑ **1990** Constitution discriminating against Indo-Fijians introduced.
- ❑ **1992** Elections. Rabuka's Fijian Political Party secures power.

F

HEALTH

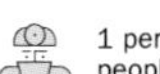 1 per 2,224 people

 Cerebrovascular and heart diseases, cancer, accidents

People living in rural areas and on the outlying islands are served by 95 nursing stations. Fiji is free of almost all tropical diseases, including malaria.

WEALTH

 Agricultural worker, 12 Fiji dollars per day; construction worker, 14 Fiji dollars per day

CONSUMER GOODS OWNERSHIP

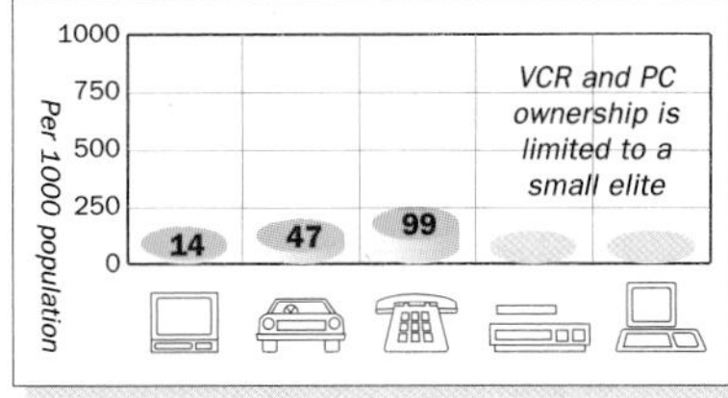

Ostentatious displays of wealth are rare; prestige derives from family and landholdings. The professional middle class, while still dominated by Indo-Fijians, is becoming more mixed.

WORLD RANKING

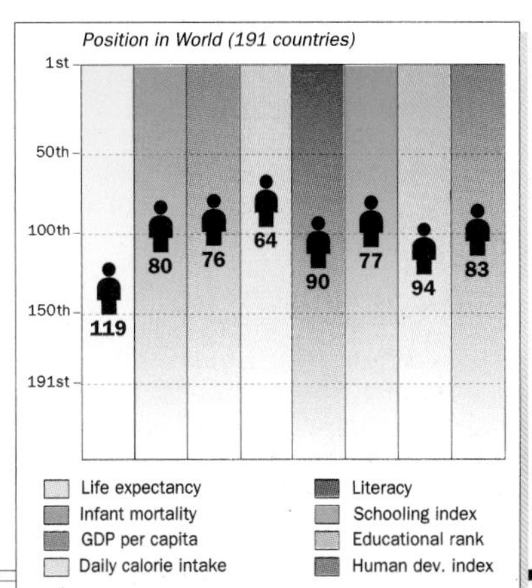

FINLAND

OFFICIAL NAME: Republic of Finland **CAPITAL:** Helsinki
POPULATION: 5 million **CURRENCY:** Markka **OFFICIAL LANGUAGES:** Finnish and Swedish

BORDERED TO THE north and west by Norway and Sweden, and to the east by Russia, Finland is a low-lying country of forests and over 60,000 lakes. Politics are based on consensus and the country has been stable despite successive short-lived coalitions. Finland was ruled by Russia until 1917, and subsequently accepted a close relationship with the Soviet Union as the price of maintaining its independence. It joined the EU in 1995. Living standards are high, but the country is recovering from a recession which, in 1990, ended a decade of record growth.

CLIMATE

WEATHER CHART

Average daily temperature — Rainfall
°C/°F J F M A M J J A S O N D cm/in
40/104 40/16
30/86 30/12
20/68 20/8
10/50 10/4
0/32 0
-10/14
-20/-4

North of the Arctic Circle the climate is extreme. Temperatures fall to –22°F in the six-month winter and rise to 80°F during the 73 days of summer midnight sun. In the south, summers are mild and short, winters are cold. The annual average temperature in Helsinki is 41F°.

COMMUNICATIONS

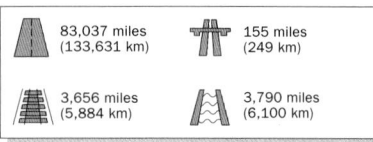

121 ships 1.02m dwt

THE TRANSPORTATION NETWORK

83,037 miles (133,631 km)
155 miles (249 km)
3,656 miles (5,884 km)
3,790 miles (6,100 km)

Finland has a well-integrated transportation system. The railroad connects with the Swedish and Russian networks. There are also frequent air services to most neighboring states. Presently, links with the Baltic countries are being improved. Internal air travel is also important, particularly north of the Arctic Circle.

With over 60,000 lakes and rivers, Finland has Europe's largest inland waterway system. Although it still carries freight, its use today is mainly recreational. Finland's international ports handle around 60 million tons a year. Kotka is the chief port for exports. Helsinki, with its five specialized harbors, handles most imports.

TOURISM

MAIN OVERSEAS ARRIVALS

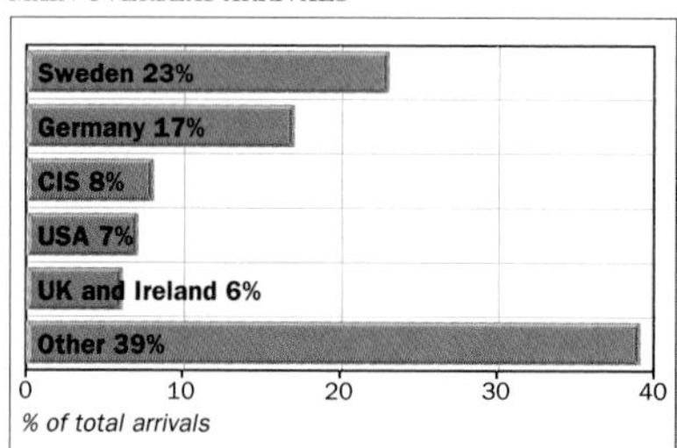

The scenery of the southern lakes and the vast forests of its Arctic north are Finland's main attractions. Helsinki is an important cultural center and hosts an annual arts festival. Its opera house has an international reputation and the capital has many first-class restaurants. Most tourists try a sauna, a Finnish invention, and the local vodka, which is reputedly among the world's finest.

Visitors come mostly from other Nordic countries and Germany. Since 1990, there has been an increase in visitors from the Baltic States and Russia. The depreciation of the markka since 1992 has helped to boost visitor numbers.

A summer's night at Lake Kilpisjärvi, "The Way of the Four Winds," which lies at the point where Finland, Sweden and Norway meet.

PEOPLE

THE URBAN/RURAL POPULATION SPLIT

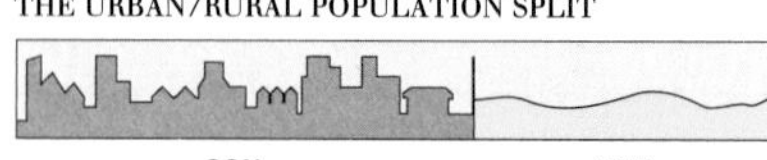

RELIGIOUS PERSUASION

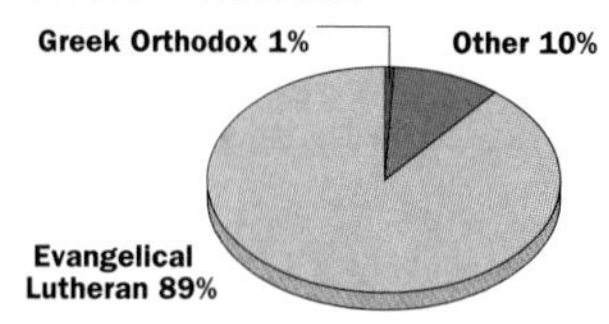

ETHNIC MAKEUP

Other (including Sami) 1%
Finn 99%

Most Finns are of Scandinavian-Baltic extraction. Finnish belongs to the small Finno-Ugric linguistic group and is a legacy of the country's earliest invaders from Asia. Although they were later ousted by the ancestors of today's Finns, their language was retained. Lappish, also a Finno-Ugric language, is spoken by the small Sami (Lapp) population, who live above the Arctic Circle. Around 6% of the population live in the Åland Islands in the southwest and speak Swedish.

More than 50% of Finns live in the five southernmost districts around Helsinki. Families tend to be close-knit, although divorce rates are high. The sauna is an integral part of everyday life; there are 1.5 million saunas among five million Finns.

Finnish women have a long tradition of political and economic participation. They were the first in Europe to get the vote, in 1906, and the first in the world able to run for parliament. Almost 50% of women now work outside the home. Both the governor of the central bank and the defense minister are women.

POPULATION AGE BREAKDOWN

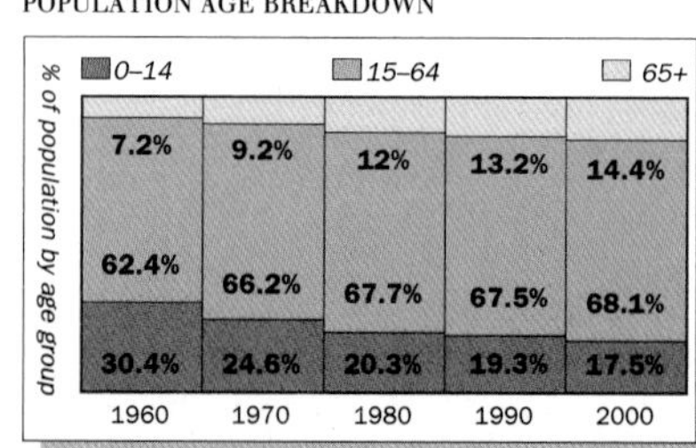

POLITICS

1995

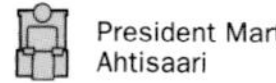

President Martti Ahtisaari

Finland's constitution combines parliamentary government with a strong presidency. The external territory of the Åland Islands has internal self-government.

MAIN POLITICAL ISSUES

EU membership

In a national referendum held in October 1994, Finland voted to join the EU. Membership was a less contentious issue than in other Nordic countries and many Finns supported entry as a way of identifying with western Europe. However, the small but influential farming community was hostile to membership because it poses a threat to farm subsidies. Further opposition stemmed from fears that public spending cuts, in particular welfare cuts, would be required to meet the economic criteria for membership.

Unemployment

The victory of SDP candidate Martti Ahtisaari in the 1994 presidential election was a sign of discontent with the conservative KESK–KOK coalition led by Prime Minister Esko Aho. Its handling of the recession resulted in record unemployment levels and welfare cuts. It also strained the traditional consensus approach to politics in Finland. Elections due in 1995 are expected to return an SDP-led coalition.

PROFILE

Proportional representation has led to government by coalition, usually dominated by the SDP or KESK. The emphasis on consensus has favored stability, but also results in slow decision-making. The parties tend to agree on aims, but not the means of achieving them.

THE STATE OF THE PARTIES

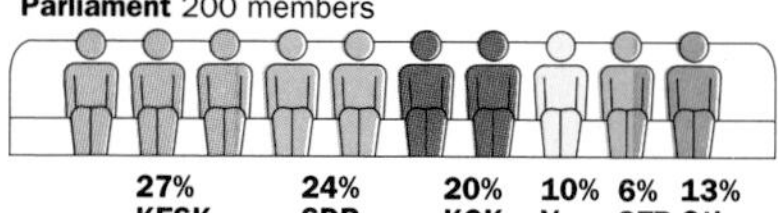

KESK = Finnish Center Party **SDP** = Finnish Social Democratic Party **KOK** = National Coalition Party **V** = Left-Wing Alliance **SFP** = Swedish People's Party **Other** = Green Union, Finnish Christian Union, Finnish Rural Party

President Martti Ahtisaari, who won the 1994 presidential election.

Prime Minister Esko Aho, leader of the KESK–KOK coalition.

WORLD AFFAIRS

After carefully balancing its relations with the Soviet Union and the West during the Cold War, Finland has now decided that its national interest lies within Western Europe. In addition to joining the EU it is also considering participation in the WEU. However, the government is also eager to avoid alienating Russia and will continue to pursue some form of special relationship with Moscow.

AID

$930m (donations)

Up 10% in 1991

Finland is one of the few donor countries to have achieved the UN target of allocating 0.7% of GDP to aid. The main recipients are countries in Southeast Asia and Africa.

CHRONOLOGY

Finland's history has been closely linked with the competing interests of Sweden and Russia.

- ❑ **1323** Treaty of Pähkinäsaari. Finland part of Swedish Kingdom.
- ❑ **1809** Treaty of Fredrikhamn, Sweden cedes Finland to Russia. Finland becomes a Grand Duchy enjoying considerable autonomy.
- ❑ **1812** Helsinki becomes capital.
- ❑ **1863** Finnish becomes an official language alongside Swedish.
- ❑ **1865** Grand Duchy acquires its own monetary system.
- ❑ **1879** Conscription law lays the foundation for a Finnish army.
- ❑ **1899** Tsar Nicholas II begins process of Russification. Labor Party founded.
- ❑ **1900** Gradual imposition of Russian as the official language begins.
- ❑ **1901** Finnish army disbanded, Finns ordered into Russian units. Disobedience campaign prevents men being drafted into the army.

F

CHRONOLOGY *continued*

- ❑ **1903** Labor Party becomes the Social Democratic Party (SDP).
- ❑ **1905** National strike forces restoration of 1899 *status quo.*
- ❑ **1906** Parliamentary reform. Universal suffrage introduced.
- ❑ **1907** SDP main party in parliament.
- ❑ **1910** Responsibility for important legislation passed to Russian Duma.
- ❑ **1917** Russian revolution allows Finland to declare independence.
- ❑ **1918** Civil war between Bolsheviks and right-wing government. Gen. Mannerheim leads the government to victory at the Battle of Tampere.
- ❑ **1919** Finland becomes a republic. Kaarlo Ståhlberg elected president with wide political powers.
- ❑ **1920** Treaty of Tartu: Soviet Union recognizes Finland's borders.
- ❑ **1921** London Convention. Åland Islands become part of Finland.
- ❑ **1939** August: Hitler-Stalin non-aggression pact gives the USSR a free hand in Finland. November: Soviet invasion. Strong Finnish resistance in ensuing Winter War.
- ❑ **1940** Invaded by USSR. Treaty of Moscow. Finland cedes one-tenth of national territory.
- ❑ **1941** Finnish troops join Germany in its invasion of the USSR.
- ❑ **1944** June: Red Army invade. August: President Ryti resigns. September: Finland, led by Marshal Mannerheim, signs armistice.
- ❑ **1946** President Mannerheim resigns, Juho Paasikivi president.
- ❑ **1948** Signs friendship treaty with the USSR. Agrees to resist any attack on the USSR made through Finland by Germany or its allies.
- ❑ **1952** Payment of $570 million in war reparations completed.
- ❑ **1955** Joins Nordic Council.
- ❑ **1956** Uhro Kekkonen, leader of the Agrarian Party, becomes president.
- ❑ **1956–1991** A series of coalition governments involving the SDP and the Agrarians, renamed the Center Party (KESK) in 1965, hold power.
- ❑ **1981** President Kekkonen resigns.
- ❑ **1982** Dr. Mauno Koivisto president.
- ❑ **1989** USSR recognizes Finnish neutrality for the first time.
- ❑ **1991** Non-socialist government elected. Budget cut as part of austerity measures.
- ❑ **1992** January: signs ten-year agreement with Russia which, for the first time since World World II, involves no military agreement. March: government applies to join the EU.
- ❑ **1994** SDP candidate, Martti Ahtisaari, elected president. Seen as a show of electoral dissatisfaction with the conservative government.
- ❑ **1995** Becomes member of EU.

DEFENSE

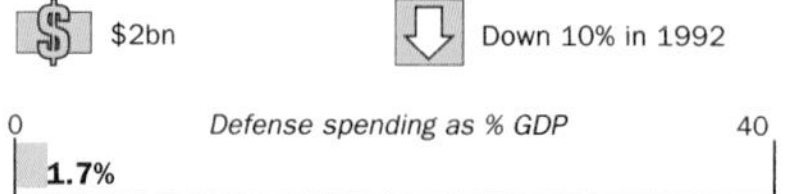

The Finnish military is small, with 32,800 troops, but there are also 700,000 active reservists and a large border guard force. Russia's instability has reinforced concern about border security, the top defense issue. Finland is reconsidering its neutrality and may opt for participation in the WEU.

FINNISH ARMED FORCES

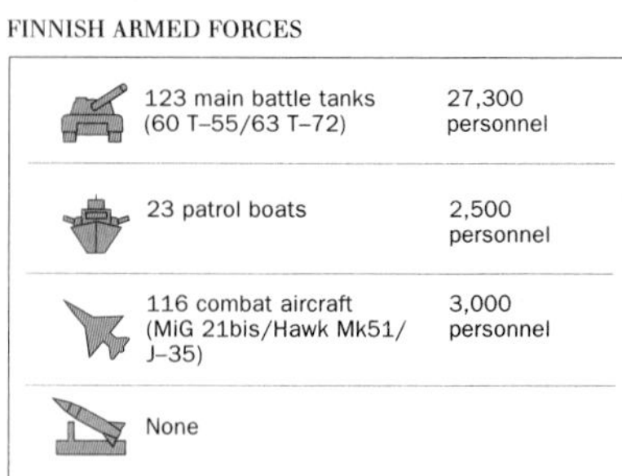

123 main battle tanks (60 T–55/63 T–72)	27,300 personnel
23 patrol boats	2,500 personnel
116 combat aircraft (MiG 21bis/Hawk Mk51/ J–35)	3,000 personnel
None	

ECONOMICS

$122bn

5.79 markkaa

SCORE CARD

- ❑ World GNP Ranking..........................25th
- ❑ GNP per Capita $24,322
- ❑ Balance of Payments....................$–5.1bn
- ❑ Inflation 1.9%
- ❑ Unemployment..................................20%

EXPORTS

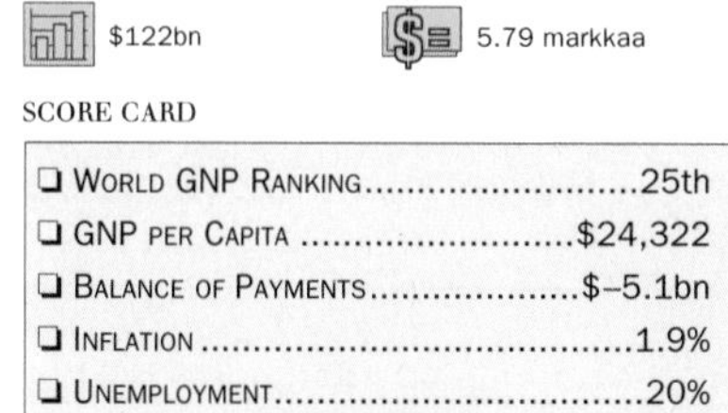

IMPORTS

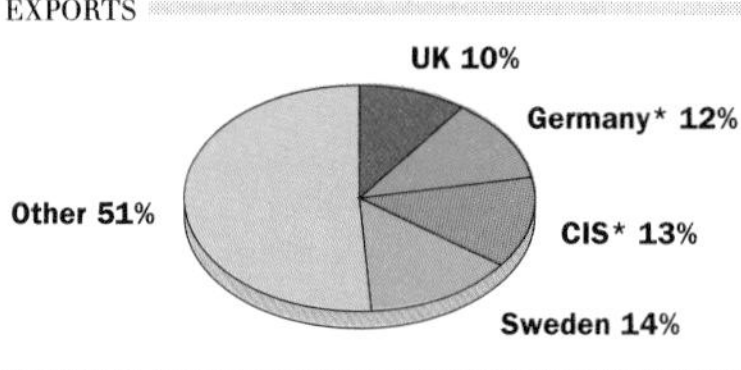

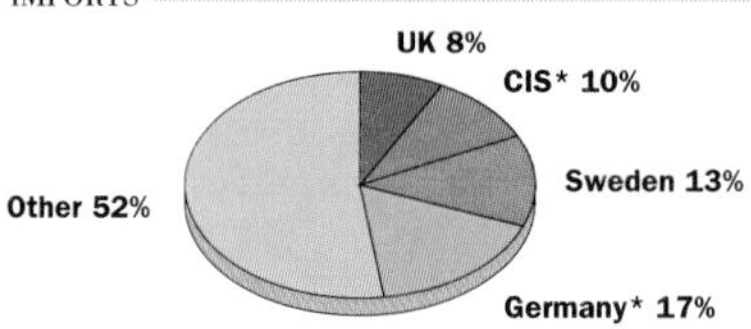

Strengths

Industry is export- and quality-oriented. Large high-tech sector. World leader in pulp and paper. Exports quick to recover from recession. Low inflation, now less than 2% a year. Improved foreign investment incentives. Gateway to Russian and Baltic economies.

Weaknesses

Severe recession following 1980s' fast growth; real GDP declined 15% during 1991–1993. High level of public sector and foreign debt, the latter 22% of GDP. Highest unemployment rate in Western Europe, up from 3.5% in 1990 to 20% in 1993. Small domestic market and peripheral position in Europe.

Profile

Finland is a market economy and still wealthy, although it is just emerging from its worst recession in 60 years. The boom years of the 1980s, when GDP expanded by almost 4% a year, came to an abrupt end in 1990. The collapse of the former Soviet Union, which had taken 28% of Finland's exports, was largely responsible for the downturn. A rapid rise in unemployment and business failures pushed up government spending. The floating of the markka in 1992 and austerity measures, including welfare benefit cuts, higher taxes and wage restraints, improved Finland's competitiveness. Exports have largely recovered. However, full recovery will take longer and unemployment is likely to stay above 15% for some years. With private investment at a ten-year low and the pressure of EU membership looming, the economy will take time to recover.

ECONOMIC PERFORMANCE INDICATOR

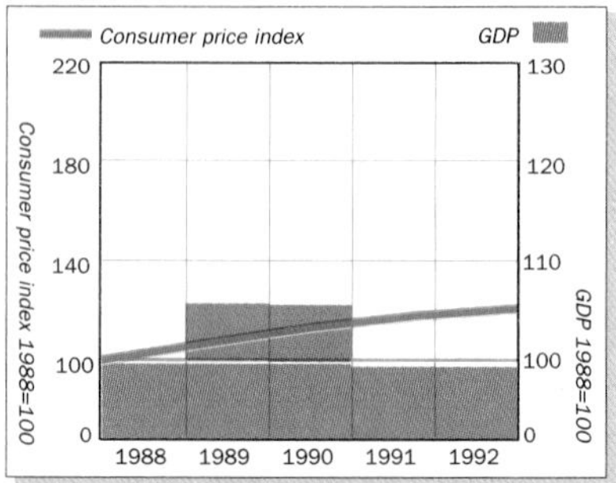

FINLAND : MAJOR BUSINESSES

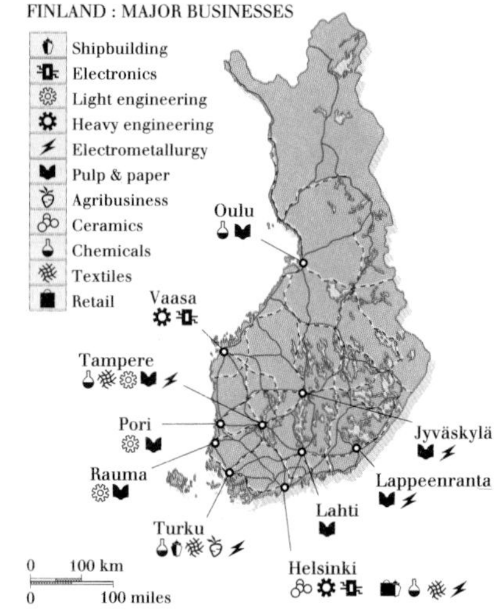

RESOURCES

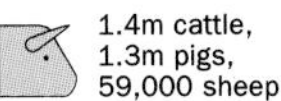

54.5bn kwh (capacity 13.2m kw)

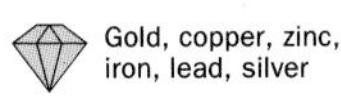

Not an oil producer; refines 200,000 b/cd

1.4m cattle, 1.3m pigs, 59,000 sheep

Gold, copper, zinc, iron, lead, silver

ELECTRICITY GENERATION

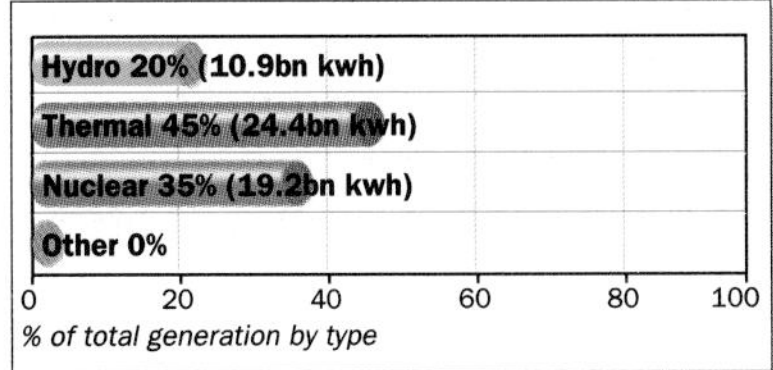

Finland's trees are its prime natural resource. Commercial forests cover 65% of the land and wood products account for 40% of exports. Finland has no oil, but has significant hydroelectric resources. Industry's high energy demands are met primarily by thermal and nuclear power. A fifth nuclear power station is planned. Oil import costs have risen since 1990, when the collapse of the USSR ended a 42-year agreement on the exchange of Finnish manufactures for Soviet oil.

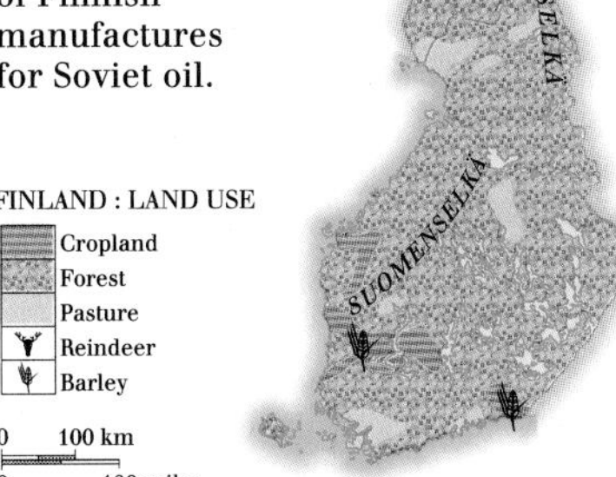

FINLAND : LAND USE

Cropland
Forest
Pasture
Reindeer
Barley

0 100 km
0 100 miles

ENVIRONMENT

2% (1% partially protected)

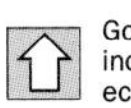

Government increasingly aware of ecological problems

ENVIRONMENTAL TREATIES

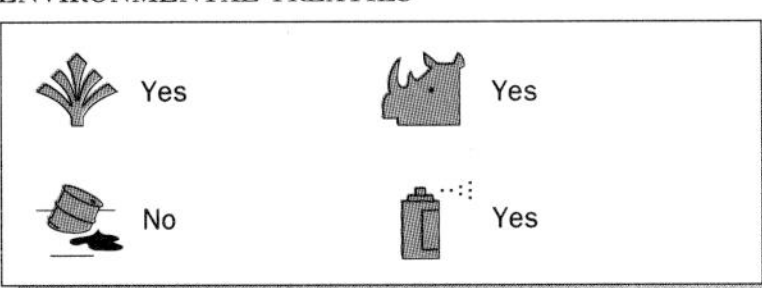

Finland has strict laws on industrial emissions. Energy efficiency is a priority; over 40% of homes are connected to district heating systems. Growing public concern about nuclear safety has led to opposition to the planned fifth nuclear plant and to proposals for the greater use of waste materials in energy generation. The government is funding nuclear safety programs in Russia. Rising levels of pollution in the Baltic are of concern.

MEDIA

There is no censorship of the media

PUBLISHING AND BROADCAST MEDIA

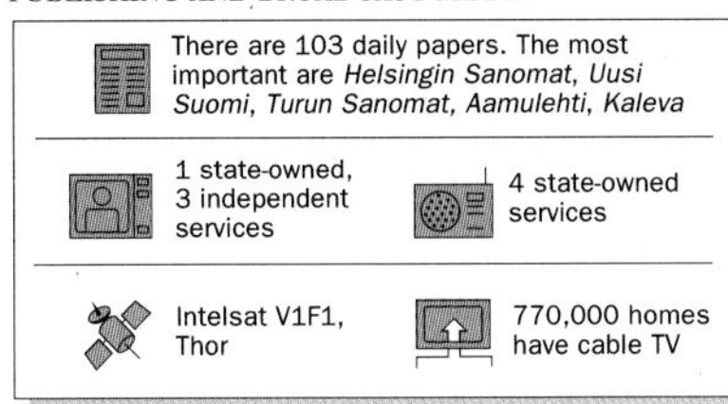

There are 103 daily papers. The most important are *Helsingin Sanomat, Uusi Suomi, Turun Sanomat, Aamulehti, Kaleva*
1 state-owned, 3 independent services
4 state-owned services
Intelsat V1F1, Thor
770,000 homes have cable TV

Nine out of ten Finns read a daily paper, the world's third-highest circulation to population ratio. Regional papers dominate; the only national is *Helsingin Sanomat*. There is no censorship, but the press shows restraint in criticizing the government.

CRIME

3,106 prisoners

Up 9% in 1990

CRIME RATES

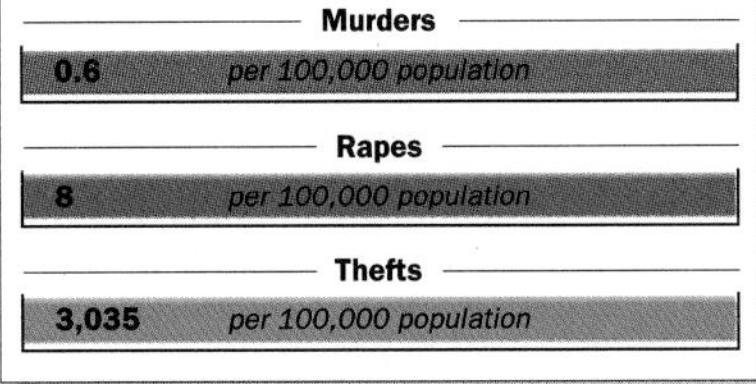

The jump in unemployment, from 3.5% in 1990 to 20% in 1993, is one cause of rising crime. There is concern about links with organized crime in Russia.

EDUCATION

100%

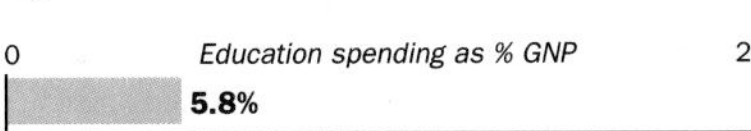

THE EDUCATION SYSTEM

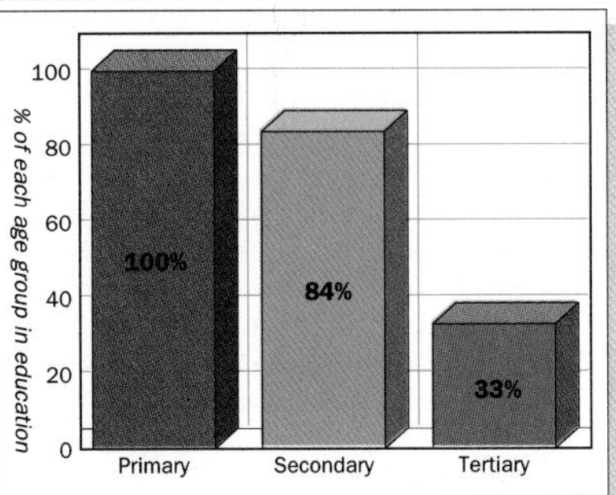

Compulsory education lasts from 7 to 16 years of age. Almost all children receive pre-school education and go on to three years of upper secondary education. Tough examinations mean that only 35% of entrants qualify to attend one of the 20 universities.

HEALTH

1 per 430 people

Cerebrovascular and heart diseases, cancer, suicides

0 *Health spending as % GNP* 25

2.5%

Spending on Finland's well-developed health care system accounts for about 10% of the state budget. Every Finn is legally guaranteed access to a local health center staffed by up to four doctors, as well as nurses and a midwife. National health insurance covers most non-hospital medical costs and hospital fees are moderate.

WEALTH

Paper machine operator, 58 markkaa per hour; general physician, 16,900 markkaa per month

CONSUMER GOODS OWNERSHIP

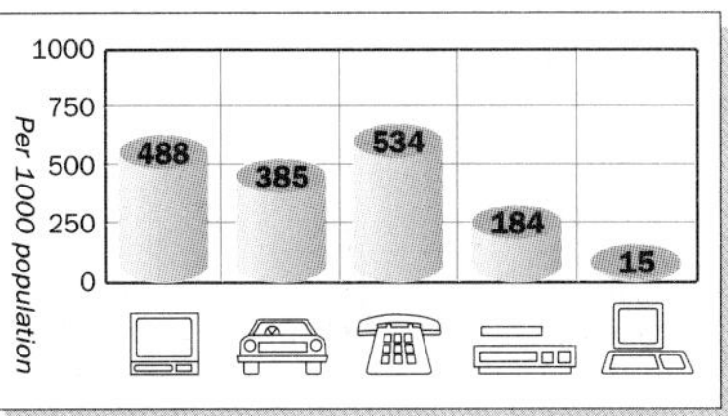

Income disparities are more marked in Finland than in the rest of Scandinavia. However, the economic boom and labor shortages of the 1980s led to a sharp rise in all living standards. Personal consumption reached Swedish levels and many families were able to take two vacations a year. Social security benefits were extended.

Since the recession began in 1990, this improvement has been reversed. Wealth disparities have also widened. Cuts in budgetary expenditure have resulted in a decline in social security benefits paid to the unemployed. Those in work have had to accept lower pay rises and higher taxes. Average real disposable income has dropped by more than 7% since 1991. Estonian immigrants form the poorest group.

WORLD RANKING

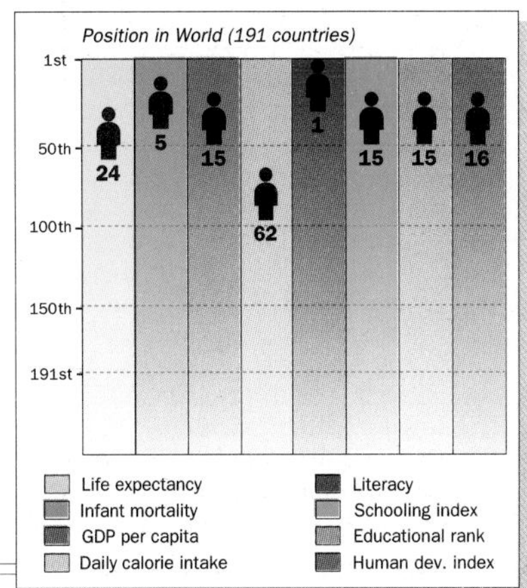

F

FRANCE

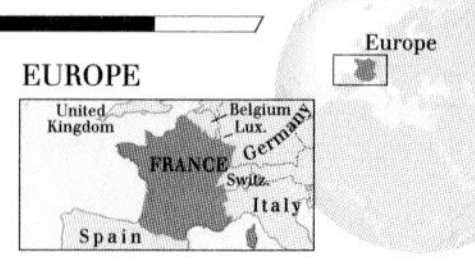

OFFICIAL NAME: The French Republic **CAPITAL:** Paris **POPULATION:** 57.2 million
CURRENCY: Franc **OFFICIAL LANGUAGE:** French **OVERSEAS TERRITORIES:** 10

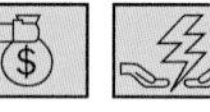

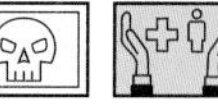

STRADDLING WESTERN EUROPE from the English Channel to the Mediterranean, France was Europe's first modern republic and built a colonial empire second only to Britain's. Today it is one of the world's major industrial powers and its fourth largest exporter. Industry is the leading economic sector, but the agricultural lobby remains powerful – French farmers are willing to mount the barricades in defense of their interests. Today, France's focus is very much toward Europe. Together with Germany it was a founder member of the European Economic Community. Following the 1992 referendum, it endorsed the Maastricht proposals which created the European Union. Paris, its capital, is generally considered one of the world's most beautiful cities. It has been home to some of the 20th century's most influential artists, writers and filmmakers.

F

Le Plessis-Bourré, Loire Valley. *The region is famous for its many chateaus, which attract thousands of visitors every year.*

CLIMATE

WEATHER CHART

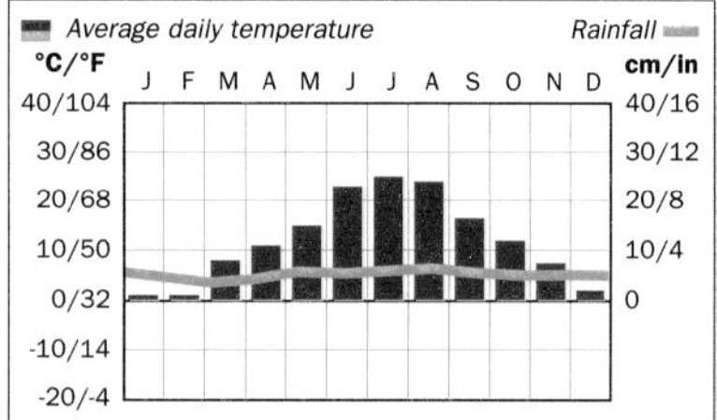

France has, in broad terms, three climates – Atlantic, Continental and Mediterranean. The northwest, particularly Brittany, is mild but damp. The east has hot summers and stormy winters. Summers in the south are dry and hot, and forest fires are common.

COMMUNICATIONS

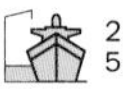

Charles de Gaulle, Paris 22.5m passengers

210 ships 5.56m dwt

THE TRANSPORTATION NETWORK

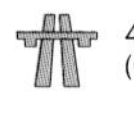

498,759 miles (804,450 sq. km)

4,142 miles (6,680 km)

21,341 miles (34,421 km)

5,270 miles (8,500 km)

Pioneers of aviation and cobuilders of the Concorde, the French today lead the world in high-speed train technology, with the TGV (*Train à Grande Vitesse*). The first TGV line, opened in 1983, does the 285-mile Paris to Lyon journey in two hours – faster, door-to-door, than air travel. TGV lines have since been built to the north and west as well as to the Channel Tunnel, which opened in 1994. It was the French, more than the British, who pressed for the tunnel to be built.

TOURISM

53.2m visitors

Up 6% in 1990

MAIN OVERSEAS ARRIVALS

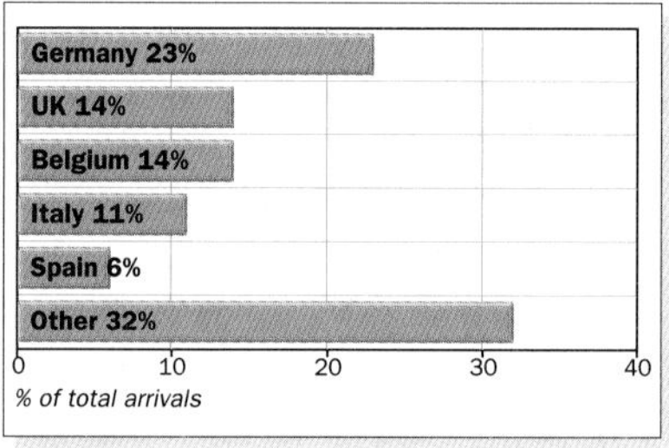

France is one of the world's leading tourist destinations. It is top of the list for the Germans and the British, and is the most popular European destination for the Japanese. The majority of French people prefer to spend their vacations in their own country, rather than traveling abroad.

Paris is the most visited European city. Its attractions include the Eiffel Tower, Notre Dame cathedral, the Pompidou Center and the Louvre, the world's largest and most popular museum.

Modern tourism was all but invented on the Côte d'Azur, when crowned heads and nobility flocked to new fashionable resorts, such as Nice, and Menton, at the end of the 19th century. Today, tourism outside Paris still focuses on the south but is more populist, and includes camping and package tours. Cannes is the venue for the world's leading film festival, as well as a growing business convention trade.

In 1992, EuroDisney opened east of Paris. However, it has not proved as popular with the public as traditional French cultural attractions, losing millions of dollars in its first year.

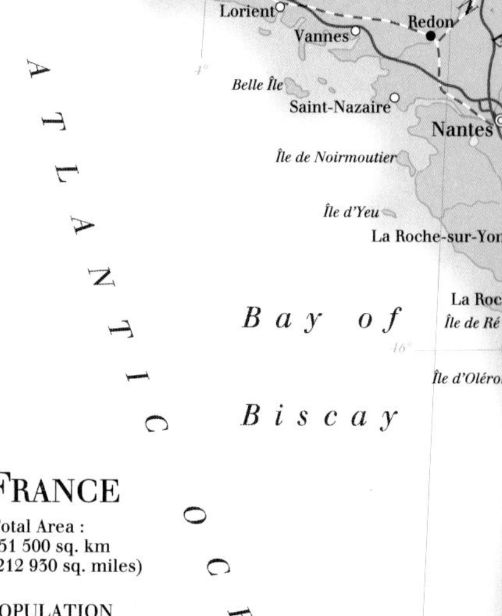

FRANCE

Total Area :
551 500 sq. km
(212 930 sq. miles)

POPULATION
over 1 000 000
over 100 000
over 50 000
over 10 000

LAND HEIGHT
3000m/9843ft
2000m/6562ft
1000m/3281ft
500m/1640ft
200m/656ft
Sea Level

N

0 100 km
0 100 miles

PEOPLE

French, Provençal, German, Breton, Catalan, Basque

269 people per sq. mile

The French, despite their strong national identity, are a great mix of peoples. Bretons, Normans, Flemmings, Alsatians, Savoyards, Provençaux, Basques and Corsicans still maintain their traditions, although today local languages are seldom spoken. France has 4.5 million people of foreign origin, nearly 40%of whom originate from southern Europe, as well as the largest Jewish community in Europe outside of Russia, numbering over 700,000.

From 1945 until the mid-1980s, France suffered relatively little from racism. Many Muslim immigrants from North Africa settled in cities such as Paris and Marseilles, becoming well-integrated in the work force. Rising unemployment over the past decade has, however, led to a rise in intolerance, reflected in the 14% vote received by the racist National Front (FN) and many North Africans feel threatened. To counter FN propaganda, many large anti-racist rallies have been held for the majority of French wish to maintain a strong liberal tradition. Unlike the North Africans, black migrants from France's present-day overseas departments are well-integrated, full French citizens. The Catholic Church, once the dominant conservative force in French society, has lost much of its influence since the 1950s. Abortion and birth control were both legalized in the 1970s despite strong opposition from the Church. Up to 50% of couples now live together before marriage and common-law marriage is legally recognized. Women and men now have identical legal rights, although women did not get the vote until 1945. Today, women are well represented in the professional sector. Edith Cresson served as France's first woman prime minister from 1991 to 1992.

THE URBAN/RURAL POPULATION SPLIT

74% 26%

POPULATION AGE BREAKDOWN

% of population by age group

	1960	1970	1980	1990	2000
65+	11.6%	12.9%	14%	13.8%	15.4%
15–64	62%	62.3%	63.7%	66.1%	65.2%
0–14	26.4%	24.8%	22.3%	20.1%	19.4%

RELIGIOUS PERSUASION

Muslim 1%, Protestant 2%, Jewish 1%, Other 6%, Roman Catholic 90%

ETHNIC MAKEUP

German 2%, Other 2%, Breton 1%, North African 3%, French 92%

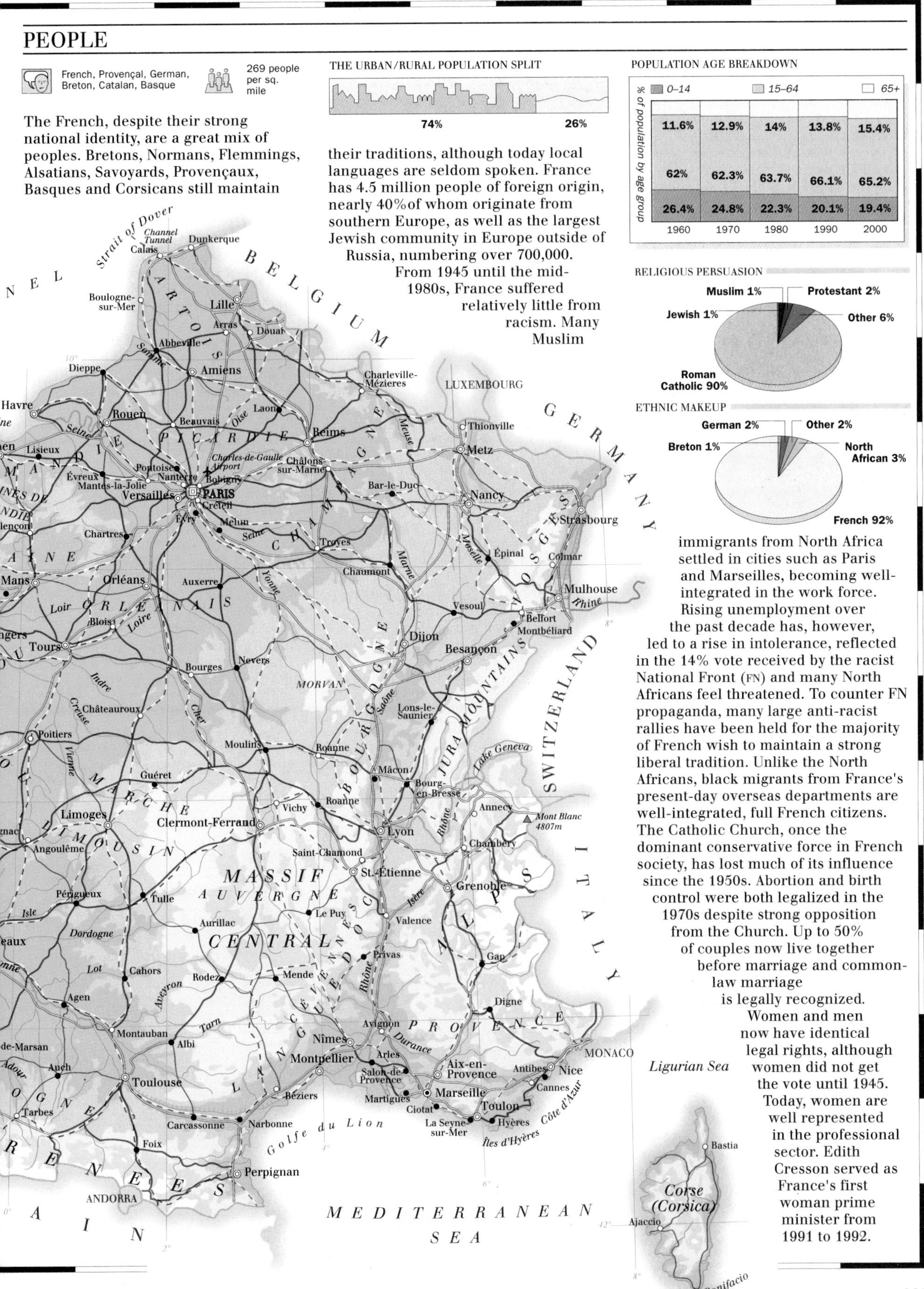

CHRONOLOGY

The French Revolution of 1789 overthrew a monarchy that had lasted for more than 1,300 years.
It ushered in periods of alternating republicanism, Napoleonic imperialism and monarchism, ending in 1870 when the founding of the Third Republic established France firmly in the republican tradition.

- ❑ **1914–1918** 1.4 million Frenchmen killed in World War I.
- ❑ **1918–1939** Economic recession and political instability; 44 governments and 20 prime ministers.
- ❑ **1940** Capitulation to Germany. Marshal Pétain heads puppet Vichy regime. General de Gaulle founds "Free French" government in London.
- ❑ **1944** Liberation of France.
- ❑ **1946–1958** Fourth Republic. Political instability; 26 governments. Nationalizations. France takes leading role in EEC formation.
- ❑ **1958** Fifth Republic founded. De Gaulle becomes president. Political stability enhanced by increased presidential powers.
- ❑ **1960** Most French colonies gain independence, retain close links with France in French Community.
- ❑ **1962** Algerian independence after bitter war with France.
- ❑ **1966** France withdraws from NATO military command.
- ❑ **1968** General strike and riots over education policy and low wages. National Assembly dissolved; Gaullist victory in June elections.
- ❑ **1969** De Gaulle resigns after defeat in referendum on regional reform, replaced by Georges Pompidou.
- ❑ **1974** Valéry Giscard d'Estaing becomes president after death of Pompidou. Center-right coalition.
- ❑ **1981** PS victory in elections; François Mitterrand president.
- ❑ **1983–1986** Differences over approach to economic recession cause dissension in left-wing coalition. PCF withdraws support.
- ❑ **1986** *Cohabitation* between socialist president and right-wing government after elections leads to return of right-wing coalition led by Jacques Chirac, who challenges presidential powers. Privatization program introduced.
- ❑ **1988** Mitterrand wins second term. PS-led coalition returns.
- ❑ **1989** Start of series of scandals, particularly involving PS politicians.
- ❑ **1991** Michel Rocard resigns as prime minister. Edith Cresson becomes first French woman prime minister
- ❑ **1993** Center-right coalition under Edouard Balladur wins elections.

POLITICS

Lower House 1998
Upper House 1995

President
Jacques Chirac

THE STATE OF THE PARTIES

National Assembly 577 members

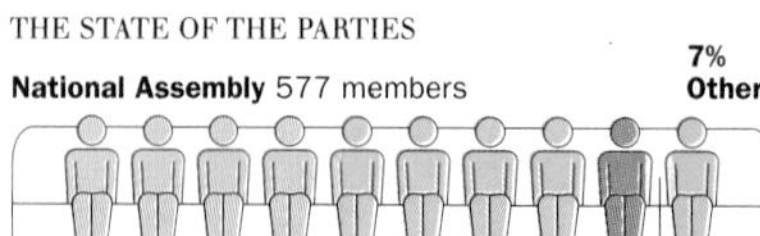

RPR = Rally for the Republic **UDF** = Union for French Democracy **PS** = Socialist Party **PCF** = French Communist Party **GRR** = Rally for the Republic Group **GS** = Socialist Group **GUCDP** = Central Union of Progressive Democrats Group **GURI** = Union of Republicans and Independents Group **GGD** = Democratic Left Group **Other** = Left Radical Movement, Communist Party

Senate 321 members

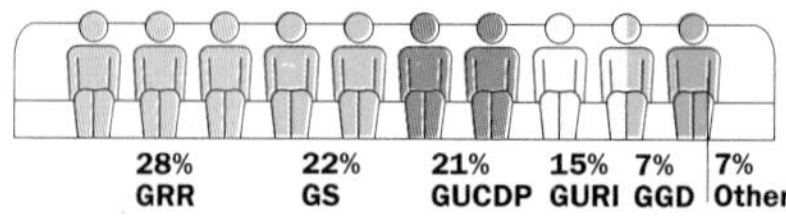

France is a multiparty democracy where the president rules in tandem with a prime minister and government chosen by the *Assemblée Nationale*. The two are elected separately and serve, respectively, seven- and five-year terms. This occasionally results in periods of *cohabitation*, where the president and *Assemblée* are of opposite political persuasions. Presidents tend to look after foreign policy and defense issues, while the *Assemblée* focuses on domestic and economic policy.

Main Political Issues

The presidential system
The experience since 1986 of periods of *cohabitation* between Socialist President Mitterrand and a right-wing government has effectively weakened the power of the presidential office. Many are convinced that presidential and *Assemblée* terms should in the future run concurrently and for the same number of years.

Racism
The problem of rising unemployment has led to the growth of racist parties, such as Jean Marie Le Pen's National Front (FN), which are threatening many of France's democratic traditions. None of the major parties has yet provided policies to combat the problem.

Reviving a strong opposition
Political scandals since 1989 have tarnished the reputation of the Socialist Party (PS), which took a beating at the polls in 1993. The French political system requires an effective opposition voice and this is currently lacking.

European integration
Before German reunification in 1990, there was a clear consensus in France on the benefits of European integration. Since then, however, support for union has cooled. Only 51% voted in favor of the Maastricht Treaty proposals in the 1992 referendum. The result may have reflected fears about the increased power of a reunified Germany within Europe.

Profile

Between 1959 and 1981, France was governed by a right-of-center coalition, first under the presidency of General de Gaulle, then Georges Pompidou and Valéry Giscard d'Estaing. The election in 1981 of François Mitterrand brought the left, including the French Communist Party (PCF), to the fore. The PS-led government nationalized many of France's most famous businesses, including the chemical company Rhône Poulenc. Local government was decentralized. However, the failure of its reflationary economic policy forced the PS to change course in 1983.

This was the most important turning point in French politics since 1958. The PS became a social democratic party, adopting the monetarist policies then in vogue. All the major French parties have since moved toward the political center, and broad agreement now exists on economic policy.

The fortunes of the far left have continued to decline. In 1945, the PCF had 25% of the vote. Today it is nearer 7%, mainly because workers no longer believe Marxism will help raise their living standards. Unemployment, however, has increased support for Jean Marie Le Pen's racist FN. The FN's share of the vote rarely rises above 14%, but it has had a disproportionate political impact, partly because of Le Pen's ability to attract publicity. One impact of the FN's rise has been tougher immigration laws.

François Mitterrand, *former president of France.*

Jacques Chirac, *elected president of France in 1995.*

Edouard Balladur, *former prime minister, succeeded by Alain Juppé in 1995.*

WORLD AFFAIRS

EU | G7 | OECD | GATT | FZ

French foreign policy has followed two, apparently contradictory, strands since the World War II – maintenance of a strongly independent line and furtherance of French interests within a united Europe. France's effective leadership of the EU meant that, until recently, it could combine the two. However, the reunification of Germany and its subsequent increased influence in the EU have led many to question the wisdom of the "what is good for Europe is good for France" policy. This shift in attitudes was seen in the Maastricht referendum, when only 51% voted for the treaty.

The keystone of foreign policy remains the containment of German power in Europe through political and monetary union, while resisting moves towards a supranational European state. France supports broadening the EU to include Scandinavia, but opposes the entry of East European states that would naturally fall within Germany's sphere of influence.

France also seeks to combat US influence in both foreign affairs and culture. It left NATO's military command in 1966, maintains an independent nuclear deterrent and provides a balance to US influence in the Middle East and Africa.

AID

$6.5bn (donations)

Down 30% in 1991

France is one of the world's major aid donors. Its motives are not simply commercial; it also wishes to maintain the influence of the French language, particularly in West Africa, which has been the main aid recipient. *Médecins sans Frontières* reflects a long French tradition of NGO aid agencies.

ECONOMICS

$1,167bn

5.90 francs

SCORE CARD

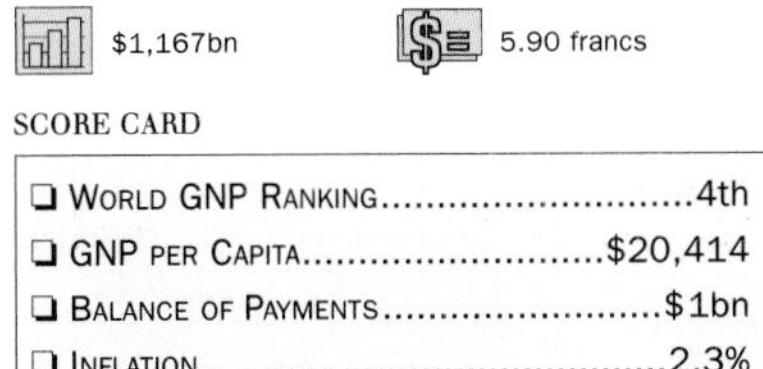

- ❑ World GNP Ranking.......4th
- ❑ GNP per Capita.......$20,414
- ❑ Balance of Payments.......$1bn
- ❑ Inflation.......2.3%
- ❑ Unemployment.......11.5%

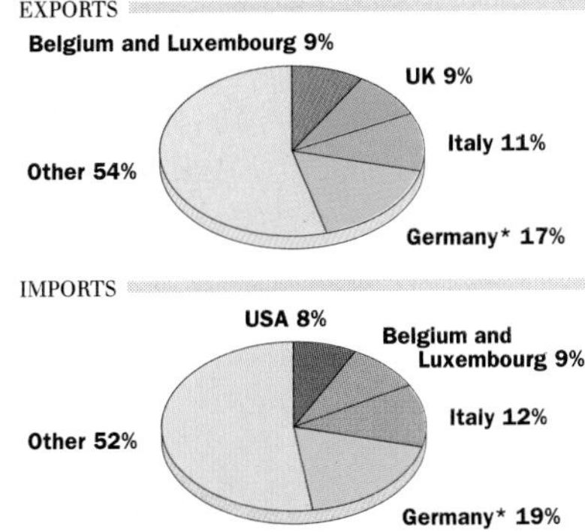

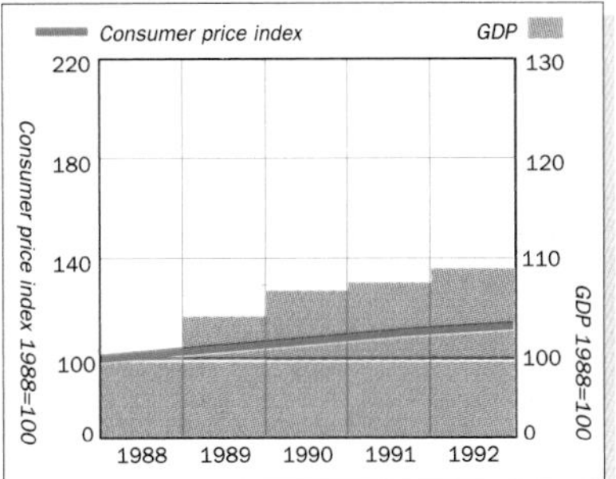

STRENGTHS

Heavy engineering, reflected in the success of the TGV and nuclear industries. Specialization in key fields such as automobiles (Renault and Citroën) and telecommunications (Alcatel). Luxury goods: France is world leader in cosmetics, perfumes and quality wines. Defense sector a major exporter, particularly of Dassault *Mirage* jets and *Exocet* missiles. French technocratic traditions mean that, unlike the USA or UK, top graduates are attracted into engineering. Most agriculture well-modernized. Docile trade unions; only 12% of the French work force is unionized.

WEAKNESSES

High unemployment, currently running at over 11%. Many sectors of industry still failing to compete due to outmoded work practices, particularly in machine tools, electric consumer durables and some textiles. Some of the major high-tech industries, such as telecommunications, partly run to further national pride, rather than on a strictly commercial basis. Despite agricultural modernization, there are still many small farms.

PROFILE

Compared to Germany and Britain, France was slow to industrialize. The 1950s and 1960s brought major changes. Protectionist France started competing in world markets and modernizing its industry with considerable success. By the 1980s, France was among the world's top three exporters. France has a long tradition of state-ownership. Between 1938 and 1945 Air France, Renault, the railroads, the coal, electricity and gas industries, large insurance companies and banks were nationalized. Between 1986 and 1988, a right-of-center government reversed the policy. But even after the massive sell-offs, much of the economy remains under state control. France is the EU's largest agricultural producer and its farmers are a powerful political lobby.

FRANCE : MAJOR BUSINESSES

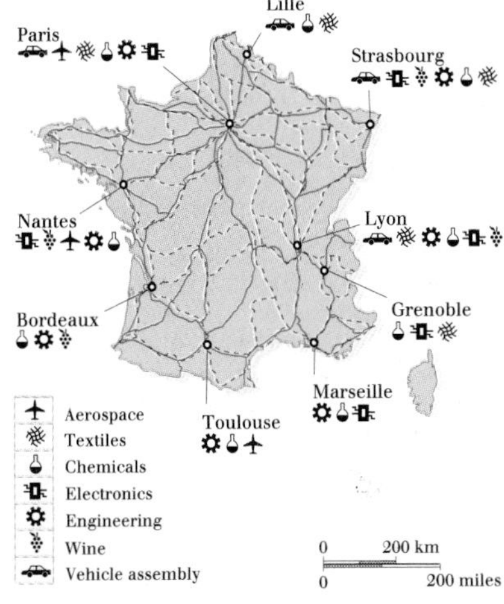

F

DEFENSE

$34.9bn

Up 1% in 1992

Defense spending as % GDP (0–40): 2.8%

FRENCH ARMED FORCES

1,343 main battle tanks (AMX-30)	260,900 personnel
2 carriers, 17 submarines, 1 cruiser, 4 destroyers and 34 frigates	64,900 personnel
808 combat aircraft (*Mirage* F-1B,-1C,-1CR/ *Jaguar/Alpha Jet*)	91,700 personnel
64 SLBM in 4 SSBN, 18 IRBM (SSBS S-3D/TN-61), 24 *Pluton* SSM launchers	

France was a founder-member of NATO, but left its military command structure in 1966 because of US domination of the alliance. France is isolated in its support for an EU-based defense force. As a result, its defense policy is still effectively defined by NATO.

The French military has historically been very strong. The influence of the army, however, is now much diminished due to the debacles of 1940 and of the 1962 Algerian War. Most young French are anti-militarist.

France has one of the world's largest defense industries, producing its own tanks, *Mirage* jets and the new *Rafale* fighter. Much of this production is exported, often controversially.

RESOURCES

419bn kwh (capacity 103m kw)

57,000 b/d (reserves 177,434,000 bbl)

21.8m cattle, 12.4m pigs, 11.9m sheep, 269,000 asses

Coal, natural gas, iron, zinc

ELECTRICITY GENERATION

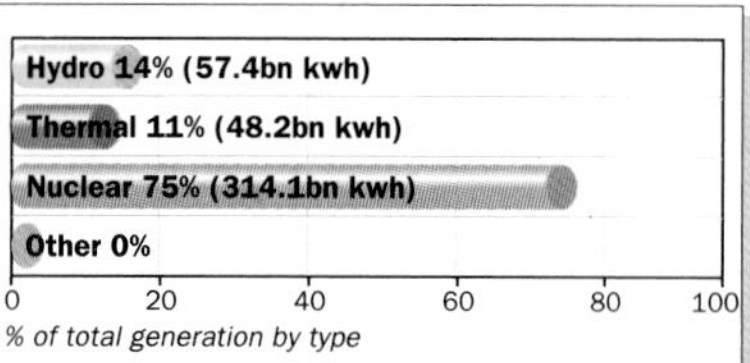

France is the world's most committed user of nuclear energy, which provides 75% of its electricity requirements. The policy reflects a desire for national energy self-sufficiency. Coal, once plentiful in the north and Lorraine, is now mostly exhausted, as are the gas fields off the southwest coast.

FRANCE : LAND USE

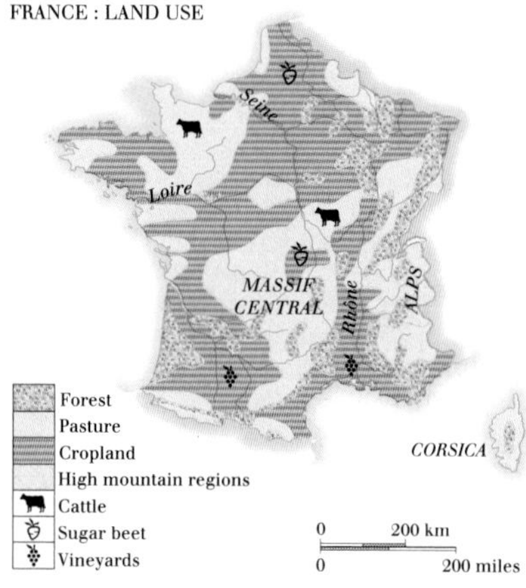

ENVIRONMENT

10% (9% partially protected)

Nuclear testing continues in Pacific

ENVIRONMENTAL TREATIES

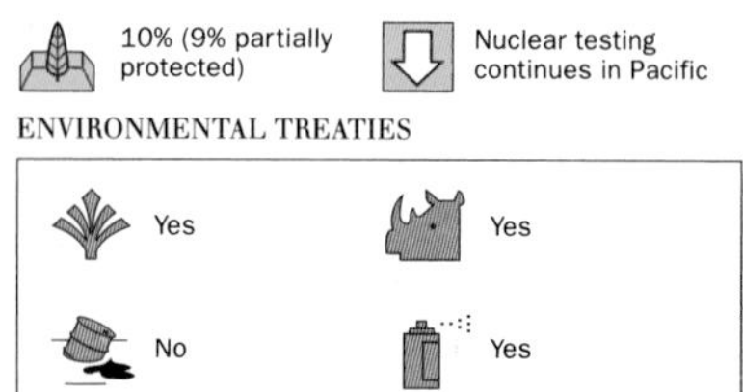

French "green" consciousness, in the past lower than that of Germans or Britons, has been rising. The Seine has been cleaned up, the size of buildings on the south coast is now controlled and air pollution is carefully monitored in Paris. The state policy of backing big projects (*gigantisme*), such as the Grande Motte tourist complex in Languedoc, has been reversed. The exception is nuclear policy. France's testing program in the Pacific continues despite strong opposition.

Regions

THE NORD-PAS DE CALAIS REGION

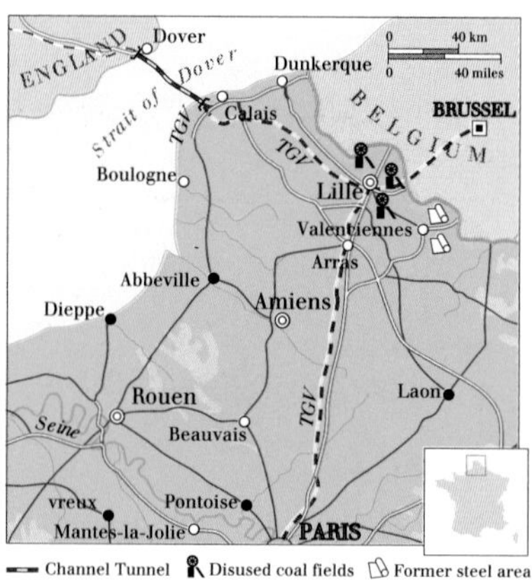

The Nord-Pas de Calais region has suffered mixed fortunes since the 1970s. Once a French industrial heartland, with Lille its foremost city, the region shed jobs and businesses at an alarming rate during the 1970s; traditional coalfields were worked out and the steel industry proved to be less competitive than its overseas rivals. By 1979, unemployment was 30% above the national average.

The arrival of the Channel Tunnel project dramatically changed the prospects for the region. French railways (SNCF) built a TGV line which connects Paris to both London and Brussels in less than three hours, providing a new focus for the region.

PARIS

Since the 1960s, the regeneration of Paris has been inextricably linked to national prestige. In 1961, the *Schéma Directeur* sought to solve congestion by creating five new towns within a 25-mile radius of the center. Meanwhile, the government set out to make Paris the architectural, scientific and cultural envy of the world. The high-tech Pompidou arts center (1977) set the tone. Under Mitterrand the process accelerated, resulting in the Arab World Institute, the Villette science center, the remodeling of the Louvre museum (including I M Pei's glass pyramid entrance) and a massive new opera house at La Bastille.

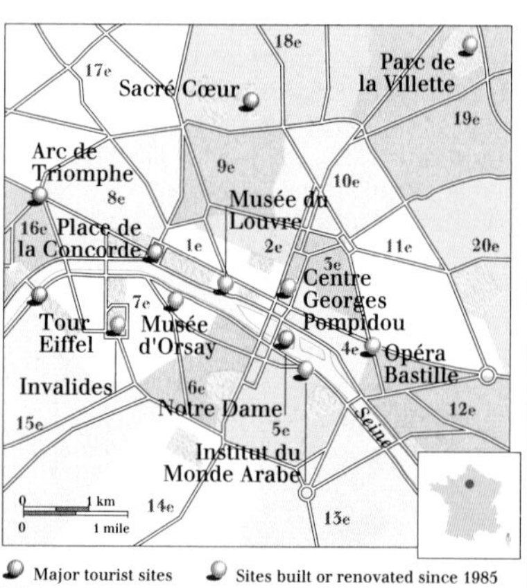

LANGUEDOC

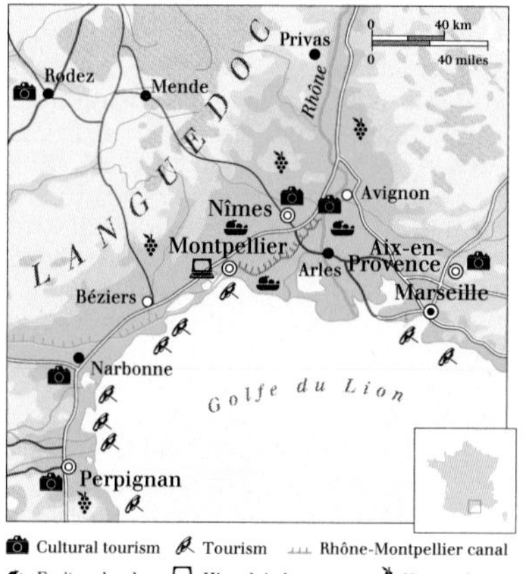

Languedoc has benefited from several initiatives in recent years. The Rhône-Montpellier canal system, Europe's biggest post-war irrigation network designed to improve yields, led to the replacement of much vine land with fruit orchards, but was not as wealth-creating as had been hoped due to cuts in EU fruit quotas.

Languedoc was also the subject of the biggest state-sponsored tourist development in history. Built to a master plan by architect George Candillis, a pupil of Le Corbusier, 280,000 new tourist beds were provided in massive resort complexes along a previously undeveloped mosquito-ridden coast. Visitor numbers have risen from 500,000 in 1965 to around four million today.

In the 1980s, Languedoc became France's leading high-tech region. IBM established its largest French manufacturing plant in Montpellier, bringing in its wake many "sun-belt" companies. The new industries have also been a great boost to the town's university, the largest in the region.

MEDIA

The media has been free of state control since the 1980s

PUBLISHING AND BROADCAST MEDIA

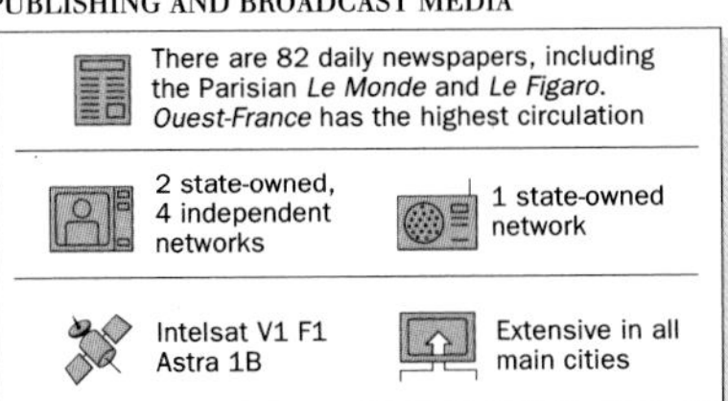

Formerly controlled and censored by the state and very timid, TV and radio were freed from direct state influence by the PS government in the 1980s. *TF1*, the primary TV network, is now privately owned and financed by advertising revenue. *France 2* is still owned by the state but is now fairly autonomous. In sharp contrast to its very strong cinema tradition, France has a weak TV service and standards are low, with many soap operas imported from the US.

Le Monde and *Libération* are the leading daily newspapers. *Le Canard Enchaîné* is the most influential satirical weekly.

CRIME

France does not publish prison figures

Up 6% in 1990

CRIME RATES

Murders	4 per 100,000 population
Rapes	8 per 100,000 population
Thefts	4,018 per 100,000 population

The French legal system is based on Roman law codified by Napoleon. The *juge d'instruction* is arguably the most important figure, a magistrate who has considerable powers in examining witnesses and assessing evidence. The press are not restricted by *sub judice* rules in reporting trials and can speak freely of suspects as though already proven guilty.

Petty crime and crimes of violence have risen sharply in recent years. Public concern about the rising crime rate helped return the right – with a law and order platform – to power in 1993. Drug trafficking through Marseilles remains a problem.

HEALTH

1 per 381 people

Liver, heart and cerebrovascular diseases, cancer

Health spending as % GNP (0–25): 9.2%

The French national health system is not entirely free. Patients pay the full cost of treatment to their physicians and are then reimbursed for 70% to 80% of the cost by an insurance company paid by the social services. Health awareness has recently risen, and the French still consume more medicine per capita than any other nation. However, the 1992 law banning smoking in public places is widely infringed. Alcoholism remains a problem, and cirrhosis of the liver is still the most common cause of death.

WEALTH

Waiter, 11,000 francs per month; senior manager, 50,000 francs per month

CONSUMER GOODS OWNERSHIP

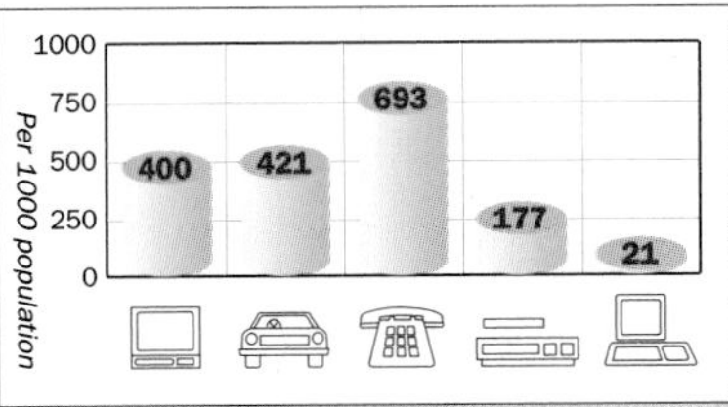

Wealth and income disparities in France are higher than in most OECD countries. The Socialists narrowed the gap a little with the introduction of the legal minimum wage (*le SMIC*). Most tax is indirect – a result of a long French tradition of income-tax evasion – which hits the poor and rich equally.

France has a fairly rigid class structure, although social mobility is increasing. The wealthy favor expensive French, German and British cars, and take exotic holidays to the Himalayas, the Andes and Polynesia.

EDUCATION

99%

Education spending as % GNP (0–25): 5.3%

THE EDUCATION SYSTEM

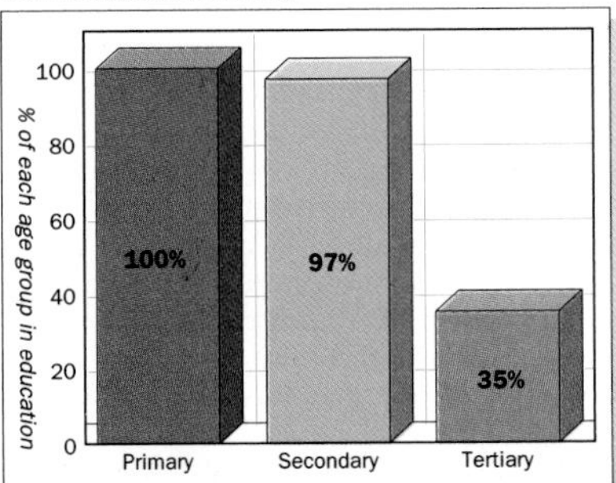

French education remains centralized, despite some relaxation of the system brought about by the student riots of 1968. The education ministry organizes the curriculum, exams and staffing, and most schools have little autonomous control over their affairs. Catholic schools, which account for 17% of the school population, are the exception. These are fee-paying but also receive large state subsidies. However, despite their relative independence, they are still obliged to follow the national curriculum.

The focus of education remains the acquisition of a broad range of knowledge, and classes are highly disciplined. French children tend to be better informed than their counterparts in other West European countries.

France has over 70 universities – 13 in Paris – and higher education bodies with 1.2 million students. Entry is not competitive, but based on passing the secondary-level exam, the *baccalauréat*. Most students attend their local university. The universities have not been given the funds or staff to cope with the huge increase in student numbers in recent years. The 150 *Grandes Écoles* are outside the university system and have just a few hundred carefully selected students each. The most influential tertiary institutions, they open the door to the top civil service and professional jobs.

***The Massif Central, Auvergne.** The Massif's lonely granite plateaus and extinct volcanoes are France's oldest rock formations.*

WORLD RANKING

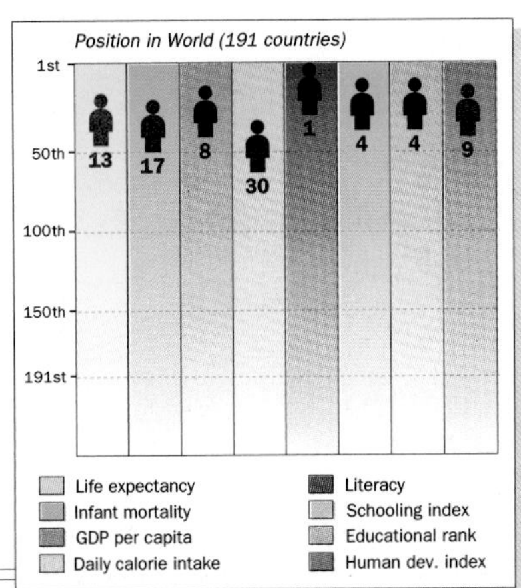

GABON

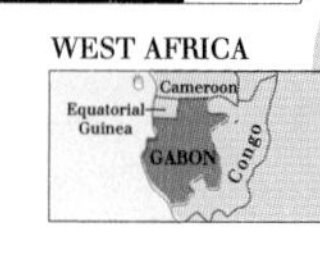

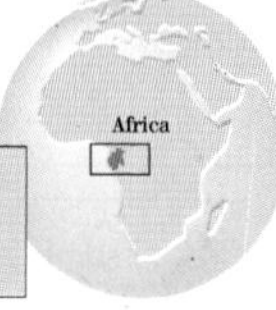

OFFICIAL NAME: The Gabonese Republic **CAPITAL:** Libreville
POPULATION: 1.2 million **CURRENCY:** CFA franc **OFFICIAL LANGUAGE:** French

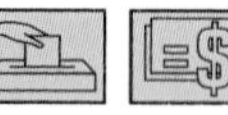

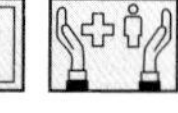

AN EQUATORIAL COUNTRY on the west coast of Africa, Gabon's major economic activity is oil. Only a small area of Gabon is cultivated and more than two-thirds constitutes one of the world's finest virgin rainforests. Gabon became independent of France in 1960. A single-party state from 1968, it returned to multiparty democracy in 1990. Gabon's population is small and the government is encouraging its increase.

CLIMATE

WEATHER CHART

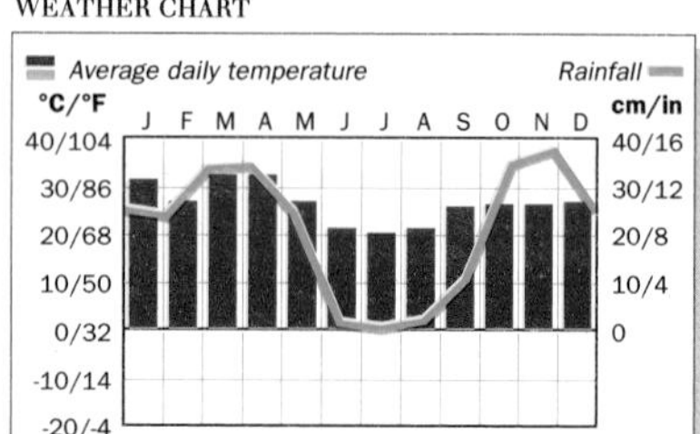

Gabon's climate is heavily equatorial, with very little distinction between seasons. The cold Benguela current lowers coastal temperatures.

COMMUNICATIONS

Léon M'Ba 611,000 passengers

7 ships 27,600 dwt

THE TRANSPORTATION NETWORK

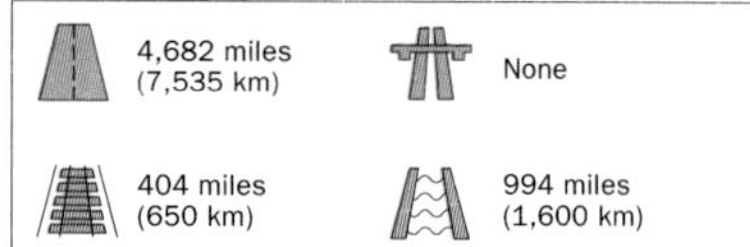

The Trans-Gabon Railroad completed in 1986, from Owendo port near Libreville to Massoukou, is the key transportation link. Air transportation is well developed and most big companies have airstrips.

TOURISM

108,000 visitors

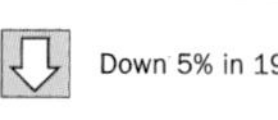
Down 5% in 1990

MAIN OVERSEAS ARRIVALS

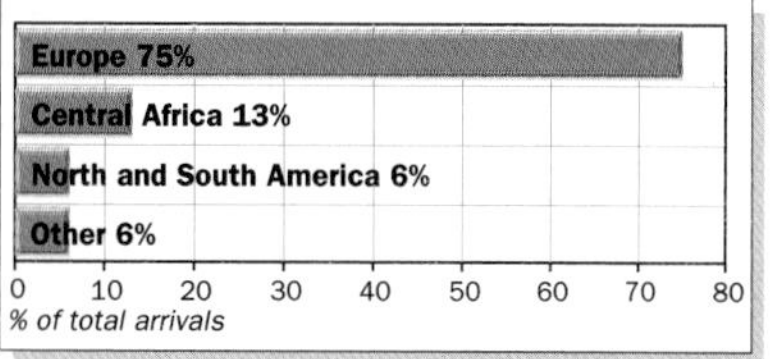

Despite Libreville's many hotels, Gabon has little tourism, in part a reflection of its lack of good beaches.

PEOPLE

Fang, French, Punu, Sira, Nzebi, Mpongwe

13 people per sq. mile

THE URBAN/RURAL POPULATION SPLIT

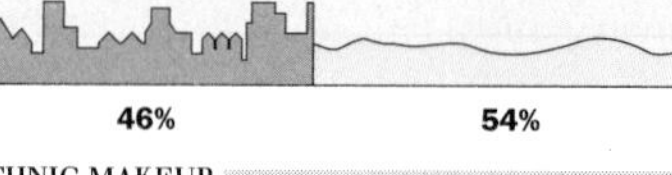

ETHNIC MAKEUP

French 2%
European and other African 9%
Bantu tribes including Fang and Bareke 89%

The largest ethnic group in Gabon is the Fang, who live mainly in the north, but they have yet to gain control of government. President Omar Bongo, himself from a sub-group of the minority Bateke in the southeast, has artfully united the common interests of other ethnic groups to keep the Fang from power. The Myene group around Port-Gentil consider themselves to be the aristocrats of Gabonese society due to their long-standing ex-colonial contacts. Oil wealth has led to the growth of a distinct bourgeoisie.

POLITICS

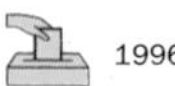
1996

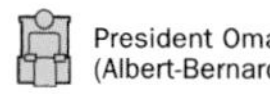
President Omar (Albert-Bernard) Bongo

THE STATE OF THE PARTIES

National Assembly 120 members

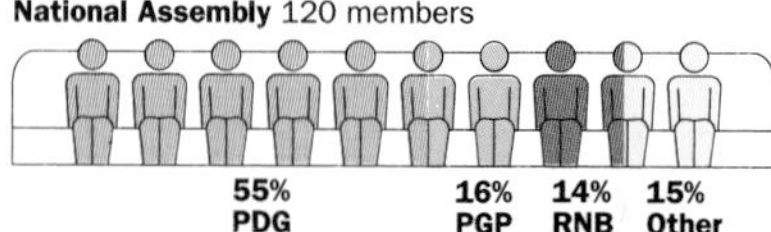

PDG = Gabonese Democratic Party **PGP** = Gabonese Progress Party **RNB** = National Rally of Lumberjacks **Other** = Association for Socialism in Gabon, Gabonese Socialist Union

Gabon has had a multiparty constitution since 1990, when a national conference paved the way for elections. The elections confirmed in power the only constitutional party of the previous 20 years – Omar Bongo's PDG. In part this was due to the divided opposition, which comprised over 30 distinct parties. In 1993, the opposition learned from the mistakes of 1990 and agreed to back only one candidate to challenge Bongo in the presidential elections. Bongo was reelected, but doubts were expressed about the fairness of the elections and future prospects for the democratic process in Gabon.

WORLD AFFAIRS

Gabon still maintains close links with France, although US companies are also making inroads into Gabon's oil-rich economy. In regional terms, Gabon remains influential in Francophone Africa, although relations farther afield, particularly with OPEC (Gabon was president in 1993), are also important.

GABON
Total Area : 267 670 sq. km (103 347 sq. miles)
POPULATION: over 100 000; over 10 000; under 10 000
LAND HEIGHT: 500m/1640ft; 200m/656ft; Sea Level
0 100 km / 0 100 miles

AID

 $142m (receipts) 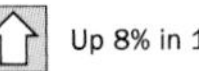 Up 8% in 1991

France is by far the major aid donor, providing two-thirds of total receipts. For a middle-income country with one of the highest GNPs per capita in the developing world, Gabon has benefited from considerable aid. Its indebtedness is the result of excessive borrowing encouraged by Western banks in the 1970s. Much aid goes to servicing this debt.

DEFENSE

 $145.8m  Down 5% in 1989

President Bongo's background in the military is reflected in Gabon's large defense budget and prestige weaponry, which includes French *Mirage* jets. Even the presidential guard has its own fleet of 12 aircraft. France guarantees Gabon's security and keeps an 800-strong garrison in Libreville; it last intervened in 1964 to suppress an attempted coup.

ECONOMICS

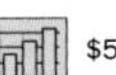 $5.4bn  295.23 CFA francs

SCORE CARD

- ❑ WORLD GNP RANKING........................111th
- ❑ GNP PER CAPITA $4,500
- ❑ BALANCE OF PAYMENTS....................$–105m
- ❑ INFLATION 2%
- ❑ UNEMPLOYMENT...........High under-employment

STRENGTHS

Oil and a relatively small population give Gabon a high per-capita GNP. Other abundant resources – including some of the world's best tropical hardwoods – are just beginning to be tapped.

WEAKNESSES

Large debt burden incurred in the 1970s. Continuing dependence on French technical assistance.

EXPORTS

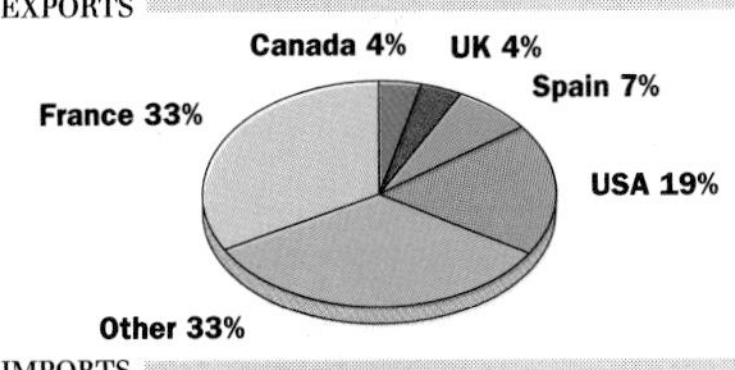

IMPORTS

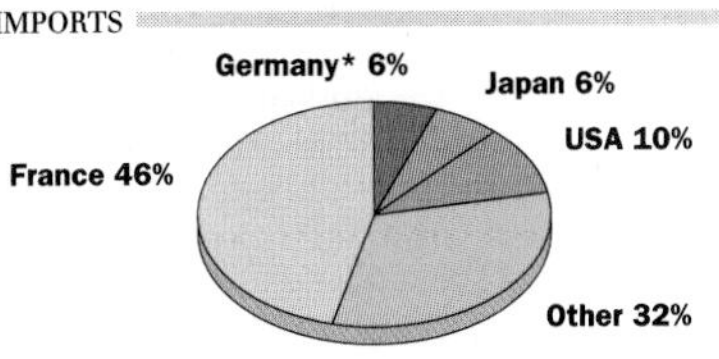

RESOURCES

 915m kwh (capacity 279,000 kw)

297,100 b/d (reserves 730,000,000 bbl)

159,000 pigs, 157,000 sheep, 27,000 cattle

Oil, manganese, uranium, gold, iron, natural gas

Oil is the major export earner. Gabon also has large deposits of uranium and over 100 years' reserves of manganese. The unexploited iron ore deposits at Bélinga are the world's largest.

ENVIRONMENT

 4% partially protected  Adoption of EU-funded pilot conservation project

The Trans-Gabon Railway has sliced through one of the world's finest virgin rainforests and has opened the interior to indiscriminate exploitation of rare woods such as oleoirme. Gabon abandoned plans for nuclear power following the 1986 Chernobyl disaster.

MEDIA

 No restrictions

PUBLISHING AND BROADCAST MEDIA

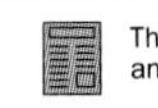 There are 2 daily newspapers, *L'Union* and *Gabon-Matin*

 1 state-owned service 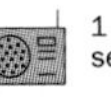 1 state-owned service

The media has become much more diverse since 1990 and Gabon now has an opposition press and *La Griffe,* a satirical weekly. *L'Union,* the state paper, carries occasional contributions from Omar Bongo, the president.

CRIME

 Gabon does not publish prison figures  Up 15% in 1990

Urban crime rates (Gabon is one of Africa's most urbanized nations) have been growing. Gabon's human rights record has improved in the last five years.

***Albert Schweitzer Hospital,** Lambaréné, on the lower Ogooué River. Schweitzer won a Nobel Prize for his pioneering work in Africa.*

CHRONOLOGY

Gabon became a French colony in 1886, administered as part of French Equatorial Africa.

- ❑ **1960** Independence. Léon M'ba president.
- ❑ **1964** Military coup. French intervene to reinstate M'ba.
- ❑ **1967** Albert-Bernard (later Omar) Bongo president.
- ❑ **1968** Single-party state instituted.
- ❑ **1990** Multiparty democracy. Omar Bongo's PDG wins elections.

G

EDUCATION

 61%

Education follows the French system. Libreville University, founded in the 1970s, now has over 2,500 students.

HEALTH

 1 per 2,000 people Heart and diarrheal diseases, pneumonia, accidents

Oil revenues have allowed substantial investment in the health service which is now among the best in Africa.

WEALTH

 Cabinet-maker, 86,000 CFA francs per month; electricity industry office clerk, 204,000 CFA francs per month

CONSUMER GOODS OWNERSHIP

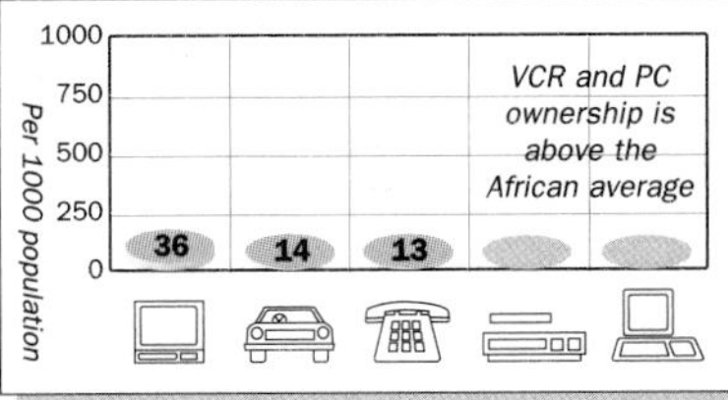

Oil wealth has led to the growth of an affluent bourgeoisie. Menial jobs are done by immigrant workers.

WORLD RANKING

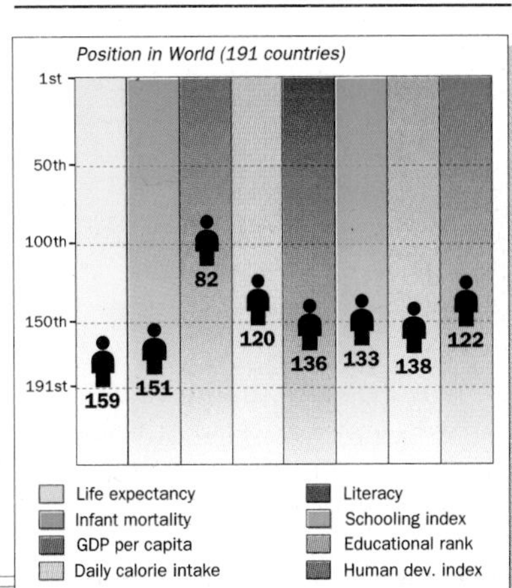

THE GAMBIA

WEST AFRICA
Africa
Senegal
GAMBIA
Mali
Guinea Bissau
Guinea

OFFICIAL NAME: Republic of The Gambia **CAPITAL:** Banjul
POPULATION: 900,000 **CURRENCY:** Dalasi **OFFICIAL LANGUAGE:** English

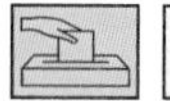

A NARROW COUNTRY, on the western coast of Africa, The Gambia had been renowned for its political stability until its government was overthrown in a coup in 1994. Agriculture accounts for 65% of its GDP, yet more Gambians are leaving rural areas for the towns, where average incomes are four times higher. Its position as an enclave within Senegal seems likely to endure following the failure of an experiment in federation in the 1980s.

G

CLIMATE

WEATHER CHART

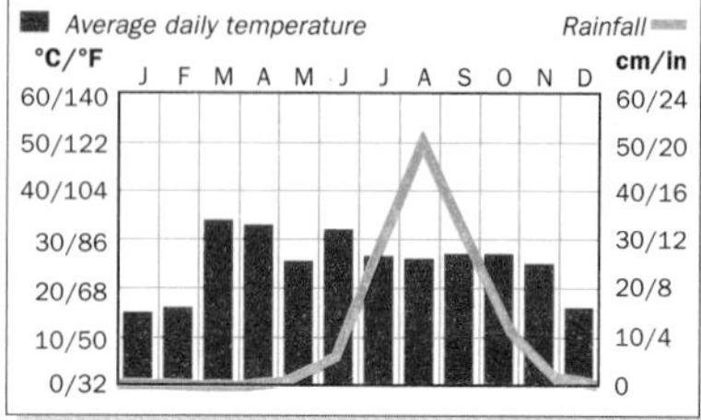

The subtropical and sunny dry season is punctuated by intermittent hot *harmattan* winds.

COMMUNICATIONS

Yundum Intl, Banjul 220,156 passengers

Has no fleet

THE TRANSPORTATION NETWORK

1,483 miles (2,386 km)

None

None

249 miles (400 km)

The Gambia River carries more traffic than the roads – ships of up to 3,000 tons can reach Georgetown. Yundum Airport was upgraded by NASA in 1989 for US space shuttle emergency landings.

TOURISM

101,419 visitors

Up 18% in 1990

MAIN OVERSEAS ARRIVALS

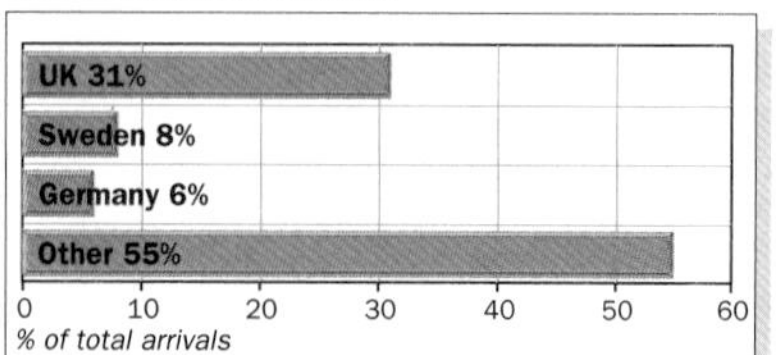

The successful tourist industry offers sunshine, beaches and resort hotel life. Most visitors are Northern Europeans escaping winter.

PEOPLE

Mandinka, Fulani, Wolof, Diola, Soninke, English

207 people per sq. mile

THE URBAN/RURAL POPULATION SPLIT

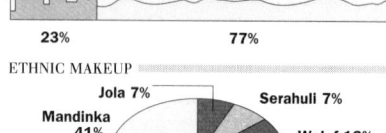

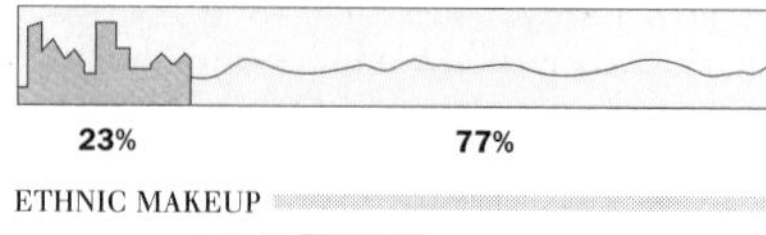

ETHNIC MAKEUP

Jola 7%
Serahuli 7%
Mandinka 41%
Wolof 13%
Fulani 14%
Other 18%

If there is any ethnic tension in The Gambia, it has come from minority resentment of the Mandinka's domination of politics. The 1962–1994 Jawara administration had, however, sought to distribute political offices fairly according to ethnic origins. The Creole community, known as the Aku, is small but socially prominent. In the early years of the tourist industry, the presence of Northern Europeans created some tension in a country that is essentially Muslim. About 85% of Gambians follow Islam although there is no official state religion. There is a yearly influx of seasonal immigrants, who come from Senegal, Guinea and Mali to grow peanuts. The Gambia is still a very poor country, with 80% of the labor force engaged in agriculture. As elsewhere in West Africa, women are active as traders.

Fishing village. *Overfishing in the waters off The Gambia and Senegal, mainly by distant nations, is a growing problem.*

POLITICS

Uncertain

President Lt Yaya Jameh

THE STATE OF THE PARTIES

House of Representatives 150 members

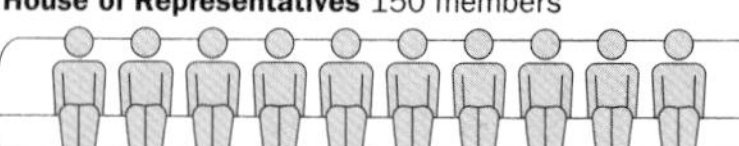

Legislative elections have been promised by Gambia's new leadership following its takeover of power in 1994

The PPP (People's Progressive Party) provided Gambia's government from 1962 until 1994, during which time the country was never a single-party state. The PPP was strongly backed by traditional rulers, especially in the Mandinka areas. The main opposition party, the NCP, was also Mandinka-led, but dependent on minority parties for support.

In 1994, however, President Jawara, leader of the PPP since 1962, was ousted in a coup led by members of the military. Sir Dawda Jawara, who had secured a fourth term of office in the 1992 presidential elections, left the country aboard a US warship. The coup's leaders claimed that it had been initiated in a bid to end corruption and pledged to preserve democracy. A new government was swiftly announced, in which several portfolios went to civil servants who had served in the former Jawara administration. The coup drew no active response from the potentially influential Senegal or Nigeria.

WORLD AFFAIRS

Relations with Senegal are crucial, especially since the collapse in 1989 of the Senegambian federation, which had been set up under pressure from the Senegalese after the rebellion of 1981. Outside West Africa, ties remain chiefly with the Commonwealth; good relations with the UK, a major aid donor, are important.

AID

$94m (receipts)

The trend is up

The Gambia's relative stability has enabled it to attract aid easily, notably from the World Bank, IMF, AfDB, the UK and Saudi Arabia. Italy and the Netherlands have given aid for health, and Japan for ferry services.

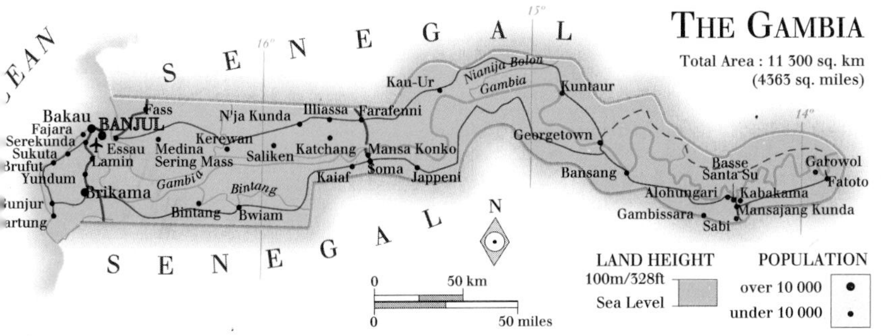

CHRONOLOGY

Mandinka traders brought Islam in the 13th century and were the main influence until the 18th century. The 1700s and 1800s saw colonial rivalry between Britain and France.

- **1888** British colony. Boundaries with France agreed in next year.
- **1959** Dawda Jawara founds PPP supported by hinterland Mandinka.
- **1962** Jawara prime minister.
- **1965** Independence.
- **1970** Republic; Jawara president.
- **1981** Senegalese troops help crush junior army officers' coup attempt.
- **1982–1989** Federated with Senegal.
- **1992** Jawara's fourth reelection.

G

DEFENSE

 $3m

No significant change from year to year

The Gambia National Army, with one infantry battalion, takes about half of the defense budget; the rest finances the 600-strong gendarmerie. Most arms are bought from the UK, although supplies are now increasingly coming from Nigeria too. A defense pact with Senegal collapsed with the federation in 1989.

ECONOMICS

 $372m

 8.39 dalasi

SCORE CARD

- World GNP Ranking........168th
- GNP per Capita........$415
- Balance of Payments........$26m
- Inflation........8.6%
- Unemployment....Widespread underemployment

Strengths

Low tariffs make The Gambia a focus of regional trade. Natural deep-water harbor at Banjul, one of the finest on the West African coast. Well-managed economy, favorably viewed by donors.

Weaknesses

Small size of country, and hence small size of market, sometimes inhibits investment. Smuggling, which deprives government of significant revenues. Lack of resources and little diversification in agriculture.

EXPORTS

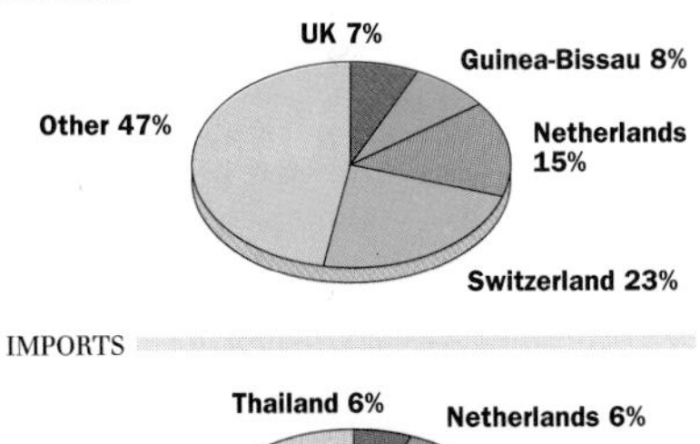

IMPORTS

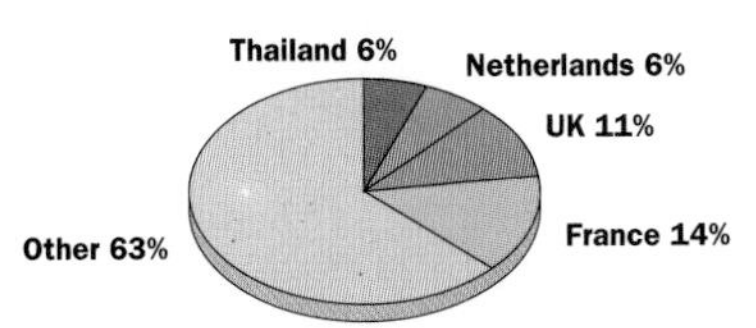

RESOURCES

 67m kwh (capacity 13,000 kw)

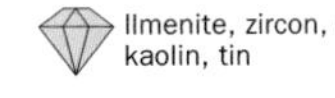

390,000 cattle, 166,000 sheep, 11,000 pigs

Ilmenite, zircon, rutile, kaolin, tin

The Gambia River is one of Africa's few good waterways, but it is underused as it is separated from its natural hinterland by the Gambia–Senegal border. Irrigation is presently provided by a single dam; plans for further dams for power generation have met with opposition. Most mineral deposits have yet to be exploited.

ENVIRONMENT

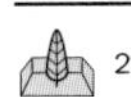 2%

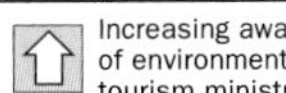

The impact of tourism on the country's environment and overfishing in Gambian waters are major concerns.

MEDIA

Very little censorship. Personal criticism of the president is tolerated

PUBLISHING AND BROADCAST MEDIA

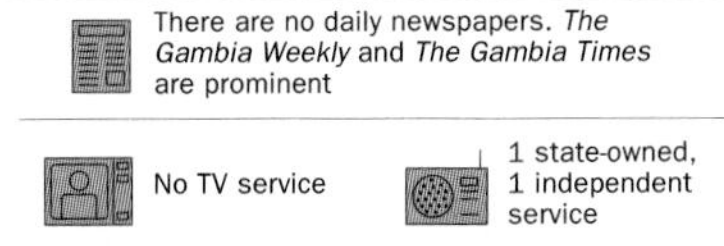

There are no daily newspapers. The Gambia Weekly and The Gambia Times are prominent
No TV service
1 state-owned, 1 independent service

The Gambian press is editorially independent. In 1988, *The Torch* carried allegations of corruption, which led to the dismissal of two ministers.

CRIME

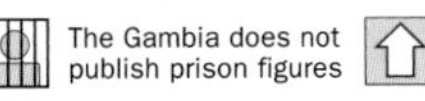

General crime levels are rising

Crime levels are relatively low in what is a peaceful society compared to many other states in the region.

EDUCATION

 27%

The literacy rate is low for the level of school enrollment – 75% in primary and 20% in secondary schools. Higher education is limited to teacher training.

HEALTH

 1 per 9,900 people

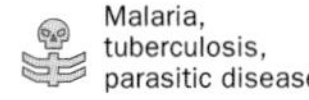

Most people have access to basic medicines, but these are no longer free. Advanced medical care in the public sector is limited. A quarter of state doctors work in the main hospital.

WEALTH

 The majority of the population is poor. Rising educational opportunites should result in greater social mobility

CONSUMER GOODS OWNERSHIP

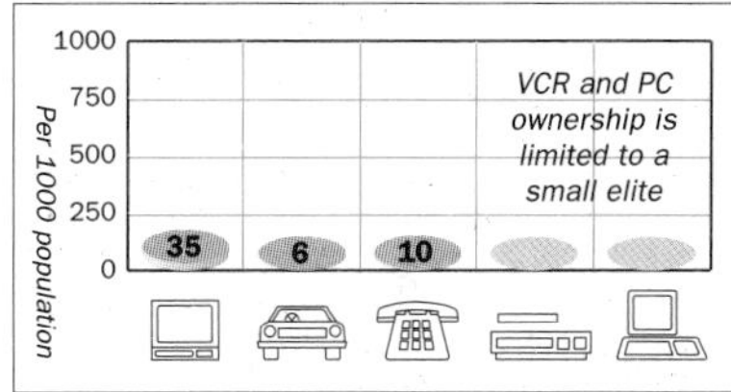

Work in professional fields and the public service has made some well-off, but wealth is not a feature of Gambian life. Unemployed young men in Banjul are seen as the poorest class.

WORLD RANKING

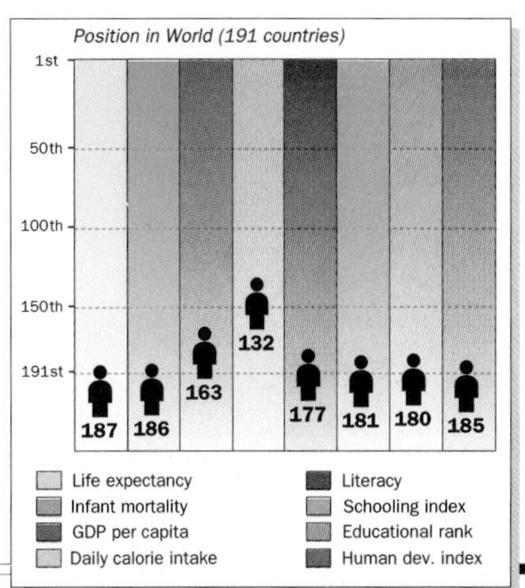

GEORGIA

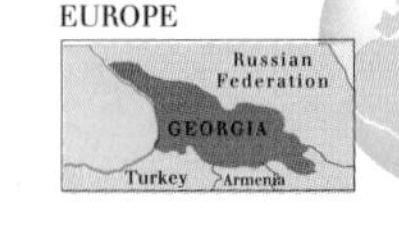

OFFICIAL NAME: Republic of Georgia **CAPITAL:** Tbilisi
POPULATION: 5.5 million **CURRENCY:** Coupon **OFFICIAL LANGUAGE:** Georgian

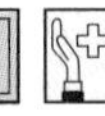

SITUATED ON THE EASTERN coast of the Black Sea, Georgia is largely mountainous. Its coastline stretches from Abkhazia in the north to Ajaria in the south. Georgia was one of the first republics to demand independence from the USSR, but has been plagued over recent years by civil war and ethnic disputes in Abkhazia and South Ossetia. The birthplace of Stalin, Georgia is primarily agricultural and is famous for its wine.

CLIMATE

WEATHER CHART

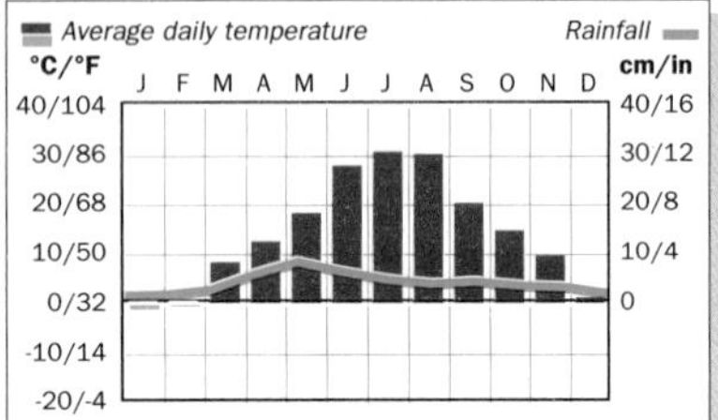

Georgia's climate is continental inland and subtropical along the coast, where grapes, citrus fruit and tea are grown.

Tbilisi, Georgia's capital since the 5th century AD. Its buildings rise in steep terraces from both banks of the River Kura.

COMMUNICATIONS

Novo Alexeyevka, Tbilisi

47 ships
1.01m dwt

THE TRANSPORTATION NETWORK

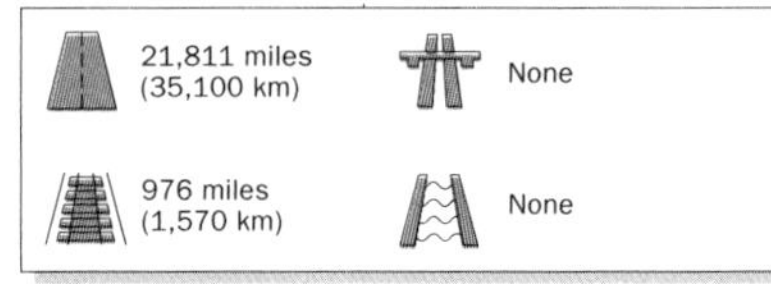

Civil war has devastated the transportation system. The autonomous republic of Ajaria maintains good communications with Turkey.

TOURISM

Flourishing Black Sea tourist trade before civil war

Sharp fall since start of civil war

MAIN OVERSEAS ARRIVALS

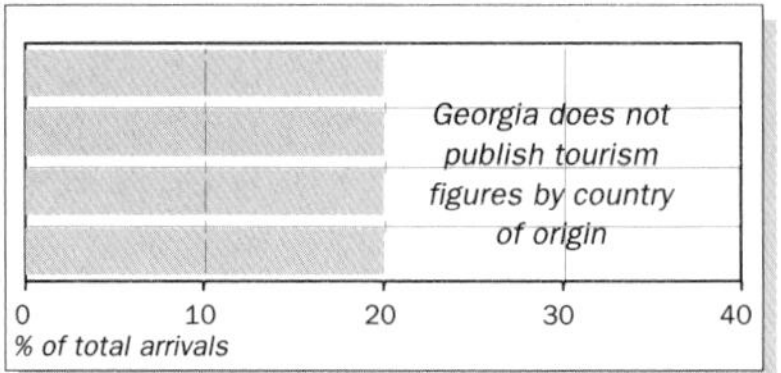
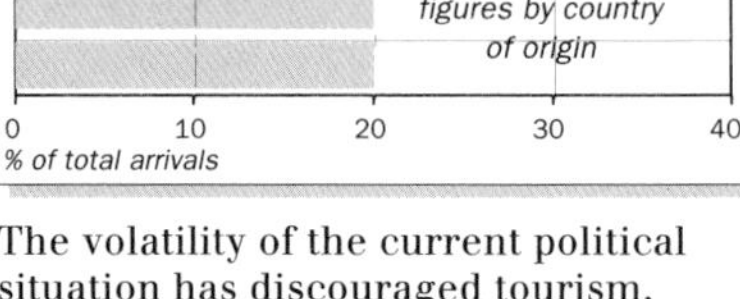

The volatility of the current political situation has discouraged tourism, although Georgia was previously a popular destination.

PEOPLE

Georgian, Russian

202 people per sq. mile

THE URBAN/RURAL POPULATION SPLIT

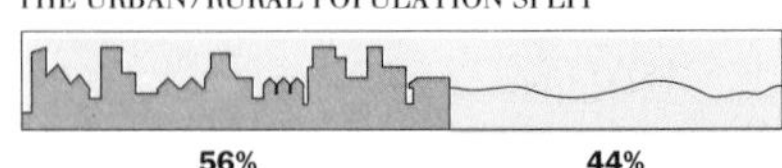

ETHNIC MAKEUP

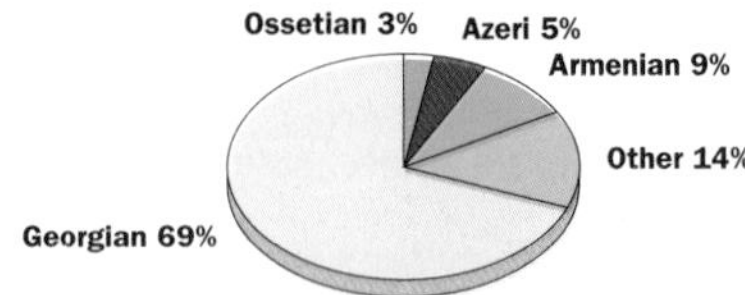

Georgia is a paternalistic society, with strong family and cultural traditions. The proportion of Georgians, who currently make up 69% of the population, is gradually increasing. Minority groups include Armenians, Russians, Azeris, Ossetians, Greeks and Abkhazians.

POLITICS

Uncertain

Chairman Eduard Shevardnadze

THE STATE OF THE PARTIES

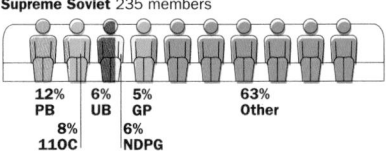

Supreme Soviet 235 members

12% PB
8% 11OC
6% UB
5% GP
6% NDPG
63% Other

PB = Peace Bloc **11OC** = 11 October Coalition **UB** = Unity Bloc **NDPG** = National Democratic Party of Georgia
GP = Green Party

Politics in Georgia are in a state of flux. An uneasy truce has followed the 1990–1993 civil war between the supporters of ex-president Zviad Gamsakhurdia, who committed suicide while under fire at the end of 1993, and troops loyal to the government. Russian military intervention on the government's side brought the fighting to an end.

In Abkhazia, another civil war is being fought as ethnic Abkhazians attempt to secede from Georgia. Georgians are being expelled from the region. Party groupings within the Supreme Soviet are unstable.

WORLD AFFAIRS

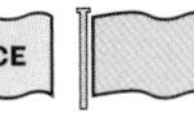
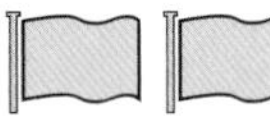

Georgia joined the CIS in 1993 in order to secure Russian military support against Gamsakhurdia.

AID

Undisclosed receipts

No obvious increase

Georgia has yet to achieve the economic and political stability that will secure IMF aid.

DEFENSE

$333.3m (est)

Sharp increase in spending owing to civil war

Georgia's military strength has been boosted by the presence of Russian troops in the country since it joined the CIS in October 1993. The Abkhazian conflict now dominates the agenda for the Georgian army. Training for the government security forces is provided by the CIA.

ECONOMICS

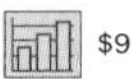
$9bn

700,000 coupons

SCORE CARD

❑ WORLD GNP RANKING	82nd
❑ GNP PER CAPITA	$1,636
❑ BALANCE OF PAYMENT	*The formal*
❑ INFLATION	*economy has*
❑ UNEMPLOYMENT	*collapsed*

STRENGTHS
Potential gateway to West for Azeri oil through pipelines over Georgian territory. Ports on the Black Sea, such as Bat'umi in Ajaria.

WEAKNESSES
Breakdown of economy due to war and severance of links with other ex-Soviet republics. Hyperinflation following introduction of coupon as parallel currency to rouble. Influence of powerful economic mafias.

EXPORTS

IMPORTS

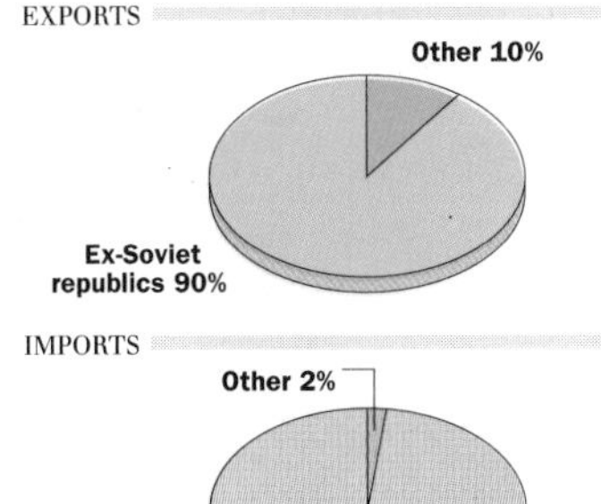

RESOURCES

14.2bn kwh (capacity 4.9m kw)

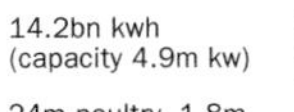
Not an oil producer and has no refineries

24m poultry, 1.8m sheep, 1.4m cattle, 1m pigs

Manganese, coal, oil, natural gas, zinc, cobalt, vanadium

Known oil reserves are as yet undeveloped and Georgia is dependent on Russia for much of its fuel and electricity supply. Cobalt and vanadium are being mined, although only in small quantities which are not easy to sell on the world market. Georgia is a predominantly agricultural country and food processing and wine production are the major industries.

ENVIRONMENT

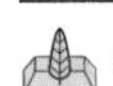
3%

No resources given to environmental initiatives

Pollution of the Black Sea is a major concern. The protection of upland pastures and hill farms from soil erosion is another key issue.

MEDIA

Government censorship is widespread

PUBLISHING AND BROADCAST MEDIA

There are 149 newspapers, 128 of which are published in Georgian. These include *Sakartvelos Respublika, Eri* and *Mamuli*

1 state-controlled network

1 state-controlled network

There is little press freedom, as the media survive on government subsidies. All TV broadcasting is controlled by the state.

CRIME

Georgia does not publish prison figures

Levels of all crime, especially organized crime, are rising

Organized crime under the control of mafia-style groups has flourished since independence in 1991. The judicial system currently favors Shevardnadze and his supporters.

EDUCATION

100%

All levels of education are now seriously underfunded. The University of Tbilisi was formerly of a high standard, with a particular reputation for the arts and economics.

HEALTH

1 per 170 people

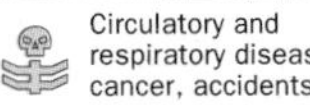
Circulatory and respiratory diseases, cancer, accidents

The health system was limited under the Soviet Union. Internal strife and a lack of resources have prevented any recent investment.

CHRONOLOGY

A Russian protectorate from 1763, Georgia was absorbed into the Russian empire in 1801. It was established as an independent state under a Menshevik socialist government in 1918.

- ❑ **1879** Stalin born in Gori.
- ❑ **1920** Recognized as an independent state by Soviet Russia.
- ❑ **1921** Soviet Red Army invades. Effectively part of USSR.
- ❑ **1922** Incorporated into the Transcaucasian Soviet Federative Socialist Republic (TSFSR).
- ❑ **1936** TSFSR dissolved.
- ❑ **1978** Public protests at threat to replace Georgian with Russian as official language.
- ❑ **1989** Pro-independence riots in Tbilisi put down by Soviet troops.
- ❑ **1990** Declares sovereignty. Shevardnadze resigns as Soviet foreign minister.
- ❑ **1991** Independence. Gamsakhurdia elected president.
- ❑ **1992** Gamsakhurdia flees Tbilisi. Shevardnadze elected chairman of Supreme Soviet and State Council.

G

WEALTH

Wealth is concentrated in Tbilisi

CONSUMER GOODS OWNERSHIP

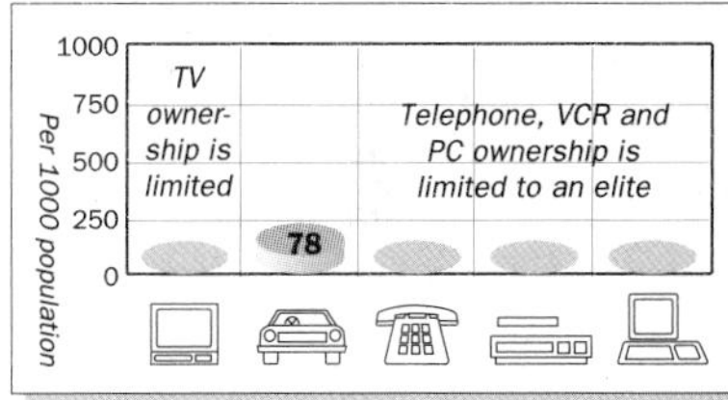

At least 80% of the population lives in poverty. There is a small, wealthy and extravagant elite.

WORLD RANKING

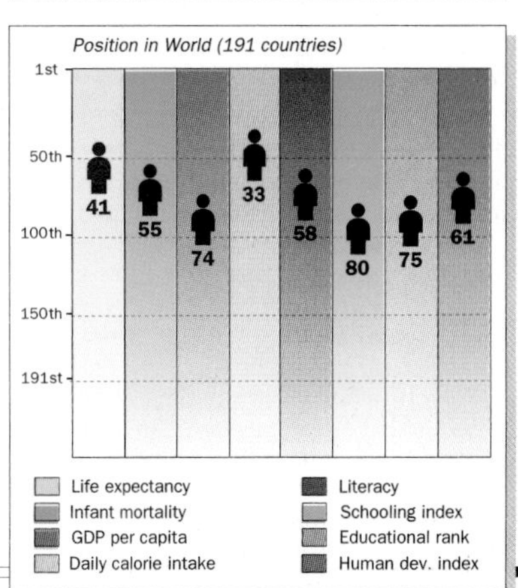

GERMANY

OFFICIAL NAME: Federal Republic of Germany **CAPITAL:** Berlin
POPULATION: 80.3 million **CURRENCY:** Deutsche Mark **OFFICIAL LANGUAGE:** German

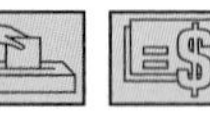

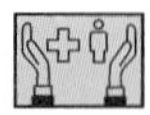

WITH COASTLINES on both the Baltic and North Seas, Germany is bordered by nine states. The north is characterized by plains and rolling hills; the south by more mountainous terrain. The most populous country in Europe after Russia, Germany is also its foremost industrial power and, after Japan, the world's second-biggest exporter. United in the 1870s, it was divided following the defeat of the Nazi regime in 1945. The western two-thirds became a free-market democracy aligned with the West; the east became a communist-ruled state in the Soviet bloc. The collapse of the East German regime in 1989 paved the way for political reunification in 1990. Social and economic unification remain elusive, however. The tensions created by differences in wealth between the east and the west dominate politics and have been exacerbated by the recent recession.

CLIMATE

WEATHER CHART

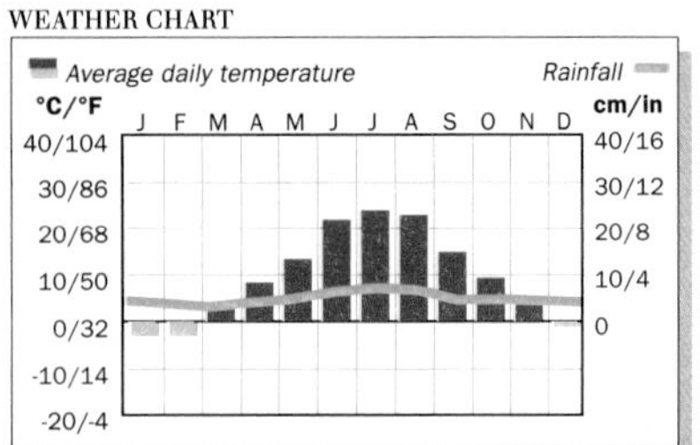

Germany has a broad climatic range. The upper Rhine Valley is very mild and suitable for wine-making. The Bayrische Alpen, the Harz Mountains and the Black Forest are, by contrast, cold with heavy snowfalls in winter.

COMMUNICATIONS

Frankfurt/Main International 28.7m passengers

720 ships 6.21m dwt

THE TRANSPORTATION NETWORK

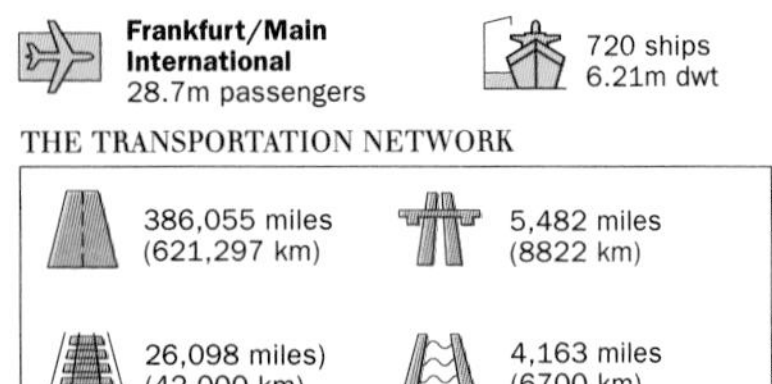

Germany virtually invented the modern highway with its 1930s *Autobahnen*, built by the Nazis primarily for military purposes. Today, the country has Europe's most elaborate highway network. Most *Autobahnen* do not have a speed limit, a contrast to the very strict speed restrictions and slow Trabant cars of former East Germany. German railroads are mostly state-owned and efficient. Its ICE lost the high-speed train race to the French TGV. Germany is now planning a 200-mile-per-hour MAGLEV train.

TOURISM

45m visitors

Down 24% in 1992

MAIN OVERSEAS ARRIVALS

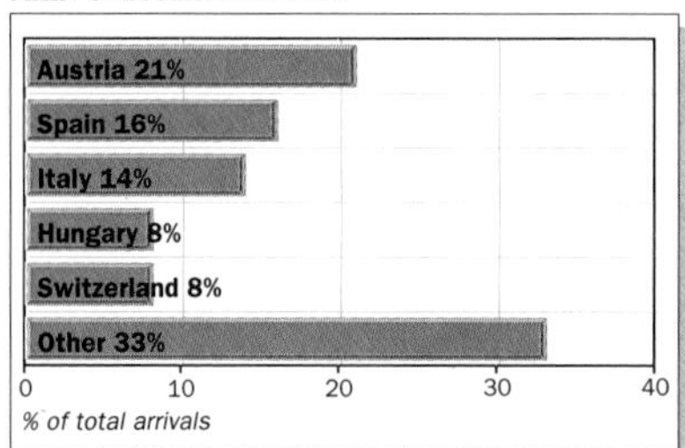

Northerly beaches and a colder climate make Germany less of a tourist draw than France or Italy. Skiing in the Bayrische Alpen, the historic castles of the Rhine Valley, the Black Forest and, for a significant number of visitors, Germany's excellent beer are all major attractions. Even before reunification, Berlin attracted many tourists with its rich cultural life and its Wall separating the West from the communist East. As the capital of reunified Germany, it is now receiving a major face-lift.

***The Stillach Valley, Allgäu Alps,** Bavaria. Germany's forests, which are found mainly in its mountain regions, are suffering badly from the effects of acid rain.*

EUROPE
Netherlands
Denmark
Belgium
GERMANY
Poland
Luxembourg
Czech Rep.
France
Switz.
Austria
Europe

GERMANY

Total Area : 356 910 sq. km (137 800 sq. miles)

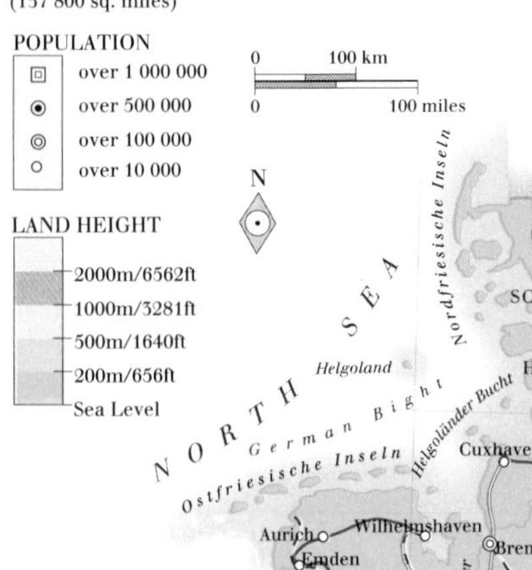

PEOPLE

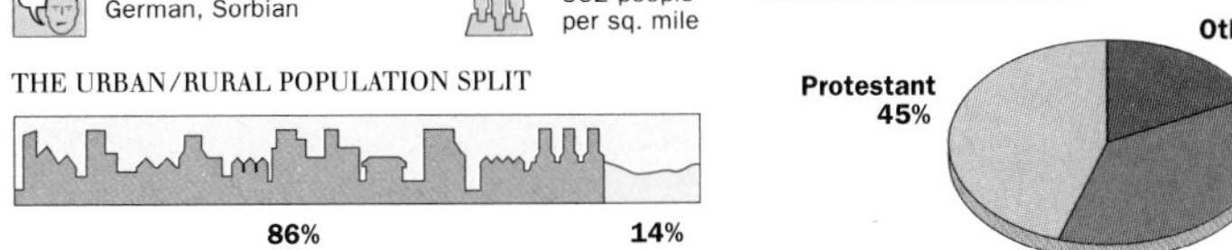

RELIGIOUS PERSUASION

Protestant 45%
Roman Catholic 37%
Other 18%

ETHNIC MAKEUP

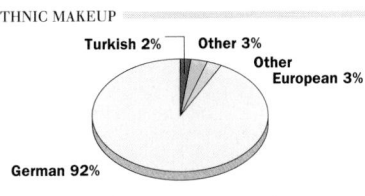

German 92%
Turkish 2%
Other 3%
Other European 3%

Germans share a common language, but they speak it with a variety of dialects, reflecting a strong sense of regionalism. Some German-speaking peoples live in neighboring Austria, France and Switzerland, but most now live in Germany. The north is still largely Protestant, while the south and southwest, particularly Bayern (Bavaria), have strong Catholic traditions. Other traditional differences between northern and southern Germans – the Prussian reputation for authoritarianism, the Bavarian for jollity – are waning, however, and most now share a common culture.

A large immigrant population, some five million people, provided much of the labor on which former West Germany's economic recovery was built. Known as *Gastarbeiter* (guest workers), they cannot easily claim full German nationality and so do not have equal rights. The 1.6 million Turks are the largest single group.

Germany's once liberal asylum laws were tightened in 1993, in response to the domestic tension created by high unemployment in the east and the huge influx of "economic" refugees from Russia, Romania and Poland following the collapse of communism. Another result of unemployment and disappointed expectations, particularly among young Germans, has been the growing support for right-wing parties and a rise in racial attacks.

Family ties in Germany are not so different from those in the USA or UK. Millions of couples live together in common-law arrangements, and while this is frowned upon by the Catholic Church, it is largely in rural districts in Bayern that traditional habits are still observed. The birth rate is one of Europe's lowest and the population would be falling were it not for the influx of immigrants since the 1950s.

Women have full rights under the law and play a bigger role in politics than in most other European countries. In 1990, they formed one-fifth of the *Bundestag* (Parliament). However, they are less well-represented in top jobs in business and industry. Germany has a tradition of strong feminism. Abortion remains a charged issue, with laws varying from region to region. After unification, women in former East Germany wanted to keep their right to abortion on demand. However, they were overruled by the constitutional court, after strong Catholic lobbying.

Despite their liberal reputation, Germans retain their formal social habits. Clear distinctions are drawn between acquaintances and good friends. Compared with the rest of Europe, there is little use of first names and many Germans generally use the formal *Sie* rather than the more familiar *du* as a form of address.

POPULATION AGE BREAKDOWN

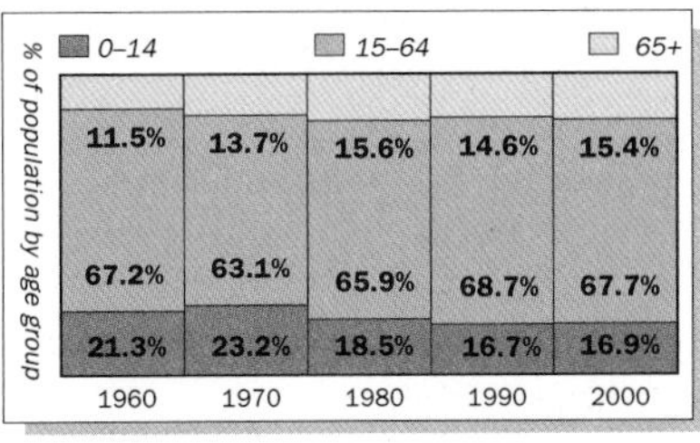

CHRONOLOGY

The Frankish Empire reached its peak under Charlemagne, crowned Holy Roman Emperor in 800. From 1273 until the 19th century, German history was tied to that of Austria's Habsburg dynasty.

- **1815** German Confederation under nominal Austrian leadership.
- **1834** Zollverein Customs Union leads to economic convergence of 18 states, including Prussia, and reflects unification aspirations.
- **1862** Otto von Bismarck appointed Prussian chancellor.
- **1864–1870** Prussians defeat Danes, Austrians and French; north German states brought under Prussian control.
- **1871** South German states join new German Empire; William I of Prussia declared emperor. France cedes Alsace and Lorraine.
- **1870s** Rapid industrialization. Bismarck's social legislation.
- **1890** Kaiser Wilhelm II accedes with aspirations for German world role; Bismarck fired.

CHRONOLOGY *continued*

- **1890s–1913** Franco-German and Anglo-German rivalries grow.
- **1914–1918** World War I.
- **1918** Germany signs armistice; Emperor flees. Weimar Republic created.
- **1919** Treaty of Versailles: Germany to lose colonies and pay reparations. Rhineland demilitarized.
- **1923** France occupies the Ruhr; financial collapse and hyperinflation.
- **1926** Joins League of Nations.
- **1929** World recession brings mass unemployment.
- **1933** Hitler appointed chancellor after Nazis become largest single party in elections. Establishes one-party rule. Withdraws from League of Nations; German rearmament.
- **1935** Nuremberg Laws; official persecution of Jews begins.
- **1936** German entry into Rhineland. Axis alliance with Italy.
- **1938** Annexation of Austria and Sudetenland.
- **1939** German invasion of Poland marks start of World War II.
- **1940** France invaded.
- **1941** USSR invaded.
- **1942–1943** German troops forced back by Red Army at Stalingrad.
- **1945** German surrender; Allied control under Soviet, UK, US and French occupation zones.
- **1949** Germany divided in two: East led by Stalinist Walter Ulbricht 1951–1971 and pro-Soviet Erich Honecker 1971–1989; West a free-market democracy.
- **1955** West Germany gains full sovereignty; joins WEU and NATO.
- **1961** Berlin Wall built.
- **1968–late 1980s** Red Army faction terrorism in West Germany.
- **1973** East and West Germany become UN members.
- **1989** Policy of Gorbachev in USSR results in fall of Berlin Wall.
- **1990** Unification of Germany. First all-German elections since 1933.

The Messeturm, Frankfurt, the tallest office building in Europe. Frankfurt is Germany's financial services center and home to many of its leading companies.

G

POLITICS

Lower House 1998

President
Roman Herzog

THE STATE OF THE PARTIES

Federal Assembly 662 members

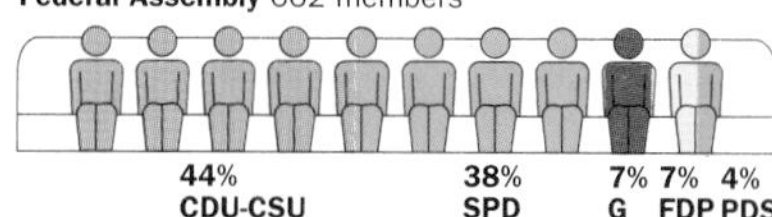

CDU-CSU = Christian Democratic Union – Christian Social Union **SPD** = Social Democratic Party **G** = Green Party
FDP = Free Democratic Party
PDS = Party of Democratic Socialism

Federal Council 68 members

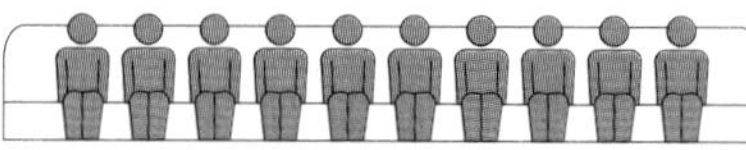

Between 3 and 6 members represent each of 16 states (*Länder*)

Germany is a federal democratic republic of 16 states, or *Länder*. The government is led by the chancellor, who is elected by the *Bundestag* (Federal Assembly). The president's role is largely ceremonial. The "Basic Law" of West Germany, drawn up in 1948, became the 1990 constitution of reunified Germany.

Main Political Issues

Reunification

Although, in 1989, 85% of Germans voted for reunification, the general rejoicing at the fall of the Berlin Wall at the end of that year has soured as the true costs of the process have become clear. Unemployment in the east has risen to 30% with the collapse of inefficient industries. In the west, taxes have gone up to pay the costs of privatization as well as a growing social security bill. However, long-term German policy remains to raise east German living standards up to the west German average.

The recession

Germans, used to constant growth since the 1950s, have been shocked by the recession that began in 1991. For the first time in living memory, car firms such as Volkswagen have been laying off workers. The recession has been doubly painful because it has coincided with the enormous and unexpected costs of reunification.

Nationalism

The problems of unemployment have led to anti-immigrant attacks and an increase in support for far-right parties. Some young Germans resent foreigners holding jobs. Turks have suffered particular vilification and were the subjects of the Rostock attack in 1992. The problem of racism is no worse than in many other European states, but is more sensitive given Germany's history.

Profile

Germany's politics remains strongly democratic and essentially stable. It has a long tradition of federative association. Before unification in 1871, Germany was a mass of separate principalities, kingdoms and city-states. This tradition was in many ways maintained by Bismarck in his unification constitution; some of the *Länder* even retained their own monarchies until 1918. The 1933–1945 Nazi period, during which the federal system was abolished, was very much a hiatus. The Allies reestablished the system in West Germany in 1945; in the east, the *Länder* were restored after reunification in 1990.

In many ways, the *Länder* are at the heart of German political life. Each *Land* has its own elected parliament and largely controls its own finances. The decentralized nature of German politics continues down to city level and below. German cities have larger budgets than their European counterparts and city mayors wield considerable power. By general consensus the system delivers efficient and commercially astute government.

Nationally, a conservative CDU–CSU coalition dominated the *Bundestag* from 1949 to 1969, followed by an SPD–FPD coalition, with Willy Brandt and Helmut Schmidt as chancellors, from 1969 to 1982. Since then, a conservative government has again been in power, led by Chancellor Helmut Kohl. The two coalitions have little to distinguish them. Their economic policies, based on low inflation, stable growth and an independent central bank, are almost identical. All parties still support the *Sozialmarktwirtschaft*, the social market economy, on which West Germany's prosperity was built.

Dr. Helmut Kohl, *Federal Chancellor and CDU chairman.*

Dr. Klaus Kinkel, *took over as foreign minister in 1992.*

Hans-Dietrich Genscher, *foreign minister 1974–1992.*

WORLD AFFAIRS

Before reunification, Germany played only a modest part in international politics. The focus of West Germany was the creation of the EU and the policy of *Ostpolitik* – improving relations with Moscow, which had 400,000 troops stationed in East Germany.

Since 1990, the emphasis has changed and a united Germany is beginning to voice a foreign policy which reflects its position as the most powerful country in Europe. It is still a leading proponent of unity. France remains its closest ally within the EU, although the relationship has cooled a little since 1990.

Germany's focus, however, has shifted eastward. It is the biggest investor in all the ex-COMECON economies, bringing the region once again under German influence.

AID

 $6.9bn (donations)  Up 5% in 1991

Unlike the USA, the UK and France, Germany's aid programs are not directly motivated by its desire for political influence in the world's poorer regions. Most are multilateral, although there is also a strong tradition of direct aid. Much comes directly from church organizations such as the Protestant *Brot für die Welt.* Many German volunteers and missionaries work overseas on aid programs.

DEFENSE

$31bn Down 4% in 1992

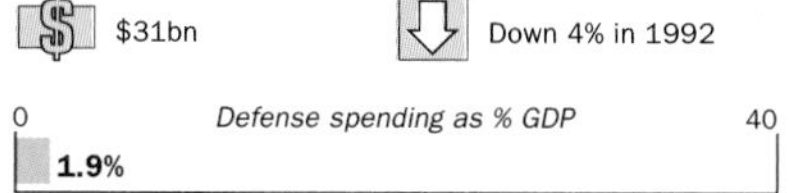

The German army, the *Bundeswehr*, is the largest in Europe. 200,000 US and British NATO troops remain stationed in Western Germany. With France, Germany has been developing the Eurocorps, a joint army of 50,000. The constitution still forbids *Bundeswehr* activity beyond the NATO area.

GERMAN ARMED FORCES

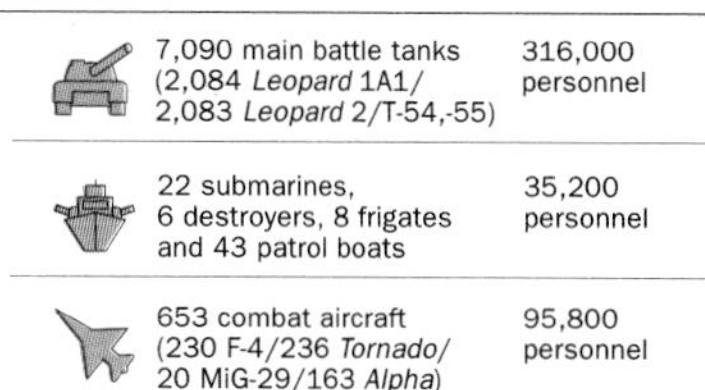

7,090 main battle tanks (2,084 *Leopard* 1A1/ 2,083 *Leopard* 2/T-54,-55)	316,000 personnel
22 submarines, 6 destroyers, 8 frigates and 43 patrol boats	35,200 personnel
653 combat aircraft (230 F-4/236 *Tornado*/ 20 MiG-29/163 *Alpha*)	95,800 personnel
None	

ECONOMICS

$1,690bn  1.65 Deutsche Marks

SCORE CARD

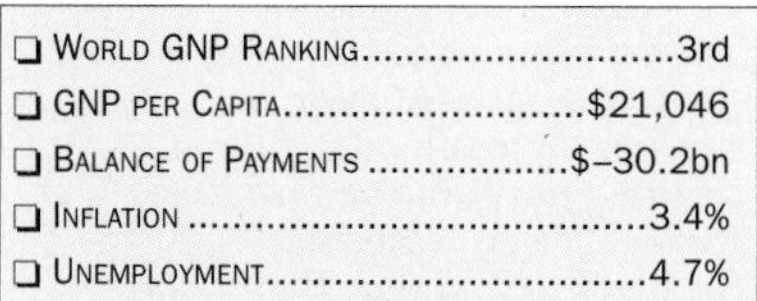

- ❑ WORLD GNP RANKING 3rd
- ❑ GNP PER CAPITA $21,046
- ❑ BALANCE OF PAYMENTS .... $-30.2bn
- ❑ INFLATION 3.4%
- ❑ UNEMPLOYMENT 4.7%

EXPORTS

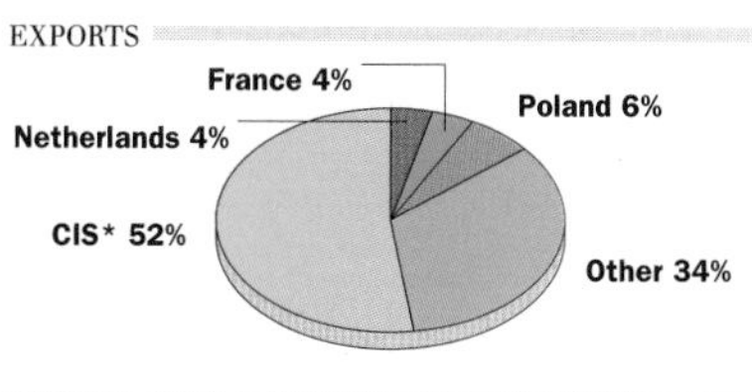

IMPORTS

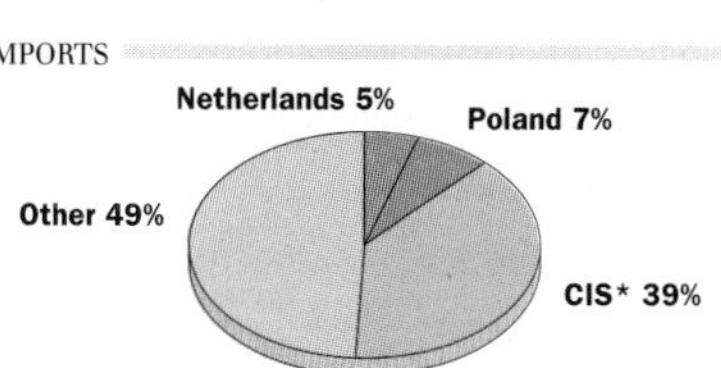

STRENGTHS

Europe's major industrial power and, until now, most successful economy. Very efficient industry benefits from Germany's low inflation environment. German workers and managers live up to their reputation for hard work, thoroughness and discipline. Strongest sectors are cars, heavy engineering, electronics and chemicals; all have massive export success.

WEAKNESSES

The east: costs of incorporating out-of-date and massively inefficient ex-communist economy underestimated.

ECONOMIC PERFORMANCE INDICATOR

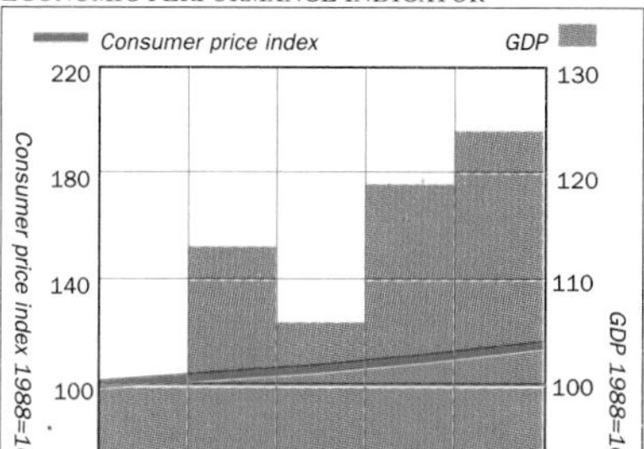

Traditionally harmonious labor relations under pressure in recent years. Growing competition from increasingly efficient, low-wage Asian economies.

PROFILE

West Germany's post-war economic recovery from a war-shattered state to become the world's third strongest economy was remarkable. US aid played its part, but equally important was the thinking behind the *Sozialmarktwirtschaft,* or social market economy. This charged the state with providing welfare and ensuring workers' rights, while leaving the economy largely in private hands.

Germany has developed little of the coordinated state and regional planning found in France. All the major banks and businesses are in private hands. One exception is Volkswagen, which is partly state-owned. The central bank, which sets interest rates and is responsible for controlling inflation, also has a large measure of independence from the government.

GERMANY : MAJOR BUSINESSES

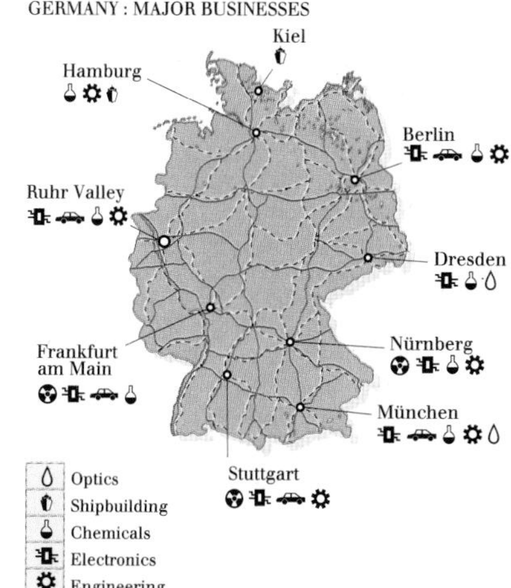

The greatest challenge for Germany remains rebuilding the east. The state privatization agency, the *Treuhand*, has now sold off 8,000 of the formerly East German state-owned concerns.

Friedrichstrasse, East Berlin. *Berlin was redesignated Germany's capital city in 1991. Redevelopment of its center has been planned.*

RESOURCES

572bn kwh (capacity 123m kw)

66,500 b/d (reserves 449,814,000 bbl)

35.1m pigs, 20.4m cattle, 4.1m sheep, 477,000 horses

Coal, natural gas, copper, salt, potash, tin, nickel

ELECTRICITY GENERATION

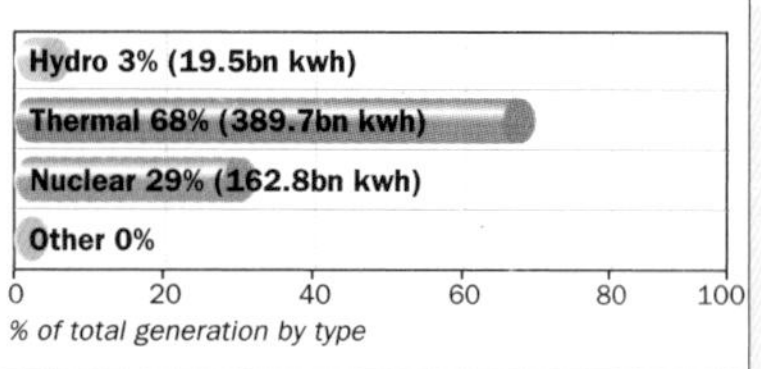

Germany has relatively few natural resources. It imports over 50% of its energy needs. Coal, the basis of its industrialization, has diminished in importance, accounting for less than 20% of energy today, compared with 51% 30 years ago. Unlike France, the former West Germany did not invest heavily in nuclear power; the accident at Chernobyl in the Ukraine strengthened the anti-nuclear lobby's case. In the east, all the Soviet-built stations have been shut down. Germany's energy conservation program is generally considered the most successful in Europe.

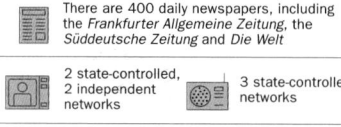

GERMANY : LAND USE

Cropland
Forest
Pasture
Vineyards
Pigs
Cattle

0 200 km
0 200 miles

NORDDEUTSCHES TIEFLAND
Elbe
Rhine
BLACK FOREST

ENVIRONMENT

16% partially protected

Successful energy conservation program

ENVIRONMENTAL TREATIES

Yes

Yes

No

Yes

Germans are among the world's most environmentally conscious people. Led by the Green Party, which emerged as a powerful political force in the 1980s, environmental campaigns have had a major influence on the policies of all the major parties. The Greens have won only a few seats in the *Bundestag*, but are far more heavily represented in *Land* parliaments and local councils.

Germany has some of the strictest pollution controls in the world, adding extra costs to businesses and forcing them to become even more efficient. Germans recycle 42% of their waste paper, reprocess 70% of their used tires and sort 50% of their glass according to color to aid recycling.

Apart from the nuclear debate, which has been vigorously fought and won by the Greens, the main concern is Germany's forests. Acid rain from car fumes and industrial pollution is suspected of killing trees in all parts of the country. Official estimates in 1986 suggesting that up to 50% of trees were sick or dying resulted in Germany becoming the first European country to insist that new cars be fitted with catalytic converters.

The east had particular problems, including the highest per capita rate of sulfer emissions in the world. These have been reduced by the shut-down of industrial plants, and the fact that the noxious Trabant cars are quickly being replaced with Western ones.

MEDIA

No political censorship

PUBLISHING AND BROADCAST MEDIA

There are 400 daily newspapers, including the *Frankfurter Allgemeine Zeitung*, the *Süddeutsche Zeitung* and *Die Welt*

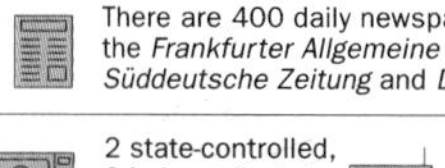
2 state-controlled, 2 independent networks

3 state-controlled networks

Intelsat V1 F1 Astra 1B

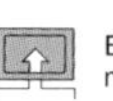
Extensive in all main cities

German TV is carefully supervised by the political parties to ensure a balance of views. The main channels, *ARD* and *ZDF*, have a reputation for safe programing, but the arrival of satellite and cable TV and competition has begun to make TV more lively. Newspapers are mostly regional and serious. An exception is *Bild Zeitung*, the right-wing, sensationalist tabloid, which sells four million copies daily.

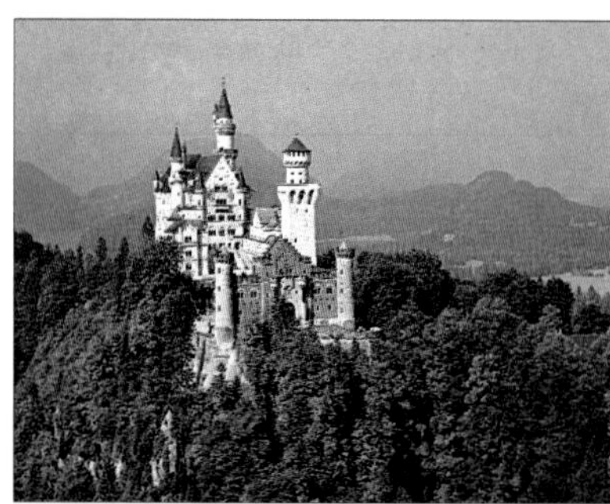

Neuschwanstein Castle in Bavaria, *one of Germany's major tourist attractions. It was built for the eccentric King Ludwig II.*

EDUCATION

99%

0 — *Education spending as % GNP* — 25
4.5%

THE EDUCATION SYSTEM

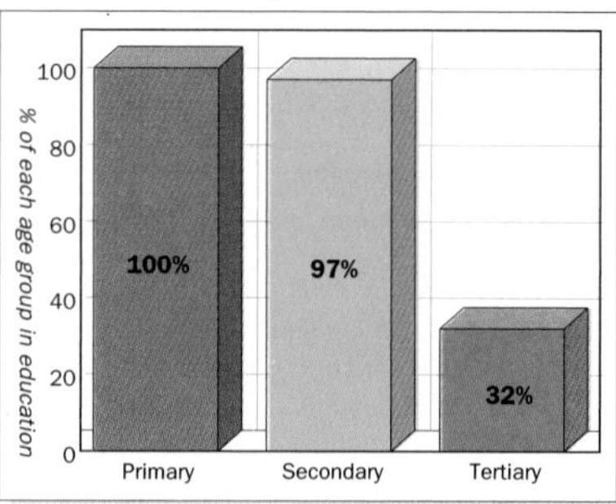

Education in Germany is run by the separate *Länder*. They coordinate their teaching policies but have full autonomy within their own borders. The German approach to education stresses academic efficiency and discipline, with few sports or cultural activities.

Those who wish to go to college attend the upper-secondary *Gymnasien* to prepare for the essential *Abitur* exam. Since this was made easier, thousands more have exercised their right to attend higher education, leading to strains on resources. Students frequently take eight years or more to complete their degrees. Research is conducted as much by firms, such as Siemens, as by universities.

CRIME

52,076 prisoners

Up 1% in 1990

CRIME RATES

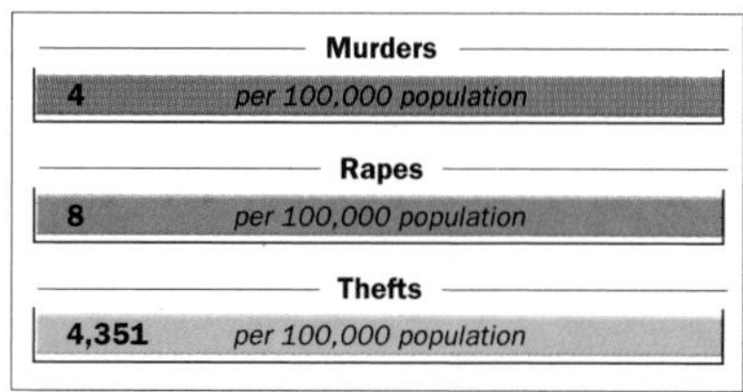

Crime rates in Germany are lower than in most other European countries. This is largely the result of a genuine respect for the law, coupled with a strong police force. Recently, however, rising unemployment has led to an increase in petty theft and a wave of violence, notably against immigrants.

German politics, once with an enviably clean reputation, have suffered several corruption scandals. Civil service corruption remains rare. People convicted under environmental laws will face ten-year jail sentences.

REGIONS

BERLIN

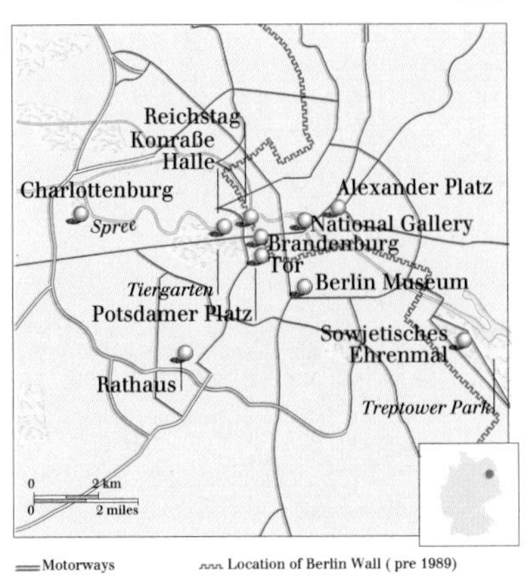

THE PROCESS OF REBUILDING Berlin as the capital of Germany began after reunification in 1990. The planning is being undertaken by an international team of architects led by Norman Foster. Much of the city was destroyed in World War II. In the Cold War years, it was split into US, UK, French and Soviet occupation zones. The first three were separated from the fourth by the notorious Berlin Wall. Many people were shot trying to cross the Wall to the western sector, which itself was an enclave within East Germany. In 1989, the almost spontaneous demolition of the Wall became a potent symbol of German reunification.

BADEN-WÜRTTEMBERG

BADEN-WÜRTTEMBERG has a long industrial tradition. It was here that Benz and Daimler invented the automobile. Its capital, Stuttgart, remains home to both Porsche and Daimler-Benz, as well as to Bosch and IBM's main European plants.

Baden-Württemberg is also a center for medium-sized precision manufacturing firms. It has emerged as a center of excellence for new technologies, including robotics and molecular industries. Lothar Späth, prime minister from 1978–1991, was largely responsible for initiatives to establish 30 new research institutes and 10 science parks, encouraging links between Stuttgart University and local industry.

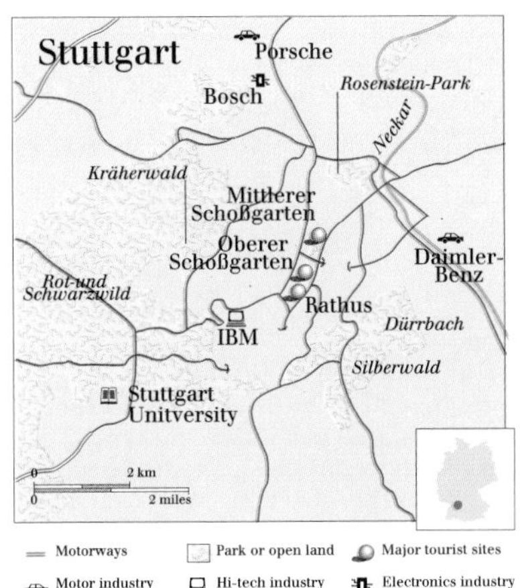

BAYERN

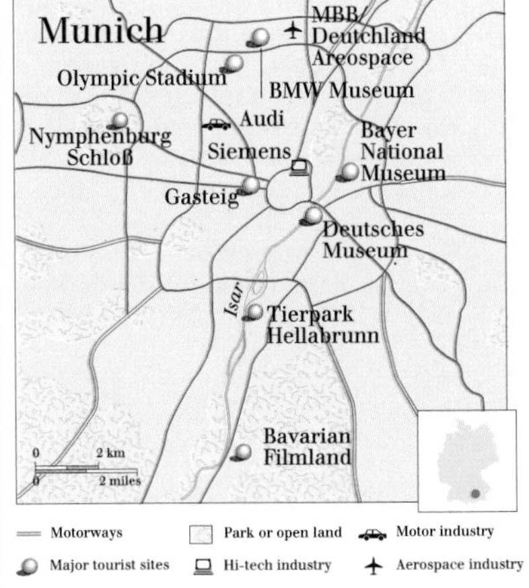

THE LARGEST of the *Länder*, Bayern (Bavaria) has a reputation for conservatism. It was one of the *Länder* to maintain its monarchy until 1918. Catholicism is stronger here than elsewhere in Germany. Liberal social and sexual habits, acceptable in most other regions, are still frowned upon in Bayern's rural districts. In its heavily agricultural economy, small farms have suffered as the subsidies provided by the EU have become less generous.

Other parts of its economy are doing well and it has been developing new high-tech industries. It is often referred to, along with Baden-Württemberg, as Germany's sunbelt. Its major firms – BMW, Siemens and Audi – have also been growing.

Munich, Bayern's capital, is the center for the German fashion, film and advertising industries, and is a center for the arts. Its now multi-purpose arts center, the *Gasteig*, opened in 1983.

HEALTH

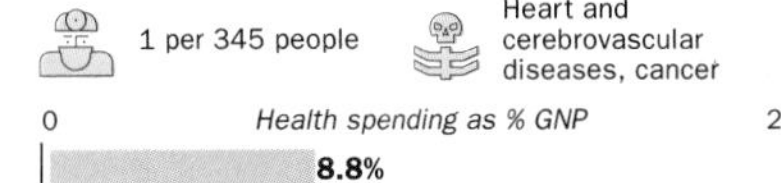

0 — Health spending as % GNP — 25

8.8%

The German social security system, first pioneered by Bismarck, is one of the most comprehensive in the world. Health insurance is compulsory and employer and employee contributions are high. Although most hospitals are run by the *Länder*, some are still owned by Germany's wealthy churches.

Germans are increasingly health-conscious, paying great attention to diet. Millions go on annual trips to the country's 200-plus spas. In the east, many are still suffering from lung diseases caused by pollution.

WEALTH

Car mechanic, 18 Deutsche Marks per hour; government official, 8,314 Deutsche Marks per month

CONSUMER GOODS OWNERSHIP

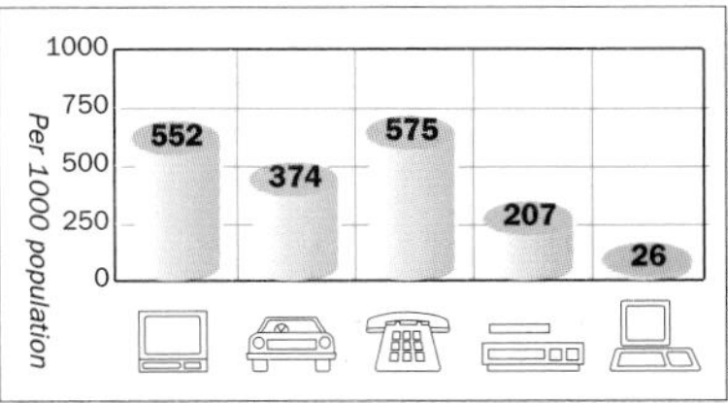

The effects of the Nazi period, which discredited many of Germany's ruling class, and the destruction of the property of millions of families in the war, account for the relatively classless nature of German society. Status is now more closely linked to wealth than to birth. In the west, disparities are less than in most of Europe; workers are generally well-paid and social security is generous. East German wages, however, are still pegged well below western rates, and there is a disproportionate number of unemployed living on welfare benefits.

WORLD RANKING

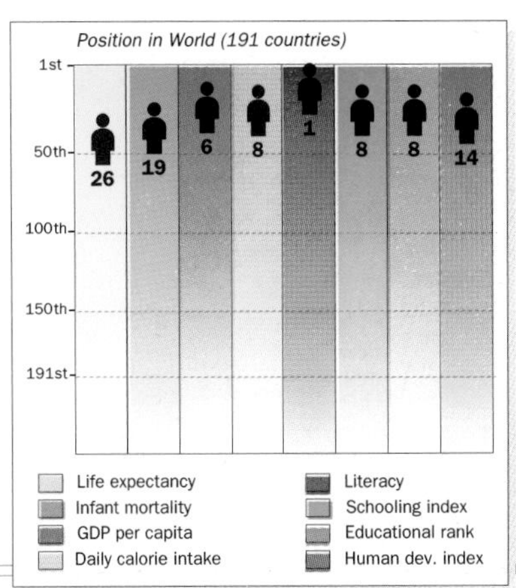

WEST AFRICA

Burkina
Togo
Ivory Coast
GHANA
Africa

GHANA

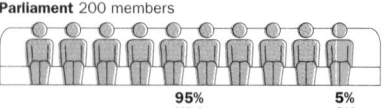

OFFICIAL NAME: Republic of Ghana **CAPITAL:** Accra
POPULATION: 16 million **CURRENCY:** Cedi **OFFICIAL LANGUAGE:** English

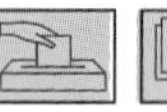

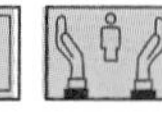

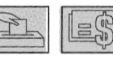

THE HEARTLAND OF THE ancient Ashanti kingdom, modern Ghana is a union of the former British colony of the Gold Coast and the British-administered part of the UN Trust Territory of Togoland. Ghana gained independence in 1957, the first British colony to do so. Its recent history has been one of intermittent military rule; the embracing of multiparty democracy in 1992 confirmed former military leader Jerry Rawlings in power.

CLIMATE

WEATHER CHART

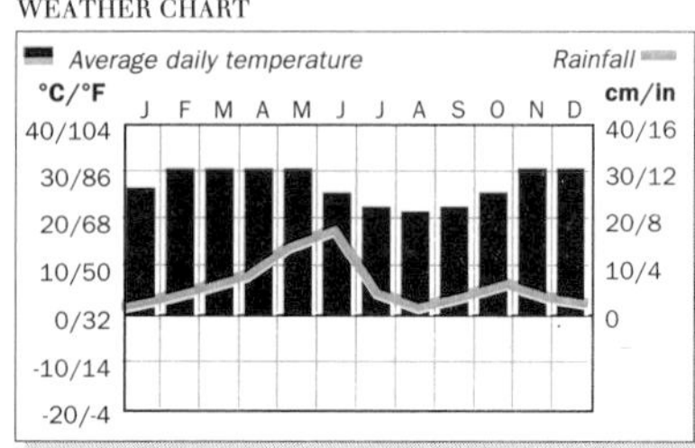

Southern Ghana has two rainy seasons: from April to July and September to November. The drier north has just one, from April to September.

COMMUNICATIONS

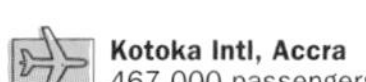

Kotoka Intl, Accra
467,000 passengers

11 ships
83,400 dwt

THE TRANSPORTATION NETWORK

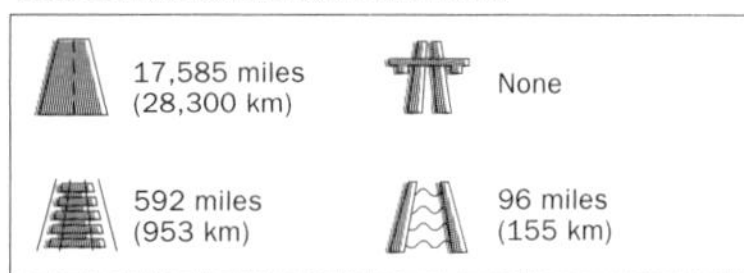

In 1983, work began to restore Ghana's roads, which had fallen into disrepair in the 1960s and 1970s; the network is now improving.

TOURISM

172,462 visitors

Up 18% in 1991

MAIN OVERSEAS ARRIVALS

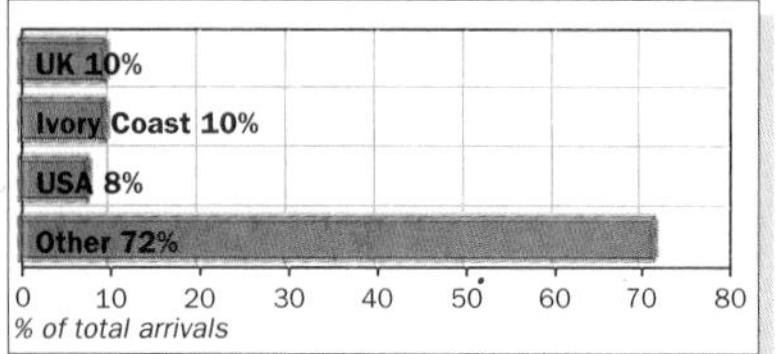

Tourism is still small-scale; most visitors come from Africa, the UK and the USA. Good beaches and old coastal forts are major attractions.

PEOPLE

Twi, Fanti, Ewe, Ga-Adangbe, Gurma, Dagomba (Dagbani)

163 people per sq. mile

THE URBAN/RURAL POPULATION SPLIT

33% 67%

RELIGIOUS PERSUASION

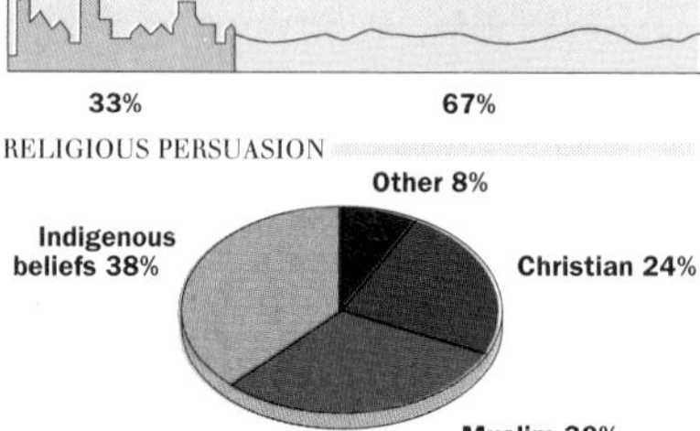

Ghana contains various cultural-linguistic groups. The largest is the Akan, who include the Ashanti and Fanti peoples. Other important groups are the Mole-Dagbani in the north, Ga-Adangbe around Accra and Ewe in the southeast. There are few tribal tensions. Family ties are strong.

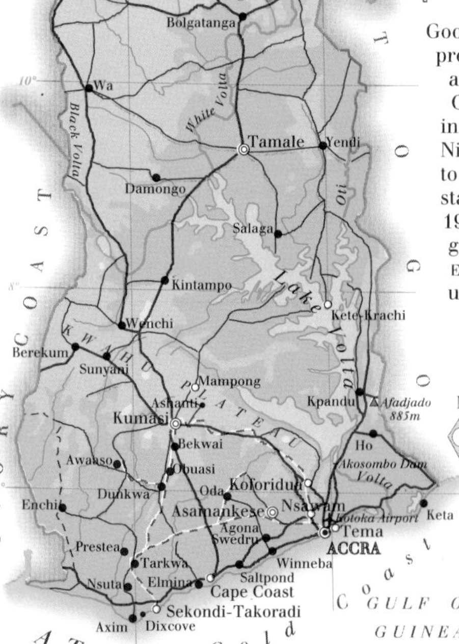

POLITICS

Uncertain

President Flt.-Lt. Jerry Rawlings

THE STATE OF THE PARTIES

Parliament 200 members

95% NDC **5% Other**

NDC = National Democratic Congress (closely linked to the former PNDC) **Other** = National Convention Party, Independent Party, Egle Party

Ghana's return to multiparty rule in 1992 marked the effective legitimization of the military government, which had previously resisted the call for greater democracy. Jerry Rawlings, a flight-lieutenant of Ewe-Scottish descent and one of the great survivors of African politics, staged coups in 1979 and 1981, and led the 1981–1992 Provisional National Defense Council military government. Rawlings emerged as a late candidate for the NDC and won 58% of the vote in the 1992 presidential elections. Opposition parties claimed malpractice but refused to contest the parliamentary elections the following month. The NDC swept the board. Opposition is still effectively outside parliament, the difference being that since 1992 political dissent is accepted.

WORLD AFFAIRS

Good relations with the West, which provides the bulk of Ghana's military and development aid, are a priority. Ghana has played a significant part in UN peacekeeping operations. After Nigeria, it is also the main contributor to the ECOWAS forces (ECOMOG) stationed in war-torn Liberia since 1990. In 1993, the Ghanaian government called unsuccessfully for ECOWAS to intervene to suppress civil unrest in Togo.

GHANA

Total Area : 238 540 sq. km (92 100 sq. miles)

LAND HEIGHT: 500m/1640ft; 200m/656ft; Sea Level

POPULATION: over 500 000; over 100 000; over 50 000; over 10 000; under 10 000

0 – 100 km; 0 – 100 miles

AID

 $724m (receipts)  Up 45% in 1991

In 1983, the PNDC began a largely successful economic recovery program backed by World Bank and IMF aid. Between 1984 and 1989, Ghana received $3.5 billion, the third largest recipient of World Bank aid after India and China.

DEFENSE

 $45.39m  Up 32% in 1990

In 1966, 1972, 1979 and 1981, the military mounted successful coups. There have also been frequent unsuccessful coups, many mounted by disaffected officers against both military and civilian governments. Outside Ghana, the army has been deployed mainly in UN and ECOWAS operations.

ECONOMICS

 $6.8bn  783.68 cedis

SCORE CARD

- ❑ WORLD GNP RANKING........96th
- ❑ GNP PER CAPITA........$425
- ❑ BALANCE OF PAYMENTS........$-377.8m
- ❑ INFLATION........18.1%
- ❑ UNEMPLOYMENT........0.5%

STRENGTHS

Cocoa, the main export crop, is cheap to produce and accounts for 15% of the world total. 1993 gold exports totaled 1 million fine ounces; the main source is the Ashanti goldfields. Bauxite – with some processed alumina – is a major export. Since 1983, economic recovery policies have raised GNP 5% a year.

WEAKNESSES

High budget deficits and debt repayments; the cedi was devalued in 1983 and has since tended to float downwards. Foreign investors generally invest solely in gold mining. Many loss-making state enterprises.

EXPORTS

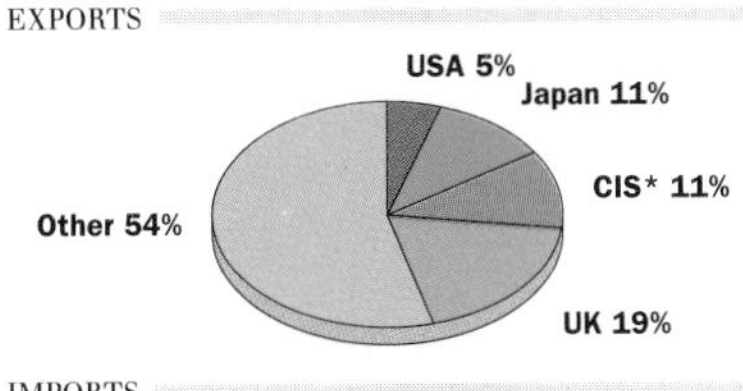

IMPORTS

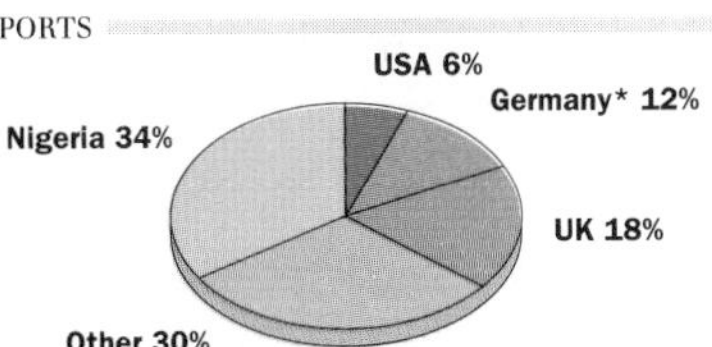

Dixcove harbor, *close to Ghana's most southerly cape. The majority of Ghanaians lead a traditional subsistence existence.*

RESOURCES

 5.3bn kwh (capacity 1.12m kw)  Reserves of 500,000 bbl; refines 26,600 b/cd

 2.2m sheep, 1.1m cattle, 559,000 pigs, 10,000 asses  Gold, diamonds, bauxite, manganese

Over the last ten years, gold production has expanded; in 1993, gold was Ghana's major export. Diamonds, bauxite and manganese are also exported. Surplus hydropower from the Volta Dam, completed in the early 1960s, is exported to Togo and Benin.

ENVIRONMENT

 5% 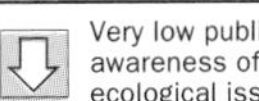 Very low public awareness of ecological issues

Cutting of wood for fuel, timber and farming has destroyed 70% of forests. Mining has devastated the surrounding land and caused serious pollution.

MEDIA

 Self-censorship by press. Overt criticism of government is not tolerated

PUBLISHING AND BROADCAST MEDIA

 There are 3 daily newspapers, the *Ghanaian Times*, the *People's Daily Graphic* and the *Evening News*

 1 state-controlled service  1 state-controlled service

New independent weeklies reflect the increase in private press ownership. Radio and TV tend to follow government reporting guidelines.

CRIME

 Ghana does not publish prison figures  Up 4% in 1990

The judiciary has little independence and the government often resorts to *ad hoc* "people's tribunals." Corruption is less of a problem than in recent years.

EDUCATION

 60%

All sectors of the education system are over-subscribed. There are a few high-quality boarding schools and four universities.

CHRONOLOGY

Finding the Ashanti uncompliant with their demands, the British sacked Kumasi, their capital, in 1874 and created the Gold Coast colony.

- ❑ **1957** Independence under authoritarian Kwame Nkrumah.
- ❑ **1964** Single-party state.
- ❑ **1966** Economy collapses. Bloodless army coup.
- ❑ **1972–1979** Corrupt "kleptocracy" of Gen. Acheampong. Executed 1979.
- ❑ **1979** Flt.-Lt. Jerry Rawlings's coup. Civilian Dr. Limann wins elections.
- ❑ **1981** Rawlings takes power again.
- ❑ **1992** Rawlings's NDC wins elections, boycott by four opposition parties.

G

HEALTH

 1 per 12,523 people  Malaria, diarrheal diseases, tuberculosis

The health of most of the population has benefited more from improvements in public hygiene than improvements in medical care.

WEALTH

The many Ghanaians who emigrated in search of better jobs remit $300 million a year – a substantial contribution to Ghana's economy

CONSUMER GOODS OWNERSHIP

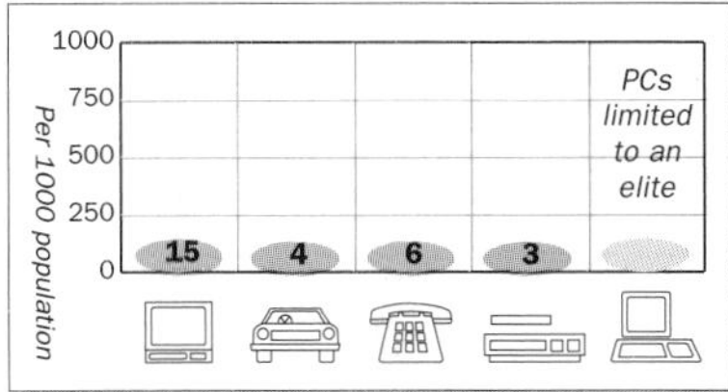

Political uncertainty brought few opportunities for advancement and many Ghanaians emigrated, but the situation is now improving. The key disparity is still between the poorer north and richer, more urban, south.

WORLD RANKING

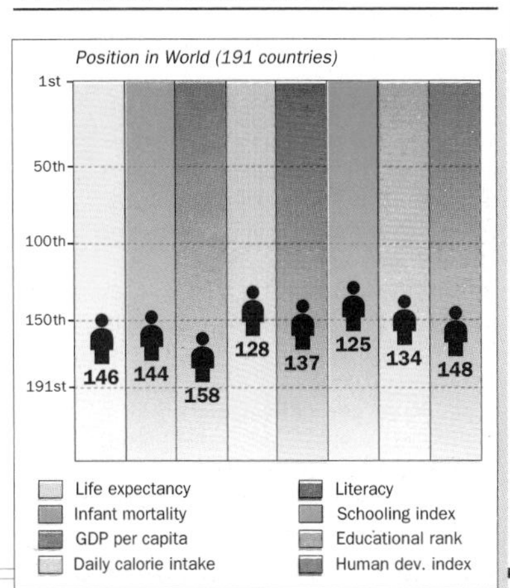

EUROPE

GREECE

OFFICIAL NAME: Hellenic Republic **CAPITAL:** Athens
POPULATION: 10.2 million **CURRENCY:** Drachma **OFFICIAL LANGUAGE:** Greek

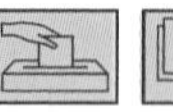

THE SOUTHERNMOST NATION of the Balkans, Greece is surrounded by the Aegean, Ionian and Cretan seas. Its territory includes over 2,000 islands. Three-fifths of the mainland is mountainous and only one-third of the land is cultivated. The country has a strong seafaring tradition and Greeks are the world's biggest ship owners. Greece is rich in minerals, including chromium, not found elsewhere in the EU. The key foreign policy concern is the Former Yugoslav Republic of Macedonia (FYRM); Greece fears its potential claim over the Greek province of Macedonia.

CLIMATE

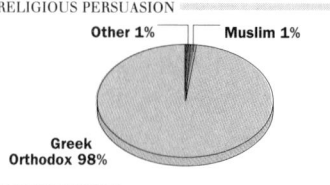

WEATHER CHART

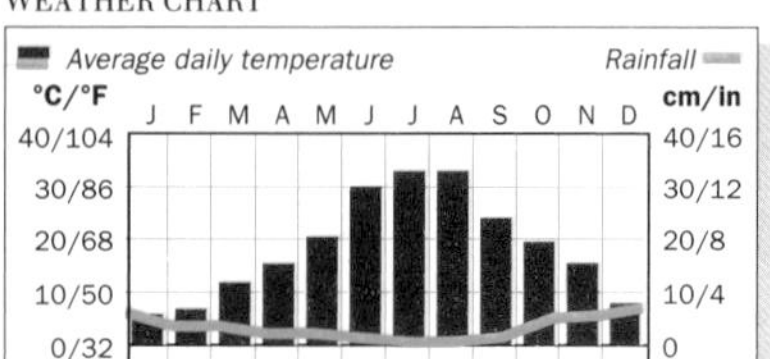

The climate varies from region to region. The northwest is alpine, while parts of Crete border on the subtropical. The large central plain experiences high summer temperatures. Water is a problem, as many rivers have been diverted underground by earthquakes.

COMMUNICATIONS

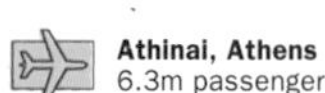
Athinai, Athens
6.3m passengers

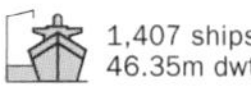
1,407 ships
46.35m dwt

THE TRANSPORTATION NETWORK

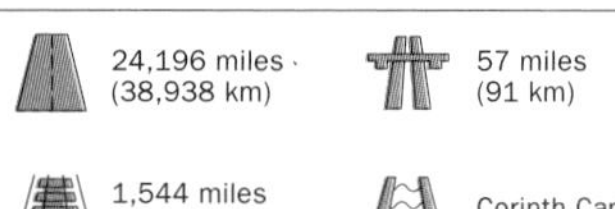

The easiest and cheapest method of transportation between the islands and the mainland is by boat or Russian-built hovercraft. Greece has a total of 444 ports, of which 123 are large enough to handle passenger or freight traffic. Of the 37 civilian airports in Greece, two-thirds are located on the islands and are also used by the military. Although the rail system is undeveloped, an inter-urban bus system and fleet of air-conditioned tourist trains offer a more extensive service. In general, Greece has a good, yet increasingly congested, road network; the number of motor vehicles is three million and rising. Piraeus is the country's main port.

TOURISM

8.2m visitors

Down 11% in 1991

MAIN OVERSEAS ARRIVALS

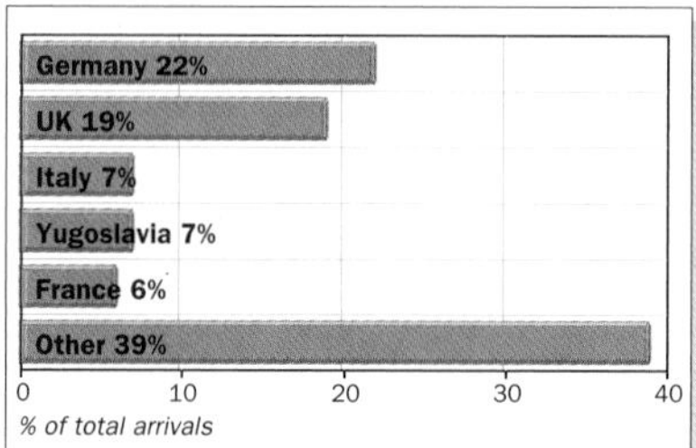

Tourism is a mainstay of the Greek economy and a major source of foreign exchange. Until recently, the government gave grants for hotel development. As a result, many third-grade hotels were built, especially on Crete and Rhodes. Smaller islands also tried to encourage tourism, but few have reliable water supplies or enough sandy beaches to attract visitors. Recently, tourism has declined, as many people have opted for cheaper vacations elsewhere. The breakup of former Yugoslavia has also deterred visitors. The Greek tourist industry is now trying to encourage visitors by upgrading its image to include sailing and conference tourism. Thessaloníki will be the European City of Culture in 1997.

Roman ruins, Dodona. *Classical sites such as this amphitheater in northwestern Greece, have helped to make tourism one of Greece's most important industries.*

PEOPLE

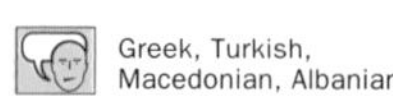
Greek, Turkish, Macedonian, Albanian

202 people per sq. mile

THE URBAN/RURAL POPULATION SPLIT

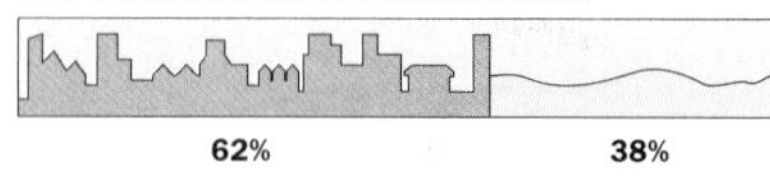

RELIGIOUS PERSUASION

Other 1% · Muslim 1% · Greek Orthodox 98%

ETHNIC MAKEUP

Other 2% · Greek 98%

Greece was for many centuries a largely agrarian and seafaring nation. The German occupation during World War II, and the civil war that followed, destroyed much of the fabric of rural life, and there was rapid urbanization between the 1950s and the 1980s. There was also extensive emigration during the 1950s and 1960s to northern Europe, Australia, the USA, Canada and southern Africa. However, many people returned to Greece in the 1980s, putting pressure on the labor market. The socialist PASOK governments of 1981–1989 spent large amounts, mostly from EU sources, on developing the infrastructure and business life of the rural regions in an attempt to halt emigration to the cities. The policy was mostly successful, but over half of the population still lives in the capital, Athens, and the main northern city, Thessaloníki.

Christianity is the main religion; 98% of the population belongs to the Greek Orthodox Church. Civil marriage and divorce only became legal in 1982. There are small minorities of Muslims, Catholics and Jews.

POPULATION AGE BREAKDOWN

% of population by age group

	1960	1970	1980	1990	2000
65+	8.3%	11.1%	13.1%	13.7%	16.9%
15–64	65.2%	64%	64.1%	66.6%	65.9%
0–14	26.5%	24.9%	22.8%	19.7%	17.2%

POLITICS

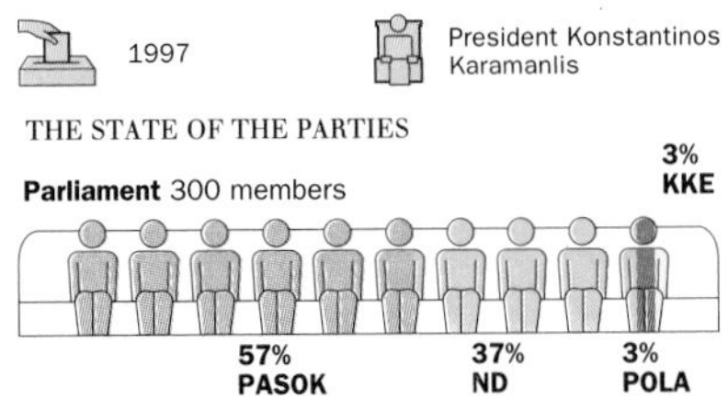

PASOK = Panhellenic Socialist Movement **ND** = New Democracy Party **POLA** = Political Spring **KKE** = Communist Party of Greece

Greece is a multiparty democracy. A military government was in power between 1967 and 1974.

MAIN POLITICAL ISSUES

Terrorism
During the 1990s, left-wing groups, notably "November 17," attacked "capitalist" targets. These included US companies and individuals of the conservative ND party. In 1990, a law was passed forbidding the publishing of alleged terrorists' views. This was abolished in 1993, but in January 1994, "November 17" ended 13 months of inaction by murdering a banker involved with the privatization of the state-owned *Ayet Iraklis* cement works.

Albanian refugees
Large numbers of Albanians of Greek descent have been entering Greece illegally since 1990. Willing to work for very low wages, they have swelled Greece's already thriving black economy. In an attempt to stem the tide, the government has embarked on an aid program in southern Albania.

PROFILE
After a financial scandal brought down the PASOK government in 1989, the ND party presented itself as the party of fiscal probity. Its policies to reduce inflation, balance the budget and curb mounting debt, though relatively successful, proved as unpopular as its privatization plans. The 1993 elections returned PASOK, and Andreas Papandreou, to power. The privatization program has been cut back, however, and economic realities have forced PASOK to continue with many of the ND's policies.

***President Karamanlis,** who began a second – and last – term in 1990.*

***Andreas Papandreou,** leader of PASOK and Prime Minister since 1993.*

WORLD AFFAIRS

Throughout the Cold War, Greece was closely allied with the West, although there are strong sympathies between the Greeks, Russians and Serbs because of their shared Orthodox heritage. Greece withdrew from the military command of NATO in 1974 in protest at the failure of the Alliance to prevent the Turkish invasion of Cyprus. It has since rejoined under a formula to negotiate with Turkey new command and control arrangements over the Aegean. These regional security issues, however, remain unresolved.

AID

Greece gives relatively little aid. It is, however, a large net receiver of regional development assistance from the EU. Total EU aid could reach $19 billion by the end of the decade. In particular, it is a major beneficiary of the EU's structural and cohesion funds. The allocation of cohesion funds for Greece are estimated to amount to around $3.5 billion over the 1993–1999 period. Some of the money has been used to reverse the decline of northeast Greece – the EU's least-developed region. EU funds make up 70% of a $370 million program to upgrade the region's road network and expand its port facilities.

GREECE

Total Area : 131 990 sq. km (50 961 sq. miles)

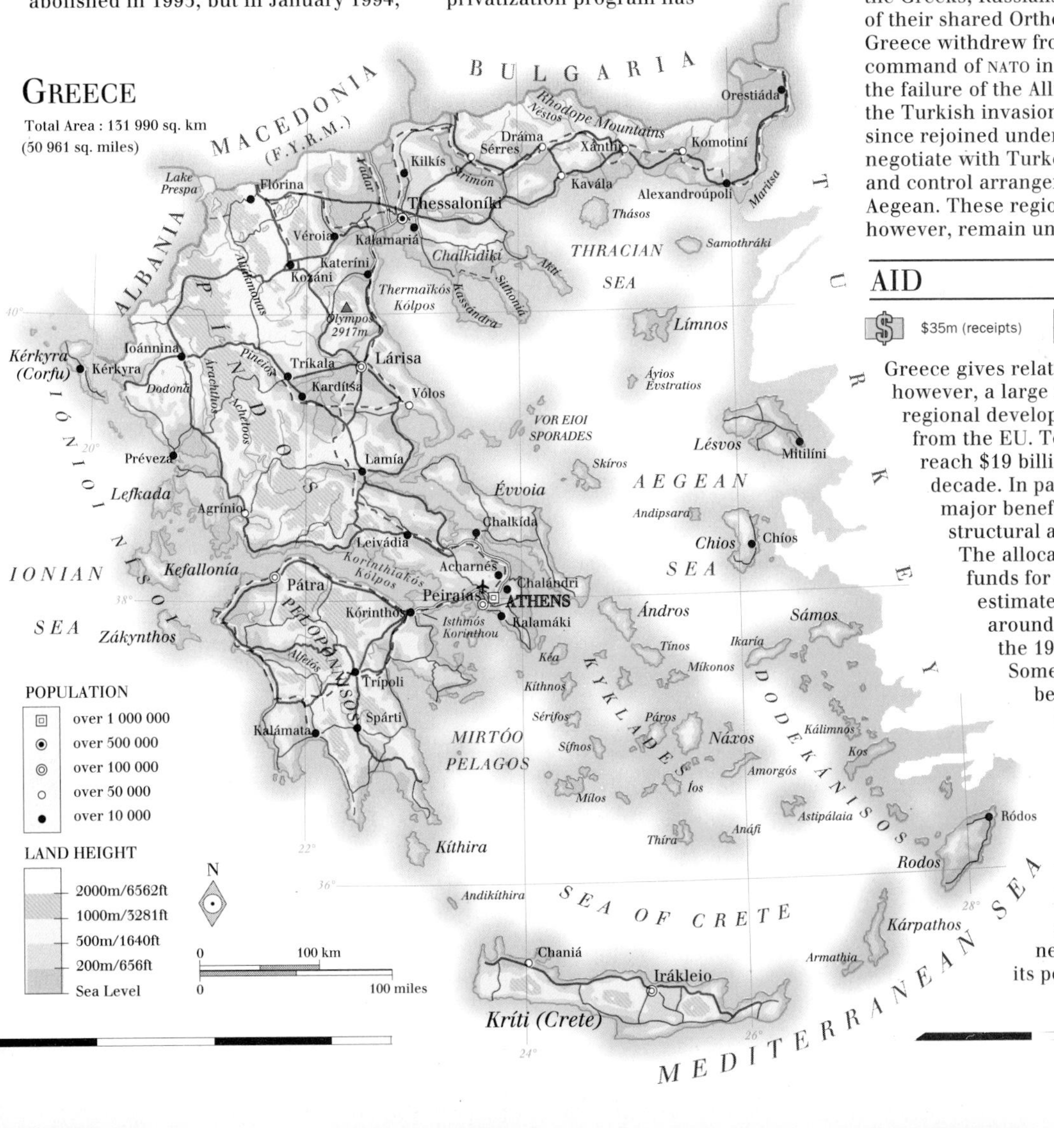

POPULATION
over 1 000 000
over 500 000
over 100 000
over 50 000
over 10 000

LAND HEIGHT
2000m/6562ft
1000m/3281ft
500m/1640ft
200m/656ft
Sea Level

0 100 km
0 100 miles

G

CHRONOLOGY

Greece was occupied by Nazi Germany between 1941 and 1944. After liberation by the Allies, communists and royalists fought a five-year civil war. This ended with communist defeat, and King Paul became the constitutional monarch.

- ❑ **1964** King Paul dies. Succeeded by son, King Constantine.
- ❑ **1967** Military coup. King in exile. Colonel Papadopoulos premier.
- ❑ **1973** Greece declared a republic, with Papadopoulos as president. Papadopoulos overthrown in military coup. Lt.-Gen. Ghizikis becomes president with Adamantios Androutsopoulos as prime minister.
- ❑ **1974** Greece leaves NATO in protest over Turkish occupation of northern Cyprus. Government falls. Constantinos Karamanlis becomes premier of Government of National Salvation. Karamanlis' ND party wins subsequent elections.
- ❑ **1975** Konstantinos Tsatsou becomes president.
- ❑ **1977** Elections. ND reelected.
- ❑ **1980** Karamanlis president. Georgios Rallis prime minister. Greece rejoins NATO.
- ❑ **1981** Socialist PASOK party wins elections. Andreas Papandreou first-ever socialist premier. Greece full member of EC.
- ❑ **1985** Proposals to limit power of president. Karamanlis resigns. Christos Sartzetakis president. Greece and Albania re-open borders, closed since 1940.
- ❑ **1985–1989** Civil unrest caused by economic austerity program.
- ❑ **1988** Cabinet implicated in financial scandal. Several leading members resign.
- ❑ **1989** Defense agreement with the USA. After inconclusive elections, Left coalition between communist KKE and EAR form government. Charilaos Florakis as president. ND join Left coalition in government. Tzannis Tzannetakis premier for three months, then succeeded by Yannis Grivas. Further election inconclusive. All-party coalition. Xenofon Zolotas prime minister.
- ❑ **1990** Coalition government collapses. ND party wins protracted elections. Mitsotakis prime minister; Karamanlis president.
- ❑ **1990–1992** Strikes against economic, educational and social security reform.
- ❑ **1992** EC persuaded to withhold recognition of Republic of Macedonia (FYRM). Maastricht Treaty on European Union ratified.
- ❑ **1993** PASOK wins general election, Andreas Papandreou premier.

DEFENSE

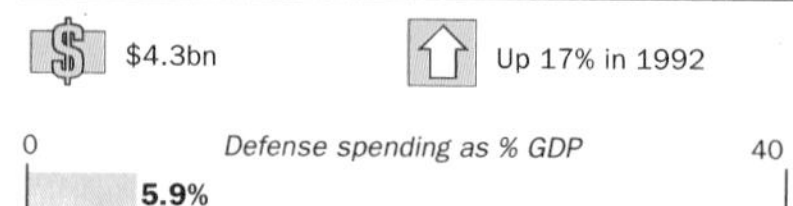

Greece spends a higher percentage of GDP on defense than any other NATO country. Its main concern is the perceived threat from Turkey. Greece is seeking full membership in the Western European Union, although this is being blocked because of disputes with Turkey.

GREEK ARMED FORCES

1,879 main battle tanks (396 M-47/1220 M-48/ 154 AMX-30)	113,000 personnel
4 frigates, 10 submarines, 9 destroyers and 37 patrol boats	19,500 personnel
381 combat aircraft (F-4E/F-5A,-B/F-104G/ F-16/F-4E	26,800 personnel
None	

ECONOMICS

$65.5bn

214.9 drachmae

SCORE CARD

❑ World GNP Ranking	35th
❑ GNP per Capita	$6,422
❑ Balance of Payments	$-1bn
❑ Inflation	15.8%
❑ Unemployment	8.9%

EXPORTS

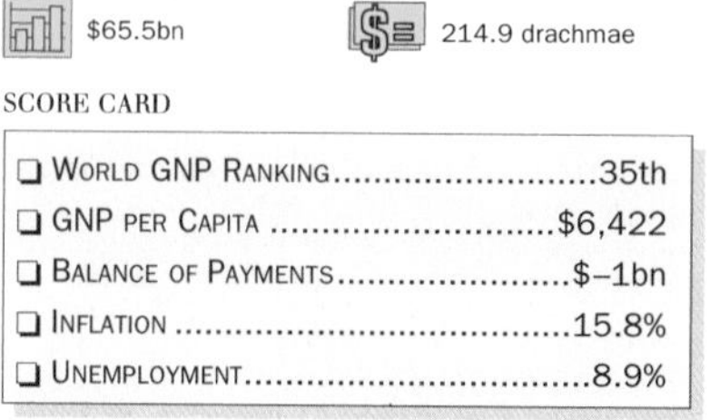

IMPORTS

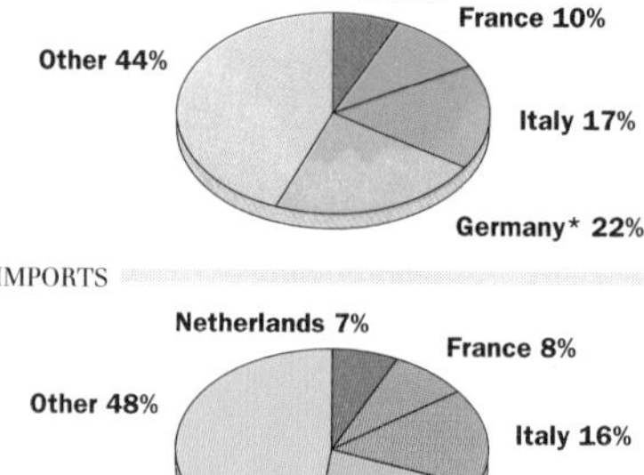

Strengths
One of the major tourist destinations in Europe. Efficient agricultural exporter. Shipping: the world's largest beneficially owned fleet.

Weaknesses
High levels of public debt. High interest rates and bureaucratic banking system discourage private initiative. State involved in almost 70% of businesses. High levels of tax evasion. Black economy accounts for 30%–50% of GDP.

Profile
Greece took longer than most other northern European countries to recover from World War II, due to years of civil strife. It was not until the 1960s that any substantial investment occurred. The Colonels' dictatorship curbed inflationary pressures through the introduction of a wage freeze. When civilian government was restored in 1974, a spate of high wage settlements and the oil price shocks of 1973 and 1979 drove

ECONOMIC PERFORMANCE INDICATOR

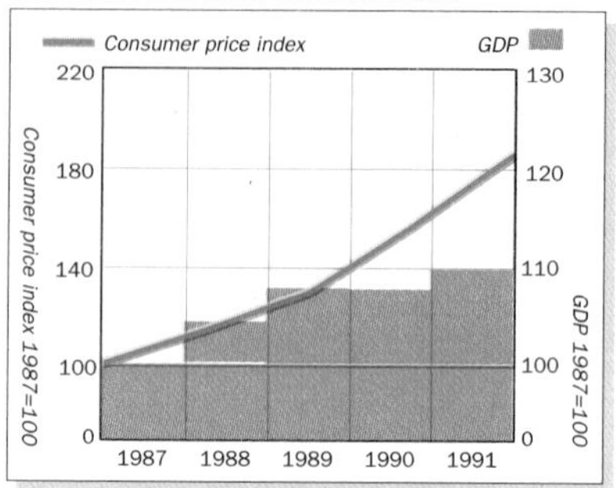

inflation to above 20%, where it hovered for some years. From 1982–1986, Greece's largest companies reported substantial losses. There was a modest return to profitability following the socialists' austerity program of 1986–1987.

In general, the return on capital has persistently been a fraction of the rate of inflation. Economic reforms in the late 1980s, however, led to a resurgence of interest in the stock exchange, which also attracts investment from the underground economy.

GREECE : MAJOR BUSINESSES

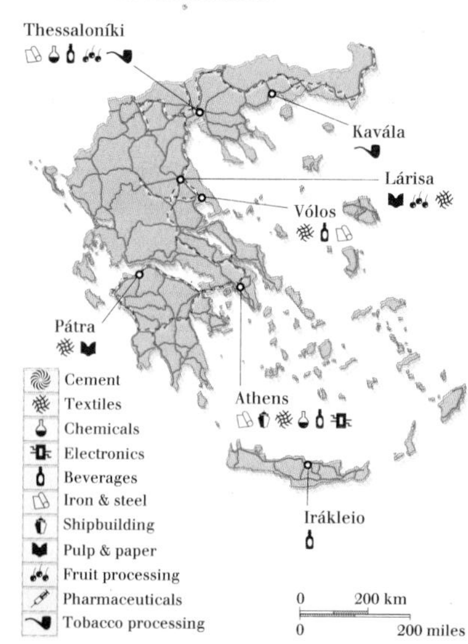

RESOURCES

35bn kwh (capacity 8.5m kw)

13,900 b/d (reserves 41,000,000 bbl)

10.4m sheep, 1.2m pigs, 731,000 cattle

Coal, iron, bauxite, oil, gas, marble, nickel, magnesite, chromium

ELECTRICITY GENERATION

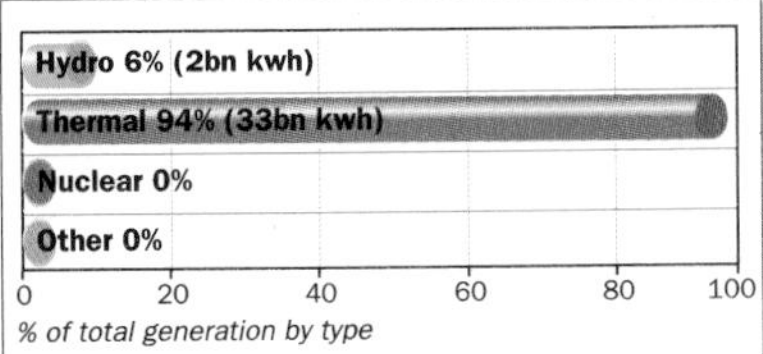

Greece has an oil and gas field off the coast of Thásos Island. Reserves may be available in its eastern waters, the ownership of which is contested by Turkey. Coal, iron and other mining contributes less than 2% to GDP. Greece is a leading producer of marble.

ENVIRONMENT

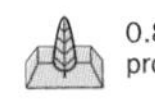
0.8% (0.2% partially protected)

Economic growth has precedence over ecological concerns

ENVIRONMENTAL TREATIES

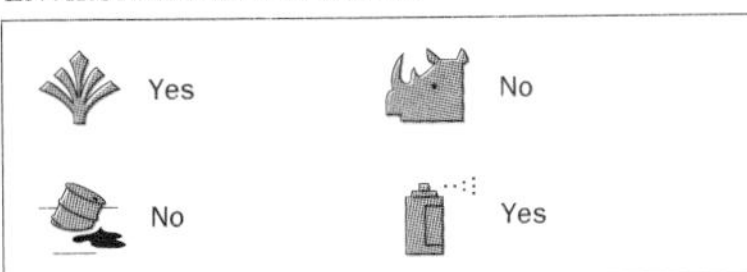

Local fishing interests have formed a highly successful anti-pollution organization known as *Helmepa*. Athens is plagued with smog known as *nefos*, which is irritating to the eyes and throat. It is also highly damaging to Greece's ancient monuments. The Parthenon in Athens has suffered more erosion in the last two decades than in the previous 2,000 years.

MEDIA

The press is free from government interference, however, the state broadcasting services are under strong government control

PUBLISHING AND BROADCAST MEDIA

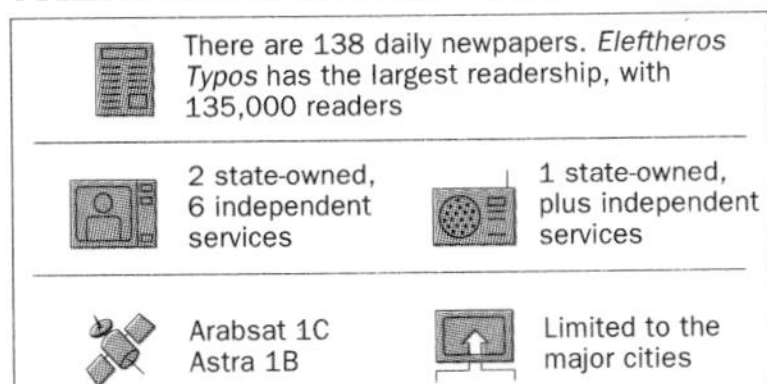

There are 138 daily newpapers. *Eleftheros Typos* has the largest readership, with 135,000 readers
2 state-owned, 6 independent services
1 state-owned, plus independent services
Arabsat 1C
Astra 1B
Limited to the major cities

The state had a monopoly on radio and TV until 1989. Commercial broadcasting has made politicians far more answerable to the electorate than ever before. It has also had a cultural impact with the import of more foreign, particularly US, programming. There are eight legal TV networks and many pirate stations.

GREECE : LAND USE

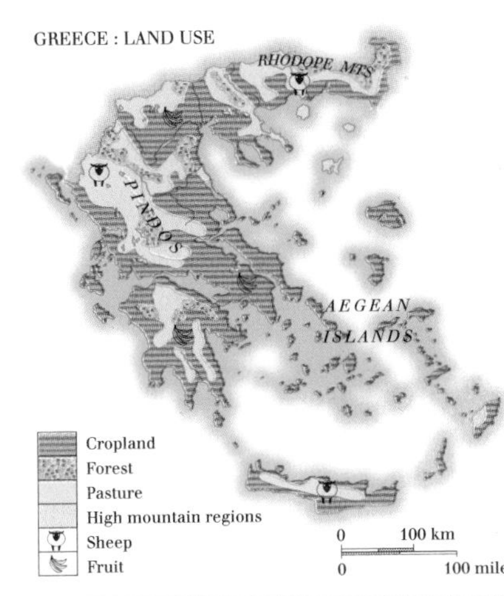

CRIME

5,008 prisoners

Up 15% in 1990

CRIME RATES

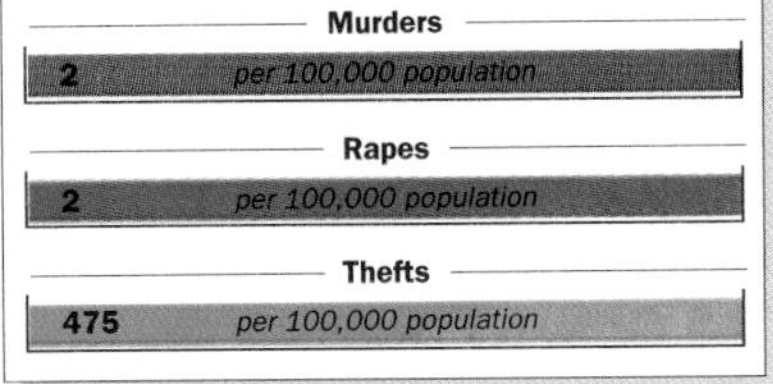

An influx of refugees from Eastern Europe, North Africa and the Far East has led to an increase in violent crime. The terrorist group November 17 has assassinated wealthy citizens.

EDUCATION

93%

0 — Education spending as % GNP — 25

2.7%

THE EDUCATION SYSTEM

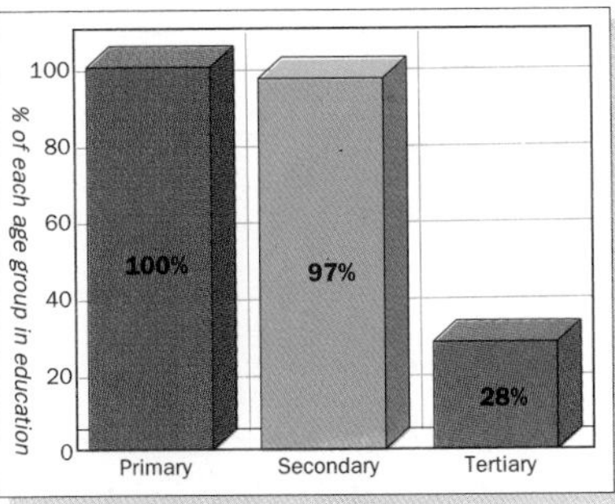

Teachers are poorly paid and qualifications are low. University places are limited and many students go abroad for higher education. Technical courses, funded by the EU, have increased since the 1990s.

HEALTH

1 per 1,067 people

Heart and cerebrovascular diseases, cancer

0 — Health spending as % GNP — 40

5.9%

The socialists (PASOK) introduced a national health service and a national pharmaceuticals industry. However, the service is short of staff and families have to perform many of the services normally expected of nurses. The New Democracy (ND) government tried to upgrade private care and to incorporate its activities with those in state hospitals. Many Greeks requiring major surgery travel to Germany, Switzerland or the UK for treatment.

WEALTH

Teacher, 120,000 drachmas a month; doctor, 230,000 drachmas a month

CONSUMER GOODS OWNERSHIP

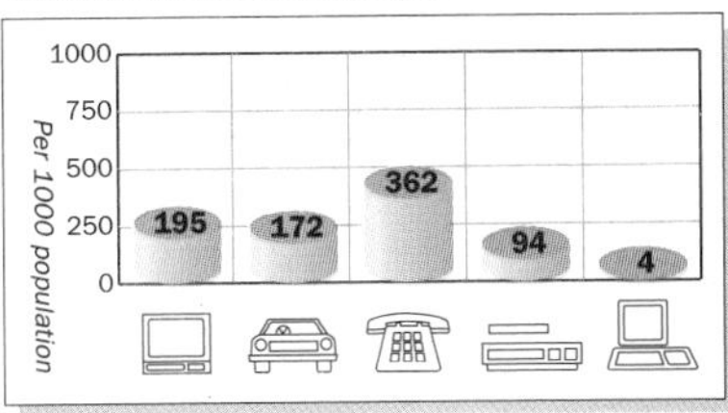

Greek society changed dramatically in the post-war period. Formerly a largely isolated agricultural community, rapid urbanization in the 1950s led to many former agricultural workers making fortunes. Many grabbed opportunities presented by the shipping industry. Among these were the prominent Niarchos and Onassis families.

The advent of the republic in 1973 reflected social changes which had occurred since the war. New wealth and success became more admired than aristocratic birth or prestige. Greece is now a socially mobile society. Living standards have improved throughout society since the 1950s.

WORLD RANKING

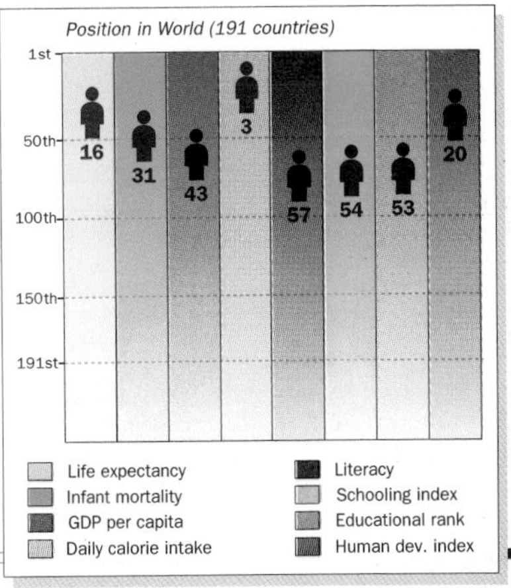

G

GRENADA

CARIBBEAN
Lesser Antilles
GRENADA
Trinidad & Tobago
Venezuela
North America

OFFICIAL NAME: Grenada **CAPITAL:** St. George's
POPULATION: 84,000 **CURRENCY:** East Caribbean dollar **OFFICIAL LANGUAGE:** English

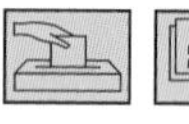

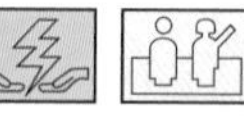

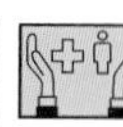
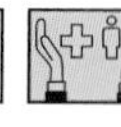

THE MOST SOUTHERLY of the Windward Islands, Grenada also includes the islands of Carriacou and Petite Martinique. It is the world's second largest nutmeg producer. Grenada became a focus of attention in 1983 when the USA, with token backing from several Caribbean states, mounted an invasion to sever its growing links with Castro's Cuba. Grenada is discussing a political union with St. Lucia, Dominica, and St. Vincent and the Grenadines.

G

CLIMATE

WEATHER CHART

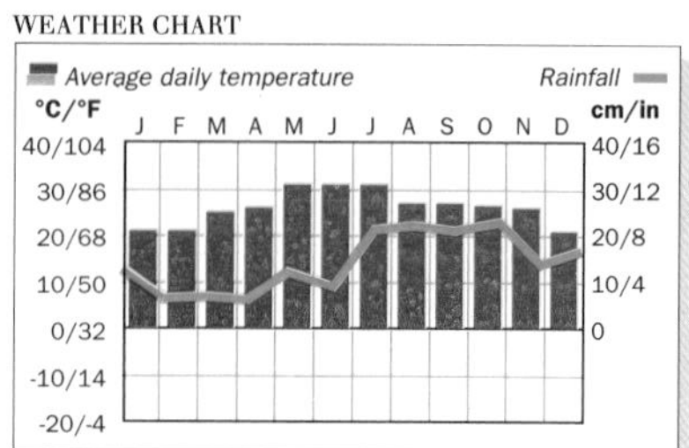

Annual rainfall ranges from 59 in. on the coast to 117 in. in the mountains. Hurricanes occur in the rainy season.

COMMUNICATIONS

Point Salines, St. George's 206,000 passengers

Has no fleet

THE TRANSPORTATION NETWORK

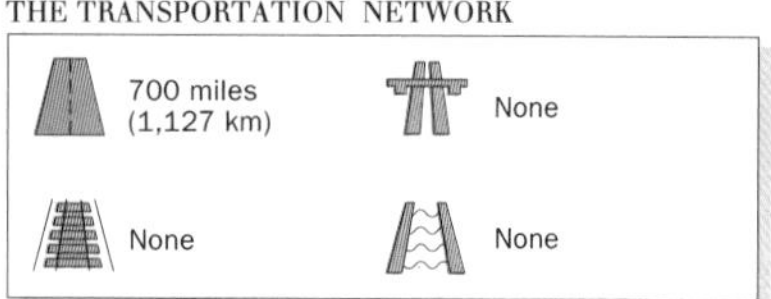

Mountain roads are frequently washed away in the rains. US aid helped to finance the international airport.

TOURISM

87,554 visitors

Up 3% in 1992

MAIN OVERSEAS ARRIVALS

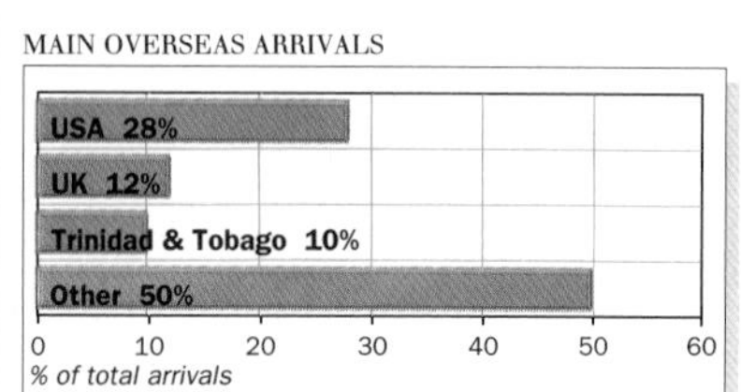

Tourism has developed since the restoration of democracy and the completion of the international airport in 1984. Large resort projects have caused serious beach erosion, in turn requiring costly coastal defenses.

PEOPLE

English, English Creole

751 people per sq. mile

THE URBAN/RURAL POPULATION SPLIT

15% 85%

RELIGIOUS PERSUASION

Other 15%
Anglican 17%
Roman Catholic 68%

Most Grenadians are descendants of Africans, brought over to work on sugar plantations between the 16th and 19th centuries. Intermarriage between this group and the small numbers of Europeans and indigenous Indians has meant that there is little racial tension. As in other Caribbean states, extended families with absentee fathers are common.

GRENADA

Total Area : 340 sq. km (131 sq. miles)

POPULATION
• over 10 000
• under 10 000

LAND HEIGHT
500m/1640ft
200m/656ft
Sea Level

Petit St Vincent I.
Petite Martinique
Windward
Carriacou
Hillsborough
Mabouya I.
Petite Dominique
Grand Bay
L'Esterre
White I.
Saline I.
Frigate I.
Large I.
Diamond I.
Les Tantes
Ronde I.
The Sisters
Caille I.
London Bridge
Sugar Loaf
Green I.
Sandy I.
Sauteurs
Bird I.
River Sallee
Victoria
Union
Mt. Rose
Hermitage
Tivoli
Mt. St Catherine 840m
Gouyave
Grenada
Grand Roy
Paradise
Concord
Grenville
Birch Grove
Brizan
Mt. Moritz
Willis
Snug Corner
Constantine
The Baide
Crochu
ST. GEORGE'S
Springs
Epping Forest
St. David's
Grande Anse
Corinth
Point Salines Airport
Westerhall Point
Glover I.
Lance aux Epines
CARIBBEAN SEA
ATLANTIC OCEAN
0 8 km
0 8 miles

POLITICS

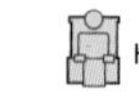

1995

HM Queen Elizabeth II

THE STATE OF THE PARTIES

House of Representatives 15 members

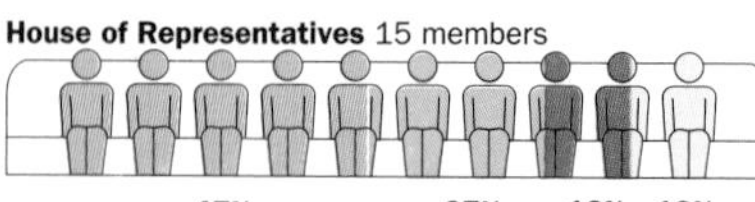

47% NDC **27% GULP** **13% TNP** **13% NNP**

NDC = National Democratic Congress **GULP** = Grenada United Labour Party **TNP** = The National Party **NNP** = New National Party

Senate 13 members

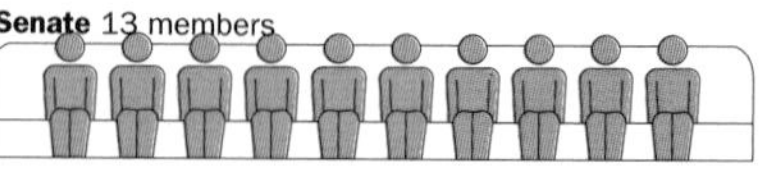

10 members chosen by the prime minister (3 after consulting various interests) and 3 by the leader of the opposition

The past 20 years have seen Grenada move toward a position of political isolation to that of being a full-fledged democracy following US policy in the Caribbean. Former prime minister Sir Eric Gairy was as well known for his eccentric requests to the UN Security Council – he once asked it to investigate UFOs on the island – as for his intimidation of political opponents with organized gangs. Gairy was overthrown in 1979 in a civilian coup by the pro-Cuba Maurice Bishop, who was in turn overthrown and then executed by the army in 1983. This coup was the pretext for the US invasion in October of that year; the primary motive was to end Cuban influence in Grenada. Elected government was restored in 1984 and the USA provided large amounts of aid for reconstruction. Politics have since been center-right and ideologically there is little to choose between the four main parties. The dominant political issue is the proposed federation between Grenada and its neighbors in the Windward Islands group: St. Lucia, Dominica, and St. Vincent and the Grenadines. Nicholas Braithwaite, the prime minister and leader of the ruling NDC, supports the proposal for union.

WORLD AFFAIRS

The main issues are the proposed federation between Grenada and the rest of the Windward Islands group, and concern that the EU may remove preferential access for Grenadian bananas. Since 1983, Grenada has supported US policy in the Caribbean.

AID

 $17m (receipts)

 Up 55% in 1991

The main aid sources are the UK, the EU and the USA. Cuba was a major donor before the 1983 invasion, helping to build the airport at Point Salines.

DEFENSE

 Minimal receipts

 Defense spending is falling

The People's Revolutionary Army, created by Maurice Bishop in the wake of his 1979 coup, was replaced in 1983 by a paramilitary defense unit trained by the USA and the UK.

ECONOMICS

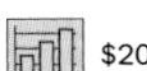 $207m

 2.70 East Caribbean dollars

SCORE CARD

❑ WORLD GNP RANKING	177th
❑ GNP PER CAPITA	$2,465
❑ BALANCE OF PAYMENTS	$-39.1m
❑ INFLATION	2.5%
❑ UNEMPLOYMENT	30%

STRENGTHS

The world's second largest producer of nutmeg after Indonesia, with 23% of the world market. Other important sectors are tourism and bananas.

WEAKNESSES

Failure to revive world nutmeg cartel with Indonesia (collapsed in 1988). Labor productivity levels are the lowest in the East Caribbean.

EXPORTS

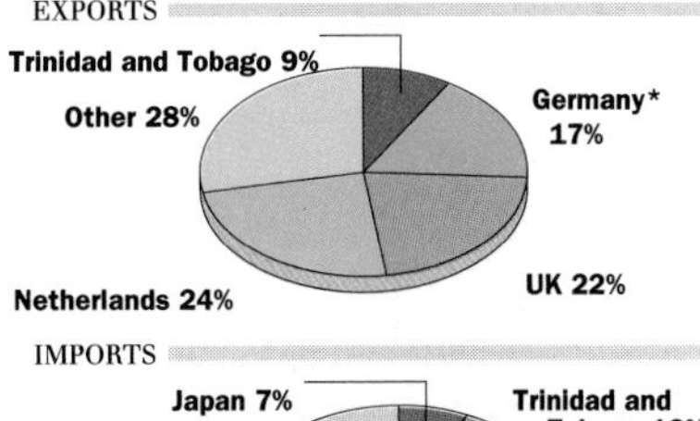

IMPORTS

Japan 7%
Trinidad and Tobago 12%
Other 37%
UK 17%
USA 27%

RESOURCES

 51m kwh (capacity 9,000 kw)

 Not an oil producer and has no refineries

 15,000 sheep, 11,000 pigs, 11,000 goats

 None

Grenada has no strategic resources and has to import most of its energy. Its major asset is the nutmeg industry, which accounts for almost one-quarter of total world production.

ENVIRONMENT

 1%

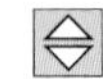 National parks legislation still inadequate

The government has recently become aware of the potential value of ecotourism, but has failed to protect some key environmental sites. The best remnant of rainforest, near Epping Forest, has not been included within an ecological protection zone.

MEDIA

 Freedom of expression guaranteed under the constitution. Little government censorship

PUBLISHING AND BROADCAST MEDIA

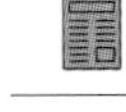 There are no daily newspapers. The *Grenadian Voice* and the *Grenada Guardian* are published weekly

 1 state-owned service

 1 state-owned station

The press in Grenada is privately owned and free from overt political interference.

CRIME

 Grenada does not publish prison figures

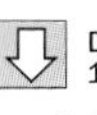 Down 53% between 1986 and 1989

Disaffected members of the disbanded People's Revolutionary Army were responsible for an increase in violent crime following the US invasion in 1983. The crime rate is now down to the Caribbean average.

EDUCATION

 90%

Education follows the former British selective 11-plus system. Most students go on to the University of the West Indies, or to college in the USA.

HEALTH

 1 per 1,625 people

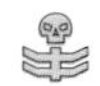 Heart diseases, cancer, nutritional disorders

After Maurice Bishop's takeover in 1979, Cuban physicians provided a basic health-care system, which did not include any dental treatment. Subsidized state hospitals now cover most areas fairly efficiently, matching the Caribbean average.

***St. George's Harbour.** The newest hotel developments are on the beaches to the south of the capital.*

CHRONOLOGY

A French colony from 1650, Grenada was captured by the British in 1762.

- ❑ **1951** Universal suffrage introduced.
- ❑ **1967** Internal self-government. Labour Party wins elections and campaigns for independence.
- ❑ **1974** Full independence from UK. Eric Gairy prime minister.
- ❑ **1979** Coup. Maurice Bishop prime minister. Growing links with Cuba.
- ❑ **1983** US invasion establishes pro-US administration.

G

WEALTH

 The disparities which existed between a few rich farmers and the majority of laborers have been reduced

CONSUMER GOODS OWNERSHIP

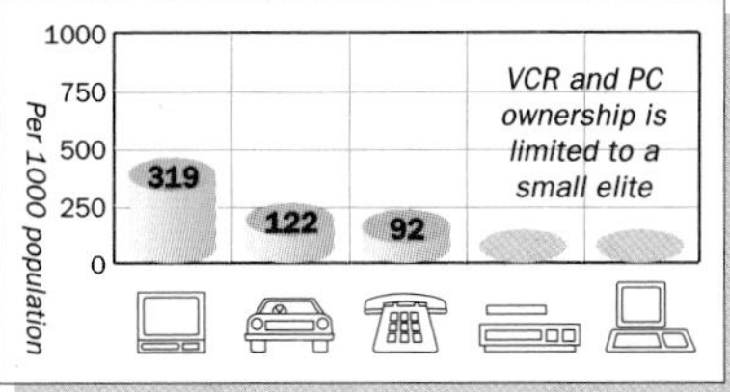

Wealth disparities on Grenada are less marked than in most Caribbean states. The wealthiest groups control the nutmeg trade.

WORLD RANKING

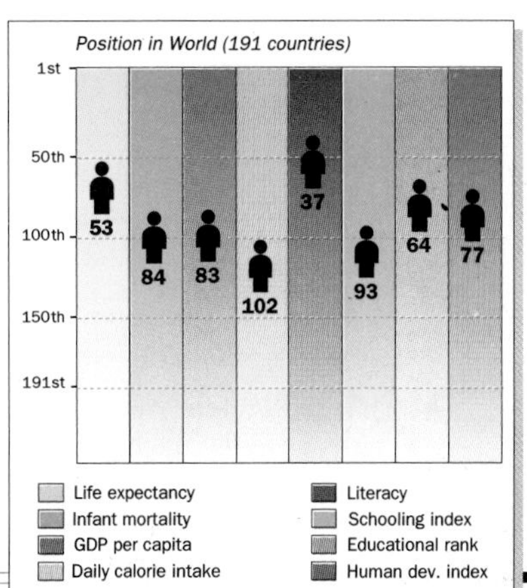

GUATEMALA

OFFICIAL NAME: Republic of Guatemala **CAPITAL:** Guatemala City
POPULATION: 9.7 million **CURRENCY:** Quetzal **OFFICIAL LANGUAGE:** Spanish

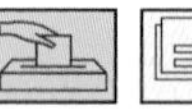

LARGEST AND MOST POPULOUS of the states of the Central American isthmus, Guatemala was home to the ancient Mayan civilization. Its fertile Pacific and Caribbean coastal lowlands give way to the highlands which dominate the country. Independent since 1838, Guatemala's history since 1954 has been one of military rule. Civilian rule returned in 1986, but 90% of people still live below the poverty line.

CLIMATE

WEATHER CHART

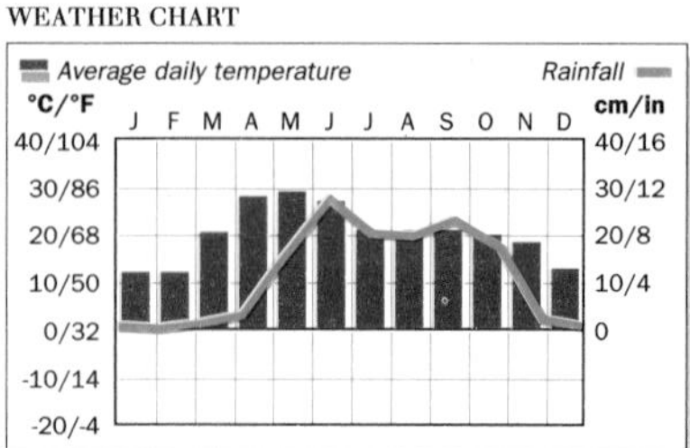

The climate varies with altitude. Daytime temperatures average 82°F in the tropical coastal regions and 68°F in the more temperate central highlands.

COMMUNICATIONS

La Aurora, Guatemala City
939,000 passengers

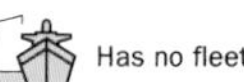

Has no fleet

THE TRANSPORTATION NETWORK

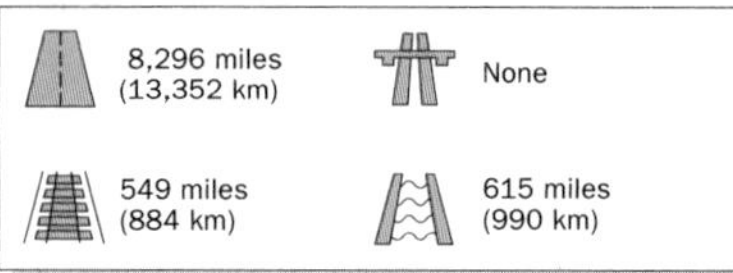

Good roads link the towns, but volcanic ash surfaces elsewhere are difficult in the wet. There are almost 400 airstrips.

TOURISM

541,025 visitors

Up 6% in 1990

MAIN OVERSEAS ARRIVALS

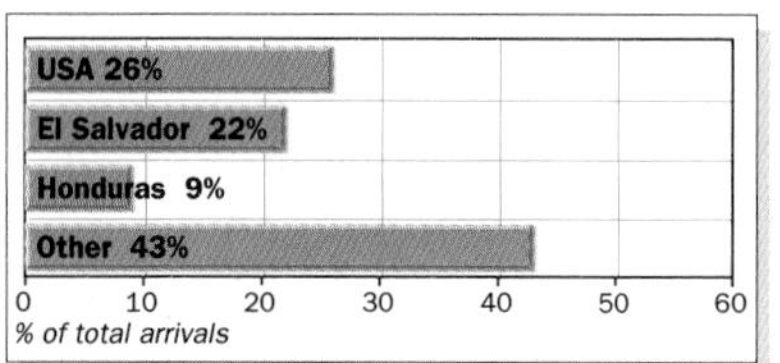

Almost destroyed by military excesses in the 1980s, tourism rapidly revived after the return to civilian rule and is now the third-largest foreign exchange earner. Mayan ruins are top attractions.

PEOPLE

Quiché, Mam, Cakchiquel, Kekchí, Spanish

220 people per sq. mile

THE URBAN/RURAL POPULATION SPLIT

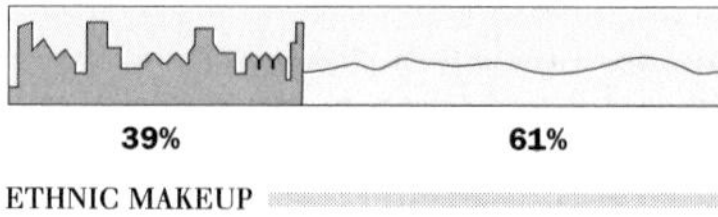

ETHNIC MAKEUP

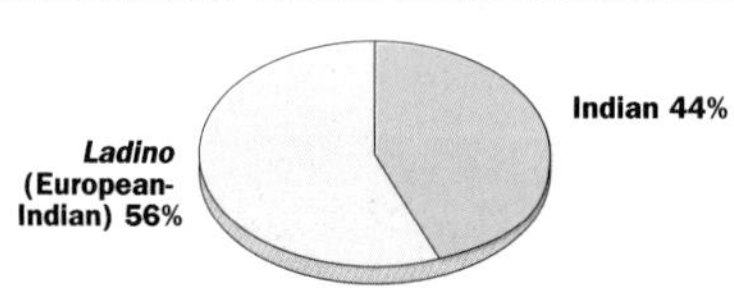

About 50% of Guatemalans are Indians, descendants of the founders of the Mayan civilization. Culture and language distinguish them from *ladino*, or non-Indian, groups. *Ladinos* include a white elite, a large mixed-race group, and now also Indians who have rejected traditional dress and language to escape oppression and marginalization. Political power and 65% of land are in the hands of a few *ladino* families. Indians mainly live in the highlands, by subsistence farming. Women are legally as well as traditionally discriminated against.

POLITICS

1995

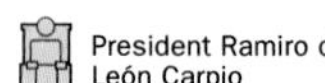

President Ramiro de León Carpio

THE STATE OF THE PARTIES

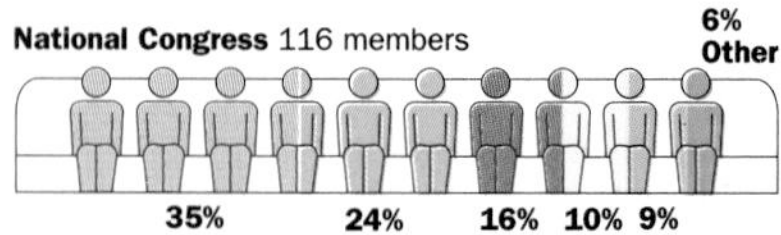

UCN = National Center Union **PDCG** = Christian Democratic Party of Guatemala **MAS** = Solidarity and Action Movement **PAN** = National Advancement Party **Coal.** = Coalition (composed of Constitutional Democratic Party, Guatemalan Republican Front, National Unity Front)

In 1954, the military, with US backing, toppled a democratic government pledged to land and social reforms. Its 32-year rule was based on the violent suppression of all opposition. The huge increase in death-squad murders and the scorched-earth campaigns against highland Indians from 1979 to 1984 led to the suspension of US support. International criticism and the wishes of moderate army factions helped bring back civilian rule in 1986. In 1993, the courts prevented President Serrano from imposing a new dictatorship. The former human rights ombudsman, Ramiro de León Carpio, was chosen to succeed him. However, he too remains dependent on military support to contain the rise in crime and continued guerrilla activity.

GUATEMALA

Total Area : 108 890 sq. km
(42 043 sq. miles)

POPULATION

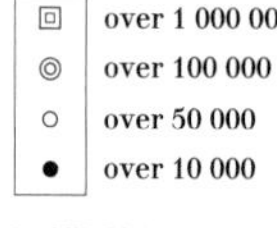

LAND HEIGHT

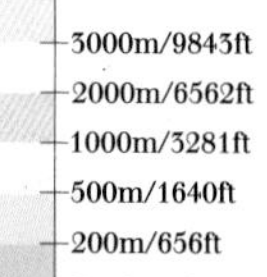

CENTRAL AMERICA
Mexico
Belize
GUATEMALA
Honduras
El Salvador
North America

WORLD AFFAIRS

OAS ECLAC LAES CACM GATT

Relations with the USA are central, but strained by human rights issues – as they were from 1979–1984. Guatemala renounced its claim to Belize in 1986.

AID

 $85m (receipts)  Down 3% in 1991

The USA was the major donor in the 1980s, but human rights concerns and changing policy in the region have led to cuts in military and economic aid in the 1990s. Donors are pushing hard for IMF-backed trade liberalization.

DEFENSE

 $94.6m  Down 13% in 1993

In 1994, the army was put in charge of internal security after police failure to contain violence and crime. Indian-dominated URNG guerrillas have been the main armed opposition since the 1980s. Most arms come from the USA.

ECONOMICS

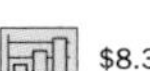 $8.3bn  5.83 quetzales

SCORE CARD

- ❑ WORLD GNP RANKING..........87th
- ❑ GNP PER CAPITA..........$856
- ❑ BALANCE OF PAYMENTS..........$–705.9m
- ❑ INFLATION..........32.8%
- ❑ UNEMPLOYMENT..........13%

STRENGTHS
Central America's largest economy. Agriculture key sector. Top exports: coffee, sugar, bananas, beef, cardamom.

WEAKNESSES
Low GDP growth and investment. Widening trade deficit. Rising inflation. Extreme inequalities in land and wealth distribution limit the domestic market and agriculture modernization.

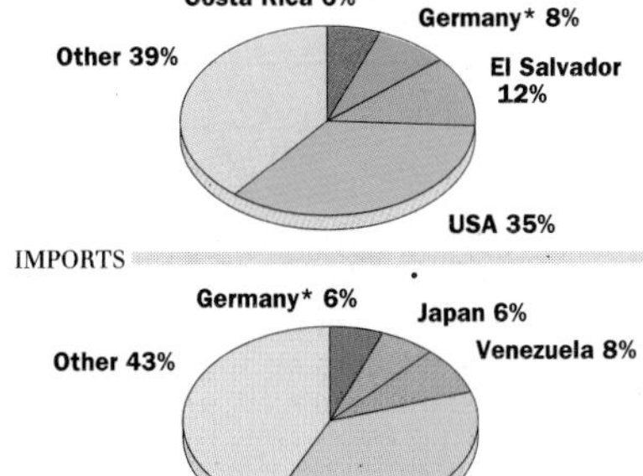

North Acropolis, Tikal, Petén. One of the largest lowland Mayan cities, Tikal was virtually abandoned by about AD 900.

RESOURCES

 2.4bn kwh (capacity 700,000 kw)

 Reserves of 27,000,000 bbl; refines 16,000 b/cd

 2m cattle, 800,000 pigs, 660,000 sheep

 Oil, antimony, lead, tungsten, nickel, copper

Agriculture provides 25% of GDP and about 70% of export earnings. Guerrilla activity has hindered exploitation of oil reserves. The Chixoy hydro-plant, which generates 65% of power, was closed by low rainfall in 1991–1992.

ENVIRONMENT

 8% (0.5% partially protected)

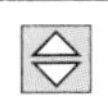 Environmental laws have been enacted but had little effect

Guatemala means "land of trees," but its rich biodiversity is endangered. Forest cover has been halved to 35% since 1954. The quetzal, the national bird, is one of 133 near-extinct species. Urban pollution and erosion are problems.

MEDIA

 The media is ostensibly free, but journalists are still subjected to beatings and death threats, despite the return to civilian rule

PUBLISHING AND BROADCAST MEDIA

 There are 8 daily newspapers, including *Prensa Libre, Siglo Veintiuno, El Gráfico* and the state *Diario de Centro América*

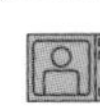 1 state-owned, 4 independent stations

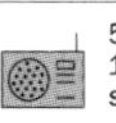 5 state-owned, 140 independent stations

Intimidation, coupled with low pay, explain the lack of critical and investigative reporting of both human rights abuses and the government.

CRIME

 Guatemala does not publish prison figures

 All types of crime are increasing

A rapid escalation in violent crime is overshadowing concern, locally, about continuing human rights abuses.

EDUCATION

 48%

The capital takes 70% of an education budget of under 2% of GDP. As a result, Guatemala has 75% rural illiteracy, the worst record in Latin America.

CHRONOLOGY

Site of the Mayan civilization, Guatemala declared independence from Spain in 1821. It became fully independent in 1838, when the Central American Federation ended.

- ❑ **1954** US-backed coup topples reformist democratic government.
- ❑ **1966–1968** Counter-insurgency war; first use of "disappearances" as a terror tactic in Latin America.
- ❑ **1978–1984** Highlands "pacification"; thousands flee to Mexico and USA.
- ❑ **1986** President Cerezo of the PDCG becomes civilian president.
- ❑ **1991** President Serrano takes over.
- ❑ **1993** Fails in attempt at personal dictatorship. Flees country. Ramiro de León Carpio chosen as president.

G

HEALTH

 1 per 1,370 people

Gastrointestinal and respiratory diseases

Mortality rates are the highest, and health spending is the lowest in Central America. Some 70% of funding goes to the capital, where 80% of doctors work. Most deaths are linked to poverty.

WEALTH

 The majority of the population lives a subsistence existence

CONSUMER GOODS OWNERSHIP

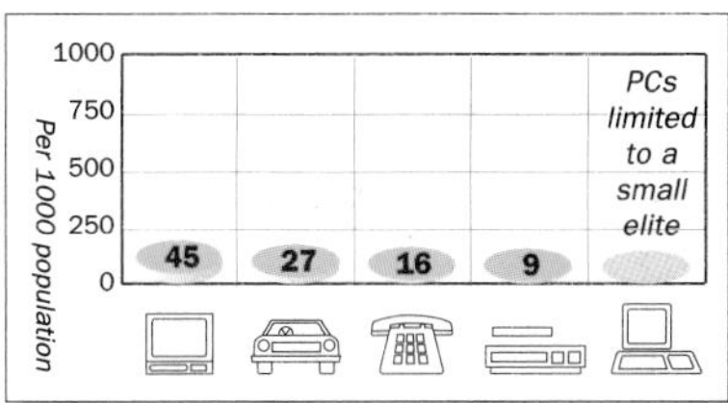

Poverty has risen since 1980 – 90% now live below the poverty line. The rich 10% control 45% of national wealth.

WORLD RANKING

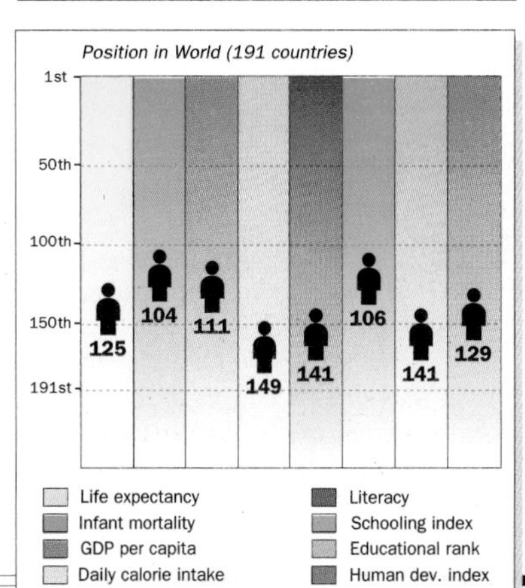

GUINEA

WEST AFRICA
Africa
Mali
Senegal
Guinea-Bissau
GUINEA
Sierra Leone
Ivory Coast

OFFICIAL NAME: Republic of Guinea **CAPITAL:** Conakry **POPULATION:** 5.9 million
CURRENCY: Guinea franc **OFFICIAL LANGUAGE:** French

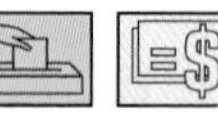
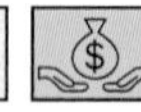

GUINEA LIES ON the western coast of Africa. Coastal plains and swamps in the west rise to densely forested or savanna highlands before sloping down to the semi-desert of the north. Since 1984, the country has been under military rule; in 1993 presidential elections were allowed.

CLIMATE

WEATHER CHART

Conakry, Guinea's capital, receives particularly heavy rainfall, with an average of 51 in. in July alone

130/51

Average daily temperature | Rainfall

°C/°F | cm/in

J F M A M J J A S O N D

60/140, 50/122, 40/104, 30/86, 20/68, 10/50, 0/32

90/35, 80/31, 70/28, 60/24, 50/20, 40/16, 30/12, 20/8, 10/4, 0

Guinea's climate is similar to that of Sierra Leone; the rainy season lasts from April to September.

COMMUNICATIONS

1 ship
100 dwt

THE TRANSPORTATION NETWORK

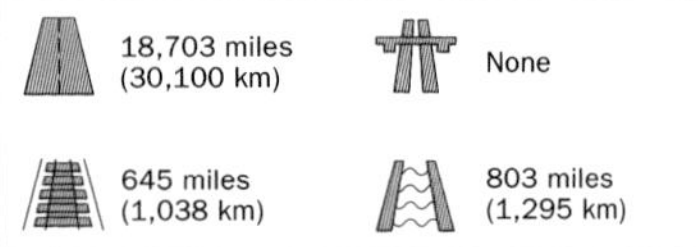

Major roads and rail lines are being rebuilt with World Bank and French aid. Much of the rail network is exclusively for the use of the bauxite industry.

A small mosque in Conakry. *Muslims make up 85% of the population; 8% are Christian. The remainder follow traditional beliefs.*

TOURISM

 5,600 visitors

 Up 24% in 1991

MAIN OVERSEAS ARRIVALS

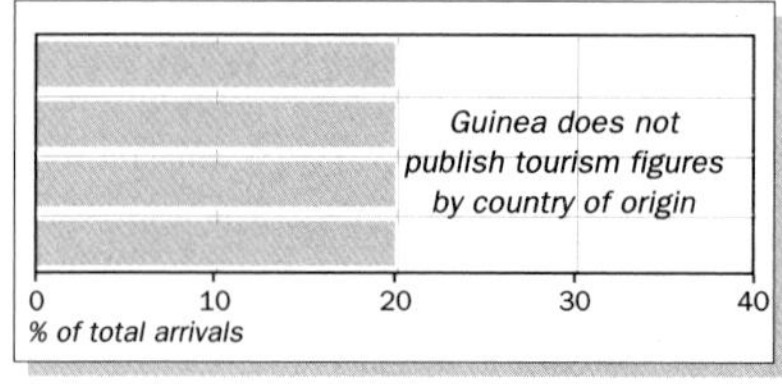

Limited infrastructure means that Guinea cannot exploit the tourist potential of its beaches, scenery and rich culture.

PEOPLE

 Fulani, Malinke, Soussou, French

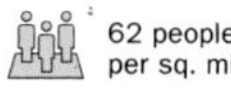 62 people per sq. mile

THE URBAN/RURAL POPULATION SPLIT

26% 74%

ETHNIC MAKEUP

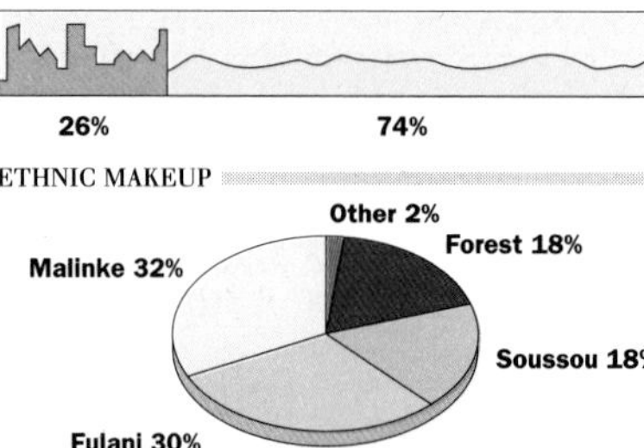

Guinea has a population of over six million people consisting of a number of ethnic groups. Since 1984, and the death of the Marxist dictator Sekou Touré, traditional rivalries have re-emerged. The largest ethnic group, the Malinke, lost the power they held under Touré, and have suffered reprisals. Today, the coastal peoples, including the Soussou, are dominant, benefiting from renewed rivalry between the two major groups – Malinke and Fulani, the latter based in the western highland region of Fouta Jallon.

Daily life in Guinea revolves around the extended family, which survived the climate of suspicion generated by paid informers under Touré. Women acquired influence within Touré's Marxist party, but a Muslim revival since 1984 has reversed this trend.

POLITICS

 1994

 President Gen. Lansana Conté

THE STATE OF THE PARTIES

Transitional Committee for National Recovery 15 members

Following the adoption of a new constitution in 1990, parliamentary elections were scheduled to take place after the 1993 presidentials

Politics in Guinea are in a state of flux. In 1984, Sekou Touré died, having headed the Marxist single-party regime of the Guinea Democratic Party (PDG) since 1958. This opened the way for the military to intervene, with promises of multiparty elections to come. In 1990, a referendum overwhelmingly approved the changes, but the military appointed a Transitional Committee to run the country. The tactic was to delay democratization for as long as possible.

When presidential elections were finally held at the end of 1993, the incumbent, Gen. Lansana Conté, won with 52% of the votes. His closest rival, the Malinke leader Alpha Condé, who had been in exile until 1992, received 20% of the votes. This was widely contested by opposition parties, which alleged the elections had been rigged. Serious violence broke out after the result was announced.

Guinea was dominated for so long by the PDG that the new parties tend to lack experience and effective organization. There is evidence that some oppression of opposition groups still exists.

WORLD AFFAIRS

Guinea is an important financial backer of ECOWAS and contributes to its multinational force in neighboring Liberia. A growing concern is balancing the interests of its two major aid donors, France and the USA.

AID

 $371m (receipts)

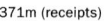

 Up 25% in 1991

In 1969, the World Bank funded the Boké bauxite project, one of its most ambitious projects at that time. Western aid dried up during the Touré years; but, since 1986, it has returned in full force, now financing more than 85% of all Guinea's development projects.

GUINEA

Total Area : 245 860 sq. km (94 926 sq. miles)

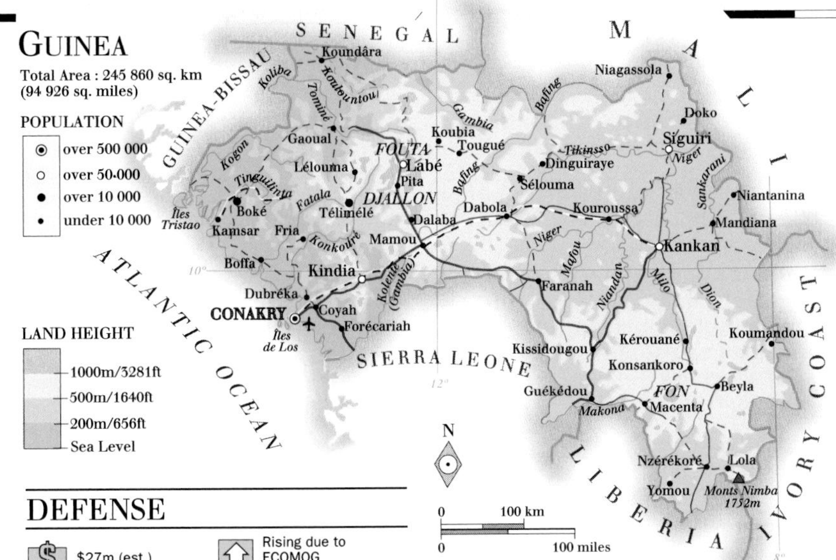

DEFENSE

 $27m (est.)

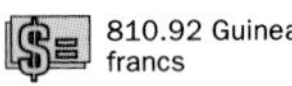 Rising due to ECOMOG commitments

Defense forces consist of a 10,000-strong army and 7,000-strong militia, which have been partly merged since the 1984 coup. China, North Korea and the Eastern bloc used to be the main arms procurement markets. Most weaponry is now supplied by France and the USA.

ECONOMICS

 $3.1bn

810.92 Guinea francs

SCORE CARD

- ❑ WORLD GNP RANKING........................123rd
- ❑ GNP PER CAPITA $480
- ❑ BALANCE OF PAYMENTS....................$-291m
- ❑ INFLATION 22.7%
- ❑ UNEMPLOYMENT....Widespread underemployment

STRENGTHS

Wide range of natural resources, including bauxite, gold, diamonds. Major iron ore deposits at Mount Nimba. Good soil and climate lead to high cash-crop yields and allow Guinea the prospect of self-sufficiency in food.

WEAKNESSES

Years of confused state control under Touré make IMF and World Bank reforms hard to implement. Limited and antiquated infrastructure.

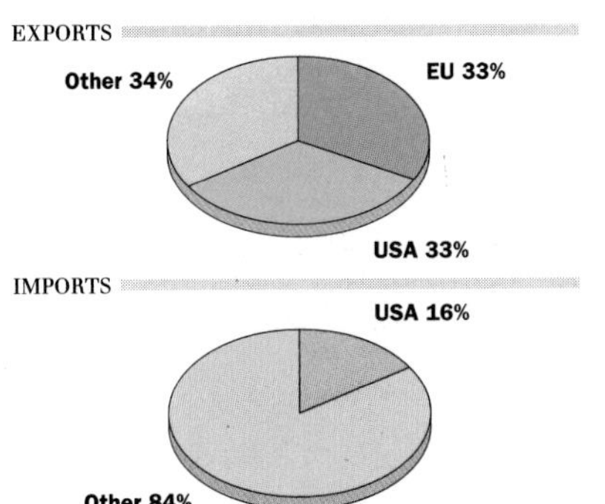

RESOURCES

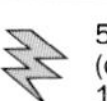 518m kwh (capacity 176,000 kw)

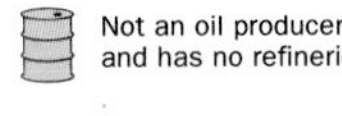

1.8m cattle, 506,000 sheep, 33,000 pigs

Bauxite, diamonds, gold, iron

Bauxite accounts for over 90% of export earnings. Guinea, with 30% of known world reserves, is the world's largest producer after Australia. Demand for electricity for bauxite processing is high. Aid from former Yugoslavia funded the dam on the Bafing River.

ENVIRONMENT

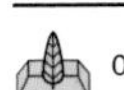 0.7%

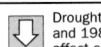

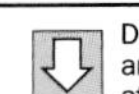 Droughts, as in 1973 and 1983, seriously affect savanna areas

Uncontrolled deforestation, particularly of rainforest areas, is the major long-term problem.

MEDIA

 Although there has been a relaxation of strict censorship, political parties are still communicating through pamphlets

PUBLISHING AND BROADCAST MEDIA

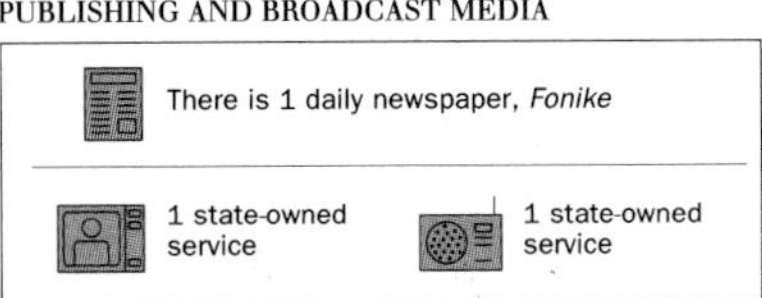

For a country of almost six million, Guinea has a limited media. There has been a relaxation in censorship. *Horoya*, the main newspaper, is a weekly.

CRIME

 Guinea does not publish prison figures

 Down 16% in 1990

The state's human rights record has not improved since 1984 and there has been an increase in political violence. Diamond smuggling is commonplace.

CHRONOLOGY

France made Guinea a colony in 1890, strongly opposed by the Fulani Muslim empire of Fouta Djallon.

- ❑ 1958 Full independence under Sekou Touré. France ends support.
- ❑ 1970 Coup attempt by Portuguese-backed exiles fails.
- ❑ 1984 Touré dies. Army coup.
- ❑ 1990 Referendum on democracy.

EDUCATION

 24%

French was readopted as the main teaching language in 1984, after Touré's decolonizing teaching experiments.

HEALTH

 1 per 10,300 people

 Malaria, diarrheal and respiratory diseases, tuberculosis

Health provision is very poor, reflected in an infant mortality rate of 144 per 1,000 live births and an average life expectancy of 42.5 years.

WEALTH

 Manual worker, 150,000 Guinea francs per month; secretary, 300,000 Guinea francs per month

CONSUMER GOODS OWNERSHIP

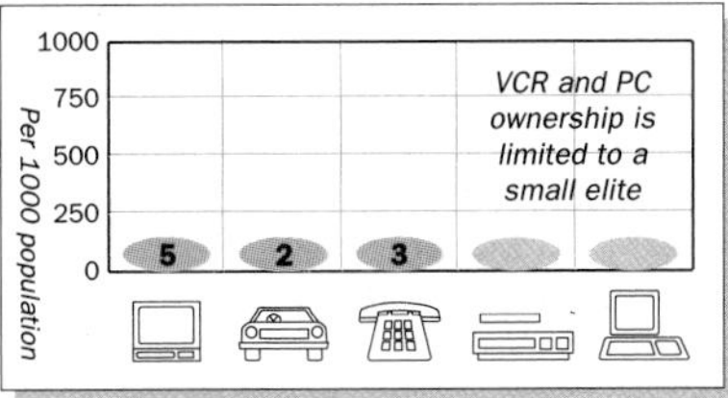

Poverty is endemic, but private enterprise has brought with it a new business class and some wealthy exiles. French and American canned foods are highly favored by the rich.

WORLD RANKING

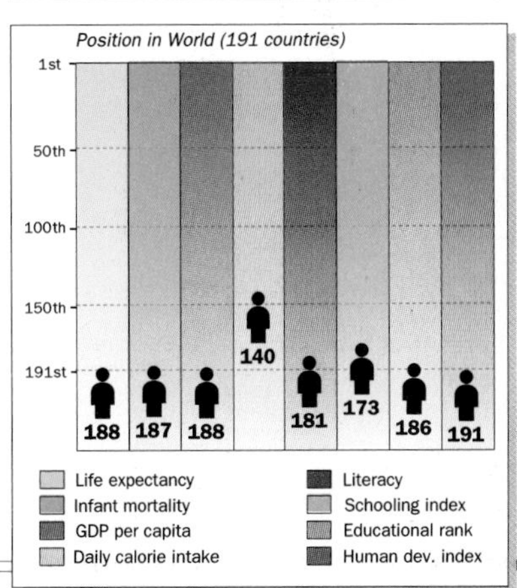

G

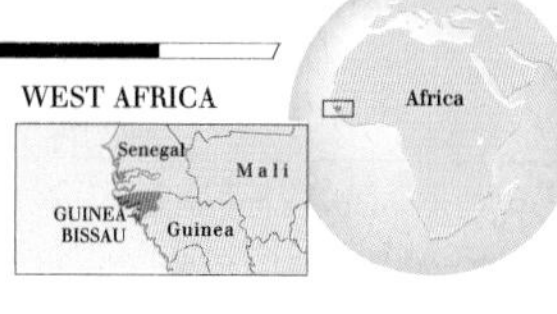

GUINEA–BISSAU

OFFICIAL NAME: Republic of Guinea-Bissau **CAPITAL:** Bissau
POPULATION: 1 million **CURRENCY:** Guinea peso **OFFICIAL LANGUAGE:** Portuguese

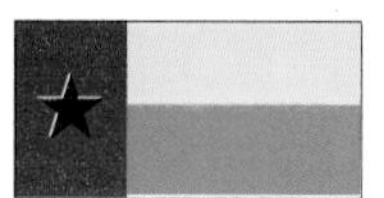

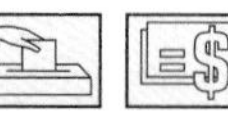

LYING ON AFRICA'S west coast, Guinea-Bissau is bordered by Senegal to the north and Guinea to the south and east. Apart from savanna highlands in the northeast, the country is low-lying. In 1974, it was the first Portuguese colony to gain independence. The ruling PAIGC initiated a process of change to multiparty democracy in 1990, as a result of which elections were held in 1994. Guinea-Bissau is one of the world's poorest countries.

G

CLIMATE

WEATHER CHART

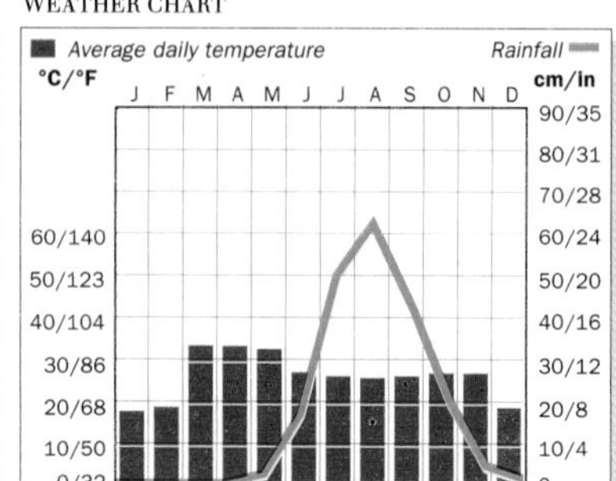

The climate is tropical. The north is affected by the Sahel, the wetter south by the Atlantic. Droughts can occur.

COMMUNICATIONS

Bissalanca International, Bissau

THE TRANSPORTATION NETWORK

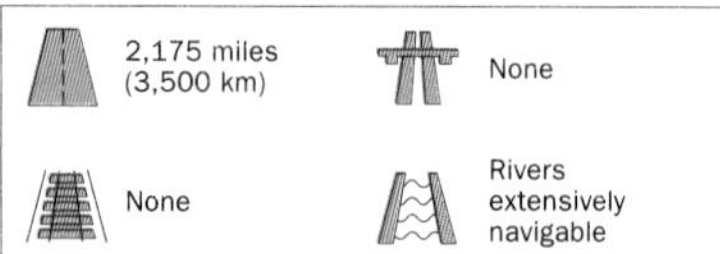

The many rivers, estuaries and islands make water transportation as important as the roads. Both are improving.

TOURISM

A small number of visitors

No significant change from year to year

MAIN OVERSEAS ARRIVALS

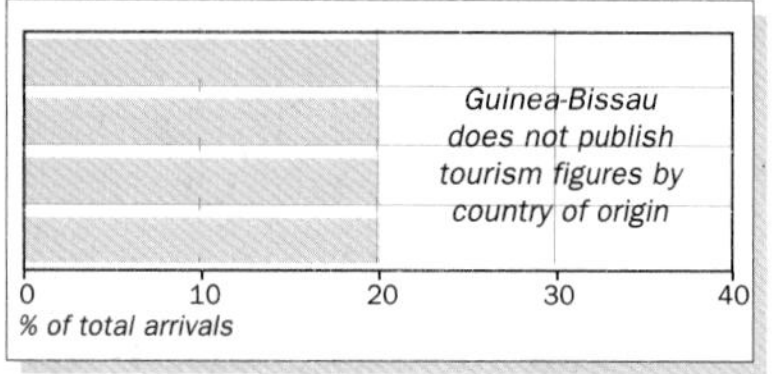

Guinea-Bissau's lack of tourist facilities make it a destination for only the most independent of travelers.

PEOPLE

Portuguese Creole, Balante, Fulani, Malinke, Portuguese

73 people per sq. mile

THE URBAN/RURAL POPULATION SPLIT

20% 80%

RELIGIOUS PERSUASION

Indigenous beliefs 1% Christian 9% Muslim 90%

About 98% of Guinea-Bissau's people come from indigenous ethnic groups. The largest is the southern Balante, who form almost one-third of the population. Mixed-race *mestiço* and European minorities make up just 2% of the population. Although small in number, the *mestiços* – many of whom derive from Cape Verde, Portugal's other former West African colony – still dominate the bureaucracy and the top ranks of the PAIGC. Resentment at this, especially among the Balante who provided most of the PAIGC troops in the independence war, was one cause of the 1980 coup. The majority of the population lives and works on small family farms, grouped in self-contained villages. The bulk of the urban population lives in the capital, Bissau.

POLITICS

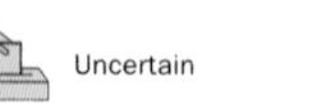
Uncertain

President Brig-Gen João Bernardo Vieira

THE STATE OF THE PARTIES

National Assembly 100 members

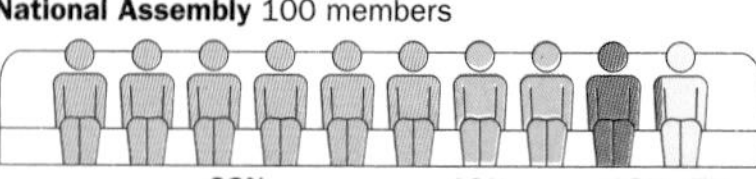

PAIGC = African Party for the Independence of Guinea-Bissau and Cape Verde **PRGB-MB** = Guinea-Bissau Resistance Party - Bafata Movement **PRS** = Party for Social Renovation

Council of State 15 members

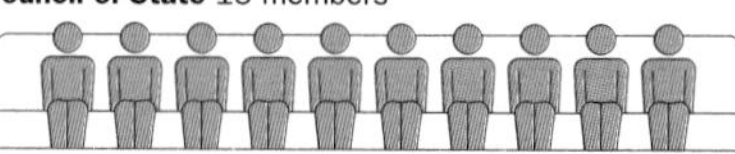

Members are elected by the National People's Assembly from among their own number

Guinea-Bissau has been ruled by the PAIGC since independence in 1974. Since 1990, it has been moving slowly toward multiparty democracy. The country's first multiparty elections were eventually held in 1994, after repeated postponements. The elections, which were declared free and fair by international observers, saw the PAIGC returned to power with an absolute majority. The opposition has, however, disputed the result and declared its intention not to participate in the new government, and continuing political instability is probable.

WORLD AFFAIRS

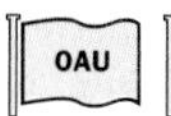

Guinea-Bissau's foreign policy is non-aligned. It trades mainly with the West. Maritime border disputes have until recently soured relations with Senegal and Guinea. Casamance separatist bases in north Guinea-Bissau are a source of tension in relations with Senegal.

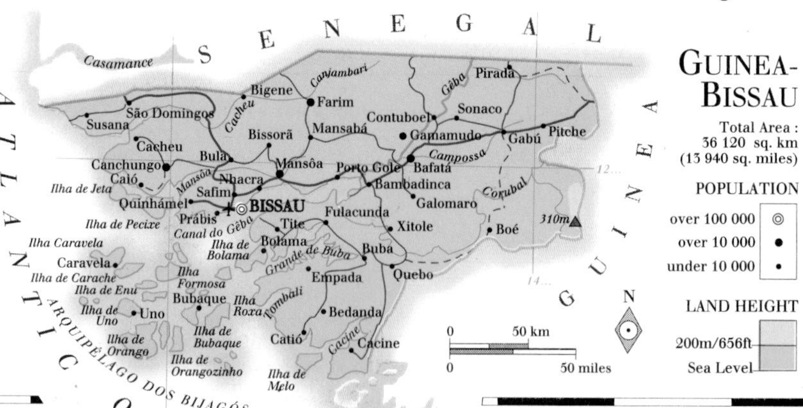

AID

 $101m (receipts)  Down 14% in 1991

Portugal is Guinea-Bissau's largest aid donor. Balance of payments support is critical to the economy. Export earnings rarely top $20 million and import and debt service costs are over $100 million. Donors, however, have largely frozen support since 1991 because of Guinea-Bissau's World Bank arrears. Although now virtually bankrupt, the government has pushed ahead with economic reforms begun in the mid-1980s in the hope of restoring aid credits. The infrastructure, education and health-care are the main targets of project aid.

DEFENSE

 $4.43m  Little change from year to year

The lower ranks of the 9,200-strong armed forces are mainly Balante from the south. Resentment at their lack of promotion and the predominance of *mestiços* in the senior ranks was a cause of the 1980 coup. Troops serve with the UN in Angola and Mozambique.

ECONOMICS

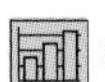 $219m 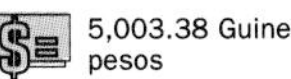 5,003.38 Guinea pesos

SCORE CARD

- ❑ WORLD GNP RANKING........................175th
- ❑ GNP PER CAPITA..............................$219
- ❑ BALANCE OF PAYMENTS.....................$-72m
- ❑ INFLATION..50%
- ❑ UNEMPLOYMENT..................................17%

STRENGTHS

Minimal at present, but good potential in fisheries and timber. Both are barely exploited. Offshore oil potential.

WEAKNESSES

Lack of sufficiency in rice staple. Few exports, mainly cashew nuts, groundnuts. Minimal industry. Lack of an entrepreneurial business class. High illiteracy. Poor state economic management.

EXPORTS

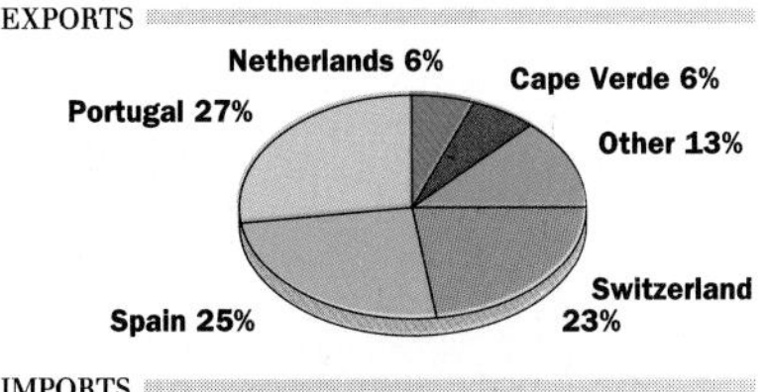

IMPORTS

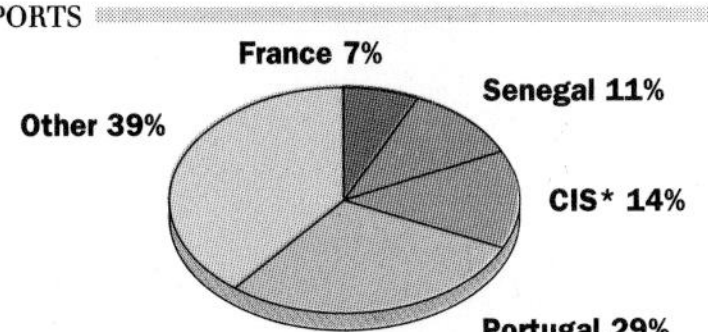

***Bafatá, the main town** in central Guinea-Bissau. It lies on the Gêba River and is also an important inland port.*

RESOURCES

 17m kwh (capacity 7,000 kw)  Not an oil producer and has no refineries

 340,000 cattle, 290,000 pigs, 205,000 sheep  Bauxite, phosphate, oil

Fish and timber are the main natural resources, but local exploitation is only 10% of the sustainable levels of 250,000 tons and 100,000 tons a year. Guinea Bissau's considerable hydro-power potential is also under-exploited.

ENVIRONMENT

 None — Economic growth has precedence over ecological concerns

Drought and locust plagues are serious natural hazards. Due to a small population and minimal industry there are few serious environmental problems.

MEDIA

 Censorship is still strong, but press freedom has increased markedly since 1991

PUBLISHING AND BROADCAST MEDIA

 There are 2 daily newspapers, *Voz da Guiné* and *Nô Printcha*, published by the government

 1 state-owned service  1 state-owned service

Only one newspaper, *Baguerra*, and one magazine, *Expresso-Bissau*, are not state-owned. Portugal helps to fund the TV service, started in 1989.

CRIME

 Guinea-Bissau does not publish prison figures 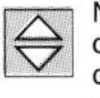 No significant change in crime levels

The death penalty was abolished in 1993. Reform of the legal system is in progress to make it more independent of the PAIGC. The government has been criticized for human rights abuses.

EDUCATION

 36%

Only 38% of children attend the rudimentary education service. Guinea-Bissau has no university.

CHRONOLOGY

The Portuguese explored the area in the 15th century. In 1879, Portuguese Guinea became a colony. A war of independence began in the 1960s, led by the PAIGC.

- ❑ **1974** Independence. PAIGC led by Luis Cabral takes power.
- ❑ **1980** Coup. João Vieira replaces Cabral.
- ❑ **1990** Vieira accepts principle of multiparty politics.
- ❑ **1991–1992** Opposition parties formed; election postponed.
- ❑ **1993** Coup attempt. Leading opposition figure João da Costa temporarily detained.

G

HEALTH

 1 per 7,310 people — Parasitic, diarrheal and communicable diseases, malaria

Guinea-Bissau's health statistics are among the world's worst, due partly to the minimal medical facilities. Average life expectancy is just 42 years; infant mortality is 180 per 1,000 live births; the maternal death rate almost one in 100.

WEALTH

 Most of the population lives in poverty

CONSUMER GOODS OWNERSHIP

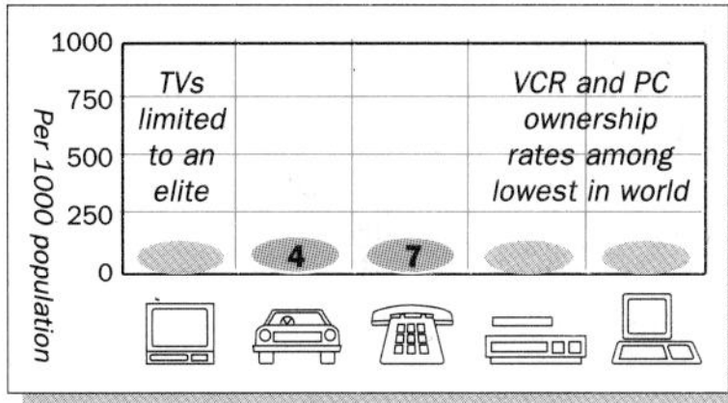

Living conditions for the majority of people are extremely poor; over 70% are unable to meet their basic needs. The tiny elite is mainly *mestiço*.

WORLD RANKING

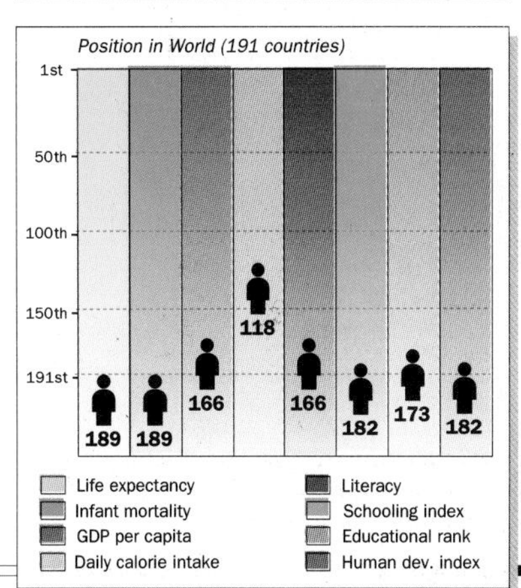

GUYANA

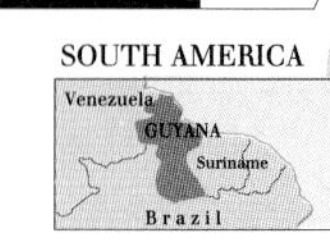

OFFICIAL NAME: Cooperative Republic of Guyana **CAPITAL:** Georgetown
POPULATION: 800,000 **CURRENCY:** Guyana dollar **OFFICIAL LANGUAGE:** English

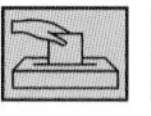

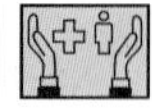

GUYANA LIES ON the northeast coast of South America, bordered by Venezuela, Brazil and Suriname. Dense interior rainforest covers 85% of its territory. Independence from Britain came in 1966. The export of four key products – bauxite, gold, rice and sugar – sustains the economy. The vast majority of Guyana's population lives on the narrow coastal plain, which is partially reclaimed from the sea.

CLIMATE

WEATHER CHART

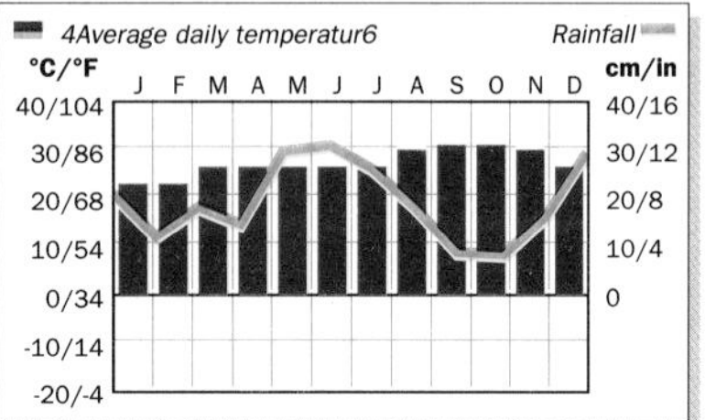

The lowlands are very humid with a constant temperature. The highlands are a little cooler, especially at night.

COMMUNICATIONS

 **Timehri Intl, Georgetown** 270,500 passengers
 11 ships 7,600 dwt

THE TRANSPORTATION NETWORK

4,763 miles (7,665 km)	None
55 miles (88 km)	3,728 miles (6,000 km)

Reliable travel into the interior is by air or river; ferries link coastal roads. The only international airport is Timehri.

TOURISM

 74,881 visitors
 Tourist numbers are increasing slowly

MAIN OVERSEAS ARRIVALS

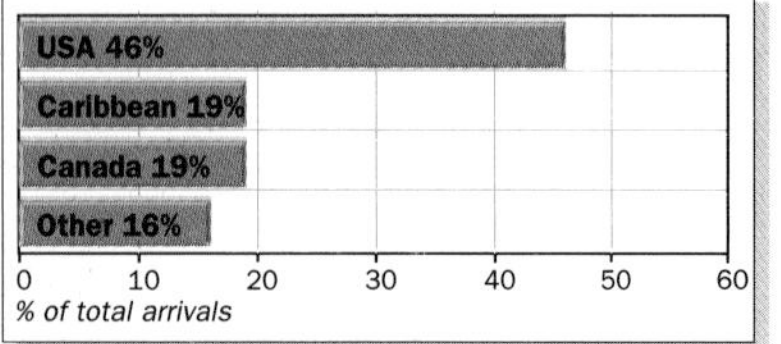

The government is eager to develop ecotourism using private investment. Guyana means "Land of Many Waters;" the Kaieteur Falls are among the world's most impressive. Old Dutch wooden architecture characterizes Georgetown.

Modest homes, Georgetown. *Most buildings there are of wood. The cathedral is one of the world's tallest freestanding wooden buildings.*

PEOPLE

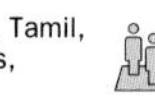
English Creole, Hindi, Tamil, Amerindian languages, English
10 people per sq. mile

THE URBAN/RURAL POPULATION SPLIT

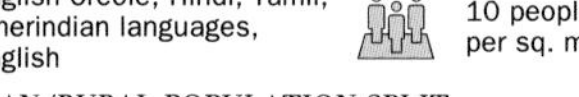

ETHNIC MAKEUP

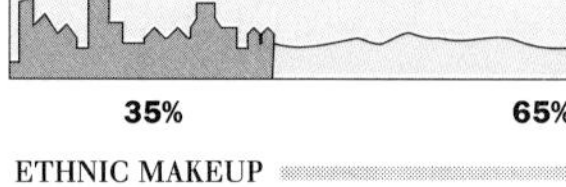

Tension exists between Afro-Guyanese, who are descended from Africans brought over between the 17th and 19th centuries, and Indo-Guyanese, descendants of South Asian laborers brought from India in the 19th century. There were a number of instances of discrimination against Indo-Guyanese during the PNC's rule.

POLITICS

THE STATE OF THE PARTIES

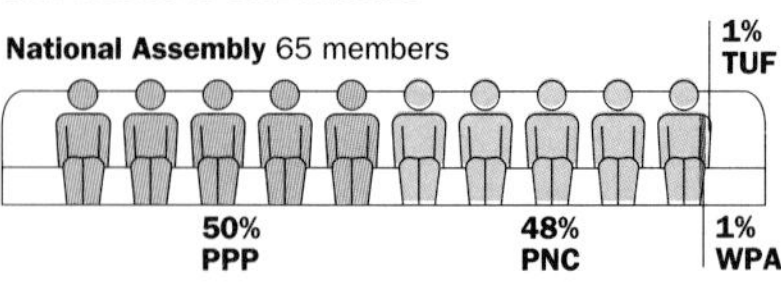

PPP = People's Progressive Party **PNC** = People's National Congress **WPA** = Working People's Alliance **TUF** = The United Force

The main power brokers in Guyana's multiparty democracy are the urban businessmen and professionals who fund the political parties. The 29-year rule of the PNC was characterized by favoritism towards the Afro-Guyanese. This was reversed with the election of the Indo-Guyanese PPP in 1992, in what international observers – and many Guyanese – saw as the first fair election since independence. As leader of the PPP, Cheddi Jagan's switch from avowed Marxism in the 1970s to free-market economics in the 1990s proved a success with voters.

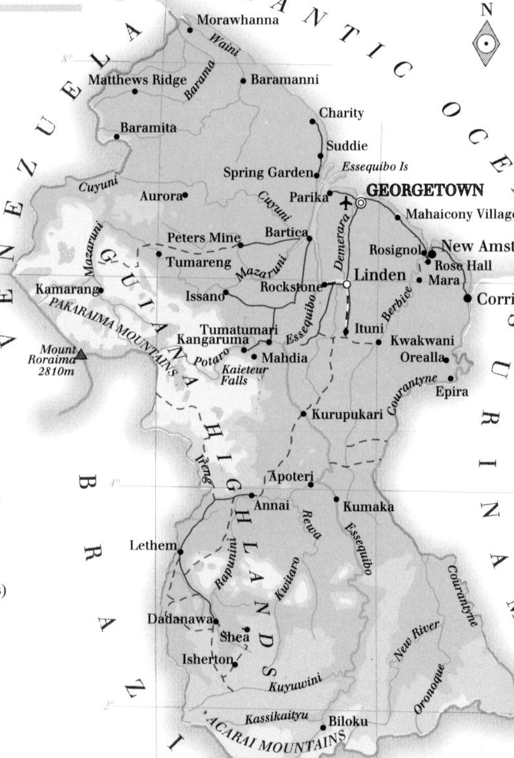

GUYANA

Total Area : 214 970 sq. km (83 000 sq. miles)

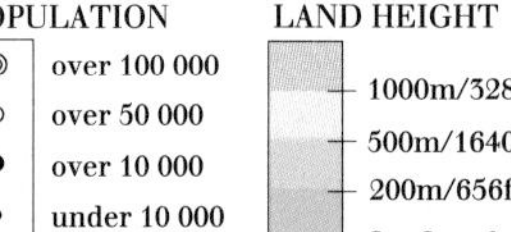

WORLD AFFAIRS

The main foreign policy concern is finding a definitive resolution to a long-standing border dispute with Venezuela, which claims the eastern two-thirds of Guyana.

AID

 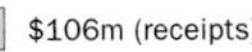 $106m (receipts)  No significant change from year to year

Most of Guyana's aid comes from the USA, EU and UK. Most aid has been in the form of development assistance and project loans.

DEFENSE

 $14.4m 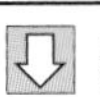 Down 50% between 1986 and 1988

The security forces, which include a 2,000-strong army, benefit from financial support and training provided by the US and UK governments.

ECONOMICS

 $233m  125.79 Guyana dollars

SCORE CARD

- ❑ WORLD GNP RANKING........................174th
- ❑ GNP PER CAPITA $300
- ❑ BALANCE OF PAYMENTS.................$-116.1m
- ❑ INFLATION 56%
- ❑ UNEMPLOYMENT....Widespread underemployment

STRENGTHS

Widespread deregulation of the economy and introduction of a floating exchange rate signal good economic prospects. Bauxite, gold, rice, sugar and diamond production. Sugar production has already increased. Overseas investment in rice and gold will lead to the further development of both sectors.

WEAKNESSES

Narrow economic base, vulnerable to price fluctuations of its main commodities. Dependence on imports.

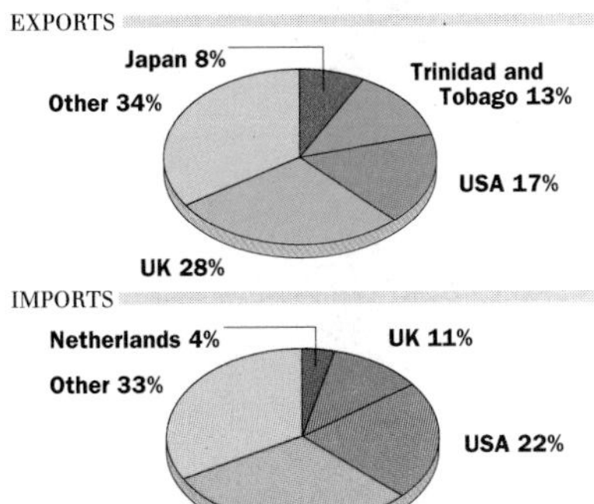

RESOURCES

 220m kwh (capacity 110,000 kw)

 Not an oil producer and has no refineries

210,000 cattle, 185,000 pigs, 120,000 sheep

 Bauxite, gold, diamonds

Gold and bauxite are the main strategic resources in Guyana. However, several companies are prospecting offshore and onshore for oil, amid reports that commercially exploitable deposits have been located. Hydroelectric power plants are planned on the many rivers.

ENVIRONMENT

 0.05%  Some controls on logging

Of major concern is the disrepair of the 18th-century sea defense system. This threatens the urbanized coastline that lies below sea level. There is a growing logging industry, although this is being kept away from parks and rainforest reserves.

MEDIA

 A relaxation of government pressure on the media has been seen in recent years

PUBLISHING AND BROADCAST MEDIA

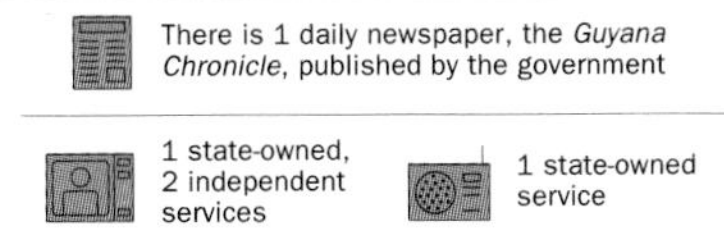
There is 1 daily newspaper, the *Guyana Chronicle*, published by the government

1 state-owned, 2 independent services

1 state-owned service

With the liberalization of the economy, which started with the Hoyte administration, there has been a relaxation of pressure on the media.

CRIME

 Guyana does not publish prison figures  Up 7% in 1984

The poorer neighborhoods of most major towns are considered unsafe to walk in by locals, especially at night. The smuggling of narcotics is an increasing problem.

EDUCATION

 96%

Education is based on the British system. Entry to high schools is by 11-plus examination. Guyana has a state-financed university, although many students go to the USA or UK.

HEALTH

 1 per 6,809 people 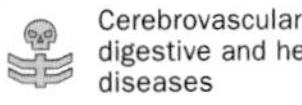 Cerebrovascular, digestive and heart diseases

Around 95% of the population have access to Guyana's mainly state-run health service. The referral system is relatively good.

CHRONOLOGY

During the 17th and 18th centuries, the Dutch founded three colonies in the region – Essequibo, Demerara and Berbice. In 1814, these came under British control, and were later combined to form the colony of British Guiana.

- ❑ **1953** First universal elections won by PPP under leadership of Dr. Cheddi Jagan; parliament later suspended by Britain.
- ❑ **1957** Forbes Burnham founds PNC.
- ❑ **1964** PNC becomes leading force in coalition government.
- ❑ **1966** Independence from Britain.
- ❑ **1973** PPP boycotts parliament, accusing PNC of electoral fraud.
- ❑ **1985** Burnham dies. Replaced by Desmond Hoyte as PNC leader.
- ❑ **1989** Foreign aid suspended; renewed calls for reform.
- ❑ **1992** Fair elections won by PPP.

G

WEALTH

 Wealth is concentrated among a few Georgetown families

CONSUMER GOODS OWNERSHIP

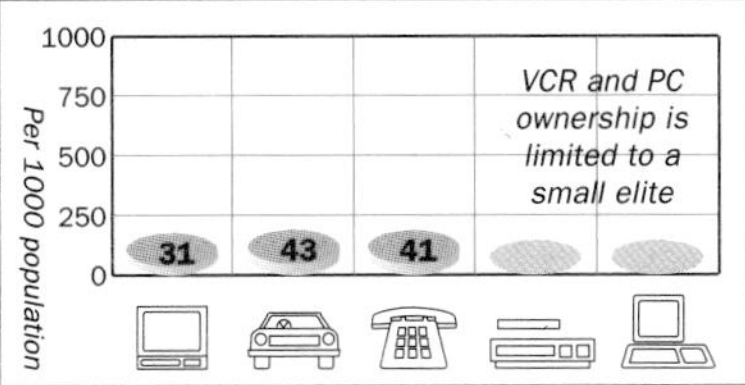

Most Guyanese enjoy a relatively similar standard of living, although there are a few very affluent urban families whose wealth is derived from business and farming. Large air-conditioned four-wheel-drive vehicles and fine whiskies are the major status symbols. The poorest group are Amerindian subsistence farmers.

WORLD RANKING

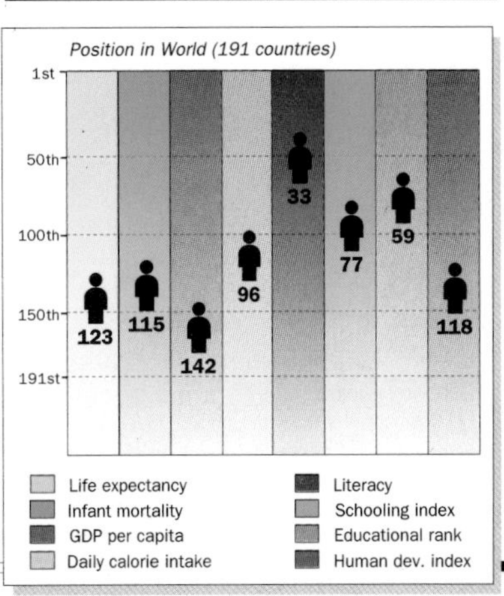

HAITI

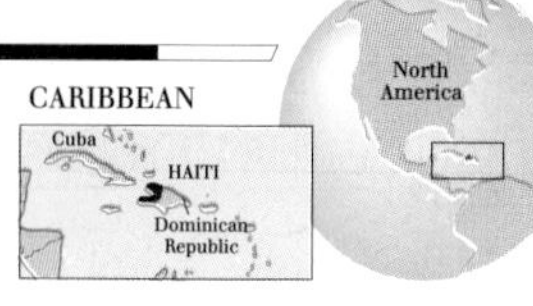

OFFICIAL NAME: Republic of Haiti **CAPITAL:** Port-au-Prince **POPULATION:** 6.5 million
CURRENCY: Gourde **OFFICIAL LANGUAGES:** French and French Creole

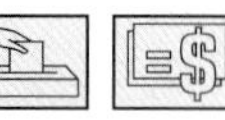

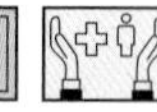

HAITI OCCUPIES THE western third of the Caribbean island of Hispaniola. Formerly a Spanish colony, it was the first Caribbean state to achieve independence, in 1804, and has been in a state of political chaos virtually ever since. Democracy did not materialize with the exile of the dictator Jean-Claude Duvalier in 1986. Elections were held in 1990, but by 1991 the military were back in power and were only ousted in 1994 through US intervention.

CLIMATE

WEATHER CHART

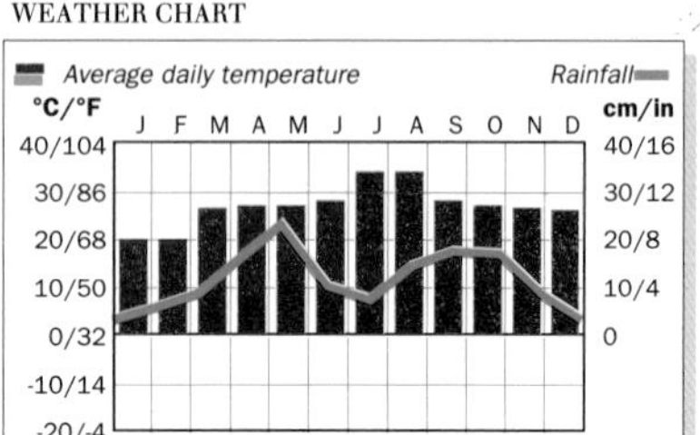

Haiti lies mostly in the rain shadow of the central mountains so is slightly less humid than average for the Caribbean.

COMMUNICATIONS

Port-au-Prince 545,000 passengers

Has no fleet

THE TRANSPORTATION NETWORK

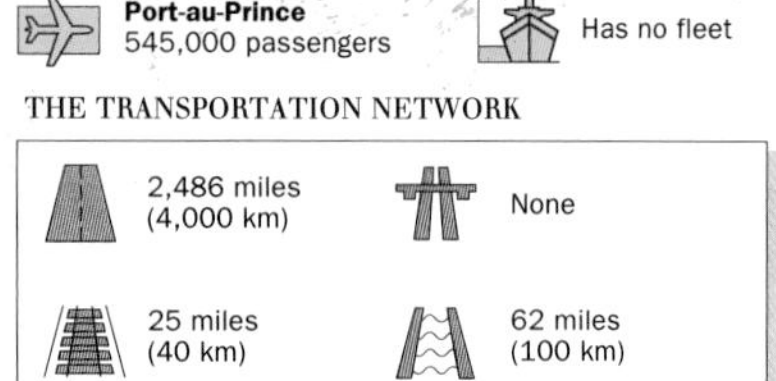

Haiti has a limited road system. Ferries provide the main transportation to the southern peninsula.

TOURISM

120,000 visitors

Down 2% in 1990

MAIN OVERSEAS ARRIVALS

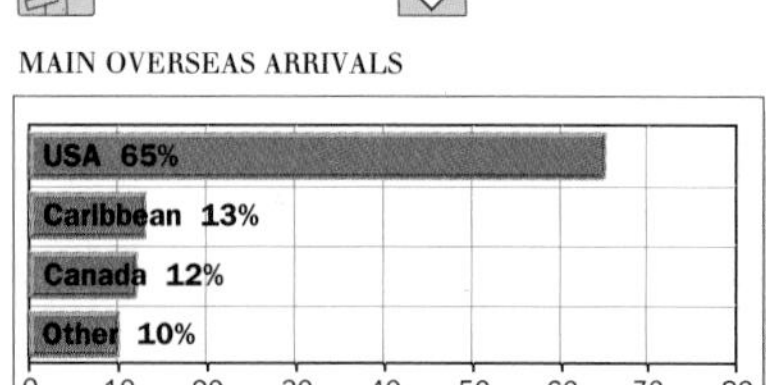

Haiti's location, history and culture provided much of its attraction for tourists in the 1960s and 1970s. The resurgence of political instability and violence in the 1980s, however, led to the industry's near collapse.

PEOPLE

French Creole, French

606 people per sq. mile

THE URBAN/RURAL POPULATION SPLIT

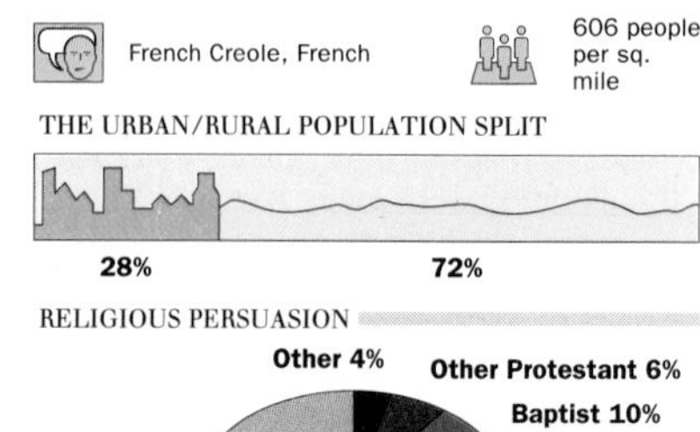

RELIGIOUS PERSUASION

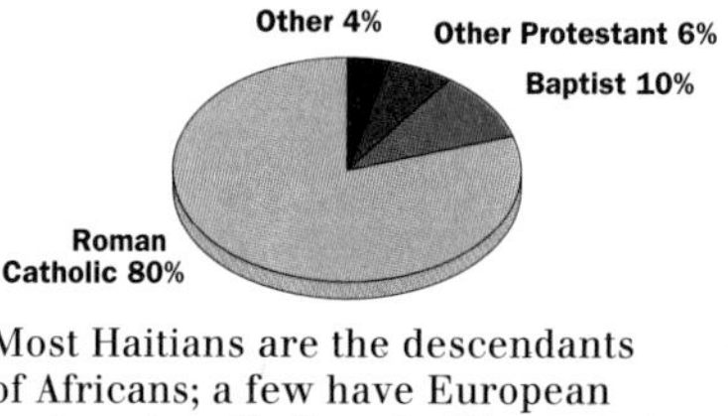

Most Haitians are the descendants of Africans; a few have European roots, primarily French. The majority of the population lives in extreme poverty: Haiti is the poorest country in the Americas; Port-au-Prince has the worst slums in the Caribbean. Social tensions run high, and focus on class rather than race. In recent years, the combination of political repression and a collapsing economy has led many to emigrate illegally to the USA, or across the border to the neighboring Dominican Republic.

POLITICS

THE STATE OF THE PARTIES

Chamber of Deputies 81 members

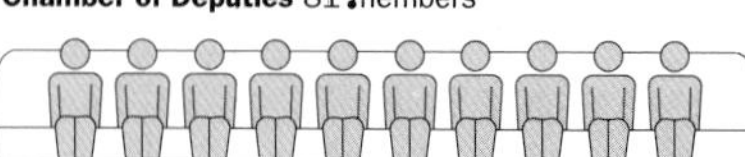

Following the return of President Aristide, elections are scheduled to take place in 1995

Senate 27 members

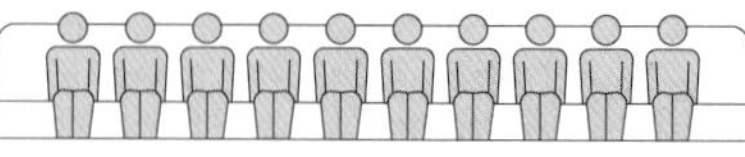

Haiti's politics have long been directly managed by the wealthy businessmen who live in palatial style above Port-au-Prince. It was this group, backed by the military, that supported the popularly detested "Baby Doc" Duvalier regime. It is this same group that, since the overthrow of Duvalier in 1986, has financed regular coups to ensure that the 1987 democratic constitution could not be implemented.

The military last intervened in 1991, following the 1990 election of Fr. Jean-Bertrand Aristide on a populist platform. Aristide was exiled by the army and his supporters suppressed. The UN's move to impose sanctions was answered by the assassination of Haiti's justice minister. In 1994, the flood of refugees fleeing the country forced the US government to step up its action. Following a period of blockade, enforced by its warships, the army was sent in to pave the way for Aristide's return to office.

HAITI

Total Area : 27 750 sq. km (10 714 sq. miles)

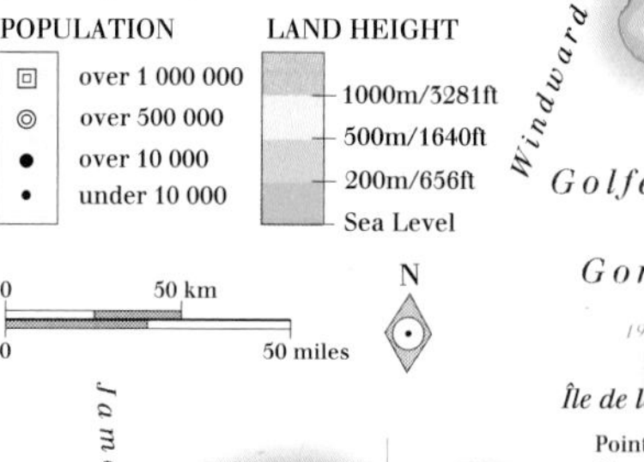

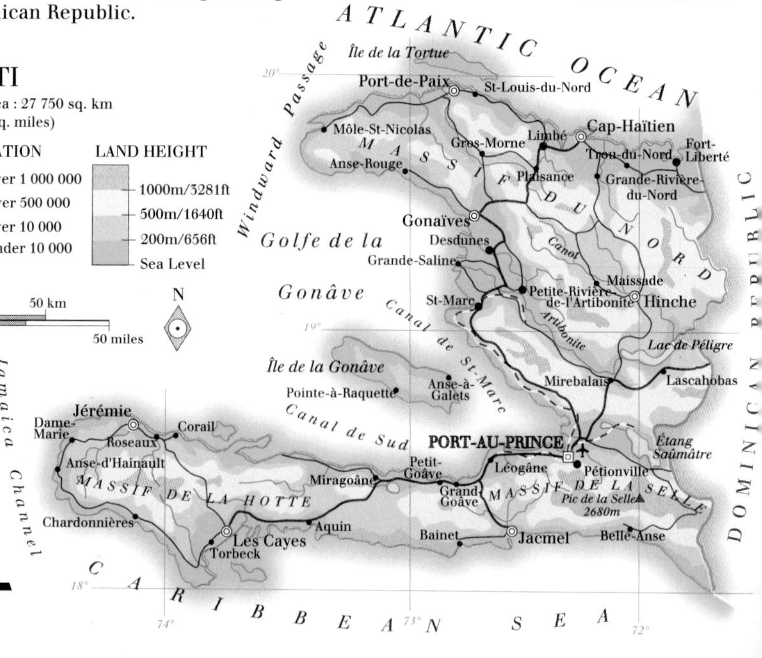

WORLD AFFAIRS

Following three years of sanctions, Haiti's economic links with the outside world have been restored. A UN force is scheduled to remain in the country until early 1996.

AID

 $500m

 New aid pledges make up for sums lost under the military

Aid was cut off following the 1991 military takeover. The USA, France and the IMF have pledged $500 million to the Aristide government, which will help smooth its resumption of power.

DEFENSE

 $29.4m

 Up 73% in 1991

Under the military government, forces were concentrated in the capital; in rural areas, its power was exerted through the *Tontons Macoutes*, who dispensed rough justice. It is planned that a new police force will be set up, trained by a US government agency.

ECONOMICS

 $2.6bn

 11.98 gourdes

SCORE CARD

- ❑ World GNP Ranking 132nd
- ❑ GNP per Capita $370
- ❑ Balance of Payments .... $-10.5m
- ❑ Inflation 15.4%
- ❑ Unemployment 5.2%

Strengths

Few, though outlook improved with lifting of sanctions. Income from coffee and from Haitians living abroad. Large profits from the transportation of narcotics to the USA.

Weaknesses

Political instability. Manufacturing collapsed following sanctions in 1991.

EXPORTS

IMPORTS

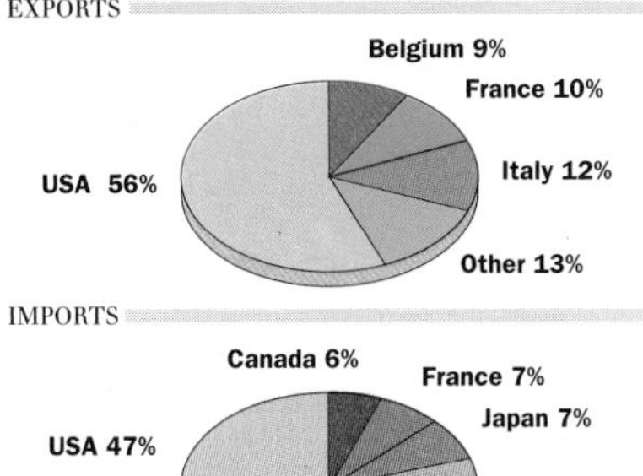

***Haiti is the poorest country in the Americas.** In remote villages, most houses are made of earth and have no windows.*

RESOURCES

 475m kwh (capacity 150,000 kw)

 Not an oil producer and has no refineries

 1.6m cattle, 950,000 pigs, 432,000 horses

 Marble, limestone, clay

Haiti has no strategic resources. Under the recent economic sanctions it had to find unofficial sources of oil; much was imported from Europe.

ENVIRONMENT

 0.4%

 Ecological initiatives hijacked for political purposes

Haiti's ecological problems receive little attention. It is one of the most environmentally degraded countries in the world; one-third of its soil is seriously eroded.

MEDIA

 Following the 1991 coup most radio stations were shut down. Newspapers, almost exclusively in French, are not accessible to most Creoles

PUBLISHING AND BROADCAST MEDIA

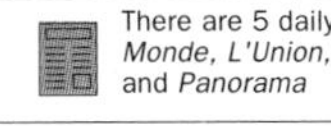 There are 5 daily newspapers, *Le Nouveau Monde, L'Union, Le Nouvelliste, Le Matin* and *Panorama*

 1 state-owned service

 1 state-owned service

The media was controlled through intimidation under the military. Given a successful transition to democracy, an open press should begin to emerge.

CRIME

 Haiti does not publish prison figures

 Crime is rising

Following the 1991 military coup, the authorities and security forces – particularly the *Attachés* – were a major source of crime, frequently terrorizing or murdering politicians and those opposed to military rule.

EDUCATION

 53%

Education, run by the state and the Roman Catholic and missionary churches, is based on the French system. The wealthy are often educated abroad.

CHRONOLOGY

In 1697, Spain ceded the west of Hispaniola to France. Ex-slave Toussaint l'Ouverture's rebellion in 1791 led to independence in 1804.

- ❑ **1915–1934** US occupation.
- ❑ **1957–1971** François "Papa Doc" Duvalier's brutal dictatorship.
- ❑ **1971** Son Jean-Claude, "Baby Doc," takes over. Slight liberalization.
- ❑ **1986** Flees. Gen. Namphy steps in.
- ❑ **1987** Elections abandoned.
- ❑ **1988** Lt.-Gen. Avril takes power.
- ❑ **1990** Father Jean-Bertrand Aristide elected but exiled in 1991 coup.
- ❑ **1994** US forces invade. Gen. Cedras ousted. Fr. Aristide reinstated.

H

HEALTH

 1 per 6,737 people

 Malaria, other parasitic diseases, tuberculosis

Most Haitians cannot afford health care. In rural areas, help is often sought from voodoo priests.

WEALTH

 One million Haitians work as cheap labor in the Dominican Republic, many in effect as slaves on the state-owned sugarcane plantations

CONSUMER GOODS OWNERSHIP

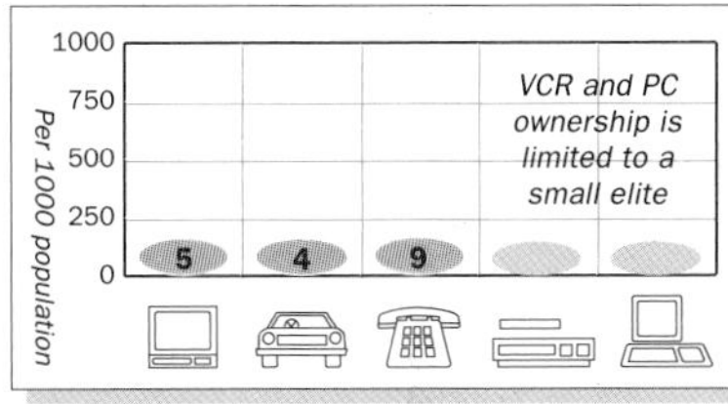

Haiti's rigid class structure maintains extreme disparities of wealth between the mass of the population, who live in slums without running water or proper sanitation, and a few affluent families. These enjoy a luxurious way of life, and educate their children in France.

WORLD RANKING

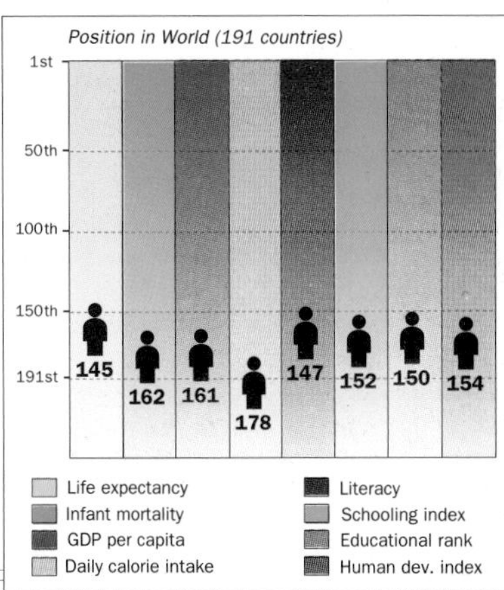

HONDURAS

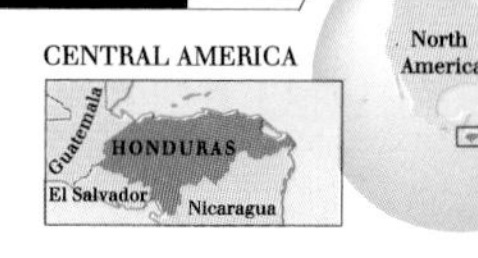

OFFICIAL NAME: Republic of Honduras **CAPITAL:** Tegucigalpa
POPULATION: 5.5 million **CURRENCY:** Lempira **OFFICIAL LANGUAGE:** Spanish

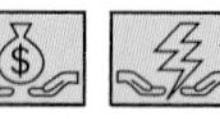

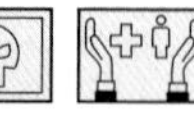

STRADDLING THE Central American isthmus, Honduras has only a short Pacific coast. Its long Caribbean shoreline includes the virtually uninhabited Mosquito Coast, while most of the rest of the country is mountainous. Honduras declared independence from Spain in 1821 and returned to civilian rule in 1981 after a succession of military governments. Honduras is one of the world's leading banana producers, but is very poor and dependent on US aid.

CLIMATE

WEATHER CHART

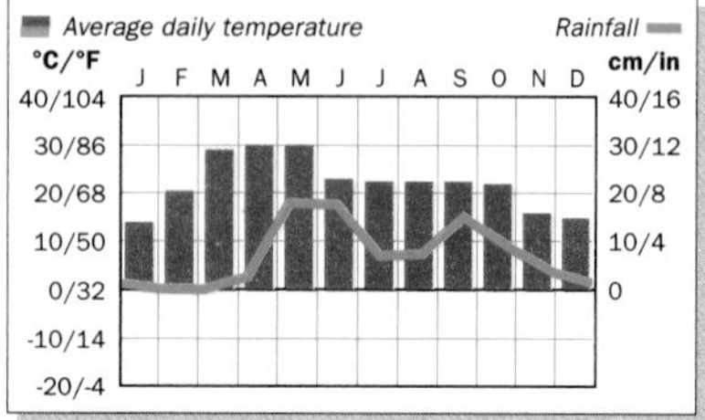

Honduras's Caribbean coast is extremely hot. The central highlands are much cooler.

COMMUNICATIONS

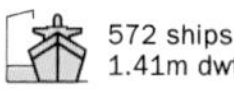

Toncontín, Tegucigalpa 404,000 passengers

572 ships 1.41m dwt

THE TRANSPORTATION NETWORK

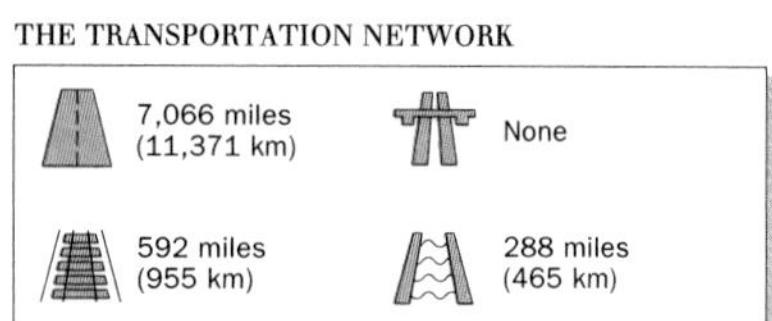

The government plans to close down the remaining railroad and improve the road system with US aid.

TOURISM

243,544 visitors

Up 8% in 1992

MAIN OVERSEAS ARRIVALS

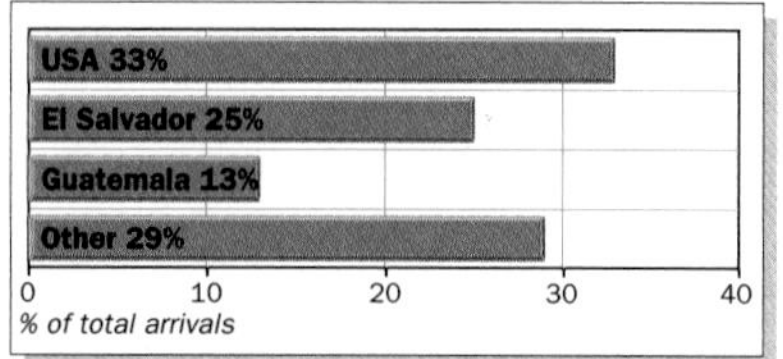

Ecotourism plans include building hotels on the virgin coastline of the Bay of Tela and lodges in the remote region inland from the Mosquito Coast. Jungle river-rafting is a growing sport among wealthy locals and foreigners.

PEOPLE

Spanish, Black Carib, English Creole

119 people per sq. mile

THE URBAN/RURAL POPULATION SPLIT

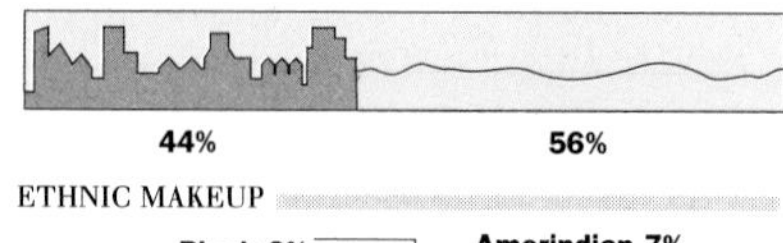

ETHNIC MAKEUP

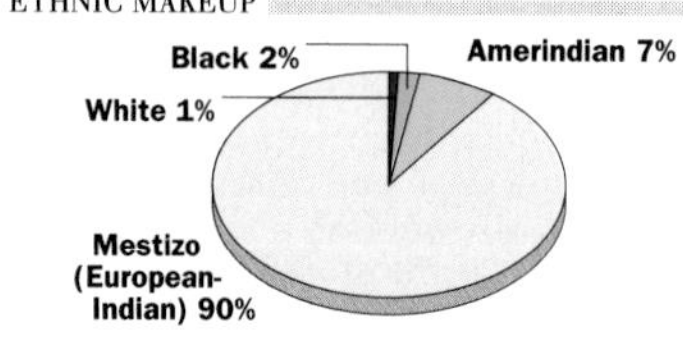

As in most of Central America, very few pure indigenous groups remain. There are an estimated 45,000 Miskito Indians, and an English-speaking black population on the Caribbean coast. Poverty is the primary cause of social tension; whites still have the best opportunities.

Honduras has one of the most unequal societies in the region: 4% of people own 60% of the land. Rural poverty and strong Roman Catholicism (93% are Roman Catholic) mean that the family is a powerful unifying force. Women's status is low; many work in domestic service.

POLITICS

1997

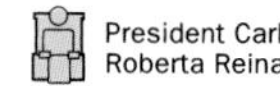

President Carlos Roberta Reina

THE STATE OF THE PARTIES

National Assembly 128 members

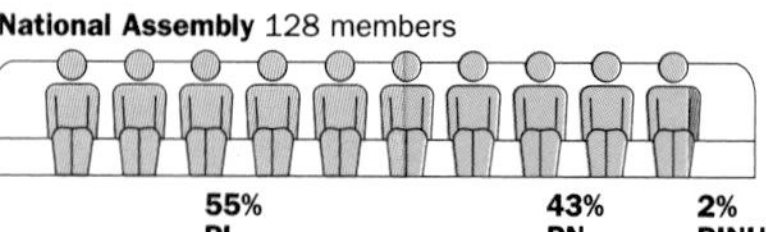

PL = Liberal Party **PN** = National Party **PINU** = Innovation and Unity Party

The main brokers in political power today are the military, the US embassy and the United Fruit Company, the biggest banana producers in Honduras.

The military held power intermittently from 1956 until 1981, when, under pressure from US President Jimmy Carter, it allowed a return to multiparty democratic civilian rule. Since then, the National and Liberal parties have alternated in power, although there are few real ideological differences between them. Presidents have tended to be weak because they can serve only one four-year term.

During the 1980s, US President Ronald Reagan effectively converted the country into a US "aircraft carrier" to counter a perceived communist threat from El Salvador and Nicaragua. The end of hostilities in these countries has meant a reduction in US aid to Honduras. The consequent shortage of funds for development leaves the new president with difficult problems. Unemployment, agrarian reform and improving the position of Honduras's landless rural poor are the main issues.

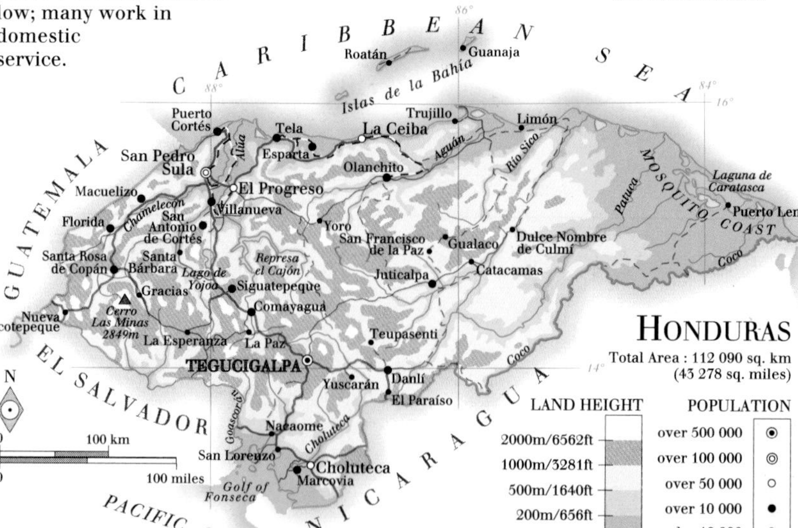

WORLD AFFAIRS

CACM

LAES

Honduras seeks to settle long-standing border disputes with El Salvador, to keep close ties with the USA and to achieve closer regional economic integration.

AID

 $275m (receipts)

 Down 39% in 1991

Peace in Central America has meant that Honduras is not of such strategic importance as it once was, and US aid has fallen.

DEFENSE

 $123.5m

 Up 3% in 1993

During the 1980s, the military repressed any internal dissent, joined maneuvers with US troops based in Honduras and backed the Nicaraguan Contras. The air force is the largest in the region. Honduras's major supplier is the USA.

ECONOMICS

 $3.1bn

 7.36 lempiras

SCORE CARD

- ❑ WORLD GNP RANKING........................121st
- ❑ GNP PER CAPITA..............................$570
- ❑ BALANCE OF PAYMENTS....................$-134m
- ❑ INFLATION.......................................28.4%
- ❑ UNEMPLOYMENT ....High underemployment

STRENGTHS
Hardwoods. Unexploited mineral deposits. Bananas. Diversification into non-traditional, high-earning agriculture – flowers and other fruit.

WEAKNESSES
Traditionally the poorest country in the region, now second to Nicaragua. Industry only 13% of GDP; industrial wages too low to spur development. Land reform has been halted. Decline in US investment.

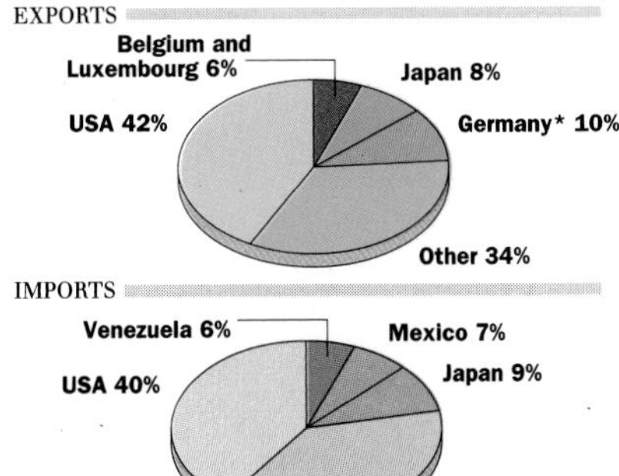

Tobacco field. Tobacco accounts for 1% of export revenues. Honduras's biggest earners are bananas, almost 40%, and coffee, 20%.

RESOURCES

 1.1bn kwh (capacity 290,000 kw)

 Not an oil producer; refines 14,000 b/cd

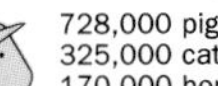 728,000 pigs, 325,000 cattle, 170,000 horses

Lead, zinc, silver, gold, copper, iron

Offshore oil exploration has begun in the north. An HEP dam in El Cajón now allows Honduras to export electricity.

ENVIRONMENT

 6% (1% partially protected)

US company wants to exploit 2.5m acres of rainforest for woodchip

Environmental groups are active, but have to face opposition from multinational commercial interests.

MEDIA

 Although the media is officially free, some journalists will accept bribes to misreport. Left-wing publications may receive death threats

PUBLISHING AND BROADCAST MEDIA

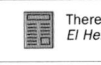

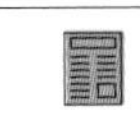 There are 4 daily newspapers, *La Prensa*, *El Heraldo*, *La Tribuna* and *El Tiempo*

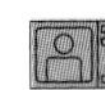 9 independent stations

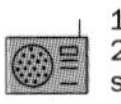 1 state-owned, 280 independent stations

Honduras TV and radio is mostly US-sourced. As a result, local coverage remains limited.

CRIME

 Honduras does not publish prison figures

 Violence in the cities, especially La Ceiba, is increasing

Drug-related crime is a major problem in Honduras. Occasional human rights abuses by the military are reported.

EDUCATION

 73%

State-run education follows the US system. The drop-out rate from secondary schools is high.

HEALTH

1 per 1,822 people

Circulatory, infectious and parasitic diseases, malaria

Only 66% of people have easy access to health services, although most infants receive basic care.

CHRONOLOGY

Honduras was a Spanish possession until 1821. In 1823, it joined the United Provinces of Central America with four neighboring nations.

- ❑ **1838** Declares full independence.
- ❑ **1890s** US banana companies set up extensive plantations.
- ❑ **1932–1949** Dictatorship of Gen. Tiburcio Carías Andino of PN.
- ❑ **1954** Elected PL president Dr. Villeda Morales deposed.
- ❑ **1957** Morales reelected.
- ❑ **1963** Military coup.
- ❑ **1969** 13-day Football War with El Salvador sparked by World Cup.
- ❑ **1980** PL wins elections but Gen. Alvarez holds real power. Military maneuvers initiated with USA.
- ❑ **1982–1983** Alvarez arrests trade unionists; death squads operate.
- ❑ **1984** Return to democracy.
- ❑ **1988** 12,000 Contra rebels forced out of Nicaragua into Honduras.
- ❑ **1990** Contra troops leave.
- ❑ **1991** Free-trade zone agreed with El Salvador.

H

WEALTH

 Plantation worker, 175 lempiras per week; high school science teacher, 415 lempiras per week

CONSUMER GOODS OWNERSHIP

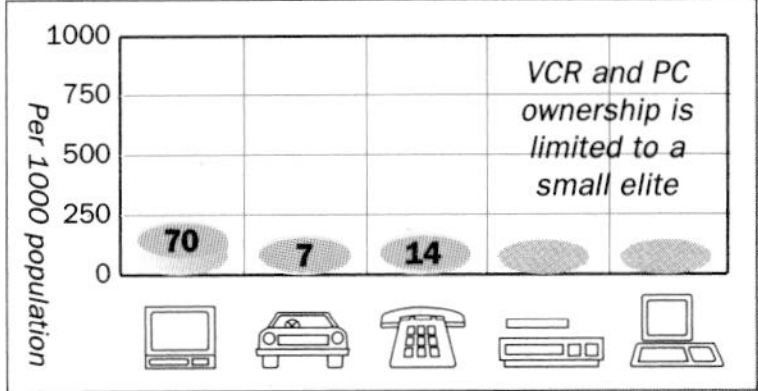

Two-thirds of the rural population live in absolute poverty. The best chance of social mobility is to join the military. Salvadorean immigrants suffer from low social status.

WORLD RANKING

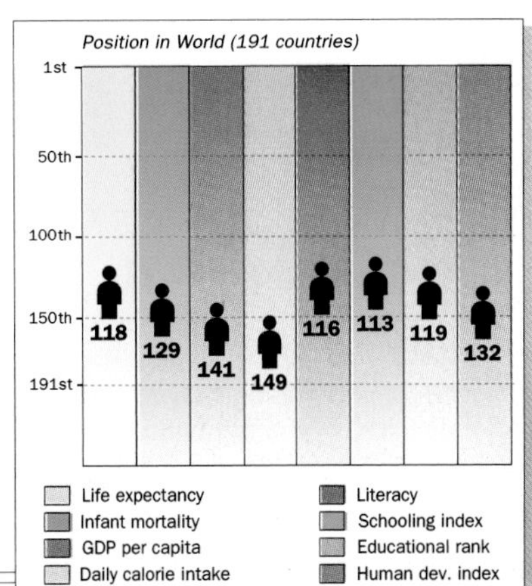

Hong Kong

Official Name: Hong Kong **Capital:** Victoria **Population:** 5.9 million
Currency: Hong Kong dollar **Official Languages:** English and Cantonese

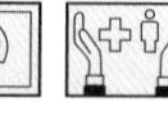

HONG KONG COMPRISES Hong Kong Island, lying off the southeastern coast of China, Kowloon and the New Territories on the mainland, and adjacent islets. Its strategic position has made it one of the world's leading trade and financial centers. In 1997, Hong Kong will revert to China, when the UK's 99-year lease on the New Territories expires. Whether its fiercely capitalist economic system will survive under Beijing's rule is the dominant political issue.

CLIMATE

WEATHER CHART

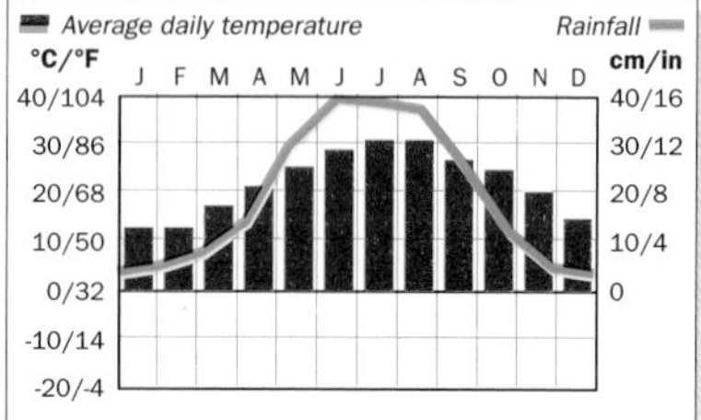

Hong Kong's climate is subtropical; it feels hotter and more humid on the streets due to the number of people.

COMMUNICATIONS

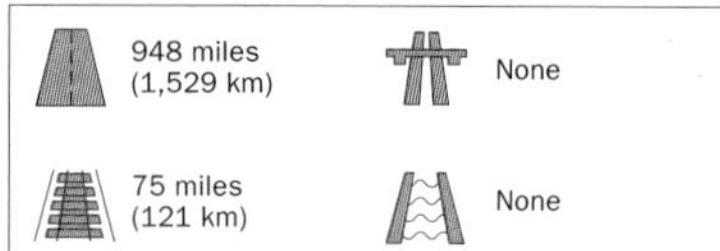

Hong Kong Intl, Kai Tak 18.69m passengers

269 ships 12.01m dwt

THE TRANSPORTATION NETWORK

948 miles (1,529 km) — None

75 miles (121 km) — None

The efficiency, cleanliness and safety of the underground Mass Transit Railway (MTR) is notable. A new airport at Chek Lap Kok is being built.

TOURISM

 5.93m visitors

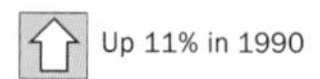 Up 11% in 1990

MAIN OVERSEAS ARRIVALS

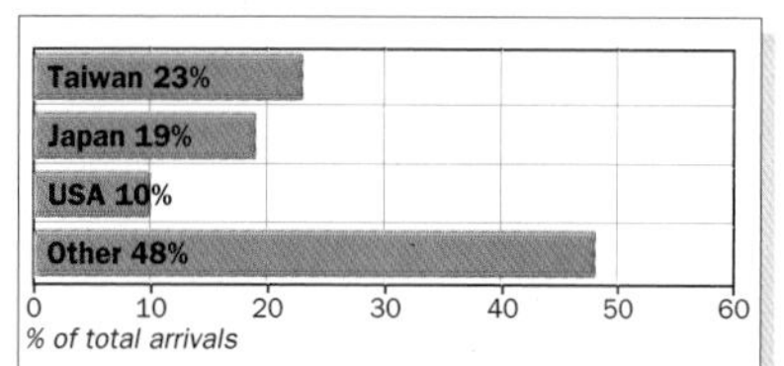

The "Manhattan of the Orient" attracts tourists with its shopping and food, and as a gateway to China and other parts of Asia. Tourism is now the third-largest foreign exchange earner.

Hong Kong Harbour and city skyline, looking across to the mainland, viewed from Victoria Peak on Hong Kong Island.

PEOPLE

 Chinese (Cantonese and Mandarin), English

 15,317 people per sq. mile

THE URBAN/RURAL POPULATION SPLIT

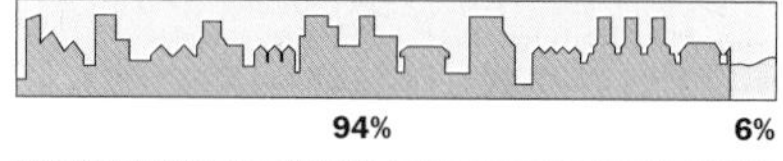

RELIGIOUS PERSUASION

Protestant 4%
Roman Catholic 5%
Other 17%
Buddhist and Daoist 74%

Ethnic tension is not a problem because of the homogeneity of the Han (Chinese) population, over 60% of whom were born in Hong Kong. Many wealthy citizens are planning to emigrate before 1997.

Hong Kong

Total Area : 1045 sq. km (403 sq. miles)

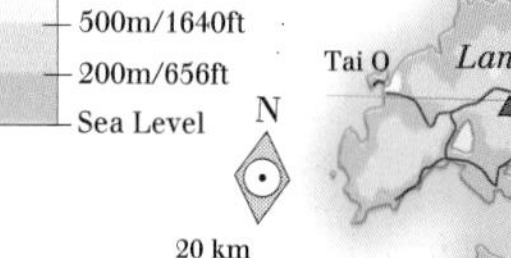

POLITICS

1995 — HM Queen Elizabeth II

THE STATE OF THE PARTIES

Legislative Council 60 members

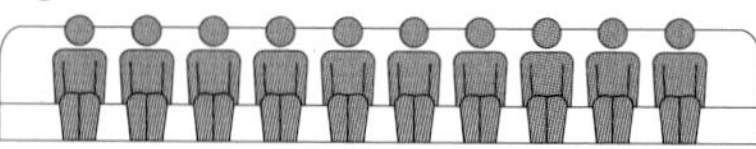

The United Democrats of Hong Kong (UDHK) won 12 of the 18 directly elected seats in the last elections in 1991. A further 21 members are elected to represent various professions and 21 are chosen by the governor

Presently a British Crown colony, Hong Kong will revert to Chinese sovereignty in 1997, when it will become a Special Administrative Region of China. The British and Chinese governments disagree about the interpretation of the 1985 Sino-British agreement and the Basic Law (Hong Kong's post-1997 constitution). Britain wants to push Hong Kong further toward elective democracy. However, Hong Kong Governor Chris Patten's policy is being undermined by his failure to conclude a deal with China, which strongly opposes any change to the *status quo*. Talks stretching to 17 rounds have failed to resolve the dispute.

Governor Patten's attempts to increase the number of elected members on the Legco (Legislative Council) have, however, speeded the formation of political parties. Prominent figures on the Hong Kong political scene include Martin Lee, leader of the UDHK, and his main rival, the leader of the Liberal Party, Allen Lee. In the 1995 Legco elections, pragmatism may lead to greater support for the Liberals, who are more acceptable to China.

ASIA
China
HONG KONG
Asia

H

WORLD AFFAIRS

WCL

As a British colony, Hong Kong's foreign policy is controlled by the UK. However, its diplomatic and economic links with other countries are extensive. The continuing Sino-British stand-off is the major issue.

AID

Minimal aid donor

Little variation from year to year

Hong Kong provides some aid to Vietnam to ease the repatriation of Vietnamese economic refugees.

DEFENSE

UK responsible for weaponry

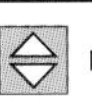

Not applicable

Hong Kong bears the manpower cost of its 10,000-strong tri national army, which is made up of Gurkhas, Hong Kong Chinese and UK personnel.

ECONOMICS

$59.2bn

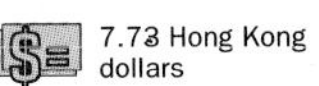

7.73 Hong Kong dollars

SCORE CARD

- ❑ WORLD GNP RANKING 37th
- ❑ GNP PER CAPITA $10,320
- ❑ BALANCE OF PAYMENTS $673m
- ❑ INFLATION 7.2%
- ❑ UNEMPLOYMENT 1.8%

STRENGTHS

Natural harbor and role as hub of East and Southeast Asian trade. Position in time zone makes Hong Kong a key global financial market.

WEAKNESSES

Dependence on China for most resources. Sensitivity to price fluctuations on international markets. Dependence on trade, especially US–China trade. Continuing uncertainty about future under Chinese rule deters some investors.

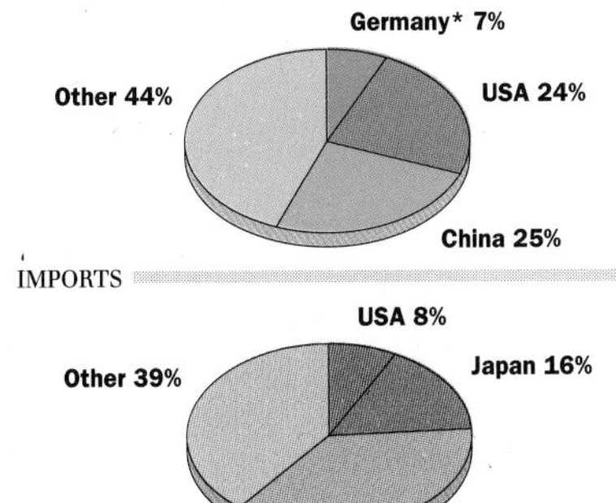

RESOURCES

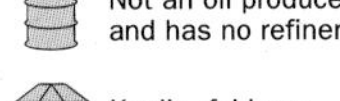

28.9bn kwh (capacity 8.3m kw)

Not an oil producer and has no refineries

350,000 pigs, 1,000 cattle, 1,000 horses

Kaolin, feldspar

Hong Kong lacks strategic resources. Energy and water have to be imported from China. Coal is imported from the Guangdong province of China in return for the export of electricity by Hong Kong's China Light and Power Company.

ENVIRONMENT

36% partially protected

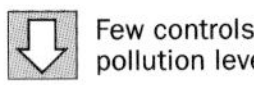

Few controls on pollution levels

Growth and urbanization have brought serious water and air pollution. The construction of the Daya Bay nuclear power station has been the focus of much public concern.

MEDIA

Some self-censorship is reportedly being exercised in the run-up to 1997. Films that might be offensive to the Chinese are not allowed on TV

PUBLISHING AND BROADCAST MEDIA

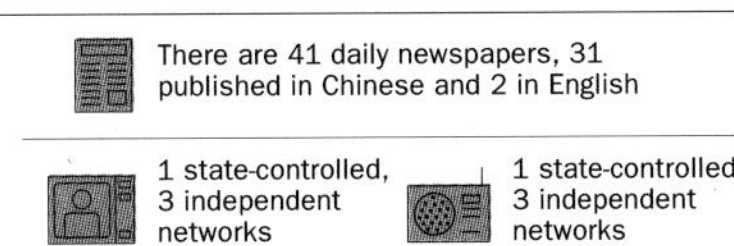

There are 41 daily newspapers, 31 published in Chinese and 2 in English
1 state-controlled, 3 independent networks
1 state-controlled, 3 independent networks

The press is divided into pro-Chinese and independent camps. Satellite broadcasting to the whole of Asia is carried out by one of Hong Kong's largest conglomerates – Hutchvision Hong Kong, which opened five Star-TV channels in 1991.

CRIME

12,095 prisoners

Up 7% in 1990

Crime is rising and becoming more violent. This is partly due to growing links with organized crime and Triad activity in China. Corruption among the elite is increasingly an issue.

EDUCATION

88%

Primary schools are oversubscribed and most can offer only two half-day sessions a week. There are three universities, where the emphasis is now on science and technology.

HEALTH

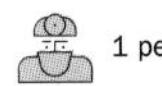

1 per 927 people

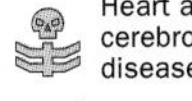

Heart and cerebrovascular diseases, cancer

Prenatal, child care and emergency services are free. Subsidies from the government keep charges for medical treatment and hospital care low.

CHRONOLOGY

Under the Treaty of Nanking in 1842, Hong Kong was ceded in perpetuity to Britain. The UK also acquired the Kowloon peninsula in 1860, and the New Territories, under a 99-year lease, in 1898.

- ❑ **1941–1945** Japanese occupation.
- ❑ **1981–1982** First wave of Vietnamese refugees arrive in Hong Kong.
- ❑ **1985** Sino-British Joint Declaration. China to regain Hong Kong sovereignty in 1997; its present social and economic systems to remain unchanged for 50 years.
- ❑ **1989** Large demonstrations following Tiananmen Square massacre in Beijing.
- ❑ **1992** Governor Chris Patten announces plans for democracy.

H

WEALTH

Shoe sewer, 170 Hong Kong dollars per day; clerk of works, 11,738 Hong Kong dollars per month

CONSUMER GOODS OWNERSHIP

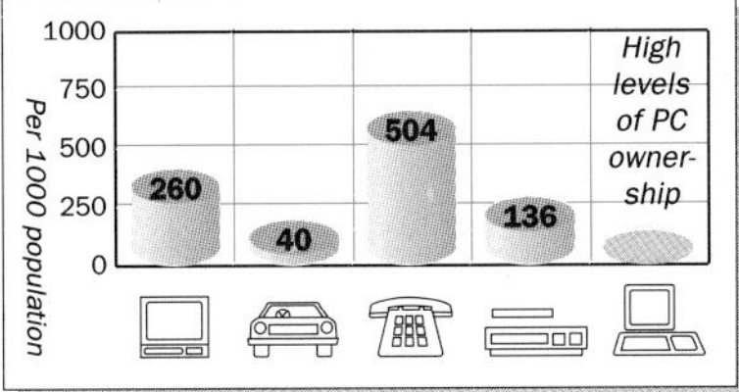

Social mobility is rapid – families who came to Hong Kong to escape communist China have achieved great wealth. Hong Kong consumers are highly status-conscious and will pay inflated prices for fashionable goods; attempts to curb car ownership by taxation have had little effect. Rich families have been able to buy citizenship overseas, allowing them to relocate, if necessary, in 1997.

WORLD RANKING

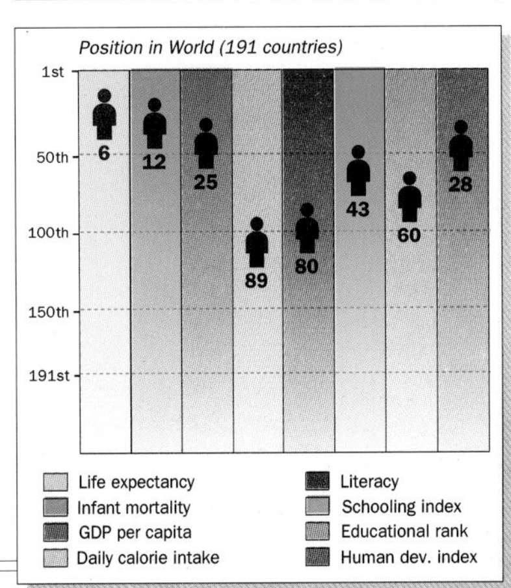

HUNGARY

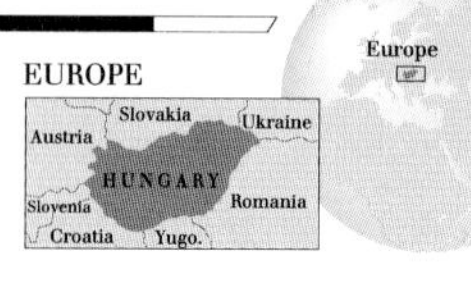

OFFICIAL NAME: Republic of Hungary **CAPITAL:** Budapest
POPULATION: 10.5 million **CURRENCY:** Forint **OFFICIAL LANGUAGE:** Hungarian (Magyar)

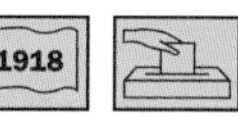

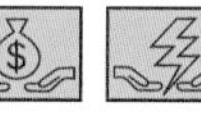

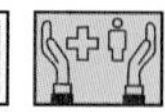

LYING AT THE HEART of Central Europe, Hungary is landlocked and has borders with seven states. Historically, Hungary has been a cosmopolitan cultural center, and during its years of market socialism was more prosperous and open to the West than the other Eastern Bloc countries. Hungary has changed its economic and political policies to develop closer ties with the EU. It now receives the lion's share of overseas investment in the former COMECON states. The treatment of the Hungarian minority in Romanian Transylvania is a major foreign policy concern.

CLIMATE

WEATHER CHART

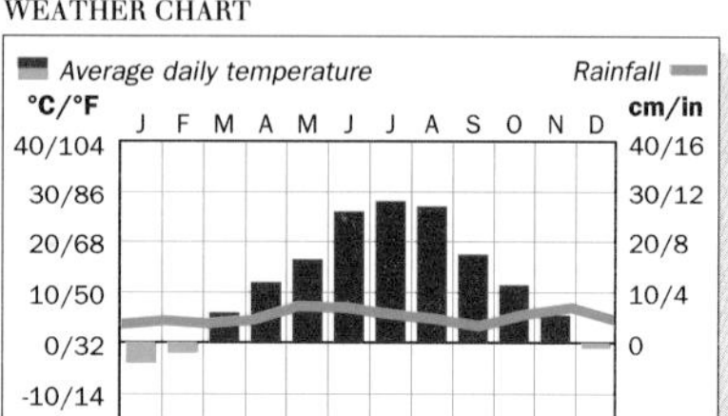

Hungary has a continental climate, with wet springs, late summers and cold, cloudy winters. There are no great differences of weather and climate within the country. Conditions in summer and winter may, however, differ from one year to the next. The transition between seasons tends to be sudden.

COMMUNICATIONS

Budapest Ferihegy
2.46m passengers

14 ships
133,000 dwt

THE TRANSPORTATION NETWORK

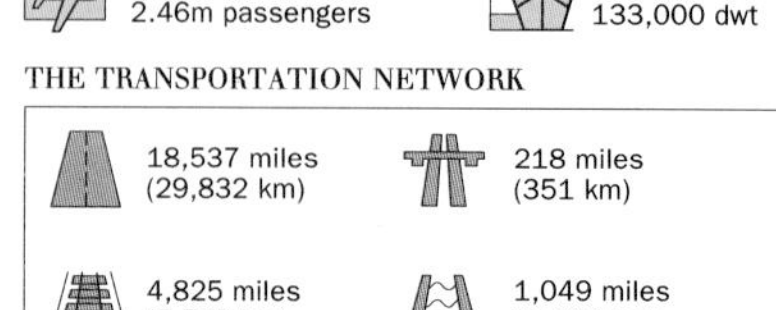

Freight travels mainly via the rail link from Budapest to the Austrian border. Most foreign investment is located along this corridor. Good roads link Hungary with Germany and Austria. The road system will be improved further once funds are available.

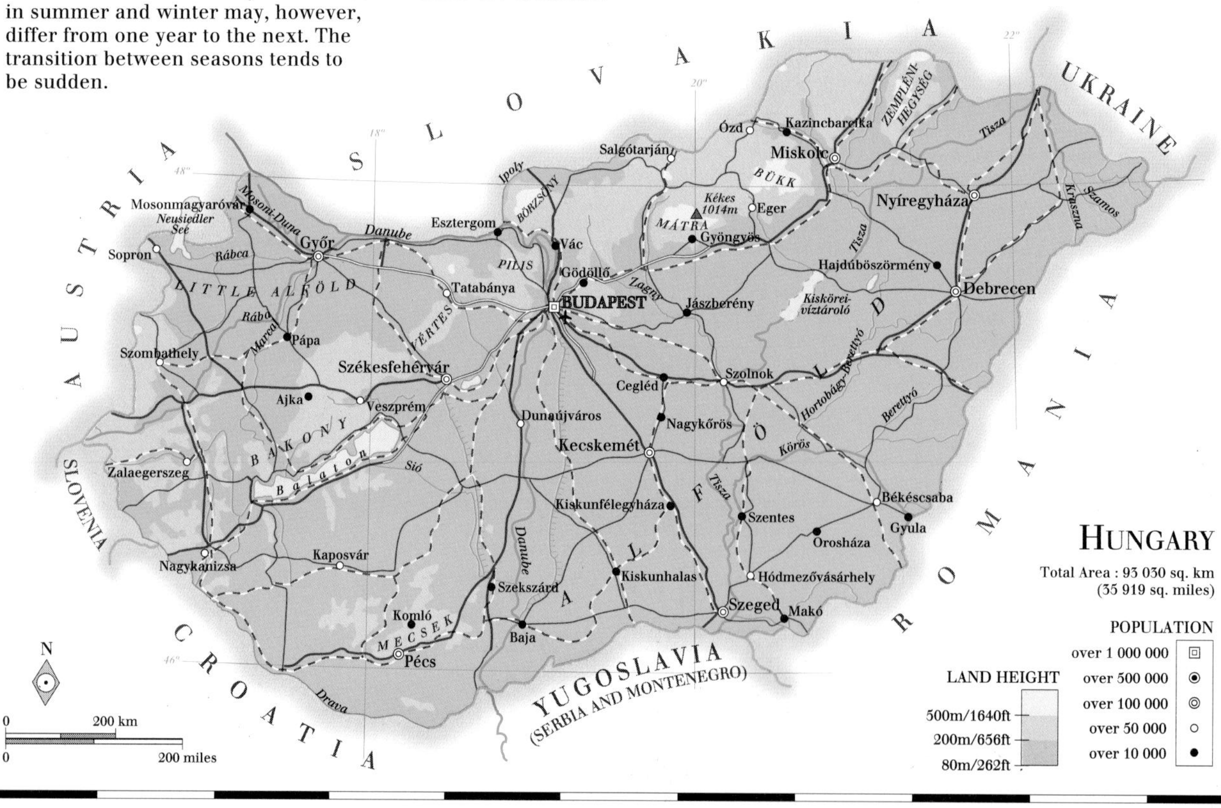

TOURISM

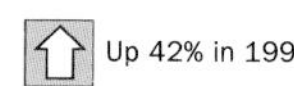

MAIN OVERSEAS ARRIVALS

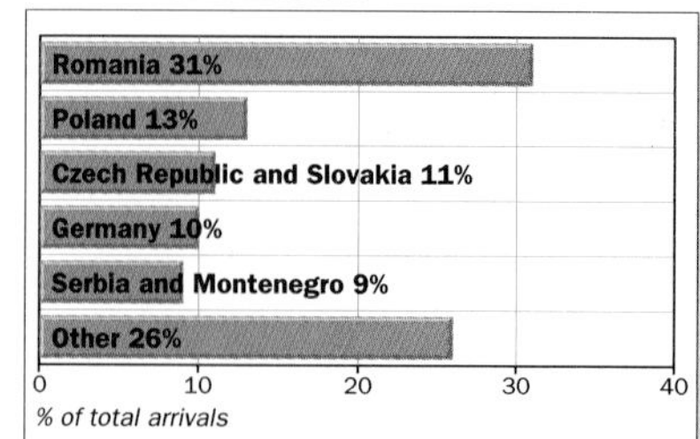

Tourism is an important source of hard currency earnings, which totaled $1.2 billion in 1993. Visitors come mainly from Eastern Europe, Germany and Austria. Since 1989, Hungary has invested heavily in tourism. The number of travel agents and hotels has risen dramatically. Lake Balaton is the traditional summer destination. In the capital city, Budapest, the baths, some of which date from the Ottoman period, are among the most popular tourist attractions. Budapest is also promoting itself as an international business convention center.

HUNGARY

Total Area : 93 030 sq. km
(35 919 sq. miles)

POPULATION
over 1 000 000
over 500 000
over 100 000
over 50 000
over 10 000

LAND HEIGHT
500m/1640ft
200m/656ft
80m/262ft

0 200 km
0 200 miles

PEOPLE

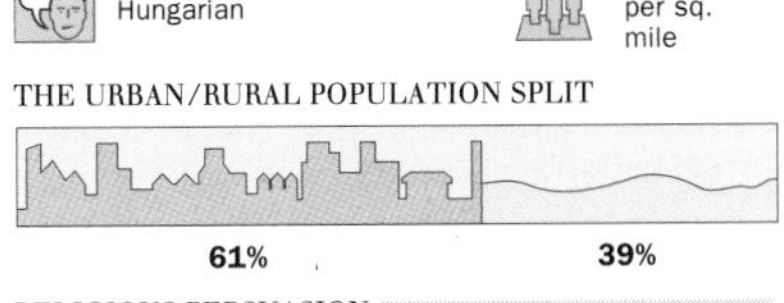

RELIGIOUS PERSUASION

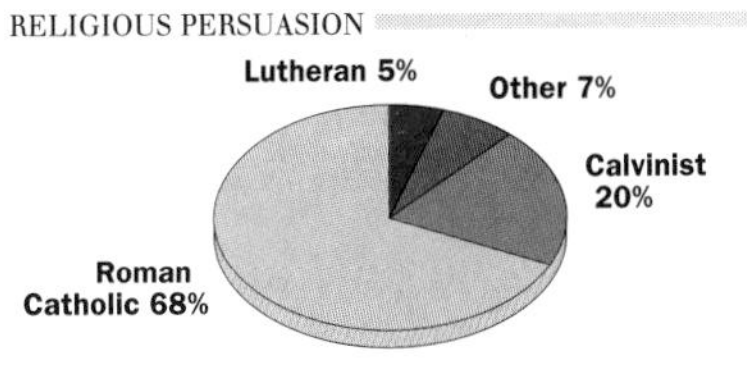

ETHNIC MAKEUP

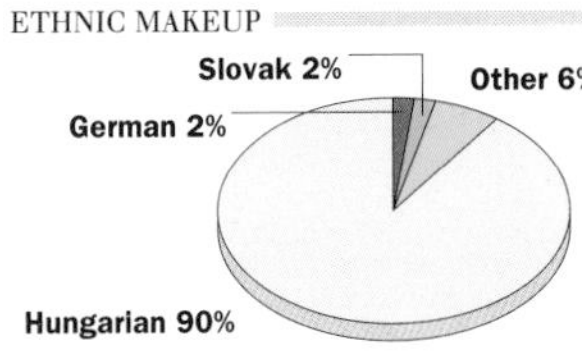

Hungary is ethnically homogeneous. There are also small minorities of Germans, Slovaks, Gypsies, Serbs, Croats and Romanians. There is little ethnic tension at home, although there is considerable concern about the treatment of Hungarian minorities in neighboring states. In terms of religion, the country is more diversified. A small Jewish community remains in Budapest. While there have been reports of isolated outbursts of anti-Semitism, prevailing opinion in Hungary remains tolerant.

Hungary suffers from a severe housing shortage. Most family homes are overcrowded, a factor that may contribute to the high rate of stress-related health disorders. Since 1989, a bourgeois class which is benefiting from the market economy has emerged. Life for the unskilled and unemployed is tougher, however, than under communism. Hungary has the highest suicide rate in the world.

POPULATION AGE BREAKDOWN

% of population by age group

	1960	1970	1980	1990	2000
65+	9%	11.6%	13.4%	13.4%	14.8%
15–64	65.7%	67.6%	64.7%	66.7%	70.6%
0–14	25.3%	20.8%	21.9%	19.9%	14.6%

POLITICS

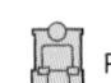

THE STATE OF THE PARTIES

National Assembly 386 members

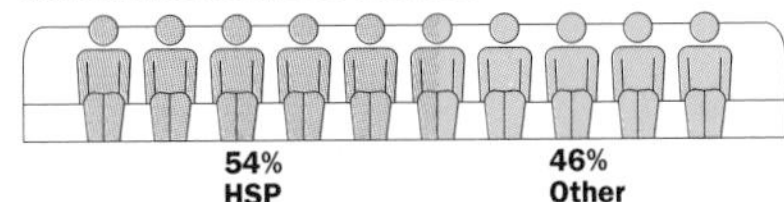

HSP = Hungarian Socialist Party (formerly HWSP = Hungarian Workers' Socialist Party) **Other** = Hungarian Democratic Forum, Alliance of Free Democrats, Independent Smallholders' Party, Federation of Young Democrats, Christian Democratic People's Party

Hungary has been a multiparty democracy since 1990.

MAIN POLITICAL ISSUES

The HSP's election promises

The clear victory of the ex-communists (the HSP) in the general elections of 1994 came as a surprise to most observers. The HSP promised voters a softer landing to the market economy, with greater social security and less unemployment. However, whether the HSP will be able to deliver its promises, given strict IMF guidelines on state spending, is now a key question.

Hungarian minorities abroad

Between 1989 and 1991, 50,000 ethnic Hungarians living abroad returned home. Many complained of poor treatment from nationalistic neighboring states. The issue has achieved prominence, particularly as Hungarians are wary of the effects of any additional competition for jobs in a tight labor market.

PROFILE

The HDF government of József Antall was installed following the elections of 1990. Until his death in 1993, Antall was a symbol of stability in Hungarian democratic politics. However, party disintegrations and the lack of an economic upturn have led to an increase in apathy and disillusionment among voters. In a 1993 poll, only 6% of Hungarians considered life to be better than under the communists.

In the May 1994 general election, voters rejected the MDF's Christian nationlist stance and voted ex-communists back into power. The victorious HSP, under Gyula Horn, pledged to work in coalition in order to ease the passage of economic and social reforms through parliament.

***President Árpád Göncz** was elected in 1990 and is head of the armed forces.*

***Gyula Horn**, ex-communist foreign minister and leader of the HSP.*

***The Hungarian parliament** buildings in Budapest, viewed across the Danube from the castle area of the city.*

WORLD AFFAIRS

Hungary was disappointed with the rebuff dealt to its applications to join NATO and the WEU; it was being offered neither full nor associate status. However, it accepted the NATO Partnership for Peace proposal of 1993.

Hungary is an associate member of the EU, and has declared its intention to acquire full membership at the earliest opportunity. A treaty of co-operation and friendship has been signed with Russia, but relations have been strained by Hungary's open courting of the West.

The most problematic relations are with Romania. For centuries, the two nations have disputed the status of the Hungarian minority in Transylvania. Relations with Slovakia are also tense.

CHRONOLOGY

The region today occupied by Hungary was first settled by the Finno-Ugrian Magyar peoples in the 8th century. In the 16th and 17th centuries it came under Austrian domination, lasting until 1867, when Austria-Hungary was formed.

- **1918** Hungarian Republic created as successor state to Austria-Hungary.
- **1919** Béla Kún leads a short-lived communist government. Romania intervenes militarily and hands power to Admiral Horthy.
- **1938-1941** Hungary gains territory from Czechoslovakia, Yugoslavia and Romania in return for supporting Nazi Germany.
- **1941** Hungary drawn into World War II on Axis side when Hitler attacks Soviet Union.
- **1944** Nazi Germany preempts Soviet advance on Hungary by invading. Deportation of Hungarian Jews and Gypsies to extermination camps begins. Soviet Red Army enters in October. Horthy forced to resign.

H

CHRONOLOGY *continued*

- ❑ **1945** Liberated by Red Army. Soviet-formed provisional government installed. Imre Nagy introduces land reform.
- ❑ **1947** Communists emerge as largest party in second post-war election.
- ❑ **1948** Forcible merger of Social Democrats with Communists to establish Hungarian Workers' Socialist Party (HWSP).
- ❑ **1949** New constitution; formally becomes People's Republic.
- ❑ **1950–1951** First Secretary Rákosi uses authoritarian powers to collectivize agriculture and industrialize the economy.
- ❑ **1953** Imre Nagy, Rákosi's rival, becomes premier and reduces political terror.
- ❑ **1955** Nagy deposed.
- ❑ **1956** Rákosi out. Student demonstrations demanding withdrawal of Soviet troops and Nagy's return become popular uprising. Nagy becomes premier; Kádár becomes First Secretary. Nagy announces Hungary will leave Warsaw Pact. Three days later, Soviet forces suppress protests. About 25,000 killed in resistance. Kádár becomes premier.
- ❑ **1958** Nagy executed following show trial.
- ❑ **1968** Kádár introduces "New Economic Mechanism" to bring market elements to socialism.
- ❑ **1986** Commemoration of the 1956 uprising broken up by police. Economists call for radical change. Democratic opposition demands Kádár's resignation.
- ❑ **1987** Party reformers establish HDF as a political movement.
- ❑ **1988** Federation of Young Democrats forms from independent student group. Kádár ousted. Environmental protests force suspension of plans for controversial Danube Dam.
- ❑ **1989** Parliament votes to allow independent political parties. Nagy rehabilitated and given full state funeral. First opposition candidate since 1947 elected in by-election. Round-table talks between HWSP and opposition. Parliament approves holding of multiparty elections.
- ❑ **1990** Multiparty elections held. HDF wins decisively and Antall's government is sworn in. Speed of economic reform hotly debated.
- ❑ **1991** Warsaw Pact dissolved. Last Soviet troops leave.
- ❑ **1993** József Antall dies. Peter Boross elected prime minister.
- ❑ **1994** Hungary agrees to NATO Partnership for Peace initiative. HSP wins general election.

AID

 $1bn (receipts)  Aid is increasing

Hungary has received World Bank loans totaling $3.4 billion since 1982. The EU is also an important source of assistance. Hungary has credit lines with the World Bank's International Finance Corporation and the EBRD. Loans are mainly used for infrastructure and energy projects.

DEFENSE

 $1.2bn Down 6% in 1992

0 *Defense spending as % GDP* 40

2.3%

Real defense spending has been halved from its 1989 level. Troop numbers have been slashed. Conventional arms and the military hierarchy have been updated to meet NATO standards. Hungary has been improving its rapid reaction forces with MiGs bought in debt-for-arms deals with Russia.

HUNGARIAN ARMED FORCES

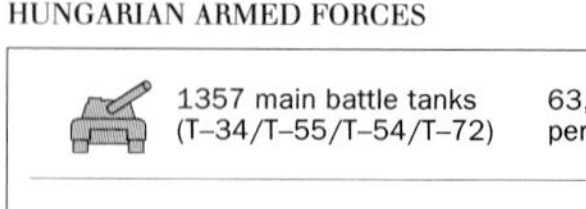

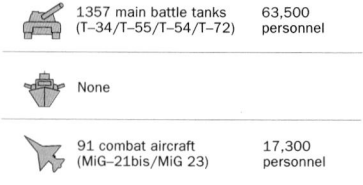

Tanks	1357 main battle tanks (T-34/T-55/T-54/T-72)	63,500 personnel
Navy	None	
Aircraft	91 combat aircraft (MiG-21bis/MiG 23)	17,300 personnel
Missiles	None	

ECONOMICS

 $28.2bn  100.75 forint

SCORE CARD

❑ World GNP Ranking	56th
❑ GNP per Capita	$2,780
❑ Balance of Payments	$-2bn
❑ Inflation	22%
❑ Unemployment	15%

EXPORTS

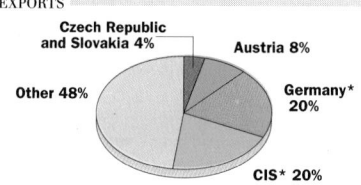

Czech Republic and Slovakia 4%
Austria 8%
Germany* 20%
CIS* 20%
Other 48%

IMPORTS

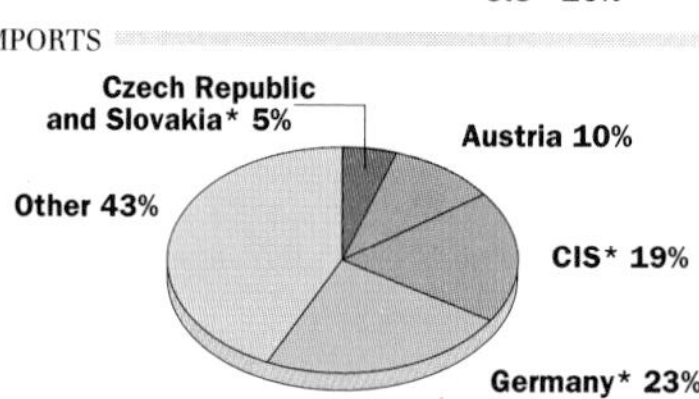

ECONOMIC PERFORMANCE INDICATOR

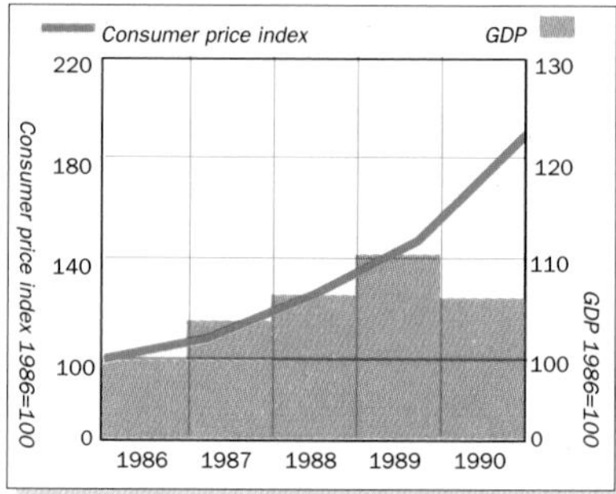

Profile

The costs of Hungary's transition to a market economy have been higher than expected. The collapse of COMECON trade caused a reorientation of trade toward Western Europe, and Hungary's economic recovery now depends largely upon trade with the EU. High tax rates make privatized assets less attractive to foreign investors.

Strengths

Openness to foreign direct investment. By 1990, Hungary had attracted half of the foreign investment coming to Eastern Europe: $5 billion. Favorable tax regime, streamlined bureaucracy and new legislation permitting fully owned subsidiaries help to attract international business.

Weaknesses

Continued lending by the banks to state-run and private firms regardless of creditworthiness has led to a crisis in the banking system. No plans to privatize banks. Downturn in overseas investment slowing privatization program.

HUNGARY : MAJOR BUSINESSES

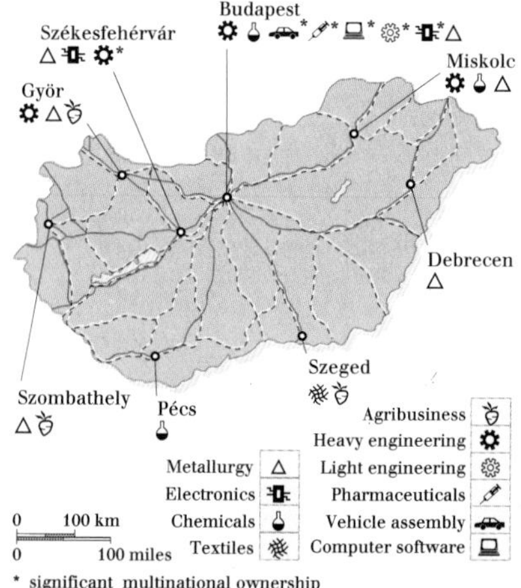

RESOURCES

ELECTRICITY GENERATION

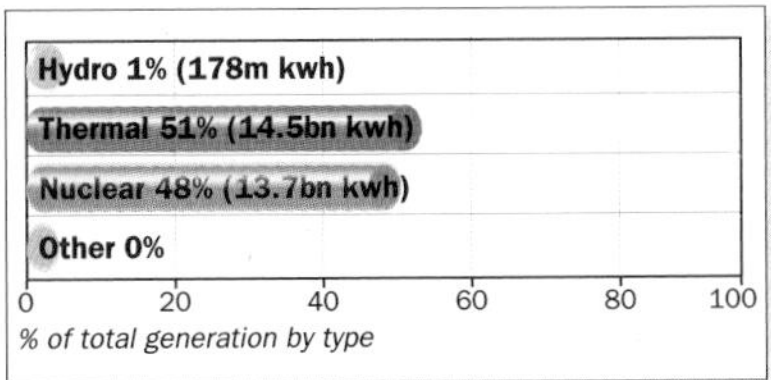

HUNGARY : LAND USE

Raba
Balaton
Danube
Tisza
ALFOLD
Forest
Pasture
Cropland
Pigs
Cereals
Vineyards - cash crop
0 100 km
0 100 miles

Hungary has bauxite, coal and fertile farmlands. Electricity companies are currently being privatized. The state holding company will retain 50% of shares, with foreign companies acquiring controlling rights with 50% or more of shares.

ENVIRONMENT

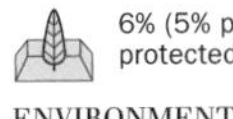

Greater awareness of environmental problems

ENVIRONMENTAL TREATIES

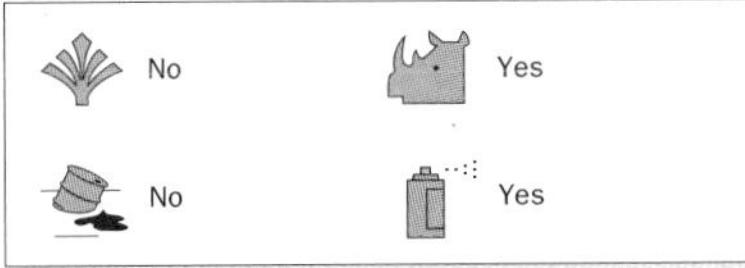

Hungary's oil reserves have a high sulfur content, which exacerbates the already serious air pollution in the industrial zones. It is estimated that 40% of Hungarians live in severely polluted areas.

Hungary's universities have an international reputation for their interdisciplinary approach to environmental science. The quality of data is high, but information has only recently become publicly accessible.

MEDIA

Little government censorship of the press

PUBLISHING AND BROADCAST MEDIA

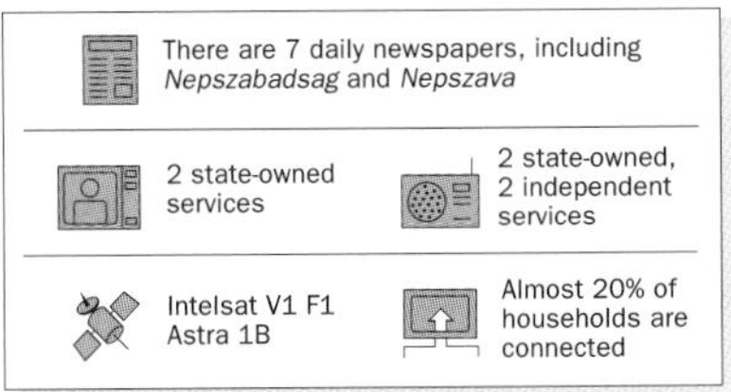

Following the end of official censorship in 1988–1989, the number of newspapers and magazines has soared. Some are foreign-owned; most are fiercely independent and critical of government policy. The TV broadcasting service is nominally independent, but in practice the state controls its news coverage. Public pressure to open frequencies to private local TV and radio networks is currently growing.

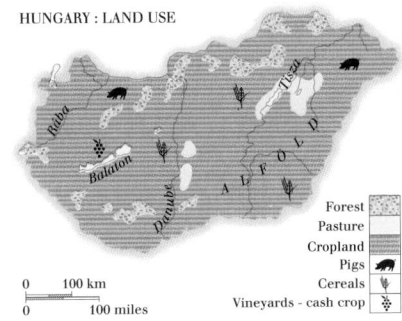

CRIME

12,373 prisoners

CRIME RATES

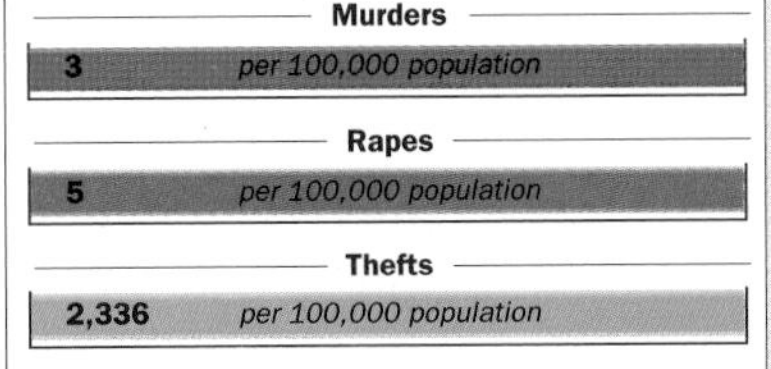

There were 288 murders in 1993. A growing proportion of these were in settling business disputes. Organized crime is also rising, and Hungary has become a money-laundering center.

EDUCATION

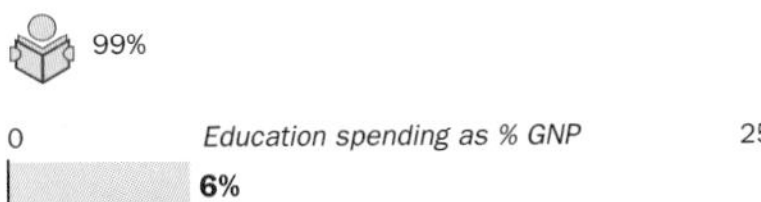

0 Education spending as % GNP 25
6%

THE EDUCATION SYSTEM

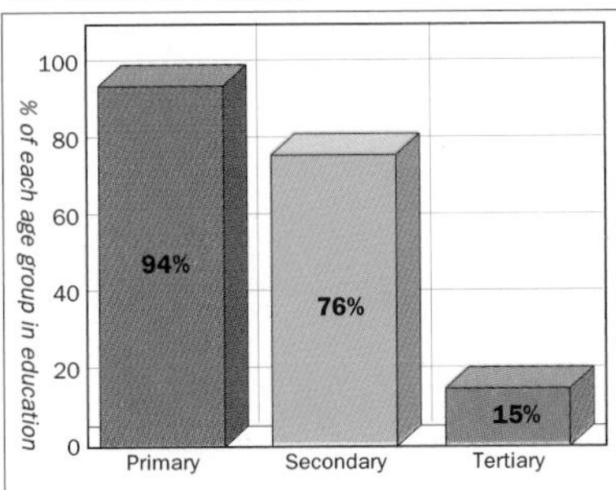

Education is free and compulsory from age six to 16. Bilingual schools are being established to provide education in the language of Hungary's ethnic minorities. There are 77 higher-education institutions – including ten universities – from which over 20,000 students graduated in 1992.

HEALTH

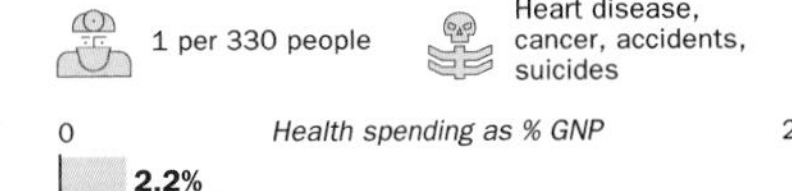

0 Health spending as % GNP 25
2.2%

Medical treatment in Hungary is free of charge to all patients, although there is a 15% charge toward the cost of prescriptions. The health service is currently underfunded and suffers from a lack of supplies. In order to jump waiting lists or to obtain better care, it is common for patients in the state health system to offer doctors gifts or bribes. The state provides sickness benefit at 75% of wages.

WEALTH

Transport worker, 16,403 forint per month; teacher, 21,928 forint per month

CONSUMER GOODS OWNERSHIP

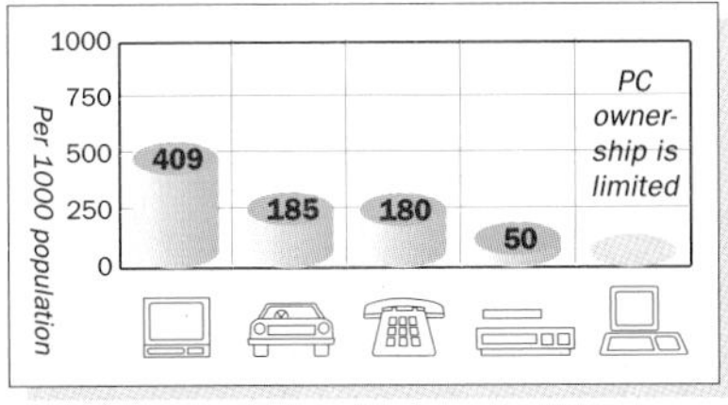

Hungary currently enjoys a higher standard of living than the other ex-COMECON countries. Around 90% of households have refrigerators, washing machines and TVs. Demand for luxury goods is rising. In 1992, Hungary was the second biggest market after Germany for BMW cars.

Real wages fell less in Hungary than in other Eastern European states. However, Hungarians have to work longer hours to pay for basic consumer goods than their Western European counterparts. Per capita GDP is still lower than that in the poorest EU state. There is also a growing sense of inequality between those working in the state and private sectors.

WORLD RANKING

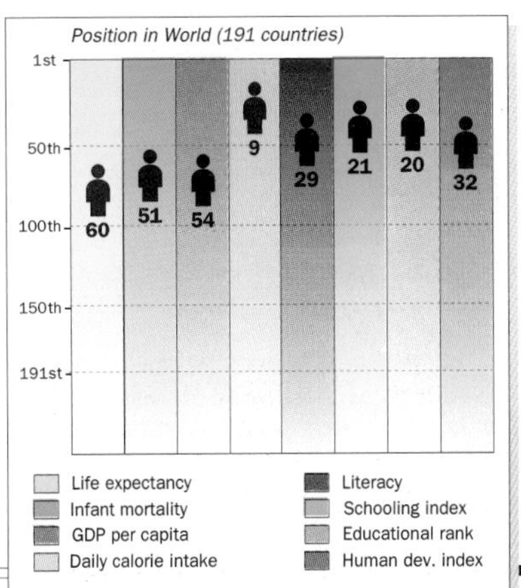

H

EUROPE

Greenland

ICELAND

Europe

ICELAND

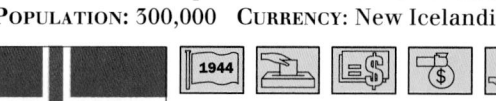

OFFICIAL NAME: Republic of Iceland **CAPITAL:** Reykjavík
POPULATION: 300,000 **CURRENCY:** New Icelandic króna **OFFICIAL LANGUAGE:** Icelandic

EUROPE'S WESTERNMOST COUNTRY, Iceland has a strategic location in the North Atlantic, just south of the Arctic Circle. Its position, on the rift where the North American and European continental plates are pulling apart, accounts for its 200 volcanoes and its numerous geysers and solfataras. Previously a Danish possession, Iceland became fully independent in 1944. Most settlements are along the coast, where ports remain ice-free in winter.

CLIMATE

WEATHER CHART

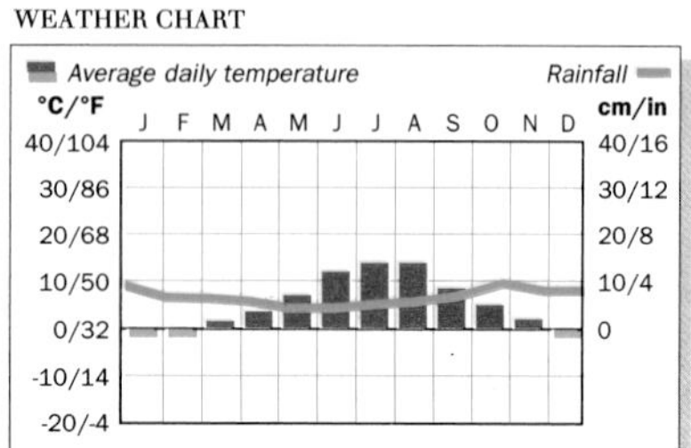

Iceland sits in the Gulf Stream. Winters are consequently mild. Summers are cool, with fine sunny days.

COMMUNICATIONS

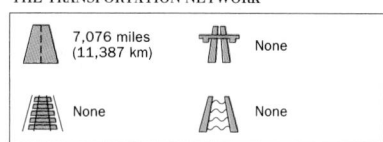

Keflavík Intl, Reykjavík
557,000 passengers

18 ships
55,300 dwt

THE TRANSPORTATION NETWORK

7,076 miles (11,387 km)

None

None

None

Icelanders rely entirely on cars, and ownership rates are among the world's highest. Most freight moves by sea. The only main road is the island ring road.

TOURISM

142,561 visitors

Down 1% in 1992

MAIN OVERSEAS ARRIVALS

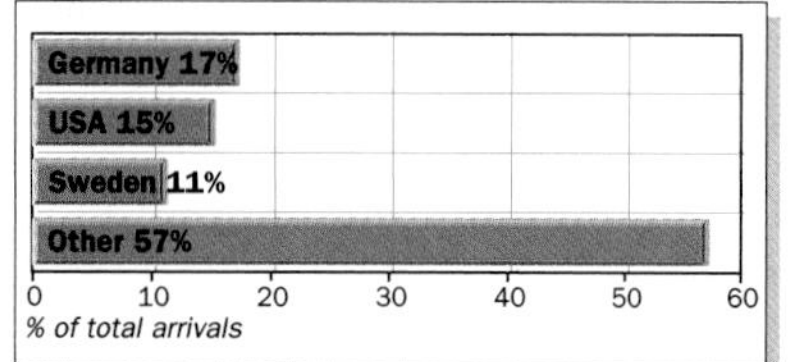

Iceland is promoting itself, especially in Japan, as an upscale destination for ecotourists, attracted by its spectacular scenery, glaciers, green valleys, fjords and hot springs.

PEOPLE

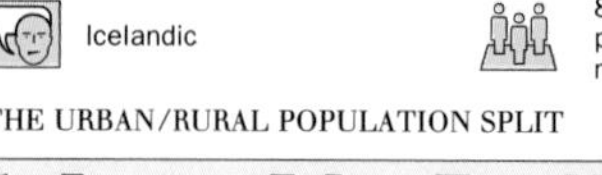

THE URBAN/RURAL POPULATION SPLIT

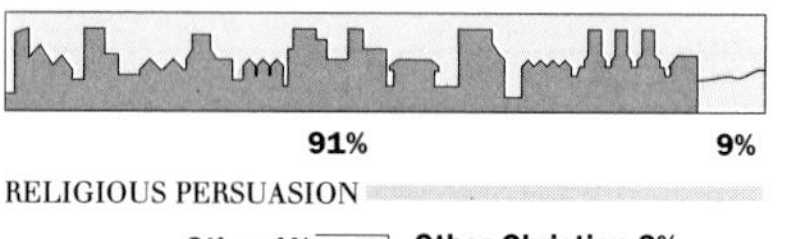

RELIGIOUS PERSUASION

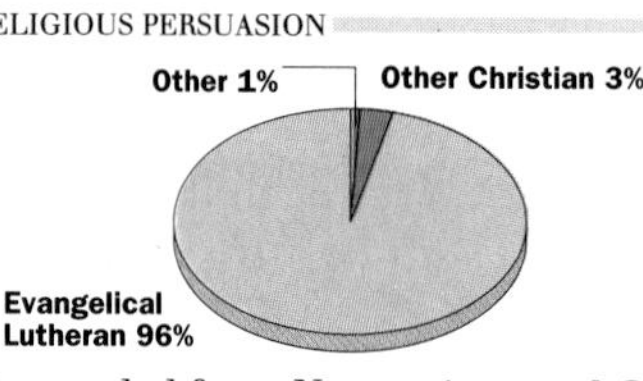

Descended from Norwegians and Celts, Icelanders form an ethnically homogeneous society; there are only 4,000 foreign residents. 96% of people follow the Evangelical Lutheran Church. Living standards are high and there are few social tensions. The main cultural influence is from the USA.

POLITICS

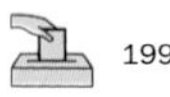

1995

President Vigdís Finnbogadóttir

THE STATE OF THE PARTIES

Parliament 63 members

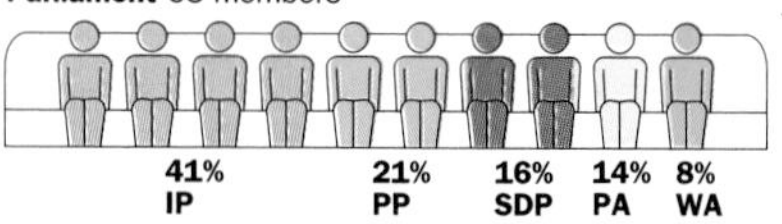

IP = Independence Party **PP** = Progressive Party
SDP = Social Democratic Party **PA** = People's Alliance
WA = Women's Alliance

From independence, Iceland was ruled by coalitions. However, in the 1980s the traditional four-party system began to splinter. In 1983, the WA was formed, and a general strike in 1984, in response to proposed tax increases, led a rebel group to leave the IP to form the Citizens' Party. By the 1991 elections, the latter had disappeared, and a new IP/SDP coalition promoted market-led reforms.

The main issues are the economic downturn and how best to manage Iceland's uneasy dependence on its major source of wealth: fish. Arguments over whether or not to join the EU were defused in 1992 with the successful negotiation of the EEA, giving Iceland access to the key EU market.

ICELAND

Total Area : 103 000 sq. km
(39 770 sq. miles)

POPULATION

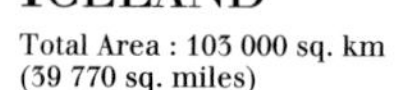

over 50 000
over 10 000
under 10 000

LAND HEIGHT

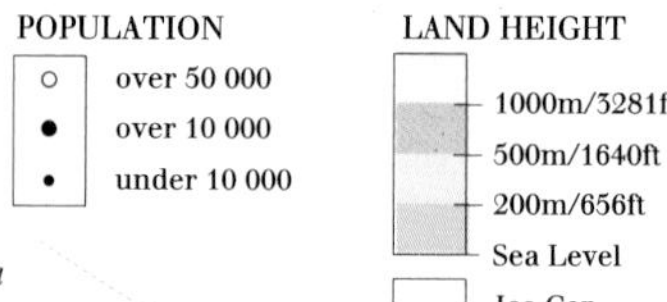

WORLD AFFAIRS

OECD

Iceland has traditionally maintained an arm's-length relationship with the EU and USA, while seeking to ensure access to both their markets. Its major disputes have been over the extension of its fishing waters. Agreements were ratified with the EEA in 1993, and with the International Whaling Commission over Iceland's wish to continue whaling.

AID

 $5.3m  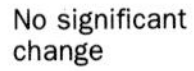 No significant change

Aid donations are modest, and form a smaller proportion of the budget than in other Scandinavian states.

DEFENSE

 Coastguard of 130 personnel only  Not applicable

Iceland has no armed forces, but is a member of NATO. The USA has 3,000 troops based at Keflavík.

ECONOMICS

 $5.9bn

71.57 New Icelandic krónur

SCORE CARD

- ❑ WORLD GNP RANKING........................107th
- ❑ GNP PER CAPITA $19,713
- ❑ BALANCE OF PAYMENTS....................$-210m
- ❑ INFLATION 4.1%
- ❑ UNEMPLOYMENT.................................4.3%

STRENGTHS
High-tech fishing industry and exclusive access to prime fishing grounds place Iceland in an almost unique position to supply EU and US markets. Very cheap geothermal power.

WEAKNESSES
Dependence on fish for 75% export earnings. Attempts to diversify have been delayed by world recession.

EXPORTS

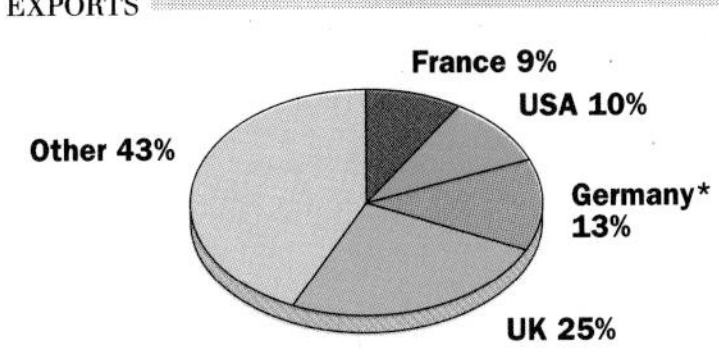

IMPORTS

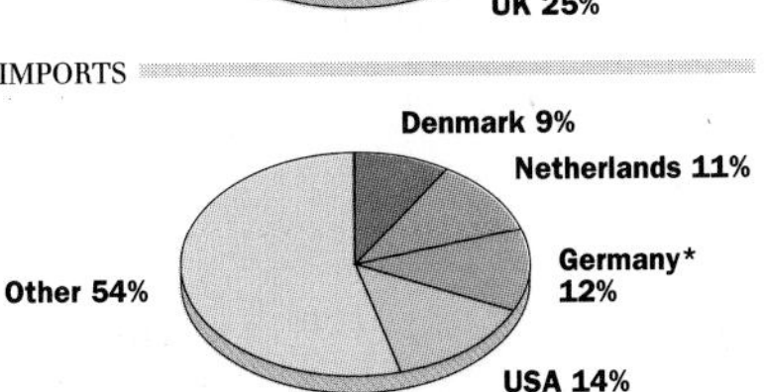

***Lava Towers**, near Lake Mývatn in northern Iceland, a region of grassy lowlands. The center consists of cold lava desert and glaciers.*

RESOURCES

 4.6bn kwh (capacity 957,000 kw)

 Not an oil producer and has no refineries

700,000 sheep, 72,000 cattle, 56,000 horses

Diatomite

Iceland has virtually no minerals. All energy needs are met by geothermal and hydroelectric sources. It has implemented measures to try to restore its once abundant fish stocks.

ENVIRONMENT

 9% (7% partially protected)

 Iceland has the largest bird sanctuary in Europe

Iceland has no nuclear or thermal power stations. The end of Soviet and US submarine operations in the Arctic Circle has removed an environmental threat. Believing that Minke whales eat valuable cod stocks, Iceland decided to resume whale hunting in 1992.

MEDIA

 Freedom of expression is guaranteed

PUBLISHING AND BROADCAST MEDIA

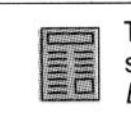 There are six daily newspapers – most support the views of one political party. *Dagbladid-Visir* has the largest circulation

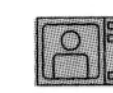 1 state-owned, 1 independent service

 1 state-owned, 1 independent service

Iceland is renowned for having one of the highest per capita newspaper circulations in the world.

CRIME

 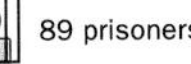 89 prisoners

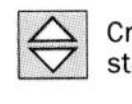 Crime rates are fairly stable

Crime rates are comparatively low. The rate of alcohol-related murders is higher than the European average.

EDUCATION

 100%

Icelanders buy more books per capita than any other nation. Education is state-run. 25% of school students go on to universities at Reykjavík or Akureyri or in the USA.

CHRONOLOGY

Iceland was first settled in the 9th century by Norwegians. It was ruled by Denmark from 1380–1944. In 1918, it became fully self-governing.

- ❑ **1940–1945** Occupied by UK and, from 1941, USA.
- ❑ **1944** Independence as a republic.
- ❑ **1949** Founder-member of NATO.
- ❑ **1951** US air base built at Keflavík despite strong local opposition.
- ❑ **1972–1976** Extends fishing limits to 50 miles; two "cod wars" with UK.
- ❑ **1975** Sets 200-mile fishing limit.
- ❑ **1980** Vigdís Finnbogadóttir elected; world's first woman head of state.
- ❑ **1985** Declares nuclear-free status.

I

HEALTH

 1 per 376 people

 Heart and cerebrovascular diseases, cancer

The state health system is free to all Icelanders. Iceland has the lowest infant mortality rate, and one of the highest longevity rates, in the world.

WEALTH

 Meat packer, 387 new Icelandic krónur per hour; bookkeeper, 638 new Icelandic krónur per hour

CONSUMER GOODS OWNERSHIP

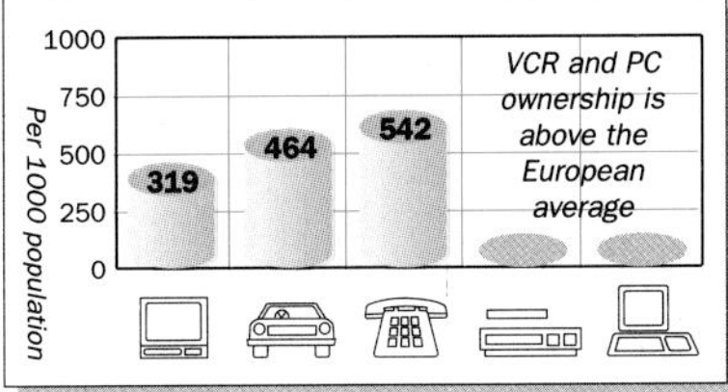

Wealth distribution is comparatively even and social mobility is high. Domestic heating, from geothermal sources, is almost free.

WORLD RANKING

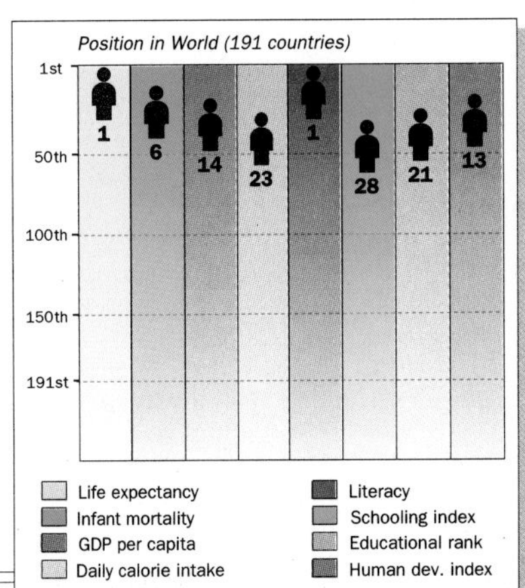

INDIA

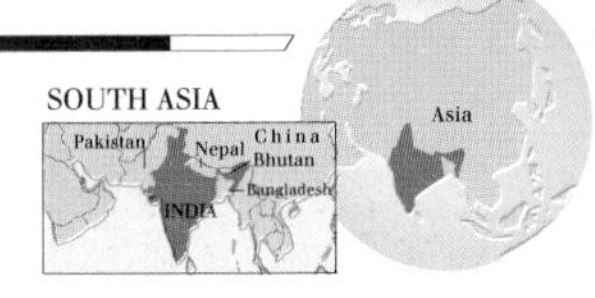

OFFICIAL NAME: Republic of India **CAPITAL:** New Delhi
POPULATION: 879.5 million **CURRENCY:** Rupee **OFFICIAL LANGUAGE:** Hindi and English

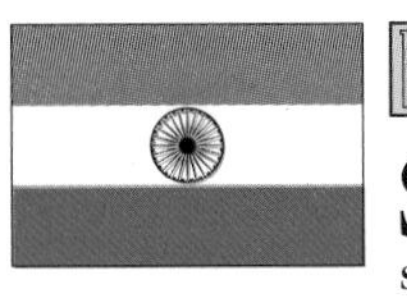

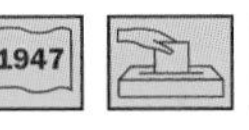

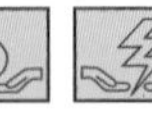

SEPARATED FROM THE REST of Asia by the Himalaya mountain range, India forms a subcontinent. As well as the Himalyas, there are two other main geographical regions, the Indo-Gangetic plain, which lies between the foothills of the Himalayas and the Vindhya Mountains, and the central-southern plateau. India is the world's largest democracy and second most populous country after China. The birthrate has recently been falling, but even at its current level India's population will probably overtake China's by 2030. After years of protectionism, India is opening up its economy to the outside world. The hope is that the free market will go some way to alleviating one of the country's major problems, poverty.

CLIMATE

WEATHER CHART

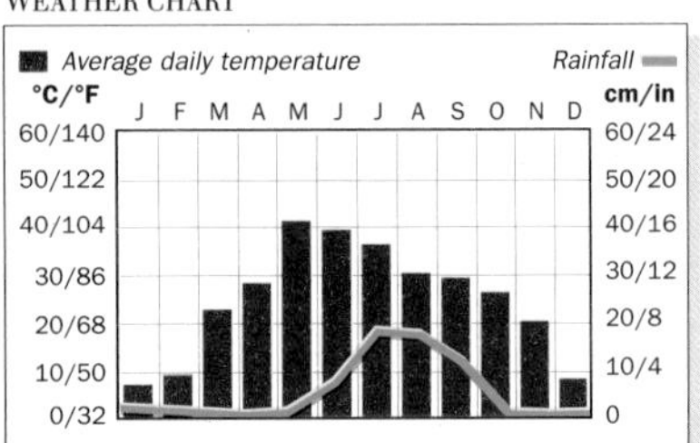

During the hot season, temperatures in the north can reach 104°F. The monsoon breaks in June and peters out in September or October. In the cool season, average temperatures are 50°F–59°F in the north and the weather is mainly dry. However, the south has a less variable climate. Madras is always hot. Average temperatures range from 75°F in January to 90°F in May and June.

COMMUNICATIONS

Bombay International 4.05m passengers

347 ships 1m dwt

THE TRANSPORTATION NETWORK

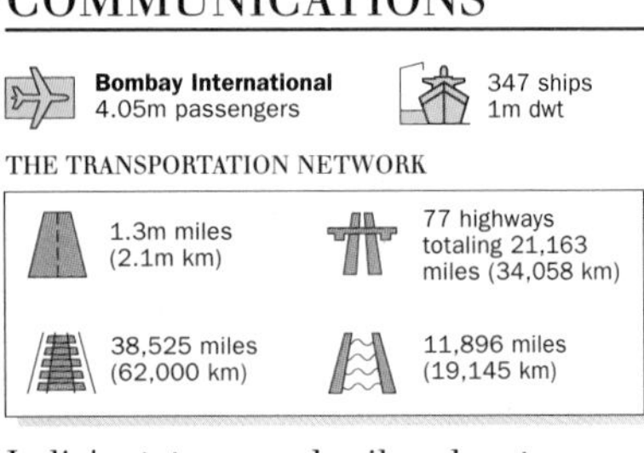

India's state-owned railroad system spans all the major cities. Rail carries 40% of passenger traffic and 65% of freight. Some routes still use steam locomotives. Intercity highways are narrow, poorly maintained and congested. Scooter and cycle rickshaws are common in urban centers. Calcutta still has rickshaws pulled by hand.

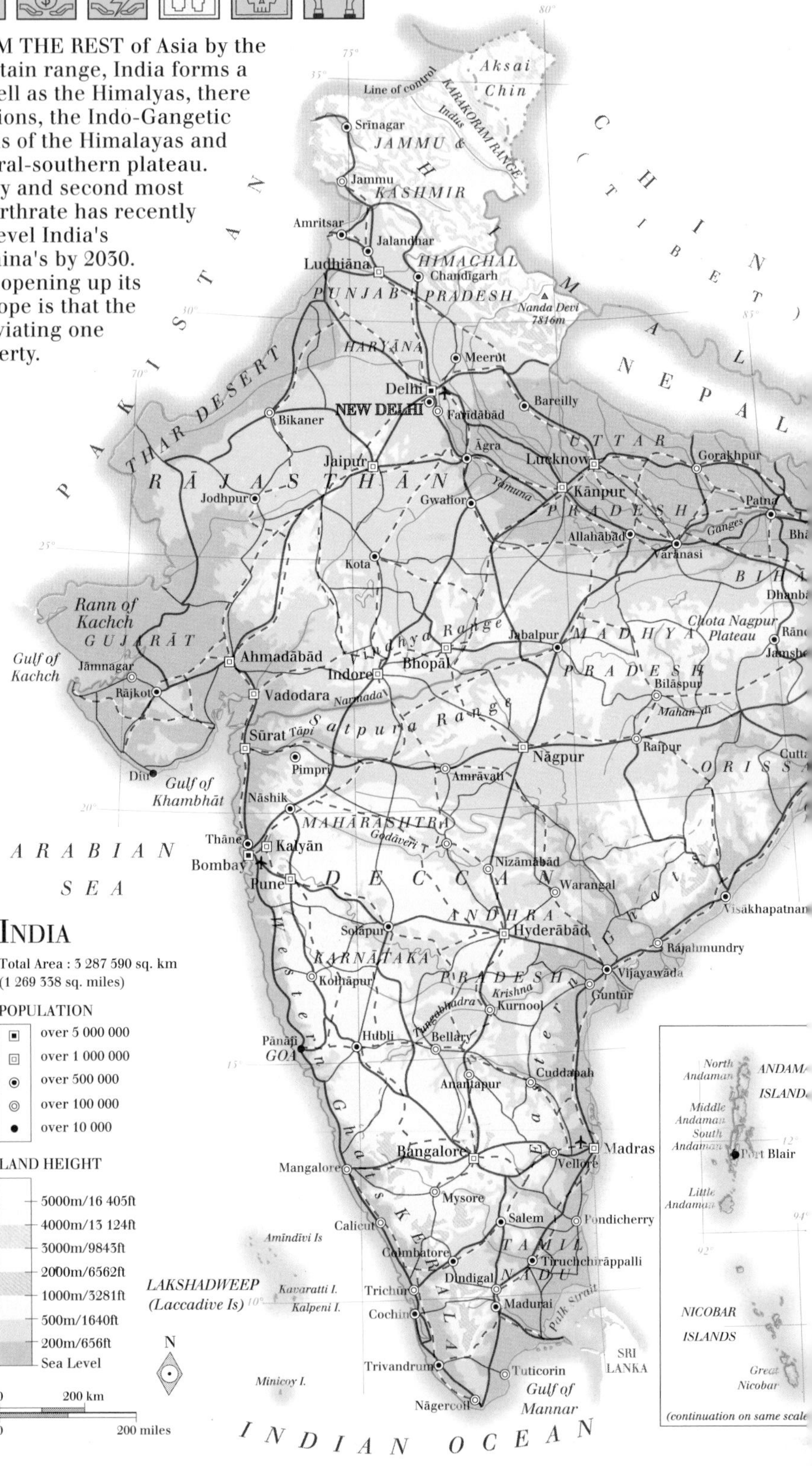

INDIA

Total Area : 3 287 590 sq. km (1 269 338 sq. miles)

POPULATION
- over 5 000 000
- over 1 000 000
- over 500 000
- over 100 000
- over 10 000

LAND HEIGHT
- 5000m/16 405ft
- 4000m/13 124ft
- 3000m/9843ft
- 2000m/6562ft
- 1000m/3281ft
- 500m/1640ft
- 200m/656ft
- Sea Level

0 200 km
0 200 miles

A religious festival. *Such festivals are a frequent occurrence and form an important part of Hindu culture.*

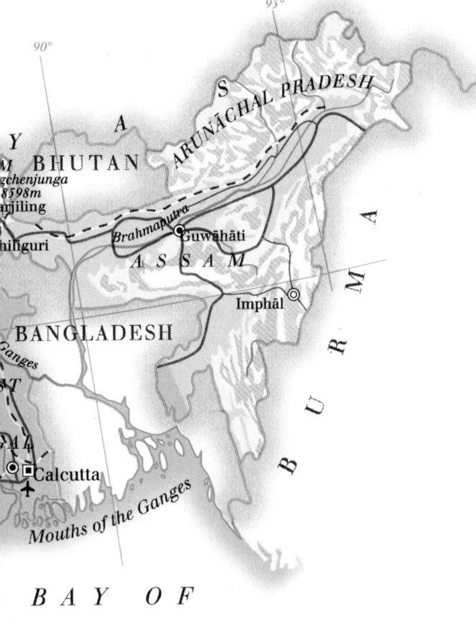

TOURISM

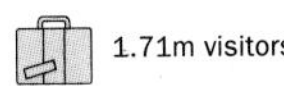
1.71m visitors

Down 2% in 1990

MAIN OVERSEAS ARRIVALS

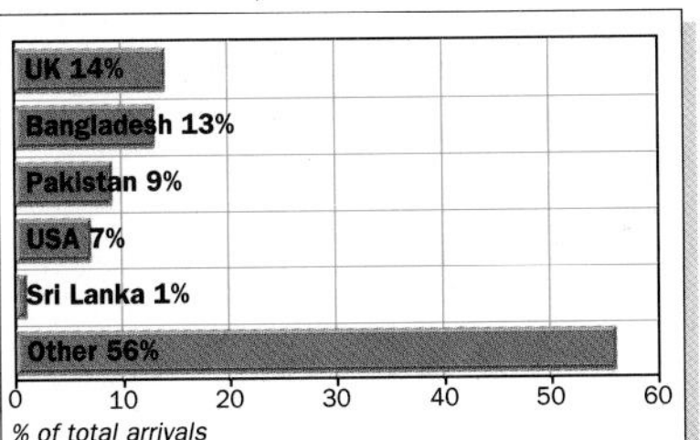

Tourism is India's sixth-largest foreign-exchange earner. More luxury hotels are now being built, and wildlife and adventure tourism are being developed. However, India still has only a small share of the world tourism market – 0.3% of the world's tourists and 1% of revenue – and is keen to expand this source of revenue and take in 2.5 million visitors by the late 1990s.

PEOPLE

Hindi, Urdu, Bengali, Marathi, Telugu, Tamil, Bihari, Gujarati, Kanarese

666 people per sq. mile

THE URBAN/RURAL POPULATION SPLIT

RELIGIOUS PERSUASION

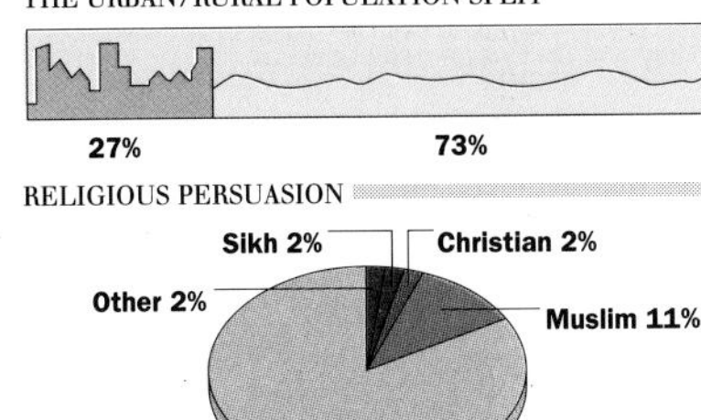

ETHNIC MAKEUP

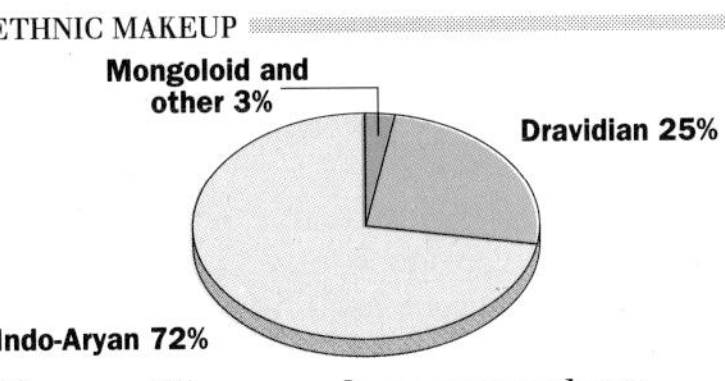

The world's second most populous country, India is home to 16% of the global population. Despite a major birth-control program, population growth has come down only slightly from 2.1% a year in the mid-1980s to 2% in 1990–1991. Today, nationwide awareness campaigns aim to promote the idea of smaller families. India's planners consider the rise in the population the most significant brake on development. Cultural and religious pressures encourage large families, however, and the extended family is seen as an essential security for old age.

The fertile rice-growing areas of the Gangetic plain and delta are very densely populated. The northern state of Uttar Pradesh has the largest population, at 139 million, followed by neighboring Bihār and the western state of Mahārāshtra. Mahārāshtra is also the most urbanized state, with 55% of its people living in towns or cities. Elsewhere, most Indians live in rural areas, although poverty continues to drive many to the swelling cities.

Some 83% of the population are Hindus. Each Hindu belongs to one of thousands of castes and sub-castes. Hindus are born into their caste and caste determines who they marry and their future status and occupation. Various attempts to reform the system have met with violent opposition.

POPULATION AGE BREAKDOWN

% of population by age group

	1960	1970	1980	1990	2000
65+	3.4%	3.7%	4%	4.5%	5.1%
15–64	56.8%	55.9%	57.5%	59%	60.4%
0–14	39.8%	40.4%	38.5%	36.5%	34.5%

CHRONOLOGY

The origins of an Indus valley civilization may be traced back to the third millennium BC. By the 3rd century BC, the Mauryan kingdom under Ashoka encompassed most of modern India. Following the Battle of Plassey in 1757, British rule – through the East India Company – was consolidated.

- ❑ **1885** Indian National Congress formed to press for political reform.
- ❑ **1919** Act of parliament for "responsible government."
- ❑ **1920–1922** Mahatma Gandhi's first civil disobedience campaign.
- ❑ **1930–1933** Further civil disobedience action.
- ❑ **1935** Government of India act.
- ❑ **1936** First elections under new constitution.
- ❑ **1942–1943** "Quit India" movement.
- ❑ **1947** August: independence and partition into India and Pakistan. Jawarhalal Nehru becomes first prime minister.
- ❑ **1948** Assassination of Mahatma Gandhi. War with Pakistan over Kashmir. India becomes a republic.
- ❑ **1951–1952** First general election won by Congress party.
- ❑ **1957** Second elections won by Congress. First elected communist government anywhere installed in Kerala.
- ❑ **1960** Bombay divided into states of Gujarat and Maharashtra.
- ❑ **1962** Congress party reelected. Brief border war with China.
- ❑ **1964** Death of Nehru. Lal Bahadur Shastri becomes prime minister.
- ❑ **1965** Second war with Pakistan over Kashmir.
- ❑ **1966** Shastri dies, Indira Gandhi (daughter of Jawarhalal Nehru) becomes prime minister.
- ❑ **1967** Congress again wins majority at elections. Opposition takes control of several states.
- ❑ **1969** Split of Congress party into two factions, the larger of which is led by Indira Gandhi.
- ❑ **1971** Indira Gandhi's Congress party wins elections. Friendship Treaty signed with USSR. Third war with Pakistan, over creation of Bangladesh; army occupies East Pakistan and recognizes it as independent state of Bangladesh.
- ❑ **1972** Simla Agreement signed with Pakistan.
- ❑ **1974** Explosion of first nuclear device in underground test.
- ❑ **1975–1977** Growing anti-government protest movement. Mass civil disobedience. State of emergency imposed. Many opposition leaders arrested. Elections postponed.

⇨

CHRONOLOGY *continued*

- **1977** General election. Congress defeated and People's Party (JD) government comes to power, with Morarji Desai as prime minister.
- **1978** New political group, Congress (Indira) – Congress (I) – formally established. Conflict within JD.
- **1979** Desai resigns.
- **1980** Indira Gandhi's C(I) wins general election.
- **1984** Unrest in Punjab. Golden Temple of Amritsar, occupied by armed Sikhs, stormed by Indian army troops. Assassination of Indira Gandhi by members of her bodyguard. Her son Rajiv becomes prime minister.
- **1985** Assam and Punjab Accords.
- **1987** Former finance and defense minister V. P. Singh expelled from C(I) and becomes leader of opposition. Following signing of accord, Indian peacekeeping force stationed in northern Sri Lanka to combat Tamil terrorists.
- **1988** Punjab unrest continues. Golden Temple in Amritsar again stormed by army.
- **1989** Blockade of Nepal following disagreement on foreign policy and migration. Sri Lankan president Premadasa orders Indian troops to leave, but new accord postpones this. Right-wing Hindu party, the BJP, wins 86 seats in elections. Minority National Front government formed with V. P. Singh as prime minister.
- **1990** Withdrawal of peacekeeping troops stationed in Sri Lanka. BJP leader Lal Advani arrested. No-confidence motion in parliament; Chandra Shekhar prime minister of minority government.
- **1991** February: Rajiv Gandhi overthrows minority government. May: Rajiv Gandhi assassinated during polling in general elections. P. V. Narasimha Rao becomes prime minister in C(I) minority government. Program of economic liberalization and reform introduced in attempt to solve huge economic problems, including balance of payments crisis. Government removes trade barriers and encourages foreign and private investment.
- **1992** Major financial scandal involving Bombay Stock Exchange. Demolition of the Babri Masjid mosque at Ayodhya by Hindu extremists. Resultant widespread violence leaves 1,200 people dead.
- **1993** Resurgence of riots leaves over 500 dead in Bombay. Explosions rock Bombay Stock Exchange.

POLITICS

THE STATE OF THE PARTIES

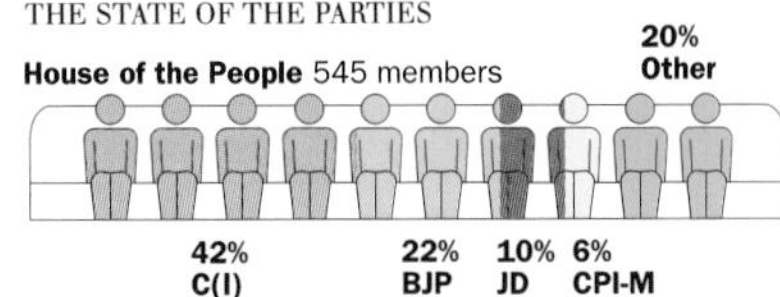

C (I) = Congress (I) **BJP** = Indian People's Party **JD** = People's Party **CPI-M** = Communist Party of India – Marxist **Other** = Communist Party of India, Telugu Nation

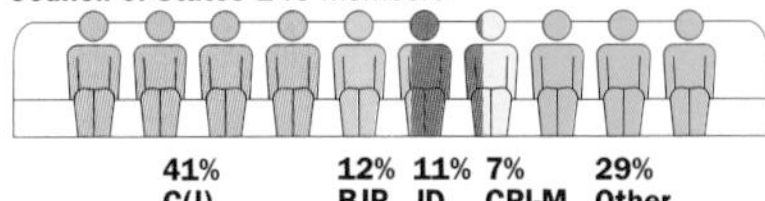

India is a multiparty democracy. The *Lok Sabha* (lower house) is directly elected by universal adult suffrage, while the *Rajya Sabha* (upper house) is indirectly elected by the state assemblies. Beyond Delhi, there are 25 states and seven union territories, each governed by a parliament and cabinet.

MAIN POLITICAL ISSUES

The "rainbow coalition"
In the recent Uttar Pradesh state assembly election, an alliance of the Samajwadi Party and the Bahujan Samaj Party secured the votes of Muslims, the lower castes and a grouping of "untouchables" (also known as *Dalits* or *Harijans*) and swept into power. The forging of this so-called "rainbow coalition" was made by promising to reserve government jobs for the lower castes. Significantly, the poor were seen to put their perceived interests above religious divisions. The win partly reflected circumstances peculiar to Uttar Pradesh, but opposition politicians nationwide see this as a way of defeating C(I) in other states.

Hindu militancy
Many observers have suggested the right-wing Hindu BJP could win the next general election. The rise of the BJP has been swift. Almost from nowhere it won 86 seats at the 1989 general election, and two years later, with its ally the *Shiv Sena*, took its tally to 123. It also formed the government in five states, including Uttar Pradesh. Most of its backing has come from the middle classes and prosperous trading and farming castes. However, voters are now beginning to question whether the BJP has defined policies other than the promotion of Hindu supremacy.

The free market
The opening up of the economy and the signing of the GATT agreement has led to large opposition-led demonstrations in Delhi and other parts of the country. The opposition contends that GATT will undermine local production in sectors such as pharmaceuticals, and lead to higher prices, which will hit the poor hardest. Aware of the potential impact of this on their vote among the poor, the C(I) announced further spending for agricultural development to tackle rural poverty in the 1994 budget.

PROFILE

Prime Minister Narasimha Rao became leader of the C(I) following the assassination of Rajiv Gandhi. He was only the second leader of India's main party not to be related to the Nehru dynasty. In the state elections of 1993, he consolidated his rule by recapturing Madhya Pradesh and the Himalayan state of Himachal Pradesh. The wins also represented the first reversal since the early 1980s for the Hindu nationalist BJP. C(I) lost ground, however, in Rājasthān and Uttar Pradesh.

C(I) continues to be the most influential party in India. It traces its origins back to the 1930s, when it was an umbrella group, with a left-of-center stance, fighting for independence. C(I) has retained its broad appeal and its members encompass businessmen as well as the poorer castes. It is the only party with a structure that allows it to organize on a national basis down to village level. Under Indira Gandhi, it adopted popular nationalization policies, yet also maintained close links with the urban capitalist elite. Rao has reshaped the party's philosophy, offering a "new vision" of the market-led open economy. Coalitions have taken power from C(I), but they rarely manage to retain it for long. State communist governments are in power in Kerala, West Bengal and Andhra Pradesh.

***P. V. Narasimha Rao**, prime minister and leader of the ruling C(I).*

***President Shankar Dayal Sharma**, who took office in July 1992.*

***Manmohan Singh**, finance minister and architect of India's liberalization.*

WORLD AFFAIRS

Delhi's overriding preoccupation in foreign policy is the divided territory of Kashmir. Disputes with Pakistan sparked two bloody wars, in 1948 and 1965. Pakistan wishes to annex largely Muslim Kashmir, and believes it would receive the support of the Kashmiri population. India is unwilling to hold a referendum or to cede any territory. The USA sees Kashmir as a potential nuclear flashpoint. It is promoting a settlement on the basis that both states limit their nuclear arsenals. However, India will not discuss nuclear weapons. It regards the Nuclear Non-proliferation Treaty as an instance of First World discrimination. Indo-US relations have recently been strained following Washington's delivery of nearly 40 F-16 jets to Pakistan, in return for a cap on its nuclear program. Relations with Beijing are now cordial.

AID

 $1.7bn (receipts)  Up 4% in 1991

India receives aid, but, unlike other countries in the region, is not dependent on it. Receipts have largely been spent on building infrastructure. The World Bank recently pulled out of the Narmada Dam project following a long campaign by environmentalists.

DEFENSE

 $6.8bn  Down 12% in 1992

0 *Defense spending as % GDP* 40

2.9%

INDIAN ARMED FORCES

3,800 main battle tanks (800 T-55/1300 T-72 1,700 *Vijayanta*)	1.1m personnel
2 carriers, 5 destroyers 21 frigates and 39 patrol boats	55,000 personnel
674 combat aircraft (80 *Jaguar* IS/MiG-21 MiG-23/MiG-29)	110,000 personnel
Nuclear capability	

India has an army of over one million men, making it the fourth largest in the world. Included in its arsenal is the recently displayed *Prithvi* missile. However, cuts in defense are forecast as the defense budget is squeezed. Much of India's foreign weaponry is outdated. Aging MiG-21s, which form a central part of the air force, are unlikely to be replaced. India produces its own *Arjun* battle tank.

ECONOMICS

 $285bn 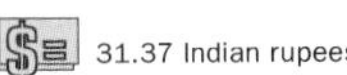 31.37 Indian rupees

SCORE CARD

- ❑ WORLD GNP RANKING........................15th
- ❑ GNP PER CAPITA..............................$324
- ❑ BALANCE OF PAYMENTS ....$-3bn
- ❑ INFLATION 9%
- ❑ UNEMPLOYMENT ...Widespread underemployment

EXPORTS

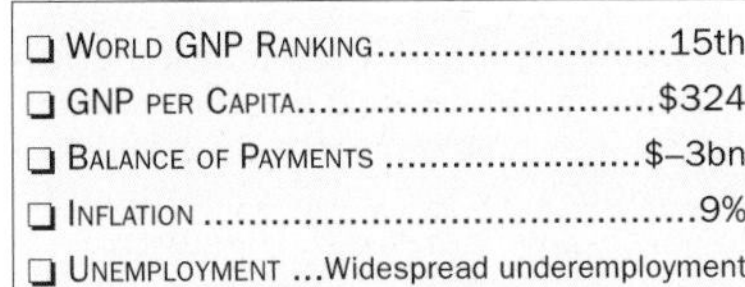

IMPORTS

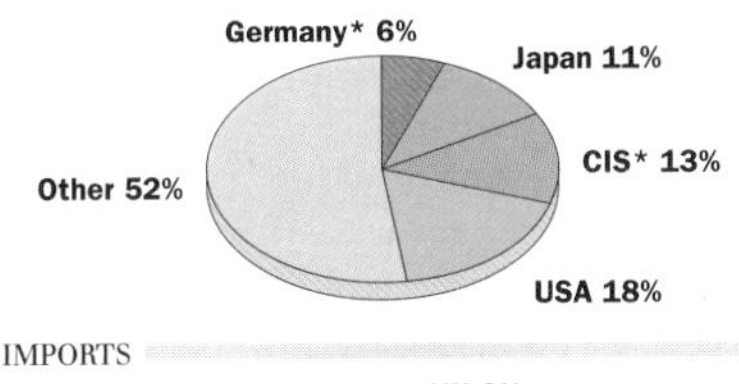

STRENGTHS

Massive home market of over 800 million people. Cheap labor. Some of the work force possess skills for new high-tech industries such as software programming. Highly efficient textile sector and garment manufacturers. Growing competitiveness on world market reflected in high export growth – up 20% in 1993. Competition is encouraging firms to manufacture to international standards.

There has been a massive rise in foreign direct investment as the economy is opened up to foreign competition; $5 billion worth of investment has been approved by government since 1991, including $3 billion in 1993. Much of this will go into the power sector. Large multinationals, such as Coca-Cola and IBM, who left in 1977 rather than dilute their equity holdings, are returning.

WEAKNESSES

Inflation rate up to 9% in 1993. Budget deficit estimated to reach 7% for the year 1993–1994. Cuts in food and industrial subsidies aimed at reducing budget deficit have added to inflationary pressure. Analysts predict inflation may soon reach double figures, and could climb higher with poor monsoon rains. Poor roads, ports and telecommunications systems and power shortages are a brake on economic growth. Mass unemployment and underemployment; urban unemployed estimated to be 37 million.

PROFILE

India's economy is undergoing radical changes. From a highly protectionist mixed economy, which succeeded in building the basis of a modern industrial state, India has converted to a free-market economy and is entering the global marketplace. A series of wide-ranging reforms, from lowering trade barriers to attracting foreign investment, have been put firmly in place. Despite strong objections from opposition parties, India will soon ratify the GATT world trade agreement.

ECONOMIC PERFORMANCE INDICATOR

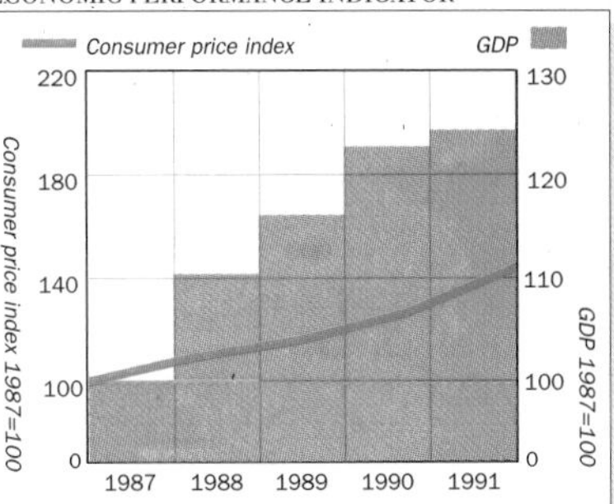

INDIA : MAJOR BUSINESSES

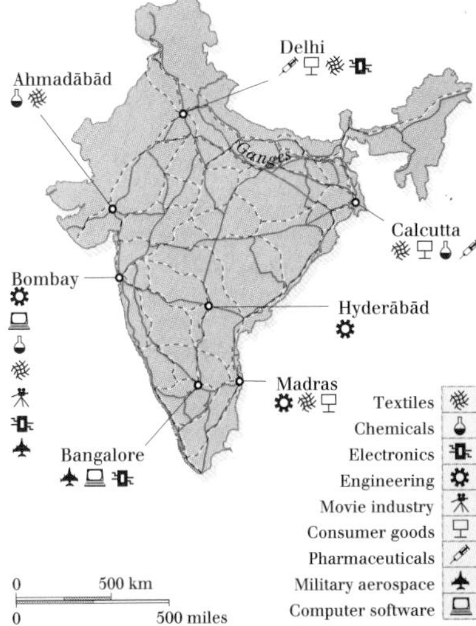

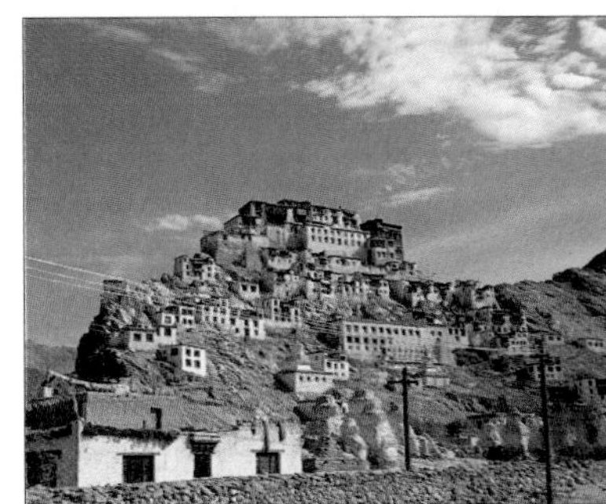

Hillside monastery in Ladakh, Kashmir, northern India. *The Ladakhi Buddhists manintain their traditional farming existence and are known for their friendliness.*

I

RESOURCES

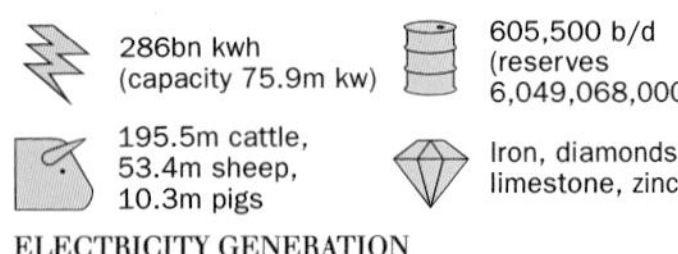

ELECTRICITY GENERATION

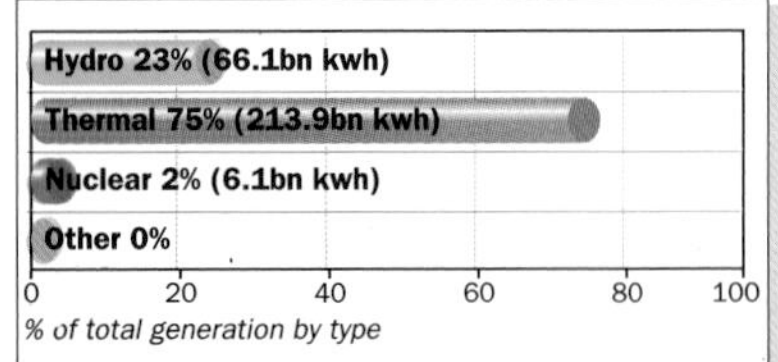

India's most significant mineral exports are iron ore and cut diamonds. There are, in addition, large coal reserves. The steel industry has recently been opened up in line with the free market reforms. Steel imports are now subject to lower duties, but the industry has so far withstood external competition, and exports have increased. However, production, which consumes up to twice as much energy as that used by some foreign competitors, is inefficient by international standards.

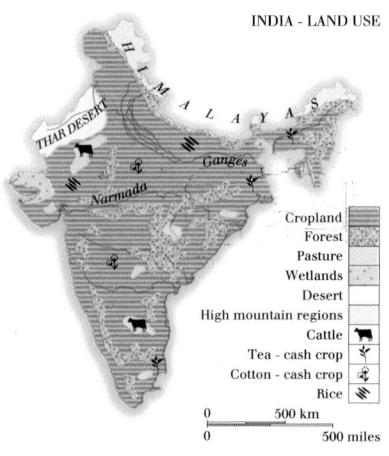

The state is currently unable to meet the country's demand for electricity. Petroleum and coal are the main sources of energy generation; however, much of these are imported. In summer, cities face acute power shortages and frequent power cuts. Attempts have been made to improve the efficiency of existing stations, and the government is planning to increase capacity by another 31,000 MW by 1997. A scheme has also been launched to attract large-scale private investment in the industry.

ENVIRONMENT

4% (3% partially protected)

Forestry programs are largely funded through foreign aid

ENVIRONMENTAL TREATIES

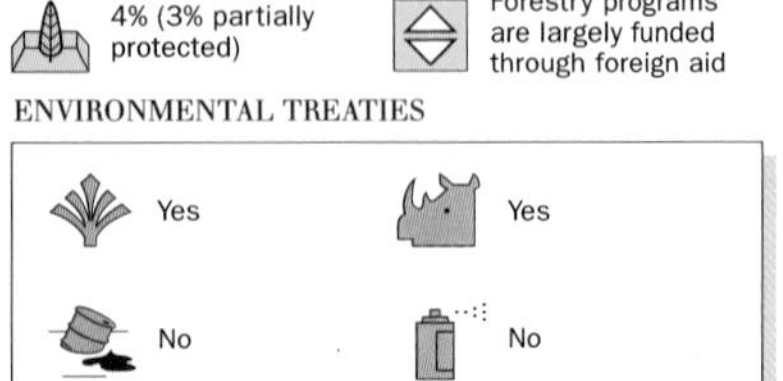

Deforestation is one of India's most pressing environmental problems. Unplanned industrial development and the pressure for more agricultural land have felled once lush tree cover and less than 11% of original forest cover remains. The effect has been a sharp rise in soil erosion, the silting up of dams, and landslides. India experienced its worst environmental accident in 1984, when an explosion at the Union Carbide plant in Bhopāl led to an escape of lethal gases. Over 2,000 died.

INDIA - LAND USE

Himalayas, Thar Desert, Ganges, Narmada

Cropland, Forest, Pasture, Wetlands, Desert, High mountain regions, Cattle, Tea - cash crop, Cotton - cash crop, Rice

0 500 km / 0 500 miles

MEDIA

Some censorship of the press. Western TV soaps and films widely considered unsuitable

PUBLISHING AND BROADCAST MEDIA

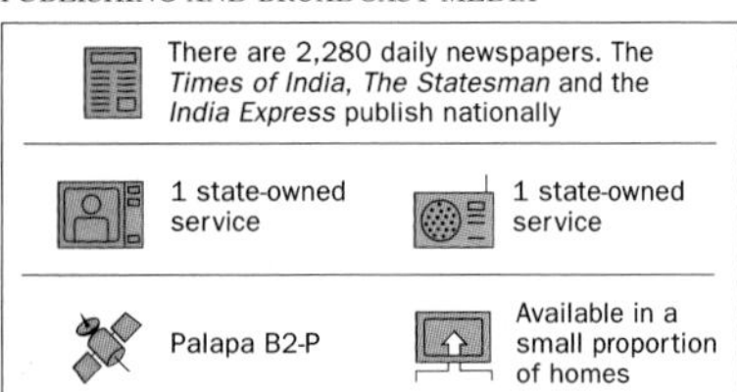

There are 2,280 daily newspapers. The *Times of India, The Statesman* and the *India Express* publish nationally
1 state-owned service
1 state-owned service
Palapa B2-P
Available in a small proportion of homes

Satellite TV is increasingly popular in India. Services range from the BBC World Service to CNN, Hindi language Zee TV and MTV, and one state-run channel. In just two years, seven million households have acquired dishes. State-run terrestrial TV has suffered as a result. Critics fear a potential Western onslaught on Indian values. Recent newspaper launches include the *Asian Age*, which is simultaneously published in London by satellite and claims to be India's first truly international paper.

CRIME

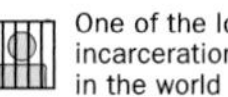

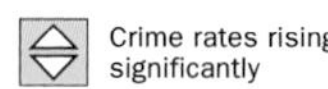

CRIME RATES

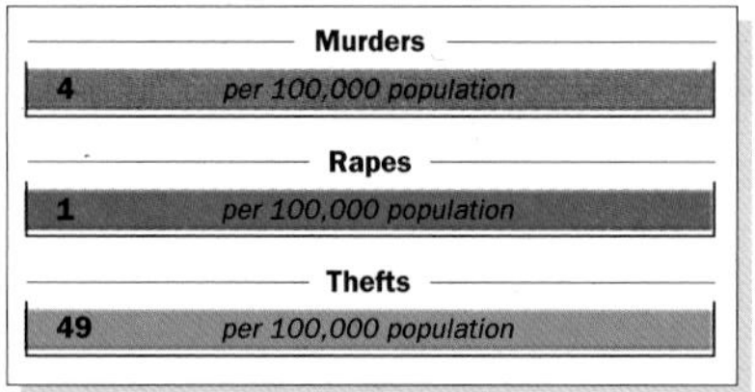

Murders
4 per 100,000 population
Rapes
1 per 100,000 population
Thefts
49 per 100,000 population

Violent crime is on the increase, particularly in the big cities. Theft has risen sharply as consumer spending increases.

Many violent criminal gangs operating in major cities such as Bombay have made vast profits from smuggling, prostitution, drugs, protection and extortion rackets, and grabbing land from the poor. Bombay's gangs have strong connections with Dubai and the Middle East; they are also said to have contacts among politicians and the police.

In large areas of central India, particularly in the region around Gwalior, *dacoits* still operate. Modeled on the *thugee* gangs of the 19th century, they are outlaws who live by highway robbery and terrorizing small rural communities.

EDUCATION

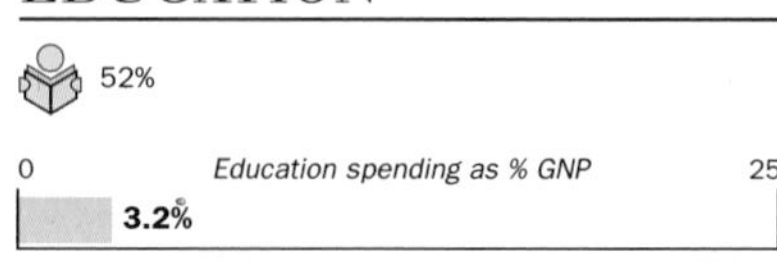

THE EDUCATION SYSTEM

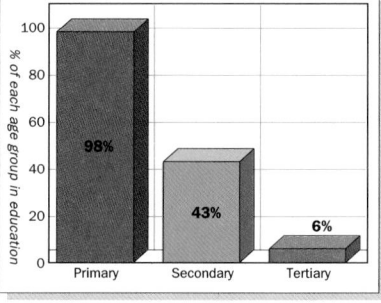

% of each age group in education: Primary 98%, Secondary 43%, Tertiary 6%

There is now a primary school in every village across the subcontinent. However, many children drop out of school to provide supplementary income for their families. There are 50 million students at secondary level, and some 10 million graduates from nearly 200 universities. Women make up 9% of those enrolled in higher education, a high percentage for a low-income economy. India has one of the largest pools of science graduates anywhere in the world. However, the 48% illiteracy rate among adults is a significant brake on development.

Corn cultivation in terraced fields in central India. *In addition to rice, wheat, sorghum, corn, millet and barley are also important cereal crops.*

REGIONS

WEST BENGAL

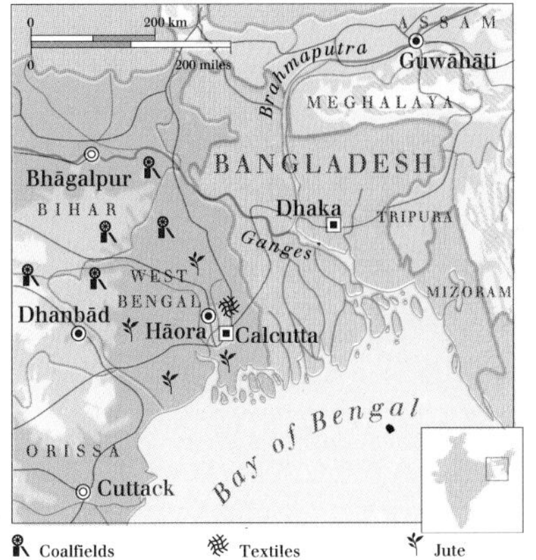

WEST BENGAL is the only region in the world with a freely elected communist government. The communists have ruled the state since 1978. Once home to 80% of the country's industry, West Bengal then became synonymous with economic decline and stagnation. However, the government has now revolutionized its economic policy, welcoming once-hated multinationals in key sectors.

Calcutta, the capital of the British Raj until 1911, has been in slow decline ever since. Over 20% of the city's 12 million people live in appalling slum conditions. Mother Theresa runs her famous mission in the city.

KARNATAKA

BANGALORE, THE CAPITAL of Karnataka, has earned itself the name of the "silicon plateau." Reputed to be South Asia's fastest-growing city, it is the home of a burgeoning electronics industry. A large pool of skilled engineering staff and comparatively low wage rates have attracted many foreign, particularly US, firms to the city.

The rich forest areas of Karnataka, particularly in the Western Ghats, include rare tracts of moist tropical deciduous forest. Vast acreages of eucalyptus trees have been planted, but most of these have been used for industrial purposes rather than to alleviate the fuelwood crisis faced by the rural poor.

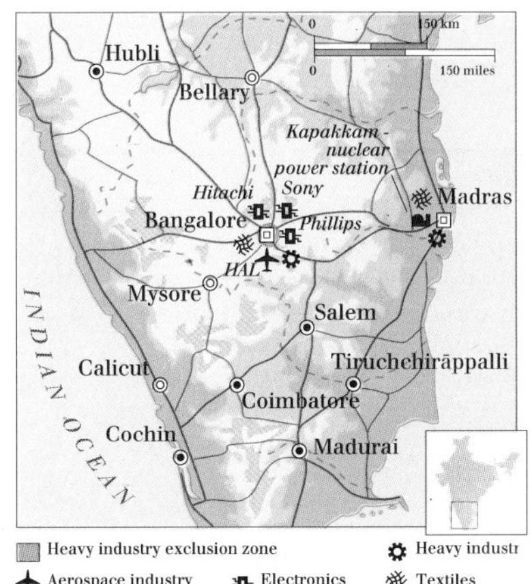

BOMBAY

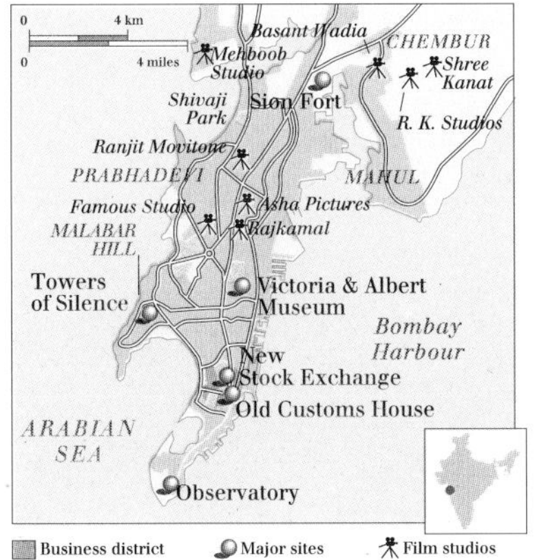

BOMBAY IS THE SYMBOL of 1990s India, with a reputation for making people rich, legally or illegally. Fast moving, cosmopolitan and rapidly expanding, it is the country's commercial capital. Central Bombay, a mixture of skyscrapers and English colonial architecture, boasts some of the highest real estate prices in the world. Dalal Street is home to the Bombay Stock Exchange, which was set up in 1875. One of the city's folk heroes is Harshad Mehta, who made a fortune selling stocks in the early 1990s, before being exposed as the man behind India's biggest-ever financial fraud.

Bombay is the center of India's movie industry, which is the world's biggest producer of feature films. Indian movies are exported to over 100 countries. The stars of what is known as "Bollywood," India's Hollywood, live in the affluent Malabar Hills neighborhood. Yet, beside this, there is also mass poverty. A 2.8 mile sprawl of shanties known as Dharavi in central Bombay is reputed to be the world's biggest slum.

HEALTH

1 per 2,400 people

Respiratory, nutritional and diarrheal diseases, malaria

0 — *Health spending as % GNP* — 25

0.8%

Malnutrition is common among the poor, and infant mortality stands at 90 per 1,000 live births. Much of this is due to preventable diseases such as diarrhea. AIDS began to spread in the mid-1980s and is now accelerating. HIV infection rates among prostitutes have increased twentyfold in seven years. A five-year program aimed at raising awareness and improving blood banks is being funded by the World Bank.

WEALTH

Field crop worker, 7–33 Indian rupees per day; office clerk, 380–875 Indian rupees per month

CONSUMER GOODS OWNERSHIP

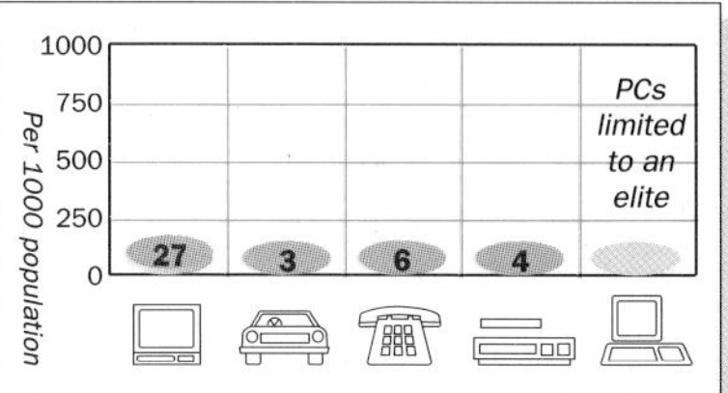

According to the government, 240 million people (30% of the population), mostly in rural areas, were living below the poverty line in the late 1980s. Recent studies dispute whether this figure is rising or falling. Extremes of wealth, particularly with the opening-up of the economy, are frequently seen alongside extremes of poverty. The middle class, who number some 150–200 million, have an exceedingly comfortable lifestyle, with servants and plush housing. Many of the slums in cities such as Bombay and Calcutta have five to nine people living in one room; few slum houses have sanitation. In Bombay alone, over 100,000 people live on the streets.

WORLD RANKING

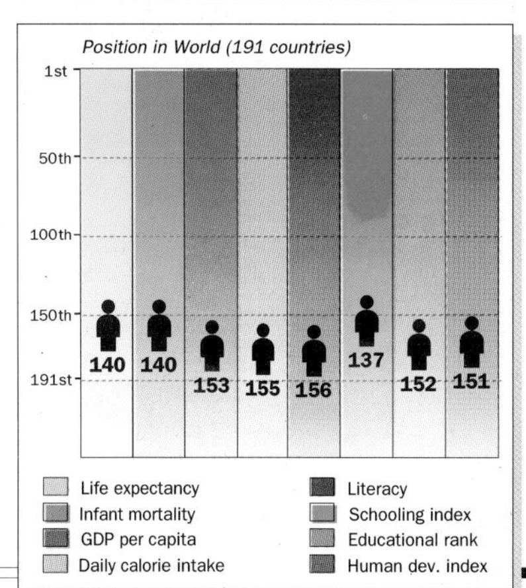

INDONESIA

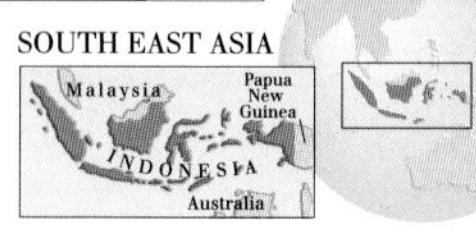

OFFICIAL NAME: Republic of Indonesia **CAPITAL:** Jakarta
POPULATION: 191.2 million **CURRENCY:** Rupiah **OFFICIAL LANGUAGE:** Bahasa Indonesia

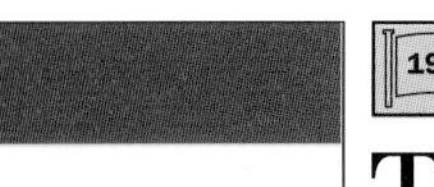

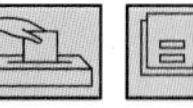

THE WORLD'S LARGEST ARCHIPELAGO, Indonesia's myriad islands stretch about 3,000 miles eastward across the Pacific, from the Malay Peninsula to New Guinea. The main islands of Sumatra, Java, Kalimantan, Irian Jaya and Sulawesi are mountainous, volcanic and densely forested. Formerly the Dutch East Indies, Indonesia achieved independence in 1949. Politics have since been dominated by the military. Demands for greater autonomy by outlying islands and for liberation by East Timor, annexed in 1975, have been forcefully opposed.

Rice terraces on Bali, *one of Indonesia's 13,677 islands and its most popular tourist destination. Rice is the staple food crop.*

CLIMATE

WEATHER CHART

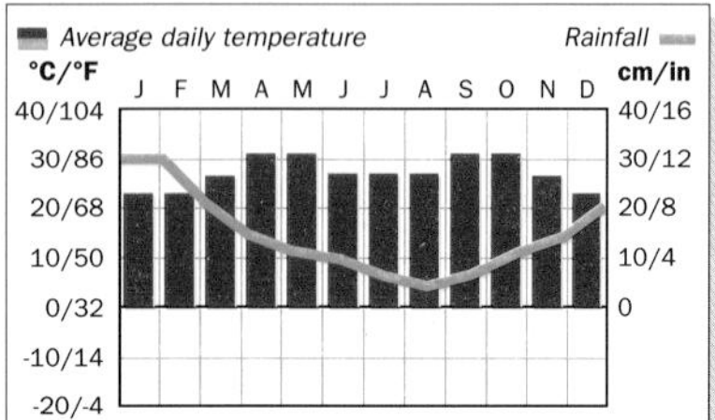

Indonesia's climate is predominantly tropical monsoon. Variations relate mainly to differences in latitude and physical structure, but hilly areas are cooler overall. Rain falls throughout the year, often in thunderstorms, but there is a relatively dry season from June to September. December to March is the wettest period, except in the Moluccas, which receive the bulk of their rain between June and September. Rainfall averages between 60 and 155 inches a year.

COMMUNICATIONS

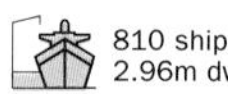

THE TRANSPORTATION NETWORK

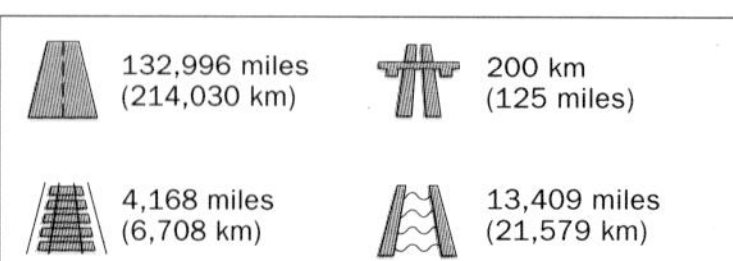

With 13,677 islands spread across over 3,000 miles and three time zones, communications are an obvious government priority. Indonesia was an early entrant into satellite communications and a countrywide, satellite-based telephone system is being installed.

Indonesia's road and shipping infrastructure is also being improved. Ports are being extended and highway projects include the recently completed Jakarta–Bandung link. The toll roads around Jakarta are contracted to President Suharto's daughter, Siti.

TOURISM

3.1m visitors

MAIN OVERSEAS ARRIVALS

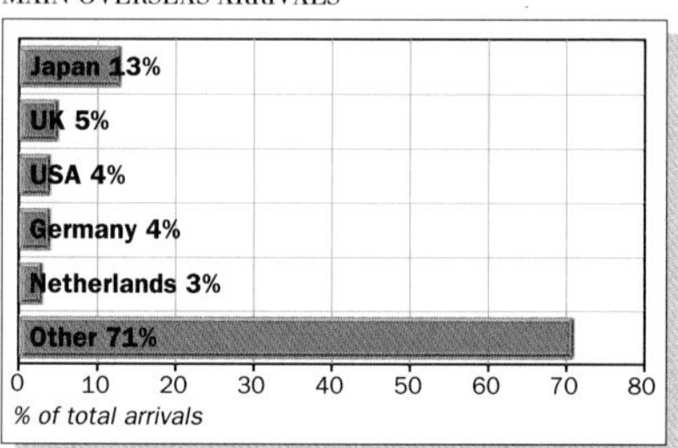

Tourism has taken off since the mid-1980s. The number of visitors increased by an average 24% a year between 1986 and 1992, to over three million. Bali, Java and Sumatra are the most popular destinations. The expansion has been underpinned by several factors, including a major investment in hotels and the opening of Bali to airlines other than the national carrier, *Garuda Indonesia.*

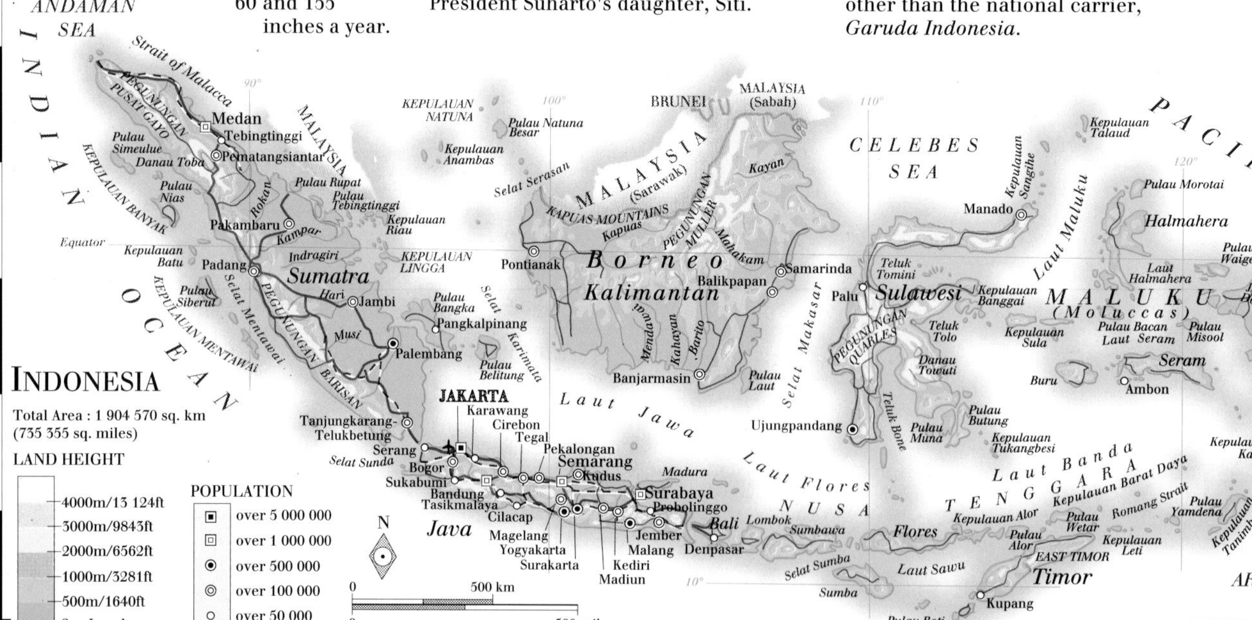

PEOPLE

Javanese, Madurese, Sundanese, Bahasa Indonesia, Dutch

243 people per sq. mile

THE URBAN/RURAL POPULATION SPLIT

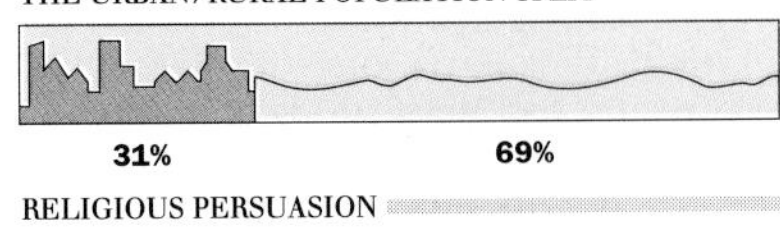

RELIGIOUS PERSUASION

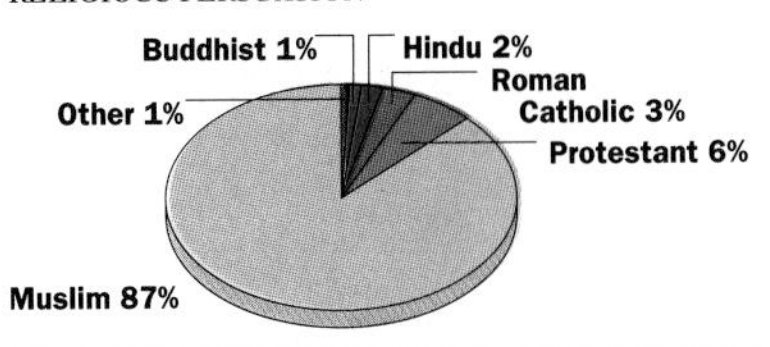

ETHNIC MAKEUP

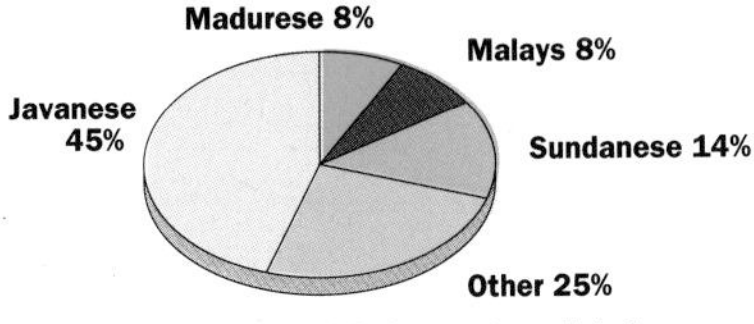

Indonesia's basic Melanesian–Malay ethnic division disguises a very diverse society. At least 250 languages or dialects are spoken. Urbanization and the national language, Bahasa Indonesia, have acted as unifying factors. The Javanese-dominated central government, however, has caused much resentment by attempting to suppress local culture and politics in order to create a national identity. The East Timoreans, the Aceh of northern Sumatra and the Papuans of Irian Jaya, denied autonomy, are all in conflict with the government.

Discrimination against the Chinese community, which has included a ban on Chinese script, has not undermined its dominance of big business.

The traditional extended family is breaking down in urban areas. There is sexual equality by law, and women are taking an increasingly active economic role – led by President Suharto's wife and daughter, both engaged in business.

POPULATION AGE BREAKDOWN

% of population by age group

	1960	1970	1980	1990	2000
65+	3.3%	3.1%	3.3%	3.9%	5.1%
15–64	56.6%	54.7%	55.7%	60.4%	63.6%
0–14	40.1%	42.2%	41%	35.7%	31.3%

WORLD AFFAIRS

Indonesia's foreign policy under General Suharto has been one of non-alignment (it became NAM chairman in 1992), tempered by the need to retain good relations with the West.

Foreign policy concerns include a continuing suspicion of China, despite the restoration of diplomatic ties in 1990. Indonesia has resolved its differences over the Timor Gap boundary with Australia, and relations have generally improved.

Internationally, the government is coming under pressure, particularly from the USA, to improve its human rights record.

AID

$1.9bn (receipts)

Up 7.5 in 1991

Indonesia relies on aid to cover its current account deficit. Japan accounts for 75% of bilateral aid; the World Bank for 58% of multilateral aid. Almost 30% of all aid is affected by "leakage," including project delays and corruption.

POLITICS

1997

President Gen. Suharto

THE STATE OF THE PARTIES

House of Representatives 500 members

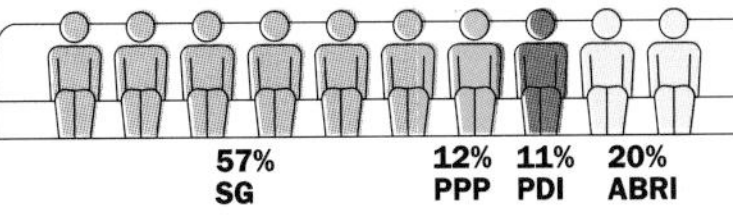

SG = Joint Secretariat of Functional Groups **PPP** = United Development Party **PDI** = Indonesian Democratic Party **ABRI** = Indonesian Armed Forces (appointed members)

People's Consultative Assembly 1,000 members

500 members of House of Representatives and 500 further members, including delegates from regional assemblies and representatives of political organizations

Indonesia is a highly-controlled semi-democracy, headed by General Suharto, who was returned for his sixth consecutive term as president in 1993.

MAIN POLITICAL ISSUE

The succession

President Suharto will be almost 77 by the next elections, and is under pressure to ensure a peaceful transition. Vice-President Try Sutrisno appears to be the military's choice, but may not be Suharto's. A key factor in his decision is expected to be the protection of his children and their extensive economic interests.

PROFILE

Indonesia's elections are invariably won by the SG, a group representing farmers, fishermen and professionals, rather than a political party. The SG is dominated by President Suharto and the armed forces. There have been only two legal opposition parties since 1972 – the Muslim-dominated United Development Party (PPP) and the Christian-oriented Indonesian Democratic Party (PDI). In practice, these operate as ineffective "partners" of government. Opposition to the Javan political elite and its centralist politics has fueled secessionist movements in Sumatra and Irian Jaya and a liberation movement on East Timor, annexed by Indonesia in 1975.

***General Suharto**, ex-army chief of staff. President since 1968.*

***Mrs. Suharto**, influential in political and business circles.*

CHRONOLOGY

On the trade route between India and China, the Indonesian archipelago, with its rich resources, has long attracted outside interest – Hindu, Buddhist, Islamic, then, from the 16th century, European. The Dutch were victors in the rivalry to exploit its strategic position,valuable spices and oil. Colonization began in the 17th century on Java. By 1910, the Dutch East Indies encompassed the whole of present-day Indonesia, except East Timor.

- **1901** Dutch introduce "ethical policy" giving limited educational and administrative opportunities to indigenous population and encourage growth of intellectual class with nationalist aspirations.
- **1912** Sarekat Islam party formed.
- **1920** Indonesian Communist Party (PKI) formed; leads revolts in West Java, 1926; Sumatra, 1927.
- **1927** Indonesian National Party formed under Dr. Sukarno.
- **1930s** Dutch repression.
- **1942–1945** Japanese occupation. Promise of autonomy in "Greater East Asia." Sukarno works with Japanese while promoting independence.
- **1945** August: three days after Japanese surrender, Sukarno declares Indonesia independent from the Netherlands.

I

CHRONOLOGY *continued*

- **1945–1949** Nationalist guerrilla war with Dutch – interspersed with negotiations – who refuse to recognize independence.
- **1949** December: independence. United States of Indonesia under President Sukarno: federation, giving limited self-government to regions. Irian Jaya stays under Dutch control until 1962.
- **1950** Federation dissolved. Unitary Republic of Indonesia.
- **1950–1957** Six governments, none able to address growing problems. Sukarno convinced country not ready for parliamentary democracy; introduces authoritarian "guided democracy," then martial law.
- **1959** Sukarno extends presidential powers. Civilian legislature replaced by military. Extreme nationalist and pro-Chinese policies. A leader of the NAM.
- **1965** Corruption of Sukarno regime, inflation and breakdown of PKI–military alliance provoke abortive military coup. PKI implicated. Mass killing of alleged PKI supporters. PKI banned.
- **1966** Sukarno forced to hand over power to army chief-of-staff General Suharto. Temporary handover becomes permanent in following year.
- **1968** Gen. Suharto becomes president. Declares "New Order": real power passes from cabinet to small group of officers. Sukarno's anti-Western stance reversed; liberal economic policies introduced.
- **1971** First elections since 1955. Government-sponsored SG wins this and all succeeding elections. Opposition parties now passive partners of government.
- **1973** Suharto reelected president; again in 1978, 1983 and 1988.
- **1975** Indonesia invades East Timor; incorporated as Indonesia's 27th province in 1976. Takeover not recognized by UN.
- **1984** Muslim protesters clash with troops in Jakarta. Start of resurgence of Islamic protest.
- **1985** Independence of East Timor declared by FRETILIN liberation front. Repressed by military.
- **1989** Growing discontent with authoritarian government; student protests, unrest in Java and Sumbawa. Demands for Suharto to retire. Low-key official response.
- **1991** New organizations, including Democratic Forum and League for Restoration of Democracy, allowed to form in response to growing demands for "openness."
- **1993** Suharto wins sixth term in office.

DEFENSE

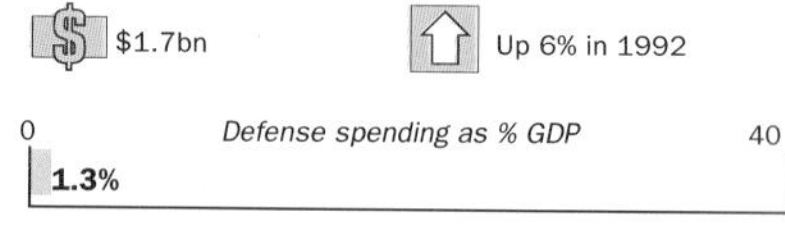

INDONESIAN ARMED FORCES

155 light tanks (125 AMX-13/30 PT-76)
215,000 personnel
2 submarines, 3 frigates and 48 patrol boats
44,000 personnel
18 combat aircraft (12 N-22 Searchmaster B/ 6 Searchmaster L)
1,000 personnel
None

The constitution enshrines the military's political role, and it remains a key influence in Indonesia. The recent "civilianization" of political parties, the bureaucracy and state companies has reduced the presence of the military in these areas, if not their influence. This was also apparent in the appointment of former supreme commander Try Sutrisno as vice-president, and thus a leading candidate to succeed Suharto. Defense spending is low by regional standards. However, "off-budget funds" often supplement official allocations. The main defense issues are currently internal security and the perceived Chinese threat.

ECONOMICS

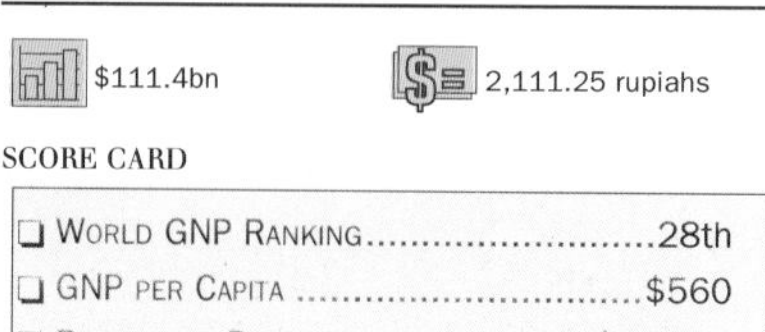

SCORE CARD

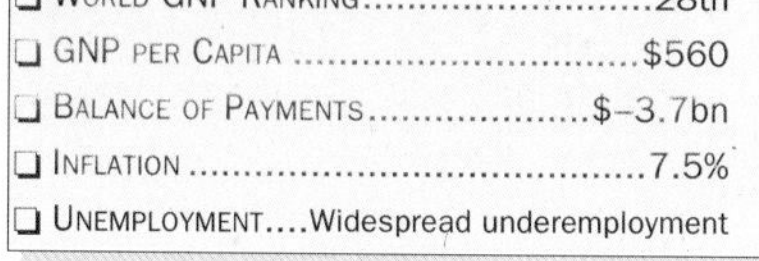

- World GNP Ranking..........................28th
- GNP per Capita..............................$560
- Balance of Payments....................$-3.7bn
- Inflation..7.5%
- Unemployment....Widespread underemployment

EXPORTS

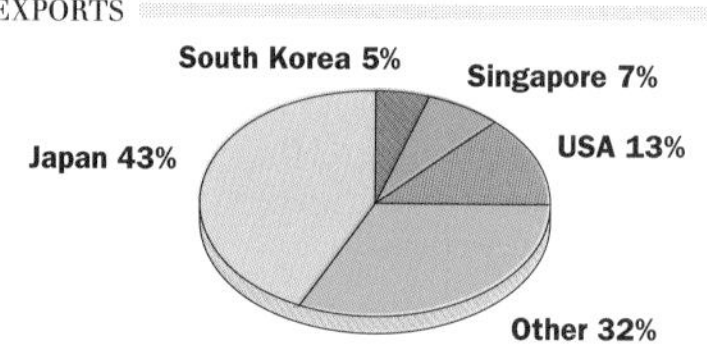

IMPORTS

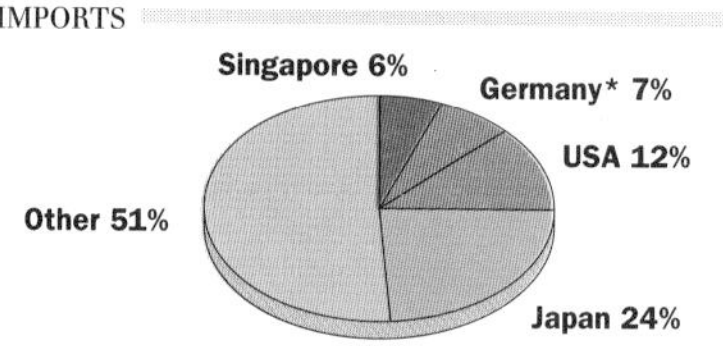

Strengths

Varied resources, especially energy. Expansion of manufacturing, including high-tech. Growth of nearly 7% a year. Cheap and plentiful labor.

Weaknesses

Red tape; corruption. State control of economy. Competition for investment from China and Vietnam. $85 billion debt burden.

ECONOMIC PERFORMANCE INDICATOR

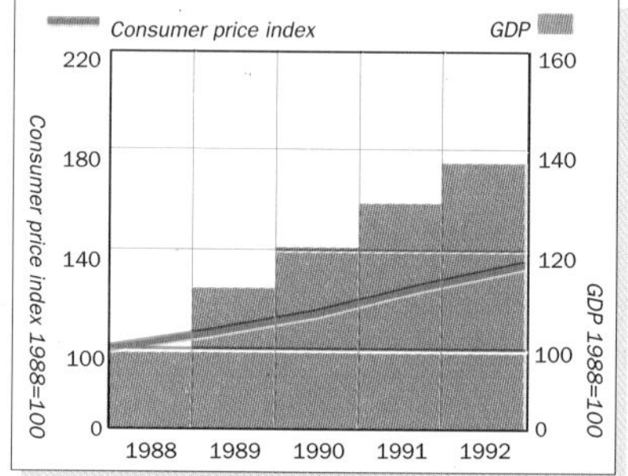

Profile

For 25 years, the economy has grown by almost 7% a year, fueled by foreign investment and oil. State-owned corporations play a significant role in the economy, which is protected against foreign competition. Non-oil exports, especially manufactured goods, are rapidly diversifying and expanding, but there is concern about the future. Oil revenues are set to decline and competition for investment from Vietnam and China is growing. However, the debt burden eats up 32% of export earnings. Government promises to cut red tape and privatize have yet to be fulfilled, reflecting conflict between advocates of deregulation and the "technologists" who argue that, in the short term, industrialization is more important than profitable state concerns.

INDONESIA : MAJOR BUSINESSES

RESOURCES

44.3bn kwh (capacity 11.48m kw)

1.4m b/d (reserves 5,779,000,000 bbl)

10.3m cattle, 6.6m pigs, 5.5m sheep

Oil, natural gas, tin, bauxite, nickel, copper, gold, coal

ELECTRICITY GENERATION

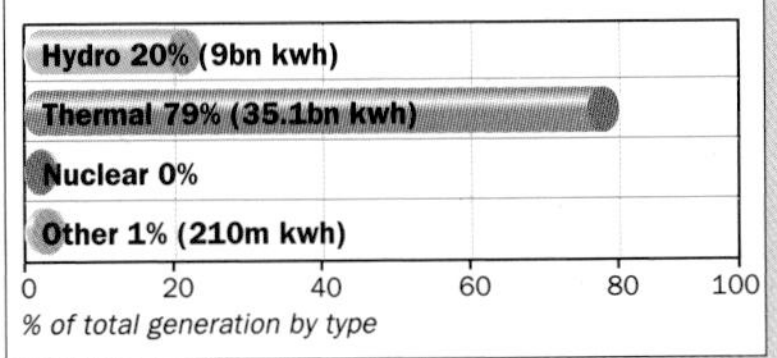

INDONESIA : LAND USE

Indonesia is rich in energy sources. Oil, which financed rapid industrialization, and liquefied natural gas (the country is the world's largest LNG exporter) are the main export earners. However, oil output is falling – down 6% in 1992 to 1.4m b/d. Combined with rapid growth in domestic energy demand, this could turn Indonesia into an oil importer in the next decade. The government is therefore encouraging the extension of exploration into remote regions. It is also considering developing geothermal and nuclear energy sources. Indonesia's other main resources are coal, bauxite and nickel, and agricultural products such as rubber and palm oil. With 75% of the land classified as forest, timber production is also significant.

ENVIRONMENT

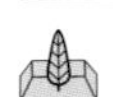

10% (3% partially protected)

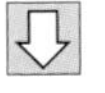

Few active restrictions on logging

ENVIRONMENTAL TREATIES

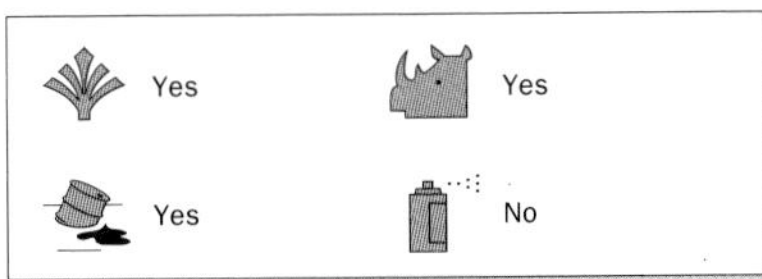

Environmental legislation is badly policed and often ignored. The worst problem relates to the protection of Indonesia's rich tropical forests, which are threatened by excessive logging. Some predict the forests could be gone in 30 years. Frequent oil spillages in the Malacca Strait are a major hazard.

MEDIA

The Indonesian press is relatively free; criticism tends to be coded to avoid official censure

PUBLISHING AND BROADCAST MEDIA

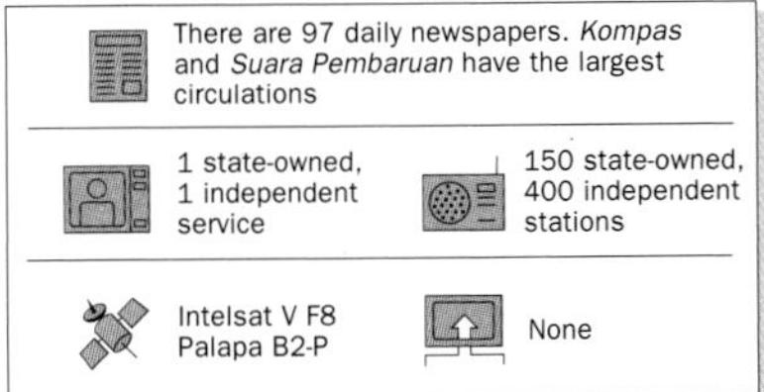

There are 97 daily newspapers. Kompas and Suara Pembaruan have the largest circulations
1 state-owned, 1 independent service
150 state-owned, 400 independent stations
Intelsat V F8 Palapa B2-P
None

Media self-censorship encourages a rich rumor-mongering tradition. The daily *Kompas* and the weekly *Tempo* are outstanding among the printed media. President Suharto's children were quick to take advantage of the 1987 decision to open TV to the private sector.

CRIME

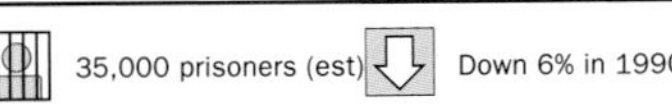

CRIME RATES

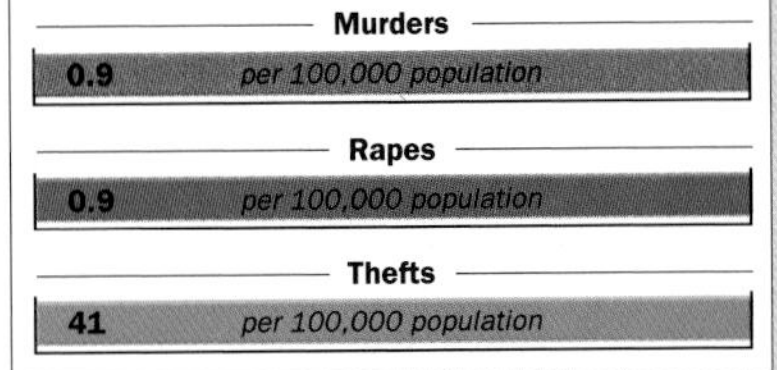

Human rights agencies are concerned about the government's violent reaction to demands for autonomy.

EDUCATION

77%

0 — Education spending as % GNP — 25

0.9%

THE EDUCATION SYSTEM

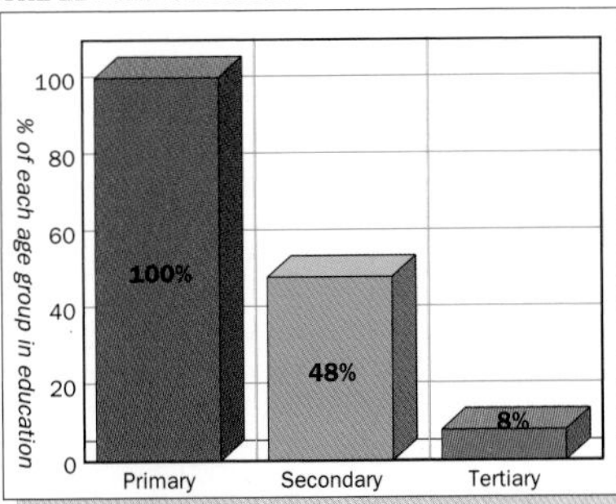

Primary education is compulsory. Secondary schooling is expanding, but is still limited in rural areas.

HEALTH

1 per 7,372 people

Lower respiratory and diarrheal diseases

0 — Health spending as % GNP — 25

0.5%

There are relatively few hospitals; about half are privately administered. However, the extensive network of clinics, down to village level, makes access to health care reasonably good. As a result, health indicators have improved significantly over the past 20 years. The death rate declined from 20 per 1,000 in 1965 to 9 per 1,000 in 1990, helping to increase life expectancy to 62 years. Infant mortality more than halved, from 128 to 61 per 1,000 live births, over the same period.

WEALTH

Agricultural worker, 100,000 rupiahs per month; engineer, 1.5m rupiahs per month

CONSUMER GOODS OWNERSHIP

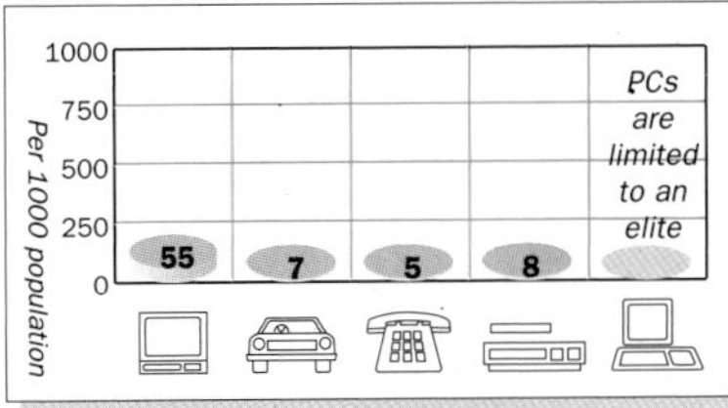

Despite its oil wealth and the rapid industrialization and improvements in agricultural productivity of the past 30 years, Indonesia is still grouped among the low-income economies by the World Bank. Health and education have improved, but many Indonesians live in relative poverty, and those on the peripheral islands, notably Irian Jaya, northern Sumatra and East Timor, live in real poverty. This reflects both a concentration of wealth in the hands of a limited number of key political and business figures, and the concentration of development and investment on the main islands, particularly on Java.

WORLD RANKING

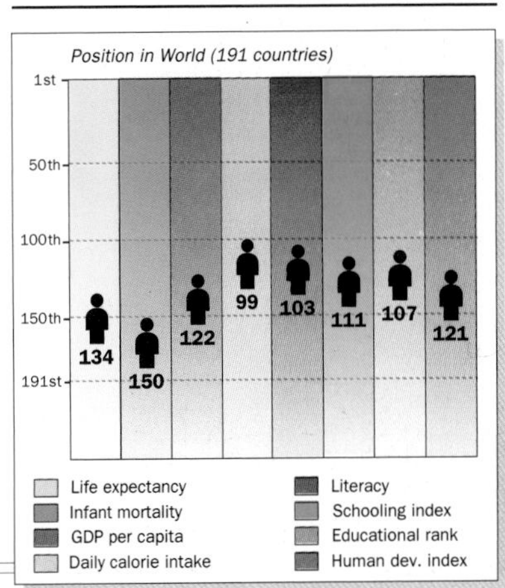

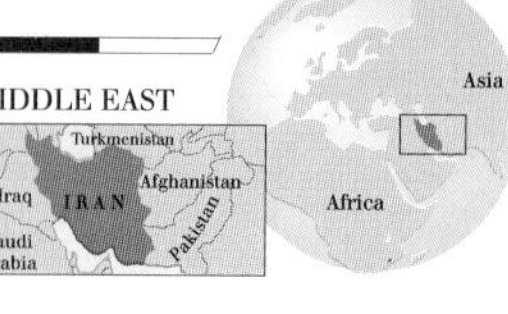

IRAN

OFFICIAL NAME: Islamic Republic of Iran **CAPITAL:** Tehran
POPULATION: 61.6 million **CURRENCY:** Iranian rial **OFFICIAL LANGUAGE:** Farsi

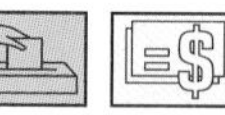

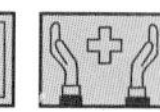

IRAN IS SURROUNDED by powerful neighbors, with republics of the former Soviet Union to the north, Afghanistan and Pakistan to the east, and Iraq and Turkey to the west. The south faces the Persian Gulf and the Gulf of Oman. Since 1979, when a revolution led by Ayatollah Khomeini deposed the Shah, Iran has become the world's largest theocracy and the leading center for militant Shi'a Islam. Iran's active support for Islamic fundamentalist movements has led to strained relations with Central Asian, Middle Eastern and North African nations, as well as with the USA.

*The **Reshteh-ye Kuhhā-ye Alborz** (Elburz Mountains). Their Caspian Sea slopes are rainy and forested; the southern slopes are dry.*

CLIMATE

WEATHER CHART

Average daily temperature — Rainfall
°C/°F: 40/104, 30/86, 20/68, 10/50, 0/32, -10/14, -20/4
J F M A M J J A S O N D
cm/in: 40/16, 30/12, 20/8, 10/4, 0

The area bordering the Caspian Sea is Iran's most temperate region. Most of the country has a desert climate.

COMMUNICATIONS

THE TRANSPORTATION NETWORK

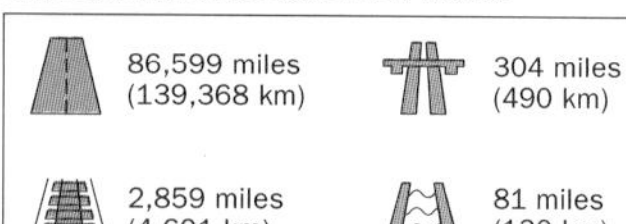

Adequate roads link main towns, but rural areas are less well served. Most freight travels by rail. A ferry runs from Bandar-e 'Abbās to the UAE.

PEOPLE

Farsi (Persian), Azerbaijani, Gilaki, Mazanderani, Kurdish, Baluchi, Arabic, Turkmen

85 people per sq. mile

THE URBAN/RURAL POPULATION SPLIT

57% 43%

RELIGIOUS PERSUASION

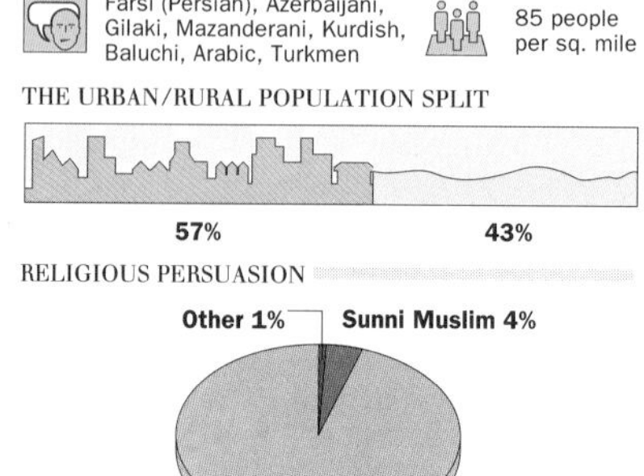

ETHNIC MAKEUP

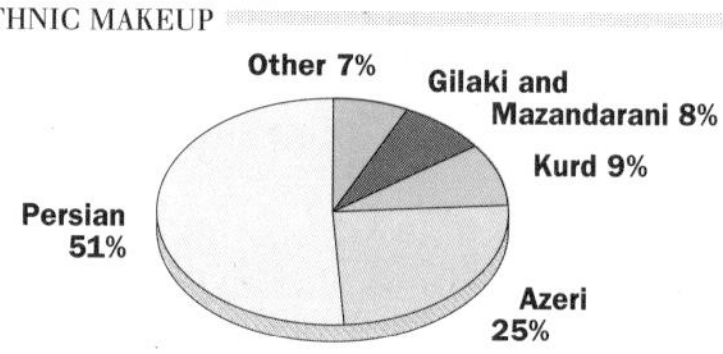

The population comprises several ethnic groups. The people of the north and center – about half of all Iranians – speak Farsi (Persian), while a further 23% speak related languages, including Kurdish in the west and Baluchi in the southeast. About a quarter of the population speaks Turkic languages, primarily the Azeris in the northwest and the Turkmen in the northeast. Smaller groups, such as the Circassians and Georgians, are found in the northern provinces.

Until the 16th century, much of Iran followed the Sunni interpretation of Islam, but since then the Shi'a sect has been dominant. Religious minorities, accounting for just 1% of the population, include followers of the Bahai faith, who suffer discrimination, Zoroastrians, Christians and Jews.

Because of the religious idealism that inspires much of Iran's political decision-making, the regime has a remarkably liberal attitude to refugees of the Muslim faith. There are nearly three million Afghan refugees scattered through 24 provinces. In Khorosan province in the east, refugees account for 23% of the population, and near the Turkish border the figure rises to 50%. Many are young, resulting in intense competition with Iranians for jobs and consequent ethnic tensions.

One of the prime aims of the 1979 Islamic revolution was to reverse the policy of female emancipation, introduced during the Shah's rule. The revolution abruptly restricted the public role of women, limiting job prospects to the medical profession and teaching. A strict dress code was enforced, obliging women to wear the ankle-length *hijab* and keep their heads covered with a scarf. However, more liberal attitudes often prevail in private, especially in affluent homes.

POPULATION AGE BREAKDOWN

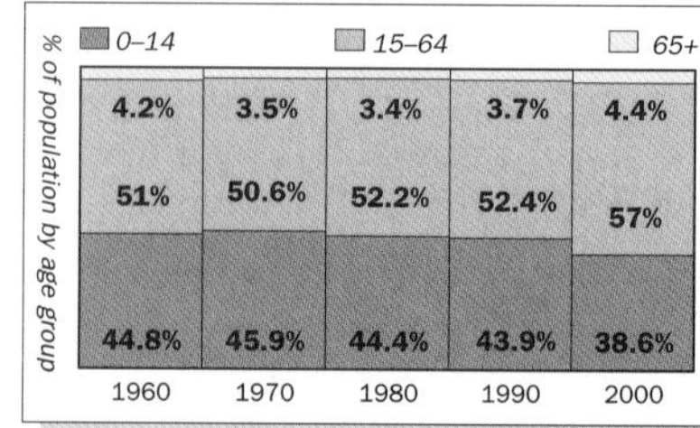

TOURISM

153,615 visitors

Up 72% in 1990

MAIN OVERSEAS ARRIVALS

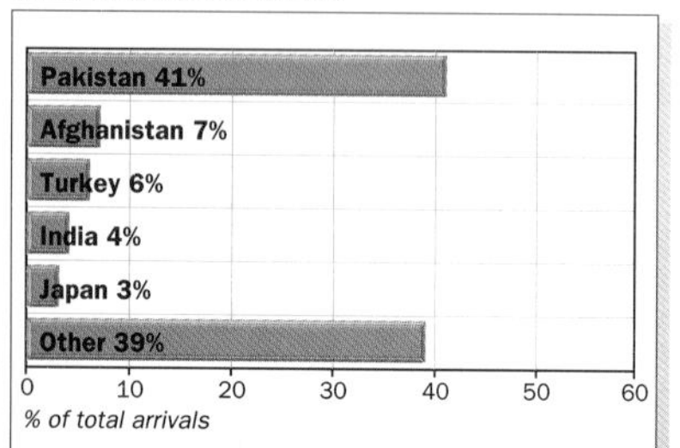

Iran's impressive historical heritage, mosques and bazaars formerly attracted sizable numbers of tourists. This flow was cut off by the 1979 revolution. Since then, adverse publicity for the regime has deterred visitors, especially from the West. In the 1990s, however, the number of business people visiting Iran has risen as the regime shows clear signs of wishing to improve its international relations. Procedures at Tehran's Mehrabad airport have been greatly speeded up and the capital's hotels have undergone some restoration.

POLITICS

1996

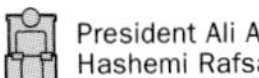
President Ali Akbar Hashemi Rafsanjani

THE STATE OF THE PARTIES

Consultative Assembly (*Majlis*) 270 members

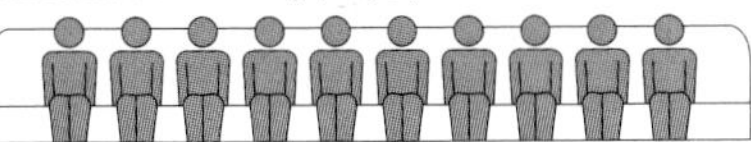

All members are elected on a non-party basis

Iran is a theocracy. An uneasy relationship exists between the mullahs (their leader exercises supreme authority, in theory) and the secular authorities, headed by an elected president.

Main Political Issue

Mosque versus secular state
The precise division of power between the mullahs and the secular state remains ill-defined. Edicts contradicting secular policy are often issued. The result is a tussle over how to run a modern economy between the conservative clergy on the one hand, and members of the assembly (*Majlis*) and reformist politicians, led by President Rafsanjani, on the other.

The mullahs remain less concerned about the effects of stagnation than the secular authorities, believing that the people's adherence to religious values is more important than their economic or material welfare. President Rafsanjani has sought to modernize the economy gradually. However, with mullahs objecting to the use of borrowed money and the import of "corrupt" Western technology, economic growth in Iran has become rather erratic.

Ayatollah Khomeini, *architect of the revolution, who died in 1989.*

President Rafsanjani, *Iran's secular leader since 1989.*

Profile

Iran's religious revolution, which brought down the monarchy, was fueled by an underprivileged people outraged at the corruption, repression and inequalities of the Shah's regime. Ayatollah Khomeini proved an effective leader of Iranian dissatisfaction. Iran's government is based on Khomeini's belief that it is the duty of the clergy, as the Prophet Mohammed's trustees on earth, to establish a just social system. Accordingly, the legislature, the executive and the judiciary may, in theory, be overruled by the religious leadership. President Rafsanjani's policies are constantly questioned by Ahmad Khomeini, son of the late Ayatollah, and by former ministers who believe in "permanent revolution" and approve of international terrorism. The mullahs remain popular among many Iranians, limiting the secular state's policy-making freedom.

I

WORLD AFFAIRS

Following the Khomeini revolution, Iran assumed international significance as the voice of militant Shi'a Islam. This was exemplified by the 1989 Salman Rushdie affair, in which Khomeini issued a *fatwa* (edict) demanding the death of the British novelist for blasphemy. Iran has attempted to foster revolution among the Shi'a minority in Saudi Arabia and has also extended its influence to the republics of the former Soviet Union, as well as to Sudan, Algeria, Egypt and Lebanon. The West views Iran's export of Islamic revolution with anxiety, but also sees the country as a buffer against Iraqi President Saddam Hussain's expansionist ambitions.

Iran's role in the Gulf has also caused controversy. Moderate Arab states were alarmed by the seizure of the islands of Abu Musa and the Tumbs from the UAE in 1970. Iran's main preoccupation, however, is Iraq, which allows *mujahideen* guerrillas to mount attacks on Iran from its territory.

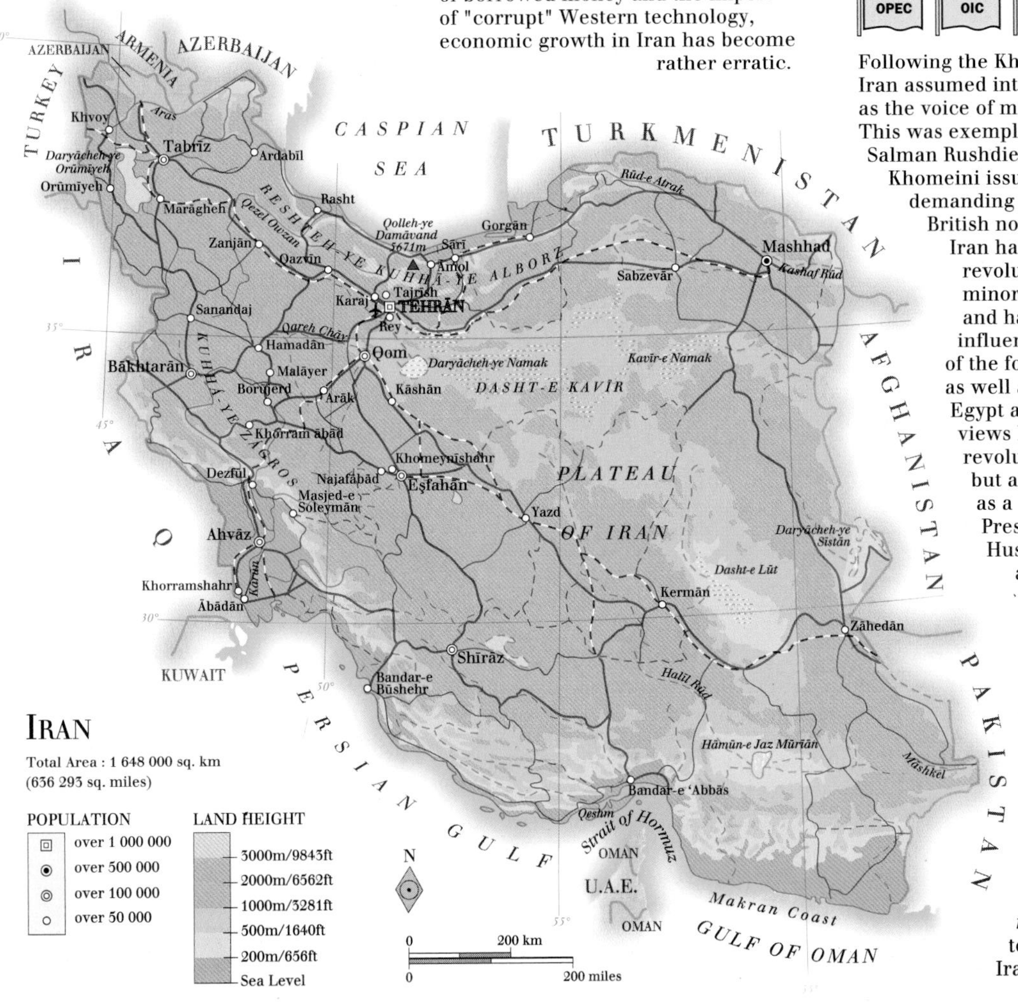

IRAN

Total Area : 1 648 000 sq. km (636 293 sq. miles)

POPULATION
- over 1 000 000
- over 500 000
- over 100 000
- over 50 000

LAND HEIGHT
- 3000m/9843ft
- 2000m/6562ft
- 1000m/3281ft
- 500m/1640ft
- 200m/656ft
- Sea Level

0 200 km
0 200 miles

CHRONOLOGY

Iran (Persia) was ruled by the Shahs as an absolute monarchy until 1906 when the first constitution was approved. The Pahlavis took power in 1925 and changed the country's name to Iran in 1935.

- ❑ **1957** SAVAK, Shah's secret police, established to control opposition.
- ❑ **1964** Ayatollah Khomeini exiled for criticisms of secular state.
- ❑ **1971** Shah celebrates 2,500th anniversary of Persian monarchy.
- ❑ **1975** Long-running dispute over access to Shatt Al Arab waterway settled with Iraq.
- ❑ **1977** Khomeini's son dies. Anti-Shah demonstrations during mourning.
- ❑ **1978** Riots and strikes. Khomeini exiled from Iraq to Paris.
- ❑ **1979** January: rising discontent; Shah goes into exile. February: Ayatollah Khomeini returns in triumph from exile in France. Islamic Revolutionary Council takes power. April: Iran declared Islamic republic. November: students seize 63 hostages at US Embassy in Tehran and demand Shah's return to face trial.
- ❑ **1980** Shah dies in exile. Start of eight-year Iran–Iraq war. Iraq invades, annulling 1975 Shatt Al Arab waterway agreement.
- ❑ **1981** US hostages released. Hojatoleslam Ali Khamenei elected president by huge majority.
- ❑ **1984** Iran captures part of marshlands around southern Iraqi island of Majnoun.
- ❑ **1985** Khamenei reelected.
- ❑ **1986** UN Security Council blames Iraq for war with Iran.
- ❑ **1987** Around 275 Iranian pilgrims killed in riots in Mecca; relations with Saudi Arabia break down.
- ❑ **1988** July: *USS Vincennes* shoots down Iranian airliner; 290 killed. August: Iran–Iraq war ends with UN-arranged ceasefire.
- ❑ **1989** February: Khomeini issues *fatwa* condemning Salman Rushdie to death for blasphemy in his novel *The Satanic Verses*. June: Khomeini dies. President Ali Khamenei appointed Supreme Religious Leader. Hashemi Rafsanjani elected president.
- ❑ **1990** Earthquake hits northern provinces, killing 45,000 people. Gulf War – Iran remains neutral.
- ❑ **1991** Iranian diplomacy helps free Western hostages in Lebanon.
- ❑ **1992** *Majlis* elections result in two-thirds support for president.
- ❑ **1993** *Fatwa* against Salman Rushdie reconfirmed. Rafsanjani reelected president.

I

AID

 $81m (receipts)

 Up 17% in 1991

As an oil exporter, Iran does not qualify for much aid. In addition, hardliners are opposed to Western aid – even in the face of disasters such as the 1990 earthquake. However, Iran receives some UN aid for its millions of refugees, who are mainly from Afghanistan, but also from Iraq, Sudan, Sri Lanka, Egypt, Palestine and India. Iran fosters the spread of Shi'a Islam by making donations for mosque building all over the world.

DEFENSE

 $4.3bn

Up 34% in 1991

0 *Defense spending as % GDP* 40

7.1%

With 528,000 men under arms, including the Revolutionary Guard Corps (*Pasdaran*), and battle experience from the war with Iraq, Iran represents a serious threat to neighboring states. Two years' military service is compulsory. The *Pasdaran* form one-third of personnel and often act as a paramilitary force to safeguard moral and behavioral standards set by the mullahs. They were used in mass frontal assaults in the war with Iraq. The navy has been weakened by clashes with Iraq and the USA.

IRANIAN ARMED FORCES

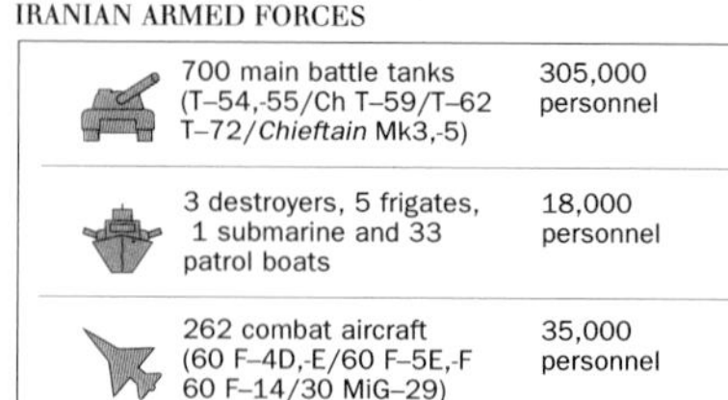

700 main battle tanks (T–54,-55/Ch T–59/T–62 T–72/*Chieftain* Mk3,-5)
305,000 personnel
3 destroyers, 5 frigates, 1 submarine and 33 patrol boats
18,000 personnel
262 combat aircraft (60 F–4D,-E/60 F–5E,-F 60 F–14/30 MiG–29)
35,000 personnel
None

ECONOMICS

$127.4bn

1,750 Iranian rials

SCORE CARD

❑ World GNP Ranking	24th
❑ GNP per Capita	$2068
❑ Balance of Payments	$–8.1bn
❑ Inflation	22.9%
❑ Unemployment	25%

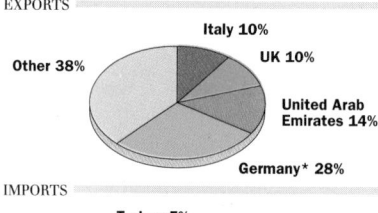

EXPORTS

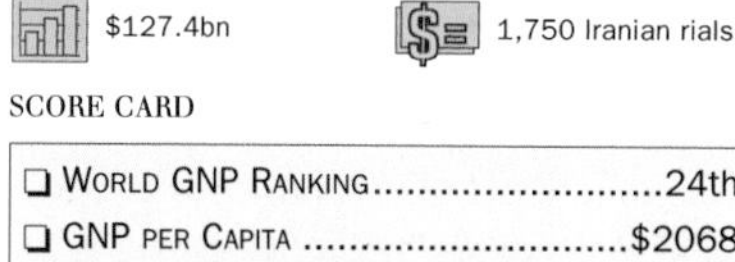

IMPORTS

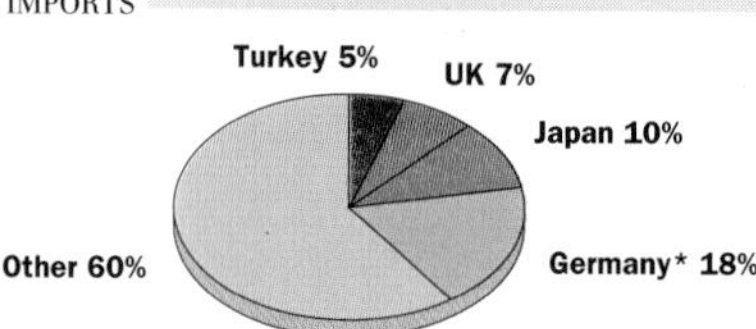

ECONOMIC PERFORMANCE INDICATOR

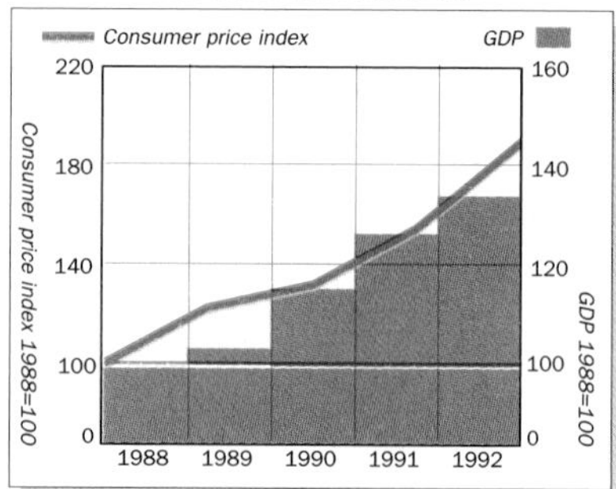

Strengths

OPEC's second-biggest oil producer. Potential for related industries and increased production of traditional exports: carpets, pistachio nuts and caviar.

Weaknesses

Theocratic government restricts contact with West, blocking acquisition of vital technology. Years of economic stagnation. High unemployment, inflation and foreign debts. Oil revenue vulnerable to market fluctuations.

Profile

Iran has few industries other than oil. The chronic shortage of foreign exchange and the costs of the long war with Iraq have accelerated a decline in living standards in the past decade.

IRAN : MAJOR BUSINESSES

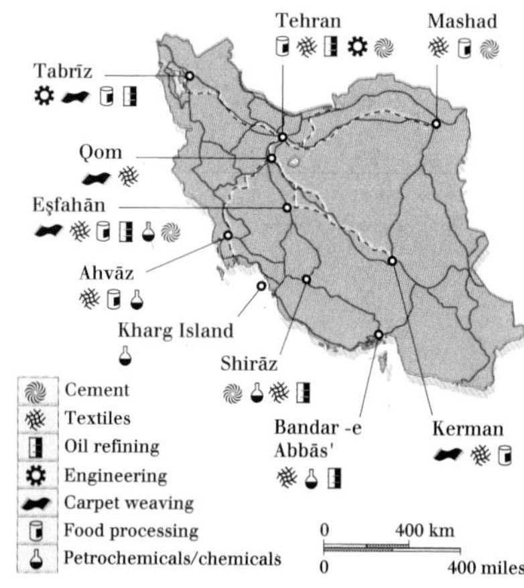

RESOURCES

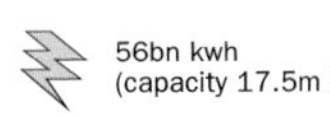

56bn kwh (capacity 17.5m kw)

3.44m b/d (reserves 92,86bn bbl)

34m sheep, 8m cattle, 1.7m asses

Iron, copper, lead, oil, zinc, chromite, coal, manganese, gypsum

ELECTRICITY GENERATION

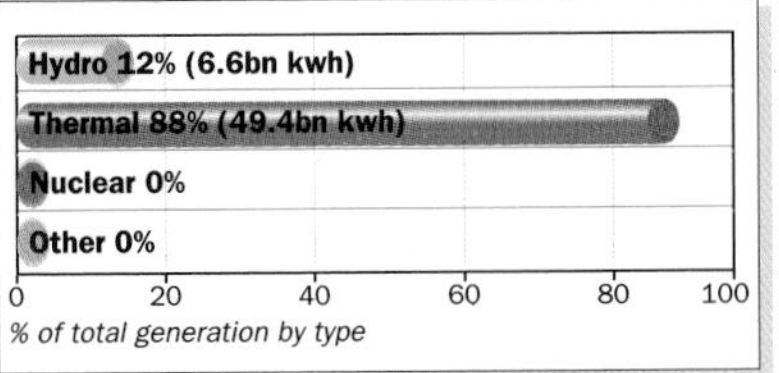

Iran has substantial oil reserves. It also has metal, coal and salt deposits, but these are relatively undeveloped. The agricultural sector is an important part of Iran's economy. Principal crops are wheat, barley, rice, sugar beet, tobacco and pistachio nuts.

Iran was once an opium exporter, but its cultivation and use has since been banned. The vodka industry has also been closed down. Enough wool is produced to supply the carpet weaving industry. Iran has insufficient livestock to supply the domestic meat market and has to import large quantities. The Caspian Sea fisheries are controlled by the state, which sells caviar for export.

IRAN : LAND USE

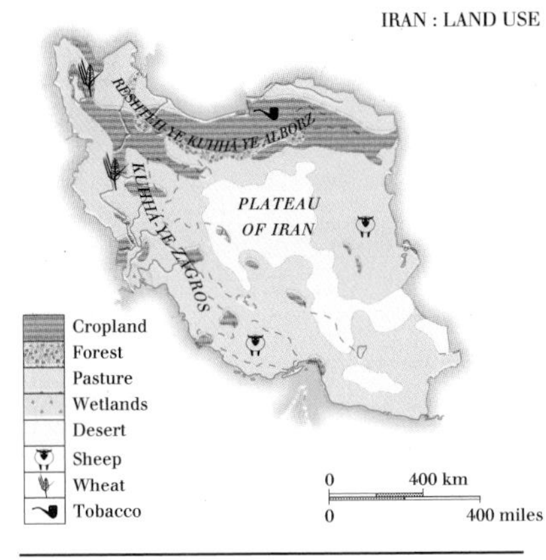

ENVIRONMENT

5% (3% partially protected)

Environmental protection is not of state concern

ENVIRONMENTAL TREATIES

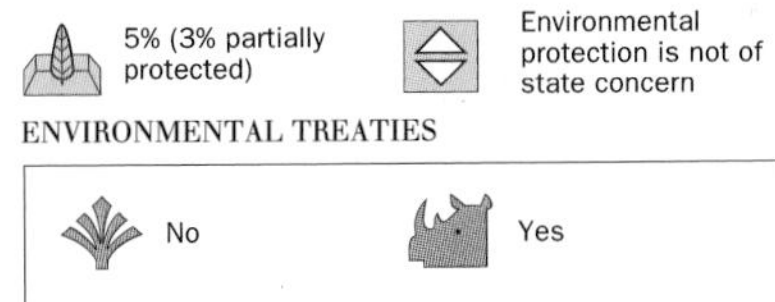

War damage to southern Iran, especially at Bandar Khomeini, the tanker terminal at Kharg Island and the refinery at Ābādān, has caused significant environmental damage. Environmental issues are not of concern to the religious leadership.

MEDIA

Censorship was introduced by the stringent Press Law of 1979. Infringement is treated as a criminal offence

PUBLISHING AND BROADCAST MEDIA

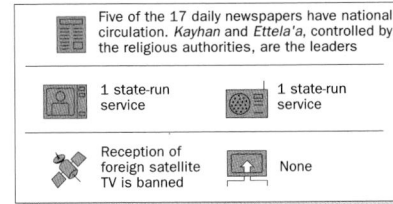

Five of the 17 daily newspapers have national circulation. *Kayhan* and *Ettela'a*, controlled by the religious authorities, are the leaders

1 state-run service

1 state-run service

Reception of foreign satellite TV is banned

None

Press freedom has been curbed. Radio and TV are state-controlled and act as a mouthpiece for the revolution. The use of satellite dishes receiving Western programs has recently been banned.

CRIME

Iran does not publish prison figures

Little change from year to year

CRIME RATES

Iran does not publish crime statistics. However, general crime rates are relatively low

Law and order is often enforced by revolutionary guards. A total of 109 offenses carry the death penalty. Executions, of both men and women, are common for political "crimes." Religious minorities are persecuted.

Iran is repeatedly accused by Western governments of sponsoring international terrorism. Iran denies these charges.

EDUCATION

54%

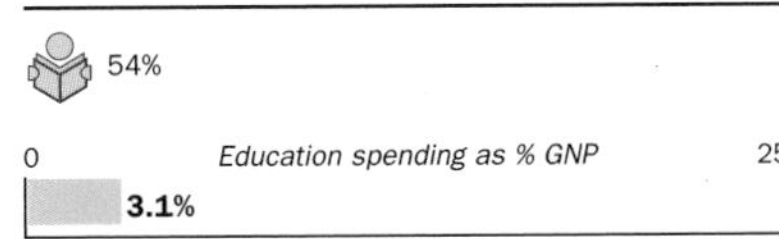

THE EDUCATION SYSTEM

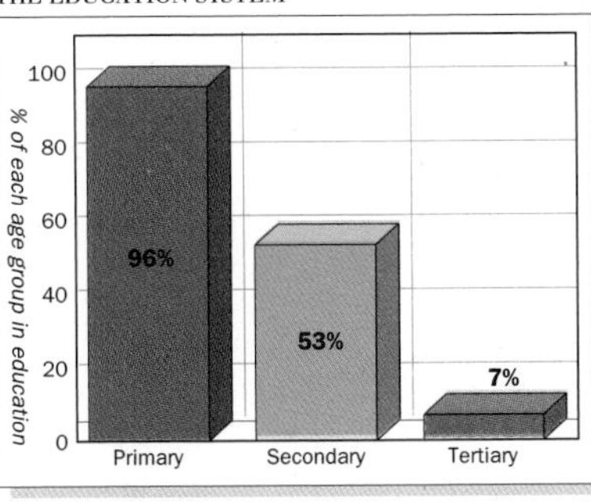

Just over half the population is literate. Education in state primary schools and universities is free. Pupils pay small fees for secondary education. There are insufficient teachers to cope with rising student numbers. Most schools have been made single-sex since 1979.

HEALTH

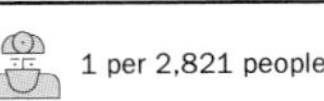

1 per 2,821 people

Heart and respiratory diseases, injuries, neonatal deaths

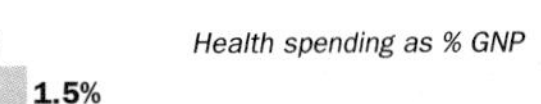

Although an adequate system of primary health care exists in the cities, conditions in rural areas are basic. The major problem facing the nation's health is the fast-growing population. Under Khomeini, producing children became a political and religious duty. The government has now introduced sterilization and contraception programs. More than 37% of children under seven are malnourished.

WEALTH

The acquisition of private wealth is discouraged

CONSUMER GOODS OWNERSHIP

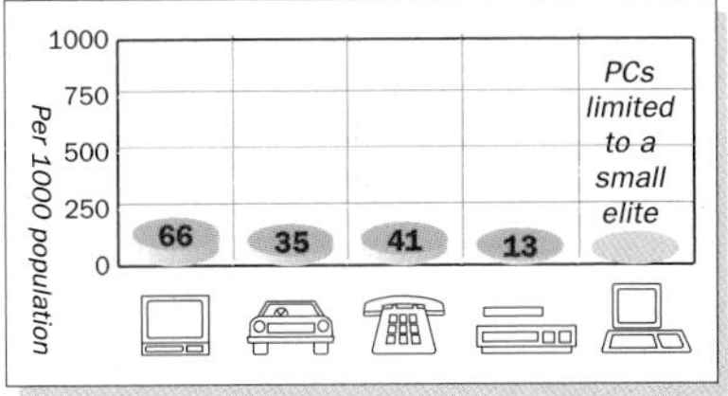

Since the 1979 revolution, living standards have declined markedly. A shortage of foreign exchange has stifled imports of consumer goods. Rationing, brought in during the war with Iraq, is still partly in force and smuggling from the Arab Gulf states is rife. One in four of the work force is unemployed. Only one in 26 Iranians possess a telephone. Official figures for income per head do not relate to conditions on the ground. In reality, oil wealth fails to reach the economically deprived. Private business, on which Iran's former prosperity was based, is discouraged by the mullahs, who have retained vital industries and services in public ownership.

WORLD RANKING

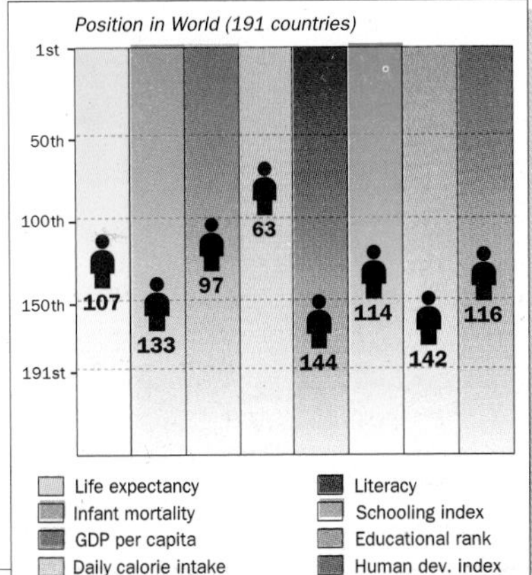

I

MIDDLE EAST

Turkey Syria IRAQ Iran Jordan Kuwait Saudi Arabia Asia Africa

IRAQ

OFFICIAL NAME: Republic of Iraq **CAPITAL:** Baghdad
POPULATION: 19.3 million **CURRENCY:** Iraqi dinar **OFFICIAL LANGUAGE:** Arabic

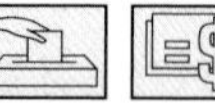

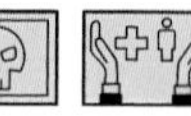

OIL-RICH IRAQ IS BISECTED by the River Euphrates and shares borders with Iran, Turkey, Syria, Jordan, Saudi Arabia and Kuwait. The fertile Euphrates Valley broadens into marshlands as it approaches the Gulf, but most of the country is desert or mountains. Iraq was the site of the ancient civilization of Babylon. Today, its borders encompass Shi'a Muslim holy shrines. Since the removal of the monarchy in 1958, Iraq has experienced considerable political turmoil. The current regime stays in power through repression.

***Golden Mosque** at Sāmarrā' on the Tigris. Among the extensive remains of its ancient city are those of the Great Mosque built in AD 847.*

CLIMATE

WEATHER CHART

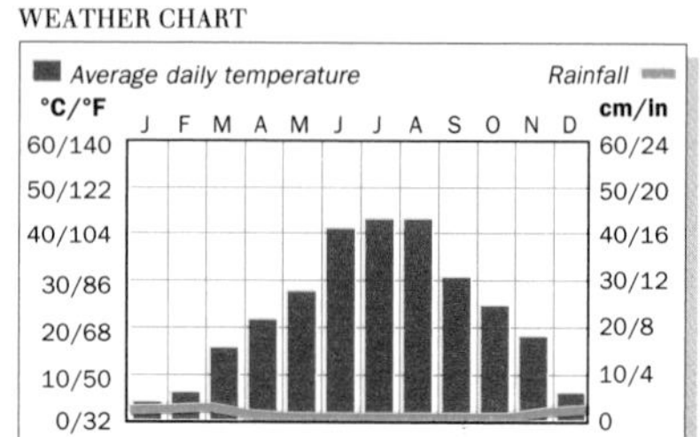

The weather is dry and rainfall is low and unreliable, except in the northeast. Iraq experiences a wide range of temperatures. The south has a desert climate, with hot, dry summers and mild winters. The summers are also dry in the north, but in mountainous Iranian and Turkish border regions winters can be harsh, with frost and heavy falls of snow. Sudden hot spells are a unique feature of winter in the center and north of the country.

COMMUNICATIONS

Saddam International, Baghdad

33 ships
136,870 dwt

THE TRANSPORTATION NETWORK

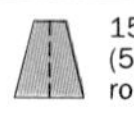
15,822 miles (5,140 paved main roads)

None

1,262 miles (2,032 km)

81 miles (130 km)

Adequate roads link main cities. Railroads provide vital arteries for the movement of goods. The land route to the Gulf states via Kuwait is closed.

TOURISM

747,000 visitors

Down 27% in 1990

MAIN OVERSEAS ARRIVALS

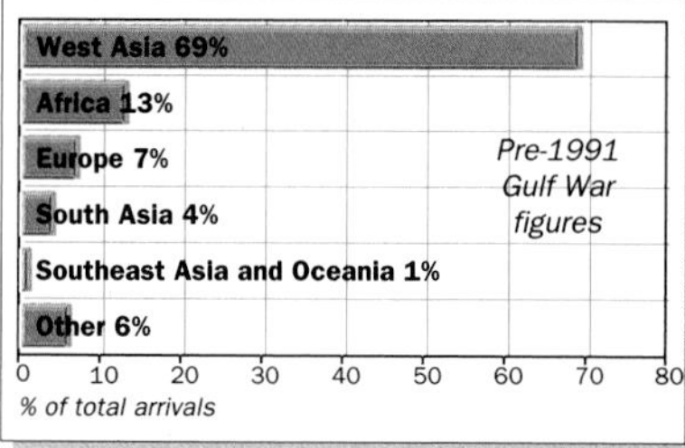

The Shi'a holy shrines in the south attract thousands of pilgrims each year. Iraq is effectively closed to Western tourists, who once visited its archaeological sites. In particular, the ruins of Babylon, and its fabled hanging gardens, were once a major tourist attraction. Westerners also used to journey to the marshlands close to the Shaṭṭ Al Arab waterway. However, this area of ecological importance is now being drained as part of a campaign to suppress the Marsh Arabs.

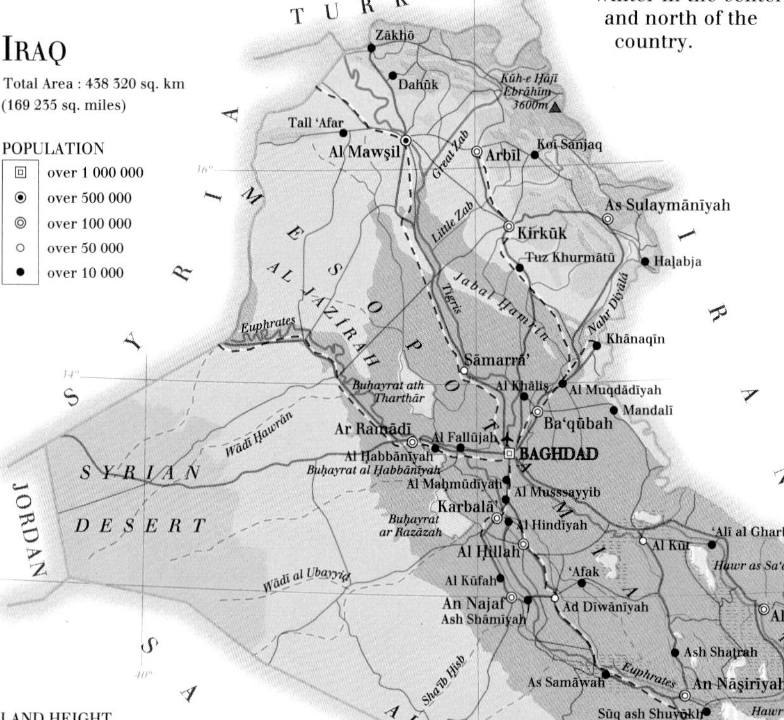

PEOPLE

 Arabic, Kurdish, Armenian, Assyrian

 111 people per sq. mile

THE URBAN/RURAL POPULATION SPLIT

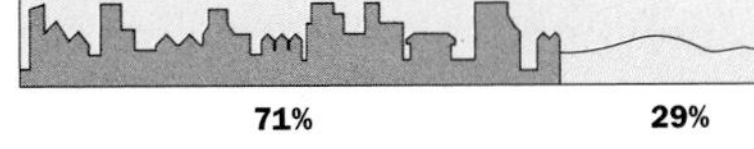

71% 29%

RELIGIOUS PERSUASION

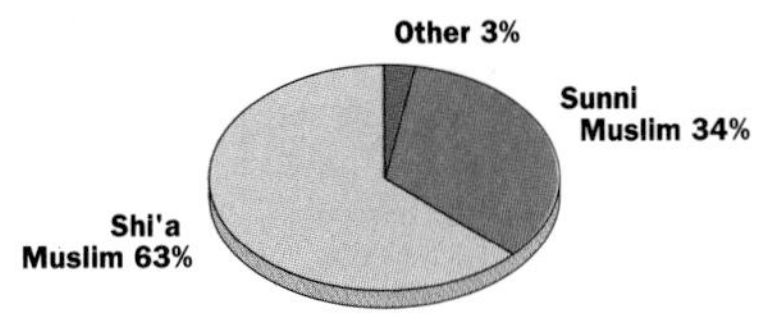

ETHNIC MAKEUP

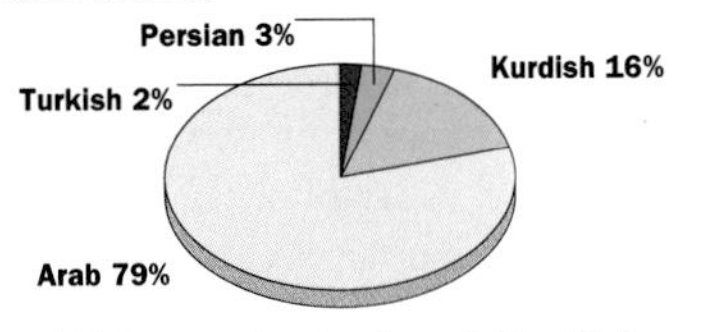

In addition to the Arab and Kurdish populations, Iraq has a small number of minority groups, such as the Turks and Persians. Over 90% of the population is Muslim, while the rest comprises a variety of Christian sects. Since the creation of Israel, most Iraqi Jews have emigrated. The Arab Muslims are divided into Sunni and Shi'a sects. The Shi'a form the largest single religious group; however, Shi'a divines do not have as intimate a connection with the people as they do in Iran and their influence on the government is limited. Since the mid-1970s, many Iraqis have moved – or been forced to move – to the cities, where some70% of the population now lives. In the marshes of the extreme south, communities of Marsh Arabs survive.

In the wake of the 1991 Gulf War, some of these attempted a rebellion against the state, which is now draining the marshes in order to destroy both the people and their culture.

POPULATION AGE BREAKDOWN

% of population by age group	1960	1970	1980	1990	2000
65+	2.4%	2.4%	2.6%	2.7%	3%
15–64	51.5%	51%	50.4%	50.9%	52.9%
0–14	46.1%	46.6%	47%	46.4%	44.1%

WORLD AFFAIRS

In 1990, Saddam Hussein embarked on a grand plan to show himself as the undisputed leader of the Arab world: the invasion of Kuwait. Saddam was counting on the West responding with sanctions rather than arms, and on Syria and Egypt not joining an Arab coalition to oppose him. A successful conclusion to the grand design would have placed Saddam in a position to control most of the oil supplies in the Gulf.

As a result of the Gulf War that followed, Iraq was economically and diplomatically isolated. Iraq was ousted from Kuwait, and sanctions were imposed. Relations with the West are now deadlocked. Iraq is effectively neutralized as a power in the region, but remains unwilling to allow UN inspection of its arsenal. No major Western state has restored diplomatic relations.

Relations with Iran are tense. Iranian guerrillas working against the regime in Tehran continue to use Iraq as a base for their operations.

POLITICS

 Uncertain

 President Saddam Hussein

THE STATE OF THE PARTIES

National Assembly 250 members

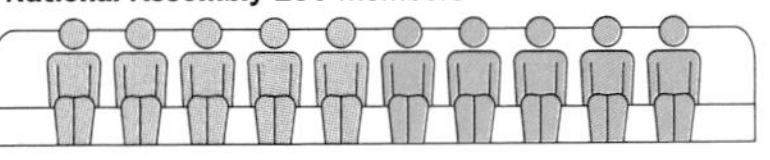

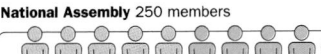

The National Assembly operates under the supervision of the Revolutionary Command Council. It is composed of Ba'athists and their supporters

Revolutionary Command Council

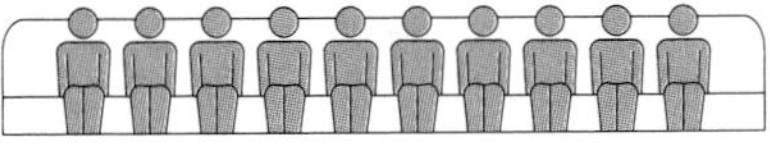

Members are appointed by the president

President Saddam Hussein has dominated Iraqi politics since overthrowing his predecessor in 1979. In theory, the highest state authority rests with the nine-member Revolutionary Command Council.

MAIN POLITICAL ISSUES

Kuwait

Iraq's invasion of Kuwait in 1990 led to UN sanctions being imposed; Iraq's overseas assets were also frozen. Despite its subsequent defeat by a US and Saudi-led coalition, the Iraqi leadership still maintains its claim to Kuwait, using it as a rallying call to unite the masses and divert attention from economic hardship. Iraq has repeatedly defied the UN's attempts to monitor its compliance with Security Council resolutions on the destruction of banned weapons. Sanctions have therefore remained in place. Numerous factories and businesses have closed as a result of the trade embargo.

Threats to the regime

Opposition is largely based outside the country and is united only in its desire to oust Saddam Hussein. The most significant groups are the Tehran-based Supreme Council for the Islamic Revolution in Iraq, which has strong backing in southern Iraq, and the Iraqi National Congress, an umbrella group with its headquarters in London.

The separatist Kurdish minority in the north of the country has been in almost continuous rebellion against Baghdad since 1962, but lacks sufficient external backing to pose a serious threat. Even Iraq's enemies do not wish to see the dismemberment of Iraq into component republics.

PROFILE

Iraq's regime – the most autocratic in the Arab world – is dominated by President Saddam Hussein and his lieutenants, mainly trusted members of his family. His cousin, Ali Hassan Al Majid, who was governor of Kuwait during the occupation, is responsible for atrocities against the Kurds.

Saddam Hussein has promoted his own extreme "personality cult." In a typical political broadcast, his name is mentioned 30 to 50 times an hour. The streets of Baghdad grind to a halt whenever the president leaves his palace. The regime remains in force through terror and the backing of the military. A vast secret service and intelligence network ensure that opposition groups are not able to organize a challenge.

***Tarek Aziz,** deputy prime minister and mediator between Iraq and the UN.*

***Saddam Hussein,** Iraq's dictatorial leader since he seized power in 1979.*

AID

 $417m (receipts)

 Up 802% in 1991

Before the Kuwait invasion, the regime received aid from various Gulf states to help pay for Iraq's war with Iran. Today, UN sanctions require that any aid to Iraq has to be covert; humanitarian supplies are allowed, however.

I

CHRONOLOGY

Iraq became independent in 1932. In 1958, the Hashemite dynasty was overthrown when King Faisal died in a coup led by the military under Brigadier Kassem. He was initially supported by the Iraqi Ba'ath Party.

- **1961** Kurdish rebellion erupts in northern Iraq. Iraq claims sovereignty over Kuwait on the eve of Kuwait's independence.
- **1963** Kassem overthrown. Colonel Abd as-Salem Muhammad Aref takes power. Kuwait's sovereignty recognized.
- **1964** Ayatollah Khomeini, future leader of Iran, takes refuge at Najaf in Iraq.
- **1966** Aref is succeeded by his brother, Abd ar-Rahman.
- **1968** Ba'athists under Ahmad Hassan Al-Bakr take power.
- **1970** Revolutionary Command Council signs manifesto on Kurdish autonomy with Kurdish leader Mulla Mustafa Barzani.
- **1972** Nationalization of Iraq Petroleum Company, owned by Western interests.
- **1973** Troops sent to fight on Syrian front against Israel.
- **1978** Iraq and Syria sign charter for economic and political union. Ayatollah Khomeini leaves Iraq for Paris.
- **1979** Saddam Hussain replaces President Al-Bakr, who is put under house arrest.
- **1980** War declared against Iran.
- **1982** President Saddam Hussain withdraws troops from Iran. Iran occupies parts of southern Iraq. Shi'a leader Mohammed Baqir Al-Hakim, exiled in Tehran, forms Supreme Council of the Islamic Revolution in Iraq.
- **1986** Armed excursion into Iran. Iraqi fighter kills 37 on *USS Stark*.
- **1988** Iraq and Iran agree cease-fire. Iraqi troops alleged to be using chemical weapons in bomb attacks on Kurdish villages.
- **1990** British journalist Farzad Bazoft hanged for spying. Iraq and Iran restore diplomatic relations. Iraq invades Kuwait, annexing emirate as its 19th province. UN imposes trade sanctions.
- **1991** Western allies launch successful 100-hour campaign to liberate Kuwait. Shi'a rebellion in southern Iraq put down.
- **1992** USA, UK, France and Russia proclaim air exclusion zone over southern Iraq.
- **1993** Iraqi attempts to recover military equipment from Kuwait provoke Western air attacks.

DEFENSE

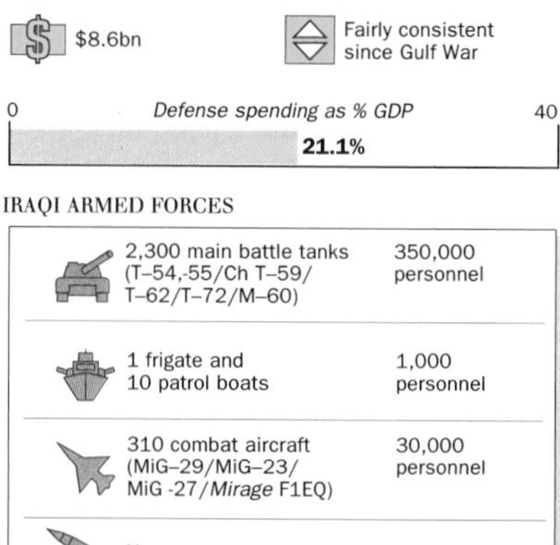

$8.6bn
Fairly consistent since Gulf War
0
Defense spending as % GDP
40
21.1%
IRAQI ARMED FORCES
2,300 main battle tanks (T-54,-55/Ch T-59/ T-62/T-72/M-60)
350,000 personnel
1 frigate and 10 patrol boats
1,000 personnel
310 combat aircraft (MiG-29/MiG-23/ MiG -27/*Mirage* F1EQ)
30,000 personnel
None

Iraq's defeat in the 100-hour US-backed UN ground campaign to free Kuwait led to the destruction of much of Iraq's arsenal. The high command has been restructured and many senior officers executed on suspicion of treason.

Iraq has now restored its defenses, but lacks the high-tech weaponry that Kuwait and Saudi Arabia have acquired since the war from US and other Western suppliers. The army is large, but contains many poorly trained conscripts. The military is mainly equipped with tanks and aircraft from the former Soviet Union and China. The air force, the most prestigious service, has some French *Mirage* fighters and US helicopters.

ECONOMICS

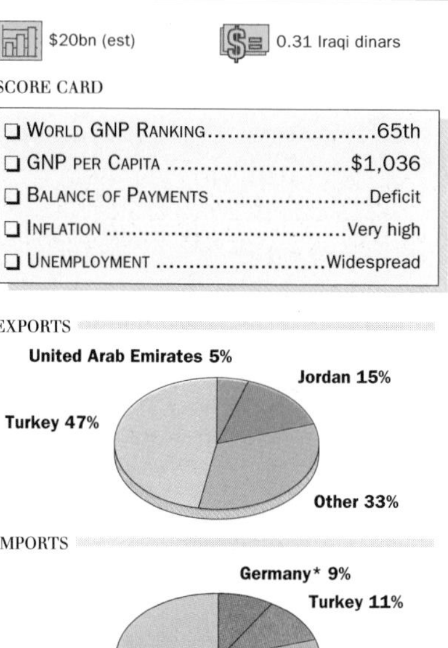

Strengths

Second-largest crude oil and natural gas reserves in OPEC. Large labor force.

Weaknesses

Inability to sell oil on the international market; UN sanctions have halved Iraq's gross national product. Once-thriving agricultural sector devastated by war.

Profile

Before 1990, Iraq was the world's third-largest oil supplier. Today, oil is being produced only for domestic consumption. Assuming an end to sanctions, however, the potential for Iraq's oil industry is massive.

Sanctions have hit Iraq hard, especially because oil sanctions are relatively easy to police and because there is currently a world oil glut. The diplomatic siege of Baghdad and the denial of Western assistance has also stifled initiatives in other sectors of the economy. Iraq was formerly rich in agriculture, but the sector was badly affected by war. Reforms to liberalize the economy have been promised, but centralized planning and state purchasing are still the norm. Participation in the thriving black market is dangerous: 42 traders were executed in 1992.

ECONOMIC PERFORMANCE INDICATOR

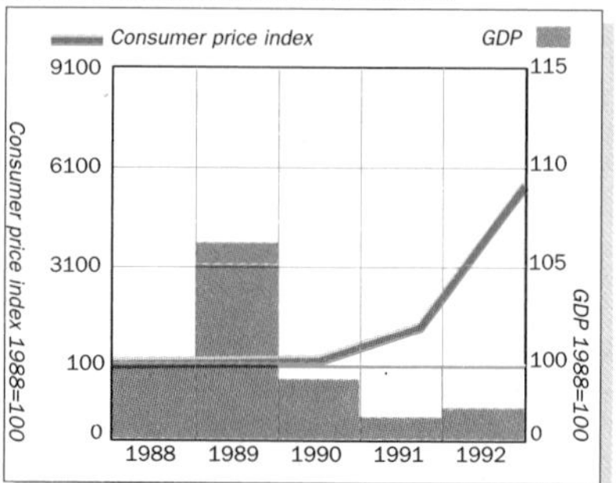

IRAQ : MAJOR BUSINESSES

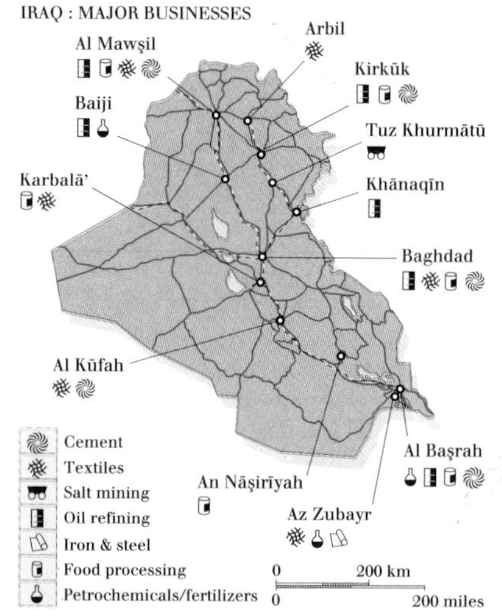

RESOURCES

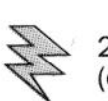
29.2bn kwh (capacity 9m kw)

402,600 b/d (reserves 100,000,000,000 bbl)

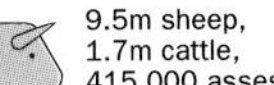
9.5m sheep, 1.7m cattle, 415,000 asses

Natural gas, sulfer

ELECTRICITY GENERATION

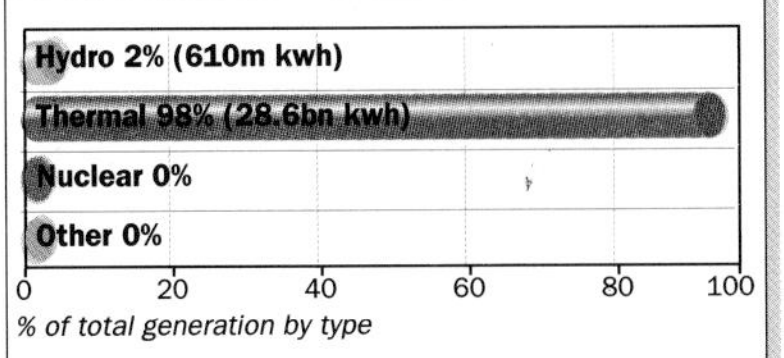

Iraq has huge reserves of oil and gas. The oil industry is controlled by the Iraqi National Oil Company. In 1990, proven reserves were conservatively estimated at 100,000 million barrels – sufficient for 97 years' production at 1989 levels of 4.5 million b/d.

Total gas reserves, three-quarters of which are associated with oil, are estimated at 2.69 billion cubic meters. Hydroelectic power is the main source of energy, though there is also a single oil-fired power station.

Before the invasion of Kuwait and the subsequent war, Iraq was supplying 80% of the world's trade in dates. Production is now sharply down. Foods are now produced simply for domestic consumption. Iraq has, however, achieved a degree of self-sufficiency in crops such as wheat, rice and sugar.

IRAQ : LAND USE

Cropland
Forest
Pasture
Wetlands
Desert
Sheep
Wheat
Dates - cash crop

MESOPOTAMIA
SYRIAN DESERT
AL HIJARAH

0 200 km
0 200 miles

ENVIRONMENT

None

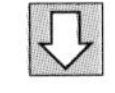
Destruction of marshlands in south

ENVIRONMENTAL TREATIES

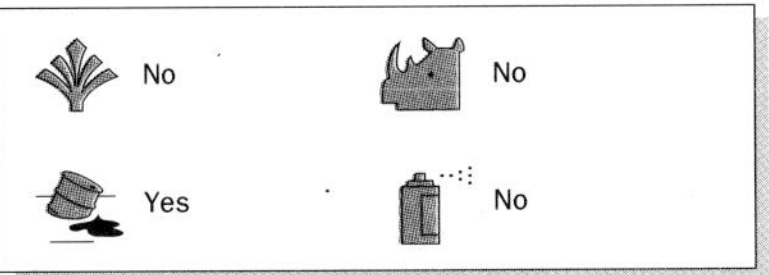

War with Iran and with the UN coalition over the Kuwaiti occupation led to massive environmental damage. Hundreds of thousands of land mines remain in the Kuwait border regions, posing lethal hazards to farmers, livestock and wild animals. The north has been affected by chemical weapons, used by the regime against the Kurds. In the south, an entire wetland ecosystem is being destroyed by an engineering program, aimed at draining the marshes for largely political reasons.

MEDIA

Tight government censorship

PUBLISHING AND BROADCAST MEDIA

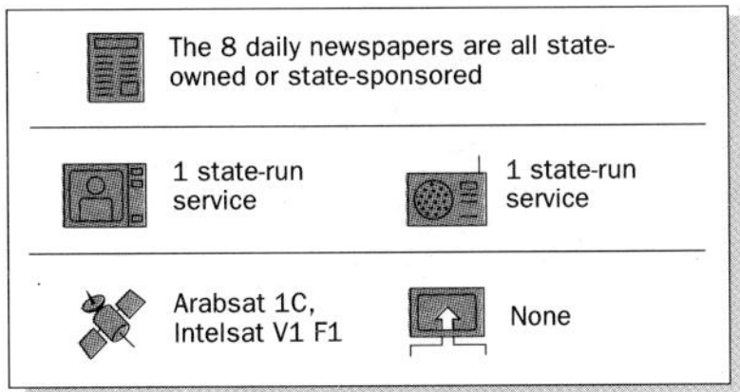

The Iraqi media is under strict state control, although rebel groups do circulate clandestine newspapers. Baghdad has four daily newspapers, one of which, the *Baghdad Times*, is in English. Members of Saddam's family control some newspapers. Foreign journalists are carefully monitored and their reports censored; those critical of the regime are refused future entry.

CRIME

Iraq does not publish prison figures

Crime is rising sharply

CRIME RATES

Crime rates are high compared with neighboring Arab states and Iran. Amnesty International has reported many cases of human rights abuses by the regime

Iraq was formerly a law-abiding society, but economic collapse has sent crime rates soaring, especially in cities. Theft has been made a capital offense, encouraging thieves to murder in order to escape detection.

EDUCATION

60%

0 — *Education spending as % GNP* — 25

3.7%

THE EDUCATION SYSTEM

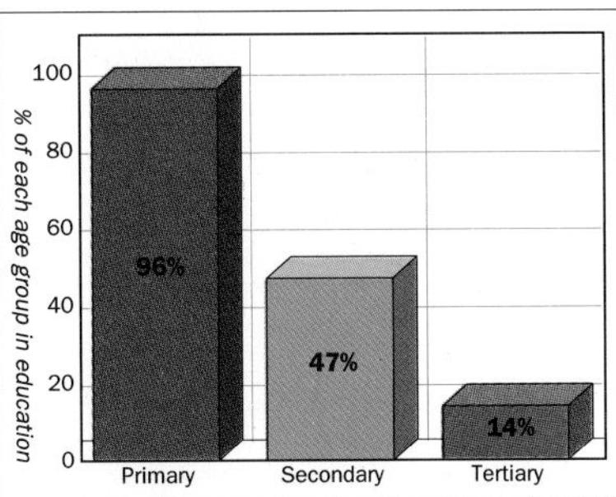

Primary and secondary education are free and universal, except in remote rural areas. There are six universities. Academics from Iraq authorized the organized plunder of antiquities and university equipment from Kuwait during the 1990 occupation.

HEALTH

1 per 1,732 people

Pneumonia, influenza, cancer, heart disease

0 — *Health spending as % GNP* — 25

0.8%

Iraqi doctors claim that the welfare of children, the sick and the elderly has suffered because of the UN embargo. Child mortality is high and the standard of hospital equipment and facilities low.

WEALTH

Few opportunities for enrichment

CONSUMER GOODS OWNERSHIP

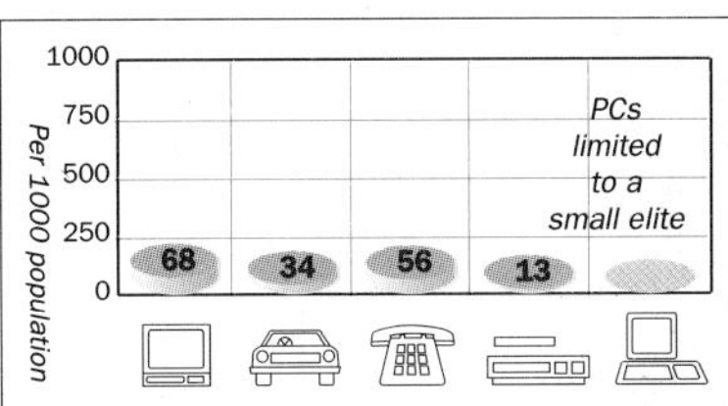

Many middle-class Iraqis and traders have taken advantage of the open border with Jordan to relocate from Baghdad to Amman.

WORLD RANKING

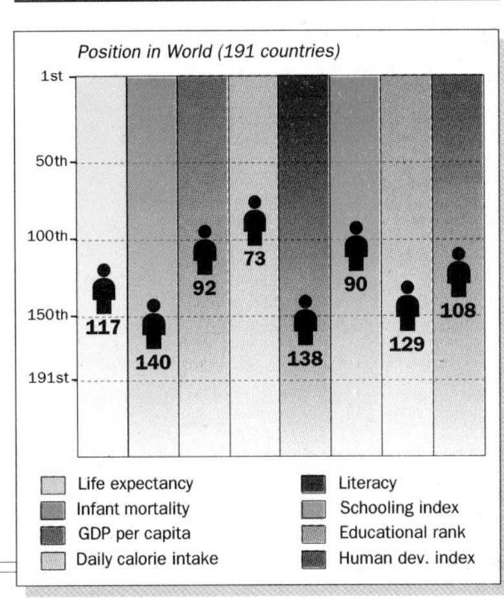

I

IRELAND

EUROPE

OFFICIAL NAME: Republic of Ireland **CAPITAL:** Dublin **POPULATION:** 3.5 million
CURRENCY: Irish pound **OFFICIAL LANGUAGES:** Irish, English

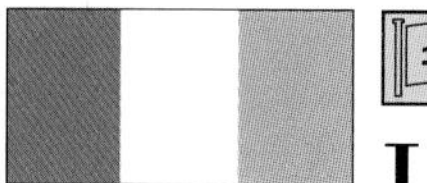

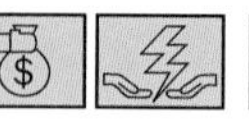

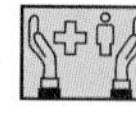

LYING IN THE ATLANTIC OCEAN, off the west coast of Great Britain, the Irish Republic occupies about 85% of the island of Ireland. Surrounded by low coastal mountain ranges, the central basin is punctuated by lakes, undulating hills and peat bogs. Centuries of struggle against English colonialism led to the formation of the Irish Free State in 1921 and full sovereignty in 1937. The political reunification of the island is a key aim of the Republic.

CLIMATE

WEATHER CHART

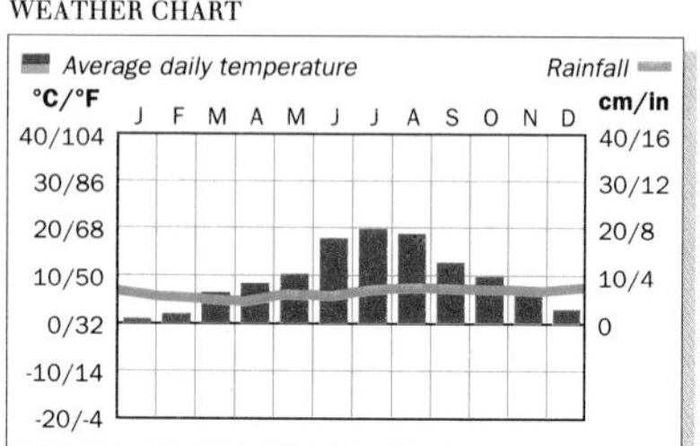

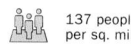

Moderated by the Gulf Stream, the Irish climate is mild, equable and wet. The mean annual temperature is 54°F.

COMMUNICATIONS

Dublin International

62 ships
189,400 dwt

THE TRANSPORTATION NETWORK

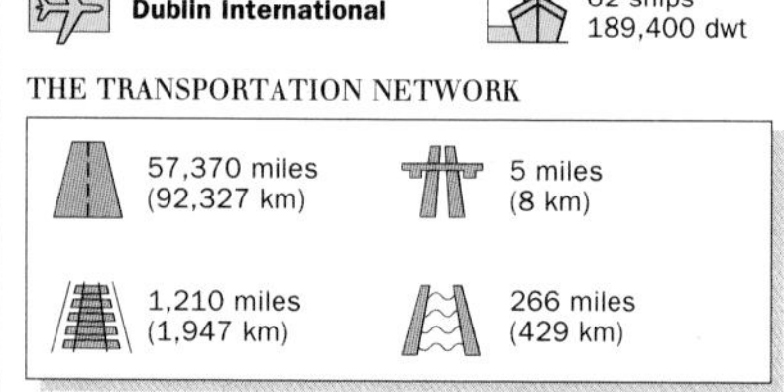

Over 40 road improvement projects are being funded by the EU. Dublin suffers from severe truck congestion.

TOURISM

3.69m visitors

Up 1% in 1991

MAIN OVERSEAS ARRIVALS

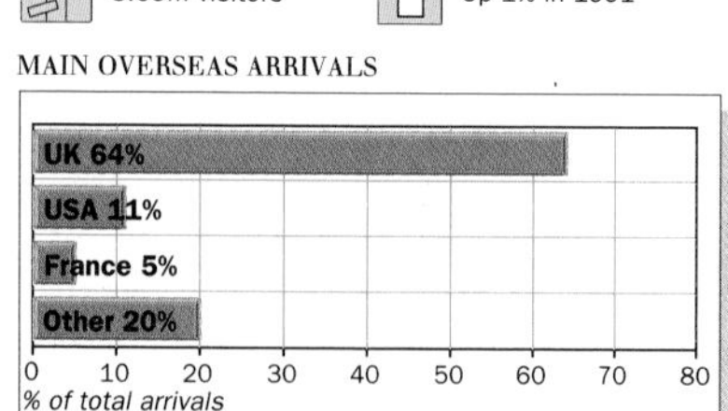

Intensive promotional campaigns have helped Ireland widen its tourist base, notably in Germany and Scandinavia. Its attractions include its scenery and "clean" environmental image, and its relaxed lifestyle.

PEOPLE

English, Irish Gaelic

137 people per sq. mile

THE URBAN/RURAL POPULATION SPLIT

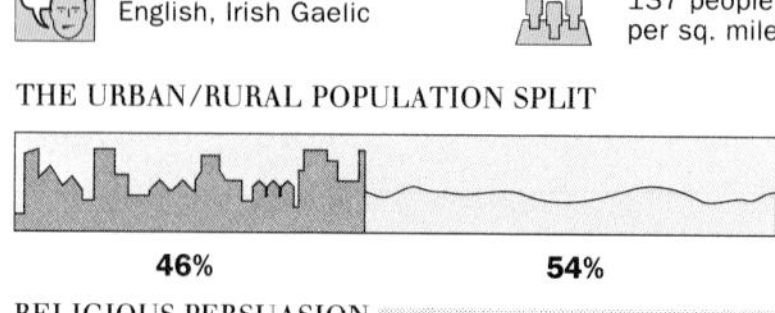

RELIGIOUS PERSUASION

Anglican 3% Other 4%

Roman Catholic 93%

The population is 95% ethnic Irish. The Catholic Church has a huge influence, opposing abortion and birth control. Many Irish still emigrate to find jobs.

POLITICS

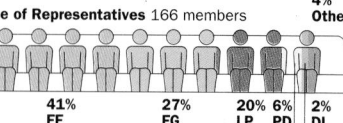

1997

President Mary Robinson

THE STATE OF THE PARTIES

House of Representatives 166 members

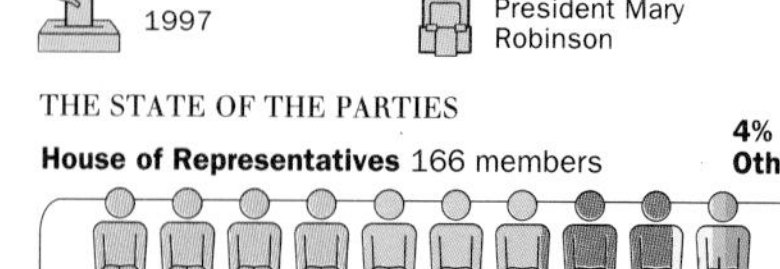

FF = Fianna Fáil (Soldiers of Destiny) **FG** = Fine Gael (United Ireland Party) **LP** = Labour Party **PD** = Progressive Democrats **DL** = Democratic Left

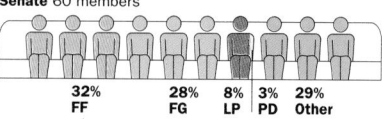

Senate 60 members

32% FF | 28% FG | 8% LP | 3% PD | 29% Other

In 1973, an FG–LP coalition took power, which saw the end of the FF as the traditional party of government – a role it had held since 1932. FF and FG–LP governments since have tended to be short-lived and, since 1989, the FF has needed PD support to govern. In December 1994 the FF–LP government fell once more and was replaced by a FG–LP–DL coalition, led by FG leader John Bruton. His government's priority will be to sustain the Northern Ireland peace process.

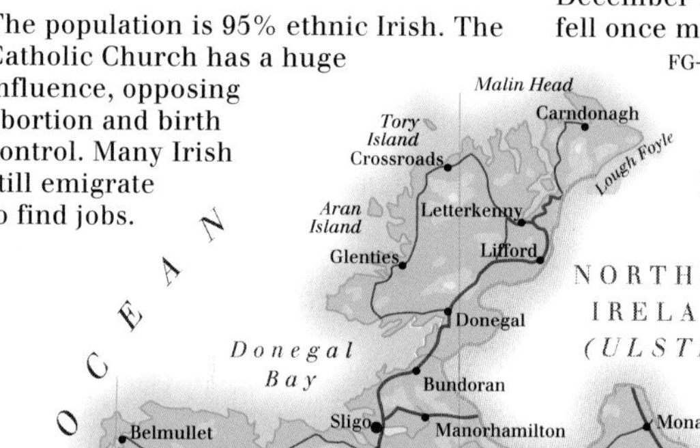

REPUBLIC OF IRELAND

Total Area: 70 280 sq. km (27 135 sq. miles)

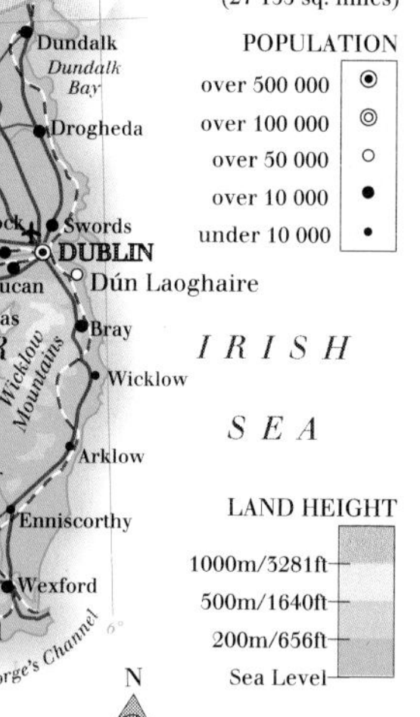

WORLD AFFAIRS

The Northern Ireland peace process, aided by the "London Declaration" and the IRA ceasefire, is the main issue.

AID

 $72m (donations)  Up 26% in 1991

Africa is the main target of Irish aid. As one of the poorer European states, Ireland is a major recipient of EU aid.

DEFENSE

  $553m  Up 14% in 1991

Ireland is determined to maintain its traditional neutrality, notwithstanding provisions within the Maastricht Treaty for a common European defense policy.

ECONOMICS

 $37.7bn  0.71 Irish pounds

SCORE CARD

- ❑ WORLD GNP RANKING........................48th
- ❑ GNP PER CAPITA.........................$10,782
- ❑ BALANCE OF PAYMENTS....................$2.6bn
- ❑ INFLATION..3.1%
- ❑ UNEMPLOYMENT..............................15.4%

STRENGTHS

One of Europe's fastest-growing economies: real GDP rose 3.5% a year 1980–1990; slightly slower 1991–1993. Trade surplus. Low inflation. Efficient agriculture, food processing industries. Rapidly expanding high-tech sector; electronics account for 25% of exports. Large recipient of EU infrastructure funding. Highly educated work force.

WEAKNESSES

Many key sectors owned by overseas multinationals. One of EU's highest unemployment rates: 15.4% overall; 28% youth unemployment. High interest rates slow investment.

EXPORTS

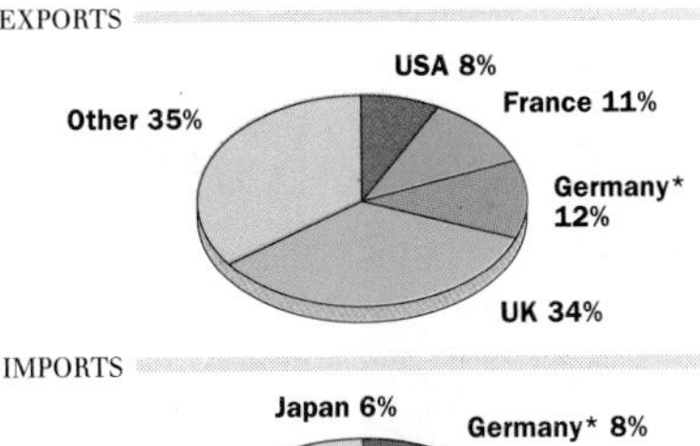

IMPORTS

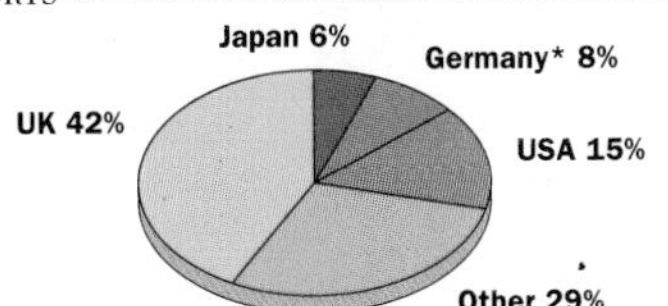

RESOURCES

 14.5bn kwh (capacity 3.8m kw)

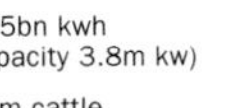 Not an oil producer; refines 56,000 b/cd

5.6m cattle, 5m sheep, 961,000 pigs

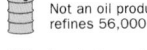

 Lead, zinc, natural gas, silver, coal

Oil has been found off the southern coast. Studies suggest this may be in commercially exploitable quantities.

ENVIRONMENT

0.4% partially protected

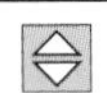 Recent anti-pollution legislation

The main environmental concerns are over-exploitation of the country's peat bogs for fuel and the recent expansion of conifer plantations. While Ireland's levels of forest cover will increase in the next few years, most new planting is of conifers. Controls on pollution were extended in 1994 with the introduction of stringent new laws.

MEDIA

 There is no official censorship, but there can be self-censorship on moral issues

PUBLISHING AND BROADCAST MEDIA

 There are seven daily newspapers. These include the *Irish Times*, the *Irish Independent* and the *Irish Press*

 1 state-owned, 1 independent service

 1 state-owned, 1 independent service

Censorship of media coverage of Sinn Féin was lifted in 1994. There is wide access to British papers, TV and radio.

CRIME

 1953 prisoners  Up 1% in 1990

Rural Ireland has the EU's lowest crime rate. Urban crime is growing and drugs are a problem in Dublin and Cork.

EDUCATION

 100%

The Catholic Church runs many schools. Trinity College, Dublin, is the most prestigious of four universities.

Clew Bay in County Mayo, on the western coast of Ireland, viewed from the slopes of neighboring Croagh Patrick.

CHRONOLOGY

English colonization, which began in 1167, was reinforced after 1558 by oppressive anti-Catholic legislation and the settlement of Scottish Protestants in the north.

- ❑ **1845–1855** Famine. One million die, 1.5 million emigrate.
- ❑ **1919–1921** Anglo-Irish war after republican Sinn Féin proclaims Irish independence.
- ❑ **1921** Irish Free State set up; north opts to stay in UK.
- ❑ **1949** Ireland becomes a republic.
- ❑ **1973** FG–LP win elections. Ends 16 years continuous FF government.
- ❑ **1992** Financial scandals. Premier Charles Haughey, FF head, resigns.
- ❑ **1994** Irish–UK talks on Northern Ireland; London Declaration.

I

HEALTH

 1 per 633 people  Heart disease, cancer

Free care is means tested. One-third of the population relies on health care insurance. Ireland has the EU's lowest per capita consumption of alcohol.

WEALTH

 Forklift truck driver, 285 Irish pounds per week; junior manager, 450 Irish pounds per week

CONSUMER GOODS OWNERSHIP

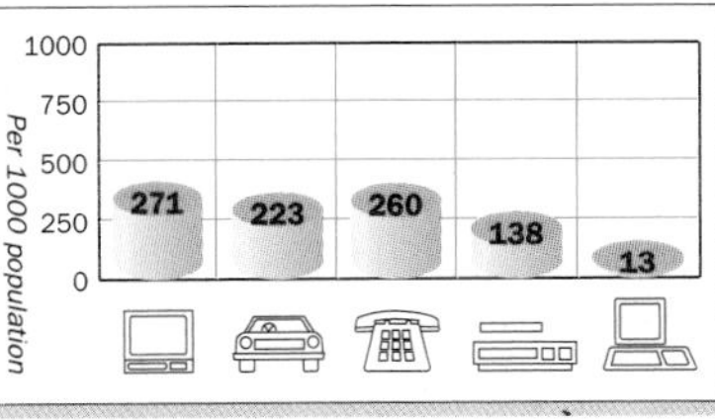

Living standards for those in jobs are rising steadily. Unemployment has, however, forced more onto welfare.

WORLD RANKING

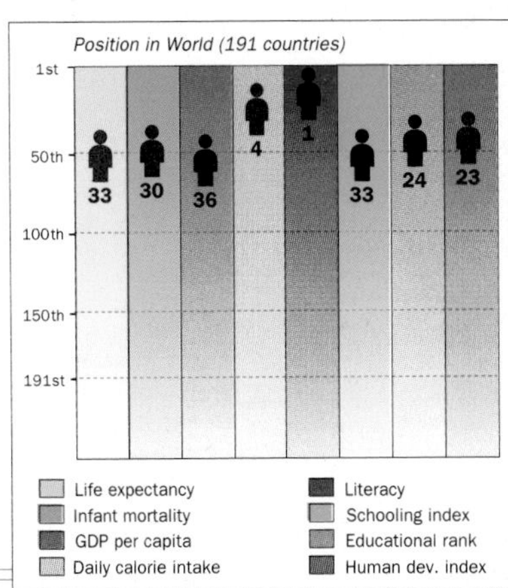

ISRAEL

MIDDLE EAST

Lebanon Syria ISRAEL Jordan Egypt Asia Africa

OFFICIAL NAME: State of Israel **CAPITAL:** Jerusalem
POPULATION: 5.3 million **CURRENCY:** New shekel **OFFICIAL LANGUAGE:** Hebrew

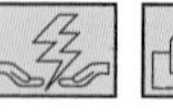

CREATED AS A NEW STATE IN 1948 with the backing of the USA and other Allied powers, Israel is bordered by Egypt, Jordan, Syria and Lebanon. Its topography varies from the HaNegev Desert in the south to the Dead Sea, the lowest point on the Earth's surface. Following wars with its Arab neighbors, Israel has unilaterally extended its original boundaries to control the West Bank, Gaza Strip, East Jerusalem and the Golan Heights.

CLIMATE

WEATHER CHART

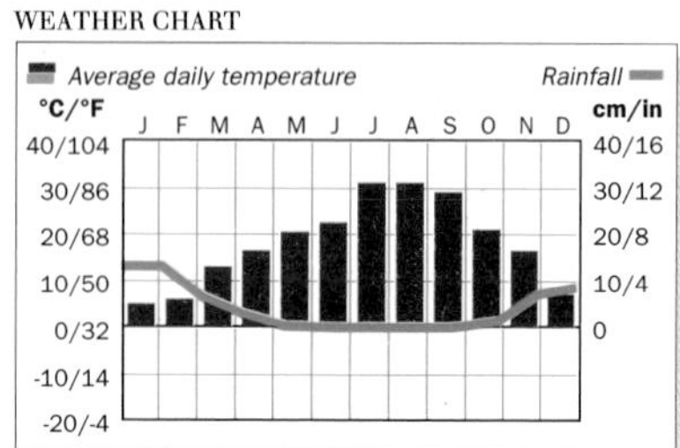

Summers are hot and dry. The wet season is between November and March, when the weather is mild.

COMMUNICATIONS

Ben-Gurion Intl, Tel Aviv-Yafo
3.5m passengers

36 ships
820,000 dwt

THE TRANSPORTATION NETWORK

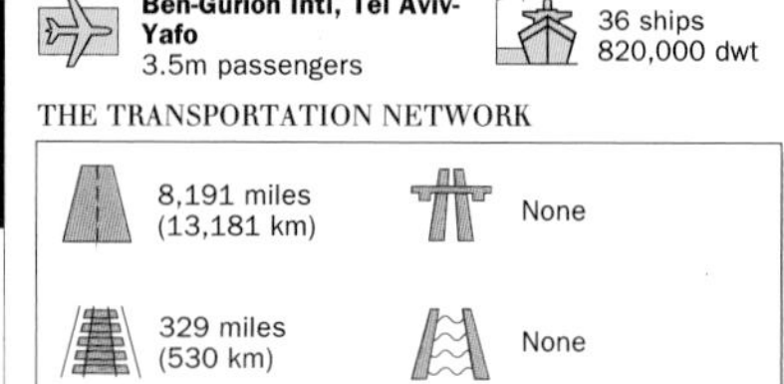

Excellent roads link all Israeli towns. Railroads are being extended, and there are three commercial ports.

TOURISM

2.28m visitors

Up 215% between 1990 and 1992

MAIN OVERSEAS ARRIVALS

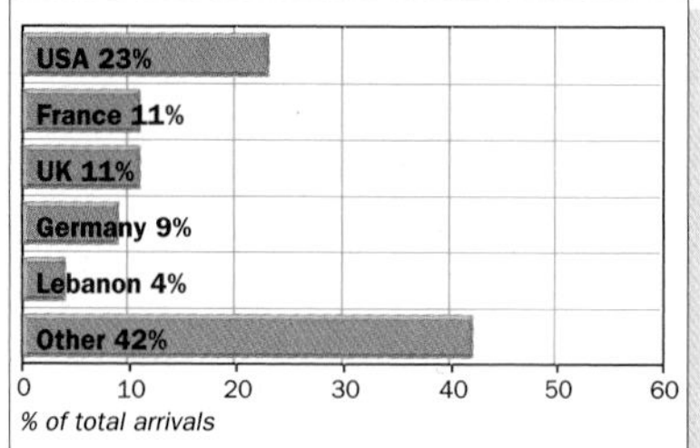

Jerusalem is the major tourist destination. Elat and the Dead Sea have been developed as beach resorts.

PEOPLE

Hebrew, Arabic, Yiddish, German, Russian, Polish, Romanian, Persian

637 people per sq. mile

THE URBAN/RURAL POPULATION SPLIT

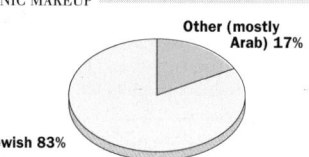

92% 8%

RELIGIOUS PERSUASION

Christian 2%
Muslim (mainly Sunni) 14%
Other 2%
Jewish 82%

ETHNIC MAKEUP

Other (mostly Arab) 17%
Jewish 83%

Large numbers of Jewish immigrants settled in Palestine before Israel was founded in 1948. After World War II, there was a massive increase in immigration. Sephardic Jews from the Middle East and the Mediterranean are now in the majority, but Ashkenazi Jews, mostly of central European origin, still dominate politics, business and social life. Thousands of Russian Jews have emigrated since 1989. Israel's Palestinian population totals some 800,000. While many take part in the democratic process, they remain sidelined in Israeli life. Those in occupied territories decline Israeli citizenship.

POPULATION AGE BREAKDOWN

% of population by age group	1960	1970	1980	1990	2000
65+	4.9%	6.7%	8.6%	8.8%	8.6%
15–64	59%	60.2%	58.2%	59.9%	63.3%
0–14	36.1%	33.1%	33.2%	31.3%	28.1%

POLITICS

1996

President Gen. Chaim Herzog

THE STATE OF THE PARTIES

Assembly 120 members

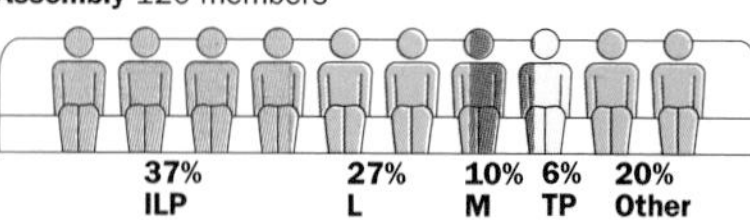

ILP = Israel Labor Party **L** = Likud (Consolidation) **M** = Meretz (composed of Ratz, Shinui, United Workers' Party) **TP** = Tzomet Party **Other** = Shas, National Religious Party, United Torah Judaism, Hadash, Moledet, Arab Democratic Party

Israel is a multiparty democracy. The prime minister and his cabinet wield executive power under the president.

MAIN POLITICAL ISSUES

Peace with the PLO
This complex issue is explained in detail on page 292.

Ethnic tensions
Rivalry between Sephardic and Ashkenazi Jews is likely to intensify, as the former, now in the majority, gain political power. Sephardic Jews already control many local councils. Russian Jewish immigrants are also demanding more representation in politics.

Religious militancy
Religious parties exert great influence in the Knesset. They seek support for religious institutions, including schools, and want changes in laws to enforce the proper observance of the Jewish faith in daily life.

PROFILE

Elected by proportional representation, Israeli governments tend to depend on minor parties for survival. The Labor coalition includes a religious party and also extreme-left, Arab-oriented parties. Political tensions are increased by confrontations between Orthodox and secular Jews, as well as between settlers and Arabs in the West Bank.

Yitzhak Rabin, Prime Minister of ruling Labor coalition since 1992.

Yasser Arafat, the militant-turned-moderate leader of the PLO.

WORLD AFFAIRS

ECE | GATT | EBRD | OAS | AG

Israel remains technically at war with all Arab states except Egypt. Regional stability may be improved by the 1993 peace accords. Links with Syria are unlikely to improve unless Israel withdraws from the Golan Heights.

AID

 $1.4bn (receipts)  Down 1% in 1991

Israel receives massive military and economic aid from the USA. Large *ad hoc* donations are also received from Jewish NGOs.

ISRAEL

Total Area : 20 700 sq. km (7992 sq. miles)

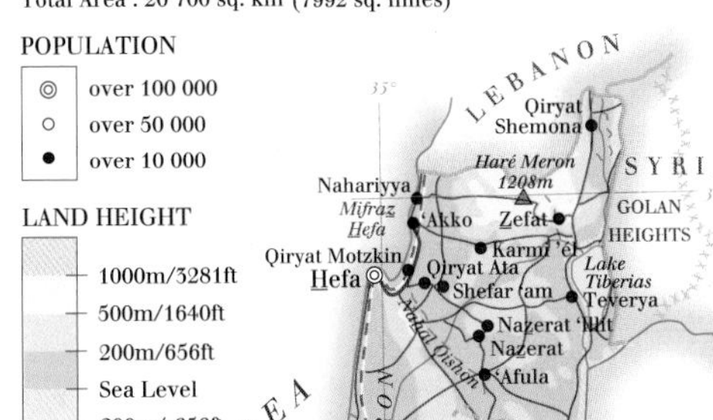

DEFENSE

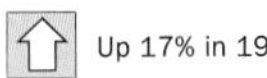
$6.8bn | Up 17% in 1992

Defense spending as % GDP (0–40): **10%**

The only Middle Eastern country with a nuclear deterrent, Israel has a small regular defense force which can be boosted by nearly 600,000 reservists. Equipped with some of the latest US technology, the forces' firepower is vastly superior to that of its Arab neighbors.

ISRAELI ARMED FORCES

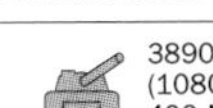
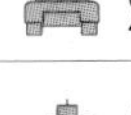

3890 main battle tanks (1080 Centurion/ 400 M-48A5/750 M-60)	134,000 personnel
3 submarines and 61 patrol boats	10,000 personnel
662 combat aircraft (112 F-4E/63 F-15/ 209 F-16/ 95 *Kfir* C2,-C7)	32,000 personnel

Widely believed that Israel has a nuclear capacity with up to 100 warheads. Delivery via *Jericho 1* and *Jericho 2* missiles

ECONOMICS

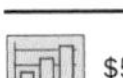 $59.1bn  2.93 new shekels

STRENGTHS

Government commitment to economic reform. Huge potential of agriculture, manufacturing and industrial products. Important banking sector. Prospect of peace in region. Sizeable aid from US government and international Jewish organizations.

WEAKNESSES

High unemployment and inflation. Large defense budget. History of regional and internal instability inhibits foreign investment. No trade with Arab neighbors.

PROFILE

Progress in the peace negotiations with the PLO would be a huge boost to the economy. The government is seeking ways to reduce state spending, which accounts for two thirds of GNP. The state owns 90% of all land and controls over 20% of all industries and services. Public companies are being privatized and there are plans to end restrictive labor practices. Agriculture is highly specialized and profitable. The state is now aiming to boost the service sector.

Despite a world recession, Israel's economy has continued to expand in the 1990s. The engine of this continued growth has been the mass immigration of Jews, many highly educated, from the former Soviet Union. Although unemployment levels have risen as a result of immigration, new skills and contacts have also helped the Israeli economy towards sustained export-led growth.

ECONOMIC PERFORMANCE INDICATOR

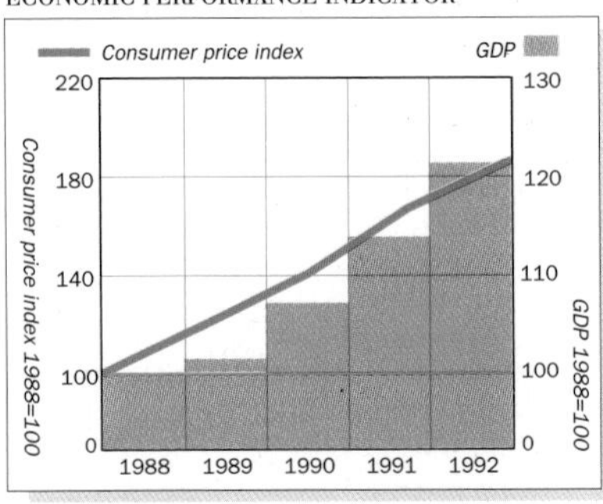

SCORE CARD

❑ WORLD GNP RANKING	38th
❑ GNP PER CAPITA	$11,151
❑ BALANCE OF PAYMENTS	$86m
❑ INFLATION	11.2%
❑ UNEMPLOYMENT	8.5%

EXPORTS

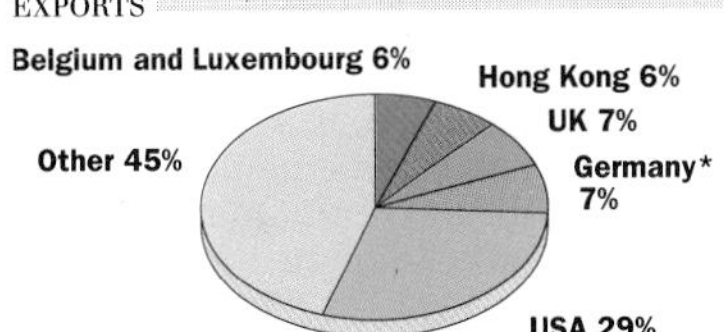

IMPORTS

UK 9% | Switzerland 9% | Other 39% | Germany* 12% | Belgium and Luxembourg 13% | USA 18%

ISRAEL : MAJOR BUSINESSES

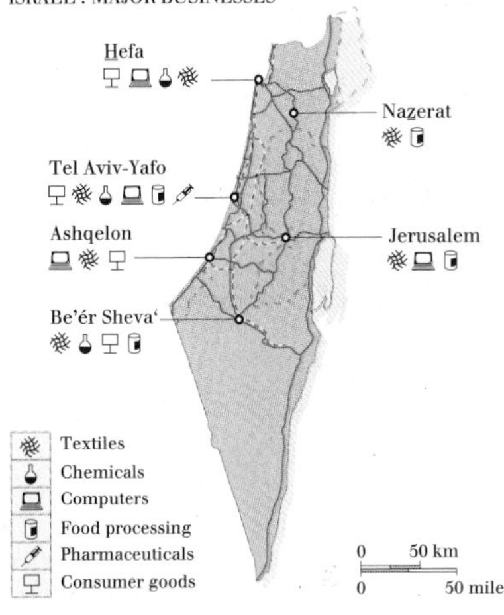

THE WEST BANK & GAZA STRIP

OCCUPIED BY ISRAELI TROOPS in the Six Day War in 1967, the West Bank and Gaza Strip were administered by Israel until 1994. The West Bank, with a land area of 2,278 sq. miles, has a population of 859,000, of whom 97% are Palestinian Arabs. Israeli settlers have encroached on much of the best land. The Gaza Strip covers only about 386 sq miles but has a population of almost 600,000 Palestinian Arabs. Both territories rely on agriculture and remittances from work in Israel. Following secret negotiations between Israel and the PLO in 1993, agreement was reached allowing limited autonomy for the Palestinians in Gaza and in an area around the town of Jericho.

WEST BANK

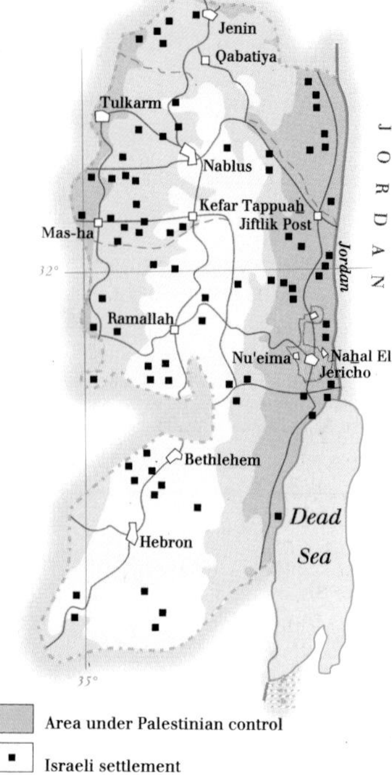

HISTORY

Israeli settlement of the West Bank began soon after the area's conquest in 1967. The Gaza Strip, the most turbulent region, was not formally incorporated into Israel until 1973.

After Egypt's President Sadat visited Israel in 1977, progress on Palestinian autonomy seemed possible. The framework agreed to at Camp David in 1978, however, failed to materialize and Israeli attitudes appeared to harden, with proposals for more Jewish settlements. By 1985, Israel had direct control of most of the West Bank. Attempts to bring peace to the region by allowing Palestinians an independent state were blocked by the PLO's refusal to recognize Israel's right to exist and Israel's refusal to negotiate with what it regarded as a terrorist group.

The frequency and violence of Arab anti-Israeli demonstrations in the Occupied Territories intensified, culminating, in January 1988, in an *intifada* (uprising) involving a strike by 120,000 Palestinians with jobs in Israel. The Israeli cabinet endorsed an "iron fist" approach by the security forces, but was divided as to long-term solutions. That year, King Hussein of Jordan abandoned links with the West Bank, allowing the PLO to declare an independent Palestinian state. The PLO also endorsed UN Resolution 242 and thus Israel's right to exist. However, only after the Rabin-led Labor coalition came to power in Israel in 1992 was progress made toward peace. At the same time, the Islamic militant group *Hamas*, opposed to any deal with Israel, was gaining support in the Occupied Territories.

GAZA STRIP

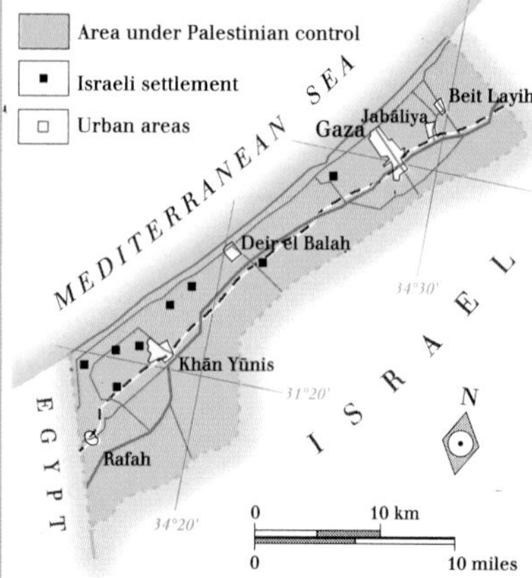

KEY ISSUES

With the annexation of the West Bank and Gaza Strip Israel was faced with the dilemma of whether to grant the Arab population citizenship or to exclude it from the democratic process. Although some right-wing Israeli leaders advocated retaining the territories, the growing power of *Hamas* demonstrated that incorporating the West Bank and Gaza into Israel was fraught with difficulty.

Much of the population in the West Bank and Gaza supports the PLO, although the organization's ranks are split. Hardliners disagree with PLO leader Yasser Arafat's moderate demands on Israel. The challenge for Israel is to maintain law and order and contain the extremists, while working to implement the 1993 Washington Accords. The problem for Arafat and his backers in the PLO is to keep a grip on the territories and to eclipse the influence of *Hamas*.

SETTLEMENT

By May 1994 only the first phase of the 1993 Accords had taken effect. The Palestinians gained home rule over the Gaza Strip and Jericho, but were a long way from their dream of an independent state with controls limited to home affairs.

Progress toward implementing the first stage of the peace plan was slow. Despite hopes that the first stage of Israeli withdrawal would start in 1993, deadlines passed without agreement until May 1994. Differences emerged over the authority of Palestinian law in the districts and the scale of a proposed amnesty for Palestinian prisoners. A number of countries, including the UK and Russia, offered to train the Palestinian police forces, which are now handling internal security in Jericho and Gaza.

However, terrorist outrages, such as the 1994 murder of 50 Palestinians in a West Bank mosque by a Zionist fanatic, and reprisal bombings by Arab militants, pose a threat to a final settlement. There is now pressure on both the PLO and Israel to make further progress.

Bethlehem, situated in the troubled West Bank, is just one of the many holy places that continue to draw visitors.

RESOURCES

20.7bn kwh (capacity 4.1m kw)

Not an oil producer; refines 221,000 b/cd

394,000 sheep, 13,000 pigs, 5,000 asses, 2,000 mules

Natural gas, potash, bromine, magnesium, salt, copper, gold

ELECTRICITY GENERATION

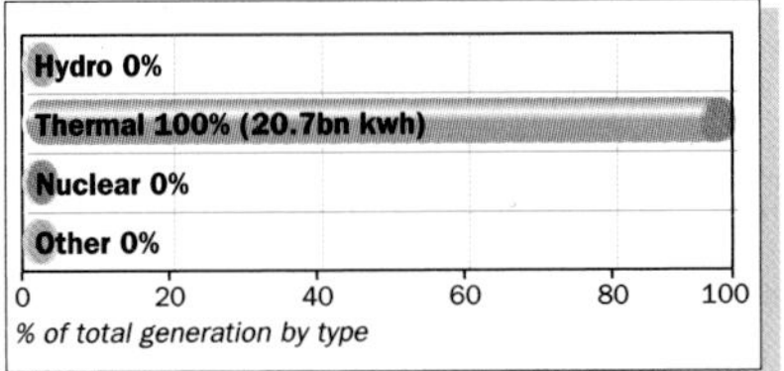

The country's most valuable deposits of minerals are potash, bromine (of which Israel is the world's largest exporter) and other salts mined near the Dead Sea. Reserves of copper ore and gold were discovered in 1988. In the coastal plain, mixed farming, vineyards and citrus groves are plentiful. Former desert areas now have extensive irrigation systems supporting specialized agriculture.

Israel's most critical resource is water. Shortages have forced Israel to purchase water, transported in plastic bags, from Turkey.

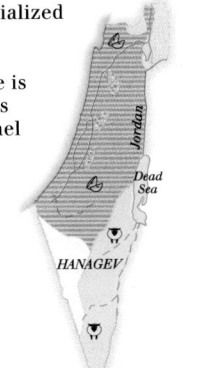

ISRAEL : LAND USE

Cropland
Forest
Pasture
Desert
Sheep
Citrus fruit - cash crop

ENVIRONMENT

10% partially protected

Consistently high standards from year to year

The government declared 1993–1994 Environment Year. It aimed to promote recycling schemes, the cleanup of rivers and improvements in Israel's urban environment.

ENVIRONMENTAL TREATIES

MEDIA

Foreign journalists are monitored. The media is constrained by extensive military and security censorship and other administrative restrictions

PUBLISHING AND BROADCAST MEDIA

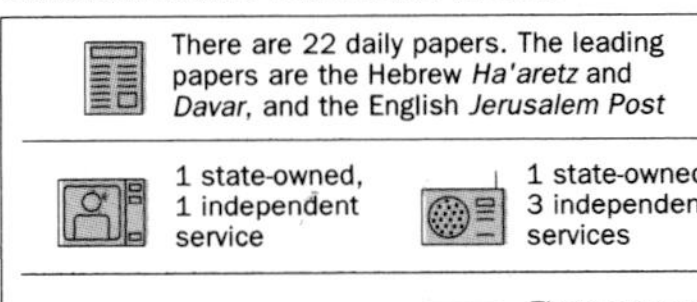

There are 22 daily papers. The leading papers are the Hebrew Ha'aretz and Davar, and the English Jerusalem Post
1 state-owned, 1 independent service
1 state-owned, 3 independent services
Arabsat 1C
Intelsat V1 F1
There are over a 1000 cable stations

The largely centrist to left-wing press has been at the forefront of support for the Arab-Israeli peace process.

CRIME

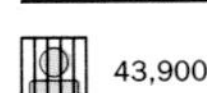

43,900 prisoners

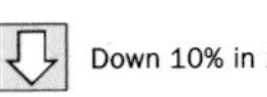

Down 10% in 1990

CRIME RATES

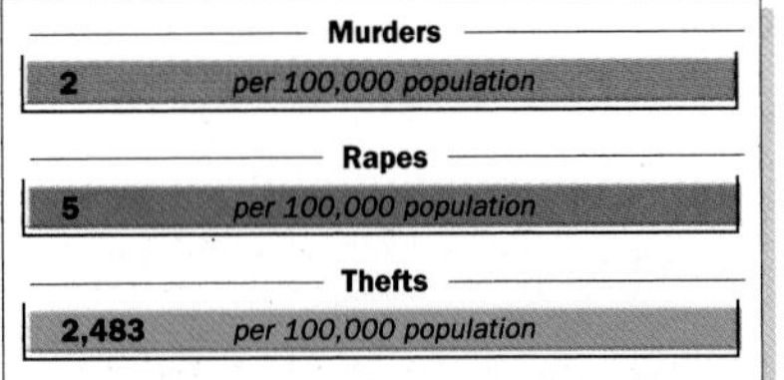

Murders
2 per 100,000 population
Rapes
5 per 100,000 population
Thefts
2,483 per 100,000 population

Terrorism by Arab, Islamic and Jewish extremists is the major problem. The army has been accused of abuses.

EDUCATION

97%

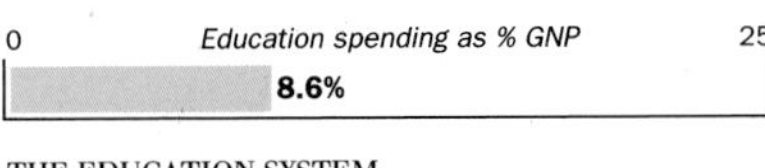

THE EDUCATION SYSTEM

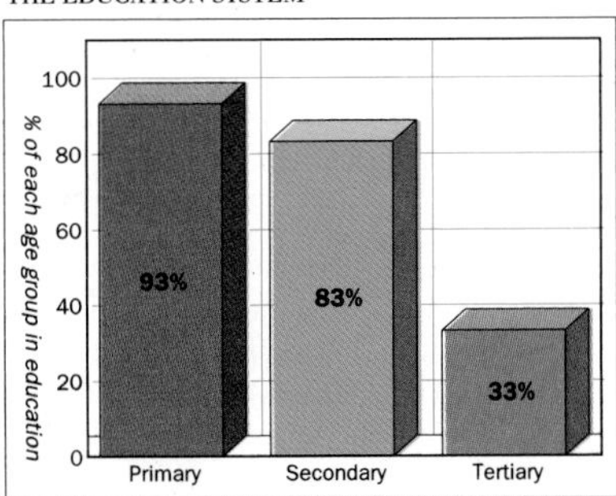

Education is free and compulsory for all between five and 16. There are both secular and religious universities. Many students study in the USA.

HEALTH

1 per 339 people

Heart and cerebrovascular diseases, cancer

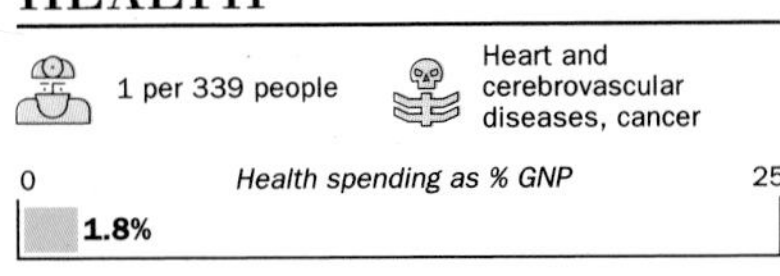

Primary health care reaches all communities. Israel's hospitals have pioneered many innovative treatments.

CHRONOLOGY

The creation of Israel in Palestine in 1948 realized the Zionist dream of a homeland for the Jewish people. However, the state was established in the face of bitter Arab opposition, leading to successive wars.

- ❑ **1967** The Six Day War with Arab states. Israel seizes the Gaza Strip, the Sinai Peninsula, the Golan Heights and the West Bank of the Jordan River. The UN Security Council adopts Resolution 242, the "land for peace" formula, calling for Israeli withdrawal in return for the right to live within secure borders.
- ❑ **1973** Egypt and Syria attack Israel and fight inconclusive 18-day war.
- ❑ **1977** Egypt's President Sadat's Jerusalem visit signals accord.
- ❑ **1979** Peace treaty signed with Egypt at Camp David, USA.
- ❑ **1982** Withdrawal from Sinai; invasion of Lebanon.
- ❑ **1993** Washington Accords signed with PLO: PLO recognition of Israel in return for autonomy for Palestinians in Gaza Strip and Jericho.
- ❑ **1994** First accords implemented.

I

WEALTH

Army officer, $1,500 per month; social worker, $800 per month

CONSUMER GOODS OWNERSHIP

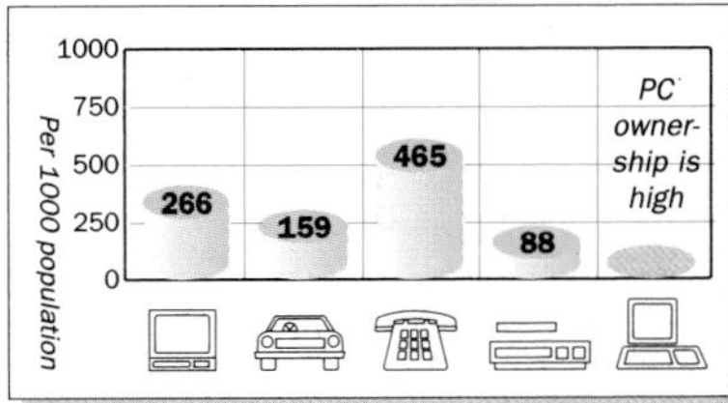

Income per head is high, but taxation is heavy. Some Israelis live in communes and shun personal material wealth.

WORLD RANKING

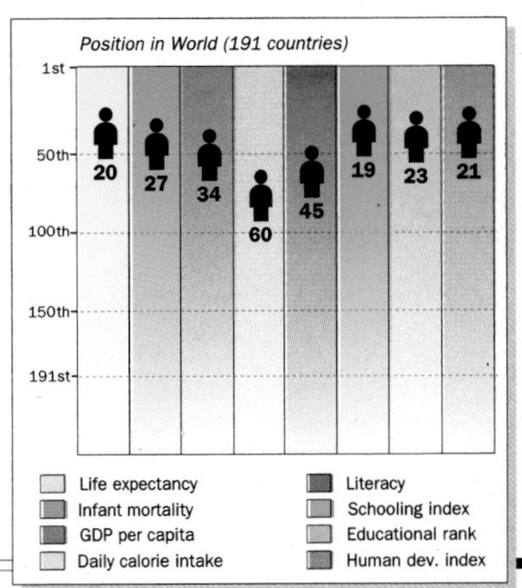

ITALY

OFFICIAL NAME: Italian Republic **CAPITAL:** Rome **POPULATION:** 57.8 million
CURRENCY: Italian lira **OFFICIAL LANGUAGE:** Italian

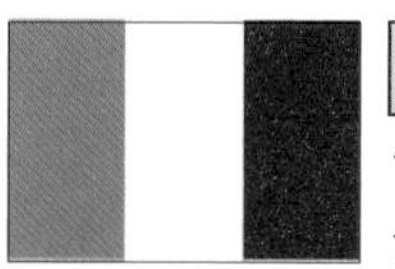

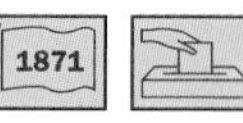

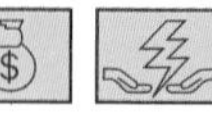

LYING IN SOUTHERN EUROPE, Italy comprises the famous boot-shaped peninsula stretching 500 miles into the Mediterranean and a number of islands – Sicily and Sardinia being the largest. The Alps form a natural boundary to the north, while the Appeninne Mountains run the length of the peninsula. The south is an area of seismic activity, epitomized by the volcanoes of Mounts Etna and Vesuvius. United under ancient Roman rule, Italy subsequently developed into a series of competing kingdoms and states, which were not fully reunited until 1870. Italian politics was dominated by the Christian Democrats (CD) from 1945 to 1992 under a system of political patronage, which extended through the judiciary, media and state businesses. Investigations into corruption from 1992 led to the demise of the CD in the elections of 1994.

CLIMATE

WEATHER CHART

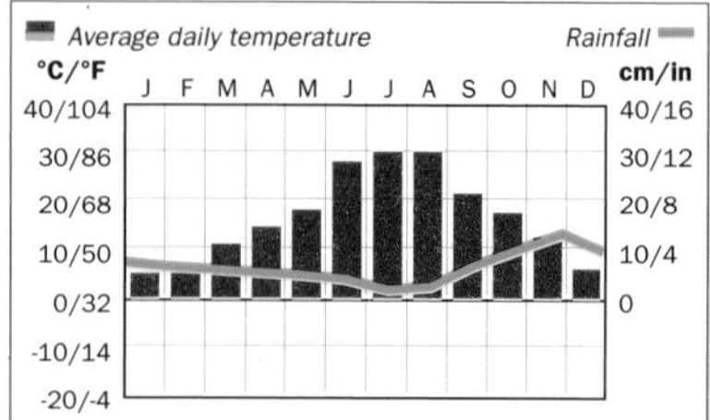

Southern Italy has a Mediterranean climate; the north is more temperate. Summers are hot and dry, especially in the south. Temperatures range from around 75°F to over 80°F in Sardinia and Sicily. Southern winters are mild; northern ones are cooler and wetter. The mountains usually experience heavy snow. The Adriatic coast suffers from cold winds such as the *bora*.

COMMUNICATIONS

Leonardo da Vinci (Fumicino), Rome
15.55m passengers

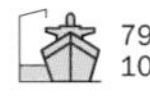

791 ships
10.13m dwt

THE TRANSPORTATION NETWORK

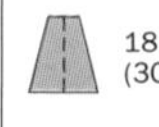

187,904 miles (302,403 km)

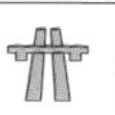

3,785 miles (6,091 km)

12,158 miles (19,566 km)

1,491 miles (2,400 km)

Many of Italy's key routes are congested. The trans-Appeninne *autostrada* (expressway) from Bologna to Florence is being doubled in size. A high-speed train program (*treno ad alta velocità* – TAV) is planned to link Turin, Milan, Venice, Bologna, Florence and Naples to Rome. Most of Italy's exports travel by road, via Switzerland and Austria. Only 16% goes by sea.

TOURISM

20.28m visitors

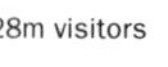

No change in 1992

MAIN OVERSEAS ARRIVALS

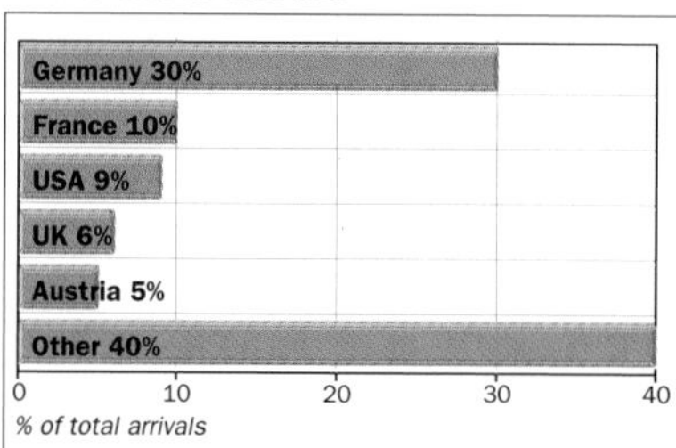

Italy has been a tourist destination since the 16th century and probably invented the concept. Roman popes consciously aimed to make their city the most beautiful in the world to attract travelers. In the 18th century, Italy was the focus of any Grand Tour. Today, its many unspoiled centers of Renaissance culture continue to make Italy one of the world's major tourism destinations. The industry accounts for 3% of Italy's GDP, and hotels and restaurants employ one million out of a working population of 21 million.

Most visitors travel to the northern half of the country, to cities such as Rome, Florence, Venice and Padova. Many are increasingly traveling to the northern lakes. Beach resorts such as Rimini attract a large, youthful crowd in summer. Italy is also growing in popularity as a skiing destination.

Fears have been expressed that tourism may be having a detrimental impact on Italy's environment. The pressure of visitors to Venice, in particular, is such that in summer one-way systems for pedestrians have to be introduced and day-trippers are often turned away.

Tuscan landscape. *Chianti wine is produced in this region, where many northern Europeans own vacation homes.*

ITALY

Total Area : 301 270 sq. km (116 320 sq. miles)

POPULATION

over 1 000 000

over 500 000

over 100 000

over 50 000

over 10 000

LAND HEIGHT

3000m/9843ft

2000m/6562ft

1000m/3281ft

500m/1640ft

200m/656ft

Sea Level

0 100 km

0 100 miles

PEOPLE

Italian, German, French, Rhaeto-Romanic, Sardinian

497 people per sq. mile

THE URBAN/RURAL POPULATION SPLIT

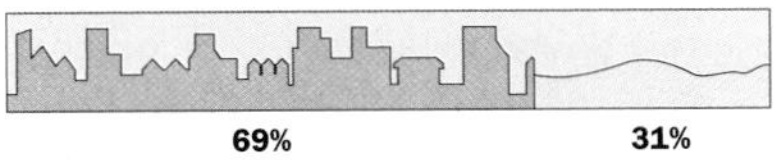

69% 31%

RELIGIOUS PERSUASION

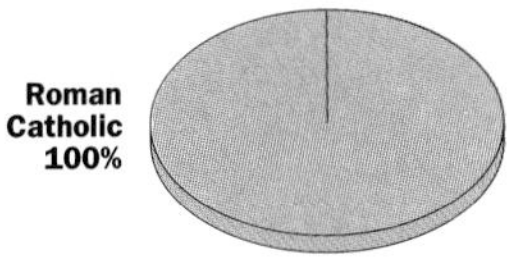

Roman Catholic 100%

ETHNIC MAKEUP

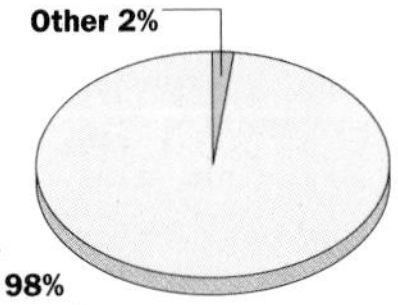

Other 2%

Italian 98%

Italy is a remarkably homogeneous society. Most Italians are Roman Catholics and Italy has far fewer ethnic minorities than its EU neighbors. Most are fairly recent immigrants from Ethiopia, the Philippines and Egypt. In the 1980s, there was a sharp rise in illegal immigration from North and West Africa, and Turkey. In response to a growth in right-wing feeling, tighter visa controls were brought in. Residency was, however, extended to illegal migrants already in Italy. Immigration was an issue at elections in 1993 and a factor in the rise of the federalist Northern League.

Difficult economic conditions caused many Italians to emigrate in the 1950s and 1960s. There are now five million Italians living abroad. About half live in other EU countries, the rest mainly in the USA, South America and Australia. Most migrants then, as now, are from the poorer south – the *Mezzogiorno.* Within Italy, prejudice still exists in the north against southern Italians.

Italians do not have a strong sense of national identity – except when it comes to sports. State institutions are viewed as inefficient and corrupt. Allegiance is to Europe, the region or community, and above all to the family. The extended family remains Italy's key social and economic support system. Most Italians live at home before marriage. Marriage rates are among the highest in Europe and divorce rates the lowest. Catholicism, however, has not stopped Italy from having the lowest birth rate and one of the highest abortion rates in the EU.

Italians tend to dress well. Their preoccupation with style reflects the traditional importance of *bella figura* – image, cutting a dash – in Italian life as much as the high living standards that most now enjoy.

POPULATION AGE BREAKDOWN

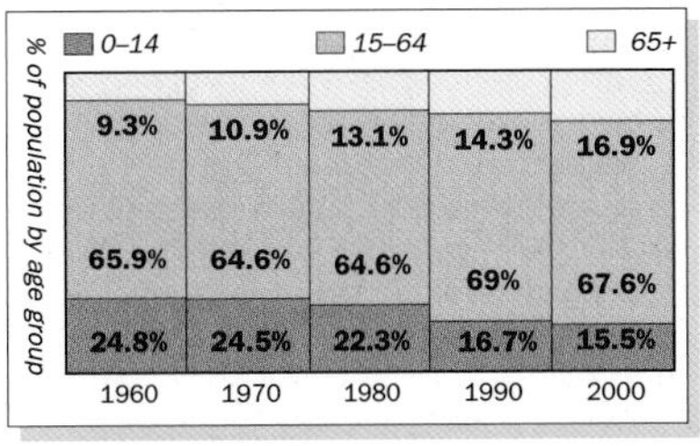

% of population by age group

	1960	1970	1980	1990	2000
65+	9.3%	10.9%	13.1%	14.3%	16.9%
15–64	65.9%	64.6%	64.6%	69%	67.6%
0–14	24.8%	24.5%	22.3%	16.7%	15.5%

CHRONOLOGY

Previously a collection of independent city states, dukedoms and monarchies, Italy became an independent unified nation in 1871.

- **1922** Mussolini asked to form government by King Victor Emmanuel III.
- **1928** One-party rule by Fascists.
- **1929** Lateran Treaties with Vatican recognize sovereignty of Holy See. Catholicism becomes state religion.
- **1936–1937** Axis formed with Nazi Germany. Ethiopia (Abyssinia) conquered.
- **1939** Albania annexed.
- **1940** Italy enters World War II on German side following fall of France.

I

CHRONOLOGY *continued*

- **1943** Invaded by Allies. Mussolini imprisoned by Victor Emmanuel III. Armistice concluded with Allies. Italy declares war on Germany.
- **1944** Christian Democratic Party (DC) formed.
- **1945** Mussolini released. Establishes puppet regime in north. Subsequently executed by Italian partisans.
- **1946** Referendum votes in favor of Italy becoming a republic.
- **1947** Italy signs peace treaty with Allies. Cedes border areas to France and Yugoslavia, Dodecanese to Greece, and gives up colonies.
- **1948** Elections. DC under De Gaspieri forms coalition with left-of-center PSDI and PLI and PRI.
- **1949** Italy founder member of NATO.
- **1950** Agreement with USA establishes US military bases on Italian soil.
- **1951** Joins European Iron and Steel Community.
- **1957** Founding member of European Community. Aided by EC funds and Marshall Aid, industrial growth accelerates.
- **1964** DC government under Aldo Moro forms coalition with PSI. Electoral support for DC falls to below 40%.
- **1969** Red Brigades, extreme left terrorist group, formed.
- **1972** Support for extreme right reaches post-war peak (9%). Rise in extreme left and right urban terrorism
- **1976** PCI support reaches a peak of 34% under Enrico Berlinguer's Eurocommunist philosophy.
- **1978** DC president Aldo Moro abducted and murdered by Red Brigades.
- **1980** Extreme right group plants bomb in Bologna railroad station, killing 84 and wounding 200.
- **1983** Center-left coalition formed under Bettino Craxi. Becomes longest serving post-war Italian government.
- **1987** Craxi government falls.
- **1990** Northern League (NL), a coalition of regionalist parties, attacks government's immigration policies and subsidies to southern Italy.
- **1992** Corruption scandal, involving the acceptance of bribes in return for public contracts, uncovered in Milan. Members of the government accused.
- **1994** General elections held. DC collapses. Coalition between *Forza Italia* and left and right-wing parties form government. December, collapses after resignation of NL ministers.

I

POLITICS

Lower house 1997
Upper house 1997

President Oscar Luigi Scalfaro

THE STATE OF THE PARTIES

Chamber of Deputies 630 members

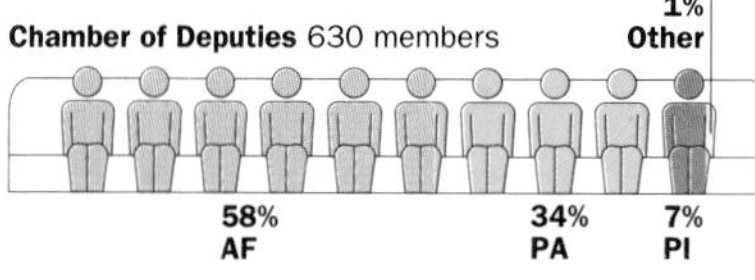

AF = Alliance for Freedom (composed of FI = Forza Italia, NL = Northern League, MSI/NA = National Alliance) **PA** = Progressive Alliance (composed of PDS = Democratic Party of the Left, RC = Reconstructed Communism, DA = Democratic Alliance, LR = La Rete, G = Green Party) **PI** = Pact for Italy (composed of PPI = Popular Party, SP = Segni Pact)

Senate 315 members

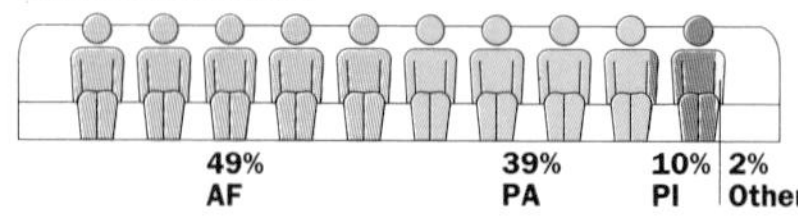

Italy is a multiparty democracy.

MAIN POLITICAL ISSUES

Corruption

The *Mani pulite*, "Clean Hand," investigations, precipitated by the 1992 revelations of illegal party financing in Milan, have revealed a network of institutionalized corruption linking the traditional parties and business. By 1994, more than 4,500 people had been arrested, many of them top public figures. Several, like Carlo de Benedetti, head of one of Italy's most prestigious firms, Olivetti, have been imprisoned. The issue, which has destroyed the old political order, will remain prominent for some years owing to the enormous backlog of cases still to be tried. Former prime minister Silvio Berlusconi was investigated in the early 1990s, but no charges were brought. To counter any conflicts of interest during his period in office, a committee was appointed to monitor the political links of his huge business empire.

Giulio Andreotti, *DC leader and prime minister six times 1976–1992.*

Umberto Bossi, *leader of the regionalist Northern League.*

Silvio Berlusconi, *former prime minister and leader of* Forza Italia.

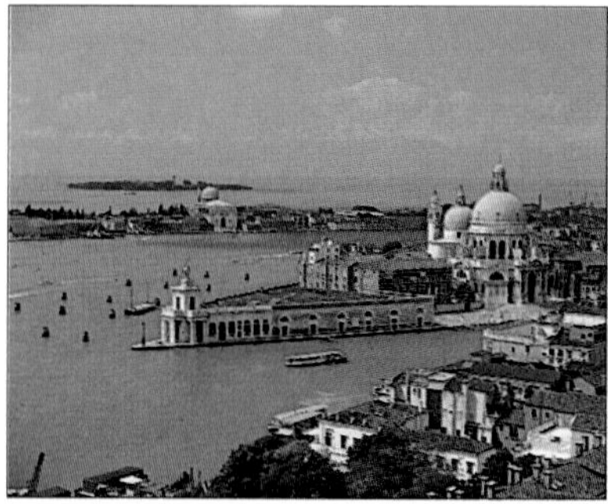

The church of Santa Maria della Salute *marks the entrance to Venice. The city state managed to retain its independence until Napoleon Bonaparte's invasion of Italy.*

Institutional Reform

Forza Italia had vowed to help the private sector by slashing red tape. The promise was popular, since Italy's extreme bureaucratization encourages corruption. The new electoral system is also widely regarded as inadequate because, like the pure proportional representation system it replaced, it does not guarantee stable government.

PROFILE

In 1993, Italy experienced its worst political crisis since 1945. The dense network of institutionalized corruption being uncovered by the *Mani pulite* investigations had discredited a whole political class – in particular the Christian Democrats (CD) and Socialists (SP). Popular disgust was seen in the disastrous results for the CD and SP in municipal elections that year. Electoral reform by an interim government, after a positive referendum on the issue, meant that in the elections in March 1994, 75% of seats would be chosen by simple majority.

The left-wing alliance headed by the PDS, the reformed communists, initially seemed likely to win. However, in January 1994, millionaire businessman Silvio Berlusconi entered the race. His *Forza Italia* went into coalition with the secessionist NL and neofascist MSI/NA, to keep the left out. The PS and CD collapsed into factions. The CD was not only disgraced, it also lost the justification for its political dominance since 1945 – keeping from power Italy's once-large Communist Party.

Berlusconi's Alliance for Freedom coalition won the elecction but its period in office was turbulent and brief. It collapsed in December 1994 when the NL withdrew from the coalition and Berlusconi, facing defeat in a no-confidence debate in parliament, resigned. A technocratic government, led by Lamberto Dini, took over in January 1995.

WORLD AFFAIRS

Since World War II, Italy has pursued a strongly Atlanticist foreign policy. Italy has also been one of the most committed members of the EU. Its strategic position in the central Mediterranean has made Italy a central member of NATO since its foundation in 1949. NATO's South European Command is based in Naples.

Since the end of the Cold War, Italy's major concern has been unrest in the Balkans. The fear that thousands of Bosnian war refugees would seek entry to Italy proved unfounded, however. The rise of Islamic fundamentalism in Algeria and the threat of a UN embargo against Libya are also of concern. Italy is highly dependent on the two North African states for its energy supplies.

AID

 $3.4bn (donations) 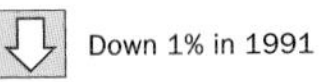 Down 1% in 1991

Italy has been targeting aid at the Balkan states and Albania. Its aim is to prevent a flood of economic migrants. Around 750 military personnel continue to operate relief in Albania; their stay has been extended indefinitely. Africa receives the bulk of development aid.

DEFENSE

 $21.2bn  Up 8% in 1992

Defense spending as % GDP (0–40): 1.7%

ITALIAN ARMED FORCES

1,220 main battle tanks (300 M-60A1/920 *Leopard*)	230,000 personnel
1 carrier, 8 submarines, 1 cruiser, 3 destroyers and 24 frigates	48,000 personnel
449 combat aircraft (80 *Tornado*/164 F-104S/ 99 G-91)	76,000 personnel
None	

The breakup of the Soviet Union and civil war in parts of former Yugoslavia have refocused Italy's defense priorities. The "New Model Defense" announced in 1992 will lead to a 23% reduction in all armed forces. The army is being remodeled for a rapid-intervention role for NATO's southern flank. The navy will be cut to fulfill Mediterranean coastal roles rather than maintaining its current oceangoing capabilities. An estimated 45% of Italy's weapons systems need to be replaced before 2000.

ECONOMICS

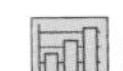 $1,134bn $ 1,712 lire

SCORE CARD

- ❑ WORLD GNP RANKING..........................5th
- ❑ GNP PER CAPITA..........................$18,550
- ❑ BALANCE OF PAYMENTS.................$-25.4bn
- ❑ INFLATION..7.1%
- ❑ UNEMPLOYMENT..............................10.4%

EXPORTS

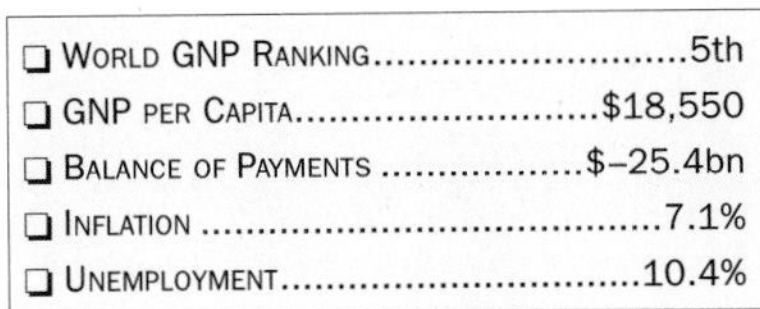

IMPORTS

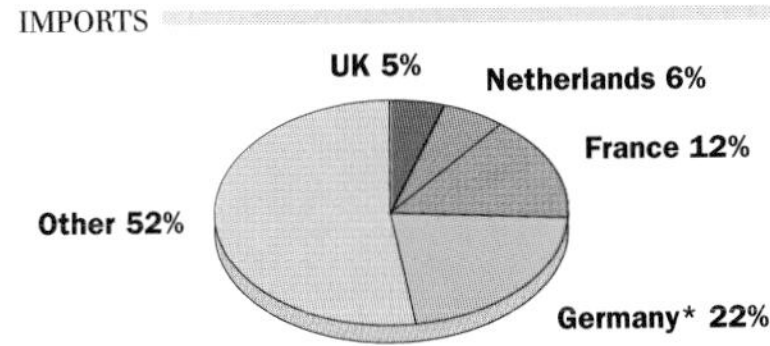

STRENGTHS

Highly competitive, innovative small to medium-size business sector. World leader in industrial and product design, textiles, and household appliances. Several highly innovative firms include Fiat (cars), Montedison (plastics), Olivetti (computers), and Benetton (fashion). Strong tourism and agriculture sectors. Weak lira a boost to exports.

WEAKNESSES

Huge public deficit and government debt; over 100% of GDP. Large and inefficient public sector. Uneven wealth distribution: north Italy far richer than the south, which suffers from high unemployment and where organized crime deters investment. Relatively small companies could find competing in a free international market hard. Heavy dependence on imported energy.

PROFILE

Since World War II, Italy has developed from a mainly agricultural society into the world's fifth industrial power, with a GDP greater than the UK's. The economy is characterized by a large state sector, a mass of family-owned businesses, relatively high levels of protectionism and strong regional differences. Compared to the other G7 economies, Italy also has relatively few multinationals.

State businesses are run mainly by two holding companies, the Institute for Industrial Reconstruction (IRI) and the National Hydrocarbons Group (ENI). IRI owns major electronics, steel, telecommunications, engineering, shipbuilding and aerospace companies.

ECONOMIC PERFORMANCE INDICATOR

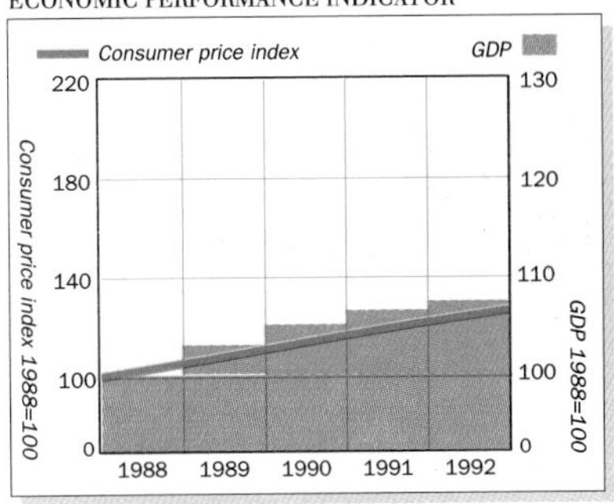

ENI is one of the world's top players in the energy and chemicals sectors.

Family-owned businesses are the backbone of Italy's private sector. They include Fiat, whose interests include jet-engines, telecommunications and bioengineering, besides cars. Similar businesses tend to congregate together. This geographical specialization encourages local competition which has translated into national success.

The *Mezzogiorno* remains the exception. It has 35% of Italy's population, but contributes only 24% of GDP. State attempts to attract new investment have met with success in areas immediately south of Rome. Elsewhere, organized crime has deterred investors and siphoned off state funds. Industrial production has stagnated and unemployment soared. Anger at the misuse of state funds in the south has been a powerful factor in the growth of the Northern League with its demands for autonomy. One-third of Italian tax revenue is generated in Italy's industrial heartland of Milan.

ITALY : MAJOR BUSINESSES

I

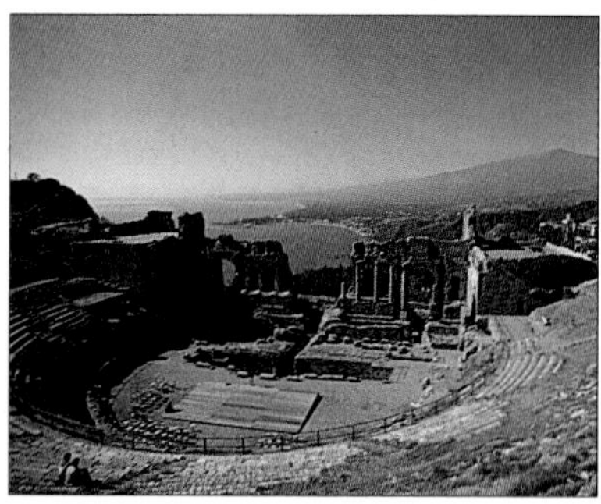

***Remains of the Greek theater** at Taormina, eastern Sicily. It was rebuilt by the Romans in the 2nd century AD. Today, the theater is the venue for an annual arts festival.*

RESOURCES

216.9bn kwh (capacity 56.5m kw)

84,200 b/d (reserves 746,977,000 bbl)

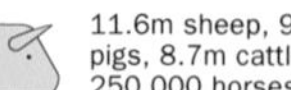

11.6m sheep, 9.4m pigs, 8.7m cattle, 250,000 horses

Lignite, pyrites, fluorspar, barytes, bauxite, lead, zinc

ELECTRICITY GENERATION

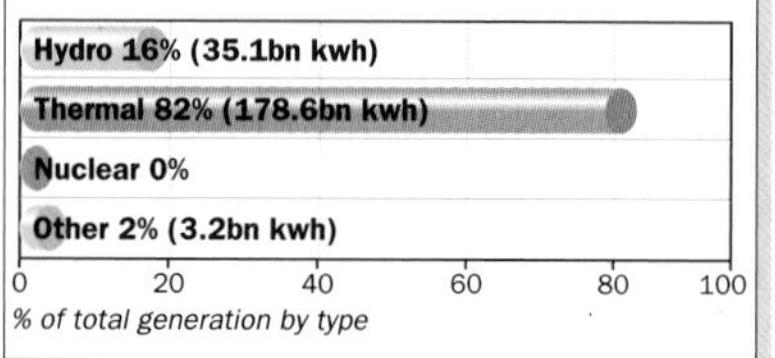

Italy has very few natural resources. It produces just 1% of its oil needs and is highly vulnerable to both fluctuations in world prices and political instability in its North African suppliers. It has reduced its exposure since 1973, when oil accounted for 71% of its needs. Even so, oil still accounts for 56% of energy consumption. Some power is generated from hydro and geothermal sources. Nuclear power was rejected in a 1987 referendum and development has in effect been abandoned. Italy's mineral assets are small and the sector contributes little to national wealth.

ITALY : LAND USE

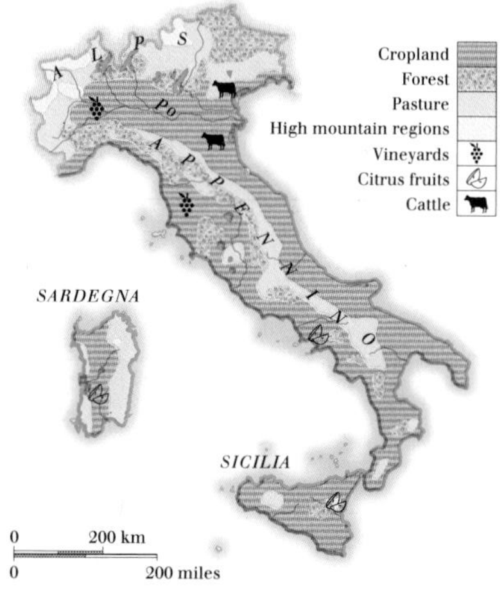

ENVIRONMENT

7% (6% partially protected)

Green issues not a priority

ENVIRONMENTAL TREATIES

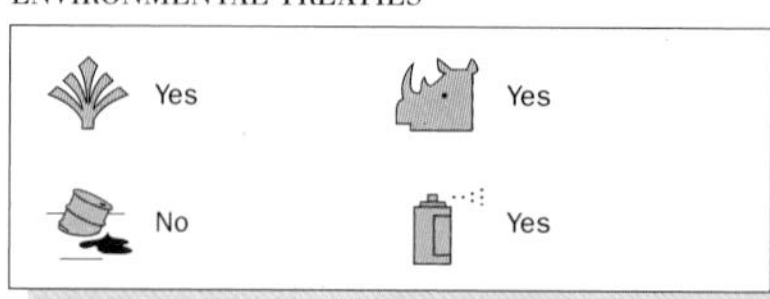

Italy has extensive environmental legislation, but, compared to other EU states, has faced problems in enforcing directives. Under the Amato administration, new measures such as energy taxes and waste recycling laws were considered. However, the government of Silvio Berlusconi was expected to be less keen to introduce environmental laws that could restrict business competitiveness.

Pollution in cities such as Naples and Rome is a major concern. Bans on traffic for up to seven hours during windless days are not uncommon. Air pollution and acid rain have also been damaging forests; 10% of trees are affected. Concern has also been expressed at the hunting of migrant birds, a popular sport in Italy, and the use by some in the fishing industry of drift nets in the Ionian Sea. Sometimes up to 20 miles long, these nets catch dolphins and turtles as well as fish. Under EU law, all drift nets over 1.5 miles long are illegal.

MEDIA

No censorship restrictions

PUBLISHING AND BROADCAST MEDIA

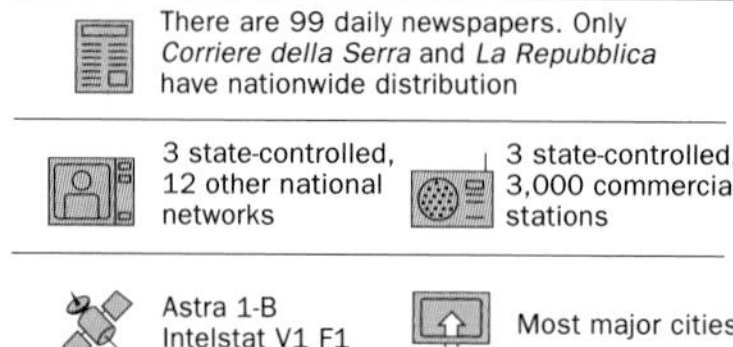

There are 99 daily newspapers. Only *Corriere della Serra* and *La Repubblica* have nationwide distribution
3 state-controlled, 12 other national networks
3 state-controlled, 3,000 commercial stations
Astra 1-B Intelstat V1 F1
Most major cities

Italy's media is dominated by a few conglomerates, notably the Fininvest Group owned by Silvio Berlusconi and Carlo de Benedetti's Ferruzzi group. It has traditionally been highly politicized. Until the exposures of the post-1992 corruption investigations brought reform, this was particularly true of the state TV RAI channels. Like the rest of the state sector, they were apportioned between the main parties: RAI 1 to the Christian Democrats, RAI 2 to the Socialists and RAI 3 to the former Communist Party. The media reflects the Italian love of sports, especially soccer. *La Gazzetta dello Sport* has one of the largest circulations of the national dailies.

CRIME

Italy does not publish prison figures

Up 22% in 1990

CRIME RATES

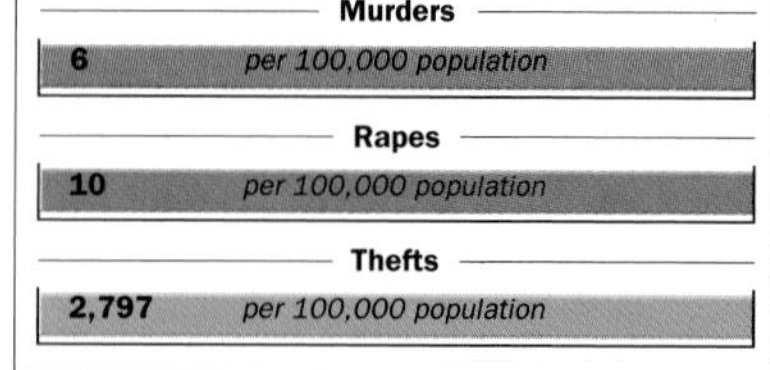

Organized crime remains Italy's most significant problem. The Mafias of Sicily, Naples and Calabria – the *Cosa Nostra*, *Camorra* and *'ndrangheta* – control wholesale agricultural markets and much of the drugs trade, bleed businesses of protection money and manipulate public works contracts and politics. Journalists and public officials delving too deeply into their activities are killed. Giovanni Falcone, the most successful anti-Mafia magistrate, was assassinated in Sicily in 1992. Estimates suggest Mafia businesses are worth \$1 billion–\$10 billion a year, on a par with US multinationals ITT and Exxon.

EDUCATION

97%

0 *Education spending as % GNP* 25

5%

THE EDUCATION SYSTEM

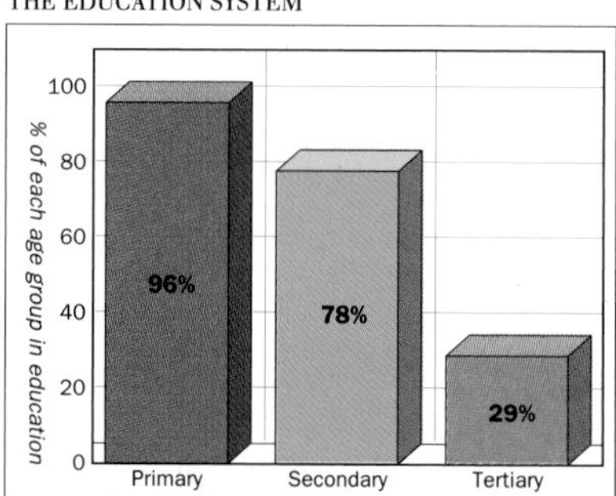

Italy's schooling is almost entirely state-run, apart from a few religious schools and elite private institutions. The pupil–teacher ratio is one of the best in Europe. In 1993, education became compulsory to the age of 16 – up from 14, bringing Italy in line with the rest of Europe. The aim was to cut the high dropout rate in schools, which in Sicily is as high as 50%.

Universities in Italy are over-subscribed – Rome has 180,000 students, only 30% of whom gain a degree. Many Italian educationalists wish to restrict entry. Another concern is the fact that Italy devotes only 1.4% of its GNP to research, compared to the European average of 2.5%.

REGIONS

MILAN

ITALY'S SECOND CITY is also its prime industrial and commercial center. The focus of the fashion, finance and publishing industries, among others, Milan and its province contribute 12% of national GDP. Its inhabitants are among the wealthiest in Europe. Since the 1970s, there has been a shift from manufacturing toward the service and high-tech sectors, which now employ 50% of the population. Many major firms have their head offices in Milan, but its economy depends on small, highly innovative businesses. The city's pride in its efficiency took a knock in 1992 when it became a focus of investigations into corruption in the awarding of public contracts.

TUSCANY

MIDWAY BETWEEN MILAN and Rome, Tuscany in many ways epitomizes Italy – certainly to the thousands of foreigners who have made it their home and the millions of tourists attracted by its beaches, hill towns and the artistic glories of its capital, Florence. It is also quintessentially Italian in that its economy depends on a myriad of small firms clustered around particular centers – such as Prato for textiles and Santa Croce for leather. Over the past 40 years, these family-run concerns have transformed Tuscany from a mainly agricultural society into a major industrial area and one of Italy's richest regions.

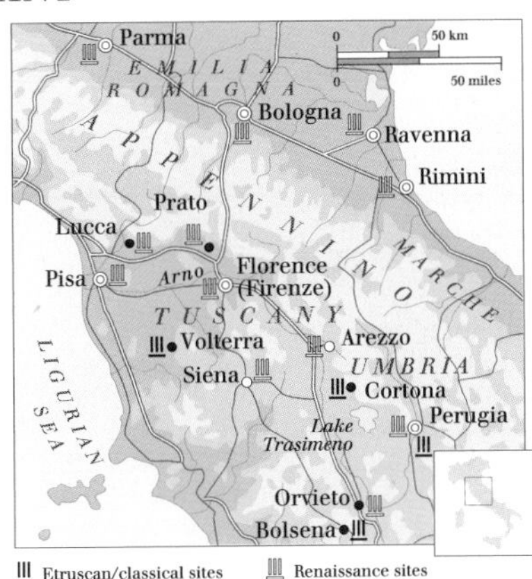

CALABRIA

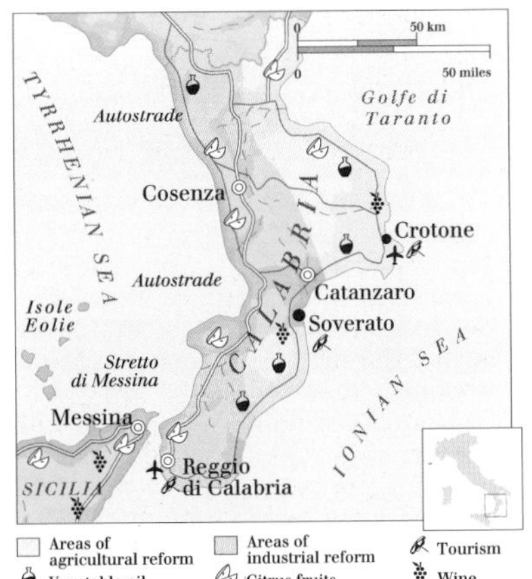

OCCUPYING THE FOOT of the Italian "boot," Calabria is region of harsh mountains. It has poor soils, virtually no industry and Italy's highest rate of unemployment. The Calabrians are Italy's poorest people, and among the poorest in Europe. To other Italians, the region is a world apart. Southern Calabria, home of the notorious *'ndrangheta* Mafia, has Europe's highest murder rate. A few Mafia-dominated communities such as Natile, San Luca and Plati have grown relatively wealthy extorting money from northern industrialists. The area is the kidnap capital of Italy. State development funds have been siphoned off by Mafia clans who control 90% of building and public works contracts. Investors, including state industries like IRI – used as pump primers in other parts of the south – have stayed away. Virtually abandoned by the state, which has made little attempt to control the *'ndrangheta*, many Calabrians have emigrated. In the years after 1945, up to one-third of Calabria's population emigrated to Australia.

HEALTH

1 per 233 people

Heart and cerebrovascular diseases, cancer

Health spending as % GNP: 0 – 25; 5%

Italy's current state-run health system was introduced in the 1970s. Standards vary as services are run by the regions, but few Italians rate their hospitals very highly. Initially free at point of use, charges were introduced in 1988. In addition to some dental and prescription costs, patients have to pay a daily hospital charge and a yearly health fee. AIDS patients are exempt.

WEALTH

Waiter, 1,533,871 Italian lire per month; journalist, 2,855,655 Italian lire per month

CONSUMER GOODS OWNERSHIP

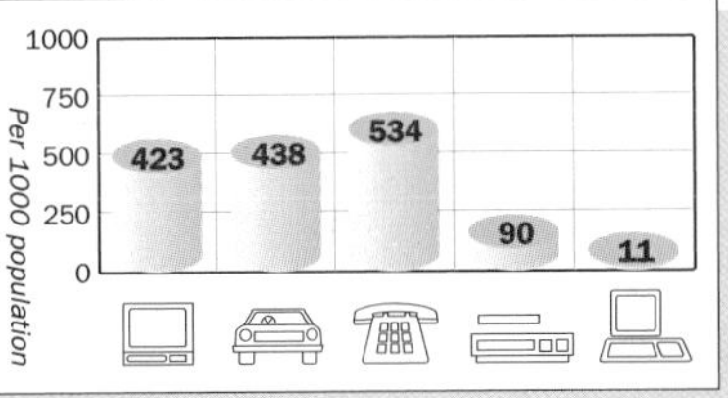

Italians, particularly in the north, are today among the world's wealthiest people in terms of disposable income. This is a result not only of economic growth, but also of the structure of Italian society.

Many Italians have more than one job. The extended families in which most people still live often have access to more than one income. Few people have mortgages, and savings and tax avoidance levels are high.

The main exceptions are in parts of the south. In places like Calabria and Naples, where investment has been lowest and unemployment is highest, many people still live in poverty. For those who do not emigrate, organized crime is usually the only source of jobs.

WORLD RANKING

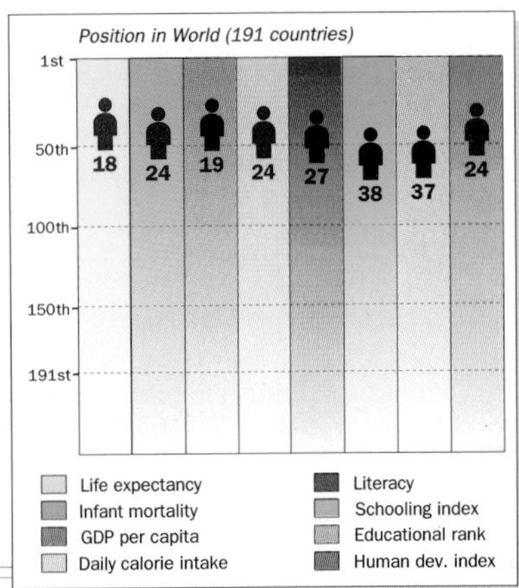

Ivory Coast

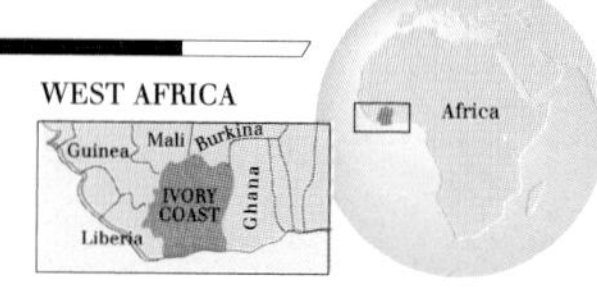

Official Name: Republic of the Ivory Coast **Capital:** Yamoussoukro
Population: 12.9 million **Currency:** CFA franc **Official Language:** French

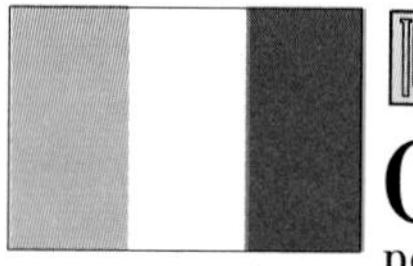

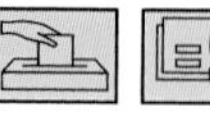

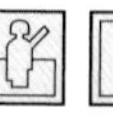

One of the larger of the West African coastal nations, the Ivory Coast remains under the powerful influence of its former colonial ruler, France; it is also called Côte d'Ivoire. Most of its population lives along the sandy coastal strip. The forested interior is sparsely populated, apart from the capital. Between independence in 1960 and his death in 1993, the Ivory Coast was ruled by President Houphouët-Boigny.

CLIMATE

WEATHER CHART

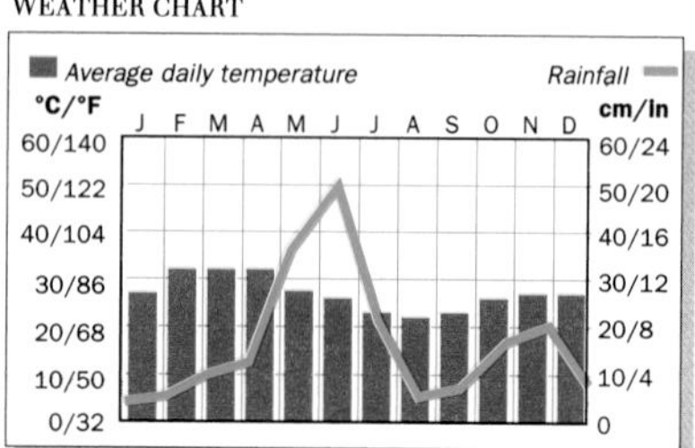

The south's four seasons – two rainy and two dry – merge in the north into a single wet season with lower rainfall.

COMMUNICATIONS

 **Abidjan-Port-Bouët** 849,000 passengers

 8 ships 93,300 dwt

THE TRANSPORTATION NETWORK

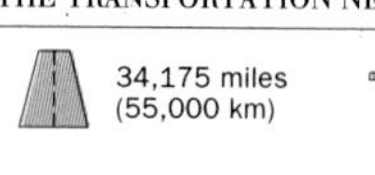 34,175 miles (55,000 km)

96 miles (155 km)

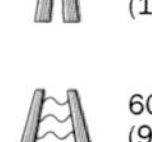 396 miles (638 km)

609 miles (980 km)

The relatively good transportation system focuses on Abidjan, the premier port of Francophone West Africa.

TOURISM

 178,000 visitors

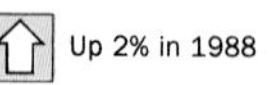 Up 2% in 1988

MAIN OVERSEAS ARRIVALS

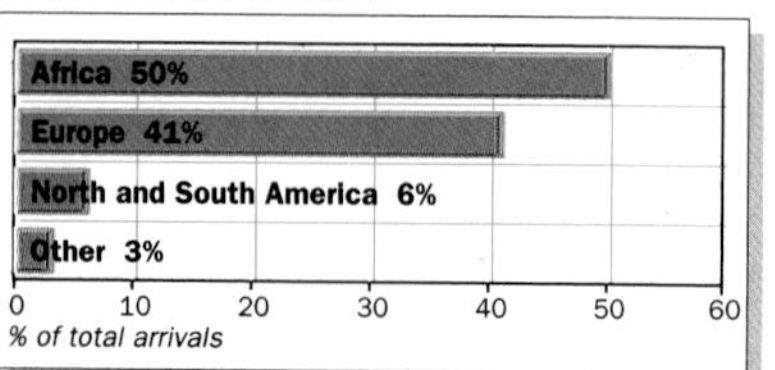

Ambitious plans for an "African Riviera" east of Abidjan and the opening of an hotel by the French *Club Méditerranée* did not boost tourism as expected. The giant Christian basilica built at Yamoussoukro is a major attraction.

PEOPLE

Akan, French, Kru, Voltaic

 96 people per sq. mile

THE URBAN/RURAL POPULATION SPLIT

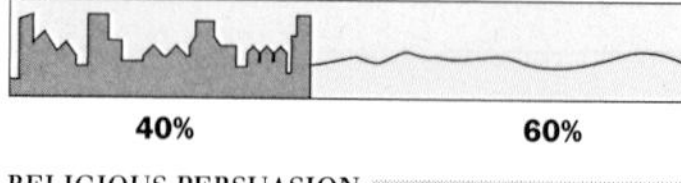

RELIGIOUS PERSUASION

Christian 12%
Muslim 25%
Indigenous beliefs 63%

Although there are more than 60 ethnic groups, the key ones are the Baoule in the center, the Agri in the east, the Senufo in the north, the Dioula in the northwest and west, the Bété in the middle west and the Dan-Yacouba in the west. Houphouët-Boigny promoted his own group, the Baoule, who number only 23% of the population. The succession of Konan Bedic, another Baoule, has annoyed many tribes, the Bété in particular. The extended family is an important force in the shantytowns of Abidjan and connects migrants with their villages. As a result of improved education, women now hold many top jobs.

POLITICS

 1995

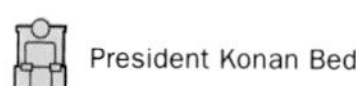 President Konan Bedic

THE STATE OF THE PARTIES

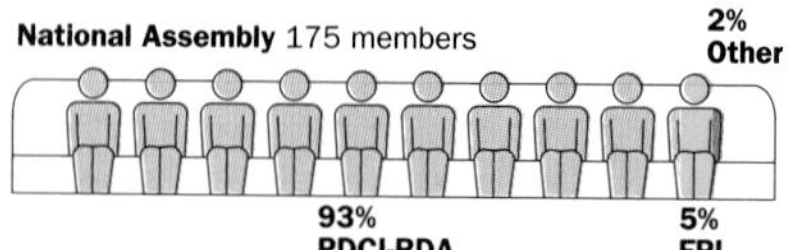

PDCI-RDA = Democratic Party of the Ivory Coast - African Democratic Rally **FPI** = Ivorian People's Front
Other = Ivorian Labor Party

The death of President Houphouët-Boigny in 1993 threw the Ivory Coast's politics into turmoil. No clear successor had been identified by the man who had run the Ivory Coast since independence. Under his rule, the Democratic Party of the Ivory Coast (PDCI) developed a monopoly on patronage which permeated all ranks of the civil service, one reason for the opposition FPI's poor showing in the country's first multiparty elections in 1990. France (the main aid donor), the business community and party barons all maintained their influence under the rule of Houphouët-Boigny, who carefully balanced competing demands. The power vacuum that followed his death left all parties with an influence in politics in a state of uncertainty at a time when the Ivory Coast had pressing economic problems to deal with. Fears were expressed that the army might decide to take a more prominent role in politics.

Ivory Coast

Total Area : 322 463 sq. km (124 503 sq. miles)

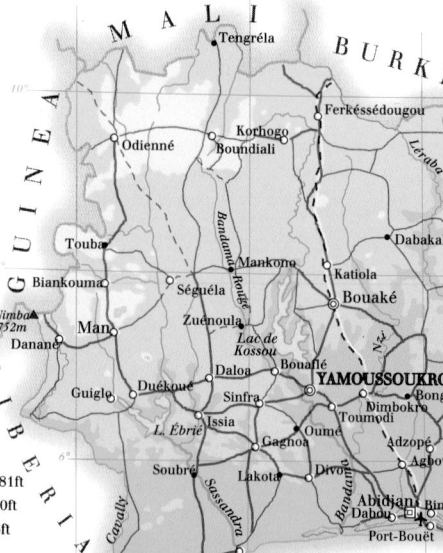

POPULATION
over 1 000 000
over 100 000
over 50 000
over 10 000
under 10 000

LAND HEIGHT
1000m/3281ft
500m/1640ft
200m/656ft
Sea Level

MALI · BURKINA · GUINEA · LIBERIA · GHANA · Ivory Coast · GULF OF GUINEA · ATLANTIC OCEAN

Tengréla · Ferkéssédougou · Odienné · Korhogo · Boundiali · Bouna · Touba · Dabakala · Mankono · Katiola · Bondoukou · Biankouma · Séguéla · Bouaké · Mount Nimba 1752m · Man · Zuénoula · Danané · Lac de Kossou · Bouaflé · YAMOUSSOUKRO · Abengourou · Guiglo · Duékoué · Daloa · Sinfra · Dimbokro · Bongouanou · Issia · Toumodi · Oumé · Gagnoa · Adzopé · Agboville · Ayamé Reservoir · Soubré · Lakota · Divo · Abidjan · Bingerville · Aboisso · Dabou · Port-Bouët · Grand-Bassam · Sassandra · San Pedro · Tabou · Cavally · Sassandra · Bandama · Bandama Rouge · Nzi · Komoé · Léraba · Black Volta · L. Ébrié

WORLD AFFAIRS

The Ivory Coast fears that the civil war in neighboring Liberia could affect its own stability. However, its main concern is balancing the demands and interests of its creditors: the US-dominated World Bank on the one hand and France on the other. Within ECOWAS, the Ivory Coast's most important relationship is with Nigeria.

AID

 $633m (receipts) 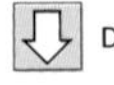 Down 9% in 1991

France donates the most aid overall. Structural adjustment loans from the World Bank have been particularly important in easing the acute debt problem. The Ivory Coast gives aid to poorer West African countries.

DEFENSE

 $185m  Fairly constant from year to year

Since independence, a defense accord has existed with France, the main supplier of equipment and trainer of officers for the 5,500-strong army. The greatest security threat is along the border with war-torn Liberia.

ECONOMICS

 $8.7bn  295.23 CFA francs

SCORE CARD

- ❑ WORLD GNP RANKING 84th
- ❑ GNP PER CAPITA $675
- ❑ BALANCE OF PAYMENTS ....$-1.4bn
- ❑ INFLATION 1%
- ❑ UNEMPLOYMENT..Lower than West African average

STRENGTHS

Diversified nature of the agricultural sector. Relatively good infrastructure. Benefits of early liberalism and attractiveness to investors.

WEAKNESSES

Major debt from over-borrowing for projects such as the Kossou Dam. Overproduction of some commodities. Political patronage system of the ruling party, which exploits farmers.

EXPORTS

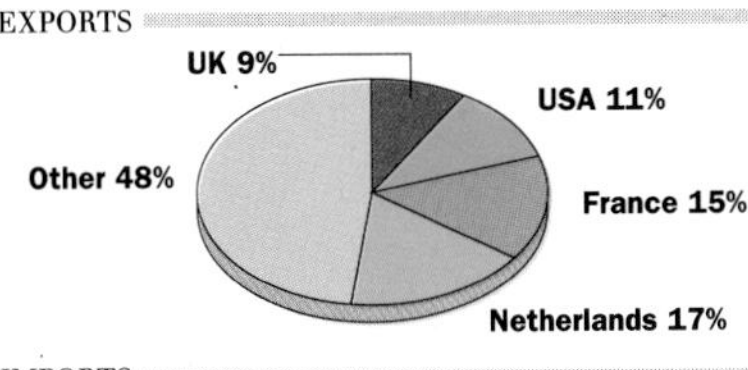

IMPORTS

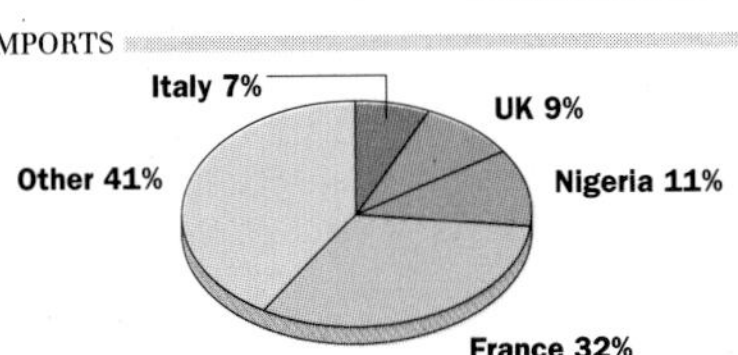

RESOURCES

 2.4bn kwh (capacity 1.17m kw)  Reserves of 100,000,000 bbl; refines 69,000 b/cd

 1m sheep, 1m cattle, 351,000 pigs, 1,000 horses  Oil, diamonds

Oil reserves have failed to meet expectations; negotiations are under way on offshore gas development.

ENVIRONMENT

 6% (0.3% partially protected)  Ban on timber exports not yet in force

The government has committed itself to a ban on timber exports when the foreign payment situation improves.

MEDIA

Despite reduction in censorship since 1990, the press is still subject to controls

PUBLISHING AND BROADCAST MEDIA

There are 2 daily newspapers, *Fraternité-Matin* and *Ivoir 'Soir*, both published by the government

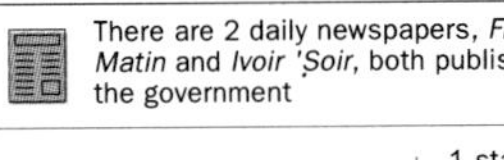 1 state-owned service — 1 state-owned, 1 independent service

The heavy censorship of the past 30 years has now eased, but there is still a hesitancy to speak out politically.

EDUCATION

 54%

A high percentage of students fail the *baccalauréat*. As expenditure has been cut, student agitation has grown.

CRIME

 The Ivory Coast does not publish prison figures  Down 52% in 1990

Crime levels are low in rural areas. However, armed robbery and violent crime are on the increase in Abidjan.

The basilica, Yamoussoukro. Built in the new capital, President Houphouët-Boigny's birthplace, it is modeled on St. Peter's, Rome.

CHRONOLOGY

One of the great trading emporia of West Africa, the Ivory Coast was made a French colony in 1893. By 1918 the French had defeated the Malinke Empire and the forest peoples of the interior.

- ❑ **1903–1935** Railroad and roads built with forced labor.
- ❑ **1946** PDCI founded as sole party.
- ❑ **1948–1950** The Dark Years; arrests and deaths in anti-French activity.
- ❑ **1960** Félix Houphouët-Boigny declares independence.
- ❑ **1970** Oil production starts.
- ❑ **1990** First contested elections: Houphouët-Boigny and PDCI win.
- ❑ **1992** First black African state to open diplomatic links with South Africa.
- ❑ **1993** Houphouët-Boigny dies.

I

HEALTH

 1 per 15,950 people  Malaria, communicable diseases, neonatal deaths

Health improved notably in the 1980s, with many more paramedical workers. Infant mortality rates are high.

WEALTH

 Metalworking machine setter, 109,500–254,300 CFA francs per month; dentist, 154,000–422,500 CFA francs per month

CONSUMER GOODS OWNERSHIP

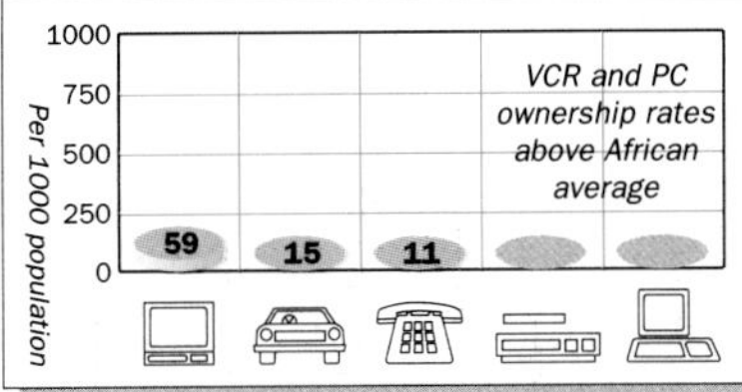

A large bourgeoisie grew rich in the boom years. Urban living standards are better than in many African countries.

WORLD RANKING

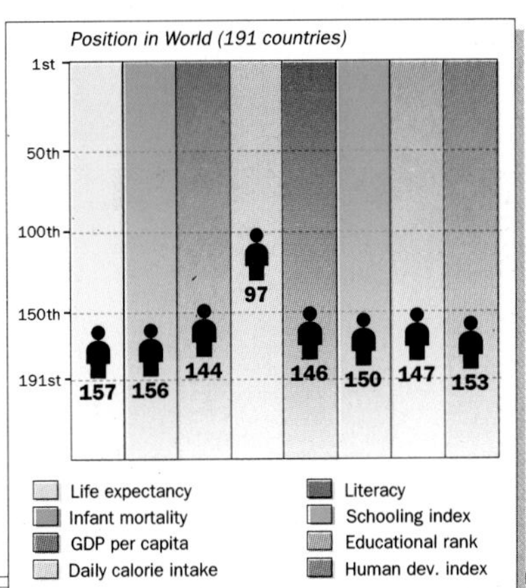

JAMAICA

OFFICIAL NAME: Jamaica **CAPITAL:** Kingston
POPULATION: 2.5 million **CURRENCY:** Jamaican dollar **OFFICIAL LANGUAGE:** English

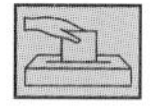

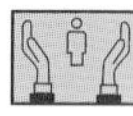

First colonized by the Spanish and then, from 1655, by the English, Jamaica is located in the Caribbean, south of Cuba. It was the first of the Caribbean island nations to become independent from colonial control in the post-war years, and remains an influential force in Caribbean politics. Jamaica is also influential in the world music scene; *reggae* and *ragga* (or *dancehall*) developed in the tough conditions of Kingston's poor districts.

CLIMATE

WEATHER CHART

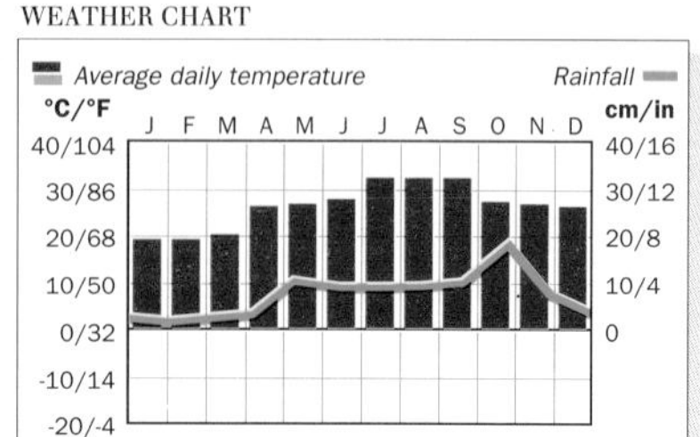

Hurricanes are likely between June and November. The hills above Kingston are the coolest spot during hot summers.

COMMUNICATIONS

4 ships 16,200 dwt

THE TRANSPORTATION NETWORK

11,309 miles (18,200 km)

None

210 miles (339 km)

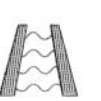

None

Jamaica has a general shortage of buses and taxis. The airports at Kingston and Montego Bay have been improved recently.

TOURISM

840,000 visitors

Up 18% in 1990

MAIN OVERSEAS ARRIVALS

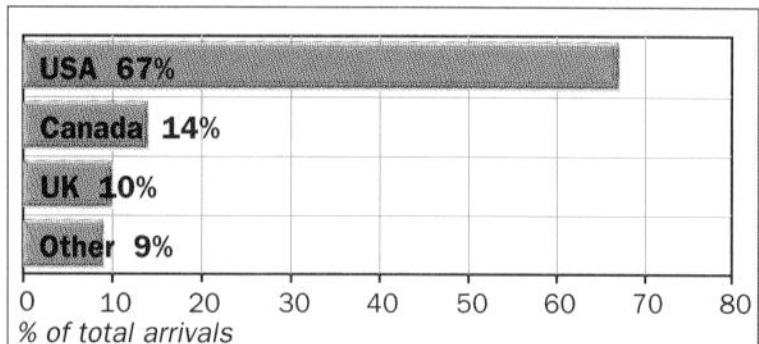

Tourism is a major industry in Jamaica. Most tourists stay in large, enclosed beach resorts. Ocho Rios and Montego Bay have the best beaches.

PEOPLE

591 people per sq. mile

THE URBAN/RURAL POPULATION SPLIT

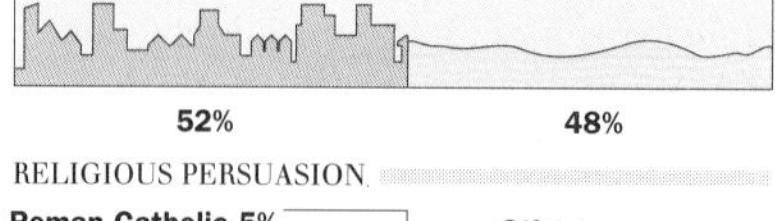

52% 48%

RELIGIOUS PERSUASION

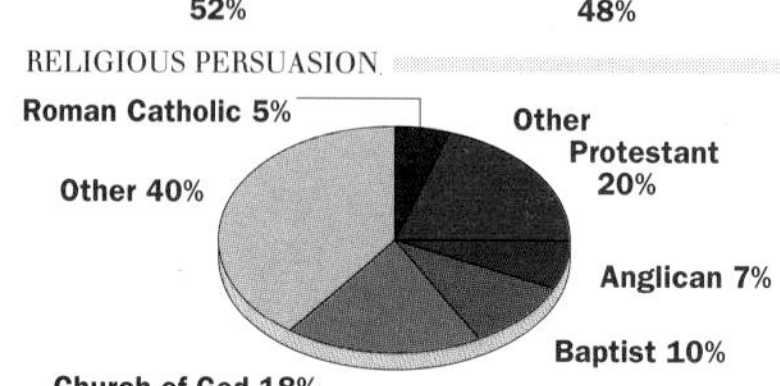

Jamaica has a broad ethnic mix. Most Jamaicans are the descendants of Africans brought to the island between the 16th and 19th centuries, but there are also minorities of Europeans, Indians, Chinese and Arabs. Jamaica is also home to the Rastafarians, worshipers of the former Emperor of Ethiopia.

Most social tension is the result of the marked disparities of wealth. The Caribbean women's rights movement arrived first in Jamaica, and today many women hold senior positions in economic and political life.

Although life revolves around the family, absentee fathers are common. Many career women are single parents by choice. Life in the ghettos of Kingston is often violent and based largely on gun law. Kingston slums have their own local dialect.

Bauxite mine and terminal, *Runway Bay. Bauxite – from which aluminum is made – is the main source of foreign income.*

POLITICS

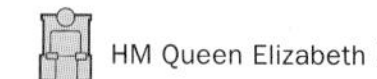

THE STATE OF THE PARTIES

House of Representatives 60 members

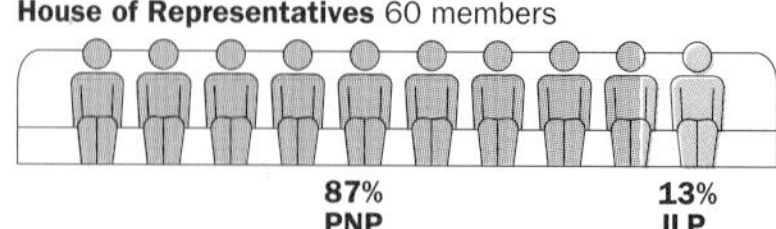

87% PNP 13% JLP

PNP = People's National Party **JLP** = Jamaica Labour Party

Senate 21 members

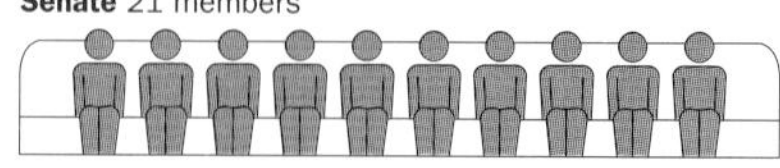

13 members chosen by the prime minister and 8 by the leader of the opposition

Jamaica's political and economic life is dominated by a few long-established and wealthy families, who fund the parties. The country's political complexion changed markedly in the late 1980s, as the ideologies of the once socialist PNP and the conservative JLP converged toward a moderate free-market economic approach.

Violence during election time is a continuing problem. Despite strong denials, some politicians retain close connections with armed gangs who control the politically important slum areas of Kingston through intimidation. When threats fail, these gangs have been known to murder political opponents.

WORLD AFFAIRS

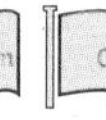

The USA is the focus of foreign policy. Jamaica cooperates with US agencies in anti-narcotics programs.

AID

$166m (receipts)

Down 61% in 1991

Most aid comes from the USA, the EU and the UK. It includes both project loans and balance of payments support.

DEFENSE

$32.52m

Up 47% in 1990

Jamaica's 5,500-strong defense force buys its arms from the USA, but is trained by the UK. Today, the defense force is used against narcotics smugglers and to break up violence during elections.

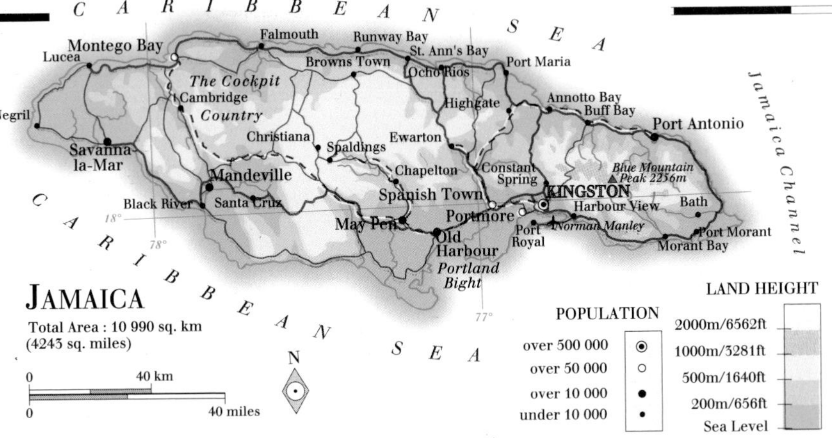

CHRONOLOGY

Spain occupied the island in 1510, wiping out the indigenous Arawak population. Britain seized the island in 1655.

- ❑ **1938** JLP founded.
- ❑ **1958–1961** West Indies Federation.
- ❑ **1962** Independence under JLP.
- ❑ **1972** PNP elected. Social and economic reforms fail; street violence begins.
- ❑ **1980** Unpopular IMF austerity measures lead to JLP election win.
- ❑ **1988** Worst ever hurricane.
- ❑ **1991** PNP back in power.

ECONOMICS

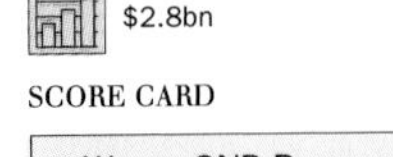

$2.8bn

28.46 Jamaican dollars

SCORE CARD

❑ World GNP Ranking	128th
❑ GNP per Capita	$1,120
❑ Balance of Payments	$–198m
❑ Inflation	60.7%
❑ Unemployment	15.7%

Strengths
A relatively broad-based economy: Mining and refining of bauxite for aluminum. Successful tourism industry. Agriculture, including sugar, bananas, rum and coffee. Light manufacturing and data processing for US companies are growing sectors.

Weaknesses
Most products are dependent on protected markets, which are under threat in both the USA and the EU.

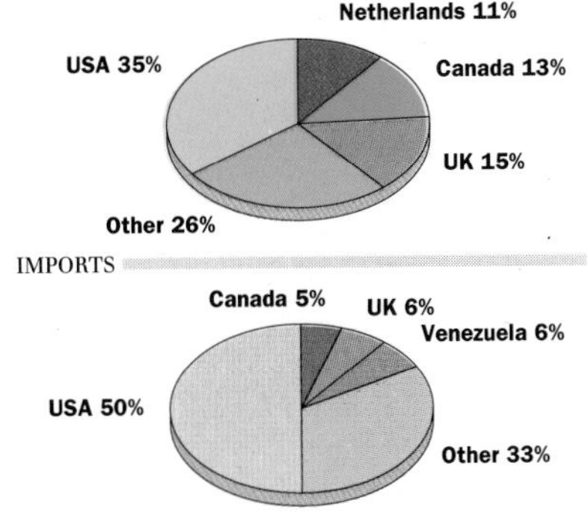

RESOURCES

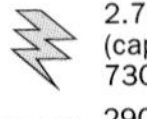

2.7bn kwh (capacity 730,000 kw)

Not an oil producer; refines 32,000 b/cd

290,000 cattle, 240,000 pigs, 23,000 asses

Bauxite, marble, gypsum, silica, clay

Jamaica is the world's third largest producer of bauxite, accounting for 11% of total global output.

ENVIRONMENT

3%

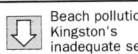

Beach pollution from Kingston's inadequate sewerage

Acidic dust from bauxite processing, the biggest heavy industry in Jamaica, is the major problem, and has led to the relocation of an entire village.

MEDIA

Freedom of expression is guaranteed under the constitution

PUBLISHING AND BROADCAST MEDIA

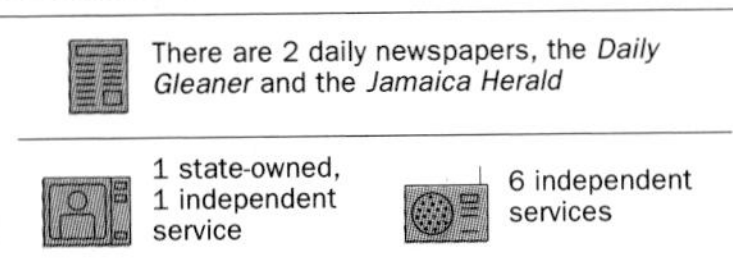

There are 2 daily newspapers, the *Daily Gleaner* and the *Jamaica Herald*

1 state-owned, 1 independent service

6 independent services

The government is in the process of loosening its hold on broadcasting. The Jamaican press is one of the most influential in the Caribbean.

CRIME

4,350 prisoners

Down 19% in 1990

Armed crime is a major problem. Many murders are the result of armed robberies linked to narcotics gangs competing for territory. Much of the world crack trade is still controlled from Jamaica. Large areas of Kingston are ruled by *Dons*, gang leaders who administer their own violent justice. The armed police are also frequently accused of the peremptory shooting of suspects.

The British Privy Council is the last court of appeal; in 1993, 80 men on death row for more than five years were reprieved in a landmark decision.

EDUCATION

98%

Education is based on the former British 11-plus selection system. Jamaica hosts the largest of the three campuses of the University of the West Indies.

HEALTH

1 per 6,687 people

Cerebrovascular and heart diseases, cancer, diabetes

The once-efficient state health service is now seriously underfunded. There are fewer doctors and nurses than in the 1980s and hospitals generally have a shortage of drugs and rudimentary medical equipment.

J

WEALTH

Miner, 1,139 Jamaican dollars per week; metal manufacturing worker, 2,840 Jamaican dollars per week

CONSUMER GOODS OWNERSHIP

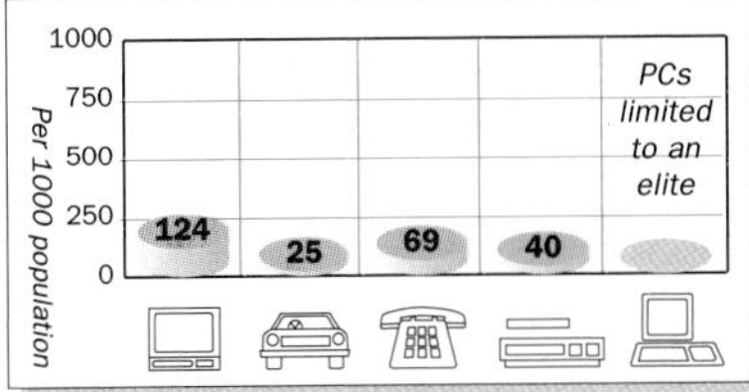

Wealth disparities are great in Jamaica, although better education has resulted in an increase in the number of black Jamaicans taking more lucrative, white-collar jobs. The poorest in Jamaica, mostly migrants from rural areas, live in the slums of Kingston.

WORLD RANKING

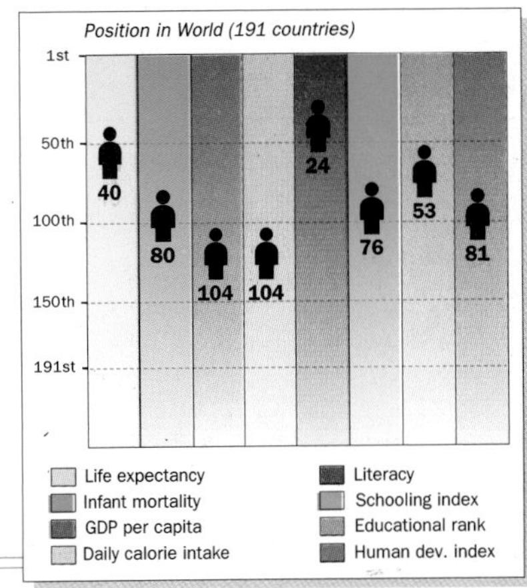

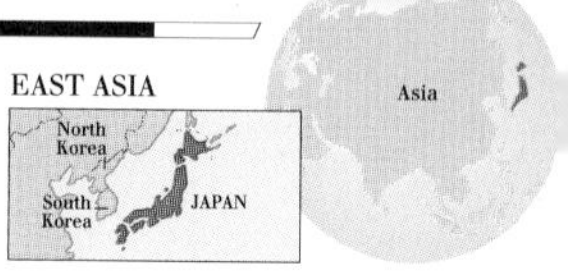

JAPAN

OFFICIAL NAME: Japan **CAPITAL:** Tokyo
POPULATION: 124 million **CURRENCY:** Yen **OFFICIAL LANGUAGE:** Japanese

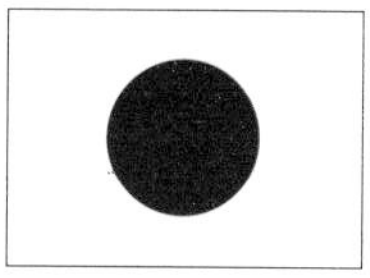

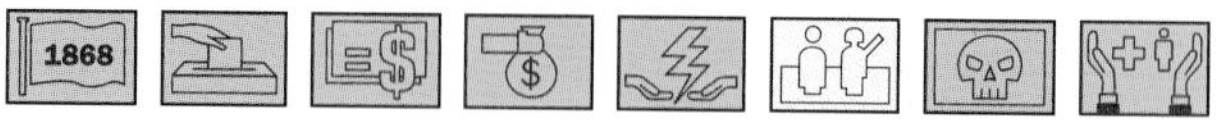

EAST ASIA
North Korea
South Korea
JAPAN
Asia

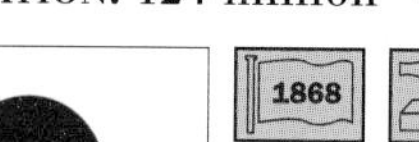

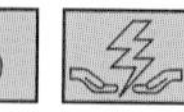

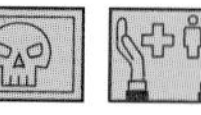

A CONSTITUTIONAL MONARCHY, with an emperor as head of state, Japan is located off the east Asian coast in the north Pacific. It comprises four principal islands, and more than 3,000 smaller islands. One chain of islands – the Kuriles in the north – is disputed with the Russian Federation. The terrain is mostly mountainous, with fertile coastal plains; over two-thirds is woodland. The Pacific coast is vulnerable to *tsunamis* – tidal waves triggered by submarine earthquakes. Most cities are located by the sea; the Kanto plain around Tokyo, Kawasaki and Yokohama is the most populous and heavily industrialized. To the north, Hokkaido is the most rural of the main islands. Japan is the world's most powerful economy, with a current trade balance of more than $100 billion per annum, and overseas investments of $240 billion.

***Traditional rice paddy** in Hokkaido. Rice farming is among the most protected sectors of the Japanese economy.*

CLIMATE

WEATHER CHART

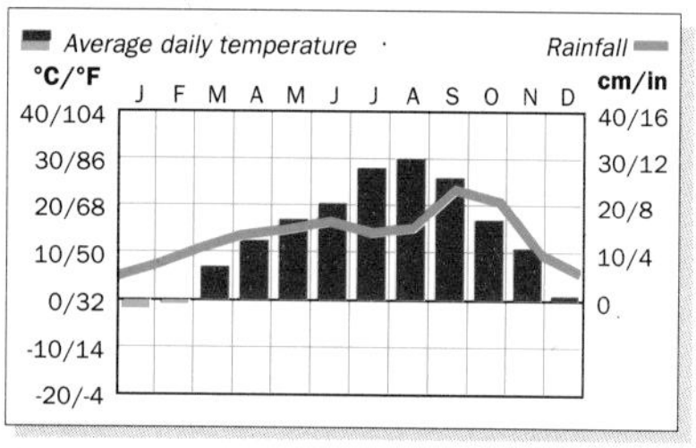

Average daily temperature · Rainfall
°C/°F · cm/in
J F M A M J J A S O N D
40/104 · 40/16
30/86 · 30/12
20/68 · 20/8
10/50 · 10/4
0/32 · 0
-10/14
-20/-4

The Sea of Japan has a moderating influence on Japan's climate. Winters are less cold than on the Asian mainland. Japan also has much higher rainfall. Spring is perhaps the most pleasant season, with warm, sunny days, but without the sultry, oppressive heat and rainfall of the summer. The freak storms and floods of August 1992 were the worst for 120 years.

COMMUNICATIONS

Narita, Tokyo 32m passengers
3,792 ships 36.34m dwt

THE TRANSPORTATION NETWORK

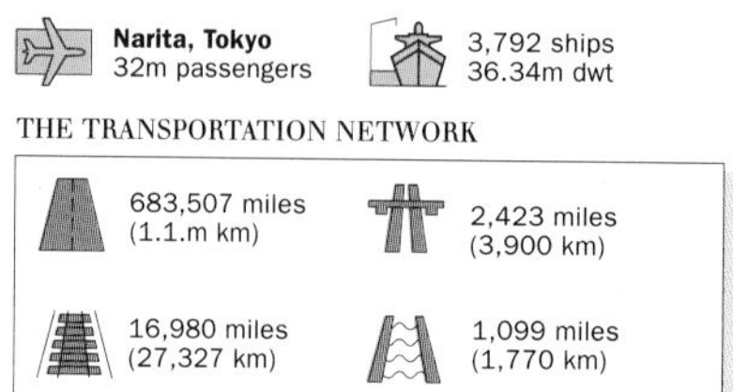

Railroads are the most important means of transportation in Japan. Known in the West as the bullet train, the *Shinkansen* is the second-fastest in the world. It is renowned as much for its reliability as for its speed. The Tokyo–Chitose air route, with six million passengers a year, is the busiest in the world.

JAPAN

Total Area : 377 800 sq. km
(145 869 sq. miles)

POPULATION

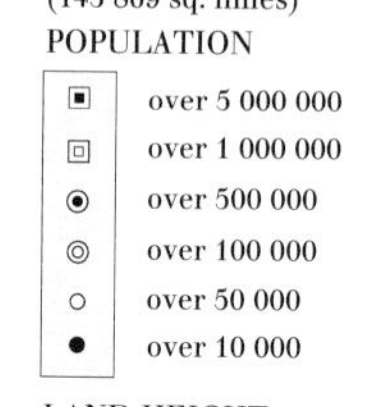

LAND HEIGHT

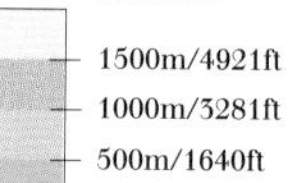

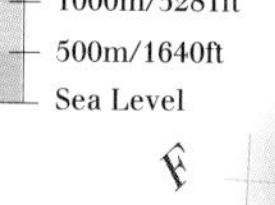

0 100 km
0 100 miles

SEA OF JAPAN
PACIFIC
HONSHU
SHIKOKU
KYŪSHŪ
Tokyo
Kawasaki
Yokohama
Nagoya
Kyōto
Ōsaka
Kōbe
Hiroshima
Fukuoka
Kitakyūshū
Sapporo

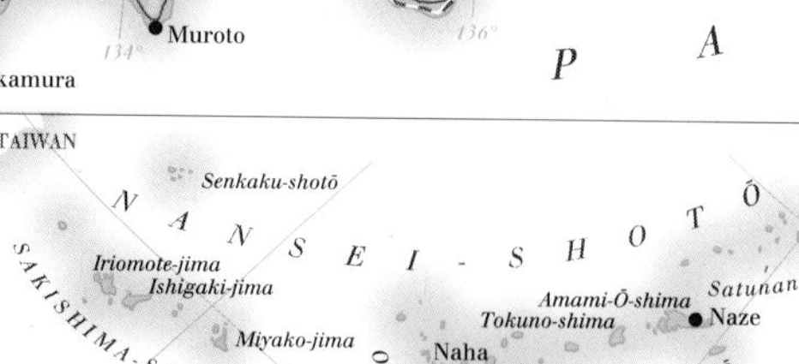

TOURISM

3.58m visitors | Up 1% in 1993

MAIN OVERSEAS ARRIVALS

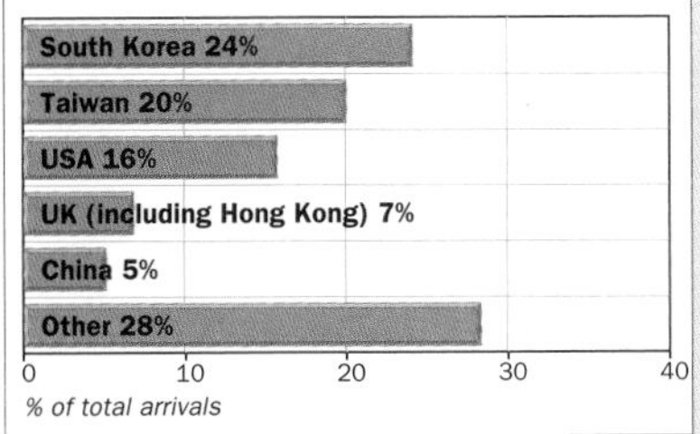

The high value of the yen makes Japan an expensive tourist destination. Attractions include the extraordinary variety of energetic high-tech urban living in Tokyo and Osaka. By contrast, rural areas such as Hokkaido are highly traditional.

A new trend in Japan is ecotourism. More than three million people a year come to look at whales, using former whaling villages such as Ogata as bases. The ancient imperial capital, Kyoto, remains the most popular tourist destination. More than 35 million people visit it every year.

***High Street, Ginza District, Tokyo** at night. Japan's well-policed cities are among the safest in the world.*

PEOPLE

Japanese, Korean, Chinese | 847 people per sq. mile

THE URBAN/RURAL POPULATION SPLIT

77% | 23%

RELIGIOUS PERSUASION

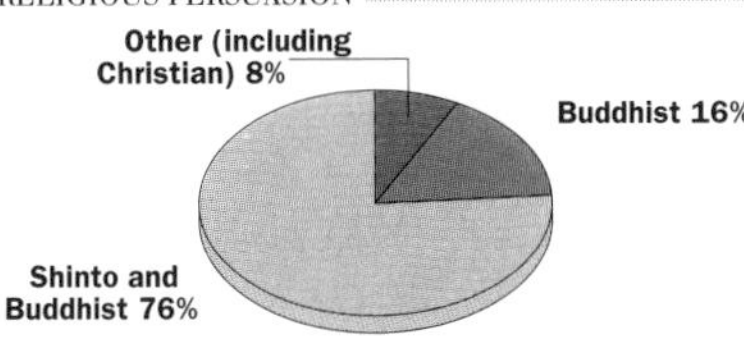

ETHNIC MAKEUP

Other (mainly Korean) 1%

Japanese 99%

Japan is one of the most racially homogeneous societies in the world. Its sense of order is reflected in the phenomenon of the lifetime employer. Many Japanese men define themselves by the company they work for rather than the job they do. An employer's influence stretches to commanding employees' social time, and even to encouraging and approving marriages.

Women mostly play a traditional role, running the home and supervising the all-important education of their children. They tend to work until the age of 26, when many will marry and continue to work part-time. Some Japanese women are, however, beginning to follow independent, long-term careers. More are entering the medical and legal fields. Japan elected its first female party leader – Takako Doi – in 1991.

There is little tradition of teenage rebellion in Japan. Whereas the young still tend to follow their parents' lifestyles, some are questioning established attitudes. They are less likely to want to work for the same company for life, and less willing to give up evenings and weekends to entertaining company clients.

Social form remains extremely important in Japanese society. Respect for elders and social and business superiors is still strong.

POPULATION AGE BREAKDOWN

% of population by age group

	1960	1970	1980	1990	2000
65+	6%	7%	9%	12%	16%
15–64	64%	69%	67%	70%	68%
0–14	30%	24%	24%	18%	16%

CHRONOLOGY

Japan's tendency to limit its contacts with the outside world ended in 1853, when a US naval squadron coerced trading concessions from the last of the Tokugawa shoguns.

- **1868** Civil war. Tokugawa regime falls. Restoration of Meiji dynasty.
- **1869** Edo renamed Tokyo. Attempts to reverse increasing Western influence.
- **1872** Modernization along Western lines introduced: the "Strong Army, Rich Country" program. *Samurai* rank abolished. Japan's strong military tradition becomes state-directed.
- **1889** Constitution modeled on Bismarck's German constitution adopted.
- **1894–1895** War with China; ends in Japanese victory.
- **1904–1905** War with Russia; ends in Japanese victory. Formosa and Korea annexed.
- **1914** Japan joins World War I on Allied side. Sees limited naval action.
- **1919** Versailles peace conference gives Japan limited territorial gains in the Pacific.
- **1920** USA limits Japanese immigration.
- **1923** Yokohama earthquake kills 140,000.
- **1927** Japan enters period of radical nationalism, and introduces the notion of a "co-prosperity sphere" in Southeast Asia under Japanese control. Interpreted in the USA as a threat to its Pacific interests.
- **1931** Manchuria invaded, placed under Japanese control and renamed Manchukuo.
- **1937** Japan launches full-scale invasion of China.
- **1938** All political parties placed under one common banner; Japan in effect ruled by militarists.
- **1939** Japan does not react to outbreak of war in Europe.
- **1940** Fall of France in Europe; Japan invades French Indochina.
- **1941** July: Japan forces Vichy government in France to sanction takeover of southern Indochina. October: USA responds with a total trade embargo, including oil, and increases the strength of the US navy relative to the Japanese. December: Japan launches attack on US fleet at Pearl Harbor. British and Dutch possessions in the Pacific invaded.
- **1942** Japan loses decisive naval battle of the Coral Sea. USA begins naval campaign in the Pacific which leads to Japan's eventual defeat at sea.

CHRONOLOGY *continued*

- **1945** Huge US bombing campaign culminates in atomic bombing of Hiroshima and Nagasaki. Soviet Union declares war on Japan. Emperor Hirohito surrenders, gives up divine status. Japan placed under US military government.
- **1945** US Gen. MacArthur installed as supreme commander of Allied Powers in Japan.
- **1947** Japanese constitution, modeled on US, but retaining the emperor in ceremonial role, introduced.
- **1949** Elections. LDP in power.
- **1950** Korean War. US army contracts lead to quick expansion of Japanese economy.
- **1952** Treaty of San Francisco. Japan regains independence. Industrial production recovers to 15% above 1936 levels.
- **1960** Ikeda economic plan announced, with aim of doubling incomes in ten years.
- **1964** Tokyo Olympics. Bullet train (*Shinkansen*) inaugurated. Japan admitted to OECD.
- **1970** Osaka Expo confirms Japan as first-rank economic power.
- **1973** Oil crisis. Economic growth cut. Government-led economic re-assessment decides to concentrate on high-tech industries.
- **1974** Ex-prime minister Sato receives Nobel prize for work on nuclear disarmament.
- **1979** Second oil crisis. Growth continues at 6% per year.
- **1982** Honda establishes first car factory in USA.
- **1983** Japanese banks account for 35% of international assets.
- **1986** Plaza Accords force upward valuation of the yen by 40%.
- **1988** Japan becomes world's largest aid donor and overseas investor.
- **1989** Death of Emperor Hirohito ends longest Japanese imperial reign. Recruit Co. bribery scandal leads to resignation of Prime Minister Noburo Takeshita. Replaced by Sosuke Uno, forced to resign over sexual scandal. Tokyo stock market crash.
- **1990** General election. LDP gains majority in lower house.
- **1992** Sagawa Kyubin scandal; resignation of LDP vice-president.
- **1993** July, LDP loses power in elections for first time in 38 years. Morihiro Hosokawa prime minister as head of seven-party coalition.
- **1994** Hokosawa resigns. Hata takes over. Coalition collapses two months later.
- **1995** January: Kobe earthquake kills over 5,000 people.

POLITICS

Lower House 1997
Upper House 1995

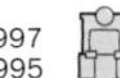

Emperor Tsegu no Miya Akihito

THE STATE OF THE PARTIES

House of Representatives 512 members

10% Shinseito

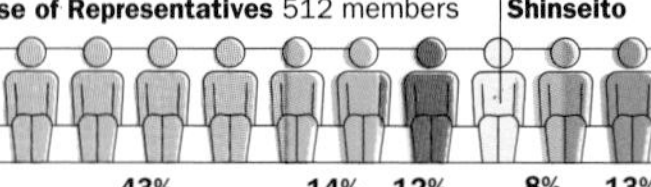

43% LDP **14% SDJP** **12% Komeito** **8% JNP** **13% Other**

LDP = Liberal Democratic Party **SDJP** = Social Democratic Party of Japan **Komeito** = Clean Government Party **Shinseito** = Japan Renewal Party **JNP** = Japan New Party **Other** = Japan Communist Party, New Harbinger Party, Democratic Socialist Party and vacant seats

House of Councillors 252 members

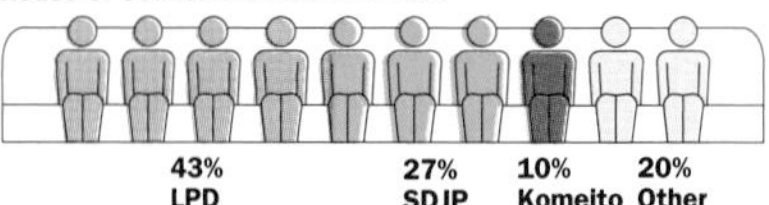

43% LPD **27% SDJP** **10% Komeito** **20% Other**

Japan is a multiparty democracy. The Emperor has a non-political role.

Main Political Issues

Reform

Japanese politics was dominated for 38 years by the ruling LDP. Politics was based on a close system of patronage, which linked big business, the bureaucracy, and the LDP in a close arrangement. The fall of the LDP in the July 1993 elections was prompted by a popular desire for reform. Groups such as Ichiro Ozawa's *Kaishin* (Innovation) are now pressing for a more Western-style system of argumentative politics. Parties with specific programs and policies are likely to emerge, replacing the LDP's patronage-based politics.

Tax reform

In April 1994, former Prime Minister Tsutomu Hata's cabinet established tax reform as one of its clearly defined policies. Hata's Japan Renewal Party wanted to raise the consumption tax to tap the resources of Japan's wealthy, retired population. However, this policy is opposed by the Social Democrats.

Tomiichi Murayama, *prime minister and head of the current LDP-SDJP coalition.*

Eijiro Hata, *international trade and industry minister under Hata.*

Koji Kakizawa, *foreign minister, ex-LDP, backed Tsutomu Hata in 1994.*

Emperor Tsegu no Miya Akihito. *He acceded in 1989 on the death of his father, Hirohito.*

The role of the military

The Japanese constitution limits its army to a defense role. In a break with tradition, Japanese forces took part in the UN peacekeeping operation in Cambodia in 1993. The Japan Renewal Party is in favor of raising Japan's international profile by increasing its contributions to UN peacekeeping operations. Conservatives of both left and right feel that Japan has been well served by its pacifist stance and that it should stick to its traditional policy of total non-intervention.

Profile

In 1993, 38 years of LDP rule in Japan came to an end. Morihiro Hosokawa took over as prime minister, helped by the fact that he was not associated with the tainted world of Tokyo politics. He headed a fragile seven-party coalition.

A string of corruption scandals had led to the LDP's fall. Four LDP prime ministers – Takeshita, Uno, Kaifu, and Miyazawa – were forced to resign because they were implicated in scandals or failed to stamp out corruption. Hosokawa's period in office was brief. He was accused of financial irregularities and resigned in 1994. However, Hosokawa did manage to pass laws on electoral reform, to apologize for Japan's war crimes, and to begin the process of institutional deregulation. His popularity ranking in 1993 reached 70%, compared with the 10% who backed the LDP in its last months in power.

Tsutomu Hata took over in April 1994. He mostly continued Hosokawa's policies and retained his cabinet. However, Hata's minority government collapsed in June 1994. A new LDP–SDJP coalition was formed, under the leadership of Tomiichi Murayama.

WORLD AFFAIRS

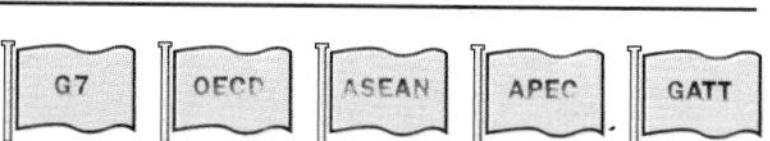

After years of limiting its role on the world stage to that of a minor power, rather than that of one of the world's most powerful economies, Japan is beginning to make its influence heard. Its eventual aim is a seat on the UN's Security Council. Tentative moves were made in 1993 with Japanese forces joining UN peacekeepers in Cambodia. The lobby that fears a resurgence of Japanese militarism is still strong, however, and wishes to avoid any foreign entanglements. In Asia, Japan is busy cultivating China, seeking to gain a prime position in the world's fastest-growing market. Disputes over the Spratly Islands – China, Brunei and Vietnam also have claims – are a likely source of future tension.

AID

 $10bn (donations)  Up 4% in 1994

Japan became the world's largest aid donor in 1991. Most aid is spent in Asia and the Pacific, particularly in the expanding economies of Thailand, Vietnam and Cambodia. Polynesian islands are beneficiaries of Japanese aid. Tokyo effectively supports their main livelihood, fishing.

DEFENSE

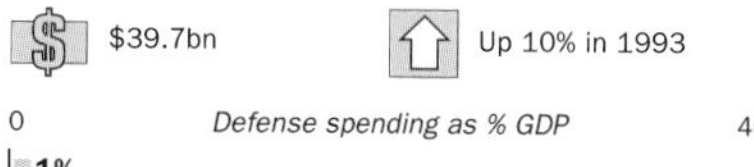

0 — *Defense spending as % GDP* — 40

1%

JAPANESE ARMED FORCES

1,200 main battle tanks (types -61,-74,-90)	156,000 personnel
7 destroyers, 55 frigates, 17 submarines and 8 patrol boats	44,000 personnel
438 combat aircraft (F-1, F-4EJ, F-15J/DJ)	46,000 personnel
None	

The defense establishment in Japan has not yet recovered from the effects of the 1941–1945 war. Any signs of military activity – even the UN peacekeeping duties that Japan undertook in Cambodia in 1993 – arouse fierce debate among pacifists. Japan's constitution forbids the use of troops abroad except in self-defense, and limits defense spending to 1% of GNP. However, Japan's economic success has allowed its armed forces to become relatively large in world terms.

ECONOMICS

 $3,337.19bn — 108.20 yen

ECONOMIC PERFORMANCE INDICATOR

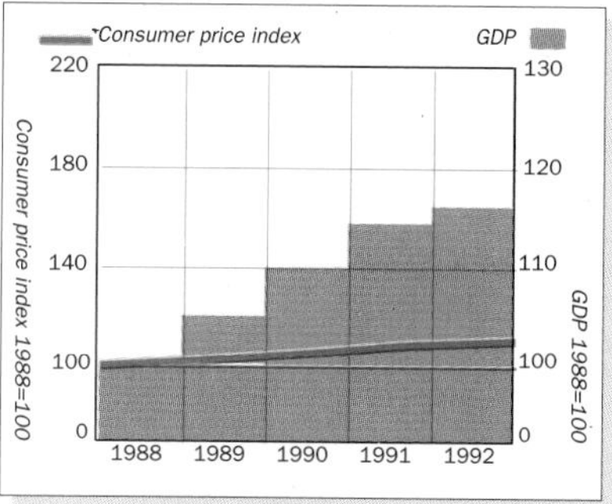

STRENGTHS
The world's most competitive producer of high-tech electronic products and cars. Commitment to long-term research and development. Talent for developing ideas from EU and USA. Global spread of business, including plants in key markets of EU and USA. Revolutionary management and production techniques continue to lead the world. *Keiretsu* – vertically integrated families of companies that agree to cooperate in business – keep non-Japanese companies out of Japanese markets.

WEAKNESSES
Heavy dependence on imported oil. Enormous, and rising, trade surplus encourages protectionism and anti-Japanese sentiment in EU and USA.

PROFILE
The Tokyo stock market crash in 1990, and particularly the collapse of the sky-high property market, ended a period of exponential growth in the Japanese economy. Industrial production fell by 8% in 1992, the sharpest drop since 1975. Corporate profits were also sharply down. The contraction in demand saw the flow of imports – particularly of European luxury products – stemmed.

However, through this slowdown, the economy continued to grow, at a rate of 2% a year. Companies did not lay off much of the labor force, and research and development spending went up. The government stepped in with a five-year economic plan ($60 billion in the first year) of infrastructure spending. The decline in imports saw Japan's trade surplus climb to $100 billion a year by 1993.

Policy is now shifting away from an almost total concentration on export-led growth, to stimulating the domestic economy. Japan is also aware that it has to relax its regulatory framework and allow in more imports, if relations with the USA and EU are not to be irreparably damaged.

Future growth is expected from new products, from wall-hung flat-screen TV sets to digital VCRs and high-speed trains. Long overdue improvements to Japanese housing will further stimulate the home economy.

SCORE CARD

❑ WORLD GNP RANKING	2nd
❑ GNP PER CAPITA	$26,912
❑ BALANCE OF PAYMENTS	$117bn
❑ INFLATION	1.9%
❑ UNEMPLOYMENT	2.1%

EXPORTS

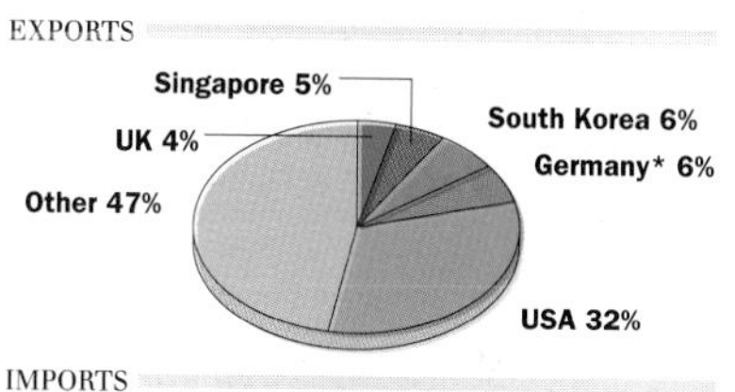

IMPORTS

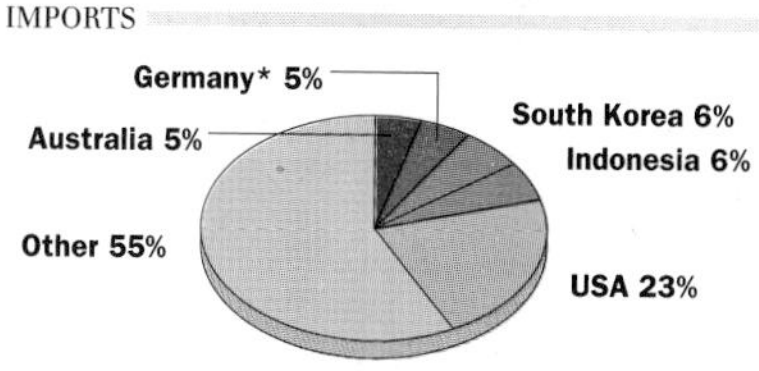

Japan's economic supremacy is likely to continue for some time. Analysts have predicted that, by 2010, Japanese GNP per capita could be over twice that of the USA.

JAPAN : MAJOR BUSINESSES

- Research & development
- Vehicle manufacture
- Heavy engineering
- Consumer goods
- Shipbuilding
- Iron & steel
- Electronics
- Chemicals
- Brewing
- Textiles
- Optics

J

RESOURCES

857.3bn kwh (capacity 194.76 billion kw)

17,000 b/d (reserves 59,850,000 bbl)

11m pigs
4m cattle
27,000 sheep

Limestone, sulfer, coal

ELECTRICITY GENERATION

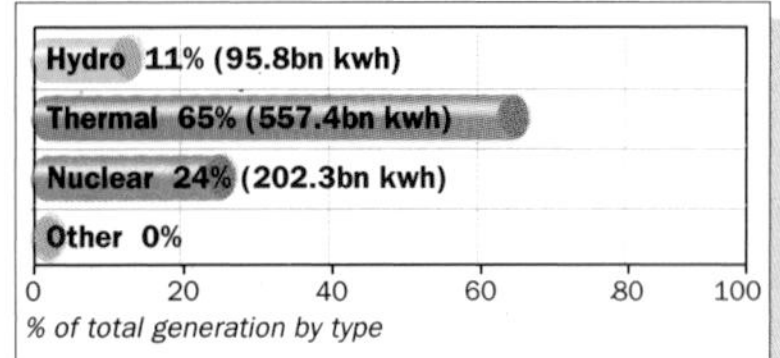

Japan has few commercially exploitable resources. Production costs make coal extraction uneconomical, and Japan has become the world's largest coal importer. In an attempt to reduce dependence on imported fuels, Japan has developed alternative sources of energy. It is now the world's fourth-biggest generator of nuclear power. However, environmentalists strongly oppose any expansion of this sector.

ENVIRONMENT

6%

Japan wishes to resume minke whale hunting

ENVIRONMENTAL TREATIES

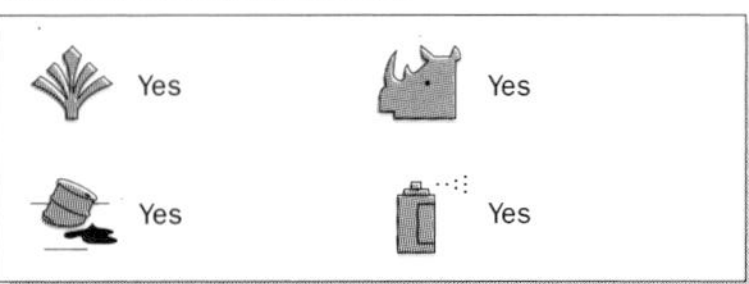

Japanese governments have seen environmental issues as a way of making an impact on the world stage. First steps were taken in 1992 to set up an International Environmental Foundation, with a budget of $12 billion for grants to encourage environmentally friendly expansion in developing countries.

Respect for nature is deeply embedded in Japan's psyche, and reflected in a long history of highly sophisticated garden design. This attitude forms the bedrock of a vigorous grass-roots ecological movement, which has succeeded in preventing development at Tokyo's Narita airport for 20 years. It also continues effective opposition to nuclear expansion. Japan supports the hunting of minke whales. It argues that there are enough whales for this not to threaten the species.

***Datsetsusan National Park**, Hokkaido. Japan's northerly island is the least populous of the main group.*

MEDIA

No political restrictions

PUBLISHING AND BROADCAST MEDIA

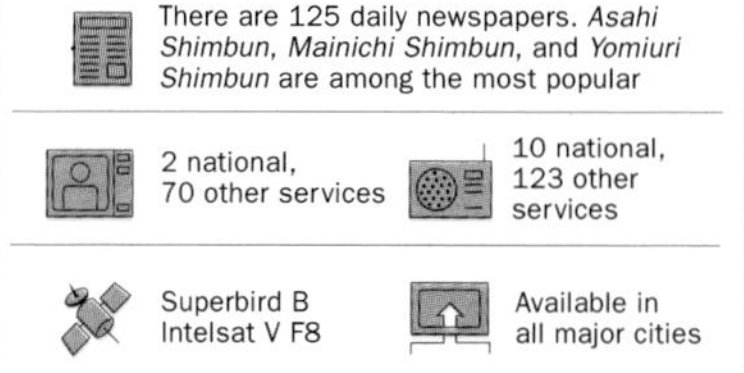

There are 125 daily newspapers. *Asahi Shimbun*, *Mainichi Shimbun*, and *Yomiuri Shimbun* are among the most popular
2 national, 70 other services
10 national, 123 other services
Superbird B Intelsat V F8
Available in all major cities

The Japanese are among the world's most avid newspaper readers. Most dailies carry serious news and are owned by large media groups which also have TV and cable interests. Weekly newspapers carry more tabloid journalism. The magazine market is huge. More than 36 billion magazines are sold in Japan every year. *Non Non*, a woman's magazine, is the best-selling title. Lifestyle magazines, encouraging the Japanese to make more use of their limited leisure time, are a growing sector of the market.

Japan is, in dollar terms, the world's second largest filmmaker after the USA. It is also Hollywood's major export market.

Japan has redefined much of the world's media. It invented the personal stereo and created the huge computer game market. In the past five years, this market has seen exponential growth. Nintendo, a leading game company, is one of the most profitable in Japan, rivaling long-established corporate giants such as Matsushita.

EDUCATION

100%.

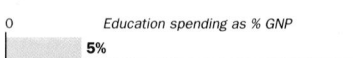

0 *Education spending as % GNP* 25
5%

THE EDUCATION SYSTEM

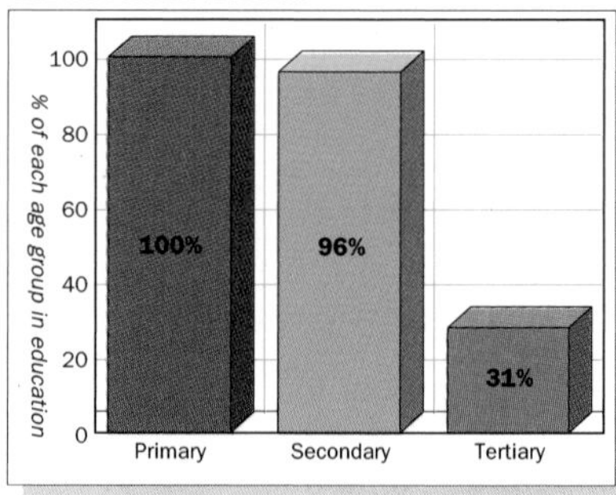

One of the key dividing lines in Japanese society is between university graduates, who get the coveted white-collar jobs for life, and non-graduates. The latter have difficulty reaching management level. The result is that the Japanese education system is highly pressurized. Competition for university places is intense, and starts with the choice of kindergarten, which the Japanese attend from the age of four. Once at university, students tend to relax – the important thing is getting in. Tokyo, Kyoto, Waseda and Keio are the most prestigious universities. Their graduates have access to top civil service and business jobs. The system succeeds in producing a uniform, and thoroughly educated, work force.

CRIME

51,829 prisoners

Up 2% in 1992

CRIME RATE

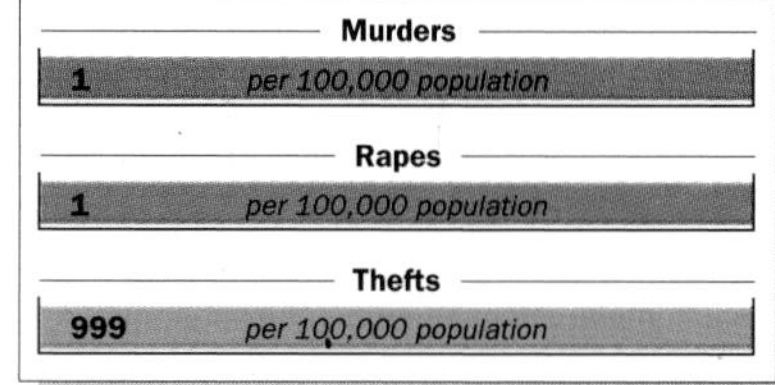

Murders
1 per 100,000 population
Rapes
1 per 100,000 population
Thefts
999 per 100,000 population

Japan has one of the lowest crime rates in the world. This is in part the result of an efficient police system. Cities are safe, with police kiosks at frequent intervals on street corners.

The major crime problem is fraud and the activities of the *kumi*, organized mafia-style syndicates whose members are known as *yakuza*. The authorities show little enthusiasm in challenging these groups, seeking to contain rather than eradicate their activities. *Kumi* are suspected of having connections with the extreme right in Japanese politics.

REGIONS

HOKKAIDO

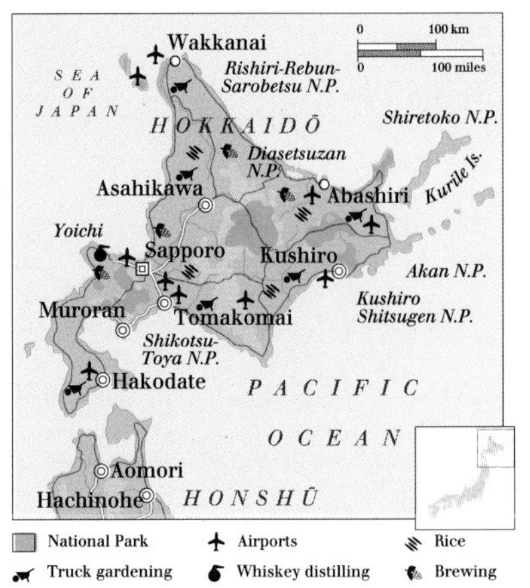

THE SECOND-LARGEST and most northerly of the four main islands, Hokkaido is Japan's biggest and most productive farming region. Its open terrain and climate is similar to the US Midwest. US advisers established wheat production here in the 1860s, and Hokkaido now produces over half of Japan's cereal needs. German-Americans from Milwaukee also established Japan's first brewery, which produces the world-famous *Sapporo* beer.

Recent government investment has encouraged high-tech industries on Hokkaido. Japan's first magnetic train (*maglev*) test track is being developed on the island.

TOKYO AND DISTRICT

THE IMMENSE concentration of Japanese wealth in Tokyo was reflected in 1988, when the value of one square mile of prime real estate in the capital was estimated to be greater than the whole of California. Unplanned expansion since 1945 has resulted in a large urban sprawl, merging Tokyo with neighboring Yokohama and Kawasaki. During the 1980s, the demands on office space resulted in a rash of new office buildings, crammed into every available piece of land. The lack of vistas – Tokyo has few parks – gives Tokyo's architecture a rather uniform feeling. Notable exceptions to this include two office buildings by the French designer Philippe Starck.

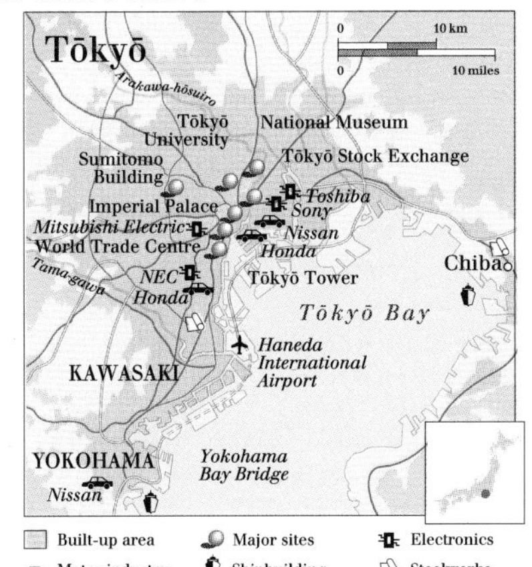

KANSAI REGION

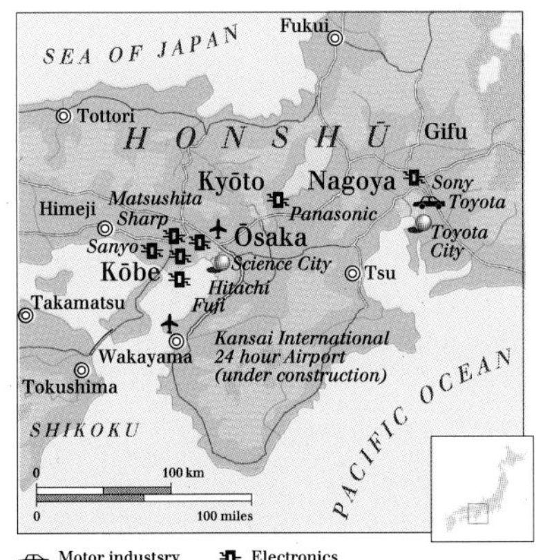

COMPRISING the six prefectures of Osaka, Hyogo, Kyoto, Shiga, Nara and Wakayama, Kansai has always had a strong regional identity. In recent years, support for a Kansai federation, with greater independence from Tokyo, has increased. Some 20 million people live here, producing 20% of Japan's textiles, 25% of its steel and 23% of its machine tools. Kansai's share of Japan's GNP exceeds the total GNP of Canada. Its industries have long been renowned for their creativity. Kansai developed the world's first desktop calculator and the first automatic ticket barrier. It is home to such world-famous companies as Matsushita, Sanyo and Sharp.

A healthy rivalry has grown up between Osaka – Kansai's main business city – and Tokyo. Osaka has sought to develop its own fashion and design industries in emulation of Tokyo. Kyoto, with its 1,400 temples and shrines, remains Japan's favorite tourist destination. Kansai International, currently being built off Kobe, will be Japan's first 24-hour international airport.

HEALTH

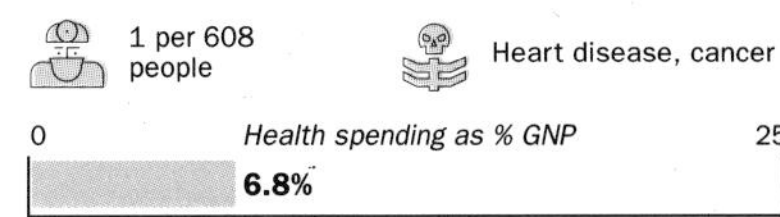

Japan has a world-class health system, which has delivered some of the highest longevity and lowest infant mortality rates in the world. Most Japanese contribute toward health costs through a national insurance program, with premiums calculated on earnings. The poorest in society receive free treatment. Japan's rapidly aging population presents a major future funding challenge.

WEALTH

Factory manager, 596,665 yen per month; machine general worker, 339,524 yen per month

CONSUMER GOODS OWNERSHIP

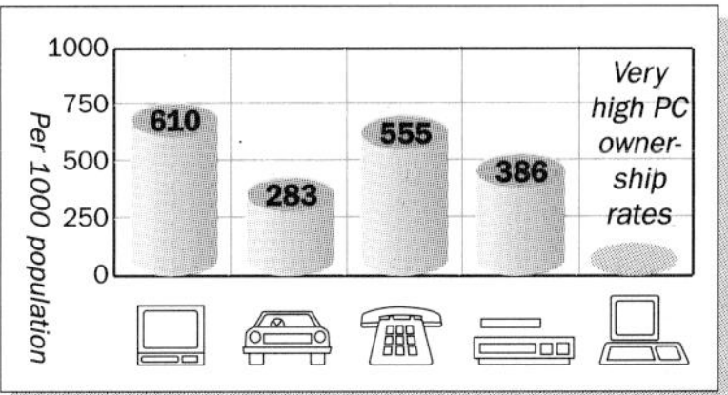

Measured in consumer goods the Japanese are wealthy; highly restrictive city parking restrictions account for the low rates of car ownership. The yen's high value makes foreign vacations, for those who can afford to take time off, relatively inexpensive. However, living costs are high – a recent survey judged Tokyo more than twice as costly as New York – and mean that most Japanese live outside the city and have a long, cramped trip into work. It is 18–25-year old girls who do best – receiving substantial financial support from their families – by avoiding the pitfalls and living at home. As a group they are reputed to have the highest disposable income in Japan.

WORLD RANKING

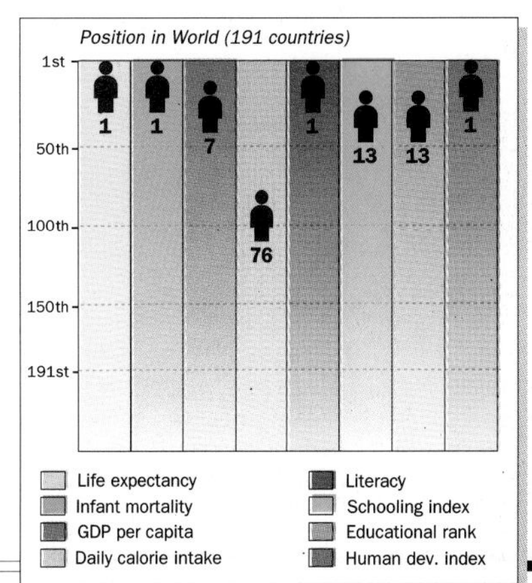

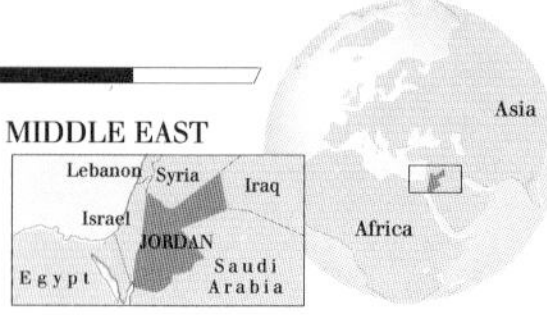

JORDAN

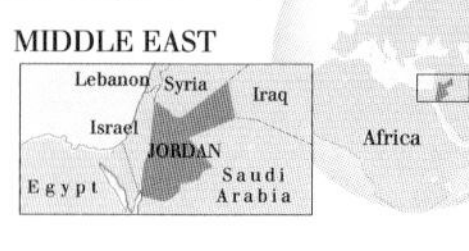

OFFICIAL NAME: Hashemite Kingdom of Jordan **CAPITAL:** Amman
POPULATION: 4.3 million **CURRENCY:** Jordanian dinar **OFFICIAL LANGUAGE:** Arabic

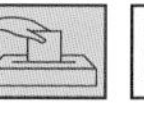

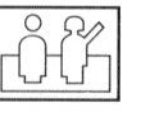

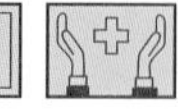

SHARING BORDERS WITH Iraq, Syria, Israel and Saudi Arabia, Jordan has just 16 miles of coastline on the Gulf of 'Aqabah. Jordanian territory legally includes the West Bank of the Jordan River and east Jerusalem, but Israel has occupied these areas since 1967. Jordan ceded its claim to the West Bank to the PLO in 1988. Phosphates and tourism associated with important historical sites such as Petra are the mainstays of the economy.

CLIMATE

WEATHER CHART

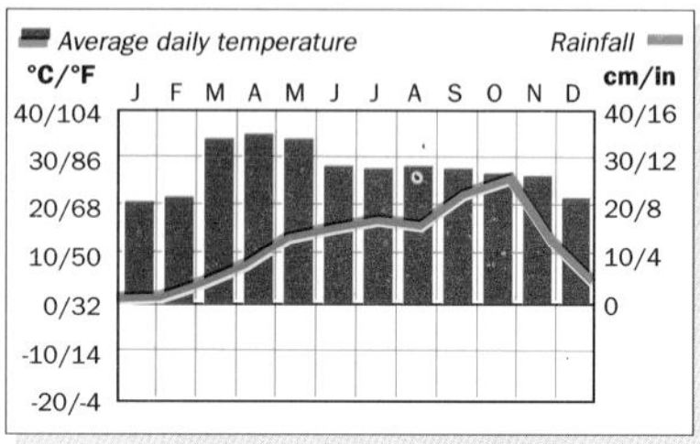

Average daily temperature — Rainfall
°C/°F — cm/in
J F M A M J J A S O N D
40/104, 30/86, 20/68, 10/50, 0/32, -10/14, -20/-4
40/16, 30/12, 20/8, 10/4, 0

Summers are hot and dry, winters cool and wet. Areas below sea level are very hot in summer and warm in winter.

COMMUNICATIONS

Queen Alia Intl, Amman 1.71m passengers

2 ships 113,600 dwt

THE TRANSPORTATION NETWORK

3,644 miles (5,865 km)

None

384 miles (618 km)

None

Adequate roads link main cities. A railroad links the Red Sea port of Al 'Aqabah with the Syrian capital, Damascus.

TOURISM

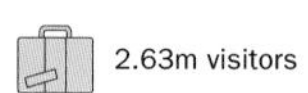

Up 16% in 1990

MAIN OVERSEAS ARRIVALS

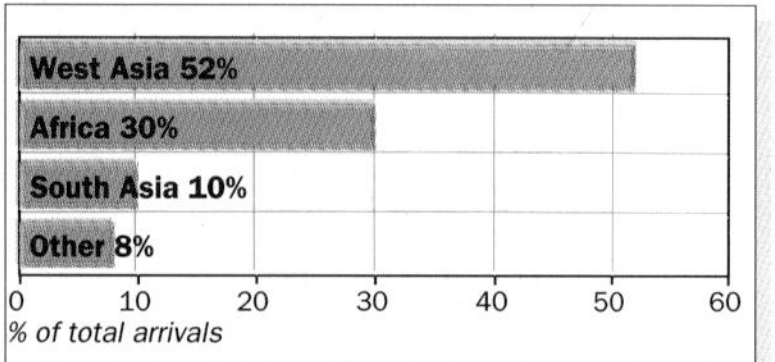

Al 'Aqabah offers fine beaches, water sports and scuba diving, while the ancient city of Petra attracts visitors interested in Roman remains. Amman is developing as a center for Arabic culture and the arts.

PEOPLE

Arabic

109 people per sq. mile

THE URBAN/RURAL POPULATION SPLIT

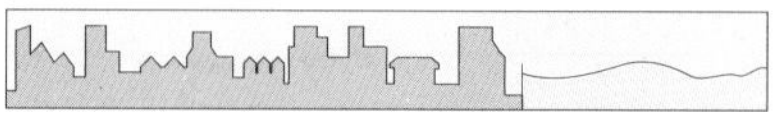

68% — 32%

ETHNIC MAKEUP

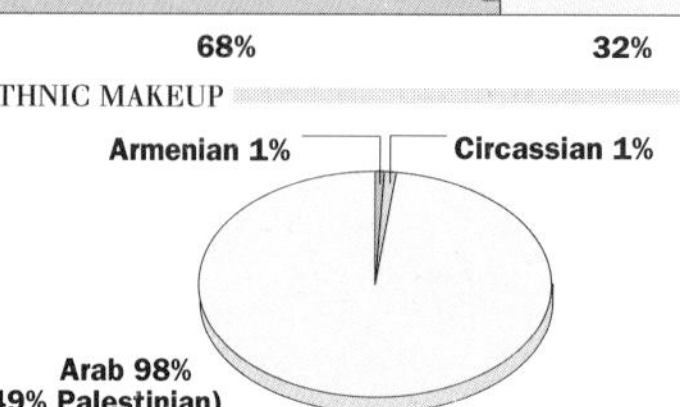

Jordan is a predominantly Muslim country drawn from Bedouin roots, with a Christian minority and a large Palestinian population. The monarchy's power base lies among the rural tribes, which also provide the backbone of the military. National identity is strong.

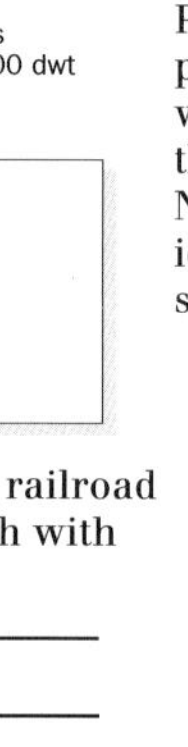

POLITICS

THE STATE OF THE PARTIES

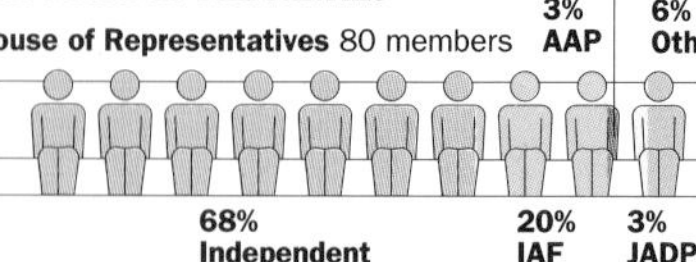

Independent = Centrist (55%), Islamicist (8%) and Leftist (5%) **IAF** = Islamic Action Front **JADP** = Jordan Arab Democratic Party **AAP** = Al Ahd Party

Senate 30 members

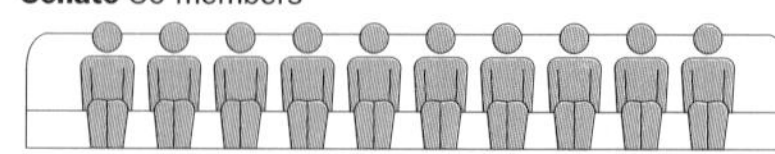

The members of the Senate are appointed by the King

King Hussein, the longest-reigning Arab ruler, retains a strong grip on government. In 1965, he eliminated any doubts over the succession by naming his technocrat brother, Hassan, as Crown Prince. Hussein has sought to promote a strong nationalism based on Jordan's tribal structure. He is also careful not to alienate Jordan's other constituencies. In 1993, he responded to calls for greater democracy by agreeing to multiparty elections. Contrary to expectations, gains were not made by fundamentalists.

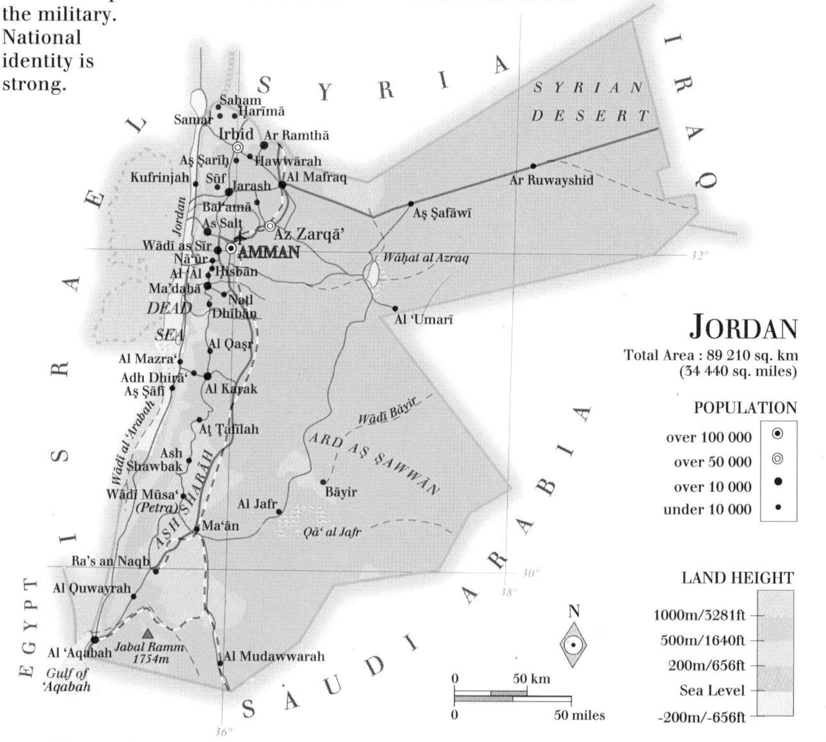

JORDAN

Total Area : 89 210 sq. km (34 440 sq. miles)

POPULATION
- over 100 000
- over 50 000
- over 10 000
- under 10 000

LAND HEIGHT
- 1000m/3281ft
- 500m/1640ft
- 200m/656ft
- Sea Level
- -200m/-656ft

0 50 km
0 50 miles

WORLD AFFAIRS

Jordan is a key player in Middle East politics. It is home to 1.7 million Palestinians. Its attitude toward the PLO has changed over the years. In 1986, it expelled the organization from Amman. However, Jordan's 1988 decision to rescind its claim to the Israeli-occupied West Bank in favor of the PLO proved decisive in bringing Israel and the PLO to the negotiating table. One result of the 1994 PLO-Israeli settlement was a settlement of Israeli-Jordanian disputes.

AID

$668m (receipts)

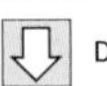
Down 25% in 1991

The Gulf states and the USA withdrew aid after Jordan backed Iraq in the Gulf war. US aid has now been restored.

DEFENSE

$508.55m

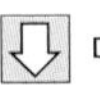
Down 12% in 1992

Jordanian forces played no part in the 1991 Gulf War. The armed forces are loyal to the monarchy. They have a reputation for thorough training and professionalism. The forces are dependent on Western support for credit in purchasing advanced arms and equipment.

ECONOMICS

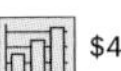
$4.5bn

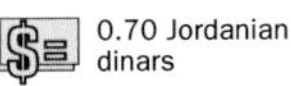
0.70 Jordanian dinars

SCORE CARD

❑ WORLD GNP RANKING	114th
❑ GNP PER CAPITA	$1,047
❑ BALANCE OF PAYMENTS	$-765m
❑ INFLATION	6.6%
❑ UNEMPLOYMENT	30%

STRENGTHS
Major exporter of phosphates and fresh foods to Gulf states. Skilled, educated and adaptable work force.

WEAKNESSES
Reliant on imports to satisfy energy requirements. Unemployment due to influx of Jordanians and Palestinians expelled from Kuwait. Tourism yet to recover from 1991 Gulf War.

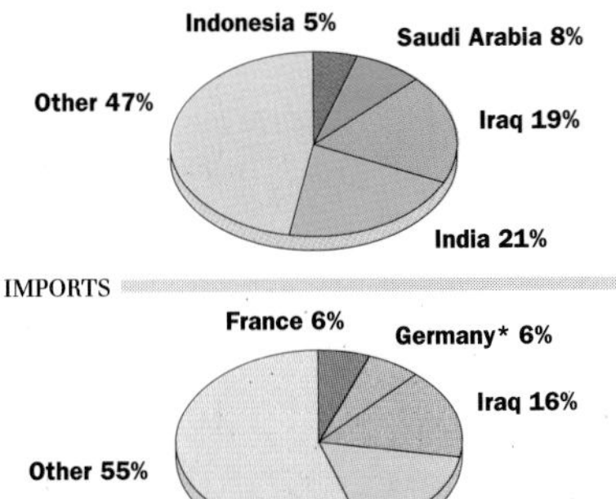

RESOURCES

3.7bn kwh (capacity 1m kw)

1,000 b/d (reserves 4,000,000 bbl)

61m poultry, 1.3m sheep, 29,000 cattle

Phosphates, potash

Oil deposits have been discovered. Phosphates, livestock and crops such as tomatoes, wheat, olives and vegetables are the main resources.

ENVIRONMENT

1% partially protected

Government pursuing vigorous conservation programs

Conservation is a government priority. Rare animals are protected and species that became extinct in the wild in the 1950s are being reintroduced into controlled environments.

MEDIA

Widespread self-censorship of the press, in accordance with government guidelines

PUBLISHING AND BROADCAST MEDIA

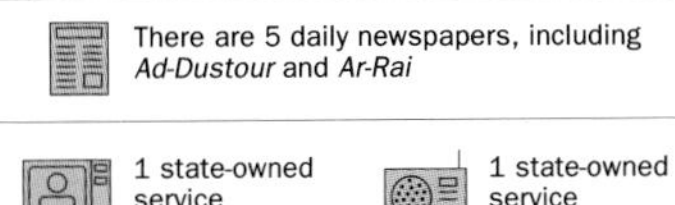
There are 5 daily newspapers, including *Ad-Dustour* and *Ar-Rai*

1 state-owned service

1 state-owned service

Radio and TV are controlled by the state. Private and publicly owned newspapers follow the government line.

CRIME

Jordan does not publish prison figures

Crime is rising

Jordan is largely peaceful. Crime levels are generally low, although theft in urban areas is rising.

EDUCATION

80%

Men and women receive the same education. Jordanian teachers work all over the Middle East.

HEALTH

1 per 842 people

Heart, digestive and respiratory diseases, accidents, cancer

Healthcare is subsidized by the government. Hospitals are distributed throughout the country.

CHRONOLOGY

King Hussein succeeded to the throne in 1952 after his father was deposed due to mental illness.

- ❑ **1958** Iraqi revolution ends Jordan's federation with Iraq.
- ❑ **1967** Israel seizes West Bank territories placed under Jordanian rule in 1949.
- ❑ **1988** King Hussein cedes claims to West Bank to PLO.
- ❑ **1993** Jordan signs protocol with Israel on future negotiations.

***The King's Highway,** seen from the castle at Al Karak. This strategic fortress was built by Crusader knights in the 12th century.*

WEALTH

The wealthiest are those closest to the King

CONSUMER GOODS OWNERSHIP

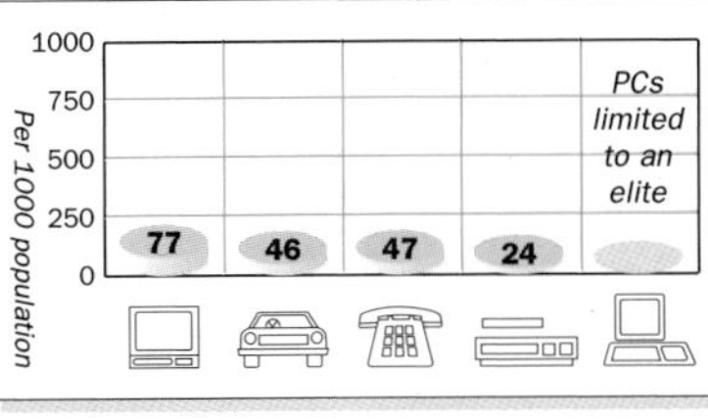

The wealthiest Jordanians are Amman-based entrepeneurs, bankers and engineers. Poverty is relatively rare.

WORLD RANKING

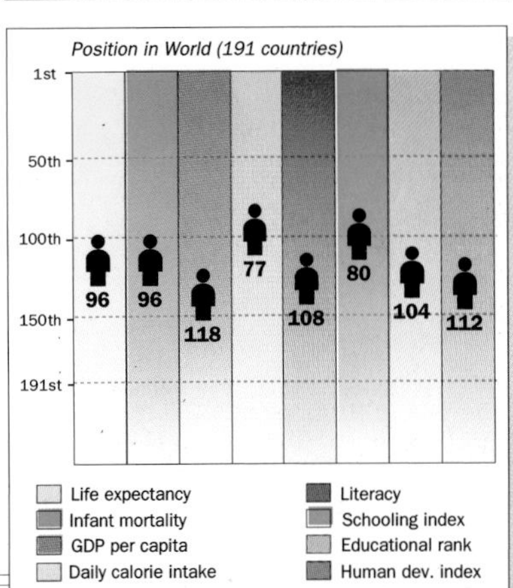

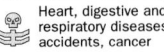

J

KAZAKHSTAN

ASIA
Russian Federation
KAZAKHSTAN
China
Uzbekistan
Kyrgyzstan
Asia

OFFICIAL NAME: Republic of Kazakhstan **CAPITAL:** Alma-Ata
POPULATION: 17 million **CURRENCY:** Tenge **OFFICIAL LANGUAGE:** Kazakh

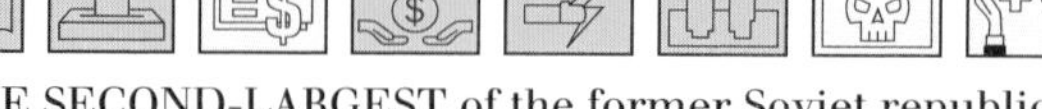

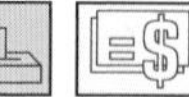

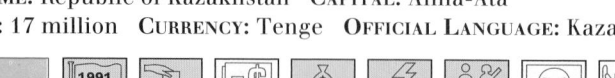

THE SECOND-LARGEST of the former Soviet republics, Kazakhstan extends almost 1,240 miles from the Caspian Sea in the west to the Altai Mountains in the east, and 806 miles north to south. It borders Russia to the north and China to the east. Kazakhstan was the last Soviet republic to declare its independence, in 1991. In 1994, elections confirmed the former-communist, Nursultan Nazarbayev, and his supporters in power. Kazakhstan is mineral-rich and has considerable economic potential. Many Western companies are seeking to exploit its natural resources.

The Altai Mountains, eastern Kazakhstan. *Subject to harsh continental winters, the Altai range is a cold, inhospitable place. Rivers carry meltwater down onto the vast steppe.*

CLIMATE

WEATHER CHART

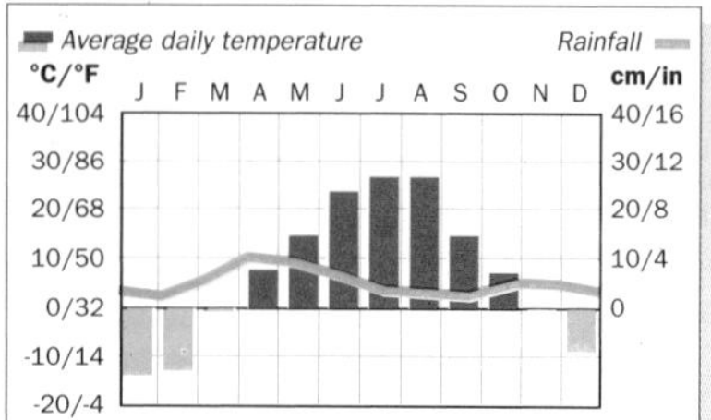

Kazakhstan has a continental climate with large temperature variations between summer and winter. Average January temperatures range from 0°F on the northern Kazakh steppe to 27°F in the deserts 806 miles to the south. July temperatures average 66°F and 86°F respectively. As the Caspian Sea never freezes, winters are mildest on Kazakhstan's southwestern coast.

COMMUNICATIONS

Small Caspian Sea merchant fleet

THE TRANSPORTATION NETWORK

102,464 miles (164,900 km)

None

8,965 miles (14,460 km)

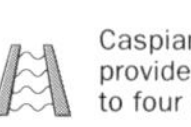

Caspian Sea provides access to four countries

Transportation is focused in the north and east, the key economic areas. The railroads link into the Russian system and most international flights go via Moscow. Extending the network and reducing dependence on Russia are priorities. There are now direct flights to Germany. A rail link with China was opened in 1992. Kazakhstan has asked Latvia for access to its Baltic ports.

TOURISM

Visitors still largely limited to business-people

Increased since the breakup of the USSR

MAIN OVERSEAS ARRIVALS

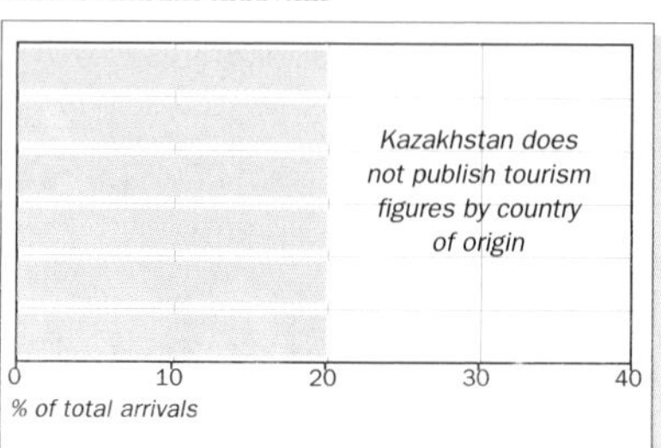

The number of visitors to Kazakhstan is increasing, but very few come solely as tourists. The majority are business travelers and a dense web of contacts with foreign companies has evolved. Of the Central Asian states, Kazakhstan has cultivated the closest links with the West. There is now a large community of foreign businesspeople living in Alma-Ata.

KAZAKHSTAN

Total Area : 2 717 300 sq. km (1 049 150 sq. miles)

PEOPLE

Kazakh, Russian, German, Uigur, Korean

16 people per sq. mile

THE URBAN/RURAL POPULATION SPLIT

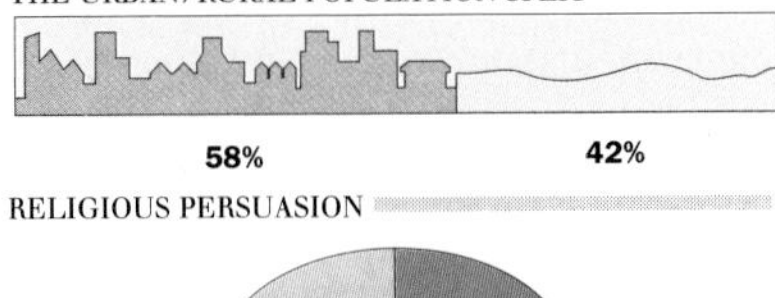

RELIGIOUS PERSUASION

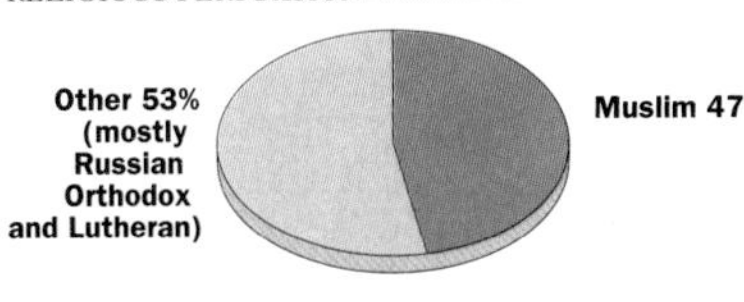

ETHNIC MAKEUP

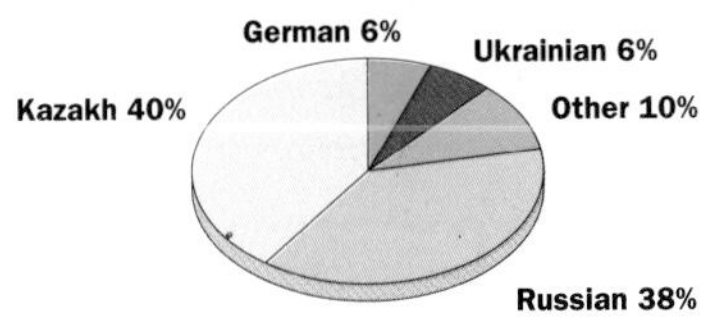

Kazakhstan's ethnic diversity is mainly a product of the forced settlement of Germans, Tatars and others during the Soviet era. Russian settlement began in the 19th century, but peaked after 1920. By 1959, ethnic Russians outnumbered Kazakhs. The balance has recently been redressed by the immigration of ethnic Kazakhs from neighboring states.

POPULATION AGE BREAKDOWN

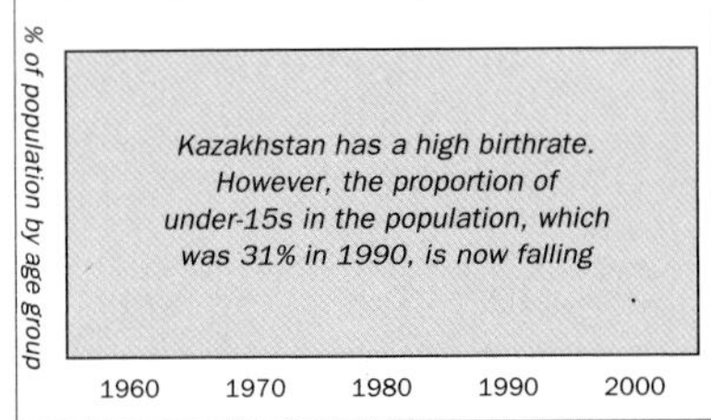

Ethnic tension has been milder than in many former Soviet states, mainly due to President Nazarbayev, who has actively encouraged a multi-ethnic nationalism, and unifying causes like the anti-nuclear movement. However, there is potential for unrest from groups like the Kazakh nationalist *Azat*, which wants northern Kazakhstan incorporated into Russia.

Only a minority of Kazakhs retain their traditional nomadic life. However, their cultural traditions, commitment to Islam and loyalty to the three Hordes (clan federations) remain strong.

POLITICS

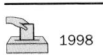

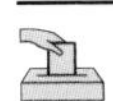
1998

President Nursultan Nazarbayev

THE STATE OF THE PARTIES

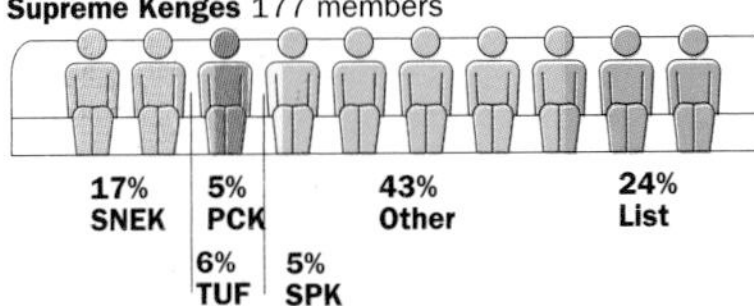

SNEK = Congress of People's Unity of Kazakhstan **TUF** = Trade Union Federation **PCK** = People's Congress of Kazakhstan **SPK** = Socialist Party of Kazakhstan **Other** = Peasant's Party, Republic Council of Women's Organizations **List** = President's List; 42 candidates elected from a list of politicians and businessmen drawn up by the president

The 1993 constitution vests legislative authority in the 177-member Supreme *Kenges* (or Soviet). The president, who must be fluent in Kazakh, has supreme executive power.

MAIN POLITICAL ISSUE

Ethnic relations

Kazakhstan's relative harmony is due to President Nazarbayev's successful efforts to balance Kazakh aspirations with the concerns of minorities, notably ethnic Russians. The constitution guarantees equal status to all groups while giving Kazakh linguistic preference. The formation of the People's Congress of Kazakhstan (PCK) as a Kazakh-dominated party to counter the Russian-dominated SPK (former communists) went some way to satisfying nationalist demands. The 1994 elections saw ethnic Kazakhs win 60% of the seats in parliament, despite forming only 40% of the population, raising ethnic Russian fears of under-representation.

PROFILE

Despite a democratic government, the president enjoys political dominance, and the patronage of the Kazakh clans is still important. Since coming to power in 1989, Nazarbayev has concentrated on reducing ethnic tension and on economic reform, reflecting his belief that growth is the best guarantor of stability. The impact of Nazarbayev's economic reforms has led to growing criticism of his government. He won a second term in early 1994, amid allegations of electoral tampering. The president's allies swept to victory in the parliamentary elections, confirming Nazarbayev's grip on power.

***President Nursultan Nazarbayev,** who steered Kazakhstan to independence.*

***Foreign Minister** Toleubai Suleimenov, the first professional diplomat in the post.*

WORLD AFFAIRS

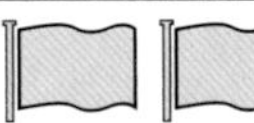

Maintaining close ties with other former Soviet republics is a priority. Kazakhstan is a leading supporter of the CIS. Relations with Russia, although strained at times by Moscow's concern over Kazakhstan's ethnic Russians, have been cemented by a 25-year cooperation treaty.

Another priority has been to develop international links and to attract foreign investment. Kazakhstan's rich mineral resources and relative ethnic stability have attracted investors from Europe, the USA and Asia. Ties with South Korea are growing particularly fast, partly reflecting President Nazarbayev's interest in South Korea's model of economic development. Relations with China remain strained, however, as Beijing has territorial claims to parts of eastern Kazakhstan.

AID

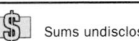

Sums undisclosed

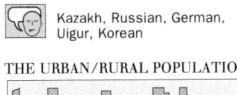

Aid levels have risen since independence

Kazakhstan joined the IMF and World Bank in 1992, and is also a member of the EBRD. Both multilateral and bilateral aid tend to be directed at supporting economic reform and providing know-how and training. The government is seeking to link the dismantling of nuclear warheads to aid payments from the West.

CHRONOLOGY

Once part of the Mongol Empire, Kazakhstan was absorbed by the Russian Empire in the 19th century. Ethnic Russians began to settle on land used by nomadic Kazakhs. Russian settlement intensified after the 1917 revolution and Kazakhstan was subjected to intensive industrial and agricultural development.

- **1916** Rebellion against the Russian rule brutally repressed.
- **1917** Russian Revolution inspires civil war in Kazakhstan between Bolsheviks, anti-Bolsheviks and Kazakh nationalists.
- **1918** Kazakh nationalists set up autonomous republic.
- **1920** Bolsheviks take control. Kirghiz Autonomous Soviet Socialist Republic (ASSR) set up within Russian Soviet Federative Socialist Republic.
- **1925** Kirghiz ASSR renamed "Kazakh ASSR."
- **1936** Kazakhstan becomes full union republic of the USSR as "Kazakh SSR."

⇨

CHRONOLOGY *continued*

- ❑ **1930s** Stalin's collectivization program leads to increase in Russian settlement and the deaths of an estimated one million Kazakhs forced to abandon their nomadic lifestyle.
- ❑ **1941–1945** Large-scale deportations of Germans, Jews, Crimean Tartars and others to Kazakhstan during World War II.
- ❑ **1950s** Intensification of heavy industry development begun in 1920s. Nuclear test site set up at Semipalatinsk in the east; 500 nuclear explosions follow before testing ends in 1991.
- ❑ **1954–1960** Khrushchev's policy to plow "Virgin Lands" for grain most vigorously followed in Kazakhstan. Russian settlement reaches a peak. Intensive plowing in this period now causing soil erosion.
- ❑ **1986** Riots in Alma-Ata after an ethnic Russian, Gennadi Kolbin, appointed head of Kazakhstan Communist Party (CPK) to replace Kazakh, Dinmukhamed Kunyev.
- ❑ **1989** June: Kolbin replaced by Nursultan Nazarbayev, an ethnic Kazakh and chair of Council of Ministers. September: political and administrative system reformed. Multiparty elections scheduled for following year.
- ❑ **1990** March: elections to Supreme Soviet. Overwhelming CPK majority. April: Nazarbayev appointed first president of Kazakhstan. October: Kazakhstan declares sovereignty.
- ❑ **1991** March: referendum on future of USSR in nine republics. Kazakhstan votes to preserve USSR as union of sovereign states. USSR authorities hand control of enterprises in Kazakhstan to Kazakh government. August: CPK ordered to cease activities in official bodies following abortive August coup in Moscow. CPK restructures itself as Socialist Party of Kazakhstan (SPK). December: independence of Republic of Kazakhstan declared. Joins CIS.
- ❑ **1992** Opposition demonstrations against continuing dominance of reformed communists in Supreme Soviet, now Supreme Kenges. Leading nationalist groups – the *Azat* movement, the Republican Party and *Jeltoqsan* – unite to form Republican Party, named *Azat*.
- ❑ **1993** January: new constitution adopted. Guarantees equal rights for all groups. December: Kazakh currency, the tenge, introduced.
- ❑ **1994** Nazarbayev wins second presidential term.

DEFENSE

 $707m

 Down 52% in 1993

0 *Defense spending as % GDP* 40

3.8%

KAZAKH ARMED FORCES

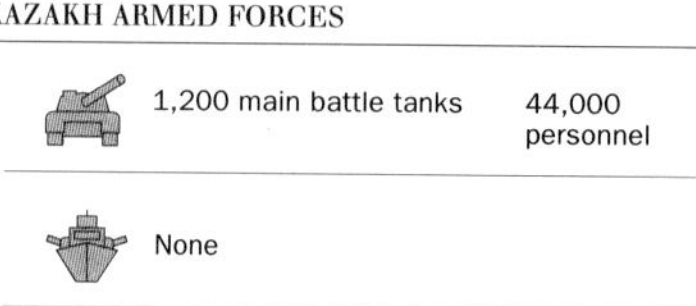

1,200 main battle tanks	44,000 personnel
None	
	140 combat aircraft (MiG-23/MiG-27/Su-24)	Undisclosed
104 ICBM (SS-18 Satan) 40 Tu-95H (ALCM equipped) under Russian control	

Kazakhstan, as the largest of the five former Soviet republics in Central Asia, has been seen as a potential guarantor of regional peace. However, the West is concerned about former Soviet nuclear warheads based in Kazakhstan. The government signed the Start I nuclear reduction treaty in 1991, but has yet to act on it. This reflects both a lack of finance, and efforts by Nazarbayev to use the weapons as a negotiating lever. In 1993, the USA agreed to provide $140 million in economic aid after Kazakhstan signed an agreement to dismantle some of its ICBMs. The government has plans to set up a national guard, mainly to protect the ruling elite. It will be trained by Russian troops.

ECONOMICS

 $41.7bn

 Tenge not convertible

SCORE CARD

- ❑ World GNP Ranking..........44th
- ❑ GNP per Capita..........$2,455
- ❑ Balance of Payments..........Deficit
- ❑ Inflation..........84%
- ❑ Unemployment..........Rising

EXPORTS

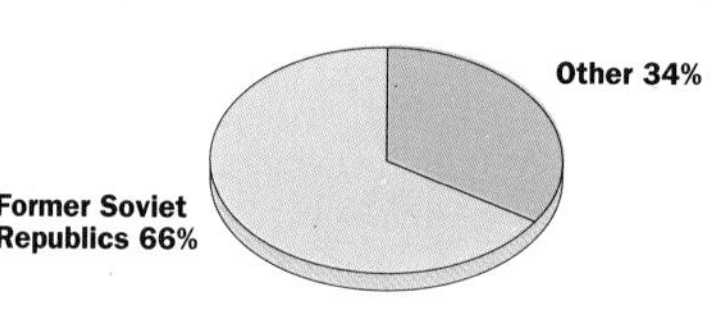

IMPORTS

Imports are largely from the Russian Federation, followed by other CIS countries and China

Strengths

Vast mineral resources, notably oil, gas, coal, gold, silver and uranium. Also bismuth and cadmium, used in electronics industry. Foreign investors attracted by early introduction of market reforms, liberal foreign investment laws and valuable resources. Joint ventures include modern processing industries and communications as well as the exploitation of oil and gas fields.

Weaknesses

Collapse of former Soviet economic and trading system. Heavy reliance on imported consumer goods. Departure from rouble zone and rapid introduction of the tenge in 1993 increased economic instability. Inefficient industrial plants. Privatization limited to small-scale enterprises.

ECONOMIC PERFORMANCE INDICATOR

Consumer prices have risen sharply since 1991. GDP is likely to rise following new foreign investment

Profile

Under Nazarbayev, Kazakhstan has moved faster than other former Soviet republics to establish a market economy. It was the first to introduce free economic zones, investment incentives and privatization. Prices have been freed, foreign trade largely decontrolled and the tax system reformed. Despite these reforms, growth has been elusive. Unemployment and inflation have risen sharply, due in large part to the impact of the collapse of the wider Soviet economy.

However, by the end of 1993, $9 billion had already been committed in foreign direct investment, mainly in the energy sector. Outdated equipment and inadequate distribution networks mean that Kazakhstan, suprisingly, has to import energy. It hopes to become self-sufficient by 2000.

KAZAKHSTAN : MAJOR BUSINESSES

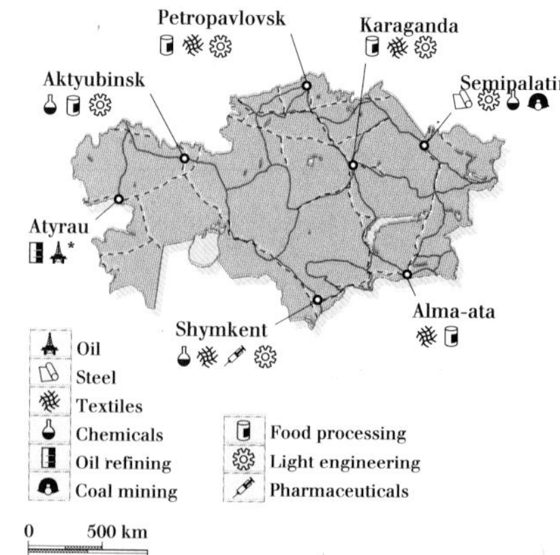

RESOURCES

81.3bn kwh (capacity 19.1m kw)

540,000 b/d Massive new oil reserves confirmed

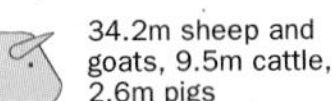

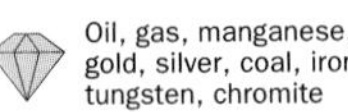

ELECTRICITY GENERATION

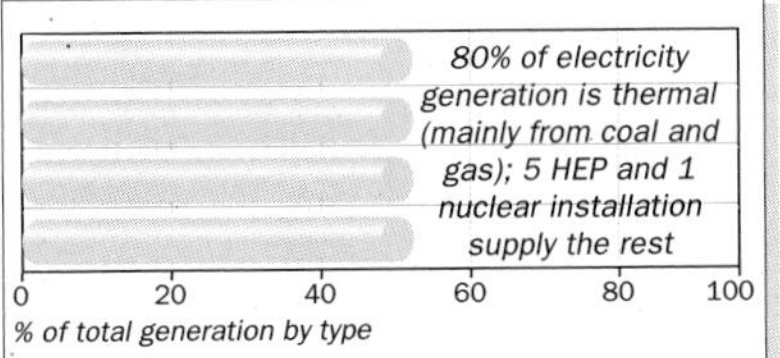

Mining is the single most important industry in Kazakhstan. Some of the world's largest oil deposits are located near the Caspian Sea. The US company Chevron signed a deal to develop the huge Tengiz oilfield in 1993. Kazakhstan also holds vast iron ore reserves, has the world's biggest chromium mine, and one of the biggest goldfields. There are plans to quadruple gold output by 1997.

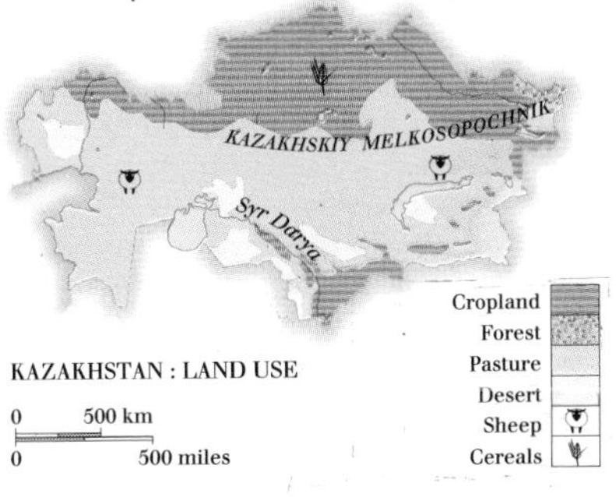

KAZAKHSTAN : LAND USE

ENVIRONMENT

None

Western pressure on government may cause improvement

ENVIRONMENTAL TREATIES

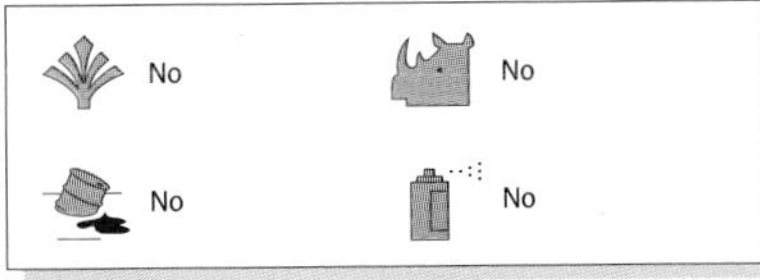

The environmental damage caused by intensive industrial and agricultural development is a major concern. The eastern cities are heavily polluted and farmlands are being eroded. The Aral Sea has been polluted by the overuse of fertilizers and has shrunk by 40% due to the diversion of rivers for irrigation.

In 1991, environmental pressure groups succeeded in ending 42 years of nuclear testing at Semipalatinsk in the northeast. The green lobby is now pressing for tighter pollution controls.

MEDIA

Censorship exists. Neither direct criticism of the president, nor the incitement of ethnic tension is tolerated

PUBLISHING AND BROADCAST MEDIA

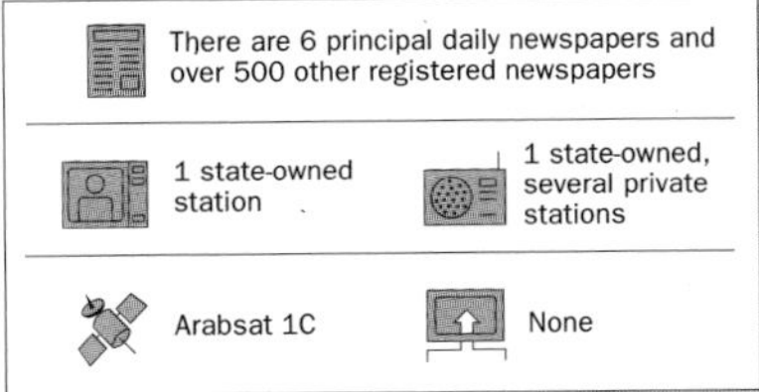

There are 6 principal daily newspapers and over 500 other registered newspapers
1 state-owned station
1 state-owned, several private stations
Arabsat 1C
None

The state-owned media competes with a range of independent publications and several privately owned radio stations. However, the government's continuing control of printing and broadcasting facilities ensures that criticism tends to be indirect. There are over 400 registered newspapers, about 40% of them in Kazakh. Turkish state TV broadcasts to Kazakhs by satellite.

CRIME

Kazakhstan does not publish prison figures

Crime levels are rising

CRIME RATES

Theft is rising more sharply than other crime

Rural people are starting to grow drug crops, mainly opium poppies, to offset falling incomes. The government has appealed for UN help to combat the problem. General crime rates are low.

EDUCATION

Lower than ex-Soviet average

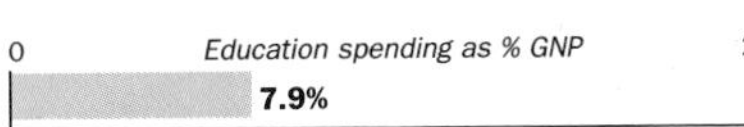

THE EDUCATION SYSTEM

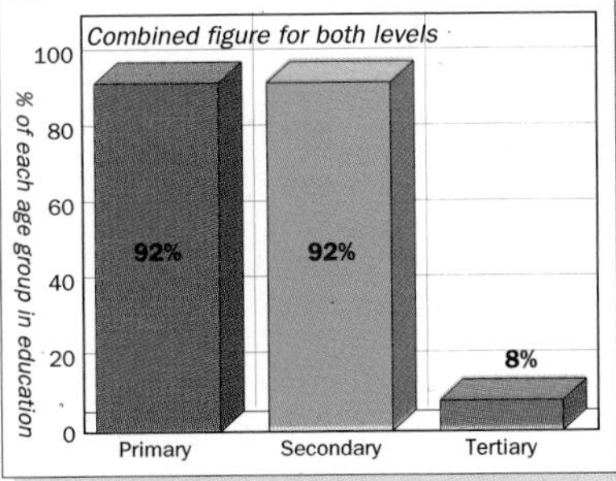

Education is based on the Soviet model. Much of teaching is still in Russian, despite the adoption of Kazakh as the state language. Kazakh-speaking teachers and Kazakh textbooks are in short supply. Literacy levels are relatively low. There are 63 higher-education institutions, and 53 medical schools.

HEALTH

1 per 245 people

Heart, cerebrovascular and respiratory diseases, cancer

0 Health spending as % GNP 25

5.8%

The health system is limited in terms of both facilities and coverage. Rural people have minimal access to clinics. As a result, Kazakhstan has the highest infant mortality rate in Central Asia. The country's size means that extending coverage, and improving the quality of care will be costly. Attempts are therefore being made to attract foreign investment into the health sector. Many doctors have emigrated to Russia.

WEALTH

The living standards of many Kazakhs has declined since independence from the USSR

CONSUMER GOODS OWNERSHIP

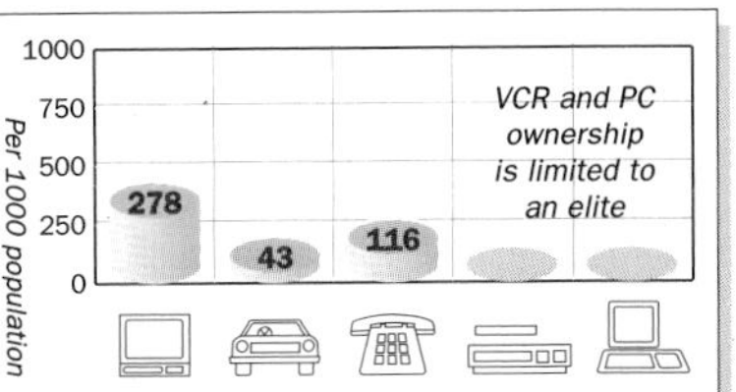

Life for the majority of Kazakhs has always been hard, and has grown even more difficult since 1989. Living standards have deteriorated and unemployment has climbed as a result of market-oriented reforms within Kazakhstan and the collapse of the wider Soviet trading system on which the country depended.

The rural population, the poorest group, has been particularly badly affected. The small wealthy elite is made up mainly of former officials within the CPK, many of whom have benefited from privatization, or belong to President Nazarbayev's clan. Foreign nationals, and their hard currency, are concentrated in the capital.

WORLD RANKING

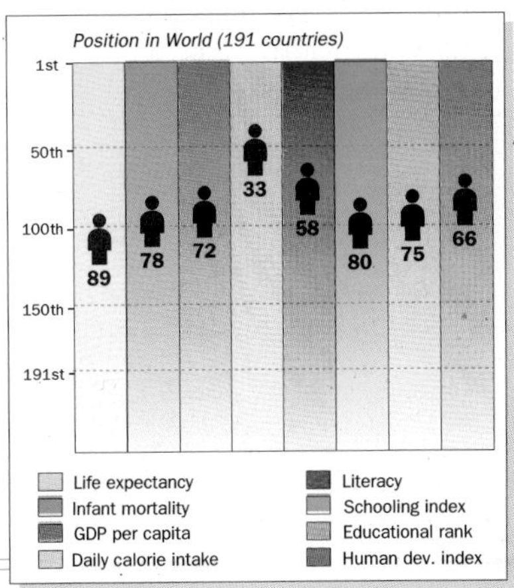

K

KENYA

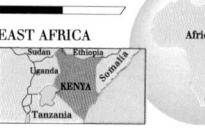

OFFICIAL NAME: Republic of Kenya **CAPITAL:** Nairobi
POPULATION: 25.2 million **CURRENCY:** Kenya shilling **OFFICIAL LANGUAGE:** Swahili

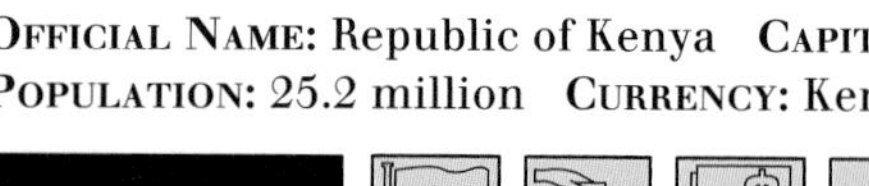

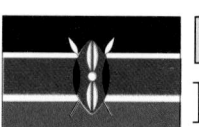

KENYA STRADDLES THE EQUATOR on Africa's east coast. Its central plateau is bisected by the Great Rift Valley. The land to the north is desert, while to the east lies a fertile coastal belt. After gaining independence from Britain in 1963, politics were dominated by Jomo Kenyatta. He was succeeded in 1978 by President Moi, who easily survived a return to multiparty elections in 1992. Ethnic violence is now the main political issue. The economic mainstays are tourism and agriculture, notably coffee and tea. Very high population growth is a key constraint on economic growth.

Kenyatta Conference Center, Nairobi. The modern skyline of the business center contrasts sharply with the slums on the city's outskirts.

CLIMATE

WEATHER CHART

Average daily temperature | Rainfall

°C/°F: 40/104, 30/86, 20/68, 10/50, 0/32, -10/14, -20/-4

J F M A M J J A S O N D

cm/in: 40/16, 30/12, 20/8, 10/4, 0

The coast and Great Rift Valley are hot and humid, the plateau interior is temperate and the northeastern desert hot and dry. Rain generally falls from April to May and October to November.

COMMUNICATIONS

Jomo Kenyatta, Nairobi 1.52m passengers

6 ships 9,900 dwt

THE TRANSPORTATION NETWORK

33,990 miles 54,700km)	None
1,698 miles (2,733 km)	Lake Victoria

Kenya's railroad, ports and main airport are being upgraded, a reflection of the importance of tourism and Kenya's role as an outlet for land-locked neighbors.

Great Rift Valley, Kenya. This huge crack in the Earth's crust runs from the Jordan river through Africa to the Zambezi River.

TOURISM

694,500 visitors

Down 3% in 1990

Tourism, which is mainly beach- and safari-oriented, is vital to the economy and a key foreign exchange earner. However, despite moving into the package vacation market during the 1980s, Kenya has seen visitor numbers decline since 1990. The main factors are world recession and the well-publicized murders of several tourists.

MAIN OVERSEAS ARRIVALS

	% of total arrivals
Germany	18%
UK	15%
Tanzania	11%
USA	9%
Italy	6%
Other	41%

0 10 20 30 40 50 60
% of total arrivals

KENYA

Total Area : 580 370 sq. km (224 081 sq. miles)

POPULATION
- over 1 000 000
- over 500 000
- over 100 000
- over 50 000
- over 10 000
- under 10 000

LAND HEIGHT
- 3000m/9843ft
- 2000m/6562ft
- 1000m/3281ft
- 500m/1640ft
- 200m/656ft
- Sea Level

N

0 100 km
0 100 miles

PEOPLE

Swahili, English, Kikuyu, Luo, Kamba

106 people per sq. mile

THE URBAN/RURAL POPULATION SPLIT

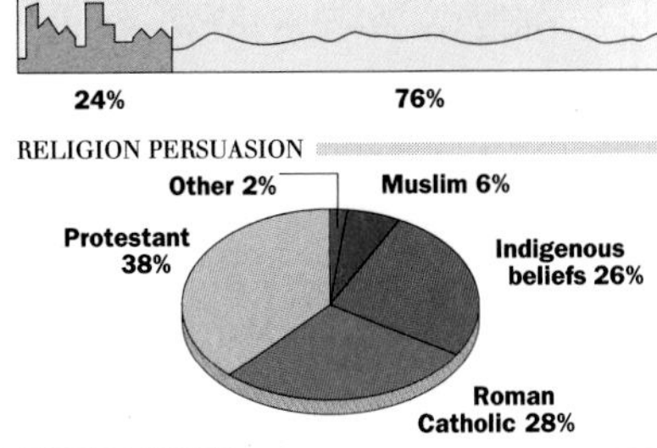

RELIGION PERSUASION

Other 2%
Muslim 6%
Protestant 38%
Indigenous beliefs 26%
Roman Catholic 28%

ETHNIC MAKEUP

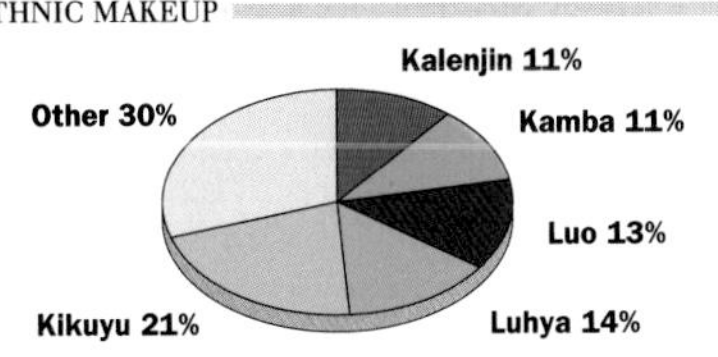

Kenya's ethnic diversity, with about 70 different groups, reflects its past as a focus of population movements. Asians, Europeans and Arabs form 1% of the population. The rural majority retains strong clan and extended family links, although these are being weakened by urban migration. Poverty and one of the world's highest population growth rates (3.5% a year) are the root causes of the land hunger which has recently been fueling a surge in ethnic violence. Much is concentrated in western Kenya, where Kikuyu are the main targets of violent attacks by Kalenjin, Masai and Pokor groups. Over 300,000 Kikuyu have also been displaced from their villages by a form of organized "ethnic cleansing" known as *majimboism*.

POPULATION AGE BREAKDOWN

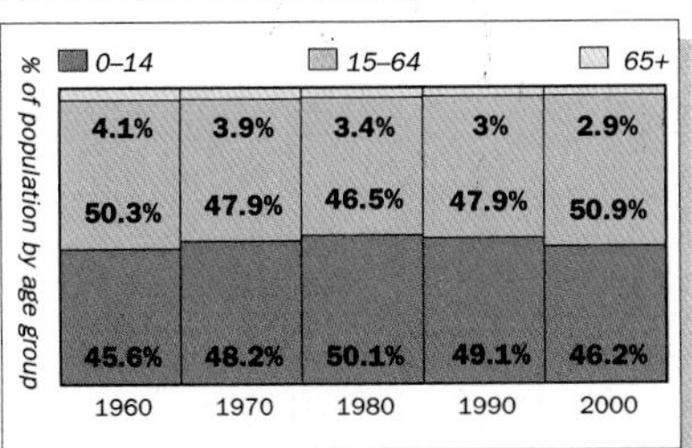

POLITICS

1997

President Daniel arap Moi

THE STATE OF THE PARTIES

National Assembly 202 members

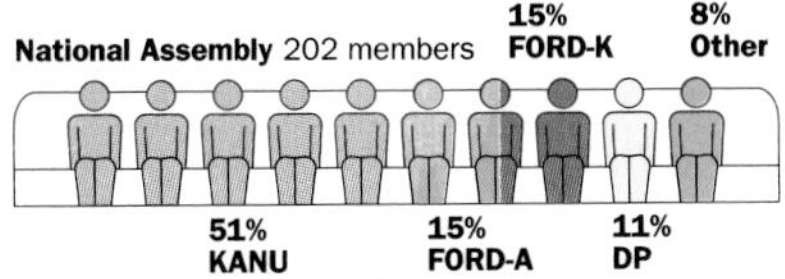

KANU = Kenya African National Union **FORD-A** = Forum for the Restoration of Democracy – Asili **FORD-K** = Forum for the Restoration of Democracy – Kenya **DP** = Democratic Party **Other** = Kenya Social Congress, Kenya National Congress

Kenya became a multiparty democracy in 1992 and has been led by President Daniel arap Moi since 1978.

MAIN POLITICAL ISSUE

Ethnic violence

The ethnic polarization of political parties in Kenya and rising poverty are fueling ethnic violence. Determined to ensure KANU dominance, President Moi, a Kalenjin, is turning the party into an alliance of smaller ethnic groups opposed to the Kikuyu. The latter are the largest ethnic group, the main victims of violence and the main supporters of the opposition. Great Rift Valley, Nyanga and Western provinces – those with most seats in parliament – are focuses of anti-Kikuyu "ethnic cleansing."

PROFILE

Kenya's status following independence as a *de facto* one-party state was formalized in 1982. President Moi's subsequent efforts to entrench KANU's power further provoked demands at home for the introduction of multiparty politics, and condemnation abroad of human rights abuses. Forced in 1992 to concede free elections, Moi helped to ensure KANU's victory by curtailing the campaign period. He has since been condemned again by the international community for manipulating ethnic conflict, part of his strategy to entrench KANU's power.

Opposition groups in Kenya remain divided, although popular pressure for reform is growing. Many are also critical of Moi's failure to improve the economy and to control corruption in the bureaucracy.

WORLD AFFAIRS

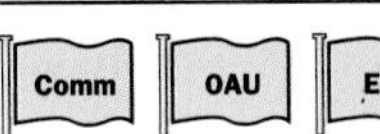

Relations with neighboring states and with key Western donors, notably the USA, are Kenya's priorities. In 1991, human rights concerns were partly responsible for a suspension of aid. Payments were restored in 1993, but made subject to an improved record. The main regional concern is the resurrection, with Uganda and Tanzania, of the East African Community, an economic zone which collapsed in 1977. The northern border dispute with Sudan over the Elemi Triangle is unresolved. Kenya lays claim to this arid piece of land which has a concentration of Christian refugees fleeing Sudanese government repression. The conflict in Somalia has also spilled over into northeast Kenya.

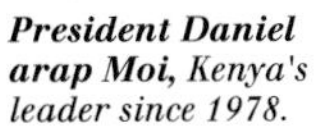

President Daniel arap Moi, Kenya's leader since 1978.

Oginga Odinga, veteran opposition leader, died in 1994.

AID

$873m (receipts)

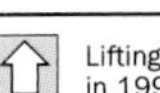
Lifting of aid freeze in 1993

Kenya has been a major recipient of aid from donors – such as the UK, Japan, the EU, the World Bank and the IMF – who are eager to support its free-market approach. Little, however, has trickled down to the majority of the population, which continues to live in poverty. This is partly because of the high proportion of aid tied to construction projects and donor-country firms and partly because of official corruption and mismanagement. Concern over both this and human rights abuses led to a freeze on aid from 1991 to 1993.

CHRONOLOGY

From the 10th century, Arab coastal settlers mixed with indigenous peoples in the region. Britain's need for a route to landlocked Uganda led to the formation in 1895 of the British East African Protectorate in the coastal region.

- **1900–1918** White settlement of interior; removal of local peoples from land.
- **1920** Interior becomes a British colony; coast remains protectorate.
- **1930** Jomo Kenyatta goes to UK; stays 14 years.
- **1944** Kenyan African Union (KAU) formed; Kenyatta returns to lead it.
- **1952–1956** *Mau Mau*, Kikuyu-led violent campaign to restore African lands. State of emergency is declared; 13,000 people killed.
- **1953** KAU banned. Kenyatta jailed.
- **1960** State of emergency ends. Tom Mboya and Oginga Odinga form KANU.
- **1961** Kenyatta freed; takes up presidency of KANU.
- **1963** KANU wins elections. Kenyatta prime minister. Full independence declared.
- **1964** Republic of Kenya formed with Kenyatta as president and Odinga as vice-president.

K

CHRONOLOGY *continued*

- ❑ **1966** Odinga defects to form Kenya People's Union (KPU).
- ❑ **1969** KANU is sole party to contest elections (also 1974). KANU Sec.-Gen. Mboya assassinated. Unrest. KPU banned and Odinga arrested.
- ❑ **1978** Kenyatta dies. Vice-President Daniel arap Moi succeeds him.
- ❑ **1982** Kenya declared a one-party state. Opposition to Moi. Abortive air-force coup. Odinga rearrested.
- ❑ **1983** Election turnout under 50%.
- ❑ **1986** Open "queue-voting" replaces secret ballot in first stage of general elections. Other measures to extend Moi's powers incite opposition.
- ❑ **1987** Government acts to suppress opposition groups. Political arrests and human rights abuses attract overseas criticism.
- ❑ **1988** Moi wins third term and extends his control over judiciary.
- ❑ **1989** Finance Minister George Saitoti replaces Vice-Pres. J. Karanja after corruption allegations. Political prisoners freed.
- ❑ **1990** Government implicated in deaths of Foreign Minister Robert Ouko and Anglican archbishop. Riots. Odinga and others form FORD, which is outlawed by government.
- ❑ **1991** Arrest of FORD leaders and attempts to stop pro-democracy demonstrations. Donors suspend aid. Moi agrees to introduce multiparty system. Ethnic violence on increase.
- ❑ **1992** FORD splits into factions led by ex-minister Kenneth Matiba and Odinga. Opposition weakness helps Moi to win December elections.
- ❑ **1994** Odinga dies.

DEFENSE

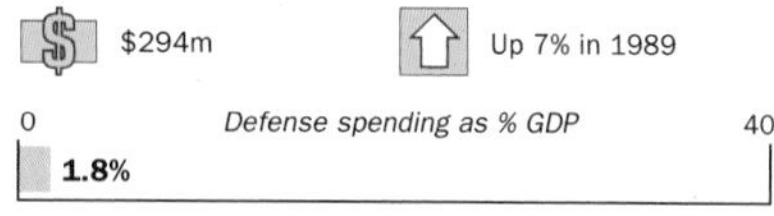

KENYAN ARMED FORCES

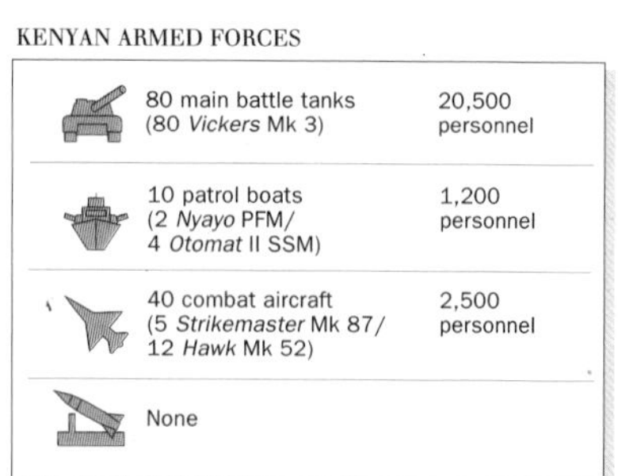

80 main battle tanks (80 *Vickers* Mk 3)	20,500 personnel
10 patrol boats (2 *Nyayo* PFM/ 4 *Otomat* II SSM)	1,200 personnel
40 combat aircraft (5 *Strikemaster* Mk 87/ 12 *Hawk* Mk 52)	2,500 personnel
None	

Destabilization of the northeastern border by the Somali civil war is the main defense issue. The military plays little part in politics.

ECONOMICS

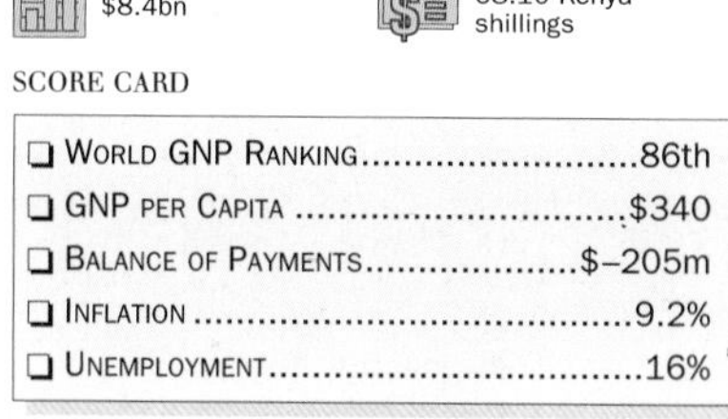

SCORE CARD

❑ WORLD GNP RANKING	86th
❑ GNP PER CAPITA	$340
❑ BALANCE OF PAYMENTS	$-205m
❑ INFLATION	9.2%
❑ UNEMPLOYMENT	16%

EXPORTS

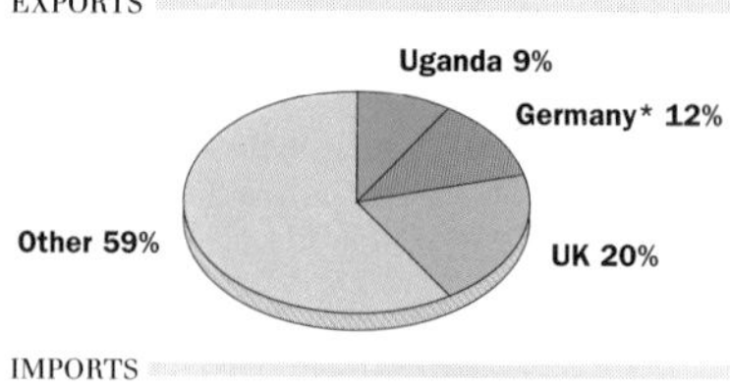

IMPORTS

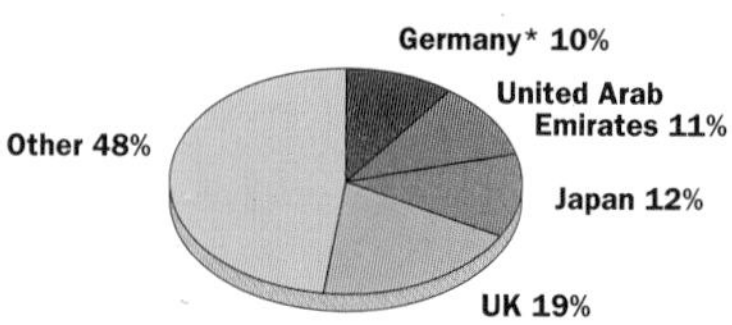

STRENGTHS
Tourism, which is the largest foreign exchange earner. Broad agricultural base, especially cash crops such as coffee and tea. East Africa's largest, most diversified manufacturing sector.

WEAKNESSES
Susceptibility of tourism, coffee and tea to fluctuating world prices. Poor recent GDP growth. High population growth of 3.5% a year. Land shortage, leading to subdivision of plots into uneconomical small units.

PROFILE
Kenya has been hailed as an example to the rest of Africa of the benefits of a mainly free-market economy. Government involvement has been relatively limited, and recently further reduced by privatization. Foreign investment has been encouraged, with some success. Tourism has developed into the leading foreign exchange earner over the past 20 years. Manufacturing now accounts for 21% of GDP, and is the most diversified sector in East Africa. However, it employs only 200,000 in formal jobs and needs to expand rapidly to provide more urban employment.

Economic growth was good by African standards during the 1980s, averaging over 4% a year. However, it was not good enough to compensate for one of the world's highest population growth rates. GDP per capita stagnated and too few jobs were created to make much impact on unemployment. The problem was intensified by urban migration and the yearly influx of thousands of school graduates into the labor market. For the majority of Kenyans, farming ever-smaller landholdings or earning a living in the informal sector, life has recently become harsher.

Other problems, including inflation, a heavy debt burden (now $7.5 billion), and growing dependence on balance of payments support came to a head in the early 1990s, when economic growth gave way to recession. Real GDP growth fell to 0.4% in 1992 and was negative in 1993. The rise in poverty-linked violence and political unrest hit tourism; earnings fell by 15% in 1992 and again in 1993. Agricultural and manufacturing output have both fallen in the past three years.

Partly as a response to pressure from donors, including the 1991–1993 freeze on balance of payments support, the government has implemented some economic liberalization measures. These include floating the Kenya shilling, raising interest rates and giving exporters direct access to their hard currency earnings. However, real growth is likely to remain elusive until Kenya overcomes two fundamental problems – the official corruption which drains vital resources, including foreign aid, and its high rate of population growth.

ECONOMIC PERFORMANCE INDICATOR

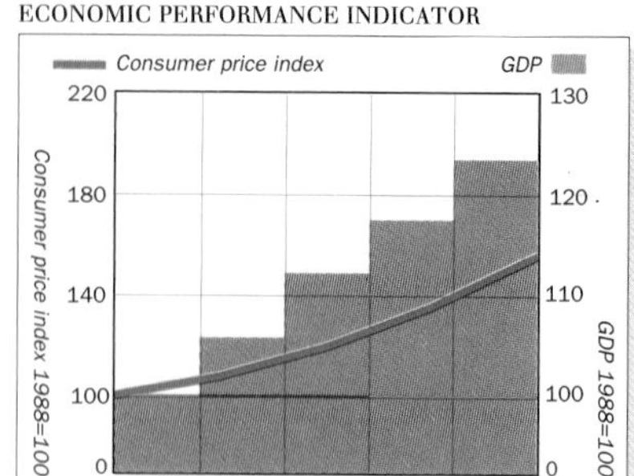

KENYA : MAJOR BUSINESSES

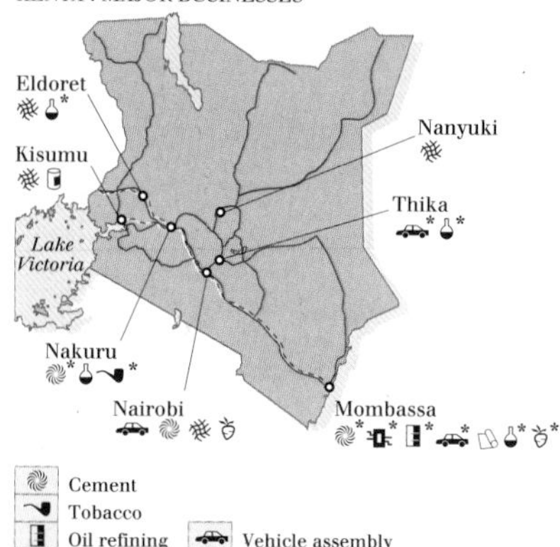

K

RESOURCES

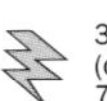

3bn kwh (capacity 723,000 kw)

Not an oil producer; refines 90,000 b/cd

13.5m cattle, 6.3m sheep, 100,000 pigs

Soda ash, fluorspar, limestone, rubies, gold, vermiculite

ELECTRICITY GENERATION

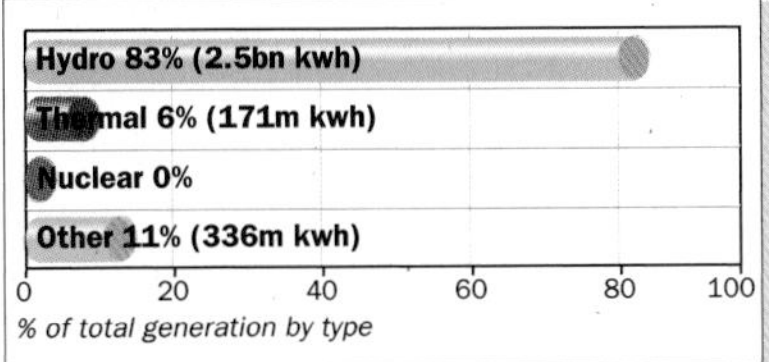

Agriculture underpins Kenya's economy and is still the largest sector, accounting for 27% of GDP. Kenya's varied topography means tropical, subtropical and temperate crops may be grown. Coffee and tea, the main export crops, have been affected by falling world prices. Efforts to reduce dependence on these crops have led to the growth of a successful export-oriented horticultural industry.

Kenya has few mineral resources and mining accounts for only 0.2% of GDP. Hydroelectric and geothermal sources are being developed to reduce energy imports – currently 70% of total requirements. Oil exploration in the Great Rift Valley and the northeast has revealed deposits in Turkana District.

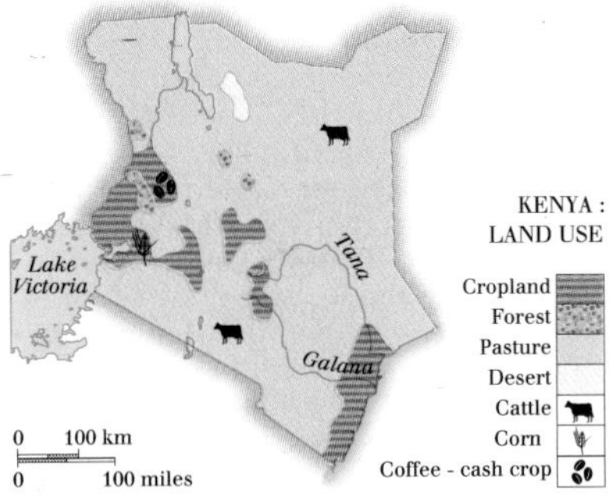

ENVIRONMENT

6%

Tourist numbers pose threat to safari park ecosystems

ENVIRONMENTAL TREATIES

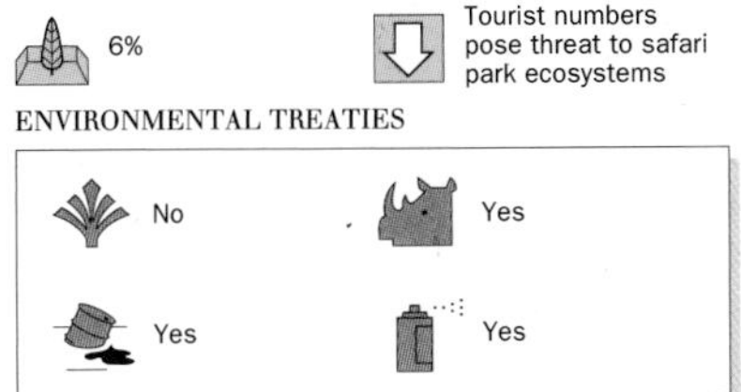

The government recognizes the importance of wildlife conservation to the tourist industry, and recent elephant protection schemes have been a success. However, initiatives to set up national reserves are competing with agriculture for land. The effect of dams on the Tana River is another concern.

MEDIA

Criticism of the government is not tolerated in practice

PUBLISHING AND BROADCAST MEDIA

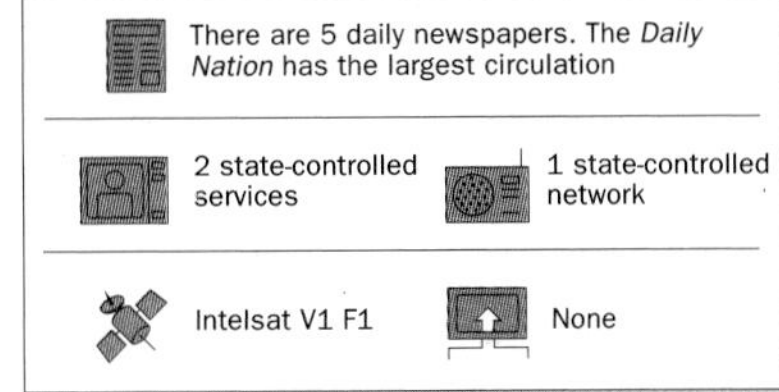

There are 5 daily newspapers. The *Daily Nation* has the largest circulation
2 state-controlled services
1 state-controlled network
Intelsat V1 F1
None

Government intolerance of criticism is long-standing and includes plays and novels as well as the media. Ngugi wa Thiongo, Kenya's most famous novelist, was exiled for his criticism of KANU.

CRIME

Kenya does not publish prison figures

Rising sharply

CRIME RATES

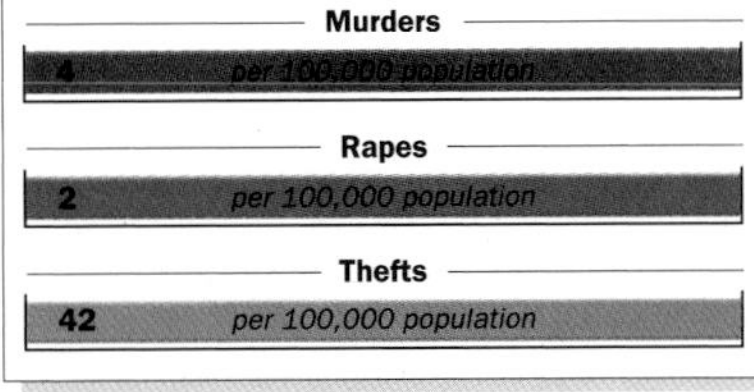

Nairobi's high crime levels are spreading countrywide, as a result of worsening poverty, ethnic violence and rising banditry in the northeast. An increase in the use of guns underlies the rapid increase in violent crime.

EDUCATION

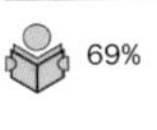

69%

0	*Education spending as % GNP*	25
6.5%		

THE EDUCATION SYSTEM

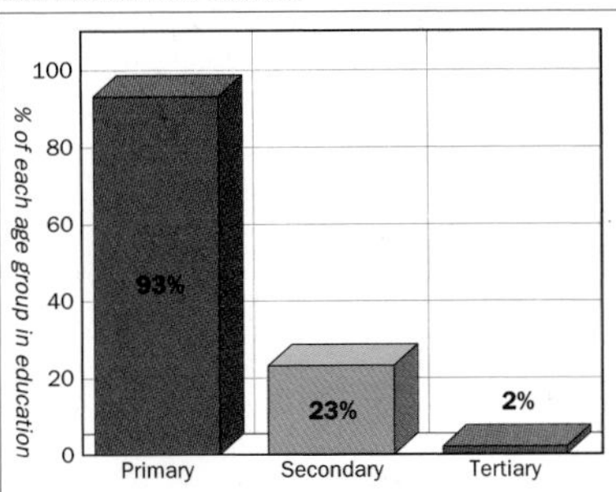

The education system is loosely based on the British model. Schooling is not compulsory, but free primary education means most children attend; the drop-out rate at the secondary level is high. In higher education the emphasis is on vocational training.

HEALTH

1 per 6,552 people

Respiratory and diarrheal diseases, malaria

0	*Health spending as % GNP*	25
2%		

The health system is a mix of state and private facilities, the latter mainly run by charities and missions. The state system has been hit by recession, worsening the already limited access of the rural majority. Poverty-related illnesses are increasing, particularly among children and women. HIV and AIDS are a growing problem among some sections of the community.

WEALTH

The majority of Kenya's rising number of poor live outside the formal economy

CONSUMER GOODS OWNERSHIP

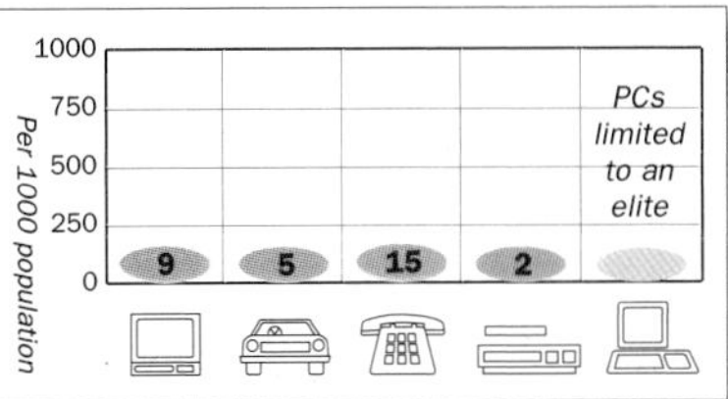

Wealth disparities in Kenya are large and growing, worsened by land hunger and migration to the cities, where jobs are few and existence depends on the informal economy. The slum dwellers of Nairobi's Amarthi Valley are among Africa's poorest, worst-nourished people. Their lives contrast with those of the country's elite – top government officials with access to patronage; white Kenyans, who derive their wealth largely from agricultural estates; and the Asian business community. Among these groups, Mercedes and the latest four-wheel-drive cars are popular, as are designer-label clothes. Wealthy Kenyans often send their children abroad for higher education.

WORLD RANKING

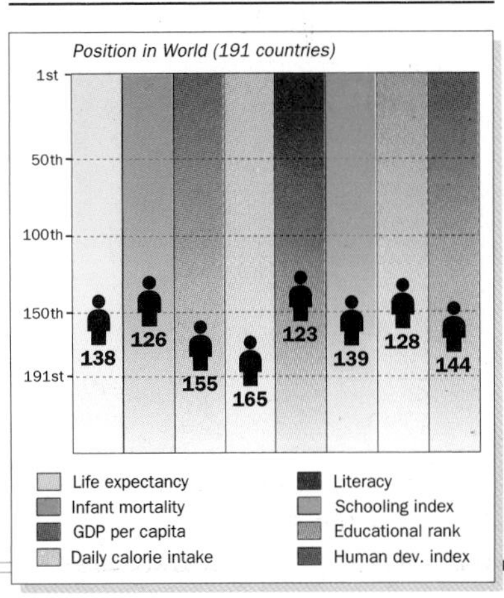

K

KIRIBATI

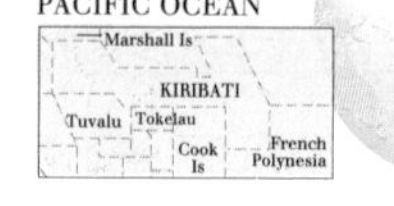

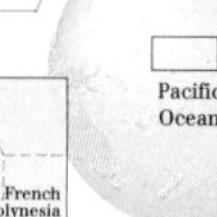

OFFICIAL NAME: Republic of Kiribati **CAPITAL:** Bairiki
POPULATION: 73,000 **CURRENCY:** Australian dollar **OFFICIAL LANGUAGE:** English

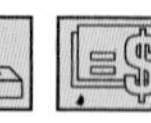

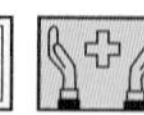

FORMERLY PART OF THE British colony of the Gilbert and Ellice Islands, the Gilberts became independent in 1979 and adopted the name Kiribati (pronounced Kiribass). British interest in the Gilberts rested solely on the exploitation of the phosphate deposits on Banaba; these ran out in 1980. In 1981 Kiribati won damages (but not the costs of litigation) from the British for decades of phosphate exploitation.

Banreaba Island, Tarawa atoll. None of the atolls is more than 26 feet high except Banaba, the main source of phosphate.

CLIMATE

WEATHER CHART

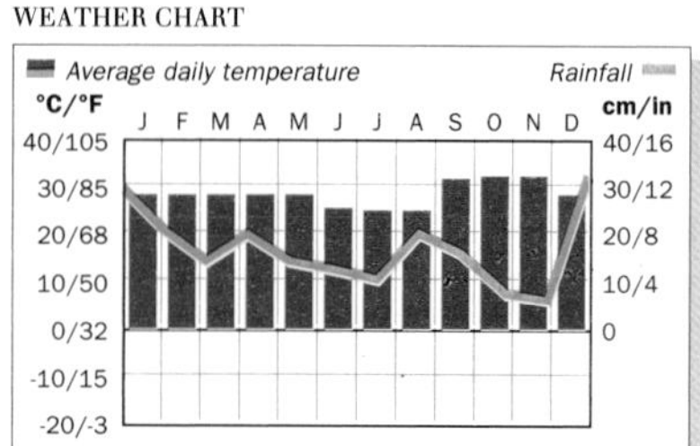

Kiribati's small land area in the vast Pacific means it often goes for months without rain. In the 1950s, a serious drought led to the resettlement of Gilbertese to the Solomon Islands.

COMMUNICATIONS

Bonriki Intl, Tarawa
51,000 passengers (est)

5 ships
2,700 dwt

THE TRANSPORTATION NETWORK

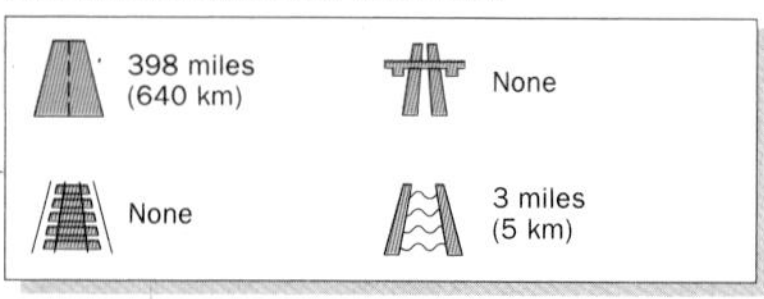

Kiribati has a limited air link with Fiji. Small-scale shipping and good satellite communications also keep it in touch with the outside world.

TOURISM

3,332 visitors

Up 21% in 1990

MAIN OVERSEAS ARRIVALS

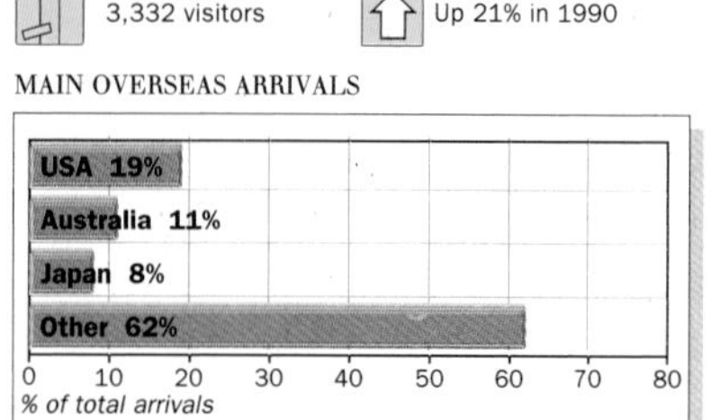

Kiritimati, which has a weekly air service to Honolulu, has been singled out for tourist development.

PEOPLE

English, Micronesian dialect

231 people per sq. mile

THE URBAN/RURAL POPULATION SPLIT

36% 64%

RELIGIOUS PERSUASION

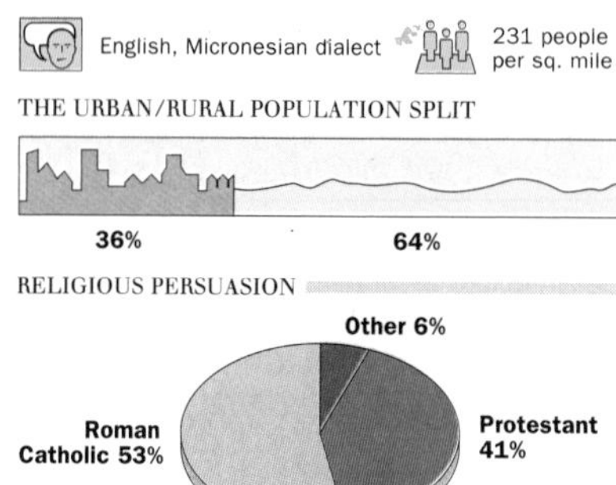

Locals still refer to themselves as Gilbertese. Apart from the inhabitants of Banaba, who employed anthropologists to establish their racial distinction, almost all Gilbertese are Micronesian. Tension with the Banabans is intense, but mostly fueled by the historic value of Banaba's phosphate deposits. Most Gilbertese are poor. Many go to Nauru as guest workers, living in barrack-room conditions, or work as merchant shipping crew. Those who stay at home go through a circular migration from the outlying islands to Tarawa, returning to see relatives. Women play a prominent role, especially on outlying islands, where they run most of the farms.

POLITICS

THE STATE OF THE PARTIES

House of Assembly 41 members

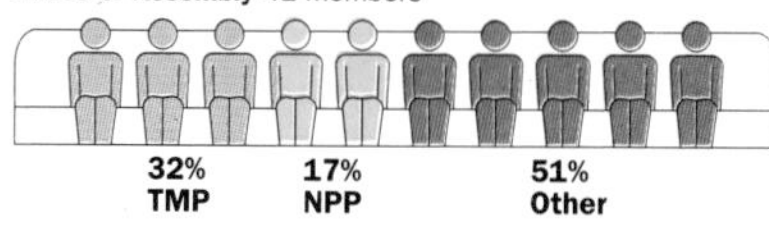

TMP = Te Maneaba Party **NPP** = National Progressive Party

The traditional chiefs still effectively rule Kiribati, through a party system based on the British model. The main concern is the economy, which is extremely vulnerable to any fluctuations in world demand for coconuts. The overpopulation of Tarawa is the other major issue. Possible restrictions on travel to the island have been discussed. Migration is partly caused by poverty and lack of opportunity on the outer islands. Plans for a wealth distribution program to reduce migration exist, but they have yet to become policy. Ieremia Tabai has been the dominant political figure of the past decade.

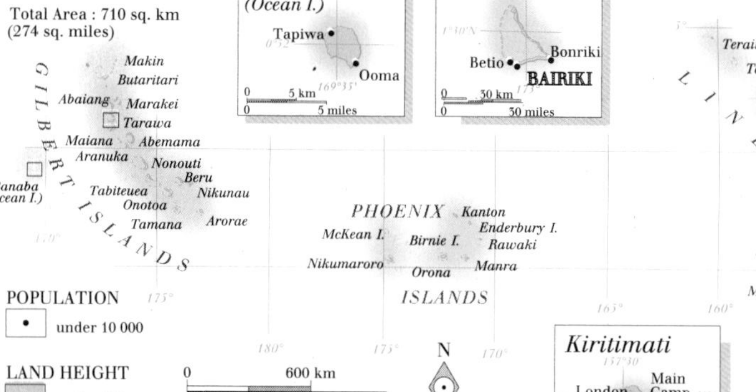

WORLD AFFAIRS

In 1986, Kiribati was a signatory to a deal between the USA and a number of Pacific Island states that resulted in the USA paying $60 million, in return for access to Pacific fishing grounds. However, the USA has yet to sign the 1982 UN Law of the Sea accords; it objects to the sections defining the ownership of migratory species such as tuna. Kiribati used to play the USSR off against the USA. The USSR was happy to pay $1.5 million for fishing leases as it allowed it to spy on US nuclear testing on the neighboring Kwajalein atoll in the Marshall Islands.

AID

 $22m (receipts)  Little change from year to year

Aid is mostly for small infrastructure projects. The causeway linking Tarawa to the airport on Bonriki, a nearby atoll, was built with Japanese aid.

DEFENSE

 Kiribati has no defense budget  Not applicable

Australia and New Zealand provide *de facto* protection, with regular anti-submarine patrols.

ECONOMICS

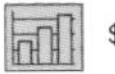 $53m  1.47 Australian dollars

SCORE CARD

- ❑ WORLD GNP RANKING........................189th
- ❑ GNP PER CAPITA $730
- ❑ BALANCE OF PAYMENTS $5.2m
- ❑ INFLATION 5.5%
- ❑ UNEMPLOYMENT................................2.8%

STRENGTHS
Subsistence economy has survived, and Kiribati has no need to import food. Coconuts provide some export income: the EU is the biggest market. Fisheries have potential, but are hampered by US fisheries policy in the Pacific.

WEAKNESSES
Banaba's phosphate deposits ran out in 1980. Isolation, and large distances between islands. Almost no economic potential.

EXPORTS

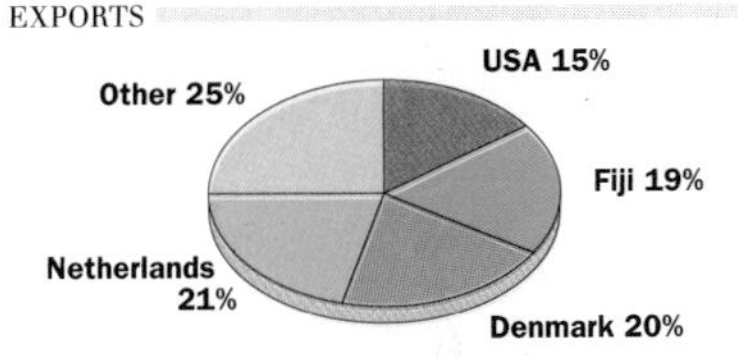

IMPORTS

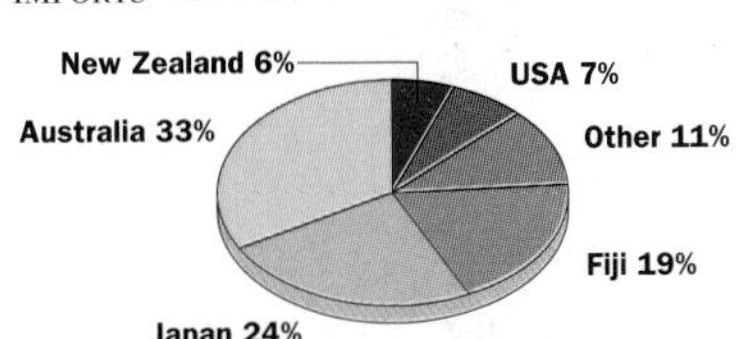

RESOURCES

 7m kwh (capacity 2,000 kw)  Not an oil producer and has no refineries

 33,100 tons Phosphate

Phosphate deposits on Banaba ran out in 1980. All energy supplies have to be imported. Underwater agriculture is being developed.

ENVIRONMENT

 39% (10% partially protected)  Refusal to allow Western toxic waste dumping

Overpopulation on Tarawa is the cause of major problems. The coral reef, which protects Tarawa from the sea and which holds important inshore fish stocks in the lagoon, is threatened by untreated effluent. Approaches have been made by international – mainly US – companies seeking to dump industrial waste into the lagoons.

MEDIA

 No restrictions on political reporting

PUBLISHING AND BROADCAST MEDIA

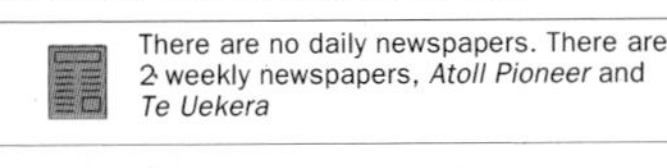
There are no daily newspapers. There are 2 weekly newspapers, *Atoll Pioneer* and *Te Uekera*

 No TV service 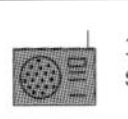 1 independent service

The main sources of news and information on Kiribati are *Pacific Islands Monthly* and *Islands' Business* magazines.

CRIME

 77 prisoners 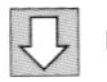 Down 46% in 1990

Crime, apart from brawls resulting from drunkenness, is minimal. The judicial system is based on the British model.

EDUCATION

 90%

Education is British-inspired. The best students go to King George V School, and on to college in Fiji.

CHRONOLOGY

The British established the phosphate-producing colony of the Gilbert and Ellice Islands in 1892.

- ❑ **1942–1943** Tarawa atoll scene of fierce US–Japanese fighting.
- ❑ **1957** First British nuclear tests take place near Kiritimati.
- ❑ **1979** Independence as two states, Kiribati (The Gilberts) and Tuvalu (The Ellice Islands).
- ❑ **1981** British agree to pay damages for almost total destruction of Banaba by phosphate mining.
- ❑ **1986** Kiribati–US fishing deal.

HEALTH

 1 per 3,938 people  Heart disease, diabetes

Most Gilbertese are healthy, thanks to the home-grown diet. Due to a lack of agricultural land, those on Tarawa are starting to import canned food, and vitamin A deficiency is a problem.

K

WEALTH

 The state is the only formal employer. Remittances from Gilbertese working in Nauru are an important source of national income

CONSUMER GOODS OWNERSHIP

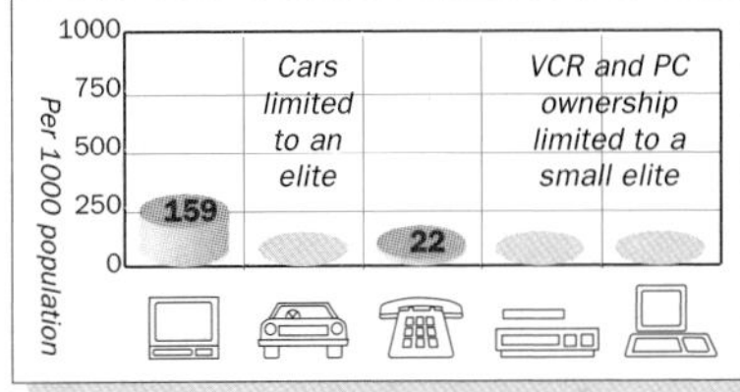

Life in Kiribati is modest. Civil servants in the capital, Bairiki, are the wealthiest group. There are a handful of cars on Tarawa, and they are confined to the single 18-mile stretch of road, from Tarawa to the airport. Most Gilbertese live by subsistence farming.

WORLD RANKING

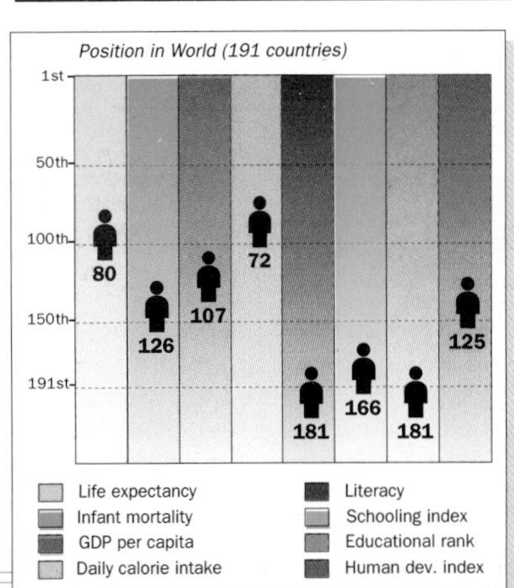

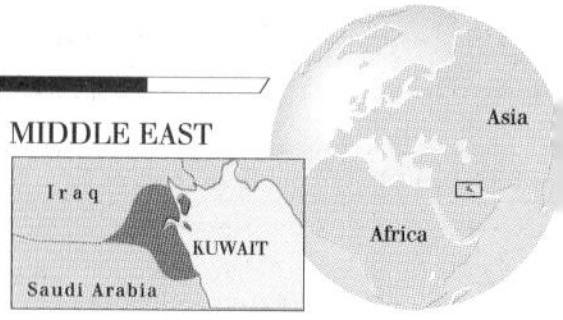

KUWAIT

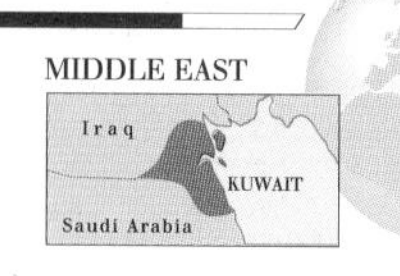

OFFICIAL NAME: State of Kuwait **CAPITAL:** Kuwait City
POPULATION: 2.1 million **CURRENCY:** Kuwaiti dinar **OFFICIAL LANGUAGE:** Arabic

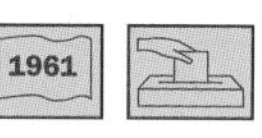

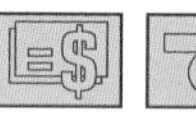

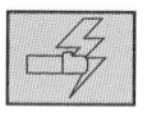

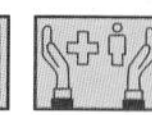

AT THE NORTHWEST EXTREME of the Persian Gulf, Kuwait is dwarfed by its neighbors Iraq, Iran and Saudi Arabia. The flat, almost featureless landscape conceals huge oil and gas reserves, which made Kuwait the world's first oil-rich state. In 1990, Iraq invaded, claiming Kuwait as its 19th province. A US-led alliance, under the aegis of the UN, expelled Iraqi forces following the Gulf War in 1991. Since its liberation, Kuwait has built a wall separating its territory from Iraq.

Saffar Towers in the business center of Kuwait City. The postwar cost of rebuilding Kuwait's economy is put at $25 billion.

CLIMATE

WEATHER CHART

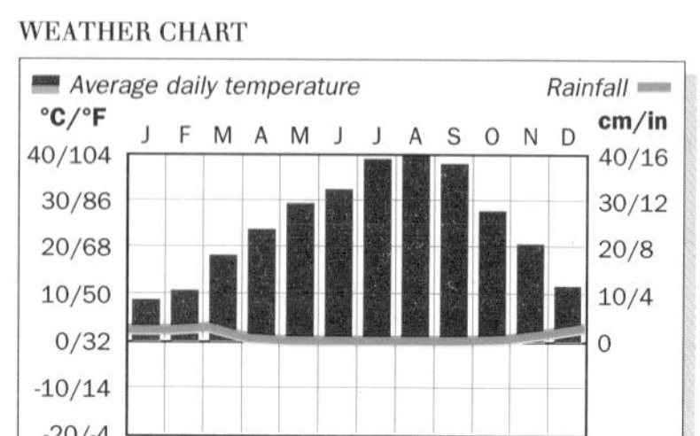

Summer temperatures can soar to over 104°F, but winters can be cold with frost at night.

COMMUNICATIONS

Kuwait Intl, Kuwait City 1.41m passengers

62 ships 3.79m dwt

THE TRANSPORTATION NETWORK

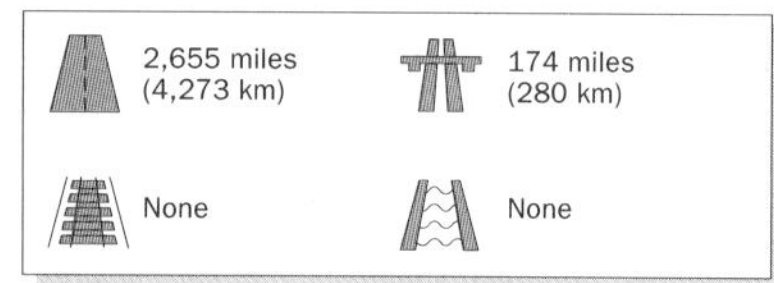

Kuwait has a system of beltways around the capital and good connecting roads to Saudi Arabia.

TOURISM

50,000 visitors

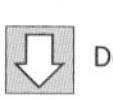
Down 44% in 1990

MAIN OVERSEAS ARRIVALS

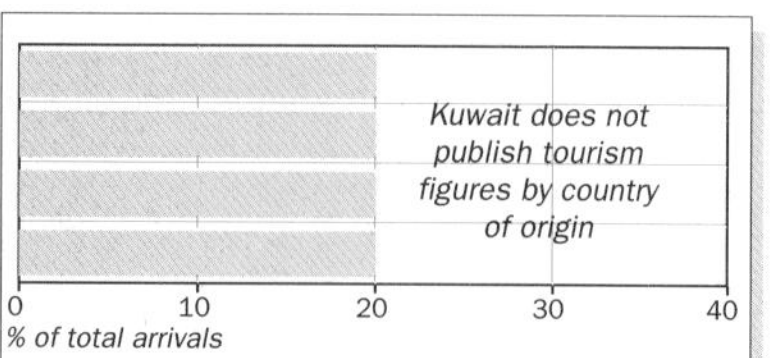

Most Westerners visit Kuwait specifically to see relatives working in the oil industry. The limited tourism from neighboring Arab states, notably Saudi Arabia, has not recovered since the 1990–1991 Gulf War.

PEOPLE

Arabic, English

290 people per sq. mile

THE URBAN/RURAL POPULATION SPLIT

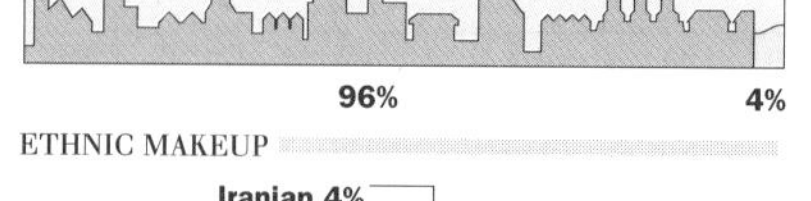

ETHNIC MAKEUP

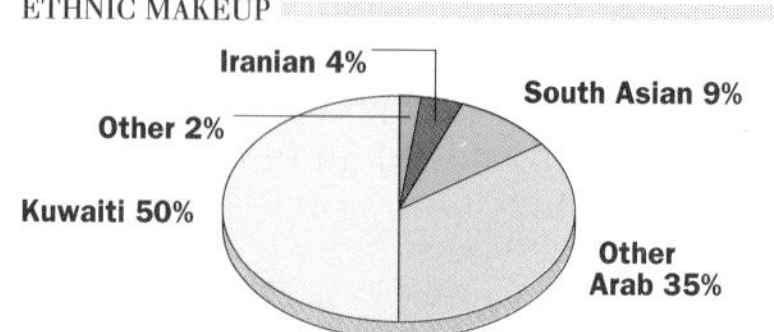

Kuwait is a fundamentalist Sunni Muslim society. Women have considerable freedom, but are not allowed to vote.

Kuwait's oil wealth has drawn in thousands of workers from India, Pakistan and other Arab countries. Before the Iraqi invasion in 1990, Kuwait had the largest Palestinian population in the Arabian peninsula. The PLO's support for Iraq's invasion led to most Palestinians being driven out. After the war, Kuwaitis vowed never again to become a minority in their own country. In 1994, native Kuwaitis only just outnumbered resident foreign nationals.

POLITICS

1996

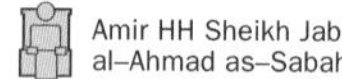
Amir HH Sheikh Jaber al-Ahmad as-Sabah

THE STATE OF THE PARTIES

National Assembly 50 members

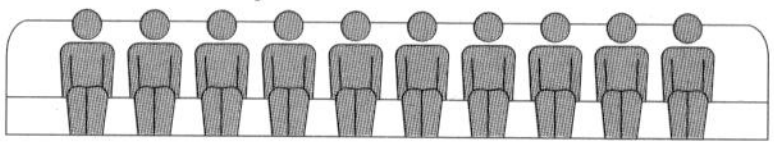

Political parties are not allowed. The members of the National Assembly are elected for a four-year term by all literate Kuwaiti males over the age of 21, except servicemen and police

In 1992, Kuwait's ruler, Amir Sheikh Jaber, restored the National Assembly and allowed a general election to take place. The franchise was restricted to male Kuwaiti nationals. Islamic and independent candidates were elected, and six deputies with opposing views to those of the government were given cabinet posts in order to create a new sense of national unity.

KUWAIT

Total Area : 17 820 sq. km (6880 sq. miles)

POPULATION
- over 100 000
- over 50 000
- over 10 000
- under 10 000

LAND HEIGHT
- 200m/656ft
- Sea Level

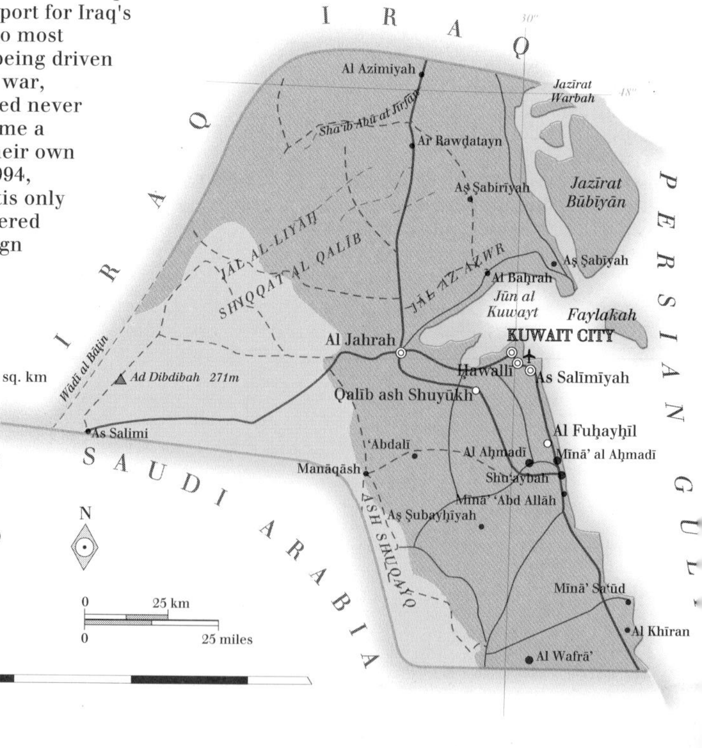

0 25 km
0 25 miles

WORLD AFFAIRS

Kuwait's strategic importance is as a major exporter of crude oil and natural gas. As such, it has always maintained very close links with the West. Since the war with Iraq, its foreign policy has become even more pro-Western. It therefore depends on its neighbor Saudi Arabia and on Western allies for its future security.

AID

 $1.7bn (donations)  Trend sharply upward

The Kuwait Fund for Arab Economic Development continued to give aid even during the invasion crisis.

DEFENSE

 $9.3bn  Up 608% in 1991

Kuwait's 11,000-strong, partly volunteer army was easily overrun by vastly superior Iraqi forces in August 1990. Since the liberation, defense pacts have been signed with the USA, the UK, France and Russia. Kuwait is rearming fast, with weapons purchased from major Western suppliers.

ECONOMICS

 $32.8bn  0.30 Kuwaiti dinars

SCORE CARD

- ❑ World GNP Ranking 51st
- ❑ GNP per Capita $16,400
- ❑ Balance of Payments $801m
- ❑ Inflation 8%
- ❑ Unemployment 1.5%

Strengths
Production of oil and gas has been restored to pre-invasion levels. Large overseas investments.

Weaknesses
Economy devastated by Iraqi "scorched-earth" policy, when oil installations were destroyed. Threat of Iraqi attack deters Western industrial investment. Skilled labor, food and raw materials have to be imported.

EXPORTS

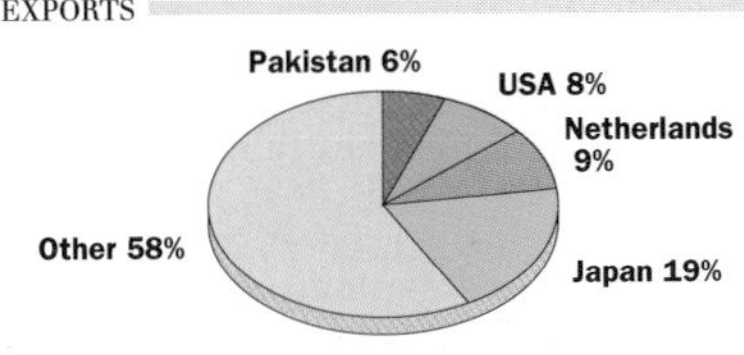

IMPORTS

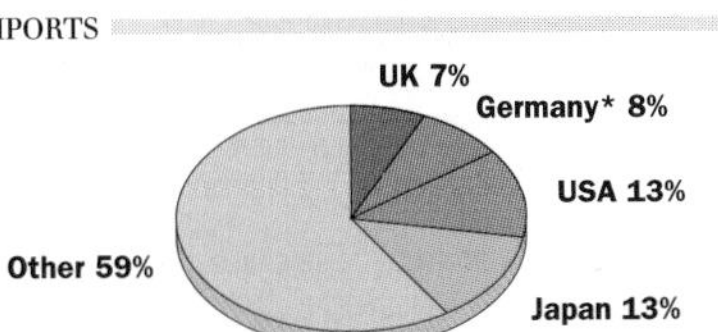

RESOURCES

20.6bn kwh (capacity 6.8m kw)

1.03m b/d (reserves 94,000,000,000 bbl)

260,000 sheep, 24,000 cattle, 6,000 camels

Oil, natural gas, salt

The oil industry is Kuwait's most profitable sector, accounting for over 80% of export earnings. It was badly hit as a result of the Gulf War, when large numbers of oil wells were deliberately set on fire, but with foreign assistance it has been quickly rehabilitated. Kuwait also possesses valuable reserves of natural gas.

ENVIRONMENT

 1.2% partially protected 

The Iraqi invasion and the subsequent war caused an ecological disaster. Although the effects did not prove as grave as some observers first feared, marine life has been damaged and many thousands of acres of cultivated land have been obliterated. Millions of land mines still litter Kuwait's border areas.

MEDIA

 There is officially no press censorship. However, the government acts swiftly against publishers who breach informal guidelines

PUBLISHING AND BROADCAST MEDIA

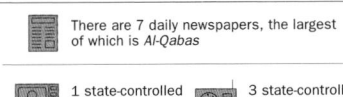

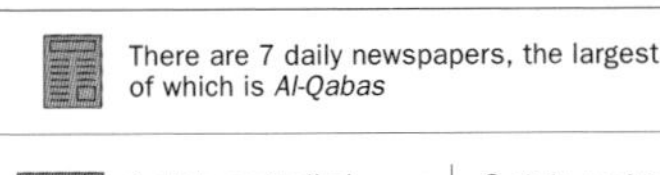

There are 7 daily newspapers, the largest of which is Al-Qabas
1 state-controlled service
3 state-controlled services

Radio and TV are state-controlled, but satellite TV is freely available. Press freedom exists in theory.

CRIME

 500 prisoners  Up 1% in 1988

Isolated acts of terrorism related to the war still occur. There have been reports of human rights abuses.

EDUCATION

 73%

Kuwaiti citizens receive free education from nursery school to college. Since liberation, more emphasis has been placed on technology in the curriculum.

CHRONOLOGY

Kuwait traces its independence to 1710, but was under British rule from the late 18th century until 1961. The government denies any historical link with Iraq.

- ❑ **1961** Independence from the UK. Iraqi claims against its sovereignty.
- ❑ **1976** The Amir suspends the National Assembly.
- ❑ **1990** Iraq invades Kuwait. The Amir flees to Saudi Arabia.
- ❑ **1991** Operation Desert Storm liberates Kuwait.
- ❑ **1992** National Assembly elections.

HEALTH

 1 per 675 people

Accidents, heart diseases, cancer, perinatal deaths

Despite theft of equipment during the Iraqi invasion, Kuwait has restored its Western-standard health-care service. Nationals receive free treatment.

WEALTH

 Most Kuwaitis have total financial security

CONSUMER GOODS OWNERSHIP

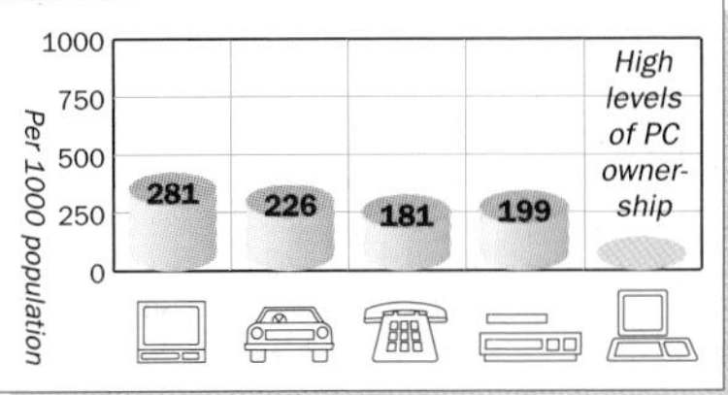

Kuwaitis enjoy high incomes and the government has repeatedly rescued citizens who have suffered stock market or other financial losses. High school and college graduates are guaranteed jobs. Capital is easily transferred abroad and there are effectively no exchange controls.

WORLD RANKING

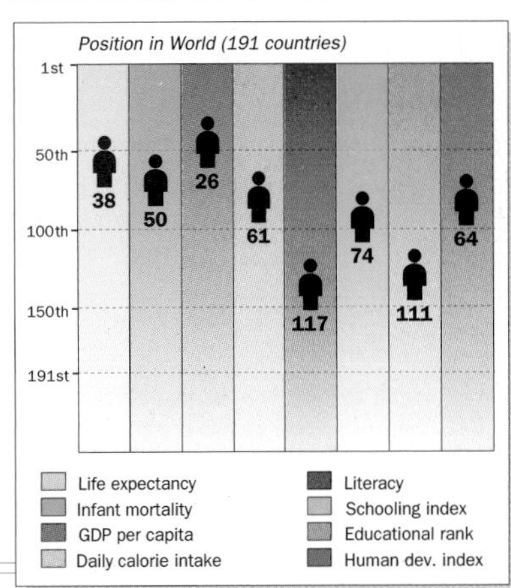

K

KYRGYZSTAN

CENTRAL ASIA

Kazakhstan
KYRGYZSTAN
Uzbekistan
Tajikistan
China
Asia

OFFICIAL NAME: Kyrgyz Republic **CAPITAL:** Bishkek
POPULATION: 4.5 million **CURRENCY:** Som **OFFICIAL LANGUAGE:** Kyrgyz

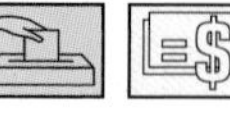

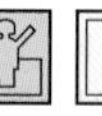

KYRGYZSTAN IS A SMALL and very mountainous nation in central Asia. It is the least urbanized of the ex-Soviet republics (the rural population is growing faster than the towns) and was among the last to develop its own cultural nationalism. Its moderate government is treading uncertainly between Kyrgyz nationalist pressures, and ensuring that the minority Russians are not alienated – they tend to possess the skills necessary to run a market-based economy.

CLIMATE

WEATHER CHART

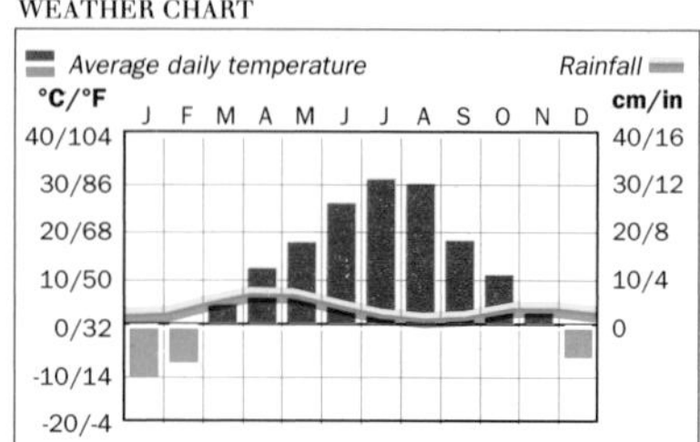

Conditions vary from permanent snow and cold deserts at altitude to hot deserts in low regions. Intermediate slopes and valleys receive some rain.

COMMUNICATIONS

Bishkek International

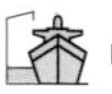
Has no fleet

THE TRANSPORTATION NETWORK

17,647 miles (28,400 km)

None

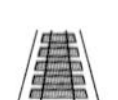
230 miles (370 km)

373 miles (600 km)

Kyrgyzstan does not have the funds to improve its poor mountain road network.

TOURISM

Mainly business visitors

Little change from year to year

MAIN OVERSEAS ARRIVALS

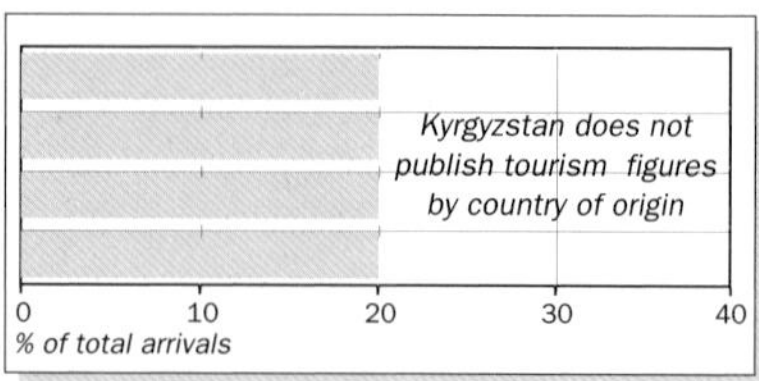

The tourist industry is undeveloped. Most visitors to Kyrgyzstan are people on business from Turkey and China in search of new contracts, or working on multilateral aid agency projects.

PEOPLE

Kyrgyz, Russian

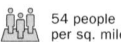

54 people per sq. mile

THE URBAN/RURAL POPULATION SPLIT

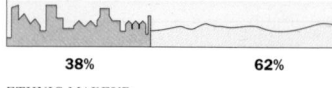

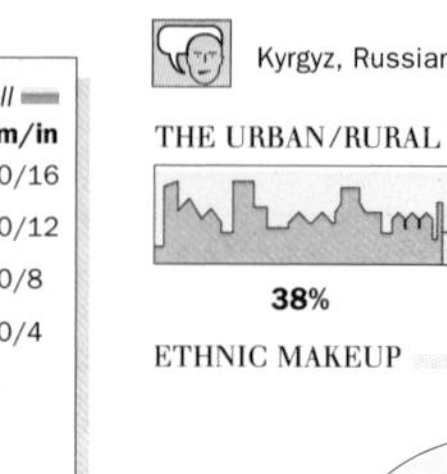

ETHNIC MAKEUP

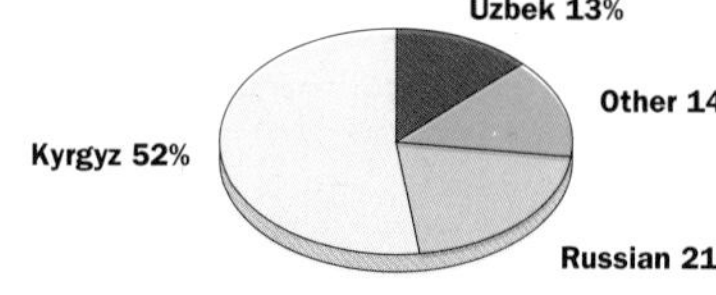

Despite claims to the contrary, Kyrgyzstan suffers from a forceful nationalism similar to that in other ex-Soviet republics. There is considerable tension between the Kyrgyz and other minorities, particularly Uzbeks. The preference given to Kyrgyz in the political system and in particular in the land laws, which exclude all others from full title, has aggravated tensions. The trend in politics is toward greater Islamicization, which is linking religion and race issues more closely and adding pressure on "foreigners," particularly Russians, to leave.

Current conditions differ radically from those in Soviet days, when the Russian community in effect ran the economy. It is only as recently as 1989 that the Kyrgyz resumed their position as the main ethnic group owing to their higher birth rate. The government is now trying to stem Russian emigration.

Loess landscape, Naryn valley. *Kyrgyzstan is dominated by the ice-capped Tian Shan Mountains, but valleys are green and fertile.*

POLITICS

Uncertain

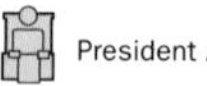
President Askar Akayev

THE STATE OF THE PARTIES

Supreme Soviet 350 members

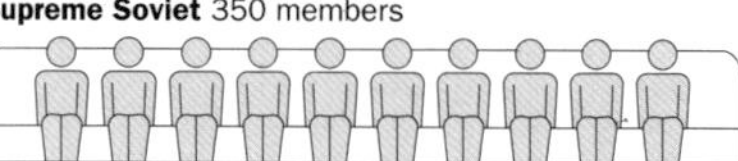

Elections are scheduled for 1995, when it has been agreed that the current terms of the president and Supreme Soviet will expire, in accordance with the 1993 constitution

Kyrgyzstan has gone further than most ex-Soviet republics in embracing political change. As the first republic to denounce the attempted coup in Moscow in 1991, it swiftly banned all the activities of the Communist Party, which now no longer exists, even under another name.

Akayev, the academic picked as a reformist president by the Supreme Soviet in 1990, has since steered a precarious course aimed at trimming from official positions the number of more extreme nationalists. These are felt to threaten the presence of minorities, whose skills are needed for Kyrgyz reconstruction. Economic policy has embraced market-led reform theories, but with few tangible results.

Although the many nationalist parties have so far failed to form a united front against the government, the broad trend in politics is still toward greater nationalism.

Ethnic tension between Kyrgyz and Uzbeks has been rising since ethnic riots in 1990 in the city of Osh, home to a large number of the Uzbek minority.

WORLD AFFAIRS

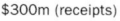

Relations with Russia are good, although Kyrgyzstan is working to reduce its dependence on it. Turkey, the second country to establish a mission in Bishkek after the USA, is developing close links aimed at restraining Iranian fundamentalist influence in the region. Relations with Uzbekistan, which supports anti-democratic forces in Kyrgyzstan, are tense.

AID

$300m (receipts)

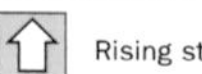
Rising steadily

The USA, Germany, Turkey and Japan are the major bilateral donors. The IMF is funding economic restructuring.

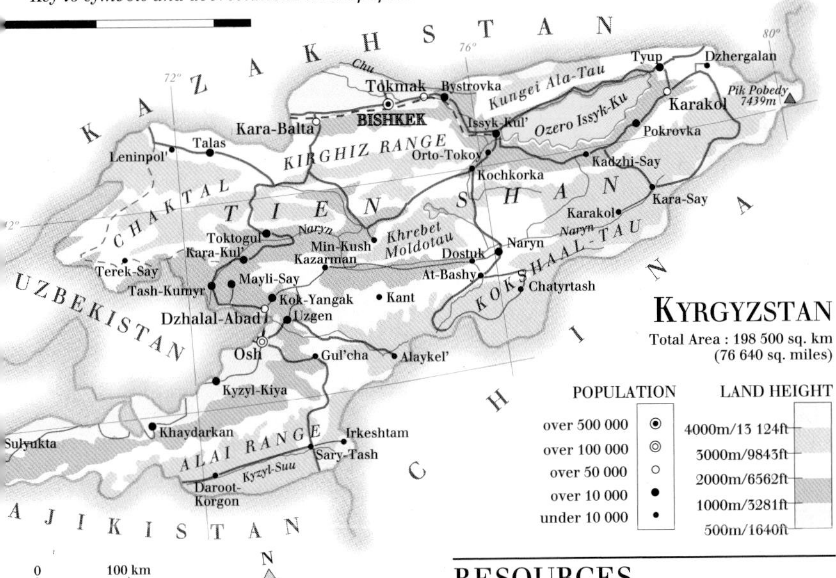

CHRONOLOGY

The Kyrgyz first developed a recognizable ethnic consciousness in the late 18th century.

- **1860s** Expansion of Russian Empire into Kyrgyz lands.
- **1916** Kyrgyz resistance to call-up to Tsar's armies fighting Germany; 120,000 Kyrgyz die in uprisings.
- **1924** Incorporated in USSR.
- **1991** Independence from USSR.

DEFENSE

 $47.1m

 No significant change

The small army, composed of the Kyrgyz remnants of the former CIS force, is weak and not influential in politics. Recruitment to a 7,000-strong National Guard was set up in 1992. Kyrgyzstan looks to its alliance with the CIS, particularly Russia, for its security.

ECONOMICS

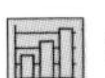 $6.9bn

 12.30 som

SCORE CARD

- World GNP Ranking 95th
- GNP per Capita $1,533
- Balance of Payments .... Deficit
- Inflation 1,500%
- Unemployment 1.5%

Strengths
Agricultural self-sufficiency. Minerals, especially gold and mercury for export. Large hydroelectric power potential.

Weaknesses
Agriculture-based economy. Economy still dominated by the state and the mentality of collective farming. Sharp economic decline since 1991 breakup of USSR, on which it depended totally for trade and supplies. Hyperinflation – high of 1,500% a year at mid-1993.

EXPORTS/IMPORTS

Trade is overwhelmingly with the Russian Federation. A smaller proportion is with other states of the former Soviet Union

RESOURCES

 15m kwh (capacity 4.1m kw)

 3,600 b/d

10.5m sheep and goats, 1.2m cattle, 440,500 pigs

Coal, antimony, gas, oil, tin, mercury, iron uranium, zinc, gold

Kyrgyzstan has small quantities of commercially exploitable coal, oil and gas and great hydroelectric power potential. Energy policy, which relies on Western aid and technology, is primarily aimed at developing these further in order to reduce dependence on supplies from Russia, and eventually to achieve self-sufficiency in energy.

ENVIRONMENT

 1%

 No funds for major initiatives

The major problem is the salination of the soil caused by excessive irrigation of cotton. Kyrgyzstan has a poor record in limiting industrial pollution.

MEDIA

 There is no censorship

PUBLISHING AND BROADCAST MEDIA

 There are 114 newspapers. The principal Kyrgyz newspapers are *Bishkek Shamy, Kyrgyz Tuusu* and *Zhashtyk Zharchysy*

 No TV service

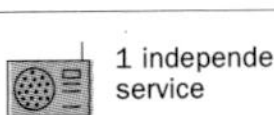

TV programming is mostly from Russia. The Kyrgyz press is the most liberal in Central Asia.

CRIME

 Kyrgyzstan does not publish prison figures

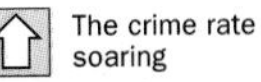

Outbreaks of violence are often the result of ethnic tensions. Economic decline is encouraging farmers to grow opium for the illegal drugs trade.

EDUCATION

 Over 90%

Replacing Russian as the main teaching language is proving an enormous task. Russian is likely to survive at higher level as the Kyrgyz language lacks key technical and scientific terms.

HEALTH

 1 per 272 people

Respiratory, heart and cerebrovascular diseases, cancer

Kyrgyzstan had one of the Soviet Union's least developed public health systems. Infant mortality remains high.

WEALTH

 Inflation is eroding the value of most salaries

CONSUMER GOODS OWNERSHIP

The old Communist Party nomenklatura, using their contacts in trade, are still the wealthiest group.

WORLD RANKING

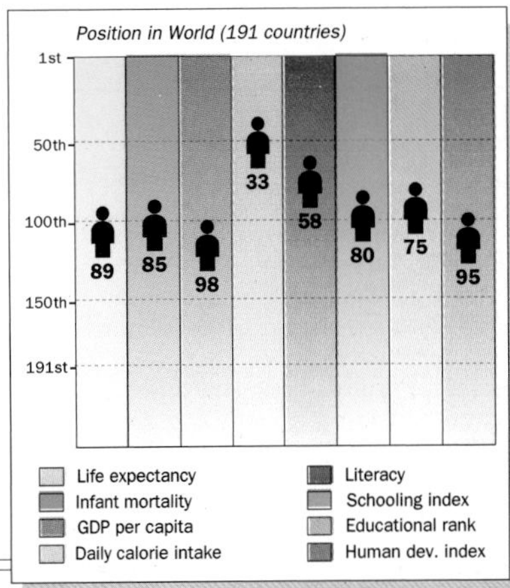

K

LAOS

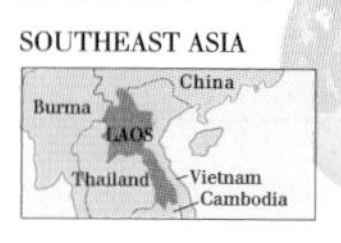

OFFICIAL NAME: Lao People's Democratic Republic
CAPITAL: Vientiane **POPULATION:** 4.3 million **CURRENCY:** Kip **OFFICIAL LANGUAGE:** Lao

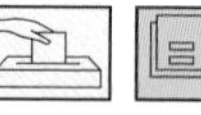

LAOS IS A LANDLOCKED country surrounded by Vietnam, Cambodia, Thailand, Burma and China. The Mekong River forms its main thoroughfare and feeds the fertile lowlands of the Mekong Valley. Laos became independent of France in 1953. It was heavily bombed by US aircraft during the Vietnam War. The communist Lao People's Revolutionary Party (LPRP) has held power since 1975. The government began introducing market-oriented reforms in 1986. A transfer of power took place in 1992 following the death of party leader Kaysone Phomvihane.

***Farm in northeastern Laos.** The only lowlands are along the Mekong River. Three-quarters of Laotians are subsistence farmers.*

CLIMATE

WEATHER CHART

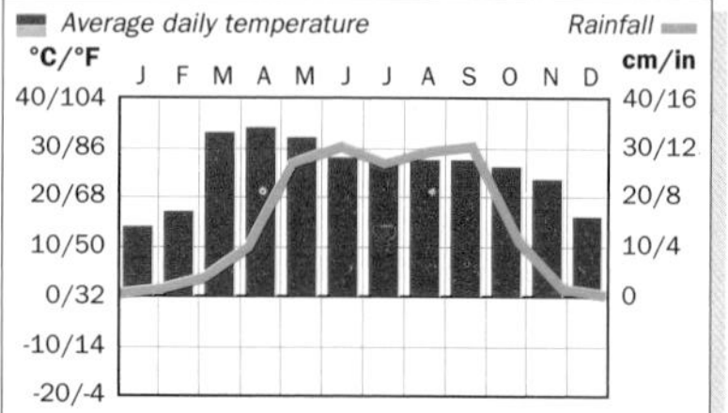

The tropical southerly monsoon brings heavy rains from May to September. For the rest of the year Laos has dry northerly winds and sunny skies.

COMMUNICATIONS

Wattay, Vientiane
165,000 passengers

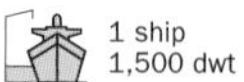
1 ship
1,500 dwt

THE TRANSPORTATION NETWORK

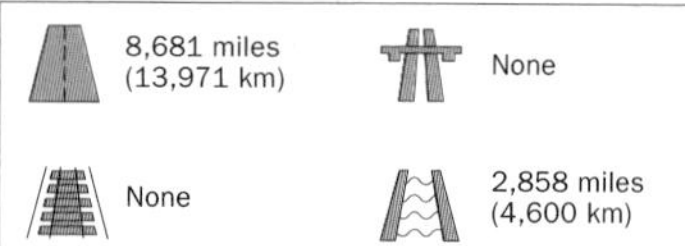

In 1994, a bridge was opened over the Mekong in Vientiane, creating the first road link between Thailand and Laos. Foreigners may enter Laos only via this route or by air to Vientiane. Other roads lead into Vietnam and Cambodia.

PEOPLE

Lao, Miao, Yao, Vietnamese, Chinese, French

44 people per sq. mile

THE URBAN/RURAL POPULATION SPLIT

Urban	Rural
19%	81%

RELIGIOUS PERSUASION

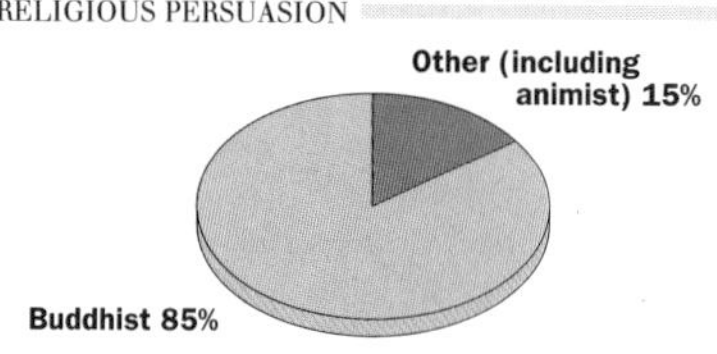

ETHNIC MAKEUP

Other 1%
Lao Soung 9%
Lao Theung 34%
Lao Loum 56%

POPULATION AGE BREAKDOWN

% of population by age group	1960	1970	1980	1990	2000
65+	2.4%	2.6%	2.8%	3%	3%
15–64	55.5%	55.1%	55.2%	53.4%	52.6%
0–14	42.1%	42.3%	42%	43.6%	44.4%

There are more than 60 ethnic groups in Laos, and this considerable diversity has hindered national integration. Society is broadly divided by altitude rather than by region.

The lowland Laotians *(Lao Loum)*, who make up the majority of the population and are mostly ethnic Lao, reside in the river valleys along the Mekong River and practice wet rice agriculture. The upland Laotians *(Lao Theung)* live in the hills above the valleys and practice slash-and-burn agriculture. Efforts by the government in Vientiane to alter this traditional form of farming, which can destroy forests and watersheds, have been resisted by the people.

Similarly, the mountain-top Laotians *(Lao Soung)*, who include the Hmong, Yao and Man groups, have resisted government efforts to introduce substitutes for traditional cash crops such as opium. The Hmong, in particular, are distanced from the Vientiane leadership. Tens of thousands fled to Thailand when the LPRP took power in 1975. Today, the government continues to face small pockets of Hmong resistance.

Two-thirds of the population speak Lao and a large number of tribal dialects are also spoken. Buddhism is the main religion, but there are some Christians and animists.

TOURISM

80,000 visitors

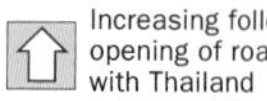
Increasing following opening of road link with Thailand

Tourists were first allowed into Laos in 1989. The government is shunning mass-market development, encouraging expensive package tours in small groups. Hotels are few, and travel outside the Vientiane area is difficult, as passes must be obtained for each province. Thai entrepreneurs are funding some new hotels.

MAIN OVERSEAS ARRIVALS

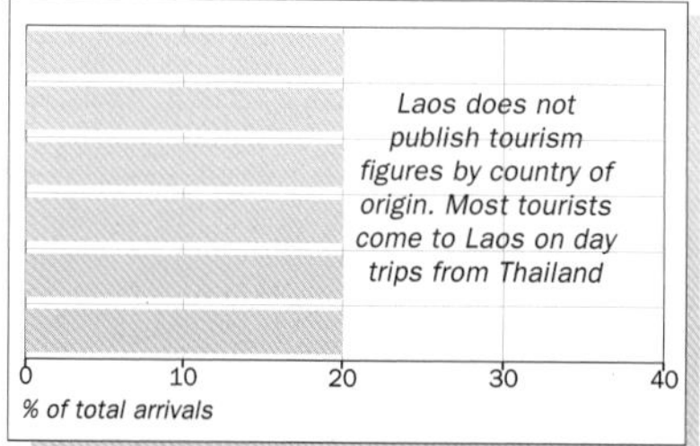

***President Nouhak Phoumsavanh,** who took office in November 1992.*

***General Khamtay Siphandon,** prime minister and head of the armed forces.*

POLITICS

Uncertain

President Nouhak Phoumsavanh

THE STATE OF THE PARTIES

National Assembly 85 members

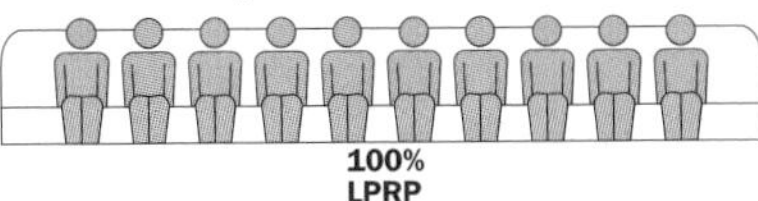

LPRP = Lao People's Revolutionary Party
Many candidates ran as independents, but all were effectively approved by the LPRP

Laos is a communist, one-party state under the direct control and administration of the LPRP.

MAIN POLITICAL ISSUES

Political reform
Reforms are currently being introduced to modernize key state functions. The country's first written constitution was adopted in 1991, and a modern legal infrastructure has been introduced.

The LPRP has begun to relax its total hold on power. The executive branch of government appears to be asserting its authority, although it still relies on the Party for broad guidelines. The legislative branch is also taking more initiative and the National Assembly is no longer simply a rubber stamp for Party edicts.

Central control
Tensions continue to be felt between the communist government in the Vientiane capital and the rural areas, where the rank and file of the LPRP and the military have their roots. There is particular resistance to central attempts to alter traditional farming methods.

PROFILE

Laos has been ruled by the same circle of communist revolutionaries since 1975. They have proved to be one of the world's most durable and closely knit hierarchies.

The vacuum left by the death of long-time Party leader, Kaysone Phomvihane, in 1992, was quickly filled by his protégés, who show no sign of deviating from the path he laid down. The military, the Party and the executive branch remain closely intertwined. Despite limited moves toward political reform, the LPRP, which is modeled on the Vietnam Communist Party, continues to dominate political life at every level.

The long-standing problem of corruption, sometimes at high levels, has become a matter of concern as Laos has opened to foreign investors. Concern that this may lead to a loss of faith has led to government crackdowns.

WORLD AFFAIRS

NAM | ADB | CP | ESCAP

Throughout the 1960s and 1970s, Vietnam was Laos's most important ally. In the 1980s, after many years of political isolation, the party leadership in Vientiane began to seek improved relations with the outside world, the West in particular. Closer ties with Japan and rapprochement with both Thailand and with former enemies, the USA and France, were secured. The motivation was mainly the need for foreign aid.

Following the collapse of communism in Eastern Europe, Laos turned to its northern neighbor, China, for ideological support and to counterbalance the growing influence of Thailand. At the same time, the government was careful not to jeopardize links with Vietnam.

In July 1992, Laos acceded to the Treaty of Amity and Concord of the Association of Southeast Asian Nation (ASEAN), marking a watershed in relations with its former adversaries in the region.

L

CHRONOLOGY

In the late 19th century France established control over the three small kingdoms of Champasak, Louangphrabang and Vientiane.

- **1893** Franco-Siamese treaty establishes French control over all territory east of the Mekong.
- **1899** Creation of a unified Laos under the French.
- **1941** Japanese seize power from Vichy French in Indochina.
- **1946** French rule resumed.
- **1950** Lao Patriotic Front, LPF, set up to oppose French rule. Gains support of newly formed communist Lao People's Party (LPP).
- **1953** Independence as a constitutional monarchy backed by France and the USA.
- **1963** LPF begins armed struggle against royal government through its armed wing, the *Pathet Lao*.
- **1964** US bombing of North Vietnamese sanctuaries in Laos; later escalated along the Ho Chi Minh trail.
- **1973** LPRP (formerly known as LPF) and royal government form a coalition after withdrawal of US forces from Indochina.
- **1975** LPRP seizes power, abolishes monarchy and proclaims Lao People's Democratic Republic. Premier Kaysone Phomvihane adopts policies for "socialist transformation" of economy.

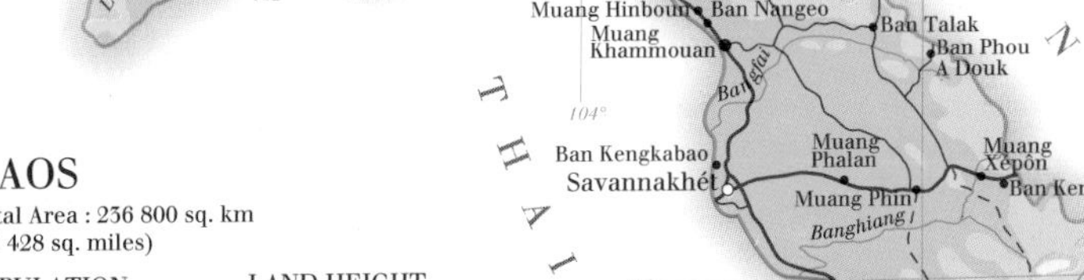

LAOS

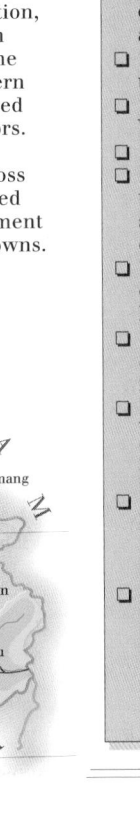

Total Area : 236 800 sq. km (91 428 sq. miles)

POPULATION
- over 100 000
- over 50 000
- over 10 000
- under 10 000

LAND HEIGHT
- 2000m/6562ft
- 1000m/3281ft
- 500m/1640ft
- 75m/246ft

0 — 100 km
0 — 100 miles

CHRONOLOGY *continued*

- **1976** Kaysone begins a series of visits to USSR and Eastern Europe.
- **1977** The Treaty of Friendship and Cooperation, providing for mutual assistance in national security, signed with Vietnam. Relations with China begin to cool.
- **1978** Resistance to collectivization. Series of natural disasters leads to rice shortages. After increasing internal dissent, the former King and Crown Prince are arrested and die in captivity. Almost 50,000 Laotians flee to Thailand.
- **1979** Softer economic line adopted and the speed of "socialist transformation" slows.
- **1983** Thirty-two state officials are convicted of corruption and anti-state activities.
- **1986** Fourth Party Congress makes market-oriented reforms.
- **1988** Brief border war fought with Thailand. Diplomatic relations restored with China.
- **1989** National elections held. All candidates approved by LPRP. Rapprochement with Thailand.
- **1990** Counter-offensives against right-wing, largely Hmong, guerrilla bases located in the outer provinces. Most agricultural collectives and state farms disbanded. Arrest of three former government officials for promoting multiparty democracy.
- **1991** A constitution providing for a National Assembly, confirming the leading role of the LPRP and enshrining the right of private ownership, is promulgated. Kaysone steps down as prime minister and takes up post of president. Khamtay Siphandon becomes prime minister.
- **1992** Death of President Kaysone. Khamtay takes over as head of the LPRP. Laos accedes to the Treaty of Amity and Concord of the ASEAN countries.
- **1994** Thai–Laos bridge opens over Mekong – first ever direct road link between the two countries.

AID

$131m (receipts)

Laos has one of the highest per capita aid inflows in the developing world. However, severe problems have been encountered in the implementation of aid programs. In the 1980s, Laos was heavily dependent on the USSR and Vietnam for aid. Today, donors include the IMF, the World Bank, the Asian Development Bank, France, Sweden, Australia and Japan.

DEFENSE

$18.94m

Increasing spending sourced from military-owned businesses

0 *Defense Spending as % GDP* 40

3.6%

The armed forces are estimated by the West to number over 50,000 personnel. This total is further swelled by a paramilitary militia. Military service is compulsory for all Laotian males for 18 months.

The military and the ruling LPRP have close links. The prime minister, Khamtay Siphandon, has long been considered the army's chief supporter in the politburo and served as defense minister from 1975 to 1991. In 1977, Laos signed a treaty with Vietnam, providing for mutual assistance in the event of a threat to national security.

LAOTIAN ARMED FORCES

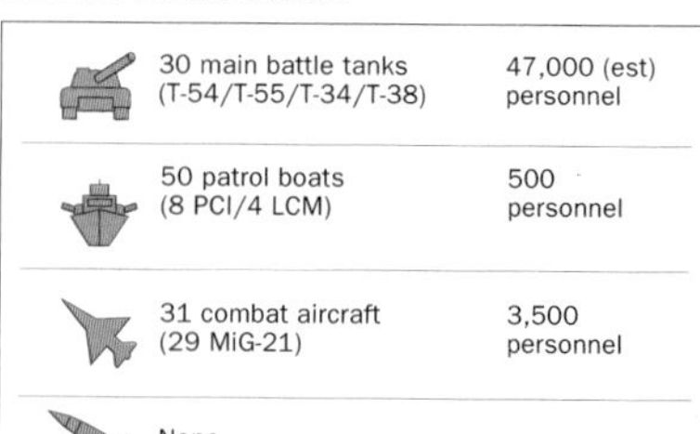

30 main battle tanks (T-54/T-55/T-34/T-38)	47,000 (est) personnel
50 patrol boats (8 PCI/4 LCM)	500 personnel
31 combat aircraft (29 MiG-21)	3,500 personnel
None	

ECONOMICS

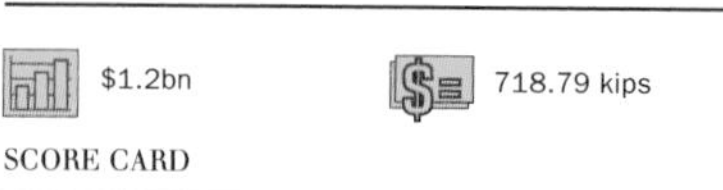

$1.2bn

718.79 kips

SCORE CARD

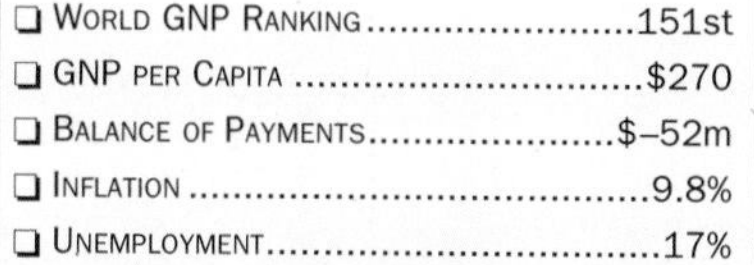

World GNP Ranking	151st
GNP per Capita	$270
Balance of Payments	$–52m
Inflation	9.8%
Unemployment	17%

EXPORTS

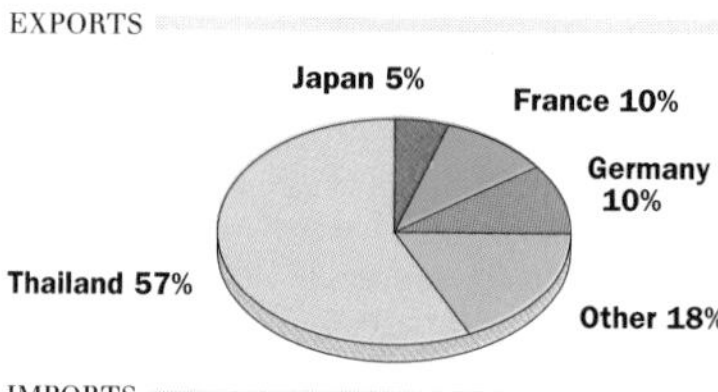

IMPORTS

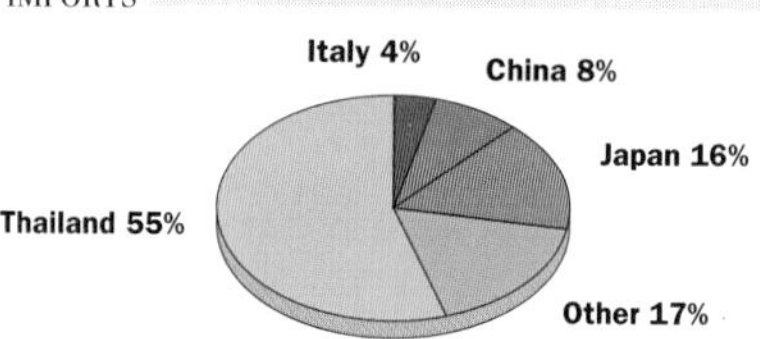

Strengths
Rising levels of overseas (mostly Thai) investment. Potential of garment manufacturing, mining, timber plantations, wood processing, tourism, banking and aviation. Minerals and possible oil and gas deposits.

Weaknesses
One of the world's 20 least-developed countries. Lack of technical expertise a major constraint to further development. Imbalance in sources of foreign investment – most is Thai. Problems in targeting aid efficiently.

Profile
The LPRP began introducing market-oriented reforms in 1986. The collapse of the Soviet Union, and the subsequent loss of Soviet aid and markets in Eastern Europe, increased the pace of this process in the early 1990s.

ECONOMIC PERFORMANCE INDICATOR

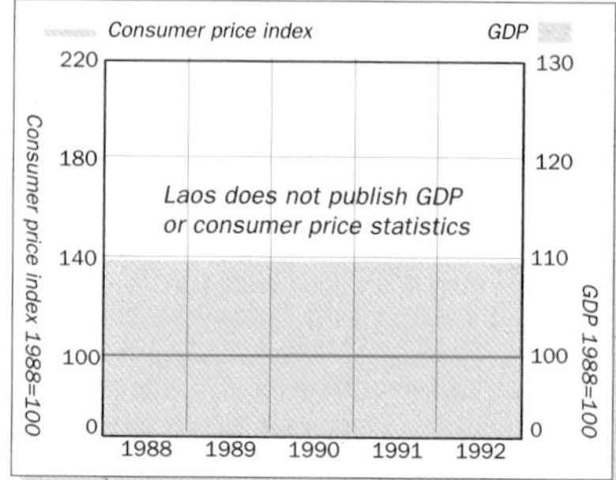

The reforms began by removing price controls on rice and other crops. This encouraged farmers to plant more and helped to establish a degree of food self-sufficiency.

In recent years, the currency has been floated, interest rates eased and trade freed from restrictions. Laos also became the first country in Indo-China to open its doors to foreign investment. However, most foreign interest has been confined to sectors that offer quick returns, such as services, and natural resource exploitation such as logging and mining. A number of state-owned companies, including the highly profitable national brewery, have recently been privatized.

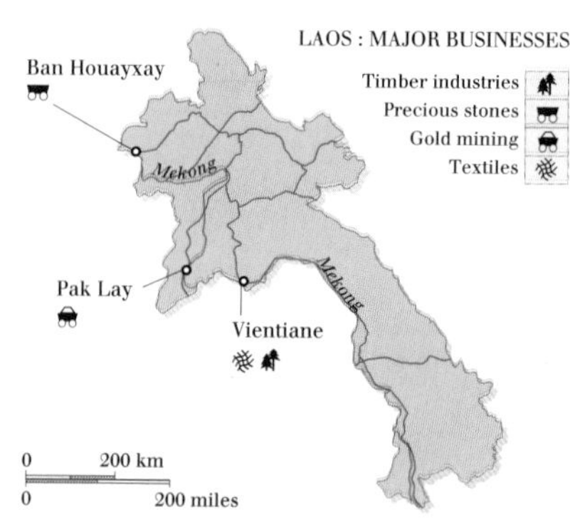

RESOURCES

Significant hydroelectricity generation

Not an oil producer and has no refineries

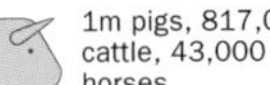
1m pigs, 817,000 cattle, 43,000 horses

Tin, gypsum, iron, copper, potash, lead, limestone, antimony

Laos's most important agricultural resources are timber and coffee. The country is rich in minerals. Important deposits include tin and gypsum (which are also exported), iron ore, copper, potash, limestone, antimony, manganese, lead and salt. An increasing number of foreign companies have been awarded concessions to mine for gold and precious stones. Two oil and gas exploration agreements with oil multinationals were also negotiated between 1990 and 1991. Laos's principal source of electricity is hydroelectric power. Surpluses are exported to Thailand.

ELECTRICITY GENERATION

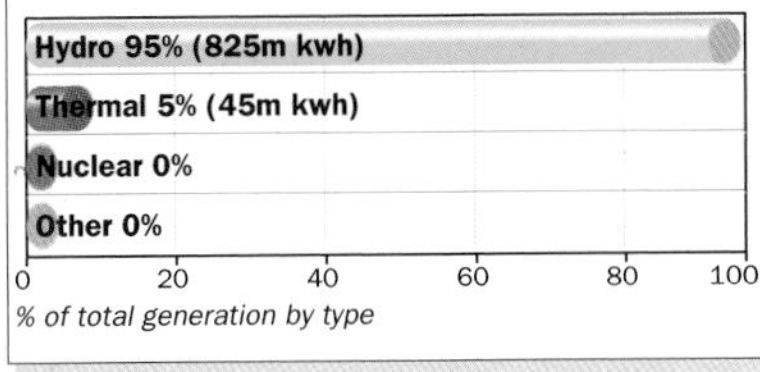

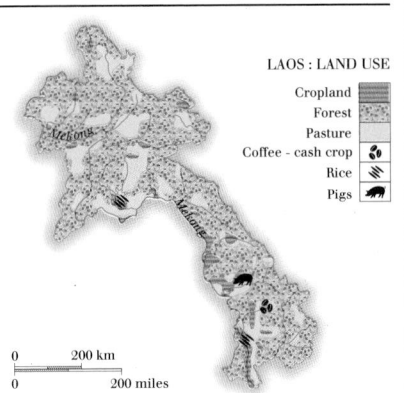

LAOS : LAND USE

Cropland
Forest
Pasture
Coffee - cash crop
Rice
Pigs

Mekong
Mekong

0 200 km
0 200 miles

ENVIRONMENT

None

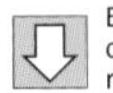
Building of more HEP dams will further reduce forest cover

Bombing and the use of defoliants in the Vietnam War did serious ecological damage. Slash-and-burn farming and illegal logging are destroying forests.

ENVIRONMENTAL TREATIES

WEALTH

Middle and high-level state officials, $20–$40 per month; trishaw drivers in Vientiane can earn nearly five times that amount

CONSUMER GOODS OWNERSHIP

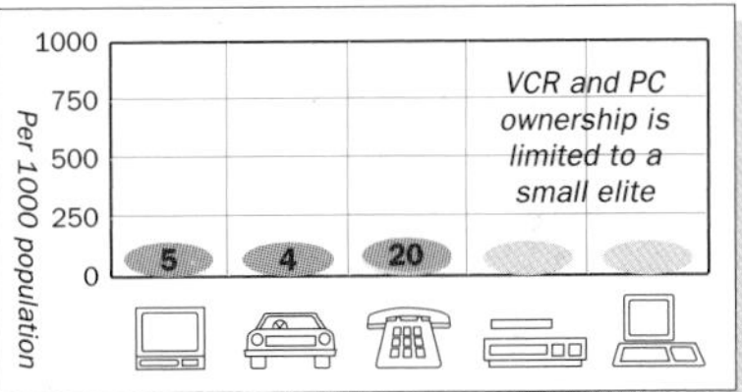

There are large inequalities of wealth in Laos. A rapidly expanding group of Laotian entrepreneurs is profiting from the liberalization of the economy. The elite live in French-style villas. Mercedes are fairly common in the capital and the number of motorcycles has doubled in the past two years.

Development is unevenly spread around the country. Many in the highlands and mountainous regions lead a subsistence existence, while farmers in the fertile Mekong Valley are relatively well-off. Most homes along the Mekong have TV sets which can receive broadcasts from Thai stations. Bribes are a key part of most bureaucrats' incomes.

MEDIA

Tight government control of media

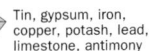

PUBLISHING AND BROADCAST MEDIA

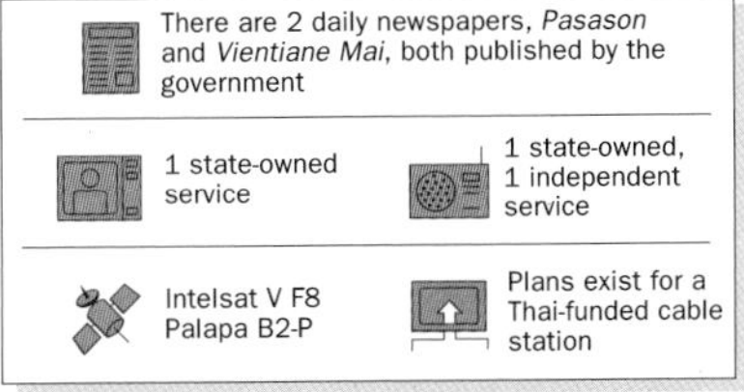

There are 2 daily newspapers, *Pasason* and *Vientiane Mai*, both published by the government
1 state-owned service
1 state-owned, 1 independent service
Intelsat V F8 Palapa B2-P
Plans exist for a Thai-funded cable station

Newspapers are owned and controlled by the party. Revelations of corruption by state officials do appear, but criticism of the Party and its leaders remains taboo. In 1990, the illegal Radio Station of the Government for the Liberation of the Lao Nation began broadcasting anti-government propaganda for four hours per day.

EDUCATION

50%

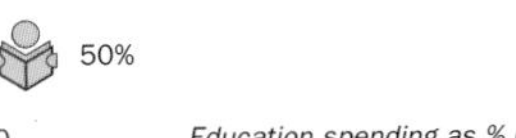

THE EDUCATION SYSTEM

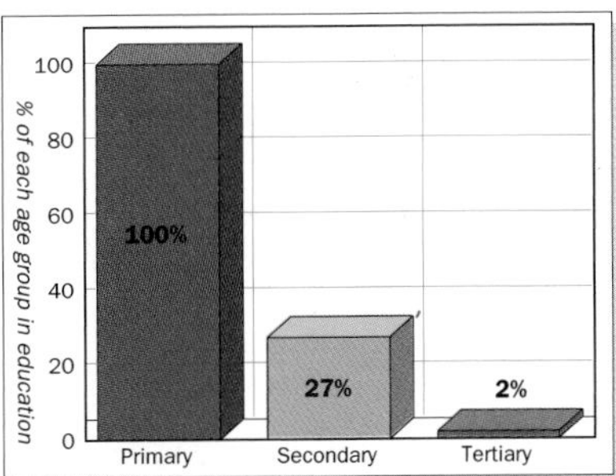

Literacy rates in Laos remain low, at 35% for women and 65% for men. However, adult education is currently being expanded and new schools are being built.

CRIME

Laos does not publish prison figures

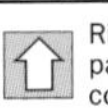
Rising overall, particularly corruption

CRIME RATES

Most crime is rising. However, the trend in mountain regions is hard to establish

Laos is the world's third largest opium producer. Since 1990 attempts have been made to combat the production and trafficking of illegal drugs. The USA is providing funds to substitute cash crops for poppies in the mountainous northeastern provinces.

HEALTH

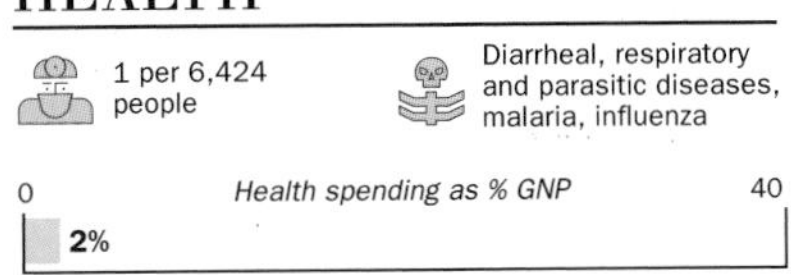

Poor sanitation and nutrition levels in most of rural Laos are reflected in the standard indicators of health and longevity. Infant mortality is over 10% and life expectancy is only 50 years. Malaria and hemorrhagic fever are on the increase.

WORLD RANKING

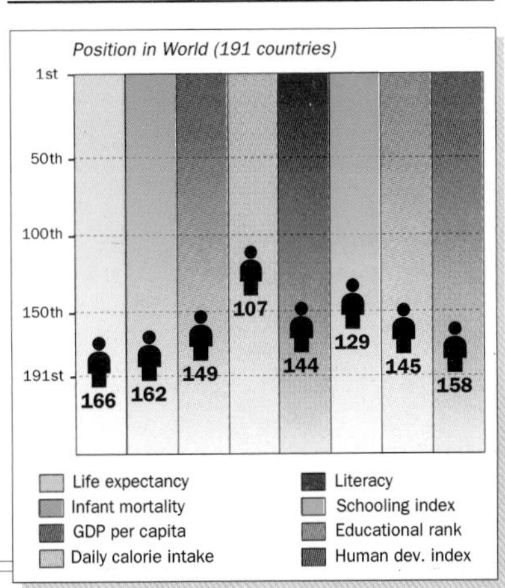

L

LATVIA

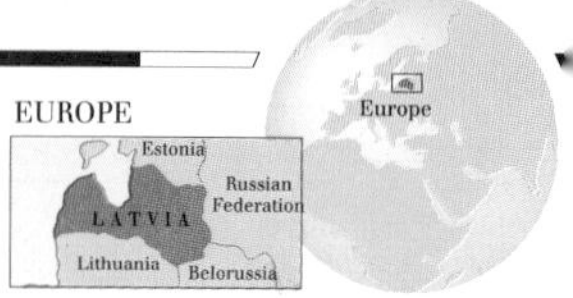

EUROPE

Estonia
Russian Federation
LATVIA
Lithuania
Belorussia
Europe

OFFICIAL NAME: Republic of Latvia **CAPITAL:** Riga
POPULATION: 2.7 million **CURRENCY:** Lats **OFFICIAL LANGUAGE:** Latvian

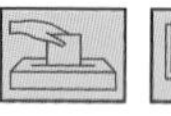

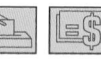

LYING BETWEEN Estonia and Lithuania, Latvia is situated on the eastern coast of the Baltic Sea. To the east it borders the Russian Federation and Belorussia. The whole country is a low-lying plain, which nowhere rises above 984 feet. Latvia's independence was recognized by Moscow in 1991. Defense-related industries and agriculture play an important role in the economy. Only 52% of the population are ethnic Latvians.

CLIMATE

WEATHER CHART

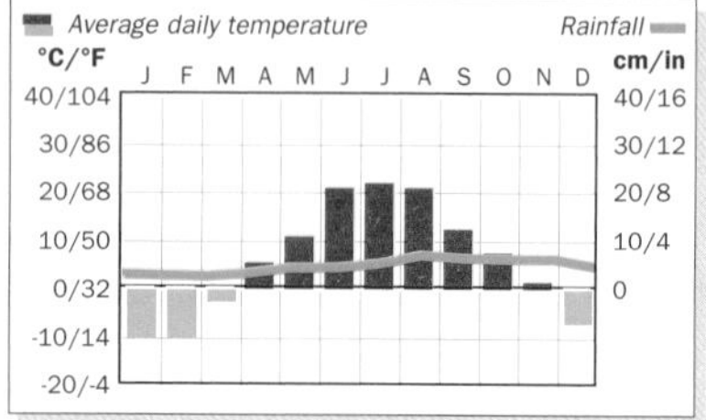

Latvia's coastal position means that the climate is temperate, with cold winters and cool summers.

The Russian Orthodox Cathedral in Riga. Used as a planetarium during the Soviet era, its interior is now being restored.

COMMUNICATIONS

Riga International

130 ships
1.34m dwt

THE TRANSPORTATION NETWORK

36,412 miles (58,600 km)

None

1,489 miles (2,397 km)

186 miles (300 km)

The planned Finland–Poland road will run through Latvia. Ports are being upgraded, particularly Ventspils and Liepāja. The EBRD is spending 10 million ECU on improvements at Riga Airport.

TOURISM

370,000 visitors

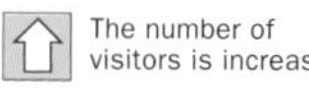
The number of visitors is increasing

MAIN OVERSEAS ARRIVALS

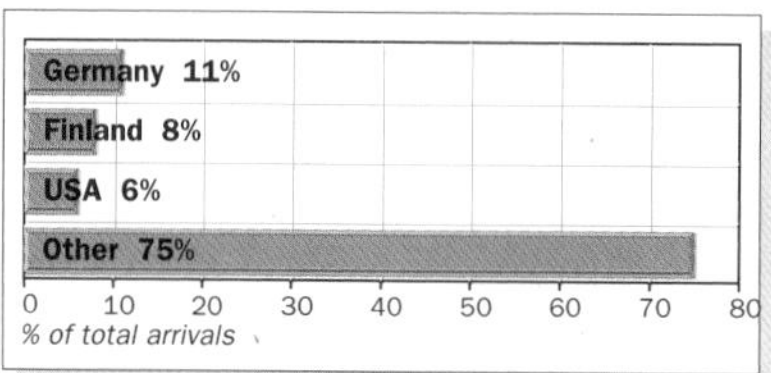

Riga is the main tourist destination, with many hotels and restaurants. Its medieval center is being restored.

PEOPLE

Latvian, Russian

109 people per sq. mile

THE URBAN/RURAL POPULATION SPLIT

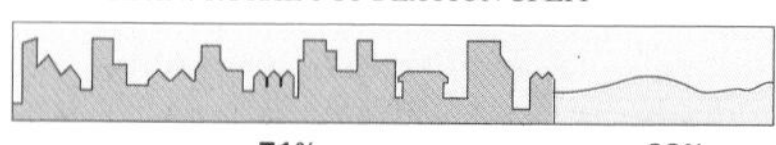

ETHNIC MAKEUP

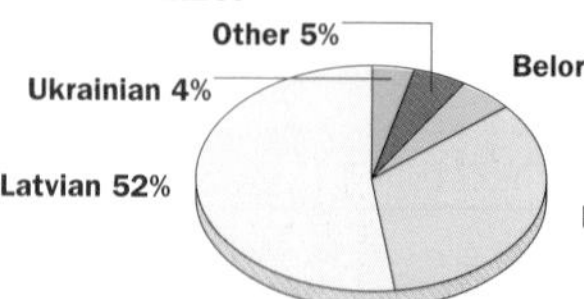

Latvians make up only 52% of the population, compared with 34% of Russians, and are a minority in the capital, Riga. Although some Latvians fear a potential cultural dilution, there is little tension between the various ethnic groups. Nevertheless, it is difficult for most ethnic Russians to become Latvian citizens. The status of women is on a par with Western Europe. The divorce rate is high.

POLITICS

1996

President Guntis Ulmanis

THE STATE OF THE PARTIES

Parliament (Saeima) 100 members

LW = Latvian Way **LNNK** = National Independence Movement of Latvia **HLRNE** = Harmony for Latvia and Rebirth for the National Economy **LZS** = Latvian Farmers' Union **ER** = Equal Rights **Other** = For the Fatherland and Freedom, Union of Christian Democrats, Democratic Center Party

The LW has become the strongest branch of the Popular Front (PLF), the group formed in 1988 to lead the campaign for Latvian autonomy under the Gorbachev regime. The political situation is now beginning to stabilize after the factionalism that followed Latvia's independence. The question of citizenship remains contentious. Full rights are only granted to those with families resident before 1940. This excluded two-thirds of the Russian minority from voting in recent general elections.

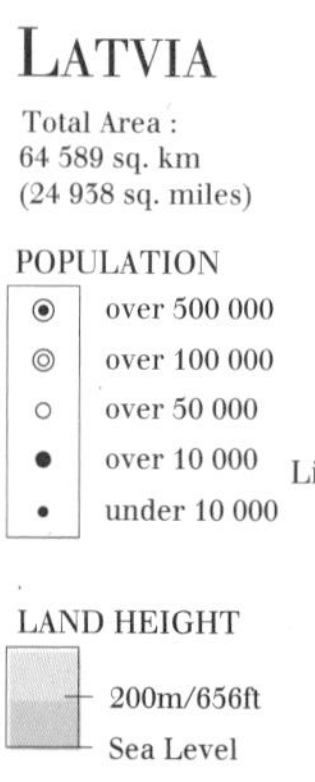

LATVIA

Total Area :
64 589 sq. km
(24 938 sq. miles)

POPULATION
over 500 000
over 100 000
over 50 000
over 10 000
under 10 000

LAND HEIGHT
200m/656ft
Sea Level

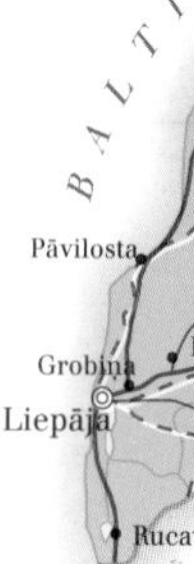

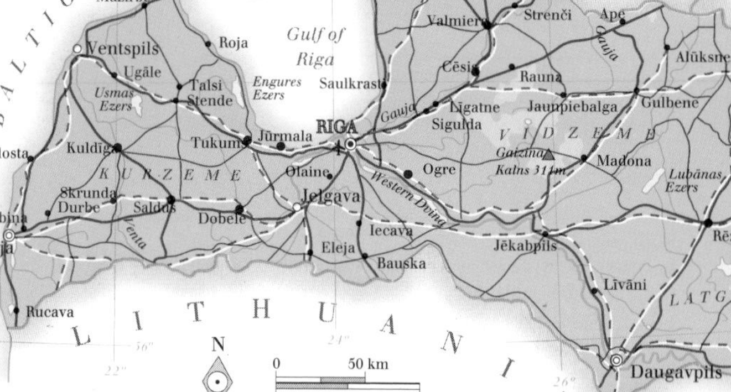

WORLD AFFAIRS

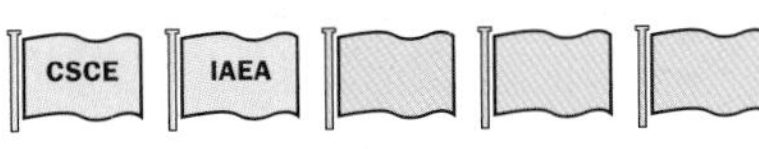

Latvia wishes to forge good relations with the EU, with the eventual aim of becoming a member. It is also eager to revive its pre-Soviet status as a country with close Western cultural and trading connections. Relations with Russia have recently cooled; Moscow's increasingly nationalistic foreign policy is the main cause.

AID

 Latvia does not publish aid receipts

 The trend is up

Aid to Latvia comes mainly from the World Bank, the IMF and the EU. Most of it goes toward improving the country's infrastructure.

DEFENSE

 $151.4m

 Rising now that Russian troops have left

Building up the military is a priority. The withdrawal of Russian troops from Latvian territory was completed in 1994. Stationed ostensibly to secure the rights of ethnic Russians, they were seen as a threat to security. Latvia is seeking closer links with Western forces and hopes to join NATO.

ECONOMICS

 $9.2bn

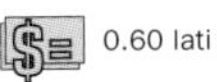 0.60 lati

SCORE CARD

❑ World GNP Ranking	81st
❑ GNP per Capita	$3,410
❑ Balance of Payments	50m
❑ Inflation	7%
❑ Unemployment	5.6%

Strengths
Well-developed industrial base, especially for defense-related industries. Numerous port facilities. Agricultural surplus.

Weaknesses
Lack of raw materials. Dependence on Russia for supplies of oil and natural gas. Slump in demand from former Soviet and East European trading partners for Latvian exports.

EXPORTS

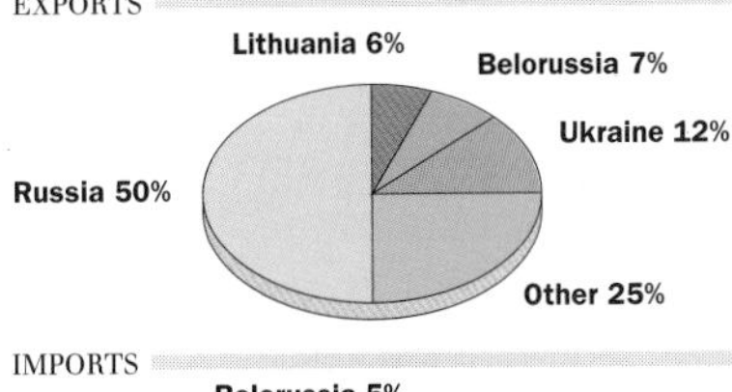

IMPORTS

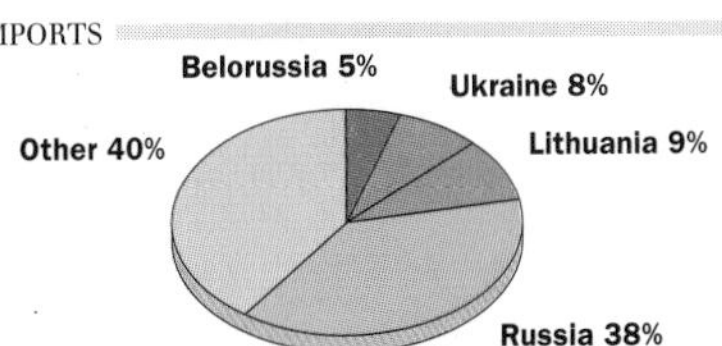

RESOURCES

 Electricity supplies are mainly imported

 Not an oil producer and has no refineries

12.2m poultry, 1.7m pigs, 1.5m cattle

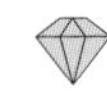 Amber, dolomite, gravel, gypsum, limestone

Latvia has no strategic resources and is dependent on imports to meet its energy requirements. In 1991, these represented almost one-third of total imports. Electricity supplies come mainly from Lithuania and Estonia, while oil is imported from Russia and Lithuania. New infrastructure is being built to broaden the supply network.

ENVIRONMENT

 3%

 Environmental issues' role in independence movement

Peat extraction – Latvia is 5% bog – has damaged the environment. Pollution of the Baltic Sea and general air and water quality are also of concern. Environmental awareness is strong. In the run-up to Latvian independence, green issues had a high profile.

MEDIA

 Officially none. Russians have restricted access to the media

PUBLISHING AND BROADCAST MEDIA

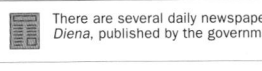

 There are several daily newspapers, including *Diena*, published by the government

 1 state-owned service

 1 state-owned service

The press is now relatively free from state interference. Previously the media was predominantly in Russian. Since 1991, the state, aiming to broaden the use of the official language, has actively promoted Latvian publications.

CRIME

 Latvia does not publish prison figures

 Crime levels are rising slightly

Levels of crime are lower than in other ex-Soviet republics, but organized crime is a growing problem.

EDUCATION

 98%

Education in Latvia is now following the German model. There are 46,000 students in higher education.

CHRONOLOGY

Latvia was dominated by Germany and, briefly, Sweden before Russia completed its conquest in 1795.

- ❑ **1917** Opposes Russian Bolshevik revolution. Declares independence.
- ❑ **1918–1920** Invaded by Bolsheviks in east and Germany in west.
- ❑ **1920** Gains independence.
- ❑ **1940** Soviet annexation.
- ❑ **1941** German occupation begins.
- ❑ **1944** Incorporated into the USSR.
- ❑ **1952** Armed resistance ends.
- ❑ **1987** Riga pro-independence rally.
- ❑ **1987** Latvian official language. PLF founded to group all reformists.
- ❑ **1989** PLF wins elections. Declaration of independence.
- ❑ **1991** Joins UN as independent state. Communist Party banned.

HEALTH

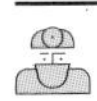 1 per 201 people

Cerebrovascular and heart diseases, cancer, accidents

The state-run health system is beset by shortages of medicine and equipment. Standards have improved little since the demise of communism.

L

WEALTH

 Secretary, 30–40 lati per month; dentist, 80 lati per month

CONSUMER GOODS OWNERSHIP

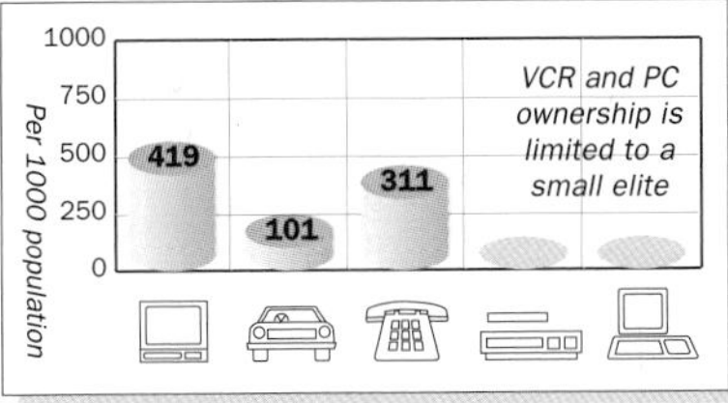

The old bureaucracy has retained its privileged status and contacts, and remains the wealthiest group.

WORLD RANKING

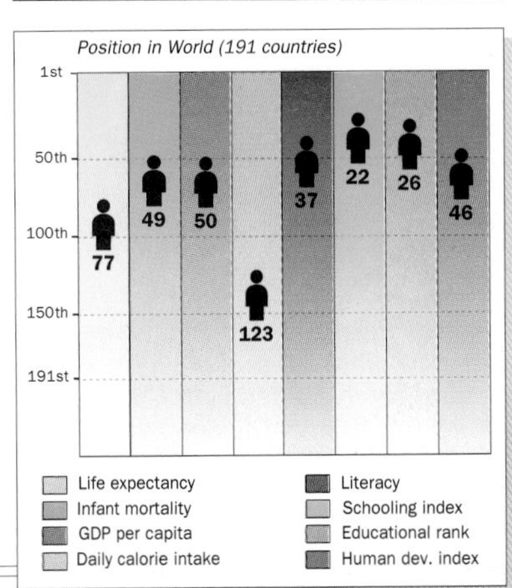

LEBANON

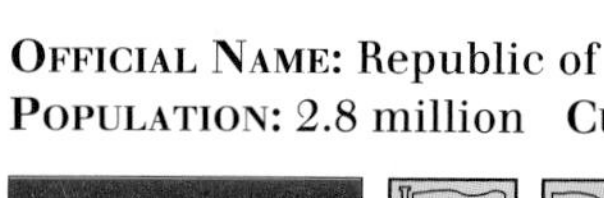

OFFICIAL NAME: Republic of Lebanon **CAPITAL:** Beirut
POPULATION: 2.8 million **CURRENCY:** Lebanese pound **OFFICIAL LANGUAGE:** Arabic

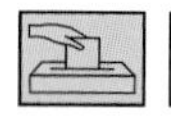

LEBANON IS DWARFED BY its two powerful neighbors, Syria and Israel. The country's coastal strip is fertile and the hinterland mountainous. Although in the minority, Maronite Christians have traditionally ruled Lebanon. A civil war between Muslim and Christian factional groups began in 1975 and threatened to lead to the breakup of the state. However, Saudi Arabia brokered a peace agreement in 1989. Elections were held in 1992.

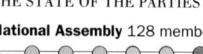

POLITICS

1996

President Elias Hrawi

THE STATE OF THE PARTIES

National Assembly 128 members

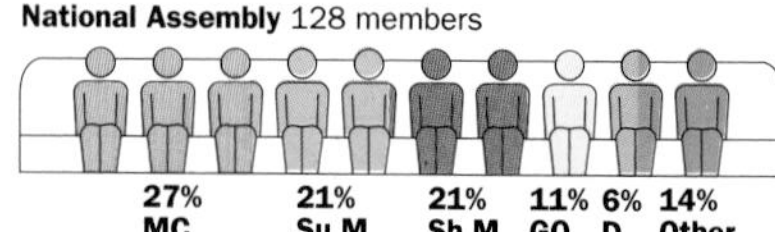

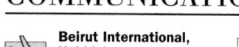

MC = Maronite Catholics **Su M** = Sunni Muslims
Sh M = Shi'a Muslims **GO** = Greek Orthodox
D = Druzes (religious sect linked to Islam)

The president must be a Maronite Christian and the prime minister a Sunni Muslim

Civil war broke out in Lebanon in 1975. The main cause was the breakdown in the Christian–Muslim consensus over the constitution, which gave Christians a disproportionate political voice. The presence of independent factions, each with its own grievances, added to the complexity of the war. Lebanon was close to fragmentation when the various factions agreed to terms for peace in Taif, Saudi Arabia, in 1989. This ended 16 years of civil war and effectively gave the Muslims more power. The elections held in 1992 were the first in 20 years. Under Prime Minister Rafiq Al-Hariri, Lebanon has achieved relative stability.

CLIMATE

WEATHER CHART

Average daily temperature — Rainfall
°C/°F: 40/104, 30/86, 20/68, 10/50, 0/32, -10/14, -20/4
J F M A M J J A S O N D
cm/in: 40/16, 30/12, 20/8, 10/4, 0

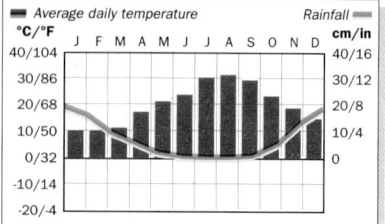

Winters are mild and summers hot, with high humidity on the coast. Snow falls on high ground in the winter.

PEOPLE

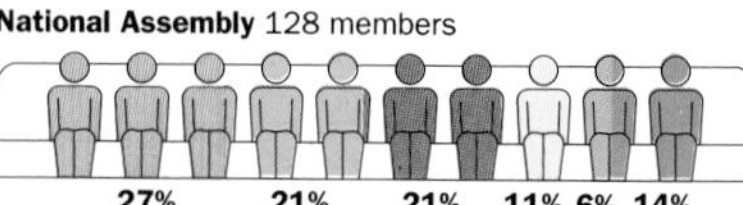
Arabic, French, Armenian, Assyrian

684 people per sq. mile

THE URBAN/RURAL POPULATION SPLIT

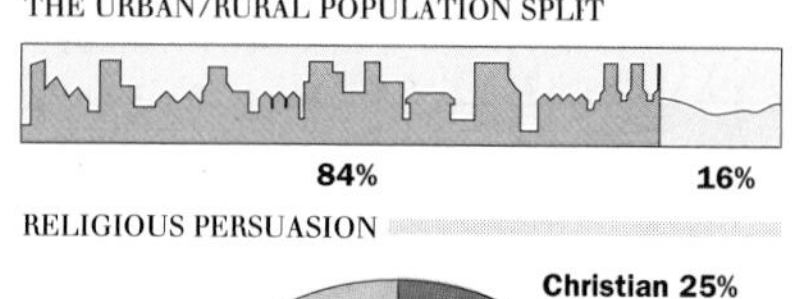

RELIGIOUS PERSUASION

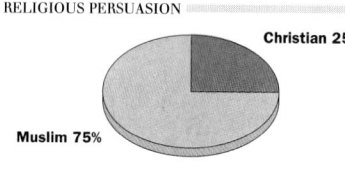

Christian 25%
Muslim 75%

The Lebanese population is fragmented religiously into sub-sects of Christians and Muslims, but retains a strong sense of national identity. There has been a large Palestinian refugee population in the country since 1948. Islamic fundamentalism is influential among poorer Shi'a Muslims.

COMMUNICATIONS

Beirut International, Kahldeh

139 ships 428,800 dwt

THE TRANSPORTATION NETWORK

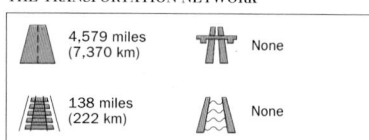

4,579 miles (7,370 km)

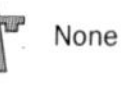
None

138 miles (222 km)

None

The redevelopment of Beirut could help it regain its position as one of the Middle East's major entrepôts.

TOURISM

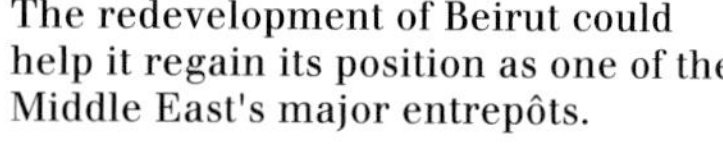
Lebanon still receives only a small number of visitors

The number of tourists is rising

MAIN OVERSEAS ARRIVALS

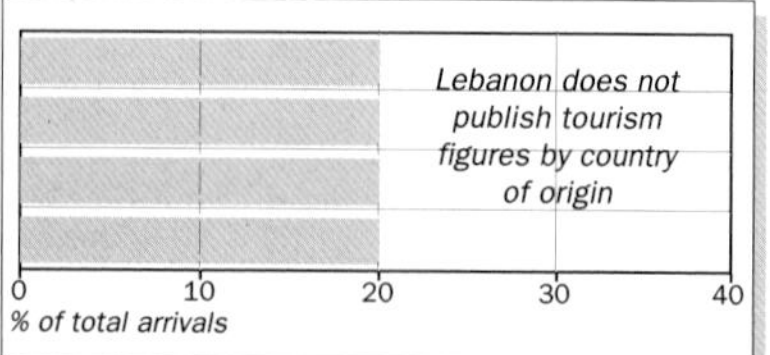

Once the playground of the Arab world where East met West, Beirut was devastated by the civil war, which ruined its profitable tourist industry. Formerly, over two million people a year visited its fine beaches and historical sites.

LEBANON

Total Area : 10 400 sq. km (4015 sq. miles)

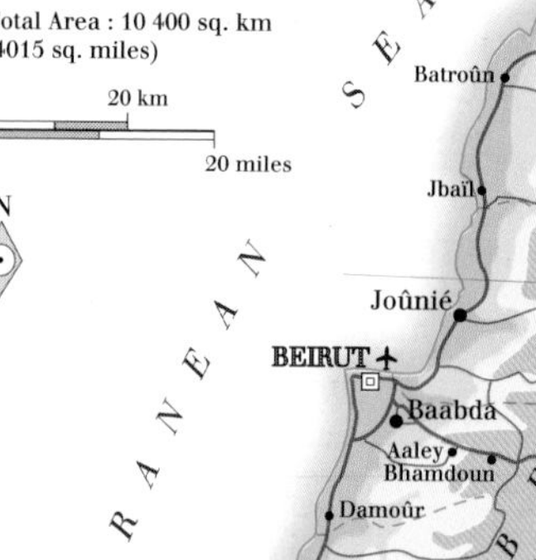

L

WORLD AFFAIRS

The civil war, hijackings, the Israeli invasion of 1982 and the Western hostage crisis brought Lebanon to the top of the international agenda in the 1980s. The 1989 Taif Agreement ended internal strife. More intractable is the Arab–Israeli dispute. The Iranian-backed *Hezbollah* militia, aided by Syria, and the Israeli-backed South Lebanon Army (SLA) still frequently clash in southern Lebanon.

AID

 $138m (receipts)

 Up 3% in 1991

The government is seeking billions of dollars to rebuild the center of Beirut and restore shattered infrastructure.

DEFENSE

 $173m

 Up 15% in 1992

Under the terms of the Taif Agreement 40,000 Syrian troops are stationed in Lebanon. Lebanon's own army has 21,000 troops. The south is controlled by the Israeli-backed South Lebanon Army. All the political factions maintain armed militias. A UN peacekeeping force attempts to police the border with Israel.

ECONOMICS

 $5.9bn

 1,835 Lebanese pounds

SCORE CARD

- ❑ WORLD GNP RANKING........................106th
- ❑ GNP PER CAPITA $2,107
- ❑ BALANCE OF PAYMENTS.................$-2,246m
- ❑ INFLATION 100%
- ❑ UNEMPLOYMENT..................................50%

STRENGTHS

Peace will allow Lebanon to regain its position as an Arab center for banking and services. Potentially a major producer of wine and fruit.

WEAKNESSES

Dependent on imported oil and gas. Infrastructure – especially in Beirut – wrecked by civil war. Agriculture still at 40% of pre-war levels. High public debt and inflation.

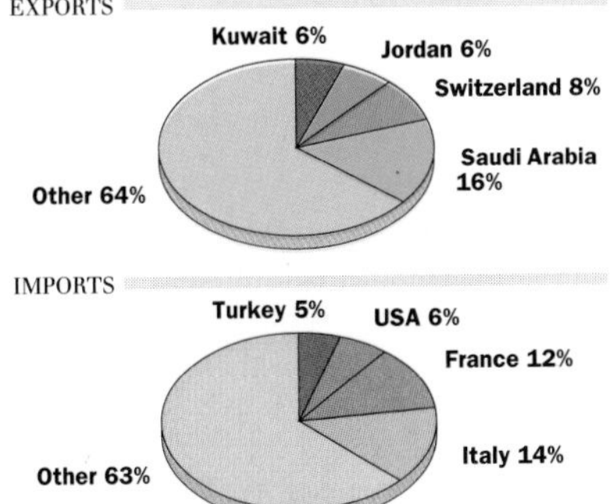

RESOURCES

 4.7bn kwh (capacity 603,000 kw)

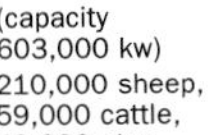 210,000 sheep, 59,000 cattle, 49,000 pigs

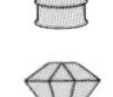 Not an oil producer; refines 37,500 b/cd

Lignite, iron ore

Wine, cotton, fruit and vegetables are the main crops. Thermal power stations are fueled by imported petroleum.

ENVIRONMENT

 0.3%

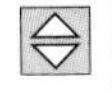 Initiatives will have to await reconstruction

Rebuilding Beirut's basic infrastructure and ridding the country of land mines are the government's priorities.

MEDIA

 The press has greater freedom than in any other country in the Arab world

PUBLISHING AND BROADCAST MEDIA

 There are 40 daily newspapers, including *Al-Anwar*, *An-Nahar*, and its French companion, *L'Orient-Le Jour*

 1 state-owned service

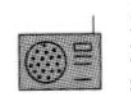 1 state-owned, 20 independent stations

Beirut could once again become a center for Arab media. However, in 1994 private TV stations were banned.

CRIME

 Lebanon does not publish prison figures

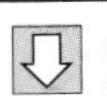 Crime is sharply down since 1989

The kidnapping of hostages and the breakdown of law and order during the civil war made Beirut a dangerous city for Western visitors. Politically motivated violence has recently declined, though the risk of urban terrorism remains. Rural areas untouched by the conflict have low levels of crime.

***The Corniche, Beirut,** due to be rebuilt by US consultant engineers and architects in a privately financed scheme.*

CHRONOLOGY

Lebanon became independent, after 20 years of French mandate, in 1944.

- ❑ **1975** Civil war erupts, stirred by Palestinian guerrillas evacuated from Jordan in 1970.
- ❑ **1982** Israel invades Lebanon and lays siege to Beirut.
- ❑ **1989** Taif Agreement brokered in Saudi Arabia. Civil war ends.
- ❑ **1991** Lebanon and Syria conclude security agreement. Release of most Western hostages secured.

EDUCATION

 80%

Lebanon has the highest literacy rate in the Arab world. However, education was severely disrupted by the war.

HEALTH

 1 per 771 people

Heart disease, infectious and parisitic diseases

An adequate system of primary health care exists. Hospital staffing is returning to pre-war levels.

WEALTH

 Minimum wage, 90 Lebanese pounds per month

CONSUMER GOODS OWNERSHIP

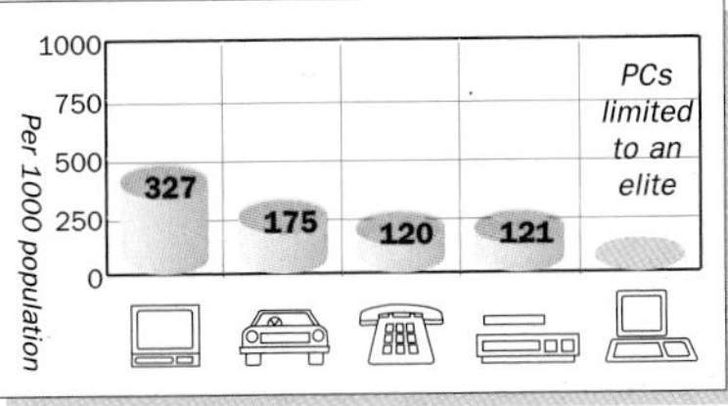

Average income per capita is low. A huge gulf exists between the poor and a small, massively rich elite.

WORLD RANKING

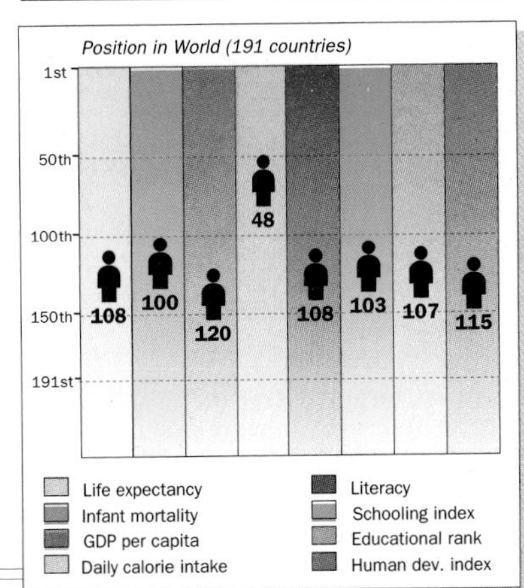

L

LESOTHO

SOUTHERN AFRICA
LESOTHO
South Africa
Africa

OFFICIAL NAME: Kingdom of Lesotho **CAPITAL:** Maseru
POPULATION: 1.8 million **CURRENCY:** Loti **OFFICIAL LANGUAGE:** English and Sesotho

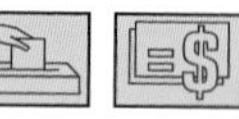

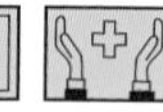

A MOUNTAINOUS AND landlocked country, Lesotho is entirely surrounded by South Africa. It is economically dependent on its neighbor, which provides all land transportation links with the outside world. The completion of the Highlands Water Scheme should bring major energy export revenues. Democratic elections in 1993 ended a period of military rule. About 38% of the male labor force are migrant workers in South Africa.

CLIMATE

WEATHER CHART

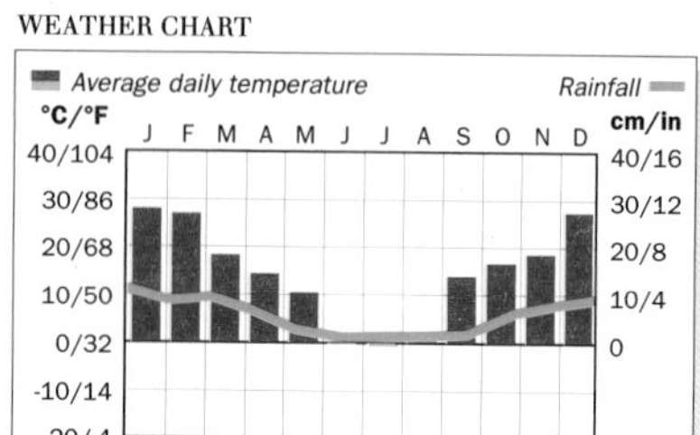

Drought is often followed by torrential rainstorms. Snow is frequent in winter in the mountains.

COMMUNICATIONS

Moshoeshoe Intl, Maseru
43,000 passengers

Has no fleet

THE TRANSPORTATION NETWORK

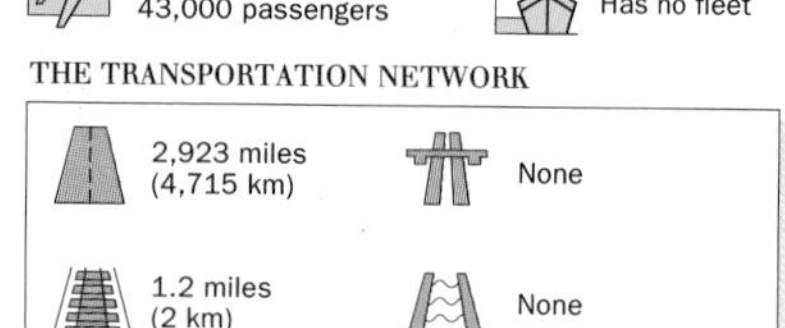

Lesotho relies on South African road and rail outlets. New roads have been constructed to service the Highlands Water Scheme.

TOURISM

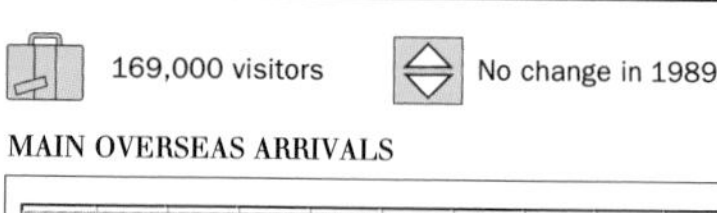

MAIN OVERSEAS ARRIVALS

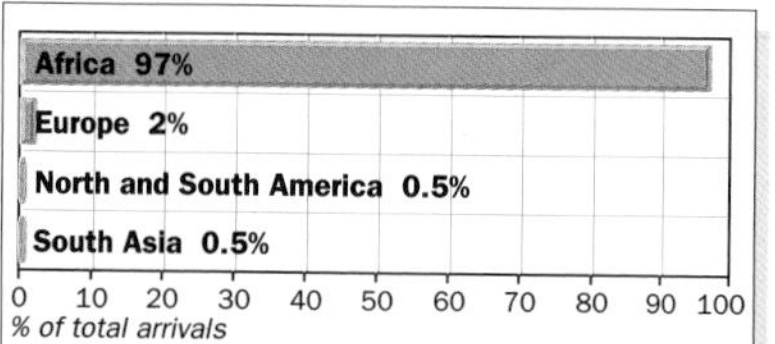

Tourism, largely based on Lesotho's spectacular mountain scenery, should benefit from South Africa's new political situation. Lakes created by Lesotho's HEP scheme will provide watersports.

PEOPLE

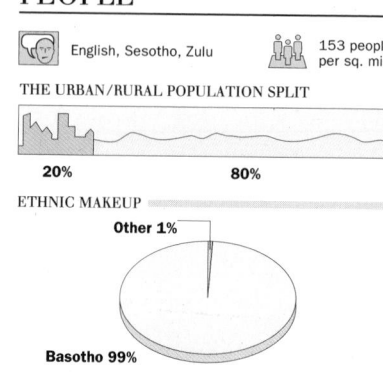

English, Sesotho, Zulu

153 people per sq. mile

THE URBAN/RURAL POPULATION SPLIT

20% 80%

ETHNIC MAKEUP

Other 1%

Basotho 99%

The overwhelming majority of the population is Basotho, though there are also Europeans and some South Asians and Taiwanese. Ethnic homogeneity and a strong sense of national identity have tended to minimize ethnic tension. However, South Asian and Chinese shopkeepers, whose control of business is resented, came under attack in riots in 1991. The export of male contract labor to South African mines means that women head 72% of households; they also run farming, regarded by Lesotho men as "women's work."

POLITICS

1998

HM King Letsie III

THE STATE OF THE PARTIES

National Assembly 65 members

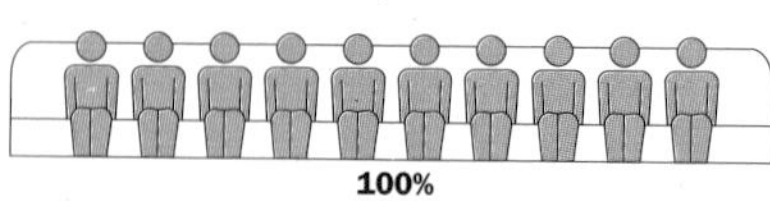

100% BCP

BCP = Basotho Congress Party

Senate 33 members

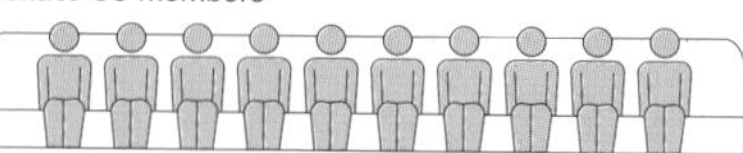

22 members are principal Chiefs and 11 are chosen by the King

The armed forces have been the key political players in Lesotho since 1986, when, following a South African blockade, Chief Jonathan's Basotho National Party (BNP) government was deposed and a military council assumed power. Colonel Elias Ramaema took over as chairman of the military council in a bloodless coup in 1991 and shortly afterward lifted the prohibition on political parties. Direct military rule ended in 1993, when free and peaceful general elections resulted in a sweeping victory for the BCP. However, a new constitutional clause gives the army precedence over the government in matters of national security, ensuring its continuing influence in politics.

The biggest single question dominating Lesotho politics is the future of the country itself as a sovereign state. Debate continues as to whether it should be integrated into a post-apartheid South Africa.

LESOTHO

Total Area : 30 350 sq. km (11 718 sq. miles)

POPULATION
over 100 000
under 10 000

LAND HEIGHT
3000m/9843ft
2000m/6562ft
1000m/3281ft

0 50 km
0 50 miles

WORLD AFFAIRS

Comm | OAU | SACU | SADC | GATT

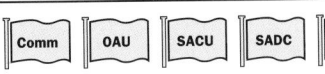

Foreign policy is dominated by the nature of Lesotho's relationship with South Africa. Lesotho currently has duty-free access for most manufactured goods to the EU and preferential access to US and Scandinavian markets.

AID

 $123m (receipts)

 Down 12% in 1991

Aid, over 50% of which comes from the Southern Africa Customs Union (SACU), is crucial to development and accounts for 26% of Lesotho's GNP. Most is concentrated in land yield projects, with the aim of making Lesotho self-sufficient in food.

DEFENSE

 $179.3m

 Increasing due to unrest

Many in the BCP are questioning the need for a 2,000-strong army, which poses a potential coup threat.

ECONOMICS

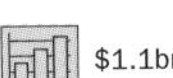 $1.1bn

 3.40 maloti

SCORE CARD

❑ World GNP Ranking	153rd
❑ GNP per Capita	$470
❑ Balance of Payments	$-70.3m
❑ Inflation	13%
❑ Unemployment	35%

Strengths
Membership of Southern Africa's Customs Union. Highlands Water Scheme, which will be a major revenue earner and employer.

Weaknesses
Economic over-dependence on South Africa. Weak agricultural sector, although it is the principal occupation. Lack of industrial development.

EXPORTS

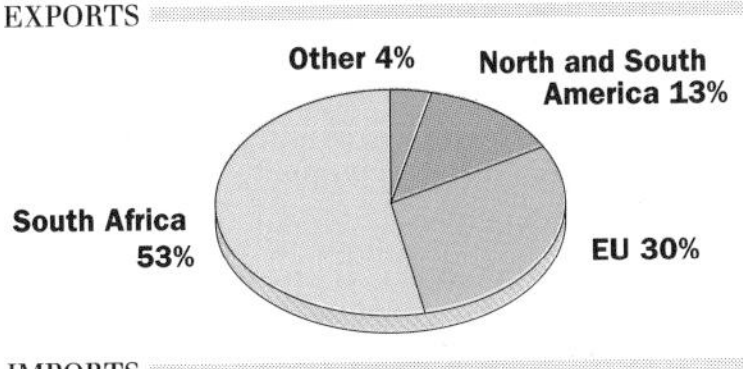

IMPORTS

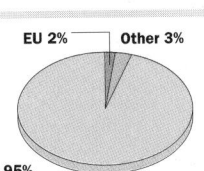

EU 2%
Other 3%
South Africa 95%

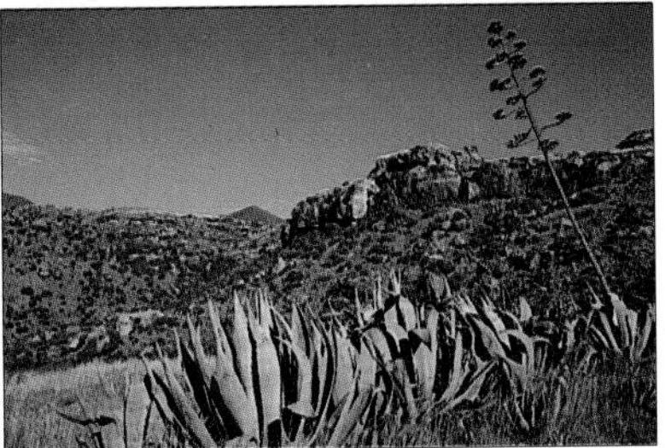

Near Mohale's Hoek in Lesotho's lowest lands, which are over 4,265 ft above sea level. This spiral aloe grows only in Lesotho.

RESOURCES

Over 90% of energy imported from South Africa

 Not an oil producer and has no refineries

 1m goats, 1m sheep, 530,000 cattle

 Diamonds

The hugely ambitious Highlands Water hydroelectric scheme will supply all of Lesotho's energy requirements; it will also supply 83 cubic yards of water per second for South African use. Diamonds are mined in the northeast.

ENVIRONMENT

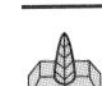 0.2% partially protected

 Government sensitive to environmental questions

Lesotho's land is seriously eroded due to the climate and overgrazing. There is also concern over the effects of the Highlands Water Scheme. The project's pylons are, however, bird-friendly, and there are schemes to protect the Maluti mountain minnow in its reservoirs.

MEDIA

 Censorship has been reduced since the previous military regime, under which the editor of the *Mirror* was deported to Kenya

PUBLISHING AND BROADCAST MEDIA

There are no daily newspapers. *Leselinyana la Lesotho* and *Moeletsi oa Basotho* are popular religious periodicals

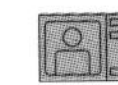 1 state-owned service

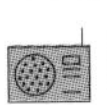 1 state-owned service

The *Mirror* is the only independent paper in Lesotho. Radio and TV broadcasts are in Sesotho and English.

CRIME

 Lesotho does not publish prison figures

 Up 34% in 1986

Crime levels are much lower than in South Africa. Robbery and corruption are problems in urban areas.

EDUCATION

 74%

Lesotho has one of the highest literacy rates in Africa, and the highest female literacy rate – 84%.

CHRONOLOGY

King Moshoeshoe I created a strong kingdom but sought British help after defeat by the Boers in 1843.

- ❑ **1884** British crown colony.
- ❑ **1966** Independent kingdom.
- ❑ **1970** PM Chief Jonathan of BNP annuls elections and bans parties.
- ❑ **1974** BCP, which had in effect won the elections, attempts coup.
- ❑ **1986** Maj.-Gen. Lekhanya leads successful military coup.
- ❑ **1990** King disagrees with military council. Exiled. Son elected King.
- ❑ **1991** Col. Ramaema seizes power.
- ❑ **1993** Free elections – BCP wins.

HEALTH

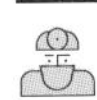 1 per 15,718 people

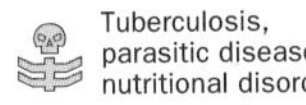 Tuberculosis, parasitic diseases, nutritional disorders

Private health organizations and NGOs are responsible for about half of all health services and are regulated by the Ministry of Health. Although the government operates a flying-doctor service, the highlands are still not adequately covered. The main endemic disease is tuberculosis.

WEALTH

 Welder, 260 maloti per month; professional nurse, 531 maloti per month

CONSUMER GOODS OWNERSHIP

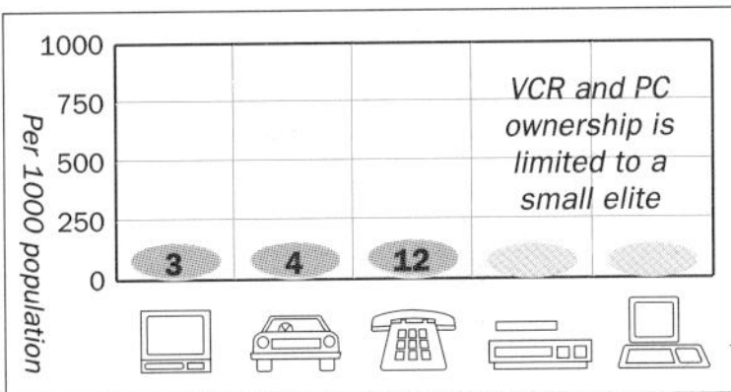

Social mobility is limited in Lesotho; the ruling elite keep a tight control on power and wealth. Over 90% of the population live below the poverty line.

WORLD RANKING

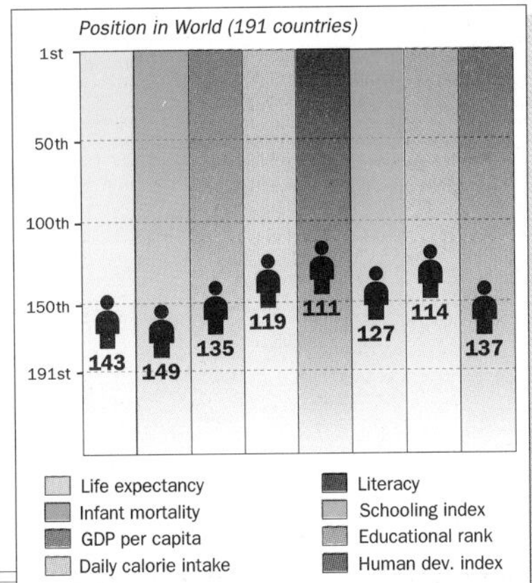

L

LIBERIA

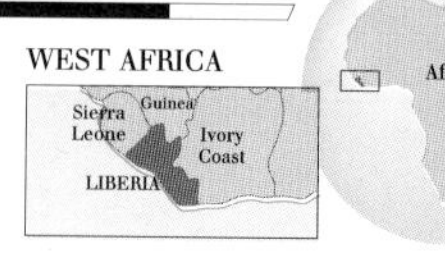

OFFICIAL NAME: The Republic of Liberia **CAPITAL:** Monrovia
POPULATION: 2.8 million **CURRENCY:** Liberian dollar **OFFICIAL LANGUAGE:** English

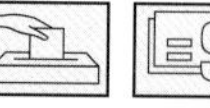

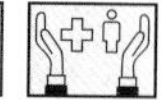

NAMED AFTER PEOPLE LIBERATED from slavery who began returning from the USA in 1816, Liberia today is a war-torn country in a state of anarchy, with private armies competing for power. Facing the Atlantic in equatorial West Africa, most of its coastline is characterized by lagoons and mangrove swamps. Inland, a grassland plateau supports the limited agriculture (just 1% of land is arable). Liberia has the world's largest flag-of-convenience merchant fleet.

CLIMATE

WEATHER CHART

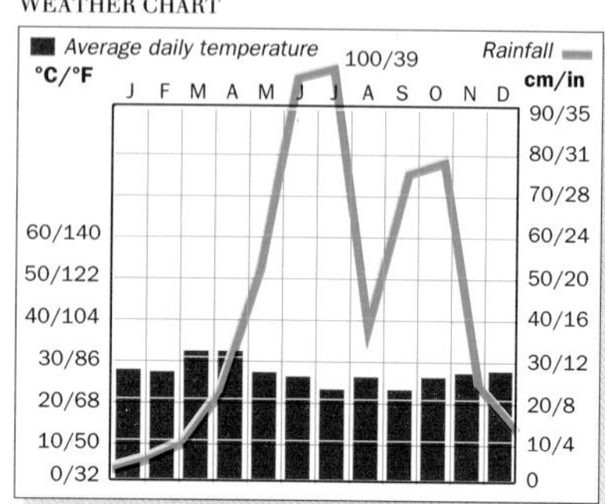

Except in the extreme southeast there is only one rainy season, from May to October. Temperatures are consistently high. During the October to March dry season when the dust-laden *harmattan* wind blows, they rise even higher inland.

COMMUNICATIONS

Roberts Field Intl, Monrovia

1,548 ships
95.9m dwt

THE TRANSPORTATION NETWORK

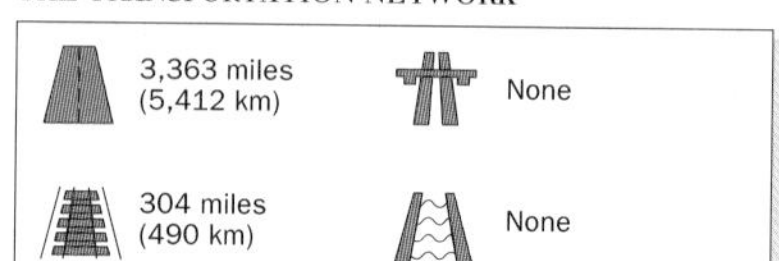

Most roads in Liberia are unpaved. The 304-mile railroad was built to transport iron ore and carries little other traffic. Roberts Field Airport was built by the USA during World War II.

TOURISM

No tourists due to war

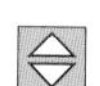
Not applicable

MAIN OVERSEAS ARRIVALS

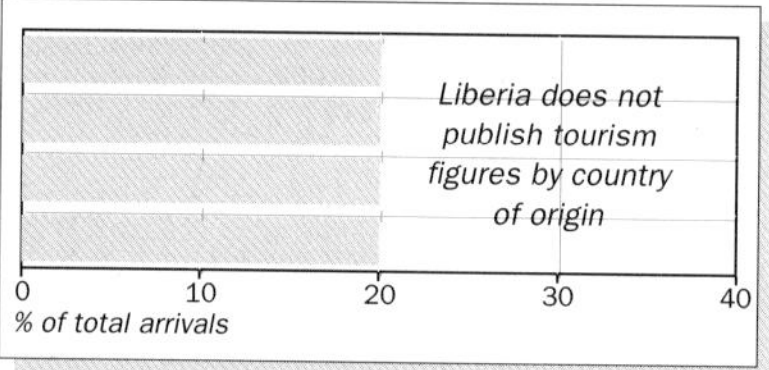

Liberia is an anarchic war zone. Few tourists visited the country before the war, and tourism has now ceased.

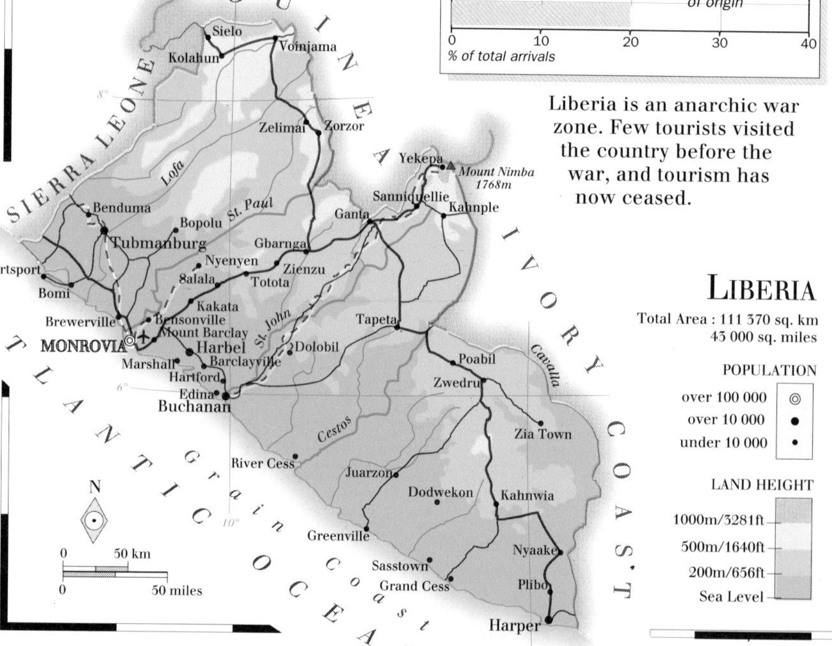

PEOPLE

Kpelle, Vai, Bassa, Kru, Grebo, Kissi, Gola, Loma, English

60 people per sq. mile

THE URBAN/RURAL POPULATION SPLIT

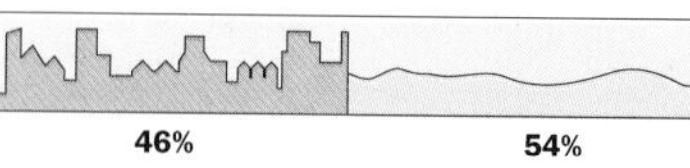

ETHNIC MAKEUP

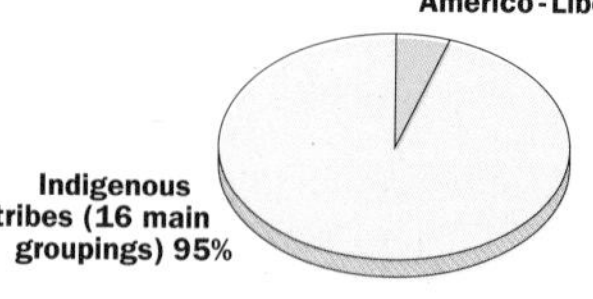

A key distinction in Liberia has been between Americo-Liberians, descendants of those freed from slavery (known as "civilized persons"), and the indigenous "tribals" majority. The latter were long held in contempt by the Americos, but intermarriage and political assimilation since 1944 have softened attitudes. Inter-tribal tension is now a problem. Conflict erupted during the 1990 invasion, when Samuel Doe's Krahn tribe exacted retribution from the Gio and Mano groups.

POLITICS

Uncertain

Dr. Amos Sawyer

THE STATE OF THE PARTIES

Interim Legislative Assembly

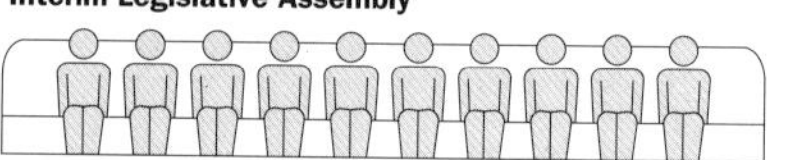

Liberia is in a state of chaos and its unelected parliament controls only the Monrovian region

Liberian politics effectively collapsed in 1990 into a chaotic, bloody and many-sided conflict, where the simple aim was the seizure of the spoils of office. The long period of Americo-Liberian rule had ended in 1980 when army sergeant Samuel Doe seized power. Doe executed the existing government and then succeeded in getting US backing. A series of armed invasions from neighboring states followed, prompting ECOWAS to send a peace-keeping force (ECOMOG) in 1990. ECOMOG turned aside from its role as peace-keeper in 1993 and launched an offensive to capture territory from the most successful of the armed groups, the National Patriotic Front of Liberia (NPFL) led by Charles Taylor. A nominal government in Monrovia has been led by Amos Sawyer since 1991. Doe was captured and executed, by a faction of the NPFL led by Prince Johnson, in 1991.

WORLD AFFAIRS

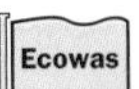

AfDB

The USA was the main foreign influence in Liberia until the arrival of ECOMOG (the army formed by Liberia's neighbors in ECOWAS), backed chiefly by Nigeria and Ghana. Burkina Faso, Ivory Coast and Libya are suspected of backing the NPFL, the main group fighting with ECOMOG for control of the country. In 1993, the UN refused a request to become involved.

AID

 $115m (receipts)  Up 95% from 1989

International agencies stopped providing aid in 1986. The USA continued giving aid to the Doe regime until 1990, despite his apparent misuse of funds.

DEFENSE

 $37.62m  Up 34% in 1989

Most of the private armies now operating in Liberia, including the official Armed Forces of Liberia (AFL), live by extortion and by intimidating local communities.

ECONOMICS

 $1.2bn  1.00 Liberian dollar

SCORE CARD

❑ WORLD GNP RANKING	152nd
❑ GNP PER CAPITA	$430
❑ BALANCE OF PAYMENTS	*The formal*
❑ INFLATION	*economy has*
❑ UNEMPLOYMENT	*collapsed*

STRENGTHS

Very few. The Firestone rubber plantation and huge LAMCO iron ore mine are under the control of the NPFL. Tropical timber, but reserves declining.

WEAKNESSES

Little commercial activity. State of anarchy since 1990 has led to collapse of the economy.

EXPORTS

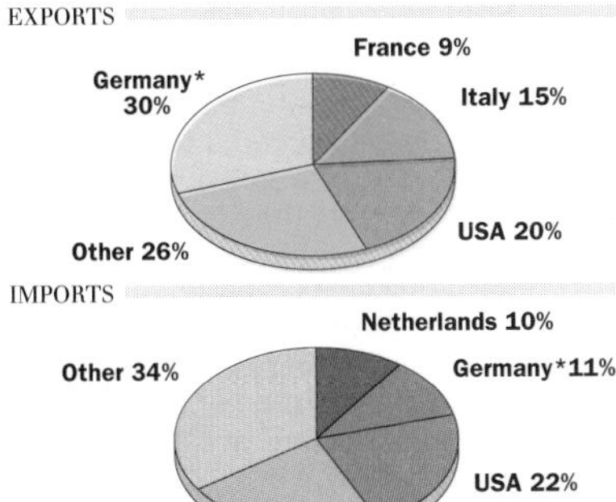

Village near Gbarnga. The Kpelle, the largest of Liberia's 16 indigenous ethnic groups, are concentrated in this part of Liberia.

RESOURCES

 565m kwh (capacity 0.33m kw)

 Not an oil producer; refines 15,000 b/cd

 240,000 sheep, 140,000 pigs, 42,000 cattle

 Iron ore, diamonds, gold, barytes, kyanite, columbite, manganese

Liberia has an estimated one billion tons of iron ore reserves at Mount Nimba. Even if peaceful conditions existed, the current state of world demand would not justify exploitation.

ENVIRONMENT

 1%  Civil war makes environmental initiatives impossible

The NPFL, and other armed groups have cut down tropical forests to finance their armies.

MEDIA

 Criticism of the government in the press was dangerous from 1980 until the fall of the Doe regime in 1991

PUBLISHING AND BROADCAST MEDIA

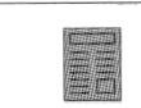 There are 2 daily newspapers: the independent *Daily Observer* and *The News*, published by the government

 1 state-owned service

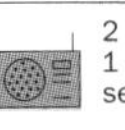 2 state-owned, 1 independent service

The Monrovia press has been freer since the fall of Doe, but distribution problems in a state of war lessen the impact of newspapers.

CRIME

 Liberia does not publish prison figures  Crime is rampant. There are no enforcing agencies

Human rights have little importance in Liberian life, and since 1990 have disappeared altogether. The warring factions have regularly massacred civilians, press-ganged armies, and displaced thousands into seeking refuge in neighboring states.

EDUCATION

 39%

Originally based on the US model, the education system has effectively collapsed during the civil war.

CHRONOLOGY

Between 1816 and 1892, 22,000 people liberated from slavery, most from the USA, resettled in Liberia.

- ❑ **1847** Established as an independent republic.
- ❑ **1926** US Firestone Rubber Company granted 405,000-hectare concession.
- ❑ **1930s** Interior brought under Monrovia's control.
- ❑ **1971** William Tolbert president.
- ❑ **1980** Coup. Tolbert assassinated by Master Sergeant Samuel Doe.
- ❑ **1990** Civil war grips whole country.
- ❑ **1991** Fall of Doe government.

HEALTH

 1 per 1,625 people  Communicable, diarrheal, parasitic and heart disease

Only the Americo-Liberian community had ready access to health care before the current state of war. Adequate care is now limited to the military.

WEALTH

 The underclass was composed of rural dwellers, but since the war started, it has encompassed most of the population

CONSUMER GOODS OWNERSHIP

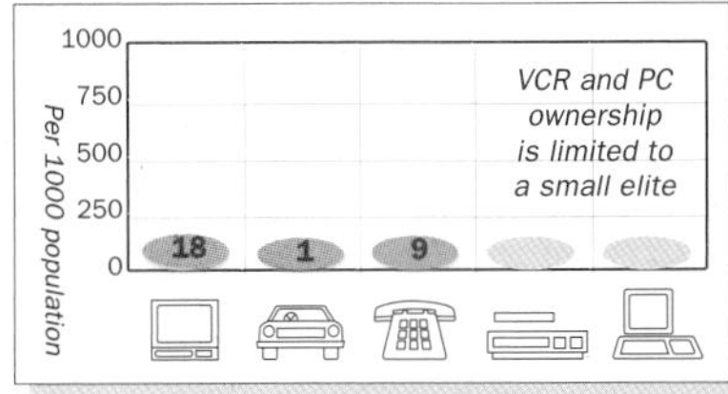

Power and wealth have a very direct connection in Liberia. Both the Americo-Liberian regimes, and Doe who replaced them, saw the state as a source of plunder in the form of well-paid jobs and kick-backs from contracts. Current warring factions seek similar power.

WORLD RANKING

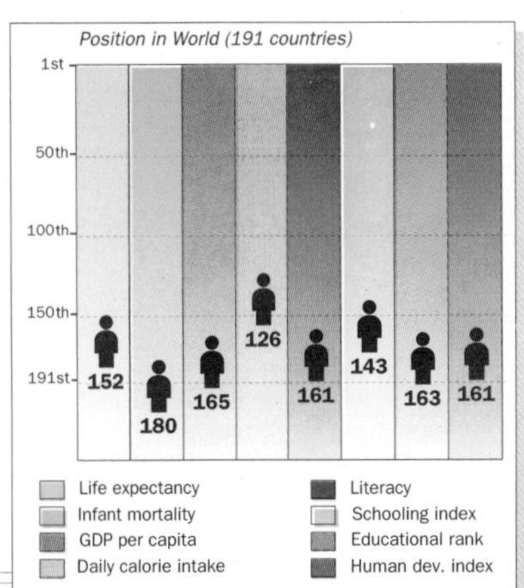

L

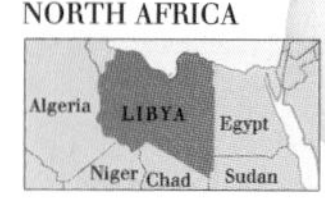

LIBYA

OFFICIAL NAME: The Great Socialist People's Libyan Arab Jamahiriya
CAPITAL: Tripoli **POPULATION:** 4.9 million **CURRENCY:** Libyan dinar **OFFICIAL LANGUAGE:** Arabic

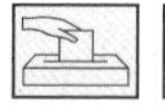

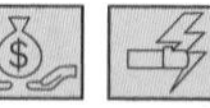

LIBYA IS SITUATED between Egypt and Algeria on the Mediterranean coast of North Africa, with Chad and Niger on its southern borders. Apart from the coastal strip and the mountains in the south, the country is desert or semi-desert. Libya's strategic position in North Africa and abundant oil and gas resources made it an important trading partner for European nations. However, it has been politically marginalized by the West for its past links with terrorist groups. Libya is also under UN sanctions for refusing to extradite two men suspected of the 1988 Lockerbie bombing.

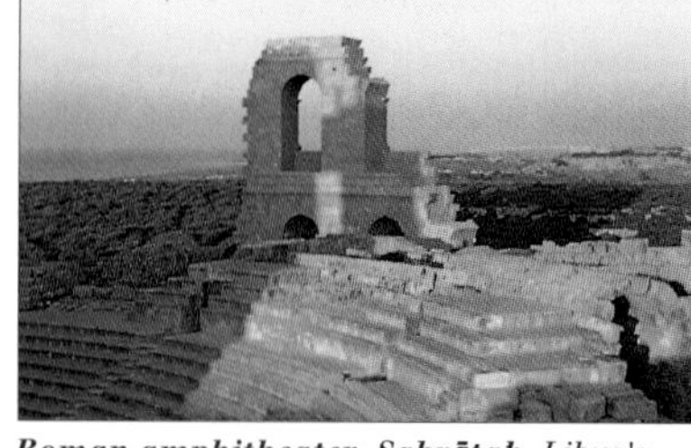

Roman amphitheater, Sabrātah. *Libya's impressive Classical heritage testifies to its importance in ancient times.*

CLIMATE

WEATHER CHART

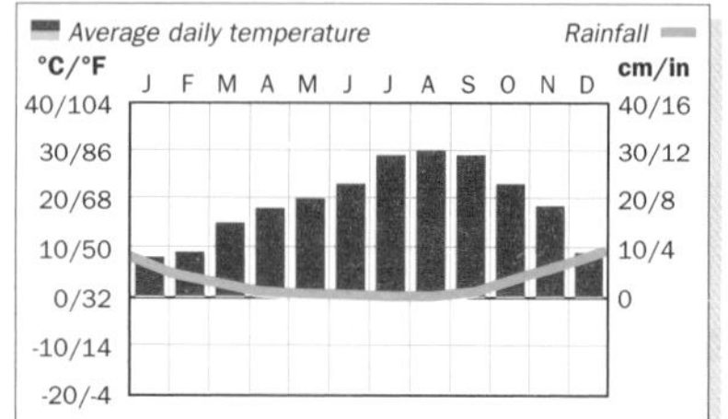

The coastal region has a warm, temperate climate, with mild, wet winters and hot, dry summers.

COMMUNICATIONS

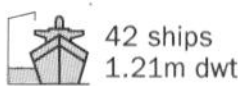

THE TRANSPORTATION NETWORK

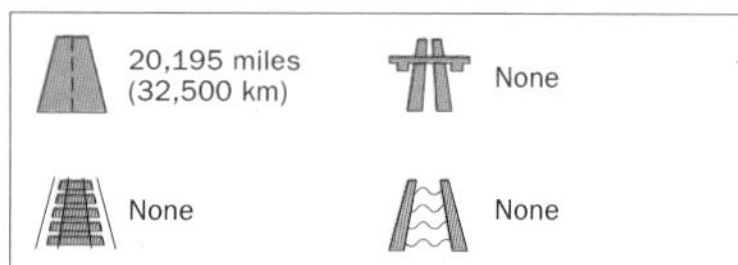

The National Coast Road runs 1,130 miles from the Tunisian to the Egyptian borders, linking the principal urban centers. There are no railroads, though some are planned. Due to UN sanctions on international flights, the major transit point is through Tunisia.

Al Kufrah Oasis. *As 90% of Libya is arid rock and sand, oases provide essential agricultural land, besides being tourist attractions.*

TOURISM

Little change from year to year

Libya possesses a rich Roman and Greek heritage, centered on the ancient Roman towns of Labdah (Leptis Magna) and Sabrātah near Tripoli, and Shaḥḥāt (Cyrene) further east. There are fine beaches at Tripoli, which is also famous for its annual International Fair. However, UN sanctions on air links with Libya have effectively closed the country to Western tourists.

MAIN OVERSEAS ARRIVALS

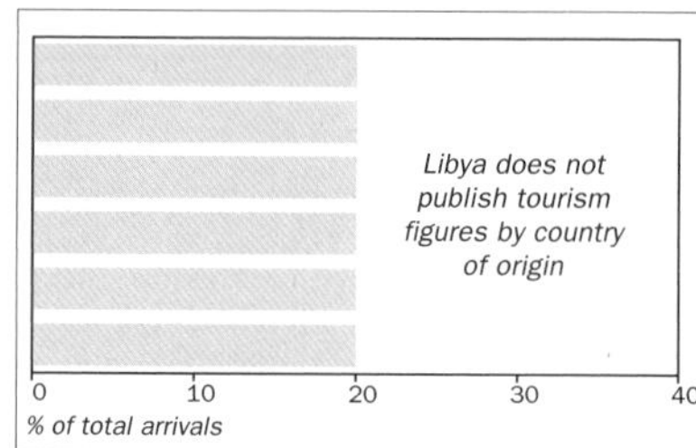

PEOPLE

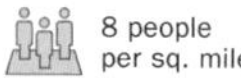

THE URBAN/RURAL POPULATION SPLIT

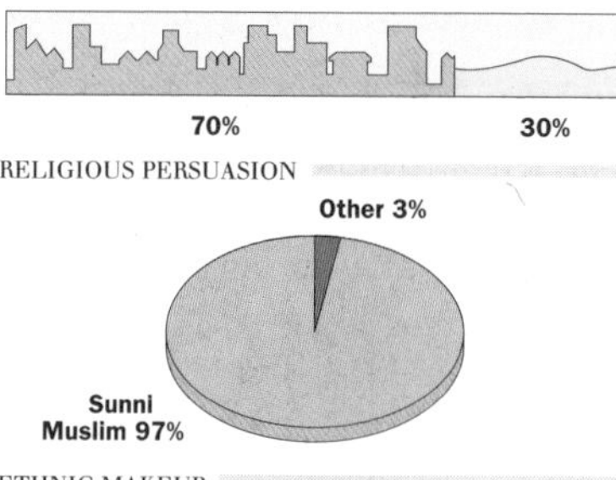

POPULATION AGE BREAKDOWN

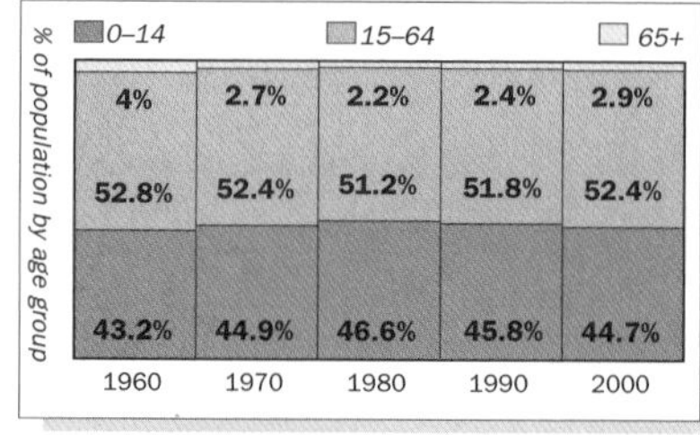

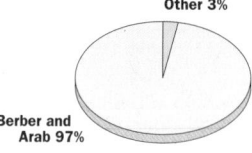

Ninety-seven percent of Libyans are of Arab and Berber origin, split into many tribal groupings. They were artificially brought together when Libya was created in 1951 by the unification of the three historic provinces of Tripolitania, Cyrenaica and the Fazzān. The pro-Western monarchy, which was set up under King Idris, perpetuated the dominance of Cyrenaican tribes and the Sanusi religious order.

The revolution of 1969 brought to the fore Arab nationalist Colonel Kaddafi, who embodied the character and aspirations of the rural Sirtica tribes from Fazzān: fierce independence, deep Islamic convictions, belief in a communal lifestyle and hatred for the urban rich. His revolution wiped out private enterprise and the middle classes, banished European settlers and Jews, undermined the function of the religious Muslim establishment and imposed a form of popular democracy through the *jamahiriya* (state of the masses). However, resentment of the regime increased as it became clear that power now lay mainly with the Sirtica tribes, especially Kaddafi's own clan, the Qadhadhfa.

The years since the revolution have seen Libya change from being largely a nation of nomads and livestock herders to a society where 70% are city-dwellers.

POLITICS

Not applicable

Col. Muammar al-Kaddafi

THE STATE OF THE PARTIES

General People's Congress 1,112 members

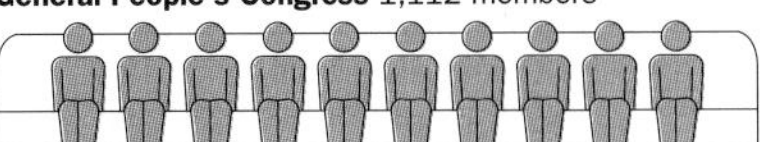

The only authorized political party is the Arab Socialist Union (ASU), from which the members of the Congress are appointed

Executive power is exercised by the General People's Committee. The General People's Congress elects the head of state, the Revolutionary Leader.

MAIN POLITICAL ISSUES

Repression

Dissidents, whether politicians, students or Islamic fundamentalists, have been violently suppressed, with public executions of alleged traitors and spies a routine occurrence. All political parties were banned in 1971. Opposition is based outside the country, notably in the Libyan Democratic Movement in Cairo, Egypt and the National Front for the Salvation of Libya in Khartoum, Sudan.

The regime's public image

In the past few years, the regime has made a deliberate effort to improve its international image. Measures have included freeing some political prisoners, allowing exiles to visit the country, and permitting foreign travel.

PROFILE

In 1977, a new form of direct democracy was promulgated, through which every adult was supposed to share in policy-making. Some 2,000 People's Congresses have sought to take Libya back to the basics of a simple Bedouin way of life. In theory, their wishes are carried out by popular committees. In practice, however, ultimate control is in the hands of Colonel Kaddafi and his collaborators from the days of the 1969 revolution, a small clique linked to the Revolutionary Leader by personal ties or kinship. These include his deputy, Major Abdessalem Jalloud. Some sources report tensions between Kaddafi and Jalloud, with the latter becoming marginalized. Kaddafi now relies on members of his own tribal clan.

Colonel Kaddafi, *Libya's leader since 1969, rejects all official titles.*

Aby Zayd Omar Durdah, *Secretary of the General People's Committee.*

WORLD AFFAIRS

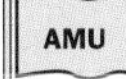

Relations between the USA and Libya have been poor ever since 1985, when CIA attempts to undermine Kaddafi's regime were publicized in the USA. Libya's support for Palestinian and other terrorists led to increasing tension, which culminated in 1986 with US bombing raids on Kaddafi's own residence, and on military and civil targets. Libya's refusal in 1990 to hand over for trial two men suspected of bombing a US airliner over Lockerbie, Scotland, resulted in UN sanctions: international air links were severed, a worldwide ban placed on arms sales to Libya and cuts made in diplomatic missions. Libya was opposed to the 1993–1994 PLO–Israeli discussions about a future Palestinian state.

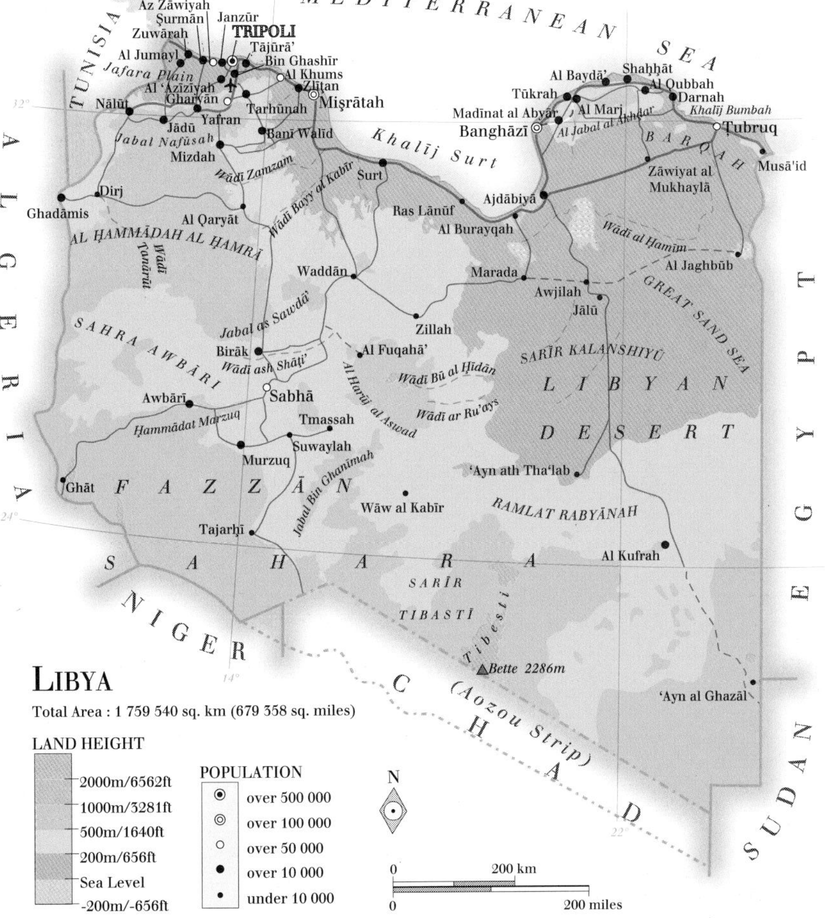

CHRONOLOGY

Italy occupied Libya and expelled the Turks in 1911. Britain and France agreed to a UN plan for an independent monarchy under King Idris in 1951.

- **1969** King Idris deposed in coup by Revolutionary Command Council led by Colonel Kaddafi. Tripoli Charter sets up revolutionary alliance with Egypt and Sudan.
- **1970** Remaining UK and US military establishments ordered out. Property belonging to Italians and Jews confiscated. Western oil company assets nationalized – a process completed in 1973.
- **1973** Libya forms abortive union with Egypt. Kaddafi launches Cultural Revolution – 1,000 intellectuals arrested. Libya occupies Aozou Strip in Chad.
- **1974** Libya forms union of Libya and Tunisia.
- **1977** Frontier clashes with Egypt. Official name changed to The Great Socialist People's Libyan Arab Jamahiriya.

⇨

L

CHRONOLOGY *continued*

- **1979** Members of Revolution Command Council replaced by elected officials. Kaddafi remains Leader of the Revolution.
- **1980** Tunisia accuses Libya of involvement in guerrilla raid on Gafsa. Exiled journalist Mohammed Ramadan killed in London by Libyan agents.
- **1981** USA shoots down two Libyan aircraft over Gulf of Sirte.
- **1984** Commandos from rebel National Salvation Front attack Kaddafi's headquarters but fail to find him. Gunman at Libyan embassy in London kills British policewoman. Libya signs Oudja Accord with Morocco for an Arab Africa Federation.
- **1985** Libya expels 30,000 foreign workers. Tunisia cuts diplomatic links.
- **1986** US aircraft bomb Libya, including Kaddafi's residence, allegedly killing his adopted daughter. 101 people killed.
- **1988** Army and police abolished. Pan-Am airliner explodes over Lockerbie, Scotland. Allegations of Libyan complicity.
- **1989** Arab Maghreb Union established with Algeria, Morocco, Mauritania and Tunisia. Libya and Chad agree to end fighting in Aozou Strip.
- **1990** USA and Germany claim Libya is making mustard gas at a plant near Rabta, south of Tripoli.
- **1990** Libya expels Palestinian splinter group led by Abu Abbas.
- **1991** Opening of first branch of Great Man-Made River project.
- **1992** UN sanctions imposed as Libya fails to extradite Lockerbie suspects. Renewed 1993.

AID

$20m (receipts)

Up 18% in 1990

As an oil-exporting state, Libya fails to qualify for international aid, despite being a developing country. In Africa during the 1970s, Colonel Kaddafi aided several well-established liberation movements and helped dissidents by training them in his Pan-African legion. He has backed African liberation movements, such as FROLINAT in Chad and financed the PLO in the Middle East, the IRA in Northern Ireland, the Moros in the southern Philippines and the Basques, Corsicans and other ethnic causes in Europe. In recent years, Kaddafi's appetite for fomenting revolution abroad has ebbed, largely due to UN sanctions and a lack of surplus resources.

DEFENSE

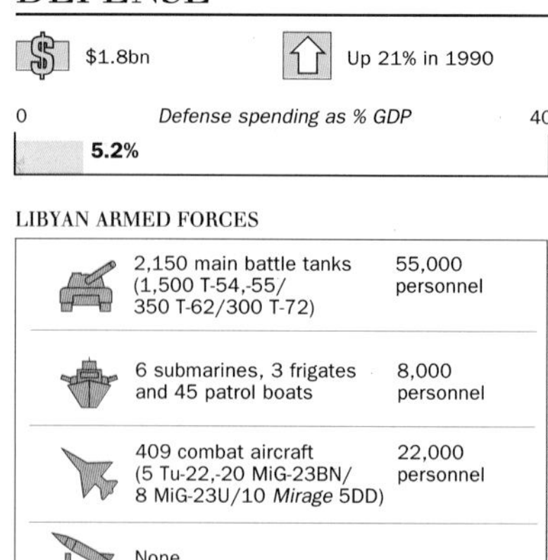

The armed forces suffered a major blow in 1987 with the loss of thousands of men and equipment worth $1.4 billion in the Chad Civil War. Libya's southern border with Chad is still disputed and skirmishes occur, especially in the Aozou Strip. The armed forces were technically abolished in 1989 and replaced with "the Armed People." Colonel Kaddafi's attempts to depoliticize the armed forces have been largely ineffective and reports of dissent within the ranks continue. As a result of a total UN ban on arms sales to Libya, first enforced in 1992, Libya's forces are largely equipped with increasingly outdated, former Soviet bloc equipment.

ECONOMICS

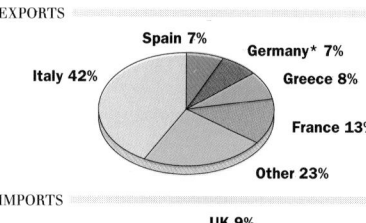

0.30 Libyan dinars

SCORE CARD

- WORLD GNP RANKING 61st
- GNP PER CAPITA $4,755
- BALANCE OF PAYMENTS .... $-800m
- INFLATION 8%
- UNEMPLOYMENT 2%

EXPORTS

Spain 7%
Germany* 7%
Italy 42%
Greece 8%
France 13%
Other 23%

IMPORTS

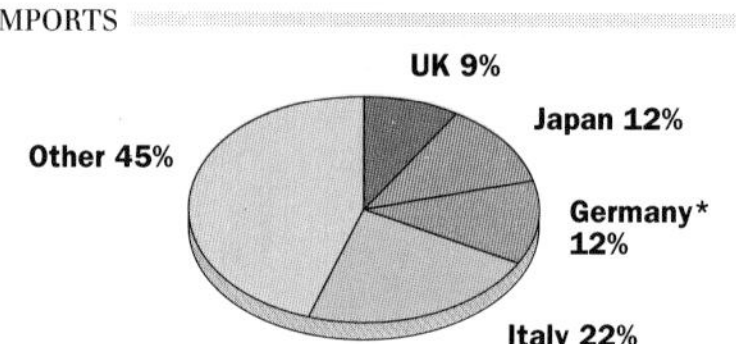

STRENGTHS
Oil and gas production. High investment in downstream industries – petrochemicals, refineries, fertilizers and aluminum smelting.

WEAKNESSES
Single-resource economy subject to oil-market fluctuations. Most food is imported. Reliance on foreign labor. Lack of water for agriculture. History of international unreliability.

PROFILE
Western oil companies had close business ties with Libya until the imposition of UN sanctions over the Lockerbie affair. If a diplomatic settlement is reached, cooperation will quickly resume. Kaddafi's most controversial economic project has been the Great Man-Made River. Started in 1984 and engineered by European and Korean companies, this project will bring underground water from the Sahara to the coast. There, it will be utilized by industry and farming. Since the 1970s, there has been an ambitious program of industrialization aimed largely at import substitution in sectors such as building materials and processed food.

ECONOMIC PERFORMANCE INDICATOR

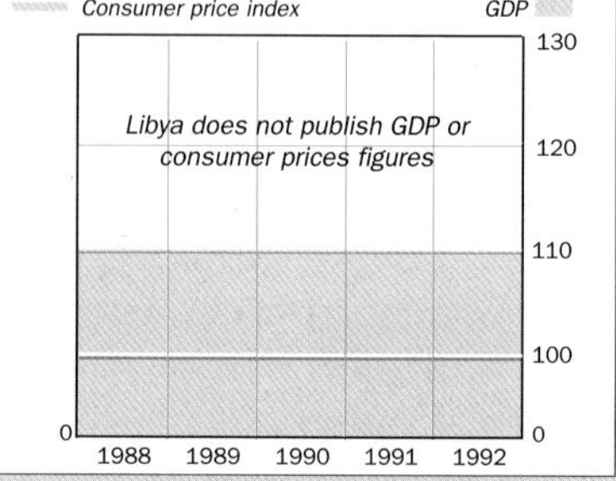

LIBYA : MAJOR BUSINESSES

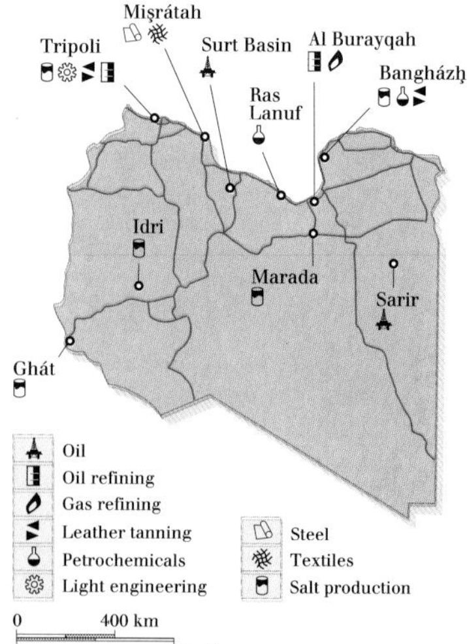

RESOURCES

19bn kwh (capacity 4.1m kw)

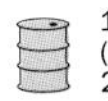
1.5bn b/d (reserves 22,800,000,000 bbl)

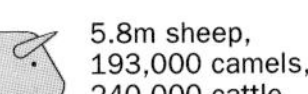
5.8m sheep, 193,000 camels, 240,000 cattle

Oil, natural gas, iron, potassium, gypsum, magnesium, sulfur

ELECTRICITY GENERATION

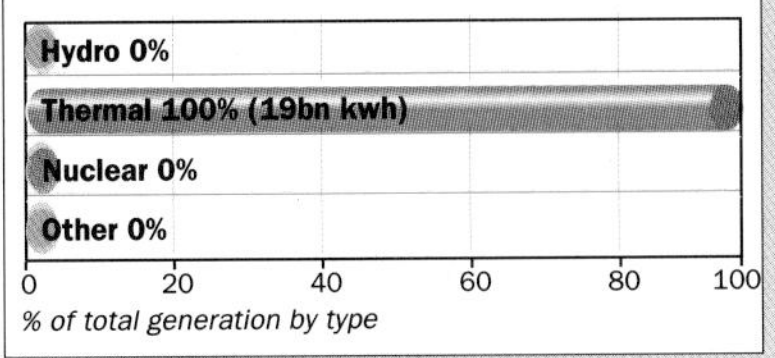

With considerable crude oil reserves, Libya is likely to remain an oil-exporting country well into the next century. Natural gas potential is more limited but, providing links are developed with other North African states, the future is assured. Libya also has reserves of iron ore, potassium, sulfur, magnesium and gypsum. With the Great Man-Made River project now running, the area of irrigated land has been increased, but 90% of Libya is desert. Animal husbandry is the basis of farming, but some cereal crops are grown, as well as dates, olives and citrus fruits. Cement production is sufficient to meet national demand and relies on local raw materials. Most other manufacturing inputs must be imported at considerable cost due to UN sanctions.

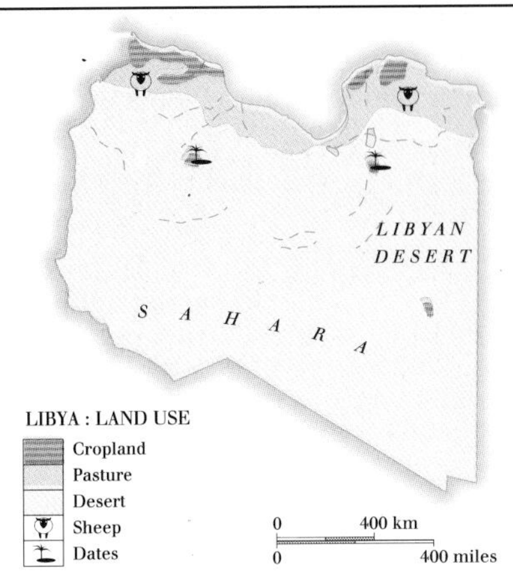

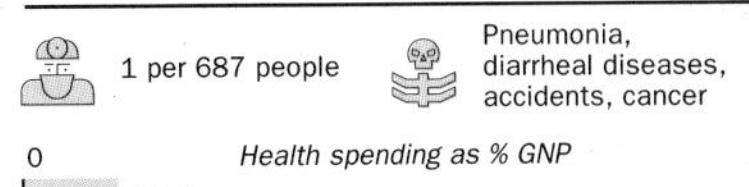

ENVIRONMENT

0.1% partially protected

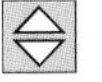
Tapping desert water may shift rather than solve problems

ENVIRONMENTAL TREATIES

The UN Development Program has described Libya as more than 90% "wasteland." Both nature and man have conspired against the environment. Apart from two coastal strips – the Jafara Plain and the Al Jabal al-Akhḑar in Cyrenaica – together with the Fazzān Oasis, most of Libya is desert. Much of the irrigated area is saline because of unwise use of naturally-occurring water from artesian wells. Seawater has penetrated the water table as far as 12 miles inland near Tripoli.

MEDIA

The media is under strict government control

PUBLISHING AND BROADCAST MEDIA

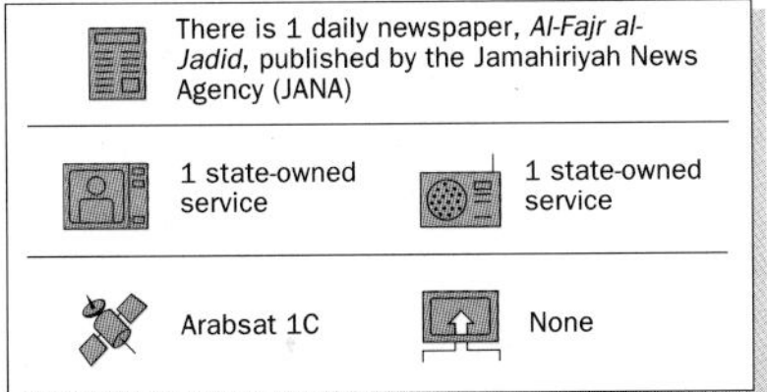

There is 1 daily newspaper, Al-Fajr al-Jadid, published by the Jamahiriyah News Agency (JANA)
1 state-owned service
1 state-owned service
Arabsat 1C
None

Libya's press and TV are a mouthpiece for the leadership. The official news agency has voiced criticism of the wealthy elite for living in closed villas sprouting with satellite dishes. The only daily newspaper is published in Arabic and has a circulation of 40,000 readers. The TV station broadcasts mainly in Arabic, with some programs in Italian, French and English.

CRIME

Libya does not publish prison figures

Down 2% in 1990

CRIME RATES

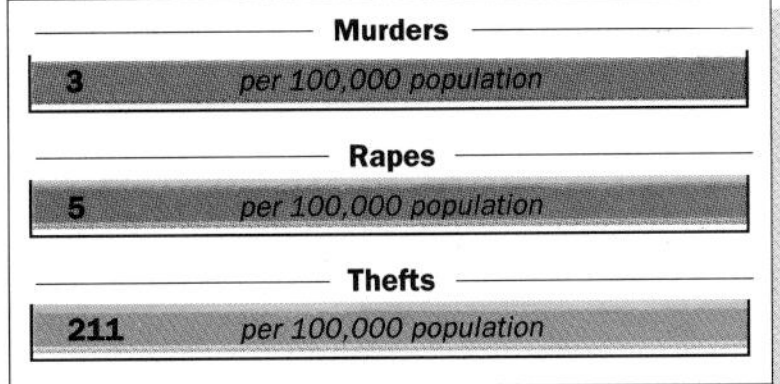

Policing is often in the hands of gangs appointed by Kaddafi's lieutenants to root out student protesters and other dissidents. Hit squads allegedly operate abroad against Libyan exiles.

EDUCATION

64%

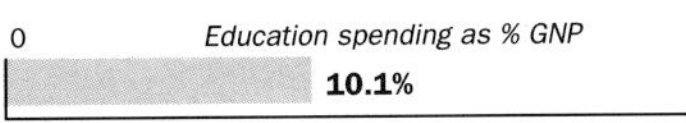

THE EDUCATION SYSTEM

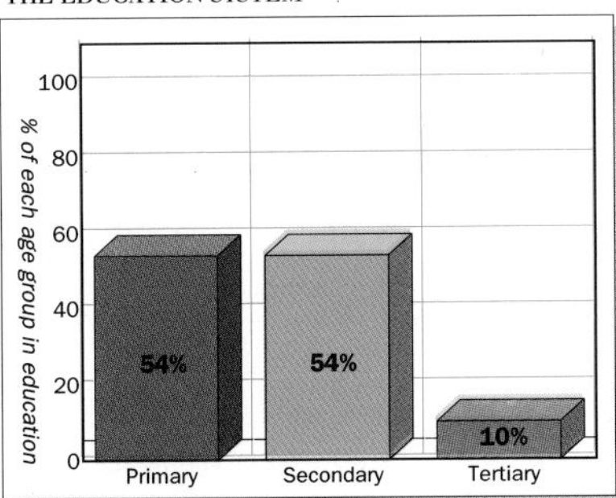

Some one million Libyans receive formal education. It is compulsory between ages 6 and 15, but varies in quality and is rudimentary in rural areas. There are universities, in Tripoli, Banghāzī and Sabhā. The literacy rate has improved from 39% in 1970 to 64% today.

HEALTH

1 per 687 people

Pneumonia, diarrheal diseases, accidents, cancer

0 Health spending as % GNP 25

3.2%

An adequate system of primary health care exists except in remote areas. Hospitals lack equipment.

WEALTH

Most Libyans have benefited little from oil wealth

CONSUMER GOODS OWNERSHIP

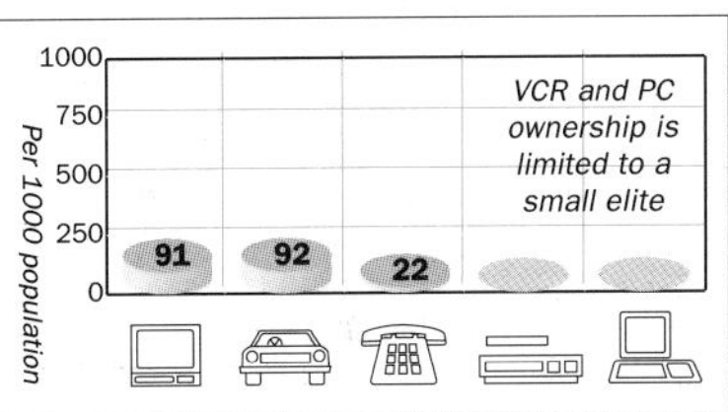

There is widespread poverty after years of import constraints. The situation has worsened as imports have dwindled due to UN sanctions. Consumer durables are the preserve of an elite.

WORLD RANKING

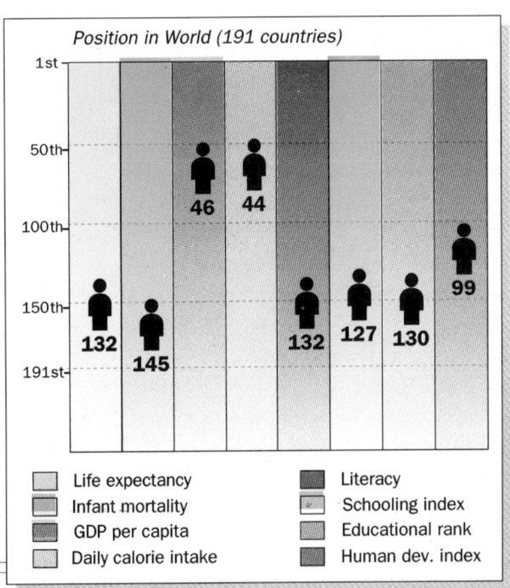

LIECHTENSTEIN

OFFICIAL NAME: Principality of Liechtenstein **CAPITAL:** Vaduz
POPULATION: 29,000 **CURRENCY:** Swiss franc **OFFICIAL LANGUAGE:** German

EUROPE
LIECHTENSTEIN Austria Switzerland Europe

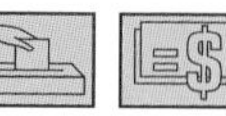

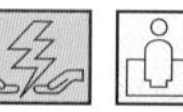

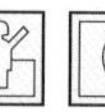

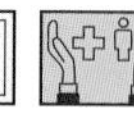

PERCHED IN THE ALPS between Switzerland and Austria, Liechtenstein is rare among small states in having both a thriving banking sector and a well-diversified manufacturing economy. It is closely allied to Switzerland, which handles its foreign relations and defense. Life in Liechtenstein is stable and conservative. Its banking secrecy laws and low taxes make it home to many overseas trusts, banks and investment companies.

CLIMATE

WEATHER CHART

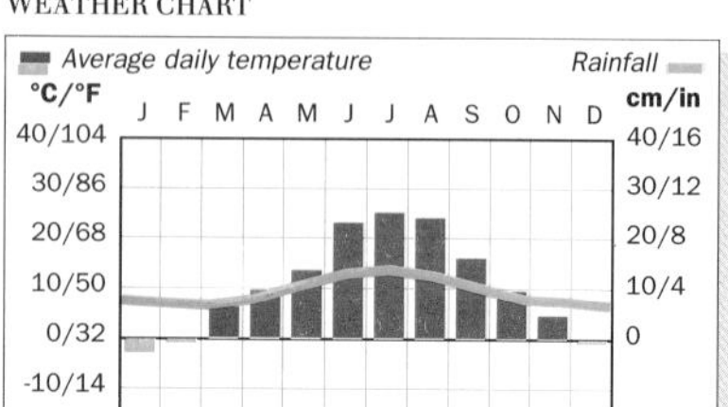

Climate varies with altitude. Excellent skiing conditions are the result of heavy settling snow from December to March. Summers are warm and dry.

COMMUNICATIONS

 None

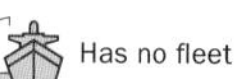 Has no fleet

THE TRANSPORTATION NETWORK

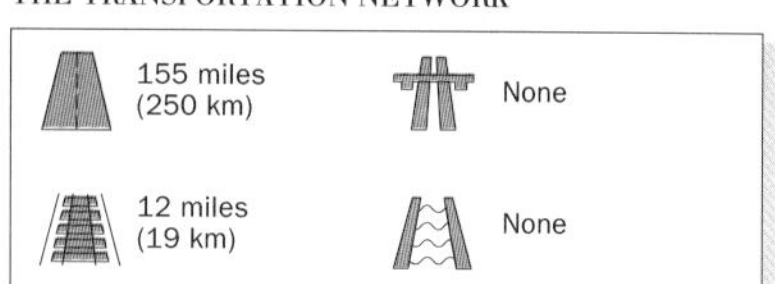

Public transportation in Liechtenstein is mostly by postal bus network. The single-track railroad has few stops. Zurich, a two-hour drive away, is the nearest airport.

TOURISM

 71,990 visitors

 Up 1% in 1992

MAIN OVERSEAS ARRIVALS

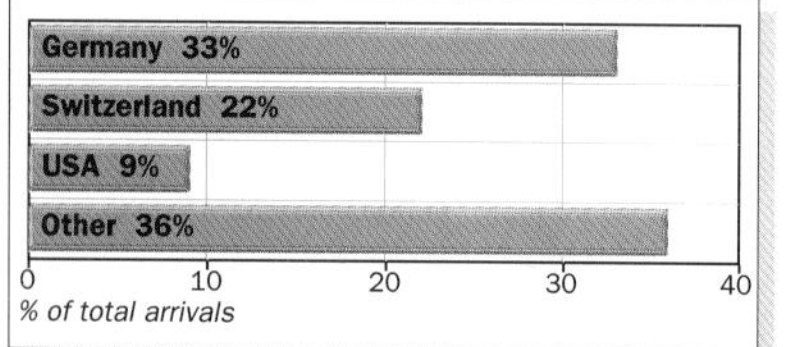

Liechtenstein's alpine scenery attracts skiers in the winter, and climbers and hikers in the summer.

PEOPLE

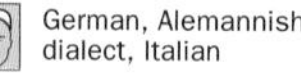

 453 people per sq. mile

THE URBAN/RURAL POPULATION SPLIT

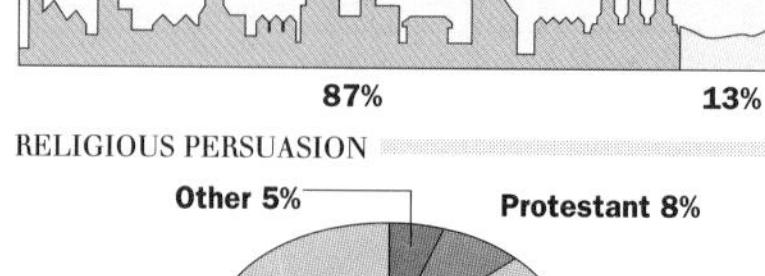

RELIGIOUS PERSUASION

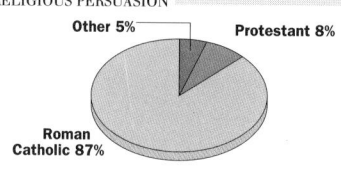

Other 5%
Protestant 8%
Roman Catholic 87%

Liechtenstein's role as a financial center accounts for the many foreign residents (over 35% of the population), of whom half are Swiss and the rest mostly German. The high standard of living results in few ethnic or social tensions. Family life is highly traditional; women received the vote only in 1984, after much controversy. A proposal the following year that equal rights for women be enshrined in the constitution was rejected in a referendum by a large majority.

POLITICS

 Prince Hans-Adam II

THE STATE OF THE PARTIES

Landtag 25 members

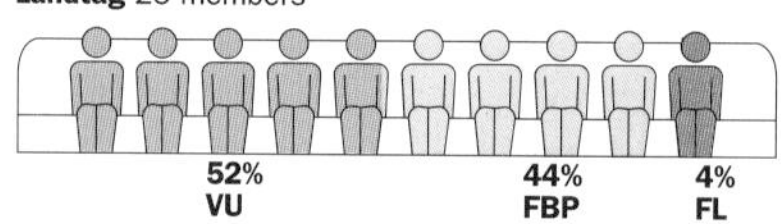

VU = Patriotic Party **FBP** = Progressive Citizens' Party
FL = Free List

Historically, the VU and the FBP have alternated as coalition leaders. However, the VU has been the leading party since 1978, except for a few brief months in 1993. An increasing use has been made of referenda to decide policy issues, such as the 1992 proposal to reduce the voting age from 20 to 18, rejected by 56% of voters.

WORLD AFFAIRS

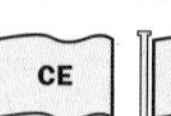

EFTA

Liechtenstein effectively gave up control of its external relations when it signed the 1924 Customs Union Treaty with Switzerland. This requires Swiss approval for any treaty arrangements between Liechtenstein and a third state. The country became a member of the UN only in 1990 and of EFTA in 1991. It is now renegotiating the Customs Union with Switzerland in order to gain entry to the EEA; a referendum on the issue was planned for 1994. Swiss rejection of EU membership in 1992 effectively ended this as a practical prospect for Liechtenstein.

AID

 Donor, but does not publish figures

 Not applicable

Although overseas aid donations are small and aid issues have little political importance, Liechtenstein has helped to fund shelter and reconstruction projects in former Yugoslavia and local development projects in Bulgaria.

LIECHTENSTEIN

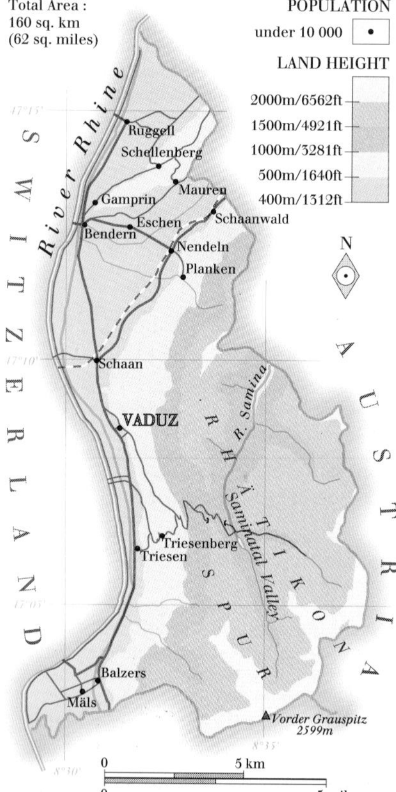

L

Alpine scenery near Vaduz. The state budget includes 2% allocated to restoring mountain vegetation and coordinating land use.

DEFENSE

 Police force of 56 men and 22 auxiliaries

 Not applicable

There has been no standing army since 1868 and there is only a small police force. *De facto* protection is provided by Switzerland. In theory, any male under 60 is liable for military service during a national emergency, although this law has never been invoked.

ECONOMICS

 $900m (est)

 1.49 Swiss francs

SCORE CARD

- ❑ WORLD GNP RANKING 157th
- ❑ GNP PER CAPITA $31,000
- ❑ BALANCE OF PAYMENTS .... Included in Swiss total
- ❑ INFLATION 5.4%
- ❑ UNEMPLOYMENT 0.1%

STRENGTHS

Stability and close association with Switzerland make Liechtenstein a favored tax haven; its lack of EU membership makes the banking sector less vulnerable to future changes in EU banking laws. The economy is well-diversified; chemicals, furniture, and the manufacture of ceramic dentures and precision instruments are all thriving sectors.

WEAKNESSES

Very few. Liechtenstein might suffer if the EU restricts imports from EFTA countries in future.

EXPORTS

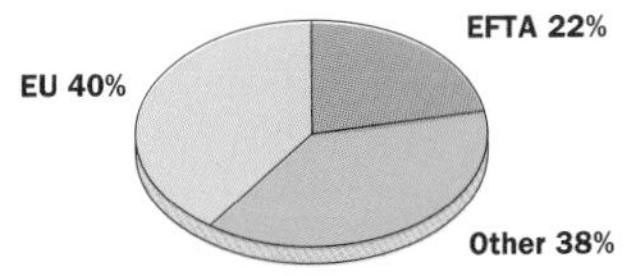

IMPORTS

With a limited domestic market, Liechtenstein's industry is export-oriented. Liechtenstein has a customs union with Switzerland and does not publish separate import figures

RESOURCES

 94% of energy requirements imported

 Not an oil producer and has no refineries

10,000 pigs, 9000 cattle, 3000 sheep

 None

Liechtenstein has to import most of its energy. Almost all of its electricity comes from German power stations.

ENVIRONMENT

 38% partially protected

 Greens won two seats in parliament in 1993

Protection of Liechtenstein's alpine scenery is high enough on the political agenda for one of the five councillors, or ministers, to have responsibility for the environment. As in Switzerland, the greatest worry is the effect of through traffic and high rates of car ownership. The 1988 experiment in providing free public bus transportation proved a failure, as Liechtensteiners remained firmly wedded to their cars.

MEDIA

 No restrictions

PUBLISHING AND BROADCAST MEDIA

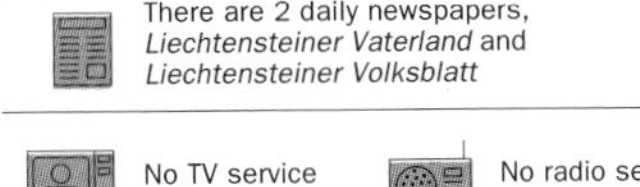

There are 2 daily newspapers, *Liechtensteiner Vaterland* and *Liechtensteiner Volksblatt*

No TV service

No radio service

The two newspapers, although free of formal state control, are both run by political parties: the *Vaterland* by the VU; the *Volksblatt* by the FBP. Both have circulations of about 8,000.

CRIME

 Liechtenstein does not publish prison figures

 Crime does not pose any great problems

Crime is a minor problem, a result of the relatively even distribution of wealth and high average living standard. Liechtenstein has also taken great care to protect its tax-haven status by careful regulation of its financial sector. There have been no major scandals, such as the BCCI collapse which tainted the reputation of its main competitor, Luxembourg.

EDUCATION

 100%

Education, modeled on the German system, includes two types of school at secondary level – the grammar-style *Gymnasium* and the *Realschule*. Liechtenstein has no university. Students go on to colleges in Austria, Switzerland and Germany, and to business schools in the USA.

CHRONOLOGY

In 1719 Liechtenstein became an independent principality of the Holy Roman Empire.

- ❑ **1805** France, under Napoleon, controls Liechtenstein's affairs.
- ❑ **1919** Switzerland replaces Austria in representing Liechtenstein's interests abroad.
- ❑ **1920** Postal union established with Switzerland.
- ❑ **1924** Liechtenstein in joint customs union with Switzerland.

HEALTH

 1 per 948 people

 Heart and respiratory diseases, cancer

Although there are few clinics and hospitals, the health system provides advanced care. Many Liechtensteiners have private health insurance arrangements, which also give them access to Swiss medical expertise. Rabies remains a significant problem.

WEALTH

 Experienced carpenter, 4,700 Swiss francs per month; primary school teacher, 4,800-7,490 Swiss francs per month

CONSUMER GOODS OWNERSHIP

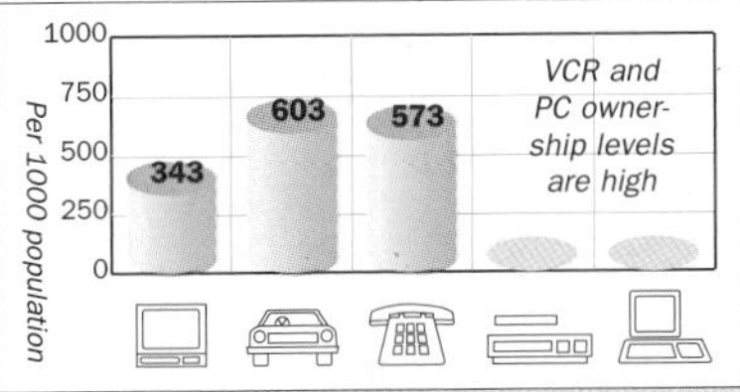

Most Liechtensteiners have a high standard of living, similar to that of the Swiss. Unlike other tax havens, such as Monaco, it does not attract the jet-set rich and private deposit accounts are not a key part of its banking business. The state welfare system is generous.

WORLD RANKING

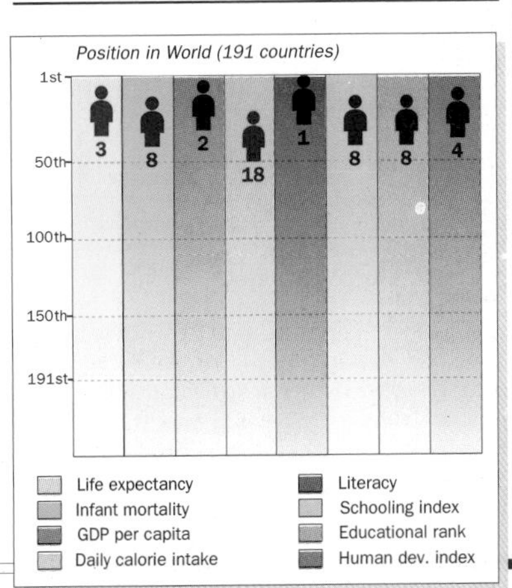

LITHUANIA

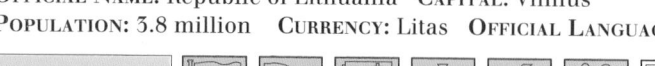

OFFICIAL NAME: Republic of Lithuania **CAPITAL:** Vilnius
POPULATION: 3.8 million **CURRENCY:** Litas **OFFICIAL LANGUAGE:** Lithuanian

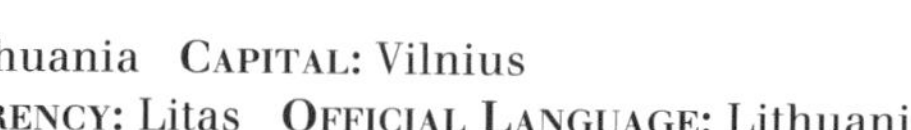

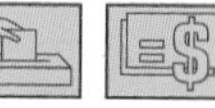

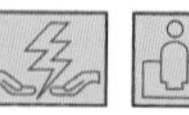

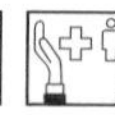

EUROPE
Russian Fed.
Latvia
LITHUANIA
Belorussia
Poland
Europe

LYING ON THE EASTERN coast of the Baltic Sea, Lithuania is bordered by Latvia, Belorussia, Poland and the Kaliningrad area of the Russian Federation. Its terrain is mostly flat with many lakes, moors and bogs. Now a multiparty democracy, Lithuania achieved independence from the former USSR in 1991. Industrial production and agriculture are the mainstays of the economy. Russia finally withdrew all its troops from Lithuania in 1993.

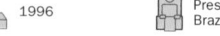

CLIMATE

WEATHER CHART

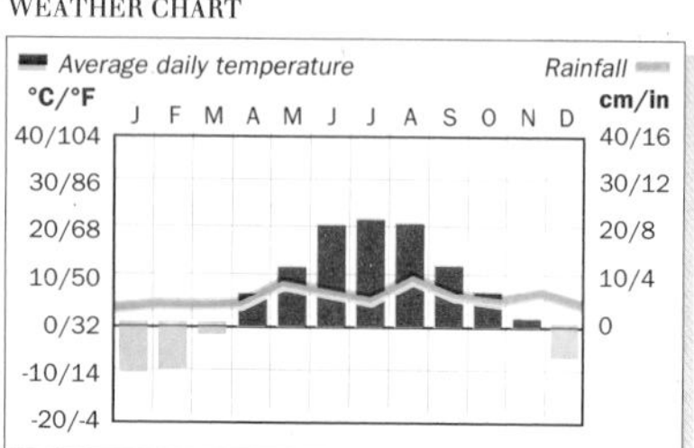

Lithuania's coastal position moderates an otherwise continental-type climate. Summers are cool.

COMMUNICATIONS

Vilnius International

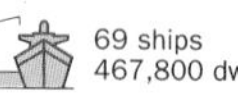
69 ships
467,800 dwt

THE TRANSPORTATION NETWORK

27,450 miles (44,177 km)

None

1,885 miles (3,033 km)

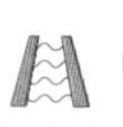
River Neman

Lithuania has an efficient rail service. Plans exist to upgrade the Soviet-built road network and port facilities.

TOURISM

Similar levels to Latvia and Estonia

The trend is up

MAIN OVERSEAS ARRIVALS

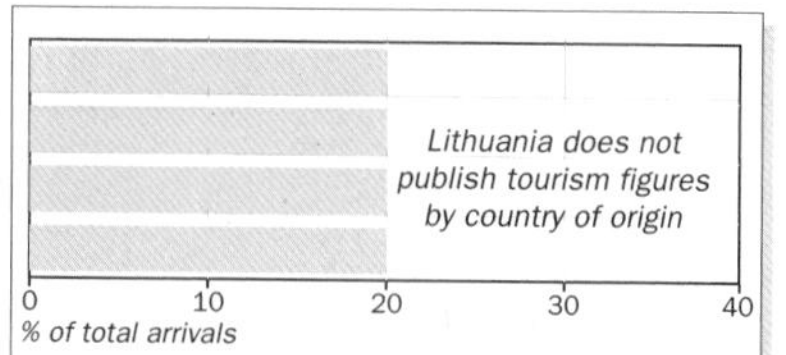

Tourism has expanded in recent years. Vilnius is well-preserved. Its historic center survived German and Russian occupation. Trakai, the capital of the Grand Duchy in the 16th century, is also popular with visitors.

PEOPLE

Lithuanian, Russian

148 people per sq. mile

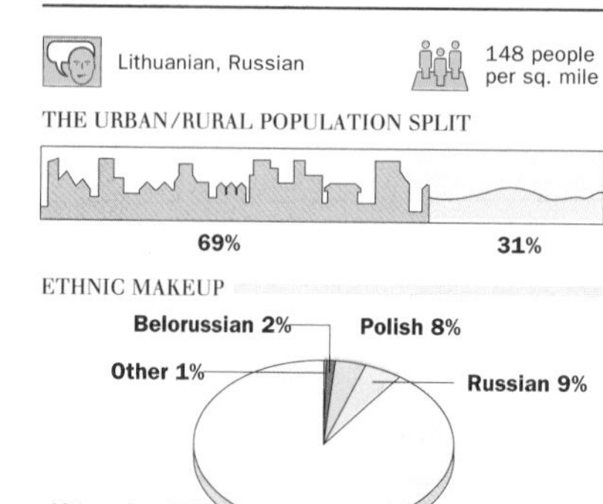

The population is made up of an 80% majority of Lithuanians, together with small groups of Russians, Poles and Belorussians. Citizenship is not a political issue in Lithuania, as it is in the other Baltic states. Ethnic relations are relatively good and inter-ethnic marriages are fairly common. Lithuania is strongly Catholic, in contrast to Protestant Latvia and Estonia. Divorce rates are high.

POLITICS

1996

President Algirdas Brazauskas

THE STATE OF THE PARTIES

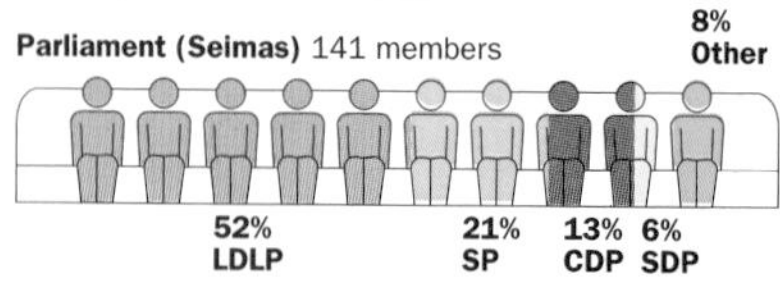

LDLP = Lithuanian Democratic Labor Party **SP** = Sajudis Party **CDP** = Christian Democratic Party **SDP** = Social Democratic Party **Other** = Union of Lithuanian Political

The elections in late 1992 resulted in a shift back to the pre-independence leadership, with the return to power of Algirdas Brazauskas and his ex-communist LDLP. This marked the end of a period of rule under the SP, led by Vytautas Landsbergis, which held office at independence in 1991. Landsbergis's leadership style had become increasingly nationalistic and autocratic, but the main reason for his defeat was a failure to tackle economic problems. Coping with the economic situation is a priority for the present government. The LDLP leadership, despite its communist past, is intently pursuing free-market and privatization policies.

Lithuania is the most politically stable of the three Baltic republics. In 1993, Russian troops left its territory, reducing fears of intervention from Moscow. Brazauskas's non-nationalist communist background has enhanced his support from the non-Lithuanian community.

LITHUANIA

Total Area : 65 200 sq. km (25 174 sq. miles)

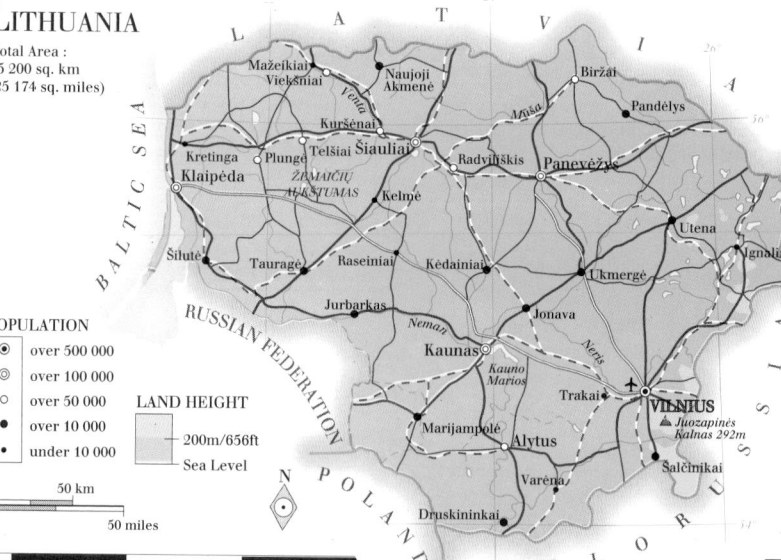

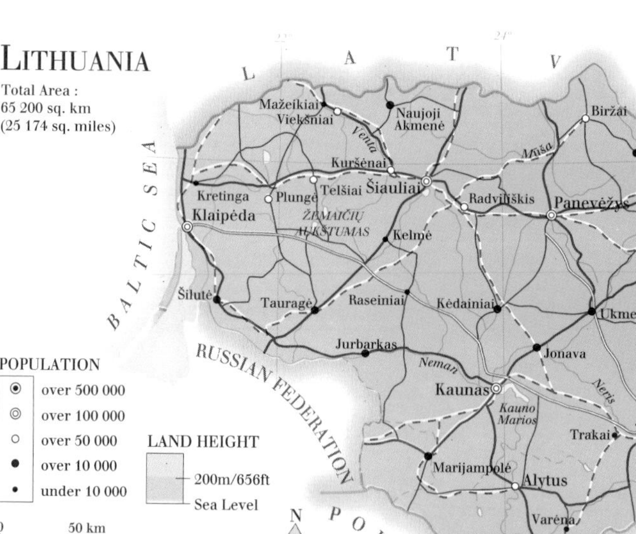

WORLD AFFAIRS

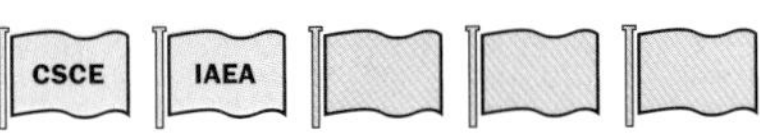

The LDLP's communist background has eased relations with Russia. In 1993, Russia withdrew its troops from Lithuanian soil. Lithuania is eager to strengthen links with the EU.

AID

 Lithuania does not publish aid receipts

 The trend is probably rising

Aid, mostly from the IMF and EU, is used for infrastructure projects and to promote private enterprise.

DEFENSE

 $588.2m

 Rising now that Russian troops have left

Lithuania's security is in the hands of its army and a National Guard formed to patrol its frontiers. However, it would be unable to defend itself against Russian attack. Most of the Russian troops who left in 1993 were relocated to neighboring Kaliningrad.

ECONOMICS

 $10.2bn

 3.89 litas

SCORE CARD

❑ WORLD GNP RANKING	77th
❑ GNP PER CAPITA	$2,685
❑ BALANCE OF PAYMENTS	Deficit
❑ INFLATION	176%
❑ UNEMPLOYMENT	0.5%

STRENGTHS
Occasional agricultural surpluses. Some exports of peat, amber, linen and light industrial goods.

WEAKNESSES
Poor raw material base. Need to import oil, natural gas and industrial products from Russia. Uncompetitive, outdated industry. Difficulty in attracting significant foreign investment. Economically the weakest Baltic state.

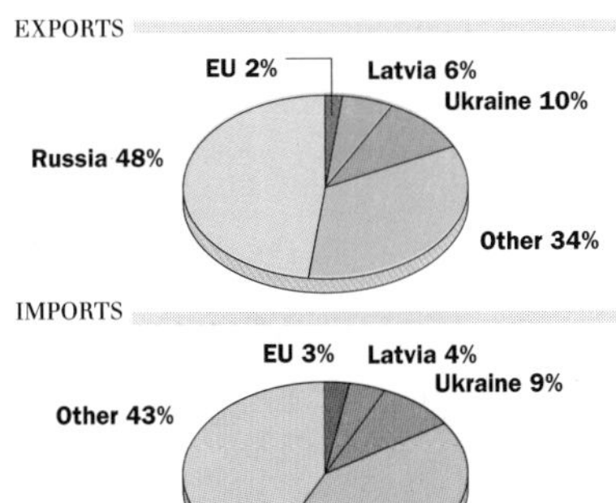

One of Lithuania's 3,000 lakes. The entire country is low-lying. Its coast, fringed by sand dunes and pine forests, is famous for amber.

RESOURCES

 Nuclear power makes up 60% of electricity production

 Not an oil producer and has no refineries

2.7m pigs, 2.4m cattle, 78,600 sheep and goats

 Sand, gravel, clay, limestone, gypsum

Lithuania has no strategic resources. Nuclear power is a major source of energy. Most of the country's oil still comes from Russia, as the supply infrastructure is in place. However, Lithuania is seeking other suppliers.

ENVIRONMENT

 2%

 Pollution in Baltic Sea

The Ignalina nuclear plant, which came on line in the mid-1980s, has experienced leakage problems. Water and air pollution levels are high. Lithuania's Baltic coast has been polluted by oil spillages.

MEDIA

 No restrictions on political reporting

PUBLISHING AND BROADCAST MEDIA

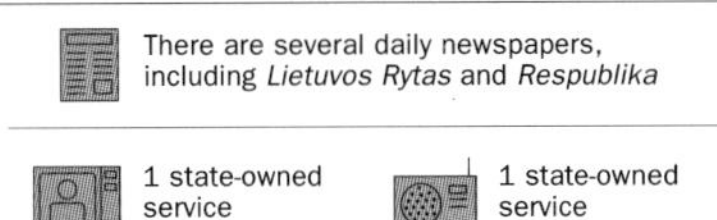

There are several daily newspapers, including *Lietuvos Rytas* and *Respublika*
1 state-owned service
1 state-owned service

The mainstream media, Russian under communism, now publishes and broadcasts mainly in Lithuanian.

CRIME

Lithuania does not publish prison figures

 Crime levels are rising slightly

Levels of crime are low compared to other parts of the former USSR. Robbery is a growing problem.

EDUCATION

 Figures not published, but among highest of ex-Soviet republics

Teaching at all levels is in Lithuanian, making access to higher education harder for minorities; 8% of the population are college graduates.

CHRONOLOGY

Russia annexed Lithuania in 1795. The suppression of rebellions in 1831 and 1863 failed to undermine its nationalist movement.

- ❑ **1915** Occupied by German troops.
- ❑ **1918** Independence declared.
- ❑ **1922** Lithuania proclaims itself a parliamentary democracy.
- ❑ **1926** Military coup leads to one-party rule.
- ❑ **1940** Annexed by Soviet Union.
- ❑ **1941–1944** Nazi occupation.
- ❑ **1945** Lithuania formally incorporated into USSR.
- ❑ **1989** Lithuanian Communist Party approves Lithuanian sovereignty. Past Soviet rule declared illegal.
- ❑ **1991** Achieves full independence.
- ❑ **1992** First multiparty elections.
- ❑ **1993** Russian troops withdraw.

HEALTH

 1 per 217 people

 Circulatory and respiratory diseases, cancer, accidents

Reforms to Lithuania's health system began in 1990 and include the legalization of private medicine.

L

WEALTH

 Traders in Vilnius are the wealthiest group

CONSUMER GOODS OWNERSHIP

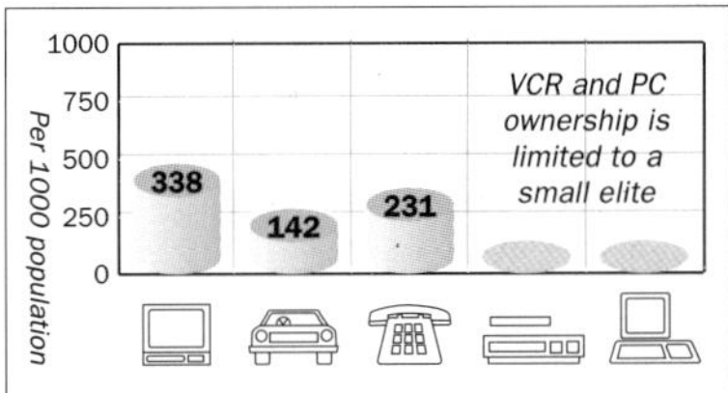

Western cars and designer goods are popular status symbols among an increasingly prosperous elite.

WORLD RANKING

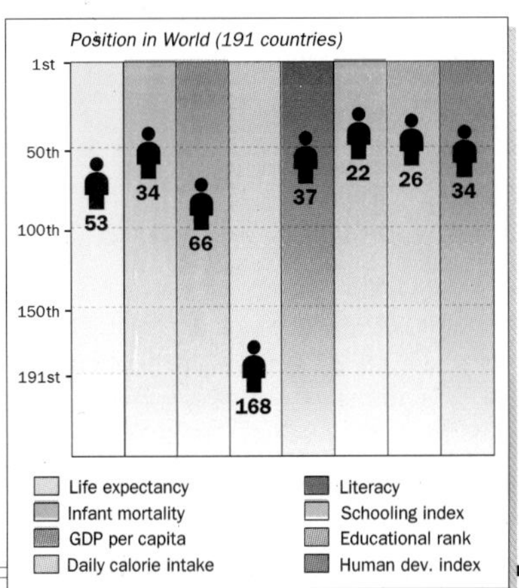

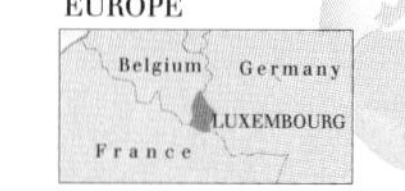

LUXEMBOURG

OFFICIAL NAME: Grand Duchy of Luxembourg **CAPITAL:** Luxembourg
POPULATION: 400,000 **CURRENCY:** Luxembourg franc **OFFICIAL LANGUAGE:** Letzeburgish

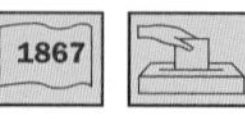

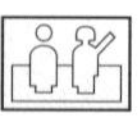

LUXEMBOURG SHARES BORDERS with the industrial regions of Germany, France and Belgium and has Europe's highest per capita income. Making up part of the plateau of the Ardennes, its countryside is undulating and forested. Its prosperity was once based on steel; before World War II it produced more per capita than the USA. Today, it is known as a tax haven and banking center, and as the headquarters of key EU institutions.

CLIMATE

WEATHER CHART

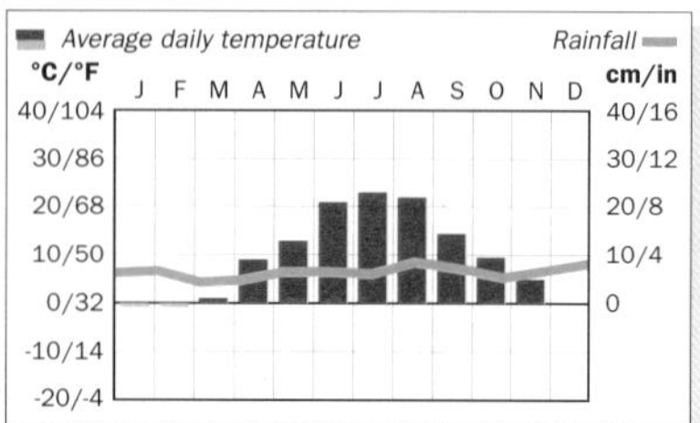

The south, where vines grow, is the warmest area. Winter is cold and snowy, especially in the Ardennes.

COMMUNICATIONS

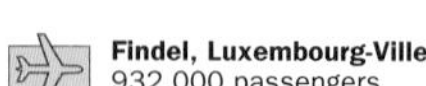
Findel, Luxembourg-Ville 932,000 passengers

52 ships 2.61m dwt

THE TRANSPORTATION NETWORK

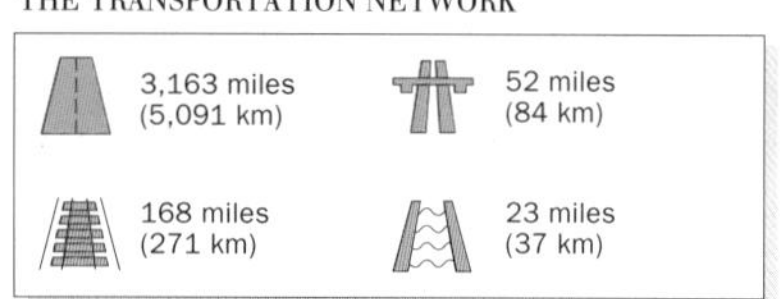

There is an excellent road network, although congestion is a problem. Rail and bus services are integrated.

TOURISM

861,284 visitors

Up 5% in 1991

MAIN OVERSEAS ARRIVALS

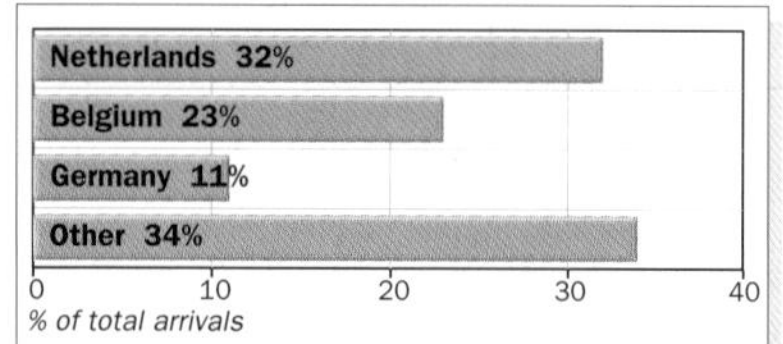

The mountains and forests, and 76 castles, many recently re-roofed, are the main attractions. The government has begun an initiative to teach foreign hotel workers the history, language and culture of the Duchy.

PEOPLE

Letzeburgish, German, French

401 people per sq. mile

THE URBAN/RURAL POPULATION SPLIT

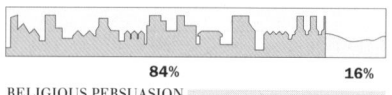

84% 16%

RELIGIOUS PERSUASION

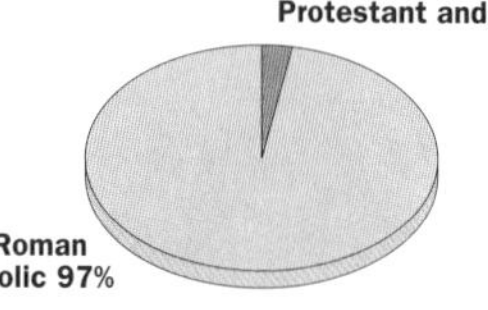

Nearly a third of Luxembourg's residents and half of its workers are foreigners. Integration has been straightforward; most are fellow Western Europeans and Catholics, mainly from Italy and Portugal. Life in Luxembourg is comfortable. Salaries are high, unemployment very low and social tensions few.

POLITICS

1999

HRH Grand Duke Jean d'Aviano

THE STATE OF THE PARTIES

Chamber of Deputies 60 members

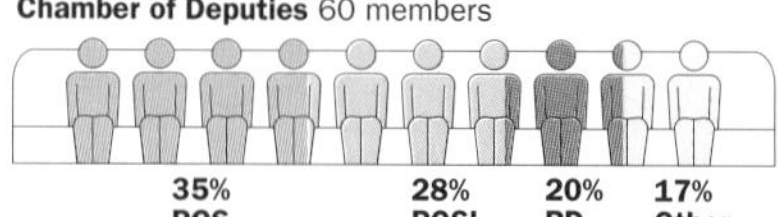

PCS = Christian Social Party **POSL** = Luxembourg Socialist Workers' Party **PD** = Democratic Party **Other** = Action Committee for Democracy and Justice, Green Alternative Party

Council of State 21 members

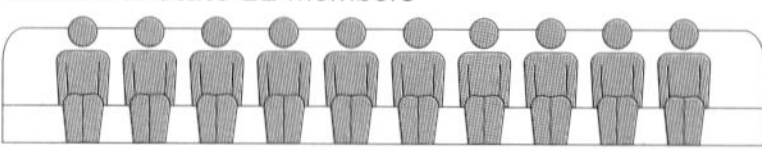

The members of the Council of State are appointed for life by the Grand Duke

Luxembourg's politics have achieved remarkable consensus, and are characterized by coalitions and long-serving prime ministers. The main political issues are now economic – raising taxes and trimming spending to cope with the economic slow-down.

WORLD AFFAIRS

Luxembourg has long been the most committed member of the EU. It was during its EU presidency that the Maastricht agreement for closer European union was brokered; Luxembourg was not only the first member state to meet all the economic, financial and legal requirements of union under Maastricht, but it also did so a year early. This commitment to the EU reflects the tremendous benefits Luxembourg has gained from membership. It is home to both the European Parliament and the Court of Justice, and its citizens enjoy the high, tax-free salaries that work in these organizations brings. In 1994, however, Luxembourg lost its bid for the European Central Bank to Frankfurt, Germany.

LUXEMBOURG

Total Area : 2586 sq. km (998 sq. miles)

N

0 10 km
0 10 miles

LAND HEIGHT: 500m/1640ft; 200m/656ft; Sea Level

POPULATION: over 50 000; over 10 000; under 10 000

Charlotte Bridge, Luxembourg. The modern road system provides excellent communications with the rest of Europe.

AID

 $39m (donations)  Up 56% in 1991

Luxembourg's aid donations, equal to only 0.35% of GNP, are largely directed toward sub-Saharan Africa.

DEFENSE

 $108m  Up 7% in 1992

Luxembourg's army numbers 800 full-time soldiers. Spending is 1.2% of GDP and has risen slightly in recent years.

ECONOMICS

 $11.8bn  36.15 Luxembourg francs

SCORE CARD

❑ World GNP Ranking	73rd
❑ GNP per Capita	$28,730
❑ Balance of Payments	Included in Belgian total
❑ Inflation	2.1%
❑ Unemployment	1.3%

Strengths
Site of EU institutions. Banking secrecy and expertise make the capital home to over 980 investment funds and 192 banks – more than in any other city in the world.

Weaknesses
International service industries account for 65% of GNP, making Luxembourg vulnerable to changing conditions overseas. Downturn in steel market.

EXPORTS

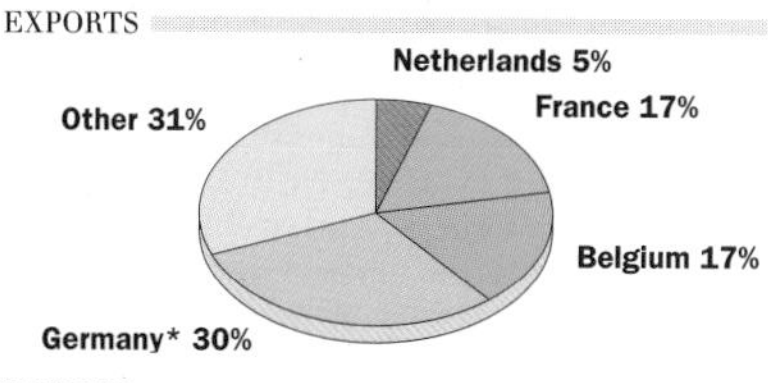

IMPORTS

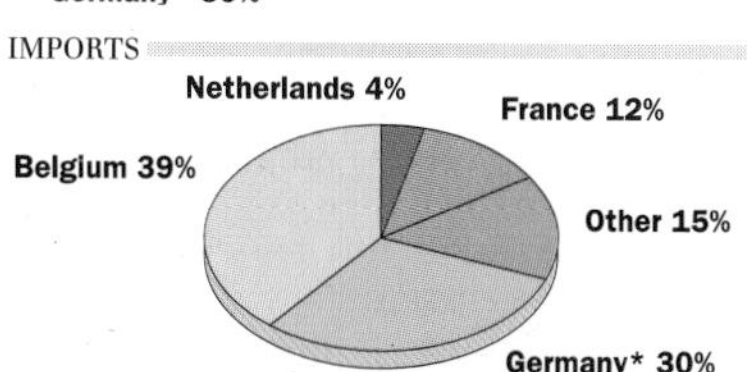

RESOURCES

 1.4bn kwh (capacity 1.24m kw)  Not an oil producer and has no refineries

 Cattle, deer, wild boar, sheep  Iron, steel

Luxembourg can meet few of its own energy needs; it produces only a small amount of hydroelectricity. The steel industry accounts for 10% of GDP.

ENVIRONMENT

 None  One of few nations active in transfrontier pollution control

Acid rain from European industry has affected about 19% of Luxembourg's trees and, in the worst cases, 30% of trees in mature stands. The Duchy is a member of an international committee on decreasing pollution of the Rhine.

MEDIA

 Freedom of expression is guaranteed by law

PUBLISHING AND BROADCAST MEDIA

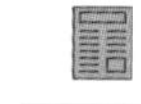 There are 4 daily newspapers. The leading newspaper, in terms of both circulation and influence, is the *Luxemburger Wort*

 1 independent service 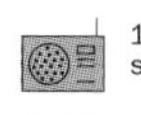 1 independent service

Broadcasting is dominated by RTL (*Radio-Television Luxembourg*), one of the largest media groups in Europe, which exports programs in a variety of languages.

CRIME

 352 prisoners  Up 4% in 1990

Luxembourg's stringent banking secrecy rules can provide a cover for both tax evasion and – as in the case of the collapsed BCCI bank, which was registered in Luxembourg – fraud.

EDUCATION

 100%

Teaching is mainly in German at primary level and French at secondary level. Higher education is limited and many students go to universities in other European countries. Training given by Luxembourg banks is reputed to be the best in Europe.

HEALTH

 1 per 529 people  Heart diseases, cancer, accidents

There are no private commercial hospitals in Luxembourg; they are run either by the state or by nuns. The fees paid by patients are refunded from the *Caisse de Maladie* (state sickness fund).

CHRONOLOGY

Throughout its history, Luxembourg has been ruled by a succession of neighboring European powers.

- ❑ **1890** Separates from Netherlands.
- ❑ **1912** End of Salic Law: Grand Duchess Marie accedes.
- ❑ **1919** Abortive republican coup.
- ❑ **1921** Economic union with Belgium. End of German ties.
- ❑ **1940–1944** Severe damage to infrastructure during resistance to German occupation.
- ❑ **1960** Benelux economic union, agreed to in 1948, comes into effect.
- ❑ **1970** Benelux customs union.
- ❑ **1989** Anti money-laundering laws.
- ❑ **1991** Luxembourg first country to ratify Maastricht Treaty.

WEALTH

 Junior salesperson, 10,000 Luxembourg francs per month; experienced sales representative, 500,000 Luxembourg francs per month

CONSUMER GOODS OWNERSHIP

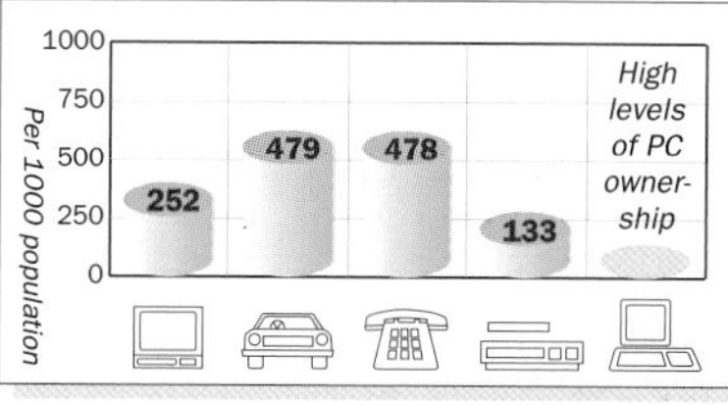

With the highest per capita income in the EU, Luxembourgers enjoy a comfortable lifestyle. In recent years, the government has been able to hand back 5% of GDP in tax relief, while simultaneously increasing public spending. Very low unemployment has led to the influx of a large number of foreign workers, mainly from other EU countries such as Portugal and Italy, to take less well-paid jobs. Financing the aging population is likely to be a burden in the future.

WORLD RANKING

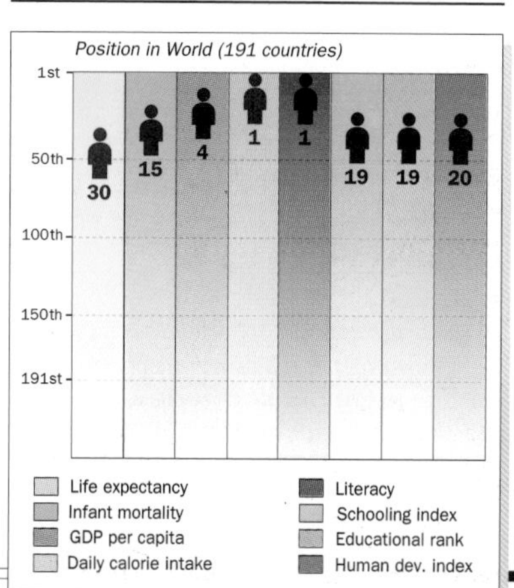

L

MACEDONIA

OFFICIAL NAME: *Former Yugoslav Republic of Macedonia* **CAPITAL:** Skopje
POPULATION: 1.9 million **CURRENCY:** Macedonian denar **OFFICIAL LANGUAGE:** *None*

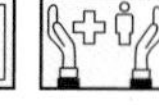

THE FORMER YUGOSLAV Republic of Macedonia (FYRM) is landlocked in southeastern Europe. The economic blockade of Serbia and Montenegro has denied the FYRM two of its most important trading partners and crippled the economy. The Greek government is hostile to the FYRM because it suspects the country may try to absorb northern Greece – also called Macedonia – in a "Greater Macedonia."

***A fisherman's hut** on Lake Dojran, which lies on the border with Greece in southeastern Macedonia and is shared by the two countries.*

CLIMATE

WEATHER CHART

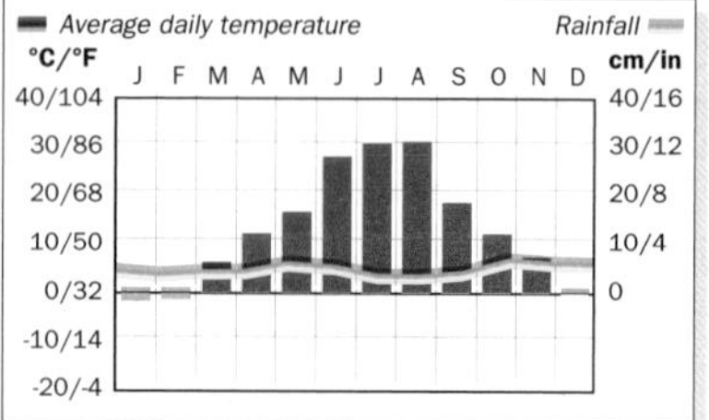

The FYRM has a continental climate, with dry autumns and wet springs. Winter snow supports skiing.

COMMUNICATIONS

 **Skopje Intl**

 Has no fleet

THE TRANSPORTATION NETWORK

 8,637 miles (13,900 km)

 None

 715 miles (1,150 km)

 None

Germany has suspended the Munich–Athens rail link, the last service linking Skopje to Western Europe.

TOURISM

 Small number of visitors only

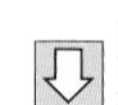 Down, due to war in Yugoslavia and political tensions

MAIN OVERSEAS ARRIVALS

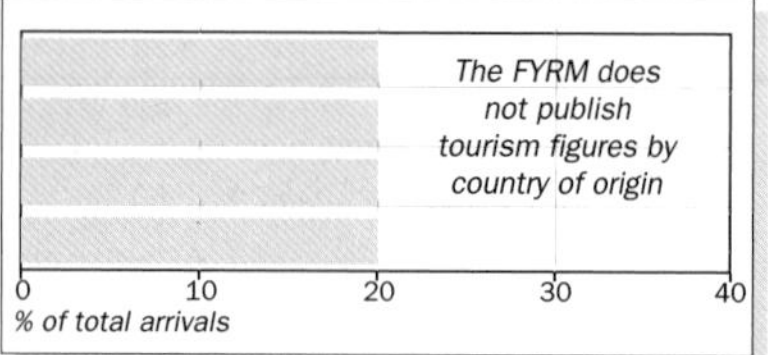

Tourism is a traditionally important income source. Lake resorts and skiing in the Šara mountains are among the attractions. However, regional political problems have reduced the number of tourists going to the FYRM.

PEOPLE

Macedonian, Serbo-Croatian

205 people per sq. mile

THE URBAN/RURAL POPULATION SPLIT

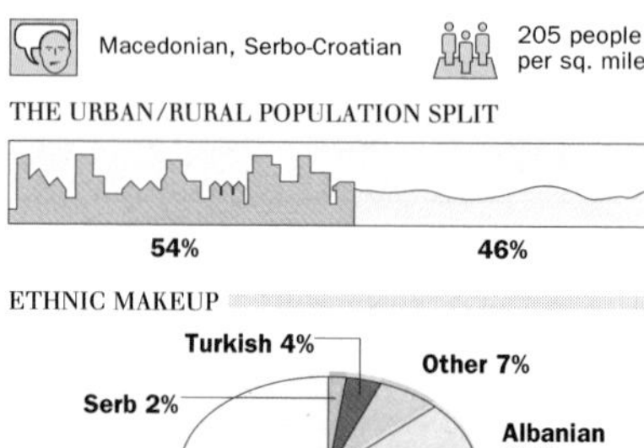

ETHNIC MAKEUP

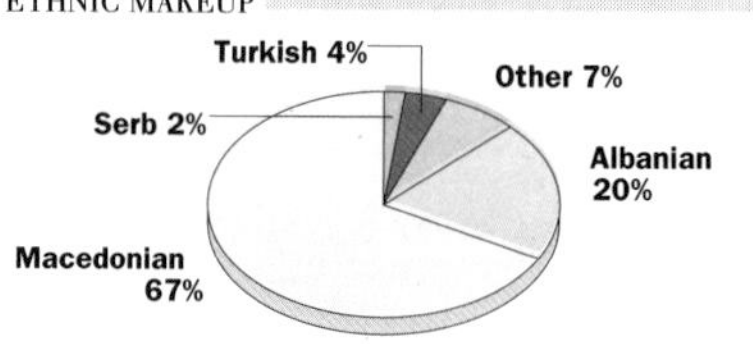

Around two-thirds of the population are ethnically Slav Macedonians. Officially 20% are Albanian, although Albanians themselves claim they account for 40%. Unlike the more publicized tensions between Serbs and Albanians in Kosovo, Slav Macedonian–Albanian stress has so far been restrained. Most Macedonians are Eastern Orthodox, but there are also a substantial number of Slavic Muslims, whose ancestors converted to Islam during the Ottoman occupation. Ethnic Albanians are mostly Muslim. There are also Roman Catholic and Jewish groups.

WORLD AFFAIRS

Greece alone has refused to recognize the state under any name that includes a reference to Macedonia.
In 1994, Greece barred the FYRM from access to the port of Thessaloníki.

AID

 Over $100m

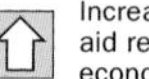 Increasing levels of aid required for economic growth

The FYRM joined the World Bank in 1993 and a $40 million loan followed. The IDA has also extended $40 million in concessional lending. A $25 million grant from the Soros Foundation has boosted foreign exchange reserves.

DEFENSE

 High, given regional tensions

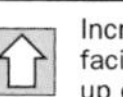 Increasing to facilitate building up of army

The army is dominated by officers who resigned from the Yugoslav army in 1992. The USA has stationed 400 troops in the FYRM to deter Serbian expansionism.

POLITICS

 1994

 President Kiro Gligorov

THE STATE OF THE PARTIES

National Assembly 120 members

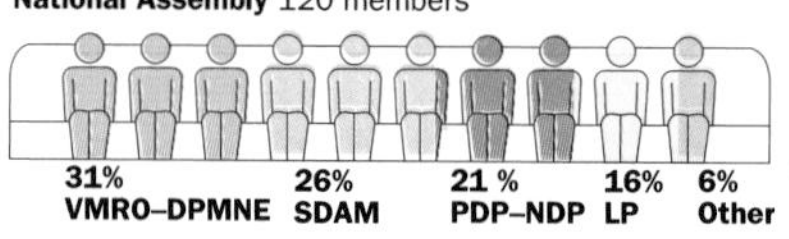

VMRO–DPMNE = Macedonian Revolutionary Organization – Democratic Party for Macedonian National Unity **SDAM** = Macedonian Social Democratic Alliance **PDP–NDP** = Democratic Prosperity Party – National Democratic Party **LP** = Liberal Party

Politics in the FYRM is fragmented along nationalist lines, and is heavily influenced by tensions in neighboring states. Although the Slav Macedonian and Albanian communities have acted with restraint, ethnic tensions are now growing. Ethnic Albanian parties are pursuing recognition as a constituent nation within the FYRM; a separatist paramilitary unit was recently detained. The Slav–Macedonian nationalist VMRO–DPMNE has been making inflammatory references to a 'Greater Macedonia'. The ruling coalition, headed by the ex-communist SDAM, attempts to steer a course between these competing forces. All political issues are overshadowed by the dispute with Greece over the state's name. Economic policy has changed little since independence and remains essentially communist.

ECONOMICS

 $2.2bn

 751.22 Macedonian denars

STRENGTHS

Strong growth in private sector. 67,000 companies have been created since independence.

WEAKNESSES

Loss of supplies and markets under UN sanctions against Serbia has paralyzed international and domestic transactions; ex-Yugoslavia accounted for the majority of exports. Key trading link broken by Greeks' refusal to allow access to port at Thessaloníki.

EXPORTS/IMPORTS

Before the imposition of UN sanctions, Yugoslavia was the FYRM's main trading partner

SCORE CARD

❑ WORLD GNP RANKING	136th
❑ GNP PER CAPITA	$1,158
❑ BALANCE OF PAYMENT	*No formal*
❑ INFLATION	*statistics*
❑ UNEMPLOYMENT	*published*

RESOURCES

 Self-sufficient in electricity production

Not an oil producer

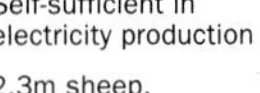 2.3m sheep, 287,000 cows, 179,000 pigs

Coal, copper, bauxite, iron, antimony, chromium, lead, zinc

Macedonia is self-sufficient in electricity production. Plants are thermal and fueled by coal.

ENVIRONMENT

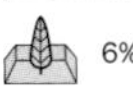 6%

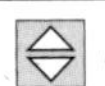 Environmental concerns not a priority

City air pollution is a serious problem. The completion of a sewage works has reduced pollution in Lake Ohrid.

FORMER YUGOSLAV REPUBLIC OF MACEDONIA

Total Area : 25 715 sq. km (9929 sq. miles)

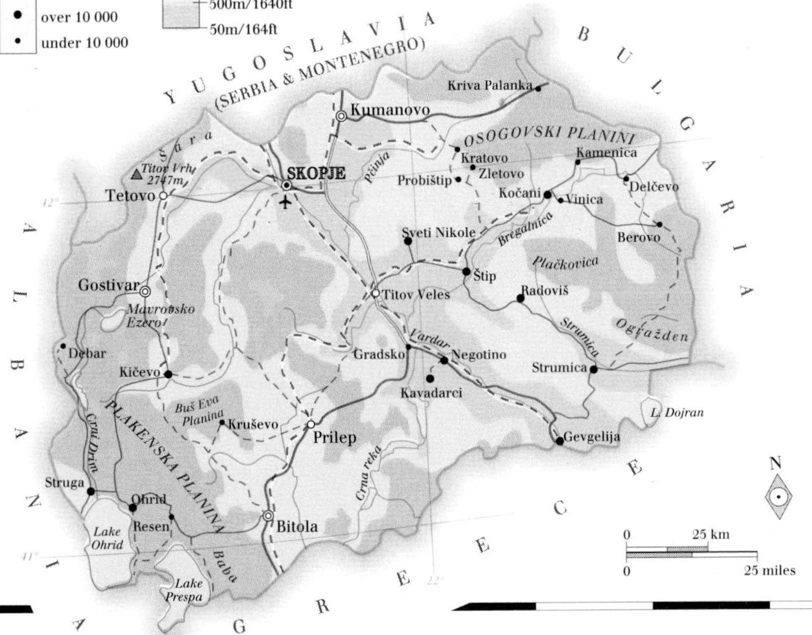

MEDIA

 No censorship restrictions

PUBLISHING AND BROADCAST MEDIA

 Newspapers include the Albanian *Flaka e Vellazerimit* and the Turkish *Birlik*, both of which are funded by the government

 1 state-owned, 1 independent service

 1 state-owned, also independent services

The free and often critical press includes the influential *Nova Makedonija* and *Rilindja Demokratika*.

CRIME

 Macedonia does not publish prison figures

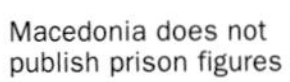

 Illegal labor market increasing rapidly

The local Albanian mafia controls the illegal trade in cigarettes, drugs, hard currencies and arms in Skopje.

EDUCATION

 93%

The education system is entirely under state control and there are no privately run schools.

CHRONOLOGY

Following the Balkan wars, Macedonia was partitioned between Greece and Serbia in 1912–1913.

- ❑ **1944** Tito establishes Republic of Macedonia and consolidates national identity, partly to counteract Bulgarian influence.
- ❑ **1945** Adoption of standardized Macedonian language.
- ❑ **1989** Communists concede multiparty elections.
- ❑ **1990** Nationalists victorious in multiparty elections.
- ❑ **1991** Independence declared. EC recognition delayed by Greeks.
- ❑ **1992** Referendum approves autonomy for Albanian-populated districts in western FYRM.

HEALTH

 1 per 523 people

 Heart and cerebrovascular diseases

In theory, the state guarantees universal health care, but effective and speedy treatment is increasingly only available in the private sector. Most pharmacies have also been privatized.

WEALTH

 The effects of war and UN sanctions have contributed to a sizable fall in living standards since 1991

CONSUMER GOODS OWNERSHIP

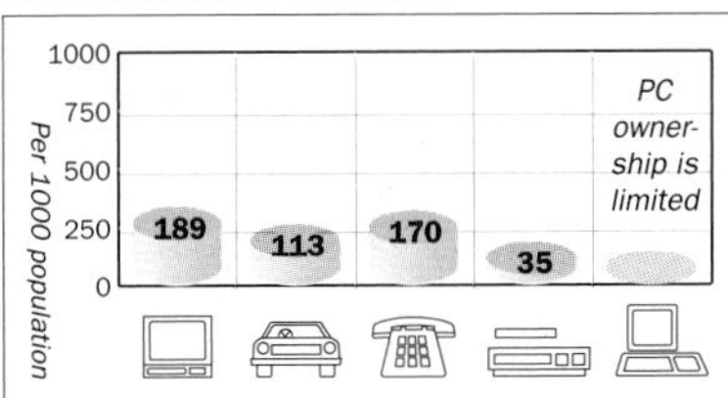

Basic food accounts for about 40% of household expenditure. Most houses and apartments are privately owned.

WORLD RANKING

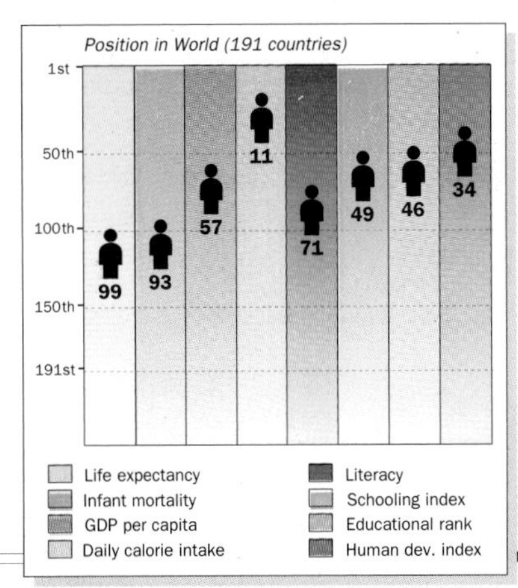

M

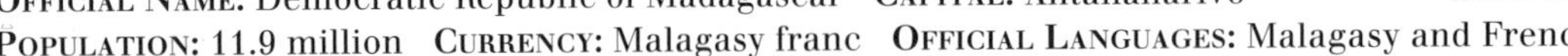

MADAGASCAR

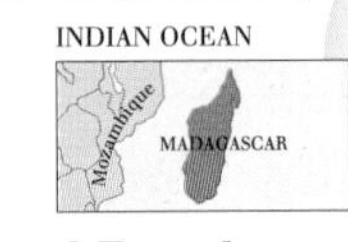

OFFICIAL NAME: Democratic Republic of Madagascar **CAPITAL:** Antananarivo
POPULATION: 11.9 million **CURRENCY:** Malagasy franc **OFFICIAL LANGUAGES:** Malagasy and French

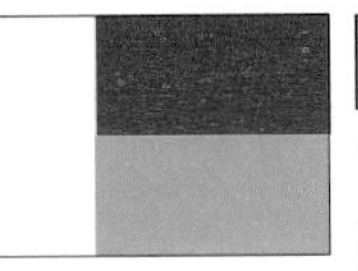
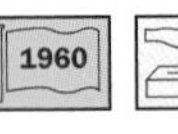

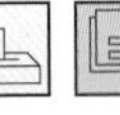

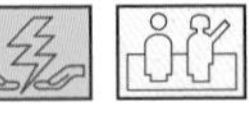

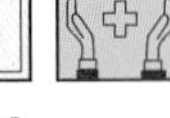
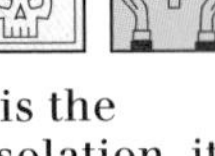

LYING IN THE INDIAN Ocean, Madagascar is the world's fourth-largest island. Due to its isolation, it is home to a host of unique wildlife and plants. To the east, the large central plateau drops precipitously through forested cliffs to the coast. On the west, gentler gradients give way to fertile plains. A former French colony, it became independent in 1960. After 18 years of radical socialism under Didier Ratsiraka, Madagascar is now a multiparty democracy struggling to rebuild an agriculturally based economy.

CLIMATE

WEATHER CHART

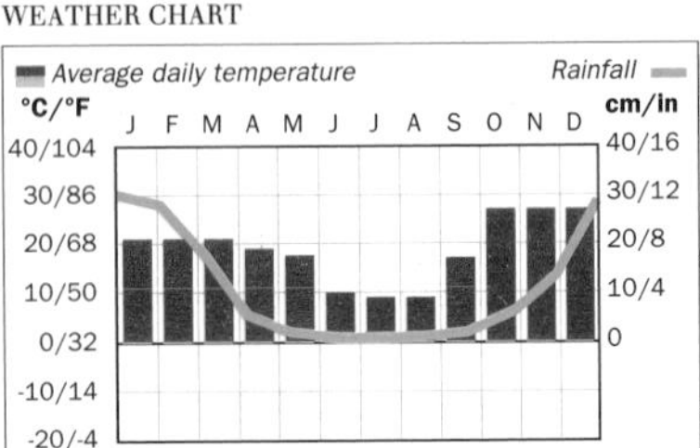

Madagascar is tropical and often hit by cyclones. The coastal lowlands are hot and mainly humid. Rainfall averages 78 in. a year in the east; but under 30 in. in the southwest. The central plateau is cooler, with 40–60 in. of rain a year.

COMMUNICATIONS

Ivato, Antananarivo
340,000 passengers (est)

18 ships
46,300 dwt

THE TRANSPORTATION NETWORK

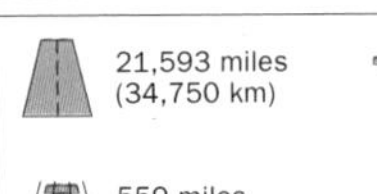
21,593 miles (34,750 km)

None

559 miles (899 km)

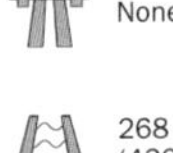
268 miles (432 km)

The extensive domestic air network is a response to the inadequacies of the road and rail systems. Many roads are impassable during the rains; the rail network is very limited. The port of Toamasina handles 70% of total traffic.

PEOPLE

Malagasy, French

52 people per sq. mile

THE URBAN/RURAL POPULATION SPLIT

24% 76%

RELIGIOUS PERSUASION

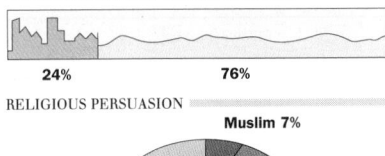

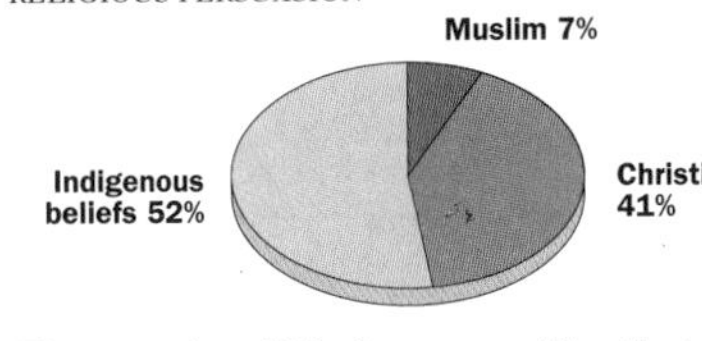

The people of Madagascar, like their language, Malagasy, are essentially Malay–Indonesian in origin. Their ancestors migrated across the Indian Ocean in successive waves from the 1st century AD. Later migrants from the African mainland intermixed and provided the many African words in Malagasy. The main ethnic division is between the plateau and *côtier* (coastal) peoples. Of more pronounced Malay extraction, the plateau Merina were Madagascar's historic rulers. They remain the social elite and largely run the government – to the resentment of the poorer *côtier* groups. Former president Didier Ratsiraka owed much of his political longevity to the fact that he is a *côtier*. The extended family is the focus of social life for the rural majority.

TOURISM

34,891 visitors

Down 34% in 1991

MAIN OVERSEAS ARRIVALS

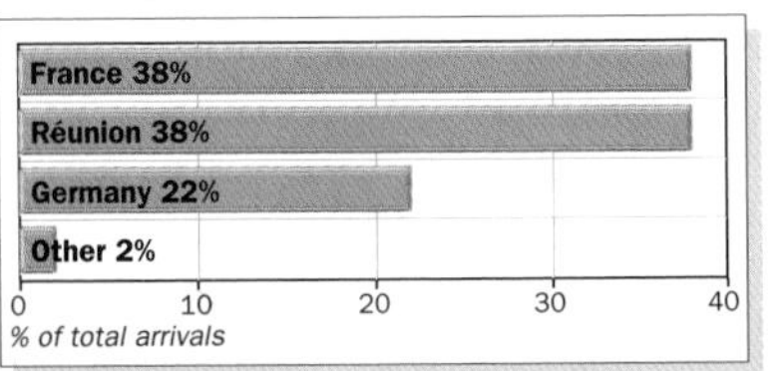

With 3,000 miles of tropical beaches and unique flora and fauna, Madagascar has excellent tourism potential. However, while the sector is now an important foreign exchange earner, it is underdeveloped. After a marked decline in 1991, tourist arrivals were expected to reach a new peak of 57,000 in 1993.

POLITICS

1998

President Albert Zafy

THE STATE OF THE PARTIES

National Assembly 138 members

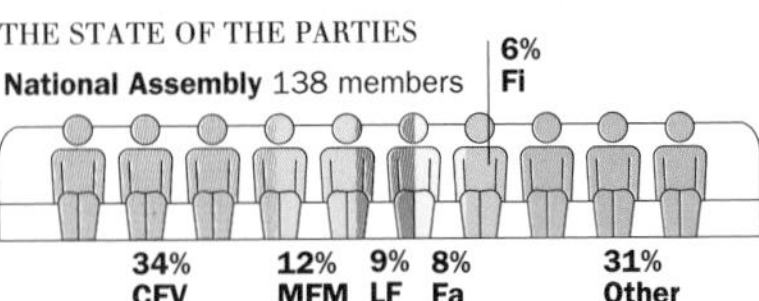

CFV = *Forces Vives* coalition **MFM** = Movement for Proletarian Power (coalition) **LF** = Leader-*Familo* **Fa** = *Famima* **Fi** = *Fihaonana*

Senate

Two-thirds of members are selected by an electoral college and the remainder appointed by the president

In 1993, 18 years of *de facto* one-party rule under Didier Ratsiraka ended when free elections were won by the *Forces Vives* (CFV) opposition coalition.

MADAGASCAR

Total Area : 587 040 sq. km (226 660 sq. miles)

POPULATION

- over 500 000
- over 100 000
- over 50 000
- over 10 000
- under 10 000

LAND HEIGHT

- 2000m/6562ft
- 1000m/3281ft
- 500m/1640ft
- 200m/656ft
- Sea Level

0 200 km
0 200 miles

WORLD AFFAIRS

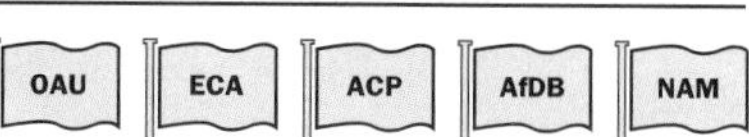

Once-close ties with Moscow and North Korea have waned since the late 1980s, as Madagascar has improved relations with its main Western trading partners, especially France and the USA. It has also increased regional links, re-establishing ties with South Africa and, in 1994, joining the east and southern Africa Preferential Trading Area (PTA).

AID

 $557m (receipts) — Down 3% in 1991

France is the top bilateral donor. The main multilateral donors are the EU and the World Bank. Most aid is now tied to economic reforms.

DEFENSE

 $36.63m

 Up 5% in 1991

A key political force, the army's priority is to maintain a stable, unitary state. In 1992, it acted against federalist *côtiers*.

ECONOMICS

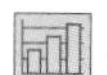 $2.85bn

 1,846.87 Malagasy francs

SCORE CARD

- ❑ WORLD GNP RANKING 127th
- ❑ GNP PER CAPITA $223
- ❑ BALANCE OF PAYMENTS .... $-182m
- ❑ INFLATION 12.7%
- ❑ UNEMPLOYMENT — Widespread underemployment

STRENGTHS

Varied agricultural base; vanilla, coffee, and clove exports. Offshore oil and gas. Prawns. Tourism.

WEAKNESSES

Losing out to cheaper vanilla exporters. Vulnerability to drought. Government reluctance to reform economy by cutting central controls and budget deficit. Not self-sufficient in rice, the food staple.

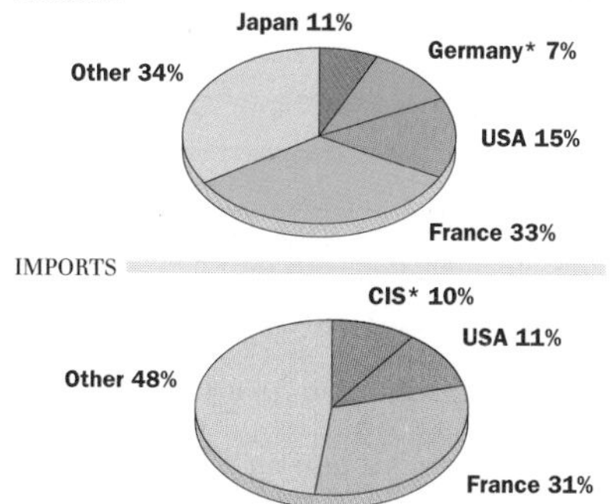

***Tôlañaro** (also known as Fort Dauphin), a port on the southeast coast. This was the area first settled by the French in the 16th century.*

RESOURCES

 566m kwh (capacity 220,000 kw)

Not an oil producer: refines 16,350 b/cd

 10.2m cattle, 1.4m pigs, 700,000 sheep

Chromite, graphite, beryl, mica, zircon, garnet, iron, bitumen

Madagascar is the world's largest vanilla exporter. Electricity is hydro-generated. Oil is imported, although offshore oil and gas have been found.

ENVIRONMENT

 2% (1% partially protected)

 Serious deforestation and soil erosion

Madagascar's environment is a unique resource; 80% of its plant and many animal species, such as the lemur, are found nowhere else. Aid donors are providing funds to fight deforestation.

MEDIA

 Censorship exists, but is limited

PUBLISHING AND BROADCAST MEDIA

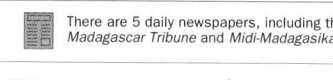

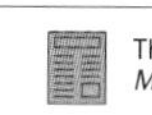 There are 5 daily newspapers, including the *Madagascar Tribune* and *Midi-Madagasikara*

 1 state-owned service

 1 state-owned service

Even before the return of multiparty democracy in 1993, there was a flourishing opposition press, including the Catholic-sponsored *La Croix*.

CRIME

 33,280 prisoners

 Crime is rising

Urban crime levels are starting to rise. The army has been criticized for human rights abuses, including the shooting of federalists in 1993.

EDUCATION

 80%

Primary education is universal. About 40% of children attend secondary school; 5% go on to higher education. Primary education is to become French-based instead of Malagasy-based.

CHRONOLOGY

Increasing European contacts after the 16th century culminated in the 1895 French invasion. Madagascar became a French colony and the Merina monarchy was abolished.

- ❑ **1947–1948** French troops kill thousands in nationalist uprisings.
- ❑ **1960** Independence.
- ❑ **1975** Didier Ratsiraka takes power with radical socialist policies.
- ❑ **1990** Political reforms allow parties other than ruling AREMA and official opposition FNDR.
- ❑ **1991** Opposition *Forces Vives* (CFV) coalition, led by Albert Zafy, set up. Mass strikes against regime.
- ❑ **1993** Ratsiraka and AREMA-FNDR coalition, named the MFM, defeated by Zafy and CFV in free elections.

HEALTH

 1 per 9,939 people

 Malaria, enteric and respiratory diseases

Private healthcare was legalized in 1993. State care is free but inadequate. Malaria is at epidemic levels. There are outbreaks of bubonic plague.

WEALTH

 Minimum wage in manufacturing, 22,000 Malagasy francs per month

CONSUMER GOODS OWNERSHIP

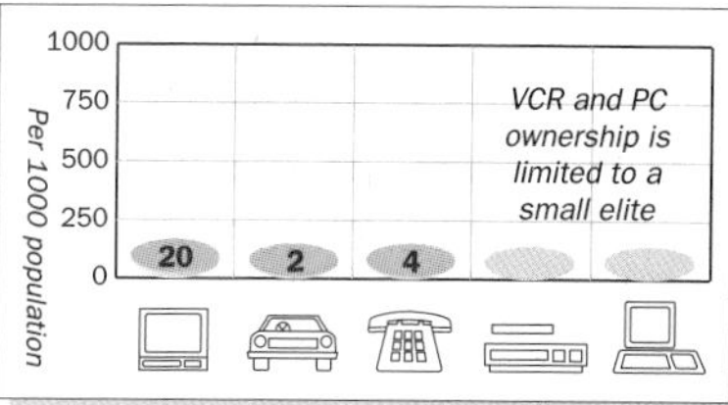

Most people are poor. However, central plateau dwellers are richer than the *côtier* farmers and fishermen.

WORLD RANKING

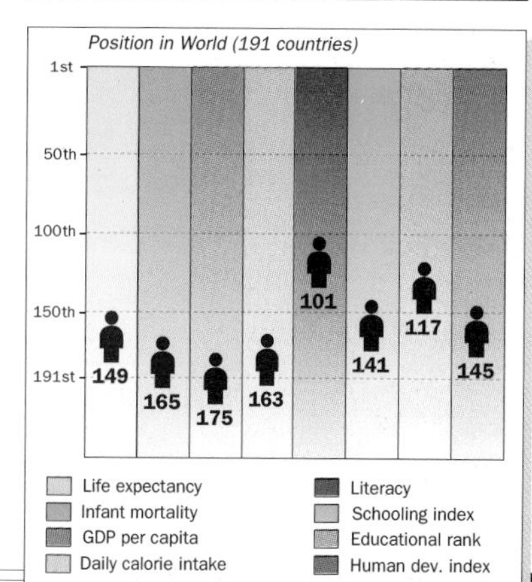

M

MALAWI

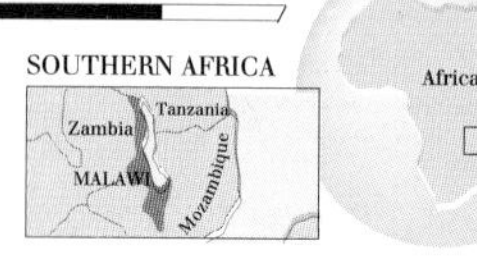

OFFICIAL NAME: Republic of Malawi **CAPITAL:** Lilongwe **POPULATION:** 10.4 million
CURRENCY: Malawian kwacha **OFFICIAL LANGUAGES:** Chewa and English

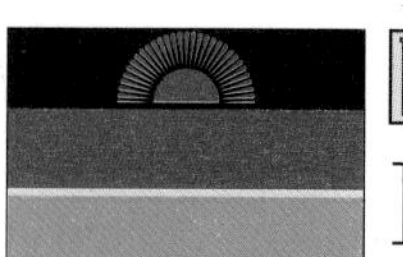

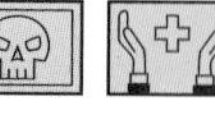

LANDLOCKED IN southeast Africa, Malawi occupies a plateau bordering the Great Rift Valley. Lake Malawi, which is 352 miles long and takes up one-fifth of the country, is among Africa's largest lakes and supports a sizeable fishing industry. Mount Mulanje is the highest mountain in East Africa. Politics in Malawi, a former British colony, are in a delicate transition period following three decades of one-party rule.

CLIMATE

WEATHER CHART

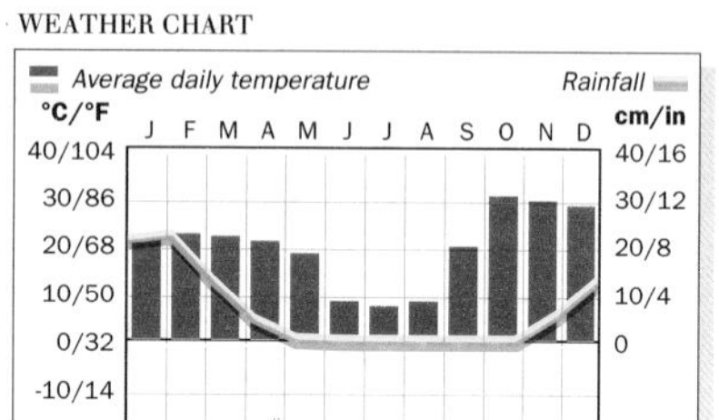

The south is hot and humid. The rest of Malawi is warm and very sunny in the dry season, but cooler in the highlands.

COMMUNICATIONS

Kamuzu Intl, Lilongwe 232,000 passengers

Has no fleet

THE TRANSPORTATION NETWORK

7,590 miles (12,215 km)

None

490 miles (789 km)

Lake Malawi, Shire River

The main road system is good, but access from rural areas is limited. The Kamuzu Highway, a key north–south link, is currently being upgraded.

TOURISM

117,069 visitors

Up 18% in 1989

MAIN OVERSEAS ARRIVALS

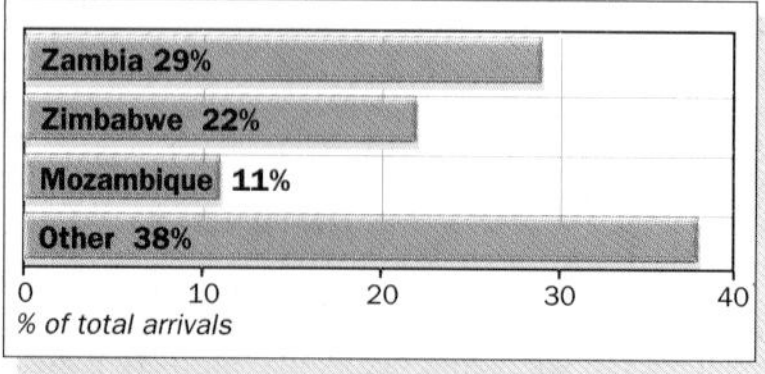

The waters of Lake Malawi, with its 500 species of fish, attract angling, wildlife and water-sports enthusiasts. The national parks and mountain lodges are also popular.

PEOPLE

Chewa, Lomwe, Yao, Ngoni, English

192 people per sq. mile

THE URBAN/RURAL POPULATION SPLIT

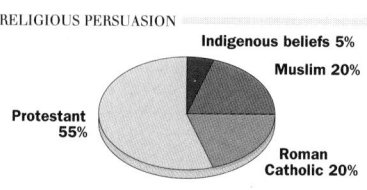

12% 88%

RELIGIOUS PERSUASION

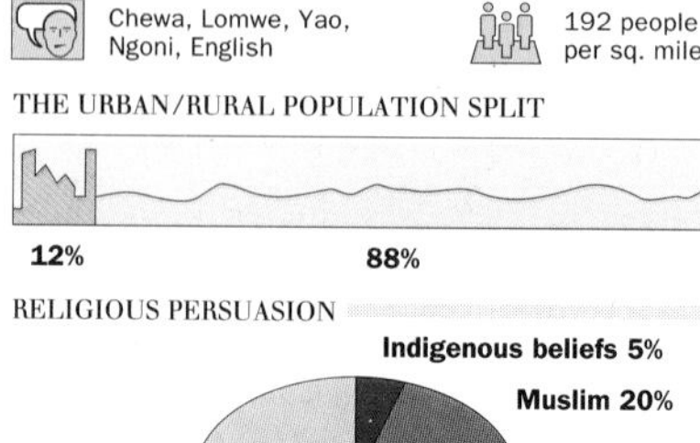

Ethnic tensions are few in Malawi, as most of the population share a common Bantu origin. The main ethnic groupings are the Chewa, Yao, Chieoka, Tonga, Tumbuka, Ngoni and Nyanja. Ethnicity has not been exploited for political ends to the extent that it has in neighboring states. However, in recent years tensions between the north and south have been rising. Northerners are increasingly disaffected by their lack of representation in politics and have become alienated from the ruling MCP.

Many of the Muslim Asians are involved in the retail trade. They have suffered some discrimination from the Banda regime. President Banda, a member of the Scottish Presbyterian Church, has promoted the expansion of Protestantism in Malawi.

***Fruit and vegetable sellers** on the Mozambique border. The south of the country is intensively cultivated.*

POLITICS

1994

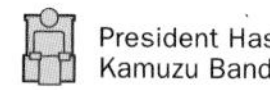
President Hastings Kamuzu Banda

THE STATE OF THE PARTIES

National Assembly 177 members

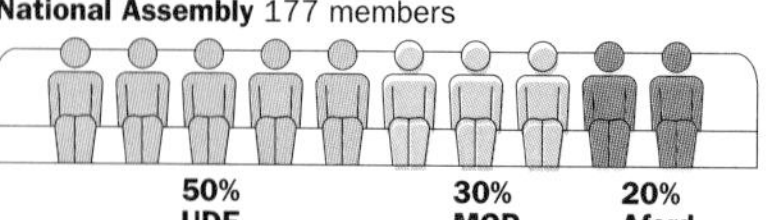

UDF = United Democratic Front **MCP** = Malawi Congress Party **Aford** = Alliance for Democracy

From independence in 1964, Malawi fell under the personalized rule of Dr. Hastings Banda. Under a single-party regime, instituted in 1966, dissent was not tolerated and torture and imprisonment without trial were common. In 1992, international aid was suspended because of the regime's poor human rights record. A referendum was held and President Banda agreed to the introduction of multiparty politics. In May 1994, presidential and legislative elections were held. The United Democratic Front (UDF), which draws most of its support from the south, scored a dramatic victory in the parliamentary elections. The UDF leader, Bakili Muluzi, also won the presidential election, bringing to a end one of the world's longest dictatorships. President Muluzi, a wealthy businessman and a former secretary-general of the MCP, recruited a number of prominent MCP politicians to the UDF, one reason for the party's good showing in the central region – a traditional MCP stronghold.

WORLD AFFAIRS

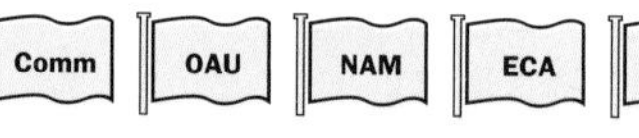

Malawi's principal concerns have been protecting its restored status as a recipient of Western aid and retaining a pragmatic relationship with South Africa. Malawi is the only black African country to have maintained full diplomatic relations with South Africa since 1967. One in ten Mozambicans fled to Malawi as refugees in the 1980s.

AID

Aid suspended in 1992

Not applicable

In May 1992, all non-humanitarian aid was suspended, with democratic change a precondition for its resumption. This action proved significant in propelling Malawi to a referendum on democracy in 1993.

M

Key to symbols and abbreviations on endpapers

DEFENSE

$22.02m

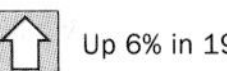
Up 6% in 1989

The 10,800-strong military has lost confidence in the ruling party and is forcing the pace of democratization. In 1993, it took the step of disarming the Young Pioneers, in what looked like the first stages of a coup. Banda heads the 6,000-strong paramilitary police force.

ECONOMICS

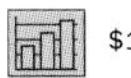
$1.8bn

4.46 kwacha

SCORE CARD

- ❑ WORLD GNP RANKING........................140th
- ❑ GNP PER CAPITA $200
- ❑ BALANCE OF PAYMENTS...................$-164m
- ❑ INFLATION 12.7%
- ❑ UNEMPLOYMENT....Widespread underemployment

STRENGTHS
Tobacco, accounting for 76% of foreign exchange earnings. Tea and sugar production. Unexploited reserves of bauxite, asbestos and coal.

WEAKNESSES
Agriculture, accounting for 80% of GDP, often hit by drought. Only 14% of GDP from industry. Small domestic market. Shortage of skilled personnel. Regional instability and refugee problem.

EXPORTS

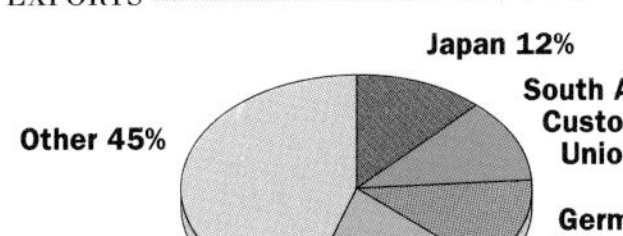

IMPORTS

Japan 9%
UK 22%
South Africa Customs Union 32%
Other 37%

RESOURCES

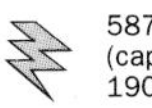
587m kwh (capacity 190,000 kw)

Not an oil producer and has no refineries

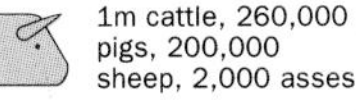
1m cattle, 260,000 pigs, 200,000 sheep, 2,000 asses

Coal, limestone, gemstones

Malawi has few strategic resources. Three hydropower plants account for 85% of electricity generating capacity, but only 3% of total energy use. Over 90% of energy needs are met from firewood as most Malawians do not have access to electricity. Malawi has reserves of bauxite and uranium, but not in commercially exploitable quantities. A deep-seam coal mine recently began production at Rumphi.

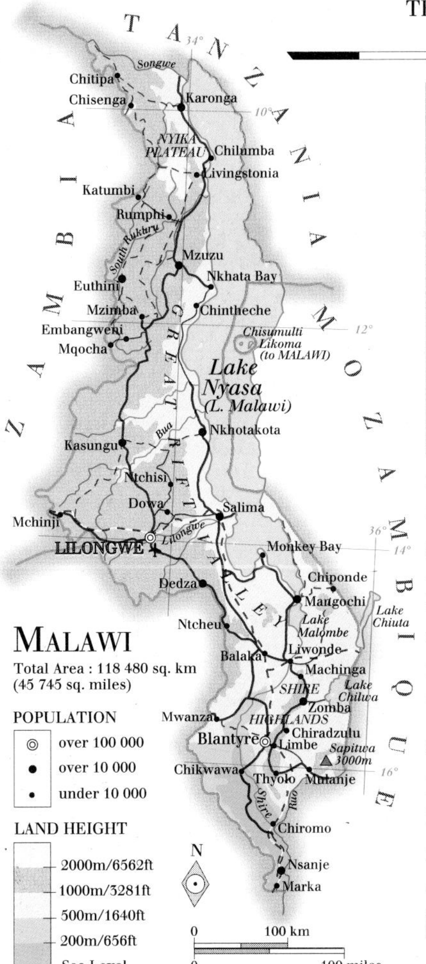

MALAWI

Total Area : 118 480 sq. km (45 745 sq. miles)

POPULATION
- ◎ over 100 000
- ● over 10 000
- • under 10 000

LAND HEIGHT
- 2000m/6562ft
- 1000m/3281ft
- 500m/1640ft
- 200m/656ft
- Sea Level

0 — 100 km
0 — 100 miles

ENVIRONMENT

11% (4% partially protected)

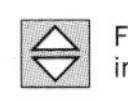
Few environmental initiatives

Drought eclipses all other problems. Agricultural production fell by 25% in 1992 due to its effects.

MEDIA

Any hint of criticism in the media is outlawed by the government

PUBLISHING AND BROADCAST MEDIA

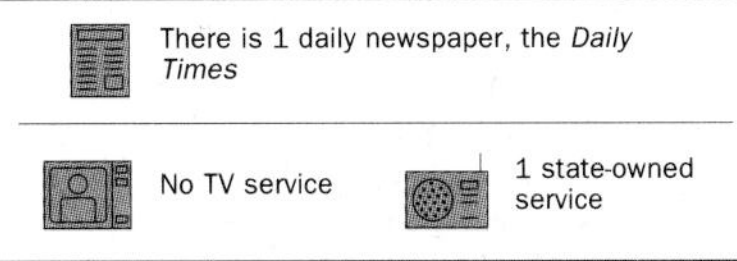

The authorities retain tight control over the press. Radio is effectively a mouthpiece for the government.

CRIME

Malawi does not publish prison figures

Up 3% in 1988

The Young Pioneers, the MCP's youth wing, have engaged in illegal violence. The proliferation of guns is contributing to an increase in armed robbery.

CHRONOLOGY

After strong Scottish missionary activity, Malawi came under British rule as Nyasaland in 1891.

- ❑ **1964** Independence under Dr. Hastings Banda.
- ❑ **1966** One-party state.
- ❑ **1967** Only African country to recognize South Africa.
- ❑ **1992** Anti-government riots. Illegal pro-democracy groups unite.
- ❑ **1993** Referendum: 63% in favor of multiparty system.

EDUCATION

52% males
31% females

Primary-level education is widespread, with 73% of boys and 60% of girls attending school regularly.

HEALTH

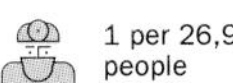
1 per 26,942 people

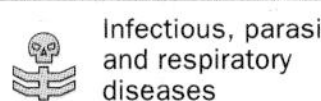
Infectious, parasitic and respiratory diseases

Access to health services is difficult; preventive care is viewed as a priority. Most doctors train abroad.

WEALTH

Most Malawians lead a subsistence existence

CONSUMER GOODS OWNERSHIP

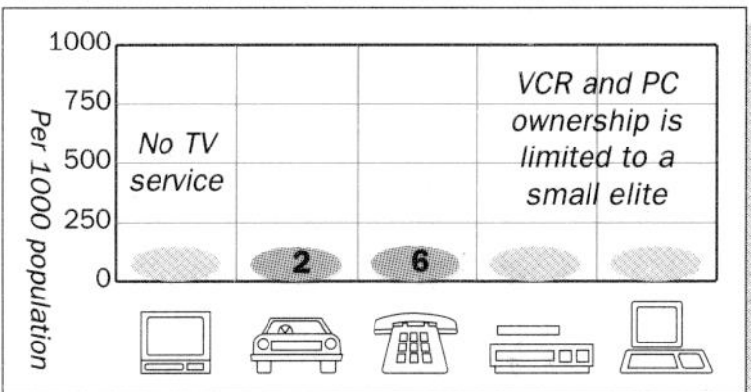

The MCP elite is the richest group. Banda allegedly has links with the Press Group consortium, which has an $250-million annual turnover.

WORLD RANKING

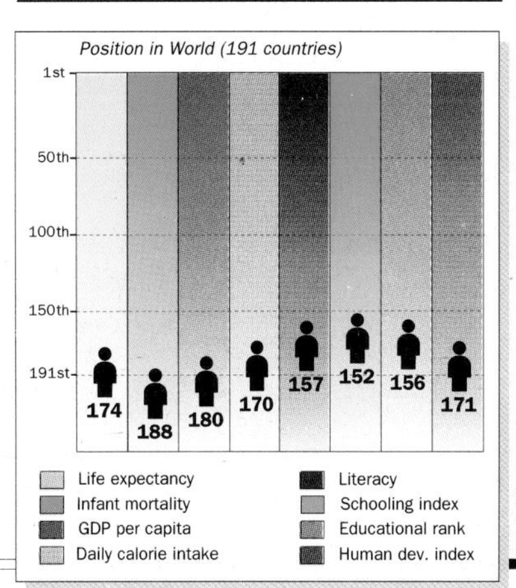

M

MALAYSIA

OFFICIAL NAME: Malaysia **CAPITAL:** Kuala Lumpur
POPULATION: 18.8 million **CURRENCY:** Ringgit **OFFICIAL LANGUAGE:** Malay

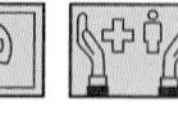

COMPRISING THE THREE separate territories of Malaya, Sarawak and Sabah, Malaysia stretches over 1,240 miles from Peninsular Malaysia to the northeastern end of the island of Borneo. It shares borders with Thailand, Indonesia and the enclave states of Singapore and Brunei. A central mountain chain divides Malaya, separating fertile western plains from a narrow eastern coastal belt. Sarawak and Sabah are characterized by swampy coastal plains rising to mountains on the border with Indonesia. Since 1987, Malaysia has been experiencing average economic growth rates of 8% a year.

CLIMATE

WEATHER CHART

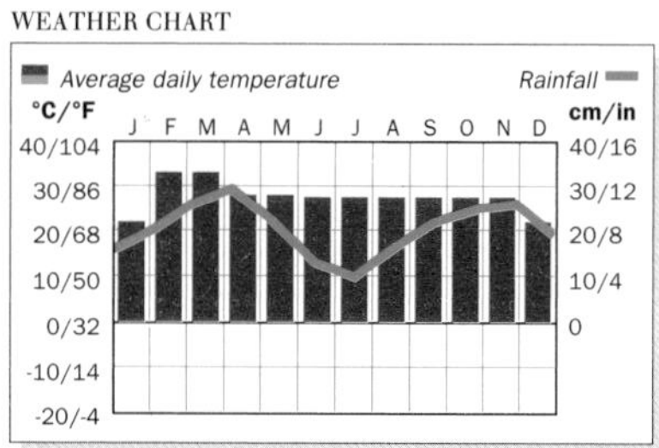

The entire country of Malaysia has an equatorial climate and experiences rainfall throughout the year; it falls on between 150 and 200 days almost everywhere. However, there are two distinct rainy seasons, when the heaviest rain falls – from March to May and from September to November. Coastal areas are also subject to the alternating southwest and northeast monsoon winds.

***Tea plantation** in the Cameron Highlands, in central-western Malaya. This region also contains one of Asia's most popular mountain resorts.*

COMMUNICATIONS

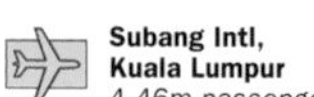

Subang Intl, Kuala Lumpur
4.46m passengers

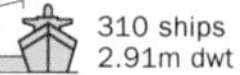

310 ships
2.91m dwt

THE TRANSPORTATION NETWORK

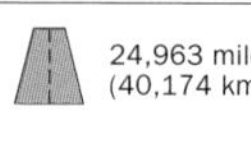

24,963 miles (40,174 km)

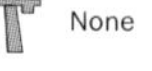

None

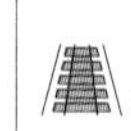

1,289 miles (2,075 km)

1,994 miles (3,209 km)

A major north–south highway is being built, and in Kuala Lumpur a new mass transit system is being constructed to extend to its outer suburbs. Malaysia's "national car," the Proton, has been a success; since 1985, national car ownership has tripled. Several ports are being updated to reduce Malaysia's current dependence on Singapore.

TOURISM

7.48m visitors

Up 54% in 1990

MAIN OVERSEAS ARRIVALS

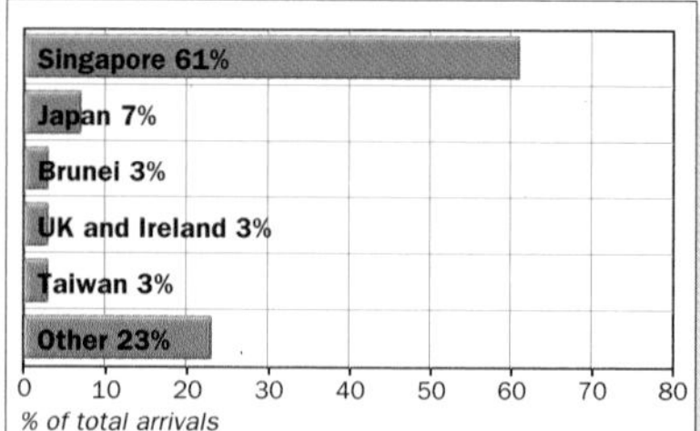

Malaysia is Southeast Asia's major tourist destination, with over seven million visitors a year. Most tourists come for the excellent tropical beaches on the east coast, to hike in the Cameron Highlands or to trek in the world's oldest rainforests in Borneo. There has recently been an increase in the international business convention trade.

By 1990, when the government ran the Visit Malaysia Year campaign, tourism had become Malaysia's third-biggest foreign exchange earner. There is still untapped potential for growth. Over half of the tourists to Malaysia are short-stay visitors from Singapore, and tourists' spending per day is less than half of that in Thailand. A second Visit Malaysia Year was launched in 1994, and a third is planned to coincide with the holding of the Commonwealth Games in Malaysia in 1998. Hotel capacity is currently growing at 10% a year and 70 new beach resorts are planned before the year 2000.

MALAYSIA

Total Area : 329 750 sq. km (127 317 sq. miles)

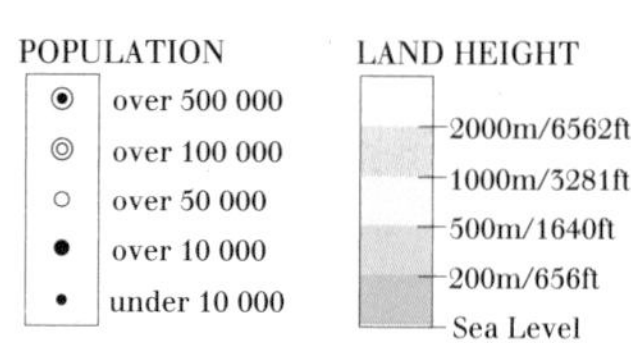

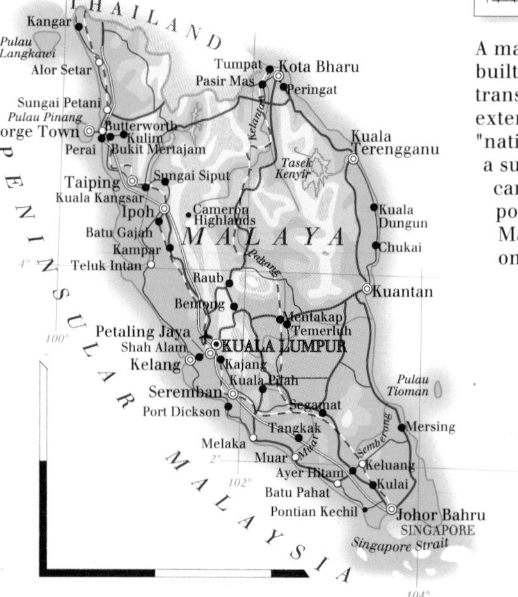

PEOPLE

Malay, Chinese, Tamil

140 people per sq. mile

THE URBAN/RURAL POPULATION SPLIT

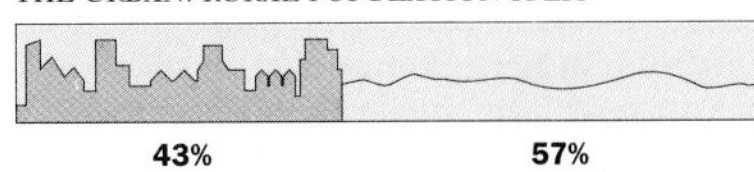

The key distinction in Malaysian society is between the indigenous Malays, termed the "Bumiputras" (literally, sons of the soil), and the Chinese. The Malays form the largest group, accounting for 47% of the population. However, the smaller Chinese population (32%) has traditionally controlled most business activity. The New Economic Policy (NEP), introduced in the 1970s, was designed to address this imbalance by offering positive opportunities to the Malays through the education system and by making jobs

RELIGIOUS PERSUASION

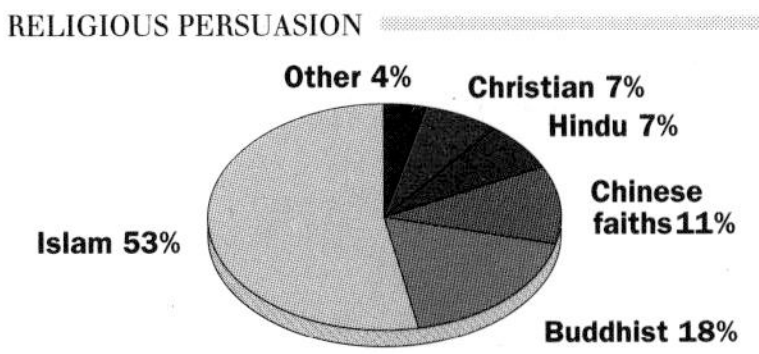

ETHNIC MAKEUP

Other 1%
Indian 8%
Indigenous tribes 12%
Malay 47%
Chinese 32%

available to them in both the state and private sectors. There are estimated to be more than one million Indonesian and Filipino immigrants in Malaysia, attracted by the country's labor

POPULATION AGE BREAKDOWN

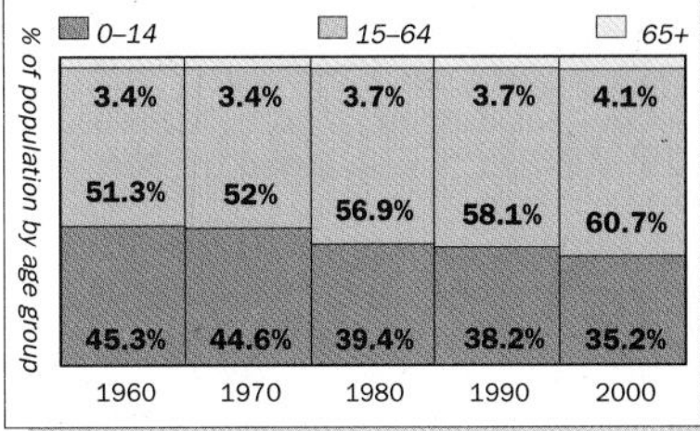

shortages and a dearth of employment in their own countries. In addition, over 200,000 Vietnamese refugees were offered asylum in Malaysia in the last decade; most have now been resettled but around 12,000 remain. In an attempt to promote Islamic tradition, Muslim Malay women have been encouraged to take the veil.

POLITICS

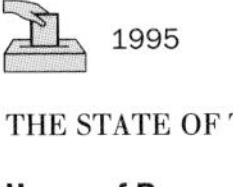

1995

HM Sultan Azlan Shah

THE STATE OF THE PARTIES

House of Representatives 180 members

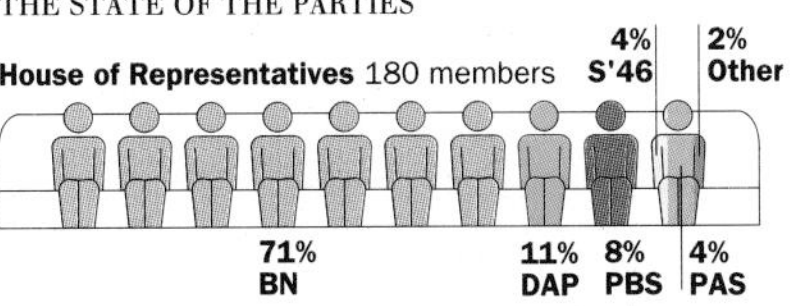

BN = National Front (coalition: principal party is UMNO = United Malays National Organization) **DAP** = Democratic Action Party **PBS** = Sabah United Party **S'46** = Spirit of '46 **PAS** = Pan-Malaysian Islamic Party

Senate 70 members

30 members elected – 2 from each of 13 State Legislative Assemblies and 2 Federal Territories – and 40 members chosen by the Head of State

Supreme power rests with the monarch, who acts on the advice of parliament. Opposition parties, while legal, are under tight control.

Main Political Issue

Malay superiority

While the current administration of Dr. Mahathir has declared that it no longer wishes to discriminate positively in favor of Malays, the Chinese community is feeling increasingly isolated. They have accused the government of corruption and uncompetitive practices, declaring that Malays are still favored in the placing of government contracts. In 1993, investment in the domestic economy by indigenous Chinese fell by an estimated 30%. The pro-Malay policy is also expressed in a more restrictive Islamic society, which further alienates the Chinese community.

Profile

Malaysia has been dominated by the UMNO since independence from Britain in 1947. In 1970, it introduced a policy of favoring Malays over the Chinese and other minorities. The party is heavily involved in business and controls a huge network of both political and economic patronage. The latter gives it and its Malay supporters a significant and growing control of the economy. The semblance of a working democracy is maintained by staged grass-roots political debate. An opposition exists, but its effectiveness is limited by the UMNO's policy of cutting funding to constituencies who vote against the party.

The success of the UMNO, and of its leader Dr. Mahathir, has been to deliver consistent economic growth and prosperity. As long as this continues, few challengers will emerge to question Mahathir's pre-eminent position in Malay political life.

Sultan Azlan Shah, *supreme head of state since 1989.*

Dr. Mahathir Mohamad, *prime minister since 1981.*

WORLD AFFAIRS

Dr. Mahathir sees himself as one of the developing world's leading voices. He maintains a strongly anti-US line in his public speeches and has chastized the West for its failure to resolve the conflict in Bosnia. His strong pro-Malay policies have in the past caused tensions with Singapore, which are exacerbated by the fact that Singapore is dependent on Malaysia for water.

AID

$459m (receipts); also a donor

Little variation from year to year

Malaysia has received soft loans from the West for large infrastructure projects. In recent years, it has also made donations. It has given aid to Bosnian Muslims and offered to take Bosnian refugees. Technical assistance has been made available to Vietnam.

M

CHRONOLOGY

The former British protectorate of Malaya, made up of 11 states, gained independence in 1957. The federation of Malaysia, incorporating Singapore, Sarawak and Sabah, was founded in 1963.

- ❑ **1965** Singapore leaves federation, reducing Malaysian states to 13.
- ❑ **1970** Malay-Chinese ethnic tension results in resignation of Prime Minister Tunku Abdul Rahman. Tun Abdul Razak, new prime minister, creates national coalition, the BN.
- ❑ **1976–1978** Guerrilla attacks by banned Communist Party of Malaya (CPM), based in southern Thailand. Cooperation between Malaysian and Thai governments leads to eventual reduction in CPM activity.
- ❑ **1976** Tun Abdul Razak dies. Succeeded by his deputy, Dato' Hussein bin Onn.
- ❑ **1977** Unrest in Kelantan following expulsion of its Chief Minister from Pan-Malaysian Islamic Party (PAS). National emergency declared. PAS expelled from BN.
- ❑ **1978** Elections consolidate BN power. PAS marginalized. Flare-up of ethnic and religious tension over government rejection of Chinese university.
- ❑ **1978–1989** Unrestricted asylum given to Vietnamese refugees.
- ❑ **1981** Dr. Mahathir Mohamad becomes Prime Minister.
- ❑ **1982** General elections return BN with increased majority.
- ❑ **1985** In Sabah state elections, BN defeated by PBS. Legality of PBS victory questioned.
- ❑ **1986** PBS wins new election and joins BN coalition. Dispute between Dr. Mahathir and his deputy, Dakuk Musa, triggers general election. BN wins, but criticism of leadership continues. Tensions increase between Malays and Chinese.
- ❑ **1987** 106 politicians from all parties suspected of Chinese sympathies detained without trial. Media censored.
- ❑ **1989** Disaffected UMNO members join PAS. Screening of Vietnamese refugees introduced. CPM sign peace agreement with Malaysian and Thai governments.
- ❑ **1990** General election. PBS leaves BN. BN wins with reduced majority.
- ❑ **1993** Assembly votes for reduction in powers, including loss of legal immunity, for the nine Sultans.
- ❑ **1994** Chief Minister of Sabah found guilty of corruption, but he and his PBS party returned in state election.

M

DEFENSE

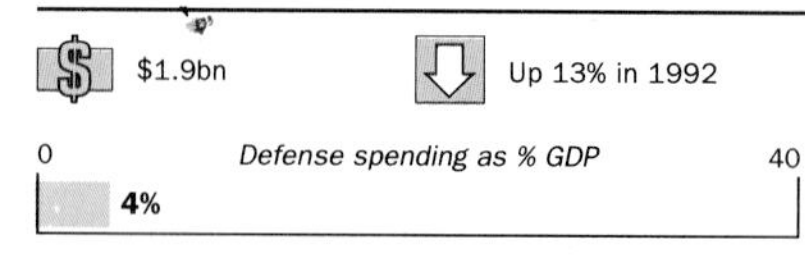

MALAYSIAN ARMED FORCES

26 light tanks (26 Scorpion (90mm))
105,000 personnel
4 frigates and 37 patrol boats
10,500 personnel
69 combat aircraft (27 A-4PTM/6TA-4/ 13 F-5E/4 F-5F)
12,000 personnel
None

The military is entirely composed of Malays. Defense spending currently accounts for 4% of GDP. There are plans to raise it to 6%, in line with neighboring Singapore. Malaysia is an important market for Western arms suppliers. The air force buys US equipment, although Malaysia has threatened to buy second-hand MiG fighters from Russia. In 1990, Malaysia expressed an interest in buying Tornado fighters from the UK. The main defense concerns are Singapore's large and highly mechanized army and growing Chinese influence in the South China Sea. Patroling East and West Malaysia is a key function of the navy, which is large by regional standards.

ECONOMICS

$55bn | 2.62 ringgits

SCORE CARD

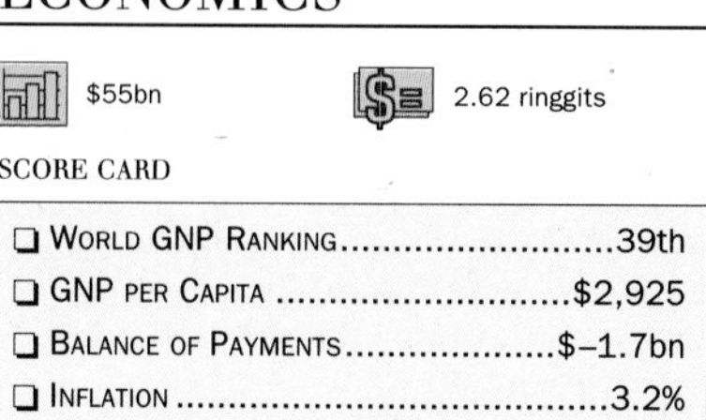

❑ World GNP Ranking	39th
❑ GNP per Capita	$2,925
❑ Balance of Payments	$-1.7bn
❑ Inflation	3.2%
❑ Unemployment	Low rate

EXPORTS

South Korea 5%
Japan 15%
Other 40%
USA 17%
Singapore 23%

IMPORTS

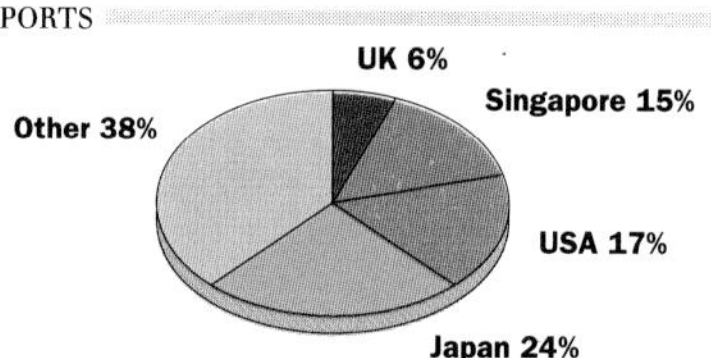

Strengths

Electronics: the world's biggest producer of disk drives. Proton car a national and international success. Heavy industries such as steel. Latex and rubber industries.

MALAYSIA : MAJOR BUSINESSES

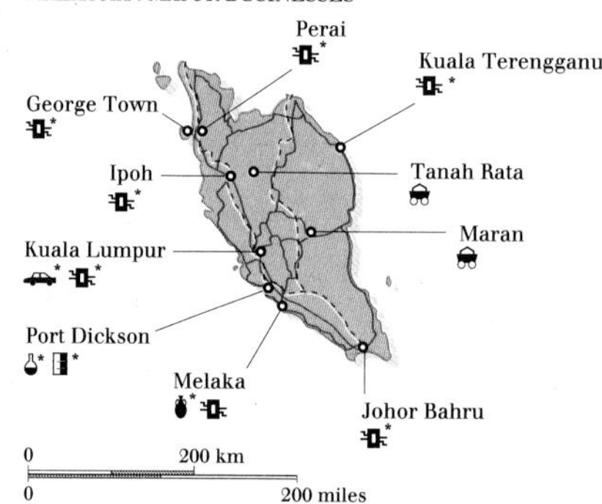

ECONOMIC PERFORMANCE INDICATOR

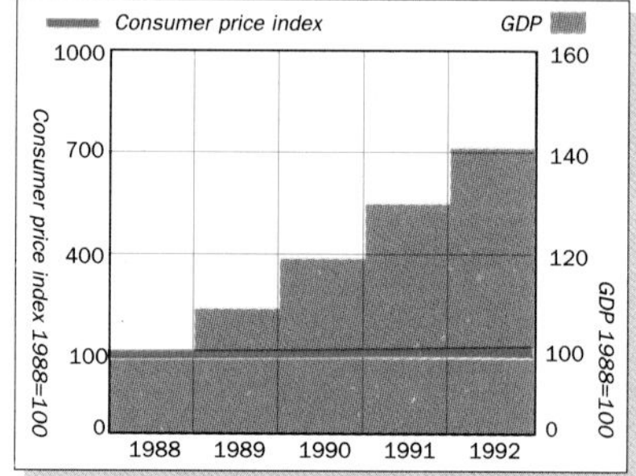

Weaknesses

Shortage of skilled labor. High interest rates deter private investors. High government budget spending. Competition from new NICs.

Profile

Growth in the economy took off in 1987. Since then, Malaysia has been expanding faster than any other Southeast Asian nation, at an average yearly rate of 8%. Much of the growth has been state-directed. In 1987, the government made a concerted push for foreign investment, which rose to a peak of 17.6 billion ringgits in 1990. The privatization of state assets was also stepped up. Goals have been set for full industrialization in a plan known as "Vision 2020."

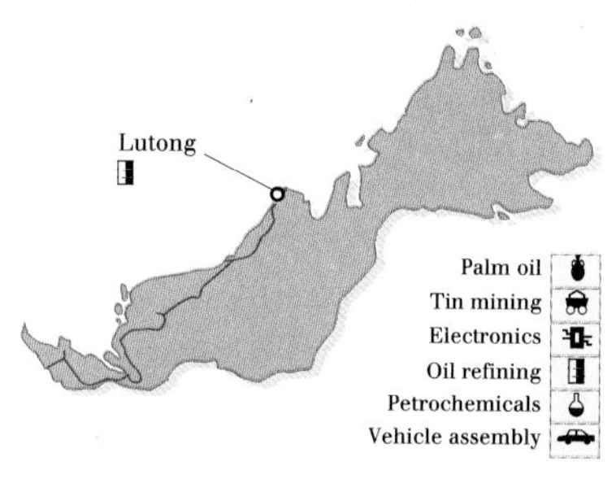

* significant multinational ownership

RESOURCES

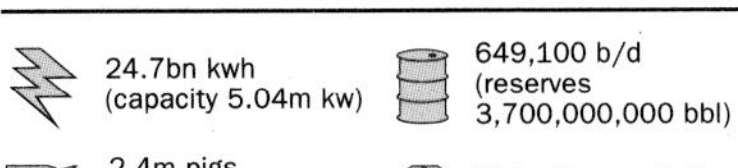

ELECTRICITY GENERATION

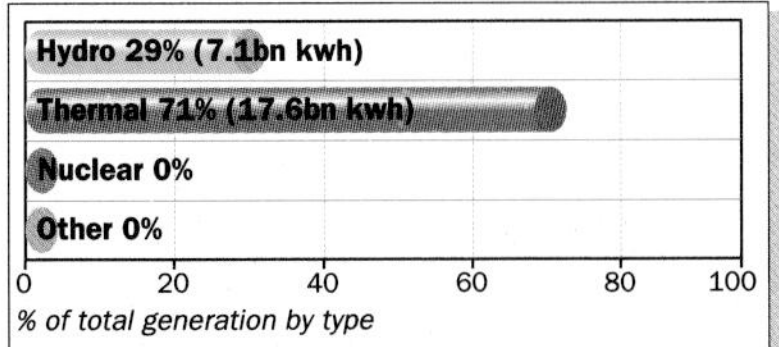

Thailand has overtaken Malaysia as the world's major rubber producer. Palm oil, of which Malaysia is the world's largest producer, is now a more important export product. Malaysia is a significant exporter of oil and natural gas. Oil reserves are offshore from Sabah and Sarawak. The good quality of the oil means that most is exported, while crude imports are refined. Malaysia accounts for nearly half of world timber exports, most of which come from Sarawak.

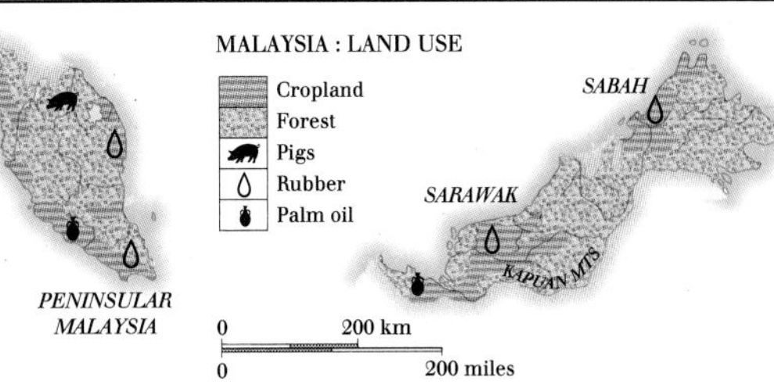

ENVIRONMENT

4% (2% partially protected)

Deforestation remains a serious problem

ECOLOGICAL TREATIES

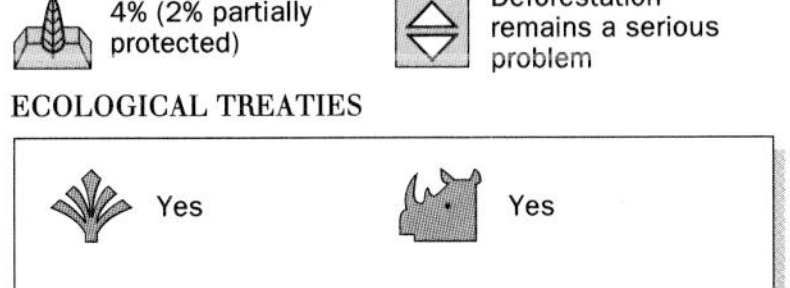

Logging is the overwhelming environmental concern of groups such as Sahabat Alam Malaysia (Friends of the Earth, Malaysia). Unprocessed log exports from Sarawak have risen from 6.7 million cubic meters in 1980 to 15.8 million cubic meters in 1991. World Bank estimates suggest that trees are being cut down at four times the sustainable rate. Indigenous forest communities such as the Penan are being destroyed and some species of wood such as Ramin are near extinction. In 1992, the state of Sarawak began to take action to diversify the economy. There is great pressure to maintain growth, however, and the profits from logging are hard to resist.

MEDIA

All news bulletins for radio and TV by Department of Broadcasting

PUBLISHING AND BROADCAST MEDIA

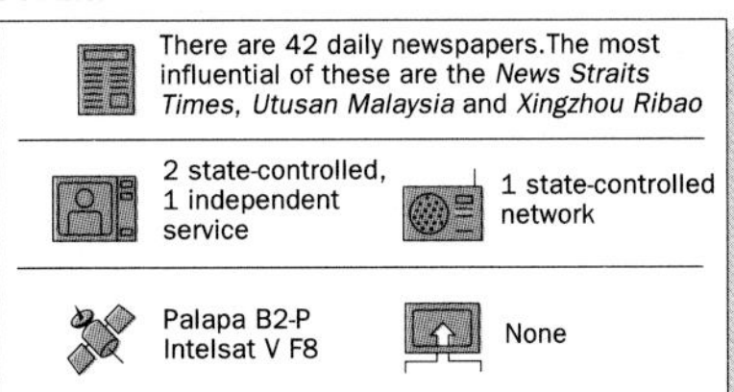

There are 42 daily newspapers.The most influential of these are the News Straits Times, Utusan Malaysia and Xingzhou Ribao
2 state-controlled, 1 independent service
1 state-controlled network
Palapa B2-P Intelsat V F8
None

Almost all newspapers in Malaysia are controlled by the UMNO, the dominant political party. The party owns the *Straits* group, which includes the most influential press. Radio and TV are also strictly controlled, under the 1987 Broadcasting Act, and Western commercials are banned. Singaporean TV can be received in the south.

CRIME

22,832 prisoners

Down 20% in 1989

CRIME RATES

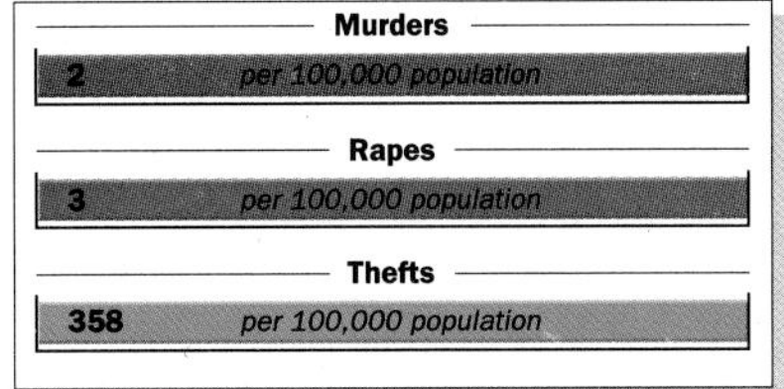

The judiciary and the ruling UMNO maintain close links. The death sentence for possession of drugs is mandatory. The state of Kelantan has attempted to implement the Islamic penal code, including stoning for adulterers and amputation for thieves.

EDUCATION

78%

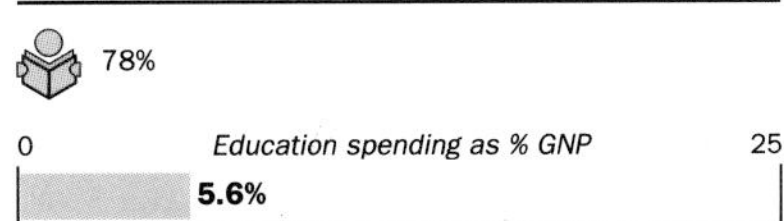

THE EDUCATION SYSTEM

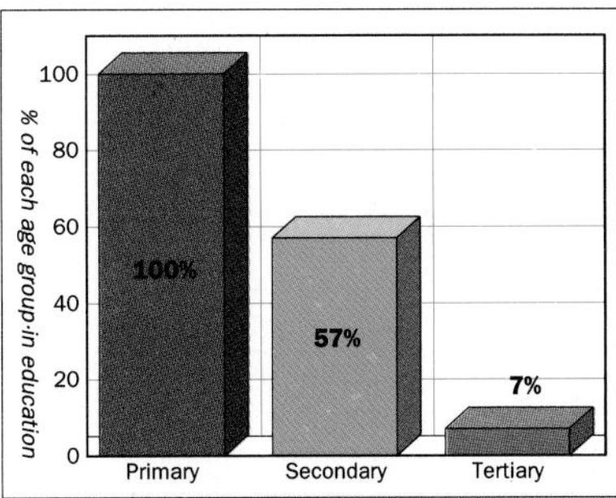

Malays are favored above other communities by a quota system which gives them preference for places in higher education. The Chinese community has its own schools. An attempt by some Chinese to establish their own private university was vetoed by the government. Many students, particularly the Chinese, complete their studies in the UK or USA.

HEALTH

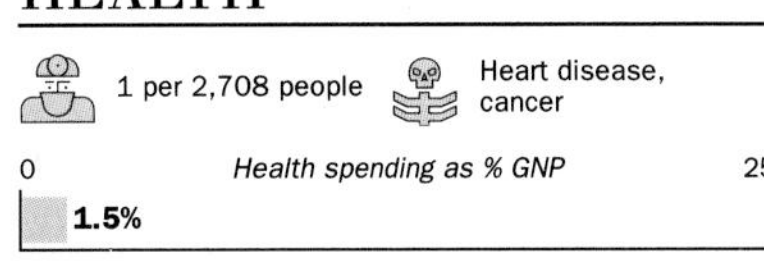

There is a sharp distinction between care in cities and the traditional medicine practiced in outlying areas.

WEALTH

Rubber tapper, 14.1 ringgits per day; electronic technician, 1,000 ringgits per month

CONSUMER GOODS OWNERSHIP

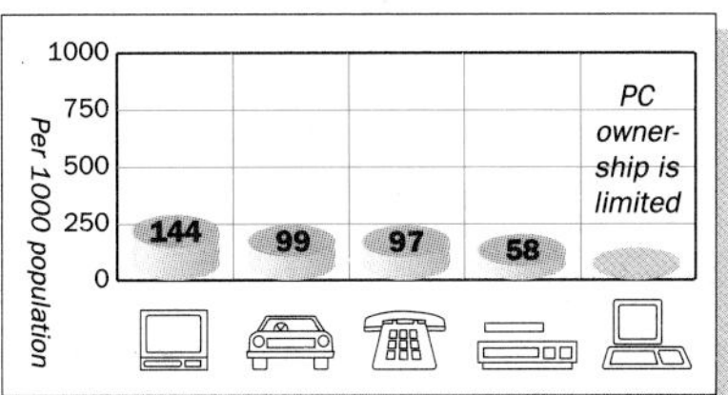

The Chinese remain the wealthiest community in Malaysia. However, following riots in 1970, the UMNO government embarked on a deliberate program of achieving 30% Malay ownership of the corporate sector. Many Malays earned quick profits from preferential privatization share allocations in the early 1990s.

WORLD RANKING

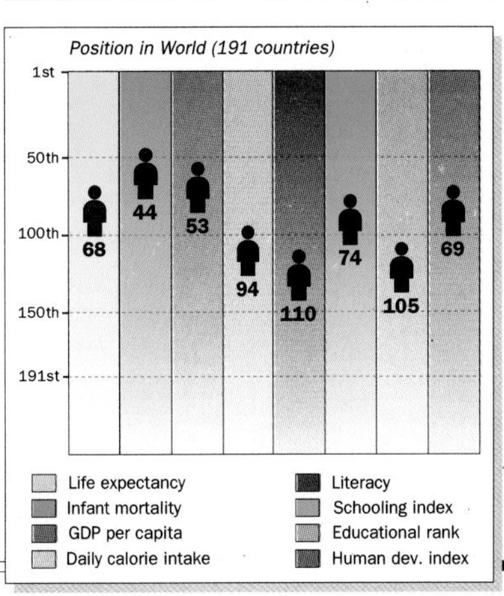

M

INDIAN OCEAN
India
Asia
MALDIVES
Sri Lanka

MALDIVES

OFFICIAL NAME: Republic of Maldives **CAPITAL:** Male'
POPULATION: 223,000 **CURRENCY:** Rufiyaa **OFFICIAL LANGUAGE:** Dhivehi

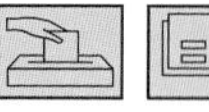

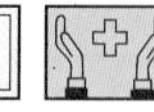

THE MALDIVES IS AN archipelago of 1,190 small coral islands set in the Indian Ocean southwest of Sri Lanka. The islands, none of which rise above 6 ft, are protected by encircling reefs or *faros*. Only 200 are inhabited. Tourism has grown in recent years, though vacation islands are separate from settler islands. In October 1993, President Maumoon Abdul Gayoom, survivor of three coup attempts, was elected for a fourth term in office.

Traditional Maldivian trading yacht. The 1,190 coral islands are grouped in natural atolls, from the Maldivian word "atolu."

CLIMATE

WEATHER CHART

Average daily temperature — Rainfall
°C/°F — cm/in
J F M A M J J A S O N D
40/104 30/86 20/68 10/50 0/32 -10/14 -20/-4
40/16 30/12 20/8 10/4 0

The Maldives has a tropical climate with abundant rainfall and high temperatures throughout the year. The northern islands are occasionally affected by violent storms caused by tropical cyclones. Most rain falls in the southern islands, from November to March.

Eight Degree Channel
Ihavandippolhu Atoll
Thiladhunmathi Atoll
Makunudhoo Atoll
North Miladummadulu Atoll
South Miladummadulu Atoll
North Maalhosmadulu Atoll
South Maalhosmadulu Atoll
Faadhippolhu Atoll
Horsburgh Atoll
Rasdu Atoll
Male' Atoll
MALE'
Ari Atoll
Felidhu Atoll
North Nilandhe Atoll
South Nilandhe Atoll
Mulaku Atoll
Kolhumadulu Atoll
Hadhdhunmathi Atoll
One and Half Degree Channel
North Huvadhu Atoll
South Huvadhu Atoll
Equatorial Channel
Equator
Fuammulah
Addu Atoll
Gan
INDIAN OCEAN

MALDIVES
Total Area : 300 sq. km (116 sq. miles)
POPULATION
over 10 000
under 10 000
LAND HEIGHT
100m/328ft
Sea Level
N
0 100 km
0 100 miles

COMMUNICATIONS

THE TRANSPORTATION NETWORK

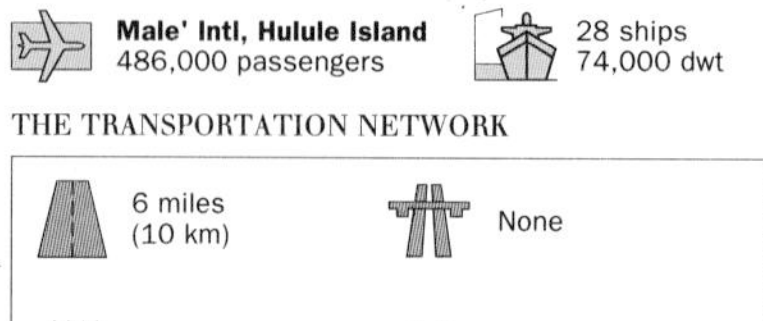

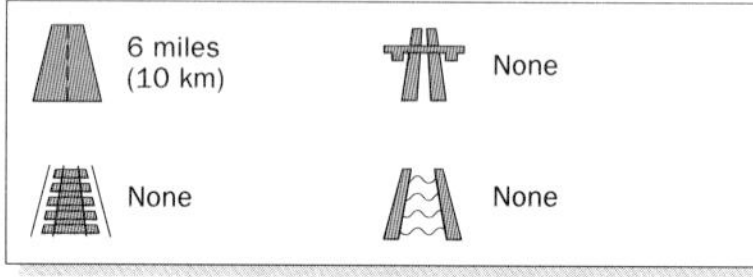

It is possible to walk across Male' Island in 20 minutes. Inter-island travel is mostly by ferry and traditional *dhoni*.

TOURISM

MAIN OVERSEAS ARRIVALS

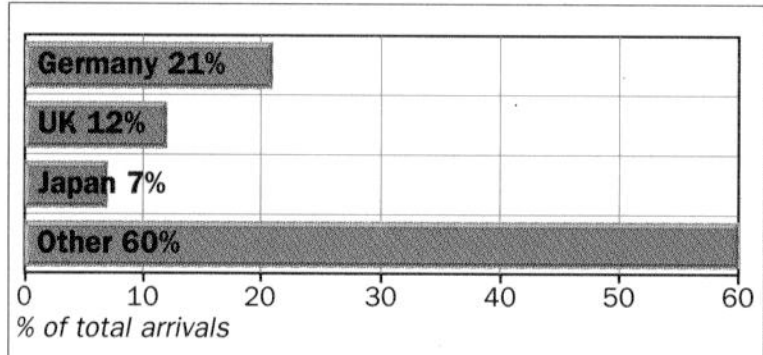

Tourism is the largest source of foreign exchange. The first resort was opened in 1972. Luxury hotels, financed by local and foreign capital, have been built on the uninhabited islands. The sea, with its many varieties of tropical fish, is a big attraction for divers.

POLITICS

THE STATE OF THE PARTIES

Citizen's Council 48 members

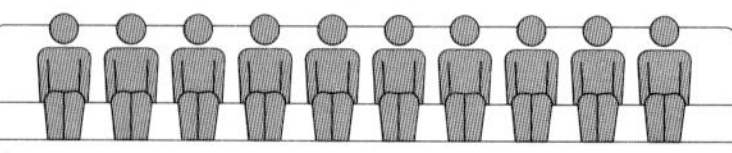

There are no political parties. 40 members are elected, 2 from Male' and 2 from each of the 19 administrative atolls. 8 members are chosen by the president

Politics in the Maldives are, in practice, restricted to a small group of influential families. Most were already dominant under the Sultanate. Politics are not based on formal parties with ideological objectives; it is organized around family and clan loyalties.

A few figures have dominated politics since independence. Former president Ibrahim Nasir was responsible for abolishing the premiership in 1975, making the presidency even more powerful. Ilyas Ibrahim, exiled to an outlying island for 15 years, and Maumoon Abdul Gayoom, a wealthy businessman, are now the main figures. Gayoom was almost defeated by Ibrahim in the 1993 elections. A new young elite, who have tasted democracy abroad, are pressing for a more liberal political system.

PEOPLE

Dhivehi (Maldivian)

1,854 people per sq. mile

THE URBAN/RURAL POPULATION SPLIT

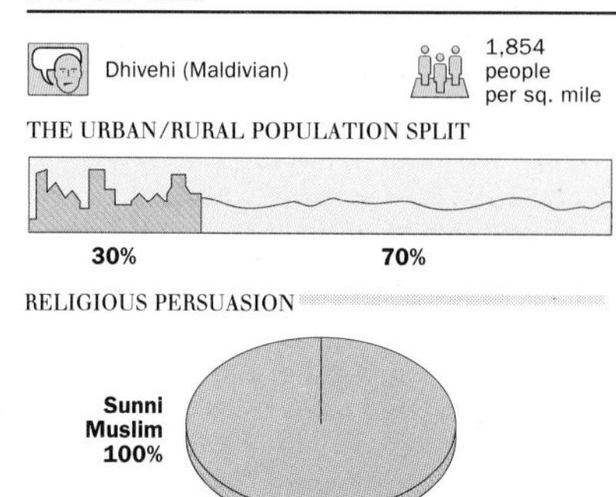

It is believed the islands were inhabited as early as 1500 BC. Aryan immigrants arrived around 500 BC. The islands were then discovered by Arab traders. The people, who are all Sunni Muslims, live on only 200 of the 1,190 islands. About 25% of the total population live on the island capital of Male'. It is estimated that 12,000 guest workers from neighboring Sri Lanka and India work in the Maldives. The country's new-found prosperity has led to the emergence of a commercial elite.

M

WORLD AFFAIRS

The Maldives is a long-standing member of the Non-Aligned Movement. The government continues to support NAM and rejects the criticism that it does not have a role to play in the post–Cold War world. The Maldives's international standing was enhanced in 1990, when it hosted the fifth SARC summit meeting, held in Male'.

AID

 $28m (receipts)

 Aid levels remain fairly constant

Aid has helped to finance development of port and airport facilities. Japan is the most important bilateral aid donor, contributing 25% of total assistance in 1991. Relief aid, principally from India, Pakistan and the USA, was given after the storms of 1991 caused $30 million damage.

DEFENSE

 Paramilitary police force only

 Not applicable

The British military presence ended in 1975, when troops were withdrawn from the staging post on Gan in the Addu atoll. The USSR's offer to lease the base was rejected, and it is now an industrial zone. The Maldives follows a policy of non-alignment.

ECONOMICS

 $101m

 11.95 rufiyaa

SCORE CARD

- ❑ WORLD GNP RANKING........185th
- ❑ GNP PER CAPITA........$455
- ❑ BALANCE OF PAYMENTS........$–38m
- ❑ INFLATION........11.4%
- ❑ UNEMPLOYMENT........2%

STRENGTHS

Growth of tourism. Fishing, especially tuna; mostly exported to the UK and Sri Lanka. Shipping. Clothing. Coconut production. Financial and commercial reforms as economy expands.

WEAKNESSES

Too dependent on fluctuating tourist industry. Growing trade deficit. Shortage of skilled labor. Small manufacturing base. Cottage industries employ 25% of work force; little scope for expansion.

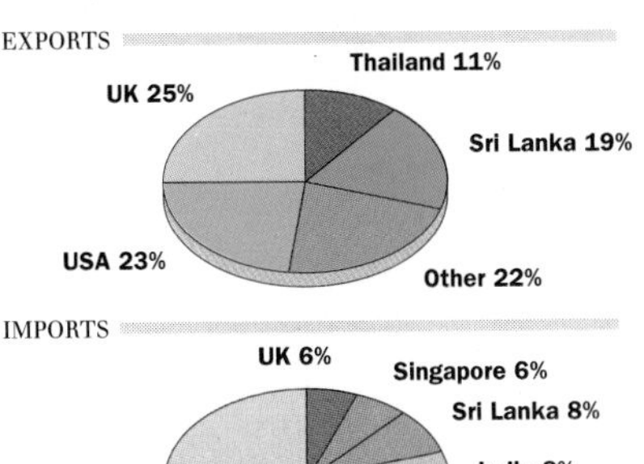

RESOURCES

 29m kwh (capacity 5,000 kw)

Not an oil producer and has no refineries

76,000 tons

 None

Natural resources include abundant stocks of fish, particularly tuna. Fishing, still carried out by the traditional pole and line method to help conserve stocks, employs over 20% of the working population. Coconut production is also important. All oil products and virtually all staple foods are imported.

ENVIRONMENT

None

Not applicable

It is believed global warming, climatic change and the rise of the sea level are threatening to submerge the islands, which have an average height of just 6 feet. A sea wall has been built around the capital island. Other environmental concerns are sewage, waste disposal and the mining of coral for building.

MEDIA

 New libel laws are being implemented by the government against journalists

PUBLISHING AND BROADCAST MEDIA

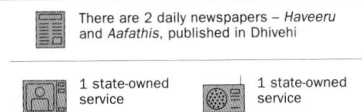

There are 2 daily newspapers – *Haveeru* and *Aafathis*, published in Dhivehi

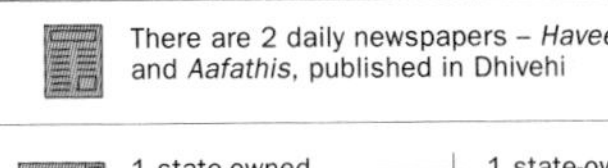

There is a marked degree of press censorship. In the past, journalists and satirists have been imprisoned. There are only two newspapers.

CRIME

 The Maldives does not publish prison figures

 Up 3% in 1990

The Maldives is a strict Islamic society. Punishment for drug crime is severe. Political prisoners are banished to outer islands. The judiciary and executive are closely linked.

CHRONOLOGY

The Maldives was a British protectorate from 1887 until its independence in 1965.

- ❑ **1932** First written constitution.
- ❑ **1968** Sultanate abolished. Declared a republic. Ibrahim Nasir elected as first president.
- ❑ **1988** Coup attempt. Suppressed by Indian troops sent over on request.
- ❑ **1993** President Gayoom reelected for fourth five-year term.

EDUCATION

 91%

Primary education has been improved. Secondary education is less developed in the outer islands; the first school outside Male' was opened in 1992.

HEALTH

 1 per 5,330 people

 Infectious and parasitic diseases

There is a lack of general equipment and facilities. Health care is less developed on the outlying islands.

WEALTH

 Private-sector secretary, 2,868 rufiyaa per month; government minister, 5,975 rufiyaa per month

CONSUMER GOODS OWNERSHIP

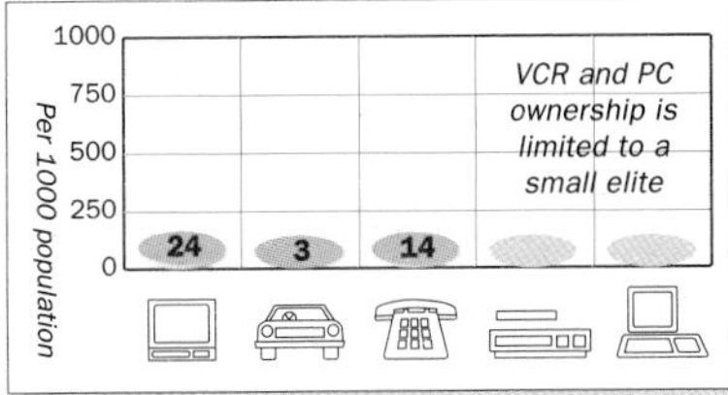

Great disparities exist between the people who live in Male' and those who live on the outer islands.

WORLD RANKING

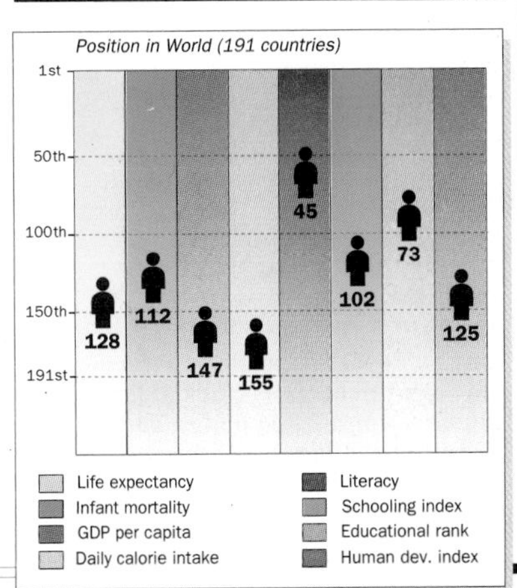

M

MALI

OFFICIAL NAME: Republic of Mali **CAPITAL:** Bamako
POPULATION: 9.8 million **CURRENCY:** CFA franc **OFFICIAL LANGUAGE:** French

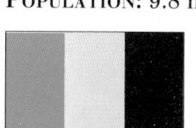

WEST AFRICA
Algeria
Mauritania
MALI
Niger
Senegal
Burkina
Guinea
Africa

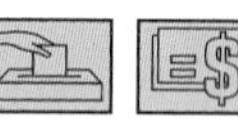

MALI IS LANDLOCKED in the heart of West Africa. Its mostly flat terrain comprises virtually uninhabited Saharan plains in the north and more fertile savanna land in the south, where most of the population lives. The Niger River irrigates the central and southwestern regions of the country. Following independence in 1960, Mali experienced a long period of largely single-party rule. It became a multiparty democracy in 1992.

CLIMATE

WEATHER CHART

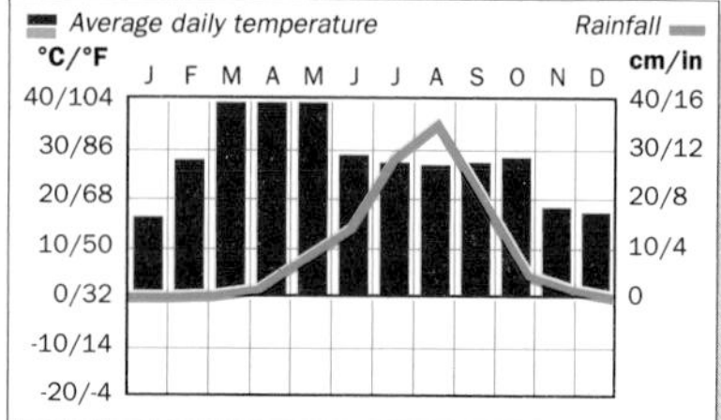

In the south, intensely hot, dry weather precedes the westerly rains. The northern half of Mali is almost rainless.

COMMUNICATIONS

THE TRANSPORTATION NETWORK

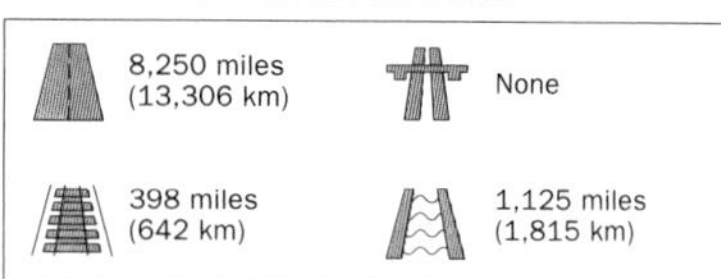

Mali is linked by rail with the port of Dakar in Senegal, and by good roads to the port of Abidjan in the Ivory Coast.

TOURISM

MAIN OVERSEAS ARRIVALS

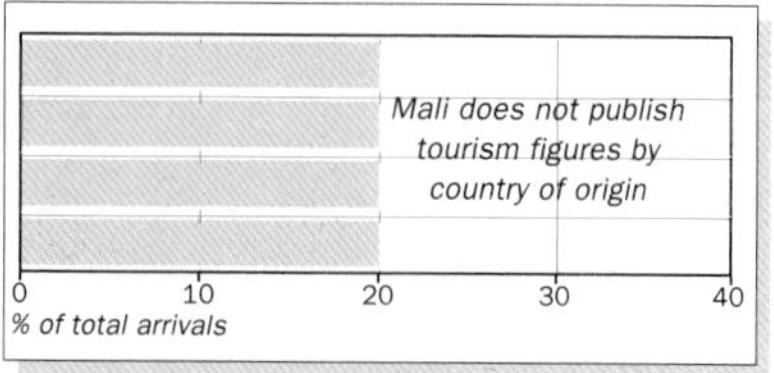

Tourism is largely safari-oriented, although the historic cities of Djénné, Gao and Mopti, lying on the banks of the Niger River, also attract visitors. A national domestic airline began operating in 1990.

PEOPLE

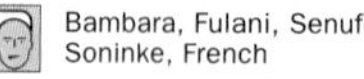

THE URBAN/RURAL POPULATION SPLIT

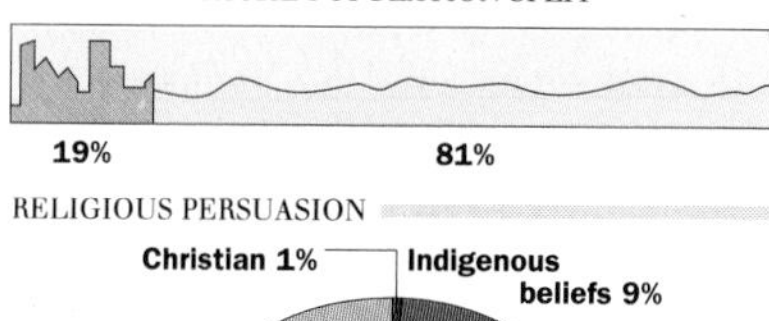

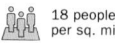

RELIGIOUS PERSUASION

Christian 1%
Indigenous beliefs 9%
Muslim 90%

Mali's most significant ethnic group, the Bambara, is also politically dominant. The Bambara speak the *lingua franca* of the Niger River, which is shared with other groups including the Malinke. The relationship betweeen the Bambara–Malinke majority and the Tuareg nomads of the Saharan north is tense and sometimes violent. As elsewhere in Africa, the extended family, often based on the village, is a vital social security system and link between the urban and rural poor. There are a few powerful women in Mali, but in general women have little status.

POLITICS

THE STATE OF THE PARTIES

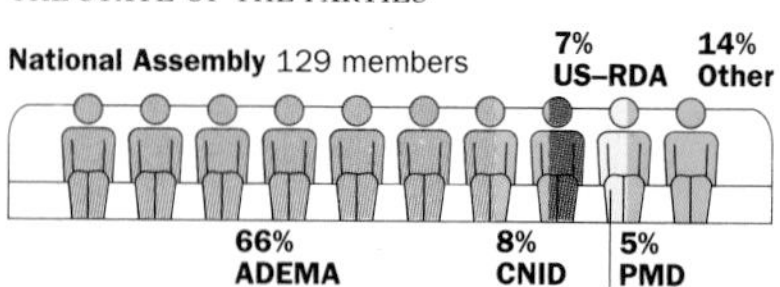

ADEMA = Alliance for Democracy in Mali **CNID** = National Committee for Democratic Initiative **US–RDA** = Sudanese Union – African Democratic Rally **PMD** = Popular Movement for the Development of West Africa **Other** = Rally for Democracy and Progress, Union for Democracy and Development

The successful transition to multiparty politics in 1992 followed the overthrow in the previous year of Moussa Traoré, Mali's dictator for 23 years. The army's role was crucial in leading the coup, while Colonel Touré, who acted as interim president, was responsible for the swift return to civilian rule in less than a year. The change marks Mali's first experience of multiparty politics. Maintaining good relations with the Tuaregs, after a peace agreement in 1991, is a key issue. However, the main challenge facing President Alpha Oumar Konaré's government is to alleviate poverty while placating the opposition, which feels that the luxury of multiparty politics is something that Mali cannot afford. As Konaré's austerity measures begin to take effect, opposition to his policies is likely to increase.

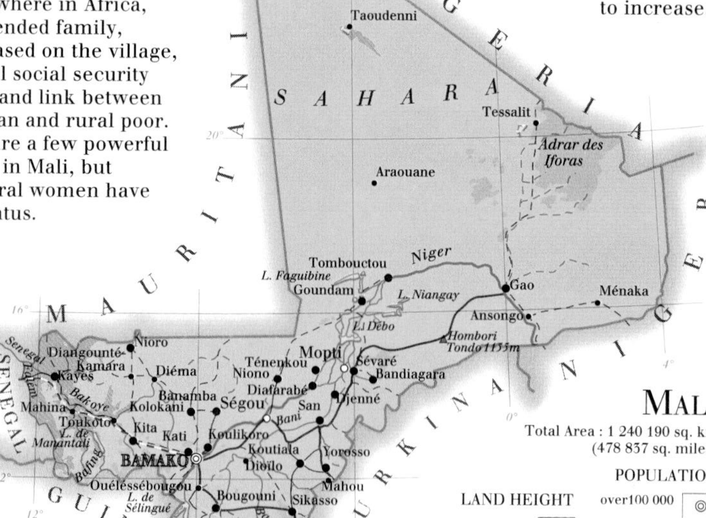

WORLD AFFAIRS

Mali concentrates on maintaining good relations with a wide variety of African neighbors, from the ECOWAS countries to the south, to its northern neighbors such as Algeria. Relations with Libya, which is suspected of inciting Tuareg revolt, are tense. Good relations with Western aid-providers are crucial.

AID

 $455m (receipts)  Up 35% in 1991

Mali is highly dependent on foreign aid, which comes from France, the EU, China, a few Arab states, the USA and international lending institutions.

DEFENSE

 $63.82m  Up 4% in 1988

Mali has traditionally had a strong army. In 1985, the air force played an important role in the war with Burkina.

ECONOMICS

 $2.8bn  295.23 CFA francs

SCORE CARD

- World GNP Ranking........129th
- GNP per capita........$285
- Balance of Payments........$-78m
- Inflation........-6.2%
- Unemployment....Widespread underemployment

Strengths
Business opportunities arising from strategic location in heart of West Africa. Niger and Senegal rivers have irrigation and HEP potential.

Weaknesses
Serious poverty and underdevelopment. Landlocked status and vast size of country present considerable communications problems. Drought-prone climate.

EXPORTS

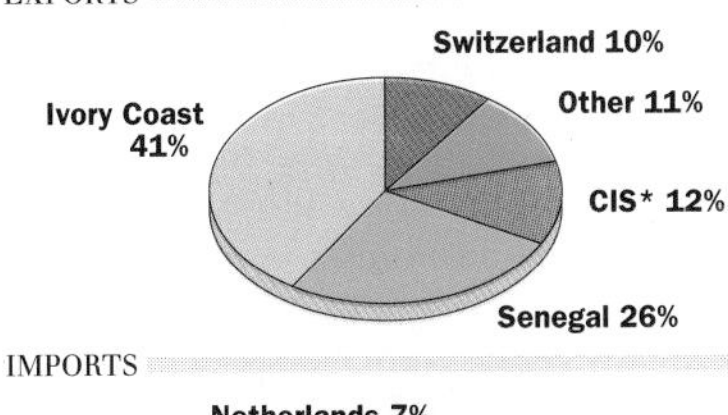

IMPORTS

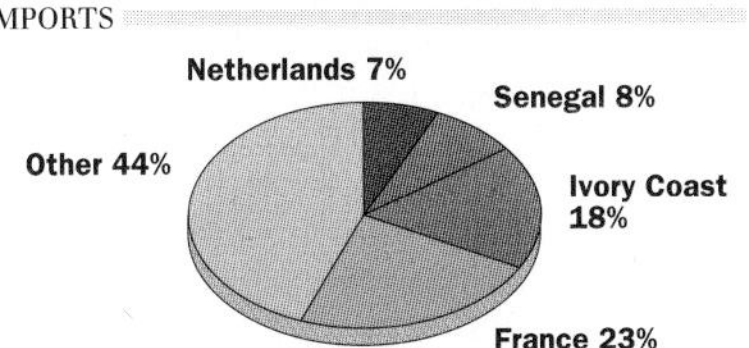

Village near Bandiagara. These low, broken hills typical of the east and southeast of Mali are the homeland of the Dogon people.

RESOURCES

 214m kwh (capacity 90,000 kw) 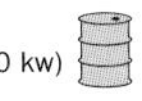 Not an oil producer and has no refineries

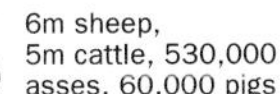 6m sheep, 5m cattle, 530,000 asses, 60,000 pigs — Gold, salt, marble, phosphate, limestone, iron, bauxite

Gold deposits are now being mined, and prospecting is under way for tungsten, diamonds and oil. The exploitation of other natural resources is hampered by Mali's poor infrastructure and land-locked situation. Almost all electricity is generated by hydroelectric power from the Selingue Dam on the Niger. When a second dam comes into operation, there should be a surplus.

ENVIRONMENT

 3% partially protected  New government takes environmental matters seriously

The 1983 drought destroyed herds and accelerated desertification and deforestation. The Selingue Dam seriously affects the levels of the Niger River, even in years of good rainfall.

MEDIA

 The constitution of 1992 guarantees freedom of expression. There are no restrictions on political reporting

PUBLISHING AND BROADCAST MEDIA

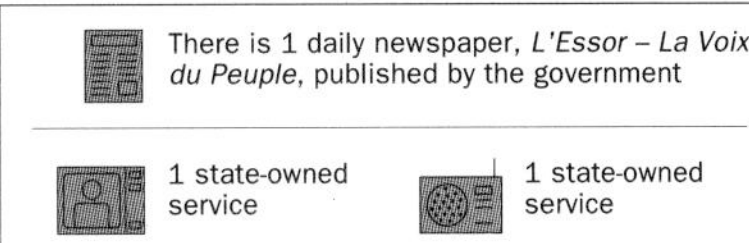

There is 1 daily newspaper, *L'Essor – La Voix du Peuple*, published by the government
1 state-owned service
1 state-owned service

Even before the coup, previously rigid controls had begun to be relaxed. The militant campaigning of the privately owned press in early 1991 was a significant factor in the overthrow of the Traoré regime.

CRIME

 Mali does not publish prison figures  Crime is rising slowly

Crime is not particularly prevalent compared with some other countries in the region, due to strong family ties and the relative lack of urbanization.In towns, robbery, juvenile delinquency, and smuggling are problems.

CHRONOLOGY

Mali was a major trans-Saharan trading empire. The French colonized the area between 1881 and 1895.

- **1960** Independence under anti-French socialist Modibo Keita.
- **1968** Armed coup; single-party state under Gen. Traoré.
- **1985** Six-day war with Burkina. ICJ splits disputed land equally.
- **1990** Democracy demonstrations.
- **1991** Traoré arrested.
- **1992** Free multiparty elections.

EDUCATION

 32%

Education in Mali is based on the French system. There are only 1,000 students in higher education – a low figure for the region.

HEALTH

 1 per 22,835 people — Malaria, pneumonia, parasitic and diarrheal diseases

An estimated 50% of the health budget is spent on an area inhabited by just 10% of the population.

WEALTH

Kindergarten teacher, 27,500 CFA francs per month; electrician, 101,500 CFA francs per month

CONSUMER GOODS OWNERSHIP

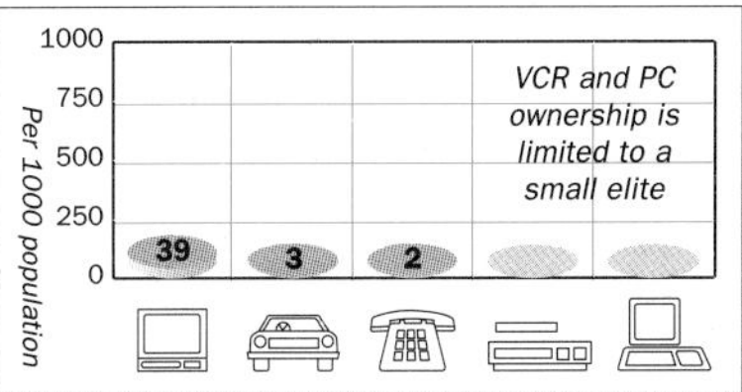

Poverty is widespread. Malians disapprove of flaunted wealth and public ostentation is rare.

WORLD RANKING

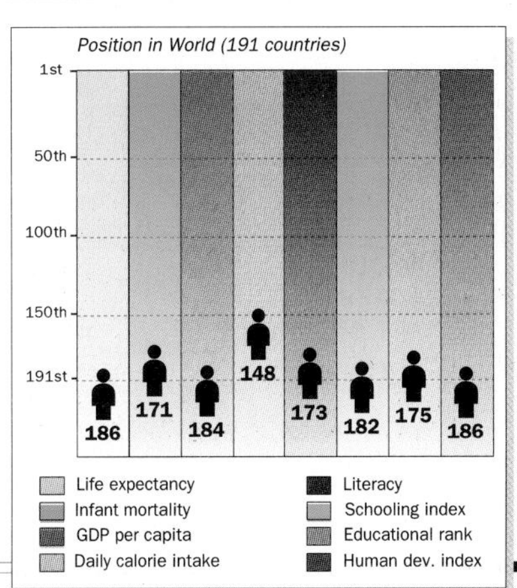

M

MALTA

EUROPE Italy Greece MALTA Tunisia Europe

OFFICIAL NAME: Republic of Malta **CAPITAL:** Valletta
POPULATION: 356,000 **CURRENCY:** Maltese lira **OFFICIAL LANGUAGES:** Maltese and English

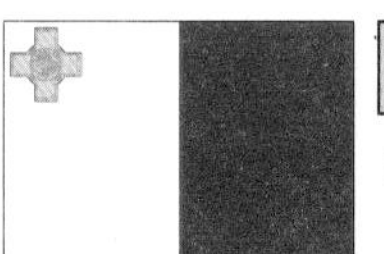

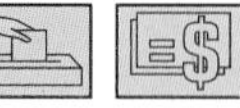

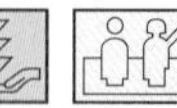

THE MALTESE ARCHIPELAGO is strategically located, lying midway between Europe and North Africa. Controlled throughout its history by successive colonial powers, Malta gained independence from the UK in 1964. The islands are mainly low-lying with rocky coastlines; only Malta, Gozo and Kemmuna are inhabited. Tourism is Malta's chief source of income, with an influx of tourists each year over two times the islands' population.

CLIMATE

WEATHER CHART

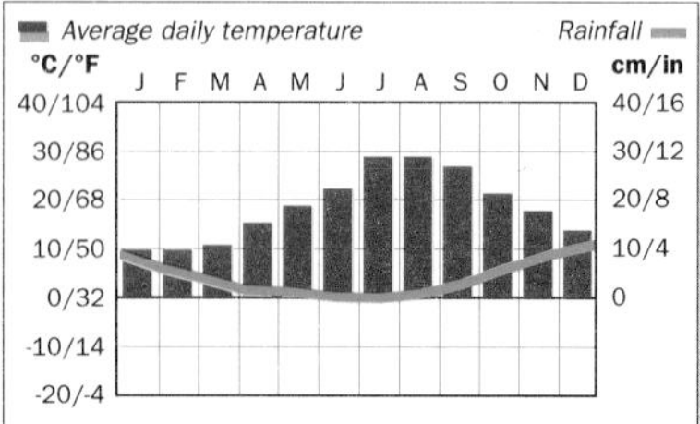

The climate is similar to that of Greece – very sunny, with at least six hours of sunshine a day, even in winter.

COMMUNICATIONS

THE TRANSPORTATION NETWORK

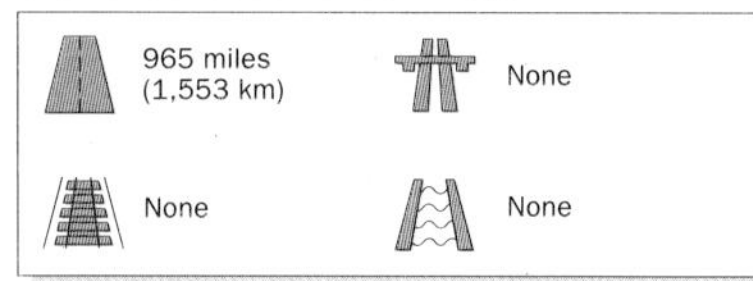

A new terminal with an annual capacity of 2.5 million passengers was recently opened at Luqa Airport. The main external sea route is to Sicily. In the summer, there is a five-minute helicopter link between the islands of Malta and Gozo, in addition to regular ferry and hovercraft services. There are regular buses on both islands.

Traditionally painted* luzzus *at St. Julian's harbor. The fish caught are now only for domestic and tourist consumption.

TOURISM

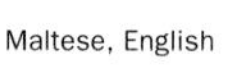

MAIN OVERSEAS ARRIVALS

UK 52%
Germany 15%
Italy 7%
Other 26%
0 10 20 30 40 50 60
% of total arrivals

Tourism is a booming industry in Malta, accounting for 30% of GNP. In addition to Malta's beaches and scenery, the government is eager to promote the historical attractions of Mdina and Valletta. Development on the quieter island of Gozo is being limited to luxury-grade hotels.

PEOPLE

Maltese, English

3,279 people per sq. mile

THE URBAN/RURAL POPULATION SPLIT

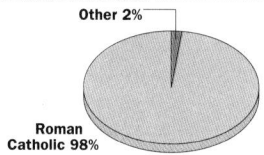

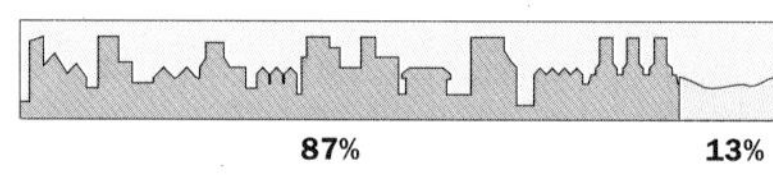

RELIGIOUS PERSUASION

Other 2%
Roman Catholic 98%

Malta's population has been subject over the centuries to diverse Arabic, Sicilian, Norman, Spanish, English and Italian influences. Today, many young Maltese go abroad to find work, especially to the USA and Australia; opportunities for them on the island are few.

The Maltese are staunch Roman Catholics – on a percentage basis more so than virtually any other nation. The remainder are mainly Anglicans, who are included within the diocese of Gibraltar. Divorce is illegal.

POLITICS

THE STATE OF THE PARTIES

House of Representatives 65 members

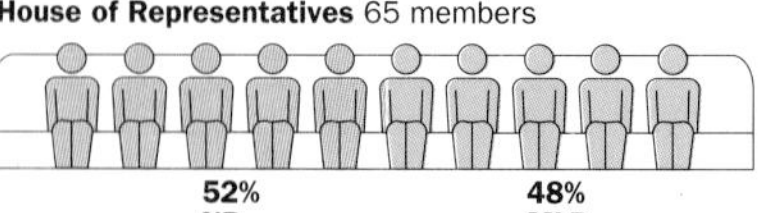

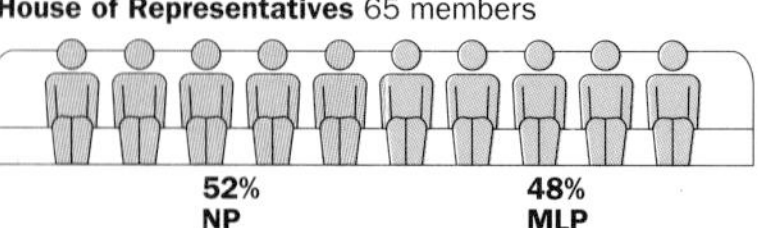

NP = Nationalist Party **MLP** Malta Labour Party

The NP, led by Dr. Fenech Adami, came to power in 1987 after 16 years of MLP rule. Adami's subsequent reelection to a second term of office in 1992 was largely due to a rise in living standards and economic growth. The Maltese were also reluctant to return to the divisive politics of the past.

Under the MLP, politics had been shaped by the leadership of the charismatic Dom Mintoff, who championed state control of industry and a strategy of international non-alignment. The NP retained the non-aligned policy and wrote it into the constitution.

In 1990, they succeeded in sealing a three-way accord between government, unions and businesses, under which wages are set in line with inflation.

The opposition is now led by Dr. Alfred Sant, a leading Maltese writer and Harvard MBA, and the MLP's traditional links with the unions have been diluted. The main current political issue is Malta's application for membership in the EU.

WORLD AFFAIRS

Malta is optimistic that it will gain entry into the EU; a formal application was made in 1990. All legislation is now drafted to EU regulations and old measures are being updated in accordance with them. Membership is expected to bring significant economic benefits; already, an estimated 75% of trade is with EU nations.

Closer links with Europe have to be balanced with Malta's traditional association with the Arab world and North Africa. Relations with Libya and the Kaddafi regime are good, although not as close as under the Labour government of Prime Minister Mintoff in the 1970s. However, a friendship treaty was recently signed between the two countries. Malta also maintains close commercial links with the CIS and China.

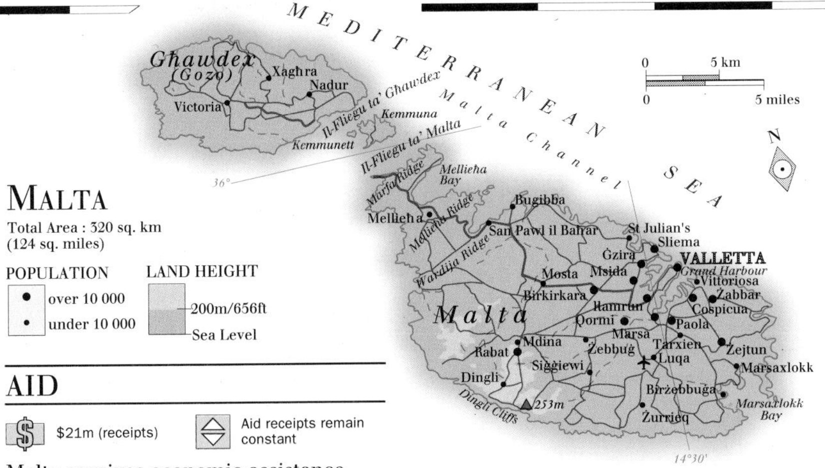

MALTA

Total Area : 320 sq. km (124 sq. miles)

POPULATION
- over 10 000
- under 10 000

LAND HEIGHT
200m/656ft
Sea Level

AID

$21m (receipts) — Aid receipts remain constant

Malta receives economic assistance under an agreement with the EU. The UK is the main bilateral source of aid.

DEFENSE

$27.7m — Up 19% in 1992

The 1,650-strong Maltese army, advised by the Libyans in the 1980s, now receives training and equipment from Italy, Germany and the UK.

ECONOMICS

 $2.6bn

 0.39 Maltese liri

SCORE CARD

- World GNP Ranking......131st
- GNP per Capita......$7,298
- Balance of Payments......$-55.4m
- Inflation......2.5%
- Unemployment......3.7%

Strengths
Tourism and naval dockyards. Programs to attract foreign high-tech industry. Offshore banking potential. Strategic position between Europe and Africa, on the main Mediterranean shipping lines.

Weaknesses
Lack of diversification at present. Cut-price competition from Africa and Asia in traditional textile industry. Need to import almost all requirements.

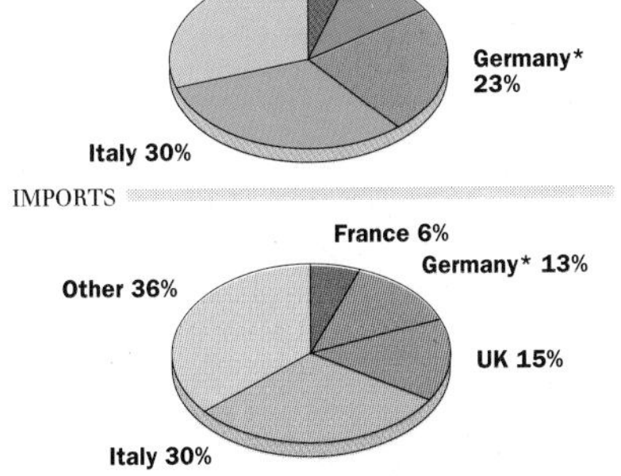

RESOURCES

 1.1bn kwh (capacity 250,000 kw)

 Not an oil producer and has no refineries

 101,000 pigs, 21,000 cattle, 6,000 sheep

Stone, sand

Electrical generating capacity is due to increase with the completion of a new 360 MW-capacity power station in 1997. Malta is dependent on desalination plants for most of its water supply. All oil has to be imported.

ENVIRONMENT

 None

 Controls on hotel developments

The main environmental concern is linked to the tourist industry. A lack of planning controls in the 1970s was responsible for unsightly beach developments. These are now tightly controlled, particularly on Gozo.

MEDIA

 Freedom of expression guaranteed under constitution

PUBLISHING AND BROADCAST MEDIA

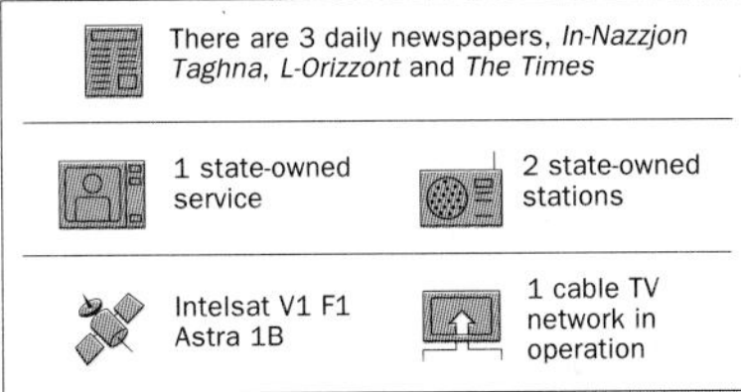

The Maltese press is largely politically oriented. Two of the three main press groups are affiliated with the NP and MLP; one is independent.

CRIME

 221 prisoners

 Up 3% in 1990

Malta's crime rates are low compared with those on the European mainland. But there has been an increase in drug transshipment and associated crimes.

CHRONOLOGY

Malta was dominated in turn by the Phoenicians, Carthaginians, Greeks and Romans; it later came under the rule of the Arabs, Norman Sicily, Spain, France and, finally, Britain.

- **1947** Internal self-government.
- **1964** Full independence from UK.
- **1971** MLP return to power, under Dom Mintoff.
- **1987** Nationalists, under Fenech Adami, in government.

EDUCATION

 96%

Spending on education is equal to 3.6% of GDP. There are 2,500 full-time students at the University of Malta in Valletta.

HEALTH

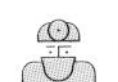 1 per 453 people

 Cerebrovascular and heart diseases, cancer, diabetes

Malta has six state-run hospitals. Around 7% of government expenditure is allocated to health services.

WEALTH

 Income per capita is below the European average

CONSUMER GOODS OWNERSHIP

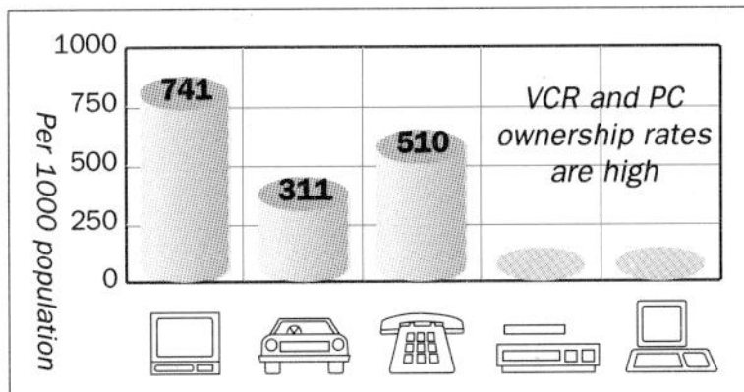

Remittances from Maltese working abroad are an important source of income for many island families.

WORLD RANKING

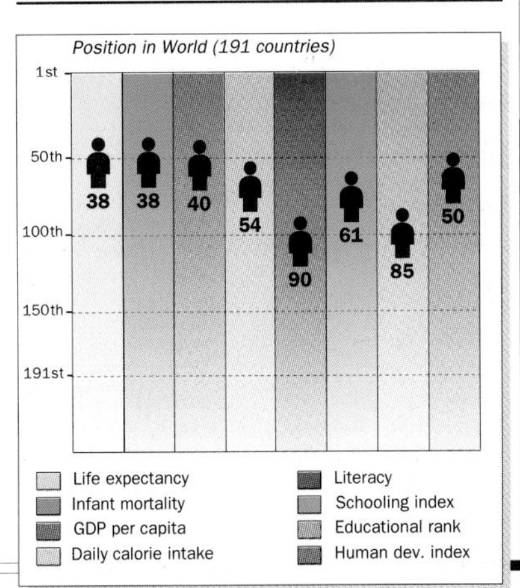

M

MARSHALL ISLANDS

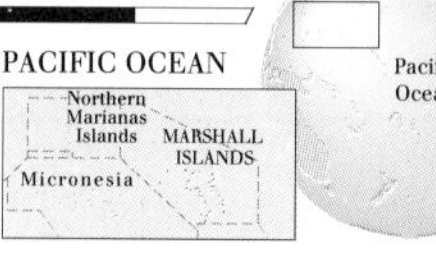

OFFICIAL NAME: Republic of the Marshall Islands **CAPITAL:** Majuro
POPULATION: 48,000 **CURRENCY:** US dollar **OFFICIAL LANGUAGES:** English and Marshallese

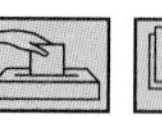

THE MARSHALL ISLANDS comprise a group of 34 widely scattered atolls in the central Pacific Ocean. These include the largest atolls in the world, formed from low coral islands with sandy beaches. Formerly under US rule as part of the Trust Territory of the Pacific Islands, the islands became self-governing in 1979. The economy is almost entirely dependent on US aid and the rent paid by the USA for its missile base on the Kwajalein atoll.

Ebeye Island in the Marshalls. *Population pressures have led to the disappearance of most tree and grass cover on the island.*

CLIMATE

WEATHER CHART

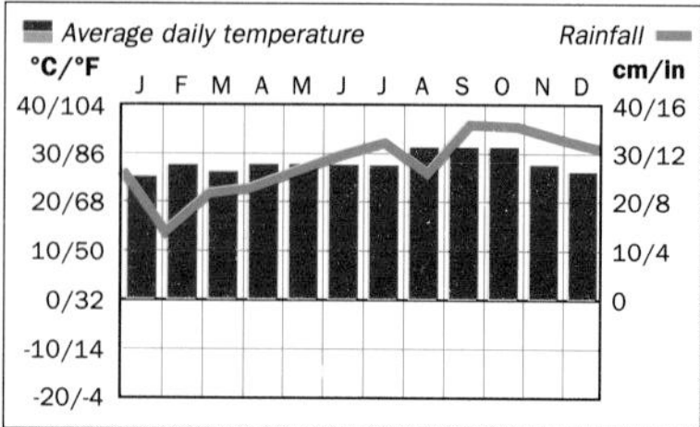

The climate is tropical oceanic. Temperatures show little seasonal variation, averaging around 85°F.

COMMUNICATIONS

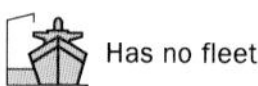
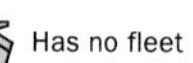

THE TRANSPORTATION NETWORK

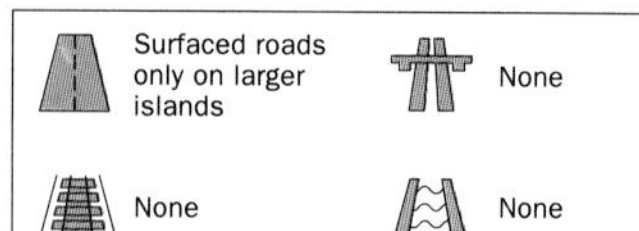

The transportation system is limited, although there is some inter-island shipping. Regular scheduled flights connect ten of the atolls.

TOURISM

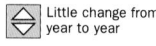

Little change from year to year

MAIN OVERSEAS ARRIVALS

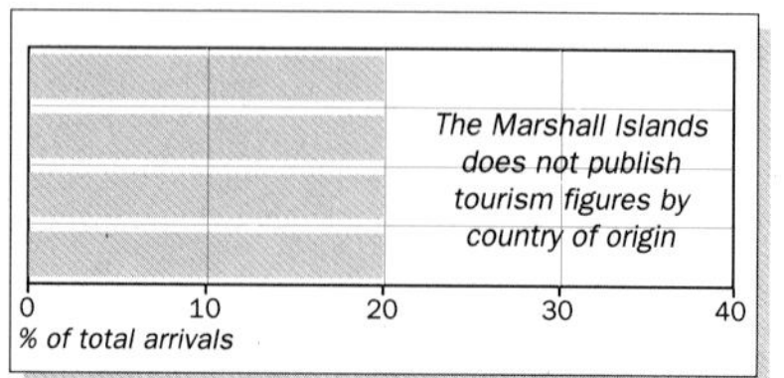

There are few hotels or amenities for tourists, though outlying islands have the potential of unspoiled beaches. Those who visit are mainly Japanese and American; many are war veterans.

PEOPLE

Marshallese, English, Japanese, German

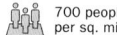

700 people per sq. mile

THE URBAN/RURAL POPULATION SPLIT

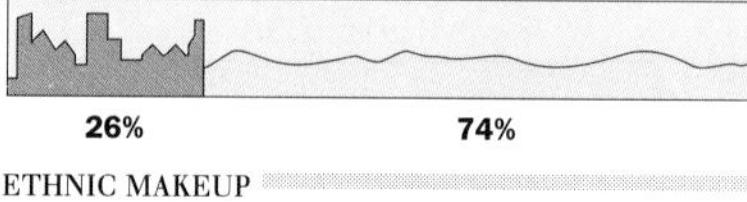

ETHNIC MAKEUP

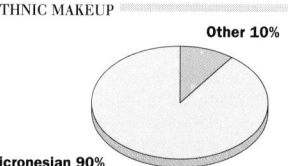

Other 10%

Micronesian 90%

Of the 34 atolls making up the Marshall Islands, 24 are inhabited. Majuro, the capital and commercial center, is home to almost half of the population, many of whom live in its overcrowded slums. The other main center of population is Ebeye, where tensions are high due to poor living conditions. Most of Ebeye's inhabitants were forcefully relocated from Kwajalein in 1947 to make way for a US missile tracking, testing and interception base; many still travel back to Kwajalein daily to work at the base. Life on the outlying islands is still centered around subsistence agriculture and fishing. Society is traditionally matrilineal.

MARSHALL ISLANDS

Total Area : 181 sq. km (70 sq. miles)

POLITICS

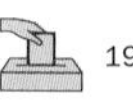

THE STATE OF THE PARTIES

Parliament (Nitijela) 33 members

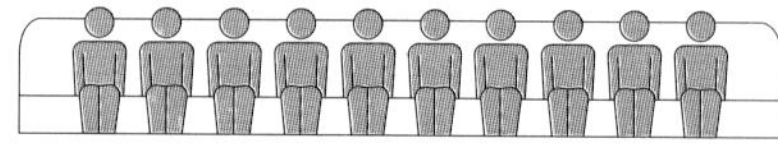

The 33 members are elected from 25 districts

Council of Chiefs 12 members

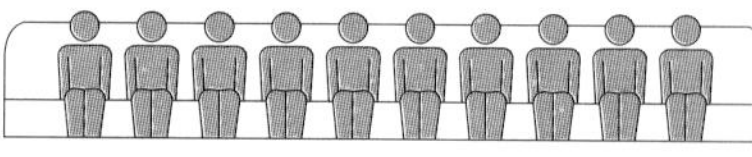

All 12 members are high chiefs

Politics are traditionally dominated by chiefs. President Amata Kabua, who has been in power since self-government began in 1979, is the islands' high chief. Members of his family hold several important government posts. There are two main political groupings, the ruling RMI and the opposition Ralik-Ratak Democratic Party. The main political issue is the islands' continuing inability to achieve financial self-sufficiency. Their economy is almost totally dependent on US aid. Discussion has centered recently on a number of projects proposed by foreign states, which could bring in additional revenue. These include a proposal for a plant to generate electricity by burning used tires and a project to use toxic waste to build a causeway on Kwajalein. The likely environmental impact of such projects is an important issue.

M

WORLD AFFAIRS

From 1947 to 1979, the islands were controlled by the USA as part of the Trust Territory of the Pacific Islands, and US influence remains strong. Under the terms of the Compact of Free Association signed in 1983, the USA is to pay $1 billion in aid over 15 years. In return, the USA has gained control of Kwajalein at a fixed rent. In addition, no further claims for compensation by victims of US nuclear testing between 1946 and 1958 will be considered.

AID

 $39m from USA

 Fairly constant from year to year

Aid from the USA accounts for around two-thirds of the islands' revenue. Australia and Taiwan also provide some assistance.

DEFENSE

 USA responsible for defense

 Not applicable

There is no defense force. All defense is provided by the USA under the Compact of Free Association. The USA does not have offensive weapons located in the Marshalls, but its navy regularly patrols the region.

ECONOMICS

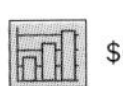 $63m

 US dollar

SCORE CARD

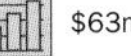

- ❑ WORLD GNP RANKING........................188th
- ❑ GNP PER CAPITA $1,313
- ❑ BALANCE OF PAYMENTS ....Deficit
- ❑ INFLATION ....Volatile
- ❑ UNEMPLOYMENT....Widespread underemployment

STRENGTHS

Aid from the USA, on which the islands are almost totally dependent. Strategic refusal by US to allow them to become impoverished, so that no other foreign power can gain influence. Copra.

WEAKNESSES

Dependence on imports, which are 11 times greater than exports. All fuel has to be imported. Vulnerability to storm damage. Large state sector employing 75% of workers.

EXPORTS/IMPORTS

The Marshall Islands' main trading partners are the USA and Japan

RESOURCES

 Electricity is provided by small diesel generators

 Not an oil producer and has no refineries

 200 tons

 Phosphates

There are few known strategic resources. Exploratory tests have revealed some high-grade phosphate deposits, but not in economically viable quantities. Small diesel generators are used for electricity production.

ENVIRONMENT

 None

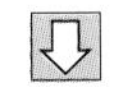 Plans for toxic waste dump

Between 1946 and 1958, Bikini and Enewetak atolls were the site of a series of US nuclear military tests. Islanders were exposed to radiation and both atolls were declared uninhabitable. The residents of Enewetak were allowed to return in 1980, following some decontamination of the land. The USA has now paid out over $101 million to victims of nuclear testing. In recent years, the Marshall Islands have been proposed as a potential toxic waste dump by both the USA and Japan. Discussions have also taken place about creating landfill sites, largely to take US household refuse.

MEDIA

 The media is generally free of censorship

PUBLISHING AND BROADCAST MEDIA

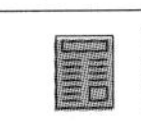 There are no daily newspapers. The one weekly newspaper, the *Marshall Islands Gazette*, is privately owned

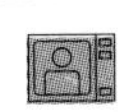 1 independent service

 1 state-controlled, 1 independent station

Radio is the main source of information in the Marshalls. There is also a subscription-only TV service. The US personnel stationed on Kwajalein have their own TV and radio stations.

CRIME

 The Marshalls does not publish prison figures

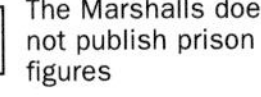

 Little change from year to year

Crime levels are generally low, although the rate is rising on Ebeye. Outlying islands are crime-free.

EDUCATION

 91%

Education is based on the US model. The number of secondary school graduates exceeds the availability of suitable employment in the Marshall Islands. Many go on to college in the USA. Small church institutions in the USA often subsidize students.

CHRONOLOGY

Following a period under Spanish rule, the Marshall Islands became a German protectorate in 1885. Japan took possession of the islands at the outbreak of the World War I. They were transferred to US control in 1945.

- ❑ **1946** US government begins a program of nuclear testing.
- ❑ **1947** UN Trust Territory of the Pacific established.
- ❑ **1961** Kwajalein becomes US army missile range, the target for ICBMs fired from California.
- ❑ **1979** Constitution approved in referendum. Government set up.
- ❑ **1986** Compact of Free Association with US operational.
- ❑ **1990** US control formally ended.

HEALTH

 1 per 2,076 people

 Respiratory, heart and diarrheal diseases

Medical facilities are rudimentary. Complex operations are performed in hospitals in Hawaii. Levels of malnutrition are high.

WEALTH

 Most Marshall Islanders live a subsistence existence

CONSUMER GOODS OWNERSHIP

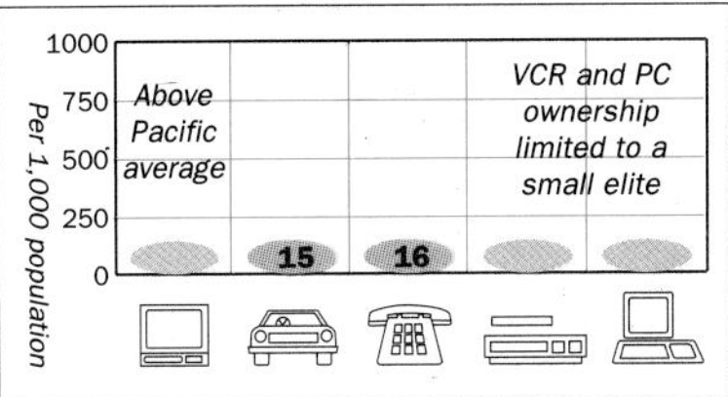

Wealth disparities are small. Very few citizens can afford luxuries such as air conditioning and cars.

WORLD RANKING

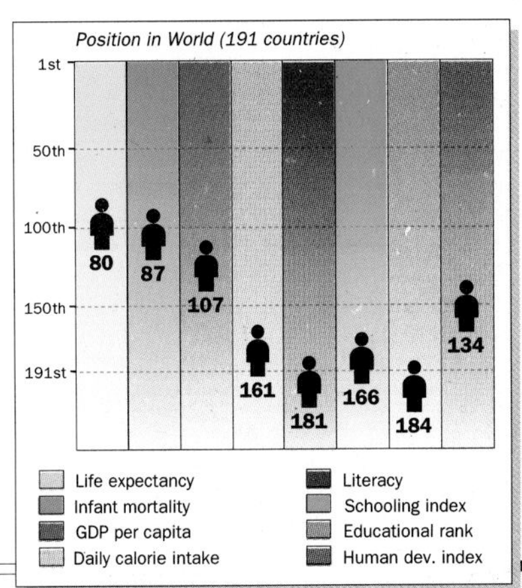

M

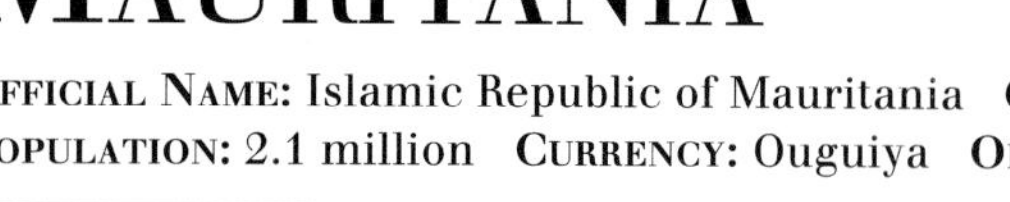

MAURITANIA

OFFICIAL NAME: Islamic Republic of Mauritania **CAPITAL:** Nouakchott
POPULATION: 2.1 million **CURRENCY:** Ouguiya **OFFICIAL LANGUAGE:** French

LOCATED IN NORTHWEST AFRICA, Mauritania is a member of both the OAU and the Arab League. Formerly a French colony, the country has taken a strongly Arab direction since 1964; today it is the Maures who control political life and dominate the minority black population. The Sahara extends across two-thirds of Mauritania's territory. The only productive land is that drained by the Senegal River in the south and southwest.

CLIMATE

WEATHER CHART

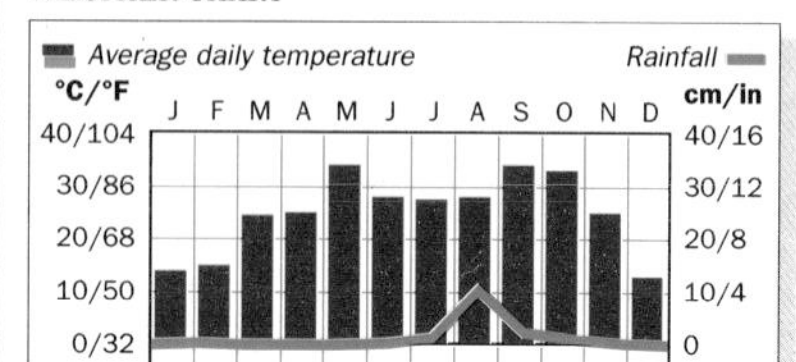

The dusty Saharan *harmattan* wind often aggravates the very hot, dry conditions. Some rain falls in the south.

COMMUNICATIONS

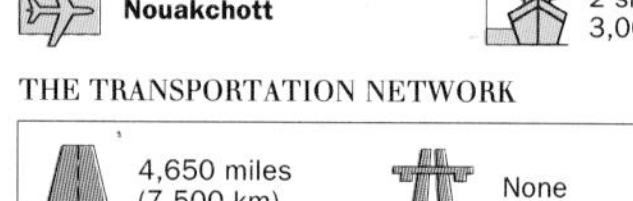

THE TRANSPORTATION NETWORK

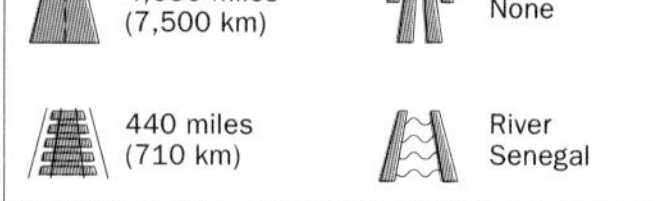

The transportation system is limited and unevenly developed. There are two major roads, but shifting sands mean they require constant maintenance.

TOURISM

12,000

No significant change from year to year

MAIN OVERSEAS ARRIVALS

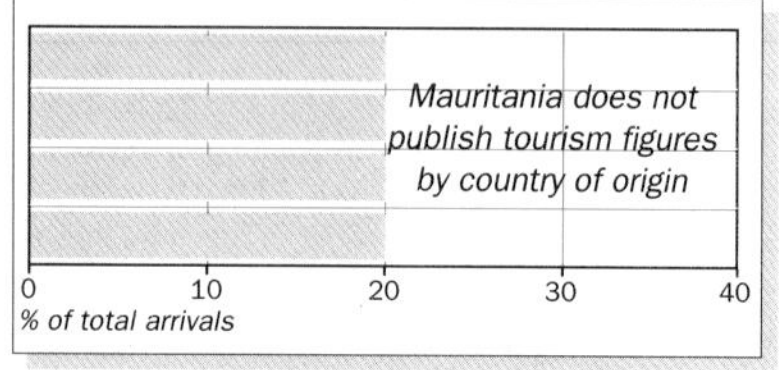

There are few tourists apart from desert safari enthusiasts. The more mountainous areas are especially dramatic, but access is difficult. Nouakchott has some hotels.

PEOPLE

Hassaniyah Arabic, Wolof, French

5 people per sq. mile

THE URBAN/RURAL POPULATION SPLIT

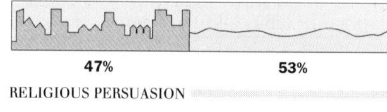

47% 53%

RELIGIOUS PERSUASION

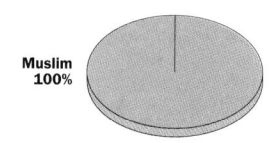

Muslim 100%

The politically dominant Maures make up about one-third of the population. The black population is composed of the Havalin, the Senegalese peoples and the Tukolor, Peulh and Wolof groups. Ethnic tension centers on the oppression of blacks by Maures. The old black bourgeoisie has now been superseded by a Maurish class; tens of thousands of blacks are estimated to be in slavery. Ethnic tension came to a head in 1989, when 200,000 Maures fled from Senegal. There were attacks on Senegalese in Mauritania and many fled or were deported to refugee camps along the Senegal River.

Family solidarity among nomads is particularly strong.

POLITICS

Lower House 1997
Upper House 1998

President Col. Maaouya Ould Sid'Ahmed Taya

THE STATE OF THE PARTIES

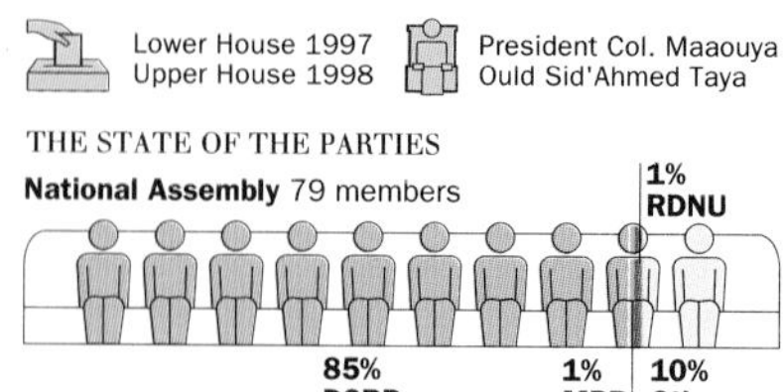

DSRP = Democratic and Social Republican Party
MPR = Mauritanian Party for Renewal RDNU = Rally for Democracy and National Unity

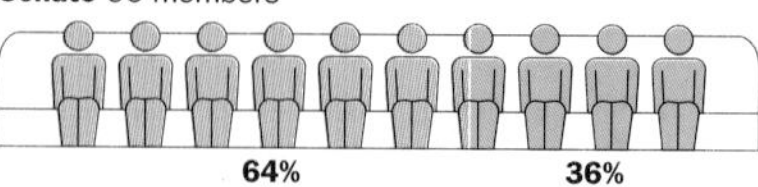

3 members are chosen to represent the interests of Mauritanians abroad

In 1991, partly because of pressure from Western aid donors, Mauritania officially returned to multiparty democracy. However, the 1992 presidential elections simply returned the incumbent military ruler, President Maaouya Ould Taya, to power. General elections were held but were boycotted by the opposition parties. These are mainly Maure-led; the blacks of the south support exiled parties, such as the Dakar-based liberation group, FLAM. The issue of ethnic relations is the central political problem, especially since a 1987 coup plot, which caused the blacks' base in the army to collapse.

MAURITANIA

Total Area : 1 025 520 sq. km (395 953 sq. miles)

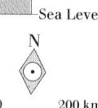

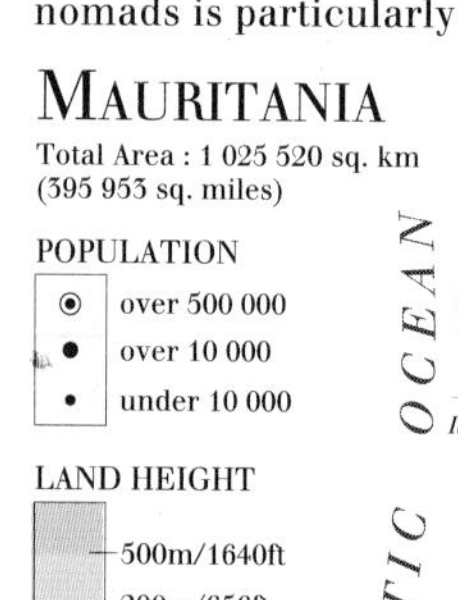

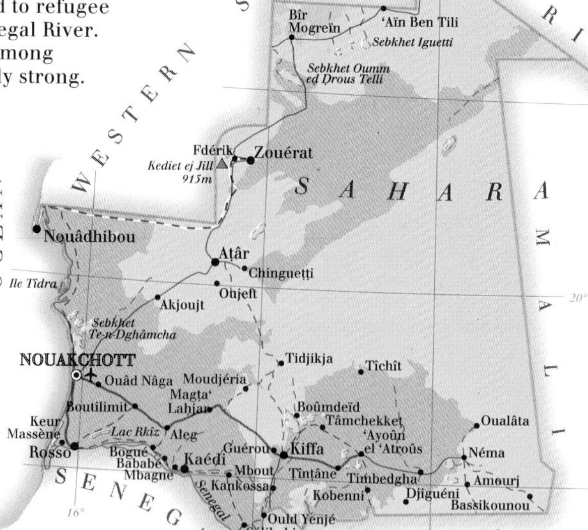

WORLD AFFAIRS

Mauritania has to maintain a delicate balance in relations with sub-Saharan Africa and the Arab world; as a result, it belongs to both ECOWAS and the Arab Maghreb Union. Relations with neighboring Senegal have improved since the conflicts of 1989.

AID

 $208m (receipts)

 Up 3% in 1991

France, Germany, the IMF, OPEC and Iraq are all donors. Most aid is used for development projects, such as the EU-funded Trans-Mauritanian Highway.

DEFENSE

 Mauritania does not publish defense budget figures

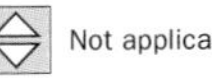 Not applicable

The 11,000-strong military is a strain on Mauritania's limited budget. Most arms procurement is still from France, but some is now from the Arab world.

ECONOMICS

 $1.1bn

 122.98 ouguiyas

SCORE CARD

❑ WORLD GNP RANKING	154th
❑ GNP PER CAPITA	$530
❑ BALANCE OF PAYMENTS	$-125m
❑ INFLATION	9.8%
❑ UNEMPLOYMENT	21%

STRENGTHS

Iron from the Cominor mine at Zouérate. Largest gypsum deposits in the world. Copper, yet to be properly exploited. Offshore fishing among the best in West Africa.

WEAKNESSES

"Debt-distressed," with a debt of nearly $2 billion – a legacy of its move to leave the Franc Zone. Poor land – two-thirds is desert. Very hot, dry climate.

EXPORTS

IMPORTS

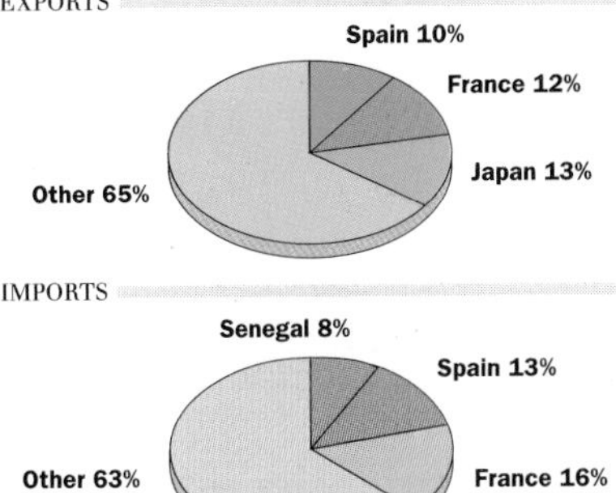

Mauritania's extreme aridity *means that only 1% of the land is arable. Two-thirds of the country is part of the Sahara Desert; sparse vegetation over the rest supports some livestock.*

RESOURCES

 140m kwh (capacity 110,000 kw)

 Not an oil producer and has no refineries

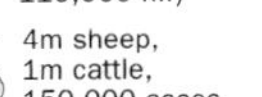 4m sheep, 1m cattle, 150,000 asses

 Iron, gypsum, copper, gold, phosphates, yttrium

Iron, which in the 1960s brought economic profitability, continues to be exploited, despite low prices on the world market. Electricity generation has expanded rapidly since the late 1960s, from 38.4m kwh in 1967 to 245m kwh in 1989, reflecting the growing needs of the minerals industries. Phosphates have been found near the Senegal River.

ENVIRONMENT

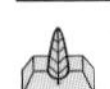 2% (0.2% partially protected)

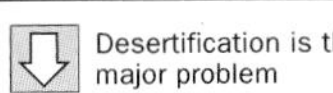 Desertification is the major problem

The chief environmental problem in Mauritania is that of the encroaching Sahara Desert, a situation worsened by the droughts of 1973 and 1983, which caused widespread loss of grazing land. The consequent exodus of people away from the land has led to Nouakchott's population increasing from 20,000 in 1960 to 500,000 today.

MEDIA

 There are still instances of censorship

PUBLISHING AND BROADCAST MEDIA

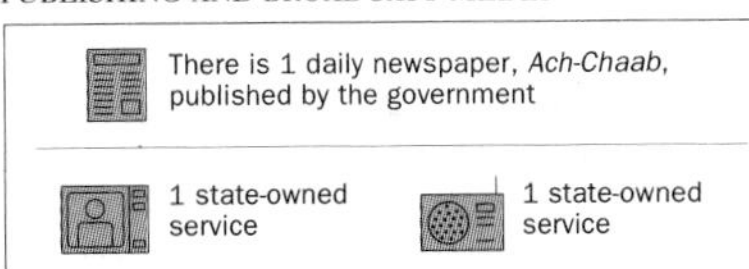

There is 1 daily newspaper, *Ach-Chaab*, published by the government
1 state-owned service
1 state-owned service

French-language press and radio is increasingly under pressure from militant Maures who are eager to promote the use of Arabic.

CRIME

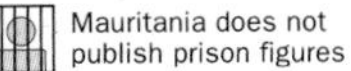 Mauritania does not publish prison figures

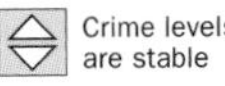 Crime levels are stable

The main problems are smuggling and robbery. Levels of violence are lower than the West African average.

CHRONOLOGY

Once part of the Islamic Almoravid state, Mauritania became a French colony in 1814.

- ❑ **1960** Independence.
- ❑ **1960** One-party state established.
- ❑ **1972** Peace with Polisario in war waged over Western Sahara.
- ❑ **1984** Col. Maaouya Ould Taya takes power in bloodless coup.
- ❑ **1992** First multiparty elections.

EDUCATION

 34%

Arabic has been compulsory in all schools since 1988, though this has met resistance from blacks. The University of Nouakchott has over 3,000 students.

HEALTH

 1 per 9,547 people

 Diarrheal and respiratory diseases, influenza, tuberculosis

Historic regional inequalities persist and the best facilities are in the capital. The overall level of care is on a par with neighboring states.

WEALTH

 Slavery officially became illegal in 1980, but much *de facto* slavery survives

CONSUMER GOODS OWNERSHIP

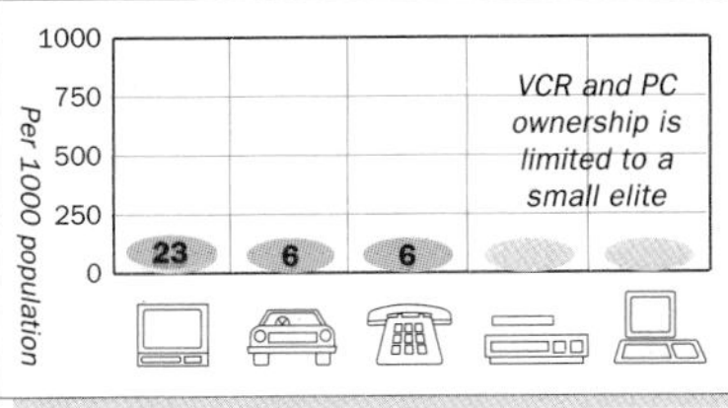

The ruling Maures form the wealthiest sector. Wealthy Maures travel to Mecca for the *haj* (Muslim pilgrimage).

WORLD RANKING

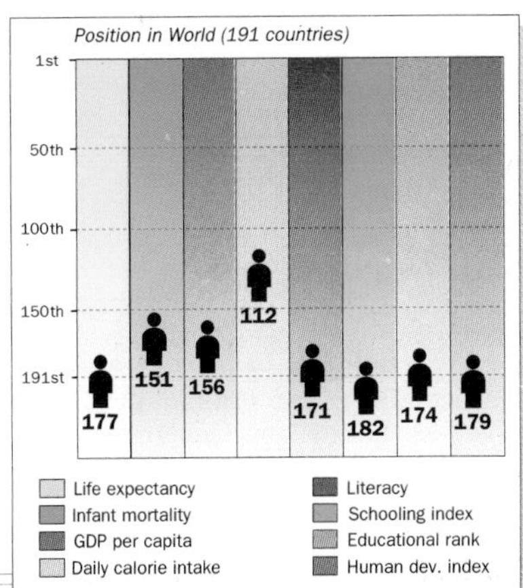

M

MAURITIUS

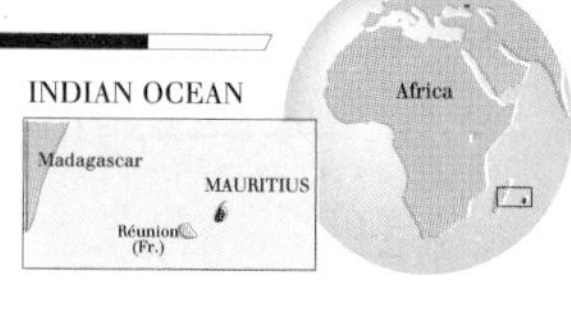

OFFICIAL NAME: Mauritius **CAPITAL:** Port Louis
POPULATION: 1.1 million **CURRENCY:** Mauritian rupee **OFFICIAL LANGUAGE:** English

THE ISLANDS THAT make up Mauritius lie in the Indian Ocean east of Madagascar. The principal island, from which the country takes its name, is of volcanic origin and surrounded by coral reefs. The outer islands, 311 mi. to the north, are Rodrigues, the Agalega Islands and the Cargados Carajos Shoals. Mauritius has enjoyed considerable economic success following recent industrial diversification and the expansion of its tourist industry.

CLIMATE

WEATHER CHART

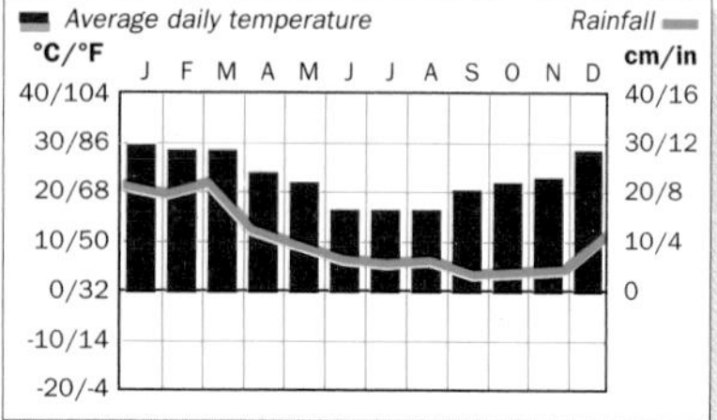

The climate is subtropical and humid. December to March are the hottest and wettest months. Tropical cyclones are an occasional threat at this time.

COMMUNICATIONS

Sir Seewoosagur Ramgoolam Intl
870,000 passengers

8 ships
166,600 dwt

THE TRANSPORTATION NETWORK

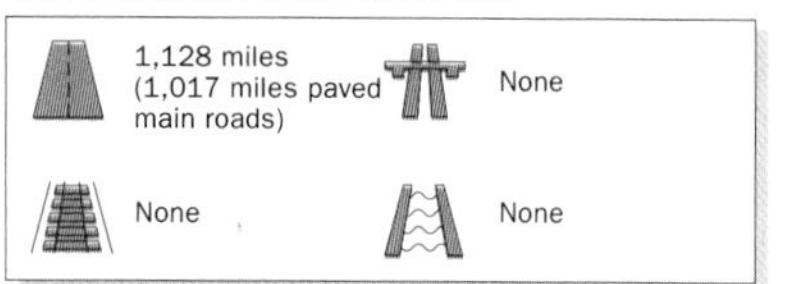

Roads are extensive, but often congested. Plans exist for a monorail link between Port Louis and Curepipe.

TOURISM

870,000 visitors

Down 1% in 1991

MAIN OVERSEAS ARRIVALS

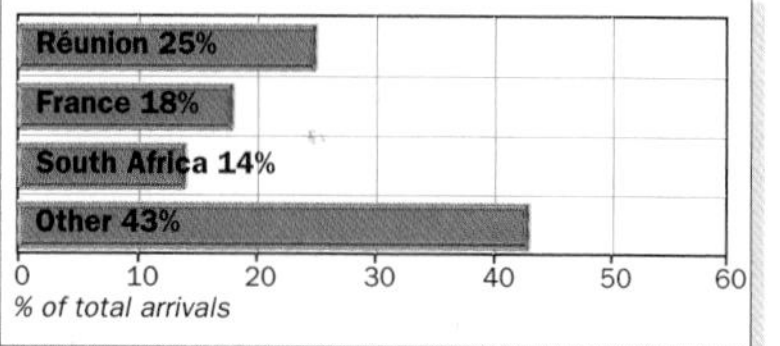

Tourism has expanded rapidly in the past decade. Spectacular beaches, water sports and big game fishing are major attractions. However, many new hotels are usually only half full.

PEOPLE

French Creole, Hindi, Urdu, Tamil, Chinese, English, French

1,380 people per sq. mile

THE URBAN/RURAL POPULATION SPLIT

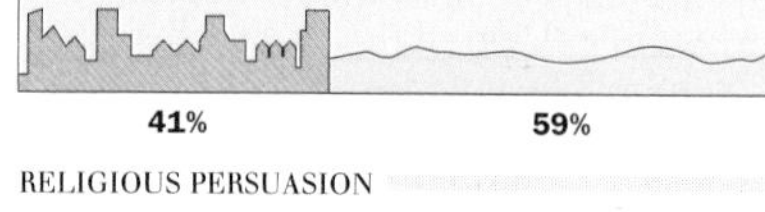

RELIGIOUS PERSUASION

Protestant 2% Other 3% Muslim 17% Hindu 52% Roman Catholic 26%

The majority of the population are the descendants of indentured laborers brought over from India in the 19th century. Creoles make up 27% of the population, while 3% are of Chinese origin. The wealthiest group is the small minority of Mauritians of French descent, who control most of business, including the sugar-cane industry.

POLITICS

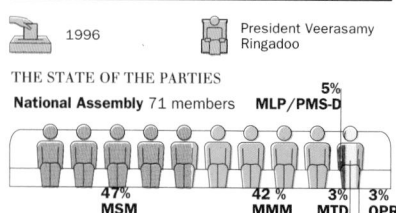

1996

President Veerasamy Ringadoo

THE STATE OF THE PARTIES

MSM = Mauritius Socialist Movement **MMM** = Mauritius Militant Movement **MLP/PMS-D** Mauritius Labour Party/ Mauritius Social-Democratic Party **MTD** = Democratic Labour Movement **OPR** = Organization of the People of Rodrigues

Mauritius became a republic in 1992. Politics are characterized by coalition governments, and are largely based on personalities. There is little ideological difference between the main parties. Government is currently in the hands of an MSM–MMM coalition. At the end of 1993, the MMM split, with one faction under the influential former finance minister, Paul Bérenger, defecting to the opposition. This has been a threat to political stability.

WORLD AFFAIRS

Comm OAU ACP ECA GATT

Mauritius is a member of the Commonwealth, but it is also seeking to develop relations with French-speaking countries. In 1993, it hosted the fifth annual summit of Francophone nations. Links with South Africa are also important.

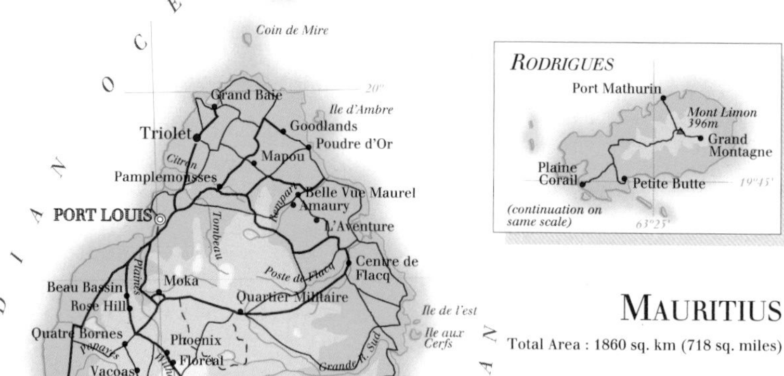

M

AID

$67m (receipts)

Down 25% in 1991

Aid is predominantly bilateral, with France and the UK as the main donors. Mauritius also receives aid from the EU, under the Lomé Convention, and other international organizations. A five-year conservation program was initiated in 1990 with assistance from the World Bank. The Bank has also promised $53 million toward the development of Port Louis as a free port.

DEFENSE

No defense force; police unit maintains internal security

Not applicable

Mauritius has no defense forces. There is, however, a special police unit to ensure internal security. Expenditure on policing accounts for 1.4% of total government spending.

ECONOMICS

$3bn

18.18 Mauritian rupees

SCORE CARD

- ❑ WORLD GNP RANKING........125th
- ❑ GNP PER CAPITA........$2,727
- ❑ BALANCE OF PAYMENTS........$-41m
- ❑ INFLATION........4.6%
- ❑ UNEMPLOYMENT........Low

STRENGTHS

Economic growth averaging 6% a year over last decade. Sugar industry, which accounts for 30% of export earnings. Export Processing Zone (EPZ), especially for clothing manufacturing. Tourism, the third largest foreign exchange earner. Highly educated work force. Potential as offshore financial center now being developed.

WEAKNESSES

Vulnerability to fluctuations in world prices for sugar. 75% of food requirements imported. Occasional cyclones mean few crops other than sugar can be grown. Remoteness. Lack of strategic resources.

EXPORTS

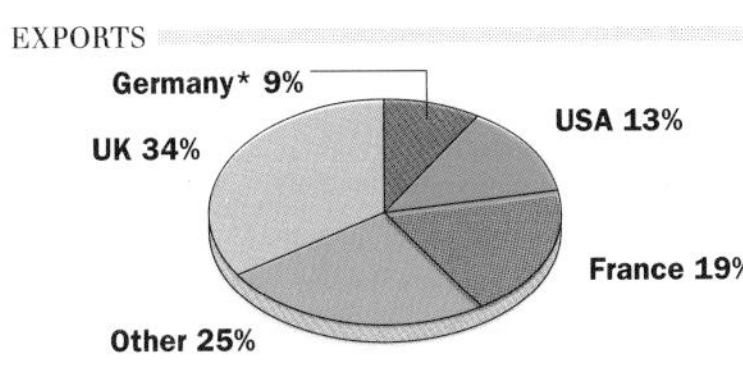

IMPORTS

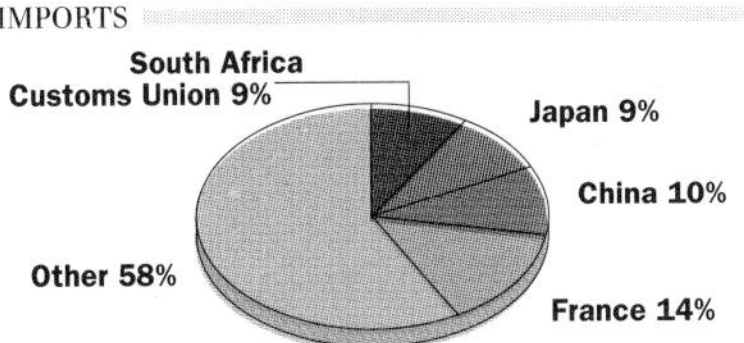

***Villagers at a water source** in the center of Mauritius Island. Mauritius's main rivers are used for hydropower generation.*

RESOURCES

770m kwh (capacity 313,000 kw)

Not an oil producer and has no refineries

34,000 cattle, 10,000 pigs, 7,000 sheep

None

Mauritius is heavily dependent on imported oil supplies. The government has put considerable investment into developing alternative energy sources, including hydroelectric power generation. Power stations fueled by bagasse (a by-product of the sugar industry) are now also in operation.

ENVIRONMENT

2% (0.1% partially protected)

New government measures to restrict development

Rapid industrialization and unchecked hotel building have caused environmental problems. Coral reefs are under threat from both coral sand mining and the discharging of untreated sewage into the sea.

MEDIA

Freedom of expression is guaranteed under the constitution. Foreign satellite TV broadcasts are subject to government approval

PUBLISHING AND BROADCAST MEDIA

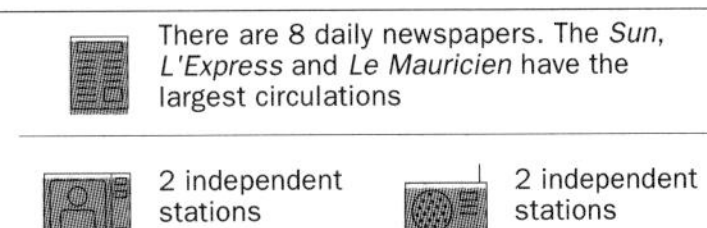
There are 8 daily newspapers. The *Sun*, *L'Express* and *Le Mauricien* have the largest circulations

2 independent stations

2 independent stations

Mauritius has an active press, subject to few regulations and with a wide readership. Newspapers are published in English, French, Creole, Hindi, Chinese and Tamil. However, opposition parties complain that TV and radio broadcasts are consistently biased toward the government.

CRIME

2,145 prisoners

Overall crime rates fairly constant from year to year

Crime rates on the main island are fairly low. There has been a small increase in thefts in the towns. Outlying islands are virtually crime-free.

CHRONOLOGY

Originally colonized by the Dutch in the 17th century, Mauritius later came under French rule. In 1810, it was captured by the British.

- ❑ **1959** First full elections.
- ❑ **1968** Independence as part of the Commonwealth. Seewoosagur Ramgoolam prime minister. Riots between Creoles and Muslims.
- ❑ **1969** MMM formed under Bérenger.
- ❑ **1992** Becomes a republic.

EDUCATION

83%

Educational provision is good and the literacy rate for Mauritians under the age of 30 is 95%. The University of Mauritius has 1,800 students.

HEALTH

1 per 1,233 people

Circulatory and respiratory diseases, cancer

Free health care is universally available. There are 14 state hospitals and six private clinics.

WEALTH

Sugar plantation worker, 13 Mauritian rupees per hour; journalist, 7,045 Mauritian rupees per month

CONSUMER GOODS OWNERSHIP

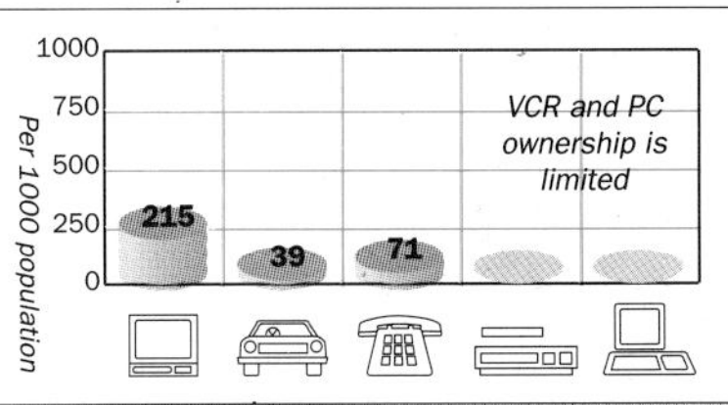

French-descended hotel and plantation owners are the wealthiest group. Government employees are well paid.

WORLD RANKING

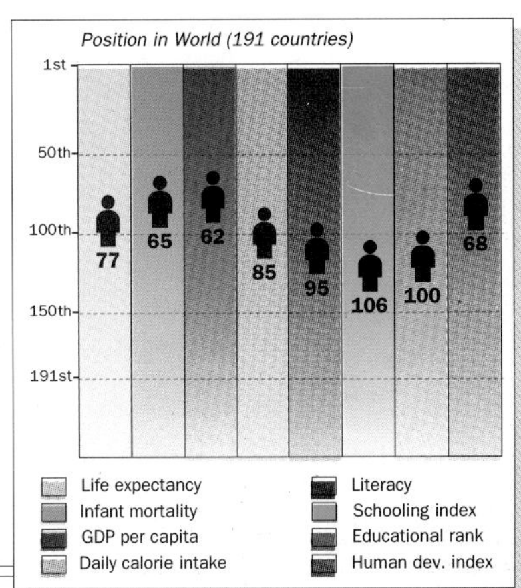

M

Mexico

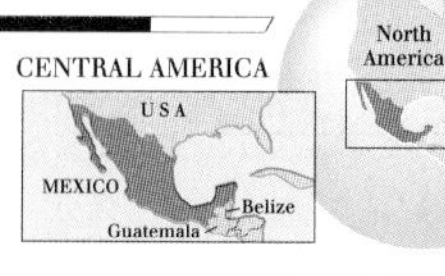

Official Name: United States of Mexico **Capital:** Mexico City
Population: 88.2 million **Currency:** Mexican new peso **Official Language:** Spanish

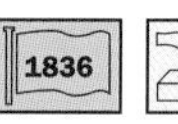

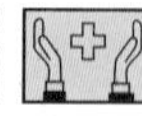

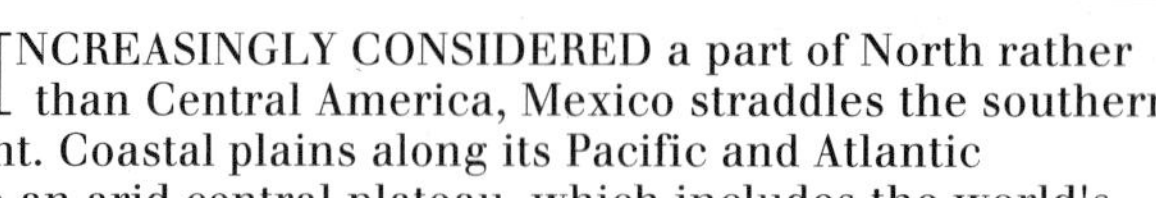

INCREASINGLY CONSIDERED a part of North rather than Central America, Mexico straddles the southern end of the continent. Coastal plains along its Pacific and Atlantic seaboards rise into an arid central plateau, which includes the world's biggest conurbation, Mexico City, built on the site of the Aztec capital, Tenochtitlán. Colonized by the Spanish for its silver mines, Mexico achieved independence in 1836. In the "Epic Revolution" of 1910–1920, in which 250,000 died, much of modern Mexico's structure was established. In 1994, Mexico signed the North American Free Trade Agreement (NAFTA).

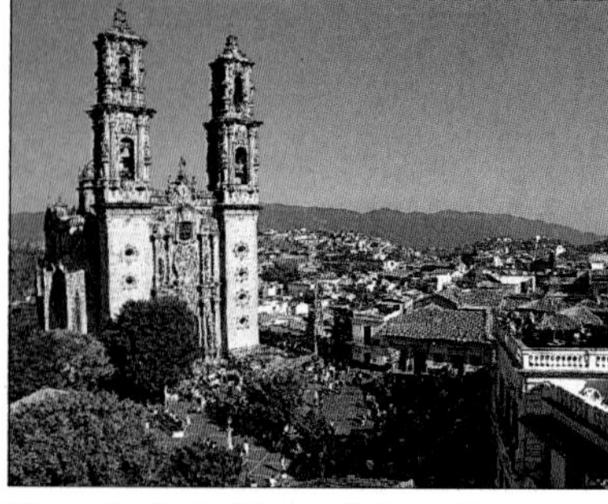

The cathedral of Santa Prisa at Taxco in Cuernavaca. It was built in Spanish churrigueresque style in the 1740s.

CLIMATE

WEATHER CHART

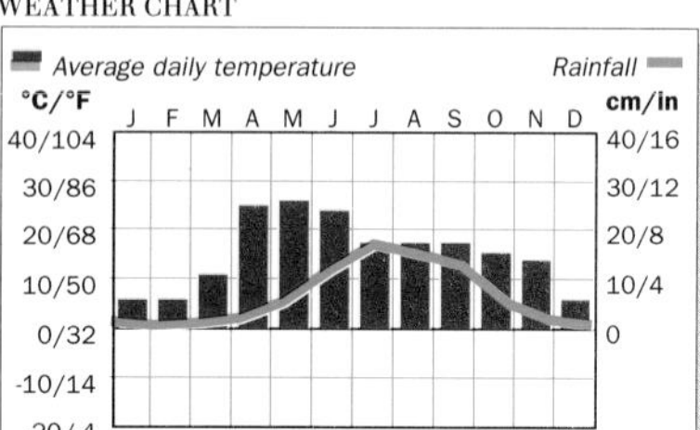

The plateau and high mountains are warm for much of the year. The Pacific coast has a tropical climate.

COMMUNICATIONS

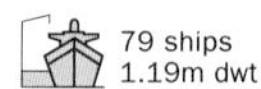

THE TRANSPORTATION NETWORK

147,300 miles (237,057 km)	1,967 miles (3,166 km)
12,655 miles (20,366 km)	1,802 miles (2,900 km)

The government has granted road building and operating concessions to private companies as part of its plans to upgrade the transportation system. A $6-billion project to build four-lane highways connecting major towns with beach resorts such as Acapulco and Puerto Vallarta is intended to increase tourism. The extensive rail network cannot be privatized without a change to the constitution.

TOURISM

6.7m visitors

Up 5% in 1993

MAIN OVERSEAS ARRIVALS

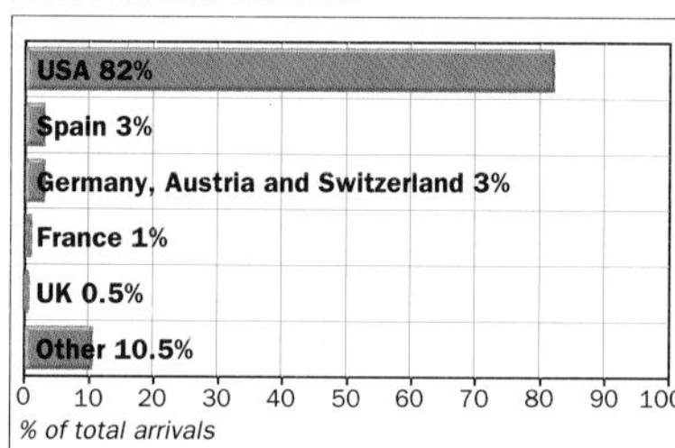

Tourism is probably Mexico's largest employment sector. Visitors are drawn to excellent beach resorts like Acapulco on the Pacific, and the new resorts of the Peninsula de Yucatán on the Atlantic Coast. Mexico also has many Aztec and Maya "World Heritage" archaeological sites. Another major tourist attraction is the many Spanish colonial cities, like Morelia and Guadalajara, which have remained virtually intact since conquest. The government has made further tourism expansion a priority. A program for improving the country's hotel infrastructure has been planned.

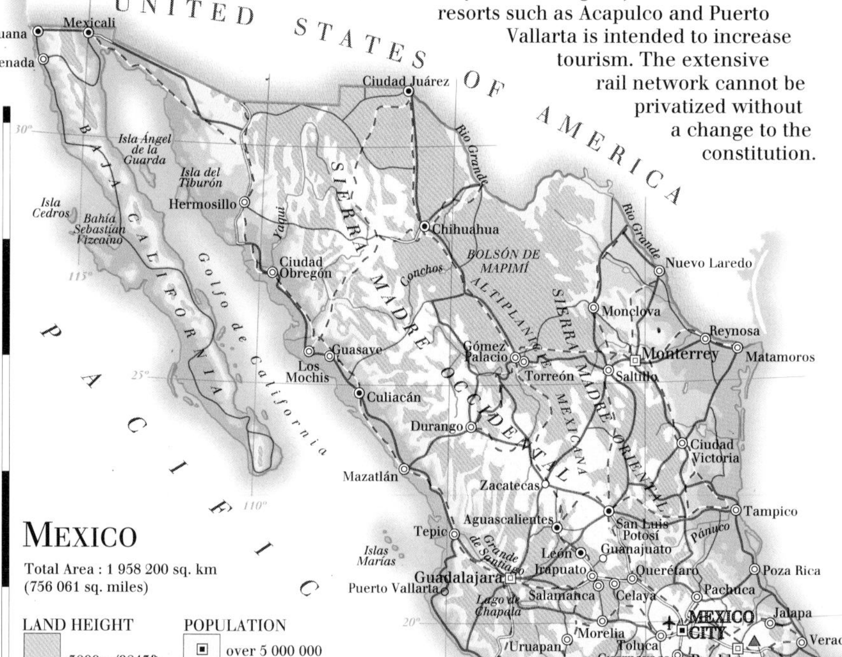

Mexico

Total Area : 1 958 200 sq. km (756 061 sq. miles)

LAND HEIGHT
- 3000m/9843ft
- 2000m/6562ft
- 1000m/3281ft
- 500m/1640ft
- 200m/656ft
- Sea Level

POPULATION
- over 5 000 000
- over 1 000 000
- over 500 000
- over 100 000
- over 50 000

PEOPLE

Spanish, Nahuatl, Maya, Zapotec, Mixtec, Otomi, Totonac, Tzotzil, Tzeltal

106 people per sq. mile

THE URBAN/RURAL POPULATION SPLIT

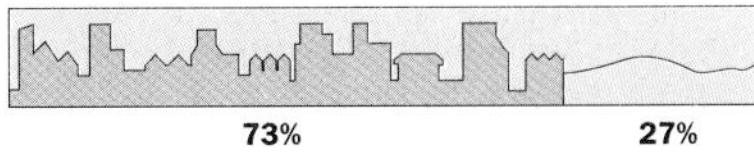

RELIGIOUS PERSUASION

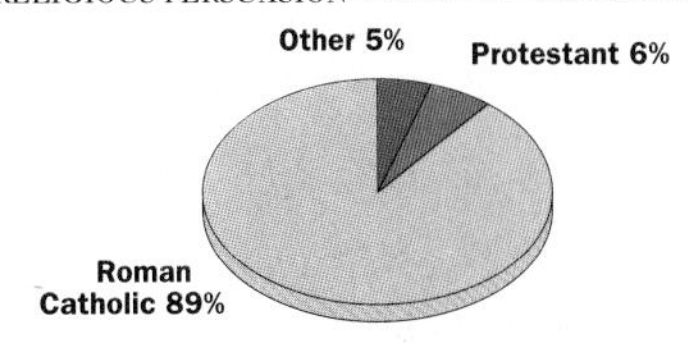

ETHNIC MAKEUP

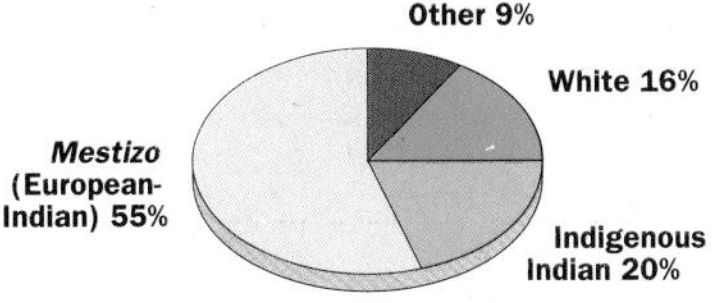

While most Mexicans are *mestizo*, it is Mexico's Indian culture which is promoted by the state. This obscures the fact that rural Indians are largely segregated from Hispanic society. The situation dates back to the Spanish colonial period and is accepted by both groups. The small black community, which is concentrated mainly along the eastern coast, is well integrated.

POPULATION AGE BREAKDOWN

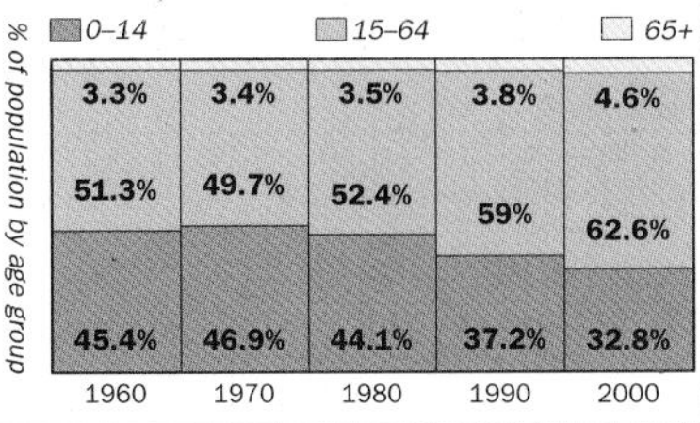

Several hundred thousand refugees recently fled to Mexico to escape Central American civil wars. They were mainly housed in camps, which were set apart from Mexican society. They are now beginning to return home.

The most pressing problem in Mexico is poverty. The 1994 Chiapas *Zapatista* guerrilla rebellion was instigated by landless Indians who had little to lose by rebelling against the state.

As in much of Latin America, men retain their dominance in business and relatively few women take part in the political process.

WORLD AFFAIRS

Mexico's most important relationship is with the USA. The signing of the NAFTA pact has effectively bound together the economies of Mexico and the USA, and cooperation is likely to develop in other areas. The agreement should also bring more US-financed jobs to poorer regions, thereby reducing the large illegal migration of Mexicans to the USA every year. Most Mexicans support NAFTA; opposition to the treaty is mainly in the USA, where workers fear losing jobs to Mexicans.

Relations with Central America could become difficult as a result. Many of Mexico's southern neighbors oppose the activities of the USA in the region. They were more comfortable with Mexico's previously independent line in foreign policy, which led it to recognize Castro's government in Cuba. Mexico's role as a mediator in Central America (it mediated in conflicts in El Salvador, Nicaragua and Guatemala) will, however, continue.

POLITICS

1997

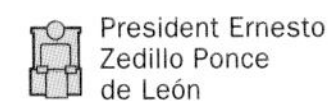

President Ernesto Zedillo Ponce de León

THE STATE OF THE PARTIES

Federal Chamber of Deputies 500 members

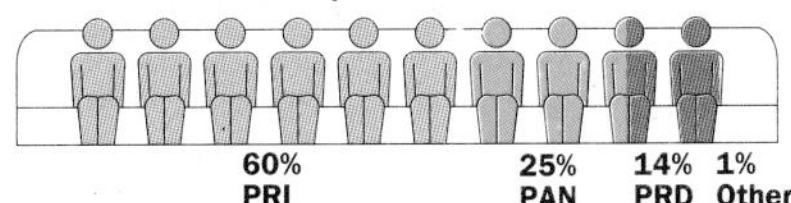

PRI = Institutional Revolutionary Party **PAN** = National Action Party **PRD** = Party of the Democratic Revolution **Other** = Labor Party, Green Party

Senate 96 members

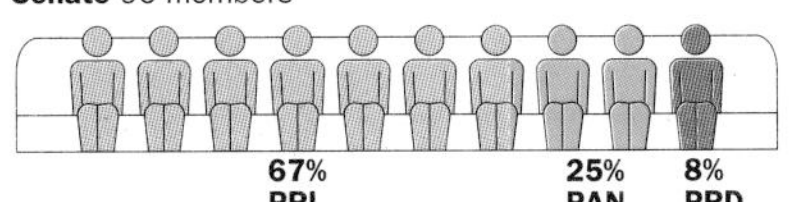

Mexico is a multiparty democracy in name. In practice, the PRI retains power by tampering with elections. The PRI has its own intelligence service.

Main Political Issues

NAFTA

The North American Free Trade Agreement (NAFTA), signed with the USA and Canada, came into force in 1994; the transition to a tariff-free zone will take 15 years. US firms will be free to establish factories anywhere in Mexico. However, Mexican firms will no longer have the protection of high tariffs and will face tough competition from more desirable US products.

Land reform

For the first time since 1917, Mexicans are now able to buy private land. Many fear that agribusinesses will replace the state as the main landowner.

Poverty

Over 16% of Mexico's population are classified as living in "extreme poverty." The Chiapas rebellion of 1994 highlighted the poverty of many rural Indian communities.

Profile

The Institutional Revolutionary Party (PRI) dominates Mexican political life at every level. Since 1929, all the governments have been PRI, and all the presidents and almost all the state governors PRI members. The only real reins on PRI power are large private industrial groups, or multinationals operating in Mexico.

Carlos Salinas de Gortari. *As president from 1988 to 1994 he reinvigorated the PRI.*

Finance Minister *Pedro Aspe Armella, who is leading privatization policies.*

AID

$183m (receipts)

Up 31% in 1991

Mexico receives minimal aid, just $2 per capita a year. Some European and US NGOs provide assistance, particularly for literacy campaigns in poorer areas.

CHRONOLOGY

The Aztec kingdom of Montezuma II was defeated in war with the Spaniard, Hernán Cortés, in 1521. By 1546, the Spaniards had discovered major silver mines at Zacatecas. Mexico, then known as New Spain, became a key part of the Spanish colonial empire.

- **1808** Napoleon invades Spain.
- **1810** Fr. Miguel Hidalgo leads abortive rising against Spanish.
- **1821** Spanish viceroy forced to leave by Agustín de Iturbide.
- **1822** Federal Republic established.
- **1823** Texas opened to US immigration.
- **1829** Spanish military expedition fails to regain control.
- **1836** The USA is the first country to recognize Mexico's independence. Spain then follows suit. Texas declares its independence from Mexico.
- **1846** War breaks out between Mexico and the USA.
- **1848** Treaty of Guadalupe Hidalgo. Mexico forced to cede almost half of its territory to the USA.

M

CHRONOLOGY *continued*

- **1848** Loses modern-day New Mexico, Arizona, Nevada, Utah, California and part of Colorado.
- **1858–1861** War of Reform won by anti-clerical Liberals.
- **1861** Mexico suspends foreign debt.
- **1862** France, Britain and Spain launch military expedition.
- **1863** French troops capture Mexico City. Maximilian of Austria established as Mexican emperor.
- **1867** Mexico recaptured by Benito Juárez. Maximilian shot.
- **1876** Porfirio Díaz president. Period of economic growth; Mexico's railroad system built.
- **1901** First year of oil production.
- **1910** Start of Epic Revolution. Provoked by excessive exploitation by foreign companies and desire for land reform.
- **1911** Díaz overthrown by Francisco Madero. Guerrilla war breaks out in north. Emilio Zapata leads peasant revolt in the south.
- **1913** Madero deposed and murdered. Civil war claims 250,000 lives.
- **1917** New constitution limits power of church. Minerals and subsoil rights reserved for the nation.
- **1926–1929** *Cristero* rebellion led by militant Catholic priests.
- **1929** National Revolutionary Party (later PRI) formed. It has held power ever since.
- **1934** General Cárdenas president. Land reform accelerated, co-operative farms established, railroads nationalized and US and UK oil companies expelled.
- **1940s** US war effort helps Mexican economy to grow.
- **1970** Accelerating population growth reaches 3% a year.
- **1982** Mexico declares it cannot repay its foreign debt of over $800 billion. IMF insists on economic reforms to reschedule the debt.
- **1984** Government violates constitution by relaxing laws on foreign investment.
- **1985** Earthquake in Mexico City. Official death toll 7,000. Costs of economic dislocation estimated at $425 million.
- **1988** Carlos Salinas de Gortari, minister of planning during the earthquake, elected president on 50.3% of the vote.
- **1990** PRI government initiates privatization program.
- **1994** Guerrilla rebellion in the Chiapas state in the south suppressed by the army. 100 dead. Mexico joins NAFTA. PRI presidential candidate Luis Colosio murdered. Ernesto Zedillo replaces him and is elected president.

M

DEFENSE

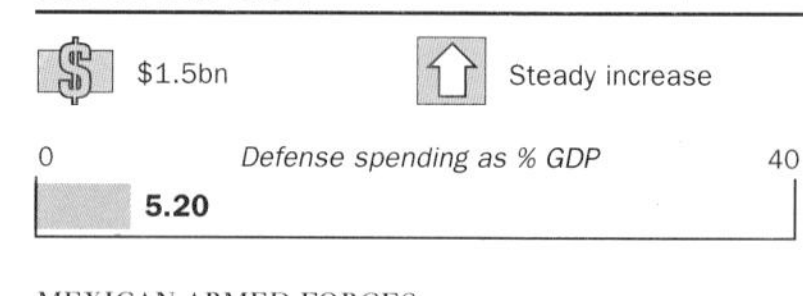

MEXICAN ARMED FORCES

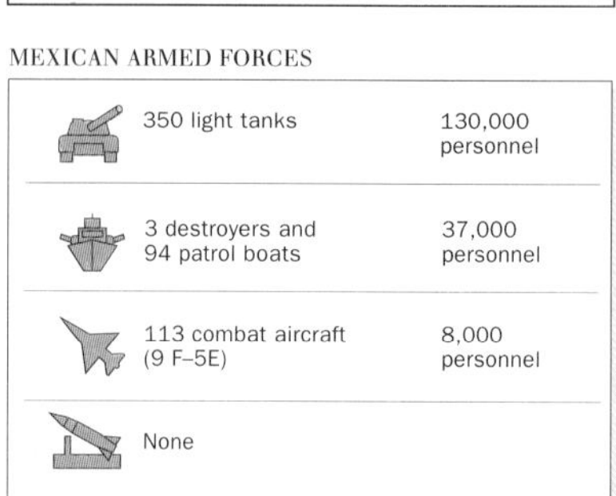

350 light tanks
130,000 personnel
3 destroyers and 94 patrol boats
37,000 personnel
113 combat aircraft (9 F–5E)
8,000 personnel
None

The Mexican military has, on the whole, kept out of politics. Although large in regional terms, Mexico has no ambitions beyond its borders and the army acts to defend internal security. Most arms procurement is from the USA and France. Some members of the military are worried that the PRI's current privatization policies could target the military for cutbacks. In 1994, the role of controlling the border with the USA was handed over to the police.

The rebellion in Chiapas in 1994 was quickly controlled by the army, acting on PRI orders. Concern was expressed by Mexicans about the brutality of the action in which 100 *Zapatistas* died.

ECONOMICS

322.1bn

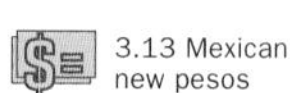

SCORE CARD

- WORLD GNP RANKING......12th
- GNP PER CAPITA......$3,660
- BALANCE OF PAYMENTS......$–22.8bn
- INFLATION......10.4%
- UNEMPLOYMENT......(Official figure) 2.6%

EXPORTS

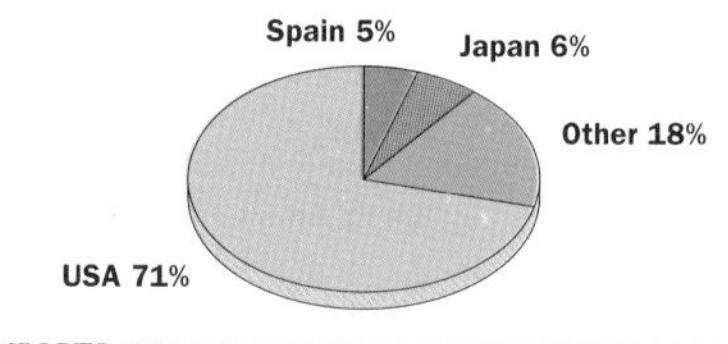

IMPORTS

Japan 4%
Germany* 5%
Other 26%
USA 65%

STRENGTHS

One of the world's largest oil producers, with substantial reserves. Extensive mineral resources – perhaps only 5% exploited to date. Inflation now under control. NAFTA agreement should boost the economy and aid stability.

WEAKNESSES

Population growth is outstripping job creation. Weak agriculture, with rural peoples lacking basic foodstuffs. Lack of development could turn Mexico into a cheap assembler of US products.

PROFILE

Traditionally the PRI ran almost every sector of the Mexican economy – around 160 major concerns. The debt crisis of the 1980s, however, forced a program of privatization. To date, banks, telecommunications and steel companies have been put up for sale.

Economic development in Mexico has been uneven, concentrated in Mexico City and the region up to the border with the USA. In the 1980s, US subsidiaries set up cheap assembly plants (*maquiladoras)* in towns close to the Río Grande which, despite slum-like living conditions, attracted a rush of migrants from the poor south. The government now hopes that one of the effects of NAFTA will be the spread of *maquiladoras* to poorer regions.

ECONOMIC PERFORMANCE INDICATOR

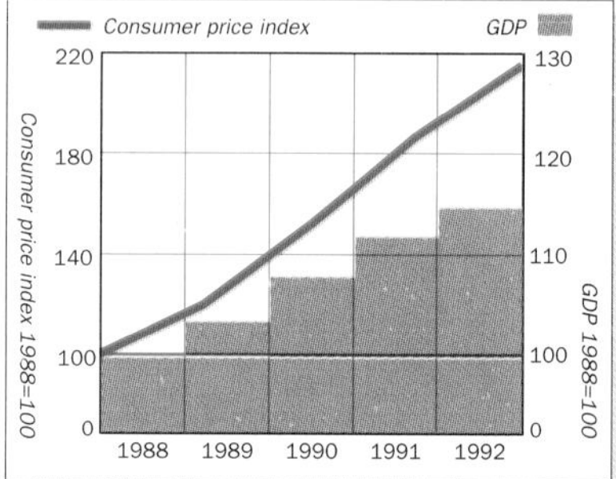

MEXICO : MAJOR BUSINESSES

RESOURCES

123bn kwh (capacity 29.3m kw)

30.9m cattle, 16.2m pigs, 6.2m horses

2.73m b/d (reserves 51,298,000,000 bbl)

Natural gas, silver, copper, fluorite, mercury, antimony

ELECTRICITY GENERATION

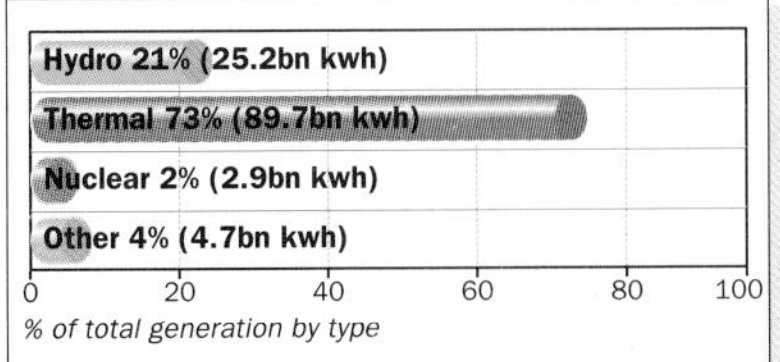

Mexico is one of the largest oil exporters outside the OPEC cartel. Most oil production comes from offshore drilling platforms in the Gulf of Mexico. The industry is state-owned and state-run by PEMEX, the world's fifth-largest oil company, employing 120,000. While the state remains in control of the oil

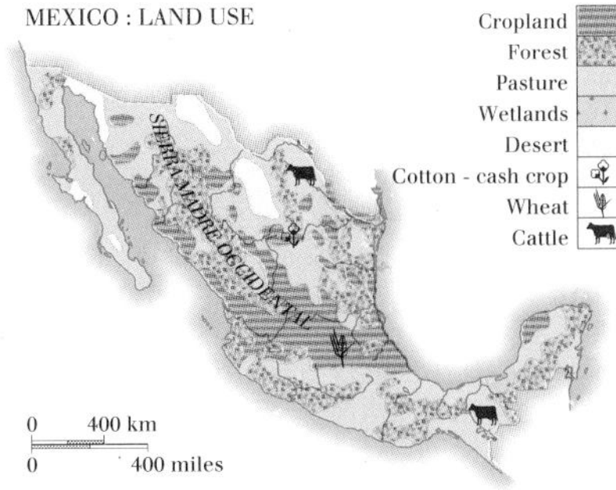

production industry (a change in the constitution is necessary to alter this) under NAFTA, US and Canadian companies will be able to break PEMEX's monopoly on supplying the domestic Mexican market. Despite its oil reserves, Mexico has embarked on a nuclear power program. Its first plant was built at Laguna Verde.

ENVIRONMENT

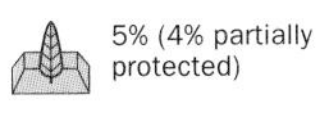

5% (4% partially protected)

NAFTA's green measures might improve poor record

ENVIRONMENTAL TREATIES

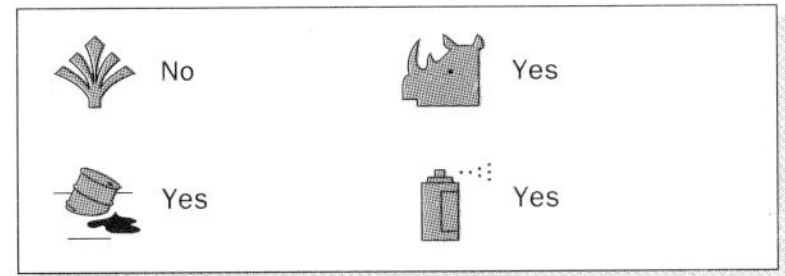

Mexico's biggest ecological problem is probably the conurbation of Mexico City. Largely unplanned growth for its 20.2 million inhabitants and the absence of environmental controls on factories have contributed to perhaps the world's worst air quality levels.

Conditions along the Mexican border are a problem. *Maquiladoras* have no environmental controls (making manufacturing there much cheaper than in the USA) and are usually surrounded by unsanitized slums. The few remaining tropical forests, in the southwest, are disappearing fast.

MEDIA

Free in practice, but power of government advertising a strong incentive against criticism. Several critical journalists have been murdered

PUBLISHING AND BROADCAST MEDIA

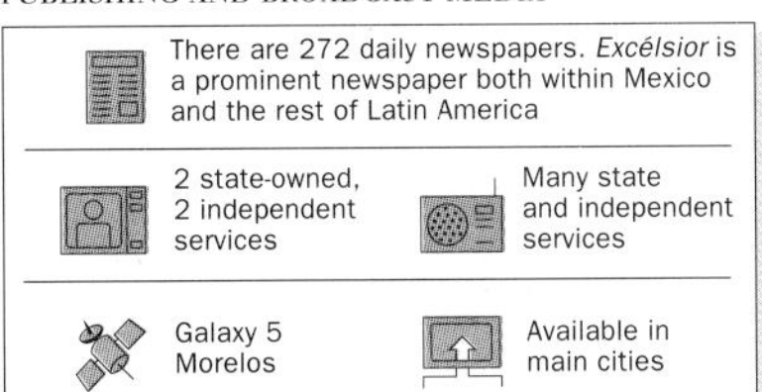

There are 272 daily newspapers. *Excélsior* is a prominent newspaper both within Mexico and the rest of Latin America
2 state-owned, 2 independent services
Many state and independent services
Galaxy 5 Morelos
Available in main cities

The state retains a tight grip on the media, frequently paying the press to run favorable front-page stories.

CRIME

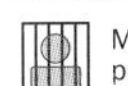

Mexico does not publish prison figures

Down 2% in 1987

CRIME RATES

Mexico does not publish murder, theft or rape statistics

Northern Mexico is a center for drug transshipments to the USA. Guns are rife and minor incidents may end in shootings. Petty offenses are usually settled by bribing the police. Mexico also has a relatively high rate of petty violence which accompanies crimes such as robbery, car theft and burglary.

EDUCATION

87%

THE EDUCATION SYSTEM

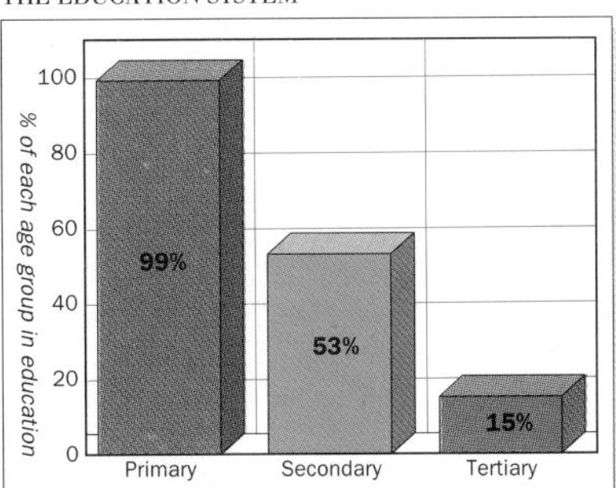

The system is a mixture of the French and US models. The public university system is well developed.

HEALTH

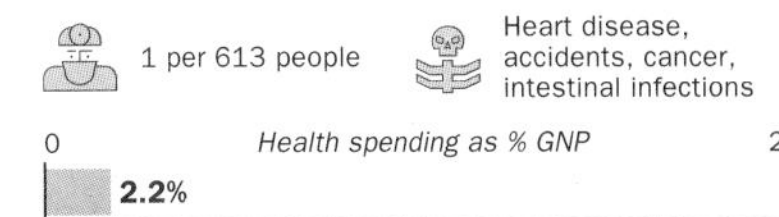

Mexico's national health-care system is rudimentary. Those in employment who pay social security receive slightly better care. Mexico has a good reputation for surgery and dentistry, but this is mostly in the private sector.

WEALTH

Plantation worker, 1,746 Mexican new pesos per day; university science professor, 3,516 Mexican new pesos per day

CONSUMER GOODS OWNERSHIP

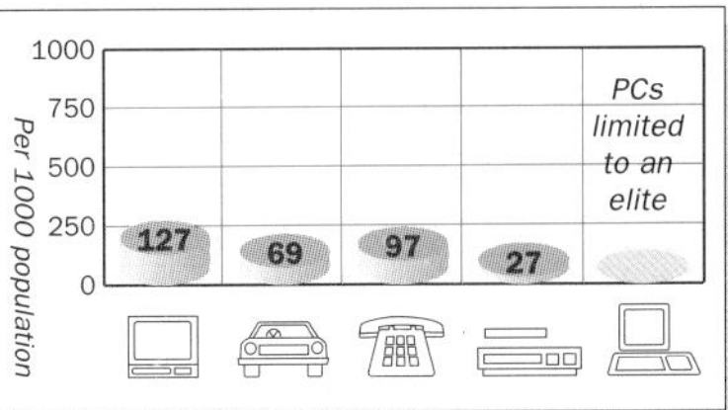

Mexico has enormous wealth disparities, from the twelve dollar-billionaires to the 16% living in extreme poverty. In the past, the wealthy did not generally pay taxes and often benefited from the large state machine. However, they now pay taxes. There is little social mobility; the old Spanish families retain their hold on government offices.

Rural Indians are probably the most disadvantaged group. In the last decade, poverty has forced them into city slums to work in factories or *maquiladoras*. Conditions are so poor that there is a very high turnover in the work force. Much of the problem resulted from Mexico's communal land laws, dating from the revolution in 1917. Without clear rights to title, the agricultural sector declined. The law was reversed in 1991 and this could result in improvements in productivity and social conditions in rural areas.

WORLD RANKING

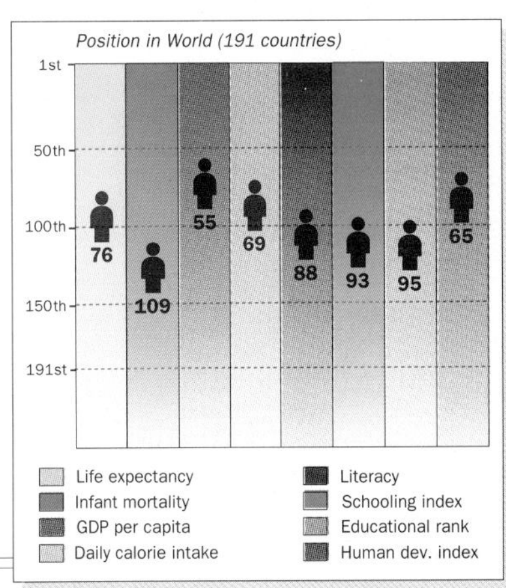

M

MICRONESIA

OFFICIAL NAME: Federated States of Micronesia **CAPITAL:** Kolonia
POPULATION: 101,000 **CURRENCY:** US dollar **OFFICIAL LANGUAGE:** English

PACIFIC OCEAN
Northern Marianas Islands
Marshall Islands
MICRONESIA
Kiribati
Pacific Ocean

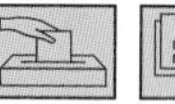
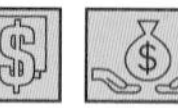

THE FEDERATED STATES of Micronesia (FSM), situated in the Pacific Ocean, encompasses all the Caroline Islands except Palau. It is composed of four main island cluster states: Pohnpei, Kosrae, Chuuk and Yap. The islands are a mixture of high volcanic and low-lying coral types. Formerly a part of the US-administered Trust Territory of the Pacific Islands, the FSM has been independent since 1979. The islands continue to receive considerable aid from the USA, which supplements the fishing and copra-based economy.

CLIMATE

WEATHER CHART

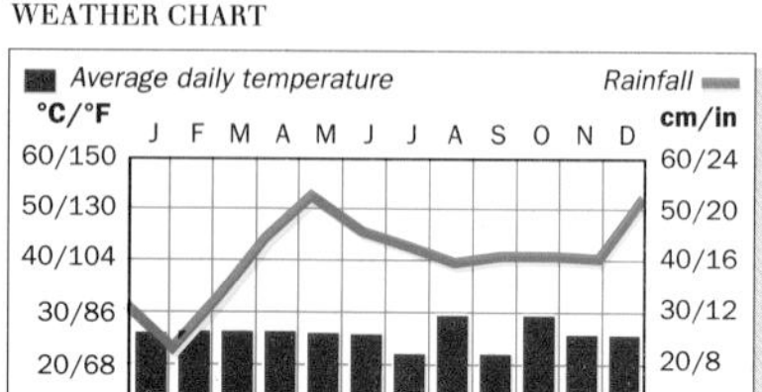

The islands are humid and fairly hot all year round, and the daily temperature range is small. Rainfall is abundant.

COMMUNICATIONS

Chuuk Intl

Has no fleet

THE TRANSPORTATION NETWORK

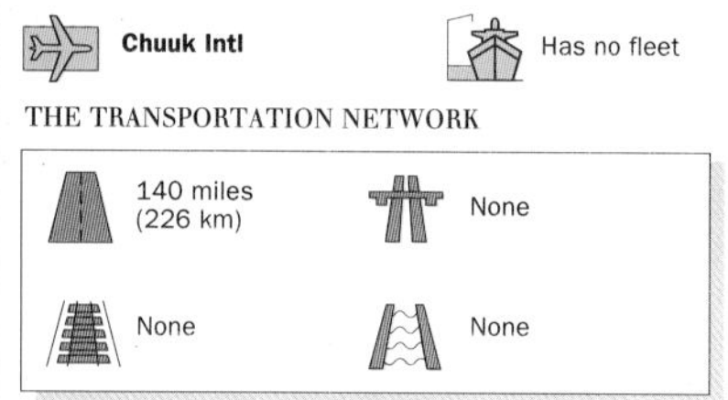

Fairly regular flights are available between the main islands. Local shipping is mainly used to transport bulk cargoes and copra.

Micronesia, aerial view of rock islands. *Like many Pacific states, Micronesia fears rising sea levels as a result of global warming.*

TOURISM

20,475 visitors

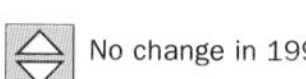
No change in 1990

MAIN OVERSEAS ARRIVALS

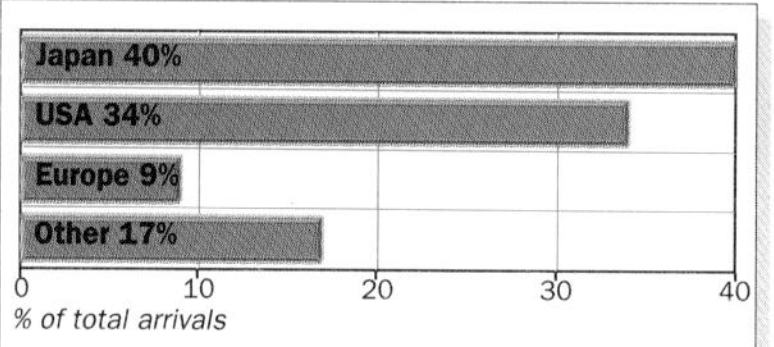

Tourism is undeveloped. Chuuk's underwater war wreckage attracts visitors, and Kosrae has good beaches. The outlying islands remain unspoiled.

PEOPLE

Trukese, Pohnpeian, Mortlockese, Losrean, English

409 people per sq. mile

THE URBAN/RURAL POPULATION SPLIT

Most Micronesians live in small village communities

RELIGIOUS PERSUASION

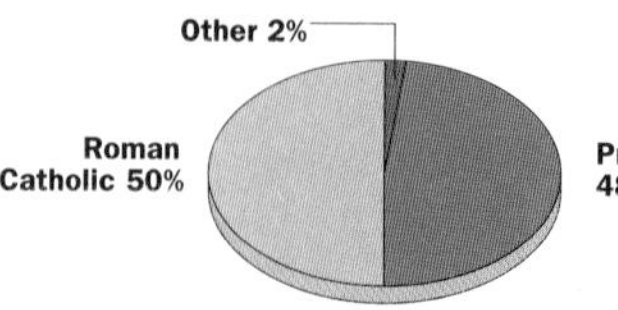

Increasing numbers of Melanesians, especially Filipino laborers, threaten to swamp the resident Micronesian population. Most islanders live without electricity or running water and many are effectively recipients of US welfare. Society is traditionally matrilineal on most of the islands.

POLITICS

1995

President Bailey Olter

THE STATE OF THE PARTIES

Congress 14 members

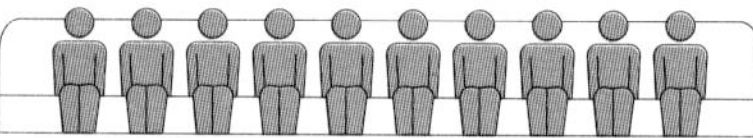

There are no political parties. The 14 senators are elected as independents, 10 for 2 years and 4 at-large senators – 1 for each state – for 4 years

The power of the traditional chiefs in politics is still very strong. Despite the existence of an elected house, it is generally accepted that the election candidates must be chiefs. Increasing Micronesia's economic independence is the key political issue. Presently, it is still heavily dependent on aid received from the USA under the Compact of Free Association, which is due for renegotiation in 2001.

WORLD AFFAIRS

Micronesia's most important relationship is with the USA, which administered the islands until 1979 as part of the Trust Territory of the Pacific Islands. The Japanese are also important, especially economically; some of the older generation still speak Japanese. Japan has provided funding for a project to widen the harbor on Yap. The FSM has developed a strong relationship with China. In 1992, President Bailey Olter made a state visit there, during which a treaty of cooperation was signed between the two countries.

AID

 12.6m (receipts)

 Little change from year to year

The USA is the principal donor of aid, which funds hospitals, schools, food stamps and construction projects.

DEFENSE

 USA responsible for defense

 Not applicable

Defense is entirely in the hands of the USA. Airstrips in the FSM were used by the USA in the Vietnam War.

ECONOMICS

 $99m

 US dollar

SCORE CARD

- ❑ WORLD GNP RANKING........................186th
- ❑ GNP PER CAPITA $980
- ❑ BALANCE OF PAYMENTS..................$-54.5m
- ❑ INFLATION ....Volatile
- ❑ UNEMPLOYMENT ....High underemployment

STRENGTHS

Access to US economy, especially for garment manufacturing through preferential trading rights. Construction industry is the largest private-sector activity. Tourism, fishing and copra production. US strategic interest in Micronesia and US budget subsidies.

WEAKNESSES

Dependence on USA for imports, especially for fuel. $30 million debt. Acute shortage of water limits development potential. High levels of underemployment.

EXPORTS

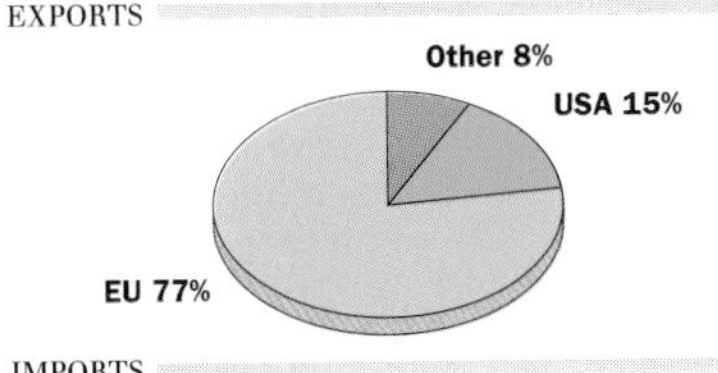

IMPORTS

The majority of imports are from the USA

RESOURCES

 Most electricity is produced by small diesel generators

Not an oil producer and has no refineries

3,634 tons

None

The FSM is entirely dependent on external sources for its energy supply. Almost all electricity is produced by small diesel generators. The main resources are copra and valuable fish stocks, especially tuna.

ENVIRONMENT

 None

 No funds for environmental initiatives

The FSM does not face pollution on the scale of that in the neighboring Marshall Islands. However, Chuuk suffers serious droughts; rationing of water to one cup per person per day is occasionally introduced for short periods. In 1992, the US government used naval vessels to transport water from Guam to alleviate the problem.

MEDIA

 No political restrictions

PUBLISHING AND BROADCAST MEDIA

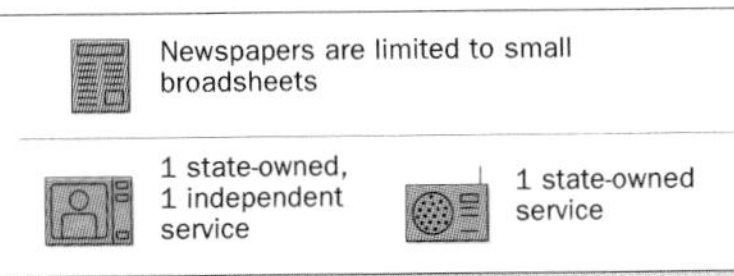

Newspapers are limited to small broadsheets
1 state-owned, 1 independent service
1 state-owned service

Television, which previously consisted of reruns of US programs, can now be received by satellite.

CRIME

 Micronesia does not publish prison figures

 Little change from year to year

On Chuuk, assault, especially alcohol-related cases, is increasing. The outlying islands are crime-free.

EDUCATION

 Probably in the region of 65%

Education is compulsory between the ages of six and 14 years. The USA provides grants for some students to attend US universities.

CHRONOLOGY

The Caroline Islands were first colonized by the Spanish, but sold to Germany in 1899. Having formed an important Japanese base during World War II, the islands were transferred to US control in 1945.

- ❑ **1947** UN Trust Territory of the Pacific Islands established.
- ❑ **1967** Demands for increased local autonomy.
- ❑ **1977** US President Carter agrees to end trusteeship by 1981.
- ❑ **1979** Becomes independent Federated States of Micronesia.
- ❑ **1986** Compact of Free Association with USA implemented.
- ❑ **1990** Official termination of trusteeship agreement.
- ❑ **1991** Joins UN.

HEALTH

 1 per 2,536 people

 Heart, cerebrovascular and intestinal diseases

Basic health care is accessible to all, but outlying islands may not have access to qualified doctors. Diabetes and drug abuse are growing problems.

WEALTH

 Minimum wage on Pohnpei, $1.35 per hour

CONSUMER GOODS OWNERSHIP

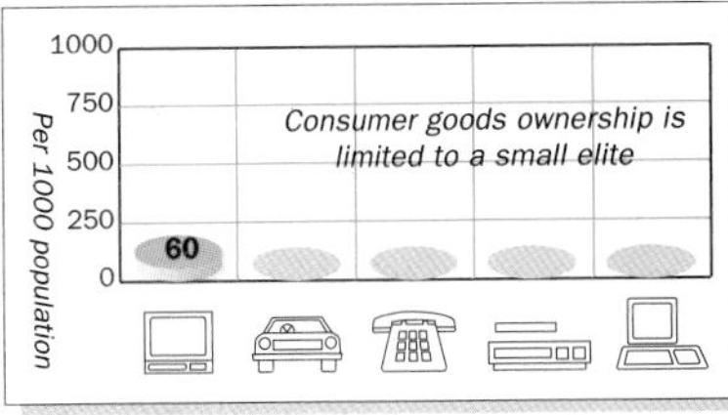

The gap between rich and poor is increasing as businessmen and local officials exploit US aid donations.

WORLD RANKING

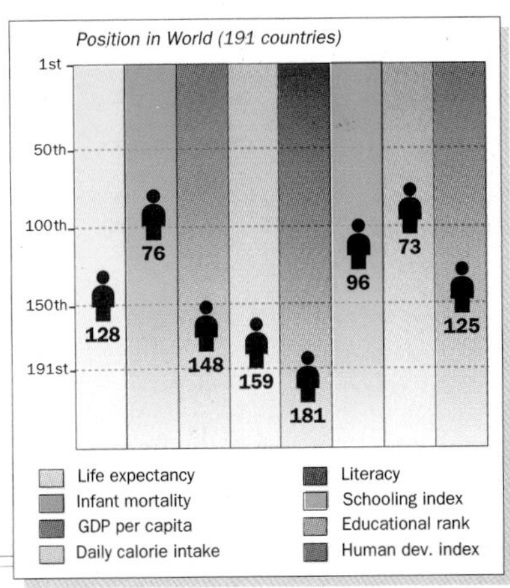

M

MOLDOVA

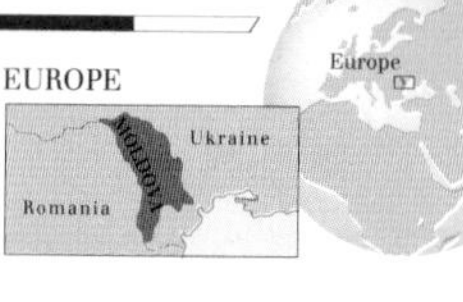

OFFICIAL NAME: Republic of Moldova **CAPITAL:** Chişinău
POPULATION: 4.4 million **CURRENCY:** Moldavian leu **OFFICIAL LANGUAGE:** Romanian

Agricultural landscape. *Warm summers and even rainfall are ideal for cereal and fruit farming. Moldova is famous for its wine.*

ONCE A PART OF ROMANIA, Moldova was incorporated into the Soviet Union in 1940. Independence in 1991 brought with it the expectation that Moldova would be reunited with Romania. In elections in 1993, however, Moldovans voted against the proposal. Moldova is mostly undulating steppe country. It is the smallest and most densely populated of the ex-Soviet republics. Most of its population is engaged in intensive agriculture.

CLIMATE

WEATHER CHART

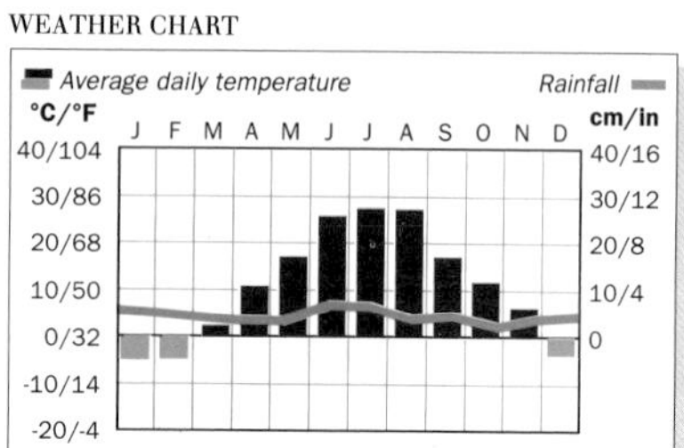

Warm summers, mild winters and moderate rainfall give Moldova an ideal climate for cultivation.

COMMUNICATIONS

Chişinău International

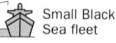

Small Black Sea fleet

THE TRANSPORTATION NETWORK

13,111 miles (21,100 km)

None

715 miles (1,150 km)

Mouth of the Danube

Moldova plans to build port facilities on the 3,000 feet of the Danube River which are its international waters.

TOURISM

Businessmen make up the majority of visitors

Moldova has seen no significant change in tourism arrivals

MAIN OVERSEAS ARRIVALS

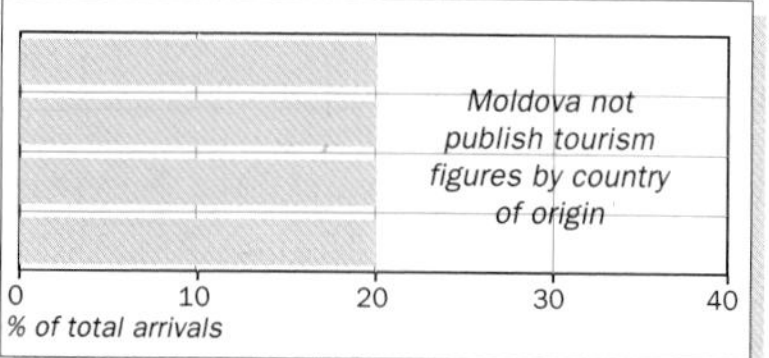

Few tourists visit Moldova. However, its relatively well-developed infrastructure could allow some expansion of tourism in the future. The vineyards and underground wine vault "streets" are the main attractions.

PEOPLE

Romanian, Russian

337 people per sq. mile

THE URBAN/RURAL POPULATION SPLIT

48% 52%

ETHNIC MAKEUP

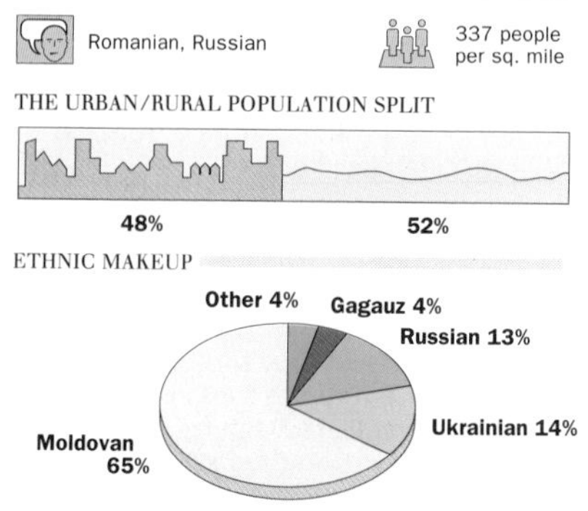

Moldovans are of the same ethnic grouping as Romanians. The southern Gagauzi (Orthodox Christian Turks), and the population of mixed Russian-Moldovan-Ukrainian parentage on the eastern bank of the Dniester, declared themselves separate republics in 1990.

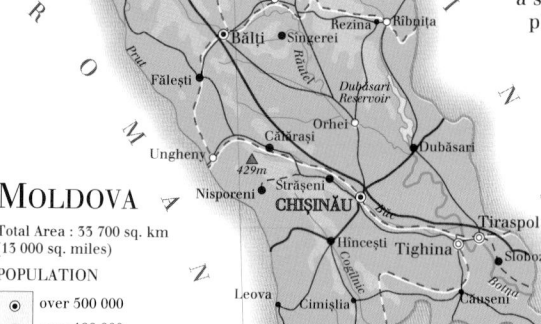

MOLDOVA

Total Area : 33 700 sq. km (13 000 sq. miles)

POPULATION

- over 500 000
- over 100 000
- over 50 000
- over 10 000
- under 10 000

LAND HEIGHT

- 200m/656ft
- 80m/262ft

0 50 km
0 50 miles

UKRAINE ROMANIA Edineţ Rîşcani Drochia Soroca Floreşti Dniester Rezina Rîbniţa Bălţi Sîngerei Prut Răut Făleşti Dubăsari Reservoir Orhei Dubăsari Călăraşi Ungheny 429m Nisporeni Străşeni CHIŞINĂU Bîc Tiraspol Hînceşti Tighina Slobozia Cogilnic Botna Căuşeni Leova Cimişlia Basarabeasca Comrat Ciadîr-Lunga Ialpug Taraclia Cahul Vulcăneşti

POLITICS

1998

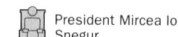

President Mircea Ion Snegur

THE STATE OF THE PARTIES

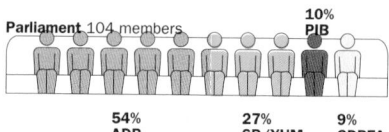

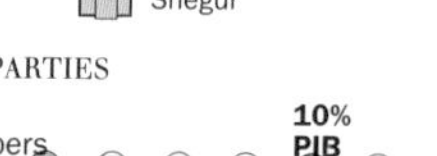

54% ADP 27% SP/YUM 9% CDPFA

ADP = Agrarian Democratic Party **SP/YUM** = Socialist Party and Yedinstvo Unity Movement **PIB** = Peasants and Intellectuals Party **CDPFA** = Christian Democratic People's Front Alliance

Moldova declared itself a multiparty democracy in 1991, but initially kept the transitional administration appointed by the last Soviet in 1990. Elections were held in February 1993 and a new constitution was drafted. The first post-independence question was whether or not Moldova should seek union with Romania. In March 1994, another election was held in which the Agrarian Democratic Party (ADP) emerged as the largest party in parliament. In a separate national plebiscite, held at the same time as the parliamentary elections, Moldovans rejected the idea of possible unification with Romania.

The secessionist republic of Transnistria (on the eastern bank of the Dniester) is seeking incorporation into the Ukraine, rather than Moldova. Furthermore, the 153,000 Gagauzi minority are still hoping for independence.

M

WORLD AFFAIRS

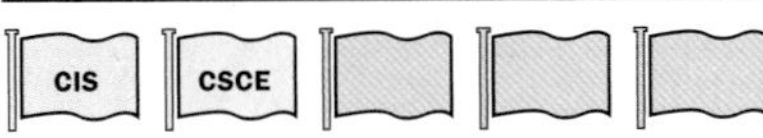

Ties with nations in the Black Sea Economic Zone are being developed. Relations with Romania have been diluted now that reunification is no longer an issue. Links with Russia are now paramount. Economic pressure from Russia persuaded Moldova to rejoin the CIS at the end of 1993. Russia still has troops stationed in Moldova.

AID

 Moldova is a net receiver of aid

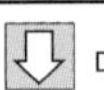 Aid receipts have risen since independence

The IMF and World Bank are supporting economic reforms. The EU, Romania, Turkey and Bulgaria are Moldova's next most important aid providers.

DEFENSE

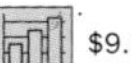 $227.8m

 Down 74% in 1992

Moldova began forming an army after independence and has signed military training agreements with Romania and Hungary. Former officers of the Soviet army are helping Transnistrian rebels.

ECONOMICS

$9.5bn

Moldovan leu not convertible

SCORE CARD

- ❑ WORLD GNP RANKING.........................80th
- ❑ GNP PER CAPITA $2,159
- ❑ BALANCE OF PAYMENTS ....Deficit
- ❑ INFLATION 27%
- ❑ UNEMPLOYMENT ...Widespread underemployment

STRENGTHS

Agriculture – notably wine, tobacco and cotton – and food processing. Light manufacturing. Good progress made in establishing markets for exports, and earning foreign exchange.

WEAKNESSES

Dependent on Russian raw materials and fuel. Most electricity imported. Isolated location and weak transportation system. Legacy of inefficient former Soviet state-run businesses. Shrinking economy as a result of privatization policies.

EXPORTS

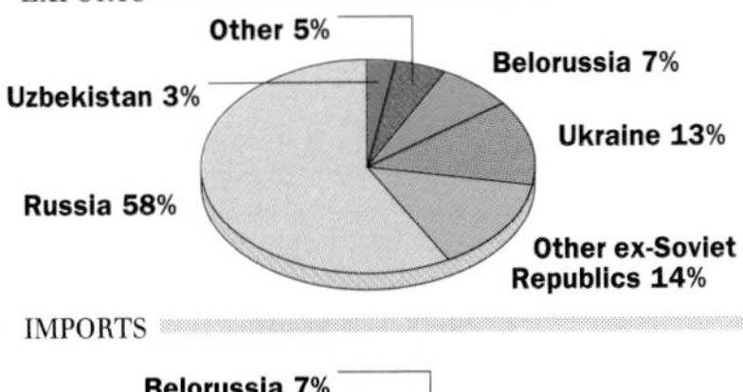

IMPORTS

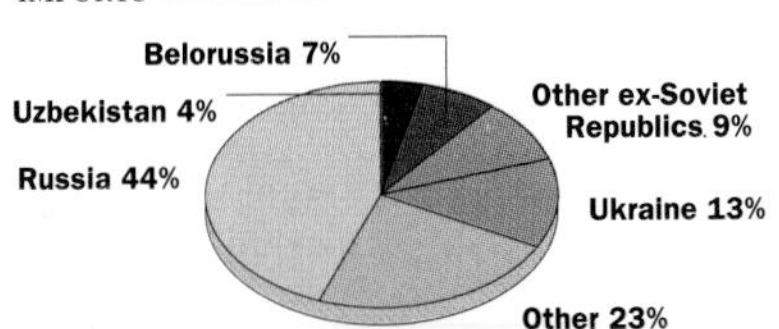

RESOURCES

 11.1bn kwh (capacity 3.1m kw)

 Oil and gas reserves not exploited

 23.6m poultry, 1.7m hogs, 1.2m sheep, 389,000 cattle

 Lignite, phosphate, gypsum, oil, natural gas

Moldova has few mineral resources. It has to import all its fuel and most of its electricity.

ENVIRONMENT

 None

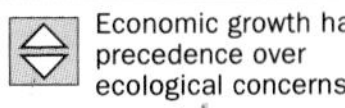

Northern Moldova is still experiencing fallout from the Chernobyl nuclear accident in 1987. Overuse of pesticides on tobacco farms is a serious problem.

MEDIA

 Media is relatively free from state control

PUBLISHING AND BROADCAST MEDIA

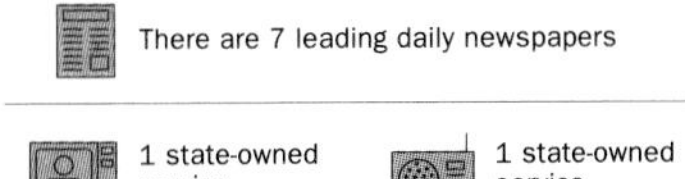

The press was privatized in 1993. The many new publications represent widely differing interest groups.

CRIME

 Moldova does not publish prison figures

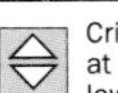 Crime levels remain at a relatively low level

Moldova still awaits a new legal system to accompany its constitution. Crime levels are generally low, but armed gangs have appeared in the south and west, and violence affects the two separatist republics.

EDUCATION

Haphazard attempts have been made to switch from a Soviet to a Romanian (French-inspired) system. Engineering is the largest university program.

HEALTH

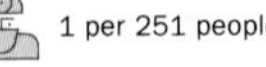

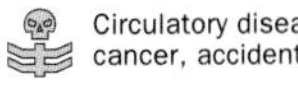

The centralized health service is poor by regional standards, with basic equipment and poorly-trained doctors.

CHRONOLOGY

Modern Moldova roughly corresponds to the eastern part of the Romanian principality of Moldova, which existed for 500 years from 1359. Most of it was annexed by Russia in 1812 as Bessarabia.

- ❑ **1918** Bessarabia joins Romania.
- ❑ **1924** Moldovan Autonomous Soviet Republic formed within USSR.
- ❑ **1940** Romania cedes Bessarabia to Ukrainian and Moldovan SSRs.
- ❑ **1941–1945** Bessarabia again under Romanian control.
- ❑ **1945** Returns to Soviet control.
- ❑ **1990** Declares sovereignty. Reunification with Romania mooted.
- ❑ **1991** Independence. Joins CIS, but then fails to ratify CIS treaty – adopts observer status.
- ❑ **1993** General election results in defeat for pro-unification parties. Moldova rejoins CIS.

WEALTH

 Increasing disparity in wealth between former-communist officials and the rest of the population

CONSUMER GOODS OWNERSHIP

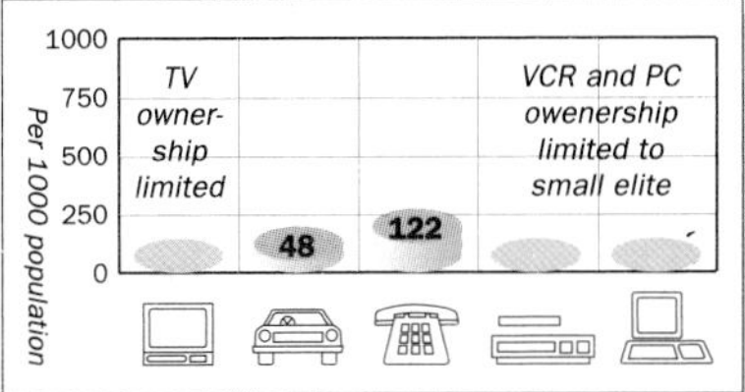

Former Communist Party officials have benefited most from the advent of capitalism. Counterfeit Turkish Napoleon brandy and Marlboro cigarettes are very popular. The ethnic Gagauzi (Orthodox Christian Turks) form the poorest group.

WORLD RANKING

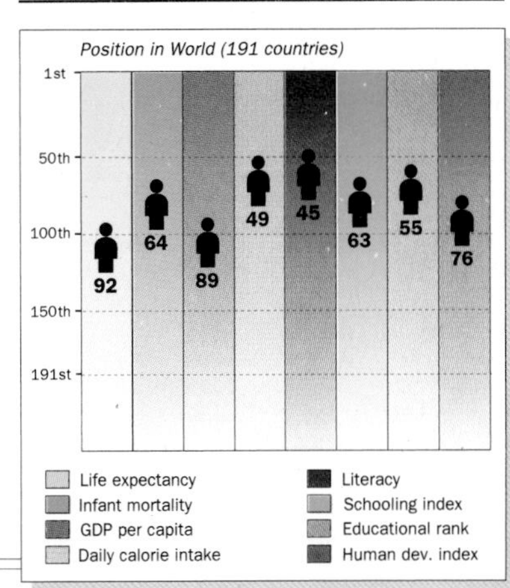

M

MONACO

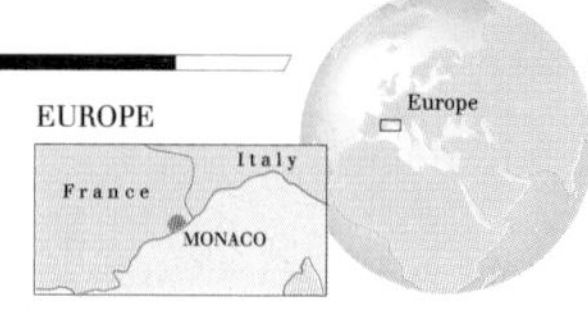

OFFICIAL NAME: Principality of Monaco **CAPITAL:** Monaco
POPULATION: 30,000 **CURRENCY:** French franc **OFFICIAL LANGUAGE:** French

MONACO IS A TINY ENCLAVE on the Côte d'Azur, in southeastern France. Its destiny changed radically in 1863 when Prince Charles III, after whom Monte Carlo is named, opened the casino. Today, Monaco is a lucrative banking and services center, as well as a tourist destination. Prince Rainier's marriage to film star Grace Kelly, and some astute management of the economy, successfully transformed Monaco into a center for the international jet-set. In 1962, the prince's absolute authority was abolished in a new, democratic constitution.

CLIMATE

WEATHER CHART

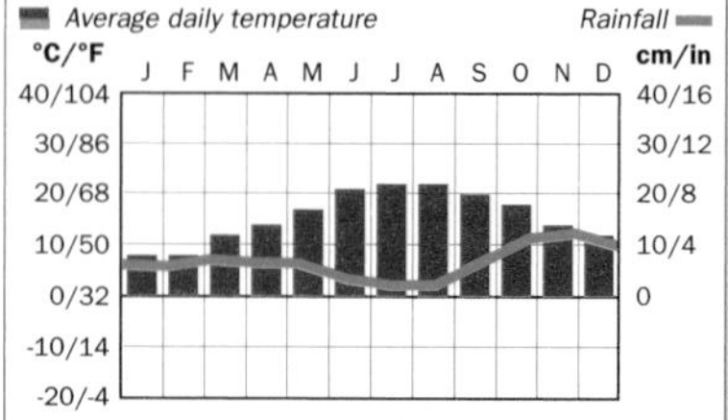

Summers are hot and dry; days with 12 hours of sunshine are not uncommon. Winters are mild and sunny.

COMMUNICATIONS

None

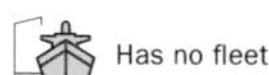
Has no fleet

THE TRANSPORTATION NETWORK

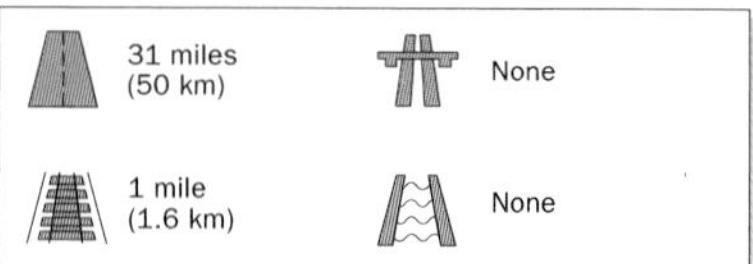

The mile-long mainline track is run by French state railroads. A helicopter shuttle links Fontvieille with Nice, the nearest airport. There are 30 miles of major roads. Monaco is an easy drive from northern Italy, the source of most of its private banking trade.

TOURISM

245,592 visitors

Up 3% in 1992

MAIN OVERSEAS ARRIVALS

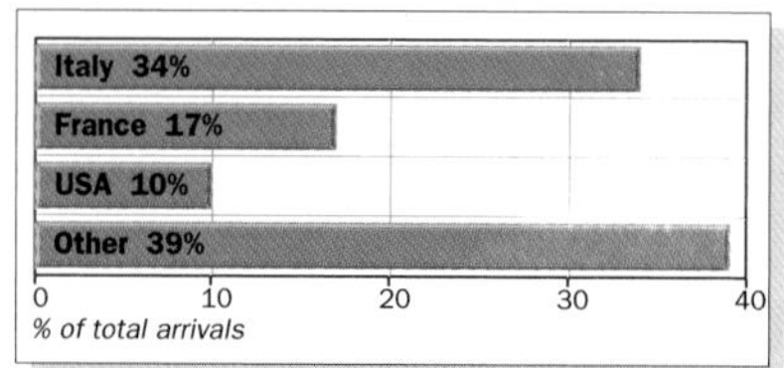

A nation of less than 30,000 people, Monaco attracts huge numbers of tourists, mainly from France and Italy. Almost all are day-trippers, coming to gamble at the casino or to sample Monaco's high life. Just 245,000 of them stay the night, but efforts are being made to improve this by attracting business and holiday visitors. A new conference center has opened and exhibition facilities are being built. Monaco is a long-time favorite destination of the rich, especially northern Italians. Spring is a key time for jet-set visitors, with several major social and sporting events: the Rose Ball (March), the Tennis Open (April) and the Grand Prix (May).

PEOPLE

French, Italian, Monégasque, English

39,681 people per sq. mile

THE URBAN/RURAL POPULATION SPLIT

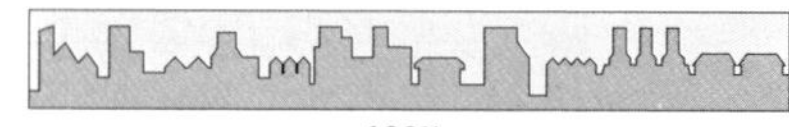

RELIGIOUS PERSUASION

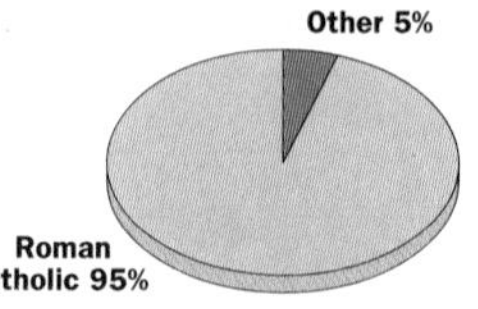

Less than one-tenth of Monaco's residents are Monégasque. Over half are French, the rest Italian, American, British and Belgian. Monégasques enjoy considerable privileges, including housing subsidies to protect them from Monaco's high property prices, and the right of first refusal before a job can be offered to a foreigner. Women have equal status, but only acquired the vote in the constitutional changes of 1962.

POLITICS

1998

HSH Prince Rainier III

THE STATE OF THE PARTIES

National Council 18 members

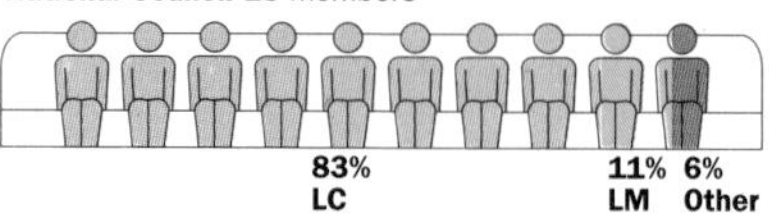

LC = Campora List **LM** = Médecin List
There are no political parties, but candidates generally enter their names through an organization

The Grimaldi princes (Rainier since 1949) have been hereditary rulers of Monaco for 700 years. The prince renounced absolute rule in the 1962 constitutional reforms. He still has considerable power and appoints the four-member executive. There are no political parties; National Council elections are based on personalities.

WORLD AFFAIRS

Monaco's key concern is to protect both banking secrecy and the liberal tax regime from EU regulation. French citizens are banned from banking in Monaco, a 1962 decision enforced by President de Gaulle, who sent troops to the border.

MONACO
Total Area : 1.95 sq. km (0.75 sq. miles)
Places of Interest
Parks and Gardens
Grand Prix Circuit
0 500 m
0 656 ft

FRANCE
Côte d'Azur
Lycée de l'Annonciade
Musée National
Larvotto
Centre de la Culture et d'Expositions
Monte-Carlo Sporting Club d'Eté
Casino
Hospitalier Grace
Railway Station
La Condamine
Centre de Congrès
Monte-Carlo
Palais du Prince
Port de Monaco
Stade Louis II
Port de Fontvieille
Palais de Justice
Ministère d'Etat
Cathédrale
MONACO
Fontvieille
Musée Océanographique
Heliport
N
7°25'

***Monte Carlo** with its luxury hotels and yacht harbor. The only space for new development is on land reclaimed from the sea.*

AID

 Monaco has no aid receipts or donations  Not applicable

Monaco neither receives nor gives aid, and the issue is not of concern to Monégasques.

DEFENSE

 France responsible for defense  Not applicable

Monaco has no armed forces and no defense budget. France, as the protecting power, bears responsibility for the defense of the principality.

ECONOMICS

  $475m (est)  5.90 French francs

SCORE CARD

- ❑ WORLD GNP RANKING........................163rd
- ❑ GNP PER CAPITA..........................$11,000
- ❑ BALANCE OF PAYMENTS...Included in French total
- ❑ INFLATION..................Included in French total
- ❑ UNEMPLOYMENT..................................0%

STRENGTHS

Banking secrecy laws and low tax rates attract over $10 billion of overseas deposits, particularly from Italy. Strong tourism sector, still fundamental to the economy. Services, including property management and overseas shipping companies' headquarters, as well as banking, account for 40% of economic turnover. Chemical, pharmaceutical, plastics, construction, electronics and printing industries.

WEAKNESSES

Banking secrecy makes Monaco vulnerable to money laundering. Some EU states wish to end Monaco's privileged tax and banking status. Lack of natural resources means Monaco is almost totally dependent on imports; lack of space could hinder growth. No agricultural land.

EXPORTS/IMPORTS

Monaco has a full customs union with France

RESOURCES

 Included within French total  Not an oil producer and has no refineries

2 tons — None

Monaco has no strategic resources and imports all its energy from France. It has no agricultural land.

ENVIRONMENT

 None  Environmental issues not paramount

Environmental questions are not a political priority, except where they might affect profitability. The quality of the environment built around the harbor occasionally arouses local passions. The important populations of red coral are under threat from land reclamation and pollution.

MEDIA

 Freedom of expression guaranteed under constitution

PUBLISHING AND BROADCAST MEDIA

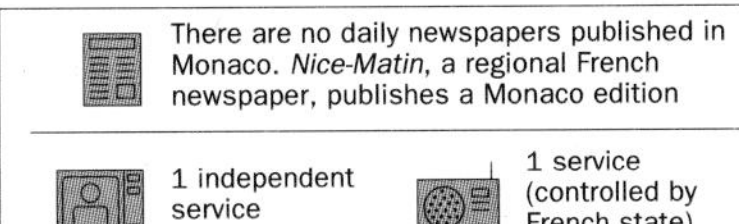
There are no daily newspapers published in Monaco. *Nice-Matin*, a regional French newspaper, publishes a Monaco edition

1 independent service — 1 service (controlled by French state)

In addition to its domestic radio and TV, Monaco receives all the mainstream French and Italian channels.

CRIME

 Monaco does not publish prison figures  Up 8% in 1990

Monaco prides itself on its relatively low crime rates and the fact that, in contrast to northern Italy, it is quite safe for the rich to sport their furs and expensive jewelry in public.

EDUCATION

 99%

The education system is essentially the same as that of France, with students studying for the *baccalauréat* exam. Most go on to universities in France but then return to claim good jobs in Monaco. The Catholic Church exerts considerable influence and is still responsible for primary schooling.

HEALTH

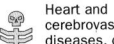

 1 per 373 people  Heart and cerebrovascular diseases, cancer

Medical care is provided by a system of private health insurance. Doctors train in France. The Princess Grace Hospital can serve 60,000 people and thus caters to patients from outside Monaco.

CHRONOLOGY

In 1297, the Grimaldis established themselves as the Principality's hereditary rulers.

- ❑ **1911** Constitution promulgated.
- ❑ **1912** Customs union with France.
- ❑ **1949** Prince Rainier III accedes to the throne.
- ❑ **1962** Constitution rewritten. End of absolute authority of the prince.
- ❑ **1963** Democratic legislative elections held for first time.
- ❑ **1982** Princess Grace dies following car accident.

WEALTH

 Due to the high cost of living in Monaco, salaries have a premium of 5% over rates of pay in the neighboring area of the Alpes-Maritimes, France

CONSUMER GOODS OWNERSHIP

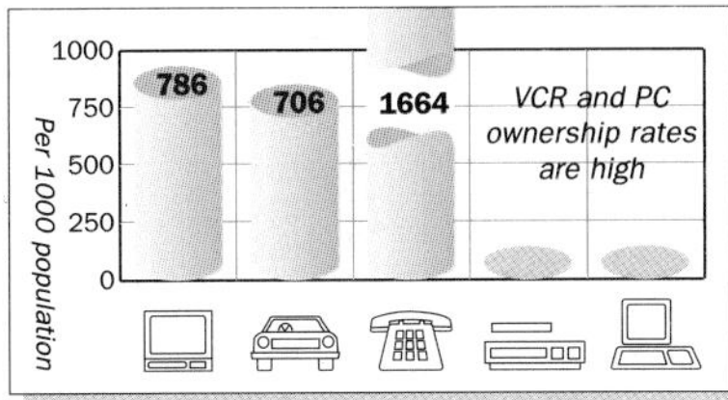

Monaco's image abroad has changed dramatically since Prince Rainier acceded in 1949. From being considered a simple gambling spot, it is now ranked as one of the world's most glamorous international jet-set destinations. In part, this was the result of Rainier's wedding to Grace Kelly, then a leading Hollywood star, which brought Monaco to the attention of US high society. More important was Rainier's work in turning Monaco into a major tax haven and an upscale resort, by making the most of its Mediterranean coastal location. Today, many tax exiles reside here, among them the Wall Street investment guru Bob Beckman.

WORLD RANKING

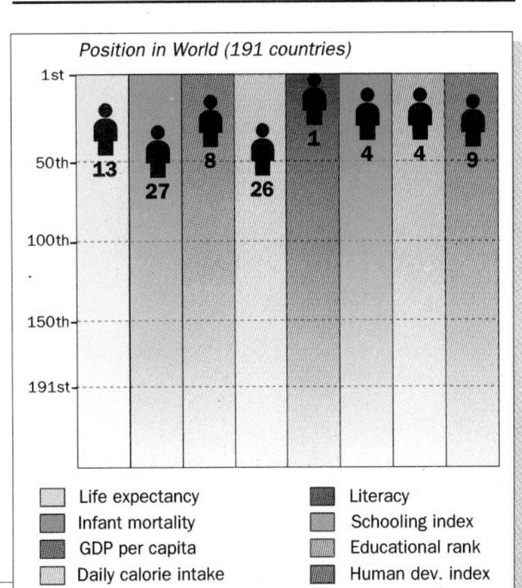

MONGOLIA

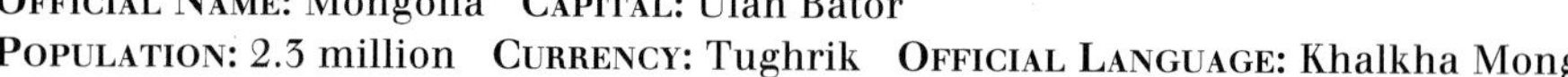

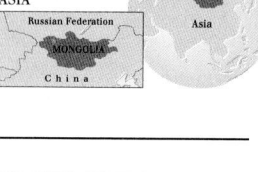

OFFICIAL NAME: Mongolia **CAPITAL:** Ulan Bator
POPULATION: 2.3 million **CURRENCY:** Tughrik **OFFICIAL LANGUAGE:** Khalkha Mongolian

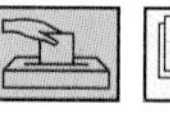

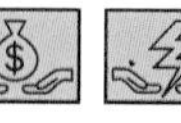

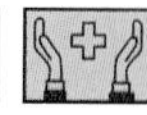

LANDLOCKED BETWEEN Russia and China, Mongolia rises from the semi-arid Gobi Desert to mountain steppe. Mongolia was unified by Ghenghis Khan in 1206 and became part of Manchu China in 1697. Independent in 1924, Mongolia became a communist state and was officially aligned with the USSR in 1936. In 1990, it became the first Asian nation to abandon communist rule; but in 1993, the former communists were voted back into power.

CLIMATE

WEATHER CHART

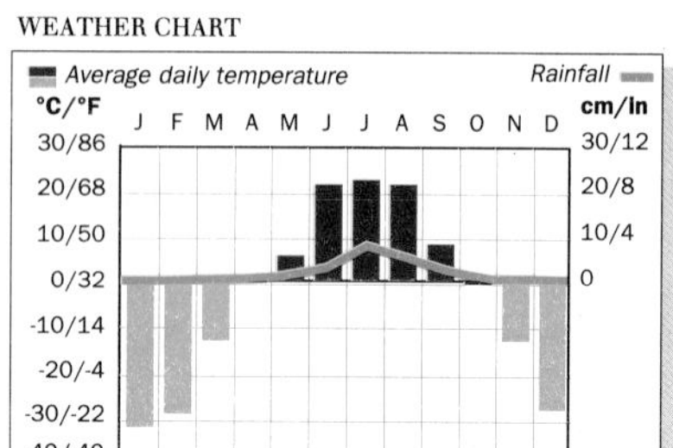

Temperatures occasionally drop to –20°F but can rise to 107°F. Sudden cold periods in early spring, known as *zud*, can kill many young livestock.

COMMUNICATIONS

Buyant-Ukhaa, Ulan Bator

Has no fleet

THE TRANSPORTATION NETWORK

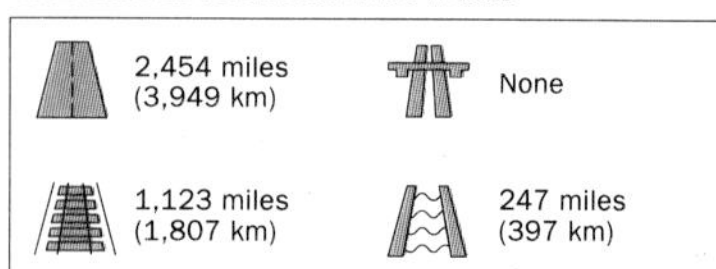

The focus of state transportation policy is shifting away from Moscow towards improved links with China and access to a Pacific port facility. Gasoline shortages have meant a large increase in the use of draft animals.

Traditional** gers **in the Gobi Desert.
Most Mongolians still choose to pursue a nomadic lifestyle, living in felt tents called gers.

TOURISM

147,236 visitors

Tourism shrank after the USSR's collapse, but is now expanding

MAIN OVERSEAS ARRIVALS

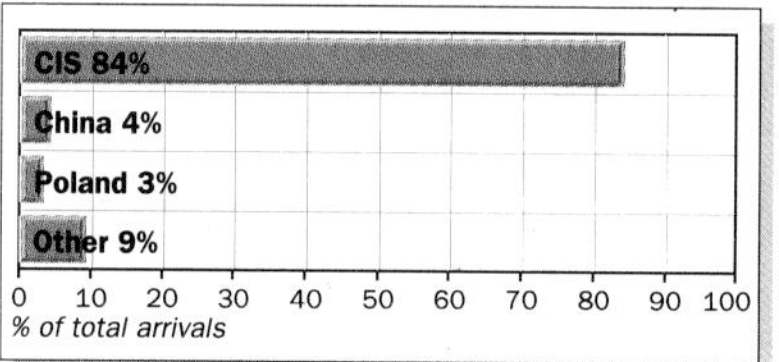

Tourism has expanded since the easing of visa restrictions in 1991. Under communism, all travel was arranged through the state agency, *Zhuuichin*, but private companies are now entering the market.

ASIA

PEOPLE

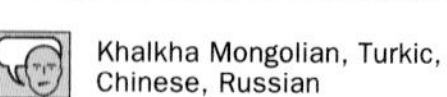

THE URBAN/RURAL POPULATION SPLIT

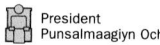

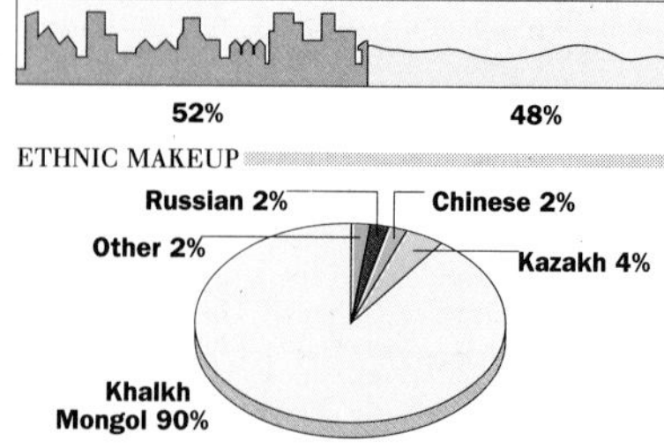

ETHNIC MAKEUP

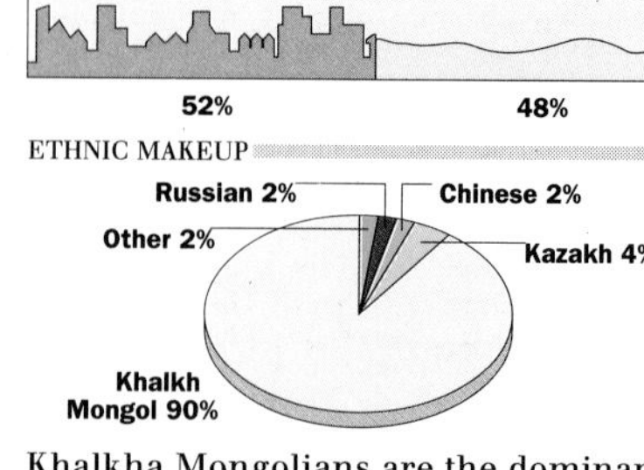

Khalkha Mongolians are the dominant ethnic group. The Kazakhs, who live in the northwest and speak a Turkic language, form the largest non-Mongol group. Since the collapse of the USSR, many Kazakhs have been emigrating to Kazakhstan. There is little indigenous ethnic tension, although there is considerable antagonism toward Chinese and Russian minorities.

POLITICS

1997
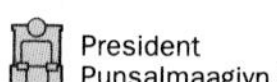
President Punsalmaagiyn Ochirbat

THE STATE OF THE PARTIES

Great Hural 76 members

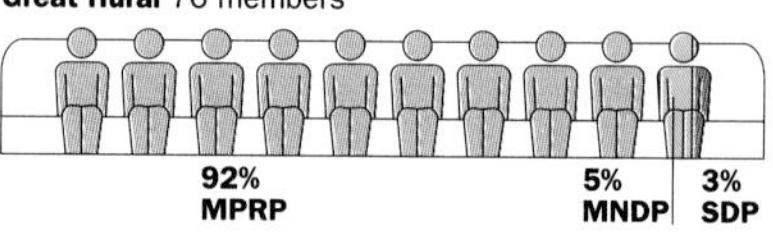

MPRP = Mongolian People's Revolutionary Party
MNDP = Mongolian National Democratic Party
SDP = Social Democratic Party

After over 50 years of Soviet-style communist rule, the advent of democracy in 1990 revolutionized Mongolian politics. Communism was banned. Political activity now functions on a constituency system. The economic results of democratic reform have been less popular and are the dominant domestic issue. In 1992, the economy shrank by 16% and Mongolians began to look back to the guaranteed housing and jobs of the communist past. The 1993 elections saw the democrats swept from power, and the renamed communists (MPRP) returned with a large majority.

MONGOLIA

Total Area : 1 565 000 sq. km (604 247 sq. miles)

0 400 km
0 400 miles

POPULATION
- over 500 000
- over 50 000
- over 10 000
- under 10 000

LAND HEIGHT
- 3000m/9843ft
- 2000m/6562ft
- 1000m/3281ft
- above 500m

RUSSIAN FEDERATION · Uvs Nuur · Ulaangom · Hövsgöl Nuur · Ölgiy · Hyargas Nuur · Mörön · Sünbaatar · Selenge · Darhan · Sharïn Gol · Erdenet · Bulgan · Dzüünharaa · Hovd · Mönh Hayrhan Uul 4362m · Dzavhan · Hangayn Nuruu · Uliastay · Orhon · ULAN BATOR · Choybalsan · Kerulen · Baganuur · Dzuunmod · Nalayh · Altay · Tsetserleg · Öndörhaan · ALTAI MOUNTAINS · Bayanhongor · Baruun-Urt · Arvayheer · Mandalgovĭ · GOBI · Saynshand · Dalandzadgad · CHINA

WORLD AFFAIRS

Since 1990, Mongolia has tried to balance China's influence with that of Japan and other east Asian states. Mongolia is seeking to improve economic and political relations with China, but there is a fear of Chinese designs on its sovereignty. Mongolia is trying to ensure its security by joining international organizations.

AID

 $320m (receipts)

 Up 113% in 1992

A large balance of payments deficit makes aid vital. The main donors are now the USA and Japan.

DEFENSE

 $130m

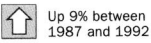

 Up 9% between 1987 and 1992

The last Soviet forces left in 1992 after the collapse of communism in Russia. The Mongolian forces have been drastically reduced and have barely any equipment. Video surveillance is being used to monitor the Chinese border.

ECONOMICS

 $1.3bn

 399.32 tughriks

SCORE CARD

- ❑ WORLD GNP RANKING........................150th
- ❑ GNP PER CAPITA $570
- ❑ BALANCE OF PAYMENTS ....$-31.3m
- ❑ INFLATION 125%
- ❑ UNEMPLOYMENT.................................2.4%

STRENGTHS

Coal and oil, although most remains untapped. Traditional farming economy still strong and supports the population efficiently in a harsh climate.

WEAKNESSES

Distance between centers. Limited infrastructure. Little manufacturing.

EXPORTS

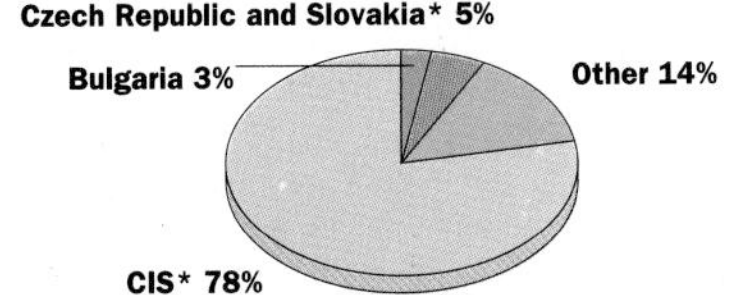

IMPORTS

RESOURCES

 3.6bn kwh (capacity 900,000 kw)

 Contracts have recently been signed with oil prospectors

 13m sheep, 2m cattle, 2m horses, 171,000 pigs

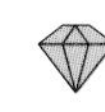 Oil, coal, copper, uranium, fluorspar, tungsten, tin, gold

Mongolia is rich in oil and many other minerals. Under communism, Mongolia's vast mineral resources were barely exploited, and prospecting has only recently begun in earnest. Known oil reserves indicate that Mongolia should meet most of its future domestic needs. Mongolia is establishing a uranium-mining joint venture with Russia.

ENVIRONMENT

 4%

 Traditional Buddhist values instill respect for nature

Industrial pollution around Ulan Bator is a concern; prevailing winds carry power station emissions over residential areas and there is a high incidence of chest diseases. The level of pollution in Lake Hövsgöl is also a serious problem.

MEDIA

 All restrictions on reporting have been removed

PUBLISHING AND BROADCAST MEDIA

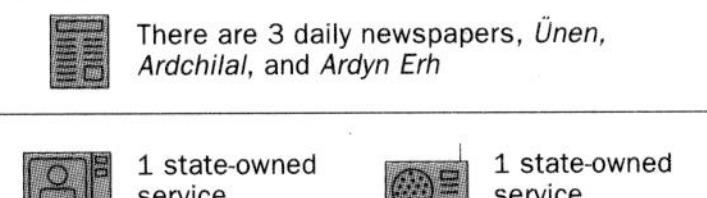
There are 3 daily newspapers, *Ünen*, *Ardchilal*, and *Ardyn Erh*

1 state-owned service

1 state-owned service

Highly restricted under communism, Mongolia's press is now strongly outspoken; there are no slander or libel laws. However, limited supplies of ink and paper restrict publications. Fuel shortages are also a problem, making distribution into remote regions prohibitively expensive.

CRIME

 Mongolia does not publish prison figures

 Crime, especially theft, is rising

Crime has risen rapidly since 1990, particularly organized crime and muggings by knife gangs. Ulan Bator is the most dangerous area, especially for foreigners; Russians, Chinese and dollar-carrying US tourists are the main targets.

EDUCATION

 89%

Education is modeled on the former Soviet system. The majority of teachers are women on low salaries. Private-sector schools emphasizing Mongol culture are beginning to open.

CHRONOLOGY

In the 17th century, the Manchus took control of Mongolia. It stayed in Chinese hands until 1911.

- ❑ **1911** Mongolian aristocracy, supported by Tsarist Russia, declares independence from China.
- ❑ **1919** China reoccupies Mongolia.
- ❑ **1921** White Russians, Chinese and communists struggle for control.
- ❑ **1924** Mongolia becomes an independent communist state.
- ❑ **1989–1990** Peaceful demonstrations in Ulan Bator demanding reform. Communists accede to request for multiparty democracy.

HEALTH

 1 per 357 people

 Heart, parasitic and respiratory diseases

Shortages of drugs and equipment have renewed interest in traditional Mongolian herbal medicine. As well as the state-run system, some Buddhist monasteries provide healthcare.

WEALTH

 Street cleaner, 4,000 tughriks per month; hospital doctor, 8,000 tughriks per month

CONSUMER GOODS OWNERSHIP

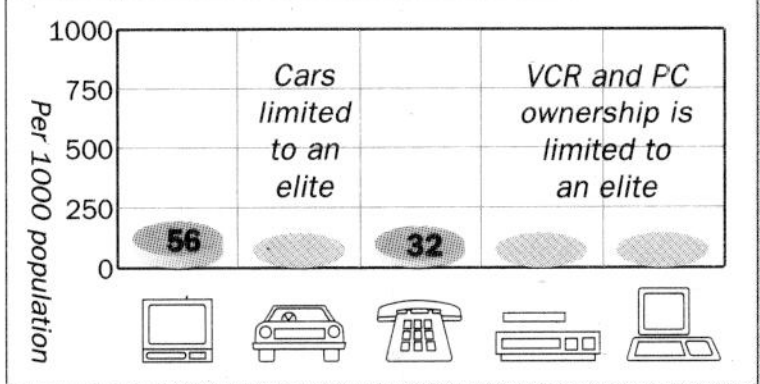

The poorest Mongolians cannot even afford to buy bread. The wealthy are those with access to dollars, often spent on shopping expeditions to China. Russian cars are favored, as parts are readily available.

WORLD RANKING

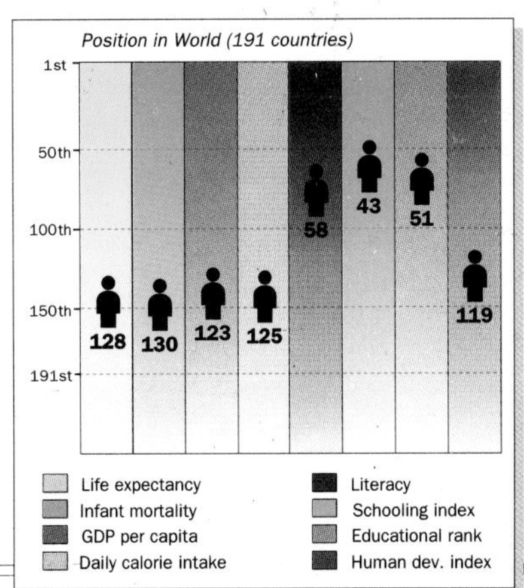

M

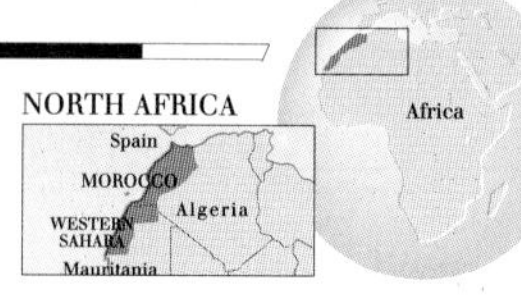

MOROCCO

OFFICIAL NAME: Kingdom of Morocco **CAPITAL:** Rabat
POPULATION: 26.3 million **CURRENCY:** Moroccan dirham **OFFICIAL LANGUAGE:** Arabic

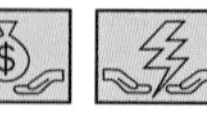

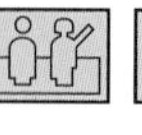

MOROCCO IS SITUATED in the north of Africa and bordered by Algeria and the Western Sahara, the future of which is to be determined by a UN-supervised referendum. Its northern regions have a Mediterranean climate, while the south comprises semi-arid desert. King Hassan's international prestige has given Morocco status out of proportion to its wealth. The main issues facing the country are the unresolved fate of the Western Sahara and the internal threat of Islamic militancy. Tourism, phosphate production and agriculture are key economic strengths.

CLIMATE

WEATHER CHART

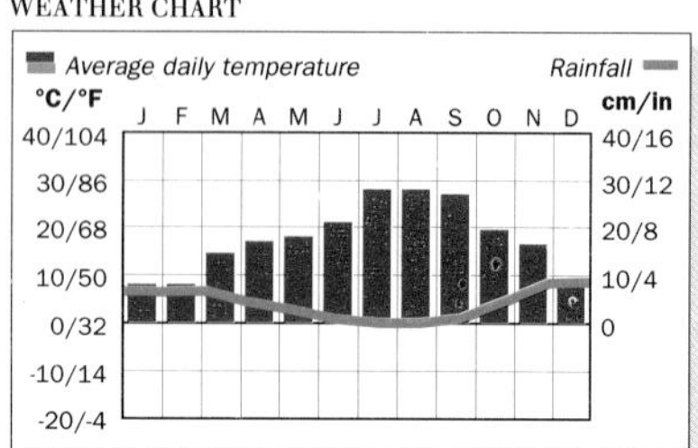

The climate ranges from warm and temperate in the north to semi-arid in the south, but temperatures are cooler in the mountains, especially in the high Atlas. During the summer, the effect of the *sirocco* and *chergui*, hot winds from the Sahara, are felt.

COMMUNICATIONS

Mohammed V, Casablanca

64 ships
483,700 dwt

THE TRANSPORTATION NETWORK

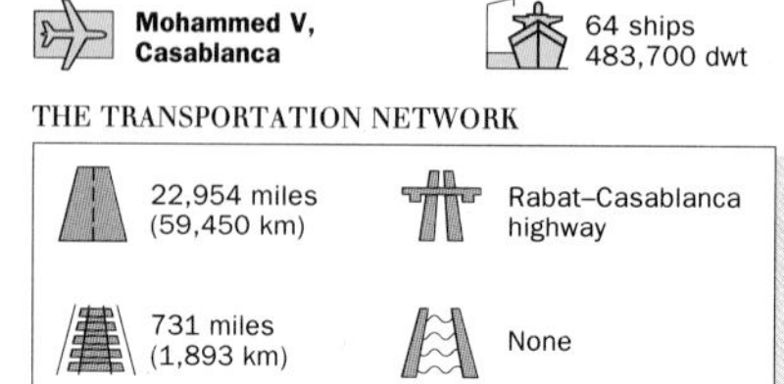

Morocco has six international airports. A highway links Rabat and Casablanca; however, roads tend to peter out in the rural areas. The railroad service is cheap, although its routes are limited.

TOURISM

3.47m visitors

Up 22% in 1989

MAIN OVERSEAS ARRIVALS

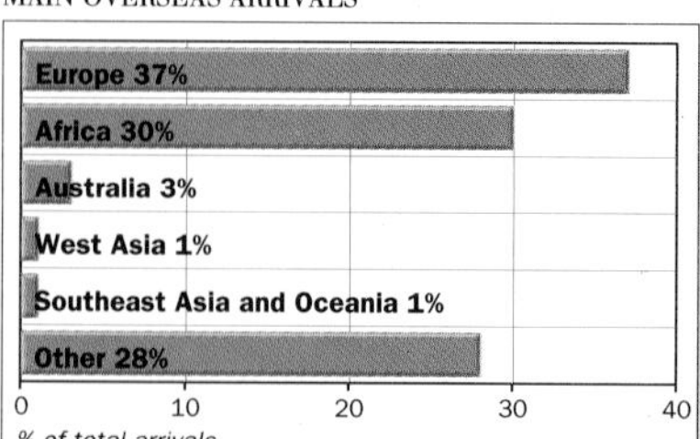

Tourism is vital to the economy. Good beaches abound; Agadir has 300 days of sunshine a year. Fès and Marrakech offer cultural interest, while the Atlas Mountains attract walkers and skiers. Desert safaris are offered in the Sahara. Most Western tourists come from France, Germany and Spain.

M

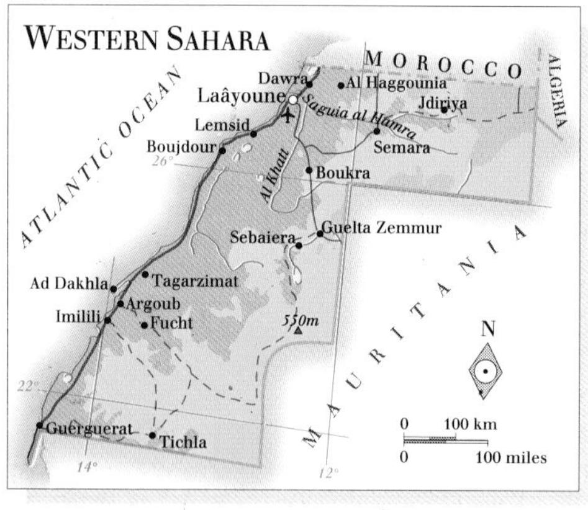

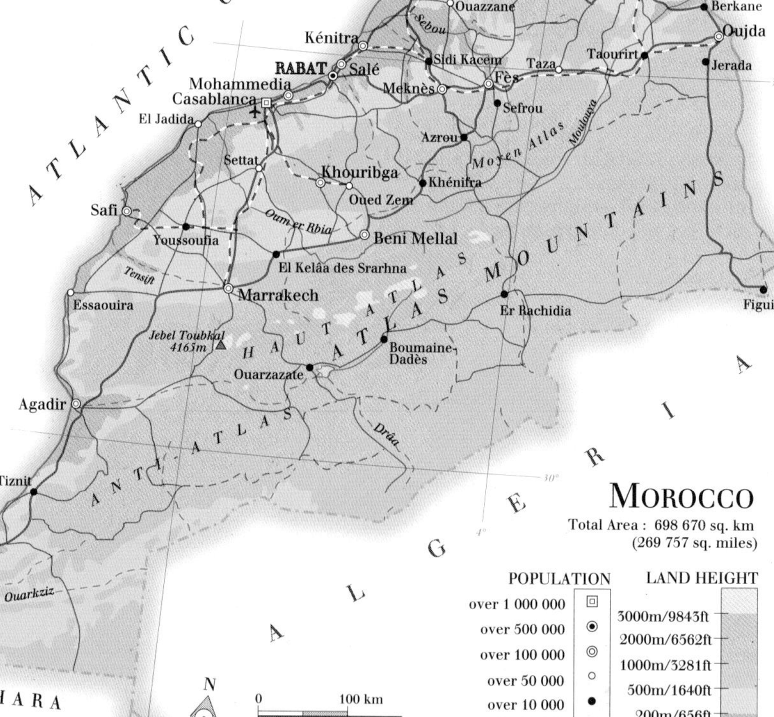

PEOPLE

Arabic, Berber (Shluh, Tamazight, Riffian), French, Spanish

145 people per sq. mile

THE URBAN/RURAL POPULATION SPLIT

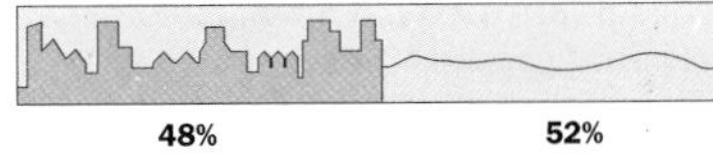

48% 52%

RELIGIOUS PERSUASION

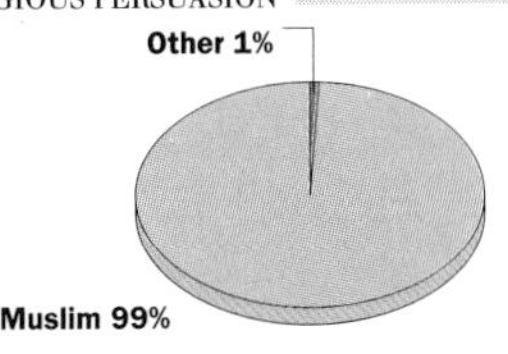

ETHNIC MAKEUP

European 1%

Arab and Berber 99%

Morocco, the westernmost of the Maghreb states, is the last refuge for descendants of the original Berber inhabitants of northwest Africa. About 35% of Moroccans are Berber-speaking. They live mainly in mountain villages, while the Arab majority inhabit the lowlands. Before independence from France, 450,000 Europeans lived in Morocco; numbers have since greatly diminished. Some 45,000 Jews enjoy religious freedom and full civil rights – a role in society unique among Arab countries. Most people speak Arabic, and French is also spoken in urban areas. Sunni Muslim is the nominal religion of most of the population. King Hassan is the spiritual leader through his position as Commander of the Faithful. The emancipation of women was slow to take root in Morocco despite advances in education and increasing freedom of social intercourse between the sexes.

POPULATION AGE BREAKDOWN

% of population by age group

	1960	1970	1980	1990	2000
65+	00%	4.2%	4.1%	3.6%	4%
15–64	00%	48.2%	52.7%	55.9%	59.1%
0–14	00%	47.6%	43.2%	40.5%	36.9%

The town of Boumaine-Dadès lies in the southern foothills of the Atlas Mountains. The region's outstanding scenery makes it one of Morocco's major tourist attractions.

POLITICS

1999

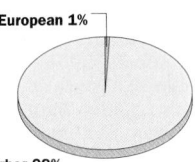

HM King Hassan II

THE STATE OF THE PARTIES

Chamber of Representatives 333 members

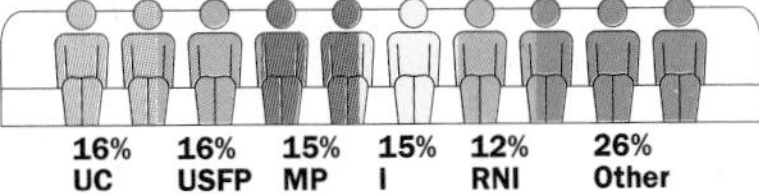

UC = Constitutional Union **USFP** = Socialist Union of Popular Force **MP** = Popular Movement **I** = Independence Party (*Istiqlal*) **RNI** = National Assembly of Independents

Morocco is a constitutional monarchy with a single assembly, to which members are elected every six years.

MAIN POLITICAL ISSUES

The succession

King Hassan is only 64 and in good health, but the power of the monarchy is such that his succession is a major concern for the wealthy business and political elite. Crown Prince Sidi Mohammad will be the next head of state, but is a less dominating figure than his father and may wield less power. Most Moroccans accept that, for the next few years, the country needs a strong, unifying force and, as a result, King Hassan is not challenged.

Islamic militancy

Mindful of the civil turmoil afflicting neighboring Algeria, the government has cracked down on Islamic militants, banning all 13 known groups. However, support for Islamic fundamentalism is increasing, especially among university students, who fear Morocco is losing its identity as an Arab, Islamic country and becoming too influenced by Europe.

PROFILE

During his long reign, King Hassan has excelled at a policy of divide and rule where political parties are concerned. Although he now allows the majority party in the elected national assembly to choose most cabinet posts, he reserves the right to terminate parliament, and to appoint or dismiss the prime minister. After the 1993 elections, the center-right emerged as the largest party. It turned down Hassan's invitation to form a government, whereupon the king himself appointed a non-party government of technocrats and politicians of liberal tendencies.

***King Hassan II**, who acceded to the throne upon the death of his father in 1961.*

***Mohammed Karim Lamrani**, prime minister for the fifth time in 1993.*

WORLD AFFAIRS

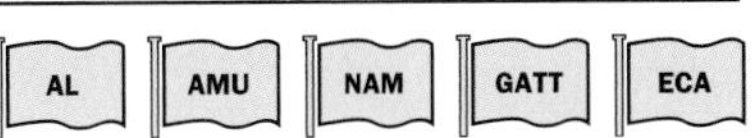

Morocco's important role in the quest for lasting peace in the Middle East was underlined by Israeli Prime Minister Yitzhak Rabin's visit to the capital Rabat following the signing of the 1993 peace accord with the Palestine Liberation Organization in Washington. King Hassan has a reputation as something of a maverick in Arab politics – he has negotiated with Israel but also heads the Jerusalem Committee of the Islamic Conference Organization – and his governments have adopted a pro-Western profile in international affairs. Morocco has also earned respect by protecting its own Jewish minority.

Despite international opposition, Morocco has occupied the former Spanish colony of Western Sahara since 1975, when King Hassan encouraged mass settlement by ordering the Green March of 350,000 people. Resistance by Polisario Front guerrillas, fighting for an independent Western Sahara, commenced in 1983 and continues, despite a UN-brokered peace plan. This rapidly foundered amid bitter disputes between the Moroccan government and the Polisario Front over voting rights to decide Western Sahara's political future.

In order to consolidate its claim on this phosphate-rich territory, Morocco has invested considerable sums to improve the Western Saharan infrastructure, employing troops to build roads and an airport in the capital, Laâyoune. An extensive program of school and hospital building has also been undertaken.

AID

$1.1bn (receipts)

Up 5% in 1991

Saudi Arabia wrote off $2.7 billion of Moroccan debt after the Gulf War. The World Bank has given help to Morocco, but the country receives little aid.

M

CHRONOLOGY

Independence from France in 1956 was only the first step in ending colonial rule for the oldest kingdom in the Arab world, even though the present Alaoui dynasty has been in power for three centuries.

- ❑ **1956** France recognizes Moroccan independence under Sultan Mohammed Ibn Yousif. Morocco joins UN. Spain renounces control over its territories, except the enclaves of Ceuta, Melilla and Ifni and territories in the south.
- ❑ **1957** Sultan Mohammed king.
- ❑ **1961** Crown Prince Hassan becomes king upon father's death.
- ❑ **1967** Morocco backs Arab cause in Six-Day War with Israel.
- ❑ **1969** Spain returns the enclave of Ifni to Morocco.
- ❑ **1971** Right-wing army officers stage abortive coup.
- ❑ **1972** King Hassan survives assassination attempt planned by defense minister and army chief.
- ❑ **1975** International Court of Justice grants self-determination to Western Saharan people. King Hassan orders Green March of 350,000 people. Moroccan forces seize Saharan capital.
- ❑ **1976** Morocco and Mauritania partition Western Sahara.
- ❑ **1979** Mauritania renounces claim to part of Western Sahara, which is added to Morocco's territory.
- ❑ **1984** King Hassan and Colonel Gaddafi of Libya sign Oujda Treaty as first step toward a Maghreb union. Morocco withdraws from OAU after criticism of its role in Western Sahara.
- ❑ **1985** Twenty-six members of left-wing Islamic Youth charged with treason. 14 sentenced to death.
- ❑ **1986** Morocco repeals Oujda Treaty with Libya.
- ❑ **1987** Completion of defensive wall around Western Sahara.
- ❑ **1988** Morocco joins UN Human Rights Commission.
- ❑ **1989** Border treaty with Algeria ratified. Arab Maghreb Union (AMU) creates no-tariff zone between Morocco, Algeria, Tunisia, Libya and Mauritania. Hassan first AMU president.
- ❑ **1990** Morocco condemns Iraq's invasion of Kuwait.
- ❑ **1991** Morocco accepts UN plan for referendum in Western Sahara.
- ❑ **1992** New constitution allows members of the majority party in parliament to choose the cabinet.
- ❑ **1993** First general election for nine years. After major parties refuse his invitation, king appoints non-party government.

M

DEFENSE

$1.1bn

Up 15% in 1992

Defense spending as % GDP (scale 0–40): 3.7%

MOROCCAN ARMED FORCES

284 main battle tanks (224 M-48A5/ 60 M-60A1)	175,000 personnel
1 frigate, 4 surface vessels and 23 patrol boats	7,000 personnel
90 combat aircraft (15 F-5E/14 *Mirage* F-1EH/15 *Mirage* F-1CH)	13,500 personnel
None	

Morocco's long struggle in the Western Sahara against Polisario Front guerrillas has given the kingdom's forces a strong reputation. Moroccans have also fought as mercenaries in the Gulf. In the 1980s, Moroccan sappers constructed a 1,550-mile defensive wall to cordon off Western Sahara in an attempt to prevent incursions from Polisario guerrillas based in Algeria.

Morocco's pro-Western stance has allowed its forces access to sophisticated weapons and training from the West, particularly the USA – unlike neighboring North African states, which are dependent on the former Soviet bloc.

The air force was formed in 1956 and flies US and European aircraft, notably *Mirage* interceptors. The navy uses Western-supplied ships, but is insignificant in regional terms.

Some 6% of national income is spent on defense – a relatively, but not prohibitively, high figure for a developing country. Military service is compulsory for 18 months.

ECONOMICS

$27.5bn

9.45 Moroccan dirhams

SCORE CARD

- ❑ World GNP Ranking 58th
- ❑ GNP per Capita $1,047
- ❑ Balance of Payments .... $-427m
- ❑ Inflation 5.7%
- ❑ Unemployment .... 19% (est)

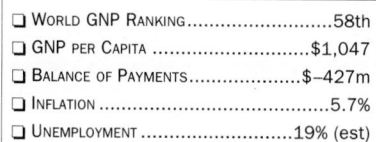

EXPORTS

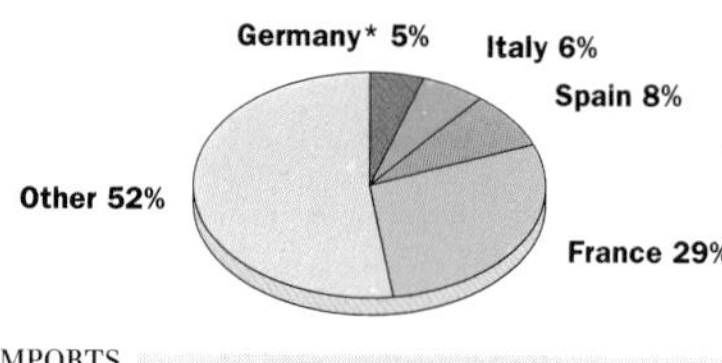

IMPORTS

Iraq 7%
USA 7%
Spain 9%
Other 53%
France 24%

Strengths

Pro-business policies and abundant labor attract foreign investment. Low inflation. Tourist industry, phosphates and agriculture all have great potential.

Weaknesses

High unemployment and population growth. Dirham not fully convertible. Droughts have hit agriculture. Cannabis production (30% of Europe's supply) complicates closer EU links.

Profile

The government has embarked on a privatization program designed to attract investment – particularly from Europe. It raised $250 million (including $100 million from Spain) in 1993 and there are plans to sell companies worth a further $2 billion by 1995. These measures have been resisted by trade unions, which have organized strikes over rising prices and deteriorating working conditions.

ECONOMIC PERFORMANCE INDICATOR

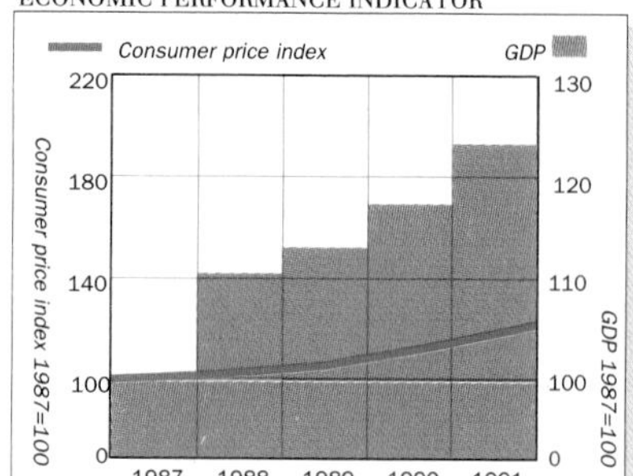

MOROCCO : MAJOR BUSINESSES

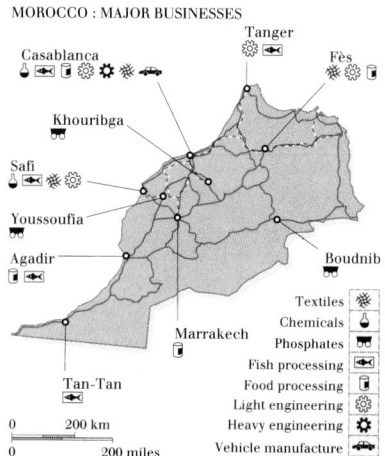

Tanger
Casablanca
Fès
Khouribga
Safi
Youssoufia
Agadir
Boudnib
Marrakech
Tan-Tan
Textiles
Chemicals
Phosphates
Fish processing
Food processing
Light engineering
Heavy engineering
Vehicle manufacture
0 200 km
0 200 miles

RESOURCES

9.6bn kwh (capacity 2.36m kw)

Not an oil producer; refines 154,600 b/cd

17.5m sheep, 3.3m cattle, 918,000 asses

Phosphates, coal, iron, barite, lead, copper, zinc

ELECTRICITY GENERATION

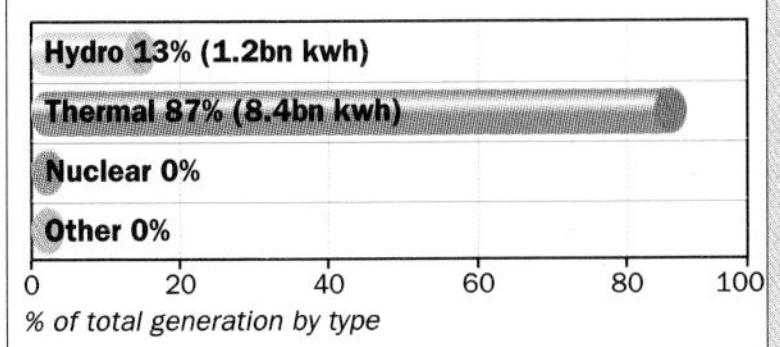

Morocco possesses 75% of the world's phosphate reserves. Other minerals include anthracite and iron ore.

Forestry is carried out in the mountains. Crops include grains, fruit, peppers, tomatoes and cut flowers.

MOROCCO : LAND USE

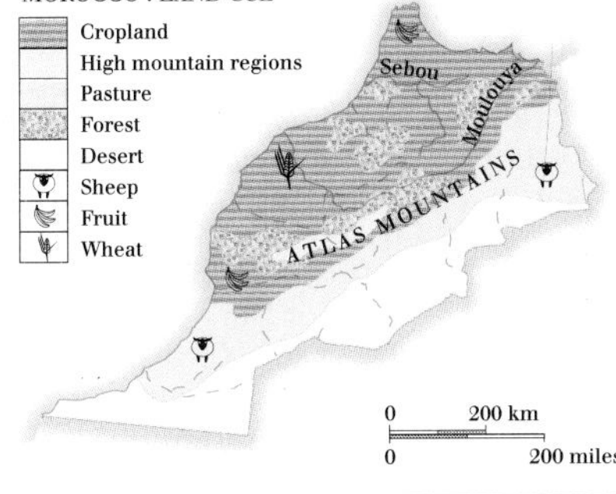

ENVIRONMENT

0.8% (0.7% partially protected)

Ecological issues are not a high priority

ENVIRONMENTAL TREATIES

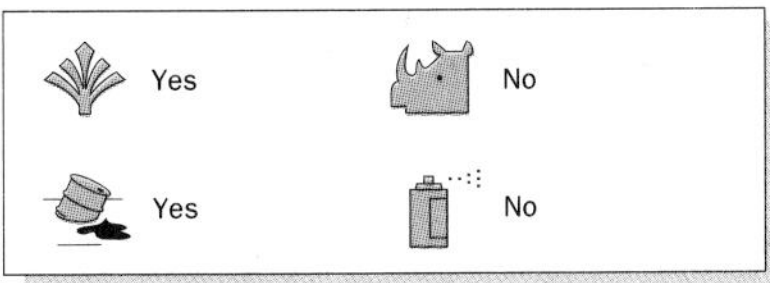

Morocco's wealth of plant and animal life has suffered severely from long periods of drought, most recently in the early 1980s and early 1990s. The unplanned development of tourist resorts is posing a threat to fragile coastal ecosystems.

CRIME

CRIME RATES

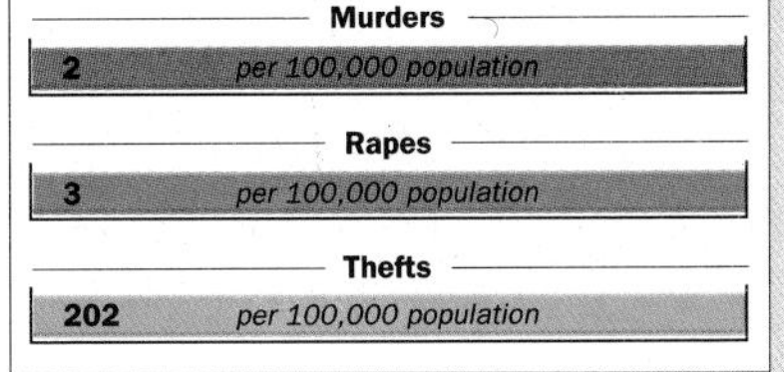

Murders
2 per 100,000 population
Rapes
3 per 100,000 population
Thefts
202 per 100,000 population

Urban crime is increasing, but muggings are rare. Apart from a 1990 strike that led to 40 deaths in Fès, Morocco has seen little civil unrest. Police watch Islamic militant activists.

MEDIA

Criticism of the king is not allowed

PUBLISHING AND BROADCAST MEDIA

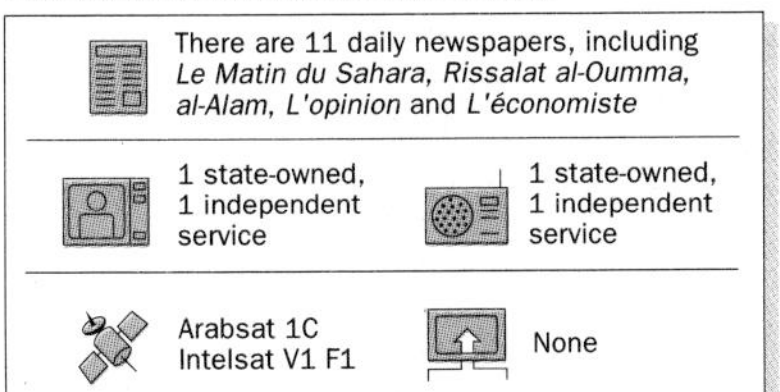

There are 11 daily newspapers, including *Le Matin du Sahara*, *Rissalat al-Oumma*, *al-Alam*, *L'opinion* and *L'économiste*
1 state-owned, 1 independent service
1 state-owned, 1 independent service
Arabsat 1C
Intelsat V1 F1
None

The media is careful to avoid criticism of King Hassan, and the reporting of current affairs tends to be cautious. The sports pages, especially the football reports, are the most dynamic sections of the newspapers – and may also contain implicit criticisms of the establishment. Newspapers are published in Arabic and French. *L'economiste* supplies the most authoritative economic information. State-owned TV began transmissions in Arabic and French in 1962. Radio broadcasts are in Arabic, Berber, French, Spanish and English from Rabat and Tangier.

EDUCATION

50%

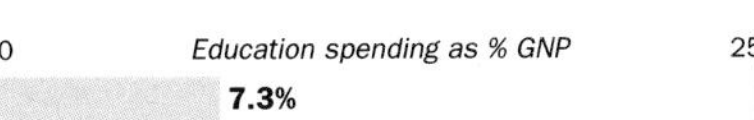

THE EDUCATION SYSTEM

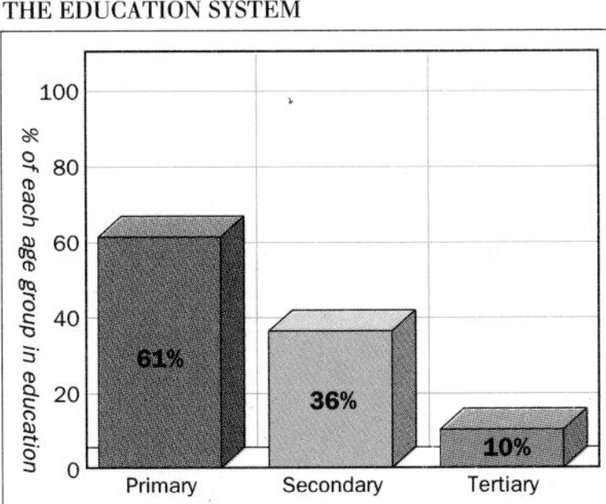

Only 25% of Morocco's rural population is literate, as opposed to 60% in the cities. The literacy level and primary school enrollment rates are well below average for countries with similar living standards. There are six universities with a combined total of 100,000 students.

HEALTH

0 *Health spending as % GNP* 25

1%

Despite recent progress, child mortality and nutritional standards for the poorest Moroccans remain well below average for countries with a similar standard of living. There is one doctor for every 4,763 Moroccans and one hospital bed for every 1,000 people. Outside the cities, primary health care is virtually non-existent; as a result people depend on traditional remedies for illnesses.

WEALTH

Factory foreman, 4,950 Moroccan dirhams per month; executive engineer, 10,981 Moroccan dirhams per month

CONSUMER GOODS OWNERSHIP

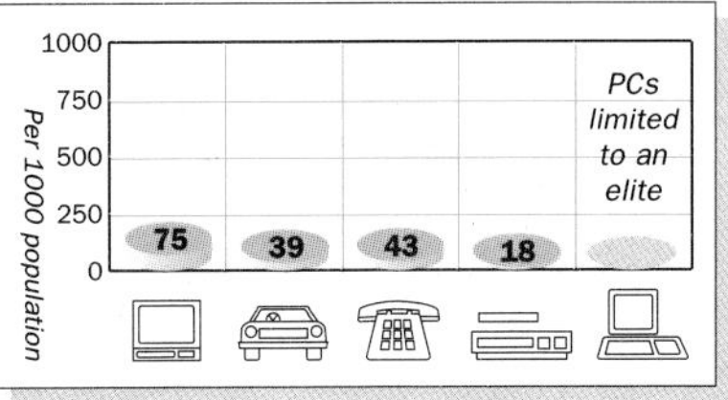

Income per head is considerably lower than in neighboring Algeria and Tunisia. One in seven Moroccans live below the poverty line – an improvement on the 1985 figure, which was one in five. About 45% of the population live in rural areas and the rural-urban gap in wealth is considerable. Drought in the 1990s accelerated the urban drift.

Unrest has largely been avoided due to Morocco's thriving informal sector. Apart from the illegal hashish trade and the smuggling of alcohol and Western goods, this provides jobs in clothing manufacturing, food processing, goods transport, and the hotel and construction industries.

WORLD RANKING

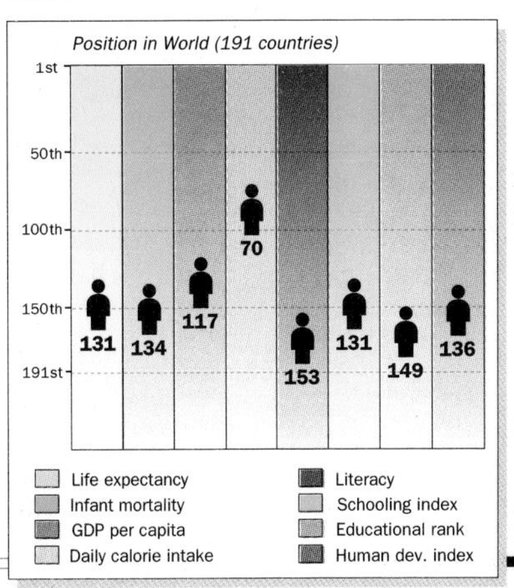

M

MOZAMBIQUE

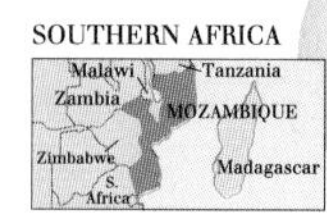

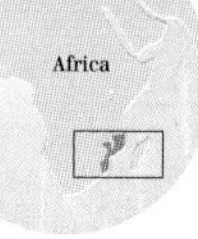

OFFICIAL NAME: Republic of Mozambique **CAPITAL:** Maputo
POPULATION: 16.1 million **CURRENCY:** Metical **OFFICIAL LANGUAGE:** Portuguese

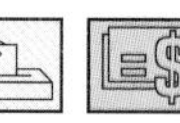

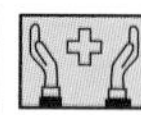

SITUATED ON THE SOUTHEAST African coast, Mozambique is bisected from east to west by the Zambezi River, which is dammed at Cahora Bassa. South of the Zambezi lies a semi-arid savanna lowland. The north-central delta provinces around Tete are the most fertile and it is here that the bulk of Mozambique's racially mixed population lives. Since its independence in 1975 from Portugal, and the accession of the Marxist FRELIMO government, Mozambique has been in a state of civil war. It has depended on international food aid for ten years, and on several occasions the disruption of food supplies has led to mass starvation. The UN brokered a tenuous peace agreement in 1992.

CLIMATE

WEATHER CHART

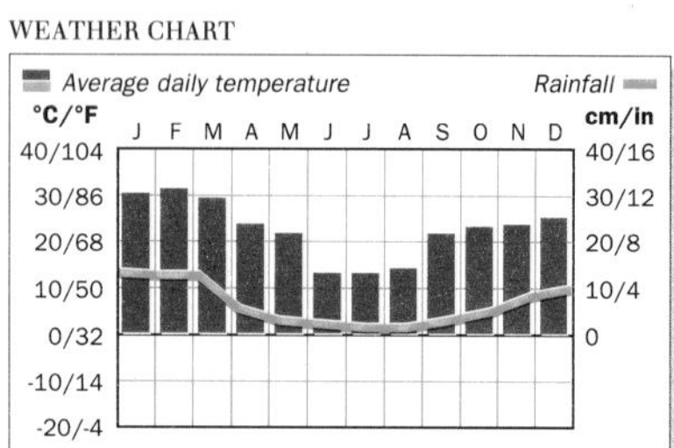

In theory, Mozambique has a rainy and a dry season. However, in the 1980s, frequent failure of the rains contributed to two disastrous famines: in 1982–1984 (when 100,000 died) and in 1986–1987. The coast south of Beira and the highlands adjoining Malawi and Zimbabwe are the wettest areas. The northern coast is dry because the moist trade winds are blocked by Madagascar. The Zambezi valley is the driest region.

COMMUNICATIONS

Maputo Intl
409,000 passengers

15 ships
24,100 dwt

THE TRANSPORTATION NETWORK

16,179 miles (26,095 km)

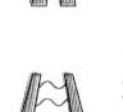

None

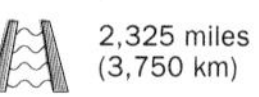

1,941 miles (3,131 km)

2,325 miles (3,750 km)

One of the biggest problems facing Mozambique is the estimated two million mines left over from the civil war, which prevent free access to many parts of the country. The hundreds of bridges destroyed in the war are slowly being rebuilt. Major improvements to road and rail links can be undertaken now the political situation is more stable. Most of Mozambique's intercontinental trade continues to pass through South African ports.

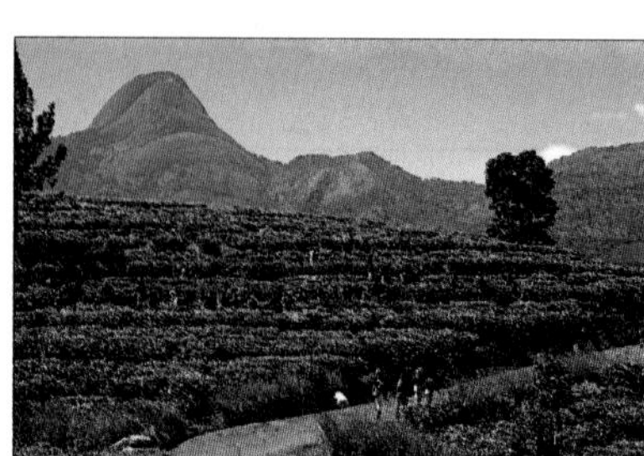

Tea picking. *Other important cash crops are cashew nuts, cotton, sugar, copra and citrus fruits. Agriculture employs 85% of workers.*

TOURISM

Tourism has still not recovered after war

No change due to effects of war

MAIN OVERSEAS ARRIVALS

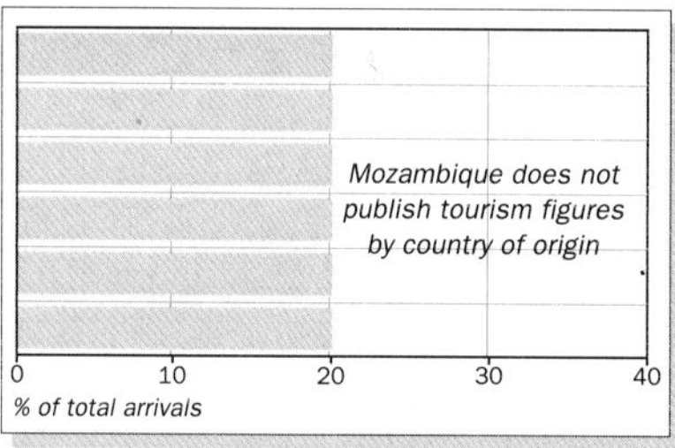

The tourist industry, which regularly used to attract around 300,000 South Africans and Rhodesians in the 1970s, has been destroyed by the war between the FRELIMO government and the Mozambique National Resistance (RENAMO) rebels. Travel outside the capital remains hazardous, and the city itself is subject to frequent power cuts and water shortages as a result of rebel activity. Tourist visas are also hard to obtain, as the government regards any outsiders with suspicion.

If political stability can be maintained, however, Mozambique will be free to exploit its excellent beaches and game reserves, which include the Gorongosa Game Park.

PEOPLE

Makua, Tsonga, Sena, Lomwe, Portuguese

52 people per sq. mile

THE URBAN/RURAL POPULATION SPLIT

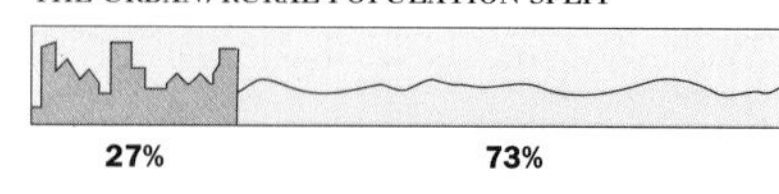

RELIGIOUS PERSUASION

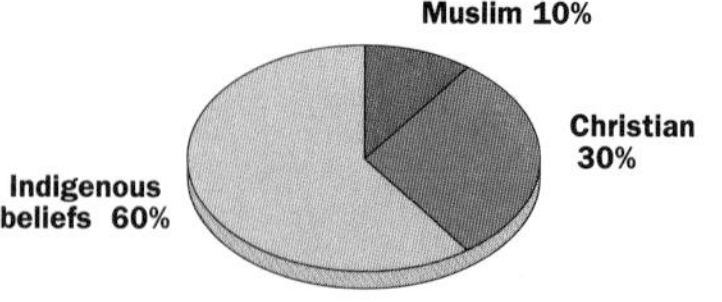

ETHNIC MAKEUP

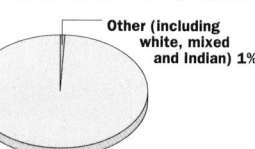

Mozambique is racially very mixed. The tensions that exist in society, however, are not between the different groups but between northerners and southerners. The government has consistently been accused of favoring the south over the north and of including more southerners in its ministries; the greater economic success of the south adds to this tension. Anti-white feelings are growing as certain "Africanist" groups are using the claim of excessive white influence in government as a means of gaining popular support.

Mozambican life is based around the extended family. In some provinces, notably Zambezia, Cabo Delgado and Tete, this is matriarchal. Polygamy is fairly widespread among those wealthy enough to take second wives. Under FRELIMO, women's rights have received particular attention. Women, who played an active part in FRELIMO armies, are now better protected by divorce, child-custody and husband-desertion laws. The Mozambican Women's Organization encourages participation in political life.

POPULATION AGE BREAKDOWN

% of population by age group	1960	1970	1980	1990	2000
65+	2.9%	3%	3.1%	3.3%	3.2%
15–64	55.7%	53.9%	53.5%	52.3%	52.2%
0–14	41.4%	43.1%	43.4%	44.4%	44.6%

M

POLITICS

1998 President Joaquim Alberto Chissano

THE STATE OF THE PARTIES

Assembly of the Republic 250 members

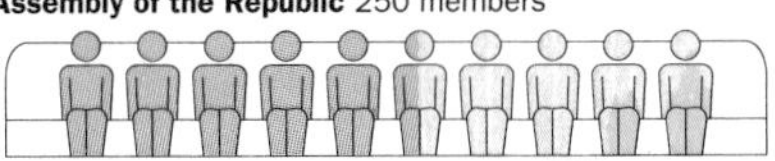

55% Frelimo **45% Renamo**

FRELIMO = Mozambican Liberation Front
RENAMO = Mozambican National Resistance Party

MAIN POLITICAL ISSUES

The move to democracy
In 1993 the UN secured, with difficulty, the $260 million and the 7,500 multinational forces required both to demobilize Mozambique's warring factions and to stage the first democratic elections.

In October 1994 elections were held, despite a last-minute threat of withdrawal by the Mozambican National Resistance party (RENAMO), and returned the Mozambican Liberation Front (FRELIMO) to power. However, support for RENAMO proved to be much stronger than anticipated. The former guerrillas won 112 of the 250 seats in the new parliament and their leader, Afonso Dhlakama polled 33% of the votes cast in the presidential election.

Reconstruction
The government now faces an enormous task in rebuilding a country ravaged by civil war, with its toll of 900,000 dead, one million refugees and an estimated 90% of the remaining population living below the poverty line.

Joaquim Chissano, president since 1986, has pushed toward political pluralism.

RENAMO leader, Afonso Dhlakama, now turning from militarism to politics.

PROFILE
Between 1977 and 1990, Mozambique was a one-party state ruled by the Soviet-backed FRELIMO, which had campaigned for independence from Portugal in the 1960s. The RENAMO rebel group, backed by Rhodesia and white South Africa, conducted a civil war to limit Soviet influence, under the guise of seeking democracy.

The changing international scene led to FRELIMO adopting a democratic constitution in 1990 and to RENAMO losing its international sponsors. The key issue now is ensuring the survival of the fragile new democracy. Although FRELIMO is the biggest party in the new parliament RENAMO is clearly a popular force and will wish to receive some benefits from 15 years of struggle. New groups, such as the anti-white PALMO, COINMO and UNAMO, are also starting to emerge.

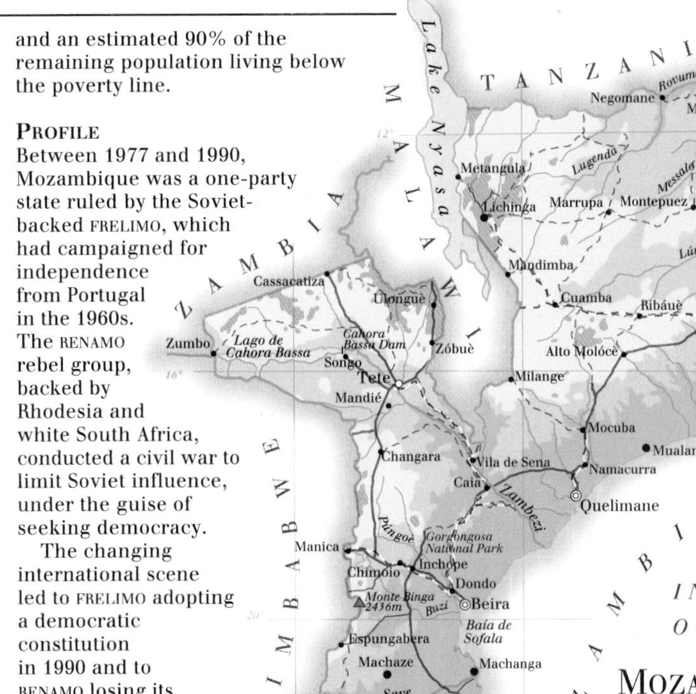

M

WORLD AFFAIRS

SADC

FLS AFDB

During the Cold War years, Mozambique was a key battleground in the conflict between Soviet-backed Marxism, and capitalism sponsored by the USA and South Africa. The result was a civil war, which devastated the country between 1977 and 1992.

A shift in the FRELIMO government's position had, however, already become apparent in the early 1980s, as Soviet aid levels became erratic. President Samora Machel then took steps toward a reconciliation with the West, which led to the USA lifting its ban on economic assistance in 1984 and Britain agreeing to provide military training for FRELIMO's forces in 1987. A peace accord was signed with South Africa in 1984. Mozambique fulfilled its obligations by expelling the ANC, but South Africa did not and continued support for RENAMO until 1990.

The UN, having brokered the peace agreement and financed the country's transition to democracy, withdrew its 6,000 peacekeepers from Mozambique in January 1995. The search for the many hidden arms caches remains incomplete.

CHRONOLOGY

The Portuguese tapped the local trade in slaves, gold and ivory in the 16th century and made Mozambique a colony in 1752. Large areas were run by private companies until 1929.

- **1962** FRELIMO founded.
- **1964** Starts war of liberation.
- **1975** Independence. Marxist FRELIMO leader Samora Machel is president. 230,000 of the 250,000 Portuguese leave, but destroy much transport and machinery.
- **1976** Resistance movement RENAMO set up in Mozambique by Rhodesians.
- **1976–1980** Mozambique closes Rhodesian border, imposes economic sanctions, and supports Zimbabwean freedom fighters. Destructive reprisals by RENAMO.

CHRONOLOGY *continued*

- **1980** South Africa takes over backing of RENAMO.
- **1982** Zimbabwean troops arrive to guard Mutare–Beira oil pipeline and road–rail route.
- **1984** Nkomati Accord: South Africa agrees to stop support for RENAMO, and Mozambique for ANC. Ineffectual. Fighting continues.
- **1986** RENAMO declares war on Zimbabwe. Tanzania sends troops and military aid to FRELIMO. President Machel dies in mystery air crash in South Africa. Joaquim Chissano replaces him.
- **1988** Nkomati Accord reactivated. Mozambicans allowed back to work in South African mines.
- **1989** Civil war estimated to have killed 600,000 and caused 405,000 children to die of malnutrition. FRELIMO drops Marxism-Leninism.
- **1990** Multiparty politics and free market economy written into new constitution. RENAMO fails to recognize it or keep ceasefire.
- **1992** Chissano and RENAMO's leader, Afonso Dhlakama, meet for first time for peace talks. Peace agreement signed in October.
- **1994** UN-led democratic elections return frelimo to power.

M

AID

$920m (receipts)

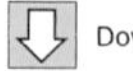
Down 2% in 1991

The economic situation left by the war has led Mozambique to launch a global campaign for assistance. Seven million Mozambicans are entirely dependent on food aid, and even the most basic economic activity relies on some form of aid. The main donor nations are Italy, the UK, the USA, Sweden, the Netherlands, Norway and, recently, South Africa – whose outlook has influenced Mozambique's turn toward a market economy. Debts from aid provided by the USSR in the late 1970s and early 1980s have been written off.

DEFENSE

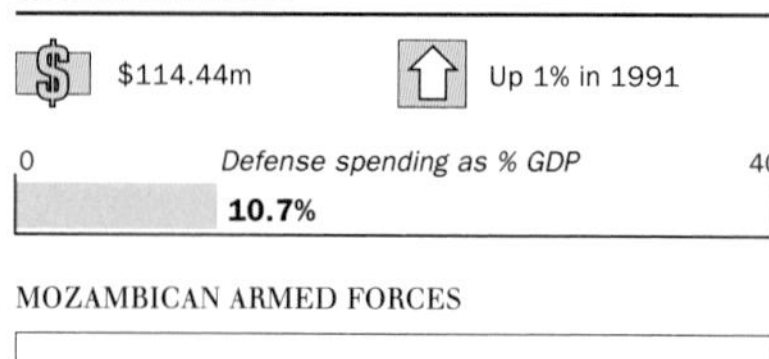

MOZAMBICAN ARMED FORCES

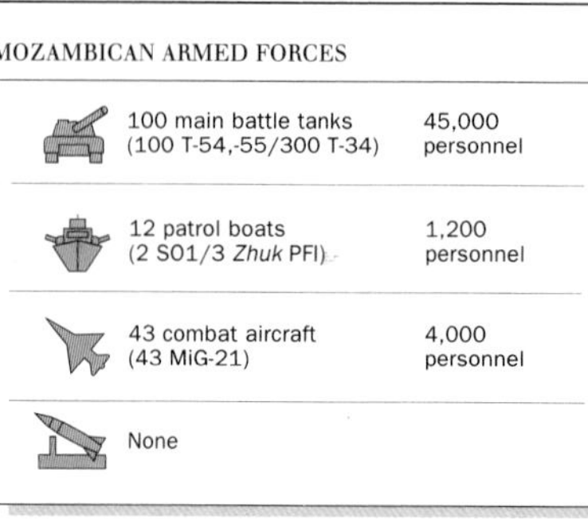

100 main battle tanks (100 T-54,-55/300 T-34)	45,000 personnel
12 patrol boats (2 S01/3 *Zhuk* PFI)	1,200 personnel
43 combat aircraft (43 MiG-21)	4,000 personnel
None	

Not surprisingly, given the civil war between 1977 and 1992, the armed forces have had a dominant role in Mozambique's affairs, swallowing on average 40% of state income. Military figures have also been prominent in the FRELIMO government, holding the Foreign Affairs, Home Affairs and Transportation posts. Since 1982, Zimbabwe has also deployed forces to secure the Beira railroad and transportation route against RENAMO attack.

The key issue now is the re-integration into civilian life and re-training of around 75,000 soldiers, whose demobilization pay will end in mid-1996. Under the UN plan, RENAMO and FRELIMO forces would form a new national army of 30,000. However, its success remains in doubt given the historical animosity between the two sides. Also, there are fears that many RENAMO units have enjoyed too much autonomy to accept any central control.

ECONOMICS

$844m

5,279.01 meticais

SCORE CARD

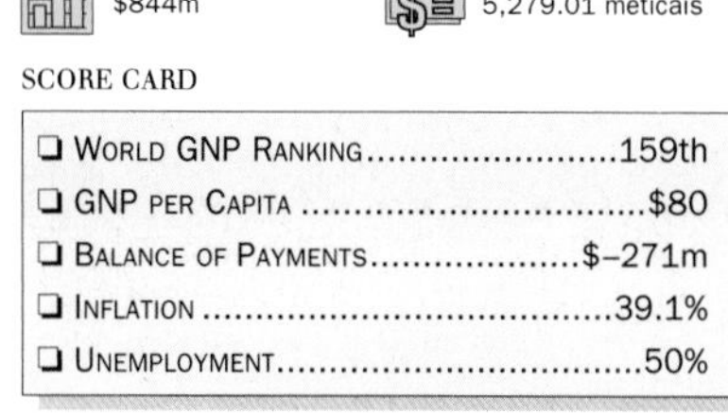

- World GNP Ranking....159th
- GNP per Capita....$80
- Balance of Payments....$-271m
- Inflation....39.1%
- Unemployment....50%

EXPORTS

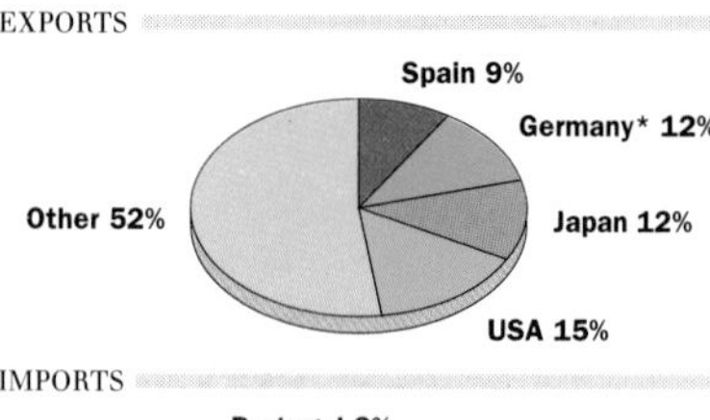

IMPORTS

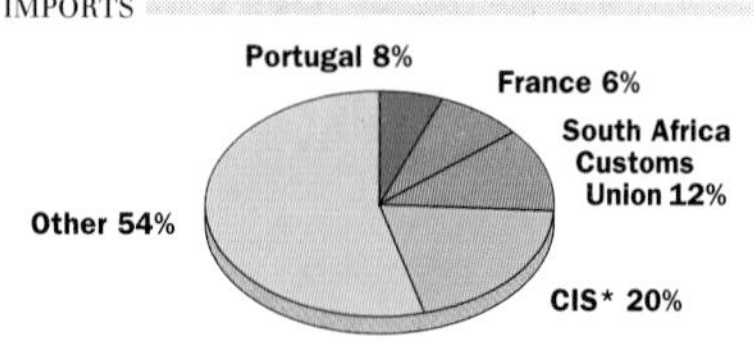

Strengths

Given the current war-ravaged conditions, Mozambique's economy has no strengths to speak of and is almost entirely dependent on foreign aid. Assuming peace prevails, Mozambique could develop the agricultural sector, which employs 85% of the workforce. The fisheries industry has great potential. Mozambique also has Africa's second largest harbor, Maputo. Modernized in 1989, it is well placed to service southern Africa's landlocked regions.

ECONOMIC PERFORMANCE INDICATOR

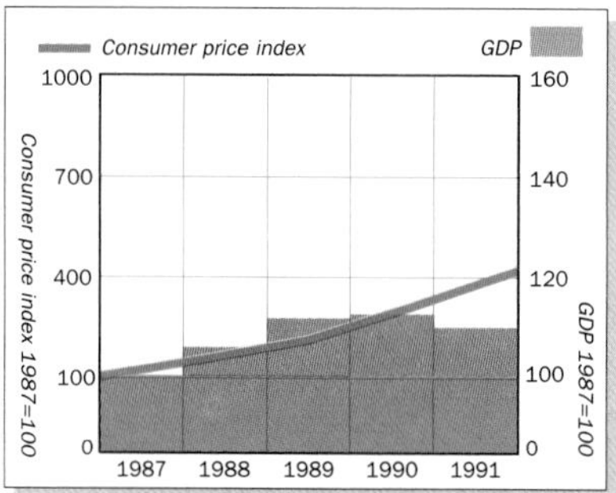

Weaknesses

Mozambique is susceptible to drought and cyclones. A war-shattered infrastructure has left the economy in a condition where overseas aid is essential to prevent at least half the population from starving. Destroyed transportation links make it impossible to exploit resources such as iron ore and bauxite. Skilled workers have sought employment in other countries; their absence will delay the return to normal economic activity. 70% of the work force remains illiterate.

Profile

Mozambique's enormous problems are further exacerbated by the failure of the socialist model in industry and agriculture and, as with many Eastern European economies, the need to learn from scratch the rules of private enterprise and the free market. Even if peaceful conditions can be assured, economic growth will be extremely slow.

MOZAMBIQUE : MAJOR BUSINESSES

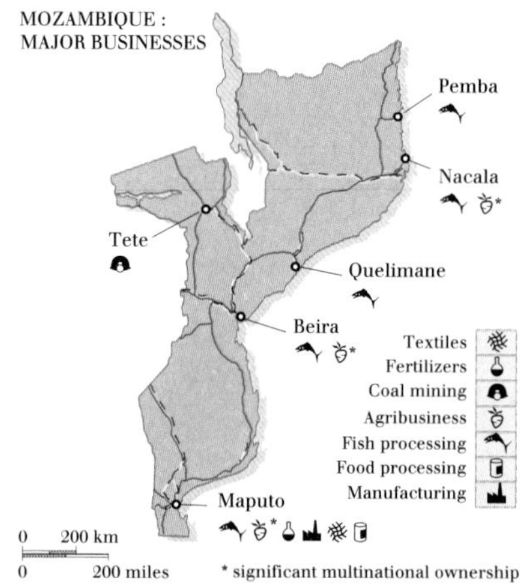

RESOURCES

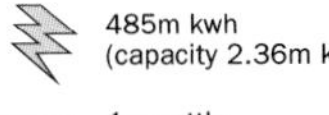

485m kwh (capacity 2.36m kw)

Not an oil producer and has no refineries

1m cattle, 165,000 pigs, 120,000 sheep

Coal, iron, tantalite, bauxite, titanium, fluorspar, zirconium

ELECTRICITY GENERATION

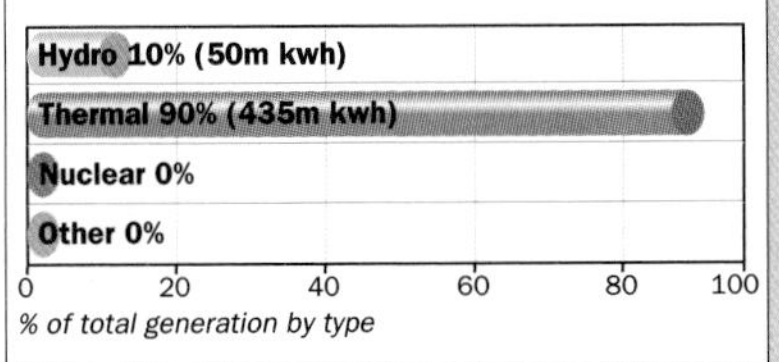

Mozambique's mineral reserves are modest and, due to the lack of useful transport links, currently unexploited.

Fishing is the most important sector (shrimp accounted for 46% of all export revenue in 1988). The government is concentrating on restoring electricity supplies.

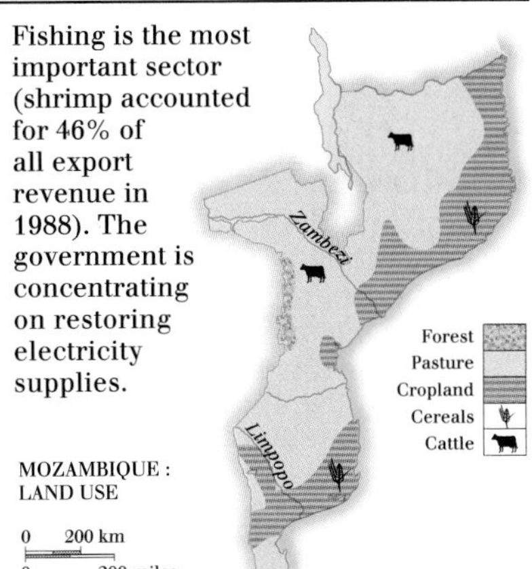

HEALTH

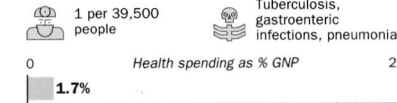

1 per 39,500 people

Tuberculosis, gastroenteric infections, pneumonia

0 *Health spending as % GNP* 25

1.7%

War casualties and almost anarchic conditions in the countryside are the major problems. 15% of the population cannot afford the drugs prescribed for them and attendance at health clinics has declined. However, preventive medicines and pre-natal care are provided free of charge. Doctors have to serve a mandatory two-year period in rural areas. In 1987, as part of the attempts at reconstruction, private clinics, which were previously banned as unsocialist, began to appear.

ENVIRONMENT

None

Peace may ease environmental pressures

ENVIRONMENTAL TREATIES

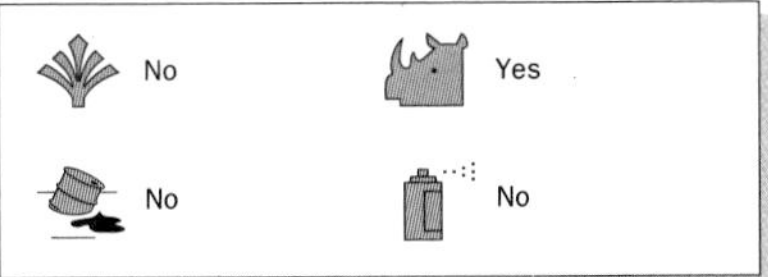

The devastating effects of perennial floods followed by droughts are Mozambique's major concern. A three-year drought between 1982 and 1984 resulted in the deaths of 100,000 and left four million close to starvation. The drought was followed in 1984 by massive flooding, which left 50,000 homeless and destroyed much of the harvest. Other ecological concerns are some way down the political agenda in the aftermath of recent conflict. An estimated 50,000 elephants were slaughtered for ivory in order to help fund RENAMO's war effort.

MEDIA

The press is now theoretically free

PUBLISHING AND BROADCAST MEDIA

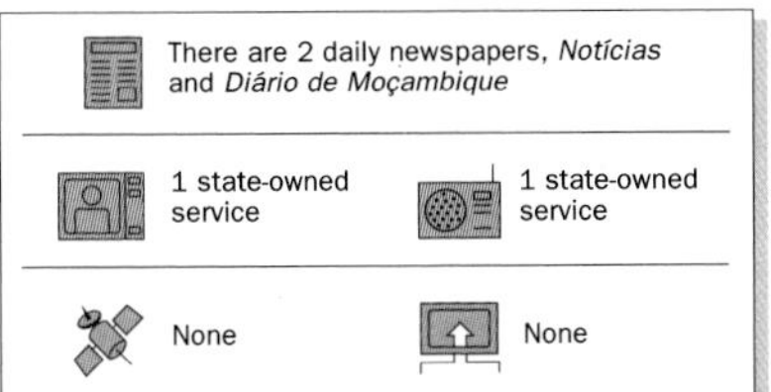

There are 2 daily newspapers, *Notícias* and *Diário de Moçambique*
1 state-owned service
1 state-owned service
None
None

The press, traditionally a FRELIMO publicity machine, was freed from restrictions by the terms of the 1990 constitution and will become more active during election periods. With only 40,000 TV sets in the whole of Mozambique, the political impact of television is minimal.

CRIME

Mozambique does not publish prison figures

Crime levels are very high and probably rising

CRIME RATES

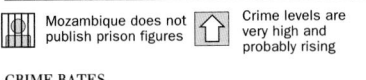

Assessment of criminality impossible due to recent war

Mozambique is awash with weapons. Banditry, frequently carried out by gangs of former soldiers, is endemic. All areas outside the main urban centers are highly dangerous and road travel is particularly unsafe. Fraud and corruption linked to the misuse of food aid are also major problems.

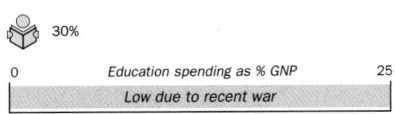

EDUCATION

30%

0 *Education spending as % GNP* 25

Low due to recent war

THE EDUCATION SYSTEM

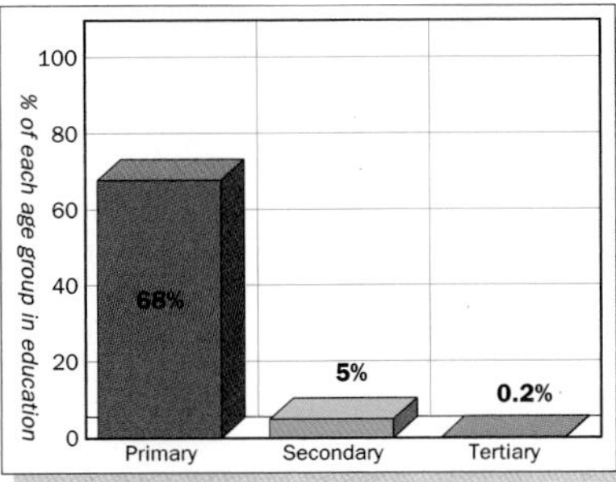

Over 3,000 schools closed between 1983 and 1990 as a direct result of the war. There were no private schools between 1977 and 1990. Students at Maputo University, which attracted many anti-apartheid academic exiles from South Africa, have to work in public service in return for their education.

WEALTH

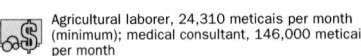

Agricultural laborer, 24,310 meticais per month (minimum); medical consultant, 146,000 meticais per month

CONSUMER GOODS OWNERSHIP

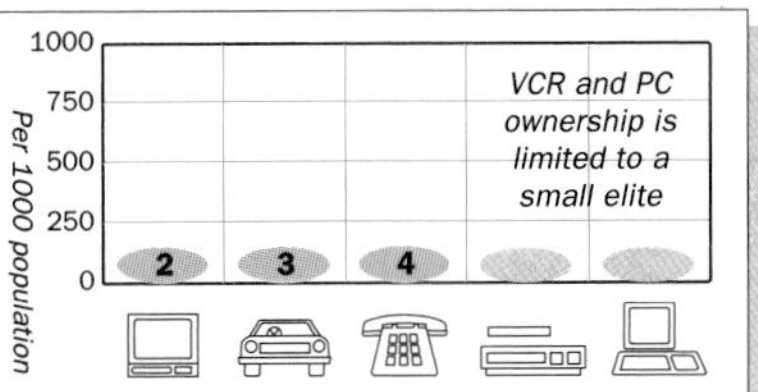

Mozambique is one of the world's poorest countries. In 1991, GNP per capita was estimated at just $80. Society is hardly stratified, as over 90% of the people live in similar impoverished conditions. Measures linked to the provision of Western aid have made conditions tougher, raising the price of rice by 600%. Only the higher echelons of FRELIMO, RENAMO and the other political parties have luxuries such as cars, air-conditioning and brick-built apartments. The slow introduction of free-market reforms will, however, increase access to consumer goods in the longer term.

WORLD RANKING

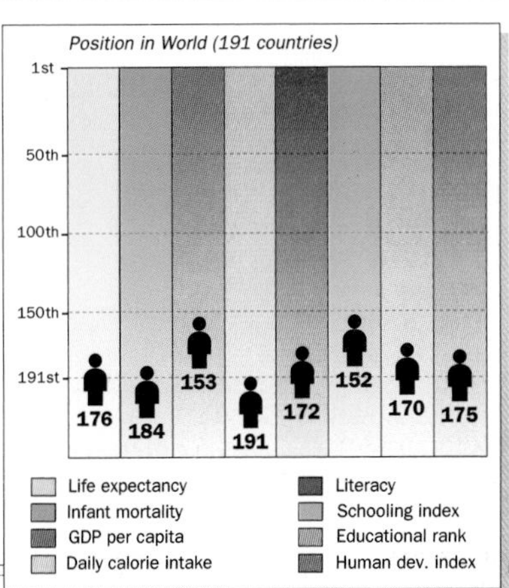

M

NAMIBIA

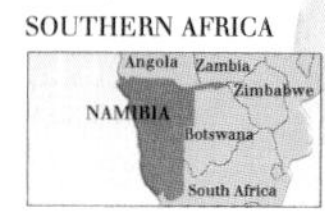

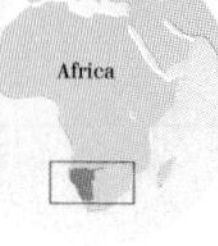

OFFICIAL NAME: The Republic of Namibia **CAPITAL:** Windhoek
POPULATION: 1.5 million **CURRENCY:** South African rand **OFFICIAL LANGUAGE:** English

LOCATED IN SOUTHWESTERN Africa, Namibia has an arid coastal strip formed by the Namib Desert. After many years of guerrilla warfare, Namibia achieved independence from South Africa in 1990. Despite the move away from apartheid, Namibia's economy remains reliant on the expertise of the small white population, a legacy of the previously poor education for blacks. Namibia is Africa's fourth largest minerals producer.

CLIMATE

WEATHER CHART

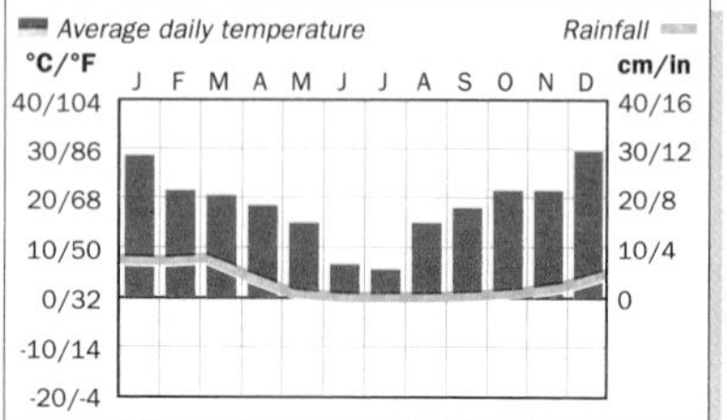

Namibia is almost rainless. The coast is usually shrouded in thick, cold fog unless the hot, very dry *berg* blows.

COMMUNICATIONS

Windhoek Intl 258,373 passengers

Has no fleet

THE TRANSPORTATION NETWORK

26,565 miles (42,760 km)

None

1,480 miles (2,382 km)

None

Large-scale industry is well served by road and rail. Plans exist to build a new harbor in Walvis Bay.

TOURISM

213,000 visitors

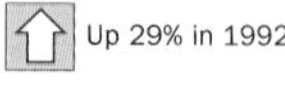

MAIN OVERSEAS ARRIVALS

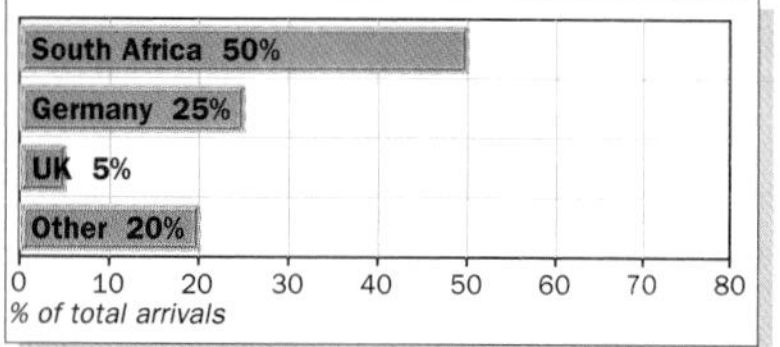

Tourists contributed only 4% to GDP in 1991. A quarter are German, many of whom come to visit Windhoek's German sector. There are plans to limit tourists to 300,000 a year to preserve Namibia's fragile desert ecology.

Spitzkoppe, west of Karibib. *Unique scenery like this is attracting increasing numbers of ecotourists to Namibia.*

PEOPLE

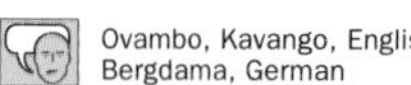

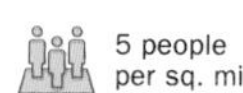

THE URBAN/RURAL POPULATION SPLIT

28% 72%

ETHNIC MAKEUP

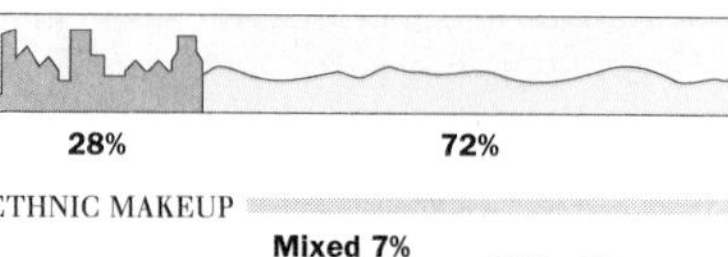

The largest ethnic group, the Ovambo, lives mostly in the north of the country. Whites – 60% of whom are Afrikaans-speakers – live mostly in Windhoek, which includes a large German community, living in comfortable, bourgeois, turn-of-the-century German houses. The strife between rival ethnic groups predicted at the time of independence in 1990 has not materialized, and Namibia has adapted well to a multiracial existence. Blacks, who are mostly subsistence farmers, have largely accepted the greater wealth of the white community.

Families are large in Namibia, and among the black community women have, on average, 6–7 children. The constitution supports sexual equality and positive discrimination in favor of women; few, however, have official jobs or own property.

POLITICS

Lower House 1999
Upper House 2000

THE STATE OF THE PARTIES

National Assembly 72 members

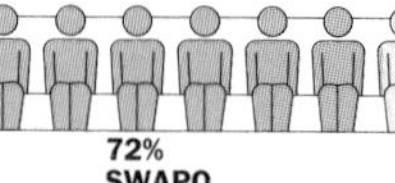

SWAPO = South West Africa People's Organization of Namibia **DTA** = Democratic Turnhalle Alliance **UDF** = United Democratic Front

National Council 26 members

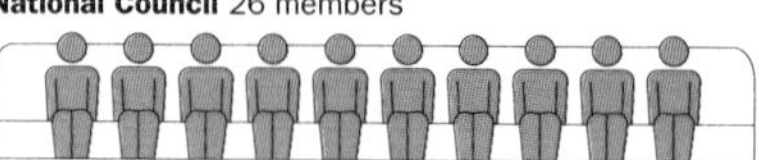

2 members are elected from among the members of each of the 13 regional councils

At independence from South Africa in 1990, Namibia switched from a system of apartheid based on ten separate homelands, to a state-wide, multiparty democracy. Since 1990, SWAPO, whose guerrilla wing fought for and won independence, has had control of the National Assembly. The Ovambo community in the north is SWAPO's main backer, although its center-left stance also gives it the support of large numbers of state employees.

SWAPO has been criticized for not moving swiftly enough to end wealth inequalities. The land reform promised in 1990 has not materialized, and whites remain in control of most areas of the economy, while unemployment among blacks is high. SWAPO's main opposition comes from the center-right DTA, a coalition of 11 parties which favors a free-market approach.

WORLD AFFAIRS

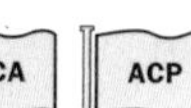

Namibia joined the UN, OAU and Commonwealth within the first few months of independence. In 1992, agreement was reached on the disputed southern border with South Africa. In August 1993 South Africa also agreed to relinquish control of the enclave of Walvis Bay – Namibia's only deep-water port.

AID

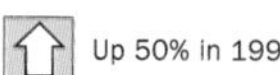

The UN provides most aid. Germany is the main unilateral donor. 31% of aid is spent on education.

NAMIBIA

Total Area : 824 290 sq. km (318 260 sq. miles)

LAND HEIGHT

2000m/6562ft
1000m/3281ft
500m/1640ft
200m/656ft
Sea Level

POPULATION

over 100 000
over 10 000
under 10 000

CHRONOLOGY

In 1915, South Africa took over the former German colony, known as South West Africa, under a League of Nations' mandate.

- ❑ **1950** South Africa refuses to give up the territory to the UN.
- ❑ **1966** Apartheid laws imposed. SWAPO begins armed struggle.
- ❑ **1968** Renamed Namibia.
- ❑ **1973** UN recognizes SWAPO.
- ❑ **1990** Independence.
- ❑ **1993** South Africa relinquishes Walvis Bay.

DEFENSE

$47.44m

Down 44% in 1990

Patrolling fishing stocks, which are frequently raided by Spanish and South African trawlers, is the main activity.

ECONOMICS

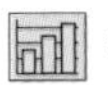
$2.1bn

3.40 South African rand

SCORE CARD

- ❑ WORLD GNP RANKING........................138th
- ❑ GNP PER CAPITA $1,240
- ❑ BALANCE OF PAYMENTS $30m
- ❑ INFLATION 11.9%
- ❑ UNEMPLOYMENT.................................40%

STRENGTHS

Varied mineral resources make Namibia the third wealthiest country in sub-Saharan Africa. Namibian waters encompass one of the world's richest offshore fishing grounds. Potential of Walvis Bay as transit point for Namibia's landlocked neighbors.

WEAKNESSES

Almost all manufactured goods have to be imported. Sensitivity to fluctuations in mineral prices. Lack of skilled labor; only 25% of Namibians participate in commercial economy.

IMPORTS / EXPORTS

Namibia has yet to publish official trade figures. South Africa remains the major source of imports and destination for exports

RESOURCES

New hydroelectric station will ensure self-sufficiency

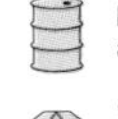
Not an oil producer and has no refineries

7m sheep, 2m cattle, 68,000 asses

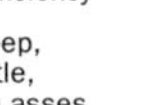
Uranium, lead, cadmium, diamonds, copper, zinc, silver

Namibia has the world's largest uranium mine, is the world's second largest lead producer, and the third largest producer of cadmium. Hydroelectric power has enormous potential; the Okavango River system carries a higher volume of water than all South Africa's rivers combined.

ENVIRONMENT

13% (2% partially protected)

More national parks planned

Illegal poaching and anthrax deposits are threatening the unique Namibian desert-adapted elephant (only 34 remain) and black rhino. Namibia has a unique, but fragile, desert ecosystem, much of which is protected. Government policy is generally sensitive to environmental issues (the annual seal-cull to protect fish stocks is an exception) and wishes to promote ecotourists rather than mass-market developments.

MEDIA

Since 1990, press freedom has been guaranteed under the constitution. Only minor criticism is tolerated in practice

PUBLISHING AND BROADCAST MEDIA

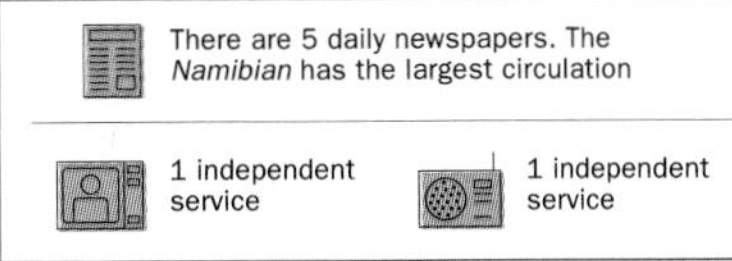
There are 5 daily newspapers. The *Namibian* has the largest circulation

1 independent service

1 independent service

The Namibian Broadcasting Corporation transmits in 11 languages, including German and English.

CRIME

Namibia does not publish prison figures

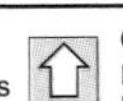
Crime is rising, particularly in urban areas

350 people held by SWAPO before independence are still unaccounted for. Ostrich smuggling to the USA is common.

EDUCATION

72%

High illiteracy rates among black adults, a legacy of apartheid, is the education system's main challenge.

HEALTH

1 per 5,008 people

Respiratory, heart and intestinal diseases

A new health ministry is trying to balance the white-oriented health service. Most areas lack safe water.

WEALTH

Returning political exiles find employment, partly because whites do not like hiring former guerrillas

CONSUMER GOODS OWNERSHIP

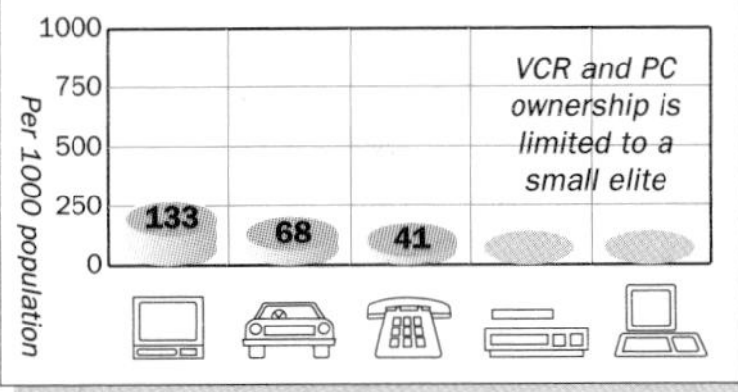

Whites still earn, on the average, 20 times more than blacks. Mercedes are the most desirable status symbol.

WORLD RANKING

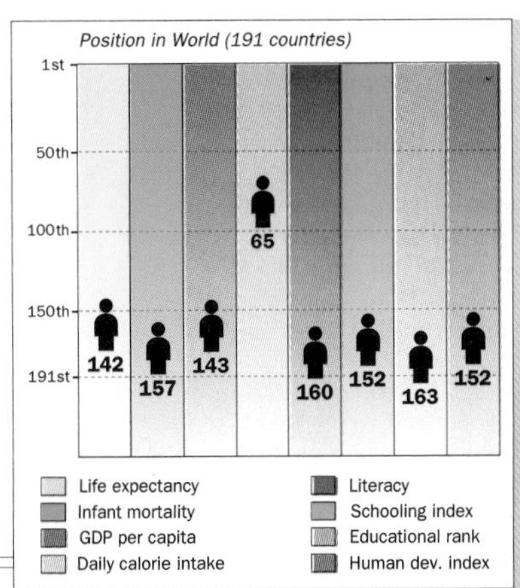

N

NAURU

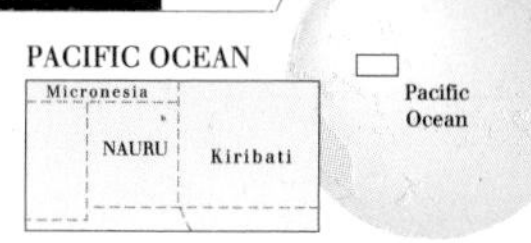

OFFICIAL NAME: The Republic of Nauru **CAPITAL:** *No official capital*
POPULATION: 9,400 **CURRENCY:** Australian dollar **OFFICIAL LANGUAGE:** Nauruan

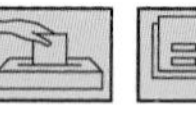

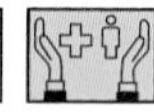

NAURU LIES IN the Pacific Ocean, 2,480 miles northeast of Australia. Formerly a British colony, Nauru was exploited for its phosphate deposits by the UK, Australia and New Zealand. Since independence in 1968, the phosphates industry has made Nauruan citizens among the wealthiest in the world. However, reserves are due to run out in 1995 and in the future, the proceeds of overseas investments will form the bulk of Nauru's income.

CLIMATE

WEATHER CHART

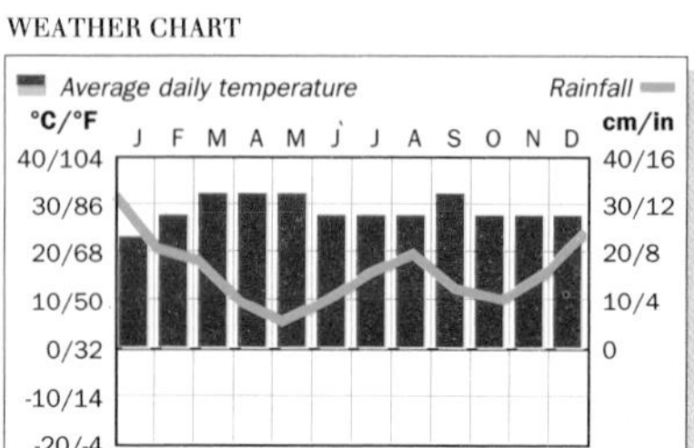

Nauru's tiny size means that rain clouds often miss the island; years may pass without rain.

COMMUNICATIONS

Nauru Island Intl 1 ship 5,800 dwt

THE TRANSPORTATION NETWORK

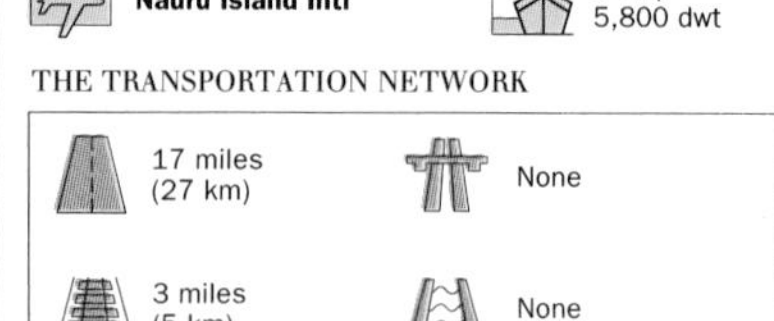

Nauru operates its own airline with Boeing 737s piloted by Australians. The Nauru Steamship Line is Nauru's main link with the outside world. However, all external travel is very expensive. Nauru has no harbor, so ships taking phosphates aboard dock with engines still running on huge concrete caissons floating out at sea. Most Nauruans can afford cars. The single circular road is often littered with abandoned cars, even expensive ones, as it is much cheaper for Nauruans to import new vehicles than attempt to repair existing ones. The number of car accident fatalities is one of the highest in the South Pacific.

TOURISM

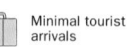

Minimal tourist arrivals

Little variation from year to year

MAIN OVERSEAS ARRIVALS

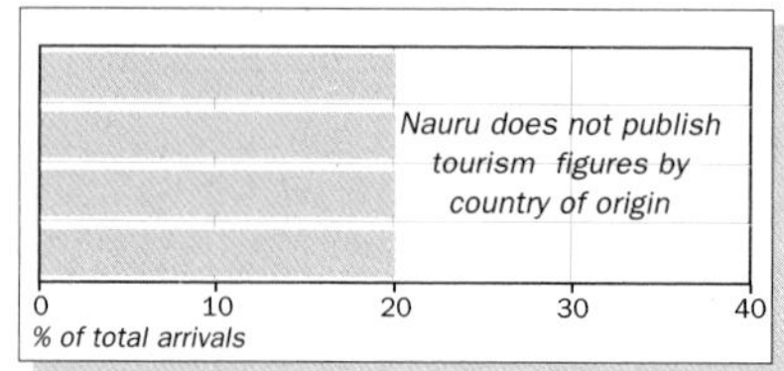

Even if Nauru had any conventional tourist attractions, the enormous cost of getting there would dissuade most tourists from making the journey. The main feature of interest on the island is the bizarre lunar landscape created by over 80 years of phosphate extraction. There are no beaches on Nauru and only a few basic hotels.

NAURU

Total Area : 21.2 sq. km (8.2 sq. miles)

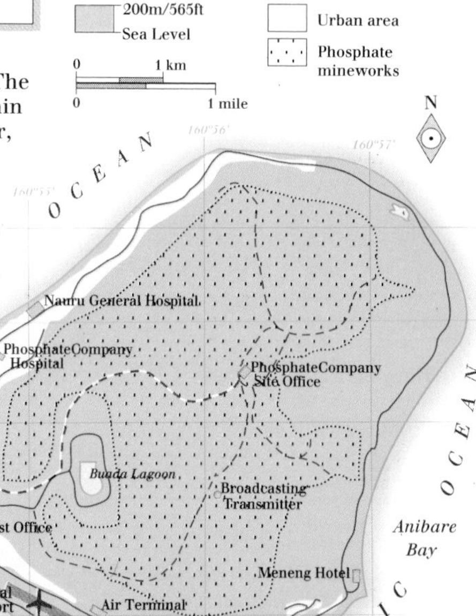

PEOPLE

Nauruan, Kiribati, Chinese, Tuvaluan, English

266 people per sq. mile

THE URBAN/RURAL POPULATION SPLIT

ETHNIC MAKEUP

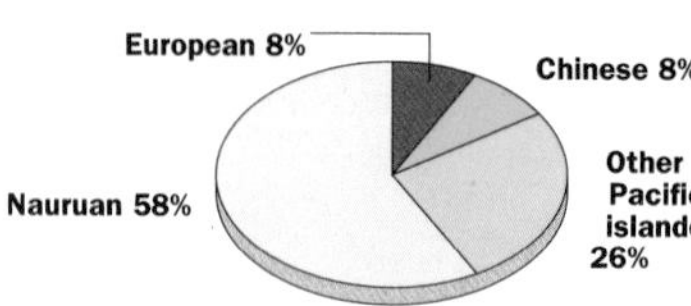

Indigenous Nauruans are a homogenous group. They do little of the tough work on the island, which is left to an imported labor force, mainly from Kiribati, who live in enclaves of male-only barracks and have few rights.

A society of just 9,400, Nauru is mostly self-regulating. There is some generational tension between younger Nauruans, who go to Australia to study, but have little incentive to do well, and their parents, who fought hard for independence. As the phosphate runs out, an increasing feeling of pointlessness is gripping the young. Many see their future in Australia or New Zealand, but are wary of a drop in living standards and of losing the luxury of sovereignty. It was the latter which led Nauruans to reject the offer of resettlement on an island off the Australian Queensland coast.

POLITICS

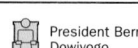

1995

President Bernard Dowiyogo

THE STATE OF THE PARTIES

Parliament 18 members

All members are elected as independents

Hammer DeRoburt, Head Chief of Nauru, became the island's first president in 1968. He dominated the political structure until a vote of no confidence forced him to resign in 1989. He was replaced by Dowiyogo, who secured his continued term in office in the 1992 elections. The traditional chiefs are still the dominant political figures. Nauru's Parliament is based on the British Westminster model. Members often switch between temporary, unstable groupings within it.

N

WORLD AFFAIRS

The case for compensation for phosphate exploitation brought by Nauru against the UK government was rejected in 1992 after the longest suit in British legal history. However, an Australian settlement in 1993 brought an immediate payment and a longer-term contribution totaling 107 million Australian dollars. Nauru's main concern is participation in the South Pacific Forum and the management of trust funds to support Nauruans when phosphate deposits run out.

AID

 Donations through the South Pacific Forum only 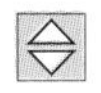 Not applicable

Nauru is neither an aid recipient nor donor, except as a member of the South Pacific Forum.

DEFENSE

 Australia responsible for defense  Not applicable

Nauru, which faces no outside threats, has no defense force. Australia, under a *de facto* arrangement, is responsible for the island's security.

ECONOMICS

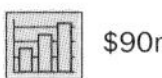 $90m  1.47 Australian dollars

SCORE CARD

- ❑ WORLD GNP RANKING........................187th
- ❑ GNP PER CAPITA..........................$10,000
- ❑ BALANCE OF PAYMENTS.......................$20m
- ❑ INFLATION..........................Low inflation rate
- ❑ UNEMPLOYMENT...........Minimal unemployment

STRENGTHS

Considerable investments in Australian and Hawaiian property and hotels. Possible future as a tax haven.

WEAKNESSES

Phosphate, the only resource, is due to run out in 1995. Phosphate mining has left 80% of the island uninhabitable and uncultivable. Nauru has been prone to poor investments, such as backing the flop London musical *Leonardo* in 1993. Nauru's flagship Melbourne skyscraper, Nauru House, has developed "concrete cancer" which is costing millions of dollars to repair.

IMPORT/EXPORTS

Nauru's only export commodity is phosphates, which it trades with Australia and New Zealand. Almost all food, drinking water and manufactured goods are imported, mostly from Australia, New Zealand, the UK and Japan

RESOURCES

 29m kwh (capacity 10,000 kw)  Not an oil producer and has no refineries

 Pigs, chickens  Guano (phosphates)

Since 1888 Nauru has been exploited by the Germans, British, Australians, New Zealanders, and recently by Nauruans themselves, for its valuable phosphate reserves. Extraction, which took out most of the center of the island, has occurred at a fast rate, and the deposits are due to run out in 1995. Nauru has no other resources. The island is entirely dependent on outside energy supplies and the cost of oil is 50% higher than the Pacific average as Nauru does not lie on any shipping routes. Most electricity is produced by small diesel generators.

ENVIRONMENT

 None 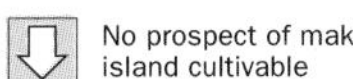 No prospect of making island cultivable

The main concern is possible fall-out from French nuclear test sites in the Pacific: Nauru lies downwind of these. Otherwise, ecological awareness is minimal. Nauruans accept that their source of wealth has effectively destroyed their island.

MEDIA

 Freedom of speech is protected by law

PUBLISHING AND BROADCAST MEDIA

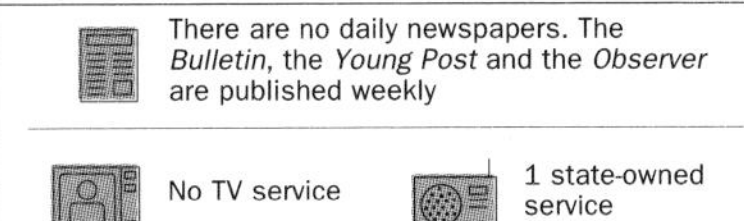

There are no daily newspapers. The *Bulletin*, the *Young Post* and the *Observer* are published weekly

No TV service

1 state-owned service

Nauru has no national TV broadcasting service; some overseas programs are made available on video.

CRIME

 Nauru does not publish prison figures  Crime levels are rising slightly

Theft is almost non-existent. Assaults and dangerous driving as a result of drunkenness are the major problems.

***Nauru is almost circular** with a single, 12-mile ring road. The overcrowded coastal strip is the sole habitable land.*

CHRONOLOGY

In 1945, the League of Nations confirmed continuing British control of Nauru, effectively approving UK phosphate exploitation.

- ❑ **1968** Independence.
- ❑ **1970** Gains control of phosphates from UK and Australia.
- ❑ **1992** Lawsuit against UK fails.

EDUCATION

 99%

Many Nauruans attend boarding school in Australia from a young age. Few go on to college.

HEALTH

 1 per 700 people  Tuberculosis, vitamin deficiencies, diabetes

A diet of processed imported foods and widespread obesity are the major problems. One-third of the population suffers from non-insulin-dependent diabetes. Industrial accidents are treated in Australia.

WEALTH

 Average white collar worker, 16,000 Australian dollars per year

CONSUMER GOODS OWNERSHIP

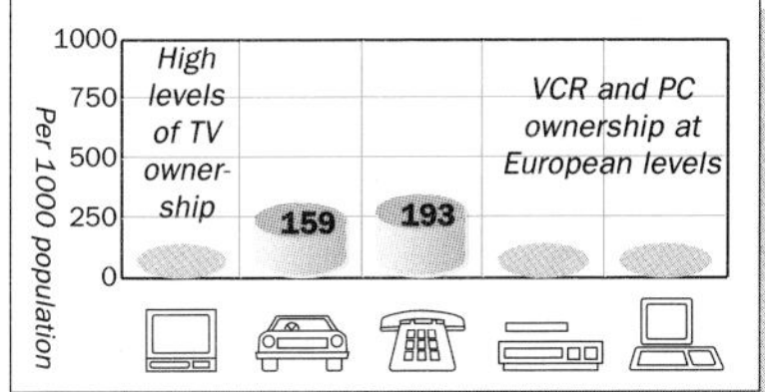

Nauru has one of the highest per capita incomes in the world. Wealth is fairly evenly distributed. Most Nauruans live in simple traditional houses and spend their money on luxury cars.

WORLD RANKING

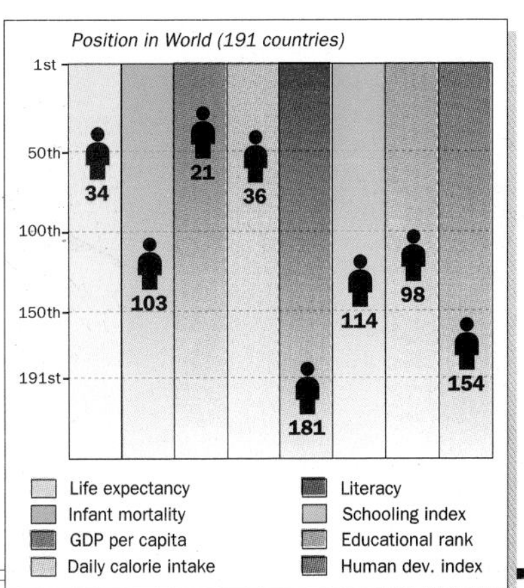

NEPAL

SOUTH ASIA

OFFICIAL NAME: Kingdom of Nepal **CAPITAL:** Kathmandu
POPULATION: 20.6 million **CURRENCY:** Nepalese rupee **OFFICIAL LANGUAGE:** Nepali

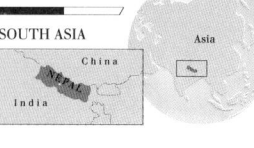

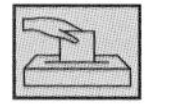

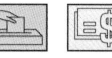

ON THE SHOULDER OF the southern Himalayas, Nepal is surrounded by India and China. It is one of the poorest countries in the world, and its largely agricultural economy is heavily dependent on the prompt arrival of the monsoon. Important new sources of income are now being developed, including hydroelectric power and tourism. In 1991, democratic elections were held for the first time since 1959, marking the end of a period of absolute rule by the king.

CLIMATE

WEATHER CHART

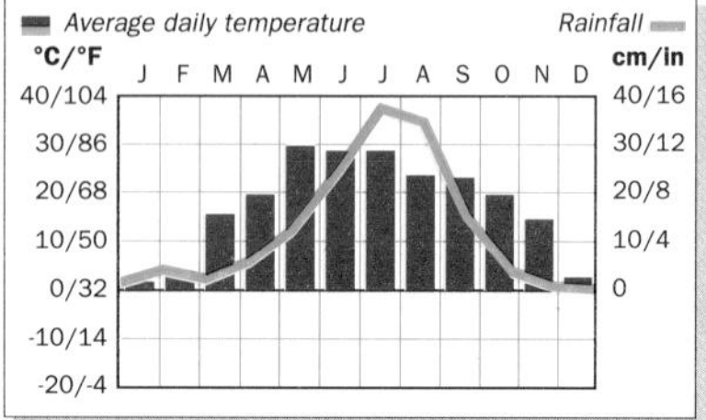

The warm July to October monsoon affects the whole country, causing flooding in the hot Terai plain, but generally decreases northward and westward. The rest of the year is dry, sunny and mild, except in the Himalayas, where valley temperatures in winter may average 14°F.

COMMUNICATIONS

Tribhuvan International, Kathmandu
800,000 passengers

Has no fleet

THE TRANSPORTATION NETWORK

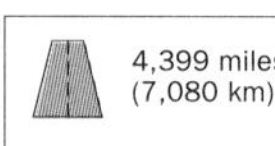

4,399 miles (7,080 km)

None

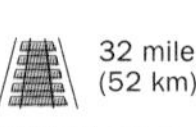

32 miles (52 km)

None

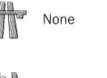

Domestic flights link the main towns. There are paved roads in the south and in the Kathmandu valley; only one runs north to China. Two short stretches of railroad cross into India.

Himalayan harvest. *The steep mountainsides and easily eroded soils mean that most fields are terraced. 90% of Nepalese are farmers.*

TOURISM

255,000 visitors

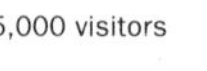

Up 6% in 1990

MAIN OVERSEAS ARRIVALS

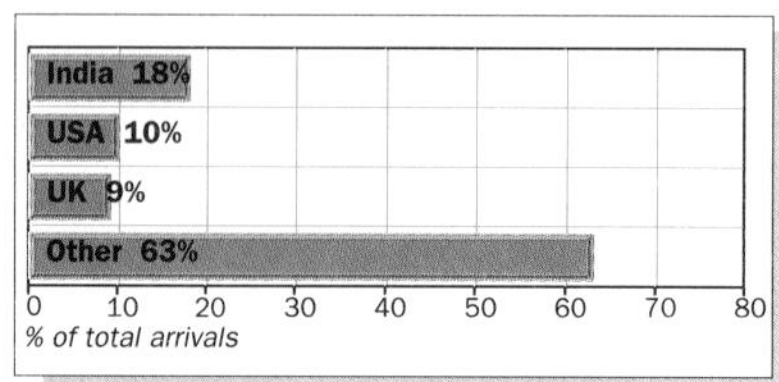

A serious conflict exists between the wish to preserve the environment and the desire for tourist revenue. Areas in the northwest were opened up to tourists in 1989, but degradation caused by 72,000 hikers a year on popular routes forced the government to set up the Annapurna Conservation Project. Firewood cutting for tourists is said to have increased deforestation, and hence soil erosion, by 10%.

PEOPLE

Nepali, Maithilli, Bhojpuri

337 people per sq. mile

THE URBAN/RURAL POPULATION SPLIT

10% 90%

RELIGIOUS PERSUASION

Muslim 3%
Other 2%
Buddhist 5%
Hindu 90%

There are few ethnic tensions despite the variety of ethnic groups, including northerners, such as the Sherpas, the inhabitants of the Terai in the south and the Newars, mostly found in the Kathmandu valley. Women's subordinate position is enshrined in property and divorce laws; Hindu women are more restricted than Sherpas and Buddhists. Polygamy is practiced in the hills.

POLITICS

Lower House 1998
Upper House 1999

HM King Birendra Bir Bikram Shah Dev

THE STATE OF THE PARTIES

House of Representatives 205 members

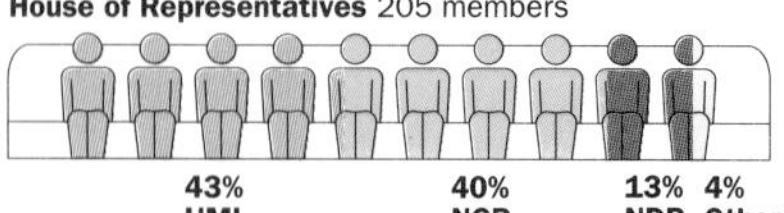

UML = Unified Marxist–Leninist Party **NCP** = Nepali Congress Party **NDP** = National Democratic Party **Other** = Nepali Sadbhavana, Nepal Workers' and Peasants' Party

National Council 60 members

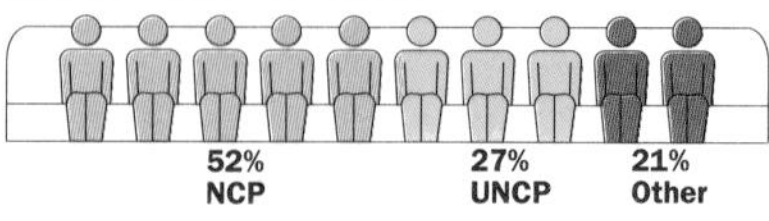

35 members elected by the House of Representatives, 15 chosen from the country's development zones, and 10 chosen by King Birendra

The end of absolute monarchy and the partyless *panchayat* system in 1990 allowed the NCP to take power in the 1991 elections. However, divisions within the NCP led to a general election in November 1994, which was won by the communist Unified Marxist–Leninist party (UML), who subsequently formed a minority government. The UML's leader Man Mohan Adhikari advocates full support of King Birendra and the pursuit of free-market policies.

WORLD AFFAIRS

The NCP is friendly toward India, on which Nepal depends for the transit of much of its trade with the outside world. Nepal regards China as a potential threat; China suspects Nepal of being used as a base by Tibetan opposition groups.

AID

$453m (receipts)

Up 5% in 1991

Nepal's strategic position has made it a focus for powerful donors, including the USA, China, India, Japan and member states of the CIS.

DEFENSE

$33.19m

Up 8% in 1991

The army is small at 35,000 men. It has no tanks, combat aircraft or armed helicopters. The limited weaponry comes from the UK and India.

N

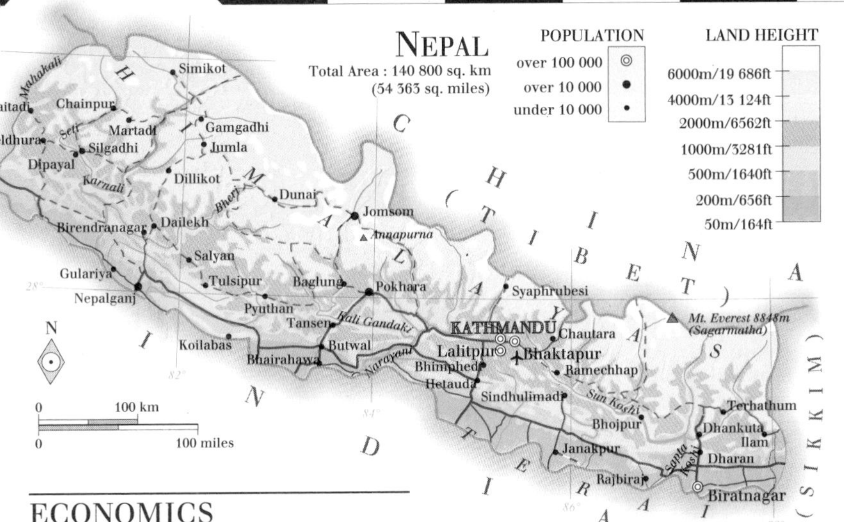

ECONOMICS

 $3.5bn

 46.30 Nepalese rupees

SCORE CARD

- ❑ World GNP Ranking........................120th
- ❑ GNP per Capita $170
- ❑ Balance of Payments................$–181.3m
- ❑ Inflation 9.1%
- ❑ Unemployment..................................5%

Strengths

Self-sufficiency in food grains in most years. Great potential for hydroelectric power generation, although little developed so far. Low debt level.

Weaknesses

Agricultural dependency; only 10% of GDP from manufacturing. Landlocked status. Low savings rate. Absence of active entrepreneurial class.

EXPORTS

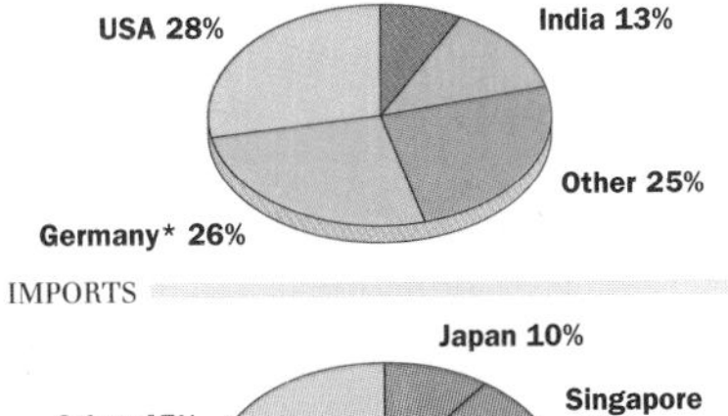

IMPORTS

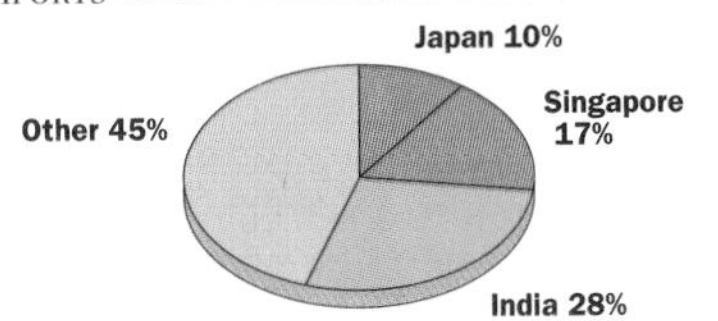

RESOURCES

 739m kwh (capacity 230,000 kw)

 Not an oil producer and has no refineries

6.3m cattle, 910,000 sheep, 548,000 pigs

 Mica, lignite, copper, cobalt, iron

There are plans to develop the large, but barely exploited, hydropower potential for domestic use and export.

ENVIRONMENT

 8% (1% partially protected)

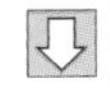 Two national parks threatened by large-scale HEP projects

Deforestation, including destruction of rhododendron forests, and the resulting soil erosion, is a serious problem. The native tiger is fast disappearing; skins are dumped by poachers who sell the bones to Chinese medicine makers.

MEDIA

 Press freedom is guaranteed under the new constitution

PUBLISHING AND BROADCAST MEDIA

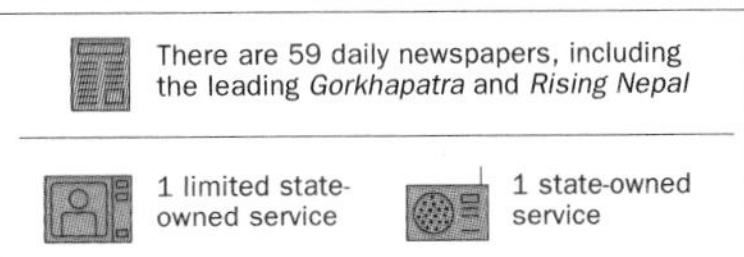

There are 59 daily newspapers, including the leading *Gorkhapatra* and *Rising Nepal*
1 limited state-owned service
1 state-owned service

The Nepal TV service began broadcasting in 1985 and 18% of the country now receives it. The press is mainly Kathmandu-based with low circulations. The *Sunday Despatch* is the paper most critical of government.

CRIME

 Nepal does not publish prison figures

 Up 11% in 1990

Petty theft and smuggling are the main problems. The legal provision for detention without trial is used and police suppression of demonstrations is often brutal.

EDUCATION

 26%

Over 80% of boys attend school in Nepal, but still only a minority of girls. Nepal's literacy rate is among the lowest in the world.

CHRONOLOGY

The foundations of the Nepalese state were laid in 1769, when King Prithvi Narayan Shah conquered the region.

- ❑ **1816–1923** Establishment of quasi-British protectorate.
- ❑ **1959** First multiparty constitution.
- ❑ **1960** King Mahendra bans all political parties and suspends the constitution.
- ❑ **1962** *Panchayat* system launched.
- ❑ **1985** Nepal is a founding member of SAARC.
- ❑ **1989–1990** "Trade and transit" dispute with India.
- ❑ **1990** Political parties reinstated.
- ❑ **1991** Multiparty elections.

HEALTH

 1 per 20,978 people

Respiratory and diarrheal diseases, maternal deaths

There are about 100 *dharmi-jhankri* (faith healers) for every health worker. Maternal mortality is high, the result of harmful traditional birth practices; a reeducation program for midwives has been established.

WEALTH

 Sawmill sawyer, 800 Nepalese rupees per month; yarn spinner, 2,500-6,000 Nepalese rupees per month

CONSUMER GOODS OWNERSHIP

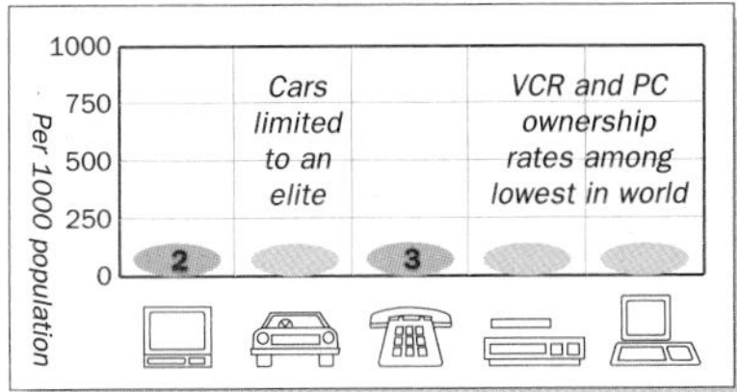

Nepal is one of the poorest countries in the world. Income per capita is less than $200 a year.

WORLD RANKING

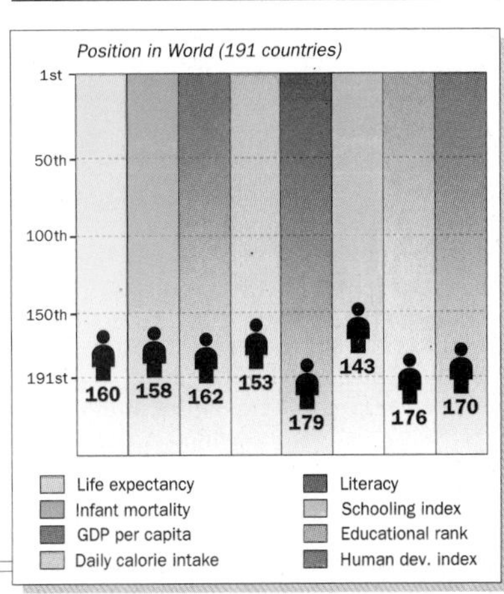

NETHERLANDS

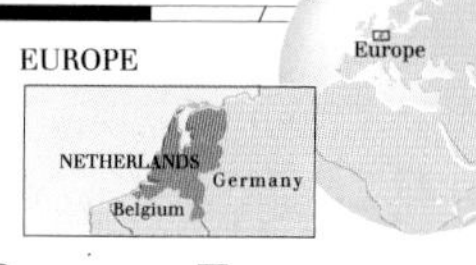

OFFICIAL NAME: Kingdom of the Netherlands **CAPITALS:** Amsterdam & The Hague
POPULATION: 15.2 million **CURRENCY:** Netherlands guilder **OFFICIAL LANGUAGE:** Dutch **OVERSEAS TERRITORIES:** 2

THE NETHERLANDS is located at the delta of five major rivers in northwest Europe. The few hills in the eastern and southern part of the country fall into a flat coastal area, bordered by the North Sea to the north and west. This area is protected by a giant infrastructure of dunes, dikes and canals, as 27% of the coast is below sea level. The Netherlands became one of the world's first confederative republics after Spain recognized its independence in 1648. Its highly successful economy has a long trading tradition and Rotterdam, its main port, is also the world's largest.

CLIMATE

WEATHER CHART

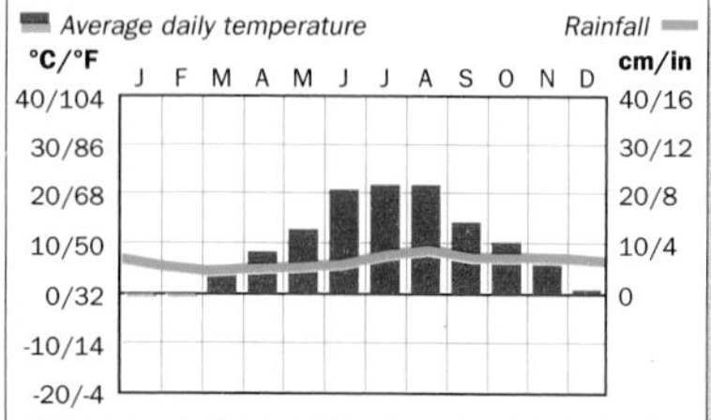

The Netherlands has a temperate climate, which is characterized by mild winters and cool summers. The country's coastal areas have the mildest climate, although northerly gales are fairly frequent, particularly in autumn and winter.

COMMUNICATIONS

515 ships
4.51m dwt

THE TRANSPORTATION NETWORK

73,572 miles (118,403 km)	1,271 miles (2,045 km)
1,757 miles (2,828 km)	3,002 miles (4,832 km)

Rotterdam, the key transshipment port for northern Europe, is also the world's largest. It is currently expanding its container capacity. The government is also expanding Schipol airport; $15 billion has been committed to make it a hub of transportation in Europe. There are plans to construct new high-speed track to allow the French TGV train to run from Brussels to Amsterdam.

TOURISM

6.2m visitors

Up 7% in 1992

MAIN OVERSEAS ARRIVALS

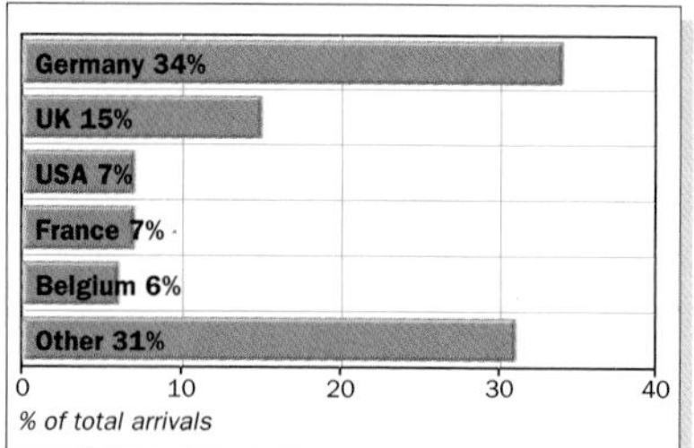

Tourism is a major business in the Netherlands. Visitors go mainly to Amsterdam, although cities such as Groningen and Maastricht are growing in popularity. Amsterdam caters for a diverse tourism market. Its world-famous museums include the Rijksmuseum, with its collection of Vermeers and Rembrandts. Amsterdam is also renowned as the sex capital of Europe. Its liberal traditions and red-light district draw millions every year.

In the past decade, the city has also become a center for the European gay community. A thriving club scene and liberal drug laws have brought an increase in partyers from neighboring countries. Special trains from Brussels to the IT club carry thousands every week during the summer.

In spring and summer, the tulip fields and North Sea beaches attract large numbers of visitors.

Windmill at Baambrugge, near Amsterdam. A century ago there were 10,000 in the country compared with today's 1,000. A protective ring of 900 mills kept Amsterdam from flooding.

PEOPLE

Dutch, Frisian

938 people per sq. mile

THE URBAN/RURAL POPULATION SPLIT

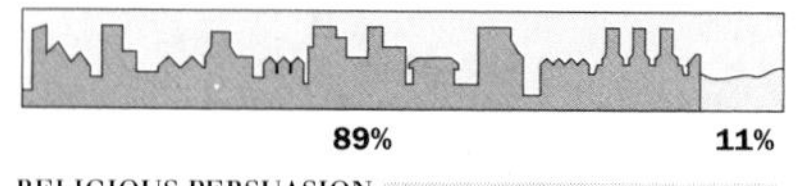

RELIGIOUS PERSUASION

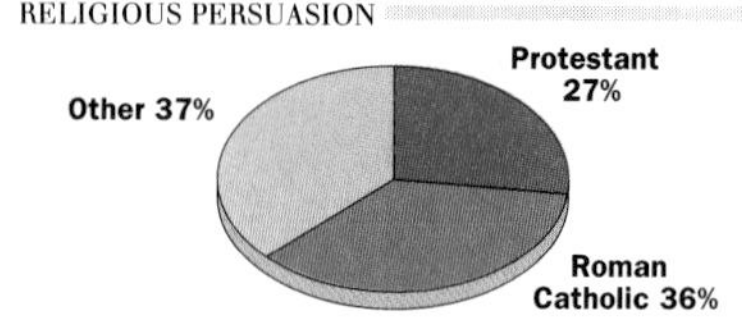

ETHNIC MAKEUP

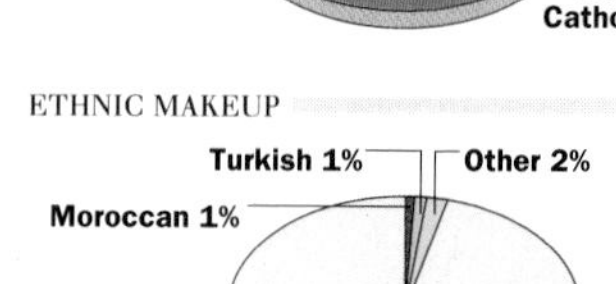
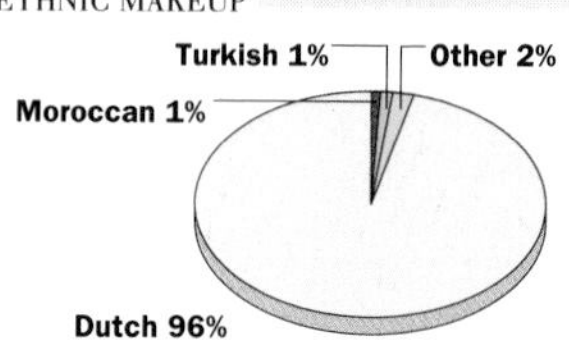

The Dutch see their country as the most tolerant in Europe. This reflects a long history of welcoming refugees seeking religious and political asylum. In the 20th century, immigrants from former colonies have settled in the Netherlands and are fully accepted as citizens. The first wave came from Indonesia, followed by settlers from the Dutch colonies in the Caribbean and South America, Suriname and the Netherlands Antilles. The small Turkish community, however, does not enjoy full citizenship, but has guest worker status similar to that of its counterparts in Germany.

The tradition of tolerance is also reflected in liberal attitudes to sexuality. Dutch homosexuals have the same rights, including the same age of consent, as heterosexuals.

The state does not try to impose a particular morality on its citizens. Drug taking is seen in the Netherlands as a matter of personal choice.

Women enjoy equal rights but they are not well represented at boardroom level.

POPULATION AGE BREAKDOWN

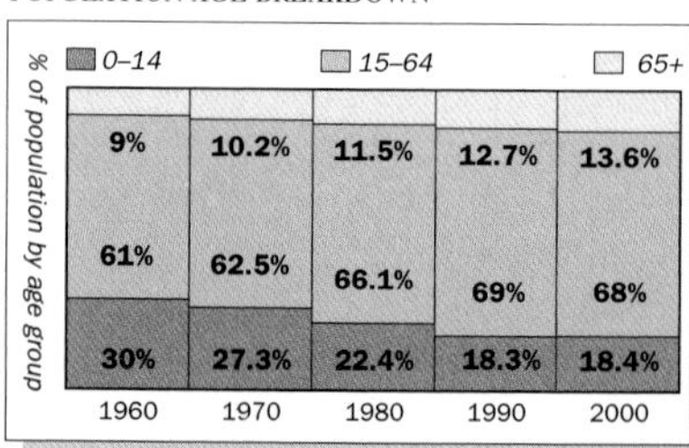

N

POLITICS

THE STATE OF THE PARTIES

Second Chamber 150 members

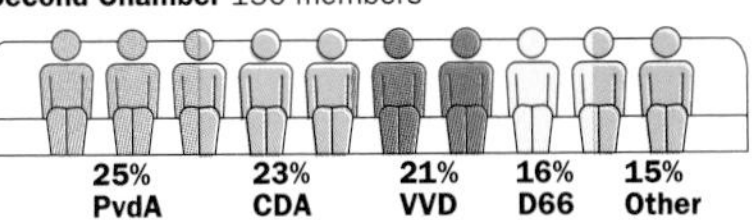

PvdA = Labor Party **CDA** = Christian Democratic Appeal **VVD** = People's Party for Freedom and Democracy **D66** = Democrats 66 **GL** = Green Front **Other** = Political Reformed Party, Reformed Political Association, Reformist Political Federation, Center Democrats

First Chamber 75 members

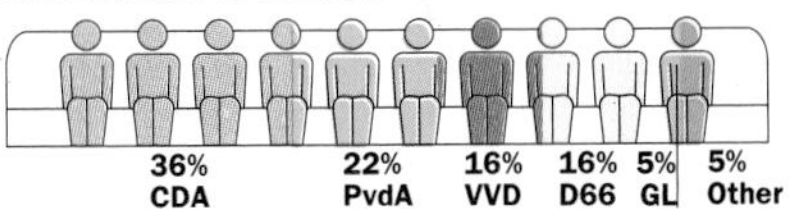

The Netherlands is a constitutional monarchy. Legislative power is vested in parliament. The monarch has only nominal power.

MAIN POLITICAL ISSUES

The future of social welfare
Even after the cutbacks of the 1980s, the Dutch still have one of the most generous welfare systems in Europe. Most political parties now accept that current levels of provision

Queen Beatrix, who acceded in 1980 and rebuilt support for the Dutch monarchy.

Wim Kok, won the 1994 elections and is the first labor Prime Minister since 1977.

cannot be maintained indefinitely. The debate is not whether to cut welfare benefits, but by how much and in which areas. The right-wing Liberal party is advocating a minimal level of provision, and the PvdA has suggested cutbacks totaling $4 billion.

Political refugees
In recent years, an increasing number of people have sought political asylum in the Netherlands. There are fears that unless immigration laws are tightened there may be a rise in support for extreme right-wing nationalist parties in the country. The mainstream parties have also begun to question whether the economy can afford the costs of housing refugees.

The fight against crime
The Dutch electorate has identified rising crime as a major concern. The prison system can no longer cope with the growing number of detainees, and many convicted criminals are being released for want of space. None of the parties has a program for reversing the trend.

PROFILE

Dutch politics are characterized by coalitions and a high degree of consensus. Most Dutch agree on the social function of government and readily accept relatively high taxes and a generous social security system. Political debate is more a question of the stress and focus of policy than of ideology. The CDA has traditionally led two-party coalition governments, either with the left-of-center PvdA or with the right-wing VVD. However, the PvdA won the 1994 elections, although both it and the CDA lost a significant number of seats.

WORLD AFFAIRS

The Netherlands has long been one of the main advocates of the EU. It supports both political and monetary integration, but failed in its attempt to rush through legislation enabling both during its EU presidency in 1992. Internationally, it has traditionally supported US and UK foreign policy, and is a member of NATO. The reunification of Germany and consequent rise in German power could see strong links with the US being weakened.

AID

As a result of tight fiscal policies, Dutch foreign aid has slightly contracted over the past few years. The Dutch government actively pursues a policy to link foreign aid and human rights. This led to a clash with Indonesia which, as a former colony, was one of the biggest receivers of Dutch support. In 1993, Indonesia turned down all Dutch aid, accusing the Netherlands of interfering in its internal affairs.

NETHERLANDS

Total Area : 37 330 sq. km (14 410 sq. miles)

CHRONOLOGY

Suppression of Protestantism by the ruling Spanish Habsburgs led to the revolt of the Netherlands and the independence of the northern provinces as a republic in 1581.

- ❑ **1813** Dutch oust French after 30 years of French rule and choose to become a constitutional monarchy.
- ❑ **1815** United Kingdom of Netherlands formed to include Belgium and Luxembourg.
- ❑ **1830** Catholic southern provinces secede as Belgium.
- ❑ **1848** New constitution – ministers to be accountable to parliament.
- ❑ **1897–1901** Wide-ranging social legislation enacted. Development of strong trade unions.
- ❑ **1898** Wilhelmina accedes to throne, so ending union with Luxembourg, where Salic Law is in force.
- ❑ **1914–1918** Dutch neutrality respected in World War I.
- ❑ **1922** Women fully enfranchised.
- ❑ **1940** Dutch attempt to maintain neutrality, but Germany invades. Fierce Dutch resistance.
- ❑ **1942** Japan invades Dutch East Indies.
- ❑ **1944–1945** "Winter of starvation."
- ❑ **1945** Liberation. International Court of Justice set up in The Hague.
- ❑ **1946** PVDA formed.
- ❑ **1946–1958** PVDA leads center-left coalitions with CVP. Marshall Aid from USA speeds reconstruction.
- ❑ **1948** Queen Juliana takes throne.
- ❑ **1949** Joins NATO. Most of East Indies colonies gain independence as Indonesia.
- ❑ **1953** 2,000 die in North Sea floods.
- ❑ **1957** Founder-member of EEC.
- ❑ **1960** Economic union with Belgium and Luxembourg comes into effect.
- ❑ **1973** PVDA wins power after 15 years spent mainly in opposition. Center-left coalition, first ever majority of left-wing ministers.
- ❑ **1980** Two main opposition Protestant parties unite in CDA. Queen Beatrix accedes to throne.
- ❑ **1977–1981** CDA–VVD coalition.
- ❑ **1982** PVDA rejects deployment of US Cruise missiles in Netherlands. CDA–VVD center-right coalition under Ruud Lubbers.
- ❑ **1989** VVD refuses to support finance for 20-year National Environment Policy (NEP). Elections. Lubbers' CDA–PVDA center-left coalition.
- ❑ **1990** NEP introduced.
- ❑ **1992** Licensed brothels and euthanasia legalized.
- ❑ **1994** Elections. PVDA heads new coalition. Politically-conservative VVD holds balance of power.

N

DEFENSE

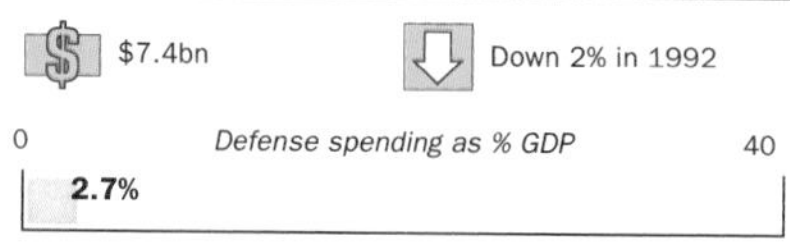

DUTCH ARMED FORCES

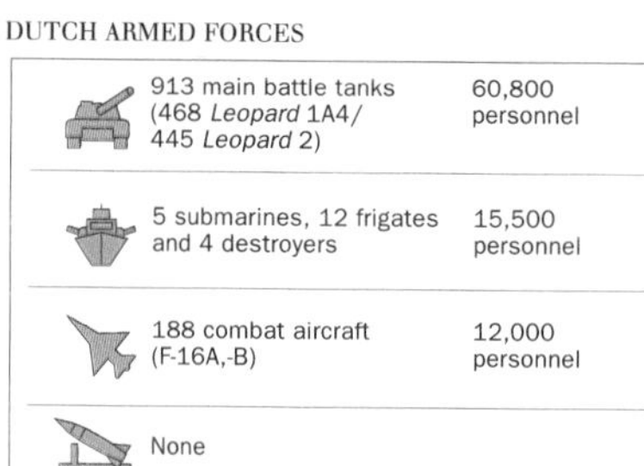

The Dutch military, which is part of NATO, is currently undergoing major restructuring. By 2000, it will have been transformed from an organization focusing on an anti-Soviet defense role into a rapidly deployable, more flexible military force. The plans include a 44% reduction in personnel and the abolition of compulsory military service. Most of the reforms affect the army, which will be reduced from three to two divisions. The Netherlands has a large defense industry, specializing in submarines, weapons systems and aircraft. The air force is equipped with US F-16s, which were partly developed with the Dutch Fokker company.

ECONOMICS

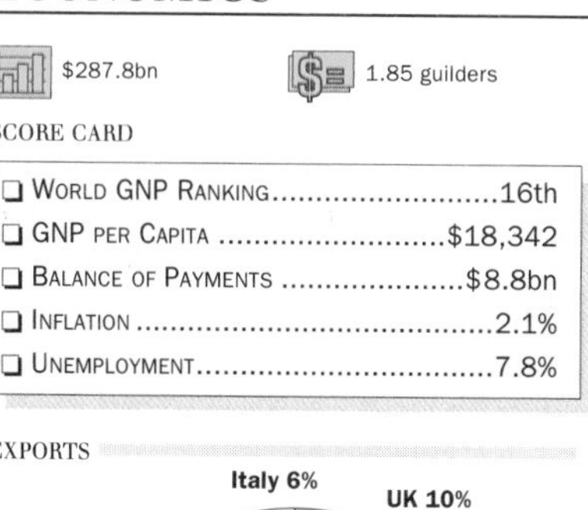

SCORE CARD

❑ World GNP Ranking	16th
❑ GNP per Capita	$18,342
❑ Balance of Payments	$8.8bn
❑ Inflation	2.1%
❑ Unemployment	7.8%

EXPORTS

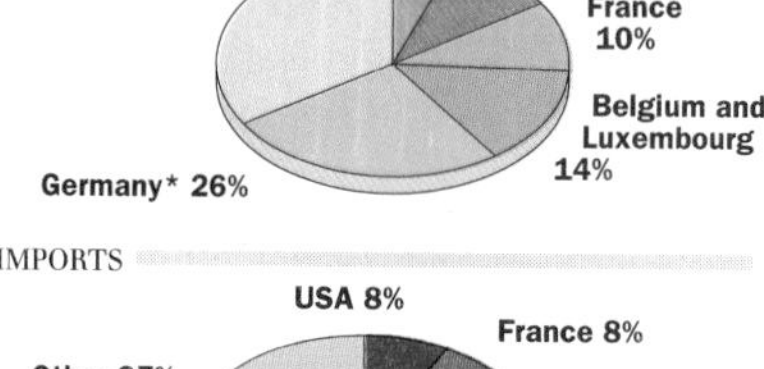

IMPORTS

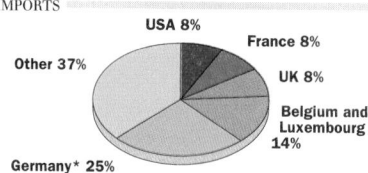

USA 8%
France 8%
Other 37%
UK 8%
Belgium and Luxembourg 14%
Germany* 25%

Strengths

Highly skilled and educated work force. Sophisticated infrastructure. Large number of blue-chip multinationals, including Philips and Shell. Strong currency, linked to the German Deutsch Mark. Low inflation. Tradition of high-tech innovation, including development of the music cassette and CD.

Weaknesses

Costly welfare system, resulting in high taxes and social insurance premiums; one-third of national income spent on social security. High labor costs.

Profile

The Dutch economy is one of the most successful in Europe. Since the 16th century, trade has been of great importance. Today, imports and exports account for over 50% of GDP. Most goods travel through Rotterdam, the world's biggest port. In addition to high-tech sectors such as electronics, telecommunications and chemicals, the Netherlands has a successful agricultural industry. Productivity rates are high and agricultural products such as cheese, vegetables, meat and flowers are significant export earners.

ECONOMIC PERFORMANCE INDICATOR

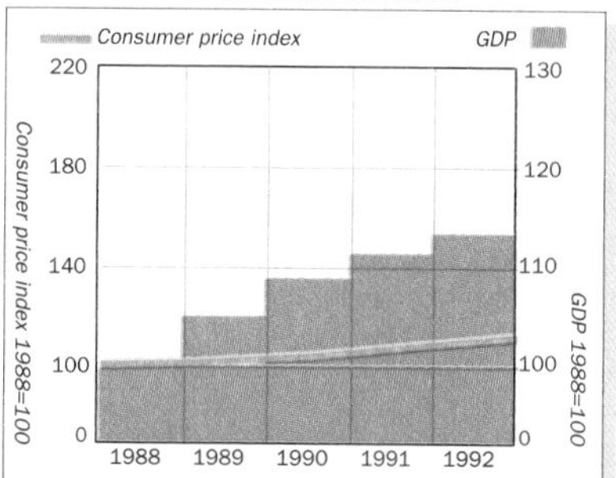

NETHERLANDS : MAJOR BUSINESSES

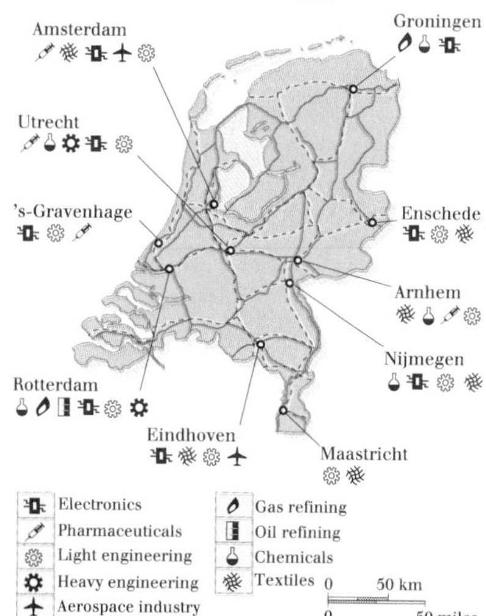

RESOURCES

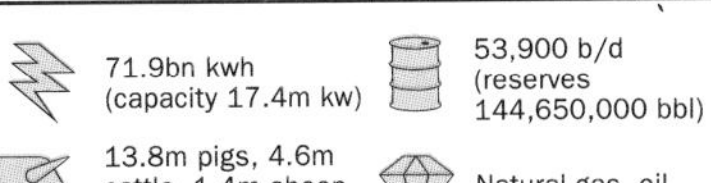

ELECTRICITY GENERATION

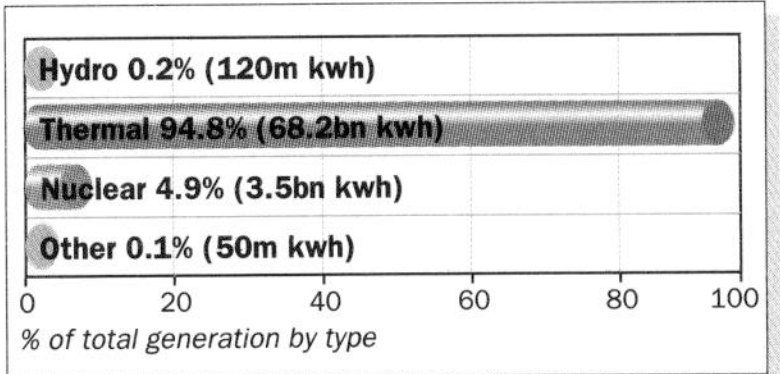

There are large natural gas reserves in the north. There is some oil production from offshore drilling in the North Sea.

NETHERLANDS : LAND USE

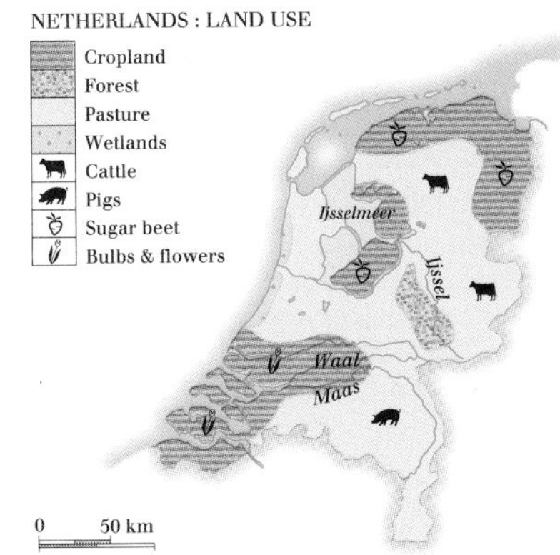

HEALTH

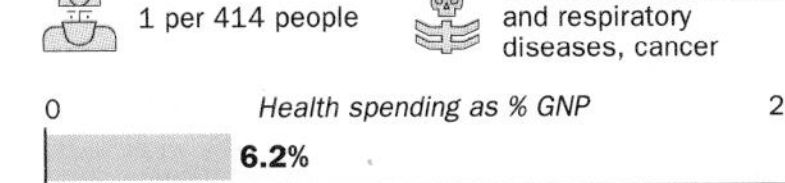

Dutch health care is almost entirely funded by the state. High spending ensures that it is among the best in the world. However, there are fears that the Dutch may have to accept lower standards in future, particularly as the population is aging. Major health problems are similar to those in the rest of western Europe. There is a higher incidence of AIDS. The Dutch are active in research in this field.

ENVIRONMENT

9% (3% partially protected)

National Environment Policy adopted in 1990

ENVIRONMENTAL TREATIES

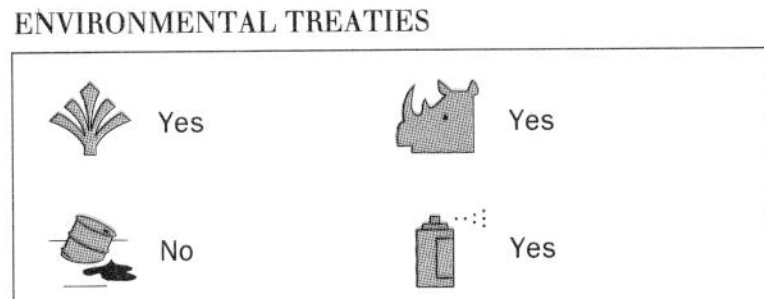

The Netherlands has a strong environmental tradition, a legacy in part of its being one of the most densely populated states in the world. NGOs such as Greenpeace are well supported and the Green Party is well represented in parliament. The Dutch recycle their domestic trash and have a good record of energy conservation.

The main concerns are halting highway building, and the proposed high-speed TGV train. The government plans that this will cross the green heartland of the Netherlands, an area known as the Randstad. It is being strongly opposed by environmentalists, who succeeded in halting a second airport north of Rotterdam.

MEDIA

Freedom of press is guaranteed by the constitution. The Netherlands has Europe's most liberal laws on censorship

PUBLISHING AND BROADCAST MEDIA

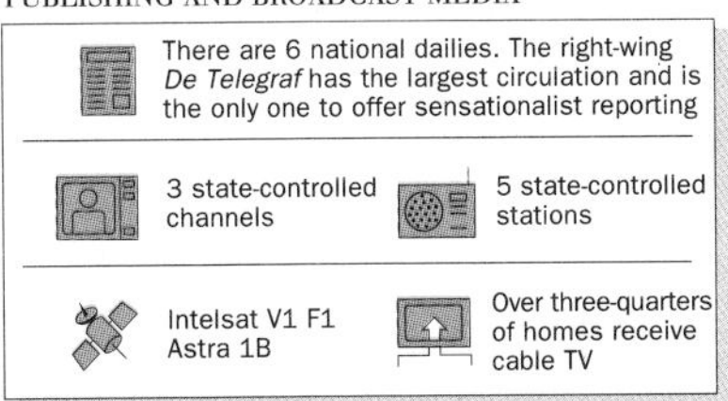

The media represents the whole social and political spectrum. Newspapers are aimed at the family and there is little sensationalist reporting. Access to cable TV is the highest in the world.

CRIME

CRIME RATES

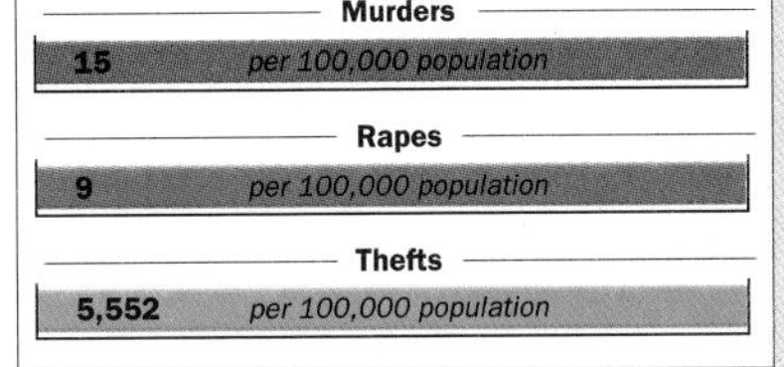

Liberal drug laws make the Netherlands a gateway for the drug trade. Several politicians have suggested decriminalizing the trade. Their aim is to reduce the crime generated by the huge profits from the business. However, such a measure would not be acceptable to the international community.

EDUCATION

99%

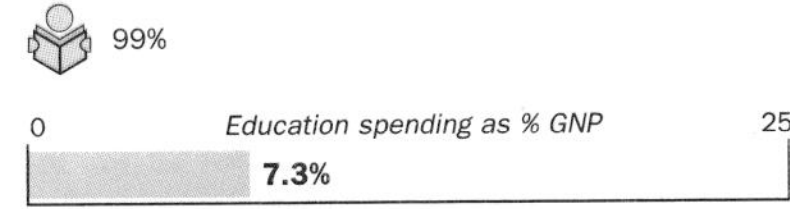

THE EDUCATION SYSTEM

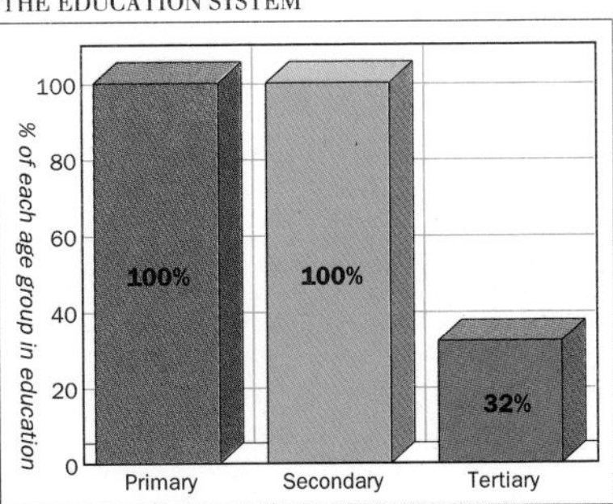

Apart from a few religious schools, all education is state-run. Corporate funding plays an important part in university research.

WEALTH

Electronic fitter, 2,248–2,387 guilders per month; journalist, 30,251–48,868 guilders per year

CONSUMER GOODS OWNERSHIP

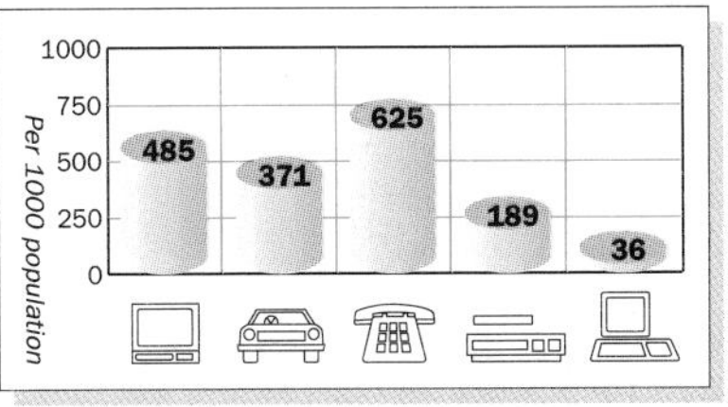

The Netherlands is, per capita, one of the richest nations in the world. The wealthiest group are oil executives, stock-market traders and businessmen. A progressive taxation system and extensive social welfare mean that wealth is quite evenly distributed. There is a small elite who have considerable inherited wealth, but extravagant displays of wealth are rare.

Class does not play a big part in Dutch society. Most citizens would consider themselves middle class. Immigrant communities are the exception; they often live on the edges of towns in deprived areas. The poorest group are illegal immigrants.

WORLD RANKING

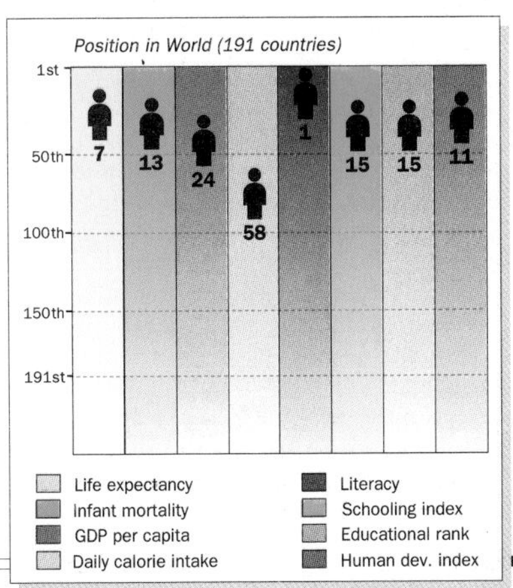

N

NEW ZEALAND

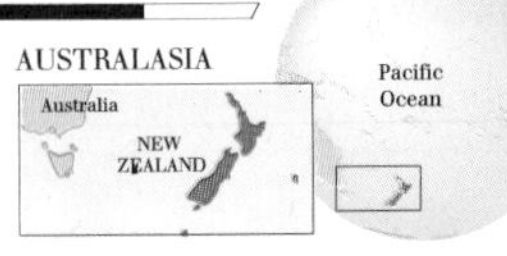

OFFICIAL NAME: The Dominion of New Zealand **CAPITAL:** Wellington
POPULATION: 3.5 million **CURRENCY:** New Zealand dollar **OFFICIAL LANGUAGE:** English **OVERSEAS TERRITORIES:** 3

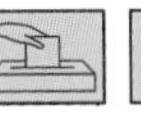

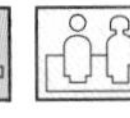

LYING IN THE SOUTH PACIFIC, 990 miles southeast of Australia, New Zealand comprises the main North and South Islands, separated by the Cook Strait, and numerous smaller islands. South Island is the more mountainous; North Island contains hot springs and geysers, and the bulk of the population. The political tradition is liberal and egalitarian, and has been dominated by the National and Labour parties. Radical, and often unpopular, reforms since 1984 have restored economic growth, speeded up economic diversification and strengthened New Zealand's position within the Pacific Rim countries.

CLIMATE

WEATHER CHART

Average daily temperature — °C/°F: 40/104, 30/86, 20/68, 10/50, 0/32, -10/14, -20/-4

Rainfall — cm/in: 40/16, 30/12, 20/8, 10/4, 0

J F M A M J J A S O N D

New Zealand's climate is generally temperate and damp, with an average temperature of 54°F. However, there are differences between the islands, which extend north–south nearly 1,240 miles. The extreme north is almost subtropical; southern winters are cold. New Zealand is windy; Wellington is known for bouts of blustery weather that can last for days.

COMMUNICATIONS

Auckland International 3.93m passengers

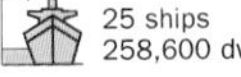
25 ships 258,600 dwt

THE TRANSPORTATION NETWORK

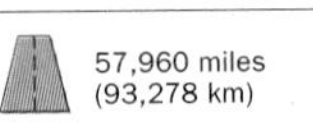

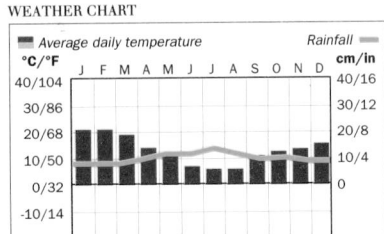

Although New Zealand's major islands are well served by transportation services, the more populous North Island has a more extensive road and rail network than South. Air and ferry services complement the land networks and provide links between North and South Islands, as well as with the numerous smaller islands. Cargo ferry services are particularly important for remote populations in the Ross Dependency. Links with the Cook Islands, Niue and the Tokelau atolls, New Zealand's associated territories, are being improved.

TOURISM

1.02 million

Up 5% in 1992

MAIN OVERSEAS ARRIVALS

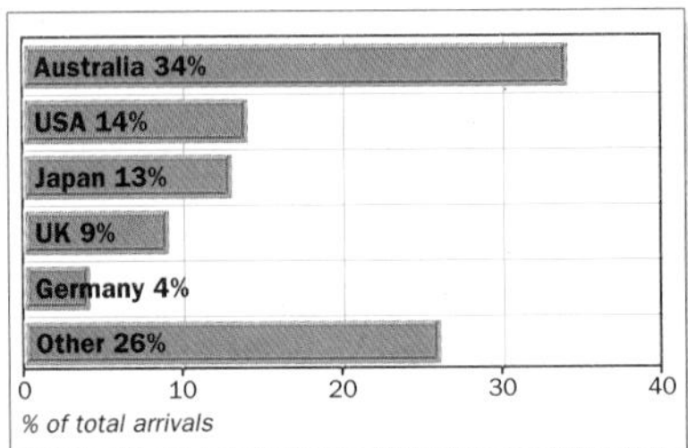

New Zealand's prime attraction is its scenery. Unspoiled and, relative to the country's size, the most varied in the world, it offers mountains, fjords and lakes, glaciers, rainforests, beaches, boiling mud pools and geysers. Other attractions are the Maori culture, and outdoor activities such as river rafting, fishing, skiing, whale watching and bungee jumping, a local invention.

Tourists come mainly from the USA, Australia, the UK, Japan and Germany. Low-cost charter flights have helped to boost visitor numbers to over one million a year. Tourism is now the largest single foreign-exchange earner, generating US$3 billion yearly. A new state tourist board has embarked on a high-profile campaign to triple visitors to three million by the year 2000.

Mount Egmont, an extinct volcano, is one of the numerous popular natural attractions of New Zealand's North Island.

PEOPLE

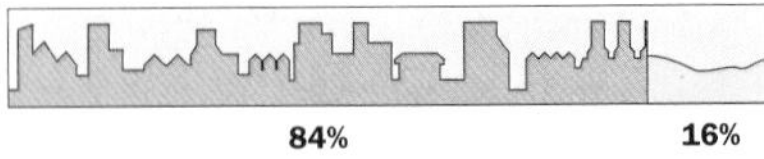

THE URBAN/RURAL POPULATION SPLIT

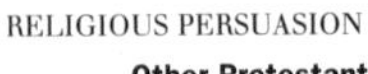

RELIGIOUS PERSUASION

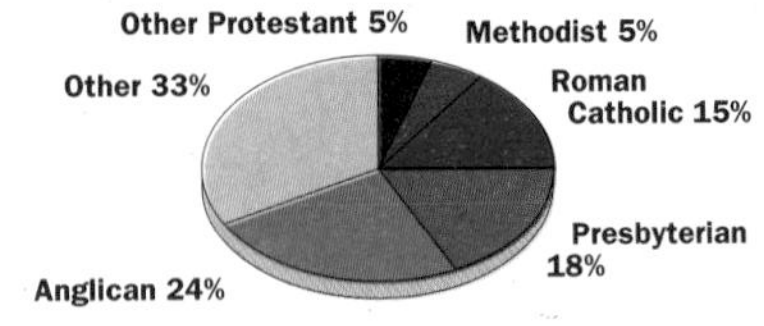

ETHNIC MAKEUP

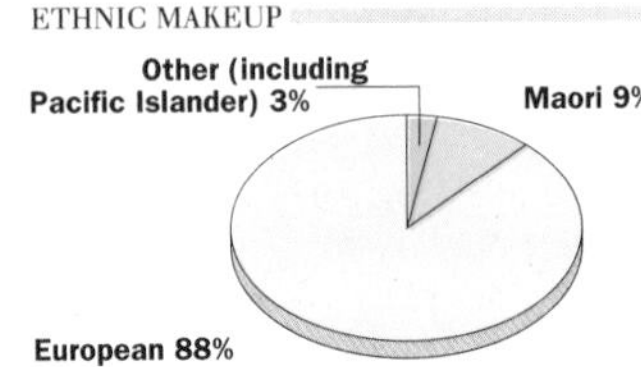

New Zealand is a country of migrants. The islands were first settled about 1,200 years ago by the Maoris as part of the Polynesian seaborne migrations. Today's majority European population is descended mainly from British migrants who settled after 1840. Recent arrivals include Asians from Hong Kong and Malaysia, and those who left Fiji following the 1987 coup.

Maoris today comprise 9% of the population. Their living and education standards are generally lower, and rates of unemployment higher, than average. Relations with the European-descended majority have been tense in recent years. The main cause has been the failure of the government to observe the terms of the 1840 Treaty of Waitangi, which protected Maori rights. In an effort to improve relations, the government reached a settlement of fishing claims with Maori leaders in 1992, and is now negotiating a settlement of land claims. New Zealand women were among the first in the world to get the vote. Today, they hold top jobs in business and politics.

POPULATION AGE BREAKDOWN

% of population by age group

	1960	1970	1980	1990	2000
65+	8.6%	8.5%	10%	10.9%	11.3%
15–64	58.5%	59.8%	63.2%	66.4%	65.3%
0–14	32.9%	31.7%	26.8%	22.7%	23.4%

POLITICS

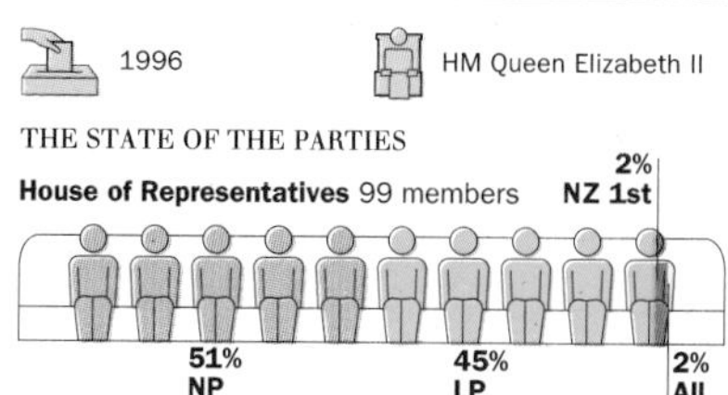

NP = National Party **LP** = Labour Party **All** = Alliance
NZ 1st = New Zealand First Party

James Bolger, NP *leader, and prime minister since 1991.*

Roger Douglas, *the creator of "Rogernomics."*

New Zealand is a single-chamber parliamentary democracy within the Commonwealth. The Cook Islands and Niue are self-governing territories.

Main Political Issues

Electoral reform

New Zealand is to shift to a system of proportional representation at the next general election, due in 1996. Popular endorsement of electoral reform in a referendum in November 1993 reflects widespread disillusionment with the NP and LP, in particular over both parties' turnabout on electoral promises during the 1980s. The German-style system, mixing constituency candidates with those identified by party, will give a much greater role to the smaller parties, which received almost 30% of the vote in the 1993 election.

Profile

Politics have been dominated by the NP and the LP under the first-past-the-post system. The period since 1984 has been one of radical reform, first of the economy under the LP and, since 1990, of welfare under the NP. Popular disaffection hardened during this period. NP and LP dissidents formed two new main parties, the Alliance and the New Zealand First Party, which took almost 30% of the vote between them at the 1993 election, and left the NP with an overall majority of only one seat.

WORLD AFFAIRS

ANZUS | Comm | APEC | OECD | GATT

A majority of New Zealanders remain strongly committed to the British crown and the Commonwealth, but the UK no longer plays a central role in New Zealand's life. The UK's involvement in the EU has forced New Zealand to reorient its trade and foreign policy toward its Pacific Rim neighbors, especially Australia. The 1983 Closer Economic Relationship (CER) treaty freed trade between the two states. Australia is now New Zealand's largest trading partner, and even closer links have been discussed in the form of an eventual political union. Relations with Asia are growing in importance. Exports to Japan are now second to those to Australia and trading relationships with other Asian states are being secured. New Zealand's anti-nuclear stance has led to its exclusion from key meetings of the ANZUS pact. Relations with France are still recovering from the 1985 bombing of the Greenpeace ship *Rainbow Warrior* by French agents in Auckland harbor.

AID

$100m (donations) — Up 47% between 1991 and 1993

Over half of New Zealand's overseas aid is bilateral. Particular areas of focus are the Pacific states and Pacific-wide organizations. New Zealand is a major supporter of the South Pacific Forum, the University of the South Pacific and the Pacific Environment Program. It also offers scholarships allowing overseas students to study or train in New Zealand.

New Zealand

Total Area : 268 680 sq. km (103 730 sq. miles)

LAND HEIGHT
2000m/6562ft
1000m/3281ft
500m/1640ft
200m/656ft
Sea Level

POPULATION
over 500 000
over 100 000
over 50 000
over 10 000
under 10 000

Chatham Is (continuation on same scale)

0 — 100 km; 0 — 100 miles

CHRONOLOGY

A former British colony, New Zealand became a dominion in 1907 and fully independent in 1947.

- **1962** Western Samoa gains independence.
- **1965** The Cook Islands become self-governing.
- **1972** Elections won by LP. Norman Kirk prime minister.
- **1973–1974** International oil crisis brings severe economic problems.
- **1974** Norman Kirk dies. William Rowling prime minister.
- **1975** Elections won by conservative NP party. Prime Minister Robert Muldoon introduces program of economic austerity.
- **1976** Immigration cut by over 80%.
- **1978** Elections; NP retains power with reduced majority.
- **1981** Elections; NP wins.
- **1984** Trade-union legislation bans "closed shops." Government pledges ban on ships carrying nuclear weapons entering ports. Election returns LP; David Lange prime minister. Waitangi Tribunal restores Auckland Harbor headland to Maori people.
- **1985** French agents sink Greenpeace ship *Rainbow Warrior* in Auckland Harbor.
- **1986** USA suspends military obligations under ANZUS Treaty.
- **1987** Elections won by LP. Controversial privatization program introduced. Legislation bans ships carrying nuclear weapons.
- **1989** Cabinet split. Lange resigns. Succeeded by Geoffrey Palmer.
- **1990** Palmer resigns because of unpopularity in polls. Replaced by Minister of Trade Michael Moore. LP defeated by NP in elections. James Bolger prime minister.
- **1991** Widespread protest over spending cuts. Two NP ministers resign.
- **1992** February: Sir Robert Muldoon resigns as minister in protest over government economic policy. April: France suspends nuclear tests in South Pacific. July: USA promises warships visiting New Zealand will no longer carry nuclear weapons. August: Waitangi Tribunal awards South Island fishing rights to Maoris. September: majority vote for electoral reform in referendum.
- **1993** May: *Jacques Cartier* first French naval ship to dock since 1985. November: elections. NP party returned with one-seat majority. As a result of referendum, proportional representation introduced for future elections.

DEFENSE

$663.4m
Down 16% in 1992
0
Defense spending as % GDP
40
1.9%
NEW ZEALAND ARMED FORCES
26 light tanks (26 Scorpion)
4,800 personnel
4 frigates and 4 patrol boats
2,400 personnel
41 combat aircraft (16 A-4K/5 TA-4K)
3,700 personnel
None

The security pact between Australia, New Zealand and the USA (ANZUS), the focus of New Zealand's defense policy since 1951, has been strained by New Zealand's refusal, since 1984, to allow nuclear warships into its ports. The USA suspended joint military exercises and preferential terms for arms purchase, forcing New Zealand to seek closer links with Australia. The 1992 announcement by the USA that its warships no longer carried nuclear weapons has paved the way for a return to more cordial relations.

Defense takes about 4.8% of government spending. The armed forces number 10,900 troops with an additional 8,500 reserves.

ECONOMICS

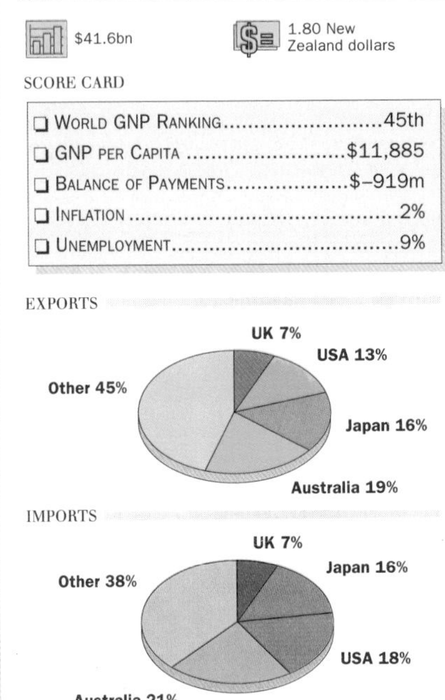

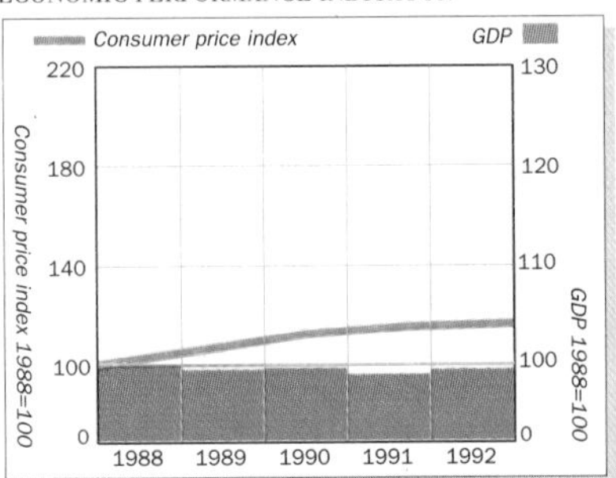

Strengths

Modern agricultural sector; world's biggest exporter of wool, cheese, butter and meat. Rapidly expanding tourist sector. Manufacturing industry growing, with emphasis on high-tech. One of world's most open economies. Rapidly expanding trade links within Pacific Rim.

Weaknesses

Public debt two-thirds of GDP, one of the highest levels outside developing world. Persistent budget and balance of payments deficits. Continuing reliance on imported manufactured goods.

Profile

Since 1984, New Zealand has changed from being one of the most regulated to one of the most open economies in the world. Radical reforms, dubbed "Rogernomics" after LP Finance Minister Roger Douglas, have helped to restore growth, cut inflation to 2% and encouraged diversification into new markets and products. The huge public debt and poor levels of private investment, however, continue to hinder sustained recovery.

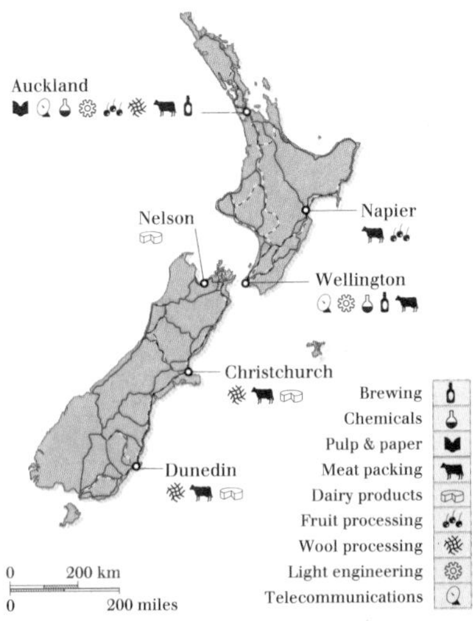

RESOURCES

30.2bn kwh (capacity 7.5m kw)

35,700 b/d (reserves 169,670,000 bbl)

55.2m sheep, 8.1m cattle, 407,000 pigs, 98,000 horses

Coal, oil, natural gas, iron, gold, silica sand

ELECTRICITY GENERATION

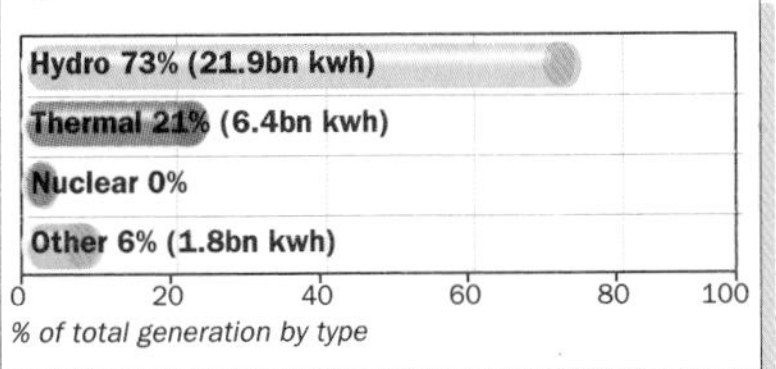

New Zealand's rich pastures, a result of even rainfall throughout the year, have traditionally been its key resource. The sheep, wool and dairy products on which the country's wealth was built are still important, but farmers are also moving into new areas. The kiwi fruit is now a thriving export. Fisheries are a growth area.

New Zealand is well-endowed with energy resources. It has coal, oil, natural gas and great hydroelectric potential.

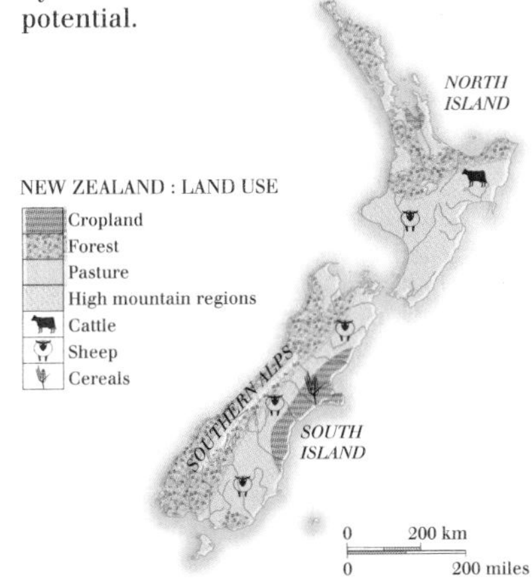

NEW ZEALAND : LAND USE

- Cropland
- Forest
- Pasture
- High mountain regions
- Cattle
- Sheep
- Cereals

ENVIRONMENT

11% (1% partially protected)

Generally high environmental awareness

ENVIRONMENTAL TREATIES

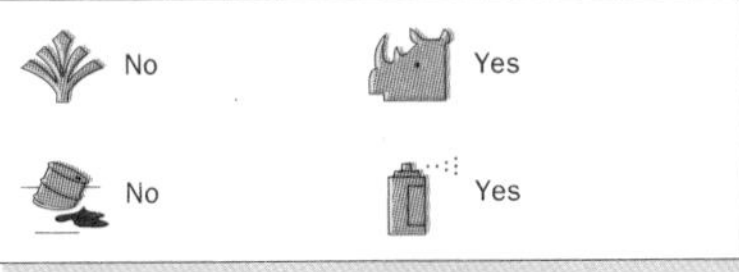

New Zealand's isolation, small population and limited industry have helped to keep it one of the world's most pollution-free countries. Ozone depletion over Antarctica competes with nuclear power as the top domestic concern. New Zealand has been a leading opponent of French nuclear testing in the Pacific and has banned nuclear warships from its ports.

MEDIA

There is no censorship of the media

PUBLISHING AND BROADCAST MEDIA

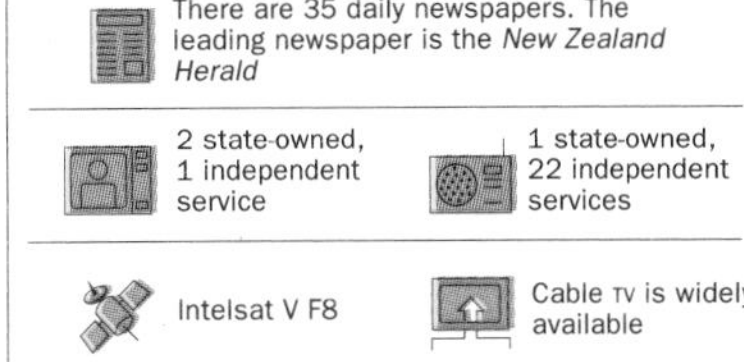

There are 35 daily newspapers. The leading newspaper is the *New Zealand Herald*
2 state-owned, 1 independent service
1 state-owned, 22 independent services
Intelsat V F8
Cable TV is widely available

The Auckland-based *New Zealand Herald* is the only daily with a national circulation; the others are primarily local papers. A third state-owned TV station is being considered.

CRIME

3,736 prisoners

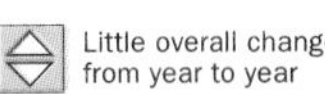

Little overall change from year to year

CRIME RATES

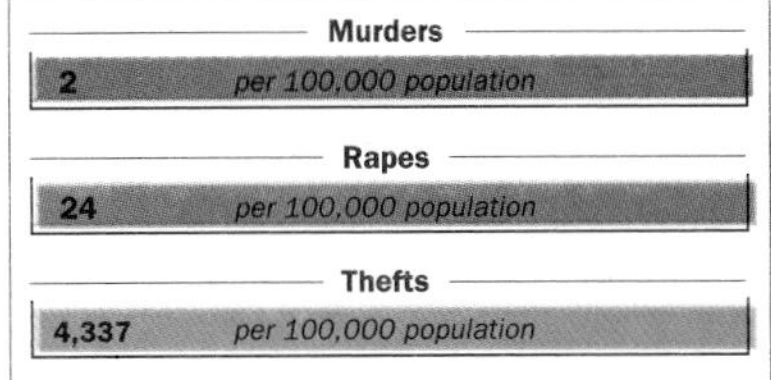

Murders
2 per 100,000 population
Rapes
24 per 100,000 population
Thefts
4,337 per 100,000 population

Crime rates in New Zealand's urban areas have increased in recent years. However, overall, the country remains one of the world's safest and most peaceful places to live.

EDUCATION

99%

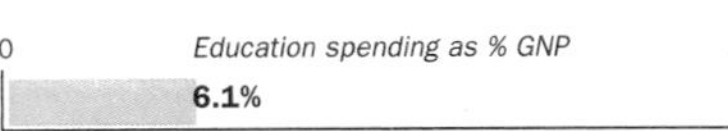

THE EDUCATION SYSTEM

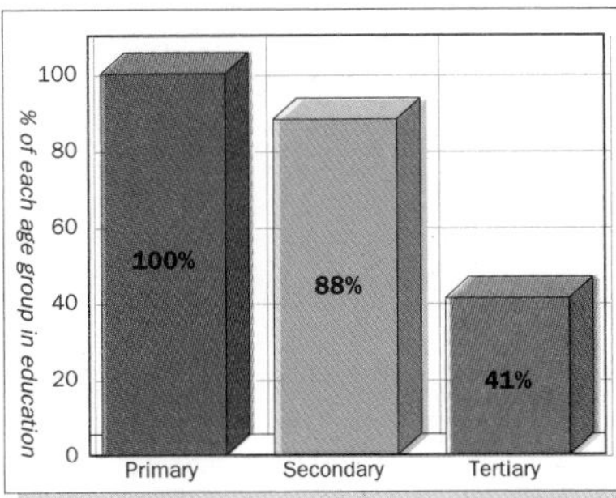

Education is compulsory between the ages of five and 16. Children start school aged five and 77% of 16-year-olds stay in full-time education. About 4% of pupils attend independent schools. The free state system is in the process of change: the government plans to give schools direct control over their finances.

HEALTH

1 per 373 people

Heart and cerebrovascular diseases, cancer

0 *Health spending as % GNP* 25

6%

New Zealand has been a world leader in the provision of public health services. In 1936, it was the first country to introduce a full welfare state. Government efforts since 1991 to impose UK-style market systems on the health service have been very unpopular. Highly controversial charges for hospital beds had to be abolished in 1993 after widespread public protests.

WEALTH

Truck parts dealer, 20,000 New Zealand dollars per year; computer sales manager, 100,000 New Zealand dollars per year

CONSUMER GOODS OWNERSHIP

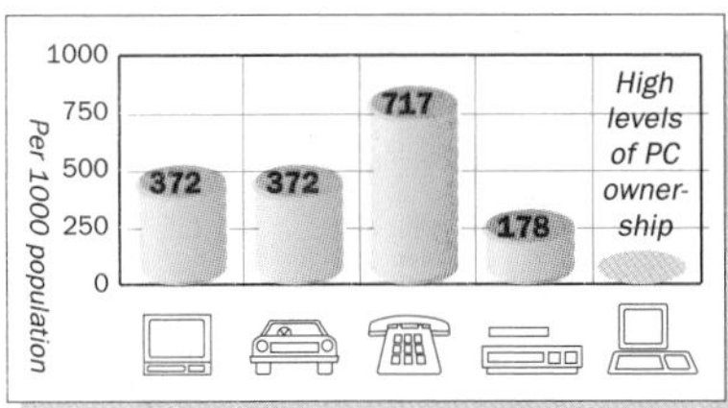

The decade since 1984 has been very difficult for New Zealanders, who are used to affluence within a generous welfare state. A rash of economic and social reforms has held back wages, raised unemployment and cut welfare benefits. Even so, average living standards are still high, and a strong egalitarian tradition means that wealth remains quite evenly distributed.

New Zealanders also enjoy one of the world's best qualities of life, in terms of access to basic necessities, and a clean, healthy urban and rural environment. Social mobility is fairly high. Wealthier people tend to spend their money on houses close to the water. Yachts are a major status symbol.

WORLD RANKING

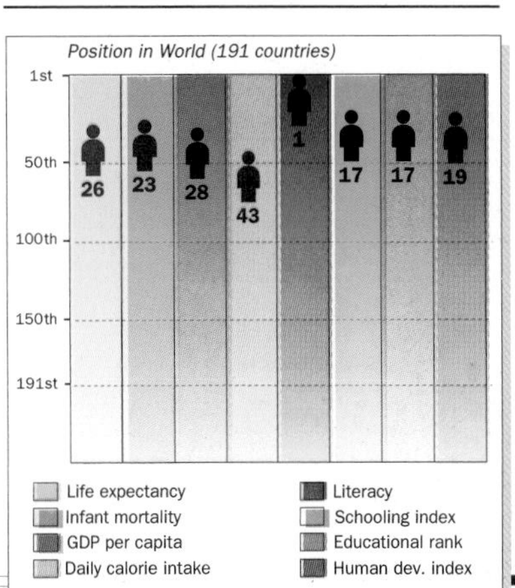

N

See also OVERSEAS TERRITORIES *p.616*

NICARAGUA

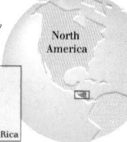

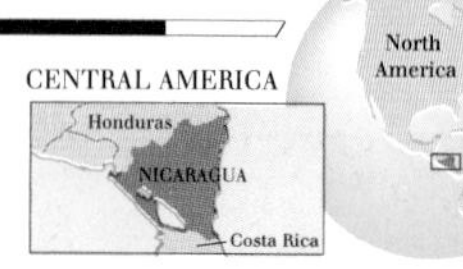

OFFICIAL NAME: Republic of Nicaragua **CAPITAL:** Managua
POPULATION: 4 million **CURRENCY:** New córdoba **OFFICIAL LANGUAGE:** Spanish

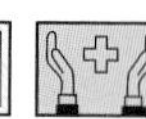

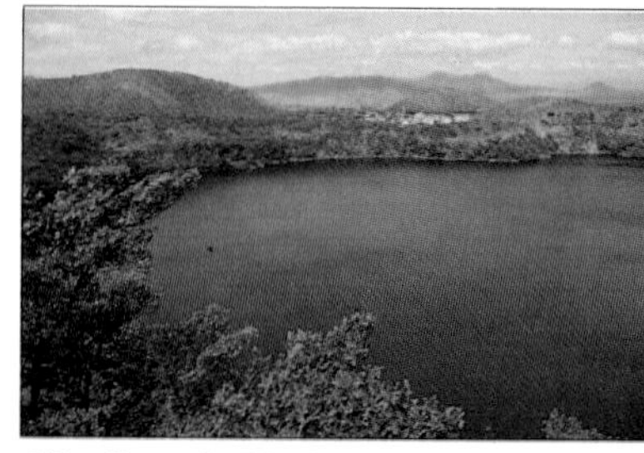

Oil refinery in Bluefields, on the Atlantic coast. Under the Sandinistas, most crude oil came from the former USSR, via Cuba.

BOUNDED BY THE Pacific Ocean to the west and the Caribbean Sea to the east, Nicaragua lies at the heart of Central America. After more than 40 years of dictatorship, the Sandinista revolution in 1978 provoked eleven years of civil war, which almost destroyed the economy. Despite unexpectedly losing free elections in 1990, the Sandinistas remain a major political force in a country where poverty and unrest are rising.

CLIMATE

WEATHER CHART

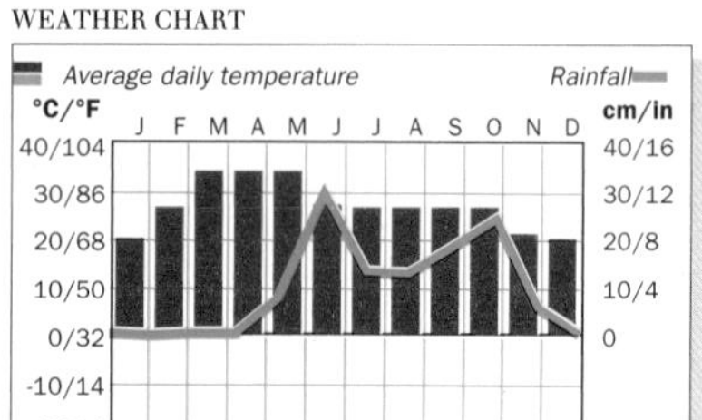

Nicaragua's climate is tropical and often violent. Hurricanes and earthquakes are an occasional threat.

COMMUNICATIONS

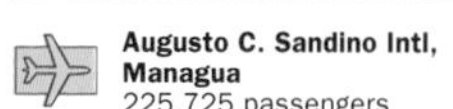

Augusto C. Sandino Intl, Managua
225,725 passengers

1 ship
1,200 dwt

THE TRANSPORTATION NETWORK

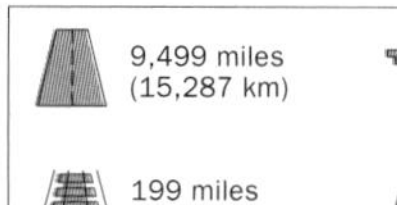

9,499 miles (15,287 km)

Pan-American Highway 239 miles (384 km)

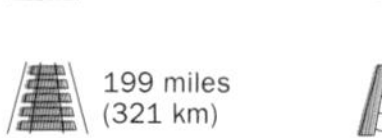

199 miles (321 km)

1,380 miles (2,220 km)

Most roads are in the Pacific region and in poor condition. The Pan-American Highway provides a key external link.

TOURISM

145,872 visitors

Nicaragua is now actively promoting leisure tourism

MAIN OVERSEAS ARRIVALS

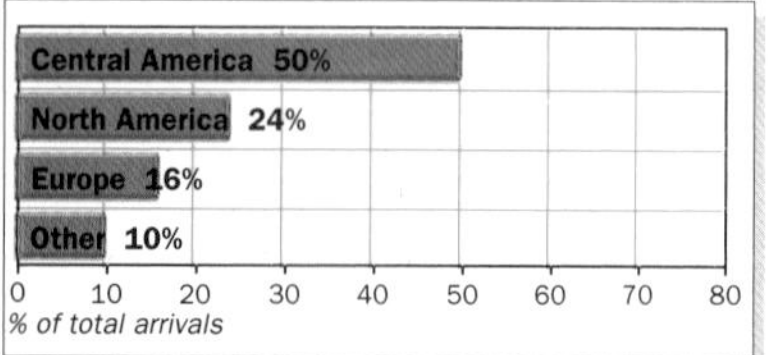

Nicaragua's tourist industry was always small. The civil war caused its near total collapse, although up to 100,000 "political tourists" visited the country every year to observe the effects of Sandinista reforms.

PEOPLE

Spanish, English Creole, Miskito

83 people per sq. mile

THE URBAN/RURAL POPULATION SPLIT

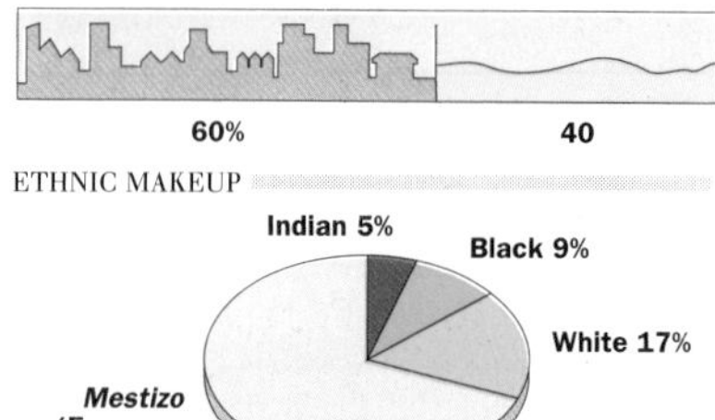

The Atlantic regions, which in 1987 achieved limited independence, are isolated from the more populous Pacific regions. The indigenous Miskito tribes and the descendants of Africans, brought over by Spanish colonists in the 18th century to work the plantations, are concentrated along the Atlantic coast, where English Creole is widely spoken. Almost 80% of the population lives in poverty. Of this group, some 20% are defined by the UN as extremely poor; between 1991 and 1992, Nicaragua's GDP per capita fell below Haiti's, normally the world's lowest. Half the population has no permanent employment and poverty has forced many women into prostitution.

POLITICS

1996

President Violeta Barrios de Chamorro

THE STATE OF THE PARTIES

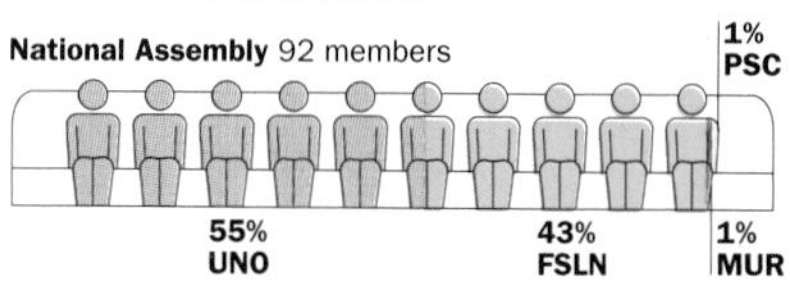

UNO = National Opposition Union **FSLN** = Sandinista National Liberation Front **MUR** = Revolutionary Unity Movement **PSC** = Social Christian Party

Nicaraguan politics are caught in a vise between right-wing pro-US parties and the left-wing Sandinistas, whose power base remains the army. Radical changes were expected after the 1990 electoral victory of Violeta Chamorro's UNO. However, her failure to revive the economy, and increasing reliance on Sandinista support, led to US threats to withhold aid. By 1993, the instability of the government was threatening a return to civil war.

NICARAGUA

Total Area : 130 000 sq. km (50 193 sq. miles)

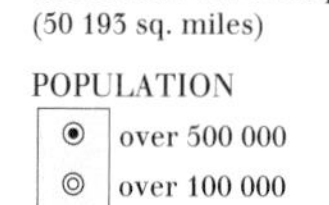

WORLD AFFAIRS

OAS CACM NAM GATT ECLAC

Nicaragua's most important, and most difficult, relationship has been with the USA. During the Sandinista years, the USA tried to overthrow the regime by providing military aid to the Contra rebels. Chamorro's 1990 election victory initially led to the resumption of US aid after years of blockade. The resurgent influence of the Sandinistas, however, led to US threats in 1993 to freeze $98 million of promised aid.

AID

 $826m (receipts)  Up 58% in 1991

The Nicaraguan economy is almost totally dependent on aid. The USA is the largest donor, but makes aid conditional on the end of Sandinista influence. Aid from the EU is more reliable. Large numbers of individually motivated foreign volunteers work in schools and hospitals.

DEFENSE

  $214.5m  Down 5% in 1992

Nicaragua's army was formed from the Sandinista forces that overthrew the Somoza regime. It grew to be the region's largest (134,000 troops) during the war with the Contras. By 1993, its numbers had fallen to 15,000. The USA has been pressing for the removal of General Humberto Ortega as leader of the Sandinista-controlled army as a condition for the resumption of full aid.

ECONOMICS

 $1.4bn  6.33 new córdobas

SCORE CARD

- World GNP Ranking....................147th
- GNP per Capita....................$350
- Balance of Payments....................$-695.4m
- Inflation....................432%
- Unemployment....................14%

Strengths
Very few. Coffee is the major export crop. Signs of cross-party support for an economic recovery program.

Weaknesses
Hyperinflation, with regular devaluations. World prices for its main exports have all fallen sharply in recent years. Banana quotas with the EU are threatened by the GATT proposals. Opposition in USA to Sandinista influence in Nicaraguan politics limits access to the key US market. Growing trade deficit and failure of successive plans to stimulate exports.

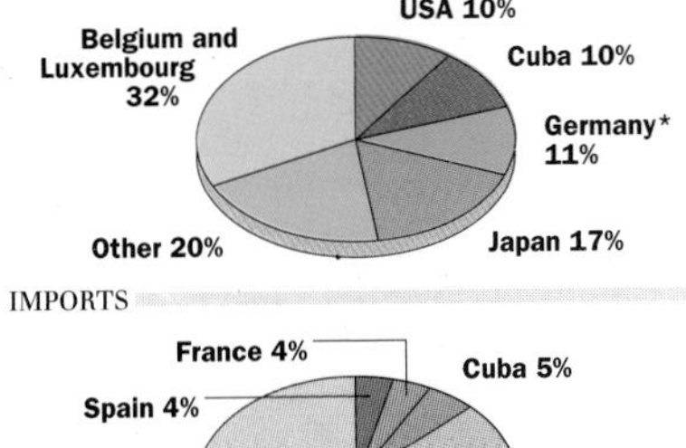

RESOURCES

 1bn kwh (capacity 400,000 kw)  Not an oil producer; refines 16,000 b/cd

2m cattle, 680,000 pigs, 250,000 horses — Gold, silver, lead, zinc

Nicaragua has no significant mineral resources and no oil. Lack of spare generator parts has led to longer and more frequent power cuts in Managua.

ENVIRONMENT

 2% (0.3% partially protected)  No efforts to check deforestation

Deforestation and natural disasters, such as the earthquake that destroyed Managua in 1974, are major problems.

MEDIA

 The press is now relatively outspoken

PUBLISHING AND BROADCAST MEDIA

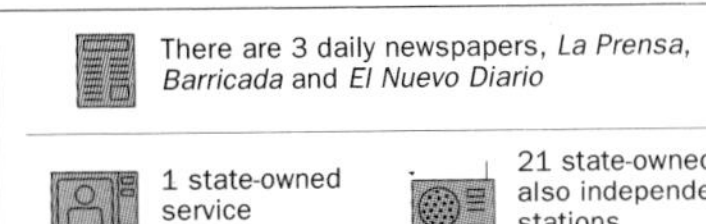

There are 3 daily newspapers, *La Prensa*, *Barricada* and *El Nuevo Diario*

1 state-owned service

21 state-owned, also independent stations

Radio is the most important medium. *Radio Mujer*, Central America's first station for women, went on air in 1992. *La Prensa*, the main daily newspaper, is owned by the Chamorro family.

CRIME

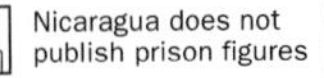 Nicaragua does not publish prison figures
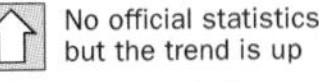 No official statistics, but the trend is up

Gun law still prevails in parts of the north, where gangs of ex-Contras and ex-Sandinistas control large areas.

CHRONOLOGY

Nicaragua became independent in 1838. Guerrilla forces, led by Gen. Sandino, opposed the US marine presence in the early 1930s.

- **1935–1979** Somoza family in power.
- **1978** Sandinista revolution overthrows Anastasio Somoza II.
- **1979–1990** Civil war between Sandinistas and US-backed Contras.

EDUCATION

 57%

The Sandinista "Literacy Crusade," which achieved dramatic results in the 1980s, has long since died away. The Jesuit-run University of Central America is one of two universities.

HEALTH

1 per 1,789 people — Diarrheal, heart and cerebrovascular diseases, pneumonia

Life expectancy in Nicaragua rose from 50 to 64 years between 1960 and 1988. Real spending on health, however, fell by 71% between 1988 and 1993, with a consequent 15% rise in child mortality.

WEALTH

 Farm laborer, 240-300 new córdobas per month, plus meals and accommodation; top executive, 6,000-12,000 new córdobas per month

CONSUMER GOODS OWNERSHIP

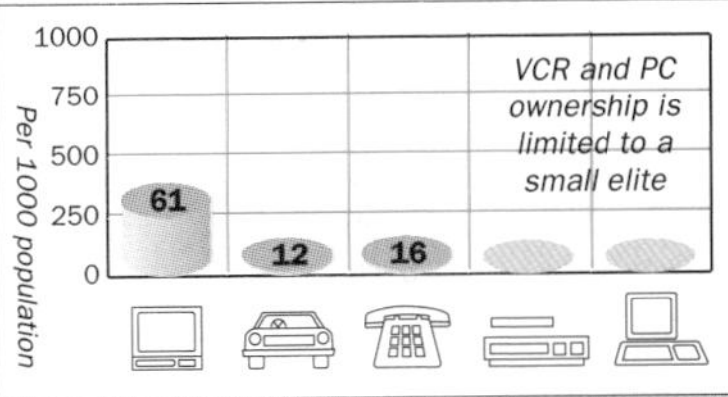

Wealthy Nicaraguans are based mainly in Miami. Some have returned under Chamorro as the "new entrepreneurs."

WORLD RANKING

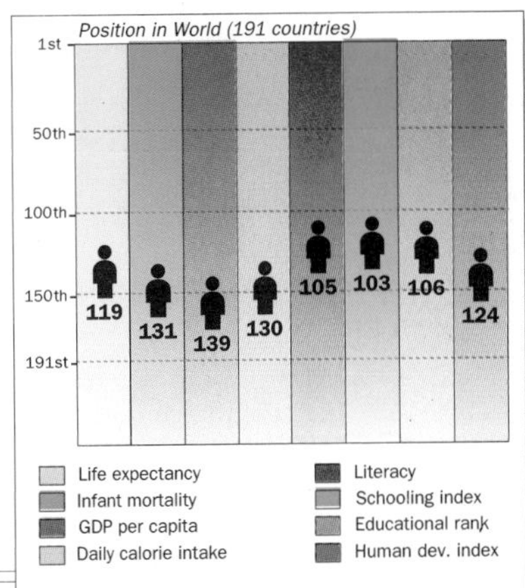

N

NIGER

WEST AFRICA

Algeria Libya Mali NIGER Chad Burkina Nigeria

Africa

OFFICIAL NAME: Republic of Niger **CAPITAL:** Niamey
POPULATION: 8.3 million **CURRENCY:** CFA franc **OFFICIAL LANGUAGE:** French

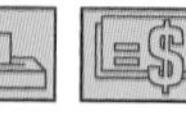

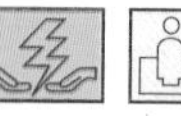

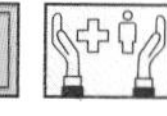

LANDLOCKED IN THE west of Africa, Niger is linked to the sea by the River Niger. The northern regions, the area around the Aïr Mountains and particularly the vast uninhabited northeast have Saharan conditions. Niger experienced ten years of economic boom in the 1970s and 1980s, when the new uranium mines brought a budget surplus, but today most Nigerois still live a harsh subsistence existence.

CLIMATE

WEATHER CHART

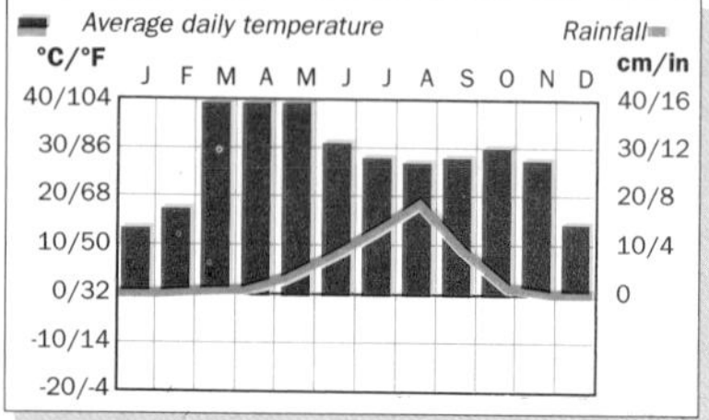

The Saharan north is virtually rainless. The south, in the Sahel belt, has an unreliable rainy season, preceded by a period of extreme daytime heat.

COMMUNICATIONS

Niamey International
74,319 passengers

Has no fleet

THE TRANSPORTATION NETWORK

24,837 miles (39,970 km)

Trans-Sahara Highway 266 miles (428 km)

None, but shares administration of Benin's railway

186 miles (300 km)

Plans to extend the railroad to Niamey from Parakou in Benin have been shelved. A bridge over the Niger, the country's second, is being built at Gaya.

TOURISM

13,071 visitors

Down 14% in 1992

MAIN OVERSEAS ARRIVALS

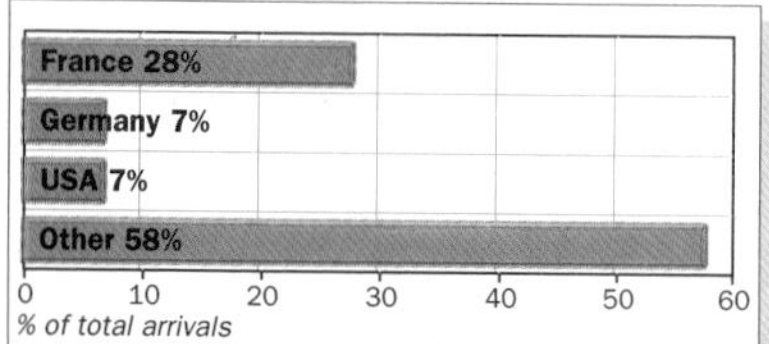

The Aïr Mountains, southern Hausa cities and Saharan Tuareg culture attract some tourists in spite of Niger's limited infrastructure and instability.

PEOPLE

Hausa, Djerma, Fulani, Tuareg, Teda, French

16 people per sq. mile

THE URBAN/RURAL POPULATION SPLIT

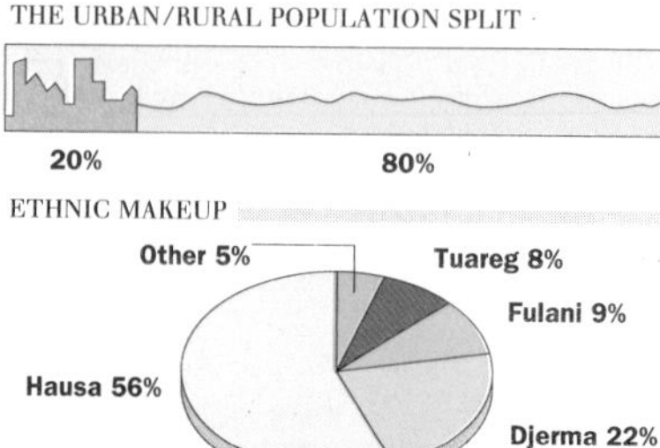

Considerable tensions exist between the Tuaregs in the north and the southern groups. The Tuaregs' sense of alienation from mainstream Niger politics has increased since the 1973 and 1983 droughts. Their herds decimated, many Tuaregs were forced away from their nomadic way of life to the towns. Northern Tuaregs responded to these pressures by mounting a low-key revolt.

A more subtle antagonism exists between the Djerma and Hausa groups. Until recently, the Djerma elite from the southwest dominated politics in Niger. Since 1993, however, control has passed to the Hausa majority.

Niger is essentially an Islamic society, having an 80% Muslim majority. Women have, on the whole, only limited rights and restricted access to education.

***Testing boating poles in the market** at Ayorou on the River Niger, the country's only major permanent watercourse.*

POLITICS

1998

President Mahamane Ousmane

THE STATE OF THE PARTIES

National Assembly 83 members

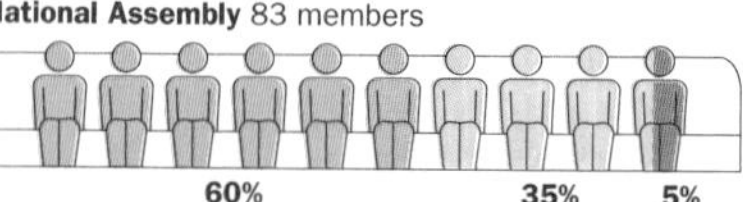

AFC = Alliance of the Forces of Change (composed of: CDS = Social Democratic Convention, PNDS = Niger Party for Unity and Democracy, ANDP = Niger Alliance for Democracy and Progress, PPN–RDA = Nigerian Progressive Party – African Democratic Rally, and two others) **MNSD** = National Movement for a Development Society **Other** = Democratic Union of Progressive Forces, Union of Democratic and Progressive Patriots

The death of the military dictator President Seyni Kountché in 1987 opened the way for the pro-democracy protests of 1990, led by students and the trade unions.

Amadou Cheiffou's interim government successfully contained a rearguard action by the military in 1992 and ran multiparty elections in 1993. The winning CDS and other parties have now forged a strong alliance (the AFC), but economic decline and a rebellion by the Tuaregs in the north are testing its permanence.

President Mahamane Ousmane is the first Hausa to lead the country.

WORLD AFFAIRS

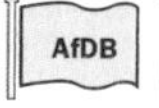

Relations with Libya and Algeria are sensitive, as Niger suspects they may be giving the Tuaregs support. The spillover into Niger of refugees loyal to Chad's ousted President Habré causes tension. Links with Nigeria will be strengthened now that Niger has a Hausa president.

AID

$376m (receipts)

Down 4% in 1991

Almost all development is aid-funded. France is the principal donor, followed by the IMF and Arab funds, and a little from Ivory Coast and Nigeria.

DEFENSE

$21m

Up 22% in 1989

Having withdrawn from politics, the military's role is now the active suppression of the Tuareg rebellion.

NIGER

Total Area : 1 267 000 sq. km (489 188 sq. miles)

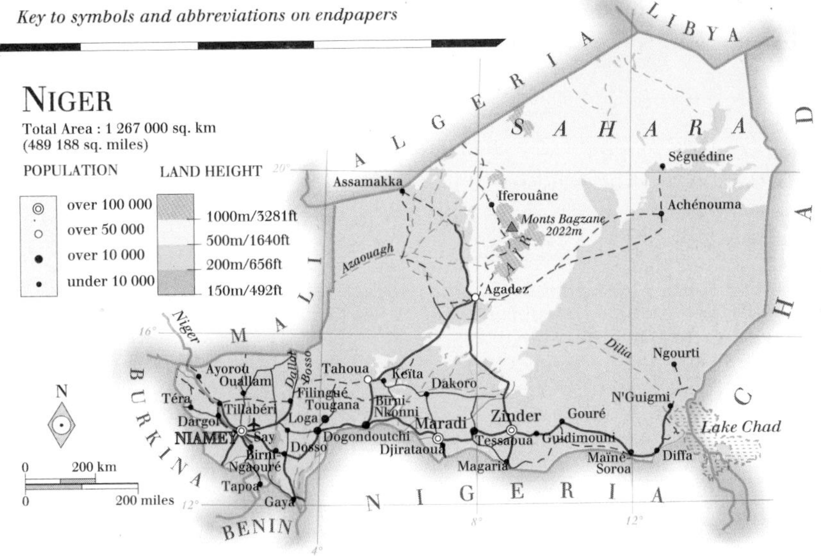

CHRONOLOGY

The powerful Islamic Sokoto Empire dissolved as the French took Niger over between 1883 and 1901.

- ❑ **1958** Autonomous republic within French community.
- ❑ **1960** Independence. Hamani Diori's one-party PPN state.
- ❑ **1968** French open uranium mines.
- ❑ **1973** Drought; 60% of livestock die; no harvest for two years.
- ❑ **1974** Military coup. Gen. Kountché bans political parties.
- ❑ **1976** First trade-balance surplus.
- ❑ **1984** New drought; River Niger dries up for first time in history. Uranium boom ends.
- ❑ **1987** Kountché dies. Gen. Saibou eases transition to democracy.
- ❑ **1990** New constitution drawn up. Tuareg rebellion becomes serious.
- ❑ **1993** Democratic elections.

ECONOMICS

 $2.3bn

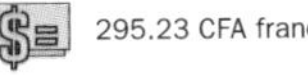 295.23 CFA francs

SCORE CARD

❑ WORLD GNP RANKING	135th
❑ GNP PER CAPITA	$280
❑ BALANCE OF PAYMENTS	$35m
❑ INFLATION	–7.8%
❑ UNEMPLOYMENT	47%

STRENGTHS

Vast uranium deposits; a few other minerals. Traditional Sahelian sense of community.

WEAKNESSES

Aid-dependent. Collapse of uranium prices in 1980s created large debt burden. Few other important minerals. Only 3% of land can be cultivated. Crops are low in value. Frequent droughts.

EXPORTS

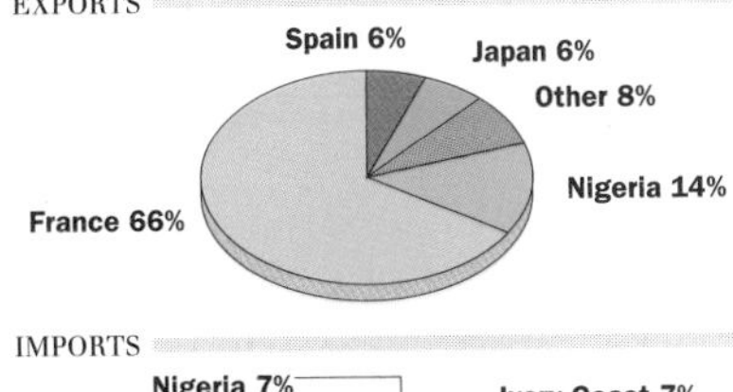

IMPORTS

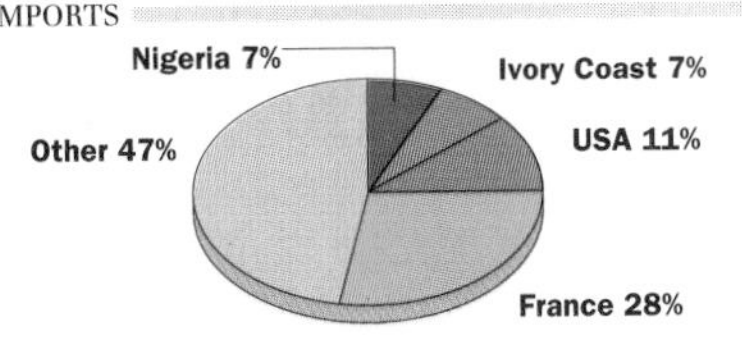

ENVIRONMENT

 8% (7% partially protected)

 Donor-funded afforestation programs

Serious droughts are increasing the rate of desertification, the problem that overrides all others in Niger.

MEDIA

 The 1992 constitution guarantees freedom of expression, but there is still an official press

PUBLISHING AND BROADCAST MEDIA

 There is 1 daily newspaper, *Le Sahel*, published by the government, and a small, influential independent press since 1990

 1 state-owned service

 1 state-owned service

The BBC World Service's Hausa programing is more influential than local French short-wave radio.

CRIME

 Niger does not publish prison figures

 Crime levels are fairly constant from year to year

Crime levels are low, although drought and Tuareg unrest have led to banditry. Smuggling to and from Nigeria is seen simply as part of the informal economy.

EDUCATION

 28%

Local languages are emphasized more strongly than in most Francophone countries. School attendance is only 30%.

RESOURCES

 163m kwh (capacity 600,000 kw)

 Not an oil producer and has no refineries

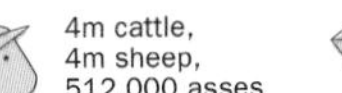 4m cattle, 4m sheep, 512,000 asses

 Uranium, tin, gypsum, coal, salt, tungsten, iron, calcium

During the 1970s, Niger's uranium mines boomed, but output collapsed in the 1980s when world prices slumped. Other mining is small-scale and oil reserves are not commercially viable. The uranium boom quadrupled electricity needs, half of which are now met by Nigeria's Kainji Dam on the Niger River.

HEALTH

 1 per 38,500 people

 Malaria, tuberculosis, meningitis, measles, malnutrition

In spite of progress in rural health care, immunization, malaria control and child nutrition are still limited.

WEALTH

 The Tuaregs are the lowest-paid social group.

CONSUMER GOODS OWNERSHIP

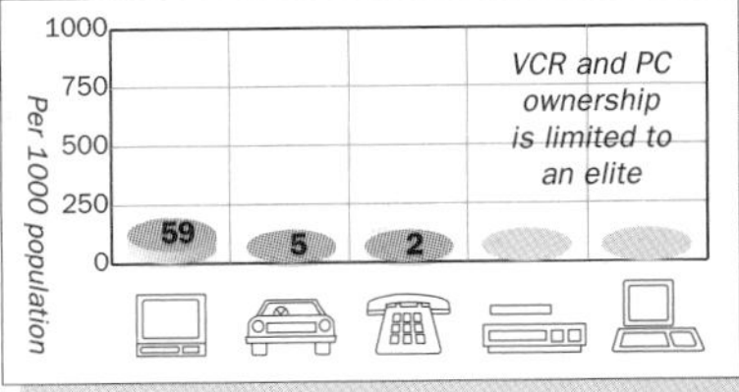

Traditional egalitarianism in Sahelian life works against private enrichment, but uranium wealth is altering values.

WORLD RANKING

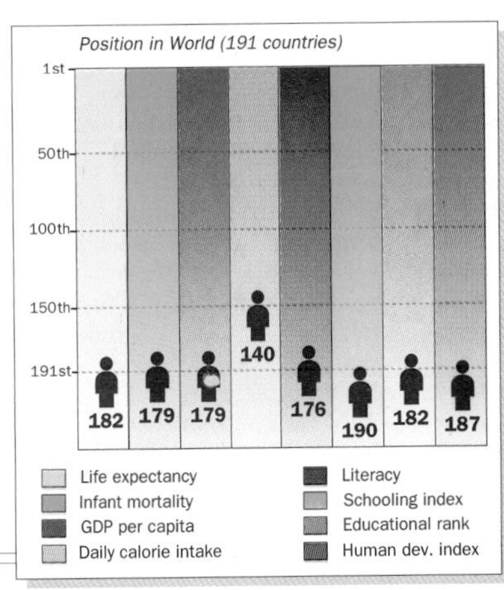

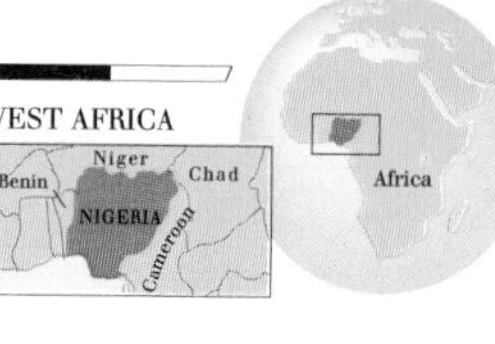

NIGERIA

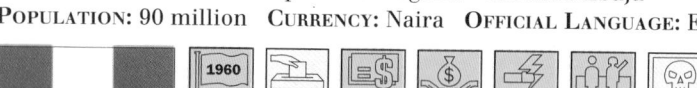

Official Name: Federal Republic of Nigeria **Capital:** Abuja
Population: 90 million **Currency:** Naira **Official Language:** English

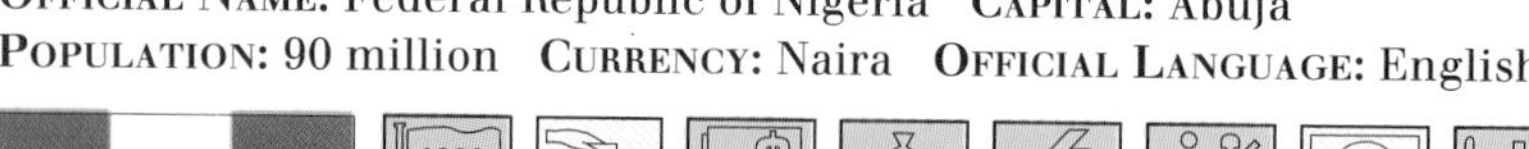

AFRICA'S MOST POPULOUS state, Nigeria gained its independence from Britain in 1960. Bordered by Benin, Niger, Chad and Cameroon, its terrain varies from tropical rainforest and swamps in the south to savanna in the north. Nigeria has been dominated by military governments since 1966. A promised return to civilian rule was aborted in 1993 when the army refused to accept the results of presidential elections. Nigeria is OPEC's fourth-largest oil producer, but it has experienced a fall in living standards since the 1970s, when it saw itself as the most dynamic African economy.

***Village beneath Tengele Peak** in Bauchi State. A large proportion of Nigerians live from subsistence agriculture.*

CLIMATE

WEATHER CHART

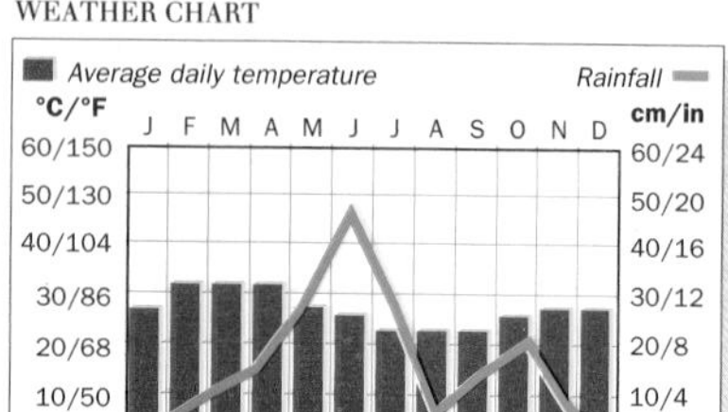

The south is hot, rainy and humid for most of the year. The arid north experiences only one, uncomfortably humid, rainy season – from May to September. Its very hot dry season is marked by the dust-laden *harmattan* wind. The Jos Plateau and the eastern highlands are cooler than the rest of Nigeria. Forcados, in the Niger delta, gets the most rain with 148 in. a year.

COMMUNICATIONS

Murtala Muhammed, Lagos 2.05m passengers

48 ships 698,300 dwt

THE TRANSPORTATION NETWORK

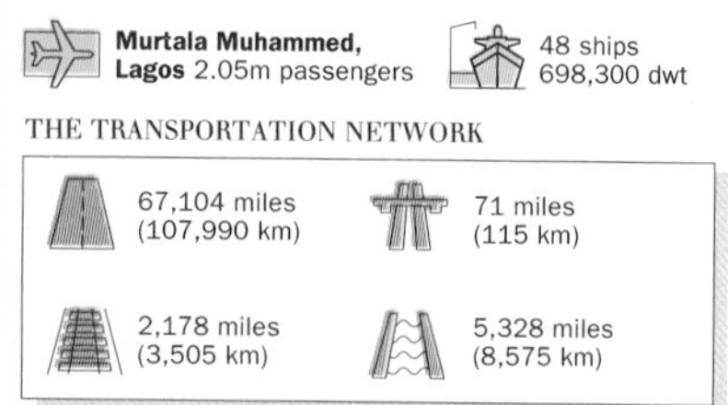

Nigeria relies almost entirely on road transportation. During the oil-boom years of the 1970s, new long-distance road links were built. Now that revenues have shrunk, maintenance is the major problem. The road accident rate is among the worst in the world. The small railroad system, built for the once-thriving bulk trade, is today very slow and badly maintained. Nigerian Airways' international operations have been privatized as Air Nigeria. The internal air market has shrunk since the prosperous years of the 1970s.

TOURISM

160,470 visitors

Down 47% in 1990

Nigeria has attempted to build a tourist industry, but with little success. Year-round tropical temperatures and poor infrastructure have limited its growth. The major deterrent to visitors, however, is crime. Travel can be hazardous, and Lagos has one of the world's highest crime rates.

MAIN OVERSEAS ARRIVALS

	% of total arrivals
Benin	27%
Niger	26%
Ghana	14%
Togo	10%
Mali	3%
Other	20%

0 10 20 30 40
% of total arrivals

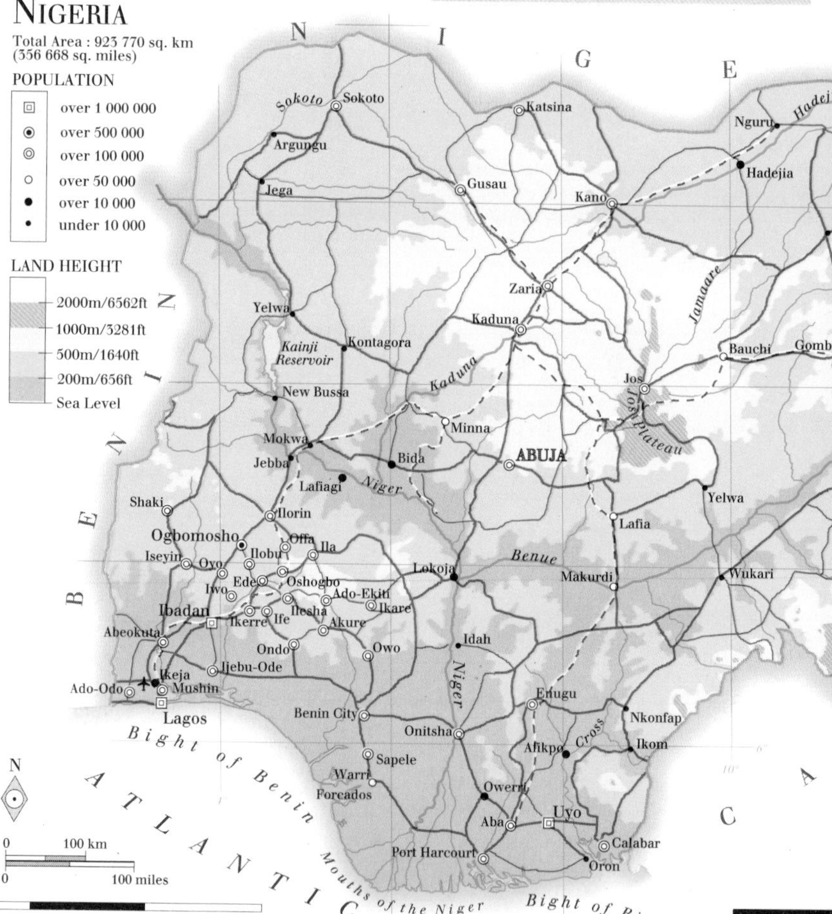

PEOPLE

Hausa, English Creole, Yoruba, Ibo, English

249 people per sq. mile

THE URBAN/RURAL POPULATION SPLIT

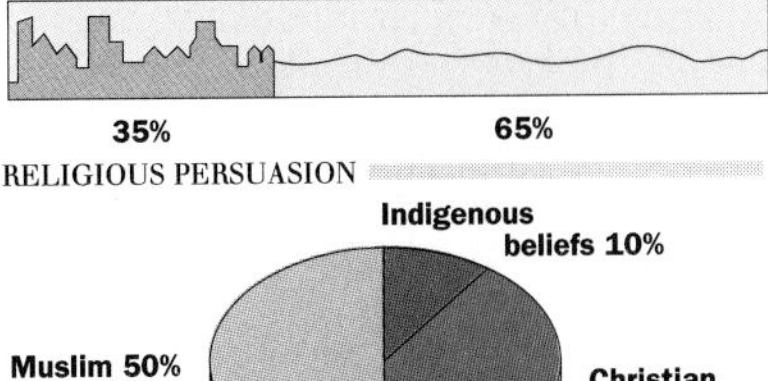

RELIGIOUS PERSUASION

Indigenous beliefs 10%
Muslim 50%
Christian 40%

ETHNIC MAKEUP

245 (est) other ethnic groups 35%
Hausa-Fulani, Yoruba and Ibo 65%

In recent years, Nigeria has largely managed to contain the passions generated by the ethnic, religious and language differences that characterize its people. There is intense rivalry between the three main ethnic groups, as well as among the 245 smaller ones. Members of one group tend to blame those of another for their problems, rather than the broader political system. Religion is a particular source of tension. Outbreaks of communal violence, particularly in the north, are frequently attributable to clashes between Muslim fundamentalists and Christian proselytizers. Except in the Islamic north, women have traditionally possessed independent economic status. In recent years they have, however, been subjected to some prejudice in professional circles.

POPULATION AGE BREAKDOWN

% of population by age group

	1960	1970	1980	1990	2000
65+	2.3%	2.4%	2.5%	2.5%	2.7%
15–64	52.3%	51.3%	50.9%	50.1%	51.3%
0–14	45.4%	46.3%	46.6%	47.4%	46%

POLITICS

Uncertain

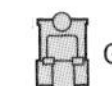
General Sanni Abacha

THE STATE OF THE PARTIES

Provisional Ruling Council

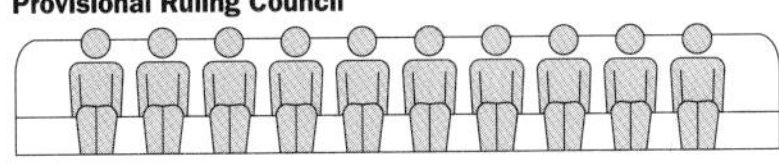

The National Assembly was dissolved in November 1993 after the resumption of military rule. Government is now by a Provisional Ruling Council of senior military figures

Nigeria is a federation, currently of 30 states, controlled by a military dictatorship. The present regime assumed formal control in November 1993 – in the wake of the aborted August elections – after dissolving the National Assembly.

MAIN POLITICAL ISSUES

Corruption

International agencies have identified corruption as a major cause of Nigeria's debt levels. Bureaucrats commonly regard holding office as a source of lucrative kickbacks from the granting of contracts. This attitude is raising anti-government feeling.

Instability

There are fears, particularly within the Western-dominated business community, that popular resentment toward the military's determination to cling to power will create serious long-term political instability.

PROFILE

A program to restore civilian government began in 1987 under President Babangida, but came to a halt in August 1993 when he annulled the results of the presidential election. Protests abroad and strikes at home persuaded Babangida to give up the presidency, and a "civilian" interim government was set up by the military.

However, the military soon resumed control under General Sanni Abacha. The interim government was swept away, along with the two political parties set up to contest the elections. General Abacha set up a Provisional Ruling Council and fired state governors, replacing them with military officers. Political activity was banned.

General Ibrahim Babangida. *Nigeria's president from 1985 to 1993.*

Moshood Abiola. *Won 1993 elections, but was prevented from taking power.*

CHRONOLOGY

Before formal colonization by the British, not begun until 1861, Nigeria was a collection of African states owing their considerable wealth to trans-Saharan and transatlantic trade. During the 18th century the principal commodity was slaves: over 15,000 people were exported annually from the Bight of Benin and another 15,000 from the Bight of Biafra.

- ❑ **1885** George Goldie's Royal Niger Company given responsibility by the UK government for the British sphere of influence along the Niger and Benue rivers. British armed forces begin coercing local rulers into accepting British rule.
- ❑ **1897** West Africa Frontier Force (WAFF) established; subjugation of the north begins.
- ❑ **1898** The Royal Niger Company's charter revoked.
- ❑ **1900** British Protectorate of Northern Nigeria established.
- ❑ **1906** Lagos incorporated into the Protectorate of Southern Nigeria.
- ❑ **1914** Protectorates of Northern and Southern Nigeria joined to form colony of Nigeria.
- ❑ **1951** Elections. Nationalists win the eastern, western and northern regions.
- ❑ **1954** New constitution establishes federal system of government.
- ❑ **1957–1958** Constitutional conferences establish timetable for independence.
- ❑ **1960** Independence. Nigeria established as a federation.
- ❑ **1961** Northern part of UK-administered UN Trust Territory of the Cameroons incorporated as part of Nigeria's northern region.
- ❑ **1966** January: first military coup, led by Maj.-Gen. Ironsi. Leading politicians murdered, including Sir Tafawa Balewa, the federal prime minister. July: counter-coup mounted by group of northern army officers believing Ironsi was representing only Eastern Region interests. Ironsi murdered. Thousands of Ibo in northern region massacred.
- ❑ **1967–1970** Civil war. Lt.-Col. Ojukwu calls for secession of oil-rich east under the new name Biafra. Over one million Nigerians die before secessionists are defeated by federal forces.
- ❑ **1970** General Gowon in power. New constitution creating 12 states from existing three.
- ❑ **1975** Gowon toppled in bloodless coup. Brigadier Murtala Mohammed takes power.
- ❑ **1976** Murtala Mohammed murdered in abortive coup.

➪

CHRONOLOGY *continued*

- **1978** Political parties legalized, on condition that they represent national, not tribal, interests.
- **1979** Elections won by Alhaji Shehu Shagari and National Party of Nigeria (NPN), marking return to civilian government.
- **1983** September: elections won again by Shagari and NPN. December: military coup. Maj.-Gen. Mohammed Buhari heads Supreme Military Council.
- **1985** Maj.-Gen. Ibrahim Babangida takes over in bloodless coup, promising a return to democracy.
- **1992** Abuja becomes capital.
- **1993** August: postponed presidential election, won by Moshood Abiola, annulled by Babangida. International protest and strikes. Babangida resigns from presidency; military sets up Interim National Government (ING) headed by Chief Adegunle Shonekan. November: ING dissolved. Military, headed by Gen. Sanni Abacha, takes over. Provisional Ruling Council set up.

WORLD AFFAIRS

Nigeria's overseas ambitions have expanded and contracted with its oil revenues. The military government of the 1970s – when oil prices were high – saw itself as Africa's leading voice. It recognized the Marxist government in Angola, was an enthusiastic sponsor of ECOWAS, and strongly opposed apartheid in South Africa. With the fall in world oil prices after 1981, this ambition was trimmed. Relations with South Africa have been restored, now that political change there is under way.

The main foreign policy concern is Nigeria's key role in the ECOWAS force that invaded war-torn Liberia in 1990. Under Babangida, Nigeria also took the lead in planning for an African Common Market, with a target date of 2025. Nigeria now has one of the non-permanent African seats on the UN Security Council.

AID

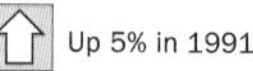

Nigeria's debt rocketed with the 1981 drop in world oil prices, and turned Nigeria from an aid donor into a major receiver of World Bank assistance. Several of the major aid agencies have expressed concern that the government may have understated its oil revenues to gain more aid.

DEFENSE

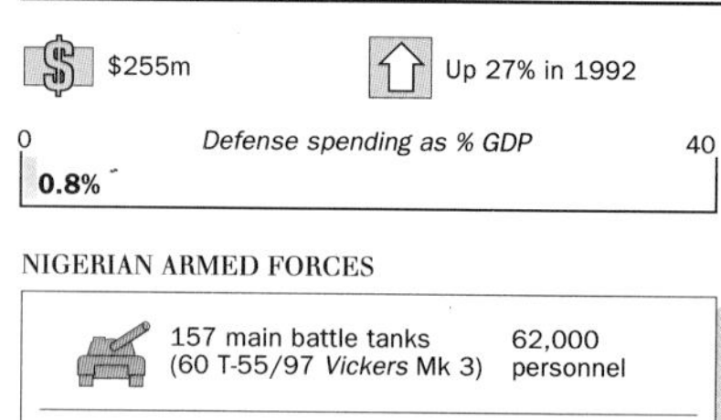

NIGERIAN ARMED FORCES

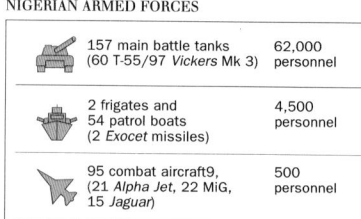

Army	157 main battle tanks (60 T-55/97 *Vickers* Mk 3)	62,000 personnel
Navy	2 frigates and 54 patrol boats (2 *Exocet* missiles)	4,500 personnel
Air force	95 combat aircraft9, (21 *Alpha Jet*, 22 MiG, 15 *Jaguar*)	500 personnel
Missiles	None	

The defense establishment in Nigeria suffers from problems caused by corruption. During Babangida's rule (1985–1993), most of the air force's prestige jets were grounded, as money for spare parts was diverted into senior officers' bank accounts. Soldiers' salaries have been steadily declining in real terms in recent years, barrack conditions have deteriorated and morale is low. However, the November 1993 restoration of military government by Defense Minister General Sanni Abacha – a key player in both the 1983 and 1985 coups – is likely to encourage expectations of improved conditions among the army rank and file.

ECONOMICS

SCORE CARD

- World GNP Ranking 57th
- GNP per Capita $311
- Balance of Payments $1.49bn
- Inflation 44.6%
- Unemployment .... *Widespread underemployment*

EXPORTS

Italy 8%
Netherlands 11%
USA 35%
France 15%
Other 31%

IMPORTS

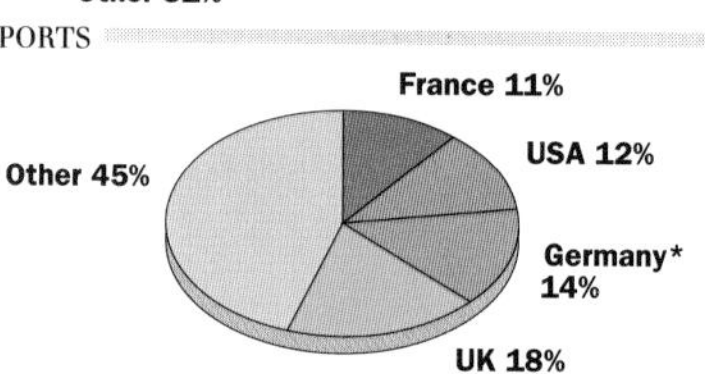

ECONOMIC PERFORMANCE INDICATOR

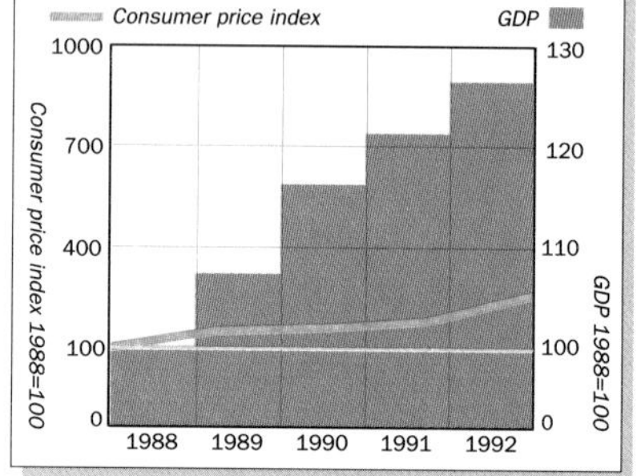

Strengths

One of world's top oil producers at 1.9 million b/d. Vast reserves of natural gas, still only partly exploited. Almost self-sufficient in food. Strong entrepreneurial class. Large domestic market of 90 million people.

Weaknesses

Over-dependence since the 1970s on oil, which accounts for 90% of export earnings and 80% of government revenue, and encourages massive state inefficiency. Advantages of a large domestic market mitigated by low per capita purchasing power and high unit transport costs. Entrepreneurs focus on trade rather than production. Only cocoa remains of Nigeria's traditional agricultural exports; it was once a major producer of tropical vegetables and fruit.

Profile

The economy has been characterized by massive government spending and the running up of debts which could not be serviced after the 1981 oil price fall. Led by the IMF, creditors want major cuts in spending – especially on loss-making public sector companies – and subsidies. Fuel subsidies alone are estimated to have cost $2.4 billion a year. Such changes are politically fraught, however. When gasoline prices were raised 400% in November 1993, there were nationwide strikes.

NIGERIA : MAJOR BUSINESSES

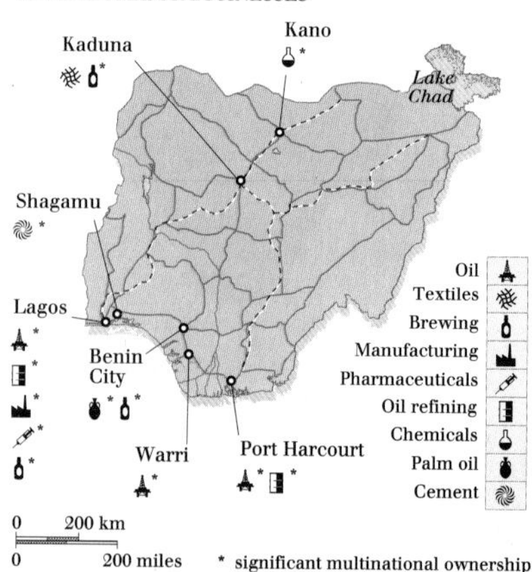

RESOURCES

9.9bn kwh (capacity 4m kw)

1.9m b/d (reserves 17,899,820,000 bbl)

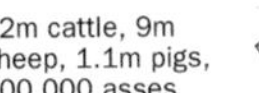
12m cattle, 9m sheep, 1.1m pigs, 700,000 asses

Oil, natural gas, coal, tin, iron, bauxite, columbite, lead

ELECTRICITY GENERATION

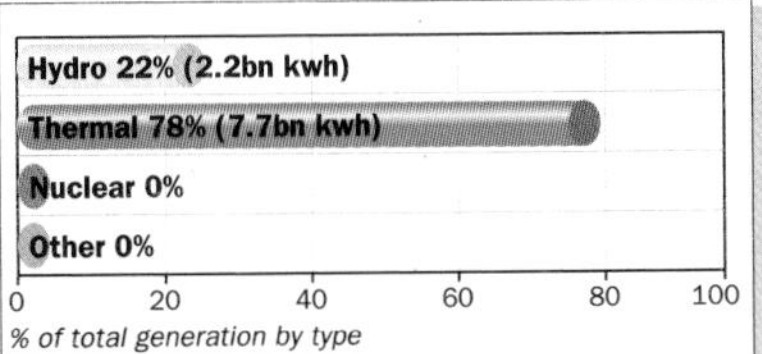

Oil has been Nigeria's main resource since the 1970s. Government policy is to increase output from 1.9 million b/d (7.5% of OPEC output) to 2.5 million b/d. Domestic demand is 300,000 b/d, much of it smuggled to neighboring countries. Nigeria's vast gas deposits are still under-exploited. The state retains 60% control of the oil and gas industry. Shell is the main foreign shareholder, but most oil multinationals are represented.

Nigeria has sizeable iron ore deposits. These are not yet utilized in the state-run steel industry; imported ore is used instead. Bauxite deposits are also currently under-exploited. There are, however, plans for establishing an aluminum industry.

NIGERIA : LAND USE

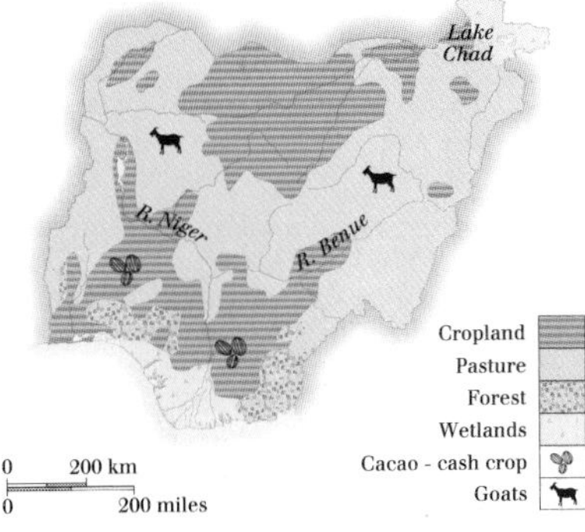

ENVIRONMENT

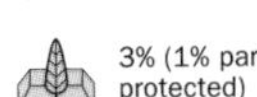
3% (1% partially protected)

No progress in controlling oilfield pollution

ENVIRONMENTAL TREATIES

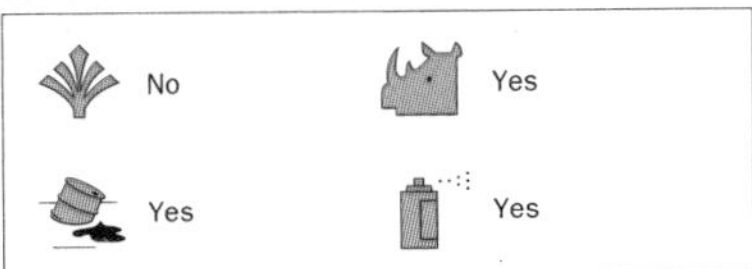

Oil industry pollution in Niger delta is a major local concern. In 1992, Shell recorded 86 protest attacks against its plants. Before the discovery of a highly toxic cargo in Lagos in 1988, Nigeria was a regular dumping ground for dangerous European chemical waste.

MEDIA

Foreign journalists have been expelled for questioning corruption in government

Nigerians are avid newspaper readers and the press is traditionally one of Africa's liveliest. However, the new military regime has made clear its unwillingness to tolerate criticism. There are over 20 English-language current-affairs periodicals.

PUBLISHING AND BROADCAST MEDIA

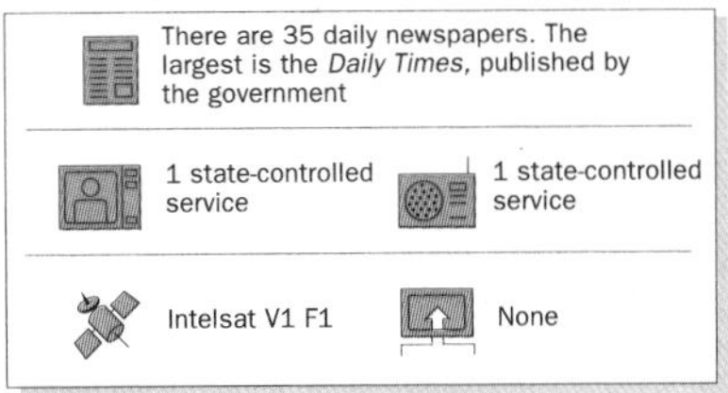

There are 35 daily newspapers. The largest is the *Daily Times*, published by the government
1 state-controlled service
1 state-controlled service
Intelsat V1 F1
None

CRIME

Nigeria does not publish prison figures

Rising. One of the highest crime rates in the world

CRIME RATES

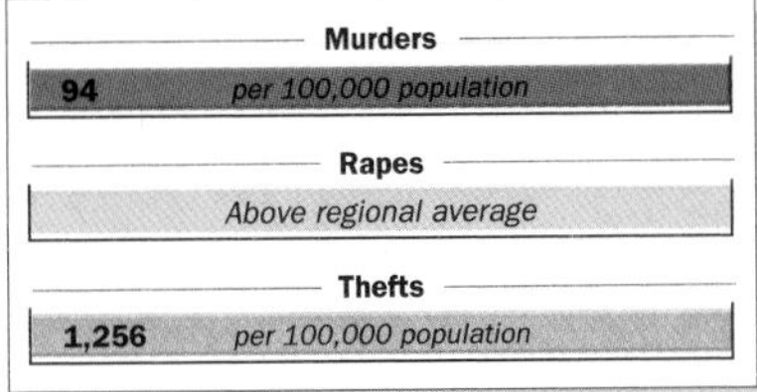

The military government frequently uses *ad hoc* tribunals for politically sensitive cases. Nigeria has one of the highest crime rates in the world. Murder often accompanies even minor burglaries. Corruption pervades the bureaucracy; the provision of kickbacks to supporters is considered routine rather than a crime. Rich Nigerians live in high-security compounds, equipped with electric fencing and patrolled by armed guards.

HEALTH

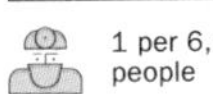
1 per 6,134 people

Yellow fever, malaria, trachoma, yaws

0 — Health spending as % GNP — 25

0.2%

The health service is concentrated in urban areas and mostly aimed at richer Nigerians. Modern medicine is not available to those living in rural areas. Health provision, with other public services, has suffered from the crisis in government revenues.

EDUCATION

51%

0 — Education spending as % GNP — 25

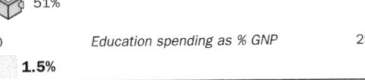

1.5%

THE EDUCATION SYSTEM

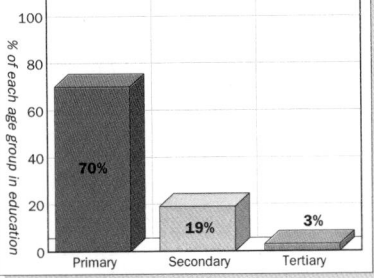

Education has suffered from the government's massive debt repayment burden. During the oil-boom years, Nigeria concentrated on creating 31 universities with prestigious medical and science schools. However, standards in primary education, which has not received the same level of investment, have fallen since the 1970s.

WEALTH

International company finance officer, 200,000 naira per year; polytechnic principal lecturer, 24,000–41,000 naira per year

CONSUMER GOODS OWNERSHIP

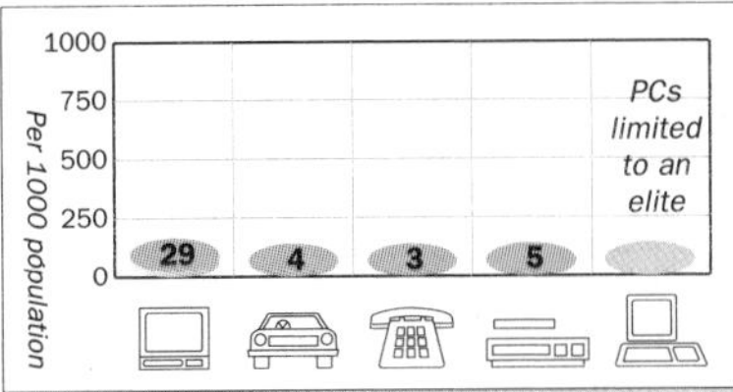

Nigerians with access to the rich pickings of political office spent on a massive scale during the oil-boom – on Maseratis, Mercedes and overseas education for their children. Much was financed by government loans. Habits have not changed with the fall in oil revenues: borrowing has simply grown.

WORLD RANKING

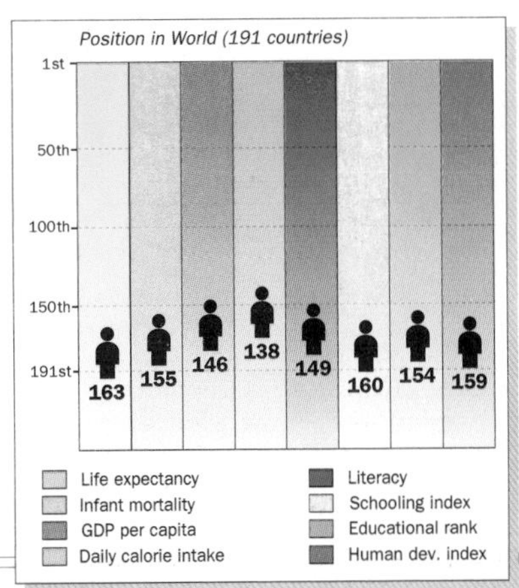

N

NORTH KOREA

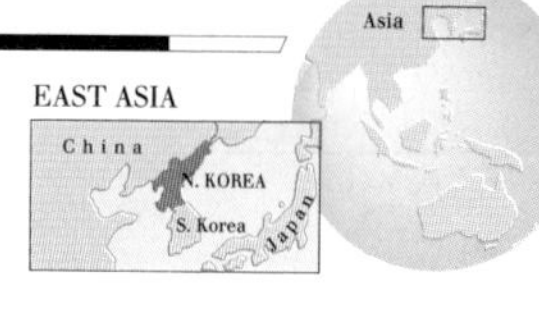

OFFICIAL NAME: Democratic People's Republic of Korea **CAPITAL:** Pyongyang
POPULATION: 22.6 million **CURRENCY:** Won **OFFICIAL LANGUAGE:** Korean

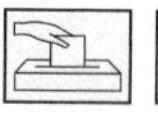
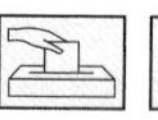

NORTH KOREA COMPRISES the northern half of the Korean peninsula and is separated from the US-dominated south close to the 38th parallel. Much of the country is mountainous; the Chaeryŏng and Pyongyang plains in the southwest are the most fertile regions. Established as an independent communist republic in 1948, North Korea remains largely isolated from the outside world. Its economy, starved of development capital, is now facing severe difficulties.

CLIMATE

WEATHER CHART

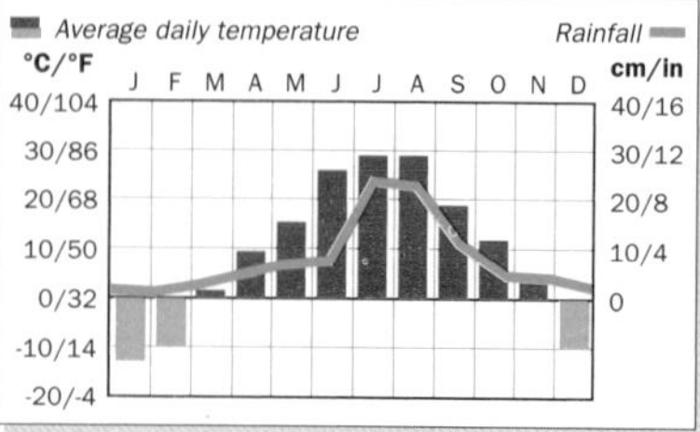

North Korea has a typically continental climate. Winters in the north can be extreme, with several months of snow.

COMMUNICATIONS

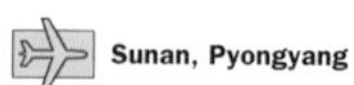
Sunan, Pyongyang

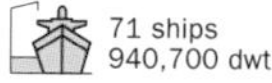
71 ships 940,700 dwt

THE TRANSPORTATION NETWORK

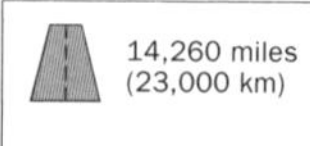

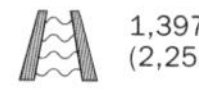

14,260 miles (23,000 km)	219 miles (354 km)
3,128 miles (5,045 km)	1,397 miles (2,253 km)

North Korea relies heavily on the antiquated railroad network built by the Japanese during their occupation. The Pyongyang–Kaesŏng motorway, completed in 1992, is open only to very limited, officially approved traffic.

TOURISM

Tourism largely banned by government

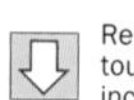
Restrictions on tourism recently increased

MAIN OVERSEAS ARRIVALS

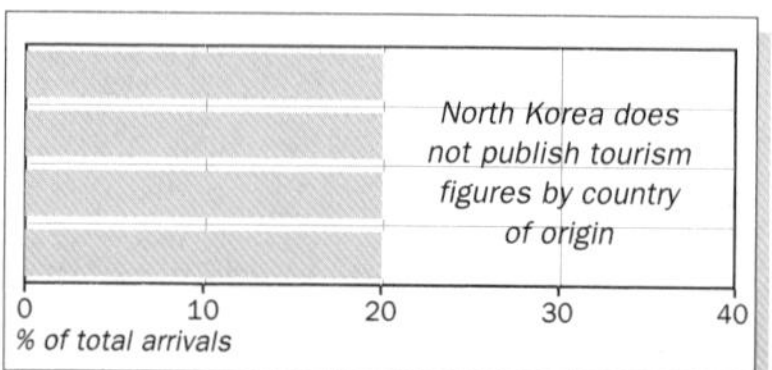

The ban on Western tourists, who had been permitted to visit the country since 1985, was reimposed in 1993.

Rice paddy. *The hot, wet summers are ideal for rice growing. Most farms are run as cooperatives.*

PEOPLE

Korean, Chinese

469 people per sq. mile

THE URBAN/RURAL POPULATION SPLIT

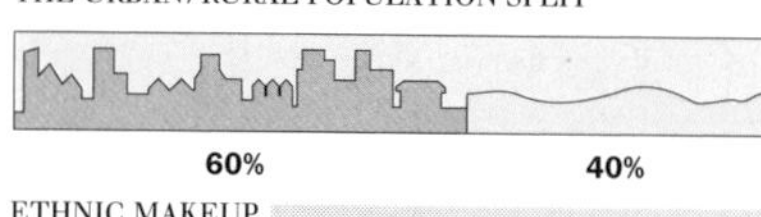

ETHNIC MAKEUP

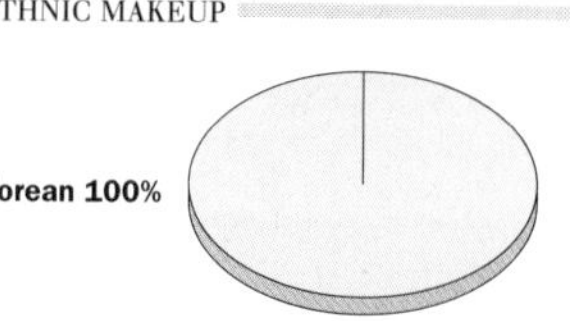

North Korea operates a strict "estate" system, by which the population is classed according to three categories: loyal, wavering and hostile. Inclusion in the first category is a prerequisite for advancement. Those deemed hostile – usually Christians and the children of landlords or of Koreans who fled to the South – have barely any rights. People live severely regulated lives. Divorce is non-existent and extra-marital sex highly frowned upon. Women form 57% of the work force, but are also expected to run the home; it is not uncommon for them to rise at 4 a.m., and end their working day at 7 p.m. From an early age, children are looked after by an extensive system of state-run nurseries. The privileged lifestyle of the communist elite – numbering only about 200,000 – is a source of considerable popular resentment.

POLITICS

Not applicable

President Kim Jong Il

THE STATE OF THE PARTIES

Supreme People's Assembly 687 members

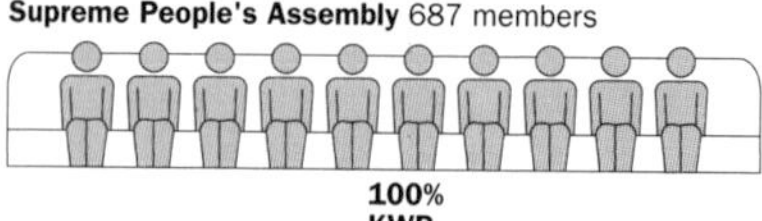

KWP = Korean Workers' Party

The KWP, with a membership of some three million, is the only legal party and its influence is felt in all parts of life. Membership is essential for advancement. Kim Il Sung, the world's longest-serving political leader, died in 1994. He had presided over the party, carefully fostering his "father of the proletariat" image, for almost 50 years. The main question now is how his son, Kim Jong Il, will handle the leadership. To date, the personality cults and concentration of power in the two men have not been challenged, and the army has remained loyal to the regime. The accession of Kim Jong Il could, however, provide a catalyst for political and economic change.

WORLD AFFAIRS

The worldwide collapse of communism has isolated North Korea. Its foreign policy is now in flux. In 1991, it joined the UN, and yet in 1992 and 1993 denied officials from the International Atomic Energy Agency (IAEA) access to suspected nuclear bomb manufacturing sites. In 1994, North Korea withdrew from the IAEA altogether. Similarly, talks have been held with South Korea about reunification, yet North and South Korean forces remain in a state of alert across the border. The 1992 recognition of South Korea by China was a major blow to North Korea, resulting in a reduction in Chinese aid, and the implicit view from Beijing that South Korea would be the dominant partner in future.

AID

$8m (receipts)

Aid has collapsed since 1991

Vital aid from the Soviet Union ended in 1991 and China ceased "friendship supplies" in 1993. Despite official denials, the aid-dependent economy has suffered badly.

N

NORTH KOREA

Total Area : 120 540 sq. km (46 540 sq. miles)

DEFENSE

 $2.8bn  Up 15% in 1992

North Korea is suspected of having a fast-track nuclear bomb program. Its advanced arms industry supplies missiles to Iran, among others.

ECONOMICS

 $29.7bn  2.15 won

SCORE CARD

- ❏ WORLD GNP RANKING 54th
- ❏ GNP PER CAPITA $1,390
- ❏ BALANCE OF PAYMENTS ....*Closed economy;*
- ❏ INFLATION ....*does not publish*
- ❏ UNEMPLOYMENT ....*any figures*

STRENGTHS

Until 1970, North Korea had a higher GNP per capita than the South. Other than minerals, strengths are now few.

WEAKNESSES

GNP has been declining by 5% a year since 1990. The loss of Soviet and Chinese aid is a major blow.

EXPORTS/IMPORTS

North Korea's main trading partners are Russia, China and Japan

RESOURCES

 53.5bn kwh (capacity 9.5m kw)

Not an oil producer; refines 42,000 b/cd

 3.2m pigs, 1.3m cattle, 380,000 sheep

 Coal, iron, lead, copper, zinc, tin, silver, gold, uranium

A shortage of electricity (blackouts are frequent) remains a major problem; a Chernobyl-type nuclear reactor remains half-built for want of Soviet aid. North Korea is relatively rich in metals, producing uranium for its nuclear program. It is also the world's ninth largest silver producer.

ENVIRONMENT

 0.5% (0.1% partially protected)

No access to state environmental information

Excessive use of fertilizers and unchecked pollution from heavy industry are the major problems.

MEDIA

Total censorship. No foreign publications permitted. Radios have fixed dials

PUBLISHING AND BROADCAST MEDIA

There are 6 daily newspapers, including the leading *Rodong Shinmun*, the party newspaper, and *Minju Choson*

1 limited state-owned service

2 state-owned services

North Korean TV consists mostly of musical shows praising the qualities of Kim Il Sung and Kim Jong Il.

CRIME

 North Korea does not publish prison figures 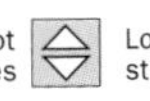 Low level of violent street crime

Corruption at all levels in dealings with the state is the major problem. The criminal code is weighted to protect the state against "subversion," rather than the rights of the individual. North Korea has a very poor human rights record and a *gulag* of over 100,000 "subversives," where whole families are sent along with those accused and where torture is routine.

CHRONOLOGY

North Korea was separated from the South after World War II.

- ❏ **1950** Korean War, as North Korea invades the South. UN troops drive invasion back to 38th parallel.
- ❏ **1953** Armistice ends Korean War.
- ❏ **1958** Kim Il Sung establishes effective absolutism.
- ❏ **1994** Withdrawal from IAEA. Kim Il Sung dies; replaced by son.

EDUCATION

95%

North Korea claims to have created over one million "intellectuals." Kim Il Sung, Pyongyang, is the only university.

HEALTH

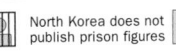

1 per 417 people

Heart diseases, cancer, digestive diseases

The free health service has raised life expectancy. The showpiece Pyongyang Maternity Hospital appears unused.

WEALTH

The 20% or so of the population classified as "hostile" live in remote areas, do the worst jobs and have little prospect of social advancement

CONSUMER GOODS OWNERSHIP

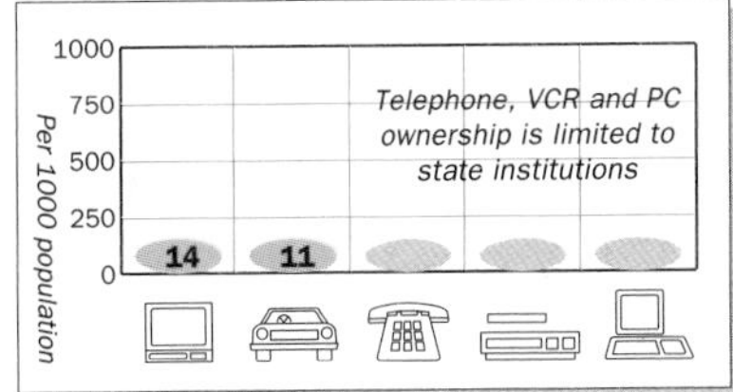

An elite within the KWP lives well, with access to specialist shops and consumer goods such as VCRs. Both private car and telephone ownership are forbidden.

WORLD RANKING

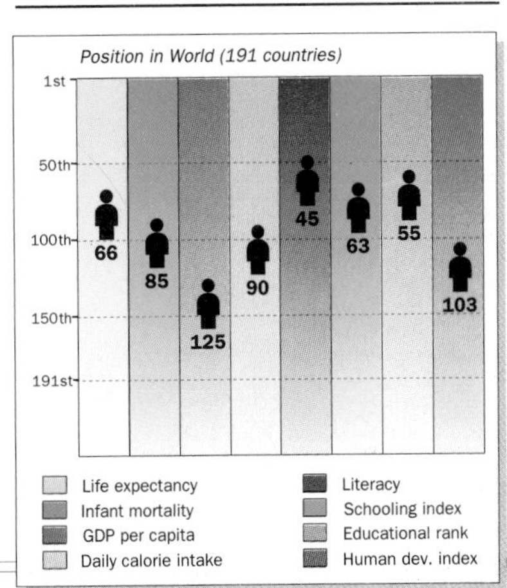

N

NORWAY

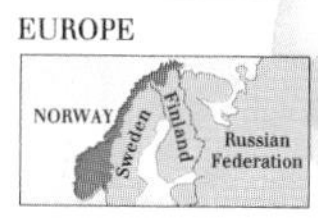

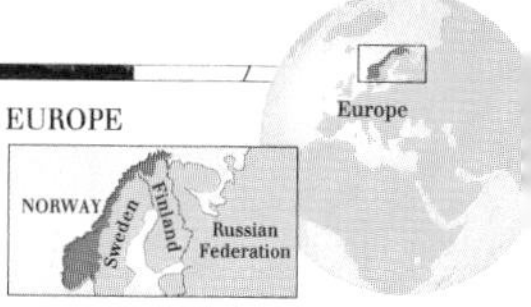

OFFICIAL NAME: Kingdom of Norway **CAPITAL:** Oslo **POPULATION:** 4.3 million
CURRENCY: Norwegian krone **OFFICIAL LANGUAGE:** Norwegian **OVERSEAS TERRITORIES:** 3

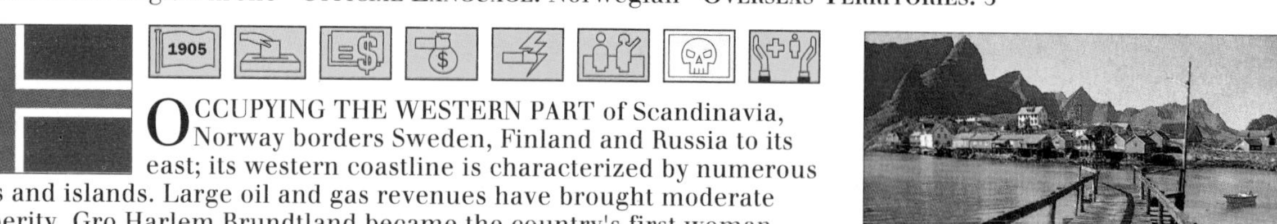

OCCUPYING THE WESTERN PART of Scandinavia, Norway borders Sweden, Finland and Russia to its east; its western coastline is characterized by numerous fjords and islands. Large oil and gas revenues have brought moderate prosperity. Gro Harlem Brundtland became the country's first woman prime minister in 1981. Despite the Europe-wide recession, Norway has managed to keep its unemployment rate below 6%. The duty of government to create conditions that enable every person to find work is enshrined in the constitution.

The village of Reine on Moskenesøya, 99 miles inside the Arctic Circle in the Lofoten Islands is popular with summer visitors.

CLIMATE

WEATHER CHART

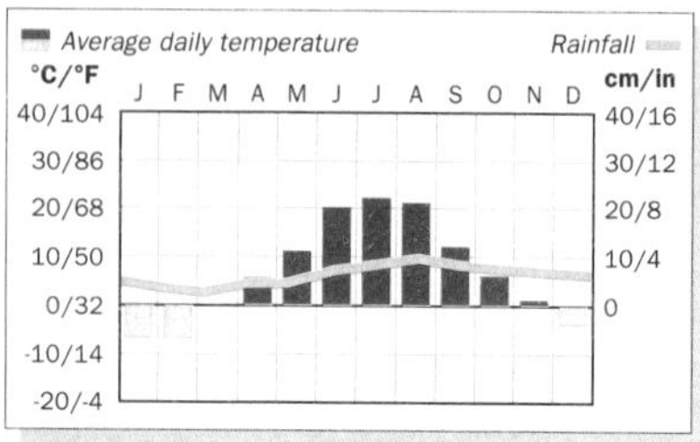

Average daily temperature — Rainfall

°C/°F — J F M A M J J A S O N D — cm/in

40/104, 30/86, 20/68, 10/50, 0/32, -10/14, -20/-4 — 40/16, 30/12, 20/8, 10/4, 0

Norway's entire west coast is kept ice-free by the warm Gulf Stream. It receives much more precipitation than the rest of the country; Bergen has a yearly average of 88 in. Norway enjoys the highest mean temperatures in Scandinavia, but in winter the temperature in Oslo can drop to–13°F.

ARCTIC OCEAN
BARENTS SEA
Magerøya
Hammerfest
Sørøya
Porsangen
Tana
Varangerfjorden
Kirkenes
Ringvassøy
Alta
Kvaløya
Tromsø
Karasjok
RUSSIAN FEDERATION
Senja
FINNMARKSVIDDA
Vesterålen
Andfjorden
Harstad
LAPLAND
FINLAND
Stamsund
Narvik
Lofoten
Vestfjorden
0 100 km
0 100 miles
Bodø
Arctic Circle
NORWEGIAN SEA
Mo
Mosjøen
Overhalla
Namsos
Trondheimsfjorden
Verdal
Steinkjer
Hitra
Trondheim
Stjørdal
Kristiansund
Støren
Molde
Ålesund
Oppdal
Røros
Ørsta
DOVREFJELL
Glomma
Glittertind 2470m
JOTUNHEIMEN
Hermansverk
Sognefjorden
Lillehammer
Gjøvik
Elverum
Voss
Gol
Hamar
Mjøsa
Stange
Bergen
Begna
Eidsvoll
Hardangerfjorden
Hønefoss
Kongsvinger
NORTH SEA
Haukeligrend
OSLO
Lillestrøm
Kongsberg
Drammen
Åkrehamn
Haugesund
Notodden
Horten
Moss
Oslofjorden
Boknafjorden
Stavanger
Skien
Sarpsborg
Sola
Sandnes
Porsgrunn
Halden
Otra
Larvik
Fredrikstad
Egersund
Sandefjord
Tønsberg
Arendal
Vennesla
Mandal
Kristiansand
Skagerrak
ATLANTIC OCEAN
SWEDEN

NORWAY

Total Area : 323 900 sq. km (125 060 sq. miles)

LAND HEIGHT

2000m/6562ft
1000m/3281ft
500m/1640ft
200m/656ft
Sea Level

POPULATION

over 100 000
over 50 000
over 10 000
under 10 000

COMMUNICATIONS

Fornebu Intl, Oslo 6.3m passengers

1,194 ships 36.52m dwt

THE TRANSPORTATION NETWORK

55,179 miles (88,800 km)

272 miles (437 km)

2,624 miles (4.223 km)

980 miles (1,577 km)

It has been impossible to extend rail links farther than Bodø, inside the Arctic Circle. To reach Lofoten or Narvik and beyond, the most common form of transportation is air. In 1988, Scandinavian Airlines Systems agreed that British Midland would take over some of SAS's UK–Norway direct routes.

The Royal Palace, Oslo, is situated near the national theater, at one end of the Karl Johanisgate, the city's main thoroughfare.

N

TOURISM

4.3m overnights. Norway does not record visitor numbers

Up 9% in 1992

Norway is a popular destination for visitors from Sweden, Germany, Denmark, the UK and the USA. Its winter tourism industry is based on skiing and has been boosted by the location of the 1994 Winter Olympics in Lillehammer. Boating along the fjords is popular with summer visitors. Areas within the Arctic Circle are a particular attraction in June, when tourists go in search of the midnight sun. Oslo has a reputation for good classical music and jazz. However, the strength of the krone and the high cost of living make Norway expensive.

MAIN OVERSEAS ARRIVALS

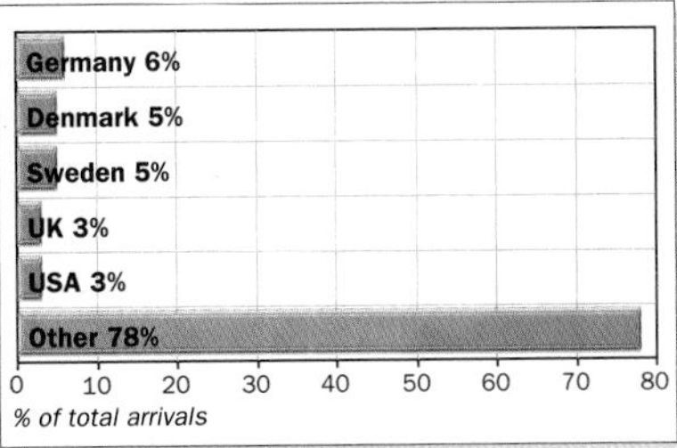

PEOPLE

Norwegian, (*Bokmå* "book language" and *Nynorsk* "new Norsk"), Lappish

34 people per sq. mile

THE URBAN/RURAL POPULATION SPLIT

75% 25%

RELIGIOUS PERSUASION

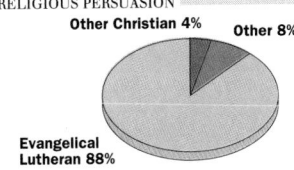

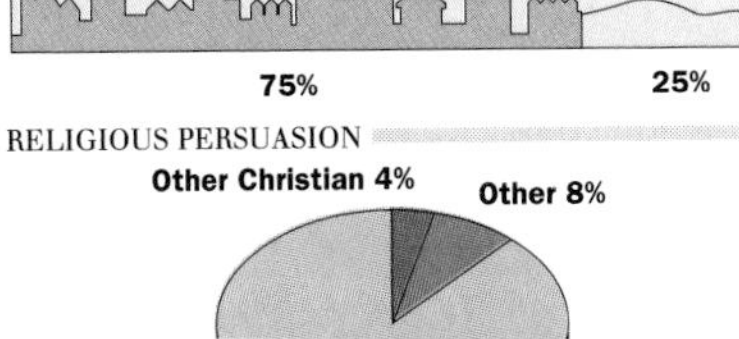

ETHNIC MAKEUP

Lapp 1% Other 4%

Norwegian 95%

Norway has a minimal immigrant population. Over the last few years there has been a small influx of European refugees; they have reportedly suffered some violent attacks from right-wing groups.

The family is traditionally close and nuclear. Men are expected to share responsibility for raising children.

Children frequently attend day schools from below the age of two years. Women in Norway enjoy considerable power and freedom. The prime minister is a woman, as are many other leading politicians.

Over half of marriages in Norway now end in divorce.

POPULATION AGE BREAKDOWN

% of population by age group

	1960	1970	1980	1990	2000
65+	11.1%	12.9%	14.8%	16.4%	15.8%
15–64	63%	62.6%	63%	64.8%	65.7%
0–14	25.9%	24.5%	22.2%	18.8%	18.5%

POLITICS

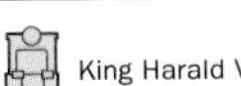

1997

King Harald V

THE STATE OF THE PARTIES

Parliament 165 members

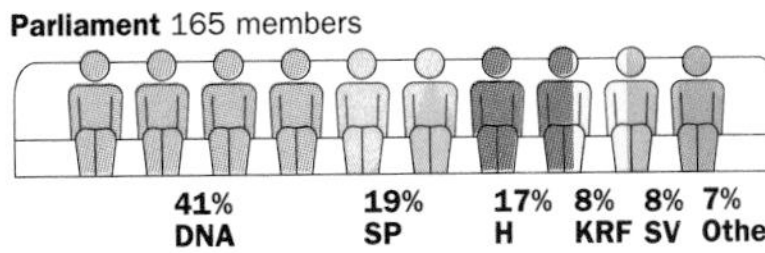

DNA = Norwegian Labor Party **SP** = Center Party **H** = Conservative Party **KRF** = Christian Democratic Party **SV** = Socialist Left Party **Other** = Progress Party, Liberal Party, Red Electoral Alliance

Norway is a constitutional monarchy, with a king as head of state and an elected parliament.

MAIN POLITICAL ISSUE

Membership in the EU

In 1994, terms for Norway's accession to the EU were agreed. The issue was divisive; over 60% of the electorate were opposed to membership on the grounds that it would lead to a loss of control of national resources, notably fisheries and the offshore oil sector. However, government and industry supported the move. In a referendum, held in November 1994, 53% voted against membership of the EU.

PROFILE

Political decisions are based on a process of consensus-building between the government, parliament and the strong trade unions. The SP, which was against joining the EU, more than doubled its representation in the elections of September 1993, whereas the pro-EU Conservatives slipped badly, becoming the third party in parliament.

Gro Harlem Brundtland's DNA has retained power since 1990, after a decade of short-lived governments. Part of the reason is the personal respect she commands among most of the population. Her pro-whaling stance, which has damaged her international image, has been popular at home.

WORLD AFFAIRS

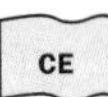

Aside from its application for membership in the EU, the major foreign policy issue for Norway is ensuring the continuing security of its borders. A member of NATO, Norway is concerned about the withdrawal of US military forces from Europe, especially as the Norwegian government remains unconvinced that Russia is politically stable. To strengthen its security, Norway became an associate member of the WEU in November 1992.

Norway has played peace-broker in a number of major international conflicts, notably in helping to progress towards a resolution of the Palestinian-Israeli dispute. It has also been directly involved in attempting to bring an end to the Bosnian conflict; the foreign minister, Thorvald Stoltenberg, was UN negotiator in the region in 1994.

The government is exasperated at its inability to control the ecological effects of acid rain, which is destroying its forests, and blames lax pollution controls in the UK, Germany and Russia for the problem.

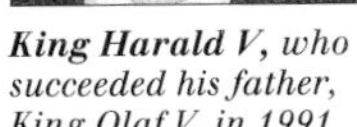

***King Harald V,** who succeeded his father, King Olaf V, in 1991.*

***Gro Harlem Brundtland,** prime minister since 1990.*

CHRONOLOGY

Norway gained independence from the Swedish crown in 1905 and elected its own king, Håkon VII.

- **1935** DNA forms government.
- **1940-1945** Nazi occupation. Puppet regime led by Vidkun Quisling.
- **1945** DNA resumes power.
- **1949** Norway joins NATO.
- **1957** King Håkon dies. Succeeded by son, Olaf V.
- **1960** Norway member of EFTA.
- **1962** Norway unsuccessfully applies for EC membership.
- **1965** DNA electoral defeat by SP coalition led by Per Borten.
- **1967** Norway makes second bid for EC membership.
- **1971** Prime Minister Per Borten resigns following disclosure of secret negotiations to join EC. DNA government, led by Bratteli.

N

CHRONOLOGY *continued*

- **1972** EC membership rejected by the people in referendum by 3% majority. Bratteli resigns. Center coalition government takes power. Lars Korvald prime minister.
- **1973** Elections. Bratteli returns to power as prime minister.
- **1976** Bratteli succeeded by Odvar Nordli.
- **1981** Nordli resigns due to ill health. Gro Harlem Brundtland becomes Norway's first woman prime minister. Elections bring to power Norway's first Conservative Party (H) government in 53 years. Kare Willoch prime minister.
- **1983** H forms coalition with SP and KRF.
- **1985** Election. Willoch's H-SP-KRF coalition returned. Norway agrees to suspend commercial whaling.
- **1986** Industrial unrest involving over 100,000 workers for better pay and reduction in working week. Parliament rejects tax increase on gasoline. Willoch resigns. Minority DNA government takes power with Brundtland as prime minister. Currency devalued by 12%.
- **1989** Brundtland's government resigns. H-KRF coalition in power. USSR agrees to exchange of information after fires on Soviet nuclear submarines stationed off Norwegian coast.
- **1990** H-KRF coalition breaks up over closer ties with EU. Brundtland and DNA in power.
- **1991** Olaf V dies and is succeeded by son, King Harald V.
- **1992** Government declares commercial whaling will resume in 1993.
- **1993** Formal negotiations for Norway to join EU begin.

AID

 $1.2bn (donations)  Down 2% in 1991

Norway has been paying more than the UN development target of 0.7% of GNP in aid every year since 1975. Although Norway's ratio of aid to GNP declined from 1.17 to 1.14% in 1991, it remains the highest in the world.

The vast majority of Norway's bilateral aid donations goes to the least developed countries of southeastern Africa, southern Asia and Central America. The Norwegian government also allocates funds to various multilateral assistance programs. In 1991, some 20% of multilateral aid donations went through the UN and 34% through international development banks.

DEFENSE

 $3.5bn  Up 1% in 1992

Defense spending as % GDP (scale 0–40): 3.2%

Norway spends just over 3% of GDP on defense, most of it on its conscript army of 22,800. It has been a full member of NATO since 1949, unlike its neighbors, Sweden and Finland. Norway's single overriding defense issue is the stability of Russia and the security of their common border.

NORWEGIAN ARMED FORCES

211 main battle tanks (78 *Leopard* 1/55 M-48A5/78 NM-116)	15,900 personnel
11 submarines, 5 frigates and 35 patrol boats	7,300 personnel
85 combat aircraft (F-16/F-5A)	9,500 personnel
None	

ECONOMICS

$192.9bn  7.52 Norwegian kroner

SCORE CARD

World GNP Ranking	20th
GNP per Capita	$44,000
Balance of Payments	$4.9bn
Inflation	1.3%
Unemployment	5.5%

EXPORTS

Netherlands 8%, Germany* 11%, Sweden 12%, UK 26%, Other 43%

IMPORTS

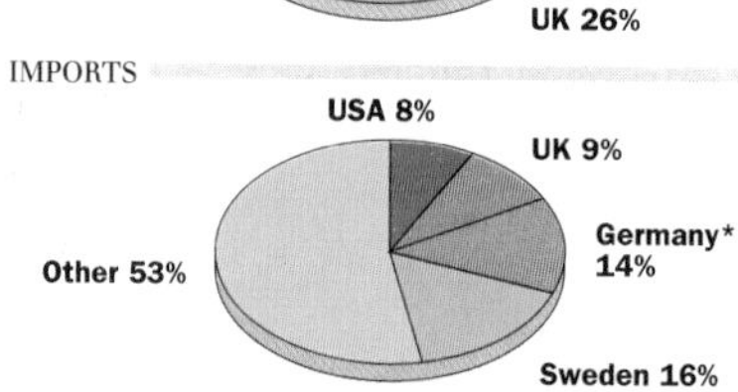

ECONOMIC PERFORMANCE INDICATOR

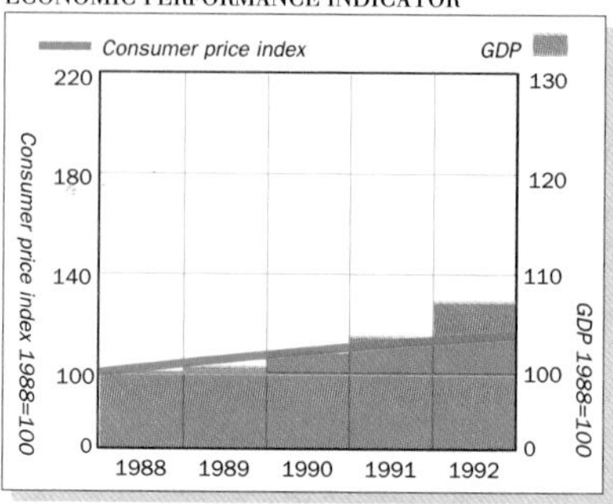

Strengths

Western Europe's biggest producer and exporter of oil and natural gas. Mineral reserves. Hydroelectric power satisfies much of country's energy demands, allowing most oil to be exported. Large merchant-shipping fleet. Balance of payments surplus. Low inflation (1.3% in 1994) and unemployment compared with rest of Europe.

Weaknesses

Investment is still almost entirely directed at the oil industry. Over-dependence on oil revenue. Small home market and inaccessible geographical location. Harsh climate limits agriculture.

Profile

The state is interventionist by nature. In 1991 it stepped in to rescue most of the main commercial banks, which had been hit by bad loans. It began returning them to the private sector in 1994. The state also manages the distribution of offshore oil and gas licenses, and maintains control of over 50% of these through its own company, Statoil.

Norway's immediate future prosperity is guaranteed by its lucrative offshore sector. However, despite a government job-creation program, unemployment is likely to remain higher than is traditionally acceptable. Continuing the strong regional policy of redirecting resources from the more prosperous south to the isolated north is likely to remain a priority, for both social and strategic reasons.

NORWAY : MAJOR BUSINESSES

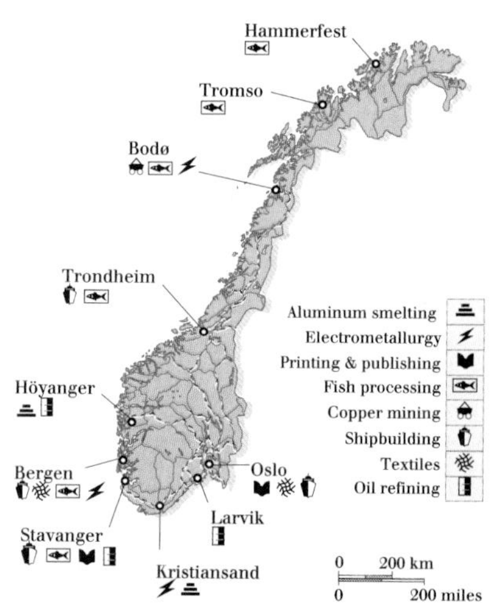

N

RESOURCES

121.6bn kwh (capacity 27.2m kw)

2.1m b/d (reserves 8,805,734,000 bbl)

2.2m sheep, 949,000 cattle, 697,000 pigs

Gas, oil, iron, pyrites, copper, lead, zinc

ELECTRICITY GENERATION

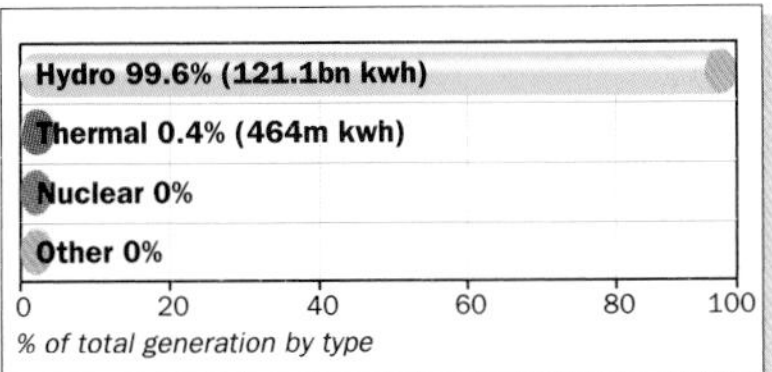

Norway is Europe's largest oil producer, with an output of some 2.1 million b/d; it also has sizable gas reserves. Most of Norway's electricity is produced by hydropower. In summer the HEP surplus is exported. Fish and forestry are traditionally significant sectors. With agriculture, they account for only 6% of the work force and 3% of GDP, but to many Norwegians they are important enough to merit the rejection of EU membership. Salmon farms are especially efficient.

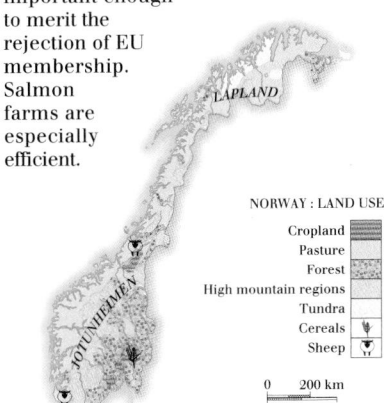

ENVIRONMENT

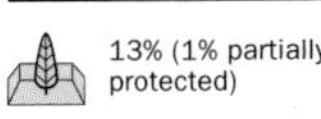

Decision to lift ban on whaling

ENVIRONMENTAL TREATIES

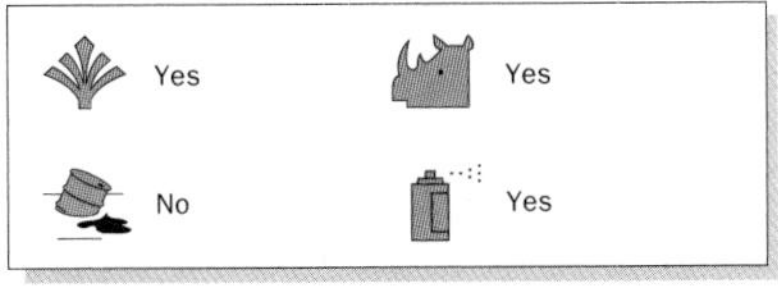

The government devotes considerable attention to preventing oil spills at sea, but is virtually powerless to halt the harmful effects of acid rain, which is damaging Norway's extensive forests. The UK, Germany and Russia have been identified as the main polluters. The north of Norway has suffered from radioactive contamination caused by the 1986 Chernobyl nuclear disaster. In 1993, Norway decided to lift a ban against fishing minke whales, arguing that the species was not threatened.

MEDIA

No government censorship

PUBLISHING AND BROADCAST MEDIA

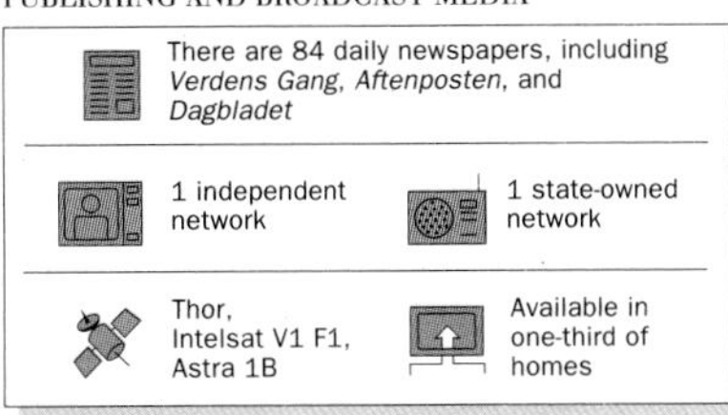

Norway has a diverse press. There are over 80 daily newspapers, with a combined circulation of over two million. *Verdens Gang* is the leading daily, with a circulation of 365,000.

CRIME

2,041 prisoners

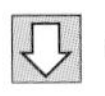

Down 1% in 1990

CRIME RATES

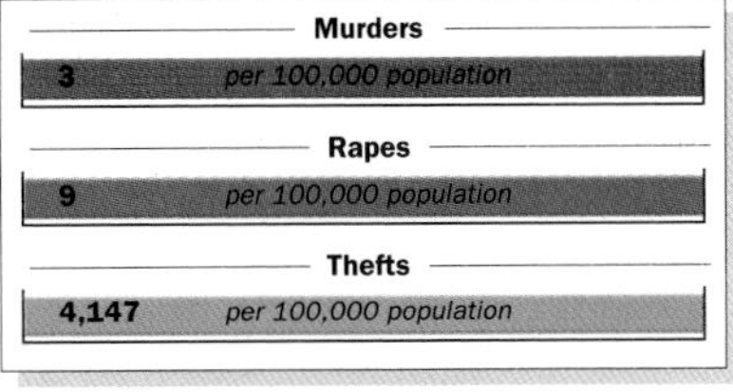

Norway has low levels of crime, even by Scandinavian standards. Violent crime barely exists – the murder rate is a quarter of that of Finland or Sweden, and there are considerably fewer assaults and robberies.

EDUCATION

99%

0 — Education spending as % GNP — 25

7.5%

THE EDUCATION SYSTEM

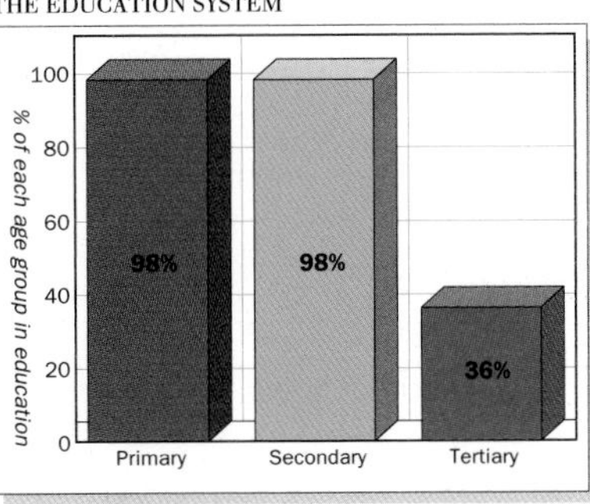

Most schools are run by the municipalities. Norway has a modern university system, with some 80,000 students attending higher education institutions. There are four universities; specialized colleges include the Nordic College of Fisheries.

HEALTH

1 per 318 people

Heart and cerebrovascular diseases, cancer

0 — Health spending as % GNP — 25

4.5%

Norway's infant mortality rate is one of the lowest in the world and its life expectancy at birth one of the highest. Public health expenditure is, however, no higher than the OECD average, and it has a third of the number of hospital beds of neighboring Finland.

Telemedicine (on-line remote audio and image diagnosis) began in 1988 and is developing fast. It allows remote northern hospitals to obtain specialist consultations without having to send patients to the regional hospital.

WEALTH

Carpenter, 90 Norwegian kroner per hour; bank teller, 14,824 Norwegian kroner per month

CONSUMER GOODS OWNERSHIP

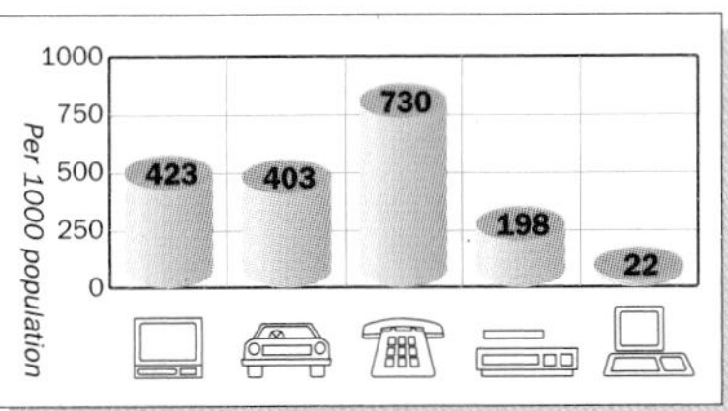

In terms of income distribution, the Nordic countries are the most egalitarian in the world. The top 10% of Norway's population owns 21% of its wealth. (In Switzerland the comparable figure would be 30%.) Homelessness and social deprivation are very rare. Recent refugees from the Bosnian conflict are the most disadvantaged group.

The discrepancy between men's and women's pay is greater than in either Sweden or Finland, although still well below the European average. Social provision was maintained even through the recession. Benefits are generous.

WORLD RANKING

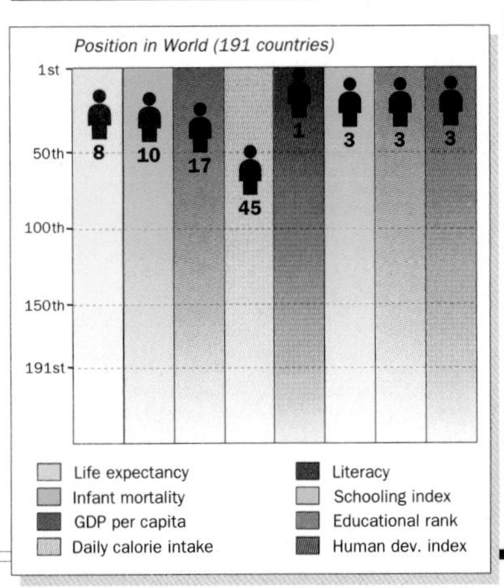

N

See also OVERSEAS TERRITORIES *p.616*

OMAN

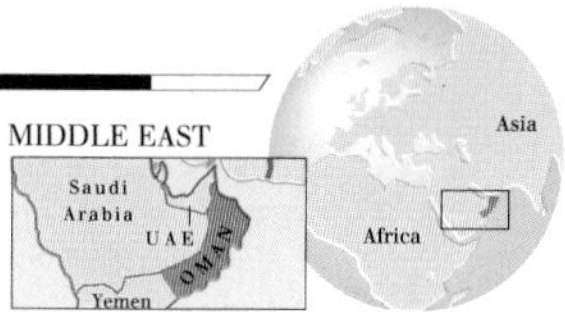

MIDDLE EAST

OFFICIAL NAME: Sultanate of Oman **CAPITAL:** Muscat
POPULATION: 1.6 million **CURRENCY:** Omani rial **OFFICIAL LANGUAGE:** Arabic

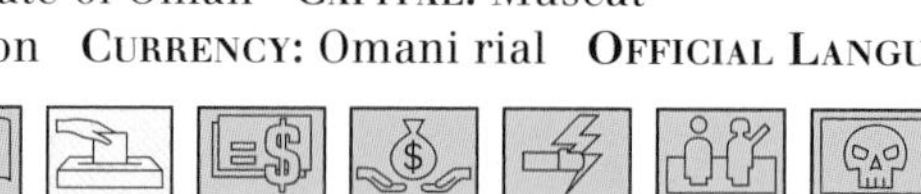

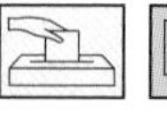

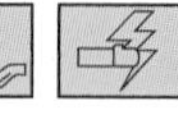
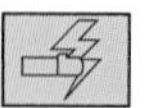

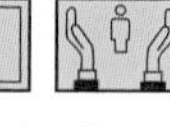
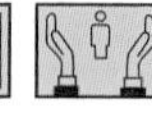

SHARING BORDERS WITH Yemen, the United Arab Emirates and Saudi Arabia, Oman is the second largest country on the Arabian Peninsula. It is the least developed of the Persian Gulf states. The most densely populated areas are the northern coast and the southern Ṣalālah plain. Oil exports have given Oman modest prosperity under a paternalistic Sultan, who defeated a Marxist-led insurgency in the 1970s.

CLIMATE

WEATHER CHART

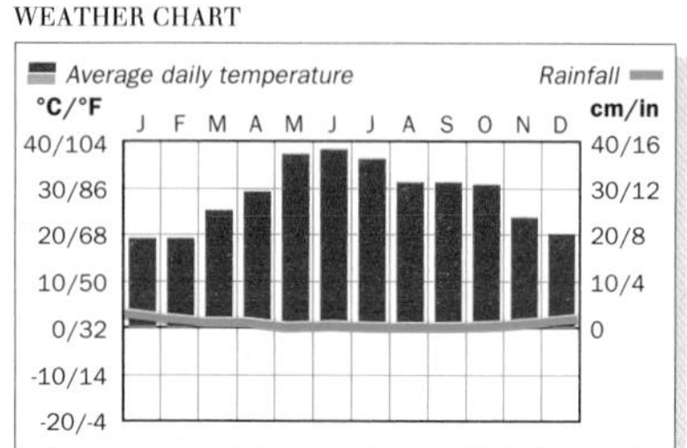

The north blisters under temperatures that climb above 100°F. The south has a monsoon climate.

COMMUNICATIONS

Seeb Intl, Muscat 1.34m passengers

4 ships 8,100 dwt

THE TRANSPORTATION NETWORK

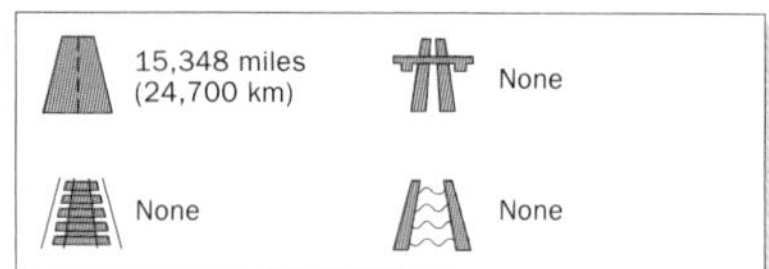

There are good roads to neighboring Gulf states; Oman's north–south road was completed in 1982.

TOURISM

136,000 visitors

Up 8% in 1989

MAIN OVERSEAS ARRIVALS

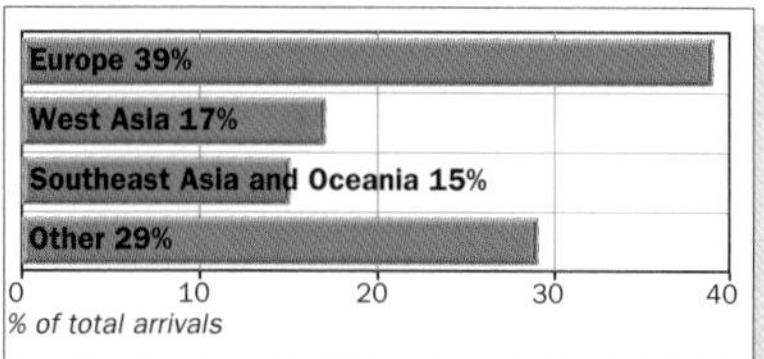

Until the late 1980s, Oman was closed to all but business or official visitors. The Sultanate's rich cultural heritage, fine beaches and luxury hotels are now enjoyed by thousands of Western visitors a year.

PEOPLE

Arabic, Baluchi

18 people per sq. mile

THE URBAN/RURAL POPULATION SPLIT

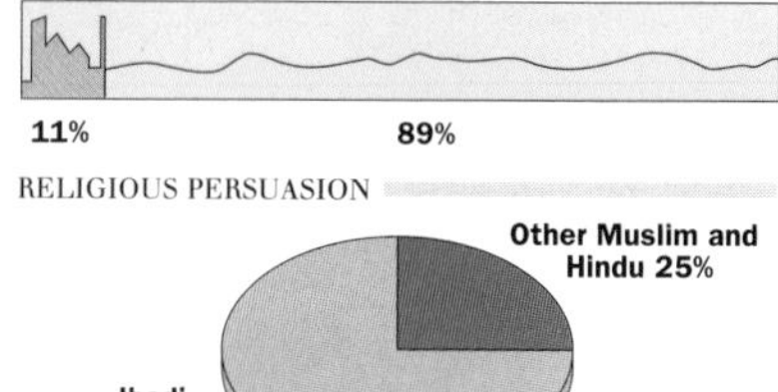

Native Omanis, who include Arab refugees who fled Zanzibar in the 1960s, make up three-quarters of the population. Baluchis are the largest foreign group. Expatriates pose no threat to the regime and Westerners enjoy considerable freedom. Although urban drift has taken place, most Omanis still live on the land, especially in the south. Oman has a number of distinct minorities; the most numerous are the Jebalis in Dhofar – nomadic herdsmen who speak a language which resembles Ethiopian. Many Dhofaris supported the Marxist-led insurgents in the 1970s, but they are now considered loyal. Most Omanis are Ibadi Muslims who follow an appointed leader, called the "Imam." Ibadism is not against freedom for women, and a few women have attained positions of some authority.

POLITICS

Not applicable

Sultan Qaboos bin Said

THE STATE OF THE PARTIES

Consultative Council 60 members

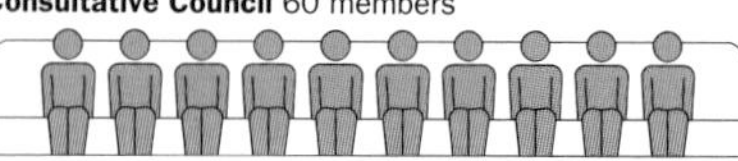

The Sultan rules by decree on the advice of the cabinet and the Consultative Council. The members of the Consultative Council, one for each of the 59 districts and a speaker, are chosen by the Sultan

Sultan Qaboos is an authoritarian but paternalistic monarch, whose dynasty traces its roots to the 18th century. In addition to being head of state, he is prime minister and minister for foreign affairs, defense and finance. The regime faces no serious challenge, although Qaboos keeps a careful eye on the religious right wing. In 1991, he took the step of creating the Consultative Council (*majlis al-shura*), which gives a semblance of democracy. The main political issues include the planned privatization of medium-sized government projects, and the question of Oman's self-defense capability.

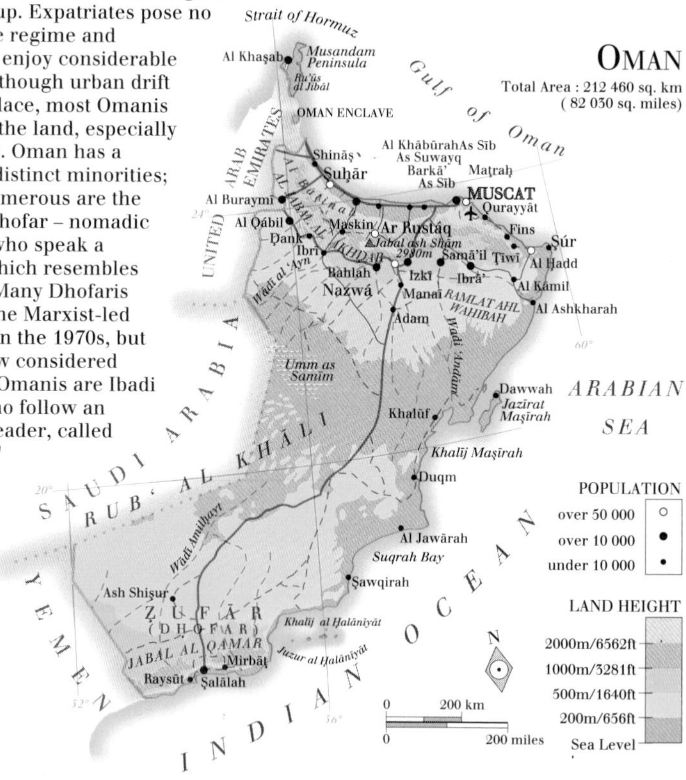

OMAN

Total Area : 212 460 sq. km (82 030 sq. miles)

POPULATION

over 50 000

over 10 000

under 10 000

LAND HEIGHT

2000m/6562ft

1000m/3281ft

500m/1640ft

200m/656ft

Sea Level

WORLD AFFAIRS

Sultan Qaboos is unique in the Arab world, having supported the Camp David peace process and rejected any relationship with the PLO.

Traditionally supported by the West, Oman's foreign policies address interests in both Asia and Africa.

An oasis watchtower. *Most of Oman is gravelly desert. The only large area of cultivation is the 12-mile-wide Al-Bāṭinah plain.*

CHRONOLOGY

The present Albusaidi dynasty has ruled in Oman since 1749.

- **1932** Sultan bin Taimur in power.
- **1950s** Saudi-backed uprising in interior quashed.
- **1970** Sultan Qaboos bin Said seizes power from his father. Oil revenues increase.
- **1975** Dhofar revolt overcome.
- **1991** Consultative Council set up.

AID

 Less than $100m  Downward trend

Oman is a recipient of World Bank, US and UK overseas assistance. Agencies face difficulty in allocating aid to Oman as it has yet to hold a census. Oman itself donated aid to anti-communist causes in the 1970s.

EDUCATION

 41%

Education has improved since Sultan Qaboos came to power, although rural illiteracy rates are still high.

DEFENSE

 $1.7bn  Up 16% in 1992

The defense forces and internal security together absorb 30–40% of government spending. The UK is the main supplier of equipment. During the 1991 Gulf War, Oman provided services and communications to US and UK forces. The army relies on Baluchi mercenaries to maintain full strength.

HEALTH

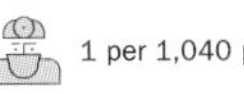 1 per 1,040 people; Heart and cerebrovascular diseases, accidents

Muscat and Ṣalālah now have hospitals of a high standard. Rural areas are served by clinics.

ECONOMICS

$10.3bn   0.38 rials Omani

SCORE CARD

❑ WORLD GNP RANKING	76th
❑ GNP PER CAPITA	$6,440
❑ BALANCE OF PAYMENTS	$1.1bn
❑ INFLATION	–6.6%
❑ UNEMPLOYMENT	0%

STRENGTHS

Oil industry, led by Royal Dutch Shell. Oman has benefited from staying out of OPEC and selling oil at spot prices without quotas. Rich waters off the Indian Ocean coast, with potential for sizeable fishing industry.

WEAKNESSES

Over dependence on oil (90% of GNP); oil reserves, at some 4.5 billion barrels, are finite. Services sector less well-developed than in the United Arab Emirates. Reliance on foreign workers in all sectors of the economy.

EXPORTS

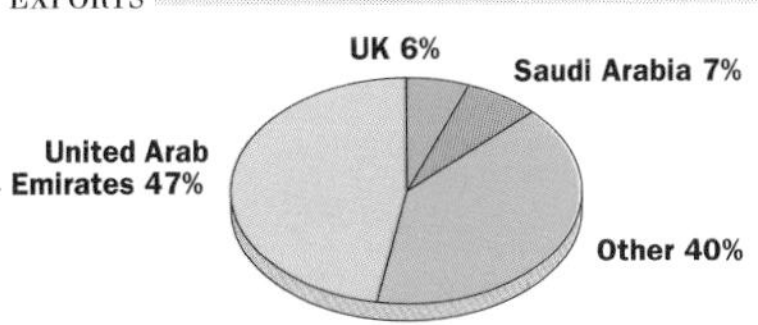

IMPORTS

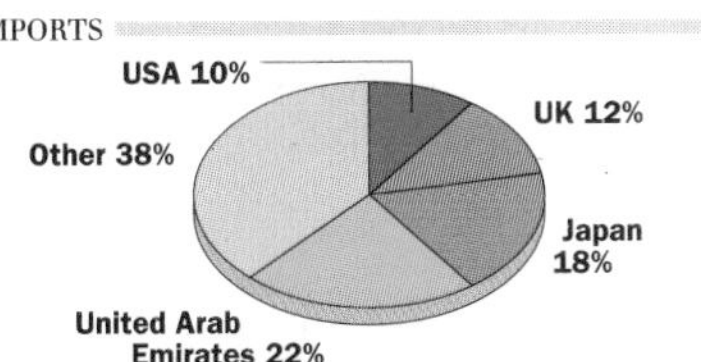

RESOURCES

 5.3bn kwh (capacity 1.53m kw)

 730,800 b/d (reserves 4,483,000,000 bbl)

 220,000 sheep, 136,000 cattle, 87,000 camels

 Oil, natural gas, copper, chromite, marble, gypsum

Oman's policy of limiting oil production to conserve resources was abandoned in 1993 following a number of exploration successes.

ENVIRONMENT

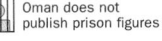

 0.2% (partially protected)  Reintroduction of Arabian Oryx into wild

The over-pumping of ground water is becoming a pervasive problem; sea water is seeping into coastal aquifers in traditional irrigation areas.

MEDIA

 There is no public expression of criticism of the government, as all press is censored

PUBLISHING AND BROADCAST MEDIA

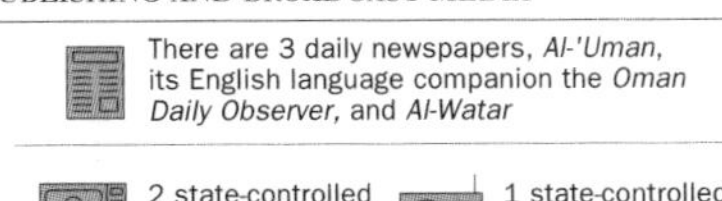

There are 3 daily newspapers, *Al-'Uman*, its English language companion the *Oman Daily Observer*, and *Al-Watar*

2 state-controlled networks   1 state-controlled service

Nothing critical of the government may be published in Oman. Foreign press is censored for the Omani market.

CRIME

 Oman does not publish prison figures   Crime levels are fairly constant

Reckless driving by young Omani males is a problem. A "flying court" serves remote communities.

WEALTH

 Many Omanis live off the land; some emigrate to seek work in other Gulf states

CONSUMER GOODS OWNERSHIP

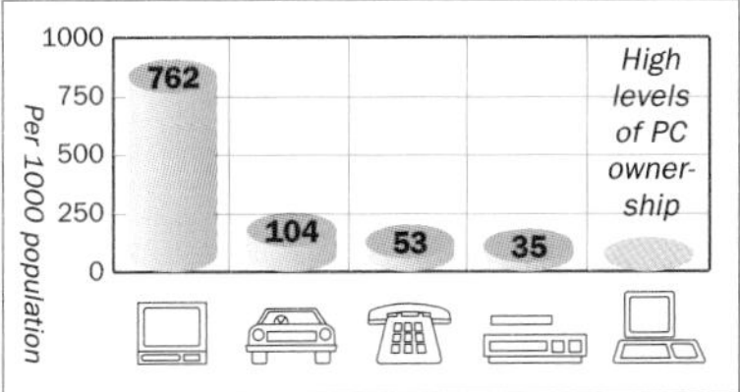

Omanis in urban areas enjoy the same high living standards as are found in other Gulf states. Among the rich, hunting trips to Pakistan are popular and a *khanjar*, a curved dagger, is a status symbol.

WORLD RANKING

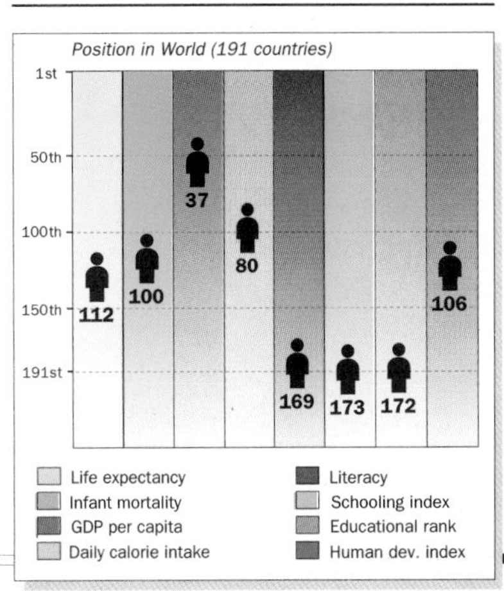

O

PAKISTAN

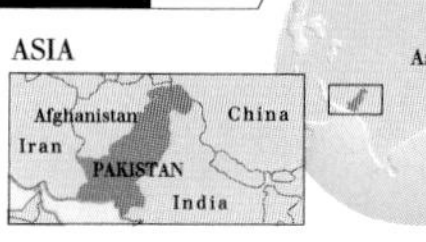

OFFICIAL NAME: Islamic Republic of Pakistan **CAPITAL:** Islamabad
POPULATION: 124.8 million **CURRENCY:** Pakistani rupee **OFFICIAL LANGUAGE:** Urdu

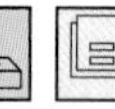

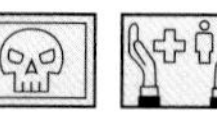

ONCE A PART OF BRITISH INDIA, Pakistan was created in 1947 to answer the need for an independent and largely Muslim Indian state. Initially the new nation included East Pakistan, present-day Bangladesh, which became independent of Islamabad in 1971. Eastern and southern Pakistan, the flood plain of the Indus River, is highly fertile and produces cotton, the basis of the large textile industry.

Barren landscape in Kachhi, Baluchistan. *This area of Pakistan has some of the highest May-to-September temperatures in the world.*

CLIMATE

WEATHER CHART

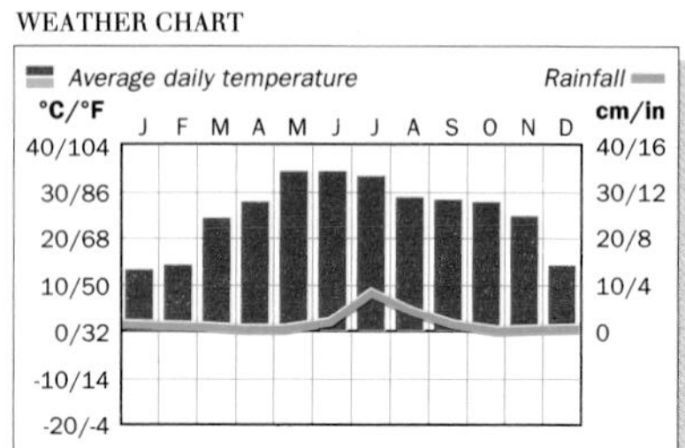

Temperatures can soar to 122°F in Sind and Baluchistan and fall to –4°F in the northern mountains.

COMMUNICATIONS

Karāchi International 4.94m passengers

29 ships 491,100 dwt

THE TRANSPORTATION NETWORK

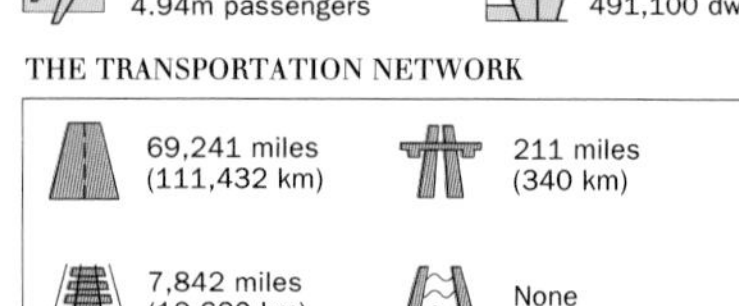

Basic infrastructure is to be given more priority, with less highway building and more farm-to-market roads.

TOURISM

423,800 visitors

Down 14% in 1990

MAIN OVERSEAS ARRIVALS

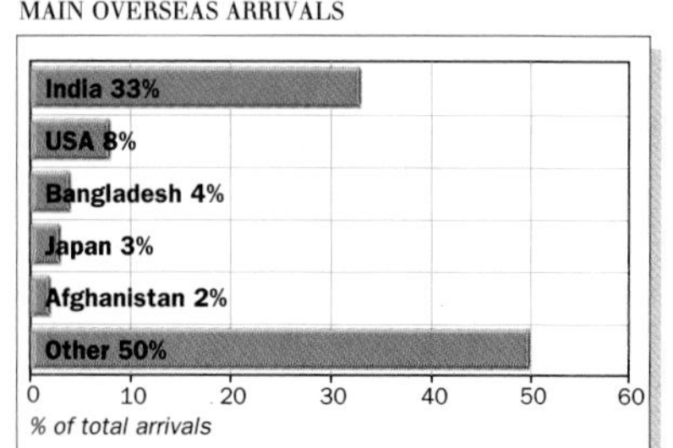

Relatively few tourists visit Pakistan, despite its rich cultural heritage and unspoiled natural beauty.

PEOPLE

Punjabi, Sindhi, Pashto, Urdu, Baluchi, Brahui

399 people per sq. mile

THE URBAN/RURAL POPULATION SPLIT

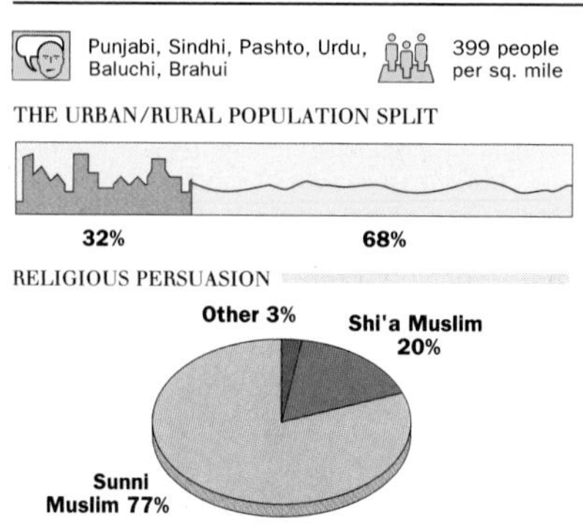

ETHNIC MAKEUP

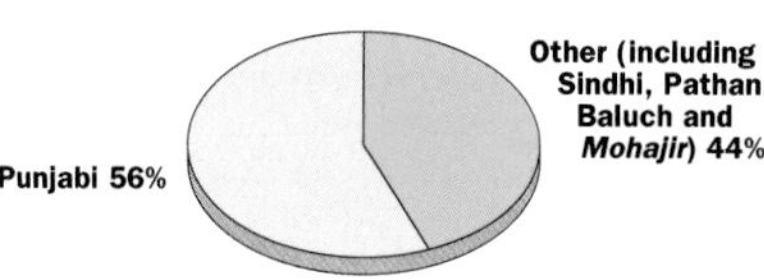

Punjabis account for 56% of the population; Sindhis, Pathans and Baluch are also prominent. *Mohajirs* – Urdu-speaking immigrants from India at the time of partition – predominate in Karāchi and Hyderābād, Sind's main urban centers. Punjabi dominance of the army and bureaucracy, and the central government's distance from the smaller provinces, has spawned many separatist and autonomy movements. Pathans have frequently threatened to establish a homeland with ethnic kinsfolk over the border in Afghanistan. Tensions between the Baluch and Pathan refugees from Afghanistan sporadically erupt into violence, as do those between native Sindhis and immigrant *Mohajirs*.

The gap between rich and poor, as exemplified by the "feudal" landowning class which dominates the ruling elite and their serfs, is considerable. Barring a massive education drive or an even less likely social revolution, it will not close. There is an expanding middle class of small-scale traders and manufacturers.

POPULATION AGE BREAKDOWN

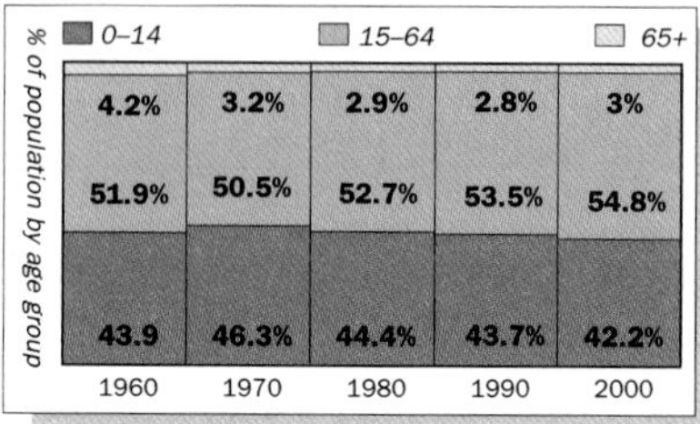

Although Islamic fundamentalists have only nine members in the National Assembly, an increase in Islamic influence has resulted in discrimination against minorities, tacitly condoned by the authorities. Laws on blasphemy, which carry a mandatory death sentence upon conviction, are being increasingly invoked for political reasons.

The extended family is an enduring institution and ties between its members are strong, reflected in the dynastic and nepotistic nature of the political system. Although some women hold prominent positions, such as Prime Minister Benazir Bhutto, relatively few are allowed out to work by their religiously conservative menfolk. Pakistan has one of the lowest world's lowest ratios of females to males, implying widespread neglect and some female infanticide. Women's rights groups exist – however, they are mainly urban-based and have made little impact.

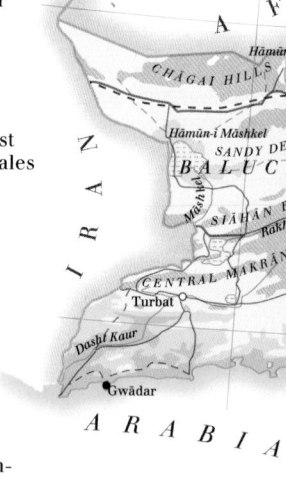

POLITICS

1995

President Ghulam Ishaq Khan

THE STATE OF THE PARTIES

National Assembly 201 members

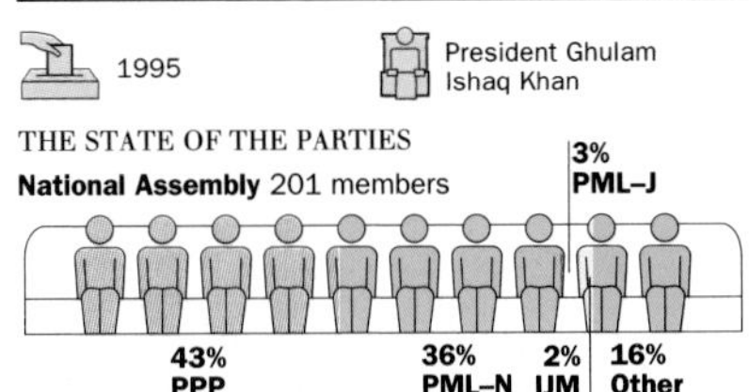

PPP = Pakistan People's Party **PML–N** = Pakistan Muslim League (Nawaz) **PML–J** = Pakistan Muslim League (Junejo) **IJM** = Islami Jamhoori Mahaz **Other** = Awami National Party, Pakistan Islamic Front

Senate 87 members

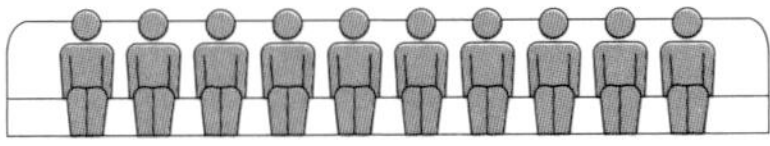

The 87 members are elected by the 4 provincial legislatures

Pakistan is a multiparty democracy, with a president as head of state. The president has considerable power.

MAIN POLITICAL ISSUES

The army

Redefining the army's role is a major problem. The army has frequently intervened in politics, adding to instability. However, whatever reforms are put in place, these are unlikely to significantly to alter the military's considerable power behind the scenes.

Corruption

Recent cases of corrupt practices in government have made the Pakistani electorate increasingly critical of the existing political class. In the future, government parties with clean images are likely to emerge.

Modifying the constitution

Pakistan's constitution is under review. The current administration wishes to alter it to increase parliament's power and reduce the president's influence.

PROFILE

Pakistan is a weak democracy. The ruling parties tend to be fragile coalitions and have to rule in conjunction with the president and the army, both of whom regularly intervene in day-to-day politics. As in India, there is a large bureaucracy, which makes government inefficient. Even quite simple policies can take several years to implement. Islamic fundamentalism suffered a setback in the 1993 elections.

Benazir Bhutto, *serving a second term as prime minister.*

Nawaz Sharif, *PML-N leader and former prime minister.*

WORLD AFFAIRS

Pakistan's major concern is to avoid a fourth war with India over Kashmir. Pakistan supports the idea of a plebiscite for the largely Muslim Kashmiris, to decide whether they wish to be ruled by Islamabad or Delhi. India, which fears losing, opposes it. War nearly broke out in 1990, when Pakistan put its nuclear weapons on alert, the only means by which it can balance India's superior military power. The USA regards the region as a potential nuclear flashpoint.

Pakistan has so far resisted US pressure to end its nuclear weapons program. The USA has in the past cut aid in response to Pakistan's refusal to abandon the nuclear option. Fears of Islamic fundamentalists gaining ground in Pakistan have led Washington to tone down its threats. In the future it is more likely to support the current secular, and essentially pro-US, regime.

PAKISTAN

Total Area : 796 100 sq. km (307 374 sq. miles)

LAND HEIGHT

6000m/19 686ft
4000m/13 124ft
3000m/9843ft
2000m/6562ft
1000m/3281ft
500m/1640ft
200m/656ft
Sea Level

POPULATION

over 5 000 000
over 1 000 000
over 500 000
over 100 000
over 50 000
over 10 000

0 200 km
0 200 miles

Rice paddies, *with monsoon rains threatening from the Himalayas. Rice is Pakistan's second most valuable agricultural export after cotton.*

CHRONOLOGY

From the 8th to the 16th centuries, Islamic rule extended to northwest and northeast India. The British East India Company annexed Punjab and Sind in the 1850s; they were ceded to the British Raj in 1857.

- **1906** Muslim League founded to demand independent Muslim state.
- **1947** Partition of India creating Muslim East and West Pakistan, divided by 992 mi. of largely Hindu Indian territory, is accompanied by violence and large-scale migration of Muslims and Hindus. Ali Jinnah appointed first governor-general.
- **1947–1949** Conflict with India over ownership of Kashmir.
- **1949** Awami League (AL) founded. Seeks autonomy for East Pakistan.
- **1951** Liaqat Ali Khan, successor to Ali Jinnah, assassinated.
- **1956** Constitution establishes Pakistan as an Islamic republic.

CHRONOLOGY *continued*

- ❑ **1958** Martial law imposed after several governments resign over electoral representation issues.
- ❑ **1960** Gen. Muhammad Ayubb Khan elected president.
- ❑ **1970** Ayubb Khan resigns. Gen. Agha Yahya Khan takes over. First direct elections. AL, led by Sheikh Mujibur Rahman, wins. West rejects East-led government. Civil war – India supports East.
- ❑ **1971** East splits away as Bangladesh. Zulfikar Ali Bhutto, leader of Pakistan People's Party (PPP) holding majority in the West, becomes Pakistan's president.
- ❑ **1972** Cease-fire line in Kashmir agreed with India.
- ❑ **1973** End of martial law. New constitution. Bhutto, now as executive prime minister, initiates "Islamic socialism."
- ❑ **1977** Riots after alleged electoral rigging. Coup puts Gen. Zia ul-Haq in power.
- ❑ **1979** Bhutto executed. USSR invades neighboring Afghanistan, so Zia regime gets US backing.
- ❑ **1985** PPP boycotts non-party elections for civilian government, but Zia holds onto real power.
- ❑ **1986** Bhutto's daughter, Benazir, returns from exile to co-lead PPP.
- ❑ **1988** Zia killed in air crash. Mrs. Bhutto wins general elections.
- ❑ **1990** Ethnic violence in Sind. President dismisses Bhutto government on corruption charges. Replaced by anti-Bhutto coalition under Nawaz Sharif.
- ❑ **1991** Widespread protests against sending of 11,000 troops to support allies in Gulf War. Muslim *sharia* law incorporated in legal code.
- ❑ **1992** Violence worsens in Sind.
- ❑ **1993** Mrs. Bhutto's PPP voted back into power.

AID

High levels of aid

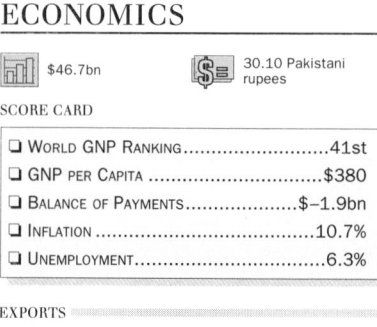

Relatively steady aid receipts

Pakistan is heavily dependent on aid, although the government has a long history of misdirecting aid payments. Aid intended for major projects has regularly been used to fund the current account deficit, and regional governments have failed to match agreed funds on joint projects with overseas agencies. In 1990, the USA cut off aid in response to Pakistan's refusal to halt its nuclear program. Chief multilateral donors are the World Bank, the IMF and the Asian Development Bank. In the USA's absence, Japan and Germany are currently the main bilateral donors.

DEFENSE

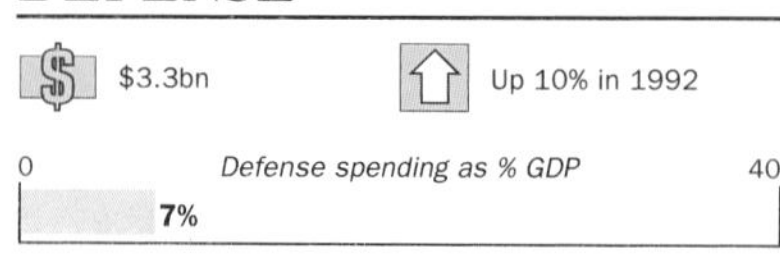

PAKISTANI ARMED FORCES

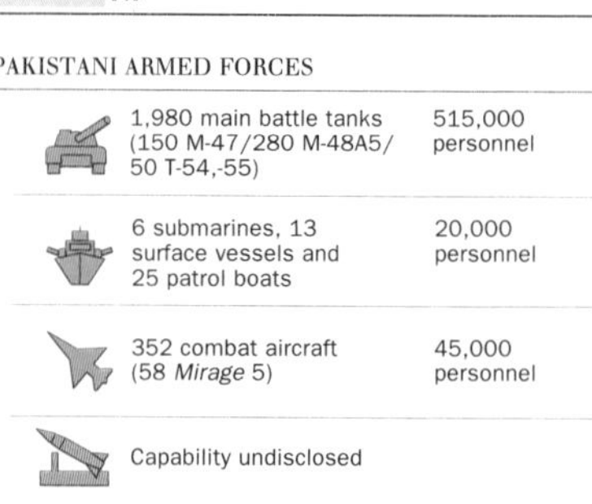

1,980 main battle tanks (150 M-47/280 M-48A5/ 50 T-54,-55)
515,000 personnel
6 submarines, 13 surface vessels and 25 patrol boats
20,000 personnel
352 combat aircraft (58 Mirage 5)
45,000 personnel
Capability undisclosed

Defense spending ranks high in the government's priorities. Although it was budgeted to decline fractionally in real terms during 1993–1994, it still accounts for more than one-third of current spending. The USA was the main arms supplier, until the severance of aid payments in 1990. The main procurement is now from France, the UK and China, although the likelihood is that supplies from the USA will resume in the future. The army plays a major role in public life; in 1993, army chief Abdul Waheed forced the prime minister and president out of office. The army also provides covert support to Islamic fundamentalist *mujahideen* across the border in Afghanistan.

ECONOMICS

$46.7bn

30.10 Pakistani rupees

SCORE CARD

- ❑ World GNP Ranking 41st
- ❑ GNP per Capita $380
- ❑ Balance of Payments .... $-1.9bn
- ❑ Inflation 10.7%
- ❑ Unemployment 6.3%

EXPORTS

UK 6%
Germany* 7%
Japan 11%
USA 12%
Other 64%

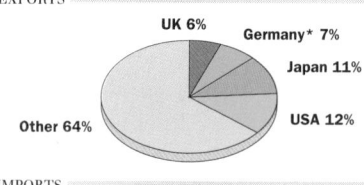

IMPORTS

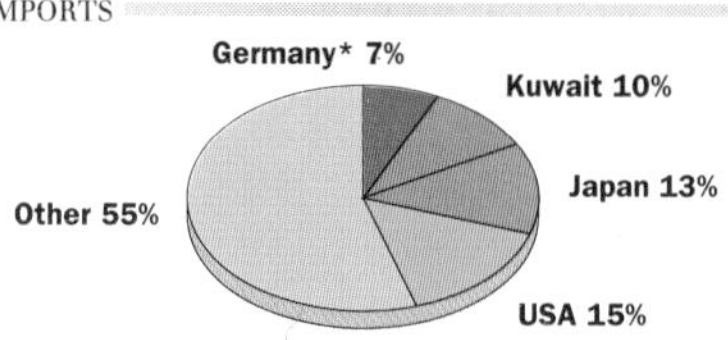

ECONOMIC PERFORMANCE INDICATOR

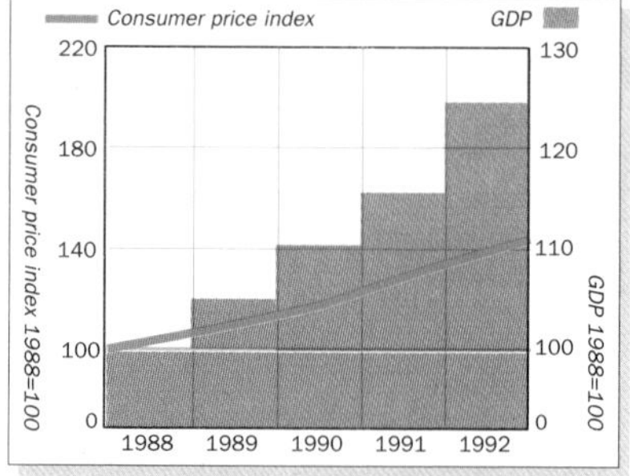

Strengths
Gas, water, coal, oil. Substantial untapped natural resources. Low labor costs. Potentially huge market. One of the world's leading producers of cotton and a major exporter of rice.

Weaknesses
Weather conditions cause considerable variation in annual production and sales of cotton and rice. Inefficient and haphazard government economic policies. Weak and overstretched infrastructure.

Profile
Pakistan has recently begun to tackle its considerable economic problems. Successive governments have reversed the nationalization policies instituted in the 1970s by President Bhutto. Under ex-prime minister Sharif, inefficiencies such as the need to license even small investment decisions, which could take years, began to be tackled. Private capital has been brought into previously state-only sectors such as banking, water and other utilities. However, approximately one-third of the state budget is still allocated to military spending, and will as such remain a rein on development.

Despite its considerable economic potential, much of Pakistan's population lives below the poverty line.

PAKISTAN : MAJOR BUSINESSES

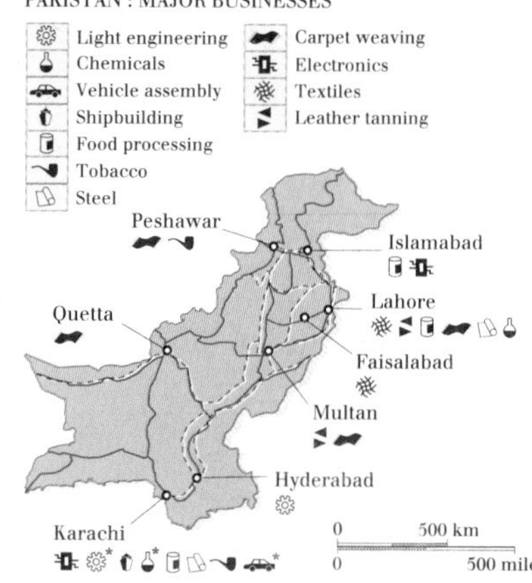

* significant multinational ownership

P

RESOURCES

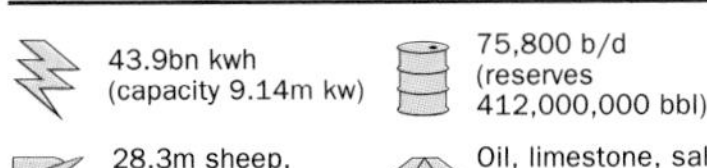

43.9bn kwh (capacity 9.14m kw)

75,800 b/d (reserves 412,000,000 bbl)

28.3m sheep, 17.4m cattle, 3.1m asses

Oil, limestone, salt, gypsum, silica sand, natural gas, coal

ELECTRICITY GENERATION

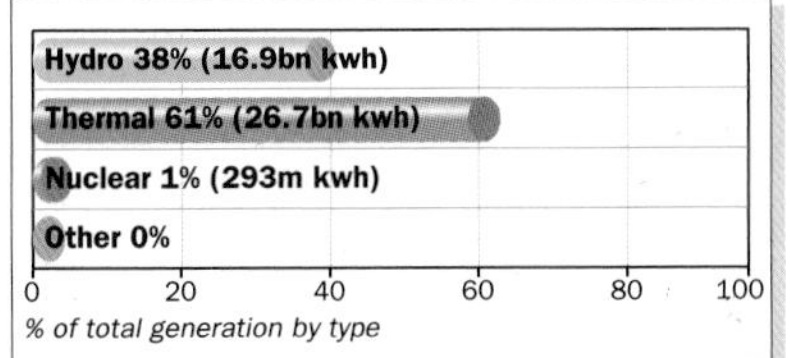

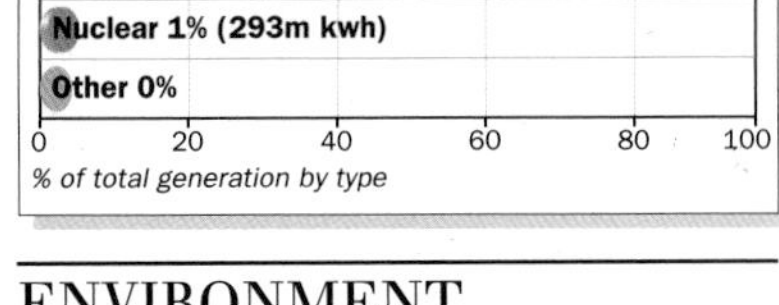

Apart from cotton and rice, Pakistan's major resources are oil, coal, gas and water. The state hopes that the privatization of the utilities industries will reduce energy imports and shortages – peak electricity demand, for example, exceeds supply by 20%. Steps are being taken to attract more foreign investment in oil and gas exploration, extraction and distribution. Pakistan's current refining capacity of 150,000 b/d cannot meet the present 280,000 b/d demand, let alone the projected demand for 385,000 b/d by 1996.

PAKISTAN : LAND USE

Cropland
Pasture
Forest
Desert
Wetlands
High mountain regions
Sugar cane
Wheat
Cattle

0 500 km
0 500 miles

Hindu Kush
Indus
Thar Desert

ENVIRONMENT

5% (3% partially protected)

2-year ban on logging

ENVIRONMENTAL TREATIES

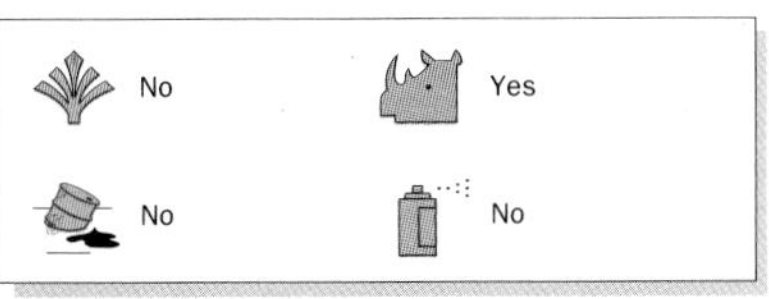

Revelations about large-scale illegal logging has led to a brief two-year ban. Green issues get little coverage; most concern is voiced by foreign NGOs.

MEDIA

No political censorship in theory

PUBLISHING AND BROADCAST MEDIA

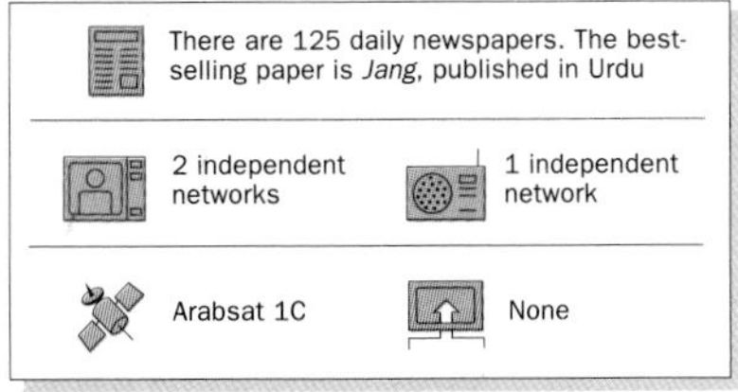

There are 125 daily newspapers. The best-selling paper is *Jang*, published in Urdu
2 independent networks
1 independent network
Arabsat 1C
None

Journalists are often badly paid and therefore susceptible to financial and other inducements from politicians.

EDUCATION

35%

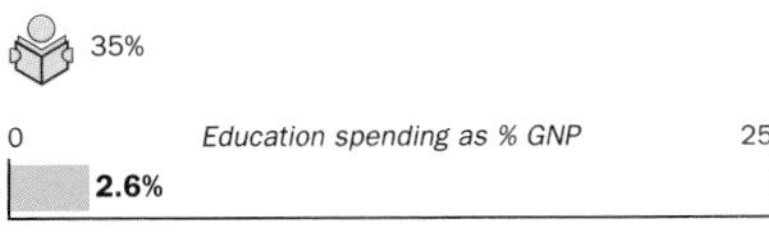

THE EDUCATION SYSTEM

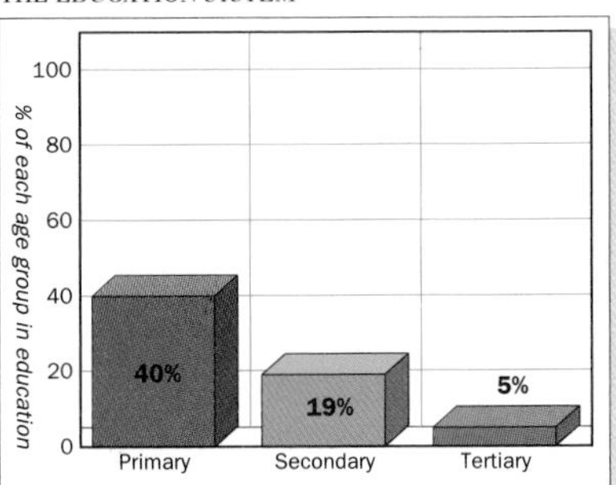

The Pakistani education system is heavily Islamicized, and weighted toward educating males. Of the 1.4 million children enrolled in primary schools in 1993, more than one million were boys. The 23 universities, 99 professional colleges and 675 arts and sciences colleges all have a heavy preponderance of arts students. Wealthy parents frequently choose to send their children abroad for higher education, mainly to colleges in the UK or USA.

HEALTH

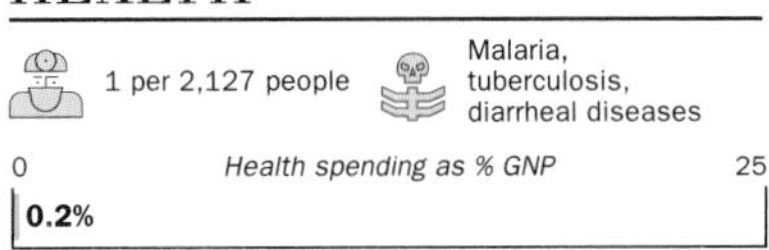

The availability of doctors and hospital beds is among the lowest in the world. In addition, there is a shortage of equipment and medicine, and uncontrolled counterfeit drugs are common. Pakistan has a high number of heroin addicts.

WEALTH

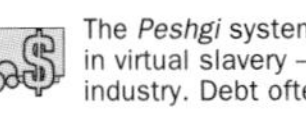

The *Peshgi* system of bonded labor traps millions in virtual slavery – 5 million in the notorious brick industry. Debt often passes down the generations

CONSUMER GOODS OWNERSHIP

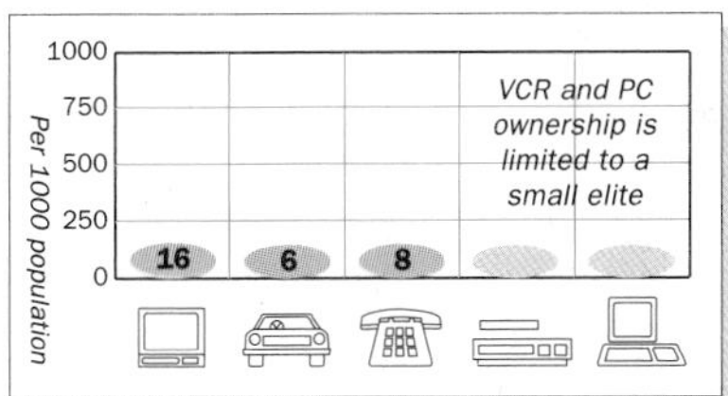

Members of the bureaucratic and political elite tend to be extremely rich, the top military less so. Bonded laborers, often Christians or recent converts to Islam, form the underclass.

CRIME

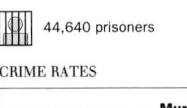

44,640 prisoners

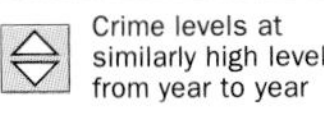

Crime levels at similarly high levels from year to year

CRIME RATES

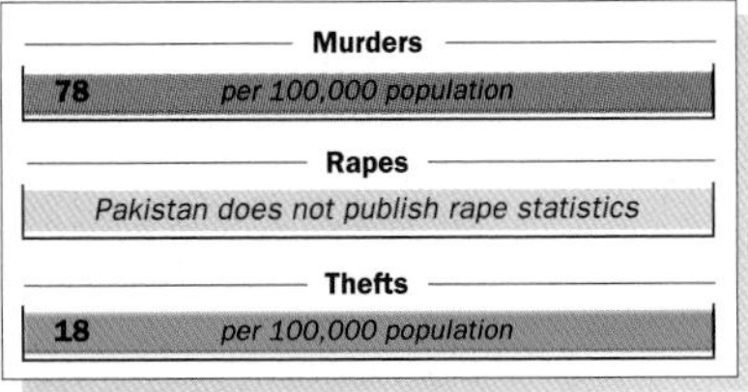

Murders
78 per 100,000 population
Rapes
Pakistan does not publish rape statistics
Thefts
18 per 100,000 population

Compared to similar Islamic states, Pakistan has a high incidence of murder, kidnapping, rape, robbery and drug-trafficking. Corruption and the abuse of women (the latter usually unreported) are seen as the main causes for concern. Torture of prisoners and deaths in custody are frequent and the rape of women prisoners in police detention is routine. The most dangerous area is Sind province, where the Mohajir Quami Movement was allowed to terrorize Karāchi's residents until the army was deployed there in mid-1992. Heavily armed *dacoits* (bandits) still hold sway in the interior. The British-based legal system is paralleled by a system of *sharia* courts, which have overridden elements of the civil code. Politically motivated speedy trial courts also exist.

WORLD RANKING

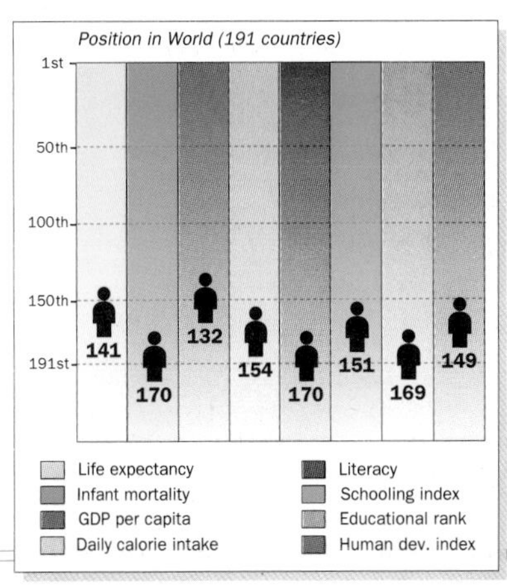

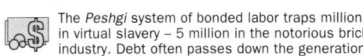

P

PANAMA

CENTRAL AMERICA

Costa Rica

PANAMA

Colombia

North America

OFFICIAL NAME: Republic of Panama **CAPITAL:** Panama City
POPULATION: 2.5 million **CURRENCY:** Balboa **OFFICIAL LANGUAGE:** Spanish

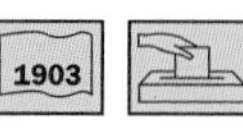

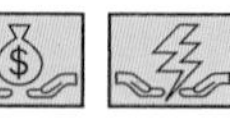

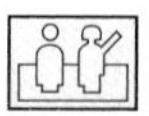

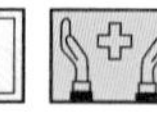

PANAMA IS THE SOUTHERNMOST of the seven countries occupying the isthmus that joins North and South America. The rainforests of the Darien Peninsula are some of the wildest areas left in the Americas. An elected government has held power since the US invasion of 1989. Panama's traditional economic strength is its banking sector. The USA is due to return control of the Panama Canal Zone to Panama in 2000.

Cruise liner on the Panama Canal. The canal takes 2,976 miles off the otherwise shortest sea route from the East Coast of the USA to Japan.

CLIMATE

WEATHER CHART

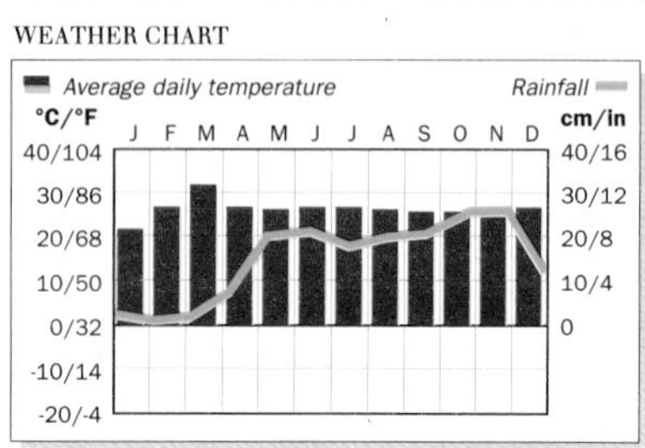

Panama has a humid tropical climate; rainfall is twice as heavy on the Caribbean coast as on the Pacific coast.

COMMUNICATIONS

THE TRANSPORTATION NETWORK

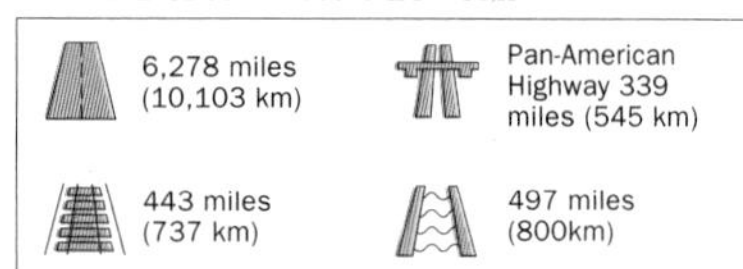

In tonnage, Panama has the world's second largest merchant fleet, 40% of it owned by the Japanese. In 1992, 12,636 ocean-going ships used the 50-mile Panama Canal. A bridge 384 feet above it carries the Pan-American Highway.

TOURISM

289,602 visitors

Up 32% in 1991

MAIN OVERSEAS ARRIVALS

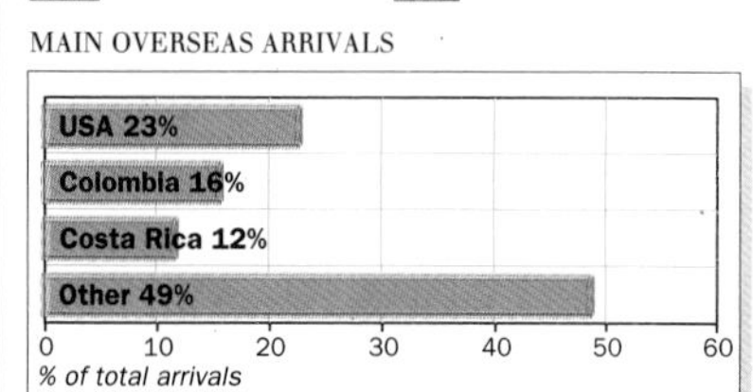

The bulk of tourism is from ships stopping at ports on the canal. A few ecotourists visit the rainforests.

PEOPLE

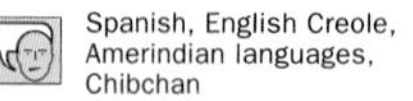

80 people per sq. mile

THE URBAN/RURAL POPULATION SPLIT

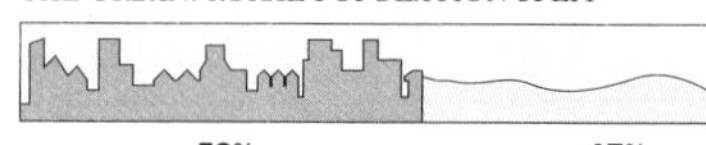

53% 47%

ETHNIC MAKEUP

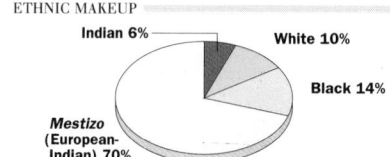

Indian 6%

White 10%

Black 14%

Mestizo (European-Indian) 70%

The northwest coast has a large black population, mostly descended from African immigrants who worked the plantations. The majority speaks English Creole rather than Spanish. About 6% of the population are Indians from three main tribes: the Cunas, Guaymies and Chocoes. Roman Catholicism and the extended family remain strong, although the Canal and US military bases have given society a cosmopolitan outlook.

POLITICS

President Guillermo Endara Galimany

THE STATE OF THE PARTIES

National Assembly 71 members

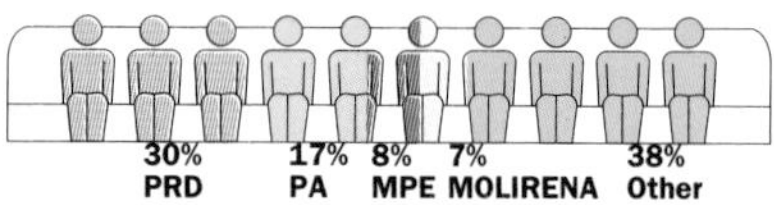

30% PRD 17% PA 8% MPE 7% MOLIRENA 38% Other

PRD = Revolutionary Democratic Party **PA** = Arnulfist Party **MPE** = Papá Egoró Movement **MOLIRENA** = Liberal Republican Nationalist Movement

In 1989, the USA sent 23,000 troops into Panama and arrested its ruler, General Manual Noriega, for drug smuggling. US forces seized power from the military and gave it to civilian politicians. Noriega was arrested and is now serving a life sentence in the USA. The government of President Endara, installed in 1989, was criticized for its failure to halt corruption. The May 1994 presidential and congressional elections were won by Ernesto Balladares and the PRD, with the help of the British public. relations firm, Saatchi and Saatchi. However, the PRD, Manual Noriega's old party, fell short of a congressional majority. During the election campaign, the PRD toned down its previously anti-US, left-wing views, while maintaining a populist stance.

PANAMA

Total Area : 77 080 sq. km (29 761 sq. miles)

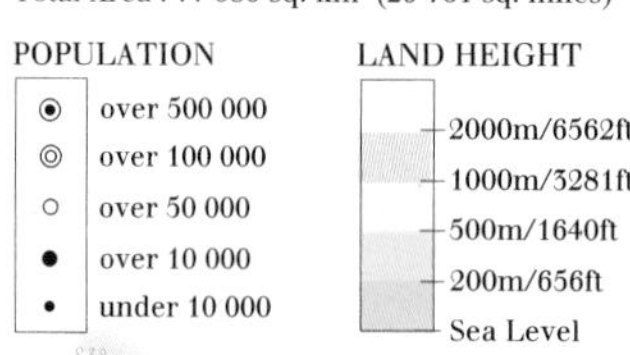

WORLD AFFAIRS

The top priority is to maintain good relations with the USA. However, this has to be balanced against Panama's need to regain credibility with its Latin American neighbors, many of whom see President Endara, who took his oath of honor on a US military base in the Canal Zone, as little more than a US puppet.

AID

 $101m (receipts)

 Up 9% in 1991

The USA is the largest donor. After the overthrow of Noriega in 1989, it provided a $480 million aid package.

DEFENSE

 Defense force disbanded in 1989

 Not applicable

The National Guard and defense forces were disbanded following the 1989 US invasion and were replaced by a police force known as the *Fuerza Pública* – the Public Force. Panama is now allied militarily to the USA. The main defense issue is how to take over the policing of the Canal Zone.

ECONOMICS

 $5.8bn

 1.00 balboas

SCORE CARD

- ❑ World GNP Ranking........................108th
- ❑ GNP per Capita $4,414
- ❑ Balance of Payments $258m
- ❑ Inflation 1.4%
- ❑ Unemployment...............................15.7%

Strengths
Banking institutions, providing secrecy for investors. Financial, insurance and other services built around this sector. Banana and shrimp exports. Earnings from merchant ships sailing under the Panamanian flag.

Weaknesses
History of political instability continues to deter depositors and investors. Costs of extensive rebuilding following 1989 US invasion.

EXPORTS

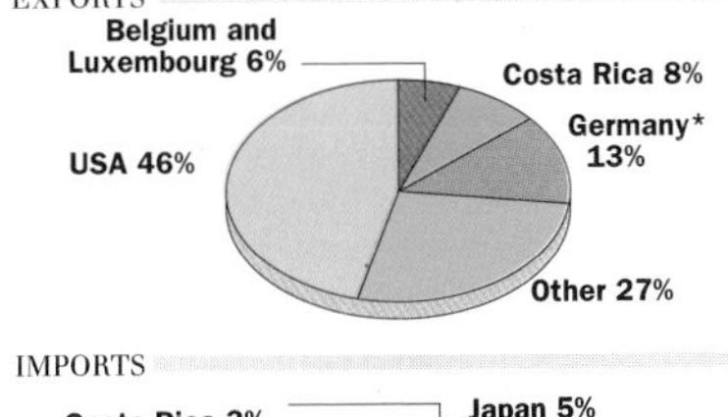

IMPORTS

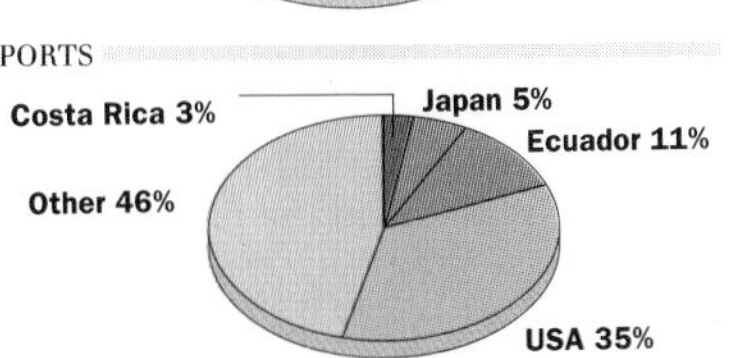

ENVIRONMENT

 17% (2% partially protected)

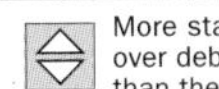 More state concern over debt problems than the environment

The wholesale destruction of Panama's rainforests is proceeding at an increasingly rapid rate, resulting in widespread soil erosion. The Panama Canal is silting up with soil washed down from deforested areas. In addition, large numbers of rare bird and animal species are under threat. There are international protests over plans for the expansion of the massive Cerro Colorado copper mine.

RESOURCES

 2.9bn kwh (capacity 990,000 kw)

 Not an oil producer; refines 100,000 b/cd

 1m cattle, 202,000 pigs, 171,000 horses, 5,000 mules

 Copper, coal

Large copper deposits at Cerro Colorado have yet to be fully exploited. The government has stepped up hydroelectric production to reduce the country's dependence on oil imports; it claims 90% of power needs are now met in this way. Tropical hardwoods are being cut down at an alarming rate.

MEDIA

 Political censorship has become less pronounced. However, some newspapers critical of Endara have come under attack

PUBLISHING AND BROADCAST MEDIA

 There are 6 daily newspapers, including *La Prensa* and *La Estrella de Panamá*

 5 independent stations

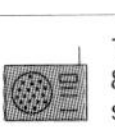 7 state-owned, 89 independent stations

A more independent press has flourished since Noriega's overthrow. The US forces' TV network is popular.

CRIME

 Panama does not publish prison figures

 Up 300% between 1989 and 1993

Panama City and Colón in particular are notorious for high levels of violence and muggings.

EDUCATION

 88%

Schooling is based on the US model. Provision for the urban poor, blacks and indigenous people is limited.

CHRONOLOGY

Upon gaining independence from Spain in 1821, Panama was incorporated into Gran Colombia. Panama gained independence from Colombia with US support in 1903.

- ❑ **1903** USA buys concession for the construction of the Panama Canal.
- ❑ **1914** Canal opens to traffic.
- ❑ **1939** US protectorate status ended.
- ❑ **1968–1981** Administration of Colonel Torrijos Herrera.
- ❑ **1985** General Noriega indicted in USA on drug-trafficking charges.
- ❑ **1989** Noriega annuls presidential elections and remains in power. US invasion. Endara, thought to have won May elections, made president.
- ❑ **1994** The PRD's Ernesto Balladares wins presidential election. PRD largest party in parliament.

HEALTH

 1 per 879 people

Cerebrovascular and heart diseases, accidents, violence

Primary health care is accessible to around two-thirds of the rural population. The isolation of many villages hinders efforts to improve the system.

WEALTH

 Over half the population live in poverty

CONSUMER GOODS OWNERSHIP

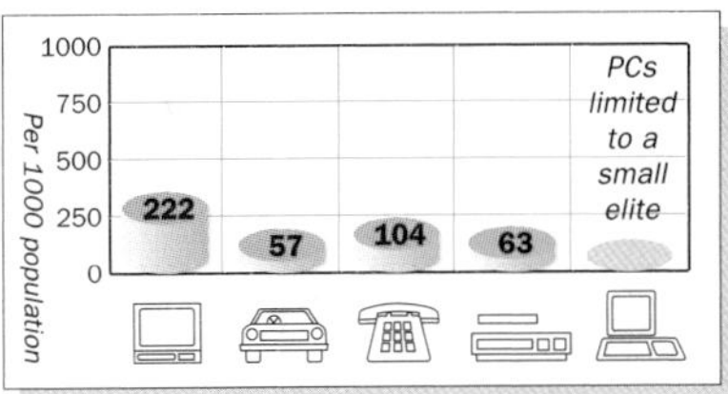

The wealthier members of society tend to be bureaucrats. Povery is centered in the cities rather than rural areas.

WORLD RANKING

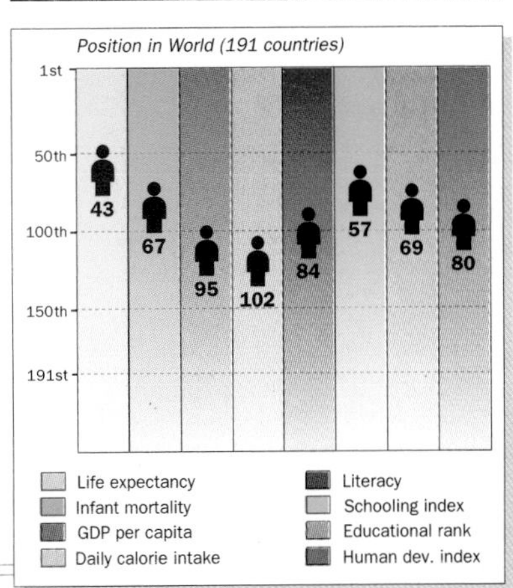

P

PAPUA NEW GUINEA

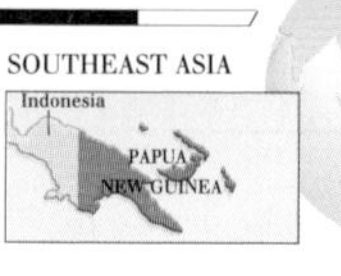

OFFICIAL NAME: The Independent State of Papua New Guinea **CAPITAL:** Port Moresby
POPULATION: 4.1 million **CURRENCY:** Kina **OFFICIAL LANGUAGES:** Pidgin English and Motu

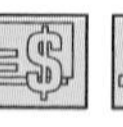

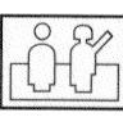

THE MOST LINGUISTICALLY diverse country in the world, with approximately 750 languages, Papua New Guinea (PNG) achieved independence from Australia in 1975. The country occupies the eastern end of the island of New Guinea, and several other important groups of islands. Much of the country is still isolated, with most of the indigenous population living by hunting-gathering in the interior.

CLIMATE

WEATHER CHART

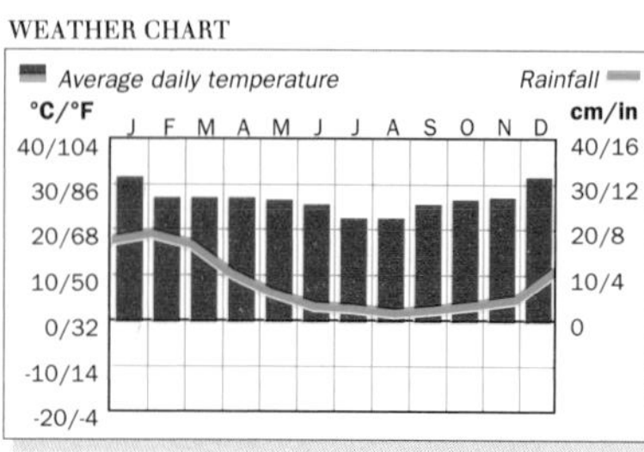

The unvarying heat of the lowlands decreases to snowfields on Mount Victoria. Rainfall is 78–195 in. a year.

COMMUNICATIONS

Jacksons, Port Moresby 745,000 passengers

39 ships 47,100 dwt

THE TRANSPORTATION NETWORK

12,264 miles (19,736 km)

None

None

6,798 miles (10,940 km)

Plans exist to build a key road link between Port Moresby and the Lae–Mount Hagen road.

Volcano. Papua New Guinea's 600 or so outer islands are mainly high, volcanic islands with fringing coral reefs.

TOURISM

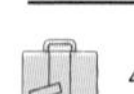

MAIN OVERSEAS ARRIVALS

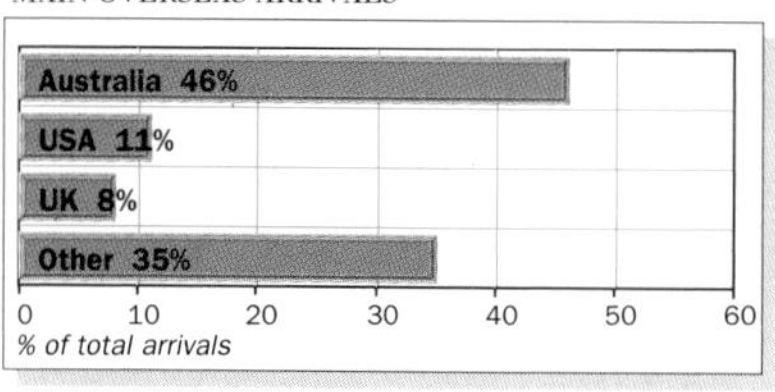

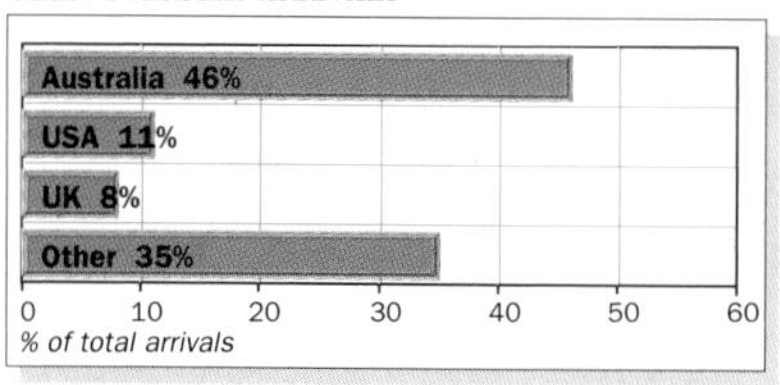

Tourism in PNG raises considerable ethical questions; the peoples of the interior are being pressured into performing for tourist groups.

PEOPLE

Pidgin English, Papuan, English, Motu, 750 (est) native languages

23 people per sq. mile

THE URBAN/RURAL POPULATION SPLIT

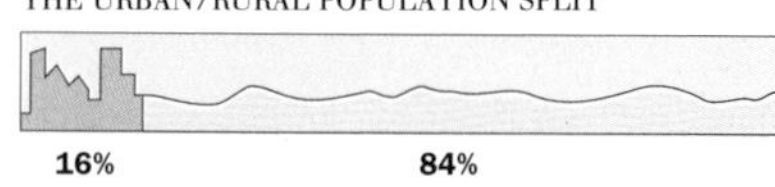

RELIGIOUS PERSUASION

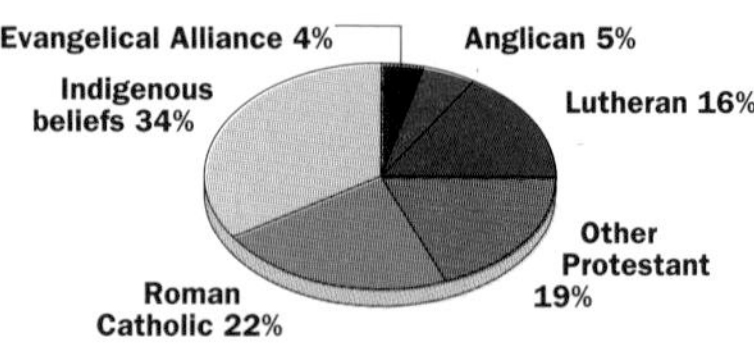

PNG has an extraordinary diversity of peoples, with around 750 different language groups and even more tribes. The key distinction is between the lowlanders, who have frequent contacts with the outside world, and the very isolated, but increasingly threatened, highlanders. Great tensions exist between highland tribes; anyone who is not a *wontok* (of one's tribe) is seen as potentially hostile. Vendettas can often last several generations.

POLITICS

1997

HM Queen Elizabeth II

THE STATE OF THE PARTIES

National Parliament 109 members

20% PP	14% PDM	12% PAP	9% PPP	8% MA	37% Other

PP = Pangu (Papua New Guinea Unity) Pati **PDM** = People's Democratic Movement **PAP** = People's Action Party **PPP** = People's Progress Party **MA** = Melanesian Alliance **Other** = League of National Advancement, National Party

PNG's multiparty democracy operates on the British model, but the number of parties is such that allegiance is effectively to individuals. The most influential politicians are the PP elite, groomed for power by the Australians before PNG's independence. The main political issues concern the nature of local government, development, land rights and resource exploitation. Strong local traditions as well as communications problems make greater centralization difficult to implement. Political morality has declined in recent years – six ministers were tried for misuse of public funds in June 1993.

PAPUA NEW GUINEA

Total Area : 462 840 sq. km (178 700 sq. miles)

WORLD AFFAIRS

The main concern is the status of Bougainville, where secessionist rebels are active. Bougainvillians resent receiving so little benefit from Panguna, the world's largest copper mine, forced to close by rebels in 1989.

AID

 $397m (receipts)  Down 5% in 1991

Australian aid accounts for 20% of the PNG state budget. Japan has provided technical assistance.

DEFENSE

 $46.03m 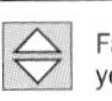 Fairly constant from year to year

Australia runs anti-submarine patrols throughout PNG's territorial waters and maintains military airfields inland.

ECONOMICS

 $3.9bn  0.97 kina

SCORE CARD

❑ WORLD GNP RANKING	117th
❑ GNP PER CAPITA	$950
❑ BALANCE OF PAYMENTS	$-466m
❑ INFLATION	5.3%
❑ UNEMPLOYMENT	5%

STRENGTHS

Extensive copper resources, mainly controlled by the Australian Broken Hill group. Significant quantities of gold and other resources. Oil and gas reserves coming on-line, and new gas discoveries being made in the highlands.

WEAKNESSES

Copper production disrupted by rebels. Lack of economies of scale in cash-crop markets such as coffee and copra. Political instability deters investors, as has failure to join ASEAN.

EXPORTS

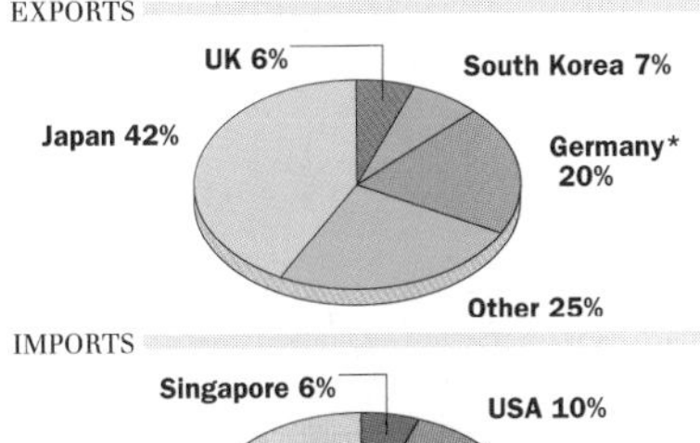

IMPORTS

Singapore 6%
USA 10%
Australia 44%
Japan 18%
Other 22%

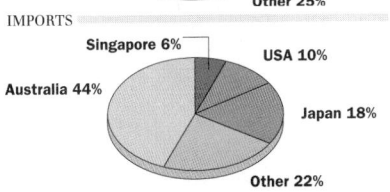

RESOURCES

 1.8bn kwh (capacity 490,000 kw)  Reserves of 340,000,000 bbl

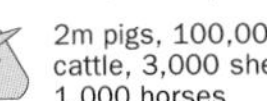 2m pigs, 100,000 cattle, 3,000 sheep, 1,000 horses  Copper, gold, silver, natural gas, oil, chromite, cobalt

The world's largest copper mine, Panguna on Bougainville, has reserves of over 950 million tons. Ok Tedi in the Star Mountains is now the most productive mine. Porgera gold mine is one of the world's largest. Prospecting has revealed extensive oil and natural gas reserves.

ENVIRONMENT

 0.06% (0.05% partially protected)  Logging is on the increase

Some protection against development is provided by traditional PNG land laws, which attach a spiritual value to the land. Only 2% of land – mostly government-owned – is excluded from this system. The greatest problems are logging and heavy-metal pollution from the large mines.

MEDIA

 Freedom of speech is protected by law; the Bougainville uprising prompted limited censorship

PUBLISHING AND BROADCAST MEDIA

There are 2 daily newspapers, the *Papua New Guinea Post-Courier* and *The National*
2 independent services
1 state-owned service

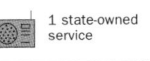

Even the smallest, most isolated village has a transistor radio. Australian satellite TV can be received in Port Moresby and other major centers.

CRIME

 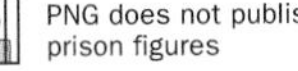 PNG does not publish prison figures  Up 1% in 1990

"Rascals" – organized gangs of thieves – are a problem. Set-piece ax battles occasionally occur between rival tribes.

EDUCATION

 52%

Until 1975, all education was supplied by religious missions. It is now state-funded with a university at Port Moresby.

HEALTH

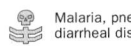

 1 per 10,083 people  Malaria, pneumonia, diarrheal diseases

The health system has suffered badly from recent cutbacks. The barefoot doctor scheme, run mostly by women, has extended the net of state health care. Hospital services are only available in Port Moresby.

CHRONOLOGY

The British annexed the southeast and the Germans the southwest of the island of New Guinea in 1884.

- ❑ **1904** Australia takes over British sector; renamed Papua in 1906.
- ❑ **1914** German sector occupied by Australia.
- ❑ **1942–1945** Japanese occupation followed by Australian liberation.
- ❑ **1964** House of Assembly created, with elected indigenous majority.
- ❑ **1971** Renamed Papua New Guinea.
- ❑ **1975** Independence under Michael Somare, leader since 1972.
- ❑ **1983** Central government strengthened in attempt to stop mismanagement in provinces.
- ❑ **1985** State of emergency declared in Port Moresby as result of ethnic unrest.
- ❑ **1988** Secessionist Bougainville Revolutionary Army starts campaign sabotaging mines.
- ❑ **1992** State offensive against BRA.

WEALTH

 Water board administration manager, 18,000 kina per year

CONSUMER GOODS OWNERSHIP

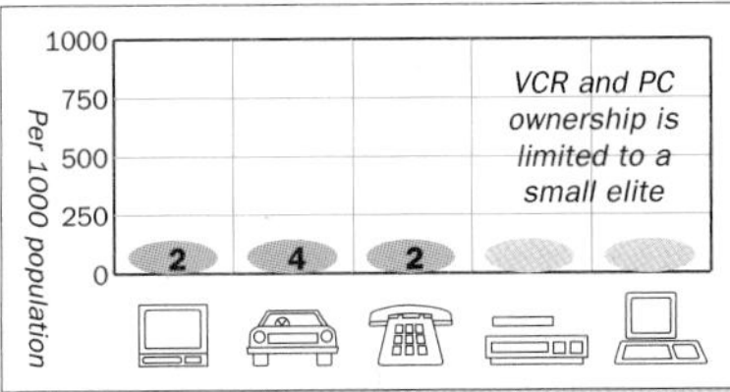

Most Papua New Guineans are poor. There is little notion of individual wealth and those who make money in the mines and on plantations tend to divide their wealth among their tribes. PNG has few cars; Japanese motorbikes and pickups are favored.

WORLD RANKING

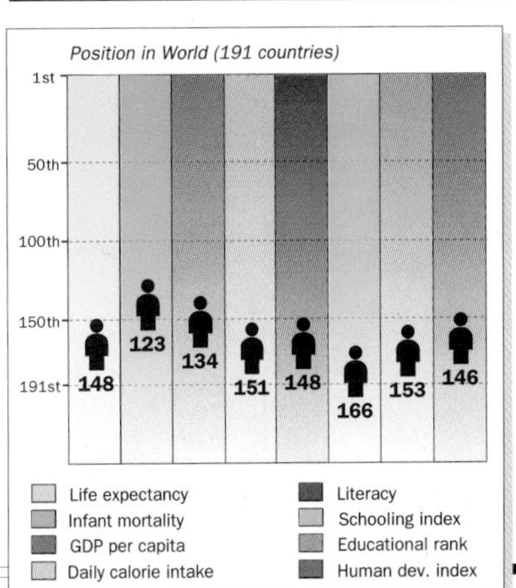

P

PARAGUAY

OFFICIAL NAME: Republic of Paraguay **CAPITAL:** Asunción
POPULATION: 4.5 million **CURRENCY:** Guaraní **OFFICIAL LANGUAGE:** Spanish and Guaraní

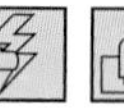
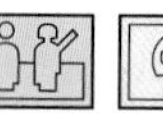
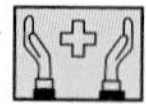

LANDLOCKED IN CENTRAL South America and a Spanish possession until 1811, Paraguay won large tracts of land from Bolivia in 1835. From then until the overthrow in 1989 of General Stroessner, South America's longest-surviving dictator, it experienced periods of anarchy and military rule. The River Paraguay divides the eastern hills and fertile plains, where 90% of people live, from the almost uninhabited Chaco in the west. Paraguay's economy is largely agricultural.

CLIMATE

WEATHER CHART

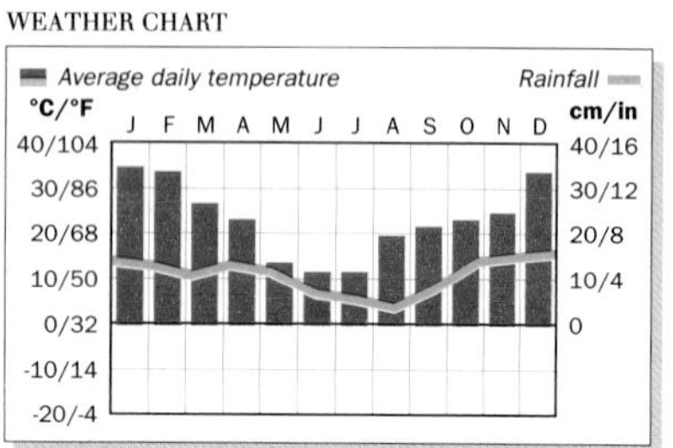

Paraguay is subtropical with all parts experiencing floods and droughts, but the Chaco is generally drier and hotter.

COMMUNICATIONS

Silvio Pettirossi Intl, Asunción 320,000 passengers

12 ships 19,100 dwt

THE TRANSPORTATION NETWORK

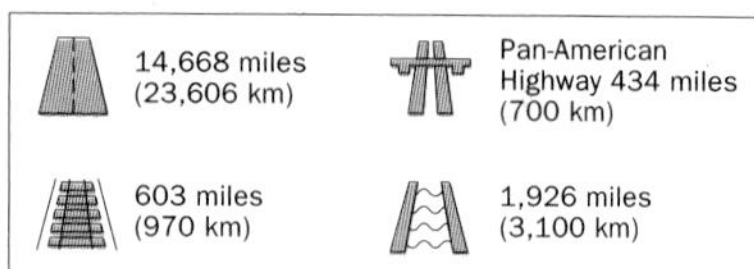

There are plans to privatize the airline and seek foreign investment to upgrade roads and the antiquated railroads.

TOURISM

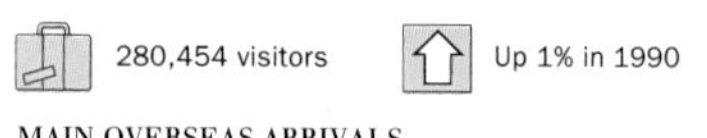

MAIN OVERSEAS ARRIVALS

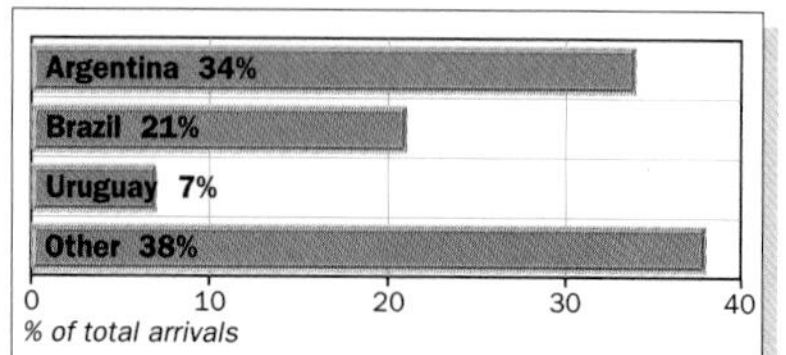

Tourism is low-level, except for large numbers of day-trippers from Brazil and Argentina, who flock to Ciudad del Este to buy cheap, mainly Far Eastern electrical goods. It is hoped the Chaco will entice ecotourists.

PEOPLE

Guaraní, Spanish

28 people per sq. mile

THE URBAN/RURAL POPULATION SPLIT

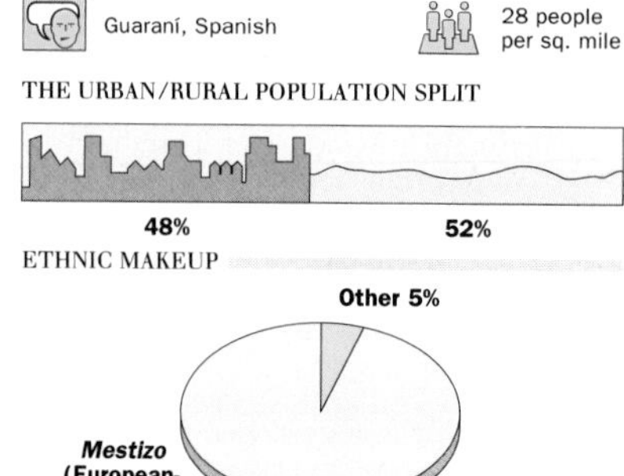

Tensions in society are minimal as most Paraguayans are of combined Spanish and native Guaraní origin. The majority are bilingual, although outside the large cities, Guaraní is spoken almost exclusively. Most people live in the southeast. The vast and almost empty Chaco is home to two-thirds of the small number of indigenous Indians, who legally own their lands but do not have control of them in practice.

POLITICS

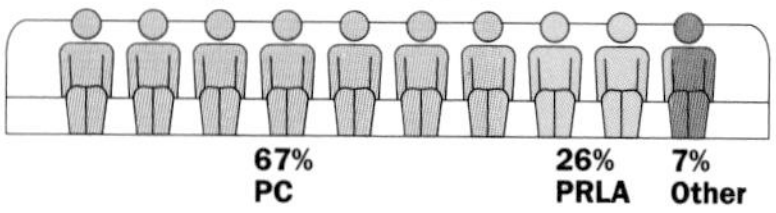

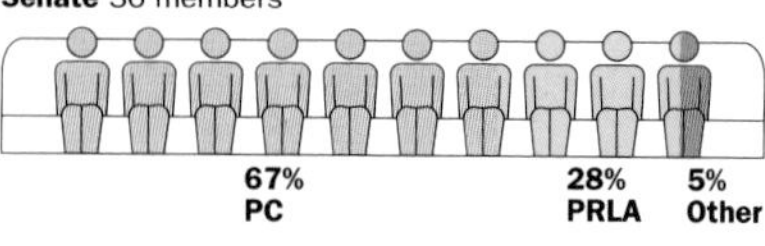

PC = Colorado Party **PRLA** = Authentic Radical Liberal Party
Other = Revolutionary Febrerista Party, Radical Liberal Party, Christian Democrat Party

Senate 36 members

67% PC | 28% PRLA | 5% Other

General Stroessner's failing health and grasp of affairs, disputes among the military elite about the succession, and economic discontent, brought General Rodríguez to power in 1989 in a one-night coup. His promise to bring in democracy was fulfilled in 1993 in the first free elections in 60 years of military rule. The PC, Stroessner's old ruling party, still received sufficient support to win both congressional and presidential elections. However, Guillermo Caballero Vargas, a leading businessman representing the PRLA and a chief exponent of free-market ideology, won half of Asunción's votes, suggesting his party may do even better in the next elections.

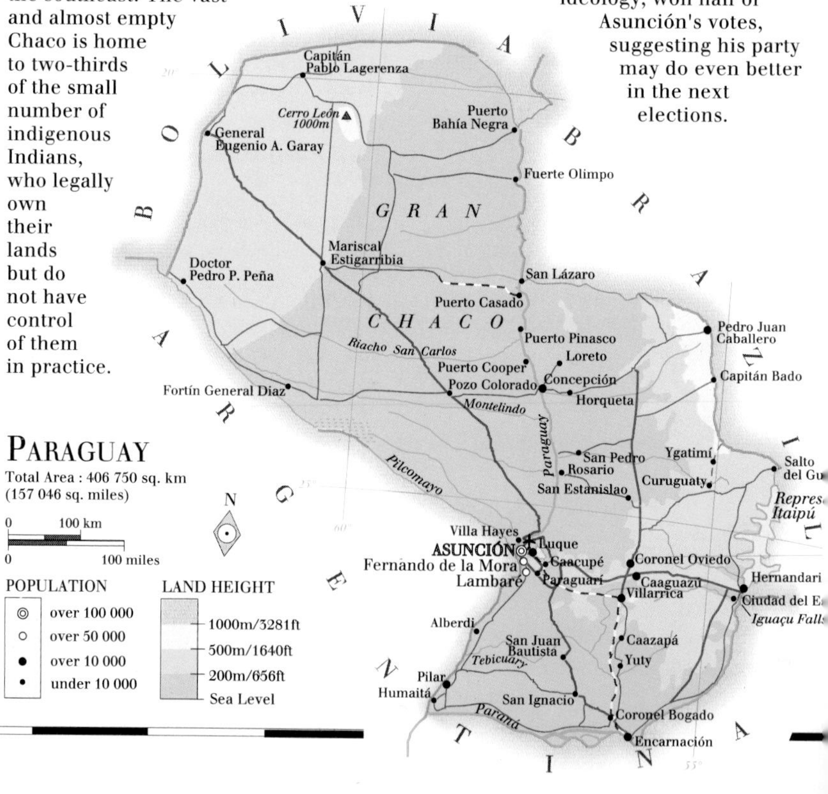

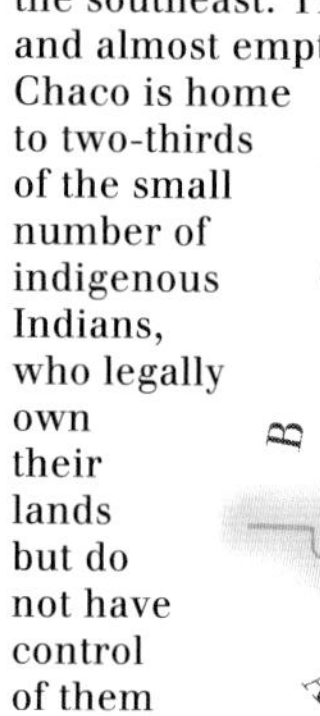

PARAGUAY

Total Area : 406 750 sq. km (157 046 sq. miles)

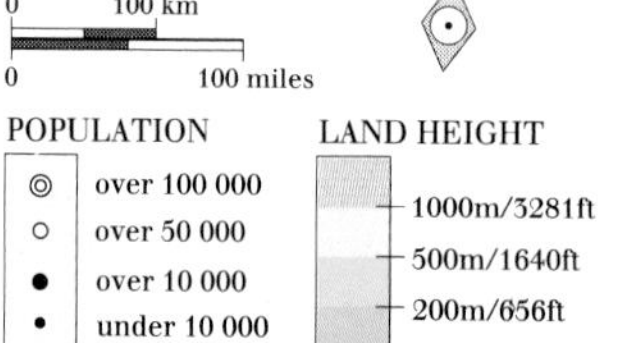

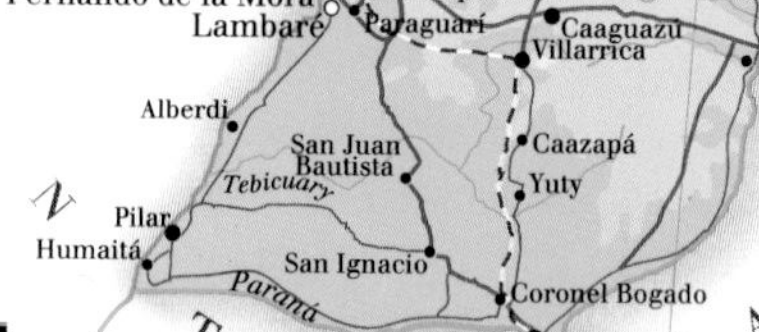

WORLD AFFAIRS

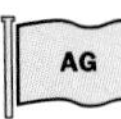

OAS | LAES | ECLAC | RG | AG

Paraguay's main aims are integration in the MERCOSUR common market and improving relations with the USA.

AID

 $144m (receipts)  Up 157% in 1991

The World Bank and IMF are the chief providers (2% of GNP). NGO charities run small programs in rural areas.

DEFENSE

 $60.59m  Up 38% in 1989

Under Stroessner, the 26,000-strong military had 42 generals and 245 colonels – a high ratio. Because it was high-ranking officers who controlled political and economic life, their full disengagement is likely to be slow. In 1992, the army chief and others were implicated in a car-smuggling scandal.

ECONOMICS

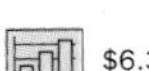 $6.3bn  1,794.96 guaranies

SCORE CARD

- ❑ WORLD GNP RANKING...:....................100th
- ❑ GNP PER CAPITA $1,400
- ❑ BALANCE OF PAYMENTS ....$–622
- ❑ INFLATION 14.6%
- ❑ UNEMPLOYMENT...................................5.1%

STRENGTHS
Electricity exporter – earnings cover oil imports. Self-sufficiency in wheat and other staple foodstuffs. Cotton (up to 50% of exports). Oilseeds, notably soya.

WEAKNESSES
Very high reliance on agriculture – 30% of GDP, 90% of exports, 45% of labor force. Has virtually no minerals. Landlocked and remote. Slow growth. Dependent on growth in neighboring countries.

EXPORTS

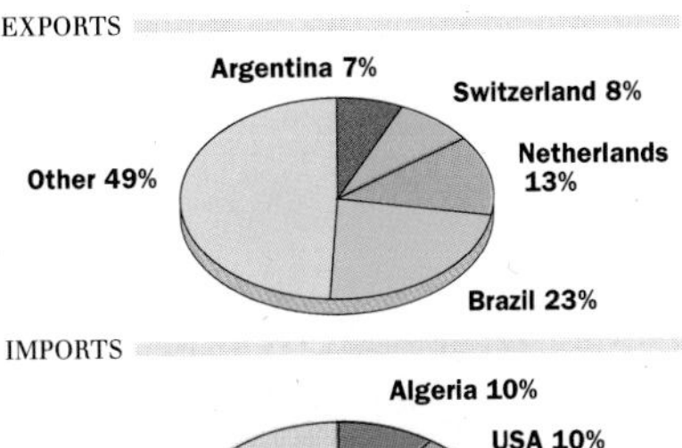

IMPORTS

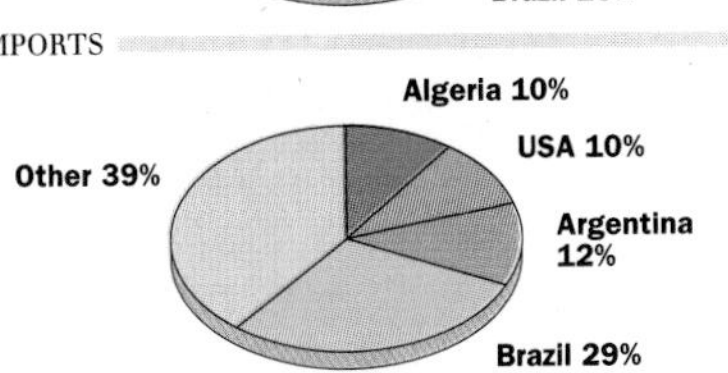

The Iguaçu Falls, on the border with Brazil and Argentina, are composed of over 20 cataracts, separated by rocks and tree-covered islands.

RESOURCES

 2.4bn kwh (capacity 5.8m kw)  Not an oil producer; refines 7500 b/cd

 8m cattle, 2.3m pigs, 449,000 sheep  Iron, manganese

The joint Paraguay–Brazil Itaipú HEP has the world's largest generating capacity. Paraguay now has an exportable electricity surplus.

ENVIRONMENT

 3% (0.1% partially protected) 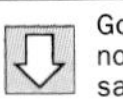 Government has no environmental safeguard policies yet

Apart from the destruction of forests for farming, the chief ecological worry is the smuggling abroad of endangered species, particularly parrots.

MEDIA

 The press is free in theory and banned newspapers have reopened, but there have been some recent instances of shootings and beatings of journalists

PUBLISHING AND BROADCAST MEDIA

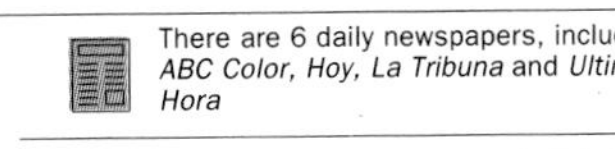 There are 6 daily newspapers, including *ABC Color, Hoy, La Tribuna* and *Ultima Hora*

 5 independent services 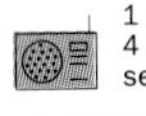 1 state-owned, 4 independent services

The media is generally sponsored by political parties. It flourished after the fall of Stroessner, publishing details of corruption and human rights abuses, but is no longer concentrating on investigative reporting.

CRIME

 Paraguay does not publish prison figures  Up 29% in 1990

Paraguay is the contraband capital of Latin America, with trade in everything from cars to cocaine. Jungle airstrips near Brazil provide a route for drugs.

EDUCATION

 90%

In 1989, an estimated 93% of children attended primary school, but only 24% secondary school. Provision is limited in remote rural areas.

CHRONOLOGY

Paraguay was controlled by Spain from 1536 until 1811.

- ❑ **1864–1870** Loses War of the Triple Alliance against Argentina, Brazil and Uruguay; bloodiest ever in Latin America.
- ❑ **1928–1935** Two Chaco Wars against Bolivia; Paraguay wins most of the disputed land.
- ❑ **1954** Gen. Alfredo Stroessner seizes power; repressive military regime.
- ❑ **1984** Opposition demonstrations.
- ❑ **1989** Stroessner deposed by Gen. Andrés Rodríguez; democracy promised.
- ❑ **1991–1993** Brazil fails to pay Itaipú electricity royalties; in 1992 alone, these were to provide 25% of national budget.
- ❑ **1993** First democratic elections.

HEALTH

 1 per 1,007 people 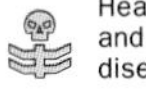 Heart, respiratory and parasitic diseases, cancer

Only one-third of the population has safe drinking water. Half of the country's hospital beds are located in Asunción.

WEALTH

 Kitchen assistant, 300,000 guaranies per month

CONSUMER GOODS OWNERSHIP

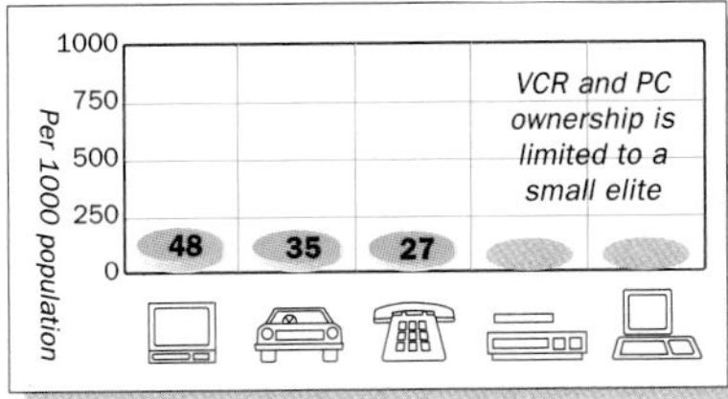

After 60 years of monopolizing lucrative state contracts, the top ranks of the military still control wealth.

WORLD RANKING

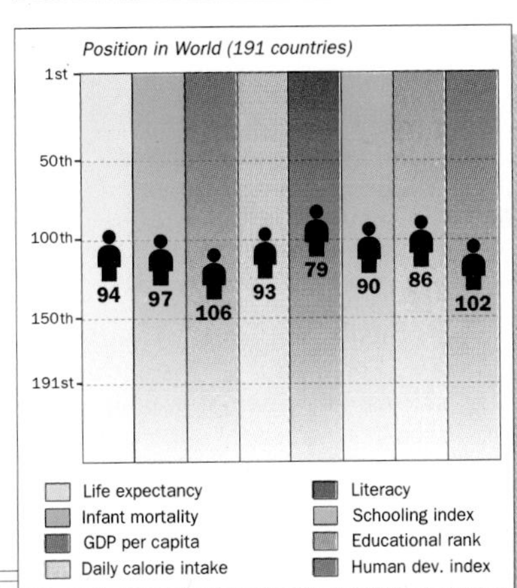

P

PERU

SOUTH AMERICA

Ecuador

Columbia

Brazil

PERU

Bolivia

Chile

South America

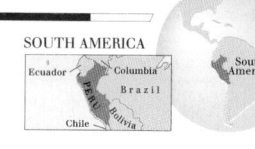

OFFICIAL NAME: Republic of Peru **CAPITAL:** Lima **POPULATION:** 22.5 million
CURRENCY: New sol **OFFICIAL LANGUAGES:** Spanish, Quechua and Aymará

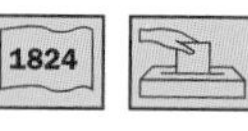

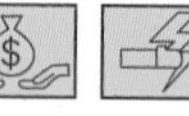

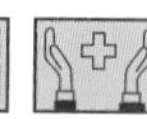

LYING JUST SOUTH OF THE EQUATOR, on the Pacific coast of South America, Peru became independent of Spain in 1824. It rises from an arid western coastal strip to the Andes, dominated in the south by volcanoes; about half of Peru's population lives in mountain regions. Its border with Bolivia to the south runs through Lake Titicaca, the highest navigable lake in the world. In 1992, Peru agreed to allow landlocked Bolivia access to the Pacific port of Ilo; the two countries are developing it into a duty-free zone.

CLIMATE

WEATHER CHART

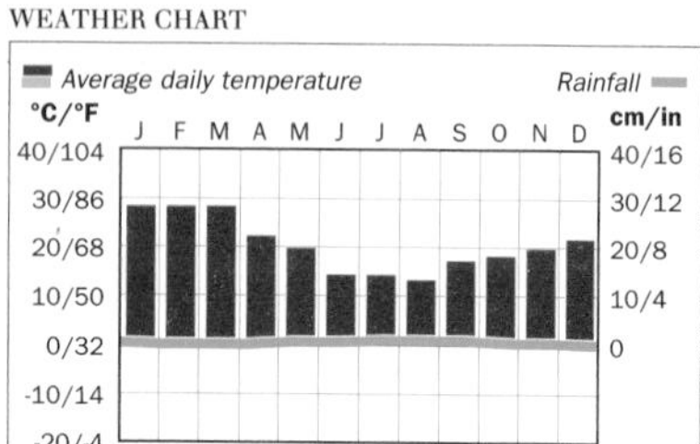

Peru has several distinct climatic regions. The arid or desert coastal region experiences the *garúa*, persistent low cloud and fog, giving Lima cool winters even though it is close to the equator. The temperate slopes of the Andes have wide daily temperature ranges and one rainy season, while the tropical Amazon Basin receives year-round rains.

COMMUNICATIONS

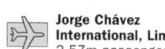

Jorge Chávez International, Lima 2.57m passengers

35 ships 519,900 dwt

THE TRANSPORTATION NETWORK

43,364 miles (69,942 km)

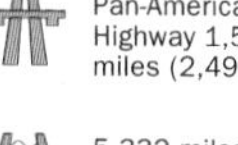

Pan-American Highway 1,547 miles (2,495 km)

1,487 miles (2,399 km)

5,332 miles (8,600 km)

The government is resurfacing some of the road network (most is unpaved and subject to landslides during the rains), and rebuilding bridges destroyed in the guerrilla war with *Sendero Luminoso*. Work has begun on a transcontinental highway from Ilo, a free port on the Pacific, via Puerto Suárez in Bolivia, to the port of Portos in Brazil. The two rail networks, the Central and Southern, are as yet unconnected. The La Oroya–Huancayo line is the world's highest stretch of standard-gauge railroad. River transportation provides major access to Iquitos in Amazonia. There are over 130 airports.

Spanish colonial church near Urubamba. *The Urubamba River, with its deep gorges, was known as the Sacred Valley to the Incas.*

TOURISM

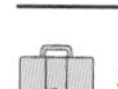

316,873 visitors

Down 5% in 1990. Still falling due to political instability

MAIN OVERSEAS ARRIVALS

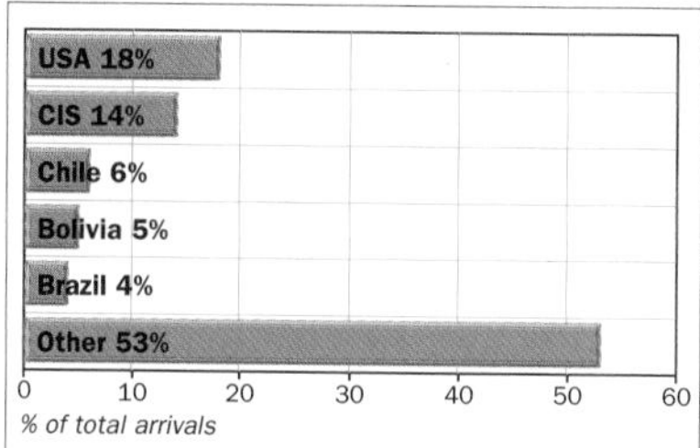

The five-day hike to Macho Picchu, the world-famous Inca city ruins in the Andes at the end of the 20-mile *Camino Inca*, is the most popular trek in South America. The trail is also visited by thousands of day-trippers. Ecotourism at lodges in the Amazon is growing. Whether this will promote conservation is disputed by some environmentalists. Many object that indigenous families are being forced to work, dance and produce handicrafts for tourists. The pre-Colombian desert areas cleared in patterns by the Nazca civilization (known as the Nazca lines) dating from the 2nd century BC, are another major attraction. However, Peru's recent political instability, visitors' fear of guerrilla activity and the relatively poor infrastructure limit tourist numbers.

PEOPLE

Spanish, Quechua, Aymará

44 people per sq. mile

THE URBAN/RURAL POPULATION SPLIT

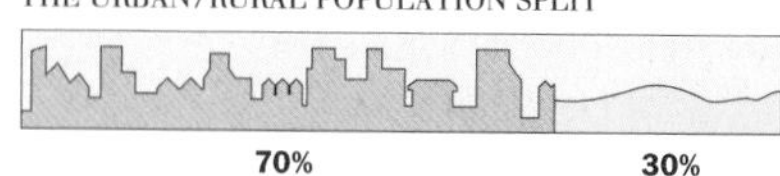

RELIGIOUS PERSUASION

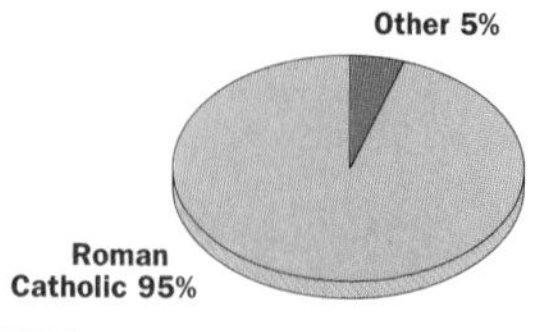

ETHNIC MAKEUP

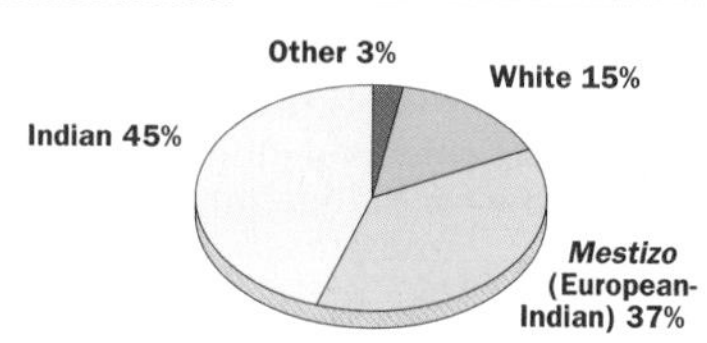

The majority of Peruvians are Indian or *mestizo*. The small group of Spanish descendants retain much of their hold on the economy, power and social standing. A few Chinese and Japanese live in the northern cities.

Most of Peru's three million Andean Indians live an existence completely detached from that of the urban residents of Lima and the coastal strip. They speak only their native Quechua and Aymará, and no Spanish. A further 250,000 Amazonian Indians live in the eastern lowlands. They, together with the small community of blacks (descendants of plantation workers), tend to suffer considerable discrimination in the towns.

The extended family remains strong. A part of traditional native Indian traditions, its role as a social bond was strengthened by Catholicism. In recent years, economic difficulties have raised its profile as the key social support system for most Peruvians. One result, however, is that society remains strongly patriarchal; feminism has had little impact in Peru.

POPULATION AGE BREAKDOWN

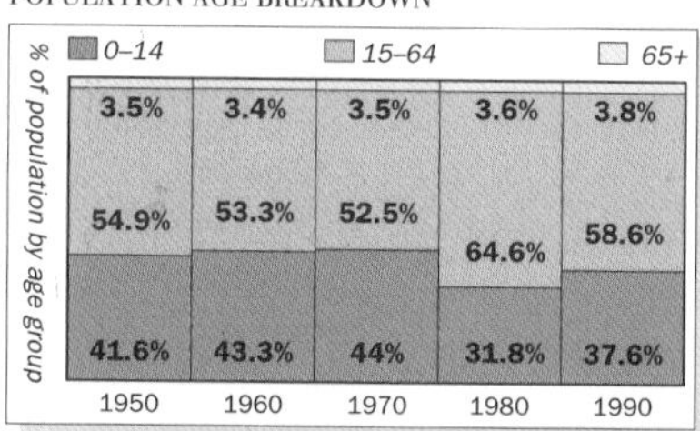

POLITICS

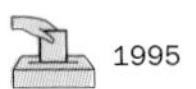
1995

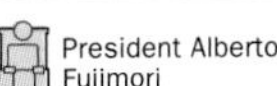
President Alberto Fujimori

President Fujimori. His dismissal of parliament was widely approved.

Leading novelist Mario Vargas Llosa, who contested the presidency in 1990.

Peru is nominally a multiparty democracy in which the president holds executive power.

MAIN POLITICAL ISSUES

Sendero Luminoso

The *Sendero Luminoso* (Shining Path) guerrilla movement has been the main cause of Peru's recent political instability. Terrorist activity in the Andes, such as the murders of 60 members of the traditionally peaceful Ashaninka tribe in 1993, have made large areas of Peru ungovernable except by military rule. In 1992, Abimael Guzmán, *Sendero*'s leader, was captured, a propaganda victory for the government. However, the Maoist group have declared they will continue their activities. President Fujimori has staked his reputation on their defeat.

THE STATE OF THE PARTIES

Democratic Constituent Congress 80 members

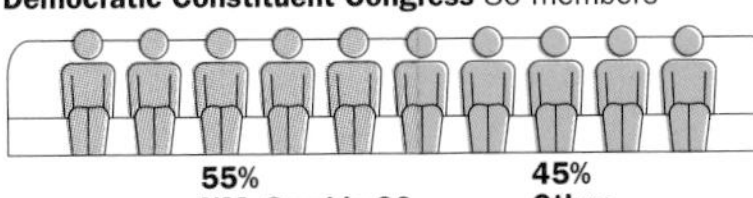

NM–Cambio-90 = New Majority–Change-90 **Other** = Popular Christian Party, Independent Moralizing Front, Renovation, Democratic Left Movement

Democracy and the president's coup

In April 1992, President Fujimori, backed by the army, dismissed parliament, replacing it with an unelected Constituent Congress. He also introduced a new constitution allowing him to run again for election in 1995. To date, most Peruvians seem to have accepted his coup as being necessary for strong government. However, Fujimori has to realize his avowed goal of destroying terrorism if he is to maintain public support.

Privatization

As in the rest of Latin America, the government is selling state assets in an attempt to reduce the level of inflation and make industry more efficient. The aim is to encourage private investment in new equipment and management, in order to force increasingly uncompetitive Peruvian businesses to modernize.

PROFILE

Peru has been run by a Constituent Congress since 1992, following President Fujimori's coup.

Fujimori broke the long tradition of large parties dominating politics, by winning the 1990 presidential elections with a loose coalition. His success demonstrated the general disenchantment that most Peruvians feel for the politics of the past three decades. The failure of successive governments to deal with *Sendero Luminoso* and human rights violations by the army were key issues in securing Fujimori's election. They also explain why voters seemed happy to accept his coup.

Behind the scenes, the army and large private business concerns still have considerable influence in political affairs.

CHRONOLOGY

Francisco Pizarro's arrival in 1532 during a war of succession between two Inca rulers marked the beginning of the Spanish colonization of Peru, and the end of the Inca Empire.

- **1821** Independence proclaimed in Lima after its capture by the Argentine liberator, José de San Martín, who had just freed Chile.
- **1824** Spain suffers final defeats at battles of Junín and Ayacucho by Simón Bolívar and Gen. Sucre, the liberators of Venezuela and Colombia.
- **1836–1839** Peru and Bolivia joined in short-lived confederation.
- **1866** Peruvian–Spanish War.
- **1879–1884** War of the Pacific. Chile defeats Peru and Bolivia. Peru loses territory in south.
- **1908** Augusto Leguía y Salcedo's dictatorial rule.
- **1919** USA starts financing public works.
- **1924** Dr. Víctor Raúl Haya de la Torre founds left-wing nationalist American Revolutionary Popular Alliance (APRA) in exile in Mexico.
- **1930** Leguía ousted. APRA moves to Peru as first political party.
- **1931–1945** APRA banned.
- **1939–1945** Moderate, pro-US civilian government.
- **1948–1956** Gen. Manuel Odría in power. APRA banned again.
- **1956–1962** Civilian government.
- **1962–1963** Two military coups.

PERU

Total Area : 1 285 220 sq. km (496 223 sq. miles)

POPULATION
- over 1 000 000
- over 500 000
- over 100 000
- over 50 000
- under 50 000

LAND HEIGHT
- 4000m/13124ft
- 2000m/6562ft
- 500m/1640ft
- Sea Level

0 100 km
0 100 miles

CHRONOLOGY *continued*

- **1963** Election of Fernando Belaúnde Terry. Land reform, but military used to suppress communist-inspired insurgency.
- **1968** Military junta takes over. Attempts to alleviate poverty. Large-scale nationalizations.
- **1975–1978** New right-wing junta.
- **1980** Belaúnde re-elected. Popular Action (AP) wins majority. Maoist guerrilla organization, *Sendero Luminoso* (Shining Path), begins armed struggle.
- **1981** Border war with Ecuador over Cordillera del Cóndor, which a 1942 protocol had given to Peru. Ecuador wants access to Amazon.
- **1982** Deaths and "disappearances" start to escalate as army cracks down on guerrillas and narcotics.
- **1985** Electoral win for left-wing APRA under Alán García Pérez.
- **1987** Peru bankrupt. Guzmán's plans to nationalize banks blocked by new *Libertad* movement led by writer Mario Vargas Llosa.
- **1990** Over 3,000 political murders. Alberto Fujimori, an independent, is elected president on an anti-corruption platform. Economic austerity program sends some food prices up 600%.
- **1991** Cholera epidemic.
- **1992** Fujimori suspends democracy in coup and establishes Constituent Congress.
- **1993** New constitution. Death penalty reintroduced.

P

WORLD AFFAIRS

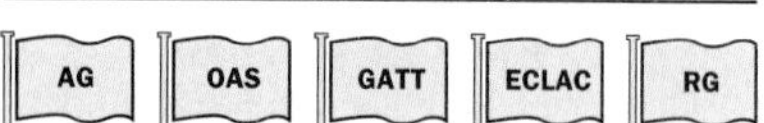

Peru's most important relationship is with the USA, its main source of aid and the most influential power in Latin America. Cooperation with the USA also extends to the war on cocaine, although the policy of eradicating the crop in the Andean foothills has largely failed; Peruvian coca production has been rising rather than falling. Peru is eager to strengthen its regional links, and those with countries on the Pacific Rim, especially Japan.

AID

 $590m (receipts)  Up 49% in 1991

Aid provided by the USA has been mostly to help combat drugs. NGOs and Catholic charities have been active on a small scale in rural areas. The World Bank promised $42 million in 1994 to help with health projects in the Andean highlands.

DEFENSE

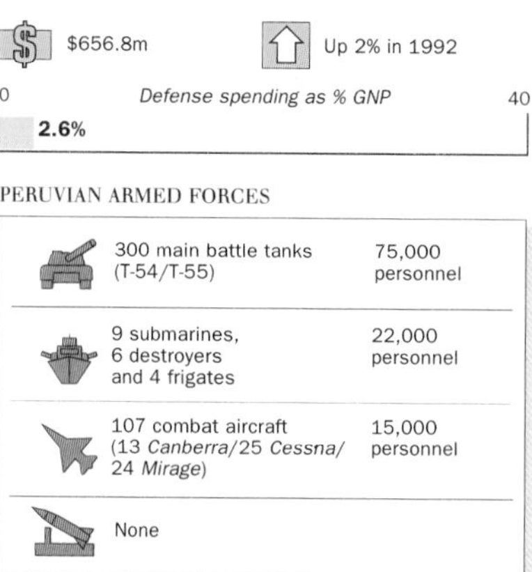

$656.8m
Up 2% in 1992
0
Defense spending as % GNP
40
2.6%
PERUVIAN ARMED FORCES
300 main battle tanks (T-54/T-55)
75,000 personnel
9 submarines, 6 destroyers and 4 frigates
22,000 personnel
107 combat aircraft (13 Canberra/25 Cessna/ 24 Mirage)
15,000 personnel
None

The military, in power from 1968 to 1980, continues to exert a direct and powerful influence in politics. Many of Peru's Andean regions are under direct military rule, the only means by which the state can combat the terrorist activities of *Sendero Luminoso.* Rule in these regions can be brutal. Amnesty International has reported cases of whole villages being punished for allegedly siding with *Sendero Luminoso*. In the same way, *Sendero Luminoso* terrorizes villagers who side with the army.

Most arms procurement by the armed forces is from the USA. Recent budgetary problems have, however, left the army under-equipped.

ECONOMICS

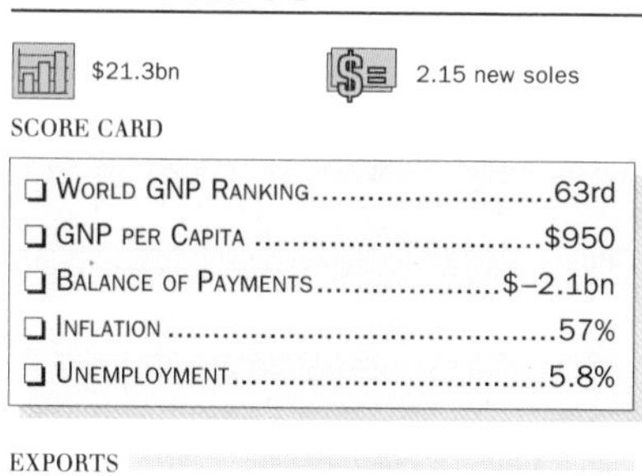

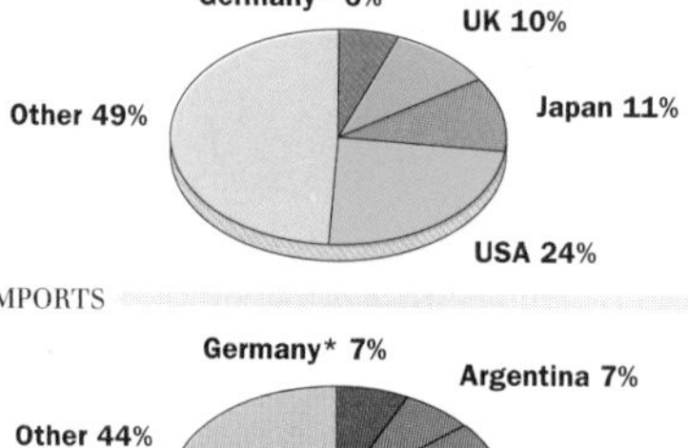

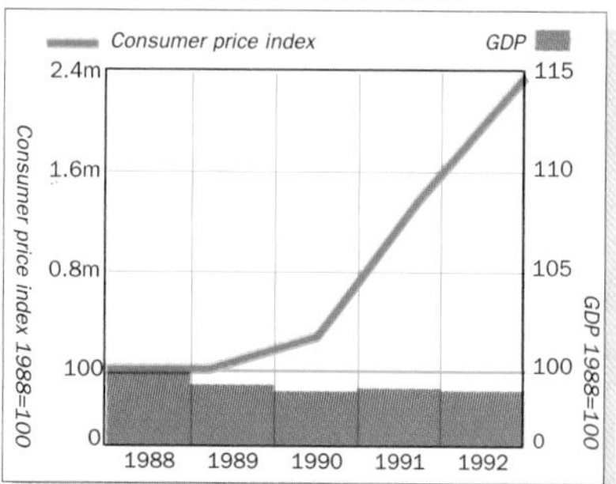

Strengths

Abundant mineral resources, including oil. Rich fish stocks in the Pacific. Wide variety of climates allowing diverse and productive agriculture; cotton and coffee are important. Well-developed textile industry.

Weaknesses

Hyperinflation in the late 1980s destroyed confidence domestically and abroad. Foreign investors discouraged by political instability and terrorism. High levels of poverty exacerbate social tensions.

Profile

Wealth and economic activity in Peru is largely confined to the cities of the coastal plain. The inhabitants of the Andean uplands are subsistence farmers or coca producers. Disrupting the coca crop has not only damaged an important local economy, but also driven the growers into the hands of guerrilla groups such as *Sendero Luminoso.*

The thrust of state economic policy has changed radically since Peru's bankruptcy under the left-wing APRA administration of President Alan García. The Fujimori government is selling off state interests in everything from copper mining and oil exploitation to ports and roads, in one of the most radical and rapid privatizations in Latin America.

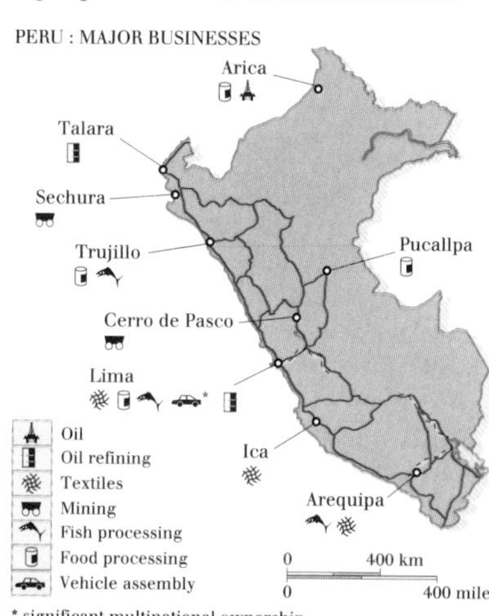

RESOURCES

13.8bn kwh (capacity 4.1m kw)

116,800 b/d (reserves 380,866,000 bbl)

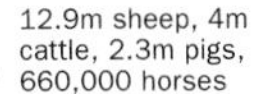

12.9m sheep, 4m cattle, 2.3m pigs, 660,000 horses

Oil, lead, zinc, silver, iron, gold, copper

ELECTRICITY GENERATION

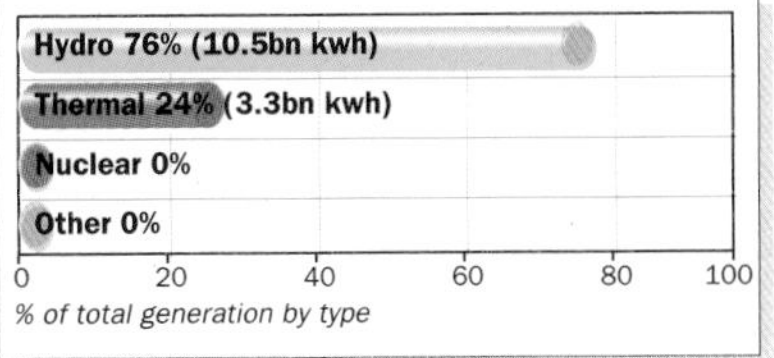

Peru is an important exporter of copper and lead. Further exploration is required to establish the true extent of its large oil reserves. The state oil concern, *PetroPeru*, is being privatized to attract new investment into the industry. The further development of hydroelectric power is a priority.

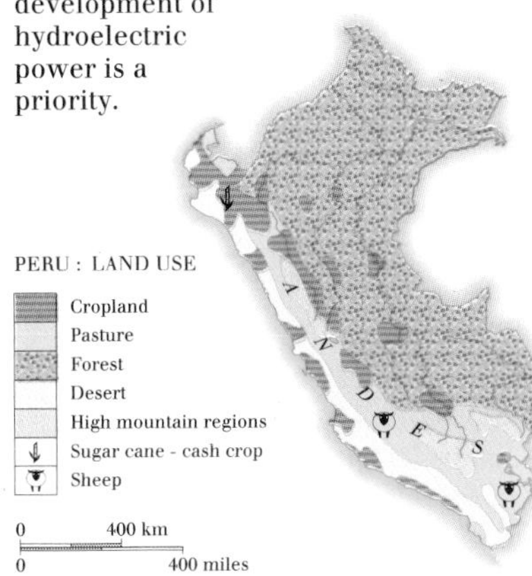

ENVIRONMENT

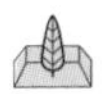

2% (0.1% parially protected)

No measures to prevent dolphin fishing

ENVIRONMENTAL TREATIES

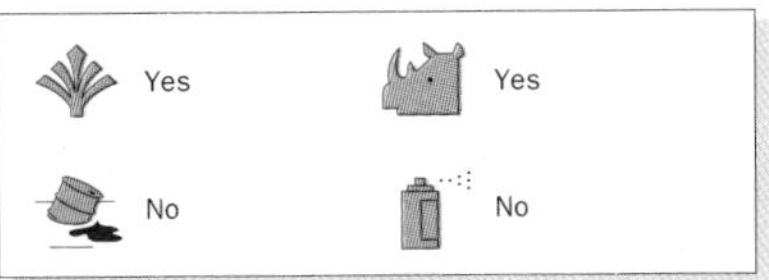

Peru's environmentalists have long been concerned about coastal industrial pollution and the activities of its fishing industry. Overfishing of anchovies almost resulted in their extinction in the 1970s. Today, attention has switched to the rise in the number of dolphins being caught in drift nets – 3,000 in 1992. Dolphin meat is being sold as a cheap alternative to pork and beef in Peruvian markets.

Concern has also turned to the coca industry. Environmentalists fear that Peru's and the USA's policy of using powerful air-sprayed herbicides to destroy the crop is adding to river pollution in the Andes.

MEDIA

Press freedom is theoretically guaranteed. In practice, the media are expected to denounce terrorists and keep silent on human rights abuses

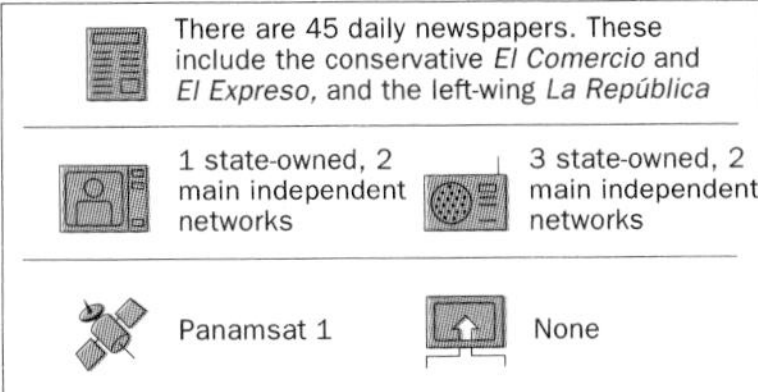

There are 45 daily newspapers. These include the conservative *El Comercio* and *El Expreso*, and the left-wing *La República*
1 state-owned, 2 main independent networks
3 state-owned, 2 main independent networks
Panamsat 1
None

Media freedom is severely restricted. Journalists and newspaper editors regularly receive death threats.

CRIME

17,368 prisoners

Up 22% in 1990

CRIME RATES

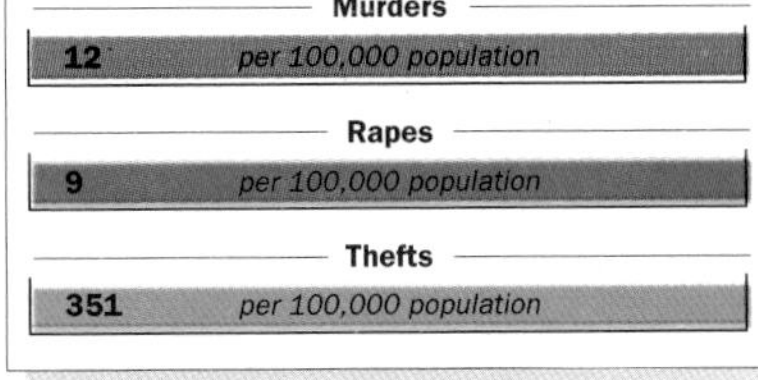

Random bombings, kidnappings and shoot-outs with security forces are still major problems in Peru. Main cities regularly have curfews and those who can afford it protect themselves with high-security homes and armed guards.

In the Andes, where *Sendero Luminoso* has been active, military law has suspended normal rights. Since 1980, over 25,000 have died as a result of guerrilla, and army, violence.

EDUCATION

95%

0 *Education spending as % GNP* 25

3.5%

THE EDUCATION SYSTEM

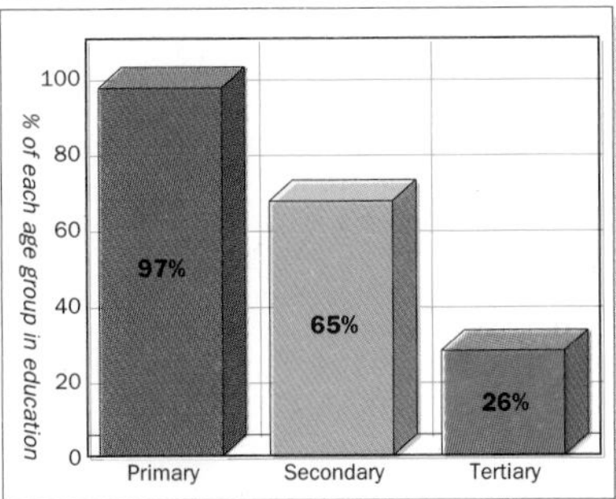

Education is based on the US system. Spending has been declining. The state and private university system is accessible to a small minority.

HEALTH

1 per 966 people

Respiratory, heart, infectious and parasitic diseases

0 *Health spending as % GNP* 25

0.8%

Peru's public health system virtually collapsed in the late 1980s. In many areas primary care is now non-existent. Advanced treatment is available only to private patients in city clinics. Goiter, a thyroid abnormality, is widespread, with a 38% prevalence among children in mountain areas; in some regions the incidence may be as high as 90%. Infant mortality is rising, the result of increasing social deprivation, diarrheal diseases and tuberculosis. Malaria is once again widespread, and cholera returned in 1991, reaching epidemic proportions by 1994.

WEALTH

Chemical industry machine operator, 45 new soles per week; journalist, 377 new soles per month

CONSUMER GOODS OWNERSHIP

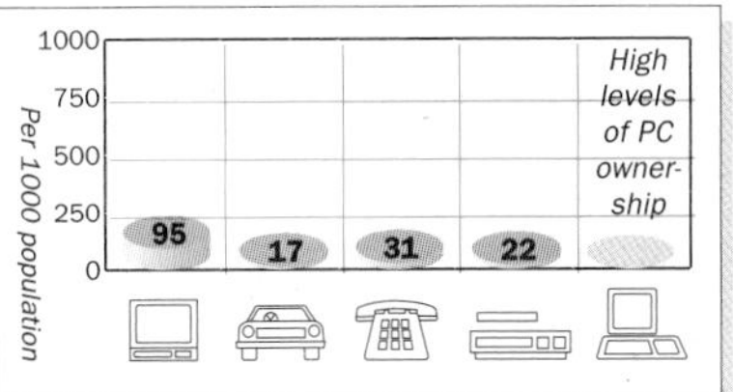

Most wealth and power in Peru is still held by old Spanish families. Indigenous peoples remain excluded from both. The wealthy in Peru live in a state of siege; a key status symbol is the number of armed guards and security cameras protecting family property. German cars – Mercedes or BMWs – are now more fashionable than American ones, while San Francisco and Miami have replaced Paris as fashionable destinations. The UN estimates that over 30% of Peruvians live below the poverty line.

WORLD RANKING

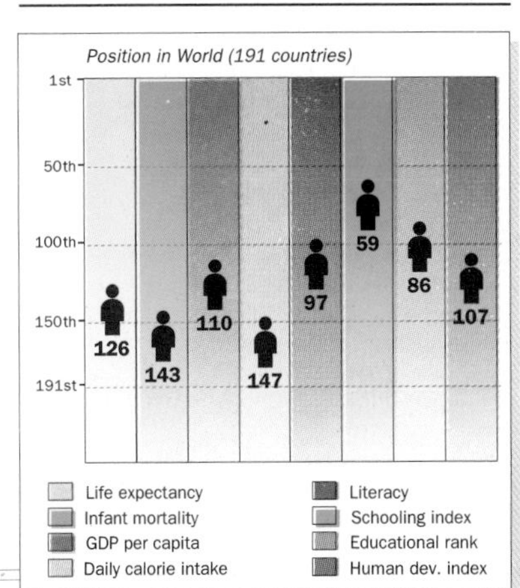

PHILIPPINES

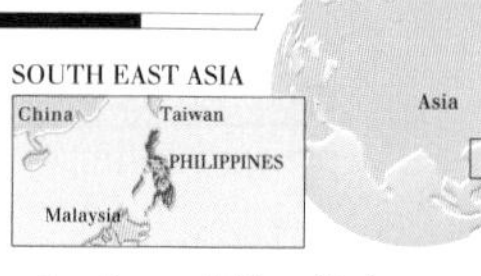

OFFICIAL NAME: Republic of the Philippines **CAPITAL:** Manila
POPULATION: 65.2 million **CURRENCY:** Philippine peso **OFFICIAL LANGUAGES:** Pilipino (Tagalog) and English

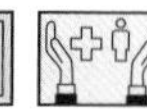

LYING IN THE WESTERN Pacific Ocean, the Philippines is the world's second largest archipelago after Indonesia. It comprises 7,107 islands, of which 4,600 are named and 1,000 inhabited. There are three main island groupings: the Luzon group, the Visayan group and the Mindanao and Sulu islands. Located on the Pacific "Ring of Fire," the Philippines is subject to frequent earthquakes and volcanic activity. Since 1992, President Fidel Ramos has worked hard to bring political stability to the country. However, economic expansion continues to fall short of the Philippines' population-growth rate.

***Bohol Island** has over 1000 of these famous mounds, also known as 'the chocolate hills'.*

CLIMATE

WEATHER CHART

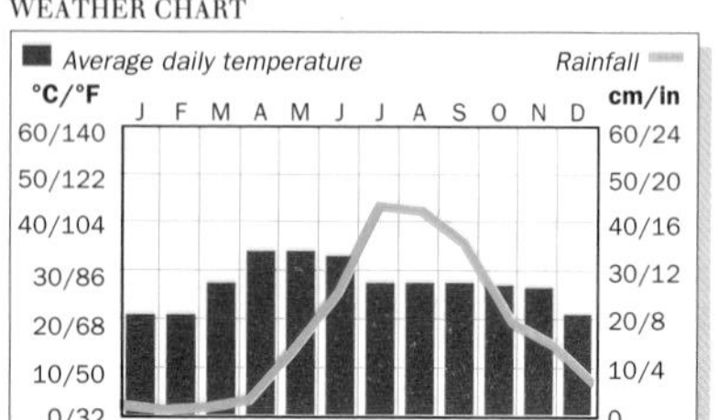

The Philippines is warm and humid all year. The rainy season lasts from June to October. Humidity falls from 85% in September to 71% in March.

TOURISM

951,365 visitors

Down 48% between 1989 and 1991

MAIN OVERSEAS ARRIVALS

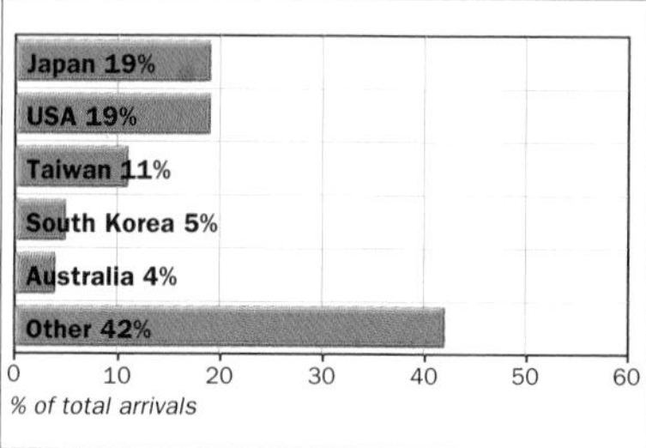

Tourism remains a smaller business in the Philippines than in the NICs of Southeast Asia. The industry is still largely based around sex-tourism. However, business may suffer when an Australian law banning its citizens from sex-tourism holidays comes into effect. Many of the islands have tourism potential. Palawan, one of the least spoiled, retains most of its tropical rainforest and coral lagoons. The rice terraces of northern Luzon are another attraction.

COMMUNICATIONS

Nino Aquino Intl, Pasay City
6.44m passengers

834 ships
13.67m dwt

THE TRANSPORTATION NETWORK

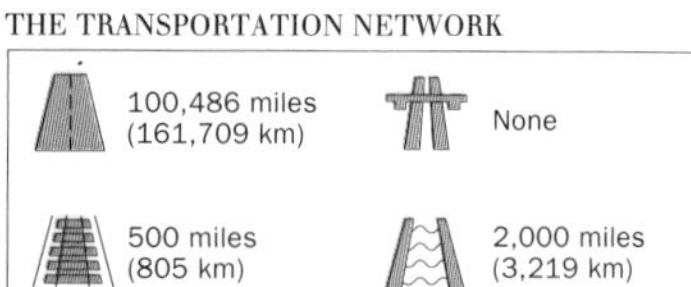

Spending on transport infrastructure has fallen by over 40% since 1984. As a result, many main roads are in need of repair. Traffic jams in Manila are a growing problem and are holding back economic growth. Air transport is the only means of getting around the islands quickly.

In 1992, the state airline, Philippines Airlines, was privatized. It is planning to buy $1.2 billion-worth of new aircraft and to add to its regional route network. Subic Bay, the USA's largest overseas base until 1992, when the US Navy decided to leave, has a prime strategic location, which the government is now exploiting. Opening onto the South China Sea, its deep natural harbor is being developed as a free port and enterprise zone. The Taiwanese are the biggest investors in this project.

PHILIPPINES

Total Area : 300 000 sq. km (777 001 sq. miles)

POPULATION
over 1 000 000
over 500 000
over 100 000

LAND HEIGHT
2000m/6562ft
1000m/3281ft
500m/1640ft
200m/656ft
Sea Level

0 200 km
0 200 miles

Batan Is · Babuyan Is · Babuyan Channel · Cordillera Central · Cagayan · Abra · Sierra Madre · Magat · Lingayen Gulf · Dagupan · Baguio · San Carlos · Luzon · Tarlac · Angeles · Cabanatuan City · San Fernando · Olongapo · Malolos · Polillo Is · Subic Bay · San Juan del Monte · MANILA · Muntinglupa · Laguna de Bay · Calagua Is · San Pablo · Lucena · Batangas · Lipa · Lubang I. · Naga · Catanduanes I. · Marinduque I. · Legaspi · Mindoro Strait · Mindoro · Burias I. · Sibuyan Sea · Busuanga I. · Calamian Group · Tablas I. · Sibuyan I. · Masbate · Calbayog · Culion I. · Semirara Is · Quiniluban Group · Jintotolo Channel · Biliran I. · Samar · Cuyo West Passage · Visayan Sea · Panay · Ormoc · Tacloban · Cuyo Is · Cuyo East Passage · Silay · Cadiz · Sagay · Leyte Gulf · Palawan · Iloilo · Bacolod · Toledo · Mandaue · Leyte · Dinagat I. · Bago · Cebu · Siargao I. · Palawan Passage · Puerto Princesa · Panay Gulf · San Carlos City · Bohol · Negros · Cagayan Is · Bohol Sea · Butuan · Cagayan de Oro · Diuata Mountains · Agusan · SULU SEA · Mindanao · Iligan · Lake Lanao · Pulangi · Tagum · Balabac I. · Balabac Strait · Davao · Zamboanga · Moro Gulf · Mount Apo 2954m · Alah · Pilas Group · Basilan I. · Davao Gulf · Pangutaran Group · Tapiantana Group · Samales Group · General Santos · Jolo I. · Jolo Group · Sarangani Is · Tapul Group · Tawi-Tawi · Tawi-Tawi Group · SULU ARCHIPELAGO · CELEBES SEA · MALAYSIA (BORNEO) · SOUTH CHINA SEA · PHILIPPINE SEA · PACIFIC OCEAN · N

PEOPLE

Pilipino, Cebuano, Hiligaynon, Samaran, Ilocano, Bikol, English

523 people per sq. mile

THE URBAN/RURAL POPULATION SPLIT

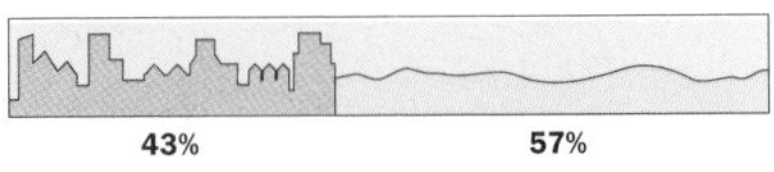

RELIGIOUS PERSUASION

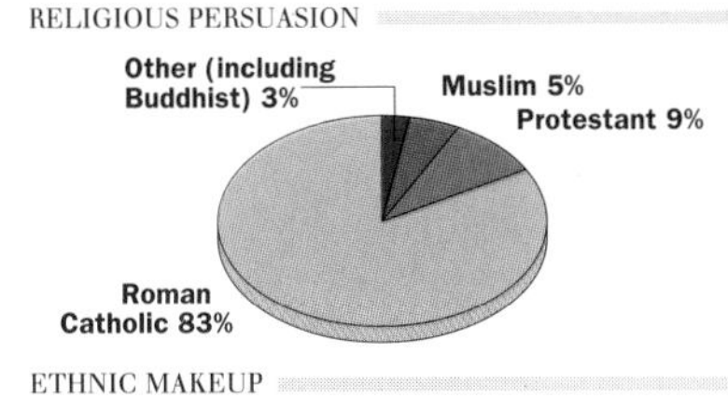

ETHNIC MAKEUP

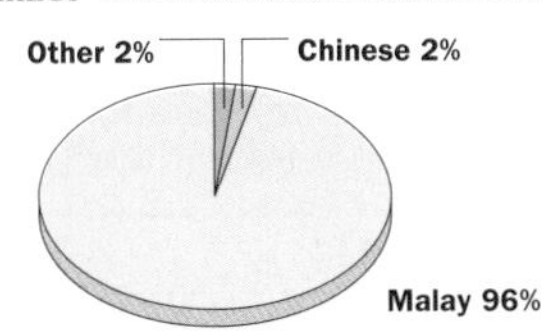

POPULATION AGE BREAKDOWN

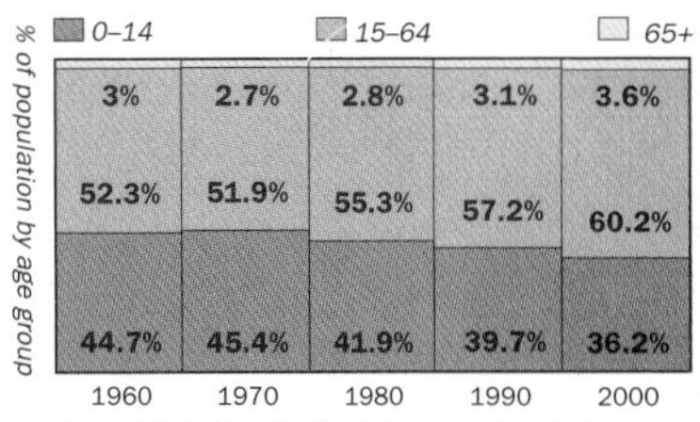

The Philippines encompasses more than 100 distinct ethnic groups. The majority of Filipinos are of Malay origin, and Christian. Most Christians belong to the Tagalog, Cebuano, Llocan, Longgo, Bicolano, Waray, Pampangueno or Pangasinense ethnic groups. They are concentrated on the main island, Luzon, and are a majority on Mindanao. Most Muslims also live on Mindanao, but many are also found in the Sulu archipelago. The Chinese minority, which was well established by 1603, has remained significant in business and trade. More than 120 Chinese schools have ensured that it has retained a distinct identity.

There are also a number of cultural minorities who practice animist religions. They include the Ifugaos, Bontocks, Kalingas and Ibalois on Luzon, the Manobo and Bukidnon on Mindanao, and the Mangyans on Palawan. Many of these groups speak Malayo-Polynesian dialects. Limited intermarriage with other peoples has meant that groups in the more remote regions have managed to retain their traditional ways of life.

The Philippines is the only Christian state in Asia; over 80% of Filipinos are Roman Catholics and the Church is the dominant cultural force in the country. It opposes state-sponsored family planning programs, designed to curb accelerating population growth, currently at 2% a year.

Women have traditionally played a prominent part in Philippine life. Inheritance laws give them equal rights with men. Many go into politics, banking and business, and in several professions women form a majority.

POLITICS

Lower House 1995
Upper House 1998

President Gen Fidel Ramos

THE STATE OF THE PARTIES

House of Representatives 250 members

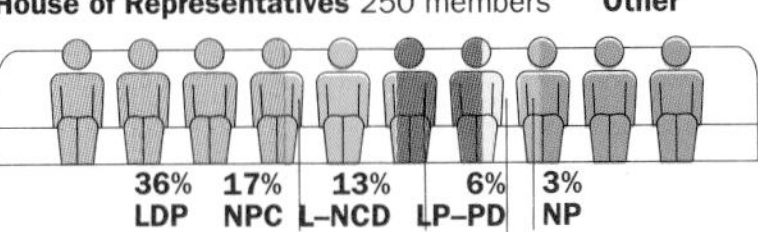

LDP = People's Power Movement of the Democratic Philippines **NPC** = National People's Coalition **L–NCD** = Power of EDSA – National Union of Christian Democrats **LP–PD** = Liberal Party – Philippine Democratic Party – Laban **NP** = Nationalist Party

Senate 24 members

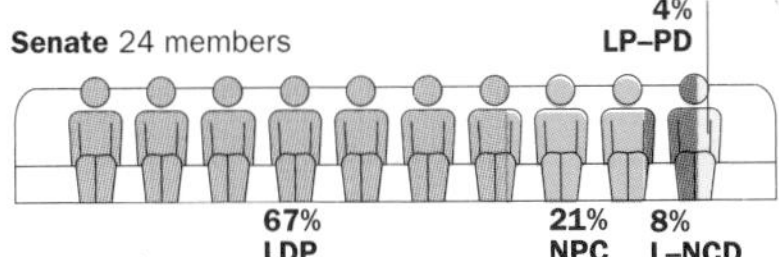

The Philippines is a multiparty democracy.

MAIN POLITICAL ISSUES

Power cuts

The 1986–1992 Aquino administration neglected investment in power stations. As a result, the Philippines suffers from widespread power cuts; in 1992 these occurred on 258 of the 297 working days. The cuts are disrupting business and deterring foreign investment in the Philippines. Under the Electric Power Crisis Law of 1993, President Ramos was given extra powers to deal with the problem. New power station projects will no longer be subject to planning controls and the president is free to raise electricity prices by dictat.

Communist and Muslim separatists

Communist and Muslim separatists have been fighting Manila governments for more than 25 years. Ten thousand armed confrontations with rebels have been recorded by the army during this period. Much of the support for secession has been fueled by the failure of successive governments to curb poverty.

Since 1992, the Ramos government has been pursuing a peace process with all armed groups. The most powerful, the communist New People's Army (NPA), is in decline. Once regarded as a heroic army of the oppressed and as an alternative to traditional politics, it has split into factions. Some wish to achieve an accommodation with the government, while other wings still adhere to their Maoist leader, Jose Maria Sison, living in exile in Holland. The Ramos government is exploiting the divisions. Its peacemaking approach was boosted by the decision of Leopoldo Mabilangan, an NPA leader, to leave the organization. He was subsequently murdered by NPA agents.

PROFILE

Democracy was restored to the Philippines in 1986. Ferdinand Marcos, in power since 1965, was in effect deposed by an army coup headed by Fidel Ramos and Marcos's defense minister, Juan Ponce Enrile. Although Marcos claimed victory, both Ramos and Enrile declared Corazon Aquino the true winner of the 1986 elections

General Fidel Ramos, *was elected president in 1992.*

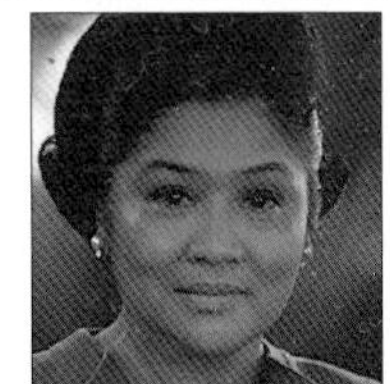
Imelda Marcos, *wife of the former dictator Ferdinand Marcos.*

and the USA decided to remove its backing for Marcos. Corazon Aquino's government succeeded in handing over power through fair elections in 1992, having survived seven coup attempts. Fidel Ramos, winner of the elections, is concentrating on achieving stability and economic growth. However, Ramos was elected on just 23% of the vote and is dependent on loose coalition arrangements in Congress. In 1994, however, opinion polls suggested 60% of the electorate approved of Ramos's performance.

WORLD AFFAIRS

Regional relationships are now paramount. The Philippines is keen to attract investment from booming ASEAN economies. The state took over US bases in 1992. US ships, however, still have rights of access to military installations in the country. Manila has established a claim to the Spratlys.

P

CHRONOLOGY

Ceded to the USA by Spain in 1898, the Philippines became self-governing in 1935. After Japanese occupation during World War II, the Philippines became an independent republic in 1946.

- ❑ **1965** Ferdinand Marcos, NP candidate, becomes president.
- ❑ **1969–1972** Marcos reelected amid malpractice allegations.
- ❑ **1972** Marcos declares martial law. Opposition leaders arrested, National Assembly suspended, press censored.
- ❑ **1977** Ex-LP leader Benigno Aquino sentenced to death. Criticism forces Marcos to delay execution.
- ❑ **1978** Elections won by Marcos's new party, New Society (KBL). Marcos president and prime minister.
- ❑ **1980** Aquino allowed to travel to USA for medical help.
- ❑ **1981** Martial law ends. Marcos re-elected president by referendum. Malpractice alleged by opposition.
- ❑ **1983** Benigno Aquino shot dead at Manila airport on return from USA. Inquiry blames military conspiracy.
- ❑ **1986** USA forces Marcos to call a presidential election. Result disputed. Army rebels led by General Fidel Ramos, and public demonstrations, bring widow of Benigno Aquino, Corazon, to power. Marcos exiled to USA. Two coups crushed by troops loyal to Aquino.
- ❑ **1987** New constitution. Aquino-led coalition wins Congress elections. Coup crushed by Aquino's troops.
- ❑ **1988** Marcos and wife, Imelda, indicted on $100 million charge for embezzlement and racketeering.
- ❑ **1989** Marcos dies in the USA. Coup attempt fails.
- ❑ **1990** Imelda acquitted of fraud charges in the USA. Earthquake in Baguio City leaves 1600 dead.
- ❑ **1991** Mt. Pinatubo erupts. US leaves Clark Air Base. Imelda Marcos returns to the Philippines.
- ❑ **1992** General Fidel Ramos wins presidential election. LDP secure most seats in parliament. US Navy leaves its bases in the Philippines.

AID

Bilateral aid makes up the majority of aid receipts

No significant variation from year to year

The Philippines' main bilateral aid donors are the USA and Japan. Large remittances are also received from Filipinos working overseas. In 1975, there were 40,000 OCWs (Overseas Contract Workers). By 1994, this had risen to 680,000. Many NGOs operate in the outlying islands.

DEFENSE

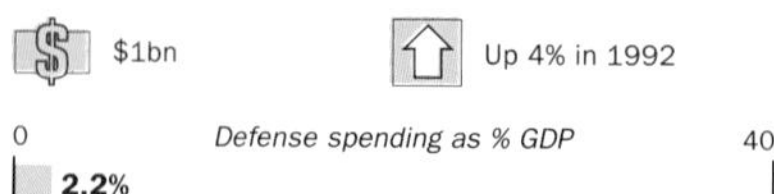

Subic Bay was the largest US base outside America and was used in both the Vietnam War and the 1991 Gulf War. The USA left Clark base in 1991, following the eruption of Mt. Pinatubo, and Subic Bay in 1992. The military retains considerable political influence; Fidel Ramos is a former army general.

PHILIPPINE ARMED FORCES

41 light tanks (41 *Scorpion*)	68,000 personnel
1 frigate and 42 patrol boats	23,000 personnel
49 combat aircraft (7 F-5-A/2 F-5-B/ 24 OV-10 *Broncos*)	15,500 personnel
None	

ECONOMICS

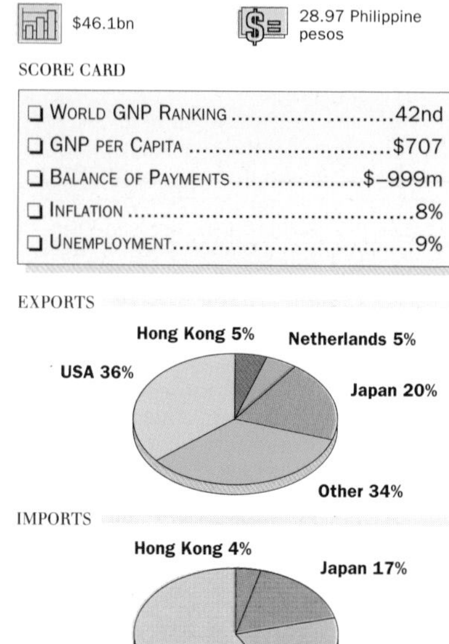

SCORE CARD

- ❑ WORLD GNP RANKING........................42nd
- ❑ GNP PER CAPITA..............................$707
- ❑ BALANCE OF PAYMENTS...................$-999m
- ❑ INFLATION..8%
- ❑ UNEMPLOYMENT..................................9%

STRENGTHS

Economy now fully open to outside investment. Agricultural productivity rising. Remittances from Filipinos working overseas are estimated at $2 billion. Well-equipped ex-US military installations with economic potential, such as Subic Bay.

WEAKNESSES

Power failures limit scope for expansion. Rudimentary infrastructure, especially transportation. Low domestic savings rates make Philippines reliant on foreign finance. $30 billion debt.

PROFILE

In the 1950s, the Philippines was one of the strongest economies in Asia. Since then, it has fallen behind once much poorer nations such as Thailand, Malaysia and South Korea. Around 50% of the population live on the poverty line. It is this poverty that has fueled many of the secessionist movements that have threatened the stability of successive governments.

ECONOMIC PERFORMANCE INDICATOR

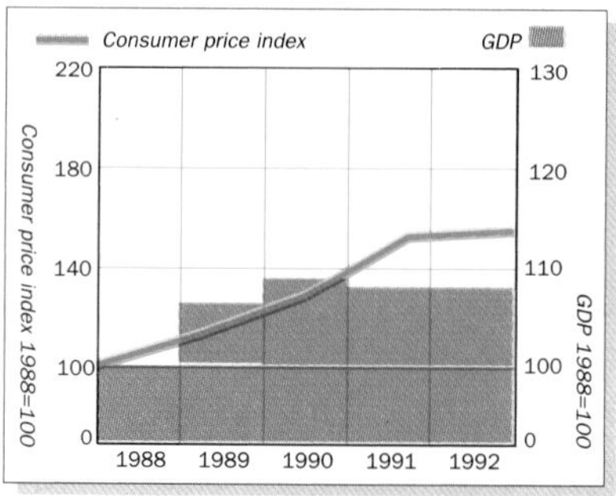

The economy is undergoing slow reform. The Ramos administration aims to emulate the success of the other Southeast Asian NICs. Backed by the IMF, it is deregulating the economy to encourage foreign investment. It is also trying to trim the power of some of the large privately run monopolies; a few families still control a major part of the economy. Long-term goals are to raise economic growth to double figures by 1998, raise the per capita income to $1,000, as opposed to the current average of $750, and to reduce those affected by poverty to 30% of the population.

PHILIPPINES : MAJOR BUSINESSES

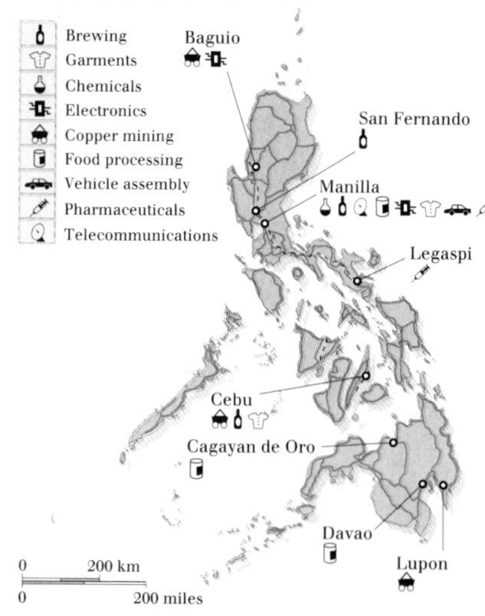

RESOURCES

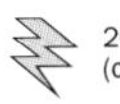
26.3bn kwh (capacity 6.87m kw)

Reserves of 147,540,000 bbl; refines 278,450 b/cd

7.8m pigs, 1.7m cattle, 300,000 horses

Coal, copper, nickel, chromium, silver, manganese, gold

ELECTRICITY GENERATION

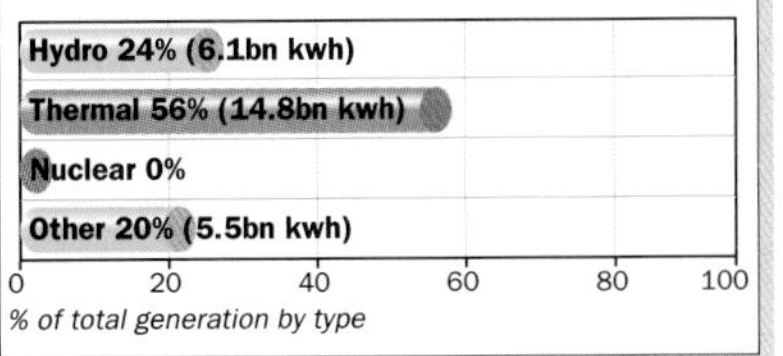

The Philippines is the world's biggest supplier of refractory chrome. Copper is also a significant export. Many areas of the country have yet to be surveyed and estimates suggest 90% of mineral potential remains undeveloped. Oil production off Palawan began in 1979. The Philippines is the world's second biggest user of geothermal power after the USA. Almost 25% of electricity on Luzon is provided by this method. In 1989, timber exports were halted. However, illegal logging and slash-and-burn farming still cause deforestation.

PHILLIPINES : LAND USE

Cropland
Forest
Pigs
Sugar cane
Coconuts

0 200 km
0 200 miles

SIERRA MADRE
LUZON
MINDANAO

ENVIRONMENT

2% (1% partially protected)

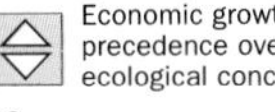
Economic growth has precedence over ecological concerns

ENVIRONMENTAL TREATIES

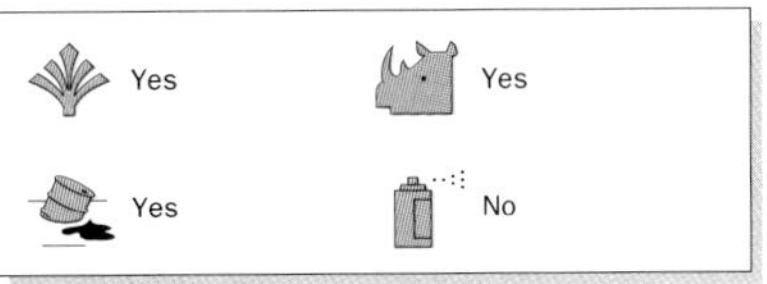

The environment has become a major issue in the Philippines. Most of the tropical rainforest has been destroyed, except for pockets such as the island of Palawan. Fishermen have dynamited unique coral habitats, and continue to use cyanide and muro-ami techniques to increase the size of their catches.

The government has recognized the costs of environmental damage. Soil run off is silting rivers and reducing the power generated by hydroelectric dams. Fast-depleting coral habitats reduce the attraction of the Philippines for tourists.

Logging has been banned, but enforcement is difficult; many loggers have their own private armies. In addition, continued use of slash-and-burn farming has aided deforestation.

MEDIA

The media practices self censorship and is inclined to be deferential to the government in power

PUBLISHING AND BROADCAST MEDIA

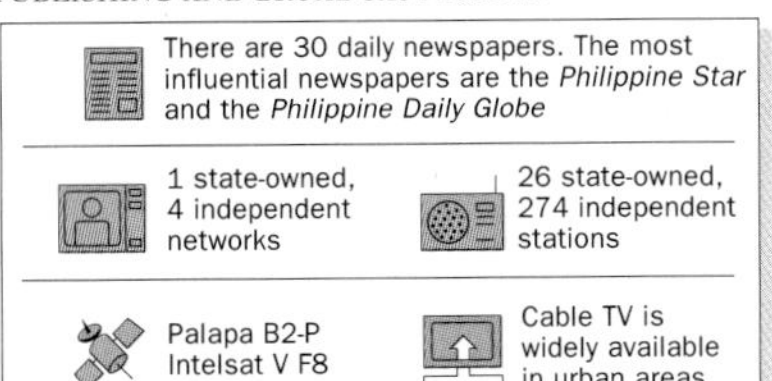

There are 30 daily newspapers. The most influential newspapers are the *Philippine Star* and the *Philippine Daily Globe*
1 state-owned, 4 independent networks
26 state-owned, 274 independent stations
Palapa B2-P Intelsat V F8
Cable TV is widely available in urban areas

The lifting of censorship following the election of Corazon Aquino in 1986 led to a burgeoning of the media. In addition to the national press, there are more than 250 regional newspapers in local dialects. State TV broadcasts in English and Filipino. Four independent television stations serve Metro Manila.

CRIME

14,525 prisoners

Down 8% in 1990

CRIME RATES

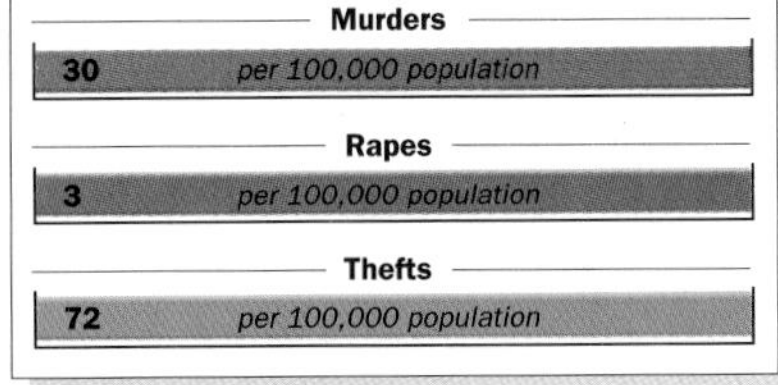

Crime rates are relatively high. Many stores have armed guards. The kidnapping of Chinese businessmen for ransom is a growing problem.

EDUCATION

90%

0 Education spending as % GNP 25

2.9%

THE EDUCATION SYSTEM

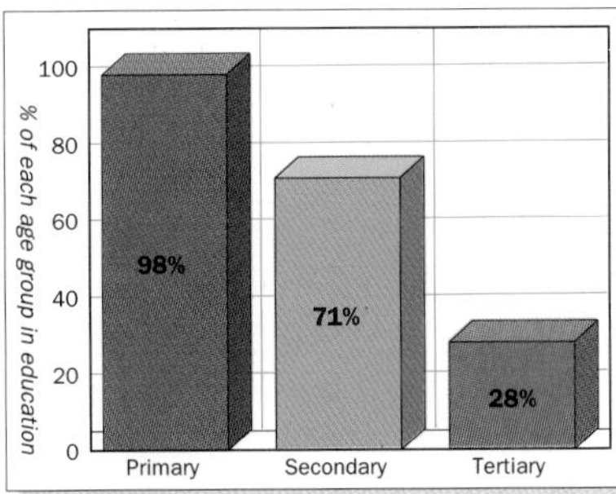

The Philippines has one of the highest literacy rates among developing countries. The education system is based on the US model, but characterized by many private schools. Sectarianism in education is common; the Chinese community has its own schools. Most colleges and universities are also run privately. The universities of San Carlos in Cebu city and Santo Tomás in Manila are Spanish colonial foundations, dating from 1595 and 1611 respectively.

HEALTH

1 per 6,413 people

Respiratory and diarrheal diseases, tuberculosis

0 Health spending as % GNP 25

0.7%

Most general hospitals are privately run. Malaria, once a major problem, has been eradicated in all but remote areas.

WEALTH

Miner, 2,986 Philippine pesos per month; teacher, 3,121 Philippine pesos per month

CONSUMER GOODS OWNERSHIP

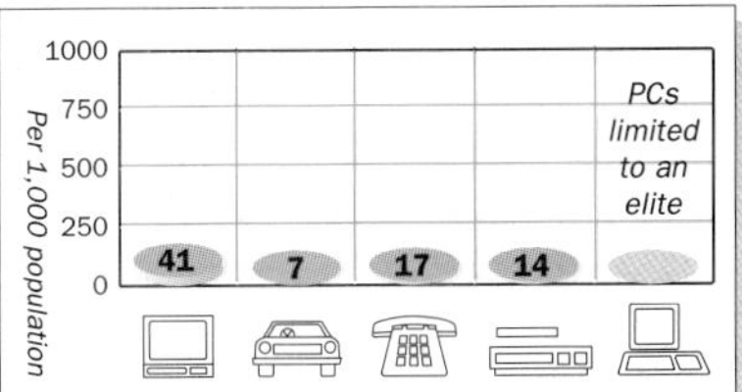

Around 50% of Filipinos live on the poverty line. Wealth remains highly concentrated in a few Manila-based business families.

WORLD RANKING

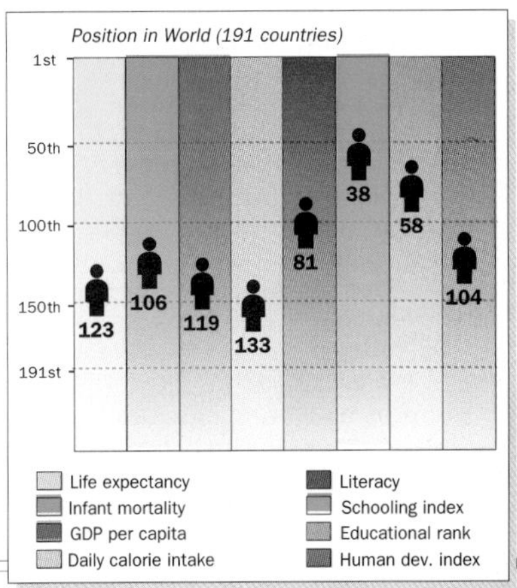

POLAND

EUROPE

Russian Fed. Lithuania Belorussia Germany POLAND Czech Republic Ukraine Slovakia

OFFICIAL NAME: Republic of Poland **CAPITAL:** Warsaw
POPULATION: 38.4 million **CURRENCY:** Zloty **OFFICIAL LANGUAGE:** Polish

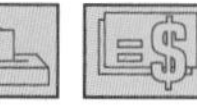

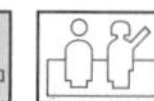

LOCATED IN THE HEART OF EUROPE, Poland's low-lying plains extend from the Baltic shore in the north to the Tatry Mountains on its southern border with the Czech Republic and Slovakia. Since the Round Table Agreement of 1989, which led to the fall of the communist regime, Poland has undergone massive social, economic and political change. It is currently experiencing rapid economic growth. Its strategic location between Western and Eastern Europe and its developing market economy could make it a major player in European politics in the years to come.

CLIMATE

WEATHER CHART

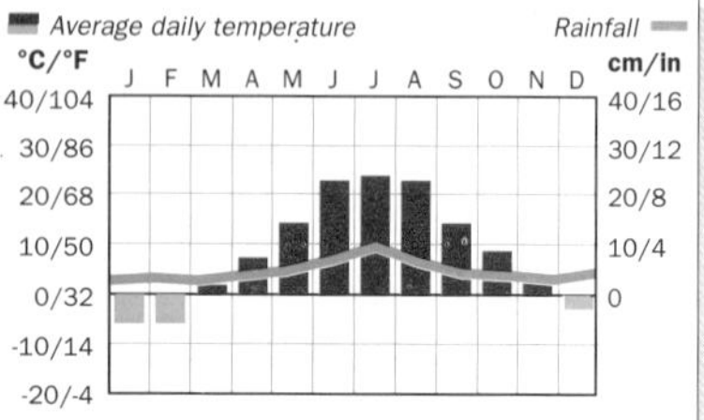

Most of the country experiences a similar climate. Summers are hot, with heavy rainfall often accompanied by thunder. Winters are severe, with snow covering the ground on the southern mountains and for as much as 60–70 days in the east.

COMMUNICATIONS

THE TRANSPORTATION NETWORK

Polish communications are in need of widespread upgrading to facilitate closer links with Western Europe. Poland is uniquely located to capture east–west and north–south trading routes. The Gdańsk–Gdynia port complex is poised to become the center of cross-Baltic trade and the Polish government is planning to build two east–west highways. A new international airport has been built near Warsaw.

A much-needed improvement of the telecommunications network is beginning, with multinationals and Polish companies forming joint ventures to bring an optical fiber network to 125,000 households in southern Poland.

The medieval administrative center of Lublin *lies in Poland's southeastern agricultural heartland.*

TOURISM

MAIN OVERSEAS ARRIVALS

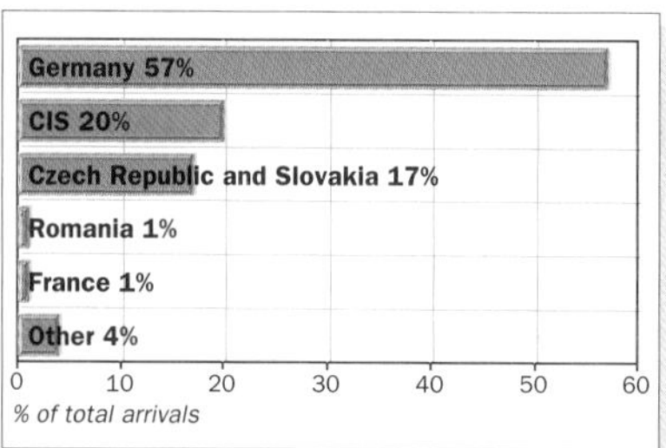

Tourism in Poland has, until recently, been targeted toward domestic or Eastern European tourists. Since 1989, however, some of the most visible signs of foreign investment have been in the hotel industry.

Despite considerable environmental problems, Poland is renowned for its skiing and hiking, especially in the Tatry Mountains. Kraków's medieval core has been preserved, while Toruń has restored its historic German Hanseatic buildings. Warsaw's historic center has been meticulously reconstructed since its destruction in 1944.

Exploiting its location between Warsaw and Berlin, Poznań has created an international exhibition and business convention industry.

PEOPLE

319 people per sq. mile

THE URBAN/RURAL POPULATION SPLIT

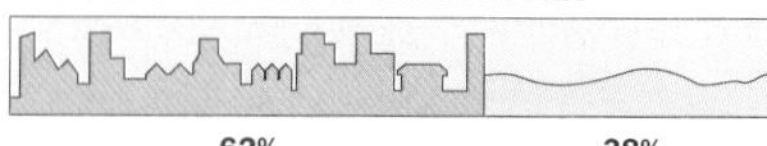

RELIGIOUS PERSUASION

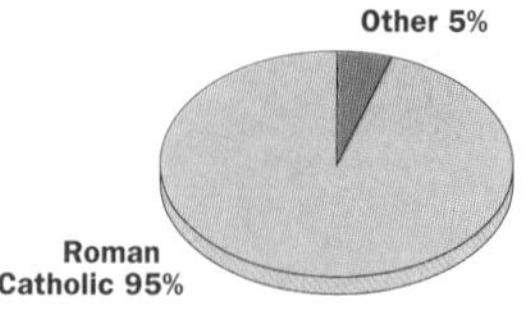

ETHNIC MAKEUP

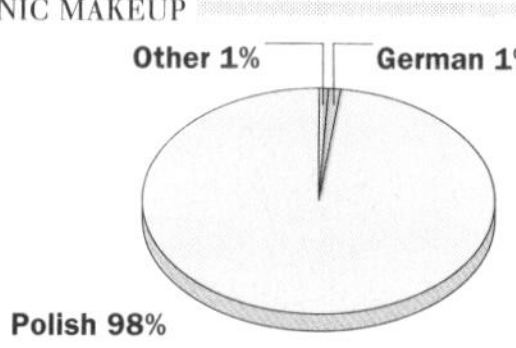

As a result of the readjustment of its borders agreed to at the Yalta Conference in 1945, Poland has few ethnic minorities. The ethnic German minority in Silesia is becoming more self-assertive, especially over the region's environmental problems, and now has special representation in parliament. The Ukrainian minority make up only 0.7% of the population. The influx of Romanian gypsies trying to enter Germany through Poland, across the River Oder, has caused considerable hostility.

The main social conflict in democratic Poland has been that between liberal, secular tendencies, and the opposing influence of the Catholic Church.

Wealth disparities are not great. The growing wealth of the entrepreneurial class is causing tension between support for the free market and the egalitarian instinct inherited from 40 years of socialism.

Polish women are prominent policy makers. Hanna Suchocka was prime minister from 1992–1993. A woman currently heads the Central Bank.

POPULATION AGE BREAKDOWN

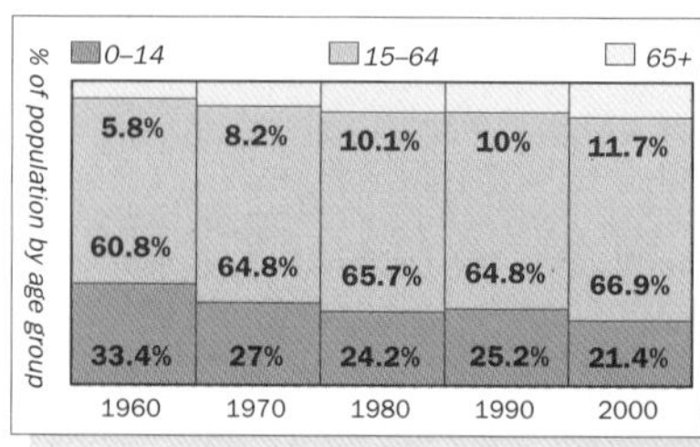

P

POLITICS

 1997  President Lech Wałęsa

THE STATE OF THE PARTIES

Parliament (*Sejm*) 460 members

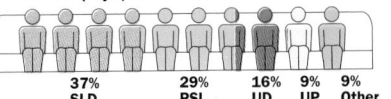

37% SLD	29% PSL	16% UD	9% UP	9% Other

SLD = Democratic Left Alliance **PSL** = Polish Peasant Party
UD = Democratic Union **UP** = Labor Union **S** = Solidarity
Other = Confederation for an Independent Poland, Non-party Bloc in Support of Reforms, German minority organizations

Senate 100 members

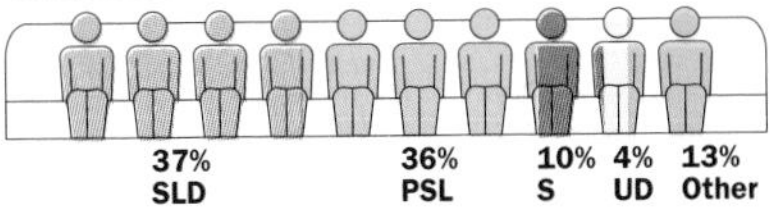

Since 1989, Poland has been a multiparty parliamentary democracy.

MAIN POLITICAL ISSUES

Coalition rule
Poland's emerging party system has been hindered by an excess of political factions and sustaining coalitions has proved difficult. Parties are required to have 5% of the vote to gain a seat and 8% to be eligible to join a coalition government.

Church–state relations
Building upon the legitimization of its authority in the martial law years, the Catholic Church has been outspoken in its views on social and political policy. Recent debates over abortion, worship in schools and values in the media have fueled a heated dialogue over the proper role of the Church in public and private life.

PROFILE

A new post-socialist constitution has yet to be drafted and the government is currently operating under a revised version of the 1952 constitution. Under its provisions, the president has considerable power; this has led to battles with the *Sejm* (parliament) over ultimate control. Frequent government changes have occurred since 1989.

The 1993 elections resulted in the ousting of the DU, the offspring of Solidarity. Government is now in the hands of the SLD and the PSL, both of which have their roots in Poland's communist past. The SLD, the successor to the Polish United Workers' Party (PUWP), supports continued economic reform. The PSL, under Prime Minister Waldemar Pawlak, represents the interests of the 30% of Poles who live off the land. This section has seen living standards decline sharply since 1989. The first months of this uneasy coalition saw Pawlak dismiss Deputy Finance Minister Stefan Kawalec over suspect share trading. Deputy Prime Minister and Financy Minister Marek Barowski then resigned in protest.

Lech Wałęsa*, president since 1990. He was imprisoned under martial law.*

Aleksander Kwasniewski*, leader of the SLD, part of the ruling coalition.*

WORLD AFFAIRS

CE | V4 | CSCE | GATT | ECE

Poland has sought to strengthen its economic and security ties with the West. Its transition to a market economy depends upon trade links and eventual economic integration with Western Europe. One of Poland's first acts as an independent nation was to apply for membership in the IMF. Developing economic and political links with the Baltics, Belarussia and the Ukraine is also seen as important.

CHRONOLOGY

Poland has Europe's second-oldest written constitution. In 1795, it was partitioned between Austria-Hungary, Germany and Russia.

- ❑ **1918** Polish state recreated.
- ❑ **1921** Democratic constitution.
- ❑ **1926–1935** Pilsudski heads military coup. Nine years of authoritarian rule. Rising ethnic intolerance.
- ❑ **1939** Molotov-Ribbentrop Pact. September: Germany invades and divides Poland with Russians.
- ❑ **1941** First concentration camps built on Polish soil.
- ❑ **1944** Warsaw Uprising: 200,000 killed in last stand against Nazis.
- ❑ **1945** Potsdam and Yalta Conferences set present borders and determine political allegiance to Soviet Union.

POLAND

Total Area : 312 680 sq. km
(120 720 sq. miles)

CHRONOLOGY *continued*

- ❑ **1947** Communists manipulate elections to gain power. Opposition dissolved and exiled.
- ❑ **1949** Communist Party absorbs socialist coalition partners and forms Polish United Workers' Party.
- ❑ **1956** Protests in Poznań erupt into riots. More than 50 killed.
- ❑ **1970** Food price increases lead to strikes and riots in the Baltic port cities. Hundreds are killed.
- ❑ **1976** Government plans to raise food prices lead to protests. Government forced to back down.
- ❑ **1979** Pope John Paul II elected. Makes triumphal visit to Poland the next year.
- ❑ **1980** A series of strikes forces the government to negotiate with Solidarity. Resulting Gdańsk Accords grant the right to strike and to form free trade unions.
- ❑ **1981** General Wojciech Jaruzelski becomes prime minister.
- ❑ **1981–1983** Martial law. Solidarity forced into underground existence. Many of its leaders, including Wałęsa, are interned.
- ❑ **1983** Wałęsa awarded Nobel Peace Prize.
- ❑ **1986** Amnesty for political prisoners, but government refuses to negotiate with Solidarity.
- ❑ **1987** Referendum rejects government austerity program.
- ❑ **1988** Industrial unrest leads to inconclusive government–Solidarity negotiations.
- ❑ **1989** PUWP agrees to hold talks with Solidarity, which is relegalized. Partially free elections are held. Solidarity candidates defeat the PUWP. First postwar non-communist government formed.
- ❑ **1990** Swift transition to market economy begins. Wałęsa elected president.
- ❑ **1991** Free elections lead to fragmented parliament.
- ❑ **1992** Last Russian troops leave.
- ❑ **1993** Reformed communists form coalition government.
- ❑ **1994** Mass privatization program implemented.

AID

$8bn promised by the 24 top industrial nations

Aid is rising

Saddled with an enormous debt from the 1980s, Poland's most important foreign assistance was the cancellation of half of its debt by the Paris Club. A London Club agreement for commercial debt is still outstanding. The IMF, EBRD and EU have all taken an active role in supporting Poland's pioneering stabilization and reform program.

DEFENSE

$2.4bn

Down 7% in 1992

Defense spending as % GDP (0–40): 2.5%

Since the demise of the Warsaw Pact, Poland has repeatedly stated its desire to join NATO, despite the West's hesitation. It recently signed the NATO-backed Partnership for Peace. Russia is a source for cut-price armaments and equipment for Poland's standing army, the largest in Europe after Russia's.

POLISH ARMED FORCES

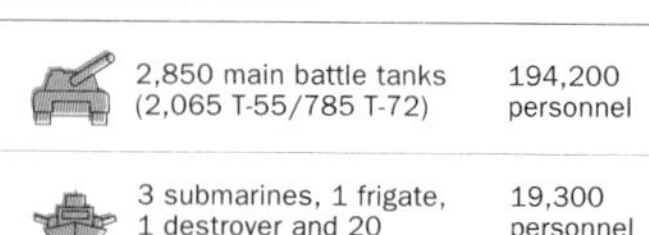

2,850 main battle tanks (2,065 T-55/785 T-72)	194,200 personnel
3 submarines, 1 frigate, 1 destroyer and 20 patrol boats	19,300 personnel
423 combat aircraft (221 MiG-21/ 37 MiG-23MF/104 Su-22)	83,000 personnel
None	

ECONOMICS

$70.6bn

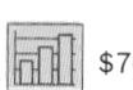

17,239 zlotys

SCORE CARD

- ❑ World GNP Ranking: 34th
- ❑ GNP per Capita: $1,838
- ❑ Balance of Payments: $-300m
- ❑ Inflation: 43%
- ❑ Unemployment: 15.7%

EXPORTS

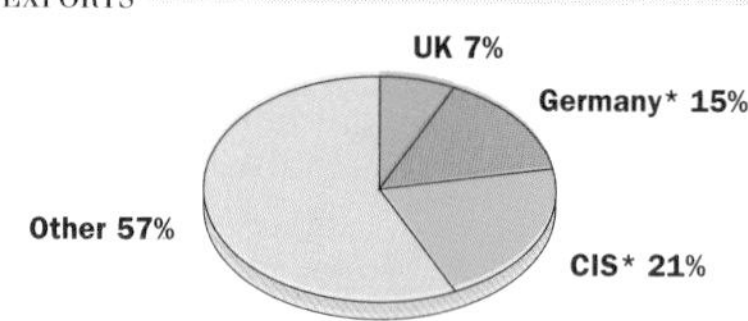

IMPORTS

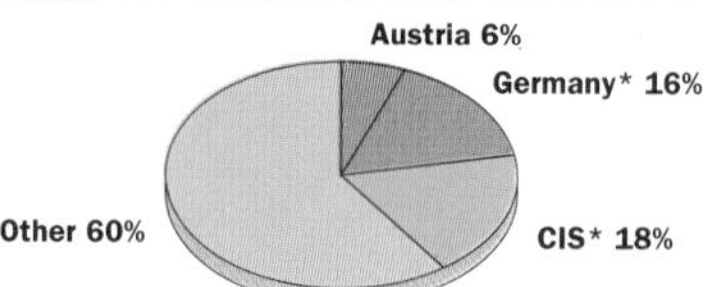

Strengths

Fastest economic growth in Europe in 1993. Steadfast implementation of economic reform since 1989 has encouraged growth of the private sector. Ability to attract foreign investment. Mass privatization scheme, including the 600 largest state-owned industries, launched in 1994.

Weaknesses

Persistent high inflation. Outdated production plant. Need to compete for foreign investment with other former COMECON states.

Profile

Poland entered deep economic crisis in the 1980s, fueled in part by high foreign debt levels. Following the change of government in January 1990, Finance Minister Leszek Balcerowicz implemented the Big Bang plan to bring about a swift transition to a market economy. Most prices were freed, trade was opened and the zloty was made convertible.

ECONOMIC PERFORMANCE INDICATOR

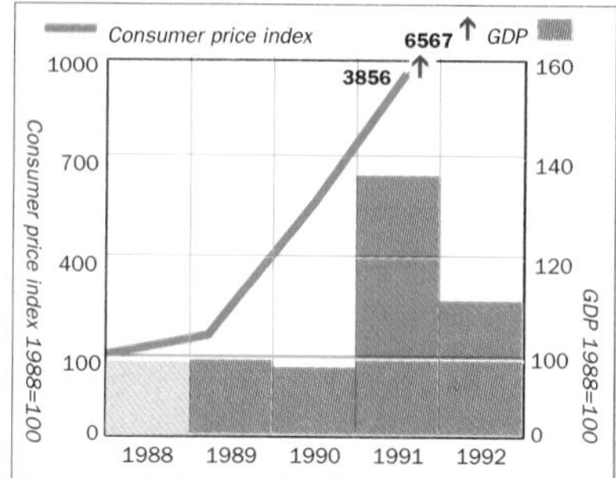

Although 40 years of communism have left considerable distortions in the economy, the framework necessary for a market economy is now being developed. The private sector now accounts for half of GNP and employs 60% of workers. Small businesses are flourishing in the previously neglected services sector. Stock and credit markets have opened and bankruptcy laws have been established. Share prices rose 900% in 1993.

Poland's economic growth and its 39 million domestic market make it attractive to foreign investors, which include companies such as Fiat, McDonalds and Proctor & Gamble.

POLAND : MAJOR BUSINESSES

RESOURCES

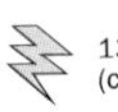

136bn kwh (capacity 30.7m kw)

Reserves of 42,208,000 bbl; refines 333,000 b/cd

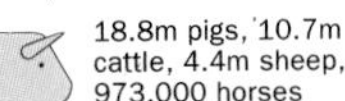

18.8m pigs, 10.7m cattle, 4.4m sheep, 973,000 horses

Coal, copper, silver, sulfur, natural gas, lead, salt, iron ore

ELECTRICITY GENERATION

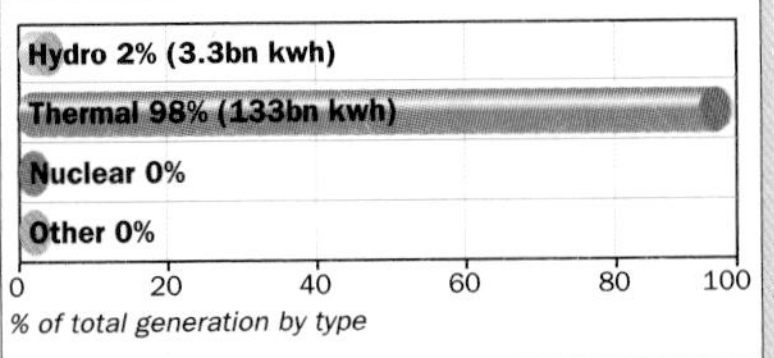

Poland has significant quantities of coal, sulfur, copper, natural gas, silver, lead and salt. With the availability of cheap fuel from Russia at an end, Poland aims to reach self-sufficiency and eventually to export fuels. Coal supplies two-thirds of electricity generation. The amounts of copper ores mined are too small to affect world markets.

POLAND : LAND USE

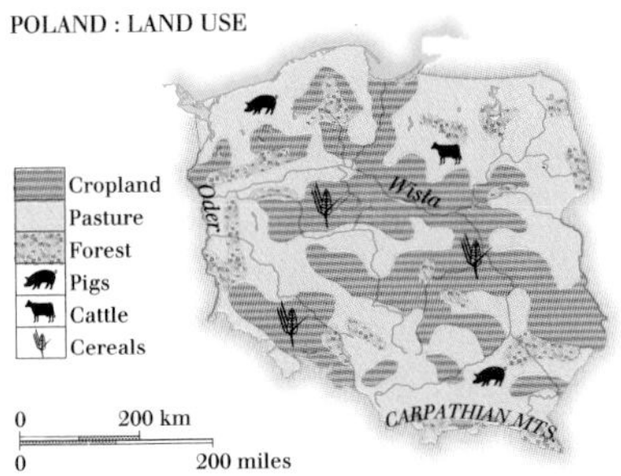

ENVIRONMENT

7% partially protected

Environmental initiatives too expensive

ENVIRONMENTAL TREATIES

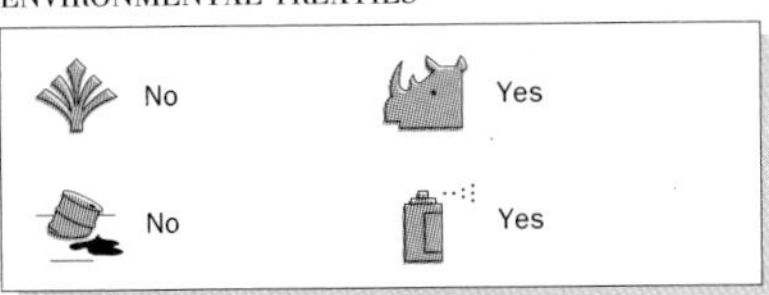

Poland faces serious pollution problems from two generations of heavy industrialization. A third of Poles live in areas regarded as extremely polluted. In the southern region of Silesia, air, water and vegetation pollution are especially severe.

The metallurgical industry and thermal electric power stations are significant sources of air pollution. Sulfur dioxide readings in Kraków can exceed legal limits by 800 times.

Only 4% of Poland's rivers have water considered fit for human consumption; 75% had been declared biologically dead by the late 1980s. Any clean-up operation would be expensive.

MEDIA

Free, but broadcast media must by law reflect Christian values

Under martial law, Poland had a vigorous underground press and this energy has survived into democracy. The leading daily, *Gazeta Wyborcza*, began as Solidarity's paper. *Nie*, a satirical weekly, is edited by the former Communist Party spokesman, Jerzy Urban.

PUBLISHING AND BROADCAST MEDIA

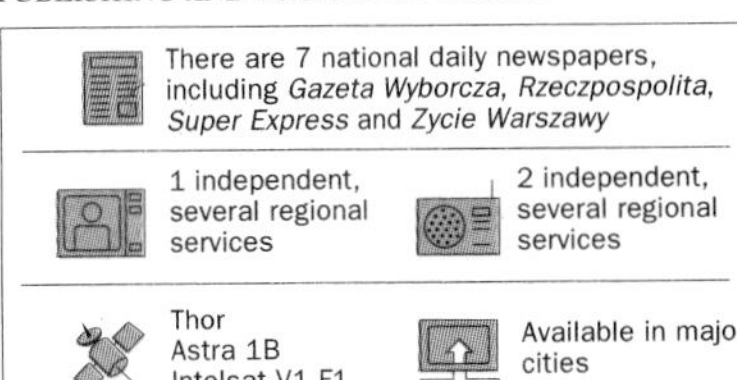

There are 7 national daily newspapers, including *Gazeta Wyborcza*, *Rzeczpospolita*, *Super Express* and *Zycie Warszawy*
1 independent, several regional services
2 independent, several regional services
Thor
Astra 1B
Intelsat V1 F1
Available in major cities

CRIME

40,321 prisoners

Levels are stable but likely to rise

CRIME RATES

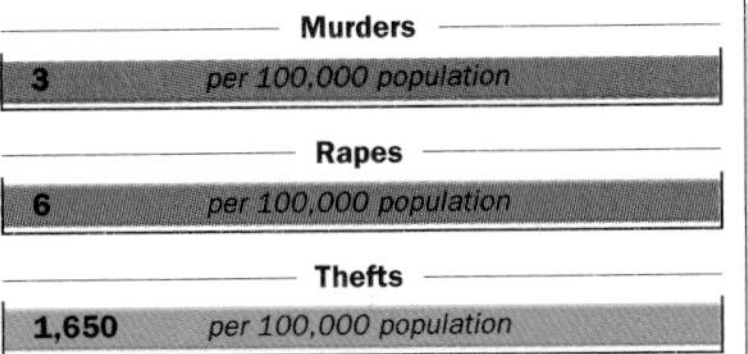

Smuggling is seen as the most significant crime problem. Warsaw is a main route for illicit as well as legal trade. Expensive cars are transferred eastward to Russia and drugs westward to Berlin. Smuggling is mostly undertaken by Poles and other Eastern Europeans. In 1993, customs seized goods worth over $660,000.

EDUCATION

99%

0 *Education spending as % GNP* 25

4.6%

THE EDUCATION SYSTEM

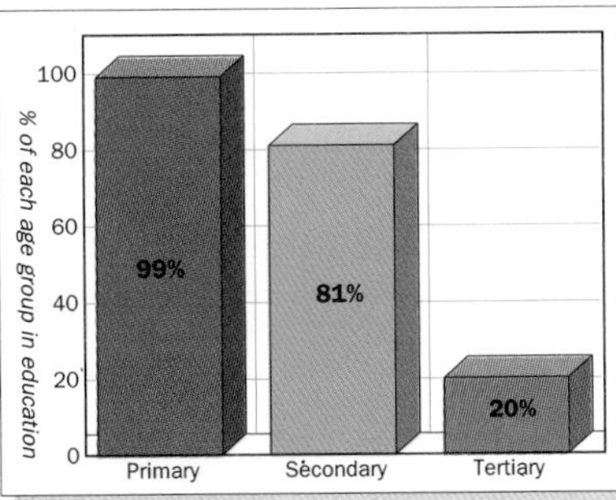

The most contentious change is the expanded influence of the Catholic Church. Religious education is mandatory in all schools, and Church-run schools are now allowed. Traditionally based on the Russian system, Polish schools are reorienting themselves toward the French model.

Universities are of a high standard, especially in mathematics and philosophy. Business schools are training badly needed managers.

HEALTH

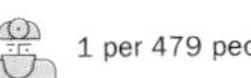

1 per 479 people

Heart and cerebrovascular diseases, cancer

0 *Health spending as % GNP* 25

4%

Free medical care is provided for workers and rural residents. Reform of the health system is being considered, as the quality of health care is regarded as inadequate. Private health care is increasingly available in cities for those who can afford it.

WEALTH

State employees are significantly worse off than those in the private sector

CONSUMER GOODS OWNERSHIP

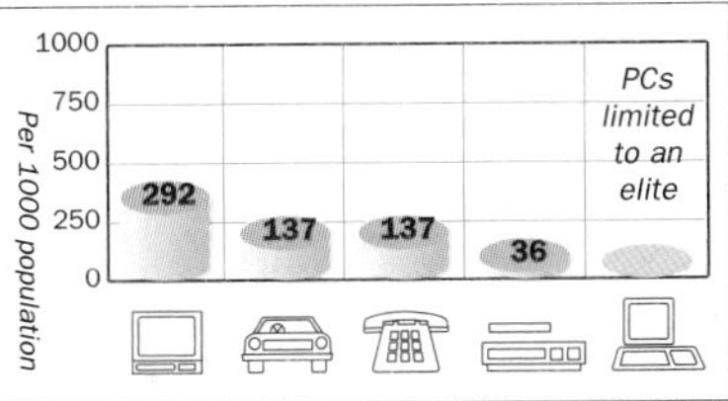

Poland began its transition to a market economy with an extremely equitable distribution of income. After 1990, real wages in industry and agriculture fell from artificially high levels and the entrepreneurial class visibly increased its wealth. Growing wealth disparities have led to resentment from those who have not benefited from reforms.

WORLD RANKING

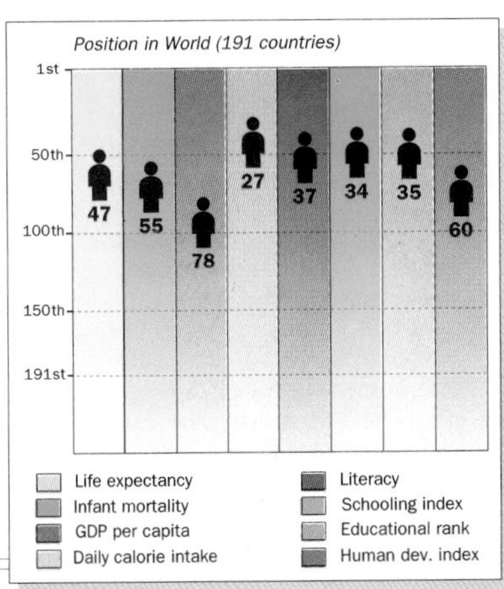

P

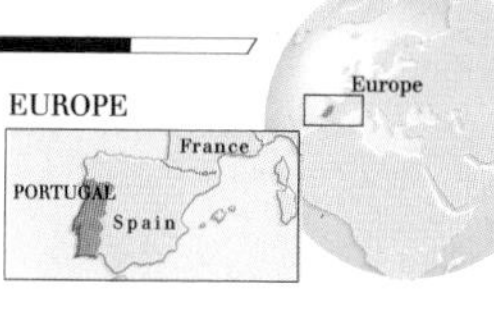

PORTUGAL

OFFICIAL NAME: Republic of Portugal **CAPITAL:** Lisbon **POPULATION:** 9.9 million
CURRENCY: Escudo **OFFICIAL LANGUAGE:** Portuguese **OVERSEAS TERRITORIES:** 1

PORTUGAL, WITH ITS long Atlantic coast, lies on the western side of the Iberian Peninsula. The River Tagus divides the more mountainous north from the lower, undulating terrain to the south. In 1974, a bloodless military coup overthrew a long-standing conservative dictatorship. Democratic elections were held in 1975 and the Armed Forces Movement withdrew from politics thereafter. The 1980s witnessed the implementation of a substantial program of socio-economic modernization. Membership in the EU since 1986 has helped to underpin this process.

Santa Marta de Penanguiao, a small village in the heart of Portugal's wine-producing region, centered around the Douro Valley.

CLIMATE

WEATHER CHART

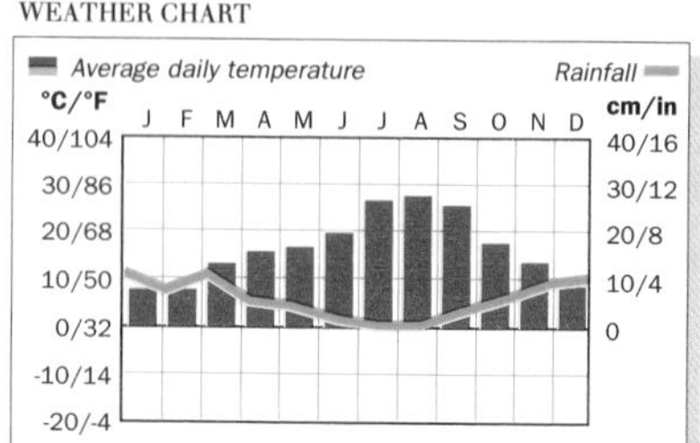

Portugal has a mild, Mediterranean climate, which is moderated by the influence of the Atlantic. Summers are hot and humid, while winters are relatively mild. Inland areas have more variable weather than coastal regions. Rainfall is generally higher in the mountainous north, while the central areas are more temperate. The southern Algarve region is predominantly dry and sunny.

COMMUNICATIONS

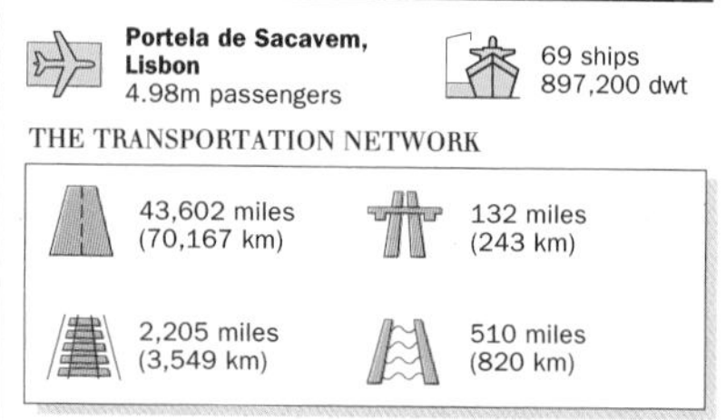

The Portuguese road system, which was formerly one of the least developed in Europe, has been extensively improved in recent years with grants from the EU. However, road links with Spain remain limited, despite a number of modernization programs. Lisbon, the densely populated capital, continues to suffer from very heavy traffic congestion, which only a major new beltway will alleviate. The railroad system is small but efficient. The national airline, TAP, is currently in financial trouble.

TOURISM

8m visitors

Up 13% in 1990

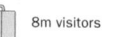

MAIN OVERSEAS ARRIVALS

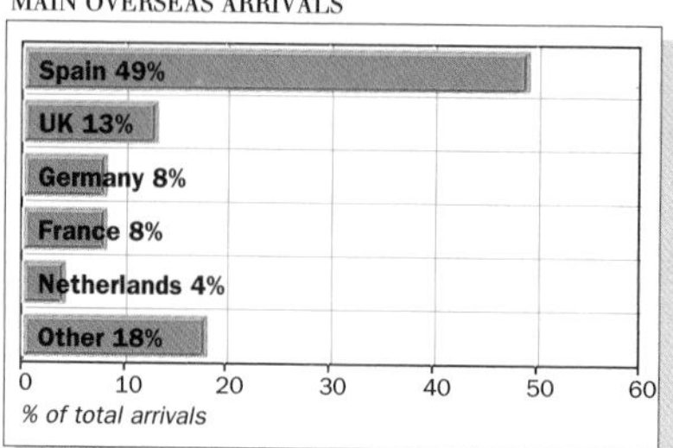

Since the 1960s, Portugal's low crime level and relatively poor economic development (reflected in low prices) have contributed to its popularity as a tourist destination. Substantial economic growth has eroded some of its appeal, but tourism is likely to remain a major income-earner. The most popular destination is the Algarve, Portugal's southernmost province, followed by the western resorts of Figueira da Foz and the Tróia Peninsula. Visitors are also attracted by Portugal's architecture, notably that dating from the Manueline period (1490–1520), and handicrafts, such as ceramics, lace and tapestries. Portugal has some of Europe's finest golf courses.

PORTUGAL

Total Area : 92 390 sq. km (35 670 sq. miles)

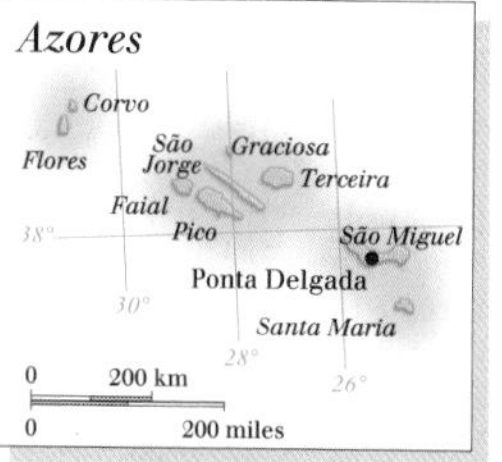

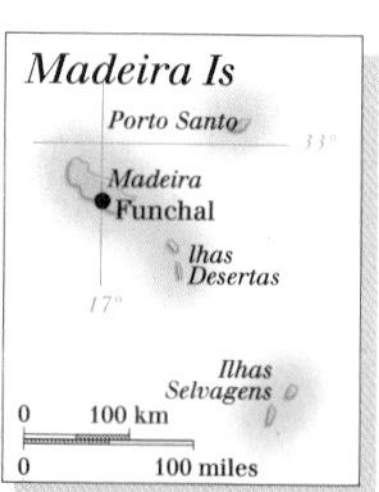

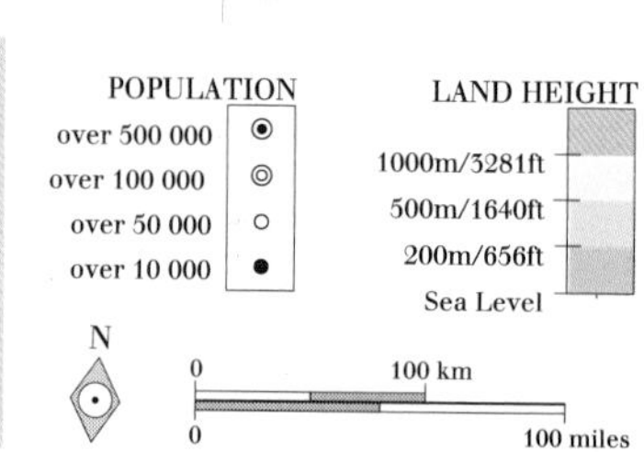

P

PEOPLE

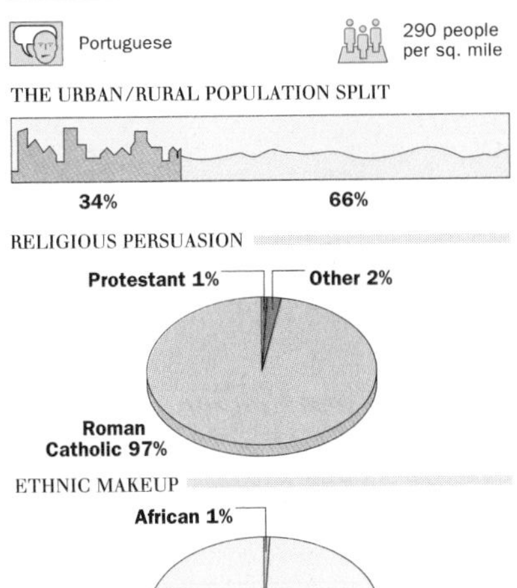

Portuguese society, once regarded as rather inward-looking, is now becoming increasingly integrated into the rest of Western Europe. Ethnic and religious tensions are limited. African immigrants, who come mainly from the former colonies, such as Angola, Mozambique and Guinea, have been assimilated into mainstream society with considerable ease.

As is true of other predominantly Catholic countries, the Church has lost much of its social influence in recent decades, as illustrated by falling birth rates and more liberal attitudes toward abortion and divorce. Nevertheless, with the exception of large urban areas, the north remains devoutly Catholic.

Family ties remain all-important. Women now have greater access to business and media jobs. Overall, democracy and rapid socio-economic change have tended to produce a more egalitarian society.

POPULATION AGE BREAKDOWN

% of population by age group

	1960	1970	1980	1990	2000
65+	8%	9.2%	10.5%	12.9%	14.4%
15–64	62.9%	62%	63.5%	65.8%	66.3%
0–14	29.1%	28.8%	26%	21.3%	19.3%

WORLD AFFAIRS

Since 1986, Portugal's foreign policy has dealt almost exclusively with the consequences of membership in the EU, from which the country has greatly benefited. It is a committed member of NATO, although its relative strategic importance has declined as a result of Spanish membership. Relations with the former African colonies are occasionally turbulent and remain a high priority, as do those with Brazil. Relations with China over the return of Macao to the latter in 1999 are cordial.

AID

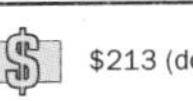

Down 11% in 1991

Portugal became an aid donor only in the early 1980s. It currently earmarks just under 0.2% of its GDP for aid to developing countries, mainly its former colonies in Africa. It is to provide $110 million to rebuild war-damaged power lines to the massive Cahora Bassa Dam in Mozambique, which has never been fully operational.

POLITICS

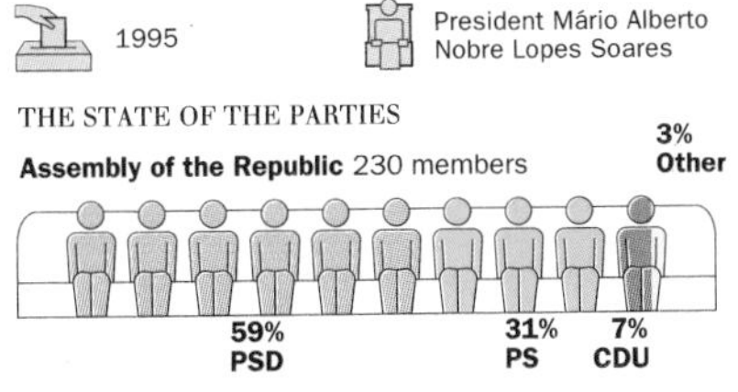

PSD = Social Democratic Party PS = Socialist Party CDU = Democratic Union Coalition (of which leading member is Portuguese Communist Party) Other = Center Democratic Party, National Solidarity Party

Portugal is a multiparty democracy.

MAIN POLITICAL ISSUES

Limiting pay rises

The government wishes to improve the state's weak financial position by keeping public sector pay rises below inflation. It proposed limiting wage rises to 2% – a cut in real terms. In 1994, the unions responded with a number of one-day strikes. The threat of rising unemployment, however, will limit demands for wage rises in the private sector.

Differences within the leadership

There have been a number of disputes between the president and the government. Prime Minister Cavaco's proposals to reform the military and to increase university fees have been opposed by President Mario Soares. Poor relations are likely to continue until the presidential elections of 1995.

PROFILE

Portugal has had almost a decade of center-right government. Close links have developed between the ruling PSD and the civil service. There are fears that this could be undermining criticism of the government. However, the highly independent stance of President Mário Soares does provide an effective opposition voice. Soares frequently uses his power of veto to delay government legislation. This is in sharp contrast to the opposition PS and CDU; both parties faced serious internal problems following their defeat in the 1991 elections.

In spite of the recent recession, the PSD face few challenges to their continued hold on power. The electorate who voted them in on their sustained record of economic growth in 1991 will, according to opinion polls, give them another term in 1995.

***Dr Mário Soares,** Portugal's socialist President since 1986, reelected in 1991.*

***Aníbal Cavaco Silva,** Prime Minister and leader of the center-right PSD.*

CHRONOLOGY

Portugal has existed as a nation state since the 11th century, although this was frequently challenged by Spain. Portugal reached its zenith in the 16th century, after which it entered a period of decline.

- **1703** Britain and Portugal sign the Methuen Treaty, facilitating the shipping of port to England.
- **1755** Earthquake destroys Lisbon.
- **1703** Joins coalition against revolutionary France.
- **1807** France invades; royal family flees to Brazil.
- **1808** British troops arrive under Wellington. Start of Peninsular War.
- **1810** French leave Portugal.
- **1820** Liberal revolution.
- **1822** King John VI returns and accepts first Portuguese constitution. His son Dom Pedro declares independence of Brazil.
- **1834** Dom Pedro returns to Portugal to end civil war and installs his daughter as Queen Mary II.
- **1856** First railroad opens.
- **1872** First industrial strike.
- **1875–1876** Republican and Socialist parties founded.
- **1890** British ultimatum ends the land connection between Angola and Mozambique.
- **1891** Republican uprising in Porto.
- **1908** Assassination of King Carlos I and heir to the throne.

P

CHRONOLOGY *continued*

- **1910** Abdication of Manuel II and proclamation of the Republic. Church and state separated.
- **1916** Portugal joins allied side in World War I.
- **1917–1918** New Republic led by Sidónio Pais.
- **1926** Army overturns republic.
- **1928** Salazar joins government as finance minister. Economy improves significantly.
- **1932** Salazar appointed Prime Minister.
- **1933** Promulgation of the constitution of the "New State," instituting right-wing dictatorship.
- **1936–1939** Salazar assists Franco in Spanish Civil War.
- **1939–1945** Portugal neutral during World War II, but lets UK use air bases in Azores.
- **1949** Founder-member of NATO.
- **1955** Joins UN.
- **1958** Américo Thómas appointed President, following the fraudulent defeat of General Delgado.
- **1961** India annexes Goa. Guerrilla warfare breaks out in Angola, Mozambique and Guinea.
- **1970** Death of Salazar, incapacitated since 1968. Succeeded by Marcelo Caetano.
- **1971** Caetano attempts liberalization.
- **1974** Carnation Revolution – the left-wing Armed Forces Movement overthrows Caetano.
- **1975** Communist takeover foiled by moderates and Mário Soares's PS.
- **1974–1975** Portuguese possessions in Africa attain independence. Some 750,000 Portuguese expatriates return to Portugal. First democratic elections.
- **1975–1976** Indonesia seizes Portuguese possession of East Timor unopposed.
- **1976** General António Eanes elected president. New socialist constitution adopted. Mário Soares appointed Prime Minister.
- **1978** Period of non-party technocratic government instituted.
- **1980** Center-right wins elections. General Eanes reelected.
- **1982** Full civilian government formally restored.
- **1983** Soares becomes caretaker prime minister; PS is majority party.
- **1985** Cavaco Silva becomes Prime Minister. Minority PSD government.
- **1986** Soares elected president. Portugal joins EC.
- **1987** Cavaco Silva wins absolute majority in parliament. Agreement to return Macao to China in 1999.
- **1991** Soares reelected President. Portugal begins talks to renegotiate US Azores air base treaty.

P

DEFENSE

$1.5bn

Up 3% in 1992

0 — Defense spending as % GDP — 40

2.2%

Portugal, a member of NATO since 1949, has a small but relatively modern navy. The army and air force are smaller and less efficient. Mounting opposition to military service is causing strains on these already semi-professional bodies. The USA is the major arms supplier. It has a strategic air base in the Azores.

PORTUGUESE ARMED FORCES

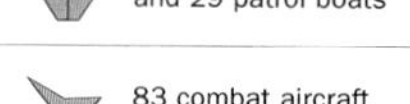

129 main battle tanks (43 M-47/86 M-48A5)	58,300 personnel
3 submarines, 11 frigates and 29 patrol boats	15,300 personnel
83 combat aircraft (A-7P/G-91R3/T1)	10,300 personnel
None	

ECONOMICS

$80bn

174.41 escudos

SCORE CARD

- World GNP Ranking 33rd
- GNP per Capita $8,081
- Balance of Payments .... $-600m
- Inflation 6.5%
- Unemployment 5.6%

EXPORTS

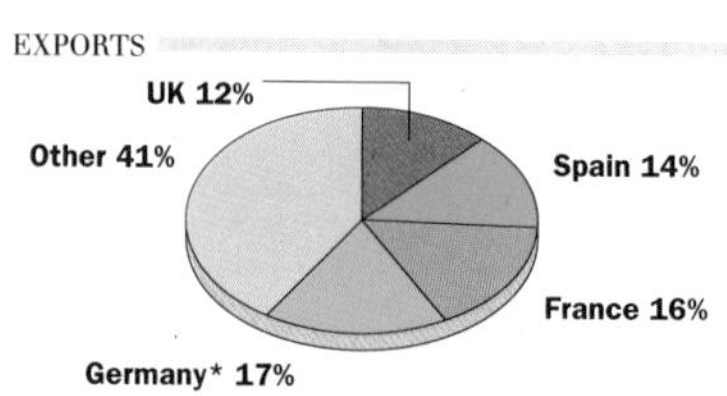

IMPORTS

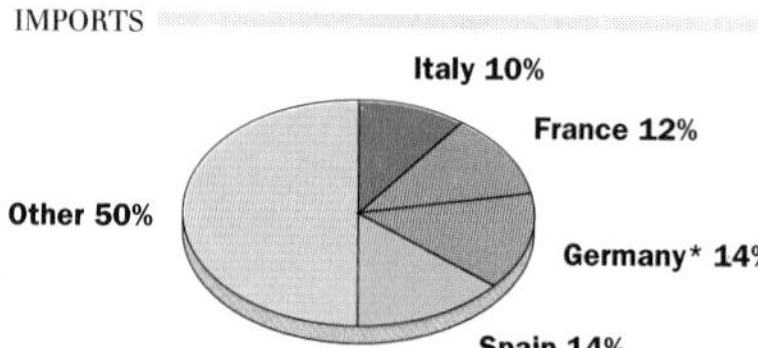

ECONOMIC PERFORMANCE INDICATOR

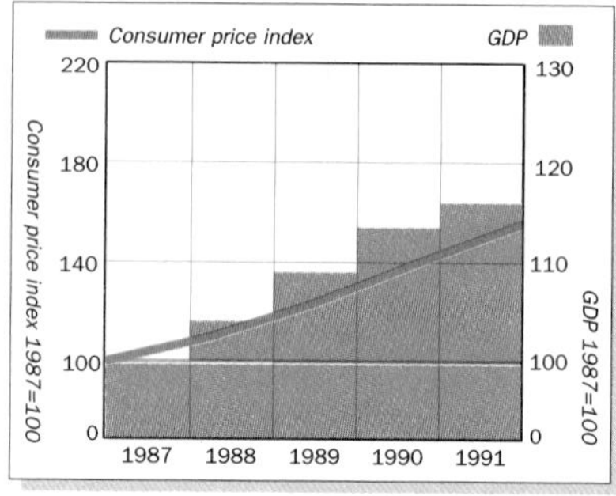

Strengths

Relatively low, though rapidly rising, labor costs. High rate of domestic and direct foreign investment, including a $3.3 billion Ford–Volkswagen vehicle-assembly plant near Lisbon, due to open 1995. Strong banking and tourism sectors. Tourism makes up 6% of GDP, the highest ratio in the EU; potential for further growth. Fast-track improvement of transport infrastructure under way. Good deep-water port at Lisbon. Wine, especially port. Tomatoes, citrus fruit, cork, sardines. Strong clothing and shoe manufacturing sectors.

Weaknesses

Large agricultural sector (5% of GDP, 10% of work force) is most inefficient in EU. Outdated farming methods, small landholdings, low crop yields. Farm products outpriced by Spain. Large budget deficit (7% of GDP in 1993). Inflation higher than EU average. Rigid labor market. High dependence on imported oil.

Profile

EU membership in 1986 brought a sharp increase in foreign investment to Portugal. Exports rose dramatically until the economy went into recession in 1991.

Despite its improved economy, Portugal has some way to go to achieve convergence with its EU partners. With an inflation rate which is 3% greater than the EU average, monetary union is a distant prospect. The government is instituting a new economic plan, "Quantum 2," which calls for budgetary and wage constraints, and industrial restructuring. Opinion polls in 1994 suggested "Quantum 2" had the backing of the Portuguese electorate.

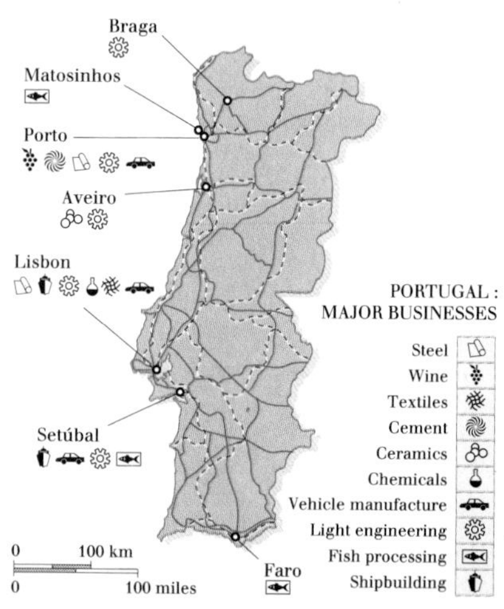

RESOURCES

28.5bn kwh (capacity 7.4m kw)

Not an oil producer; refines 294,000 b/cd

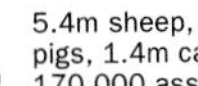

5.4m sheep, 2.3m pigs, 1.4m cattle, 170,000 asses

Limestone, granite, marble, copper

ELECTRICITY GENERATION

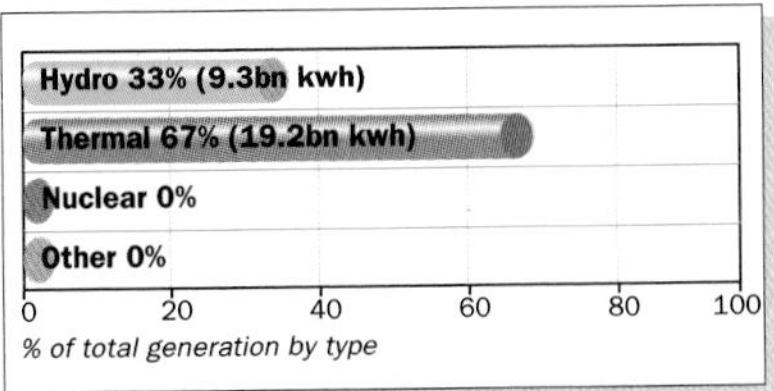

Portugal has been plagued by a lack of natural resources, including water. Mining has historically been important, notably for wolfram, copper and tin. Industry has relied on small coal deposits and large oil imports. Portugal hopes to build HEP stations, and aims to pipe natural gas from Algeria by 1996.

PORTUGAL : LAND USE

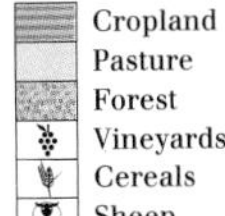

ENVIRONMENT

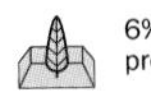

6% partially protected

Fast modernization balanced by new conservation concern

ENVIRONMENTAL TREATIES

The unrestricted development of tourist resorts in the Algarve and the huge investment in new harbor, road and bridge developments are having detrimental effects on natural habitats. EU agricultural grants for projects such as draining meadows, and monoculture afforestation, notably of *Eucalyptus* and *Pinus*, are degrading biodiversity. Much toxic waste is dumped on any available land as few official controls or infill sites exist. New waste management regulations are being planned.

MEDIA

There is full freedom from censorship and the press is entirely independent

PUBLISHING AND BROADCAST MEDIA

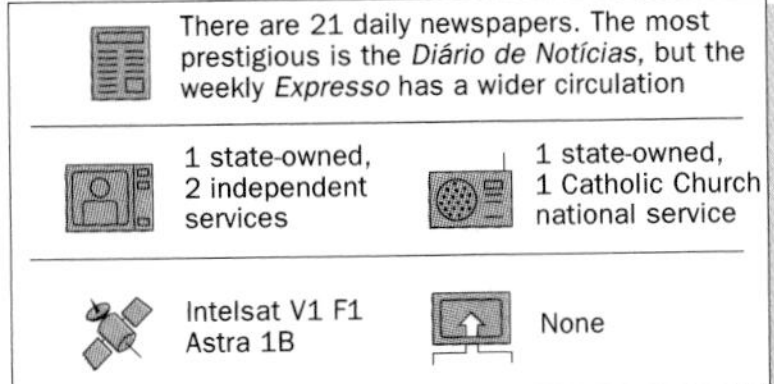

There are 21 daily newspapers. The most prestigious is the *Diário de Notícias*, but the weekly *Expresso* has a wider circulation
1 state-owned, 2 independent services
1 state-owned, 1 Catholic Church national service
Intelsat V1 F1
Astra 1B
None

Newspaper circulation figures are among the lowest in Europe and most papers have regional rather than national distribution. Radio and TV are therefore the main source of news, in part reflecting Portugal's low literacy rate. In 1992, two independent TV stations began broadcasting, breaking the state's monopoly. Most English-language footage is not dubbed.

CRIME

8181 prisoners

Up 9% in 1990

CRIME RATES

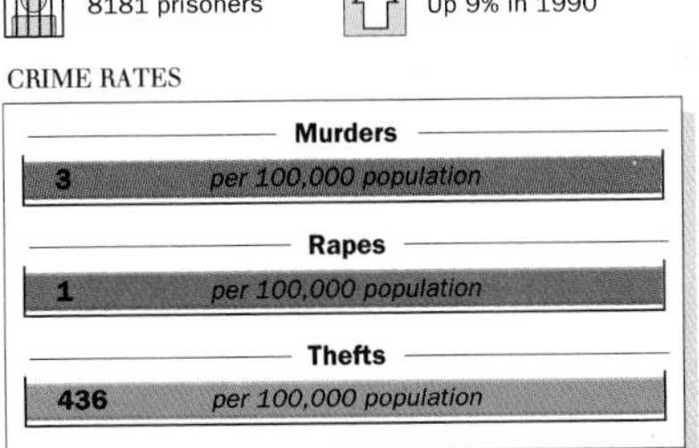

Compared with most West European countries, Portugal still enjoys a remarkably low crime rate. However, drug-trafficking and related offenses are on the rise.

EDUCATION

85%

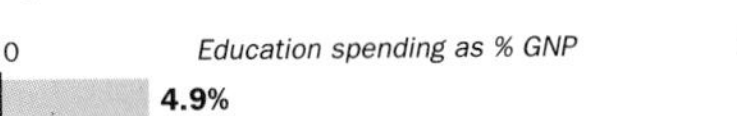

THE EDUCATION SYSTEM

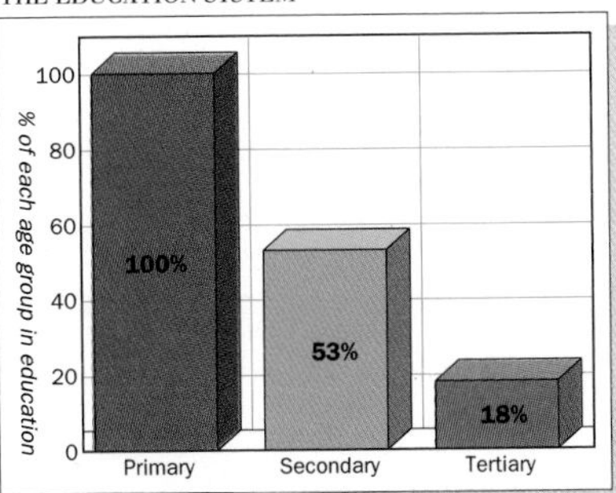

Free state education is available to all pupils between ages three and 15, although the pre-school stage up to age six is not compulsory. Middle-class parents rely heavily on private schools. State universities are large and oversubscribed. There are several prestigious private universities.

HEALTH

1 per 412 people

Cancer, heart and cerebrovascular diseases, accidents

0 — Health spending as % GNP — 25

3.5%

The public health system is free, but it suffers from underfunding. However, Portugal's larger urban hospitals are modern and well-equipped.

Private health-care plans are both affordable and good value. Over 40% of the population use the private system. In spite of high tobacco and wine consumption, the Portuguese are a healthy nation, with similar life expectancy rates to neighboring Spain.

WEALTH

Shop assistant, 1.7m escudos per year; managing director, 11.3m escudos per year

CONSUMER GOODS OWNERSHIP

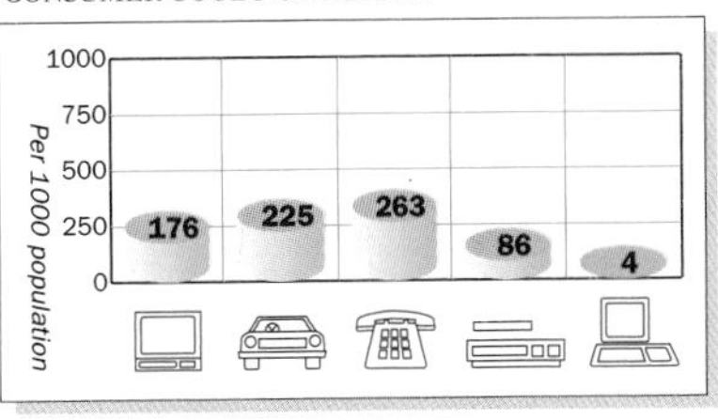

Wealth differentials in Portugal are smaller than in most EU countries. The bloodless military coup of 1974 led to many wealthy families transferring their assets abroad, or leaving Portugal altogether. The 1976 constitution enshrined socialist goals, and subsequent governments introduced limited wealth redistribution measures.

Many long-standing Portuguese families have seen the value of their assets fall with the dramatic drop in land prices since 1986. However, those with land with tourist development potential, such as golf courses, have made large profits. Much wealth generated by new businesses leaves Portugal, as most are foreign-owned.

WORLD RANKING

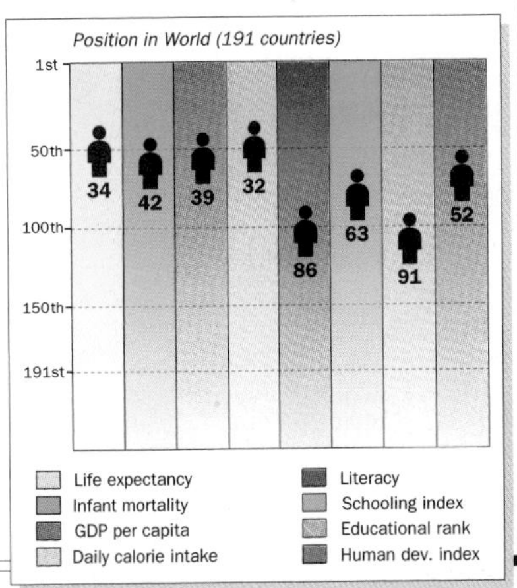

P

QATAR

MIDDLE EAST

OFFICIAL NAME: State of Qatar **CAPITAL:** Doha
POPULATION: 500,000 **CURRENCY:** Qatar riyal **OFFICIAL LANGUAGE:** Arabic

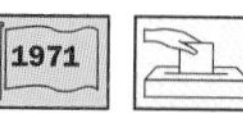

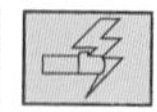

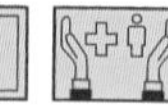

PROJECTING NORTH FROM the Arabian peninsula into the Persian Gulf, Qatar has land borders with Saudi Arabia and the United Arab Emirates, and a disputed sea border with Bahrain. Most of the country is flat, semi-arid desert. Qatar is a founding member of OPEC and its plentiful oil and natural gas reserves make it one of the wealthiest states in the region. The country enjoys political stability under the rule of the 15,000-strong Al Thani clan.

CLIMATE

WEATHER CHART

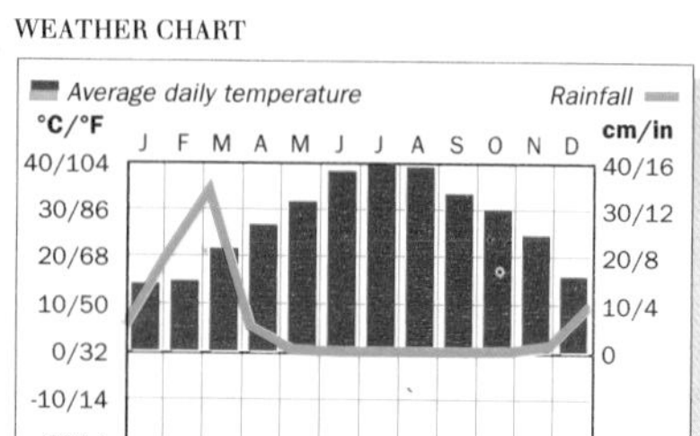

The climate is hot and humid with midsummer temperatures reaching 111°F. Rainfall is rare.

COMMUNICATIONS

Doha International 1.1m passengers (est)

23 ships 593,600 dwt

THE TRANSPORTATION NETWORK

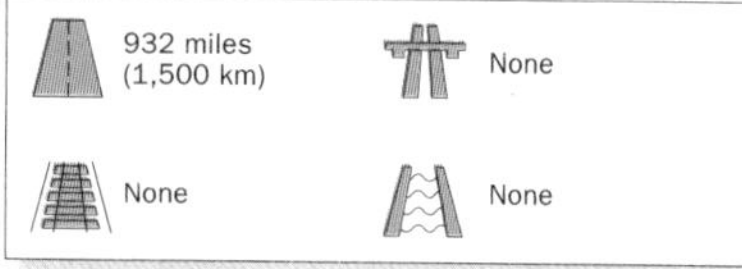

A good road network links Qatar to its neighbors. A new international airport in Doha is scheduled for 1997.

TOURISM

Small-scale tourism

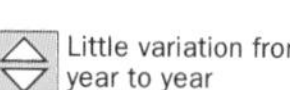
Little variation from year to year

MAIN OVERSEAS ARRIVALS

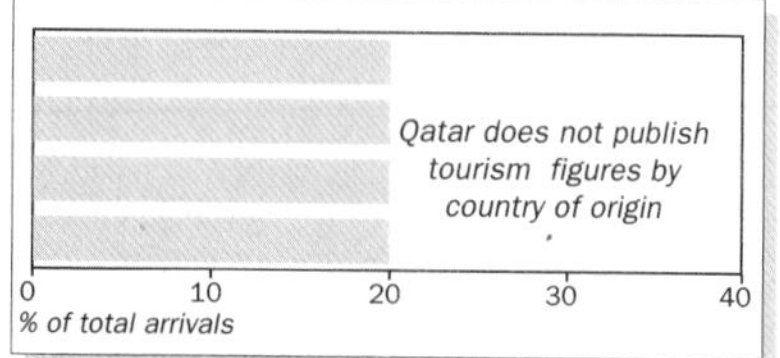

Qatar attracts several thousand European visitors a year, who enjoy unspoiled beaches, duty-free shopping, modern hotels and the desert hinterland. Alcohol is permitted in five-star hotels for non-Muslims.

PEOPLE

Arabic

93 people per sq. mile

THE URBAN/RURAL POPULATION SPLIT

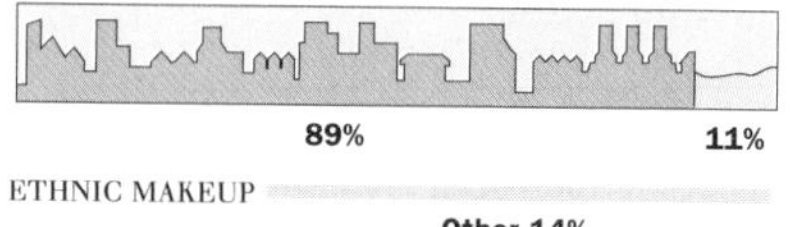

ETHNIC MAKEUP

Other 14%
Arab 40%
Iranian 10%
Pakistani 18%
Indian 18%

Only one in five Qataris is native-born. Most of the population are guest workers from the Indian subcontinent, Iran and the northern African countries. Expatriates enjoy a high standard of living and take no part in politics.

Qataris are followers of the Wahhabi interpretation of Sunni Islam and espouse conservative religious views. However, women are not obliged to wear the veil and can have drivers licenses. Expatriate Christians are allowed freedom to worship but not to promote Christianity.

Since the advent of oil wealth, the Qataris, who were formerly nomadic Bedouins, have become a nation of city-dwellers. Almost 90% of the population now inhabit the capital of Doha and its suburbs. As a result, northern Qatar is dotted with depopulated and abandoned villages.

Doha, the capital. *Although desert covers the whole country, Qatar now grows most of its own vegetables by tapping ground water.*

POLITICS

Not applicable. Absolute rule by an Amir

Amir Sheikh Khalifa bin Hamad Al Thani

THE STATE OF THE PARTIES

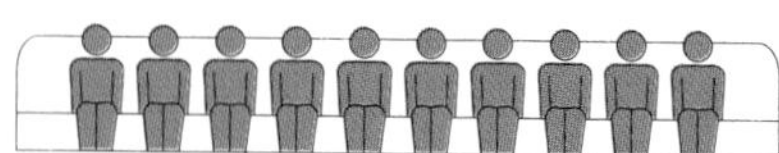

Qatar is an absolute monarchy and has no legislature. The Amir rules with the assistance of the Council of Ministers and the Advisory Council

Qatar is a traditional emirate. Its government and religious establishment is dominated by Amir Sheikh Khalifa, who took power in a bloodless coup in 1972. His designated successor is his son, Sheikh Hamad. Although the Al Thani family has several sub-groups, the Amir and his immediate relatives are unchallenged.

The largely middle-class pro-democracy movement has called for reform of the 35-member Advisory Council. The Amir's response has been to introduce more technocrats into the cabinet. However, he maintains a tight rein on finance, personally signing all government checks over 250,000 Qatar riyals.

WORLD AFFAIRS

OPEC AL   

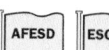

Qatar sided with Iraq in the Iran-Iraq War (1980–1988). However, during the Gulf War against Iraq (1990–1991), it hosted UN forces and its soldiers fought at the battle of Khafji. The Amir is eager to retain strong links with Western states, notably the UK and the USA. Within the quotas set by OPEC, Qatar has supported a moderate oil price. It has firmly resisted claims against its territory by Bahrain and has sought to strengthen ties with the Islamic Republic of Iran. In 1992, a ten-year defense agreement was signed with the USA, despite Saudi Arabia's disapproval. Qatar is a founding member of the Gulf Cooperation Council, established in 1981 as an economic union with Saudi Arabia, Kuwait, the United Arab Emirates, Oman and Bahrain.

AID

Qatar now gives minimal aid

Sharp fall in donations

Qatar was a generous aid donor to developing countries during the 1970s and early 1980s, but levels have fallen sharply as a result of lower oil prices.

Q

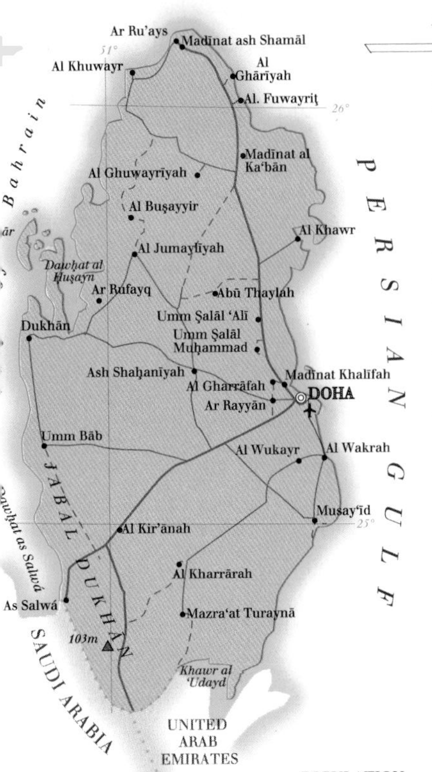

QATAR

Total Area : 11 000 sq. km (4247 sq. miles)

DEFENSE

$934.1bn

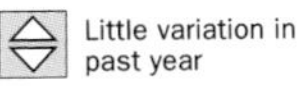
Little variation in past year

The 9,000-strong armed forces are too small to play a significant role in Qatari affairs, even in the event of political turmoil. A ten-year defense agreement with the USA provides for joint exercises, the stockpiling of American equipment and US access to bases.

RESOURCES

4.6bn kwh (capacity 1.41m kw)

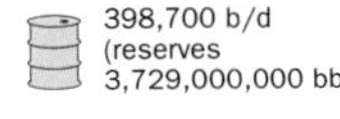
398,700 b/d (reserves 3,729,000,000 bbl)

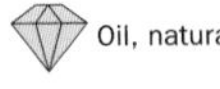
2m chickens, 128,000 sheep, 78,000 goats

Oil, natural gas

Qatar has the third-smallest reserves of crude oil within OPEC, but it has abundant reserves of gas, including the world's largest non-associated gas field, known as North Field.

ENVIRONMENT

None

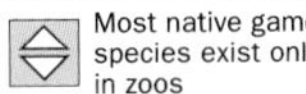
Most native game species exist only in zoos

The desert hinterland supports little plant or animal life. Oil pollution has damaged marine life. On land, game has been hunted out and most native species are extinct in the wild.

MEDIA

The press is subject to censorship

PUBLISHING AND BROADCAST MEDIA

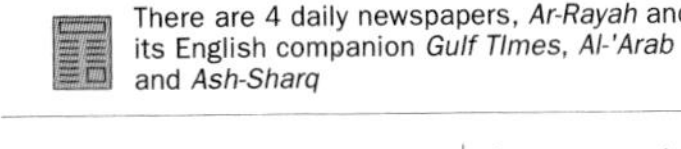
There are 4 daily newspapers, *Ar-Rayah* and its English companion *Gulf Times*, *Al-'Arab* and *Ash-Sharq*

1 state-owned service

2 state-owned networks

There is total political censorship. The foreign media is also censored for good taste. Satellite TV channels are freely available.

CRIME

6,285 prisoners

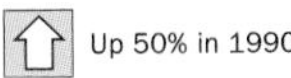
Up 50% in 1990

Traditional Islamic punishments have deterred crime. However, drug-trafficking is on the increase. The incidence of street crime is low.

CHRONOLOGY

The ruling Al Thanis date back to the 18th century. An offshoot of the Khalifa family of Bahrain, they came under first Turkish, then British, dominance.

- ❑ **1971** Independence from the UK.
- ❑ **1972** Accession of Amir Khalifa.
- ❑ **1981** Qatar joins Gulf Cooperation Council.

EDUCATION

76%

Education is free from primary to university level. The government finances students to study overseas.

HEALTH

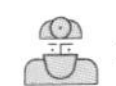
1 per 561 people

Heart, circulatory and infectious diseases, cancer

Primary health care is free to Qataris. Hospitals operate to Western standards of care and the government also funds treatment abroad.

WEALTH

Poverty is very rare in Qatar

CONSUMER GOODS OWNERSHIP

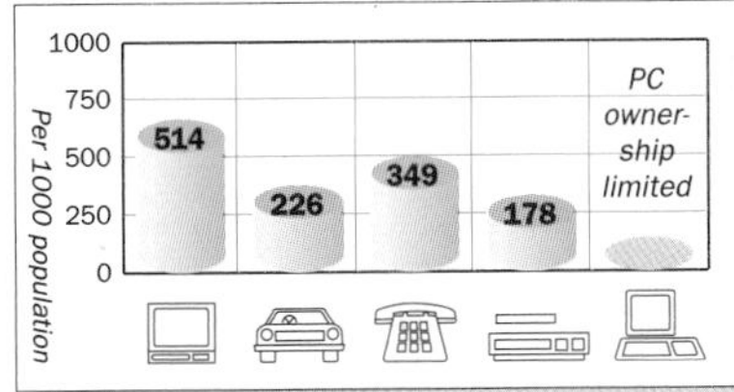

Qataris have a very high income per capita, no income tax, free public services and the government guarantees jobs for high-school graduates. There are no exchange controls.

ECONOMICS

$7bn

3.63 Qatar riyals

SCORE CARD

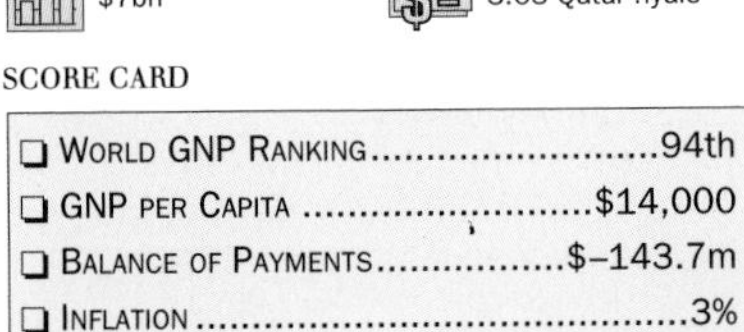

❑ WORLD GNP RANKING	94th
❑ GNP PER CAPITA	$14,000
❑ BALANCE OF PAYMENTS	$-143.7m
❑ INFLATION	3%
❑ UNEMPLOYMENT	0%

STRENGTHS

A steady supply of crude oil and huge gas reserves, plus related industries. Modern infrastructure.

WEAKNESSES

Dependence on foreign work force. All raw materials and most foods are imported. Virtually all water has to be desalinated. Government has large foreign reserves, but new industries depend on cementing agreements with foreign partners. Potential threat to security from Iraq and Iran makes some multinationals wary of investment.

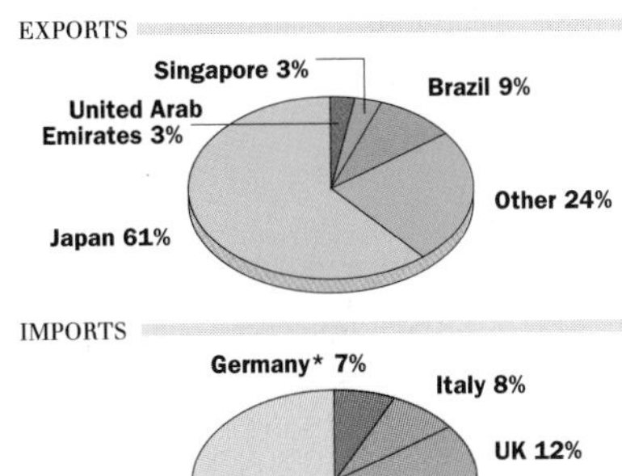

WORLD RANKING

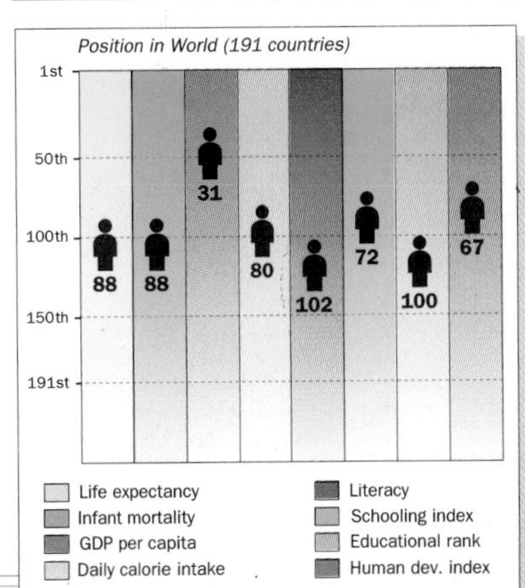

Q

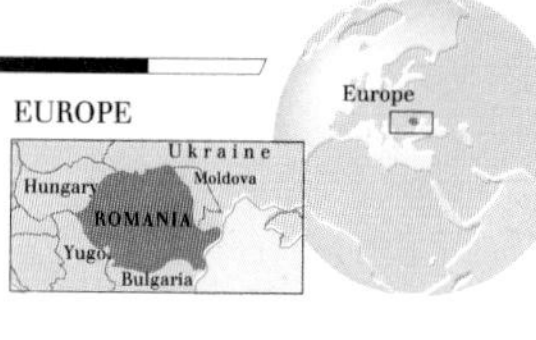

ROMANIA

OFFICIAL NAME: Romania **CAPITAL:** Bucharest
POPULATION: 23.3 million **CURRENCY:** Leu **OFFICIAL LANGUAGE:** Romanian

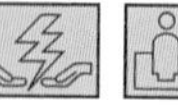

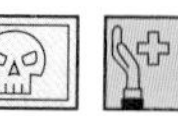

ROMANIA LIES ON THE Black Sea coast, with the Danube as its southern border. The eastern Carpathian Mountains form an arc across the country, curving around the upland basin of Transylvania. Long dominated by the Ottoman, Russian and Hapsburg empires, Romania became an independent monarchy in 1878. After World War II, the monarchy was supplanted by a communist People's Republic, which was headed by Nicolae Ceauşescu from 1965. A coup in 1989 resulted in Ceauşescu's execution. Romania is now a limited democracy, converting slowly to a free-market economy.

Village in northeastern Romania, *in the foothills of the Carpathian Mountains, close to the border with Ukraine. Corn and wheat are Romania's main crops.*

CLIMATE

WEATHER CHART

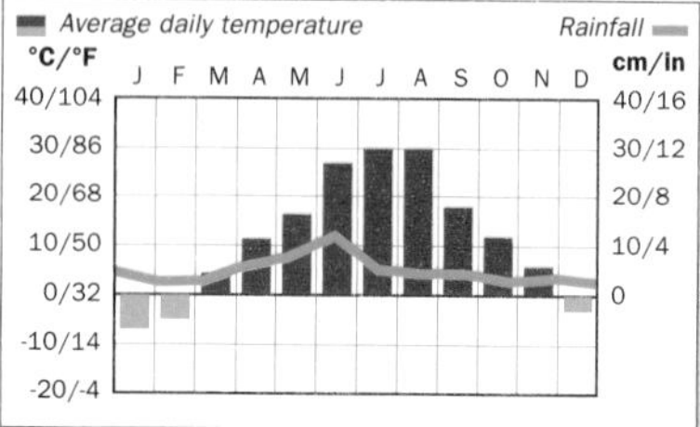

Romania has a continental climate with two growing seasons. Rainfall is generally moderate, with most falling in spring and early summer. Very heavy spring rains occasionally destroy new crops. Snow is frequent in winter, which can be bitterly cold.

COMMUNICATIONS

Bucharest-Otopeni Intl
1m passengers

261 ships
4.13m dwt

THE TRANSPORTATION NETWORK

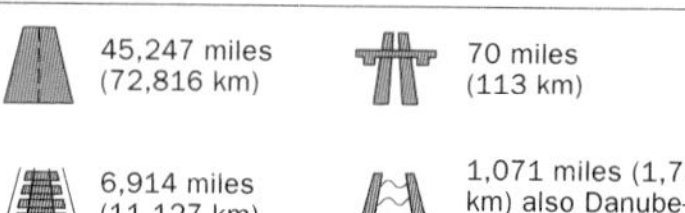

Outdated infrastructure is a major obstacle to Romania's development. Work on a subway for Bucharest, on new highways and on the almost-complete Danube–Black Sea Canal was stopped in 1989. US interests have proposed increasing the regional role of the port of Constanţa.

TOURISM

5.8m visitors

Up 17% in 1992

MAIN OVERSEAS ARRIVALS

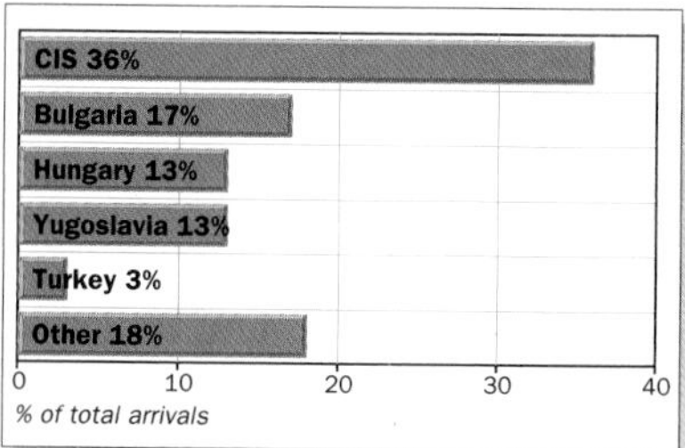

The Black Sea, Danube delta and Carpathian Mountains are the primary natural attractions, while Transylvania has a rich historical heritage. However, tourist facilities are generally poor. Under Ceauşescu, the need for foreign currency meant that tourists came before Romanians in accommodation priorities. Today, privatization of property and an acute housing shortage have reduced accommodation available to visitors. By 1992, tourism was no longer a net foreign exchange earner for Romania.

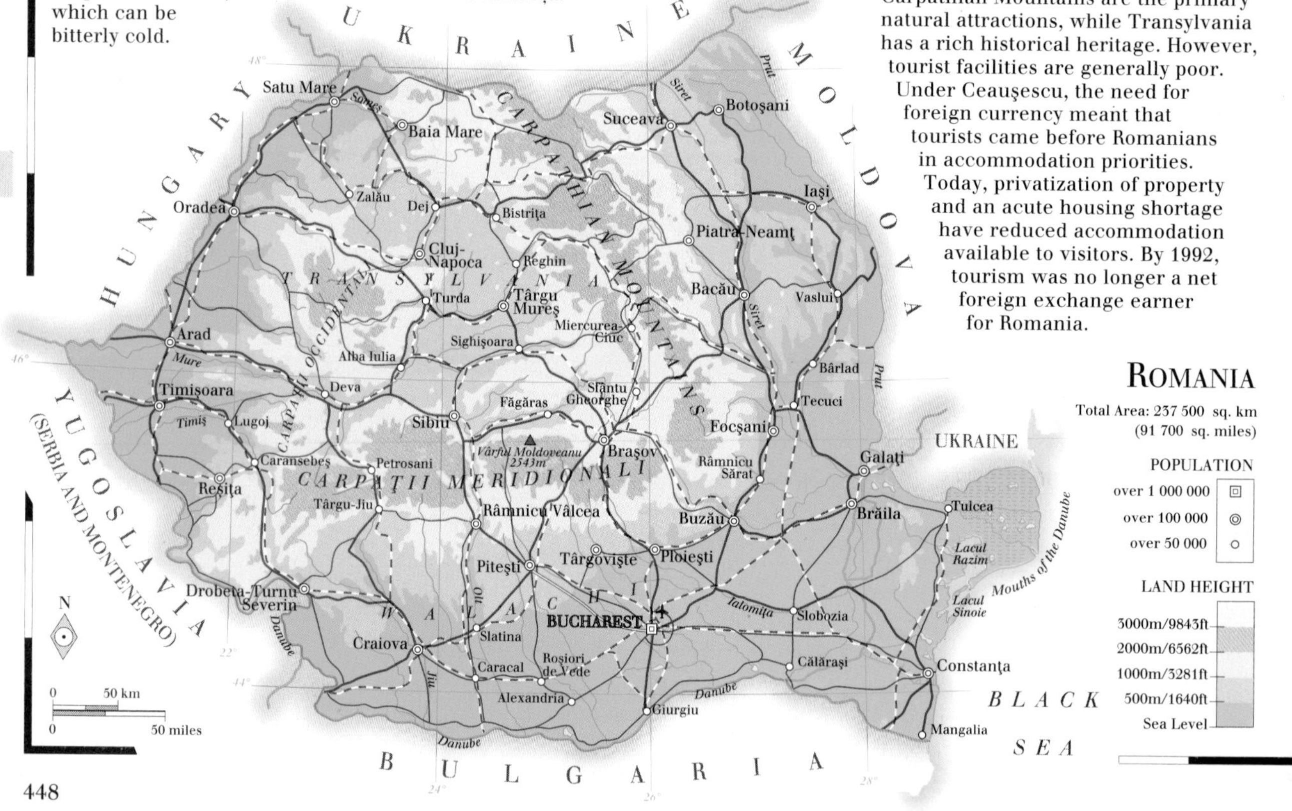

ROMANIA

Total Area: 237 500 sq. km (91 700 sq. miles)

POPULATION
over 1 000 000
over 100 000
over 50 000

LAND HEIGHT
3000m/9843ft
2000m/6562ft
1000m/3281ft
500m/1640ft
Sea Level

0 50 km
0 50 miles

PEOPLE

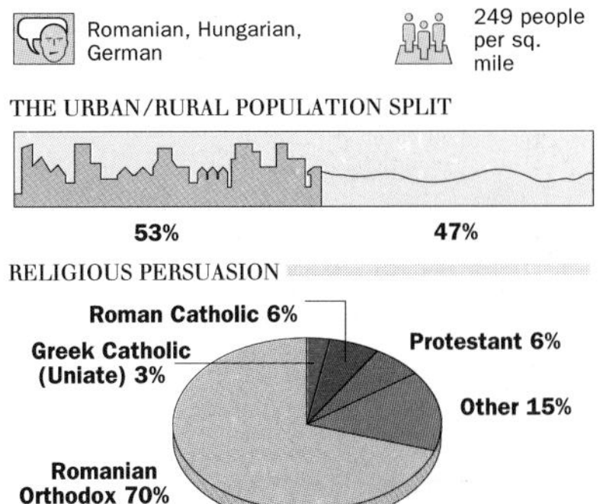

ETHNIC MAKEUP

Other 2% Hungarian 9%

Romanian 89%

Since 1989, there has been a rise in Romanian nationalism, aggravated by the hardships brought by economic reform and accompanying austerity measures. The incidence of ethnic violence has also risen, particularly toward Gypsies and Hungarians. Ethnic Hungarians form the largest minority group in Romania. They are partly protected by the influence of the Hungarian state, whereas the Gypsies do not have any similar support and tend to suffer greater discrimination.

Romania's population is currently decreasing. This is due to rising emigration since 1989, mainly for economic reasons, and to a falling birthrate since the early 1990s. The latter trend is in sharp contrast to the 1980s, when the Ceauşescu regime enforced a "pro-natalist" policy, by banning contraception and abortion. The government also imposed taxes on childless adults or on those with fewer than four children and obliged married women to have monthly fertility examinations. The birthrate rose accordingly. However, the population as a whole did not rise significantly, due to an increase in Romania's mortality rate. Abortion was legalized in 1989; maternal death rates have recently declined.

POPULATION AGE BREAKDOWN

% of population by age group

	1960	1970	1980	1990	2000
65+	6.7%	8.6%	10.3%	10.3%	12.6%
15–64	65.2%	65.4%	63.1%	66.3%	66.2%
0–14	28.1%	26%	26.6%	23.4%	21.2%

WORLD AFFAIRS

While making efforts to remain on good terms with the former Soviet states, Romania is building closer links with Western Europe. In 1993, it signed an association agreement with the EU.

Relations with Hungary are tense. Despite pressure from Budapest, Romania has resisted the demands of the Hungarian minority in Transylvania for greater autonomy.

After 1989, unification with Moldova was a distinct possibility, as Romanians are of the same ethnic group as Moldovans. However, the issue was quashed in 1993 when Moldova voted for closer links with the CIS. Romania has followed UN policy on Yugoslavia, adhering to sanctions despite the negative effects on its own economy.

AID

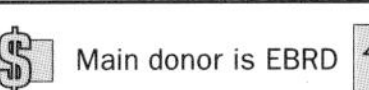

Increasing aid from EBRD and IMF

There has been some delay in receiving IMF and World Bank aid. Romania does not want to conform to IMF economic directives. Aid is being used to improve telecommunications and mechanize the privatized – but undercapitalized – agricultural sector.

POLITICS

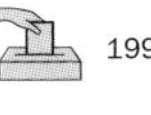

President Ion Iliescu

THE STATE OF THE PARTIES

Chamber of Deputies 341 members

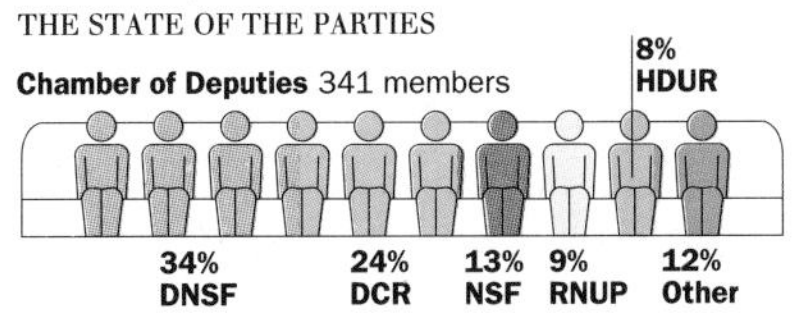

DNSF = Democratic National Salvation Front **DCR** = Democratic Convention of Romania (composed of: Christian Democrat National Peasants' Party, Party of the Civic Alliance, National Liberal Party – Democratic Convention, National Liberal Party – Youth Wing, Romanian Social Democratic Party, Romanian Ecology Party) **NSF** = National Salvation Front **RNUP** = Romanian National Union Party **HDUR** = Hungarian Democratic Union of Romania **Other** = Greater Romania Party, Socialist Labor Party, Agrarian Democratic Party of Romania

Senate 143 members

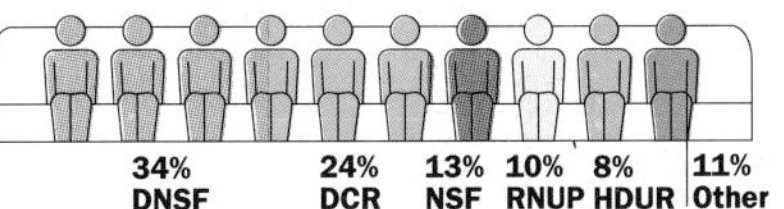

In 1991, Romania voted to become a multiparty democracy headed by a directly elected president, who may not belong to any political party.

MAIN POLITICAL ISSUES

Economic performance

The poor performance of the economy has exerted pressure on the minority government. General strikes in early 1994 expressed popular discontent with falling living standards, and the seeming inability of the government to develop a coherent economic policy.

Ethnic tensions

Ethnic tensions are rising in Romania. The far right has made political gains and nationalism is increasingly accepted. In 1993, elements of the extreme right were advocating labor camps for ethnic minorities. Gypsies are becoming victims of violent, racially motivated attacks.

PROFILE

Romania's 1989 revolution left an old communist elite in power. Unlike Poland, Hungary and Czechoslovakia, Romania did not have an organized group ready to introduce real democracy, with the skills necessary to create a vibrant market economy. Democracy is in place on the surface, but political intimidation and ballot-rigging remain commonplace.

While many state assets have been privatized, most have remained in the hands of people tied to the ruling political clique. The DNSF government retains the support of conservative groups, such as miners and rural workers.

President Ion Iliescu succeeded Ceauşescu and was reelected in 1992.

Nikolae Vacaroiu, an economist who became prime minister in 1992.

CHRONOLOGY

Many of Romania's foreign policy tensions are the legacy of its long history of redrawn borders. Former territories are resisting reunification, primarily on economic grounds.

- **1859** Unification of Moldova and Wallachia forms basis of future Romania.
- **1878** Independence, but at cost of losing Bessarabia to Russia.
- **1916–1918** Enters World War I on Allied side. At end of war, gains substantial territory, including Transylvania from Hungary.

R

CHRONOLOGY *continued*

- **1924** Communists banned in unstable political arena. Rise of fascist "Iron Guard."
- **1938** King Carol establishes royal autocracy.
- **1940** Under extreme pressure, territory ceded to Soviet Union, Bulgaria and Hungary. Iron Guard stages coup. King Carol abdicates in favor of son, Michael. Tripartite Pact with Germany.
- **1941** Enters war on Axis side, hoping to recover Bessarabia from the Soviets.
- **1944** Romania switches sides as Soviet troops reach border.
- **1945** Soviet-backed regime installed. Romanian Communist Party plays an increasing role.
- **1946** Paris Peace Conference gives Romania Transylvania but not Bessarabia, which goes to Soviets, who also demand huge reparations. Communist-led National Democratic Front wins majority in disputed election results.
- **1947** King Michael forced to abdicate.
- **1948–1953** Centrally planned economy put in place.
- **1953** Leaders of Jewish community prosecuted for Zionism.
- **1958** Soviet troops withdraw.
- **1964** Prime Minister Gheorghiu-Dej declares national sovereignty. Proposes joint COMECON planning to lessen Soviet economic control.
- **1965** Ceauşescu becomes party secretary after death of Gheorghiu-Dej.
- **1968–1980** Condemnation of Soviet invasion of Czechoslovakia; successful courting of USA and EC.
- **1982** Ceauşescu vows to pay off foreign debt.
- **1987** Brasov party headquarters ransacked in riot, which is forcibly suppressed.
- **1989** Demonstrations, in which many killed by security forces. Armed forces join with opposition in National Salvation Front (NSF) to form government. Ion Iliescu declared president. Ceauşescu summarily tried and shot.
- **1990** Elections held, in which NSF victorious. Amnesty for political prisoners.
- **1991** New constitution, providing for market reform, approved in referendum.
- **1992** Second free elections. NSF splits into two factions: DNSF and NSF. DNSF forms minority government.
- **1993** No-confidence motion fails.
- **1994** Largest general strike since 1989, demanding faster pace of economic reform.

R

DEFENSE

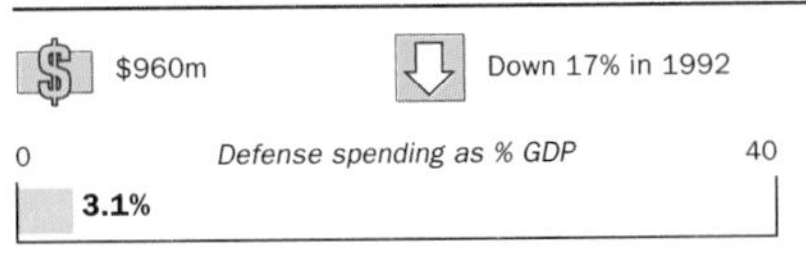

The military received limited funding under the Ceauşescu regime and troops were routinely deployed as cheap labor. Since the demise of the Warsaw Pact, Romania has not sought close ties with NATO. The weak economy means that military expenditure will fall further in future.

ROMANIAN ARMED FORCES

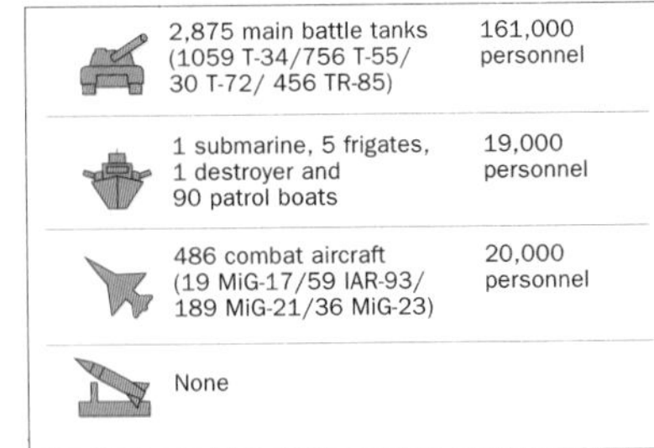

2,875 main battle tanks (1059 T-34/756 T-55/ 30 T-72/ 456 TR-85)
161,000 personnel
1 submarine, 5 frigates, 1 destroyer and 90 patrol boats
19,000 personnel
486 combat aircraft (19 MiG-17/59 IAR-93/ 189 MiG-21/36 MiG-23)
20,000 personnel
None

ECONOMICS

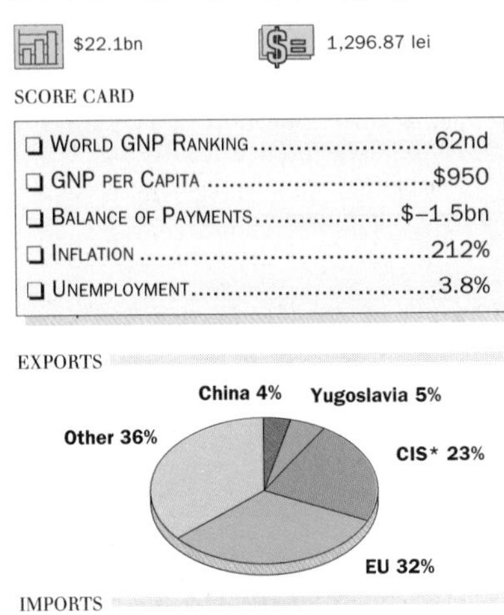

$22.1bn
1,296.87 lei
SCORE CARD
World GNP Ranking 62nd
GNP per Capita $950
Balance of Payments ....$-1.5bn
Inflation 212%
Unemployment 3.8%
EXPORTS
China 4%
Yugoslavia 5%
Other 36%
CIS* 23%
EU 32%

IMPORTS

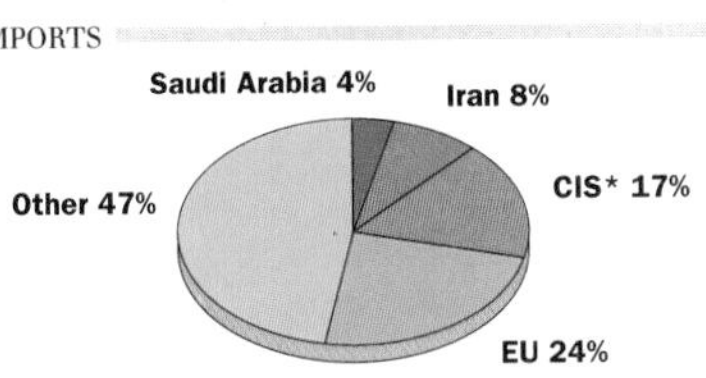

STRENGTHS
Large number of foreign joint ventures. Tourism potential.

WEAKNESSES
Slow transition from centrally planned to market economy. Delays in implementing economic reform. Low foreign investment levels. Large bureaucracy.

PROFILE
Few economic reforms have been undertaken in Romania compared with other former communist Eastern European states. While all have suffered from recession in the reform process, Romania's has been the most severe, and there appears to be little prospect of improvement in the near future. Pressure for reform is strongest in the chemical, petrochemical, metal, transportation and food industries.

Only a small minority is doing well economically. Real wages have also fallen since the change of regime, and are continuing to do so. Farming began to be privatized in 1989 and by 1994, 80% of farmland was in private hands. It remains severely undermechanized. Agricultural processing is still under state control, and output levels have fallen, notably in meat products.

Romania was the first Eastern European country to open its economy to foreign investment, allowing 100% foreign ownership from 1990. The number of joint ventures – 21,000 – is the highest in Eastern Europe, but most are small-scale. Foreign investment is hindered by bureaucracy and doubts about the country's stability. However, both imports and exports rose in 1993. The EU is now Romania's main trading partner.

ECONOMIC PERFORMANCE INDICATOR

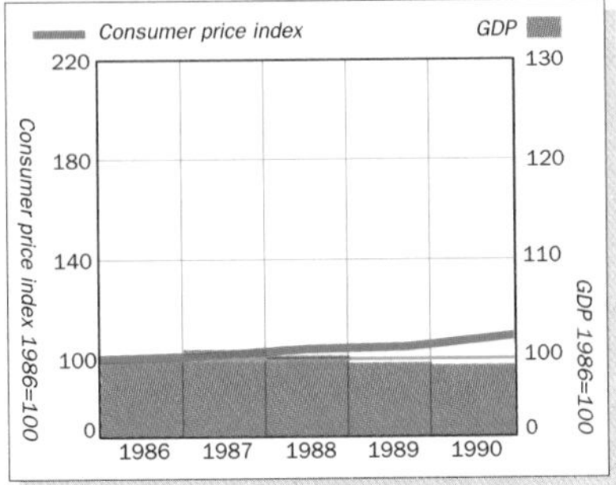

ROMANIA : MAJOR BUSINESSES

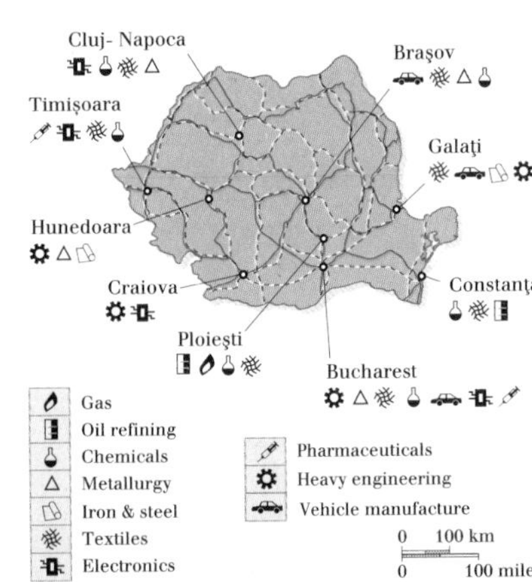

RESOURCES

64.3bn kwh (capacity 22.9m kw)

138,300 b/d (reserves 1,588,754,000)

16.2m sheep, 14.4m pigs, 6.4m cattle

Coal, salt, iron, natural gas, methane, bauxite, copper, lead, zinc, oil

ELECTRICITY GENERATION

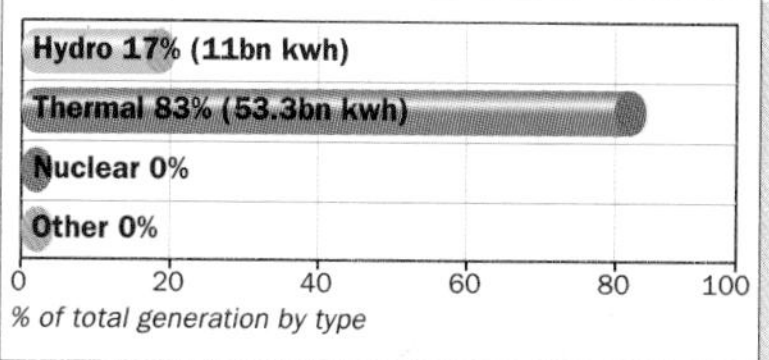

Romania has oil and gas reserves, but production is insufficient to meet domestic demand. Production from onshore fields fell during the 1980s as reserves were depleted, and oil imports have risen substantially since 1989. Efforts are being concentrated on developing offshore reserves in the Black Sea and several drilling platforms are now in operation. Romania has opened up exploration and processing to foreign investors, including Middle Eastern and CIS companies.

The electricity supply is outdated and has been insufficient to meet national demand for the last 20 years. The development of a nuclear power industry has been scrapped because of the lack of available funds.

Deposits of other minerals are small and contribute little to export earnings.

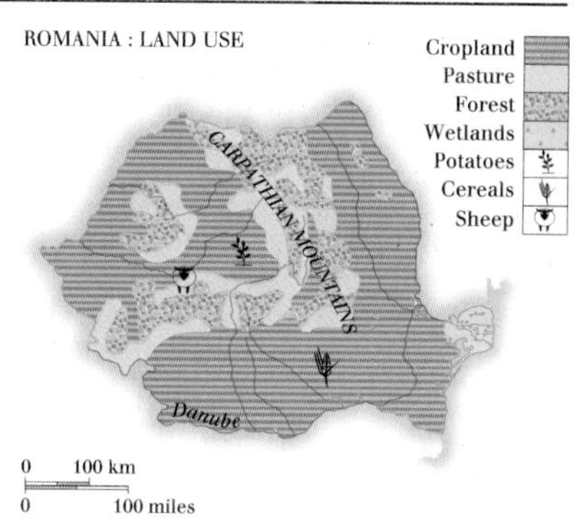

ENVIRONMENT

5% (4% partially protected)

Rising public awareness, but no funds available

ENVIRONMENTAL TREATIES

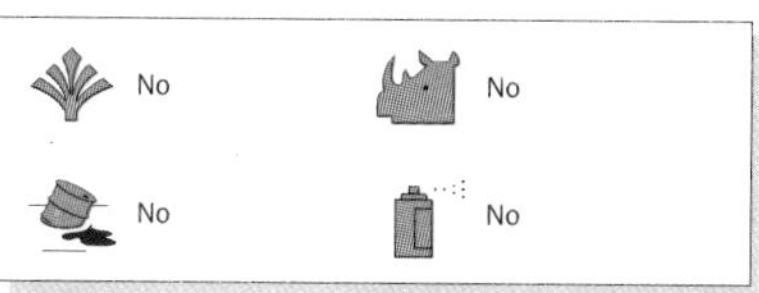

The south is the region with the most serious pollution problems. Cement-plant and power-station emissions have been linked to respiratory diseases. The incidence of birth defects has risen in the vicinity of the artificial fiber plant in Suceava. Industrial water pollution is also a major problem, aggravated by insufficient purification facilities. However, nature conservation is currently receiving more attention. The Danube delta has been identified as a site for a biosphere reserve.

MEDIA

No restrictions on political reporting

PUBLISHING AND BROADCAST MEDIA

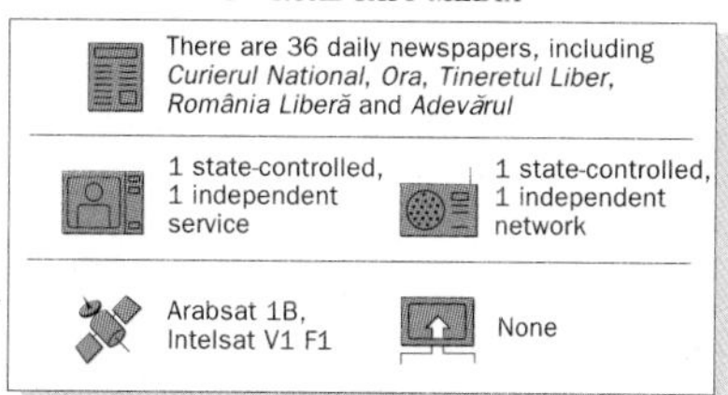

There are 36 daily newspapers, including *Curierul National, Ora, Tineretul Liber, România Liberă* and *Adevărul*
1 state-controlled, 1 independent service
1 state-controlled, 1 independent network
Arabsat 1B, Intelsat V1 F1
None

Restrictions were lifted on the press in 1989. The number of publications is now over 1,600. The main dailies are *România Liberă* and *Adevărul*, as well as the tabloid *Tineretul Liber*. The broadcast media are still largely under government control, but the debut of the first independent TV station has provided viewers with an alternative news source.

CRIME

41,300 prisoners

Up 31% in 1990

CRIME RATES

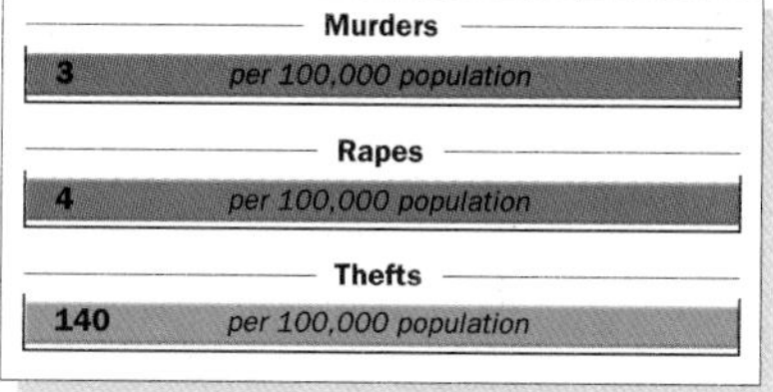

The black economy is the primary source of income for a third of the population. Levels of tax evasion are estimated to be among the highest in the world.

EDUCATION

96%

0 Education spending as % GNP 25

2.1%

THE EDUCATION SYSTEM

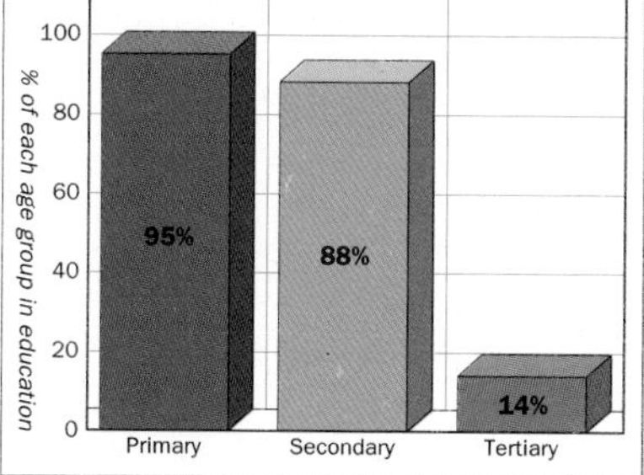

Primary and secondary school attendance is 90%, lower than the European average. University enrollment is no longer restricted. The number of students in higher education has risen by nearly a third since 1989, temporarily alleviating high unemployment among young adults.

HEALTH

1 per 555 people

Heart, cerebrovascular and respiratory diseases, cancer

0 Health spending as % GNP 25

2.5%

Romania's life expectancy is, jointly with Albania's, the lowest in Europe; at 71 years; in the worst polluted parts of Transylvania it is 61 years. Its TB rate is also the highest in Europe.

WEALTH

Coal miner, 19,349 lei per month; dentist, 9,900 lei per month

CONSUMER GOODS OWNERSHIP

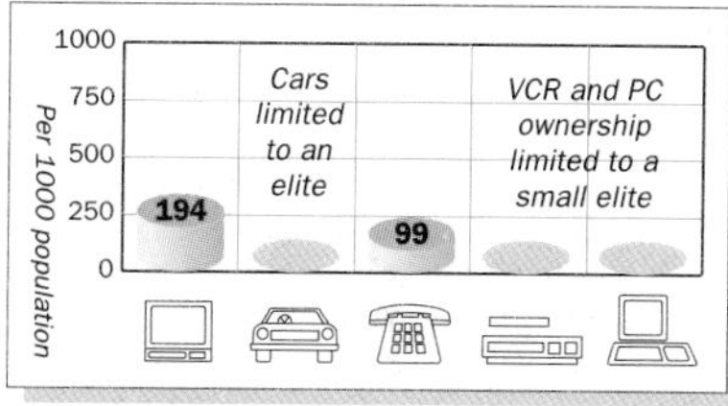

Wealth distribution has changed little since the fall of the Ceauşescu regime in 1989. The ruling ex-communist clique is still the richest group, and is determined to maintain its economic as well as political position.

WORLD RANKING

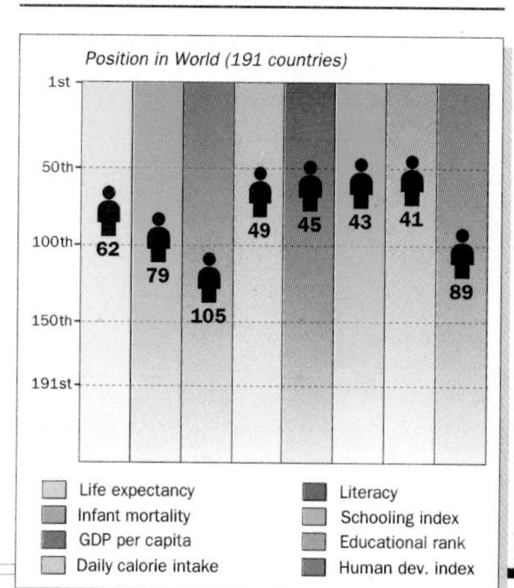

R

Russian Federation

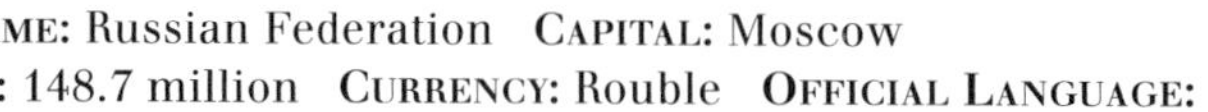

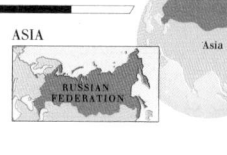

Official Name: Russian Federation **Capital:** Moscow
Population: 148.7 million **Currency:** Rouble **Official Language:** Russian

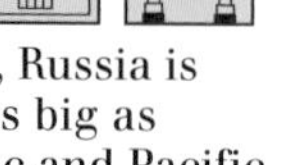

WITH A TERRITORY of 6 million sq. miles, Russia is the world's largest state, almost twice as big as either the USA or China. Bounded by the Arctic and Pacific Oceans on its northern and eastern coasts, it also has land boundaries with 13 countries. With the formal dissolution of the USSR in 1991, Russia became an independent sovereign state. Within the CIS, it maintains a traditionally dominant role in Central Asia and Eurasia. Ethnic Russians make up 80% of the population, but there are around 150 smaller ethnic groups, many with their own national territories within Russia's borders. The growth of regionalism is a major political issue. The situation is complicated by the fact that many of these territories are rich in key resources such as oil, gas, gold and diamonds.

The Kremlin, Moscow. *Rebuilt in 1475 by Ivan the Great, who commissioned architects from Pskov and Italy, it is enclosed by walls 1.5 miles long and lies on the Moscow River.*

CLIMATE

WEATHER CHART

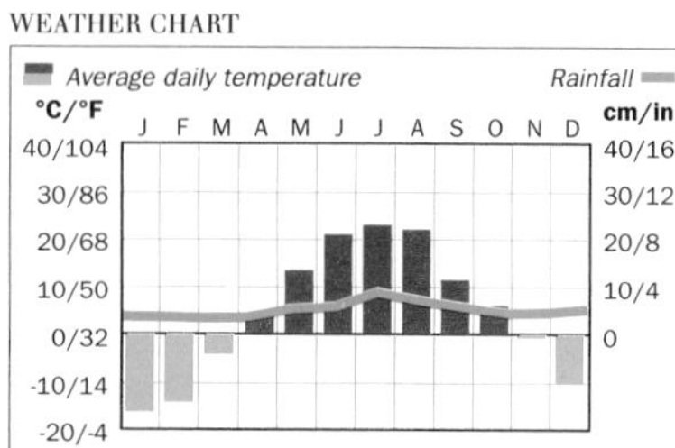

Russia has a cold continental climate, characterized by two widely divergent main seasons. Spring and autumn are very brief periods of transition between warm summers and freezing winters. The country is open to the influences of the Arctic and Atlantic to the north and west. However, mountains to the south and east prevent any warming effects from the Indian and Pacific Oceans from filtering across. Severe winters characterize most regions. Winter temperatures vary little from north to south, but fall sharply in eastern regions. The January temperature of –94°F recorded at Verkhoyansk in Siberia is the world record low outside Antarctica.

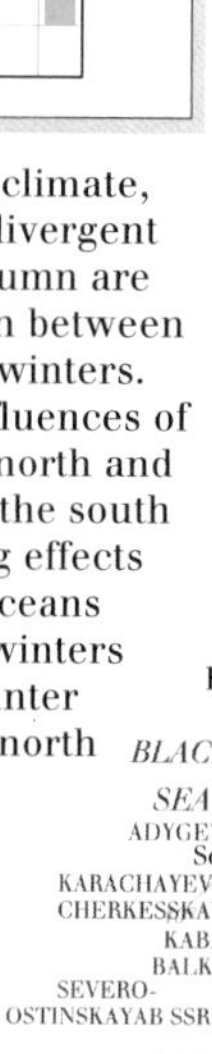

Russian Federation

Total Area :
17 400 286 sq. km
(6 592 800 sq. miles)

POPULATION

- over 5 000 000
- over 1 000 000
- over 500 000
- over 100 000
- over 50 000
- over 10 000

LAND HEIGHT

- 3000m/9843ft
- 2000m/6562ft
- 1000m/3281ft
- 500m/1640ft
- 200m/656ft
- Sea Level
- -200m/-656ft

N

0 500 km

0 500 miles

Housing in Moscow. *Living conditions in major cities are cramped, with two families often sharing one small apartment.*

R

COMMUNICATIONS

Sheremetyevo, Moscow
9.31m passengers

1,662 ships
13.98m dwt

THE TRANSPORTATION NETWORK

530,066 miles
(854,000 km)

None

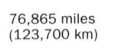

54,115 miles
(87,090 km)

76,865 miles
(123,700 km)

Russia has a comprehensive transportation network. Cities are served by good trolley and bus systems and Moscow has one of the most impressive subway systems in the world. In rural areas, car ownership is still low and the population relies on an extensive bus service. However, since 1991, all systems have seen some decline. The railroads, which were already declining in the Soviet era, are seriously overburdened and accidents and delays are increasing. About 20% of the railroad track should be renewed annually owing to frost and other damage. Shortage of funds means this is no longer done. Roads are also deteriorating, especially in major cities, but inter-urban highways are also affected. Crime is growing on railroads – notably the Trans-Siberian – and roads.

Since 1991, many new airlines have been set up as routes are privatized. However, Aeroflot, the previous state monopoly airline, is still the largest. Now called Russian International Airlines on overseas routes, it uses Boeing aircraft on flights from Moscow to London, Paris, Frankfurt, New York and Tokyo.

Standards on international routes are generally high. However, the safety record of internal routes is declining.

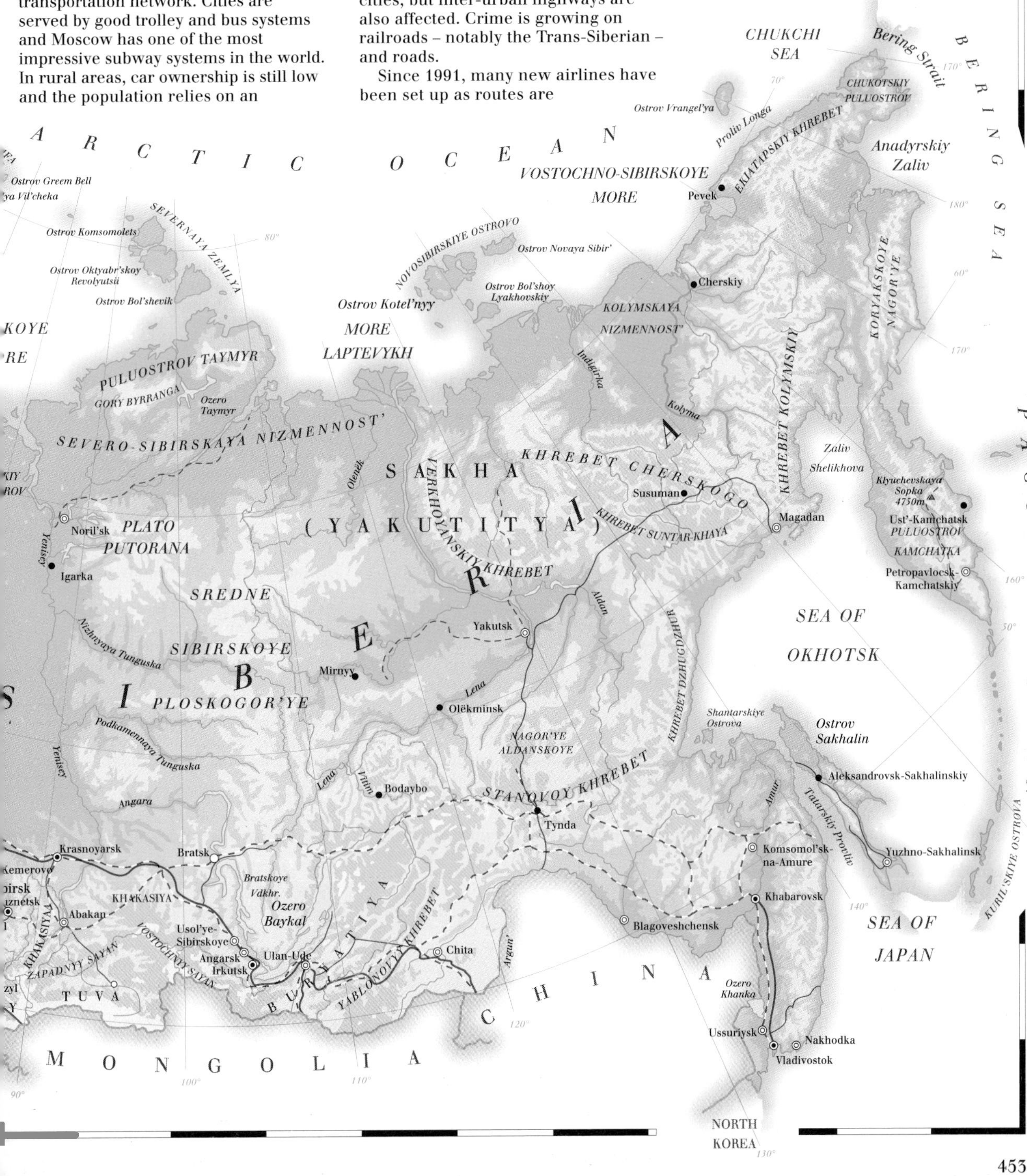

R

TOURISM

3m visitors

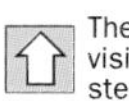
The number of visitors is increasing steadily

MAIN OVERSEAS ARRIVALS

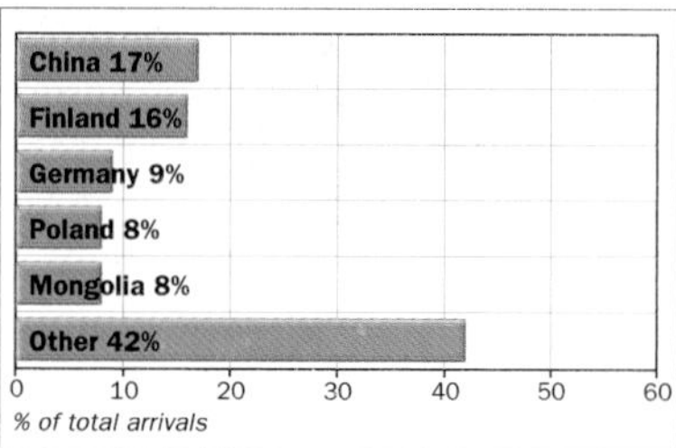

The privatization and breakup of *Intourist*, the previous monopoly tourist agency, has led to a vast expansion of tourism opportunities in Russia; each region is eager to earn hard currency and to attract rich visitors. At the luxury end of the market, trips from St. Petersburg to Tashkent are now available on former President Brezhnev's official train. River trips down the Volga and visits to medieval monasteries are increasingly popular. Tourists can also experience life in a Russian forest, or fish for salmon in the Kola peninsula. The defense sector has opened up to tourism and now offers flights in MiG jets, or drives in T-84 Russian tanks.

Moscow and St. Petersburg remain favorite destinations. Hotels in both cities tend either to cater for the well-off visitor, or to be of a basic standard. The St. Petersburg region is also increasingly explored. Novgorod has many fine churches and the Pskov area is celebrated as the setting for many of Pushkin's works, including *Eugene Onegin* and *Boris Godunov*.

Many parts of Russia remain inaccessible to most tourists. The communist ban on foreigners visiting the Urals has only recently been lifted, but the area still has very few facilities. However, resorts such as Sochi on the Black Sea have experienced a building boom, including the 2,500-room *Dagomys* Acapulco-style hotel complex.

PEOPLE

Russian

23 people per sq. mile

THE URBAN/RURAL POPULATION SPLIT

74% 26%

RELIGIOUS PERSUASION

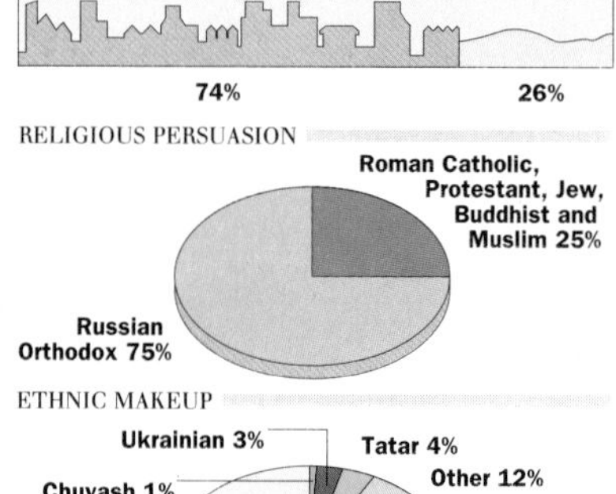

ETHNIC MAKEUP

Ukrainian 3%
Tatar 4%
Other 12%
Chuvash 1%
Russian 80%

In the former Soviet Union, Russians accounted for just over 50% of the population, but in Russia they are an overwhelming majority. Significant numbers of Russians still live in some of the neighboring Central Asian republics, notably, in Ukraine and Latvia. However, a rise in nationalism throughout the former USSR has persuaded many central Asian Russians to return to Russia.

Within Russia there has also been some increase in ethnic tension. There are 57 nationalities with their own territories within the federation and 95 nationalities without a territory (although these groups make up only 6% of the population).

Social life in Russia has not changed significantly since the demise of communism. However, with the lifting of censorship, there has been a greater expression of sexuality as well as of political and religious views. While there has been some increase in the availability of pornography and prostitution, this is mostly confined to major urban centers. There has been some revival of both the Russian Orthodox and Muslim faiths. However, Church attendance is still below Western levels. One marked change of which Russians speak is the growing importance attached to money. The mutual support systems of extended friendships are now in decline.

The position of women has changed little since the fall of communism. Many have suffered from the rise in unemployment, but this reflects the demise of many part-time or badly paid jobs, rather than a gender-motivated change in Russian society. Most Russians' very modest living standards have been maintained and retail sales in Russia are rising. Compared with the West, unemployment remains low, at an estimated 5% of the population.

POPULATION AGE BREAKDOWN

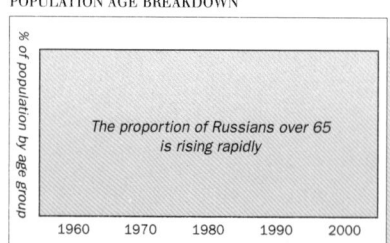

% of population by age group

The proportion of Russians over 65 is rising rapidly

1960 1970 1980 1990 2000

POLITICS

Uncertain

President Boris N. Yeltsin

THE STATE OF THE PARTIES

State *Duma* 450 members

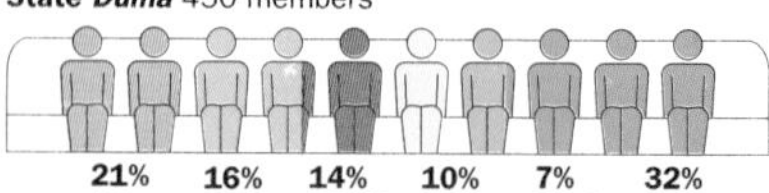

RC = Russia's Choice **LDPR** = Liberal Democratic Party of Russia **CPRF** = Communist Party of the Russian Federation **APR** = Agrarian Party of Russia **Y-B-L** = Yavlinsky-Boldyrev-Lukin bloc **Other** = Party of Russian Unity and Accord, Women of Russia, Democratic Party of Russia

Federal Council 178 members

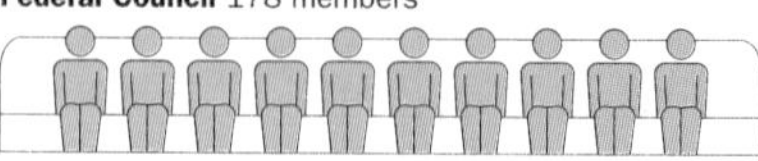

2 members are elected to represent each of 89 regions and republics

Russia has a democratically elected parliament under the leadership of an executive president.

Main Political Issues

Living standards

Russians are disillusioned at the failure of politicians to improve their living standards. The securities that used to underpin life – long-term employment, guaranteed housing and a basic diet – have been swept away. The decline has hit certain vulnerable groups – particularly the old – rather than the population as a whole.
However, there are signs that conditions may be improving. Retail sales in Russia rose consistently in the 18 months to mid-1994.

Crime

Crime has risen alarmingly since the collapse of communism. It is no longer safe to walk the streets of St. Petersburg or Moscow after dark. Bureaucratic corruption is now open and rising – officials demand payment for most services. Vladimir Zhirinovsky's promise to crush crime is a major reason behind his recent electoral success, particularly from the newly emerging middle class.

Disaffection with reform

Many Russians are disappointed with President Yeltsin's period in power and

President Yeltsin, *backed the reformers who lost heavily in the 1993 elections.*

Vladimir Zhirinovksy, *leader of the ultra-right Liberal Party.*

R

POLITICS *continued*

his attempts at reform. Mindful of the changing popular mood, parties no longer use the word "reform" but speak of "stabilization."

Russia's loss of Great Power status
Under communism, Russians took a great pride in their country's role in the world. The collapse of the economy and Russia's withdrawal from a global role has badly dented this pride. For many Russians, accepting Western aid and technology is a reminder of Russia's loss of status. The result is that politicians such as Zhirinovsky, who are promising to restore Russia's prestige, are gaining popular support.

PROFILE
The elections of 1993 confirmed a shift in the popular mood in Russia away from the pro-Yeltsin, pro-Western reformers toward the New Right reform policies advocated by Vladimir Zhirinovsky's Liberal Party.

President Yeltsin dissolved the Congress of People's Deputies in October 1993 in order to break a deadlock in parliament which was impeding the government's program. However, against Yeltsin's expectations, Russia's Choice lost votes while Vladimir Zhirinovky's Liberal Party saw a sharp increase in support. Following the elections, the key pro-Yeltsin reformers, Gaidar and Fyodorov, resigned. Yeltsin's loss of support in the *Duma* was clearly illustrated by the decision of Russian MPs to release the men behind the October 1993 attempted coup, in February 1994.

The rise of Zhirinovsky at the elections was significant. His Liberal Party's program has been likened to that of the National Socialists in 1930s Germany. Zhirinovsky is offering a New Right vision of Russia. He is not anti-reform, but proposes radical modernization. Much of his rhetoric attempts to inflame passions against ethnic minorities including the Azeris, Chechens and Armenians. He opposes Yeltsin's pro-Western stance. Zhirinovsky is emerging as a leading contender for the presidential elections of 1996.

***Yegor Gaidar**, one of the leading reformers in the Russian parliament.*

***Defense Minister Grachev**, in effect controls the Russian Army.*

The other significant change in 1993 was the increasingly aggressive attitude of the regions toward central government. The 89 regions in Russia are resentful that they do not have full control of their resources, while the former republics of the USSR now do. They also resented the Yeltsin-backed restrictions following the October 1993 coup attempt. Yeltsin's recent loss of influence could lead to the revival of a parliamentary debate on how a more federal Russia should work.

The future of Russian politics now depends on the ability of politicians to achieve economic growth. There was sharp change in policy following the elections. In 1994, the *Duma* decided to ignore strict IMF economic guidelines by increasing subsidies to the inefficient state sector. The policy is unlikely to be reversed before the elections of 1996.

WORLD AFFAIRS

During 1992 and 1993 Russia displayed little independent initiative in foreign affairs and allied itself closely to the USA. Its weak economy and a need for regular infusions of hard currency put it in no position to antagonize the Western powers and Japan.

However, since the 1993 elections, Russia has developed a more independent foreign policy. In February 1994, Russia brokered a withdrawal of Serbian heavy weapons around Sarajevo in Bosnia. This move brought Russia back again as a lead player in the Balkans, where Serbia is its traditional ally. Moscow also announced that its security guarantees to North Korea, should the South invade, remained in place. In March 1994, Russia disagreed with the USA on how to get the PLO-Israeli peace talks back on track after the Hebron massacre. This signaled an independent Russian Middle East policy for the first time since independence. During the Gulf War of 1990-91 Russia had been happy to follow the US line in the region. The expense of pursuing a global policy, however, has led to a total Russian withdrawal from Africa and the rest of the developing world.

Russia remains the overwhelmingly dominant partner in the CIS. It regards the successor states of the USSR as the "near abroad" and maintains troops in most of them. The policy is motivated in part by the need to protect the many Russians living in these states. Many of the CIS regimes are run by ex-communists with close links with Moscow.

***St. Basil's Cathedral, Moscow.** It was built in 1555-1561 to celebrate Ivan the Terrible's capture of the Tatar stronghold of Kazan. The exterior domes were decorated in the 1670s.*

AID

 $1bn

 Aid is rising

Russia has received about $1 billion from the IMF. However, failure to meet IMF economic criteria will restrict further loans. The EBRD has offered $300 million of credit; loans of up to $30,000 are available to small concerns. A similar fund invests in equities of newly privatized companies.

DEFENSE

 29.1bn

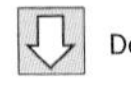 Down 27% in 1993

Defense spending as % GDP (scale 0–40): 5%

RUSSIAN ARMED FORCES

25,000 main battle tanks (T-54/-55, T-62, T-64A, T-72, T-80/-M9)	1m personnel
2 carriers, 219 submarines, 29 cruisers,24 destroyers, 114 frigates	300,000 personnel
3,600 combat aircraft (MiG 29, MiG 27, MiG 25, MiG-23, Su-27, Su-24)	170,000 personnel
1,204 ICBM, 52SSBN, 1,700 APC, 100 ABM	

In 1991, Russia inherited armed forces of 2.7 million men, of which 2.1 million were within its borders. However, it proved incapable of affording such a large army. By 1994, the forces had fallen to 1.2 million. Draft-dodging has also increased. In 1992, the army lost 35,000 officers and another 16,000 resigned in the first four months of 1993. Defense budgets have also been reduced. Spending on strategic nuclear forces is now limited to the physical protection of warheads. Early warning and space programs have also been sharply reduced. The navy has been the worst affected, and Russia's northern and Pacific fleets are inactive and deteriorating fast. No agreement has yet been reached with Ukraine over who owns the Black Sea fleet. The air force suffers from fuel shortages.

Regions

MOSCOW

Moscow, Russia's capital, administrative center and the seat of parliament, has a population of 8,801,500. It is now the most Westernized of Russia's cities. In practice, it functions almost like an independent city state. Market reforms have proceeded faster in Moscow than in any other Russian city and, in the December 1993 local elections, Russia's Choice, the pro-reform party, won a majority in the city *Duma*. Privatization of housing, stores and enterprises has been swift, but this has led to a rapid increase in corruption and crime. According to its forceful mayor, Yury Luzhkov, the city is almost bankrupt as the Russian government has failed to pay Moscow 250 billion roubles in central grants. A new tax of 0.1% of turnover in the Moscow Inter-Bank Currency Exchange has been imposed to raise revenue, much to the annoyance of businessmen.

CHECHNYA

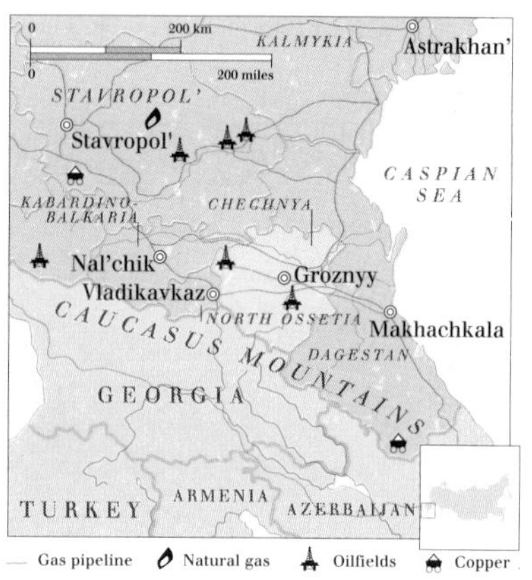

Located in the southwest of Russia, Chechnya region is dominated by the Chechens, the largest of the North Caucasian nationalities. In 1991 Chechnya declared itself independent of Russian rule and appointed its own president and government. An attempt to overthrow President Gen. Dzhokar Dudayev and replace him with a Moscow-approved leader failed and in December 1994 President Yeltsin, despite much political opposition, sent troops to capture Chechnya's capital, Grozny. The mission was incompetently executed and Russian troops faced fierce and prolonged resistance from Chechen forces before the city finally fell in February 1995.

ST. PETERSBURG

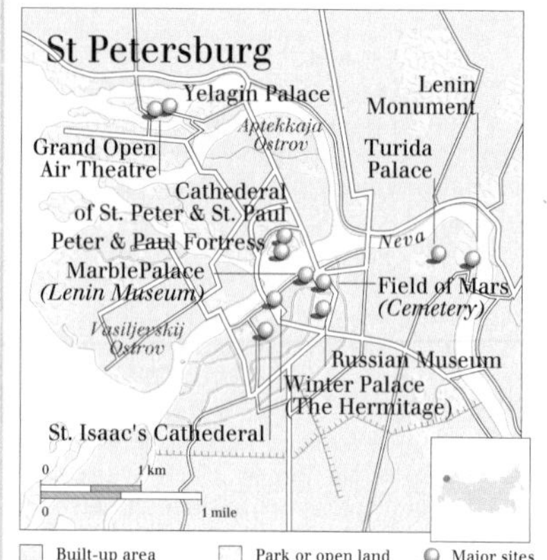

Built by Peter the Great in the 18th century to emulate European capitals, St. Petersburg is still considered one of the most beautiful cities in Russia. Its magnificent Versailles-influenced architecture includes The Hermitage, home to one of the world's greatest art collections. It was the storming of its Winter Palace in 1917 which marked the start of the Revolution.

The city's various name changes reflect key periods in Russian history. In 1914, anti-German sentiment resulted in the more Slavic name of Petrograd. In 1924, the city became Leningrad, as a tribute to Lenin who died that year. In 1991, the restoration of St. Petersburg was a snub to Russia's years under the Communist Party.

St. Petersburg has faced greater problems than Moscow during its transition to a market economy. Its industry is dominated by companies supplying the defense sector.

KRASNOYARSK KRAI

Covering 14% of Russian territory, but with a population of only 3.1 million, Krasnoyarsk Krai is seeking greater autonomy from Moscow. The region has huge hydrocarbon and mineral reserves and wishes to establish greater control over the wealth that they produce. Over 60% of Siberia's oil and gas and a quarter of all Russian coal is found in the region. Krasnoyarsk Krai also accounts for most of Russia's nickel exports. Agriculture is a strong sector. With 8.1 million acres of fertile arable land, the region is a net exporter of farming produce and has 18% of Russia's huge timber reserves.

More than 100 distinct nationalities live in Krasnoyarsk Krai. The majority are Russian. Nearly a third of the population lives in the capital, Krasnoyarsk, which began expanding in the 19th century following the discovery of gold in the region. The arrival of the Trans-Siberian railroad and the relocation of industries to the city during World War II were a further boost.

In 1989, protests by the Krasnoyarsk residents managed to prevent the construction of the world's largest nuclear waste dump, which threatened to pollute the Yenisey River.

TYUMEN

Located in western Siberia. Tyumen *Oblast* (region) has considerable economic potential. In October 1993, the region produced 21.3 million tons of oil, bucking the Russian trend for declining oil output. Natural gas output is also increasing.

Deutsche Bank has extended the region a DM1 billion ($650 million) credit package. The region planned to export one million tons of oil annually to Germany between 1993 and 1995. The credit was also to be used to develop consumer goods and agribusiness in the region. A further DM1 billion credit to develop the oil and gas industry is being negotiated.

Tyumen also possesses the huge Yamal peninsula gas deposits. Much of its production is already exported to western Europe through pipelines. Another pipeline (via Poland) is currently being built.

As Tyumen realizes its economic potential, so secession will become an increasingly popular prospect for the region. The state government is already in conflict with Moscow over how much of its economic and resource wealth must be delivered to the national treasury.

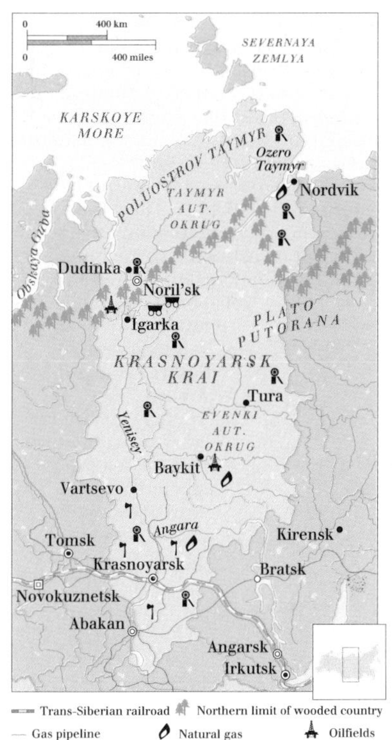

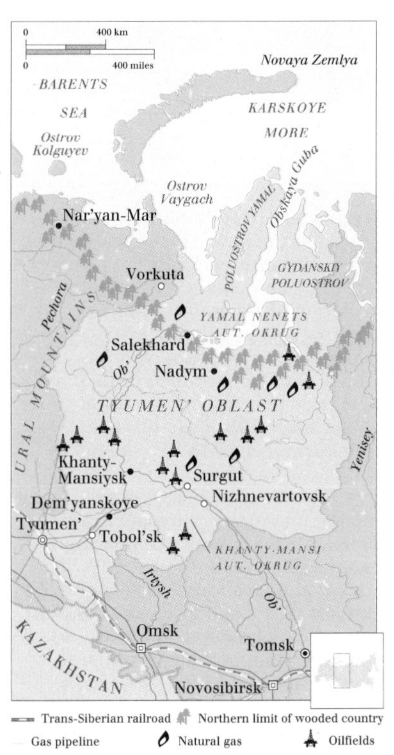

ECONOMICS

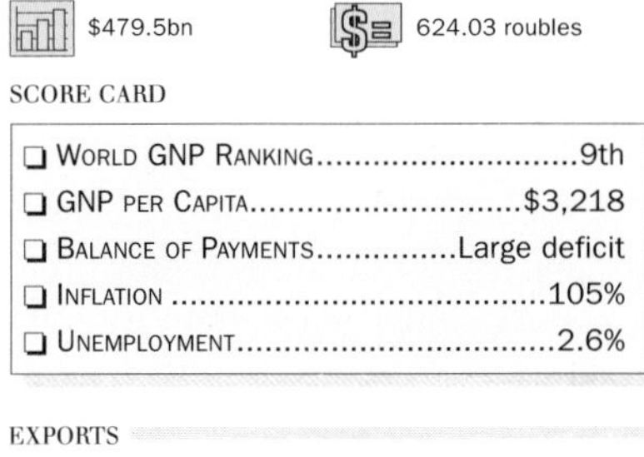

SCORE CARD

- ❑ WORLD GNP RANKING............................9th
- ❑ GNP PER CAPITA.............................$3,218
- ❑ BALANCE OF PAYMENTS...............Large deficit
- ❑ INFLATION 105%
- ❑ UNEMPLOYMENT..................................2.6%

EXPORTS

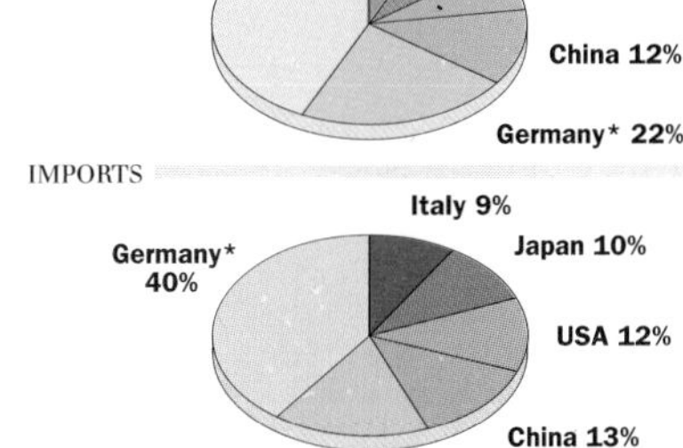

IMPORTS

STRENGTHS

Huge natural resources; in particular hydrocarbons, precious metals, fuel, timber. Enormous engineering and scientific base. Some dynamic small joint-stock enterprises. Privatization is proceeding fast; by July 1994, it will embrace 60% of large-scale industry and agriculture. Huge potential for oil and natural gas.

WEAKNESSES

Many company directors are asset-stripping privatized companies. Most are adjusting to a market economy unwillingly. Many of the skills developed under communism are not relevant in a competitive economy. Lack of adequate legal infrastructure making establishing property rights and trading transactions difficult. Russian companies have an estimated $32 billion in Western bank accounts and the outflow of capital is estimated at $1 billion monthly. New commercial sector has to meet costs of its own security as police protection is now inadequate.

ECONOMIC PERFORMANCE INDICATOR

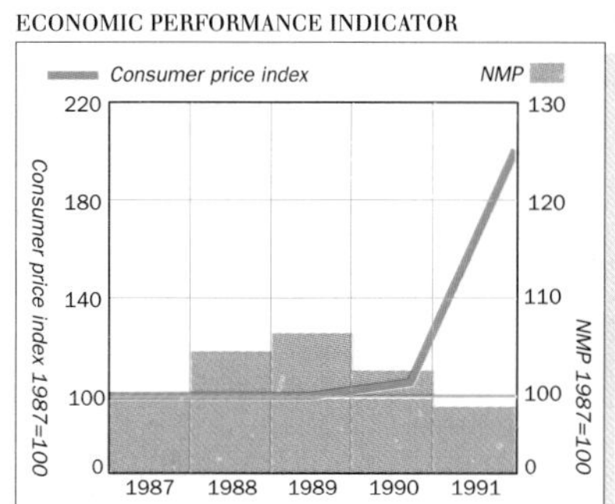

PROFILE

In 1988, President Gorbachev began a program of introducing market principles to Russia's command economy. The result by 1991 was a fall in industrial output of 19%. Russian currency reserves were spent in an attempt to cover up the collapse and $10 billion was appropriated from Russian company deposits in the state bank. Foreign currency reserves fell to $21 million. By the end of 1991, the formal economy had almost collapsed and some estimates suggested output was down by 40%.

The next crop of reformers, backed by Yeltsin and led by Gaidar, liberalized prices. Massive inflation was the result, but goods and food were once again readily available. However, Russia's huge unprofitable industrial concerns were not broken up. Many continue to supply goods for which there is little demand. The largest item of government spending remains the 10% of GDP spent on subsidies – a larger amount than on education and defense put together.

RUSSIAN FEDERATION : MAJOR BUSINESSES

R

CHRONOLOGY

The first Russian state (Rus) was in present-day Ukraine. Occupation by the Tatars (1240–1480) left a mark on the Russian language and character. From the 17th century, rule was under the Romanovs.

- **1904–1905** Russian war against Japan; ends in defeat for Russia.
- **1905** Revolution.
- **1909–1914** Rapid expansion of economy.
- **1914** Enters World War I against Germany.
- **1917** February Revolution; abdication of Nicholas II. October Revolution; Bolsheviks take over with Lenin as leader.
- **1918** July: Nicholas II and family murdered.
- **1918–1920** Civil war.
- **1921** New Economic Policy; retreat from socialism.
- **1922** USSR established.
- **1924** Lenin dies. Struggle for leadership, eventually won by Stalin, follows.
- **1928** First Five-Year Plan begins; forced industrialization and collectivization.
- **1929** Trotsky is first banished to Kazakhstan, then deported to Turkey.
- **1936–1938** Show trials and campaigns against actual and suspect members of opposition. Millions sent to *gulags* in Siberia and elsewhere. Forced labor; purges widespread.
- **1939** Hitler-Stalin pact gives USSR Baltic states, eastern Poland and Bessarabia.
- **1941** Germany attacks USSR. Stalin unprepared. December: Battle of Moscow is first German defeat.
- **1943** February: great Soviet victory at Stalingrad.
- **1944–1945** Soviet offensive penetrates Balkans.
- **1945** January: Yalta agreement recognizes eastern and southeastern Europe as Soviet zone of influence; four-power occupation of Germany. August: Potsdam agreement; intends Germany to be ruled as whole, but it quickly breaks up into east and west. USSR dominant European power.
- **1947** Cold War begins; Stalin on defensive and fears ideological penetration of Western and capitalist values.
- **1953** Stalin dies.
- **1956** Hungarian uprising against Soviet occupation. Moscow crushes uprising and reinstates Imre Nagy as Prime Minister. Krushchev's "secret speech" attacking Stalin at Party congress.

RESOURCES

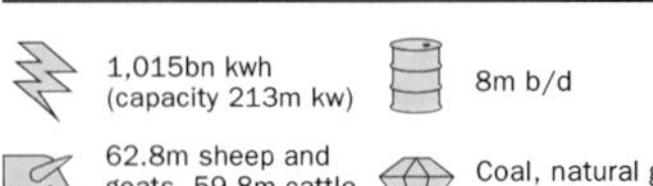

ELECTRICITY GENERATION

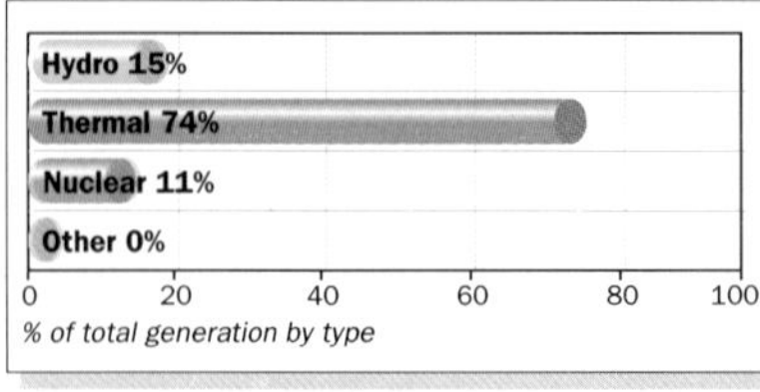

RUSSIAN FEDERATION : LAND USE

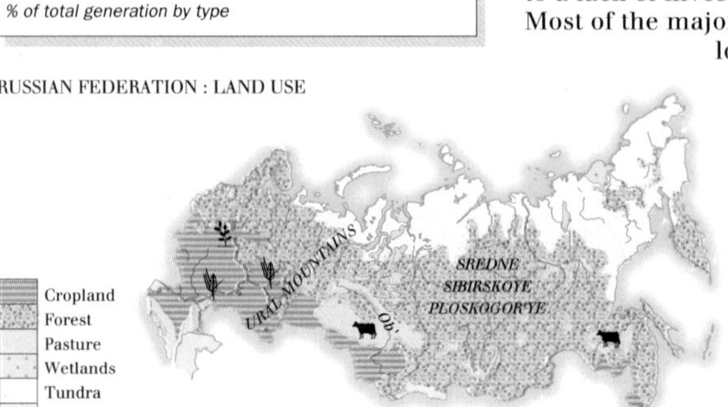

Russia is a leading world producer of oil, natural gas and electricity, among other resources. Confirmed reserves make Russia the world's leading country in terms of hydrocarbons, gold, precious metals, diamonds and timber.

Unlike some of the other republics of the ex-USSR, Russia has not opened its resources up to foreign concerns. It does not wish to lose any control to Western multinationals. They are consequently underexploited owing to a lack of investment and technology. Most of the major resources are also located in national territories such as Tatarstan and Sakha Yakutia in Siberia. The regions' desire for greater autonomy has turned the ownership of these resources into a delicate political issue.

ENVIRONMENT

 1% (of USSR)

 Few environmental protection laws are being passed

ENVIRONMENTAL TREATIES

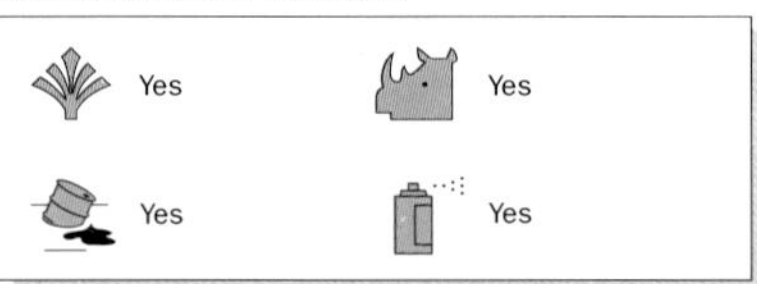

Awareness of Russia's environmental problems has risen sharply since the demise of communism. However, the resources, political will and know-how to tackle them are still lacking. While Russia now has an active "green" movement, it did not gain significant support at the 1993 general elections.

Each region has its own particular problems. The north suffers from the effects of nuclear dumping in the Barents Sea. More than 17,000 contaminated containers were dumped there by the Russian navy, including the old nuclear reactor from the icebreaker *Lenin*. Thousands of tons of chemical weapons have been dumped in the Baltic, although their exact location has not been revealed. The Volga River in Central Russia is so polluted and diverted by dam-building that many fish species are now extinct. The worst problems are probably in the Urals and the cities of European Russia. Chemical and heavy industrial plants still lack adequate protection. Most do not treat their effluents at all.

MEDIA

 No political restrictions, although temporary censorship may occur

PUBLISHING AND BROADCAST MEDIA

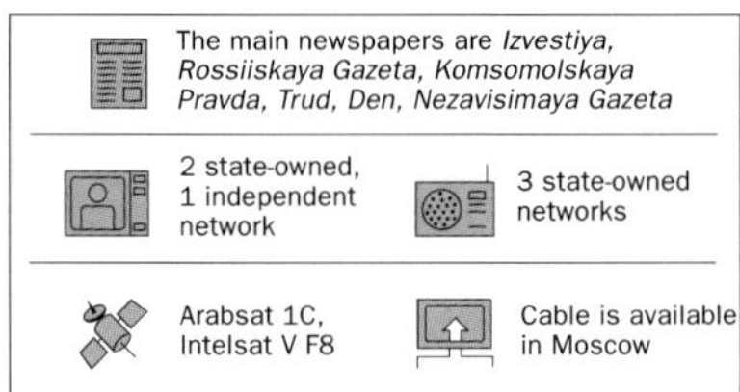

The main newspapers are *Izvestiya, Rossiiskaya Gazeta, Komsomolskaya Pravda, Trud, Den, Nezavisimaya Gazeta*
2 state-owned, 1 independent network
3 state-owned networks
Arabsat 1C, Intelsat V F8
Cable is available in Moscow

Russians have traditionally been avid newspaper readers. This is reflected in the number of titles. In 1990, there were 4,808 daily newspapers with a total circulation of 166 million copies compared to a population of 149 million. Since then, however, the number of titles has fallen dramatically, largely due to a rise in the cost of paper. The old state daily, *Pravda*, is barely surviving and is partly dependent on subsidies from the Greek Communist Party. After the October 1993 right-wing coup attempt many newspapers were banned. Most are now reappearing although often under new names. The regional and local press is also growing in importance. State TV is now the most important news source and less biased than under communism. It remains under the control of supporters of President Yeltsin. Many Russians now have satellite dishes and tune in to CNN and other Western channels.

CHRONOLOGY *continued*

- **1957** Krushchev consolidates power. Sputnik launched.
- **1961** April: Yuri Gagarin first man in space.
- **1962** October: Cuban Missile Crisis between USSR and USA brings world close to nuclear war.
- **1964** Krushchev ousted in coup, replaced by Leonid Brezhnev.
- **1975** Helsinki Final Act; confirms European frontiers as at end of World War II. Soviets agree to human rights as legitimate concern of international community.
- **1979** Invades Afghanistan. Beginning of new Cold War.
- **1982** Brezhnev dies. Yuri Andropov takes over.
- **1984** Andropov dies and is succeeded by Chernenko.
- **1985** Chernenko dies. Gorbachev in power. Beginning of *perestroika*, era of new political thinking and the breakup of the USSR. First of summits with US President Reagan in Geneva, which lead to arms reduction treaties and détente between the superpowers. Nationality conflicts surface.
- **1988** Law of State Enterprises in operation. More power for enterprises; this leads to greater inflation and dislocation of economy.
- **1990** Gorbachev becomes president of the Soviet Union. First partly freely elected parliament (Supreme Soviet) meets.
- **1991** Boris Yeltsin elected president of Russia. August: attempted coup by right-wing elements against Gorbachev successfully opposed by Yeltsin and Muscovites. CIS established; demise of USSR.
- **1992** Beginning of economic shock therapy; rapid price rises.
- **1993** September: Yeltsin decrees dissolution of Supreme Soviet. October: Yeltsin uses force to disband parliament. December: elections return conservative, anti-reform State *Duma*.

Tundra in Russia's far east. *Russia has some of the largest uninhabited tracts of land in the world.*

CRIME

Russia does not publish prison figures  Rising dramatically

CRIME RATES

Rates for all types of crime are rising dramatically

Crime is now a formidable problem in Russia, and the police cannot keep up with its rise. Reported murders in the first nine months of 1993 rose to 33,798, up 47% on the previous year.

Most murders are the result of inter-gang violence. Muggings in the larger cities are sharply up. Corruption and mafia-style activity are also widespread. Protection rackets, prostitution, smuggling operations and drugs are the Russian mafia's sources of profit. Russian crime bosses are beginning to fund similar activities in Western Europe, using banks as fronts. In outlying areas, especially Siberia, Westerners are increasingly the victims of violent car theft. The rise in crime has become a major issue for most Russians. Parties such as Zhirinovsky's LDPR, who are promising to stamp crime out, are gaining popular support.

EDUCATION

 99%

Education spending as % GNP (0–25): **7.9%**

THE EDUCATION SYSTEM

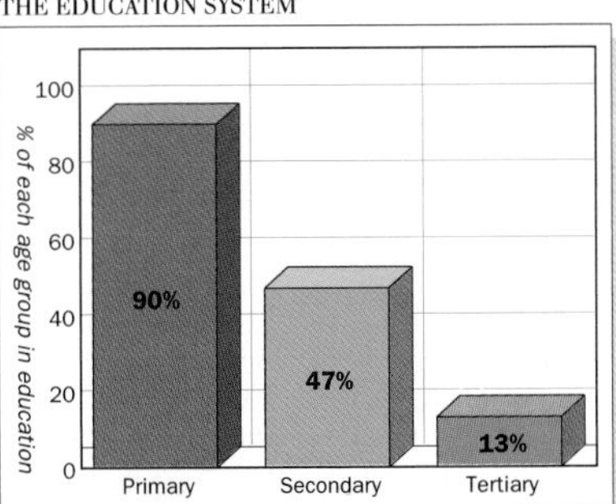

Russian education still follows the Soviet model. While there has been some attempt at historical revisionism, this has been hampered by a lack of funds to pay for new books. Many private academies have sprung up – such as those run by the Orthodox Church – often offering courses in English and German. German, in particular, has made a comeback in Moscow as a key commercial language. Higher education is now underfunded. Prestigious institutions such as the Academy of Sciences have cut staff and research. Most academics now have to rely on extra-mural earnings.

HEALTH

1 per 213 people | Heart, respiratory and cerebrovascular diseases, cancer

Health spending as % GNP (0–25): *Minimal health spending*

Until 1991, state enterprises provided considerable health care for their employees. This is now disappearing as companies are privatized and seek to cut costs. Local authorities have few resources to take over these responsibilities. Bribing medical staff to obtain treatment is commonplace and there is a lack of pharmaceutical products and drugs. Hospital patients are normally fed by their relatives.

WEALTH

It is estimated that 35% of the population now lives below the poverty line

CONSUMER GOODS OWNERSHIP

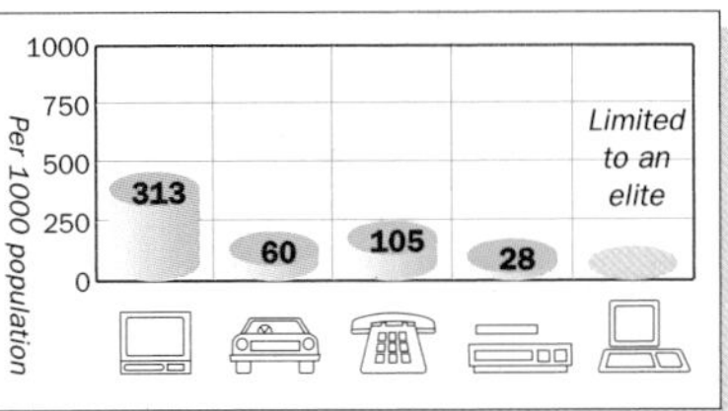

Wealth disparities in Russia are increasing rapidly. A small minority of the population has made huge profits from marketization. About 10% are thought to have benefited in some way. There is a growing number of dollar millionaires who flaunt their wealth, especially in Moscow. Russia is now the biggest buyer of Rolls-Royce cars, while BMWs, Mercedes and Volvos are relatively common in Moscow and St. Petersburg. A considerable amount of wealth is now deposited abroad, however. There are now thousands of Russian offshore bank accounts; Northern Cyprus is a favorite location. The bosses of organized crime are Russian society's wealthiest group.

WORLD RANKING

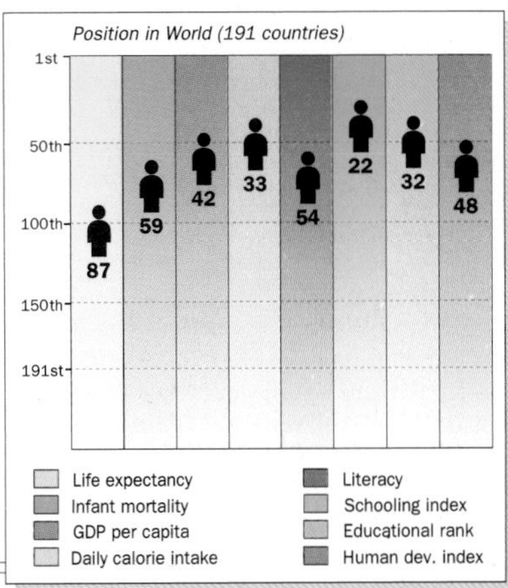

RWANDA

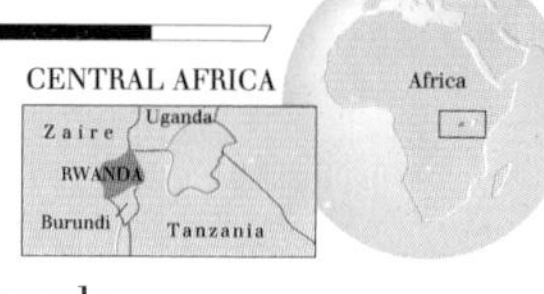

OFFICIAL NAME: Republic of Rwanda **CAPITAL:** Kigali
POPULATION: 7 million **CURRENCY:** Rwanda franc **OFFICIAL LANGUAGES:** French, Kinyarwanda

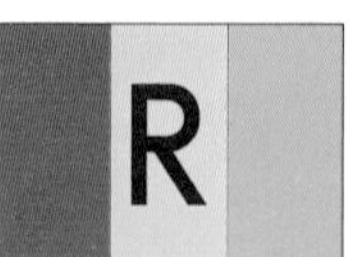

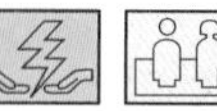
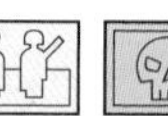

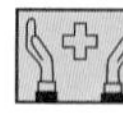

LYING JUST SOUTH OF THE EQUATOR in east-central Africa, landlocked Rwanda is 992 miles from the nearest port. Since independence in 1962, ethnic tensions have dominated politics. In 1994, the death of the president in a plane crash led to a breakout of ethnic violence in which an estimated 500,000 Rwandans died. Over half of the surviving population is displaced; many are living in refugee camps in neighboring countries.

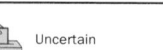

POLITICS

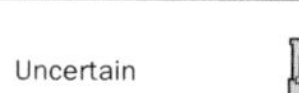

THE STATE OF THE PARTIES

Parliament

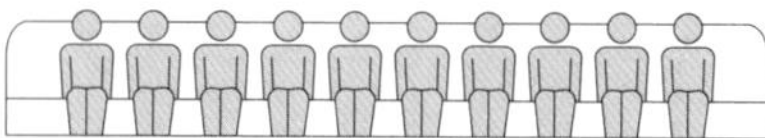

There are no plans for elections following the recent conflict. Until early 1994 the Hutu-dominated MRNDD (National Republican Movement for Development and Democracy) had been in control of a transitional government

With the introduction of a new constitution in 1991, Rwanda attempted to come to terms with its ethnic divisions by moving toward a multiparty system. The changes were precipitated in 1990 by the invasion of a rebel army of exiled Tutsi, the FPR (Rwandan Patriotic Front). In 1992, a transitional coalition of the MRNDD and internal opposition parties was formed to negotiate peace with the FPR before organizing elections.

However, all arrangements were thrown into turmoil following the death of the president in a plane crash in 1994. The FPR army mounted an attack to take control of the capital from the government. An estimated 500,000 died and more than 2 million Hutus fled as refugees in the conflict, in which the FPR eventually gained control of the country. Hutus have been allocated most of the key posts in the new government, including the presidency.

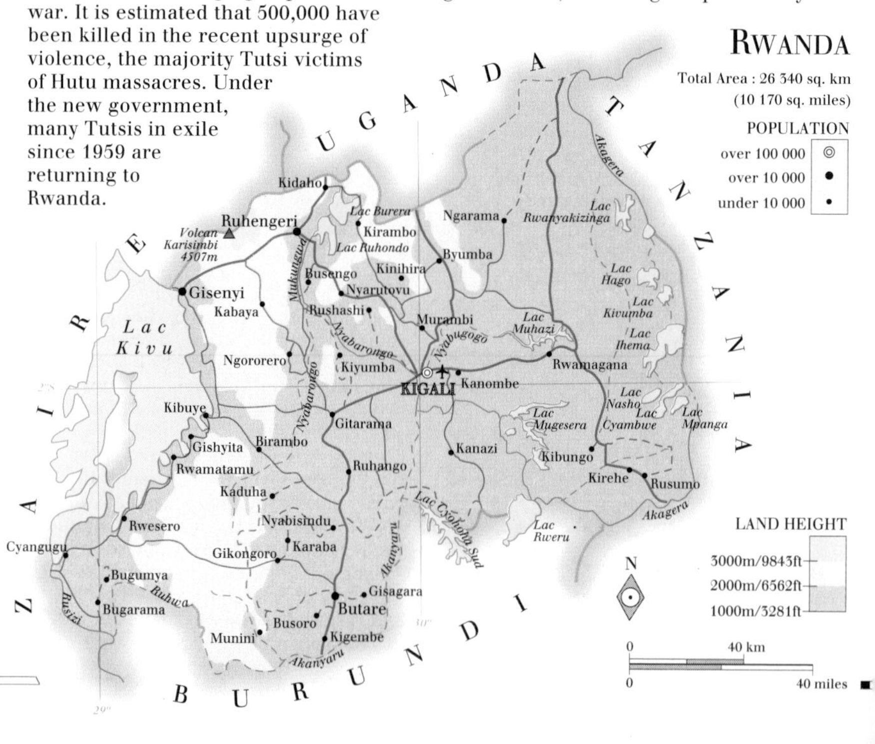

CLIMATE

WEATHER CHART

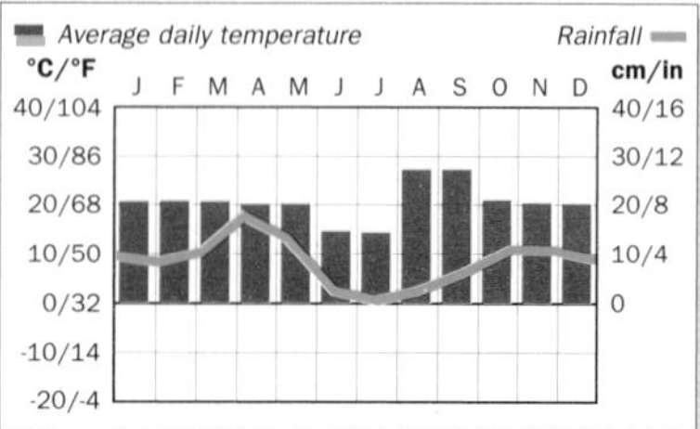

Rwanda's climate is tropical, tempered by altitude. Two wet seasons allow for two harvests each year.

COMMUNICATIONS

THE TRANSPORTATION NETWORK

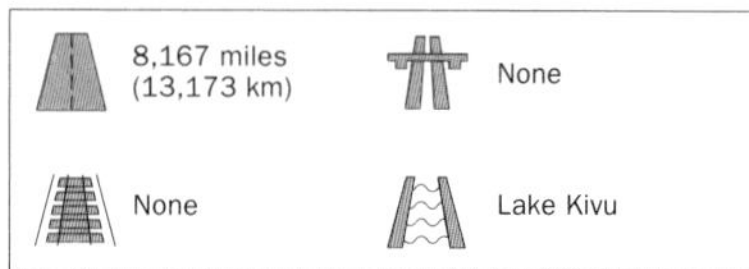

The road network is well developed. The international airport near Kigali was completed in 1986.

TOURISM

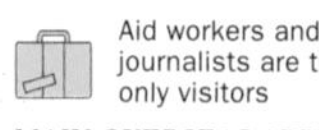

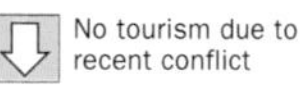

MAIN OVERSEAS ARRIVALS

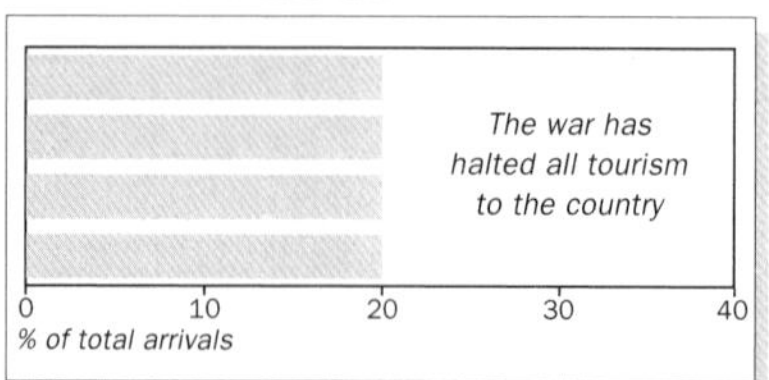

All tourism has ceased as a result of the civil war. When peace is secured, Rwanda may be able to regain its status as a destination for wealthy wildlife enthusiasts. Top attractions are the mountain gorillas and Lake Kivu.

PEOPLE

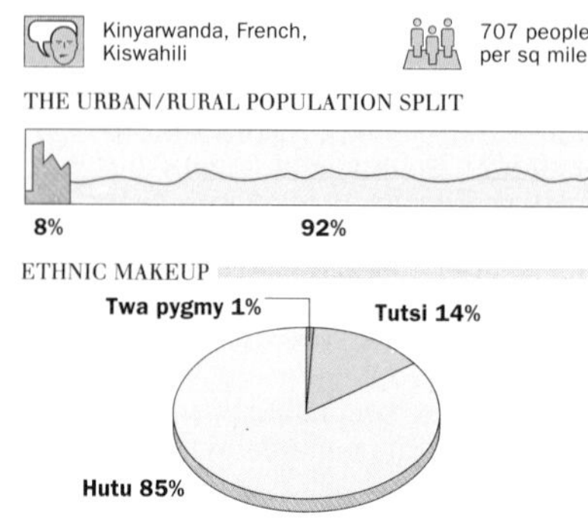

The Hutu and Tutsi are the main groups; the Twa pygmies, the original inhabitants, have been marginalized. For over 500 years, the cattle-owning Tutsi were politically dominant, oppressing the land-owning Hutu majority. In 1959, violent revolt led to a reversal of the roles. The two groups have since been waging a spasmodic war. It is estimated that 500,000 have been killed in the recent upsurge of violence, the majority Tutsi victims of Hutu massacres. Under the new government, many Tutsis in exile since 1959 are returning to Rwanda.

RWANDA

Total Area : 26 340 sq. km (10 170 sq. miles)

POPULATION
over 100 000
over 10 000
under 10 000

LAND HEIGHT
3000m/9843ft
2000m/6562ft
1000m/3281ft

0 40 km
0 40 miles

WORLD AFFAIRS

The breakout of inter-ethnic violence in 1994 led to the collapse of the peace process. Over 2 million Rwandans fled into neighboring Zaire, Tanzania and Burundi. French troops established a "safe zone" in the west of the country.

AID

 $351m (receipts)  Up 20% in 1991

The breakout of ethnic violence led to the suspension of all formal aid payments. Several UN aid workers were slaughtered by troops. Humanitarian agencies are active in the camps which house over 2 million refugees.

DEFENSE

 $36.63m  Defense spending is rising

The former Rwandan army, which underpinned MRNDD power, has sought refuge in Zaire, where it has been allowed to regroup.

ECONOMICS

 $1.6bn  144.4 Rwanda francs

SCORE CARD

- ❑ World GNP Ranking........144th
- ❑ GNP per Capita........$213
- ❑ Balance of Payments........$-34.1m
- ❑ Inflation........9.5%
- ❑ Unemployment.....Few have formal employment

Strengths
Currently none. Assuming peace, Rwanda produces coffee. Possible oil and gas reserves.

Weaknesses
Ethnic violence has suspended all economic activity. The 1,000-mile journey to both Kenyan and Tanzanian ports imposes high transportation costs. Rwanda has few resources.

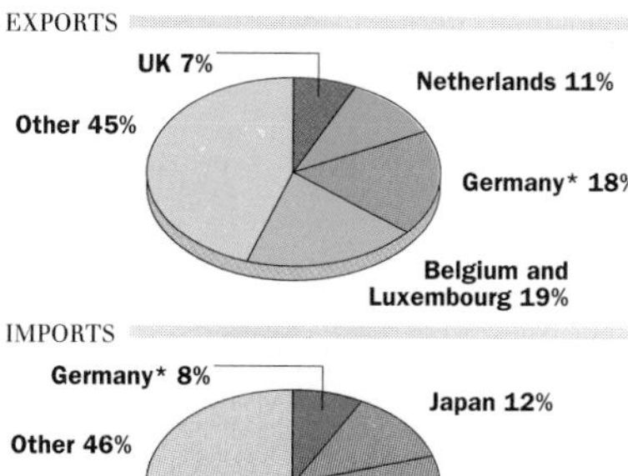

Terraced hillside. *Before the war, Rwanda was the most densely populated country in Africa and its land intensively cultivated.*

RESOURCES

 176m kwh (capacity 60,000 kw)  Not an oil producer and has no refineries

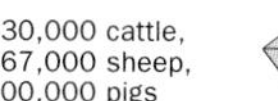 630,000 cattle, 367,000 sheep, 100,000 pigs — Tin, tungsten, gold, columbo-tantalite, beryl, methane

Gas deposits in Lake Kivu are likely to be explored with Zaire. Only 20% of urban homes are on the national power grid.

ENVIRONMENT

  12% 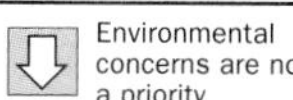 Environmental concerns are not a priority

Soil erosion and forest loss are the major environmental problems, the effects of war aside. The tourist industry underpinned the preservation of the mountain gorilla.

MEDIA

 Under the MRNDD-led government there were many instances of opposition journalists being harassed and arrested

PUBLISHING AND BROADCAST MEDIA

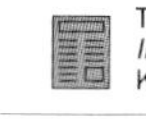 There are no daily newspapers. The weekly *Imvaho* and *La Relève* are published in Kinyarwanda and French respectively

 1 state-controlled service 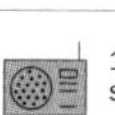 1 state-controlled service

The media has been used as an important propaganda tool by both sides in the civil war.

CRIME

 Rwanda does not publish prison figures  Down 33% in 1990.

Previously benefiting from a low crime rate, an orgy of inter-ethnic violence broke out in 1994 leaving an estimated 500,000 dead. Hundreds of thousands survived by fleeing the country.

EDUCATION

 50%

Schools are administered by the state and Christian missions. Primary education is officially compulsory, but only 60% of children attend; just 6% go on to secondary schooling.

CHRONOLOGY

The Hutu majority began to arrive in the 14th century; the warrior Tutsi in the 15th. From 1890, German and then Belgian colonizers acted to reinforce Tutsi dominance.

- ❑ **1962** Independence under Hutu-led government.
- ❑ **1960s** Tutsi revolt; massacres by Hutu; thousands of Tutsi in exile.
- ❑ **1973** Army head Gen. Habyarimana takes power in bloodless coup.
- ❑ **1975** One-party state under MRNDD.
- ❑ **1990** Invasion by Tutsi FPR; MRNDD forced to move toward democracy.
- ❑ **1992–1993** Transitional coalition to negotiate peace. Elections planned.
- ❑ **1994** President Habyarimana dies in plane crash. Breakout of ethnic violence between Tutsi and Hutu.

HEALTH

 1 per 33,170 people 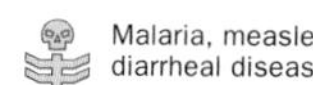 Malaria, measles, diarrheal diseases

Rwanda has a network of 34 hospitals and 188 health centers. This should mean the majority have easy access to care, although treatment is rarely free.

WEALTH

 Most Rwandans live a subsistence existence

CONSUMER GOODS OWNERSHIP

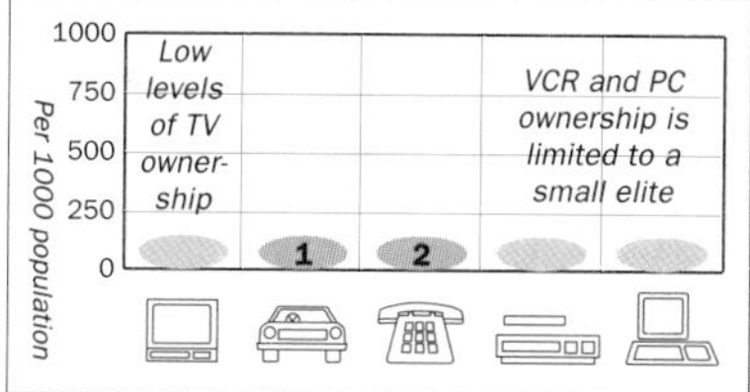

Wealth is limited to the political elite. Most Rwandans are poor farmers; Twa pygmies and refugees are poorer still.

WORLD RANKING

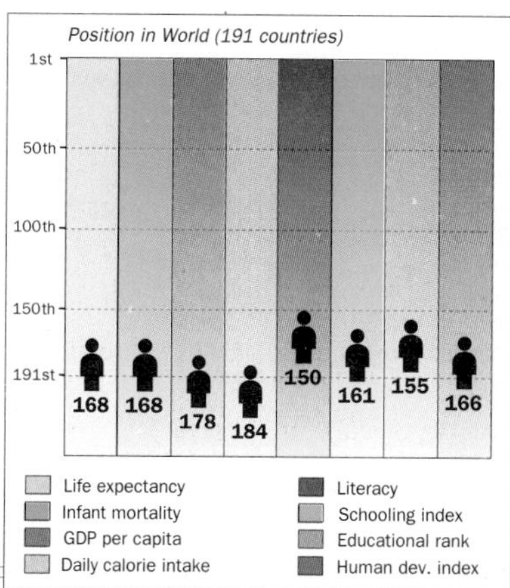

ST. KITTS & NEVIS

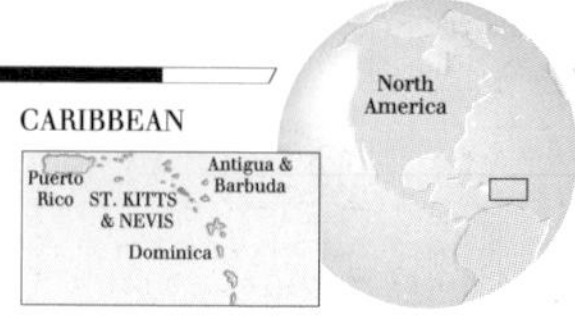

OFFICIAL NAME: Federation of Saint Christopher and Nevis **CAPITAL:** Basseterre
POPULATION: 44,000 **CURRENCY:** East Caribbean dollar **OFFICIAL LANGUAGE:** English

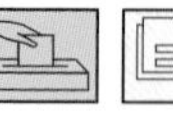

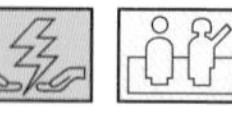

ONE OF THE CARIBBEAN'S most popular tourist destinations, St. Kitts and Nevis, a former British colony, lies at the northern end of the Leeward Islands chain. St. Kitts is of volcanic origin; Mount Liamuiga, a dormant volcano with a crater 745 feet deep, is the highest point on the island. Nevis is separated from St. Kitts by a 2-mile-wide channel and is the lusher but less developed of the two islands. In the 18th century its renowned hot and cold springs gave Nevis a reputation as "the Spa of the Caribbean."

CLIMATE

WEATHER CHART

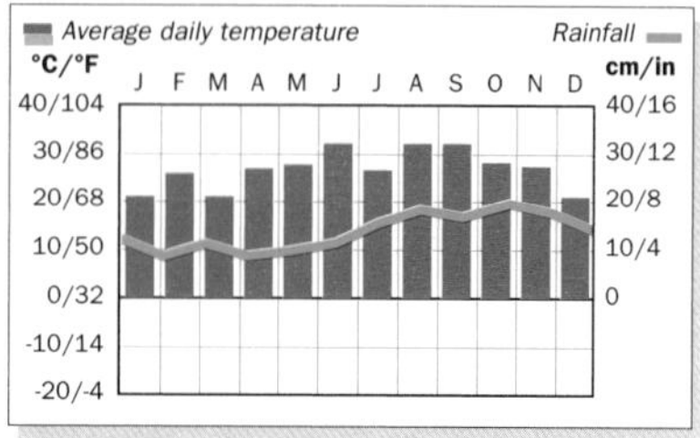

A combination of high temperatures, trade breezes, and moderate rainfall in summer account for St. Kitts' typically Caribbean climate.

COMMUNICATIONS

Golden Rock, Basseterre

1 ship
600 dwt

THE TRANSPORTATION NETWORK

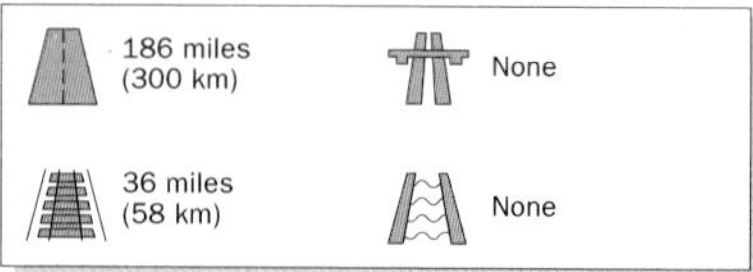

Most roads on the islands skirt the coast, with just a few crossing through the interior. The government is planning to build a road to the isolated southern tip of St. Kitts. The airport on St. Kitts takes large jets; Nevis's airport accepts only small propeller aircraft. Regular ferries connect both islands.

The southeastern peninsula of St. Kitts, looking across to Nevis in the background, on a typical December evening.

TOURISM

75,789 visitors

Up 5% in 1990

MAIN OVERSEAS ARRIVALS

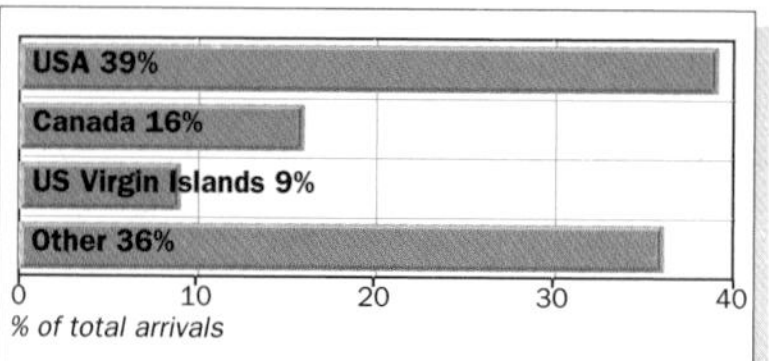

Over the past 20 years, St. Kitts has targeted the mass US tourist market. With improvements in communications, in particular plans to open up the southern peninsula of St. Kitts Island, the industry should continue to grow. Most visitors come for the beaches, the sun and the Caribbean mood, although in recent years safaris to see local wildlife and mineral springs have operated from isolated hotels in the hills. On St. Kitts, the old Brimstone Hill fortress has been converted into a museum, as has the Nevis birthplace of Alexander Hamilton, one of the architects of the US constitution.

PEOPLE

English, English Creole

396 people per sq. mile

THE URBAN/RURAL POPULATION SPLIT

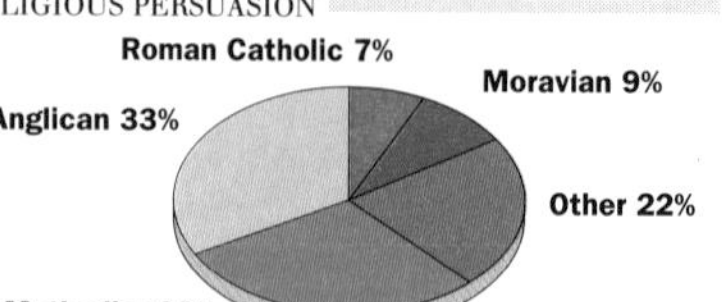

RELIGIOUS PERSUASION

Roman Catholic 7%
Moravian 9%
Anglican 33%
Other 22%
Methodist 29%

Most of the population is descended from Africans brought over in the 17th century; intermarriage has blurred other racial lines. There is opposition to government plans to grant citizenship to 3,000 Hong Kong business executives in exchange for investment in the islands.

POLITICS

THE STATE OF THE PARTIES

National Assembly 14 members

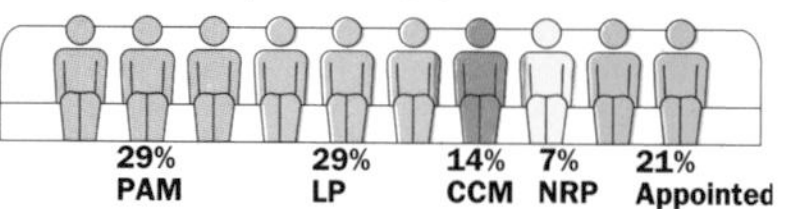

PAM = People's Action Movement **LP** = Labour Party
NRP = Nevis Reformation Party **CCM** = Concerned Citizens' Movement

Based on the British system, political funds are provided by urban professionals (for the PAM) and, unusually for the Caribbean, trade unions (for the LP). Political differences are those of style rather than policy, except for occasional calls for greater autonomy from the NRP.

ST. KITTS & NEVIS

Total Area : 360 sq. km (139 sq. miles)

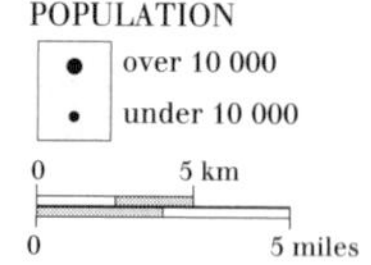

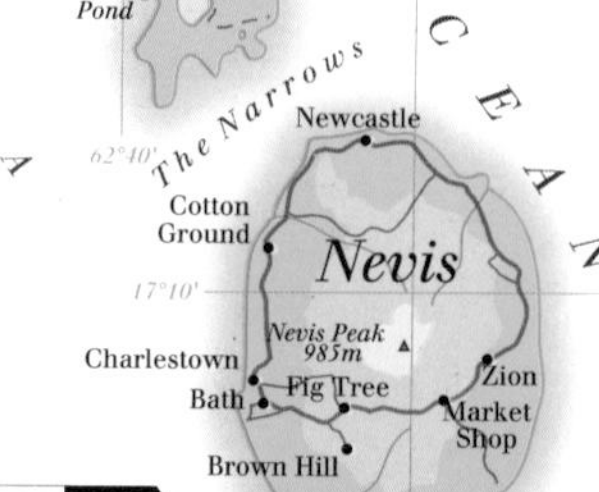

WORLD AFFAIRS

Maintaining preferential access to EU and US markets for its sugar is the main concern. St. Kitts is not interested in the political union proposed by its Windward Islands neighbors.

AID

 $7m (receipts)  Up 17% in 1991

Aid, mostly from the USA, the EU and the UK, is very important, particularly project aid – such as the funding of the road to St. Kitts' southern peninsula. Donors are also providing support for economic diversification.

DEFENSE

 Army duties undertaken by Volunteer Defense Force  Not applicable

An army existed for six years before it was disbanded to cut government expenditure in 1981. A small paramilitary unit remains within the police; it made a token appearance with US forces during the 1983 invasion of Grenada.

ECONOMICS

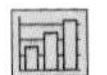 $185m 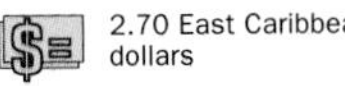 2.70 East Caribbean dollars

SCORE CARD

- ❑ WORLD GNP RANKING........................180th
- ❑ GNP PER CAPITA............................$4,200
- ❑ BALANCE OF PAYMENTS...................$–49.7m
- ❑ INFLATION..6.4%
- ❑ UNEMPLOYMENT...................................8%

STRENGTHS

Sugar industry, currently UK-managed, with preferential access to US and EU markets. Tourism, the source of recent growth, is set to expand further.

WEAKNESSES

Dependence on sugar cane industry, which is sensitive to fluctuating world market prices.

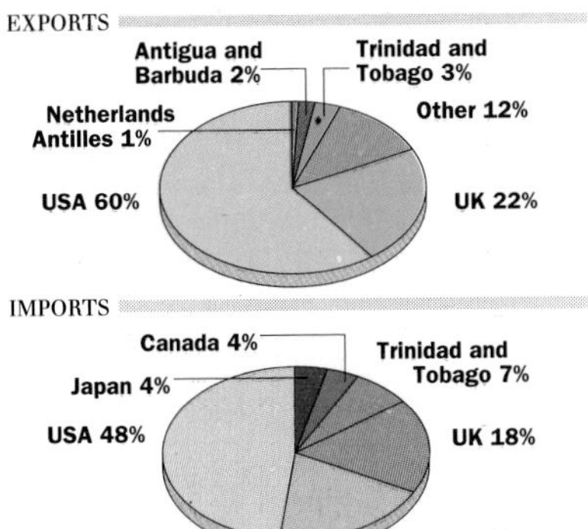

RESOURCES

 37m kwh (capacity 15,000 kw)

 Not an oil producer and has no refineries

15,000 sheep, 5,000 cattle, 4,000 pigs

 None

St. Kitts has no strategic resources. Almost all energy has to be imported, mainly oil from Venezuela and Mexico. Sugar output is insignificant in world terms. New crops, such as Sea Island cotton on Nevis, are being introduced. Offshore fishing has potential.

ENVIRONMENT

 10% New laws protecting monkeys

Hurricanes are the greatest environmental threat. The islands caught only the tail end of Hurricane Hugo in 1989, but it caused severe damage to the sugar crop and power supplies. As in the rest of the Caribbean, benefits from encouraging tourism must be set against potential ecological damage. The government has shown sensitivity, with strict preservation orders on the remaining rainforest and on indigenous monkeys.

MEDIA

 No political restrictions

PUBLISHING AND BROADCAST MEDIA

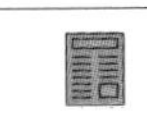 There are no daily newspapers. The two main weekly newspapers are *The Democrat* and the *Labour Spokesman*

 1 state-owned station

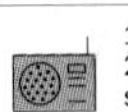 1 state-owned, 2 independent stations

The media has little political independence, but this is not due to government interference. The funding for the two weekly newspapers is provided by the political parties.

CRIME

 St. Kitts does not publish prison figures  Down 7% in 1988

The judicial system is based on British common law. The police force is trained by officers from London's Scotland Yard. Rape, burglary and armed robbery are the main concerns; murder is rare. In 1993, there were allegations that the political parties were arming their activists.

EDUCATION

 82%

Education is based on the old British 11-plus selective system and is mostly state-run. Students attend the regional University of the West Indies, or go on to colleges in the USA and UK.

CHRONOLOGY

A British colony since 1783 and part of the Leeward Islands Federation until 1956, St. Kitts and Nevis achieved independence in 1983.

- ❑ **1932** St. Kitts-Nevis-Anguilla Labour Party formed to campaign for independence.
- ❑ **1967** Internal self-government.
- ❑ **1980** Anguilla formally separates from St. Kitts & Nevis.
- ❑ **1983** Independence from UK.
- ❑ **1989** Hurricane Hugo destroys sugar crop.

HEALTH

 1 per 1,593 people 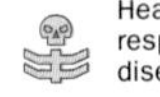 Heart and respiratory diseases, cancer

The government-run health service now provides rudimentary care on both St. Kitts and Nevis. Doctors and other medical specialists train at the University of the West Indies. Some of the wealthier use private doctors and health clinics for treatment.

WEALTH

 There is no great disparity of wealth on the islands, although urban professionals enjoy a higher standard of living than rural cane farmers

CONSUMER GOODS OWNERSHIP

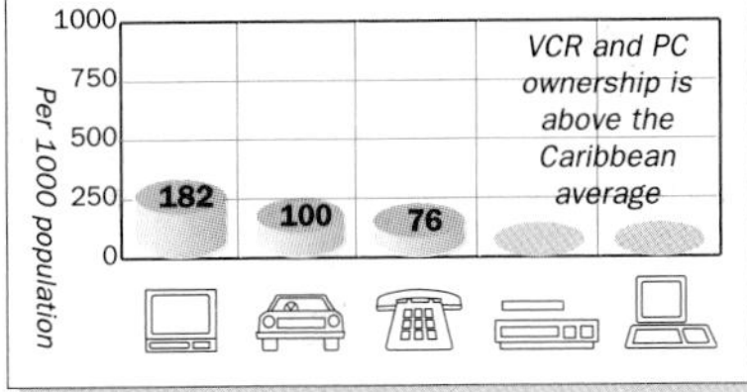

Native professionals and civil servants have replaced expatriates over the past 20 years. They are now the best-paid group, but there are no great extremes of income. Status symbols include Japanese cars and satellite dishes.

WORLD RANKING

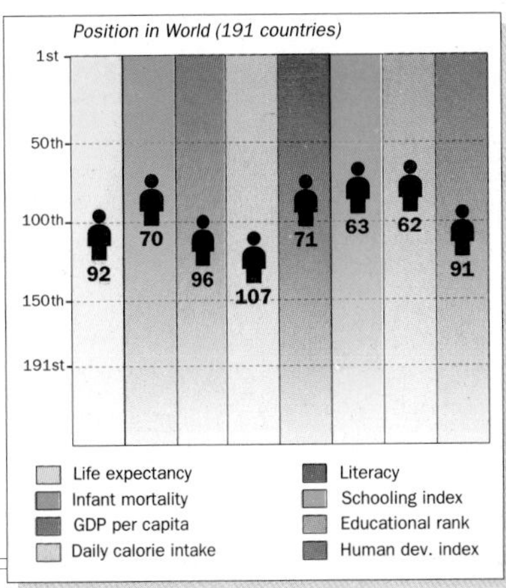

St. Lucia

Official Name: Saint Lucia **Capital:** Castries
Population: 153,000 **Currency:** East Caribbean dollar **Official Language:** English

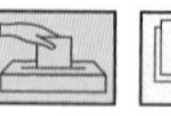

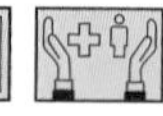

St. Lucia is one of the most beautiful islands of the Windward group of the Antilles. The twin Pitons, south of Soufrière, are one of the most striking natural features in the Caribbean. Ruled by the French and British at different times in its past, St. Lucia retains the character of both. A multiparty democracy, it lives by banana growing and beach and cruise-ship tourism. Its unspoiled rainforest makes it a popular ecotourist destination.

CLIMATE

WEATHER CHART

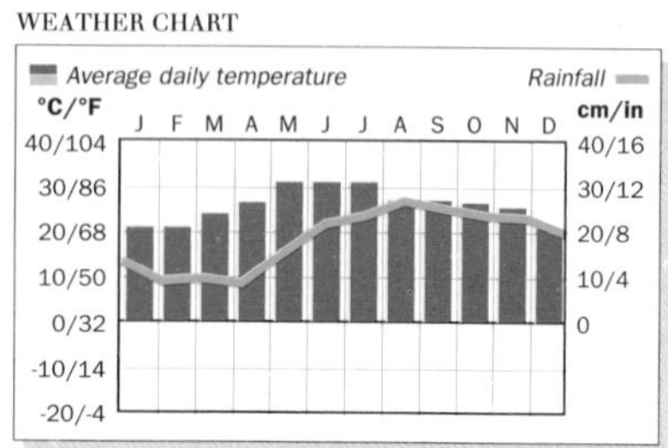

The dry season, from January to April, brings intense heat to sheltered parts of St. Lucia. During the rainy season, short warm showers can occur daily. Rainfall is highest in the mountains.

COMMUNICATIONS

 **Hewanorra Intl, Vieux-Fort** 245,000 passengers

 2 ships 900 dwt

THE TRANSPORTATION NETWORK

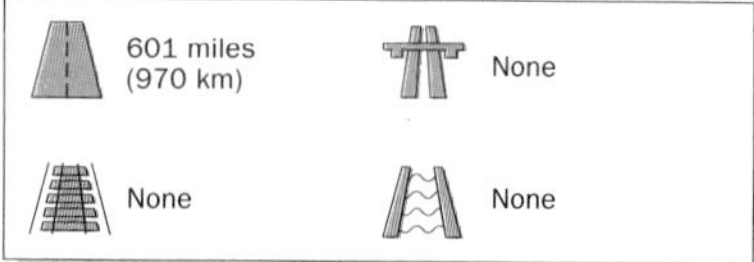

There are no railroads and roads are confined to the west and southeast coasts, making the mountainous interior inaccessible except on foot or mule. The main airport (Hewanorra International) accepts jumbo jets.

One of the twin Pitons south of Soufrière, marking the entrance to the Jalousie Plantation harbor.

TOURISM

 146,578 visitors

 Up 5% in 1990

MAIN OVERSEAS ARRIVALS

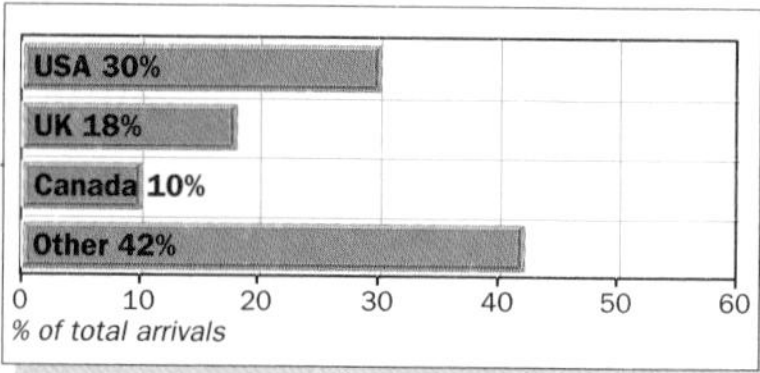

Tropical beaches and typical Caribbean towns, such as Soufrière, have long made St. Lucia a favorite Caribbean tourist destination. Ecotourism into the island's rainforest and volcanic interior is growing, and with it local resistance to the over-development of the island.

PEOPLE

 English, French Creole

 632 people per sq. mile

THE URBAN/RURAL POPULATION SPLIT

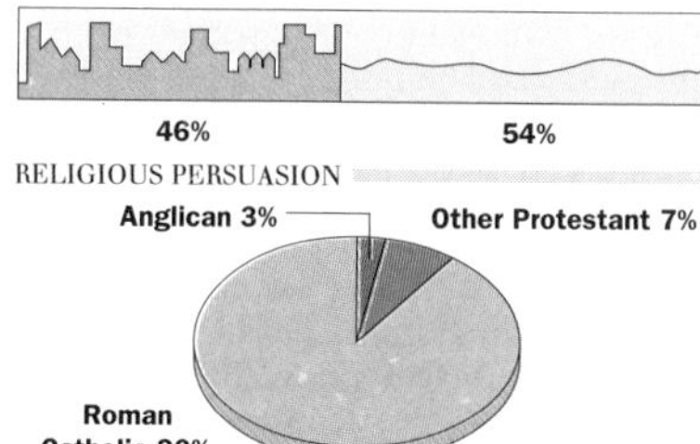

St. Lucia now has a rich, tension-free racial mix of descendants of Africans, Carib Indians and European settlers. Despite relaxed attitudes, family life is still important to most St. Lucians, many of whom are practicing Roman Catholics. The nuclear family is the norm, but in rural districts, where women run many of the farms, absentee fathers are fairly common. In recent years, women have had greater access to university education and are moving into the legal, medical and financial professions.

POLITICS

 1997

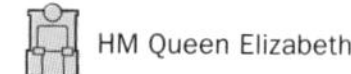

THE STATE OF THE PARTIES

House of Assembly 17 members

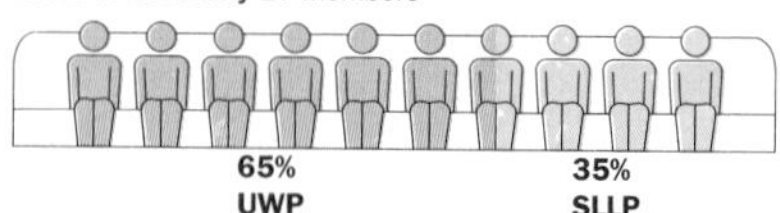

UWP = United Workers' Party **SLLP** = St. Lucia Labour Party

Senate 11 members

11 members appointed by the governor-general, including 6 appointed with the advice of the prime minister and 3 with the advice of the leader of the opposition

Politics have been dominated for the past decade by two brothers-in-law: John Compton, head of the UWP, and Julian Hunte, leader of the SLLP. The UWP favors the planned Windward Islands' federation. The SLLP opposes federation on the grounds that Compton will use it to retain power.

WORLD AFFAIRS

St. Lucia has traditionally backed US policy against left-wing regimes in the Caribbean, and openly supported the US invasion of Grenada in 1983. Relations with Washington have soured, however, following US pressure on the EU to remove its preferential treatment of bananas from the Caribbean. St. Lucia cannot compete with cheaper fruit from South America. The other main issue is a proposed Windward Islands Federation with Dominica, Grenada and St. Vincent, which will require ratification.

AID

 $20m (receipts)

 Up 122% in 1991

The US, the EU, and, in particular, the UK are the main donors. Most aid is in the form of project loans.

DEFENSE

 Police force has special service unit for defense purposes

 Not applicable

A police force of 500 is supported by a small paramilitary unit. Training is provided by the USA and the UK.

ST. LUCIA

Total Area : 620 sq. km (239 sq. miles)

POPULATION
- over 10 000
- under 10 000

LAND HEIGHT
- 500m/1640ft
- 200m/656ft
- Sea Level

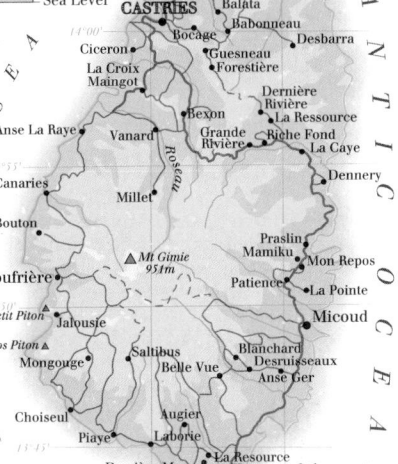

RESOURCES

104m kwh (capacity 22,000 kw)

Not an oil producer and has no refineries

16,000 sheep, 13,000 cattle, 12,000 pigs

None

St. Lucia has no mineral resources and imports most of its energy. Plans exist to develop geothermal energy from the hot springs in the volcanic interior.

ENVIRONMENT

2% partially protected

Decision to allow development on Jalousie Plantation

St. Lucians are proud of their island and environmental questions arouse fierce debate. In recent years, the greatest controversy has surrounded the decision to allow a luxury hotel development on the ecologically important Jalousie Plantation, which encompasses the extraordinary twin Pitons and includes an important Amerindian archeological site. The issue illustrates a key problem in St. Lucia, where business pressures to develop tourism can outweigh vital environmental concerns. One notable conservation success has been the St. Lucian parrot. In 1978, there were 150 birds; strict laws against the trade in parrots ensured that by 1992 numbers had risen to 400.

CHRONOLOGY

In the 17th and 18th centuries, St. Lucia, which provided an excellent naval raiding base in the Caribbean, was fought over by France and Britain. Ownership alternated between the two before it was finally ceded to Britain in 1814. French influence survives in St. Lucian patois and the local cuisine.

- **1958** Joins West Indies Federation.
- **1964** Sugar growing ceases.
- **1967** Gains internal autonomy.
- **1979** Gains independence and joins Commonwealth.
- **1990** Anti-drug force established.
- **1990** Establishes body with Dominica, Grenada and St. Vincent to discuss forming a Windward Islands Federation.

HEALTH

1 per 2,429 people

Heart and respiratory diseases, cancer

Health care has improved since the 1960s. State hospitals are supplemented by private clinics.

WEALTH

Factory worker, 99 East Caribbean dollars per week; communications office worker, 380 East Caribbean dollars per week

CONSUMER GOODS OWNERSHIP

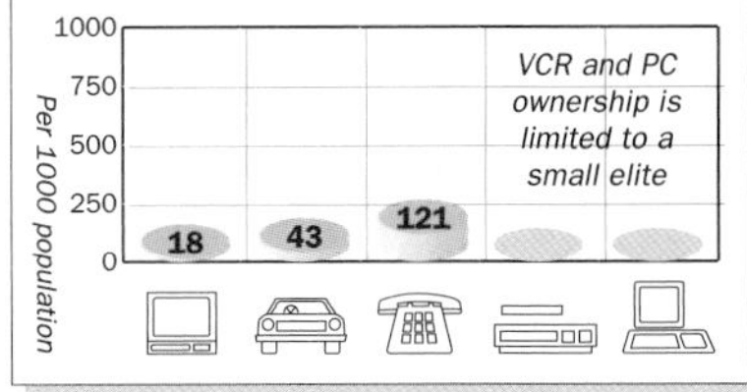

The big banana growers and hotel owners are the richest members of St. Lucian society. Japanese cars are particularly favored.

ECONOMICS

$456m

2.70 East Caribbean dollars

SCORE CARD

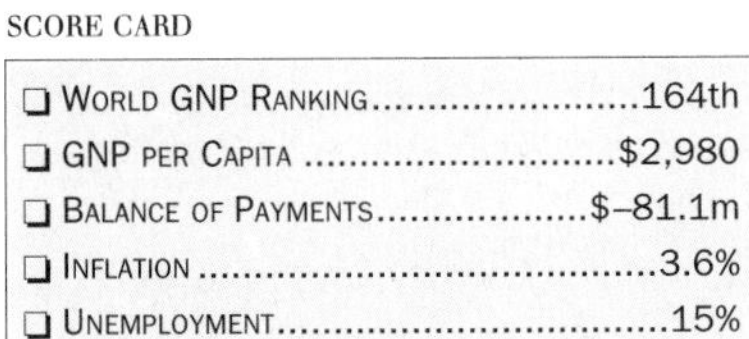

❑ WORLD GNP RANKING	164th
❑ GNP PER CAPITA	$2,980
❑ BALANCE OF PAYMENTS	$-81.1m
❑ INFLATION	3.6%
❑ UNEMPLOYMENT	15%

STRENGTHS

Banana crop, currently with preferential access to EU, and tourism.

WEAKNESSES

Most tourist resorts are foreign-owned; profits do not directly benefit St. Lucia.

EXPORTS

IMPORTS

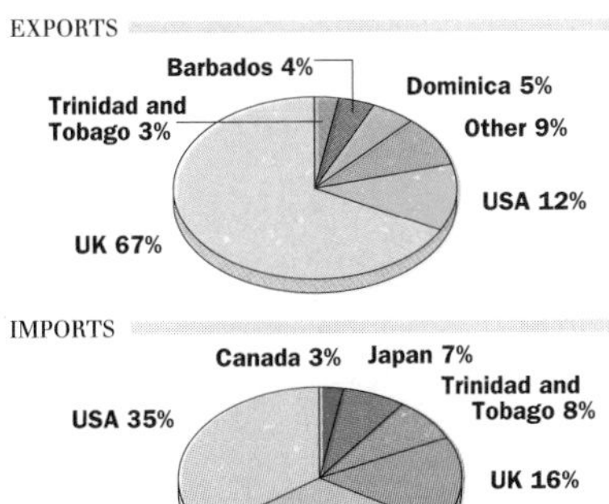

MEDIA

Generally free, although some government sensitivity about phone-in radio programs

PUBLISHING AND BROADCAST MEDIA

There are no daily newspapers. The *Star* and the *Voice of St. Lucia* are published bi-weekly
1 independent service
1 state-owned, 1 independent service

The privately owned press is free from government intervention. It is possible to receive TV programs from US, Mexican and some Caribbean stations.

CRIME

1,016 prisoners

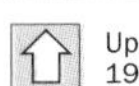
Up 17% between 1985 and 1989

There are no particularly dangerous areas on the island. Murder is rare and burglary is regarded by the locals as a major crime. The police force is trained by the UK and the USA.

EDUCATION

88%

Education is based on the British system. St. Lucia has the most Nobel laureates per capita in the world – Sir Arthur Lewis (economics) and Derek Walcott (literature) are both St. Lucians.

WORLD RANKING

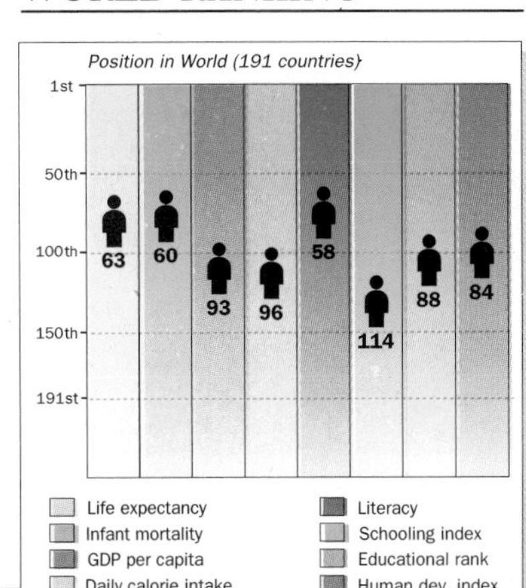

S

ST. VINCENT & THE GRENADINES

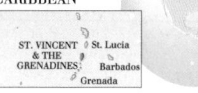

CARIBBEAN

ST. VINCENT & THE GRENADINES · St. Lucia · Barbados · Grenada · North America

OFFICIAL NAME: Saint Vincent and the Grenadines **CAPITAL:** Kingstown
POPULATION: 117,000 **CURRENCY:** East Caribbean dollar **OFFICIAL LANGUAGE:** English

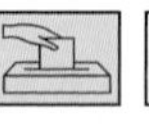

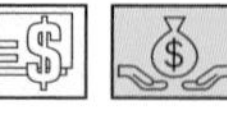

AMONG THE MOST ATTRACTIVE of the Windward Islands group, St. Vincent and the Grenadines is renowned as the Caribbean playground of the international jet-set. Tourism and bananas are the economic mainstays, and St. Vincent is also the world's largest arrowroot producer. St. Vincent is mostly volcanic; the one remaining active volcano, Mount Soufrière, last erupted in 1979. The Grenadines are flat, mainly bare coral reefs.

CLIMATE

WEATHER CHART

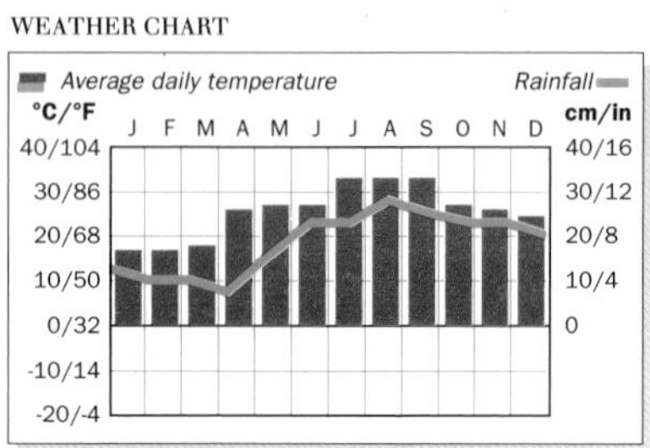

Constant trade winds moderate St. Vincent's tropical climate. Rainfall is heaviest during the summer months. Tropical depressions and hurricanes are likely between June and November.

COMMUNICATIONS

Arnos Vale, Kingstown

595 ships 6.96m dwt

THE TRANSPORTATION NETWORK

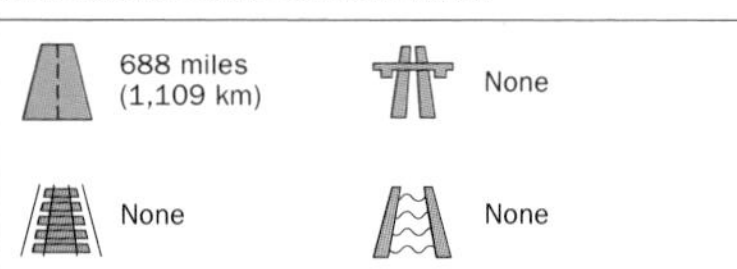

The government plans to extend St. Vincent's limited road network with coastal and interior roads. Also under construction is a shipyard and marina, financed by a German bank and the government. In 1992, an airport taking executive jets was completed on Bequia.

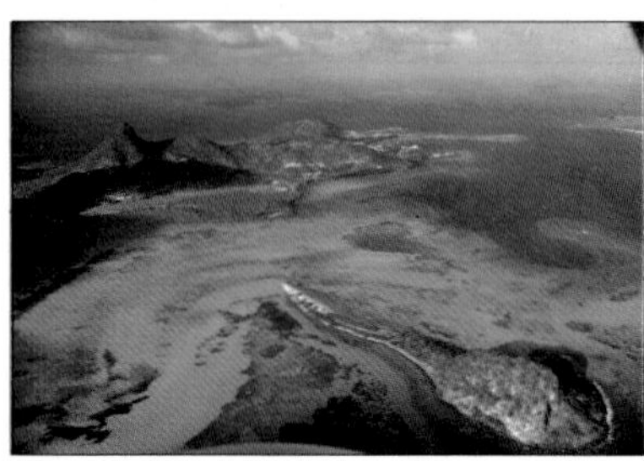

Aerial view of Union Island *in the Grenadines chain. The government is developing the island as a major yachting center.*

TOURISM

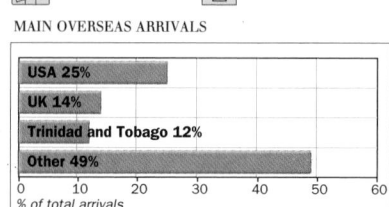

53,316 visitors

Up 3% in 1992

MAIN OVERSEAS ARRIVALS

	% of total arrivals
USA	25%
UK	14%
Trinidad and Tobago	12%
Other	49%

Tourism is targeted at the jet-set and cruise-ship rather than the mass market, and is concentrated on the Grenadines. Mustique, the most famous destination, is frequented by Mick Jagger and Princess Margaret, among others. Union Island is developing as a playground for the yachting rich. On St. Vincent, the pre-Columbian Amerindian petroglyphs at Layou are a major archaeological attraction.

PEOPLE

English, English Creole

712 people per sq. mile

THE URBAN/RURAL POPULATION SPLIT

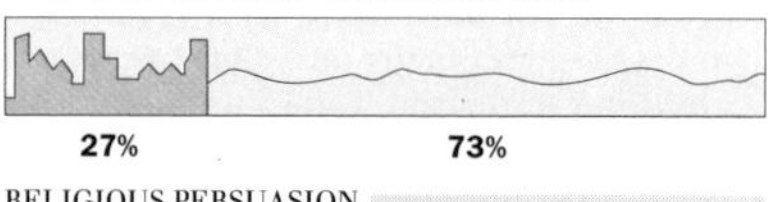

RELIGIOUS PERSUASION

Anglican 42%, Other 19%, Roman Catholic 19%, Methodist 20%

Family life on St. Vincent is heavily influenced by the strong Anglican Church. Racial tensions are minimal, and because of intermarriage the original communities of descendants of African slaves, Europeans and the few indigenous Caribs can no longer be distinguished. Many locals fear that traditional St. Vincent life is being threatened by the expanding tourist industry.

POLITICS

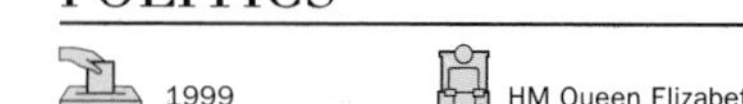

THE STATE OF THE PARTIES

National Assembly 21 members

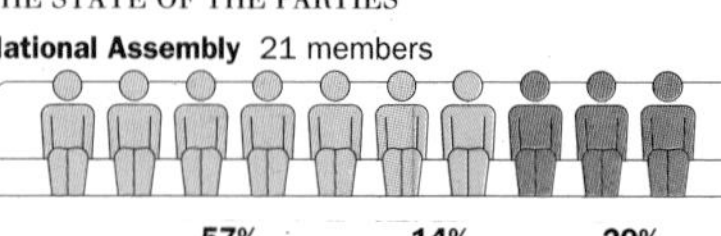

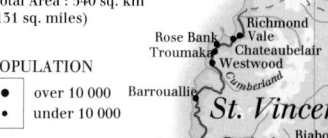

57% NDP · **14% SVLP-MNU** · **29% Appointed**

NDP = New Democratic Party **SVLP-MNU** = Saint Vincent Labour Party – Movement for National Unity

Prime Minister James Mitchell's NDP confirmed its political dominance with a clean sweep of seats at the 1989 elections. The opposition parties remain weak and short of funds; the top banana growers support the NDP. The main issue is the proposed Windward Islands Federation, which Mitchell favors. He has his eye on the federal presidency.

ST. VINCENT & THE GRENADINES

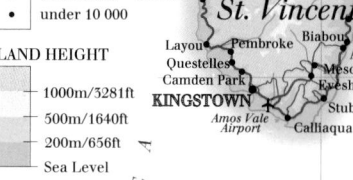

Total Area : 340 sq. km (131 sq. miles)

POPULATION
- ● over 10 000
- • under 10 000

LAND HEIGHT
- 1000m/3281ft
- 500m/1640ft
- 200m/656ft
- Sea Level

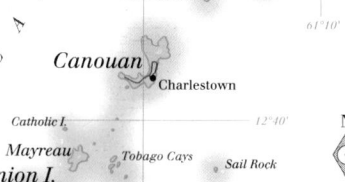

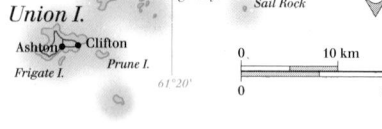

La Soufrière 1234m · Richmond Vale · Rose Bank · Troumaka · Chateaubelair · Westwood · Barrouallie · St. Vincent · Layou · Pembroke · Biabou · Questelles · Camden Park · Mesopotamia · Evesham · KINGSTOWN · Stubbs · Amos Vale Airport · Calliaqua · CARIBBEAN SEA · Port Elizabeth · Bequia · Derrick · Isle à Quatre · Battowia · Baliceaux · The Pillories · Lovell Village · Mustique · Rabbit I. · Petite Mustique · Savan I. · Petite Canouan · Canouan · Charlestown · Catholic I. · Mayreau · Tobago Cays · Sail Rock · Union I. · Ashton · Clifton · Frigate I. · Prune I. · 0 10 km · 0 10 mi

S

WORLD AFFAIRS

Usually excellent relations with Washington – St. Vincent supported the US invasion of Grenada in 1983 – have been put under strain by the USA's efforts to pressurize the EU into deregulating its trade, which currently favors Caribbean banana growers.

AID

 $16m (receipts)

 Up 78% in 1991

Aid is important in helping to stabilize the country's external finances. The USA and the EU are the main providers of project loans, the UK of grant aid.

DEFENSE

 $3.2m

 No significant change from year to year

St. Vincent has no army. A 500-strong police force, trained by the USA and UK, is part of the Windward and Leeward Islands' Regional Security System.

ECONOMICS

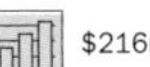 $216m

 2.70 East Caribbean dollars

SCORE CARD

- ❑ WORLD GNP RANKING......................176th
- ❑ GNP PER CAPITA...........................$1,845
- ❑ BALANCE OF PAYMENTS..................$-9.02m
- ❑ INFLATION.......................................5.8%
- ❑ UNEMPLOYMENT.................................40%

STRENGTHS
Bananas, with preferential access to the EU, and tourism. East Caribbean dollar provides currency stability. St. Vincent is the world's largest producer of arrowroot starch.

WEAKNESSES
Little diversification. St. Vincent is vulnerable to US moves to deregulate the world banana market.

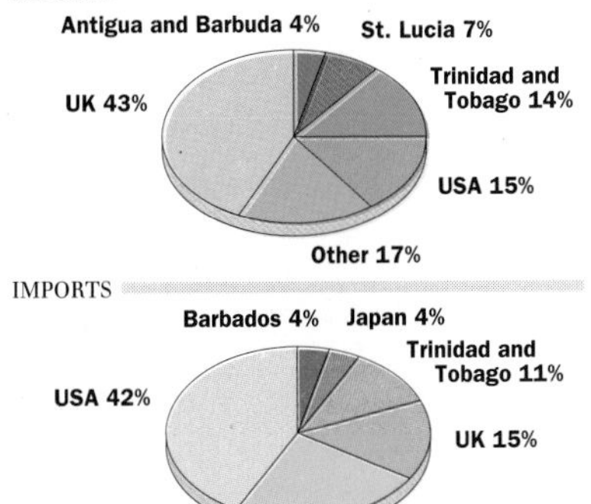

RESOURCES

48m kwh (capacity 14,000 kw)

 Not an oil producer and has no refineries

15,000 sheep, 9,000 pigs, 7,000 cattle

None

There is a hydroelectric plant on the Cumberland River. Virtually all other energy requirements have to be imported. Some of the Grenadines have no fresh water sources.

ENVIRONMENT

21% (including marine and semi-protected areas)

 New airport on Bequia

Hurricanes are the main environmental threat; Hurricane Emily destroyed 70% of the banana crop in 1987. For years, the inaccessibility of St. Vincent and the Grenadines meant that tourism was a minor environmental threat. The attraction of islands such as Mustique was based on their untouched, idyllic landscape. Mustique remains well protected – building has been restricted to 30 houses and further development is limited as fresh water has to be shipped in. On Bequia, the new airport and the associated increase in visitors are seen as a mixed blessing. Commercial whaling is a contentious issue.

MEDIA

 Journalists and radio news editors have been subjected to government intimidation

PUBLISHING AND BROADCAST MEDIA

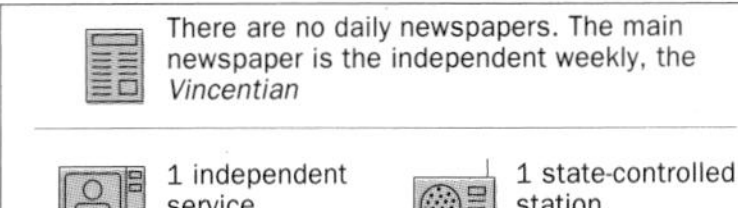

There are no daily newspapers. The main newspaper is the independent weekly, the *Vincentian*
1 independent service
1 state-controlled station

Only one of the four weekly papers is privately owned; the rest are published by political parties. Freedom of the press is written into the constitution.

CRIME

 281 prisoners

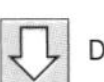 Down 3% in 1990

The judicial system on St. Vincent is based on British common law. Rape and robbery are the main local concerns, although on the outlying islands both incidents are very rare.

EDUCATION

 85%

State schools follow the old British 11-plus selective system. There are a few private schools. College students go on to the regional University of the West Indies in Jamaica, although increasing numbers are also studying in the USA and the UK.

CHRONOLOGY

In 1795, the local Carib population staged a revolt against the British, who deported them, leaving a largely black African population.

- ❑ **1951** Universal suffrage.
- ❑ **1969** Internal self-government.
- ❑ **1972** James Mitchell premier; holds balance of power between People's Political Party (PPP) and St. Vincent Labour Party (SVLP).
- ❑ **1974** Coalition of PPP and SVLP.
- ❑ **1979** Milton Cato, head of coalition; leads St. Vincent to full independence from Britain. La Soufrière volcano erupts.
- ❑ **1989** General election; NDP, founded by James Mitchell in 1975, takes all seats.

HEALTH

 1 per 3,216 people

 Heart and respiratory diseases, cancer

Doctors train at the University of the West Indies. The system is a mixture of state and private hospitals and clinics; facilities are scarcer on the Grenadines.

WEALTH

 Wealth is quite evenly dispersed, although large banana growers and established urban professionals tend to be more affluent

CONSUMER GOODS OWNERSHIP

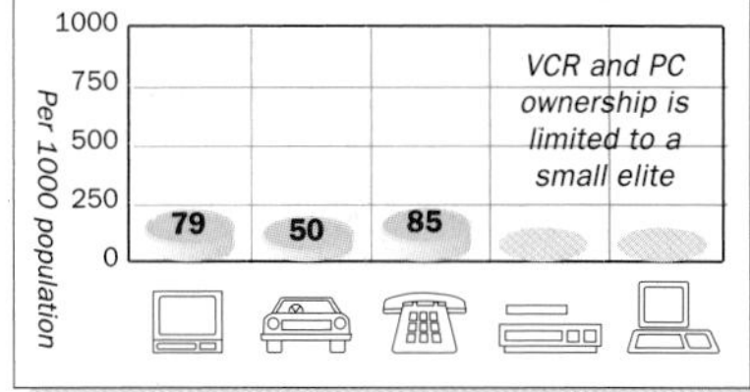

Jet-set wealth is very evident in the Grenadines, particularly on Union Island and Mustique. The local rich favor Jeeps and motor yachts.

WORLD RANKING

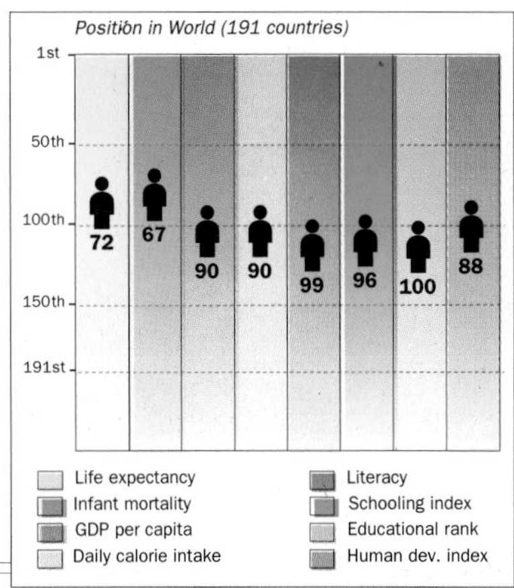

S

EUROPE

SAN MARINO

Italy

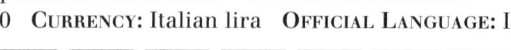

Europe

San Marino

Official Name: Republic of San Marino **Capital:** San Marino
Population: 22,000 **Currency:** Italian lira **Official Language:** Italian

PERCHED ON THE SLOPES of Mount Titano in the Italian Appennines, San Marino is, after Nauru, the world's smallest republic. It has maintained its independence since the 4th century AD. The territory is divided into nine castles, or districts. One-third of the San Marinese population lives in the northern town of Serravalle. San Marino's mainstays are agriculture, tourism and limited industry. Italy effectively controls most of its affairs.

San Marino's second fortress, the Cesta, *built in the 13th century, dominates the republic from its highest pinnacle, 2,477 ft. above sea level.*

CLIMATE

WEATHER CHART

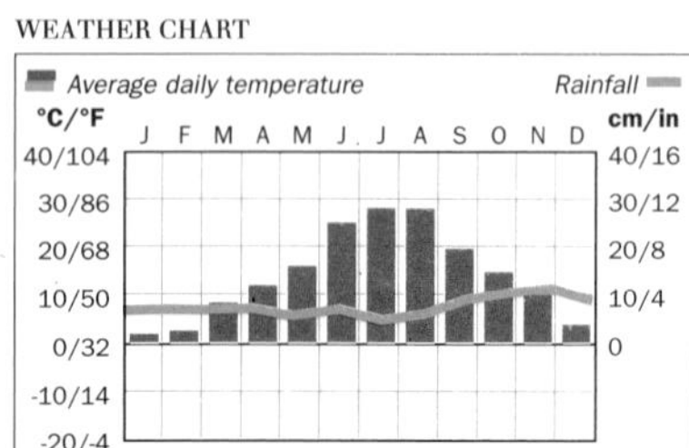

San Marino's Mediterranean climate is moderated by cool sea breezes and its height above sea level. In summer temperatures can reach 80°F, while in winter they fall to 20°F. Rainfall is more common in the winter months.

COMMUNICATIONS

None

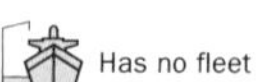
Has no fleet

THE TRANSPORTATION NETWORK

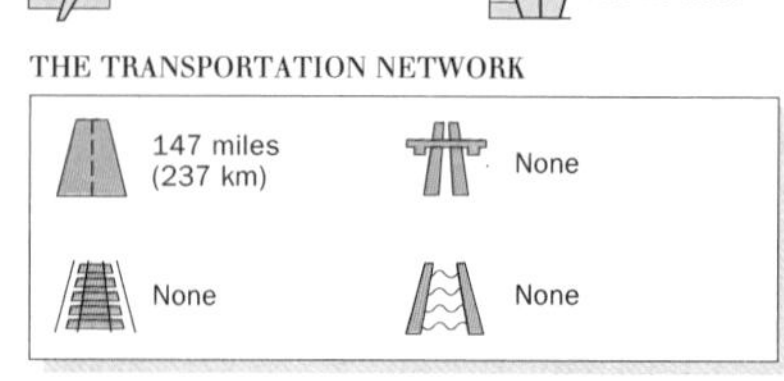

The 15-mile highway to Rimini, which has the closest airport, is San Marino's most important link. Congestion is a major problem, particularly during the annual *Mille Miglia* car rally. A funicular railroad climbs the east side of Mount Titano. The railroad to Rimini, closed since 1945, is being rebuilt.

PEOPLE

Italian

935 people per sq. mile

THE URBAN/RURAL POPULATION SPLIT

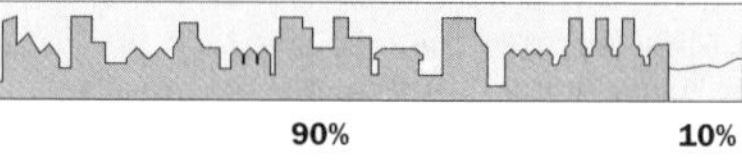

90% 10%

RELIGIOUS PERSUASION

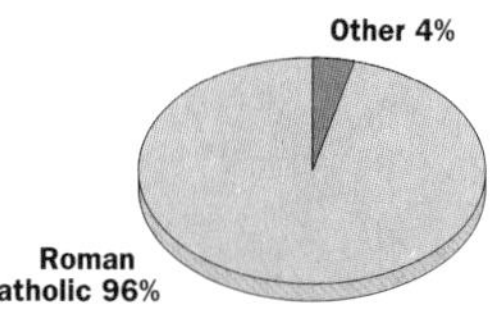

San Marino is a tightly-knit society. Foreigners must have resided in the republic for at least 30 years to gain citizenship. Women gained the vote in 1960, but were not able to stand for public office until 1973. Twenty thousand San Marino citizens are resident abroad, mainly in Italy.

TOURISM

2.73m visitors

Down 12% in 1992

Tourism is the mainstay of San Marino's economy, contributing 60% of government revenue. Tourist-related activities provide employment for 20% of the workforce, who cater to the three million visitors annually who come to sample its folklore and museums, and to explore the fortifications of Mount Titano.

The Titano fortresses of *la Rocca, la Cesta* and *Montale,* built during the Middle Ages, command superb views and are the main attractions. Many visitors to San Marino are day-trippers from Italy. The Republic's tourist industry is boosted by the close proximity of two international airports, in Rimini and Pisa.

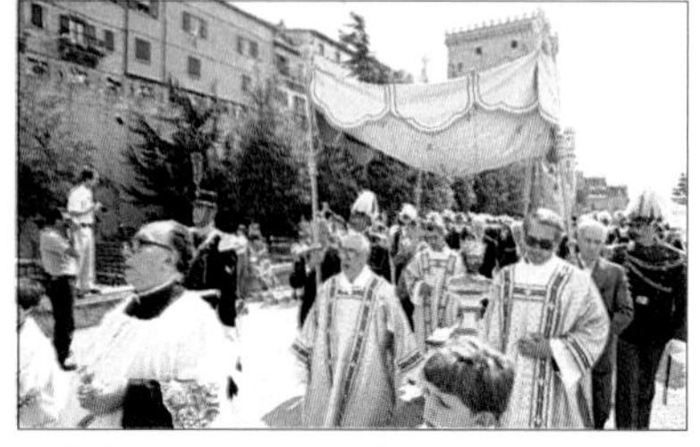

Religious procession. *The official state religion of San Marino is Roman Catholicism, in contrast to Italy, which has no state religion.*

MAIN OVERSEAS ARRIVALS

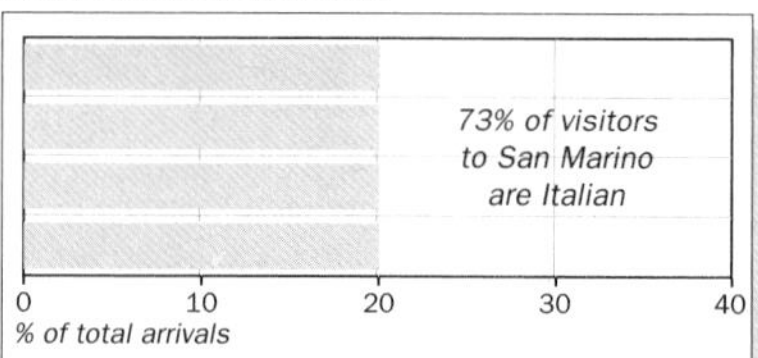

Efforts have been made to attract business meetings and conferences with extensive publicity in the Italian media. There are plans for a new high-tech conference hotel.

The San Marino tourist bureau is also attracting thousands of sports enthusiasts to the republic by hosting a series of top international athletic events. In March, both the Rimini–San Marino Marathon and the *Mille Miglia* veteran car meeting are held. May heralds the San Marino Grand Prix, when thousands of Formula One fans descend on the country. June, meanwhile, attracts more motor-racing fans for the World Motocross Championships.

San Marino

Total Area : 61 sq. km (24 sq. miles)

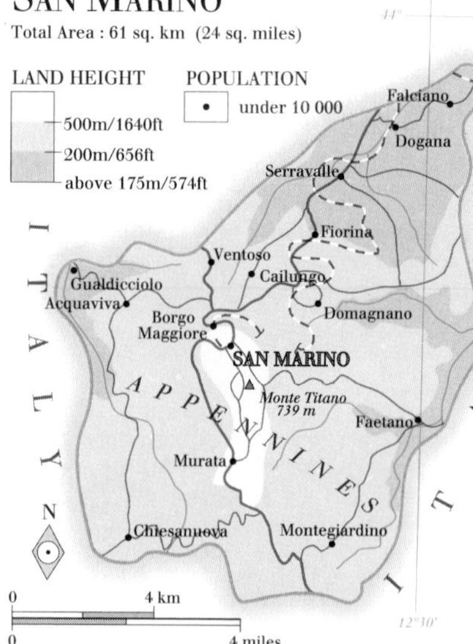

S

POLITICS

1998

Two Captains-Regent jointly hold office for a six month period

San Marino is a parliamentary democracy. The party system is parallel to Italy's, with regular coalition governments. The PDCS holds the majority of seats in the Great and General Council and governs in coalition with the PSS. The communists have been in decline since 1957.

THE STATE OF THE PARTIES

Great and General Council 60 members

PDCS = San Marino Christian Democrat Party
PSS = San Marino Socialist Party **PDP** = Democratic Progress Party **PDA** = Popular Democratic Alliance
DM = Democratic Movement **CR** = Communist Reformation

WORLD AFFAIRS

Foreign affairs are effectively decided by Italy, on which San Marino is entirely dependent. In 1992, San Marino acquired a seat at the UN.

AID

Neither an aid donor nor receiver

Not applicable

San Marino does not receive aid. However, annual subsidies from Italy and free access to the Italian market are essential to the economy.

DEFENSE

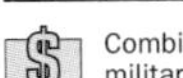
Combined voluntary military forces

Not applicable

San Marino has a small territorial army and fortification guards. There is no compulsory military service, but males aged 16–55 may be called up in a national emergency.

ECONOMICS

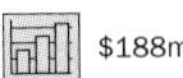
$188m

1,712 Italian lira

SCORE CARD

- ❑ WORLD GNP RANKING........................179th
- ❑ GNP PER CAPITA $8,545
- ❑ BALANCE OF PAYMENTS ....Within Italian total
- ❑ INFLATION 6.1%
- ❑ UNEMPLOYMENT...............................4.3%

STRENGTHS
Tourism, providing 60% of government revenue. Light industry, notably mechanical engineering and clothing, with emphasis on sportswear and high-quality prestige lines.

WEAKNESSES
Need to import all raw materials.

EXPORTS/IMPORTS

Does not publish independent trade statistics; trade movements are included in the Italian totals

RESOURCES

No electricity generation

Not an oil producer and has no refineries

Small numbers of cattle, pigs, sheep and horses

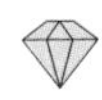
None

San Marino has to import all its energy from Italy. It has no exploitable mineral resources, now that the stone quarry on Mount Titano has been exhausted.

ENVIRONMENT

None

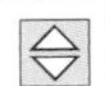
Farming poses a threat to remaining indigenous woodland

Mount Titano is a unique limestone outcrop in the surrounding Italian plain and thus has a very localized ecosystem.

MEDIA

There is full freedom of expression

PUBLISHING AND BROADCAST MEDIA

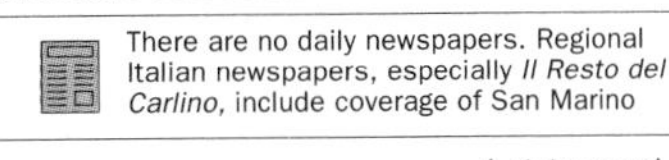
There are no daily newspapers. Regional Italian newspapers, especially *Il Resto del Carlino*, include coverage of San Marino

1 state-owned service

1 state-owned, 1 independent service

In 1993, a local TV station, *San Marino RTV*, began broadcasting. Sanmarinese can also receive Italian TV.

CRIME

San Marino does not publish prison figures

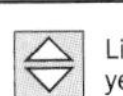
Little change from year to year

San Marino has a low crime rate. Justice, except in minor civil cases, is administered by the Italian legal system.

EDUCATION

98%

The government spends 13% of the budget on education. Students can go on to Italian universities.

HEALTH

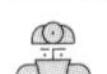
1 per 375 people

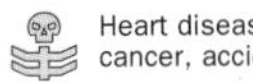
Heart disease, cancer, accidents

San Marino's hospital provides a limited health service. Those people requiring difficult operations are normally taken to Rimini for treatment.

CHRONOLOGY

Founded in the 4th century, the Republic of San Marino became one of many medieval Italian city-states. It refused to join the unified Italian state created in 1861.

- ❑ **1862** San Marino signs friendship treaty with Italy.
- ❑ **1914–1918** San Marino fights for Italy in World War I.
- ❑ **1940** Supports Axis powers and declares war on the Allies.
- ❑ **1943** Declares neutrality shortly before Italy surrenders.
- ❑ **1960** Women obtain the vote.
- ❑ **1978** Coalition between San Marino Communist Party (PCS) and PSS – sole communist-led government in Western Europe.
- ❑ **1986** Financial scandals lead to a new PDCS–PCS government.
- ❑ **1988** Joins Council of Europe.
- ❑ **1990** PCS renames itself the Democratic Progress Party (PDP).
- ❑ **1992** San Marino joins the UN. The collapse of communism in Europe sees the PDCS–PDP alliance replaced by a PDSC–PSS coalition government.
- ❑ **1993** May: general election.

WEALTH

Similar wealth levels to those in northern Italy

CONSUMER GOODS OWNERSHIP

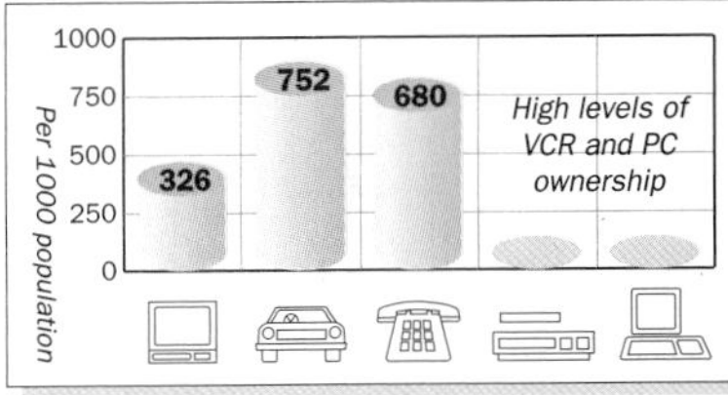

Living standards are similar to those of northern Italy. The unemployment rate of 4% is below the Italian average.

WORLD RANKING

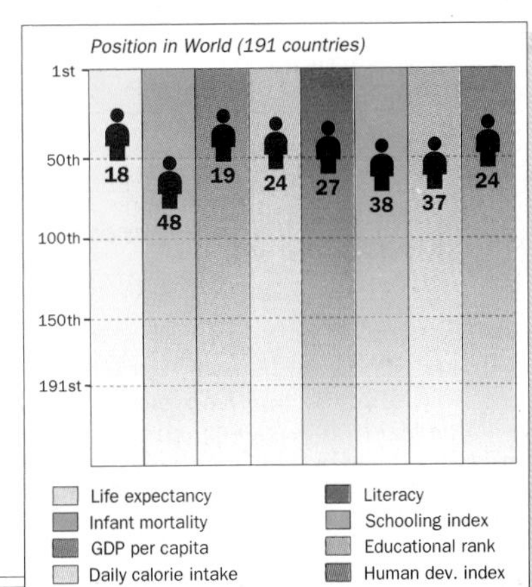

S

Sao Tome & Principe

WEST AFRICA

Principe · SAO TOME & PRINCIPE · São Tomé · Equatorial Guinea · Gabon · Africa

OFFICIAL NAME: Democratic Republic of Sao Tome and Principe **CAPITAL:** São Tomé
POPULATION: 124,000 **CURRENCY:** Dobra **OFFICIAL LANGUAGE:** Portuguese

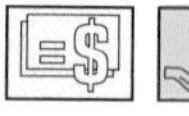

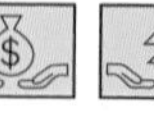

COMPOSED OF the main islands of São Tomé and Príncipe and surrounding islets, the republic of Sao Tome and Principe is situated off the western coast of Africa. In 1975, a classic Marxist single-party regime was established following independence from Portugal, but a referendum in 1990 resulted in a 72% vote in favor of democracy. Sao Tome's main concerns are to rebuild relations with Portugal and to seek closer ties with the EU and the USA.

CLIMATE

WEATHER CHART

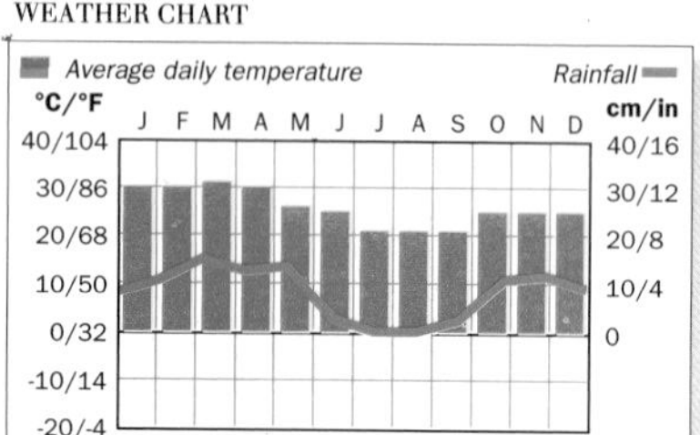

The hot, humid islands straddle the equator. Annual rainfall is 195 in. in the southwest and 39 in. in the north.

COMMUNICATIONS

São Tomé Intl 23,000 passengers (est)

2 ships 1,300 dwt

THE TRANSPORTATION NETWORK

236 miles (380 km) · None

None · None

After years of neglect, road repairs and the upgrading of São Tomé's airport began in the late 1980s.

TOURISM

MAIN OVERSEAS ARRIVALS

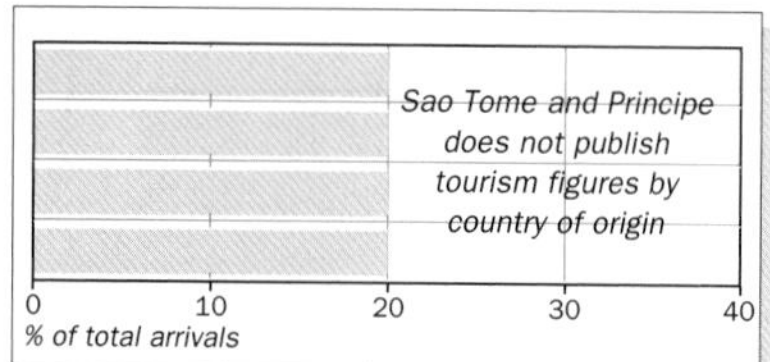

Tourism is still small-scale, attracting wealthy Gabonese and Europeans. Despite recent foreign investment, tourism on a sizeable scale will take decades to develop. The country's first modern hotel opened in 1986.

PEOPLE

Portuguese Creole, Portuguese

313 people per sq. mile

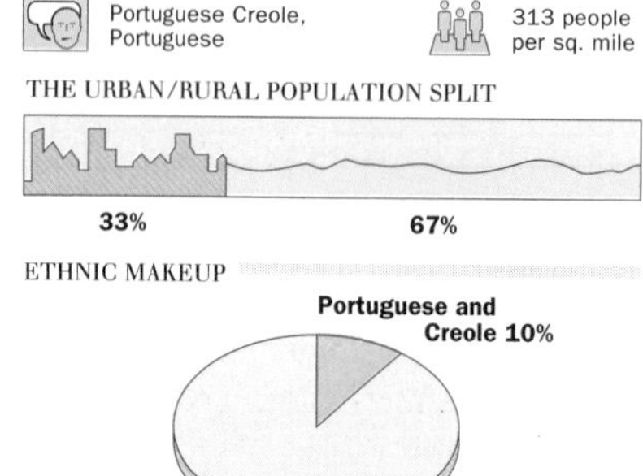

The population is entirely descended from immigrants, as the islands were uninhabited when the Portuguese arrived in 1470. As the Portuguese settled, they imported Africans as slaves to work the sugar and cocoa plantations. The abolition of slavery in the 19th century, and the departure of 4,000 Portuguese at independence, have resulted in a population which is 10% Portuguese and Creole and 90% black African, although Portuguese culture predominates. Blacks run the political parties. Society is well integrated and free of racial prejudice. The main conflicts relate to class or differing ideologies. The extended family still offers the best, if not the only, form of social security. Women have a higher status than in most other African countries; many hold prominent positions in professional fields.

Lush vegetation on Sao Tome. *The tropical climate is slightly moderated by the cool Benguela current.*

POLITICS

1995

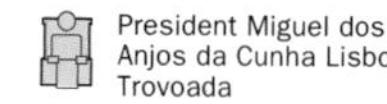

THE STATE OF THE PARTIES

National People's Assembly 55 members

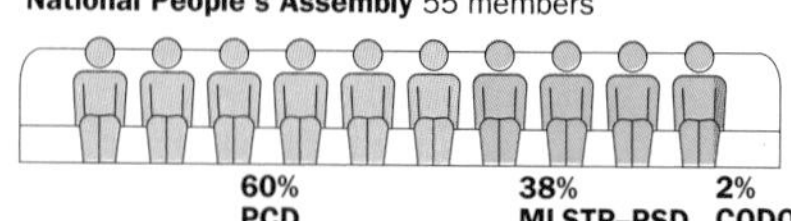

PCD = Democratic Convergence Party **MLSTP–PSD** = Movement for the Liberation of Sao Tome and Principe – Social Democratic Party **CODO** = Democratic Opposition Coalition

In 1990, a new multiparty constitution swept away the Marxist single-party state that had existed since the republic's independence in 1975. In the 1991 elections the PCD defeated the MLSTP–PSD, the former ruling party, whose new name reflects its change of ideology. The next few years will show whether or not the PCD dismantles socialism. Most parties are now grouped around personalities. Former leader, Pinto da Costa, steered the way to multiparty politics. However, he withdrew from the 1990 presidential elections, leaving as sole candidate Miguel Trovoada, who returned from 11 years' exile to stand successfully as an independent. The most important pressure groups in politics now are the Roman Catholic Church (harassed under Marxism) and the trade unions. The main political concerns are to uphold the multiparty system and stimulate growth in the economy.

WORLD AFFAIRS

Sao Tome has achieved rapprochement with Portugal and seeks to maintain links with other ex-Portuguese colonies, notably Angola. It has always had close ties with Gabon and, while not dropping its ex-communist links, is seeking closer relations with other CEEAC countries, France and the USA.

AID

$48m (receipts)

Up 30% in 1991

Sao Tome has one of the highest aid-to-population ratios in Africa. Joining the Lomé Convention in the 1970s has proved advantageous: Sao Tome has found new sources of aid fairly easily since the demise of communism worldwide. The World Bank and IMF are the main donors.

S

DEFENSE

 Defense budget not disclosed

 Probably constant from year to year

Since independence, the armed forces have figured prominently in national life. They have put down several attempted coups, notably in 1978, after which 2,000 Angolan troops plus Soviet and Cuban advisers were invited in, and in 1988. The national armed forces are still believed to number 2,000, which is large for the size of the population. Aid donors are pressing for a reduction. With the collapse of the Eastern bloc, Sao Tome now receives military assistance from the USA.

RESOURCES

 15m kwh (capacity 6,000 kw)

 Not an oil producer and has no refineries

 4,000 cattle, 3,000 pigs, 2,000 sheep

None

Sao Tome has no mineral resources, although oil prospecting began in 1990. Almost all energy needs, apart from firewood, are met by oil imported from Angola. Sao Tome is very fertile; cocoa estates are finally back to pre-1975 productivity and crop diversification is now a priority. Principe has better ports, but its wild scenery makes it more suitable for tourism than farming.

CHRONOLOGY

The entire pre-independence history of the islands was as a Portuguese colony exploited by plantation owners.

- **1972–1973** Strikes by plantation workers. Liberation movement set up in Gabon is recognized by UN.
- **1975** Independence as Marxist state. Plantations nationalized.
- **1978** Attempted coup suppressed.
- **1984** Declares itself non-aligned.
- **1990** New democratic constitution.

ECONOMICS

 $37m

 239.59 dobras

SCORE CARD

- World GNP Ranking 191st
- GNP per Capita $300
- Balance of Payments .... $-26.3m
- Inflation 25%
- Unemployment .... Widespread underemployment

EXPORTS

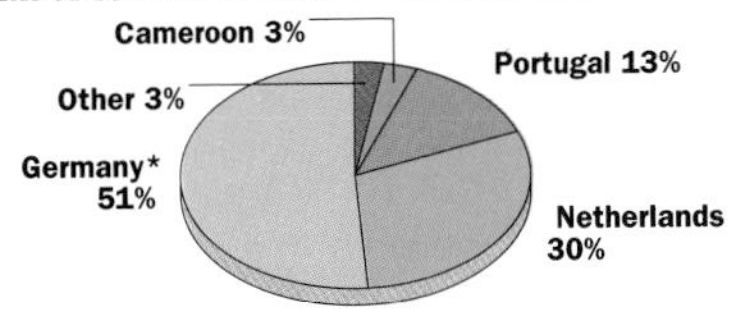

IMPORTS

Angola 11%
Portugal 27%
Belgium and Luxembourg 16%
Germany* 24%
Other 22%

STRENGTHS

Legacy of Portuguese-built infrastructure. Potential for tourism, agricultural and fisheries development. Ability to attract substantial aid.

WEAKNESSES

90% of export earnings from cocoa. Skillful diplomacy has attracted high levels of aid, although mismanagement of these funds has resulted in severe debt. Weak currency.

EDUCATION

 57%

Education is compulsory for 6–12-year-olds. All staff at the one technical and three secondary schools are foreigners.

HEALTH

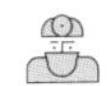 1 per 2,819 people

Respiratory, diarrheal and parasitic diseases

Although health care is not free, Sao Tome has a better system of basic care than other ex-colonial African countries.

WEALTH

 Workers on the cocoa plantations form the poorest group

CONSUMER GOODS OWNERSHIP

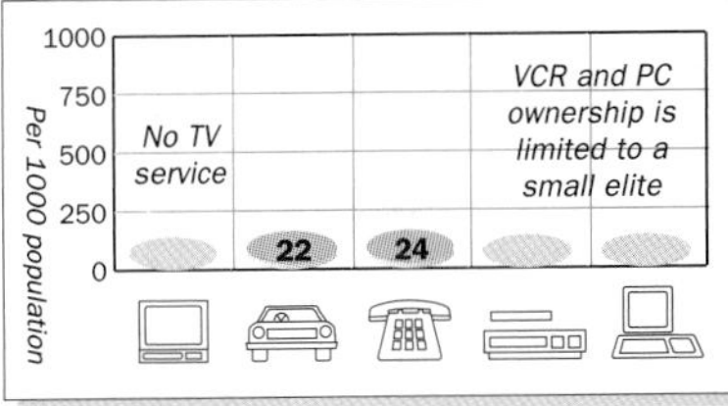

Wealth disparities are not conspicuous. There is a growing business class. Cocoa workers are the poorest group.

SAO TOME & PRINCIPE

Total Area : 964 sq. km (372 sq. miles)

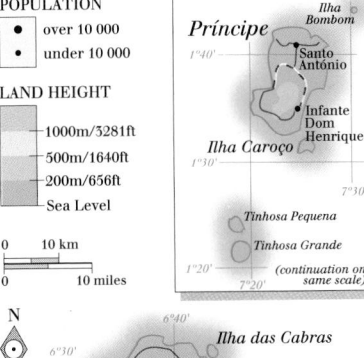

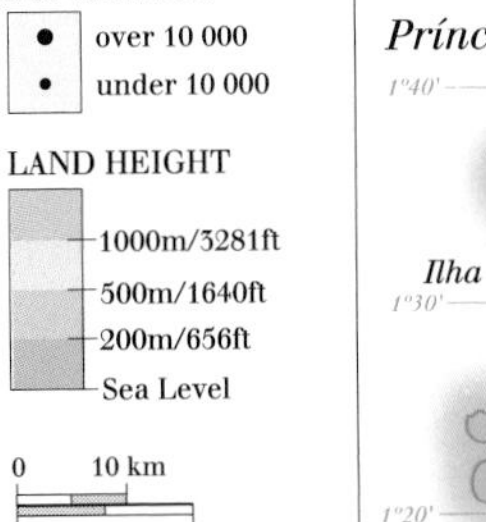

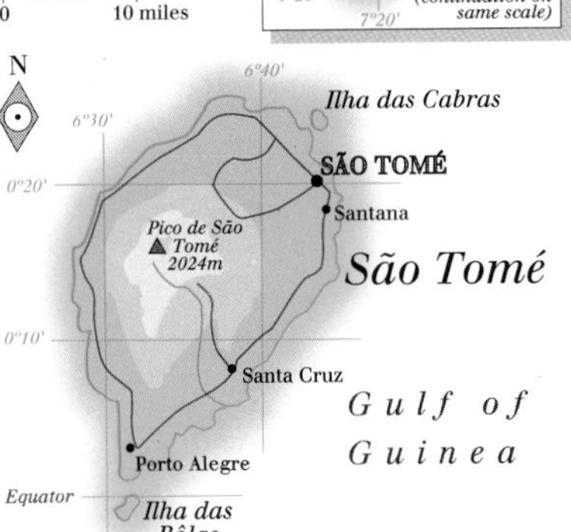

ENVIRONMENT

 None

 No attempt to curb deforestation and soil erosion

Fish conservation, deforestation for firewood and potential tourism expansion are the major issues.

MEDIA

 The press was strictly controlled until 1988, but censorship rules have now been relaxed

PUBLISHING AND BROADCAST MEDIA

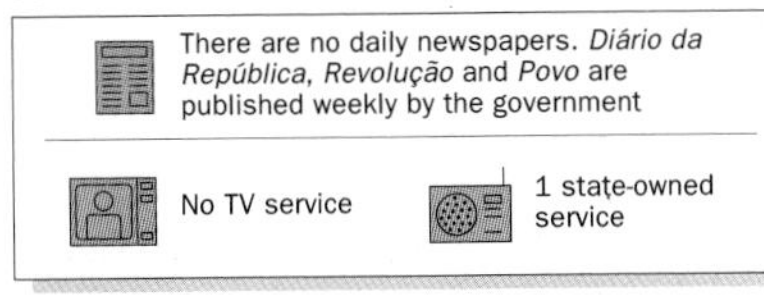

There are no daily newspapers. *Diário da República*, *Revolução* and *Povo* are published weekly by the government
No TV service
1 state-owned service

The strict censorship of the Marxist regime began to be relaxed in 1988. Radio ownership is high for Africa.

CRIME

 Sao Tome does not publish prison figures

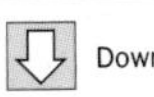 Down 20% in 1988

Crime levels are fairly low due to the tightly knit nature of the community. Urban robbery is a problem.

WORLD RANKING

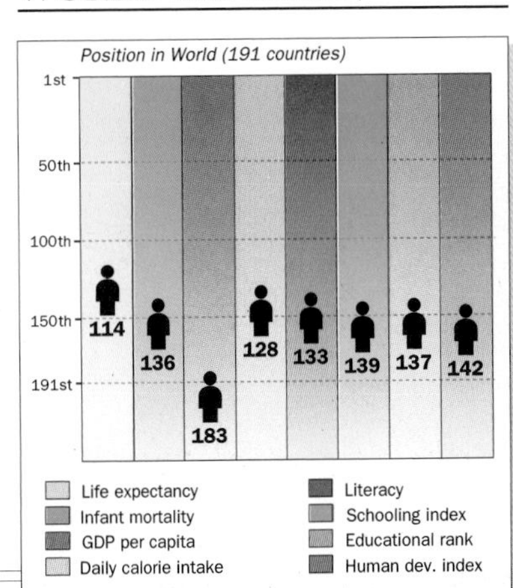

S

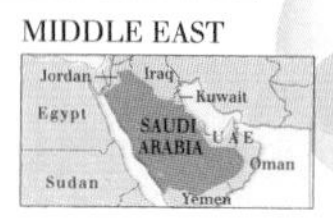
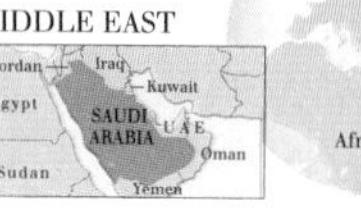

SAUDI ARABIA

OFFICIAL NAME: Kingdom of Saudi Arabia **CAPITAL:** Riyadh
POPULATION: 15.9 million **CURRENCY:** Saudi riyal **OFFICIAL LANGUAGE:** Arabic

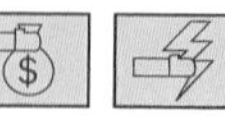

OCCUPYING MOST OF THE Arabian Peninsula, Saudi Arabia covers an area as large as Western Europe. Over 95% of its land is desert, with the most arid part, known as the "Empty Quarter," or Rub al Khali, in the southeast. Saudi Arabia has the world's largest oil and gas reserves as well as major refining and petrochemicals industries. It includes Islam's holiest cities, Medina and Mecca, visited each year by two million Muslims performing the pilgrimage known as the *haj*. The Al-Saud family have been Saudi Arabia's absolutist rulers since 1932.

CLIMATE

WEATHER CHART

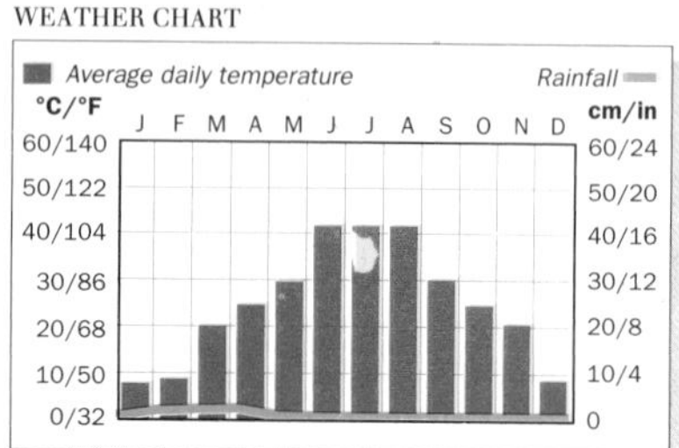

The kingdom's only reliable rainfall is in the southern Asir province, which makes agriculture there viable. The central plateau requires deep artesian wells to water crops. Inland, summer temperatures often soar above 118°F, but in winter, especially in the northwest, they may fall to freezing point.

COMMUNICATIONS

King Abdul Aziz International, Jiddah 3.65m passengers

108 ships 1.25m dwt

THE TRANSPORTATION NETWORK

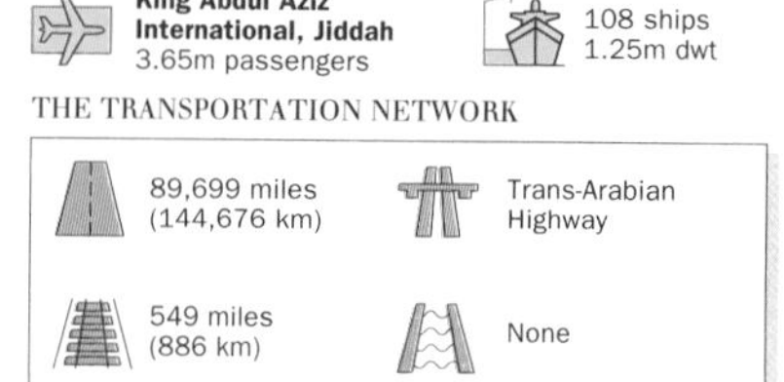

Since the advent of oil wealth in the 1970s, a modern transportation infrastructure has been created, linking the main centers to the Gulf States, Jordan and Egypt.

TOURISM

827,000 pilgrims

Up 8% in 1990

MAIN OVERSEAS ARRIVALS

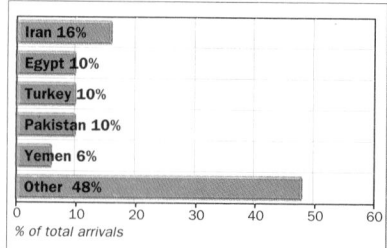

	% of total arrivals
Iran	16%
Egypt	10%
Turkey	10%
Pakistan	10%
Yemen	6%
Other	48%

Saudi Arabia does not encourage foreign tourism. Only Muslim pilgrims, businesspeople and foreign workers are permitted entry. Non-Muslims are banned from the holy cities. Over two million Muslims perform the *haj* (pilgrimage) in the twelfth month of the Arabic year. Muslims are expected to carry out the *haj* at least once in their life, and strict quotas have had to be imposed to avoid massive overcrowding. Many choose Jiddah as a base from which to begin the pilgrimage. The *umra*, or little pilgrimage, has also become popular, as it can be made at any time of year. The royal family has spent $2.5 billion in recent years on improving facilities at Medina and Mecca. Excellent scuba diving exists on the Red Sea, especially at Jīzān in the south of the country.

SAUDI ARABIA

Total Area : 2 149 690 sq. km (829 995 sq. miles)

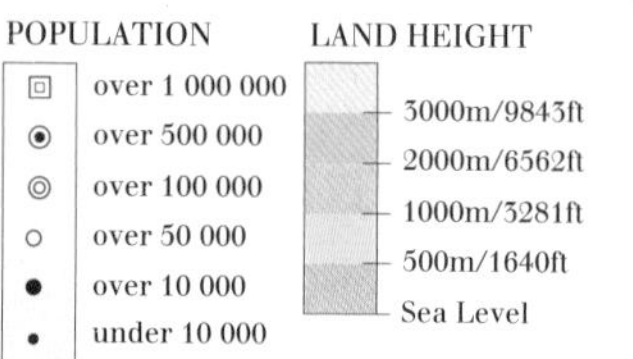

Network of modern road junctions spread out across the landscape near Mecca.

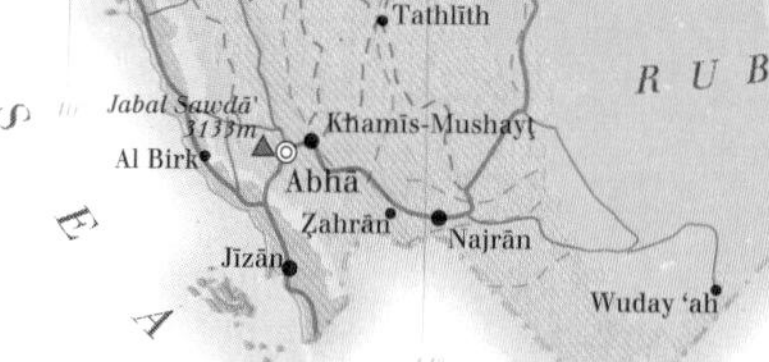

PEOPLE

Arabic

18 people per sq. mile

THE URBAN/RURAL POPULATION SPLIT

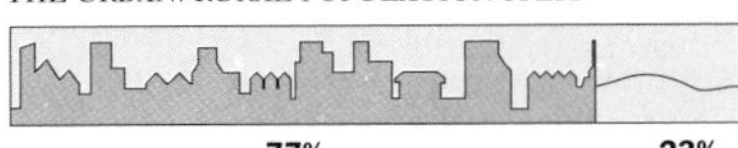

RELIGIOUS PERSUASION

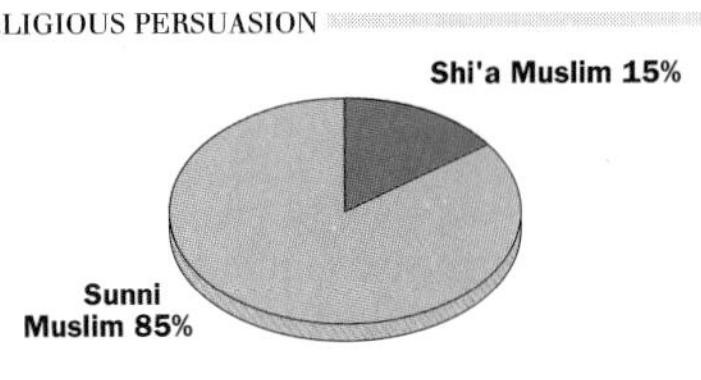

ETHNIC MAKEUP

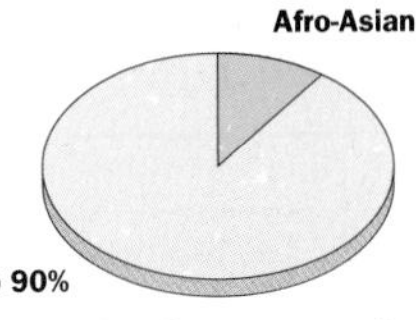

The Saudis take their name from the ruling Al-Saud family. They were united by conquest between 1902 and 1932 by King Abd al-Aziz Al Sa'ud, who expelled the Turks.

The vast majority of Saudis are Sunni Muslims who follow the *wahhabi* (puritan) interpretation of Islam and embrace *sharia* (Muslim) law in their daily lives.

The politically dominant Nejadi tribes from the central plateau around Riyadh are Bedouin in origin. The Hejazi tribes from southern and western Saudi Arabia, who have a more cosmopolitan, mercantile background, have largely been displaced from politics. In the eastern province there is a Shi'a minority of some 300,000, many of whom are employed in the oilfields.

Women are obliged to wear the veil, cannot hold drivers licenses and have no role in public life. They are effectively barred from the workplace except as teachers and nurses.

POPULATION AGE BREAKDOWN

% of population by age group

	1960	1970	1980	1990	2000
65+	3.3%	3.2%	2.8%	2.6%	2.6%
15–64	53.4%	52.3%	53%	52.1%	51.7%
0–14	43.3%	44.5%	44.2%	45.3%	45.7%

WORLD AFFAIRS

Saudi Arabia's strategic importance is derived entirely from its oil reserves and worldwide investments. The Kingdom of Saudi Arabia is among the top ten trading partners of nearly every industrialized country in the world. Relations with the USA are particularly close. Although foreign reserves have fallen because of the cost of liberating Kuwait in 1991, the Saudis remain important institutional investors with significant amounts invested in the West.

The Saudi reaction to Iraq's invasion of Kuwait in 1990 demonstrated the Sa'uds' determination to maintain the current *status quo* in the Middle East. Saudi Arabia helped to persuade other Arab states of the need to evict Iraq from Kuwait. It gave sanctuary to the Kuwaiti royal family and offered its military bases to the Western allies. More Saudi troops fought in the UN's Operation Desert Storm than did troops from any other Arab country.

The guardian of Mecca, Saudi Arabia has immense importance as the spiritual center for more than a billion Muslims all over the world.

POLITICS

Not applicable

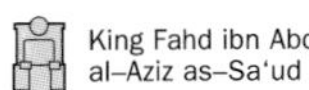
King Fahd ibn Abd al-Aziz as-Sa'ud

THE STATE OF THE PARTIES

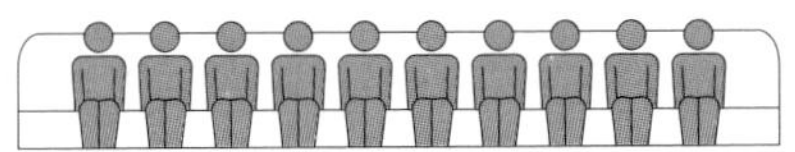

Saudi Arabia is an absolute monarchy. The King rules with the assistance of an appointed Council of Ministers

Saudi Arabia is an absolute monarchy. A 60-man Consultative Assembly *(majlis ashoura)* is appointed by the King.

MAIN POLITICAL ISSUES

Questioning the ruling family

Following the 1991 Gulf War, a civil rights campaign emerged to challenge the authority of the ruling family, demanding closer adherence to Islamic values. The movement objected to the presence of US troops on Saudi territory and the consequent exposure to "corrupt" Western culture; particular outrage was felt at the presence of women soldiers. The Sa'uds moved swiftly to quash the protest. Academics and civil servants behind the movement were imprisoned.

The religious establishment

The ruling family has the support of the religious establishment, led by the *ulema*, a convocation of Islamic scholars in *sharia* law. In the 1980s, King Fahd adopted the title Guardian of the Two Holy Shrines to emphasize his commitment to the defense of Islam. The King consults the Supreme Council of *Ulema* on moral and political issues. King Fahd has often suppressed his modernizing tendencies, following the *Ulema*'s advice.

PROFILE

The royal family rules by carefully manipulating appointments in all sectors of government. Frequent changes of personnel within the armed forces ensure that officers do not build personal followings. All influential cabinet portfolios, apart from those of oil and religious affairs, are held by princes.

Absolutist rule means that domestic politics are virtually non-existent. The regime retains feudal elements: weekly *majlis*, or councils, are held where citizens can present petitions or grievances to leading members of the royal family. Large cash sums are often dispensed at these meetings.

The legitimacy of the regime is built on its adherence to Islamic values, and the backing of the *ulema*. It is the stress on Islam that colors Saudi life most. The 5,000-strong *mutawa* (religious police) enforce the five-times-a-day call to prayer when businesses must close. During Ramadan the *mutawa* are especially active.

AID

$3.7bn (donations)

Up 315% in 1990

Through the Saudi Fund for Development, the kingdom makes generous loans and grants to other Arab and developing countries, mainly for infrastructure projects. Saudi Arabia promotes Islam through charitable foundations, especially in Africa, Asia and the former Soviet Union. The royal purse also supports scientific and medical research. Since the liberation of Kuwait in 1991, Saudi Arabia has given large sums to countries that supported the Allies, notably Egypt, Syria, Morocco and Turkey. In addition, the Saudi government substantially reimbursed the USA and UK for the cost of their expeditionary forces, as well as favoring companies from the Allied powers for reconstruction contracts.

King Fahd ibn Abd al-Aziz as-Sa'ud *acceded to the Saudi throne in 1982.*

Sheikh Muhammad Ali Aba al-Khail, *Saudi Arabia's Minister of Finance.*

CHRONOLOGY

The unification of Saudi Arabia under King Abd al-Aziz (Ibn Sa'ud) was achieved in 1932. The kingdom remains the only country in the world named after its royal family.

- ❑ **1937** Oil reserves discovered near Riyadh.
- ❑ **1939** Ceremonial start of oil production at Az Zahran.
- ❑ **1945** Abdel Aziz meets US President Roosevelt on *USS Quincy* in the Red Sea.
- ❑ **1953** King Sa'ud succeeds upon the death of his father, Abdel Aziz.
- ❑ **1964** King Sa'ud abdicates in favor of his brother, Faisal.
- ❑ **1967** Saudi forces join with those of Jordan and Iraq against Israel during Six Day War.
- ❑ **1969** Air Force officers stage an abortive coup against King Faisal.
- ❑ **1973** Saudi Arabia imposes an oil embargo on Western supporters of Israel.
- ❑ **1975** King Faisal assassinated by a deranged nephew and is succeeded by his brother Khaled.
- ❑ **1979** Muslim fundamentalists led by Juhaiman ibn Seif al-Otaibi seize the Grand Mosque in Mecca and proclaim a *Mahdi* (messiah) on the first day of the Islamic year 1400.
- ❑ **1981** Formation of Gulf Cooperation Council, with secretariat in Riyadh.
- ❑ **1982** King Fahd succeeds upon the death of his brother, King Khaled. Promises to create consultative assembly.
- ❑ **1986** Opening of King Fahd Causeway to Bahrain. Sheikh Yamani fired as oil minister.
- ❑ **1987** Diplomatic relations with Iran deteriorate after 402 people die in riots involving Islamic fundamentalists in Mecca during the *haj* (pilgrimage).
- ❑ **1989** Saudi Arabia signs non-aggression pact with Iraq. Saudi Arabia brokers political settlement to Lebanese civil war.
- ❑ **1990** Kuwaiti royals seek sanctuary in Taif after Iraqi invasion.
- ❑ **1990–1991** US, UK, French, Egyptian and Syrian forces assemble in Saudi Arabia for Operation Desert Storm. Public executions are halted.
- ❑ **1991** Iraqis seize border town of Al Khafji, but are driven out by Saudi, US and Qatari forces.
- ❑ **1992** King Fahd pays for British girl Laura Davies to have heart transplant in USA.
- ❑ **1993** King Fahd appoints 60-man Consultative Assembly.

DEFENSE

$36bn | Up 53% in 1991

Defense spending as % GDP (0–40): 13.2%

SAUDI ARABIAN ARMED FORCES

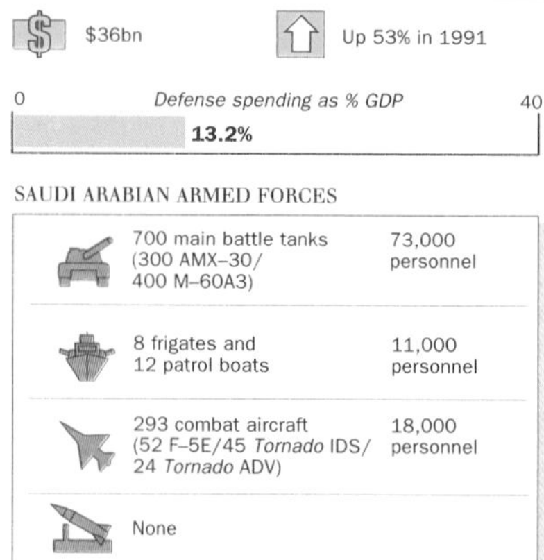

700 main battle tanks (300 AMX–30/ 400 M–60A3)	73,000 personnel
8 frigates and 12 patrol boats	11,000 personnel
293 combat aircraft (52 F–5E/45 *Tornado* IDS/ 24 *Tornado* ADV)	18,000 personnel
None	

The liberation of Kuwait boosted the armed forces' prestige. Military equipment is purchased mostly from the USA, UK and France. Weapons systems are advanced and include *Patriot* missiles and AWACS early warning radar. However, skilled foreign personnel operate many of these: 1,000 US Air Force troops are employed to keep AWACS flying. The air force is the elite branch of the military. It had one brief period of politicization in 1969 when officers attempted a coup. The paramilitary National Guard is drawn from tribal supporters of the Al-Sa'ud regime. Its commander-in-chief is the Crown Prince rather than the defense minister.

ECONOMICS

$105.1bn | 3.75 Saudi riyals

SCORE CARD

- ❑ World GNP Ranking........................30th
- ❑ GNP per Capita...........................$6,610
- ❑ Balance of Payments..................$–19.4bn
- ❑ Inflation...5%
- ❑ Unemployment..................................0%

EXPORTS

Singapore 5%
France 5%
Japan 9%
USA 26%
Other 55%

IMPORTS

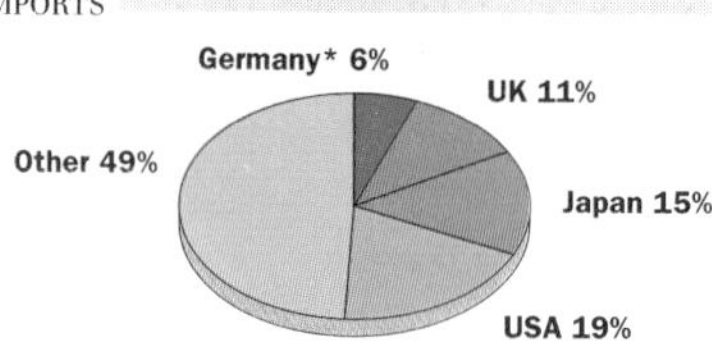

Strengths

Vast oil and gas reserves. World-class associated industries. Accumulated surpluses and steady current income. Large income from two million annual pilgrims to Mecca.

Weaknesses

Lack of skilled workers. Food production requires heavy subsidy. Most consumer items and industrial raw materials imported.

Profile

Since the 1970s, strenuous efforts have been made to shift the economy away from its dependence on oil exports and to provide employment for young Saudis. While most investment in oil is from the government, Saudi entrepreneurs have become more involved in secondary industries. Saudi financial markets are poorly developed, however, due to religious inhibitions about paying or receiving interest. Saudi Aramco, the Middle East's largest employer, controls the national oil industry and has ambitious plans for new exploration. Large sums have been spent on giving Saudi Arabia a US-standard infrastructure, with the aim of providing the basis for a manufacturing economy. The economy, however, remains dependent on foreign workers.

ECONOMIC PERFORMANCE INDICATOR

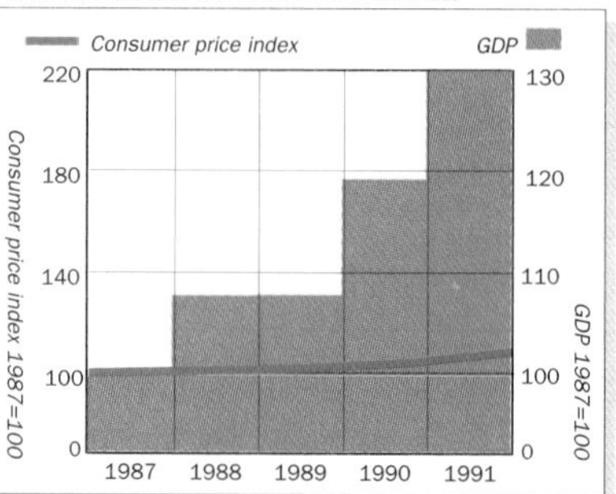

SAUDI ARABIA : MAJOR BUSINESSES

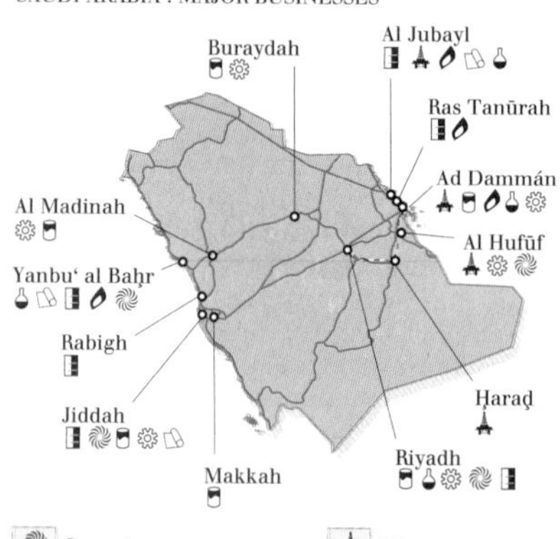

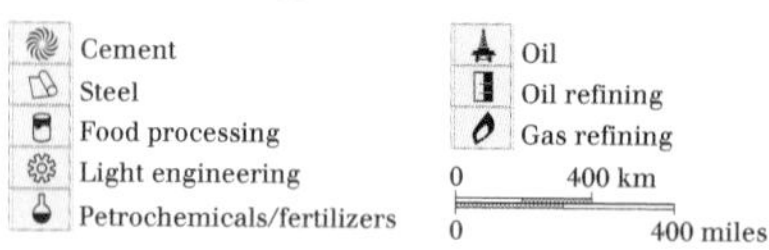

RESOURCES

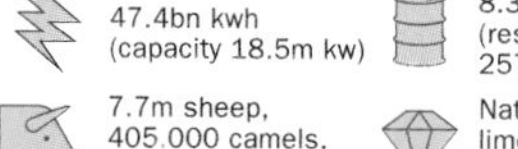

47.4bn kwh (capacity 18.5m kw)

8.38m b/d (reserves 257,842,000,000 bbl)

7.7m sheep, 405,000 camels, 250,000 cattle

Natural gas, limestone, gypsum, marble, clay, salt

ELECTRICITY GENERATION

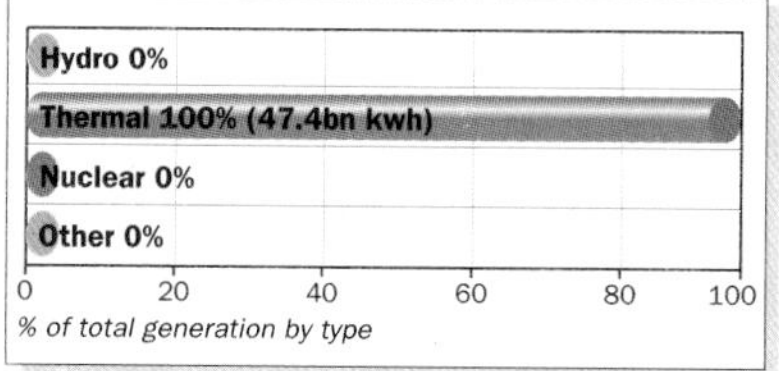

Home to the world's biggest oil and gas reserves, Saudi Arabia plays a key role in the global economy and is among the top ten traders of all the world's major industrialized nations.

SAUDI ARABIA : LAND USE

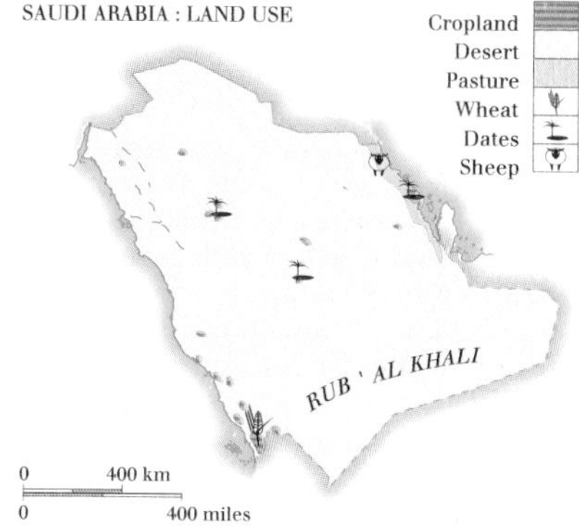

ENVIRONMENT

9% partially protected

Little environmental legislation

ENVIRONMENTAL TREATIES

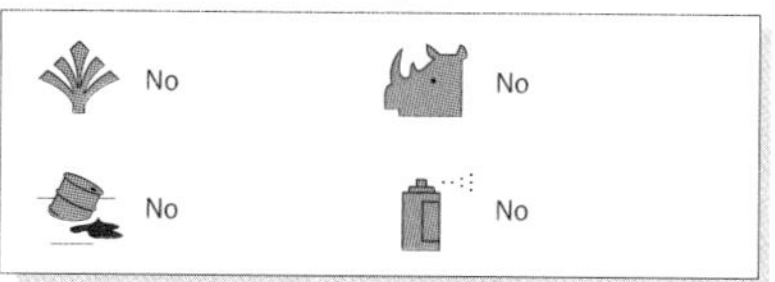

Pollution in the Gulf and Red Sea has threatened some wildlife and their habitats, as have hunters using high-velocity rifles and off-road vehicles. The government has taken steps to confine manufacturing to industrial estates. Environmental legislation is, nevertheless, poorly developed, although planning controls apply in the major cities.

MEDIA

Control of the media is achieved through the Ministry of Information, which controls the national news agency and the broadcasting services

PUBLISHING AND BROADCAST MEDIA

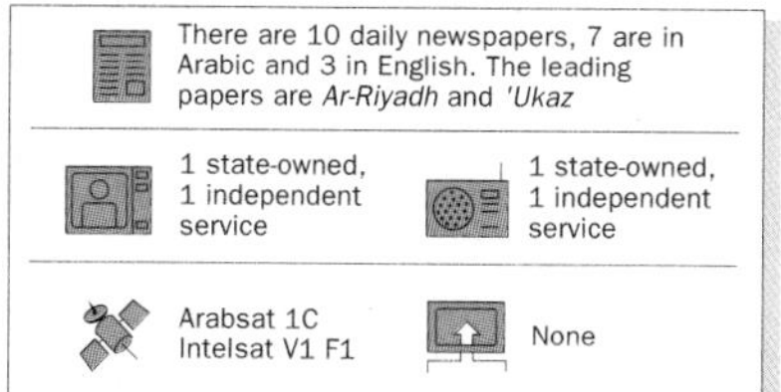

There are 10 daily newspapers, 7 are in Arabic and 3 in English. The leading papers are *Ar-Riyadh* and *'Ukaz*
1 state-owned, 1 independent service
1 state-owned, 1 independent service
Arabsat 1C Intelsat V1 F1
None

The government imposes total censorship and insists on strict morality in the Saudi press. In 1994, private citizens were banned from owning satellite dishes, reflecting the state's wish to keep CNN out of Saudi homes. Saudi publishers play a leading role in the Arabic media, however. *Sharq Al Awsat* (The Middle East), published in Saudi Arabia is considered one of the leading Arabic dailies. Saudi investors have bought the influential press agency United Press International.

CRIME

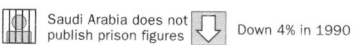

Saudi Arabia does not publish prison figures

Down 4% in 1990

CRIME RATES

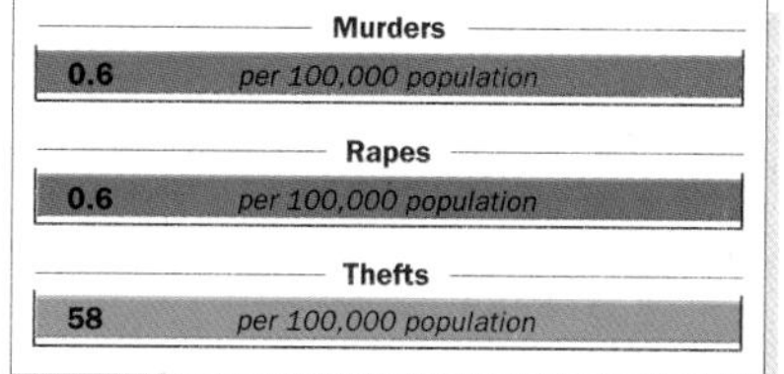

Strict Islamic punishments – stoning for adultery, amputation for stealing and beheading for murder – deter crime. Amnesty International has condemned the high number of public executions.

EDUCATION

62%

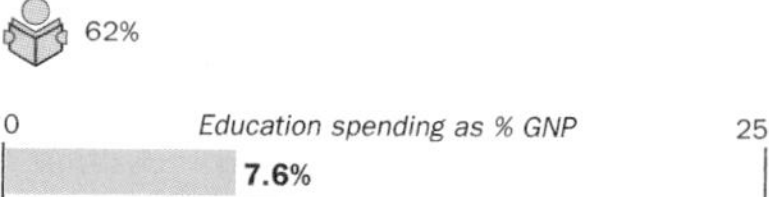

THE EDUCATION SYSTEM

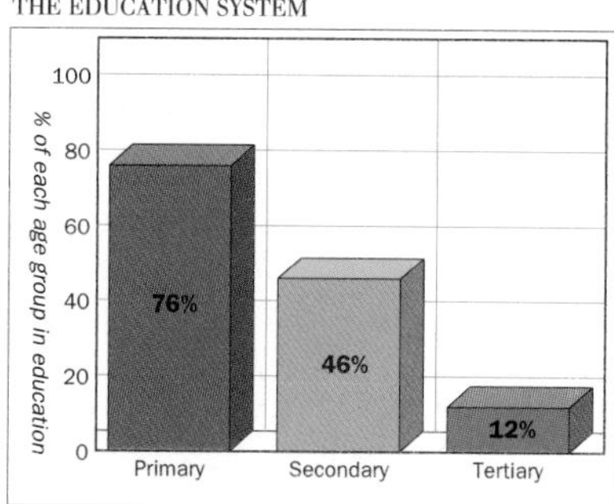

In the 1950s, the then Crown Prince Faisal persuaded the religious establishment to give women equal opportunities in education. Much government money has gone into higher education and Islamic universities, though many Saudis still travel abroad to complete their studies.

HEALTH

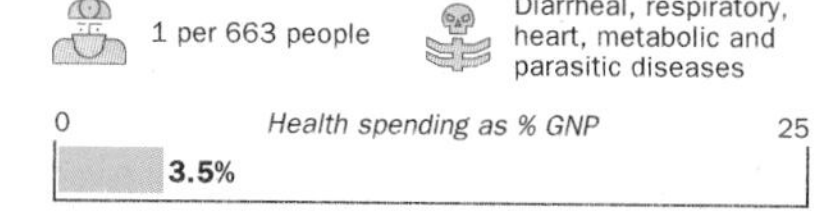

0 *Health spending as % GNP* 25

3.5%

In the 1970s, resources were committed to building a network of modern hospitals at the expense of primary health care. Large sums have been spent on Western expertise. The private sector has also been encouraged. Many Saudis are still sent overseas for treatment by the government, especially for transplant operations, which pose some ethical problems for religious leaders.

WEALTH

Top US surgeon (on contract), 267,023 Saudi riyals per year

CONSUMER GOODS OWNERSHIP

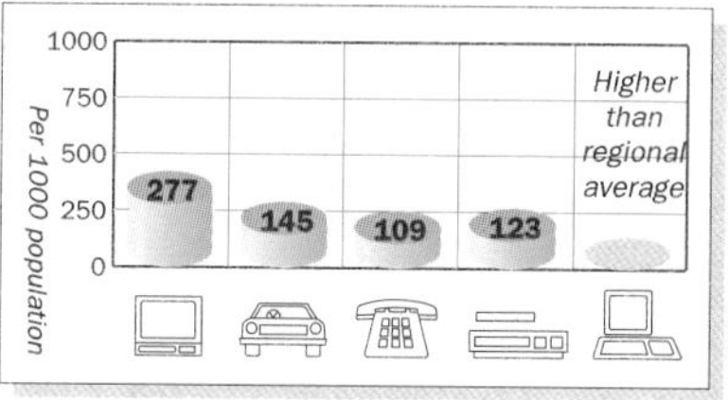

Saudi citizens are among the most prosperous in the world. The Al-Sa'uds have used their wealth to create a cradle-to-grave welfare system. Ownership of TVs, telephones and VCRs is among the world's highest. The distribution of wealth is carefully controlled by the royal family through the *majlis* system. Petitioners attend weekly assemblies held by prominent royals and beg favors, which are usually granted. There is no stock market, although shares in public companies are traded privately. Many Saudis refuse to accept interest on deposits with banks, but Islamic banks offer profit-sharing investment plans as an alternative.

WORLD RANKING

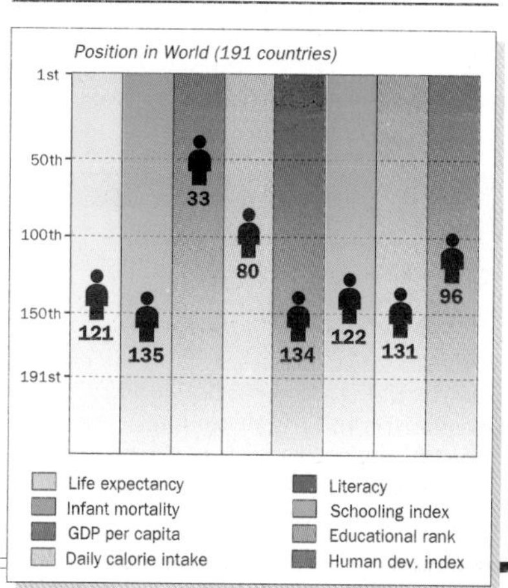

S

SENEGAL

OFFICIAL NAME: Republic of Senegal **CAPITAL:** Dakar
POPULATION: 7.7 million **CURRENCY:** CFA franc **OFFICIAL LANGUAGE:** French

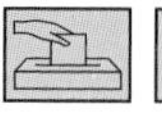

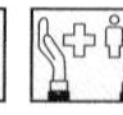

SENEGAL'S CAPITAL, Dakar, lies on the westernmost cape of Africa. The country is mostly low, with open savanna and semi-desert in the north and thicker savanna in the south. After independence from France in 1960, Senegal was ruled for 20 years by its first president, Léopold Senghor, who maintained a system of virtual single-party rule. Full multipartyism was introduced in the 1980s. Fishing and tourism are important industries.

CLIMATE

WEATHER CHART

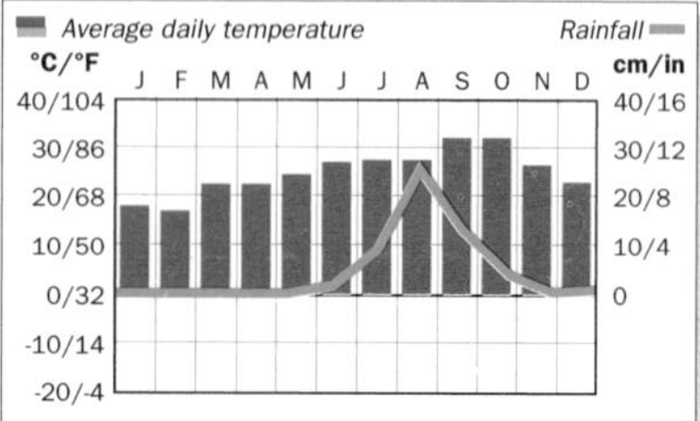

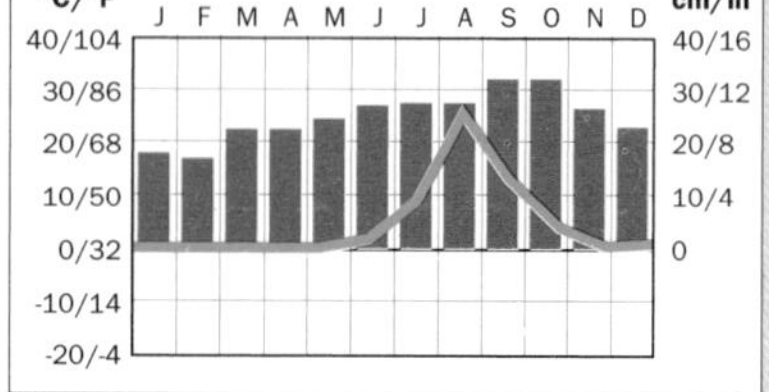

The coastal regions, which project into the path of the northern trade winds, are remarkably cool given their latitude.

COMMUNICATIONS

Dakar-Yoff Intl
772,719 passengers

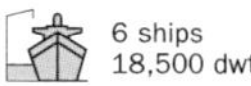

6 ships
18,500 dwt

THE TRANSPORTATION NETWORK

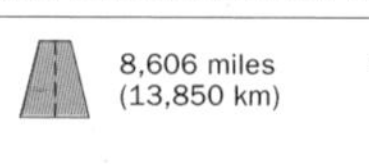

8,606 miles (13,850 km)

None

737 miles (1,186 km)

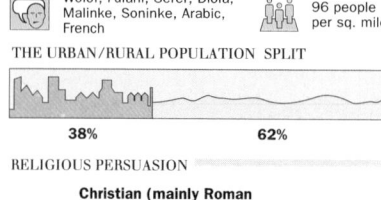

559 miles (900 km)

Dakar is too large a port for Senegal alone. It also serves the hinterland of Mali, southern Mauritania and Guinea. The key rail link to Bamako, Mali's capital, was built in the 1920s.

TOURISM

233,512 visitors

Down 5% in 1991

MAIN OVERSEAS ARRIVALS

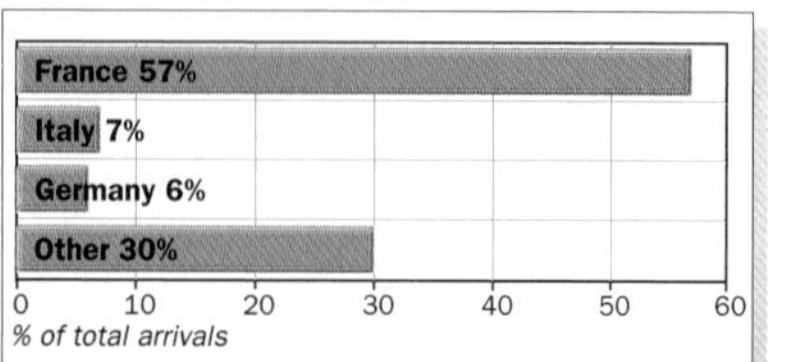

In addition to French package tours to coastal resorts, tours for African-Americans to Gorce, an old slave island, are increasing.

PEOPLE

Wolof, Fulani, Serer, Diola, Malinke, Soninke, Arabic, French

96 people per sq. mile

THE URBAN/RURAL POPULATION SPLIT

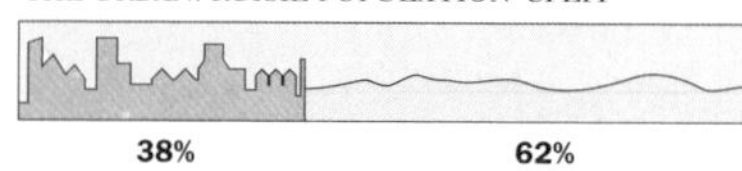

RELIGIOUS PERSUASION

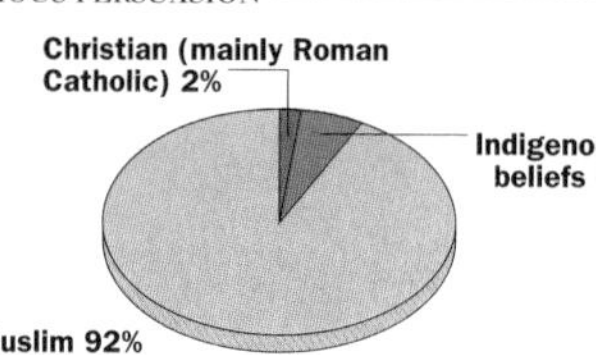

Senegal has a fairly well-developed sense of nationhood, and intermarriage between groups has reduced ethnic tensions. Groups can still be identified regionally, however. Dakar is a Wolof area, the Senegal River is dominated by the Toucouleur, the Malinke mostly live in the east, and the Diola in Casamance. The Diola have felt excluded from the political process, and this has led to unrest in Casamance. A French-influenced class system is still prevalent and has become increasingly apparent in recent years.

POLITICS

1998

President Abdou Diouf

THE STATE OF THE PARTIES

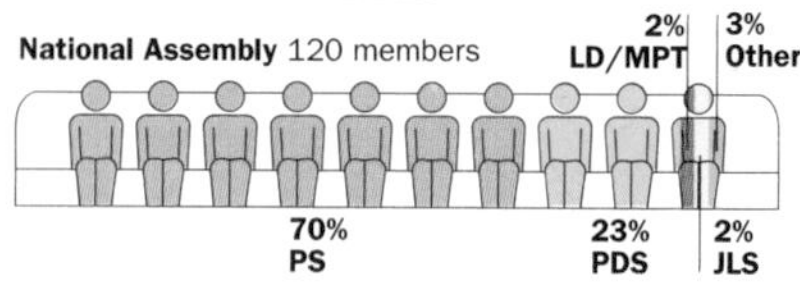

PS = Senegalese Socialist Party **PDS** = Senegalese Democratic Party **LD/MPT** = Democratic League/ Movement for the Labor Party **JLS** = "Let Us Unite" coalition **Other** = Independence and Labor Party, Senegalese Democratic Union – Renovation

Senegal is a multiparty democracy and freedom of association is respected. However, the PS has been in power since the 1950s, albeit under different names, and has spread its influence deep into the civil service, judiciary and local government, making opposition difficult. The main issue is the economy; the collapse of the AOF hit Senegal hard as it lost important markets, especially for Dakar's port. Other problems include the separatist movement in anti-Islamic Casamance, and discontent in the northeast, where drought and refugees from Mauritania are leading to tension.

WORLD AFFAIRS

Senegal's most important relationship is with France, which provides high levels of aid; whether these will be maintained is Senegal's major concern. Relations with Mauritania have improved since tension was caused by the expulsion of 200,000 Mauritanians in 1989. A border dispute with Guinea-Bissau remains unresolved. Relations with the USA are good.

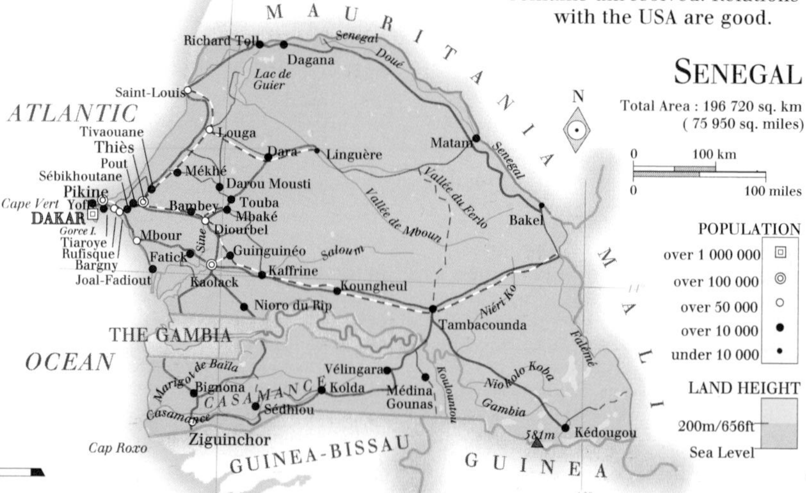

AID

 $577m (receipts)  Down 27% in 1991

Senegal is one of the highest recipients of aid per capita in Africa, mostly from France, the EU and the World Bank. Aid receipts are used to import 400,000 tons of rice annually, but are also absorbed in administration costs, helping to finance the sizeable civil service. Senegal has given small aid donations to African liberation movements, including the ANC.

***The mosque in Touba,** religious capital of the Muslim Mouride sect, which was founded in 1887 in Senegal's groundnut-growing district.*

CHRONOLOGY

France colonized Senegal, a major entrepôt from the 15th century, in 1890. Dakar was the capital of French West Africa.

- ❑ **1885** Gambia split off as British enclave within Senegal.
- ❑ **1960** Independence under socialist president Léopold Sédar Senghor.
- ❑ **1966** One-party state.
- ❑ **1976** Three-party system.
- ❑ **1981** Abdou Diouf president. Full multiparty politics restored.

DEFENSE

 $154.5m  Up 38% in 1991

Senegal receives protection from France, which maintains an important naval base at Dakar. By African standards the defense budget is small, and the army is not heavily involved in politics – Senegal has never had a coup. Senegal sent troops to Operation Desert Storm in 1991. Preventing assistance from Guinea-Bissau to Casamance separatists is the main current concern.

ECONOMICS

 $6.2bn  295.23 CFA francs

SCORE CARD

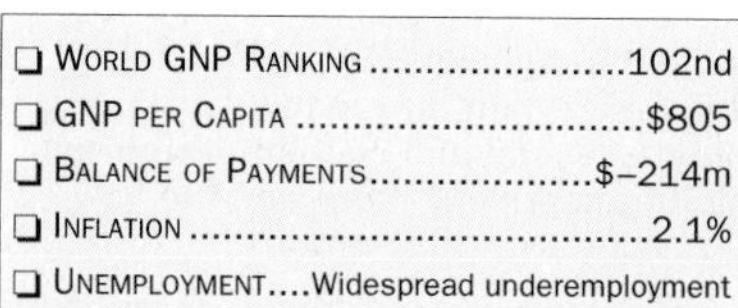

❑ WORLD GNP RANKING	102nd
❑ GNP PER CAPITA	$805
❑ BALANCE OF PAYMENTS	$-214m
❑ INFLATION	2.1%
❑ UNEMPLOYMENT	Widespread underemployment

STRENGTHS

Skilled work force is highly educated and motivated. Dakar port linked to the interior by good French-built infrastructure. Also a conference venue.

WEAKNESSES

Few natural resources are exploited, other than groundnuts, phosphates and fish. The Gambia River remains unbridged, making access to the oil-rich Casamance region difficult.

EXPORTS

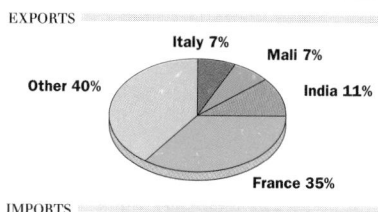

Italy 7%
Mali 7%
India 11%
France 35%
Other 40%

IMPORTS

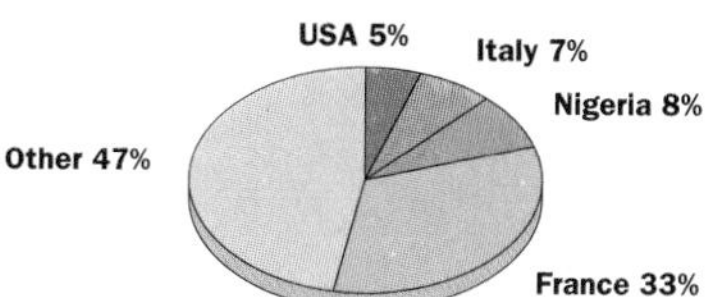

EDUCATION

 38%

Illiteracy is the major challenge faced by the system. There are two universities – at Dakar and St.-Louis.

HEALTH

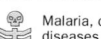

 1 per 16,909 people; Malaria, diarrheal diseases

Senegal's state health system is rudimentary. Rich Senegalese are well served by private clinics.

WEALTH

 Most Senegalese lead a subsistence existence

CONSUMER GOODS OWNERSHIP

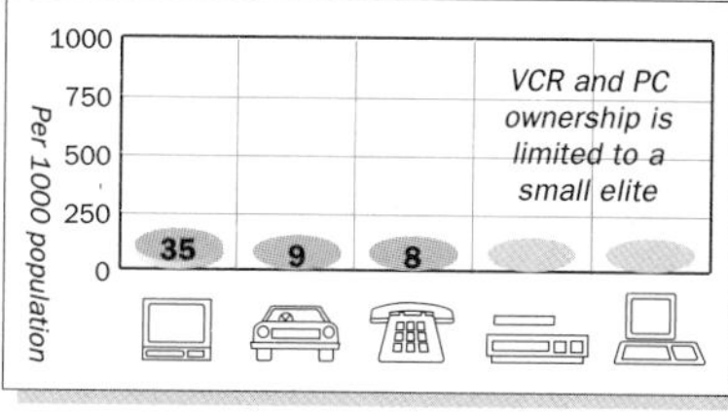

Wealth disparities are considerable and poverty widespread. Those close to the government are the wealthiest group.

RESOURCES

 684m kwh (capacity 231,000 kw)

 Not an oil producer; refines 22,600 b/cd

3.9m sheep, 2.7m cattle, 490,000 pigs

 Phosphates, bauxite, salt, natural gas, marble, iron, copper

Senegal's electricity capacity is largely dependent on imported fuel; cheaper supplies are expected to become available soon from the Manantali dam in Mali. Initial explorations suggest oil reserves may exist off Casamance.

MEDIA

Opposition parties have limited access to the TV station. Together they are permitted 50% of viewing time; the rest goes to the ruling party

PUBLISHING AND BROADCAST MEDIA

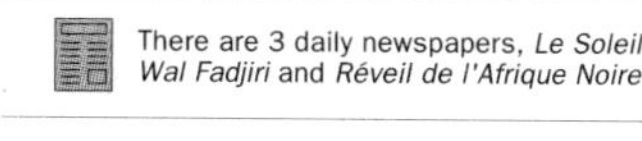

There are 3 daily newspapers, *Le Soleil*, *Wal Fadjiri* and *Réveil de l'Afrique Noire*

1 state-owned service

1 state-owned service

The independent media flourished with multiparty politics. Senegal had the first satirical journal in Africa with the founding of *Le Politicien* in 1978.

ENVIRONMENT

 11% (6% partially protected); Damming of the Senegal River

The damming of the Senegal River has caused concern that traditional farming practices, which rely on seasonal floods, may be disrupted. Two major droughts in 1973 and 1983 led to the advance of the Sahara Desert in the west of the country.

CRIME

 Senegal does not publish prison figures  Down 42% in 1990

Senegal has comparatively low crime rates, although levels are on the increase in Dakar and the surrounding shantytowns, where gangs are based.

WORLD RANKING

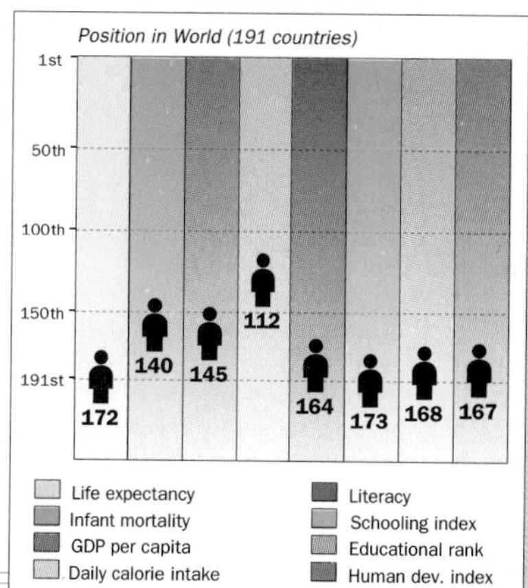

S

SEYCHELLES

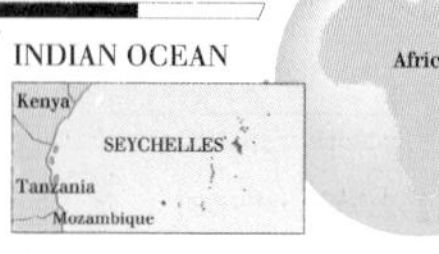

OFFICIAL NAME: Republic of the Seychelles **CAPITAL:** Victoria
POPULATION: 68,000 **CURRENCY:** Seychelles rupee **OFFICIAL LANGUAGE:** Creole

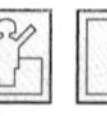

COMPRISING 115 ISLANDS in the Indian Ocean, the Seychelles support unique flora and fauna, including the giant tortoise and the world's largest seed, the *coco-de-mer*. Formerly a UK colony and then under one-party rule, the Seychelles became a multiparty democracy in 1993. The economy is reliant on tourism.

POLITICS

1998

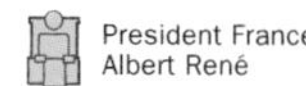
President France Albert René

THE STATE OF THE PARTIES

National Assembly 33 members

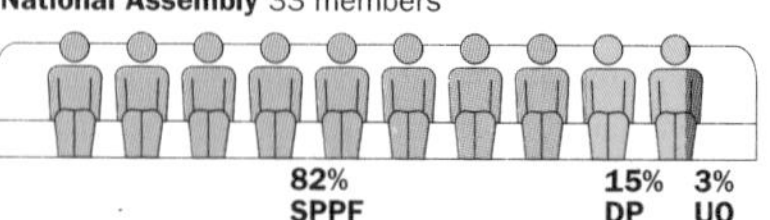

SPPF = Seychelles People's Progressive Front
DP = Democratic Party **UO** = United Opposition

In 1993, the Seychelles returned to multiparty democracy after 16 years of one-party socialist rule under President René. As prime minister, he had seized complete power in a coup just one year after independence. Divisions within the opposition in the 1993 elections resulted in René being confirmed as president. His old party, renamed the SPPF, received the majority vote. In a major change of ideology and policy, the government has made wide-ranging social and economic reforms, including privatizations and the legalization of trade unions.

WORLD AFFAIRS

OAU | Comm

The Seychelles has pursued a non-aligned policy. However, its strategic location has encouraged competing world powers to seek its friendship. Trade accords exist with other Indian Ocean states.

CLIMATE

WEATHER CHART

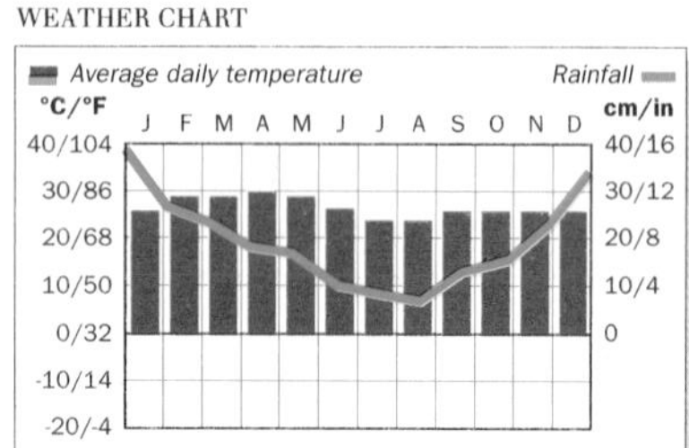

The islands have a tropical oceanic climate, with only small temperature variations.

COMMUNICATIONS

Seychelles Intl, Mahé
155,000 passengers

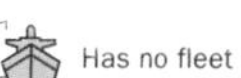
Has no fleet

THE TRANSPORTATION NETWORK

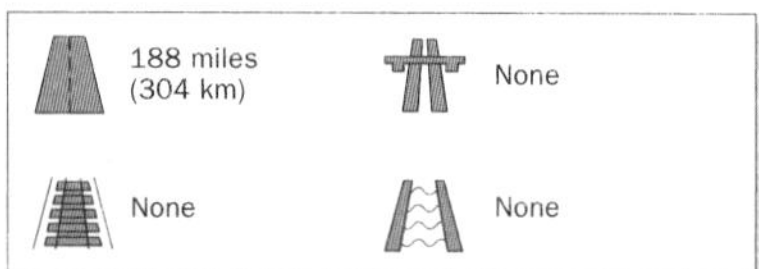

The current focus is on building airstrips – nine islands now have them, improving roads on tourist islands and renewing the public transportation fleet.

TOURISM

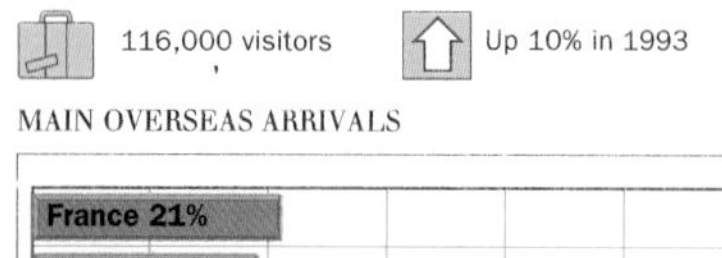
116,000 visitors

Up 10% in 1993

MAIN OVERSEAS ARRIVALS

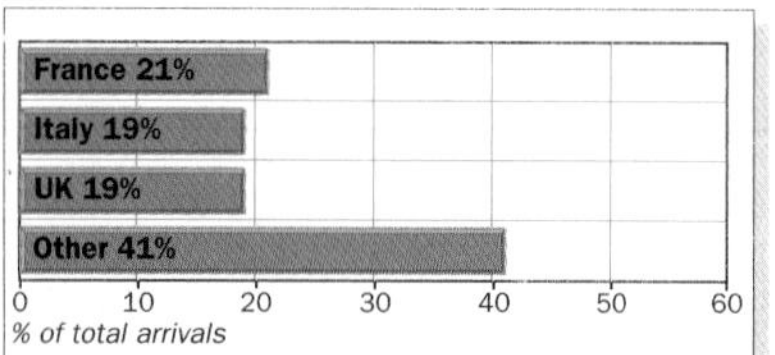

The opening of an international airport on Mahé in 1971 has made tourism the mainstay of the economy. New hotels are now being built with private foreign investment, but development must comply with strict laws to protect the islands' beauty and unique wildlife.

PEOPLE

French Creole, English, French

389 people per sq. mile

THE URBAN/RURAL POPULATION SPLIT

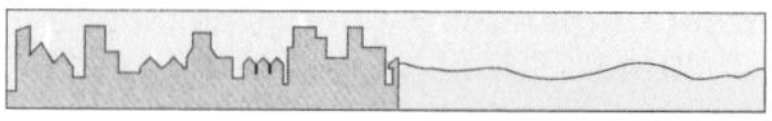

52% 48%

RELIGIOUS PERSUASION

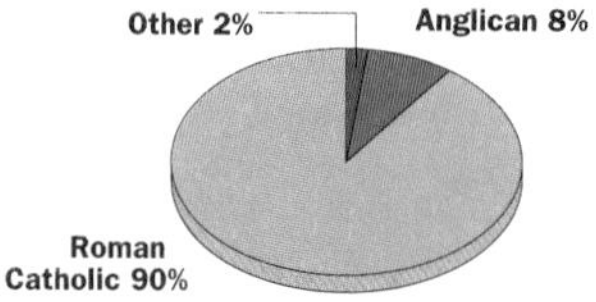

Other 2%
Anglican 8%
Roman Catholic 90%

The Seychelles were uninhabited before French settlers arrived in the 1770s. Today, the population is markedly homogeneous, as a result of intermarriage between different ethnic groups. The Creoles are the descendants of the French settlers and the Africans who were settled in the islands by subsequent British administrators.

There are small Chinese and Indian minorities. Almost 90% of Seychellois live on Mahé. Population growth has been very low, as about 1,000 people a year have been emigrating. The new democracy may reverse this trend.

SEYCHELLES

Total Area : 280 sq. km (108 sq. miles)

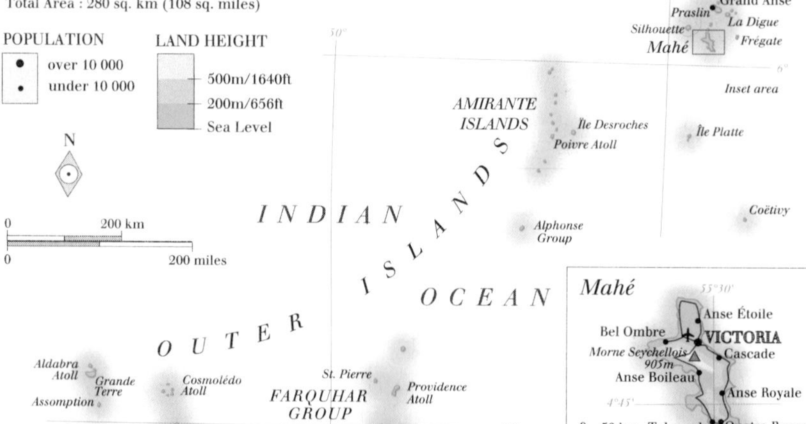

AID

 $20m (receipts)  Down 43% in 1991

There is growing support for development projects from multilateral agencies, notably the EU and the Arab Development Fund. Bilateral aid, which used to be the main type of assistance, comes mostly from France and the USA. The UK, Australia and Japan are also sizeable donors.

DEFENSE

 $15.92m  Up 28% in 1991

Seychelles has a 1,100-strong army, and a paramilitary guard of almost equal size. The latter includes a small coast guard made up of air and sea forces. The army, set up in 1977, was initially trained by Tanzania, and Tanzanian troops were brought in for three years after a coup attempt in 1981. North Korea provided advisors until 1989.

ECONOMICS

 $380m 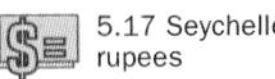 5.17 Seychelles rupees

SCORE CARD

- ❑ WORLD GNP RANKING........................167th
- ❑ GNP PER CAPITA $5,588
- ❑ BALANCE OF PAYMENTS $34.6m
- ❑ INFLATION 3.3%
- ❑ UNEMPLOYMENT....................................9%

STRENGTHS

Tourism. Fishing, especially shrimp, and tuna: the latter is canned for export. Profitable re-export trade. Copra. Cinnamon. Tea.

WEAKNESSES

Growing trade and budget deficits in 1990s due to drop in tourism following 1991 Gulf War, spending on hosting 1993 Indian Ocean Games and costs of four recent elections. High debt servicing costs. Reliance on food imports, especially for tourist industry. Copra production declining. Significant reliance on expatriate labor.

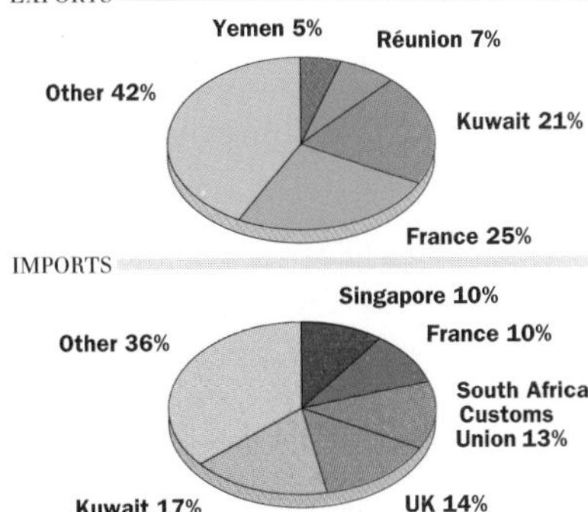

One of the 40 central islands. These are mostly mountainous, with lush vegetation, and are the only granitic islands in the world.

RESOURCES

 85m kwh (capacity 22,000 kw)  Not an oil producer and has no refineries

15,000 pigs, 2,000 cattle  Guano, salt, granite, natural gas

The Seychelles has virtually no mineral resources. All mineral fuel is imported. It is used to generate the power on the three islands that have an electricity supply system. Natural gas finds have spurred oil exploration.

ENVIRONMENT

 95%   Strict state controls to conserve land and marine ecosystems

The Seychelles has been praised for its commitment to conservation. It is the sole country to possess two natural World Heritage sites.

MEDIA

 Freedom of expression has been permitted since 1992

PUBLISHING AND BROADCAST MEDIA

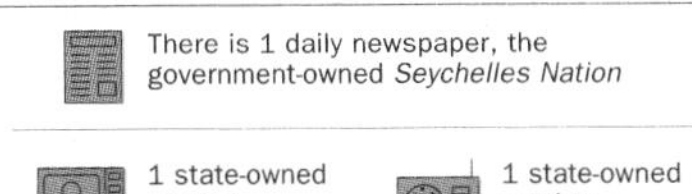

There is 1 daily newspaper, the government-owned *Seychelles Nation*
1 state-owned service
1 state-owned service

The state broadcasting company has been reorganized and is now ostensibly free of government control. Private periodicals are now permitted.

CRIME

 1,060 prisoners  Up 4% in 1990

Violent crime is rare in the Seychelles. The main concern is the increasing rate of petty theft.

EDUCATION

 57%

Private schools have been allowed since 1993. National Youth Service has been reduced from two years to one, but is still mandatory for entry to higher education.

CHRONOLOGY

The French claimed the islands in 1756. French-British rivalry for control ended when France ceded them to the UK in 1815.

- ❑ **1952** Political parties formed, led by F. A. René (pro-independence) and James Mancham (pro-UK rule).
- ❑ **1965** UK returns Desroches, Aldabra and Farquhar islands, which are leased to USA to 1976.
- ❑ **1976** Independence. Coalition with Mancham president, René premier. US tracking station set up on Mahé.
- ❑ **1977** René takes over in coup.
- ❑ **1979** One-party socialist state.
- ❑ **1979–1987** Several coup attempts.
- ❑ **1992** Politicians in exile return.
- ❑ **1993** Democratic elections.

HEALTH

 1 per 1,404 people  Heart and cerebrovascular diseases, cancer

State health care is free. Private medicine is to be allowed for the first time under the government's new social legislation.

WEALTH

 Plantation worker, 9 Seychelles rupees per month; dentist, 23 Seychelles rupees per month

CONSUMER GOODS OWNERSHIP

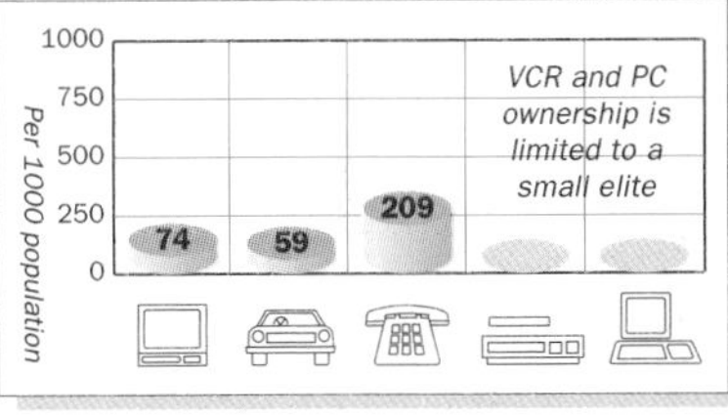

Living standards are the highest among OAU nations. There are no slums and the welfare system caters to all.

WORLD RANKING

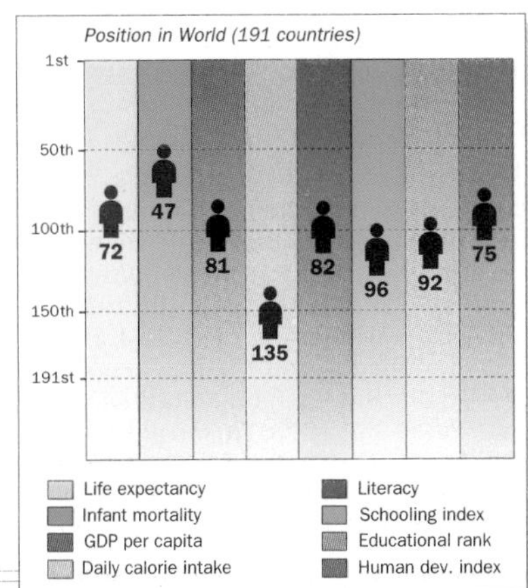

S

SIERRA LEONE

WEST AFRICA
Guinea
SIERRA LEONE
Ivory Coast
Liberia
Africa

OFFICIAL NAME: Republic of Sierra Leone **CAPITAL:** Freetown
POPULATION: 4.4 million **CURRENCY:** Leone **OFFICIAL LANGUAGE:** English

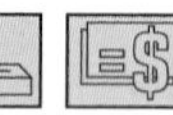

THE WEST AFRICAN STATE of Sierra Leone was first colonized by the British in 1787 as a settlement for Africans freed from slavery. Bordered by Guinea and Liberia, its terrain rises from flat, coastal lowlands to mountains in the northeast. The military government that seized power in 1992 promised, but has yet to deliver, a swift return to civilian rule. One of the world's poorest countries, Sierra Leone's main export is diamonds.

CLIMATE

WEATHER CHART

Average daily temperature / Rainfall
°C/°F — cm/in
J F M A M J J A S O N D
Left axis: 0/32, 10/50, 20/68, 30/86, 40/104, 50/122, 60/140
Right axis: 0, 10/4, 20/8, 30/12, 40/16, 50/20, 60/24, 70/28, 80/31, 90/35

Rainfall on the coast can be as high as 195 in. a year, making Sierra Leone one of the wettest places in coastal West Africa. Humidity is consistently high – about 80% – during the rainy season. The dusty, northeasterly *harmattan* wind often blows during the hotter dry season from November to April. The northeastern savannas are drier, with 74–98 in. of rain a year, but are one of the hottest areas.

COMMUNICATIONS

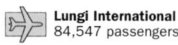

Lungi International 84,547 passengers

6 ships 4,500 dwt

THE TRANSPORTATION NETWORK

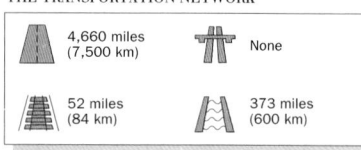

4,660 miles (7,500 km)	None
52 miles (84 km)	373 miles (600 km)

Little progress has been made in improving Sierra Leone's roads. The 186-mile narrow-gauge railroad was abandoned in 1971 as uneconomic, although 52 miles of track still run to the closed iron ore mines at Marampa. Having failed in 1987, Sierra Leone's national airline resumed flights – to Paris only – in 1991. The airport is across the estuary from the capital. The only link between the two is a limited ferry service.

TOURISM

89,334 visitors

Down 7% in 1992

MAIN OVERSEAS ARRIVALS

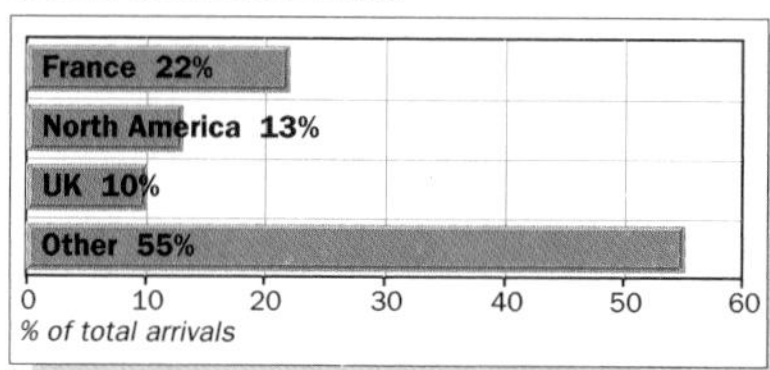
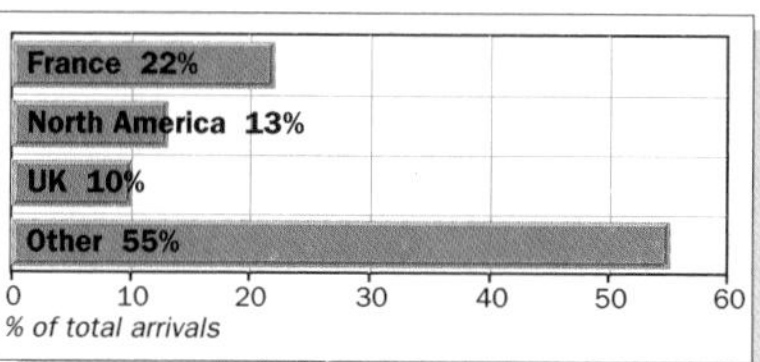

Sierra Leone attracts few tourists, apart from occasional cruise-ship calls. Internal turmoil and instability mean that plans to develop tourism cannot progress at the moment. Among the top potential attractions are the beaches along the Freetown peninsula, which are virtually undeveloped.

PEOPLE

Mende, Temne, Krio, English

153 people per sq. mile

THE URBAN/RURAL POPULATION SPLIT

32% 68%

ETHNIC MAKEUP

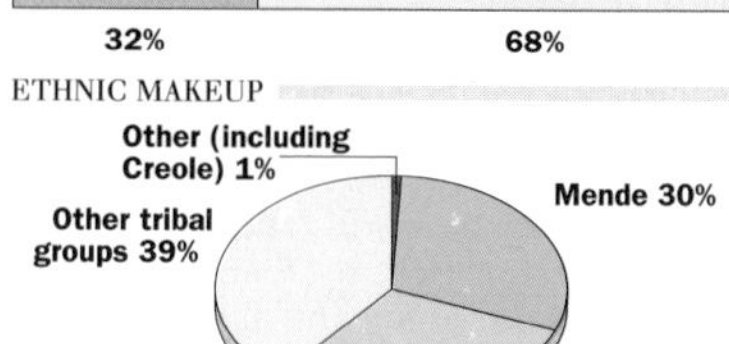

Freetown, as its name suggests, was founded as a settlement for people freed from slavery. Its citizens' British and North American origins account for Sierra Leone's strongly anglicized Creole culture. Ethnic groups gained political control in 1951.

POLITICS

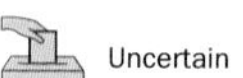

Uncertain

Capt. Valentine Strasser

THE STATE OF THE PARTIES

House of Representatives

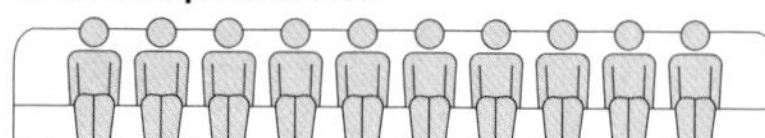

The legislature was dissolved following a coup in April 1992

The role of government is largely limited to maintaining the military and police. Its energy is now focused on suppressing rebel activity by Liberian troops who entered the country in 1991, and Sierra Leonean rebels who have since joined them. The army chief, General Momoh, succeeded President Siaka Stevens on his retirement in 1985 and made moves to end Stevens' one-party system. However, a coup of junior army officers led by Captain Valentine Strasser halted the process. Strasser promised, but has yet to deliver, an early return to civilian rule.

SIERRA LEONE

Total Area : 71 740 sq. km (27 699 sq. miles)

LAND HEIGHT
1000m/3281ft
500m/1640ft
200m/656ft
Sea Level

POPULATION
over 100 000
over 10 000
under 10 000

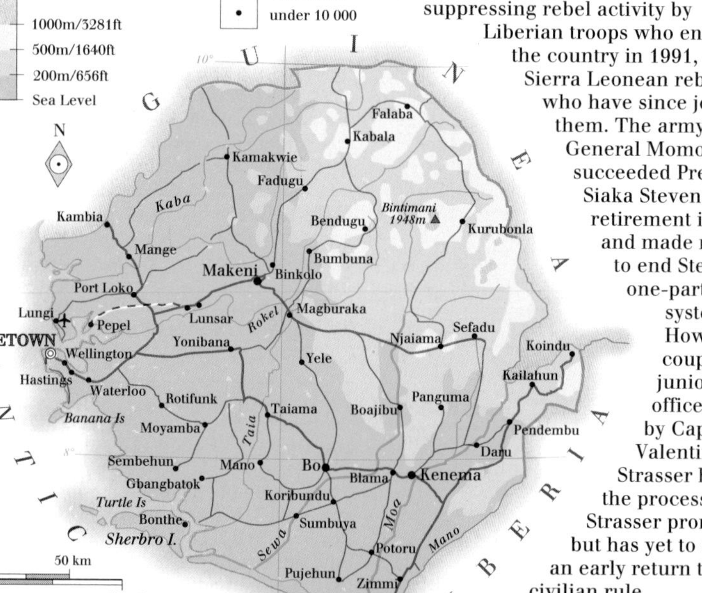

S

WORLD AFFAIRS

Ecowas | Comm | OAU | GATT | NAM

The main concern is that the civil war in neighboring Liberia will create increasing instability in Sierra Leone.

AID

 $105m (receipts)

 Up 62% in 1991

Sierra Leone has not been able to fulfill the terms of the aid package agreed with the IMF in 1989. Instead, funds have been diverted to cope with refugees from Liberia, internal migrants fleeing the rebellion in the southeast, and the near collapse of public services.

DEFENSE

 $5.15m

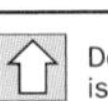 Defense spending is rising

After its last intervention in politics in 1968, the army resumed a central role in the 1992 coup. It has little credibility, however, as a fighting force.

ECONOMICS

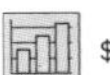 $625m

 549.07 leones

SCORE CARD

- ❑ World GNP Ranking 161st
- ❑ GNP per Capita $145
- ❑ Balance of Payments .... $-95m
- ❑ Inflation 80.8%
- ❑ Unemployment .... Endemic

Strengths
Diamonds, although much of the output is smuggled out. Some bauxite and rutile production.

Weaknesses
Inefficient government, which has proposed a tax on imports by overseas charities working in Sierra Leone. Rebel fighting affects the most productive areas of the country, including diamond fields.

EXPORTS

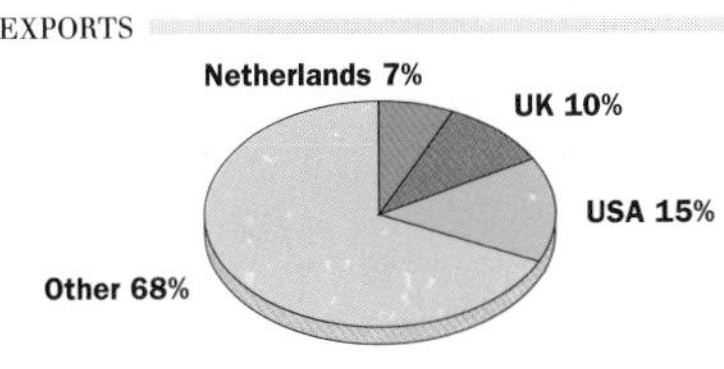

IMPORTS

Netherlands 9%
USA 10%
Germany* 10%
UK 13%
Other 58%

RESOURCES

 224m kwh (capacity 130,000 kw)

 Not an oil producer; refines 10,000 b/cd

 330,000 cattle, 330,000 sheep, 50,000 pigs

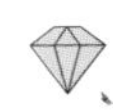 Diamonds, rutile, bauxite, gold, titanium

The large diamond deposits need fresh investment, as areas currently being mined are becoming depleted. The southeast is the most fertile region.

ENVIRONMENT

 1% partially protected

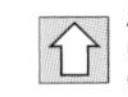 Attempt to establish university conservation course

Strain is being placed on the land and on other natural resources to support the growing population.

MEDIA

 Close government supervision of media. Journalists sometimes imprisoned

PUBLISHING AND BROADCAST MEDIA

 There are no daily newspapers. The *New Breed*, published by the government, has the largest circulation of the 11 weeklies

 1 state-owned service

 1 state-owned service

Freetown's Creole population is well served by the broad range of periodicals published there. The 1992 coup curbed rising press freedom.

CRIME

 Sierra Leone does not publish prison figures

 Crime is rising

Illegal diamond mining and smuggling is one of the most lucrative crimes, in which several government members have been implicated. Sierra Leoneans do not have confidence in the legal system. In December 1992, 26 people were executed for allegedly planning a coup, despite the fact that some were in jail at the time.

EDUCATION

 21%

Freetown has a long tradition of education and its university, Fourahbay College, became affiliated with Durham University in the UK in 1876. In recent times, its students have often been active in political dissent. Educational provision has deteriorated with the economic situation over the last decade.

HEALTH

1 per 13,153 people

 Communicable diseases, malaria, malnutrition, childbirth

Only traditional health care is available outside the capital. Average life expectancy is 41.5 years; only three other countries share such a low figure.

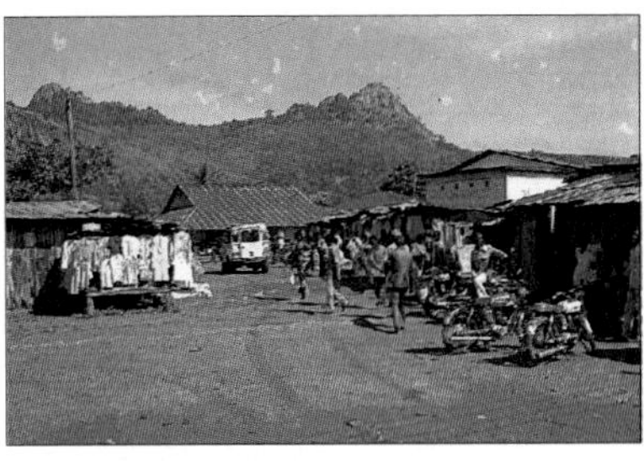

The main street, Kabala. *In 1993, Sierra Leone was second from bottom of the UN's Human Development Index.*

CHRONOLOGY

Freetown was founded in 1787 and became a British colony in 1808; the interior was annexed in 1896.

- ❑ **1961** Independence.
- ❑ **1968** Siaka Stevens prime minister.
- ❑ **1978** Single-party republic under Stevens. National bankruptcy.
- ❑ **1991** Liberian rebels invade Sierra Leone in protest at its participation in ECOWAS force in Liberia. Sierra Leonean rebels join the fighting.
- ❑ **1992** Army coup installs Captain Strasser. Executions after alleged counter-coup widely criticized.

WEALTH

 Most Sierra Leoneans lead a subsistence existence

CONSUMER GOODS OWNERSHIP

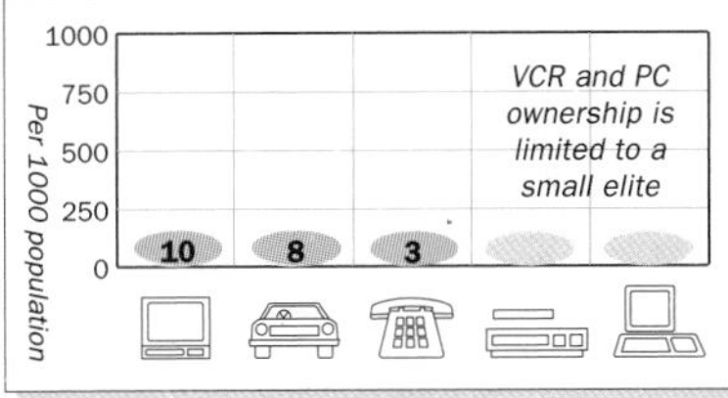

Most of the population is impoverished. Wealth is almost exclusively associated with political power and influence.

WORLD RANKING

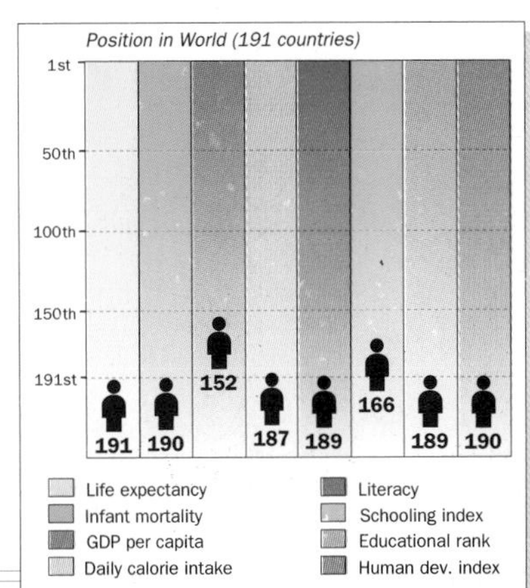

S

SOUTHEAST ASIA

Malaysia

SINGAPORE

SINGAPORE

OFFICIAL NAME: Republic of Singapore **CAPITAL:** Singapore City

POPULATION: 2.9 million **CURRENCY:** Singapore dollar **OFFICIAL LANGUAGES:** Malay, Chinese, Tamil and English

AN ISLAND STATE linked to the southernmost tip of the Malay peninsula by a causeway, Singapore was largely uninhabited between the 14th and 18th centuries. In 1819, an official of the British East India Company, Stamford Raffles, recognized the island's strategic position on key trade routes and established Singapore as a trading settlement. Today, Singapore is still one of the most important entrepôts in Asia.

CLIMATE

WEATHER CHART

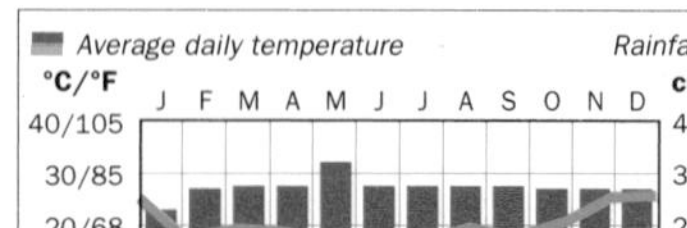

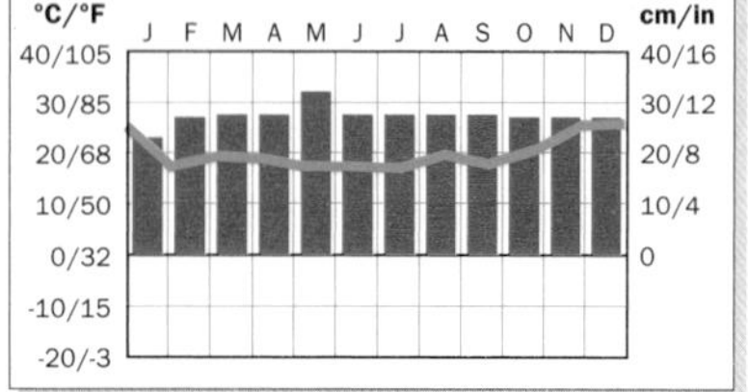

The only variations in the hot, wet and humid climate are the airless months of September and March, when the trade winds change direction.

COMMUNICATIONS

Changi International
1.49m passengers

600 ships
15.45m dwt

THE TRANSPORTATION NETWORK

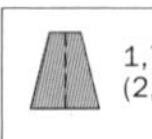

1,742 miles (2,810 km)

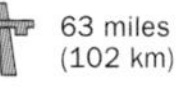

63 miles (102 km)

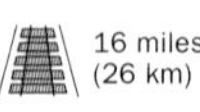

16 miles (26 km)

None

The Mass Rapid Transit System (subway), completed in 1991, is among the world's most efficient. Space for new roads has run out and monthly auctions are held to sell certificates entitling people to buy from a quota of new cars. The vast port at Pasir Panjang is being expanded on reclaimed land.

The financial center. *More than a quarter of Singapore's GDP is generated by financial and business services.*

TOURISM

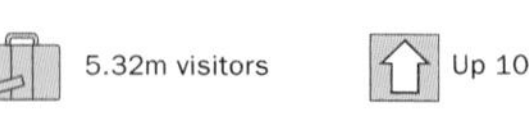

5.32m visitors

Up 10% in 1990

MAIN OVERSEAS ARRIVALS

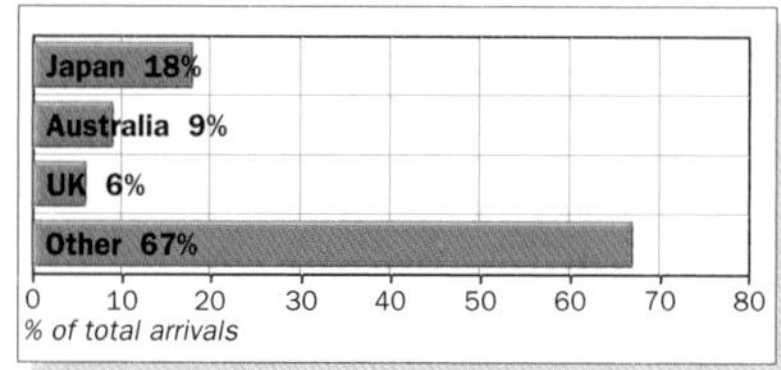

The Chinatown district is recognized as a picturesque tourist asset and its buildings are being restored. The other main attractions are shopping and golf; Singapore has one of the highest densities of golf courses in the world.

PEOPLE

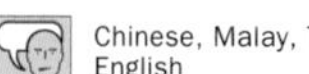

Chinese, Malay, Tamil, English

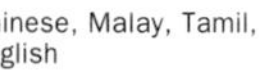

11,124 people per sq. mile

THE URBAN/RURAL POPULATION SPLIT

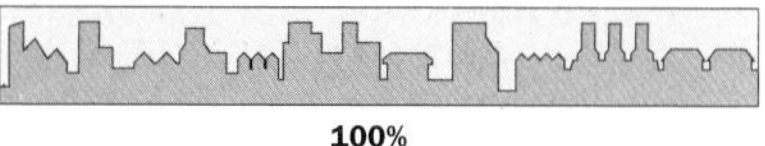

100%

ETHNIC MAKEUP

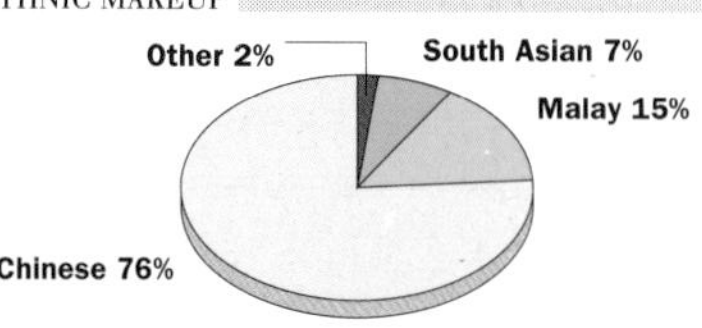

Singapore is dominated by the Chinese, who make up 76% of the community; the old English-speaking Straits Chinese and newer Mandarin-speakers are now well integrated. Indigenous Malays are generally the poorest group. Serious race riots erupted in the 1950s, but today there is little overt ethnic tension. There is a significant foreign workforce in Singapore; a recent labor shortage has forced the government to try to attract scientists from the CIS, Eastern Europe and Hong Kong. Society is highly regulated and government campaigns to improve public behavior are frequent.

POLITICS

1996

President Ong Teng Cheong

THE STATE OF THE PARTIES

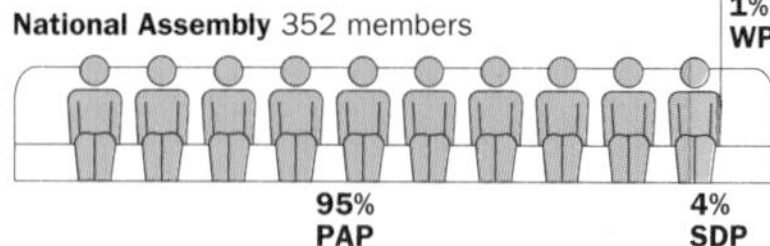

PAP = People's Action Party **SDP** = Singapore Democratic Party **WP** = Workers' Party

Singapore is a multiparty democracy, although the ruling People's Action Party (PAP) effectively controls all parts of the political process and much of the economy. Following a constitutional amendment in 1993, Ong Teng Cheong became the first president to be directly elected by the people of Singapore.

The government promotes the development of Singapore on the basis of a strong free-market economy, while continuing to place emphasis on social welfare. There are plans to create a national ideology ("shared values") based on Confucian traditions.

The PAP saw its share of the vote fall from 84% in 1968 to 61% in 1991, and there were signs that the party had lost support among the Chinese working class, its traditional backer. However, it is unlikely that the party, which has given Singaporeans one of the highest living standards in the world, will lose its grip on power.

WORLD AFFAIRS

Singapore has established diplomatic links with China, while continuing to maintain close economic ties with Taiwan. Relations with Indonesia were improved following the establishment of joint military training facilities.

AID

Singapore has no aid receipts or donations

Not applicable

Aid is simply not an issue in Singapore. The state does not provide aid to any states in Southeast Asia.

DEFENSE

$2.1bn

Up 19% in 1991

Singapore is the most heavily armed state in the region. Defense accounts for 46% of current expenditure.

S

ECONOMICS

$39.2bn

1.61 Singapore dollars

SCORE CARD

- ❑ WORLD GNP RANKING........................47th
- ❑ GNP PER CAPITA.......................$12,310
- ❑ BALANCE OF PAYMENTS...................$2.9bn
- ❑ INFLATION..................................2.3%
- ❑ UNEMPLOYMENT.............................1.9%

STRENGTHS

Massive accumulated wealth – reserves are over $60 billion – derived from success as an entrepôt and center of high-tech industries. Huge state enterprises, such as TAMESEK, with over 450 companies, have proved highly flexible in responding to market conditions. Singapore produces 50% of the world's computer disk drives; the world leader in new biotechnologies.

EXPORTS

Thailand 7%

Hong Kong 7%

Other 43%

Japan 9%

Malaysia 13%

USA 21%

IMPORTS

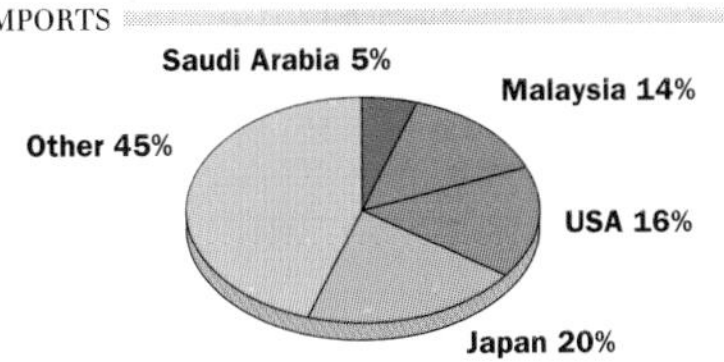

WEAKNESSES

Dependence on Malaysia for water. All food and energy has to be imported. Skills shortages in some key areas, especially engineering. Lack of land is restraining further development.

CHRONOLOGY

In 1819, Sir Stamford Raffles set up a trading post in the village of Singapore; by 1826 it was Britain's colonial center in Southeast Asia.

- ❑ **1869** Suez Canal opens; start of Singapore's sustained trade boom.
- ❑ **1942–1945** Japanese occupation.
- ❑ **1959** Lee Kuan Yew and PAP elected. PAP in power ever since.
- ❑ **1965** Independence.

RESOURCES

15.6bn kwh (capacity 3.4m kw)

Not an oil producer; refines 1.03m b/cd

12,600 tons

Granite

Singapore has no strategic resources and has to import almost all the energy and food it needs. Its main resources, on which its wealth as a center of commerce has been built, are its strategic position and its people.

ENVIRONMENT

4% partially protected

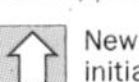

New clean city initiatives

There is a small green belt around the causeway. Singapore sees itself as a world leader in providing the perfect urban environment. There is no litter, thanks to instant heavy fines; chewing gum is banned by law.

MEDIA

The press is completely regulated

PUBLISHING AND BROADCAST MEDIA

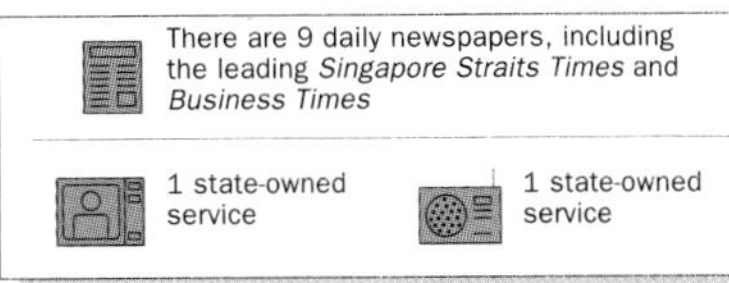

The government is very sensitive to any criticism that might reflect badly on Singapore as a business center. The *Asian Wall Street Journal* was closed for a period for hinting at problems in the stock-exchange clearing system.

CRIME

6,470 prisoners

Down 9% in 1990

Crime is limited and punishment can be severe. The Triads are no longer a problem; the main issue is intellectual piracy.

EDUCATION

90%

Education is not compulsory, but attendance at both primary and secondary schools is high. There are two universities and five colleges.

HEALTH

1 per 753 people

Circulatory and respiratory diseases, cancer

Singapore has an efficient modern health system. Incentives exist aimed at preserving the extended family, so that the elderly are cared for at home.

WEALTH

Live-in maid, 500 Singapore dollars per month; experienced secretary, 5,000 Singapore dollars per month

CONSUMER GOODS OWNERSHIP

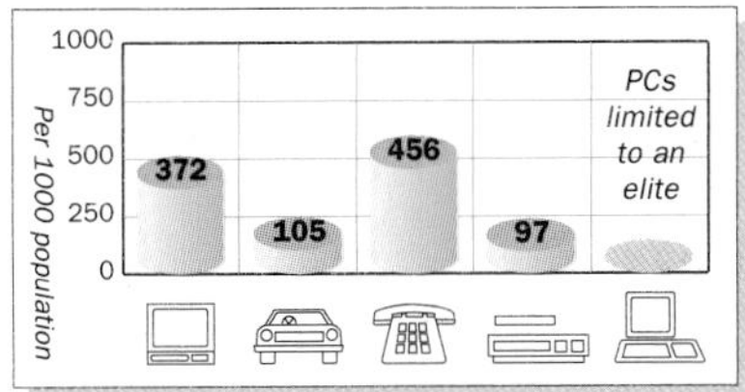

The Chinese and Indians live very well, although their party-allocated flats are not luxurious by Western standards. The Malays are the poorest group.

S

WORLD RANKING

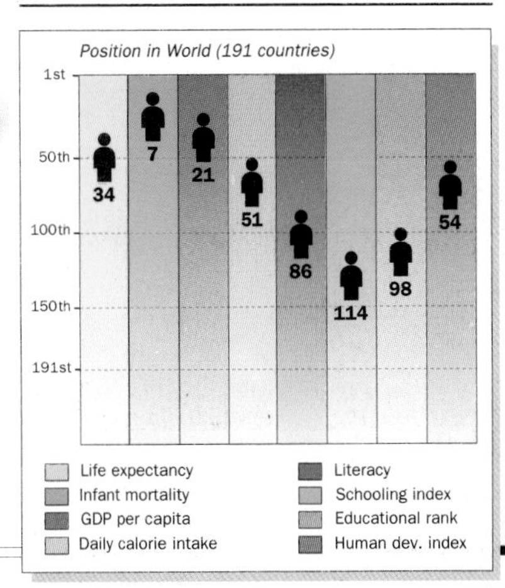

SINGAPORE

Total Area : 620 sq. km (239 sq. miles)

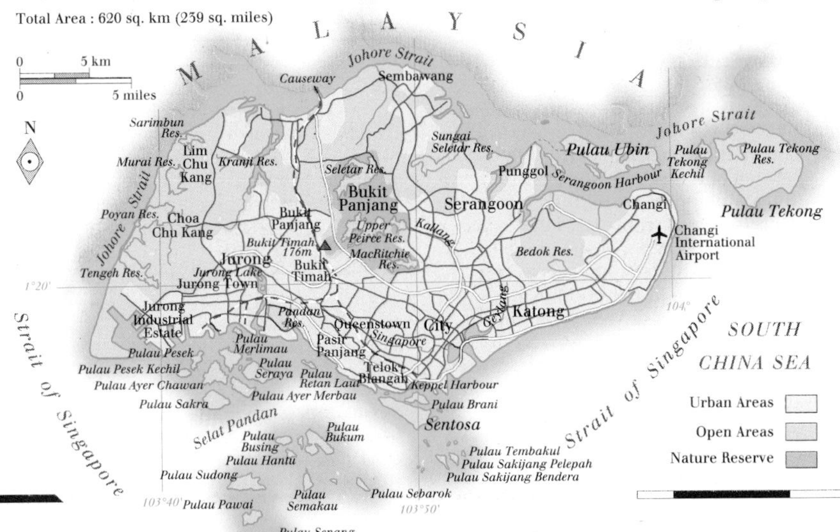

SLOVAKIA

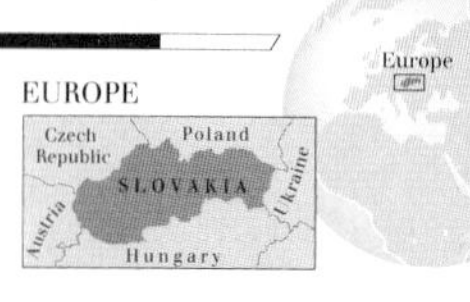

OFFICIAL NAME: Slovak Republic **CAPITAL:** Bratislava
POPULATION: 5.3 million **CURRENCY:** Slovak koruna **OFFICIAL LANGUAGE:** Slovak

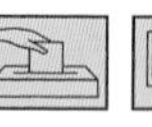

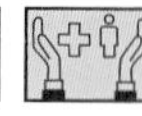

SLOVAKIA IS BORDERED BY the Czech Republic, Austria, Poland, Hungary and the Ukraine. Southern lowlands contrast with the Carpathian mountain range, which extends along the Polish border. An independent democracy since 1993, Slovakia is the less-developed half of the former Czechoslovakia. It is facing difficulties in making its industry-based economy efficient.

Levoča, in northeastern Slovakia, dates from the 13th century and still retains its medieval street plan and town walls.

CLIMATE

WEATHER CHART

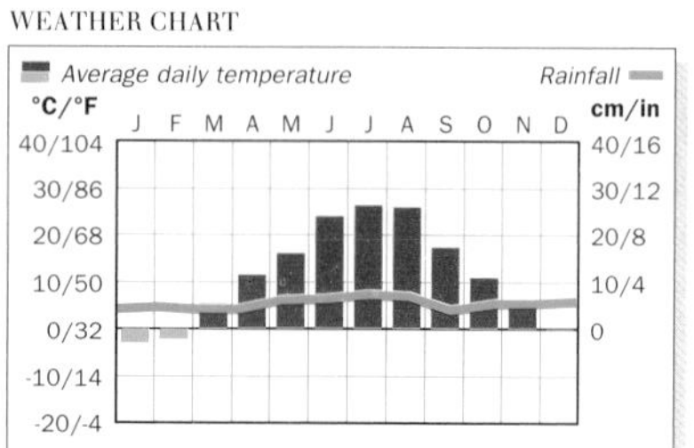

Slovakia has a continental climate. Snowfalls are heavy in winter, while summers are moderately warm.

COMMUNICATIONS

Ivánka, Bratislava

THE TRANSPORTATION NETWORK

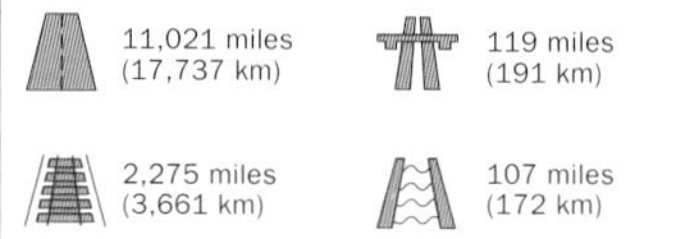

Establishing transportation links with Austria, the main route to Central and Western Europe, is vital. The horse and cart is still used in rural areas.

TOURISM

750,000 visitors (est)

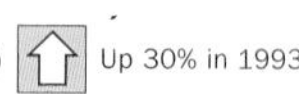

MAIN OVERSEAS ARRIVALS

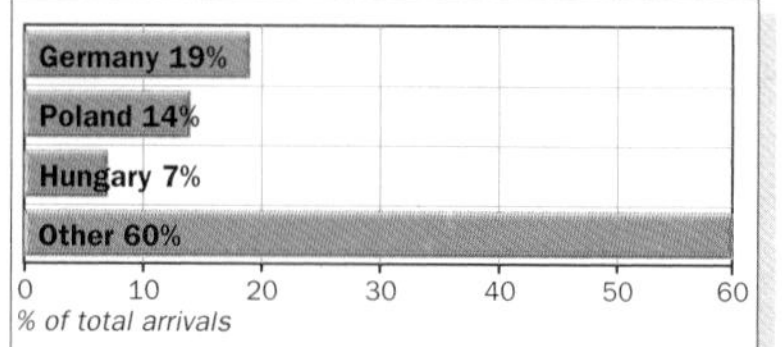

The Tatra Mountains are popular with skiers, hikers and cave explorers. Most of the tourist industry has been privatized, but the government plans to retain partial control of Slovakia's many thermal-spring health spas.

PEOPLE

Slovak, Hungarian, Czech

280 people per sq. mile

THE URBAN/RURAL POPULATION SPLIT

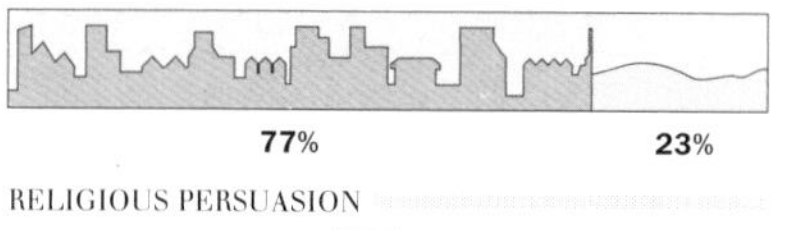

RELIGIOUS PERSUASION

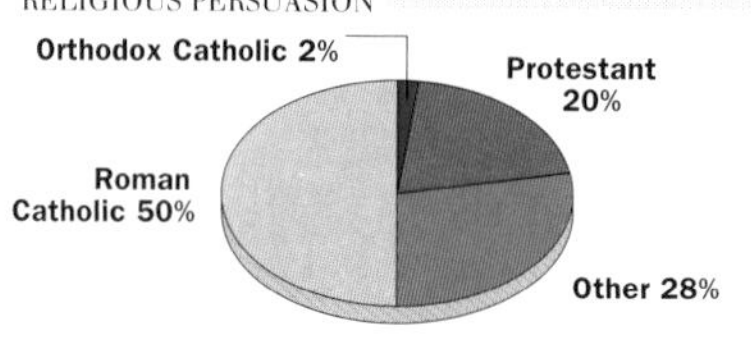

Slovaks dominate society, but 9% of the population is Hungarian and there is a large Gypsy minority. Tension has increased between the Slovaks and Hungarians, particularly over the directive that Hungarians should adopt Slovak name endings. Before independence, many skilled Slovaks took senior jobs in Prague, but few have returned to help structure the new Slovakia. Roman Catholicism remains a powerful social force.

POLITICS

1998

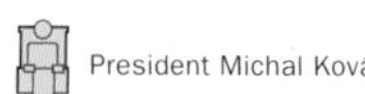
President Michal Kováč

THE STATE OF THE PARTIES

National Council of the Slovak Republic 150 members

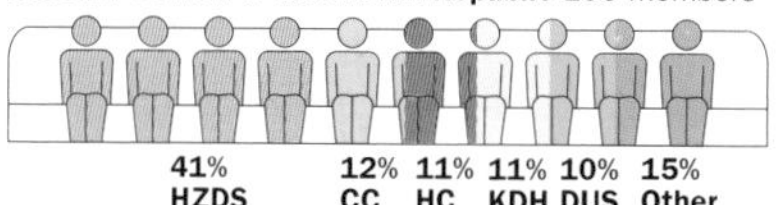

HZDS = Movement for a Democratic Slovakia
CC = Common Choice bloc **HC** = Hungarian Coalition
KDH = Christian Democratic Movement **DUS** = Democratic Union of Slovakia **Other** = Association of Workers of Slovakia, Slovak National Party

The move to independence in 1993 was more a result of Czech than Slovak policies. Slovak leader Vladimír Mečiar was bargaining with Prague not for independence, but for more power within a federation. However, Klaus, the Czech leader, offered Slovakia continued membership of the federation on Czech terms or else separation.

Slovakian politics are now in flux. Parties that once represented Slovak interests within Czechoslovakia are having to define new objectives in a mostly Slovak context. In March 1994, Mečiar was ousted from the premiership in a no-confidence vote. However, in elections later in that year his HZDS again won over a third of the vote. The Hungarian minority has its own parties, but the 300,000 Gypsies have no official representation.

WORLD AFFAIRS

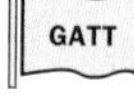

Relations with Hungary are strained over Slovakia's unilateral decision to complete the Gabcikovo Dam, and the treatment of the Hungarian minority in Slovakia. Slovakia is working to raise its international profile.

AID

Significant receipts

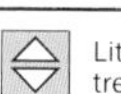
Little change in trends

Aid is of particular importance due to the lack of inward foreign investment. The IMF and EU are the main donors.

DEFENSE

119.4m

A new Slovak army, one-third of the Czechoslovak army, has been formed. Slovakia recently acquired some weapons from Russia, but lack of finance remains a major problem.

RESOURCES

Over 50% of electricity is nuclear-generated

Produces very small quantities of crude oil

13.3m poultry, 576,000 pigs, 546,000 cattle

Coal, lignite, gas, oil, antimony, copper, iron, mercury, zinc

Slovakia is planning to export power from the massive Gabcikovo Dam on the Danube River.

S

SLOVAKIA

Total Area : 49 500 sq. km (19 100 sq. miles)

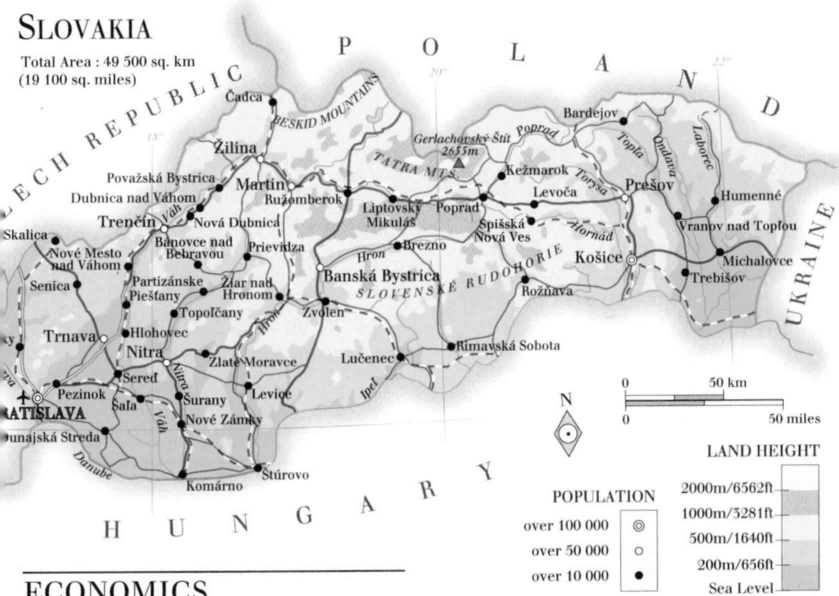

CHRONOLOGY

Formerly part of the Austro-Hungarian Empire, Slovakia joined with the Czech Lands to form the Republic of Czechoslovakia in 1918.

- ❑ **1920** Treaty of Trianon sets Czechoslovakian borders.
- ❑ **1939-1945** Separate Slovak state under pro-Nazi Fr. Jozef Tiso.
- ❑ **1945** Restoration of pre-war Czechoslovak state.
- ❑ **1947** Communists seize power.
- ❑ **1968** "Prague Spring": brief period of political tolerance and reform, ended by Warsaw Pact invasion.
- ❑ **1969** Federal system introduced.
- ❑ **1989** Demonstrations initiate process leading to democracy.
- ❑ **1990** Free multiparty elections.
- ❑ **1993** Jan 1: separate Slovak and Czech states established.

ECONOMICS

10.1bn (est)   32.78 Slovak koruny

SCORE CARD

- ❑ WORLD GNP RANKING..........78th
- ❑ GNP PER CAPITA..........$1,910
- ❑ BALANCE OF PAYMENTS..........Deficit
- ❑ INFLATION..........21% (est)
- ❑ UNEMPLOYMENT..........18%

STRENGTHS

Potential for tourism, particularly skiing in the Tatras, once hotel infrastructure is upgraded.

WEAKNESSES

Legacy of status as less-developed part of Czechoslovakia. Loss of subsidies from Czech Republic. Economy's narrow emphasis on heavy engineering and arms manufacture; collapse of COMECON markets for these have hit Slovakia very hard. Unemployment high, since Slovak economy is not competitive in European markets. Lack of foreign investors. Many skilled Slovaks in areas such as banking and policy-making have remained in the Czech Republic.

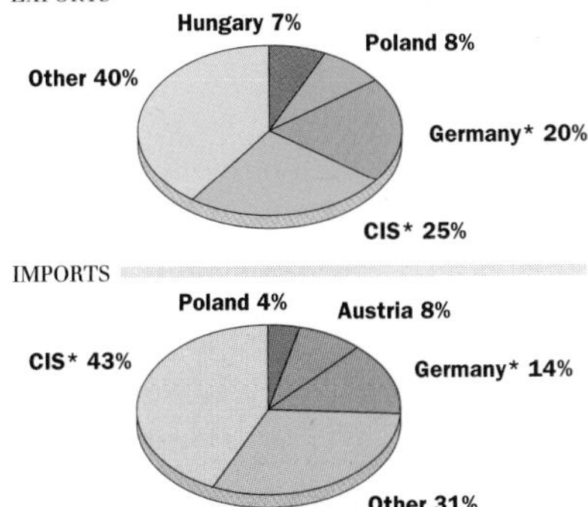

ENVIRONMENT

 10%   Acid rain from power stations has damaged forests

Levels of industrialization are not as great, and pollution not as serious, as in the neighboring Czech Republic.

MEDIA

 Press freedom is generally assured, though access is limited for minorities

PUBLISHING AND BROADCAST MEDIA

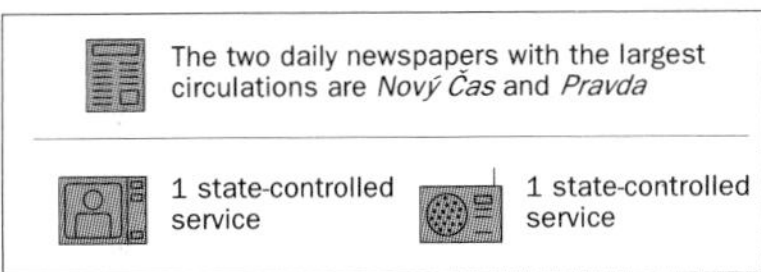

The two daily newspapers with the largest circulations are *Nový Čas* and *Pravda*
1 state-controlled service
1 state-controlled service

Hungarians, who make up 9% of the population, are now demanding access to the media; Gypsies have practically no media coverage.

CRIME

 Slovakia does not publish prison figures    Up 33% in 1993

The state is launching a major initiative to prevent Slovakia from being used as a route by smugglers bringing uranium out of the Ukraine and Russia, Semtex explosives out of the Czech Republic and illegal drugs from the Far East.

EDUCATION

 93%

Schooling is reverting to the pre-1939 Slovakian traditions. Rural areas are not well served by the education system. There is a modern university in Bratislava.

HEALTH

 1 per 294 people    Cancer, heart and cerebrovascular diseases, accidents

Although limited, the health service is of a higher standard than in most of the ex-COMECON states.

WEALTH

 Secretary, 4,000 Slovak koruny per month; lawyer, 20,000 Slovak koruny per month

CONSUMER GOODS OWNERSHIP

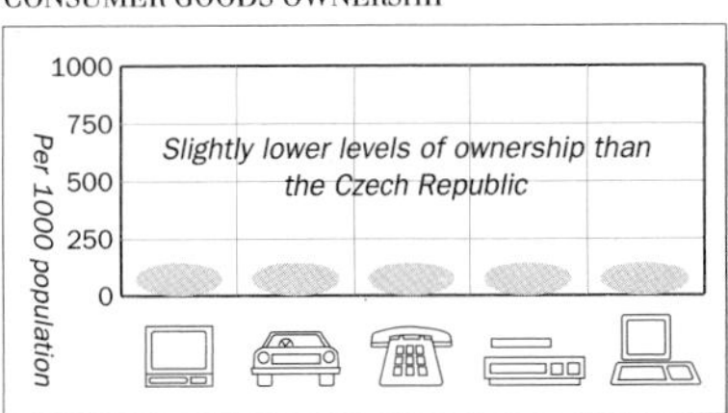

Western goods are very popular with the newly emerging elite. The rural workers are the poorest group.

WORLD RANKING

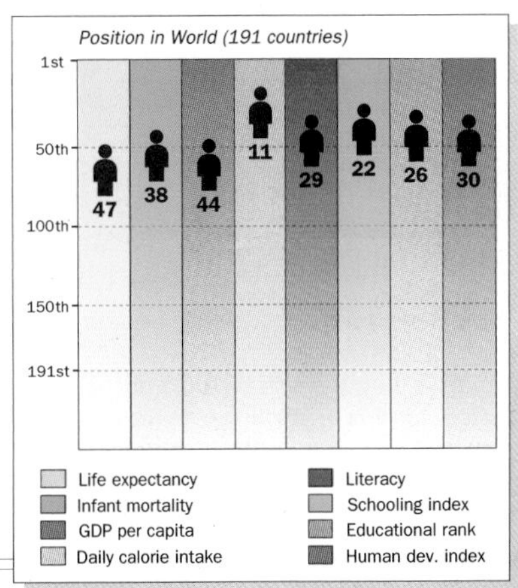

S

SLOVENIA

OFFICIAL NAME: Republic of Slovenia **CAPITAL:** Ljubljana
POPULATION: 1.9 million **CURRENCY:** Tolar **OFFICIAL LANGUAGE:** Slovene

EUROPE

Austria Hungary Italy SLOVENIA Croatia

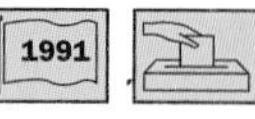

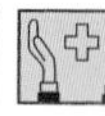
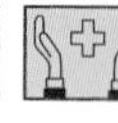

OF ALL THE FORMER Yugoslav republics, Slovenia has the closest links with Western Europe. Located at the northeastern end of the Adriatic Sea, this small, alpine country controls some of Europe's major transit routes. Its economy has been badly affected by the collapse of Yugoslavia, and it has struggled to develop economic ties with the West. Slovenia's transition to independence in 1991 avoided the violence associated with the breakup of Yugoslavia.

CLIMATE

WEATHER CHART

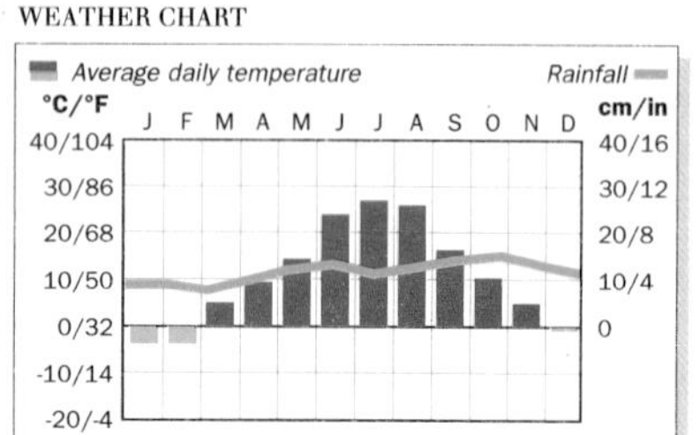

Slovenia's interior has a continental climate. Its small coastal region has a mild Mediterranean climate.

COMMUNICATIONS

 Ljubljana International  2 ships 200 dwt

THE TRANSPORTATION NETWORK

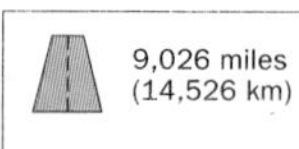

742 miles (1,196 km)

None

Slovenia is strategically situated at some of Europe's major crossroads. In addition, its Adriatic ports provide Austria with its main maritime outlets.

TOURISM

 298,700 visitors 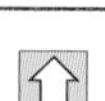 Tourism has grown since 1991

MAIN OVERSEAS ARRIVALS

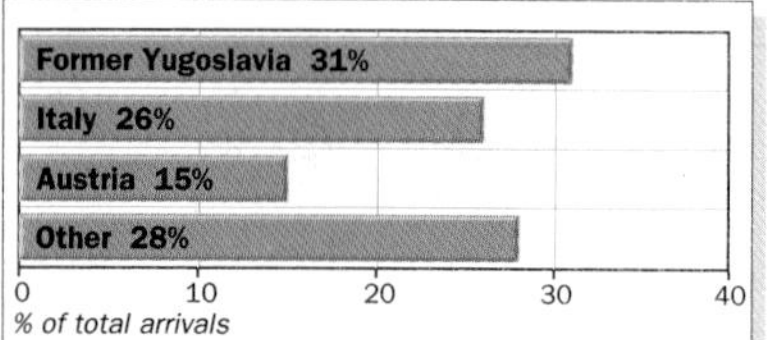

Slovenia hopes "village tourism" will bring visitors to rural towns and farms, as well as to its mountains and beaches. However, large numbers of tourists are still put off by the war in Bosnia.

PEOPLE

Slovenian, Serbo-Croatian

254 people per sq. mile

THE URBAN/RURAL POPULATION SPLIT

49% 51%

ETHNIC MAKEUP

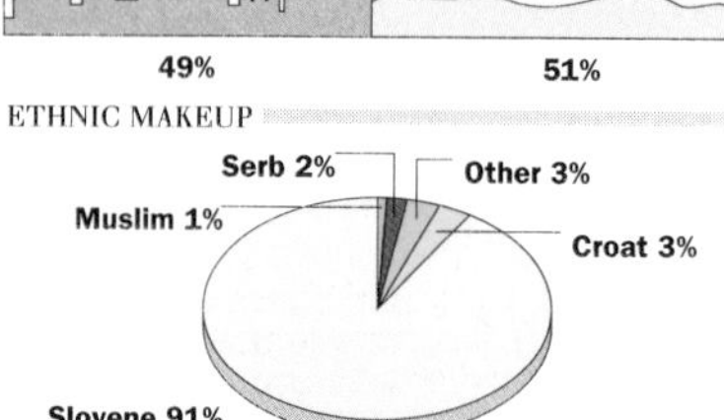

Slovenia is ethnically homogeneous: 91% are Slovene. There are also small communities of Italians and Hungarians. The Slovene language is sufficiently different from Serbo-Croatian to foster a separate identity from its Yugoslav neighbors. Slovenia has traditionally identified more with the alpine countries to the west than its Balkan neighbors. Access to Italy and Austria during the 1970s and 1980s encouraged a separatist movement. These factors, combined with a well-developed economy, aided Slovenia's relatively peaceful secession from the former Yugoslavia in 1991.

POLITICS

1996 President Milan Kučan

THE STATE OF THE PARTIES

National Assembly 90 members

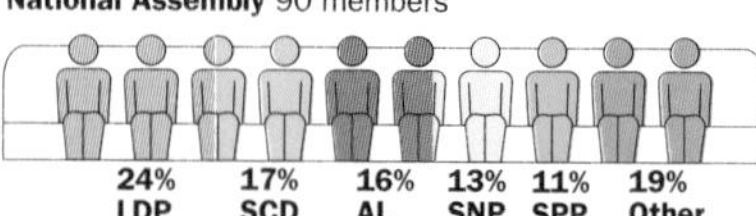

LDP = Liberal Democratic Party **SCD** = Slovenian Christian Democrats **AL** = Associated List **SNP** = Slovenian National Party **SPP** = Slovenian People's Party **Other** = Democratic Party of Slovenia, Greens of Slovenia, Social Democratic Party of Slovenia

National Council 40 members

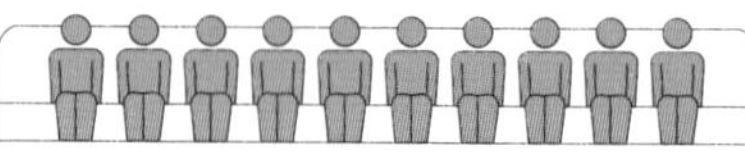

22 members are elected and 18 are chosen by an electoral college to represent various interests

Following its independence, a broad consensus on political reforms existed in Slovenia. This consensus has begun to evaporate. In December 1992, an LDP-led coalition government was elected, headed by Janez Drnovsek. His ability to transform Slovenia into a full market economy is being questioned. A major weakness is his government's dependence on the support of the largely ex-communist AL. The AL is using its influence to promote social policies with popular appeal that run contrary to Drnovsek's proposed reforms. Differences have also emerged among the coalition partners over the pace and impact of market reforms.The result is that economic and institutional change in Slovenia is proceeding slowly.

S

SLOVENIA

Total Area : 20 250 sq. km (7820 sq. miles)

WORLD AFFAIRS

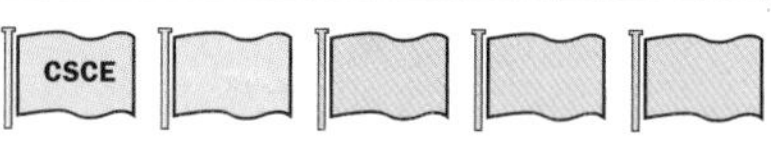

Slovenia has stated its intention to apply for membership in EFTA, the EU and GATT. Disputes with Croatia over fishing rights have now been settled.

AID

 Attraction of aid a major government concern

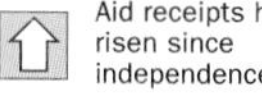 Aid receipts have risen since independence

Recent agreements with the EU and the IMF have set up lines of credit. Aid is being targeted at infrastructural improvements and education projects.

DEFENSE

 $170m

 Spending has risen to protect Slovenian sovereignty

Slovene troops successfully held off federal Yugoslav army attacks following secession in 1991. A small air force is being developed.

ECONOMICS

 12bn (est)

 121.20 tolar

SCORE CARD

- ❑ WORLD GNP RANKING 72nd
- ❑ GNP PER CAPITA $6,300
- ❑ BALANCE OF PAYMENTS $764m
- ❑ INFLATION 22.9%
- ❑ UNEMPLOYMENT.................................. 13%

EXPORTS

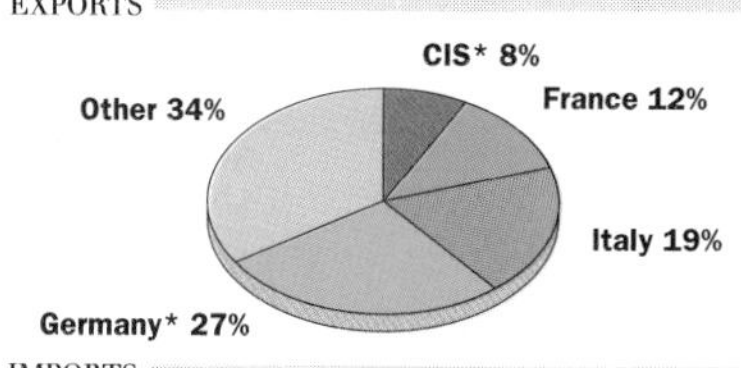

IMPORTS

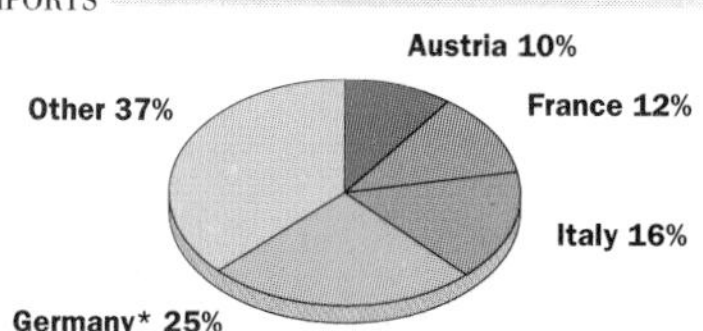

STRENGTHS

Competitive manufacturing industry. Prospects for growth in electronics industry. Well-developed tourist sector. Czech demand for Slovenia's consumer goods exports. Well placed to supply ex-Yugoslavia when sanctions lifted.

WEAKNESSES

Rising real labor costs may stifle output growth. Highest wages in central Europe. Persistent wage pressures may fuel inflation. Rising unemployment. Privatization process has been slow.

Lake Bled in the Julian Alps, which lie astride the Slovenian–Italian border. The lake is a popular tourist destination.

RESOURCES

 12,669m kwh

Not an oil producer; refines 14,700 b/cd

484,000 cattle
529,000 pigs
28,000 sheep

coal, lignite, lead, zinc, uranium, silver, mercury

Slovenia has come under pressure from Austria to close the nuclear plant in Krsvo, which provides one-third of Slovenia's power. It has deposits of brown coal and lignite, but they are difficult to extract and of poor quality.

ENVIRONMENT

 4%

Some industrial pollution

Slovenes were in the vanguard of former Yugoslavia's environmental movement. Protecting the country's alpine ecology is a priority.

MEDIA

 The media is free from government interference

PUBLISHING AND BROADCAST MEDIA

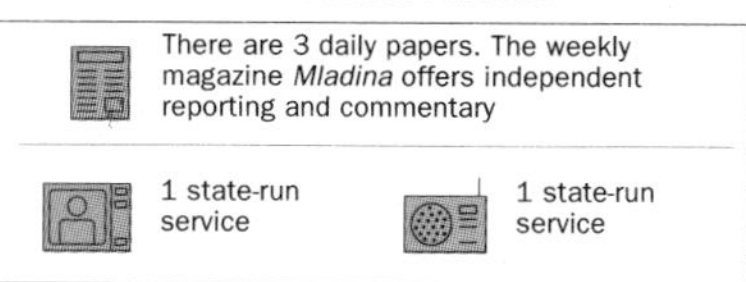

There are 3 daily papers. The weekly magazine *Mladina* offers independent reporting and commentary
1 state-run service
1 state-run service

The Slovene-language media actively worked to undermine Yugoslav institutions during the secession crisis, reinforcing the sense of national identity.

CRIME

 Slovenia does not publish prison figures

 Low crime levels for region. Little change from year to year

Slovenia has traditionally been a transit point for drug smuggling into Western Europe. The trade has declined since the UN imposed sanctions on Serbia.

EDUCATION

 99%

School is compulsory from 7 to 15 years, and standards are high. In 1992, there were over 30,000 students in higher education. The university at Ljubljana was founded in 1595.

CHRONOLOGY

Slovenia was part of the Austro-Hungarian Empire until 1918. It was the first republic to secede from the Federal Republic of Yugoslavia.

- ❑ **1918** Slovenia joins Yugoslav kingdom.
- ❑ **1949** Tito's break with Moscow. Opens borders with the West.
- ❑ **1989** Parliament confirms right to secede. Calls multiparty elections.
- ❑ **1990** Control over army asserted, referendum approves secession.
- ❑ **1991** Independence declared. Yugoslav federal army attacks held off. EU-brokered cease-fire.
- ❑ **1992** EU recognizes Slovenia. First multiparty elections held. Milan Kučan elected president.
- ❑ **1993** Member of IMF and IBRD.

HEALTH

 1 per 523 people

 Cerebrovascular and heart diseases, cancer

National health care in Slovenia uses health centers and outpatient clinics to increase accessibility for patients.

WEALTH

 Slovenia has the highest wages among the former Yugoslav republics

CONSUMER GOODS OWNERSHIP

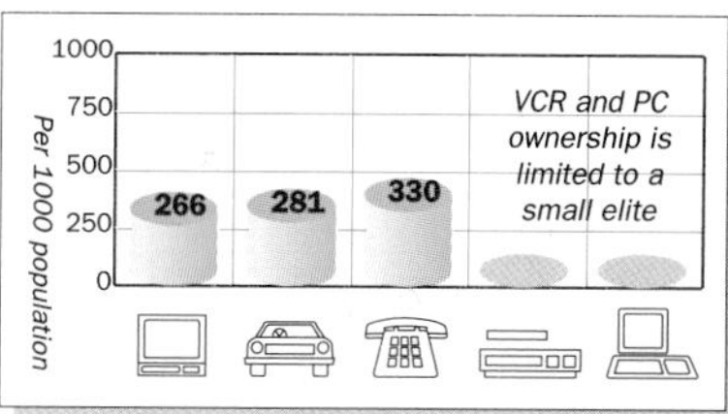

Slovenia was the most advanced and highly industrialized of the six Yugoslav republics. Average net monthly wages in 1993 were equivalent to $400.

WORLD RANKING

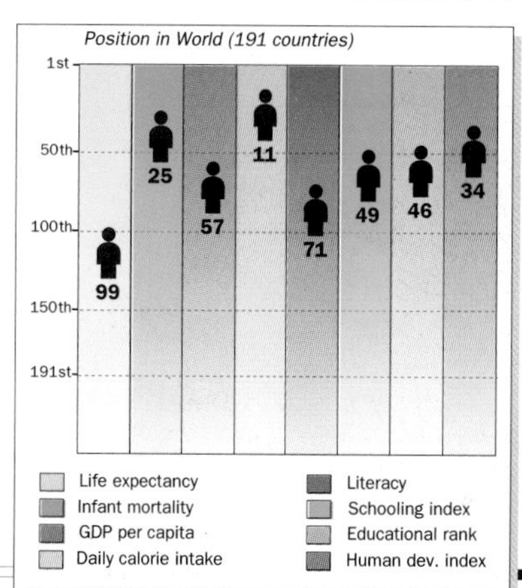

S

SOLOMON ISLANDS

PACIFIC OCEAN
Papua New Guinea
Nauru
SOLOMON ISLANDS
Tuvalu
Pacific Ocean

OFFICIAL NAME: Solomon Islands **CAPITAL:** Honiara
POPULATION: 300,000 **CURRENCY:** Solomon Islands dollar **OFFICIAL LANGUAGE:** English

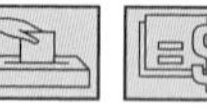
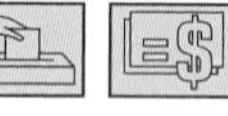

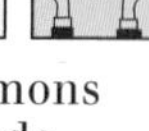

SCATTERED OVER 289,000 sq. miles, the Solomons archipelago consists of several hundred islands. Most of the population live on the six largest islands – Guadalcanal, Malaita, New Georgia, Makira, Santa Isabel and Choiseul. The Solomons have been settled since at least 1000 BC and the Spanish reached the islands in 1568. They gained independence from Britain in 1978. Most of the Solomons are coral reefs. Just 1% of the islands' land area is cultivable.

CLIMATE

WEATHER CHART

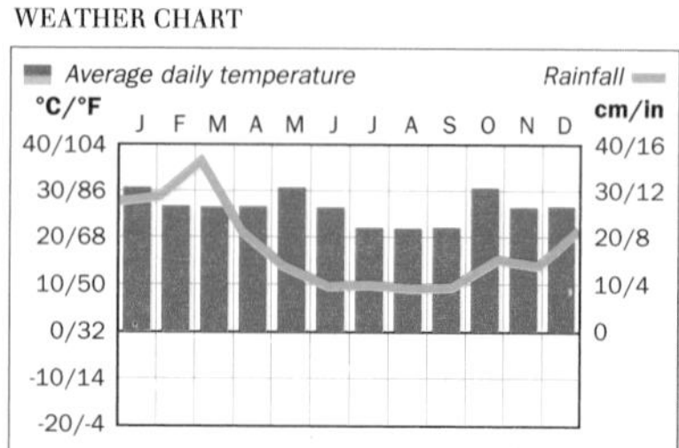

There is little variation in the humid, hot subtropical climate, but ferocious cyclones can occur in the rainy season.

COMMUNICATIONS

Henderson, Honiara
22,000 passengers

2 ships
600 dwt

THE TRANSPORTATION NETWORK

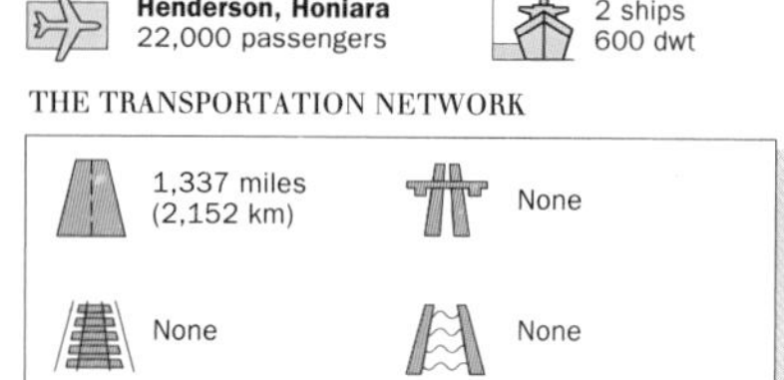

The airport on Guadalcanal was begun by the Japanese and completed by the USA during World War II. Most airfields are simple grass strips.

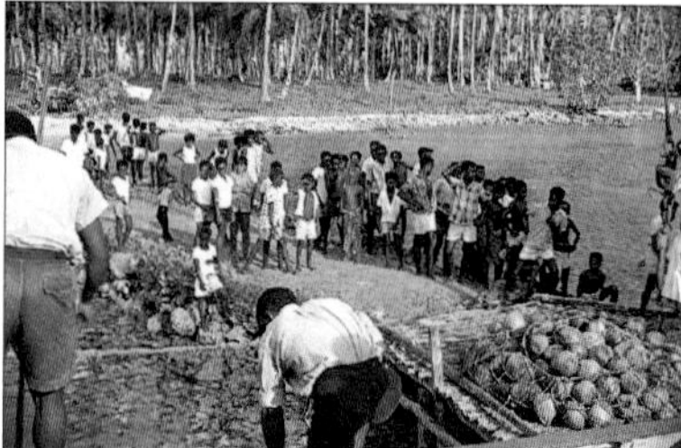

Unloading seed coconuts *near Munda on New Georgia in the Solomons' southern chain of islands. Coconuts are by far the largest and most commercially important crop.*

TOURISM

11,105 visitors

Up 21% in 1991

MAIN OVERSEAS ARRIVALS

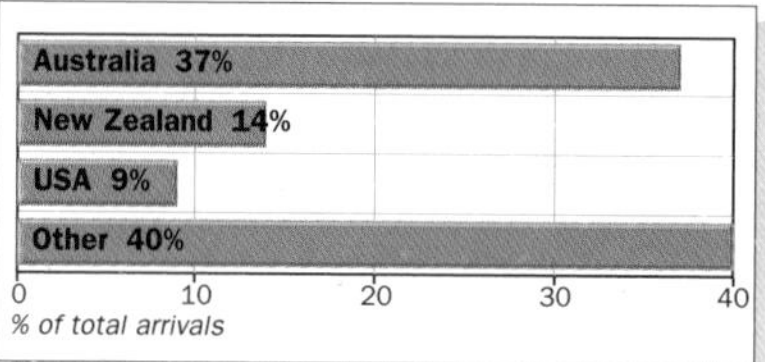

More tourists are expected now that Boeing 747 jets can land at the main airport. Guadalcanal, a key battle site of World War II in the Pacific, has seen a decline in visitors in recent years. Outlying islands cater to visitors wishing to "go native."

PEOPLE

English, Pidgin English, Melanesian Pidgin

28 people per sq. mile

THE URBAN/RURAL POPULATION SPLIT

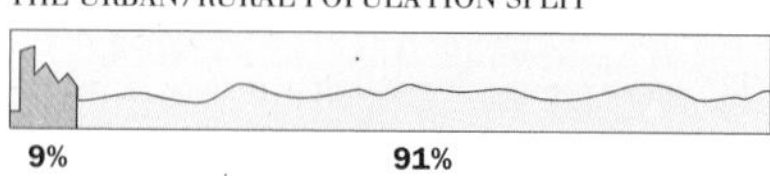

RELIGIOUS PERSUASION

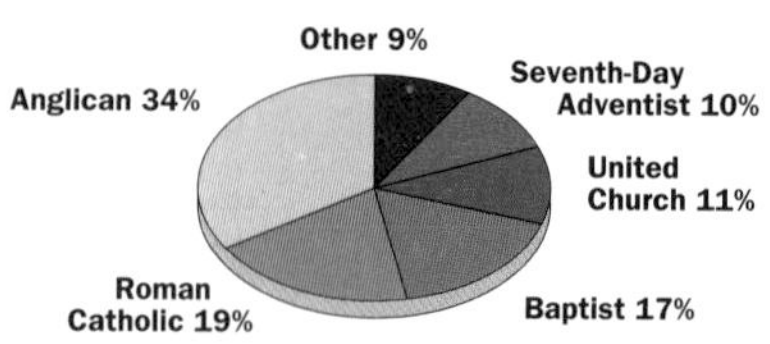

Almost all Solomon Islanders are Melanesian. In 1957, large numbers of Gilbertese were resettled in the Solomons following a hurricane; a few stayed on and today form a small, distinct community. Over 50 dialects are spoken in the Solomons, a state of 326,000 people spread over 1,000 miles. As in other Melanesian island states, villagers are expected to share their wealth with their *wontoks*, or clan. Almost all islanders are nominally Christian. Most also maintain their traditional animist beliefs.

POLITICS

1997

HM Queen Elizabeth II

THE STATE OF THE PARTIES

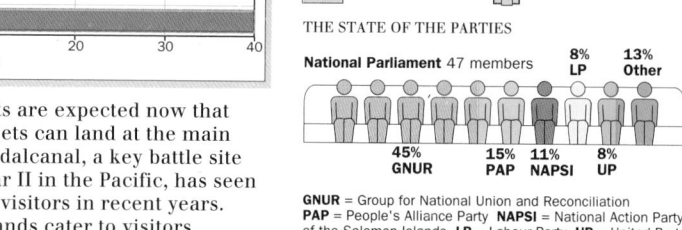

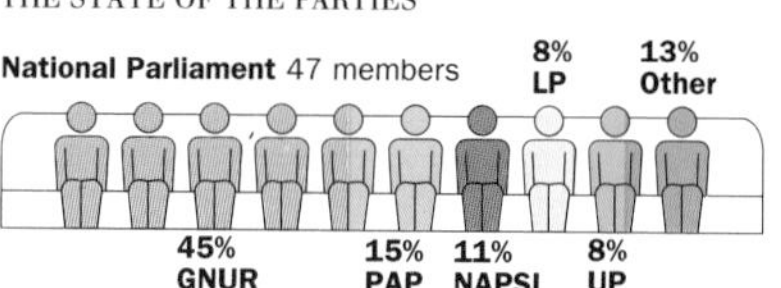

GNUR = Group for National Union and Reconciliation
PAP = People's Alliance Party **NAPSI** = National Action Party of the Solomon Islands **LP** = Labour Party **UP** = United Party

The Solomons' parliament is based on the British model. Unlike other Pacific states, there is no one class of chiefs which dominates the political process. It is prominent figures in village life – known locally as "big men" – who stand as candidates. They are usually in parliament for just one term, as elections tend to result in a large turnover of members. Party arrangements within parliament are fluid and coalitions unstable. Women do not take part in the political process. How to reverse the decline in the economy is the main political issue.

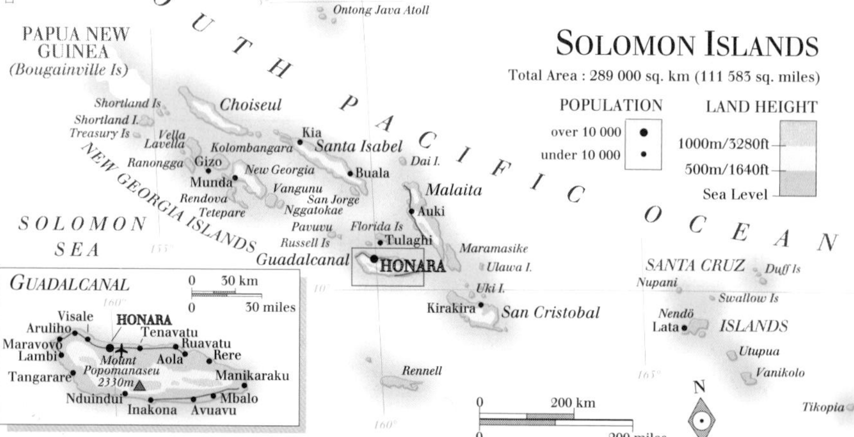

WORLD AFFAIRS

The main issue is the status of Bougainville in neighboring Papua New Guinea (PNG). Geographically part of the Solomons, Bougainville, which includes the world's largest copper mine, became part of PNG as a result of an Anglo-German colonial deal. Honiara gives tacit support to the Bougainvillian secessionist groups.

AID

 $40m (receipts)

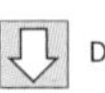 Down 9% in 1991

The refocusing of Australian aid payments away from the Pacific islands toward Asia has already affected the Solomons' economy. However, Australia has provided cyclone relief and helped restore airfields. Australian NGOs are active. Japan gives technical aid related to the fishing industry.

DEFENSE

 Australia responsible for defense

 Not applicable

The Solomons has no armed forces. Australia provides *de facto* protection and two fast patrol boats which are used to protect fisheries from Taiwanese and Okinawan poachers. However, the huge distances which have to be covered mean that their effectiveness is limited.

ECONOMICS

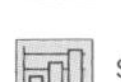 $234m

 3.19 Solomon Islands dollars

SCORE CARD

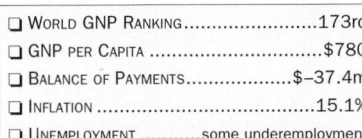

- ❑ WORLD GNP RANKING........................173rd
- ❑ GNP PER CAPITA $780
- ❑ BALANCE OF PAYMENTS...................$–37.4m
- ❑ INFLATION 15.1%
- ❑ UNEMPLOYMENT ....some underemployment

EXPORTS

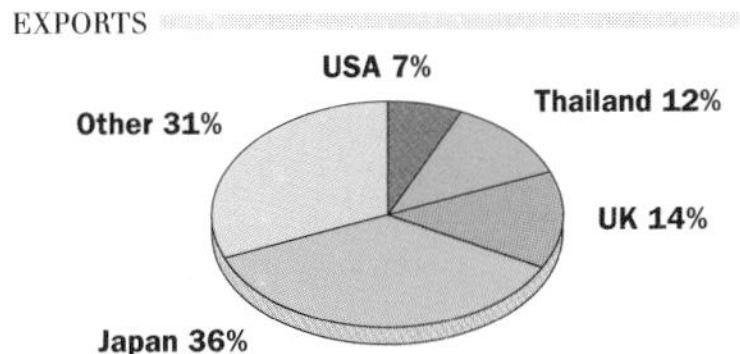

IMPORTS

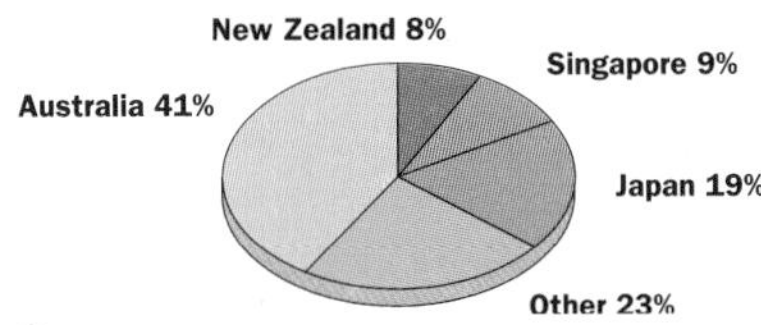

STRENGTHS

Copra and timber. Survival of subsistence agriculture; Solomon Islanders are self-sufficient in food. Modest diversification of economy into oil palm and cocoa.

WEAKNESSES

Copra industry increasingly unproductive. Opposition to over-exploitation of timber. Dependence on imported energy. Location away from main Pacific sea and air routes.

RESOURCES

 30m kwh (capacity 10,000 kw)

 Not an oil producer and has no refineries

 52,000 pigs, 13,000 cattle

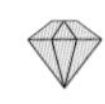 Gold, copper, bauxite, lead, zinc, silver, cobalt, phosphates

Bauxite deposits have been discovered on Rennett Island. In addition, there are traces of gold and copper on Guadalcanal, but not in commercially exploitable quantities. Most energy has to be imported.

ENVIRONMENT

 None

Successful environmental campaigns

The environmental movement is strong in the Solomons. It persuaded the government that exploiting bauxite on Rennett would destroy the island. It is currently mounting a fierce campaign against the tropical timber industry.

MEDIA

 Minimal government interference

PUBLISHING AND BROADCAST MEDIA

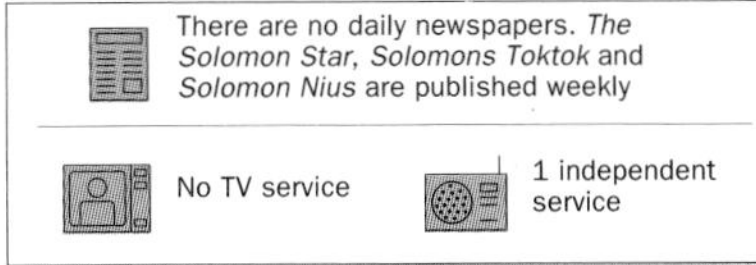

There are no daily newspapers. *The Solomon Star, Solomons Toktok* and *Solomon Nius* are published weekly

No TV service

1 independent service

The one radio station broadcasts in English and Pidgin. Islanders oppose TV, believing it would dilute their culture.

CRIME

 Solomon Islands does not publish prison figures

 Crime rate rising

There has been a small increase in crime on Honiara. Most offenses are alcohol-related.

CHRONOLOGY

Settled since before 1000 BC by Melanesian peoples, the Solomons became a British colony in 1893.

- ❑ **1900** Britain acquires northern Solomons from Germany. Copra industry established.
- ❑ **1942** Occupied by Japanese forces.
- ❑ **1943** Japan loses control to USA following fierce fighting.
- ❑ **1978** Independence from UK.
- ❑ **1986** Cyclone: massive damage.

EDUCATION

 60%

Education is modeled on the British system. Students may go on to the University of the South Pacific in Fiji.

HEALTH

1 per 8,812 people

Not available

The main hospital is in Honiara. Known as "Number 9," it was built as a military hospital by the US army during World War II.

WEALTH

 Most islanders are subsistence farmers

CONSUMER GOODS OWNERSHIP

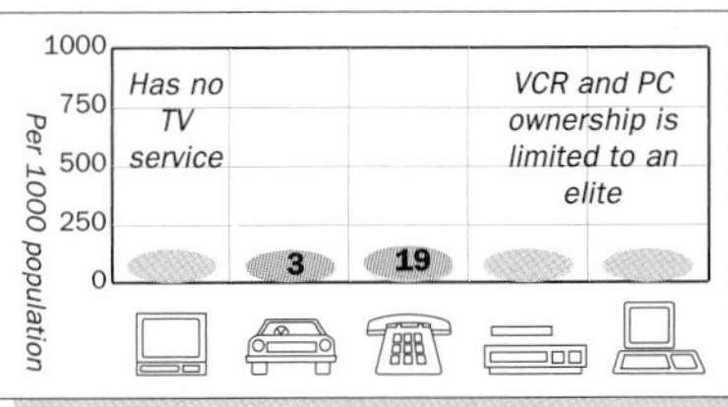

Solomon Islanders in government jobs are the wealthiest group. Outlying islands are extremely poor.

WORLD RANKING

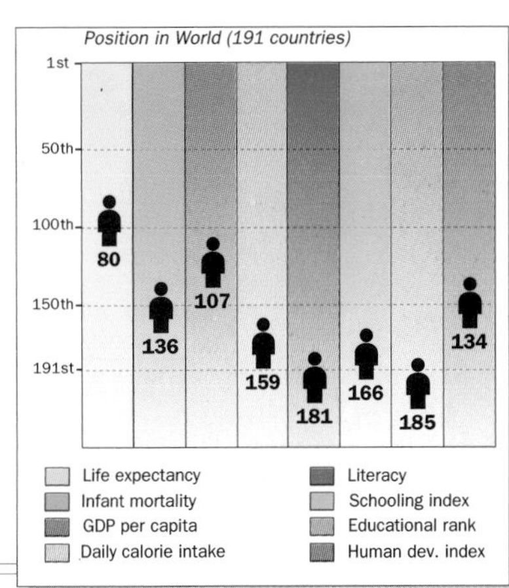

S

SOMALIA

OFFICIAL NAME: Somali Democratic Republic **CAPITAL:** Mogadishu
POPULATION: 9.2 million **CURRENCY:** Somali shilling **OFFICIAL LANGUAGES:** Somali and Arabic

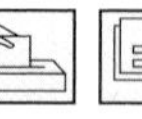

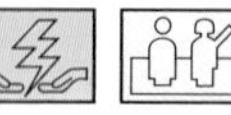

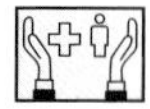
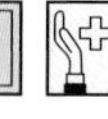

OCCUPYING THE HORN OF AFRICA, Italian Somaliland and British Somaliland were united in 1960 to form an independent Somalia. The land is semi-arid except in the more fertile south. Years of clan-based civil war have resulted in the collapse of central government. By 1992, drought and the conflict had created the worst mass starvation and refugee crisis ever to face the UN.

CLIMATE

WEATHER CHART

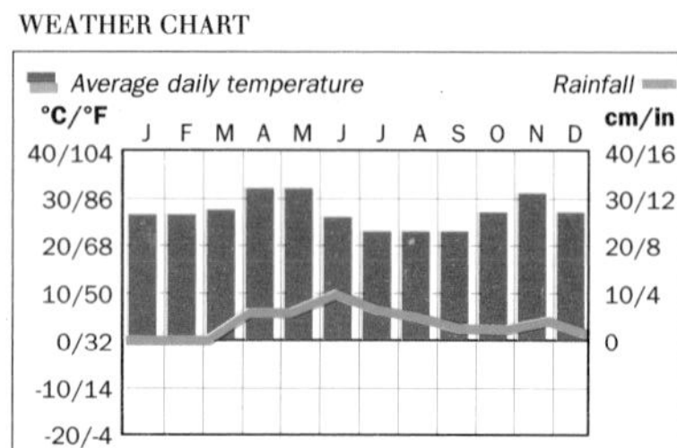

Somalia is very dry. The northern coast is very hot and humid, the eastern less so. The interior has some of the world's highest yearly mean temperatures.

COMMUNICATIONS

Mogadishu International 5 ships 12,800 dwt

THE TRANSPORTATION NETWORK

About 50% of Somalis are nomads for whom the camel is the principal means of transportation. In 1990, the IDA agreed to repair the road network, but by 1994 no work had started on the seven-year project.

TOURISM

Urban and rural instability deters tourism

Not applicable

MAIN OVERSEAS ARRIVALS

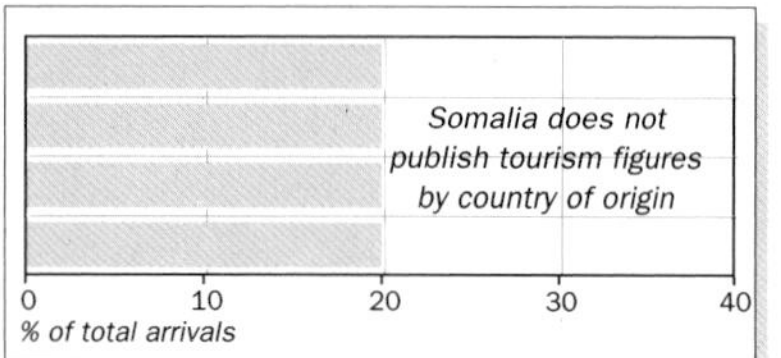

Aid workers, foreign journalists and UN peace-keepers are the only visitors. Land mines are a hazard.

Baydhabo market. *Although subsistence farming supports most people, 2.8 million war refugees needed Red Cross food aid in 1992.*

PEOPLE

Somali, Arabic, English, Italian

31 people per sq. mile

THE URBAN/RURAL POPULATION SPLIT

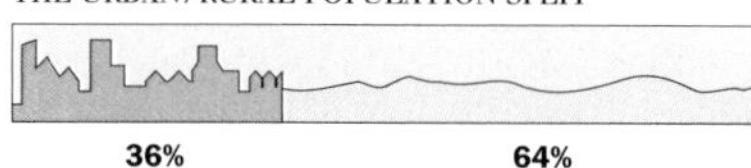

RELIGIOUS PERSUASION

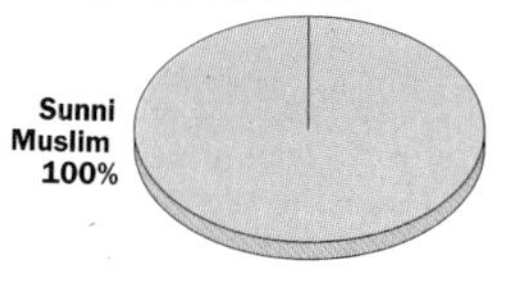

The clan system is at the root of all social, political and commercial issues in Somalia. Shifting allegiances characterize its structure – a tendency stifled by Siad Barre's dictatorship but revived after his fall in 1991. His undermining of the traditional brokers of justice, the elders, contributed to the present power vacuum, while his persecution of the Issaqs led to Somaliland's secession in 1991. However, the entire population is ethnic Somali and national identity remains strong; widespread opposition to the US-led UN peace-keeping force reflects this.

POLITICS

Uncertain

Interim President Ali Mahdi Mohamed

THE STATE OF THE PARTIES

National Assembly 123 members

There has been no prospect of organizing new elections since the overthrow of Siad Barre, although an attempt has been made to draft a new democratic constitution

Somalia is no longer the undivided republic it was under its dictator, President Siad Barre. Civil war started in the north in the 1980s and spread as other opposition groups took up arms against his regime. He eventually fled the capital in early 1991. The subsequent civil war in the south and the self-proclaimed independence of Somaliland in the north in May that year have meant that the unitary state has effectively ceased to exist. In spite of UN intervention led by the USA, southern Somalia is almost entirely in the grip of warring clan factions and opportunist warlords. Chief among them are the two United Somalia Congress (USC) faction leaders, General Aideed, who was instrumental in ousting Siad Barre, and Ali Mahdi, who unilaterally declared himself president. Now that fighting has stopped in Somaliland, the region awaits international recognition.

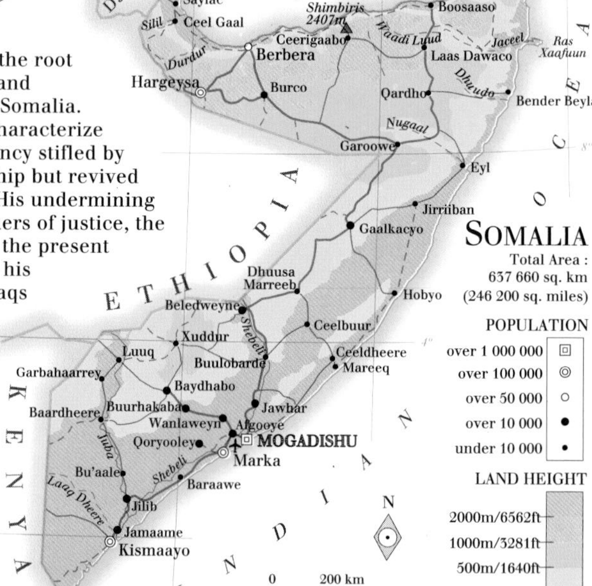

WORLD AFFAIRS

The central questions are whether the UN should extend its peace-keeping and humanitarian roles and effectively run the country, and whether self-declared Somaliland will gain international recognition, with borders in line with those of former British Somaliland. Even though fighting has stopped there, no help other than emergency aid is being provided because the region lacks official status.

AID

 $428m (receipts)  Up 1% in 1990

Mass starvation among the Somali population in 1991 finally prompted the UN into launching a large-scale humanitarian aid effort. US forces have been drafted in under the UN to protect aid convoys from attacks by armed gangs.

DEFENSE

 $18.05m  Down 61% in 1989

Somalia is awash with weapons supplied by both the USA and the former USSR during the Cold War.

ECONOMICS

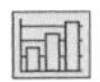 $835m  2,615.58 Somali shillings

SCORE CARD

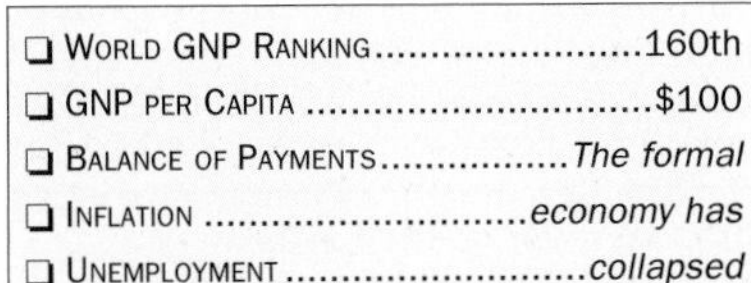

❑ WORLD GNP RANKING	160th
❑ GNP PER CAPITA	$100
❑ BALANCE OF PAYMENTS	*The formal*
❑ INFLATION	*economy has*
❑ UNEMPLOYMENT	*collapsed*

STRENGTHS

Very few. Export of livestock to Arabian Peninsula resumed in the north. Inflow of money from Somalis living abroad. Growing market in stolen food aid.

WEAKNESSES

Every commodity, except arms, in extremely short supply. The south has little economic potential. Effects of drought include death of nomads' livestock herds.

EXPORTS

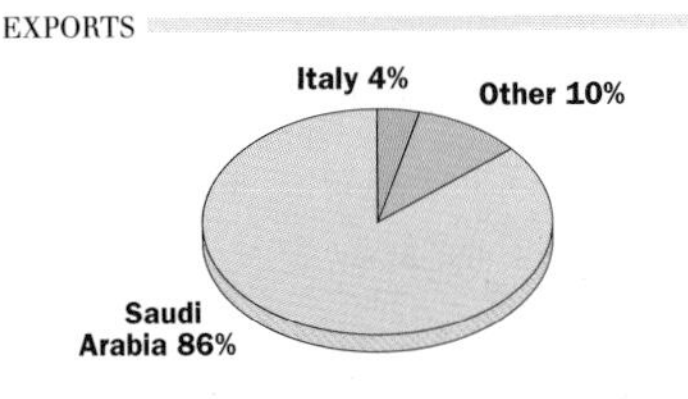

IMPORTS

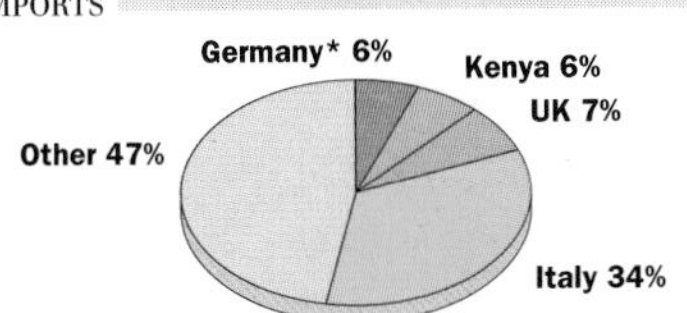

RESOURCES

 230m kwh (capacity 60,000 kw)  Not an oil producer; refines 10,000 b/cd

 21.1m goats, 13.8m sheep, 6.8m camels — Salt, tin, zinc, copper, gypsum, manganese, uranium, iron

Commercially exploitable minerals remain untapped. Oil experts are confident of discovering large offshore reserves in the north.

ENVIRONMENT

 0.3% partially protected  Nomadic lifestyle by definition in tune with the environment

Human deprivation and starvation caused by the effects of drought and war on land and livestock outweigh all other ecological considerations.

MEDIA

 Following the overthrow of the Siad Barre regime, independent newspapers have been established

PUBLISHING AND BROADCAST MEDIA

Two Radio Mogadishu stations run by the two main USC factions – Ali Mahdi's and General Aideed's – existed until US forces destroyed Aideed's. There are few newspapers, as paper is currently in very short supply.

CRIME

 Somalia does not publish prison figures — Widespread breakdown of law and order since 1991

Armed clan factions (some, in remoter regions, engaged in family feuds rather than the war) and bandits rule large areas. Police forces exist in some cities but, with few resources, dare not risk confrontation with warlords. Muslim *sharia* law, now the *de facto* system, is run in a makeshift fashion by elders.

EDUCATION

 24%

The system collapsed during the civil war. There were reports of improvised open-air schools starting up again in urban areas in 1993. Somali has been a written language only since 1972.

CHRONOLOGY

The lands of the Somalis became UK and Italian colonies in the 1880s.

- ❑ **1941–1950** UK rules both areas.
- ❑ **1960** Unification at independence.
- ❑ **1964** Somalia's claim to Ogaden leads to war with Ethiopia.
- ❑ **1969** Gen. Siad Barre seizes power.
- ❑ **1977–1978** Attack on Ethiopia fails.
- ❑ **1981** Two opposition groups based in Ethiopia begin guerrilla war.
- ❑ **1987** Reconciliation with Ethiopia induces Somali National Movement group to occupy north.
- ❑ **1991** Siad Barre ousted. War degenerates into clan chaos. Mass starvation. Somaliland secedes.
- ❑ **1992** Warlords plunder food aid. US sends in military with UN backing.
- ❑ **1994** US troops withdrawn.

HEALTH

 1 per 4,640 people  Diarrheal, communicable and parasitic diseases

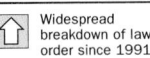

The state-run system has collapsed entirely. A few very rudimentary facilities are run by foreign workers.

WEALTH

 The subsistence existence of the nomads (the bulk of the population) contrasts with the Somali warlords' wealth, won by armed force

CONSUMER GOODS OWNERSHIP

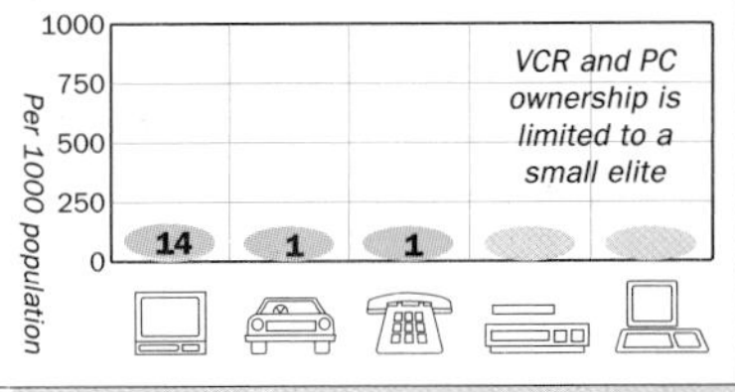

Rich pickings are available for bandits and warlords in the aid-stealing racket. In Somaliland, ministers survive from money sent by relatives living overseas.

WORLD RANKING

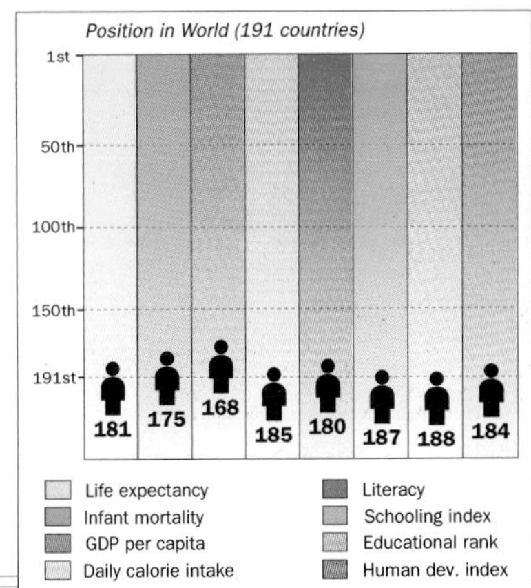

S

SOUTH AFRICA

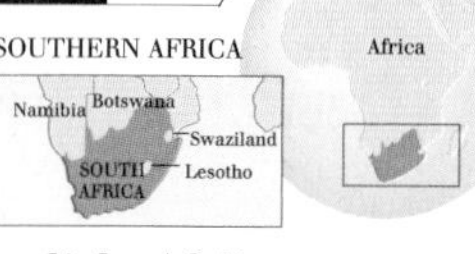

OFFICIAL NAME: Republic of South Africa **CAPITALS:** Pretoria, Cape Town, Bloemfontein
POPULATION: 37.4 million **CURRENCY:** Rand **OFFICIAL LANGUAGES:** 11 African languages, English, Afrikaans

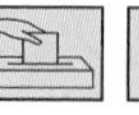

RICH IN NATURAL RESOURCES, South Africa comprises a central plateau, or *veld*, bordered to the south and west by the Drakensberg Mountains. After eight decades of white minority rule, and racial segregation under the apartheid policy since 1948, South Africa held its first multiracial, multiparty elections in 1994. The revolution in South Africa's politics began in 1990, when President F. W. De Klerk legalized black freedom groups and began dismantling apartheid. The African National Congress (ANC), under Nelson Mandela, is now the leading political movement.

***Nelson Mandela,** who became president of South Africa in April 1994.*

***F. W. De Klerk.** He dismantled apartheid legislation during his presidency.*

CLIMATE

WEATHER CHART

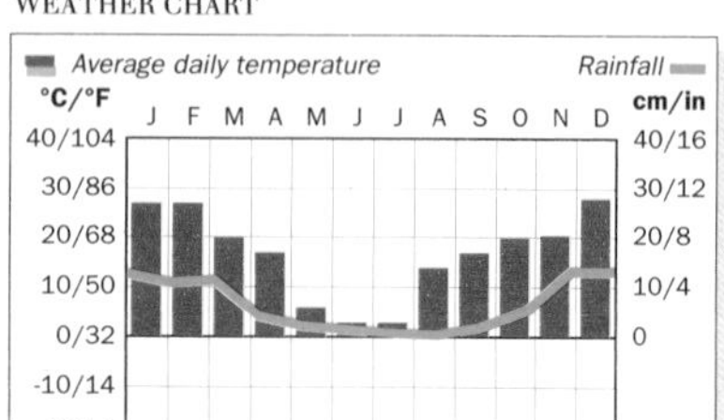

Despite the moderating effects of oceans on three sides, South Africa's warm temperate climate is dry; 65% of the country has less than 50 cm of rain a year. Drought is a periodic hazard.

TOURISM

MAIN OVERSEAS ARRIVALS

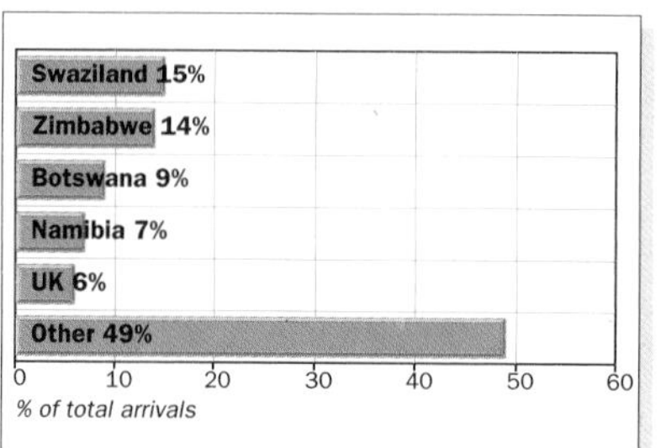

South Africa has a huge potential for tourism. Its attractions range from beaches to mountains, from prize-winning vineyards to internationally renowned wildlife reserves. The Kruger National Park is perhaps the most diverse in the world, with 137 species of mammal and 450 species of bird. This potential, however, has yet to be fully realized. South Africa's isolation during the apartheid era kept tourist numbers down. Today, the key constraints on efforts to expand tourism are political uncertainty and the rising level of violent crime.

COMMUNICATIONS

Jan Smuts International, Johannesburg
4.5m passengers

6 ships
200,500 dwt

THE TRANSPORTATION NETWORK

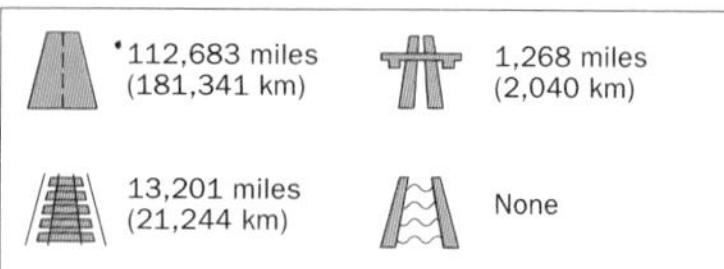

The further expansion of port capacity is a priority. Improvements to the road network are aimed in part at reducing accidents: South Africa has one of the world's worst road death rates.

***Vineyard backed by** the dramatic mountains of Cape Province. The lifting of trade sanctions has provided a major boost to the South African wine industry.*

PEOPLE

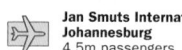

Afrikaans, Zulu, Xhosa, Tswana, Sotho, Pedi, English, Swazi, Venda, Bushman

75 people per sq. mile

THE URBAN/RURAL POPULATION SPLIT

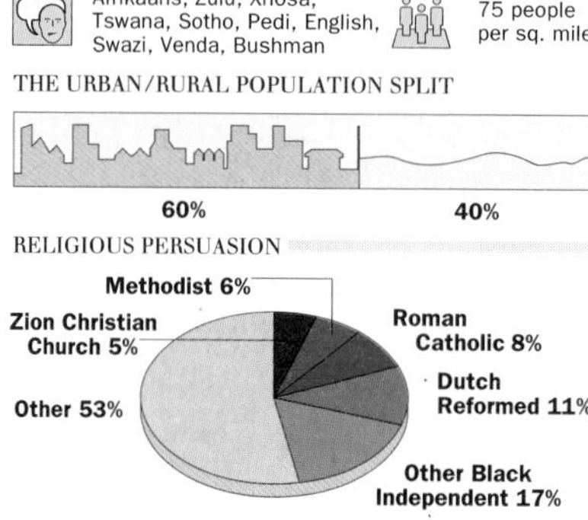

ETHNIC MAKEUP

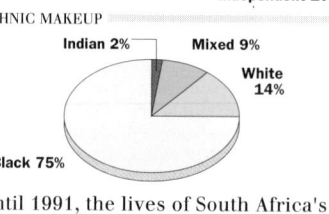

Indian 2%
Mixed 9%
White 14%
Black 75%

Until 1991, the lives of South Africa's many ethnic groups were structured by apartheid, the system of racial segregation controlled by the white minority. The Dutch-descended Afrikaners dominated politics; the English-speaking whites the economy. The black majority was marginalized socially and politically.

The extended family has been undermined by regulations forcing men to migrate for work, leaving their wives and children in the rural areas. A small black middle class has grown up, but most black South Africans are underemployed.

Ethnic tension remains high in the transition period following the dismantling of apartheid. This has led to demands for independent homelands by some Zulus and whites.

The decline of the male-dominated Afrikaner political culture will allow women, who already play an increasingly important economic role, to move to the center of politics. Around 40% of ANC election candidates were female. The new constitution guarantees equality of the sexes.

POPULATION AGE BREAKDOWN

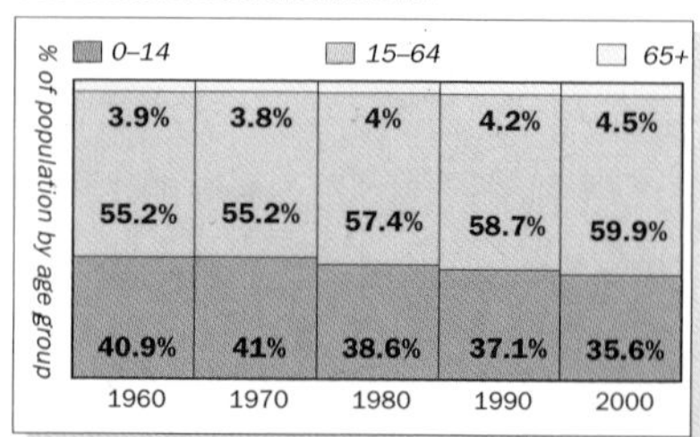

POLITICS

1998

President Nelson Rolihlahla Mandela

THE STATE OF THE PARTIES

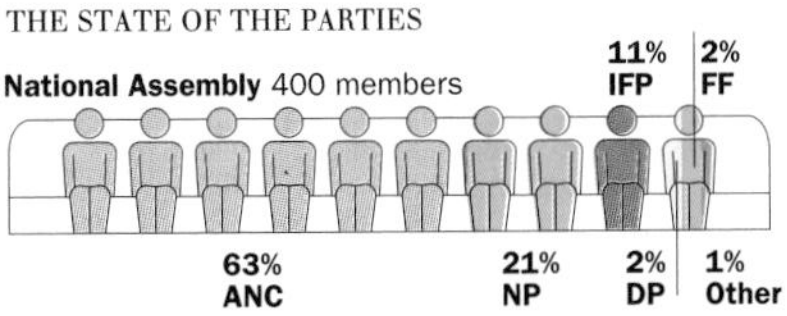

National Assembly 400 members

11% **IFP** · **2%** **FF**

63% **ANC** · **21%** **NP** · **2%** **DP** · **1%** **Other**

ANC = African National Congress **NP** = National Party
IFP = Inkatha Freedom Party **DP** = Democratic Party
FF = Freedom Front Other = Pan African Congress (**PAC**), African Christian Democratic Party

Senate 90 members

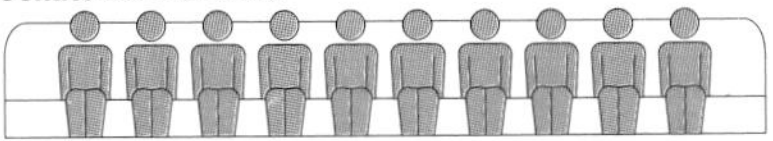

10 members elected by each of 9 regional legislatures

South Africa became a multiparty democracy following elections in 1994.

Main Political Issues

Maintaining unity

In April 1994, South Africa confounded the proponents of violence and ethnic division to hold peaceful elections which brought its first multiracial government to power. The challenge facing the new ANC-dominated administration is to ensure that, while pursuing the aspirations of the black majority, it does not marginalize South Africa's minorities. The white far right and Chief Buthelezi's *Inkatha* have the potential to resume violent destabilization if they feel their interests are not being addressed.

Role of the security forces

The loyalty of the security forces to the new government is uncertain. There was plenty of evidence, notably from the 1994 Goldstone Commission, of police and military involvement in pre-election violence. A particular problem for the police, long seen as the agents of apartheid, is to evolve into a neutral crime-prevention force.

Profile

The 1994 elections put an end to over 45 years of white rule by the NP. Its leader, F. W. De Klerk, played a central role with ANC leader Nelson Mandela in the transition to multiracial democracy. The NP came second in the polls but well behind the ANC, which only just missed the two-thirds majority it needed to govern alone. The ANC now dominates the Unity government. Its main challenge, apart from maintaining national unity, will be to reconcile the demands of its activists for jobs and better living standards, while encouraging foreign investment.

WORLD AFFAIRS

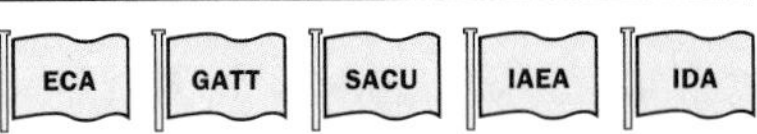

After several decades of political isolation and economic sanctions, South Africa is to be readmitted to the UN and the Commonwealth. Its priority now is to attract new international investors and to encourage the return of the many who disinvested during the 1980s. The end of apartheid brought an end to hostility from South Africa's neighbors. Improving relations with them and with the non-aligned countries is also important. Membership of the Southern African Development Community (SADC) is being discussed, although existing members are concerned that South Africa's economic domination of the region could lead to its taking over the organization. A regional security alliance has also been mooted. Evidence that rogue army and civilian elements are involved with UNITA in the renewed Angolan civil war has been an embarrassment to the government.

SOUTH AFRICA

Total Area : 1 221 040 sq. km (471 443 sq. miles)

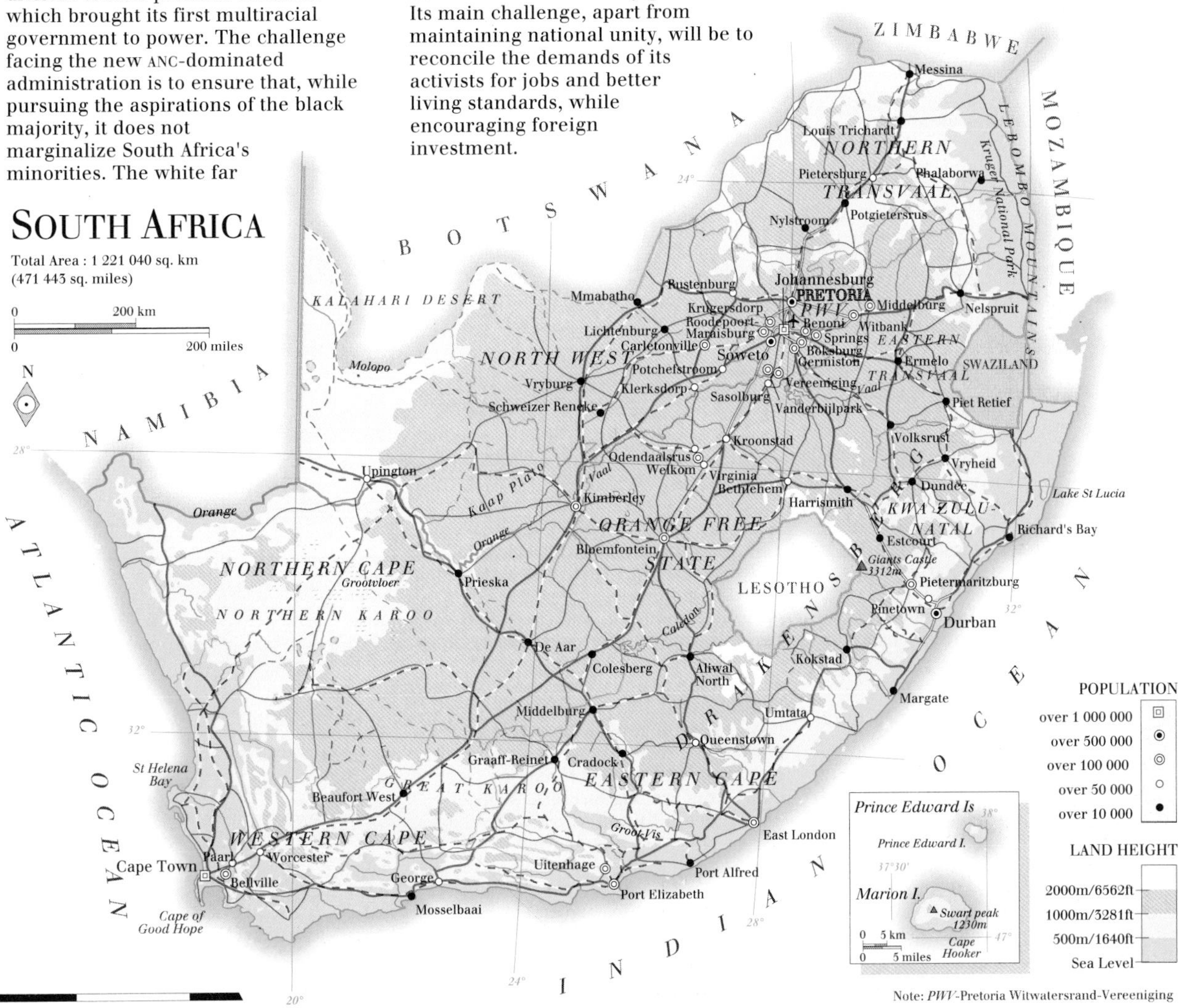

0 200 km
0 200 miles

POPULATION
over 1 000 000
over 500 000
over 100 000
over 50 000
over 10 000

LAND HEIGHT
2000m/6562ft
1000m/3281ft
500m/1640ft
Sea Level

Note: *PWV*-Pretoria Witwatersrand-Vereeniging

AID

$849 million (est) in 1993 — Increasing with end of political isolation

South Africa was cut off from almost all aid, particularly from the World Bank and IMF, during the apartheid years. It is now trying to persuade donors to provide the massive financial aid needed to support reconstruction, in particular for job creation and social infrastructure programs.

CHRONOLOGY

Until 1652, South Africa was peopled by Bantu-speaking groups and Bushmen. Then, Dutch settlers arrived. British colonizers followed in the 18th century.

- **1899–1902** Boer War with Britain.
- **1910** Union of South Africa set up as British dominion; white monopoly of power formalized.
- **1912** ANC formed.
- **1934** Independence.
- **1948** NP takes power; apartheid segregationist policy introduced.
- **1958–1966** Dr Hendrik Verwoerd prime minister. "Grand Apartheid" policy implemented.
- **1959** Pan African Congress (PAC) formed in split from ANC.
- **1960** Sharpeville massacre. ANC, PAC banned. South Africa becomes republic; leaves Commonwealth.
- **1964** Nelson Mandela, a senior leader of the ANC, jailed.
- **1976** Soweto uprisings sparked by attempts to force black schools to teach Afrikaans; hundreds killed.
- **1978** P. W. Botha prime minister.
- **1984** New constitution: Indians and Coloreds get some representation. Growing black opposition.
- **1985** State of emergency introduced. International sanctions.
- **1989** F. W. De Klerk replaces P. W. Botha as president. Elections underline white conservative hostility to change.
- **1990** De Klerk legalizes ANC and PAC; frees Nelson Mandela.
- **1990–1993** International sanctions gradually withdrawn.
- **1991** Multiparty Convention for a Democratic South Africa (CODESA) begins negotiating new political structure.
- **1992** De Klerk wins whites-only referendum. June–August: "Mass Action;" ANC breaks off talks over government veto on CODESA. September: talks resume. De Klerk and Mandela work together on transition process.
- **1993** Transitional timetable takes shape. Mandela and De Klerk win Nobel Peace Prize.
- **1994** April: multiracial elections.

DEFENSE

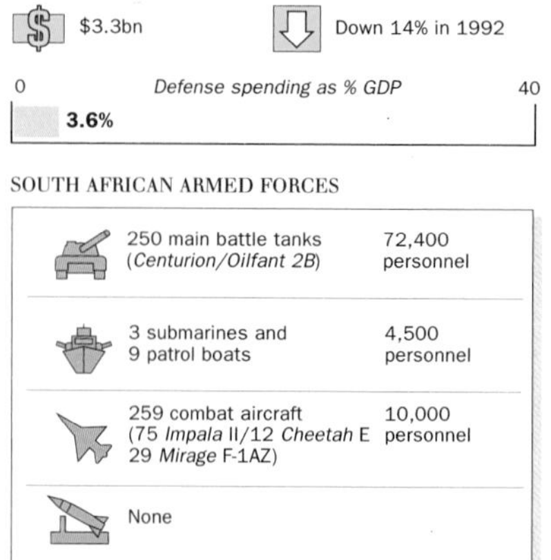

$3.3bn — Down 14% in 1992

Defense spending as % GDP (0–40): 3.6%

SOUTH AFRICAN ARMED FORCES

250 main battle tanks (*Centurion/Olifant 2B*)	72,400 personnel
3 submarines and 9 patrol boats	4,500 personnel
259 combat aircraft (75 *Impala* II/12 *Cheetah* E 29 *Mirage* F-1AZ)	10,000 personnel
None	

The government is trying to turn the South African Defense Force (SADF), the enforcer of apartheid, into a body loyal to a multiracial government. The process has included cuts in defense spending, an end to the SADF's policy-making role and changes in top personnel. The possibility of a security alliance with South Africa's former opponents in the region has been proposed. A major test will be the integration of the armed wings of the ANC and PAC. Rogue SADF elements involved in political violence and former officers in the racist far-right may threaten the outcome of reform.

Sanctions encouraged a major arms industry. South Africa is now the world's twelfth leading arms exporter.

ECONOMICS

$90.4bn — 3.06 rand

SCORE CARD

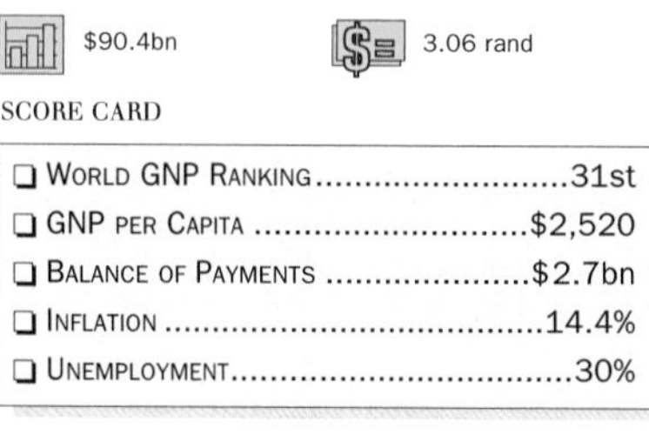

World GNP Ranking	31st
GNP per Capita	$2,520
Balance of Payments	$2.7bn
Inflation	14.4%
Unemployment	30%

EXPORTS

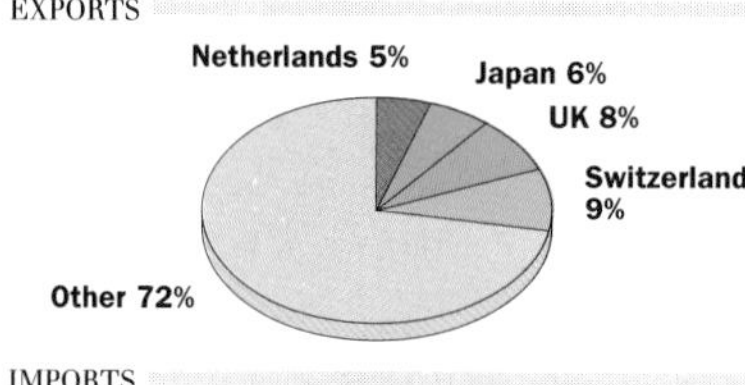

IMPORTS

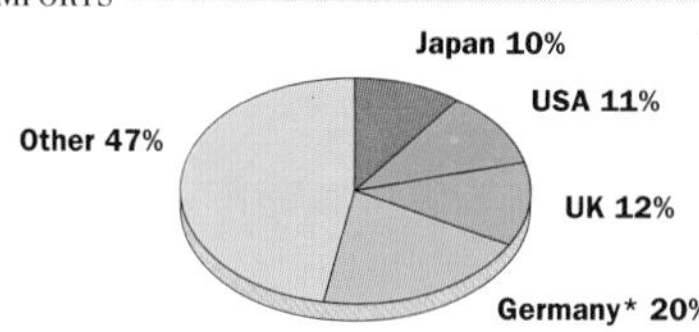

STRENGTHS

Africa's largest and most developed economy; highly diversified with modern infrastructure. Strong financial sector for mobilizing investment. Growing manufacturing sector, at present accounting for 23% of GDP. Varied resource base, particularly of strategically important minerals.

WEAKNESSES

Risks of political instability deter foreign investment. Growth too low to provide resources to overcome deprivation among black majority. Black unemployment growing by 2.5% a year. High population growth.

PROFILE

South Africa has a large and diverse private sector, much of it controlled by multinationals. International sanctions forced the government to play a central economic role through state corporations in the 1980s. This is now being reduced in a series of privatizations. The ANC has declared its intention to work with big business in order to revivify the economy and develop the townships.

ECONOMIC PERFORMANCE INDICATOR

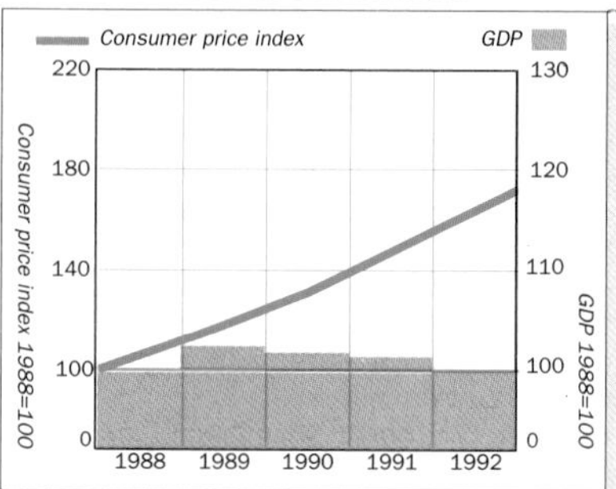

SOUTH AFRICA : MAJOR BUSINESSES

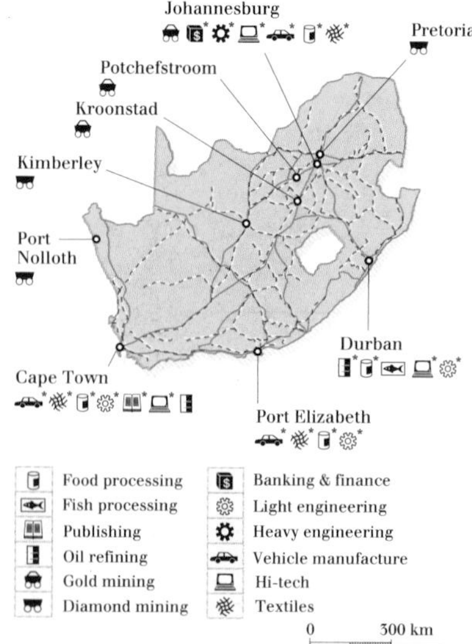

RESOURCES

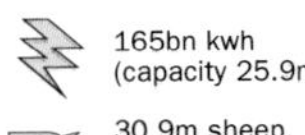

Not an oil producer; refines 430,500 b/cd

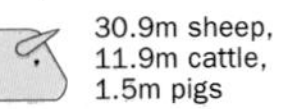

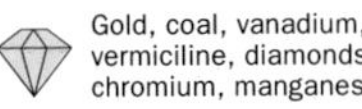

ELECTRICITY GENERATION

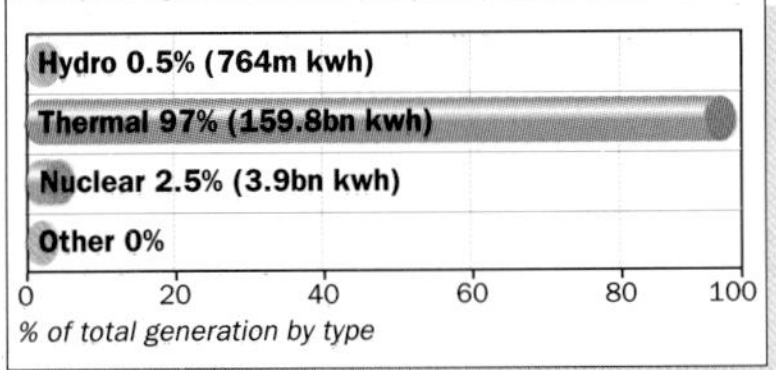

South Africa has some of the continent's richest natural resources, in particular minerals. Its dominance of the world market in gold and diamonds was central to its survival of sanctions during apartheid. Over the past century, 47% of the world's gold has come from South Africa. Today's output of 670 tons a year accounts for 30% of the world total. South Africa is the single largest producer of manganese metal, chrome ore, vanadium and vermiciline.

South Africa lacks oil reserves, and sanctions-busting was costly. Its huge coal reserves are used to generate 87% of electricity and to make oil. The priority is to bring the 80% of black homes without electricity into the national grid. Agriculture is varied.

SOUTH AFRICA : LAND USE

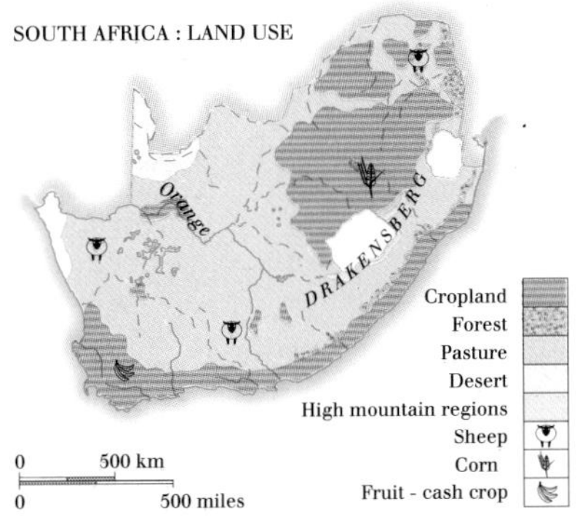

ENVIRONMENT

6% (4% partially protected)

Environmental legislation not a priority

ENVIRONMENTAL TREATIES

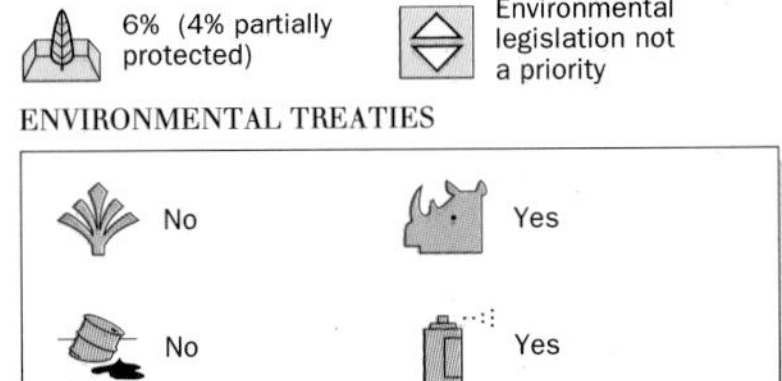

Natural disasters, notably floods and drought, are a hazard. The main concern is protecting rich and varied animal species. Environmental measures could conflict in future with the demands of economic growth.

MEDIA

Censorship regulations imposed under apartheid have been largely dismantled since 1990

PUBLISHING AND BROADCAST MEDIA

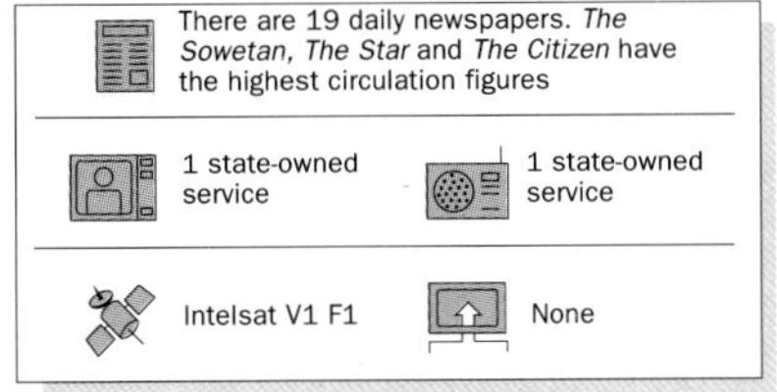

There are 19 daily newspapers. The Sowetan, The Star and The Citizen have the highest circulation figures
1 state-owned service
1 state-owned service
Intelsat V1 F1
None

The end of censorship is reflected in the press, which ranges from far-left to extreme-right. TV programming is now more balanced and diverse.

CRIME

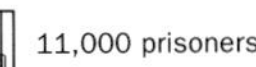

Rapid rise in violent crime

CRIME RATES

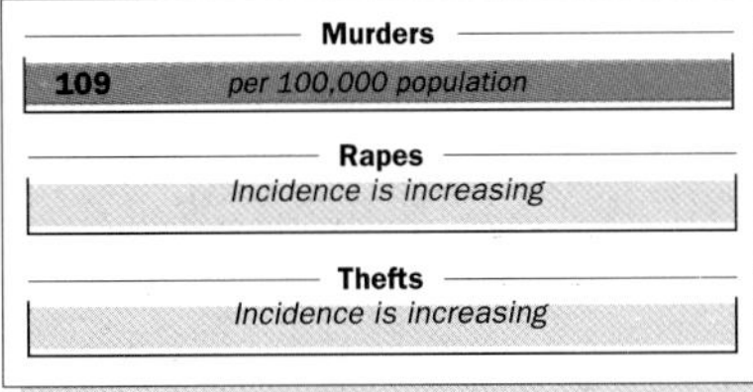

South Africa is the world's most dangerous country (besides war zones), with 40,000 murders a year. Despite its high profile, political violence accounts for only 10% of the total. The rise in levels of murder, armed robbery and muggings has led to a boom in the personal security industry.

EDUCATION

59%

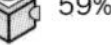

THE EDUCATION SYSTEM

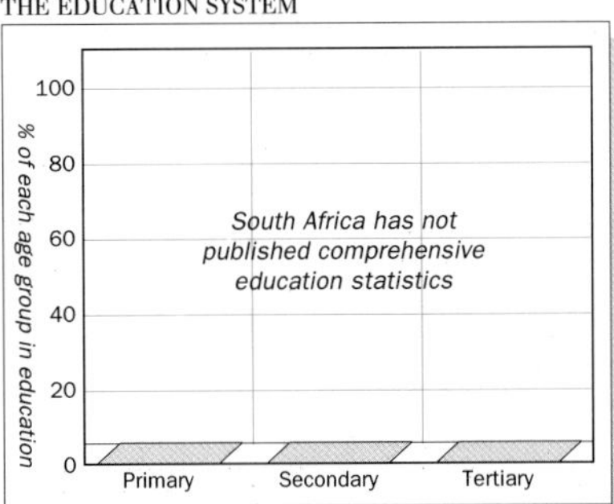

Education has been desegregated, but most black children are still restricted to underfunded schools. Upgrading education is a priority if employment prospects for blacks are to meet their requirements.

HEALTH

1 per 1,340 people

Heart, respiratory and diarrheal disease, cancer, road deaths

0 *Health spending as % GNP* 25

0.6%

Health services were desegregated in 1990, but have yet to be restructured and expanded to give all people equal access to care. The per capita figures on provision of medical facilities hide a strong bias toward whites and urban areas, where 80% of doctors work. The limited provision for rural black South Africans, in particular, is reflected in mortality figures. Of every 1,000 black children born, 200 die before the age of five, compared with the sub-Saharan average of 165 per 1,000.

WEALTH

Salaries among whites are substantially higher than among blacks

CONSUMER GOODS OWNERSHIP

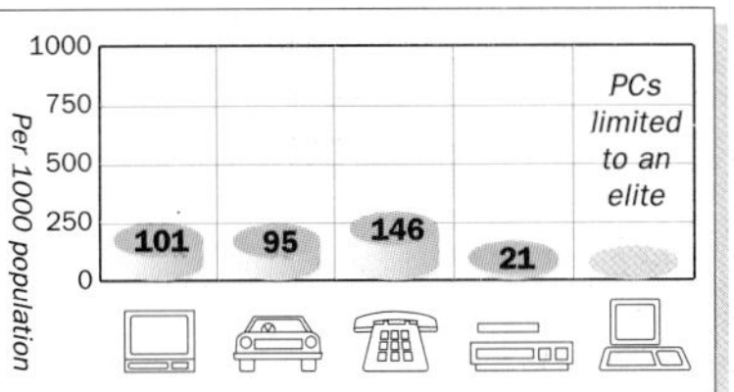

In South Africa, the black majority is the poorest group. Wealth disparities are marked. At the top, the white elite enjoys one of the world's highest standards of living, on a par with that of California. In contrast, black living standards are among Africa's poorest. Half of black adults are unemployed. Most blacks have been deprived of decent housing, education and health facilities. In between are the Asian and mixed race communities, given more privileges under apartheid's strict racial hierarchy, and a very small black middle class. Reducing these disparities will be the new government's priority.

WORLD RANKING

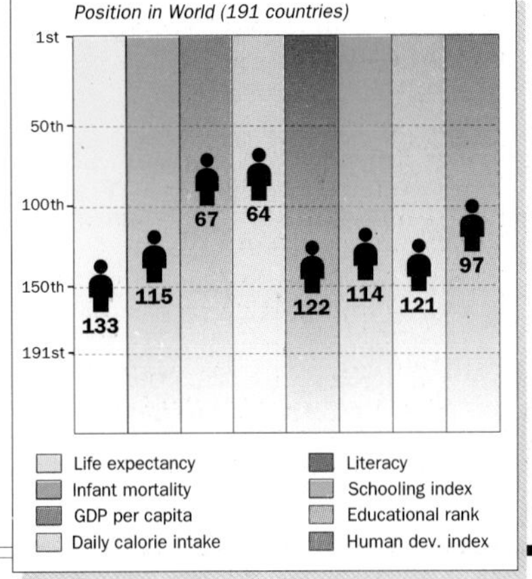

South Korea

Official Name: Republic of Korea **Capital:** Seoul
Population: 44.2 million **Currency:** Won **Official Language:** Korean

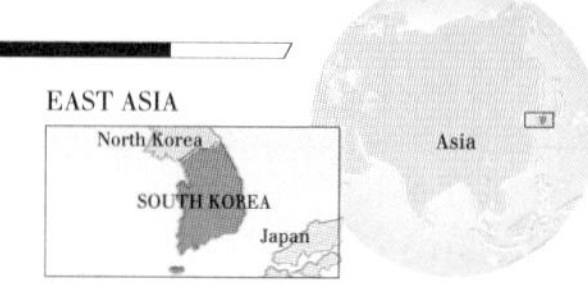

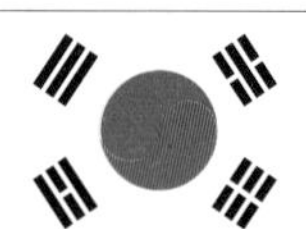

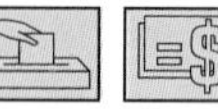
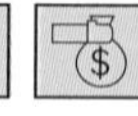

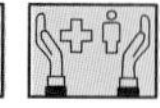

South Korea occupies the southern half of the Korean peninsula in East Asia. Over 80% of its terrain is mountainous and two-thirds is forested. Rice is the major agricultural product, grown by over 85% of South Korea's three million farmers. Most of the urban population lives along the coastal plains. Under US sponsorship, South Korea was separated from the communist North after World War II. In 1991, the two states discussed reunification. However, South Korea remains suspicious that the North may be planning a military takeover.

CLIMATE

WEATHER CHART

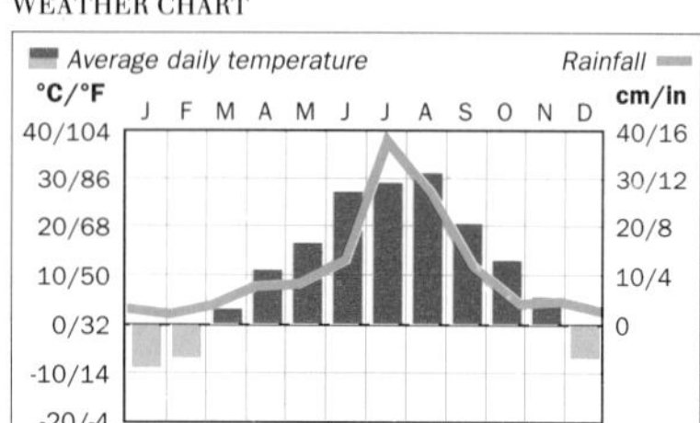

South Korea has four distinct seasons. Winters are dry and can be bitterly cold. Summers are hot and humid. The island of Cheju-do has a tropical climate.

COMMUNICATIONS

Kimpo Intl, Seoul 21.33m passengers

645 ships 1.34m dwt

THE TRANSPORTATION NETWORK

34,659 miles (55,778 km)

963 miles (1,550 km)

4,011 miles (6,456 km)

1,000 miles (1,609 km)

South Korea has a highly integrated transportation policy. Massive investments have been made in all aspects of communications. In 1968, a nationwide expressway network was inaugurated. Mainly toll-based, it now joins most major urban centers. Air travel, an easy way to get around the mountainous interior, has expanded rapidly. Competition for Korean Air (KAL) has come with the licensing of a second airline, Asiana. The increase in air traffic has brought forward plans to replace Kimpo International with a new airport.

South Korea has perhaps the world's best public transportation system. Buses, trains, boats and planes are integrated in one timetable. All systems have a reputation for punctuality. A $14-billion high-speed rail link is being built between Seoul and Pusan.

TOURISM

2.96m visitors

Up 8% in 1990

MAIN OVERSEAS ARRIVALS

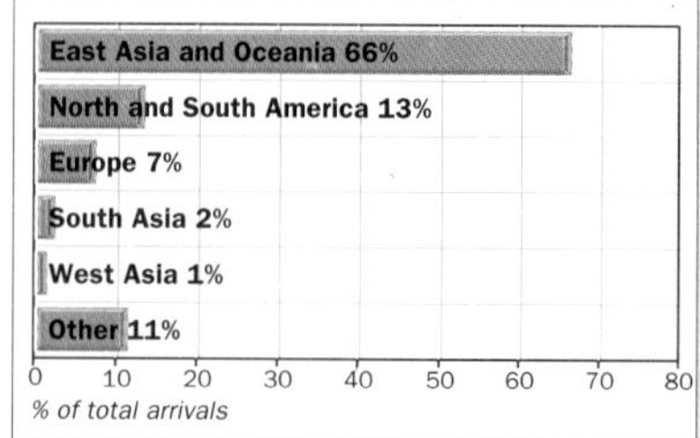

Overseas tourism to South Korea has increased tenfold since 1969. Most visitors are Japanese, who come for the golf and Seoul's nightlife.

Cheju-do Island is a favored honeymoon destination. 13% of all tourists are visiting relatives; this would once have meant relations serving with the US army. Today, Los Angeles-based Korean-Americans make up the greatest proportion of visitors. However, despite the publicity generated by the 1988 Olympics, and the decision to make 1994 "Visit Korea Year," South Korea is still not seen in the West as a prime tourist destination.

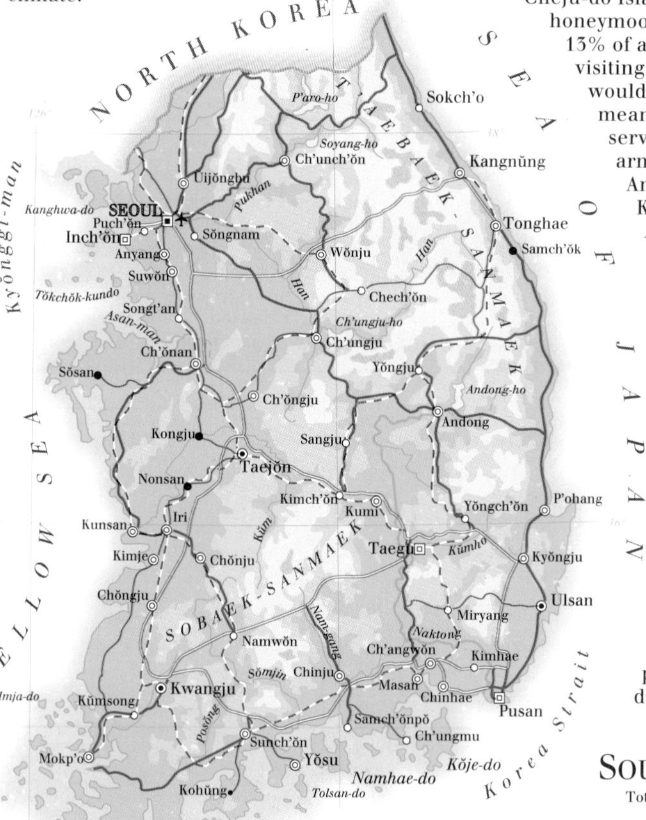

South Korea
Total Area : 99 020 sq. km (38 232 sq. miles)

POPULATION
over 5 000 000
over 1 000 000
over 500 000
over 100 000
over 50 000
over 10 000
under 10 000

LAND HEIGHT
1000m/3281ft
500m/1640ft
200m/656ft
Sea Level

N

0 50 km
0 50 miles

PEOPLE

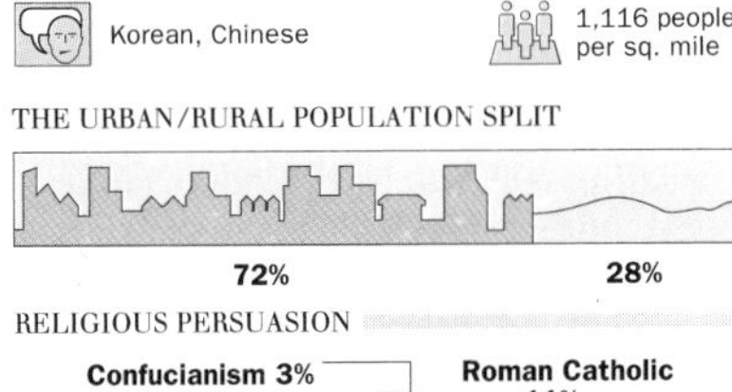

RELIGIOUS PERSUASION

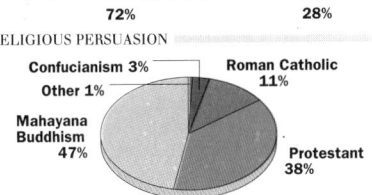

Confucianism 3%
Roman Catholic 11%
Other 1%
Mahayana Buddhism 47%
Protestant 38%

ETHNIC MAKEUP

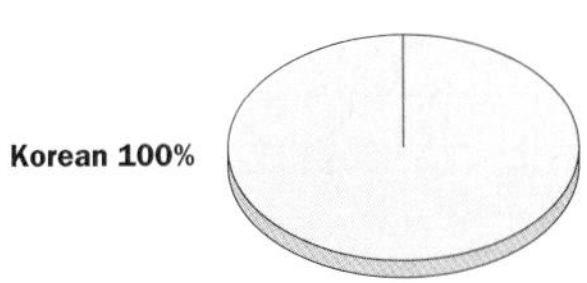

South Korea, like the North, is unusual in having been inhabited by one ethnic group for the last 2,000 years. There is a tiny Chinese community, but this is diminishing as most emigrate to Taiwan. One result of economic growth has been an increase in illegal immigrants from the poorer Asian countries who take menial jobs that Koreans now refuse. Family life is a central and clearly defined part of Korean society. Most Koreans can trace their ancestry back thousands of years. This is significant as those of the same surname group (rather than the same surname – 60% of Koreans are called Lee, Kim or Pak) may not marry. Pressure on housing has led to an increase in nuclear families, as urban apartments do not have room for the traditional household of three generations. Women play a traditional role in society: it is still not respectable for those who are married to have a job or career.

POPULATION AGE BREAKDOWN

% of population by age group

	1960	1970	1980	1990	2000
65+	3.3%	3.3%	3.8%	4.8%	6.4%
15–64	54.8%	54.7%	62.2%	69.5%	71.6%
0–14	41.9%	42%	34%	25.7%	22%

POLITICS

THE STATE OF THE PARTIES

National Assembly 299 members

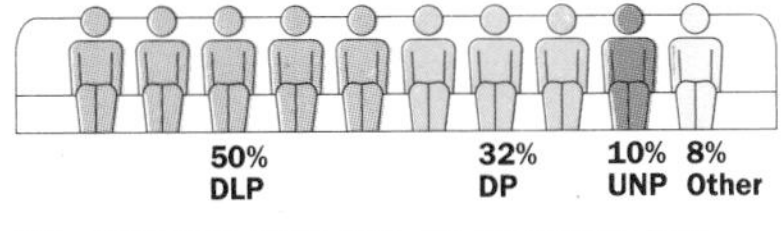

DLP = Democratic Liberal Party **DP** = Democratic Party **UNP** = Unification National Party **Other** = New Political Reform Party

Officially a democracy since its inception, in practice South Korea was ruled by military dictators until 1987, when the Sixth Republic established multiparty democratic politics.

MAIN POLITICAL ISSUES

Corruption
President Kim Young-Sam's anti-corruption program has been popular with voters, and has succeeded in purging his enemies. Pushing the process too far, however, risks antagonizing the military and splitting his party.

The economy
South Korea's growth slowed to 4.8% in 1992 – poor by Korean standards. The debate is moving in favor of state intervention in the economy.

Faction-led parties
South Korea's political parties are highly factionalized and fragmented, and regroup often. Voters are beginning to demand unified parties that represent clearer ideological positions.

PROFILE

South Korea's politics changed radically in 1987 when President Roh Tae-Woo instituted a genuine transition to democracy, including, for the first time, direct elections for president, a parliament with enhanced powers and a free press.

In 1993, the first non-military leader in 30 years, President Kim Young-Sam became president. He quickly appointed a new head of the army staff, thereby establishing his independence from the military. Searching tax audits have also been used to embarrass political opponents. A reform drive in 1994 was aimed at rooting out corruption in all areas of government.

Kim Young-Sam, veteran democratic activist and president since 1993.

Roh Tae-Woo, a former general and president between 1988 and 1993.

WORLD AFFAIRS

Since the 1950s, relations with North Korea have been the major concern of foreign policy. These remain unresolved. North Korea has recently shown a new willingness to consider reunification, while simultaneously, South Korea suspects, pursuing an aggressive nuclear program. South Korea is also concerned that the North Korean economy may be about to suffer an East German-style collapse, which would seriously increase the social and economic costs of union. Relations with China, once an important ally of North Korea, have improved and are being cemented by trade. Japan is also a major trading partner, although South Koreans harbor resentment over the 1910–1945 Japanese occupation.

AID

$110m (donations)

Once a massive recipient of US aid, and then from 1965 of Japanese war reparations, South Korea has in recent years become an aid donor. Aid is primarily used to further foreign policy, such as the $3-billion sweetener to the CIS to promote good relations with Russia and Central Asia.

CHRONOLOGY

The Yi dynasty, founded in Seoul in 1392, ruled the kingdom of Korea until 1910. However, Korea became a vassal state of China in 1644.

- **1860** Korea reacts to French and British occupation of Peking by preventing Western influence.
- **1864–1907** Taewon'gun's rule. Korea remains the "Hermit Kingdom."
- **1894–1895** Social and religious revolt. Rebels defeat government, which invites Chinese help. Japanese seize power. Sino-Japanese War – Japanese win.
- **1896** King seeks Russian help.
- **1904–1905** Russo-Japanese War. Japan conquers Korea.
- **1910** Japan annexes Korea.
- **1919** Independence protests all over Korea violently suppressed.
- **1945** US and Soviet armies arrive. Korea split at 38°N. South comes under *de facto* US rule.
- **1948** Republic of South Korea created.
- **1948** Elections. Liberals' leader Dr. Syngman Rhee becomes president. Leads increasingly authoritarian regime.

S

CHRONOLOGY *continued*

- **1950** Hostilities between North and South, each aspiring to rule a united Korea. North invades South sparking Korean War. US, with UN backing, enters on South's side, China on North's. In 1951, China takes Seoul, but is pushed back to 38°N. 600,000 die in South.
- **1953** Armistice. Border re-set at ceasefire line, close to 38°N
- **1960** Syngman Rhee resigns in face of popular revolt.
- **1961** New military coup. Junta led by Park Chung-Hee.
- **1963** Pressure for civilian government. Park reelected as president (also in 1967, 1971). Massive economic development in 1960s–1970s. All mineral resources in North Korea, so South concentrates on manufactures and huge export drive.
- **1965** Links restored with Japan.
- **1966** Sends 45,000 troops to fight for South Vietnam.
- **1972** Martial law stifles political opposition. New constitution with greater presidential powers.
- **1979** Park assassinated. Gen Chun Doo-Huan, intelligence chief, leads coup. Kim Young-Sam, opposition leader, expelled from parliament.
- **1980** Chun chosen as president. Kim Dae-Jong and other opposition leaders arrested.
- **1985** Freer elections held. New Democratic Party (NDP), wins strong support.
- **1986** Car exports start.
- **1987** Domestic and international pressure for democracy. Roh Tae-Woo, Chun's chosen successor, elected president.
- **1988** Olympic Games in Seoul. Restrictions on foreign travel lifted.
- **1990** Government party and two opposition parties, including Kim Young-Sam's, merge to form DLP. Those opposed to merger form DP.
- **1991** South Korea joins UN. Reunification discussions with North.
- **1992** Links with China established.

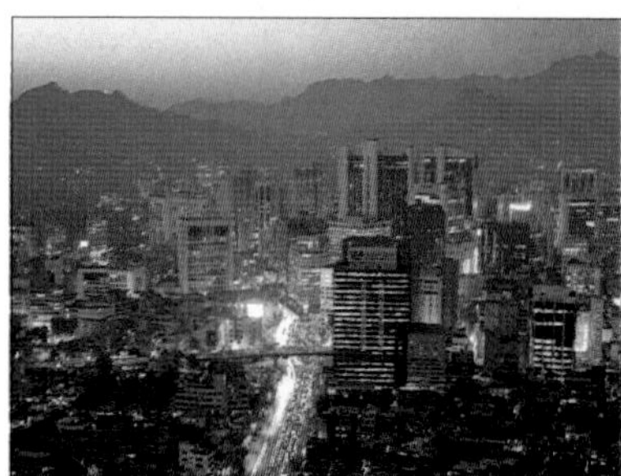

Seoul lit up at night. *The city is home to more than 10.5 million people – one-quarter of South Korea's population. Seoul means "capital."*

S

DEFENSE

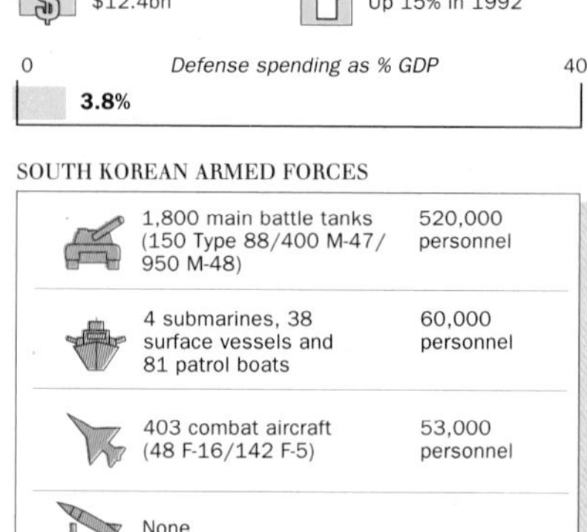

$12.4bn
Up 15% in 1992
0
Defense spending as % GDP
40
3.8%
SOUTH KOREAN ARMED FORCES
1,800 main battle tanks (150 Type 88/400 M-47/ 950 M-48)
520,000 personnel
4 submarines, 38 surface vessels and 81 patrol boats
60,000 personnel
403 combat aircraft (48 F-16/142 F-5)
53,000 personnel
None

Since Kim Young-Sam came to power, the role of the military has been sharply downgraded. A campaign to root out corruption in arms procurement and investigations into past military involvement in politics have forced 40 generals to retire.

The main defense concern is the North Korean regime. South Korea has fewer troops, tanks, artillery and aircraft than the North, but it claims parity in having superior technology and the presence of 35,000 US troops permanently based on its territory. However, recent US computer simulations have questioned whether South Korea can resist an invasion by the North's one-million-strong army.

ECONOMICS

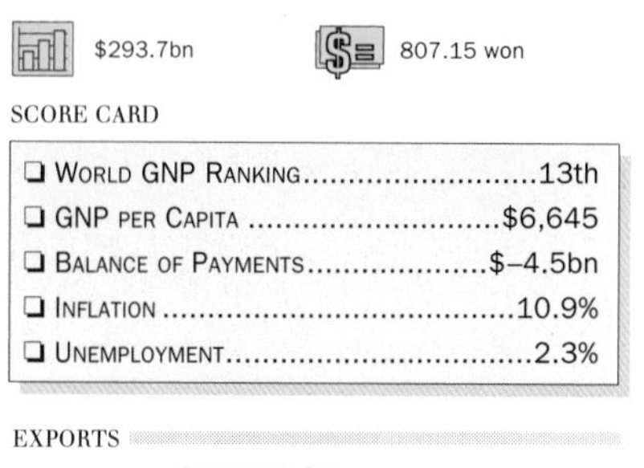

$293.7bn 807.15 won

SCORE CARD

World GNP Ranking	13th
GNP per Capita	$6,645
Balance of Payments	$–4.5bn
Inflation	10.9%
Unemployment	2.3%

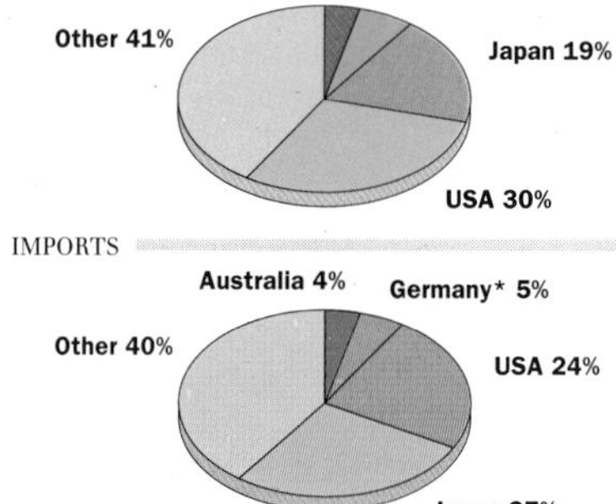

ECONOMIC PERFORMANCE INDICATOR

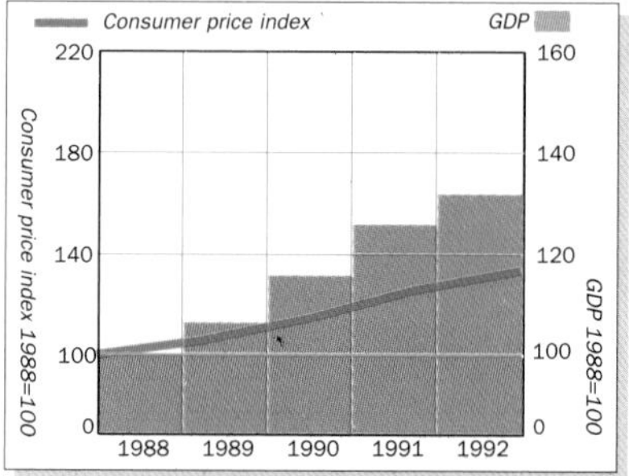

STRENGTHS
The world's most successful shipbuilder, with 45% of the market. Continuing benefits of highly valued yen, which make Korean exports more competitive than Japan's. Strong demand from China for Korean goods, particularly cars.

WEAKNESSES
Work force beginning to demand better working conditions. State sector is still a burden on the economy. Japanese plants in other Southeast Asian countries, particularly Indonesia, offering strong competition.

PROFILE
The first decades of the South Korean economic miracle were the result of centralized planning. Conglomerates known as *chaebol*, such as Samsung, achieved impressive growth rates in strategic industries such as car manufacture, shipbuilding and semi-conductors. The three largest *chaebol* had sales of $180 billion. South Korea's work force, well-educated but cheaper than Japan's, and cheap state credit, gave Korea a competitive edge. The government now aims to encourage foreign investment and to concentrate on smaller industries, which it sees as the key to maintaining current growth.

SOUTH KOREA : MAJOR BUSINESSES

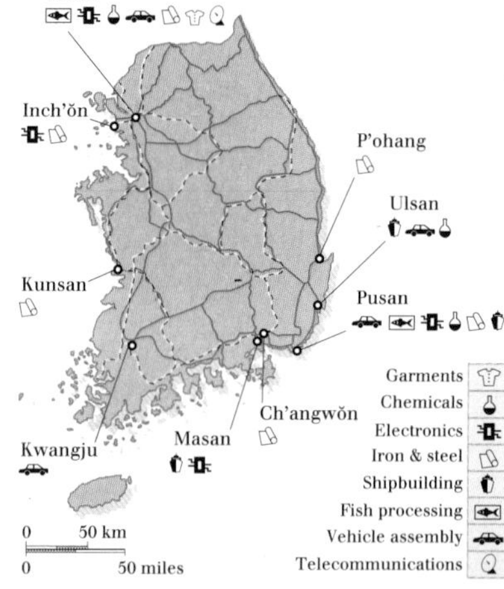

RESOURCES

118.7bn kwh (capacity 24.1m kw)

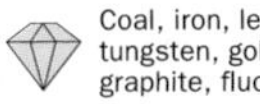
Not an oil producer; refines 1.15m b/cd

4.8m pigs, 2m cattle, 4,000 horses

Coal, iron, lead, zinc, tungsten, gold, graphite, fluorite

ELECTRICITY GENERATION

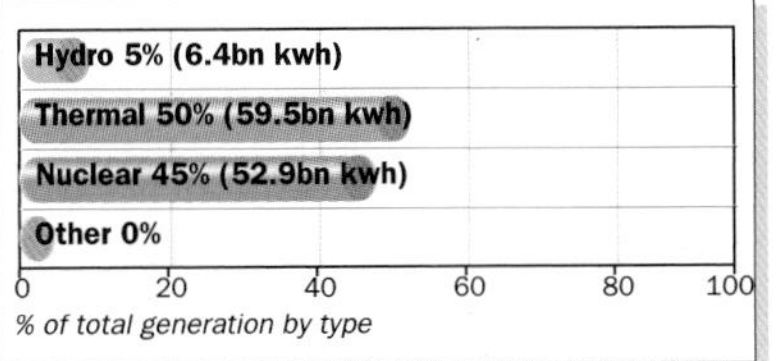

South Korea has embraced nuclear power for generating electricity. Nine nuclear reactors are already in operation, with a combined generating capacity of nearly 8,000 MW. One reactor a year is scheduled to come into production between 1991 and 1995. This will add a further 4,740 MW of capacity to the national grid. South Korea has to import all its oil.

Agriculture remains a highly protected sector. Plans announced in 1994 to open up the rice market led to massive demonstrations in Seoul.

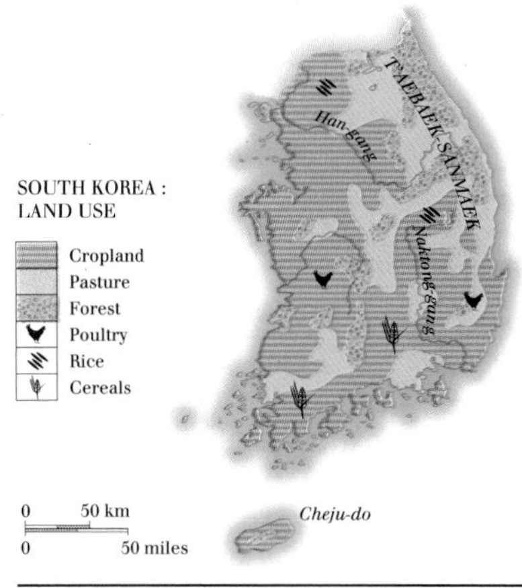

ENVIRONMENT

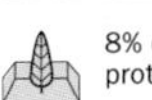
8% (7% partially protected)

Environmental protection is not yet of primary concern

ENVIRONMENTAL TREATIES

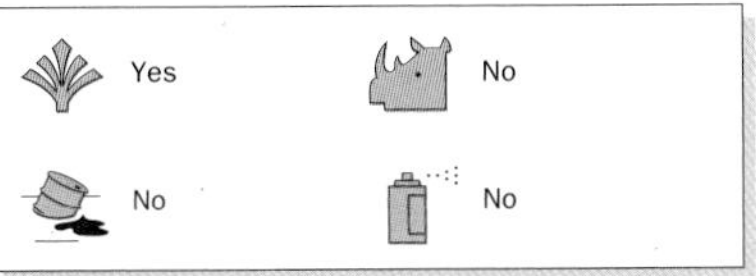

Environmental groups in Southeast Asia have expressed concern at South Korea's fast-track nuclear power program. The country's rapid industrialization and modernization has resulted in a number of environmental problems. Urban areas, particularly Seoul, suffer from air pollution owing to the widespread use of low-grade coal for heating and industry. In rural areas, many rivers have been polluted by fertilizers and chemicals.

CRIME

52,371 prisoners

Up 1% in 1986

CRIME RATES

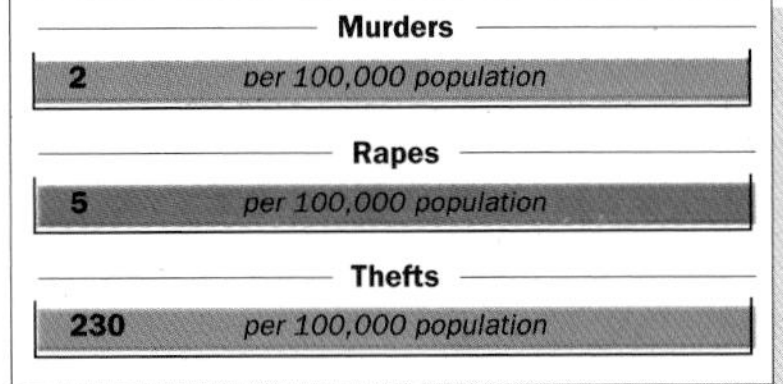

The government has begun to treat corruption as a crime. Otherwise, crime rates are relatively low and cases of violent crime uncommon. Since 1987, the internal security forces' operations have been restricted, although left-wing activists are still harassed. Striking workers and student demonstrators are subjected to tear gas and other methods of crowd control.

HEALTH

1 per 1,066 people

Cancer, heart and cerebrovascular diseases

0	Health spending as % GNP	25
0.4%		

The health service has improved in line with economic growth and now offers most advanced treatments. Health indicators such as infant mortality and longevity have improved accordingly.

WEALTH

Dentist 3m won per month; secretary 800,000 won per month

CONSUMER GOODS OWNERSHIP

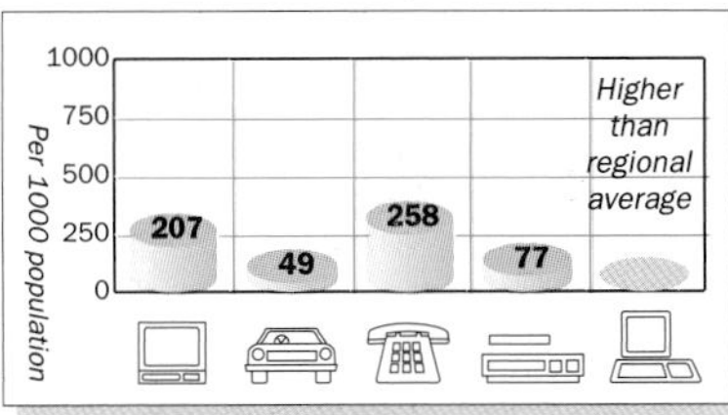

Most South Koreans have benefited from economic growth. However, the Cholla region remains the poorest.

MEDIA

The media is free of direct governmental interference

PUBLISHING AND BROADCAST MEDIA

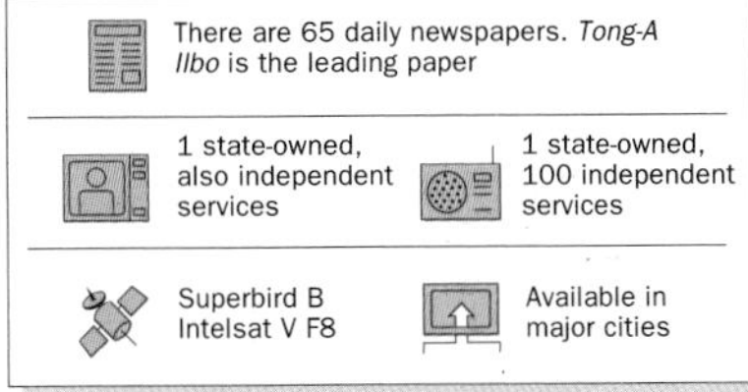

There are 65 daily newspapers. Tong-A Ilbo is the leading paper
1 state-owned, also independent services
1 state-owned, 100 independent services
Superbird B
Intelsat V F8
Available in major cities

South Korea's media has been freed of most restrictions since the advent of full multiparty democracy. However, criticisms of the armed forces are still frowned upon and journalists tend to avoid the subject of the role of the military in society altogether. Caution also has to be exercised in reporting facts about North Korea. In the past, South Korean journalists who have made favorable mention of President Kim Il Sung's communist regime in North Korea have suffered harassment and intimidation.

EDUCATION

96%

0	Education spending as % GNP	25
3.6%		

THE EDUCATION SYSTEM

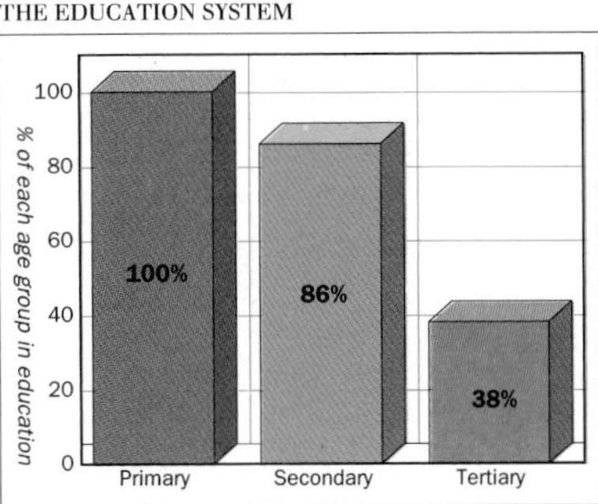

South Korea embarked on a concentrated education program in the 1950s. The high priority given to education contributed greatly to South Korea's subsequent economic success. Higher education enrollment is 38%, one of the highest rates in the world.

WORLD RANKING

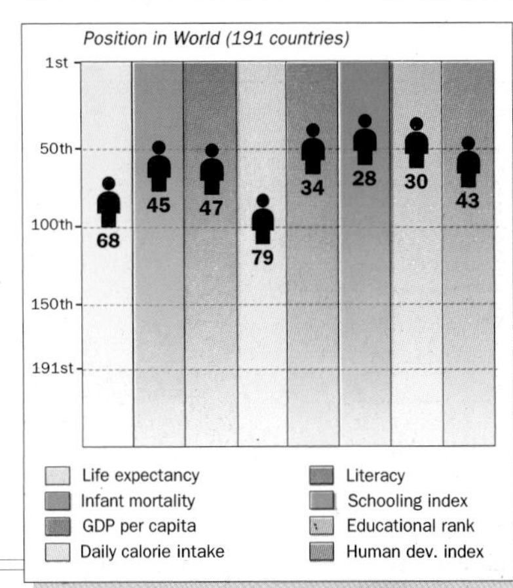

S

SPAIN

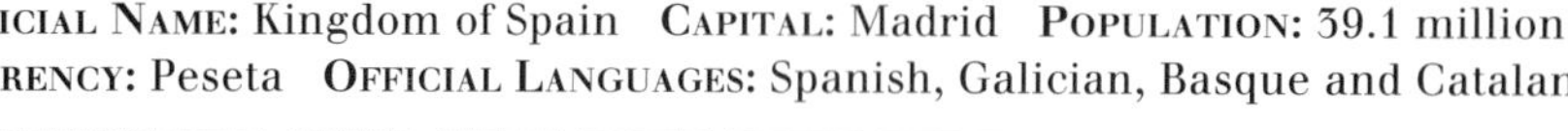

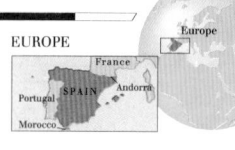

OFFICIAL NAME: Kingdom of Spain **CAPITAL:** Madrid **POPULATION:** 39.1 million
CURRENCY: Peseta **OFFICIAL LANGUAGES:** Spanish, Galician, Basque and Catalan

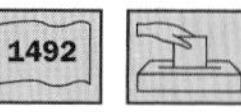

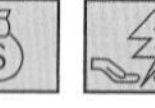

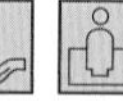

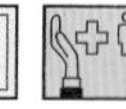

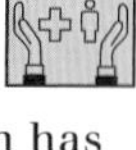

SITUATED IN SOUTHWESTERN EUROPE, Spain has a wet Atlantic and a dry Mediterranean coast. It is dominated by a central plateau drained by the Duero, Tagus and Guadiana rivers. Since the death of General Franco in 1975, Spain has managed a rapid and relatively peaceful transition to democracy under the supervision of King Juan Carlos I. In recent years, it has been governed by a succession of socialist administrations led by Felipe González. Since joining the EC in 1986, there has been an increasing devolution of power to the regions.

Alcaudete, Jaén Province, *in the Andalusian Mountains between Granada and the River Guadalquivir. The ruined castle is Moorish.*

CLIMATE

WEATHER CHART

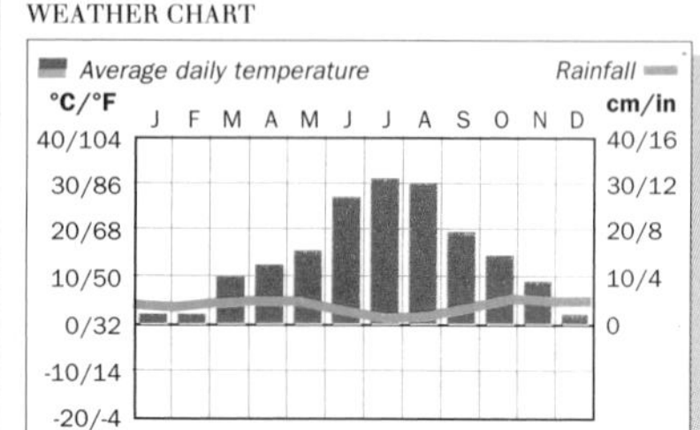

The central plateau, or *meseta*, endures an extreme climate. Coastal areas are milder, and wetter in the north than in the south.

COMMUNICATIONS

THE TRANSPORTATION NETWORK

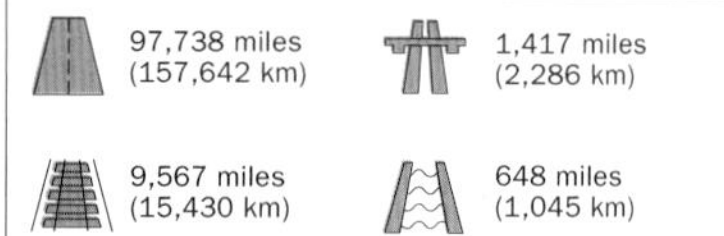

In 1992, Spain completed the *AVE*, a French *TGV*-style high-speed train linking Madrid and Seville. Spain's road accident rate remains high.

PEOPLE

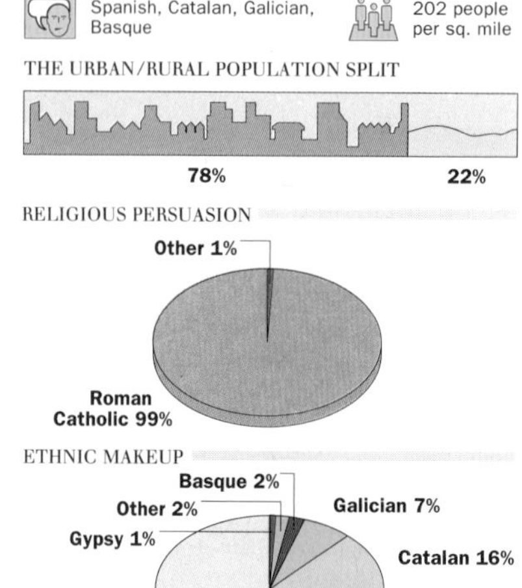

A vigorous ethnic regionalism in Spain, suppressed under Franco, has been increasing as the influence of Spain's EU partners becomes more apparent. The declining influence of the Catholic Church has meant that Spain now has one of the lowest birthrates in Europe. However, many traditional features of Spanish life remain. While attitudes toward sexuality are now relaxed, church-going remains popular. The divorce rate is extremely low and family ties remain strong, with young males living at home until their late 20s.

POPULATION AGE BREAKDOWN

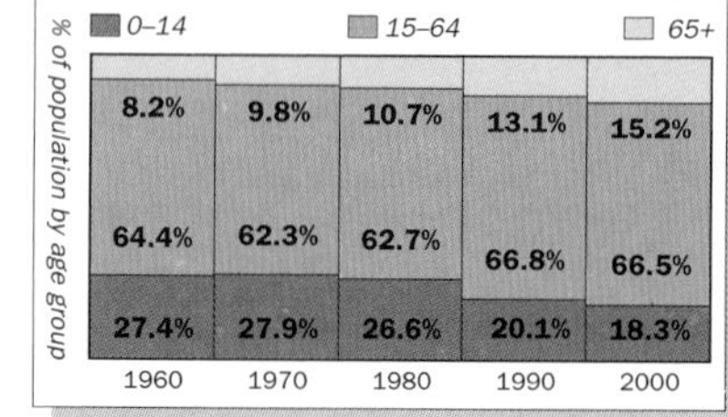

Economic growth from the 1970s led to a change in the composition of society. Spain began to attract substantial numbers of immigrants, mainly from Latin America and North Africa. However, the economic downturn in the early 1990s led to a rise in racial tensions and racism, a pattern echoed in France.

Spanish women are becoming increasingly emancipated. They have also become more influential in politics, currently making up 15% of the Spanish Congress, a higher proportion than in any other West European country.

TOURISM

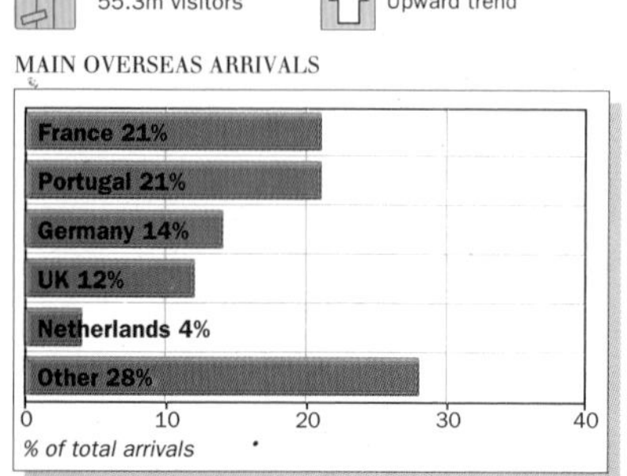

Tourism accounts for 10% of Spain's GDP, and employs one in ten Spaniards. In 1989–1991, the industry suffered significant losses due to competition from cheaper destinations. Spain is now concentrating on attracting higher-spending cultural tourists. Inland destinations, with their greater cultural, artistic and culinary appeal, are being promoted above beach resorts. The Olympics and Expo '92 provided a huge boost for Barcelona and Seville; tourism to both has since risen sharply.

POLITICS

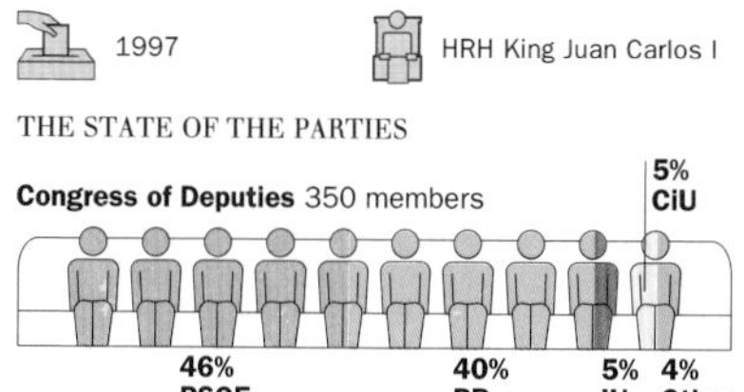

PSOE = Spanish Socialist Workers' Party PP = Popular Party
IU = United Left CiU = Convergence and Union
PNV = Basque National Party **Other** = Canary Islands Coalition, United People, Republican Left of Catalonia, Regionalist Party, Basque Solidarity, Valencian Union

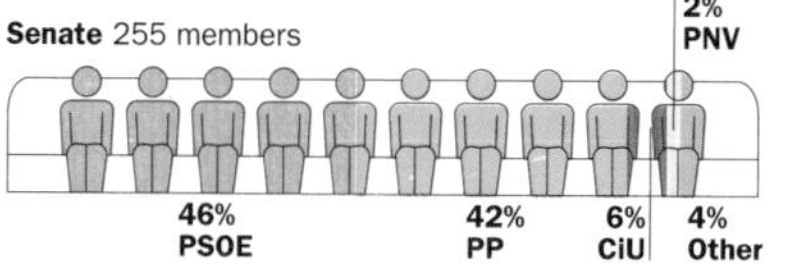

Since 1978, Spain has been a semi-federal, multiparty parliamentary monarchy.

MAIN POLITICAL ISSUES

Power struggles in the PSOE

The power struggle between *renovadores* (reformers) and *guerristas* (followers of former deputy Prime Minister Alfonso Guerra) is threatening to tear apart Spain's ruling party, the PSOE, while preventing its leader Felipe González, from selecting a successor. Having failed to win a working majority in June 1993, González needs the support of Catalan nationalists to see through his economic reforms.

Increasing regionalism

Spain has 17 autonomous regions, all vying for greater funds or independence from Madrid. Many have bypassed central government to borrow their own funds on the international money markets and are close to breaching their legal debt limits, set at 25% of revenue. The PSOE's need for Catalan support in the *Cortes* will test the ability of the center to keep control. The Catalans are demanding ever greater autonomy and even a direct line to Brussels.

PROFILE

Spain has been dominated for the past 11 years by Felipe González's PSOE. After such a long period in power, however, the boundaries between party and state have become blurred. The *Cortes* (parliament) cannot check executive power, and political disputes are often left to the judiciary. Ideological issues no longer sharply divide the main parties, and they hold similar views on economic policy and EU membership.

Though hardly on the Italian scale, political corruption – often related to the financing of parties – has been a problem, undermining voters' faith in Spain's political system.

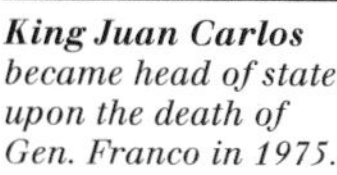

King Juan Carlos *became head of state upon the death of Gen. Franco in 1975.*

Felipe González Márquez, *Prime Minister since 1982 and PSOE leader.*

WORLD AFFAIRS

The Spanish government remains an enthusiastic member of the EU in spite of current difficulties. Spain is not eager to enlarge the EU to include Scandinavia or Central Europe, which it sees as a threat to its own position within the Union. Elsewhere, Spain has sponsored an Ibero-American Community of Nations (a Hispanic Commonwealth), which held its third summit meeting in Brazil in July 1993. Anxious to establish itself as a major international player, Spain has contributed troops to the UN peace-keeping force in the former Yugoslavia, and aspires to a seat on the UN Security Council.

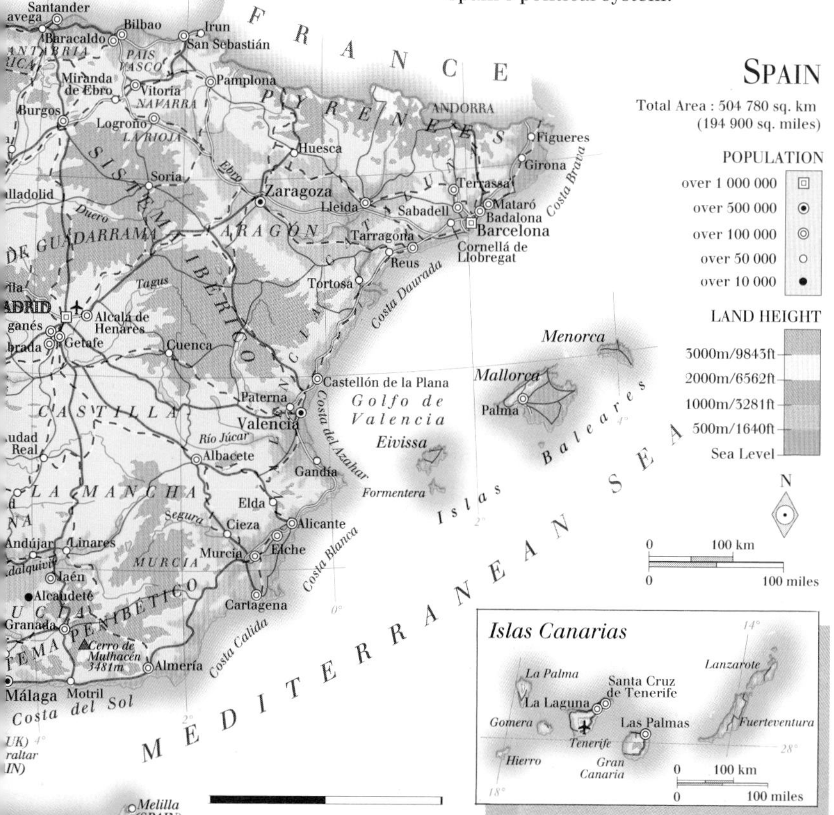

CHRONOLOGY

United under Ferdinand and Isabella in 1492, Spain became a dominant force in Europe. A long period of economic and political decline followed, however. By the mid-19th century, Spain lagged behind many other European countries in stability and prosperity.

- ❑ **1874** Constitutional monarchy restored under Alfonso XII.
- ❑ **1879** Spanish Socialist Workers' Party (PSOE) founded.
- ❑ **1881** Trade unions legalized.
- ❑ **1885** Death of Alfonso XII.
- ❑ **1898** Defeat in war with USA results in loss of Cuba, Puerto Rico and the Philippines.
- ❑ **1909** Barcelona's "tragic week" of anti-clerical riots.
- ❑ **1914–1918** Spain neutral in First World War.
- ❑ **1921** Spanish army routed by Berbers in Spanish Morocco.
- ❑ **1923** Coup by General Primo de Rivera accepted by King Alfonso XIII. Military dictatorship.
- ❑ **1930** General Primo de Rivera dismissed by monarchy.

⇨

CHRONOLOGY *continued*

- ❑ **1931** Second Republic proclaimed. Alfonso XIII flees Spain.
- ❑ **1933** Center-right coalition wins general election.
- ❑ **1934** Asturias uprising quashed by army. Failure of attempt to form Catalan state.
- ❑ **1936** Popular Front wins elections. Right-wing military uprising against the Republic. Gen. Franco subsequently appointed leader.
- ❑ **1939** Franco wins civil war which claims 300,000 lives.
- ❑ **1940** Franco meets Hitler, but does not enter Second World War.
- ❑ **1946** UN condemns Franco regime.
- ❑ **1948** Spain excluded from Marshall Plan.
- ❑ **1950** UN lifts veto.
- ❑ **1953** Concordat with Vatican. Spain grants USA military bases.
- ❑ **1955** Spain joins UN.
- ❑ **1959** Adoption of Stabilization Plan, prelude to rapid economic growth in the 1960s.
- ❑ **1962** Franco government applies for eventual membership in EEC.
- ❑ **1969** Franco names Juan Carlos, grandson of Alfonso XIII, as his successor.
- ❑ **1970** Spain signs preferential trade agreement with EEC.
- ❑ **1973** Prime Minister Carrero Blanco assassinated by Basque separatists. Succeeded by Arias Navarro.
- ❑ **1975** Death of Franco. Proclamation of King Juan Carlos I.
- ❑ **1976** King replaces Arias Navarro with Adolfo Suárez.
- ❑ **1977** First democratic elections since 1936 won by Suárez's Democratic Center Union.
- ❑ **1978** New constitution declares Spain a parliamentary monarchy.
- ❑ **1981** Leopoldo Calvo Sotelo replaces Suárez. King foils military coup. Calvo Sotelo takes Spain into NATO.
- ❑ **1982** Felipe González wins landslide victory for PSOE.
- ❑ **1986** January: Spain joins EC. March: González wins referendum on keeping Spain in NATO.
- ❑ **1992** Olympic Games held in Barcelona, Expo '92 in Seville.
- ❑ **1993** PSOE wins general election.

AID

$1.2 billion (donations)

Up 219% between 1991 and 1993

Spain became a donor in 1977, and currently earmarks 0.4% of GDP for aid to developing countries (mainly in Latin America), slightly above average for Western Europe.

DEFENSE

$7.4bn

Down 10% in 1992

0 Defense spending as % GDP 40

1.6%

Spain has a substantial, largely state-owned defense industry, which exports light weapons, ammunition and small aircraft to countries such as Indonesia and Chile. Spain is a co-partner with the UK, Germany, Italy and France in the EF-2000 fighter aircraft project.

SPANISH ARMED FORCES

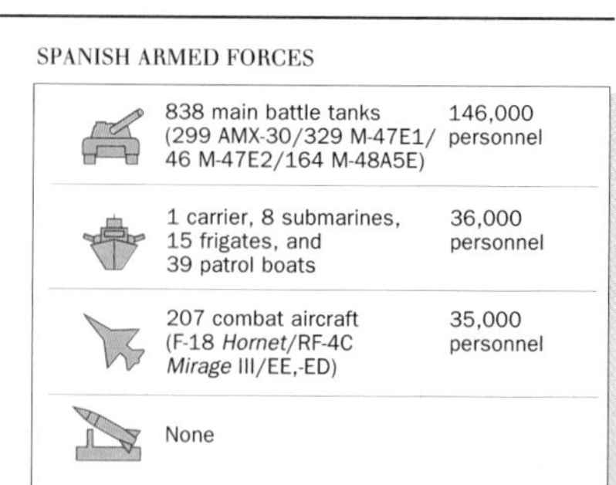

838 main battle tanks (299 AMX-30/329 M-47E1/ 46 M-47E2/164 M-48A5E)
146,000 personnel
1 carrier, 8 submarines, 15 frigates, and 39 patrol boats
36,000 personnel
207 combat aircraft (F-18 Hornet/RF-4C Mirage III/EE,-ED)
35,000 personnel
None

ECONOMICS

$486.6bn

114.55 pesetas

SCORE CARD

- ❑ World GNP Ranking 8th
- ❑ GNP per Capita $12,455
- ❑ Balance of Payments .... $-22bn
- ❑ Inflation 5.3%
- ❑ Unemployment 19.5%

EXPORTS

UK 9%
Italy 11%
Germany* 14%
France 21%
Other 45%

IMPORTS

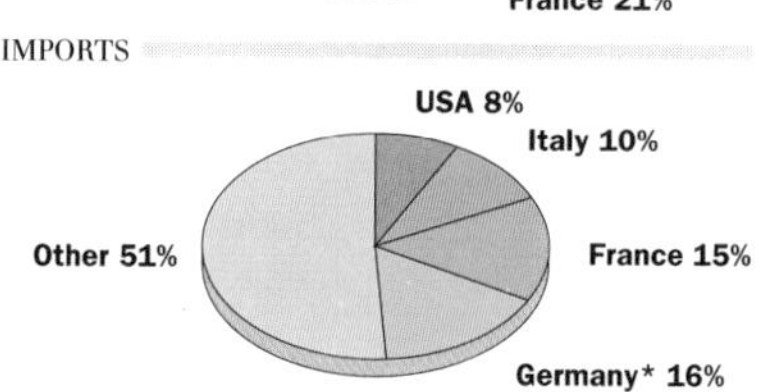

ECONOMIC PERFORMANCE INDICATOR

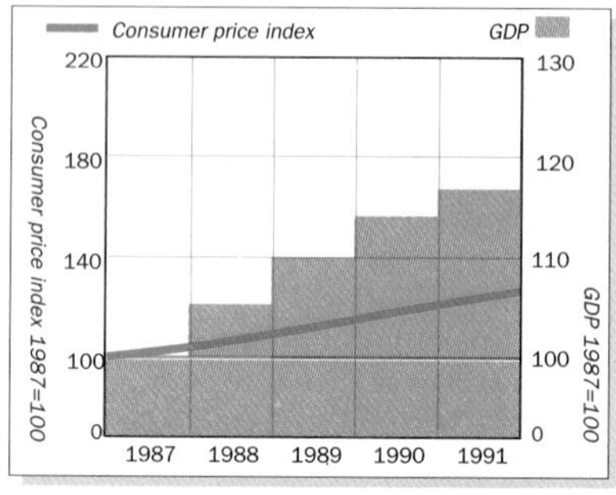

Strengths

Spain's labor force is well qualified and relatively low labor costs are still an advantage, though less so than before. Improvements in transportation and communications will continue to attract foreign investment. Potential for domestic growth is Spain's major asset.

Weaknesses

The massive foreign penetration of the Spanish economy and absence of Spanish multinationals pose long-term problems. Low investment in research and development; a rigid labor market (which trade unions are reluctant to reform); a concentration in declining industries; and low productivity – notably in agriculture – are major weaknesses. Spain's percentage of economically active people is lower than in the rest of the EU.

Profile

Since joining the EC in 1986, the government's main economic goal has been real convergence with the major European economies. This seemed possible in the period 1986–1991, when Spain enjoyed the highest investment-led output growth in the OECD. By 1991 GDP per capita stood at almost 80% of the EC average. In 1992, however, Spain plunged into recession along with its major trading partners. In 1992–1993, three devaluations of the peseta, by a total of 18%, just managed to keep it in the ERM.

Whatever happens to the EU, González remains committed to convergence, and is pinning his hopes on wage moderation, labor market reforms and increased productivity.

SPAIN : MAJOR BUSINESSES

S

RESOURCES

151bn kwh (capacity 43.3m kw)

20,700 b/d (reserves 22,518,000 bbl)

24.3m sheep, 16.7m pigs, 5.2m cattle

Coal, oil, iron, uranium, mercury, fluorspar, gypsum

ELECTRICITY GENERATION

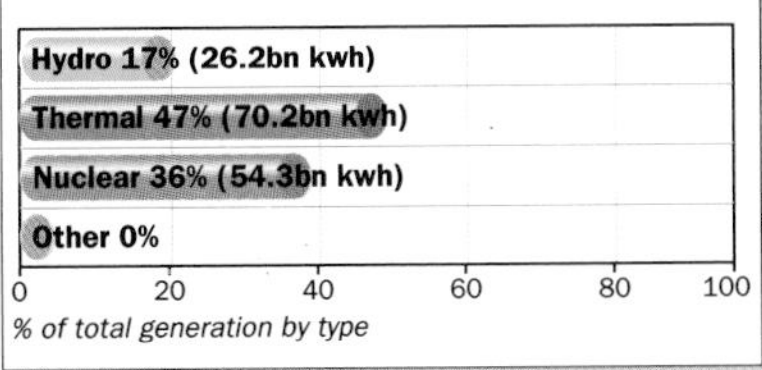

Spain has always been hampered by a lack of natural resources, including water, and is heavily dependent on imported oil and gas. Contrary to popular belief, food products such as fruit and vegetables constitute only 13% of its exports. Spain has one of the world's largest fishing fleets, but EU restrictions have reduced its catches.

SPAIN : LAND USE

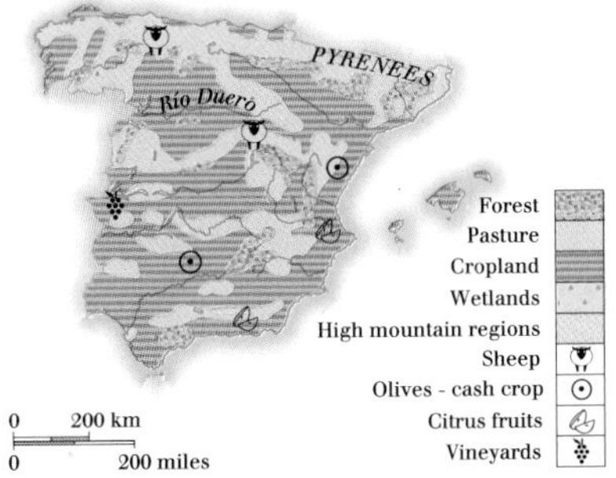

ENVIRONMENT

7% partially protected

Consciousness is rising. Highly active green NGOS

ENVIRONMENTAL TREATIES

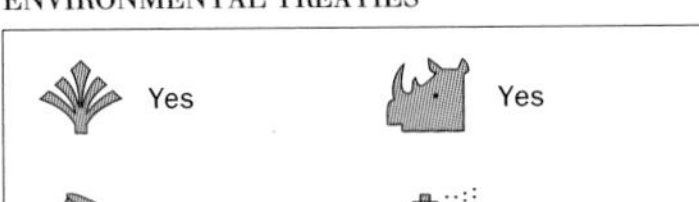

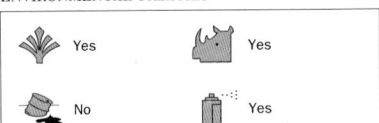

Although Spain paid little attention to environmental matters until very recently, public opinion is becoming increasingly demanding. A national tree-planting project has been initiated to reduce soil erosion, but its benefits have been offset by losses from increasingly frequent intentional forest fires. Spain has more land with national park status than any other European country, and there are plans to double the number. However, rising visitor numbers and tourist developments inside the parks, as in the Coto Doñana wetlands in the south, are damaging their integrity. A large new dam project is threatening the habitat and hence the survival of Spain's last brown bears.

MEDIA

Freedom of expression, though TV is vulnerable to government pressure

PUBLISHING AND BROADCAST MEDIA

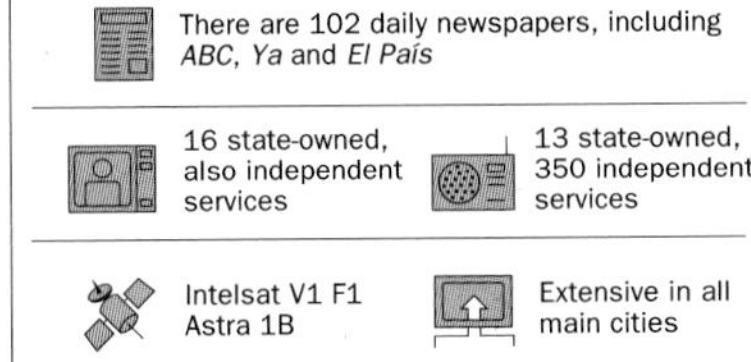

There are 102 daily newspapers, including *ABC*, *Ya* and *El País*
16 state-owned, also independent services
13 state-owned, 350 independent services
Intelsat V1 F1
Astra 1B
Extensive in all main cities

Despite the large number of daily newspapers, readership is among the lowest in Europe. Both public and private TV are popular. Radio is generally high-quality.

CRIME

29,344 prisoners

Down 2% in 1990

CRIME RATES

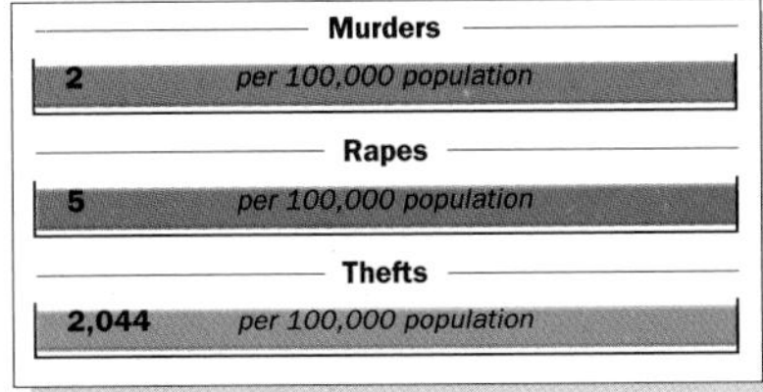

Spain is a major crossroad in the world narcotics trade and drug-related crime is rising. Rape is increasing (or reported more often), while property-related crime is stable.

EDUCATION

96%

0 *Education spending as % GNP* 25

3.2%

THE EDUCATION SYSTEM

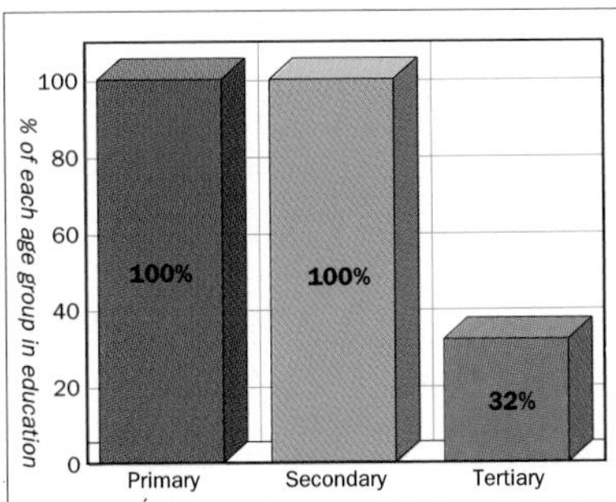

Primary and secondary schooling, 35% of it private but widely affordable, is compulsory. Universities are over-subscribed. Most teaching is lecture-based. Top students with parental funding and good English are increasingly completing their education abroad, often in the USA.

HEALTH

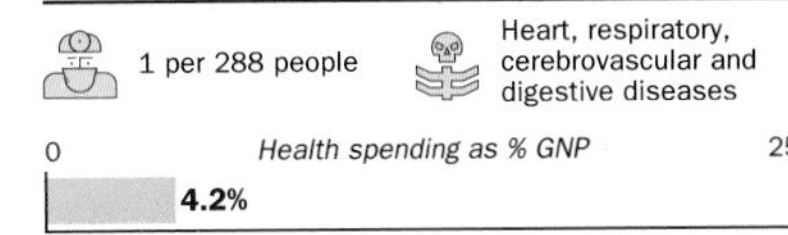

Public health care is high-quality and readily available, and public hospitals are generally considered to be better than private ones. In spite of very high tobacco and alcohol consumption, Spain has a healthy population, possibly due to its Mediterranean diet. The incidence of AIDS, however, is the second highest in Europe.

WEALTH

Cleaner, 100,000 pesetas per month; company director, 1m pesetas per month

CONSUMER GOODS OWNERSHIP

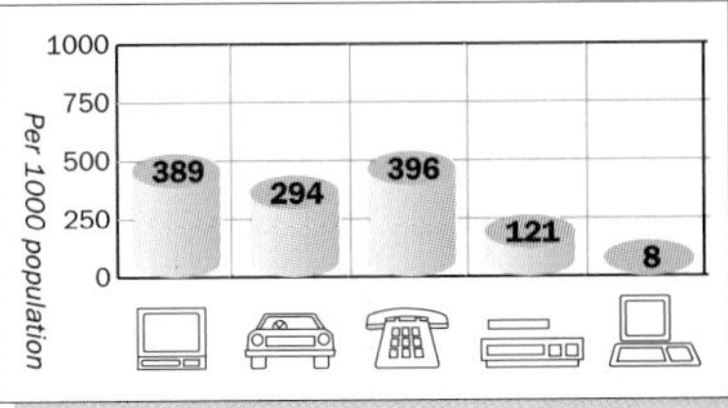

In the late 1980s, it became fashionable in Spain to compete openly, make money and consume. The country's rapid economic growth at the time greatly enriched the professional and managerial classes. The latter became the best-paid, in real terms, in Europe. Some became media celebrities, such as the banker Mario Conde of Banesto, and began to rival soccer players in popularity. In spite of high taxes, the rich became richer and more ostentatious. Spain quickly developed into an important market for luxury cars and yachts; a personal bodyguard also became a status symbol.

The recession of the early 1990s, however, changed attitudes, as Spain was afflicted with one of the highest unemployment rates in Europe.

WORLD RANKING

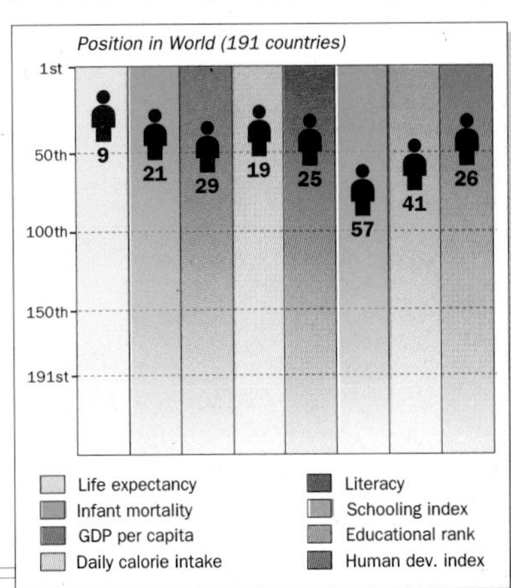

S

SRI LANKA

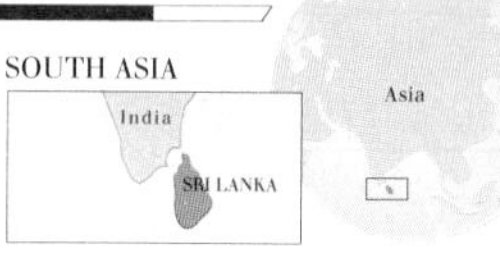

OFFICIAL NAME: Democratic Socialist Republic of Sri Lanka **CAPITAL:** Colombo
POPULATION: 17.7 million **CURRENCY:** Sri Lanka rupee **OFFICIAL LANGUAGE:** Sinhalese

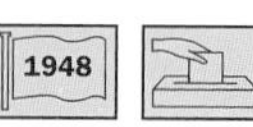

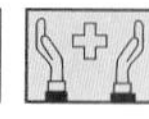

SEPARATED FROM INDIA by the Palk Strait, Sri Lanka comprises one large island and several coral islets to the northwest known as Adam's Bridge. The main island is dominated by rugged central uplands. The fertile plains to the north are dissected by rivers and bordered to the southeast by the Mahaweli Ganga River. Sri Lankan affairs are dominated by the conflict between the government and the Tamils, who are fighting for an independent state.

CLIMATE

WEATHER CHART

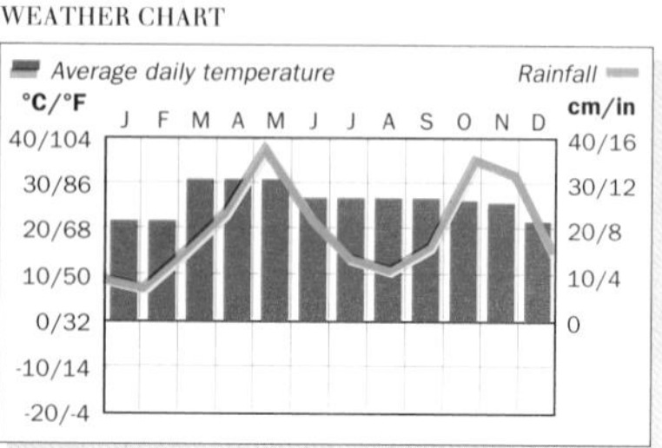

The climate is tropical, with afternoon breezes on the coast and cooler air in the highlands. The northeast is driest.

COMMUNICATIONS

THE TRANSPORTATION NETWORK

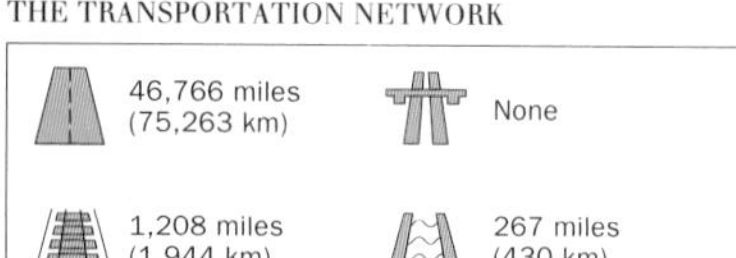

Main roads are crowded and slow, but those to resorts are being improved. Air Lanka now flies non-stop to Europe.

TOURISM

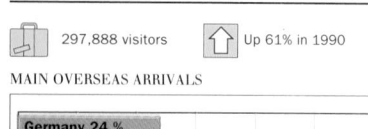

297,888 visitors

MAIN OVERSEAS ARRIVALS

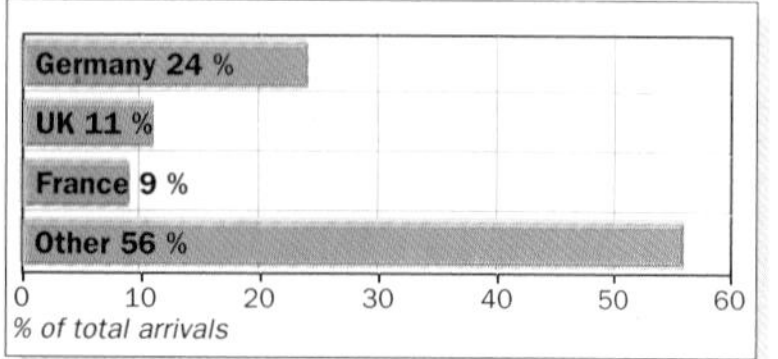

Tourism, which halved between 1983 and 1989, is growing again, but hotels are rundown and in short supply. Buddhist centers such as Kandy are major attractions. Sri Lanka is a popular gay tourist destination.

PEOPLE

Sinhalese, Tamil, Sinhalese-Tamil, English

679 people per sq. mile

THE URBAN/RURAL POPULATION SPLIT

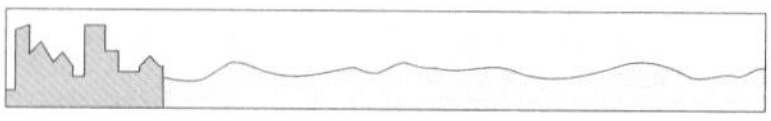

21% 79%

ETHNIC MAKEUP

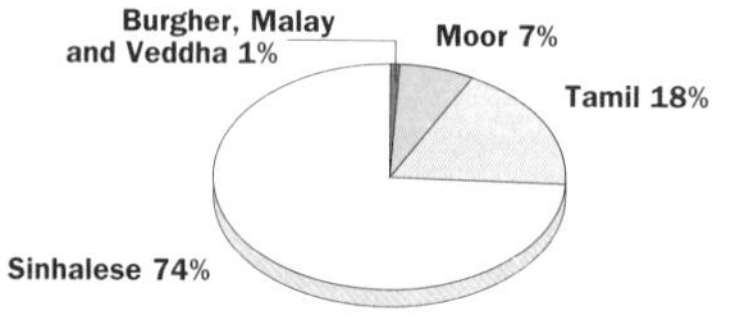

Burgher, Malay and Veddha 1%
Moor 7%
Tamil 18%
Sinhalese 74%

Ethnic tensions between the minority Tamils and majority Sinhalese erupted into civil war in 1983. The Tamils were the minority group favored by the British colonists. When the British left, laws were passed to redress the balance by favoring the Sinhalese. As a result, Tamils feel sidelined, and support for secessionism has grown. The conflict also has a religious dimension – most Sinhalese are Buddhist, while Tamils are mostly Muslim or Hindu.

SRI LANKA

Total Area : 65 610 sq. km (25 332 sq. miles)

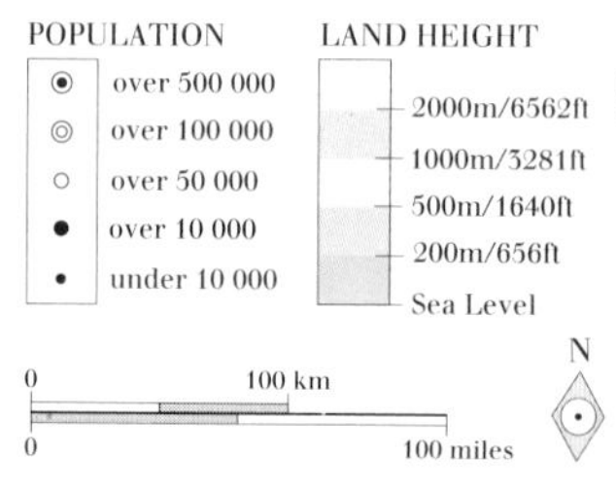

POLITICS

2000

President Dingiri Banda Wijetunga

THE STATE OF THE PARTIES

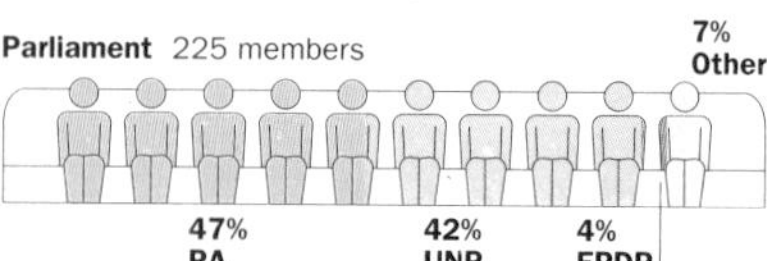

PA = People's Alliance (of which main party is SLFP = Sri Lankan Freedom Party) **UNP** = United National Party **EPDP** = Eelam People's Democratic Party **Other** = Sri Lankan Muslim Congress, Tamil United Liberation Front, Democratic People's Liberation Front

The Tamil-Sinhalese conflict colors all political debate. In 1983, civil war erupted between the Liberation Tigers of Tamil Eelam (LTTE or Tamil Tigers) and the government. The LTTE wants an independent state in the north and east. The government is committed to keeping Sri Lanka unified and has resisted federalism. The most recent peace efforts collapsed in 1990 and were followed by an army campaign in which 10,000 died. On May 1, 1993, President Ranasinghe Premadasa was assassinated. In 1993 and 1994 the army, which is growing in political influence, captured significant LTTE towns in the Jaffna Peninsula.

WORLD AFFAIRS

Relations with India are paramount. The 1987 Indo–Sri Lankan accords led to Indian troops playing a peace-keeping role. They became embroiled in fighting the LTTE, however, and were forced to pull out. The LTTE is suspected of being behind the assassination of Indian president Rajiv Gandhi in 1992.

AID

 $814m (receipts)

 Up 21% in 1991

Canada, the Netherlands and the UK have threatened to freeze aid unless Sri Lanka's human rights record improves.

DEFENSE

 $450.06m

 Up 6% in 1991

Defeating the LTTE is the overwhelming concern. Sri Lanka's chief arms suppliers are the UK, India and China. The LTTE smuggles arms from India.

ECONOMICS

 $8.67bn

 46.00 Sri Lanka rupees

SCORE CARD

- WORLD GNP RANKING..........85th
- GNP PER CAPITA..........$489
- BALANCE OF PAYMENTS..........$–267.6m
- INFLATION..........11%
- UNEMPLOYMENT..........14.4%

STRENGTHS
The world's largest tea exporter. Export Processing Zones and state privatization programs attracting foreign investment. Manufacturing now accounts for 60% of exports; in 1980 the figure was 15%. Tourism; potential for further growth.

WEAKNESSES
Civil war a drain on government funds and deters investors and many tourists.

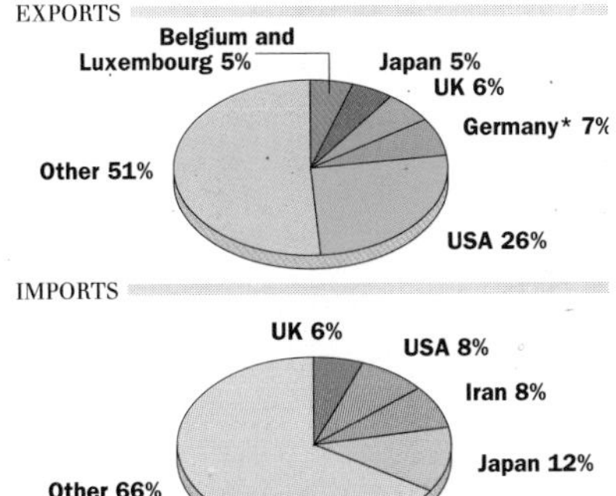

A peak in central Sri Lanka, close to the country's highest mountain, Pidurutalagala, which reaches 8,280 feet.

RESOURCES

3.2bn kwh (capacity 1.29m kw)

Not an oil producer; refines 50,000 b/cd

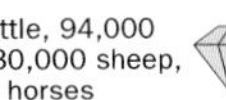

2m cattle, 94,000 pigs, 30,000 sheep, 1,000 horses

Gemstones, graphite, iron, monazite, uranium, ilmenite

Sri Lanka has to import all its oil. Hydropower supplies 75% of electricity; droughts are frequent and supplies can be erratic. Sri Lanka is eager to diversify power sources and is turning to coal-powered generation.

ENVIRONMENT

 12% (4% partially protected)

 Deforestation is under control

Sri Lanka has successfully promoted its national parks. The government is very aware of the benefits to tourism of a protected environment.

MEDIA

 Little press freedom due to Tamil–Sinhalese conflict. Government is able to enact emergency controls

PUBLISHING AND BROADCAST MEDIA

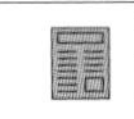 There are 16 daily newspapers, including the *Daily News, Davasa, Dinamina, Lankadipa* and *Dinapathi*

 2 state-owned services

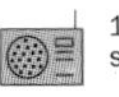 1 state-owned service

The press is not critical of the government. Much is owned by the Sinhalese Lake House Group. Tamils have their own newspapers.

CRIME

 14,128 prisoners

 Down 23% in 1990

Both the army and the LTTE have been accused of human rights abuses. The civil war has claimed at least 30,000 lives since 1983. LTTE members carry cyanide capsules in case of arrest.

EDUCATION

 88%

Sri Lanka has the highest literacy rate of any developing nation. Many Sri Lankans attend US universities.

CHRONOLOGY

Sri Lanka has been inhabited by the Tamils and Sinhalese since before the 6th century. Named Ceylon under the British Empire, the island became independent in 1948.

- **1948** Indian Tamil workers stripped of suffrage and citizenship rights.
- **1956** SLFP wins election on platform to make Sinhalese the sole language. Civil disobedience by Tamils. Anti-Tamil pogroms.
- **1970** Maoist Sinhalese JVP rebellion in south put down.
- **1972** Name changed to Sri Lanka.
- **1983** Civil war erupts between Tamil LTTE and Sinhalese.
- **1989** JVP insurgency ends.
- **1990** Failed peace talks.
- **1993** President Premadasa assassinated.

HEALTH

 1 per 7,255 people

 Suicide, heart attacks, cancer, pneumonia, strokes

Years of government funding have resulted in an accessible, fee-free system. Ayurvedic medicine is popular.

WEALTH

 Plantation worker, 6 Sri Lanka rupees per hour; hotel receptionist, 16 Sri Lanka rupees per hour

CONSUMER GOODS OWNERSHIP

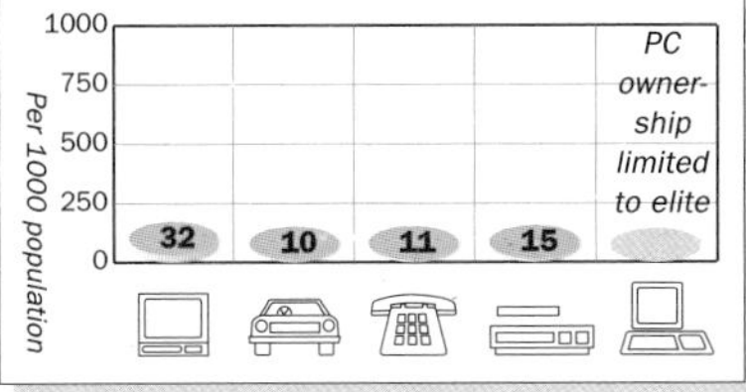

Economic growth has created a new class of wealthy Sinhalese. Tamil tea workers are the poorest group.

WORLD RANKING

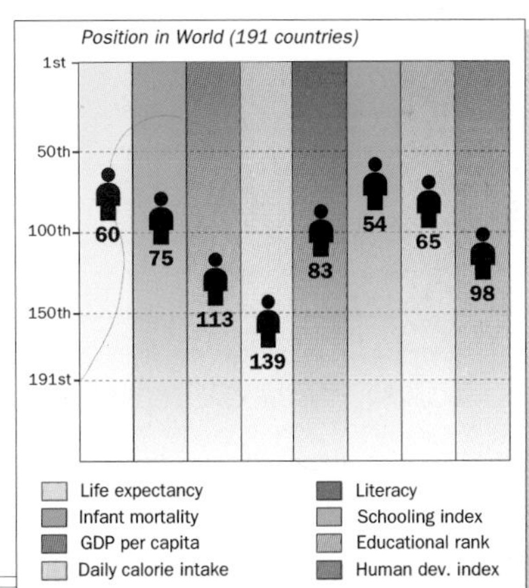

S

SUDAN

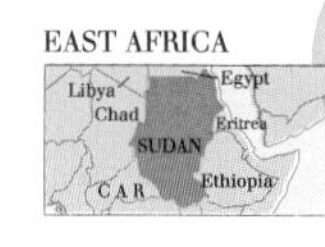

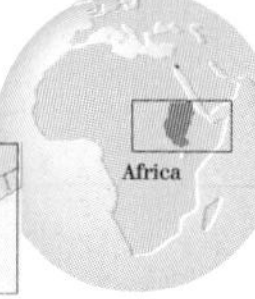

OFFICIAL NAME: Republic of Sudan **CAPITAL:** Khartoum
POPULATION: 26.7 million **CURRENCY:** Sudanese dinar **OFFICIAL LANGUAGE:** Arabic

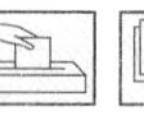

BORDERING THE RED SEA, Sudan is the largest country in Africa. Its landscape changes from desert in the north to lush tropical in the south, with grassy plains and swamps in the center. Tensions between the Arab north and African south have led to two civil wars since independence from British and Egyptian rule in 1956. The second of these conflicts remains unresolved. In 1989, an army coup installed a military Islamic fundamentalist regime.

***Camel caravan in the dry north.** Due to periodic drought coupled with war disruption, Sudan requires large amounts of food aid.*

CLIMATE

WEATHER CHART

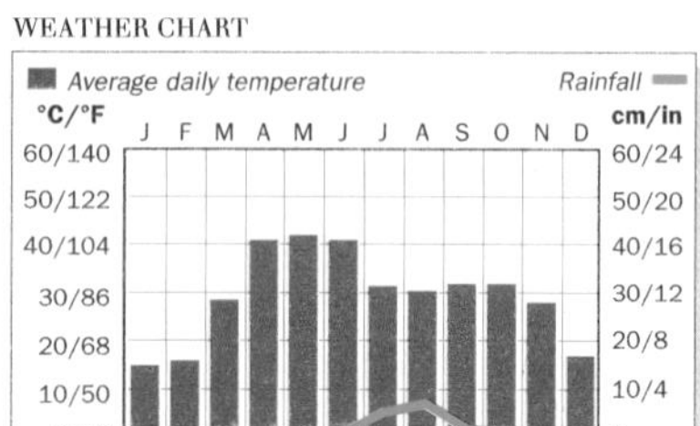

Sudan's northern half is hot, arid desert with constant dry winds. The rest has a rainy season varying from two months in the center to eight in the south.

COMMUNICATIONS

Khartoum International

7 ships
62,100 dwt

THE TRANSPORTATION NETWORK

The Port Sudan–Khartoum railroad and road are Sudan's most important links. There are few other roads, but Iran is financing a Rabak–Malakal highway. Civil war has stopped all Nile shipping.

TOURISM

32,789 visitors

Up 44% in 1990

MAIN OVERSEAS ARRIVALS

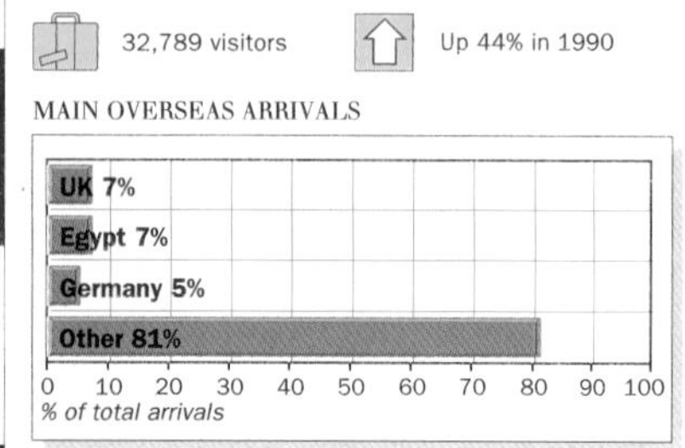

Tourism has now almost ceased due to political unrest and civil war. Visitors are mostly aid workers or businesspeople.

PEOPLE

Arabic, Dinka, Nuer, Nubian, Beja, Zande, Bari, Fur, Shilluk, Lotuko

26 people per sq. mile

THE URBAN/RURAL POPULATION SPLIT

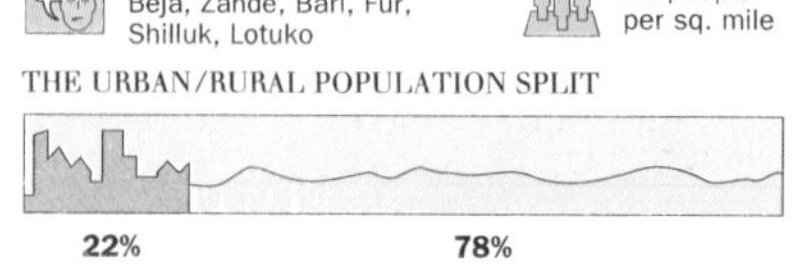

RELIGIOUS PERSUASION

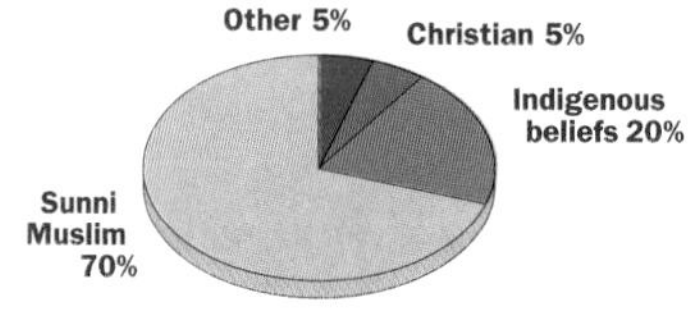

Sudan has a large number of ethnic and linguistic groups. About two million Sudanese are nomads. The major social division, however, is between the Arabized Muslims in the north and the mostly African, largely animist or Christian population in the south. Attempts to impose Arab and Islamic values throughout Sudan have been the root cause of the civil war that has ravaged the south since 1983. However, the rebels have now split into two factions, pitting southern Sudan's small ethnic groups against the Dinka, the south's largest tribe. There are some non-Arab groups in the north and the densely-populated Darfur region. Women not wearing Islamic dress can suffer harassment or even public flogging.

POLITICS

1995

Lt.-Gen. Omar Hassan Ahmad al-Bashir

THE STATE OF THE PARTIES

National Assembly 300 members

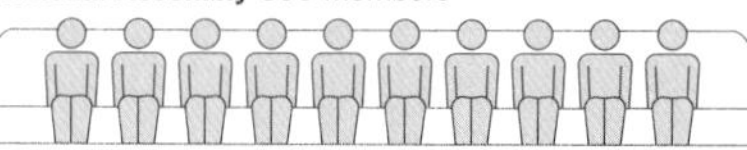

A transitional government was appointed in 1992 to prepare the country for elections

The military regime headed by General al-Bashir took over in a coup in 1989. It banned all political parties except the the National Islamic Front (NIF), which emerged as the force behind the coup. Its leader, Dr. Hassan al-Turabi, does not hold ministerial office, but is Sudan's most influential figure. A strict policy of Arabization and Islamicization, including *sharia* law, has been imposed, but is ineffective in the southern areas held by non-Muslim rebels. Dissent elsewhere has been violently crushed. Many opposition leaders are in exile.

SUDAN

Total Area : 2 505 581 sq. km
(9 674 048 sq. miles)

0 400 km
0 400 miles

LAND HEIGHT
2000m/6562ft
1000m/3281ft
500m/1640ft
200m/656ft
Sea Level

POPULATION
over 500 000
over 100 000
over 50 000
over 10 000
under 10 000

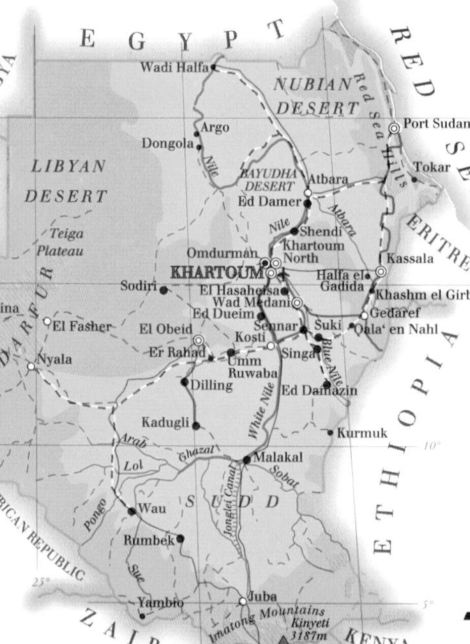

WORLD AFFAIRS

Since Sudan's support for Iraq in the 1991 Gulf War, relations with the West have almost ceased and ties with the Arab world have deteriorated. Only Iran, Yemen and Libya maintain friendly relations.

AID

 $887m (receipts)  Up 8% in 1991

Sudan's only substantial bilateral aid comes from Iran. IMF funding ceased in 1990. Sudan depends on food aid.

DEFENSE

 $320m 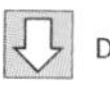 Down 44% in 1990

The NIF controls the military and police and has its own paramilitary militia. Sudan's 68,000-strong army is engaged in fighting the two factions of the southern Sudanese People's Liberation Army, numbering up to 50,000 men.

ECONOMICS

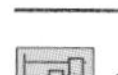 $7.2bn 

SCORE CARD

- ❑ World GNP Ranking....93rd
- ❑ GNP per Capita....$269
- ❑ Balance of Payments....$–1.5bn
- ❑ Inflation....200%
- ❑ Unemployment....Widespread underemployment

Strengths
Cotton, gum arabic, sesame, sugar, gold.

Weaknesses
Low industrialization. Lack of foreign exchange for importing energy and spare parts for industry. Little transportation infrastructure. Huge distances between towns. Civil war prevents exploitation of oil reserves. Drought. Alienation of Arab donors and investors.

EXPORTS

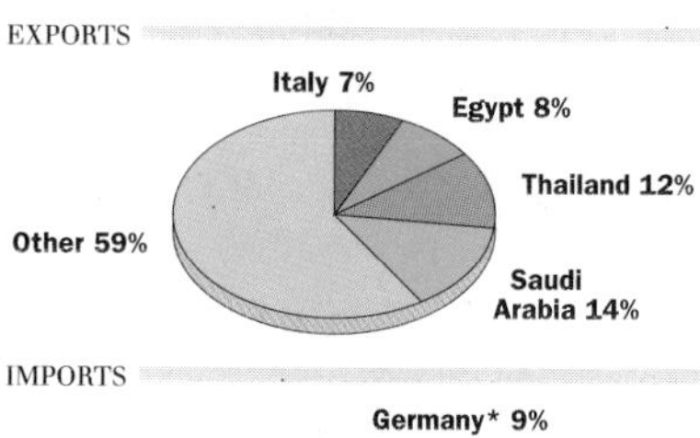

IMPORTS

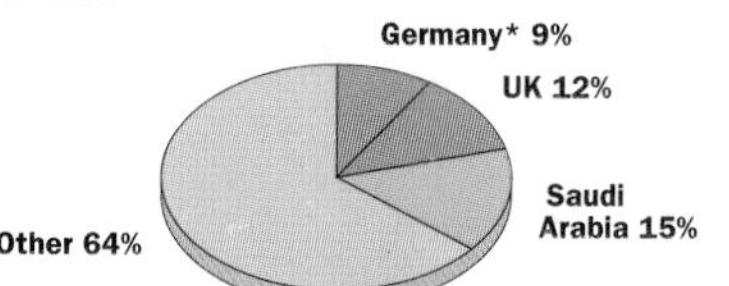

RESOURCES

 1.33m kwh (capacity 500,000 kw)

 Reserves of 300,000,000 bbl; refines 21,700 b/cd

 20.5m cattle, 20m sheep, 2.8m camels

Oil, gas, gold, copper, gypsum, marble, mica, silver, chromium, zinc

Large oil and gas reserves were found in the south in the 1980s, but civil war has prevented their exploitation. The half-thermal, half-hydroelectric generating capacity is insufficient and week-long power cuts are frequent. Gold mining has expansion potential.

ENVIRONMENT

 4% (0.3% partially protected)  Desertification is increasing

Work on the Jonglei Canal to straighten the White Nile was halted in 1986. If it was completed, environmentalists believe the world's largest swamp in the Sudd Plain would dry up, destroying wildlife and intensifying desertification.

MEDIA

 Tight government control of the media

PUBLISHING AND BROADCAST MEDIA

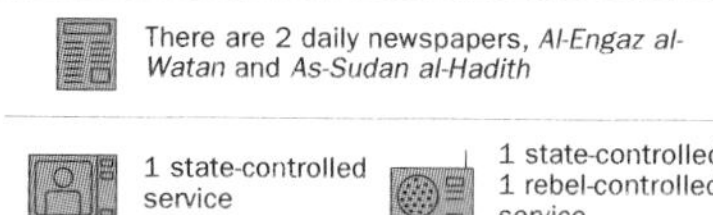

The media were relatively free from 1985 to 1989, but all are now controlled by the government or the army.

CRIME

 Sudan does not publish prison figures  Up 10% in 1986

Anti-government dissent is often suppressed by violence, and torture by the security forces is widespread. In 1993, the UN condemned Sudan's poor human rights record.

EDUCATION

 27%

In 1991, measures were introduced to Islamicize education. Primary school children must have two years of Islamic religious instruction, and men wishing to go to college must first serve for a year in the NIF's People's Militia.

HEALTH

 1 per 9,345 people  Infectious and parasitic diseases

As most health funds are tied to urban hospitals, health service standards in rural areas are basic. The civil war has led to an increase in communicable diseases, especially leishmaniasis.

CHRONOLOGY

Northern Sudan was taken by Egypt in 1821, the south by Britain in 1877.

- ❑ **1882** British invade Egypt.
- ❑ **1883** Muslim revolt in Sudan led by Muhammad Ahmed, the Mahdi.
- ❑ **1898** Mahdists defeated. Anglo-Egyptian condominium set up.
- ❑ **1955** Rebellion in south starts 17 years of civil war.
- ❑ **1956** Independence as republic.
- ❑ **1958–1964** Army runs Sudan.
- ❑ **1965** Civilian revolution, elections.
- ❑ **1969** Army coup led by Col. Nimeri.
- ❑ **1971** Nimeri President.
- ❑ **1972** South gets limited autonomy.
- ❑ **1973** Sudanese Socialist Union (former communist) sole party.
- ❑ **1978** Supports Egypt–Israel peace.
- ❑ **1983** Southern rebellion resumes. *Sharia* law imposed. Nimeri's proposal that Sudan become a formal Islamic state is rejected.
- ❑ **1984** Devastating drought.
- ❑ **1986** Army coup restores civilian government.
- ❑ **1989** Gen. al-Bashir takes over.
- ❑ **1991** *Sharia* penal code instituted. Sudan backs Iraq in Gulf War.

WEALTH

 Most of the population lives a subsistence existence

CONSUMER GOODS OWNERSHIP

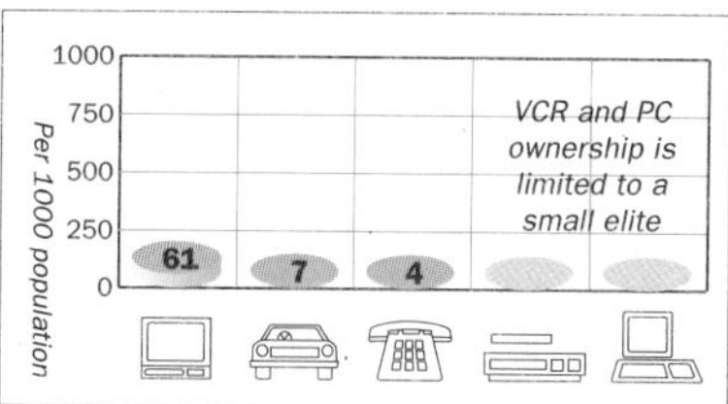

Wealth is limited to the NIF and southern rebel elites. Most of the population struggles to survive.

WORLD RANKING

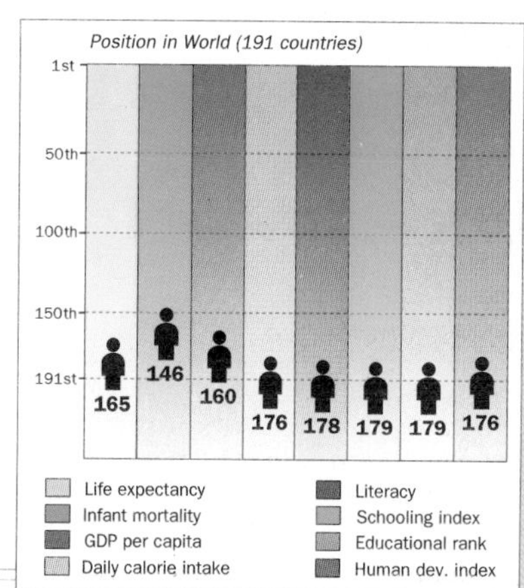

S

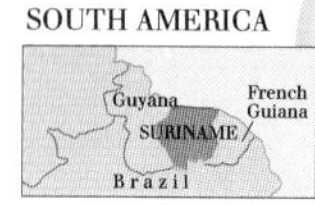

SURINAME

OFFICIAL NAME: Republic of Suriname **CAPITAL:** Paramaribo
POPULATION: 425,000 **CURRENCY:** Suriname guilder **OFFICIAL LANGUAGE:** Dutch

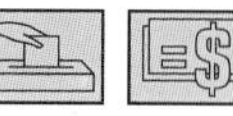

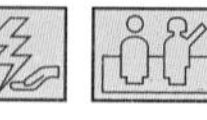

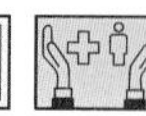

LOCATED ON THE NORTH COAST of South America, Suriname is bordered by Guyana, French Guiana and Brazil. The interior is rainforested highlands; most people live near the coast. In 1975, after almost 300 years of Dutch rule, Suriname became independent. The Netherlands is still its main aid supplier, and home to one-third of Surinamese. Multiparty democracy was restored in 1991, after almost eleven years of military rule.

Congested street in Paramaribo. *It boasts 18th- and 19th-century Dutch architecture and the Caribbean's largest mosque.*

CLIMATE

WEATHER CHART

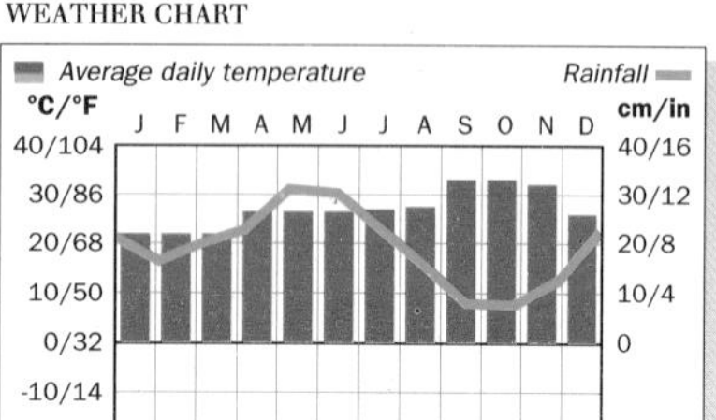

Suriname's tropical climate is cooled by the trade winds. The temperature averages 80°F. Rainfall varies from 9 to 18 inches between coast and interior.

COMMUNICATIONS

Johann Pengel Intl, Paramaribo
175,000 passengers

7 ships
14,300 dwt

THE TRANSPORTATION NETWORK

5,687 miles (9,153 km)

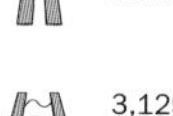
None

98 miles (157 km)

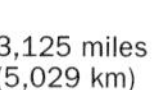
3,125 miles (5,029 km)

The road network runs east–west and focuses on the coast and its immediate hinterland. Rivers provide the main north–south links. The vast interior relies on water or air transportation.

TOURISM

MAIN OVERSEAS ARRIVALS

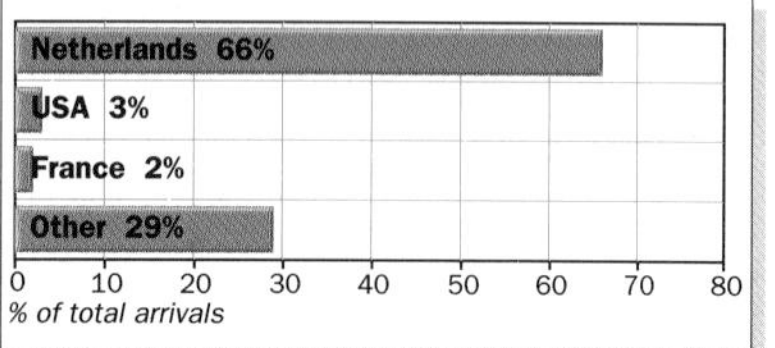

Tourism is undeveloped. Travelers outside Paramaribo are advised to carry their own hammock and food.

PEOPLE

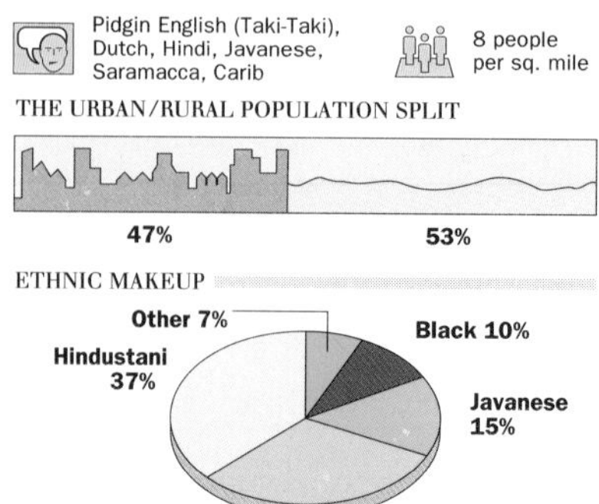

About 200,000 Surinamese, one-third of the ethnically diverse population, has emigrated since 1975. Of those still in Suriname, 90% live near the coast. The rest live in very scattered rainforest communities. About 7,000 are native Amerindians. The remainder are *bosnegers* – the descendants of runaway African slaves. They fought the Creole-dominated government in the 1980s. Many Indians and Javanese work in farming.

POLITICS

1996

President Ronald Venetiaan

THE STATE OF THE PARTIES

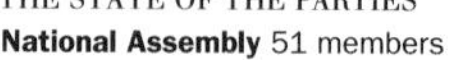

National Assembly 51 members

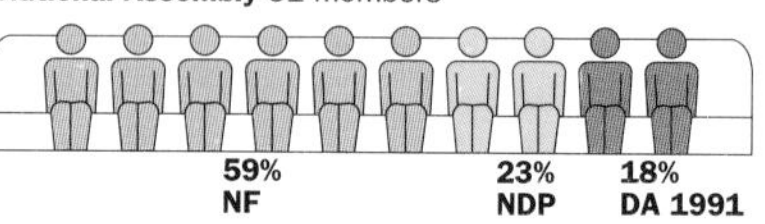

NF = New Front (composed of: NPS = Suriname National Party, VHP = Progressive Reform Party, KTPI = Party for National Unity and Solidarity, SPA = Suriname Labor Party) **NDP** = National Democratic Party **DA 1991** = Democratic Alternative 1991

Council of State 15 members

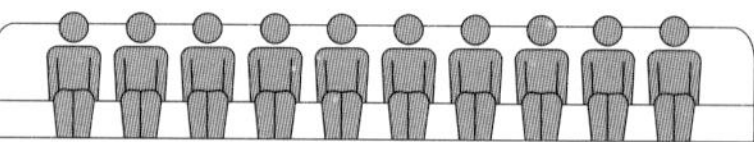

Representatives of trade unions, armed forces and elected political parties

The democratically elected coalition that took power in 1991 is dominated by traditional, ethnically-based parties: the Creole NPS, the Indian VHP and the Indonesian KTPI. The opposition NDP is led by Desi Bouterse, former head of the military regime that ruled from 1980 to 1988. Bouterse was also the force behind the 1990 coup, which ended Suriname's first attempt to return to democracy, and is still a key political player.

WORLD AFFAIRS

NAM

Relations with the Netherlands and the USA, Suriname's key aid and trading partners, have eased since the return to democracy in 1991. They were strained during the 1980s when both stopped aid in response to the military regime's human rights abuses. Integration into the Caribbean region and better links with India and Indonesia are priorities.

AID

 $40m (receipts)

 Down 30% in 1991

The Netherlands is the largest donor. The economy was badly hit by aid suspensions from 1982 to 1988 over human rights abuses and after the 1990 coup. Humanitarian aid resumed in 1992. Other aid is still frozen.

DEFENSE

 $67m

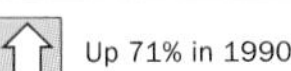 Up 71% in 1990

Under Colonel Desi Bouterse, the army has played a dominant political role since 1980. Bouterse resigned as army head in 1992, but military intervention remains a threat. A six-year civil war against *bosneger* rebels ended in 1992.

ECONOMICS

$1.6bn

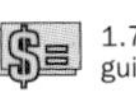 1.79 Surinam guilders

SCORE CARD

- World GNP Ranking........143rd
- GNP per Capita........$3,880
- Balance of Payments........$31.9m
- Inflation........30%
- Unemployment........16.5%

Strengths
Bauxite. Rainforest potential, notably timber. Oil. Agricultural exports: rice, bananas, citrus fruits. Shrimp exports.

Weaknesses
Over-dependence on declining bauxite reserves and Dutch aid. Government failure to reform monetary system. Continued budget deficit is extending aid freeze and exacerbating associated economic recession. Net food importer.

EXPORTS

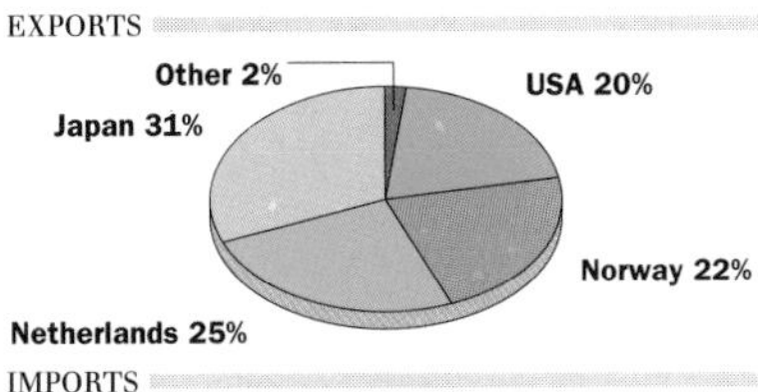

IMPORTS

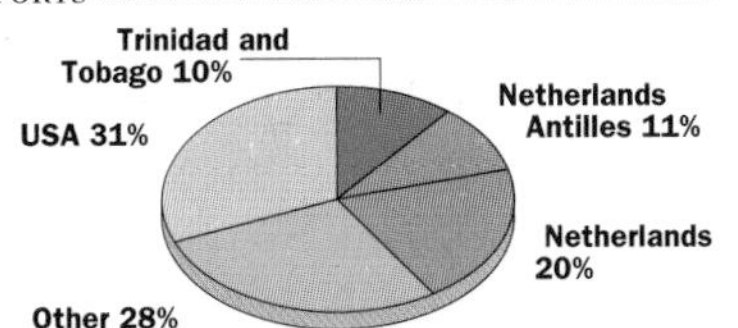

RESOURCES

1.4bn kwh (capacity 420,000 kw)

 Not an oil producer; refines 4,700 b/cd

89,000 cattle, 25,000 pigs, 8,000 sheep

Bauxite, iron, manganese, copper, nickel, platinum, gold

Suriname is the world's sixth-largest bauxite producer. Aluminum and bauxite account for over 75% of export earnings, but the sector has been hit by civil war and poor world prices. Oil production started in 1982, near Paramaribo. Exploitation of Suriname's rainforests has barely begun. Rice and fruit are the key agricultural products.

ENVIRONMENT

 4% partially protected

 Economic growth has precedence over ecological concerns

Many of the 13 nature reserves were damaged in the civil war. *Bosneger* and Amerindian rainforest communities are becoming more militant in demanding control over their lands as commercial interest in the forests' potential grows.

MEDIA

 Censorship has eased since the return to democratic government in 1991

PUBLISHING AND BROADCAST MEDIA

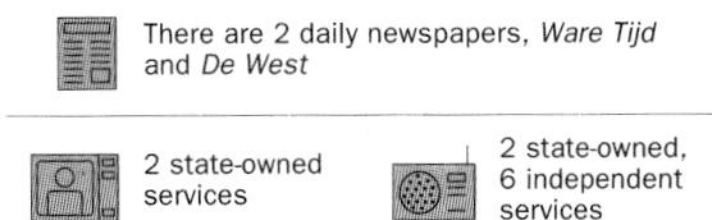

There are 2 daily newspapers, *Ware Tijd* and *De West*

2 state-owned services

2 state-owned, 6 independent services

The radio stations broadcast in a number of languages. Dutch is used by the daily newspapers and TV stations.

CRIME

 Suriname does not publish prison figures

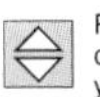 Relatively high crime levels from year to year

The human rights abuses associated with the military regime have largely ended. President Venetiaan has also tried to clamp down on cocaine and illegal arms smuggling, which became a major problem during the 1980s.

EDUCATION

 95%

Education is free and includes adult literacy programs. There is a long tradition of higher education, but most graduates now live in the Netherlands.

CHRONOLOGY

Around 300 years of Dutch rule began in 1667, when Britain swapped its colony in Suriname for Nieuw Amsterdam (New York).

- **1975** Independence.
- **1980** Coup. Lt.-Col. Desi Bouterse heads military government.
- **1982** 15 opposition leaders executed. Dutch suspend aid.
- **1986–1992** *Bosneger* rebel war.
- **1988** Coalition led by President Shankar takes power after free elections. Dutch resume aid.
- **1990** Coup. Dutch suspend aid.
- **1991** Free elections. Coalition led by President Venetiaan.
- **1992** Dutch resume humanitarian aid. Bouterse resigns as army head.

HEALTH

 1 per 1,798 people

 Circulatory diseases, accidents, violence

Urban medical facilities are relatively good. In the interior, they are basic and provided largely by mission stations.

WEALTH

 Deep sea fisherman, 600–850 Suriname guilders per month; chemical industry foreman, 2,890–4,700 Suriname guilders per month

CONSUMER GOODS OWNERSHIP

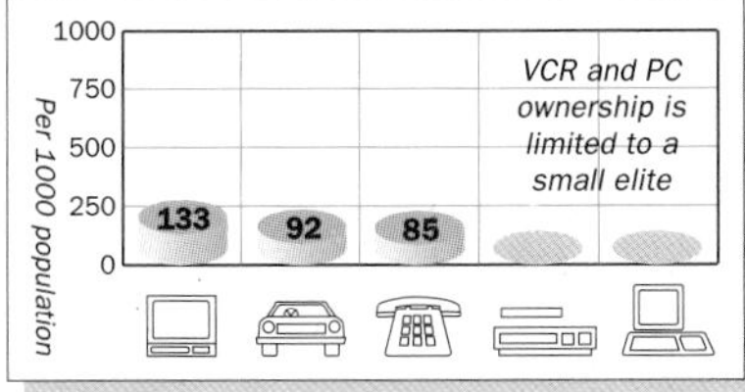

Living standards have fallen since 1982, due to the effects of aid suspension and civil war. Urban Creoles dominate the rich elite. Amerindians and *bosnegers* are the poorest groups.

WORLD RANKING

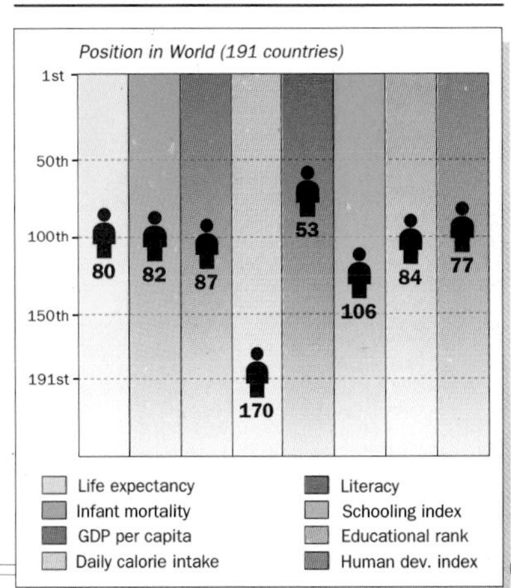

S

SWAZILAND

SOUTHERN AFRICA

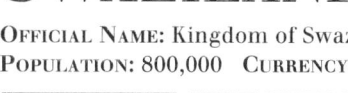

OFFICIAL NAME: Kingdom of Swaziland **CAPITAL:** Mbabane
POPULATION: 800,000 **CURRENCY:** Lilangeni **OFFICIAL LANGUAGES:** Siswati and English

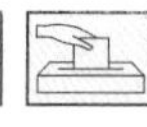

THE TINY SOUTHERN AFRICAN kingdom of Swaziland, bordered on three sides by South Africa and to the east by Mozambique, comprises mainly upland plateaus and mountains. Governed by a strong hereditary monarch, Swaziland is a country in which tradition is being challenged by demands for modern multiparty government. King Mswati III, crowned in 1986, has overhauled the electoral process, but has yet to legalize party politics.

CLIMATE

WEATHER CHART

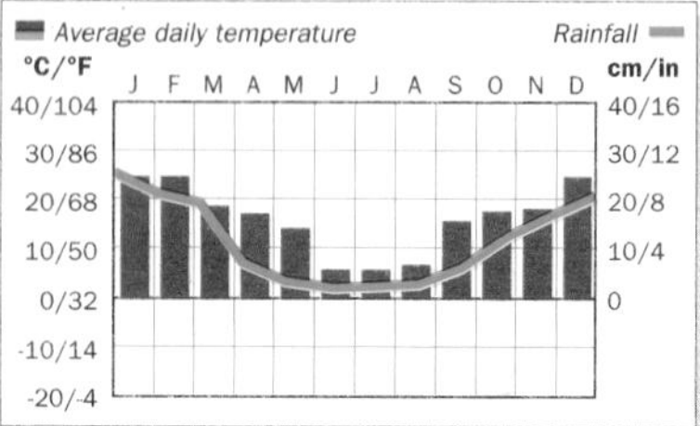

Swaziland is temperate. Temperatures rise and rainfall declines as the land descends eastward, from high to low *veld.* The Low Veld is prone to drought.

COMMUNICATIONS

Matsapa, Manzini
93,000 passengers

Has no fleet

THE TRANSPORTATION NETWORK

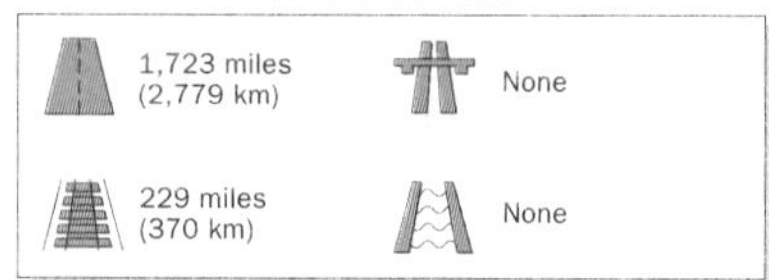

A sharp rise in road traffic has led to a focus on road improvement projects. The railroad, which runs to Mozambique and South Africa, mainly carries exports.

TOURISM

287,796 visitors

Up 3% in 1990

MAIN OVERSEAS ARRIVALS

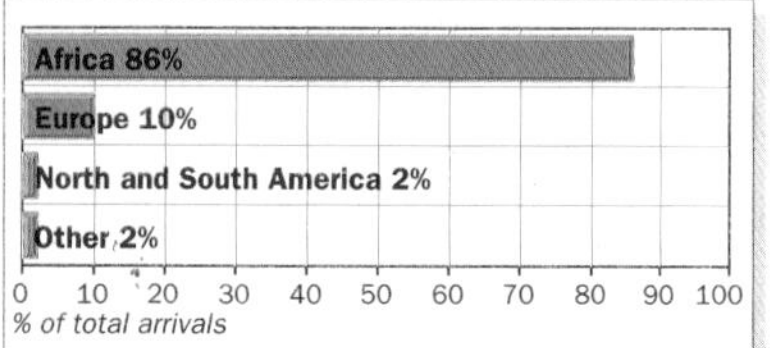

Swaziland's attractions are its game reserves, mountain scenery and, for the South Africans who make up more than 70% of tourists, its casinos.

The outskirts of Mbabane. It lies on the High Veld, where traditional cattle farming has become more difficult due to overgrazing.

PEOPLE

Siswati, English, Zulu

119 people per sq. mile

THE URBAN/RURAL POPULATION SPLIT

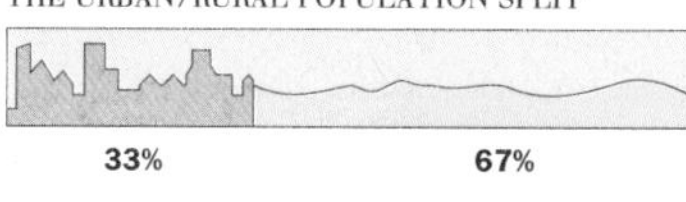

RELIGIOUS PERSUASION

Indigenous beliefs 40%
Christian 60%

Over 95% of the population belong to the Swazi ethnic group, making Swaziland one of Africa's most homogeneous states. It is also one of the most conservative, although it is now coming under pressure from urban-based modernizers. Its political system actively promotes Swazi tradition and is dominated by a powerful monarchy. Society is patriarchal and focused around the clan and chiefs. Both are also politically important. Polygamy is tolerated. Women farm and may vote, but have little economic or political power. The exception is the Queen Mother, the "Great She Elephant," whose influence was demonstrated during the interregnum of the mid-1980s.

POLITICS

1999

HM King Mswati III

THE STATE OF THE PARTIES

House of Assembly 65 members

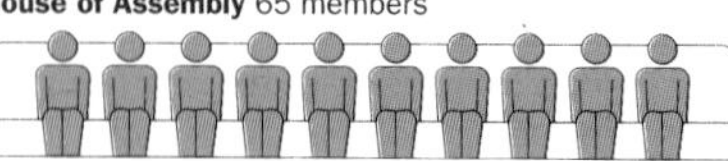

55 members are elected by traditional communities, or Tinkhundla, from candidates nominated by the chiefs. 10 are appointed by the King

Senate 30 members

10 members are selected by the House of Assembly from among its own members, and 20 are appointed by the King

Politics are dominated by a strong executive monarchy, and rivalries within the royal Dlamini clan. The King's traditional advisers act as a counter to the cabinet. Constitutional reform introduced direct elections to the House of Assembly in 1993. There is growing pressure for the King to legalize political parties and move toward multiparty democracy.

SWAZILAND

Total Area : 17 360 sq. km (6703 sq. miles)

POPULATION
- over 50 000
- over 10 000
- under 10 000

LAND HEIGHT
- 1000m/3281ft
- 500m/1640ft
- 200m/656ft
- Sea Level

0 25 km
0 25 miles

WORLD AFFAIRS

AfDB

Swaziland's economic dependence on South Africa means good relations with the Republic are the top priority. It has had to balance membership of SADC with the need to not alienate Pretoria. A secret security pact was agreed with South Africa in 1982. With 134,000 Mozambican refugees, Swaziland is also eager to see peace in that country.

AID

 $54m (receipts)

 Up 66% between 1989 and 1991

Balance of payments aid is important. Project aid has been targeted at the development of the Matsapha industrial estate, roads and social projects. Donors have generally looked favorably upon Swaziland. The EU, Germany, the USA, the UK and the World Bank are important donors.

DEFENSE

 $12.68m

 Up 12% in 1992

The Swaziland Defense Force has only 5,000 troops. Although it does not play an overt political role, its loyalty is to the monarch and the *status quo*.

ECONOMICS

 $960m

 3.40 emalangeni

SCORE CARD

❑ WORLD GNP RANKING	156th
❑ GNP PER CAPITA	$1,200
❑ BALANCE OF PAYMENTS	$25.3m
❑ INFLATION	13%
❑ UNEMPLOYMENT	Widespread underemployment

STRENGTHS

Economy quite diversified and buoyant; grew 4.5% a year during 1980s. Manufacturing 32% of GDP. Investment rules attractive. Sugar 33% of export earnings. Wood pulp. Debt service low: only 3.5% of export earnings in 1991.

WEAKNESSES

Sugar vulnerable to changes in world prices. Exports at risk through regional instability; most go through Mozambique. Dependence on South Africa for jobs, revenue, investment, electricity. Small plots of land and lack of land titles hinder farm modernization. High population growth.

EXPORTS

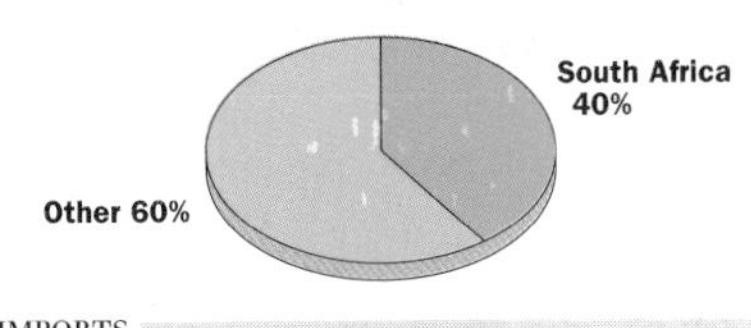

IMPORTS

Other 8%

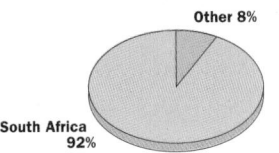

South Africa 92%

RESOURCES

Over half of power supply imported from South Africa

 Not an oil producer and has no refineries

 660,000 cattle, 33,000 sheep, 23,000 pigs

 Coal, diamonds, gold, asbestos, cassiterite, iron, beryl

Swaziland's main export is sugarcane. Wood pulp, coal and asbestos are also exported. The HEP station at Lupholo-Ezulwim, completed in the 1980s, will reduce energy imports from South Africa.

ENVIRONMENT

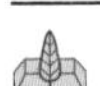 3% partially protected

 Recognized as important for tourism

The main threat is land shortage, due to high population growth. In an effort to combat the problem, family planning programs are being introduced.

MEDIA

 The media is strictly controlled. Editors must get permission before publishing sensitive articles

PUBLISHING AND BROADCAST MEDIA

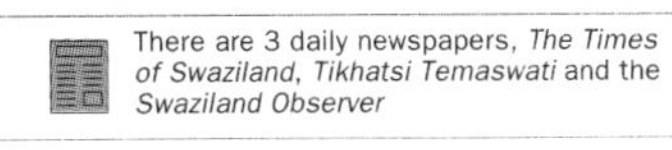
There are 3 daily newspapers, *The Times of Swaziland*, *Tikhatsi Temaswati* and the *Swaziland Observer*

 1 state-owned service

 1 state-owned, 3 independent services

The Times of Swaziland and *Swaziland Observer* are independent, but the press is generally respectful of the monarch and the royal Dlamini clan.

CRIME

 Swaziland does not publish prison figures

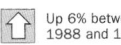

Up 6% between 1988 and 1990

The crime rate is low, but rising. An influx of illegal weapons brought in by refugees has boosted armed crime.

EDUCATION

 68%

Education is not compulsory. Parents pay fees at all levels. Even so, primary enrollment is about 82%. Drop-out rates at secondary level are high.

CHRONOLOGY

Swaziland became a British protectorate in 1903.

- ❑ **1964** Limited self-government under King Sobhuza II.
- ❑ **1968** Independence.
- ❑ **1973** King bans political activity, repeals constitution.
- ❑ **1978** New constitution confirms King's executive, legislative control.
- ❑ **1982** King Sobhuza dies. Queen Mother becomes regent for Prince Makhosetive, aged 14. Power struggle between modernists and traditionalists in royal Dlamini clan.
- ❑ **1986** Prince Makhosetive crowned King Mswati III.
- ❑ **1992** King allows some electoral reform. Refuses to remove ban on political parties.
- ❑ **1993** Elections under new system.

HEALTH

 1 per 7,971 people

 Diarrheal and respiratory diseases

There is no national health service and the network of facilities is rudimentary. Health takes 7% of budget spending.

WEALTH

 Half the population lives below the UN poverty line

CONSUMER GOODS OWNERSHIP

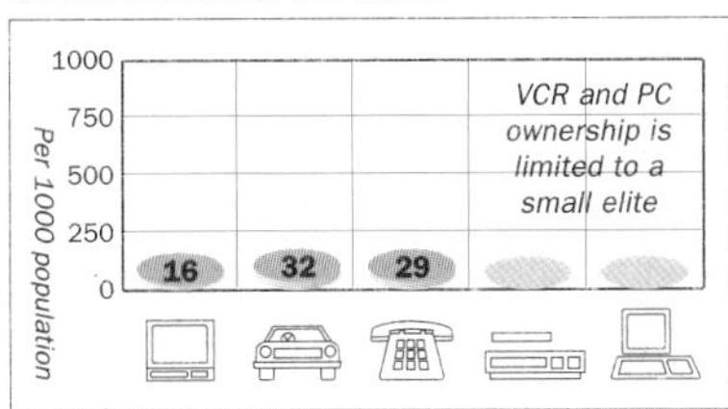

About 50% of Swazis live below the UN poverty line. The royal Dlamini clan enjoys Western luxuries and travel.

WORLD RANKING

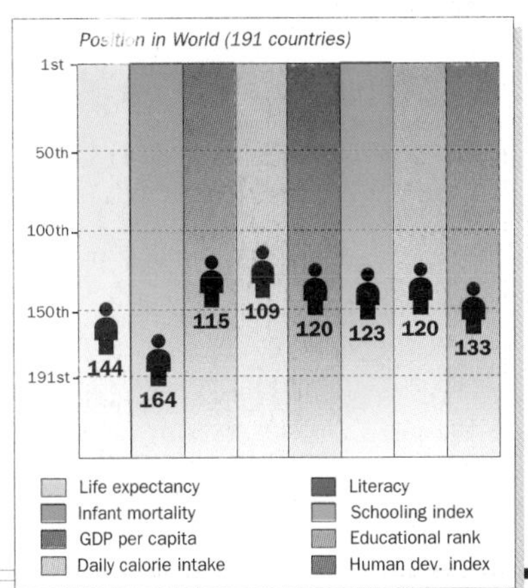

S

SWEDEN

EUROPE

Europe

Norway Finland SWEDEN Denmark

OFFICIAL NAME: Kingdom of Sweden **CAPITAL:** Stockholm
POPULATION: 8.6 million **CURRENCY:** Swedish krona **OFFICIAL LANGUAGE:** Swedish

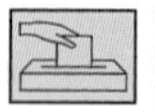

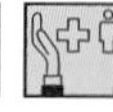

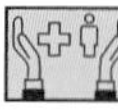

SITUATED ON THE Scandinavian Peninsula, between Norway and Finland, Sweden is a densely forested country with numerous lakes. The north of Sweden falls within the Arctic Circle. Much of the south is fertile and widely cultivated. Sweden has one of the most extensive welfare systems in the world, and is among the world's leading proponents of equal rights for women. Its economic strengths include high-tech industries and car manufacturers such as Volvo and Saab. Sweden, Europe's fourth largest country, joined the EU in 1995.

CLIMATE

WEATHER CHART

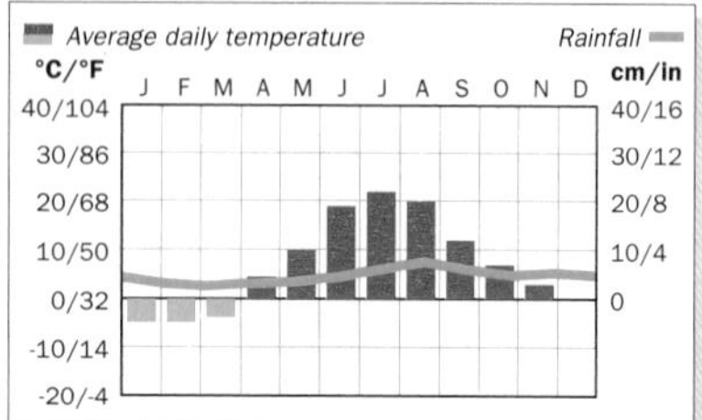

Sweden has a largely continental climate. The Baltic Sea often freezes in winter, making the east coast much colder than the west. Summers are cool everywhere, with temperatures varying surprisingly little between northern and southern regions.

COMMUNICATIONS

Arlanda, Stockholm
14.82m passengers

273 ships
3.35m dwt

THE TRANSPORTATION NETWORK

82,877 miles (133,673 km)

580 miles (936 km)

6,945 miles (11,202 km)

1,272 miles (2,052 km)

Maintaining and improving transportation links is a key issue. Swedish governments have traditionally spent large amounts on infrastructure. Spending on transportation is also seen as a way of boosting the economy as a whole. A new $20-billion program was recently announced, which will finance road, rail and port development.

Sweden's biggest single transportation project is a $5 billion bridge across The Sound, which will provide a road link to Denmark and to the rest of Europe. A rail link between Arlanda Airport and Stockholm is also planned. By law, cars must travel with their headlights on at all times.

TOURISM

6.1m overnights. Sweden does not record visitor numbers

Up 3% in 1993

MAIN OVERSEAS ARRIVALS

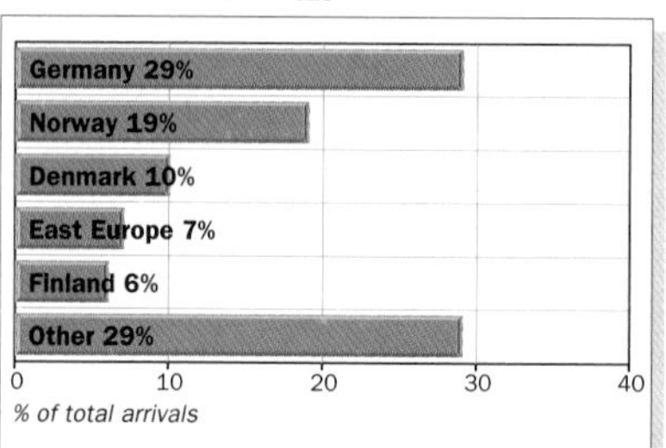

Sweden expanded rapidly as a tourist destination in the 1970s and 1980s. Stockholm, the capital, is renowned for its palaces. The international success of Abba in the 1970s boosted its vibrant nightlife. Visitors to the capital are typically young and affluent.

Although Sweden has fewer lakes than Finland, and lacks Norway's dramatic scenery, it still has a variety of natural attractions. The mountains of the "Midnight Sun" lie north of the Arctic Circle, while the southern coast has many white sandy beaches. Some are attracted to the vast tracts of deserted landscape and the simple country communal living. Despite the relatively high cost of travel to Sweden, tourism now accounts for 5% of GDP.

A crofter's holding in Darlana, *Central Sweden, an area which is more than 50% forested. The timber and paper industries account for almost 20% of Sweden's exports.*

PEOPLE

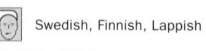

Swedish, Finnish, Lappish

49 people per sq. mile

THE URBAN/RURAL POPULATION SPLIT

84% 16%

RELIGIOUS PERSUASION

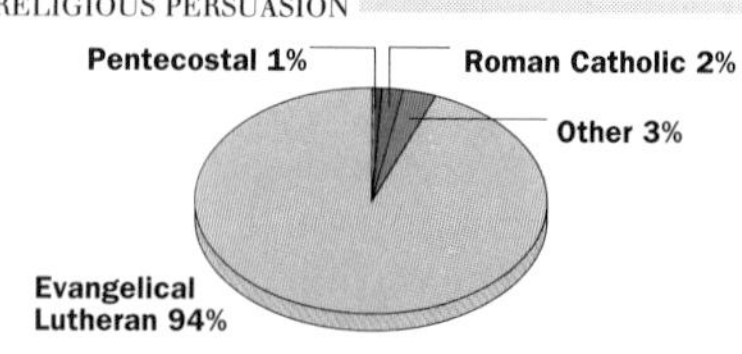

ETHNIC MAKEUP

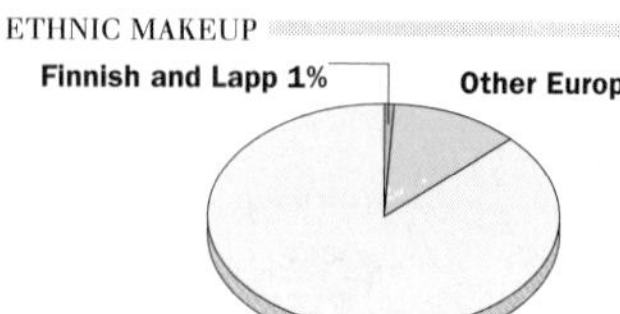

As in all of Scandinavia, the nuclear family forms the basis of society. The birthrate is low with, on average, less than two children per family. Marriage is declining, and cohabitation outside marriage is common.

Swedish society has an egalitarian tradition. The role of the state is seen as the provision of conditions allowing each individual, male or female, to gain economic independence through employment. Sweden's welfare system is also one of the most extensive in the world. However, in the early 1990s, recession reduced benefits, and mothers in particular now face increasing difficulties with the closure of childcare facilities. Women make up nearly half of the work force, one of the highest proportions in Europe.

While Sweden has generous asylum laws, immigration is tightly controlled. Racial tensions are minimal, although there have been instances of right-wing attacks on Bosnian refugees.

A 15,000-strong minority of Sami (or Lapps) live in northern Sweden. Their traditional way of life is protected.

POPULATION AGE BREAKDOWN

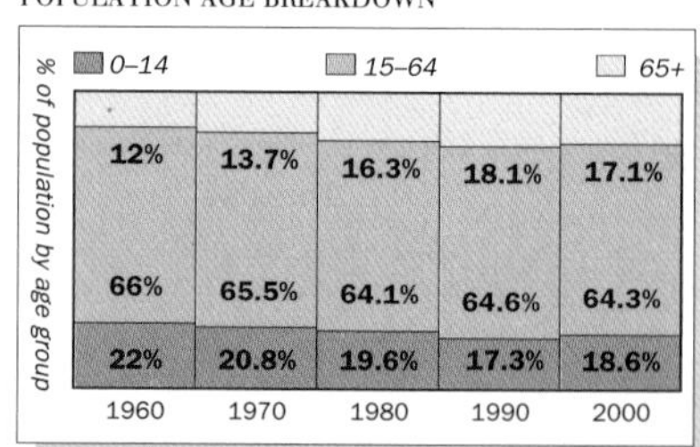

S

POLITICS

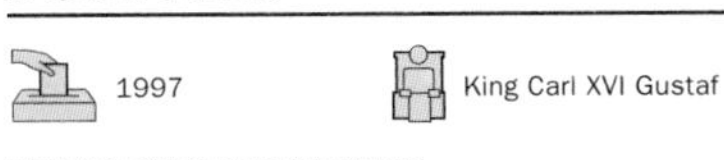

THE STATE OF THE PARTIES

Parliament (Riksdag) 349 members

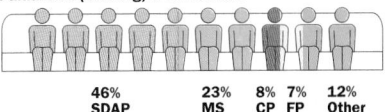

46% SDAP	23% MS	8% CP	7% FP	12% Other

SDAP = Social Democratic Labor Party
MS = Moderate Party **CP** = Center Party **FP** = Liberal Party
Other = Green Party, Left Party, Christian Democratic Party

Sweden is a constitutional monarchy with an elected parliament under the leadership of the prime minister.

MAIN POLITICAL ISSUES

EU membership
In March 1994, Sweden agreed terms to join the EU. A referendum was held in November that year in which 52% voted in favor of membership.

High cost of the welfare state
The cost of Sweden's welfare system has brought about an enormous budget deficit, equivalent to 15% of GDP in 1993. The government has to steer a difficult course between raising taxes and cutting benefits.

PROFILE

Swedish politics have traditionally been split between the monolithic Social Democrats (SDAP) and trade unions on the left, and a host of moderate center and right-wing parties. Since the 1930s, the Social Democrats have governed every term with the exception of 1976–1982 and 1991–1994. The marked shift to the right in Swedish politics seen in 1991 was reversed in the 1994 elections. These saw a swing back in favor of the Social Democrats, although the party failed to gain an absolute majority in parliament. Ingvar Carlsson, SDAP leader, elected to form a minority government.

Carl XVI Gustaf, ascended the throne in 1973. His role is purely ceremonial.

Carl Bildt, leader of the Moderate Party, was prime minister from 1991 to 1994.

SWEDEN

Total Area : 449 960 sq. km (173 730 sq. miles)

POPULATION
- over 1 000 000
- over 100 000
- over 50 000
- over 10 000

LAND HEIGHT
- 1000m/3281ft
- 500m/1640ft
- 200m/656ft
- Sea Level

N

0 100 km
0 100 miles

WORLD AFFAIRS

Recently, Sweden's main foreign policy concern has been obtaining membership in the EU; terms were settled in 1994. Since the collapse of the Soviet Union, Sweden has also altered its traditionally neutral stance. Membership in the Western European Union and even NATO are being considered. This contrasts sharply with Prime Minister Olof Palme's period in office in the 1980s, when Sweden was a vociferous critic of the USA's antagonistic policy toward the USSR. In 1993–1994 Sweden participated in the UN peace-keeping force in the former Yugoslavia.

AID

 $2.1bn (donations)  Up 5% in 1991

Sweden runs a very active development aid program, to which 1% of GDP is allocated. The majority of bilateral aid goes to African countries.

CHRONOLOGY

Sweden's history has been closely linked to the control of the Baltic Sea and its highly profitable trade routes. Under the house of Vasa, Sweden became a major power, controlling much of the Baltic region. By the 18th century, however, Sweden's position had been eroded by its regional rivals, particularly Russia.

- **1814–1815** Congress of Vienna. Sweden cedes territory to Russia and Denmark. Period of 180 years of unbroken peace begins.
- **1844** Oscar I becomes king.
- **1859** Carl XV ascends the throne.
- **1865–1866** Minister of Justice Louis De Greer reforms the Riksdag into a bicameral parliament.
- **1872** Oscar II ascends the throne.
- **1905** Norway gains independence from Sweden.
- **1907** Gustav V becomes king.

⇨

CHRONOLOGY *continued*

- **1911** First Liberal government.
- **1914** Government resigns over defense policy.
- **1914–1917** Sweden remains neutral though it supplies Germany. Allied blockade.
- **1917** Food shortages. Conservative government falls. Nils Edén forms a Liberal government which limits exports contributing to German war effort.
- **1919** Universal adult suffrage.
- **1921** Finland gains Åland Islands, retribution for Sweden's war role.
- **1932** Severe recession. Social Democrat government elected under Per Albin Hansson.
- **1939–1945** Sweden neutral. Grants transit rights to German forces.
- **1945–1976** Continuing Social Democratic rule under Tage Erlander shuns "Functional Socialism." Establishes Sweden as world's most advanced welfare state, and one of the most affluent.
- **1950** Gustav VI Adolf becomes king.
- **1953** Nordic Council member.
- **1959** Founder-member of EFTA.
- **1969** Erlander succeeded by Olof Palme as prime minister.
- **1973** Carl XVI Gustav on throne.
- **1975** Major constitutional reform. Riksdag becomes unicameral with a 3-year term. Role of monarchy reduced to ceremonial functions.
- **1976** SDAP lose power. Non-socialist coalition led by Thorbjörn Fälldin in government.
- **1978** Fälldin resigns over issue of nuclear power. Ola Ullsten prime minister.
- **1979** Fälldin prime minister again.
- **1982** Elections. SDAP forms minority government. Palme prime minister.
- **1986** Palme shot dead. His deputy, Ingvar Carlsson, prime minister. Police fail to find assassin.
- **1989** Palme murder suspect acquitted.
- **1990** Carlsson introduces moderate austerity package. Cuts government spending, raises indirect taxes.
- **1991** July: Sweden applies to join the EU. September: SDAP remains largest party but is unable to form government; Carlsson resigns. October: Carl Bildt, leader of the Moderate Party (MS), forms coalition of non-socialist parties.
- **1992** Austerity measures succeed in reducing inflation. November: SDAP refuses to support further cuts in government expenditure.
- **1993** Negotiations for EU membership begin. MS coalition survives vote of no confidence.
- **1994** Terms of EU membership settled. Referendum finds majority in favor of joining EU.

DEFENSE

$6.2bn
Up 6% in 1992
0
Defense spending as % GDP
40
2.5%
SWEDISH ARMED FORCES
885 main battle tanks (340 Strv-101/110 Strv-102,-104 *Centurion*)
43,000 personnel
12 submarines and 41 patrol boats
9,500 personnel
499 combat aircraft (79 AJ-37/18 SK-37/ 65 J-35/11 SK-35C)
7,500 personnel
None

Sweden maintains a sophisticated, powerful military force. Government spending is concentrated on defense, reflecting Sweden's need to protect its neutrality. Most weaponry, including Saab fighter jets and Bofor anti-aircraft guns, is supplied by its advanced home defense industry. Regular anti-submarine patrols are maintained in the Baltic and North Seas.

With the end of the Cold War, strategic priorities have changed. Sweden feels less bound to its neutral stance and is considering future membership in the Western European Union and even NATO. Mutual security cooperation agreements are also being discussed with the Baltic States.

ECONOMICS

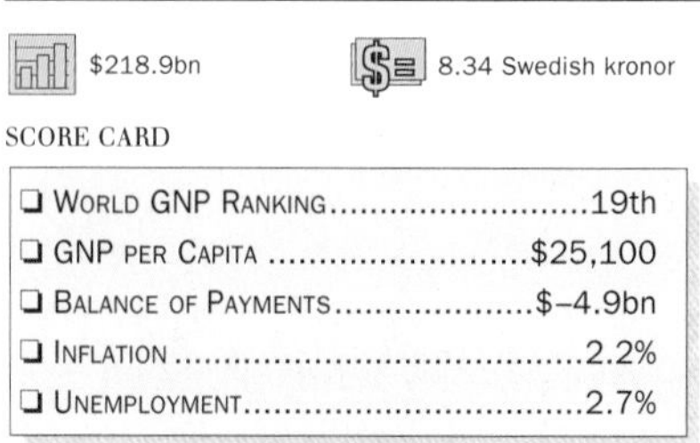

$218.9bn
8.34 Swedish kronor
SCORE CARD
World GNP Ranking..........19th
GNP per Capita..........$25,100
Balance of Payments..........$-4.9bn
Inflation..........2.2%
Unemployment..........2.7%

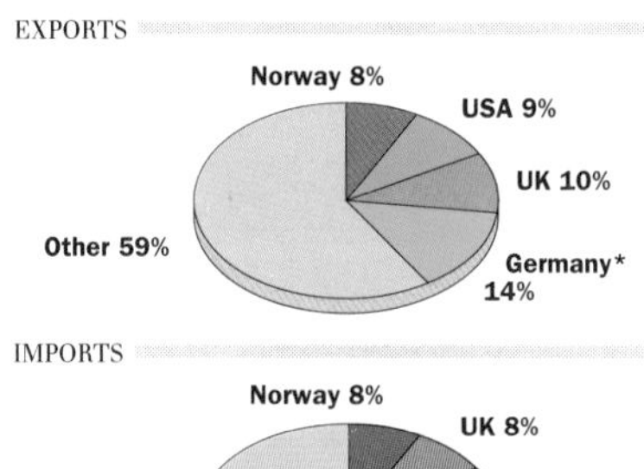

Strengths
Companies of global importance, including Ericsson, Saab, Volvo, Electrolux and SKF, the world's biggest roller-bearing manufacturer. Highly developed and constantly updated infrastructure. Sophisticated technology. Skilled labor force is virtually bilingual in English.

Weaknesses
Uncompetitive labor costs, although this is beginning to change slowly. Highest taxation in the OECD, accounting for over 60% of GDP. Peripheral location, raising costs for producers and exporters.

Profile
The state plays a significant role in the economy, but tends to restrict its role to services and infrastructure.

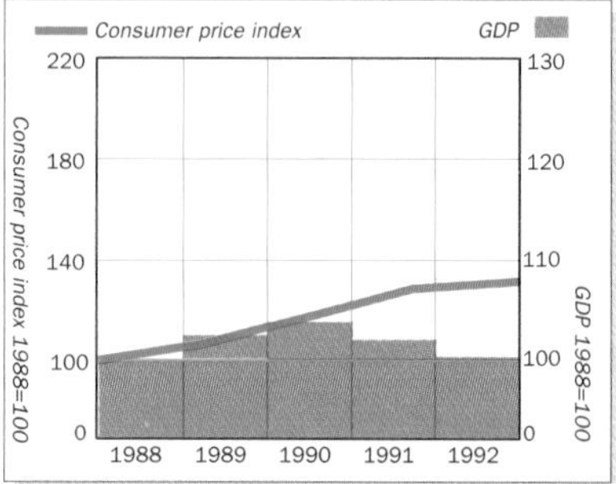

Sweden's industrial giants have mostly been private-sector companies.

The early 1990s witnessed a shift in government economic policy. Some elements of the post-war consensus on the social role of government were abandoned in favor of measures designed to help business. However, the hoped-for result of greater growth was not achieved, and unemployment and the overall cost of welfare rose. Sweden's balance of payments deficit is now the highest in the OECD. The deficit will have to be financed by improved business performance and higher taxation.

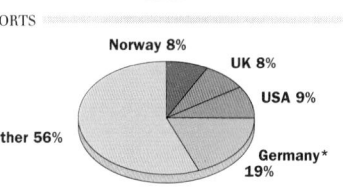

RESOURCES

146.5bn kwh (capacity 34.2m kw)

Not an oil producer; refines 427,500 b/cd

2.3m pigs, 1.7m cattle, 401,000 sheep

Iron, uranium, copper, lead, zinc, silver

ELECTRICITY GENERATION

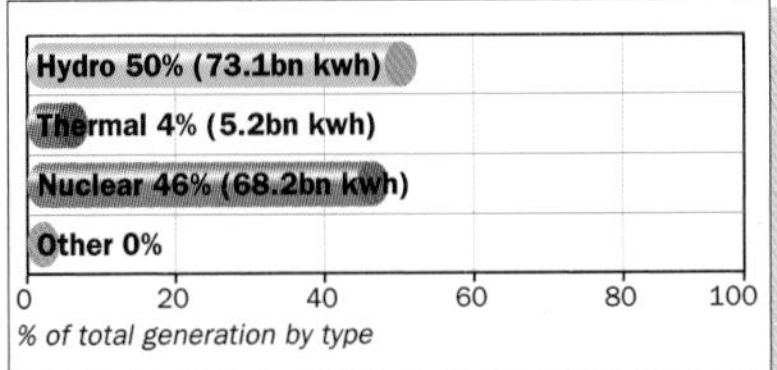

Sweden is rich in minerals, pig iron, copper and silver. While mining and quarrying account for only 0.3% of GDP, they underpin other industrial sectors. Despite its abundant uranium deposits, making up 80% of the European total, Sweden has only four nuclear power stations. The government has ordered that nuclear power be phased out by the year 2010. As a result, Sweden is importing energy from Germany, some of it from nuclear reactors.

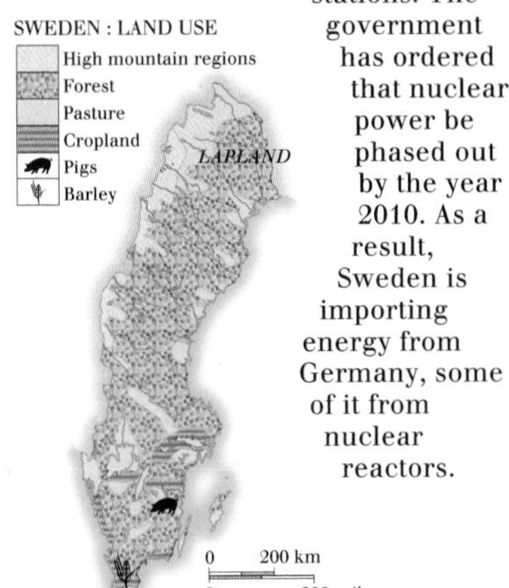

ENVIRONMENT

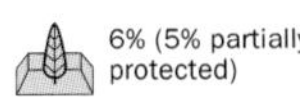

6% (5% partially protected)

Environmental policy is a high priority

ENVIRONMENTAL TREATIES

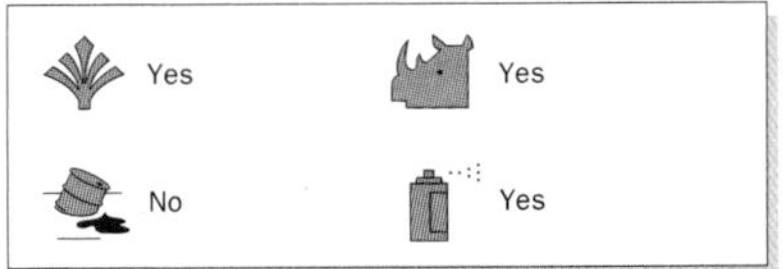

Since the Environment Protection Act of 1969, investment in environmental protection measures has totaled 20 billion kronor. Sweden has blamed the considerable acid-rain damage to forests and lakes on airborne sulfur dioxide from factories in Western Europe. Swedish nuclear reactors are said to be very safe, with filtered venting systems designed to retain 90% of all radioactivity released in the event of a core meltdown.

MEDIA

Government censorship is non-existent

PUBLISHING AND BROADCAST MEDIA

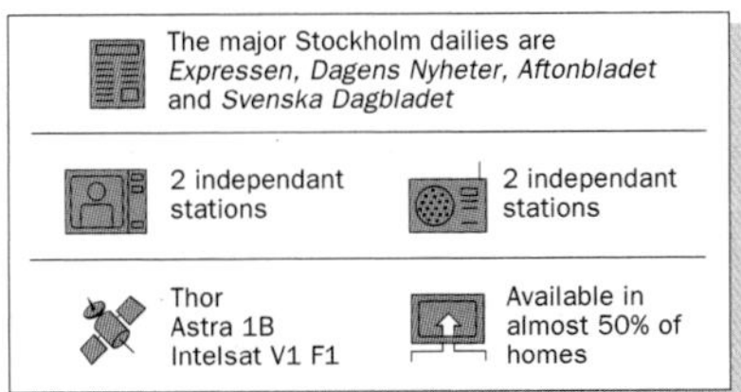

The major Stockholm dailies are *Expressen, Dagens Nyheter, Aftonbladet* and *Svenska Dagbladet*
2 independant stations
2 independant stations
Thor
Astra 1B
Intelsat V1 F1
Available in almost 50% of homes

Radical viewpoints are rarely expressed in the Swedish press. The influence of the major daily newspapers is largely confined to Stockholm, as the provinces have a strong press of their own. Six companies control almost all of Sweden's magazines. Political parties finance many newspapers.

CRIME

4,716 prisoners

Up 6% in 1990

CRIME RATES

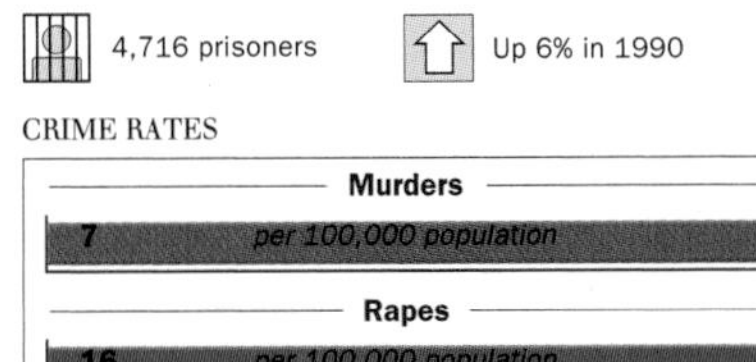

Crime rates are below the European average, although they are the highest among Scandinavian countries. Assault, rape and theft are growing problems, especially in the cities.

EDUCATION

99%

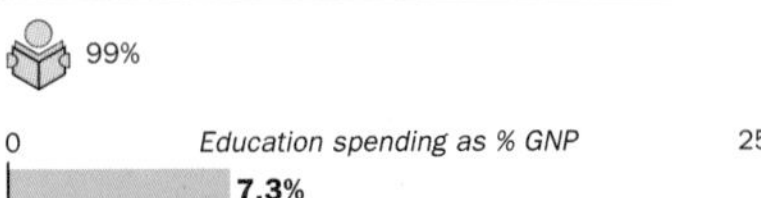

THE EDUCATION SYSTEM

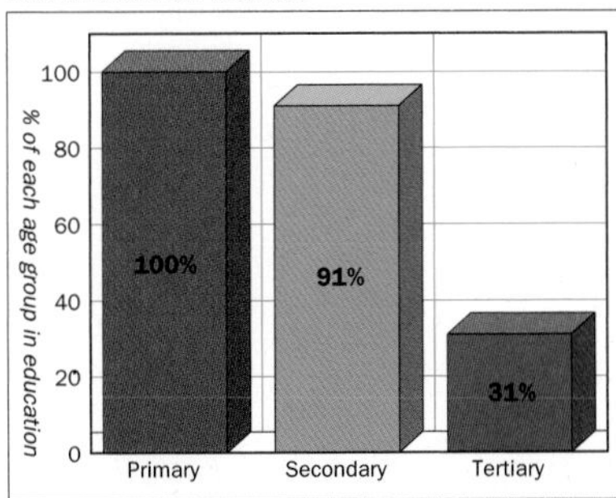

Coeducational comprehensive schools are the norm. The higher education system is freely available to most of the population, and many adults return to college to do further study.

HEALTH

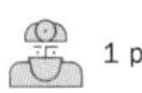

1 per 355 people

Heart and cerebrovascular diseases, cancer

0 *Health spending as % GNP* 25

7.5%

Sweden's health care system is comprehensive and of a universally high standard. However, since 1991, it has been under review in an attempt to cut government spending. Almost 25% of surgical beds have been closed and 30,000 jobs cut. Sweden is now among the lowest spenders on health as a proportion of GNP in the OECD. Reforms in 1994 gave individuals the right to choose their own doctors, and allowed doctors and specialists to set up private practices.

WEALTH

Sawmill sawyer, 86 kronor per hour; accountant, 21,649 kronor per month

CONSUMER GOODS OWNERSHIP

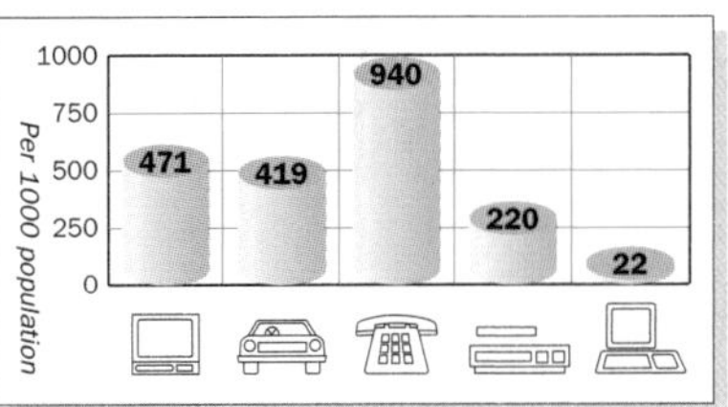

Sweden has minimal income disparities and Swedish executives are generally paid less than their counterparts in France, Germany and Italy. Social competition and a sense of hierarchy are limited compared with other European states or the USA. Despite cuts in services, the welfare system still provides some of the best health, unemployment and pension provisions in Europe.

Swedes are enthusiastic overseas property buyers, particularly of villas in Italy and the south of France. Net overseas per capita investment remains among the highest in the world.

WORLD RANKING

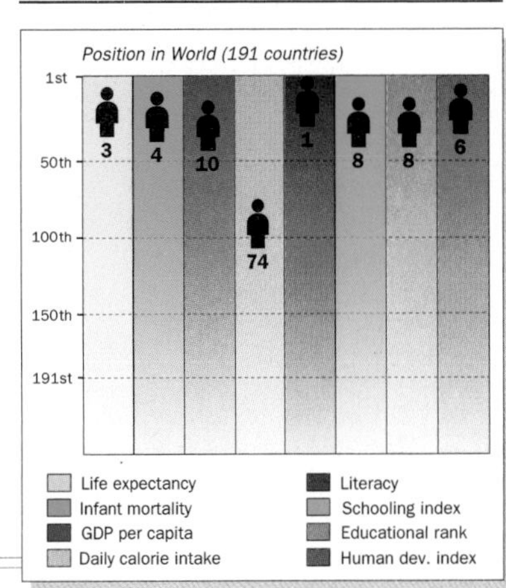

S

SWITZERLAND

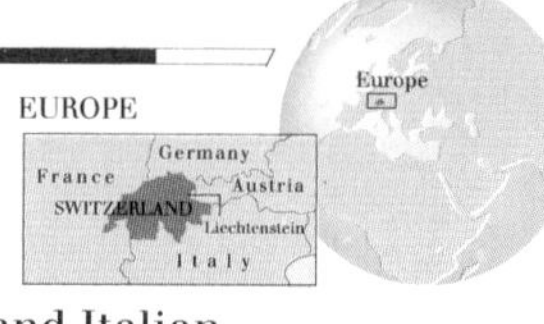

OFFICIAL NAME: Swiss Confederation **CAPITAL:** Bern
POPULATION: 6.8 million **CURRENCY:** Swiss franc **OFFICIAL LANGUAGES:** German, French and Italian

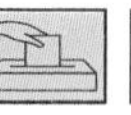

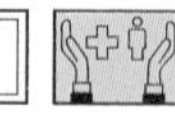

SWITZERLAND LIES AT THE CENTER of Western Europe geographically, but outside it politically. Sometimes called Europe's water tower, it is the source of Western Europe's largest rivers: the Po, the Rhine, the Rhône and the Inn-Danube. Switzerland has managed to retain its neutral status through every major European conflict since 1815. It has also built one of the world's most prosperous economies. The central issue now facing the country is whether or not to join the process of greater European political and economic integration.

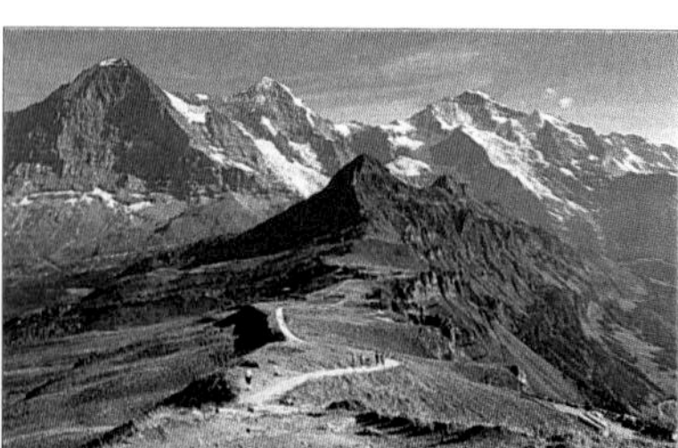

***The Eiger in the Berner Oberland.** In 1994, a referendum voted to ban all commercial truck traffic from the Swiss Alps as of 2004.*

CLIMATE

WEATHER CHART

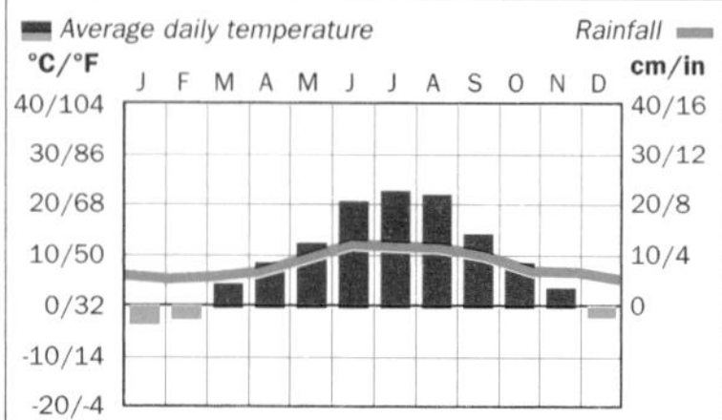

Temperature and weather vary enormously, not only with the seasons, but also because of the huge variations in altitude, and the country's location in the center of Europe. On the plateau north of the Alps, where most of the population lives, summers are warm and winters dry, cool and often foggy. South of the Alps, it is considerably warmer and sunnier. Strong southerly winds, or *föhn*, can bring summer-like weather even in winter.

COMMUNICATIONS

Kloten, Zürich
12.28m passengers

24 ships
604,800 dwt

THE TRANSPORTATION NETWORK

44,179 miles (71,099 km)

941 miles (1,515 km)

3,236 miles (5,208 km)

751 miles (1,208 km)

Switzerland is a major European freight transit route. Pollution caused by trucks is a major concern. The NEAT project, approved in 1992, will provide two new high-speed rail lines linking Basel and Milan, designed so that trucks will be carried on trains. Estimates suggest it will cost three times as much to build as the Channel Tunnel.

TOURISM

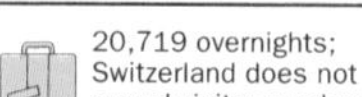
20,719 overnights; Switzerland does not record visitor numbers

Down 3% in 1991

MAIN OVERSEAS ARRIVALS

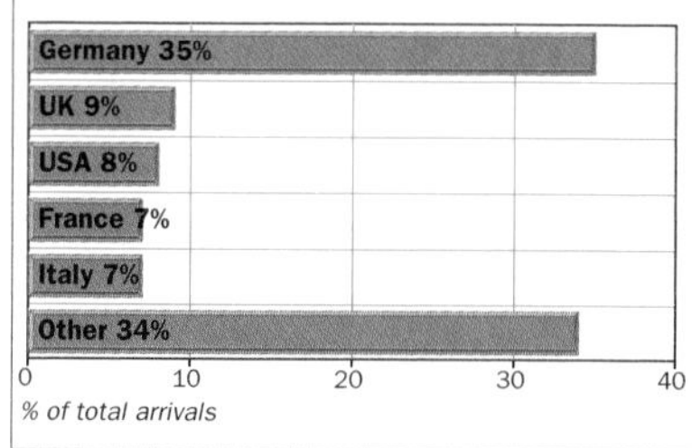

Tourism is Switzerland's third largest industry. About 350,000 Swiss earn their living from it, and in 1992 tourism accounted for 6% of GNP. The Alps are the main attraction, drawing winter and summer tourists from around the world. However, several factors have led to the recent downturn in the industry. Warmer winters have resulted in a shorter skiing season. The rise in value of the Swiss franc has made Switzerland an expensive destination, and Austria is offering tough competition.

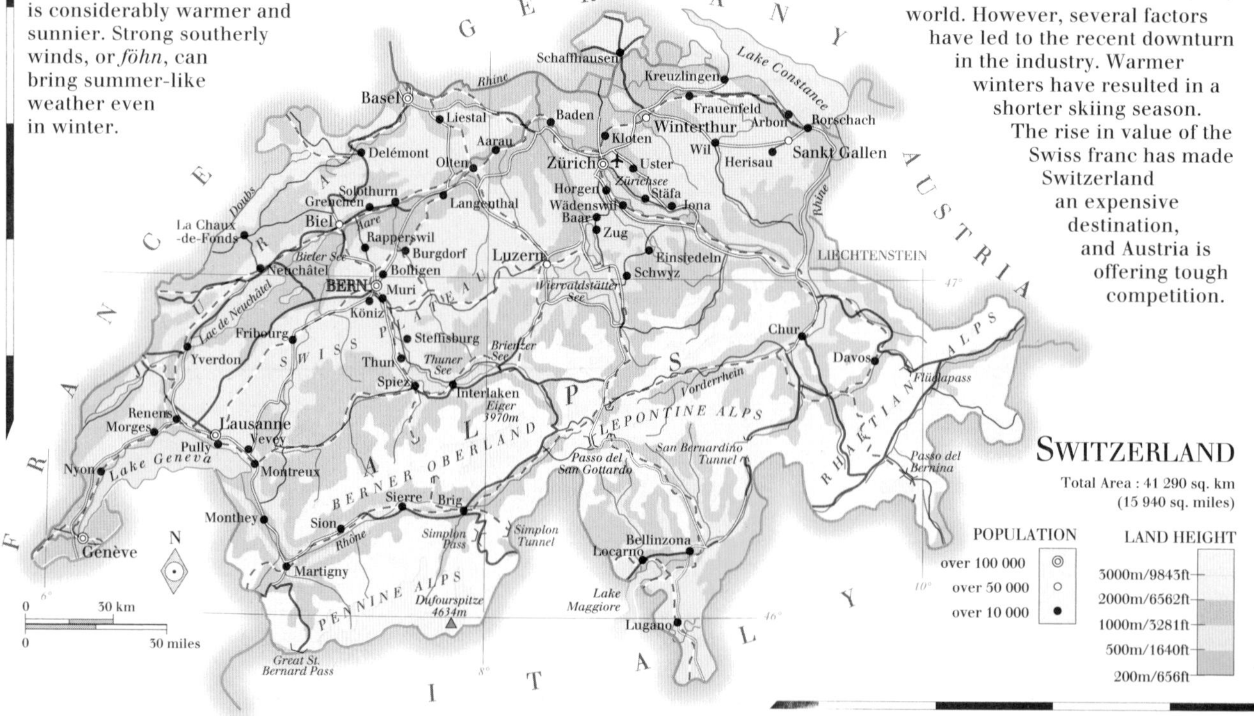

SWITZERLAND

Total Area : 41 290 sq. km (15 940 sq. miles)

POPULATION
over 100 000
over 50 000
over 10 000

LAND HEIGHT
3000m/9843ft
2000m/6562ft
1000m/3281ft
500m/1640ft
200m/656ft

0 30 km
0 30 miles

PEOPLE

 German, Swiss German, French, Italian, Romansch

 414 people per sq. mile

THE URBAN/RURAL POPULATION SPLIT

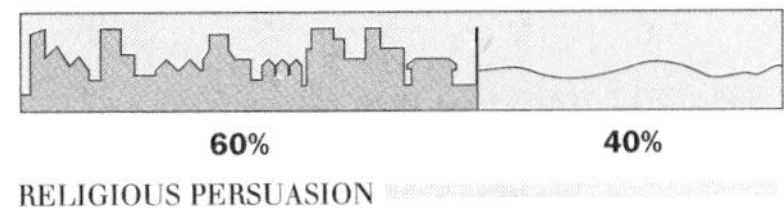
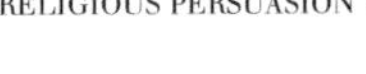

RELIGIOUS PERSUASION

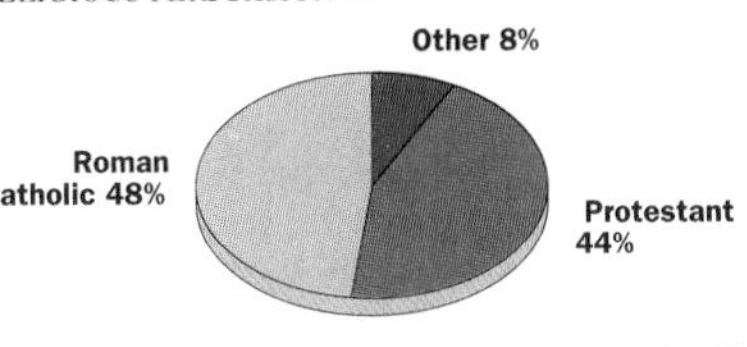

ETHNIC MAKEUP

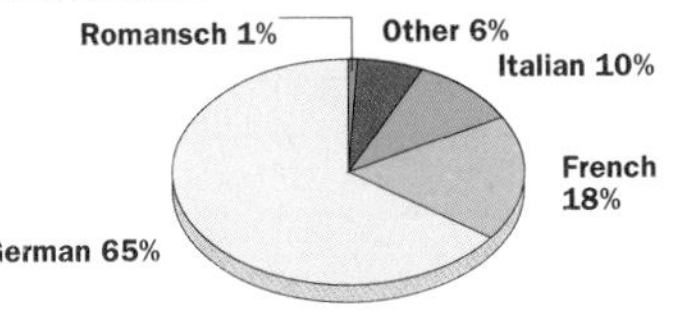

Switzerland is composed of distinct Italian-Swiss, French-Swiss and German-Swiss linguistic groups. About 40,000 in the canton of Grisons speak Romansch. The German-Swiss are in the majority. They are a tightly-knit community, with a dialect that is impenetrable to most outsiders. In recent years the three groups have grown further apart. The French-Swiss, in favor of joining the EU, are opposed by the German-Swiss. In Ticino, originally an Italian-Swiss canton, a political party has emerged to champion Italian-Swiss interests. There has also been a rise in tension between Swiss and guest workers. The fear that the Swiss are losing jobs to recent immigrants is commonly cited. Swiss society retains strong conservative elements. Two half-cantons granted women the vote in federal elections only in 1989 and 1990. Marriage rates are high and divorce less common than in most other European states.

POPULATION AGE BREAKDOWN

% of population by age group

	1960	1970	1980	1990	2000
65+	10.1%	12.6%	13.8%	15%	16.3%
15–64	65.7%	63.6%	66.5%	68.6%	66.9%
0–14	24.2%	23.8%	19.7%	16.4%	16.8%

WORLD AFFAIRS

The basis of Switzerland's foreign policy remains its neutrality. Geneva has retained its position as a center for many international organizations. The UN has its European headquarters there, and it is also home to the Red Cross. The city is often chosen as a site for diplomatic negotiations: the Camp David accords, START nuclear reduction treaties, and attempts to resolve the conflict in the former Yugoslavia were all negotiated in Geneva.

Switzerland has chosen not to join the process for closer European integration. It turned down membership in the EEA and voted by referendum in 1992 against joining the EU. Many believe, however, that the economic case for joining the union will become overwhelming once Switzerland's EFTA partners – Austria and the Scandinavian states – become members. Opponents of integration argue that Switzerland's seeming isolation will enhance its role as an international tax haven.

***Otto Stich**, of the Social Democratic Party, President of Switzerland for 1994.*

***Adolf Ogi**, of the Swiss People's Party, was President the previous year.*

POLITICS

 1995

One of seven Federal Council members annually made president

THE STATE OF THE PARTIES

National Council 200 members

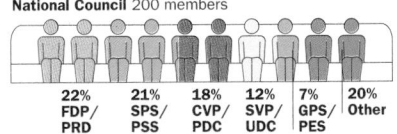

22% FDP/PRD	21% SPS/PSS	18% CVP/PDC	12% SVP/UDC	7% GPS/PES	20% Other

FDP/PRD = Radical Democratic Party **SPS/PSS** = Social Democratic Party **CVP/PDC** = Christian Democratic People's Party **SVP/UDC** = Swiss People's Party **GPS/PES** = Green Party **LPS/PLS** = Liberal Party

Council of States 46 members

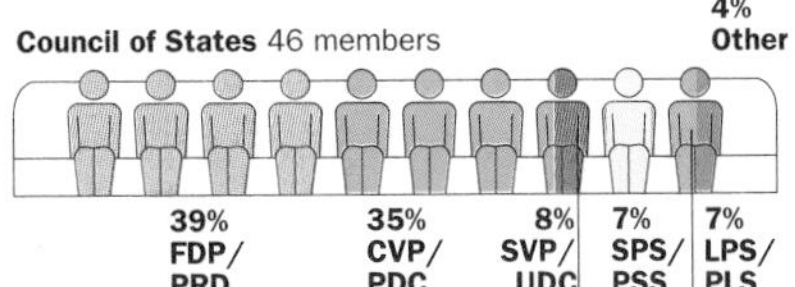

Switzerland is a federal democratic republic with 26 autonomous cantons.

MAIN POLITICAL ISSUES

Hard drugs

Public anxiety has been growing over the rise in drug-related crime; Zürich, where most addicts and dealers congregate, has one of the biggest open drug scenes in Europe. The federal government decided to act in 1994, after the marginal right-wing SVP gained seats on Zürich's council. To the dismay of civil rights activists, tough new measures limiting the rights of asylum seekers were introduced. The aim was to make it harder for drug dealers from the former Yugoslavia to do business in Switzerland.

European integration

Almost all of the country's prominent politicians and business leaders favor joining the EU, but voters remain sharply divided. The Swiss are strongly attached to their decentralized style of government and fear that this would be lost within the EU. There are also fears that in a barrier-free Europe, Switzerland's high standards of living would fall because of a large influx of immigrants.

PROFILE

The same four-party coalition has been in power in Switzerland since 1959. This explains the consistency of Switzerland's domestic and foreign policies and the slow rate of political change. Politics have recently become more contentious, however, with voting patterns becoming more polarized. Divisive issues are those concerning drugs and membership in the EU. Both right-wing and green minority parties have recently gained more seats in parliament.

Switzerland's political system is unique in Europe. Important decisions are all made on the results of referenda. A petition of more than 100,000 signatures can also force a referendum on any issue.

CHRONOLOGY

The autonomy of the Swiss cantons was curtailed by the Habsburg Empire in the 11th century. In 1291, the three cantons of Unterwalden, Schwyz and Uri set up the Perpetual League to pursue Swiss liberty. Joined by other cantons, they succeeded in 1499 in gaining virtual independence. The Habsburgs retained a titular role.

- ❑ **1648** Peace of Westphalia ending 30 Years' War, in which Switzerland played no active part, recognizes full Swiss independence.
- ❑ **1798** Invaded by French.
- ❑ **1815** Congress of Vienna after Napoleon's defeat confirms Swiss independence and establishes its neutrality. Geneva and Valais join Swiss Confederation.

S

CHRONOLOGY *continued*

- ❑ **1848** New constitution – central government given more powers, but cantons' powers guaranteed.
- ❑ **1857** Joined by Neuchâtel.
- ❑ **1864** Henri Dumant founds International Red Cross in Geneva.
- ❑ **1874** Referendum established as important decision-making tool.
- ❑ **1888** Swiss Socialist Party founded.
- ❑ **1894** FDP/PRD founded.
- ❑ **1912** Conservative Party founded, later to become CVP/PDC.
- ❑ **1914–1918** Plays humanitarian role in World War I.
- ❑ **1917** Farmers and burghers found SVP/UDC.
- ❑ **1919** Proportional representation. Ensures future political stability.
- ❑ **1920s** New Swiss Communist Party gains little support.
- ❑ **1920** Joins League of Nations.
- ❑ **1939–1945** Neutral again. Refuses to join UN in 1945.
- ❑ **1959** Founder-member of EFTA. Present four-party coalition comes to power, taking over FDP/PRD dominance of government.
- ❑ **1967** Right-wing groups make electoral gains, campaigning to restrict entry of foreign workers.
- ❑ **1971** Most women granted right to vote in federal elections.
- ❑ **1984** Parliament approves application for UN membership. Dr. Elisabeth Kopp is first woman minister (justice minister).
- ❑ **1986** Referendum rejects UN membership. New laws to restrict numbers of immigrants.
- ❑ **1987** Green Party wins its first two seats in parliament.
- ❑ **1988** Dr. Kopp resigns over her alleged violation of secrecy of information laws.
- ❑ **1990** Dr. Kopp. acquitted. Case revealed that Public Prosecutor's office held secret files on 200,000 people. Violent demonstrations. State security laws amended.
- ❑ **1991** Large increase in attacks on asylum-seekers' hostels.
- ❑ **1992** Joins IMF and World Bank. Referendum votes against joining EEA (only French cantons and one German canton vote in favor).

AID

$863m (donations)

Up 15% in 1991

Switzerland ranks fairly high among developed countries as an aid donor, with total disbursements amounting to 0.5% of the country's GDP in 1992. However, a large part – some 40% – of its aid is conditional upon the recipients buying Swiss goods and services.

DEFENSE

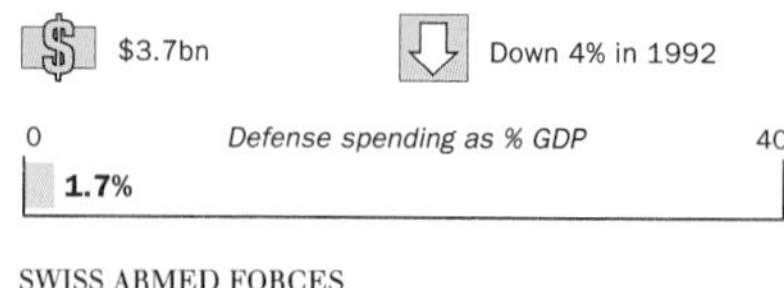

SWISS ARMED FORCES

812 main battle tanks (275 Pz-87 *Leopard* 2/ 143 Pz-61/195 Pz-68)	565,000 personnel
None	
Air Corps (part of army) 242 combat aircraft (80 *Hunter* F-58/7 T-68)	60,000 personnel
None	

Switzerland has one of the largest armed forces in Europe. Military service and further training at intervals is compulsory for males, up to the age of 50. The army is organized so that 600,000 conscripts can be called up and armed in a few hours. The army still uses skis, bicycles and horses to protect the Alps. Bridges and tunnels are mined with explosives in accordance with a defense strategy drafted earlier this century. However, as in the rest of Europe, force numbers are being cut in response to the end of the Cold War. By 1995, the army will be two-thirds its current size. Switzerland is also considering allowing its armed troops to join UN peacekeeping operations.

ECONOMICS

$225.9bn

1.50 Swiss francs

SCORE CARD

- ❑ World GNP Ranking......................17th
- ❑ GNP per Capita.......................$33,221
- ❑ Balance of Payments....................$17bn
- ❑ Inflation.......................................3%
- ❑ Unemployment..................................5%

EXPORTS

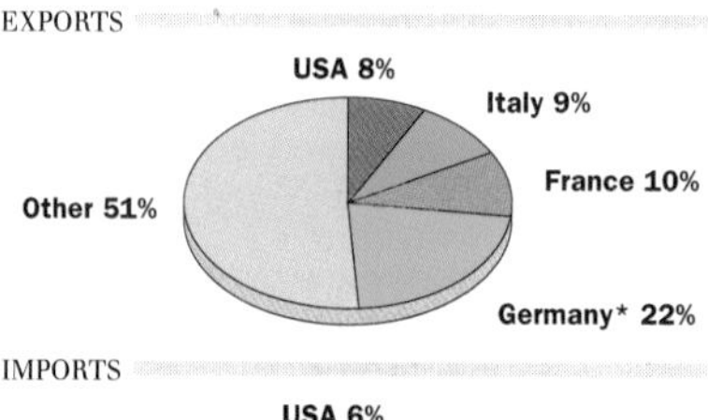

IMPORTS

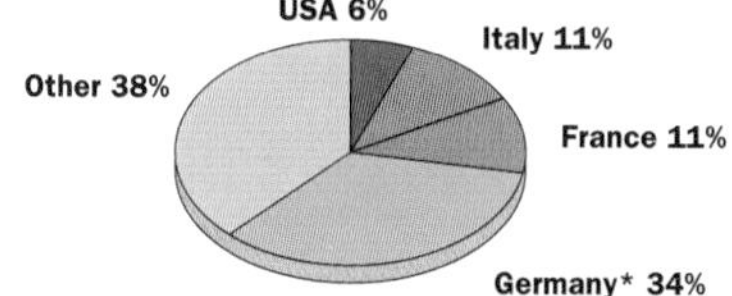

Strengths
Highly skilled work force. Reliable provider of services; key to strength of banking sector. Strong machine tools and precision engineering. Powerful chemicals and banking multinationals; banking secrecy laws attract foreign capital. Ability to innovate to capture mass markets, typified by Swatch watch and proposed Swatch car.

Weaknesses
Protected cartels result in many over-priced goods. Highly subsidized agricultural sector. 35% withholding tax on income earned in Switzerland by non-residents stifles direct foreign investment in business.

Profile
The Swiss economy is widely diversified, with 61% of GDP coming from services and 26% from industry. The country has an outsized banking sector, thanks to its outstanding success in attracting capital for investment. Almost half of the world's investment capital placed outside the investor's own country is in Switzerland. It is also home to some large multinational enterprises.

ECONOMIC PERFORMANCE INDICATOR

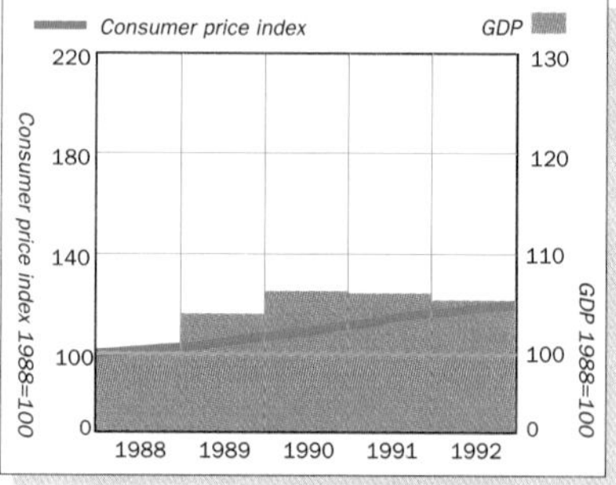

SWITZERLAND : MAJOR BUSINESSES

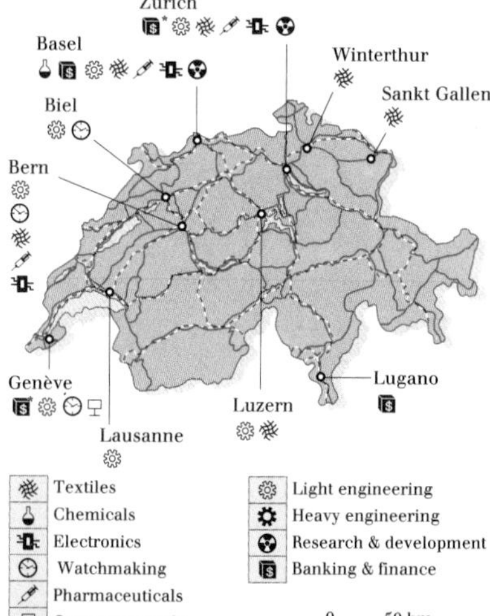

RESOURCES

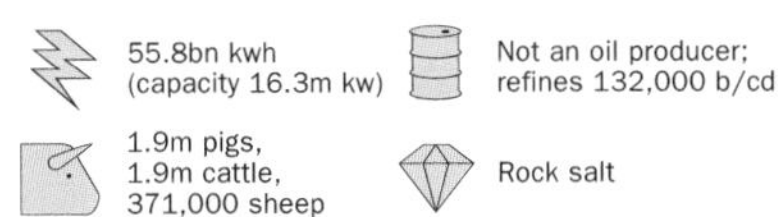

ELECTRICITY GENERATION

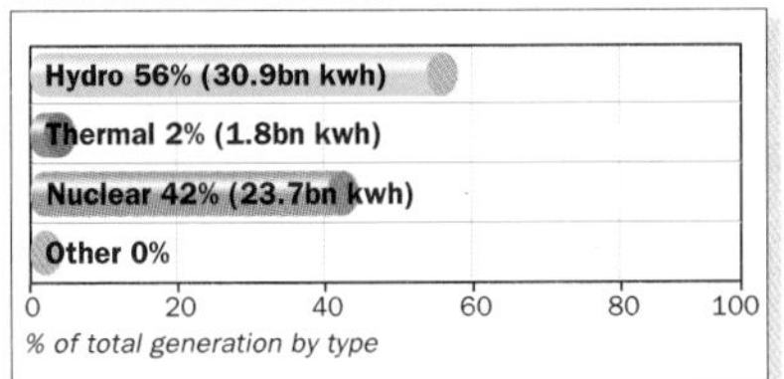

Switzerland is poor in natural resources, having no valuable minerals in commercially exploitable quantities. Over half of its electricity comes from hydropower, while five nuclear plants supply most of the rest. This allows spending on imported oil and coal to be kept to a minimum – they account for less than 4% of the total import bill. The Chernobyl accident inspired large-scale anti-nuclear power demonstrations and a sixth plant was canceled. However, a referendum approved continued use of existing plants.

SWITZERLAND : LAND USE

Cropland
Forest
Pasture
High mountain regions
Cattle
Vineyards

Rhine
JURA
ALPS
Lake Geneva
Rhône

0 50 km
0 50 miles

ENVIRONMENT

18% partially protected

Strong state commitment to conservation

ENVIRONMENTAL TREATIES

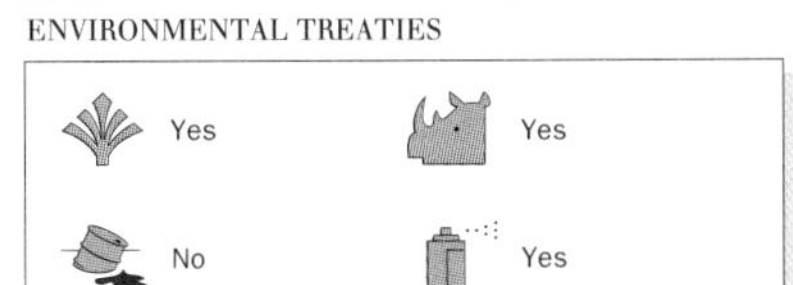

The Swiss are among the most environmentally conscious people in the world and are willing to back their convictions with money: the Basel–Milan tunnel plan was approved by referendum, despite the estimated $13.3bn cost. The planners aim to achieve a total ban on truck transit traffic by 2004, although some argue that a ban will not be necessary, as trucks traveling on trains will cut two hours off the Basel–Milan journey. The Swiss are avid recyclers and taxation is used to encourage this. A carbon dioxide tax was also proposed in 1994.

MEDIA

Freedom of expression is guaranteed

PUBLISHING AND BROADCAST MEDIA

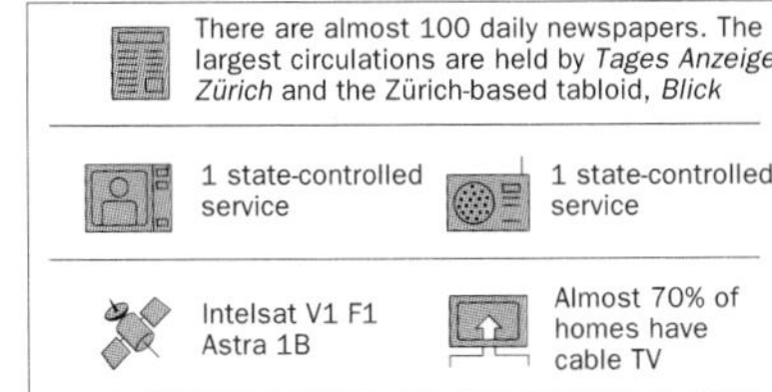

There are almost 100 daily newspapers. The largest circulations are held by *Tages Anzeiger Zürich* and the Zürich-based tabloid, *Blick*
1 state-controlled service
1 state-controlled service
Intelsat V1 F1
Astra 1B
Almost 70% of homes have cable TV

The Swiss media is broadly organized along regional lines and reflects the country's linguistic divisions. The state-owned German, French and Italian language TV and radio stations tend to focus on the interests of their specific communities. German, Italian and French satellite TV is widely available. Few newspapers have national coverage; *Tribune de Genève* and *Neue Zürcher Zeitung* are exceptions.

CRIME

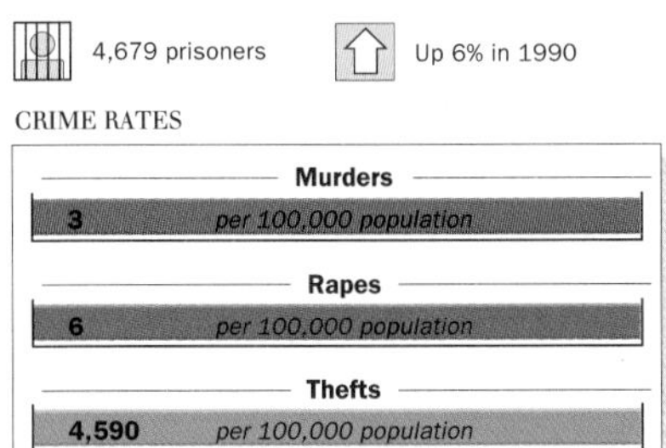

Crime rates are low by international standards. However, muggings and burglaries are on the rise. Much of the growth is drug-related. More cases of banking secrecy laws attracting laundered funds are coming to light.

EDUCATION

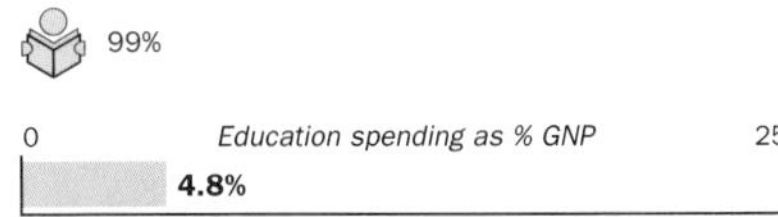

THE EDUCATION SYSTEM

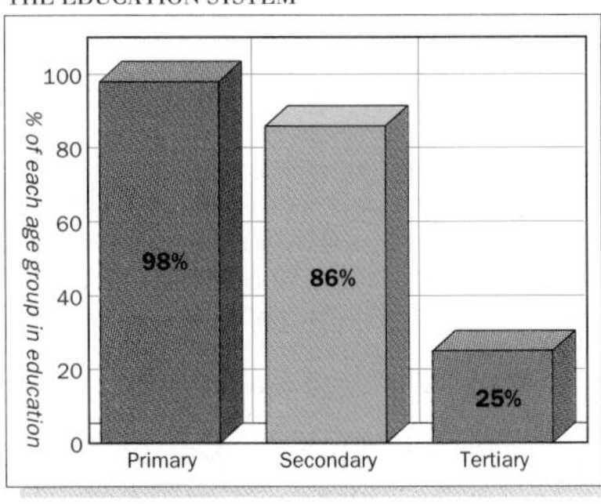

Most students over the age of 16 are encouraged to take up vocational studies. Training is thorough and is usually combined with three or four years' apprenticeship in the student's chosen field. The higher education institutions have the funds to attract top European academics. Zurich's Federal Technological Institute has gained an international reputation for its computer programming research.

HEALTH

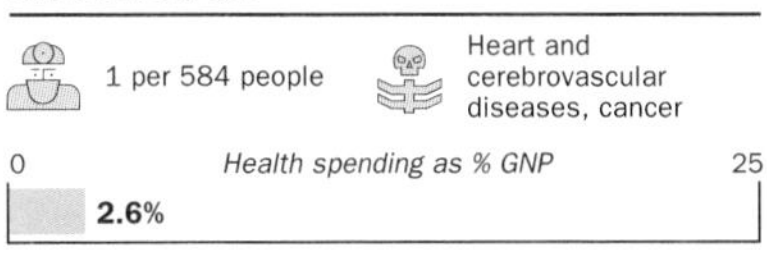

The health system is among the most efficient and pioneering in the world. Health costs are covered by compulsory insurance plans.

WEALTH

Chambermaid, 2,875 Swiss francs per month; top chef, 12,000 Swiss francs per month

CONSUMER GOODS OWNERSHIP

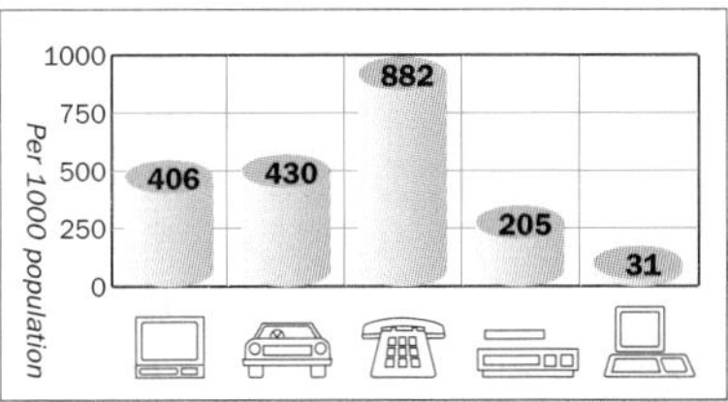

Switzerland is the world's wealthiest country – its per capita income is more than $33,000. Wages are relatively high, although the cost of living is also well above the European average. Many workers choose to live in France and commute across the border. The land market is highly regulated.

WORLD RANKING

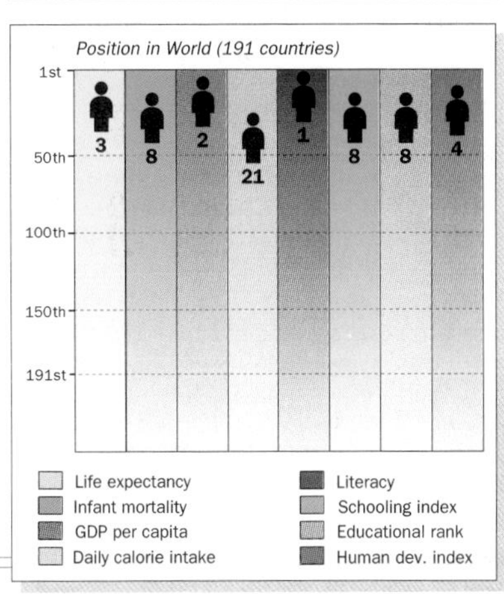

S

MIDDLE EAST
Turkey · SYRIA · Lebanon · Israel · Jordan · Iraq · Asia · Africa

SYRIA

OFFICIAL NAME: Syrian Arab Republic **CAPITAL:** Damascus
POPULATION: 13.3 million **CURRENCY:** Syrian pound **OFFICIAL LANGUAGE:** Arabic

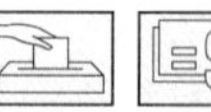

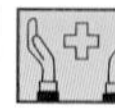

SYRIA SHARES BORDERS with Lebanon, Israel, Jordan, Iraq and Turkey. Many Syrians regard their country as an artificial creation of French colonial rule, which lasted from 1920 to 1946. They identify instead with a Greater Syria encompassing Lebanon, Jordan and Palestine. Since independence, Syria's foreign relations have been turbulent, although President Assad's authoritarian Ba'athist regime has brought a measure of internal stability.

CLIMATE

WEATHER CHART

Average daily temperature · Rainfall
°C/°F: 40/104, 30/86, 20/68, 10/50, 0/32, -10/14, -20/-4
cm/in: 40/16, 30/12, 20/8, 10/4, 0
J F M A M J J A S O N D

The coastal climate is Mediterranean, with mild, wet winters and dry, hot summers. Away from the coast, the country is increasingly arid, with some desert areas. In the mountains, snow is common in winter. Most of the country receives less than 10 inches of rainfall a year and, away from the coast, rainfall is very unpredictable.

COMMUNICATIONS

Damascus International 1.5m passengers

94 ships 231,000 dwt

THE TRANSPORTATION NETWORK

18,444 miles (29,682 km)

442 miles (712 km)

1,192 miles (1,918 km)

418 miles (672 km)

The road network is adequate in the cities, but unreliable in rural areas, especially during the winter wet season. State-run and privately owned bus services operate from Damascus and Aleppo to most towns. Roads are integrated with the railroads, which carry over four million passengers a year and are vital to freight transport. Damascus is the main international airport and Latakia the main port.

TOURISM

562,000 visitors

Up 37% in 1990

MAIN OVERSEAS ARRIVALS

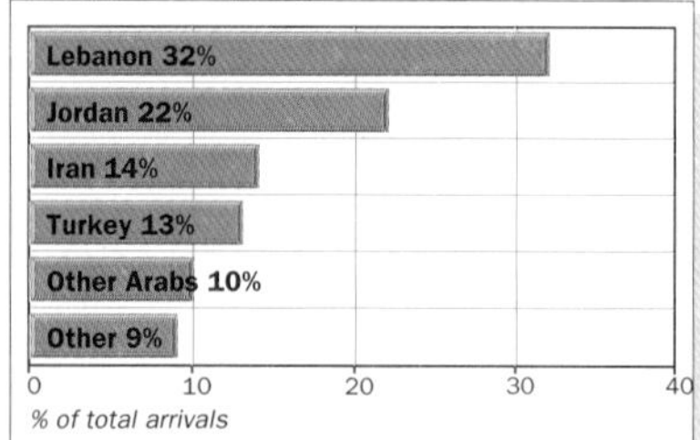

Years of political turbulence, allegations of human rights abuses committed by the Assad government and strict, complex, travel regulations retarded the development of tourism. However, just before the 1990–1991 Gulf War, Syria began to compete in popularity as a holiday destination with other Middle Eastern states. Modern hotels were built in most main cities and facilities improved to cater for growing numbers of Western visitors. Following the war, tourist numbers dropped sharply, but they are now gradually recovering. Syria's main attractions are the antiquities of Damascus – the oldest inhabited city in the world – and Aleppo and Palmyra, with their covered markets (*soukhs*), mosques and baths. Syria has a wealth of castles dating back to the Crusades and sites associated with the advent of Islam. In addition, there are as many as 3,500 as yet unexcavated archaeological sites. Syria's Mediterranean coastline has fine beaches, and there are mountain resorts in Latakia.

***The ancient city of Palmyra,** in Syria's central region, possesses some of the Middle East's finest Classical monuments.*

PEOPLE

Arabic, French, Kurdish, Armenian, Circassian, Turkmen, Assyrian, Aramaic

186 people per sq. mile

THE URBAN/RURAL POPULATION SPLIT

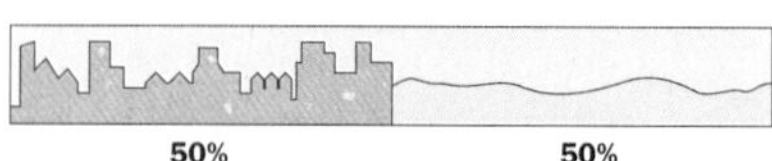

RELIGIOUS PERSUASION

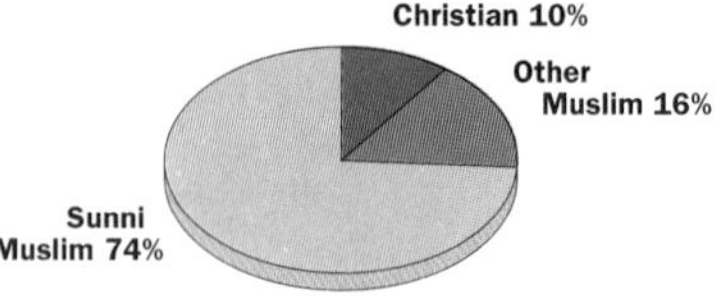

ETHNIC MAKEUP

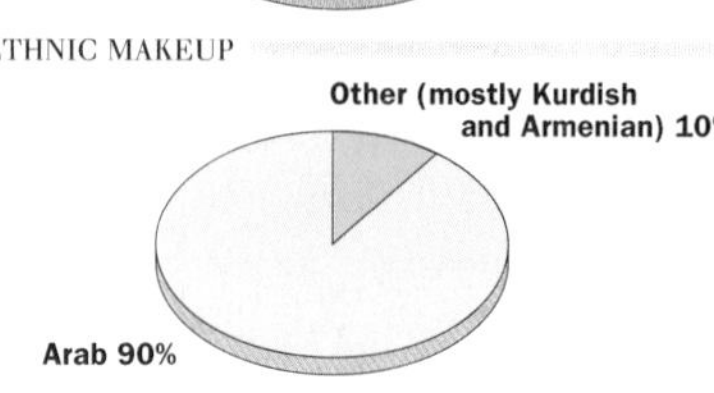

Most Syrians live within 60 miles of the coast, where the largest cities are sited. About 90% are Muslim. They include the politically dominant Alawis, based in Latakia and Tartous provinces. There is also a sizable Christian minority. In the west and north a mosaic of groups exists, including Kurds, Turkish-speaking communities and Armenians, the latter based in cities. Damascus, Al Qamishli and Aleppo have small Jewish communities, and there are three villages where Aramaic is spoken. In addition, some 300,000 Palestinian refugees have settled in Syria. Minorities were initially attracted to the ruling Ba'ath Party because of its emphasis on the state over sectarian interests. However, disputes between factions led to the Shi'a Muslim Alawis taking control, fostering resentment among the Sunni Muslim majority.

The emancipation of women, promoted by the Ba'ath regime in the late 1960s, has been carried forward under President Assad. His first woman cabinet minister was appointed in 1976.

POPULATION AGE BREAKDOWN

% of population by age group

	1960	1970	1980	1990	2000
65+	3.8%	4.4%	3.2%	2.6%	2.6%
15–64	51.8%	46.7%	49.3%	49.1%	50.9%
0–14	44.4%	48.9%	47.5%	48.3%	46.5%

S

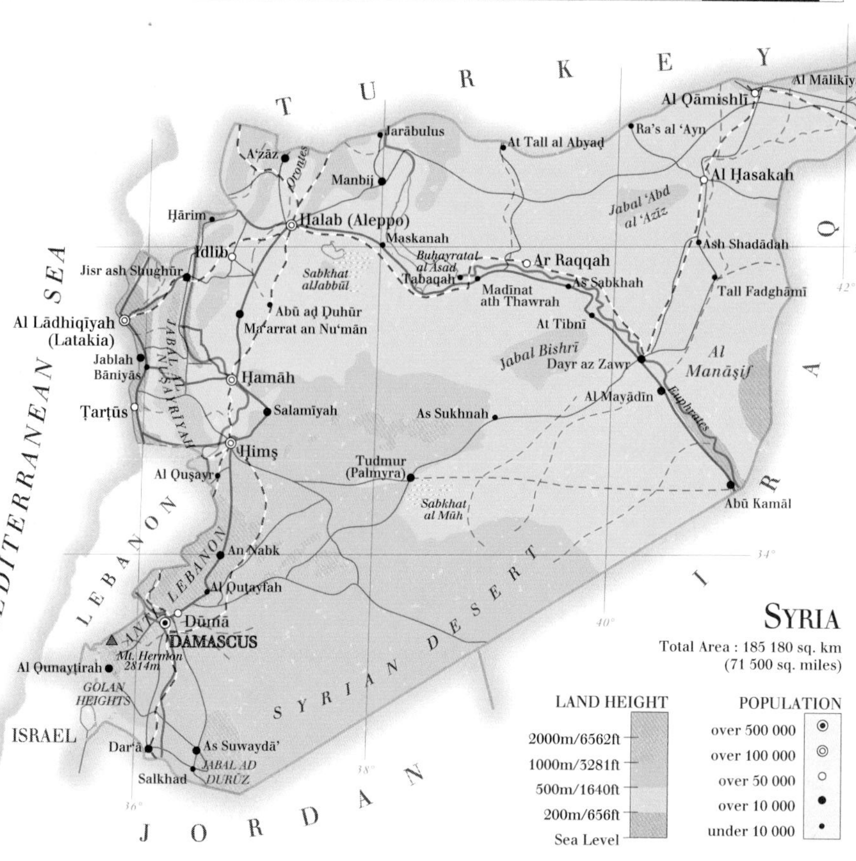

POLITICS

Uncertain

President Lt.-Gen. Hafiz al-Assad

THE STATE OF THE PARTIES

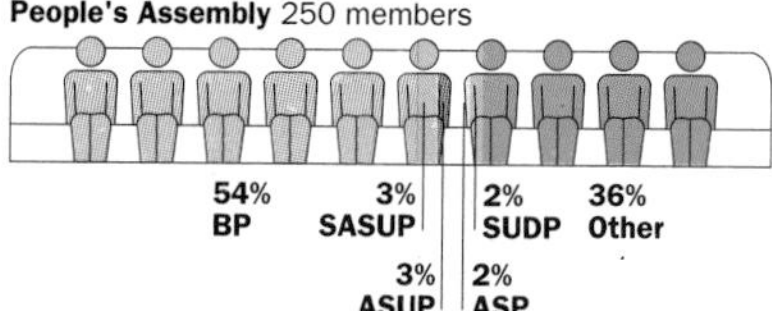

BP = Ba'ath Party **SASUP** = Syrian Arab Socialist Party **ASUP** = Arab Socialist Unionist Party **ASP** = Arab Socialist Party **SUDP** = Socialist Unionist Democratic Party **Other** = Communist Party

Syria is, in practice, a single-party, national socialist state. Its military-backed leader since 1971 has been President Assad, a lifelong Ba'ath Party militant, dedicated to its campaign for Arab revival.

MAIN POLITICAL ISSUES

Human rights

The Syrian regime is under international pressure to improve its human rights record. Allegations of oppression of the country's Jews and opposition Sunni Islamic fundamentalists, and also of links with international terrorist groups are widespread. The EU has suspended aid payments until conditions improve.

Political pluralism

President Assad remains the dominant political figure and he and his military-backed regime, drawn mainly from the Shi'a Alawi grouping, keep a tight hold on power. Again under international pressure, Assad has made promises to permit more political parties, but they remain unfulfilled. Assad was sworn in for another seven-year term in 1992.

PROFILE

The Ba'athist military swept to power in 1963 with a vision of uniting all Arab nations under one, Syrian-dominated socialist system. The coup ended the power of city elites and promoted citizens from rural areas. The state became the main employer.

When Assad came to power in 1971, he consolidated the Ba'ath Party as the major political force. Unrest among Islamic militants was crushed, and Assad focused on foreign affairs in a bid to make Syria a major power.

Syria initially found a Ba'athist ally in Iraq, and the two countries embarked on a plan for union in 1978. Relations soon foundered amid mutual charges over interference in each other's internal affairs – to the extent that, alone among Arab nations, Syria backed Iran in the Iran–Iraq War.

WORLD AFFAIRS

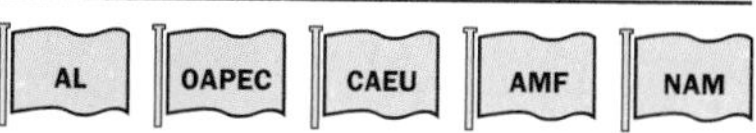

Following Egypt's 1979 accord with Israel, Syria sees itself as the major barrier to Israel's regional dominance. Syria has extended its influence over Lebanon (where it has achieved a high degree of control), Jordan and the Palestinians, as well as seeking alliances with North African states. The biggest single issue between Syria and Israel remains the occupation of the strategically vital Golan Heights, seized by Israel during the Six Day War in 1967. Under the 1993 Washington peace accord between Israel and the PLO, it was suggested that the Heights should become a demilitarized zone. Syria, however, insists on their return.

Syria faced international isolation in the 1980s because of the Assad government's alleged backing of terrorists. It regained a measure of respect in 1990 by securing the release of Western hostages in Lebanon from Shi'a militants. Assad followed up this diplomatic triumph by backing the Western allies in the 1990–1991 Gulf War, contributing troops to liberate Kuwait from Iraqi forces. Syria's involvement in the Gulf War was vital in legitimizing the action in the eyes of the Arab world. Syria has now emerged as a major ally of the West in containing Iraqi expansionism.

AID

$1.2bn (exceptional receipts)

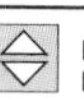

Likely to return to low annual level

Syria has historically received little aid, due to its human rights record and substantial oil income. However, one-off payments totaling $2 billion in 1992 and $1.2 billion in 1993 were received after the Gulf War, mainly from Saudi Arabia and the Gulf states, but with contributions from the West and Japan.

***President Assad,** who was elected for a fourth term of office in 1992.*

***Mahmoud az-Zoubi,** who became Prime Minister of Syria in 1990.*

CHRONOLOGY

Complete independence from France was achieved in 1946. From 1958–1961, Syria merged with Egypt to form the United Arab Republic.

- ❑ **1963** Ba'athist military junta, the National Council of the Revolutionary Command, seizes power. Maj.-Gen. Amin al-Hafiz president.
- ❑ **1966** Military junta of radical Ba'ath Party members seizes power.
- ❑ **1967** Israel overruns Syrian positions above Lake Tiberias, seizes Golan Heights and occupies Quneitra. Syria boycotts Arab Summit and rejects compromise with Israel.
- ❑ **1970** Hafiz al-Assad seizes power in "corrective coup."
- ❑ **1971** Assad elected president for seven-year term.
- ❑ **1973** New constitution approved by plebiscite confirming Ba'ath Party as dominant force. War launched with Egypt against Israel to regain territory lost in 1967. Further territory lost to Israel.
- ❑ **1976** Syria intervenes militarily to quell fighting in Lebanon with a peacekeeping mandate from Arab League.
- ❑ **1977** Relations broken off with Egypt after President Sadat's visit to Jerusalem.
- ❑ **1978** National charter signed with Iraq for union. President Assad returned for second term.
- ❑ **1980** Membership of Muslim Brotherhood made capital offense. Treaty of Friendship with USSR.
- ❑ **1981** Israel formally annexes Golan Heights. Charter with Iraq collapses.
- ❑ **1982** Islamic extremist uprising in Hama crushed; thousands killed. Israel invades Lebanon; Syrian missiles in Bekaa Valley destroyed.
- ❑ **1985** Assad reelected president. USA claims Syrian links to airport bombings at Rome and Vienna.
- ❑ **1986** Syrian complicity alleged in planting of bomb aboard Israeli airliner in London. EU, except for Greece, imposes sanctions.
- ❑ **1989** Diplomatic relations re-established with Egypt.
- ❑ **1990** Troops take part in Operation Desert Storm to liberate Kuwait from Iraqi forces. UK restores diplomatic relations after Syrian help in freeing Western hostages in Lebanon.
- ❑ **1991** Damascus Declaration aid and defense pact signed with Egypt, Saudi Arabia, Kuwait, the UAR, Qatar, Bahrain and Oman.
- ❑ **1992** Assad reelected president.

DEFENSE

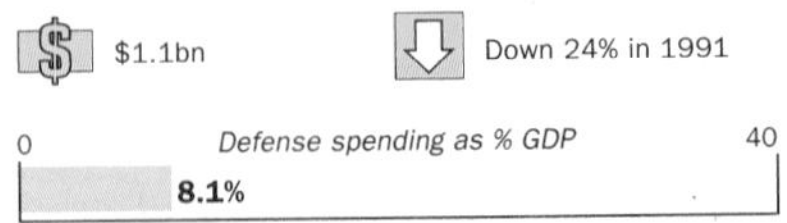

Having fought four wars against Israel since 1948, Syria is the Arab world's strongest military power after Egypt. There is no political mechanism to challenge the dominance of the military. With more than 400,000 troops and nearly 50% of government income spent on weapons, Syria is a formidable power. The military is mostly equipped with weapons obtained from the former Soviet Union.

During the 1980s, Syrian forces fought off a series of Israeli encroachments in the region, and also foiled Israeli attempts to control Lebanon. Syria remains the power Israel fears most.

SYRIAN ARMED FORCES

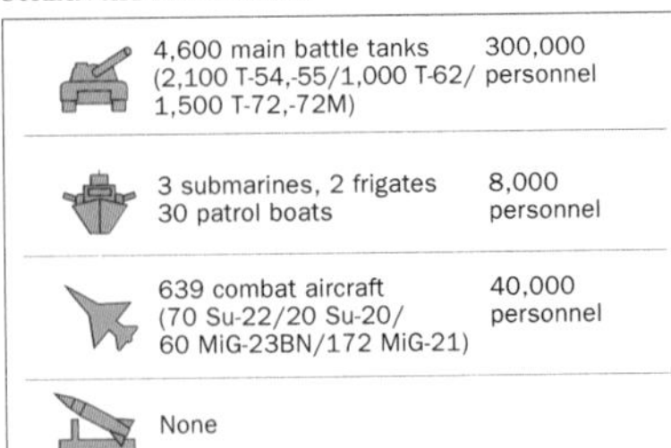

4,600 main battle tanks (2,100 T-54,-55/1,000 T-62/ 1,500 T-72,-72M)
300,000 personnel
3 submarines, 2 frigates 30 patrol boats
8,000 personnel
639 combat aircraft (70 Su-22/20 Su-20/ 60 MiG-23BN/172 MiG-21)
40,000 personnel
None

ECONOMICS

$16.2bn

20.96 Syrian pounds

SCORE CARD

- ❑ World GNP Ranking..........66th
- ❑ GNP per Capita..........$1,218
- ❑ Balance of Payments..........$1.8bn
- ❑ Inflation..........40% (est)
- ❑ Unemployment..........Fairly low

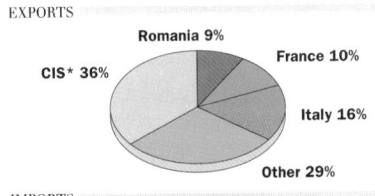

EXPORTS

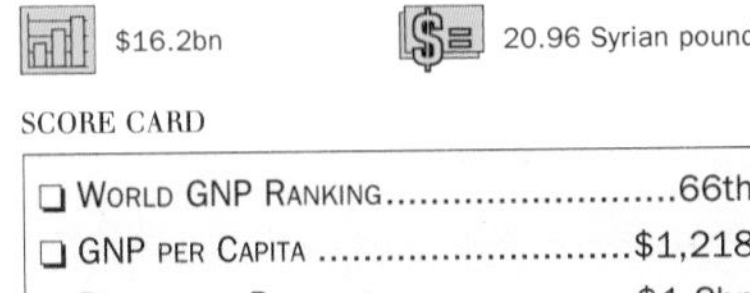

IMPORTS

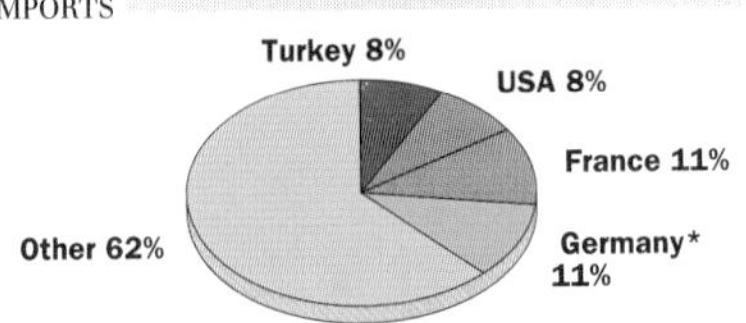

Strengths

Exporter of crude oil – production increasing as a result of new oil strikes. Manufacturing base has grown. Thriving agricultural sector.

Weaknesses

High defense spending is a major drain on economy. Large black market. High inflation. Economy dominated by inefficient state-run companies. Autocratic regime deters foreign investment. High population growth.

Profile

Billions of dollars flowed into the Syrian economy from the USA, Japan, the EU, Saudi Arabia and other Gulf states following the 1990–1991 Gulf War. This cash injection, along with increased oil revenue, led to rapid growth. Also, a decision to divert water from the Euphrates River toward fertile plains, rather than using it to irrigate poorer land, led to a rise in agricultural output. However, long-term economic prospects remain uncertain. The large public sector, which employs 20% of the work force, makes little contribution to the economy. State controls have inhibited private enterprise and investment and have created a booming black market. Turkey's plans to draw water from the Euphrates threaten farming in Syria.

ECONOMIC PERFORMANCE INDICATOR

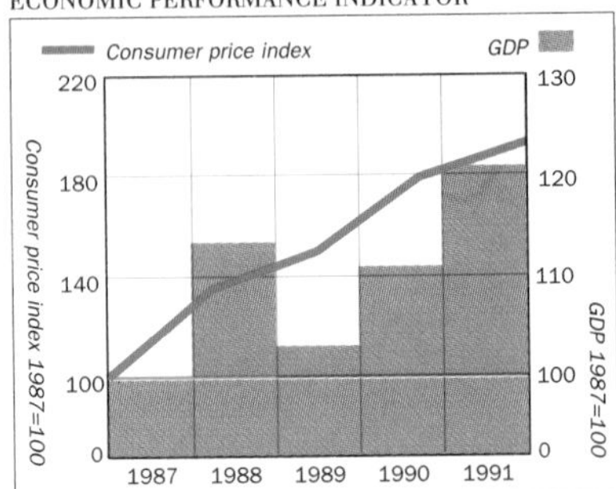

SYRIA : MAJOR BUSINESSES

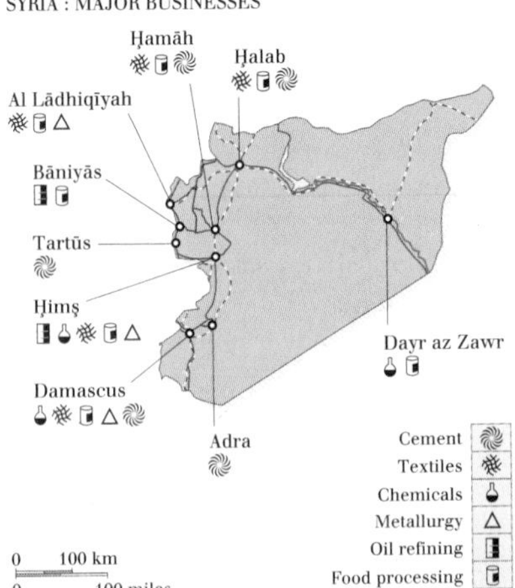

RESOURCES

10.6bn kwh
(capacity 3.7m kw)

531,100 b/d
(reserves 1,7bn bbl)

13.9m sheep,
756,000 cattle,
177,000 asses

Phosphate, oil,
natural gas, iron

ELECTRICITY GENERATION

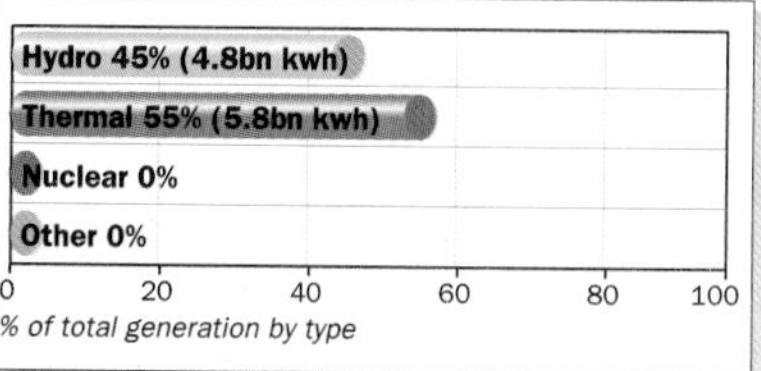

Syria has large supplies of oil, mostly good quality light crude, which was discovered along the Euphrates in the 1980s. Gas was found in substantial quantities near Palmyra. Syria's other important minerals are phosphates and iron ore. Hydroelectric power satisfies most energy requirements. The manufacturing base is largely made up of oil-derived industries, including plastics and chemicals, textiles and food products. Cotton is the main cash crop, but fruit and vegetables are also grown. Livestock, especially sheep and goats, supports the rural economy.

SYRIA : LAND USE

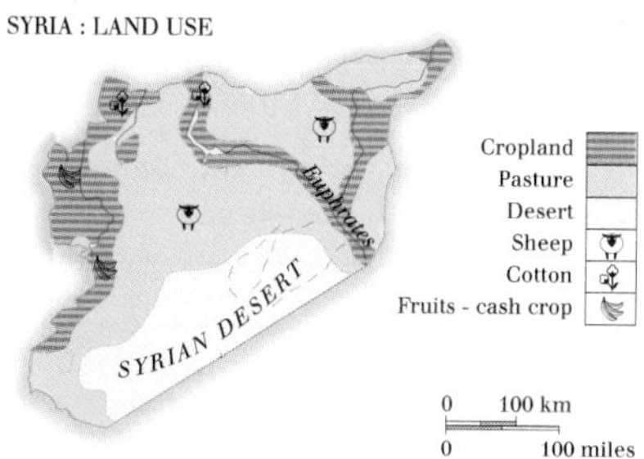

ENVIRONMENT

None

Few conservation initiatives

ENVIRONMENTAL TREATIES

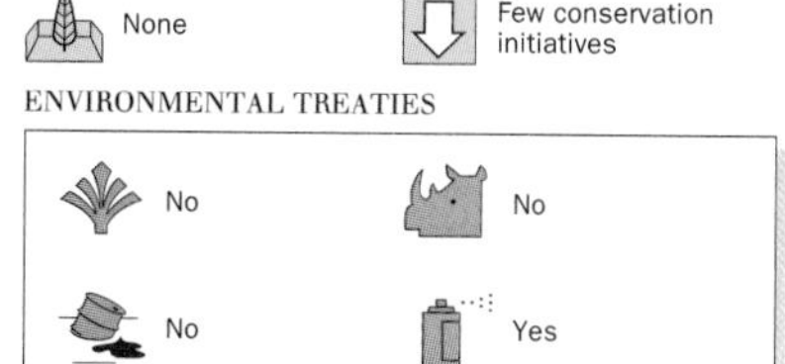

The Assad regime's most expensive and controversial environmental project has been the Euphrates Dam, power station and irrigation network at Tabaqah. The dam's vast man-made reservoir, Lake Buḩayrat al Asad, engulfed some 300 villages and destroyed 62,000 acres of fertile farmland. Syria's industrial program has on occasion damaged the environment. A giant cement factory, built by the East Germans at Tartus in the mid-1970s, has been held responsible for polluting a valuable stretch of Mediterranean coastline.

MEDIA

The media is under strict government control

Virtually all daily newspapers, which include the English language *Syria Times*, are state-owned or have government affiliations. Radio and TV, the news agency SANA, press distribution and advertising companies are also controlled by the regime. There is no freedom of information.

CRIME

Syria does not publish prison figures

Up 30% in 1990

CRIME RATES

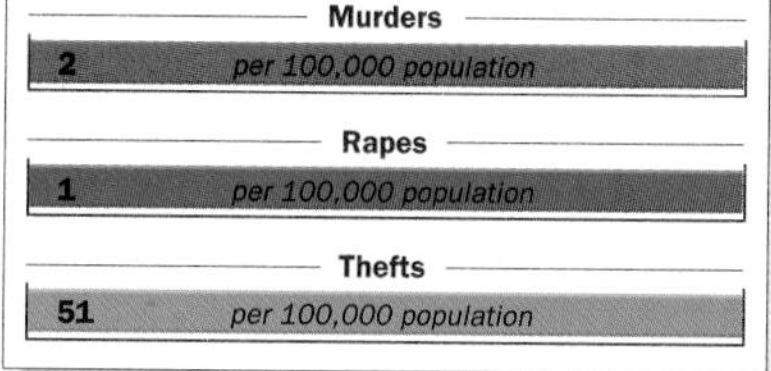

There is no truly independent judiciary. The powerful security services exercise arbitrary powers of arrest and detention. There are widespread reports of torture in custody. Politicians overthrown by President Assad in the 1970s are still held in the prison-fortress of Mezze in Damascus.

EDUCATION

64%

0 Education spending as % GNP 25

4.1%

THE EDUCATION SYSTEM

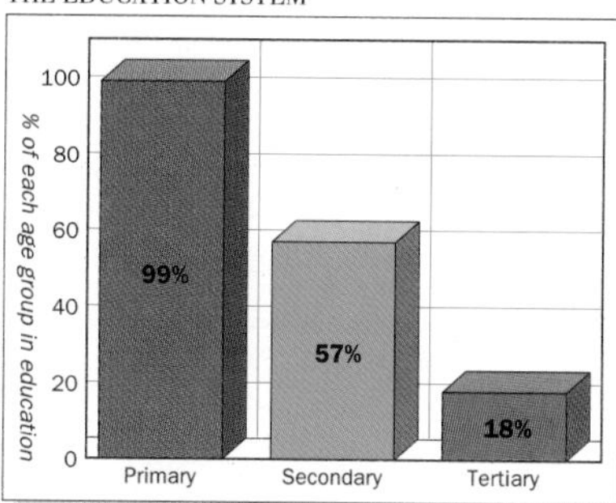

A free and compulsory system of primary education for all was a priority of the Ba'ath Party when it came to power. Under Assad, co-education for boys and girls began in the cities and spread to rural areas. Higher education is provided by seven universities, notably at Damascus, Aleppo, Tishrin and Ḩimş. There are over 130,000 university students. Education ranks second – though by a considerable margin – to defense in government expenditure.

PUBLISHING AND BROADCAST MEDIA

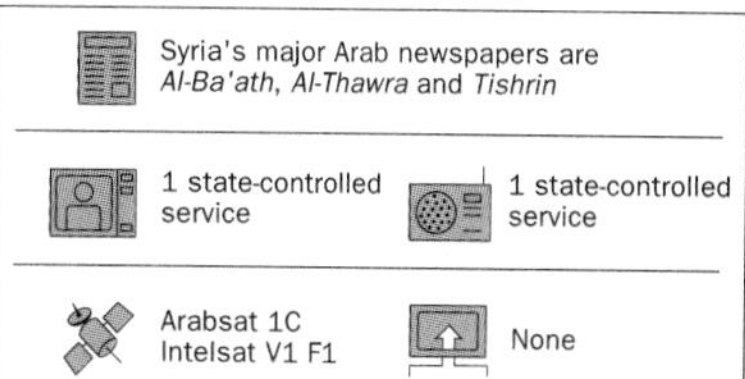

Syria's major Arab newspapers are Al-Ba'ath, Al-Thawra and Tishrin
1 state-controlled service
1 state-controlled service
Arabsat 1C
Intelsat V1 F1
None

HEALTH

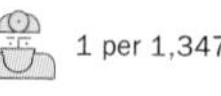
1 per 1,347 people

Heart, respiratory, digestive, infectious and parasitic diseases

0 Health spending as % GNP 25

0.4%

An adequate system of primary health care has been set up since the Ba'ath Party came to power. Treatment is free for those unable to pay. However, hospitals often lack modern equipment and medical services are in need of further investment.

WEALTH

Very large gap between rich and poor

CONSUMER GOODS OWNERSHIP

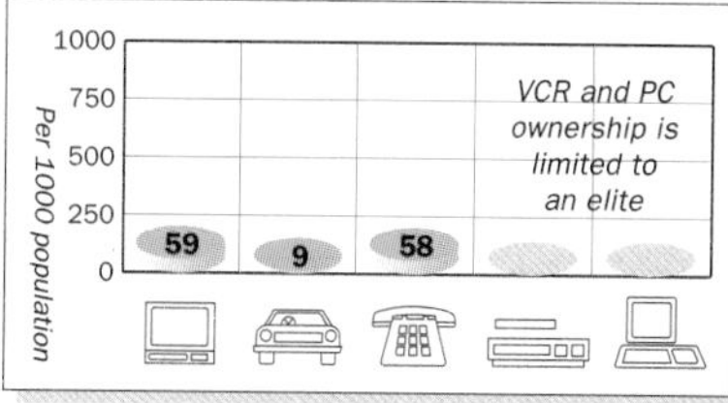

Syria is far from the equitable society that early Ba'ath Party thinkers envisioned. The gulf between rich and poor is widening. Syria's political elite, many of whom live in the West Malki suburb of Damascus, is more numerous and richer than ever before. Palestinian refugees and the urban unemployed make up the poorest groups.

WORLD RANKING

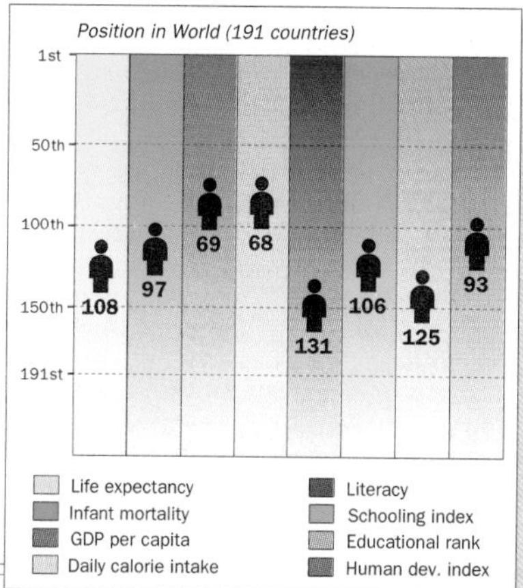

S

TAIWAN

SOUTHEAST ASIA
China
TAIWAN
Asia

OFFICIAL NAME: Republic of China (Taiwan) **CAPITAL:** Taipei
POPULATION: 20.8 million **CURRENCY:** New Taiwan dollar **OFFICIAL LANGUAGE:** Northern Chinese (Mandarin)

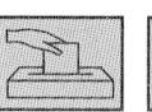

THE ISLAND REPUBLIC of Taiwan lies 80 miles off the southeast coast of mainland China. Formerly known as Formosa, the Republic of China (Taiwan) was established in 1949 by Chiang Kai-shek's Kuomintang (KMT), which was expelled from government in Beijing (then Peking) by the communists under Mao. The KMT still claims to be the sole legitimate ruler of all China, while Beijing considers Taiwan to be one of its provinces. Taiwan is dominated by a mountain region that runs north to south and covers two-thirds of the island. The lowlands are highly fertile, cultivated mostly with rice, and densely populated. In 1986, Taiwan adopted democracy in place of *de facto* military rule. The KMT has been in power since 1949.

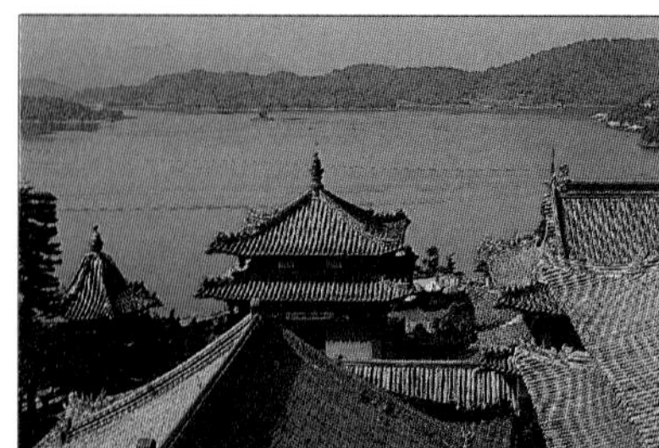

***Wen Wu Temple**, on the shores of Sun Moon Lake in the mountains of central Taiwan – a region famous for its many temples.*

CLIMATE

WEATHER CHART

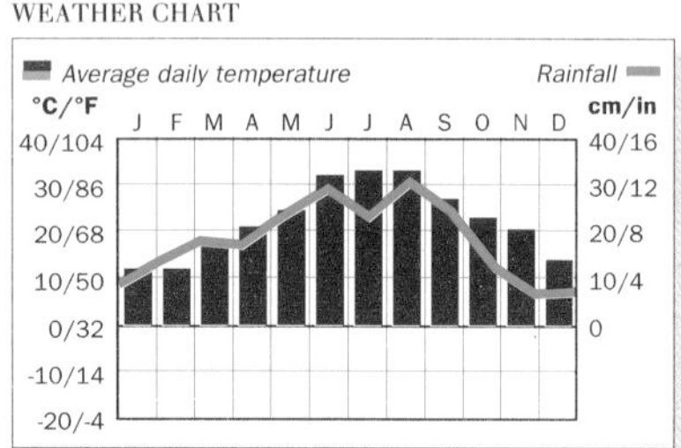

Taiwan has a tropical monsoon climate similar to that of the southern Chinese mainland. Typhoons from the South China Sea between July and September bring the heaviest rains.

TOURISM

1.93m visitors

Down 3% in 1990

MAIN OVERSEAS ARRIVALS

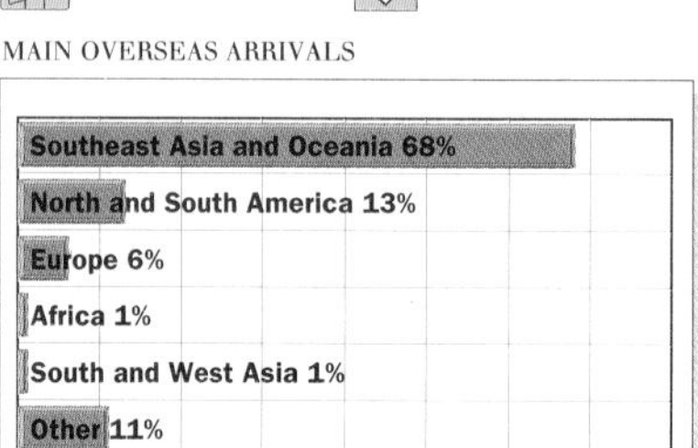

Taiwan is not a major tourist destination and has only recently begun to target tourists in the USA and Japan. As part of the most recent six-year-plans, hotels are being upgraded and tourist facilities at international airports are being improved. The major attraction is the Palace Museum in Taipei, which includes the massive treasure looted by the Nationalists from Beijing. Only 5% can be shown at any one time. Sex tourism is an important business in Taipei, and is second only to Bangkok's. Sex establishments masquerade as barbershops.

COMMUNICATIONS

Chiang Kai Shek Intl, Taoyuan

239 ships
8.93m dwt

THE TRANSPORTATION NETWORK

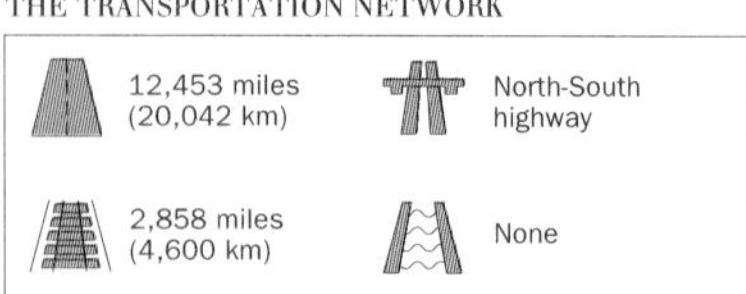

Taiwan is implementing several major transportation infrastructure projects as part of the latest six-year economic plan. Subway and rapid transit systems are being built in Taipei and Kaohsiung. Several new roads are planned, including north–south and east–west cross-island highways. The plan is motivated by the fear that congestion will restrain future growth. Most urban Taiwanese currently ride motor scooters, but transportation planners anticipate a sharp increase in car ownership over the next decade. The bicycle is not as popular in Taiwan as in mainland China. However, Taiwan is the world's biggest bicycle producer, exporting mostly to Europe and the USA.

PEOPLE

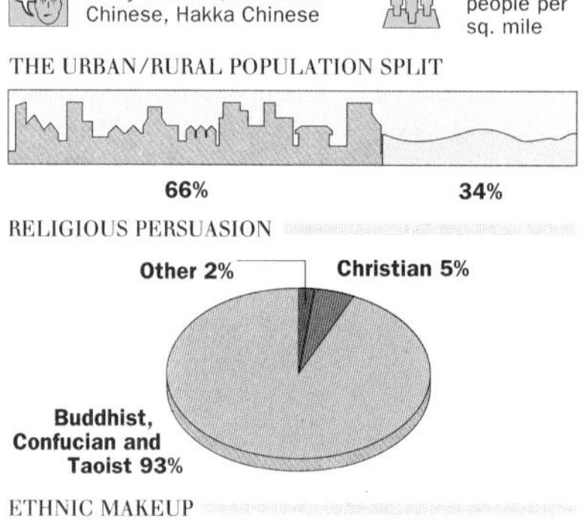

ETHNIC MAKEUP

Aborigine 2%
Mainland Chinese 14%
Indigenous Chinese 84%

Most Taiwanese are Han Chinese, descendants of the 1644 migration of the Ming dynasty from mainland China. The 100,000 Nationalists, who arrived in 1949, established themselves as a ruling class and monopolized the most prestigious jobs in the civil service. This led to considerable resentment from the local inhabitants, but as the 1947 generation have aged, local Taiwanese have entered the political process.

There is little ethnic tension in Taiwan, although the indigenous minorities who live in the eastern hills do suffer considerable discrimination.

As in the rest of Southeast Asia, the extended family is still important and provides a social-security net for the elderly. However, the trend is toward European-style nuclear families, partly a result of housing shortages. Women are not well-represented in the political process, but are prominent in business and the civil service.

POPULATION AGE BREAKDOWN

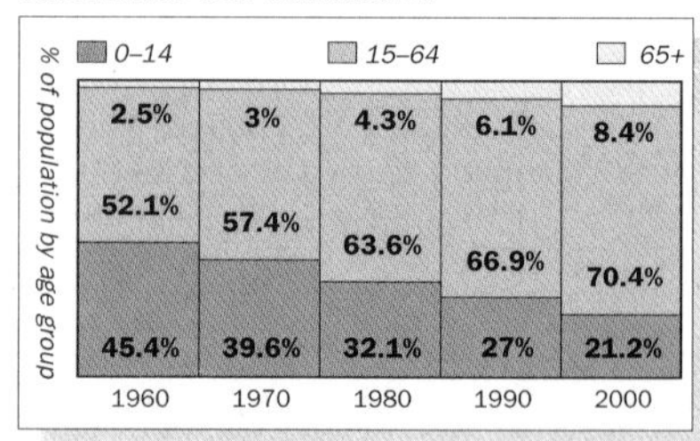

T

POLITICS

Lower House 1995 | President Lee Teng-hui

THE STATE OF THE PARTIES

National Assembly 405 members

79% KMT | 18% DPP | 3% Other

KMT = National Party of China
DPP = Democratic Progressive Party

Legislative Yuan 161 members

63% KMT | 31% DPP | 6% Other

Until 1986, Taiwan was effectively a one-party state. Today, it is a fully functioning multiparty democracy.

MAIN POLITICAL ISSUES

Relations with China
Relations with China have a significant influence on Taiwanese domestic politics. Beijing has made clear its desire to see the Nationalists remain in power in Taiwan. It has threatened invasion should the DPP come to power. This has dissuaded many from voting for the DPP. Beijing objects to the DPP's policy of claiming independence from China, because it belies the Nationalists' claim to be the true government of the mainland. The Nationalists' policy sustains the idea that China is still a unitary state that includes Taiwan. The DPP's stance directly contradicts this. The issue is likely to dominate the 1995 elections.

Elective presidency
The president is currently elected by a caucus of the National Assembly. Suggestions that the office should be directly elected arose because, until 1992, the caucus was dominated by a traditional gerontocracy from the generation of 1947. The caucus is now composed of much younger members, but most commentators believe the president will be directly elected by 1998. The effect will be to weaken the office of president and strengthen that of prime minister.

Li Yuan-zu, vice-president of Taiwan

Lee Teng-hui, president since 1988, reelected in 1990.

Corruption
Many voters associate corruption with democracy. Part of the reason is the open fraud that has surrounded elections, with candidates buying votes at polling booths. The issue is increasingly discussed in political debates.

PROFILE

Between 1949 and 1986, Chiang Kai-shek's KMT monopolized political power in Taiwan and ruled by strict martial law. In 1986, Gen. Chiang Ching-kuo, Chiang Kai Shek's son and successor, decided to pave the way for democracy. Free multiparty elections were first held in December 1986.

TAIWAN

Total Area : 36 179 sq. km (13 969 sq. miles)

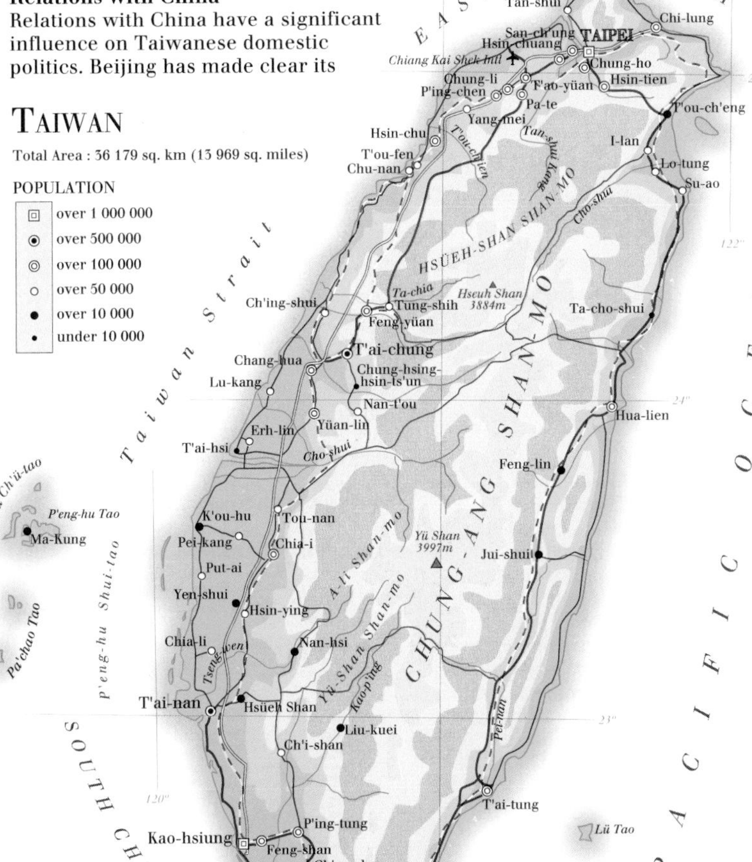

POPULATION
- over 1 000 000
- over 500 000
- over 100 000
- over 50 000
- over 10 000
- under 10 000

LAND HEIGHT
- 3000m/9843ft
- 2000m/6562ft
- 1000m/3281ft
- 500m/1640ft
- 200m/656ft
- Sea Level

WORLD AFFAIRS

Taiwan is diplomatically isolated. States wishing to do business with China cannot have relations with Taipei, which still claims to be the official government of the mainland as well as of Taiwan. Taipei has to conduct its overseas relations via trade delegations rather than embassies and cannot gain representation at the UN. States which recently severed relations were Saudi Arabia in 1991 and South Korea in 1992. Just before becoming South Africa's leader, Nelson Mandela also stated his intention to do so.

Relations with the USA have been difficult since Washington was forced to recognize China at the UN in 1972. Taiwan effectively lost its status as a US client state, and the US 6th Fleet was removed from the Taiwan Strait. US security guarantees to Taiwan have been ambiguous ever since.

China continues to recognize Taiwan only as a province of the mainland.

AID

Substantial donations to small Pacific states

Little change from year to year

Taiwan has a large aid fund devoted to small Pacific Island states. Aid donations are, in practice, an exchange for the fact that states such as Kiribati, Tuvalu and Tonga are among the few nations that have granted Taiwan diplomatic recognition. They have also represented Taiwan's interests in the UN since 1972, when it lost its seat following the US recognition of China.

DEFENCE

$9.7bn

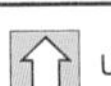

Up 5% in 1992

Defense spending as % GDP (scale 0–40): 5.4%

Taiwan, with a relatively small population, has the fifth-largest army in the world. The main concern is a possible invasion by China. Taiwan is eager to buy the very latest air force technology. Worries about US loyalty have led Taipei to purchase French *Mirage* fighters in addition to their F-16s.

CHINESE (TAIWANESE) ARMED FORCES

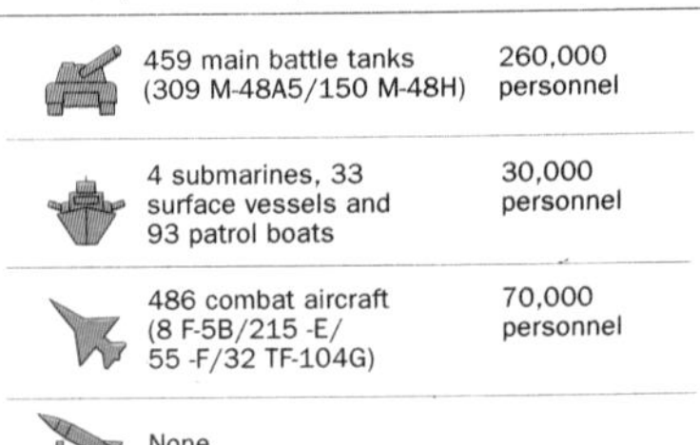

459 main battle tanks (309 M-48A5/150 M-48H)
260,000 personnel
4 submarines, 33 surface vessels and 93 patrol boats
30,000 personnel
486 combat aircraft (8 F-5B/215 -E/ 55 -F/32 TF-104G)
70,000 personnel
None

CHRONOLOGY

Following the 1949 communist revolution in China, Gen. Chiang Kai-shek's nationalist KMT party sought refuge in the island province of Taiwan. The KMT saw the revolution as illegal and itself as the sole rightful Chinese government.

- ❑ **1971** People's Republic of China replaces Taiwan at UN and on UN Security Council.
- ❑ **1973** Taipei's KMT regime rejects Beijing's offer of secret talks on reunification of China.
- ❑ **1975** President Chiang Kai-shek dies. His son, Gen. Chiang Ching-kuo becomes KMT leader. Dr. Yen Chia-kan president.
- ❑ **1979** USA severs relations with Taiwan in favor of People's Republic of China. However, arms sales to Taiwan continue.
- ❑ **1981** Beijing's terms for reunification rejected.
- ❑ **1984** President Chiang reelected.
- ❑ **1986** Political reforms: KMT permits other political parties in Taiwan, ends martial law and permits visits to Chinese mainland for "humanitarian" purposes for first time in 38 years. In 1988, Chinese are allowed to visit Taiwan on same basis.
- ❑ **1988** Lee Teng-hui becomes president.
- ❑ **1989** April: KMT considers reconciliation with Beijing under the formula of "one China, two governments." June: ruthless suppression of student dissent by communist regime ends rapprochement.
- ❑ **1990** Lee Teng-hui reelected president. KMT formally ends state of war with People's Republic.
- ❑ **1991** DPP opposition drafts alternative constitution for Taiwan as an independent state. Policy causes outrage among KMT regime and also in Beijing. KMT reelected with large majority.
- ❑ **1993** Beijing proposes talks on reunification.

ECONOMICS

$162bn

25.41 New Taiwan dollars

SCORE CARD

❑ WORLD GNP RANKING	22nd
❑ GNP PER CAPITA	$7,990
❑ BALANCE OF PAYMENTS	$10,866m
❑ INFLATION	3%
❑ UNEMPLOYMENT	1.4%

EXPORTS

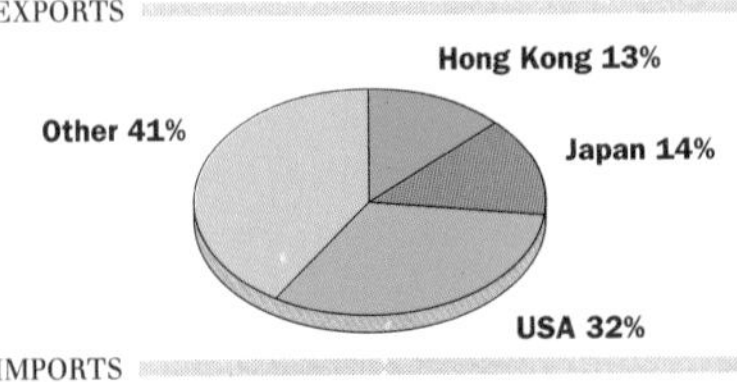

IMPORTS

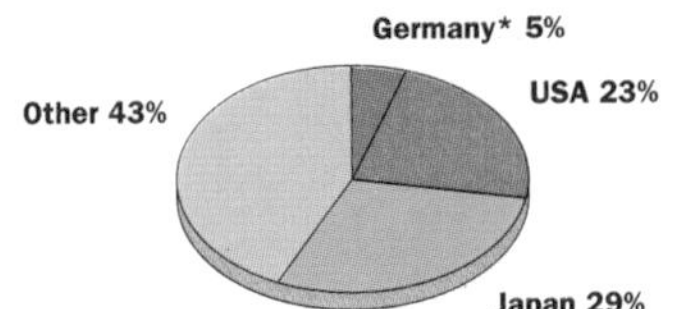

STRENGTHS

Highly educated and ambitious work force, many US-trained and educated, with an inside knowledge of the US market. Manufacturing economy based on small companies that have proved extremely adaptable to changing market conditions. Track record of capturing major markets. Taiwan was successively the world's biggest TV producer, watch producer, PC producer and running shoe manufacturer. Economy in massive surplus, allowing it to invest in burgeoning Southeast Asian economies.

WEAKNESSES

Taiwan's small economic units lack the muscle of Japanese and Western multinationals; they are consequently unable to follow predatory pricing policies. Weak research and development: economy has no tradition of coming up with new products or creating new markets. Unresponsive banking system.

ECONOMIC PERFORMANCE INDICATOR

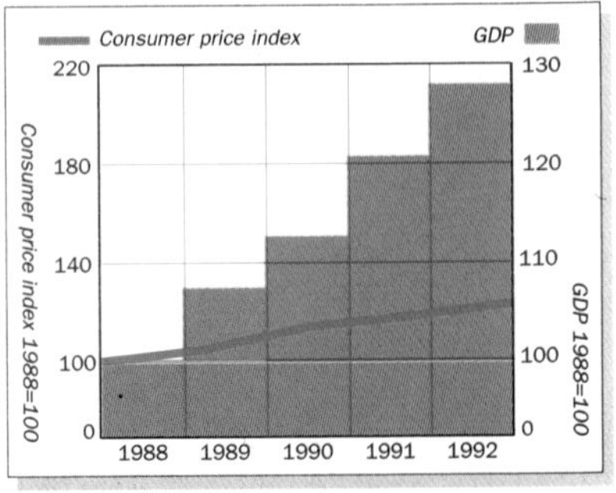

PROFILE

Taiwan is one of the world's most successful economies. Its impressive growth rates, second only to Japan's, will probably not be sustained in the next decade, yet the economy is still expected to grow by 6%–7% a year. The economy retains a strong element of state direction, reflecting the KMT's Soviet economic training. All-embracing six-year plans state targets to be achieved. Taiwan is now investing abroad and is responsible for over 60% of inward investment in China since 1990.

TAIWAN : MAJOR BUSINESSES

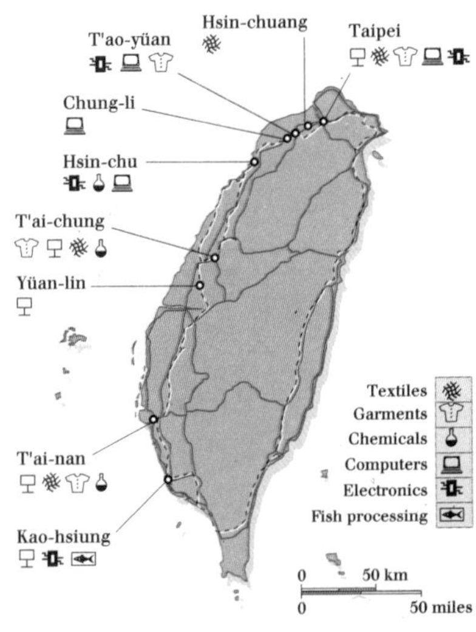

RESOURCES

Not available

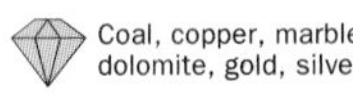
Not an oil producer; refines 542,500 b/cd

77m chickens, 10.6m ducks, 8.6m pigs

Coal, copper, marble, dolomite, gold, silver

ELECTRICITY GENERATION

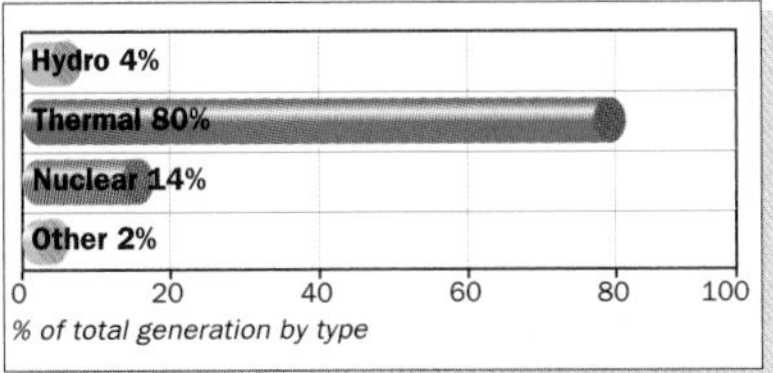

Taiwan has few strategic resources and its mineral industry is not a significant foreign exchange earner. All oil supplies are imported, mostly from Saudi Arabia and Kuwait. The proportion of electricity generated by nuclear power is the highest in the world and Taiwan is a major buyer of South African uranium. Hydroelectric power is also an important sector. Taiwan's fishing industry is highly successful and is a major supplier to the huge Japanese market. Fishermen are often accused of plundering Atlantic fishing grounds.

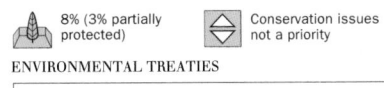

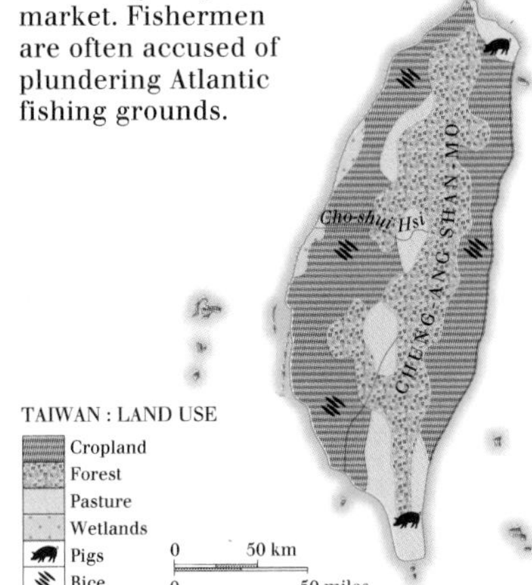

ENVIRONMENT

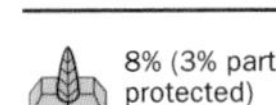
8% (3% partially protected)

Conservation issues not a priority

ENVIRONMENTAL TREATIES

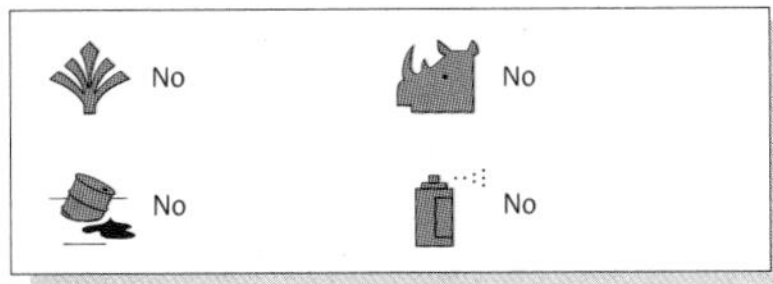

Environmental concerns have not been a priority in Taiwan's dash for growth. Cities have grown fast without many planning controls and factories have few pollution laws to comply with. Taiwan's fishing industry has also been criticized for the use of long-line techniques which trap dolphins, and for plundering other nations' fishing grounds without regard to stock levels.

MEDIA

Criticism of the government is discouraged

PUBLISHING AND BROADCAST MEDIA

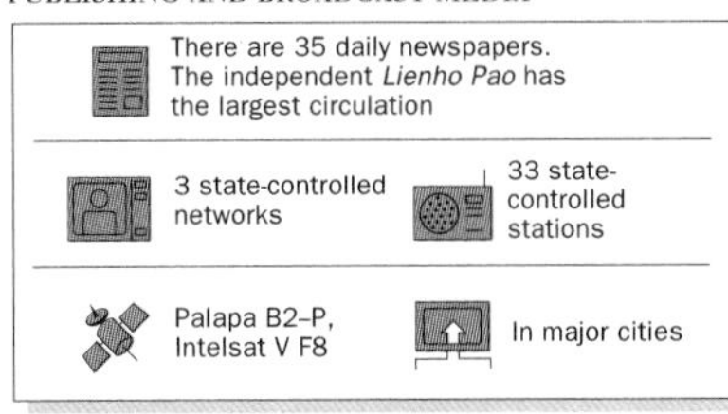

There are 35 daily newspapers. The independent *Lienho Pao* has the largest circulation
3 state-controlled networks
33 state-controlled stations
Palapa B2-P, Intelsat V F8
In major cities

The rigid state control that used to exist over the media has been relaxed. Opposition parties now have access to the state media. Before the 1990s, press with simplified Chinese characters was banned, thus excluding all publications from the mainland. Taiwan has a large domestic TV and film industry.

CRIME

Taiwan does not publish prison figures

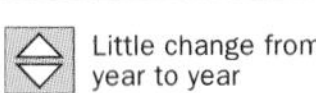
Little change from year to year

CRIME RATES

Most Taiwanese are highly conscious of crime. However, rates are low by US or European standards

Since the end of martial law in 1986, most political prisoners have been released. Taiwan does not suffer from organized crime to the extent found in Hong Kong or Japan. Counterfeit CDs are a major business.

EDUCATION

92%

0 — Education spending as % GNP — 25

3.6%

THE EDUCATION SYSTEM

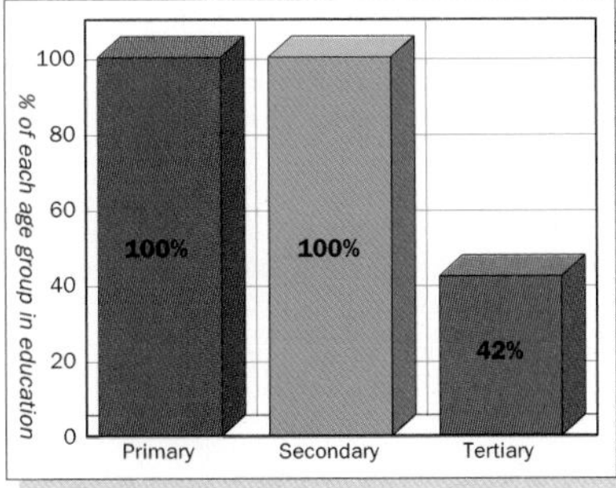

The education system is the same as that found on the mainland and was inspired by 1922 reforms suggested to Beijing by Bertrand Russell and John Dewey. Higher education attendance is one of the highest in the world. Schools have lavish facilities and equipment. Many Taiwanese study in the USA.

HEALTH

1 per 913 people

Cerebrovascular and heart diseases, hypertension

0 — Health spending as % GNP — 25

Higher than regional average

Most health provision in Taiwan is in the private sector. Taiwanese take out elaborate health insurance policies and must prove coverage before treatment is provided. Health facilities are on a par with the best in the world and Taiwanese enjoy a high life expectancy, similar to that in Sweden or Japan. The incidence of AIDS is in line with the Southeast Asian average.

WEALTH

Most Taiwanese are comfortably off

CONSUMER GOODS OWNERSHIP

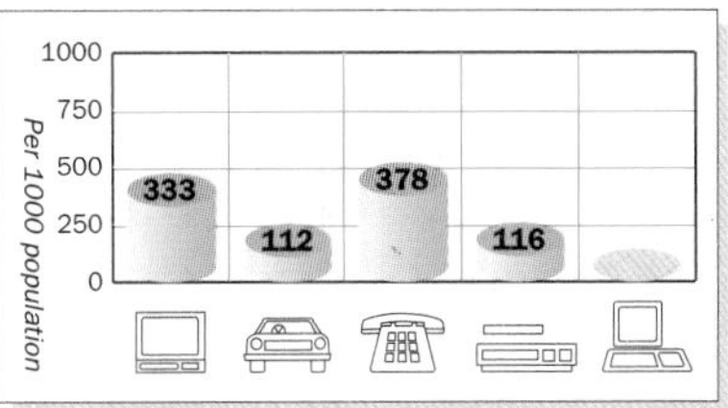

Until 1987, Taiwan had the largest cash reserves of any nation in the world. This reflected the closed nature of its markets and the success of the export economy. Taiwanese have shared in much of this wealth. Inequalities of income distribution are comparatively small, and a high degree of social cohesion has been achieved. In part, this is the result of the land reforms of the 1950s, which gave agricultural workers control of the land while compensating landowners and encouraging them to set up businesses in the cities. Today, most Taiwanese would describe themselves as middle class. Taiwan is perhaps the most consumerist society on earth; conspicuous consumption is celebrated.

WORLD RANKING

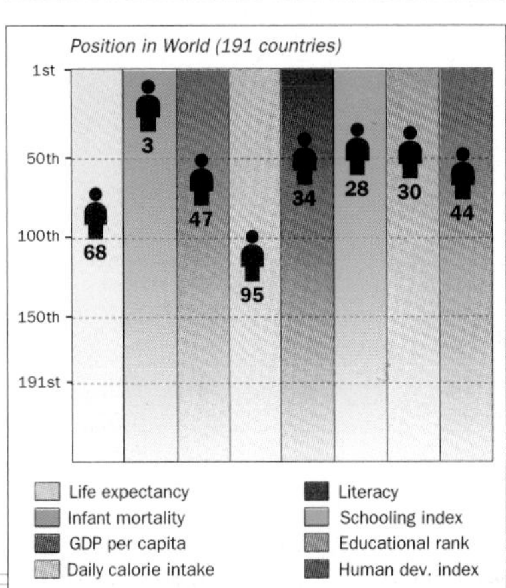

T

CENTRAL ASIA

Uzbekistan Kyrgyzstan TAJIKISTAN China Afghanistan Asia

TAJIKISTAN

OFFICIAL NAME: Republic of Tajikistan **CAPITAL:** Dushanbe
POPULATION: 5.6 million **CURRENCY:** Rouble **OFFICIAL LANGUAGE:** Tajik

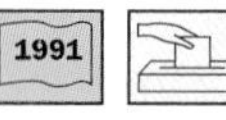

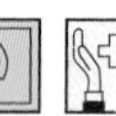

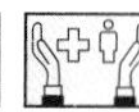

TAJIKISTAN LIES ON the western slopes of the Pamirs in Central Asia. The Tajiks' language and traditions are similar to those of Iran rather than of Turkic Uzbekistan. Tajikistan decided to declare independence only when neighboring Soviet republics declared theirs in late 1991. The republic has since been split by armed conflict between the communist government, backed by Russia and the Uzbeks, and Tajik Islamic rebels.

The Varzob Gorge, north of Dushanbe. Half of the country is over 9,843ft. above sea level.

CLIMATE

WEATHER CHART

Average daily temperature · Rainfall

°C/°F: 40/104, 30/86, 20/68, 10/50, 0/32, -10/14, -20/-4
J F M A M J J A S O N D
cm/in: 40/16, 30/12, 20/8, 10/4, 0

Rainfall is low in the valleys. In mountainous areas winter temperatures can fall below –50°F.

COMMUNICATIONS

Dushanbe Intl
Passenger figures not published

Has no fleet

THE TRANSPORTATION NETWORK

17,709 miles (28,500 km)

None

298 miles (480 km)

124 miles (200 km)

Tajikistan has good cross-border roads and well-maintained airfields, the result of its use as a staging post by Soviet forces during the Afghan War. The best way to visit the mountainous interior is by air.

TOURISM

Almost no tourists

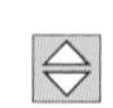

Little change from year to year

MAIN OVERSEAS ARRIVALS

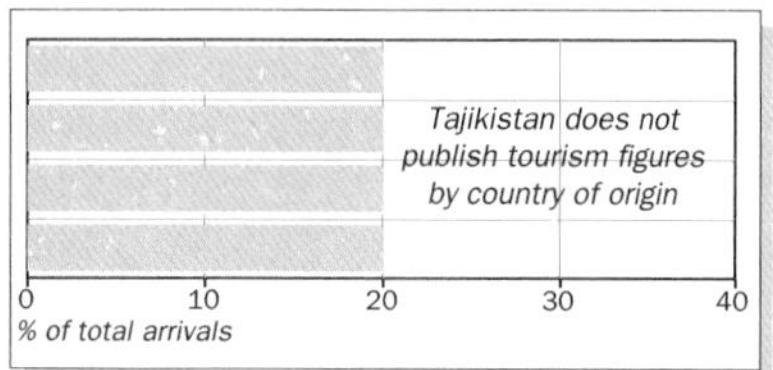

The conflict in Tajikistan makes travel almost impossible. Journalists from the West are often attacked.

PEOPLE

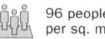

Tajik, Russian

96 people per sq. mile

THE URBAN/RURAL POPULATION SPLIT

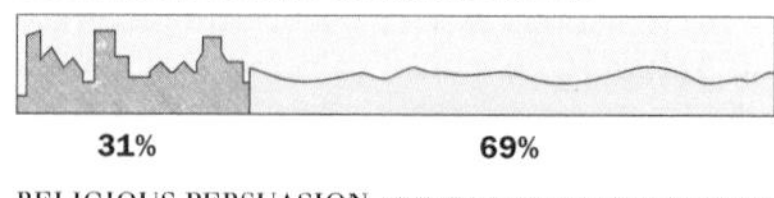

RELIGIOUS PERSUASION

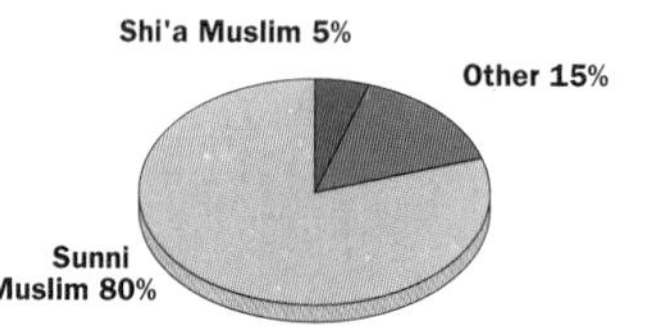

The main ethnic conflict in Tajikistan is between the Tajiks and Uzbeks – peoples of Persian and Turkic origin, respectively. As in neighboring Uzbekistan, however, Russians are discriminated against and their ranks have thinned from 400,000 in 1989 to around 200,000 today. By 1990, the 35,000-strong German minority had left. The struggle between Dushanbe-based communists and Islamic militants in the central and eastern regions has displaced over 60,000 refugees into Afghanistan, whose own Tajik population numbers over one million. Attempts to repatriate the refugees in 1993 failed.

POLITICS

Uncertain

President Imamali Sharipovich Rahmonov

THE STATE OF THE PARTIES

Supreme Soviet 230 members

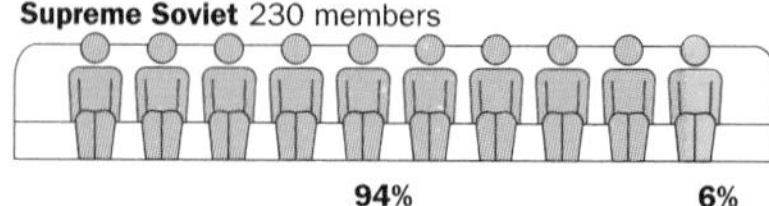

94% CPT **6% Other**

CPT = Communist Party of Tajikistan
Genuine opposition was banned at the elections of 1990. Other main parties are the Democratic Party of Tajikistan, the Islamic Renaissance Party (IRP) and Rebirth

The communist candidate won free presidential elections following independence in 1991. Nine months later Dushanbe was taken over by a coalition of democrats and Muslims, but the capital was retaken by pro-government forces in December 1992. The presidency was abolished and the Chairman of the Supreme Soviet became head of state. In 1993–1994 the communists began to regain control of the largely rebel east, but resistance continued from Afghanistan, despite the presence of 3,500 Russian troops on the Tajik side of the border.

TAJIKISTAN

Total Area : 143 100 sq. km (55 251 sq. miles)

POPULATION
- over 500 000
- over 100 000
- over 50 000
- over 10 000
- under 10 000

LAND HEIGHT
- 4000m/13 124ft
- 3000m/9843ft
- 2000m/6562ft
- 1000m/3281ft
- 500m/1640ft
- 200m/656ft

UZBEKISTAN KYRGYZSTAN CHINA AFGHANISTAN PAKISTAN
Khudzhand Kanibadam Isfara Nau Ura-Tyube Ayni Zeravshan Pendzhikent Dzhirgatal' Garm Navabad Karakul' Pik Kommunizma 7495m DUSHANBE Gissar Kofarnikhon Kalaikhum Murgab Kudara Tursunzade Nurek Yavan Dangara Kulyab Kalininabad Kurgan-Tyube Kolkhozabad Vakhsh Moskovskiy Parkhar Dusti Shaartuz Nizhniy Pyandzh Pyandzh Rushan Kyzylrabot Khorog Dzhelandy Ishkashim
TURKESTAN RANGE GISSAR RANGE KURAMA RANGE KHREBET PETRA PERVOGO SARIKOL RANGE PAMIRS Fergana Valley
Kayrakkumskoye Vdkhr.
0 100 km · 0 100 miles

WORLD AFFAIRS

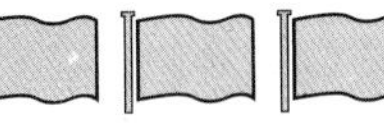

Russia has a common interest with the communist government in Tajikistan in sidelining Islamic fundamentalism and lends military support; it provided border guards in 1993 to prevent cross-border incursions from neighboring Afghanistan. Tacit support also comes from the USA, which is eager to limit the influence of Iranian-backed fundamentalists worldwide. The government does not stress the link with the USA, however, fearing that this may encourage Iran, and possibly Pakistan, to promote the Islamic fundamentalist IRP.

AID

 Precise figures not available, but mostly military aid

Steep increases due to war with rebel forces

The government in Dushanbe is reliant on Russian and Uzbek military aid in its fight with the Afghan-based rebels.

DEFENSE

 $882.4m

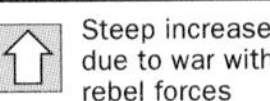 Steep increase due to war with rebel forces

The Tajik armed forces are weak; it is Russian forces who are winning the war against the rebels. The rebels are effectively cut off in the Fergana Valley. The only road bridge has been blown up by the government.

ECONOMICS

 $5.7bn

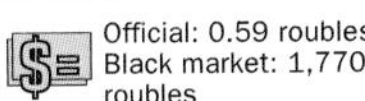 Official: 0.59 roubles
Black market: 1,770 roubles

SCORE CARD

- ❑ WORLD GNP RANKING......................109th
- ❑ GNP PER CAPITA..........................$1,020
- ❑ BALANCE OF PAYMENTS........No formal economy
- ❑ INFLATION......................................100%
- ❑ UNEMPLOYMENT..Only 40% in formal employment

STRENGTHS

Few, although Tajikistan has 14% of known world uranium reserves. Hydroelectric power has considerable potential. Carpet-making.

WEAKNESSES

Formal economy on verge of collapse. Dependence on barter economy. No central planning. Little diversification in agriculture; only 6% of land is arable. Skilled Russians leaving. Production in all sectors in decline.

EXPORTS

IMPORTS

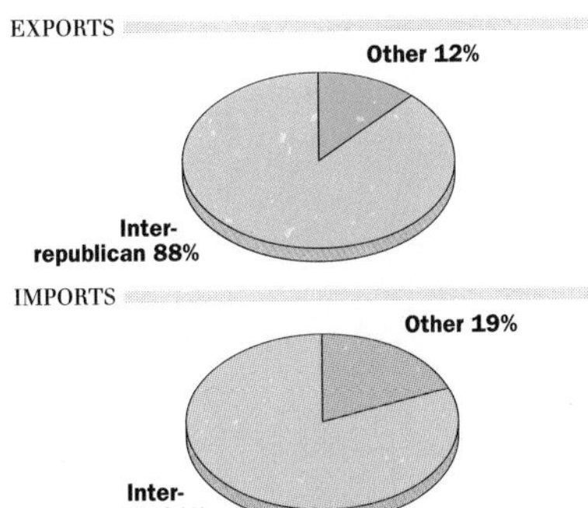

RESOURCES

 HEP supplies 75% of domestic energy requirements

 3600 b/d

 3.4m sheep and goats, 1.4m cattle, 212,200 pigs

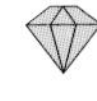 Uranium, gold, iron, lead, mercury, tin

Tajikistan has one key resource – uranium – which accounted for 30% of the USSR's total production before 1990. The end of the nuclear arms race has reduced its value, however. Most of Tajikistan is bare mountain and just 6% of the land can be used for agriculture. Industry is concentrated in the Fergana Valley, close to the Uzbek border.

ENVIRONMENT

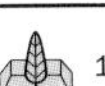 1%

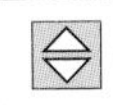 No resources for environmental measures

Landslides are a problem, frequently cutting off villages. Excessive irrigation for cotton production has led to salination of the soil, with consequent reduced crop yields.

MEDIA

 Journalists who criticize the government may be risking their lives

PUBLISHING AND BROADCAST MEDIA

There are 74 newspapers, 66 of which are published in Tajik, including *Djavononi Todjikiston, Sadoi mardum* and *Tochikistoni*

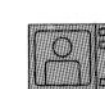 1 state-controlled service

 1 state-controlled service

The media are totally controlled by the communist government. There have been a few cases of critical journalists dying in suspicious accidents.

CRIME

 Tajikistan does not publish prison figures

 Crime has been rising dramatically

Only very remote areas are free from violence perpetrated by armed gangs. Many political prisoners are still held in prison awaiting charges and trials.

EDUCATION

 Tajikistan does not publish literacy figures

The university at Dushanbe has been weakened by the departure of its Russian academics.

CHRONOLOGY

In the 19th century Tajikistan was a collection of semi-independent principalities, some under Russian control, others under the influence of the Emirate of Bukhara.

- ❑ **1918** Bolsheviks take control of northern provinces of Tajikistan.
- ❑ **1921** Bolsheviks capture Dushanbe.
- ❑ **1925** Soviets gain control of whole of Tajikistan.
- ❑ **1940** Cyrillic script introduced.
- ❑ **1989** Tajik replaces Russian as official language. Arabic script taught in schools.
- ❑ **1991** Full independence from Moscow achieved.

HEALTH

 1 per 362 people

 Heart, cerebrovascular, respiratory, infectious and parasitic diseases

Tajikistan's health service has always been poor. The infant mortality rate before 1990 was one of the highest in the USSR.

WEALTH

 A minority are formally employed. Most Tajiks live by herding cattle

CONSUMER GOODS OWNERSHIP

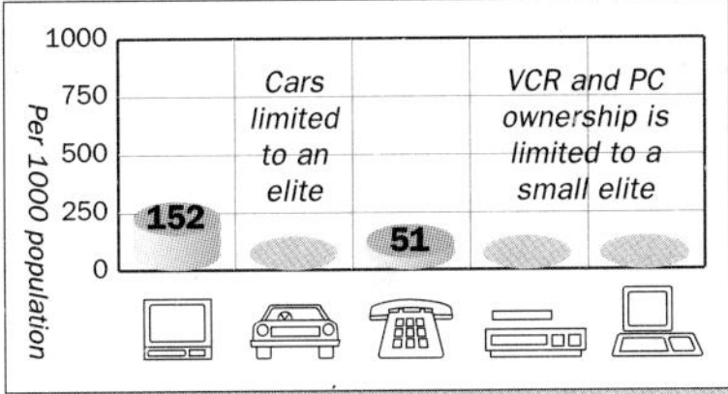

Around 87% of Tajiks live below the UN-defined poverty line. The war has made conditions even harder. The old communist bureaucrats are still the wealthiest group.

WORLD RANKING

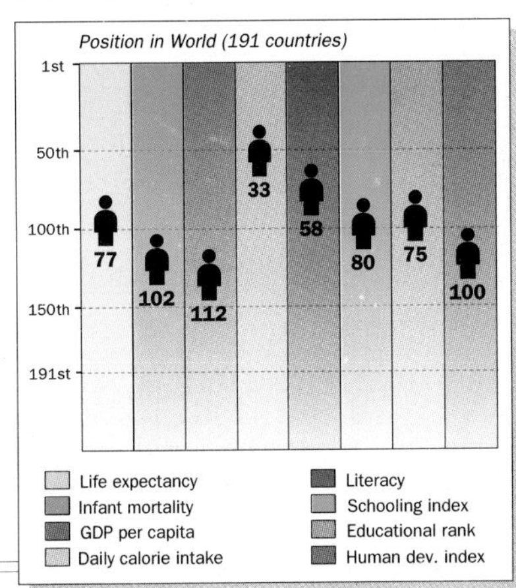

T

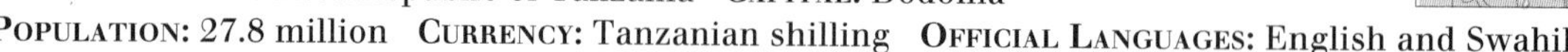

TANZANIA

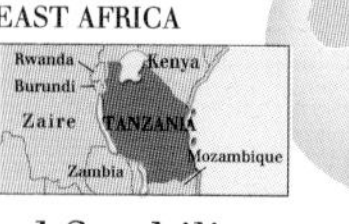

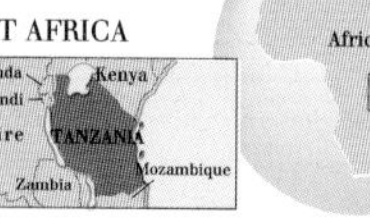

OFFICIAL NAME: United Republic of Tanzania **CAPITAL:** Dodoma
POPULATION: 27.8 million **CURRENCY:** Tanzanian shilling **OFFICIAL LANGUAGES:** English and Swahili

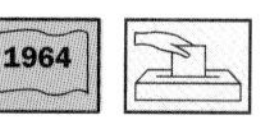

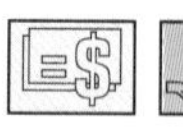

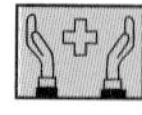

TANZANIA LIES BETWEEN KENYA and Mozambique on the East African coast. Formed by the union of Tanganyika and Zanzibar, Tanzania comprises a coastal lowland, volcanic highlands and the Great Rift Valley. It includes Mount Kilimanjaro, Africa's highest peak. Tanzania was led by the socialist Julius Nyerere from 1962 until his retirement in 1985. The trend in politics now is away from socialism and toward greater democracy.

Arusha National Park. *Lying within the* Ngurdoto *volcanic crater, the park has herds of buffaloes, rhinos, elephants and giraffes.*

CLIMATE

WEATHER CHART

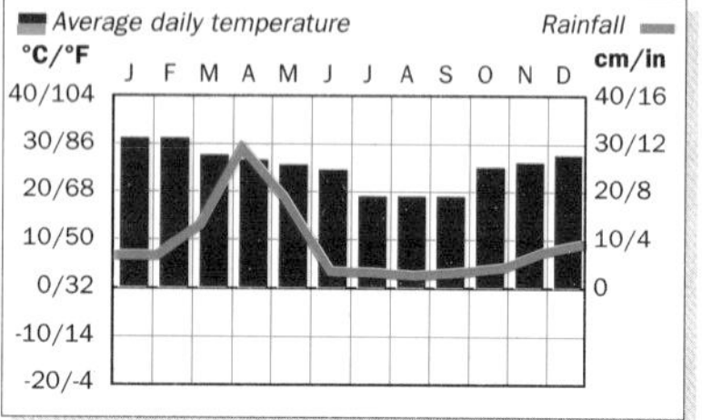

The coast and Zanzibar are tropical. The central plateau is semi-arid and the highlands are semi-temperate.

COMMUNICATIONS

Dar es Salaam Intl
453,000 passengers

15 ships
45,200 dwt

THE TRANSPORTATION NETWORK

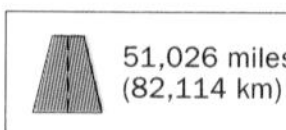

51,026 miles (82,114 km)

None

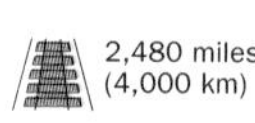

2,480 miles (4,000 km)

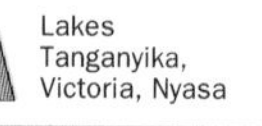

Lakes Tanganyika, Victoria, Nyasa

The roads, railroads and ports are being upgraded. An $870-million program to improve 70%of Tanzania's main roads is due for completion in 1996.

TOURISM

186,000 visitors

Up 22% in 1991

MAIN OVERSEAS ARRIVALS

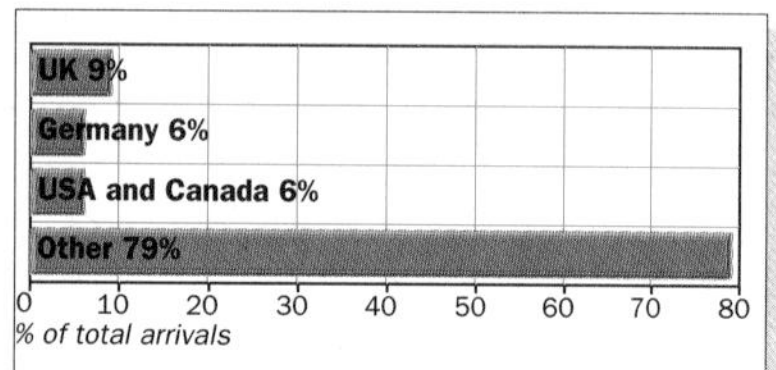

One-third of Tanzania is national park or game reserve. The Ngorongoro Crater and the Serengeti Plain are top attractions. Tourist numbers have risen sharply since 1990.

PEOPLE

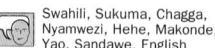

Swahili, Sukuma, Chagga, Nyamwezi, Hehe, Makonde, Yao, Sandawe, English

75 people per sq. mile

THE URBAN/RURAL POPULATION SPLIT

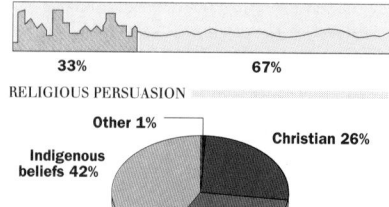

33% 67%

RELIGIOUS PERSUASION

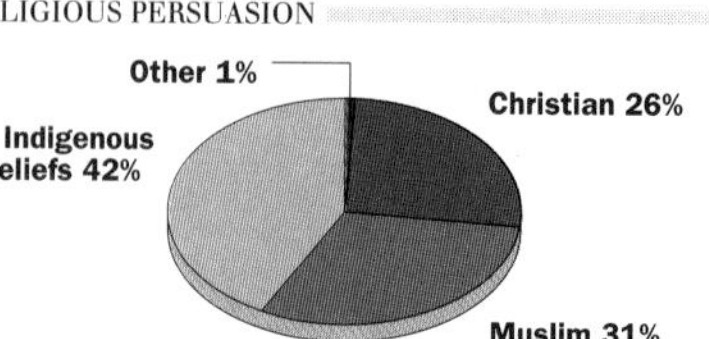

For many Tanzanians the family is the focus of traditional rural life. About 99% belong to one of 120 small ethnic Bantu groups. The remaining 1% comprises Arab, Asian and European minorities. The use of Swahili as a *lingua franca* has helped make ethnic rivalries almost non-existent.

POLITICS

1995

President Ali Hassan Mwinyi

THE STATE OF THE PARTIES

National Assembly 291 members

100% CCM

CCM = Revolutionary Party of Tanzania

Now in voluntary retirement, Julius Nyerere was the dominant force in Tanzanian politics for 21 years. He founded the ruling party, the CCM, and his philosophy of African socialism guided Tanzania's development. Ali Hassan Mwinyi succeeded Nyerere as president in 1985, and as CCM chairman in 1990. He has overseen a gradual relaxation of socialist policies, and introduced reforms which are moving Tanzania toward multiparty elections. The key political problem is Zanzibar. Many Zanzibaris have never accepted the 1964 union of the island with Tanganyika and separatists are a growing force.

WORLD AFFAIRS

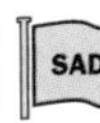

Tanzania plays a role in both eastern and southern Africa. An active member of the SADC, it was a base for the ANC during its anti-apartheid struggle. Relations with Kenya and Uganda have warmed since 1985 and there is talk of reviving the East African Community. A large influx of Burundian refugees has strained links with Burundi.

AID

 $1.1bn (receipts)

 Down 6% in 1991

Tanzania is heavily dependent on aid to help offset a severe balance-of-payments deficit. Most aid is now linked to an IMF-backed economic reform program. Infrastructure projects and the agricultural sector are the main recipients of aid.

DEFENSE

 $110.2m

 Down 8% between 1987 and 1989

Defense accounts for 15% of budget spending. The armed forces are closely linked with the ruling CCM. There is a 100,000-strong citizens' reserve force.

ECONOMICS

 $2.5bn

 475.19 Tanzanian shillings

SCORE CARD

❑ World GNP Ranking	134th
❑ GNP per Capita	$90
❑ Balance of Payments	$–284m
❑ Inflation	18.9%
❑ Unemployment	25%

STRENGTHS
Coffee, cotton, sisal, tea. Cloves from Zanzibar, the world's third largest producer. Diamonds. State commitment to reforms which have cut inflation and the budget deficit. Rise in inward investment. A return to positive growth.

WEAKNESSES
Growth still too low to increase per capita income. Shortage of foreign exchange. Poor credit and equipment limit agricultural development.

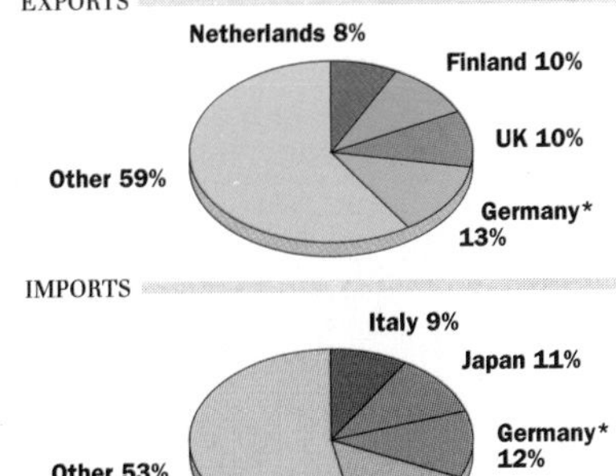

RESOURCES

 830m kwh

 Not an oil producer; refines 17,000 b/cd

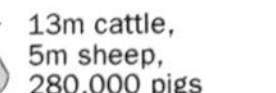 13m cattle, 5m sheep, 280,000 pigs

Natural gas, oil, iron, diamonds, gold, salt, phosphates, coal, gypsum, kaolin, tin

Agriculture, including livestock and forestry, is the key economic resource. It accounts for 60% of GDP and 80% of employment and exports. Forests cover 50% of Tanzania. More than 90% of energy demand is met from wood and charcoal. Hydropower provides 70% of electricity and is being expanded. To reduce oil imports, which take 40% of export earnings, Tanzania is starting to exploit offshore gas at Songo Songo. Oil has been discovered off Pemba Island.

ENVIRONMENT

 14% (10% partially protected)

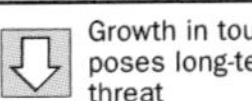 Growth in tourism poses long-term threat

The demand for firewood is a threat to forests. Tourism's demands have to be carefully balanced with those of delicate wildlife environments, like the Ngorongoro Crater and the Serengeti.

MEDIA

 Censorship is now minimal. There has been a great increase in the number of independent publishers

PUBLISHING AND BROADCAST MEDIA

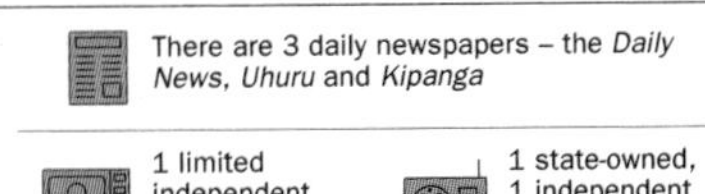

There are 3 daily newspapers – the Daily News, Uhuru and Kipanga
1 limited independent service
1 state-owned, 1 independent service

The daily press is state-owned. Much of the independent press is in Swahili. Only Zanzibar has TV.

CRIME

 Tanzania does not publish prison figures

 Up 4% in 1990

Crime levels are low, although theft in Dar es Salaam has risen. Tanzania's human rights record is good.

EDUCATION

 89%

Primary education is free; secondary students pay fees. Only 50% of children attend primary and 4% secondary school, but adult literacy campaigns maintain high levels of literacy.

CHRONOLOGY

The mainland became the German colony of Tanganyika in 1884. The Sultanate of Zanzibar became a British protectorate in 1890.

- ❑ **1918** Tanganyika British mandate.
- ❑ **1961** Tanganyika independent.
- ❑ **1962** Nyerere becomes president.
- ❑ **1963** Zanzibar independent.
- ❑ **1964** Zanzibar signs union with Tanganyika to form Tanzania.
- ❑ **1977** One-party state. Mainland and Zanzibari parties form CCM.
- ❑ **1985** Nyerere resigns as president. President Mwinyi, former vice-president, begins relaxation of Nyerere's socialist policies.
- ❑ **1990** Nyerere resigns from CCM chair. Mwinyi becomes new chairman.
- ❑ **1992** Political parties allowed.

HEALTH

 1 per 19,775 people

 Diarrheal and respiratory diseases, malaria

Basic medical care is provided by the state and Christian missions. Rural areas are served by local clinics.

WEALTH

 Most Tanzanians lead a subsistence existence

CONSUMER GOODS OWNERSHIP

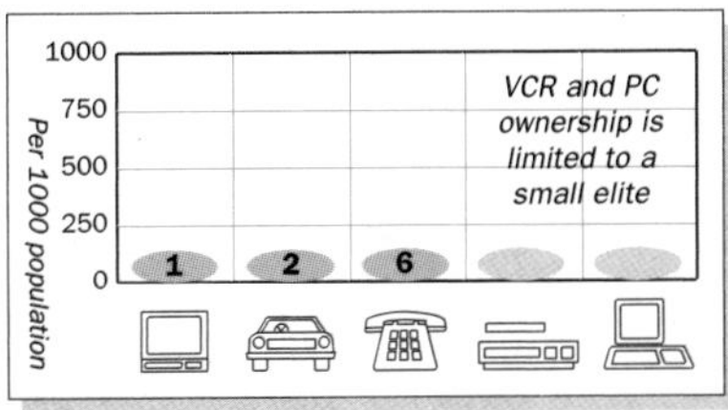

The majority of Tanzanians are subsistence farmers. The wealthy elite is small, and composed mainly of Asian and Arab business families.

WORLD RANKING

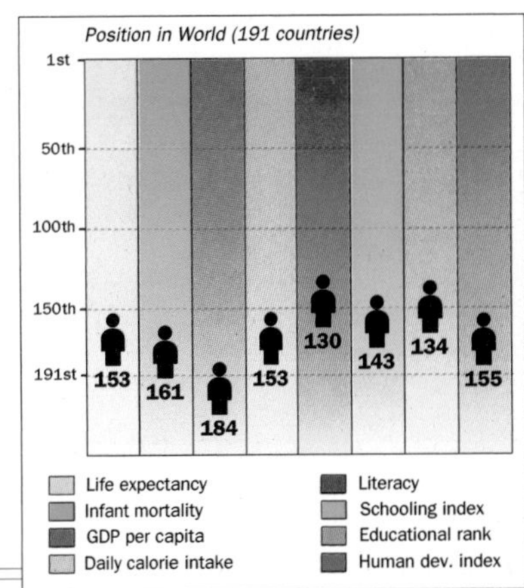

T

THAILAND

OFFICIAL NAME: Kingdom of Thailand **CAPITAL:** Bangkok
POPULATION: 56.1 million **CURRENCY:** Baht **OFFICIAL LANGUAGE:** Thai

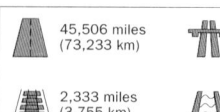

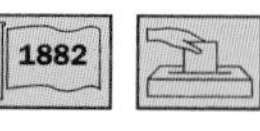

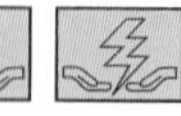

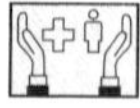

THAILAND LIES BETWEEN the Indian and Pacific oceans in Southeast Asia. The north, the western border with Burma and the long Isthmus of Kra are mountainous. The central plain is the most fertile and densely populated area, while the low northeastern plateau is the poorest region. Thailand has been an independent kingdom for most of its history and, since 1932, a constitutional monarchy with alternating military and civilian governments. Continuing rapid industrialization is resulting in massive congestion in Bangkok and a serious depletion of natural resources.

SOUTHEAST ASIA
Burma Laos THAILAND Cambodia
Asia

CLIMATE

WEATHER CHART

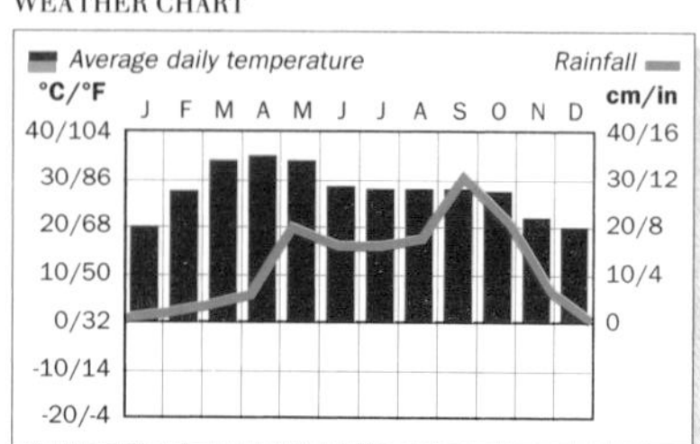

Thailand's tropical monsoon climate has three seasons – a hot sultry period, rains from May to October, and a dry, cooler season from November to March.

COMMUNICATIONS

Don Muang International, Bangkok 14.33m passengers

283 ships 1.28m dwt

THE TRANSPORTATION NETWORK

45,506 miles (73,233 km)

None

2,333 miles (3,755 km)

2,300 miles (3,701 km)

Bangkok suffers from huge traffic jams. An elevated railroad and a highway to the airport are being built, but will have little impact on the problem. Good US-built roads run to the north and east. The Chao Phraya River carries most freight.

Island in the Andaman Sea. The over-development of Thailand's best-known resorts is pushing tourism into more remote locations.

TOURISM

5.7m visitors

Up 11% in 1993

MAIN OVERSEAS ARRIVALS

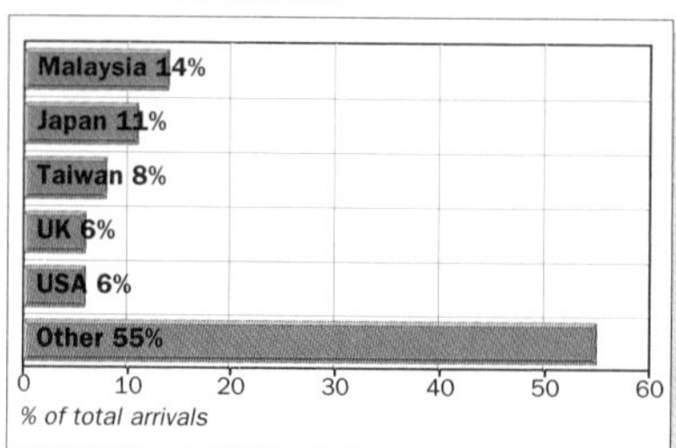

Tourism is an important contributor to the Thai economy. Tourist numbers fell in the early 1990s as a result of both the worldwide recession and local over-development during the 1980s boom. Although the number of arrivals recovered in 1993, visitors are tending to seek the less developed resorts. Bangkok's hotel occupancy rates are still falling as yet more hotels are built. Pattaya beach resort has seen such uncontrolled development that sea pollution is now a serious problem, and opposition to the intrusion of large numbers of tourists is growing among northern hill tribes.

Although prostitution is illegal, Bangkok and Pattaya are centers for sex tourism, which thrives despite the state's embarrassment at its effect on Thailand's image. Japanese and German men are among the main clients and Burmese girls are increasingly recruited as prostitutes. Child prostitution is also a major problem.

There has been a boom in golf tourism, especially among the Japanese. The large number of new golf courses that are under construction will make Thailand the largest golf destination in Asia. The vast amounts of water needed to maintain the courses is aggravating Thailand's serious water shortage.

PEOPLE

Thai, Chinese, Malay, Khmer, Mon, Karen, Miao

275 people per sq. mile

THE URBAN/RURAL POPULATION SPLIT

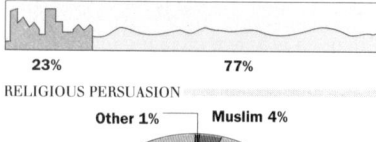

23% 77%

RELIGIOUS PERSUASION

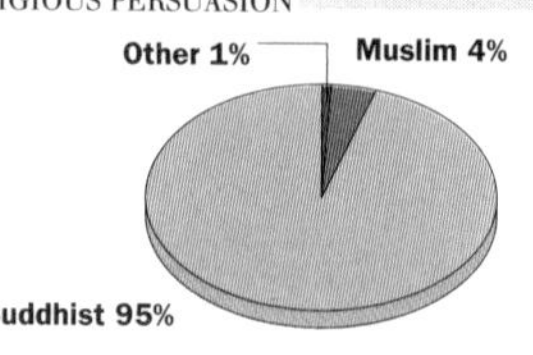

ETHNIC MAKEUP

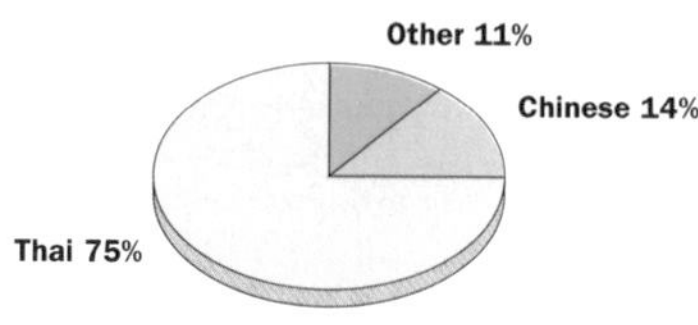

There is little ethnic tension in Thailand – Buddhism is a great binding force. The majority of Thais follow Theravada Buddhism, although the reformist Asoke Santi Buddhist sect, which advocates a new moral austerity, is gaining influence. Its principles have been espoused by one of the leading opposition parties, the Palang Dharma (PD), led by the governor of Bangkok, which seeks to clean up politics.

The far north and northeast are home to about 600,000 hill tribespeople with their own languages, and to permanently settled refugees from Laos, mostly of the Hmong tribal group.

The large Chinese community is the most assimilated in Southeast Asia. Sino-Thais are particularly dominant in agricultural marketing. Most of Thailand's one million Muslim Malays live in the south. They feel stronger affinity with Muslims in Malaysia than with Thai culture, and this has given rise to a secessionist movement.

Women are important in business, but their involvement in national politics is limited.

POPULATION AGE BREAKDOWN

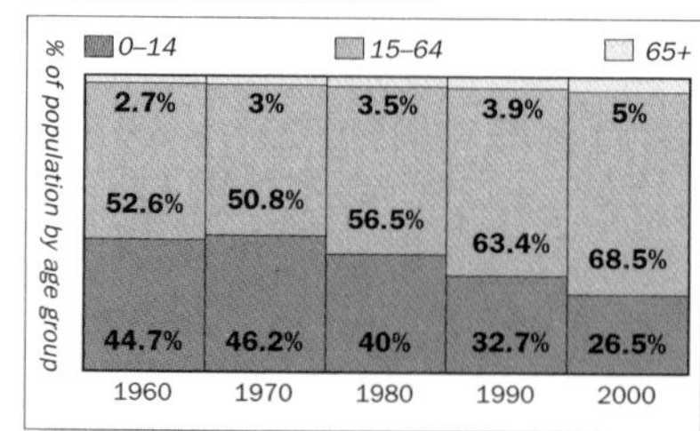

T

POLITICS

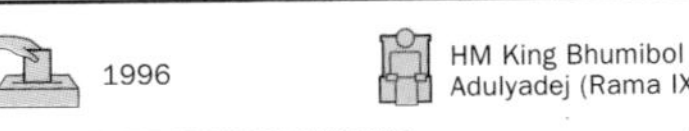

THE STATE OF THE PARTIES

House of Representatives 360 members

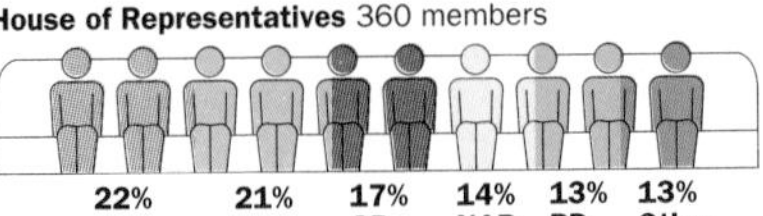

DP = Democrat Party **CT** = Thai Nation **CP** = National Development **NAP** = New Aspiration Party **PD** = Righteous Force **Other** = Social Action Party

Senate 270 members

The members of the Senate are nominated

Thailand is a parliamentary democracy. The King is head of state. Despite his position as a constitutional monarch, he has immense personal prestige. Criticism of the King is not tolerated.

MAIN POLITICAL ISSUES

The military–democratic cycle
Thailand has been ruled by alternating military and civilian governments since 1932. When pro-military parties chose an unelected army general as prime minister in 1992, there were large demonstrations in Bangkok. The army's heavy-handed attempts to suppress them led to the King's personal intervention. He ordered General Suchinda to step down and the constitution was amended. It now states that any prime minister must be an elected member of parliament. Since then, the military has been subdued. The moderate DP and its allies won the elections in 1992, prompting hopes that the military–civilian cycle has been broken.

Congestion in Bangkok
A major issue is the concentration of industry and commerce in the Bangkok area. Uncontrolled development has left it with traffic congestion that is among the world's worst and a serious hindrance to economic activity. Bangkok is also one of the world's few major cities without a mass transit system. However, an elevated highway to the airport is nearing completion and agreement has been reached on a skytrain.
In 1993, the government began offering incentives for relocating industry to the provinces. This is also intended to help distribute wealth more evenly – up to 60% of GDP is generated in the Bangkok area.

THAILAND

Total Area : 513 120 sq. km (198 116 sq. miles)

LAND HEIGHT	POPULATION
2000m/6562ft	over 5 000 000
1000m/3281ft	over 1 000 000
500m/1640ft	over 100 000
200m/656ft	over 50 000
Sea Level	over 10 000

HM King Bhumibol Adulyadej. He stepped in to resolve the political crisis in 1992.

Chuan Leekpai, Prime Minister and leader of the Democrat Party.

Water
The national water shortage, caused by rapid industrialization, is so acute that it is affecting industrial and farm output.

PROFILE
The Thai political process is highly personalized. Parties are focused on individuals, who dispense patronage or represent business interest groups, and seldom have strong ideologies. Due to the large number of parties, it is rare for one party to achieve a parliamentary majority. Personality clashes are common and often make coalitions unstable. Lack of coordination between coalition partners hinders major policy decisions, notably on improvements to Bangkok's transportation.
The Senate is heavily pro-military, although in 1992 its powers were curtailed; retired military figures are prominent in most political parties. Communists are no longer a political force. The only internal threat, barring a new military coup, is from Muslim separatists in the south.

WORLD AFFAIRS

Thailand has friendly relations with China and Burma. Many Thai logging concerns, often run by the military, have been active in Burma since Thailand's 1988 logging ban at home. Following border disputes, relations with Laos and Cambodia are improving, as are those, more tentatively, with the traditional enemy, Vietnam. Thailand supported Khmer guerrilla resistance to the Vietnamese regime in Cambodia in the 1980s.
Thailand, Indonesia and Malaysia have begun liberalizing trade to promote development in southern Thailand, Sumatra and northern Malaysia – regions all distant from their respective capitals.
Thailand maintains close relations with the USA, despite some tension over intellectual property rights and minor trade issues, but no longer has any US military bases on its territory.

AID

 $722m (receipts)  Down 4% in 1991

The World Bank and Japan are the largest aid donors. Thailand has imposed a ceiling on foreign borrowing to keep its debt stable.

CHRONOLOGY

Thailand emerged as a kingdom in the 13th century and by the late 17th century its capital, then Ayudhya, was the largest city in Southeast Asia. In 1767, Burmese invaders destroyed the city. In 1782, the present Chakri dynasty and a new capital, Bangkok, were founded.

- **1855** King Mongut signs Bowring trade treaty with British – Thailand never colonized by Europeans.
- **1868–1910** King Chulalongkorn westernizes Thailand. Laos and Cambodia, taken by Thailand 1824–1851, ceded to France.
- **1917** Enters World War I on Allies' side.
- **1925** King Prajadhipok begins absolute rule.
- **1932** Bloodless military–civilian coup. Constitutional monarchy.
- **1933** Military takes full control.
- **1941** Japanese invade. Government collaborates. Free-Thai movement aids Allies.
- **1944** Pro-Japanese prime minister Phibun voted out of office.
- **1945** Exiled King Ananda returns.
- **1946** Ananda assassinated. King Bhumibol accedes.
- **1947** Military coup. Phibun back.
- **1957** New military coup. Constitution abolished.
- **1965** Allows USA to use Thai bases in Vietnam War. Start of foreign investment and industrialization.
- **1969** Military leaders allow new constitution and elected parliament.
- **1971** Army suspends constitution.
- **1973–1976** Student riots lead to interlude of democracy.
- **1976** New military takeover.
- **1979** Vietnam invades Cambodia. Thailand backs Khmer resistance.
- **1980–1988** Gen. Prem Tinsulanond Prime Minister. Partial democracy restored. Center-right coalition.
- **1988** Elections. Gen. Chatichai Choonhaven, right-wing CT leader, is prime minister.
- **1991** Military accuses government of corruption and takes over in coup. Civilian Anand Panyarachun is caretaker premier.
- **1992** Elections. Gen. Suchinda named premier. Demonstrations. King forces Suchinda to step down and reinstalls Anand. September: moderates win new elections.

DEFENSE

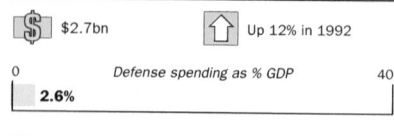

$2.7bn — Up 12% in 1992

Defense spending as % GDP (scale 0–40): 2.6%

THAI ARMED FORCES

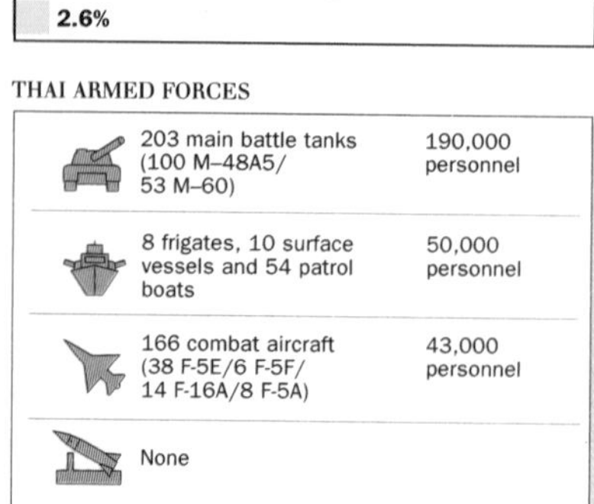

203 main battle tanks (100 M–48A5/ 53 M–60)
190,000 personnel
8 frigates, 10 surface vessels and 54 patrol boats
50,000 personnel
166 combat aircraft (38 F-5E/6 F-5F/ 14 F-16A/8 F-5A)
43,000 personnel
None

The military has either ruled Thailand, or played a prominent role in politics, since 1932. Its last intervention was its takeover of power in 1991. Now it plays an important role in the appointed Senate, which has blocking powers over legislation, and retired military figures are prominent in the major political parties.

Since 1986, spending has focused on the navy and air force. China, Germany and Spain are supplying naval vessels, the UK, USA and Russia, aircraft.

The main defense concerns are border disputes with Cambodia, Burma and Laos, the Muslim secessionist movement in the south, and piracy and fishing disputes in the South China Sea.

ECONOMICS

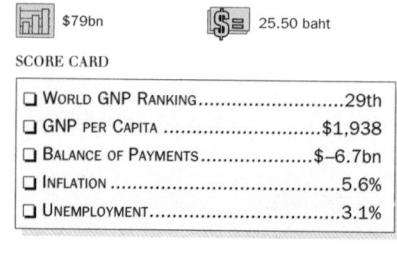

$79bn — 25.50 baht

SCORE CARD

World GNP Ranking	29th
GNP per Capita	$1,938
Balance of Payments	$–6.7bn
Inflation	5.6%
Unemployment	3.1%

EXPORTS

IMPORTS

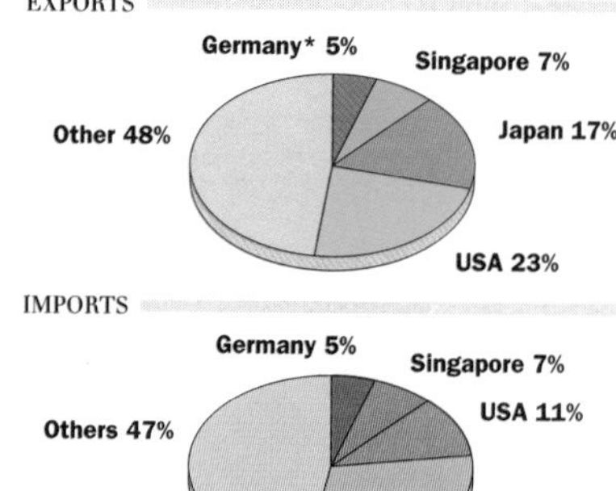

ECONOMIC PERFORMANCE INDICATOR

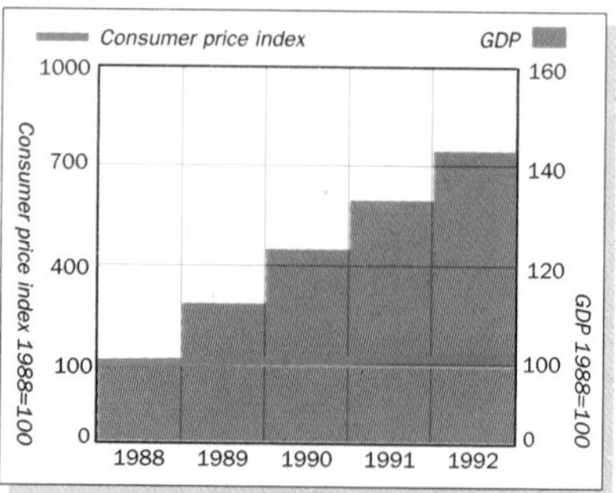

Strengths
Success of export-based and import-substituting manufacturing. Rapid economic growth. Natural gas. Tourism. Chief world exporter of rice and rubber.

Weaknesses
Concentration of economic activity in Bangkok. Severe lack of transportation infrastructure there. Inadequate water storage facilities affecting agricultural output and industrial development. 60% of population in low-profit farming.

Profile
Thailand's economy has been growing at over 9% a year since 1988, driven by a combination of a steady rise in manufacturing and rising levels of overseas investment in industry, especially from Japanese companies. Economic policy is concentrating on further industrialization, and on developing the finance and service sectors. A major problem is that as Thai wages rise, Thailand is facing ever stiffer competition from China and Vietnam where labor is cheaper. However, not enough Thais have the skills to enable the country to move into high technology on a large scale, though it is a big producer of integrated circuits and electronics goods.

THAILAND : MAJOR BUSINESSES

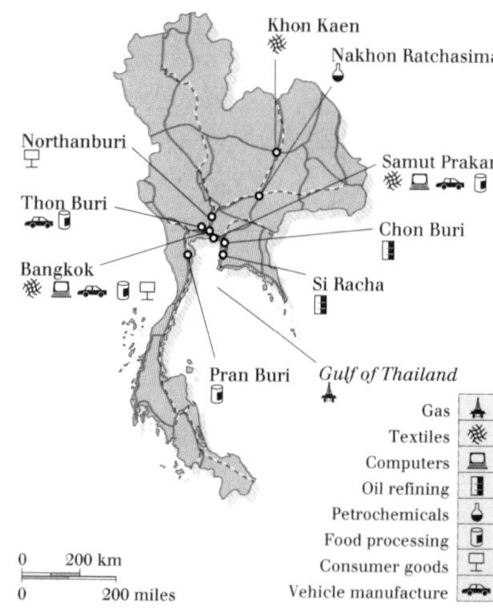

T

RESOURCES

46.2bn kwh (capacity 9.72m kw)

50,800 b/d (reserves 241,900,000 bbl)

5.3m cattle, 4.7m pigs, 156,000 sheep

Tin, lignite, gas, gems, oil, tungsten, lead, zinc, antimony, potash

ELECTRICITY GENERATION

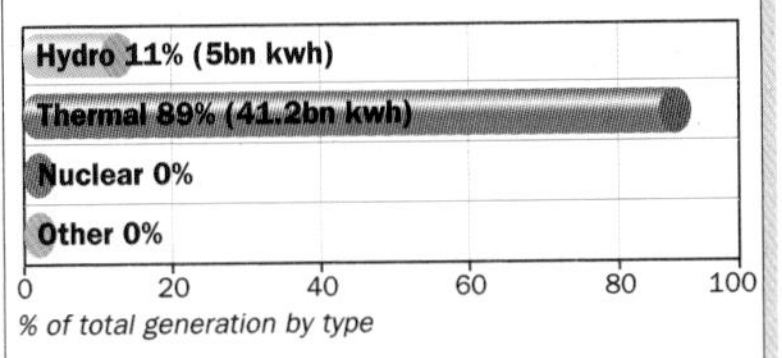

% of total generation by type

Thailand has minimal crude oil and has rejected the nuclear option in favor of speeding up development of its large natural gas fields. It also has significant lignite deposits for power generation. World demand for Thailand's tin has declined, but recent gold and copper finds offer new potential. Thailand has valuable gemstone deposits. It is also the world's biggest shrimp producer.

THAILAND : LAND USE

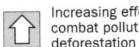

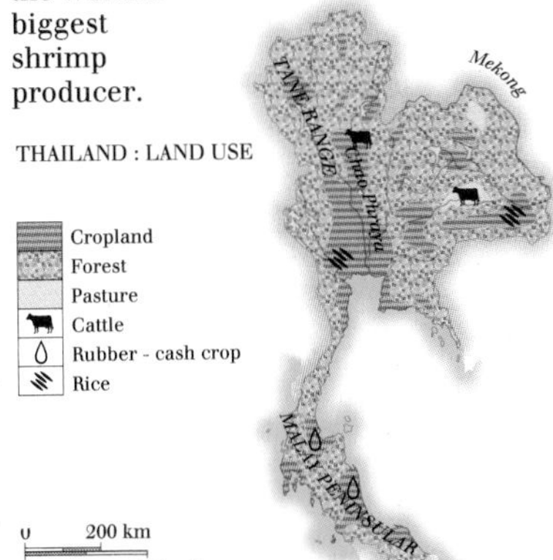

ENVIRONMENT

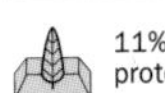

11% (5% partially protected)

Increasing efforts to combat pollution and deforestation

ENVIRONMENTAL TREATIES

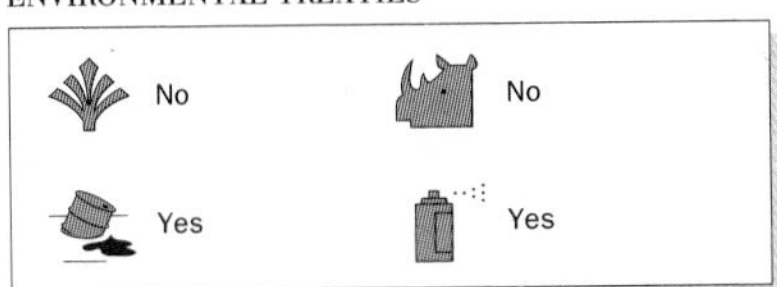

Deforestation, especially of the watersheds in the north, has led to the increasing severity of both floods and droughts. Particularly serious flooding in the south resulted in a total logging ban in 1988. Illegal logging still continues, however. Reafforestation projects, some criticized for using single quick-growing species, will not solve the national water shortage. There is evidence of growing official concern about pollution levels. The worst polluting factories are being forced to move out of Bangkok and new factories are not allowed to use CFCs.

MEDIA

Criticism of the King is not tolerated

PUBLISHING AND BROADCAST MEDIA

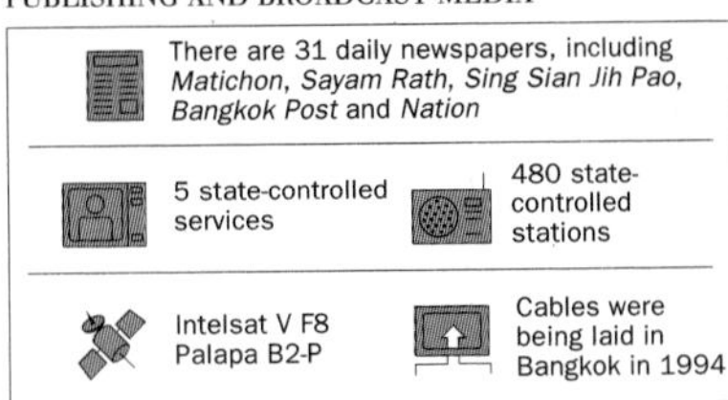

There are 31 daily newspapers, including *Matichon, Sayam Rath, Sing Sian Jih Pao, Bangkok Post* and *Nation*
5 state-controlled services
480 state-controlled stations
Intelsat V F8
Palapa B2-P
Cables were being laid in Bangkok in 1994

Newspapers now enjoy a high level of freedom in political reporting. Two of the five TV stations are run by the military. A fast expansion of cable-TV networks is planned.

CRIME

73,296 prisoners

Up 335% in 1990

CRIME RATES

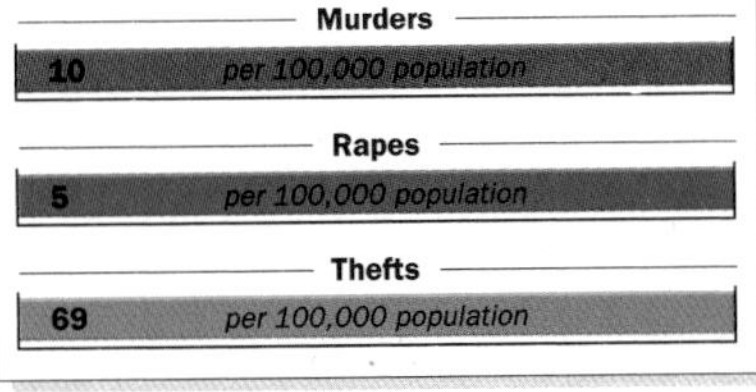

Political imprisonment has been almost non-existent since the early 1980s. There is some police involvement in crime, however, and extra-judicial killings and poor treatment of prisoners in police detention are quite common.

The King has inspired an opium-substitution crop program. The government has cracked down on music, software and video piracy.

EDUCATION

93%

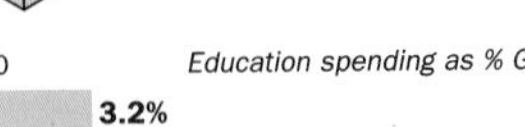

THE EDUCATION SYSTEM

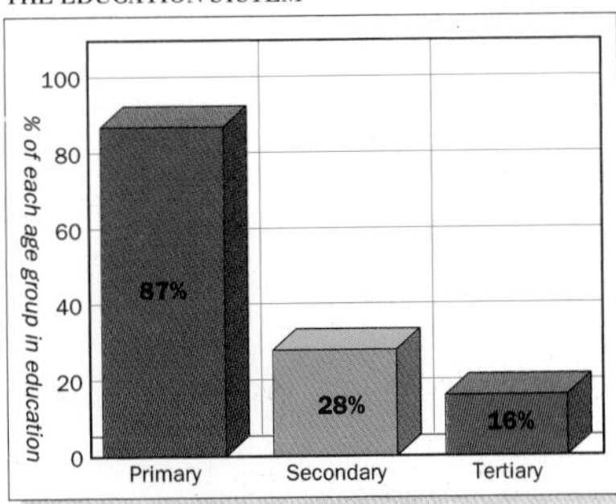

In 1993, the first steps were taken to make schooling compulsory for nine years instead of six.

HEALTH

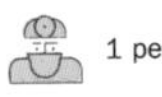

1 per 4,843 people

Heart diseases, gastroenteritis

0 *Health spending as % GNP* 25

1.1%

High-quality health care is heavily concentrated in Bangkok. Most of the 75% of the population who live in rural areas have access to primary health care. Trained personnel are aided by village health volunteers, monks, teachers and traditional healers. In 1993, the decision was taken to improve the skills of primary health workers, rather than increase the number of fully-trained doctors, as a means to improve rural health care.

The government operates a system whereby the poor can apply annually for a certificate entitling them to free healthcare. However, estimates suggest 30% of users can afford to pay.

High-profile family planning programs are slowing population growth, and sex education programs among prostitutes are aimed at combating the spread of AIDS.

WEALTH

Employment of child labor is widespread

CONSUMER GOODS OWNERSHIP

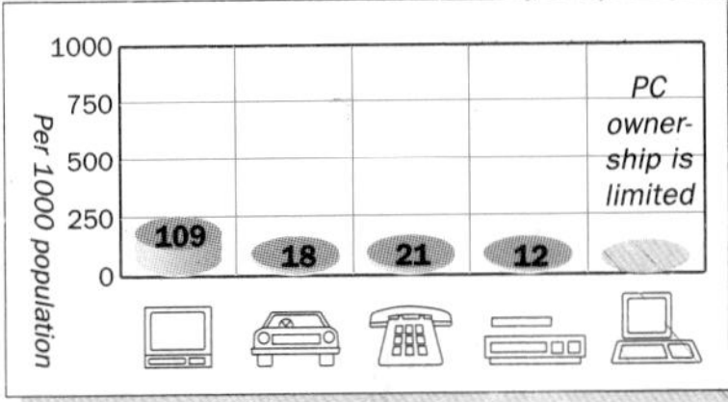

The government is trying to spread the great concentration of people and wealth from Bangkok to the provinces. The northeast is particularly poor. The gap between rich and poor is greater in Thailand than in other industrializing Southeast Asian states.

WORLD RANKING

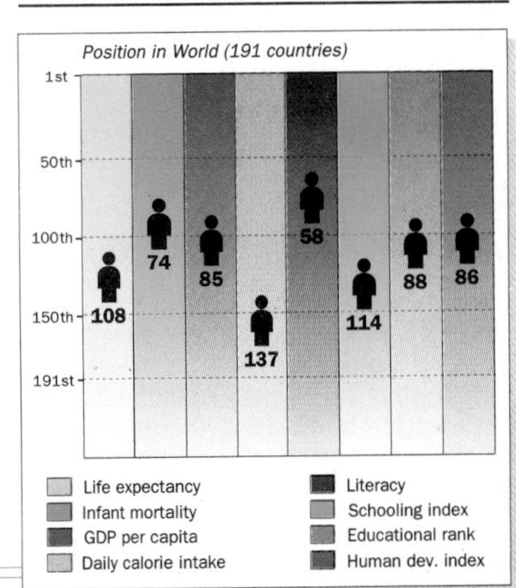

T

TOGO

WEST AFRICA

OFFICIAL NAME: Togolese Republic **CAPITAL:** Lomé
POPULATION: 3.8 million **CURRENCY:** CFA franc **OFFICIAL LANGUAGES:** French, Kabye and Ewe

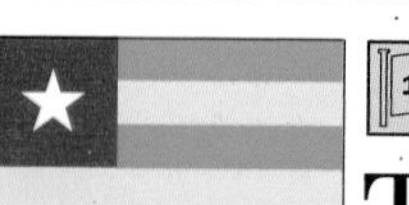

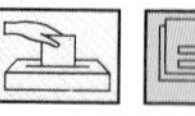

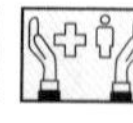

TOGO IS SANDWICHED between Ghana and Benin in West Africa. A central forested region is bounded by savanna lands to the north and south. Togo exploits its position, and the port of Lomé, to act as an entrepôt for West African trade. The 1993 and 1994 elections were the first since independence.

CLIMATE

WEATHER CHART

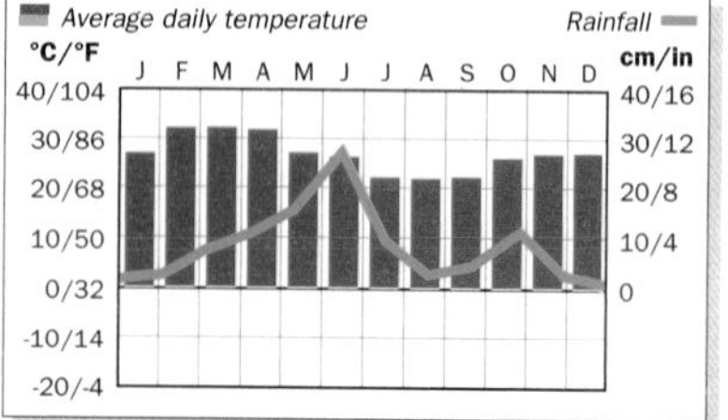

Togo has a typical Gulf of Guinea climate – very hot and humid on the coast and drier inland.

COMMUNICATIONS

Tokoin, Lomé
168,981 passengers

21 ships
20,600 dwt

THE TRANSPORTATION NETWORK

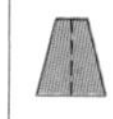
4,688 miles (7,545 km)

None

326 miles (525 km)

None

Improving the already good road network and Lomé's port facilities are priorities, given Togo's role as an entrepôt. The only railroad runs from Lomé to Kpalimé.

TOURISM

65,098 visitors

Negligible tourism since 1990

MAIN OVERSEAS ARRIVALS

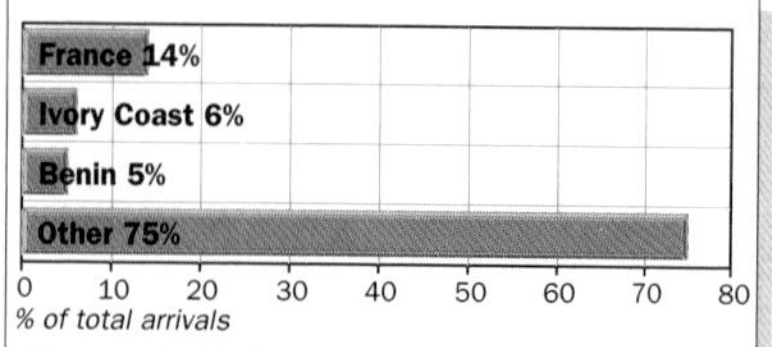

There is some package tourism, mainly French and German, to coastal tourist villages and hotels built during the expansion program of the 1980s. However, since 1990 most tourists have been deterred by the political crisis.

PEOPLE

Ewe, Kabye, Gurma, French

161 people per sq. mile

THE URBAN/RURAL POPULATION SPLIT

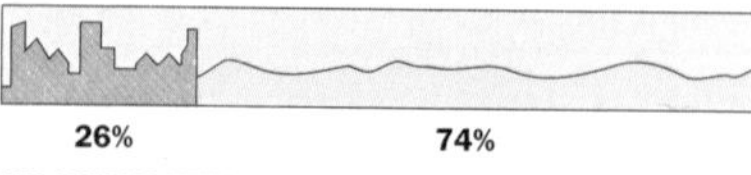

RELIGIOUS PERSUASION

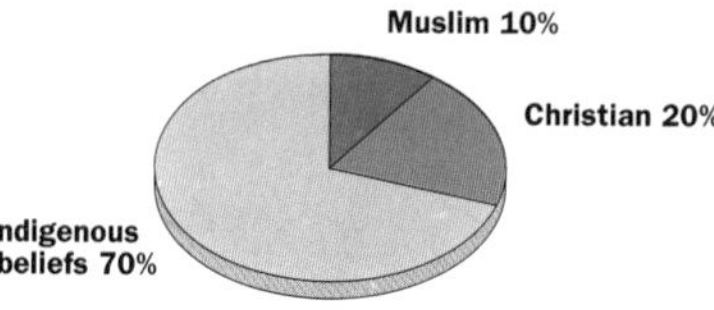

A bitter divide has existed between north and south since before independence. Most southern resentment is directed toward a minority in the north, the Kabye people from the Kabye Plateau, because of their domination of the military. The Kabye and other northerners in turn resent their own underdevelopment in contrast to the high development, especially educationally, of all southerners. The dominant southern group is the Ewe, who make up more than 40% of the population.

As elsewhere in Africa, the extended family is important and tribalism and nepotism are key factors in everyday life. Some Togolese ethnic groups, such as the Mina, have matriarchal societies. The "Nana Benz," the market-women of Lomé market, who control the retail trade, have considerable private money. Politics, however, remain a male preserve.

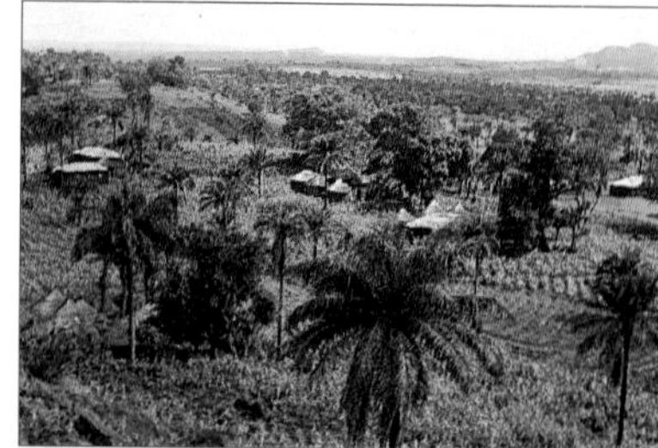

Kabye cultivations near Kara, *in northern Togo. The main food crops grown are cassava, yams and corn.*

POLITICS

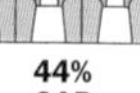
1999

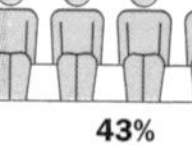
President Gen. Gnassingbe Eyadéma

THE STATE OF THE PARTIES

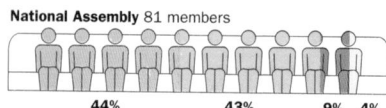

National Assembly 81 members

CAR = Action Committee for Renewal **RPT** = Rally of the Togolese People **UTD** = Togolese Union for Democracy **Other** = Union of Young Democrats, New Force Coordination

Politics have been dominated for two decades by General Gnassingbe Eyadéma, who took power at the head of a military government in 1967. The army is the main power broker, notably the small group of officers from Pya on the Kabye Plateau.

A democracy movement has been gathering momentum since 1990, when serious rioting occurred in Lomé. Many unofficial parties sprang up and were legitimized early in 1991, although since then they have been struggling against Eyadéma's efforts to claw back his power. Multiparty presidential elections held in 1993 confirmed Eyadéma in power. However, these were boycotted by some opposition candidates in protest over the exclusion from the elections of Gilchrist Olympio, an arch-opponent of Eyadéma and son of a former president. Legislative elections held early in 1994 saw a close contest between the CAR and Eyadéma's RPT. However, results in three constituencies have since been declared invalid, and further elections are scheduled for later in the year.

WORLD AFFAIRS

The priority now is to maintain traditional links, especially with France, in spite of the crisis. For the past two years, Eyadéma's foreign policy has competed with that of the democratic forces seeking allies in Europe, the USA and West Africa.

AID

$204m (receipts)

Down 15% in 1991

Development projects have suffered from recent aid suspensions by donors including the USA and the EU. Prior to this, Togo had a good record in project implementation, despite occasional cases of political interference.

T

TOGO

Total Area : 56 790 sq. km (21 927 sq. miles)

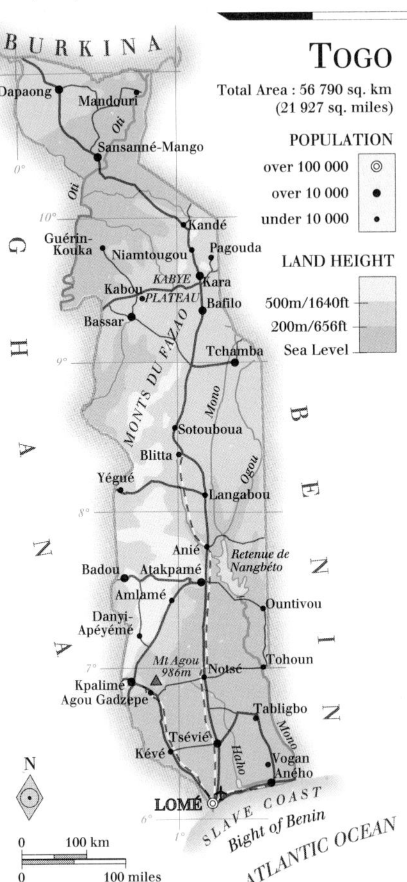

DEFENSE

 $47.44m

 Down 5% in 1991

The military has an important role in Togo, and spending on defense is high. Modern equipment is supplied mainly by France, Germany and the USA. Potential intervention by Ghana is regarded as a primary defense issue. France guarantees Togo's security through a defense accord.

RESOURCES

 41m kwh (capacity 34,000 kw)

 Not an oil producer and has no refineries

1.1m sheep, 433,000 pigs, 246,000 cattle

 Phosphates, iron, chromite, bauxite

Phosphates are Togo's most important resource. Exploration for oil is under way, but none has yet been found. The Nangbeto Dam, constructed jointly with Benin and opened in 1988, has reduced dependence on Ghana for energy.

ENVIRONMENT

 11%

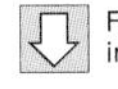 Few ecological initiatives taken

Ecologists have been critical of the transformation of nature reserves into hunting grounds for the military elite. Other problems include coastal erosion around Aneho and desertification.

MEDIA

 The total censorship that existed prior to 1990 has eased. However, the new independent press is subject to severe intimidaton

PUBLISHING AND BROADCAST MEDIA

 Daily newspapers include *Togo Presse*, published by the government

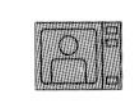 1 state-owned service

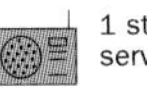 1 state-owned service

With the arrival of the democracy movement, a number of privately owned newspapers have sprung up.

CRIME

 Togo does not publish prison figures

 Theft on increase in the capital

Togo is normally relatively peaceable. However, crime has inevitably increased during the recent periods of unrest. Robberies, in particular, are on the increase in the capital.

CHRONOLOGY

After colonization by Germany in 1894, Togoland was divided between France and the UK in 1914.

- ❑ **1960** French part independent as Togo (UK part joined to Ghana).
- ❑ **1967** Eyadéma's bloodless coup.
- ❑ **1969** One-party state.
- ❑ **1993** Presidential elections.
- ❑ **1994** Close result between CAR and RPT in fraudulent elections.

EDUCATION

 43%

Schooling is based on the French model. The university in Lomé has over 4,000 students.

HEALTH

 1 per 8,700 people

Malaria, diarrheal, infectious and parasitic diseases

A favored target of foreign aid, Togo's health care system is relatively well-structured.

WEALTH

 Agricultural worker, 16,500 CFA francs per month; bank employee, 57,964 CFA francs per month

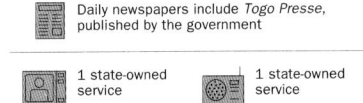

CONSUMER GOODS OWNERSHIP

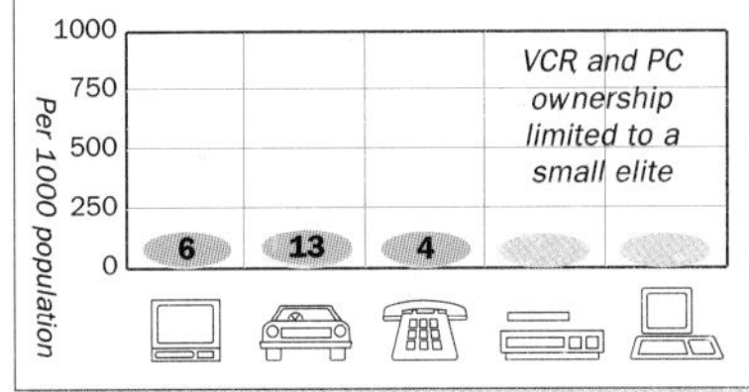

Considerable wealth disparities exist between the political and business classes, and Togolese who work the land. Between these extremes, the urban class is relatively prosperous.

ECONOMICS

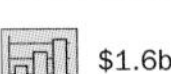 $1.6bn

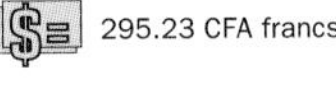 295.23 CFA francs

SCORE CARD

- ❑ WORLD GNP RANKING........145th
- ❑ GNP PER CAPITA........$421
- ❑ BALANCE OF PAYMENTS........$-97m
- ❑ INFLATION........3.3%
- ❑ UNEMPLOYMENT........2%

STRENGTHS

Efficient civil service. Ideal location for role as entrepôt, based on Lomé port. Proceeds of widespread smuggling. Resourcefulness of entrepreneurs, notably market women. Phosphate deposits have the world's highest mineral content. Self-sufficient in basic foodstuffs. Diverse range of food crops.

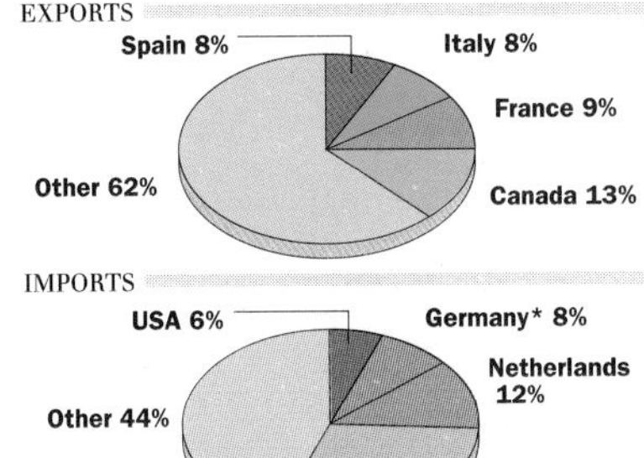

WEAKNESSES

Smuggling-dependent economy could easily be disrupted by border closure with Ghana. Limited internal market due to size of country. Lack of natural resources.

WORLD RANKING

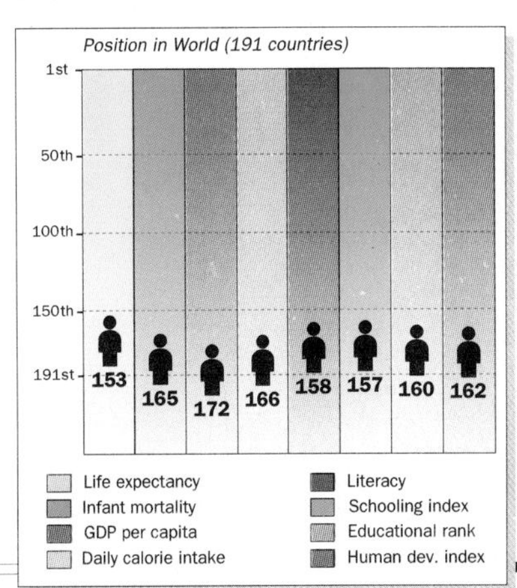

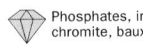

T

PACIFIC OCEAN
Wallis & Fortuna
Western Samoa
American Samoa
TONGA
Fiji
Niue
Pacific Ocean

TONGA

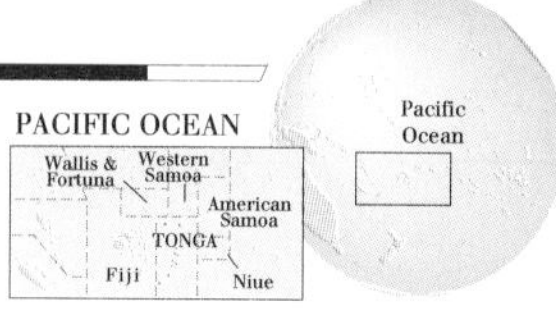

OFFICIAL NAME: Kingdom of Tonga **CAPITAL:** Nuku'alofa
POPULATION: 94,000 **CURRENCY:** Pa'anga **OFFICIAL LANGUAGE:** Tongan

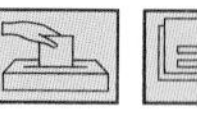

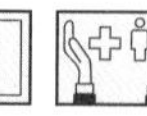

LOCATED IN THE SOUTH PACIFIC northeast of New Zealand, Tonga is an archipelago of 170 islands. These are divided into three main groups: Vava'u, Ha'apai and Tongatapu. Tonga's easterly islands are generally low and fertile; those in the west are higher and volcanic in origin. Tonga's economy is based on agriculture, especially coconut, cassava and passion fruit production. Politics are effectively controlled by the King.

CLIMATE

WEATHER CHART

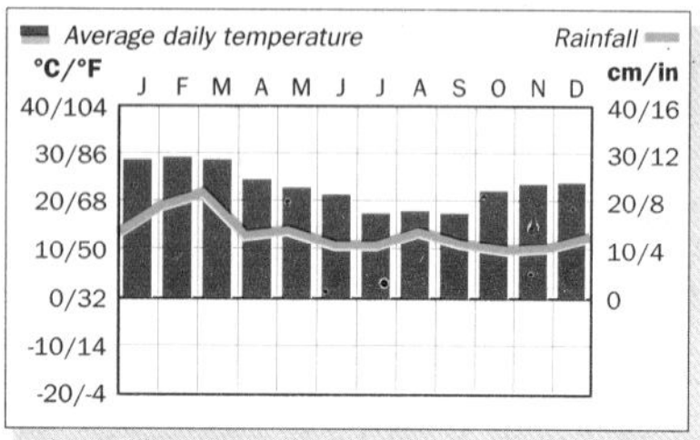

Average daily temperature — Rainfall
°C/°F — cm/in
J F M A M J J A S O N D
40/104, 30/86, 20/68, 10/50, 0/32, -10/14, -20/-4
40/16, 30/12, 20/8, 10/4, 0

Tonga has a tropical oceanic climate, with year-round temperatures ranging between 68°F and 86°F.

COMMUNICATIONS

Fua'amotu International, Tongatapu
67,000 passengers

8 ships
13,200 dwt

THE TRANSPORTATION NETWORK

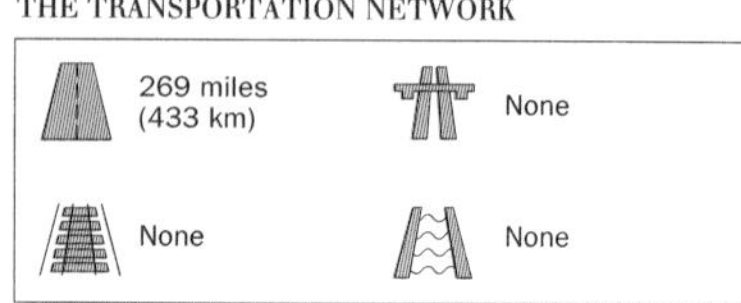

Japanese and other foreign aid is currently financing a major port development in Nuku'alofa.

TOURISM

MAIN OVERSEAS ARRIVALS

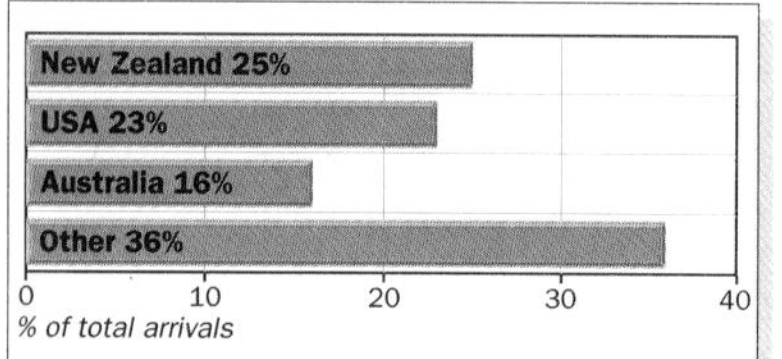

Tonga's main attractions are its tropical beaches. Tourist numbers, mainly from New Zealand and the USA, are increasing slowly. However, fears have been expressed that too many visitors may erode traditional Tongan culture.

Mountainous scenery typical of Tonga's westerly islands. Tonga's 170 islands are scattered over a wide expanse of the South Pacific. Only 45 are inhabited.

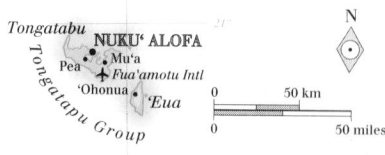

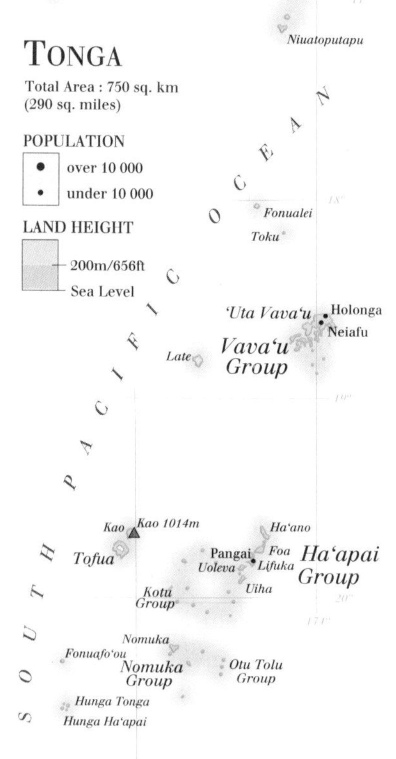

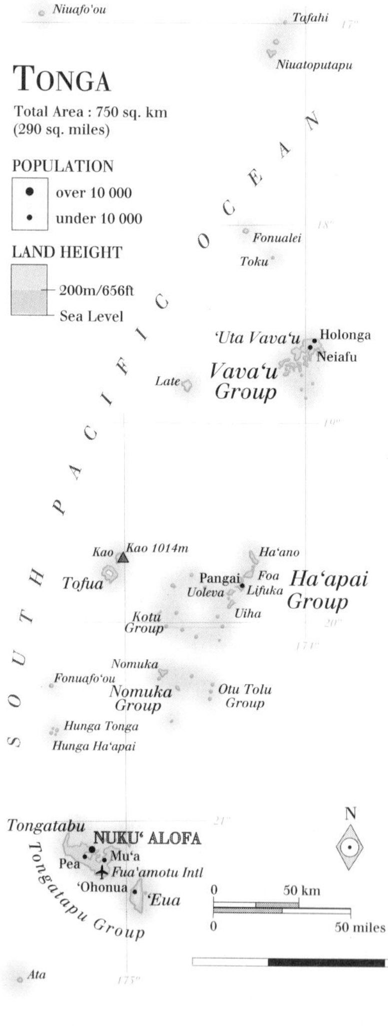

PEOPLE

English, Tongan

THE URBAN/RURAL POPULATION SPLIT

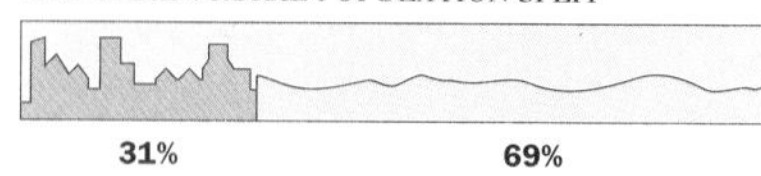

RELIGIOUS PERSUASION

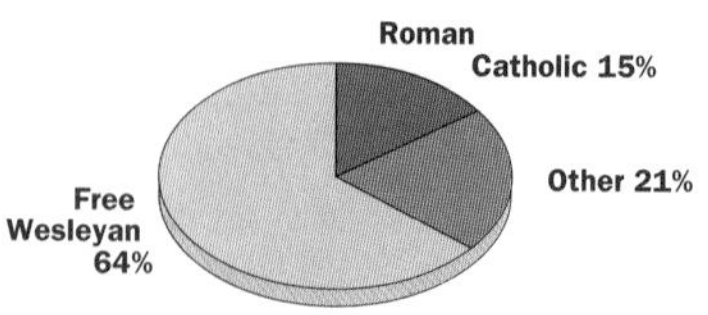

Tonga has strong ethnic ties with eastern Fiji and there has traditionally been considerable population movement between the two states. Tongans tend to see themselves as unique among Pacific islanders as they were never fully colonized and retain their monarchy.

Respect for traditional values and institutions remains high. Tongans are strong church-goers; the Wesleyan, Roman Catholic and Mormon churches are influential and often fund education. However, a new generation of Western-educated Tongans is questioning some traditional attitudes.

POLITICS

1996

HM King Taufa'ahau Tupou IV

THE STATE OF THE PARTIES

Legislative Assembly 31 members

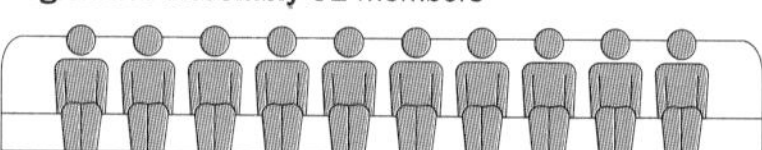

The Legislative Assembly comprises the King, the 12 members of the Privy Council, 9 hereditary nobles chosen by their peers and 9 elected members

The main power brokers in Tongan politics are the King, the noble establishment and the landowners. King Tupou IV effectively heads his government, frequently exercising kingly powers. The legislative assembly defers to his judgement and the King has taken the initiative in instigating several development projects. These initiatives, including recent talks on possible Libyan investment in oil exploration, are undertaken without reference to the government.

Younger Westernized Tongans are now increasingly questioning the role of the monarchy. When the current King dies, calls for change are likely to accelerate.

WORLD AFFAIRS

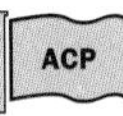

Tonga has historically fallen within New Zealand's sphere of influence. It is a member of the SPARTECA trade agreement, which includes Australia and New Zealand. Tonga is one of the few states in the region not to endorse the South Pacific Nuclear Free Zone.

AID

 Significant aid receipts

 Fairly constant

Aid finances major infrastructure projects; Australia, the USA, New Zealand, the EU and the ADB are major donors. Significant amounts were recently plowed into oil exploration, but without success.

DEFENSE

 $2m

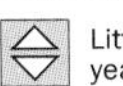 Little variation from year to year

Tonga has a small defense force, which includes both regulars and reserves. 5% of the state budget is currently allocated to defense.

ECONOMICS

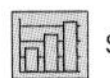 $139m

 1.47 pa'anga

SCORE CARD

- ❑ WORLD GNP RANKING........................184th
- ❑ GNP PER CAPITA $1,500
- ❑ BALANCE OF PAYMENTS.....................$-1.4m
- ❑ INFLATION 10.6%
- ❑ UNEMPLOYMENT.................................13%

STRENGTHS
Range of subsistence agriculture. Commercial production of coconut, cassava and passion fruit.

WEAKNESSES
Off main shipping routes. Exports in direct competition with rest of South Pacific region. Many productive Tongans live abroad.

EXPORTS

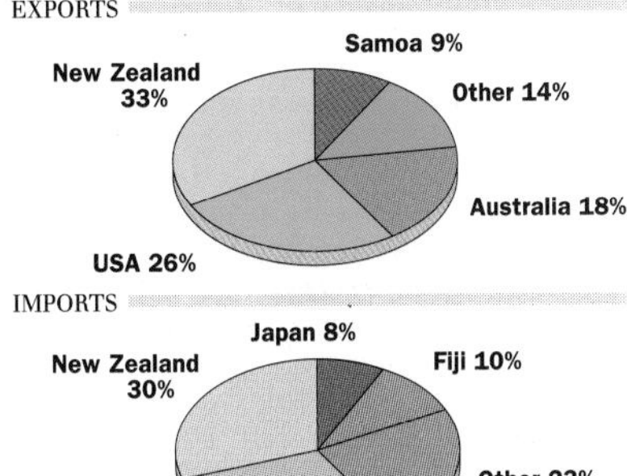

RESOURCES

 22m kwh (capacity 7,000 kw)

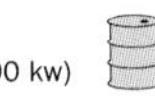 Not an oil producer and has no refineries

 81,000 pigs, 11,000 horses, 9,000 cattle

 None

Tonga has no strategic or mineral resources. Electricity is generated from imported fuel, which is brought ashore in uneconomical 44-gallon units. Recent exploration has failed to identify any oil reserves.

ENVIRONMENT

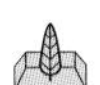 None

 Environmental issues not of particular concern

Tonga does not suffer from serious environmental problems, although it is occasionally afflicted by natural disasters, such as the 1982 typhoon. Commercial activity has made little impact on the environment.

MEDIA

 Censorship tends to be self-imposed. Outspoken slander or attacks on the King are not acceptable

PUBLISHING AND BROADCAST MEDIA

 There are no daily newspapers. Weeklies include the *Conch Shell* and the *Tonga Chronicle*

 No TV service

 1 independent service

There are five main newspapers. The *Conch Shell* has a circulation of around 10,000. The *Tonga Chronicle* is published by the government.

CRIME

 58 prisoners

 Rising levels of theft

Crime rates are generally low, partly due to the strong influence of the family. However, offenses such as breaking and entering have increased with rising unemployment levels among young Tongans.

EDUCATION

 93%

Education is based on the Australian and New Zealand models and church participation in schools is high. The 'Atenisi Institute offers university-level courses. A few students go on to the University of the South Pacific in Fiji.

HEALTH

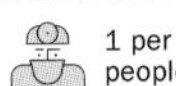
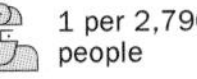 1 per 2,790 people

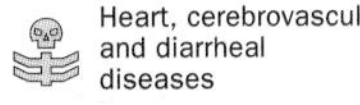 Heart, cerebrovascular and diarrheal diseases

Tonga has some modern health care facilities. However, patients have to be flown out to Australia or New Zealand for sophisticated surgery.

CHRONOLOGY

Originally discovered by the Polynesians, Tonga was visited by the Dutch in the 17th century and Captain Cook in the 18th. In the latter half of the 19th century, during the reign of King George Tupou I, the islands became a unified state after a period of civil war.

- ❑ **1875** First constitution established by King George Tupou I.
- ❑ **1900** Concern over German ambitions in region leads to signing of Treaty of Friendship and Protection with UK.
- ❑ **1918–1965** Reign of Queen Salote Tupou III.
- ❑ **1958** Greater autonomy from UK enshrined in Friendship Treaty.
- ❑ **1965** King Taufa'ahau Tupou IV accedes upon mother's death.
- ❑ **1970** Independence within British Commonwealth.
- ❑ **1988** Treaty allowing US nuclear warships right of transit through Tongan waters signed.
- ❑ **1990** Court case starts against government over sale of passports to Hong Kong citizens.

WEALTH

 Remittances from Tongans living overseas are important for the local economy

CONSUMER GOODS OWNERSHIP

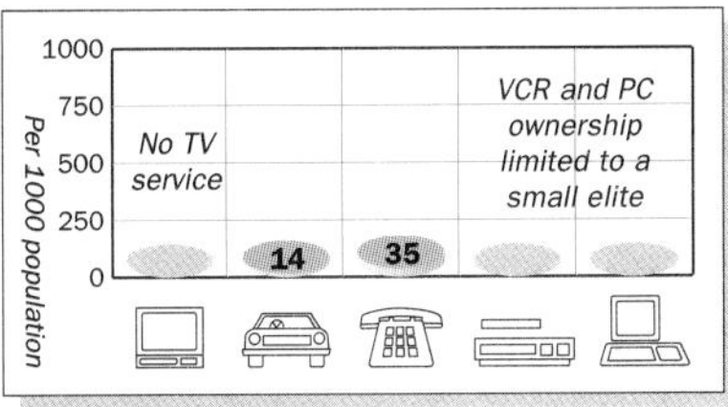

Tongans indulge in few ostentatious displays of wealth. The rich provide financial support for relatives.

WORLD RANKING

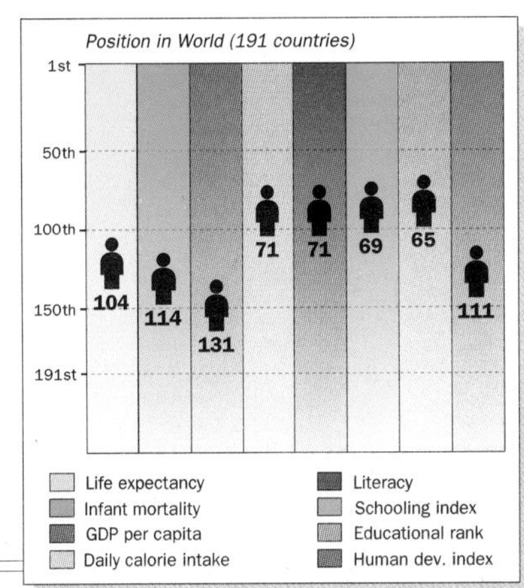

T

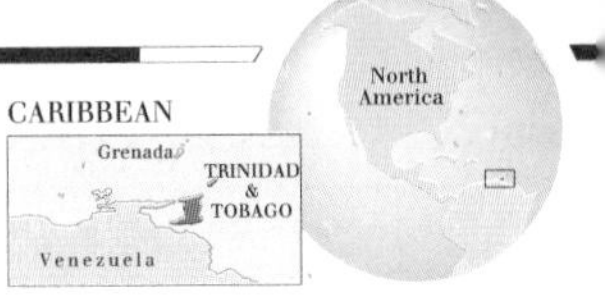

TRINIDAD & TOBAGO

OFFICIAL NAME: Republic of Trinidad and Tobago **CAPITAL:** Port-of-Spain
CURRENCY: Trinidad and Tobago dollar **POPULATION:** 1.3 million **OFFICIAL LANGUAGE:** English

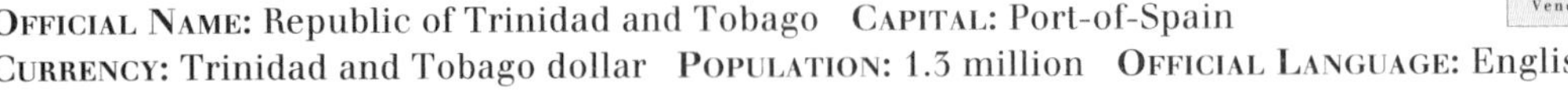

CARIBBEAN
Grenada
TRINIDAD & TOBAGO
Venezuela
North America

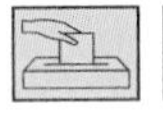

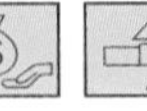

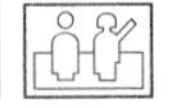

THE TWO ISLANDS of Trinidad and Tobago are the most southerly of the Caribbean Windward Islands and lie just 9 miles off the Venezuelan coast. They gained joint independence from Britain in 1962 and Tobago was given internal autonomy in 1987. The spectacular mountain ranges and large swamps are rich in tropical flora and fauna. Pitch Lake on Trinidad is the world's largest natural reservoir of asphalt.

CLIMATE

WEATHER CHART

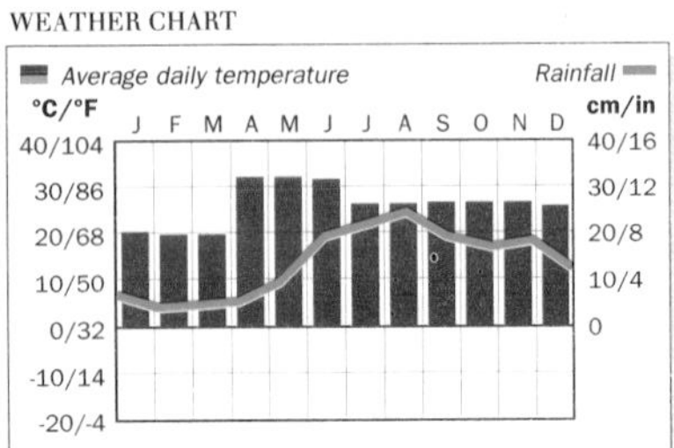

The islands are a little warmer than others in the Caribbean and escape the hurricanes, which pass by to the north.

COMMUNICATIONS

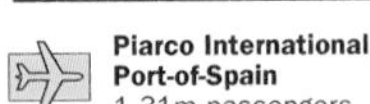

Piarco International, Port-of-Spain
1.31m passengers

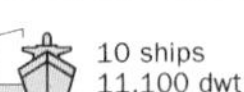

10 ships
11,100 dwt

THE TRANSPORTATION NETWORK

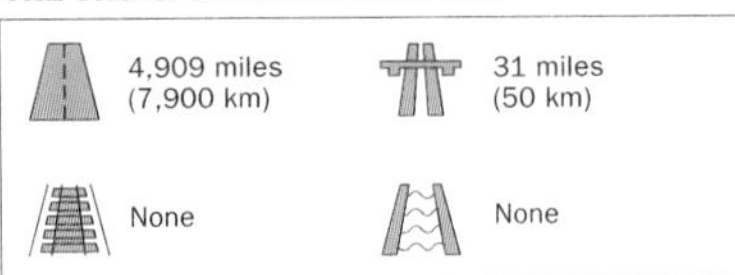

The road network is well developed. Trinidadians get around the islands in private taxis or by "maxi-taxi," minibuses with set routes, which can be hailed at any point on the roadside.

TOURISM

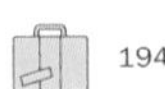

194,021 visitors

No change in 1990

MAIN OVERSEAS ARRIVALS

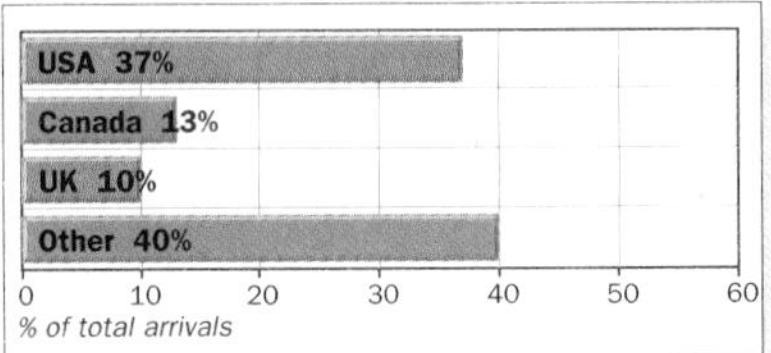

Sidetracked by its concentration on the oil sector, Trinidad was one of the last Caribbean states to develop its tourism potential. Tourism is concentrated on Tobago (said to be the model for the island in *Robinson Crusoe*), renowned for its wildlife, including over 500 species of butterfly.

TRINIDAD & TOBAGO

Total Area : 5130 sq. km (1981 sq. miles)

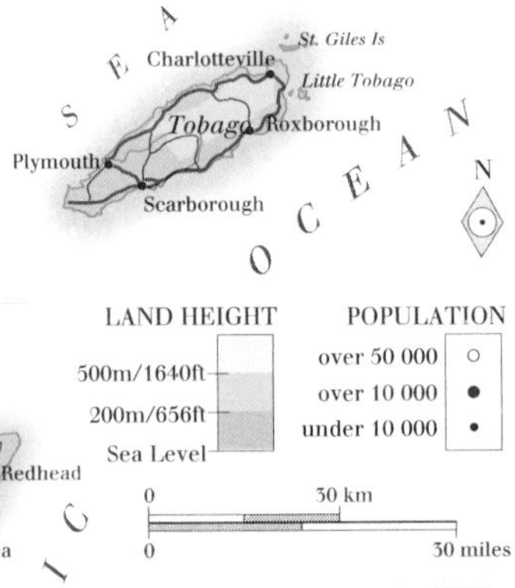

LAND HEIGHT
500m/1640ft
200m/656ft
Sea Level

POPULATION
over 50 000
over 10 000
under 10 000

0 30 km
0 30 miles

PEOPLE

English Creole, English, Hindi, French, Spanish

624 people per sq. mile

THE URBAN/RURAL POPULATION SPLIT

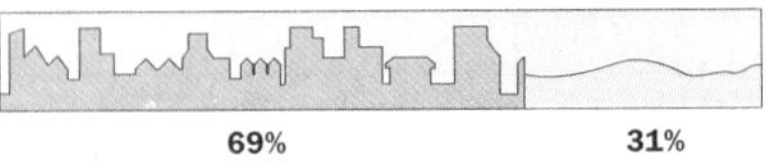

69% 31%

ETHNIC MAKEUP

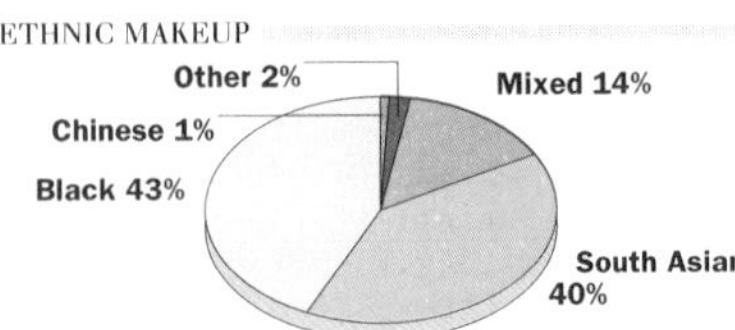

Trinidad's South Asian community is the largest in the Caribbean, and holds on to its Muslim and Hindu inheritance. The open discussion of race issues in Trinidad goes some way to dissipating latent tensions between the black and South Asian Trinidadians.

POLITICS

1996

President Noor Mohammed Hassanali

THE STATE OF THE PARTIES

House of Representatives 36 members

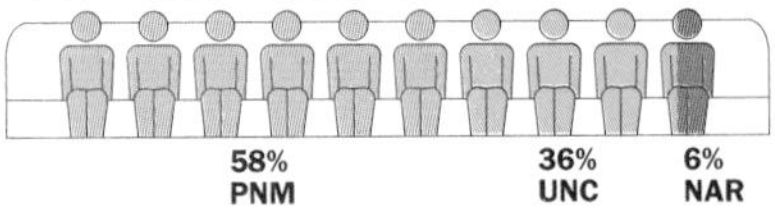

58% PNM 36% UNC 6% NAR

PNM = People's National Movement **UNC** = United National Congress **NAR** = National Alliance for Reconstruction

Senate 31 members

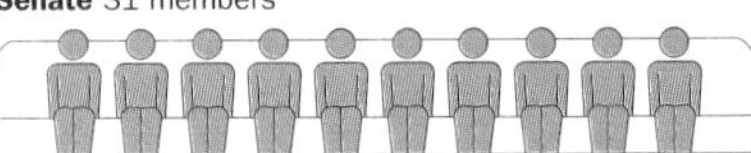

16 members chosen by the prime minister, 6 by the leader of the opposition, and 9 by the president

Trinidad has lacked a major political figure since the death of Eric Williams, the autocratic PNM leader, who led the country to independence in 1962. After 29 years of PNM rule, politics have recently become fragmented, and dominated by the race issue. Black Trinidadians have clearly expressed their opposition to any South Asian Trinidadian becoming prime minister, a view strengthened by a 1990 coup attempt by the Black Muslim sect.

Tobago's white sand beaches, *verdant landscape and natural anchorages have enabled it to develop a thriving tourist industry.*

T

WORLD AFFAIRS

In 1994, Trinidad expressed a wish to improve economic ties with the Group of Three: Venezuela, Colombia and Mexico. This was a direct response to Mexico joining NAFTA. The major foreign policy issue is the dispute with neighboring Venezuela over sea boundaries, important for establishing both fishing and marine oil rights.

AID

 Minimal

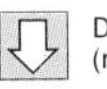 Down from $18m (receipts) in 1990

Trinidad has a strong economy, and little need of aid. Minimal sums are received from the EU.

DEFENSE

  $74m

 Up 25% between 1989 and 1992

Defense forces comprise a 2,500-strong army and coastguard. The latter is used to patrol fishing grounds.

ECONOMICS

 $4.5bn

 5.51 Trinidad and Tobago dollars

SCORE CARD

- ❑ WORLD GNP RANKING........................113th
- ❑ GNP PER CAPITA...........................$3,470
- ❑ BALANCE OF PAYMENTS..................$-16.7m
- ❑ INFLATION.....................................16.5%
- ❑ UNEMPLOYMENT.................................22%

STRENGTHS

Oil, which accounts for 70% of export earnings. Gas is increasingly being exploited to support new industries, such as nitrogenous fertilizer manufacture. Tourism, particularly on Tobago, is being developed.

WEAKNESSES

The economy is still insufficiently diversified and highly sensitive to world oil price movements.

EXPORTS

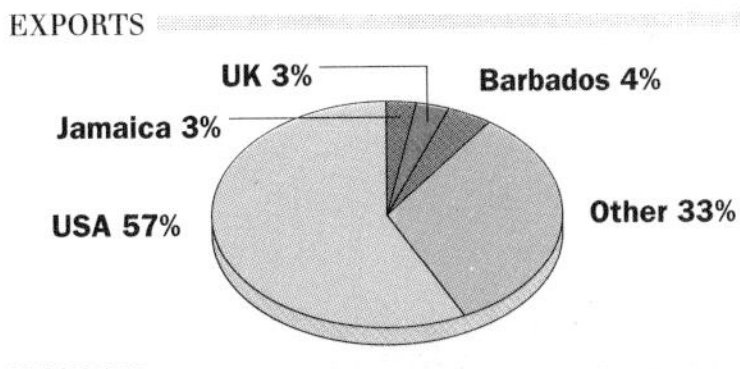

IMPORTS

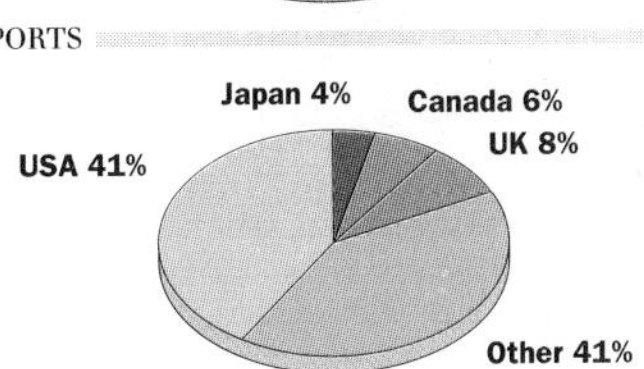

RESOURCES

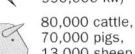

 3.5bn kwh (capacity 990,000 kw)

 136,500 b/d (reserves 572,600,000 bbl)

 80,000 cattle, 70,000 pigs, 13,000 sheep

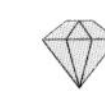 Oil, natural gas, natural asphalt

Oil and gas are Trinidad's major resources. Government policy is to continue increasing both production and refinery output.

ENVIRONMENT

 3% partially protected

Greater environmental consciousness

Spillages from oil tankers, which pose a serious threat to coastal conservation areas such as the Caroni Swamp with its 500 species of butterflies, are the major concern. Oil spills are also threatening some tourist beaches.

MEDIA

 No restrictions on political reporting

PUBLISHING AND BROADCAST MEDIA

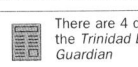

 There are 4 daily newspapers, including the *Trinidad Express* and the *Trinidad Guardian*

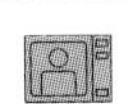 1 state-owned service

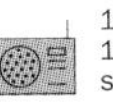 1 state-owned, 1 independent service

New TV and radio stations have sprung up since broadcasting license rules were relaxed in 1992. Most TV programing is from US networks.

CRIME

 2,387 prisoners

 Down 3% in 1990

Crime in Trinidad is higher than in most of its Caribbean neighbors, and most towns have unsafe areas at night. A proposal to abolish the death penalty has been strongly opposed by locals.

EDUCATION

 96%

Education is based on the British 11-plus system. Most students go on to the University of the West Indies; Trinidad hosts the St. Augustine campus. However, wealthy Trinidadians go to universities in the USA.

HEALTH

 1 per 1,213 people

 Cerebrovascular and heart diseases, cancer, diabetes

Oil wealth has given Trinidad a better public health service than most Caribbean states, and more private clinics, mainly serving the expatriate community. However, treatment delays are seen as a growing problem. 98% of the population has safe water.

CHRONOLOGY

Britain seized Trinidad from Spain in 1797 and Tobago from France in 1802. They were unified in 1888.

- ❑ **1956** Dr. Eric Williams founds PNM and wins general elections: main support from blacks. Indian population supports opposition.
- ❑ **1958** Joins West Indian Federation; leaves in 1961.
- ❑ **1962** Independence.
- ❑ **1970** Black Power demonstrations cause brief state of emergency.
- ❑ **1980** Tobago gets own House of Assembly; internal autonomy 1987.
- ❑ **1986** NAR coalition wins elections, but fails to halt economic decline.
- ❑ **1988** Baseo Panday dismissed from Cabinet; forms left-wing UNC.
- ❑ **1990** Premier taken hostage in failed fundamentalist coup.
- ❑ **1991** PNM elected back to power.

WEALTH

 Welder, 16 Trinidad and Tobago dollars per hour; government computer programmer, 2,640 Trinidad and Tobago dollars per month

CONSUMER GOODS OWNERSHIP

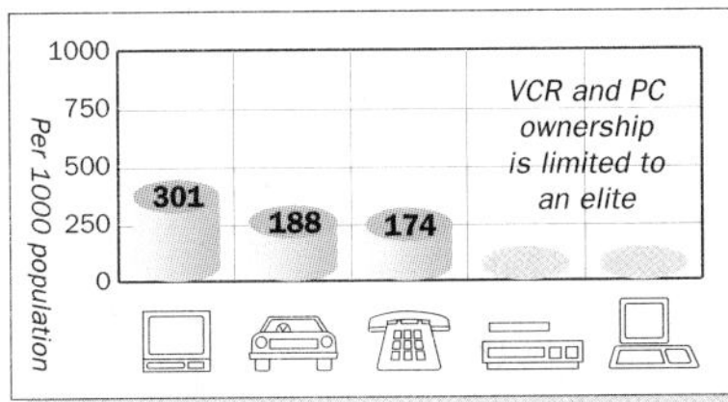

Wealth disparities between the affluent oil-rich business elite, many of whom are expatriate, and farm laborers are marked in Trinidad. During the oil-boom years of the 1970s, Trinidad was proportionately the world's biggest importer of Scotch whiskey. Today, rural poverty in the interior, particularly among South Asian Trinidadian farmers, is a growing problem.

WORLD RANKING

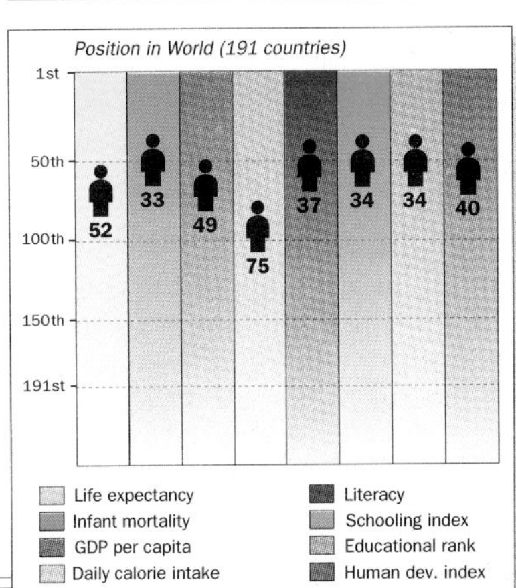

T

TUNISIA

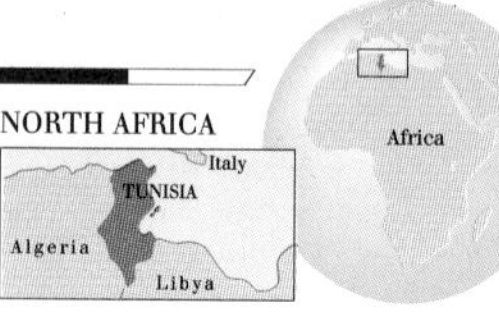

OFFICIAL NAME: Republic of Tunisia **CAPITAL:** Tunis
POPULATION: 8.4 million **CURRENCY:** Tunisian dinar **OFFICIAL LANGUAGE:** Arabic

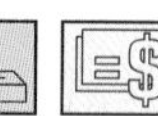

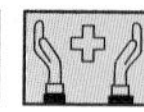

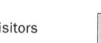

NORTH AFRICA'S SMALLEST country, Tunisia lies sandwiched between Libya and Algeria. The populous north is mountainous, fertile in places and has a long Mediterranean coastline. The south is largely desert. Habib Bourguiba ruled the country from its independence in 1956 until his downfall in a bloodless coup in 1987. Under President Ben Ali, the government has since been moving toward multiparty democracy, but faces a challenge from Islamic fundamentalists. Closer ties with the EU, Tunisia's main trading partner, are a priority. Manufacturing and the important tourism sector are expanding.

CLIMATE

WEATHER CHART

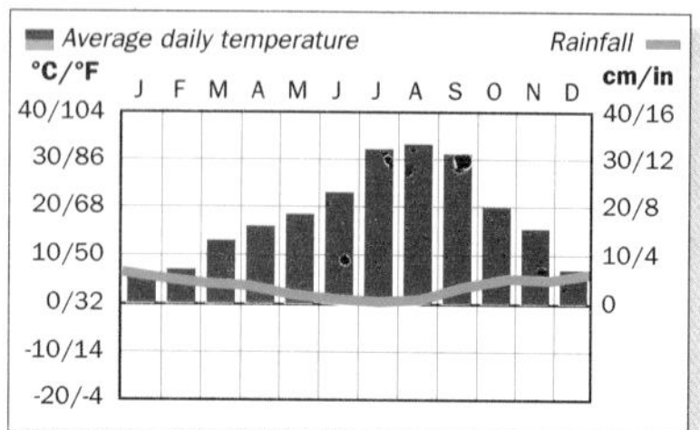

Tunisia is hot in summer. The north is often wet and windy in winter. The far south is arid. The spring brings the dry, dusty *chili* wind from the Sahara.

COMMUNICATIONS

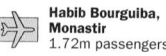

Habib Bourguiba, Monastir
1.72m passengers

28 ships
227,900 dwt

THE TRANSPORTATION NETWORK

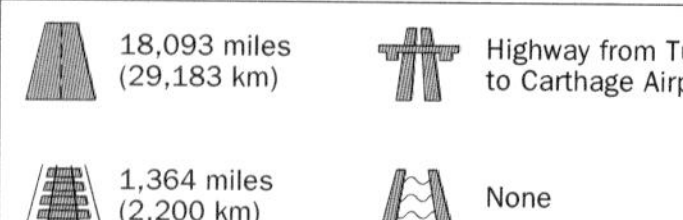

Tunisia has six international airports. A highway from Tunis to Carthage Airport opened in 1993. A light metro in Tunis and a rail link from Gafsa to Gabès are being built. The southern third of the country has few roads.

TOURISM

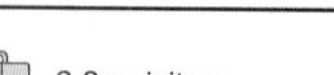

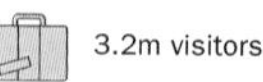

MAIN OVERSEAS ARRIVALS

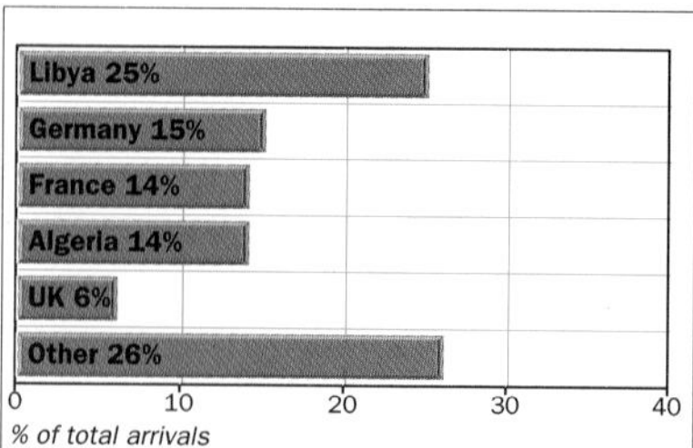
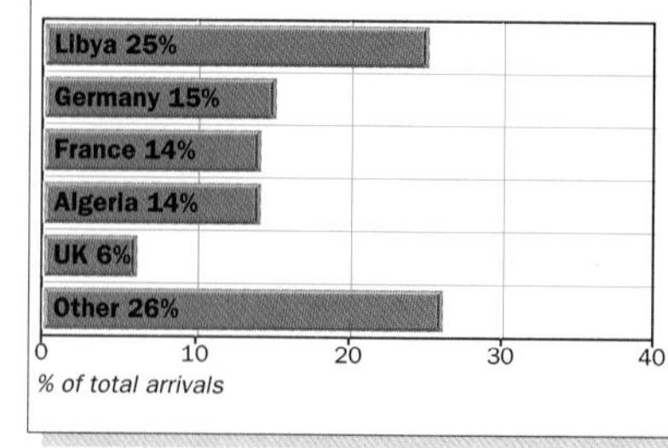

Tourists have flocked to Tunisia since the 1960s, attracted by its winter sunshine, beaches, desert and Roman remains. One of the Mediterranean's cheapest package destinations, Tunisia attracts up to 1.8 million European visitors a year. However, numbers were hit in 1990–1991 by the Gulf War and the fear of attacks by Islamic militants. Tourism employs 190,000 people and is a focus of investment. Capacity has doubled since 1980 to 140,000 beds and is set to top 200,000 beds by the year 2000. However, concern about the environmental impact is growing.

PEOPLE

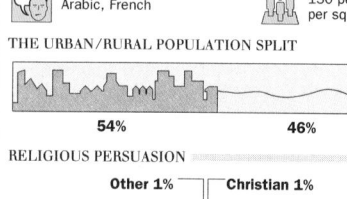

Arabic, French

130 people per sq. mile

THE URBAN/RURAL POPULATION SPLIT

54% 46%

RELIGIOUS PERSUASION

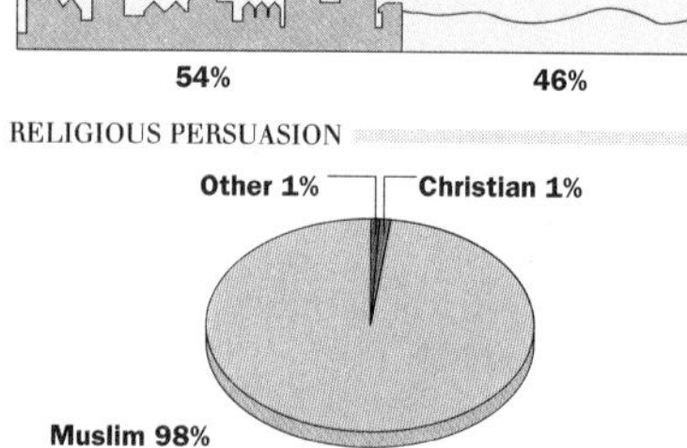

ETHNIC MAKEUP

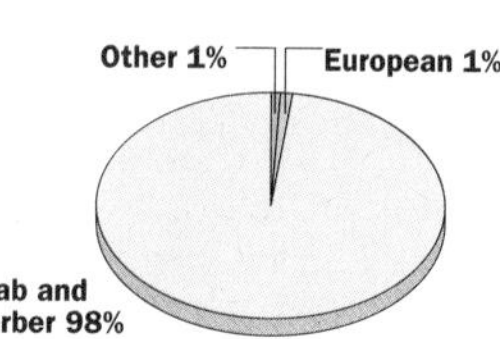

The population is almost entirely of Arab and Berber descent, although there are Jewish and Christian minorities. Many Tunisians still live in extended family groups, in which three or four generations are represented.

Tunisia has traditionally been one of the most liberal Arab states. The 1956 Personal Statutes Code of President Bourguiba gave women better rights than in any other Arab country. Further legislation has since given women the right to custody of children in divorce cases, made family violence against women punishable by law, and helped divorced women to get alimony. Family planning and contraception have been freely available since the early 1960s. Now Tunisia's population grows by only 16,000 a year. Women make up 25% of the total workforce and 35% of the industrial workforce. Company ownership by women is steadily increasing; politics, however, remain exclusively a male preserve.

These freedoms are threatened by the growth in recent years of Islamic fundamentalism, which also worries the mainly French-speaking political and business elite who wish to strengthen links with Europe.

The Ben Ali regime, although not as repressive as its predecessor, has been criticized for its actions against Islamic activists, particularly the banned *Al-Nahda* party. Amnesty International has detailed a number of human rights abuses, mainly against female members of *Al-Nahda*.

POPULATION AGE BREAKDOWN

% of population by age group	1960	1970	1980	1990	2000
65+	4.2%	3.8%	3.8%	4%	4.8%
15–64	52.5%	49.9%	54.5%	58%	62.2%
0–14	43.3%	46.3%	41.7%	38%	33%

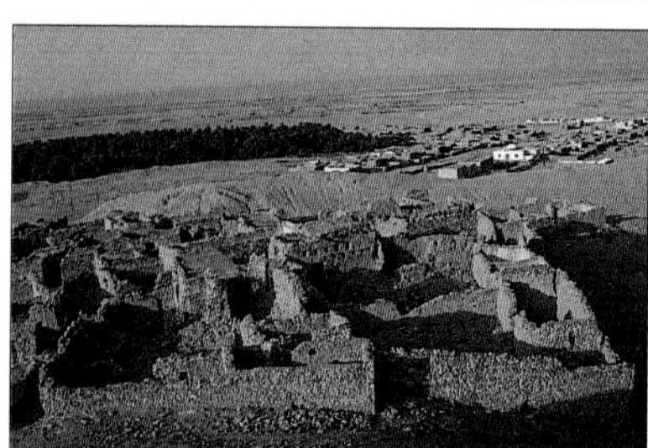

Roman remains at the village of La-Kesra *in the Tozeur region, a low-lying area of oases in western central Tunisia.*

T

POLITICS

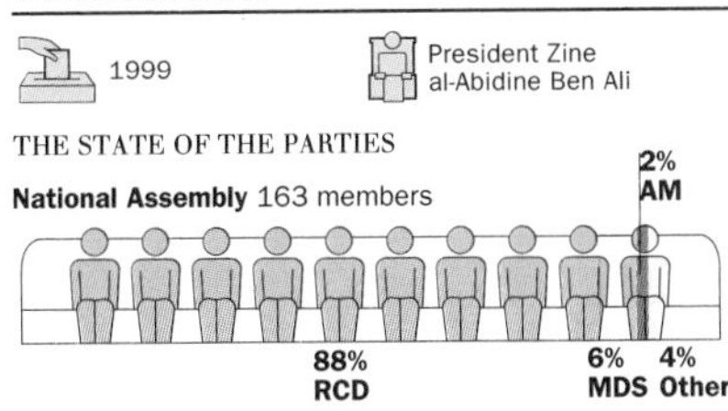

RCD = Constitutional Democratic Assembly **MDS** = Social Democratic Party **AM** = *Attajdid* Movement **Other** = Democratic Union, Popular Unity Party

Legally a multiparty democracy since 1988, Tunisia is still dominated by the RCD and President Ben Ali.

President Ben Ali, *became head of state in 1987.*

Dr. Hamed Karoui, *was appointed prime minister in 1988.*

MAIN POLITICAL ISSUES

Fundamentalism

The RCD has clamped down on Islamic fundamentalists, particularly the outlawed *Al-Nahda*, or Renewal Party. In 1991, 500 *Al-Nahda* members were arrested following a failed coup, thought to be inspired by fundamentalists. Its leader, Rachid Gannouchi, is now in exile.

Social reform

The RCD sees social programs aimed at reducing unemployment as a way to combat the spread of Islamic militancy. The expansion of women's rights is also likely to continue, balanced by steps toward Arabization.

PROFILE

President Ben Ali has made strong efforts to draw opposition parties into government. The political system has been liberalized with, for example, the abolition of the life presidency and state security court. Press freedom has also been increased. The aim of the 1994 election was to form a national coalition against the outlawed Islamic fundamentalists. A complex proportional representation system ensured an overwhelming victory for the RCD, in addition to a limited degree of political plurality.

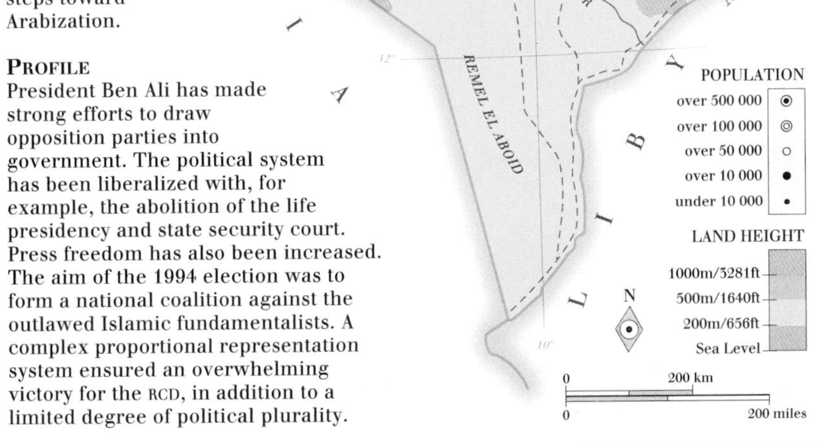

WORLD AFFAIRS

A foreign policy priority is to strengthen contacts with the West, which have generally been good because of Tunisia's liberal economic and social policies. Attention is focused on ties with the EU, the main outlet for Tunisia's agricultural exports.

Tunis has been host to the PLO since the organization was expelled from Lebanon. Relations with other Arab states, particularly Kuwait and Saudi Arabia, were soured by Tunisia's support for Iraq in the Gulf War. The government would like to see them restored to their former amicability. There is concern over the possible effects of the political success of Islamic fundamentalism in neighboring Algeria. Relations with Libya are improving, helped by the fact that Tunisia has been turning a blind eye to sanction-busters operating through its territory.

CHRONOLOGY

Tunisia has been home to the Zenata Berbers since earliest times and its history is linked to the rise and fall of the Mediterranean-centered empires. Carthage (near present-day Tunis), founded in the 9th century BC, became the hub of a 1,000-year Phoenician trading empire which linked European and African trading networks. Tunisia was then incorporated into the Roman, Byzantine, Arab, Ottoman and, finally, French empires.

- ❑ **1883** La Marsa Treaty makes Tunisia a French protectorate, ending its semi-independence. Bey of Tunis remains monarch.
- ❑ **1900** Influx of French and Italian settlers begins.
- ❑ **1920** Destour (Constitution) Party formed; calls for self-government.
- ❑ **1935** Habib Bourguiba forms Neo-Destour (New Constitution) Party.
- ❑ **1943** Defeat of Axis powers by British troops restores French rule.
- ❑ **1955** Internal autonomy. Bourguiba returns from exile.
- ❑ **1956** Independence. Bourguiba elected prime minister. Personal Statutes Code gives rights to women. Family planning introduced.
- ❑ **1957** The Bey is deposed. Tunisia becomes a republic with Bourguiba as first president.
- ❑ **1964** Neo-Destour becomes the only legal political party; changes its name to Destour Socialist Party (PSD). Moderate socialist economic program is introduced.

⇨

CHRONOLOGY *continued*

- **1969** Agricultural collectivization program, begun 1964, abandoned.
- **1974** Bourguiba becomes president for life. Trade unions disagree with PSD over economic policy.
- **1974–1976** Hundreds imprisoned for belonging to "illegal organizations."
- **1978** Trade union movement, UGTT, holds 24-hour general strike; over 50 killed in clashes. UGTT leadership replaced with PSD loyalists.
- **1980** Guerrillas attack Gafsa in western Tunisia; government forces quickly regain control. New prime minister Muhammed Mazli ushers in greater political tolerance.
- **1981** Elections. Opposition groups allege electoral fraud after failing to win enough votes to entitle them to recognition as parties.
- **1984** Widespread riots after food price increases.
- **1986** General Zine al-Abidine Ben Ali becomes interior minister. Four Muslim fundamentalists sentenced to death.
- **1987** Fundamentalist leader Rachid Gannouchi arrested. Ben Ali becomes prime minister; takes over presidency after doctors certify Bourguiba senile. PSD becomes the RCD.
- **1988** Most political prisoners released. Constitutional reforms introduce multiparty system and abolish life presidency. Two opposition parties legalized.
- **1989** Elections. RCD wins all seats. Ben Ali president. Fundamentalists take 13% of vote. Gannouchi, now leader of banned Islamic *Al-Nahda* party, goes into exile.
- **1990** Tunisia backs Iraq over invasion of Kuwait. Clampdown on fundamentalists intensifies.
- **1991** Abortive coup blamed on *Al-Nahda*; over 500 arrests.
- **1993** Agreement on electoral reform paves way for opposition parties to participate equally with RCD in 1994 elections.

T

AID

$322m (receipts)

Down 18% in 1991

France is the major single donor, providing 22% of bilateral aid. Italy, Germany, the World Bank and the African Development Bank are other important sources of assistance. Oil-rich Arab states, including Saudi Arabia and Kuwait, have suspended their aid programs to Tunisia since 1990 because of its pro-Iraq stance in the Gulf War. Tunisia's total external debt is equivalent to 62% of GNP, making receipts crucial to its development.

DEFENSE

$508.7m

Up 17% in 1992

Defense spending as % GDP: 3.3% (scale 0–40)

Despite its small size – 35,000 troops, 26,400 of them conscripts – the military holds the reins of power behind the scenes of the Ben Ali regime. The army is equipped with US weapons. Border security and potential instability in neighboring Libya and Algeria are Tunisia's main defense concerns.

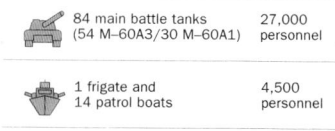

TUNISIAN ARMED FORCES

84 main battle tanks (54 M-60A3/30 M-60A1)	27,000 personnel
1 frigate and 14 patrol boats	4,500 personnel
38 combat aircraft (15 F-5E,-5F)	3,500 personnel
None	

ECONOMICS

$15.3bn

1.04 dinars

SCORE CARD

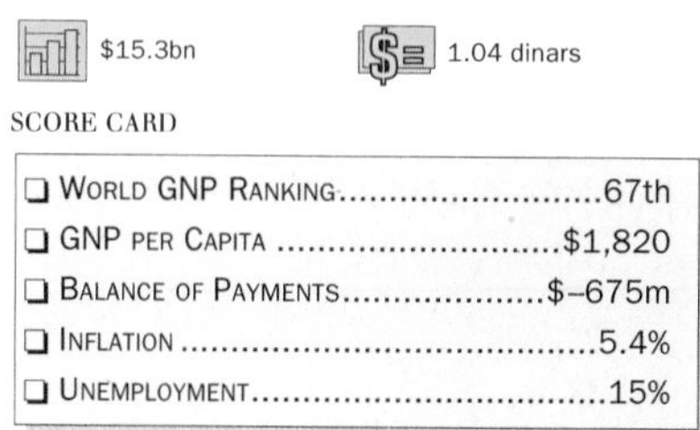

World GNP Ranking	67th
GNP per Capita	$1,820
Balance of Payments	$-675m
Inflation	5.4%
Unemployment	15%

EXPORTS

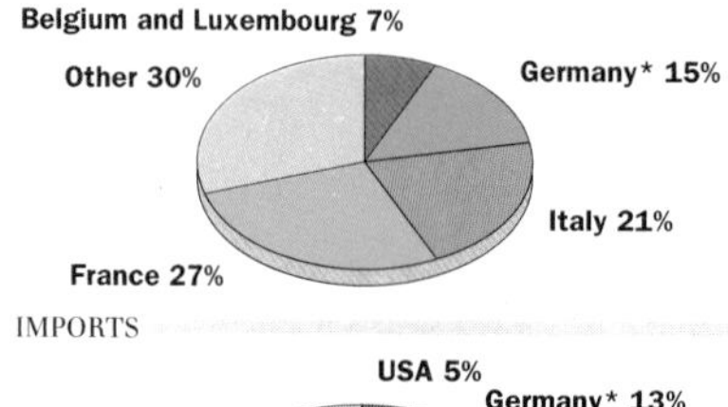

IMPORTS

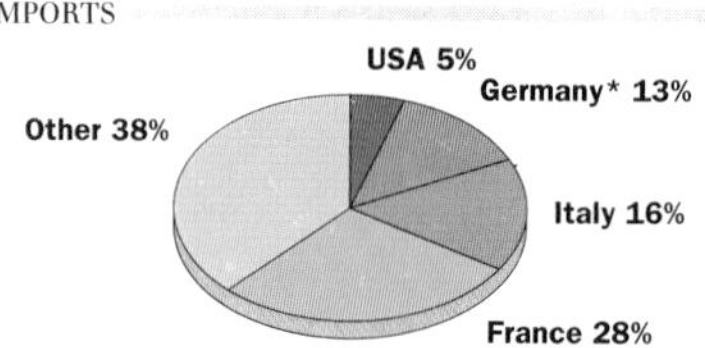

Strengths

A well-diversified economy, despite limited resources. Tourism. Oil and gas exports. Manufacturing is expanding. European investment.

Weaknesses

Dependence on growth of drought-prone agricultural sector. Growing domestic energy demand on oil and gas resources.

Profile

Since it began a process of structural adjustment in 1988, supported by the IMF and World Bank, Tunisia has become an increasingly open, market-oriented economy. Helped by good harvests, real growth averaged almost 6% a year between 1989 and 1993. The budget deficit has been cut to under 2% of GDP, from around 4% in the late 1980s. Prices have been freed, most state companies privatized and import barriers reduced.

The government has also begun a search for foreign investment, which is targeted to triple by 1996. High investment levels are essential if Tunisia is to reach its goal of providing an extra 313,000 jobs for young people over the next two years, let alone cutting the overall 15% unemployment rate. Another problem is the balance of payments, which relies on fluctuating tourism receipts to offset a trade deficit. The government must also balance the demands of growth with those of Tunisia's expanding middle class for better social provisions. Negotiations to increase trading opportunities with the EU, already Tunisia's main trading partner, have begun.

ECONOMIC PERFORMANCE INDICATOR

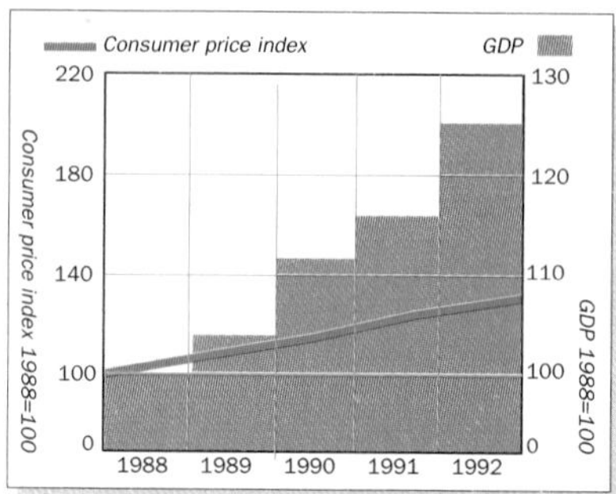

TUNISIA : MAJOR BUSINESSES

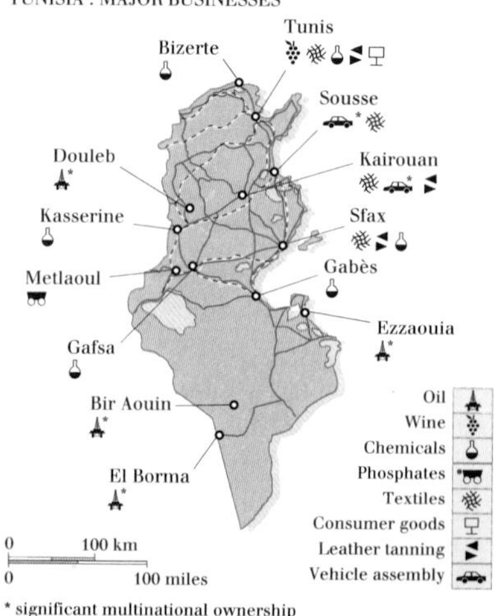

RESOURCES

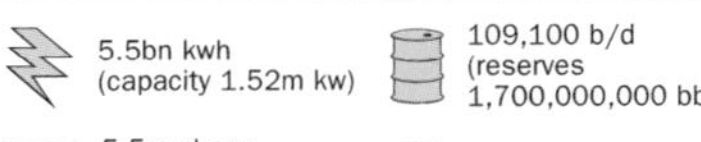

ELECTRICITY GENERATION

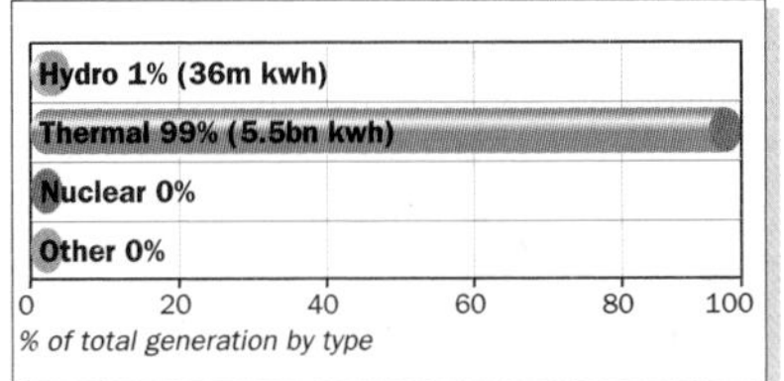

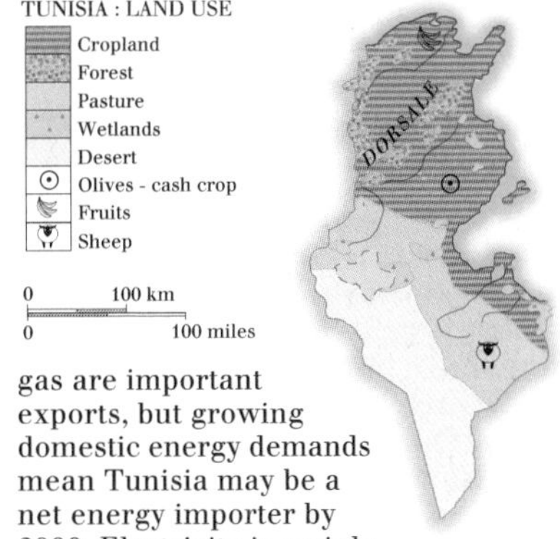

Tunisia is one of the world's leading producers of phosphates for fertilizers, mainly from mines near Gafsa. Oil and gas are important exports, but growing domestic energy demands mean Tunisia may be a net energy importer by 2000. Electricity is mainly thermal, with some hydropower.

HEALTH

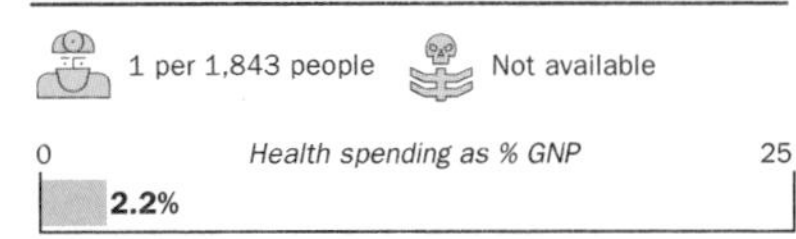

Well-developed family planning facilities have almost halved Tunisia's birth rate over the past 30 years. The population growth rate has dropped from 3.2% to 1.9% – the lowest in the region. The mortality rate has been more than halved, to around 48,000 a year, reflecting the extension of free medical services to over 70% of the population. Services lack sophistication, but an umbrella of primary care facilities covers all but the most isolated rural communities.

ENVIRONMENT

0.3%

Mass tourism is an ecological threat

ENVIRONMENTAL TREATIES

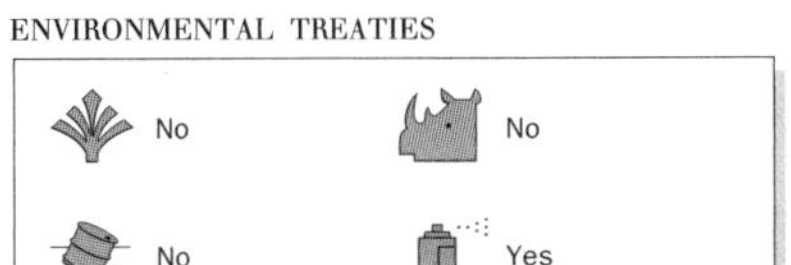

Desertification is a serious problem in the largely arid central and southern regions. However, the dominant environmental issue is the rapid expansion of tourism since the 1980s. Large, insensitively designed hotel and resort developments, which do not fit in with the local architecture, are spoiling coastal areas such as the Isle of Jerba and Hammamet. Tourism is also making an impact on the fragile desert ecology of the south, previously protected by its isolated position.

CRIME

CRIME RATES

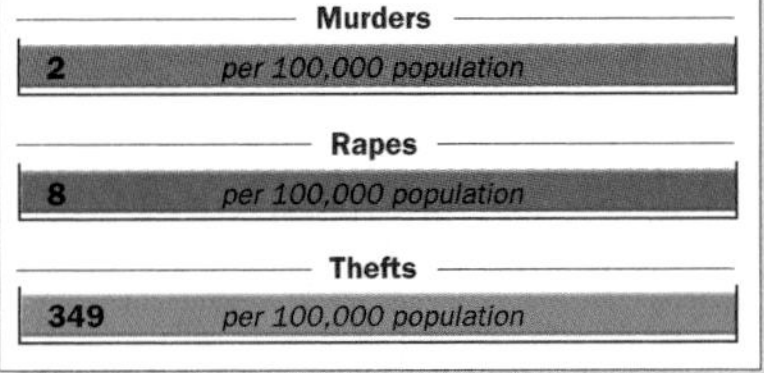

Street crime is unusual. Tunisia has a good human rights record. However, there were reports of the severe maltreatment of hundreds of Islamic fundamentalists, detained without trial by the authorities, following the abortive coup in 1991.

WEALTH

Waiter, 0.8 dinars per hour; journalist, 1.7 dinars per hour

CONSUMER GOODS OWNERSHIP

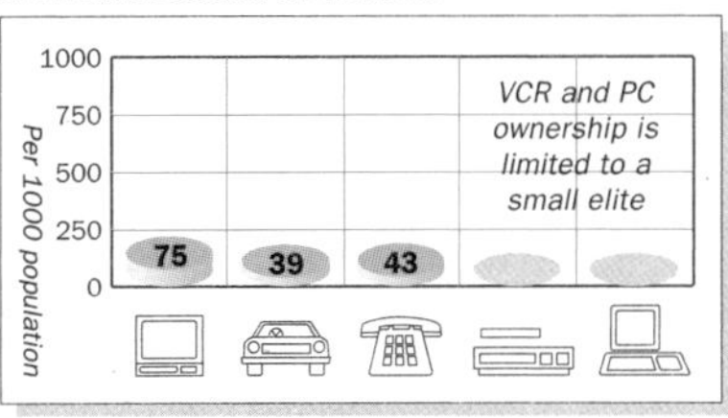

Today 7% of Tunisians are estimated to live in absolute poverty. In 1970 it was 30%. The poorest tend to live in the urban shantytowns, or *bidonvilles*. The Western-oriented elite has links to government or business. Social security covers sickness, old age and maternity, but not unemployment, currently at 15%. The government is concerned that unemployment is encouraging the spread of Islamic fundamentalism. Economic growth is its medium-term solution to the problem. Special projects are being set up in the most deprived urban areas to offset the worst effects of poverty.

MEDIA

The press has enjoyed considerable freedom since 1987, but government still interferes at times

PUBLISHING AND BROADCAST MEDIA

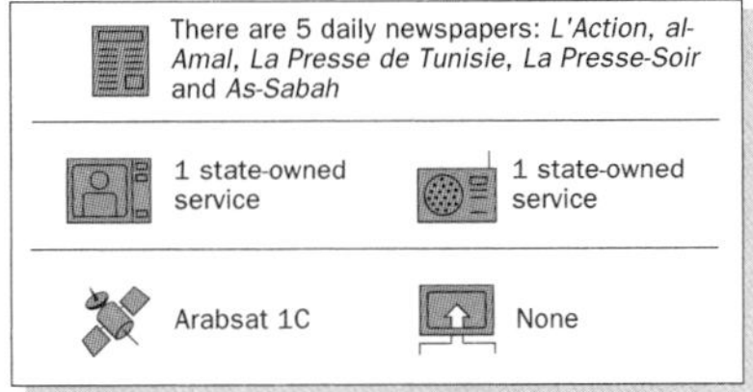

There are 5 daily newspapers: L'Action, al-Amal, La Presse de Tunisie, La Presse-Soir and As-Sabah
1 state-owned service
1 state-owned service
Arabsat 1C
None

Reforms since the late 1980s have in theory increased press freedom in Tunisia, a country traditionally considered a source of liberal ideas in the Arab world. In practice, government restrictions remain. The foreign press is also occasionally banned, but the arrival of satellite TV from Europe has meant that people can receive a wide range of programs in their homes.

EDUCATION

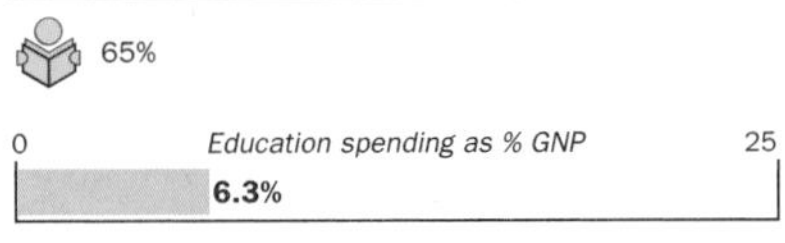

THE EDUCATION SYSTEM

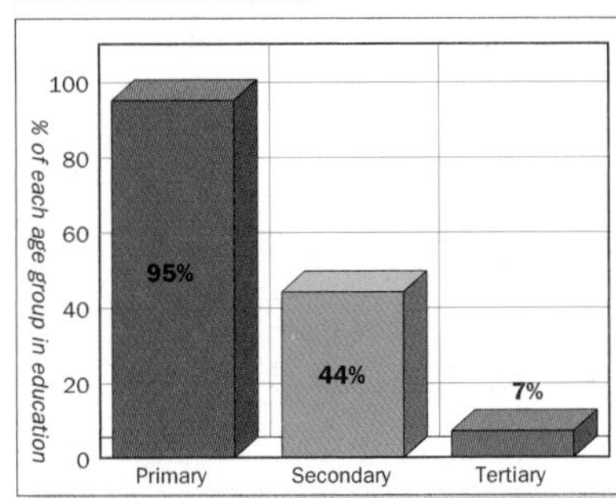

Education is not compulsory, but about 80% of school-age children attend school. French is taught from the second year of primary school and is used almost exclusively in higher education. There are two universities.

WORLD RANKING

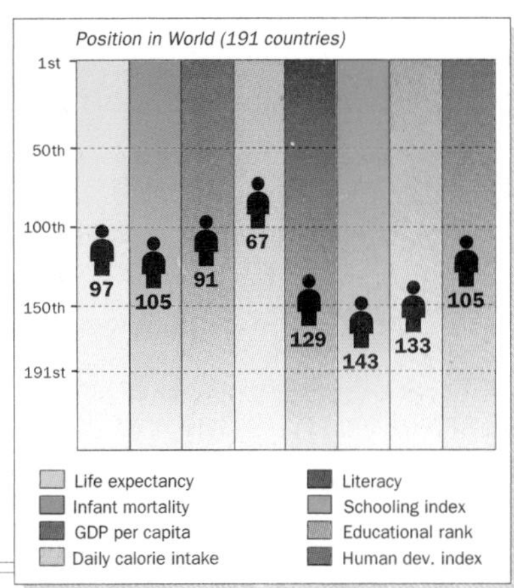

T

TURKEY

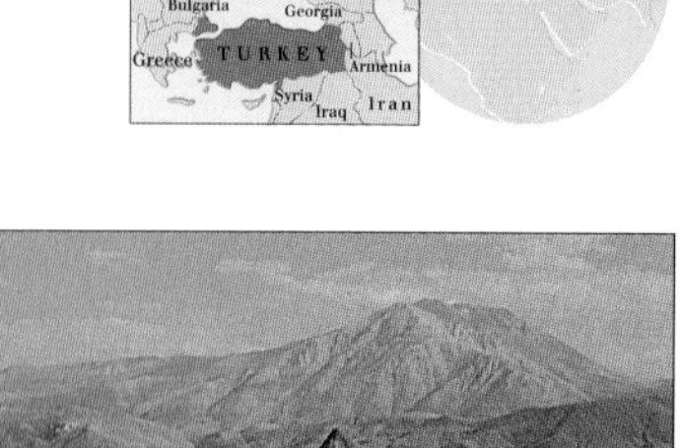

OFFICIAL NAME: Republic of Turkey **CAPITAL:** Ankara
POPULATION: 58.4 million **CURRENCY:** Turkish lira **OFFICIAL LANGUAGE:** Turkish

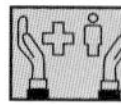

A SECULAR ISLAMIC STATE, Turkey occupies the peninsula of Asia Minor and the region of Eastern Thrace in Europe. It thus controls the entrance to the Black Sea, which is straddled by Turkey's largest city, Istanbul. The majority of Turks live in the western half of the country. The eastern and southeastern reaches of the Anatolia Plateau are Kurdish regions. Turkey's strategic location gives it significant influence in the Mediterranean, Black Sea and Middle East. Since the breakup of the USSR, Turkey has also been developing trading links with Central Asia.

The island of Akdamar, eastern Anatolia. *Surrounded by Lake Van, the island is the site of the 10th-century Church of the Holy Cross.*

CLIMATE

WEATHER CHART

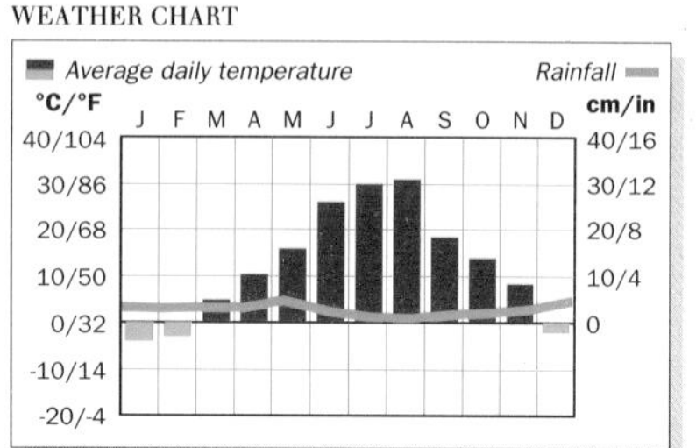

Coastal regions have a Mediterranean climate. The interior has cold, snowy winters and hot, dry summers.

COMMUNICATIONS

Atatürk Intl, Ankara
10m passengers

703 ships
6.88m dwt

THE TRANSPORTATION NETWORK

36,740 miles (59,128 km)

513 miles (826 km)

5,244 miles (8,439 km)

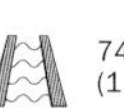
746 miles (1,200 km)

The rail system is well-developed. Plans exist for a $4-billion rail tunnel under the Boêazi, and for a high-speed link between Istanbul and Ankara. More highways are planned, including a road bridge across the Dardanelles.

PEOPLE

Turkish, Kurdish, Arabic, Circassian, Armenian, Greek, Georgian, Ladino

186 people per sq. mile

THE URBAN/RURAL POPULATION SPLIT

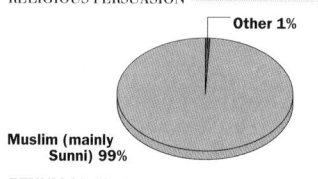

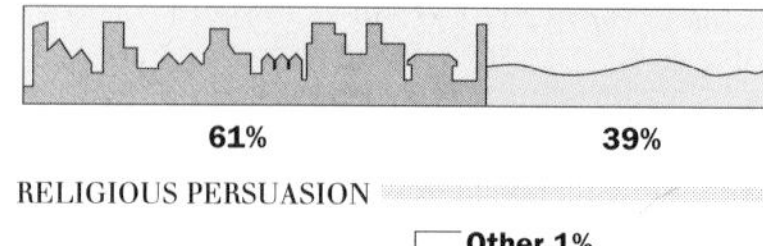

RELIGIOUS PERSUASION

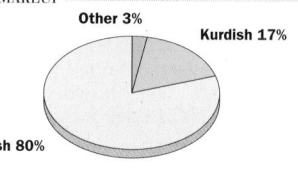

Other 1%
Muslim (mainly Sunni) 99%

ETHNIC MAKEUP

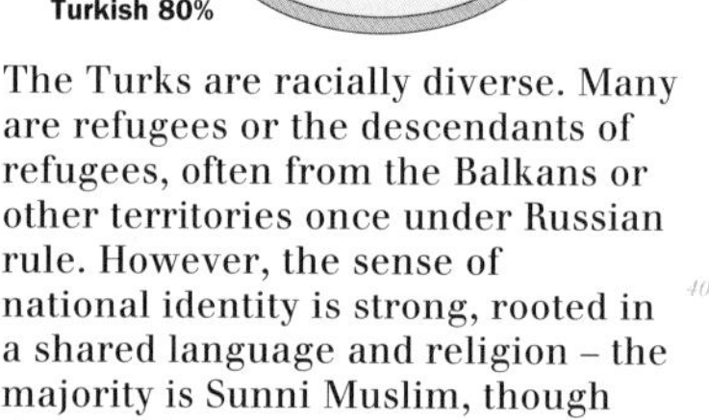

The Turks are racially diverse. Many are refugees or the descendants of refugees, often from the Balkans or other territories once under Russian rule. However, the sense of national identity is strong, rooted in a shared language and religion – the majority is Sunni Muslim, though there is a fast-growing Shi'a community in central Anatolia. The largest minority – 2.5 million – are the Kurds while some 500,000 people, mainly in the southeast, are Arabic speakers. Women have equal rights and Turkey's first woman prime minister came to power in 1993.

POPULATION AGE BREAKDOWN

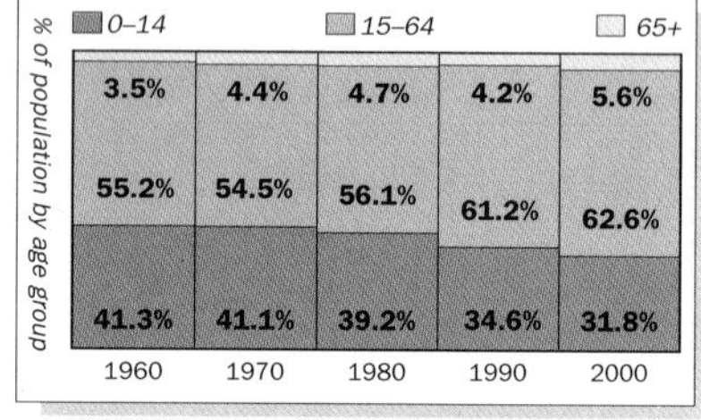

TOURISM

7.8m visitors

Up 41% in 1992

As well as major Classical sites such as Ephesus and Troy on the Aegean coast, Turkey is rich in antiquities of both the Ottoman and Byzantine periods. Istanbul is a magnet for shoppers, especially collectors of antiques and carpets. Southern Turkey has fine beaches. Tourism is a major foreign currency earner. Hotels are now being built to higher standards.

MAIN OVERSEAS ARRIVALS

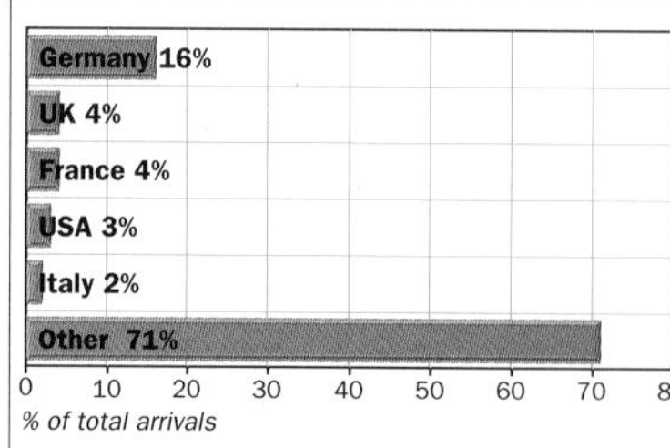

T

POLITICS

1996

President Süleyman Demirel

THE STATE OF THE PARTIES

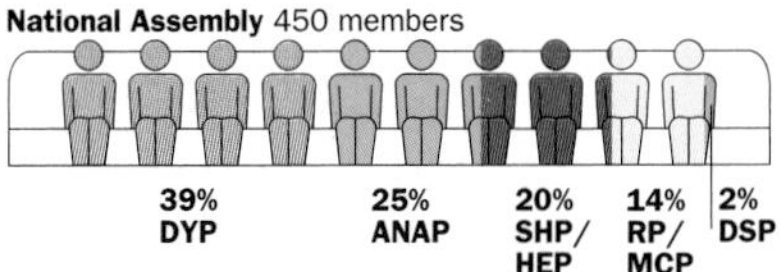

DYP = True Path Party **ANAP** = Motherland Party **SHP** = Social Democratic Populist Party **HEP** = People's Labor Party **RP** = Welfare Party **MÇP** = Nationalist Labor Party **DSP** = Democratic Left Party

Per the 1982 constitution, Turkey is a multiparty republic with a national assembly elected every five years. The president serves a seven-year term and appoints the prime minister.

MAIN POLITICAL ISSUES

Islamic fundamentalism

In the municipal elections of 1994, the Islamic fundamentalist RP took 18% of the vote. The backers of the RP are mostly the poor of Turkey's urban slums. However, the RP's rise represents a growing challenge from below to the Westernizing secularist path that Turkey has been following since Atatürk's rule. Whether the fundamentalists can be contained within the democratic framework is now a central issue in Turkish politics.

Kurdish separatists

Turkey's southeastern region has been the scene of a bitter civil war since 1984. Kurdish secessionists are led by the Kurdistan Workers Party (PKK). Thousands have died in conflict with the Turkish army. The PKK agreed to a cease-fire in 1993 and declared that they no longer wished for secession, but for recognition of Kurdish rights within Turkey. There is pressure on the government, which has spent $7 billion on containing the conflict, to reach a settlement.

PROFILE

In recent years, political parties have proliferated in Turkish politics. They encompass center, right and left, social democrat and extremes of neo-fascists, socialists and Islamic radicals. Party distinctions are often highly artificial and frequently have more to do with personalities than politics.

With Süleyman Demirel's accession to the presidency in 1993, the leadership of the ruling center-right DYP was won by an ex-economics professor, Mrs. Tansu Çiller, whose personal popularity helped lead the DYP to a narrow win in the 1994 elections. In practice, there is often little to distinguish the DYP from the second-largest party, ANAP. The DYP draws its support mainly from the small towns of Anatolia and the Aegean, while ANAP is strongly supported by Istanbul's business community.

Under former Prime Minister Turgut Özal, Muslim fundamentalists were allowed a greater voice in politics. However, should their popularity increase to the point where Turkey's pro-Western secularism is threatened, the army could once more step in to run the government.

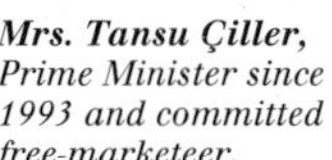
Mrs. Tansu Çiller, *Prime Minister since 1993 and committed free-marketeer.*

Turgut Özal, *who died in 1993, presided over several years of prosperity.*

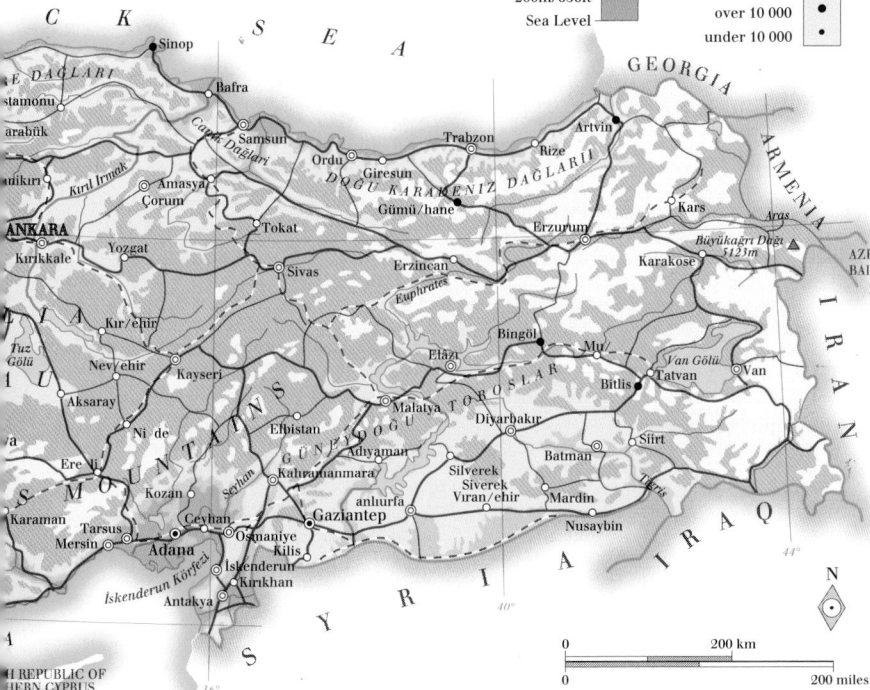

TURKEY

Total Area : 779 450 sq. km(300 950 sq. miles)

LAND HEIGHT	POPULATION
3000m/9843ft	over 5 000 000
2000m/6562ft	over 1 000 000
1000m/3281ft	over 500 000
500m/1640ft	over 100 000
200m/656ft	over 50 000
Sea Level	over 10 000
	under 10 000

0 200 km
0 200 miles

WORLD AFFAIRS

With the end of the Cold War, Turkey's strategic value as NATO's first Western line of defense against the USSR has diminished. Turkey is now redefining its world role by exploring closer ties with neighboring states. In 1992, Turkey hosted the first meeting of the Black Sea Economic Cooperation Region, involving Greece, Albania and several former Soviet republics. The government has also tried to mediate between Armenia and Azerbaijan.

As a base for operations against Iraq in the 1991 Gulf War, Turkey gave valuable assistance to the Western-led coalition, and was rewarded with economic aid. Membership in the EU, once a cherished goal, is now accepted as a distant prospect. Greece will oppose Ankara's membership as long as Turkey continues to occupy northern Cyprus. Trading links with the EU are close, however, and Turkey will join the EU customs union in 1995.

AID

$1.6bn (receipts)

Up 30% in 1991

Turkey has a foreign debt of over $50 billion and is a net recipient of aid. The government received over $4 billion in grants and credits after the Gulf War, mainly from Saudi Arabia, Kuwait and Japan. Turkey supports peace between Israel and the Palestinians and has promised the West Bank $52 million in cash and credits.

T

CHRONOLOGY

Following the collapse of the Ottoman Empire and Turkey's defeat in World War I, nationalist Mustafa Kemal Atatürk deposed the ruling sultan in 1922, declaring Turkey a republic in 1923.

- **1924** Religious courts abolished.
- **1928** Islam no longer the state religion.
- **1934** Women given the vote. Western-style surnames adopted.
- **1938** President Ataturk dies. Succeeded by Ismet Inonu.
- **1945** Turkey declares war on Germany and joins UN.
- **1947** Military assistance agreement signed with USA.
- **1952** Turkey admitted to Council of Europe and NATO.
- **1960** Army stages coup against ruling Democratic Party and suspends National Assembly.
- **1961** Fresh elections held after new constitution is approved by referendum. Party politics restored.
- **1963** Association agreement signed with EEC.
- **1974** After clashes between Greek and Turkish Cypriots, Turkish troops invade Cyprus and occupy northern part of the island.
- **1980** Armed forces overthrow the Demirel government's Justice Party and suspend party politics. Turkey under military rule for three years.
- **1982** New constitution enforced after referendum.
- **1983** General election won by Turgut Özal's Motherland Party.
- **1984** Ambassadors exchanged with "Turkish Republic of Northern Cyprus." Kurdish separatist PKK launch guerrilla war in southeast provinces.
- **1987** Turkey applies for full membership in EC.
- **1989** EC delays consideration of full membership until completion of single European market. Strained relations with Bulgaria over assimilation policy, which results in influx of 300,000 Turkish refugees.
- **1990** Allied powers permitted to operate air strikes against Iraq from Turkish bases. Escalating clashes between security forces and PKK.
- **1991** Iraqi Kurds, fleeing Iraqi army, try to cross Turkish border. Elections won by DYP, led by Süleyman Demirel.
- **1992** Turkey joins Black Sea alliance. Racist attacks on Turkish workers in Germany.
- **1993** Demirel elected president. Mrs. Çiller becomes DYP leader and Prime Minister. Ceasefire with PKK breaks down and conflict resumes.

DEFENSE

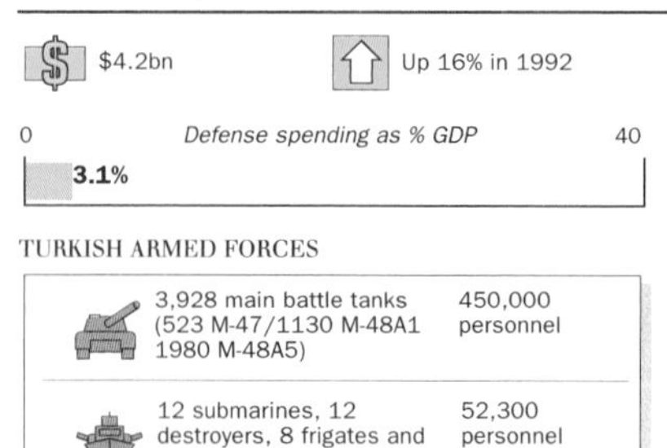

TURKISH ARMED FORCES

3,928 main battle tanks (523 M-47/1130 M-48A1 1980 M-48A5)	450,000 personnel
12 submarines, 12 destroyers, 8 frigates and 47 patrol boats	52,300 personnel
573 combat aircraft (F-16C,-D/F-5/F-4E/F-104)	58,000 Personnel
None	

The army has, on occasion, intervened in Turkish politics (the last time was the 1980 military coup), and its leaders often determine the shape of governments. With 18 months' service compulsory for all males at age 20, Turkey is a sizeable military power. However, defense spending is slightly below average. Thanks to NATO membership, Turkey has access to Western arms suppliers. The air force flies F-16 fighters, the navy has German-made frigates, and the army is supplied with modern battle tanks. Over 20,000 troops have been deployed to fight Kurdish separatists based in northern Iraq and in Turkey's own southeastern provinces.

ECONOMICS

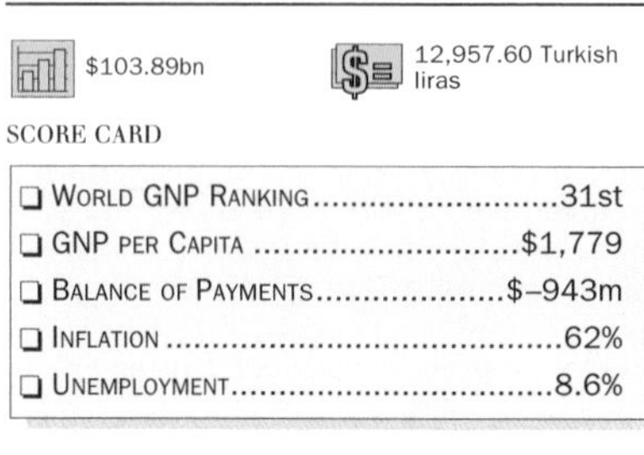

SCORE CARD

- WORLD GNP RANKING 31st
- GNP PER CAPITA $1,779
- BALANCE OF PAYMENTS .... $-943m
- INFLATION 62%
- UNEMPLOYMENT 8.6%

EXPORTS

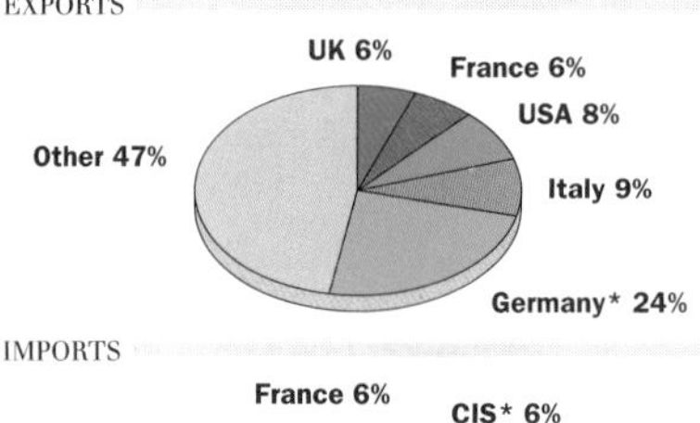

IMPORTS

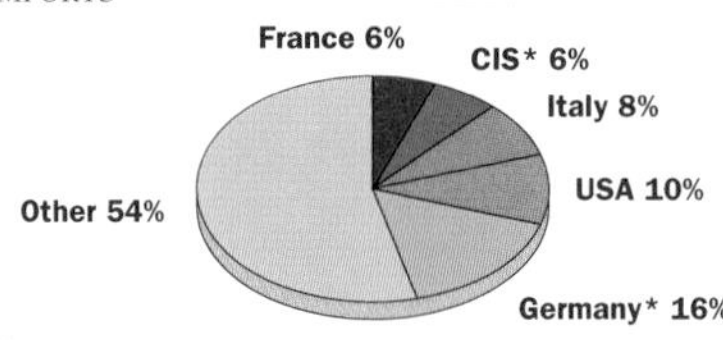

STRENGTHS

Liberalized economy resulted in the highest growth rate in the OECD in early 1990s. Self-sufficient in agriculture. Textiles, manufacturing and construction sectors competitive on world markets. Tourism industry.

WEAKNESSES

High inflation and unemployment. Many companies protected from external competition by high tariff barriers, due to come down when Turkey joins EU customs union in 1995. Shortage of investment capital. High costs of civil war with Kurds. Many sectors of state-owned economy making huge losses: $3 billion in 1993.

PROFILE

Turkey's economy began its dramatic growth in the early 1980s when a

ECONOMIC PERFORMANCE INDICATOR

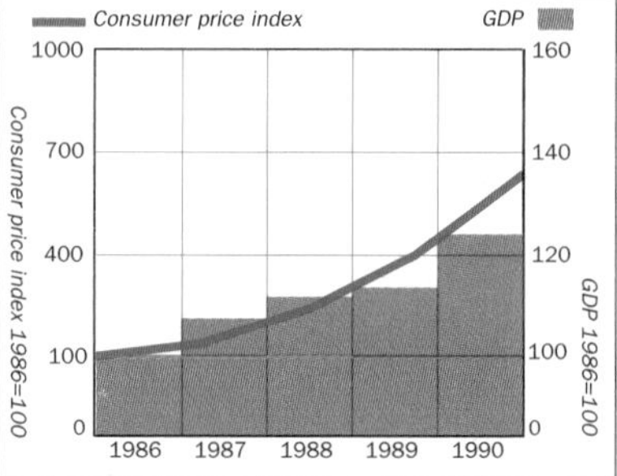

process of liberalization and increased competition began. The result was an unprecedented growth in exports. Turkey also has foreign currency reserves of $17 billion. However, the cost of rapid expansion has been high inflation, and government spending has not been brought under control. Public finances are also burdened by the loss-making state sector, low tax income and an annual population growth of 2.1%.

TURKEY : MAJOR BUSINESSES

T

RESOURCES

57.5bn kwh (capacity 16.3m kw)

82,300 b/d (reserves 474,761,000 bbl)

34.9m sheep, 13.1m goats, 11.8m cattle

Chromium, copper, borax, coal, natural gas, bauxite, iron

ELECTRICITY GENERATION

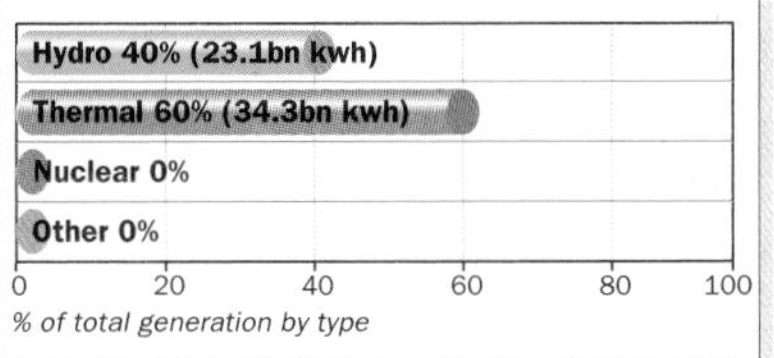

In the mid-1980s Turkey launched the Southeastern Anatolian Projects. Harnessing the waters of the Euphrates and Tigris rivers, massive dams will allow the irrigation of 4.2 million acres of land. Eighteen HEP stations will further increase Turkey's generating capacity.

Turkey produces oil in Garcan and Raman, and some local refining takes place as well. The eastern Asian provinces are rich in minerals, such as chromium, of which Turkey is the world's largest producer.

TURKEY : LAND USE

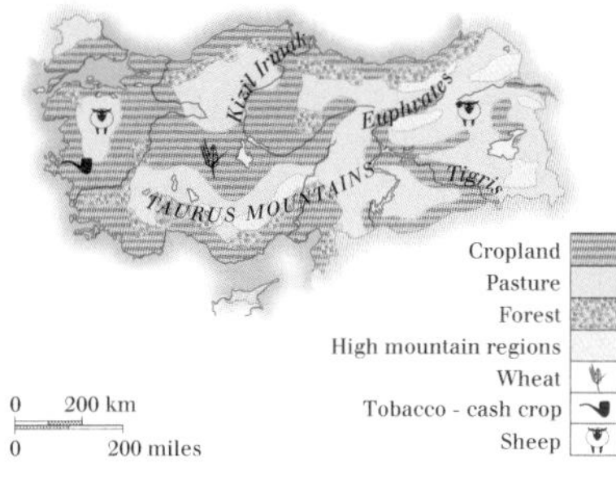

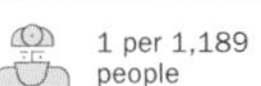

ENVIRONMENT

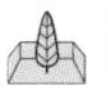
0.4% (0.1% partially protected)

Yacht-tourism threat to marine ecosystems in south and west

ENVIRONMENTAL TREATIES

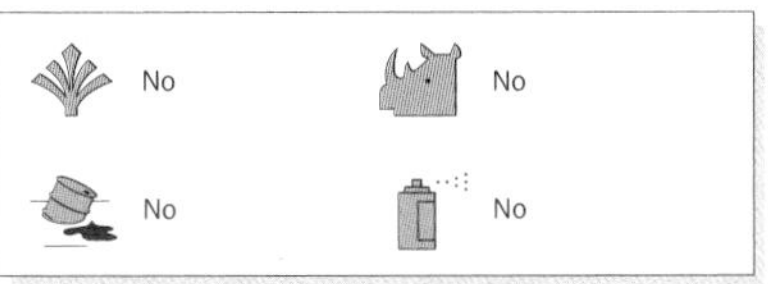

Turkey's program of dam-building on the Tigris and Euphrates has met with international condemnation, particularly from Syria and Iraq, whose rivers will suffer reduced flow rates as a result. Concern has also been expressed over plans to build a nuclear power plant. Much of the western coast has been spoiled by lack of planning and by uncontrolled tourist developments.

CRIME

51,800 prisoners

Down 6% in 1990

CRIME RATES

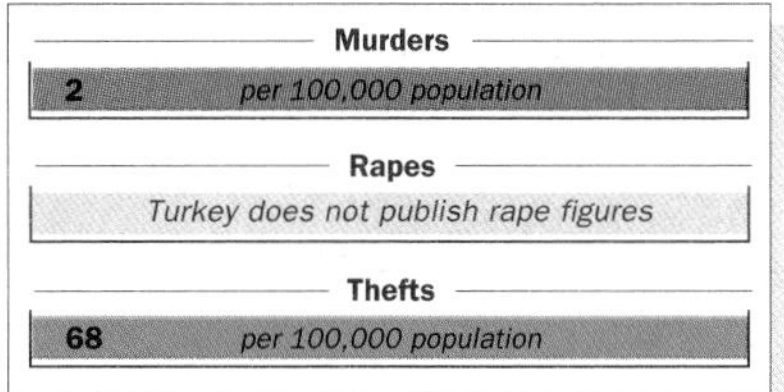

Most crime levels are stable or falling slightly, although there has been an increase in drug-related crime. The routine torture of prisoners by the police was an issue in the 1995 elections and the government intends to limit the force's powers.

HEALTH

1 per 1,189 people

Heart, cerebrovascular, respiratory and digestive diseases

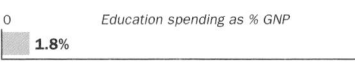

0 *Health spending as % GNP* 25

1.5%

Turkey has an adequate national system of primary healthcare. By Western standards, however, hospitals are under-equipped.

WEALTH

Tanner, 4,535 Turkish liras per hour; chemical engineer, 2.53m Turkish liras per month

CONSUMER GOODS OWNERSHIP

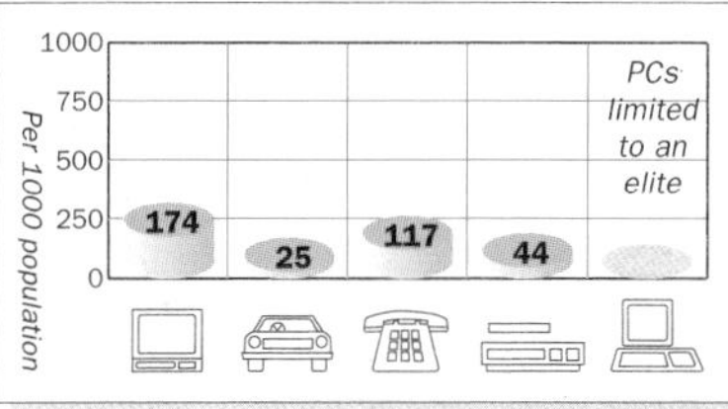

The economic expansion of the 1980s has created a new class of wealthy entrepreneurs. However, due to high inflation, many on fixed incomes have fared badly in the last decade. Many Turks have chosen to work abroad as guest workers in Germany and the Netherlands.

MEDIA

Harsh laws inhibit freedom of expression

PUBLISHING AND BROADCAST MEDIA

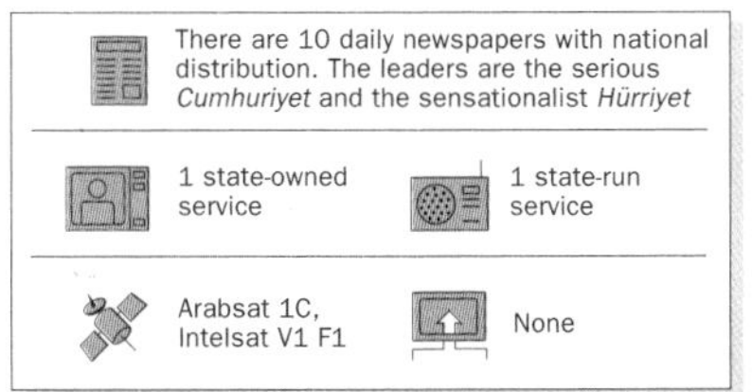

There are 10 daily newspapers with national distribution. The leaders are the serious *Cumhuriyet* and the sensationalist *Hürriyet*
1 state-owned service
1 state-run service
Arabsat 1C, Intelsat V1 F1
None

The Turkish press is diverse, vigorous and largely privately owned, but political debate is subject to censorship laws dating back to the 1980 military coup. Espousing the Kurdish cause is banned. Although Islam is the dominant religion, the media is not subject to the moral censorship found in the Gulf states. Almost all Istanbul newspapers are printed in Ankara and Izmir on the same day. Four have circulations of over 300,000 copies.

As an addition to programing offered by the state-owned Turkish Radio and Television Corporation, many Turks are now buying satellite dishes to receive foreign broadcasts.

EDUCATION

81%

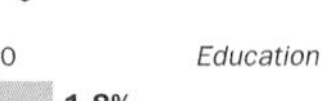

THE EDUCATION SYSTEM

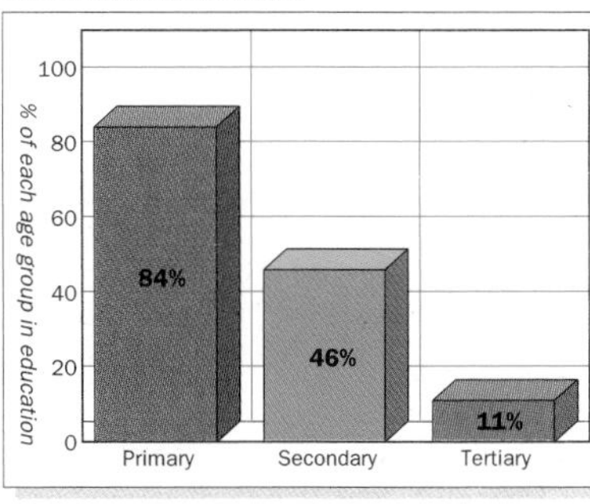

With the formation of the Turkish republic, all educational establishments were nationalized. In 1928, a Turkish alphabet was introduced using Latin characters. Turkey spends 10% of its state budget on education – a relatively high figure. Engineering is usually the strongest department in Turkey's many universities.

WORLD RANKING

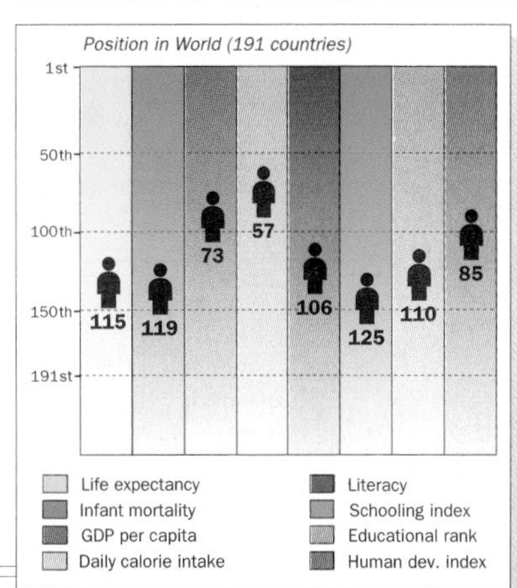

T

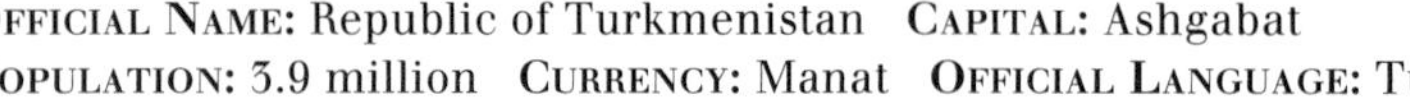

TURKMENISTAN

OFFICIAL NAME: Republic of Turkmenistan **CAPITAL:** Ashgabat
POPULATION: 3.9 million **CURRENCY:** Manat **OFFICIAL LANGUAGE:** Turkmen

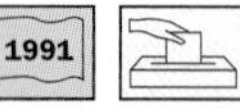

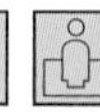

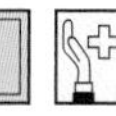
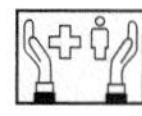

ORIGINALLY THE POOREST state among the former Soviet republics, Turkmenistan has adjusted better than most to independence, exploiting the market value of its abundant natural gas supplies. A largely Sunni Muslim area, Turkmenistan is part of the former Turkestan, the last expanse of Central Asia incorporated into Tsarist Russia. Much of life is still based on tribal relationships. Turkmenistan is isolated – telephones are rare and TV barely available.

CLIMATE

WEATHER CHART

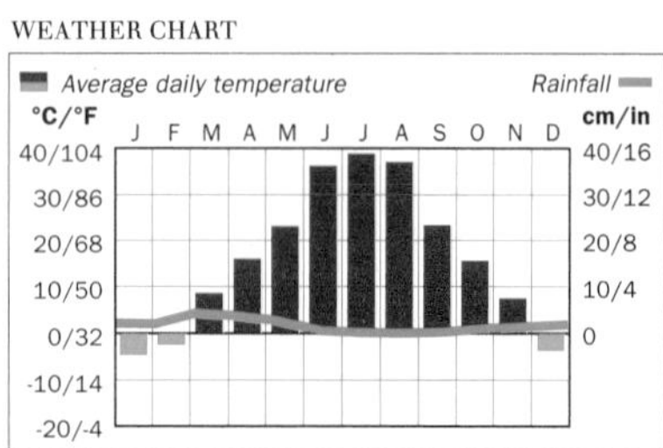

Most of Turkmenistan is arid desert. Only 2% of the total land area is suitable for agriculture.

COMMUNICATIONS

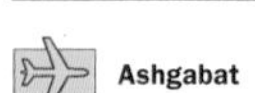

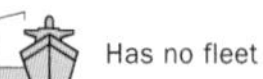

THE TRANSPORTATION NETWORK

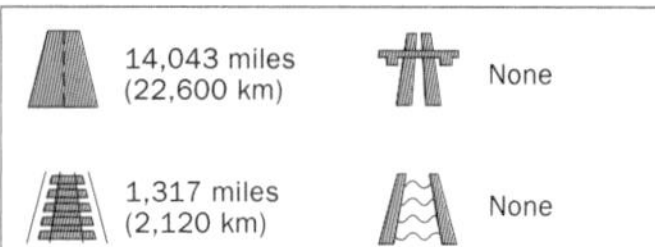

The road and rail links to Teheran will be the first to be upgraded. There are plans to modernize Ashgabat Airport.

TOURISM

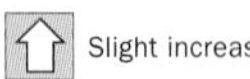

MAIN OVERSEAS ARRIVALS

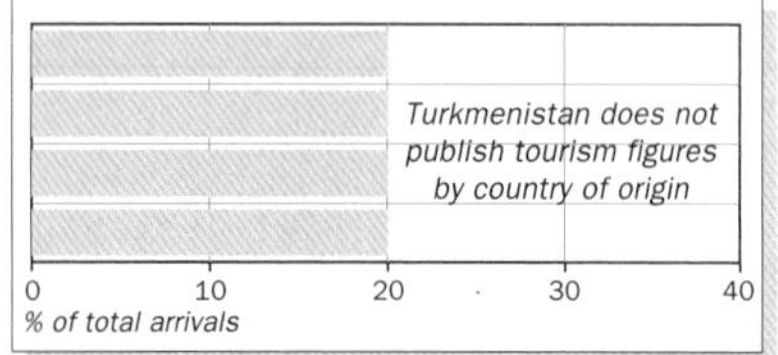

Most visitors are businessmen attracted by the state's stability under President Niyazov. Turkmenistan may become a popular tourist area in the future; traditional Turkmen Muslim monuments are slowly being restored.

Kara Kum Canal zone: salt flats and the Kopetdag Mountains on the Iranian border. The Kara Kum is Turkmenistan's largest desert.

PEOPLE

THE URBAN/RURAL POPULATION SPLIT

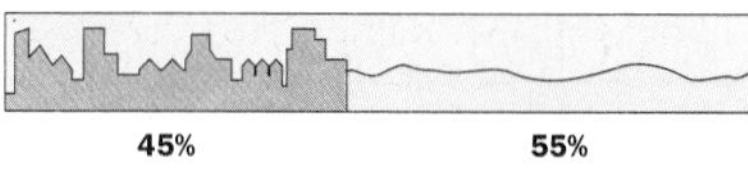

RELIGIOUS PERSUASION

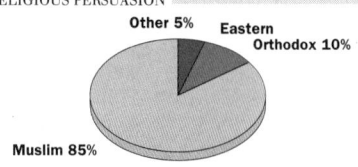

Other 5%
Eastern Orthodox 10%
Muslim 85%

Before Tsarist Russia annexed Turkmenistan in 1884, the Turkmen were a largely nomadic tribal people. The tribal unit remains strong – the largest tribes are the Tekke in the center, the Ersary on the eastern Afghan border and the Yomud in the west. It is tribal conflicts among the Turkmen, rather than tensions with the two main minorities – Russians and Uzbeks – that are a source of strife. Paradoxically, this has meant that since independence from Moscow, there has been less virulent nationalism than in other ex-Soviet republics. Since 1989, Turkmenistan has been rehabilitating its traditional language and culture, as well as reassessing its history. Islam is once more central to the Turkmen, although few make the *haj* (pilgrimage) to Mecca and many continue to maintain a cult of ancestors.

CENTRAL ASIA

Kazakhstan
Uzbekistan
TURKMENISTAN
Iran
Afghanistan
Asia

POLITICS

1999

THE STATE OF THE PARTIES

Parliament 50 members

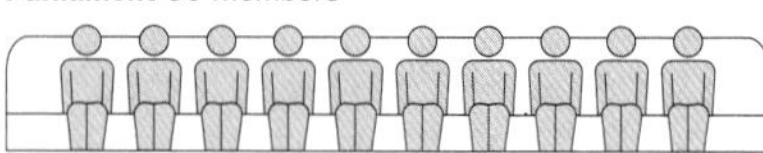

Elections were held on December 11 1994. All candidates were returned unopposed – most belonged to the one permitted political party, The Democratic Party of Turkmenistan (the former Communist Party)

People's Council

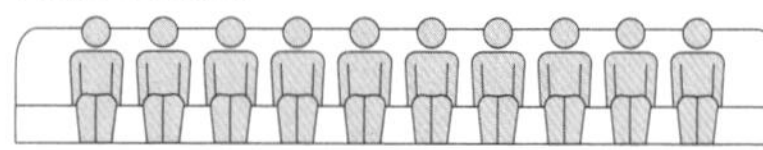

Comprises 60 elected members,the members of the Council of Ministers and others

Officially, Turkmenistan became a multiparty democracy in 1990. As in other ex-Soviet states, however, the old communist nomenklatura still controls the political process: the communists renamed themselves the Democratic Party of Turkmenistan in 1991. The DPT has maintained the communist suspicion of the Islamic fundamentalism promoted by Iran. President Niyazov has developed an extreme personality cult. He sustains his popularity with such measures as providing free electricity and water.

The main political concern is to prevent the social and nationalistic conflicts that have blighted other CIS republics. Broad policy is communist. Russian remains the bureaucratic language, and gas revenues are still used to subsidize inefficient industry and agriculture.

WORLD AFFAIRS

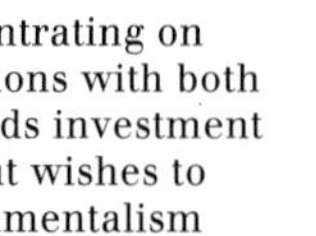

Turkmenistan is concentrating on establishing good relations with both Iran and Turkey. It needs investment from both countries, but wishes to avoid the Islamic fundamentalism promoted by the Iranians. President Niyazov opposes economic union with the CIS, fearing this would compromise Turkmenistan's control of its gas fields.

AID

Aid is mostly concentrated in the oil and gas industries and comes from Turkey, Iran, Switzerland and Germany.

T

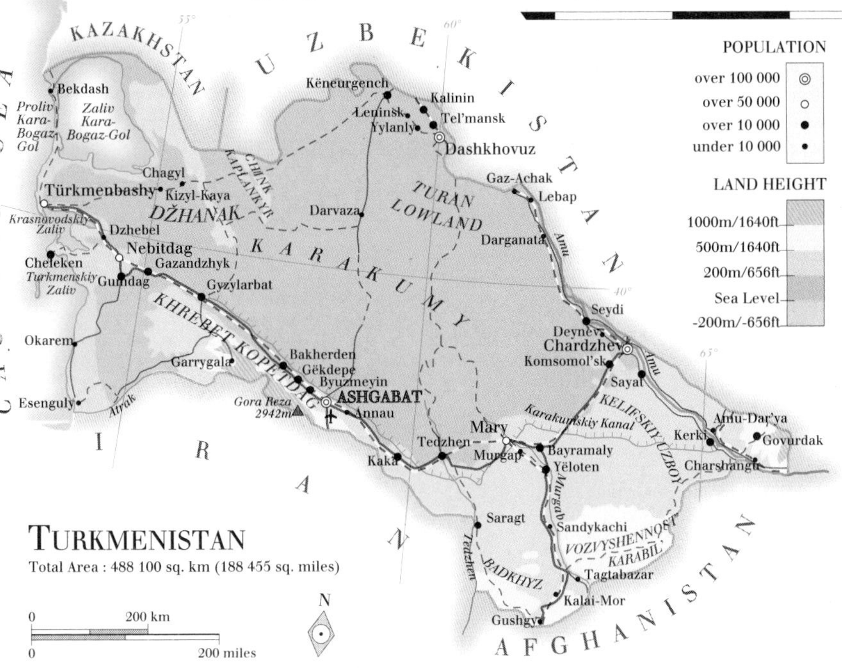

TURKMENISTAN

Total Area : 488 100 sq. km (188 455 sq. miles)

CHRONOLOGY

The nomadic peoples of Western Turkestan came under Russian imperial control from the 1850s.

- ❑ **1881** Russians found Askhabad (present-day Ashgabat).
- ❑ **1906** Mass colonization starts.
- ❑ **1924** Turkestan divided into five republics including Turkmenistan.
- ❑ **1940** Cyrillic replaces Turkish.
- ❑ **1948** Earthquake destroys capital.
- ❑ **1991** Independence from USSR.

DEFENSE

 $6.4bn

 Little change in defense spending

Compared to other states in the region, Turkmenistan is reasonably stable. Its army is under joint control with Russia, on whom it depends for defense.

ECONOMICS

 $6.4bn

 Official exchange rate not established

SCORE CARD

- ❑ WORLD GNP RANKING..........................98th
- ❑ GNP PER CAPITA $1,650
- ❑ BALANCE OF PAYMENTS $2,553m
- ❑ INFLATION 90%
- ❑ UNEMPLOYMENT................................2.5%

STRENGTHS

Cotton and gas. Turkmenistan was the USSR's major supplier of cotton and supplied 12% of gas. Hard currency trading has meant that real prices are being paid for these commodities for the first time – under the USSR only 1% of profits returned to Turkmenistan.

WEAKNESSES

Cotton monoculture means most food has to be imported. The least industrialized ex-Soviet state: most plant dates back to the 1920s.

EXPORTS/IMPORTS

Most imports and exports are still from and to Russia and other CIS republics. However, Turkmenistan is beginning to establish a wide range of Western contacts

RESOURCES

 15.8bn kwh

 101,200 b/d

 5.4m sheep and goats, 774,000 cattle

 Potassium, sulfur, sodium sulfate

During the Soviet years most Turkmen agriculture was turned over to cotton – seen by Moscow as a strategic crop.

ENVIRONMENT

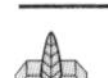 2.3%

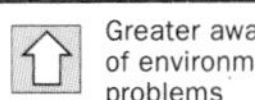 Greater awareness of environmental problems

The building of the Kara Kum Canal, hailed as a progressive move by Moscow in 1958, has drained 35% of the Aral Sea's water, leading to an increase in unproductive salinated soil.

MEDIA

 The government controls all media. Censorship is widespread

PUBLISHING AND BROADCAST MEDIA

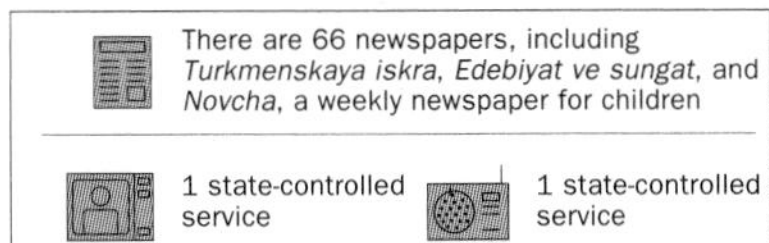

Iranian and Afghan radio stations, beaming in Islamic programs, are popular. TV is only available in cities.

CRIME

 Turkmenistan does not publish prison figures

 Increasing levels of theft

Levels of crime are low compared with neighboring ex-Soviet republics. Theft, however, is on the increase.

EDUCATION

 Literacy rate among lowest of ex-Soviet republics

The Turkmen language and literature (banned until 1987) are now on the syllabus. However, Russian schools still have the highest standards.

HEALTH

 1 per 274 people

 Cerebrovascular, heart and respiratory diseases

Highly polluted water is a major health hazard; only 35% of the population have a treated water supply.

WEALTH

 The unemployed and the old form the poorest group. The extended family system and subsidies often prevent absolute poverty

CONSUMER GOODS OWNERSHIP

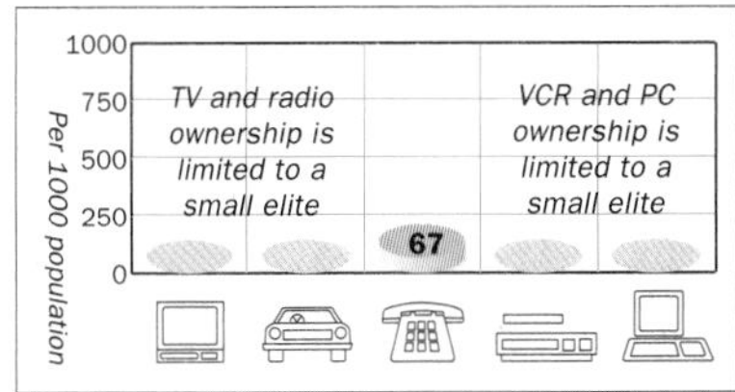

The ex-communist bureaucrats are still the richest group. They enjoy Japanese and Korean luxury goods.

WORLD RANKING

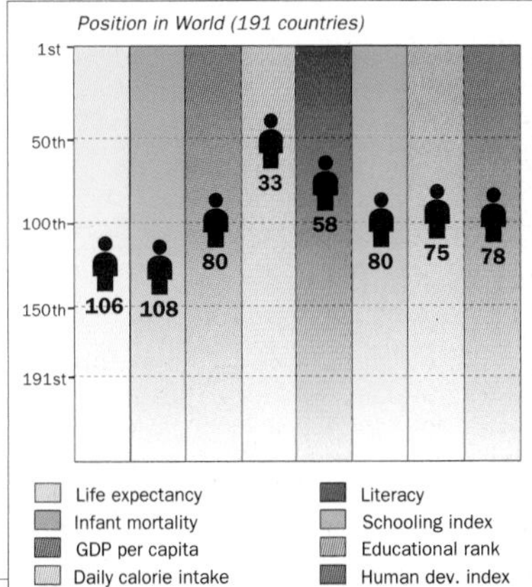

T

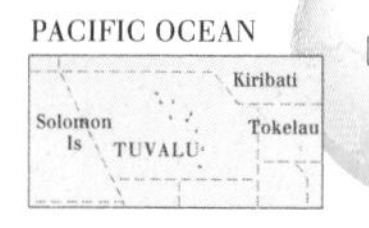

TUVALU

OFFICIAL NAME: Tuvalu **CAPITAL:** Funafuti **POPULATION:** 9,061
CURRENCIES: Australian dollar, Tuvaluan dollar **OFFICIAL LANGUAGE:** *No official language*

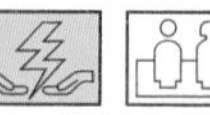

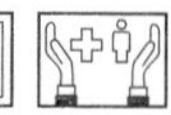

ONE OF THE WORLD'S SMALLEST, most isolated states, Tuvalu lies 650 mi. north of Fiji in the central Pacific. A chain of nine coral atolls, 360 mi. long, it has a land area of just over 65 sq. mi. As the Ellice Islands, it was linked to the Gilbert Islands as a British colony until independence in 1978. Politically and socially conservative, Tuvaluans live by subsistence farming and fishing.

CLIMATE

WEATHER CHART

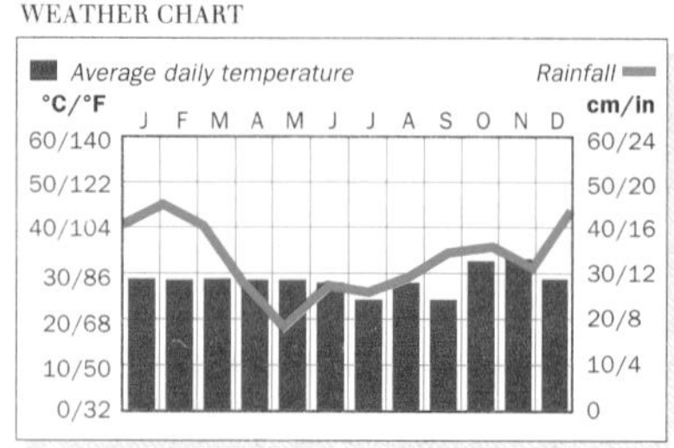

Although average humidity exceeds 90%, the climate is pleasantly warm. The mean annual temperature is 84°F. The October–March hurricane season brings many violent storms.

COMMUNICATIONS

There is an airstrip on Funafuti

5 ships 15,800 dwt

THE TRANSPORTATION NETWORK

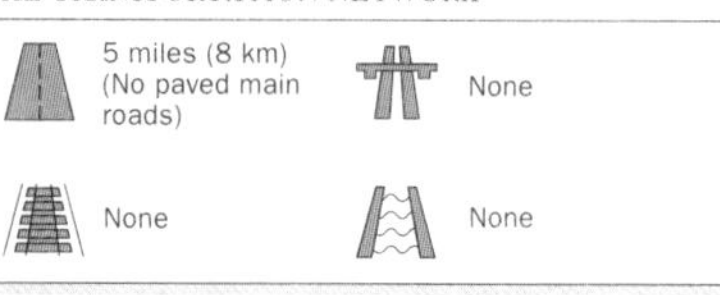

A ferry links the atolls. There are air links with Kiribati and Fiji. Funafuti and Nukufetau have deep-water berths.

TOURISM

976 visitors

Little change from year to year

MAIN OVERSEAS ARRIVALS

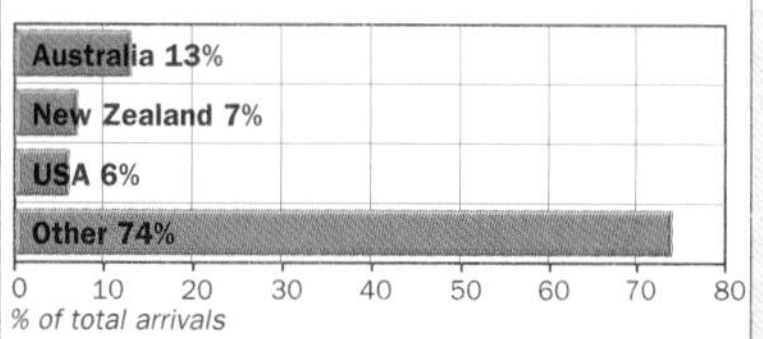

Unspoiled and lapped by some of the world's warmest waters, these remote coral atolls have few visitors. Tourism plans focus round the recently paved airstrip and Taiwanese investment in Tuvalu's only hotel, on Funafuti.

PEOPLE

Tuvaluan, Kiribati, English

943 people per sq. mile

THE URBAN/RURAL POPULATION SPLIT

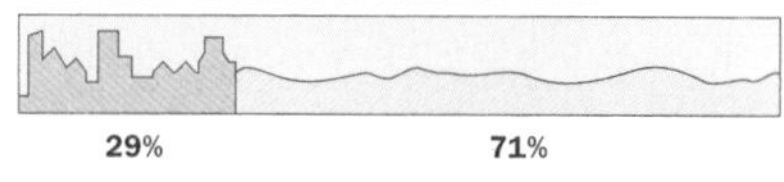

RELIGIOUS PERSUASION

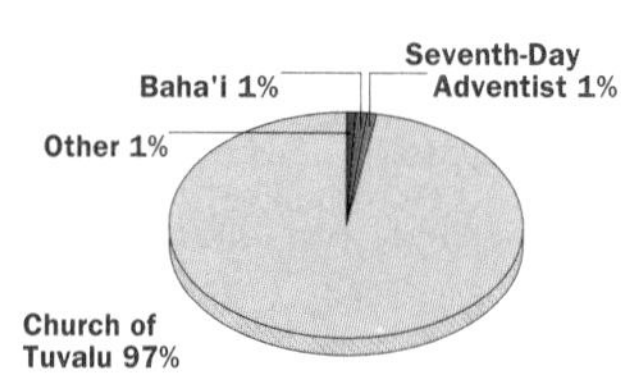

Around 95% of Tuvaluans are Polynesian. Their ancestors came from Tonga and Samoa 2,000 years ago. Nui atoll has Micronesian influences. There is an I-Kiribati community on Funafuti; many Tuvaluans who worked in Kiribati took local wives. All nine islands are inhabited. However, over 40% of the population now lives on Funafuti, pushing its population density to almost 4,000 per sq. mile. Life is still communal, traditional and hard. Droughts are common and fresh water is precious. About 80% of people depend on subsistence farming, digging special pits out of the coral to grow most of the islands' limited range of crops. Fishing is also important, and Tuvaluans have a reputation as excellent sailors. Some 2,000 Tuvaluans work overseas, many in Nauru's phosphate mines, others as merchant seamen.

***Tuvalu's soil** is porous, but sufficiently fertile to support coconut palms, pandanus and salt-tolerant plants. Fresh water supply is limited.*

POLITICS

1997 HM Queen Elizabeth II

THE STATE OF THE PARTIES

Parliament 12 members

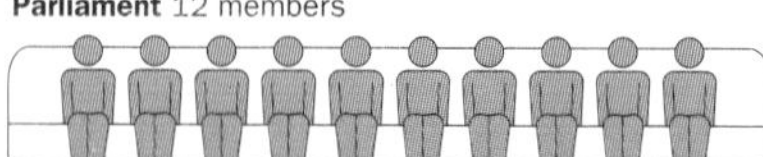

There are no political parties. All members are Independent candidates

The 12 MPs, elected every four years, are independents who work in loose political associations. The prime minister, an MP elected by parliament, works with a cabinet of up to four other MPs. After the 1993 elections, MPs were evenly divided between the two men who had dominated politics for most of the post-independence period, Tomasi Puapua and Bikenibeu Paeniu. After a second general election, Puapua pulled out of the premiership contest. Paeniu was then defeated by Kamuta Laatasi, BP Oil's manager in Tuvalu. Day-to-day administration is in the hands of elected councils on each island.

WORLD AFFAIRS

Agreements have been signed with Taiwan, Korea and the USA allowing their boats to exploit Tuvalu's fish-rich 3.2 million sq. mile exclusive economic zone in return for licensing fees. British criticism of the government's economic policy and Tuvaluan attacks on the pace of UK aid disbursements have strained relations with the former colonial power since 1990.

AID

$7m (receipts)

Not available

With import costs more than 400 times export earnings, aid is crucial to Tuvalu. Most importantly, in 1987 a trust fund was set up, with $A41 million in grants from Australia, New Zealand and the UK, to provide a regular income for Tuvalu. The first two are still major donors. The UK is reducing its aid as support from Taiwan and Japan grows.

DEFENSE

There are no armed forces

Not available

Tuvalu has no military. Internal security is the responsibility of the small police force.

T

ECONOMICS

$46m

1.46 Australian dollars

SCORE CARD

- ❑ WORLD GNP RANKING.......................191st
- ❑ GNP PER CAPITA..............................$530
- ❑ BALANCE OF PAYMENTS.......................Deficit
- ❑ INFLATION...8%
- ❑ UNEMPLOYMENT.................................Low

STRENGTHS

Exclusive economic zone: a source of income, through fishing license fees, and jobs; possible mineral potential. Regular income from trust fund. Sustainable subsistence economy.

WEAKNESSES

World's smallest economy. Physical isolation. Few exports: copra, stamps, garments. Few potential new income sources. Dependence on imports and aid. Remittances set to fall as Nauru phosphate mines nearly worked out.

EXPORTS

Tuvalu does not publish export figures by country of destination

IMPORTS

UK 5%

Japan 3%

New Zealand 11%

Australia 41%

Other 40%

CHRONOLOGY

The former Ellice Islands, together with the Gilbert Islands, were annexed by the UK in 1892.

- ❑ **1974** Islanders vote to separate from Micronesian Gilbertese.
- ❑ **1978** Ellice Islands become independent Tuvalu.
- ❑ **1987** Tuvalu Trust Fund set up.
- ❑ **1993** MPs fail to agree on prime minister after September elections. Second elections called. Kamuta Laatasi becomes prime minister.

HEALTH

1 per 1,750 people

Malaria, diarrheal, infectious and parasitic diseases

Concerted efforts since independence to improve healthcare facilities and programs have cut the incidence of communicable diseases. However, infant mortality rates remain high and life expectancy, at 59 years, is still well below the Pacific average of 71 years.

RESOURCES

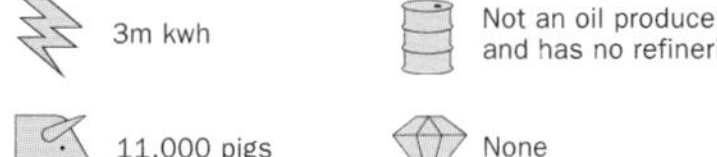

3m kwh

Not an oil producer and has no refineries

11,000 pigs

None

Tuvalu's resource potential lies solely in the waters of its 3.2 million sq. miles exclusive economic zone (EEZ). Its rich fish stocks are being exploited mainly by foreign boats in return for licensing fees. However, Japan has donated fishing boats to Tuvalu and deep-water fishing is being developed. Hopes of valuable mineral reserves have been raised by the discovery of an undersea mountain in the EEZ. Solar energy is being developed to cut the use of petrol for power generation. Fuel accounts for about 14% of import costs.

ENVIRONMENT

None

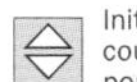

Initiatives counterbalanced by population pressure

Efforts to protect the environmentally fragile atolls include reafforestation and solar energy projects. On Funafuti, population pressure is leading to overfishing in the atoll lagoon. The "greenhouse effect" is a major concern since climate changes attributed to it are blamed for a steep rise in cyclone frequency. Any rise in sea levels induced by global warming would quickly drown the atolls.

MEDIA

There is no censorship of the media

PUBLISHING AND BROADCAST MEDIA

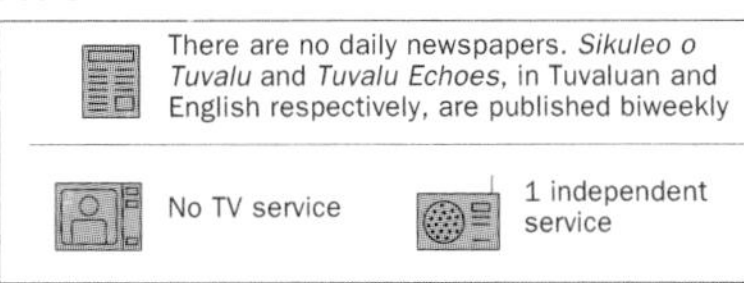

There are no daily newspapers. *Sikuleo o Tuvalu* and *Tuvalu Echoes*, in Tuvaluan and English respectively, are published biweekly

No TV service

1 independent service

Two biweekly papers and a religious monthly, *Te Lama*, are the only publications.

WEALTH

Small wealth disparities

CONSUMER GOODS OWNERSHIP

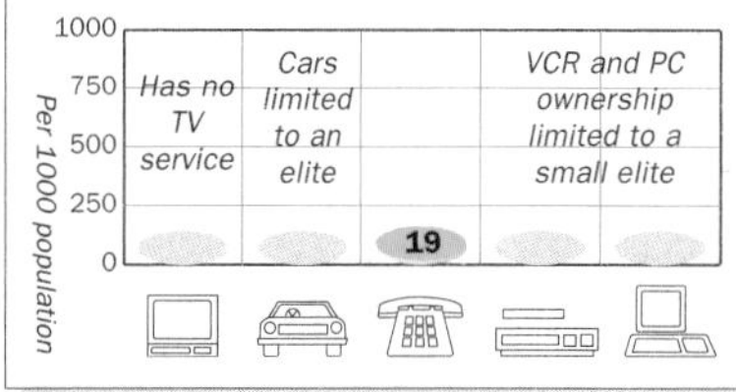

Although living standards are very low, traditional social support systems mean extreme poverty is rare. Most people rely on subsistence agriculture and fishing, supplemented by remittances from expatriate Tuvaluans.

TUVALU

Total Area : 26 sq. km (10 sq. miles)

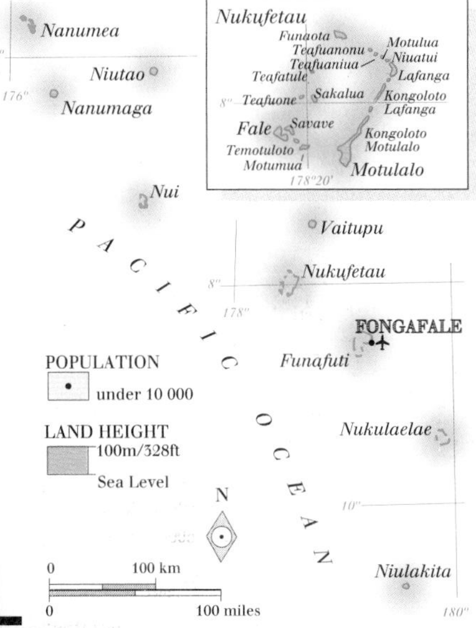

CRIME

Tuvalu does not publish prison figures

Little change from year to year

Crime is minimal and the result mainly of alcohol-related violence, particularly during the weekends.

EDUCATION

95%

Each island has a primary school. The secondary school and a marine training school are based on Funafuti. There are 20 state-funded students at the University of the South Pacific.

WORLD RANKING

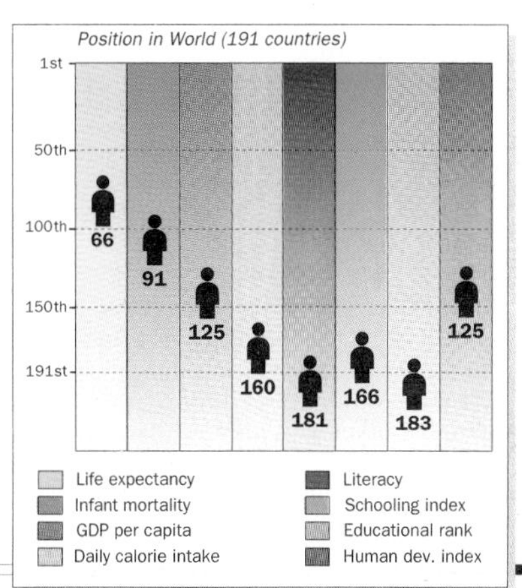

T

UGANDA

OFFICIAL NAME: Republic of Uganda **CAPITAL:** Kampala
POPULATION: 18.7 million **CURRENCY:** New Uganda shilling **OFFICIAL LANGUAGE:** English

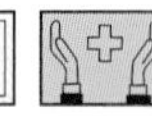

AN EAST AFRICAN COUNTRY of fertile upland plateau and mountains, Uganda has outlets to the sea through Kenya and Tanzania. Its history from independence in 1962 until 1986 was one of ethnic strife. Since 1986, under President Museveni, peace has been restored and steps taken to rebuild the economy and democracy.

Kampala, Uganda's capital. *It lies in the country's most populated region close to Lake Victoria, the world's third-largest lake.*

CLIMATE

WEATHER CHART

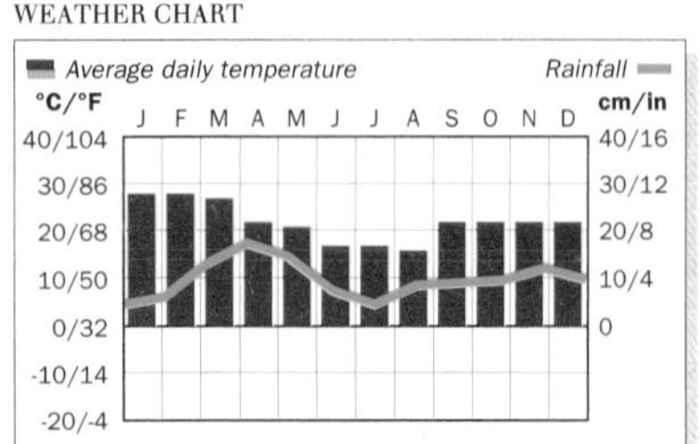

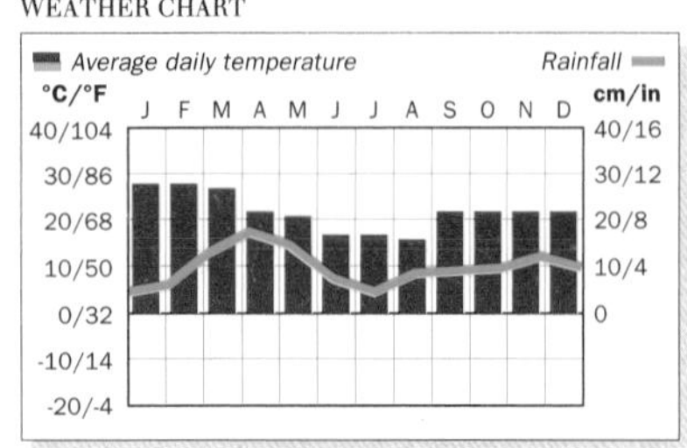

Altitude and the influence of Lake Victoria moderate Uganda's equatorial climate. Spring is the wettest season.

COMMUNICATIONS

Entebbe International
122,000 passengers

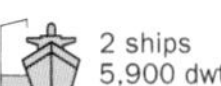
2 ships
5,900 dwt

THE TRANSPORTATION NETWORK

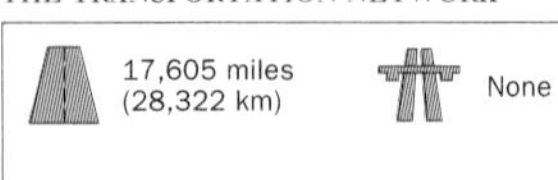
17,605 miles (28,322 km)

None

764 miles (1,230 km)

Lake Victoria

The government is rebuilding the transportation infrastructure with the help of international aid.

TOURISM

82,151 visitors

Up 11% in 1992

MAIN OVERSEAS ARRIVALS

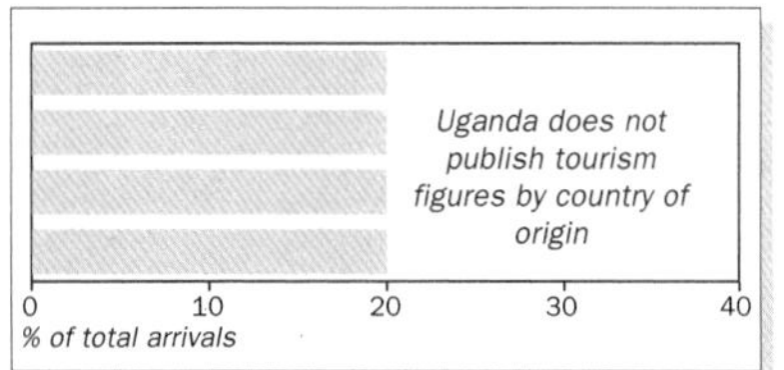

The tourist industry is recovering with the return of stability. Visitors are mainly high-spending independent travelers. Major attractions are Uganda's lakes and mountains, notably the rugged Ruwenzori range, better known as the Mountains of the Moon.

PEOPLE

Luganda, Nkole, Chiga, Lango, Acholi, Teso, Lugbara, English

207 people per sq. mile

THE URBAN/RURAL POPULATION SPLIT

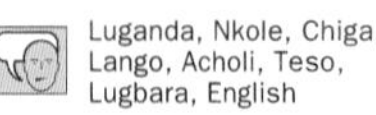

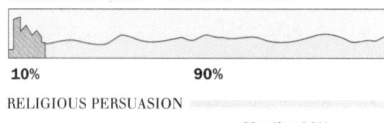

10% 90%

RELIGIOUS PERSUASION

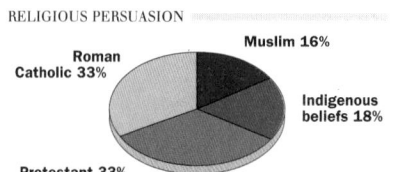

Roman Catholic 33%
Muslim 16%
Indigenous beliefs 18%
Protestant 33%

The predominantly rural population consists of 13 main ethnic groups. Traditional animosities, manipulated by ex-presidents Amin and Obote, underlay the ethnic conflict which has marred Uganda's history. Since 1986, President Museveni has worked hard for reconciliation. In 1993, he allowed the restoration of Uganda's four historical monarchies.

POLITICS

1995

THE STATE OF THE PARTIES

National Resistance Council 278 members

The National Resistance Council is to remain as the legislative body until elections take place, following the expected drafting of a new constitution

Uganda is due to return to multiparty democracy in 1995. Since 1986, President Museveni has run a "no-party democracy," with political parties represented in a broadly based government, but banned from campaigning. Overcoming ethnic tension is now the main issue. In the 1970s and 1980s, ethnic conflict destroyed the economy and resulted in the death of almost one million Ugandans. The new constitution will involve a federal system with boundaries based on the old kingdoms. The hope in Uganda is that political parties will also broaden their traditional ethnically based support and that the military, key power brokers in the past, will stay out of politics.

UGANDA

Total Area : 235 880 sq. km (91 073 sq. miles)

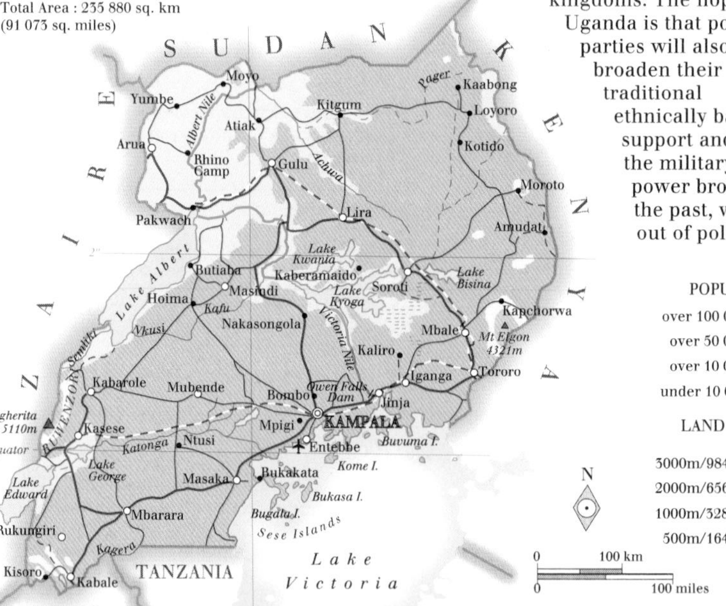

U

WORLD AFFAIRS

GATT

Relations with Sudan and Rwanda are strained. Internal conflicts in both countries have resulted in a large influx of refugees into Uganda. Occasional border tensions have led to incursions by the Zairian military. Relations with Tanzania and Kenya are improving; the three nations are discussing reforming the former East African Community.

AID

 $525m (receipts)  Down 5% in 1991

Aid, mainly from the World Bank and the IMF, has been rising since 1986, encouraged by Uganda's adoption of economic liberalization and private sector investment policies. Aid has focused on balance of payments support and the rehabilitation of the key transportation sector.

CHRONOLOGY

Uganda's ancient kingdoms were combined in a British protectorate, the "jewel" in Britain's crown, from 1893 to independence in 1962.

- ❑ **1962–1971** Milton Obote in power.
- ❑ **1971–1986** Ethnic strife. Economic collapse first under Idi Amin, then from 1980, under Obote.
- ❑ **1986** President Museveni in power. Ethnic strife ends. Moves toward democracy.

DEFENSE

 $73.29m  Down 1% in 1991

Since 1986, the military's political role has been downgraded. The National Resistance Army, the official armed force, is being reduced in size and its ethnic base broadened. The pre-1986 army, dominated by northern Acholi and Langi groups, was responsible for many atrocities under Amin's rule. Security in border areas is the priority.

ECONOMICS

 $3.1bn  1,131.73 new Uganda shillings

SCORE CARD

- ❑ World GNP Ranking........................122nd
- ❑ GNP per Capita...............................$190
- ❑ Balance of Payments....................$-118m
- ❑ Inflation.......................................23.3%
- ❑ Unemployment....Widespread underemployment

Strengths
Agriculture. Coffee brings in 93% of export earnings. Potential for more export crops. Road system is being repaired. Pro-investment policies.

Weaknesses
Recent ethnic conflict has left a generation lacking skills. Coffee vulnerable to world price fluctuations. High transportation costs.

EXPORTS

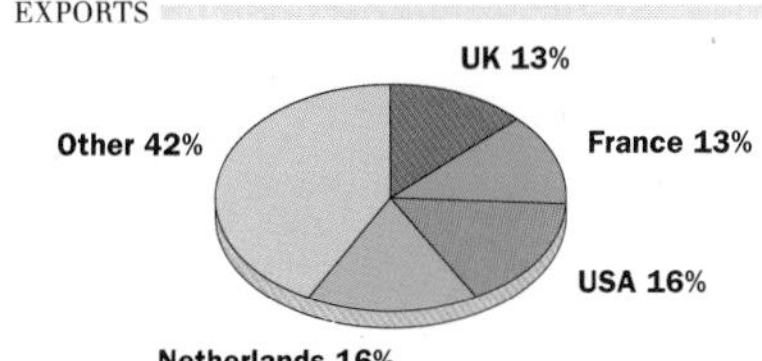

IMPORTS

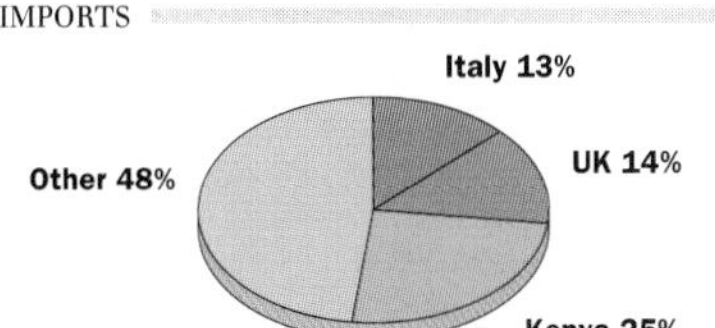

RESOURCES

 603m kwh (capacity 162,000 kw)  Not an oil producer and has no refineries

4.2m cattle, 1.8m sheep, 460,000 pigs  Copper, cobalt, tin apatite, magnetite, tungsten, gold

Mineral resources are varied but barely exploited. Uganda has sizeable copper deposits. The mines, closed under Obote, are now being reopened. Gold and cobalt mining is also due to resume and oil exploration is under way. Hydroelectric output is being expanded, notably at Owen Falls, with the aim of replacing 50% of oil imports.

ENVIRONMENT

 8% (4% partially protected)  Rising environmental awareness

Uganda's priority is economic reconstruction, but ecological issues are not ignored. Construction of a huge hydroelectric power station at the Kabalega Falls was canceled recently, following strong local environmental objections to the choice of site.

MEDIA

 The press has been free since 1986. Comment likely to cause ethnic tension is banned

PUBLISHING AND BROADCAST MEDIA

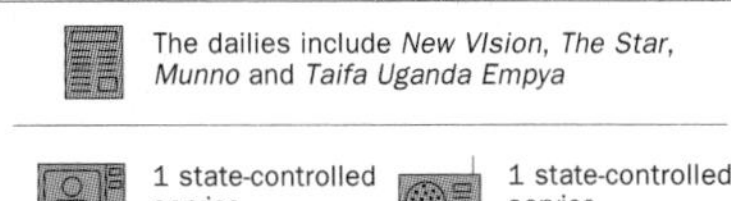

The dailies include *New Vision, The Star, Munno* and *Taifa Uganda Empya*
1 state-controlled service
1 state-controlled service

The 13 daily and weekly papers cover the political and religious spectrum; eight are published in English. Only the *New Vision* is government-controlled.

CRIME

 10,080 prisoners  Low levels; fairly stable from year to year

Crime levels are far lower than in neighboring Kenya, although theft in Kampala is a growing problem. Uganda now has one of the best human rights records in Africa.

EDUCATION

 48%

Education is not compulsory and all schools charge fees. Only 10% of pupils go on to secondary school.

HEALTH

 1 per 22,291 people  Malaria, respiratory and diarrheal diseases, measles

The health system, badly hit by war and the loss of foreign personnel, is slowly being rebuilt. AIDS-related illness is a major problem in some areas.

WEALTH

 Most Ugandans live a subsistence existence

CONSUMER GOODS OWNERSHIP

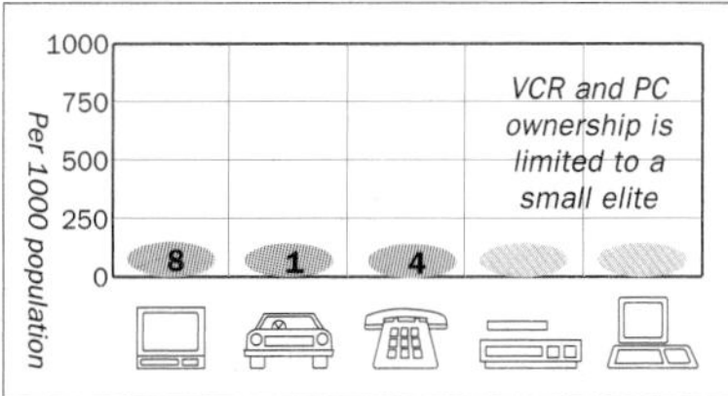

Uganda has a small, but growing middle class. Those close to the government form the wealthiest group.

WORLD RANKING

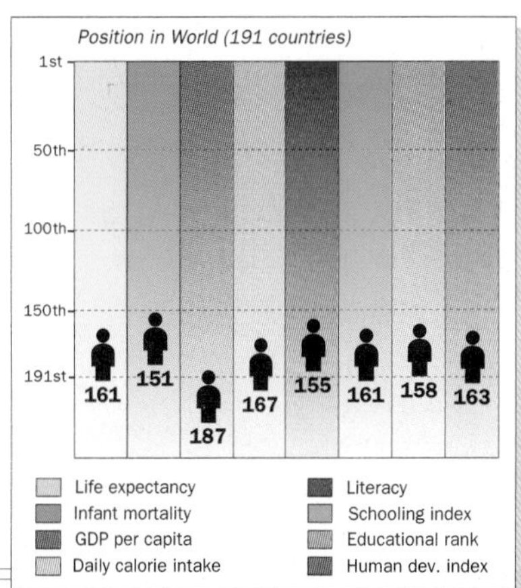

U

UKRAINE

OFFICIAL NAME: Ukraine **CAPITAL:** Kiev
POPULATION: 51.9 million **CURRENCY:** Karbovanets **OFFICIAL LANGUAGE:** Ukrainian

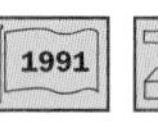

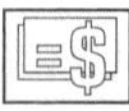

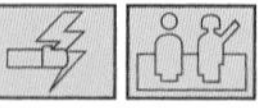

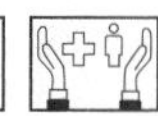

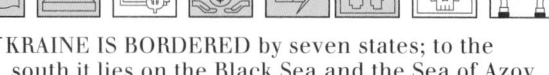

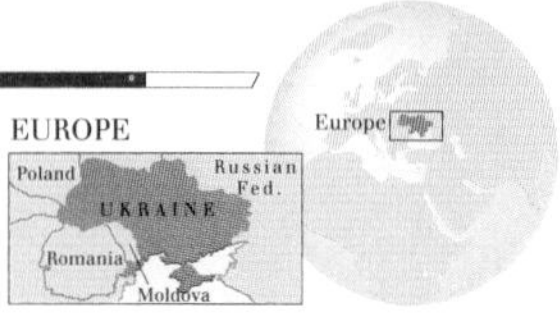

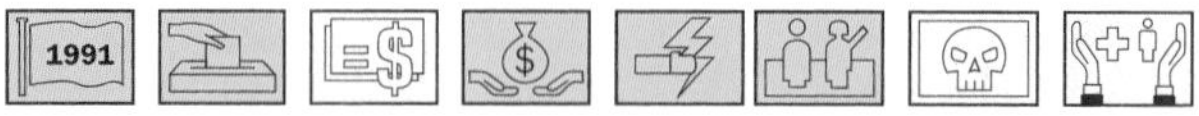

UKRAINE IS BORDERED by seven states; to the south it lies on the Black Sea and the Sea of Azov. An independent Ukrainian state was established in 1918, but was overrun in the same year by Soviet forces from the east and Polish forces from the west. In 1991, Ukraine again became an independent state. The country has historically been divided between the nationally conscious and Ukrainian-speaking west (which was not under Russian occupation until Word War II) and the east, which has a large ethnic Russian population.

***View toward the Cathedral** of the Assumption in Kharkiv. Many Ukrainian cities are equipped with elaborate trolley networks.*

CLIMATE

WEATHER CHART

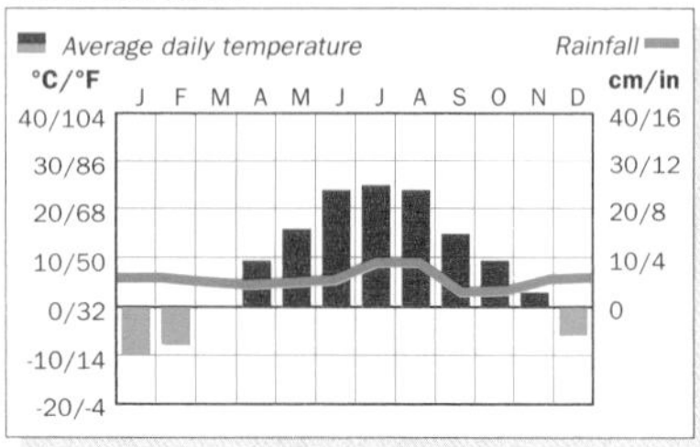

Average daily temperature — Rainfall
°C/°F — cm/in
J F M A M J J A S O N D
40/104, 30/86, 20/68, 10/50, 0/32, -10/14, -20/-4
40/16, 30/12, 20/8, 10/4, 0

Ukraine has a continental climate, with the exception of the southern coast of Crimea, which has a Mediterranean climate. There are four distinct seasons.

COMMUNICATIONS

Boryspiel Intl, Kiev

2 ships
4,800 dwt

THE TRANSPORTATION NETWORK

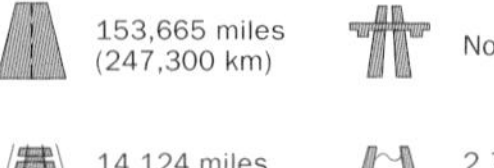

Transportation within major cities includes Soviet-style subway systems and trolley networks. There are plans to improve the main highway linking Kiev and L'viv. The rail system is in need of extensive upgrading.

TOURISM

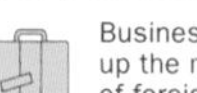
Businessmen make up the majority of foreign visitors

No significant change in tourism figures

MAIN OVERSEAS ARRIVALS

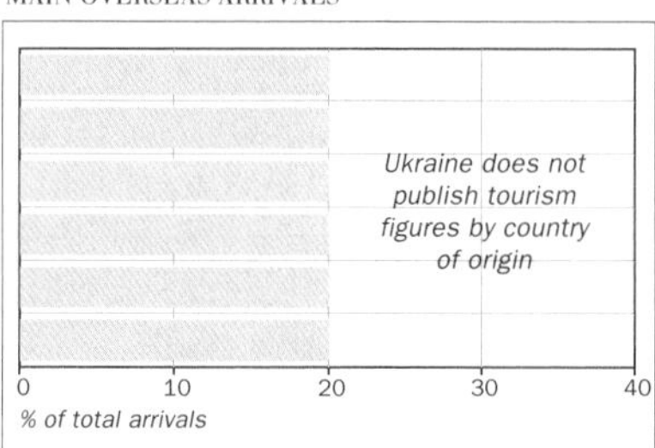

Among potential tourist attractions are warm resort areas in Crimea and the south, and the Carpathian Mountains. The government has maintained a highly regulated system of managing tourism. Western visitors are deterred by the expensive Soviet-style hotels they are required to use.

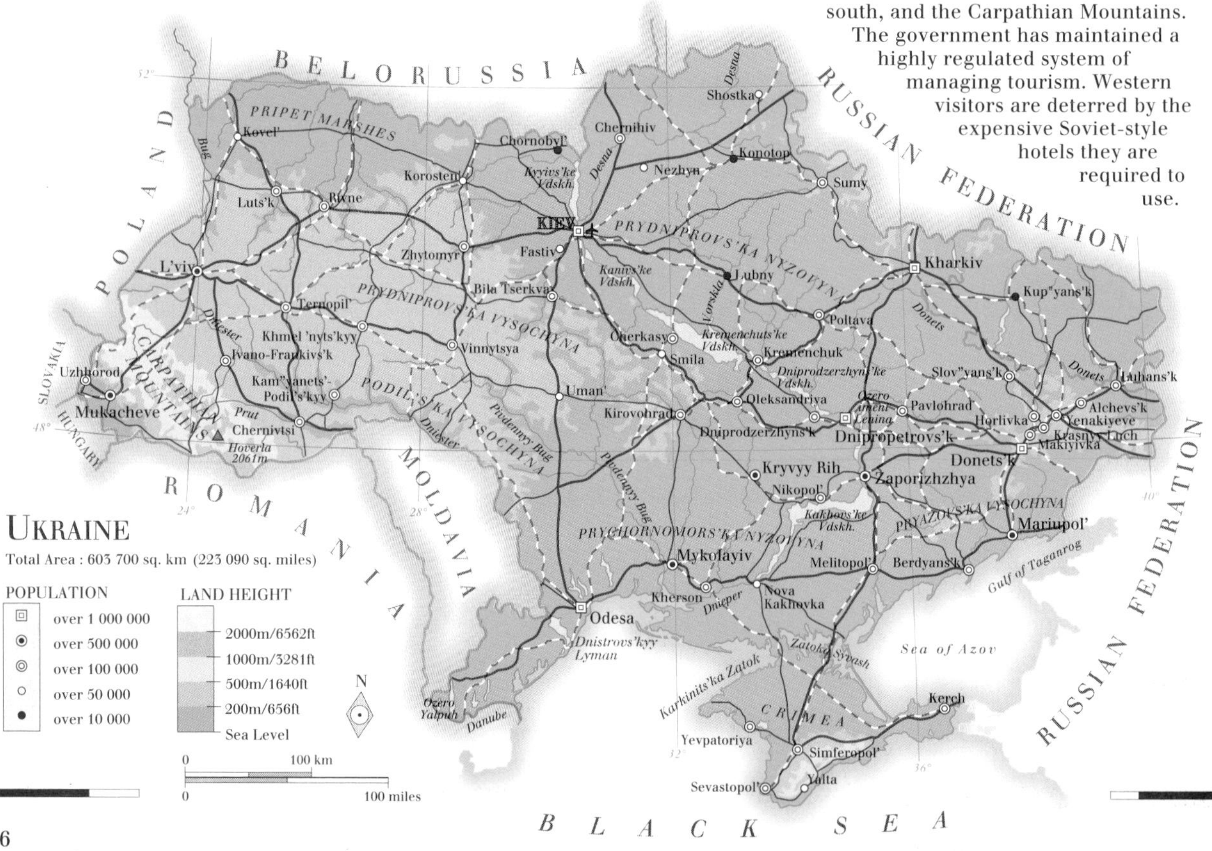

UKRAINE

Total Area : 603 700 sq. km (223 090 sq. miles)

POPULATION
- over 1 000 000
- over 500 000
- over 100 000
- over 50 000
- over 10 000

LAND HEIGHT
- 2000m/6562ft
- 1000m/3281ft
- 500m/1640ft
- 200m/656ft
- Sea Level

0 100 km
0 100 miles

PEOPLE

 Ukrainian, Russian, Tartar

 223 people per sq. mile

THE URBAN/RURAL POPULATION SPLIT

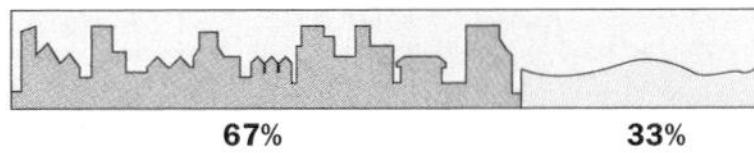

RELIGIOUS PERSUASION

Ukrainian Orthodox is the dominant religion of the Ukraine. It has three branches, those under the Moscow and Kiev Patriarchates and the Autocephalous branch. There are also small Catholic, Protestant and Jewish groups

ETHNIC MAKEUP

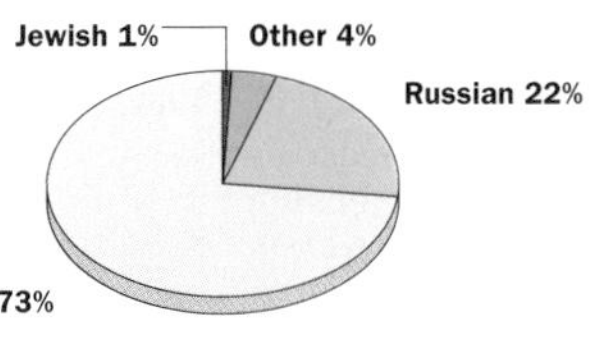

In the cities and countryside of western Ukraine, Ukrainians make up over 90% of the population. However, in several of the large cities of the east and south, Russians form a majority. The large Russian population in these areas is a legacy of 19th-century industrialization, and more recent migration during the Soviet-era. At independence, most Russians accepted Ukrainian sovereignty. However, tensions are now rising as both groups adopt more extremist nationalist policies.

In Crimea, relations between Russians, ethnic Ukrainians and Tartars are becoming increasingly tense. Crimea has a majority Russian population, but is also home to the Tartars, a Turkic-speaking people. The Tartars were deported *en masse* to the eastern USSR under Stalin in 1945. They have been returning to the region since 1990 and now comprise roughly 10% of its population.

POPULATION AGE BREAKDOWN

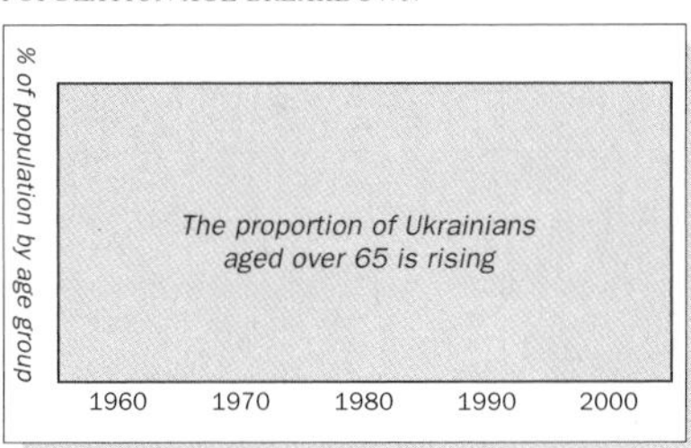

Leonid Plyushch, *chairman of the Ukrainian parliament.*

Leonid Kravchuk, *president 1991–1994. He tried to postpone democratic elections.*

WORLD AFFAIRS

The main foreign policy threat to Ukraine is Russia. Ukrainian commentators have expressed the fear that if the Crimea or pro-Russian regions in Ukraine demand unification with Russia, this could spark a civil war in Ukraine with the risk of Russian intervention. Alternatively, should extremist Russian nationalists, such as Vladimir Zhirinovsky, come to power in Moscow, it is possible they would try to incorporate Ukraine into Russia.

Ukraine's internal instability and the increasingly aggressive stance of Russia toward it has been a source of concern to the US government. The Clinton administration has demonstrated a growing willingness to support the state both politically and economically. Germany and other European states also support Ukraine as a buffer to Russia. However, it is unlikely that this support will extend to accepting Ukrainian EU membership.

POLITICS

 1998

Leonid Kuchma

THE STATE OF THE PARTIES

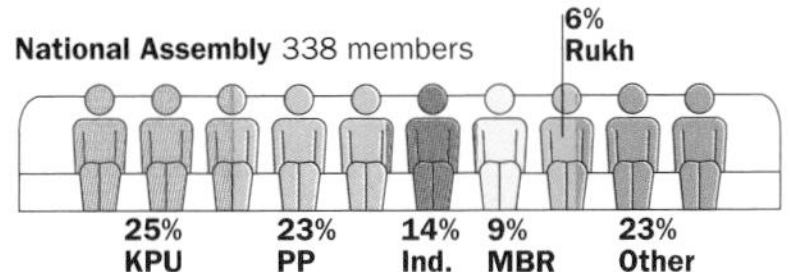

KPU = Ukrainian Communist Party **PP** = Party of Power **Ind.** = Independents **MBR** = Interegional Block for Reform **Rukh** = Ukrainian People's Movement **Other** = Ukrainian Socialist Party, Ukrainian Peasants Party, Congress of Ukrainian Nationalists, Ukrainian Republican Party, Crimean Communist Party, Ukrainian National Assembly, Ukrainian Democratic Party, New Wave

Ukraine has been a multiparty democracy since 1991.

MAIN POLITICAL ISSUES

Economic reform

Western and central Ukraine are generally more in favor of economic reform than the eastern regions, which prefer continued support for their subsidy-dependent economy. This division was illustrated by the strong showing of the communist and socialist parties in eastern regions in the 1994 elections.

Relations with Russia

Western Ukrainians are vehement in their opposition to closer ties with Russia, while such ties are supported by their eastern counterparts. In a referendum in March 1994, citizens in the Donetsk region voted for closer links with the CIS, and in favor of introducing Russian as a joint official language. Likewise, in Crimea, voters have demanded dual Russian–Ukrainian citizenship and closer economic integration.

Potential destabilization

Some commentators fear that the growing antagonism between nationalist and anti-nationalist groups could spark a civil war. Conflict could arise in Crimea, which is dominated by ethnic Russians. In 1994, the Crimean parliament issued another declaration of independence from Kiev. Kiev responded with an ultimatum, but failed to act on its threat. The situation remains unresolved. Tension is rising in other regions with large Russian minorities, such as the Donbass.

PROFILE

Ukraine has yet to develop a strong democratic party system. Individuals – generally local potentates, such as enterprise directors or collective farm chairmen – are very influential. Around 30 parties competed in the 1994 elections, while more than half of the candidates ran as independents. The dominant figure in politics from 1990 to 1994 was Leonid Kravchuk. He became president at independence in 1991, but was ousted in the 1994 presidential elections by Leonid Kuchma.

CHRONOLOGY

In 1240, Kiev was conquered by the Mongols. The Ukrainian Cossacks later came under the domination of Lithuania, Poland and Russia.

- **1918** Independent Ukrainian state established in the aftermath of the collapse of Russian and Austrian empires. Brest-Litovsk Treaty signed with Germany.
- **1919** Red Army invades. Ukrainian Soviet Socialist Republic is proclaimed.
- **1920** Poland invades. Western Ukraine comes under Polish occupation.
- **1922** USSR founded; Ukrainian SSR is one of founder-members.
- **1922–1930** Cultural revival results from "Ukrainianization" policy adopted by Lenin to pacify national sentiment.

U

CHRONOLOGY *continued*

- **1932–1933** "Ukrainianization" policy reversed. Stalin's government induces man-made famine to eliminate Ukraine as source of opposition to his regime. Seven million die.
- **1939** Carpatho-Ukraine declares its independence from Slovakia. Soviet Union invades Poland and incorporates ethnic Ukrainian territories of Poland into the Ukrainian SSR.
- **1941** Germany invades USSR. Activities of Ukrainian nationalists suppressed by Germans. Seven and a half million Ukrainians die by end of World War II.
- **1942** Nationalists form Ukrainian Insurgent Army, which wages war against both Germans and Soviets.
- **1954** Crimea ceded to Ukrainian SSR.
- **1972** Widespread arrests of intellectuals and dissidents by Soviet state. Shcherbitsky, a Brezhnevite, replaces moderate reformer Shelest as head of Communist Party of Ukraine (CPU).
- **1986** World's worst nuclear disaster takes place at Chernobil' nuclear power station north of Kiev.
- **1989** First major coalminers' strike in Donbass. Pro-Gorbachev Ivashko becomes head of CPU.
- **1990** July: Ukrainian parliament declares the Ukrainian SSR to be a sovereign state. Leonid Kravchuk replaces Ivashko as leader.
- **1991** January: Crimea declared an autonomous republic within Ukrainian SSR. August: government declares full independence, conditional on approval by referendum. December: over 90% of population approve move in referendum. CPU banned.
- **1993** Major strike in Donbass results in costly settlement, which exacerbates budget deficit and stimulates inflation. Karbovanets enters hyperinflation. CPU re-established at congress in Donetsk.
- **1994** First President of Crimea, Yuri Meshkov, elected on platform of Crimean independence and closer ties with Russia. March–April: first democratic elections in independent Ukraine take place.

AID

Further aid is dependent on economic reform

No significant change

Ukraine has received assistance from Western countries in training a new administrative elite, and in modernizing telecommunications infrastructure.

DEFENSE

$4.3bn

No significant change in 1992

Defense spending as % GDP (scale 0–40): **0.4%**

UKRAINIAN ARMED FORCES

5,700 main battle tanks (1,100 T-54, 400 T-62, 2,500 T-64,1300 T-72)
217,000 personnel
Black Sea Fleet controlled jointly with Russia
3,000 personnel
900 combat aircraft (MiG-21, MiG-23, MiG-27)
171,000 personnel
166 ICBMs

Ukraine is still a member of the CIS, but is consolidating its own forces because of fear about rising Russian willingness to intervene in other ex-Soviet republics. The main focus of defense spending is the modernization of weaponry. Ukraine has recently brought out a new version of the Soviet T-72 tank and is planning to update its fleet.

In late 1993, the Ukrainian parliament agreed to ratify the START-1 nuclear disarmament treaty. In March 1994, Ukraine transferred a number of nuclear warheads to Russia, in accordance with the agreement.

The long-smouldering dispute between Ukraine and Russia over control of the Black Sea Fleet has not yet been decisively resolved. Ukraine now seems likely to reverse its decision to give up ownership of the Fleet in return for debt relief from Russia. Further negotiations were held in 1994, but with little tangible result.

ECONOMICS

$189.5bn

18,231 karbovanets

SCORE CARD

- WORLD GNP RANKING..........27th
- GNP PER CAPITA..........$2,326
- BALANCE OF PAYMENTS..........Large deficit
- INFLATION..........79.3%
- UNEMPLOYMENT..........2%

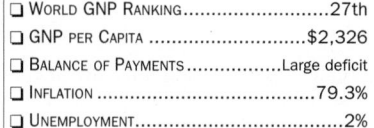

EXPORTS

Other 18%
Ex-Soviet republics 82%

IMPORTS

Other 18%
Ex-Soviet republics 82%

STRENGTHS
Well-educated work force. Good public transportation infrastructure within cities. Technological potential, especially in aerospace and computers; many research institutes in these areas. Long-term potential for extensive grain and food export. Minerals.

WEAKNESSES
Failure to reform centrally planned economy following collapse of Soviet Union. Hyperinflation. Anti-reform political elites. Inefficient, subsidized manufacturing industries. Corruption.

PROFILE
While privatization of large enterprises has scarcely begun, there has been some privatization of small industries in the larger cities. Many traders and street vendors have sprung up in Kiev and other major cities. Agriculture, however, is still hindered by an entrenched collective farm system.

ECONOMIC PERFORMANCE INDICATOR

UKRAINE : MAJOR BUSINESSES

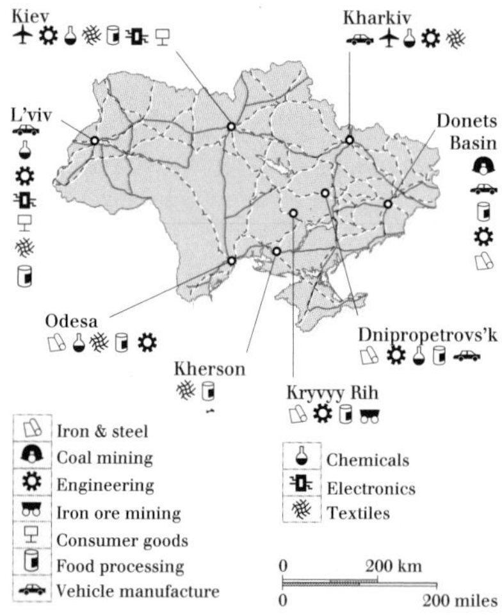

U

RESOURCES

 251bn kwh

 Small-scale oil production

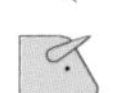 24.6m cattle, 19.4m pigs, 8.4m sheep and goats

 Coal, iron, oil, natural gas, manganese, lignite, peat, mercury

ELECTRICITY GENERATION

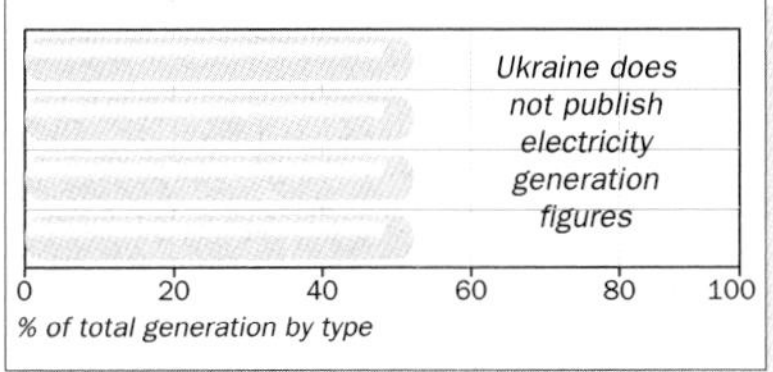

Ukraine's most successfully exploited fuel resource is coal. Most coal is mined in the Donets'k basin or the Donbass, around Donets'k and Luhans'k. There are also smaller reserves in western Ukraine, in the L'viv-Volhynia coal basin. Production has, however, been declining since the 1970s, and the industry has been hit by strikes since 1989. In 1992, production stood at 134 million tons a year.

Production of natural gas has also been declining since the 1970s. There are some uranium deposits, but Ukraine does not yet have the facilities to produce fuel for its own nuclear reactors. Oil production has not been carried out on a large scale, although there are significant untapped reserves in the Donbass and in the Carpathian Mountains in the west.

UKRAINE : LAND USE

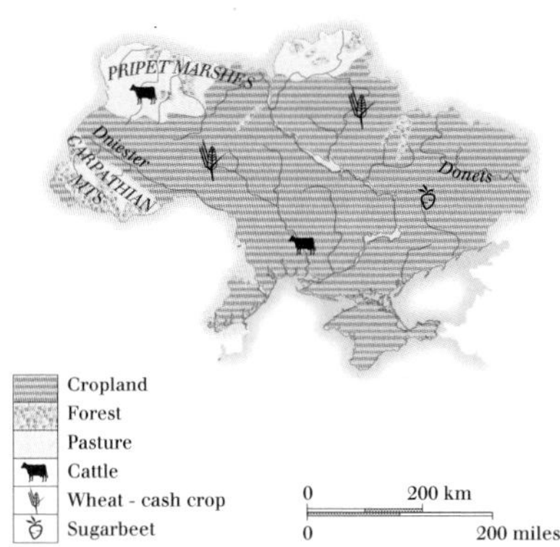

ENVIRONMENT

 0.8%

 Widespread contamination from Chernobil' incident

ENVIRONMENTAL TREATIES

No

No

No

No

As a result of the Chernobil' nuclear disaster – the worst nuclear accident in history – four millon Ukrainians now live in dangerously radioactive areas and 12% of arable land is contaminated. Children who live in areas with high radiation levels are sent by the state to summer camps in uncontaminated areas.

The government has now turned back to nuclear production because of the rising cost of Russian oil imports. In 1994, reactors from the Chernobil' plant were still being used to produce nuclear power.

Industrial pollution is widespread. Air pollution from coal and chemicals industries in the Donbass region remains particularly high.

CRIME

 Ukraine does not publish prison figures

 Most crime is rising

CRIME RATES

Most types of crime have increased since the demise of the USSR

The deteriorating state of the economy, and a general breakdown in law and order following the collapse of the Soviet system, have led to a steady increase in crime rates. The police suffers from underfunding and has proved unable to control the increase. Corruption is now rampant in all areas of the economy. The mafia is thought to be even more influential in Ukraine than in neighboring Russia. Foreigners are targets for muggings.

HEALTH

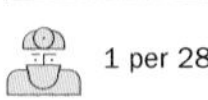 1 per 288 people

Cerebrovascular and heart diseases, cancer

0 *Health spending as % GNP* 25

25% *(includes education spending)*

The health ministry keeps a registry of all those affected by the Chernobil' disaster, including the 134,000 young army recruits who participated in the initial clean-up operation.

WEALTH

 In 1991, 41% of Ukrainians were living below the poverty line

CONSUMER GOODS OWNERSHIP

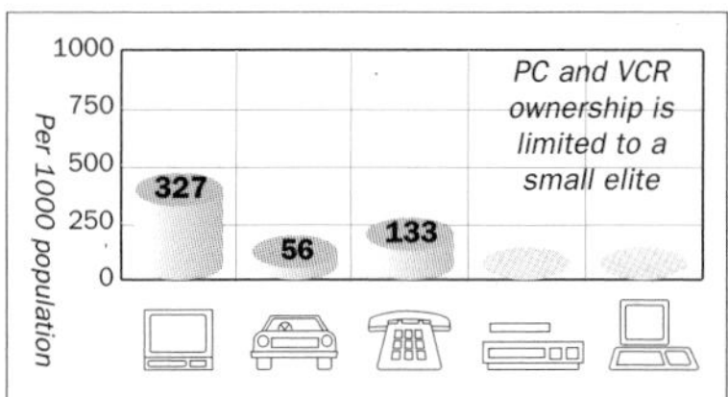

Ukraine has a small well-off elite, which has grown rich from business, corruption or mafia activities.

EDUCATION

 96%

0 *Education spending as % GNP* 25

25% *(includes health spending)*

THE EDUCATION SYSTEM

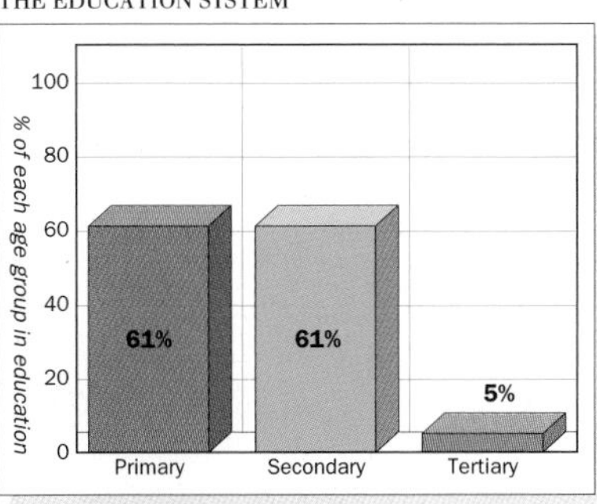

In eastern regions, most university teaching is in Russian; in western ones, in Ukrainian. Some schools in the west no longer teach Russian.

MEDIA

 There is no tradition of investigative journalism

PUBLISHING AND BROADCAST MEDIA

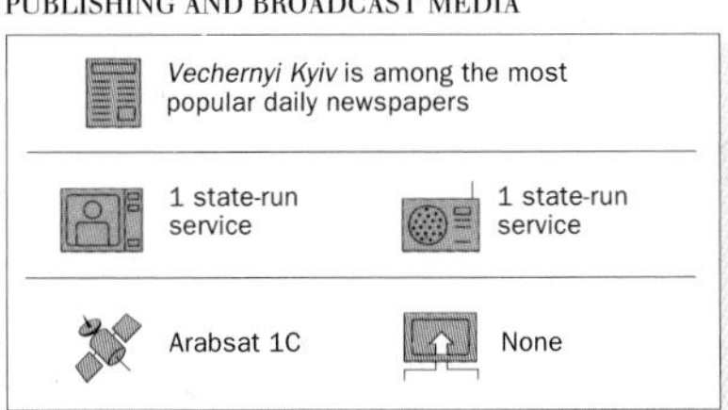

Vechernyi Kyiv is among the most popular daily newspapers
1 state-run service
1 state-run service
Arabsat 1C
None

A number of independent, mass-circulation newspapers are now published. Local TV stations reflect regional political differences.

WORLD RANKING

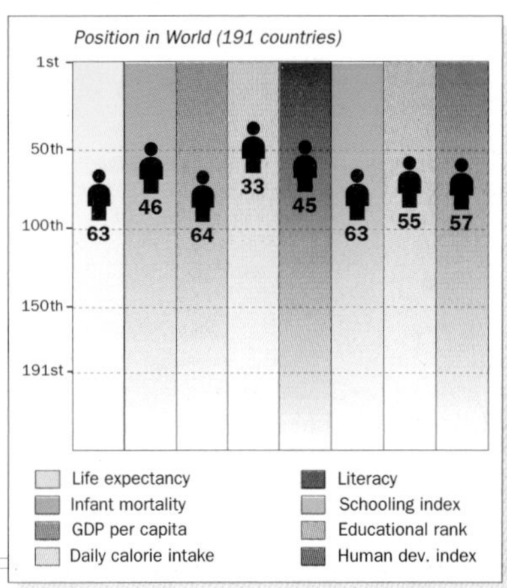

UNITED ARAB EMIRATES

OFFICIAL NAME: United Arab Emirates **CAPITAL:** Abu Dhabi
POPULATION: 1.9 million **CURRENCY:** UAE dirham **OFFICIAL LANGUAGE:** Arabic

MIDDLE EAST

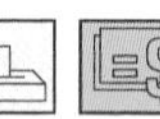

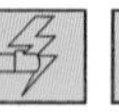

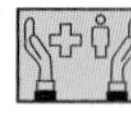

THE ARAB WORLD'S only working federation, the United Arab Emirates (UAE) shares borders with Oman, Saudi Arabia and Qatar, as well as a disputed maritime boundary with Iran. The UAE is mostly semi-arid desert relieved by occasional oases. The cities, watered by extensive irrigation systems, have lavish greenery. The UAE's economic prosperity once relied on pearls, but it is now a sizeable gas and oil exporter, and has a growing services sector.

CLIMATE

WEATHER CHART

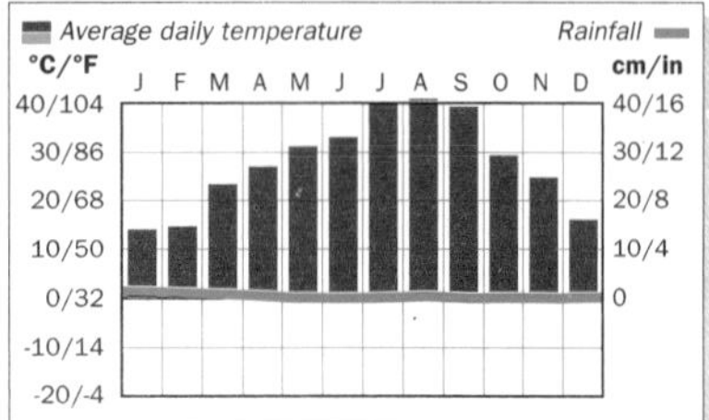

Although rainfall is minimal, summers are humid. Sand-laden *shamal* winds often blow in winter and spring.

COMMUNICATIONS

Abu Dhabi International 1.01m passengers

THE TRANSPORTATION NETWORK

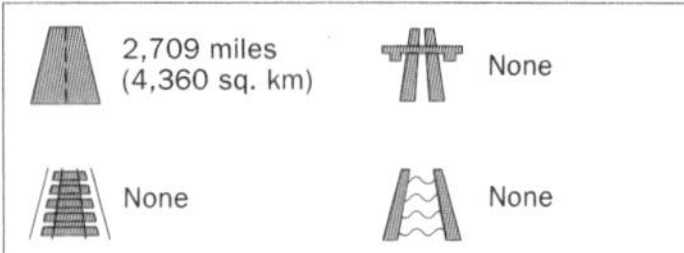

The roads are good, though littered with wrecked cars. Five of the seven emirates have international airports.

TOURISM

345,000 visitors

MAIN OVERSEAS ARRIVALS

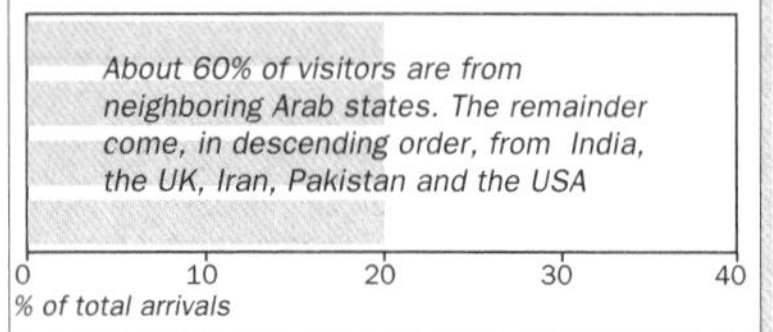

About 60% of visitors are from neighboring Arab states. The remainder come, in descending order, from India, the UK, Iran, Pakistan and the USA
0
10
20
30
40
% of total arrivals

Until the mid-1980s, tourism was minimal. Led by Dubai, the UAE has now launched initiatives to attract visitors during the northern winter for sunshine, heritage, water sports, desert safaris and duty-free shopping.

PEOPLE

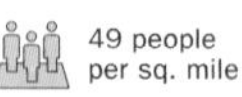

49 people per sq. mile

THE URBAN/RURAL POPULATION SPLIT

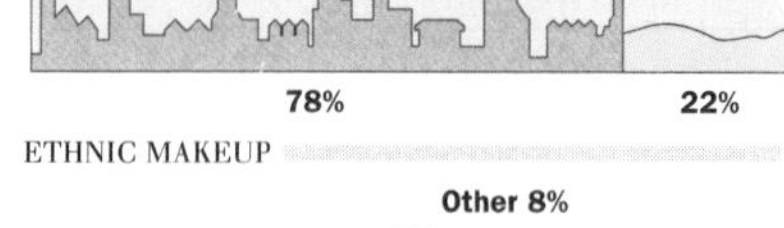

ETHNIC MAKEUP

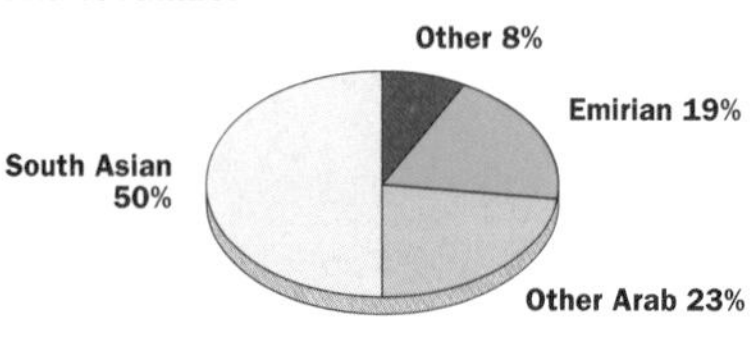

UAE nationals are largely city dwellers, with Abu Dhabi and Dubai the dominant centers. They are outnumbered by expatriates who flocked to the country in the 1970s during the oil boom; UAE nationals make up one-fifth of the population.

UAE citizens are mostly conservative Sunni Muslims of Bedouin descent. There is a Shi'a community in Dubai with links to Iran. The Western expatriate community is permitted a virtually unrestricted lifestyle. Islamic fundamentalism, however, is a growing force among the young.

Poverty is rare in the UAE. The government remains the biggest employer. Women in theory enjoy equal rights with men.

POLITICS

Not applicable

THE STATE OF THE PARTIES

Federal National Council 40 members

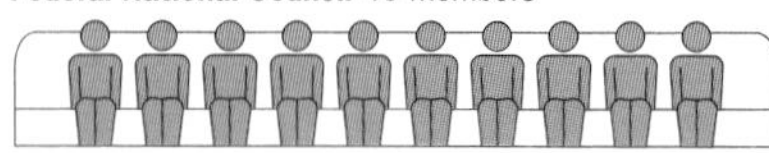

The 40 members are appointed by the emirates. There are no political parties

Supreme Council of Rulers 7 members

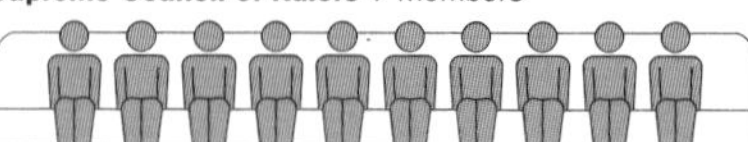

The Supreme Council of Rulers, composed of the rulers of the 7 emirates, has overall authority

The UAE's seven emirates – Abu Dhabi, Dubai, Sharjah, Ras al Khaimah, Ajman, Umm al Qaiwain and Fujairah – are dominated by their ruling families. The main personalities are the ruler of Abu Dhabi and UAE President Sheikh Zayed, and the Maktoum brothers who control Dubai.

President Zayed has relaunched the advisory Federal National Council in response to criticism about the lack of democracy. The growth of Islamic fundamentalism is also a concern. The freedoms granted to Westerners have aroused some anger but, for economic reasons, are unlikely to be withdrawn.

UNITED ARAB EMIRATES

Total Area : 83 600 sq. km (32 278 sq. miles)

POPULATION
over 100 000
under 10 000

LAND HEIGHT
1000m/3281ft
500m/1640ft
Sea Level

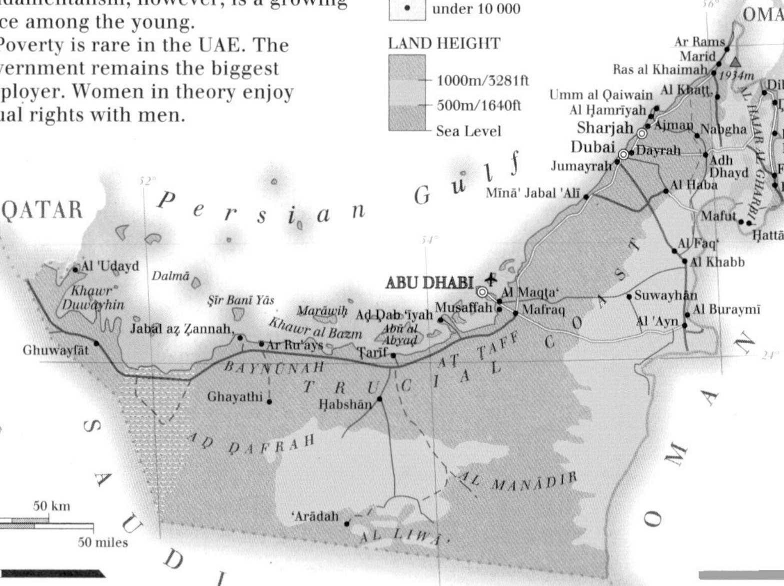

WORLD AFFAIRS

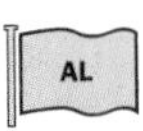

The UAE is well known as an advocate of moderation within the Arab world. It maintains close links with most OECD economies, especially the UK and the USA. In 1992, conflict flared when Iran seized control of three islands in the Strait of Hormuz. Attempts are being made to settle the dispute through diplomacy.

AID

 $588m (donations)  Down 34% in 1991

Once a generous donor to developing countries, the UAE's contributions have fallen because of weak energy prices.

DEFENSE

 $1.6bn  Up 3% in 1991

At 55,000, the UAE's forces are too small and too scattered among the emirates to pose a threat to the traditional rulers. Although they are well equipped, training is limited and recruits largely drawn from other Arab states and the Indian subcontinent. During the 1991 Gulf crisis, UAE air bases were used by UN forces for strikes against Iraq.

ECONOMICS

 $32.8bn  3.67 UAE dirhams

SCORE CARD

❑ WORLD GNP RANKING	52nd
❑ GNP PER CAPITA	$17,500
❑ BALANCE OF PAYMENTS	$4bn
❑ INFLATION	1.1%
❑ UNEMPLOYMENT	0.4%

STRENGTHS

Oil and gas reserves are the fourth biggest in OPEC. Service industries have been developed to support the economy when the wells run dry.

WEAKNESSES

Lack of skilled labor. Most raw materials and foodstuffs have to be imported. Water resources scarce as ground water is depleted.

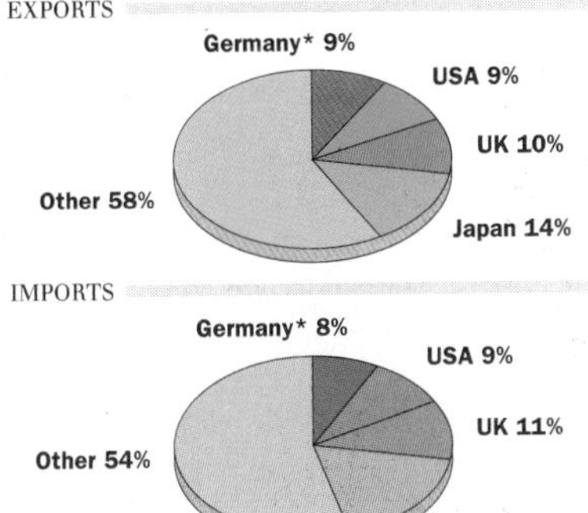

RESOURCES

 13.6bn kwh (capacity 4.66m kw)  2.3bn b/d (reserves 98,100,000,000 bbl)

 580,000 goats, 260,000 sheep, 115,000 camels  Oil, natural gas

The UAE is a major exporter of crude oil and natural gas; Abu Dhabi in particular has abundant reserves. Oil production is the largest economic sector and accounts for 89% of export revenues. Mīnā' Jabal 'Alī in Dubai is the world's largest man-made port and has attracted companies from 58 countries.

ENVIRONMENT

 None 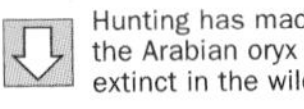

Despite its harsh desert climate, the UAE has a rich variety of plant and animal life; rare species, however, are threatened by hunting.

MEDIA

 Western print media are censored for taste and political correctness

PUBLISHING AND BROADCAST MEDIA

There are 8 daily newspapers. The leading Arabic newspaper is *Al-Ittihad. Emirates News* is its English-language counterpart

1 state-owned, 2 independent services

2 state-owned, 1 independent service

Radio and TV are state-run; satellite TV is unrestricted. The privately owned press follows censorship guidelines.

CRIME

 The UAE does not publish prison figures  Up 9% in 1987

Street crime and muggings are rare. However, Dubai has a reputation as a transit point for drugs.

***An oasis village**, inland from Fujairah, now accessible through a well-developed network of new roads.*

CHRONOLOGY

The UAE was influenced by the Portuguese and the Ottomans, but British control became dominant in the 19th century.

- ❑ **1971** The UK withdraws as protecting power and the UAE federation is formed.
- ❑ **1991** UAE offers bases to Western forces after Kuwait is invaded.

EDUCATION

 68%

UAE citizens enjoy free education from nursery to college. The government funds overseas student scholarships.

HEALTH

 1 per 1,619 people  Circulatory and respiratory diseases, cancer

A high-standard system of primary health care is in place for all UAE citizens, with hospitals able to perform most operations.

WEALTH

 Poverty is rare in the UAE

CONSUMER GOODS OWNERSHIP

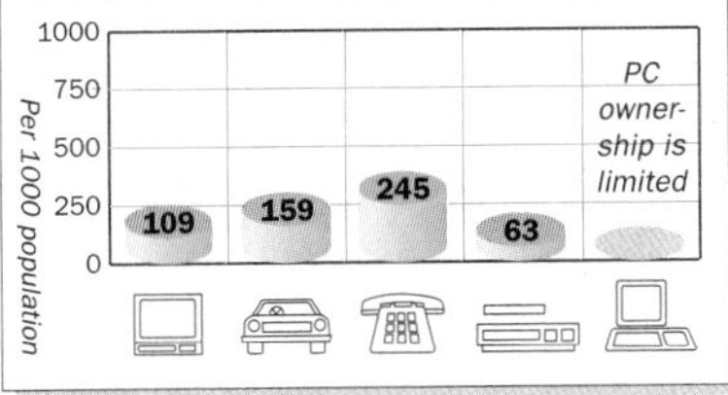

UAE nationals have one of the highest incomes per capita in the world. There is no income tax and oil revenues subsidize public services. Government policies encourage entrepreneurs.

WORLD RANKING

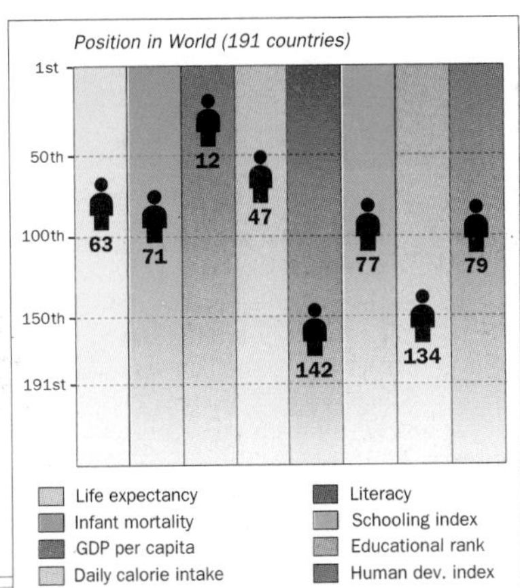

U

UNITED KINGDOM

OFFICIAL NAME: United Kingdom of Great Britain and Northern Ireland **CAPITAL:** London
POPULATION: 57.7 million **CURRENCY:** Pound sterling **OFFICIAL LANGUAGE:** English **OVERSEAS TERRITORIES:** 15

LYING IN NORTHWESTERN EUROPE, the United Kingdom (UK) occupies the major portion of the British Isles. It includes the nations of England, Scotland and Wales, the consitutionally distinct region of Northern Ireland and several outlying islands. Its only land border is with the Republic of Ireland. The UK is separated from the European mainland by the English Channel and North Sea. To the west lies the Atlantic Ocean. Most of the population lives in towns and cities and, in England, is fairly well distributed. The most densely populated region is the southeast. Scotland is the wildest region, with the Highlands less populated today than in the 18th century. The UK became a member of the EEC (later the EU) in 1973. Most of its trade is now with its European partners, although membership in the UN Security Council gives it a prominent role in international diplomacy.

CLIMATE

WEATHER CHART

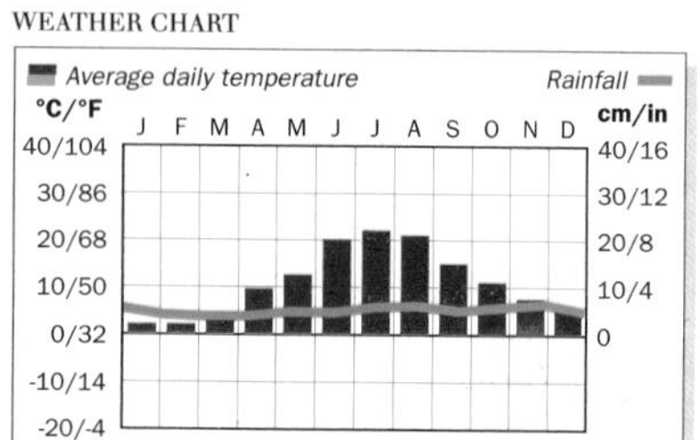

The UK has a generally mild, temperate, and highly changeable climate. Rain, regarded as synonymous with Britain's weather, is fairly well distributed throughout the year. The west is generally wetter than the east, and the south warmer than the north. The most extreme weather conditions occur in the mountains of Scotland, Wales and northern England.

COMMUNICATIONS

Heathrow, London
42.65m passengers

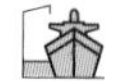
447 ships
6.62m dwt

THE TRANSPORTATION NETWORK

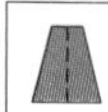
221,529 miles (356,517 km)

1,922 miles (3,093 km)

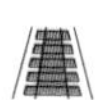
10,304 miles (16,583 km)

1,988 miles (3,200 km)

Since the 1960s, Britain has built an extensive system of expressways, including the world's busiest beltway, the M25. The main link to Scotland is being upgraded to expressway standard. British Rail was reorganized in 1993 ready for its flotation on the stock market. In 1994, the Channel Tunnel opened, although Britain has yet to build a high-speed rail link to London.

TOURISM

18.5m visitors

Up 8% in 1992

MAIN OVERSEAS ARRIVALS

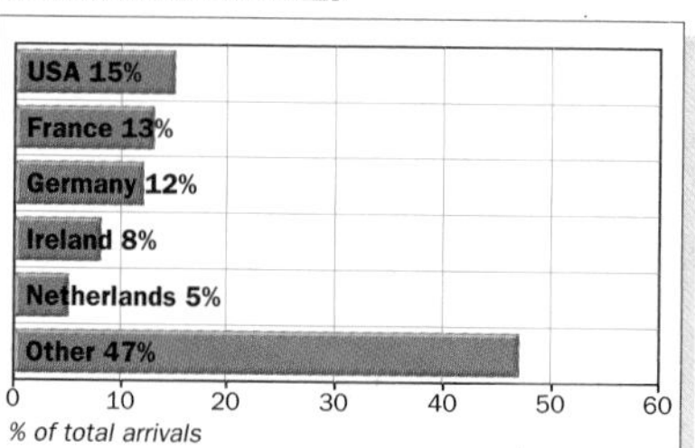

Tourism is among the UK's most important industries and a growing source of employment. London, with its art galleries, theaters and historical buildings, remains the major destination. However, many visitors choose to bypass the capital and head straight for the Roman splendors of Bath, the Shakespearean theater of Stratford-upon-Avon, medieval York or the Highlands of Scotland. Americans are the main visitors to the UK, although fear of terrorism and recession in the USA have recently dissuaded some from making the trip.

View of Oxford, with the Clarendon Building and Sheldonian Theatre in the foreground. The 17th-century Sheldonian (right) was one of Sir Christopher Wren's first commissions.

PEOPLE

English, Welsh, Scottish, Gaelic

616 people per sq. mile

THE URBAN/RURAL POPULATION SPLIT

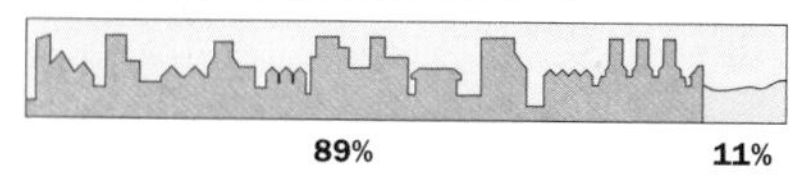

RELIGIOUS PERSUASION

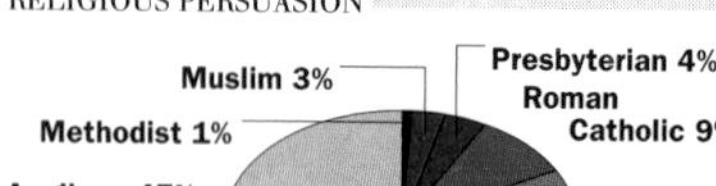
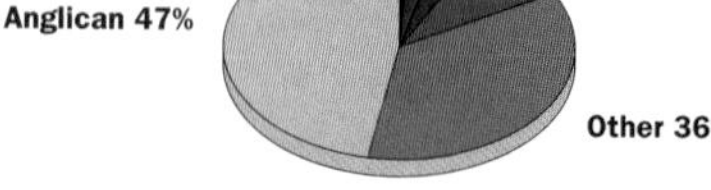

ETHNIC MAKEUP

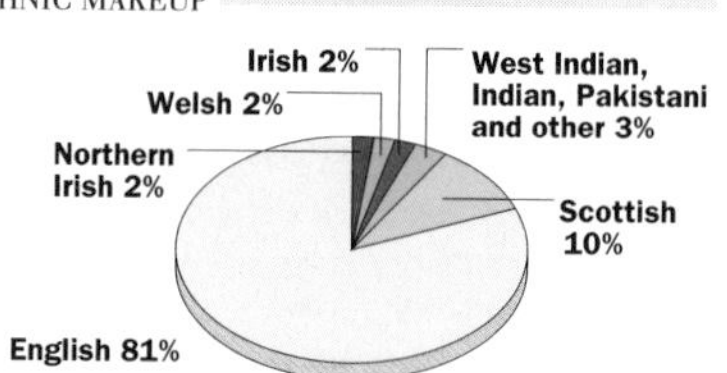

The UK is the 17th most populous state in the world. The Scottish and Welsh minorities are ethnically and culturally distinct. Both remain recognizable nations and the Scots retain their own legal and educational systems.

Britain's ethnic minorities account for less than 5% of the total population. Over 50% were born in Britain. The ethnic population is concentrated in the inner cities, where there are problems of deprivation and social stress. Women in the Bangladeshi community in particular, suffer from poor education and isolation from society. However, significant progress has been made in tackling racial disadvantage since the 1970s and there is very little support for racist politics.

Marriage is in decline in the UK. Over 30% of births now occur out of wedlock, compared with 12% in 1980. However, many of these births are to cohabiting couples. Around 17% of families with children under the age of 18 are one-parent families, compared with 6% in Italy and 25% in the USA.

POPULATION AGE BREAKDOWN

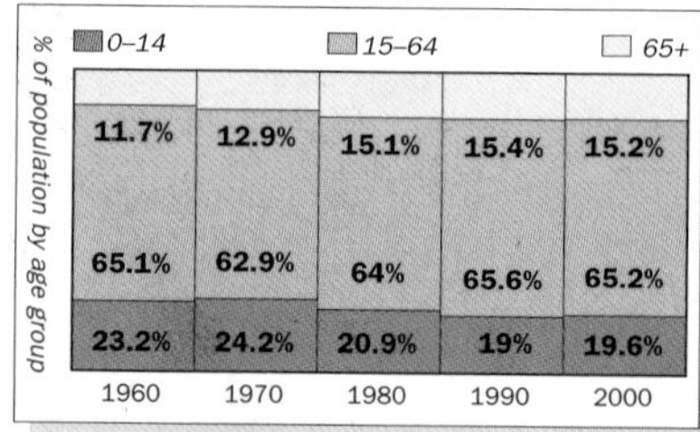

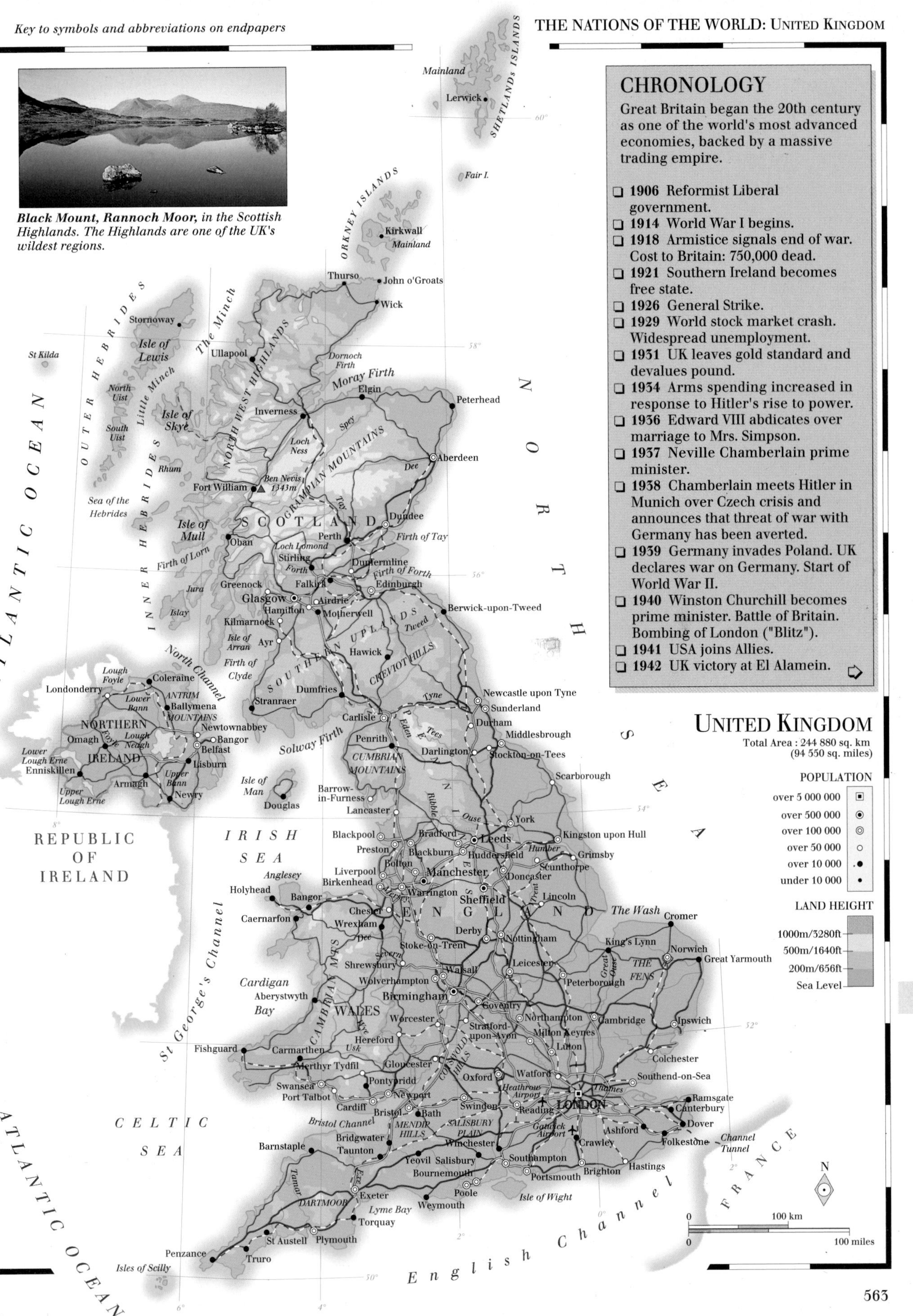

Black Mount, Rannoch Moor, *in the Scottish Highlands. The Highlands are one of the UK's wildest regions.*

CHRONOLOGY

Great Britain began the 20th century as one of the world's most advanced economies, backed by a massive trading empire.

- **1906** Reformist Liberal government.
- **1914** World War I begins.
- **1918** Armistice signals end of war. Cost to Britain: 750,000 dead.
- **1921** Southern Ireland becomes free state.
- **1926** General Strike.
- **1929** World stock market crash. Widespread unemployment.
- **1931** UK leaves gold standard and devalues pound.
- **1934** Arms spending increased in response to Hitler's rise to power.
- **1936** Edward VIII abdicates over marriage to Mrs. Simpson.
- **1937** Neville Chamberlain prime minister.
- **1938** Chamberlain meets Hitler in Munich over Czech crisis and announces that threat of war with Germany has been averted.
- **1939** Germany invades Poland. UK declares war on Germany. Start of World War II.
- **1940** Winston Churchill becomes prime minister. Battle of Britain. Bombing of London ("Blitz").
- **1941** USA joins Allies.
- **1942** UK victory at El Alamein.

CHRONOLOGY *continued*

- ❑ **1944** 6 June: D-Day launches invasion of German-occupied France.
- ❑ **1945** End of World War II. War costs 330,000 British lives. LP government comes to power on social welfare platform.
- ❑ **1946** Government begins nationalization of Bank of England, railroads, coal and utilities. Begins departure from former colonies.
- ❑ **1947** India granted independence.
- ❑ **1948** UK founder-member of UN Security Council. "Austerity Olympics" held in London. National Health Service established.
- ❑ **1949** UK founder-member of NATO.
- ❑ **1956** Suez crisis. UK intervenes in Suez Canal Zone but forced to withdraw by USA.
- ❑ **1957** US nuclear missiles accepted on UK soil.
- ❑ **1960** UK founder-member of EFTA.
- ❑ **1961** UK application to join EC rejected by French President De Gaulle.
- ❑ **1965** Winston Churchill dies.
- ❑ **1968** Abortion and homosexuality legalized.
- ❑ **1969** British troops sent into Ulster. Peace Wall between Protestant and Catholic communities erected.
- ❑ **1970** Age of majority cut to 18. CUP in power under Edward Heath. 8.8m work days lost in strike action.
- ❑ **1973** UK joins EEC. Oil crisis. Industry placed on three-day week following strikes by utility workers and miners.
- ❑ **1974** LP government, under Harold Wilson, concedes miners' demands and strikes end. High inflation.
- ❑ **1975** Margaret Thatcher becomes CUP leader. Referendum ratifies EEC membership. First North Sea oil pipeline in operation.
- ❑ **1976** "Cod War" with Iceland.
- ❑ **1979** CUP wins election.
- ❑ **1980** Anti-US Cruise missiles protests. Rising unemployment and inner-city riots.
- ❑ **1981** CUP launches privatization program.
- ❑ **1982** Unemployment three million. Argentina invades Falklands. Islands retaken by UK task force.
- ❑ **1983** Tax-cutting policies. CUP wins general election.
- ❑ **1985** Anglo-Irish Accord: attempt to resolve Ulster's "troubles."
- ❑ **1986** Financial services market deregularized ("Big Bang").
- ❑ **1987** CUP wins third election in a row. First black MP in Parliament.
- ❑ **1988** PanAm airliner blown up by terrorists over Lockerbie, Scotland.
- ❑ **1990** John Major takes over as CUP leader. UK joins Gulf War.
- ❑ **1992** CUP wins election.

POLITICS

1997

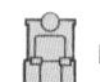
HM Queen Elizabeth II

THE STATE OF THE PARTIES

House of Commons 651 members

3% LDP

52% CUP — 42% LP — 3% Other

CUP = Conservative and Unionist Party **LP** = Labour Party **LDP** = Liberal Democratic Party **Other** = Ulster Unionists, Scottish National Party, Plaid Cymru

House of Lords 1,199 members

The House of Lords is an unelected body of spiritual, judicial, hereditary and life peers appointed by the Queen. 39% are Conservative peers, 10% Labour peers, 5% Liberal Democratic peers, 23% are independent and 23% have an unspecified allegiance

The UK is a multiparty democracy. The monarch holds no real power.

MAIN POLITICAL ISSUES

Europe

The question of whether the UK should pursue the goal of a Federal Europe has split the ruling CUP. The anti-EU faction is concerned that the EU is undemocratic and wasteful. The pro-EU faction believes that the UK has no choice but to follow the majority of European states who want federation, if it is to influence the nature of the UK's most important market.

The economy

There is now a broad consensus between the major parties on economic policy. The LP no longer believes in renationalizing privatized industries, and the CUP has toned down the pro-market rhetoric of the Thatcher years. However, the ruling CUP has been blamed for the recession and for raising taxes in 1994. Opinion polls suggest that both factors have led to a rise in support for the LP.

Health

The creation of an internal market in the National Health Service (NHS) has been opposed by doctors and voters. Many fear that the CUP may have plans to privatize the service. Most voters remain attached to the idea of an NHS that is free to all at point of use.

Northern Ireland (Ulster)

The most recent manifestation of sectarian conflict between Northern Ireland's Protestant and Catholic communities began in 1969. The Catholic community backs unification with the Irish Republic. The majority Protestant community wishes to remain part of the UK. Terrorism in the province by Catholic and Protestant groups has been widespread and the Catholic Provisional Irish Republican Army (IRA) took its campaign of terror to the British mainland. In 1994, both factions declared a ceasefire, pending negotiations with both the UK and Irish governments. This was greeted as a tentative, though positive step, although all four parties acknowledge that reaching a power-sharing agreement would be a long and painful process.

Margaret Thatcher, *prime minister 1979–1990; leader of the CUP 1975–1990.*

John Major, *leader of the CUP, became prime minister in 1990.*

John Smith, *LP leader from 1992, died suddenly of a heart attack in 1994. He was replaced by Tony Blair.*

PROFILE

Margaret Thatcher's 1979 election victory ushered in 15 years of CUP rule, and monetarist and privatization policies. The opposition LP lost four elections in a row, but moved to the political center, abandoning policies of high taxation and renationalization.

In 1990, Margaret Thatcher was forced from office and replaced by John Major, who won the elections of 1992. Neil Kinnock resigned as LP leader and was replaced by John Smith.

However, by 1994, Major's popularity had plummeted and the CUP lost heavily in local elections in May. LP leader John Smith died suddenly of a heart attack.

Vauxhall Cross, *a postmodern office building by Terry Farrel on the River Thames. Farrel has had more influence on London's skyline than any architect since Wren.*

WORLD AFFAIRS

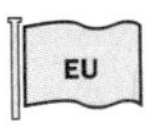

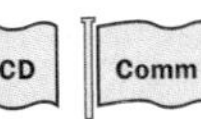

The UK owes much of its prominence in world affairs to its seat on the UN Security Council. However, since 1945, it has followed a largely US line in its foreign policy. It was a founder-member of NATO and maintained front-line troops in West Germany during the Cold War. In 1991, it was a major partner in UN Operation Desert Storm to evict Iraqi forces from Kuwait.

The UK signed the Maastricht Treaty in 1992, committing itself to eventual political and monetary union with its EU partners.

Relations with China over the hand-over of Hong Kong have been tense. Beijing has objected to British attempts to introduce democracy to the colony.

AID

 $3.2bn (donations) 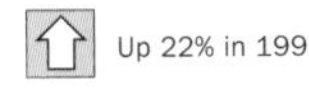 Up 22% in 1991

Britain gives rather less aid than the European average. Its current donations of 0.3% of GNP are well below the target 0.7% for industrialized nations. Current policy is to freeze the aid program until 1995 and to cut bilateral aid to countries in sub-Saharan Africa. Aid fell sharply during the 1980s. Three-quarters goes to developing countries; India and Bangladesh are the biggest recipients.

Aid is not a highly politicized issue in the UK. However, the country is home to some prominent NGOs, including Oxfam. The Voluntary Service Overseas (VSO) organization sends people to share their skills in developing countries. In 1985, the Live Aid rock concert in London highlighted the plight of Ethiopia's devastating famine.

DEFENSE

 $41.2bn  Down 2% in 1992

0 *Defense spending as % GDP* 40

4.2%

BRITISH ARMED FORCES

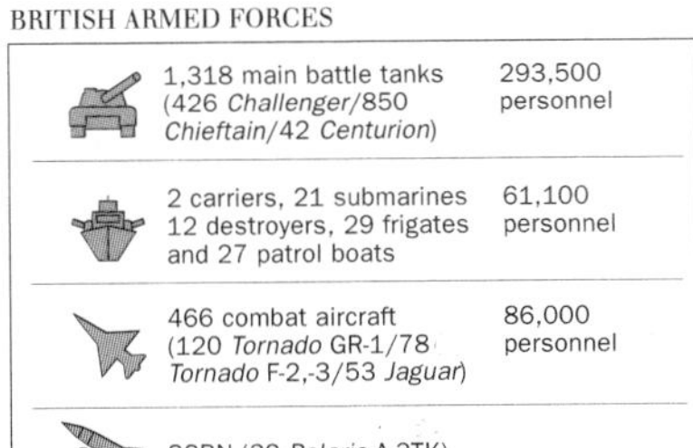

1,318 main battle tanks (426 *Challenger*/850 *Chieftain*/42 *Centurion*)	293,500 personnel
2 carriers, 21 submarines 12 destroyers, 29 frigates and 27 patrol boats	61,100 personnel
466 combat aircraft (120 *Tornado* GR-1/78 *Tornado* F-2,-3/53 *Jaguar*)	86,000 personnel
SSBN (32 *Polaris* A-3TK)	

The UK's defense spending as a proportion of GNP is one of the highest in the OECD. However, as a response to the end of the Cold War, the 1990 Options for Change program was implemented in 1993. The army and navy came in for the greatest cuts in personnel and equipment orders. The UK's independent nuclear deterrent was scaled down. The emphasis now is on creating rapid reaction forces and fulfilling the UK's UN commitments.

The UK is one of the world's leading arms exporters. Major buyers include Middle Eastern states and the booming economies of Southeast Asia.

ECONOMICS

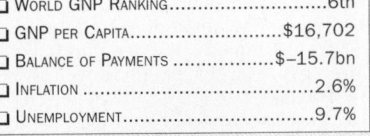

 $964bn  0.68 pounds sterling

SCORE CARD

- ❑ WORLD GNP RANKING........................6th
- ❑ GNP PER CAPITA..........................$16,702
- ❑ BALANCE OF PAYMENTS.................$-15.7bn
- ❑ INFLATION.......................................2.6%
- ❑ UNEMPLOYMENT...............................9.7%

EXPORTS

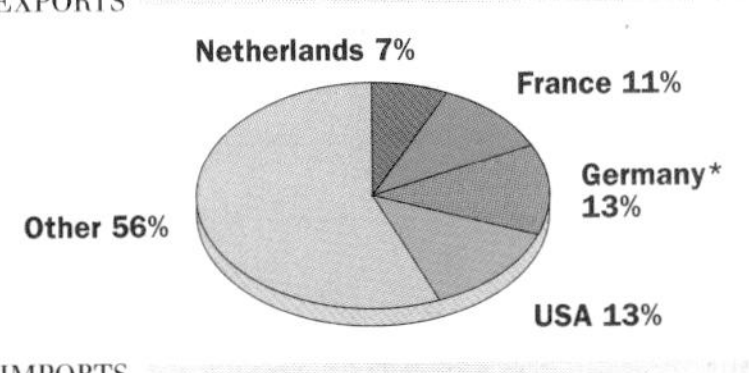

IMPORTS

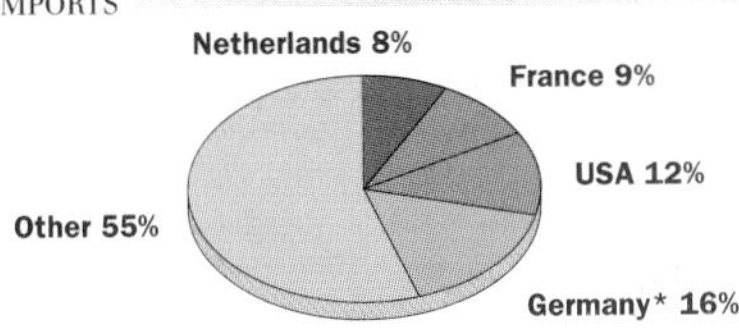

STRENGTHS

World leader in financial services, pharmaceuticals and defense industries. Successful aerospace sector. Precision engineering and high-tech sectors, including telecommunications. Strong energy sector based on North Sea oil and gas production. Flexible working practices and lower wage rates than France, Germany or Scandinavia. The EU's largest recipient of inward investment. Strong multinational sector, with companies such as Glaxo, ICI, RTZ, BAT and Hanson.

WEAKNESSES

Decline of some key manufacturing sectors since 1970s, including cars and household goods. Much of industry still working with outmoded machinery. Past propensity for inflation. High levels of consumer and government debt. Quick-return mentality of many investment decisions does not create the culture to sustain long-term growth.

PROFILE

Manufacturing is still the largest sector of the UK economy, although its importance has declined as the services and energy sectors have grown. During the 1980s, there was a sharp decline in heavy industries such as steel and engineering, located mostly in the Midlands and the North, while sectors such as financial services expanded rapidly in the south. A sharp recession led to a 2.5% decline in GDP in 1991. The subsequent revival was sluggish. By 1994, non-oil GDP was growing by 1.5% a year.

ECONOMIC PERFORMANCE INDICATOR

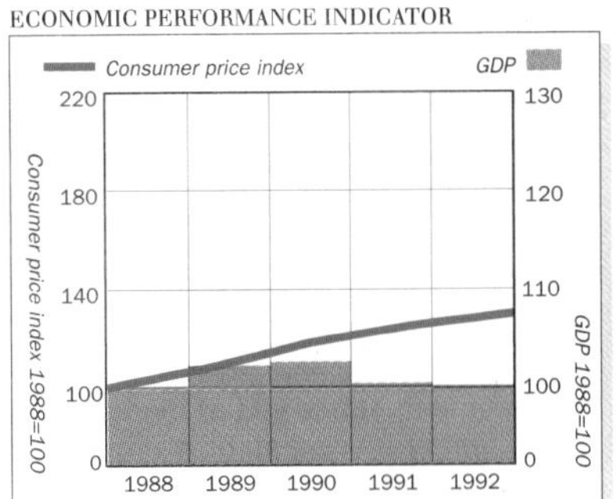

UNITED KINGDOM : MAJOR BUSINESSES

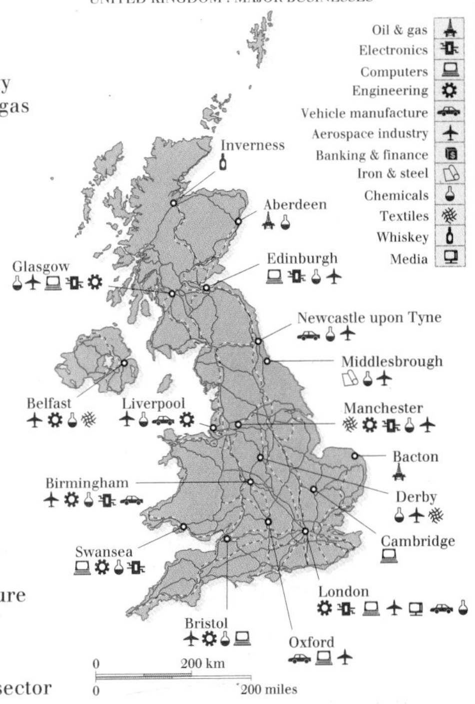

RESOURCES

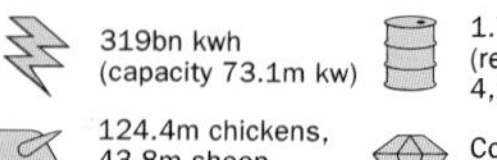

124.4m chickens,
43.8m sheep,
12.1m cattle

Coal, limestone,
natural gas

ELECTRICITY GENERATION

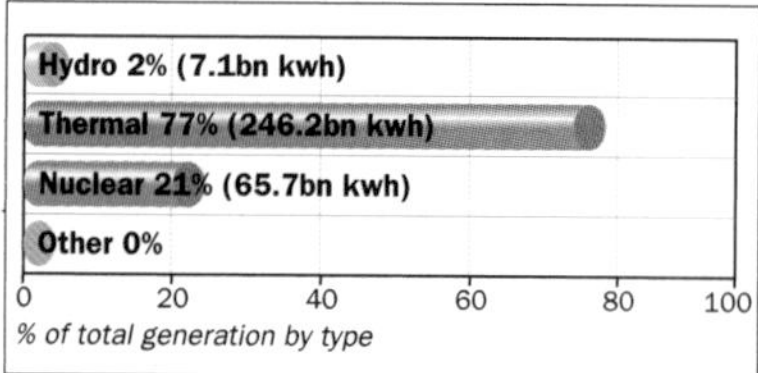

The UK has the largest energy resources of any EU state. The country's energy position is bolstered by substantial oil and gas reserves offshore on the Continental Shelf in the North Sea. Drilled under difficult conditions, the oil is of a high grade. Revenues from taxes on oil companies have been a major contributor to government finances, averaging around $12 billion a year. The oil is expected to last at least until 2010.

Coal reserves are also sizeable, and at current rates could meet Britain's energy needs well into 2400. However, the privatization of the electricity industry resulted in the industry switching from coal to gas-fired power stations. The consequent fall in demand for coal has resulted in the closure of all but 14 mines.

The UK produces few other minerals in significant quantities. Tin workings in the West Country and gold mines in Wales and Scotland have mostly been mined out.

UNITED KINGDOM : LAND USE

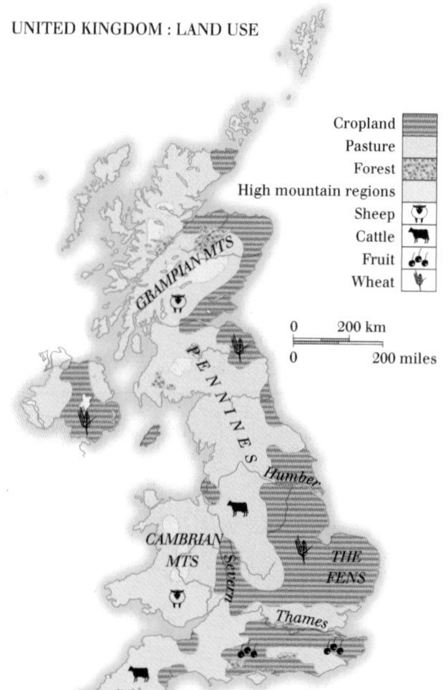

ENVIRONMENT

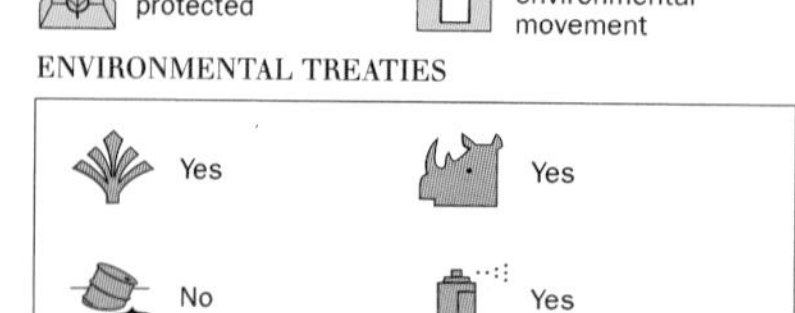

ENVIRONMENTAL TREATIES

	Yes		Yes
	No		Yes

Environmental issues have come to the fore and are increasingly a political issue in the UK in the 1990s. Plans for the building of Thorp, a massive new nuclear reprocessing plant, have met with heated opposition. Sellafield, where the plant is due to be built, is already the largest single source of civil radioactive discharge in Europe. The UK's beaches have been condemned by the EU for their high levels of sewage pollution. Meanwhile, several road building projects are the focus of vigorous local opposition campaigns.

MEDIA

No political restrictions

PUBLISHING AND BROADCAST MEDIA

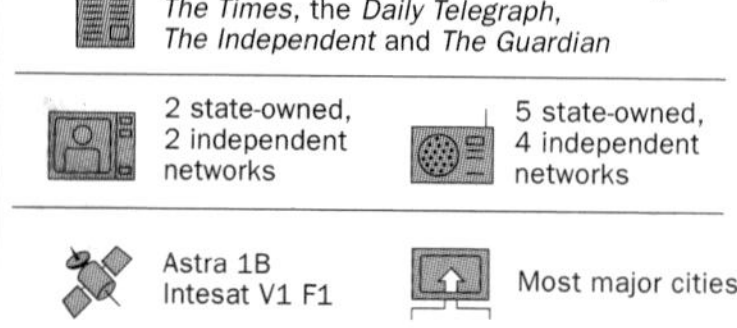

More newspapers are sold per capita in the UK than in any other European country. Newspapers are owned mostly by large media corporations, such as News International and, while free from censorship, tend to express right-of-center political views. The arrival of satellite TV has led to plans for a deregulated market and increased competition for the highly protected British Broadcasting Corporation (BBC). The BBC's *World Service* remains an influential international news source.

***The Welsh coal industry** has virtually disappeared. Wales now has the highest percentage of small business start-ups, relative to the population, of any part of the UK.*

CRIME

52,169 prisoners

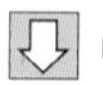
Down 8% in 1990

CRIME RATES

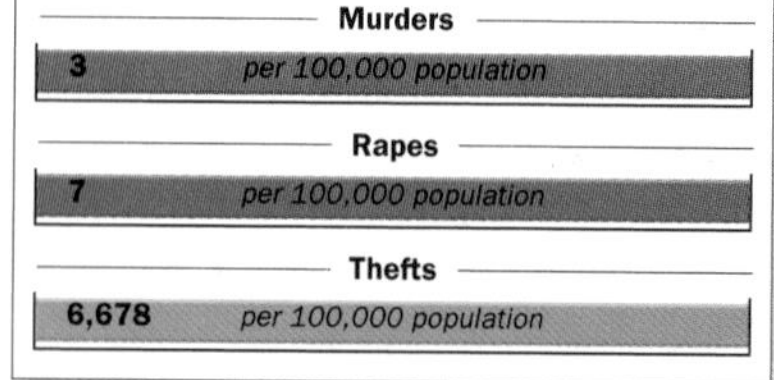

Crime has risen sharply in the UK since the 1970s. The largest increase has been in burglary; car theft rates are the highest in Europe and higher than the USA's. Most crime is opportunistic and committed by young males. In the inner cities there is a growing crime problem fueled by drug dependency.

The UK has one of the highest prison populations in Europe. CUP plans for tougher sentencing will result in a further increase in numbers by 2000.

EDUCATION

99%

0 Education spending as % GNP 25

5%

THE EDUCATION SYSTEM

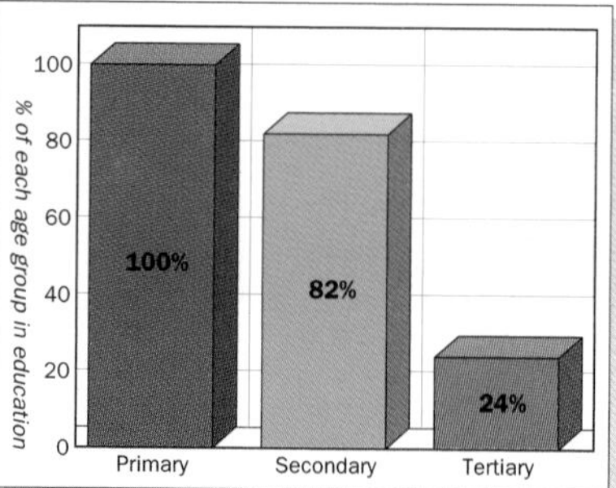

Once based on an elitist system of grammar schools, with membership decided by a competitive examination at the age of 11, the British state system underwent extensive reform in the 1970s and 1980s. Standards, however, declined sharply. The 1988 Education Reform Bill attempted to reverse falling standards by introducing a program of required courses. The state system is used by 94% of children. The rest attend private schools known as public schools. In Northern Ireland, many schools are segregated along religious (Catholic or Protestant) lines.

Compared with its EU partners, relatively few UK students proceed to higher education. Entry to universities is highly competitive and dependent on grades achieved in the end of school A-level exams. Oxford and Cambridge are the most prestigious universities.

REGIONS

SCOTLAND

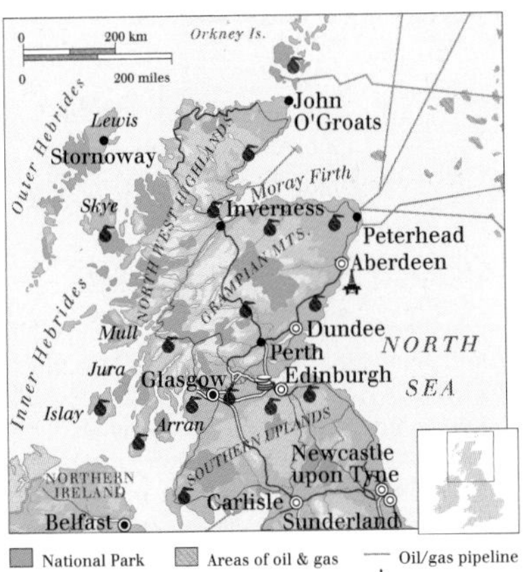

ALTHOUGH RULED FROM Westminster since 1707, Scotland is still very much a separate nation. It has its own legal and educational systems; its own church and banknotes. It is also one of the most pro-EU parts of the UK, believing closer integration would bring not only economic but also political benefits – notably devolution. Only a minority of Scots want independence, but most would like Scotland to have more control over its affairs. Mining and heavy industry are all but dead. Offshore oil helped fuel growth in the 1980s. New industry is proving hard to attract – a result of Scotland's peripheral positon in Europe.

TYNESIDE

TYNESIDE IN NORTHEAST England is slowly emerging from decades of decline. Like neighboring Wearside and Teeside, it depended on shipbuilding and heavy industry, and on a few large companies which employed successive generations of families. Today, little of that economic base is left, decimated by recession and by competition from cheaper producers. Instead, disused docks and derelict factory sites are being turned into business parks. Foreign investors have included prominent Japanese firms such as Nissan; Scandinavia and the EU are also well represented. A symbol of returning prosperity is Gateshead's huge Metro Centre – the UK's most profitable retail center.

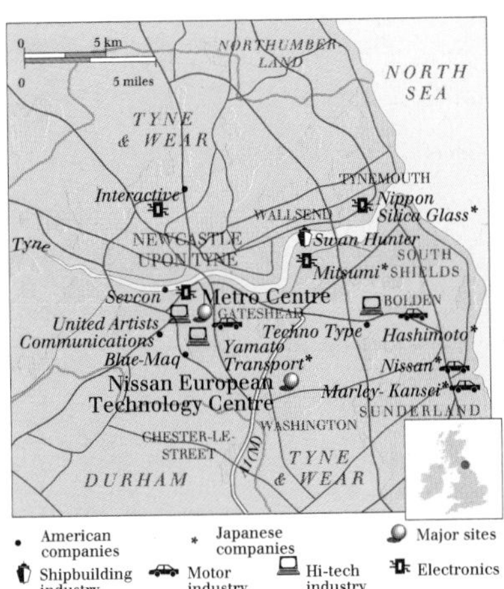

LONDON

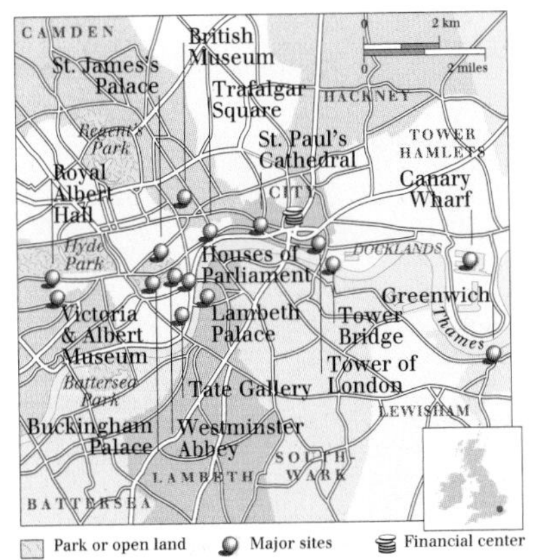

THE FIRST OF THE WORLD'S mega-cities, the UK's capital today is home to 6.8 million people. London is the seat of government and dominates the country's political, financial and cultural life. The flight of industry to cheaper locations outside the capital means London depends mainly on service industries. Tourism and retail services are important, but the capital's $84 billion economy is underpinned by the financial sector.

Focused on the City of London, the site of the Roman city, this sector carries out 20% of all global banking transactions and is also the location of much international commodity trade. Following the deregulation of the market ("Big Bang") in the 1980s, the City expanded rapidly. Recession in the early 1990s, however, saw many job losses and dented profits.

Much of London was rebuilt in the 1980s and early 1990s, including the major East End development of Canary Wharf.

HEALTH

1 per 1,719 people

Heart, cerebrovascular and respiratory diseases, cancer

Health spending as % GNP (0–25): **5.1%**

The majority of health care is provided by the National Health Service (NHS), which is financed by central government and free to all residents. The system is efficient – the UK spends a smaller proportion of its GNP on health than Germany, France or Italy. However, the pressures of an aging population are reflected in long waiting lists for non-essential operations.

WEALTH

Sanitation worker, 221 pounds sterling per week; accountant, 446 pounds sterling per week

CONSUMER GOODS OWNERSHIP

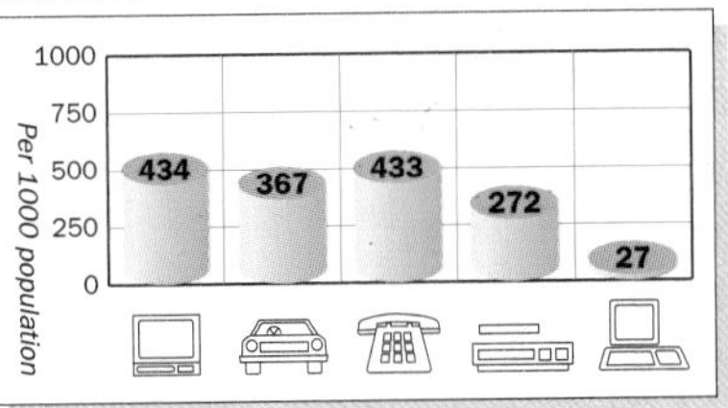

Income inequality in the UK was higher in 1994 than in 1884, when records first began. In part, this is the result of the reductions in taxation for higher earners introduced under the Thatcher administration. The purchasing power of salaries rose sharply during the 1980s and early 1990s. However, in the same period unemployment tripled whilst the value of state benefits fell. The value of the old age pension has fallen sharply.

Wealth remains well-hidden in the UK. Considerable amounts are invested on the stock market, overseas, or in the Lloyds' insurance market. A series of disastrous losses at Lloyds between 1991 and 1993 severely dented the fortunes of many investing families.

WORLD RANKING

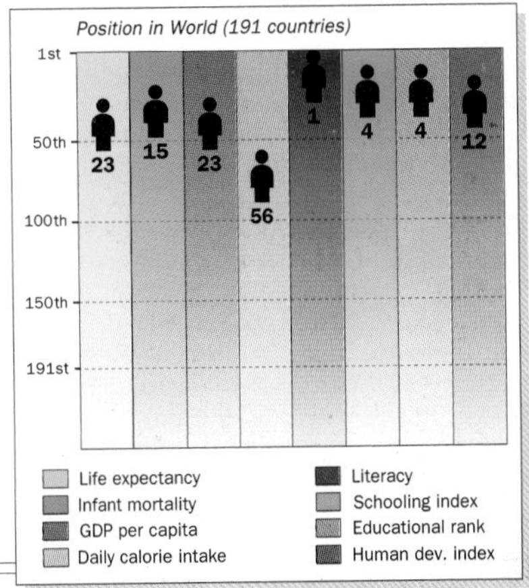

U

See also OVERSEAS TERRITORIES *p.616*

UNITED STATES

NORTH AMERICA

OFFICIAL NAME: United States of America **CAPITAL:** Washington, DC
POPULATION: 255.2 million **CURRENCY:** US dollar **OFFICIAL LANGUAGE:** English **OVERSEAS TERRITORIES:** 14

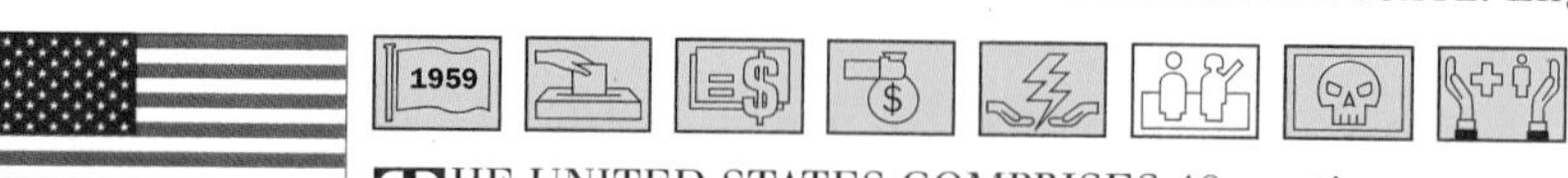

THE UNITED STATES COMPRISES 48 contiguous states, bounded by Canada and Mexico, and the outlying states of Alaska and Hawaii. Alone of the nations that encompass a great landmass, it is neither overpopulated (like China and India), underpopulated (like Australia), nor held hostage to extremes of climate or topography (like Russia and Brazil). The USA also stands apart from most other nations in that it is founded neither on ethnic unity nor within natural geographical boundaries, but instead on the appeal of some powerful ideas. Democracy and liberty, in both a political and an economic sense, continue to be the guiding lights of the USA – as they were for its founders over 200 years ago.

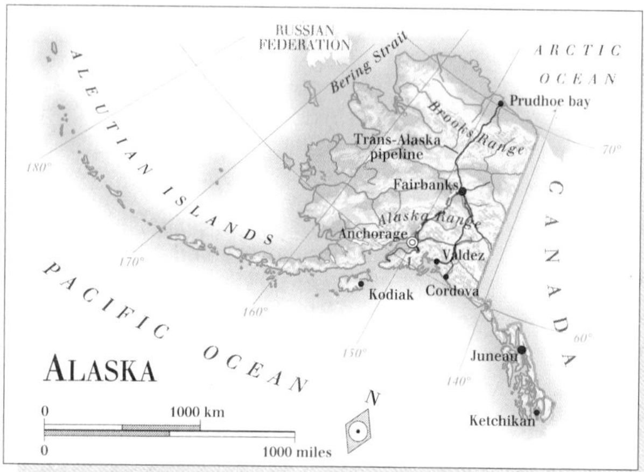

CLIMATE

WEATHER CHART

Average daily temperature — Rainfall
°C/°F: 40/104, 30/86, 20/68, 10/50, 0/32, -10/14, -20/-4
J F M A M J J A S O N D
cm/in: 40/16, 30/12, 20/8, 10/4, 0

Spanning a continent, and extending far into the Pacific Ocean in Alaska and Hawaii, the USA displays a full range of climatic conditions. Mean annual temperatures range from 84°F in Florida to –18°F in Alaska. Except for New England, Alaska and the Pacific Northwest, summer temperatures are higher than in Europe. Southern summers are humid; in the southwest they are dry. Winters are particularly severe in the western mountains and plains and in the Midwest – where the Great Lakes can freeze. The Atlantic northeast can experience heavy snow from November to April. The USA's weather is frequently dramatic. Tornadoes, cyclones, floods, thunderstorms and droughts are common.

The AT & T building, New York, a notable example of postmodern architecture by the influential US architect Philip Johnson.

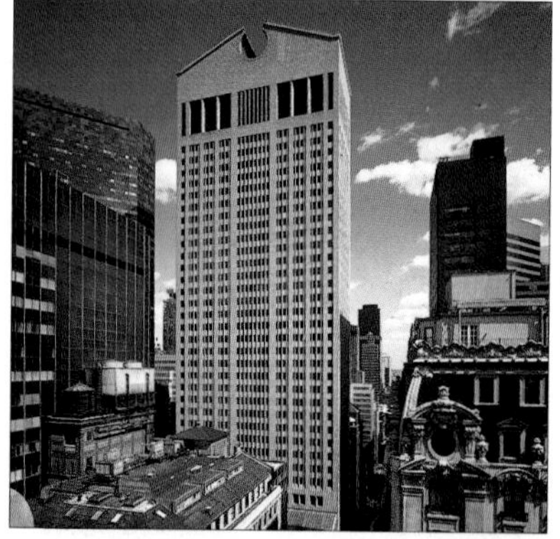

PACIFIC OCEAN
Kauai
Lihue
Niihau
Oahu
Wahiawa
Kaneohe
Honolulu
Molokai
Wailuku
Maui
HAWAII
Hilo
Hawaii
0 200 km
0 200 miles

COMMUNICATIONS

John F Kennedy, New York 29.79m passengers

502 ships 22.44m dwt

THE TRANSPORTATION NETWORK

3.96m miles (6.37m km)

52,419 miles 84,361 km

167,964 miles (270,312 km)

25,482 miles (41,009 km)

Extensive river systems such as the Mississippi–Missouri provided early transportation networks for the USA. Today, it has the world's cheapest, most extensive internal air network and a good system of interstate highways.

The rail network is poorly developed, by European standards, and carries mostly freight. Since Henry Ford began mass production in Detroit nearly 90 years ago, Americans have been wedded to the car. In 1919, Ford sold one million cars. Today, there are over 255 million cars in the USA. Many cities, such as Los Angeles, have come to depend on the car; the USA now accounts for more than half of the world's car trips. Cheap gasoline has underpinned this growth. In the long term, the prospect of dependence on oil imports, as domestic supplies run out, could force a review of the car's role.

The Mittens, Monument Valley, Arizona. *These striking natural rock formations are created by erosion of red sandstone. The Valley is home to the Navajo people.*

UNITED STATES

Total Area : 9 372 610 sq. km (3 618 760 sq. miles)

POPULATION

- over 5 000 000
- over 1 000 000
- over 500 000
- over 100 000
- over 50 000
- over 10 000
- under 10 000

LAND HEIGHT

- 3000m/9843ft
- 2000m/6562ft
- 1000m/3281ft
- 500m/1640ft
- 200m/656ft
- Sea Level

0 400 km

0 400 miles

ATLANTIC OCEAN

GULF OF MEXICO

TOURISM

 45.6m visitors  Up 2% in 1993

MAIN OVERSEAS ARRIVALS

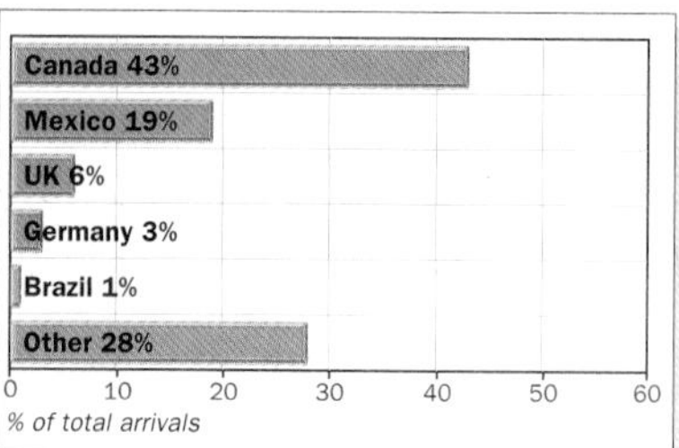

Tourism is an important industry, catering to ever-growing demand from both foreign visitors and Americans themselves. The number of overseas visitors has doubled in the past 15 years, reflecting the relative weakness of the dollar and the deregulation of air fares. Domestic tourism has expanded just as rapidly, as real incomes have risen. In 1993, over two billion trips were made within the USA.

The top tourist destinations include Florida's Disney World – with over 20 million visitors a year – Niagara Falls, Las Vegas, New York, San Francisco, LA and Hollywood, the Grand Canyon, New Orleans, Atlantic City and Washington. All the states have their own attractions, however, and most court tourists. Tourism is a major generator of jobs, especially in areas of industrial decline, like the northeast.

Tourism's rapid expansion has also brought some problems. The 367 parks and sites run by the National Parks Service (NPS) have been particular casualties. Visitor numbers have more than doubled since 1970, to a record 275 million in 1992. To try and reduce pressure on the most popular areas, NPS lands have been doubled in area since 1976, to 126,566 sq. miles. Even so, there is still bumper-to-bumper traffic in Yellowstone Park, and a seven-year waiting list for a raft ride down the Grand Canyon.

PEOPLE

 English, Spanish, Italian, German, French, Polish, Chinese, Tagalog, Greek  70 people per sq. mile

THE URBAN/RURAL POPULATION SPLIT

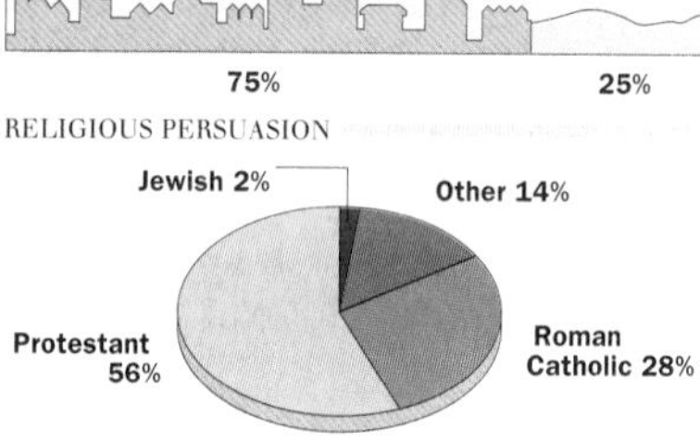

ETHNIC MAKEUP

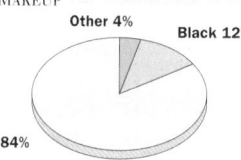

Other 4%
Black 12%
White 84%

Unlike Western Europe, the USA is experiencing a population boom. This is a consequence of the least understood, but arguably most important aspect of modern America – immigration.

Although the ideology of the "melting pot" suggests that the USA has always been a country of immigrants, from the 1920s to the 1960s this was not the case. Fewer immigrants came to the USA in the 1950s than in the 1850s. However, since the mid-1960s, and especially since 1980, the USA has undergone an astonishing immigration boom. During the 1980s, probably ten million immigrants (legal and illegal) settled in the country, more than in any other single decade. The new immigrants are disproportionately drawn from Asia and Latin America. In the 1980s, more than two million immigrants came from Mexico alone.

Most of the available evidence suggests that Asians and Latinos assimilated into US society at the same rate as Poles and Italians did three generations ago. The critical variable for this is "out-marriage" – the rate of marriage outside an ethnic group.

There is concern that the growth of immigration will marginalize the position of American blacks, who increasingly find they have to compete both politically and economically with the newer immigrants. In some communities, such as Los Angeles, this is already a source of tension.

For all the importance of immigration, though, it remains possible that by 2050 the majority of Americans (about 65%) will still be non-Latino whites. They are also likely to remain religious. Americans are consistently shown to place a much higher premium on the value of religion than most other nationalities.

POPULATION AGE BREAKDOWN

% of population by age group	1960	1970	1980	1990	2000
65+	9.2%	9.8%	11.3%	12.6%	12.8%
15–64	59.7%	61.9%	66.2%	66%	67%
0–14	31.1%	28.3%	22.5%	21.4%	20.2%

POLITICS

 1996  President William Jefferson Clinton

THE STATE OF THE PARTIES

House of Representatives 435 members

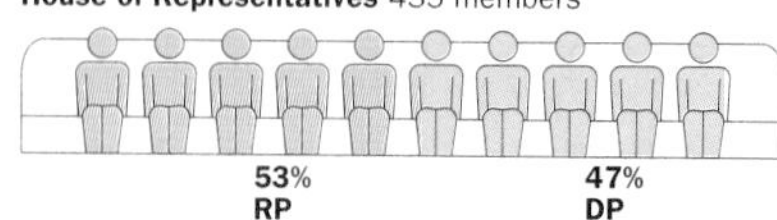

RP = Republican Party **DP** = Democratic Party
There are also two independent members of the House of Representatives

Senate 100 members

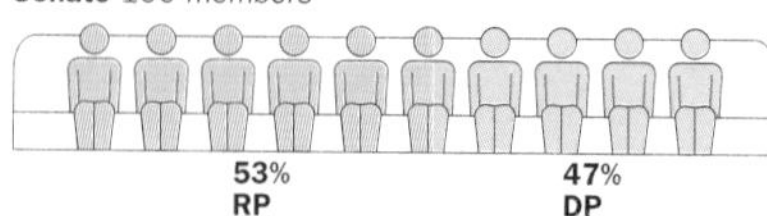

The USA has a federal democratic government. Under this system, many important issues are dealt with by the states. The federal government, for example, does not have a central role in education or urban development.

Main Political Issues

Crime, race and poverty

The USA has seen its crime rates soar for 20 years. At the same time parts of its cities have faced increasing social problems. The black community, which makes up 60% of those living in poor districts, faces particular problems. Both rates of criminality and crime victims are higher in the black community than in any other.

A priority over the next ten years will be finding a way of regenerating the cities where the poorest live. This is most likely to be achieved by a combination of new economic opportunities and programs that give poor people more power over their own lives (for example, by self-management of public housing projects). If it fails in this effort, the country runs the risk of having a permanently disaffected section of the population living within its major cities.

Health

The USA is wrestling with a health-care system whose costs are increasing faster than private or public budgets can tolerate, and which gives patchy

President Bill Clinton *was elected to office in November 1992.*

Albert Gore Jr., *Vice President. He is a keen promoter of environmental issues.*

POLITICS *continued*

service to clients. The costs of health care are currently growing at twice the rate of the rest of the economy. The aim of the proposed legislation is to make health care free to all citizens at the point of access. However, there is considerable debate as to how this should be funded. According to the president's preferred option, employers would foot at least 80% of the bill of their employees' health costs. Regional bodies would be set up from which all but employees of the largest companies would choose from between at least three health-care schemes. An alternative favored by some liberal Democrats in Congress is the adoption of the Canadian model, under which costs are met out of direct taxation.

Foreign policy
In the post-Cold War world, the USA has to decide how and in what circumstances to project its unique power abroad. The USA is not by nature isolationist, but historically has required convincing in order to play the role of global policeman. As demands on US military personnel and logistics continue to grow, so will the domestic consequences of these demands.

The Clinton presidency
The Clinton administration has been beset by minor irritants, which commentators suggest are distracting the president. The president's personal life has been closely scrutinized by the press amidst a number of opportunistic lawsuits. The mid-term elections in November 1994 saw a surge of support for Republican candidates, resulting in Republican majorities in both the House of Representatives and the Senate.

PROFILE
In modern times, the Republican Party has dominated the presidency and the Democratic Party the Congress. The election of Bill Clinton at the end of 1992 was meant to end the resultant "gridlock" between the executive and legislative branches. However, Congress has become such a power in its own right that it is at least as important to the country's domestic agenda as Clinton.

In the 1950s and 1960s, some of the most momentous decisions in the country were in fact made in the Supreme Court. However, the big legal issues – such as ending racial discrimination – were taken long ago, and the Court is now retreating to a much less salient position in US politics.

A fundamental consensus on economic and foreign policy continues to exist between the USA's two main political parties.

***Warren Christopher** holds the position of secretary of state.*

***Hillary Clinton.** The First Lady is orchestrating health-care reforms.*

WORLD AFFAIRS

The USA's attitude to international affairs has been colored by two facts. First, it is protected from the rest of the world by two great oceans. Second, its immediate neighbors – Canada and Mexico – have historically been benign. As a result, for much of its history the USA has enjoyed the luxury of being able to choose the extent of its involvement in the affairs of others.

For most of the first half of the 20th century it pursued an isolationist policy, becoming only reluctantly involved in World Wars I and II. After 1945, however, it swapped isolationism for involvement. The UN was headquartered in New York, and the USA took its seat on the Security Council. As leader of one side of the struggle between democracy and communism, the USA helped to set up NATO, and subsequently played an active part in the defense of Western Europe. For the USA, the Cold War was most immediate – and costly – in the Korean and Vietnam Wars. The heavy death toll and shock of defeat in Vietnam kept the USA out of military involvement overseas for over a decade. Instead, it concentrated on diplomacy – with particular success in China and the Middle East – and on supporting the opponents of left-wing regimes in the developing world, as in Nicaragua.

The collapse of the eastern bloc after 1989 has led to a renewed debate over foreign policy. In particular, as the only remaining superpower, the USA has to determine the scope of its foreign responsibilities in an era when its own survival is no longer threatened. At times in the early 1990s, it appeared set to take on the role of world policeman, taking a lead in the interventions in Kuwait and Somalia. However, as its subsequent problems in Somalia indicated – and lack of clear policy on Bosnia and Haiti confirmed – the USA is still uncertain about its role in the post-Cold War world.

***Manhattan Island,** bounded by the Hudson and East Rivers. New York's two main clusters of skyscrapers are found in the financial district and in midtown Manhattan.*

AID

 $9.4bn (donations)  Down 17% in 1991

The USA gives proportionately little foreign aid, and such aid as it does give is perennially held hostage to special pleading in Congress. The lion's share goes to Israel and Egypt, although of late there has been substantial assistance to the countries of the former USSR and Eastern Europe.

DEFENSE

 $277.2bn Down 2% in 1993

Defense spending as % GDP (scale 0–40): 5.1%

AMERICAN ARMED FORCES

15,629 main battle tanks (896 M-48A5/2, 155 M-60 A3/7, 422 M-1/M-1A1)	674,800 personnel
110 submarines, 12 carriers, 45 destroyers, 83 frigates and 30 patrol boats	546,650 personnel
3,485 combat aircraft (F15, F15E, F16D/D, F-111, A-10, F-4G, F-117)	499,300 personnel
25 SSBN (with 504 missiles)	

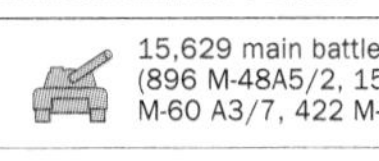

The enormous US military-industrial complex dates from the years since 1945. Before then, the armed forces were small in number, poorly equipped and rapidly dismantled at the end of wars. Defense spending has peaked three times since 1945: at the time of the Korean War in the 1950s, during the 1965–1975 Vietnam War and again in the defense build-up of 1979–1986.

A combination of the end of the Cold War and need to cut the budget deficit means defense spending has been cut in the 1990s. In real terms, it is now at its lowest level since 1945. This is having one unanticipated but troubling side effect. The armed forces are the area where blacks have found it easiest to gain top positions. As the military shrinks, so do the opportunities for black American advancement.

U

Regions

THE GREAT LAKES

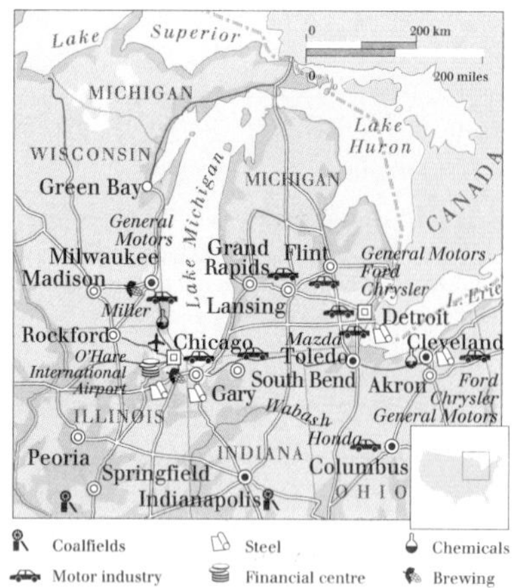

WITH A total area of 94,500 sq. mi, Lakes Erie, Huron, Michigan, Superior and Ontario form the world's largest expanse of fresh water. The Great Lakes provide a natural transportation system, which enabled the adjacent Midwest states to become the USA's leading industrial and agricultural area in the 19th century. Agriculture is still important, especially in Wisconsin and Minnesota; the Minneapolis grain exchange is the USA's largest cash commodity market. The region's heavy industries have suffered badly since the early 1980s, hit by overseas competition and the shift toward the high-tech sector. Even so, Detroit, home of Ford, is still the USA's leading vehicle producer. Chicago, once known for its stock markets and the Mob, is now one of the USA's leading cultural centers – and is still its transportation hub.

SILICON VALLEY

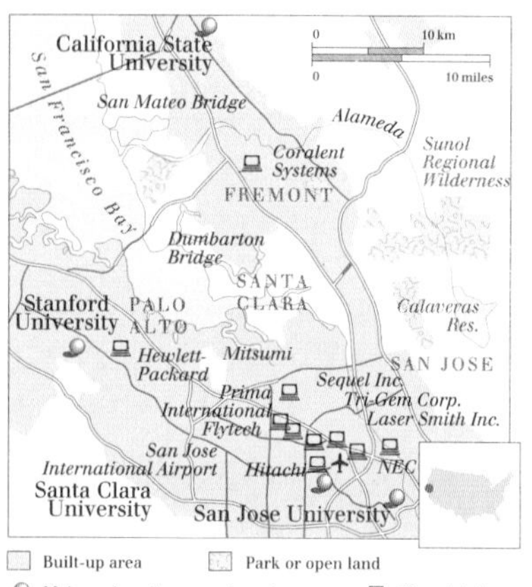

LOCATED IN northern California, Silicon Valley has it origins in the years before World War II. By the early 1960s it had developed into a center of high-tech innovation and entrepreneurialism. Home to scores of established companies – including Hewlett-Packard and Apple – Silicon Valley has lost little of its early spirit. It still generates many imaginative young enterprises. Hewlett-Packard has had recently to face stiff competition from newcomers, such as Sun Microsystems. Apple, too, has had to undertake significant restructuring to meet the demands of the 1990s market. Many Asian, European and Latin American immigrants have been drawn by the region's industry, which has a reputation for extracting the maximum from its work force. Workers often have a stake in their company through stock ownership. Local universities, in particular Stanford, have played an important role in developing the new technology on which the Valley thrives.

HOUSTON

The Texas Medical Center, Houston. *It is equipped with an array of up-to-the-minute high-tech facilities.*

AMERICA'S fourth city, Houston has been the center of the oil industry since 1901. However, oil is lessening in importance, as Houston, like the rest of Texas, turns to high-tech industries. In 1980, just 16% of its economy was not dependent on oil; today it is 40%. Houston has two main attractions for investors like computer giant Compaq: the Lyndon B. Johnson Space Center, home to the space shuttle program, and the Texas Medical Center, the world's largest medical complex. The resulting concentration of research facilities, scientists and engineers has enabled Houston to develop as a top applied and bio-technology center.

THE SOUTH

IN THE 1940S THE SOUTH almost seemed to be another country. Thanks to abundant cheap labor, its agriculture was still tied to cotton. With a few exceptions, such as Birmingham, Alabama, industry had never taken root. The "Jim Crow" laws epitomized a bitter racial division. World War II started a transformation process. Industry developed along the Gulf Coast, in towns like Mobile. The cotton harvest was mechanized. Not least, the federal government extended its powers into the South in the battle to end legally sanctioned racial discrimination. Since the 1970s, the South has been one of the fastest-growing areas of the USA. Its population has increased by over 33% and many industries have moved south. The core states of the "Confederate" South, however, have done less well. In

NEW YORK

NEW YORK, the "Big Apple," is the largest city in the USA and has been the gateway city for repeated waves of immigrants. During most of the first two centuries of the Republic, New York was its capital for everything but politics. It is a huge and in many ways still vibrant city, partly because it is currently experiencing a new influx of immigrants – this time from Asia and Russia. Its collar of suburbs has a population greater than that of Belgium. However, the extent of the city's decay is evident – more so in the outer boroughs than in Manhattan, where most of its tourist attractions are located. In terms of pop culture, art, sport, business and recreation, New York has never loomed less large within the USA than it does now.

SEATTLE

LARGEST CITY of the Pacific Northwest state of Washington, Seattle has a dramatic location – bounded to the west by the Puget Sound and to the east by Lake Washington. The economic boom years of the 1980s saw large numbers of immigrants and new businesses attracted to the region. The businesses included Microsoft, the world's leading software manufacturer. Yet, despite the arrival of a different style of industry, Boeing is still the largest employer in the Seattle area. With its newfound wealth, Seattle has swiftly changed from a backwater near America's northwest border with Canada into a cosmopolitan city. Its lively downtown area recently gained international fame as the birthplace of "grunge" music.

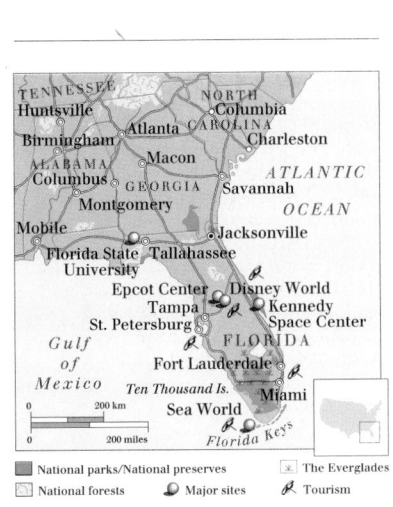

National parks/National preserves
National forests
Major sites
The Everglades
Tourism

addition, areas such as West Virginia, already among the poorest in the USA, stagnated and lost population.

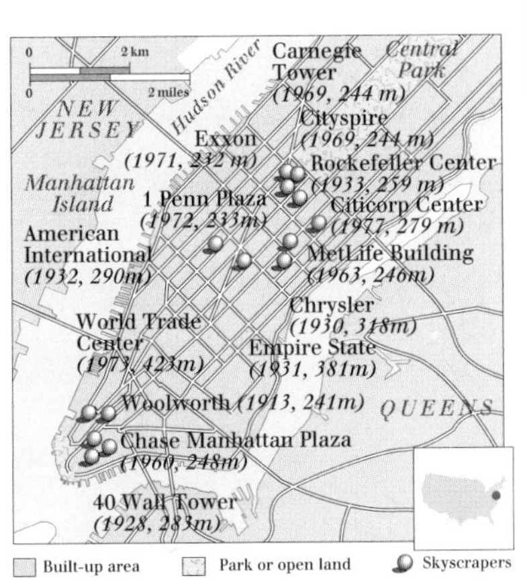

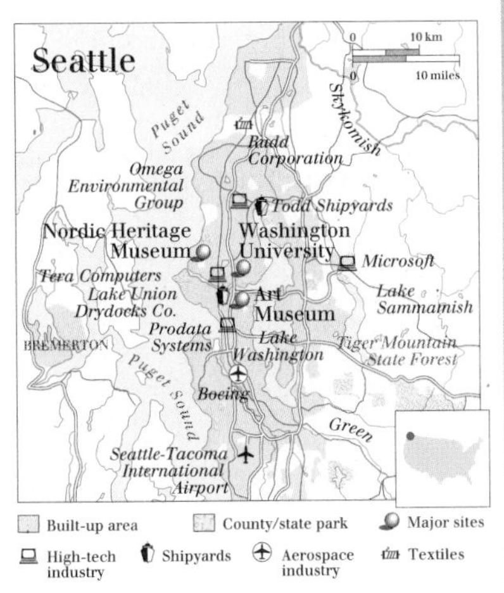

ECONOMICS

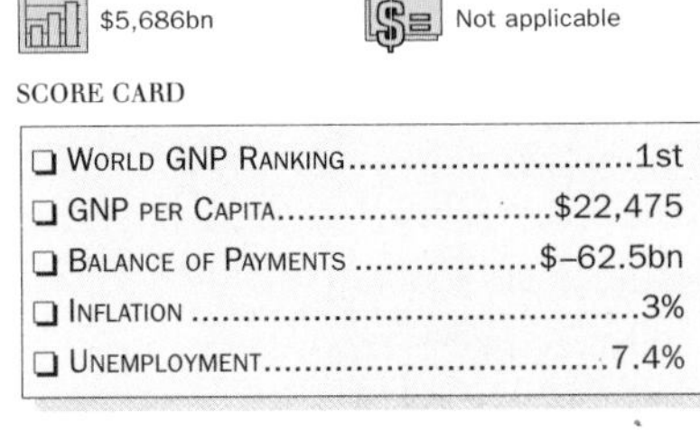

$5,686bn

Not applicable

SCORE CARD

❑ WORLD GNP RANKING	1st
❑ GNP PER CAPITA	$22,475
❑ BALANCE OF PAYMENTS	$-62.5bn
❑ INFLATION	3%
❑ UNEMPLOYMENT	7.4%

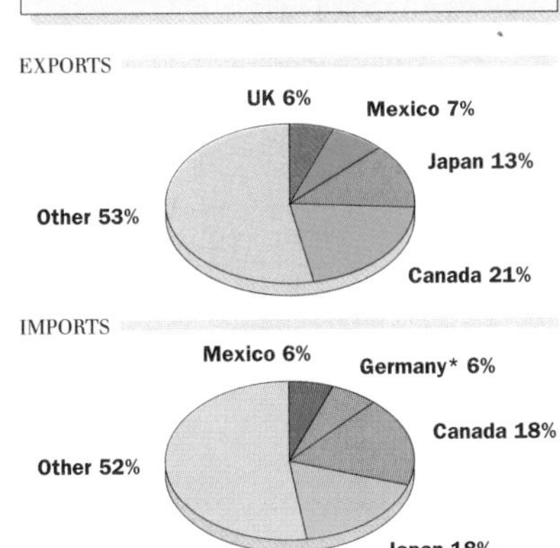

STRENGTHS

The world's largest economy. Wealth of natural resources, including energy, raw materials and foods. Strong high-tech base and world-leading research and development. Sophisticated service sector, as well as advanced and competitive manufacturing industry. World-class multinationals such as Ford, GM, Exxon and IBM. Global leader in computer software. Entrepreneurial business ethic. High quality of post-graduate education, especially related to application of high-tech to business. Global dominance of US culture a major boost to US manufactures.

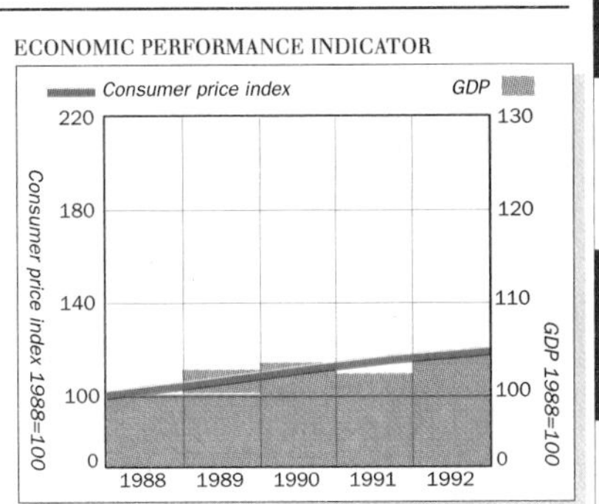

WEAKNESSES

Dramatic fall in manufacturing employment over last 20 years; though manufacturing sector has remained constant as a share of GDP over that period. Post-war economic boom was built on the back of low-skilled, high-waged employment in areas such as car industry. Tough competition from Japan, the rest of Asia and EU, particularly in future leading-edge technologies. Lower savings rate than many competitors. World's largest debtor nation.

PROFILE

In 1945, the USA accounted for about 50% of world output, in 1994 for about 25%. That is not, as Americans often think, a sign of failure, but a clear indication that the 1940s and 1950s were unusual years. The current total of 25% is about the same share of the world market which the USA had in 1914, when it was already the world's greatest economy.

The USA has become a great exporter, and continues to have both a stable political system and a uniquely strong combination of skilled labor and natural resources. Its economic potential will continue to outstrip that of any other nation for the foreseeable future.

UNITED STATES : MAJOR BUSINESSES

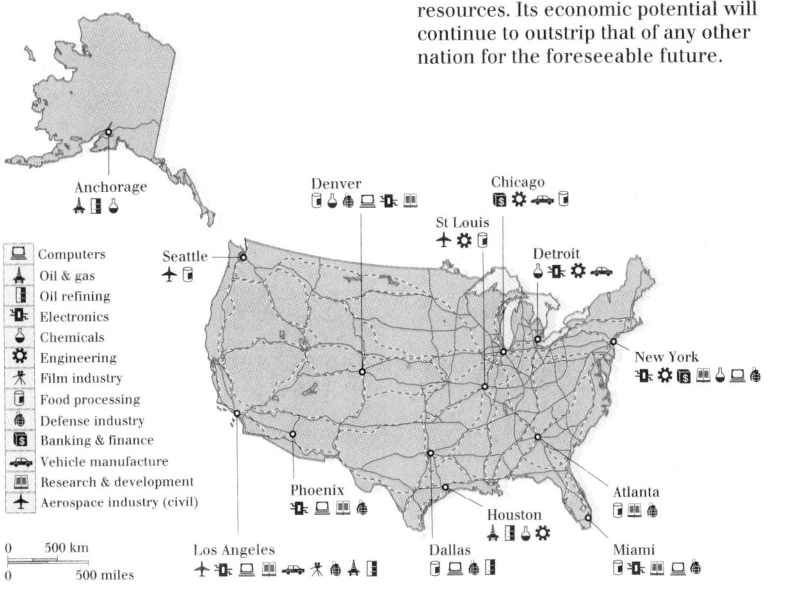

U

CHRONOLOGY

At the beginning of the 17th century, British settlers began to establish colonies on the eastern seaboard. After a successful war for independence (1775–1781), Britain recognized the independence of the 13 colonies. The Constitution of 1787 joined the original states to establish the USA. Following the victory of the northern states in the 1861–1865 Civil War, slavery was abolished throughout the USA. The 19th century saw a series of conflicts in which native Americans were dispossessed of their land.

- ❑ **1917** Enters World War I.
- ❑ **1929** New York stock market collapse; economic depression.
- ❑ **1941** Japanese attack on Pearl Harbor. Enters World War II.
- ❑ **1950–1953** Korean War.
- ❑ **1954** Supreme Court rules racial segregation in schools is unconstitutional. Blacks, seeking constitutional rights, start campaign of civil disobedience.
- ❑ **1959** Alaska and Hawaii become 49th and 50th states of the USA .
- ❑ **1961** John F. Kennedy becomes president. Promises to provide aid to South Vietnamese. Relations with Cuba deteriorate; US-backed invasion defeated at Bay of Pigs.
- ❑ **1962** Discovery of Soviet missile bases on Cuba; serious threat of war with USSR averted.
- ❑ **1963** November: Kennedy assassinated. Lyndon Baines Johnson president. Effects on economy of increased defense and social expenditure begin to be felt.
- ❑ **1964** US involvement in Vietnam stepped up. Civil Rights Act guarantees blacks constitutional equality.
- ❑ **1968** Martin Luther King assassinated.
- ❑ **1969** Republican Richard Nixon takes office as president. Growing public opposition to Vietnam War.
- ❑ **1972** Nixon reelected. Makes historic visit to China. Relations with USSR also improve.
- ❑ **1973** Withdrawal of US troops from Vietnam; 58,000 US troops dead.
- ❑ **1974** August: Nixon resigns following "Watergate" scandal: revelation that his campaign team had organized breakin to DP headquarters. Succeeded by Vice President Gerald Ford.
- ❑ **1976** Democrat Jimmy Carter elected president.
- ❑ **1978** Conclusion of US-sponsored "Camp David" agreement between Egypt and Israel.
- ❑ **1979** Seizure of US hostages in Tehran, Iran.

⇨

RESOURCES

ELECTRICITY GENERATION

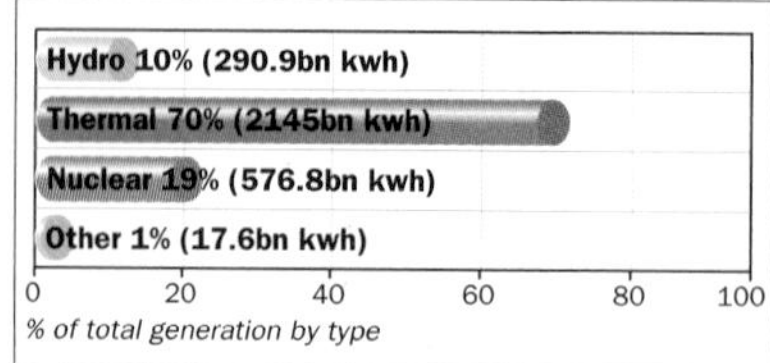

The USA has an abundance of natural resources, including oil, although the country is a net oil importer. There are massive deposits of coal in the western states – where almost all mining is open-pit – and substantial mineral deposits in the mountains and intramontane basins.

Environmental concerns have prevented the development of new sources of nuclear power since the accident at Three Mile Island in 1979. Environmentalism has also forced the timber industry to retreat from the Pacific Northwest, especially from Washington State. It has moved to the south, where great stands of pine are harvested as if they were fields of wheat. The USA has harnessed hydroelectric power in the past; today, imports of hydro-power from Canada are commonplace.

By comparison with Western Europe, the USA is not intensively farmed. The huge size of farms in the Midwest and West has allowed both arable and livestock farming to be based upon a low-input for low-output model.

UNITED STATES : LAND USE

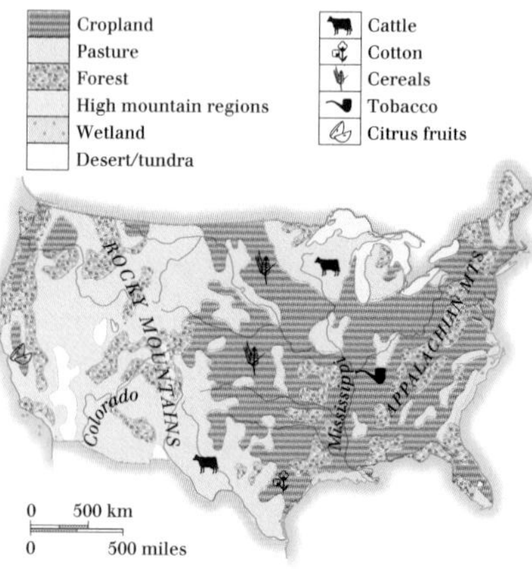

ENVIRONMENT

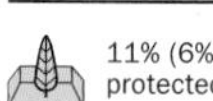

11% (6% partially protected)

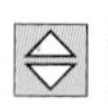

Political opposition to environmental causes

ENVIRONMENTAL TREATIES

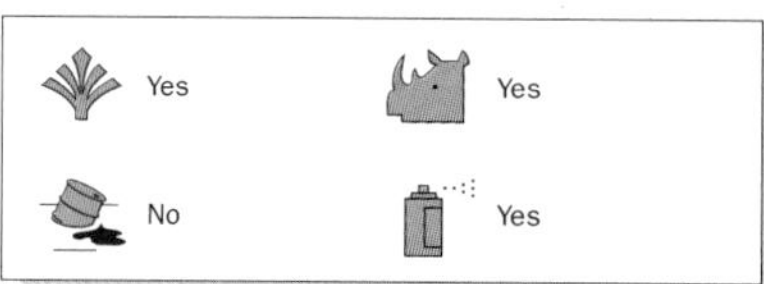

Although the USA came early to environmentalism, it has in some respects been overtaken by countries such as Germany. Food packaging is astonishingly wasteful and many cars are still "gas-guzzlers." As the suburban sprawl testifies, its wide open spaces have engendered a somewhat cavalier attitude to aspects of the environment.

To an extent which has not been true elsewhere, the ecological movment has been challenged politically. Protection necessarily involves the regulation of market activities; in the USA such a move is always contentious. The intramontane West is a battleground between those who want to maintain its beauty, and those who advocate "wise use" – in practice this often means giving ranchers and miners free rein. Environmental teaching is, however, strong in schools.

MEDIA

Freedom of press guaranteed in constitution

PUBLISHING AND BROADCAST MEDIA

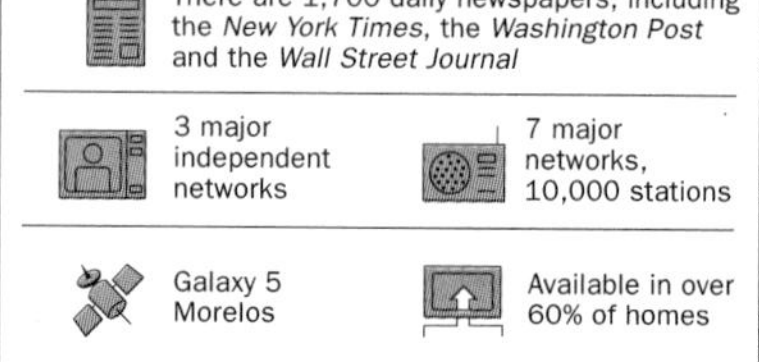

There are 1,700 daily newspapers, including the *New York Times*, the *Washington Post* and the *Wall Street Journal*
3 major independent networks
7 major networks, 10,000 stations
Galaxy 5 Morelos
Available in over 60% of homes

Mass media as a phenomenon was born in the USA. No other society on earth has ever had anything quite like American network TV. And no other society has so easily moved into the world of multichannel TV; homes with 50 or more channels are commonplace. Newspapers, however, are having a difficult time. With a few exceptions, newspapers are local, not national. They tend to have very low cover prices and to gain most of their revenue from advertising. This business is under increasing threat from cable TV and other outlets. Many companies are exploring multimedia opportunities, investing in ways of providing on-line news, information and other services.

U

CHRONOLOGY *continued*

- ❑ **1980** Ronald Reagan wins election for Republicans. Adopts tough anti-communist foreign policy.
- ❑ **1983** Military invasion of Grenada.
- ❑ **1985** Retaliatory air strikes against Libyan cities. Relations with USSR improve; first of three summits between Reagan and Mikhail Gorbachev.
- ❑ **1986** Iran-Contra affair revealed.
- ❑ **1987** Intermediate Nuclear Forces Treaty signed by USA and USSR.
- ❑ **1988** Republican George Bush, Vice President under Reagan, defeats Democrat Michael Dukakis in election.
- ❑ **1989** Sending of 23,000 troops to Panama – to overthrow government and arrest General Noriega on drug-trafficking charges – condemned by UN Security Council.
- ❑ **1990** Normalization of relations with Nicaragua, following defeat of Sandinista government in election. USA and six other nations agree to give aid to USSR to finance transition to market economy. USA takes leading role in international opposition to Iraqi invasion of Kuwait. NATO and Warsaw Pact group sign Treaty on Conventional Armed Forces in Europe.
- ❑ **1991** January: Operation Desert Storm launched against Iraq. Multinational forces include 43,000 US ground troops. USA and USSR sign START arms reduction treaty.
- ❑ **1992** Riots in Los Angeles and other cities; brings to light issue of disaffected black youth. Bush–Yeltsin summit agrees further arms reductions. Democrat Bill Clinton defeats Bush in election.
- ❑ **1993** US participates in selective bombing of Iraqi missile sites. 24,000 US troops sent to Somalia as part of US-led UN force. Reducing budget deficit and reforming health care among main objectives of new Clinton administration. US troops withdrawn from Somalia.

Snow-capped mountains rise from cattle pastures in Montana. *There are about 100 million head of cattle in the USA.*

CRIME

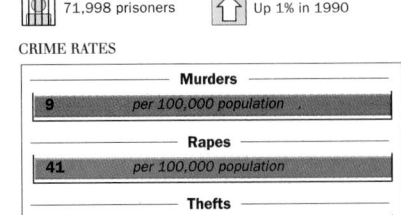

71,998 prisoners | Up 1% in 1990

CRIME RATES

Murders	9 per 100,000 population
Rapes	41 per 100,000 population
Thefts	5,346 per 100,000 population

The USA has seen a 20-year long crime wave. Violent crime – especially murder – is much more common than in other developed countries. This is the case even in relatively well-off parts of the country. Seattle, for example, which by US standards is a peaceful city, has a murder rate seven times that of Birmingham, England.

The rate of incarceration for drug crimes in the USA is much higher than in most Western countries – and the conditions worse. Capital punishment has made a strong comeback since the 1980s, especially in the South. Texas is the state that carries out most executions; most of the liberal "northern tier" states, by contrast, have abolished the death penalty.

EDUCATION

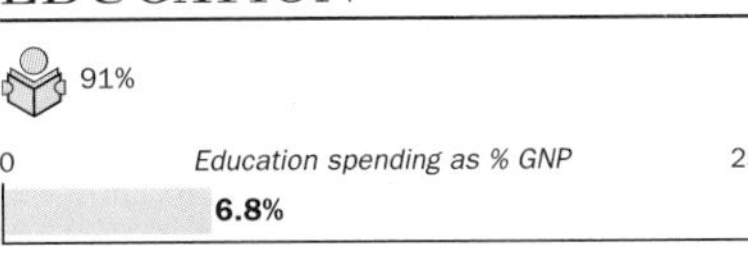

THE EDUCATION SYSTEM

% of each age group in education	Primary	Secondary	Tertiary
	100%	88%	60%

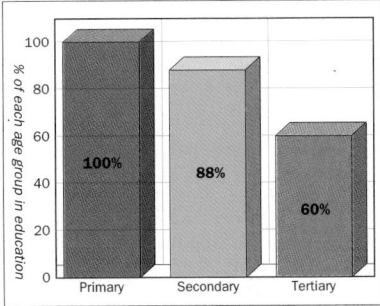

Education in the USA is primarily the responsibility of the state governments. A series of recent reports have been critical of standards in US high schools. Yet, all accept that US universities are world class.

Private education is a rapidly developing sector. Though the number of pupils in private education does not appear to have increased much in the last generation, this is misleading. While the number of Catholic private schools has shrunk, non-denominational fee-paying schools have been founded to take their place.

HEALTH

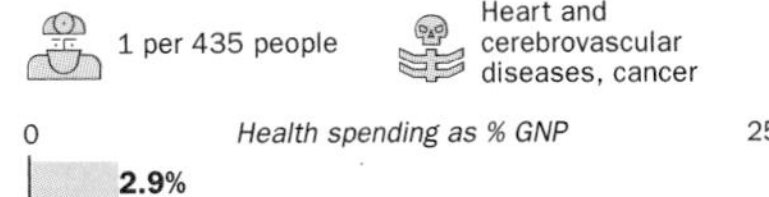

0 — Health spending as % GNP — 25: **2.9%**

The US health system is subject to enormous disparities. At one level, sophisticated techniques are available to those with insurance (which they typically receive from their employer). The Texas Medical Center, in Houston, the epitome of high-tech medicine, has a budget equivalent to that of some small countries. On the other hand, infant mortality statistics in some parts of the country are at near-African levels.

Partly because of these disparities, reform has become a major political issue. But it has also been driven by the skyrocketing cost of care – the health sector now accounts for more than an eighth of the total economy.

WEALTH

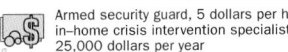

Armed security guard, 5 dollars per hour; in-home crisis intervention specialist, 25,000 dollars per year

CONSUMER GOODS OWNERSHIP

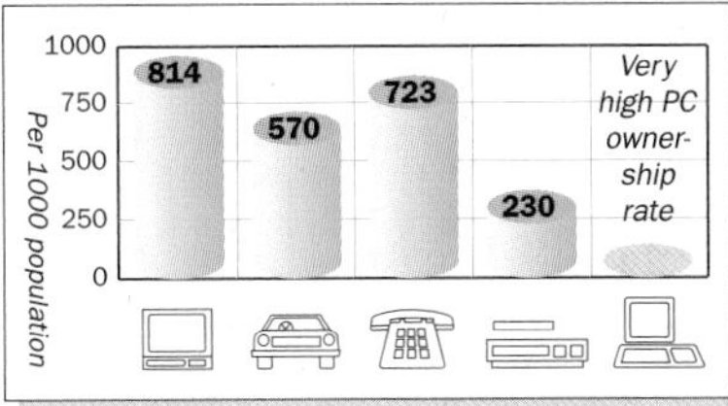

Between 1945 and 1973, all sectors of the population got richer. Since then, however, a new pattern has emerged. Those who finished high school have continued to see their standard of living increase, while those who did not have not seen an improvement for a generation. In a way that has not been seen for more than fifty years, the "education effect" is leading to noticeable class divisions.

WORLD RANKING

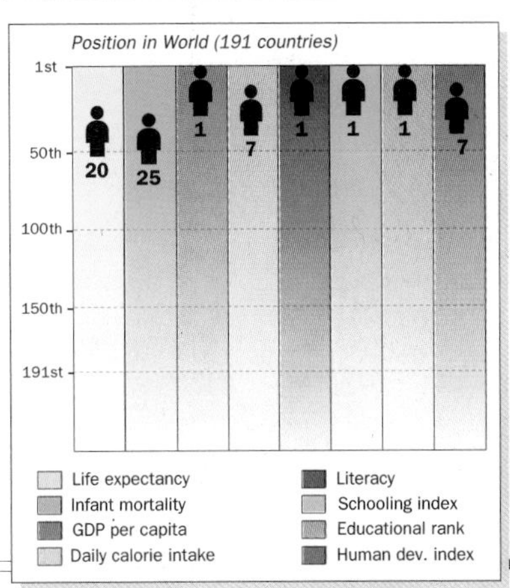

U

URUGUAY

OFFICIAL NAME: Eastern Republic of Uruguay **CAPITAL:** Montevideo
POPULATION: 3.1 million **CURRENCY:** New Uruguayan peso **OFFICIAL LANGUAGE:** Spanish

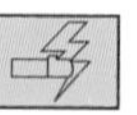

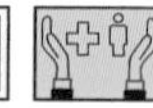

URUGUAY IS THE SMALLEST country in South America. Its capital, Montevideo, is an Atlantic port on the River Plate, lying across the river from Buenos Aires, Argentina's capital. Uruguay became independent in 1828, after nearly 150 years of Spanish and Portuguese control. Decades of liberal government ended in 1973 with a military coup that was to result in 12 years of dictatorship, during which 400,000 people emigrated. Most have since returned. Almost the entire lowlying landscape is devoted to the rearing of livestock, especially cattle and sheep. Uruguay is the world's second biggest wool exporter. Tourism and offshore banking now bring in substantial foreign earnings.

Uruguayan grasslands. *Rich pasture covers three-quarters of the country, ideal for cattle and sheep. Animals and animal products account for over one-third of export earnings.*

CLIMATE

WEATHER CHART

Average daily temperature / Rainfall

°C/°F: 40/104, 30/86, 20/68, 10/50, 0/32, -10/14, -20/-4
cm/in: 40/16, 30/12, 20/8, 10/4, 0
J F M A M J J A S O N D

Uruguay has one of the most benign climates in the world. It is uniformly temperate over the whole country. Winters are mild, frost is rare and it never snows. Summers are generally cool for these latitudes and heat is rare. The moderate rainfall tends toward heavy showers, leaving most days sunny.

COMMUNICATIONS

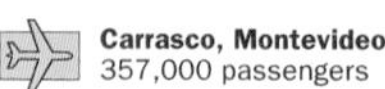

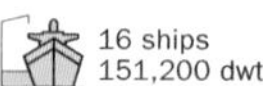

THE TRANSPORTATION NETWORK

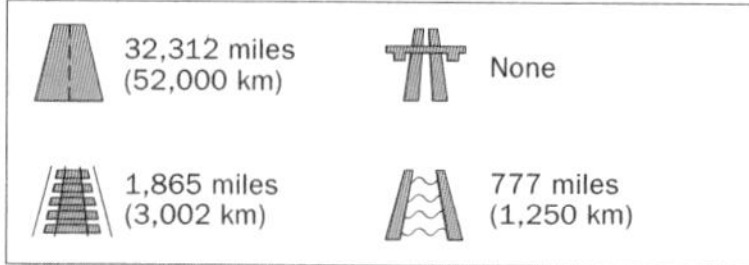

Uruguay's transportation plans for the 1990s center on privatization. The government has sold off its share in the national bus industry – there are extensive internal and international coach and bus services – and has closed down all passenger railroad services. There is a plan to build a road tunnel from Montevideo to Buenos Aires under the River Plate, but this will take many years to complete.

TOURISM

Up 24% in 1989

MAIN OVERSEAS ARRIVALS

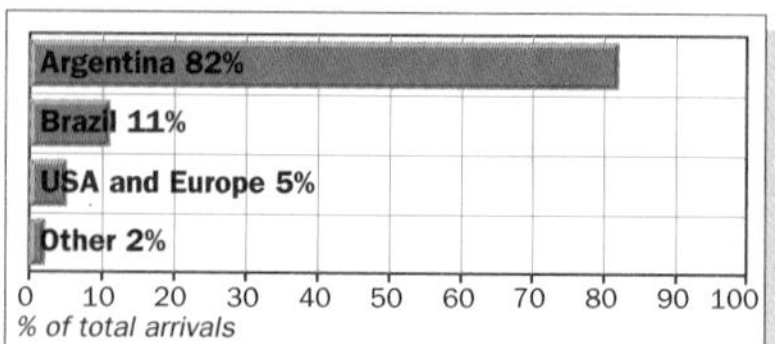

Most visitors to Uruguay travel through Montevideo to the sandy beaches near the River Plate estuary. Although the old Spanish fortifications of Montevideo have been destroyed, the city retains a colonial atmosphere. Punta del Este, 86 miles east of the capital, Uruguay's major beach resort, is served by direct flights from Buenos Aires.

PEOPLE

Spanish

47 people per sq. mile

THE URBAN/RURAL POPULATION SPLIT

86% 14%

RELIGIOUS PERSUASION

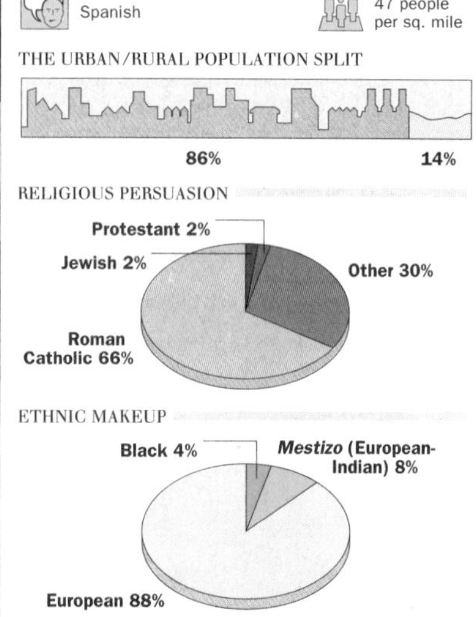

Most Uruguayans are second or third generation European, mostly of Spanish or Italian descent. There are also some *mestizos* and a small minority of people descended from Africans or immigrants from Brazil, who live in or around the capital of Montevideo or near the Brazilian border. All indigenous Amerindian groups became integrated in the *mestizo* population by the mid-19th century. The population's unusual degree of homogeneity – and the fact that it is small compared to the amount of land – means that ethnic tensions are few. The birth-rate is low for Latin America.

The considerable prosperity derived from cattle ranching allowed Uruguay to become a welfare state long before any other Latin American country. In spite of Uruguay's serious economic decline since the end of the 1950s, there is still a sizeable, if less prosperous, middle class. A clear sign of the country's economic and social deterioration during the years of military dictatorship was the unprecedented growth of shantytowns around Montevideo.

Although a Roman Catholic country, Uruguay is liberal in its attitude toward religion and all forms are tolerated. Divorce is legal. Women are regarded as equal to men and able to vote. There is no capital punishment.

POPULATION AGE BREAKDOWN

% of population by age group

Age group	1960	1970	1980	1990	2000
65+	8.1%	8.9%	10.5%	11.6%	12.7%
15–64	64%	63.2%	62.6%	62.6%	63.4%
0–14	27.9%	27.9%	26.9%	25.8%	23.9%

U

POLITICS

Lower House 1999
Upper House 1999

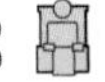

President Julio María Sanguinetti

THE STATE OF THE PARTIES

Chamber of Deputies 99 members

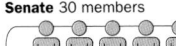

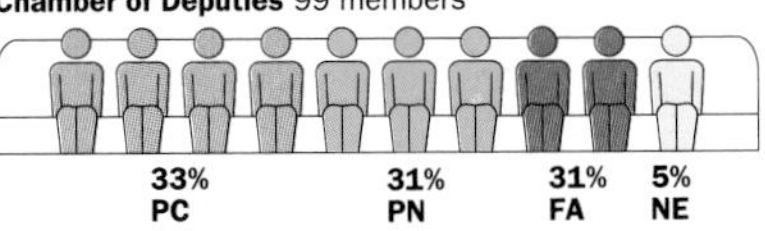

PC = Colorado Party (*Colorados*) **PN** = National Party (*Blancos*) **FA** = Broad Front **NE** = New Space

Senate 30 members

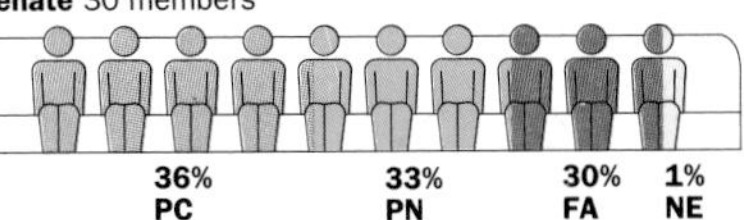

Uruguay is a multiparty presidential democracy.

MAIN POLITICAL ISSUES

Modernization and privatization
After 20 years of military dictatorship and transitional government, Uruguay is seeking the best way of modernizing the state and state-run institutions. The central political question is whether or not privatization will help to reverse economic decline.

The aging population
Uruguay's long-established welfare system is under strain from the increasing proportion of elderly people in the population. The emigration of young workers to Europe and Argentina is exacerbating the problem.

PROFILE

The elections of 1984 marked Uruguay's return to democracy. The winning Colorado (Liberal) Party addressed some human rights issues, but its attempts to reverse economic recession met with fierce trade-union opposition. The 1989 elections resulted in an uneasy coalition between the *Colorados* and the conservative *Blancos*. Labor unrest has continued, fueled by popular anger over the privatization of public companies. New free-market economic policies are also hampered by a law declaring that, if 25% of the electorate agree, a referendum must be held on new legislation.

Luis Alberto Lacalle Herrera, *president from 1990–1994.*

President Julio María Sanguinetti, *who took office in March 1995.*

WORLD AFFAIRS

After many years of political isolation and economic decline, Uruguay's chief foreign policy concern is achieving regional integration with Argentina, Brazil and Paraguay in MERCOSUR, the common market of southern South America. This should come into full operation in 1996. Uruguay is already part of a continental defense alliance with other Latin American countries and the USA. However, it has some unresolved border problems with Brazil. Uruguay allowed the UK to use its ports during the Falklands conflict.

In 1991, Uruguay and the USA signed a legal-assistance treaty to allow easier access to the bank accounts of those suspected of laundering the proceeds of drug-trafficking. This had increasingly been carried out through Montevideo's offshore banking sector.

AID

 $51m (receipts) 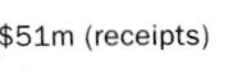  Up 9% in 1991

Uruguay is a minimal recipient of aid, and aid plays little part in the Uruguayan economy.

CHRONOLOGY

The Spaniards were the first to colonize the area north of the River Plate. In 1680, the Portuguese also founded a colony there, at Colonia del Sacramento, thus starting 150 years of rivalry between the colonial powers for control of the territory.

- ❑ **1726** Spaniards found Montevideo. By end of century, whole country is divided into large cattle ranches.
- ❑ **1808** Montevideo declares independence from Buenos Aires.
- ❑ **1811** Patriotic rancher and local caudillo, José Gervasio Artigas, fends off Brazilian attack.
- ❑ **1812–1820** Uruguayans, known as *Orientales* ("Easterners," from the eastern side of the River Plate) fight wars against Argentinian and Brazilian invaders. Brazil finally takes Montevideo.
- ❑ **1827** Gen. Lavallejo defeats Brazilians with Argentine help.
- ❑ **1828** Seeing trade benefits that an independent Uruguay would bring as a buffer state between Argentina and Brazil, Britain mediates and secures Uruguayan independence.
- ❑ **1836** Start of large-scale European immigration.

⇨

CHRONOLOGY *continued*

- **1838–1865** *La Guerra Grande* civil war between *Blancos* (Whites, future conservative party) and *Colorados* (Reds, future liberals).
- **1865–1870** Colorado president, Gen. Venancio Flores, takes Uruguay into War of the Triple Alliance against Paraguay.
- **1872** Peace under military rule. *Blancos* strong in country, *Colorados* in city.
- **1890s** Violent strikes by immigrant trade unionists against landed elite enriched by massive European investment in ranching.
- **1903–1907** Reformist Colorado, José Batllé y Ordóñez, president.
- **1911–1915** Batllé serves second term in office. *Batllismo* creates the only welfare state in Latin America with pensions, social security and free education and health service; also pursues nationalizations, disestablishment of Church, abolition of death penalty.
- **1933** Military coup. Opposition groups excluded from politics.
- **1942** President Alfredo Baldomir dismisses government and tries to bring back proper representation.
- **1939–1945** Neutrality.
- **1951** New constitution replaces president with nine-member council. Decade of great prosperity follows until world agricultural prices plummet. Sharp drop in foreign investment.
- **1958** *Blanco* party wins elections for first time in 93 years.
- **1962** Tupamaro urban guerrilla group founded. Its campaign of terrorism continues until 1973.
- **1964** Large trade unions unite.
- **1966** Presidency reinstated. *Colorados* back in power.
- **1967** Jorge Pacheco president. Tries to stifle opposition to tough anti-inflation policies.
- **1973** Military coup. Promises to encourage foreign investment counteracted by denial of political freedom and brutal repression of the left; 400,000 emigrate.
- **1974** EEC bans meat imports.
- **1984** Military agrees to step down. Elections held.
- **1985** Dr. Julio Sanguinetti (Colorado) president.
- **1986** Those guilty of human rights abuse granted amnesty.
- **1988** Drought; one million cattle die.
- **1989** Referendum endorses amnesty in interests of stability. Fully free elections won by Lacalle Herrera and *Blancos*. Attempt to include Colorado ministers fails.
- **1991** Signs MERCOSUR agreement.
- **1992** Referendum forces partial repeal of privatization plans.

DEFENSE

$260m

Fairly stable from year to year

0 Defense spending as % GDP 40

2.7%

The military withdrew from power in 1984 and has since respected civilian rule. However, secret right-wing groups linked to the military – a few members are said to be officers on active duty – have carried out terrorist attacks against the government. A 1986 law virtually blocked investigations into "disappearances," killings and torture during the dictatorship, but there is still public pressure to bring guilty officers to trial. The defense budget is low; most equipment is bought from the USA and less sophisticated weaponry from Brazil.

URUGUAYAN ARMED FORCES

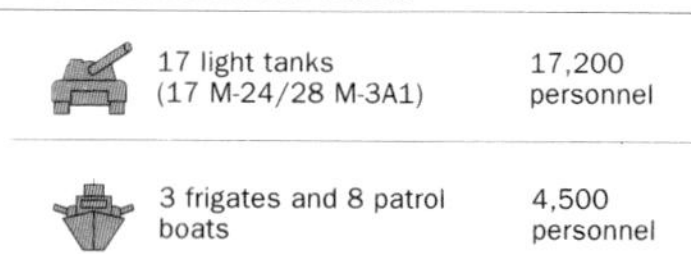

17 light tanks (17 M-24/28 M-3A1)	17,200 personnel
3 frigates and 8 patrol boats	4,500 personnel
37 combat aircraft (12 A37B/6 IA-58B)	3,000 personnel
None	

ECONOMICS

$11.2bn

4.45 new Uruguayan pesos

SCORE CARD

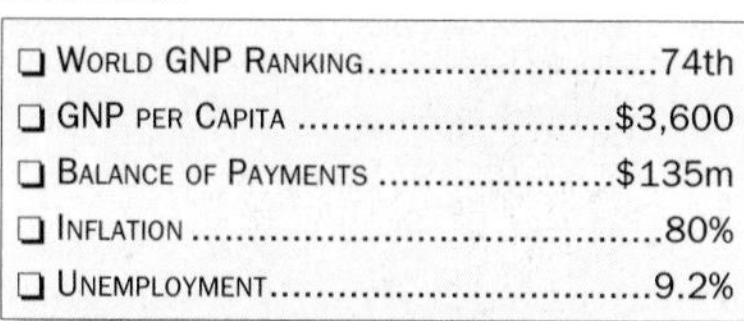

World GNP Ranking	74th
GNP per Capita	$3,600
Balance of Payments	$135m
Inflation	80%
Unemployment	9.2%

EXPORTS

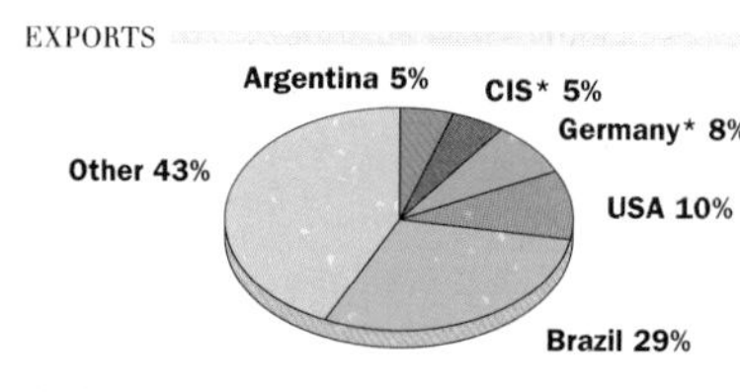

IMPORTS

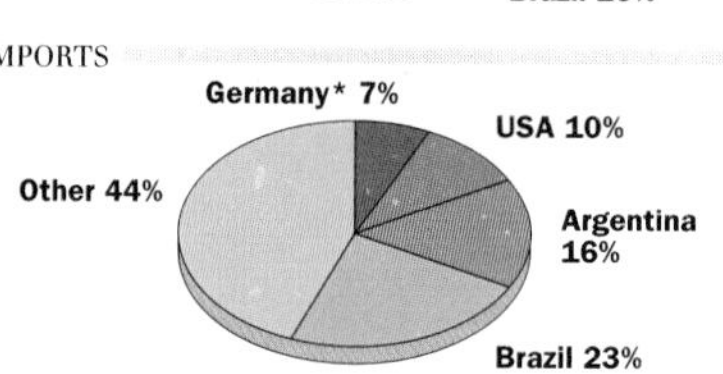

ECONOMIC PERFORMANCE INDICATOR

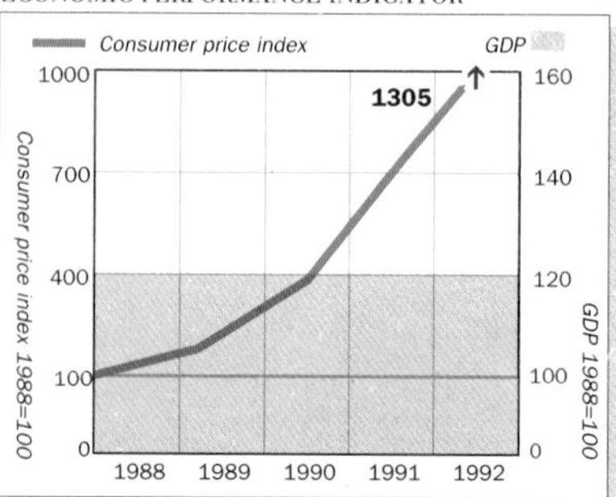

STRENGTHS
Substantial earnings as offshore banking center. Buoyant tourism. Fertile grasslands. World's second-biggest wool exporter.

WEAKNESSES
No oil or minerals except for agate, amethysts, unexploited gold deposits and small quantities of iron ore. Little progress in industrialization. Low world agricultural prices.

PROFILE
Uruguay is traditionally an agricultural economy. Three-quarters of the country is rich pasture, supporting livestock. Much of the rest is devoted to crops. Farming, which formerly brought great wealth to Uruguay, still employs about 15% of the labor force, accounting for about 10% of GDP. Livestock and animal products, especially meat and wool, account for over one-third of export earnings. In addition, manufacturing, which accounts for 25% of GDP, is farm-based. However, tourism has now overtaken both in terms of economic importance. Most economic activity – and half the population – is concentrated in Montevideo. Much of the economy is still state-controlled, including all the largest companies. In 1992, voters rejected a large part of President Herrera's privatization program in a referendum.

URUGUAY : MAJOR BUSINESSES

U

RESOURCES

7.4bn kwh (capacity 1.68m kw)

Not an oil producer; refines 28,500 b/cd

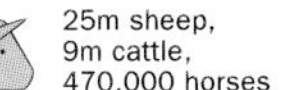

25m sheep, 9m cattle, 470,000 horses

Agate, amethyst, gold, iron

Most of Uruguay is farmland; much is given over to cattle and sheep. Rice is the country's only significant crop on the world market. Mineral resources may be considerable but, despite optimistic geological surveys, are yet to be exploited. Small quantities of building materials and jewelry-quality agate and amethysts are mined.

ELECTRICITY GENERATION

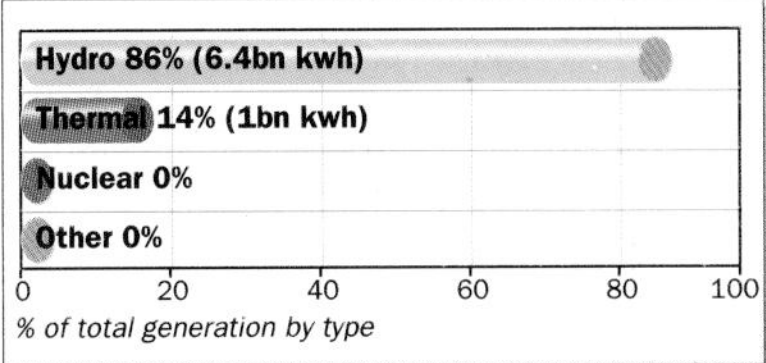

Hydroelectric power generates 86% of the country's electricity. Its export offsets Uruguay's total dependency on imported oil.

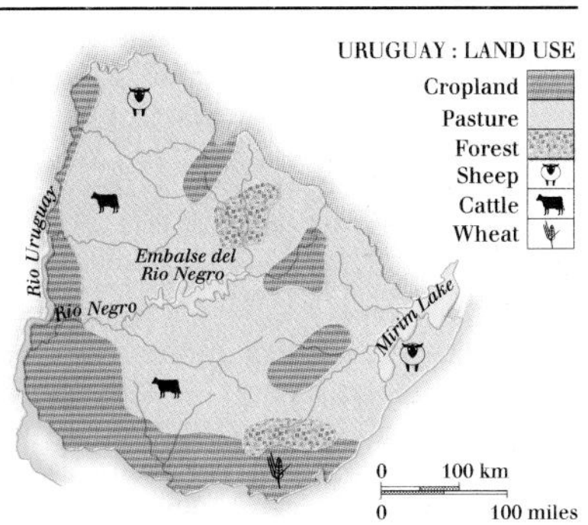

ENVIRONMENT

0.2% (0.1% partially protected)

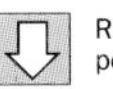

Rising riverine pollution

ENVIRONMENTAL TREATIES

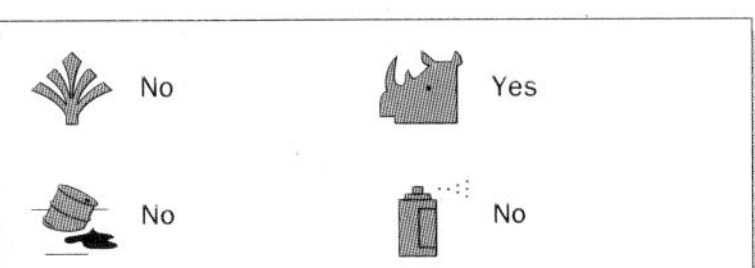

Pollution of the country's two main rivers, the Uruguay and the River Plate, is of increasing concern.

MEDIA

Full freedom of expression is guaranteed by the constitution

PUBLISHING AND BROADCAST MEDIA

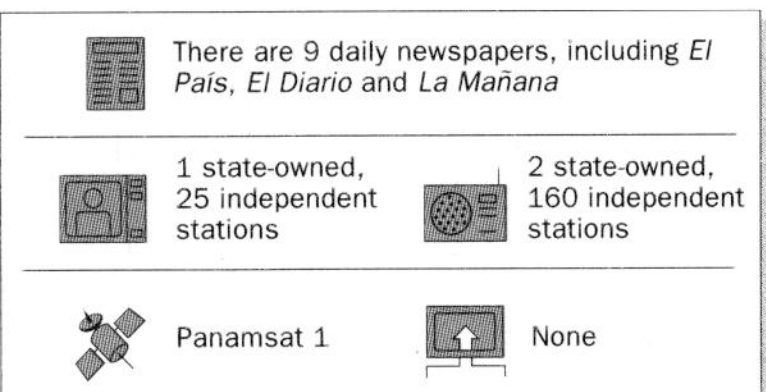

There are 9 daily newspapers, including *El País*, *El Diario* and *La Mañana*
1 state-owned, 25 independent stations
2 state-owned, 160 independent stations
Panamsat 1
None

The press is now relatively free. *El País* supports the *Blancos* (PN), while *La Manaña* backs the *Colorados* (PC).

CRIME

1,910 prisoners

Up 29% in 1990

CRIME RATES

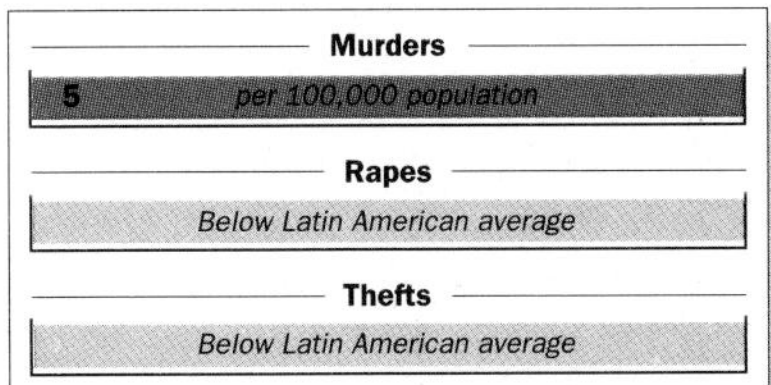

Crime levels in Uruguay are low, particularly compared with its neighbors Brazil and Argentina. Domestic theft is the main problem. Bribery is not common.

EDUCATION

96%

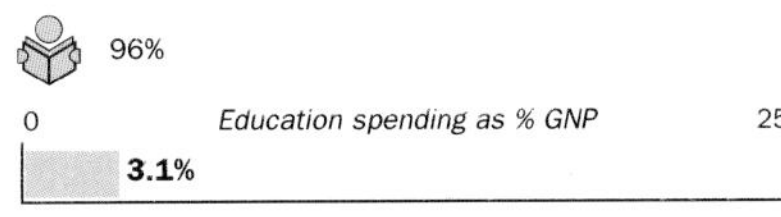

THE EDUCATION SYSTEM

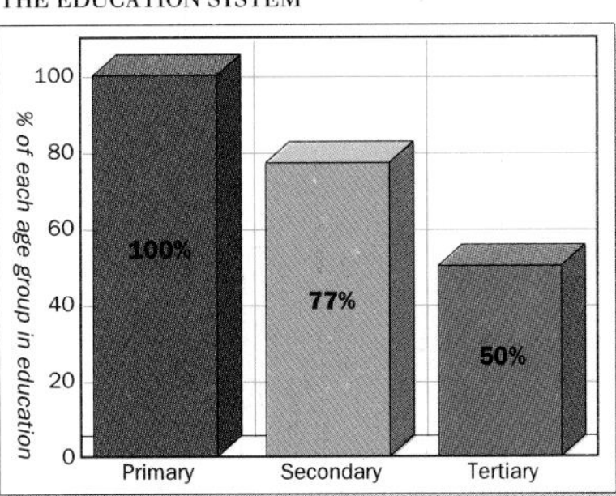

Education is inspired by the French *lycée* system. Up to secondary level (12 years) it is paid for by the state and is compulsory for all children between the ages of six and 14. Uruguay boasts the highest literacy rate (around 96%) in South America. Both state and private schools follow the same curriculum; private schools are monitored by the government. However, in poor rural areas, facilities are rudimentary. Uruguay has two state-funded universities. The children of wealthy Uruguayans tend to complete their studies in the USA.

HEALTH

1 per 341 people

Cerebrovascular and heart diseases, cancer, accidents

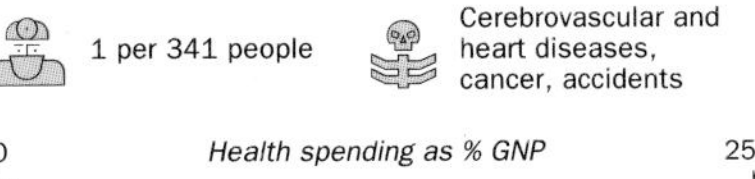

Most Uruguayans have easy access to health services. The average life expectancy of 72 years is the highest in South America. Public services cater to 40% of the population and the private sector to the remaining 60%. Despite opposition, the government is attempting to privatize some state medical establishments.

WEALTH

Grain miller, 4,860 new Uruguayan pesos per hour; medical general practitioner, 20,400 new Uruguayan pesos per hour

CONSUMER GOODS OWNERSHIP

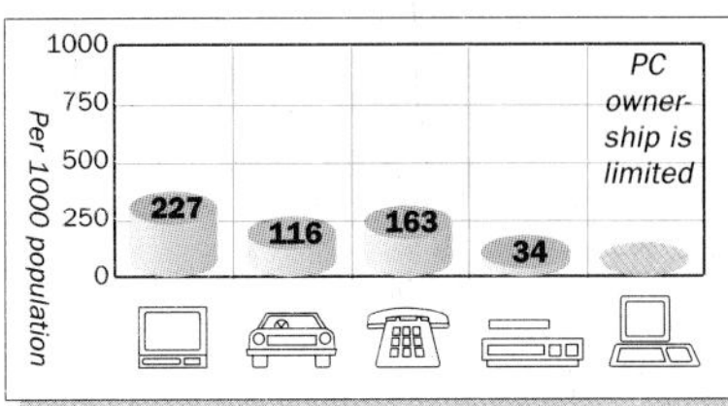

Uruguay possesses the social mobility typical of countries created through decades of large-scale immigration. Many professionals come from modest backgrounds. The wealthy tend to be landowners or employed in the financial sector. They still look toward Europe, rather than the USA, for luxury goods and the latest fashions. They travel to Europe for their vacations or visit Uruguay's coastal resorts, such as Punta del Este. The most common status symbol is a Mercedes car.

The most deprived sections of Uruguayan society are the urban poor of Montevideo, a large proportion of whom are of mixed African and European descent, and the rural poor, who have little or no land of their own.

WORLD RANKING

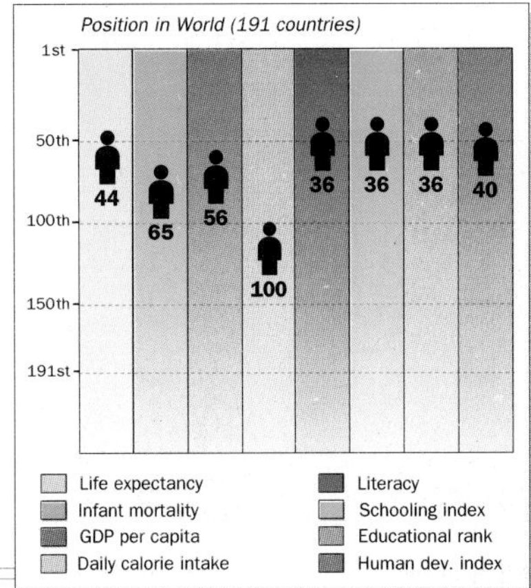

U

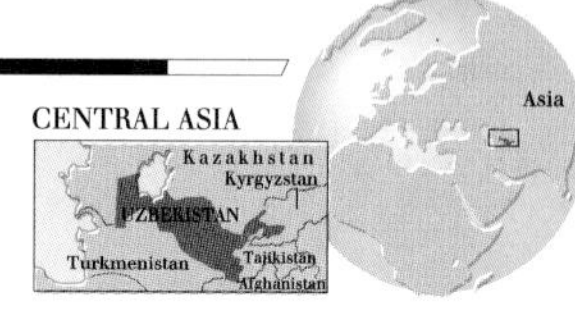

UZBEKISTAN

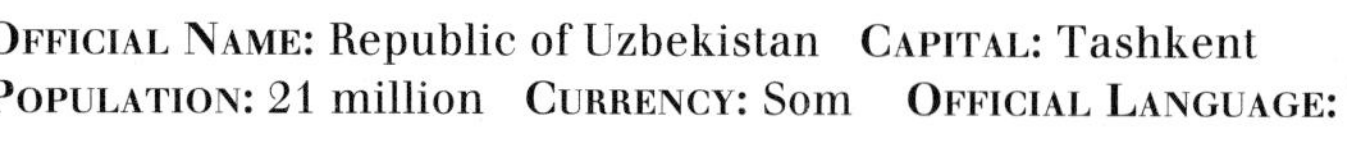

OFFICIAL NAME: Republic of Uzbekistan **CAPITAL:** Tashkent
POPULATION: 21 million **CURRENCY:** Som **OFFICIAL LANGUAGE:** Uzbek

SHARING THE ARAL SEA coastline with its northern neighbor, Kazakhstan, Uzbekistan has common borders with five countries, including Afghanistan to the south. It is the most populous Central Asian republic and has considerable natural resources. Uzbekistan contains the ancient Muslim cities of Samarkand, Bukhara, Khiva and Tashkent. The dictatorship of President Karimov has prevented the spread of Islamic fundamentalism.

CLIMATE

WEATHER CHART

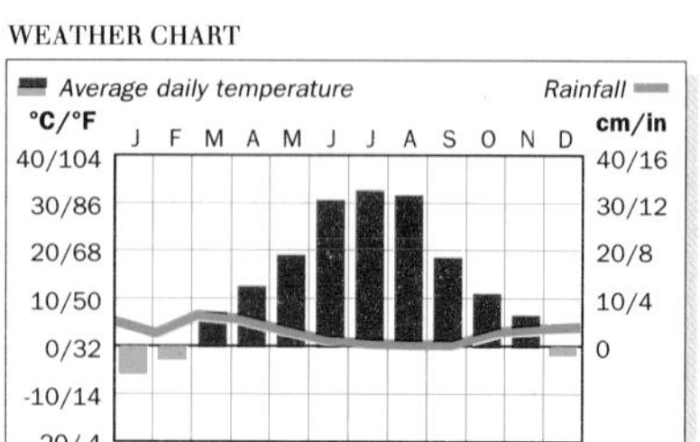

Uzbekistan has a harsh continental climate. Summers can be extremely hot and dry. Large areas of the country are desert.

COMMUNICATIONS

THE TRANSPORTATION NETWORK

Uzbekistan has a well-developed transportation system. An extensive network of buses serves country areas while good Soviet-style systems of trolley buses and trolleys operate in the major cities. Road and rail networks have, however, deteriorated since 1991, and are concentrated in the south and east. The national airline, the *Uzbek Khavo Yullan* (Uzbekistan Airways), is operated by a Pakistani company.

TOURISM

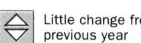

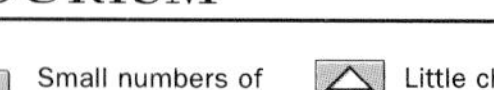

MAIN OVERSEAS ARRIVALS

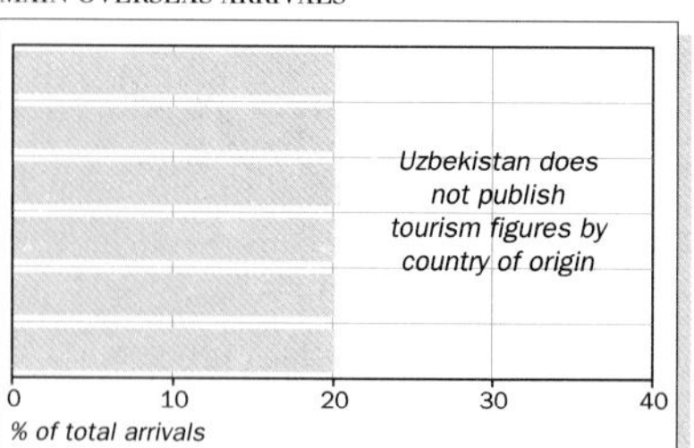

Uzbekistan has considerable tourist potential. Bukhara, once a trading center on the silk route, is famous worldwide for its architecture and carpet-making. To Muslims, it is second only to Mecca as a religious center. Muslims unable to undertake the *haj* (pilgrimage) to Mecca can become *hajis* by visiting Bukhara seven times instead. The city of Samarkand was built in the 14th century by Tamburlaine, and is home to the monumental gateway of the Shir Dar Madrasa, which vies with India's Taj Mahal as one of the most beautiful buildings in the Islamic world.

UZBEKISTAN

Total Area : 1 138 910 sq. km (439 733 sq. miles)

LAND HEIGHT	POPULATION
3000m/9843ft	over 1 000 000
2000m/6562ft	over 100 000
1000m/3281ft	over 50 000
500m/1640ft	over 10 000
200m/656ft	

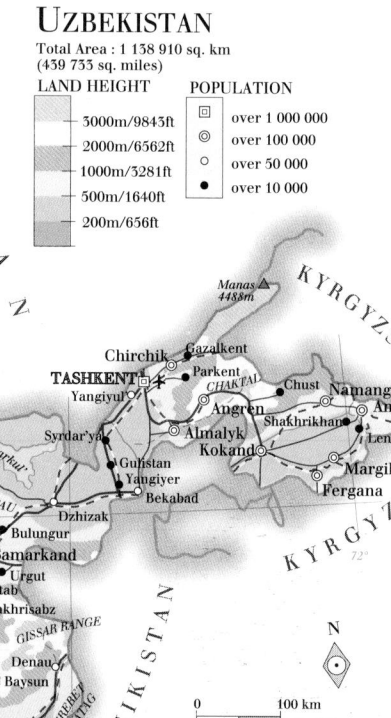

KAZAKHSTAN · ARAL SEA · USTYURT PLATEAU · TURAN LOWLAND · KYZYL KUM · TURKMENISTAN · KYRGYZSTAN · TAJIKISTAN · AFGHANISTAN · Muynak · Chimbay · Takhtakupyr · Kungrad · Amu · Khodzheyli · Nukus · Takhiatash · Uchkuduk · Zarafshan · Beruni · Urgench · Turtkul' · Khiva · Manas 4488m · Chirchik · Gazalkent · Parkent · CHAKTAL · TASHKENT · Yangiyul' · Chust · Namangan · Andizhan · Angren · Almalyk · Shakhrikhan · Leninsk · Kokand · Syrdar'ya · Gulistan · Yangiyer · Bekabad · Margilan · Fergana · Ozero Aydarkul' · Nurata · Lyangar · KHREBET NURATAU · Navoi · Gizhduvan · Gazli · Bukhara · Kagan · Aktash · Kattakurgan · Dzhizak · Bulungur · Samarkand · Urgut · Karakul' · Kitab · Shakhrisabz · Kasan · Karshi · GISSAR RANGE · Denau · Baysun · KHREBET BABATAG · Dzharkurgan · Termez · N · 0 100 km · 0 100 miles

Mosque in Samarkand. The city remained an Islamic stronghold, despite communist attempts at suppression, when Uzbekistan formed part of the Soviet Union.

PEOPLE

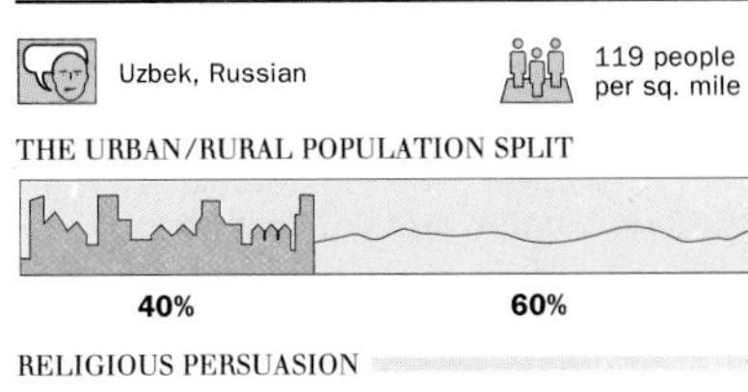

RELIGIOUS PERSUASION

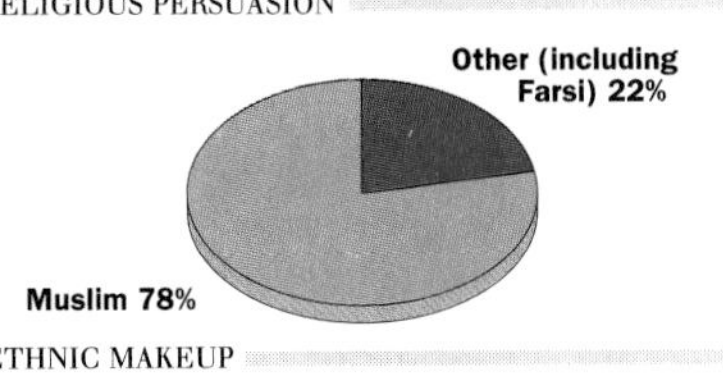

ETHNIC MAKEUP

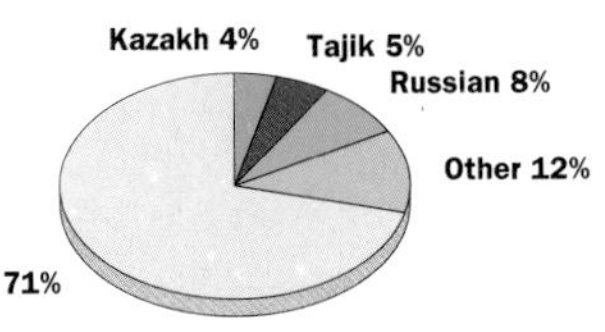

Among ex-Soviet republics, Uzbekistan has a relatively complex makeup. In addition to the Uzbeks, Russians, Tajiks and Kazakhs, there are small minorities of Tatars and Karakalpaks. The proportion of Russians has been declining since the 1970s, when net emigration of Russians began. Tensions among ethnic groups have the potential to create regional and racial conflict. The authoritarian nature of the Karimov leadership has so far prevented these antagonisms from becoming violent. Incidents such as the 1989 and 1990 clashes between Meskhetian Turks and Uzbeks are rare. The removal of the Communist Party's leadership has meant that Uzbek society has reverted to traditional social patterns based on family, religion, clan and region, rather than on membership of the party. Independence has done little to alter the minor role of women in politics. Arranged marriages are still the custom in the countryside.

POPULATION AGE BREAKDOWN

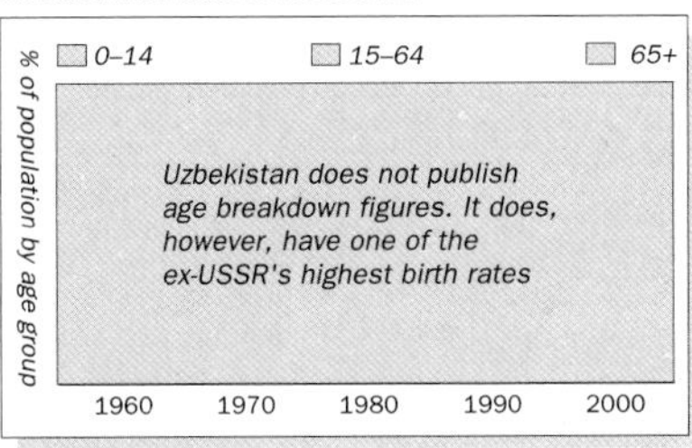

POLITICS

1994

President Islam Karimov

THE STATE OF THE PARTIES

Supreme Soviet 500 members

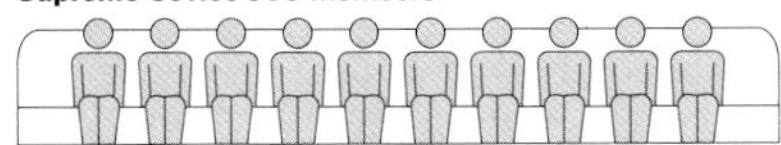

The People's Democratic Party of Uzbekistan (the former Communist Party) is the ruling party. Elections to a new Supreme Assembly, due to replace the Supreme Soviet, are scheduled for 1994

Uzbekistan is in effect run by a presidential dictatorship.

Main Political Issues

Islamic fundamentalism

The civil war in neighboring Tajikistan has made the Karimov leadership wary of Islamic fundamentalism taking hold in Uzbekistan. The Uzbek constitution stipulates the separation of Islam and the state, and Islam has been carefully kept out of politics.

Regionalism

Uzbekistan's high birthrate is placing pressure on limited agricultural resources. There have been calls for secession from some regions wishing to stop large numbers of people moving from poorer areas. In the Fergana Valley, one of the most densely populated regions, there have been a number of violent incidents.

Profile

President Karimov's People's Democratic Party of Uzbekistan has not been willing to devolve or share power.

A constitution adopted in December 1992, a year after the country attained formal independence, appeared to allow for the development of multiparty politics along Western lines. However, it also gave the President greater powers than before. Karimov subsequently banned a number of opposition parties, including the nationalist *Birlik* (Unity) movement and the Islamic Renaissance Party. The only legal opposition party, *Erk* (Will), lost its license with the Ministry of Justice in 1993.

Opposition is now almost entirely underground. Arbitrary imprisonment and even physical intimidation are being used against suspected enemies of the regime. Karimov's avoidance of overtly nationalist rhetoric gives him the support of the Russian minority.

***Islam A. Karimov**, first elected President in 1990; reelected, by referendum, the following year.*

WORLD AFFAIRS

Unlike neighboring Turkmenistan, Kyrgyzstan and Tajikistan, Uzbekistan has the resources to allow it to follow a relatively independent foreign policy. The Karimov leadership has used this to promote Uzbekistan as the leading central Asian state. It has established itself as the CIS power base in the region, and has even proposed a central Asian common market. The silk route used to run through Samarkand and Tashkent and, in a modern revival of the connection, Uzbekistan sees itself once more as a key link between Europe and China.

Relations with Turkey are also developing. Where Western companies have difficulty in sealing contracts in Uzbekistan, Turkish companies have been commissioned to build vital installations such as telecommunications. Many young Uzbeks are also being sent to Turkey to study business practice.

The crucial relationship, however, remains that with Russia, which has 100,000 troops stationed in the country. These are a key part of Karimov's ability to stay in power. Moscow backs him because it approves of his anti-nationalist approach to domestic politics.

CHRONOLOGY

Part of the great Mongol empire, present-day Uzbekistan was incorporated into the Russian Empire between 1865 and 1876. Russification of the area was superficial, and it was not until Soviet rule that significant Slav immigration occurred. A further influx of Slavs into Uzbekistan occurred during Stalin's program of forced collectivization.

- **1917** Soviet power established in Tashkent.
- **1918** Turkestan Autonomous Soviet Socialist Republic (ASSR), incorporating present-day Uzbekistan, proclaimed.
- **1923–1941** Language changed four times, from Arabic alphabet to Latin, then based on Iranized Tashkent, and finally replaced by Cyrillic.
- **1924** Basmachi rebels who resisted Soviet rule crushed. Uzbek SSR founded (which, until 1929, included the Tajik ASSR).
- **1925** Repressive campaign against Islamic religion. All Muslim schools and mosques forced to close. Retains autonomous status.

U

CHRONOLOGY *continued*

- **1936** Karakalpak ASSR (formerly part of the Russian Soviet Federative Socialist Republic) incorporated into the Uzbek SSR.
- **1937** Akmal Ikramov, first secretary of the Uzbek Communist Party (CPUZ), and Prime Minister Faizulla Khodzhaev, purged by Stalin.
- **1941–1945** Industry and Slavs evacuated to Uzbekistan from war zone in eastern USSR during World War II. Leads to considerable economic growth.
- **1959** Sharaf Rashidov becomes first secretary of CPUZ. Retains position until 1983.
- **1983** Yuri Andropov becomes President in Moscow. Begins campaign to root out corruption in government. CPUZ specially targeted. Massive corruption scandal uncovered in cotton procurement industry. The USSR's largest anti-corruption purge results in the replacement of 40 out of 65 party secretaries. In effect, an entirely new generation of Central Asian officials installed. Uzbekistan's managerial elite now the youngest in the USSR.
- **1989** First non-communist political movement, Unity Party *(Birlik)*, formed but not officially registered. June: clashes between Meskhetian Turks and indigenous Uzbek population of Fergana Valley in eastern Uzbekistan; more than 100 dead. October: *Birlik* campaign leads to Uzbek being declared the official language.
- **1990** March: Islam Karimov becomes executive president of the new Uzbek Supreme Soviet. Sovereignty declared. Further interethnic fighting in Fergana Valley. 320 killed.
- **1991** 31 August: independence proclaimed. September: Republic of Uzbekistan adopted as official name. October: Uzbekistan signs treaty establishing economic community with seven other former Soviet republics. November: Communist Party of Uzbekistan restructured as the People's Democratic Party of Uzbekistan (PDPU). Karimov remains its leader. December: Karimov confirmed in post of president with 86% of total votes. Uzbekistan joins the CIS.
- **1992** Price liberalization provokes student riots in Tashkent. New post-Soviet constitution adopted along Western democratic lines. All religious parties banned. September: Uzbekistan sends troops to Tajikistan to suppress violence and strengthens border controls.

U

AID

 $123m (receipts)

 Likely to rise

A lack of commitment to economic stabilization or reform and the abuse of human rights have generally deterred bilateral aid donors. However, in 1993, the World Bank contributed $23 million and the EBRD $100 million to assist in the restructuring of small enterprises.

DEFENSE

 Low

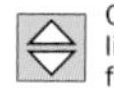 Currently stable, but likely to rise as national forces are established

0 *Defense spending as % GDP* 40

Uzbekistan does not publish defense spending figures

Uzbekistan has a 700-strong National Guard, which generally acts as the personal army of Karimov. The army is trained by Russian officers whereas the police are Turkish-trained. Russian troops are still based on Uzbek territory to protect the Russian minority and as part of Moscow's security strategy.

UZBEK ARMED FORCES

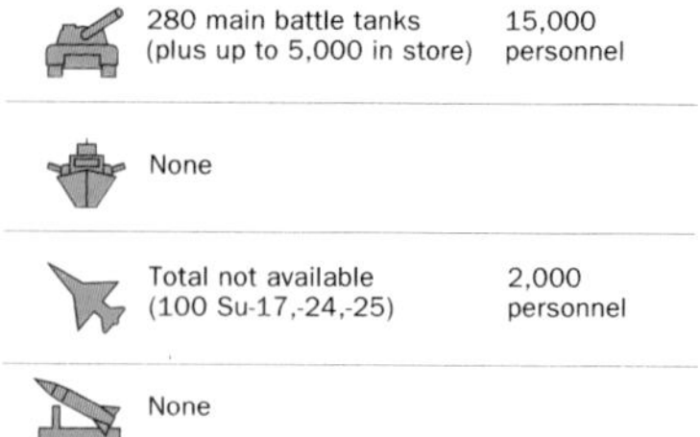

Tanks	280 main battle tanks (plus up to 5,000 in store)	15,000 personnel
Navy	None	
Air force	Total not available (100 Su-17,-24,-25)	2,000 personnel
Missiles	None	

ECONOMICS

 $28.26bn

 20,000 som

SCORE CARD

- World GNP Ranking..........55th
- GNP per Capita..........$1,346
- Balance of Payments..........$-60m
- Inflation..........600%
- Unemployment..........6.9%

EXPORTS/IMPORTS

Trade is overwhelmingly with the Russian Federation and neighboring states of the former Soviet Union

ECONOMIC PERFORMANCE INDICATOR

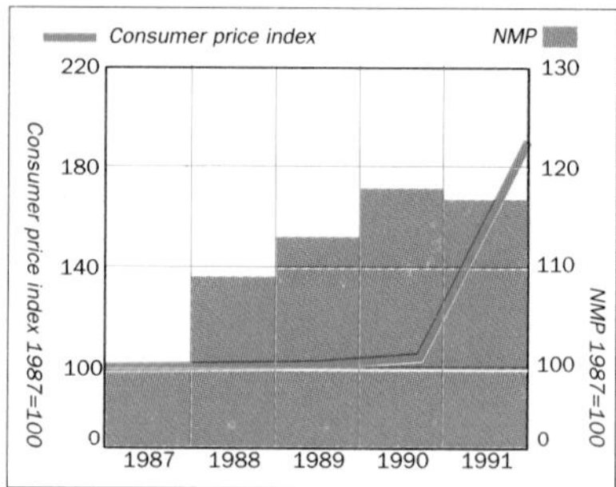

Strengths
Gold: Uzbekistan was the USSR's second largest producer. Well-developed cotton market. Considerable unexploited deposits of oil and natural gas. Current production of natural gas makes significant contribution to electricity generation. Manufacturing tradition includes agricultural machinery and central Asia's only aviation factory.

Weaknesses
Dependent on Russia, Kazakhstan and at times the USA for grain, as Uzbekistan produces only 25% of its domestic requirements. Little progress on privatization. Very limited economic reform. Cotton production depends on massive, environmentally damaging irrigation programs.

Profile
Uzbekistan's economy remains predominantly agricultural. Tashkent became an industrial area following the evacuation of industry from the western USSR states during World War II. Privatization is unlikely to be speeded up while the ex-communists are in power. The gold sector, however, has been opened up to joint ventures with US companies. Uzbekistan also hopes that eager foreign interest in its unexploited energy resources will result in large investments.

UZBEKISTAN : MAJOR BUSINESSES

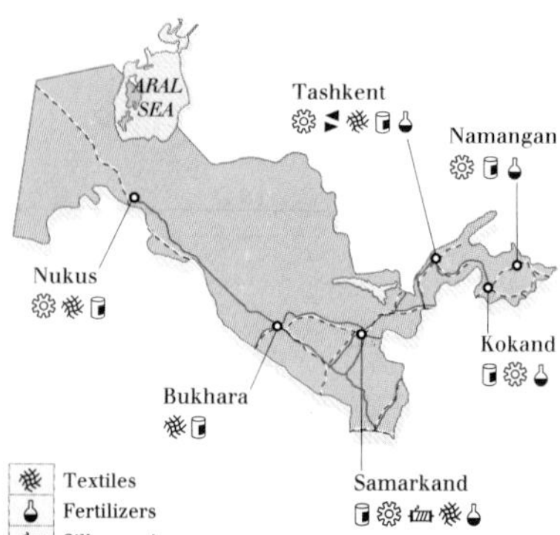

RESOURCES

50.9bn kwh (capacity 11.9m kw)

50,600 b/d

8.8m sheep and goats, 4.2m cattle, 742,900 pigs

Natural gas, coal, oil, gold, uranium, copper, tungsten, bauxite

ELECTRICITY GENERATION

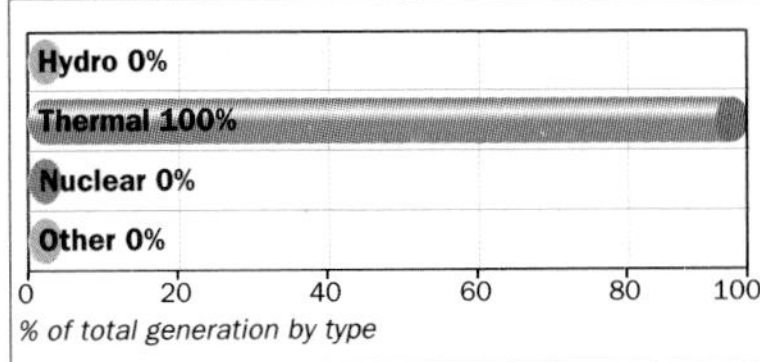

As well as containing the world's largest single gold mine, at Murantau, Uzbekistan has large deposits of natural gas, petroleum, coal and uranium. An important oilfield was discovered in 1992 in the Namangan region and production will rise with further investment. Most gas production is currently used domestically, but gas could also become a strong export.

Cotton is the main focus of agriculture: Uzbekistan is the world's fourth-largest producer. A post-independence decision to diversify was reversed when the value of cotton as a commodity on the world market became clear. Fruit, silk cocoons and vegetables for Moscow's markets are also of rising importance.

UZBEKISTAN : LAND USE

ARAL SEA

KYZYL KUM

Cropland
Pasture
Forest
High mountain regions
Desert
Wetlands
Sheep
Cotton - cash crop

0 200 km
0 200 miles

ENVIRONMENT

Minimal

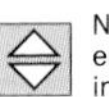

No major environmental initiatives under way

ENVIRONMENTAL TREATIES

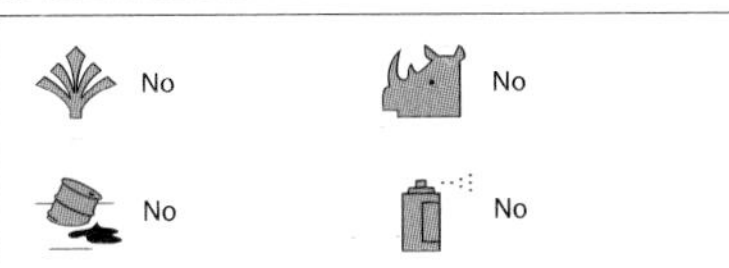

Under Soviet rule, Uzbekistan's cotton industry became one of the largest in the world. The irrigation schemes required to sustain the crop were ill-conceived and have wreaked considerable environmental damage. Soil salination is now a major problem. The Aral Sea has also been seriously depleted. From 23,875 sq. miles in 1974, it is expected to have shrunk to an area of only 9,034 sq. miles by 2000. The almost indiscriminate use of fertilizers and pesticides to raise production has also heavily polluted many Uzbek rivers.

MEDIA

The media operates under tight political and religious censorship

PUBLISHING AND BROADCAST MEDIA

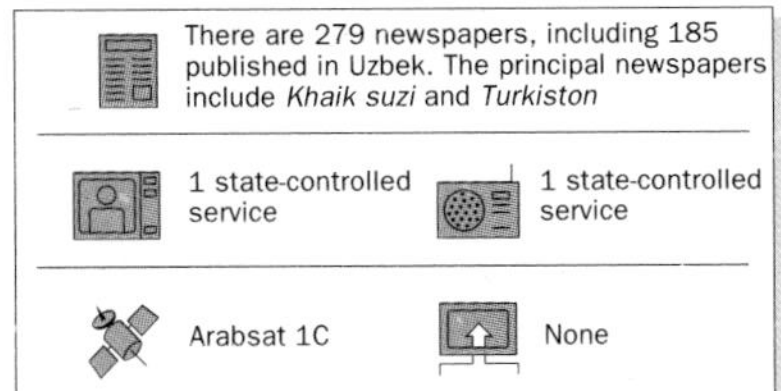

There are 279 newspapers, including 185 published in Uzbek. The principal newspapers include *Khaik suzi* and *Turkiston*
1 state-controlled service
1 state-controlled service
Arabsat 1C
None

In effect, Uzbekistan has no independent media. The press supports the personality cult and policies of Karimov. All opposition press is censored. Expression of Islamic and nationalist opinion is also forbidden, and any journalists suspected of promoting such views are repressed. Russian-language newspapers imported from Moscow are censored.

CRIME

Uzbekistan does not publish prison figures

Crime is rising

CRIME RATES

All categories of crime are rising, especially in areas of high unemployment such as the Fergana Valley

A decline in living standards has meant a general increase in crime. Many of the rural population grow drug plants, particularly opium poppies, to supplement their falling incomes. Unofficial Islamic courts set up by disaffected young men in the Fergana Valley are an indication of growing Muslim opposition to the government.

EDUCATION

Over 90%

0 *Education spending as % GNP* 25

7.9%

THE EDUCATION SYSTEM

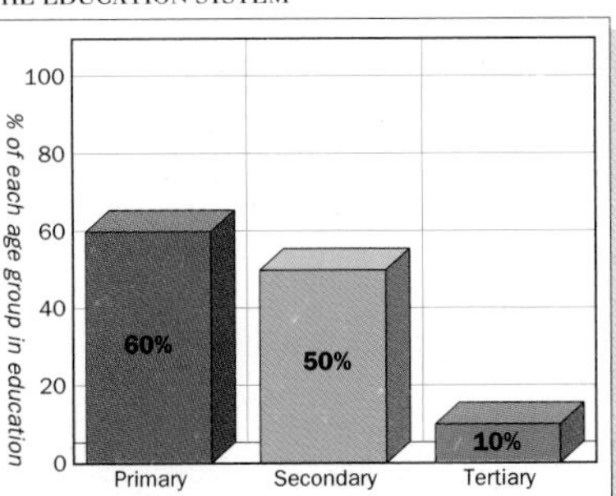

The system still follows the Soviet model, although some instruction is in Uzbek. In the late 1980s, a few ethnic Tajik schools appeared in large cities along with a university in Samarkand. They were virtually all closed down in 1992 as a result of a decline in relations between the leaderships of Uzbekistan and Tajikistan.

HEALTH

1 per 275 people

Circulatory and respiratory diseases, accidents, cancer

0 *Health spending as % GNP* 25

Uzbekistan does not publish health spending figures

The health service has been declining since the dissolution of the USSR. Some rural areas are not served at all. Serious respiratory diseases among cotton growers are increasing.

WEALTH

There is a very large disparity of wealth between rich and poor

CONSUMER GOODS OWNERSHIP

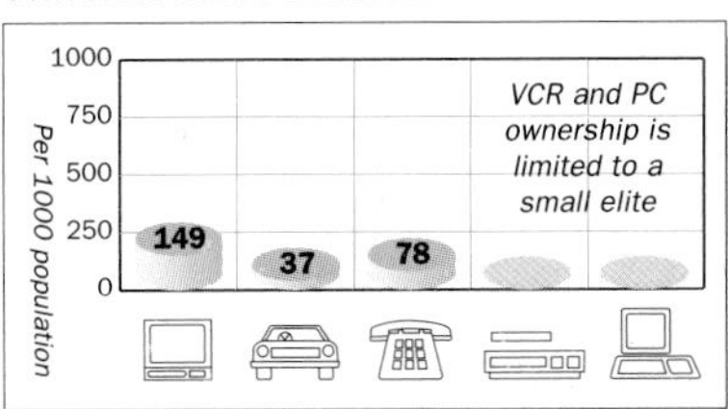

Former communists are still the wealthiest group as they retain control of the economy. Many rural poor live below the poverty line.

WORLD RANKING

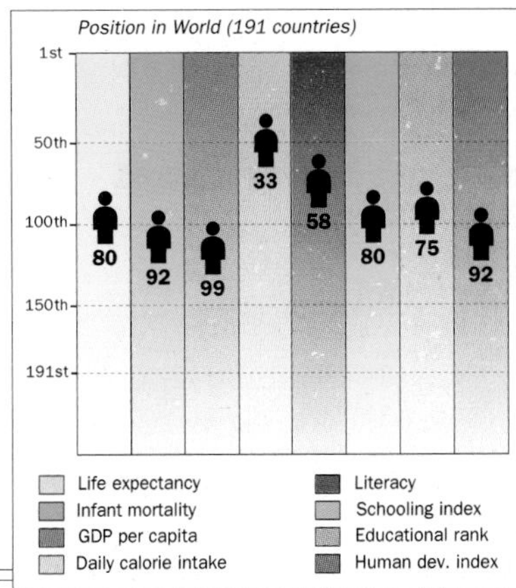

U

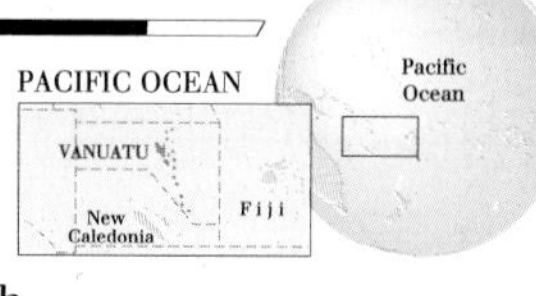

VANUATU

OFFICIAL NAME: Republic of Vanuatu **CAPITAL:** Port-Vila
POPULATION: 163,000 **CURRENCY:** Vatu **OFFICIAL LANGUAGES:** Bislama, English and French

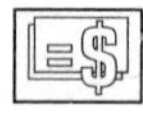

AN ARCHIPELAGO strung out over 800 miles of the South Pacific, Vanuatu lies 620 miles west of Fiji. Mountainous and volcanic in origin, only 12 of the 82 islands are of significant size – Espiritu Santo and Malakula are the largest. The capital, Port-Vila, is on Éfaté. Formerly the New Hebrides – ruled jointly by France and Britain from 1906 – Vanuatu became independent in 1980. Politics since independence in 1980 has been democratic but volatile.

CLIMATE

WEATHER CHART

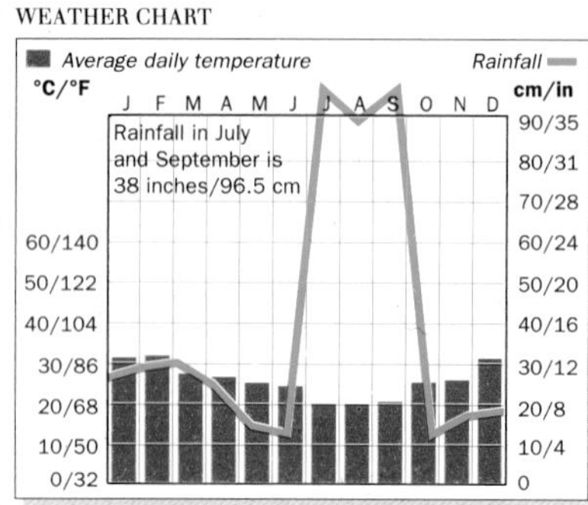

The climate is tropical and hot. Rainfall and temperatures decrease north to south. Cyclones occur November–April.

COMMUNICATIONS

 **Bauerfield, Port-Vila**

THE TRANSPORTATION NETWORK

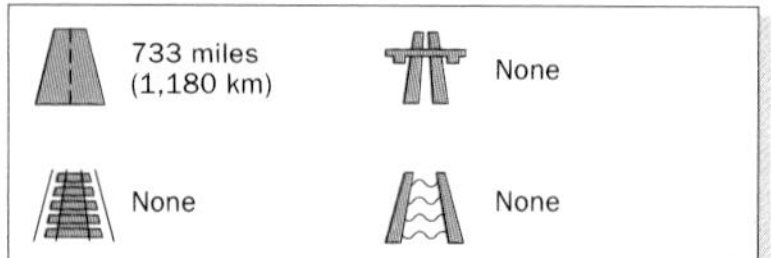

Frequent air and shipping services link the islands. State-owned Air Vanuatu flies to Australia and New Zealand.

TOURISM

 42,673 visitors

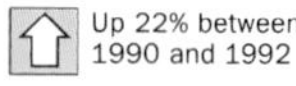

MAIN OVERSEAS ARRIVALS

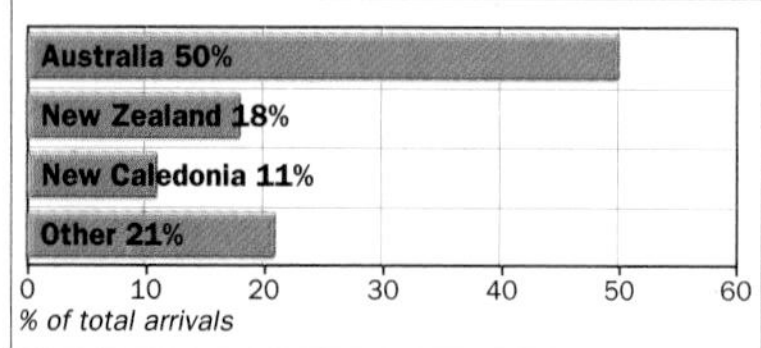

Tourism is the fastest-growing sector of the economy, accounting for 40% of GDP. There are plans to expand hotel capacity and international air links.

PEOPLE

Bislama (Melanesian pidgin), English, French

31 people per sq. mile

THE URBAN/RURAL POPULATION SPLIT

21% 79%

RELIGIOUS PERSUASION

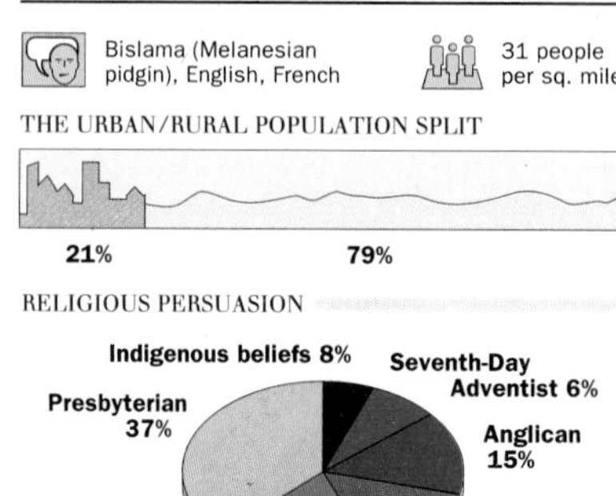

Indigenous Melanesians, ni-Vanuatu, comprise 98% of the population. Of Vanuatu's 82 islands, 67 are inhabited, but 80% of people live on 12 main islands. One in eight ni-Vanuatu now lives in Port-Vila. However, 75% of the population still live by subsistence agriculture.

Vanuatu is home to some of the Pacific's most traditional peoples and local social and religious customs are strong. With 105 indigenous languages, Vanuatu boasts the world's highest per capita density of languages. Bislama pidgin is the *lingua franca*.

Women have lower social status than men and bride price is still commonly paid. Many educated women refuse to marry because of loss of property rights. To boost equality, primary schools must now take 50% girls.

Vanuatu's unspoilt beaches are one of the reasons for the upsurge in the tourist industry.

POLITICS

1995

THE STATE OF THE PARTIES

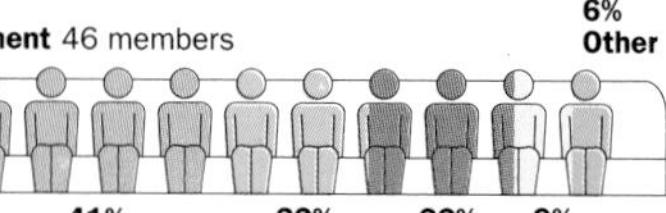

UMP = Union of Moderate Parties **VP** = Vanua'aku Party (Our Land Party) **NUP** = National United Party **MPP** = Melanesian Progressive Party

The government of Vanuatu was formerly shared by France and Britain. Political instability in the islands was one of the reasons which contributed to France's reluctance – not shared by the UK – to grant independence in 1980. The anti-French stance of the Vanua'aku Party (Our Land Party – VP), which governed from 1980–1991, was reinforced by French support for the short-lived secession of Espiritu Santo in 1980. Rivalries and splits in the VP culminated in a constitutional crisis in 1988, when President Sokomanu backed former VP secretary-general Barak Sope's efforts to oust Prime Minister Walter Lini. They failed and Fred Timakata became president. Lini's increasingly autocratic stance led to his dismissal by the VP in 1991.

Elections that year saw the victory of the opposition UMP. The UMP then formed a coalition with the NUP, set up by Lini, and began to repair relations with Paris. Strains in the coalition led to a stalemated election for a new president when Timakata's term ended in 1994. Parliamentary speaker Alfred Maseng became acting president.

WORLD AFFAIRS

Vanuatu was the first South Pacific nation to gain full membership in the Non-Aligned Movement. Relations with Australia are close. Those with France have improved since 1991.

AID

 $48m (receipts)

 Down 2% in 1991

Grant aid is equivalent to 30% of GDP, making Vanuatu Melanesia's most aid-dependent state. Leading donors include Australia, New Zealand, the UK and France. France cut aid twice in the 1980s after alleged interference in Vanuatu's internal affairs.

DEFENSE

 There are no military forces

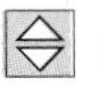 Not applicable

There is a small paramilitary force. Papua New Guinean troops helped to end the 1980 secessionist movement on Espiritu Santo under a defense agreement signed after independence.

ECONOMICS

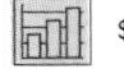 $193m

 122.86 vatu

SCORE CARD

- ❑ WORLD GNP RANKING........................178th
- ❑ GNP PER CAPITA $1,184
- ❑ BALANCE OF PAYMENTS..................$–17.1m
- ❑ INFLATION 4.3%
- ❑ UNEMPLOYMENT ....Low rate

STRENGTHS

Expanding services sector, including tourism and offshore finance, now accounts for 68% of GDP. Subsistence farming and small-scale cash cropping give majority of population a livelihood. Low foreign debt. GDP increasing.

WEAKNESSES

Large trade and budget deficits. Heavy import–export duties – to compensate for no direct taxes – increase domestic prices and deter exports. Declining prices for two largest exports: copra and cocoa. Limited outlets for new crop exports.

EXPORTS

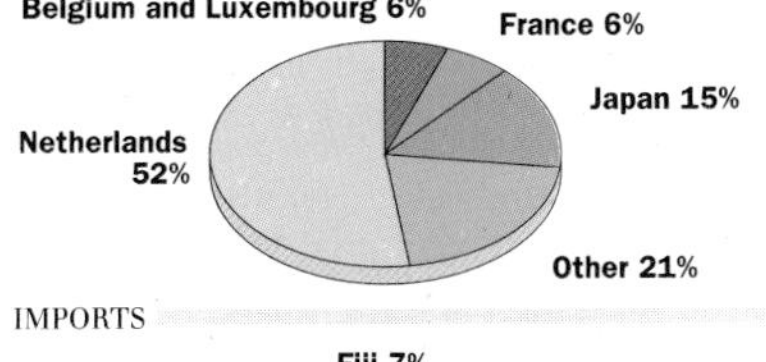

IMPORTS

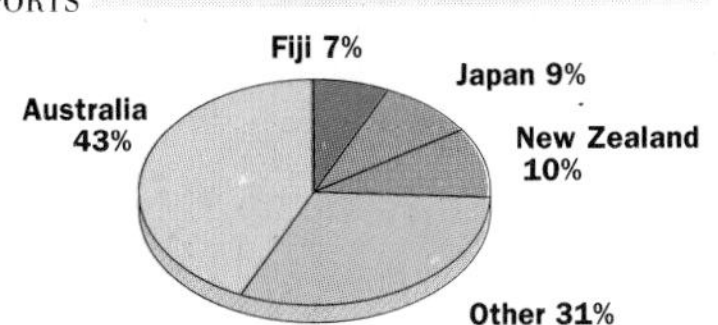

RESOURCES

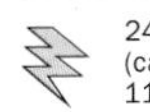 24m kwh (capacity 11,000 kw)

 Not an oil producer and has no refineries

 117,000 cattle, 80,000 pigs, 4,000 horses

 None

Vanuatu's main resources are its arable land – only 17% is utilized – and its forests and waters. These could be exploited by the tourist, timber and fishing industries. New export crops are being explored to offset declining copra and cocoa exports. Beef is of growing importance. Nuclear-power development was banned under 1983 legislation.

VANUATU

Total Area : 12 190 sq. km (4707 sq. miles)

POPULATION
over 10 000
under 10 000

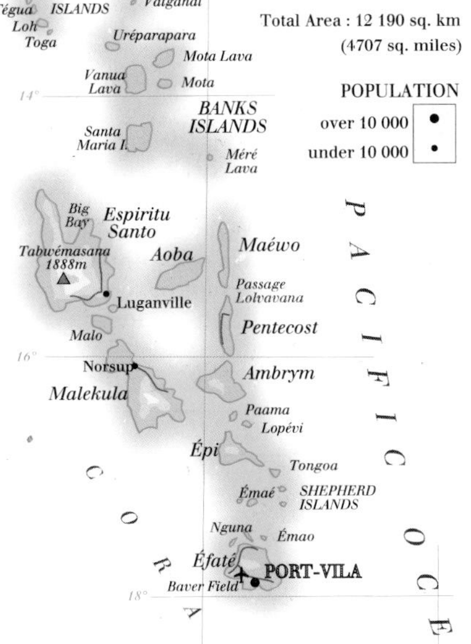

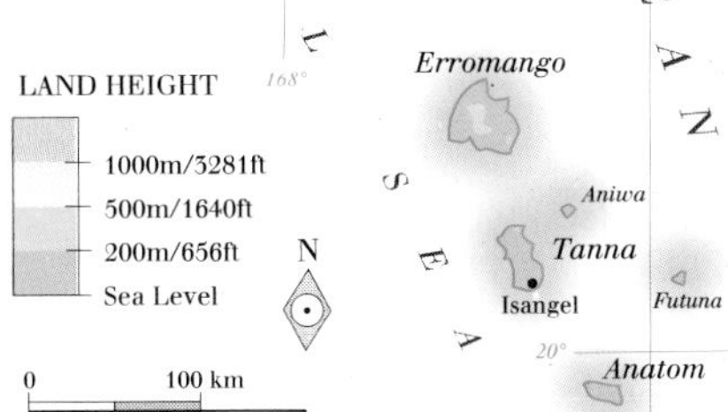

ENVIRONMENT

 None

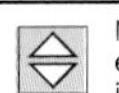 No serious environmental imbalances

Logging is growing, but 75% of the rainforest remains. Population growth is high at 3.2% a year, but not yet a major problem. Introduced diseases and the labor trade reduced the population from some 500,000 in 1800 to 40,000 in 1920; it is still recovering.

MEDIA

 There is no censorship

PUBLISHING AND BROADCAST MEDIA

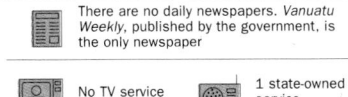

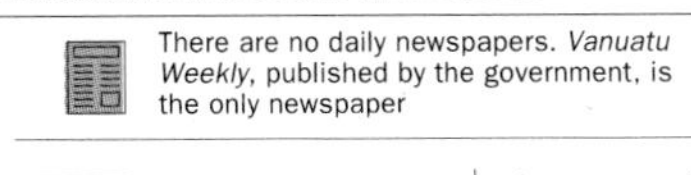

The dour *Vanuatu Weekly* is published in the three official languages. There is also a monthly, *Pacific Islands Profile*.

CRIME

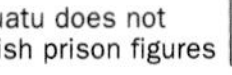 Vanuatu does not publish prison figures

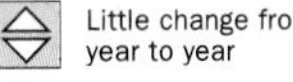 Little change from year to year

Domestic violence is a problem, but otherwise Vanuatu is almost crime-free – unlike other Melanesian states.

CHRONOLOGY

In 1906, Britain and France set up the New Hebrides under joint rule.

- ❑ **1980** Secessionism on Espiritu Santo mars independence; Walter Lini of VP is prime minister.
- ❑ **1980–1991** VP retains power amid political infighting and instability.
- ❑ **1991** UMP forms coalition with NUP set up by Lini in split from VP.
- ❑ **1994** Electoral college fails to elect new president.

EDUCATION

 53%

The abolition of fees has helped to boost primary enrolment to 85%. Secondary enrolment is under 20%.

HEALTH

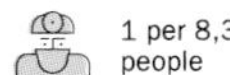 1 per 8,344 people

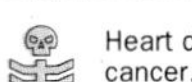 Heart diseases, cancer, malaria

A network of rural clinics and village health workers has helped to improve health levels. Nominal fees are charged.

WEALTH

 Wealth disparities are small among the indigenous population

CONSUMER GOODS OWNERSHIP

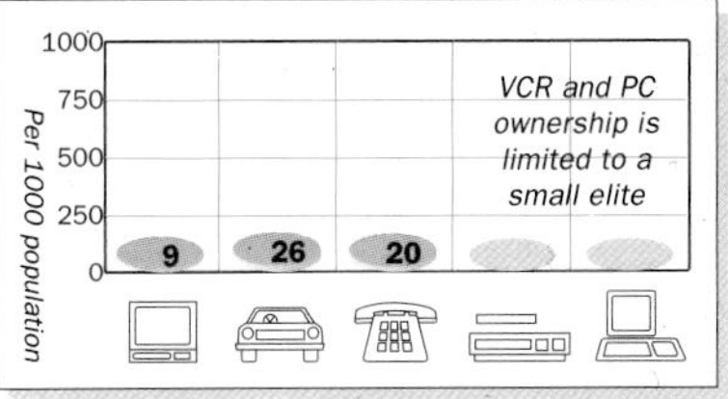

The dominance of subsistence farming and small-scale cash cropping has helped to prevent extreme poverty. The rich are mainly non-ni-Vanuatu.

WORLD RANKING

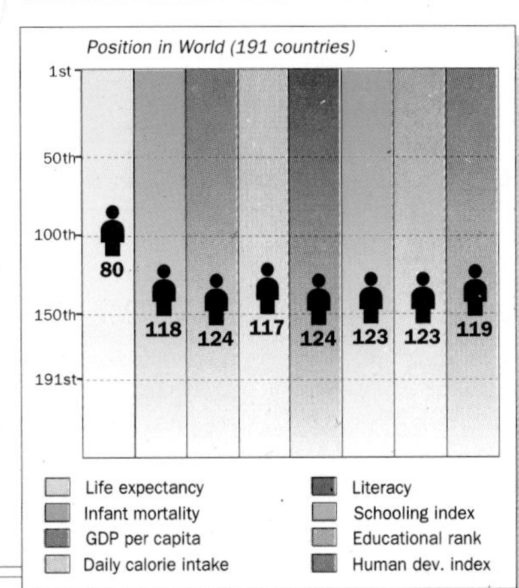

V

EUROPE

Europe

Italy

VATICAN CITY

VATICAN CITY

OFFICIAL NAME: State of the Vatican City **CAPITAL:** *Not applicable*
POPULATION: 1,000 **CURRENCY:** Lira **OFFICIAL LANGUAGES:** Italian and Latin

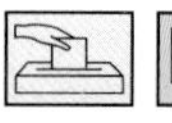

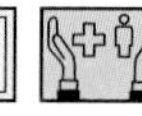

THE VATICAN CITY lies close to the Tiber in central Rome and is a fully independent state. It also includes ten other buildings in Rome and the Pope's residence at Castel Gandolfo. As the Holy See, it is the seat of the Catholic Church, deriving its income from investments and voluntary contributions known as Peter's Pence.

***The buildings and gardens** of the Vatican City. St. Peter's Basilica was built from 1506 to 1626 on the traditional site of St. Peter's tomb.*

CLIMATE

WEATHER CHART

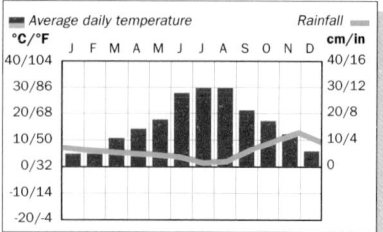

Average daily temperature — *Rainfall*

°C/°F — J F M A M J J A S O N D — cm/in

40/104, 30/86, 20/68, 10/50, 0/32, -10/14, -20/-4 — 40/16, 30/12, 20/8, 10/4, 0

Winters are mild, although November is particularly gray, and summers are hot.

COMMUNICATIONS

Heliport for official visitors

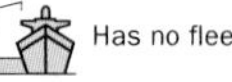

Has no fleet

THE TRANSPORTATION NETWORK

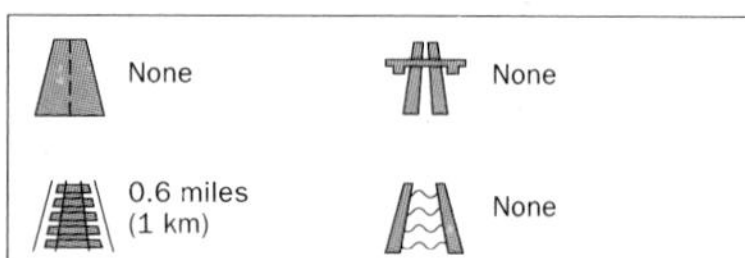

The railroad is only used for carrying freight. Official visitors are transferred from Rome airport by helicopter.

TOURISM

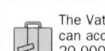

The Vatican Museums can accommodate 20,000 visitors daily

Little change from year to year

MAIN OVERSEAS ARRIVALS

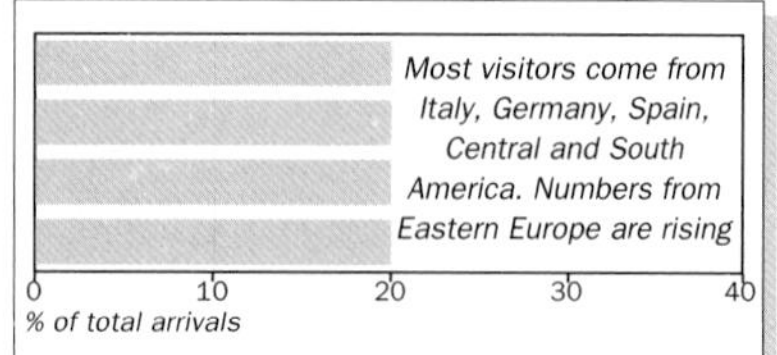

Almost all tourists who visit Rome visit the Vatican, while others come as pilgrims. Up to 100,000 hear the Pope's annual Easter Message in St. Peter's Square. The Vatican's art collections are among the greatest in the world. Years of restoration work on the Sistine Chapel frescoes were completed in 1994.

PEOPLE

Italian, Latin

5,887 people per sq. mile

THE URBAN/RURAL POPULATION SPLIT

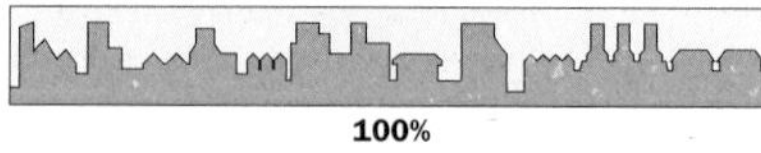

100%

RELIGIOUS PERSUASION

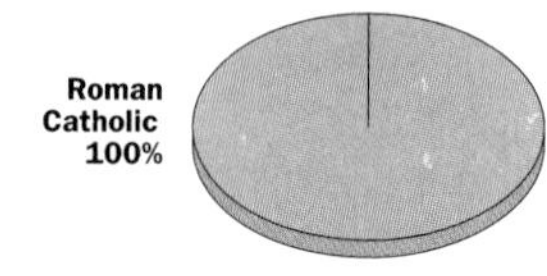

The Vatican has about 1,000 permanent inhabitants, including several hundred lay persons, and employs a further 3,400 lay staff. Citizenship can be acquired through stable residence and holding an office or job within the City. A citizen's family can gain residence only by authorization.

The Pope is spiritual head of almost 18% of the world's population. The countries with the largest number of Roman Catholics are Brazil, Mexico, Italy, the USA and the Philippines.

VATICAN CITY

Total Area : 0.44 sq. km (0.17 sq. miles)

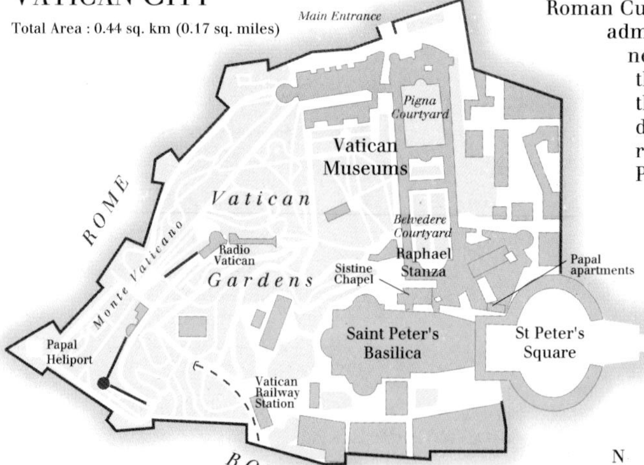

POLITICS

On death of reigning Pope

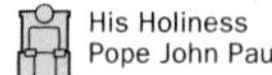

THE STATE OF THE PARTIES

Sacred College of Cardinals 162 members

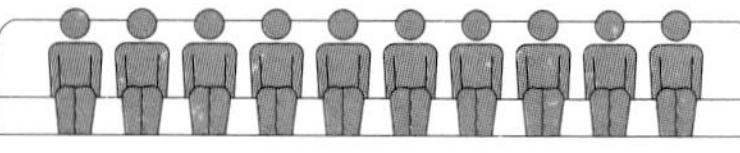

The Cardinals are divided into 3 orders, Bishops, Priests and Deacons

The Vatican City operates in the manner of an elected monarchy, as the reigning Pope has supreme executive, legislative and judicial powers, and holds office for life. He is elected by 120 members of the College of Cardinals, who vote until one candidate for the position of Supreme Pontiff achieves a two-thirds majority.

The administration of the Vatican City State, of which the Pope is temporal head, is conducted by the Pontifical Commission. The Holy See, which is the governing body of the Catholic Church worldwide and of which the Pope is spiritual head, is governed by the Roman Curia, the Church's administrative network. It is the Holy See that maintains diplomatic relations abroad. Pope John Paul II, elected in 1978, is the first non-Italian Pope since 1523.

V

WORLD AFFAIRS

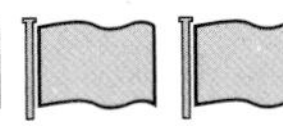

The Vatican maintains a neutral stance in world affairs and has observer status in many international organizations. It has mediated in many conflicts, notably achieving the 1993 peace agreement in Mozambique. Pope John Paul II has traveled more extensively than any other Pope to promote peace, overcome religious and racial discrimination, support the rights of minorities, whether foreign or indigenous, and to spread Roman Catholicism. The Holy See now has diplomatic relations with Russia and other former Soviet-bloc nations, and in 1993 the Pope re-established the Catholic Church in previously atheist Albania.

AID

 Undisclosed

 Undisclosed

Aid is donated through the Pope's Charities (The Holy Childhood Association, for example, distributes $15 million a year for children's causes), through funds donated for use at the Pope's discretion, and through religious orders acting under papal charter.

DEFENSE

 Ceremonial Swiss Guard only

 No significant change from year to year

The Vatican is strictly neutral territory. Under the 1954 Hague Convention, it is recognized as "a moral, artistic and cultural patrimony worthy of being respected as a treasure for all mankind."

ECONOMICS

 Not applicable

 1,473.41 Italian lira

SCORE CARD

- ❑ World GNP Ranking .... *The Vatican*
- ❑ GNP per Capita .... *does not have*
- ❑ Balance of Payments .... *a national*
- ❑ Inflation .... *economy in the*
- ❑ Unemployment .... *usual sense*

Strengths

Istituto per le Opere di Religione has assets of $3–$4 billion. Voluntary contributions from Catholics worldwide (Peter's Pence). Interest on investments. Gold reserves in Fort Knox, USA. Stamp and coin issues.

Weaknesses

Growing budgetary deficit (over $90 million): losses incurred by Vatican radio and newspaper, foreign Papal visits, high running costs of buildings, administration and diplomatic missions. Repayment of creditors from Banco Ambrosiano bankruptcy in 1982.

EXPORTS/IMPORTS

The Vatican produces no goods for export. All commodities are imported, mainly from Italy

RESOURCES

 None

 None

 None

None

The Vatican imports all its energy. It has no farmland as its area is restricted to buildings and their formal gardens.

ENVIRONMENT

 None

 Vatican has set up the St. Francis Prize for the Environment

The Vatican is increasingly concerned about the need to balance development and conservation. In 1993, the Pope urged a gathering of scientists to press colleagues worldwide to inform people on the need to protect the environment.

MEDIA

 The Vatican regards freedom of expression as a fundamental human right. The Vatican's media promotes the Catholic Church's beliefs and views

PUBLISHING AND BROADCAST MEDIA

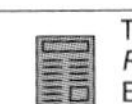 There is one daily newspaper, *L'Osservatore Romano*, which is also published weekly in 5 European languages, and monthly in Polish

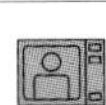 1 state-owned service

 1 state-owned service

The Vatican produces its own religious TV programs, but has no transmitter. Its radio broadcasts in 37 languages.

CRIME

 There are no prisons in the Vatican City

 Minimal crime levels

The only crime to have rocked the Vatican in recent years was the alleged implication of three of the Vatican Bank's officials in the Italian Banco Ambrosiano's fraudulent bankruptcy. Italy's Supreme Court ruled that Vatican affairs were beyond its jurisdiction.

EDUCATION

 100%

The University, founded by Gregory XIII, is renowned for its theological and philosophical learning. There are 79,141 primary and 31,406 secondary Catholic schools around the world.

CHRONOLOGY

The Vatican is located in Rome because tradition held that St Peter was buried on the site of the Church of Constantine, which was pulled down in the Renaissance to make way for the building of St Peter's Basilica. The Vatican has been the Pope's usual residence since 1417, when the pontiffs returned from Avignon in France at the end of the 39 years of Great Schism.

- ❑ **1870** Italy occupies Papal States – 16,000 sq. miles in central Italy.
- ❑ **1929** Lateran Treaty – Italy recognizes Vatican City as independent state.
- ❑ **1978** Cardinal Karol Wojtyła Pope.
- ❑ **1981–1982** Attempts on Pope's life.
- ❑ **1983** New Church legal code.
- ❑ **1984** Catholicism disestablished as Italian state religion.
- ❑ **1985** Catholic Catechism revised for first time since 1566.
- ❑ **1989** Pope appoints first bishop to Belorussia – the first in 60 years in the former Soviet Union.
- ❑ **1992** Formal acknowledgment that Galileo wrongly condemned.
- ❑ **1993** Chinese sanction first official publication of full Bible in Chinese.

HEALTH

Pope's own doctor is in permanent residence at Vatican

Heart and cardiovascular diseases, cancer

The Catholic Church runs 5,617 hospitals, 14,748 dispensaries, 774 leprosariums and 17,519 homes for the sick, the aged and orphans worldwide.

WEALTH

 Vatican employees earn salaries on a par with those in Rome

CONSUMER GOODS OWNERSHIP

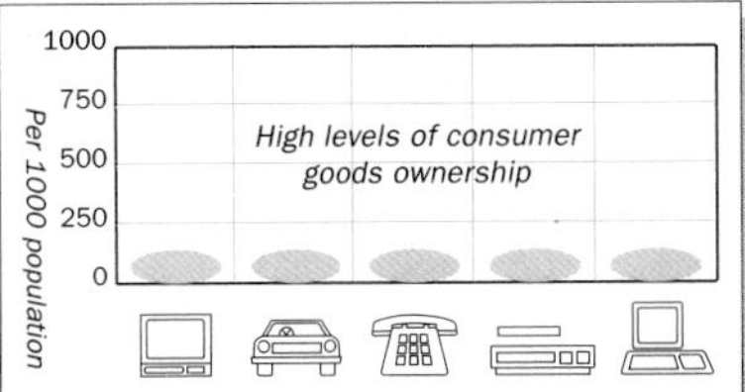

The wealth of the Vatican is primarily that of the Church. Its art treasures may not be sold. It is not known how much personal wealth its citizens have.

WORLD RANKING

The Pope and his Vatican staff enjoy one of the highest standards of living in the world

V

VENEZUELA

OFFICIAL NAME: Republic of Venezuela **CAPITAL:** Caracas
POPULATION: 20.2 million **CURRENCY:** Bolívar **OFFICIAL LANGUAGE:** Spanish

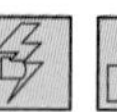

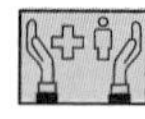

LOCATED ON THE northern coast of South America, Venezuela's vast central plain is drained by the Orinoco, while the Guiana Highlands dominate the southwest of the country. A Spanish colony until 1811, Venezuela has been lauded as Latin America's most stable democracy. Recent political upheavals have, however, led to fears of instability. The country with one of the largest known oil deposits outside the Middle East still has much of its population living in shantytown squalor.

Carlos Andrés Pérez, *AD leader who was deposed from the presidency in 1993.*

Dr Rafael Caldera Rodríguez, *who won the presidency for a second time in 1994.*

CLIMATE

WEATHER CHART

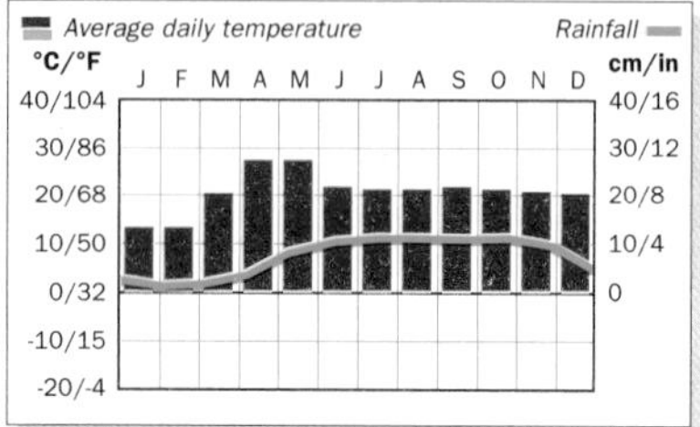

The hot Maracaibo coast is surprisingly dry; the Orinoco *llanos* are alternately parched or flooded. Uplands are cold.

TOURISM

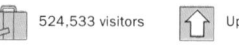

524,533 visitors

Up 27% in 1990

MAIN OVERSEAS ARRIVALS

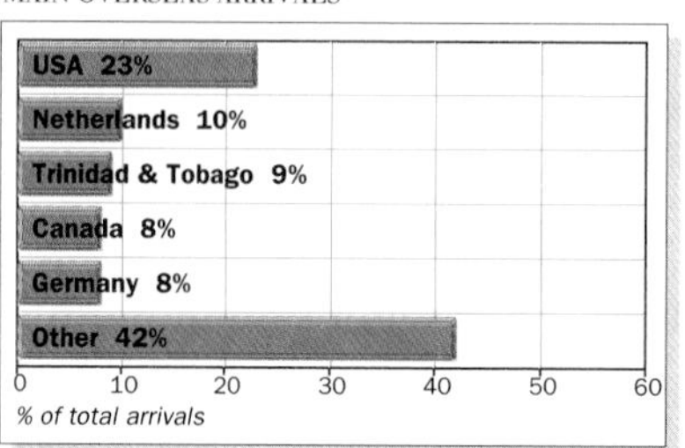

Tourism is still a relatively minor industry in Venezuela, but one with enormous potential. Venezuela has many beaches that are the equal of any Caribbean island's, and a fascinating jungle interior. For many years, the high value of the bolívar made Venezuela an expensive destination but, after the devaluation of 1983, it became one of the cheapest in the Caribbean. Now the government is privatizing its state-run hotels and seeking to attract foreign investment.

COMMUNICATIONS

Simón Bolívar, Caracas
6.48m passengers

75 ships
1.21m dwt

THE TRANSPORTATION NETWORK

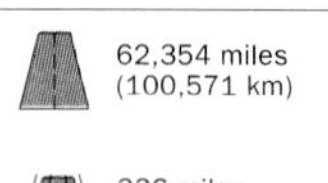

62,354 miles (100,571 km)

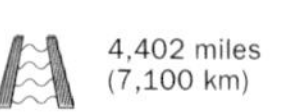

Pan-American Highway 800 miles (1,290 km)

336 miles (542 km)

4,402 miles (7,100 km)

A massive road-building program in the 1960s was designed to serve the oil and aluminum industries. The French-designed Caracas subway is one of the world's most efficient. A new $1-billion, 50-mile railroad/port system is being built on Lake Maracaibo to service the expanding oil-refining industry.

The Orinoco. Its huge llanos *(plains) are grazed by five million cattle, which are herded down close to the river in the dry season.*

PEOPLE

Spanish, Amerindian languages

54 people per sq. mile

THE URBAN/RURAL POPULATION SPLIT

91% 9%

RELIGIOUS PERSUASION

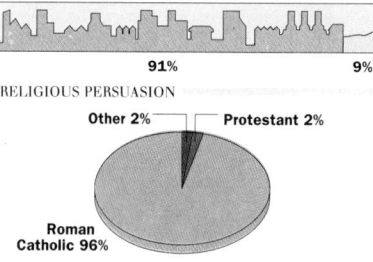

Other 2%
Protestant 2%
Roman Catholic 96%

ETHNIC MAKEUP

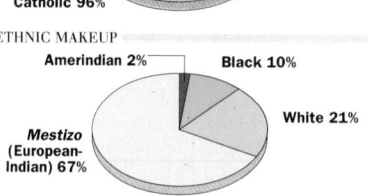

Amerindian 2%
Black 10%
White 21%
Mestizo (European-Indian) 67%

Venezuela is the most highly urbanized society in Latin America, with most of its population living in cities, mainly in the north of the country. Venezuela has traditionally been seen as Latin America's "melting pot," with large-scale immigration from Italy, Portugal, Spain and all over Latin America. There is little of the white Hispanic aristocracy that survives in Colombia and Ecuador. The small number of native Indians, such as the Yanomami, live in remote and inaccessible regions, and are often little touched by modern life.

Most of the black population, descended from Africans brought over to work the cacao industry in the 19th century, live along the Caribbean coast.

Oil wealth has brought comparative prosperity, but life in the *barrios* (shantytowns), which sprawl over the hillsides around Caracas, is one of extreme poverty. Discontent peaked in the food riots of 1991, which forced the government to initiate poverty programs. The oil boom accelerated change for women, who today find employment in all professions. Politics, however, remains a male preserve. Oil wealth has also brought Americanization – boxing and baseball are among the most popular sports.

POPULATION AGE BREAKDOWN

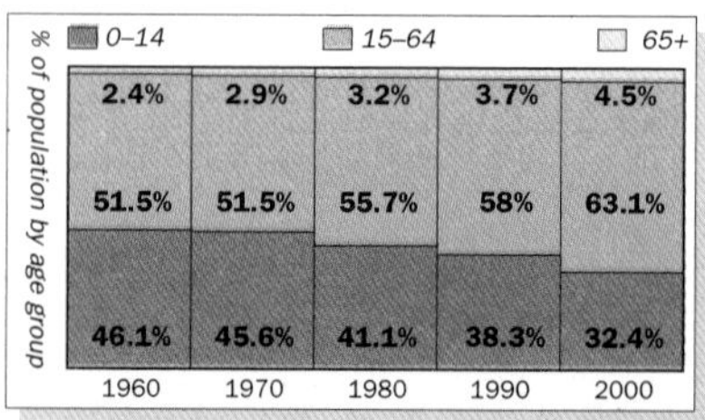

V

VENEZUELA

Total Area : 912 050 sq. km (352 143 sq. miles)

POPULATION

- over 1 000 000
- over 500 000
- over 100 000
- over 50 000
- over 10 000

LAND HEIGHT

- 3000m/9843ft
- 2000m/6562ft
- 1000m/3281ft
- 500m/1640ft
- Sea Level

Projected Railway

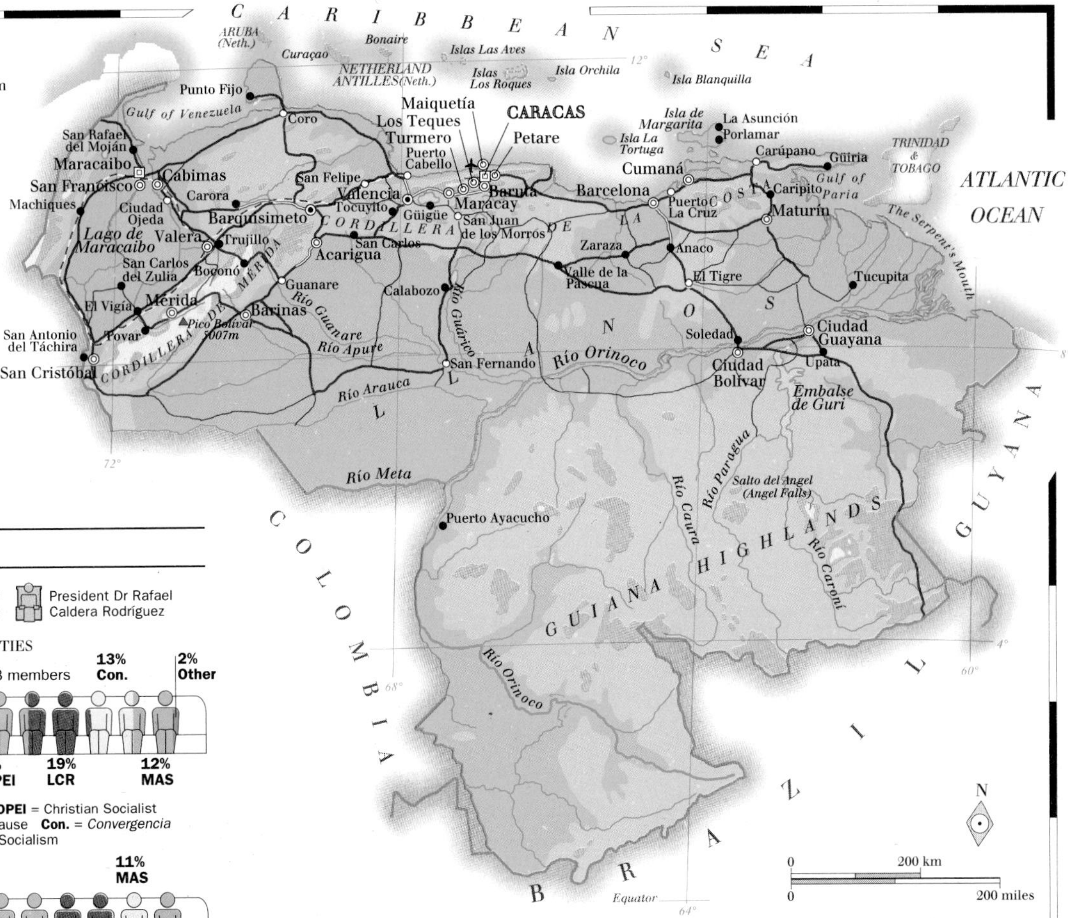

POLITICS

Lower House 1999
Upper House 1999

President Dr Rafael Caldera Rodríguez

THE STATE OF THE PARTIES

Chamber of Deputies 203 members

27% **AD** — **27%** **COPEI** — **19%** **LCR** — **12%** **MAS** — **13%** **Con.** — **2%** **Other**

AD = Democratic Action **COPEI** = Christian Socialist Party **LCR** = The Radical Cause **Con.** = *Convergencia* **MAS** = Movement Towards Socialism

Senate 53 members

34% **AD** — **28%** **COPEI** — **17%** **LCR** — **11%** **MAS** — **10%** **Con.**

Venezuela is a democracy, with multiparty elections.

MAIN POLITICAL ISSUES

Corruption

Corruption, the issue which led to the ousting of Carlos Andrés Pérez in 1993, has been a feature of Venezuelan political life. Jaime Lusinchi, ex-president and previous AD leader, was more profligate than most, reputedly squandering more than $8.5-billion buying political favors in his last two years in office.

Trimming the state sector

For decades, Venezuelan governments spent on an enormously wasteful scale, with the assumption that petro-dollars would keep flowing. The decline in oil revenues has left the state unable to fulfill its commitments without sharp cutbacks, which will meet with fierce resistance from the large number of state employees.

PROFILE

Venezuela's democracy is looking more fragile than a decade ago, in part due to the failure of successive regimes to tackle poverty. Three hundred died in anti-price-rise riots in Caracas in 1991, and in 1992 the leader of an abortive coup was declared a national hero by *barrio* dwellers. In 1993, Carlos Andrés Pérez, who had taken office in 1989 and had grown increasingly unpopular for his austerity measures, was deposed by Congress on corruption charges which have yet to be proven.

WORLD AFFAIRS

Venezuela has traditionally been seen as pro-US, since the USA was the destination of most of its oil exports and the source of its imports. There was little reaction to the US removal of Manuel Noriega from power in Panama in 1989. Currently working at easing US–Cuban relations, Venezuela is also actively encouraging Cuba to join the Organization of American States.

Venezuela has disputed borders with Colombia (fighting almost erupted in 1987) and Guyana, its much smaller neighbor, claiming 32,820 square miles of its oil, iron and gold-rich territory.

CHRONOLOGY

Venezuela was the first of the Spanish imperial colonies to repudiate Madrid's authority under the guidance of the revolutionary, Simón Bolívar, in 1811.

- **1821** Battle of Carabobo finally overthrows Spanish rule and leads to consolidation of independence within Gran Colombia (Venezuela, Colombia and Ecuador).
- **1830** Gran Colombia collapses. José Antonio Páez rules Venezuela; coffee planters effectively in control.
- **1870** Guzmán Blanco in power. Attracts foreign investment to build railroad system.
- **1908** General Juan Vicente Gómez dictator; oversees development of oil industry.
- **1935** Vicente Gómez falls from power. Increasing mass participation in political process.
- **1945** Military coup overthrows General Isías Medina Angarita. Rómulo Betancourt of the Democratic Action party (AD) takes power as leader of a civilian-military junta.

V

CHRONOLOGY *continued*

- ❑ **1948** February: AD wins elections, with novelist Rómulo Gallegos as presidential candidate.
- ❑ **1948** November: Gallegos overthrown in military coup. Marcos Pérez Jiménez forms government, with US and military backing.
- ❑ **1958** January: general strike. Admiral Wolfgang Larrázabal leads military coup deposing Jiménez government.
- ❑ **1958** December: free elections. Betancourt, newly returned from exile, wins presidential election as AD candidate. Anti-communist campaign mounted. A few state welfare programs introduced.
- ❑ **1960** Movement of the Revolutionary Left (MIR) splits off from AD and begins anti-government activities.
- ❑ **1961** Venezuela becomes a founder member of OPEC.
- ❑ **1962** Communist-backed guerrilla warfare attempts repetition of Cuban revolution in Venezuela. Fails to gain support among the peasantry.
- ❑ **1963** Raúl Leoni (AD) elected president – the first democratic transference of power in Venezuelan history. Anti-guerrilla campaign continues.
- ❑ **1966** Unsuccessful coup attempt by supporters of former president, Pérez Jiménez.
- ❑ **1969** Elections. Dr. Rafael Caldera Rodríguez of the Social Christian Party (COPEI) becomes president. Continues Leoni policies.
- ❑ **1973** Elections. Carlos Andrés Pérez wins back power for AD. Oil and steel industries nationalized. World oil crisis. Venezuelan currency peaks in value against the US dollar.
- ❑ **1978** Elections won by Dr. Luis Herrera Campíns for COPEI. Disastrous economic programs, and failure of huge Workers' Bank.
- ❑ **1983** Elections. AD victory under Jaime Lusinchi. Fall in world oil prices leads to cuts in state welfare programs. Student and union unrest.
- ❑ **1988** Carlos Andrés Pérez wins elections for AD. Fails to deliver populist election promises.
- ❑ **1991** Caracas food riots; 300 dead.
- ❑ **1993** Carlos Andrés Pérez falls and is put on trial for corruption.

AID

 Minimal receipts

 No change from year to year

Venezuela receives minimal aid; assistance from Germany and Spain is in the form of small NGO projects.

DEFENSE

 $1.6bn

Up 300% in 1991

Defense spending as % GDP (0–40): 3.1%

The army is under-equipped and badly paid, with only 34,000 men including conscripts. Having been largely absent from politics for three decades, it regained prominence in the attempted coups of 1992, headed by relatively junior officers who identified with the squeeze on the middle classes.

VENEZUELAN ARMED FORCES

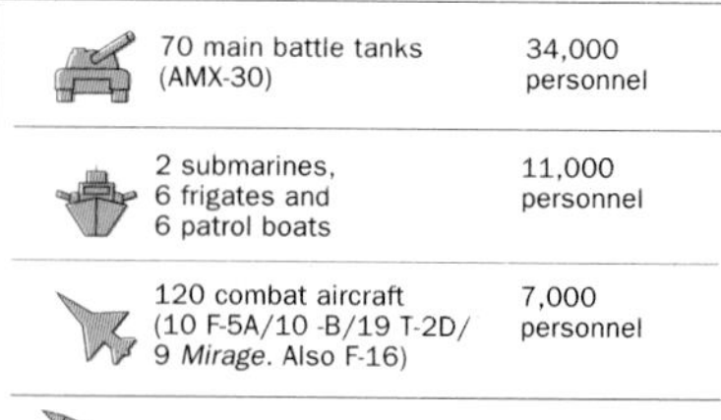

70 main battle tanks (AMX-30)	34,000 personnel
2 submarines, 6 frigates and 6 patrol boats	11,000 personnel
120 combat aircraft (10 F-5A/10 -B/19 T-2D/ 9 *Mirage*. Also F-16)	7,000 personnel
None	

ECONOMICS

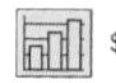 $59.5bn

106.20 bolivares

SCORE CARD

- ❑ World GNP Ranking.........................36th
- ❑ GNP per Capita $2,945
- ❑ Balance of Payments....................$-3.4bn
- ❑ Inflation 33.1%
- ❑ Unemployment.................................8.4%

EXPORTS

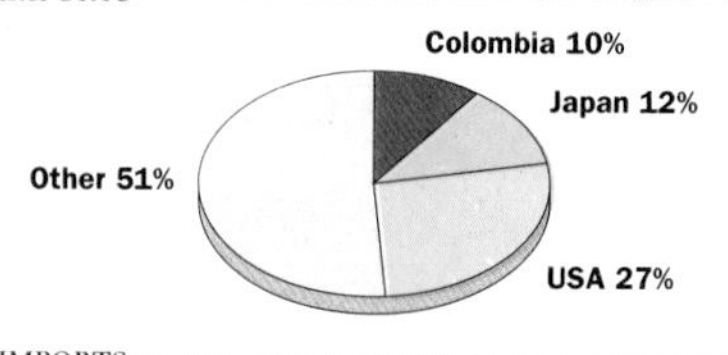

IMPORTS

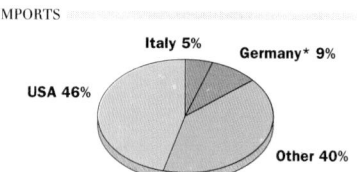

Italy 5%
Germany* 9%
USA 46%
Other 40%

Strengths

The largest proven oil deposits outside the Middle East and CIS. Massive reserves of coal, bauxite, iron and gold. Successful development of new bitumen fuel, Orimulsion, produced in the Orinoco delta. Considerable foreign investment in all these sectors, led by US and giant Japanese concerns such as Mitsubishi. World's most efficient producer of high-grade aluminum.

Weaknesses

Huge, cumbersome state sector; despite some privatization, large areas of the state sector are still over-manned and inefficient. Poor public services, which, despite Venezuela's wealth during the oil-boom years, have been badly maintained. Major infrastructure renewal is now long overdue. Widespread tax evasion, and lack of political will to reform tax regime (Venezuela, thanks to large subsidies, has the lowest gasoline prices in the world) dents government revenues.

ECONOMIC PERFORMANCE INDICATOR

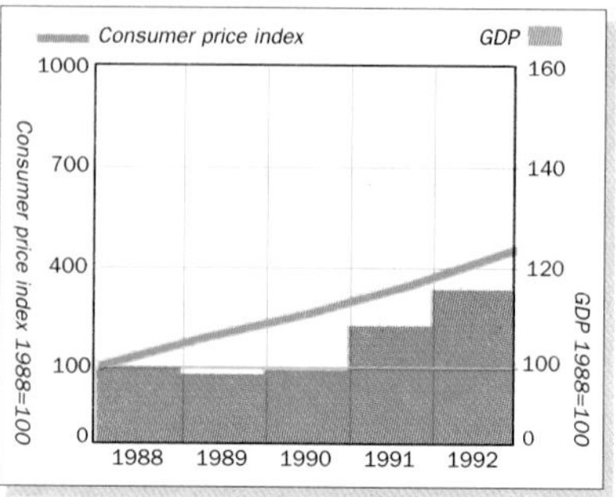

Profile

Venezuela is an economic paradox. One of the strongest economies in Latin America, its government finances are in a poor state. A culture of non-accountability has been created due to years of politically motivated patronage in state-owned industries and government bureaucracies. A program of privatization and cutting state spending has begun to tackle the problem, but too slowly to make a real impact. Conditions for the poor have not improved, and violent food riots in Caracas in 1991 highlighted their plight. This unrest, along with fears of a military coup, has had the effect of deterring future investors.

VENEZUELA : MAJOR BUSINESSES

V

RESOURCES

61bn kwh (capacity 18.6m kw)

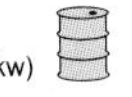

2.29m b/d (reserves 62,650,000,000 bbl)

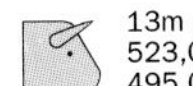

13m cattle, 3m pigs, 523,000 sheep, 495,000 horses

Oil, bauxite, iron, natural gas, coal, gold

ELECTRICITY GENERATION

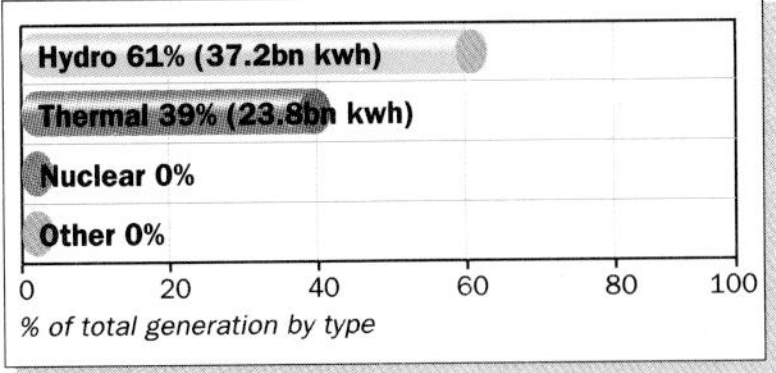

Venezuela has a remarkable diversity of resources. It has proven oil reserves of 62 billion barrels, vast quantities of coal, iron ore, bauxite and gold, and cheap hydroelectric power. Huge investment programs are currently under way to raise production in all these sectors. Oil companies are also increasing refining capacity. A $10-billion refining expansion program is due for completion in 1996. The state oil company, PDVSA, is also investing in coal – particularly the Guanare fields – to raise annual production from 1.5 to 20 million tons.

Venezuela has begun exploitation of a new bitumen-based fuel from the Orinoco, Orimulsion; commercially exploitable reserves are estimated at 270 billion barrels. The world's most efficient producer of aluminum, Venezuela aims to be the biggest by the year 2000.

VENEZUELA : LAND USE

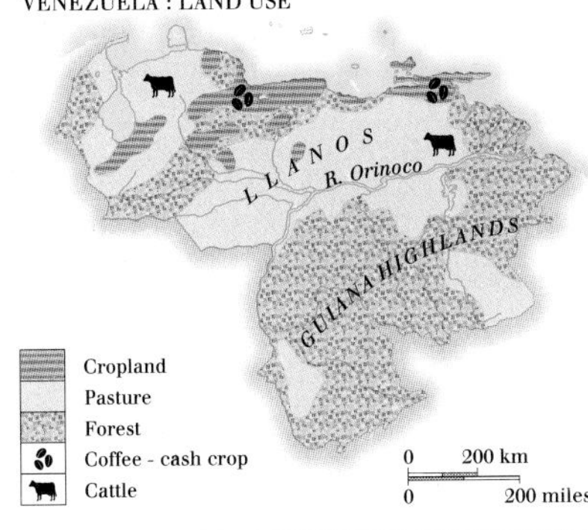

ENVIRONMENT

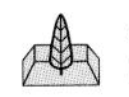

31% (16% partially protected)

Ecology studies are now part of the school curriculum

ENVIRONMENTAL TREATIES

The destruction of the last remaining rainforests and the oil pollution of Lake Maracaibo are the main concerns.

MEDIA

Attempts have been made to intimidate any press which is critical of the government

PUBLISHING AND BROADCAST MEDIA

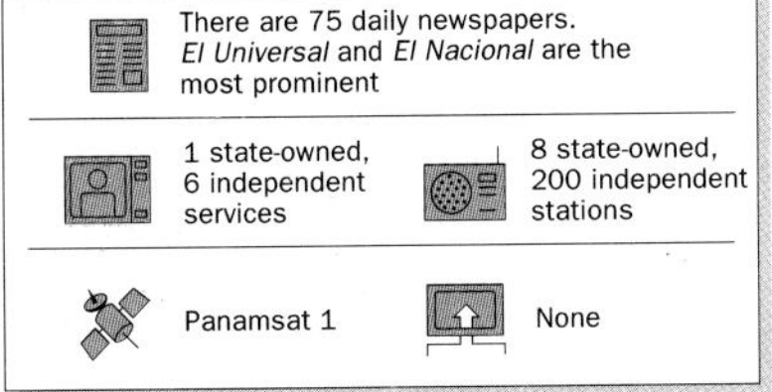

There are 75 daily newspapers. *El Universal* and *El Nacional* are the most prominent
1 state-owned, 6 independent services
8 state-owned, 200 independent stations
Panamsat 1
None

Most of the press is independent of the main political parties. Venezuelan soap operas vie with Mexican rivals for dominance.

CRIME

32,000 prisoners

Up 4% in 1988

CRIME RATES

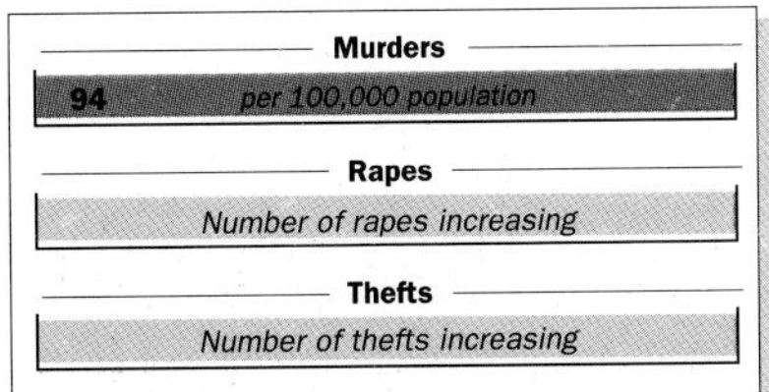

Murders
94 per 100,000 population
Rapes
Number of rapes increasing
Thefts
Number of thefts increasing

Venezuela is generally less violent than neighboring countries, though drug-related crime is on the increase. Cattle smuggling to Colombia is common.

EDUCATION

88%

0 *Education spending as % GNP* 25

4.2%

THE EDUCATION SYSTEM

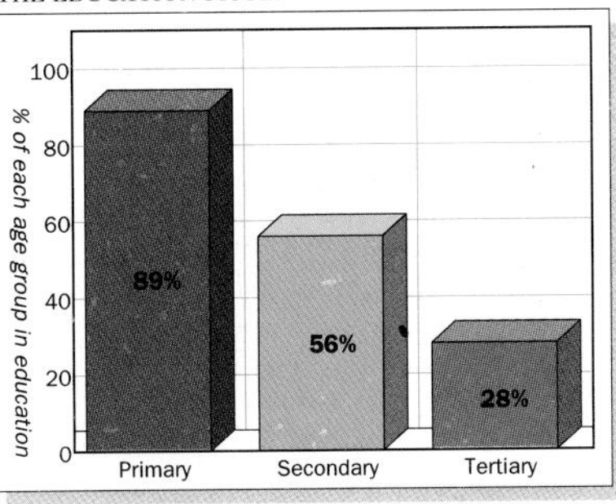

The state education system suffers from a shortage of qualified teachers, and from recent cuts in the state education budget.

HEALTH

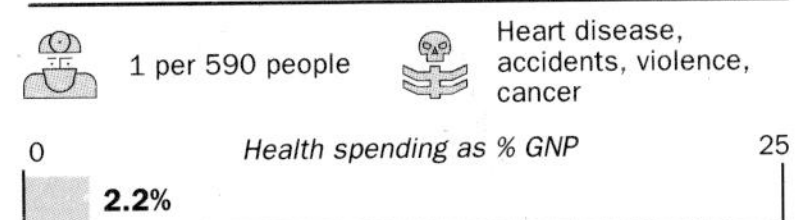

The health service, although still comparatively good, has suffered along with other public services from poor management in the 1970s and 1980s and the cuts introduced by the Pérez government in the 1990s.

Most healthcare is concentrated in the towns, and people from indigenous communities often have to travel long distances to receive treatment. Venezuela has a reputation for innovative plastic surgery.

WEALTH

Miner, 276 bolívares per day; electronics draughtsman, 17,000 bolívares per month

CONSUMER GOODS OWNERSHIP

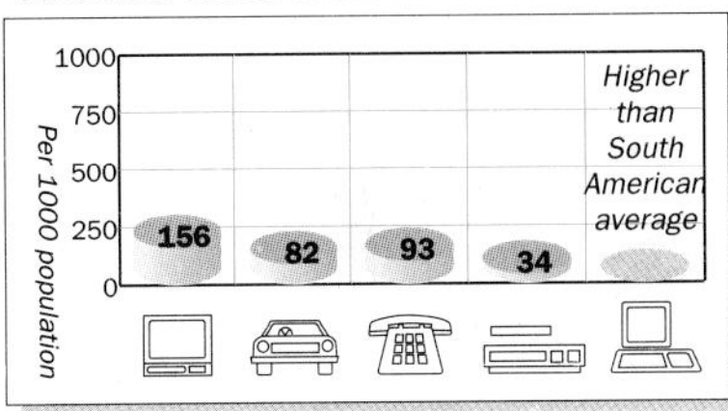

In 1973, when there were just 4.3 bolívares to the US dollar, Venezuela was the world's biggest importer of Chivas Regal Whisky and French champagne, and it was cheaper to spend the weekend in Miami than in Caracas.

Living standards have fallen since the collapse in world oil prices. However, wealth remains concentrated among Venezuelans connected to the government and a few industrialists.

The poorest section of society, dependent on the welfare state, has suffered particularly from austerity measures introduced in an attempt to cut the budget deficit. Recent moves to tighten income tax collection (most Venezuelans evade it) have hit the salaried middle classes.

WORLD RANKING

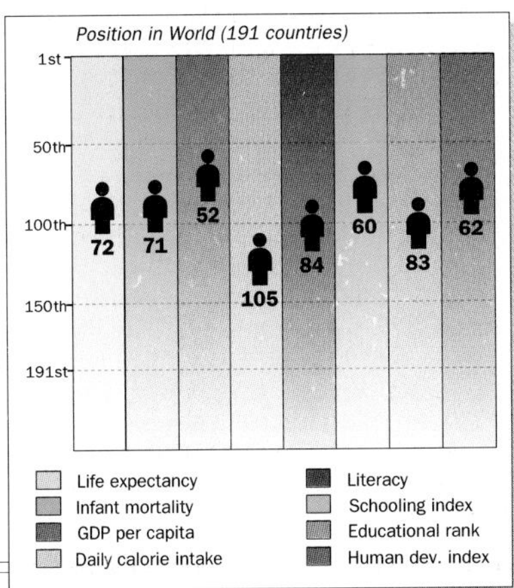

VIETNAM

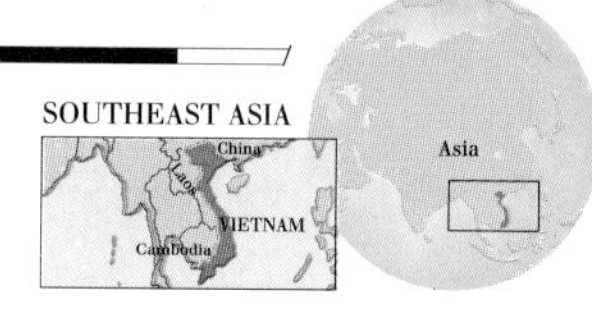

OFFICIAL NAME: Socialist Republic of Viet-Nam **CAPITAL:** Hanoi
POPULATION: 67.8 million **CURRENCY:** New dông **OFFICIAL LANGUAGE:** Vietnamese

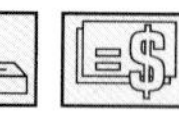

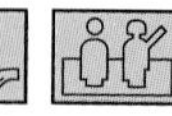

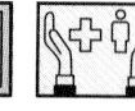

LOCATED ON THE EASTERN COAST of the Indochinese peninsula, over half of Vietnam is dominated by a heavily forested mountain range, the Chaîne Annamitique. The most populated areas, which are also the most intensively cultivated, are along the Red and Mekong rivers. Partitioned after World War II, the communist north reunited the country after the world's longest 20th-century conflict, the 1962–1975 Vietnam War. Today, Vietnam is a single-party state ruled by the Communist Party. Since 1986, the regime has followed a liberal economic policy known as *doi moi* (renovation).

CLIMATE

WEATHER CHART

Vietnam has a sharply contrasting climate. The north has cool winters, while the south is tropical with even temperatures all year round. The central provinces are affected by typhoons. The most intensively cultivated areas are the deltas of the Red and Mekong rivers, which are respectively subject to drought and heavy flooding.

COMMUNICATIONS

Tan Son Naht Intl, Ho Chi Minh City

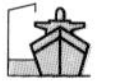
184 ships 597,300 dwt

THE TRANSPORTATION NETWORK

53,253 miles (85,700 km)

None

1,616 miles (2,600 km)

11,000 miles (17,702 km)

Rebuilding infrastructure destroyed during the war is still the priority. A key project is likely to be the reconstruction of Highway 1, linking Hanoi and Ho Chi Minh City (formerly Saigon). Ports and railroads will also require rehabilitation, and construction has begun on two new port facilities, at Vung Tau in the south and Cai Lan in the north. Trains travel slowly in Vietnam, with an average speed of around 9 miles an hour. The journey from Hanoi to Ho Chi Minh City takes three days.

TOURISM

300,000 visitors

Up 16% in 1991

MAIN OVERSEAS ARRIVALS

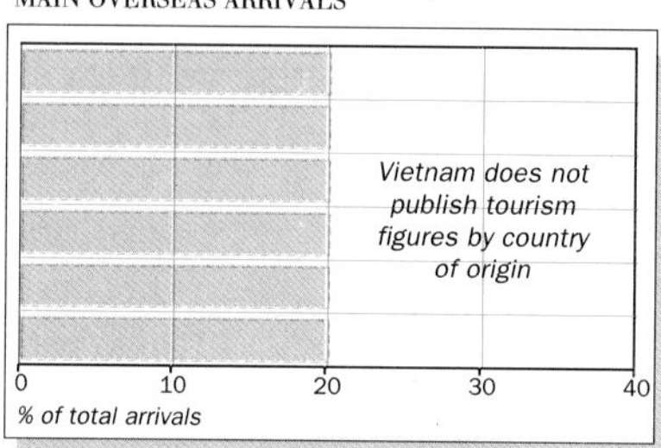

Russians, East Europeans and backpackers from the West made up the bulk of the 400,000 or so tourists Vietnam received each year during the 1980s. Other travelers were either on business, or overseas Vietnamese, *Viet Kie*, visiting relatives.

Since 1990, the government has opened the way to large-scale tourism. Massive investment is now going into hotels, and an official target of three million tourists a year by 2000 has been set. For the moment, Vietnam's appeal rests on its unspoiled Asian way of life and areas of spectacular natural beauty such as Ha Long Bay on the Red River delta. It is estimated that earnings from tourism in 1993 stood at $200 million.

Boats moored near Nha Trang. *A network connecting Vietnam's main ports provides an important internal communications link.*

PEOPLE

Vietnamese, Chinese, Thai, Khmer, Muong, Nung, Miao, Yao, Jarai

523 people per sq, mile

THE URBAN/RURAL POPULATION SPLIT

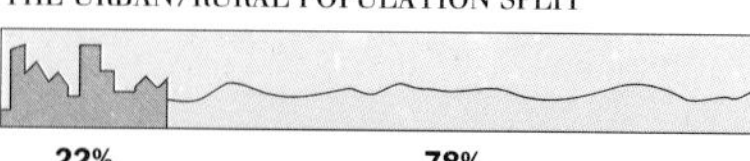

RELIGIOUS PERSUASION

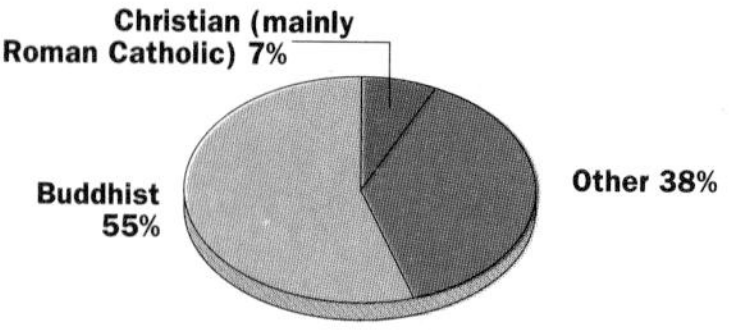

ETHNIC MAKEUP

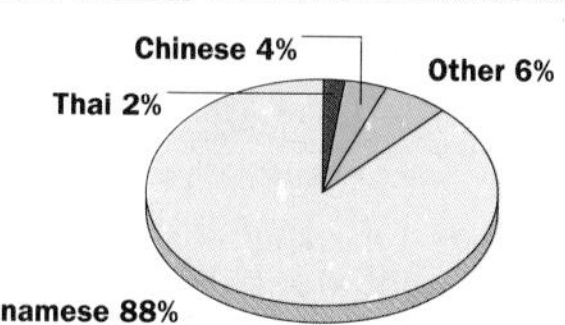

Overseas Chinese constitute the largest minority group in Vietnam, and were subject to considerable discrimination in the early years of the communist takeover. The Saigon Chinese, with their Taiwanese links, were viewed as corrupt bourgeoisie, while the northern Mountain Chinese were suspected as a fifth column for China's ambitions in Vietnam. Various other mountain minorities (*Montagnards*), who have a history of collaboration with the French and Americans and who continued armed resistance, were also sidelined by the regime in Hanoi. Today, the main source of tension is the resettling of lowlanders in mountain regions, which is putting pressure on limited farming and forest resources.

Women outnumber men, largely because of war deaths. They form a high proportion of the industrial work force (during the war they were the majority), but have not received any greater political voice. There are still no women in the Politburo.

Family life is strong and is based on kinship groups within village clans.

POPULATION AGE BREAKDOWN

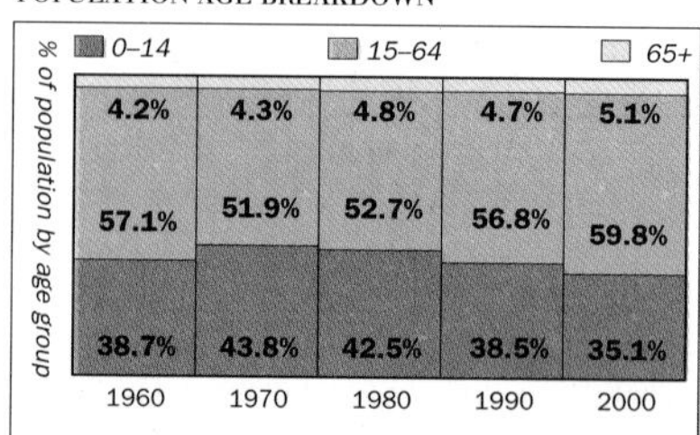

***General Le Duc Anh,** President since 1992.*

***Vo Van Kiet,** prime minister of Vietnam.*

POLITICS

 1997

 President Gen. Le Duc Anh

THE STATE OF THE PARTIES

National Assembly 395 members

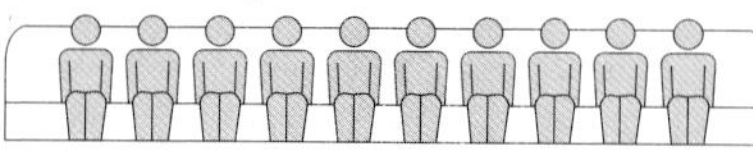

Elections were last held in 1992, following a change in the constitution of the same year.

Vietnam is a single-party communist state.

MAIN POLITICAL ISSUES

Economic reform
Vietnam is attempting to make the transition from a centrally planned to a market economy without the political liberalization that has characterized the transition in Eastern Europe.

Resisting political reform
The founders of the Communist Party have transferred power to the younger generation, who formed the vanguard in the wars against the French and Americans in the 1950s–1970s. They are unwilling to give up the power won by force of arms by democratizing the political process.

PROFILE
Politically, Vietnam still operates according to a traditional communist system. The 13-member Politburo, elected by the 146-strong Central Committee, is still the most powerful body. Power filters down to state-enterprise managers, all of whom are members of the Party. However, maintaining the Communist Party's legitimacy, when the central plank of economic ideology has been removed, will not be easy. Already there are signs of "multipartyists" pressing for reform.

VIETNAM

Total Area : 329 560 sq. km (127 243 sq. miles)

POPULATION
- over 1 000 000
- over 500 000
- over 100 000
- over 50 000
- over 10 000
- under 10 000

LAND HEIGHT
- 2000m/6562ft
- 1000m/3281ft
- 500m/1640ft
- 200m/656ft
- Sea Level

0 100 km

0 100 miles

WORLD AFFAIRS

Vietnam's economic liberalization has led to improvements in its relationship with the USA. In 1993, Washington finally lifted its aid embargo, allowing the World Bank to start investing in reconstruction and US companies to bid for contracts. Relations with the ex-colonial power, France, have also improved; a French company is upgrading Vietnam's telephone system.

The removal of Vietnamese troops from neighboring Cambodia in 1989 led to improved relations with China. In 1992, the two countries resolved their dispute over oil rights in the South China Sea.

AID

 $190m

 up 47% in 1990

The Vietnamese invasion of Cambodia in 1978 halted all aid from China, Japan and the West, with the exception of Scandinavian countries. Vietnam turned to the Soviet Union, which financed the large trade deficit until 1985. The USA resumed humanitarian aid in 1992 and removed economic restrictions in 1993. Aid now provides for 89% of all capital expenditure.

CHRONOLOGY

From 1825, the brutal persecution of the Catholic community, originally converted by French priests in the 17th century, gave France the excuse to colonize Cochin-China, Annam and Tonkin, and then merge them with Laos and Cambodia.

- **1920** *Quoc ngu* (Roman script) replaces Chinese script.
- **1930** Ho Chi Minh founds Indochina Communist Party.
- **1940** Japanese invade but tolerate Vichy administration until 1945.
- **1941** Viet Minh resistance founded in exile in China; aided by USA.
- **1945** Viet Minh take Saigon and Hanoi. Emperor abdicates. Republic with Ho Chi Minh as president.
- **1946** French (rearmed by UK) re-enter. First Indochina War.
- **1954** French defeated at Dien Bien Phu. Vietnam divided at 17°N. USSR supports North; USA arms South. Communist opposition in South secretly armed by North down Ho Chi Minh Trail.
- **1960** Groups opposed to President Diem's repressive regime in South unite as Viet Cong.
- **1961** USA sends in military advisors.

V

CHRONOLOGY *continued*

- ❑ **1964** US Congress approves war.
- ❑ **1965** Gen. Nguyen Van Thieu takes over military government of South. First US combat troops arrive; in three years, they number 500,000.
- ❑ **1965–1968** Operation Rolling Thunder – intense bombing of North by South and USA.
- ❑ **1967** Anti-war protests start in USA and elsewhere.
- ❑ **1968** Tet (New Year) Offensive – 105 towns attacked simultaneously in South with infiltrated arms. Viet Cong suffer serious losses. Peace talks begin. USA eases bombing and starts withdrawing troops.
- ❑ **1969** Ho Chi Minh dies. War intensifies again in spite of talks.
- ❑ **1970** USA begins secret attacks in Laos and Cambodia and new mass bombing of North to try to stop arms reaching Viet Cong.
- ❑ **1972** 11-day Christmas Campaign is heaviest US bombing of war.
- ❑ **1973** Paris Peace Agreements signed, but fighting continues.
- ❑ **1974** One million refugees flee the North.
- ❑ **1975** Fall of Saigon to combined forces of North and Provisional Revolutionary (Viet Cong) Government of South. Further one million flee after end of war.
- ❑ **1976** Vietnam united as Socialist Republic of Vietnam, with Le Duan continuing to hold the real power as General Secretary of Communist Party. Saigon renamed Ho Chi Minh City.
- ❑ **1977** Vietnam begins incursions into Kampuchea (Cambodia).
- ❑ **1978** Thousands of ethnic Chinese flee Vietnam.
- ❑ **1979** Nine-Day War with China. Chinese troops destroy everything for 25 miles inside Vietnam. Chinese pushed back. Vietnam ousts Pol Pot in full-scale invasion of Kampuchea and installs friendly regime. "Boat-people" (illegal emigrants) now creating crisis of international proportions. At UN conference, Vietnam agrees to allow legal emigration, but exodus continues.
- ❑ **1986** Nguyen Van Linh appointed General Secretary. Initiates liberal economic *doi moi* (renovation) policy.
- ❑ **1987** Fighting in Thailand as Vietnam pursues Kampuchean resistance fighters across border.
- ❑ **1989** Troops leave Cambodia.
- ❑ **1991** Open anti-communist dissent made a criminal offense.
- ❑ **1992** Revised constitution allows foreign investment, but essential role of Communist Party is unchanged.

DEFENSE

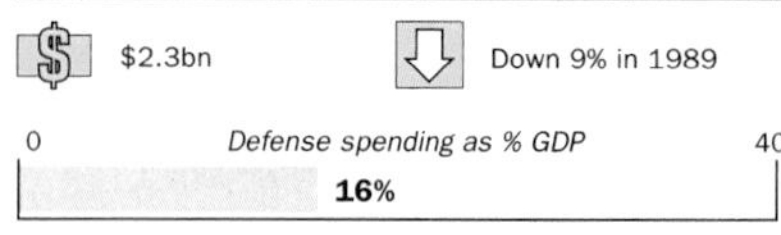

Since the withdrawal from Cambodia in 1989 (only the Khmer Rouge suggests that the withdrawal has not occurred), the focus of defense spending has moved to the navy, a reflection of growing tensions in the South China Sea. Vietnam's "volunteer force" in Laos has also been much reduced.

VIETNAMESE ARMED FORCES

1,300 main battle tanks (T-34,-54,-55/T-62/ Ch Type-59/M-48A3)	70,000 personnel
7 frigates and 55 patrol boats	42,000 personnel
185 combat aircraft (20 Su-17/40 Su-22)	15,000 personnel
None	

ECONOMICS

$15.2bn — 10,882 new dông

SCORE CARD

- ❑ World GNP Ranking.........................68th
- ❑ GNP per Capita $224
- ❑ Balance of Payments...................$-213m
- ❑ Inflation 4%
- ❑ Unemployment...................................5%

EXPORTS

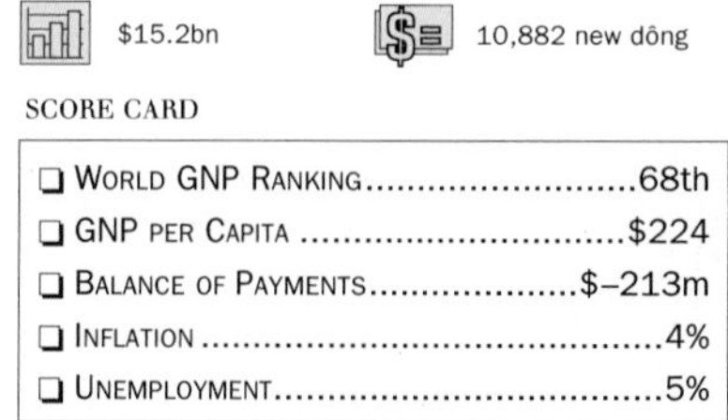

IMPORTS

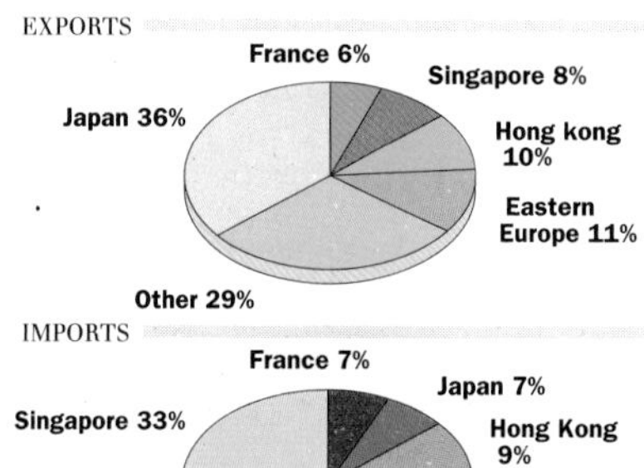

Strengths

Diverse resource base. Location in East Asia. Much lower labor costs than second-tier NICs such as Malaysia and Thailand.

Weaknesses

Weak economic institutions will make transition to a full market economy difficult. Enormous task of reconstruction after war; dependent on aid from the West, Japan and China.

Profile

Vietnam is already being billed by some commentators as the next Asian "tiger." The prospect is still distant, though the potential certainly exists. Mineral resources, located mostly in the north, and a resumption of Western aid to the capital-starved economy, are the foundations on which the adoption of a full market economy will be based. The major concerns are the need to develop the private sector and to maintain inflation at a tolerable level. It is now running at 4%, compared with 600% in 1987–1988. The tax net also needs to be widened if government finances are to be set on a proper footing.

Even before the collapse of the Soviet Union, there was a widespread acceptance in Vietnam that the centrally planned economy had problems. The encouragement of private enterprise began in 1988. Between 1988 and 1993, foreign investors proposed new projects worth over $6.8 billion. Exports, including rice, textiles and seafood, grew at 30% a year over the same period. In 1993, the economy grew by over 8.3%. The government has set a target of doubling Vietnam's GDP in the next decade.

ECONOMIC PERFORMANCE INDICATOR

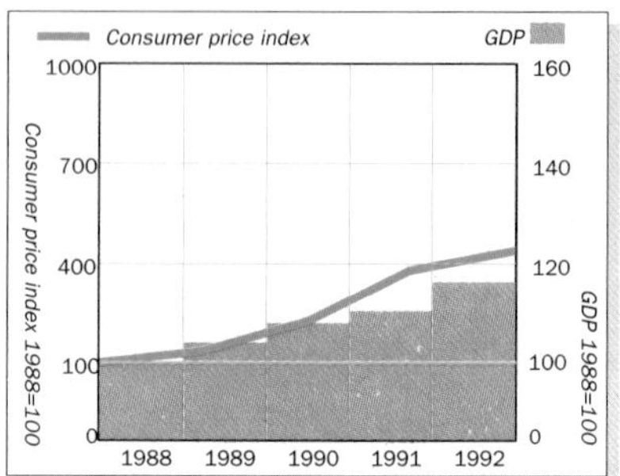

VIETNAM : MAJOR BUSINESSES

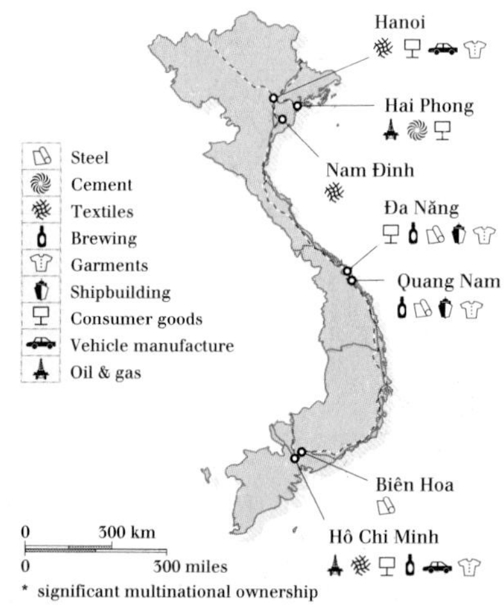

RESOURCES

8.7bn kwh (capacity 1.32m kw)

99,100 b/d (reserves 500,000,000 bbl)

12.2m pigs, 3.2m cattle, 2.8m buffaloes

Coal, oil, tin, zinc, iron, antimony, apatite, salt, bauxite

ELECTRICITY GENERATION

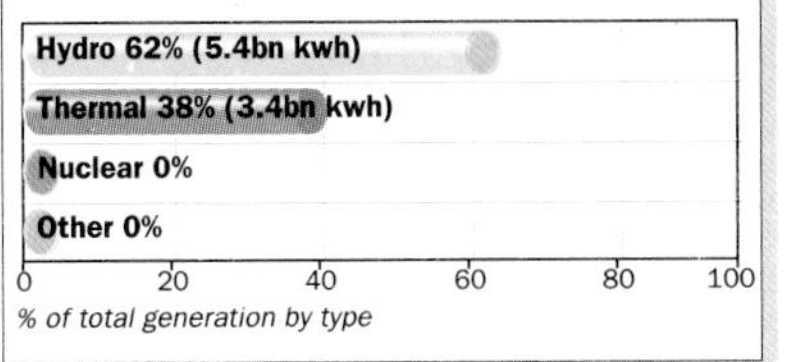

Vietnam is the world's third-largest exporter of rice, after Thailand and the USA. Oil production at 99,100 b/d is negligible by world standards, but sufficient to make it Vietnam's biggest export earner. Oil and gas exploitation is undertaken by VietSovPetro, a joint venture with Russia. However, Vietnam is linking up with new partners, including the Australian company BHP and British Gas. Mobil Oil is also signing new deals, having abandoned its interests in the face of advancing communist troops in 1975. Vietnam has considerable unexploited gas reserves in the South China Sea; gas from the only producing field currently has to be flared off.

Northern Vietnam has a surplus of electricity. A new power line will make this available to the South.

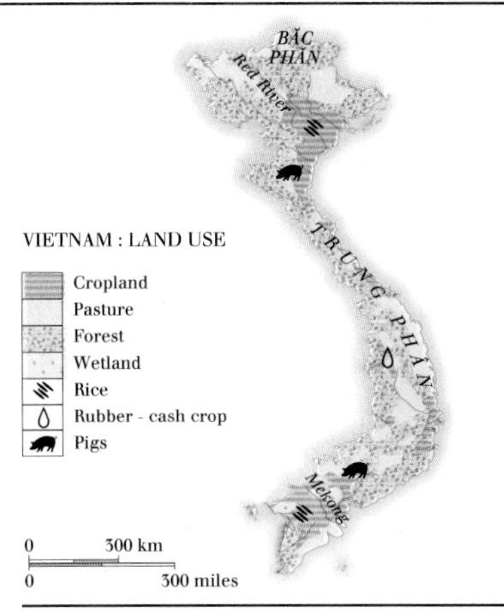

ENVIRONMENT

3% (2% partially protected)

Environmental issues are not a priority

ENVIRONMENTAL TREATIES

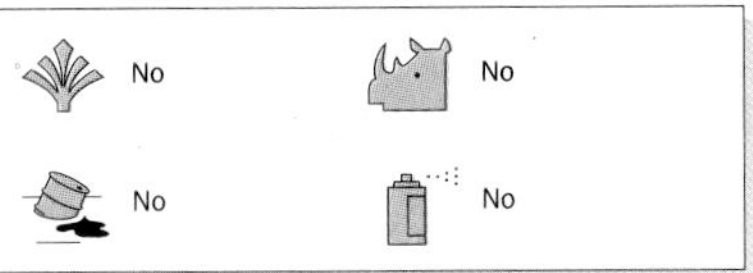

Vietnam is still counting the massive environmental cost of the Vietnam War. Seven million tons of bombs were dropped, and the defoliant chemical Agent Orange was sprayed over 4.2 million acres. In addition to the bridges, industrial zones and irrigation works destroyed, 50% of Vietnam's forests were seriously damaged and 5% wiped out. Continuing deforestation is now the major problem. Each year, 494,000 acres are lost, with consequential soil erosion and flooding.

CRIME

Vietnam does not publish prison figures

Increase in petty theft

CRIME RATES

Rates of murder and rape remain farirly constant. Theft has risen slightly

The judicial system is based on the Soviet model. Although the reeducation camps established after liberation have now closed, religious and political dissidents are still held without trial.

Petty theft from foreigners is a problem in the major cities. There has been a sharp rise in corruption since economic liberalization.

Religious tensions have given rise to recent disturbances. In one incident, supporters of the Buddhist minority clashed with the police in Hué.

HEALTH

1 per 2,882 people

Cardiovascular diseases, cancer, malaria

0 — *Health spending as % GNP* — 25

Minimal health spending

Vietnam's main medical achievements are the development of a vaccine for Hepatitis B, and the extraction of artemisinin (an anti-malarial drug) from the indigenous Thanh Hao tree.

WEALTH

Wealth disparities are small

CONSUMER GOODS OWNERSHIP

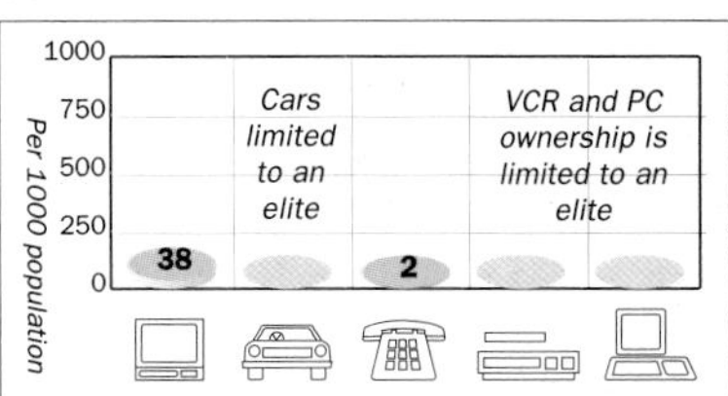

The Party remains the route to advancement. Ostentatious displays of wealth are still frowned upon.

MEDIA

Some political restrictions

PUBLISHING AND BROADCAST MEDIA

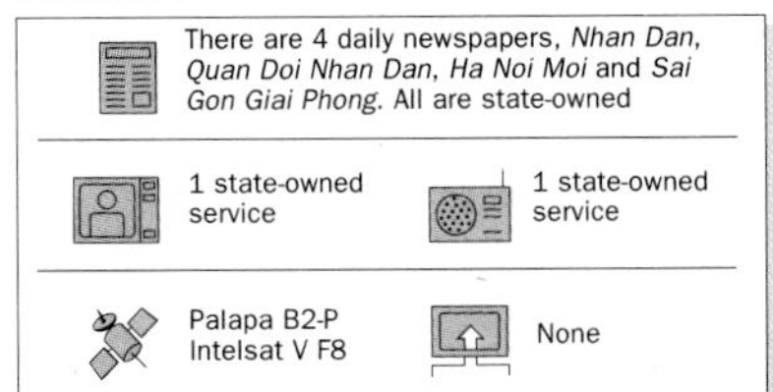

There are 4 daily newspapers, *Nhan Dan, Quan Doi Nhan Dan, Ha Noi Moi* and *Sai Gon Giai Phong*. All are state-owned
1 state-owned service
1 state-owned service
Palapa B2-P Intelsat V F8
None

Although the media is tightly regulated and all editors have to be Party members, criticism of the authorities is still possible. The weekly *Tuoi Tre* is known for its investigative reporting, and even *Nhan Dan*, the Party newspaper, has been known to expose laxity in the system, especially in the judiciary. The army daily, *Quan Doi Nhan Dan*, is the most hardline paper.

EDUCATION

88%

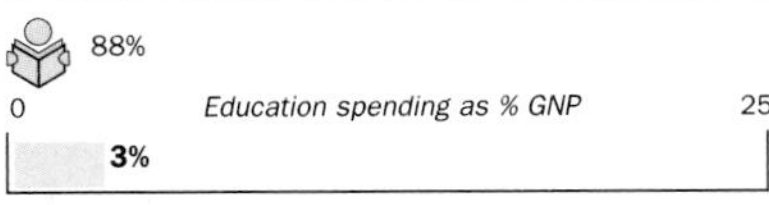

THE EDUCATION SYSTEM

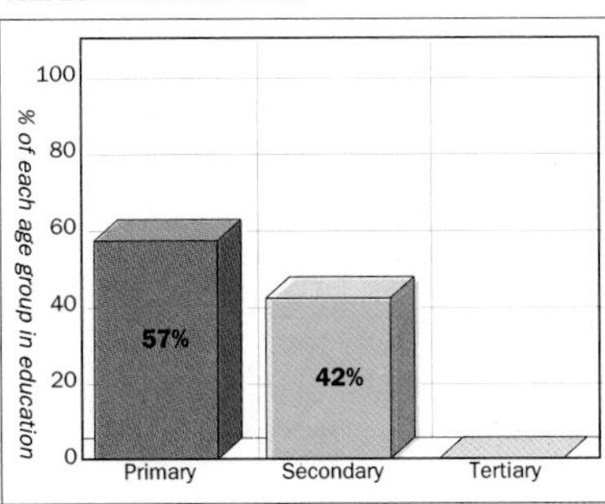

Fees for education have recently been introduced, and enrollment is falling. Vietnamese universities have a strong liberal arts tradition.

WORLD RANKING

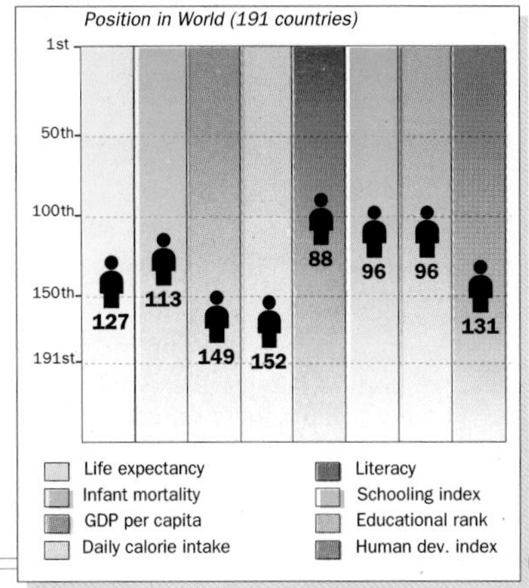

V

WESTERN SAMOA

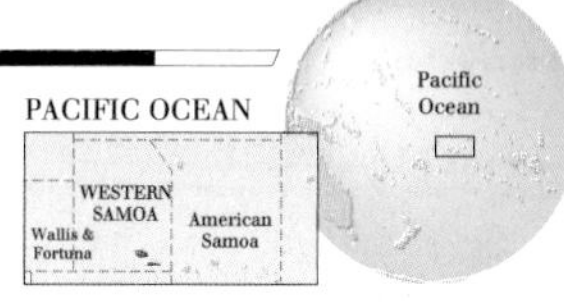

OFFICIAL NAME: Independent State of Western Samoa **CAPITAL:** Apia
POPULATION: 169,000 **CURRENCY:** Tala **OFFICIAL LANGUAGES:** Samoan, English

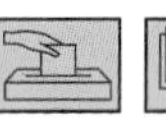

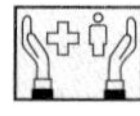

WESTERN SAMOA LIES IN THE HEART of the South Pacific, 1,500 miles north of New Zealand. Four of its nine volcanic islands are inhabited – Apolima, Manono, Sava'ai, the largest, and Upolu, home to 72% of the population. Rainforests cloak the mountains; vegetable gardens and coconut plantations thrive around the coasts. A German protectorate until 1914, Western Samoa was then administered by New Zealand until its independence in 1962.

CLIMATE

WEATHER CHART

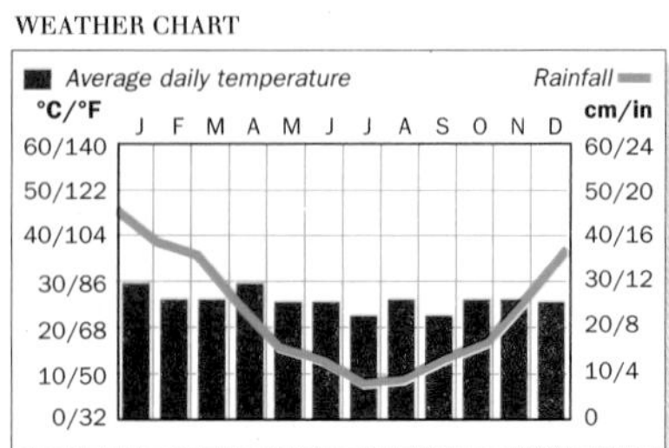

The climate is humid and temperatures rarely drop below 75°F. December to March is the hurricane season.

COMMUNICATIONS

Faleolo Apia 191,727 passengers

3 ships 5,800 dwt

THE TRANSPORTATION NETWORK

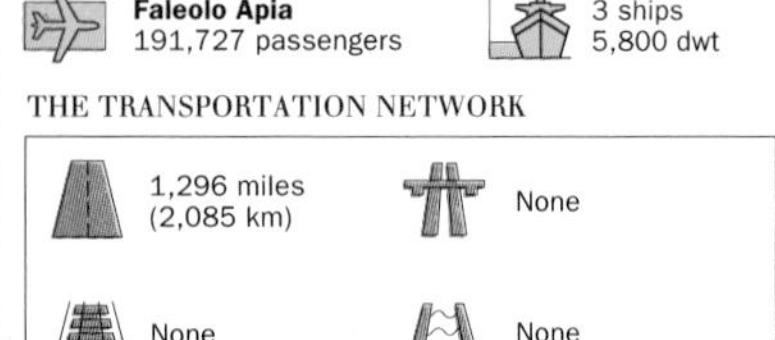

The port of Apia has been upgraded with Japanese aid. International links are mainly by air. Ferries provide inter-island connections.

TOURISM

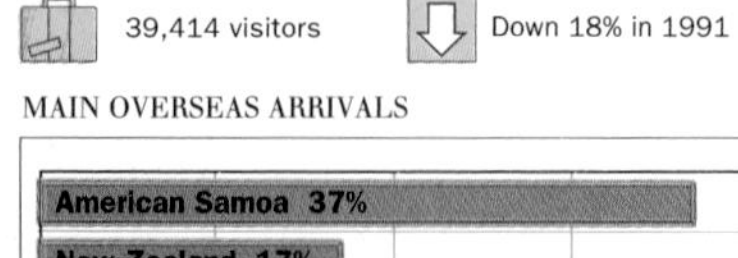

MAIN OVERSEAS ARRIVALS

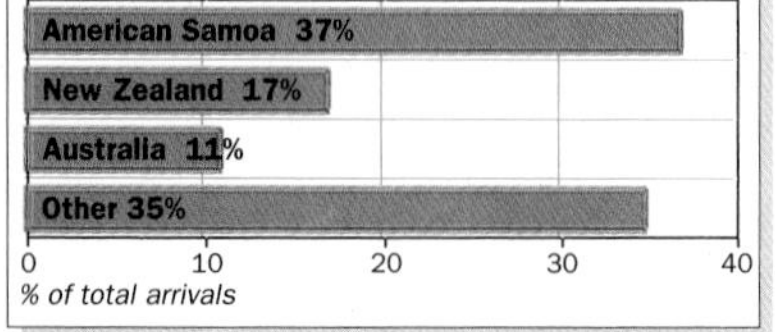

Concern that the Samoan way of life would be disrupted has limited tourism development until recently. Efforts now to improve facilities reflect the need to increase national revenues.

PEOPLE

Samoan, English

60 people per sq. mile

THE URBAN/RURAL POPULATION SPLIT

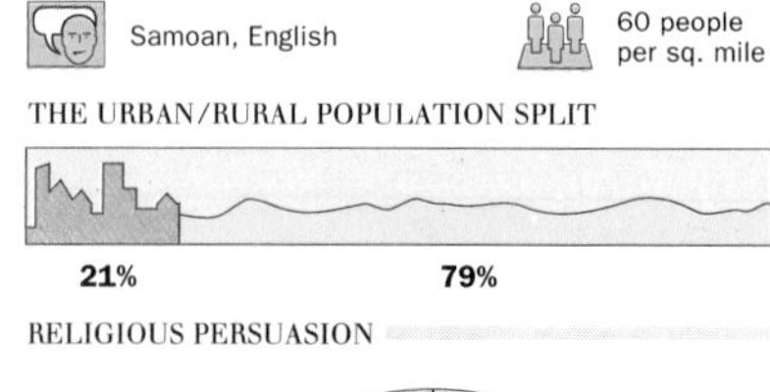

RELIGIOUS PERSUASION

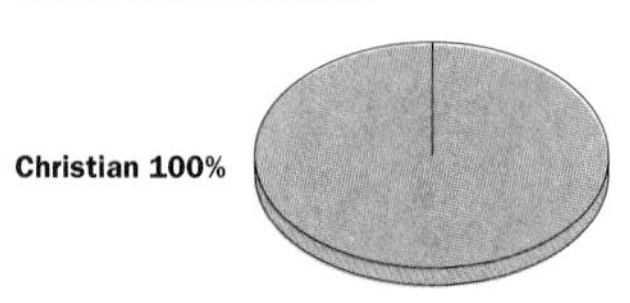

Ethnic Samoans – around 93% of the population – are the world's second-largest Polynesian group, after the Maoris. The *fa'a Samoa*, Samoan way of life, is communal and formalized. Extended family groups, in which most people live, own 80% of the land, and are not permitted to sell it. Each family is headed by a *matai*, or elected chief, who looks after its political and social interests. Large-scale migration to New Zealand and the USA reflects a lack of jobs and the attractions of Western life. Conflict between the *fa'a Samoa* and modern life is strongest among the young, who have a high suicide rate.

POLITICS

1996

H.H. Malietoa Tanumafili II

THE STATE OF THE PARTIES

Legislative Assembly 49 members

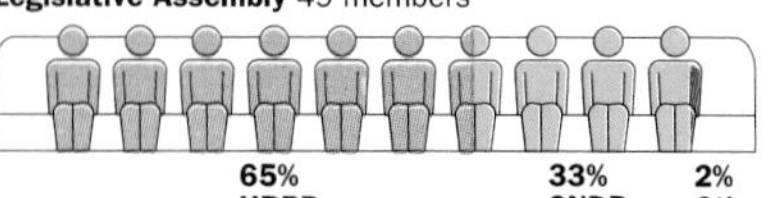

HRPP = Human Rights Protection Party
SNDP = Samoa National Development Party

The conservatism of the *fa'a Samoa*, reinforced by the Church's influence, has underpinned Western Samoa's political stability. Allegiance to the two main parties is quite fluid, and politics have as much to do with personalities as policies. Until 1990, only the 1,800 elected chiefs, or *matai*, could vote for the 47 ethnic Samoan seats; the other two seats are elected by non-Samoans. Universal suffrage was introduced at the 1991 elections, although only *matai* may run for the *fono*, or parliament. Following the elections, Fiame Naomi, a woman chief, became the country's first female cabinet minister.

WORLD AFFAIRS

SPF | SPC | Comm | ACP | ADB

New Zealand is Western Samoa's main trading partner. However, a steady tightening of controls on Samoan immigrants has at times strained relations with Wellington. Australia, the USA and EU are also important trading partners. Ties with Tokyo are growing, linked to Japanese investment.

AID

$52m (receipts)

Up 89% between 1989 and 1991

Australia, Japan, New Zealand and the EU are the main donors. With import costs 12 times export earnings and a heavy debt burden, aid is vital to the survival of the economy.

WESTERN SAMOA

Total Area : 2840 sq. km (1097 sq. miles)

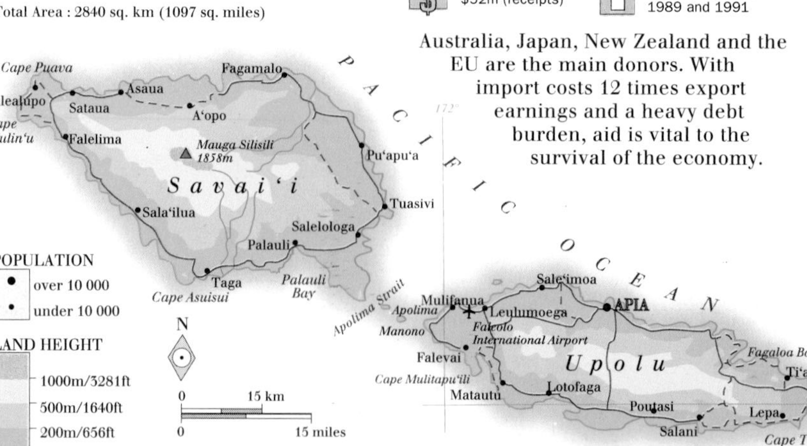

DEFENSE

 Western Samoa has no army and few police

 Not applicable

New Zealand looks after defense, under a 1962 treaty. Internal order is mostly maintained by the chiefs, or *matai*.

ECONOMICS

 $152m

 2.60 tala

SCORE CARD

- ❑ WORLD GNP RANKING 182nd
- ❑ GNP PER CAPITA $900
- ❑ BALANCE OF PAYMENTS ....$–29.2m
- ❑ INFLATION 9.7%
- ❑ UNEMPLOYMENT ....Underemployment

STRENGTHS

Light manufacturing growing; in 1992, it accounted for 75% of export earnings. Attracting foreign, especially Japanese, firms. Services growing rapidly since 1989 launch of offshore banking. Tropical agriculture; taro, coconut cream, cocoa, copra are main exports.

WEAKNESSES

Chronic balance of trade and payments deficits; dependence on aid and expatriate remittances. Declining agricultural exports. Clash between communal *fa'a Samoa* and donor pressure for market-style reforms.

EXPORTS

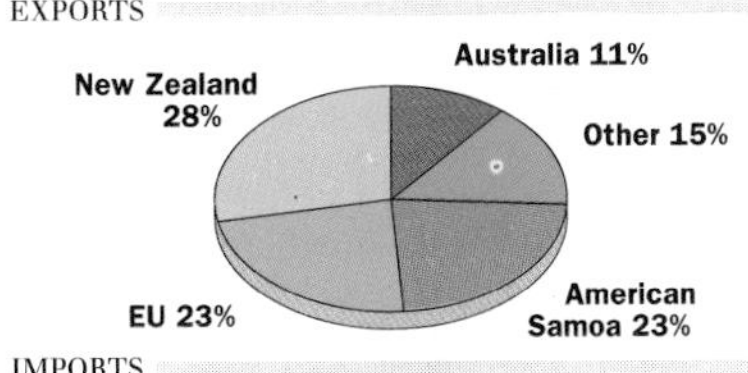

IMPORTS

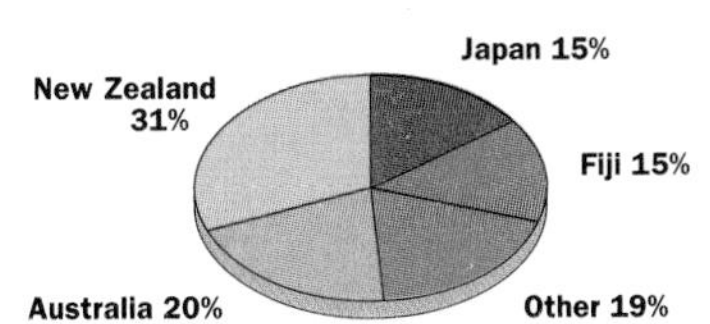

RESOURCES

 46m kwh (capacity 19,000 kw)

 Not an oil producer and has no refineries

 55,000 pigs, 29,000 cattle, 7,000 asses

 None

With no minerals, Western Samoa's main resources are its forests and tropical agriculture. The rainforests in lower lying areas are increasingly exploited for timber. Mahogany and teak plantations are being developed. The volcanic soils, particularly on Upolu, allow a wide range of staple and export crops to be grown. Two-thirds of the population works in agriculture.

***Apia, the capital**, on Upolu, Western Samoa's second-largest island. It has a central volcanic range of mountains and many rivers.*

ENVIRONMENT

 None

 Rainforests are increasingly under threat from logging

Efforts to increase revenues are putting the environment under pressure – 80% of lowland rainforest has been replaced by plantations. Overhunting and loss of habitat have endangered rare species of fruitbat and pigeon. Foreign firms have proposed environmentally damaging projects such as waste disposal plants, but these have so far been rejected.

MEDIA

 Fairly open criticism of the government is possible

PUBLISHING AND BROADCAST MEDIA

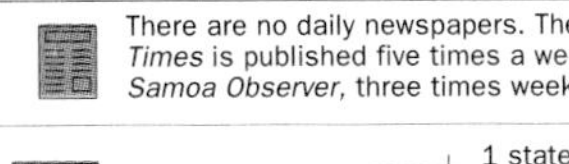 There are no daily newspapers. The *Samoa Times* is published five times a week; the *Samoa Observer*, three times weekly

 No TV service

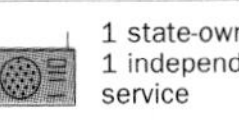 1 state-owned, 1 independent service

American Samoan TV, linking with the US networks, is widely received. A state-owned service is being set up.

CRIME

 Western Samoa does not publish prison figures

 Little change from year to year

Alcohol-related violence is a problem, especially on weekends; otherwise violent crime is almost unknown. Theft is increasing in urban areas.

EDUCATION

 98%

Education is based on the New Zealand system. School attendance is universal and literacy levels high. A university was established in 1988. Scholarships are available for study abroad.

HEALTH

 1 per 3,685 people

 Heart and cerebro-vascular diseases, pneumonia, suicide

The Samoan preference for being big married well with traditional diets. Diabetes and heart disease are rising as people change to Western-style foods.

CHRONOLOGY

Polynesians settled Samoa in about 1000 BC. Western rivalry after 1830 led to the 1899 division of the islands into German Western and American Eastern Samoa.

- ❑ **1914** New Zealand occupies Western Samoa. Administers first for League of Nations, then for UN.
- ❑ **1962** Becomes first independent Polynesian nation.
- ❑ **1990** Cyclone Ofa leaves 10,000 homeless. A year later, Cyclone Val causes worse damage, kills 12.
- ❑ **1991** HRPP retains power in first election under universal adult suffrage; follows positive 1990 referendum. Parliamentary term raised from three to five years.

WEALTH

 Many in the private sector earn only the statutory minimum of 1.25 tala per hour

CONSUMER GOODS OWNERSHIP

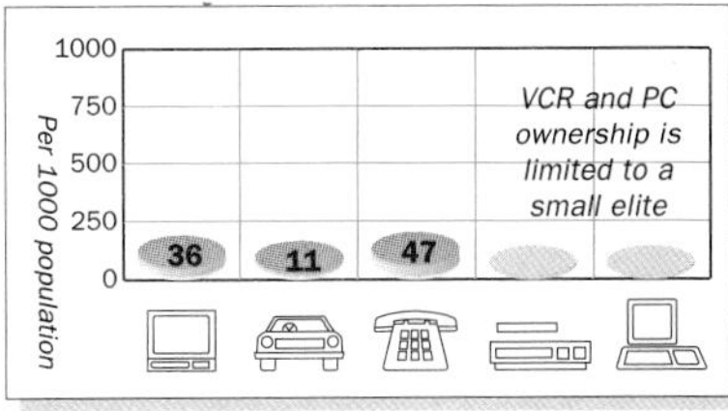

One of the world's least developed nations according to the UN, Western Samoa has the lowest wage and highest unemployment rates in Oceania. As a result, emigration is high. Some 60,000 Samoans live in New Zealand, 50,000 in the USA and 10,000 in neighboring American Samoa, where generous US support makes life much easier. Most people depend on subsistence farming and the remittances of relatives for their livelihood. Two-thirds of those with a job work for the government.

WORLD RANKING

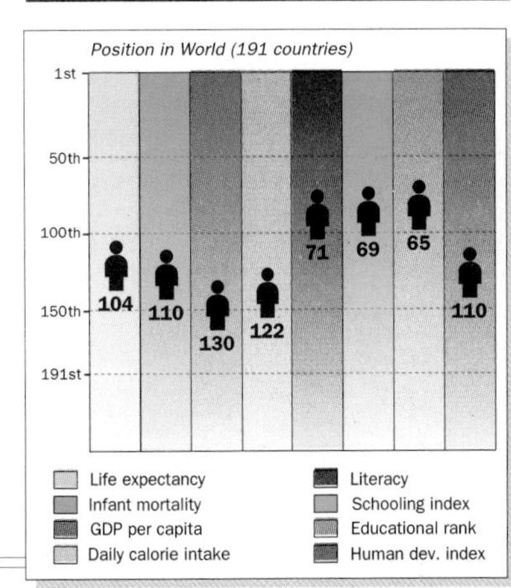

W

YEMEN

MIDDLE EAST
Saudi Arabia · Oman · Eritrea · YEMEN · Djibouti · Asia · Africa

OFFICIAL NAME: Republic of Yemen **CAPITAL:** Sana
POPULATION: 12.5 million **CURRENCY:** Yemen rial, Yemeni dinar **OFFICIAL LANGUAGE:** Arabic

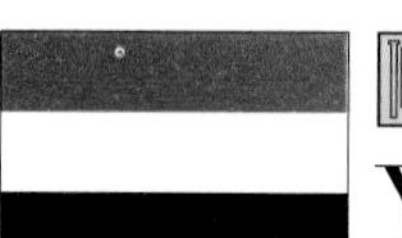

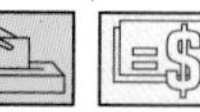
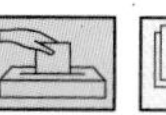

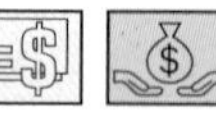
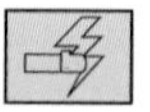
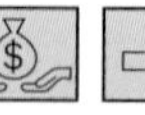
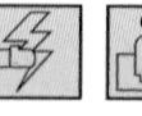

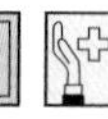

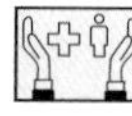

YEMEN IS LOCATED in southern Arabia between Saudi Arabia and Oman. The north is mountainous, with a fertile strip along the Red Sea. The south is largely arid mountains and desert. Yemen was formerly two countries, The Yemen Arab Republic in the north and The People's Democratic Republic of Yemen in the south, which united in 1990. The poorer south, with its capital in Adan, was the Arab world's only Marxist state after British rule ended in 1967. The north was run from Sana by successive military regimes, following a coup against the royalist imamate in 1962.

CLIMATE

WEATHER CHART

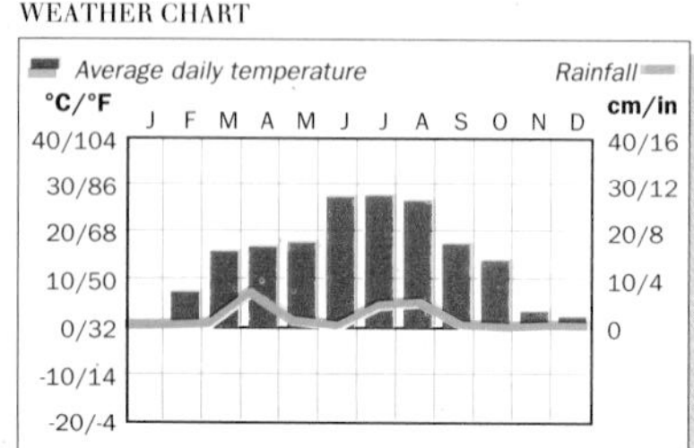

The desert climate is modified by altitude, which affects temperatures by as much as 54°F. Rainfall is greatest in northwest and central Yemen.

COMMUNICATIONS

Sana International
624,000 passengers

7 ships
9,700 dwt

THE TRANSPORTATION NETWORK

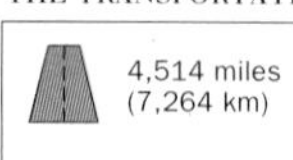
4,514 miles (7,264 km)

None

None

None

Adan's position at the entrance to the Red Sea makes it a key shipping port. The main cities are linked by adequate roads, but many rural areas are inaccessible. Sana and Adan are served by international airlines.

***Hilltop village** in northern Yemen, showing traditionally decorated, multistory houses built from mud bricks.*

TOURISM

55,000 visitors

Tourism has risen since 1990

MAIN OVERSEAS ARRIVALS

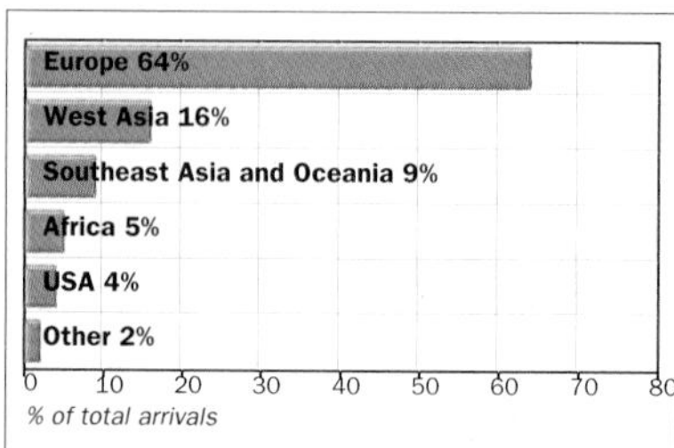

Believed to be the home of the legendary Queen of Sheba, Yemen attracts tourists interested in Arab society, architecture, archaeology and historical remains. The Romans called Yemeni Arabia "Felix" because of its fertile farmlands and dominance in the frankincense trade. Yemen was the second country, after Saudi Arabia, to convert to Islam.

Southern Yemen has been open to Western visitors only since 1990. Its run-down infrastructure and lack of hotels, especially on the coast, have hindered tourism. Sana, a walled medieval city, is the more interesting center for tourists. It has impressive architecture, particularly tall stone-and-terracotta Arab houses, and the palaces of the former imamate. Despite being over 600 miles away from the capital, the Marib Dam, built in ancient times, is another major attraction.

German and French tourists were the first to travel in numbers to North Yemen, when specialist tour companies began to offer adventure vacations during the 1980s. Tourism is on the rise, despite growing reports of terrorism and kidnapping.

Tourists are subject to a ban on the consumption of alcohol, except in five-star hotels. Whisky and beer are available on the black market, which operates out of Djibouti.

PEOPLE

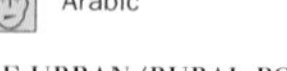
Arabic

57 people per sq. mile

THE URBAN/RURAL POPULATION SPLIT

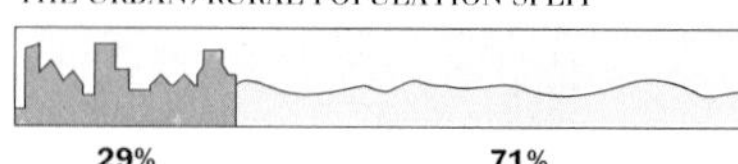

RELIGIOUS PERSUASION

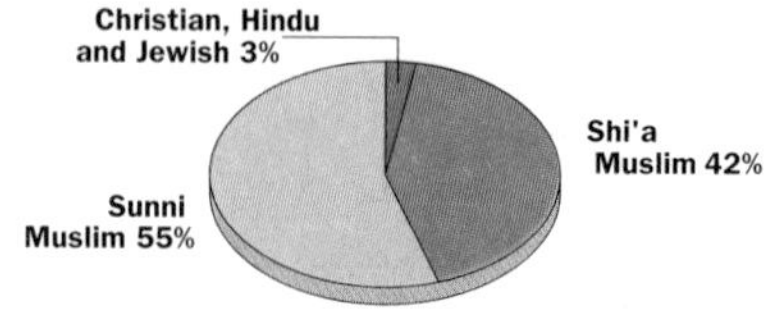

ETHNIC MAKEUP

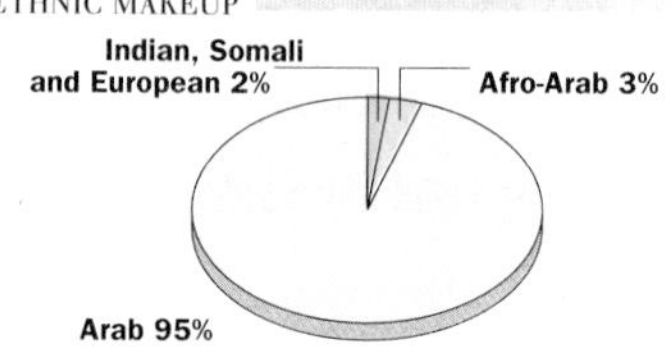

Yemenis are almost entirely of Arab and Bedouin descent, although there is a dwindling Jewish minority. The majority are Sunni Muslims, of the Shafi sect. In the north, many people have close family ties in Saudi Arabia. Many Yemenis consider Saudi's Asir province to be part of Yemen.

Agriculture employs more than half of the population. Many Yemenis sought jobs in Saudi Arabia and the Gulf states during the 1970s oil boom. More than one million worked in Saudi Arabia, most as manual laborers and farmhands. Their expulsion, a result of Yemen's support for Iraq's invasion of Kuwait in 1990, has raised unemployment within Yemen.

In rural areas and in the north, Islamic orthodoxy is strong and most women wear the veil. In the south, however, women still claim the freedoms they had under the Marxist regime, especially in urban areas.

Tension continues to exist between the south, led by the cosmopolitan city of Adan, and the more conservative north. Clashes between their former armies escalated into civil war in 1994.

POPULATION AGE BREAKDOWN

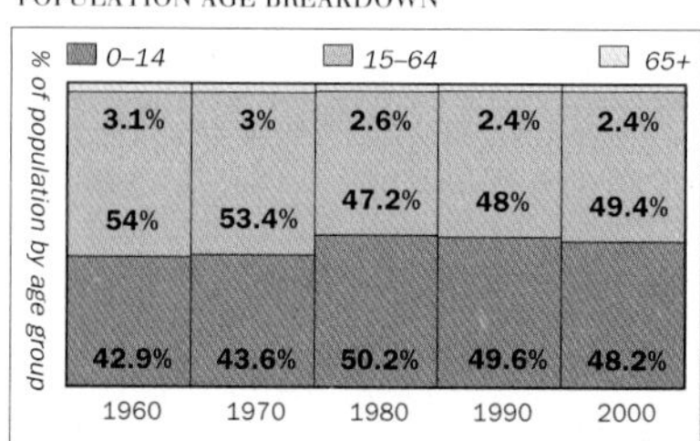

Y

YEMEN

Total Area : 527 970 sq. km
(203 849 sq. miles)

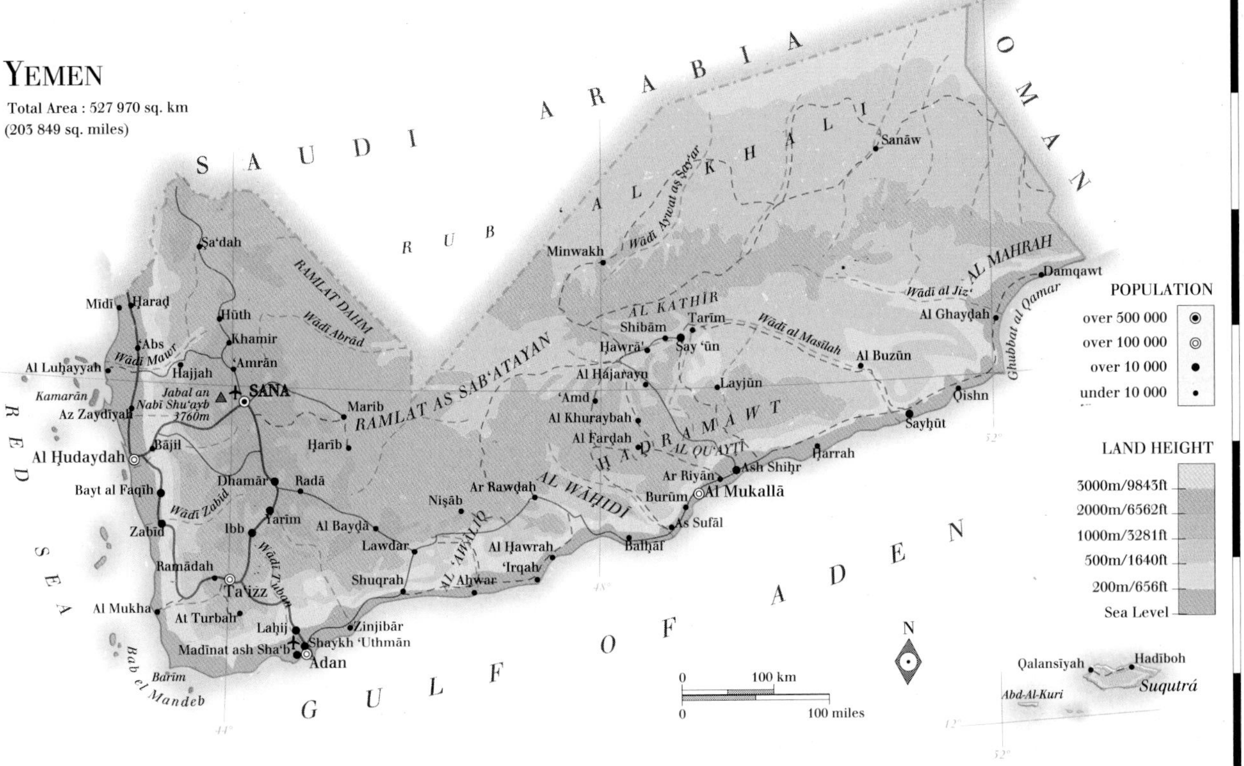

POPULATION

over 500 000
over 100 000
over 10 000
under 10 000

LAND HEIGHT

3000m/9843ft
2000m/6562ft
1000m/3281ft
500m/1640ft
200m/656ft
Sea Level

0 100 km
0 100 miles

POLITICS

THE STATE OF THE PARTIES

House of Representatives 301 members

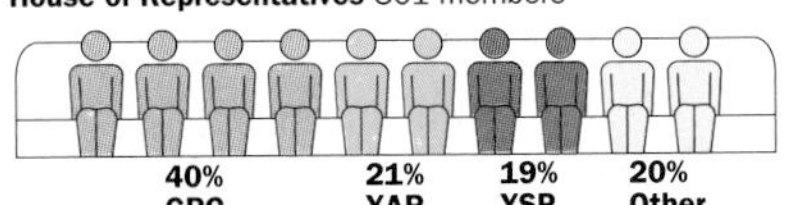

GPC = General People's Congress **YAR** = Yemeni Alliance for Reform **YSP** = Yemeni Socialist Party **Other** = Arab Socialist Ba'ath Party, Truth Party

Yemen is a multiparty democracy. The president retains executive power while the House of Representatives holds legislative power.

MAIN POLITICAL ISSUES

Instability

The 1993 general election resulted in a government of national unity being formed. However, the merger of South and North Yemen has been under severe strain since then. Growing animosity between the Yemen Socialist Party (YSP), which formerly ruled in Adan, and the conservative hierarchy in Sana led to the outbreak of full-blown civil war in May 1994.

Saudi interference

In the run up to the elections, there were bombings and attacks on leading politicians. Since the Gulf War, political relationships with Saudi Arabia have been strained, raising suspicions that the latter is funding northern dissidents.

PROFILE

The merger of North and South Yemen in 1990 united Yemenis under one ruler for the first time since 1735. At first, President Ali Saleh, who had had difficulty controlling the north even before the union with the socialist regime in Adan, skillfully maintained unity. Then, in the spring of 1994, tensions mounted following an assassination attempt on a political supporter of Saleh's, Hassan Makki. Amid accusations from the South that President Saleh was attempting to overthrow Vice President al-Baidh, the former leader of South Yemen, civil war broke out. Most of the fighting was centered in the South, in particular around the port of Adan, which became the scene of mass evacuations by European workers. By July 1994, the fighting had died down and the South's attempted secession had been quashed.

Ali Abdullah Saleh, *former North Yemen president, now leader of the unified Yemen.*

Ali Salem al-Baidh, *vice-president and former leader of South Yemen.*

CHRONOLOGY

From the 9th century AD the Zaydi dynasty ruled Yemen, until their defeat by the Ottoman Turks in 1517. The Turks were expelled by the Zaydi Imams in 1636.

- **1839** Britain occupies Aden.
- **1918** Yemen secures independence.
- **1937** Aden made a Crown Colony, the hinterland a Protectorate.
- **1962** Army coup. Imam deposed and Yemen Arab Republic (YAR) declared in the North.
- **1962–1970** Northern civil war between royalists and republicans.
- **1963** Aden and Protectorate united to form Federation of South Arabia.
- **1967** British troops leave Aden.
- **1970** South Yemen renamed the People's Democratic Republic of Yemen (PDYR). Republicans victorious in the North.
- **1971** Civilian elections in the YAR.
- **1972** September: war between YAR and PDYR. October: peace signed.
- **1974** Army coup in YAR.
- **1975** Sultan of Oman defeats PDYR-backed revolt in Dhofar province.
- **1978** Lt.-Col. Ali Saleh YAR president. Coup in PDYR. Radical Abdalfattah Ismail in power.
- **1979** February: war breaks out. March: peace. October: PDYR signs 20-year treaty with USSR.
- **1980** Ismail replaced by moderate Ali Muhammed.

Y

CHRONOLOGY *continued*

- **1982** President of PDYR Ali Muhammed signs peace treaty with the Sultan of Oman.
- **1984** YAR signs 20-year cooperation treaty with USSR.
- **1986** January: coup attempt against President Muhammed in PDYR develops into civil war. Rebels take control of Adan. February: rebels install Haydar Al Attas as president. July: presidents of PDYR and YAR meet.
- **1987** Oil production starts in YAR.
- **1988** YAR holds elections for a consultative council, Muslim brotherhood gains influence.
- **1989** Unification process speeds up dramatically. June: telephone links established. July: PDYR publishes a program of free-market reforms. November: YAR and PDYR sign agreement to unify the two states. December: constitution of unified Yemen published.
- **1990** January: restrictions on travel between YAR and PDYR end. Growing opposition to unification inside Yemen from fundamentalists against the secular constitution. May 22: unification of PDYR and YAR. Ali Saleh becomes president of the Republic of Yemen. August: Yemen criticizes Western response to the Iraqi invasion of Kuwait.
- **1991** Yemeni guest workers expelled by Saudi Arabia in retaliation for Yemen's position over the Iraqi invasion of Kuwait. Arab states boycott independence celebrations.
- **1992** Assassinations and political unrest delay elections until April 1993. Economic decline.
- **1993** April: elections leave the ruling parties still in power. Islamic fundamentalists gain influence in President Saleh's government.

WORLD AFFAIRS

Yemen's links with Saudi Arabia and the West have still not recovered from the support Yemen gave to Iraq during the Gulf War. Yemen's relationship with Oman has improved with the signing of a border agreement in 1992.

AID

 $313m (receipts)  Down 23% in 1991

Yemen receives limited backing from the World Bank and Western aid agencies. Aid from Gulf states depends on Yemen abandoning ties with Iraq.

DEFENSE

 $935m 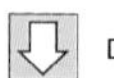 Down 12% in 1992

Defense spending as % GDP (scale 0–40): 13%

Following unification, mutual suspicion slowed down the integration of North and South Yemen's defense forces. Sporadic, bitter clashes have taken place, most notably in 1994. In the past, Soviet weapons were bought by both governments, although the north also possesses US arms.

YEMENI ARMED FORCES

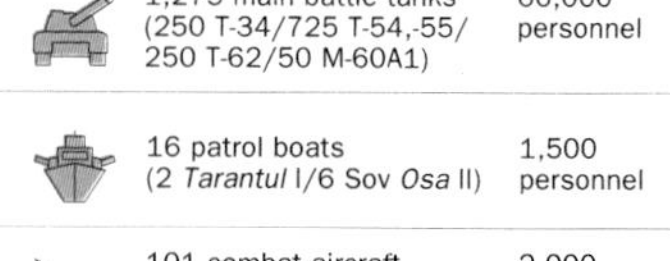

Army	1,275 main battle tanks (250 T-34/725 T-54,-55/ 250 T-62/50 M-60A1)	60,000 personnel
Navy	16 patrol boats (2 *Tarantul* I/6 Sov *Osa* II)	1,500 personnel
Air force	101 combat aircraft (11 F-5E/111 Su-20, -22/188 MiG-21)	2,000 personnel
Missiles	None	

ECONOMICS

$7.3bn  0.46 Yemeni dinars 16.47 Yemen rials

SCORE CARD

- World GNP Ranking: 91st
- GNP per Capita: $585
- Balance of Payments: $-579m
- Inflation: 70%
- Unemployment: 13%

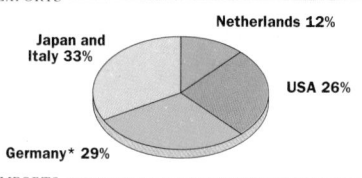

ECONOMIC PERFORMANCE INDICATOR

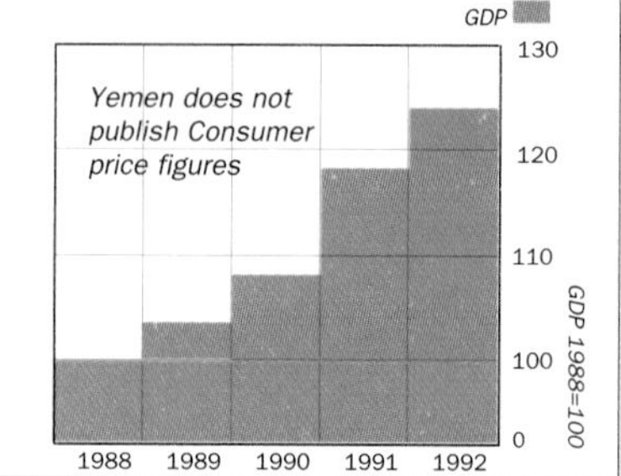

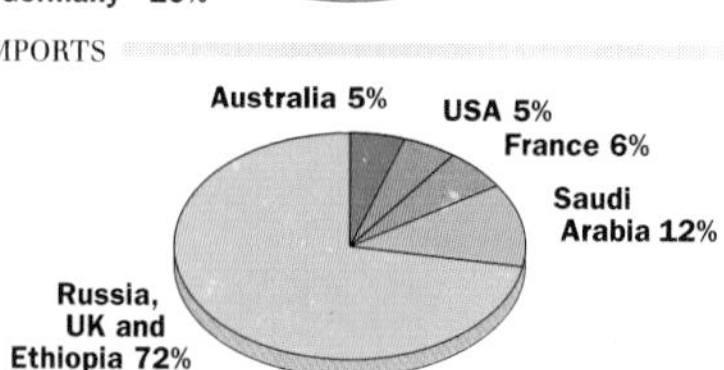

STRENGTHS

Rising oil production. Salt mining. Deposits of copper, gold, lead, zinc and molybdenum. Industries include oil refining, chemicals and food products.

WEAKNESSES

Political instability deters foreign investment. Well-organized black market undermines tax base. Large balance of payments deficit. Overall dependence on subsistence agriculture.

PROFILE

Yemen's unification in 1990 was designed to transform the economy. High expectations were placed on the exploitation of large oil and natural gas reserves, discovered in 1984. Exports of oil began in 1987. Plans were also made to encourage industrial investment around the port of Adan. Both these policies for regeneration suffered severe setbacks as a result of the 1990–1991 Gulf War. In addition, the expulsion of over one million Yemeni guest workers from Saudi Arabia imposed a huge burden on the economy and ended the flow of workers' remittances.

Economic crisis forced the government to reduce expenditure and subsidies on certain staple foods. This provoked widespread civil unrest and encouraged many farmers to switch from food crops, such as wheat, to growing the more profitable narcotic plant *qat*. As a result, Yemen has increasingly had to import foodstuffs.

In line with its free-market reforms, the government has encouraged joint-venture deals with Western oil firms. Some companies were deterred by bandits, who stole equipment and kidnapped personnel for ransom. The evacuation of skilled foreign workers due to an outbreak of civil war in 1994 will hit the economy hard.

YEMEN : MAJOR BUSINESSES

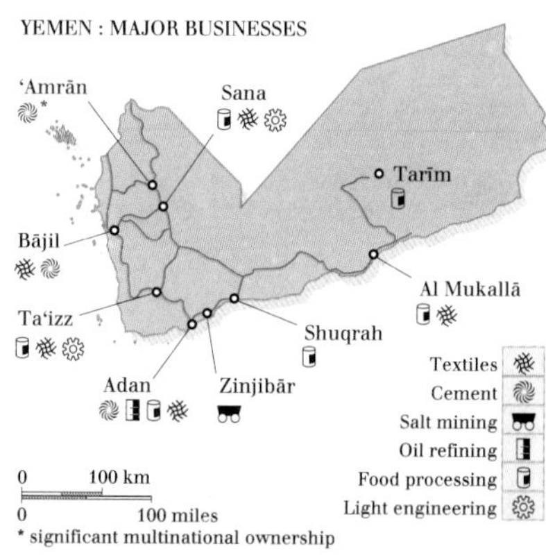

Y

RESOURCES

1.7bn kwh (capacity 800,000 kw)

450,000 b/d (reserves 4,000,000,000 bbl)

3.7m sheep, 1.2m cattle, 690,000 asses

Oil, natural gas, salt, molybdenum, zinc, gold, lead, copper

ELECTRICITY GENERATION

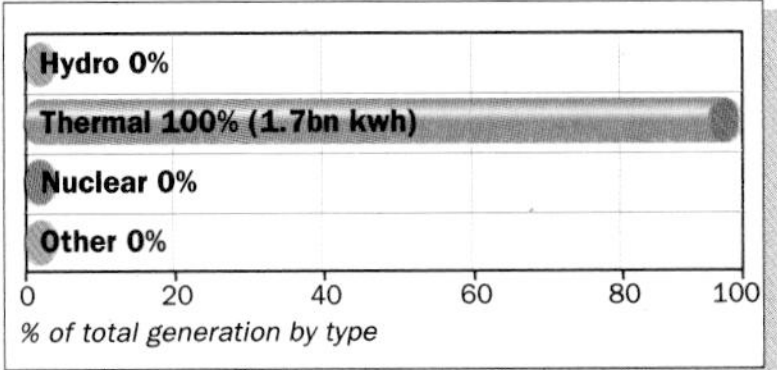

There are considerable reserves of oil and gas. Crude oil production has reached 450,000 b/d. It would be more but for Western companies' reluctance to offend Saudi Arabia, whose relations with Yemen are strained. Despite attacks by bandits, exploration is continuing in many areas. Salt is the only other mineral that is commercially exploited at present, and its production continues to grow steadily.

The agricultural sector employs 55% of the working population and accounts for 22% of GDP. Cotton is grown as a cash crop. There is also some forestry and hunting for animal skins. Livestock and livestock products, such as dairy produce and hides, are the economic mainstays of the north.

Yemen's rich fishing grounds in the Arabian Sea have been developed. They now provide a major source of earnings, despite poor equipment.

YEMEN : LAND USE

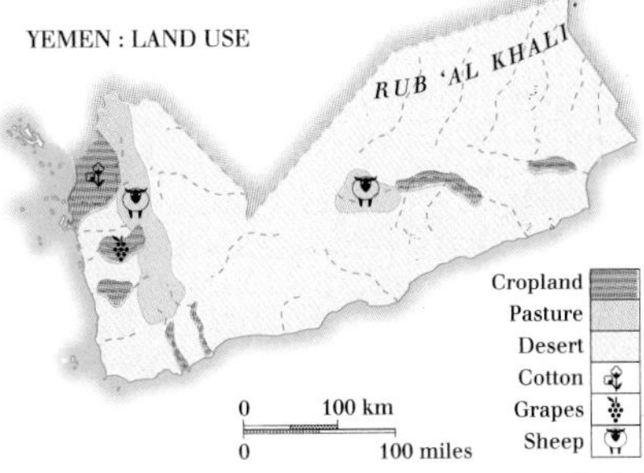

ENVIRONMENT

None

Environmental issues not a major concern

ENVIRONMENTAL TREATIES

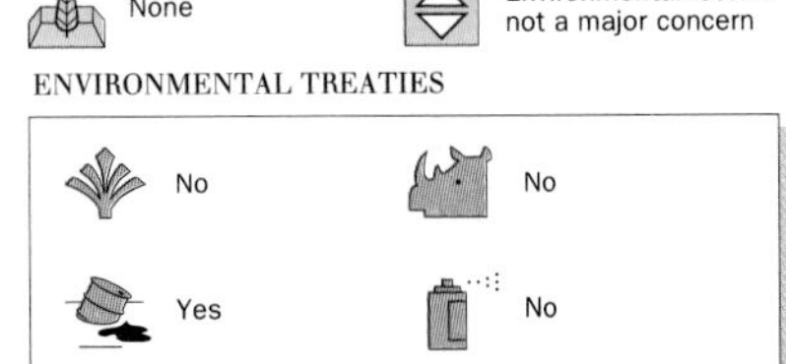

Yemen's low economic development has resulted in large untouched areas of land. However, game animals are under severe threat from hunters.

MEDIA

The media is under tight government control

PUBLISHING AND BROADCAST MEDIA

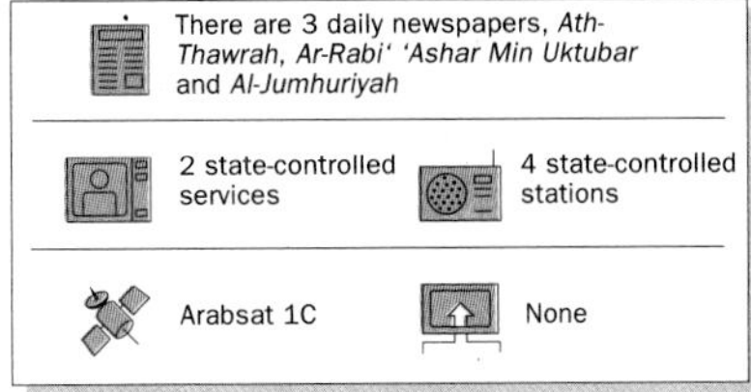

There are 3 daily newspapers, *Ath-Thawrah, Ar-Rabi' 'Ashar Min Uktubar* and *Al-Jumhuriyah*
2 state-controlled services
4 state-controlled stations
Arabsat 1C
None

CRIME

Yemen does not publish prison figures

Crime is rising

CRIME RATES

Threat of civil war makes normal law enforcement problematic

Political assassinations have long been a feature of Yemeni life and continue to threaten political stability. Formal law enforcement does not often operate far outside the main cities. As a result, Western companies face the double risk of their personnel being kidnapped and their equipment being stolen by Bedouin raiding parties. To combat the latter, many vehicles have their roofs marked so that police can readily identify them from the air and, if necessary, track down thieves.

EDUCATION

39%

0 *Education spending as % GNP* 25

6.1%

THE EDUCATION SYSTEM

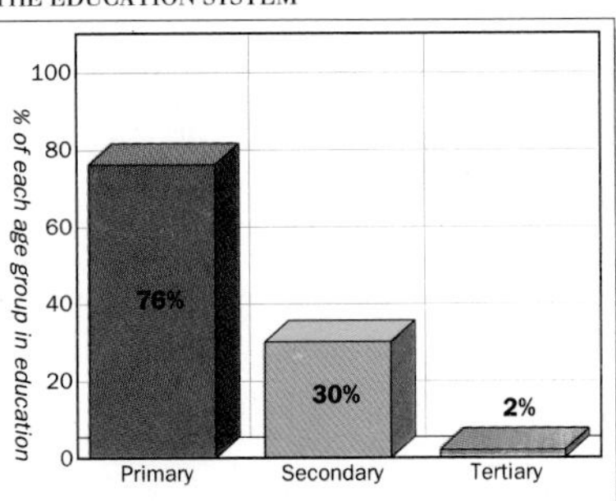

Some 80% of the population have no formal education. Schooling barely extends into the rural areas. Illiteracy is especially high among women: 75% cannot read or write. There are fewer than 10,000 students at Yemen's two universities in Sana and Adan. Yemen also has some technical colleges.

Yemen has a long, distinguished tradition of intellectual debate, but the press is poorly developed. The government keeps a tight control on the media and vets the entry of foreign journalists. TV and radio are state-controlled and have a limited range around the principal cities. Satellite TV is not generally available. The ownership of radios and TVs is low, with only a small minority of the population owning a TV.

HEALTH

1 per 5,531 people

Diarrheal diseases, tuberculosis, malaria, bilharzia

0 *Health spending as % GNP* 25

1.5%

The major cities have an adequate primary healthcare system. Rural areas are less well served. Yemen has only one doctor for every 5,531 people. Infant mortality is high for the Middle East at 12%. Life expectancy is 52 years for men and 56 for women.

WEALTH

Most Yemenis lead a subsistence existence

CONSUMER GOODS OWNERSHIP

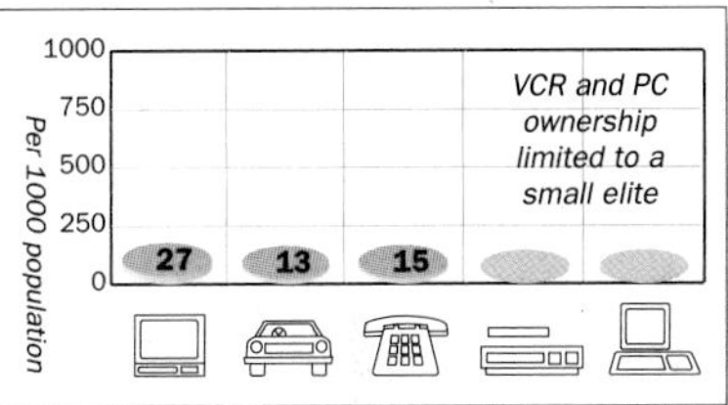

Most Yemenis have experienced a reduced standard of living since Saudi Arabia expelled its Yemeni workers. The lack of jobs in other Gulf states has added to unemployment levels. Except for a small elite, the ownership of consumer goods is low.

WORLD RANKING

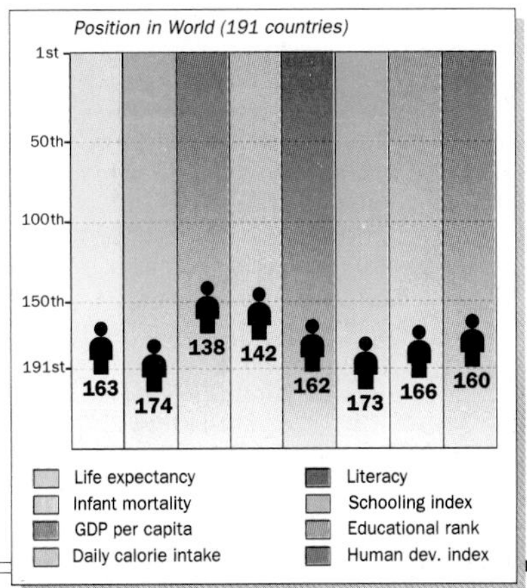

Y

YUGOSLAVIA (SERBIA & MONTENEGRO)

OFFICIAL NAME: Federal Republic of Yugoslavia **CAPITAL:** Belgrade
POPULATION: 10.4 million **CURRENCY:** Dinar **OFFICIAL LANGUAGE:** Serbo-Croatian

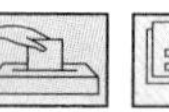
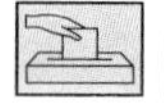

THE SELF-PROCLAIMED Federal Republic of Yugoslavia (FRY), comprising the republics of Serbia and Montenegro, lays claim to being the successor state to the former Yugoslavia. Serbia is vilified in the international community for its role in the ongoing conflict in the region and the FRY has been denied recognition by most countries. UN sanctions imposed in 1992 have taken a tremendous economic toll. Nationalism among the Hungarian minority in the autonomous region of Vojvodina and, in particular, among Albanians in Kosovo, is a further source of tension.

CLIMATE

WEATHER CHART

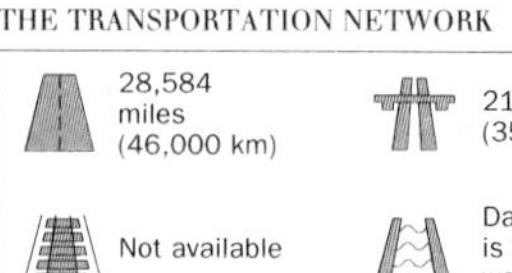

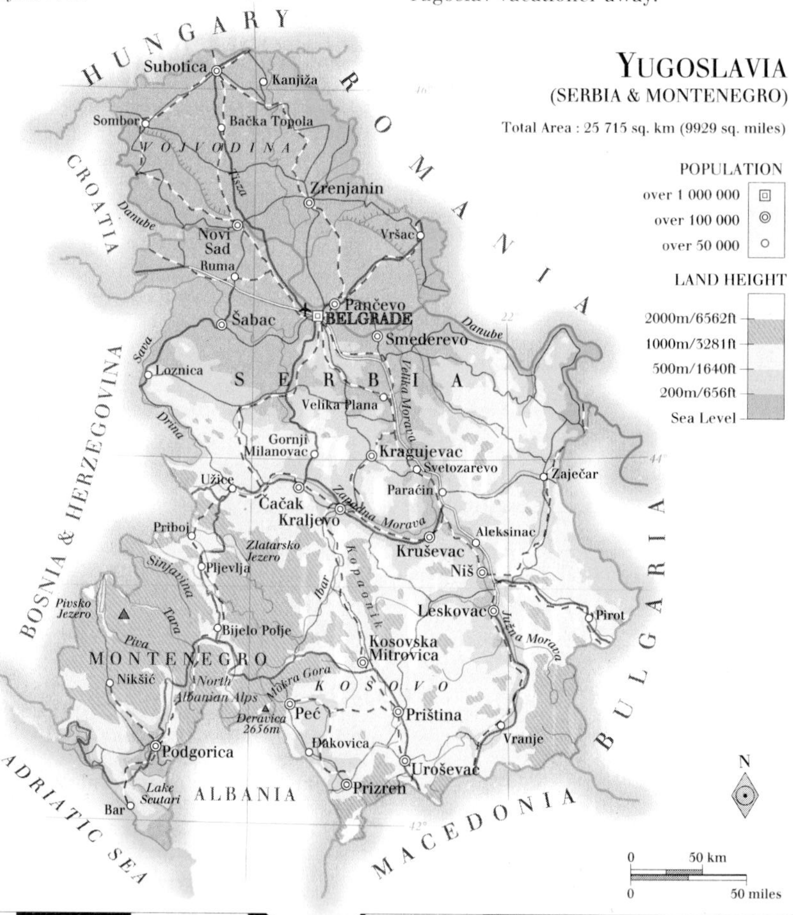

The former Yugoslavia's mountain scenery and fine beaches attracted more than five million tourists a year before 1991.

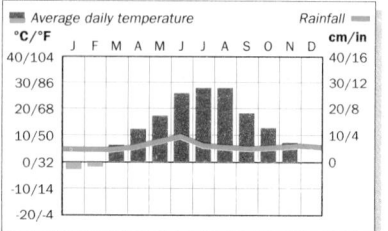

The climate is continental inland and Mediterranean along the Montenegrin coast. Summers are hot and springs rainy. Winters are cold, with heavy snowfalls. In July and August the average daily maximum in Belgrade is 82°F, while in January it is 37°F.

COMMUNICATIONS

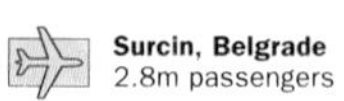

THE TRANSPORTATION NETWORK

28,584 miles (46,000 km)	217 miles (350 km)
Not available	Danube River is the major waterway

About one-third of railroads in the FRY is electrified. However, the important rail link to Greece, one of Serbia's main trading links, has been cut since 1993 as a result of international economic sanctions. Most goods are still available in the shops, but are brought into the country by illegal trade.

Roads in Serbia are manned by small groups of soldiers carrying AK47s. Yugoslavia issues transit visas relatively freely and travel on the main Budapest–Sofia highway through Serbia has resumed. Although Yugoslavia is fairly safe for foreign travelers and harassment by the military is rare, most travelers choose to take longer routes through neighboring countries.

TOURISM

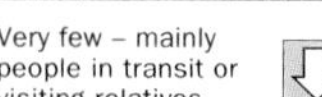

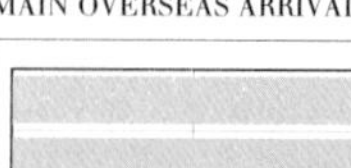

MAIN OVERSEAS ARRIVALS

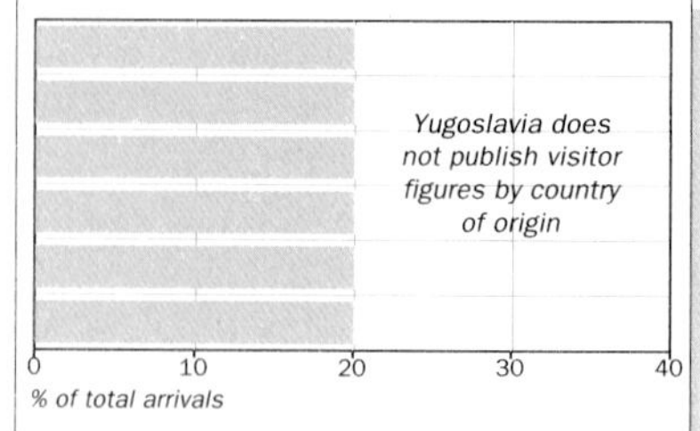
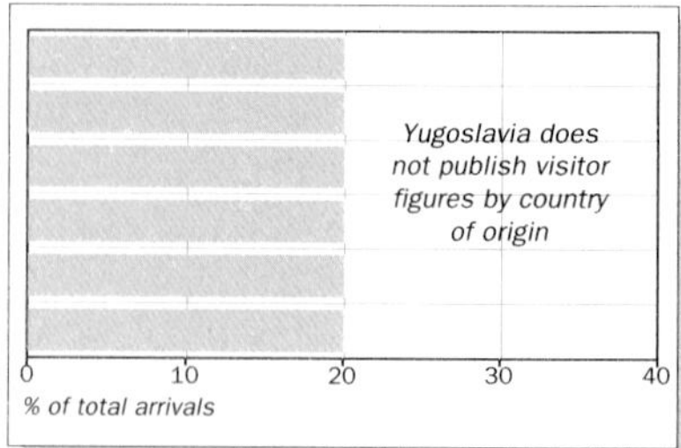

Serbia has never been a center of tourism. The Montenegrin coast, however, has renowned beaches. The imposition of UN sanctions means that foreign tourism has ceased. Montenegrin tourism is monopolized by Serbians, particularly by the political and criminal elements of the Serbian elite. The impact of recession and hyperinflation has kept the average Yugoslav vacationer away.

YUGOSLAVIA
(SERBIA & MONTENEGRO)
Total Area : 25 715 sq. km (9929 sq. miles)

POPULATION
over 1 000 000
over 100 000
over 50 000

LAND HEIGHT
2000m/6562ft
1000m/3281ft
500m/1640ft
200m/656ft
Sea Level

PEOPLE

Serbo-Croatian

1,046 people per sq. mile

THE URBAN/RURAL POPULATION SPLIT

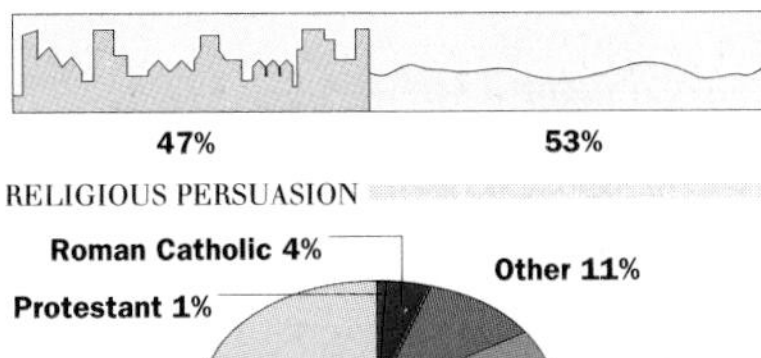

RELIGIOUS PERSUASION

Roman Catholic 4%
Other 11%
Protestant 1%
Muslim 19%
Orthodox Catholic 65%

ETHNIC MAKEUP

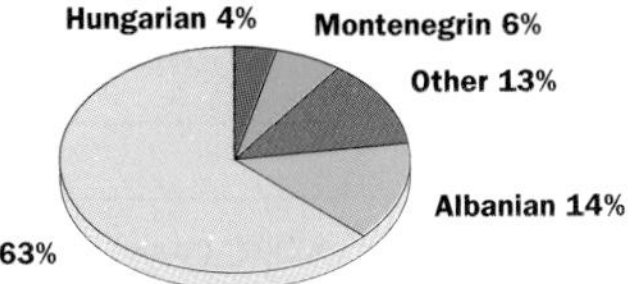

The social order in the FRY is disintegrating. The professional classes have effectively been driven out of Serbia; 100,000 have left since the dissolution of federal Yugoslavia. The absence of a middle class is likely to be most strongly felt when sanctions are eventually lifted; the lack of educated and experienced professionals may affect the prospects for economic recovery. An estimated two-thirds of the population are currently living below subsistence level. Many people are suffering from malnutrition, and health problems are aggravated by biting cold winters. A modest estimate of a household's basic consumption needs costs three times the average wage. Those relying on state pensions are faring the worst. At the end of 1993, real monthly pensions were virtually worthless – about $1.90 – and pensioners in Belgrade were reported to be committing suicide at a rate of four a week.

POPULATION AGE BREAKDOWN

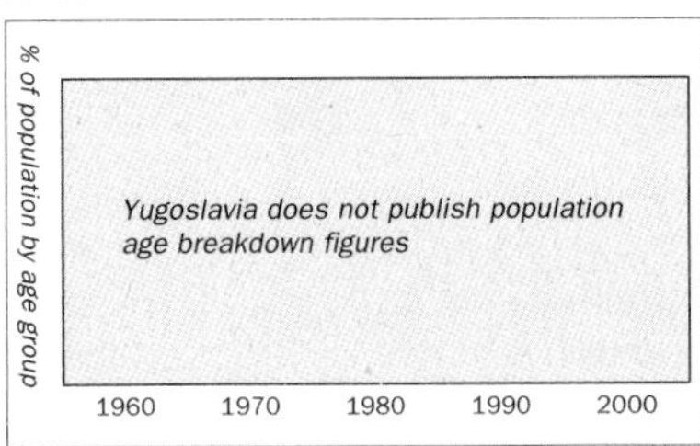

POLITICS

 Uncertain

 President

THE STATE OF THE PARTIES

Chamber of Citizens 138 members

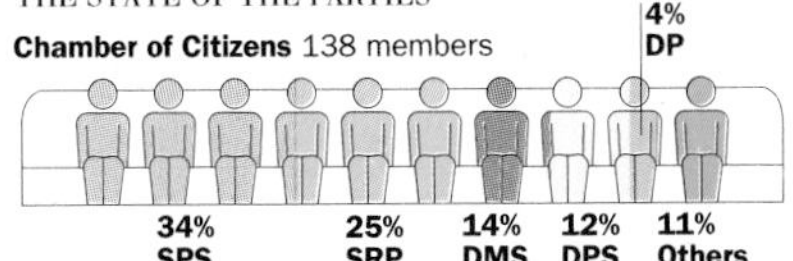

SPS = Socialist Party of Serbia **SRP** = Serbian Radical Party **DMS** = Democratic Movement of Serbia **DPS** = Democratic Party of Socialists **DP** = Democratic Party

Chamber of Republics 40 members

Composed of 40 members from Serbia and Montenegro selected on a proportional basis to reflect the composition of Serbia's and Montenegro's republican legislatures

Serbia and Montenegro each have a single-chamber, democratically elected parliament and a president. Each also contributes members to the bicameral Federal Assembly.

MAIN POLITICAL ISSUES

Inter-republican conflict

Montengro has recently been showing greater independence from Serbia in decision making, in response to internal pressure and a need to secure its position within the Federal Republic. Serbia, in turn, has sought to undermine the authority of President Bulatović. In the summer of 1993, Serbia instigated a trade war with its smaller neighbor, focusing on energy and food. Montenegro responded with cuts in the exports of raw materials, such as bauxite, which are essential to Serbian industry, particularly the armaments sector.

Minority government in Serbia

The Serbian parliament remains unstable. In the 1993 elections, the Socialists enlarged their share of seats from 101 to 123, leaving them still three seats short of an absolute majority.

PROFILE

Serbia is the stronger political player and, as Serbian president, Milošević is at the center of policy making. In Montenegro, the DPS government elected in 1992 formed a coalition with all the parties except the SRS, despite having themselves received a clear majority.

Radoje Konić, who replaced Milan Panić as federal prime minister in 1993.

Slobodan Milošović, Serbian president and the FRY's major political influence.

WORLD AFFAIRS

UN economic sanctions against the FRY have isolated it from the international community, and foreign affairs center on the states of the former Yugoslavia. The exact nature of the links with Bosnian Serbs is intentionally obscured, but it is widely accepted that Bosnian Serb troops receive considerable support from Serbia. An open declaration of support for integrating seized lands into a "Greater Serbia" would torpedo hopes of a peaceful settlement. Fighting continues over the region of Krajina, which is within Croatian territory, but is considered by President Milošević to be within the Serb sphere of influence. Slovenia and Serbia have disputed the division of federal Yugoslav property. The existence of a strong Hungarian minority in Vojvodina and the more explosive tensions which surround the Albanian minority in Kosovo complicate relations with neighboring states, Hungary and Albania.

AID

 Only humanitarian aid

 None likely until peace settlement

All aid has been suspended with other economic relations. It is unlikely that recovery from the economic devastation which the FRY has sustained will be possible without international assistance.

CHRONOLOGY

The Serbs were defeated by the Turks at the Battle of Kosovo in 1389. Parts of the region later came under the control of the Austrian Habsburg empire.

- **1878** Full independence gained by Serbia and Montenegro at Congress of Berlin.
- **1918** Joint Kingdom of Serbs, Croats and Slovenes created.
- **1929** King Alexander of Serbia assumes absolute powers over state; changes name to Yugoslavia.
- **1941** Germans launch surprise attack. Rival resistance groups: Chetniks (Serb royalist) and Partisans (communist, under Tito).
- **1945** Federal People's Republic of Yugoslavia founded with Tito as prime minister. Vojvodina and Kosovo provinces gain autonomy within Serbia.
- **1948** Tito breaks with Stalin.
- **1950** Workers' councils give employees voice on economy.

CHRONOLOGY *continued*

- **1951** Farmers permitted to sell produce on free market.
- **1955** Detente between Yugoslavia and the USSR.
- **1973** April: economic cooperation agreement signed with West Germany. October: agreement of noninterference signed with Soviet Union. December: Croat nationalists purged from party leadership and government.
- **1974** New constitution decentralizes government. Vojvodina and Kosovo given status within Serbia.
- **1980** Tito dies. Succeeded by collective presidency.
- **1981** Unrest among Kosovo Albanians; state of emergency declared.
- **1985** Serbian intellectuals publish memorandum listing Serb grievances within Yugoslavia.
- **1986** Slobodan Milošević becomes leader of communist party in Serbia (SPS).
- **1987** Government wage freeze in attempt to combat inflation. Scandals lead to banking system crisis.
- **1988** Emergency party meeting proposes economic and social reforms. Belgrade protests against economic austerity. Mikulić government brought down over budget failure.
- **1989** Kosovo Albanians protest presence of Serb police unit; crackdown leads to loss of autonomy for province. King Nicholas I reburied in Montenegro. 600th anniversary of Battle of Kosovo.
- **1990** December: Milošević and Socialist party victorious in elections in Serbia. Communists win presidency and dominate assembly in multiparty elections in Montenegro.
- **1992** EC recognizes breakaway republics of Croatia, Slovenia and Bosnia-Herzegovina. UN sanctions imposed. Ibrahim Rugova elected president of self-declared Republic of Kosovo. Failure of Vance-Owen plan for Bosnia. Milošević defeats Prime Minister Milan Panić and is reelected president, but socialists lose absolute majority. Momir Bulatović wins Montenegrin presidency.
- **1993** Radical deputy Vuk Drasković arrested, but released after international protests. Ultra-nationalist Seselj calls successful vote of no confidence. Socialists improve parliamentary standing in December elections. New EU initiative in peace talks over Bosnia.

DEFENSE

$3.8bn

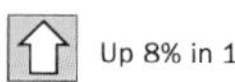

Up 8% in 1992

Defense spending as % GDP (0–40): 5%

SERBIAN ARMED FORCES

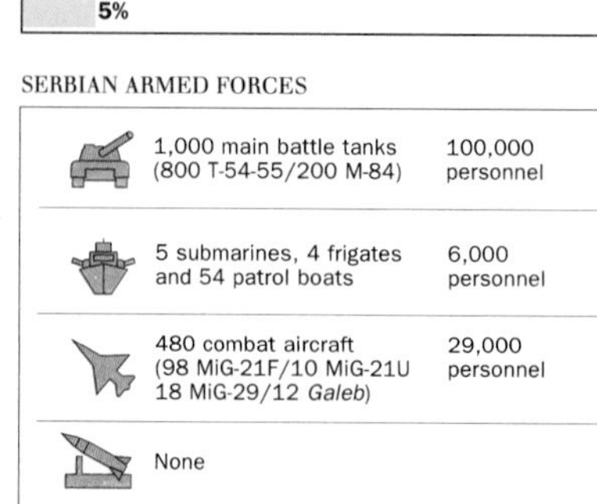

1,000 main battle tanks (800 T-54-55/200 M-84)
100,000 personnel
5 submarines, 4 frigates and 54 patrol boats
6,000 personnel
480 combat aircraft (98 MiG-21F/10 MiG-21U 18 MiG-29/12 Galeb)
29,000 personnel
None

The Serbian desire to reduce Bulatović's influence has resulted in the disestablishment of republican defense and foreign ministries in favor of the Serbian-controlled federal bodies. Montenegro has resisted the initiative.

The Serbian military has been more visible as an actor in the conflict in former Yugoslavia. Serbia was traditionally the center of armaments manufacture in the former republic. Its military hardware industry has enabled Serbia to arm itself without being dependent upon imports. The need to create money to pay for domestically produced weapons was a major factor in the crippling hyperinflation of 1993.

ECONOMICS

13.5bn

Dinar on 1:1 par with the Deutsch Mark

SCORE CARD

World GNP Ranking	69th
GNP per Capita	1,298
Balance of Payments	Deficit
Inflation	High
Unemployment	25%

EXPORTS

Imports and exports have effectively been cut off as a result of UN sanctions

Strengths

Serbian machinery exports have found a niche selling their low-priced goods to their poorer neighbors despite sanctions. Even after adding the cost of sanctions-bending bribes, Serbian machines are still price-competitive.

Weaknesses

Virtual economic collapse following imposition of sanctions; effect on fuel-supply particularly hard-hitting. Severe disruption of food-distribution networks, leading to shortages, a barter economy and widespread hunger.

Profile

Following the transition to a multiparty system, a short-lived reformist government began to implement privatization, fiscal reform and a reorganization of the banking sector. The war in Bosnia has since devastated these initiatives. Sanctions, which have cut off imports and exports, have decimated the emerging private sector as well as the state sector. The hyperinflation of 1992–1993 – inflation reached an hourly rate of 0.7% in December 1993 – pushed the economy to the verge of complete collapse.

ECONOMIC PERFORMANCE INDICATOR

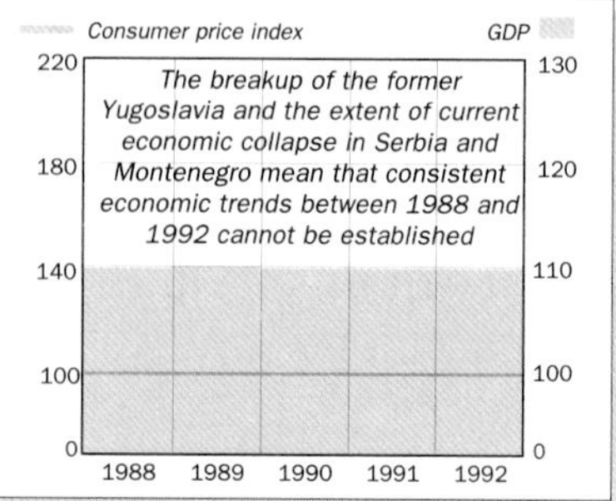

Savings were rendered worthless and any incentive to invest in the economy was destroyed. Output levels in 1993 fell to a third of 1990 levels and Deutsch Marks assumed the position of almost legal tender. The 1994 stabilization plan is based on the creation of a "super dinar" pegged to the Deutsch Mark. However, it will be difficult to implement without IMF backing or a cut in spending.

YUGOSLAVIA : MAJOR BUSINESSES

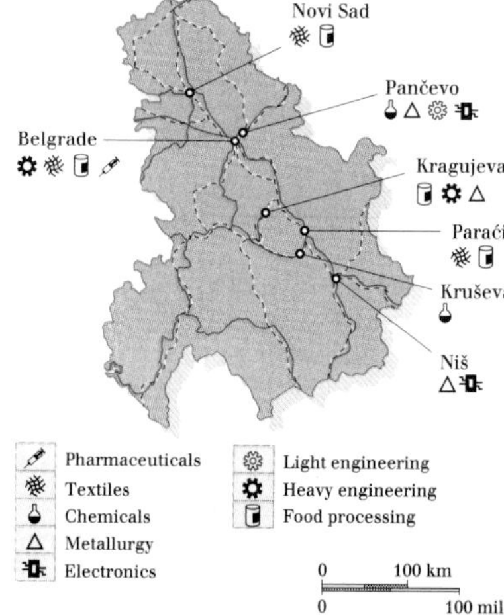

Y

RESOURCES

42m kwh (capacity 8.85m kw)

Not an oil producer

Cattle, sheep, goats

Coal, bauxite, iron, lead, copper, zinc

ELECTRICITY GENERATION

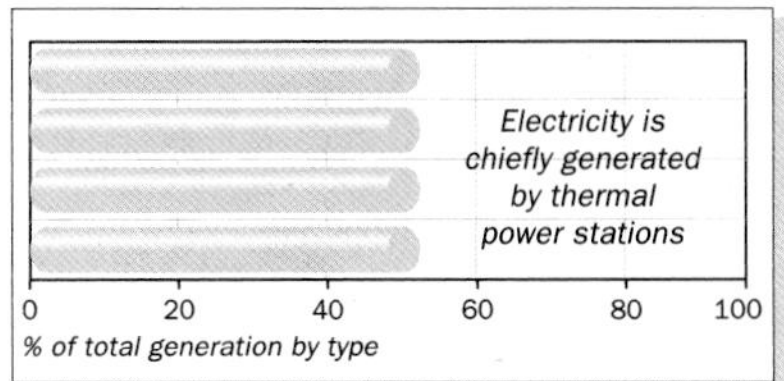

The FRY has attained self-sufficiency in coal and electricity production. The latter comes mainly from hydroelectric or coal-fired plants. Vojvodina caters for one-third of oil needs.

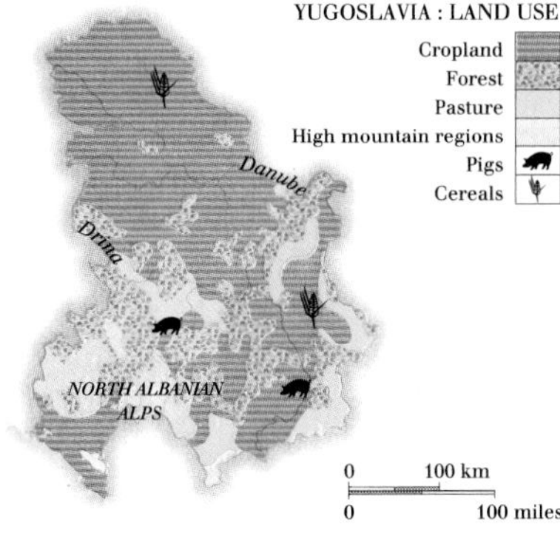

ENVIRONMENT

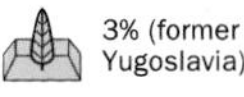

3% (former Yugoslavia)

Environmental issues currently receive low priority

ENVIRONMENTAL TREATIES

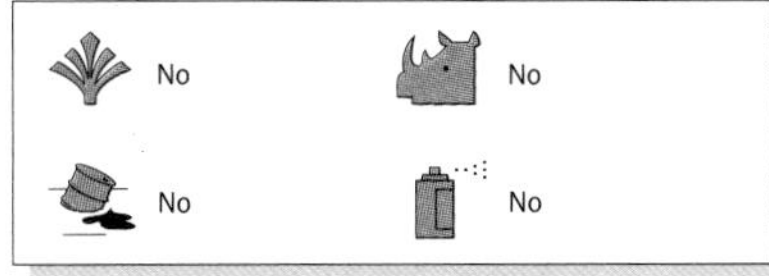

In Serbia, ecological awareness peaked in the late 1980s. The Ecological Forum sought to pursue the cross-border implications of pollution. Organized resistance in Montenegro to the Tara River dam project partially succeeded, in that the dam was moved upstream from a scenic canyon. The biosphere reserve at Durmitor National Park preserves unique wetlands.

MEDIA

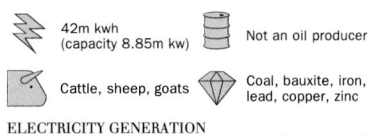

Independent TV and radio stations have been targets of harassment and police raids

PUBLISHING AND BROADCAST MEDIA

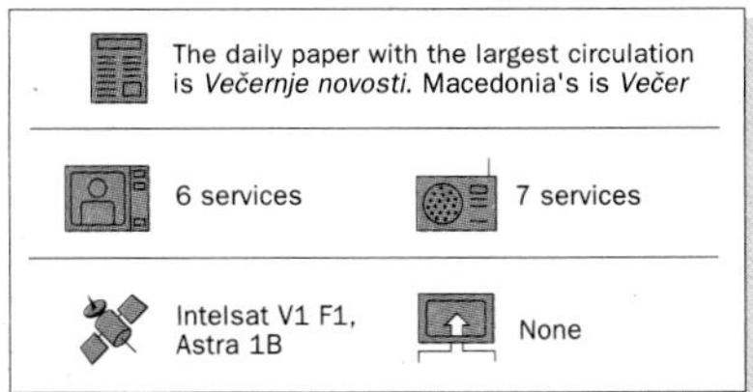

The daily paper with the largest circulation is *Večernje novosti*. Macedonia's is *Večer*
6 services
7 services
Intelsat V1 F1, Astra 1B
None

Public opinion continues to be shaped by the state-regulated broadcast media, on which most of the population is dependent for news coverage. There is also an independent press which provides news and commentary. Notable publications include *Vreme* and *Borba* in Serbia, and *Monitor* in Montenegro. *Tanjug*, the official news agency, was purged in 1991 to eliminate criticism of the regime. Independent TV and radio stations are only receivable in the Belgrade area.

CRIME

Serbia does not publish prison figures

No change in current high crime levels

CRIME RATES

Civil disorder and the proliferation of weapons has led to a sharp rise in all categories of crime, including extortion

Economic crime, from currency trading to black-market goods, has boomed. An estimated 40% of all economic activity takes place in the illegal market. Formerly on the main east–west smuggling route, Montenegro's drugs trade has been disrupted by sanctions. Fears are that Serbian militia will turn to mafia-type extortion operations.

EDUCATION

89%

0 *Education spending as % GNP* 25

Yugoslavia does not publish education spending figures

THE EDUCATION SYSTEM

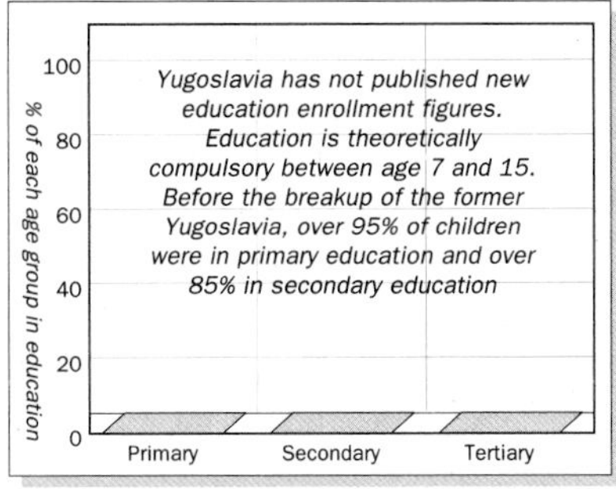

The education system is in crisis. Since the outbreak of war, some wealthy families have used hard currency earnings to send their children abroad to complete their secondary education. Literacy rates in Kosovo are below average for the FRY, at 82%. There are six universities and 37 colleges.

HEALTH

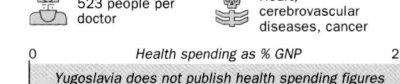

523 people per doctor

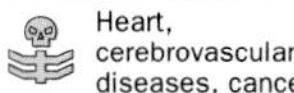

Heart, cerebrovascular diseases, cancer

0 *Health spending as % GNP* 25

Yugoslavia does not publish health spending figures

Isolation from former trading partners has affected the quality of the health service, despite the exemption of medicines and medical supplies from sanctions. Most medicines are unaffordable to the general population, and mortality rates among infants and the elderly have risen dramatically.

WEALTH

Average wage, $12 per month

CONSUMER GOODS OWNERSHIP

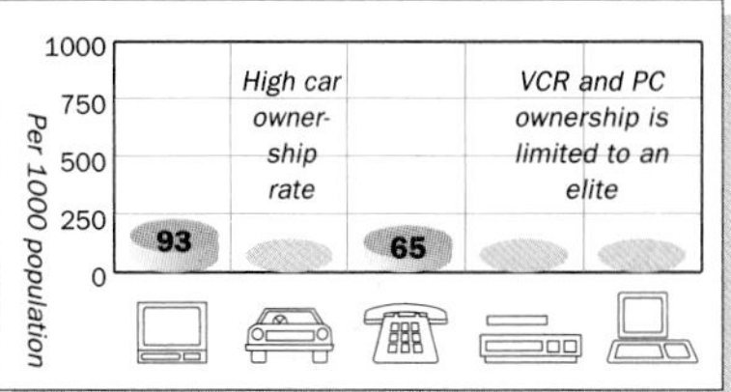

The country as a whole has been impoverished as a result of sanctions, but those who have managed to hang on to hard currency savings are at an advantage. Since the imposition of sanctions, real incomes have fallen to a tenth of what they were in 1990. Yet, food prices in Belgrade are higher than in much of Western Europe. Many people were financially destroyed by the loss of their dinar savings in the bank collapses of 1992. Those who are presently amassing wealth are largely doing so by exploiting the chaos of war through the black market. One of the few areas of business expansion in recent years has been in exploiting markets for goods which were previously imported. The few rich buy sanctions-busting goods illegally imported from Western Europe.

WORLD RANKING

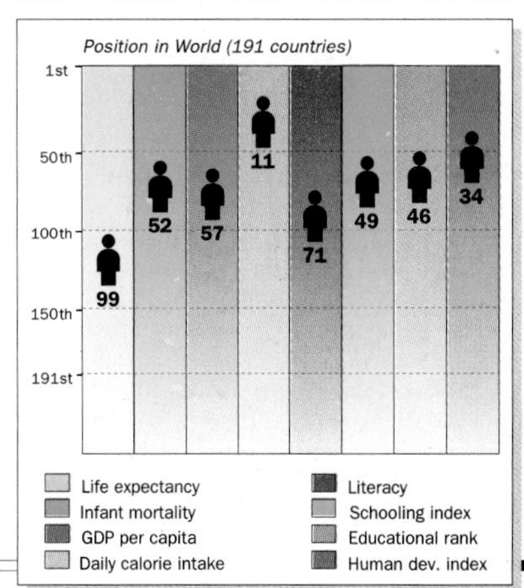

Y

ZAIRE

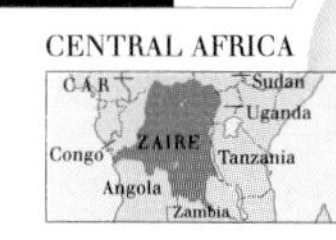

OFFICIAL NAME: Republic of Zaire **CAPITAL:** Kinshasa
POPULATION: 39.9 million **CURRENCY:** New zaire **OFFICIAL LANGUAGE:** French

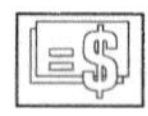

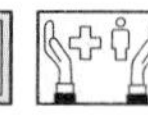
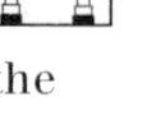

LYING IN EAST-CENTRAL Africa, Zaire is one of the continent's largest countries. The rainforested basin of the Congo River occupies 60% of the country; its estuary provides Zaire's only sea access. The former Belgian Congo became independent in 1960 and was immediately plunged into civil war. President Mobutu took power in 1965, renamed the country Zaire and instituted an increasingly corrupt and unpopular regime. His reluctance to see through the transition to multiparty democracy, begun in 1990, has left Zaire with two governments and a disintegrating economy.

The Zaire River is navigable for 994 miles and provides one of the most convenient ways of traveling in the country.

CLIMATE

WEATHER CHART

Average daily temperature — Rainfall
°C/°F — cm/in
J F M A M J J A S O N D
40/104, 30/86, 20/68, 10/50, 0/32, -10/14, -20/-4
40/16, 30/12, 20/8, 10/4, 0

Zaire's climate is tropical and humid. Temperatures average 77°F and vary little through the year. Annual rainfall is around 60–80 inches; mountainous areas are wetter. The equator passes through the north of the country, causing marked regional variations. To its south, well-differentiated wet and dry seasons last from October to May and June to September respectively. North of the equator, a short dry season lasts from December to February; the rest of the year is wet.

COMMUNICATIONS

N'Djili, Kinshasa
525,000 passengers

2 ships
15,900 dwt

THE TRANSPORTATION NETWORK

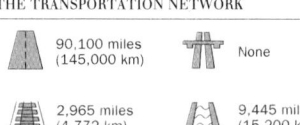

90,100 miles (145,000 km)

None

2,965 miles (4,772 km)

9,445 miles (15,200 km)

The Congo (known locally as the Zaire) and its many tributaries provide the main means of communication. Zaire's size and the fact that most of it is covered by dense rainforest have severely limited the development of road and rail networks. Many forest settlements are inaccessible except by air. Road maintenance, always poor, has virtually ceased outside the main towns since 1990, isolating even more settlements away from the main rivers.

TOURISM

51,422 visitors

Up 30% in 1989

MAIN OVERSEAS ARRIVALS

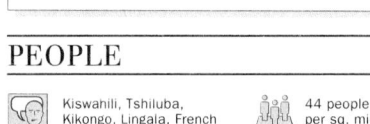

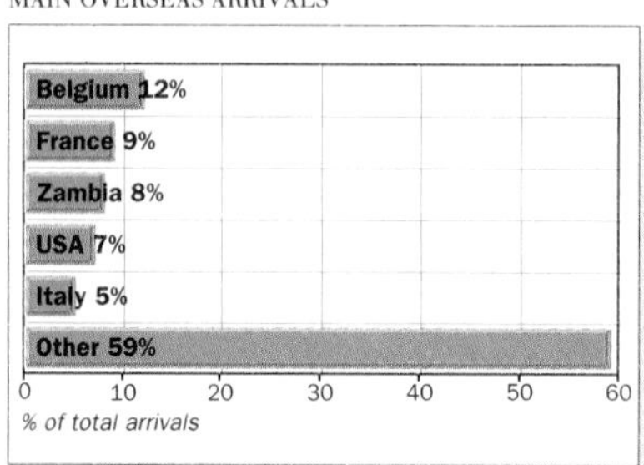

Zaire's attractions lie in its scenery, wildlife and the vibrant music of Kinshasa's many bands. Paramount is the Congo, 10 miles wide in places and Africa's longest river after the Nile. President Mobutu's regime, however, has not encouraged tourism. Official restrictions on foreigners traveling around the country, combined with negligible tourism facilities outside the towns, have kept all but a few independent travelers away. Most of these have avoided Zaire since 1990 and the once-large number of business visitors has also collapsed.

PEOPLE

Kiswahili, Tshiluba, Kikongo, Lingala, French

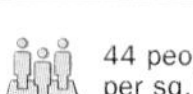

44 people per sq. mile

THE URBAN/RURAL POPULATION SPLIT

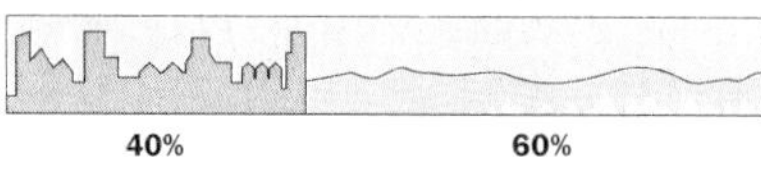

RELIGIOUS PERSUASION

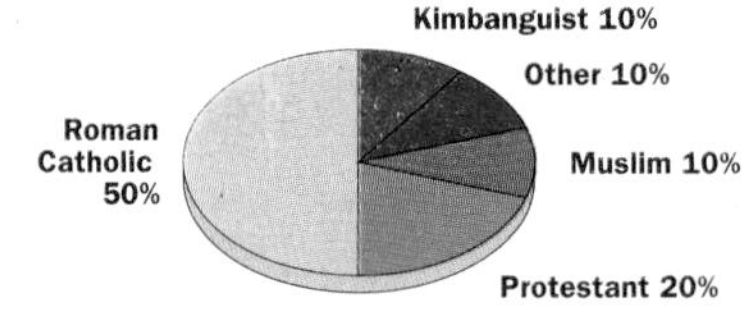

ETHNIC MAKEUP

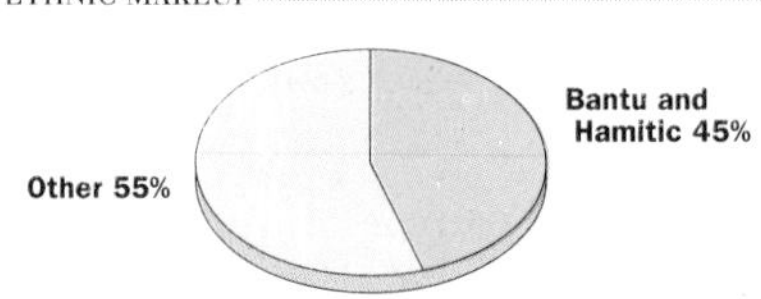

Zaire is ethnically diverse, with more than 12 main groups and around 190 smaller ones. The largest group is of Bantu origin, but there are also large Hamitic and Nilotic populations, mainly in the north and northeast. Zaire's original inhabitants, the forest Pygmies, today form a tiny and marginalized group. The population is very unevenly distributed. The Shaba mining area and major urban centers are densely populated, while the rainforests have a density of less than 8 people per sq. mile. Those in remoter areas have always lived on the margins of the cash economy. Since 1990, however, hyperinflation has forced the majority into a subsistence lifestyle.

President Mobutu managed to contain ethnic tensions inherited from the colonial period during most of his rule. Since 1990, however, there have been outbreaks of ethnic violence and "cleansing," notably in Shaba Kivu and Kasai provinces. Over 6,000 people were reported to have been killed in clashes during 1993. Belgium has accused Mobutu of encouraging ethnic strife to delay democratic change.

POPULATION AGE BREAKDOWN

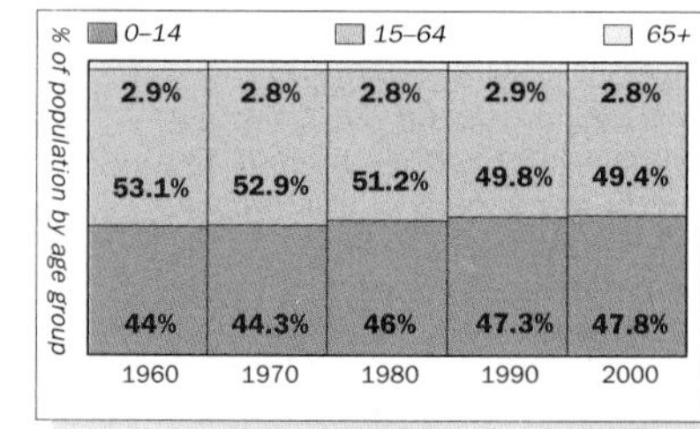

ZAIRE

Total Area : 2 345 410 sq. km (905 563 sq. miles)

POPULATION

- over 1 000 000
- over 500 000
- over 100 000
- over 50 000
- over 10 000
- under 10 000

LAND HEIGHT

- 2000m/6562ft
- 1000m/3281ft
- 500m/1640ft
- 200m/656ft
- Sea Level

0 400 km

0 400 miles

POLITICS

Uncertain

President Marshal Mobutu Sese Seko

THE STATE OF THE PARTIES

National Legislative Council 210 members

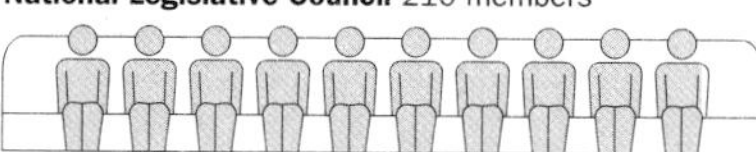

Zaire has two opposing governments. President Mobutu's administration is now opposed by a 435–member transitional legislature known as the High Council of the Republic (HCR). The HCR has appointed Etienne Tshisekedi as prime minister in opposition to the president and his government

President Mobutu Sese Seko has ruled Zaire since 1965.

MAIN POLITICAL ISSUE

Ending the political crisis

The fundamental problem facing Zaire is how to force President Mobutu to fulfill his 1990 promise of instituting a multiparty democracy. All his actions since have made clear his intention to hang on to power at all costs. He has refused to surrender control of the treasury and security forces, or accept the High Council and its government, and has set up a puppet alternative. This has combined to create a political vacuum in which violence flourishes while the economy falls apart.

PROFILE

From 1965 to 1989, President Mobutu's absolute rule combined repression with astute political manipulation. In 1990, growing internal opposition and foreign pressure led him to announce moves to multiparty democracy. A National Executive Council, dominated by the Sacred Union coalition of opposition parties, was set up to negotiate a new constitution. In December 1992, it transformed itself into the High Council, a 435-member interim parliament which backed Etienne Tshisekedi as head of a transitional government. Rejecting this attack on his power, Mobutu set up his own government in 1993, headed by Faustin Birindwa. Tshisekedi has popular and international support; Mobutu controls the treasury and army.

Etienne Tshisekedi, *the High Council's choice as premier.*

President Mobutu, *who is under pressure to resign.*

WORLD AFFAIRS

For almost 25 years, President Mobutu's anticommunism made Zaire one of the leading African allies of the West, and of the USA in particular. Western economic and military aid – which included sending troops to help suppress the 1977 and 1978 invasions by exiles based in Angola – played a critical role in sustaining his regime. In return, he guaranteed Western access to Zaire's mineral wealth and provided Angola's US-backed UNITA rebels with bases during the 1980s.

At the same time, however, Mobutu's political astuteness enabled him to maintain close ties with several communist states, notably China. Relations with African neighbors were more problematic, complicated by Mobutu's support for UNITA and for Morocco's annexation of Western Sahara. From 1984 to 1986, Zaire withdrew from the OAU in protest over its support of Western Saharan independence.

Since the late 1980s, the changing political situation in eastern Europe, combined with growing concerns about human rights abuses and corruption in Zaire, has led to a fundamental shift in attitudes to Mobutu. Most countries have stopped all but humanitarian aid since 1990. Belgium, France, the USA and EU, formerly Mobutu's closest allies, now view him as an embarrassment. Backing the High Council and its nominated government, led by Etienne Tshisekedi, they are involved in efforts to resolve the country's political crisis and persuade Mobutu to step down.

AID

 $823m (receipts)

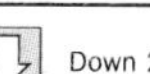 Down 23% in 1990

Zaire's importance to the West during the Cold War brought it aid revenues on a large scale. Between 1970 and 1989, it received $8.3 billion in economic aid – including $1.1 billion from the USA and $6.9 billion from other OECD states – as well as large-scale military assistance. Changing political priorities led the USA to act on long-deferred problems of human rights abuses and misappropriation of aid by President Mobutu. In 1990, it suspended all but humanitarian aid; most other donors quickly followed suit. In 1992, the IMF declared Zaire "non cooperative," ending any chances of rescheduling its $10 billion foreign debt. Aid will not be resumed until Mobutu goes and a new, democratic government is installed.

CHRONOLOGY

Modern Zaire was the site of the Kongo and other powerful African kingdoms and a focus of the slave trade. Belgium's King Leopold II claimed most of the Congo basin after 1876.

- **1885** Congo Free State (CFS) founded as King Leopold's private fief; start of brutal colonization.
- **1908** Belgium takes over CFS after international outcry. Renamed Belgian Congo.
- **1960** Independence of Republic of Congo. Katanga (Shaba) province secedes. The UN intervenes.
- **1963** Katanga secession collapses.
- **1964** Belgian troops help crush new revolts in center and east.
- **1965** General Joseph-Désiré Mobutu seizes power.
- **1970** Mobutu elected President; makes his Popular Revolutionary Movement (MPR) sole legal party.
- **1971** Country renamed Zaire.
- **1972** Africanization of names. Becomes Mobutu Sese Seko.
- **1977–1978** Two invasions by former Katanga separatists repulsed with Western help.
- **1982** Opposition parties set up Union for Democracy and Social Progress (UDPS).
- **1986–1990** Mobutu implements numerous cabinet reshuffles in face of growing popular unrest and foreign criticism of widespread human rights abuses.
- **1990** Belgium suspends aid after security forces kill democracy demonstrators. April: Mobutu announces transition to multiparty rule. UDPS legalized.
- **1991** Strikes, mass rallies continue. July: 130 opposition parties form Sacred Union coalition. August: National Conference (NC) convened. September: Belgian and French troops evacuate foreigners during rioting. UDPS leader Etienne Tshisekedi heads short-lived "crisis government" formed by Mobutu.
- **1992** January: NC suspended. April: NC reconvenes and assumes sovereign powers. August: Tshisekedi made Prime Minister by NC. December: Mobutu fires Tshisekedi who refuses to go; NC dissolves itself; elects 435-member High Council of the Republic (HCR).
- **1993** February: HCR endorses Tshisekedi. March: Mobutu appoints Faustin Birindwa as head of alternative government. October: compromise agreement on transitional constitution and government collapses when Mobutu faction refuses to accept Tshisekedi as interim premier.

DEFENSE

$66.82m | Up 44% in 1988

Defense spending as % GDP (0–40): 1%

Zaire's military has played a key role in keeping President Mobutu in power and has been responsible for widespread human rights abuses. The Israeli-trained presidential guard is the elite force. Ordinary troops, poorly equipped and poorly paid, have taken to rioting, looting and extortion.

ZAIREAN ARMED FORCES

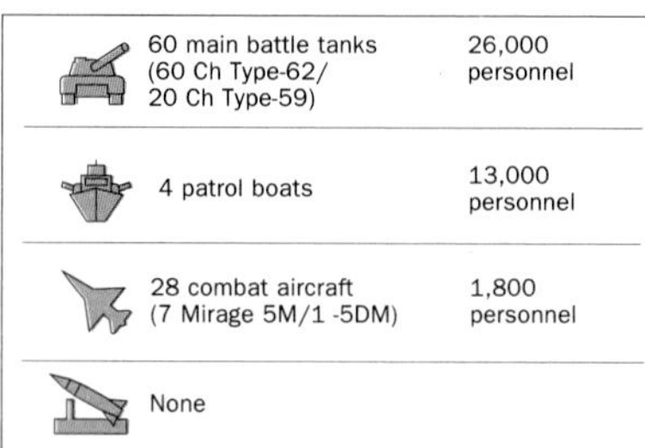

60 main battle tanks (60 Ch Type-62/ 20 Ch Type-59)
26,000 personnel
4 patrol boats
13,000 personnel
28 combat aircraft (7 Mirage 5M/1 -5DM)
1,800 personnel
None

ECONOMICS

$8.1bn | 249.00 new zaires

SCORE CARD

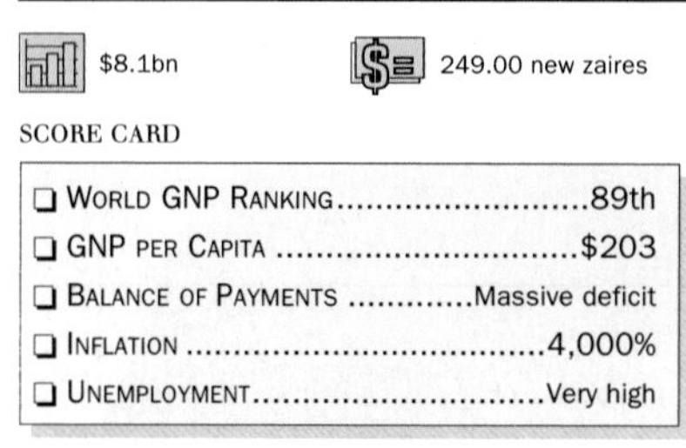

World GNP Ranking	89th
GNP per Capita	$203
Balance of Payments	Massive deficit
Inflation	4,000%
Unemployment	Very high

EXPORTS

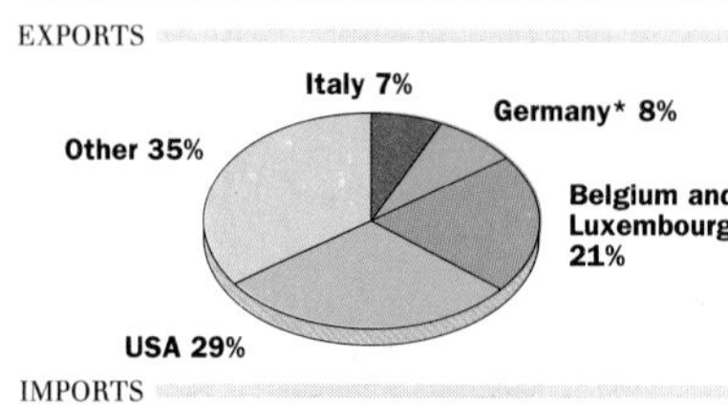

IMPORTS

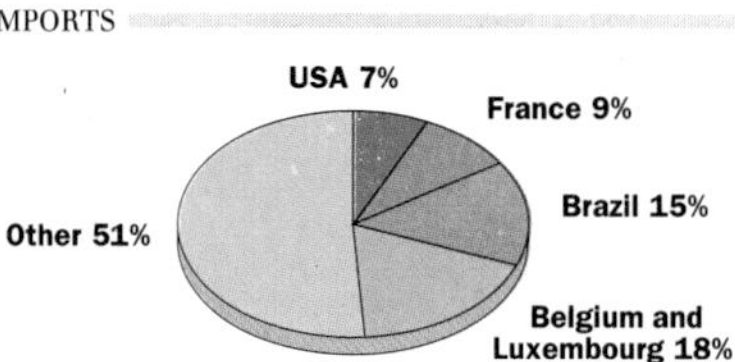

Strengths

Rich resource base. Minerals – notably copper, cobalt, diamonds – provide 85% of export earnings. Energy: oil; possibly Africa's largest hydro-power potential. Rich soil; much unutilized arable land. Trade surplus in normal years.

Weaknesses

Legacy of 25 years of mismanagement and corruption: $10 billion foreign debt; withdrawal of crucial foreign aid; inadequate, disintegrating social and transport infrastructures; lack of food self-sufficiency. Political instability. Hyperinflation. Loss of export income. Withdrawal of foreign investment.

Profile

In the early 1990s, political instability, combined with the legacies of 25 years of mismanagement, had brought the economy near to collapse. Real GDP growth in 1990–1993 averaged –8% a year; in 1993 it topped –12%. The budget deficit is at record levels, in part due to hyperinflation, which was not

ECONOMIC PERFORMANCE INDICATOR

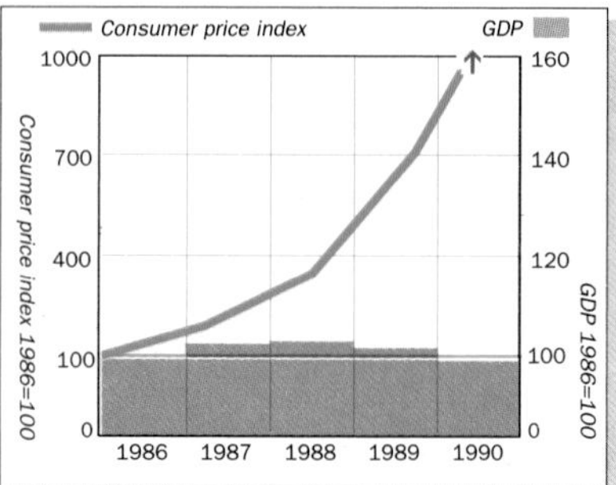

ended by the introduction of the new zaire – worth 3 million old zaires – in late 1993. Lack of spares and power cuts have closed many mines and halted most other industry. Strikes and riots over plummeting living standards have hastened the flight of foreign capital. Subsistence farming and petty trade keep most people going. But even if political stability is restored, Zaire's immediate outlook is grim. Resumption of large-scale aid and debt relief, essential to rebuild the economy, will depend on difficult reforms and paying off arrears to the IMF and other creditors. In the long term, Zaire's rich resources hold out hope of prosperity.

ZAIRE : MAJOR BUSINESSES

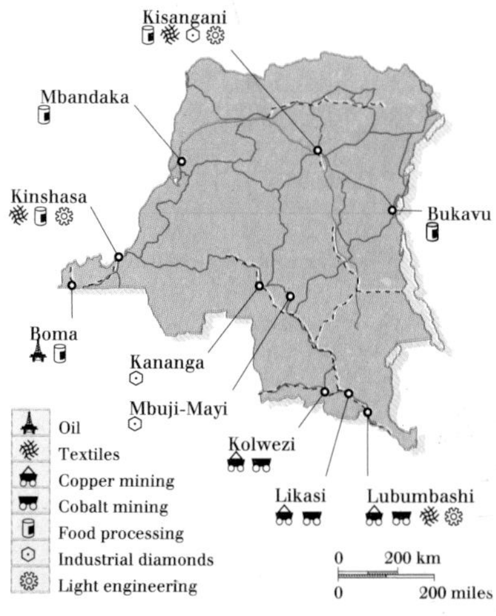

RESOURCES

6.2bn kwh (capacity 2.83m kw)

26,200 b/d (reserves 187bn bbl)

3m goats, 1.5m cattle, 890,000 sheep

Copper, diamonds, oil cobalt, zinc, uranium, manganese, tin, gold

ELECTRICITY GENERATION

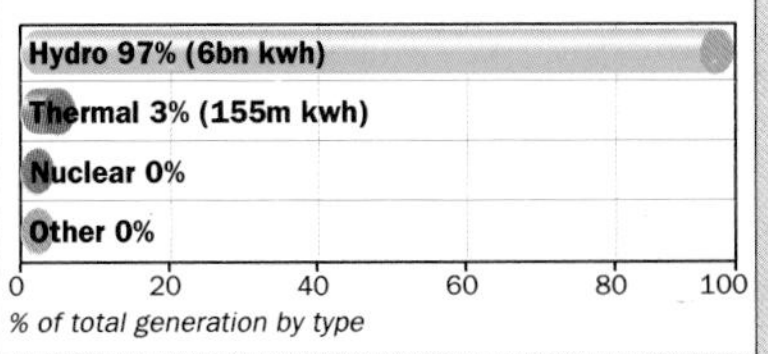

With its huge mineral, agricultural and energy resources Zaire should be rich. Instead, mismanagement and, since 1990, political instability have reduced it to one of the world's poorest states. Copper, cobalt and diamonds provide almost 80% of export earnings. In the 1980s, Zaire was the world's largest cobalt exporter and second-largest industrial diamond exporter. Since 1990, copper and cobalt output has collapsed and diamond smuggling is booming. Zaire has oil reserves, but its energy wealth lies in its HEP potential, which could supply much of Africa if fully exploited. Lack of maintenance has, instead, shut down many turbines and most urban areas face power cuts. Despite rich soils and the fact that 80% of people are involved in farming, Zaire is not self-sufficient in food.

ZAIRE : LAND USE

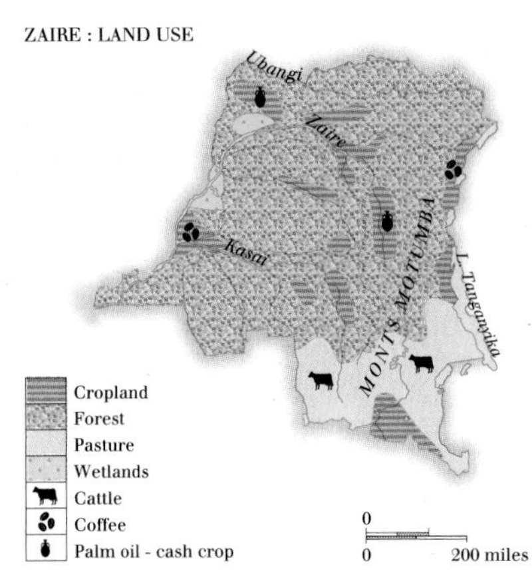

ENVIRONMENT

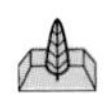

4%

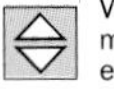
Vast size of country means many ecosystems are intact

ENVIRONMENTAL TREATIES

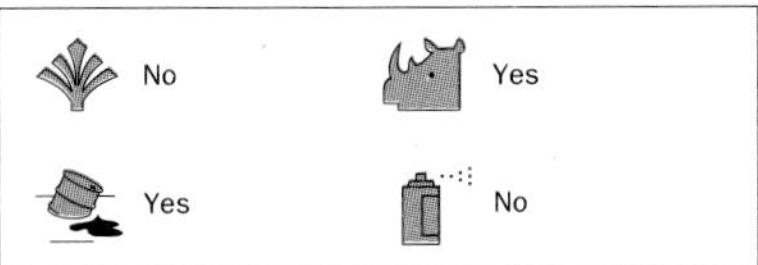

The predominantly virgin rainforests covering over 60% of Zaire comprise almost 6% of the world's and 50% of Africa's remaining woodlands. They are home to important populations of several endangered species, including gorillas. Zaire's poor transportation network has so far prevented large-scale commercial exploitation, but fire wood clearance is a problem. The collapse since 1990 of many urban refuse and sewage disposal systems has led to major health and pollution problems.

MEDIA

Press censorship has relaxed since 1990, but journalists critical of the regime still face harassment, including arrest

PUBLISHING AND BROADCAST MEDIA

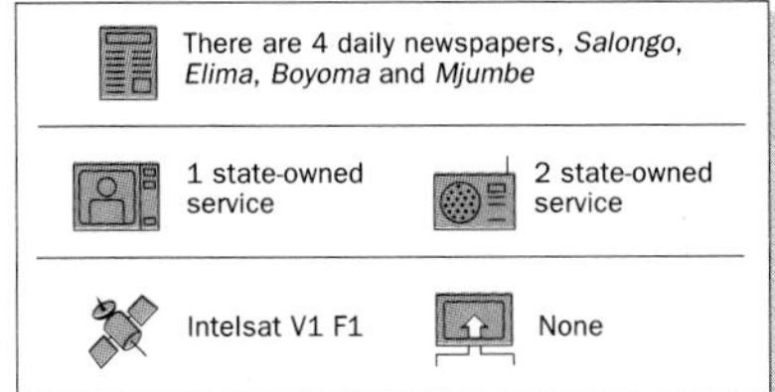

There are 4 daily newspapers, Salongo, Elima, Boyoma and Mjumbe
1 state-owned service
2 state-owned service
Intelsat V1 F1
None

In contrast to the broadcast media, the press is privately owned. Coverage of the opposition has widened since 1990, but press criticism of President Mobutu or the security forces is still generally muted. One newspaper's Kinshasa offices were burned down in 1993 after it published a strongly anti-Mobutu article. Overtly critical journalists face arrest or other reprisals.

CRIME

Zaire does not publish prison figures

Violence and crime have risen rapidly since 1990

CRIME RATES

All types of crime are on the increase

Political crisis and economic collapse have exacerbated Zaire's long-standing problems of corruption and human rights abuses. Violence and crime of all kinds, including extortion, robbery, rape and murder, are on the increase. Many murders are attributed to the security forces and politically linked death squads, as are the occasional "disappearances." Ethnic violence, suppressed after 1965, has resurfaced, particularly in the south.

EDUCATION

60%

0 *Education spending as % GNP* 25

0.9%

THE EDUCATION SYSTEM

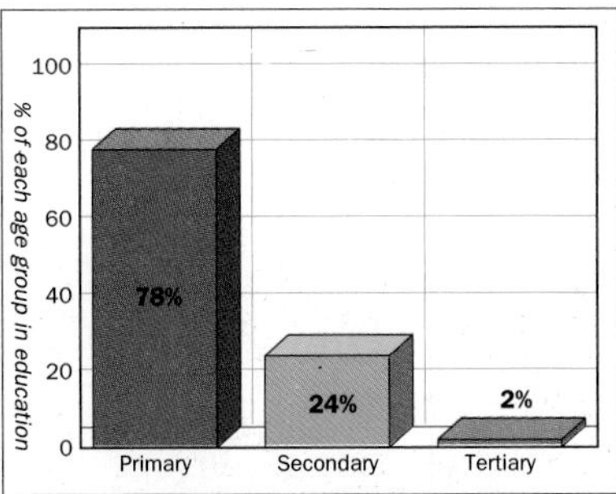

State educational provision, like health care, is patchily distributed and has faced sharp budget cuts since 1980. As a result, about 70% of schooling is now provided by the Catholic Church.

HEALTH

1 per 13,540 people

Malaria, respiratory and diarrheal diseases

0 *Health spending as % GNP* 25

0.8%

State services, long underfunded, have virtually collapsed. Disease and death rates are rising, especially in rural areas. HIV/AIDS is a significant problem.

WEALTH

A large majority of the population lives a subsistence existence

CONSUMER GOODS OWNERSHIP

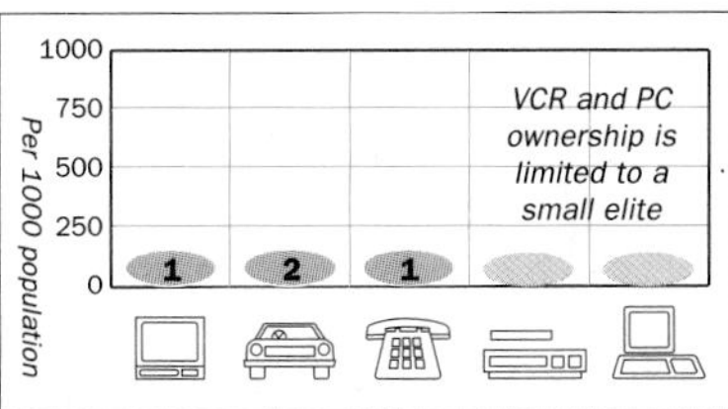

President Mobutu is one of the world's richest men, worth an admitted $50 million and an estimated $5 billion. Most Zaireans live in poverty.

WORLD RANKING

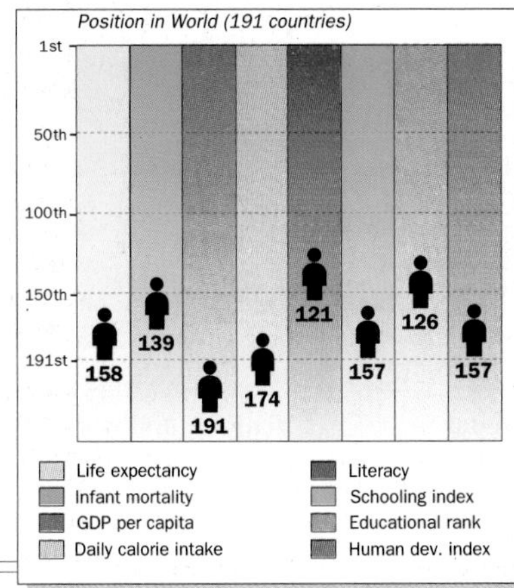

Z

ZAMBIA

SOUTHERN AFRICA
Zaire Tanzania Angola ZAMBIA Malawi Mozambique Zimbabwe Africa

OFFICIAL NAME: Republic of Zambia **CAPITAL:** Lusaka
POPULATION: 8.6 million **CURRENCY:** Zambian kwacha **OFFICIAL LANGUAGES:** English, Bemba and Nyanja

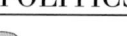

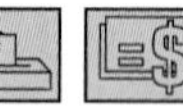

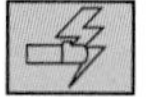

LYING IN THE HEART of southern Africa, Zambia is a country of upland plateaus, bordered to the south by the Zambezi River. Its economic fortunes are tied to the copper industry. Falling copper prices in the late 1970s, and then the growing inaccessibility of remaining reserves, have led to a severe decline in the economy. In 1991, Zambia achieved a peaceful transition from single-party rule to multiparty democracy.

CLIMATE

WEATHER CHART

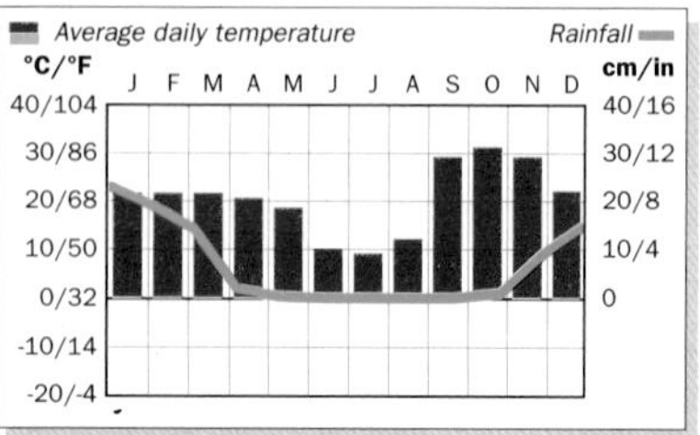

Zambia has a tropical climate, with rains from November to April. The southwest is prone to drought.

COMMUNICATIONS

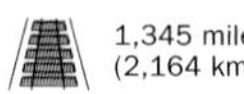 **Lusaka International** 590,000 passengers
 Has no fleet

THE TRANSPORTATION NETWORK

23,215 miles (37,360 km)	None
1,345 miles (2,164 km)	1,398 miles (2,250 km)

The priorities are privatizing Zambia Airways and rehabilitating the rail and road networks. The poor state of rural roads hampers harvest collections and undermines food self-sufficiency plans.

TOURISM

 171,507 visitors  Up 22% in 1991

MAIN OVERSEAS ARRIVALS

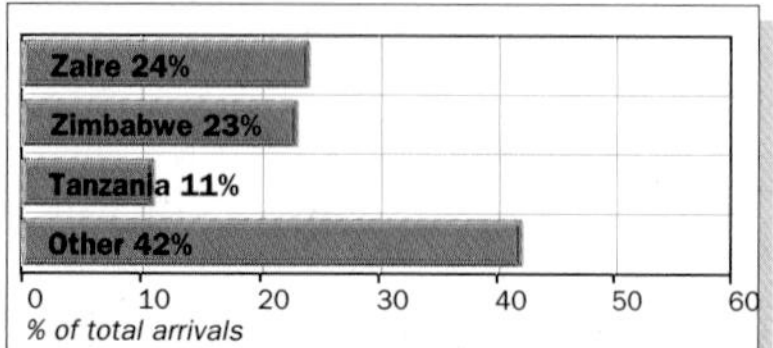

Wildlife, the Victoria Falls and white-water rafting on the Zambezi are Zambia's main attractions. Expansion plans are being hit by funding shortages.

PEOPLE

 Bemba, Nyanja, Tonga, Kaonde, Lunda, Luvale, Lozi, English

 28 people per sq. mile

THE URBAN/RURAL POPULATION SPLIT

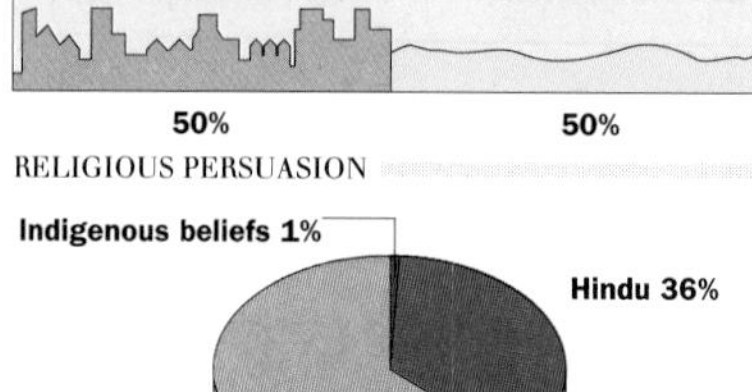

Although ethnically heterogeneous, with more than 70 different groups, Zambia has been less affected by ethnic tension than many African states. The largest ethnic group, about 18% of the population, is the Bemba, who live in the northeast and predominate in the central Copperbelt. Other major groups are the southern Tonga people, the eastern Nyanja, and the Lozi who live to the west.

Zambia is one of Africa's most urbanized countries, with many third- and fourth-generation town dwellers in the Copperbelt, the main urban area. Urban life has done little to change the traditionally subordinate role of women in the family and politics. They are, however, increasingly involved in business, and three women hold cabinet posts. The rural population lives mainly by subsistence farming.

Victoria Falls, *known to Africans as* Musi-o-Tunyi (*The Smoke That Thunders*). *Spray from the falls can be seen 19 mi. away.*

POLITICS

 Lower House 1996 — President Frederick Chiluba

THE STATE OF THE PARTIES

National Assembly 150 members

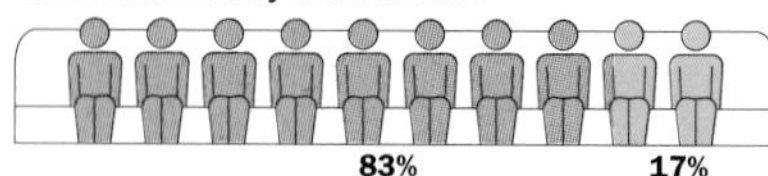

MMD = Movement for Multiparty Democracy
UNIP = United National Independence Party

House of Chiefs 27 members

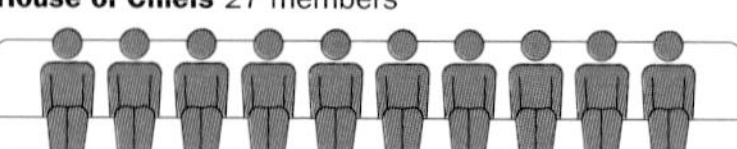

Composed of 27 chiefs representing 8 provinces

The 1991 defeat of Dr. Kenneth Kaunda and the UNIP in the first multiparty elections for 19 years expressed popular discontent with the state of the economy and official corruption. President Chiluba and the MMD government have since made little headway in revitalizing the economy, despite socially painful reforms. There have also been renewed allegations of top-level corruption. In 1993, UNIP and MMD dissidents set up the National Party to challenge the dominant political position of the MMD.

WORLD AFFAIRS

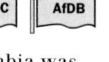

Under President Kaunda, Zambia was one of Africa's leading opponents of the South African apartheid regime. The MMD is now seeking close links with reformed South Africa.

AID

 $884m (receipts)  Up 82% in 1991

Aid levels, mainly from the EU and the World Bank, are high. Most is used to support the restructuring of the economy away from the declining mining sector. Donors are concerned about levels of bureaucratic corruption and the need to strengthen democracy.

DEFENSE

 $213.4m  Up 15% in 1990

A large budget means the 24,000-strong armed forces are well-equipped. Security on the border with Angola is the main defense concern.

ECONOMICS

$1.8bn

652.69 Zambian kwacha

SCORE CARD

- ❏ WORLD GNP RANKING........................139th
- ❏ GNP PER CAPITA..............................$210
- ❏ BALANCE OF PAYMENTS........................$1m
- ❏ INFLATION.......................................155%
- ❏ UNEMPLOYMENT ...Widespread underemployment

STRENGTHS

Potential for self-sufficiency in food; also for export of wide range of crops. Arable land underutilized. Minerals, notably copper, cobalt and coal. Commitment of government to market-oriented reform.

WEAKNESSES

Dependence on copper for 80% of export earnings. Domestic reserves rapidly declining. Poor outlook for world copper prices. Shortage of finance for restructuring due to large deficit in balance of payments. Rescheduling payments on $7.6-billion debt take most export earnings. High inflation. Low productivity.

EXPORTS

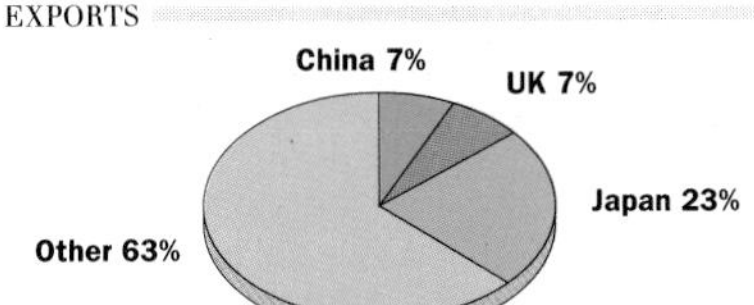

IMPORTS

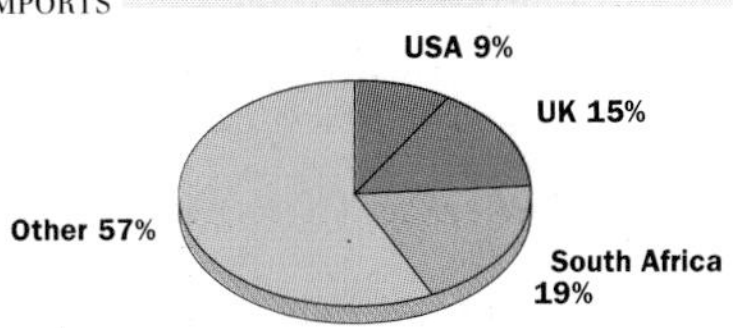

RESOURCES

 7.8bn kwh (capacity 2.44m kw)

 Not an oil producer; refines 23,750 b/cd

 2.8m cattle, 200,000 pigs, 85,000 sheep

 Copper, cobalt, coal, zinc, lead, gold, emeralds, amethyst

Despite declining reserves, copper is still the key resource; Zambia is the world's fifth-largest producer. It also has good hydropower resources.

ENVIRONMENT

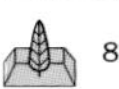 8%

 Official involvement in conservation projects increasing

Drought is a recurrent hazard. Rhinos are almost extinct as a result of poaching. Revenues from legal hunting are being channeled into villages to encourage support for conservation.

MEDIA

 Little press censorship by government

PUBLISHING AND BROADCAST MEDIA

 There are 3 daily newspapers – the *Times of Zambia*, the *Daily Mail* and the *Daily Express*

 1 state-controlled service

 1 state-controlled service

The state-owned *Times* and *Daily Mail* face increasing competition from independents like the *Weekly Standard*.

CRIME

 Zambia does not publish prison figures

 Rising rapidly since 1990

Cases of violent crime, burglary and rape are rising rapidly, particularly in major towns such as Lusaka and Ndola.

ZAMBIA

Total Area : 752 610 sq. km (290 563 sq. miles)

POPULATION

- ⦿ over 500 000
- ◎ over 100 000
- ○ over 50 000
- ● over 10 000
- • under 10 000

LAND HEIGHT

- 1000m/3281ft
- 500m/1640ft
- 200m/656ft

0 200 km

0 200 miles

CHRONOLOGY

Former Northern Rhodesia was developed by Britain solely for its copper resources. Dr. Kenneth Kaunda and the UNIP took power at Zambian independence in 1964.

- ❏ **1972** UNIP one-party government.
- ❏ **1980** Attempted coup fails.
- ❏ **1982-1991** Austerity measures introduced. Corruption scandals. Pressure for democracy grows.
- ❏ **1991** Democratically elected MMD government comes to power.

EDUCATION

 73%

Primary education is compulsory. New fees for secondary students will hit the already low attendance rate of 15%.

HEALTH

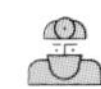 1 per 8,437 people

 Respiratory infections, diarrheal diseases, malaria

Austerity measures have resulted in health service cutbacks and a rise in the use of traditional medicines.

WEALTH

 Copper miner, 3,880 Zambian kwacha per year; computer programmer in insurance, 196,982 Zambian kwacha per year

CONSUMER GOODS OWNERSHIP

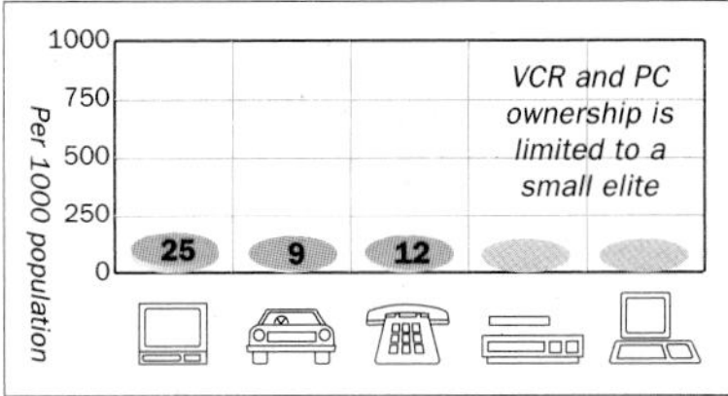

Declining profits from copper mining mean that per capita GDP is $400 lower now than upon independence in 1964.

WORLD RANKING

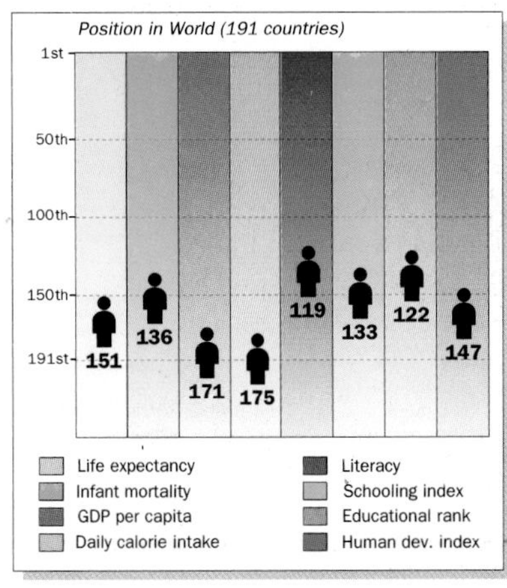

Z

ZIMBABWE

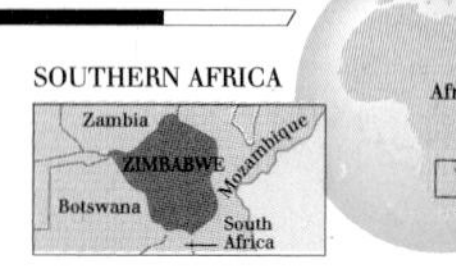

OFFICIAL NAME: Republic of Zimbabwe **CAPITAL:** Harare **POPULATION:** 10.6 million
CURRENCY: Zimbabwe dollar **OFFICIAL LANGUAGE:** English

SITUATED IN SOUTHERN AFRICA, Zimbabwe is bordered by South Africa, Botswana, Zambia and Mozambique. The upland center is crisscrossed by rivers which flow into Lake Kariba and the Zambezi River. The Zambezi possesses Zimbabwe's most spectacular natural feature, the Victoria Falls. Formerly the British colony of Southern Rhodesia, the country achieved independence in 1980 after a struggle between the white minority, led by Prime Minister Ian Smith, and the black majority, represented by Robert Mugabe's and Joshua Nkomo's Patriotic Front (PF).

The Kariba Dam, which has created the vast Lake Kariba on the Zambezi River, lies on Zimbabwe's northwest border with Zambia.

CLIMATE

WEATHER CHART

Average daily temperature / Rainfall
°C/°F: 40/104, 30/86, 20/68, 10/50, 0/32, -10/14, -20/-4
cm/in: 40/16, 30/12, 20/8, 10/4, 0
J F M A M J J A S O N D

Due to its altitude, Zimbabwe is comparatively temperate for a country in the tropics; humidity is also low. The rainy season occurs between November and March. But, with the exception of the eastern highlands, rainfall is erratic and drought is common. Annual rainfall ranges from 55 inches in the Eastern Highlands to 15 inches in the Limpopo Valley.

COMMUNICATIONS

Harare International
1.02m passengers

Has no fleet

THE TRANSPORTATION NETWORK

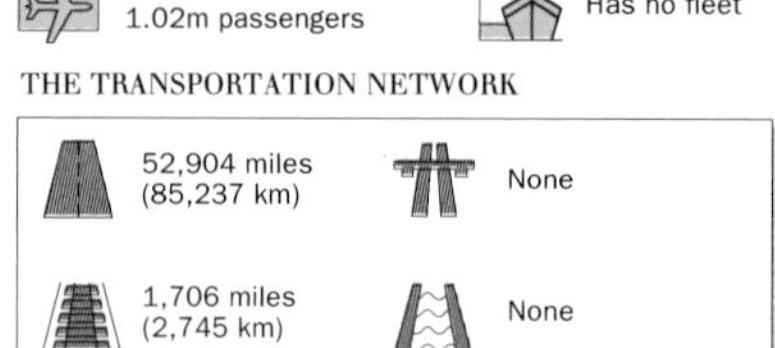

Public transportation is a high priority. Policies include developing and updating railroads, and increasing the number of international air links.

TOURISM

552,686 visitors

Up 27% in 1990

MAIN OVERSEAS ARRIVALS

Country	% of total arrivals
South Africa	39%
Zambia	29%
UK and Ireland	8%
Mozambique	6%
USA and Canada	3%
Other	15%

0 10 20 30 40
% of total arrivals

Tourists visit Zimbabwe for both cultural and safari vacations. Principal attractions are the Victoria Falls, the Kariba Dam and the many national parks. Great Zimbabwe ruins near Masvingo and World's View in the Matopo Hills are of special interest. Adventure trips are being developed, with canoeing and white-water rafting on the Zambezi, and trout fishing and climbing in the eastern highlands. Harare and Victoria Falls have conference facilities. The government does not intend to make Zimbabwe a destination for mass-market tourism, due to fears of environmental damage. However, the lure of foreign exchange has encouraged the development of holiday complexes around Victoria Falls, such as Elephant Hills. Import controls relating to the tourist industry have been deregulated. A two-tier pricing structure now prevails with locals paying less; foreigners must pay in hard currencies.

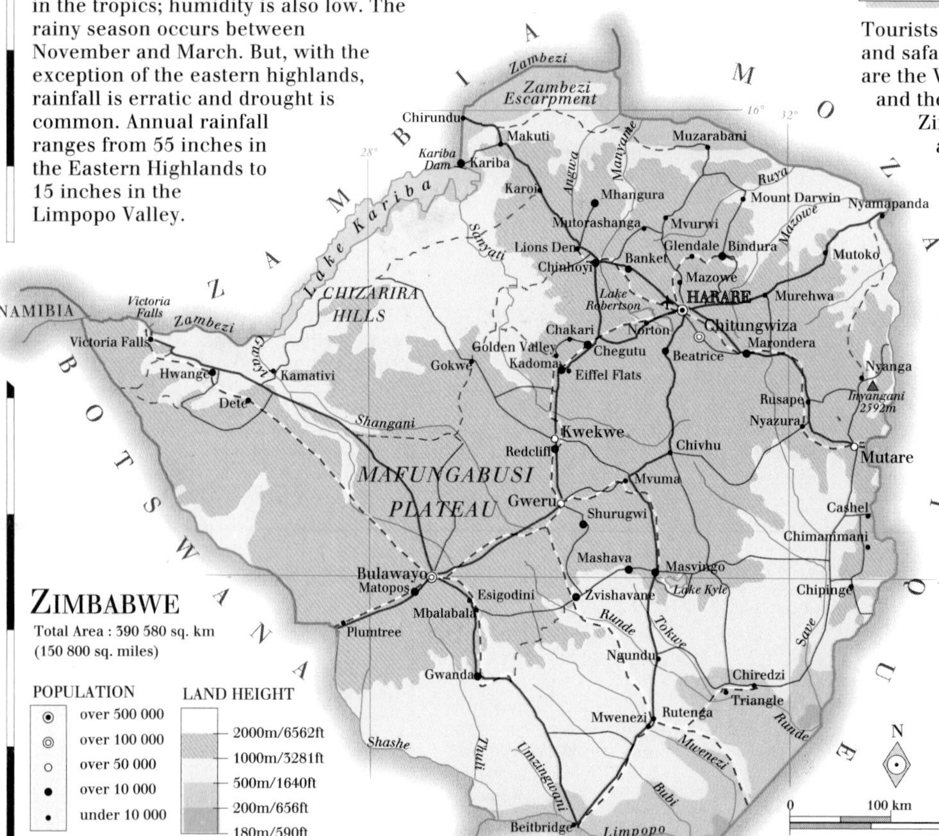

PEOPLE

 Shona, Ndebele, English  65 people per sq. mile

THE URBAN/RURAL POPULATION SPLIT

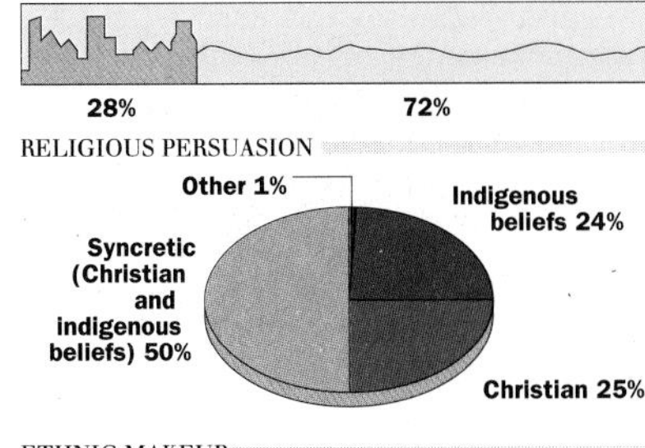

ETHNIC MAKEUP

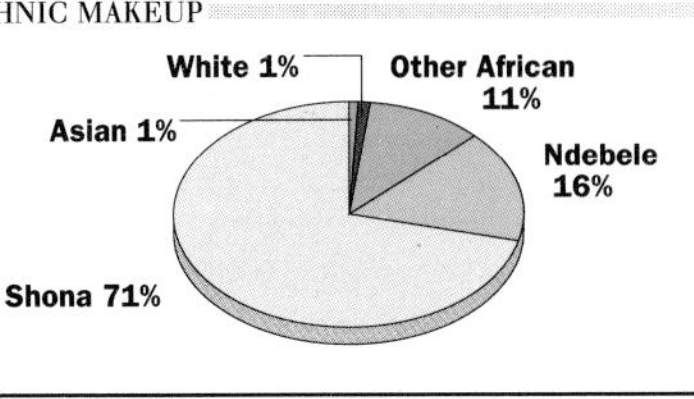

There are two main ethnic groups – the Ndebele (popularly known as the Matabele) in the north and the Shona (known as the Mashona) in the south. The Mashona outnumber the Matabele by about four to one. Europeans and Asians comprise 2% of the population.

Tension between the Matabele and the Mashona was rife in the 1980s. This was caused by the attempt of President Mugabe's ruling Zimbabwe African National Union (ZANU–PF), linked to the Mashona, to suppress the leading opposition party, the Zimbabwe African People's Union (ZAPU–PF), linked with the Matabele. The conflict was most intense in 1983, when the army killed 1,500 Matabele. Tension abated following the Unity Accord of 1987 and the 1990 appointment of ZAPU-PF leader Joshua Nkomo as vice president.

As a legacy of colonial rule, whites are still generally far more affluent than blacks. This imbalance has been somewhat redressed by government policies to increase black education and white-collar employment.

Families are large; almost half of the population is under 15. Zimbabwean society is traditionally patriarchal, but the number of women managers is growing, and individuals such as Sally Mugabe, late wife of the president, have achieved political prominence.

POPULATION AGE BREAKDOWN

% of population by age group

	1960	1970	1980	1990	2000
65+	2.9%	2.7%	2.6%	2.7%	2.8%
15–64	50.6%	48.2%	49.6%	52.6%	53.2%
0–14	46.5%	49.1%	47.8%	44.7%	44%

POLITICS

1995 President Robert Gabriel Mugabe

THE STATE OF THE PARTIES

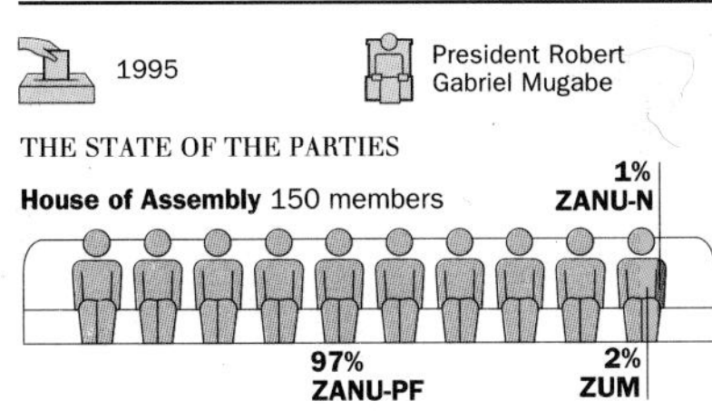

ZANU-PF = Zimbabwe African National Union – Patriotic Front **ZUM** = Zimbabwe Unity Movement **ZANU-N** = Zimbabwe African National Union – Ndonga

Zimbabwe is constitutionally a multiparty state. 80% of MPs are elected and serve five-year terms. Every six years, parliament elects the president, who is eligible for reelection.

MAIN POLITICAL ISSUES

Political repression

At independence, the PF was a coalition of ZANU, led by Robert Mugabe, and ZAPU, led by Joshua Nkomo. As ZANU-PF became more powerful, the coalition split and ZAPU-PF supporters resorted to guerrilla activity. This continued until 1987, when a unity agreement was signed with Nkomo, later made vice president. With the main opposition party absorbed, Mugabe, now president, attempted to assert a one-party, socialist state. These plans were abandoned in 1991 and other parties have since emerged. But repression continues: student dissension has been quashed and the civil service is closed to non-supporters of the ruling party.

Land redistribution

In an attempt to redistribute wealth from the white to the black community, the government introduced the Land Acquisition Act in 1992. This allowed the compulsory purchase of white-owned farmland. The Act provoked a storm of protest, including allegations of corruption, and was suspended.

PROFILE

The ruling ZANU-PF appears to have lost direction following the collapse of the Eastern Bloc and the end of apartheid in South Africa. The influence of its once-dominant leader, Robert Mugabe, is waning, but he has no clear successor.

Opposition parties include the Forum for Democratic Reform, advocating an open, free-market society, and the United Front Party, an uneasy coalition of politicians from the pre-1980 period. These include Edgar Tekere, Reverend Sithole and Ian Smith.

Robert Mugabe, *elected prime minister in 1980 and president in 1987.*

Simon Muzenda, *senior vice president. Joshua Nkomo is joint vice president.*

AID

 $393m (receipts)  Up 16% in 1991

In January 1992, the IMF agreed to the equivalent of $484 million to support an economic and financial reform program. Zimbabwe is also to receive $117 million in grants, over five years, from the EU. Bilateral donors, including the UK, France, Germany, Denmark and the USA, intend their aid to be used to sustain the local economy and to be directed at small farmers. However, the government directs much of it toward large industrial projects. In the 1980s, Zimbabwe sent food to help relieve famine in Ethiopia.

WORLD AFFAIRS

Zimbabwe stresses close cooperation with its neighbors, in the context of SADC and the Preferential Trade Area for East and South Africa, and has consistently followed a policy of non-alignment. President Mugabe was chairman of the Non-Aligned Movement from 1985 to 1989. His regime had an activist stance against South Africa and apartheid. Since the 1990 freeing of Nelson Mandela, relations have improved; however, a consistent policy is still evolving.

For ideological reasons and to maintain access to the sea via the Beira corridor, the government began providing military assistance to the socialist Mozambican government against the RENAMO guerrillas in 1982. President Mugabe then played a major mediating role, resulting in a peace accord in August 1992. In 1993, 150 troops were sent to Somalia to begin training exercises with the USA.

CHRONOLOGY

In 1953, the British colony of Southern Rhodesia (Zimbabwe) became part of the Federation of Rhodesia and Nyasaland with Northern Rhodesia (Zambia) and Nyasaland (Malawi).

- ❑ **1959** African National Congress (ANC), led by Joshua Nkomo, banned.
- ❑ **1961** Nkomo forms ZAPU.
- ❑ **1962** ZAPU banned. Racial segregationist Rhodesian Front (RF) wins elections. Winston Field prime minister.
- ❑ **1963** African nationalists in Northern Rhodesia and Nyasaland demand dissolution of Federation. ZANU, offshoot of ZAPU, formed by Rev. Sithole and Robert Mugabe.
- ❑ **1964** Ian Smith new RF prime minister. British conditions for independence, including majority rule, rejected. ZANU banned.
- ❑ **1965** May: RF reelected. November: state of emergency declared (renewed every year until 1990). Smith makes unilateral declaration of independence. UK imposes economic sanctions. ANC, ZANU and ZAPU begin guerrilla war.
- ❑ **1970** Rhodesia declared republic.
- ❑ **1974** RF regime agrees to ceasefire terms with African nationalists.
- ❑ **1975–1979** Intermittent negotiations between British government, the RF and African nationalists to reach constitutional settlement.
- ❑ **1976** ZANU and ZAPU unite into Patriotic Front (PF).
- ❑ **1977** PF backed by "frontline" African states: Mozambique, Tanzania, Botswana and Zambia.
- ❑ **1979** Internal settlement drafted by Ian Smith and moderate African nationalists. Rejected by PF.
- ❑ **1979** Constitution signed.
- ❑ **1980** Independence. Following violent election campaign, Robert Mugabe becomes prime minister of ZANU–PF/ZAPU–PF coalition. Relations severed with South Africa.
- ❑ **1983–1984** Unrest in Matabeleland, ZAPU-PF's power base.
- ❑ **1985** Elections return ZANU–PF, with manifesto to create one-party state. Many ZAPU–PF members arrested.
- ❑ **1987** Unrest in Matabeleland. June: ban on ZAPU–PF. September: provision for white seats in parliament abolished. November: ban on ZAPU–PF lifted. December: ZANU–PF and ZAPU–PF sign unity agreement (merge in 1989). Mugabe elected president.
- ❑ **1990** Elections won by ZANU–PF. Mugabe reelected president.
- ❑ **1991** Mugabe abandons plan for one-party state.

DEFENSE

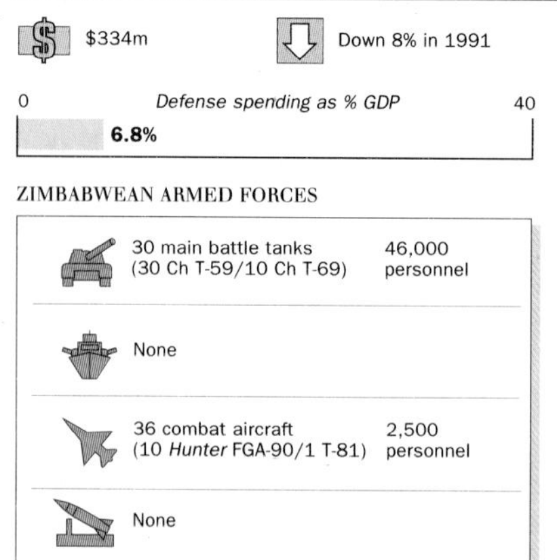

$334m
Down 8% in 1991
0
Defense spending as % GDP
40
6.8%
ZIMBABWEAN ARMED FORCES
30 main battle tanks (30 Ch T-59/10 Ch T-69)
46,000 personnel
None
36 combat aircraft (10 Hunter FGA-90/1 T-81)
2,500 personnel
None

The military appears to be under the complete control of President Mugabe, who is Commander-in-Chief of the armed forces. In the early 1980s, however, some soldiers deserted to fight government forces in the Matabele bush. They provided the nucleus of dissident movements that plagued the regime until the Unity Accord of 1987. Zimbabwe receives military aid and training from the UK and South Korea. Because of Zimbabwe's policy of non-alignment, it has not entered into any formal military alliances. However, it has supported the Mozambican regime against RENAMO guerrillas and backed the US-led operation in Somalia.

ECONOMICS

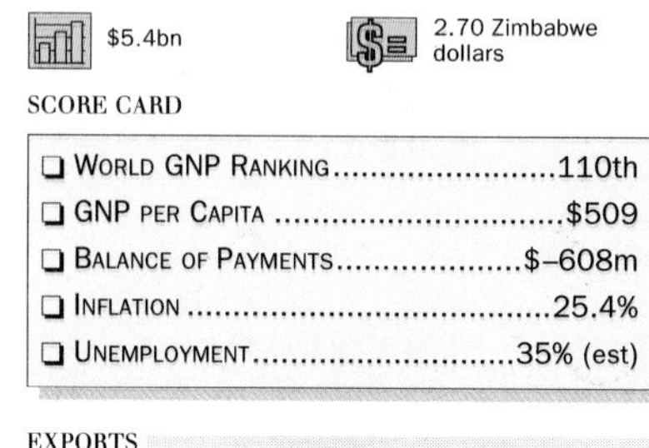

$5.4bn
2.70 Zimbabwe dollars
SCORE CARD
❑ World GNP Ranking........110th
❑ GNP per Capita........$509
❑ Balance of Payments........$-608m
❑ Inflation........25.4%
❑ Unemployment........35% (est)

EXPORTS

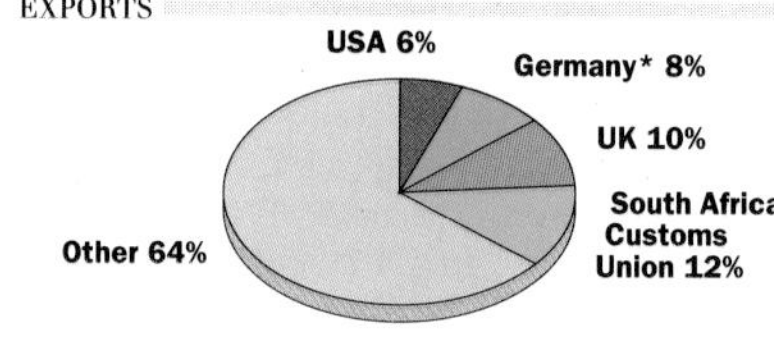

IMPORTS

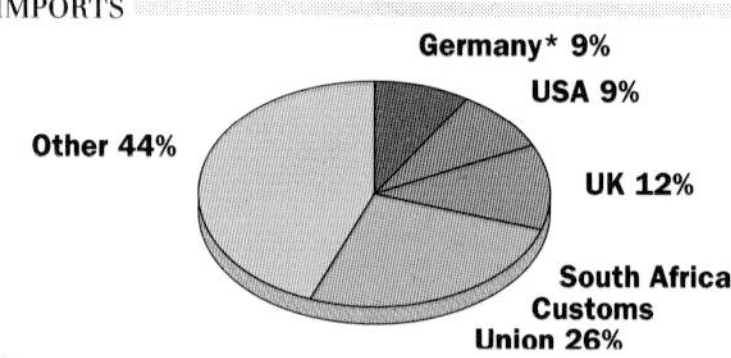

STRENGTHS

The most broadly based African economy after South Africa. Sound infrastructure. Unrivaled international credit rating in sub-Saharan Africa, due to careful policy of debt-servicing in 1980s. Virtual self-sufficiency in food and energy.

WEAKNESSES

Drought has hit agriculture, and also industry, due to reduction in output of hydroelectric power. Large balance of payments and budgetary deficits. High inflation; unemployment over 30%. Belated moves toward market-oriented economy.

PROFILE

In the 1980s, the government's verbal commitment to socialist policies was, in practice, tempered by pragmatism. The main aim was to correct the imbalance between black and white incomes. In 1991, faced with growing balance of payments problems and a need to create jobs, the government embarked on a five-year structural adjustment program which marked a radical reassessment of priorities. This move to a more market-oriented economy has had heavy social costs, pushing up unemployment and inflation, while leading to cuts in social welfare.

ECONOMIC PERFORMANCE INDICATOR

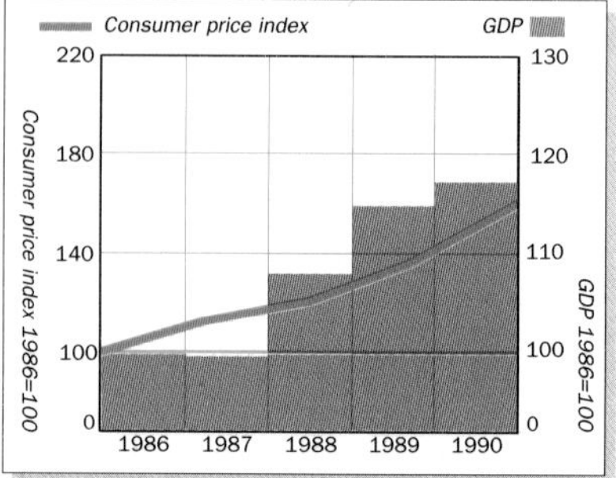

ZIMBABWE : MAJOR BUSINESSES

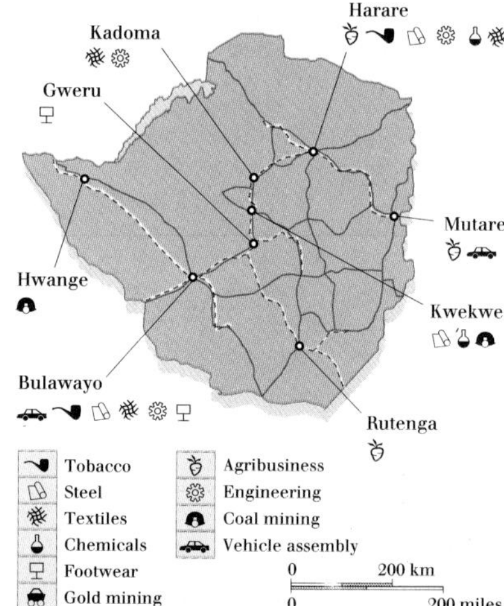

Z

RESOURCES

9.6bn kwh (capacity 2.04m kw)

Not an oil producer and has no refineries

6.5m cattle, 610,000 sheep, 237,000 pigs

Gold, coal, asbestos, nickel, copper, silver, iron, emeralds, lithium

ELECTRICITY GENERATION

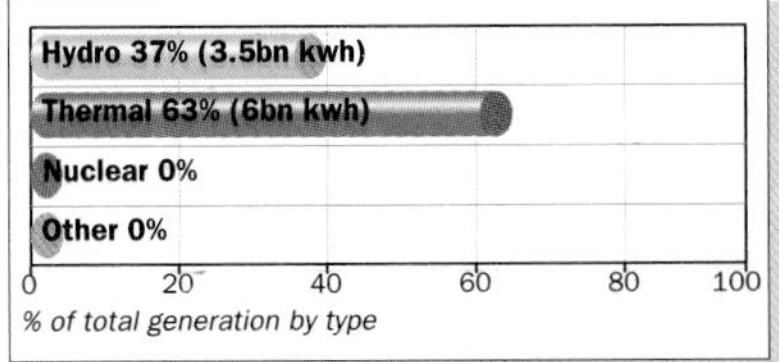

Almost 40% of Zimbabwe's electricity needs are met by hydropower, notably from the Kariba Dam, jointly owned with Zambia. The state power company is seeking to maximize capacity and to undertake long-term development. In 1991, the government agreed to the construction of an extension facility at Kariba South, and a joint HEP station at Bartoka Gorge with Zambia. An oil pipeline from Beira, Mozambique, to Mutare is being extended to Harare. Coal mining is expanding in Hwange to exploit deposits of 400 million tons.

ZIMBABWE : LAND USE

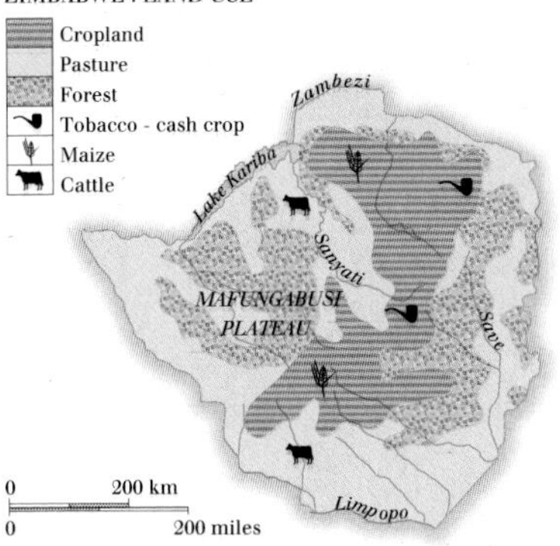

ENVIRONMENT

8% (1% partially protected)

Zimbabwe still suffers the after-effects of drought

ENVIRONMENTAL TREATIES

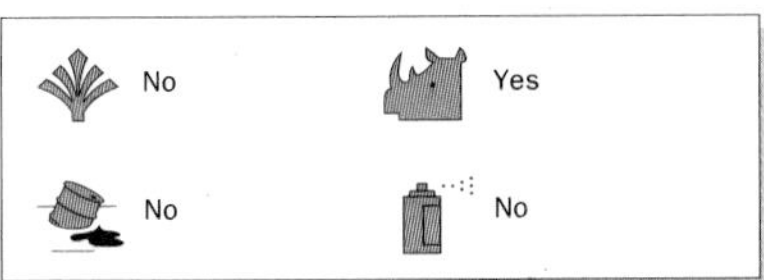

The 1991–1992 drought left half the population in need of drought relief, and swallowed 20% of public spending.

In communal areas, the land is suffering from overpopulation and overstocking. Deforestation, soil erosion and deterioration of wildlife and water resources are widespread.

Measures have been taken to protect the black rhinoceros, including moving animals to safer areas and combating poaching – patrols have killed 150 poachers since 1986. The government also supports a plan for dehorning rhinos – the horn is the poachers' main target. In 1992, Zimbabwe argued that elephants no longer required special protection. However, the Convention on International Trade in Endangered Species disagreed. It claimed that much poaching still exists, and accused the army of collusion.

CRIME

21,000 prisoners

Up 15% in 1990

CRIME RATES

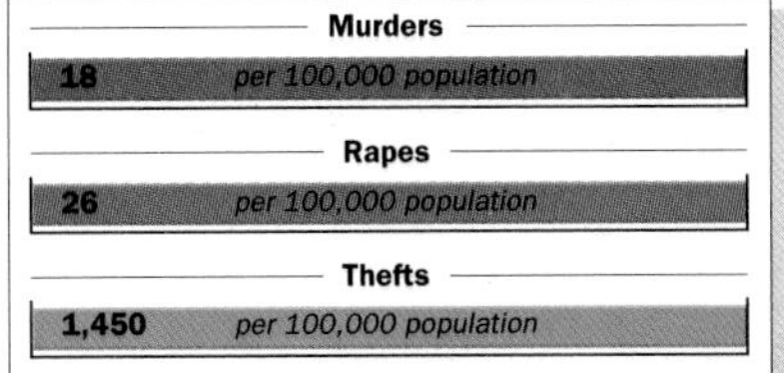

Urban areas have a high incidence of murder and drug-related offenses. With the worsening economic climate, crime is increasing in rural areas. The secret service, the Central Intelligence Organization, has faced international criticism for its alleged abuses of human rights.

HEALTH

1 per 7,180 people

Malnutrition, pneumonia, malaria, diarrheal diseases

0 *Health spending as % GNP* 25

3.7%

Free to those on less than a minimum wage, the health system is short of expertise and staff. The government has been slow to react to the spread of AIDS. In 1991, 28.5% of the work force were reported to be HIV positive.

WEALTH

Bus driver, 600 Zimbabwe dollars a month; school teacher, 1,500 Zimbabwe dollars a month

CONSUMER GOODS OWNERSHIP

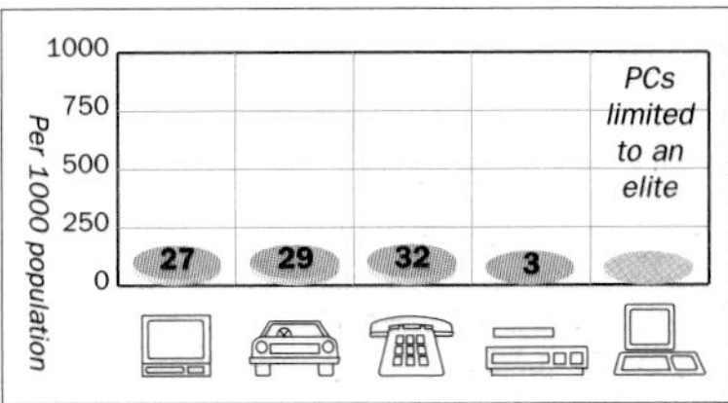

In the 1980s, "Growth with Equity" policies lessened the gap between blacks and whites. Growth now has priority over wealth redistribution.

EDUCATION

67%

0 *Education spending as % GNP* 25

8.5%

THE EDUCATION SYSTEM

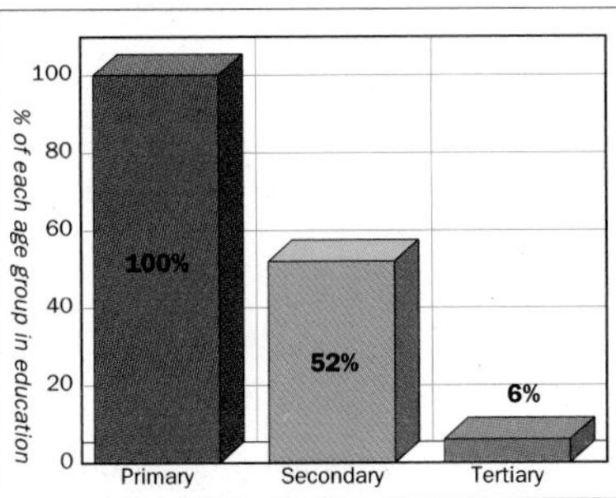

Education is compulsory. After reforms in 1991 and 1992, fees were introduced for primary and secondary education. Schooling is based on the British system and instruction is in English. The emphasis is now on vocational training to create a work force with the skills in agriculture, medicine and engineering that Zimbabwe needs.

MEDIA

There is no official censorship

PUBLISHING AND BROADCAST MEDIA

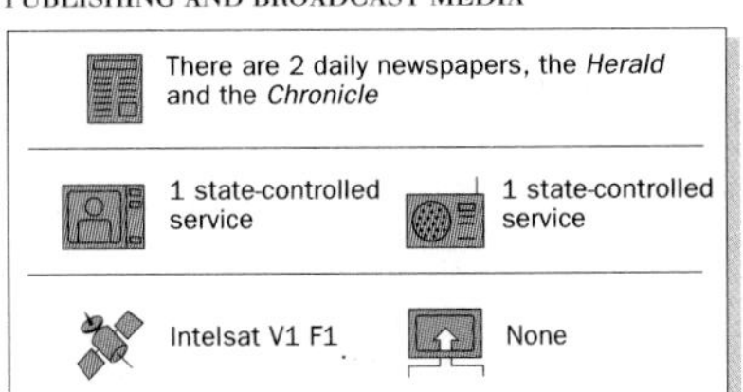

There are 2 daily newspapers, the Herald and the Chronicle
1 state-controlled service
1 state-controlled service
Intelsat V1 F1
None

The press is free, but the state has a controlling interest in the two main newspapers. There are, however, a great number of politically independent smaller newspapers and periodicals.

WORLD RANKING

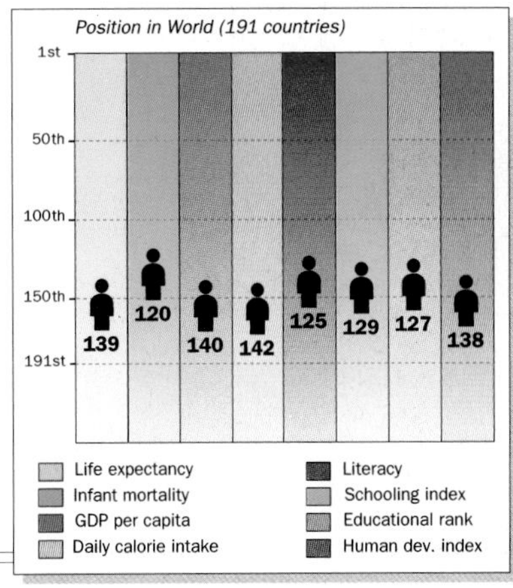

Z

OVERSEAS TERRITORIES & DEPENDENCIE

DESPITE THE RAPID process of decolonization since 1945 (pages 46-49), roughly 10 million people around the world still live under the protection of France, Australia, Denmark, New Zealand, Norway, Portugal, the UK, the USA or the Netherlands. The continued existence of these territories from the colonial era is a result of economic, historical or political reasons. Hong Kong, for instance, will revert to China in 1997 for historical reasons. Others await political developments, such as referenda, which will determine their future status. Some territories are retained because of their strategic or economic importance. Finally, a large group of territories are considered too small, remote or weak to be able to survive as independent nations.

UNITED KINGDOM

The UK still has the largest number of overseas territories in the world. They are split into Crown colonies, Crown dependencies and dependent territories. The distinction between them is largely constitutional, since most sustain a large degree of local autonomy. Britain generally operates a policy of non-interference. If a territory expresses a constitutional desire for formal independence then it may have it, as long as it can form a viable independent country.

Svalbard (to Norway)
BARENTS SEA
Jan Mayen (to Norway)
Faeroe Islands (to Denmark)
NORWAY
BALTIC SEA
NORTH SEA
Isle of Man (to UK)
UNITED KINGDOM
DENMARK
NETHERLANDS
Channel Islands: Guernsey and Jersey (to UK)
FRANCE
EUROPE
PORTUGAL
Gibraltar (to UK)
MEDITERRANEAN SEA
ASIA
SEA OF JAPAN
YELLOW SEA
EAST CHINA SEA
Hong Kong (to UK)
Macao (to Portugal)
Paracel Islands (Disputed)
Northern Mariana Islands (to US)
Guam (to US)
SOUTH CHINA SEA
Spratly Islands (Disputed)
Palau (to US)
AFRICA
ARABIAN SEA
British Indian Ocean Territory (to UK)
Ascension (Administered by St Helena)
Cocos (Keeling) Islands (to Australia)
Mayotte (to France)
JAVA SEA
ARAFURA SEA
Christmas Island (to Australia)
Ashmore & Cartier Islands (to Australia)
St Helena (to UK)
Réunion (to France)
Europa (Administered by Réunion)
Bassas da India (Administered by Réunion)
ATLANTIC OCEAN
INDIAN OCEAN
AUSTRALIA
Tristan da Cunha (Administered by St Helena)
Gough Island (Administered by St Helena)
Amsterdam Island
St. Paul Island
French Southern & Antarctic Territories (France)
Crozet Islands
Kerguelen
Heard & McDonald Islands (to Australia)
Bouvet Island (to Norway)

French Southern and Antarctic territories are not included in the following section. Any territories which involve an Antarctic claim are not shown.

NEW ZEALAND

New Zealand's government has no desir to retain any overseas territories. However, the economic weakness of its dependent territory Tokelau and its free associated states, Niue and the Cook Islands, has forced New Zealand to remain responsible for their foreign policy and defense.

nited States of America

nerica's overseas territories have been seen as
rategically useful, though expensive, links with
s "backyards." The USA has, in most cases, given
e local population a say in deciding its own
atus. Thus, three former US-administered UN
rust Territories have been, or are being, granted
ll sovereignty. A US Commonwealth territory
as a greater level of independence than that of a
S unincorporated or external territory.

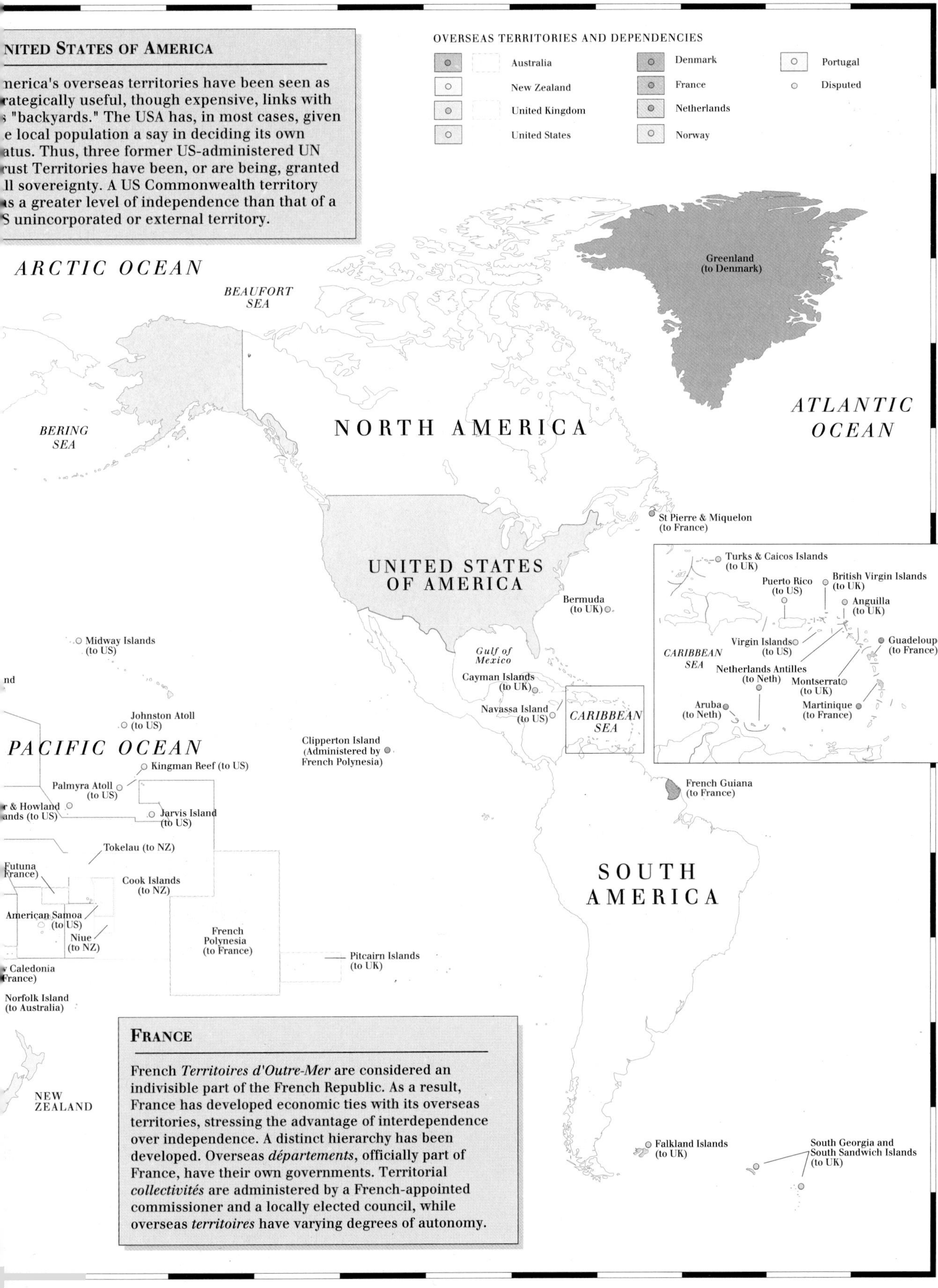

OVERSEAS TERRITORIES AND DEPENDENCIES

Australia
New Zealand
United Kingdom
United States
Denmark
France
Netherlands
Norway
Portugal
Disputed

ARCTIC OCEAN
BEAUFORT SEA
BERING SEA
NORTH AMERICA
Greenland (to Denmark)
ATLANTIC OCEAN
St Pierre & Miquelon (to France)
UNITED STATES OF AMERICA
Bermuda (to UK)
Gulf of Mexico
Cayman Islands (to UK)
Navassa Island (to US)
CARIBBEAN SEA
Turks & Caicos Islands (to UK)
Puerto Rico (to US)
British Virgin Islands (to UK)
Anguilla (to UK)
Virgin Islands (to US)
Guadeloupe (to France)
CARIBBEAN SEA
Netherlands Antilles (to Neth)
Montserrat (to UK)
Aruba (to Neth)
Martinique (to France)
Midway Islands (to US)
nd
Johnston Atoll (to US)
PACIFIC OCEAN
Clipperton Island (Administered by French Polynesia)
Kingman Reef (to US)
Palmyra Atoll (to US)
r & Howland ands (to US)
Jarvis Island (to US)
French Guiana (to France)
Tokelau (to NZ)
Futuna rance)
Cook Islands (to NZ)
SOUTH AMERICA
American Samoa (to US)
Niue (to NZ)
French Polynesia (to France)
Pitcairn Islands (to UK)
Caledonia rance)
Norfolk Island (to Australia)
NEW ZEALAND
Falkland Islands (to UK)
South Georgia and South Sandwich Islands (to UK)

France

French *Territoires d'Outre-Mer* are considered an indivisible part of the French Republic. As a result, France has developed economic ties with its overseas territories, stressing the advantage of interdependence over independence. A distinct hierarchy has been developed. Overseas *départements*, officially part of France, have their own governments. Territorial *collectivités* are administered by a French-appointed commissioner and a locally elected council, while overseas *territoires* have varying degrees of autonomy.

AMERICAN SAMOA

STATUS: Unincorporated territory of the USA **CLAIMED:** 1900

CAPITAL: Pago Pago **POPULATION:** 50,923 **DENSITY:** 622 per sq. mile

AMERICAN SAMOA consists of five volcanic islands and two coral atolls in the southern Pacific Ocean. It has a tropical climate with an average annual rainfall of 200 inches. Typhoons and tropical storms are common from December to March.

Samoans are among the last remaining true Polynesians. *Fa'a Samoa* – meaning the Samoan way of life – still directs Samoan society. The extended family, the *aiga*, forms the base of Samoan life, with chiefs still holding a central role in government. This has created tension, however, with a younger generation attracted by the lifestyle of *fa'a America*. As a result, many young Samoans have emigrated to the USA. One-fifth of all tuna consumed in the USA passes through Pago Pago's canneries, which employ 25% of the population. Recently, in an effort to diversify the economy, the American Samoan government has tried to encourage the development of other light industries and tourism.

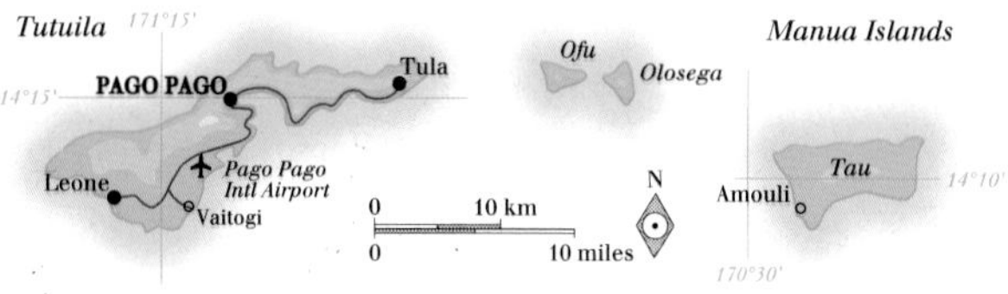

ANGUILLA

STATUS: British dependent territory **CLAIMED:** 1650

CAPITAL: The Valley **POPULATION:** 8,960 **DENSITY:** 241 per sq. mile

ANGUILLA is situated at the northern end of the Leeward Islands, in the Caribbean. It has a subtropical climate, with heat and humidity tempered by trade winds. In 1967 Anguillans refused to follow St. Kitts and Nevis into independence, preferring instead to retain the economic stability that came with dependent status. Since then the People's Progressive Party, renamed the Anguilla National Alliance in 1980, has dominated politics. Its leader and Chief Minister, Emile Gumbs, has pursued a policy of developing the tourist sector and attracting foreign investment, particularly in the offshore banking industry. However, stricter laws introduced in the 1990s forced a subsequent contraction in the sector. Lobster fishing continues to provide the majority of export earnings.

The island of Sombrero, 30 miles north of Anguilla, is also part of the territory.

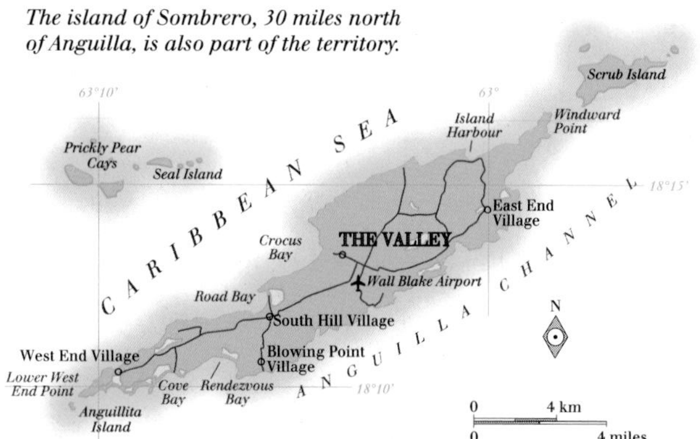

ARUBA

STATUS: Autonomous part of the Netherlands **CLAIMED:** 1643

CAPITAL: Oranjestad **POPULATION:** 62,365 **DENSITY:** 837 per sq. mile

ONE OF THE SMALLEST islands in the Dutch Caribbean, Aruba lies 16 miles off the coast of Venezuela. It has a tropical climate moderated by constant trade winds sweeping in from the Atlantic.

Formerly part of the Netherlands Antilles, Aruba became a separate dependency in 1986. However, as Aruba approaches independence in 1996, the Netherlands has voiced concern over the island's security and the danger of it becoming a base for drug-trafficking. Furthermore, the Aruban government, led by Nelson Oduber, has questioned the desirability of full independence, citing high unemployment and economic instability. For these reasons, the date of independence may well be postponed. The economy, formerly dependent on oil refining, has diversified, with tourism and offshore finance now the most important sectors. The oil refinery, which closed in 1985, was reopened at reduced capacity in 1990 by Coastal Oil of Texas.

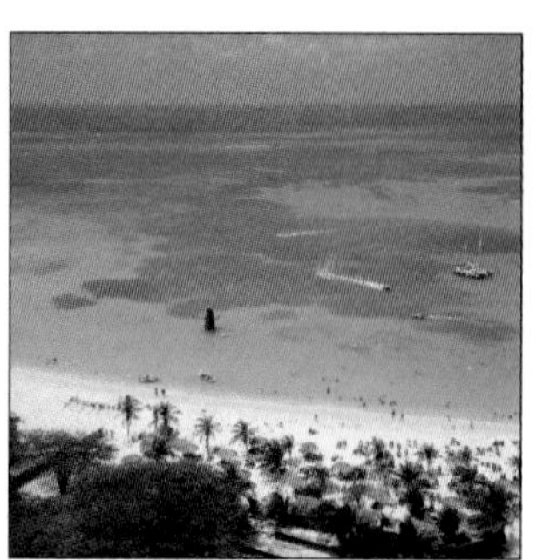

Palm Beach, Aruba, also known as the Turquoise Coast, lies on the western side of the island. The beach stretches for 6 miles and is the site of a low-rise beach resort.

ASHMORE & CARTIER IS.

STATUS: Australian external territory **CLAIMED:** 1978

CAPITAL: None **POPULATION:** None

LYING IN THE Timor Sea, the three Ashmore Islets and Cartier Island are separated by 37 miles of water, and cover a land area of 2 sq. miles. They are governed from Darwin, capital of the Northern Territories, nearly 500 miles to the west. Under an agreement with the Australian government, the sand and coral islands' waters are fished by Indonesians. However, reports of overfishing have led the government to monitor their activities. In 1983 Ashmore Reef was made a nature reserve.

BAKER & HOWLAND IS.

STATUS: Unincorporated territory of the USA **CLAIMED:** 1856

CAPITAL: None **POPULATION:** None

THE UNINHABITED Baker and Howland Islands lie 1,612 miles southwest of Hawaii, in the Pacific Ocean. The USA's interest in the two coral islands centered on rich guano deposits, which were worked out by 1891. The islands were again inhabited between 1936 until 1942, becoming a stop for trans-Pacific flights. They are now a refuge for over a million birds.

LAND HEIGHT | above Sea Level | 200m/656ft | 500m/1640ft | 1000m/3281ft | 1500m/4572ft | above 2000m/6562ft

BERMUDA

STATUS: British Crown colony **CLAIMED:** 1612

CAPITAL: Hamilton **POPULATION:** 58,433 **DENSITY:** 2,857 per sq. mile

SITUATED OVER 550 miles off the coast of South Carolina, Bermuda consists of a chain of over 150 coral islands. The Gulf Stream, flowing between Bermuda and America's eastern seaboard, keeps the climate mild and humid.

Bermuda is racially mixed; some 60% of the population are of African origin, the rest are mostly of European extraction. Racial tension, which existed in the 1960s and 1970s, has declined in the face of a more representative electoral system which was established after a Royal Commission visited Bermuda in 1978.

Despite changes made to the constitution in 1979, all elections have been won by the moderate, conservative United Bermuda Party (UBP). Its leader, and the island's premier, John Swan, is an advocate of eventual independence from the UK.

However, the electorate seems content to practice *de facto* independence. The UBP's prime current concerns are economic and environmental issues, as well as the growing problem of drug-trafficking. Despite its small size and few resources, Bermuda has one of the highest per capita incomes in the world. Tourism accounts for 55% of the island's GDP. Bermuda is a leading insurance market and also operates one of the world's largest flag-of-convenience shipping fleets.

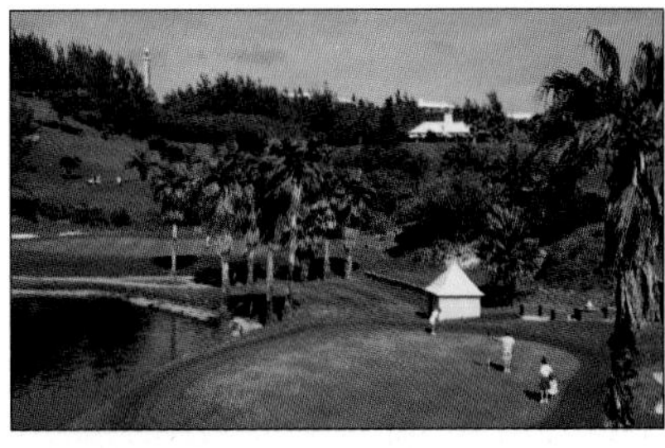

***Bermuda** has one of the highest densities of golf courses in the world. Eight courses have been developed in all.*

BOUVET ISLAND

STATUS: Norwegian dependency **CLAIMED:** 1927

CAPITAL: NONE **POPULATION:** None

A VOLCANIC, ice-covered island in the South Atlantic Ocean, Bouvet lies 992 miles north of Antarctica. Because it lies north of the Antarctic Circle it is not covered by the Antarctic Treaty. A royal decree, issued in 1971, made the whole island a nature reserve. Bouvet Island regularly plays host to scientific expeditions from Norway.

BRITISH INDIAN OCEAN TERRITORY

STATUS: British dependent territory **CLAIMED:** 1814

CAPITAL: Diego Garcia **POPULATION:** 3,400 **DENSITY:** 124 per sq. mile

THE BRITISH Indian Ocean Territory, or Chagos Islands, lie in the middle of the Indian Ocean. The coral atolls, previously used for copra production, are now uninhabited, except for the US-UK military base on Diego Garcia – a vital link in US plans to ensure a strategic capability in the Persian Gulf. The UK has agreed to cede the islands to Mauritius when they are no longer required for military purposes.

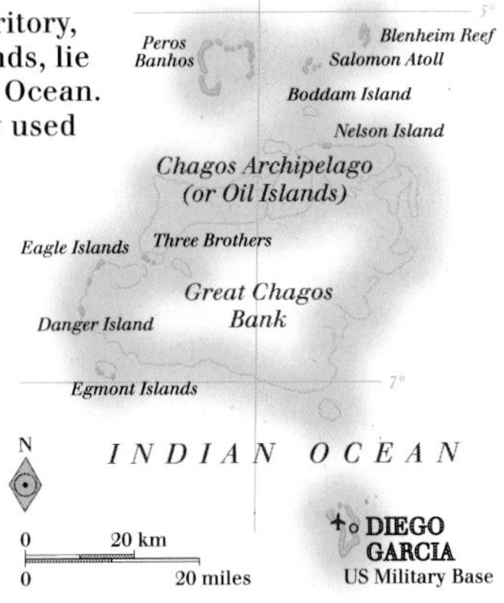

BRITISH VIRGIN ISLANDS

STATUS: British dependent territory **CLAIMED:** 1672

CAPITAL: Road Town **POPULATION:** 16,644 **DENSITY:** 282 per sq. mile

AN ARCHIPELAGO OF 40 Caribbean islands, 15 of them inhabited, the British Virgin Islands lie at the eastern end of the Greater Antilles. The islands' tropical climate has encouraged the development of tourism, now the islands' major economic activity. The local government has also developed the Virgin Islands as an offshore tax haven. However, a number of scandals involving companies registered in the islands resulted in strict legislation and a contraction of the sector in the 1990s. In recent years, a major political issue has been the rise in illegal immigration.

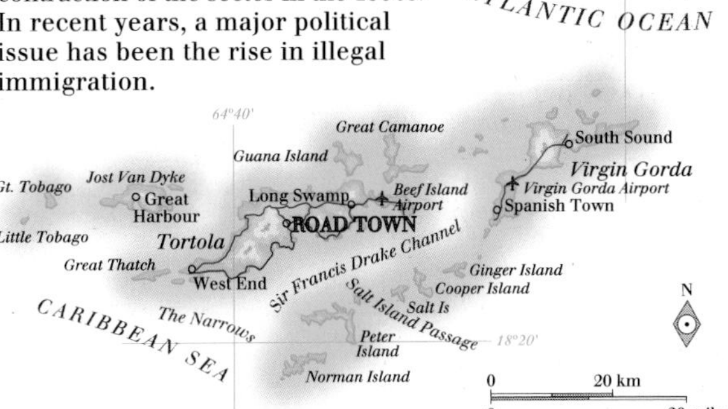

CAYMAN ISLANDS

STATUS: British dependent territory **CLAIMED:** 1670
CAPITAL: George Town **POPULATION:** 25,355 **DENSITY:** 254 per sq. mile

THE LARGEST OF Britain's remaining territories in the Caribbean, the Cayman Islands are situated 185 miles northwest of Jamaica. Convinced that the islands' economic prosperity is directly linked to the stability its dependent territory status gives, the islanders recently shelved plans to rewrite the constitution to give themselves greater autonomy from London. The islands are one of the world's largest offshore financial centers. Nearly 24,000 companies have been attracted by the lack of income tax and foreign-exchange controls. However, tourism underpins the economy, providing 70% of GDP.

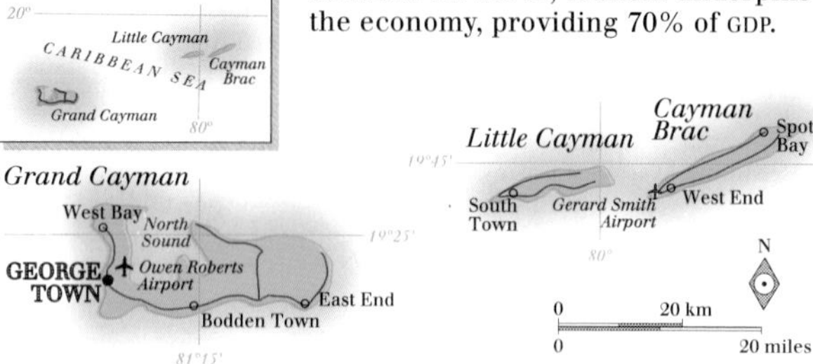

CHRISTMAS ISLAND

STATUS: Australian external territory **CLAIMED:** 1958
CAPITAL: Flying Fish Cove **POPULATION:** 1,275 **DENSITY:** 23 per sq. mile

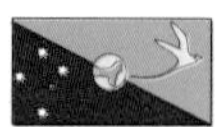

SO NAMED because it was sighted on Christmas Day in 1643, the island lies in the Indian Ocean, 185 miles south of Java. It was inhabited by labor imported to mine rich phosphate deposits. As a result, the population is mostly Malay and Chinese. Since 1990, the islanders have enjoyed an economic boom. The mine – closed in 1987 – has been reopened and a tourist complex has been built.

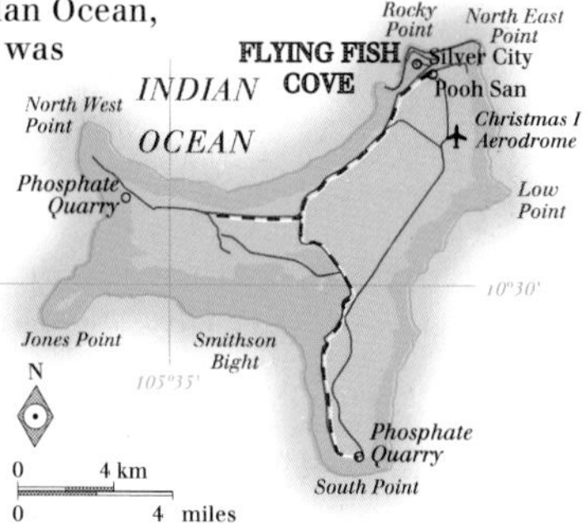

COCOS (KEELING) ISLANDS

STATUS: Australian external territory **CLAIMED:** 1955
CAPITAL: West Island **POPULATION:** 647 **DENSITY:** 119 per sq. mile

IN ALL, 27 coral atolls make up the Cocos (Keeling) Islands. They are situated in the Indian Ocean, roughly half way between Australia and Sri Lanka. The population is split between the European-dominated West Island and the Malays on Home Island. Coconuts are the sole cash crop and are grown throughout the atolls. The sale of postage stamps for foreign currency was stopped in the 1990s.

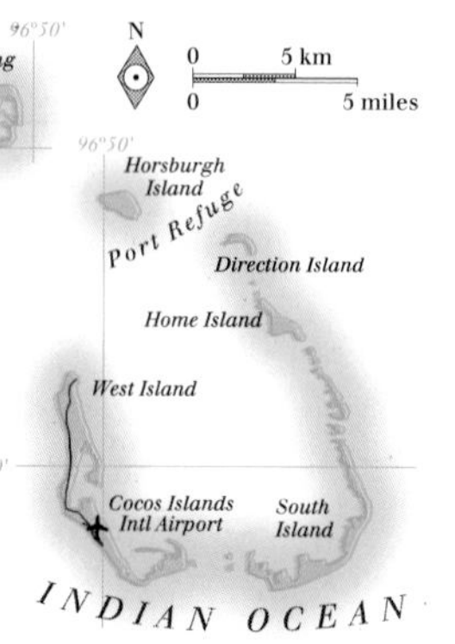

COOK ISLANDS

STATUS: Territory in free association with New Zealand **CLAIMED:** 19
CAPITAL: Avarua **POPULATION:** 18,547 **DENSITY:** 202 per sq. mile

LYING 2,170 MILES NORTHEAST of New Zealand, the Cook Islands are a combination of 24 coral atolls and volcanic islands. The islands achieved self-government in 1965 and have adopted a diverse approach to their economy. Extensive clam and pearl farming, and an ostrich farm, have been developed alongside tourism and banking. With the breakup of the ANZUS alliance in 1986, the Cook Islands declared their neutrality as doubts grew over New Zealand's ability to defend them. In 1991, the territory signed a friendship treaty with France which provided for French surveillance of its territorial waters.

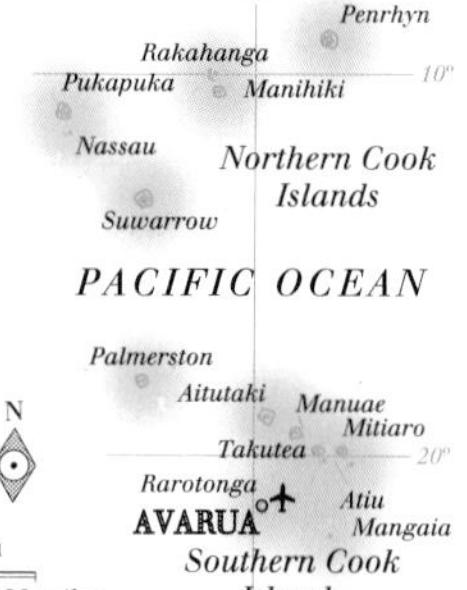

CORAL SEA ISLANDS

STATUS: Australian external territory **CLAIMED:** 1969
CAPITAL: None **POPULATION:** 3

THE TERRITORY OF THE Coral Sea Islands is a group of reefs and islands scattered over an area of nearly 400,000 sq. miles off the east coast of Queensland, Australia. Uninhabited except for a manned weather station on Willis Island, the islands function as a large nature reserve. They provide sanctuary, in particular, to a number of rare seabirds and turtles.

FAEROE ISLANDS

STATUS: Self-governing territory of Denmark **CLAIMED:** 1380
CAPITAL: Tórshavn **POPULATION:** 47,310 **DENSITY:** 88 per sq. mile

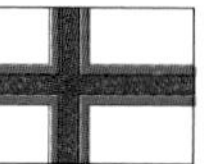

MIDWAY BETWEEN Scotland and Iceland in the North Atlantic, the Faeroe Islands have a moderate climate for their latitude – the result of the warm Gulf Stream current. Home rule since 1948 has given the Faeroese a strong sense of national identity – they voted against joining the EC with Denmark in 1973. In the face of international criticism, they have also continued their traditional cull of pilot whales and bottlenosed dolphins. Sheep farming is common, although fishing has had the strongest influence in shaping Faeroese society. As Denmark moves toward closer integration with the EU, which has a strict fisheries policy, internal pressure is growing for complete independence. However, as the islands' economy depends on Danish subsidies, this appears unlikely in the near future.

LAND HEIGHT above Sea Level 200m/656ft 500m/1640ft 1000m/3281ft 1500m/4572ft above 2000m/6562ft

FALKLAND ISLANDS

STATUS: British dependent territory **CLAIMED:** 1832
CAPITAL: Stanley **POPULATION:** 2,121 **DENSITY:** 0.5 per sq. mile

SITUATED IN THE South Atlantic Ocean, more than 7,440 miles from Britain, the Falkland Islands are influenced by the cold Antarctic current. The main islands of East and West Falkland and the hundreds of outlying islands have a cool, temperate climate with frequent strong winds.

The islands gained international renown with the Argentine invasion, and subsequent British recapture, in 1982. Since then, the British government has invested heavily in a "Fortress Falklands" policy. A new runway and military base were built at Mount Pleasant to house an enlarged garrison. Sovereignty over the Falklands, however, continues to exert a negative influence on Anglo-Argentine relations. The islanders, for their part, are determined to maintain the *status quo*.

Since the Falklands War the economy of the islands has prospered. Falklanders invested heavily in schools, roads and tourism in a fresh drive for a strong identity. By 1987 the Falklands had become financially solvent due to the sale of fishing licences. However, sales of cheaper, less restrictive licenses by Argentina forced a slump in fishing revenues. In addition, a fall in wool prices began to affect the living standards of the predominantly sheep-farming community. The islands' prospective fortunes were revived, and mass unemployment and emigration avoided, by the discovery of large oil reserves in their territorial waters. However, many islanders fear that the lure of oil will reawaken Argentina's desire to control the Falklands.

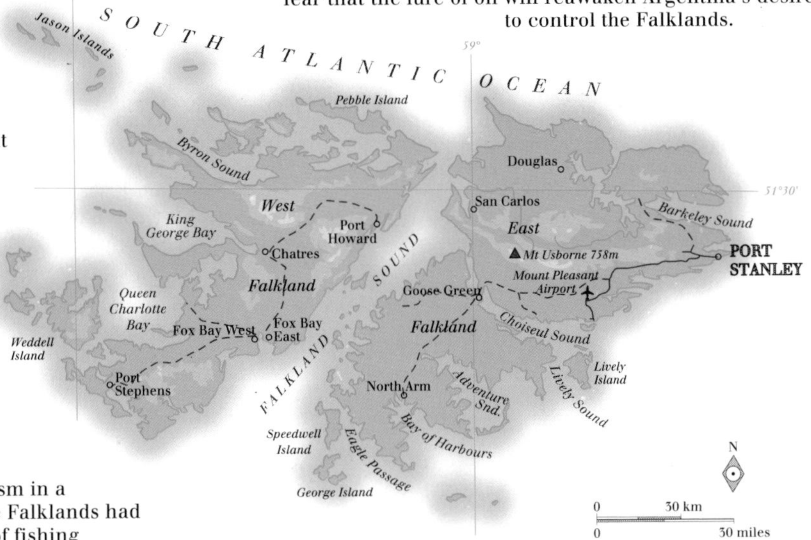

FRENCH GUIANA

STATUS: French overseas department **CLAIMED:** 1817
CAPITAL: Cayenne **POPULATION:** 114,808 **DENSITY:** 2.5 per sq. mile

SANDWICHED BETWEEN Brazil and Suriname on the northeast coast of South America, French Guiana is South America's only remaining colony. A belt of coastal marsh, and an interior of equatorial jungle, combine in a location which was, for years, notorious for the offshore penal colony, Devil's Island. The rainforest is particularly rich in flora and fauna. It harbors over 400,000 species, including more different kinds of birds than the whole of Europe.

Concentrated near the coast, the population is ethnically mixed. There are some 5,000 Indians and many descendants of African slaves.

A campaign for greater autonomy in the late 1970s and early 1980s led to limited decentralization of power to a regional council. The ruling Guianese Socialist Party (GSP) has maintained its hold on the regional council in the face of a divided opposition.

As French Guiana confronts growing economic and social instability, the people have become increasingly vocal in their condemnation of the French government's perceived indifference to their country's problems. Accordingly, the GSP has campaigned for greater autonomy from France in such important areas as transportation, immigration, education and health.

As an overseas *département* of metropolitan France, French Guiana is also a region of the EU. Despite this, the economy is heavily dependent on France for aid, food and manufactured goods. It has a number of valuable natural resources and also tourist potential, but these are yet to be fully exploited because of a lack of skilled labor and investment, and an underdeveloped infrastructure. One asset, however, which has made French Guiana strategically important to France, is the European Space Agency rocket launch facility for the Ariane rocket at Kourou.

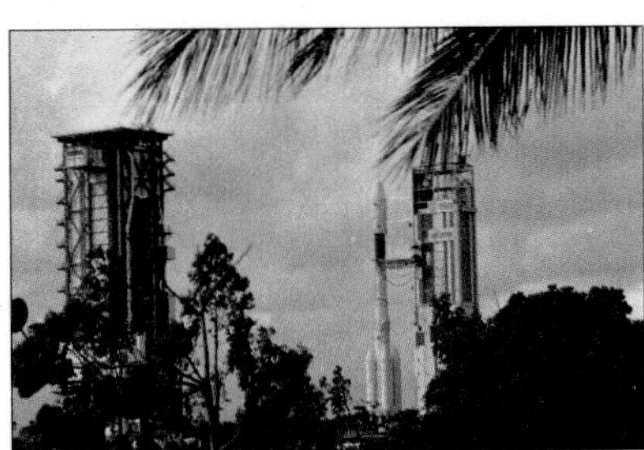

***Kourou** was selected for the launch of the Ariane rocket because of its equatorial site. The town has grown from 800 to 15,000 people.*

POPULATION  under 5000 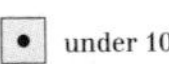 under 10 000  over 10 000  over 50 000  over 100 000 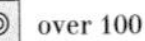 Urban areas AIRPORTS 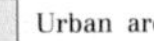 International  Local 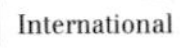

French Polynesia

Status: French overseas possession **Claimed:** 1843
Capital: Papeete **Population:** 199,031 **Density:** 124 per sq. mile

A MYRIAD of 130 South Pacific islands and coral atolls combine to form French Polynesia, in an area the size of Europe. The average annual temperature varies between 68°F and 84°F, with annual rainfall of over 58 inches. Nearly 75% of the population live on the main island of Tahiti. The Polynesian majority have seen their simple, self-sufficient economy transformed into one dependent on the French military and tourism. Nuclear testing on Mururoa Atoll created many jobs. Testing stopped in 1992, however, and unemployment has risen as a result. In addition, the French administration has developed the islands with little regard for local opinion. In response, the Polynesian majority has increased calls for greater autonomy, a reduction in tourism and a program for rebuilding indigenous trade. However, the 20,000, mainly French, expatriate workers oppose any change.

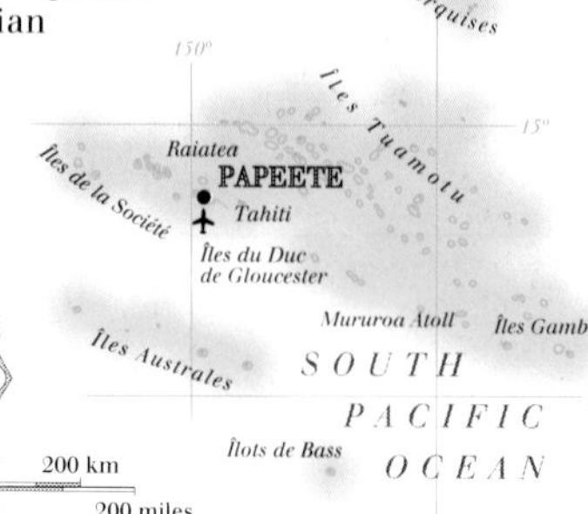

Gibraltar

Status: British Crown colony **Claimed:** 1713
Capital: Gibraltar **Population:** 28,074 **Density:** 11,186 per sq. mile

GUARDING THE western entrance to the Mediterranean, Gibraltar has traditionally survived on military and marine revenues. However, as Britain has cut its defense spending, the UK's military presence on the Rock has declined. In response, Gibraltarians have developed a vibrant offshore banking industry, although 70% of employment still remains in the public sector. Politics are dominated by the issue of Gibraltar's relationship with Britain and Spain. As the UK's role diminishes, Gibraltar's chief minister, Joe Bossano, has called for independence under EU sponsorship. However, this seems unlikely while Spain continues to press for control over the Rock.

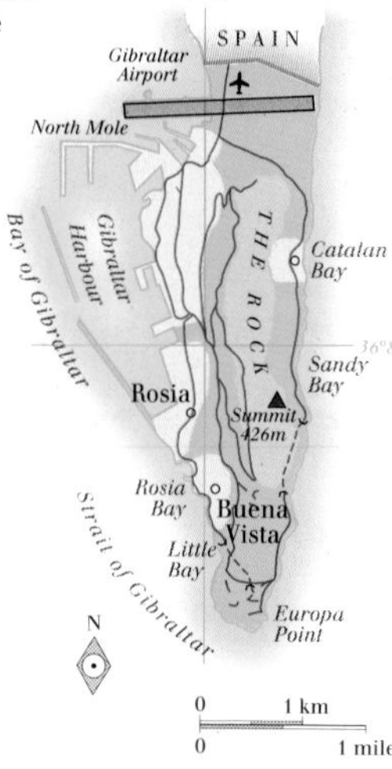

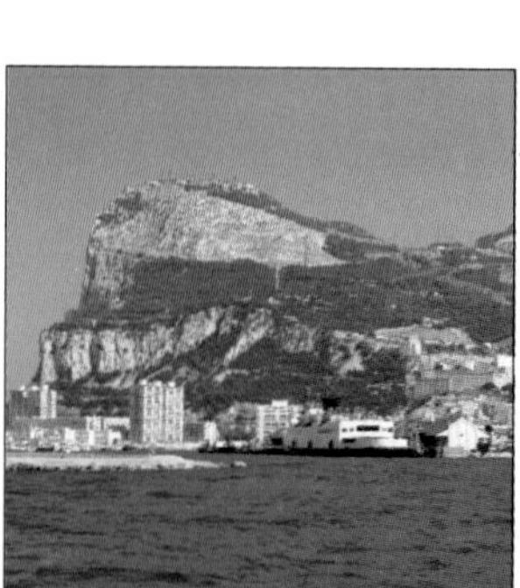

The Rock of Gibraltar. *The British built 143 caves, 30 miles of roads and as many miles of tunnels for defensive purposes.*

Greenland

Status: Self governing territory of Denmark **Claimed:** 1380
Capital: Nuuk **Population:** 55,385 **Density:** 0.06 per sq. mile

THE WORLD'S LARGEST island, Greenland is situated in the North Atlantic and surrounded by seas that are either frozen or cooled by cold Arctic currents. The island has an Arctic climate and much of its land is permanently covered in ice. Granted home rule in 1979, Greenlanders are an independent people – a mix of Innuit and European in origin. Younger islanders are increasingly rejecting the traditional subsistence lifestyle by moving to towns. This move away from self-sufficiency, allied to a decline in the important fishing industry, has placed a heavy burden on Greenland's advanced welfare system.

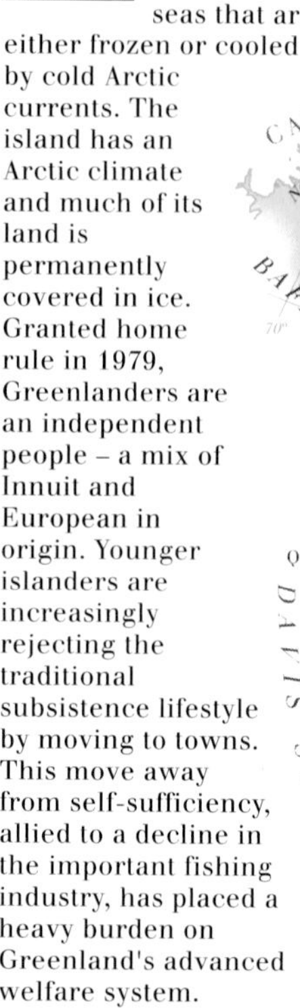

Guadeloupe

Status: French overseas department **Claimed:** 1635
Capital: Basse-Terre **Population:** 387,034 **Density:** 562 per sq. mile

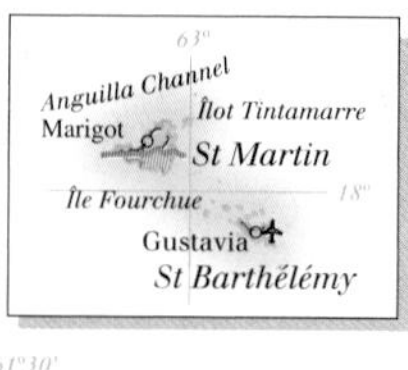

GUADELOUPE lies at the northern end of the Windward Islands in the Caribbean. It could become independent, but instead prospers from a developed infrastructure and large amounts of French and EU aid. However, tensions are growing between the local population, who demand more autonomy, and the expatriate bureaucracy who impose the regulations of mainland France. Exports of the major cash crop, bananas, have been hit by the loss of special advantages under the Single European Act.

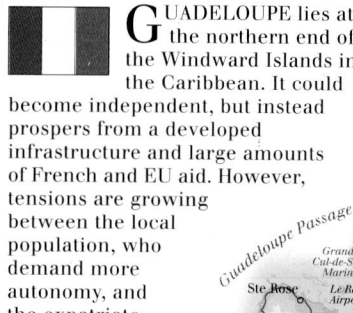

LAND HEIGHT: above Sea Level; 200m/656ft; 500m/1640ft; 1000m/3281ft; 1500m/4572ft; above 2000m/6562ft; Ice Cap

GUAM

STATUS: Unincorporated territory of the USA **CLAIMED:** 1898
CAPITAL: Agaña **POPULATION:** 133,152 **DENSITY:** 629 per sq. mile

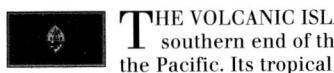

THE VOLCANIC ISLAND of Guam lies at the southern end of the Mariana Archipelago in the Pacific. Its tropical climate has encouraged tourism, although it lies in a region where typhoons are common. Guam's indigenous Chamorro people, who comprise just under half the population, dominate the island's political and social life. They are famous for a set of facial expressions, called "eyebrow," which virtually constitutes a language of its own. The US military base, covering one-third of the island, has made Guam strategically important to the USA. Military spending and tourism revenues have given islanders a high living standard. The influx of American culture and *mores* has, however, threatened to upset Guam's social stability.

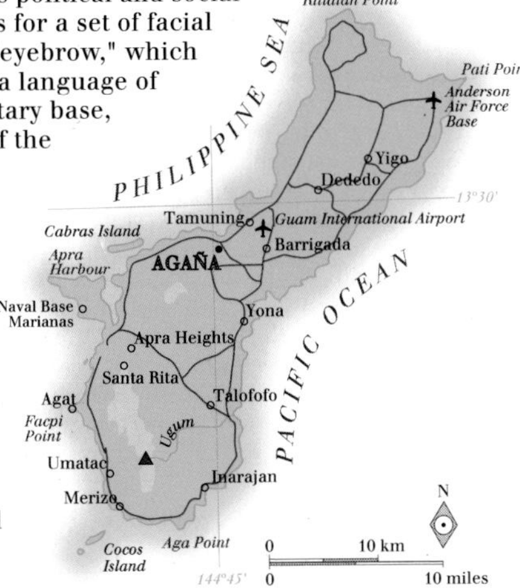

GUERNSEY

STATUS: British Crown dependency **CLAIMED:** 1066
CAPITAL: St. Peter Port **POPULATION:** 58,867 **DENSITY:** 2,347 per mile

LYING 30 MILES off the coast of France, Guernsey and its dependencies form the northwestern part of the Channel Islands. Some of the islands are too small for people to need cars, and life continues in an unhurried manner that has changed little through the centuries. The islanders guard this lifestyle with strict residential laws. Guernsey's mild climate has encouraged the development of tourism and market gardening as major industries.

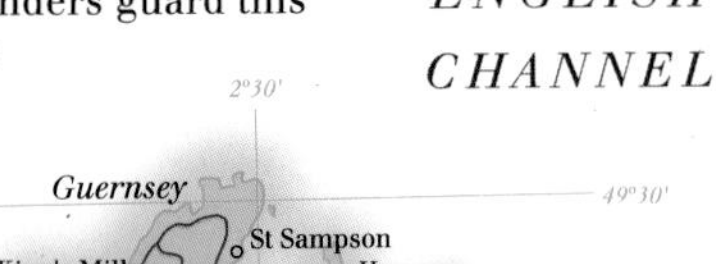

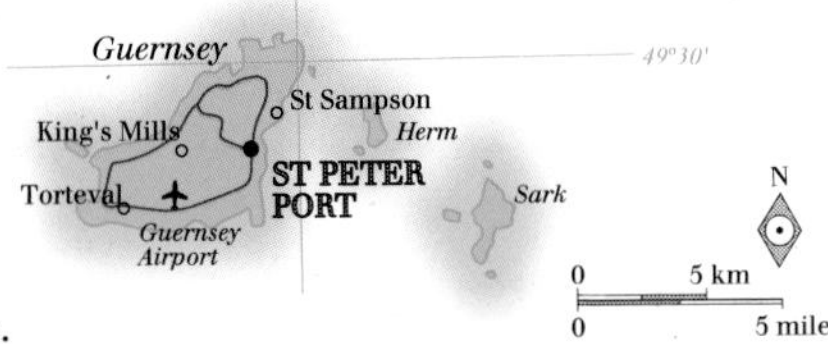

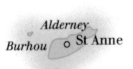

HEARD & MACDONALD IS.

STATUS: Australian external territory **CLAIMED:** 1947
CAPITAL: None **POPULATION:** None

SITUATED 2,480 miles southwest of Australia in the Indian Ocean, the Heard and Macdonald Islands are ice-covered, volcanic rock outcrops. Their principal use is for scientific research. Because of Heard Island's unique location – it offers direct access to the world's main oceans – it was chosen in 1991 as the site of an experiment to monitor global warming using soundwaves.

ISLE OF MAN

STATUS: British Crown dependency **CLAIMED:** 1765
CAPITAL: Douglas **POPULATION:** 69,788 **DENSITY:** 316 per sq. mile

LYING HALFWAY between England and Northern Ireland in the Irish Sea, the Isle of Man has been inhabited for centuries by the Celtic Manx people. Established by the Vikings in the ninth century, the Manx parliament, the Tynwold, has autonomy from the UK in a number of matters, including taxation. The islanders have used this independence to establish a thriving financial and business sector, which has aided employment as the traditional industries of agriculture and fishing decline. The Manx culture received a boost in 1993 when the local language, which was in danger of dying out, began being taught in the island's schools again. The Calf of Man is uninhabited and is administered as a nature reserve.

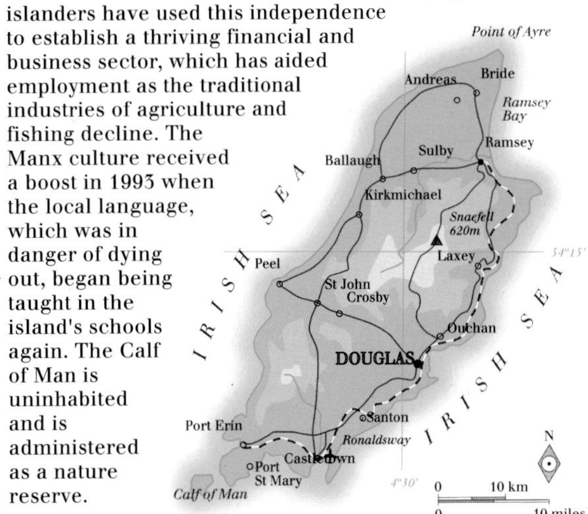

Isle of Man's TT motorcycle race. *Thousands of bikers come each year to see the island's famous Touring Trophy race. It is run on a 38-mile circuit of the island.*

JAN MAYEN

STATUS: Norwegian dependency **CLAIMED:** 1929
CAPITAL: None **POPULATION:** None

THE MOUNTAINOUS, volcanic island of Jan Mayen lies 558 miles northwest of Norway, in the Arctic Ocean. The island's only resource is its rich fishing grounds. These were the subject of a long dispute with Greenland over fishing rights and possibly also oil and gas deposits. The International Court of Justice helped the two parties reach a compromise in 1993.

JARVIS ISLAND

STATUS: Unincorporated territory of the USA **CLAIMED:** 1856
CAPITAL: None **POPULATION:** None

A SMALL CORAL island, less than 2 miles long and one mile wide, Jarvis Island is located 1,240 miles south of Honolulu. It remains uninhabited, although scientists do occasionally visit. The island is managed primarily as a nesting, roosting and foraging site for seabirds and shorebirds.

Jersey

Status: British Crown dependency **Claimed:** 1066
Capital: St. Helier **Population:** 82,809 **Density:** 1,847 per sq. mile

THE BAILIWICK OF JERSEY, the largest of the Channel Islands, lies some 12 miles from the coast of Normandy in France. The island has a mild climate due to the Gulf Stream, as well as fine beaches and more sunshine than anywhere in the British Isles.

Jersey has its own legislative and taxation systems which are a blend of the French and British versions. It also has one of the oldest legislative bodies in the world, the Jersey States Assembly. There are no political parties; members run as independents. The islanders have used their autonomy from the UK to develop the economy as an offshore tax haven. Historically, agriculture has been Jersey's most important industry, with dairy cows its most famous export. Over the past 50 years, however, farming has been eclipsed by the rise of finance and tourism. The growth of these sectors, and rigid controls on the rights of residency, have ensured high living standards for most of the inhabitants. Jersey also plays host to a large Portuguese community who work in the island's tourist industry.

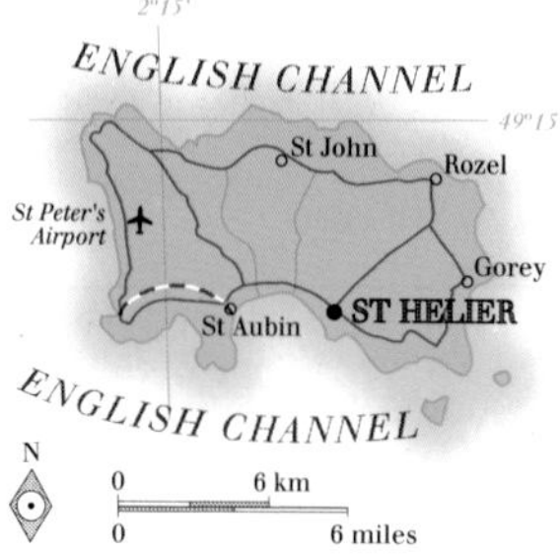

Johnston Atoll

Status: Unincorporated territory of the USA **Claimed:** 1858
Capital: None **Population:** 1,375 **Density:** 1,272 per sq. mile

JOHNSTON ATOLL lies 713 miles southwest of Hawaii. The atoll consists of a coral reef, two highly-modified natural islands, Johnston and Sand, and two completely artificial islands, Akau and Hikina. The US military has drastically altered the islands and little of the original habitat remains. They have, in the past, been used for nuclear-weapons tests and storing nerve gases. However, the atoll is now used for a chemical-weapons disposal project by the US government. The islands are inhabited by US government personnel and civilian contractors who support the plant.

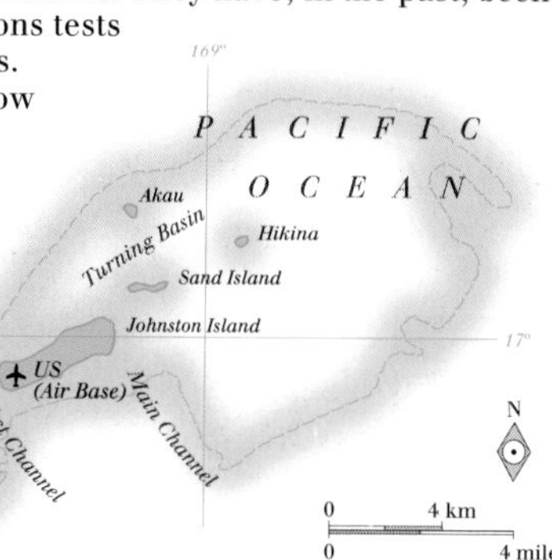

Kingman Reef

Status: Unincorporated territory of the USA **Claimed:** 1856
Capital: None **Population:** None

A barren, triangular reef, just over 3 feet in elevation, Kingman Reef lies 930 miles southwest of Hawaii. The reef is 9 miles long and 5 miles wide. Only the eastern end of it now remains above water. There is no land flora but it is rich in marine life. The reef is administered by the US Navy.

Macao

Status: Special territory of Portugal **Claimed:** 1557
Capital: Macao **Popn:** 355,693 **Density:** 51,181 per sq. mile

THE PORTUGUESE ENCLAVE of Macao is situated on the South China coast, at the mouth of the Pearl River. It comprises a small area of mainland and two nearby islands, linked to the mainland by bridge and causeway. A subtropical climate brings high humidity and the possibility of typhoons sweeping in from the South China Sea.

Macao is scheduled to become a Special Administrative Region of China in 1999. In contrast to the problems being experienced by the British in Hong Kong, Macao's preparations for Chinese sovereignty have been relatively smooth, primarily because all Macanenes have been offered Portuguese passports. Tension has, however, developed between the skilled elite and the merchants who support China's takeover in 1999. In local legislative elections in 1992 the pro-China candidates secured half of the directly elected seats in the 23-seat assembly.

Macao has always suffered by comparison with Hong Kong, just 17 miles to the east. While Hong Kong has developed into an advanced capitalist economy, Macao is traditionally characterized by stagnation, corruption and bureaucratic inefficiency. However, the economy of Macao is now booming in the build-up to 1999. The government has been able to diversify the economy away from a dependency on gambling, although its casinos still lure hundreds of thousands of visitors a year. An international airport is being built on reclaimed land to aid economic development, and Macao is now a major center for making cheap, finished goods for export. Its factories use cheap Chinese labor to produce anything from fireworks to artificial flowers.

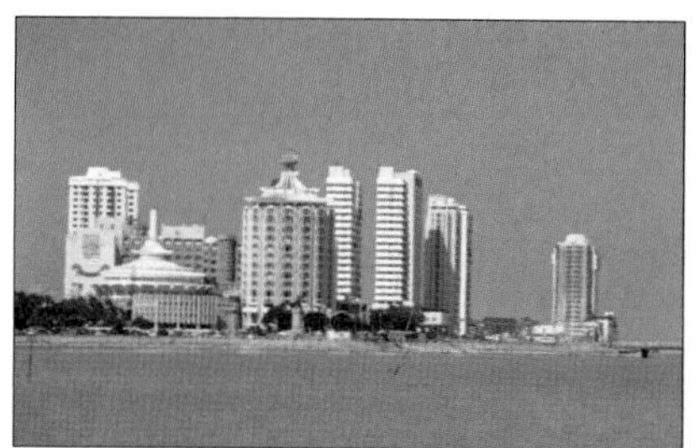

Macao's skyline is dominated by large hotels and casinos which provide the territory with an important source of revenue.

MARTINIQUE

STATUS: French overseas department **CLAIMED:** 1635
CAPITAL: Fort-de-France **POPN:** 359,579 **DENSITY:** 847 per sq. mile

CHRISTOPHER COLUMBUS called Martinique "The most beautiful country in the world." It lies in the eastern Caribbean and is dominated by the dormant volcano Mont Pelée. The island is also situated in the Caribbean's hurricane belt and has therefore suffered an average of one natural disaster every five years. Nearly 90% of the population is of African or mixed ethnicity. However, economic power remains in the hands of the *Bekes* (descendants of white colonial settlers), who own most of the agricultural land. In addition, the bureaucracy is largely staffed by expatriates. This situation has led to outbreaks of violence and increased popular demands for more autonomy. The French government responded with some measures to increase the island's autonomy. However, the islanders are acutely aware that their high living standards are dependent on French subsidies. The economy relies on tourism and the production of sugar cane and bananas. EU reductions in subsidies has forced the island to diversify its economy.

MAYOTTE

STATUS: French territorial collectivity **CLAIMED:** 1843
CAPITAL: Mamoudzou **POPN:** 94,410 **DENSITY:** 655 per sq. mile

PART OF THE Comoros Archipelago, Mayotte lies about 4,960 miles from France, between Madagascar and the East African coast. The Mahorais are strongly in favor of maintaining their links with France, despite widespread poverty, endemic unemployment and a cost of living twice that of France. The main political movement has demanded that Mayotte be given the status of a French *département*. They hope that this would bring more aid to develop their largely agricultural economy. The expense involved has led France to oppose the idea. The French have, however, invested in an airport and port. It is hoped these will foster the growth of an upscale tourist sector.

MIDWAY ISLANDS

STATUS: Unincorporated territory of the USA **CLAIMED:** 1867
CAPITAL: None **POPULATION:** 453 **DENSITY:** 236 per sq. mile

NAMED BECAUSE OF its position on the route between California and Japan, Midway is a coral atoll at the western end of the Hawaiian islands. The scene of a major World War II battle, the atoll comprises two large islands, totaling over 1.5 sq. miles, and several smaller ones. Midway functions as a naval air base and wildlife refuge. The population is limited to military personnel and civilian contractors.

MONTSERRAT

STATUS: British dependent territory **CLAIMED:** 1632
CAPITAL: Plymouth **POPULATION:** 11,852 **DENSITY:** 290 per sq. mile

MONTSERRAT IS PART of the Leeward Islands chain in the eastern Caribbean. Luxuriant flora and a tropical climate have made the island a tourist destination for the rich and famous. However, Montserrat's mountainous terrain, and hurricanes such as Hugo in 1989, have impeded its agricultural development. In response, the government has also developed the island as a financial and data-processing center, although recent economic activity has been dominated by rebuilding infrastructure destroyed by Hugo. Independence, which dominated local politics in the late 1980s, fell into abeyance after the hurricane and a financial scandal involving local politicians.

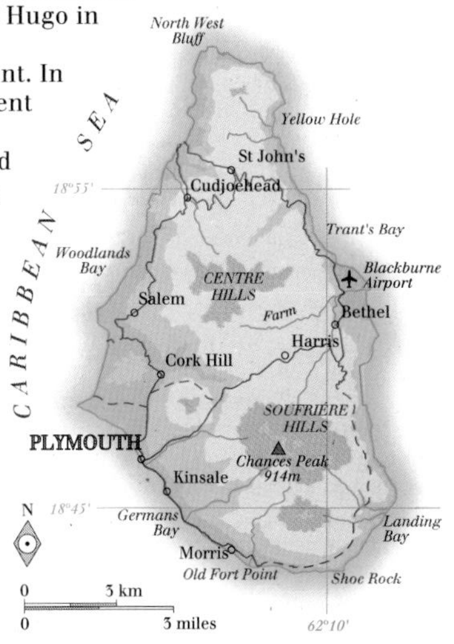

Monserrat is known as the Caribbean's "emerald isle" because of its luxuriant flora and the islanders' Irish heritage.

NAVASSA ISLAND

STATUS: Unincorporated territory of the USA **CLAIMED:** 1856
CAPITAL: None **POPULATION:** None

AN UNINHABITED rocky outcrop, Navassa Island lies halfway between Cuba and Haiti, in the Caribbean. The island, also claimed by Haiti, is occasionally used by Haitians fishing the local waters. They also sometimes hunt the island's goats. Navassa has an automatic lighthouse which is run by the US Coast Guard.

POPULATION ○ under 5000 ● under 10 000 ● over 10 000 ○ over 50 000 ◎ over 100 000 ▢ Urban areas AIRPORTS ✈ International ✈ Local

NETHERLANDS ANTILLES

STATUS: Autonomous part of the Netherlands **CLAIMED:** 1816
CAPITAL: Willemstad **POPN:** 191,311 **DENSITY:** 619 per sq. mile

THE NETHERLANDS Antilles are composed of two Caribbean island groups. Curaçao – the richest and wealthiest island – and Bonaire lie just off the Venezuelan coast, and Saba and St. Eustatius and the Dutch part of St. Maarten lie 500 miles to the north. The islands have given the Dutch government, which donates $160 million in aid annually, a number of problems. These include financial scandals, arguments over the federation's future and – particularly on the four smaller islands – political instability and allegations of drug-trafficking. In 1993, Curaçao's population opted to remain in the federation.

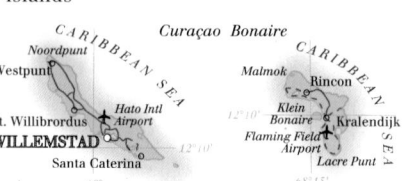

NEW CALEDONIA

STATUS: French overseas territory **CLAIMED:** 1853
CAPITAL: Nouméa **POPULATION:** 164,173 **DENSITY:** 23 per sq. mile

NEW CALEDONIA, or as the indigenous Kanaks call it, Kanaky, is an island group 930 miles off the northeast coast of Australia. Tension between the Kanaks and the Caldoches, the francophile expatriate population, over socioeconomic inequalities and independence, have resulted in a long history of political violence. By the 1988 Matignon Accord, the French government took over the administration of the territory for a year in order to introduce economic reforms and address Kanak grievances. Political prisoners were released and a referendum on independence promised for 1998. However, after the year was up, racial violence flared up and political resentments resurfaced. Nickel mining – the territory produces 25% of world output – tourism and agriculture have greatly enriched the economy, but there are considerable contrasts in living standards between rich and poor, with unemployment high among young Kanaks.

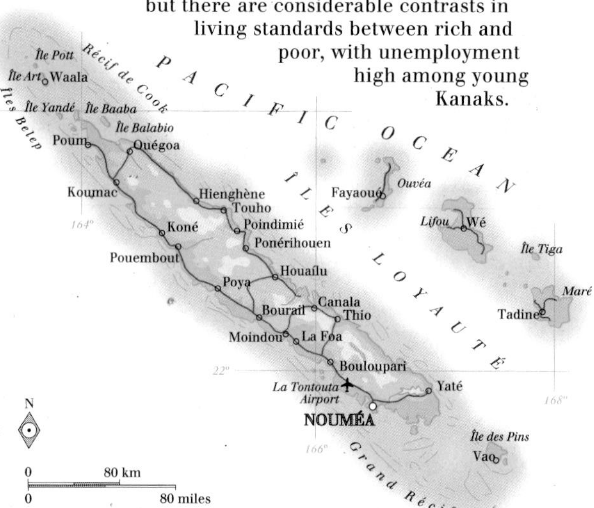

NIUE

STATUS: Territory in free association with New Zealand **CLAIMED:** 1
CAPITAL: Alofi **POPULATION:** 2,239 **DENSITY:** 23 per sq. mile

THE WORLD'S largest coral island, Niue, lies 1,300 miles northeast of New Zealand. The subsistence economy produces a variety of tropical fruits, while tourism and the sale of postage stamps provide foreign currency. Despite the island's paradise image, nearly 10,000 Niueans, frustrated by the lack of job prospects on Niue, live in New Zealand. In the hope of stopping further emigration, New Zealand has invested heavily in the economy. However, inefficient use of aid and cyclone damage have held back growth.

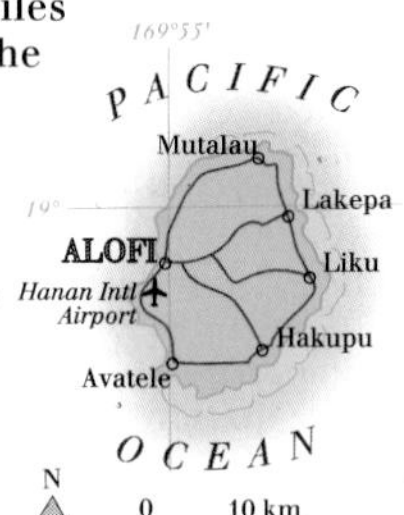

NORFOLK ISLAND

STATUS: Australian external territory **CLAIMED:** 1774
CAPITAL: Kingston **POPULATION:** 1,912 **DENSITY:** 143 per sq. mile

INHABITED by descendants of the *HMS Bounty* mutineers and more recent Australian migrants, Norfolk Island lies 868 miles east of Australia. The islanders speak a hybrid language, mixing West Country English, Gaelic and ancient Tahitian. They enjoy a fair degree of autonomy, and in 1991 rejected a plan to become part of the Australian federal state. Tourists, attracted by the climate and unique flora, have brought islanders a relatively high standard of living.

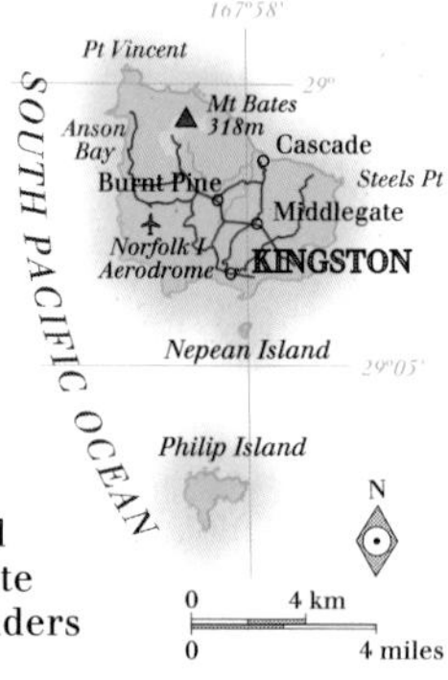

NORTHERN MARIANA IS.

STATUS: Commonwealth territory of the USA **CLAIMED:** 1947
CAPITAL: Saipan **POPULATION:** 43,345 **DENSITY:** 590 per sq. mile

UNLIKE OTHER UN trust territories in the Western Pacific who opted for independence in 1987, the Northern Marianas preferred to retain links with the USA. However, local politicians have begun to question their new status. While US aid fueled an economic boom during the 1980s, it failed to benefit the local Chamorro population. In addition, tourism has speeded the decline of the traditional subsistence economy.

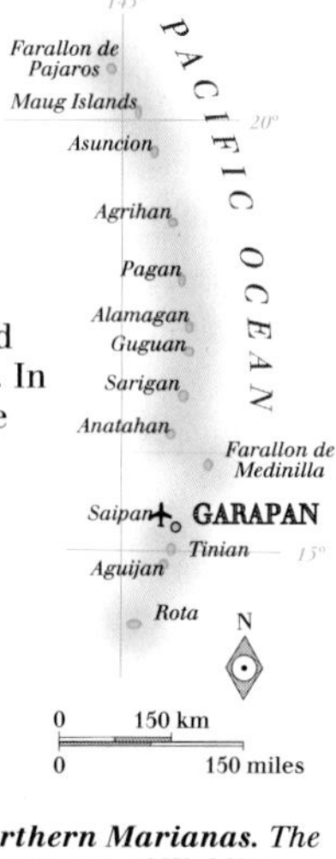

Rota, Northern Marianas. The limestone outcrop of Wedding Cake Mountain overlooks the small village of Songsong.

LAND HEIGHT above Sea Level 200m/656ft 500m/1640ft 1000m/3281ft 1500m/4572ft above 2000m/6562ft

PALAU

STATUS: Former US-administered UN trust territory **CLAIMED:** 1947
CAPITAL: Koror **POPULATION:** 16,386 **DENSITY:** 83 per sq. mile

THE PALAU archipelago, a group of over 200 islands, eight of which are inhabited, was the last remaining UN trust territory in the Pacific administered by the USA, until 1994. The previous year, after eight referenda, the Palauan people voted for independent statehood in free association with the USA. This compact, which had been held up by a local ban on the disposal of nuclear, chemical and biological weapons, was enacted in October 1994. The economy operates on a subsistence level, the principal crops being coconuts and cassava. Revenue from fishing licenses and tourism provide Palau with foreign currency. With a warm, though rainy, climate and outstanding coastlines, the tourism potential of Palau is considerable.

However, the islands' isolation and lack of facilities pose considerable problems for further tourism development.

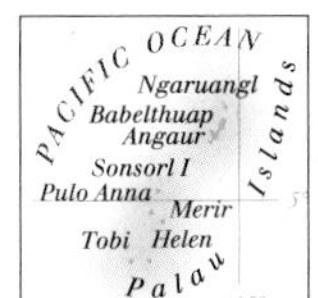

PARACEL ISLANDS

STATUS: Disputed **CLAIMED:** Not applicable
CAPITAL: Woody Island **POPN:** Unknown **DENSITY:** Unknown

OCCUPIED BY CHINESE FORCES, but also claimed by Taiwan and Vietnam, the Paracel Islands are a small collection of coral atolls, situated some 250 miles east of Vietnam, in the South China Sea. Subject to frequent typhoons and with a tropical climate, the Paracels are at the center of a regional dispute over the vast reserves of oil and natural gas that are believed to lie beneath their territorial waters. China has built port facilities and an airport on Woody Island to support its claim.

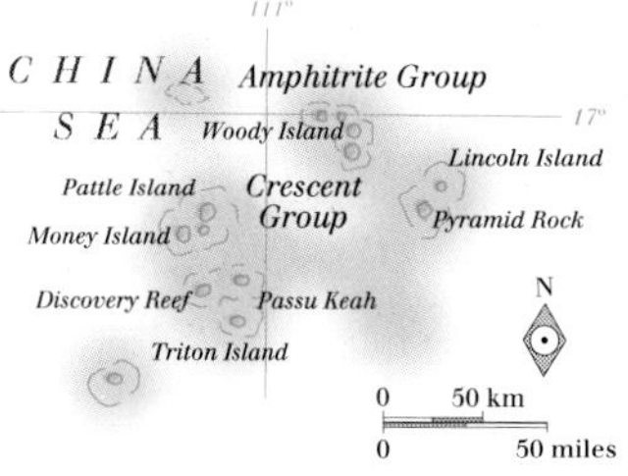

PALMYRA ATOLL

STATUS: Unincorporated territory of the USA **CLAIMED:** 1898
CAPITAL: None **POPULATION:** None

A PRIVATELY OWNED, uninhabited collection of 50 islets, Palmyra Atoll is situated some 1,000 miles southwest of Hawaii. Administered by the USA since 1898, the atoll is covered in dense vegetation, including coconut palms, which have prospered in its hot and humid climate. In 1990, a Hawaiian property developer took out a 75-year lease on Palmyra from its owners, the Fullard-Leo brothers. Plans exist to turn the atoll into a tourist and residential complex, which will promote a "get away from it all" image.

PITCAIRN ISLANDS

STATUS: British dependent territory **CLAIMED:** 1887
CAPITAL: Adamstown **POPULATION:** 52 **DENSITY:** 31 per sq. mile

PITCAIRN, a group of volcanic South Pacific islands, is Britain's most isolated dependency. Pitcairn Island provided the last refuge for the *HMS Bounty* mutineers. Emigration continues to be a major problem for the Pitcairners, who depend on regular airdrops from New Zealand and periodic visits by supply vessels. The economy operates by barter, fishing and subsistence farming. Postage stamp sales provide foreign currency earnings. Mineral exploitation could boost the economy in the future.

PUERTO RICO

STATUS: Commonwealth territory of the USA **CLAIMED:** 1898
CAPITAL: San Juan **POPN:** 3.5 million **DENSITY:** 1,026 per sq. mile

THE MOST POPULOUS of the US overseas territories, Puerto Rico lies in the Caribbean between the Dominican Republic and the Virgin Islands. The island, which is split by a central mountain range, has a tropical climate that attracts growing numbers of tourists. In 1993, the population voted by a narrow majority to maintain the current compromise between statehood and independence. The result was seen as a personal blow to governor Pedro Rossello, who campaigned to make Puerto Rico the USA's 51st state. The population has one of the highest living standards in the region. Tax incentives, cheap labor and its role as an export processing zone have encouraged many businesses to the the island. As a result, industries – like electronics and petrochemicals – have overtaken agriculture as the major economic activity.

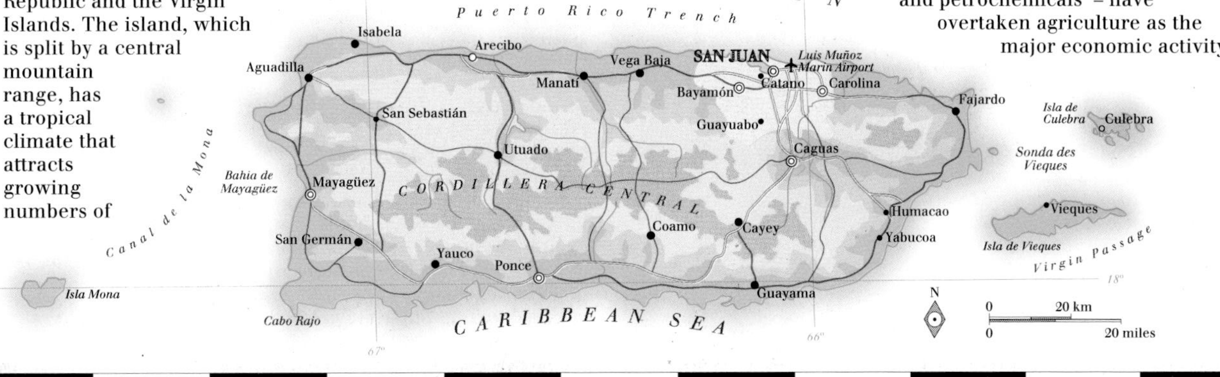

POPULATION ○ under 5000 ● under 10 000 ● over 10 000 ○ over 50 000 ◎ over 100 000 Urban areas AIRPORTS International Local

RÉUNION

STATUS: French overseas department **CLAIMED:** 1638
CAPITAL: Saint-Denis **POPULATION:** 597,828 **DENSITY:** 616 per sq. mile

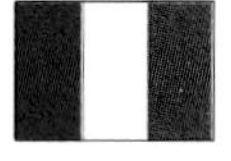

THE LARGE VOLCANIC island of Réunion, 500 miles east of Madagascar, provides France with an important strategic presence – and a large military base – in the Indian Ocean. Its mountainous interior has forced the majority of the population to live along the coast. Socioeconomic differences between the poorer black community and the wealthier Indian and European groups raised ethnic tensions in the past, resulting in severe rioting in 1991. The French government responded with a series of measures, applicable to all overseas *départements*, to raise economic and social conditions to those of France itself. Réunion's main crop is sugarcane.

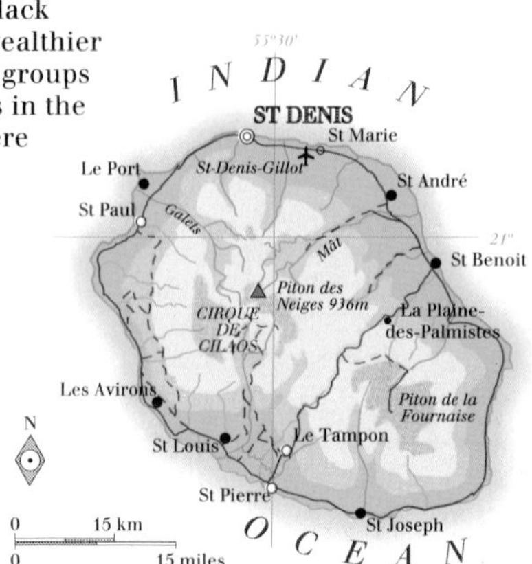

ST. PIERRE & MIQUELON

STATUS: French territorial collectivity **CLAIMED:** 1604
CAPITAL: St. Pierre **POPULATION:** 6,392 **DENSITY:** 68 per sq. mile

ST. PIERRE & Miquelon is a group of barren islands, just off the south coast of Newfoundland, Canada. The islands are surrounded by some of the world's richest fishing grounds. Their inhabitants have traditionally earned a living from fishing, and servicing foreign trawler fleets, off the coast. A long-running and sometimes bitter dispute between Canada and France over fishing and mineral rights was settled in 1992. The ruling, which was generally deemed to be in Canada's favor, has led the French authorities to diversify the economy by developing port facilities and encouraging tourism.

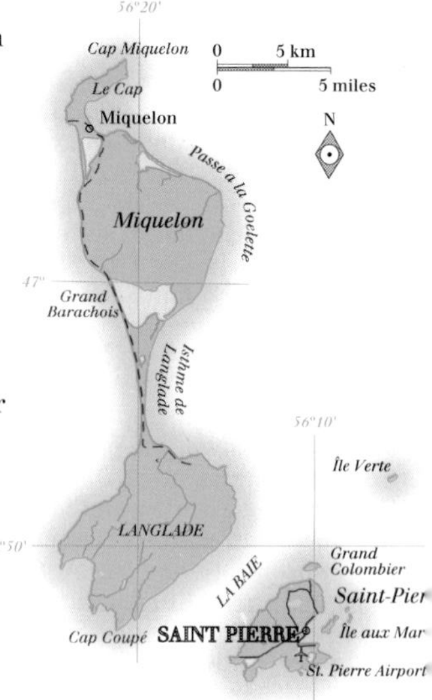

ST. HELENA & DEPENDENCIES

STATUS: British dependent territory **CLAIMED:** 1673
CAPITAL: Jamestown **POPN:** 7,000 (est) **DENSITY:** 57 per sq. mile

TOGETHER, the islands of St. Helena, Tristan da Cunha and Ascension form Britain's main dependency in the South Atlantic. St. Helena, the principal island, is the last remaining dependency to need budgetary aid from the UK. The island's main economic activities, fishing, livestock farming – and the sale of handicrafts – cannot support the population. As a result, underemployment is a major problem on St. Helena. Opportunities seem to be better on its dependencies and many St. Helenians have been forced to seek work on Ascension Island. Some were also employed building Mount Pleasant Airport on the Falklands. No resident population is allowed on Ascension Island, which operates as a military base and communications center. It is an integral part of the air-bridge supplying the Falklands. Tristan da Cunha, a volcanic island 1,240 miles to the south of St. Helena, is inhabited by a small, closely knit farming community.

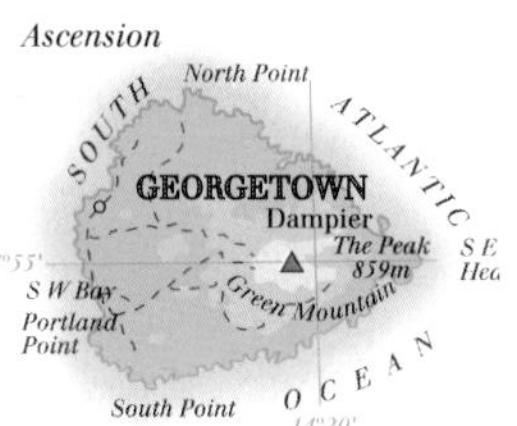

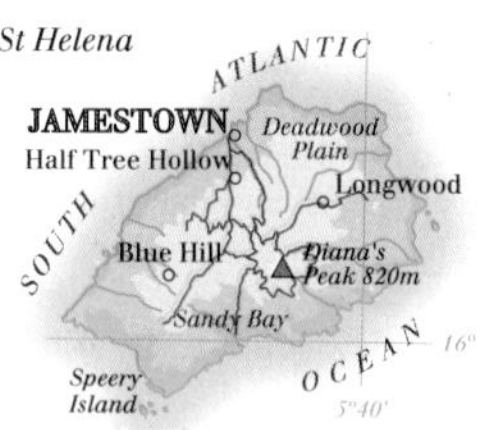

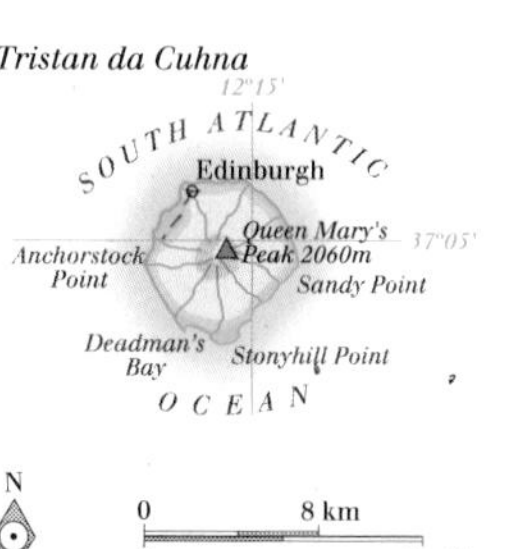

SOUTH GEORGIA & SOUTH SANDWICH ISLANDS

STATUS: British dependent territory **CLAIMED:** 1775
CAPITAL: Grytviken **POPULATION:** Unknown

THE SOUTH Atlantic island of South Georgia, briefly occupied by Argentine forces during the Falklands War, has a small UK garrison at Grytviken and a British Antarctic Survey base. The volcanic South Sandwich Islands, 465 miles to the southeast, are uninhabited. The territory is increasingly visited by eco-tourists, attracted by the abundant wildlife.

SPRATLY ISLANDS

STATUS: Disputed **CLAIMED:** Not applicable
CAPITAL: None **POPULATION:** Unknown

SCATTERED across a large area of the South China Sea, the reefs, islands and atolls that make up the Spratly Islands have become one of Southeast Asia's most serious security issues. Claimed, all or in part, by China, Taiwan, Vietnam, Brunei, Malaysia and the Philippines, 44 of the larger islands now have garrisons from some of the claimant nations. The reasons for this interest, and the occasional skirmishes, are twofold. Strategically, the islands control some of the world's most important shipping lanes. In addition, surveys suggest that some of the largest oil and gas reserves yet found lie in the Spratlys' territorial waters.

SVALBARD

STATUS: Norwegian dependency **CLAIMED:** 1920
CAPITAL: Longyearbyen **POPN:** 3,116 **DENSITY:** 0.13 per sq. mile

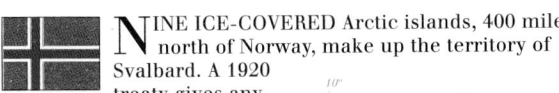

NINE ICE-COVERED Arctic islands, 400 miles north of Norway, make up the territory of Svalbard. A 1920 treaty gives any country the right to exploit Svalbard's mineral resources. Today's population, mostly Norwegian and Russian coal miners, lives in harsh conditions. However, falling coal reserves and the end of the Cold War have begun to test Norway's strong attachment to the islands.

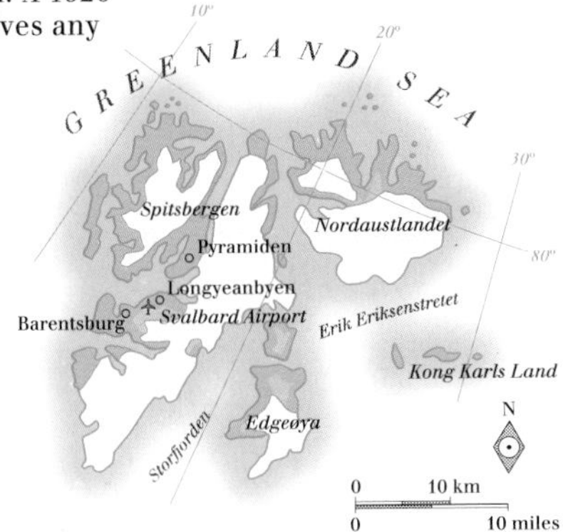

TOKELAU

STATUS: New Zealand dependent territory **CLAIMED:** 1926
CAPITAL: None **POPULATION:** 1,760 **DENSITY:** 433 per sq. mile

ACCORDING to a 1989 UN report, this South Pacific island will disappear under the sea in the 21st century unless action is taken to stop global warming. In 1990, in another blow for the islanders, a cyclone destroyed crops and wrecked Tokelau's infrastructure. The New Zealand government has, however, made efforts to spur development. A tuna cannery and the sale of fishing licenses has raised revenue, and a catamaran link between the atolls has increased the islands' tourist potential. However, its small size and continued economic weakness still makes independence unlikely.

TURKS & CAICOS ISLANDS

STATUS: British dependent territory **CLAIMED:** 1766
CAPITAL: Cockburn Town **POPN:** 12,350 **DENSITY:** 75 per sq. mile

SITUATED 25 miles south of the Bahamas, the Turks and Caicos Islands is a group of 30 low-lying islands, eight of which are inhabited. Services dominate the economy, particularly tourism and offshore banking. Many skilled islanders seek work in the Bahamas. Haitian refugees form the poorest segment of society.

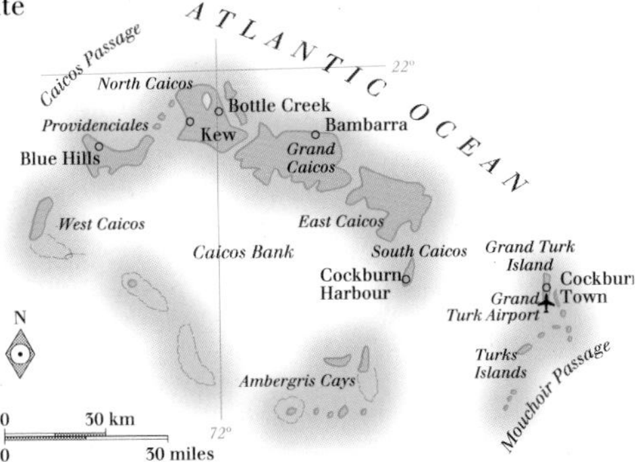

VIRGIN ISLANDS (US)

STATUS: Unincorporated territory of the USA **CLAIMED:** 1917
CAPITAL: Charlotte Amalie **POPN:** 101,809 **DENSITY:** 743 per sq. mile

THE US VIRGIN Islands are a collection of 53 volcanic islands, just to the east of Puerto Rico. Most of the population – a mix of African and European ethnic groups – live on the main islands of St. John, St. Thomas and St. Croix. Tourism is the principal industry, although St. Croix has also used federal aid to develop industry. It has one of the world's largest oil refineries.

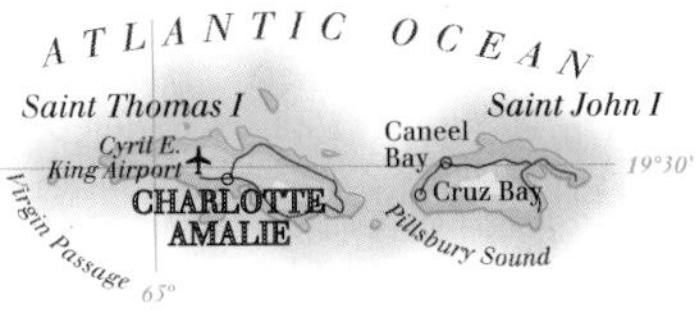

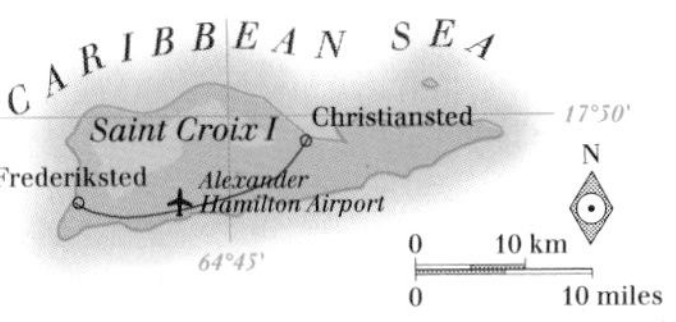

St. Thomas, US Virgin Islands, is a major stop-off for Caribbean cruise ships. Tourists are attracted by the island's duty-free shopping.

WAKE ISLAND

STATUS: Unincorporated territory of the USA **CLAIMED:** 1898
CAPITAL: None **POPULATION:** 381 **DENSITY:** 153 per sq. mile

FORMED BY the rim of an extinct underwater volcano, Wake Island's strategic importance has declined since the end of the Vietnam War. It is now used as an emergency airstrip for trans-Pacific flights, and as a stopover for cargo planes.

WALLIS & FUTUNA

STATUS: French overseas territory **CLAIMED:** 1842
CAPITAL: Mata Uta **POPULATION:** 13,705 **DENSITY:** 130 per sq. mile

UNLIKE FRANCE'S other overseas territories in the South Pacific, the inhabitants of Wallis and Futuna have little desire for greater autonomy. The islands' subsistence economy produces a variety of tropical crops, while expatriate remittances and the sale of licenses to Japanese and Korean fishing fleets provide foreign exchange. Futuna was hit by an earthquake in 1993.

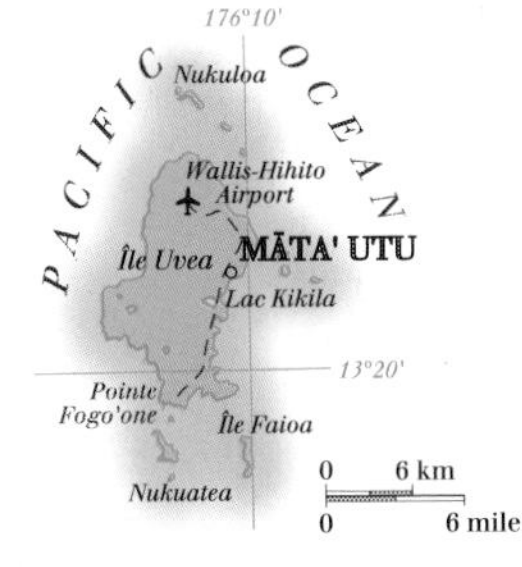

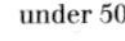

3

GLOBAL ISSUES

WORLD POPULATION
HUNGER & DISEASE
THE WORLD ECONOMY
ETHNICITY AND THE NATION STATE
THE WORLD ENVIRONMENT
GLOBAL COMMUNICATIONS
SECURITY & DEFENSE
GLOBAL TOURISM
THE FINAL FRONTIERS

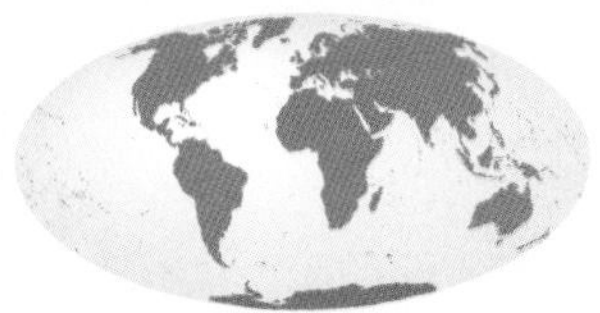

WORLD POPULATION

WORLD POPULATION, 5.4 billion people in 1992, is projected to rise to 8-10 billion people by 2025. It is estimated that population will stabilize at around 8-12 billion people after 2050. Despite a decline in total world fertility, population will increase in countries that are in the process of industrialization. There is little indication that fertility is set to decline in the least developed countries, presently comprising some 0.5 billion people. These densely populated regions of the world lack the infrastructure and resources needed to cope with growing populations. On the other hand, birth rates in the industrialized countries of Europe, in Japan and in the USA, have fallen to the point where they fail to replace deaths.

WORLD POPULATION DISTRIBUTION

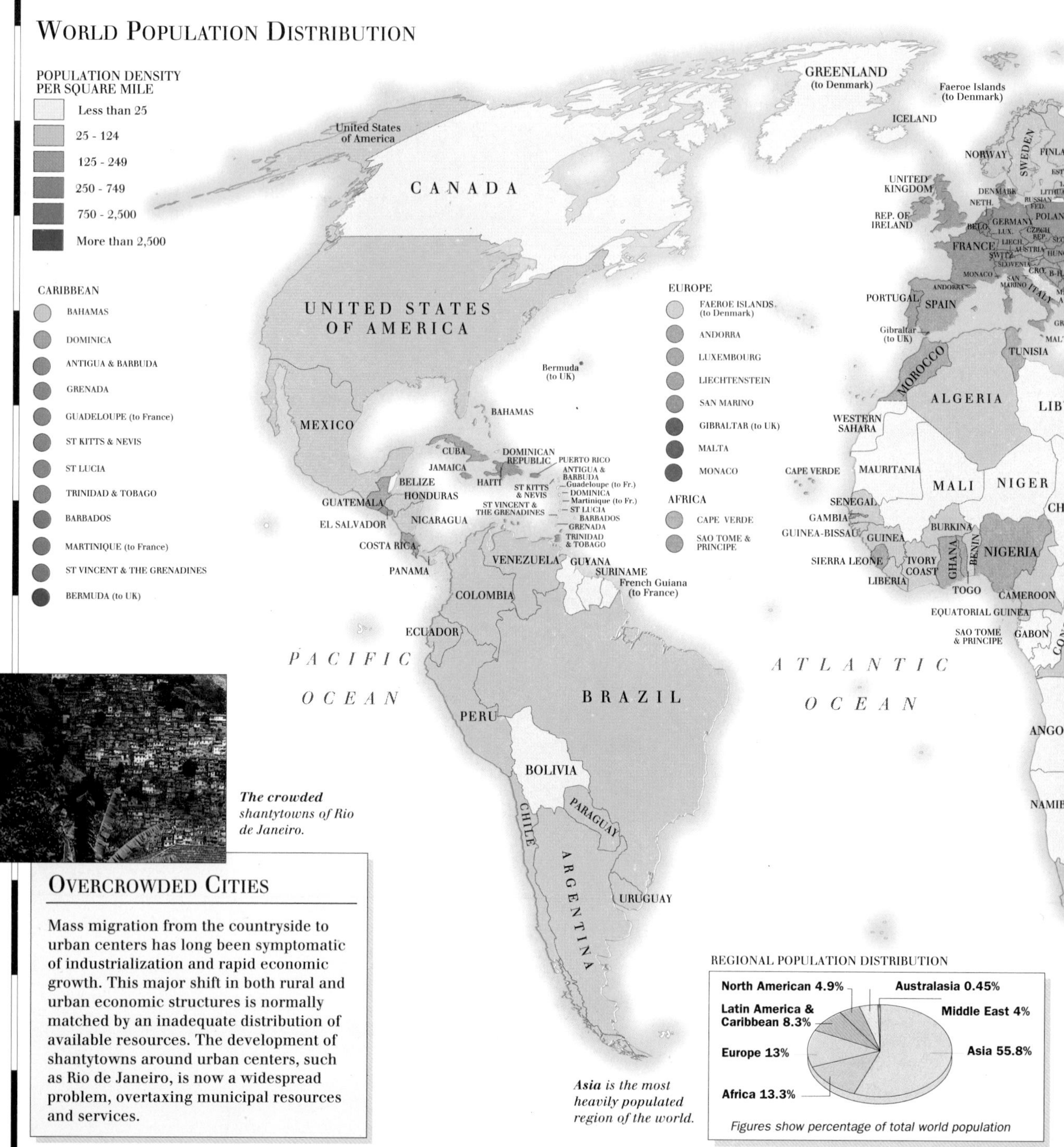

The crowded shantytowns of Rio de Janeiro.

OVERCROWDED CITIES

Mass migration from the countryside to urban centers has long been symptomatic of industrialization and rapid economic growth. This major shift in both rural and urban economic structures is normally matched by an inadequate distribution of available resources. The development of shantytowns around urban centers, such as Rio de Janeiro, is now a widespread problem, overtaxing municipal resources and services.

Asia is the most heavily populated region of the world.

The intensively farmed *rural landscape of the Netherlands.*

The Netherlands

One of the most densely populated countries of Europe, the Netherlands also remains one of the wealthiest. Over the centuries, a balance between resources and population has been achieved which allows for a sustainable growth of the economy, of individual wealth and of living conditions. The pressure of a large population on limited quantities of land has led to massive land reclamation projects. From as early as the 16th century, land has been taken back from the sea – initially for agriculture, but also today for industrial plant and residential development.

FERTILITY RATES

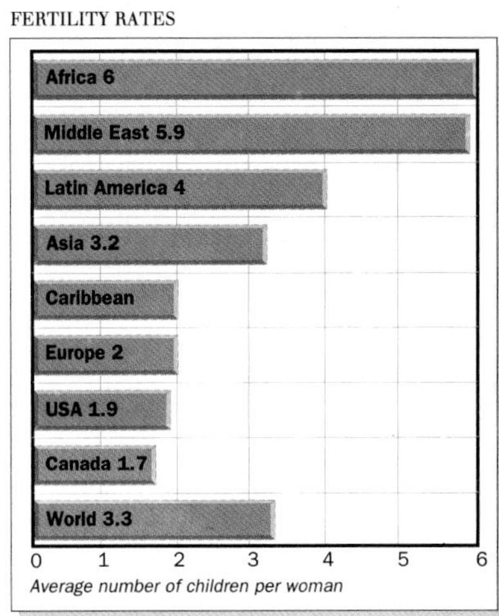

Fertility *has declined throughout the industrialized world and is highest in Africa.*

PACIFIC OCEAN
- FIJI
- SOLOMON ISLANDS
- VANUATU
- WESTERN SAMOA
- KIRIBATI
- MICRONESIA
- TONGA
- NAURU

MIDDLE EAST
- BAHRAIN

INDIAN OCEAN
- COMOROS
- SEYCHELLES
- MALDIVES
- MAURITIUS

ASIA
- MACAO (to Portugal)
- HONG KONG (to UK)
- SINGAPORE

A nomadic *goatherder in northwest Somalia.*

Pastoral Nomadism

Traditional ways of life, in which a balance between population numbers and natural resources had achieved equilibrium, are now under threat. Since the mid-1980s a succession of droughts in the Sahel and civil wars in Sudan, Ethiopia, Eritrea and Somalia have disrupted the traditional balance between population and resources in this region.

HUNGER AND DISEASE

THE RECENT PAST has seen an unparalleled increase in food production and availability. However, underlying global success there is marked regional inequality; drought, conflict and natural catastrophes can have disastrous effects on the ability of people to feed themselves. Current estimates are that nearly 800 million people, almost all in the developing countries, do not have enough food to meet their basic nutritional needs. A third of children in developing countries suffer growth faltering, mainly because of under-nutrition. Undernourished children are handicapped in their intellectual development, fall ill more easily and have lower physical productivity as adults.

WORLD INFANT MORTALITY

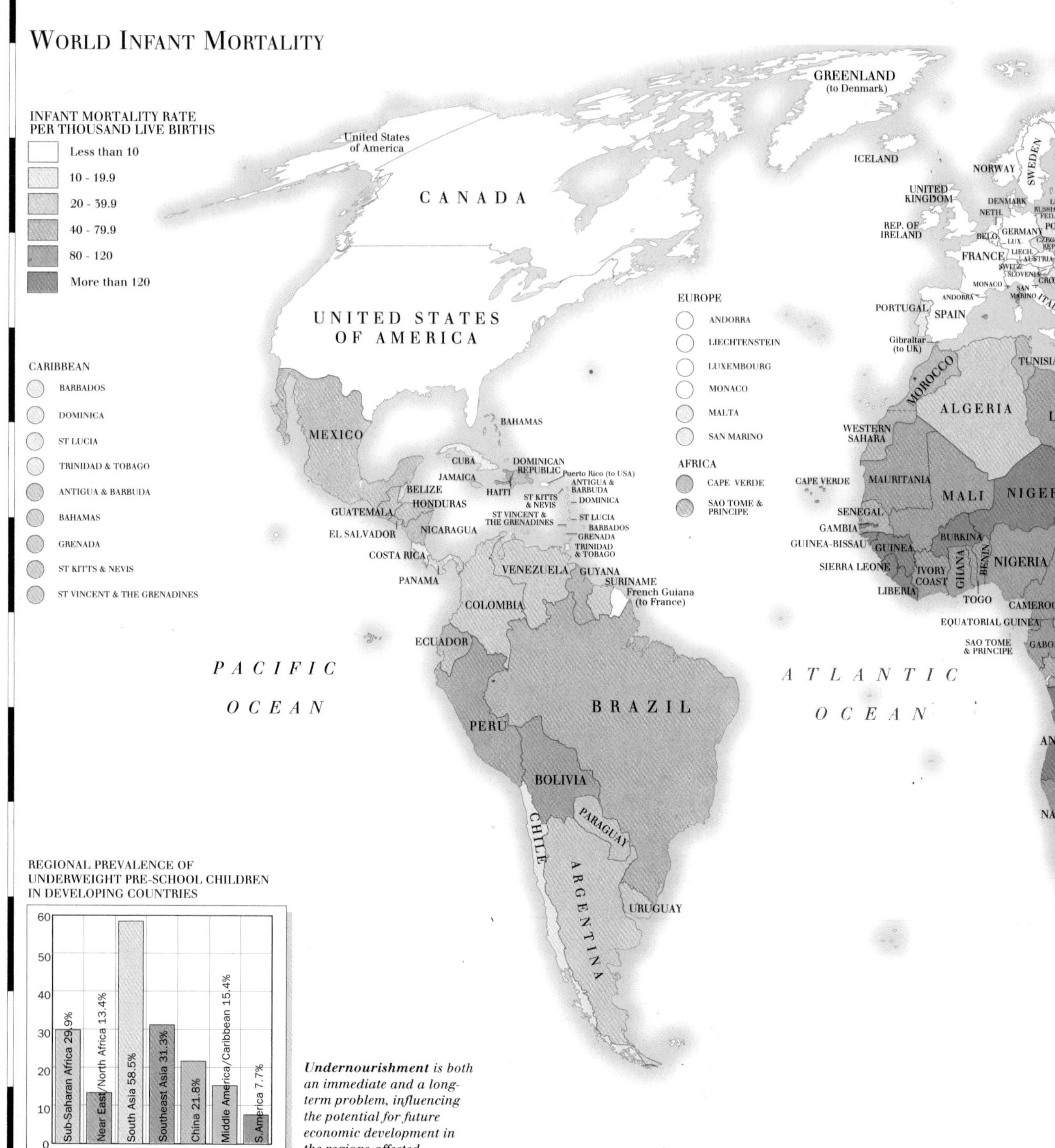

Undernourishment is both an immediate and a long-term problem, influencing the potential for future economic development in the regions affected.

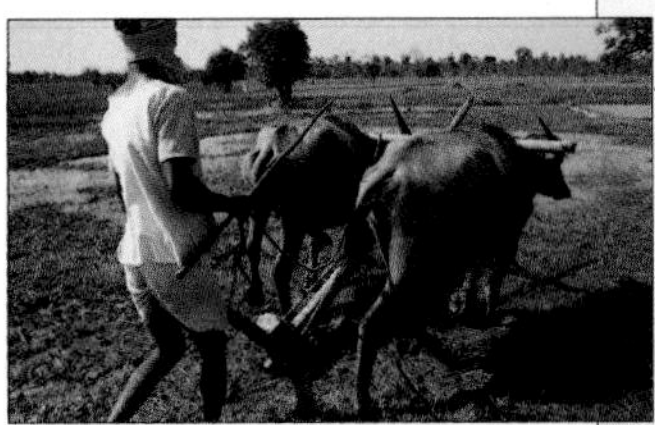

Poor soil, inadequate technology, *lack of water control and infestation by pests are all problems afflicting farmers on marginal land in Asia.*

POVERTY

Rural poverty, especially in Asia and Africa, is associated with hunger and malnutrition. People who are reduced to subsistence farming on unproductive land are most at risk. Their children are more likely to be undernourished, and are prone to infections such as dysentery and respiratory and parasitic diseases. Improving the food supply is not the only solution: better access to health services, improved health education and sanitation, the promotion of breast feeding and immunization are all important priorities.

CONFLICT

Conflict is increasingly a cause of hunger. In 1993-1994, approximately 80% of food aid worldwide was being directed to relieve distress in man-made rather than natural disasters – in Somalia, Angola, Liberia, southern Sudan, Rwanda, Afghanistan and Cambodia. Breakdown of civil order and infrastructure in war zones makes food aid distribution hazardous and inadequate. Refugees are forced to become landless – cultivated land is neglected indefinitely, compounding the difficulties of recovery.

The distribution *of food to refugees in war zones is often disrupted by the fighting. Food frequently disappears onto the black market, never reaching the starving.*

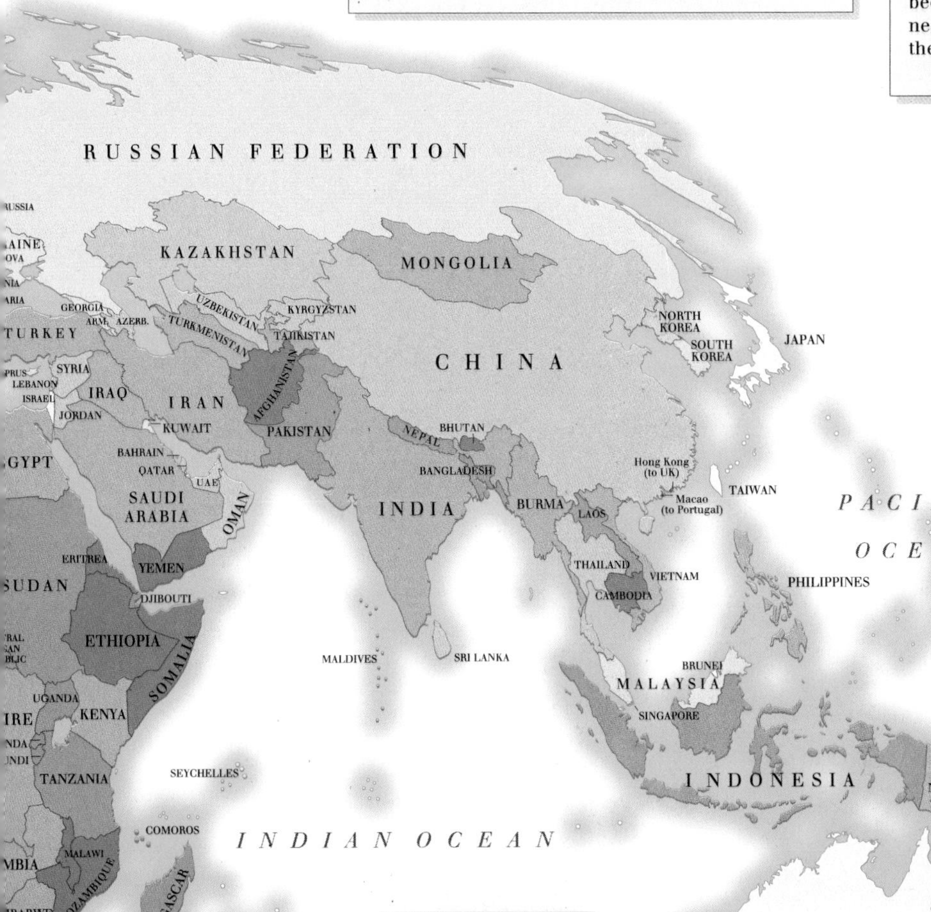

RUSSIAN FEDERATION
KAZAKHSTAN
MONGOLIA
GEORGIA
ARM.
AZERB.
UZBEKISTAN
KYRGYZSTAN
TURKMENISTAN
TAJIKISTAN
TURKEY
SYRIA
LEBANON
ISRAEL
IRAQ
JORDAN
IRAN
AFGHANISTAN
KUWAIT
PAKISTAN
CHINA
NORTH KOREA
SOUTH KOREA
JAPAN
NEPAL
BHUTAN
BAHRAIN
QATAR
UAE
BANGLADESH
SAUDI ARABIA
OMAN
INDIA
BURMA
LAOS
Hong Kong (to UK)
Macao (to Portugal)
TAIWAN
YEMEN
ERITREA
SUDAN
DJIBOUTI
ETHIOPIA
SOMALIA
THAILAND
VIETNAM
CAMBODIA
PHILIPPINES
PACIFIC OCEAN
MALDIVES
SRI LANKA
BRUNEI
MALAYSIA
SINGAPORE
UGANDA
KENYA
TANZANIA
SEYCHELLES
INDONESIA
PAPUA NEW GUINEA
SOLOMON IS
COMOROS
INDIAN OCEAN
MALAWI
MOZAMBIQUE
MADAGASCAR
MAURITIUS
SWAZILAND
LESOTHO
AUSTRALIA
New Caledonia (to France)
NEW ZEALAND

PACIFIC OCEAN
- FIJI
- MICRONESIA
- KIRIBATI
- NAURU
- SOLOMON ISLANDS
- TONGA
- VANUATU
- WESTERN SAMOA

MIDDLE EAST
- BAHRAIN

INDIAN OCEAN
- SEYCHELLES
- MAURITIUS
- MALDIVES
- COMOROS

ASIA
- HONG KONG (U K)
- SINGAPORE

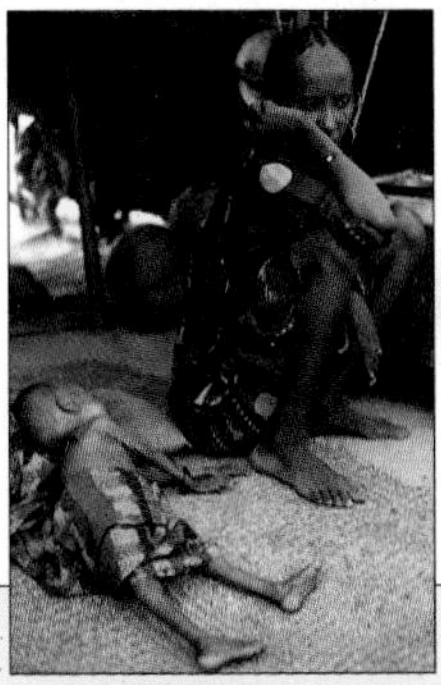

A combination *of war and famine in Ethiopia has brought starvation to catastrophic levels.*

STARVATION IN AFRICA

Although food production in Africa has actually increased since the 1970s, per capita food production has fallen, and dependence on food imports and foreign aid has increased. In 1992, more than 40 million Africans were faced with the threat of famine, and nearly half of sub-Saharan Africa's population is facing food shortages.

THE WORLD ECONOMY

THE PATTERN OF THE GLOBAL ECONOMY frequently relates to an underlying equation, the relationship between population and available resources. Japan, for example, has a much "bigger" economy than the former Soviet Union, or India or Latin America as a whole. Such imbalances occur because economies differ enormously in their living standards, the productivity of their agriculture and in the value of their markets. A close comparison of economic performance can be measured on a Purchasing Power Parity (PPP) basis, which tells us how much is produced and consumed in different countries when their prices are compared as exactly as possible.

NATIONAL ECONOMIC PERFORMANCE

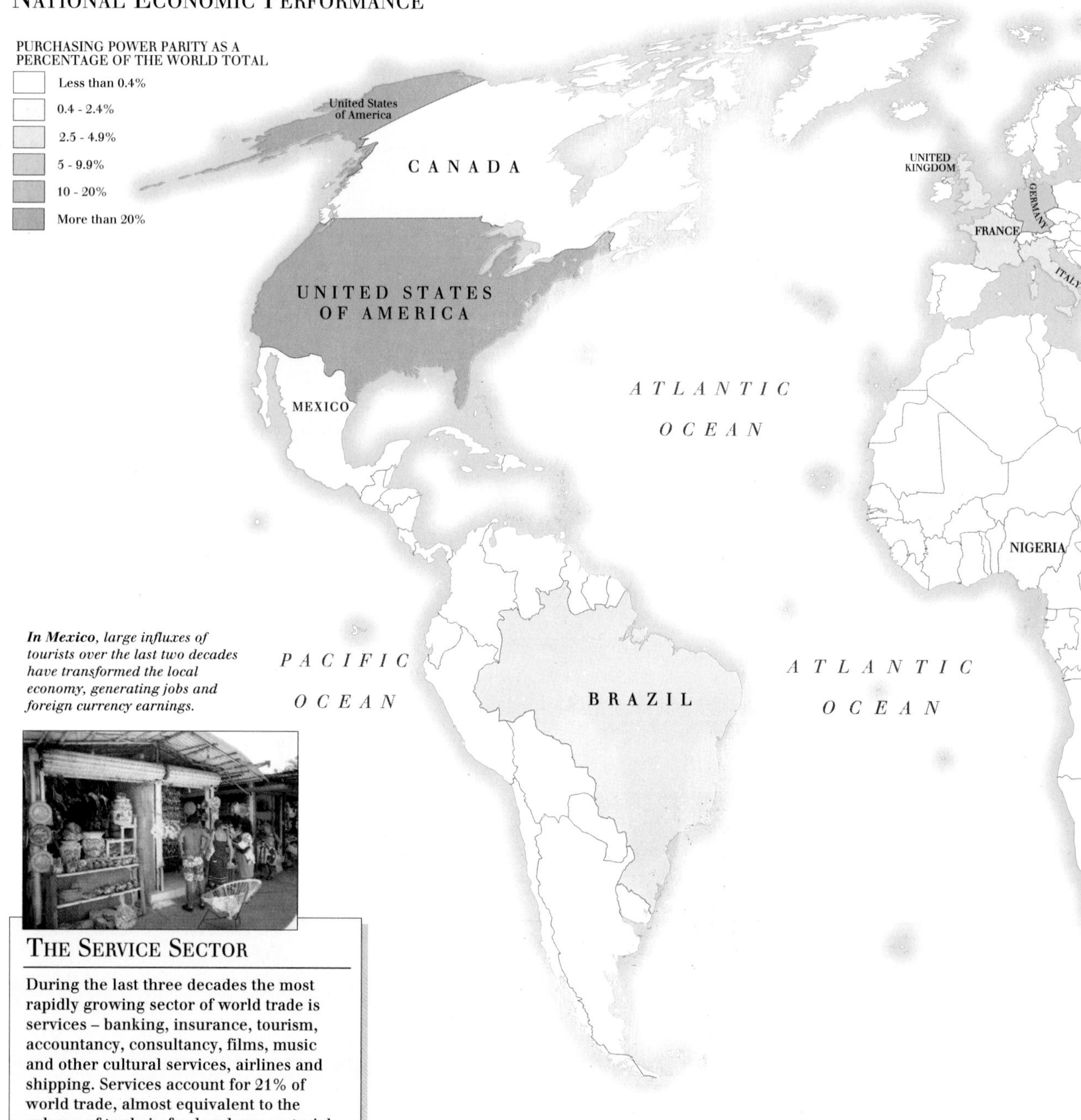

In Mexico, large influxes of tourists over the last two decades have transformed the local economy, generating jobs and foreign currency earnings.

THE SERVICE SECTOR

During the last three decades the most rapidly growing sector of world trade is services – banking, insurance, tourism, accountancy, consultancy, films, music and other cultural services, airlines and shipping. Services account for 21% of world trade, almost equivalent to the volume of trade in food and raw materials.

WORLD TRADE

For most of the post-war period, trade has expanded more rapidly than the world economy – in 1991 global import trade alone accounted for $400 billion. Trade has acted as a dynamic influence in economics, helping to pull up growth. In 1992, manufactures made up around 57% of world trade, raw materials and food 22% and services 21%. Trade takes place predominantly between the rich countries of northern Europe, Japan and the USA.

***Baltimore** is a container port where large quantities of cargo are shipped to worldwide markets. Seaborne trade accounts for more than 80% of the total volume of world trade.*

PACIFIC RIM

The "Four Dragons" of the Pacific Rim – South Korea, Taiwan, Hong Kong and Singapore – are high-growth areas, forging ahead with rapid export-led industrialization. Growth rates in the region over the last three decades have consistently been double or triple those of the USA or Western Europe. Low labor costs, stable governments and encouragement of foreign investment have all contributed to this spectacular growth.

***South Korea** has become a major industrial power, specializing in shipbuilding, car manufacture, and high technology – computers and communications equipment.*

RUSSIAN FEDERATION
INE
UZBEKISTAN
URKEY
CHINA
SOUTH KOREA
JAPAN
IRAN
PACIFIC OCEAN
YPT
SAUDI ARABIA
Hong Kong (to UK)
TAIWAN
INDIA
THAILAND
SINGAPORE
INDONESIA
INDIAN OCEAN
AUSTRALIA

THE WORLD'S TOP EXPORTERS 1992

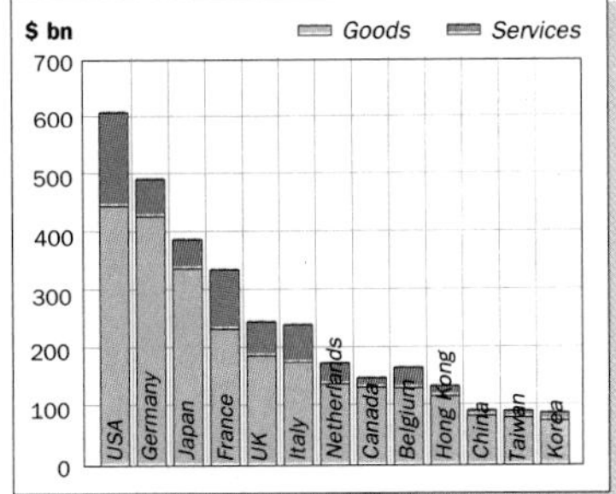

***Manufactured goods** still dominate the export market, but service industries account for an increasingly large sector in the developed world.*

Ethnicity and the Nation State

With the end of the Cold War, long-standing alliances and conflicts based on ideological differences – ideas of "left" and "right" – have disappeared into the background. However, others based on some form of cultural identity or ethnicity, whether it is derived from language, religion, color, clan, tribe or cultural tradition, have seemingly proliferated. Very few nation states can claim to have a homogenous identity. Almost all possess minorities. In some cases, alienation between a minority of the population and the majority may lead to the breakup of a nation state. In others, a sense of cultural identity spans several countries: this is known as "pan-ethnicity."

Nations Within Nations

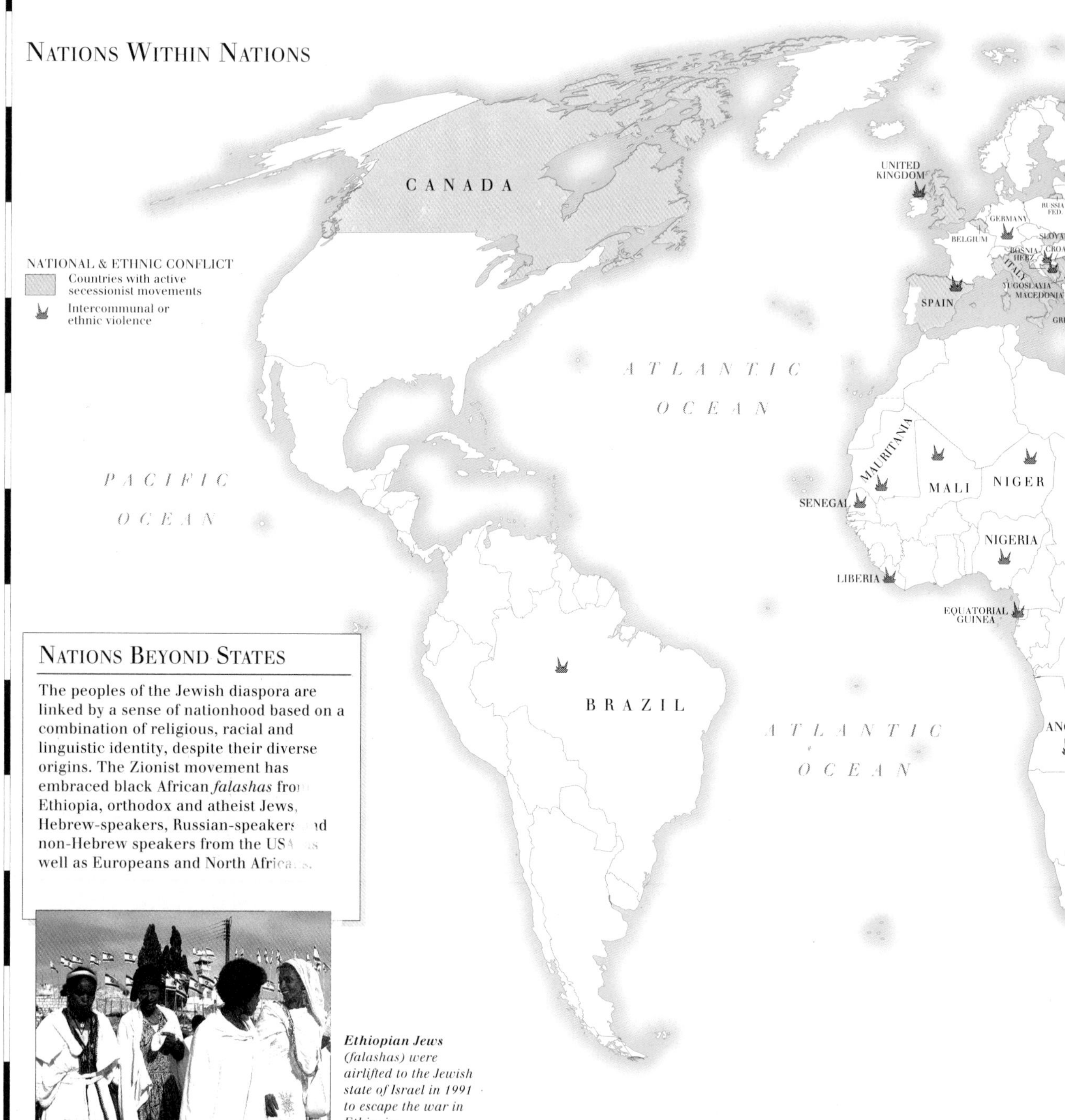

Nations Beyond States

The peoples of the Jewish diaspora are linked by a sense of nationhood based on a combination of religious, racial and linguistic identity, despite their diverse origins. The Zionist movement has embraced black African *falashas* from Ethiopia, orthodox and atheist Jews, Hebrew-speakers, Russian-speakers and non-Hebrew speakers from the USA as well as Europeans and North Africans.

Ethiopian Jews *(falashas) were airlifted to the Jewish state of Israel in 1991 to escape the war in Ethiopia.*

Ulster protestants *commemorate the English victory against the Irish in 1690. The "marching season" is often a trigger for sectarian violence.*

RELIGIOUS LOYALTIES

Religion can be a politically unifying force, as well as a source of friction with other religions and denominations. In the Irish Republic, Catholics make up the majority of the population, while Protestants dominate in Ulster. More than in any other country in western Europe, people's daily lives are shaped by their religion, and an acute sense of the roots of their differences has resulted in continuing inter-communal conflict.

***Political posters** in northern Spain keep the issue of Basque separatism high on the political agenda. So far, the Spanish government has failed to deal effectively with the question.*

PAN-ETHNICITY

Sometimes, groups that straddle different countries feel a sense of nationhood, which cannot yet be realized in a nation state. There are many examples of ethnic minorities trying to secede, in many cases drawing sustenance from co-religionists or ethnic brethren across borders. In Europe, for example, the Basque people hope for a pan-ethnic Basque state within a federal EU. In West Asia, both the Kurds and the Palestinians aspire to national sovereignty.

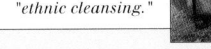

***Iraq's Marsh Arabs** have fallen victim to a campaign of "ethnic cleansing."*

ETHNIC CLEANSING

Minority ethnic groups are frequently at risk because of their religious, cultural or linguistic differences. Extreme forms of persecution, forced relocation or genocide, known as "ethnic cleansing," have recently been witnessed in Iraq, Iran, Bosnia and Rwanda.

The World Environment

Each day 50 to 100 species of plant and animal become extinct – it is now internationally recognized that conservation of the world's remaining wildlife and ecosystems is an urgent priority. In many countries, legislation is ensuring that land is protected from urbanization and agriculture – the two greatest threats to the environment. However, environmental protection legislation is much more apparent in the countries of the developed world. In the developing countries, pressure on land and resources creates more urgent priorities: environmental protection is often dependent on grants and aid from the developed world, and foreign currency-earners such as tourism take precedence over conservation.

Global Conservation

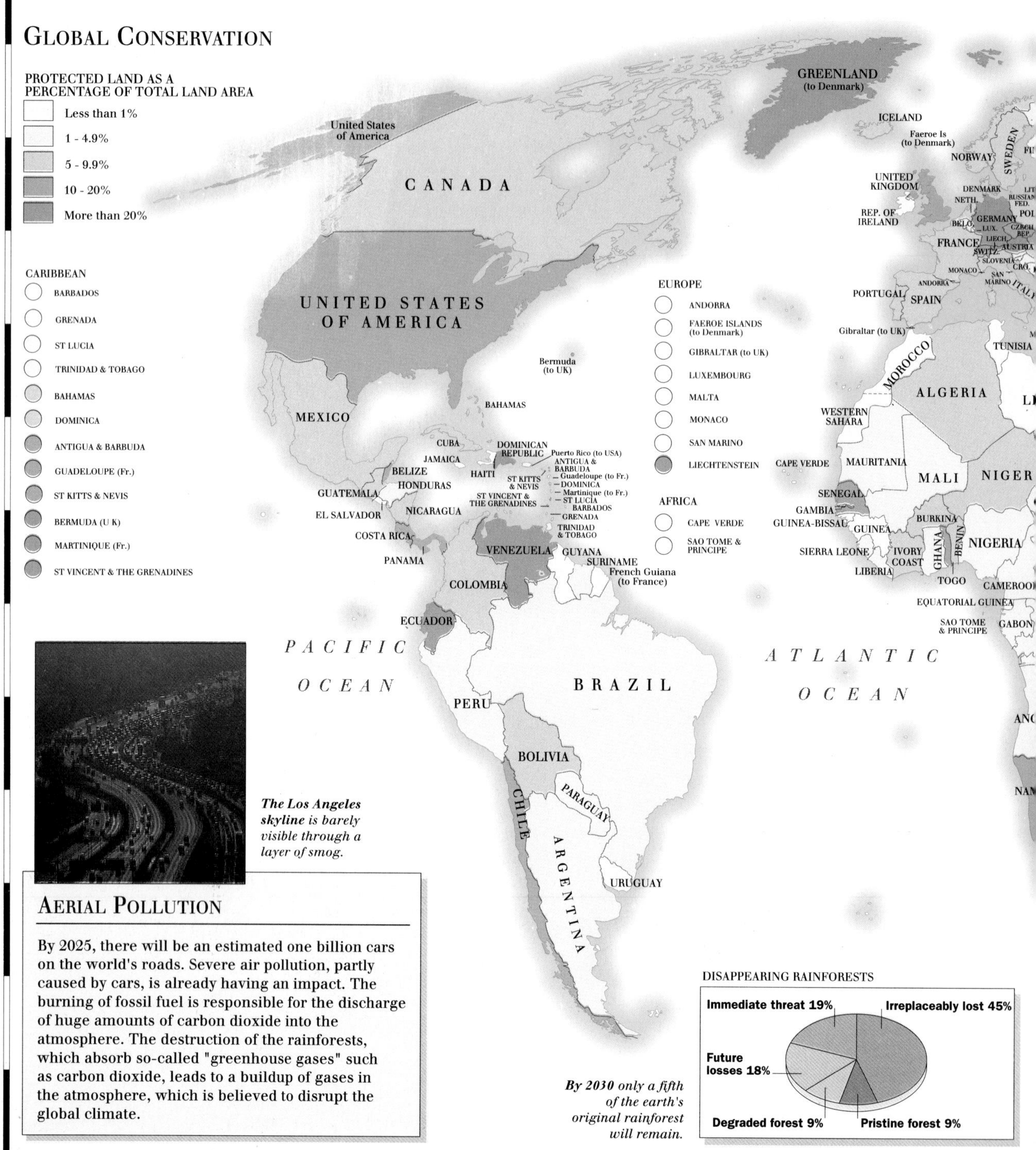

***The Los Angeles skyline** is barely visible through a layer of smog.*

Aerial Pollution

By 2025, there will be an estimated one billion cars on the world's roads. Severe air pollution, partly caused by cars, is already having an impact. The burning of fossil fuel is responsible for the discharge of huge amounts of carbon dioxide into the atmosphere. The destruction of the rainforests, which absorb so-called "greenhouse gases" such as carbon dioxide, leads to a buildup of gases in the atmosphere, which is believed to disrupt the global climate.

***By 2030** only a fifth of the earth's original rainforest will remain.*

Water Resources

Global demand for water – for industrial, agricultural and domestic use – has increased five-fold since 1950. In many parts of the world, water resources are contaminated by industrial waste and pollution, while dams and irrigation schemes transform river and floodplain ecoystems. Localized drought, spread of water-borne diseases, and contaminated drinking water are all major problems.

***The Aral Sea** has shrunk by 23,000 sq. miles as a result of schemes to irrigate the cotton fields of Uzbekistan.*

***The tropical rainforests** of Malaysia. Rainforests contain more than 20% of all the known natural species of plants and animals living on Earth.*

Rainforest

It is thought that there are some 4.5 million plant and animal species, two-thirds of which are to be found in the tropics, with an abundance living in the equatorial rainforests. This diversity of plant and animal life is increasingly threatened by the destruction of the rainforest. Commercial logging and clearing forests for agriculture, ranching and mineral exploitation are destroying the rainforest at the rate of more than 60,000 square miles each year.

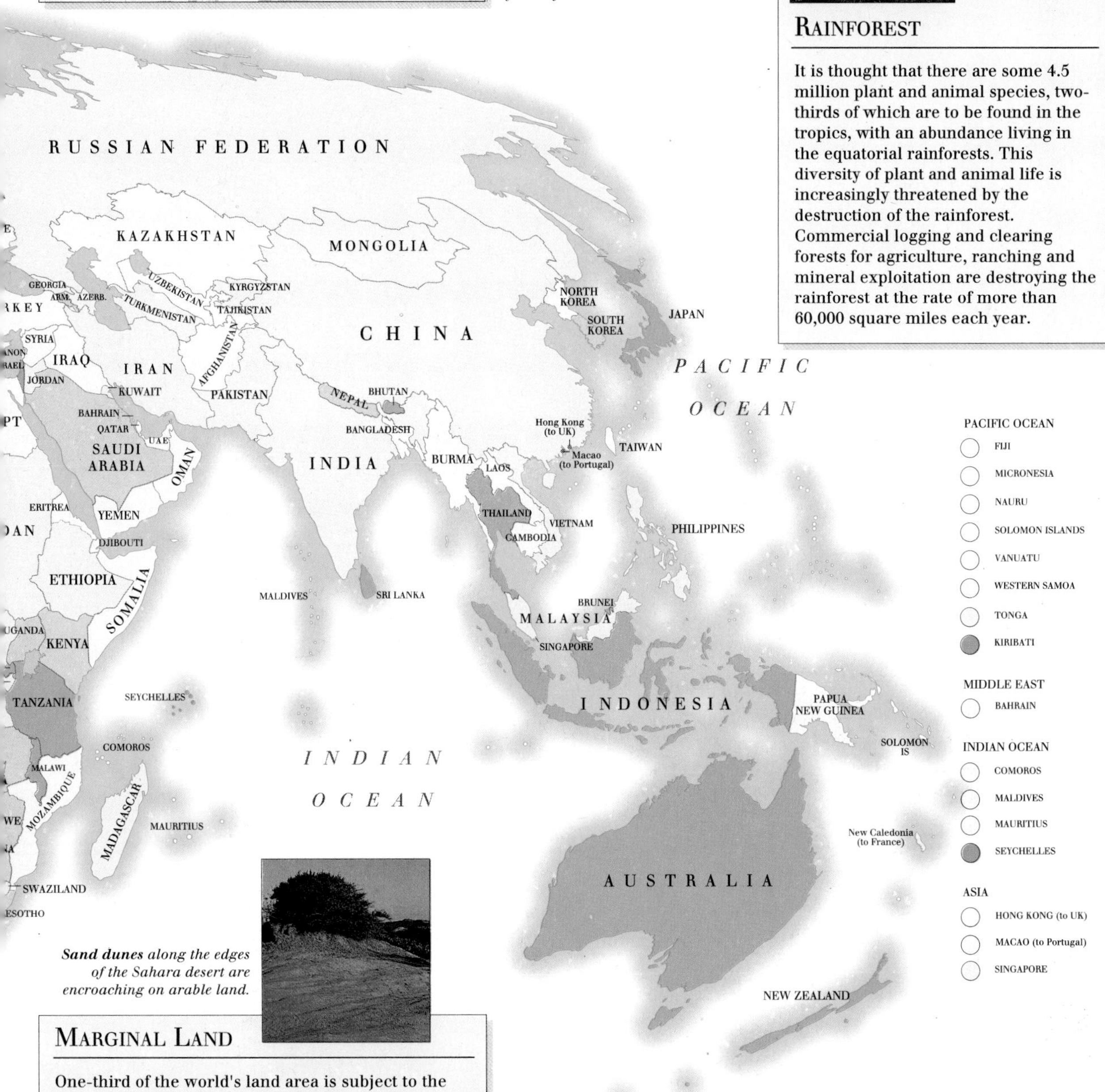

RUSSIAN FEDERATION
KAZAKHSTAN
MONGOLIA
GEORGIA
ARM.
AZERB.
UZBEKISTAN
TURKMENISTAN
KYRGYZSTAN
TAJIKISTAN
NORTH KOREA
SOUTH KOREA
JAPAN
CHINA
SYRIA
IRAQ
IRAN
AFGHANISTAN
JORDAN
KUWAIT
PAKISTAN
NEPAL
BHUTAN
BAHRAIN
QATAR
UAE
SAUDI ARABIA
OMAN
BANGLADESH
INDIA
BURMA
LAOS
Hong Kong (to UK)
Macao (to Portugal)
TAIWAN
PACIFIC OCEAN
ERITREA
YEMEN
DJIBOUTI
ETHIOPIA
SOMALIA
THAILAND
VIETNAM
CAMBODIA
PHILIPPINES
MALDIVES
SRI LANKA
BRUNEI
MALAYSIA
SINGAPORE
UGANDA
KENYA
TANZANIA
SEYCHELLES
INDONESIA
PAPUA NEW GUINEA
SOLOMON IS
COMOROS
MALAWI
MOZAMBIQUE
MADAGASCAR
MAURITIUS
INDIAN OCEAN
New Caledonia (to France)
AUSTRALIA
SWAZILAND
ESOTHO
NEW ZEALAND

PACIFIC OCEAN
- FIJI
- MICRONESIA
- NAURU
- SOLOMON ISLANDS
- VANUATU
- WESTERN SAMOA
- TONGA
- KIRIBATI

MIDDLE EAST
- BAHRAIN

INDIAN OCEAN
- COMOROS
- MALDIVES
- MAURITIUS
- SEYCHELLES

ASIA
- HONG KONG (to UK)
- MACAO (to Portugal)
- SINGAPORE

***Sand dunes** along the edges of the Sahara desert are encroaching on arable land.*

Marginal Land

One-third of the world's land area is subject to the risk of soil erosion and desertification – in the absence of other fuels, wood and charcoal burning destroys the forests, removing topsoils and hastening the encroachment of the desert. The onward march of desert can be halted by expensive tree-planting programs and better land management.

Global Communications

WHEN ASKED what had caused the collapse of communism in eastern Europe, Polish President Lech Waleşa pointed to a television set. "It all came from there," he said. Undoubtedly, the globalization of television and printed news has wrought dramatic changes in the world. In addition, a revolution in digital technology has created a truly global village.

Television viewers can now receive hundreds of channels by satellite, watch movies and the latest news, shop, book tickets and access databanks. With the help of optical fiber cables, the conduits of digital information, and increasingly compatible software, computer users can now communicate across geographical borders.

Global Satellite Television Coverage

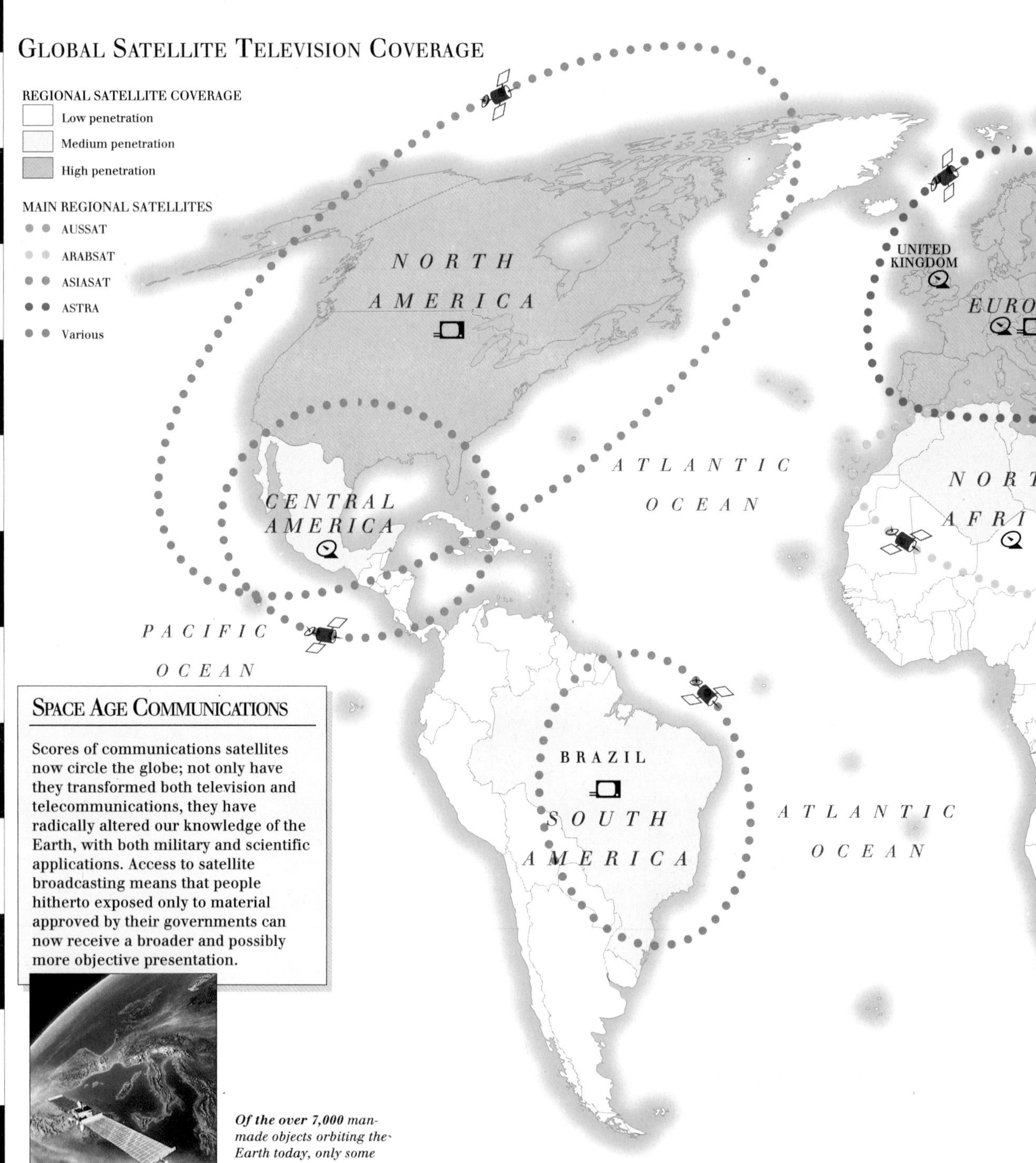

Space Age Communications

Scores of communications satellites now circle the globe; not only have they transformed both television and telecommunications, they have radically altered our knowledge of the Earth, with both military and scientific applications. Access to satellite broadcasting means that people hitherto exposed only to material approved by their governments can now receive a broader and possibly more objective presentation.

Of the over 7,000 man-made objects orbiting the Earth today, only some 500 are satellites.

A bicycle wheel on a Delhi rooftop picks up television signals. Used to makeshift technology, Indians are unwilling to pay for satellite.

GLOBAL VILLAGE

Since 1980, the number of television sets in the world nearly tripled to one billion. Multimedia empires are currently competing for the vast satellite audiences (and lucrative advertising revenues) of the developing world. While there is resistance to the endless diet of Western popular culture broadcast by satellite, which is thought to corrupt traditional values, many governments are powerless to stop the spread of satellites.

GLOBAL BREAKDOWN OF INTERNET HOSTS

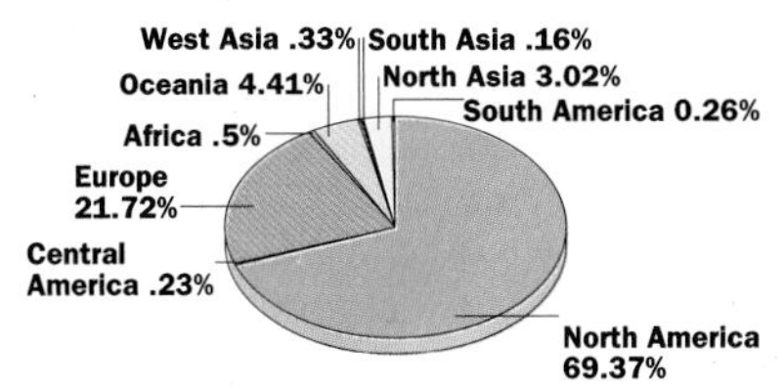

Total numbers of Internet hosts: 2.2 million

The "information highway" enables information of all kinds – textual, graphical, still and moving pictures – to be transformed into computer language and transmitted through communications channels (telephone lines, optical fibers) to a personal computer. Internet is an open access computer network with over 20 million users. A host is an exchange point at which a networked group of users may access the Internet. Some 80 countries are connected to the Internet.

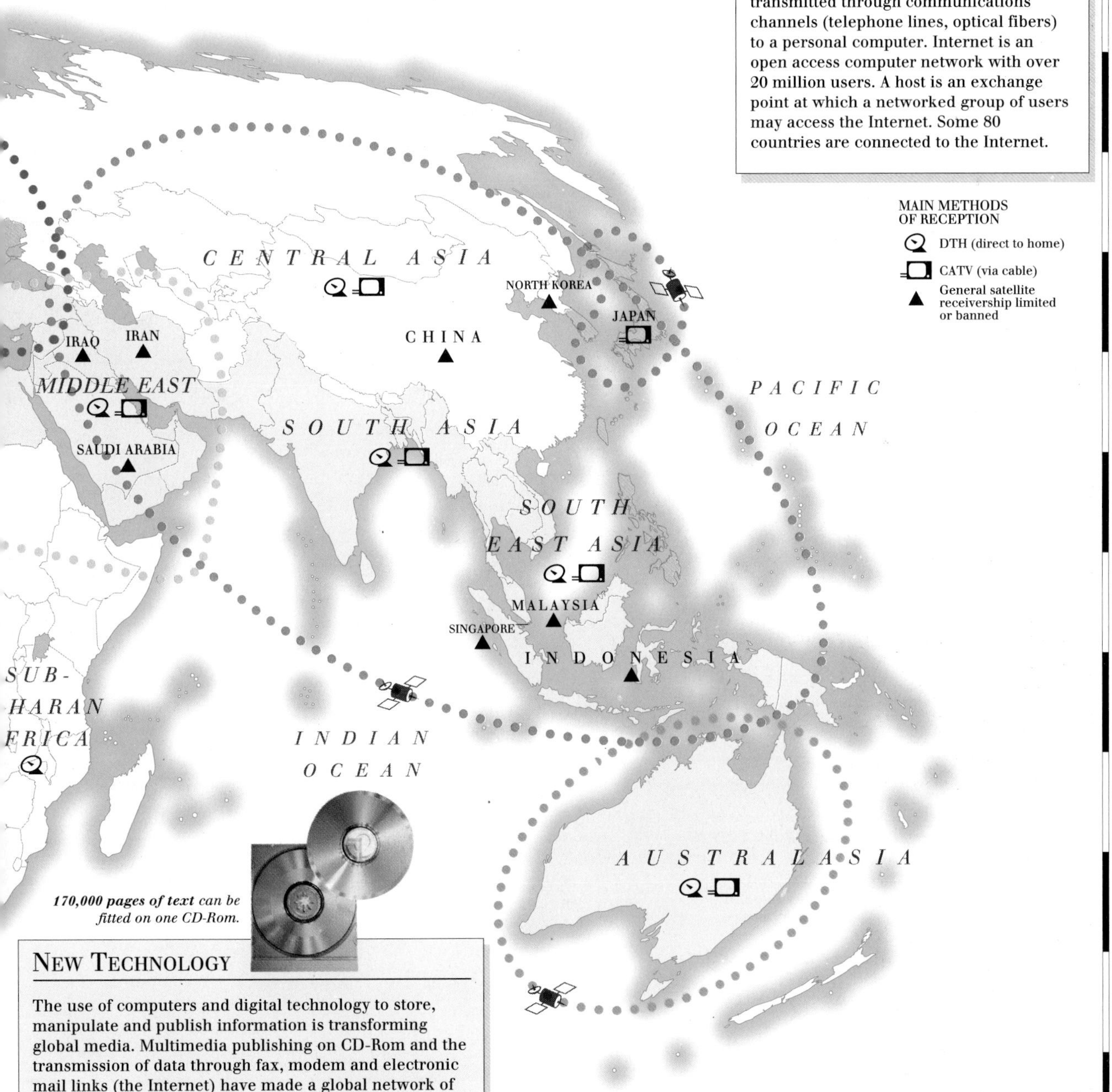

MAIN METHODS OF RECEPTION

- DTH (direct to home)
- CATV (via cable)
- General satellite receivership limited or banned

CENTRAL ASIA

NORTH KOREA

JAPAN

IRAQ

IRAN

CHINA

MIDDLE EAST

SOUTH ASIA

SAUDI ARABIA

PACIFIC OCEAN

SOUTH EAST ASIA

MALAYSIA

SINGAPORE

INDONESIA

SUB-SAHARAN AFRICA

INDIAN OCEAN

AUSTRALASIA

170,000 pages of text can be fitted on one CD-Rom.

NEW TECHNOLOGY

The use of computers and digital technology to store, manipulate and publish information is transforming global media. Multimedia publishing on CD-Rom and the transmission of data through fax, modem and electronic mail links (the Internet) have made a global network of information available to the private home. This technology will radically alter the way in which we communicate, learn and think.

Security and Defense

THE POST-COLD WAR PERIOD has produced a range of threats to the principal states of the international community. Ethnic conflict within states, mass migration and environmental hazards provide examples of new insecurities with potential for conflict of a very different sort from its Cold War counterpart. The spectacle of Yugoslavia's collapse into warring factions and the breakup of the Soviet Union were the most dramatic examples of the decline of the state as a source of security for its citizens and as a pillar of world order. Today, while orthodox diplomacy still has its place, recognition of the inability of the state to cope alone makes multilateral solutions imperative.

Global Defense and Conflict

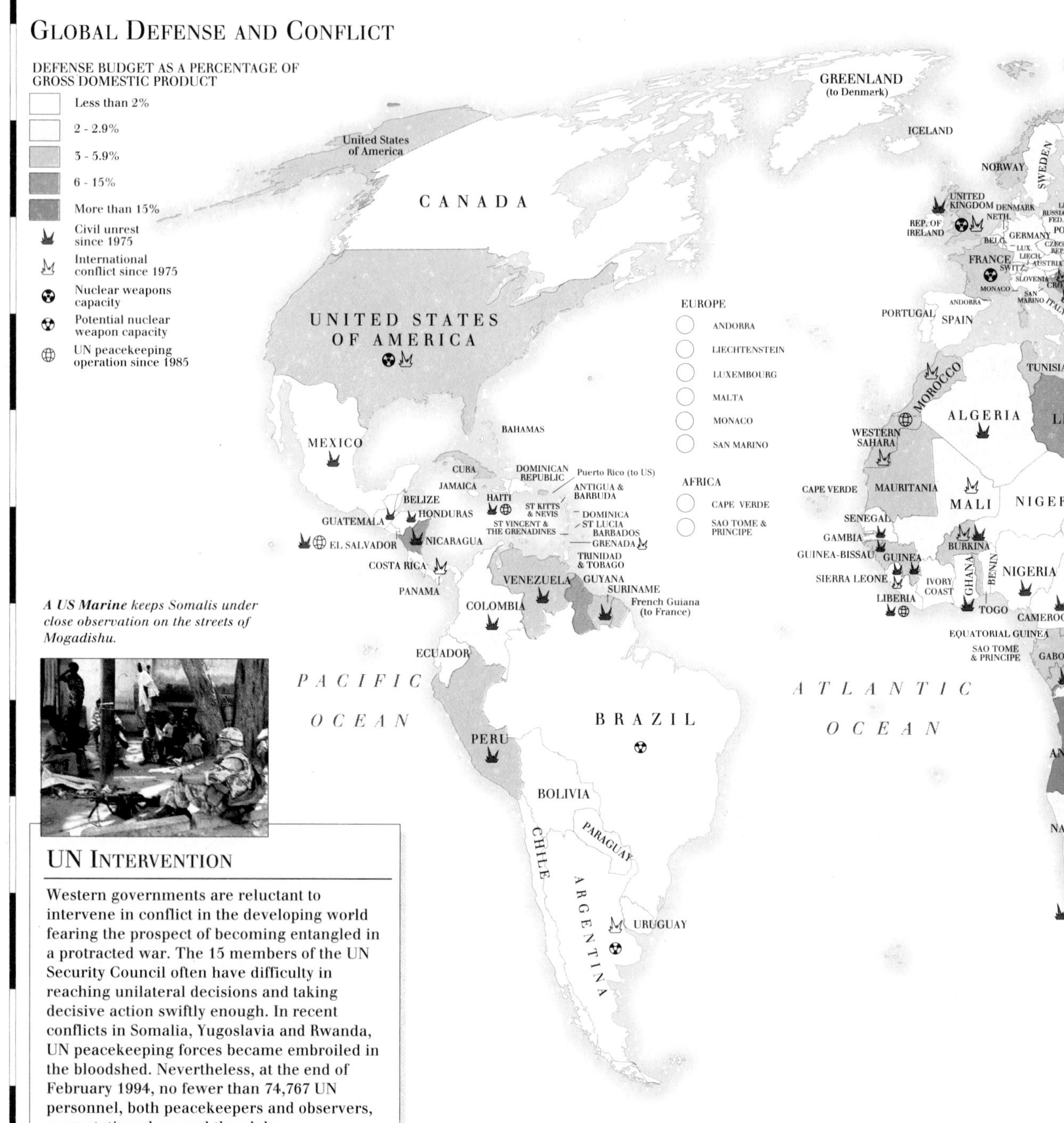

*A **US Marine** keeps Somalis under close observation on the streets of Mogadishu.*

UN Intervention

Western governments are reluctant to intervene in conflict in the developing world fearing the prospect of becoming entangled in a protracted war. The 15 members of the UN Security Council often have difficulty in reaching unilateral decisions and taking decisive action swiftly enough. In recent conflicts in Somalia, Yugoslavia and Rwanda, UN peacekeeping forces became embroiled in the bloodshed. Nevertheless, at the end of February 1994, no fewer than 74,767 UN personnel, both peacekeepers and observers, were stationed around the globe.

THE ARMS RACE

After World War II, international power was concentrated in the hands of two superpowers, the USA and USSR, and their military and economic allies. Potential all-out conflict was effectively contained by the nuclear deterrent. Today, the collapse of the Soviet Union and the diminishing economic and political power of the USA have led to fundamental changes in the power balance. The developing economies of Asia are now acquiring nuclear capability.

***An array of weaponry** once paraded through the streets of Moscow on each anniversary of the Bolshevik October revolution.*

GULF CONFLICT

In 1990, Iraq's President Saddam Hussain invaded the small oil-rich nation of Kuwait. This event led to rare accord among members of the United Nations Security Council, and troops were sent to the Gulf. The ensuing war (1990-1991) is a prime example of successful military intervention by the UN. However, the political objective was clear and limited: to drive the Iraqis out of Kuwaiti territory – defending one state against aggression by another.

***The oil wells of Kuwait** blazed for many months after the Gulf conflict, causing enormous environmental damage.*

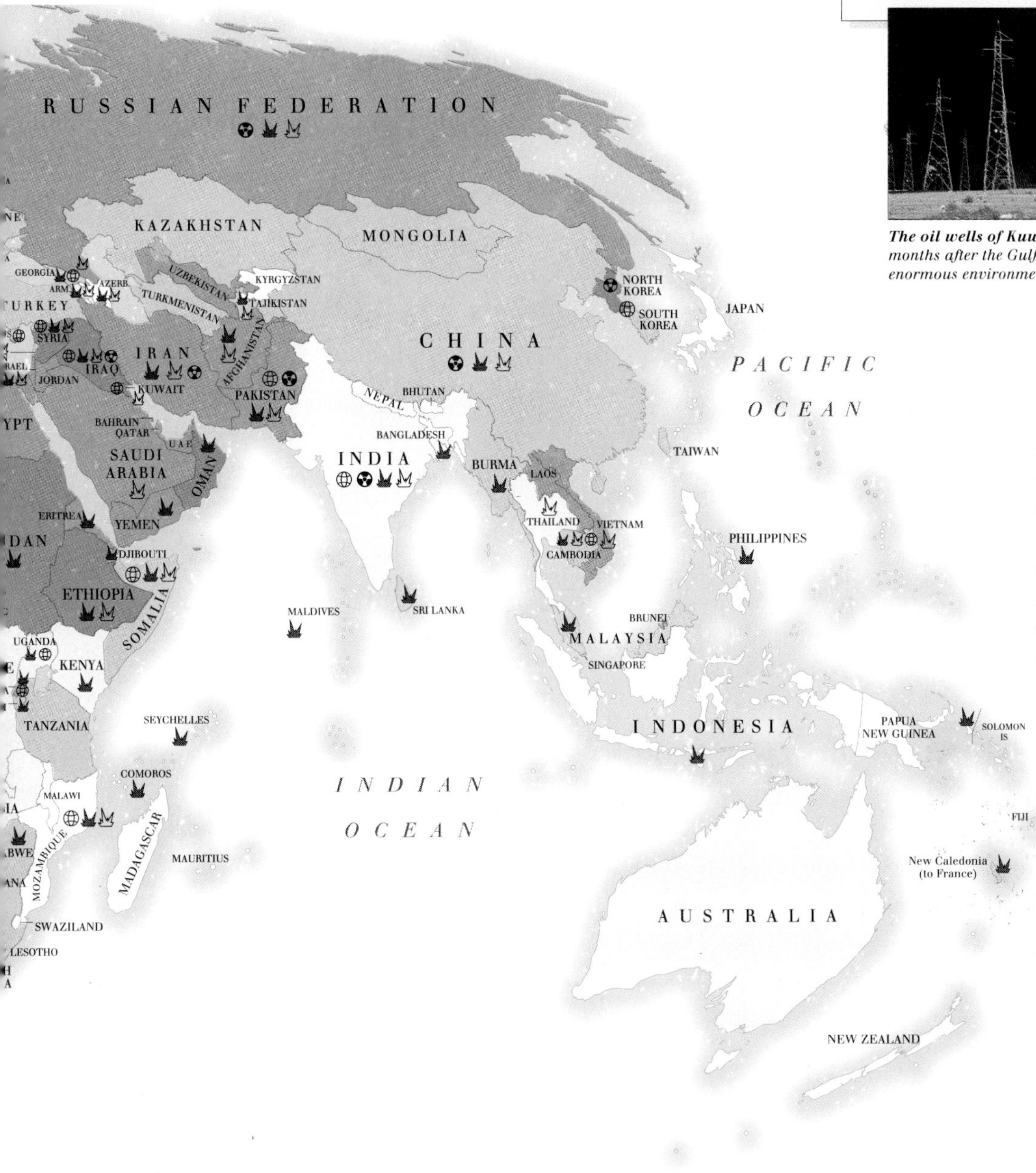

RUSSIAN FEDERATION

KAZAKHSTAN

MONGOLIA

GEORGIA

ARM.

AZERB.

UZBEKISTAN

KYRGYZSTAN

TURKMENISTAN

TAJIKISTAN

NORTH KOREA

SOUTH KOREA

JAPAN

TURKEY

SYRIA

IRAN

IRAQ

JORDAN

KUWAIT

AFGHANISTAN

PAKISTAN

CHINA

NEPAL

BHUTAN

PACIFIC OCEAN

BAHRAIN

QATAR

U.A.E.

SAUDI ARABIA

OMAN

BANGLADESH

INDIA

BURMA

LAOS

TAIWAN

ERITREA

YEMEN

THAILAND

VIETNAM

CAMBODIA

PHILIPPINES

DJIBOUTI

ETHIOPIA

SOMALIA

MALDIVES

SRI LANKA

BRUNEI

MALAYSIA

SINGAPORE

UGANDA

KENYA

TANZANIA

SEYCHELLES

INDONESIA

PAPUA NEW GUINEA

SOLOMON IS

COMOROS

MALAWI

INDIAN OCEAN

MOZAMBIQUE

MADAGASCAR

MAURITIUS

FIJI

New Caledonia (to France)

SWAZILAND

LESOTHO

AUSTRALIA

NEW ZEALAND

PACIFIC OCEAN

KIRIBATI

MICRONESIA

NAURU

SOLOMON ISLANDS

TONGA

VANUATU

WESTERN SAMOA

FIJI

MIDDLE EAST

BAHRAIN

INDIAN OCEAN

COMOROS

MALDIVES

MAURITIUS

SEYCHELLES

ASIA

SINGAPORE

GLOBAL TOURISM

TOURISM IS THE WORLD'S biggest industry. In 1990 there were 425 million tourists worldwide; this number is expected to rise to 937 million by 2010. With improved transportation, cheaper flights and increased leisure time, many of the countries of the developing world are rapidly becoming tourist meccas. Since the 1960s, mass tourism has become increasingly specialized, encompassing sporting and adventure vacations as well as ecological tours. Although the tourist industry employs 127 million people worldwide, the benefits of tourism are not always felt at a local level, where jobs are often low paid and menial. Unregulated growth of tourism is causing both environmental and social damage.

THE GLOBAL TOURIST INDUSTRY

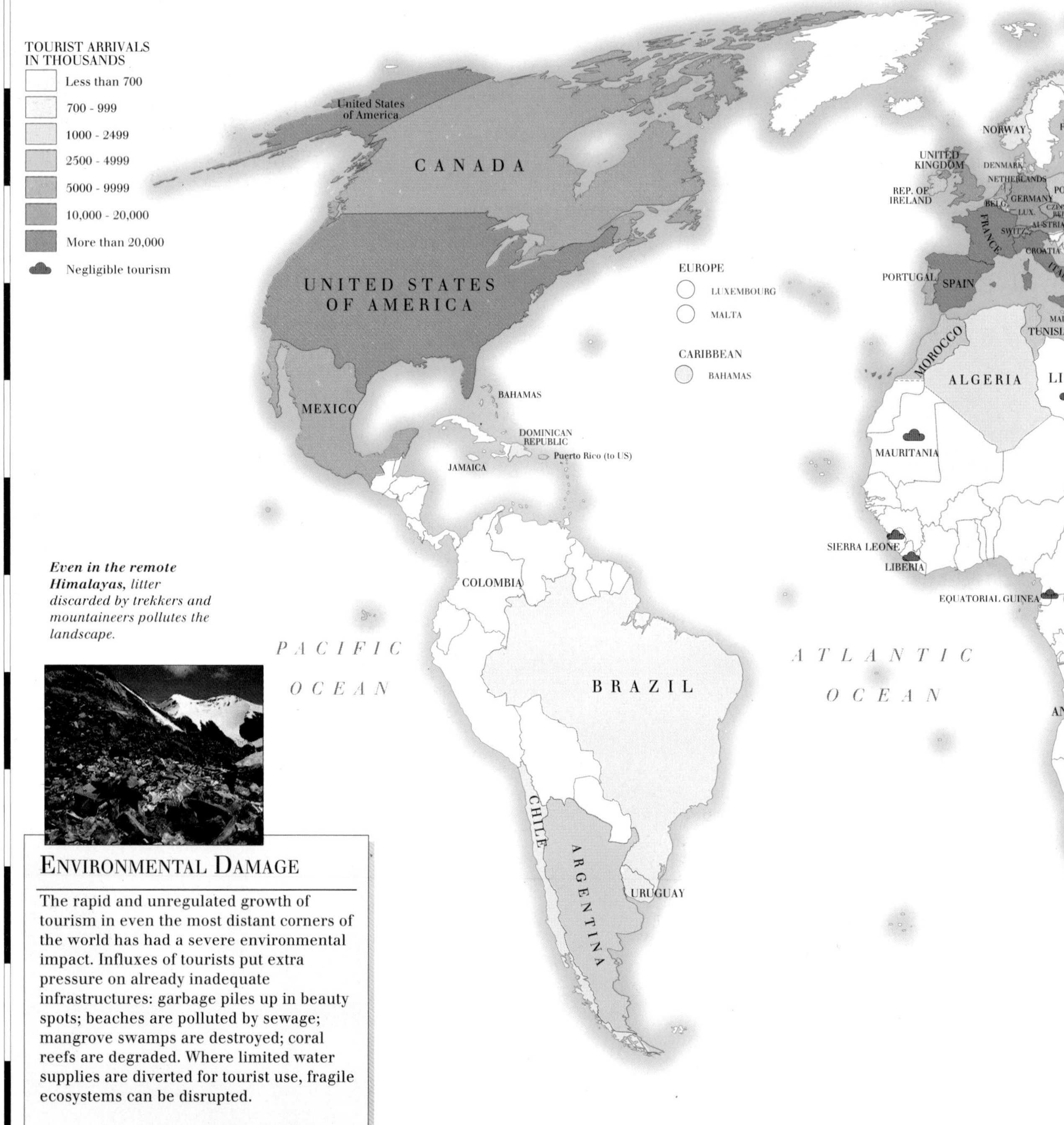

Even in the remote Himalayas, litter discarded by trekkers and mountaineers pollutes the landscape.

ENVIRONMENTAL DAMAGE

The rapid and unregulated growth of tourism in even the most distant corners of the world has had a severe environmental impact. Influxes of tourists put extra pressure on already inadequate infrastructures: garbage piles up in beauty spots; beaches are polluted by sewage; mangrove swamps are destroyed; coral reefs are degraded. Where limited water supplies are diverted for tourist use, fragile ecosystems can be disrupted.

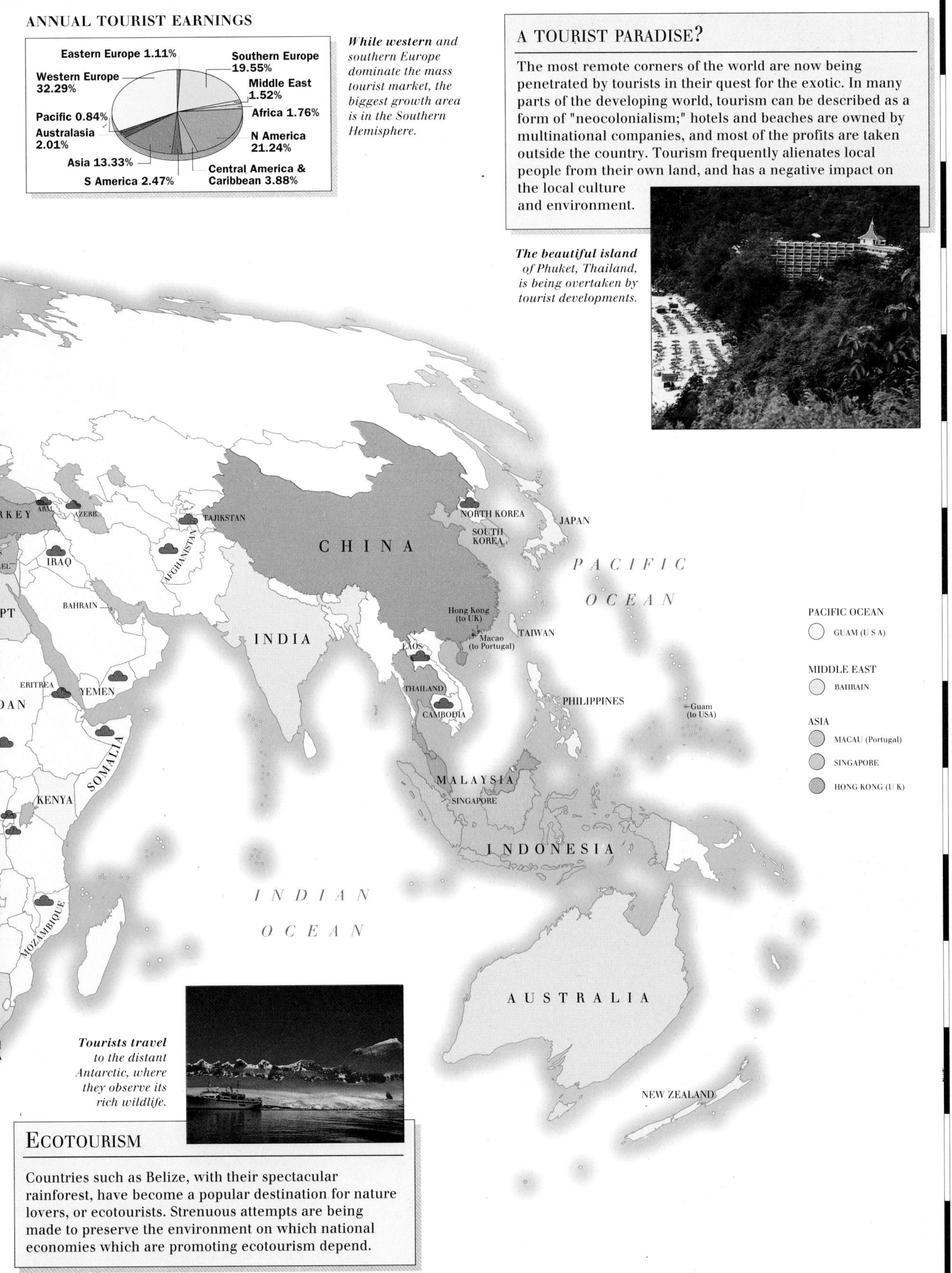

While western and southern Europe dominate the mass tourist market, the biggest growth area is in the Southern Hemisphere.

A TOURIST PARADISE?

The most remote corners of the world are now being penetrated by tourists in their quest for the exotic. In many parts of the developing world, tourism can be described as a form of "neocolonialism;" hotels and beaches are owned by multinational companies, and most of the profits are taken outside the country. Tourism frequently alienates local people from their own land, and has a negative impact on the local culture and environment.

***The beautiful island** of Phuket, Thailand, is being overtaken by tourist developments.*

***Tourists travel** to the distant Antarctic, where they observe its rich wildlife.*

ECOTOURISM

Countries such as Belize, with their spectacular rainforest, have become a popular destination for nature lovers, or ecotourists. Strenuous attempts are being made to preserve the environment on which national economies which are promoting ecotourism depend.

The Final Frontiers

Respect for national sovereignty and the international recognition of national boundaries is a principle central to the United Nations Charter. Nevertheless, there are over 60 disputed borders or territories in the world today; while many of these can be settled by peaceful arbitration, some are sources of international conflict. Ownership of valuable natural resources is a common reason for such disputes, although ethnic concerns provide frequent bloody flashpoints. The legacy of colonial mapmakers, notably in Africa, where inadequate knowledge and political pragmatism led to many arbitrary borders, has caused problems, while territorial acquisitions in long-settled wars can sour international relations.

International Territorial Disputes

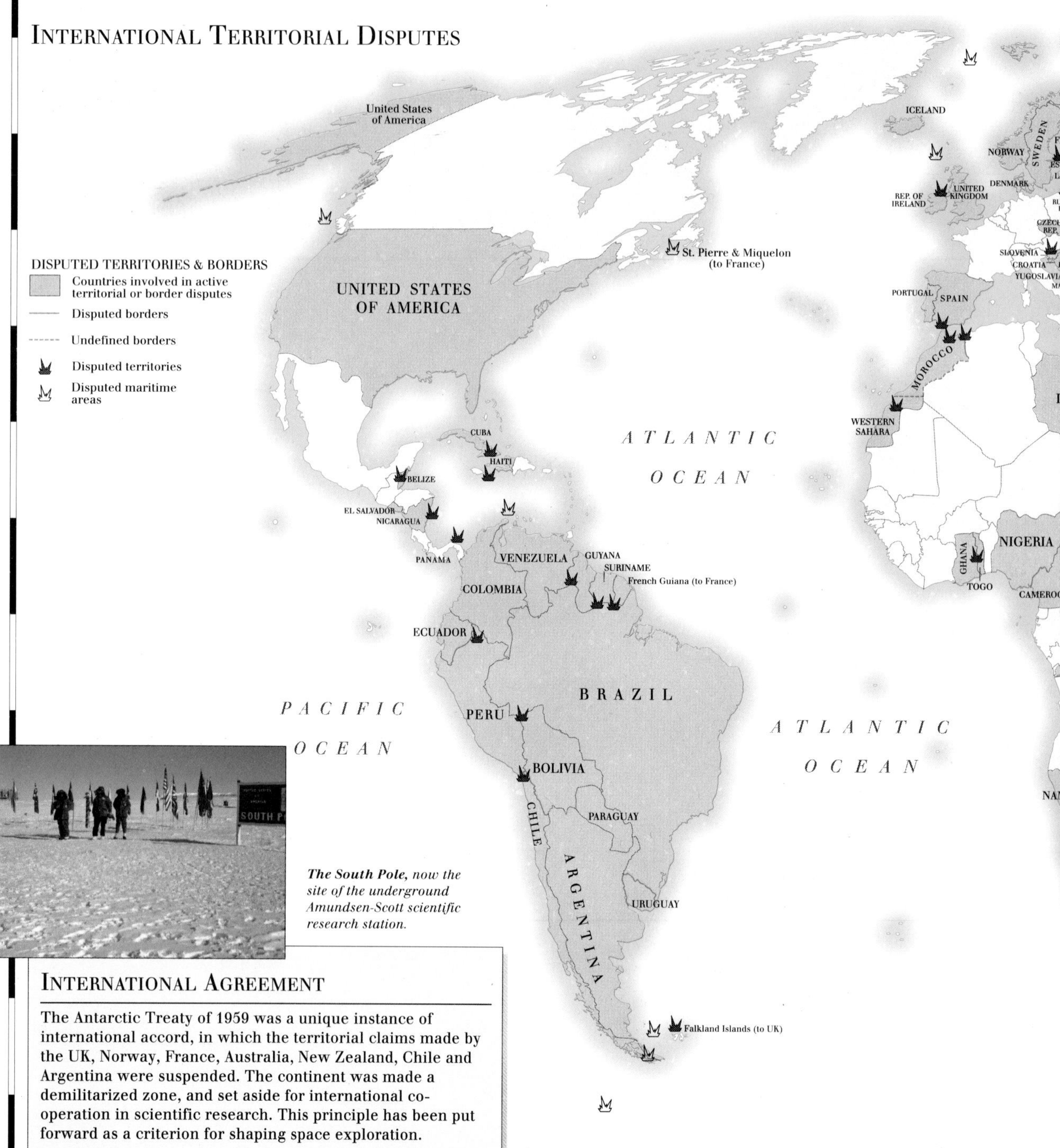

The South Pole, now the site of the underground Amundsen-Scott scientific research station.

International Agreement

The Antarctic Treaty of 1959 was a unique instance of international accord, in which the territorial claims made by the UK, Norway, France, Australia, New Zealand, Chile and Argentina were suspended. The continent was made a demilitarized zone, and set aside for international co-operation in scientific research. This principle has been put forward as a criterion for shaping space exploration.

Occupied Territory

After its creation in 1948, Israel expanded its territory to include the West Bank and Gaza Strip (1967), Sinai (1956, 1967-82) and the Golan Heights (1967). Israel has sustained a program of settlement and administrative control in these occupied territories, claiming that the West Bank at least was an integral part of biblical Israel.

***An Israeli** settlement under construction on the West Bank.*

Military borders

The current border between North and South Korea, which follows the ceasefire line of the 1950–1953 war, is one of the world's few remaining 'military' borders. While the border itself is a DMZ (demilitarized zone) and is administered by United Nations forces, the areas immediately to the north and south of the border zone are heavily fortified and constantly patrolled by armed troops while propaganda messages are broadcast over the barbed wire.

***The border** between North and South Korea , administered by UN forces.*

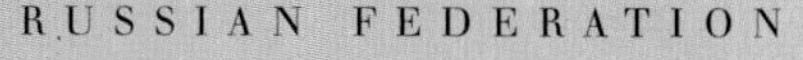

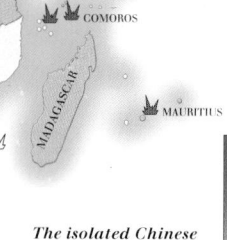

The isolated Chinese occupying force on one of the Spratly Islands.

Territorial Claims

Ambitious territorial claims are often advanced when the presence of rich mineral deposits is suspected. The Spratly Islands in the South China Sea, the site of potential oil and natural gas reserves, have been claimed by China, Vietnam, Taiwan, Brunei, Malaysia and the Philippines since a wartime claim by the Japanese was relinquished in 1951. Some claimants have even posted small military garrisons to the islands.

4

INDEX~ GAZETTEER

INTERNATIONAL ORGANIZATIONS
GEOGRAPHICAL PLACE NAMES
GLOSSARY OF GEOGRAPHICAL TERMS
GLOSSARY OF ABBREVIATIONS
A-Z INDEX~GAZETTEER

INTERNATIONAL ORGANIZATIONS

THIS LISTING PROVIDES definitions for all international organizations referred to, often by acronym, in the Atlas. (All political parties are defined under the Politics heading within each national entry.)

The definitions are followed by the date of establishment or foundation, an indication of membership where appropriate and a summary of the organization's aims and functions.

ABEDA
Arab Bank for Economic Development in Africa
established 1974
members – 18 Arab nations; promotes economic development

ACC
Arab Cooperation Council
established 1989
members – Egypt, Iran, Jordan, Yemen; promotes Arab economic cooperation

ACP
African, Caribbean and Pacific Countries
established 1976; *members* – 70 nations; preferential economisc and aid relationship with the EU.

ADB
Asian Development Bank
established 1966
members – 36 Asian-Pacific nations, 16 non-regional members; encourages regional development

AfDB
African Development Bank
established 1963
members – 50 African nations, 25 non-African nations; encourages African economic development

AFESD
Arab Fund for Economic and Social Development
established 1968
members – 21 Arab nations; promotes social and economic development

AG
Andean Group
established 1969
members – Bolivia, Colombia, Ecuador, Peru and Venezuela; promotes development through integration

AL
Arab League
established 1945
members – 21 Arab nations; forum to promote Arabic cooperation on social, political and military issues

AMF
Arab Monetary Fund
established 1976
members – 19 nations plus the PLO; promotes monetary and economic cooperation

AMU
Arab Maghreb Union
established 1989
members – Algeria, Libya, Mauritania, Morocco, Tunisia; promotes integration and economic cooperation among North African Arab states

ANC
African National Congress (originally the South African Native National Congress)
established 1912; political movement whose primary aim was to establish black majority rule in South Africa

ANZUS
Australia–New Zealand–United States Security Treaty
established 1951; implements trilateral security agreement

APEC
Asia-Pacific Economic Cooperation
established 1989
members – 15 Pacific Rim nations; promotes regional cooperation

ASEAN
Association of South East Asian Nations
established 1967
members – Brunei, Indonesia, Malaysia, Singapore, Thailand; promotes economic, social and cultural cooperation

BBC
British Broadcasting Corporation
established 1922; largest news broadcaster in the world.

BCCI
Bank of Credit and Commerce International
established 1972; Luxembourg-based bank that collapsed in 1992

BCIE
Central American Bank for Economic Integration
established 1960
members – Costa Rica, El Salvador, Guatemala, Honduras, Nicaragua; promotes economic integration and development in Central America

BDEAC
Central African States Development Bank
established 1975
members – Cameroon, Central African Republic, Chad, Congo, Equatorial Guinea, France, Gabon, Germany, Kuwait; furthers economic development

Benelux
Benelux Economic Union
established 1958
members – Belgium, Luxembourg, Netherlands; develops economic ties between member nations

BSEC
Black Sea Economic Cooperation Zone
established 1922
members – Albania, Armenia, Azerbaijan, Bulgaria, Georgia, Greece, Moldavia, Romania, Russia, Turkey, Ukraine; furthers regional stability through economic cooperation

CACM
Central American Common Market
established 1960
members – Costa Rica, El Salvador, Guatemala, Honduras, Nicaragua; furthers economic ties between members

CAEU
Council of Arab Economic Unity
established 1957
members – 11 Arab nations plus the PLO; encourages economic integration

Caricom
Caribbean Community and Common Market
established 1973
members – 13 Caribbean nations; fosters economic ties in the Caribbean

CBSS
Council of the Baltic Sea States
established 1992
members – Denmark, Estonia, Finland, Germany, Latvia, Lithuania, Norway, Poland, Russia, Sweden; promotes cooperation among Baltic Sea states

CDB
Caribbean Development Bank
established 1969
members – 20 Caribbean nations, 5 non-Caribbean nations; regional development

CE
Council of Europe
established 1949
members – 29 European nations; promotes unity and quality of life in Europe

CEEAC
Economic Community of Central African States
established 1983
members – 11 Central African nations; promotes regional cooperation and aims to establish Central African common market

CEI
Central European Initiative
established 1991 (evolved from Hexagonal Group)
members – Austria, Bosnia & Herzegovina, Croatia, Czech Republic, Hungary, Italy, Poland, Slovakia, Slovenia, Yugoslavia; promotes economic and political cooperation

CG
Contadora Group *see* RG

CIA
Central Intelligence Agency
established 1944
Agency in USA responsible for external security

CILSS
Permanent Interstate Committee for Drought Control in the Sahel
established 1973
members – Burkina, Cape Verde, Chad, Gambia, Guinea-Bissau, Mali, Mauritania, Niger, Senegal; promotes prevention of drought and crop failure in Sahel region

CIS
Commonwealth of Independent States
established 1991
members – Armenia, Belorussia, Kazakhstan, Kyrgyzstan, Moldova, Russia, Tajikistan, Turkmenistan, Ukraine, Uzbekistan; promotes interstate relationships

Comm
Commonwealth (evolved from British Empire)
established 1931
members – 48 nations; develops relationships and contacts between members

CP
Colombo Plan
established 1951
members – 26 nations; encourages economic and social development in Asia-Pacific region

CSCE
Conference on Security and Cooperation in Europe
established 1972
members – 52 nations; organization that attempts to reduce tensions associated with the Cold War

CNN
Cable News Network
established 1980; worldwide satellite-broadcast 24-hour TV news channel

EADB
East African Development Bank
established 1967
members – Kenya, Tanzania, Uganda; encourages economic development

EBRD
European Bank for Reconstruction and Development
established 1991
members – 58 nations; helps transition of former communist European states to market economies

EC
European Community
see EU

ECA
Economic Commission for Africa
established 1958
members – 52 nations; regional commission of UN's Economic and Social Council

ECE
Economic Commission for Europe
established 1947
members – 44 nations; regional commission of UN's Economic and Social Council

ECLAC
Economic Commission for Latin America and the Caribbean
established 1948
members – 41 nations, including those from outside Latin America; regional commission of the UN's Economic and Social Council

ECOWAS
Economic Community of West African States
established 1975
members – 17 nations; promotes closer regional economic cooperation

EEC
European Economic Community *see* EU

EFTA
European Free Trade Association
established 1960
members – Austria, Finland, Iceland, Norway, Sweden, Switzerland; promotes economic cooperation

ESCAP
Economic and Social Commission for Asia and the Pacific
established 1947 (as Economic Commission for Asia and the Far East)
members – 46 nations; regional commission of UN's Economic and Social Council

ESCWA
Economic and Social Commission for Western Asia
established 1973 (as Economic Commission for Western Asia)
members – Bahrain, Egypt, Iraq, Jordan, Kuwait, Lebanon, Oman, Qatar, Saudi Arabia, Syria, UAE, Yemen, PLO; regional commission of UN's Economic and Social Council

EU
European Union
established 1965; formerly known as EEC (European Economic Community) and EC (European Community)
members – Belgium, Denmark, France, Germany, Greece, Ireland, Italy, Luxembourg, Netherlands, Portugal, Spain, UK. Austria, Finland, and Sweden joined in Jan 1995, following national referenda. Seeks to establish integrated European common market, and eventual federation

FLS
Front Line States
established 1975
members – Angola, Botswana, Mozambique, Namibia, Tanzania, Zambia, Zimbabwe; group whose aim was to achieve black majority rule in South Africa

FZ
Franc Zone
members – 15 nations; aims to form monetary union among nations whose currencies are linked to the French franc.

GATT
General Agreement on Tariffs and Trade
established 1947
members – 104 nations; aims to establish international free trade through multilateral trade agreements

GCC
Gulf Cooperation Council
established 1981
members – Bahrain, Kuwait, Oman, Qatar, Saudi Arabia, UAE; promotes cooperation in economic, political and military affairs

G7
Group of 7
established 1985
members – Canada, France, Germany, Italy, Japan, UK, US; organization of the seven major Western powers

Hexagonal Group *see* CEI

IAEA
International Atomic Energy Agency
established 1956
members – 115 nations; promotes and monitors peaceful use of atomic energy

IBRD
International Bank for Reconstruction and Development (also known as the World Bank)
established 1945
members – 117 nations; UN agency providing economic development loans

ICJ
International Court of Justice
established 1945
15 judges; primary judicial organ of UN. All major legal systems are represented

IDA
International Development Association
established 1960
members – 147 nations; UN agency providing loans for low-income countries

IDB
Islamic Development Bank
established 1973
members – 45 nations; promotes Islamic social aid and development

IGADD
Inter-Governmental Authority on Drought and Development
established 1986
members – Djibouti, Ethiopia, Kenya, Somalia, Sudan, Uganda; promotes cooperation on drought-related matters

IMF
International Monetary Fund
established 1944
members – 175 nations; UN agency concerned with world monetary stability and economic development

IWC
International Whaling Commission
established 1946
members – 40 nations; reviews conduct of whaling throughout world. Coordinates and funds whale research

IOC
Indian Ocean Commission
established 1982
members – Comoros, France, Madagascar, Mauritius, Seychelles; promotes regional cooperation

IOC
International Olympic Committee
established 1894
members – 168 nations; promotes Olympic ideals and administers the Olympic games

LAES
Latin American Economic System
established 1975
members – 26 Latin American nations; promotes economic and social development through regional cooperation

LAIA
Latin American Integration Association
established 1980
members – Argentina, Bolivia, Brazil, Chile, Colombia, Ecuador, Mexico, Paraguay, Peru, Uruguay, Venezuela; promotes free regional trade

MERCOSUR
Southern Cone Common Market
established 1991
members – Argentina, Brazil, Paraguay, Uruguay; promotes economic cooperation

NACC
North Atlantic Cooperation Council
established 1991
members – 38 nations; forum for cooperation on political and security issues

NAFTA
North American Free Trade Agreement;
established 1994
members – Canada, Mexico, USA; free-trade zone

NAM
Non-Aligned Movement
established 1961
members – 103 nations; fosters political and military cooperation away from traditional Eastern or Western blocs

NASA
National Aeronautics and Space Administration
established 1958;
US government body that develops manned and unmanned space programs

NATO
North Atlantic Treaty Organization
established 1949
members – Belgium, Canada, Denmark, France, Germany, Greece, Iceland, Italy, Luxembourg, Netherlands, Norway, Portugal, Spain, Turkey, UK, USA; promotes mutual defense cooperation

NC
Nordic Council
established 1952
members – Denmark, Finland, Iceland, Norway, Sweden; promotes cultural and environmental cooperation in Scandinavia

OAPEC
Organization of Arab Petroleum Exporting Countries
established 1968
members – Algeria, Bahrain, Egypt, Iraq, Kuwait, Libya, Qatar, Saudi Arabia, Syria, Tunisia, UAE; organization dealing with petroleum pricing for Arab world

OAS
Organization of American States
established 1948
members – 35 nations; promotes security, economic and social development in the Americas

OAU
Organization of African Unity
established 1963
members – 52 African nations; promotes unity and cooperation

OECD
Organization for Economic Cooperation and Development
established 1961
members – 24 nations; forum for economic development

OECS
Organization of Eastern Caribbean States
established 1981
members – Antigua & Barbuda, Dominica, Grenada, Montserrat, St. Kitts & Nevis, St. Lucia, St. Vincent & the Grenadines; promotes political, economic and defense cooperation

OIC
Organization of the Islamic Conference
established 1969
members – 48 nations; furthers Islamic solidarity and cooperation

Opanal
Agency for the Prohibition of Nuclear Weapons in Latin America and the Caribbean
established 1967
members – 26 nations; promotes peaceful use of atomic energy

OPEC
Organization of Petroleum Exporting Countries
established 1960
members – Algeria, Gabon, Indonesia, Iran, Iraq, Kuwait, Libya, Nigeria, Qatar, Saudi Arabia, UAE, Venezuela; cartel aiming to coordinate oil prices

PLO
Palestine Liberation Organization
established 1964; seeks to create an independent Palestinian state

RG
Rio Group
established 1948 (evolved from Contradora Group)
members – Argentina, Bolivia, Brazil, Chile, Colombia, Ecuador, Mexico, Paraguay, Peru, Uruguay, Venezuela; forum for Latin American issues

SAARC
South Asian Association for Regional Cooperation
established 1985
members – Bangladesh, Bhutan, Maldives, Nepal, Pakistan, Sri Lanka; encourages economic, social, and cultural cooperation

SACU
Southern African Customs Union
established 1969
members – Bophuthatswana, Botswana, Ciskei, Lesotho, Namibia, South Africa, Swaziland, Transkei, Venda; to promote cooperation in trade and customs matters among southern African states and homelands

SADC
Southern African Development Community
established 1992
members – Angola, Botswana, Lesotho, Malawi, Mozambique, Namibia, Swaziland, Tanzania, Zambia, Zimbabwe; promotes economic integration

SPARTECA
South Pacific Regional Trade and Economic Cooperation Agreement
established 1981
members – 15 nations; aims redress unequal trade relationship of Australia and New Zealand with Pacific island economies

SPC
South Pacific Commission
established 1948
members – 27 nations; promotes regional cooperation in economic and social matters

SPF
South Pacific Forum
established 1971
members – 15 nations; develops regional political cooperation

UN
United Nations
established 1945
members – 184 nations; all countries in the world represented except Kiribati, Nauru, Switzerland (Observer status only), Taiwan, Tonga, Tuvalu, Vatican City (Observer status only); aims to maintain international peace and security and to promote cooperation over economic, social, cultural and humanitarian problems

UNDP
United Nations Development Program
established 1965
members – 48 nations; provides technical assistance for economic development

UNHCR
United Nations Office of the High Commissioner for Refugees
established 1951
members – 46 nations; encourages humane treatment of refugees

UNESCO
United Nations Scientific and Cultural Organization
established 1945
members – 172 nations; encourages cooperation in education, science and culture

UNSC
United Nations Security Council
established 1945
members – China, France, Russia, UK, USA; 10 non-permanent members for 2-year terms; seeks to maintain international peace and security

UNTAC
United Nations Transitional Authority in Cambodia
established 1992
members – 31 nations; founded by UNSC to aid setting up of elections and maintenance of peace in Cambodia

WCL
World Confederation of Labor
established 1924 (as International Federation of Christian Trade Unions)
members – 94 nations; promotes labor movements internationally

WEU
Western European Union
established 1954
members – Belgium, France, Italy, Germany, Luxembourg, Netherlands, Portugal, Spain, UK; organization for mutual defense and political union

WHO
World Health Organization
established 1946
members – 180 nations; UN agency specializing in health matters

Geographical Place Names

THE CHOICES confronting a map-maker when deciding which place-name style to use on a map are surprisingly varied. The criteria adopted may be affected by a range of factors: the existence of foreign and native language forms of a place name (London, Londres, Londra), variant spellings used within the country itself (Gent, Gand) and the existence of completely different language forms for international features (the English Channel, La Manche).

In addition to these, political expedience, simple clarity and the use to which the published map may be put are all factors that need consideration.

The revision of place-name forms and spellings, which is a continuing administrative activity worldwide, adds a further dimension of complexity to the subject. Since the collapse of Soviet communism, for instance, place names in Russia have been altered to expunge traces of communist ideology (the most famous being the 1991 reversion of Leningrad to its pre-1914 name, St. Petersburg). In many former Soviet republics, Russian names have been replaced with native language forms (notably in Ukraine, Belorussia, Georgia and Armenia).

Standardized Arabic forms and spellings have been instituted throughout most of the Arab world, although in some of the former French North African colonies, such as Algeria, the adoption of standardized Arabic names has been hindered by the persistent use of French forms in practice.

The Maps

The maps in the Nations of the World section of the Atlas have used the most up-to-date reference sources available to provide local name forms and spellings, that is to say those used within the country. In an age when international travel, on vacation or on business, is commonplace, this criterion seems the most appropriate.

English conventional forms have been used for all international features (such as sea areas between countries, and cross-border mountain ranges); for all country names (the Index~Gazetteer provides local forms and spellings, while commonly used alternative names, such as Burma/Myanmar are also made clear in the national A-Z entry) and for all capital cities. The Index~Gazetteer provides a fully cross-referenced system that will guide the reader the short distance from the English conventional "Florence" to the local "Firenze," as used on the maps.

English conventional forms also appear on all the maps in The World Today and Global Issues. These maps have not been indexed, as all contemporary places featured are more usefully and accurately identified on the national maps.

The Index~Gazetteer

The Index~Gazetteer lists all names that appear on the maps in the Nations of the World section of the Atlas. Physical features are defined as such, as are countries and those administrative or regional names included on the maps; all other names are those of population centers. Location is given by page number, then country, and is narrowed down by positional reference as N(orth), S(outh), E(ast), W(est) or C(entral), or combinations of these as appropriate.

Following each main entry name are given: variant spellings of the name most commonly found; its previous name or names; and such foreign-language forms of the name as are pertinent to modern history since 1940. This is the cut-off date generally adopted, permitting the inclusion of all place-name changes made during or after World War II. Exceptionally, name changes made in Russia and other countries of the former Soviet Union before 1940 are given, since many old names in these countries are now being restored.

The following pages provide a glossary of foreign geographical terms (656–657) that occur in the main entry names, and a comprehensive glossary of abbreviations (658) used in the Index~Gazetteer and throughout the Atlas.

Glossary of Geographical Terms

THE GLOSSARY FOLLOWING lists all the geographical terms occurring on the maps and in the main-entry names in the Index~Gazetteer. These terms may precede, follow or be run together with the proper element of the name. In those cases where they precede it, the term is reversed for indexing purposes – thus Poluostrov Yamal is indexed as Yamal, Poluostrov.

KEY
Geographical term *Language,* Term

A
Å *Danish, Norwegian,* River
Alpen *German,* Alps
Altiplanicie *Spanish,* Plateau
Älv(en) *Swedish,* River
Anse *French,* Bay
Archipiélago *Spanish,* Archipelago
Arcipelago *Italian,* Archipelago
Arquipélago *Portuguese,* Archipelago
Aukštuma *Lithuanian,* Upland

B
Bahía *Spanish,* Bay
Baía *Portuguese,* Bay
Baḩr *Arabic,* River
Baie *French,* Bay
Bandao *Chinese,* Peninsula
Banjaran *Malay,* Mountain range
Batang *Malay,* Stream
-berg *Afrikaans, Norwegian,* Mountain
Birket *Arabic ,* Lake
Boğazı *Turkish,* Lake
Bucht *German,* Bay
Bugten *Danish,* Bay
Buḩayrat *Arabic,* Lake, reservoir
Buḩeiret *Arabic,* Lake
Bukit *Malay,* Mountain
-bukta *Norwegian,* Bay
bukten *Swedish,* Bay
Burnu *Turkish,* Cape, point
Buuraha *Somali,* Mountains

C
Cabo *Portuguese,* Cape
Cap *French,* Cape
Cascada *Portuguese,* Waterfall
Cerro *Spanish,* Mountain
Chaîne *French,* Mountain range
Chau *Cantonese,* Island
Chāy *Turkish,* River
Chhâk *Cambodian,* Bay
Chhu *Tibetan,* River
-chŏsuji *Korean,* Reservoir
Chott *Arabic,* Salt lake, depression
Ch'ün-tao *Chinese,* Island group
Chuôr Phnum *Cambodian,* Mountains
Cordillera *Spanish,* Mountain range
Costa *Spanish,* Coast
Côte *French,* Coast
Cuchilla *Spanish,* Mountains

D
Dağı *Azerbaijani, Turkish,* Mountain
Dağları *Azerbaijani, Turkish,* Mountains
-dake *Japanese,* Peak
Danau *Indonesian,* Lake
Đao *Vietnamese,* Island
Daryā *Persian,* River
Daryācheh *Persian,* Lake
Dasht *Persian,* Plain, desert
Dawḩat *Arabic,* Bay
Dere *Turkish,* Stream
Dili *Azerbaijani,* Spit
-do *Korean,* Island
Dooxo *Somali,* Valley
Düzü *Azerbaijani,* Steppe
-dwīp *Bengali,* Island

E
Embalse *Spanish,* Reservoir
Erg *Arabic,* Dunes
Estany *Catalan,* Lake
Estrecho *Spanish,* Strait
-ey *Icelandic,* Island
Ezero *Bulgarian, Macedonian,* Lake

F
Fjord *Danish,* Fjord
-fjorden *Norwegian,* Fjord
-fjørdhur *Faeroese,* Fjord
Fleuve *French,* River
Fliegu *Maltese,* Channel
-fljór *Icelandic,* River

G
-gang *Korean,* River
Ganga *Nepali, Sinhala,* River
Gaoyuan *Chinese,* Plateau
-gawa *Japanese,* River
Gebel *Arabic,* Mountain
-gebirge *German,* Mountains
Ghubbat *Arabic,* Bay
Gjiri *Albanian,* Bay
Gol *Mongolian,* River
Golfe *French,* Gulf
Golfo *Italian, Spanish,* Gulf
Gora *Russian, Serbian,* Mountain
Gory *Russian,* Mountains
Guba *Russian,* Bay
Gunung *Malay,* Mountain

H
Ḩadd *Arabic,* Spit
-haehyŏp *Korean,* Strait
Haff *German,* Lagoon
Hai *Chinese,* Sea, bay
Ḩammādat *Arabic,* Plateau
Hāmūn *Persian,* Lake
Hawr *Arabic,* Lake
Hāyk' *Amharic,* Lake
He *Chinese,* River
Helodrano *Malagasy,* Bay
-hegység *Hungarian,* Mountain range
Hka *Burmese,* River
-ho *Korean,* Lake
Hô *Korean,* Reservoir
Ḫolot *Hebrew,* Dunes
Hora *Belorussian,* Mountain
Hrada *Belorussian,* Mountains, ridge
Hsi *Chinese,* River
Hu *Chinese,* Lake

I
Île(s) *French,* Island(s)
Ilha(s) *Portuguese,* Island(s)
Ilhéu(s) *Portuguese,* Islet(s)
Irmak *Turkish,* River
Isla(s) *Spanish,* Island(s)
Isola (Isole) *Italian,* Island(s)

J
Jabal *Arabic,* Mountain
Jāl *Arabic,* Ridge
-järvi *Finnish,* Lake
Jazīrat *Arabic,* Island
Jazīreh *Persian,* Island
Jebel *Arabic,* Mountain
Jezero *Serbo-Croatian,* Lake
Jiang *Chinese,* River
-joki *Finnish,* River
-jökull *Icelandic,* Glacier
Juzur *Arabic,* Islands

K
Kaikyō *Japanese,* Strait
-kaise *Lappish,* Mountain
Kali *Nepali,* River
Kalnas *Lithuanian,* Mountain
Kalns *Latvian,* Mountain
Kang *Chinese,* Harbor
Kangri *Tibetan,* Mountain(s)
Kaôh *Cambodian,* Island
Kapp *Norwegian,* Cape
Kavīr *Persian,* Desert
K'edi *Georgian,* Mountain range
Kediet *Arabic,* Mountain
Kepulauan *Indonesian, Malay,* Island group
Khalîg, Khalīj *Arabic,* Gulf
Khawr *Arabic,* Inlet
Khola *Nepali,* River
Khrebet *Russian,* Mountain range
Ko *Thai,* Island
Kolpos *Greek,* Bay
-kopf *German,* Peak
Körfäzi *Azerbaijani,* Bay
Körfezi *Turkish,* Bay
Kõrgustik *Estonian,* Upland
Koshi *Nepali,* River
Kowtal *Persian,* Pass
Kūh(hā) *Persian,* Mountain(s)
-kundo *Korean,* Island group
-kysten *Norwegian,* Coast
Kyun *Burmese,* Island

L
Laaq *Somali,* Watercourse
Lac *French,* Lake
Lacul *Romanian,* Lake
Lago *Italian, Portuguese, Spanish,* Lake
Laguna *Spanish,* Lagoon, Lake
Laht *Estonian,* Bay
Laut *Indonesian,* Sea
Lembalemba *Malagasy,* Plateau
Lerr *Armenian,* Mountain

Lerrnashght'a *Armenian,* Mountain range
Les *Czech,* Forest
Lich *Armenian,* Lake
Liqeni *Albanian,* Lake
Lumi *Albanian,* River
Lyman *Ukrainian,* Estuary

M

Mae Nam *Thai,* River
-mägi *Estonian,* Hill
Maja *Albanian,* Mountain
-man *Korean,* Bay
Marios *Lithuanian,* Lake
-meer *Dutch,* Lake
Melkosopochnik *Russian,* Plain
-meri *Estonian,* Sea
Mifraẕ *Hebrew,* Bay
Monkhafad *Arabic,* Depression
Mont(s) *French,* Mountain(s)
Monte *Italian, Portuguese,* Mountain
More *Russian,* Sea
Mörön *Mongolian,* River

N

Nagor'ye *Russian,* Upland
Naẖal *Hebrew,* River
Nahr *Arabic,* River
Nam *Laotian,* River
Nehri *Turkish,* River
Nevado *Spanish,* Mountain (snow-capped)
Nisoi *Greek,* Islands
Nizmennost' *Russian,* Lowland, plain
Nosy *Malagasy,* Island
Nur *Mongolian,* Lake
Nuruu *Mongolian,* Mountains
Nuur *Mongolian,* Lake
Nyzovyna *Ukrainian,* Lowland, plain

O

Ostrov(a) *Russian,* Island(s)
Oued *Arabic,* Watercourse
-oy *Faeroese,* Island
-øy(a) *Norwegian,* Island
Oya *Sinhala,* River
Ozero *Russian, Ukrainian,* Lake

P

Passo *Italian,* Pass
Pegunungan *Indonesian, Malay,* Mountain range
Pelagos *Greek,* Sea
Penisola *Italian,* Peninsula
Peski *Russian,* Sands
Phanom *Thai,* Mountain
Phou *Laotian,* Mountain
Pi *Chinese,* Point
Pic *Catalan,* Peak
Pico *Portuguese, Spanish,* Peak
Pik *Russian,* Peak
Planalto *Portuguese,* Plateau
Planina, Planini *Bulgarian, Macedonian, Serbo-Croatian,* Mountain range
Ploskogor'ye *Russian,* Upland
Poluostrov *Russian,* Peninsula
Potamos *Greek,* River
Proliv *Russian,* Strait
Pulau *Indonesian, Malay,* Island
Pulu *Malay,* Island
Punta *Portuguese, Spanish,* Point

Q

Qāʻ *Arabic,* Depression
Qolleh *Persian,* Mountain

R

Raas *Somali,* Cape
-rags *Latvian,* Cape
Ramlat *Arabic,* Sands
Ra's *Arabic,* Cape, point, headland
Ravnina *Bulgarian, Russian,* Plain
Récif *French,* Reef
Represa (Rep.) *Spanish, Portuguese,* Reservoir
-rettō *Japanese,* Island chain
Riacho *Spanish,* Stream
Riban' *Malagasy,* Mountains
Rio *Portuguese,* River
Río *Spanish,* River
Riu *Catalan,* River
Rivier *Dutch,* River
Rivière *French,* River
Rowd *Pashtu,* River
Rūd *Persian,* River
Rudohorie *Slovak,* Mountains
Ruisseau *French,* Stream

S

Sabkhat *Arabic,* Salt marsh
Şaḩrā' *Arabic,* Desert
Samudra *Sinhala,* Reservoir
-san *Japanese, Korean,* Mountain
-sanchi *Japanese,* Mountains
-sanmaek *Korean,*
Sarīr *Arabic,* Desert
Sebkha, Sebkhet *Arabic,* Salt marsh, depression
See *German,* Lake
Selat *Indonesian,* Strait
-selkä *Finnish,* Ridge
Selseleh *Persian,* Mountain range
Serra *Portuguese,* Mountain
Serranía *Spanish,* Mountain
Shaʻīb *Arabic,* Watercourse
Shamo *Chinese,* Desert
Shan *Chinese,* Mountain(s)
Shan-mo *Chinese,* Mountain range
Shaţţ *Arabic,* Distributary
-shima *Japanese,* Island
Shiqqat *Arabic,* Depression
Shui-tao *Chinese,* Channel
Sierra *Spanish,* Mountains
Sơn *Vietnamese,* Mountain
Sông *Vietnamese,* River
-spitze *German,* Peak
Štít *Slovak,* Peak
Stoeng *Cambodian,* River
Stretto *Italian,* Strait
Su Anbarı *Azerbaijani,* Reservoir
Sungai *Indonesian, Malay,* River
Suu *Turkish,* River

T

Tal *Mongolian,* Plain
Tandavan' *Malagasy,* Mountain range
Tangorombohitr' *Malagasy,* Mountain massif
Tao *Chinese,* Island
Tassili *Berber,* Plateau, mountain
Tau *Russian,* Mountain(s)
Taungdan *Burmese,* Mountain range
Teluk *Indonesian, Malay,* Bay
Terara *Amharic,* Mountain
Tog *Somali,* Valley
Tônlé *Cambodian,* Lake
Top *Dutch,* Peak
-tunturi *Finnish,* Mountain
Turʻat *Arabic,* Channel

V

Väin *Estonian,* Strait
-vatn *Icelandic,* Lake
-vesi *Finnish,* Lake
Vinh *Vietnamese,* Bay
Vodokhranilishche (Vdkhr.) *Russian,* Reservoir
Vodoskhovyshche (Vdskh.) *Ukrainian,* Reservoir
Volcán *Spanish,* Volcano
Vozvyshennost' *Russian,* Upland, plateau
Vrh *Macedonian,* Peak
Vysochyna *Ukrainian,* Upland
Vysočina *Czech,* Upland

W

Waadi *Somali,* Watercourse
Wādī *Arabic,* Watercourse
Wāḩat, Wâhat *Arabic,* Oasis
Wald *German,* Forest
Wan *Chinese,* Bay
Wyżyna *Polish,* Upland

X

Xé *Laotian,* River

Y

Yarımadası *Azerbaijani,* Peninsula
Yazovir *Bulgarian,* Reservoir
Yoma *Burmese,* Mountains
Yü *Chinese,* Island

Z

Zaliv *Bulgarian, Russian,* Bay
Zatoka *Ukrainian,* Bay
Zemlya *Russian,* Bay

Glossary of Abbreviations

THIS GLOSSARY provides a comprehensive guide to the abbreviations used in this Atlas, and in the Index~Gazetteer.

A

abbrev. abbreviated
ABM anti-ballistic missile(s)
ACP African, Caribbean and Pacific countries
AD admin. Anno Domini
Afr. Afrikaans
Alb. Albanian
ALCM air-launched Cruise missile(s)
Amh. Amharic
anc. ancient
APC armored personnel carrier(s)
approx. approximately
Ar. Arabic
Arm. Armenian
ASSR Autonomous Soviet Socialist Republic
Aust. Australian
Az. Azerbaijani
Azerb. Azerbaijan

B

bbl billion barrels
Basq. Basque
BC before Christ
b/cd barrels per calendar day
b/d barrels per day
Bel. Belorussian
Ben. Bengali
Ber. Berber
B-H Bosnia-Herzegovina
bn billion (one thousand million)
BP British Petroleum
Bret. Breton
Brig Brigadier
Brit. British
Bul. Bulgarian
Bur. Burmese

C

C central
C. Cape
°C degrees (Centigrade)
Cam. Cambodian
Cant. Cantonese
Capt Captain
CAR Central African Republic
Cast. Castilian
Cat. Catalan
Chin. Chinese
CIS Commonwealth of Independent States
CITES Convention on International Trade in Endangered Species of wild flora and fauna
cm centimeter(s)
Cmdr Commander
Col Colonel
Cro. Croat
Cz. Czech
Czech Rep. Czech Republic

D E

Dan. Danish
dept. department
dev. development
Dom. Rep. Dominican Republic
Dr Doctor
Dut. Dutch
dwt dead weight tonnage
E east
EC see EU
EEC see EU
EEZ Exclusive Economic Zone
ECU European Currency Unit
EMS European Monetary System
Eng. English
est estimated
Est. Estonian
EU European Union (previously European Community [EC], European Economic Community [EEC])

F G

°F degrees Fahrenheit
Faer. Faeroese
Fij. Fijian
Fin. Finnish
Fr Father
Fr. French
Fris. Frisian
ft. foot/feet
FYRM Former Yugoslav Republic of Macedonia
FZ Franc Zone
g gram(s)
Gael. Gaelic
Gal. Galician
GDP Gross Domestic Product (the total value of goods and services produced by a country excluding income from foreign countries)
Gen General
Geor. Georgian
Ger. German
Gk Greek
GNP Gross National Product (the total value of goods and services produced by a country)

H I

Heb. Hebrew
HEP hydroelectric power
HH His/Her Highness
Hind. Hindi
hist. historical
HM His/Her Majesty
HMS His/Her Majesty's ship
HRH His/Her Royal Highness
HSH His/Her Serene Highness
Hung. Hungarian
I. Island
ICBM intercontinental ballistic missile(s)
Icel. Icelandic
in. inch(es)
In. Innuit (Eskimo)
Ind. Indonesian
Intl International
Ir. Irish
IRBM intermediate-range ballistic missile(s)
Is Islands
It. Italian
ITTA International Tropical Timber Agreement

J K L

Jap. Japanese
Kaz. Kazakh
kg kilogram(s)
Kir. Kirghiz
km kilometer(s)
km² square kilometer (singular)
Kor. Korean
Kurd. Kurdish
kw kilowatt(s)
kwh kilowatt hour(s)
L. Lake
Lao. Laotian
Lapp. Lappish
Lat. Latin
Latv. Latvian
Liech. Liechtenstein
Lith. Lithuanian
LNG liquefied natural gas
Lt Lieutenant
Lux. Luxembourg

M N

m million/meter(s)
Mac. Macedonian
Maced. Macedonia
Maj Major
Mal. Malay
Malg. Malagasy
Malt. Maltese
mi. mile(s)
Mong. Mongolian
Mt. Mountain
Mts Mountains
N north
Nep. Nepali
Neth. Netherlands
NGO Non-Governmental Organization
NIC Newly Industrialized Country
Nic. Nicaraguan
Nor. Norwegian
NZ New Zealand

P Q R

Pash. Pashtu
PC personal computer
Per. Persian
PNG Papua New Guinea
Pol. Polish
Poly. Polynesian
Port. Portuguese
prev. previously
Rep. Represa (Spanish, Portuguese for reservoir)
Rep. Republic
Res. Reservoir
Rev Reverend
Rmsch. Romansch
Rom. Romanian
Rus. Russian
Russ. Fed. Russian Federation

S

S south
SALT Strategic Arms Limitation Treaty
SCr. Serbo-Croatian
Serb. Serbian
Sinh. Sinhala
SLBM submarine-launched ballistic missile(s)
Slvk. Slovak
Slvn. Slovene
Som. Somali
Sp. Spanish
sq. square
SSBN nuclear-fueled ballistic-missile submarine(s)
SSM surface-to-surface missile(s)
St., St Saint
START Strategic Arms Reduction Treaty
Strs. Straits
Swa. Swahili
Swe. Swedish
Switz. Switzerland

T U

Taj. Tajik
Th. Thai
Thai. Thailand
Tib. Tibetan
Turk. Turkish
Turkm. Turkmenistan
TV television
UAE United Arab Emirates
Uigh. Uighur
UK United Kingdom
Ukr. Ukrainian
UN United Nations
UNCLOS United Nations Convention on the Law of the Sea
Urd. Urdu
US/USA United States of America
USS United States Ship
USSR Union of Soviet Socialist Republics
Uzb. Uzbek

V W X Y

var. variant
VCR videocassette recorder
Vdkhr. Vodokhranilishche (Russian for reservoir)
Vdskh. Vodoskhovyshche (Ukrainian for reservoir)
Vtn. Vietnamese
W west
Wel. Welsh
Yugo. Yugoslavia

INDEX

A

Allada *108* S Benin
Al Lādhiqīyah *521 Eng.* Latakia. W Syria
Allahābād *270* NE India
Allanmyo *135* W Burma
'Allâqi, Wâdi el *202 var.* Wādī al 'Allāqi. Dry watercourse of SE Egypt
All Awash Island *466* island of E St Vincent & the Grenadines
Allenstein *see* Olsztyn
Allentown *569* Pennsylvania, NE USA
Al Liwā' *560* oasis region of SW United Arab Emirates
All Saints *68* C Antigua, Antigua & Barbuda
Al Lubnān *see* Lebanon
Al Luḩayyah *599* W Yemen
Al Ma'āmīr *91* NE Bahrain
Alma-Ata *312 Rus./Kaz.* Almaty. ❖ of Kazakhstan, SE Kazakhstan
Almada *442* W Portugal
Al Madīnah *472 Eng.* Medina. W Saudi Arabia
Al Mafraq *310 var.* Mafraq. N Jordan
Al Mahdīyah *see* Mahdia
Al Maḩmūdīyah *284 var.* Mahmudiya. C Iraq
Al Mahrah *599* mountains of E Yemen
Al Majma'ah *472* C Saudi Arabia
Al Mālikīyah *91* W Bahrain
Al Mālikīyah *521 var.* Dayrīk. NE Syria
Almalyk *580 Uzb.* Olmaliq. E Uzbekistan
Al Mamlakah *see* Morocco
Al Manādir *560 var.* Al Manadir. Desert region of Oman and United Arab Emirates
Al Manāmah *see* Manama
Al Manāşif *521* mountains of E Syria
Al Manşūrah *see* El Manşûra
Al Maqţa' *560* C United Arab Emirates
Al Marj *339 var.* Barka, *It.* Barce. NE Libya
Al Marsá *see* La Marsa
Almaty *see* Alma-Ata
Al Mawşil *284 Eng.* Mosul. N Iraq
Al Mayādīn *521 Fr.* Meyadine. E Syria
Al Mazra' *310 var.* Al Mazra'ah. W Jordan
Almelo *397* E Netherlands
Almendra, Embalse de *501* reservoir of NW Spain
Almere *397* C Netherlands
Almería *501* S Spain
Al Mīnā' *see* El Mina
Al Minyā *see* El Minya
Al Miqdādīyah *see* Al Muqdādīyah
Almirante *424* W Panama
Al Mubarraz *472* NE Saudi Arabia
Al Mudawwarah *310* SW Jordan
Al Muḩammadīyah *91 var.* Umm aş Şabbān. Island of NW Bahrain
Al Muḩarraq *91 var.* Moharek, Muharraq, Jazirat al Muharraq. Bahrain
Al Mukallā *599 var.* Mukalla. SE Yemen
Al Mukhā *599 Eng.* Mocha. SW Yemen
Al Muknīn *see* Moknine
Al Munastīr *see* Monastir
Al Muqdādīyah *284 var.* Al Miqdādīyah. C Iraq
Al Mussayyib *284* C Iraq
Al Obayyid *see* El Obeid
Alofi *626* ❖ of Niue, W Niue
Alofi, Île *629* island of Île Futuna, N Wallis & Futuna
Alohungari *233* E Gambia
Alor, Kepulauan *276* island group of E Indonesia
Alor, Pulau *276* island of E Indonesia
Alor Setar *354 var.* Alur Setar, Alor Star. NW Peninsular Malaysia
Alost *see* Aalst
Alotau *426* SE Papua New Guinea
Aloupos *187 var.* Çiftlik Dere. River of NW Cyprus
Alpen *see* Alps
Alpes *see* Alps
Alphen aan de Rijn *397* W Netherlands
Alphonse Group *478* island group of C Seychelles
Alpi *see* Alps
Alps *82, 225, 294, 516 It.* Alpi, *Fr.* Alpes, *Ger.* Alpen. Mountain range of C Europe
Al Qābil *418 var.* Qabil. NW Oman
Al Qaḑārif *see* Gedaref
Al Qāhirah *see* Cairo
Al Qal'ah al Kubrá *see* Kalaa Kebira
Al Qāmishlī *521 var.* Kamishli. NE Syria
Al Qaryah *91* NE Bahrain
Al Qaryāt *339* NW Libya
Al Qaşr *310* W Jordan
Al-Qaşrayn *see* Kasserine
Al Qayrawān *see* Kairouan
Al Qubayyāt *see* Qoubaiyat
Al Qubbah *339* NE Libya
Al Quds *see* Jerusalem
Al Quşayr *521 var.* El Quseir, *Fr.* Kousseir. W Syria
Al Quţayfah *521 var.* Quţayfah, Quteife, *Fr.* Kouteifé. SW Syria
Al Quwayrah *310 var.* Makhfar al Quwayrah, El Quweira. SW Jordan
Als *190 Ger.* Alsen. Island of S Denmark
Alsace *255* cultural region of NE France
Alsen *see* Als
Al Shahaniyah *see* Ash Shaḩanīyah
Alt *see* Olt
Alta *414* NE Norway
Altai Mountains *380* mountain range of C Asia
Altay *162 Chin.* A-le-t'ai, *prev.* Ch'eng-hua, *var.* Chenghwa, *Mong.* Sharasume. Xinjiang Uygur Zizhiqu, NW China
Altay *380* W Mongolia
Altay, Respublika *453* autonomous republic of C Russia
Alt de la Coma Pedrosa, Pic *62* mountain of NW Andorra
Altkanischa *see* Kanjiža
Alto Molócuè *387* C Mozambique
Alto Paraná *see* Paraná
Alt-Schwanenburg *see* Gulbene
Altsohl *see* Zvolen
Altun Shan *162 var.* Altyn Tagh. Mountain range of Xinjiang Uygur Zizhiqu, NW China
Altyn Tagh *see* Altun Shan
Alu *see* Shortland Island
Al Ubayyiḑ *see* El Obeid
Al 'Udayd *560 var.* Al Odaid. W United Arab Emirates
Alūksne *330 Ger.* Marienburg. NE Latvia
Al 'Ulā *472* NW Saudi Arabia
Al 'Umarī *310* C Jordan
Al Uqşur *see* Luxor
Al Wafrā' *322* SE Kuwait
Al Wāḩāt al Khārijah *see* El Wâhât el Khârga
Al Wajh *472* NW Saudi Arabia
Al Wakrah *447 var.* Wakra. E Qatar
Al Wukayr *447 var.* Al Wukair. E Qatar
Alyat *see* Älät
Alyaty-Pristan' *see* Älät
Alytus *344 Pol.* Olita. S Lithuania
Al Zubair *see* Az Zubayr
Amadora *442* W Portugal
Amakusa-shotō *304* island group to the W of Kyūshū, SW Japan
Amala *316* river of SW Kenya
Amami-Ō-shima *304* island of Amami-shotō, SW Japan
Amami-shotō *304* island group of Nansei-shotō, SW Japan
Amara *see* Al 'Amārah
Amarapura *135* C Burma
Amasia *74 Rus.* Amasiya, *var.* Amasija. NW Armenia
Amasya *547* N Turkey
Amatique, Bahía de, *250* bay of the Gulf of Honduras
Amaury *368* NE Mauritius
Amazon *121, 171, 431 Sp.* Amazonas. River of South America
Amazonia *120* physical region of C South America
Ambalangoda *504* SW Sri Lanka
Ambalavao *350* S Madagascar
Ambam *144* S Cameroon
Ambanja *350* N Madagascar
Ambato *200* C Ecuador
Ambatondrazaka *350* E Madagascar
Ambergris Cay *102* island of NE Belize
Ambergris Cays *629* island group of S Turks and Caicos Islands
Ambilobe *350* N Madagascar
Amblève *99* river of E Belgium
Ambo *see* Hāgere Hiywet
Amboasary *350* S Madagascar
Ambohidratrimo *350* C Madagascar
Ambon *276 prev.* Amboina. Ambon, C Indonesia
Ambositra *350* C Madagascar
Ambre, Ile d' *368* Island of NE Mauritius
Ambriz *64* NW Angola
Ambrym *585 var.* Ambrim. Island of E Vanuatu
'Amd *599* C Yemen
Ameland *397* island of Waddeneilanden, N Netherlands
American Samoa *618* unincorporated territory of the USA, Pacific Ocean.
Amersfoort *397* C Netherlands
Amherst *see* Kyaikkami
Amiens *225* N France
Amilḩayt, Wādī *418 var.* Wādī Umm al Ḩayt. Seasonal watercourse of SW Oman
Amindivi Islands *270* island group of Lakshadweep, SW India
Amioun *332 var.* Amyūn. N Lebanon
Amirante Islands *478 var.* Amirantes Group. Island of C Seychelles
Amlamé *537* C Togo
Amman *310 Ar.* 'Ammān. ❖ of Jordan, NW Jordan
Ammochostos *see* Gazimağusa
Ammochostos Bay *see* Famagusta Bay
Amnok *see* Yalu
Āmol *281 var.* Amul. N Iran
Amorgós *245* island of SE Greece
Amouli *618 var.* Tau. Tau, E American Samoa
Amourj *366* SE Mauritania
Ampara *504* E Sri Lanka
Amphitrite Group *627* island group of N Paracel Islands
'Amrān *599* W Yemen
Amrāvati *270 prev.* Amraoti. C India
Amritsar *270* N India
Amstelveen *397* W Netherlands
Amsterdam *397* ❖ of the Netherlands, C Netherlands
Amstetten *82* N Austria
Am Timan *156* SE Chad
Amu Darya *53, 528, 550, 580 Turkm.* Amyderya, *Uzb.* Amudaryo. River of C Asia
Amudat *554* E Uganda
Amul *see* Āmol
Amund Ringnes Island *146* island of Sverdrup Islands, N Canada
Amundsen Gulf *146* gulf of the Beaufort Sea, on the NW coast of Canada
Amundsen-Scott *66* US research station at the South Pole, Greater Antarctica, Antarctica
Amundsen Sea *66* sea of the Pacific Ocean, off Antarctica
Amur *163, 453 Chin.* Heilong Jiang. River of China and Russia
Amyderya *see* Amu Darya
Amyūn *see* Amioun
An Abhainn Mhór *see* Blackwater
Anaco *589* NE Venezuela
Anadolu Dağları *see* Doğu Karadeniz Dağlarıı
Anadyr, Gulf of *see* Anadyrskiy Zaliv
Anadyrskiy Zaliv *453 Eng.* Gulf of Anadyr. Gulf of Bering Sea, bordering NE Russia
Anáfi *245* island of SE Greece
Anaiza *see* 'Unayzah
Analalava *350* N Madagascar
Analamaitsa Plateau *350* plateau of NE Madagascar
Anambas, Kepulauan *276* island group to the NW of Borneo, W Indonesia
Anan *304* Shikoku, SW Japan
Anantapur *270* S India
Anápolis *121* S Brazil
Anarjokka *see* Inarijoki
Anatahan *626* island of C Northern Mariana Islands
Anatolia Plateau *546* plateau of C Turkey
Anatom *585 var.* Aneityum, *prev.* Kéamu. Island of S Vanuatu
An Bhearú *see* Barrow
An Bhóinn *see* Boyne
Anchorage *568* Alaska, USA
Ancona *295* C Italy
Andalucia *500-501* autonomous community of S Spain
Andaman Islands *270* island group of SE India
Andaman Sea *135, 276, 533* sea of Indian Ocean, to the SW of Burma and Thailand
'Andām, Wadi *418* seasonal desert watercourse of E Oman
Andapa *350* NE Madagascar
Andaung Pech *see* Bâ Kêv
Andenne *99* SE Belgium
Anderson Air Force Base *623* NE Guam
Andes *71, 112, 159, 171, 200, 431* mountain range of South America, running the entire length of the west coast
Andfjorden *414* fjord of NE Norway
Andijon *see* Andizhan
Andikíthira *245* island of S Greece
Andipsara *245* island of E Greece
Andizhan *580 var.* Andižan, *Uzb.* Andijon. E Uzbekistan
Andkhvoy *53* N Afghanistan
Andoany *350 prev.* Hell-Ville. N Madagascar
Andong *496 Jap.* Antō. E South Korea
Andong-ho *496* reservoir of E South Korea
Andorra *62-63* officially Principality of Andorra. Country of SW Europe divided into 7 admin. units (parishes)
Andorra la Vella *62* ❖ of Andorra, W Andorra
Andreas *623* N Isle of Man
Andreas, Cape *see* Apostolos Andreas, Cape
Andria *295* S Italy
Androna, Lembalemba Ambanin' *350 var.* Plateau de l'Androna. Plateau of N Madagascar
Ándros *245* island of SE Greece
Andros Island *88* island of W Bahamas
Andros Town *88* Andros Island, Bahamas
Andújar *501* SW Spain
Anegada *619* island of NE British Virgin Islands
Aného *537 var.* Anécho, *prev.* Petit-Popo. S Togo
Aneityum *see* Anatom
Änew *see* Annau
An Fheoir *see* Nore
Anfile Bay *210* bay of the Red Sea to the E of Eritrea
Angara *453* river of C Russia
Angarsk *453* C Russia
Angaur *627* island of S Palau
Ånge *513* C Sweden

Angel *see* Úhlava
Ángel de la Guarda, Isla *370* island of NW Mexico
Angeles *435* Luzon, N Philippines
Angers *225* NW France
Ângk Tasaôm *141* *prev.* Angtassom. S Cambodia
Anglesey *563* *Wel.* Môn. Island of NW Wales, UK
Angmagssalik *622* SE Greenland
Angoche *387* E Mozambique
Angola *64-65* officially Republic of Angola, *prev.* People's Republic of Angola. Country of Central Africa divided into 18 admin. units (provinces)
Angora *see* Ankara
Angoram *426* N Papua New Guinea
Angoulême *225* W France
Angra Pequena *see* Lüderitz
Angren *580* E Uzbekistan
Angtassom *see* Ângk Tasaôm
Anguilla *618* British dependent territory of the Caribbean Sea. ❖ The Valley.
Anguilla Cays *88* islets of W Bahamas
Anguilla Channel *618, 622* channel of the Caribbean Sea between Anguilla and St-Martin
Anguilles *368* river of S Mauritius
Anguillita Island *618* island of S Anguilla
Angwa *612* river of Mozambique and Zimbabwe
Anhui *163* *var.* Anhwei. Province of E China
Anhwei *see* Anhui
Anibare Bay *392* bay of the Pacific Ocean, E Nauru
Anié *537* C Togo
Añisoc *208* *var.* Añisok. NE Río Muni, Equatorial Guinea
Añisok *see* Añisoc
Aniwa *585* island of S Vanuatu
Anjou *224-225* cultural region of NW France
Anju *413* W North Korea
Ankara *547* *prev.* Angora. ❖ of Turkey, C Turkey
Ankaratra, Tangorombohitr' *350* *var.* Ankaratra Range. Mountains of C Madagascar
An Laoi *see* Lee
Ânlong Vêng *141* NW Cambodia
An Mhuir Cheilteach *see* Celtic Sea
Annaba *59* *prev.* Bône. NE Algeria
An Nabk *521* *var.* Nebk, El Nebk, *Fr.* Nébeck. SW Syria
An Nafūd *472* desert region of N Saudi Arabia
Annai *256* SW Guyana
An Najaf *284* *var.* Najaf. C Iraq
Annam *see* Trung Phân
Annapolis *569* Maryland, E USA
Anna, Pulo *627* island of S Palau
Annapurna *395* mountain massif of C Nepal
An Nāqūrah *see* En Nâqaoûra
Ann Arbor *569* Michigan, NC USA
An Nás *see* Naas
An Nāṣirīyah *284* *var.* Nasiriya. SE Iraq
Annau *551* *Turkm.* Änew. S Turkmenistan
Annecy *225* E France
An Nīl al Abyaḍ *see* White Nile
An Nīl al Azraq *see* Blue Nile
Annotto Bay *303* E Jamaica
An Nuwaydirāt *91* NE Bahrain
Anṣāb *see* Niṣāb
Anse-à-Galets *258* Île de la Gonâve, Haiti
Anseba *210* seasonal river of W Eritrea
Anse Boileau *478* Mahé, Seychelles
Anse-d'Hainault *258* SW Haiti
Anse Étoile *478* Mahé, Seychelles
Anse Ger *465* SE St Lucia
Anse La Raye *465* NW St Lucia
Anse-Rouge *258* NW Haiti
Anse Royale *478* *var.* Anse Royal. Mahé, Seychelles
Anshan *163* *var.* An-shan. Liaoning, NE China
Anson Bay *626* bay of the South Pacific Ocean, NW Norfolk Island
Ansongo *360* E Mali
Antakya *547* *var.* Hatay. S Turkey
Antalaha *350* NE Madagascar
Antalya *546* *prev.* Adalia. SW Turkey
Antalya Körfezi *546* *var.* Gulf of Adalia, *Eng.* Gulf of Antalya. Gulf of the Mediterranean Sea
Antananarivo *350* *prev.* Tananarive. ❖ of Madagascar, C Madagascar
Antarctica *66-67* largely ice-covered continent centred on the South Pole. Though not internationally recognized the following territorial claims have been made: Argentine Antarctica Sector, Australian Antarctic Territory, British Antarctic Territory, Chilean Antarctic Territory, Queen Maud Land (*Nor.*) Dronning Maud Land, Ross Dependency (*NZ*), Terre Adélie (*Fr.*)
Antequera *501* S Spain
Antibes *225* SE France
Antigua *see* Antigua Guatemala
Antigua *68* island of Lesser Antilles which, with Barbuda, forms Antigua & Barbuda
Antigua and Barbuda *68-69* island state of the West Indies, divided into 6 admin. units (parishes)
Anti-Atlas *382* mountain range of SW Morocco
Antigua Guatemala *250* *var.* Antigua. SW Guatemala
Anti-Lebanon Mountains *332, 521* *Fr.* Anti-Liban, *Ar.* Al Jabal ash Sharqī, *var.* Jebel esh Sharqi. Mountain range of Lebanon and Syria
Anti-Liban *see* Anti-Lebanon
Antivari *see* Bar
Antō *see* Andong
Antofagasta *159* N Chile
Antongila, Helodrano *350* *var.* Baie d'Antongil, Antongil Bay. Bay to the NE of Madagascar
Antrim Mountains *563* mountain range of NE Northern Ireland, UK
Antseranana *see* Antsirañana
An tSionainn *see* Shannon
Antsirabe *350* C Madagascar
Antsirañana *350* *var.* Antseranana, Antsirane, *prev.* Diégo-Suarez. N Madagascar
An tSiúir *see* Suir
Antsla *212* *Ger.* Anzen. SE Estonia
An tSláine *see* Slaney
Antsohihy *350* N Madagascar
An-tung *see* Dandong
Antwerp *see* Antwerpen
Antwerpen *99* *Eng.* Antwerp, *Fr.* Anvers. N Belgium
Anuradhapura *504* N Sri Lanka
Anuta *488* *var.* Cherry I. Island of E Solomon Islands
Anvers *see* Antwerpen
Anyang *496* NW South Korea
Anzen *see* Antsla
Aoba *585* *var.* Omba, Ambae. Island of C Vanuatu
Aola *488* NE Guadalcanal, Solomon Is
Aomori *304* Honshū, N Japan
A'opo *596* Sauai'i, Western Samoa
Aorangi *see* Mount Cook
Aosta *294* N Italy
Ao Thai *see* Thailand, Gulf of
Aouk *154, 156* river of Central African Republic and Chad
Aozou *156* N Chad
Aozou Strip *156, 339* disputed region of N Chad, claimed by Libya
Apaporis *171* river of Brazil and Colombia
Aparan *74* C Armenia
Apartadó *171* NW Colombia
Apatity *252* NW Russia
Apatou *621* NW French Guiana
Ape *330* NE Latvia
Apeldoorn *397* C Netherlands
Apenrade *see* Åbenrå
Apéyémé *see* Danyi-Apéyémé
Apia *596* ❖ of Western Samoa, Upolu, Western Samoa
Apitiri, Monts *621* mountain range of S French Guiana
Apoera *508* NW Suriname
Apolima *596* Upolu, Western Samoa
Apolima Strait *596* strait between Savai'i and Upolu, Western Samoa
Apo, Mount *435* mountain of Mindanao, S Philippines
Apopa *207* C El Salvador
Apostolos Andreas, Cape *187* *var.* Cape Andreas, Zafer Burnu. Cape of Cyprus
Apoteri *256* C Guyana
Appalachian Mountains *569* mountain range of E USA
Appennines *294, 468* *It.* Appennino. Mountain range of C Italy
Appennino *see* Appennines
Appikalo *508* S Suriname
Approuague, l' *621* river of E French Guiana
Apra Harbour *623* harbour of W Guam
Apra Heights *623* W Guam
Apsheronskiy Poluostrov *see* Abşeron Yarımadası
Apure *589* river of W Venezuela
Apurímac *431* river of S Peru
Aqaba *see* Al 'Aqabah
Aqaba, Gulf of *202, 291, 310* *var.* Gulf of 'Aqabah, Gulf of Elat, *Ar.* Khalīj al 'Aqabah. Gulf of Red Sea between Egypt and Jordan
'Aqabah, Gulf of *see* Aqaba, Gulf of
Āqchah *53* *var.* Āqcheh. N Afghanistan
Aqmola *see* Akmola
Aqtaū *see* Aktau
Aqtöbe *see* Aktyubinsk
Aquila *see* L'Aquila
Aquila degli Abruzzi *see* L'Aquila
Aquin *258* SW Haiti
'Arabah, Wādī al *291, 310* *Heb.* Ha'Arava. Dry watercourse of Israel and Jordan
Arabian Gulf *see* Persian Gulf
Arabian Sea *418, 420-421* sea of the Indian Ocean between Arabia and India
'Arab, Baḥr al *see* Arab, Bahr el
Arab, Bahr el *506* *var.* Baḥr al 'Arab. River of S Sudan
'Arabī, Khalīj al *see* Persian Gulf
Arab Sahara *see* Sahara
'Arab, Shaṭṭ al *284* *Per.* Arvand Rūd. River of Iran and Iraq
Aracaju *121* E Brazil
Árachthos *245* *prev.* Árakhthos. River of W Greece
Arad *448* W Romania
'Arad *291* S Israel
'Arād *91* NE Bahrain
'Arādah *560* SW United Arab Emirates
Aradhippou *187* *var.* Aradippou. SE Cyprus
Arafura Sea *77, 276* sea of the Indian Ocean between Australia and New Guinea
Aragac *see* Aragats Lerr
Aragats Lerr *74* *var.* Aragac. Mountain of W Armenia
Aragón *501* autonomous community of E Spain
Araguaia *121* *var.* Araguaya. River of C Brazil
Araguaya *see* Araguaia
Aragvi *234* river of C Georgia
Arai *304* Honshū, C Japan
Arainn Mhór *see* Aran Island
Arāk *281* NW Iran
Arakan Yoma *135* mountain range of W Burma
Araks *see* Aras
Aral Sea *312, 580* *Kaz.* Aral Tengizi, *Rus.* Aral'skoye More, *Uzb.* Orol Dengizi. Inland sea of Kazakhstan and Uzbekistan
Aral'sk *312* *var.* Aral. SW Kazakhstan
Aral Tengizi *see* Aral Sea
Aran Island *288* *Ir.* Arainn Mhór. Island of NW Ireland
Aran Islands *288* island group of W Ireland
Aranos *391* SE Namibia
Aranuka *320* island of the Gilbert Is, W Kiribati
Aranyosmarót *see* Zlaté Moravce
Arao *304* Kyūshū, SW Japan
Araouane *360* N Mali
Arapey Grande *577* river of N Uruguay
Ararat *74* S Armenia
Ararat, Mount *see* Büyükağrı Dağı
Aras *74, 86, 281, 547* *Arm.* Arak's, *Per.* Rūd-e Aras, *Rus.* Araks, *Turk.* Aras Nehri. River of SW Asia
Arauca *171* NE Colombia
Arauca *589* river of Colombia and Venezuela
Arawa *426* Bougainville I, Papua New Guinea
Ārba Minch' *215* SW Ethiopia
Arbatax *294* Sardegna, W Italy
Arbīl *284* *var.* Irbīl, Erbil, *Kurd.* Hawlēr. N Iraq
Arbon *516* NE Switzerland
Arcalis *62* NW Andorra
Archangel *see* Arkhangel'sk
Arctic Bay *146* N Canada
Arctic Ocean *146, 414, 453* *Nor.* Nordishavet, *Rus.* Severnyy Ledovityy Okean. Ocean surrounding North Pole, between N America, N Europe and N Asia
Arctowski *66* Polish research station of South Shetland Islands, Antarctica
Arda *128* river of Bulgaria and Geece
Ardabīl *281* *var.* Ardebil. NW Iran
Arḍ aş Şawwān *310* *var.* Ardh es Suwwān. Plain of C Jordan
Ardennes *99, 346* plateau of W Europe
Arecibo *627* N Puerto Rico
Arel *see* Arlon
Arenal, Laguna *178* lake of NW Costa Rica
Arenas *424* SW Panama
Arendal *414* S Norway
Arensburg *see* Kuressaare
Arequipa *431* SE Peru
Arezzo *295* C Italy
Argentina *70-73* officially Republic of Argentina. Country of S South America divided into 23 admin. units (22 provinces, 1 district)
Arghandāb, Daryā-ye *53* river of S Afghanistan
Argirocastro *see* Gjirokastër
Argo *506* N Sudan
Argoub *382* W Western Sahara
Argun' *453* river of China and Russia
Argungu *408* NW Nigeria
Argyle, Lake *77* salt lake of NW Australia
Argyrokastron *see* Gjirokastër
Århus *190* *var.* Aarhus. C Denmark
Ariamsvlei *391* S Namibia
Ariana *543* *var.* Aryānah, L'Ariana. N Tunisia
Ari Atoll *358* atoll of C Maldives
Arica *159* N Chile
Aride, Île *478* island of the Inner Islands, NE Seychelles
Arīḥā *see* Jericho
Arima *540* N Trinidad, Trinidad & Tobago
Arinsal *62* NW Andorra
Arinsal, Riu d' *62* river of NW Andorra
Aripuanã *120* river of W Brazil
Arizona *568* state of SW USA
Arkalyk *312* *Kaz.* Arqalyk. C Kazakhstan

Axim *242* S Ghana
Axios *see* Vadar
Ayabe *304* Honshū, C Japan
Ayacucho *431* S Peru
Ayaguz *312 Kaz.* Ayaköz. E Kazakhstan
Ayaköz *see* Ayaguz
Ayamé Reservoir *300* reservoir of E Ivory Coast
Ayamiken *208* NW Río Muni, Equatorial Guinea
Āybak *53 var.* Aibak, Haibak. NE Afghanistan
Aydarkul', Ozero *580 Uzb.* Aydarkŭl. River of E Uzbekistan
Aydın *546* SW Turkey
Ayer Chawan, Pulau *483* island of SW Singapore
Ayer Hitam *354* S Peninsular Malaysia
Ayer Merbau, Pulau *483* island of SW Singapore
Ayers Rock *see* Uluru
Ayeyarwady *see* Irrawaddy
Ayia Napa *187 var.* Agia Napa. E Cyprus
Ayios Amvrosios *see* Esentepe
Áyios Eustratios *245* island of E Greece
Ayios Ioannis *187 var.* Agios Ioannis. SW Cyprus
Ayios Seryios *see* Yeniboğaziçi
Ayios Theodhoros *see* Çayirova
'Ayn al Ghazāl *339* SE Libya
'Ayn ath Tha'lab *339* C Libya
Ayni *528 var.* Ajni. W Tajikistan
Ayorou *407* W Niger
'Ayoûn el 'Atroûs *366 var.* Aïoun el Atroûss. SE Mauritania
Ayr *563* W Scotland, UK
Ayre, Point of *623* headland on the N coast of Isle of Man
Ayrs' *312* S Kazakhstan
Āysha *215* NE Ethiopia
Aytos *128 var.* Aitos, Ajtos. E Bulgaria
Ayutthaya *533 var.* Phra Nakhon Si Ayutthaya. C Thailand
Aywat aş Şay'ar, Wādī *599* seasonal river of N Yemen
Azaha, Costa del *501* coastal region of E Spain
Azaouagh *407 var.* Azaouak. River of W Niger
Azaouak *see* Azaouagh
Azärbaycan *see* Azerbaijan
A'zāz *521* NW Syria
Azbine *see* Aïr
Azerbaijan *86-87* officially Azerbaijani Republic, *Az.* Azärbaycan, *prev.* Azerbaijan SSR. Country of SE Caucasus divided into 66 admin. units (rayons)
Āzezo *215* NW Ethiopia
Azimabad *see* Patna
Azizbekov *see* Vayk'
Azogues *200* S Ecuador
Azores *442 Port.* Arquipélago dos Açores, *var.* Açores. Island group of W Portugal
Azoum *156* river of SE Chad
Azov, Sea of *452, 556 Ukr.* Azovs'ke More, *Rus.* Azovskoye More. Area of Black Sea between Russia and Ukraine
Azovs'ke More *see* Azov, Sea of
Azovskoye More *see* Azov, Sea of
Azraq, Bahr el *see* Blue Nile
Azraq, Wāḩat al *310* oasis of N Jordan
Azrou *382* C Morocco
Azua *198* SE Dominican Republic
Azuero, Península de *424* peninsula of S Panama
Azul *71* E Argentina
Azur, Côte d' *225* coastal region of SE France
'Azza *see* Gaza
Az Zāb al Kabīr *see* Great Zab
Az Zāb aş Şaghīr *see* Little Zab
Aẓ Ẓahrān *472 Eng.* Dhahran. NE Saudi Arabia
Az Zallāq *91* W Bahrain
Az Zarqā' *310* NW Jordan
Az Zāwiyah *339* NW Libya
Azzel Matti, Sebkha *59 var.* Sebkra Azz el Matti. Salt flat of C Algeria
Az Zaydīyah *599* W Yemen
Az Zilfī *472* C Saudi Arabia
Az Zubayr *284 var.* Al Zubair. SE Iraq

B

Ba *see* Sông Da Rang
Ba *218 prev.* Mba. Viti Levu, W Fiji
Baa Atoll *see* South Maalhosmadulu Atoll
Baaba, Île *626* island of Îles Belep, W New Caledonia
Baabda *332 var.* B'abdā. C Lebanon
Baalbek *332 var.* Ba'labakk. E Lebanon
Baar *516* N Switzerland
Baardheere *490 var.* Bardere, *It.* Bardera. SW Somalia
Baarle-Hertog *99* exclave of N Belgium
Bába *349 var.* Buševa Planina. Mountain range of Greece and FYR Macedonia
Bababé *366* SW Mauritania
Babahoyo *200 prev.* Bodegas. C Ecuador
Bābā, Kūh-e *53* mountain range of C Afghanistan
Bāb al Mandab *see* Bab el Mandeb
Babatag, Khrebet *580 var.* Hrebet Babatag. Mountains of Tajikistan and Uzbekistan
Bab el Mandeb *194, 599 Ar.* Bāb al Māndab. Strait connecting the Gulf of Aden and Red Sea, between Djibouti and Yemen
Babelthuap *627* island of E Palau
Babian Jiang *see* Black River
Babonneau *465* N St Lucia
Babruysk *104 Rus.* Bobruysk. E Belorussia
Babuyan Channel *435* channel connecting South China Sea and Pacific Ocean
Babuyan Islands *435* island of N Philippines
Bacan, Pulau *276 prev.* Batjan. Island of Maluku, E Indonesia
Bacău *448* NE Romania
Bắc Bô, Vinh *see* Tongking, Gulf of
Bắc Giang *593* N Vietnam
Bach Long Vi, Đao *593* island of N Vietnam
Bačka Topola *602 Hung.* Topolya, *prev.* Bácstopolya. N Serbia, Yugoslavia
Bac Liêu *593 var.* Vinh Loi. S Vietnam
Bacolod *435* Negros, C Philippines
Bac Phân *593 var.* Tonkin, Tongking. Cultural region of N Vietnam
Bácstopolya *see* Bačka Topola
Badajoz *500* W Spain
Badalona *501* E Spain
Badas *126* W Brunei
Baden *82 var.* Baden bei Wien. NE Austria
Baden *516* N Switzerland
Bad Ischl *82* C Austria
Bādiyat ash Badkhyz *551 var.* Badhyz, *Turkm.* Bathyz. Region of S Turkmenistan
Bādiyat ash Shām *see* Syrian Desert
Badkhyz ash Shām *see* Syrian Desert
Badou *537* W Togo
Badulla *504* C Sri Lanka
Badyarada 'Adméd *see* Aden, Gulf of
Baetic Mountains *see* Penibético, Sistema
Bafang *144* W Cameroon
Bafatá *254* C Guinea-Bissau
Baffin Bay *147, 622* bay of the Atlantic Ocean, between Baffin Island, NE Canada and Greenland
Baffin Island *147* island of NE Canada
Bafia *144* C Cameroon
Bafilo *537* NE Togo
Bafing *253, 360* headstream of the Senegal river, Guinea and Mali
Bafoussam *144* W Cameroon
Bafra *547* N Turkey
Baga *409* NE Nigeria
Bagaces *178* NW Costa Rica
Bagamoyo *530* E Tanzania
Baganuur *380* C Mongolia
Baghdad *284 var.* Bagdad, *Ar.* Baghdād. ❖ of Iraq, C Iraq
Bāgherhat *93* SW Bangladesh
Baghlān *53* NE Afghanistan
Baghramyan *74 var.* Bagramyan. W Armenia
Baglung *395* C Nepal
Bago *435 var.* Bago City. Negros, C Philippines
Bago *see* Pegu
Bagoé *360* river of Ivory Coast and Mali
Bagramyan *see* Baghramyan
Baguio *435* Luzon, N Philippines
Bagzane, Monts *407* mountain of N Niger
Bahamas *88-89* officially Commonwealth of the Bahamas. Island state of the W Atlantic Ocean
Baharden *see* Bakherden
Bahāwalpur *421 var.* Bhawalpur. E Pakistan
Bāherden *see* Bakherden
Bahía Blanca *71* E Argentina
Bahía de Caráquez *see* Caráquez
Bahía, Islas de la *260* island group to the N of Honduras
Bahir Dar *215 var.* Bahr Dar. NW Ethiopia
Bahlah *418 var.* Bahla. N Oman
Bahrain *90-91* officially State of Bahrain, *Ar.* Al Baḩrayn, *prev.* Bahrein. Country of the Persian Gulf divided into 9 admin. units (municipalities and regions)
Bahrain, Gulf of *91, 447 var.* Khalīj al Baḩrayn. Area of the Persian Gulf, off the E coast of Arabian Peninsula
Bahrām Chāh *53* SW Afghanistan
Bahr Dar *see* Bahir Dar
Bahrein *see* Bahrain
Baia Mare *448 Hung.* Nagybánya, *Ger.* Neustadt. N Romania
Baïbokoum *156* S Chad
Baicheng *163 var.* Pai-ch'eng, *prev.* T'aon-an. Jilin. NE China
Baidoa *see* Baydhabo
Baikal, Lake *see* Baykal, Ozero
Baile Átha Cliath *see* Dublin
Bailey's Bay *619* bay of the North Atlantic Ocean, N Bermuda
Bailundo *64 Port.* Vila Teixeira da Silva. C Angola
Bainet *258* S Haiti
Bā'ir *see* Bāyir
Bairiki *320* S Tarawa, Kiribati
Baitadi *395* W Nepal
Baitou Shan *see* Paektu-san
Baiyuda *see* Bayudha Desert
Baja *264* S Hungary
Baja California *370 Eng.* Lower California. Peninsula of NW Mexico
Bājil *599* W Yemen
Bajo Boquete *see* Boquete
Bajos de Haina *198* S Dominican Republic
Bajram Curri *57* N Albania
Bajura *see* Martadi
Bakala *154* C Central African Republic
Bakau *233* W Gambia
Bakel *476* E Senegal
Bâ Kêv *141 var.* Bo Kheo, *prev.* Andaung Pech. NE Cambodia
Bakherden *551 prev.* Bakharden, *var.* Baharden, *Turkm.* Bäherden. SW Turkmenistan
Bākhtarān *281 prev.* Kermānshāh, Qahremānshahr. W Iran
Bakı *see* Baku
Bakı Komissarı *86 Rus.* Imeni 26 Bakinskikh Komissarov. SE Azerbaijan
Bakkaflói *268* area of the Norwegian Sea
Bakony *264 Eng.* Bakony Mountains. Mountain range of W Hungary
Bakoumba *230* SE Gabon
Bakoye *360 var.* Bakoy. Headstream of the Senegal river, W Mali
Baku *86 Az.* Bakı, *var.* Baky. ❖ of Azerbaijan, E Azerbaijan
Bakwanga *see* Mbuji-Mayi
Balabac Island *435* island of W Philippines
Balabac Strait *355, 435* strait connecting the South China Sea and Sulu Sea
Balabio, Île *626* island of W New Caledonia
Balaka *353* S Malawi
Balakovo *452* W Russia
Bal'amā *310* NW Jordan
Bālā Morghāb *53* NW Afghanistan
Balata *465* N St Lucia
Balaton *264 var.* Lake Balaton, *Ger.* Plattensee. Lake of W Hungary
Balbina, Represa *120* reservoir of NW Brazil
Balboa *424* C Panama
Balcarce *71* E Argentina
Balclutha *401* S South Island, New Zealand
Bâle *see* Basel
Baleares, Islas *501 Eng.* Balearic Islands. Island group of E Spain
Balearic Islands *see* Islas Baleares
Balḩāf *599* S Yemen
Balho *194* NW Djibouti
Bali *227* island of C Indonesia
Baliceaux *466* island of C St Vincent & the Grenadines
Balıkesir *546* W Turkey
Balikpapan *276* Borneo, C Indonesia
Balimo *426* SW Papua New Guinea
Balkan Mountains *128 Bul.* Stara Planina. Mountain range of Bulgaria and Yugoslavia
Balkh *53* N Afghanistan
Balkhash *312 Kaz.* Balqash. SE Kazakhstan
Balkhash, Ozero *312 Eng.* Lake Balkhash, *Kaz.* Balqash Köl. Lake of SE Kazakhstan
Balla Balla *see* Mbalabala
Ballarat *77* SE Australia
Ballari *see* Bellary
Ballaugh *623* NW Isle of Man
Balleny Islands *66* island group to the N of Victoria Land, Antarctica
Ballina *288* NW Ireland
Ballymena *563* Northern Ireland, UK
Balqash *see* Balkhash
Balqash Köl *see* Balkhash, Ozero
Balsas *370 var.* Mexcala. River of S Mexico
Balsas *424* river of SE Panama
Bălţi *376 Rus.* Bel'tsy. N Moldavia
Baltic Port *see* Paldiski
Baltic Sea *212, 221, 237, 330, 344, 439, 513 Rus.* Baltiskoye, *Ger.* Ostee. Sea of the Atlantic Ocean between Scandinavia and NE Europe
Baltimore *569* Maryland, E USA
Baltischport *see* Paldiski
Baltiski *see* Paldiski
Baltiskoye More *see* Baltic Sea
Baluchistan *420-421* administrative region of SW Pakistan
Balzar *200* W Ecuador
Balzers *342* S Liechtenstein
Bamako *360* ❖ of Mali, SW Mali
Bambadinca *254* C Guinea-Bissau
Bambama *176* SW Congo
Bambari *154* C Central African Republic

Battowia *466* island of C St Vincent & the Grenadines
Batu Gajah *354* W Peninsular Malaysia
Batu, Kepulauan *276* *prev.* Batoe. Island group to the W of Sumatra, W Indonesia
Bat'umi *234* W Georgia
Batu Pahat *354* *prev.* Bandar Penggaram. S Peninsular Malaysia
Bat Yam *291* C Israel
Bauchi *408* NE Nigeria
Baumann, Pic *see* Agou, Mont
Baures *112* river of NE Bolivia
Bauru *121* S Brazil
Bauska *330* *Ger.* Bauske. S Latvia
Bautzen *237* E Germany
Bavarian Alps *82, 237* *Ger.* Bayerische Alpen. Mountain range of Austria and Germany
Bawku *242* N Ghana
Baxoi *162* Xizang Zizhiqu, W China
Bayamo *182* SE Cuba
Bayamón *627* NE Puerto Rico
Bayanhongor *380* C Mongolia
Bayano, Lago *424* lake of E Panama
Baydhabo *490* *var.* Isha Baydhabo, *It.* Baidoa. SW Somalia
Bayerische Alpen *see* Bavarian Alps
Bāyir *310* *var.* Bā'ir. C Jordan
Bāyir, Wādī *310* *var.* Wādī Bā'ir. Dry watercourse of C Jordan
Baykal, Ozero *453* *Eng.* Lake Baikal. Lake of S Russia
Bay, Laguna de *435* lake of Luzon, N Philippines
Baynūnah *560* desert region of W United Arab Emirates
Bayonne *224* SW France
Bayram-Ali *see* Bayramaly
Bayramaly *551* *prev.* Bayram-Ali, *var.* Bajram-Ali. SE Turkmenistan
Bayrūt *see* Beirut
Baysun *580* *var.* Bajsun, *Uzb.* Boysun. SE Uzbekistan
Bayt al Faqīh *599* W Yemen
Bayt Lahm *see* Bethlehem
Bayudha Desert *506* *var.* Baiyuda, Şahrā' Bayyūḑah. Desert of NE Sudan
Bayy al Kabīr, Wādī *339* dry watercourse of NW Libya
Bayyūḑah, Şahrā' *see* Bayudha Desert
Bazardüzü Dağ *86* *Rus.* Gora Bazardyuzyu. Mountain of N Azerbaijan
Bazargic *see* Dobrich
Bazgrad *128* NE Bulgaria
Bazin *see* Pezinok
Bcharré *332* *var.* Bsharrī. NE Lebanon
Beagle Channel *159* channel connecting Pacific Ocean and Atlantic Ocean
Beata, Isla *198* island of SW Dominican Republic
Beatrice *612* NE Zimbabwe
Beau Bassin *368* W Mauritius
Beaufort Sea *146* sea of the Arctic Ocean to the N of North America
Beaufort West *493* *Afr.* Beaufort-Wes. Western Cape, SW South Africa
Beauvais *225* N France
Béchar *59* *prev.* Colomb-Béchar. W Algeria
Bécs *see* Vienna
Bedanda *254* S Guinea-Bissau
Bedok Reservoir *483* E Singapore
Be'ér Sheva' *291* S Israel
Begamganj *93* SE Bangladesh
Begna *414* river of S Norway
Begovat *see* Bekabad
Behagle *see* Laï
Beibu Wan *see* Tongking, Gulf of
Beida *see* Al Baydā'
Beijing *see* Peking
Beira *387* C Mozambique
Beirut *332* *var.* Beyrouth, Bayrūt. ❖ of Lebanon, W Lebanon
Beruit, Pulau *354* island of W Borneo, Malaysia
Beitbridge *612* S Zimbabwe
Beit Lahiya *291, 292* NE Gaza Strip
Beja *442* SE Portugal
Béja *543* *var.* Bājah. N Tunisia
Béjaïa *59* *prev.* Bougie. N Algeria
Bejhi *421* *var.* Beji. River of W Pakistan
Bekaa Valley *see* El Beqaa
Bekabad *580* *prev.* Begovat, *Uzb.* Bekobod. SE Uzbekistan
Bek-Budi *see* Karshi
Bekdash *551* *var.* Bekdaš. NW Turkmenistan
Békéscsaba *264* SE Hungary
Bekobod *see* Bekabad
Bekwai *242* C Ghana
Bélabo *144* C Cameroon
Belait, Sungai *126* river of C Brunei
Belarus *see* Belorussia
Bela Vista *387* S Mozambique
Belaya Tserkov' *see* Bila Tserkva
Belbeis *see* Bilbeis
Belcher Is *147* island group in Hudson Bay, C Canada
Beledweyne *490* *var.* Belet Huen, *It.* Belet Uen. C Somalia
Belém *121* *prev.* Pará. N Brazil
Belep, Îles *626* island group of W New Caledonia
Belfast *563* Northern Ireland, UK
Belfort *225* NE France
Belgium *98-101* officially Kingdom of Belgium. Country of W Europe divided into 9 admin. units (provinces)
Belgian Congo *see* Zaire
Belgorod *452* W Russia
Belgrade *602* *SCr.* Beograd. ❖ of Yugoslavia, N Serbia, Yugoslavia
Belgrano II *66* Argentinian research station of Greater Antarctica, Antarctica
Belice *see* Belize City
Beligrad *see* Berat
Beli Manastir *181* *Hung.* Pélmonostor. NE Croatia
Belitoeng *see* Belitung, Pulau
Belitung, Pulau *276* *prev.* Belitoeng, Billiton. Island to the SE of Sumatra, W Indonesia
Belize *102* river of Belize and Guatemala
Belize *102-103* Country of Central America divided into 6 admin units (districts)
Belize City *102* *Sp.* Belice. E Belize
Beljak *see* Villach
Bellary *270* *Hind.* Ballari. S India
Bella Unión *577* N Uruguay
Belle-Anse *258* S Haiti
Belle Île *224* island of NW France
Bellenz *see* Bellinzona
Belleplaine *97* N Barbados
Belle Vue *465* S St Lucia
Bellevue Chopin *196* S Dominica
Belle Vue Maurel *368* NE Mauritius
Bellingshausen *66* CIS research station of South Shetland Islands, Antarctica
Bellinzona *516* *Ger.* Bellenz. S Switzerland
Bello *171* NW Colombia
Bello Horizonte *see* Belo Horizonte
Belluno *295* N Italy
Bellville *493* Western Cape, SW South Africa
Belmanier *196* N Dominica
Belmopan *102* ❖ of Belize, C Belize
Belmullet *288* NW Ireland
Belo Horizonte *121* *prev.* Bello Horizonte. SE Brazil
Bel Ombre *368* SW Mauritius
Bel Ombre *478* Mahé, Seychelles
Belorussia *104-107* officially Republic of Belarus, *var.* Belarus, *prev.* Belorussian SSR, *Rus.* Belorus kaya SSR. Country of Europe divided into 6 admin. units (oblasts)
Belorusskaya Gryada *see* Byelruskaya Hrada
Beloshchel'ye *see* Nar'yan-Mar
Belostok *see* Białystok
Belo Tsiribihina *350* *var.* Belo-Tsiribihina, Belo-sur-Tsiribihina. W Madagascar
Belovár *see* Bjelovar
Beloye More *221, 452* *Eng.* White Sea. Sea of Arctic Ocean, bordering NW Russia
Bel'tsy *see* Bălţi
Belukha, Gora *312* mountain of E Kazakhstan and Russia
Bembèrèkè *108* *var.* Bembéréké. N Benin
Benaco *see* Garda, Lago di
Benares *see* Vārānasi
Ben Arous *543* *var.* Bin Arūs. N Tunisia
Bender Beyla *490* *var.* Bandarbeyla, Bender Beila. NE Somalia
Bender Cassim *see* Boosaaso
Bendern *342* NW Liechtenstein
Bendery *see* Tighina
Bendigo *77* SE Australia
Bendugu *480* N Sierra Leone
Benduma *336* NW Liberia
Benemérita de San Cristóbal *see* San Cristóbal
Beneški Zaliv *see* Gulf of Venice
Benešov *188* W Czech Republic
Benevento *295* S Italy
Bengal, Bay of *93, 135, 271, 504* bay of the Indian Ocean
Bengasi *see* Banghāzī
Bengbu *163* *var.* Peng-pu. Anhui, E China
Benghazi *see* Banghāzī
Benguela *64* *var.* Benguella. W Angola
Bengweulu *see* Bangweulu, Lake
Benha *202* *var.* Banhā. N Egypt
Beni *112* river of N Bolivia
Beni *607* NE Zaire
Beni Mellal *382* C Morocco
Benin *108-109* officially Republic of Benin, *prev.* Dahomey. Country of W Africa divided into 6 admin. units (departments)
Benin, Bight of *108, 408, 537* area of the Gulf of Guinea
Benin City *408* SW Nigeria
Beni Suef *202* *var.* Banī Suwayf. N Egypt
Bénitiers, Ile aux *368* SW Mauritius
Benito *see* Mbini
Ben Nevis *563* mountain of C Scotland, UK
Benoni *493* Pretoria-Witwatersrand-Vereeniging, NE South Africa
Be, Nosy *350* *var.* Nossi-Bé. Island of N Madagascar
Bénoué *see* Benue
Bénoy *156* S Chad
Benque Viejo del Carmen *102* *var.* Benque Viejo. W Belize
Bense *196* N Dominica
Bensheim *236* SW Germany
Bensonville *336* *prev.* Bentol. W Liberia
Bent Jbaïl *332* *var.* Bint Jubayl. S Lebanon
Bentol *see* Bensonville
Bentong *354* *var.* Bentung. C Peninsular Malaysia
Bên Tre *593* *var.* Truc Giang. S Vietnam
Benue *144, 408* *Fr.* Bénoué. River of Cameroon and Nigeria
Benxi *163* *var.* Pen-ch'i, Penki. Liaoning, NE China
Beograd *see* Belgrade
Beqa *218* *prev.* Mbengga. Island to the S of Viti Levu, W Fiji
Bequia *466* island of C St Vincent & the Grenadines
Beragala *504* SE Sri Lanka
Berat *57* *var.* Berati, *SCr.* Beligrad. C Albania
Beraun *see* Berounka
Berbera *490* NW Somalia
Berbérati *154* SW Central African Republic
Berbice *256* river of NE Guyana
Berd *74* NE Armenia
Berdyans'k *556* *Rus.* Berdyansk, *prev.* Osipenko. SE Ukraine
Bereeda *490* *var.* Bareeda, *It.* Bereda. NE Somalia
Berekua *196* S Dominica
Berekum *242* W Ghana
Berettyó *264* river of Hungary and Romania
Berezina *see* Byerazino
Berezino *see* Byerazino
Berezniki *452* W Russia
Bergamo *294* N Italy
Bergen *414* SW Norway
Bergen *see* Mons
Berg en Dal *508* NE Suriname
Bergen op Zoom *397* SW Netherlands
Bergisch Gladbach *236* W Germany
Beringen *99* NE Belgium
Bering Sea *453* *Rus.* Beringovo More. Sea of Pacific Ocean between NE Asia and NW North America
Bering Strait *453, 568* *Rus.* Beringov Proliv. Strait connecting Bering Sea and Chukchi Sea, between NE Russia and Alaska, USA
Berkane *382* NE Morocco
Berkeley Sound *621* area of the South Atlantic Ocean, NE Falkland Islands
Berlin *237, 241* ❖ of Germany, NE Germany
Bermuda *619* British Crown colony of the North Atlantic Ocean. ❖ Hamilton.
Bermudian Landing *102* C Belize
Bern *516* *Fr.* Berne. ❖ of Switzerland, W Switzerland
Bernal *431* NW Peru
Bernberg *237* C Germany
Berner Oberland *516* *Eng.* Bernese Oberland. Mountain range of SW Switzerland
Bernina, Passo del *516* mountain pass of SE Switzerland
Béroubouay *see* Gbéroubouè
Beroun *188* W Czech Republic
Berounka *188* *Ger.* Beraun. River of W Czech Republic
Berovo *349* E FYR Macedonia
Berry Islands *88* island group of N Bahamas
Bertoua *144* E Cameroon
Beru *320* island of the Gilbert Is, W Kiribati
Beruni *580* *var.* Biruni, *Uzb.* Beruniy. W Uzbekistan
Beruniy *see* Beruni
Berwick-upon-Tweed *563* NE England, UK
Besalampy *350* NW Madagascar
Besançon *225* E France
Beskiden *see* Beskid Mountains
Beskid Mountains *485* *var.* Beskids, *Slvk.* Beskydy, *Ger.* Beskiden, *Pol.* Beskidy. Mountain range of C Europe
Beskra *see* Biskra
Bessarabka *see* Basarabeasca
Beszterce *see* Bistriţa
Besztercebánya *see* Banská Bystrica
Betanzos *112* S Bolivia
Bétérou *108* *var.* Betérou. C Benin
Bethanien *391* *var.* Bethanie, Bethany. S Namibia
Bethel *625* E Montserrat
Bethesda *68* SE Antigua, Antigua & Barbuda
Bethlehem *493* Orange Free State, C South Africa
Bethlehem *291, 292* *Heb.* Bet Leḥem, *Ar.* Bayt Lahm. C West Bank
Betio *320* Tarawa, W Kiribati
Bétou *176* N Congo
Bet Shemesh *291* C Israel

C

Caicos Passage *88, 629* strait of the Atlantic Ocean, between the Bahamas and Caicos Islands
Cai Lan *593* N Vietnam
Caille Island *248* island to the N of Grenada island, Grenada
Cailungo *468* N San Marino
Caió *254* W Guinea-Bissau
Cairns *77* NE Australia
Cairo *202* *Ar.* Al Qāhirah, *var.* El Qâhira. N Egypt
Cajamarca *431* *prev.* Caxamarca. NW Peru
Cajón, Represa el *260* reservoir of W Honduras
Çakilli Dere *see* Yialias
Čakovec *181* *Hung.* Csáktornya, *Ger.* Csakathurn, *prev.* Tschakathurn. N Croatia
Calabar *408* S Nigeria
Calabozo *589* C Venezuela
Calabrai *299* S Italy
Calagua Islands *435* island group of N Philippines
Calais *225* N France
Calama *159* N Chile
Calamian Group *435* island group of W Philippines
Calandula *64* *var.* Kalandula. NW Angola
Calanscio Sand Sea *see* Kalanshiyū, Sarīr
Călăraşi *448* SE Romania
Călăraşi *376* *var.* Călăras, *Rus.* Kalarash. C Moldova
Calbayog *435* Samar, W Philippines
Calceta *200* W Ecuador
Calcutta *102* N Belize
Calcutta *271* E India
Calcutta *508* N Suriname
Caldas da Rainha *442* W Portugal
Caledon *334, 493* river of Lesotho and South Africa
Caleta Olivia *71* SE Argentina
Calf of Man *632* island of S Isle of Man
Calgary *146* SW Canada
Calhau *152* São Vincente, N Cape Verde
Cali *171* W Colombia
Calibishie *196* N Dominica
Calicut *270* *var.* Kozhikode. S India
Calida, Costa *501* coastal region of SE Spain
California *568* state of W USA
California, Golfo de *370* gulf of the Pacific Ocean
Călilabad *86* *Rus.* Dzhalilabad, *var.* Džalilabad, *prev.* Astrakhan-Bazar. S Azerbaijan
Callao *431* W Peru
Calliaqua *466* S St Vincent, St Vincent & the Grenadines
Caltanissetta *295* Sicilia, S Italy
Cama *198* river of C Dominican Republic
Camabatela *64* NW Angola
Camacupa *64* *Port.* General Machado. C Angola
Camagüey *182* *prev.* Puerto Príncipe. C Cuba
Camagüey, Archipiélago de *182* island group of N Cuba
Ca Mau *593* *var.* Quan Long. S Vietnam
Cambay, Gulf of *see* Khambhat, Gulf of
Cambodia *140-143* officially State of Cambodia, *Cam.* Kampuchea, *prev.* People's Democratic Republic of Kampuchea. Country of SE Asia divided into 20 admin. units (provinces)
Cambrian Mountains *563* mountain range of Wales, UK
Cambridge *303* NW Jamaica
Cambridge *401* C North Island, New Zealand
Cambridge *563* E England, UK
Cambridge Bay *146* Victoria Island, NW Canada
Cambrouze *621* N French Guiana
Cambulo *64* NE Angola
Camden Park *466* SW St Vincent, St Vincent & the Grenadines
Cameron Highlands *354* highlands of C Peninsular Malaysia
Cameroon *144-145* officially Republic of Cameroon, *Fr.* Cameroun. Country of W Africa divided into 10 admin. units (provinces)
Camiri *112* S Bolivia
Camopi *621* river of SE French Guiana
Camopi *621* E French Guiana
Camotes Islands *435* island group of E Philippines
Campana *71* E Argentina
Campbell River *146* Vancouver Island, SW Canada
Campeche *370* SE Mexico
Campeche, Bahía de *370* *var.* Gulf of Campeche. Bay of the Gulf of Mexico
Campeche, Gulf of *see* Campeche, Bahía de
Câm Pha *593* N Vietnam
Campina Grande *121* E Brazil
Campinas *121* S Brazil
Campine *see* Kempen
Campobasso *295* S Italy
Campo Grande *121* SW Brazil
Campos *121* *var.* Campo dos Goitacazes. SE Brazil
Campossa *254* river of E Guinea-Bissau
Cam Ranh *593* SE Vietnam
Camrose *146* SW Canada
Canada *146-151* *prev.* British North America. Country of North America, divided into 12 admin. units (10 provinces, 2 territories)
Cañada de Gómez *71* C Argentina
Canadian *569* river of SW USA
Canadian Shield *see* Laurentian Plateau
Çanakkale *546* W Turkey
Canakkale Boğazi *546* *Eng.* Dardanelles. Strait connecting Marmara Denizi and Aegean Sea
Canala *626* C New Caledonia
Canarias, Islas *501* *Eng.* Canary Islands. Islands of the Atlantic Ocean, part of Spain.
Canaries *465* W St Lucia
Canarreos, Archipiélago de los *182* island group of W Cuba
Canary Islands *see* Canarias, Islas
Cañas *178* NW Costa Rica
Canberra *77* ❖ of Australia, SE Australia
Canchungo *254* *prev.* Teixeira Pinto. W Guinea-Bissau
Cancuén *see* Santa Isabel
Candia *see* Irákleio
Canea *see* Chaniá
Caneel Bay *629* Saint John Island, E Virgin Islands
Canelones *577* *var.* Guadalupe. S Uruguay
Canguzo *see* Cankuzo
Canik Dağları *547* mountain range of N Turkey
Canillo *62* C Andorra
Canjambari *254* river of N Guinea-Bissau
Çankırı *547* N Turkey
Cankuzo *138* *var.* Canguzo. E Burundi
Cannes *225* SE France
Canoas *121* S Brazil
Cano, Pico do *152* mountain of Fogo, S Cape Verde
Canot, Rivière *258* river of C Haiti
Canouan *466* island of S St Vincent & the Grenadines
Cantabria *501* autonomous community of N Spain
Cantábrica, Cordillera *500-501* mountains of N Spain
Cantaro *540* N Trinidad, Trinidad & Tobago
Canterbury *563* SE England, UK
Canterbury Bight *401* area of the Pacific Ocean, SE New Zealand
Canterbury Plains *401* plain of C South Island, New Zealand
Cân Thơ *593* S Vietnam
Canton *see* Guangzhou
Canton Island *see* Kanton
Cao Băng *593* N Vietnam
Cape Breton Island *147* *Fr.* Île du Cap-Breton. Island of SE Canada
Cape Coast *242* *prev.* Cape Coast Castle. S Ghana
Cape Domesnes *see* Kolkasrags
Capellen *346* SW Luxembourg
Cape Palmas *see* Harper
Capesterre *622* Marie-Galante, S Guadeloupe
Capesterre-Belle-Eau *622* S Guadeloupe
Cape Town *493* *Afr.* Kaapstad. Legislative capital of South Africa, Western Cape, SW South Africa
Cape Verde *152-153* officially Republic of Cape Verde, *Port.* Ilhas do Cabo Verde. Country of volcanic islands in the Atlantic Ocean divided into 14 admin. units (districts)
Cape York *77* N Australia
Cape York Peninsula *77* peninsula of N Australia
Cap-Haïtien *258* *var.* Le Cap. N Haiti
Capitán Arturo Prat *66* Chilian research station of South Shetland Islands, Antarctica
Capitán Bado *428* E Paraguay
Capitán Pablo Lagerenza *428* *var.* Mayor Pablo Lagerenza. N Paraguay
Capodistria *see* Koper
Capri, Isola di *295* island of S Italy
Caprivi Concession *see* Caprivi Strip
Caprivi Strip *118, 391* *prev.* Caprivi Concession, *Ger.* Caprivizipfel. Finger of territory of NE Namibia
Caprivizipfel *see* Caprivi Strip
Cap Saint-Jacques *see* Vung Tau
Caquetá *171* river of S Colombia
CAR *see* Central African Republic
Caracal *448* S Romania
Caracas *589* ❖ of Venezuela, N Venezuela
Carache, Ilha de *254* island of W Guinea-Bissau
Caracollo *112* W Bolivia
Caransebes *448* W Romania
Caráquez *200* *prev.* Bahía de Caráquez. W Ecuador
Caratasca, Laguna de *260* lagoon on the E coast of Honduras
Caravela *254* Ilha Caravela, Guinea-Bissau
Caravela, Ilha *254* island of Arquipélago dos Bijagós, W Guinea-Bissau
Carbonia *294* SW Sardegna, Italy
Carcassonne *225* S France
Cardamom, Chaîne des *see* Krâvanh, Chuŏr Phmun
Cardamom Mountains *see* Krâvanh, Chuŏr Phmun
Cárdenas *182* NW Cuba
Cardiff *563* *Wel.* Caerdydd. S Wales, UK
Cardigan Bay *563* bay of W Wales, UK
Cardona *577* SW Uruguay
Cardonagh *288* N Ireland
Čardžou *see* Chardzhev
Carenage *540* NW Trinidad, Trinidad & Tobago
Caribbean Sea *178, 258, 618, 619, 627* arm of the Atlantic Ocean, Central America
Caripito *589* NE Venezuela
Carlton, The *88* *var.* Abraham Bay. Mayaguana, Bahamas
Carletonville *493* North West, N South Africa
Carlisle *563* NW England, UK
Carlow *288* SE Ireland
Carlsruhe *see* Karlsruhe
Carmarthen *563* *Wel.* Caerfyrddin. W Wales, UK
Carmelo *577* *var.* Carmelo del Este. SW Uruguay
Carmona *178* W Costa Rica
Carmona *see* Uíge
Carnavon *76* W Australia
Carnegie, Lake *76* salt lake of W Australia
Carnot *154* W Central African Republic
Caroço, Ilha *471* island to the S of Príncipe, Sao Tome & Principe
Carolina *627* NE Puerto Rico
Caroline Island *320* island of the Line Is, E Kiribati
Caroni *540* river of N Trinidad, Trinidad & Tobago
Caroní *589* river of E Venezuela
Carora *589* NW Venezuela
Carpathian Mountains *188, 439, 448, 556* *var.* Carpathians, *Ger.* Karpaten, *Cz./Pol.* Karpaty. Mountain range of E Europe
Carpaţii Meridionali *448* *var.* South Carpathians, *Eng.* Transylvanian Alps. Mountain range of C Romania
Carpaţii Occidentali *448* mountain range of W Romania
Carpentaria, Gulf of *77* gulf of the Arafura Sea, on the coast of N Australia
Carrantual *see* Carrauntoohill
Carrara *294* N Italy
Carrauntoohill *288* *var.* Carrauntohil, *Ir.* Carrantual. Mountain of SW Ireland
Carriacou *248* island to the north of Grenada, Grenada
Carrick on Shannon *288* N Ireland
Carson City *568* Nevada, W USA
Carstensz, Puntjak *see* Jaya, Puncak
Cartagena *171* NW Colombia
Cartagena *501* SE Spain
Cartago *171* W Colombia
Cartago *178* C Costa Rica
Carúpano *589* NE Venezuela
Casablanca *382* *Ar.* Dar el Beida. NW Morocco
Casamance *476* cultural region of SW Senegal
Casamance *476* river of SW Senegal
Cascade *626* NE Norfolk Island
Cascade *478* Mahé, Seychelles
Cascade Range *568* mountain range of Canada and USA
Casey *66* Australian research station of Greater Antarctica, Antarctica
Caseyr, Raas *490* *var.* Ras Aser, *prev.* Cape Guardafui. Cape on the NE coast of Somalia
Cashel *612* E Zimbabwe
Casilda *71* C Argentina
Ca *593* river of Laos and Vietnam
Casper *569* Wyoming, NW USA
Caspian Sea *86* *Az.* Xäzär Dänizi, *Rus.* Kaspiyskoye More, *Per.* Daryā-ye Khazar, Baḩr-e Khazar, *Kaz.* Kaspiy Tengizi. Shallow inland sea between W Asia and E Europe
Cassacatiza *387* NW Mozambique
Cassai *see* Kasai
Cassel *see* Kassel
Cassiar Mountains *146* mountain range of W Canada
Castellamare di Stabia *295* S Italy
Castellón de la Plana *501* *Cat.* Castelló de la Plana. E Spain
Castelo Branco *442* C Portugal
Castelvetrano *295* Sicilia, S Italy
Castiliano *152* São Nicolau, N Cape Verde
Castilla *431* NW Peru
Castilla-La Mancha *501* autonomous community of NE Spain

Cheju *496 Jap.* Saishū. Cheju-do, South Korea
Cheju-do *496 prev.* Quelpart, *Jap.* Saishu. Island of S South Korea
Cheju Strait *496 var.* Chejuhaehyop, Cheju-Haehyop. Strait connecting the Korea Strait and Yellow Sea
Chek Chue *262 var.* Stanley. S Hong Kong
Chekiang *see* Zhejiang
Chek Lap Kok *262* W Hong Kong
Chek Mun Hoi Hap *262* NE Hong Kong
Cheleken *551 var.* Čeleken. W Turkmenistan
Chelkar *312* W Kazakhstan
Chelyabinsk *452* C Russia
Chemin Grenier *368* S Mauritius
Chemnitz *237 prev.* Karl-Marx-Stadt. E Germany
Chemulpo *see* Inch'ŏn
Ch'eng-chou *see* Zhengzhou
Chengchow *see* Zhengzhou
Chengdu *163 var.* Chengtu. Sichuan, SW China
Chenghsien *see* Zhengzhou
Ch'eng-hua *see* Altay
Chenghwa *see* Altay
Chenkaladi *504* E Sri Lanka
Cheoc Van, Baía de *624* bay of the South China Sea, S Macao
Cheom Ksan *see* Chŏâm Khsant
Chepo *424* NE Panama
Cher *225* river of C France
Cherbourg *225* NW France
Cheren *see* Keren
Cherepovets *452* W Russia
Chergui, Chott ech *59* salt lake of NW Algeria
Chergui, Île *543 Ar.* Jazirat ash Sharqi. Island of E Tunisia
Cherikaw *104* E Belorussia
Cherkasy *556 Rus.* Cherkassy. C Ukraine
Cherne More *see* Black Sea
Chernivtsi *556 Rus.* Chernovtsy, *Rom.* Cernăuţi, *Ger.* Czernowitz. W Ukraine
Chernobil' *556 var.* Chernobyl. N Ukraine
Chernobyl *see* Chernobil'
Cherno More *see* Black Sea
Cherry Island *see* Anuta
Cherskiy *453* NE Russia
Cherskogo, Khrebet *453* mountain range of NE Russia
Cherso *see* Cres
Cherson *see* Kherson
Cherven-Bryag *128 var.* Červen brjag. NW Bulgaria
Chester *563* NW England, UK
Chetumal, Bahia *102 var.* Chetumal Bay. Bay of the Caribbean Sea
Chetumal Bay *see* Chetumal, Bahia
Cheung Chau *262* SW Hong Kong
Cheviot Hills *563* hills of England and Scotland, UK
Ch'ew Bahir *215 var.* Lake Stefanie. Lake of SW Ethiopia
Cheyenne *569* Wyoming, NW USA
Chhlong *see* Phumĭ Chhlong
Chhuk *see* Phumĭ Chhuk
Chhukha *110* SW Bhutan
Chia-i *525 var.* Chiayi, Kiayi, *Jap.* Kagi. W Taiwan
Chia-li *525 var.* Kiali, *Jap.* Kari. W Taiwan
Chia-mu-ssu *see* Jiamusi
Chiang-hsi *see* Jiangxi
Chiang Mai *533 var.* Chiengmai. NW Thailand
Chiang-su *see* Jiangsu
Chiat'ura *234* C Georgia
Chiba *304* Honshū, SE Japan
Chibuto *387* S Mozambique
Chicago *569* Illinois, C USA
Chīchāwatni *421* E Pakistan
Chichicastenango *250* W Guatemala
Chichigalpa *404* W Nicaragua
Ch'i-ch'i-ha-erh *see* Qiqihar
Chiclayo *431* NW Peru
Chicoutimi *147* SE Canada
Chicualacuala *387* SW Mozambique
Chiemsee *237* lake of SE Germany
Chiesanuova *468* SW San Marino
Chih-fu *see* Yantai
Chihli *see* Hebei
Chihli, Gulf of *see* Bo Hai
Chi-hsi *see* Jixi
Chihuahua *370* NW Mexico
Ch'ikhareshi *234* N Georgia
Chikwawa *353* SW Malawi
Chilanga *611* S Zambia
Chilaw *504* W Sri Lanka
Chile *158-161* officially Republic of Chile. Country of South America divided into 13 admin. units (12 regions and 1 metropolitan area)
Chile Chico *159* W Chile
Chilika Lake *270* lake of E India
Chililabombwe *611* C Zambia
Chi-lin *see* Jilin
Chillán *159* C Chile
Chilliwack *146* SW Canada
Chiloé, Isla de *159 var.* Isla Grande de Chiloé. Island of W Chile
Chilumba *353 prev.* Deep Bay. N Malawi
Chi-lung *525 var.* Keelung, *Jap.* Kirun. N Taiwan
Chilwa, Lake *353 var.* Lake Shirwa, *Port.* Lago Chirua. Lake of SE Malawi
Chimaltenango *250* W Guatemala
Chimanimani *612 prev.* Mandidzudzure, *prev.* Melsetter. E Zimbabwe
Chimbay *580 var.* Čimbaj, *Uzb.* Chimboy. NW Uzbekistan
Chimborazo *200* mountain of C Ecuador
Chimbote *431* W Peru
Chimboy *see* Chimbay
Chimishliya *see* Cimişlia
Chimkent *see* Shymkent
Chimoio *387* C Mozambique
China *162-169* officially People's Republic of China, *Chin.* Zhonghua Renmin Gonghe Guo, *var.* Chung-hua Jen-min Kung-ho-kuo, *prev.* Chinese Empire (until January 1912). Country of E Asia divided into 30 admin. units (22 provinces, 5 autonomous regions, 3 province-level municipalities)
Chinan *see* Jinan
Chinandega *404* W Nicaragua
Chincha Alta *431* SW Peru
Chin-chiang *see* Quanzhou
Chin-chou *see* Jinzhou
Chinchow *see* Jinzhou
Chin-do *496 Jap.* Chin-tō. Island of SW South Korea
Chindwin *135* river of NW Burma
Ch'ing Hai *see* Qinghai Hu
Chinghai *see* Qinghai
Chingola *611* C Zambia
Ch'ing-shui *525 var.* Tsingshui, *Jap.* Kiyomizu. W Taiwan
Ching-Tao *see* Qingdao
Chinguetti *366* C Mauritania
Chinhae *496 Jap.* Chinkai. S South Korea
Chinhoyi *612 var.* Sinoia. N Zimbabwe
Chinhsien *see* Jinzhou
Chiniot *421* NE Pakistan
Chinit *141 var.* Chinit. River of C Cambodia
Chinju *496 Jap.* Shinshū. S South Korea
Chinkai *see* Chinhae
Chink Kaplankyr *551* ridge of NW Turkmenistan
Chinko *154* river of E Central African Republic
Chintheche *353 var.* Chinteche. N Malawi
Chin-tō *see* Chin-do
Chios *245 prev.* Khíos. Island of E Greece
Chíos *245 prev.* Khíos, *It.* Scio, *Turk.* Sakis-Adasi. Chios, E Greece
Chipata *611 prev.* Fort Jameson. E Zambia
Chipinge *612 prev.* Chipinga. E Zimbabwe
Chiponde *353* SE Malawi
Chiquimula *250* SE Guatemala
Chiquimulilla *250* S Guatemala
Chiradzulu *353* S Malawi
Chirang *110* S Bhutan
Chirchik *580 var.* Čirčik, *Uzb.* Chirchiq. E Uzbekistan
Chire *see* Shire
Chiredzi *612* SE Zimbabwe
Chirilagua *207* SE El Salvador
Chiriquí *424* W Panama
Chiriquí, Golfo de *424* gulf of the Pacific Ocean to the SW of Panama
Chiriquí Grande *424* W Panama
Chiriquí, Laguna de *424* lagoon of W Panama
Chiromo *353* S Malawi
Chirongui *625* S Mayotte
Chirripó Grande, Cerro *178* mountain of E Costa Rica
Chirua, Lago *see* Chilwa, Lake
Chirundu *612* N Zimbabwe
Chisenga *353* NW Malawi
Ch'i-shan *525 var.* Kishan, *Jap.* Kizan. SW Taiwan
Chishtiān Mandi *421* E Pakistan
Chisimaio *see* Kismaayo
Chişinău *376 var.* Kishinev. ❖ of Moldova, C Moldova
Chissioua Mtsamboro *625* island of NW Mayotte
Chita *453* C Russia
Chitipa *353 prev.* Fort Hill. NW Malawi
Chitose *305* Hokkaidō, N Japan
Chitré *424* S Panama
Chittagong *93 Ben.* Chāttagām. SE Bangladesh
Chittagong Hills *93* hilly region of S Asia
Chitungwiza *612 prev.* Chitangwiza. NE Zimbabwe
Chiuta, Lake *353* lake of SE Malawi
Chivhu *612 prev.* Enkeldoorn. C Zimbabwe
Chixoy *250 var.* Río Negro, Salinas. River of Guatemala and Mexico
Chizarira Hills *612* hilly region of NW Zimbabwe
Chkalov *see* Orenburg
Chlef *59 prev.* El Asnam, Orléansville, *var.* Ech Cheliff, Ech Chleff. NW Algeria
Choa Chu Kang *483* area of W Singapore
Chŏâm Khsant *141 prev.* Cheom Ksan. N Cambodia
Choiseul *465* SW St Lucia
Choiseul *488 var.* Lauru. Island of the W Solomon Islands
Choiseul Sound *621* area of the South Atlantic Ocean, E Falkland Islands
Cholo *see* Thyolo
Choluteca *260* S Honduras
Choluteca *260* river of S Honduras
Choma *611* S Zambia
Chomo Lhari *110* mountain of NW Bhutan
Chomutov *188 Ger.* Komotau. NW Czech Republic
Ch'ŏnan *496 Jap.* Tenan. W South Korea
Chon Buri *533* C Thailand
Chone *200* W Ecuador
Ch'ŏngch'ŏn *413* river of W North Korea
Ch'ŏngjin *413* NE North Korea
Chŏngju *413* W North Korea
Chŏngju *496 prev.* Chŏngup, *Jap.* Seiyu. SW South Korea
Ch'ŏngju *496 var.* Chŏngju. C South Korea
Chongqing *163 var.* Chungking, Ch'ung-ching, Yuzhou. Sichuan, SW China
Chongwe *611* E Zambia
Chŏnju *496 Jap.* Zenshū. SW South Korea
Chorne More *see* Black Sea
Chorzów *439 Ger.* Königshütte. S Poland
Chōsen-kaikyō *see* Korea Strait
Chōshū *see* Ch'ao-chou
Cho-shui Hsi *525* river of W and NE Taiwan
Chota Nagpur Plateau *270* plateau of NE India
Choybalsan *380* E Mongolia
Christchurch *401* E South Island, New Zealand
Christiana *303* C Jamaica
Christiania *see* Oslo
Christian, Point *627* headland of Pitcairn Island, S Pitcairn Islands
Christiansand *see* Kristiansand
Christianshåb *622 var.* Qasigiangguit. W Greenland
Christiansted *629* Saint Croix, S Virgin Islands (US)
Christiansund *see* Kristiansund
Christmas Island *620* Australian external territory of the Indian Ocean. ❖ Flying Fish Cove.
Christmas Island *see* Kiritimati
Chrysochou Bay *see* Khrysokhou Bay
Chu *312 Kaz.* Shū. SE Kazakhstan
Chu *325 var.* Ču, *Kir.* Chüy. River of Kazakhstan and Kyrgyzstan
Chu *593* river of Laos and Vietnam
Chuādānga *93* W Bangladesh
Ch'uan-chou *see* Quanzhou
Chubek *see* Moskovskiy
Ch'u-chiang *see* Shaoguan
Chucunaque *424* river of E Panama
Chudskoye Ozero *see* Peipus, Lake
Chūgoku-sanchi *304* mountain range of Honshū, W Japan
Chuí *see* Chuy
Chukai *354 var.* Cukai. E Peninsular Malaysia
Chukchi Sea *453 Rus.* Chukotskoye More. Sea of Arctic Ocean between NE Asia and NW N America
Chukotskiy Poluostrov *453 Eng.* Chukchi Peninsula. Peninsula of NE Russia
Chulucanas *431* NW Peru
Chumphon *533* S Thailand
Chu-nan *525* NW Taiwan
Ch'unch'ŏn *496 Jap.* Shunsen. N South Korea
Chung-ang Shan-mo *525* mountain range of C Taiwan
Ch'ung-ching *see* Chongqing
Chung-ho *525* N Taiwan
Chung-hsing-hsin-ts'un *525* W Taiwan
Chung-hua Jen-min Kung-ho-kuo *see* China
Ch'ungju *496 Jap.* Chūshū. C South Korea
Ch'ungju-ho *496* reservoir of C South Korea
Chungking *see* Chongqing
Chung-li *525 Jap.* Chūreki. N Taiwan
Ch'ungmu *496* S South Korea
Chunya *530* SW Tanzania
Chuquícamata *159* N Chile
Chur *516 It.* Coira, *Rmsch.* Cuera, *Fr.* Coire. E Switzerland
Church Cay *466* cay of E St Vincent & the Grenadines
Churchill *146* C Canada
Church Village *97* SE Barbados
Chūreki *see* Chung-li
Chūshū *see* Ch'ungju
Chust *580 var.* Čust. E Uzbekistan
Chuuk Islands *375 var.* Hogoley Islands. Island group of C Micronesia
Chuvashskaya, Respublika *452* autonomous republic of W Russia
Chuy *577 var.* Chuí. SE Uruguay
Ciadîr-Lunga *376 var.* Ceadâr-Lunga, *Rus.* Chadyr-Lunga. S Moldova

Ciceron *465* NW St Lucia
Cicia *218 prev.* Thithia. Island of the Lau Group, E Fiji
Cidade Velha *152* Santiago, S Cape Verde
Ciego de Ávila *182* C Cuba
Ciénaga *171* N Colombia
Cienfuegos *182* C Cuba
Cieza *501* SE Spain
Çiftlik Dere *see* Aloupos
Cifuentes *182* C Cuba
Cikobia *218 prev.* Thikombia. Island to the N of Vanua Levu, N Fiji
Cilacap *276 prev.* Tjilatjap. Java, C Indonesia
Cill Airne *see* Killarney
Cill Choinnigh *see* Kilkenny
Cilli *see* Celje
Cill Mhantáin *see* Wicklow
Čimbaj *see* Chimbay
Cimişlia *376 Rus.* Chimishliya. S Moldova
Cina Selatan, Laut *see* South China Sea
Cincinnati *569* Ohio, NE USA
Ciney *99* SE Belgium
Ciotat *225* SE France
Čirčik *see* Chirchik
Cirebon *276 prev.* Tjirebon. Java, C Indonesia
Cirque de Cilaos *628* mountain range of W Réunion
Cirquenizza *see* Crikvenica
Ciskei Bantustan 'self-governing homeland' comprising 2 non-contiguous territories of E Cape Province, South Africa; created in 1981, abolished in 1994
Citlaltépetl *370 var.* Pico de Orizaba, Volcán Citlaltépetl. Mountain of SE Mexico
Citlaltépetl, Volcán *see* Citlaltépetl
Citron *621* NW French Guiana
Citron *368* river of NW Mauritius
Ciudad Arce *207* W El Salvador
Ciudad Bolívar *589* E Venezuela
Ciudad de Guatemala *see* Guatemala City
Ciudad del Este *428 prev.* Puerto Presidente Stroessner. SE Paraguay
Ciudad de México *see* Mexico City
Ciudad de Panama *see* Panama City
Ciudad Guayana *589* E Venezuela
Ciudad Juárez *370* NW Mexico
Ciudad Obregón *370* NW Mexico
Ciudad Ojeda *589* NW Venezuela
Ciudad Real *501* C Spain
Ciudad Trujillo *see* Santo Domingo
Ciudad Victoria *370* C Mexico
Civitavecchia *295* C Italy
Clarence *401* river of NE South Island, New Zealand
Clarence Island *66* island of South Shetland Islands, Antarctica
Clarence Town *88* Long Island, Bahamas
Clermont-Ferrand *225* C France
Clervaux *346* N Luxembourg
Cleveland *569* Ohio, NE USA
Clifden *288* W Ireland
Clifton *196* NW Dominica
Clifton *466* Union I, St Vincent & the Grenadines
Clonmel *288 Ir.* Cluain Meala. S Ireland
Cluj-Napoca *448 prev.* Cluj, *Hung.* Kolozsvár, *Ger.* Klausenburg. NW Romania
Clutha *401* river of SW South Island, New Zealand
Clyde, Firth of *563* estuary of the river Clyde, SW Scotland, UK
Coamo *627* S Puerto Rico
Coast Mountains *146 Fr.* Chaîne Côtière. Mountain range of Canada and USA
Coast Range *568* mountain range of NW USA
Coast Ranges *568* mountain range of SW USA
Coatepeque *250* W Guatemala
Coatepeque, Lago de *207* lake of W El Salvador
Coatzacoalcos *370 prev.* Puerto México. SE Mexico
Cobán *250* C Guatemala
Cobija *112* NW Bolivia
Cochabamba *112* C Bolivia
Cochin *270 var.* Kochi. S India
Cockburn Harbour *629* South Caicos, E Turks and Caicos Islands
Cockburn Town *88* Great Exuma I, Bahamas
Cockburn Town *629* Grand Turk Island, SE Turks and Caicos Islands
Cockpit Country, The *303* physical region of NW Jamaica
Coco *404 var.* Segovia. River of N Nicaragua
Coco *260 var.* Wangkí, Segovia. River of Honduras and Nicaragua
Cocobeach *230* NW Gabon
Coco, Isla del *178* island of SW Costa Rica
Cocoli *see* Corubal
Cocos (Keeling) Islands *620* Australian external territory of the Indian Ocean. ❖ West Island
Cocos Island *623* island group of S Guam
Codrington *68* C Barbuda, Antigua & Barbuda
Codrington Lagoon *68* W Barbuda, Antigua & Barbuda
Coeroeni *see* Corantijn
Coëtivy *478* island of E Seychelles
Coffs Harbour *77* E Australia
Cogîlnic *376 var.* Cogâlnic, *Rus.* Kogil'nik. River of SE Moldova
Cognac *225* W France
Cogo *see* Kogo
Cohoha *see* Cyohoha-Sud Lac
Coiba, Isla de *424* island of SW Panama
Coihaique *159 var.* Coyhaique. S Chile
Coimbatore *270* S India
Coimbra *442* W Portugal
Coin de Mire *368 Eng.* Gunners Quoin. Island of N Mauritius
Coira *see* Chur
Coire *see* Chur
Coi, Sông *see* Red River
Cojutepeque *207* C El Salvador
Colchester *563* E England, UK
Coleraine *563* Northern Ireland, UK
Colesberg *493* Northern Cape, C South Africa
Colihaut *196 var.* Kulihao. W Dominica
Collie *76* SW Australia
Collingwood Bay *426* bay of the Solomon Sea to the E of Papua New Guinea
Colmar *225 Ger.* Kolmar. NE France
Cöln *see* Köln
Coloane *624* Coloane, S Macao
Coloane *624* island of S Macao
Cologne *see* Köln
Colomb-Béchar *see* Béchar
Colombia *170-173* officially Republic of Colombia. Country of South America divided into 32 admin. units (departments)
Colombo *504* ❖ of Sri Lanka, W Sri Lanka
Colón *182* NW Cuba
Colón *424 prev.* Aspinwall. N Panama
Colón, Archipiélago de *see* Galapagos Islands
Colonia *see* Kolonia
Colonia del Sacramento *577* SW Uruguay
Colorado *178* river of NE Costa Rica
Colorado *569* river of Texas, SC USA
Colorado *569* river of SW USA
Colorado *568-569* state of SW USA
Colorados, Archipiélago de los *182* island group of NW Cuba
Colorado Springs *569* Colorado, SW USA
Columbia *568* river of NW USA
Columbia *569* South Carolina, SE USA
Columbia, District of *569* federal district of NE USA
Columbus *569* Georgia, SE USA
Columbus *569* Ohio, NE USA
Columbus Channel *540* channel connecting the Atlantic Ocean and Gulf of Paria
Colville Channel *401* channel linking the Bay of Plenty and Hauraki Gulf, N of North Island, New Zealand
Comarapa *112* C Bolivia
Comas *431* W Peru
Comayagua *260* W Honduras
Comendador *198 prev.* Elías Piña. W Dominican Republic
Comer *see* Como, Lago di
Comilla *93 Ben.* Kumillā. E Bangladesh
Commissioner's Point *619* headland of Ireland Island North, W Bermuda
Communism Peak *see* Pik Kommunizma
Como *294* N Italy
Comodoro Rivadavia *71* SE Argentina
Como, Lago di *294 var.* Lario, *Eng.* Lake Como, *Ger.* Comer See. Lake of N Italy
Comoros *174-175* officially Federal Islamic Republic of the Comoros. Island group of the Indian Ocean, between Madagascar and the African mainland, divided into 3 admin. units (districts)
Comrat *376 Rus.* Komrat. S Moldova
Conakry *253* ❖ of Guinea, SW Guinea
Concepción *112* E Bolivia
Concepción *159* C Chile
Concepción *428 var.* Villa Concepción. C Paraguay
Concepción *see* Riaba
Concepción de La Vega *see* La Vega
Conchos *370* river of NW Mexico
Concord *248* W Grenada island, Grenada
Concord *569* New Hampshire, NE USA
Concordia *71* E Argentina
Condado *182* C Cuba
Côn Dao *593 var.* Con Son. Island of S Vietnam
Condroz *99* physical region of SE Belgium
Congo *64, 176, 607 var.* Zaire, Kongo, Lualaba. River of C Africa
Congo *176-177* officially Republic of the Congo. Country of C Africa divided into 9 admin. units (regions)
Congo Basin *607* drainage basin of C Africa
Con, Loch *see* Conn, Lough
Connaught *288* province of W Ireland
Connecticut *569* state of NE USA
Conn, Lough *288 Ir.* Loch Con. Lake of NW Ireland
Consolación del Sur *182* W Cuba
Constance, Lake *82, 236, 516 Ger.* Bodensee. Lake of C Europe
Constanţa *448 Ger.* Konstantza, *Turk.* Köstence, *var.* Küstendje, *Eng.* Constanza. SE Romania
Constantine *59 Ar.* Qoussantîna, *var.* Qacentina, NE Algeria
Constantine *248* SW Grenada island, Grenada
Constantinople *see* Istanbul
Constant Spring *303* SE Jamaica
Constanza *198* C Dominican Republic
Contagem *121* SE Brazil
Contuboel *254* NE Guinea-Bissau
Cook Islands *620* territory in free association with New Zealand, Pacific Ocean. ❖ Avarua.
Cook, Mount *401 prev.* Aorangi. Mountain of W South Island, New Zealand
Cook, Récif de *626* reef of the Pacific Ocean, N New Caledonia
Cook Strait *401 var.* Raukawa. Strait between North and South Islands of New Zealand, connecting the South Pacific Ocean and Tasman Sea
Cooper Creek *77 var.* Barcoo, Cooper's Creek. River of C Australia
Cooper Island *619* island of SE British Virgin Islands
Copacabana *112* W Bolivia
Copenhagen *190 Dan.* København. ❖ of Denmark, Sjælland, E Denmark
Copiapó *159* N Chile
Coppename *508 var.* Koppename. River of C Suriname
Coppermine *146 var.* Qurlurtuuq. NW Canada
Coquilhatville *see* Mbandaka
Coquimbo *159* N Chile
Corail *258* SW Haiti
Coral Harbour *147* Southampton Island, NE Canada
Coral Sea *77, 585, 426* sea of the Pacific Ocean between Australia and Papua New Guinea
Corantijn *256, 508 var.* Coeroeni, Corentyne, Courantyne. River of Guyana and Suriname
Córdoba *71* C Argentina
Córdoba *501 var.* Cordoba, *Eng.* Cordova. SW Spain
Cordova *568* Alaska, USA
Corentyne *see* Corantijn
Corfu *see* Kérkyra
Corinth *see* Kórinthos
Corinth *248* SE Grenada island, Grenada
Corinth, Gulf of *see* Korinthiakós Kólpos
Corinth, Isthmus of *see* Korínthou, Isthmós
Corinto *404* W Nicaragua
Coriole *see* Qoryooley
Corisco, Isla de *208* Island of SW Equatorial Guinea
Cork *288 Ir.* Corcaigh. S Ireland
Cork Hill *625* W Montserrat
Corleone *295* Sicilia, S Italy
Cornellá de Llobregat *501* E Spain
Corner Brook *147* Newfoundland, E Canada
Corn Exchange *334* NW Lesotho
Corn Islands *see* Maíz, Islas
Cornwallis Island *146* island of Parry Islands, N Canada
Coro *589 var.* Santa Ana de Coro. NW Venezuela
Corocoro *112* W Bolivia
Coromandel Peninsula *401* peninsula of NE North Island, New Zealand
Coronel Bogado *428* S Paraguay
Coronel Oviedo *428* SE Paraguay
Çorovodë *57 var.* Çorovoda, Corovoda. SE Albania
Corozal *102* N Belize
Corrib, Lough *288 Ir.* Loch Corrib. Lake of W Ireland
Corrientes *71* NE Argentina
Corriverton *256* E Guyana
Corriza *see* Korçë
Corse *225 Eng.* Corsica. Island of SE France
Corsica *see* Corse
Cortés *178* SE Costa Rica
Corubal *254 var.* Cocoli, Rio Grande. River of W Africa
Çorum *547* N Turkey
Corvallis *568* Oregon, NW USA
Corvo *442 var.* Ilha do Corvo. Island of the Azores, Portugal
Cosenza *295* S Italy
Cosmolédo Atoll *478* atoll of the Aldabra Group, SW Seychelles
Cospicua *363* E Malta
Costa, Cordillera de la *589 var.* Cordillera de Venezuela. Mountain range of N Venezuela
Costa Rica *178-179* officially Republic of Costa Rica. Country of Central America divided into 7 admin. units (provinces)

D

Direction Island *620 var.* Pulu Tikus. Island of E Cocos Islands
Dirē Dawa *215* E Ethiopia
Diriamba *404* SW Nicaragua
Dirj *339* NW Libya
Dirk Hartog Island *76* island of W Australia
Disappointment, Lake *76* salt lake of W Australia
Discovery Bay *262* W Hong Kong
Discovery Reef *627* reef of the China Sea, W Paracel Islands
Disna *see* Drysa
Disûq *202 var.* Disūq. N Egypt
Diu *270* W India
Diuata Mountains *435* mountain range of Mindanao, S Philippines
Diva *see* Piva
Divinópolis *121* SE Brazil
Divisa *424* S Panama
Divo *300* S Ivory Coast
Diwaniya *see* Ad Dīwanīyah
Diyālá *284 Per.* Rūdkhāneh-ye Sīrvān, Sirwan. River of Iran and Iraq
Diyarbakır *547* SE Turkey
Dizful *see* Dezfūl
Dja *144* river of SE Cameroon
Djailolo *see* Halmahera
Djakarta *see* Jakarta
Djakovica *see* Đakovica
Djakovo *see* Đakovo
Djamâa *59* NE Algeria
Djambala *176* W Congo
Djambi *see* Hari
Djambi *see* Jambi
Djanet *59 prev.* Fort Charlet. SE Algeria
Djawa *see* Java
Djéblé *see* Jablah
Djelfa *59 var.* El Djelfa. N Algeria
Djéma *154* E Central African Republic
Djember *see* Jember
Djénné *360 var.* Jenné. C Mali
Djérablous *see* Jarābulus
Djerba *see* Jerba, Île de
Djerba *see* Houmt Souk
Djerem *144 var.* Djérem. River of C Cameroon
Djevdjelija *see* Gevgelija
Djibo *132* N Burkina
Djibouti *194 var.* Jibuti. ❖ of Djibouti, E Djibouti
Djibouti *194-195* officially Republic of Djibouti, *var.* Jibuti, *prev.* French Territory of the Afars and Issas 1967-77, French Somaliland -1967. Country of East Africa divided into 5 admin. units (districts)
Djidjel *see* Jijel
Djidjelli *see* Jijel
Djiguéni *366* SE Mauritania
Djirataoua *407* S Niger
Djisr el Choghour *see* Jisr ash Shughūr
Djoua *176* river of Congo and Gabon
Djoué *176* river of S Congo
Djougou *108* W Benin
Djúpivogur *268* SE Iceland
Dmitriyevsk *see* Makiyivka
Dnieper *556 Bel.* Dnyapro, *Ukr.* Dnipro, *Rus.* Dnepr. River of E Europe
Dniester *376, 556 Rom.* Nistru, *Rus.* Dnestr, *Ukr.* Dnister. River of Moldova and Ukraine
Dniprodzerzhyns'k *556 Rus.* Dneprodzerzhinsk, *prev.* Kamenskoye. E Ukraine
Dniprodzerzhyns'ke Vodoskhovyshche *556 Rus.* Dneprodzerzhinskoye Vodokhranilische. Reservoir of C Ukraine
Dnipropetrovs'k *556 Rus.* Dnepropetrovsk, *prev.* Ekaterinoslav. E Ukraine
Dnistrovs'kyy Lyman *556 Rus.* Dnestrovskiy Liman. Inlet of the Black Sea, SW Ukraine
Dnyapro *see* Dnieper
Doba *156* S Chad
Dobele *330 Ger.* Doblen. W Latvia
Doberai, Jazirah *276 Dut.* Vogelkop. Region of Irian Jaya, E Indonesia
Doboj *116* N Bosnia & Herzegovina
Dobrich *128 var.* Dobrič, *prev.* Tolbukhin, *Rom.* Bazargic. NE Bulgaria
Dobrush *104* SE Belorussia
Doctor Pedro P. Peña *428* W Paraguay
Dodekánisos *245 prev.* Dhodhekánisos, *var.* Noties Sporádes, *Eng.* Dodecanese. Island group of SE Greece
Dodoma *530* ❖ of Tanzania, C Tanzania
Dodona *245* site of ancient city, N Greece
Dodwekon *336 var.* Dudwiokahn. SE Liberia
Doetinchem *397* SE Netherlands
Dogana *468* NE San Marino
Dogondoutchi *407* SW Niger
Doğu Karadeniz Dağlarıı *547 var.* Anadolu Dağları. Mountain range of NE Turkey
Doha *447 Ar.* Ad Dawḩah. ❖ of Qatar, E Qatar
Dohuk *see* Dahuk
Doko *253* NE Guinea
Dolisie *see* Loubomo
Dolobil *336* C Liberia
Dolomites *see* Dolomitiche, Alpi
Dolomitiche, Alpi *295 var.* Dolomiti, *Eng.* Dolomites. Mountain range of N Italy
Dolo Odo *215 var.* Dollo Odo, Dolo. S Ethiopia
Dolores *250* N Guatemala
Dolores *577* W Uruguay
Domagnano *468* NE San Marino
Domel Island *see* Letsok-aw I
Dominica *196-197* officially Commonwealth of Dominica. Country of the West Indies divided into 10 admin. units (parishes)
Dominica Channel *see* Martinique Passage
Dominican Republic *198-199* Country of the West Indies divided into 30 admin. units (1 national district and 29 provinces)
Dominica Passage *622* passage of the Caribbean Sea, N Guadeloupe
Domoni *174* SE Anjouan, Comoros
Don *452* river of W Russia
Donau *see* Danube
Doncaster *563* N England, UK
Dondo *64* NW Angola
Dondo *387* C Mozambique
Donegal *288* N Ireland
Donegal Bay *288 Ir.* Bá Dhún na nGall. Bay of the Atlantic Ocean, to the N of Ireland
Donets *556 Rus.* Severskiy Donets, *Ukr.* Sivers'kyy Donets'. River of E Ukraine
Donets'k *556 prev.* Stalino, *Rus.* Donetsk. E Ukraine
Donga *144* river of Cameroon and Nigeria
Đông Ha *593* C Vietnam
Đông Hơi *593* C Vietnam
Dong Nai *593 var.* Donnai, Dong-nai, Dong Noi. River of S Vietnam
Dongola *506 var.* Dunqulah, Donqola N Sudan
Dongou *176* NE Congo
Dong Rak, Phanom *see* Dang Rak, Phanom
Dongting Hu *163 var.* Tung-t'ing Hu. Lake of SE China
Donostia *see* San Sebastián
Doornik *see* Tournai
Dorada, Costa *see* Daurada, Costa
Dordogne *225* river of SW France
Dordrecht *397* SW Netherlands
Dori *132* N Burkina
Dornbirn *82* W Austria
Dornoch Firth *563* estuary of the river Dornoch, NE Scotland, UK
Dorpat *see* Tartu
Dorra *194* NW Djibouti
Dorsale *543* mountain range of N Tunisia
Dortmund *236* W Germany
Dos D'Âne *196* N Dominica
Dospad Dagh *see* Rhodope Mountains
Dos Puntas, Cabo *208* cape on the W coast of Río Muni, Equatorial Guinea
Dosso *407* SW Niger
Dostuk *325* C Kyrgyzstan
Douai *225* N France
Douala *144 var.* Duala. SW Cameroon
Double Headed Shot Cays *88* islets of W Bahamas
Doubs *516 var.* Le Doubs. River of France and Switzerland
Doudoub Bololé *194* S Djibouti
Doué *476* river of N Senegal
Douglas *621* East Falkland, NE Falkland Islands
Douglas *563, 623* ❖ of Isle of Man, SE Isle of Man
Douma *see* Dūmā
Douro *see* Duero
Dover *563 Fr.* Douvres. SE England, UK
Dover *569* Delaware, E USA
Dover, Strait of *225 var.* Straits of Dover, *Fr.* Pas de Calais. Strait connecting the English Channel and North Sea between England and France
Dovrefjell *414* mountain of SW Norway
Dowa *353* C Malawi
Dōzen *304* island to the N of Honshū, W Japan
Drâa *382* seasonal river of S Morocco
Drac *see* Durrës
Draç *see* Durrës
Dragon's Mouths, The *540 Sp.* Bocas del Dragón. Strait connecting the Caribbean Sea and Gulf of Paria
Dra, Hamada du *59 var.* Haut Plateau du Dra, Hammada du Drâa. Desert region of W Algeria
Drakensberg *334, 493* mountain range of Lesotho and South Africa
Drake Passage *159* passage connecting Pacific Ocean and Atlantic Ocean between South America and Antarctica
Dráma *245 var.* Dhráma. NE Greece
Drammen *414* S Norway
Drangajökull *268* glacier of NW Iceland
Drava *82, 181, 264, 486 Eng.* Drave, *Hung.* Dráva, *Ger.* Drau, *SCr.* Drava. River of C Europe
Dresden *237* E Germany
Drina *116, 602* river of Bosnia & Herzegovina and Yugoslavia
Drin Gulf *see* Drinit, Gjiri i
Drinit *57 var.* Drin. River of NW Albania
Drinit, Gjiri i *57 var.* Pellg i Drinit, Drin Gulf. Gulf of the Adriatic Sea, NW Albania
Drinit të Zi *57, 349 var.* Drin i Zi, *Eng.* Black Drin, *SCr.* Crni Drim. River of Albania and FYR Macedonia
Drin i Zi *see* Drinit të Zi
Drinos *57* river of S Albania
Drissa *104* river of Belorussia and Russia
Drobeta-Turnu Severin *448 prev.* Turnu Severin. SW Romania
Drochia *376 Rus.* Drokiya. N Moldavia
Drogheda *288 Ir.* Droichead Átha. E Ireland
Drontheim *see* Trondheim
Druskininkai *344 Pol.* Druskieniki. S Lithuania
Drysa *104 Rus.* Disna. River of Belorussia and Lithuania
Dschang *144* W Cameroon
Duala *see* Douala
Duarte, Pico *198* mountain of C Dominican Republic
Dubai *560 Ar.* Dubayy. NE United Arab Emirates
Dubăsari *376 Rus.* Dubossary. NE Moldova
Dubăsari Reservoir *376* reservoir of NE Moldova
Dubawnt *146* river of C Canada
Dubbo *77* E Australia
Dublanc *196* NW Dominica
Dublin *288 Ir.* Baile Átha Cliath. ❖ of Ireland, E Ireland
Dubnica nad Váhom *485 Hung.* Máriatölgyes, *prev.* Dubnicz. NW Slovakia
Dubnicz *see* Dubnica nad Váhom
Dubossary *see* Dubăsari
Dubréka *253* SW Guinea
Dubrovnik *181 It.* Ragusa. SE Croatia
Duc de Gloucester, Îles du *622* island group of C French Polynesia
Ducie Island *627* island of E Pitcairn Islands
Ducos *625* C Martinique
Dudelange *346* S Luxembourg
Dudo, Uadi *see* Dhuudo
Dudwiokahn *see* Dodwekon
Duékoué *300* W Ivory Coast
Duero *442, 500-501 Port.* Douro. River of Portugal and Spain
Duesseldorf *see* Düsseldorf
Duff Islands *488* small island group within Santa Cruz Is, Solomon Is
Dufourspitze *516* mountain of S Switzerland
Dugi Otok *181 It.* Isola Lunga. Island of W Croatia
Duinkerden *see* Dunkerque
Duisburg *236* W Germany
Duitama *171* C Colombia
Duitse Bocht *see* German Bight
Dukhān *447* W Qatar
Dukhan Heights *see* Dukhān, Jabal
Dukhān, Jabal *447 var.* Dukhan Heights. Hilly region of SW Qatar
Dukhan, Jabal *see* Dukhān, Jabal ad
Dukhān, Jabal ad *91 var.* Dukhan Heights, Jabal Dukhan. Mountain of C Bahrain
Dukou *see* Panzhihua
Dulce, Golfo *see* Izabal, Lago de
Dulce Nombre de Culmí *260* Honduras
Dulit, Banjaran *354 var.* Dulit Range. Mountain range of W Borneo, Malaysia
Duluth *569* Minnesota, NC USA
Dūmā *521 Fr.* Douma. SW Syria
Dumfries *563* SW Scotland, UK
Dumistān *91* NW Bahrain
Dumont D'Urville *66* French research station of Greater Antarctica, Antarctica
Dumyât *202 Eng.* Damietta. N Egypt
Düna *see* Western Dvina
Dünaburg *see* Daugavpils
Dunai *395* W Nepal
Dunaj *see* Danube
Dunaj *see* Vienna
Dunajská Streda *485 Hung.* Dunaszerdahely. SW Slovakia
Dunapentele *see* Dunaújváros
Dunărea *see* Danube
Dunării, Delta *see* Danube, Mouths of the
Dunaszerdahely *see* Dunajská Streda
Dunaújváros *264 prev.* Sztálinváros, *prev.* Dunapentele. C Hungary
Dunavska Ravnina *128 Eng.* Danubian Plain. Lowland region of N Bulgaria
Dundalk *288 Ir.* Dún Dealgan. NE Ireland

F

Foyle *563* river of Ireland and UK
Foyle, Lough *288, 563* *Ir.* Loch Feabhai. Inlet of the Atlantic Ocean, Ireland and UK
Fraile Muerto *577* E Uruguay
Frakštát *see* Hlohovec
France *224-229* officially French Republic. Country of Europe divided into 22 admin. units (regions, comprising 96 départements)
Franceville *see* Massoukou
Francistown *118* NE Botswana
Franconian Jura *see* Fränkische Alb
Frankfort *569* Kentucky, C USA
Frankfurt am Main *236* *Eng.* Frankfort on the Main, Frankfurt. SW Germany
Frankfurt an der Oder *237* E Germany
Fränkische Alb *237* *Eng.* Franconian Jura. S Germany
Frantsa-Iosifa, Zemlya *452-453* *Eng.* Franz Josef Land. Island group of N Russia
Fraser *146* river of SW Canada
Fraser Island *77* *var.* Great Sandy Island. Island of E Australia
Frauenburg *see* Saldus
Frauenfeld *516* NE Switzerland
Fray Bentos *577* W Uruguay
Fredericia *190* Jylland, SW Denmark
Fredericton *147* SE Canada
Frederiksdal *622* *var.* Narsaq Kuyalleq. S Greenland
Frederikshavn *190* Jylland, N Denmark
Frederiksted *629* Saint Croix, S Virgin Islands
Fredrikshald *see* Halden
Fredrikstad *414* S Norway
Freemans *68* C Antigua, Antigua & Barbuda
Freeport *88* *var.* Freeport-Lucaya. Bahamas
Freetown *68* SE Antigua, Antigua & Barbuda
Freetown *480* ❖ of Sierra Leone, W Sierra Leone
Frégate *478* island of the Inner Islands, NE Seychelles
Freiburg *see* Fribourg
Freiburg im Breisgau *236* *var.* Freiburg. SW Germany
Freistadtl *see* Hlohovec
Fremantle *76* SW Australia
French Guiana *621* *var.* Guyane. French overseas département of N South America. ❖ Cayenne.
French Polynesia *622* French overseas possession of the Pacific Ocean. ❖ Papeete.
French Somaliland *see* Djibouti
French Sudan *see* Mali
French Territory of the Afars and Issas *see* Djibouti
French Togoland *see* Togo
Fria *253* W Guinea
Fribourg *516* *Ger.* Freiburg. W Switzerland
Friedek-Místek *see* Frýdek-Místek
Friedrichshafen *236* S Germany
Friendly Islands *see* Tonga
Frigate Island *248* island to the S of Carriacou, Grenada
Frigate Island *466* island of SW St Vincent & the Grenadines
Frisches Haff *see* Vistula Lagoon
Frobisher Bay *see* Iqaluit
Frome, Lake *77* salt lake of S Australia
Front Range *see* Maluti
Frunze *see* Bishkek
Frýdek - Místek *188* *Ger.* Friedek - Mistek. SE Czech Republic
Fuammulah *358* *var.* Gnaviyani Atoll. Atoll of S Maldives
Fu-chien *see* Fujian
Fu-chou *see* Fuzhou
Fucht *382* W Western Sahara
Fuenlabrada *501* C Spain
Fuerte Olimpo *428* NE Paraguay
Fuerteventura *501* island of Islas Canarias, SW Spain
Fuglafjørdhur *620* *var.* Fuglefjord. Eysturoy, N Faeroe Islands
Fugloy *620* *var.* Fuglø. Island of NE Faeroe Islands
Fu-hsin *see* Fuxin
Fujairah *560* *Ar.* Al Fujayrah. NE United Arab Emirates
Fuji *304* Honshū, SE Japan
Fujian *163* *var.* Fukien, Fu-chien. Province of SE China
Fuji-san *304* mountain of Honshū, SE Japan
Fujisawa *304* Honshū, SE Japan
Fukuchiyama *304* Honshū, C Japan
Fukue *304* island of Gotō-rettō, SW Japan
Fukue *304* Gotō-rettō, SW Japan
Fukui *304* Honshū, C Japan
Fukuoka *304* Kyūshū, SW Japan
Fukushima *304* Honshū, N Japan
Fukuyama *304* Honshū, W Japan
Fulacunda *254* C Guinea-Bissau
Fulaga *218* island of the Lau Group, E Fiji
Fulda *236* C Germany
Fullarton *540* SW Trinidad, Trinidad & Tobago
Funabashi *304* Honshū, SE Japan
Funafuti *see* Fongafale
Funafuti *553* coral atoll of C Tuvalu
Funaota *553* islet of Nukufetau, Tuvalu
Funchal *442* Madeira, Madeira Islands, Portugal
Fünen *see* Fyn
Fünfkirchen *see* Pécs
Funhalouro *387* SE Mozambique
Furna *152* Brava, S Cape Verde
Furnas, Represa de *121* reservoir of SE Brazil
Furneaux Group *77* island group of SE Australia
Furstenwald *237* NE Germany
Fusan *see* Pusan
Fushun *163* Liaoning, NE China
Futa Jallon *see* Fouta Djallon
Futuna *585* island of S Vanuatu
Futuna, Île *629* island of N Wallis & Futuna
Fuwairet *see* Al Fuwayriţ
Fuxin *163* *var.* Fu-hsin, Fusin. Liaoning, NE China
Fuzhou *163* *var.* Foochow, Fu-chou. Fujian, SE China
Füzuli *86* *Rus.* Fizuli SW Azerbaijan
Fyn *190* *Ger.* Fünen. Island of C Denmark

G

Gaafu Alifu Atoll *see* North Huvadhu Atoll
Gaafu Dhaalu Atoll *see* South Huvadhu Atoll
Gaalkacyo *490* *var.* Galka'yo, *It.* Galcaio. C Somalia
Gabela *64* W Angola
Gabès *543* *var.* Qābis. C Tunisia
Gabès, Gulf of *543* gulf of the Mediterranean Sea to the E of Tunisia
Gablonz an der Neisse *see* Jablonec nad Nisou
Gabon *230-231* officially Gabonese Republic. Country of West Africa divided into 9 admin. units (provinces)
Gaborone *118* *prev.* Gaberones. ❖ of Botswana, SE Botswana
Gabriel, Ilot *368* *Eng.* Gabriel Island. Island of N Mauritius
Gabrovo *128* C Bulgaria
Gabú *254* *prev.* Nova Lamego. E Guinea-Bissau
Gaeta, Golfo di *295* *var.* Gulf of Gaeta. Gulf of the Tyrrhenian Sea, on the W coast of Italy
Gaferut *375* island of C Micronesia
Gafsa *543* *var.* Qafşah. W Tunisia
Gagnoa *300* C Ivory Coast
Gagra *234* NW Georgia
Gaherré *194* NE Djibouti
Gahnpa *see* Ganta
Gaibānda *93* NW Bangladesh
Gaillimh *see* Galway
Gailtaler Alpen *82* mountain range of S Austria
Gairdner, Lake *77* salt lake of S Australia
Gaiziņ *see* Gaizina Kalns
Gaizina Kalns *330* *var.* Gaiziņ. Mountain of E Latvia
Gâlâfi *194* W Djibouti
Galana *316* river of SE Kenya
Galapagos Islands *200* *var.* Tortoise Islands, *Sp.* Archipiélago de Colón. Island group of W Ecuador in the Pacific Ocean
Galaţi *448* *Ger.* Galatz. E Romania
Galaymor *see* Kalai-Mor
Galcaio *see* Gaalkacyo
Gales Point *102* E Belize
Galets *628* river of NW Réunion
Galgóc *see* Hlohovec
Galibi *508* NE Suriname
Galicia *501* NW Spain
Galilee, Sea of *see* Tiberias, Lake
Galle *504* *prev.* Point de Galle. SW Sri Lanka
Gällivare *513* N Sweden
Gâlma *see* Guelma
Galomaro *254* C Guinea-Bissau
Galway *288* *Ir.* Gaillimh. W Ireland
Galway Bay *288* *Ir.* Cuan na Gaillimhe. Bay of the Atlantic Ocean, to the W of Ireland
Gamamudo *254* NE Guinea-Bissau
Gamba *230* SW Gabon
Gambia *232-233* officially The Gambia, Republic of the The Gambia. Country of W Africa divided into 6 admin. units (divisions)
Gambia *233, 253, 476* *Fr.* Gambie. River of W Africa
Gambier, Îles *622* island group of E French Polynesia
Gambissara *233* E Gambia
Gamboma *176* E Congo
Gamboula *154* SW Central African Republic
Gamgadhi *395* *var.* Gum. W Nepal
Gamlakarleby *see* Kokkola
Gammouda *see* Sidi Bouzid
Gampaha *504* W Sri Lanka
Gamprin *342* NW Liechtenstein
Gâm *593* river of N Vietnam
Gan *358* C Maldives
Ganaane *see* Juba
Gäncä *86* *Rus.* Gyandzha, *prev.* Kirovabad, Yelisavetpol. W Azerbaijan
Gand *see* Gent
Gandajika *607* S Zaire
Gandía *501* E Spain
Ganges *93, 270-271* *Ben.* Padma, *Hind.* Ganga. River of S Asia
Ganges, Mouths of the *93, 271* large delta area of Bangladesh and India
Gansu *163* *var.* Kansu. Province of NW China
Ganta *336* *var.* Gahnpa. NE Liberia
Gao *360* E Mali
Gaoua *132* SW Burkina
Gaoual *253* N Guinea
Gap *225* E France
Garabogazköl Bogazy *see* Kara-Bogaz-Gol, Proliv
Garagum *see* Karakumy
Garagum Kanaly *see* Karakumskiy Kanal
Garam *see* Hron
Garamszentkereszt *see* Žiar nad Hronom
Garango *132* C Burkina
Garapan *626* ❖ of Northern Mariana Islands, Saipan, S Northern Mariana Islands
Garbahaarrey *490* *It.* Garba Harre. SW Somalia
Garda, Lago di *294* *var.* Benaco, *Eng.* Lake Garda. Lake of N Italy
Gardēz *53* *var.* Gardeyz. E Afghanistan
Gardner Island *see* Nikumaroro
Gardo *see* Qardho
Garissa *316* E Kenya
Garm *528* C Tajikistan
Garmo Peak *see* Kommunizma, Pik
Garonne *225* river of SW France
Garoowe *490* *var.* Garoe. N Somalia
Garoua *144* *var.* Garua. N Cameroon
Garowol *233* E Gambia
Garrygala *551* *prev.* Kara-Kala. SW Turkmenistan
Garsen *316* SE Kenya
Gary *569* Indiana, C USA
Garyllis *187* river of S Cyprus
Garzón *171* SW Colombia
Gasan-Kuli *see* Esenguly
Gasa Tashi Thongmen *110* NW Bhutan
Gascogne *224-225* *Eng.* Gascony. Cultural region of SW France
Gascogne, Golfe de *see* Biscay, Bay of
Gascony *see* Gascogne
Gaspé, Péninsule de *147* *var.* Péninsule de la Gaspésie. Peninsula of SE Canada
Gasteiz *see* Vitoria
Gat *see* Ghat
Gata *152* Boa Vista, E Cape Verde
Gata, Cape *187* cape of S Cyprus
Gatooma *see* Kadoma
Gatún, Lago *424* reservoir of C Panama
Gau *218* *prev.* Ngau. Island to the E of Viti Levu, C Fiji
Gauhāti *see* Guwāhāti
Gauja *330* *Ger.* Aa. River of N Latvia
Gaulette *196* E Dominica
Gävle *513* E Sweden
Gaya *407* SW Niger
Gaza *291, 292* *Heb.* 'Azza, *Ar.* Ghazzah. NE Gaza Strip
Gaz-Achak *551* *Turkm.* Gazojak. NE Turkmenistan
Ghazāl, Baḥr al *see* Ghazal, Bahr el
Ghazal, Bahr el *506* *var.* Baḥr al Ghazāl. River of S Sudan
Gazalkent *580* *Uzb.* Ghazalkent. E Uzbekistan
Gazandzhyk *551* *var.* Kazandzhik, *Turkm.* Gazanjyk. W Turkmenistan
Gaza Strip *291, 292* *Ar.* Qita Ghazzah. Disputed territory of SW Asia
Gaziantep *547* *prev.* Aintab. S Turkey
Gazimağusa *187* *var.* Famagusta *Gk* Ammochostos. E Cyprus
Gazimağusa Körfezi *see* Famagusta Bay
Gazli *580* S Uzbekistan
Gbangbatok *480* SW Sierra Leone
Gbarnga *336* C Liberia
Gbéroubouè *108* *var.* Béroubouay. N Benin
Gdańsk *439* *Ger.* Danzig. N Poland
Gdan'skaya Bukhta *see* Danzig, Gulf of
Gdańsk, Gulf of *see* Danzig, Gulf of
Gdańska, Zatoka *see* Danzig, Gulf of
Gdynia *439* *Ger.* Gdingen. N Poland
Gêba *254* river of W Africa
Gêba, Canal do *254* canal of W Guinea-Bissau
Geçitkale *187* *var.* Lefkoniko. NE Cyprus

Gedaref *506* *var.* Al Qaḍārif, El Gedaref. E Sudan
Gedser *190* Falster, SE Denmark
Geel *99* NE Belgium
Geelong *77* SE Australia
Gege *510* SW Swaziland
Geghama Lernashght'a *74* *Rus.* Gegamskiy Khrebet. Mountain range of C Armenia
Geita *530* NW Tanzania
Gëkdepe *551* *prev.* Geok-Tepe, *Turkm.* Gökdepe. SW Turkmenistan
Gela *295* Sicilia, S Italy
Gelang *see* Geylang
Geleen *397* S Netherlands
Gelib *see* Jilib
Gelsenkirchen *236* W Germany
Gemena *607* NW Zaire
Genalē Wenz *see* Juba
Geneina *506* *var.* Al Junaynah, Ajjinena. W Sudan
General Bernardo O'Higgins *66* Chilean research station of Antarctic Peninsula, Antarctica
General Carrera, Lago *see* Buenos Aires, Lago
General Eugenio A. Garay *428* *var.* Fortín General Eugenio Garay, *prev.* Yrendagüé. NW Paraguay
General J.F. Uriburu *see* Zárate
General Machado *see* Camacupa
General Santos *435* Mindanao, S Philippines
Gênes *see* Genova
Geneva, Lake *225, 516* *Fr.* Lac Léman, *var.* Le Léman, Lac de Genève, *Ger.* Genfer See. Lake of France and Switzerland
Genève *516* *Eng.* Geneva, *Ger.* Genf, *It.* Ginevra. SW Switzerland
Genk *99* *var.* Genck. NE Belgium
Gennargentu, Monti del *295* mountain of Sardegna, W Italy
Genova *294* *Eng.* Genoa, *Fr.* Gênes. N Italy
Genova, Golfo di *294* *Eng.* Gulf of Genoa. Gulf of the Ligurian Sea, on the W coast of Italy
Genovesa, Isla *200* island of N Galapagos Is, Ecuador
Genshū *see* Wŏnju
Gent *99* *Eng.* Ghent, *Fr.* Gand. NW Belgium
Geokchay *see* Göyçay
Geok-Tepe *see* Gëkdepe
Georga, Zemlya *452* *Eng.* George Land. Island of Zemlya Frantsa-Iosifa, N Russia
George *493* Western Cape, S South Africa
George Island *621* island of S Falkland Islands
George, Lake *554* lake of SW Uganda
George Land *see* Zemlya Georga
Georgenburg *see* Jurbarkas
George Town *88* San Salvador, Bahamas
George Town *354* *var.* Penang, Pinang. NW Peninsular Malaysia
George Town *620* ❖ of Cayman Islands, Grand Cayman, W Cayman Islands
Georgetown *628* ❖ of Ascension Island, W Ascension Island
Georgetown *233* E Gambia
Georgetown *256* ❖ of Guyana, NE Guyana
Georgetown *466* NE St Vincent & the Grenadines
Georgeville *102* W Belize
Georgia *569* state of SE USA
Georgia *234-235* officially Republic of Georgia, *Geor.* Sak'art'velo, *Rus.* Gruziya, *prev.* Georgian SSR, *Rus.* Gruzinskaya SSR. Country of E Europe divided into 65 admin units (raioni)
Georgi Dimitrov, Yazovir *128* reservoir of C Bulgaria
Georg von Neumayer *66* German research station of Greater Antarctica, Antarctica
Gera *237* C Germany
Geral de Goiás, Serra *121* mountain range of E Brazil
Geraldton *76* W Australia
Gereshk *53* SW Afghanistan
Gerlachovský Štít *485* *var.* Gerlachovka, *Ger.* Gerlsdorfer Spitze. Peak of Poland and Slovakia
German Bight *236* *Ger.* Deutsche Bucht, *Dut.* Duitse Bocht. Bay of the North Sea
German East Africa *see* Tanzania
German Southwest Africa *see* Namibia
German Ocean *see* North Sea
Germans Bay *625* bay of the Caribbean Sea on the SW coast of Montserrat
Germany *236-241* officially Federal Republic of Germany, *Ger.* Deutschland. Country of Western Europe divided into 16 admin. units (Länder)
Germering *237* S Germany
Germiston *493* *var.* Pretoria-Witwatersrand-Vereeniging, NE South Africa
Getafe *501* C Spain
Gevgelija *349* *var.* Đevđelija, Djevdjelija, *Turk.* Gevgeli. SE FYR Macedonia
Geylang *483* *var.* Gelang. River of SE Singapore
Geylegphug *110* S Bhutan
Ghadāmis *339* *var.* Rhadames. NW Libya
Ghana *242-243* officially Republic of Ghana. Country of W. Africa divided into 10 admin. units (regions)
Ghanongga *see* Ranongga
Ghanzi *118* W Botswana
Ghap'an *see* Kapan
Gharbi, Île *543* *Ar.* Jazirat al Gharbi. Island of E Tunisia
Ghardaïa *59* N Algeria
Gharsa, Chott el *543* *var.* Shaṭṭ al Gharsah. Salt lake of W Tunisia
Gharyān *339* NW Libya
Ghāt *339* *var.* Gat. W Libya
Ghawdex *see* Gozo
Ghawdex, Il-Fliegu ta' *363* *Eng.* North Comino Channel. Strait of Mediterranean Sea between Gozo and Kemmuna, NW Malta
Ghayathi *560* W United Arab Emirates
Ghazal *156* *var.* Soro. Seasonal river of C Chad
Ghazalkent *see* Gazalkent
Ghaznī *53* E Afghanistan
Ghazzah *see* Gaza
Ghelîzâne *see* Relizane
Ghent *see* Gent
Gherra, Sebkhet el *543* salt flat of NE Tunisia
Ghijduwon *see* Gizhduvan
Ghilizane *see* Relizane
Ghimbi *see* Gīmbī
Ghochas *see* Gochas
Ghukasyan *see* Ashots'k
Ghūrīān *53* W Afghanistan
Ghuwayfāt *560* *var.* Gheweifat. W United Arab Emirates
Giahel, Uadi *see* Jaceel
Giamame *see* Jamaame
Giants Castle *493* mountain of Lesotho and South Africa.
Gibeon *391* S Namibia
Gibraltar *501, 622* British Crown Colony, to the S of Spain
Gibraltar, Bay of *622* *var.* Bahía de Algeciras. Bay of the Atlantic Ocean on the W coast of Gibraltar
Gibraltar Harbour *622* W Gibraltar
Gibraltar, Strait of *382, 501, 622* *Sp.* Estrecho de Gibraltar. Strait connecting the Atlantic Ocean and Mediterranean Sea, between Gibraltar and Morocco
Gibson Desert *76-77* desert of W Australia
Gifu *304* Honshū, C Japan
Giggiga *see* Jijiga
Gihororo *138* C Burundi
Gijón *501* NW Spain
Gikongoro *460* SW Rwanda
Gilbert Islands *182* island group of W Kiribati
Gilf Kebir Plateau *202* *Ar.* Haḍabat al Jilf al Kabīr. Plateau of SW Egypt
Gilgit *421* river of N Pakistan
Gilolo *see* Halmahera
Gīmbī *215* *It.* Ghimbi. W Ethiopia
Gimie, Mount *465* mountain of C St Lucia
Gimma *see* Jīma
Ginda *210* C Eritrea
Ginevra *see* Genève
Ginger Island *619* island of SE British Virgin Islands
Giohar *see* Jawhar
Giran *see* I-lan
Girardot *171* C Colombia
Giraudel *196* S Dominica
Girba, Khashm el *506* *var.* Khashm al Qirbah, Khashim Al Qirba. E Sudan
Girgenti *see* Agrigento
Girne *187* *var.* Keryneia, Kyrenia. N Cyprus
Girón *171* N Colombia
Girona *501* E Spain
Girsun *547* NE Turkey
Gisagara *460* S Rwanda
Gisborne *401* E North Island, New Zealand
Giseifu *see* Ŭijŏngbu
Gisenyi *460* *var.* Gisenye. NW Rwanda
Gishyita *460* W Rwanda
Gissar *528* W Tajikistan
Gissar Range *528, 580* *Rus.* Gissarskiy Khrebet. Mountains of Tajikistan and Uzbekistan
Gissarskiy Khrebet *see* Gissar Range
Gisuru *138* *prev.* Kisuru. E Burundi
Gitanga *138* *prev.* Kitanga. S Burundi
Gitarama *460* C Rwanda
Gitega *138* *prev.* Kitega. C Burundi
Giulie, Alpi *see* Julian Alps
Giurgiu *448* S Romania
Give *190* Jylland, W Denmark
Giyon *215* *var.* Wehso. C Ethiopia
Gîza *see* El Gîza
Gizhduvan *580* *var.* Giždųvan, *Uzb.* Ghijduwon. S Uzbekistan
Gizo *488* New Georgia Is, Solomon Is
Gjakovë *see* Đakovica
Gjirokastër *57* *var.* Gjirokastra, *prev.* Gjinokastër, Gjinokastra, *It.* Argirocastro, *Gk* Argyrokastron. S Albania
Gjoa Haven *146* King William Island, N Canada
Gjøvik *414* S Norway
Gkreko, Cape *see* Greco, Cape
Glåma *see* Glomma
Glanvilles *68* E Antigua, Antigua & Barbuda
Glanvillia *196* NW Dominica
Glasgow *563* W Scotland, UK
Glazoué *108* S Benin
Glendale *612* NE Zimbabwe
Glenties *288* N Ireland
Glina *181* NE Croatia
Glittertind *414* *var.* Glittertinden. Mountain of S Norway
Gliwice *439* *Ger.* Gleiwitz. S Poland
Głogów *439* *Ger.* Glogau. W Poland
Glomma *414* *var.* Glommen, Glåma. River of S Norway
Gloucester *563* C England, UK
Glover Island *248* *var.* Ramier I. Island to the S of Grenada island, Grenada
Glubokoye *see* Hlybokaye
Gmundner See *see* Traunsee
Gnaviyani Atoll *see* Fuammulah
Goascorán *207* river of El Salvador and Honduras
Goascorán *260* river of SW Honduras
Goat Island *68* island to the N of Barbuda, Antigua & Barbuda
Goba *215* *var.* Gobba. S Ethiopia
Gobabis *391* E Namibia
Gobi *163, 380* desert of China and Mongolia
Goce Delčev *see* Gorna Oryakhovitsa
Gochas *391* *var.* Ghochas. SE Namibia
Go Công *593* S Vietnam
Godāveri *270* river of C India
Godhavn *622* *var.* Qeqertarsuaq, W Greenland
Göding *see* Hodonín
Gödöllő *264* N Hungary
Godoy Cruz *71* W Argentina
Godwin Austen, Mount *see* K2
Goedgegun *see* Nhlangano
Goelette, Passe a la *628* channel of the Atlantic Ocean, to the E of Miquelon, Saint Pierre and Miquelon
Goeree *397* island of SW Netherlands
Goes *397* SW Netherlands
Goettingen *see* Göttingen
Gogounou *108* N Benin
Goiânia *121* *prev.* Goyania. S Brazil
Gökdepe *see* Gëkdepe
Gokwe *612* NW Zimbabwe
Gol *414* S Norway
Golan Heights *291* disputed territory of SW Syria
Gold Coast *77* E Australia
Gold Coast *243* coastal region of W Africa
Golden Bay *401* bay on the coast of N South Island, New Zealand
Golden Valley *612* N Zimbabwe
Goldingen *see* Kuldīga
Golfito *178* SE Costa Rica
Gollel *see* Lavumisa
Golmud *162* *var.* Golmo, *Chin.* Ko-erh-mu. Qinghai, W China
Golungo Alto *64* NW Angola
Goma *607* NE Zaire
Gombe *408* E Nigeria
Gomel' *see* Homyel'
Gomera *501* island of Islas Canarias, SW Spain
Gómez Palacio *370* NW Mexico
Gonaïves *258* W Haiti
Gonâve, Golfe de la *258* gulf of the Caribbean Sea to the W of Haiti
Gonâve, Île de la *258* W Haiti
Gonder *215* *var.* Gondar. NW Ethiopia
Gondomar *442* NW Portugal
Goodenough Island *426* *var.* Morata. Island of SE Papua New Guinea
Good Hope *196* E Dominica
Good Hope, Cape of *493* *Afr.* Kaap die Gooie Hoop. Coastal feature of SW South Africa
Goodlands *368* NE Mauritius
Goose Bay *see* Happy Valley-Goose Bay
Goose Green *621* East Falkland, C Falkland Islands
Gopālpur *93* N Bangladesh
Gorakhpur *270* NE India
Gorce Island *476* island of W Senegal
Gore *401* S South Island, New Zealand
Goré *156* S Chad
Gorē *215* W Ethiopia
Gorey *624* E Jersey
Gorgān *281* *var.* Gurgan. N Iran
Gori *234* C Georgia
Goris *74* SE Armenia
Gorki *see* Horki
Gor'kiy *see* Nizhniy Novgorod
Görlitz *237* E Germany
Gorlovka *see* Horlivka
Gorna Dzhumaya *see* Blagoevgrad
Gorna Oryakhovitsa *128* *var.* Gorna Orjahovica. N Bulgaria
Gornji Milanovac *602* C Serbia, Yugoslavia

H

Halas *see* Kiskunhalas
Haldefjäll *see* Haltiatunturi
Halden *414 prev.* Fredrikshald. S Norway
Halditjåkko *see* Haltiatunturi
Halfa el Gadida *506 var.* New Halfa, Halfa Al Jadida. E Sudan
Halfmoon Bay *401* Stewart Island, SW New Zealand
Half Tree Hollow *628* N St Helena
Halifax *147* SE Canada
Halīl Rūd *281* river of SE Iran
Halla-san *496 Jap.* Kanra-san. Mountain of Cheju-do, S South Korea
Halle *237* C Germany
Hallein *82* N Austria
Halley *66* UK research station of Greater Antarctica, Antarctica
Hall in Tirol *82 var.* Hall. W Austria
Hall Islands *375* island group of C Micronesia
Hall Peninsula *147* peninsula of Baffin Island, NE Canada
Halls Creek *77* NW Australia
Halmahera *276 prev.* Djailolo, Jailolo, Gilolo. Island of Maluku, E Indonesia
Halmahera, Laut *276* sea of the Pacific Ocean, E Indonesia
Halmstad *513* SW Sweden
Ḩalq al Wādī *see* La Goulette
Hälsingborg *see* Helsingborg
Haltiatunturi *221 Swe.* Haldefjäll, *prev.* Halditjåkko, *Nor.* Reisduoddarhalde. Mountain of Finland and Norway
Ḩamad *see* Madīnat Ḩamad
Hamada *304* Honshū, W Japan
Hamadān *281* NW Iran
Hamada Town *see* Madīnat Ḩamad
Ḩamāh *521* W Syria
Hamamatsu *304* Honshū, C Japan
Hamar *414* S Norway
Hambantota *504* SE Sri Lanka
Hamburg *237* N Germany
Ḩamḑ, Wādī al *472* dry watercourse of W Saudi Arabia
Hämeenlinna *221 Swe.* Tavastehus. SW Finland
Hamersley Range *76* mountain range to the W of Australia
Hamgyŏng-sanmaek *413* mountain range of N North Korea
Hamhŭng *413* C North Korea
Hami *162 Uigh.* Kumul, *var.* Qomul. Xinjiang Uygur Zizhiqu. NW China
Hamilton *619* C Bermuda
Hamilton *147* S Canada
Hamilton *401* C North Island, New Zealand
Hamilton *563* C Scotland, UK
Ḩamīm, Wādī al *339* dry watercourse of NE Libya
Hamm *236* W Germany
Hammamet *543 var.* Ḩammāmāt. N Tunisia
Hammamet, Golfe de *543* gulf of the Mediterranean Sea to the E of Tunisia
Hammam Lif *543 var.* Ḩammām al Anf. N Tunisia
Ḩammār, Hawr al *284* lake of SE Iraq
Hammerfest *414* NE Norway
Ḩamrīn, Jabal *284* mountain range of N Iraq
Hamriya *see* Al Ḩamrīyah
Hamrun *363* C Malta
Hāmūn, Daryācheh-ye *see* Sīstān, Daryācheh-ye
Han *496 Jap.* Kan-kō. River of N South Korea
Hanábana *182* river of C Cuba
Hânceşti *see* Hînceşti
Handan *163 var.* Han-tan. Hebei, NE China
Handeni *530* E Tanzania
Handréma, Baie de *625 var.* Mandréma Bay. Bay of the Indian Ocean on the N coast of Mayotte
HaNegev *291 Eng.* Negev. Desert of S Israel
Hanga Roa *159* Easter I, W Chile
Hangayn Nuruu *380* mountain range of W Mongolia
Hangzhou *163 var.* Hangchow, Hang-chou. Zhejiang, E China
Hanka, Lake *see* Khanka, Lake
Hanko *221 Swe.* Hangö. SW Finland
Hankow *see* Wuhan
Hannover *236 Eng.* Hanover. NW Germany
Hanöbukten *513* bay of the Baltic Sea to the S of Sweden
Hanoi *593 Vtn.* Ha Nôi. ❖ of Vietnam, N Vietnam
Hanover *see* Hannover
Hanstholm *190* Jylland, NW Denmark
Han-tan *see* Handan
Hantu, Pulau *483* island of SW Singapore
Hāora *271 prev.* Howrah. E India
Haouach, Ouadi *156* dry watercourse of E Chad
Happy Valley-Goose Bay *147 prev.* Goose Bay. E Canada
Hapsal *see* Haapsalu
Ḩaraḑ *472 var.* Haradh. E Saudi Arabia
Ḩaraḑ *599* N Yemen
Hara Laht *212* bay of the Gulf of Finland, on the coast of N Estonia
Harare *612 prev.* Salisbury. ❖ of Zimbabwe, NE Zimbabwe
Haraze-Mangueigne *156* SE Chad
Harbel *336* W Liberia
Harbin *163 var.* Ha-erh-pin, *prev.* Pinkiang. Heilongjiang, NE China
Harbours, Bay of *621* bay of the South Atlantic Ocean, SE Falkland Islands
Harbour View *303* E Jamaica
Hardangerfjorden *414* fjord of SW Norway
Hardap Dam *391* dam of C Namibia
Haré Meron *291* Mountain of N Israel
Hārer *215* E Ethiopia
Hargeysa *490* NW Somalia
Hari *276 var.* Batang Hari, *prev.* Djambi. River of Sumatra, W Indonesia
Ḩarīb *599* W Yemen
Hari Kurk *212* channel of Baltic Sea, between the island of Hiiumaa and Estonia mainland
Ḩārim *521* NW Syria
Ḩarīmā *310* N Jordan
Haringhat *93* river of SW Bangladesh
Harīrūd *53* river of C Asia
Harīrūd *see* Tedzhen
Harmanli *see* Kharmanli
Harper *336 var.* Cape Palmas. S Liberia
Ḩarrah *599* SE Yemen
Harrington Sound *619* bay of the North Atlantic Ocean, N Bermuda
Harris *625* E Montserrat
Harrisburg *569* Pennsylvania, NE USA
Harrismith *493* Orange Free State, E South Africa
Harstad *414* NE Norway
Hartford *336* SW Liberia
Hartford *569* Connecticut, NE USA
Hartley *see* Chegutu
Harz *237 var.* Harz Mountains. Mountain range of C Germany
HaSharon *291 Eng.* Plain of Sharon. Plain of C Israel
Haskovo *see* Khaskovo
Haspengouw *see* Hesbaye
Hasselt *99* NE Belgium
Hassetché *see* Al Ḩasakah
Hastings *97* SW Barbados
Hastings *401* SE North Island, New Zealand
Hastings *480* W Sierra Leone
Hastings *563* SE England, UK
Hatay *see* Antakya
Hātia *93* river and one of the main mouths of the Ganges, S Bangladesh
Hato Mayor *198* E Dominican Republic
Ḩattā *560* E United Arab Emirates
Hattiesburg *569* Mississippi, SE USA
Hattieville *102* E Belize
Hat Yai *533 var.* Ban Hat Yai. S Thailand
Haud *215 var.* Hawd. Plateau of Somalia and Ethiopia.
Haugesund *414* SW Norway
Hau Hoi Wan *262 Eng.* Deep Water Bay. Bay to the NW of Hong Kong
Haukeligrand *414* SW Norway
Haukivesi *221* lake of SE Finland
Hauraki Gulf *401* gulf on the N coast of North Island, New Zealand
Hau *593* river of SW Vietnam
Haut Atlas *382 Eng.* High Atlas. Mountain range of C Morocco
Haute-Sangha *see* Mambéré-Kadéi
Hautes Fagnes *99 Ger.* Hohes Venn. Mountain range of Belgium
Haute Sûre, Lac de la *346* reservoir of NW Luxembourg
Haut Plateau du Dra *see* Dra, Hamada du
Hauts Plateaux *59* plateau of NW Algeria
Havana *182 var.* La Habana. ❖ of Cuba, NW Cuba
Havířov *188* E Czech Republic
Havlíčkův Brod *188 prev.* Německý Brod, *Ger.* Deutsch-Brod. S Czech Republic
Hawaii *568* island of Hawaiian group, Hawaii, USA, C Pacific
Hawaii *568* non-contiguous state of USA, C Pacific
Ḩawallī *322* E Kuwait
Hawash *see* Awash
Hawea, Lake *401* W South Island, New Zealand
Hawera *401* SW North Island, New Zealand
Hawick *563* S Scotland, UK
Hawke Bay *401* bay of the South Pacific Ocean, on the SE coast of North Island, New Zealand
Hawlēr *see* Arbīl
Ḩawmat as Sūq *see* Houmt Souk
Ḩawrā' *599* C Yemen
Ḩawrān, Wādī *284* dry watercourse of W Iraq
Hawwārah *310 var.* Huwwāra. N Jordan
HaYarden *see* Jordan
Hay River *146* W Canada
Ḩayyān, Ra's *91 var.* Ra's Hayyān. Cape of E Bahrain
Hebei *163 var.* Hopei. Province of NE China
Hebrides, Sea of the *563* sea of the Atlantic Ocean to the NW of UK
Hebron *291, 292 Ar.* Al Khalil. S West Bank
Heerenveen *397* NE Netherlands
Heerlen *397* S Netherlands
Ḩefa *291* N Israel
Ḩefa, Mifraẕ *291 Eng.* Bay of Haifa. Bay of the Mediterranean Sea
Hefei *163 var.* Hofei, *hist.* Luchow. Anhui, E China
Heichin *see* P'ing-chen
Heidelberg *236* SW Germany
Heihe *163 prev.* Ai-hun. Heilongjiang, NE China
Hei-ho *see* Nagqu
Heilbronn *236* SW Germany
Heiligenkreuz *see* Žiar nad Hronom
Heilong Jiang *see* Amur
Heilongjiang *163 var.* Heilungkiang, Hei-lung-chiang. Province of NE China
Heimaey Island *268 var.* Heimaey, Heimaæy. Island of S Iceland
Heitō *see* P'ing-tung
Helen *627* island of S Palau
Helena *568* Montana, NW USA
Helgoland *236 Eng.* Heligoland. Island of NW Germany
Helgoländer Bucht *236 var.* Helgoland Bay, Heligoland Bight. Bay of the North Sea
Hell-Ville *see* Andoany
Helmand, Daryā-ye *53* river of Afghanistan and Iran
Helmond *397* S Netherlands
Helsingborg *513 prev.* Hälsingborg. S Sweden
Helsingør *190 Eng.* Elsinore. Sjælland, E Denmark
Helsinki *221 Swe.* Helsingfors. ❖ of Finland, S Finland
Ḩelwân *202 var.* Ḩulwān, Ḩilwān. N Egypt
Henan *163 var.* Honan. Province of C China
Henderson Island *627* island of N Pitcairn Islands
Hendū Kosh *see* Hindu Kush
Hengduan Shan *162* mountain range of SW China
Hengelo *397* E Netherlands
Hengyang *163* Hunan, S China
Hentiesbaai *391* W Namibia
Henzada *135* SW Burma
Heradhsvötn *268* river of C Iceland
Herāt *53* W Afghanistan
Heredia *178* C Costa Rica
Hereford *563* C England, UK
Herisau *516 Fr.* Hérisau. NE Switzerland
Héristal *see* Herstal
Herm *623* island of S Guernsey
Hermannstadt *see* Sibiu
Hermansverk *414* SW Norway
Hermel *332 var.* Hirmil. NE Lebanon
Hermitage *248* C Grenada island, Grenada
Hermon, Mount *521 Ar.* Jabal ash Shaykh. Mountain of SW Syria
Hermosillo *370* NW Mexico
Hernád *see* Hornád
Hernandarias *428 prev.* Tacurupucú. SE Paraguay
Herne *236* W Germany
Herning *190* Jylland, W Denmark
Herstal *99 Fr.* Héristal. E Belgium
Herzliyya *291* C Israel
Herzogenbusch *see* 's-Hertogenbosch
Hesbaye *99 Dut.* Haspengouw. Physical region of C Belgium
Hesperange *346* SE Luxembourg
Hestur *620* island of C Faeroe Islands
Hetauda *395* C Nepal
Hida-sammyaku *304* mountain range of Honshū, C Japan
Hienghène *626* W New Caledonia
Hierro *501 var.* Ferro. Island of Islas Canarias, SW Spain
High Atlas *see* Haut Atlas
Highgate *303* NE Jamaica
High Island Reservoir *262* reservoir of E Hong Kong
Highlands, The *68* highlands of Barbuda, Antigua & Barbuda
High Point *619* headland of W Bermuda
High Veld *see* Northern Karoo
Higüey *198 var.* Salvaleon de Higüey. E Dominican Republic
Hiiumaa *212 var.* Hiiuma, *Ger.* Dagden, *Swed.* Dagö. Island of W Estonia
Hikina *624* island, NE Johnston Atoll
Hildesheim *236* NW Germany
Hilla *see* Al Ḩillah
Hillaby, Mount *97* mountain of Barbados
Hillerød *190* Sjælland, E Denmark
Hillsborough *248* W Carriacou, Grenada
Hilo *568* Hawaii, USA
Hilversum *397* C Netherlands
Ḩilwan *see* Ḩelwân
Himachal Pradesh *270* state of N India
Himalayas *110, 162, 270, 395* mountain range of S Asia

I

Ibarra *200 var.* San Miguel de Ibarra. N Ecuador
Ibb *599* W Yemen
Ibbenbüren *236* NW Germany
Ibenga *176* river of N Congo
Ibérico, Sistema *501 var.* Cordillera Ibérica, *Eng.* Iberian Mountains. Mountains of NE Spain
Ibiza *see* Eivissa
Ibo *see* Sassandra
Iboundji *230* C Gabon
Ibrā' *418* N Oman
Ibrī *418* NW Oman
Irbīl *see* Arbīl
Ibusuki *304* Kyūshū, SW Japan
Içá *120* river of NW Brazil
Ica *431* SW Peru
Iceflavík *see* Keflavík
Îçel *see* Mersin
Iceland *268-269* officially Republic of Iceland, *Icel.* Ísland. Country of the North Atlantic Ocean divided into 8 admin. units (regions)
Ichinomiya *304* Honshū, C Japan
Ichinoseki *304* Honshū, N Japan
Idah *408* S Nigeria
Idaho *568* state of NW USA
Idaho Falls *568* Idaho, NW USA
Idensalmi *see* Iisalmi
Idfu *202 var.* Idfū, Edfu. SE Egypt
Idi Amin, Lac *see* Edward, Lake
Idlib *521* NW Syria
Idrija *486 It.* Idria. W Slovenia
Idzhevan *see* Ijevan
Iecava *330* C Latvia
Ieper *99 Fr.* Ypres. W Belgium
Ifalik *375* atoll of C Micronesia
Ife *408* SW Nigeria
Iferouâne *407* N Niger
Iferten *see* Yverdon
Iganga *554* SE Uganda
Igarka *453* N Russia
Igatimí *see* Ygatimí
Iglau *see* Jihlava
Iglesias *294* Sardegna, W Italy
Igló *see* Spišská Nová Ves
Ignalina *344* E Lithuania
Iguaçu, Salto do *121 Sp.* Cataratas del Iguazú, *prev.* Victoria Falls. Waterfall of Argentina and Brazil
Iguetti, Sebkhet *366* salt lake of N Mauritania
Ihavandippolhu Atoll *358 var.* Ihavandiffulu Atoll. Atoll of N Maldives
Ihema, Lac *460* lake of Burundi and Rwanda
Ihosy *350* S Madagascar
Iida *304* Honshū, C Japan
Iijoki *221* river of C Finland
Irbīl *see* Arbīl
Iisalmi *221 Swe.* Idensalmi. C Finland
Ijebu-Ode *408* SW Nigeria
Ijevan *74 Rus.* Idzhevan, *var.* Idževan. N Armenia
IJssel *397 var.* Yssel. River of C Netherlands
IJsselmeer *397 prev.* Zuider Zee. Lake of N Netherlands
Ikare *408* SW Nigeria
Ikaría *245* island of SE Greece
Ikast *190* Jylland, W Denmark
Ikeja *408* SW Nigeria
Ikerre *408 var.* Ikerre-Ekiti. SW Nigeria
Iki *304* island to the NW of Kyūshū, SW Japan
Ikom *408* S Nigeria
Ikopa *350* river of N Madagascar
Ila *408* W Nigeria
Ilam *395* W Nepal
I-lan *525 Jap.* Giran. NE Taiwan
Ile *see* Ili
Ilebo *607 prev.* Port Francqui. W Zaire
Ilesha *408* SW Nigeria
Ilha Solteira, Represa de *121* reservoir of S Brazil
Ili *312 Kaz.* Ile. River of China and Kazakhstan
Iligan *435* Mindanao, S Philippines
Ilirska Bistrica *486* SW Slovenia
Il'jaly *see* Yylanly
Illapel *159* C Chile
Illiassa *233* NW Gambia
Illinois *569* state of C USA
Ilobasco *207* C El Salvador
Ilobu *408* W Nigeria
Iloilo *435* Panay, C Philippines
Ilopango, Lago de *207* volcanic lake of C El Salvador
Ilorin *408* W Nigeria
Īluh *see* Batman
Il'yaly *see* Yylanly
Imatong Mountains *506* mountains of S Sudan
Imatra *221* SE Finland
Imeni 26 Bakinskikh Komissarov *see* Bakı Komissarı
Imilili *382* W Western Sahara
İmişli *86 Rus.* Imishli, Imišli. C Azerbaijan
Imja-do *496* island of SW South Korea
Imola *295* N Italy
Imperatriz *121* NE Brazil
Imperia *294* N Italy
Impfondo *176* NE Congo
Imphāl *271* E India
Ina *304* Honshū, C Japan
Inakona *488* S Guadalcanal, Solomon Is
In Aménas *59 var.* I-n-Amenas, In Amnas. E Algeria
Inárajan *623* SE Guam
Inarijärvi *221 Swe.* Enareträsk, *Lapp.* Aanaarjävri. Lake of N Finland
Inarijoki *221 Nor.* Anarjokka. River of Finland and Norway
Inawashiro-ko *304* lake of Honshū, N Japan
Inbhear Mór *see* Arklow
Inch'ŏn *496 prev.* Chemulpo, *Jap.* Jinsen. NW South Korea
Inchope *387* C Mozambique
Incles *62* river of NE Andorra
Independence *102* SE Belize
Inderagiri *see* Indragiri
India *270-275* officially Republic of India, *Hind.* Bharat. Country divided into 32 admin. units (25 states and 7 union territories)
Indiana *569* state of C USA
Indianapolis *569* Indiana, C USA
Indian Desert *see* Thar Desert
Indian Ocean *66, 620* ocean bounded to the W by Africa, to the E by Australia and to the S by Antarctica
Indigirka *453* River of NE Russia
Indonesia *276-279* officially Republic of Indonesia, *Ind.* Republik Indonesia, *prev.* United States of Indonesia, Dutch East Indies, Netherlands East Indies. Country of SE Asia divided into 25 admin. units (24 provinces and 1 autonomous district)
Indonesian Borneo *see* Kalimantan
Indore *270* NW India
Indragiri *276 var.* Inderagiri. River of Sumatra, W Indonesia
Indre *225* river of C France
Indus *270, 421* river of S Asia
Indus, Mouths of the *421* river delta of S Pakistan
Infante Dom Henrique *471* SE Príncipe, Sao Tome & Principe
Ingolstadt *237* S Germany
Inguri *see* Enguri
Ingushetiya, Respublika *452* autonomous republic of SW Russia
Ingwavuma *see* Nggwavuma
Inhambane *387* S Mozambique
I-ning *see* Yining
Inírida *171* river of E Colombia
Inis *see* Ennis
Inland Sea *304 var.* Seto Naikai. Sea of the Pacific Ocean between Honshū and Shikoku, W Japan
Inn *82, 237* river of C Europe
Inner Channel *102 var.* Main Channel. Inlet of W Caribbean Sea
Inner Hebrides *563* island group of NW Scotland, UK
Inner Islands *478 var.* Central Group. Island group of NE Seychelles
Inner Mongolian Autonomous Region *see* Nei Mongol Zizhiqu
Innsbruck *82* W Austria
Inrin *see* Yüan-lin
In Salah *59 var.* I-n-Salah. C Algeria
Insein *135* S Burma
Intelewa *508* S Suriname
Interlaken *516* SW Switzerland
Inthanon, Doi *533* mountain of NW Thailand
Intipucá *207* SE El Salvador
Inuvik *146* NW Canada
Invercargill *401* SW South Island, New Zealand
Inverness *563* N Scotland, UK
Inyanga *see* Nyanga
Inyangani *612* mountain of E Zimbabwe
Inyazura *see* Nyazura
Ioánnina *245 var.* Janina, Yannina. W Greece
Iolotan' *see* Ëloten
Ionian Islands *see* Iónioi Nísoi
Ionian Sea *57, 245, 295 Gk* Iónio Pélagos, *It.* Mar Ionio. Area of the Mediterranean Sea, between Italy and SE Europe
Ionio, Mar *see* Ionian Sea
Iónioi Nísoi *245 Eng.* Ionian Islands. Island group of W Greece
Iori *234* river of Azerbaijan and Georgia
Íos *245* island of SE Greece
Iowa *569* state of C USA
Ipeľ *see* Ipoly
Ipiales *171* SW Colombia
Ipoh *354* W Peninsular Malaysia
Ipoly *264, 485 Slvk.* Ipeľ, *Ger.* Eipel. River of Hungary and Slovakia
Ippy *154* C Central African Republic
Ipswich *77* E Australia
Ipswich *563* E England, UK
Iqaluit *147 prev.* Frobisher Bay. Baffin Island, NE Canada
Iquique *159* N Chile
Iquitos *431* N Peru
Irákleio *245 Eng.* Candia, *prev.* Iráklion. Crete, S Greece
Iran *280-283* officially Islamic Republic of Iran, *prev.* Persia. Country of SW Asia divided into 24 admin. units (provinces)
Iran, Pegunungan *355 var.* Iran Mountains. Mountain range of Borneo, Indonesia and Malaysia
Iran, Plateau of *281* plateau of C Iran
Irapuato *370* C Mexico
Iraq *284-287* officially Republic of Iraq, *Ar.* 'Irāq. Country of SW Asia divided into 18 admin. units (governorates)
Irbe Strait *212 Est.* Kura Kurk, *prev.* Irbe Väin, *Latv.* Irbes Šaurums. Strait connecting the Baltic Sea and Gulf of Riga
Irbid *310* N Jordan
Ireland Island North *619* island of W Bermuda
Ireland Island South *619* island of W Bermuda
Ireland, Northern *see* Northern Ireland
Ireland, Republic of *288-289* officially Republic of Ireland, Éire. Country of W Europe divided into 26 admin. units (counties)
Ireng *256 var.* Maú. River of Brazil and Guyana
Irgalem *see* Yirga 'Alem
Iri *496 Jap.* Riri. W South Korea
Irian *see* New Guinea
Irian Jaya *276-277 Eng.* West Irian, *prev.* Dutch New Guinea. Province of W Indonesia
Iringa *530* C Tanzania
Iriomote-jima *304* island of Sakishima-shotō, SW Japan
Iriri *121* river of N Brazil
Irish Sea *288, 563, 623 Ir.* Muir Eireann. Sea of the Atlantic Ocean between Ireland and UK
Irkeshtam *325 var.* Irkeštam. SW Kyrgyzstan
Irkutsk *453* C Russia
Irmak *547* river of N Turkey
Iroise *224* area of the Atlantic Ocean to the NW of France
'Irqah *599* SW Yemen
Irrawaddy *135 var.* Ayeyarwady. River of C Burma
Irrawaddy, Mouths of the *135* delta area of SW Burma
Irrsee *82* lake of N Austria
Irtysh *312, 452 Kaz.* Ertis. River of Kazakhstan and Russia
Irun *501* N Spain
Iruñea *see* Pamplona
Isabela *627* NW Puerto Rico
Isabela, Isla *200* island of SW Galapagos Is, Ecuador
Isachsen *146* Ellef Ringnes Island, N Canada
Ísafdhardjúp *268* inlet of the Atlantic Ocean, NW Iceland
Isangel *585* Tanna, Vanuatu
Isa Town *see* Madīnat 'Īsá
Isalo, Tangorombohitr' *350* mountains of SW Madagascar
Ischia, Isola d' *295* island of S Italy
Ise *304* Honshū, C Japan
Isefjord *190* fjord of Sjælland, E Denmark
Isembe *138 var.* Shembe. S Burundi
Isére *225* river of SE France
Iseyin *408* W Nigeria
Isfara *528* N Tajikistan
Ísfjördhur *268* NW Iceland
Isha Baydhabo *see* Baydhabo
Isherton *256* S Guyana
Ishigaki-jima *304* island of Sakishima-shotō, SW Japan
Ishikari *305* river of Hokkaidō, N Japan
Ishim *312 Kaz.* Esil. River of Kazakhstan and Russia
Ishinomaki *304* Honshū, N Japan
Ishkashim *528* S Tajikistan
Ishurdi *93* W Bangladesh
Isidoro Noblia *577* NE Uruguay
Isiolo *316* C Kenya
Isiro *607* NE Zaire
Iskeçe *see* Xánthi
İskele *187 var.* Trikomo. E Cyprus
İskenderun *547 Eng.* Alexandretta. S Turkey
İskenderun Körfezi *547 Eng.* Gulf of Alexandretta. Gulf of the Mediterranean Sea
Iskŭr *128* river of NW Bulgaria
Iskŭr, Yazovir *128* reservoir of W Bulgaria
Islāmābād *421* ❖ of Pakistan, NE Pakistan
Island Harbour *618* bay of the Caribbean Sea on the N coast of Anguilla
Islay *563* island of Inner Hebrides, W Scotland, UK
Isle *225* river of SW France
Ismâ'ilîya *202 var.* Al Ismā'īlīyah, *Eng.* Ismaila. N Egypt
Isna *202 var.* Isnā, Esna. SE Egypt
Isoka *611* NE Zambia
Isonzo *see* Soča.
Ispahan *see* Eşfahān
İsparta *547* SW Turkey

Israel *290-293* officially State of Israel, *Heb.* Yisra'el. Country of SW Asia divided into 6 admin. units (districts).
Issano *256* C Guyana
Issia *300* SW Ivory Coast
Issyk-Kul' *325 prev.* Rybach'ye, *Kir.* Ysyk-Köl. NE Kyrgyzstan
Issyk-Ku, Ozero *325 var.* Issiq Köl. Lake of NE Kyrgyzstan
Istanbul *547 prev.* Constantinople, *Turk.* İstanbul, *Bul.* Tsarigrad. NW Turkey
İstanbul Boğazı *547* Karadeniz Boğazi, *Eng.* Bosporus. Strait connecting Marmara Denizi and Black Sea
Istra *181 Eng.* Istria. Peninsula of SE Europe
Istria *see* Istra
Itabuna *121* E Brazil
Itagüí *171* NW Colombia
Itaipú, Represa de *121, 428* reservoir of Brazil and Paraguay
Italy *294-299* officially The Italian Republic, *It.* Italia, Repubblica Italiana. Country of S Europe divided into 20 admin. units (regions)
Itany *see* Litani
Itassi *see* Vieille Case
Iténez *see* Guaporé
Itonamas *112* river of NE Bolivia
Itremo *350 var.* Massif de l'Itremo. Mountain range of C Madagascar
Ivakoany, Massif de l' *see* Ivakoany
Itsamia *174* S Mohéli, Comoros
Itsandra *174* W Grande Comore, Comoros
Itu Aba Island *628* island of W Spratly Islands
Ituni *256* C Guyana
Iturup *305* disputed island of Kurile Islands, SE Russia
Ivakoany *350 var.* Massif de l'Ivakoany. Mountain range of SE Madagascar
Ivalojoki *221* river of N Finland
Ivano-Frankivs'k *556 Rus.* Ivano-Frankovsk, *prev.* Stanislav, *Pol.* Stanisławów, *Ger.* Stanislau. W Ukraine
Ivatsevichy *104* SW Belorussia
Ivindo *230* river of C Africa
Iviza *see* Eivissa
Ivoire, Côte d' *see* Ivory Coast
Ivory Coast *300 Fr.* Côte d'Ivoire. Coastal region of S Ivory Coast
Ivory Coast *300-301 Fr.* Côte d'Ivoire. Country of W Africa divided into 34 admin. units (departments)
Ivujivik *147* NE Canada
Iwakuni *304* Honshū, W Japan
Iwaki *304* Honshū, N Japan
Iwo *408* SW Nigeria
Iwŏn *413* E North Korea
Ixcán *250* river of Guatemala and Mexico
Izabal, Lago de *250 prev.* Golfo Dulce. Lake of E Guatemala
Izhevsk *452 prev.* Ustinov. W Russia
Izkī *418* N Oman
İzmir *547 prev.* Smyrna. W Turkey
İzmit *547 var.* Kocaeli. NW Turkey
Izuhara *304* Tsushima, W Japan
Izumo *304* Honshū, W Japan
Izu-shotō *304* island group to the SE of Honshū, SE Japan

J

Jabal aẓ Ẓannah *560 var.* Jebel Dhanna, W United Arab Emirates
Jabāliya *291, 292* NE Gaza Strip
Jabalpur *270 prev.* Jubbulpore. C India
Jabat *364 var.* Jabwot Island. Island of S Marshall Islands
Jabbul, Sabkhat al *521* salt-flat of NW Syria
Jablah *521 var.* Jeble, *Fr.* Djéblé. W Syria
Jablanica *57* mountain range of E Albania
Jablonec nad Nisou *188 Ger.* Gablonz an der Neisse. N Czech Republic
Jaboatão *121* E Brazil
Jabwot Island *see* Jabat
Jaceel *490 It.* Uadi Giahel. Seasonal river of NE Somalia
Jackson *569* Mississippi, SE USA
Jacksonville *569* Florida, SE USA
Jacmel *258 var.* Jaquemel. S Haiti
Jaco *178* SW Costa Rica
Jacob *see* Nkayi
Jacobābād *421* SW Pakistan
Jadotville *see* Likasi
Jadransko More *see* Adriatic Sea
Jādū *339* NW Libya
Jaén *501* SW Spain
Jafara Plain *339* plain of Libya and Tunisia
Jaffna *504* N Sri Lanka
Jaffna Lagoon *504* lagoon of N Sri Lanka
Jafr, Qā' al *310 var.* El Jafr. Salt pan of S Jordan
Jägala *212 var.* Jägala Jõgi. River of N Estonia
Jägerndorf *see* Krnov
Jagodina *see* Svetozarevo
Jaguarão *see* Yaguarón
Jailolo *see* Halmahera
Jaipur *270 prev.* Jeypore. N India
Jaipur Hāt *93* NW Bangladesh
Jajce *116* W Bosnia & Herzegovina
Jakar *110* C Bhutan
Jakarta *276 prev.* Djakarta, *Dut.* Batavia. ❖ of Indonesia, Java, C Indonesia
Jakobshavn *622 var.* Ilulissa, W Greenland
Jakobstad *221 Fin.* Pietersaari. W Finland
Jakobstadt *see* Jēkabpils
Jalal-Abad *see* Dzhalal-Abad
Jalālābād *53* E Afghanistan
Jalandhar *270 prev.* Jullundur. N India
Jalapa *370 var.* Jalapa Enríquez, *prev.* Xalapa. SE Mexico
Jalapa *250* C Guatemala
Jalousie *465* SW St Lucia
Jālū *339* NE Libya
Jaluit *364* island of S Marshall Islands
Jamaame *490 It.* Giamame. S Somalia
Jamaare *408* river of NE Nigeria
Jamaica *302-303* island state of the West Indies, divided into 14 admin. units (parishes)
Jamaica Channel *258, 303* channel of the Caribbean Sea between Haiti and Jamaica
Jamālpur *93* N Bangladesh
Jambi *276 prev.* Djambi, *var.* Telanaipura. Sumatra, W Indonesia
Jambol *see* Yambol
Jamdena *see* Yamdena, Pulau
James Bay *147* inlet of Hudson Bay, C Canada
Jamestown *628* ❖ of St Helena, N St Helena
Jamestown *see* Holetown
Jammāl *see* Jemmel
Jammerbugten *190* bay to the NW of Denmark
Jammu *270* N India
Jāmnagar *270 prev.* Navangar. W India
Jämsä *221* S Finland
Jamshedpur *270* E India
Jamuna *93* lower course of the Brahmaputra, N Bangladesh
Jamundá *see* Nhamundá
Janakpur *395* E Nepal
Janela *152* Santo Antão, N Cape Verde
Jangijul *see* Yangiyul'
Janīn *see* Jenin
Janina *see* Ioánnina
Janow *see* Jonava
Jantra *see* Yambol
Janzūr *339* NW Libya
Japan *304-309* country of E Asia, divided into 47 admin. units (prefectures)
Japan, Sea of *304, 413, 453, 496 Rus.* Yapanskoye More. Sea of Pacific Ocean, between E Asia and Japan
Jappeni *233* C Gambia
Japurá *120 var.* Yapurá. River of Brazil and Colombia
Jaquemel *see* Jacmel
Jarabacoa *198* C Dominican Republic
Jarābulus *521 var.* Jerablus, *Fr.* Djérablous. N Syria
Jarash *310 var.* Jerash. NW Jordan
Jarbah, Jazīrat *see* Jerba, Île de
Jardines de la Reina, Archipiélago de los *182* island group of S Cuba
Jarej District *364* district of Majuro, SE Marshall Islands
Jari *121 var.* Jary. River of N Brazil
Jarīd, Shaṭṭ al *see* Jerid, Chott el
Jaroměř *188* NE Czech Republic
Jarqŭrghon *see* Dzharkurgan
Jars, Plain of *see* Xiangkhoang, Plateau de
Järvenpää *221 Swe.* Träskända. S Finland
Jason Islands *621* island group of NW Falkland Islands
Jassy *see* Iaşi
Jastrzębie Zdrój *439* S Poland
Jászberény *264* NE Hungary
Jauf *see* Al Jawf
Jaunpiebalga *330* NE Latvia
Java *276 var.* Jawa, *prev.* Djawa. Island of C Indonesia
Javan *528 var.* Yavan. W Tajikistan
Javari *120-121 var.* Yavarí. River of Brazil and Peru
Java Sea *see* Jawa, Laut
Jawa *see* Java
Jawa, Laut *276 Eng.* Java Sea. Sea of the Pacific Ocean, C Indonesia
Jawhar *490 var.* Jowhar, *It.* Giohar. S Somalia
Jayapura *277 prev.* Sukarnapura, *Dut.* Hollandia. Irian Jaya, E Indonesia
Jay Dairen *see* Dalian
Jaya, Puncak *277 prev.* Puntjak Sukarno, Puntjak Carstensz. Mountain of Irian Jaya, E Indonesia
Jazā'ir, Ra's al *91* cape of SW Bahrain
Jaz Murian, Hamun-e *281* lake of SE Iran
Jazzīn *see* Jezzine
Jbaïl *332 var.* Jubayl. W Lebanon
Jdiriya *382* NE Western Sahara
Jebba *408* W Nigeria
Jebel *see* Dzhebel
Jebel, Bahr el *see* White Nile
Jebel Dhanna *see* Jabal aẓ Ẓannah
Jeble *see* Jablah
Jedda *see* Jiddah
Jeffara *543 var.* Al Jifārah. Physical region of SE Tunisia
Jefferson City *569* Missouri, C USA
Jega *408* NW Nigeria
Jehegnadzor *see* Yeghegnadzor
Jēkabpils *330 Ger.* Jakobstadt. SE Latvia
Jelenia Góra *439 Ger.* Hirschberg in Riesengebirge. SW Poland
Jelgava *330 Ger.* Mitau. C Latvia
Jember *276 prev.* Djember. Java, C Indonesia
Jemmel *543 var.* Jammāl. N Tunisia
Jemo *364* island of C Marshall Islands
Jena *237* C Germany
Jendouba *543 var.* Jundūbah. NW Tunisia
Jenin *291, 292 var.* Janīn, *Ar.* Jinīn. N West Bank
Jenné *see* Djénné
Jennings *68* W Antigua, Antigua & Barbuda
Jenny *508* N Suriname
Jequitinhonha *121* river of E Brazil
Jerablus *see* Jarābulus
Jerada *382* NE Morocco
Jerash *see* Jarash
Jerba *see* Houmt Souk
Jerba, Île de *543 var.* Djerba, Jazīrat Jarbah. Island of E Tunisia
Jérémie *258* SW Haiti
Jerevan *see* Yerevan
Jerez de la Frontera *500* SW Spain
Jericho *291, 292 Heb.* Yeriḥo, *Ar.* Arīḥā. E West Bank
Jerid, Chott el *543 var.* Shaṭṭ al Jarīd. Salt lake of SW Tunisia
Jermuk *74 Rus.* Dzhermuk. SE Armenia
Jersey *224, 624* British Crown dependency of the English Channel. ❖ St Helier.
Jerusalem *291, 292 Ar.* Al Quds, *Heb.* Yerushalayim. ❖ of Israel, Israel and West Bank
Jesenice *486 Ger.* Assling. NW Slovenia
Jesselton *see* Kota Kinabalu
Jessore *93* W Bangladesh
Jesús Menéndez *182* SE Cuba
Jeta, Ilha de *254* island of W Guinea-Bissau
Jevlah *see* Yevlax
Jeypore *see* Jaipur
Jezercës, Maja e *57 var.* Jezerce. Mountain of N Albania
Jezzine *332 var.* Jazzīn. S Lebanon
Jhālakāti *93* S Bangladesh
Jhang *421 var.* Jhang Sadar, Jhang Sadr. NE Pakistan
Jhelum *421* NE Pakistan
Jhelum *421* river of India and Pakistan
Jhenida *93* W Bangladesh
Jiamusi *163 var.* Chia-mu-ssu, Kiamusze. Heilongjiang, NE China
Jiangsu *163 var.* Kiangsu, Chiang-su. Province of E China
Jiangxi *163 var.* Kiangsi, Chiang-hsi. Province of SE China
Jibuti *see* Djibouti
Jičin *188* N Czech Republic
Jiddah *472 Eng.* Jedda. W Saudi Arabia
Jiddah *91* island of NW Bahrain
Jidd Ḥafṣ *91 var.* Judd Ḥafṣ. N Bahrain
Jiftilik Post *292* E West Bank
Jiguaní *182* SE Cuba
Jihlava *188 Ger.* Iglau. S Czech Republic
Jijel *59 var.* Djidjel, *prev.* Djidjelli. NE Algeria
Jijiga *215 It.* Giggiga. E Ethiopia
Jilf al Kabīr, Haḍabat al *see* Gilf Kebir Plateau
Jilib *490 It.* Gelib. S Somalia
Jilin *163 var.* Kirin, Chi-lin, *prev.* Yungki. Jilin, NE China
Jilin *163 var.* Kirin, Chi-lin. Province of NE China
Jīma *215 var.* Jimma, Ft. Gimma. SW Ethiopia
Jimaní *198* W Dominican Republic
Jinan *163 var.* Chinan, Tsinan. Shandong, E China
Jinīn *see* Jenin
Jinja *554* S Uganda
Jinotega *404* C Nicaragua
Jinotepe *404* S Nicaragua
Jinsen *see* Inch'ŏn
Jintotlolo Channel *435* channel connecting Mindoro Strait and Visayan Sea
Jinzhou *163 var.* Chin-chou, Chinchow, *prev.* Chinhsien. Liaoning, NE China
Jipijapa *200* W Ecuador

Jiquilisco *207* S El Salvador
Jiquilisco, Bahia de *207* bay of the Pacific Ocean to the S of El Salvador
Jirriiban *490 prev.* Ceel Xamurre, *It.* El Hamurre. E Somalia
Jisr ash Shughūr *521* *var.* Djisr el Choghour. NW Syria
Jiu *448 Ger.* Schyl, *Hung.* Zsily. River of S Romania
Jiulong *see* Kowloon
Jixi *163 var.* Chi-hsi. Heilongjiang, NE China
Jīzān *472 var.* Qīzān. S Saudi Arabia
Jizuka *304* Kyūshū, SW Japan
Jiz', Wādī al *599* dry watercourse of E Yemen
Jizzakh *see* Dzhizak
Jleeb, Shagat Al *see* Qalīb, Shiqqat al
Jleeb al Shuyoukh *see* Qalīb ash Shuyūkh
Joal-Fadiout *476 prev.* Joal. W Senegal
João Barrosa *152* Boa Vista, E Cape Verde
João Pessoa *121 prev.* Paraíba. E Brazil
Jo-ch'iang *see* Ruoqiang
Joden Savanne *508* NE Suriname
Jodhpur *270* NW India
Joel's Drift *334* N Lesotho
Joensuu *221* SE Finland
Jõgeva *212 Ger.* Laisholm. C Estonia
Jogjakarta *see* Yogyakarta
Johannesburg *493* Pretoria-Witwatersrand-Vereeniging, NE South Africa
John o'Groats *563* N Scotland, UK
Johnsons Point *68* SW Antigua, Antigua & Barbuda
Johnson, Rapides *607* rapids of Zaire and Zambia
Johnston Atoll *624* unincorporated territory of the USA, Pacific Ocean.
Johnston Island *624* island of S Johnston Atoll
Johor Bahru *354* SE Peninsular Malaysia
Johore Strait *483* strait connecting Strait of Malacca and South China Sea
Joinville *121 var.* Joinvile. S Brazil
Jolo Group *435* island group of Sulu Archipelago, SW Philippines
Jolo Island *435* island of Jolo Group, SW Philippines
Jomsom *395* W Nepal
Jona *516* NE Switzerland
Jonava *344 Ger.* Janow. C Lithuania
Jones Point *620* headland on the W coast of Christmas Island
Jonglei Canal *506* canal of S Sudan
Jönköping *513* S Sweden
Jonquière *147* SE Canada
Jordan *291, 292, 310 Ar.* Urdunn, *Heb.* HaYarden. River of SW Asia
Jordan *310-311* officially Hashemite Kingdom of Jordan, *Ar.* Al Urdunn. Country of SW Asia divided into 8 admin. units (governorates)
Jos *408* C Nigeria
José Batlle y Ordóñez *577* C Uruguay
José E. Bisanó *198* N Dominican Republic
José Pedro Varela *577* SE Uruguay
Joseph Bonaparte Gulf *77* gulf of Timor Sea on the coast of NW Australia
Jos Plateau *408* C Nigeria
Jos Sudarso *see* Yos Sudarso, Pulau
Jost Van Dyke *619* island of W British Virgin Islands
Jotunheimen *414* mountains of SW Norway
Joûnié *332 var.* Juniyah. W Lebanon
Jovellanos *182* NW Cuba
Jozini Dam *510* reservoir of South Africa and Swaziland
Jsahaya *304* Kyūshū, SW Japan
Juan Fernández Islands *159* island group of W Chile
Juan L. Lacaze *577 prev.* Sauce. SW Uruguay
Juarzon *336 var.* Juazohn. SE Liberia
Juazeiro do Norte *121* E Brazil
Juazohn *see* Juarzon
Juba *215, 490 Som.* Jubba, *var.* Ganaane, *Amh.* Genale Wenz, *It.* Guiba. River of Ethiopia and Somalia
Juba *506 var.* Jūbā. S Sudan
Jubba *see* Juba
Jubbulpore *see* Jabalpur
Júcar *501* river of C Spain
Juclà, Estany de *62* lake of NE Andorra
Judd Ḥafş *see* Jidd Ḥafş
Judenburg *82* C Austria
Juigalpa *404* S Nicaragua
Jui-shui *525* E Taiwan
Juiz de Fora *121* SE Brazil
Jujuy *see* San Salvador de Jujuy
Juliaca *431* SE Peru
Julian Alps *486 Ger.* Julische Alpen, *It.* Alpi Giulie, *Slvn.* Julijske Alpe. Mountains of NW Slovenia
Juliana Top *508* mountain of C Suriname
Julianehåb *622 var.* Qaqortoq. S Greenland
Jullundur *see* Jalandhar
Jumayrah *560 var.* Jumeirah. NE United Arab Emirates
Jumla *395* E Nepal
Jumna *see* Yamuna
Jundūbah *see* Jendouba
Juneau *568* Alaska, USA
Jungbunzlau *see* Mladá Boleslav
Junín *71* E Argentina
Junk Bay *see* Tseung Kwan O
Juntas *178* W Costa Rica
Junten *see* Sunch'ŏn
Juozapinės Kalnas *344* mountain of SE Lithuania
Jupiá, Represa de *121* reservoir of S Brazil
Jura *563* island of Inner Hebrides, W Scotland, UK
Jura *225, 516 var.* Jura Mountains. Mountain range of France and Switzerland
Juraguá *182* C Cuba
Jura Mountains *see* Jura
Jurbarkas *344 Ger.* Jurburg, *var.* Georgenburg. W Lithuania
Jūrmala *330* NW Latvia
Jurong Lake *483* lake of W Singapore
Jurong Town *483* W Singapore
Juruá *120* river of Brazil and Peru
Juruena *120* river of W Brazil
Jutiapa *250* S Guatemala
Juticalpa *260* C Honduras
Jutland *see* Jylland
Juventud, Isla de la *182* *var.* Isla de Pinos, *Eng.* Isle of Pines. Island of W Cuba
Južna Morava *602* river of SE Serbia, Yugoslavia
Jwaneng *118* S Botswana
Jylland *190 Eng.* Jutland. Island of W Denmark
Jyrgalan *see* Dzhergalan
Jyväskylä *221* S Finland

K

K2 *421 Eng.* Mount Godwin Austen. Mountain of China and Pakistan
Kaabong *554* NE Uganda
Kaafu Atoll *see* Male' Atoll
Kaaimanston *508* NW Suriname
Kaakhka *see* Kaka
Kaala *see* Caála
Kaapstad *see* Cape Town
Kaba *480 var.* Little Scarcies. River of Guinea and Sierra Leone
Kabakama *233* E Gambia
Kabala *480* N Sierra Leone
Kabale *554* SW Uganda
Kabalega Falls *see* Murchison Falls
Kabara *218 prev.* Kambara. Island of the Lau Group, E Fiji
Kabardino-Balkarskaya, Respublika *452* autonomous republic of S SW Russia
Kabarnet *316* W Kenya
Kabarole *554* W Uganda
Kabaya *460* NW Rwanda
Kaberamaido *554* C Uganda
Kabinda *607* SE Zaire
Kabinda *see* Cabinda
Kābol *see* Kābul
Kabompo *611* W Zambia
Kabompo *611* river of W Zambia
Kabou *537* N Togo
Kābul *53 Per.* Kābol. ❖ of Afghanistan, E Afghanistan
Kabul *53, 421* river of Afghanistan and Pakistan
Kabuye *138* N Burundi
Kabwe *611* C Zambia
Kabye Plateau *537* plateau of E Togo
Kachch, Gulf of *270* *var.* Gulf of Cutch, Gulf of Kutch. Gulf of Arabian Sea to the W of India
Kachhi *421* lowland region of C Pakistan
Kadan Island *135 prev.* King I. Island of S Burma
Kadavu *218 prev.* Kandavu. Island to the S of Viti Levu, SW Fiji
Kadavu Passage *218* channel of the Pacific Ocean between Kadavu and Vitu Levu, Fiji
Kadéï *144, 154* river of Cameroon and Central African Republic
Kadoma *612 prev.* Gatooma. C Zimbabwe
Kadugli *506 var.* Kāduqlī. S Sudan
Kaduha *460* SW Rwanda
Kaduna *408* C Nigeria
Kaduna *408* river of N Nigeria
Kadzharan *see* K'ajaran
Kadzhi-Say *325 Kir.* Kajisay. NE Kyrgyzstan
Kaédi *366* S Mauritania
Kaélé *144* N Cameroon
Kaesŏng *413* S North Korea
Kaewieng *see* Kavieng
Kafan *see* Kapan
Kāfar Jar Ghar *53* mountain range of C Afghanistan
Kaffrine *476* C Senegal
Kafr el Dauwâr *202 var.* Kafr ad Dawwār. N Egypt
Kafr el Sheikh *202* *var.* Kafr ash Shaykh. N Egypt
Kafu *554 var.* Kafo. River of W Uganda
Kafue *611* river of C Zambia
Kafue *611* SE Zambia
Kaga Bandoro *154* *prev.* Fort-Crampel. C Central African Republic
Kagan *580 Uzb.* Kogon. S Uzbekistan
Kaganovichabad *see* Kolkhozabad
Kagera *see* Akagera
Kagi *see* Chia-i
Kâğıthane *547* NW Turkey
Kagoshima *304* Kyūshū, SW Japan
Kagul *see* Cahul
Kahama *530* NW Tanzania
Kahayan *276* river of Borneo, C Indonesia
Kahnple *336* NE Liberia
Kahnwia *336* SE Liberia
Ká-Hó, Baía de *624* bay of the South China Sea, SE Macao
Kahramanmaraş *547 var.* Marash, Maraş. S Turkey
Kaiaf *233* S Gambia
Kaieteur Falls *256* waterfall of C Guyana
Kaifeng *163* Henan, C China
Kai, Kepulauan *276 prev.* Kei Islands. Island group of Maluku, E Indonesia
Kaikoura *401* NE South Island, New Zealand
Kailahun *480* E Sierra Leone
Kainan *304* Honshū, C Japan
Kainji Reservoir *408* reservoir of W Nigeria
Kaipara Harbour *401* harbour of NW North Island, New Zealand
Kaiperi Island *270* island of Lakshadweep, SW India
Kairouan *543 var.* Al Qayrawān. N Tunisia
Kaiserslautern *236* SW Germany
Kaitaia *401* NW North Island, New Zealand
Kajaani *221 Swe.* Kajana. C Finland
Kajana *see* Kajaani
Kajang *354* W Peninsular Malaysia
K'ajaran *74 Rus.* Kadzharan, *var.* Kadžaran. SE Armenia
Kajisay *see* Kadzhi-Say
Kaka *551 prev.* Kaakhka, *var.* Kaachka. S Turkmenistan
Kakamega *316* W Kenya
Kakata *336* C Liberia
Kakhovs'ke Vodokhovyshche *556* *Rus.* Kakhovskoye Vodokhranilische. Reservoir of SE Ukraine
Kakia *see* Khakhea
Kakogawa *304* Honshū, C Japan
Kakshaal-Too, Khrebet *see* Kokshaal-Tau
Kalaa Kebira *543 var.* Al Qal'ah al Kubrá. N Tunisia
Kalabo *611* W Zambia
Kalahari Desert *118, 391, 493* desert region of southern Africa
Kalaikhum *528* C Tajikistan
Kalai-Mor *551 Turkm.* Galaymor. SE Turkmenistan
Kalamáki *245 prev.* Kalmákion. SE Greece
Kalamariá *245 prev.* Kalamaria. N Greece
Kalámata *245 prev.* Kalámai. S Greece
Kalandula *see* Calandula
Kalang *see* Kallang
Kalanshiyū, Sarīr *339* *var.* Calanscio Sand Sea. Desert region of E Libya
Kalarash *see* Călăraşi
Kalasin *533 var.* Muang Kalasin. NE Thailand
Kalāt *53 var.* Qalāt. S Afghanistan
Kalāt *421 var.* Kelat. W Pakistan
Kalbā *560 var.* Kalba, NE United Arab Emirates
Kaldakvísl *268* river of C Iceland
Kalemie *607 prev.* Albertville. SE Zaire
Kalgan *see* Zhangjiakou
Kalgoorlie *76* SW Australia
Kali Gandaki *395* river of C Nepal
Kalima *607* E Zaire
Kalimantan *276 Eng.* Indonesian Borneo. Region of Borneo, administered by Indonesia
Kálimnos *245* island of SE Greece
Kalinin *551* N Turkmenistan
Kalininabad *528* SW Tajikistan
Kaliningrad *452* W Russia
Kalinino *see* Tashir
Kalinkavichy *104 Rus.* Kalinkovichi. SE Belorussia
Kaliro *554* SE Uganda
Kalisz *439 Ger.* Kalisch. C Poland
Kalixälv *513* river of NE Sweden
Kalkandelen *see* Tetovo
Kalkfeld *391* NW Namibia
Kallang *483 var.* Kalang. River of C Singapore
Kallaste *212 Ger.* Krasnogor. E Estonia
Kallavesi *221* lake of SE Finland
Kalmar *513* S Sweden
Kalmykiya, Respublika *452* autonomous republic of SW Russia
Kalomo *611* S Zambia
Kalsoy *620 var.* Kalsø. Island of N Faeroe Islands
Kalu Ganga *504* river of S Sri Lanka
Kalulushi *611* C Zambia

Kalundborg *190* Sjælland, C Denmark
Kalungwishi *611* river of N Zambia
Kalutara *504* SW Sri Lanka
Kaluwawa *see* Fergusson Island
Kalyān *270* W India
Kama *607* E Zaire
Kamai *156* N Chad
Kamaishi *305* Honshū, N Japan
Kamakwie *480* NW Sierra Leone
Kamālia *421* NE Pakistan
Kamanjab *391* NW Namibia
Kamarān *599* island of W Yemen
Kamarang *256* W Guyana
Kamativi *612* W Zimbabwe
Kambar *421* *var.* Qambar. SW Pakistan
Kambara *see* Kabara
Kamchatka, Poluostrov *453* *Eng.* Kamchatka Peninsula. Peninsula of NE Russia
Kamchiya *128* *var.* Kamčija. River of E Bulgaria
Kamenets-Podol'sk *see* Kam"yanets'-Podil's'kyy
Kamenets-Podol'skiy *see* Kam"yanets'-Podil's'kyy
Kamenica *349* NE FYR Macedonia
Kamenskoye *see* Dniprodzerzhyns'k
Kamina *607* S Zaire
Kamishli *see* Al Qāmishlī
Kamloops *146* SW Canada
Kammersee *see* Attersee
Kamnik *486* *Ger.* Stein. C Slovenia
Kamo *74* C Armenia
Kamp *82* river of N Austria
Kampala *554* ❖ of Uganda, S Uganda
Kampar *354* W Peninsular Malaysia
Kampar *276* river of Sumatra, W Indonesia
Kampo *see* Ntem
Kampong Batang Duri *126* NE Brunei
Kampong Benutan *126* C Brunei
Kampong Bukit Sawat *126* C Brunei
Kampong Bunut *126* N Brunei
Kâmpóng Cham *141* *prev.* Kompong Cham. S Cambodia
Kâmpóng Chhnăng *141* C Cambodia
Kampong Jerudong *126* N Brunei
Kâmpóng Khleăng *141* *prev.* Kompong Kleang. NW Cambodia
Kampong Kuala Abang *126* C Brunei
Kampong Kuala Balai *126* SW Brunei
Kampong Labi *126* S Brunei
Kampong Labu *126* NE Brunei
Kampong Lumut *126* W Brunei
Kampong Paring *126* N Brunei
Kampong Parit *126* N Brunei
Kâmpóng Saôm *141* *var.* Kompong Som, *prev.* Sihanoukville. SW Cambodia
Kâmpóng Saôm, Chhâk *141* *Fr.* Baie de Kompong Som. Bay of the Gulf of Thailand on the SW coast of Cambodia
Kâmpóng Spoe *141* *prev.* Kompong Speu. S Cambodia
Kampong Sukang *126* S Brunei
Kampong Tanajor *126* C Brunei
Kampong Teraja *126* S Brunei
Kâmpóng Thum *141* *prev.* Kompong Thom. C Cambodia
Kâmpôt *141* S Cambodia
Kampuchea *see* Cambodia
Kamsar *253* W Guinea
Kam"yanets'-Podil's'kyy *556* *Rus.* Kamenets-Podol'skiy, *prev.* Kamenets-Podol'sk. W Ukraine
Kanacea *218* *prev.* Kanathea. Taveuni, N Fiji
Kanacea *218* island of the Lau Group, E Fiji
Kananga *607* *prev.* Luluabourg. SW Zaire
Kanazawa *304* Honshū, C Japan
Kanazi *460* SE Rwanda
Kandahār *53* *var.* Qandahār. S Afghanistan
Kandavu *see* Kadavu
Kandé *537* NE Togo
Kandi *108* N Benin
Kandrian *426* New Britain, E Papua New Guinea
Kandy *504* C Sri Lanka
Kaneohe *568* Oahu, Hawaii, USA
Kanevskoye Vodokhranilische *see* Kanivs'ke Vodoskhovyshche
Kang *118* C Botswana
Kangar *354* NW Peninsular Malaysia
Kangaroo Island *77* island of S Australia
Kangaruma *256* C Guyana
Kangchenjunga *271* *var.* Kanchenjunga. Mountain of NE India
Kanggye *413* N North Korea
Kanghwa-do *496* *Jap.* Kōka-tō. Island of NW South Korea
Kangnŭng *496* *Jap.* Kōryō. NE South Korea
Kango *230* NW Gabon
Kanibadam *528* N Tajikistan
Kani, Baie de *625* *var.* Kani Bay. Bay of the Mozambique Channel on the SW coast of Mayotte
Kanivs'ke Vodoskhovyshche *556* *Rus.* Kanevskoye Vodokhranilische. Reservoir of C Ukraine
Kanjiža *602* *prev.* Stara Kanjiža, *Ger.* Altkanischa, *Hung.* Magyarkanizsa, Ókanizsa. N Serbia, Yugoslavia
Kankan *253* E Guinea
Kankesanturai *504* N Sri Lanka
Kan-kō *see* Han
Kankossa *366* S Mauritania
Kanli Dere *see* Pedhieos
Kanmaw Island *135* *var.* Kettharin I, Kisseraing. Island of S Burma
Kano *408* N Nigeria
Kanombe *460* C Rwanda
Kanoya *304* Kyūshū, SW Japan
Kānpur *270* *prev.* Cawnpore. N India
Kanra-san *see* Halla-san
Kansas *569* state of C USA
Kansas City *569* Kansas, C USA
Kant *325* C Kyrgyzstan
Kantipur *see* Kathmandu
Kanton *320* *var.* Abariringa, Canton I, *prev.* Mary I. Island of the Phoenix Is, C Kiribati
Kanyaru *see* Akanyaru
Kanye *118* S Botswana
Kao *538* island of W Tonga
Kao *538* mountain of Kao, Tonga
Kaôh Nhêk *141* E Cambodia
Kao-hsiung *525* *var.* Kaohiung, *Jap.* Takao. SW Taiwan
Kaolack *476* *var.* Kaolak. W Senegal
Kaolak *see* Kaolack
Kaolan *see* Lanzhou
Kaoma *611* W Zambia
Kao-p'ing Hsi *525* river of C Taiwan
Kapan *74* *var.* Ghap'an. *Rus.* Kafan. SE Armenia
Kapchorwa *554* E Uganda
Kapenguria *316* W Kenya
Kapfenberg *82* C Austria
Kapingamarangi *375* atoll of S Micronesia
Kapiri Mposhi *611* C Zambia
Kapiti Island *401* island to the S of North Island, New Zealand
Kapka, Massif du *156* mountains of E Chad
Kaposvár *264* SW Hungary
Kaproncza *see* Koprivnica
Kapsabet *316* W Kenya
Kapsukas *see* Marijampolė
Kapuas *276* *prev.* Kapoeas. River of Borneo, C Indonesia
Kapuas Mountains *276, 354* *Ind.* Pegunungan Kapuas Hulu. Mountain range of Indonesia and Malaysia
Kara *537* *var.* Lama-Kara. NE Togo
Karaba *460* SW Rwanda
Kara-Balta *325* NW Kyrgyzstan
Karabil', Vozvyshennost' *551* region of SE Turkmenistan
Kara-Bogaz-Gol, Zaliv *551* NW Turkmenistan
Kara-Bogaz-Gol, Proliv *551* *Turkm.* Garabogazköl Bogazy. Strait of the Caspian Sea, on the NW coast of Turkmenistan
Karabük *547* N Turkey
Karachayevo-Cherkesskaya SSR *452* autonomous republic of SW Russia
Karāchi *421* S Pakistan
Karadeniz *see* Black Sea
Karadeniz Boğazi *see* İstanbul Boğazi
Karaferiye *see* Véroia
Karaganda *312* *Kaz.* Qaraghandy. C Kazakhstan
Karaitivu *504* N Sri Lanka
Karaj *281* NW Iran
Karak *see* Al Karak
Kara-Kala *see* Garrygala
Karaklin *see* Vanadzar
Karakol *325* *var.* Karakolka. E Kyrgyzstan
Karakol *325* *prev.* Przheval'sk, *var.* Prževalsk. NE Kyrgyzstan
Karakoram Range *270, 421* mountain range of C Asia
Karakose *547* NE Turkey
Kara-Kul' *325* *Kir.* Kara-Köl. W Kyrgyzstan
Karakul' *580* *Uzb.* Qorakŭl. S Uzbekistan
Karakul' *528* E Tajikistan
Karakul', Ozero *528* lake of E Tajikistan
Karakumskiy Kanal *551* *Turkm.* Garagum Kanaly. Canal of SE Turkmenistan
Karakumy *551* *Eng.* Kara Kum, *Turkm.* Garagum, *var.* Qara Qum. Desert region of C Turkmenistan
Karaman *547* S Turkey
Karamay *162* *var.* Karamai, *Chin.* K'o-la-ma-i. Xinjiang Uygur Zizhiqu, NW China
Karamea Bight *401* area of the Tasman Sea, on the NW coast of South Island, New Zealand
Kara-Say *325* E Kyrgyzstan
Karasburg *391* S Namibia
Kara Sea *see* Karskoye More
Karasjok *414* NE Norway
Kara Su *see* Mesta, Néstos
Karatau *312* *Kaz.* Qarataū. S Kazakhstan
Karatsu *304* Kyūshū, SW Japan
Karavastasë, Laguna e *57* *var.* Kënet' e Karavastas, Kravasta Lagoon. Lagoon of W Albania
Karawang *276* *prev.* Krawang. Java, C Indonesia
Karawanken *82* *Slvn.* Karavanke. Mountain range of C Europe
Karbalā' *284* *var.* Kerbala. C Iraq
Kardítsa *245* C Greece
Kärdla *212* *Ger.* Kertel. Hiiumaa, Estonia
Kareliya, Respublika *452* autonomous republic of NW Russia
Karen *see* Hua-lien
Kari *see* Chia-li
Kariba *612* N Zimbabwe
Kariba Dam *612* dam at NE end of Lake Kariba, on Zambezi river, NW Zimbabwe
Kariba, Lake *611, 612* reservoir of Zambia and Zimbabwe
Karibib *391* C Namibia
Karimama *108* N Benin
Karimata, Selat *276* strait connecting Laut Jawa and the South China Sea, E Indonesia
Karisimbi, Volcan *460* *var.* Mount Karisimbi. Mountain of Rwanda and Zaire
Karkaralinsk *312* E Kazakhstan
Karkar Island *426* island of NE Papua New Guinea
Karkinits'ka Zatoka *556* *Rus.* Karkinitskiy Zaliv. Gulf of the Black Sea, S Ukraine
Karleby *see* Kokkola
Karl-Marx-Stadt *see* Chemnitz
Karlö *see* Hailuoto
Karlovac *181* *Ger.* Karlstadt, *Hung.* Károlyváros. N Croatia
Karlovo *128* *prev.* Levskigrad. C Bulgaria
Karlovy Vary *188* *Ger.* Karlsbad, *var.* Carlsbad. W Czech Republic
Karlsbad *see* Karlovy Vary
Karlskrona *513* S Sweden
Karlsruhe *236* *var.* Carlsruhe. SW Germany
Karlstad *513* SW Sweden
Karlstadt *see* Karlovac
Karmi 'él *291* N Israel
Karnali *395* *var.* Kauriala. River of W Nepal
Karnobat *128* E Bulgaria
Karoi *612* N Zimbabwe
Károlyváros *see* Karlovac
Karonga *353* N Malawi
Karonje, Mount *138* mountain of W Burundi
Karpasia *187* *var.* Karpas Peninsula. Peninsular of NE Cyprus
Karpaten *see* Carpathian Mountains
Kárpathos *245* island of SE Greece
Karpaty *see* Carpathian Mountains
Karrānah *91* N Bahrain
Kars *547* NE Turkey
Karshi *580* *var.* Karši, *prev.* Bek-Budi, *Uzb.* Qarshi. S Uzbekistan
Karskoye More *453* *Eng.* Kara Sea. Sea of Arctic Ocean, bordering N Russia
Kartala *174* mountain of Grande Comore, Comoros
Kartung *233* W Gambia
Kārūn *281* river of W Iran
Karungu Bay *316* bay of Lake Victoria, to the SW of Kenya
Karuzi *138* C Burundi
Karviná *188* *Ger.* Karwin. E Czech Republic
Karzakkān *91* NW Bahrain
Kas *547* SW Turkey
Kasai *64, 607* *var.* Kassai, Cassai. River of Angola and Zaire
Kasama *611* N Zambia
Kasan *580* *Uzb.* Koson. S Uzbekistan
Kasane *118* N Botswana
Kasari *212* river of W Estonia
Kasbegi *see* Qazbegi
Kaschau *see* Korice
Kasese *554* SW Uganda
Kashaf Rūd *281* river of NE Iran
Kāshān *281* NW Iran
Kashgar *see* Kashi
Kashi *162* *Uigh.* Kashgar. Xinjiang Uygur Zizhiqu, NW China
Kashiwa *304* Honshū, SE Japan
Kashiwazaki *304* Honshū, N Japan
Käsmark *see* Kežmarok
Kasongo *607* E Zaire
Kaspi *234* C Georgia
Kaspiyskoye More *see* Caspian Sea
Kaspiy Tengizi *see* Caspian Sea
Kassa *see* Košice
Kassai *see* Kasai
Kassala *506* *var.* Kassalā, Kasala. E Sudan
Kassándra *245* peninsula of NE Greece
Kassel *236* *prev.* Cassel. C Germany
Kasserine *543* *var.* Al-Qaşrayn. W Tunisia
Kassikaityu *256* river of S Guyana
Kastamonu *547* N Turkey
Kastsyukovichy *104* E Belorussia
Kasugai *304* Honshū, C Japan
Kasulu *530* W Tanzania
Kasumiga-ura *304* lake of Honshū, SE Japan
Kasungu *353* C Malawi
Kasupe *see* Machinga

Katchang *233* C Gambia
Kateríni *245* N Greece
Katete *611* E Zambia
Katha *135* N Burma
Katherina, Gebel *202* *var.* Jabal Katrīnah, *Eng.* Mt. Catherine. Mountain of NE Egypt
Kathmandu *395* *prev.* Kantipur. ❖ of Nepal, C Nepal
Kati *360* SW Mali
Katima Mulilo *391* *var.* Ngweze. NE Namibia
Katiola *300* C Ivory Coast
Kat O Chau *262* NE Hong Kong
Katonga *554* river of SW Uganda
Katowice *439* *Ger.* Kattowitz. S Poland
Katrīnah, Jabal *see* Katherina, Gebel
Katsina *408* N Nigeria
Kattakurgan *580* *Uzb.* Kattaqŭrghon. SE Uzbekistan
Kattegat *190, 513* strait between Denmark and Sweden
Katumbi *353* NW Malawi
Katwijk aan Zee *397* W Netherlands
Kauai *568* island of Hawaii, USA, C Pacific
Kaufbeuren *237* S Germany
Kaunas *344* *Ger.* Kauen, *Pol.* Kowno, *Rus.* Kovno. C Lithuania
Kauno Marios *344* reservoir of S Lithuania
Kauriala *see* Karnali
Kau Sai Chau *262* E Hong Kong
Kaushany *see* Căuşeni
Kau-Ur *233* N Gambia
Kavadarci *349* S FYR Macedonia
Kavajë *57* *It.* Cavaia. W Albania
Kavála *245* *prev.* Kaválla. NE Greece
Kavango *see* Cubango
Kavaratti Island *270* island of Lakshadweep, SW India
Kavengo *see* Cubango
Kavieng *426* *var.* Kaewieng. New Ireland I, Papua New Guinea
Kavīr, Dasht-e *281* desert region of N Iran
Kavirondo Gulf *see* Winam Gulf
Kavkaz *see* Caucasus
Kawagoe *304* Honshū, SE Japan
Kawambwa *611* N Zambia
Kawasaki *304* Honshū, SE Japan
Kaya *132* C Burkina
Kayagangiri, Mont *154* mountain of W Central African Republic
Kayan *276* river of Borneo, C Indonesia
Kayan *135* S Burma
Kayangel Islands *627* island group of N Palau
Kayanza *138* N Burundi
Kayes *360* W Mali
Kayl *346* S Luxembourg
Kayogoro *138* S Burundi
Kayrakkumskoye Vodokhranilishche *528* reservoir of NW Tajikistan
Kayseri *547* C Turkey
Kayts *504* island of N Sri Lanka
Kazakh *see* Qazax
Kazakhskiy Melkosopochnik *312* *Eng.* Kazakh Uplands. Uplands of C Kazakhstan
Kazakhstan *312-315* officially Republic of Kazakhstan, *Kaz.* Qazaqstan, *prev.* Kazakh SSR. *Rus.* Kazakhskay SSR. Country of C Asia divided into 19 admin. units (provinces)
Kazakh Uplands *see* Kazakhskiy Melkosopochnik
Kazan' *452* W Russia
Kazandzhik *see* Gazandzhyk
Kazanlŭk *128* *var.* Kazanlăk, Kazanlik. C Bulgaria
Kazan-rettō *304* *Eng.* Volcano Islands. Island group to the SE of Honshū, SE Japan
Kazarman *325* C Kyrgyzstan
Kazbek *234* mountain of N Georgia
Kazi Magomed *see* Qazimämmäd
Kazincbarcika *264* NE Hungary
Kazvin *see* Qazvin
Kéa *245* island of SE Greece
Kéamu *see* Anatom
Kebili *543* *var.* Qibilī. C Tunisia
Kebnekaise *513* mountain of N Sweden
Kecskemét *264* C Hungary
Kėdainiai *344* C Lithuania
Kediet ej Jill *366* *var.* Kediet Ijill, Kédia d'Idjil. Mountain of NW Mauritania
Kediri *276* Java, C Indonesia
Kédougou *476* SE Senegal
Keeling Islands *see* Cocos Islands
Keelung *see* Chi-lung
Keetmanshoop *391* S Namibia
Kefallonía *245* *prev.* Kefallinía, *Eng.* Cephalonia. Island of W Greece
Kefar Sava *291* C Israel
Kefar Tappuah *292* C West Bank
Keflavík *268* *var.* Iceflavik. W Iceland
Kegalla *504* *var.* Kegalle. C Sri Lanka
Kegel *see* Keila
Kei Islands *see* Kai, Kepulauan
Keijō *see* Seoul
Keila *212* *Ger.* Kegel. NW Estonia
Keila *212* *var.* Keila Jõgi. River of NW Estonia
Keishū *see* Kyŏngju
Kéita *156* *var.* Doka. River of S Chad
Keïta *407* SW Niger
Keitele *221* lake of C Finland
Kékes *264* mountain of N Hungary
Kelang *354* *var.* Klang, *prev.* Port Swettenham. W Peninsular Malaysia
Kelantan *354* river of N Peninsular Malaysia
Kelbia, Sebkhet *543* *var.* Sabkhat Kalbīyah. Salt flat of NE Tunisia
Këlcyrë *57* *var.* Këlcyra. S Albania
Kelifskiy Uzboy *551* region of SE Turkmenistan
Kéllé *176* W Congo
Kelmė *344* NW Lithuania
Kélo *156* SW Chad
Kelowna *146* SW Canada
Keluang *354* *var.* Kluang. SE Peninsular Malaysia
Kembolcha *215* *var.* Kombolcha. N Ethiopia
Kémerovo *453* *prev.* Shcheglovsk. C Russia
Kemi *221* NW Finland
Kemijärvi *221* N Finland
Kemijoki *221* river of NW Finland
Kemiö *see* Kimito
Kemmuna *363* island of NW Malta
Kemmunett *363* island of NW Malta
Kempen *99* *Fr.* Campine, *Ger.* Kempenland. Heathland of NE Belgium
Kempten *237* S Germany
Kenema *480* SE Sierra Leone
Këneurgench *551* *prev.* Kunya-Urgench, Kunja-Urgenč, *Turkm.* Köneür gench. N Turkmenistan
Kénitra *382* *prev.* Port Lyautey. NW Morocco
Kenmare *288* SW Ireland
Kentau *312* S Kazakhstan
Kentucky *569* state of C USA
Kenya *316-319* officially Republic of Kenya. Country of E Africa divided into 7 admin. units (provinces)
Kenya, Mount *see* Kirinyaga
Keppel Harbour *483* harbour, S Singapore
Keppel Island *see* Niuatoputapu
Kerava *221* *Swe.* Kervo. S Finland
Kerch *556* *Rus.* Kerch'. SE Ukraine
Kerema *426* S Papua New Guinea
Keren *210* *var.* Cheren. C Eritrea
Kerewan *233* W Gambia
Kericho *316* W Kenya
Kerio *316* river of W Kenya
Kerkenah, Îles *543* *var.* Kerkenna Islands, *Ar.* Juzur Qarqannah. Island group of E Tunisia
Kerki *551* SE Turkmenistan
Kerkrade *397* S Netherlands
Kérkyra *245* *prev.* Kérkira, *Eng.* Corfu. Island of W Greece
Kérkyra *245* *Eng.* Corfu, *prev.* Kérkira. W Greece
Kermān *281* *var.* Kirman. SE Iran
Kermānshāh *see* Bākhtarān
Kerora *210* N Eritrea
Kérouané *253* SE Guinea
Kertel *see* Kärdla
Kerulen *380* *var.* Herlen Gol. River of China and Mongolia
Kervo *see* Kerava
Keryneia *see* Girne
Kesen'-numa *305* Honshū, N Japan
Késmárk *see* Kežmarok
Kesra *543* *var.* Kisrah. NW Tunisia
Keta *242* SE Ghana
Ketchikan *568* Alaska, USA
Kete-Krachi *242* *var.* Kete Krakye. E Ghana
Kétou *108* SE Benin
Kettharin Island *see* Kanmaw Island
Keur Massène *366* SW Mauritania
Kévé *537* SW Togo
Kew *629* North Caicos, NW Turks and Caicos Islands
Kežmarok *485* *Ger.* Käsmark, *Hung.* Késmárk. NE Slovakia
Khabarovsk *453* SE Russia
Khabura *see* Al Khaburah
Khachmas *see* Xaçmaz
Khairpur *421* S Pakistan
Khakasiya, Respublika *453* autonomous republic of C Russia
Khakassk *see* Abakan
Khakhea *118* *var.* Kakia. S Botswana
Khalándrion *see* Chalándri
Khalkidhikí *see* Chalkidikí
Khalkís *see* Chalkída
Khalūf *418* *var.* Al Khaluf. S Oman
Khambhat, Gulf of *270* *Eng.* Gulf of Cambay. Gulf of Arabian Sea to the W of India
Khamir *599* *var.* Khamr. W Yemen
Khamīs Mushayţ *472* S Saudi Arabia
Khānābād *53* NE Afghanistan
Khānaqīn *284* E Iraq
Khānewāl *421* NE Pakistan
Khanh Hung *see* Soc Trăng
Khanka, Lake *163, 453* *var.* Lake Hanka, *Rus.* Ozero Khanka, *Chin.* Xingkai Hu, Hsing-K'ai Hu. Lake of China and Russia
Khanka, Ozero *see* Khanka, Lake
Khankendy *see* Xankändi
Khānpur *421* SE Pakistan
Khanty-Mansiysk *452* *prev.* Ostyako-Voguls'k. C Russia
Khān Yūnis *291, 292* *Ar.* Khan Yunus. Gaza Strip
Kharâb, Ghoubbet el *194* bay at the head of Golfe de Tadjoura, E of Djibouti
Kharanah *see* Al Kir'ānah
Khāriān *421* NE Pakistan
Kharīţ, Wādi el *202* *var.* Wādī al Kharīţ. Dry watercourse of SE Egypt
Kharkiv *556* *Rus.* Khar'kov. NE Ukraine
Kharmanli *128* *var.* Harmanli. S Bulgaria
Khartoum *506* *var.* Al Khurţūm. ❖ of Sudan, C Sudan
Khartoum North *506* *var.* Al Khurţūm al Baḩrī. E Sudan
Khasab *see* Al Khaşab
Khāsh Rūd *53* river of W Afghanistan
Khashuri *234* C Georgia
Khaskovo *128* *var.* Haskovo. S Bulgaria
Khatt *see* Al Khaţţ
Khawr al Bazm *560* *var.* Khor al Bizm. Inlet of the Persian Gulf, on the coast of United Arab Emirates
Khawr al 'Udayd *447* *var.* Khor al Udeid. Inlet of the Persian Gulf on the coast of SE Qatar
Duwayhin, Khawr *560* inlet of the Persian Gulf, on the coast of United Arab Emirates
Khawr Fakkān *560* *var.* Khor Fakkan. NE United Arab Emirates
Khaydarkan *325* *var.* Khaydarken, Hajdarken. SW Kyrgyzstan
Khazar, Baḩr-e *see* Caspian Sea
Khazar, Daryā-ye *see* Caspian Sea
Khenchela *59* *var.* Khenchla. NE Algeria
Khénifra *382* C Morocco
Kherson *556* *var.* Cherson. S Ukraine
Khezqazghan *see* Zhezkazgan
Khíos *see* Chíos
Khiva *580* *Uzb.* Khiwa. W Uzbekistan
Khmel 'nyts'kyy *556* *Rus.* Khmel'nitskiy, *prev.* Proskurov. W Ukraine
Khodzhent *see* Khudzhand
Khodzheyli *580* *Uzb.* Khujayli. W Uzbekistan
Khoi *see* Khvoy
Khojend *see* Khudzhand
Kholm *53* N Afghanistan
Khomeynīshahr *281* *prev.* Homāyūnshahr. W Iran
Khoms *see* Al Khums
Khong Sedone *see* Muang Khôngxédôn
Khon Kaen *533* *var.* Muang Khon Kaen. N Thailand
Khor al Udeid *see* Khawr al 'Udayd
Khôr 'Angar *194* NE Djibouti
Khorixas *391* NW Namibia
Khorog *528* *var.* Horog. S Tajikistan
Khorramābād *281* W Iran
Khorramshahr *281* *prev.* Khūnīnshahr. W Iran
Khotan *see* Hotan
Khouribga *382* C Morocco
Khowst *53* E Afghanistan
Khoyniki *104* SE Belorussia
Khrysokhou Bay *187* *var.* Chrysochou Bay. Bay of the Mediterranean Sea, on the NW coast of Cyprus
Khudzhand *528* *prev.* Leninabad, Khodzhent, Khojend. NW Tajikistan
Khujayli *see* Khodzheyli
Khulna *93* SW Bangladesh
Khūnīnshahr *see* Khorramshahr
Khurīyā Murīyā, Jazā'ir *see* Ḩalānīyāt, Juzur al
Khurramshahr *see* Khorramshahr
Khushāb *421* NE Pakistan
Khvoy *281* *var.* Khoi. NW Iran
Khyber Pass *53, 421* mountain pass connecting Afghanistan with Pakistan
Kia *488* SW Santa Isabel, Solomon Is
Kiamusze *see* Jiamusi
Kiangsi *see* Jiangxi
Kiangsu *see* Jiangsu
Kiayi *see* Chia-i
Kibondo *530* NW Tanzania
Kibre Mengist *215* *var.* Adola. S Ethiopia
Kibungo *460* *var.* Kibungu. SE Rwanda
Kibuye *460* W Rwanda
Kičevo *349* W FYR Macedonia
Kidaho *460* NW Rwanda
Kiel *237* N Germany
Kiel Bay *190, 237* *Ger.* Kieler Bucht. Bay of the Baltic Sea
Kielce *439* S Poland
Kieler Bucht *see* Kiel Bay
Kieta *426* Bougainville I, Papua New Guinea
Kiev *556* *Ukr.* Kyyiv, *Rus.* Kiyev. ❖ of Ukraine, N Ukraine
Kiffa *366* S Mauritania
Kigali *460* ❖ of Rwanda, C Rwanda
Kigembe *460* S Rwanda
Kigoma *530* W Tanzania
Kigwena *138* SW Burundi

Kikila, Lac *629* lake of Île Uvea, S Wallis & Futuna
Kihnu Island *212* island of SW Estonia
Kikládhes *see* Kyklades
Kikori *426* river of C Papua New Guinea
Kikwit *607* W Zaire
Kilchu *413* NE North Korea
Kili *364* island of S Marshall Islands
Kilien Mountains *see* Qilian Shan
Kilifi *316* SE Kenya
Kilima *138* N Burundi
Kilimanjaro *530* mountain of NE Tanzania
Kilingi-Nõmme *212 Ger.* Kurkund. S Estonia
Kilinochchi *504* N Sri Lanka
Kilis *547* S Turkey
Kilkee *288* W Ireland
Kilkenny *288 Ir.* Cill Choinnigh. SE Ireland
Kilkís *245* N Greece
Kilkoch *288* E Ireland
Killarney *288 Ir.* Cill Airne. SW Ireland
Kilmarnock *563* W Scotland, UK
Kilosa *530* C Tanzania
Kilwa Masoko *530* SE Tanzania
Kimbe *426* New Britain , Papua New Guinea
Kimberley *493* Northern Cape, C South Africa
Kimberley Plateau *76* plateau of NW Australia
Kimch'aek *413 prev.* Sŏngjin. E North Korea
Kimch'ŏn *496* C South Korea
Kimhae *496* SE South Korea
Kimito *221 Swe.* Kemiö. Island of SW Finland
Kimje *496* SW South Korea
Kinabatangan *354* river of NE Borneo, Malaysia
Kinabalu, Gunung *354* mountain of N Borneo, Malaysia
Kindamba *176* S Congo
Kindia *253* SW Guinea
Kindu *607* C Zaire
Kineshma *452* W Russia
King George Bay *621* bay of the South Atlantic Ocean, W Falkland Islands
King George Land *66* island of South Shetland Islands, Antarctica
King Island *77* island of SE Australia
King Island *see* Kadan I
Kingissepp *see* Kuressaare
King's Lynn *563* E England, UK
King's Mills *623* SW Guernsey
Kingston *147* SE Canada
Kingston *303* ❖ of Jamaica, E Jamaica
Kingston *626* ❖ of Norfolk Island, S Norfolk Island
Kingston upon Hull *563 var.* Hull. NE England, UK
Kingstown *466* ❖ of St Vincent & the Grenadines, SW St Vincent
King William Island *146 var.* King William. Island of N Canada
Kinihira *460* N Rwanda
Kinkala *176* S Congo
Kinneret-Negev Conduit *291* canal of S Israel
Kinsale *625* SW Montserrat
Kinshasa *607 prev.* Léopoldville. ❖ of Zaire, W Zaire
Kintampo *242* C Ghana
Kinyeti *506* mountain of S Sudan
Kioa *218* island to the E of Vanua Levu, N Fiji
Kipengere Range *530* SW Tanzania
Kipushi *607* SE Zaire
Kirakira *488* San Cristobal I, Solomon Islands
Kirambo *460* N Rwanda
Kirdzhali *see* Kŭrdzhali
Kirehe *460* SE Rwanda
Kirghizia *see* Kyrgyzstan
Kirghiz Range *325 Rus.* Kirgizskiy Khrebet, *prev.* Alexander Range. Mountain range of Kazakhstan and Kyrgyzstan
Kirghiz Steppe *312* plain of W Kazakhstan
Kiribati *320-321* officially Republic of Kiribati. Country of the Pacific Ocean
Kırıkhan *547* S Turkey
Kırıkkale *547* C Turkey
Kirin *see* Jilin
Kirinyaga *316 var.* Mount Kenya. Extinct volcano of C Kenya
Kiritimati *320 var.* Christmas I. Island of the Line Is, E Kiribati
Kiriwina Islands *426 var.* Trobriand Is. Island group of SE Papua New Guinea
Kirkenes *414* NE Norway
Kirklareli *547* NW Turkey
Kirkmichael *623* W Isle of Man
Kirkpatrick, Mount *66* mountain of Greater Antarctica, Antarctica
Kirkūk *284 var.* Karkūk. N Iraq
Kirkwall *563* Orkney Islands, N Scotland, UK
Kirman *see* Kermān
Kirov *452 prev.* Vyatka. W Russia
Kirovabad *see* Gäncä
Kirovakan *see* Vanadzor
Kirovohrad *556 prev.* Kirovo, Zinov'yevsk, Yelizavetgrad. C Ukraine
Kirşehir *547* C Turkey
Kirthar Range *421* mountain range of S Pakistan
Kirun *see* Chi-lung
Kiruna *513* N Sweden
Kirundo *138 var.* Kirundu. N Burundi
Kiryū *304* Honshū, SE Japan
Kisangani *607 prev.* Stanleyville. NE Zaire
Kishan *see* Ch'i-shan
Kishinev *see* Chişinău
Kishiwada *304* Honshū, C Japan
Kishorganj *93* NE Bangladesh
Kisii *316* SW Kenya
Kisitwe *138* N Burundi
Kiskörei-víztároló *264* reservoir of E Hungary
Kiskunfélegyháza *264 prev.* Félegyháza. C Hungary
Kiskunhalas *264 prev.* Halas. S Hungary
Kismaayo *490 var.* Kismayu, Chisimayu, *It.* Chisimaio. S Somalia
Kisoro *554* SW Uganda
Kisseraing *see* Kanmaw Island
Kissidougou *253* S Guinea
Kistna *see* Krishna
Kisumu *316 prev.* Port Florence. W Kenya
Kisuru *see* Gisuru
Kita *360* W Mali
Kitab *580 Uzb.* Kitob. SE Uzbekistan
Kitakami *304* Honshū, N Japan
Kitakyūshū *304* Kyūshū, SW Japan
Kitale *316* W Kenya
Kitami *305* Hokkaidō, N Japan
Kitanga *see* Gitanga
Kitchener *147* S Canada
Kitega *see* Gitega
Kitgum *554* N Uganda
Kíthira *245* island of S Greece
Kíthnos *245* island of SE Greece
Kitinen *221* river of N Finland
Kitob *see* Kitab
Kitobe *138* N Burundi
Kit Stoddart's *462* SE St Kitts, St Kitts & Nevis
Kittitian Village *462* SE St Kitts, St Kitts & Nevis
Kitui *316* S Kenya
Kitwe *611 var.* Kitwe-Nkana. C Zambia
Kitzbühler Alpen *82* mountain range of W Austria
Kiunga *426* W Papua New Guinea
Kivalo *221* physical region of C Finland
Kiviõli *212* NE Estonia
Kivoga *138* C Burundi
Kivu, Lac *see* Kivu, Lake
Kivu, Lake *460, 607 Fr.* Lac Kivu. Lake of Rwanda and Zaire
Kivumba, Lac *460* lake of E Rwanda
Kiyev *see* Kiev
Kiyevskoy Vodokhranilische *see* Kyyivs'ke Vodoskhovyshche
Kiyomizu *see* Ch'ing-shui
Kiyumba *460* C Rwanda
Kizan *see* Ch'i-shan
Kizyl-Arvat *see* Gyzylarbat
Kizyl-Kaya *551 var.* Kizyl-Kaja, Gyzylgaya. NW Turkmenistan
Kjølen *see* Kölen
Kladno *188* NW Czech Republic
Klagenfurt *82* S Austria
Klaipėda *344 Ger.* Memel. NW Lithuania
Klaksvík *620* Bordhoy, N Faeroe Islands
Klang *see* Kelang
Klarälven *513* river of SW Sweden
Klatovy *188* W Czech Republic
Klausenburg *see* Cluj-Napoca
Klein Bonaire *626* island to the W of Bonaire, S Netherlands Antilles
Klerksdorp *493* North West, N South Africa
Klirou *187* W Cyprus
Ključ *116* NW Bosnia & Herzegovina
Klosterneuburg *82* NE Austria
Kloten *516* N Switzerland
Kluang *see* Keluang
Klyuchevskaya Sopka *453* Mountain of NE Russia
Knezha *128 var.* Kneža. NW Bulgaria
Knin *181* S Croatia
Knittelfeld *82* C Austria
Knox Atoll *see* Narikrik
Knoxville *569* Tennessee, SE USA
Knud Rasmussen Land *622* physical region of N Greenland
Kōbe *304* Honshū, C Japan
København *see* Copenhagen
Kobenni *366* S Mauritania
Koblenz *236* W Germany
Kobryn *104 Rus.* Kobrin. SW Belorussia
Kocaeli *see* İzmit
Kočani *349* NE FYR Macedonia
Kočevje *486 Ger.* Gottschee. S Slovenia
Kōchi *see* Cochin
Kochi *304* Shikoku, SW Japan
Kochkor *see* Kochkorka
Kochkorka *325 Kir.* Kochkor. NE Kyrgyzstan
Koddiyar Bay *504* bay of the Indian Ocean, on the NE coast of Sri Lanka
Kodiak *568* Alaska, USA
Koedoes *see* Kudus
Koeln *see* Köln
Ko-erh-mu *see* Golmud
Koes *391* SE Namibia
Koetai *see* Mahakam
Kofarnikhon *528 prev.* Ordzhonikidzeabad. W Tajikistan
Kofinou *see* Kouklia
Koforidua *242* SE Ghana
Køge *190* Sjælland, E Denmark
Kogil'nik *see* Cogîlnic
Kogo *208 var.* Cogo, *prev.* Puerto Iradier. SW Equatorial Guinea
Kogon *253* river of W Guinea
Kogon *see* Kagan
Kŏgŭm-do *496* island of S South Korea
Kohāt *421* N Pakistan
Kohtla-Järve *212* NE Estonia
Kohŭng *496* S South Korea
Koilabas *395* W Nepal
Koimbani *174* E Grande Comore, Comoros
Koindu *480* E Sierra Leone
Koi Sanjaq *284 var.* Kūysanjaq, Koysanjaq. N Iraq
Kŏje-do *496 Jap.* Kyōsai-tō. Island of S South Korea
Kokand *580 var.* Khokand, *Uzb.* Qŭqon. E Uzbekistan
Kōka-tō *see* Kanghwa-do
Kokchetav *312 var.* Kökshetaū. N Kazakhstan
Kokemäenjoki *221* river of SW Finland
Kök-Janggak *see* Kok-Yangak
Kokkina *187 var.* Erenköy. W Cyprus
Kokkola *221 Swe.* Karleby, *prev.* Gamlakarleby. W Finland
Koko Nor *see* Qinghai Hu
Kokshaal-Tau *325 Rus.* Khrebet Kakshaal-Too. Mountain range of China and Kyrgyzstan
Kökshetaū *see* Kokchetav
Kokstad *493* Kwazulu Natal, E South Africa
Kok-Yangak *325 var.* Kok-Jangak, *Kir.* Kök-Janggak. SW Kyrgyzstan
Kolahun *336* N Liberia
K'o-la-ma-i *see* Karamay
Kola Peninsula *see* Kol'skiy Poluostrov
Kolda *476* S Senegal
Kolding *190* Jylland, W Denmark
Kölen *513 Nor.* Kjølen. Mountains of N Sweden
Kolenté *253* river of Guinea and Sierra Leone
Kolga Laht *212* bay of the Gulf of Finland, on the coast of N Estonia
Kolguyev, Ostrov *452* Island of NW Russia
Kolhāpur *270* SW India
Kolhumadulu Atoll *358 var.* Kolumadulu Atoll, Thaa Atoll. Atoll of S Maldives
Kolia *629* Île Futuna, N Wallis & Futuna
Koliba *253* river of NW Guinea
Kolín *188 Ger.* Kolin. C Czech Republic
Kolkasrags *330 prev.* Cape Domesnes. Cape of NW Latvia
Kolkhozabad *528 var.* Kolhozabad, *prev.* Kaganovichabad, Tugalan. SW Tajikistan
Kolmar *see* Colmar
Köln *236 var.* Koeln, *prev.* Cöln, *Eng.* Cologne. W Germany
Kolokani *360* W Mali
Kolombangara *488 var.* Nduke. New Georgia Is, Solomon Islands
Kolonia *375 var.* Colonia. ❖ of Micronesia, Pohnpei, Micronesia
Kolonjë *see* Ersekë
Kolonyama *334* NW Lesotho
Kolozsvár *see* Cluj-Napoca
Kolpa *486 SCr.* Kupa, *Ger.* Kulpa. River of S Slovenia
Kol'skiy Poluostrov *452 Eng.* Kola Peninsula. Peninsula of NW Russia
Koltur *620* island of C Faeroe Islands
Kolumadulu Atoll *see* Kolhumadulu Atoll
Kolwezi *607* S Zaire
Kolyma *453* river of NE Russia
Kolyma Lowland *see* Kolymskaya Nizmennost'
Kolymskaya Nizmennost' *453 Eng.* Kolyma Lowland. Lowland region of NE Russia
Kolymskiy, Khrebet *453 Eng.* Kolyma Range. Mountain range of NE Russia
Komanit, Liqeni i *57* lake of N Albania
Komárno *485 Ger.* Komorn, *Hung.* Komárom. SW Slovakia
Komárom *see* Komárno
Komati *510* river of SE Africa
Komatsu *304* Honshū, C Japan
Kombissiri *132 var.* Kombissiguiri. C Burkina

Kubango *see* Cubango
Kuching *354* W Borneo, Malaysia
Kūchnay Darvīshān *53* SW Afghanistan
Kuçovë *57 var.* Kuçova, *prev.* Qyteti Stalin. C Albania
Kudara *528 var.* Gudara. E Tajikistan
Kudat *355* NE Borneo, Malaysia
Kudus *276 prev.* Koedoes. Java, C Indonesia
Kuei-chou *see* Guizhou
Kuei-Yang *see* Guiyang
K'u-erh-lo *see* Korla
Kufranja *see* Kufrinjah
Kufrinjah *310 var.* Kufranja. NW Jordan
Kuhmo *221* E Finland
Kuito *64 Port.* Silva Porto. C Angola
Kuivastu *212 Ger.* Kuiwast. Muhu, Estonia
Kujang *413* W North Korea
Kujū-san *304* mountain of Kyūshū, SW Japan
Kukës *57 var.* Kuksi, Kukësi. NE Albania
Kukong *see* Shaoguan
Kulai *354* SE Peninsular Malaysia
Kula Kangri *110* mountain of N Bhutan
Kuldīga *330 Ger.* Goldingen. W Latvia
Kuldja *see* Yining
Kulihao *see* Colihaut
Kulim *354* NW Peninsular Malaysia
Kullorsuaq *622* NW Greenland
Kulyab *528* SW Tajikistan
Kum *see* Qom
Kŭm *496 Jap.* Kin-kō. River of W South Korea
Kumagaya *304* Honshū, SE Japan
Kumaka *256* SE Guyana
Kumamoto *304* Kyūshū, SW Japan
Kumanovo *349* N FYR Macedonia
Kumasi *242* C Ghana
Kumayri *see* Gyumri
Kumba *144* W Cameroon
Kumbo *144* NW Cameroon
Kŭmch'ŏn *413* S North Korea
Kum-Dag *see* Gumdag
Kumho *496* river of SE South Korea
Kumi *496* C South Korea
Kumillā *see* Comilla
Kumo *408* E Nigeria
Kŭmsong *496 prev.* Naju *Jap.* Rashū. SW South Korea
Kumul *see* Hami
Kunashir *305* disputed island of Kurile Islands, SE Russia
Kunda *212* N Estonia
Kunda *212 var.* Kunda Jõgi. River of NE Estonia
Kundiawa *426* C Papua New Guinea
Kunduz *53 var.* Kondūz, Qondūz, Kondoz. NE Afghanistan
Kuneitra *see* Ali Qunayṭirah
Kunene *see* Cunene
Kungei Ala-Tau *325 Rus.* Khrebet Kyungëy Ala-Too, *Kir.* Küngöy Ala-Too. Mountain range of Kazakhstan and Kyrgyzstan
Kungrad *580 Uzb.* Qŭnghirot. NW Uzbekistan
Kungsbacka *513* SW Sweden
Kunlun Shan *162* mountain range of W China
Kunming *163 var.* K'un-ming.Yunnan, SW China
K'un-ming *see* Kunming
Kunoy *620 var.* Kunøisland. Island of N Faeroe Islands
Kunsan *496 var.* Gunsan, *Jap.* Gunzan. W South Korea
Kuntaur *233* NE Gambia
Kunu *413* W North Korea
Kunya-Urgench *see* Këneurgench
Kuop *375* atoll of C Micronesia
Kuopio *221* C Finland
Kupa *see* Kolpa
Kupang *276 prev.* Koepang. Timor, C Indonesia
Kupiano *426* SE Papua New Guinea
Kup'yans'k *556* E Ukraine
Kura *86, 234 Az.* Kür. River of Azerbaijan and Georgia
Kura Kurk *see* Irbe Strait
Kurama Range *528 Rus.* Kuraminskiy Khrebet. Mountain range of C Asia
Kurashiki *304* Honshū, W Japan
Kürdämir *86 Rus.* Kyurdamir. C Azerbaijan
Kŭrdzhali *128 var.* Kirdzhali. S Bulgaria
Kure *304* Honshū, W Japan
Küre Dağları *546* mountain range of N Turkey
Kuressaare *212 prev.* Kingissepp, *Ger.* Arensburg. SW Estonia
Kurgan-Tyube *528* W Tajikistan
Kuria Maria Islands *see* Ḩalānīyāt, Juzur al
Kuria Muria Bay *see* Ḩalānīyāt, Khalīj al
Kurīgrām *93* N Bangladesh
Kurile Islands *see* Kuril'skiye Ostrova
Kuril'sk *305* Kurile Islands, SE Russia
Kuril'skiye Ostrova *305, 453 Eng.* Kurile Islands. Partially disputed island group of E Russia
Kurkund *see* Kilingi-Nõmme
Kurmuk *506* SE Sudan
Kurnool *270* S India
Kurram *421* river of Afghanistan and Pakistan
Kuršėnai *344 var.* Kuršenaj, Kuršenai. NW Lithuania
Kuru *110* river of E Bhutan
Kurubonla *480* NE Sierra Leone
Kurume *304* Kyūshū, SW Japan
Kurunegala *504* C Sri Lanka
Kurupukari *256* C Guyana
Kurzeme *330 Eng.* Courland. Region of W Latvia
Kusaie *see* Kosrae
Kushiro *305* Hokkaidō, N Japan
Kushiro *305* river of Hokkaidō, N Japan
Kushka *see* Gushgy
Kushmurun *312* N Kazakhstan
Kusho *see* Kwangju
Kushtia *93* W Bangladesh
Kusŏng *413* W North Korea
Kussharo-ko *304* lake of Hokkaidō, N Japan
Kustanay *312 var.* Kustanai, Kustanaj. N Kazakhstan
Küstendje *see* Constanţa
Kusu Island *see* Tembakul, Pulau
Kütahya *547 prev.* Kutaiah. W Turkey
Kutai *see* Mahakam
K'ut'aisi *234* W Georgia
Kūt al 'Amārah *see* Al Kūt
Kut al Imara *see* Al Kūt
Kutch, Gulf of *see* Kachch, Gulf of
Kuthuleni *510* NW Swaziland
Kutina *181* NE Croatia
Kuŭm *413* SE North Korea
Kuusamo *221* E Finland
Kuusankoski *221* S Finland
Kuwait *322-323* officially State of Kuwait. Country of SW Asia divided into 5 admin units (governorates)
Kuwait Bay *322* bay of the Persian Gulf, on the coast of E Kuwait
Kuwait City *322 var.* Al Kuwayt. ❖ of Kuwait, E Kuwait
Kuybyshev *see* Samara
Kuybyshevskoye Vodokhranilishche *452 Eng.* Kuybyshev Reservoir. W Russia
Kūysanjaq *see* Koi Sanjaq
Kuyuwini *256* river of S Guyana
Kvændrup *190* Fyn, S Denmark
Kvaløya *414* island of NE Norway
Kvareli *see* Qvareli
Kvarner *181 It.* Quarnero. Gulf of the Adriatic Sea, to the W of Croatia
K'vemo K'edi *234* SE Georgia
Kwa *607* river of W Zaire
Kwahu Plateau *242* plateau of Ghana
Kwai Chung *262* C Hong Kong
Kwajalein *364* island of C Marshall Islands
Kwakoegron *508* N Suriname
Kwakwani *256* E Guyana
Kwale *316* S Kenya
Kwando *see* Cuando
Kwangchow *see* Guangzhou
Kwangju *496 var.* Kwangchu, Guangju *Jap.* Kōshū. SW South Korea
Kwango *64, 607 Port.* Cuango. River of Angola and Zaire
Kwangsi Chuang Autonomous Region *see* Guangxi
Kwangtung *see* Guangdong
Kwangyuan *see* Guangyuan
Kwania, Lake *554* lake of C Uganda
Kwanza *see* Cuanza
Kwazulu Natal *493* province of E South Africa
Kweichow *see* Guizhou
Kweisui *see* Hohhot
Kweiyang *see* Guiyang
Kwekwe *612 prev.* Que Que. C Zimbabwe
Kwenge *607* river of Angola and Zaire
Kwiranda *138* W Burundi
Kwitaro *256* River of C Guyana
Kwito *see* Cuito
Kwun Tong *262* SE Hong Kong
Kyabé *156* S Chad
Kyaikkami *135 var.* Amherst. SE Burma
Kyaiklat *135* S Burma
Kyaikto *135* S Burma
Kyaukpyu *135* W Burma
Kyaukse *135* C Burma
Kyklades *245 prev.* Kikládhes, *Eng.* Cyclades. Island group of SE Greece
Kyle, Lake *612* reservoir of SE Zimbabwe
Kymijoki *221* river of S Finland
Kyoga, Lake *554 var.* Lake Kioga. Lake of C Uganda
Kyŏnggi-man *413, 496* bay of the Yellow Sea off NW South Korea
Kyŏnghŭng *413* NE North Korea
Kyŏngju *496 Jap.* Keishū. SE South Korea
Kyŏngsŏng *see* Seoul
Kyōsai-tō *see* Kŏje-do
Kyōto *304* Honshū, C Japan
Kyperounda *187 var.* Kyperounta. C Cyprus
Kypros *see* Greece
Kyrenia *see* Girne
Kyrgyzstan *324-325* officially Kyrgyz Republic, *var.* Kirghizia, *prev.* Republic of Kyrgyzstan, *prev.* Kirghiz SSR, Kirgizskaya SSR. Country of C Asia divided into 6 admin. units (oblasts)
Kythrea *see* Degirmenlik
Kyungëy Ala-Too, Khrebet *see* Kungei Ala-Tau
Kyurdamir *see* Kürdämir
Kyūshū *304* island of SW Japan
Kyustendil *128* W Bulgaria
Kyyiv *see* Kiev
Kyyivs'le Vodoskhovyshche *556 Rus.* Kiyevskoy Vodokhranilische. Reservoir of NW Ukraine
Kyzyl *453* C Russia
Kyzyl-Kiya *325 var.* Kyzyl-Kija, *Kir.* Kyzyl-Kyya. SW Kyrgyzstan
Kyzyl Kum *580 var.* Kizil Kum, *Uzb.* Qizilqum. Desert region of Kazakhstan and Uzbekistan
Kyzylrabot *528* E Tajikistan
Kyzyl-Suu *325 var.* Kyzylsu. River of Kyrgyzstan and Tajikistan
Kzyl-Orda *312 Kaz.* Qyzylorda. SW Kazakhstan

L

Laagen *see* Lågen
Laaland *see* Lolland
Laamu Atoll *see* Hadhdhunmathi Atoll
Laas Dawaco *490 var.* Las Dawa'o, Laz Daua. N Somalia
Lâ'assa *194* NE Djibouti
La Asunción *589* Isla de Margarita, Venezuela
Laâyoune *382* NW Western Sahara
La Baie *628* channel of the Atlantic Ocean between Saint Pierre and Miquelon, S Saint Pierre and Miquelon
Labasa *218 prev.* Lambasa. Vanua Levu, N Fiji
Labe *see* Elbe
Labé *253* NW Guinea
Laborec *485 Hung.* Laborca. River of E Slovakia
Laborie *465* S St Lucia
Labrador *147* cultural region of E Canada
Labrador City *147* E Canada
Labrador Sea *147* area of the Atlantic Ocean, off E Canada
La Brea *540* SW Trinidad, Trinidad & Tobago
Labuan *see* Victoria
Labuan, Pulau *355* island of N Borneo, Malaysia
Labuk *355* river of NE Borneo, Malaysia
Labuk, Telukan *355 var.* Labuk Bay. Bay of the Sulu Sea, on the NE coast of Borneo, Malaysia
Labutta *135* SW Burma
La Caye *465* E St Lucia
Laccadive Islands *see* Lakshadweep
La Ceiba *260* N Honduras
Lacepede Bay *77* bay on the coast of SE Australia
Lac Giao *see* Buôn Ma Thuôt
La Chaux-de-Fonds *516* W Switzerland
Lachlan *77* river of SE Australia
La Chorrera *424* C Panama
La Concepción *424* W Panama
La Condamine *378* W Monaco
la Cortinada *62* NW Andorra
La Coruña *see* A Coruña
Lacre Punt *626* headland of Bonaire, S Netherlands Antilles
La Croix Maingot *465* NW St Lucia
La Cruz *178* NW Costa Rica
La Désirade *622* island of E Guadeloupe
La Digue *478* island of the Inner Islands, NE Seychelles
Ladoewani *508* C Suriname
Ladoga, Lake *see* Ladozhskoye Ozero
Ladozhskoye Ozero *221, 452 Eng.* Lake Ladoga. Lake of NW Russia
Lae *364* island of W Marshall Islands
Lae *426* E Papua New Guinea
Læsø *190* island of N Denmark
La Esperanza *260 var.* La Esperanza Intibucá. SW Honduras
Lafanga *553* islet of Nukufetau, Tuvalu
La Fe *see* Santa Fé
La Fé *182* W Cuba
Lafia *408* C Nigeria
Lafiagi *408* W Nigeria
La Foa *626* S New Caledonia
Lagarfljót *see* Lögurinn
Lagdo, Lac de *144* lake of N Cameroon
Lågen *414 var.* Laagen. River of S Norway
Lages *121* S Brazil
Laghouat *59* N Algeria
Lagone *see* Logone
Lagos *408* SW Nigeria
La Goulette *543 var.* Ḩalq al Wādī. N Tunisia
Lagunillas *112* SE Bolivia

Lemsid *382* NW Western Sahara
Le Murge *295* mountain range of S Italy
Lemvig *190* Jylland, W Denmark
Lena *453* River of E Russia
Lengoué *176* *var.* Bokiba. River of C Congo
Lenin *see* Leninsk
Lenina, Ozero imeni *556* lake of E Ukraine
Leninabad *see* Khudzhand
Leninakan *see* Gyumri
Leningrad *see* St. Petersburg
Leningradskaya *66* CIS research station of Greater Antarctica, Antarctica
Leninogorsk *312* E Kazakhstan
Leninpol' *325* NW Kyrgyzstan
Leninsk *580* *prev.* Assake. E Uzbekistan
Leninsk *551* *Turkm.* Lenin. N Turkmenistan
Leninsk *see* Chardzhev
Lenkoran' *see* Länkäran
Lennox, Isla *159* S Chile
Léo *132* SW Burkina
Leoben *82* C Austria
Léogâne *258* S Haiti
León *370* *var.* León de los Aldamas. C Mexico
León *501* NW Spain
León *404* W Nicaragua
Leonardville *391* E Namibia
Leonarisso *see* Ziyamet
León, Cerro *428* mountain of NW Paraguay
Leonding *82* N Austria
Leone *618* Tutuila, W American Samoa
Léopold II, Lac *see* Mai-Ndombe, Lac
Léopoldville *see* Kinshasa
Leova *376* *Rus.* Leovo. SW Moldova
Lepa *596* Upolu, Western Samoa
Lepel' *see* Lyepyel'
Lépontiennes, Alpes *see* Lepontine Alps
Lepontine, Alpi *see* Lepontine Alps
Lepontine Alps *516* *Fr.* Alpes Lépontiennes, *It.* Alpi Lepontine. Mountain range of SE Switzerland
Le Port *628* NW Réunion
Le Puy *225* SE France
Léraba *132, 300* river of Burkina and Ivory Coast
Léré *156* SW Chad
Leribe *see* Hlotse
Lérida *see* Lleida
Le Robert *625* E Martinique
Lerwick *563* Mainland, Shetland Islands, NE Scotland, UK
Les Abymes *622* C Guadeloupe
Les Anses-D'Arlets *625* SW Martinique
Les Avirons *628* W Réunion
Lesbos *see* Lésvos
Les Cayes *258* SW Haiti
les Escaldes *62* C Andorra
Les Gonaïves *see* Gonaïves
Lesh *see* Lezhë
Lesina *see* Hvar
Leskovac *602* SE Serbia, Yugoslavia
Lesotho *334-335* officially Kingdom of Lesotho, *prev.* Basutoland. Country of Africa divided into 10 admin. units (districts)
Les Saintes *622* island group of S Guadeloupe
Lesser Antarctica *66* physical region of Antarctica
Lesser Caucasus *86, 234* *Rus.* Malyy Kavkaz. Mountain range of SW Asia
Lesser Khingan Range *see* Xiao Hinggan Ling
Lesser Sunda Islands *see* Nusa Tenggara
Les Tantes *248* islands to the N of Grenada island, Grenada
L'Esterre *248* SW Carriacou, Grenada
Lésvos *245* *var.* Lesbos. Island of E Greece
Le Tampon *628* SW Réunion
Lethbridge *146* SW Canada
Lethem *256* *prev.* Rupununi. SW Guyana
Leticia *171* S Colombia
Leti, Kepulauan *276* island group of Maluku, E Indonesia
Letir Ceanainn *see* Letterkenny
Letpadan *135* SW Burma
Letsok-aw Island *135* *var.* Letsutan Island, *prev.* Domel Island. Island of S Burma
Letsutan Island *see* Letsok-aw Island
Letterkenny *288* *Ir.* Letir Ceanainn. N Ireland
Lettland *see* Latvia
Lëtzebuerg *see* Luxembourg
Leucas *see* Lefkada
Leulumoega *596* Upolu, Western Samoa
Leung Sheun Wan Chau *262* E Hong Kong
Leuven *99* *Fr.* Louvain, *Ger.* Löwen. C Belgium
Léva *see* Levice
Le Vauclin *625* SE Martinique
Levera Island *see* Sugar Loaf
Leverkusen *236* W Germany
Levice *485* *Ger.* Lewenz, Hung. Léva. SW Slovakia
Levin *401* S North Island, New Zealand
Levkás *see* Lefkada
Levoča *485* *Ger.* Leutschau, Hung. Lőcse. NE Slovakia
Levskigrad *see* Karlovo
Levuka *218* Ovalau, C Fiji
Lewenz *see* Levice
Lewis, Isle of *563* island of Outer Hebrides, NW Scotland, UK
Lewiston *568* Idaho, NW USA
Lewiston *569* Maine, NE USA
Lexington *569* Kentucky, C USA
Leyte *435* island of E Philippines
Leyte Gulf *435* gulf of the Pacific Ocean, E Philippines
Lezhë *57* *var.* Lezha, *prev.* Lesh, Leshi. NW Albania
Lhasa *162* *var.* La-sa. Xizang Zizhiqu, W China
Lhaviyani Atoll *see* Faadhippolhu Atoll
Lhuntshi *110* E Bhutan
Lhut, Uadi *see* Luud, Waadi
Liamuiga, Mount *462* *var.* Mount Misery. Mountain of C St Kitts, St Kitts & Nevis
Liangyungang *163* *var.* Xinpu, Lien-yun. Jiangsu, E China
Liaodong Bandao *163* *var.* Liaotung Peninsula. Peninsula of NE China
Liaoning *163* *hist.* Shenking, Fengtien. Province of NE China
Lib *364* island of C Marshall Islands
Liban, Jebel *332* *Eng.* Lebanon, Mount Lebanon, *Ar.* Jabal Lubnān. Mountain range of C Lebanon
Libau *see* Liepāja
Liberec *188* *Ger.* Reichenberg. N Czech Republic
Liberia *178* NW Costa Rica
Liberia *336-337* officially Republic of Liberia. Country of West Africa, divided into 9 admin. units (counties)
Liberta *68* S Antigua, Antigua & Barbuda
Libertad *577* S Uruguay
Libertad *102* *prev.* Pembroke Hall. N Belize
Librazhd *57* *var.* Librazhdi. E Albania
Libreville *230* ❖ of Gabon, NW Gabon
Libya *338-341* officially Socialist People's Libyan Arab Jamahiriya, *prev.* Libyan Arab Republic. Country of N Africa, the current administrative structure is not clear
Libyan Desert *202, 339, 506* *Ar.* Aş Şahrā' al Lībīyah. Desert of N Africa
Libyan Plateau *202, 339* *Ar.* Aḍ Ḍiffah. Plateau of Egypt and Libya
Licata *295* Sicilia, S Italy
Lichinga *387* N Mozambique
Lichtenburg *493* North West, N South Africa
Lida *104* W Belorussia
Lido di Ostia *295* C Italy
Liechtenstein *342-343* officially Principality of Liechtenstein. Country of C Europe divided into 11 admin. units (communes)
Liège *99* *Dut.* Luik, *Ger.* Lüttich. E Belgium
Liegnitz *see* Legnica
Lieksa *221* E Finland
Lien-yun *see* Liangyungang
Lienz *82* W Austria
Liepāja *330* *Ger.* Libau. W Latvia
Lier *99* *Fr.* Lierre. N Belgium
Liestal *516* N Switzerland
Lievenhof *see* Līvāni
Lifford *288* N Ireland
Lifou *626* island, Îles Loyauté, E New Caledonia
Lifuka *538* island of Ha'apai Group, Tonga
Līgatne *330* NE Latvia
Ligure, Appennino *294* mountain range of N Italy
Ligure, Mar *see* Ligurian Sea
Ligurian Sea *225, 294* *It.* Mar Ligure, *Fr.* Mer Ligurienne. Area of the Mediterranean Sea, between France and Italy
Lihue *568* Kauai, Hawaii, USA
Lihula *212* *Ger.* Leal. W Estonia
Liivi Laht *see* Riga, Gulf of
Likasi *607* *prev.* Jadotville. SE Zaire
Likiep *364* island of C Marshall Islands
Likouala *176* river of NW Congo
Likouala aux Herbes *176* river of E Congo
Liku *626* E Niue
Lille *225* *Dut.* Rijssel. N France
Lillebælt *190* *Eng.* Little Belt, *var.* Lille Bælt. Straits between Fyn and Jylland, SW Denmark
Lillehammer *414* S Norway
Lillestrøm *414* S Norway
Lilongwe *353* ❖ of Malawi, W Malawi
Lilongwe *353* river of W Malawi
Lima *431* ❖ of Peru, W Peru
Limassol *187* *var.* Lemesos. SW Cyprus
Limbe *353* S Malawi
Limbe *144* *prev.* Victoria. SW Cameroon
Limbé *258* N Haiti
Lim Chu Kang *483* area of NW Singapore
Limerick *288* *Ir.* Luimneach. SW Ireland
Limfjorden *190* fjord of Jylland, NW Denmark
Límni Megáli Préspa *see* Prespa, Lake
Limni Prespa *see* Prespa, Lake
Límnos *245* *var.* Lemnos. Island of E Greece
Limoges *225* C France
Limón *178* E Costa Rica
Limón *260* NE Honduras
Limon, Mont *368* mountain of Rodrigues, Mauritius
Limousin *225* cultural region of C France
Limpopo *118, 387, 390, 612* *var.* Crocodile. River of southern Africa
Limulunga *611* W Zambia
Linakeng *334* E Lesotho
Linares *159* C Chile
Linares *501* S Spain
Lincoln *563* E England, UK
Lincoln *569* Nebraska, C USA
Lincoln Island *627* island of E Paracel Islands
Linden *256* E Guyana
Lindi *607* river of NE Zaire
Lindi *530* SE Tanzania
Line Islands *182* island group of E Kiribati
Lingayen Gulf *435* gulf of the South China Sea, N Philippines
Lingga, Kepulauan *276* island group to the E of Sumatra, W Indonesia
Linguère *476* N Senegal
Linköping *513* S Sweden
Linyanti *118* river of Botswana and Namibia
Linz *82* N Austria
Lion, Golfe du *225* *Eng.* Gulf of Lions. Gulf of the Mediterranean Sea to the S of France
Lions Den *612* N Zimbabwe
Lipa *435* Luzon, N Philippines
Lipari Islands *see* Eolie, Isole
Lipari, Isola *295* island of S Italy
Lipari, Isole *see* Eolie, Isole
Lippstadt *236* W Germany
Lipsk *see* Leipzig
Liptovský Mikuláš *485* *Ger.* Liptau-Sankt-Nikolaus, *Hung.* Liptószentmiklós. C Slovakia
Lira *554* N Uganda
Liranga *176* E Congo
Liri *295* river of C Italy
Lisala *607* N Zaire
Lisbon *442* *Port.* Lisboa. ❖ of Portugal, W Portugal
Lisburn *563* Northern Ireland, UK
Lisieux *225* NW France
Lismore *77* E Australia
Lissa *see* Vis
Litani *508, 621* *var.* Itany. River of French Guiana and Suriname
Litani *332* river of C Lebanon
Litaven *see* Lithuania
Litavra *see* Lithuania
Lithgow *77* SE Australia
Lithuania *344-345* officially Republic of Lithuania, *Lith.* Lietuva, *Ger.* Litauen, *Pol.* Litwa, *Rus.* Litva, *prev.* Lithuanian SSR, *Rus.* Litovskaya SSR. Country of E Europe divided into 44 admin. units (districts)
Litla Dimun *620* island of S Faeroe Islands
Little Abaco *88* island of N Bahamas
Little Alföld *264* plain of Hungary and Slovakia
Little Andaman *270* island of Andaman Islands to the SE of India
Little Barrier Island *401* island to the N of North Island, New Zealand
Little Belt *see* Lillebælt
Little Cayman *620* island of C Cayman Islands
Little Coco Island *135* island of SW Burma
Little Inagua *88* island of S Bahamas
Little Minch *563* strait of the Atlantic Ocean , NW Scotland, UK
Little Rock *569* Arkansas, SC USA
Little Scarcies *see* Kaba
Little Sound *619* bay of the North Atlantic Ocean, W Bermuda
Little Tobago *619* island of W British Virgin Islands
Little Tobago *540* *var.* Bird of Paradise Island. Island to the E of Tobago, Trinidad & Tobago
Little Zab *284* *Ar.* Zāb aş Şaghīr, *Kurd.* Zē-i Kōya. River of Iran and Iraq
Litva *see* Lithuania
Litwa *see* Lithuania
Liu-ch'iu Yü *525* island of SW Taiwan
Liu-kuei *525* S Taiwan
Liuzhou *163* *var.* Liu-chou, Liuchow. Guangxi, S China
Livadhi *187* *var.* Leivadi. River of W Cyprus

Līvāni 330 Ger. Lievenhof. SE Latvia
Lively Island 621 island of E Falkland Islands
Lively Sound 621 area of the South Atlantic Ocean, E Falkland Islands
Liverpool 563 NW England, UK
Lívingston 250 E Guatemala
Livingstone 611 var. Maramba. S Zambia
Livingstonia 353 N Malawi
Livno 116 SW Bosnia & Herzegovina
Livojoki 221 river of C Finland
Livonia see Vidzeme
Livorno 294 Eng. Leghorn. C Italy
Liwonde 353 S Malawi
Liyāḩ, Jāl al 322 ridge of NW Kuwait
Ljouwert see Leeuwarden
Ljubelj see Loibl Pass
Ljubljana 486 var. Lyublyana, Ger. Laibach, It. Lubiana. ❖ of Slovenia, C Slovenia
Ljubrlj see Loibl Pass
Ljungan 513 river of C Sweden
Ljusnan 513 river of C Sweden
Llallagua 112 SW Bolivia
Lleida 501 Cast. Lérida. NE Spain
Llolleo 159 C Chile
Lloydminster 146 SW Canada
Lô 593 river of China and Vietnam
Loaita Island 628 island of W Spratly Islands
Loangwa see Luangwa
Lobatse 118 var. Lobatsi. S Botswana
Lobaye 154 river of SW Central African Republic
Lobito 64 W Angola
Lob Nor see Lop Nur
Locarno 516 Ger. Luggarus. S Switzerland
Lôc Ninh 593 SW Vietnam
Locri 295 S Italy
Lőcse see Levoča
Lod 291 var. Lydda. C Israel
Lodge 462 NE St Kitts, St Kitts & Nevis
Lodja 607 C Zaire
Lodwar 316 NW Kenya
Łódź 439 Rus. Lodz. C Poland
Loei 533 var. Muang Loei. N Thailand
Lofa 336 var. Loffa. River of Guinea and Liberia
Lofoten 414 var. Lofoten Islands. Islands of NE Norway
Loga 407 W Niger
Logan, Mount 146 mountain of NW Canada
Logone 144, 156 var. Lagone. River of Cameroon and Chad
Logroño 501 N Spain
Lögurinn 268 var. Lagarfljót. Lake of E Iceland
Loh 585 Torres Islands, N Vanuatu
Loibl Pass 82 var. Ljubelj, Ger. Loiblpass, Slvn. Ljubrlj. Mountain pass of Austria and Slovenia
Loikaw 135 E Burma
Loir 225 river of NW France
Loire 225 river of C France
Loita Hills 316 hilly region of SW Kenya
Loja 200 S Ecuador
Lökbatan 86 Rus. Lokbatan. E Azerbaijan
Lokeren 99 NW Belgium
Lokitaung 316 NW Kenya
Løkken 190 Jylland, NW Denmark
Lokoja 408 C Nigeria
Lokossa 108 S Benin
Loksa 212 Ger. Loxa. N Estonia
Lol 506 river of S Sudan
Lola 253 SE Guinea
Lolland 190 prev. Laaland. Island of S Denmark
Lolotique 207 SE El Salvador
Lolvavana, Passage 585 strait between Maewo and Pentecost, C Seychelles
Lom 128 prev. Lom-Palanka. NW Bulgaria
Lom 144 river of Cameroon and Central African Republic
Lomahasha 510 NE Swaziland
Lomami 607 river of C Zaire
Lomas de Zamora 71 E Argentina
Lombok 276 island of Nusa Tenggara, C Indonesia
Lomé 537 ❖ of Togo, S Togo
Lomond, Loch 563 lake of C Scotland, UK
Lom Sak 533 var. Muang Lom Sak. N Thailand
Londiani 316 W Kenya
London 563, 567 ❖ of United Kingdom
London 147 S Canada
London 320 Kiritimati, E Kiribati
London Bridge 248 island to the N of Grenada island, Grenada
Londonderry 563 var. Derry. Northern Ireland, UK
Londrina 121 S Brazil
Longa, Proliv 453 Eng. Long Strait. Strait connecting Chukchi Sea and East Siberian Sea, between NE Asia and NW North America
Long Bay 619 bay of the North Atlantic Ocean, E Bermuda
Long Bay 619 bay of the North Atlantic Ocean, W Bermuda
Longford 288 Ir. Longphort. C Ireland
Long Island 619 island of W Bermuda
Long Island see Arop Island
Long Island 88 island of C Bahamas
Long Island 68 island to the N of Antigua, Antigua & Barbuda
Longmont 569 Colorado, SW USA
Longoni, Baie de 625 var. Longoni Bay. Bay of the Indian Ocean on the N coast of Mayotte
Longphort see Longford
Longreach 77 E Australia
Long Strait see Longa, Proliv
Long Swamp 619 Tortola, C British Virgin Islands
Longwood 628 E St Helena
Long Xuyên 593 SW Vietnam
Longyearbyen 629 Spitsbergen, W Svalbard
Lonhlupheko 510 E Swaziland
Lons-le-Saunier 225 E France
Loop Head 288 promontory on the W coast of Ireland
Lop Buri 533 C Thailand
Lopévi 585 island of C Vanuatu
Lopez, Cap 230 W Gabon
Lop Nur 162 var. Lop Nor, Lob Nor, Chin. Lo-pu Po. Lake of Xinjiang Uygur Zizhiqu, NW China
Lo-pu Po see Lop Nur
Lora, Hāmūn-i- 420 salt marsh of W Pakistan
Lord Howe Island see Ontong Java Atoll
Lorengau 426 var. Lorungau, Manus I, Papua New Guinea
Lorentz 277 river of Irian Jaya, E Indonesia
Loreto 428 C Paraguay
Lorian Swamp 316 swamp E Kenya
Lorient 224 W France
Lorn, Firth of 563 inlet of Atlantic Ocean, W Scotland, UK
Lorraine 255 cultural region of NE France
Los Amates 250 E Guatemala
Los Andes 159 C Chile
Los Angeles 568 California, W USA
Los Ángeles 159 C Chile
Losap 375 atoll of C Micronesia
Los Chiles 178 NW Costa Rica
Los, Îles de 253 Island group to the SW of Guinea
Lošinj 181 It. Lussino. Island of W Croatia
Loslau see Wodzisław Śląski
Los Mochis 370 W Mexico
Losonc see Lučenec
Losontz see Lučenec
Los Roques, Islas 589 island group of N Venezuela
Los Teques 589 N Venezuela
Lot 225 river of S France
Lotofaga 596 Upolu, Western Samoa
Lo-tung 525 Jap. Ratō. NE Taiwan
Louang Namtha 327 var. Luong Nam Tha. N Laos
Louangphrabang 327 var. Luang Prabang. C Laos
Loubiere 196 SW Dominica
Loubomo 176 prev. Dolisie. S Congo
Loudima 176 S Congo
Louéssé 176 river of SW Congo
Louga 476 NW Senegal
Loughrea 288 W Ireland
Louis Gentil see Youssoufia
Louisiade Archipelago 426 island group of SE Papua New Guinea
Louisiana 569 state of SC USA
Louis Trichardt 493 Northern Transvaal, NE South Africa
Louisville 569 Kentucky, C USA
Louisville 102 N Belize
Loukoléla 176 E Congo
Loum 144 W Cameroon
Louna 176 river of SE Congo
Louny 188 NW Czech Republic
Lourenço Marques see Maputo
Lourenço Marques, Baía de see Maputo, Baía de
Louvain see Leuven
Lovech 128 var. Loveč. NW Bulgaria
Lovell Village 466 Mustique, St Vincent & the Grenadines
Lóvua 64 N Angola
Lowell 569 Massachusetts, NE USA
Löwen see Leuven
Lower Bann 563 river of Northern Ireland, UK
Lower California see Baja California
Lower Carlton 97 NW Barbados
Lower Hutt 401 S North Island, New Zealand
Lower Lough Erne 563 lake of Northern Ireland, UK
Lower Mortlocks 375 island group of C Micronesia
Lower Rhine see Neder-Rijn
Lower Tunguska see Nizhnyaya Tunguska
Lower West End Point 618 headland on the SW coast of Anguilla
Low Point 620 headland on the E coast of Christmas Island
Loyada 194 E Djibouti
Loyauté, Îles 626 island group of E New Caledonia
Loyoro 554 NE Uganda
Loznica 602 W Serbia, Yugoslavia
Lualaba 607 var. Zaire, Fr. Loualaba. River of E Zaire
Luampa 611 river of W Zambia
Luanda 64 ❖ of Angola, NW Angola
Luang Prabang see Louangphrabang
Luang Prabang Range 327 mountain range of W Laos
Luangwa 611 Port. Aruângua. River of Mozambique and Zambia
Luanshya 611 C Zambia
Luapula 607, 611 river of Zaire and Zambia
Luar, Pulu see Horsburgh Island
Luba 208 prev. San Carlos. W Bioko, Equatorial Guinea
Lubānas Ezers 330 lake of E Latvia
Lubang Island 435 island of N Philippines
Lubango 64 Port. Sá da Bandeira. SW Angola
Lubao 607 SE Zaire
Lübeck 237 N Germany
Lubelska, Wyżyna 439 plateau of SE Poland
Lubiana see Ljubljana
Lublin 439 Rus. Lyublin. E Poland
Lubnān, Jabal see Liban, Jebel
Lubny 556 C Ukraine
Lubumbashi 607 prev. Élisabethville. SE Zaire
Luca 112 SW Bolivia
Lucala 64 NW Angola
Lucan 288 Ir. Leamhcán. E Ireland
Lucano, Appennino 295 mountain range of S Italy
Lucapa 64 var. Lukapa. NE Angola
Lucea 303 NW Jamaica
Lucena 435 Luzon, N Philippines
Lučenec 485 Hung. Losonc, Ger. Losontz. C Slovakia
Lucerne see Luzern
Lucerne, Lake of see Vierwaldstätter See
Luchow see Hefei
Lucie 508 Suriname
Łuck see Luts'k
Lucknow 270 Hind. Lakhnau. N India
Lüderitz 391 prev. Angra Pequena. SW Namibia
Ludhiāna 270 N India
Ludwigshafen 236 var. Ludwigshafen am Rhein. SW Germany
Luebo 607 SW Zaire
Luena 64 Port. Luso. E Angola
Lufira, Lac de Retenue de la 607 var. Lac Tshangalele. Lake of SE Zaire
Lugano 516 Ger. Lauis. S Switzerland
Luganville 585 Espiritu Santo, Vanuatu
Lugards Falls 316 waterfall of SE Kenya
Lugenda 387 river of N Mozambique
Luggarus see Locarno
Lugh Ganana see Luuq
Lugo 501 NW Spain
Lugoj 448 W Romania
Lugusi see Ruguzi
Luhans'k 556 Rus. Lugansk, prev. Voroshilovgrad. E Ukraine
Luiana 64 river of SE Angola
Luichow Peninsula see Leizhou Bandao
Luik see Liège
Luimneach see Limerick
Luján 71 C Argentina
Lu-kang 525 var. Lu-chiang, Jap. Rokkō. W Taiwan
Lukapa see Lucapa
Lukenie 607 river of C Zaire
Lukhalweni 510 S Swaziland
Lukusashi 611 river of C Zambia
Luleå 513 NE Sweden
Luleälv 513 river of NE Sweden
Lulonga 607 river of NW Zaire
Lulua 607 river of S Zaire
Luluabourg see Kananga
Lumbo 387 NE Mozambique
Lumi 426 NW Papua New Guinea
Lumphăt 141 prev. Lomphat. NE Cambodia
Lumpungu see Rumpungu
Lund 513 S Sweden
Lunga 611 river of Zambia
Lunga, Isola see Dugi Otok
Lungi 480 W Sierra Leone
Lungkiang see Qiqihar
Lungwebungu 611 river of Angola and Zambia
Luninyets 104 Rus. Luninets. SW Belorussia
Lunsar 480 W Sierra Leone
Lunsemfwa 611 river C Zambia
Luong Nam Tha see Louang Namtha
Luoyang 163 Henan, C China
Luque 428 S Paraguay
Lúrio 387 NE Mozambique
Lúrio 387 river of NE Mozambique
Lusaka 611 ❖ of Zambia, SE Zambia
Lushnjë 57 var. Lushnja. C Albania
Luso see Luena
Lussino see Lošinj
Lustenau 82 W Austria
Lusutfu 510 var. Usutu, Great Usutu. River of southern Africa

M

Malacca, Strait of *276* strait connecting the Andaman Sea and South China Sea between Malay Peninsula and Sumatra, SE Asia
Malacka *see* Malacky
Malacky *485* *Hung.* Malacka. W Slovakia
Maladzyechna *104* *Rus.* Molodechno, *Pol.* Molodeczno. NW Belorussia
Málaga *501* S Spain
Malagarasi *138, 530* *var.* Muragarazi. River of Burundi and Tanzania
Malagasy Republic *see* Madagascar
Malaita *488* *var.* Mala, Island of C Solomon Islands
Malakal *506* *var.* Malakāl. S Sudan
Malambo *171* N Colombia
Malang *276* SE Java, Indonesia
Malange *see* Malanje
Malanje *64* *var.* Malange. NW Angola
Malanville *108* NE Benin
Mälaren *513* lake of SE Sweden
Malatya *546* SE Turkey
Malawi *352-353* officially Republic of Malawi, *prev.* Nyasaland, Nyasaland Protectorate. Country of S Africa divided into 3 admin. units (regions)
Malawi, Lake *see* Nyasa, Lake
Malaya *see* Peninsular Malaysia
Malāyer *281* NW Iran
Malay Peninsula *533* peninsula of Malaysia and Thailand
Malaysia *354-357* *prev.* the separate territories of Federation of Malaya, Singapore (left 1965), Sarawak and Sabah (North Borneo). Country of SE Asia divided into 15 admin. units (13 states, 2 federal territories)
Maldegem *99* NW Belgium
Malden Island *320* island of the Line Is, E Kiribati
Maldives *358-359* Officially Republic of Maldives, Maldivian Divehi. Country of the Indian Ocean divided into 19 admin. units (districts)
Maldonado *577* S Uruguay
Male' *358* *var.* Male. ❖ of Maldives, Male' Atoll, C Maldives
Male *see* Male'
Male' Atoll *358* *var.* Kaafu Atoll. Atoll of C Maldives
Malebo Pool *see* Stanley Pool
Malékoula *see* Malekula
Malekula *585* *var.* Malakula, *prev.* Mallicolo. Island of W Vanuatu
Mali *360-361* officially Republic of Mali, *prev.* Sudanese Republic, French Sudan. Country divided into 8 admin. units (7 regions and 1 capital district)
Malibamatso *334* river of C Lesotho
Mali Hka *135* river of N Burma forming a headstream of the Irrawaddy river
Malindi *316* SE Kenya
Malines *see* Mechelen
Malinga *230* SE Gabon
Malin Head *288* headland on the N coast of Ireland
Mallāq, Wādī *see* Mellègue, Oued
Mallawi *202* *var.* Mallawī. C Egypt
Mallicolo *see* Malekula
Mallorca *501* *Eng.* Majorca. Island of the Islas Baleares, E Spain
Mallow *288* *Ir.* Magh Ealla. SW Ireland
Malmédy *99* E Belgium
Malmö *513* S Sweden
Malmok *626* headland of Bonaire, S Netherlands Antilles
Malo *585* island of W Vanuatu
Maloelap *364* island of E Marshall Islands
Malolo *218* island of the Mamanuca-i-ra Group, W Fiji
Malolos *435* Luzon, N Philippines
Maloma *510* S Swaziland
Malombe, Lake *353* lake of SE Malawi
Małopolska *439* plateau of S Poland
Maloti Mountains *see* Maluti
Malpasso *198* SW Dominican Republic
Mäls *342* S Liechtenstein
Malta *363* island of the Mediterranean Sea, with Gozo and Kemmuna forms the state of Malta
Malta *362-363* officially Republic of Malta. Country of the Mediterranean Sea
Malta Channel *363* *It.* Canale di Malta. Strait of Mediterranean Sea between Malta and Sicily
Maltahöhe *391* S Namibia
Malta, Il-Fliegu ta' *363* *Eng.* South Comino Channel. Strait of Mediterranean Sea between Kemmuna and Malta islands, NW Malta
Maluku *276* *prev.* Spice Islands, *Eng.* Moluccas. Island group of E Indonesia
Maluku, Laut *276* *Eng.* Molucca Sea. Sea of the Pacific Ocean, E Indonesia
Malung *513* C Sweden
Maluti *334* *var.* Maluti Mountains, Maloti Mountains, Front Range. Mountain range of C Lesotho
Malvinas, Islas *see* Falkland Islands
Malyy Kavkaz *see* Lesser Caucasus
Mamanuca-i-ra Group *218* islands of W Fiji
Mamates *334* NW Lesotho
Mambéré *154* river of SW Central African Republic
Mambili *176* river of W Congo
Mamer *346* SW Luxembourg
Mamfé *144* W Cameroon
Mamiku *465* E St Lucia
Mamoré *112* river of Bolivia and Brazil
Mamou *253* W Guinea
Mamoudzou *625* ❖ of Mayotte, N Mayotte
Mampong *242* C Ghana
Mamţalah, Ra's al *see* Mummaţalah, Ra's al
Mamuno *118* W Botswana
Man *300* W Ivory Coast
Mana *621* NW French Guiana
Manado *276* *prev.* Menado. Celebes, C Indonesia
Managua *404* ❖ of Nicaragua, W Nicaragua
Managua, Lago de *404* W Nicaragua
Manaḩ *418* *var.* Bilād Manaḩ. N Oman
Manakara *350* SE Madagascar
Mana *621* river of C French Guiana
Manama *91* *Ar.* Al Manāmah. ❖ of Bahrain, NE Bahrain
Manambaho *350* seasonal river of NW Madagascar
Manambolo *350* river of W Madagascar
Mananjary *350* SE Madagascar
Manantali, Lac de *360* reservoir of W Mali
Manāqīsh *322* *var.* Manageesh. S Kuwait
Manas *580* mountain of NE Uzbekistan
Manatí *627* N Puerto Rico
Manaus *120* *prev.* Manáos. NW Brazil
Manbij *521* *Fr.* Membidj. N Syria
Manchester *563* N England, UK
Manchester *569* New Hampshire, NE USA
Man-chou-li *see* Manzhouli
Manda Island *316* island of SE Kenya
Mandal *414* SW Norway
Mandalay *135* N Burma
Mandalgovĭ *380* S Mongolia
Mandali *284* E Iraq
Mandaue *435* Cebu, C Philippines
Mandera *316* NE Kenya
Mandeville *303* SW Jamaica
Mandiana *253* E Guinea
Mandi Būrewāla *421* *var.* Būrewāla. E Pakistan
Mandidzudzure *see* Chimanimani
Mandié *387* NW Mozambique
Mandimba *387* N Mozambique
Mandji *230* C Gabon
Mandouri *537* N Togo
Manfredonia *295* S Italy
Manga *132* C Burkina
Mangai *607* W Zaire
Mangaia *620* island of Southern Cook Islands, S Cook Islands
Mangalia *448* SE Romania
Mangalmé *156* SE Chad
Mangalore *270* SW India
Mangde *110* river of S Bhutan
Mange *480* NW Sierra Leone
Mango *see* Sansanné-Mango
Mango *see* Mago
Mangoche *see* Mangochi
Mangochi *353* *var.* Mangoche, *prev.* Fort Johnson. SE Malawi
Mangoky *350* river of SW Madagascar
Mangula *see* Mhangura
Mangyshlak *312* W Kazakhstan
Mania *350* river of C Madagascar
Manica *387* *var.* Vila de Manica. W Mozambique
Manihiki *620* island of Northern Cook Islands, N Cook Islands
Manikaraku *488* E Guadalcanal, Solomon Is
Manikganj *93* C Bangladesh
Manila *435* *var.* Manilla City. ❖ of the Philippines, Luzon, N Philippines
Manisa *546* *prev.* Saruhan. W Turkey
Man, Isle of *563, 623* British Crown dependency of the Irish Sea
Manitoba *146* province of S Canada
Manizales *171* W Colombia
Manjimup *76* SW Australia
Mankayane *510* *var.* Mankaiana. W Swaziland
Mankono *300* C Ivory Coast
Mankulam *504* N Sri Lanka
Mannar *504* *var.* Manar. NW Sri Lanka
Mannar, Gulf of *270, 504* gulf of Indian Ocean, to the S of India
Mannar Island *504* island to the N of Sri Lanka
Mannheim *236* SW Germany
Mano *480* SW Sierra Leone
Mano *480* river of Liberia and Sierra Leone
Manombo Atsimo *350* *var.* Manombo. SW Madagascar
Manono *596* Upolu, Western Samoa
Manono *607* SE Zaire
Manorhamilton *288* N Ireland
Manp'o *413* *var.* Manp'ojin. NW North Korea
Manra *320* *var.* Sydney I. Island of the Phoenix Is, C Kiribati
Mansa *611* *prev.* Fort Rosebery. N Zambia
Mansabá *254* NW Guinea-Bissau
Mansajang Kunda *233* E Gambia
Mansa Konko *233* C Gambia
Mansion *462* NE St Kitts, St Kitts & Nevis
Mansôa *254* W Guinea-Bissau
Mansôa *254* river of W Guinea-Bissau
Manta *200* W Ecuador
Mantes-la-Jolie *225* *prev.* Mantes-sur-Seine, Mantes-Gassicourt. N France
Mantova *294* *Eng.* Mantua, *Fr.* Mantoue. N Italy
Mantsonyane *334* C Lesotho
Manuae *620* island of Southern Cook Islands, S Cook Islands
Manua Islands *618* island group of E American Samoa
Manukau Harbor *401* harbor of W North Island, New Zealand
Manurewa *401* N North Island, New Zealand
Manus Island *426* *var.* Great Admiralty I. NE Papua New Guinea
Manyame *612* *var.* Hunyani, *Port.* Panhame. River of Mozambique and Zimbabwe
Manyame, Lake *612* *prev.* Robertson, Lake. Reservoir of N Zimbabwe
Manyara, Lake *530* lake of NE Tanzania
Manyoni *530* C Tanzania
Manzanillo *182* SE Cuba
Manzhouli *163* *var.* Man-chou-li. Nei Mongol Zizhiqu, NE China
Manzil Bū Ruqaybah *see* Menzel Bourguiba
Manzil Tamīm *see* Menzel Temime
Manzini *510* *prev.* Bremersdorp. C Swaziland
Mao *156* W Chad
Mao *198* NW Dominican Republic
Maoke, Pegunungan *277* *Dut.* Sneeuw-gebergte, *Eng.* Snow Mountains. Mountain range of Irian Jaya, E Indonesia
Mapoteng *334* NW Lesotho
Mapou *368* N Mauritius
Maputo *387* *prev.* Lourenço Marques. ❖ of Mozambique, S Mozambique
Maputo, Baía de *387* *var.* Baía de Lourenço Marques, *Eng.* Delagoa Bay. Bay on the coast of Mozambique
Mara *256* E Guyana
Maracaibo *589* NW Venezuela
Maracaibo, Lago de *589* inlet of Caribbean Sea, NW Venezuela
Maracay *589* N Venezuela
Marada *339* N Libya
Maradi *407* S Niger
Marāgheh *281* *var.* Maragha. NW Iran
Marahoul *see* Bandama Rouge
Marajó, Baía de *121* N Brazil
Marajó, Ilha de *121* island of N Brazil
Marakabei *334* *var.* Marakabeis. C Lesotho
Marakei *320* island of the Gilbert Is, W Kiribati
Maralal *316* C Kenya
Maralik *74* W Armenia
Maramasike *488* island of E Solomon Is
Maramba *see* Livingstone
Marambio *66* Argentinian research station near Antarctic Peninsula, Antarctica
Maramvya *138* SW Burundi
Marandellas *see* Marondera
Marañón *431* river of N Peru
Marash *see* Kahramanmaraş
Maravovo *488* W Guadalcanal, Solomon Is
Marāwiḩ *560* *var.* Merawwah. Island of W United Arab Emirates
Marburg *see* Maribor
Marburg an der Lahn *236* W Germany
Marcal *264* river of W Hungary
Marche *225* cultural region of C France
Marche-en-Famenne *99* SE Belgium
Marchena, Isla *200* island of N Galapagos Is, Ecuador
Marchfield *97* SE Barbados
Mar Chiquita, Lago *71* lake of C Argentina
Marcounda *see* Markounda
Marcovia *260* S Honduras
Mardān *421* N Pakistan
Mar del Plata *71* E Argentina
Mardin *547* SE Turkey
Maré *626* island, Îles Loyauté, E New Caledonia
Mareeq *490* *var.* Mereeg, *It.* Meregh. E Somalia
Marek *see* Dupnitsa
Marfa Ridge *363* ridge of NW Malta
Margarita, Isla de *589* island of N Venezuela

Margate *493* Kwazulu Natal, SE South Africa
Margherita, Lake *see* Ābaya Hāyk'
Margherita Peak *554, 607* mountain of Uganda and Zaire
Margilan *580 var.* Margelan, *Uzb.* Marghilon. E Uzbekistan
Māragow, Dasht-e- *53* desert of SW Afghanistan
Mari *187* S Cyprus
Marianao *182* NW Cuba
Marías, Islas *370* Island of W Mexico
Maria-Theresiopel *see* Subotica
Máriatölgyes *see* Dubnica nad Váhom
Mar'ib *599* W Yemen
Maribo *190* Lolland, S Denmark
Maribor *486 Ger.* Marburg. NE Slovenia
Marid *560* NE United Arab Emirates
Marie Byrd Land *66* physical region of Greater Antarctica, Antarctica
Marie-Galante *622* island of SE Guadeloupe
Mariehamn *221 var.* Maarianhamina. Aland, Finland
Mariel *182* NW Cuba
Marienburg *see* Alūksne
Mariental *391* S Namibia
Marigot *622* St. Martin, N Guadeloupe
Marigot *196* NE Dominica
Marigot de Baïla *476* river of SW Senegal
Mariguana *see* Mayaguana
Marijampolė *344 prev.* Kapsukas. S Lithuania
Marília *121* S Brazil
Marinduque Island *435* island of C Philippines
Maringá *121* S Brazil
Marins, Île aux *628* island of SE Saint Pierre and Miquelon
Marion Island *493* island of Prince Edward Islands , S South Africa
Ionio, Mar *see* Ionian Sea
Maripasoula *621* W French Guiana
Mariscal Estigarribia *428* NW Paraguay
Marisule Estate *465* N St Lucia
Maritsa *128, 245 var.* Marica, *Gk* Évros, *Turk.* Meriç. River of SE Europe
Mariupol' *556 prev.* Zhdanov. SE Ukraine
Mariy El, Respublika *452* autonomous republic of W Russia
Märjamaa *212 Ger.* Merjama. W Estonia
Marjayoun *332 var.* Marj 'Uyūn. S Lebanon
Marka *490 var.* Merca. S Somalia
Marka *353* S Malawi
Market Shop *462* SE Nevis, St Kitts & Nevis
Markounda *154 var.* Marcounda. NW Central African Republic
Marlánské Lázně *188* W Czech Republic
Marmara Denizi *546 Eng.* Sea of Marmara. Sea to the NW of Turkey
Marmaris *546* SW Turkey
Marne *225* river of NE France
Marneuli *234* S Georgia
Maro *156* S Chad
Maroantsetra *350* NE Madagascar
Maromokotro *350* mountain of N Madagascar
Marondera *612 var.* Marandellas. NE Zimbabwe
Maroni *505, 621 Dut.* Marowijne. River of French Guiana and Suriname
Maros *see* Mureş
Marosvásárhely *see* Târgu Mureş
Maroua *144* N Cameroon
Marovoay *350* NW Madagascar
Marowijne *see* Maroni
Marqūbān *91* NE Bahrain
Marquises, Îles *622* island group of N French Polynesia
Marrakech *382 var.* Marakesh, *Eng.* Marrakesh, *prev.* Morocco. W Morocco
Marrupa *387* N Mozambique
Marsa *363* C Malta
Marsá al Burayqah *see* Al Burayqah
Marsabit *316* N Kenya
Marsala *295* Sicilia, S Italy
Marsaxlokk *363* SE Malta
Marsaxlokk Bay *363* inlet on the SW coast of Malta
Marseille *225 prev. Eng.* Marseilles. SE France
Marshall *336* W Liberia
Marshall Islands *364-365* officially Republic of the Marshall Islands. Country of the Pacific Ocean divided into 33 admin. units (districts)
Marsh Harbour *88* Great Abaco, Bahamas
Martaban *135* SE Burma
Martadi *395 var.* Bajura. W Nepal
Martigny *516* SW Switzerland
Martigues *225* SE France
Martin *485 prev.* Turčianský Svätý Martin, *Ger.* Sankt Martin, *Hung.* Turócszentmárton. NW Slovakia
Martinique *625* French overseas department of the Caribbean Sea. ❖ Fort-de-France.
Martinique Passage *196 var.* Dominica Channel, Martinique Channel. Passage connecting the Atlantic Ocean and Caribbean Sea between Dominica and Martinique
Martuni *74* E Armenia
Marungu *607* mountain range of SE Zaire
Mary *551 prev.* Merv. SE Turkmenistan
Maryborough *77* E Australia
Mary Island *see* Kanton
Maryland *569* state of E USA
Marzūq *see* Murzuq
Masai Steppe *530* grassland of NW Tanzania
Masaka *554* SW Uganda
Masākin *see* M'saken
Masally *see* Massılı
Masampo *see* Masan
Masan *496 prev.* Masampo. S South Korea
Masasi *530* SE Tanzania
Masatepe *404* SW Nicaragua
Masaya *404* S Nicaragua
Masbate *435* island of C Philippines
Mascara *59 var.* Mouaskar. NW Algeria
Maseru *334* ❖ of Lesotho, W Lesotho
Mas-ha *292* W West Bank
Mashava *612 prev.* Mashaba. SE Zimbabwe
Mashhad *281 var.* Meshed. NE Iran
Māshkel *281, 420 var.* Rūd-i Māshkel, Māshkīd. River of Iran and Pakistan
Māshkel, Hāmūn-i *420* salt marsh of Iran and Pakistan
Māshkīd *see* Māshkel
Mashtagi *see* Mastaği
Masīlah, Wādī al *599* dry watercourse of E Yemen
Masindi *554* W Uganda
Masinga Reservoir *316* reservoir of C Kenya
Masirah, Gulf of *see* Maşīrah, Khalīj
Maşīrah, Jazīrat *418 var.* Masirah, Masira. Island of E Oman
Maşīrah, Khalīj *418 var.* Gulf of Masirah. Bay of the Arabian Sea, E Oman
Masis *74* SW Armenia
Masjed Soleymān *281 var.* Masjed-e Soleymān, Masjid-i Sulaimān. W Iran
Masjid-i Sulaimān *see* Masjed Soleymān
Maskall *102* NE Belize
Maskanah *521 var.* Meskene. N Syria
Maskin *418 var.* Miskin. N Oman
Mask, Lough *288 Ir.* Loch Measca. Lake of W Ireland
Ma *593* river of Laos and Vietnam
Massa *294* N Italy
Massachusetts *569* state of NE USA
Massacre *196* W Dominica
Massawa *210 Amh.* Mits'iwa. E Eritrea
Massawa Channel *210* channel of the Red Sea between Dahlak Archipelago and mainland Eritrea
Massenya *156* SW Chad
Massif Central *225* plateau region of C France
Massılı *86 Rus.* Masally. S Azerbaijan
Massoukou *230 var.* Masuku, *prev.* Franceville. E Gabon
Maştağa *86 Rus.* Mastaga, *var.* Maštaga, Mashtagi. E Azerbaijan
Masterton *401* S North Island, New Zealand
Masuda *304* Honshū, W Japan
Masunga *118* NE Botswana
Masvingo *612 prev.* Nyanda, *prev.* Fort Victoria. SE Zimbabwe
Mât *628* river of NE Réunion
Matacawa Levu *218* island of the Yasawa Group, NW Fiji
Matadi *607* W Zaire
Matagalpa *404* C Nicaragua
Matale *504* C Sri Lanka
Matam *476* NE Senegal
Matamoros *370* E Mexico
Matanzas *182* NW Cuba
Matara *504* S Sri Lanka
Mataró *501* E Spain
Mataura *401* river of SW South Island, New Zealand
Matautu *596* Upolu, Western Samoa
Matá 'Utu *629 var.* Mata Uta. ❖ of Wallis & Futuna, Île Uvea, S Wallis & Futuna
Matela's *334* W Lesotho
Matelot *540* NE Trinidad, Trinidad & Tobago
Matiguas *404* C Nicaragua
Matina *178* E Costa Rica
Matit *57 var.* Mat. River of C Albania
Mato Grosso, Planalto de *121* plateau of C Brazil
Matopos *612* SW Zimbabwe
Matosinhos *442 prev.* Matozinhos. NW Portugal
Mátra *264* mountain range of N Hungary
Maţraḩ *418 var.* Mutrah. NE Oman
Matrûh *202 var.* Maţrūḩ. NW Egypt
Matsapha *510 var.* Matsapal, Mtsapa. C Swaziland
Matsieng *334* W Lesotho
Matsue *304* Honshū, W Japan
Matsumato *304* Honshū, C Japan
Matsusaka *304* Honshū, C Japan
Matsuyama *304* Shikoku, SW Japan
Matthews Ridge *256* N Guyana
Matthew Town *88* Great Inagua, Bahamas
Mattsee *82* lake of N Austria
Matuku *218* island to the SE of Viti Levu, S Fiji
Maturín *589* NE Venezuela
Mauga Silisili *596 var.* Mount Silisili. Mountain of NW Western Samoa
Maug Islands *626* island group of N Northern Mariana Islands
Maui *568* island of Hawaii, USA, C Pacific
Maun *118* C Botswana
Mauren *342* NE Liechtenstein
Maurice *see* Mauritius
Maú *see* Ireng
Mauritania *366-367* officially Islamic Republic of Mauritania, *Ar.* Mūrītānīyah. Country of W Africa divided into 12 admin. units (regions)
Mauritius *368-369* officially Republic of Mauritius, *Fr.* Maurice. Country of Indian Ocean divided into 9 admin. units (districts)
Mavrovsko Ezero *349* lake of W FYR Macedonia
Mawlaik *135* NW Burma
Mawlamyine *see* Moulmein
Mawr, Wādī *599* dry watercourse of NW Yemen
Mawson *66* Australian research station of Greater Antarctica, Antarctica
Mayaguana *88* Island of S Bahamas
Mayaguana Passage *88* passage between Crooked I and Mayaguana, Bahamas
Mayagüez *627* W Puerto Rico
Mayagüez, Bahia *627* bay of the Caribbean Sea on the W coast of Puerto Rico
Mayaluka *510* SE Swaziland
Maya Mts *102* mountain range of Belize and Guatemala
Mayarí *183* SE Cuba
Maych'ew *215 var.* Mai Chio, *It.* Mai Ceu. N Ethiopia
Maydī *see* Midī
Mayence *see* Mainz
Mayenne *225* river of NW France
Mayli-Say *325 Kir.* Mayly-Say. W Kyrgyzstan
Mayly-Say *see* Mayli-Say
Maymyo *135* N Burma
Mayoko *176* SW Congo
Mayor Pablo Lagerenza *see* Capitán Pablo Lagerenza
Mayotte *625* French territorial collectivity of the Indian Ocean. ❖ Mamoudzou.
May Pen *303* S Jamaica
Mayreau *466* island of SW St Vincent & the Grenadines
Mayumba *230* S Gabon
Mazabuka *611* S Zambia
Mazagan *see* El Jadida
Mazār-e Sharīf *53* N Afghanistan
Mazaruni *256* river of N Guyana
Mazatenango *250* SW Guatemala
Mazatlán *370* W Mexico
Mažeikiai *344* NW Lithuania
Mazirbe *330* NW Latvia
Mazowe *612 prev.* Mazoe. NE Zimbabwe
Mazowe *612 var.* Mazoe. River of Mozambique and Zimbabwe
Mazra'at Turaynā *447 var.* Traina Garden. S Qatar
Mazury *439* region of NE Poland
Mazyr *104 Rus.* Mozyr'. SE Belorussia
Mba *see* Ba
Mbabane *510* ❖ of Swaziland, NW Swaziland
Mbacké *see* Mbaké
Mbagne *366* SW Mauritania
Mbaïki *154 var.* M'Baiki. SW Central African Republic
Mbakaou, Lac de *144* lake of C Cameroon
Mbaké *476 var.* Mbacké. W Senegal
Mbala *611 prev.* Abercorn. NE Zambia
Mbalabala *612 prev.* Balla Balla. SW Zimbabwe
Mbale *554* E Uganda
Mbalmayo *144 var.* M'Balmayo. S Cameroon
Mbalo *488* SE Guadalcanal, Solomon Is
Mbam *144* river of NW Cameroon
Mbandaka *607 prev.* Coquilhatville. NW Zaire
Mbanga *144* W Cameroon
M'Banza Congo *64 Port.* São Salvador do Congo. NW Angola

Mbanza-Ngungu 607 W Zaire
Mbarara 554 SW Uganda
Mbatiki see Batiki
Mbé 144 N Cameroon
Mbengga see Beqa
M'Béni 174 NE Grande Comore, Comoros
Mbeya 530 SW Tanzania
Mbigou 230 C Gabon
Mbilua see Vella Lavella
Mbinga 530 S Tanzania
Mbini 208 W Río Muni, Equatorial Guinea
Mbini 208 prev. Benito. River of Equatorial Guinea and Gabon
Mbomo 176 NW Congo
Mbomou see Bomu
Mbour 476 W Senegal
M'Bout see Mbout
Mbout 366 var. M'Bout. S Mauritania
Mbrès 154 C Central African Republic
Mbuji-Mayi 607 prev. Bakwanga. S Zaire
Mbulu 530 N Tanzania
Mbulungwane 510 S Swaziland
Mbuluzi 510 var. Black Umbeluzi. River of Mozambique and Swaziland
Mbutha see Buca
Mchinji 353 prev. Fort Manning. W Malawi
McKean Island 182 island of the Phoenix Is, C Kiribati
M'Clintock Channel 146 var. McClintock Channel. Channel between Prince of Wales Island and Victoria Island, N Canada
McMurdo 66 US research station near Ross Shelf, Antarctica
Mdina 363 W Malta
Mead, Lake 568 reservoir of SW USA
Measca, Loch see Mask, Lough
Mecca see Makkah
Mechelen 99 Fr. Malines. C Belgium
Mecheria 59 var. Mechriyya. NW Algeria
Mecklenburger Bucht 237 bay of the Baltic Sea, on the N coast of Germany
Mecsek 264 mountain range of SW Hungary
Medan 276 Sumatra, E Indonesia
Medawachchiya 504 N Sri Lanka
Médéa 59 var. Lemdiyya, El Mediyya. N Algeria
Medellín 171 NW Colombia
Médenine 543 var. Madanīyīn. SE Tunisia
Medford 568 Oregon, NW USA
Medicine Hat 146 SW Canada
Medina see Al Madīnah
Médina Gonassé see Médina Gounas
Médina Gounas 476 var. Médina Gonassé. S Senegal
Medina Sering Mass 233 W Gambia
Mediterranean Sea 225, 291, 546 Fr. Mer Méditerranée. Sea of the Atlantic Ocean, enclosed by N Africa, SW Asia and S Europe
Medjerda see Mejerda, Oued
Medoc 224 cultural region of SW France
Médouneu 230 N Gabon
Meekatharra 76 W Australia
Meemu Atoll see Mulaku Atoll
Meenen see Menen
Meerut 270 N India
Meghna 93 river of S Bangladesh
Meghri 74 var. Megri. SE Armenia
Mehdia see Mahdia
Meherpur 93 W Bangladesh
Meheso see Mī'ēso
Me Hka see Nmai Hka
Mehtarlām 53 var. Methariam, Meterlam. E Afghanistan
Meiganga 144 NE Cameroon
Meiktila 135 C Burma
Meissen 237 E Germany
Mejerda, Monts de la 543 var. Monts de la Medjerda, Monts de la Majardah. Mountain range of Algeria and Tunisia
Mejerda, Oued 543 var. Medjerda, Wādī Majardah. River of Algeria and Tunisia
Méjico see Mexico
Mejit 364 island of NE Marshall Islands
Mékambo 230 NE Gabon
Mek'elē 215 var. Makale. N Ethiopia
Mekerrhane, Sebkha 59 var. Sebkra Mekerrhane, Sebkha Meqerghane. Salt flat of C Algeria
Mékhé 476 NW Senegal
Meknès 382 N Morocco
Mekong 135, 141, 162, 327, 533, 593 Chin. Lancang Jiang, var. Lan-ts'ang Chiang, Cam. Mékôngk, Lao. Mènam Khong, Th. Mae Name Khong, Vtn. Sông Tiên Giang, Tib. Za Qu, var. Dza Chu. River of SE Asia
Mekong Delta 593 delta of S Vietnam
Mékrou 108,132 river of W Africa
Melah, Oued el 543 var. Wādī al Milḩ. Dry watercourse of W Tunisia
Melah, Sebkhet el 543 var. Sabkhat al Milḩ. Salt flat of SE Tunisia
Melaka 354 var. Malacca. SW Peninsular Malaysia
Melbourne 77 SE Australia
Meleda see Mljet
Melekeiok 627 C Palau
Melfi 156 S Chad
Melilla 382, 501 enclave of Spain, NE Morocco
Melitopol' 556 SE Ukraine
Melle 236 NW Germany
Mellègue, Oued 543 var. Wādī Mallāq. River of Algeria and Tunisia
Mellerud 513 SW Sweden
Mellieħa 363 NW Malta
Mellieħa Ridge 363 ridge of Malta island, Malta
Mělník 188 NW Czech Republic
Melo 577 E Uruguay
Melo, Ilha de 254 var. Melho Island. Island of S Guinea-Bissau
Melsetter see Chimanimani
Melun 225 N France
Melville Hall 196 river of N Dominica
Melville Island 77 island of N Australia
Melville Island 146 island of Parry Islands, N Canada
Melville Islands see St. Giles Islands
Melville Peninsula 147 peninsula of N Canada
Melville Sound see Viscount Melville Sound
Memel see Neman
Memel see Klaipėda
Memphis 569 Tennessee, SE USA
Menabe 350 physical region of W Madagascar
Menado see Manado
Ménaka 360 E Mali
Mènam Khong see Mekong
Menbij see Manbij
Mendawai 276 river of Borneo, C Indonesia
Mende 225 S France
Mendi 426 C Papua New Guinea
Mendip Hills 563 hills of W England, UK
Mendoza 71 W Argentina
Menen 99 prev. Meenen, Fr. Menin. W Belgium
Menongue 64 Port. Serpa Pinto. C Angola
Menorca 501 Eng. Minorca. Island of the Islas Baleares, E Spain
Mentakap 354 var. Mentakab. C Peninsular Malaysia
Mentawai, Kepulauan 276 island group to the W of Sumatra, Indonesia
Mentawai, Selat 276 strait of the Indian Ocean between Pulau Siberut and Sumatra, W Indonesia
Menzel Bourguiba 543 prev. Ferryville, var. Manzil Bū Ruqaybah. N Tunisia
Menzel Temime 543 var. Manzil Tamīm. N Tunisia
Meppel 397 NE Netherlands
Merawwah see Marāwiḩ
Merca see Marka
Mercedes 71 C Argentina
Mercedes 71 NE Argentina
Mercedes 71 E Argentina
Mercedes 577 W Uruguay
Mercedes Umaña 207 SE El Salvador
Meregh see Mareeq
Méré Lava 585 Banks Islands, N Vanuatu
Mergui 135 SE Burma
Mergui Archipelago 135 island group of S Burma
Meriç see Maritsa
Mérida 370 E Mexico
Mérida 501 W Spain
Mérida 589 W Venezuela
Mérida, Cordillera de 589 var. Sierra Nevada de Mérida. Mountain range of W Venezuela
Meridian 569 Mississippi, SE USA
Merir 627 island of S Palau
Merizo 623 SW Guam
Merjama see Märjamaa
Melrhir, Chott 59 var. Chott Melghir. Salt lake of E Algeria
Merlimau, Pulau 483 island of SW Singapore
Merredin 76 SW Australia
Mersa Fatma 210 E Eritrea
Mersa Teklay 210 N Eritrea
Mersch 346 C Luxembourg
Mersey 563 river of NW England, UK
Mersin 547 var. İçel. S Turkey
Mersing 354 SE Peninsular Malaysia
Merthyr Tydfil 563 S Wales, UK
Meru 316 C Kenya
Merv see Mary
Meshed see Mashhad
Meskene see Maskanah
Mesopotamia 284 historical region of SW Asia
Mesopotamia 466 SE St Vincent, St Vincent & the Grenadines
Messalo 387 var. Mualo. River of NE Mozambique
Messina 295 var. Messana. Sicilia, S Italy
Messina 493 Northern Transvaal, NE South Africa
Messina, Stretto di 295 Eng. Strait of Messina. Strait connecting the Ionian Sea and Tyrrhenian Sea, between mainland Italy and Sicilia
Mesta see Néstos
Mestghanem see Mostaganem
Mestia 234 var. Mestiya. N Georgia
Meta 171, 589 river of Colombia and Venezuela
Meta Incognita Peninsula 147 peninsula of Baffin Island, NE Canada
Metangula 387 N Mozambique
Metapán 207 NW El Salvador
Metema 215 NW Ethiopia
Meterlam see Mehtarlām
Methariam see Mehtarlām
Metković 181 SE Croatia
Metu 215 var. Mattu, Mettu. W Ethiopia
Metz 225 NE France
Meuse 99, 225, 397 var. Maas. River of W Europe
Mexcala see Balsas
Mexiana, Ilha 121 island of N Brazil
Mexicali 370 NW Mexico
Mexicana, Altiplanicie 370 Eng. Plateau of Mexico, Mexican Plateau. Plateau of N Mexico
Mexico 370-373 officially United States of Mexico, Sp. Estados Unidos Mexicanos, Méjico. Country of North or Central America divided into 31 admin. units (states).
Mexico City 370 Sp. Ciudad de México. ❖ of Mexico, C Mexico
Mexico, Gulf of 182, 370 Sp. Golfo de México. Gulf of the Atlantic Ocean, on the SE coast of North America
Mexico, Plateau of see Mexicana, Altiplanicie
Meyadine see Al Mayādīn
Meymaneh 53 var. Maimana. NW Afghanistan
Mezdra 128 NW Bulgaria
Mfanganu Island 316 var. Mfangano Island. Island of Lake Victoria, SW Kenya
Mfouati 176 S Congo
Mhangura 612 var. Mangula. N Zimbabwe
Mhlambanyatsi 510 W Swaziland
Mhlosheni 510 S Swaziland
Mhlume 510 NE Swaziland
Mhlumeni 510 NE Swaziland
Miami 569 Florida, SE USA
Miānwāli 421 NE Pakistan
Michalovce 485 Ger. Grossmichel, Hung. Nagymihály. E Slovakia
Michigan 569 state of NC USA
Michigan, Lake 147, 569 Lake of NC USA
Micomeseng see Mikomeseng
Micoud 465 SE St Lucia
Micronesia 374-375 officially Federated States of Micronesia. Country of the Pacific Ocean divided into 4 admin. units (states)
Middelburg 397 SW Netherlands
Middelburg 493 Eastern Cape, S South Africa
Middelburg 493 Eastern Transvaal, NE South Africa
Middelfart 190 Fyn, SW Denmark
Middle Andaman 270 island of Andaman Islands to the SE of India
Middle Atlas see Moyen Atlas
Middlegate 626 C Norfolk Island
Middle Island 462 W St Kitts, St Kitts & Nevis
Middlesbrough 563 NE England, UK
Middlesex 102 E Belize
Mīdī 599 var. Maydī. NW Yemen
Miercurea-Ciuc 448 Hung. Csíkszereda. C Romania
Mieres 501 NW Spain
Mī'ēso 215 var. Miesso, Meheso. C Ethiopia
Migongo 138 E Burundi
Mikhaylovgrad see Montana
Mikhaylovka 452 W Russia
Mikkeli 221 Swe. Sankt Michel. S Finland
Mikomeseng 208 var. Micomeseng. NE Río Muni, Equatorial Guinea
Míkonos 245 island of SE Greece
Mikuni-sammyaku 304 mountain range of Honshū, N Japan
Milagro 200 SW Ecuador
Milange 387 N Mozambique
Milano 294, 299 Eng. Milan, Ger. Mailand. N Italy
Milas 546 SW Turkey
Mildura 77 SE Australia
Mil Düzü 86 Rus. Mil'skaya Step'. Physical region of C Azerbaijan
Milgis 316 var. Malgis. River of C Kenya
Mili 364 island of SE Marshall Islands
Milḩ, Baḩr al see Razāzah, Buḩayrat ar
Milḩ, Wādī al see Melah, Oued el
Millet 465 C St Lucia
Millstätter See 82 lake of S Austria
Milo 253 river of E Guinea
Milondo, Mont 230 mountain of C Gabon

Mílos *245* island of SE Greece
Mil'skaya Step' *see* Mil Düzü
Milton Keynes *563* C England, UK
Milwaukee *569* Wisconsin, NC USA
Milyang *see* Miryang
Mimongo *230* C Gabon
Mīnā' 'Abd Allāh *322* *var.* Mina Abdulla. E Kuwait
Mīnā' al Aḥmadī *322* *var.* Mina Ahmadi. E Kuwait
Mīnā' Jabal 'Alī *560* NE United Arab Emirates
Minas *577* S Uruguay
Mīnā' Sa'ūd *322* *var.* Mīnā' Su'ūd. SE Kuwait
Minas de Corrales *577* N Uruguay
Minas de Matahambre *182* W Cuba
Minatitlán *370* SE Mexico
Minbu *135* W Burma
Minch, The *563* strait of the Atlantic Ocean, between Outer Hebrides and Scotland
Mincivan *86* *Rus.* Mindzhivan. SW Azerbaijan
Mindanao *435* island of S Philippines
Mindanao Sea *see* Bohol Sea
Mindelo *152* *var.* Porto Grande. São Vincente, N Cape Verde
Mindoro *435* island of C Philippines
Mindoro Strait *435* strait connecting South China Sea and Sulu Sea
Mindouli *176* S Congo
Mindživan *see* Mincivan
Mingäçevir *86* *Rus.* Mingechaur *var.* Mingečaur. C Azerbaijan
Mingäçevir Su Anbarı *86* *Rus.* Mingechaurskoye Vodokhranilishche. Reservoir of NW Azerbaijan
Mingala *154* SE Central African Republic
Mingãora *421* *var.* Mingora, Mongora. N Pakistan
Mingechaurskoye Vodokhranilishche *see* Mingäçevir Su Anbarı
Ming-Kush *see* Min-Kush
Minho *see* Miño
Minicoy Island *270* island of Lakshadweep, SW India
Min-Kush *325* *Kir.* Ming-Kush. C Kyrgyzstan
Minna *408* C Nigeria
Minneapolis *569* Minnesota, NC USA
Minnesota *569* state of NC USA
Miño *442, 500* *Port.* Minho. River of Portugal and Spain
Minorca *see* Menorca
Minot *569* North Dakota, NC USA
Minsk *104* ❖ of Belorussia, C Belorussia
Minto Reef *375* atoll of C Micronesia
Minvoul *230* N Gabon
Minwakh *599* N Yemen
Miquelon *628* N Saint Pierre and Miquelon
Miquelon *628* island of N Saint Pierre and Miquelon
Miquelon, Cap *628* cape of the Atlantic Ocean on the coast of Miquelon, N Saint Pierre and Miquelon
Miragoâne *258* SW Haiti
Miranda de Ebro *501* N Spain
Mirbāṭ *418* *var.* Marbat. SW Oman
Mirebalais *258* C Haiti
Miri *354* NW Borneo, Malaysia
Mirim Lagoon *121, 577* *var.* Lake Mirim. Lagoon of Brazil and Uruguay
Mirim, Lake *see* Mirim Lagoon
Mirnyy *453* C Russia
Mirnyy *66* CIS research station of Greater Antarctica, Antarctica
Mīrpur *see* New Mīrpur
Mirs Bay *262* *Cant.* Tai Pang Wan. Bay to the NE of Hong Kong
Mirtóo Pelagos *245* *Eng.* Mirtoan Sea. Area of the Mediterranean Sea, S Greece
Miryang *496* *var.* Milyang *Jap.* Mitsuō. SE South Korea
Misery, Mount *see* Liamuiga, Mount
Miskito Coast *see* Mosquito Coast
Miskitos, Cayos *404* island group of NE Nicaragua
Miskolc *264* NE Hungary
Misool, Pulau *276* island of Maluku, E Indonesia
Mişrātah *339* *var.* Misurata. N Libya
Mississippi *569* river of C USA
Mississippi *569* state of SE USA
Missoula *568* Montana, NW USA
Missouri *569* river of NC USA
Missouri *569* state of C USA
Misurata *see* Mişrātah
Mitau *see* Jelgava
Mitchell *77* river of NE Australia
Mitiaro *620* island of Southern Cook Islands, S Cook Islands
Mitilíni *245* *var.* Mytilene. Lésvos, E Greece
Mito *304* Honshū, SE Japan
Mitre Island *see* Fatutaka
Mitrovica *see* Kosovska Mitrovica
Mitrovicë *see* Kosovska Mitrovica
Mitsamiouli *174* N Grande Comore, Comoros
Mits'iwa *see* Massawa
Mitsoudjé *174* SW Grande Comore, Comoros
Mitsuyō *see* Miryang
Mitú *171* SE Colombia
Mitumba, Monts *607* *var.* Chaîne des Mitumba, Mitumba Range. Mountain range of E Zaire
Mitzic *230* N Gabon
Miyako *305* Honshū, N Japan
Miyako-jima *304* island of Sakishima-shotō, SW Japan
Miyakonojō *304* Kyūshū, SW Japan
Miyazaki *304* Kyūshū, SW Japan
Miyoshi *304* Honshū, W Japan
Mizdah *339* *var.* Mizda. NW Libya
Mjøsa *414* *var.* Mjøsen. Lake of SE Norway
Mkhondvo *510* *var.* Mkondo. River of South Africa and Swaziland
Mladá Boleslav *188* *Ger.* Jungbunzlau. N Czech Republic
Mlanje *see* Mulanje
Mljet *181* *It.* Meleda. Island of S Croatia
Mmabatho *493* North West, N South Africa
Mmathethe *118* S Botswana
Mnjoli Dam *510* reservoir of NE Swaziland
Mo *414* NE Norway
Moa *480* river of W Africa
Moa *183* SE Cuba
Moabi *230* SW Gabon
Moala *218* island to the SE of Viti Levu, S Fiji
Moamba *387* SW Mozambique
Moanda *230* SE Gabon
Moba *607* E Zaire
Mobaye *154* S Central African Republic
Mobile *569* Alabama, SE USA
Moca *198* N Dominican Republic
Moçambique *387* island and settlement of NE Mozambique
Moçâmedes *see* Namibe
Moce *218* island of the Lau Group, E Fiji
Mocha *see* Al Mukhā
Mochudi *118* S Botswana
Mocímboa da Praia *387* *var.* Vila de Mocímboa da Praia. N Mozambique
Môco *64* *var.* Serra Môco, Morro de Môco. Mountain of W Angola
Mocoa *171* SW Colombia
Mocuba *387* E Mozambique
Modena *294* NW Italy
Mödling *82* NE Austria
Modohn *see* Madona
Modriča *116* N Bosnia & Herzegovina
Moe *77* SE Australia
Moen *see* Weno
Möen *see* Møn
Moena *see* Muna, Pulau
Moengo *508* NE Suriname
Moers *236* W Germany
Moesi *see* Musi
Moeskroen *see* Mouscron
Mogadishu *490* *Som.* Muqdisho, *It.* Mogadiscio. ❖ of Somalia, S Somalia
Mogador *see* Essaouira
Mogilëv *see* Mahilyow
Mogotón, Pico *404* mountain of NW Nicaragua
Mohales Hoek *334* SW Lesotho
Mohammadia *59* *var.* El Mohammaidia. NW Algeria
Mohammedia *382* *prev.* Fédala. NW Morocco
Moharek *see* Al Muḥarraq
Mohéli *174* *var.* Mwali. Island of Comoros
Mohn *see* Muhu
Moihani *174* S Mohéli, Comoros
Moindou *626* C New Caledonia
Mõisaküla *212* *Ger.* Moiseküll. S Estonia
Moïssala *156* S Chad
Moka *368* C Mauritius
Mokhotlong *334* NE Lesotho
Mokil *375* atoll of E Micronesia
Moknine *543* *var.* Al Muknīn. NE Tunisia
Mokp'o *496* *Jap.* Moppo. SW South Korea
Mokra Gora *602* mountain range of SW Serbia, Yugoslavia
Mokwa *408* W Nigeria
Moldau *see* Vltava
Moldavia *see* Moldova
Molde *414* SW Norway
Moldotau, Khrebet *325* mountain range of C Kyrgyzstan
Moldova *376-377* officially Republic of Moldova, *var.* Moldavia, *prev.* Moldavian SSR, *Rus.* Moldavskaya SSR. Country of E Europe divided into 40 admin. units (districts)
Molepolole *118* S Botswana
Môle-St-Nicolas *258* NW Haiti
Molineux *462* NE St Kitts, St Kitts & Nevis
Möll *82* river of S Austria
Mölndal *513* SW Sweden
Molodechno *see* Maladzyechna
Molodeczno *see* Maladzyechna
Molodezhnaya *66* CIS research station of Greater Antarctica, Antarctica
Molokai *568* island of Hawaii, USA, C Pacific
Molopo *118, 493* seasonal river of southern Africa
Molotov *see* Severodvinsk
Molotov *see* Perm'
Moloundou *144* SE Cameroon
Moluccas *see* Maluku
Molucca Sea *see* Maluku, Laut
Mombasa *316* SE Kenya
Môn *see* Anglesey
Møn *190* *prev.* Möen. Island of SE Denmark
Mona, Canal de la *198, 627* channel connecting the Atlantic Ocean and Caribbean Sea, between Dominican Republica and Puerto Rico
Monaco *378-379* officially Principality of Monaco. Country of W Europe divided into 4 admin. units (quarters)
Monaco *see* München
Monaghan *288* *Ir.* Muineachán. NE Ireland
Monagrillo *424* S Panama
Mona, Isla *627* island of SW Puerto Rico
Monapo *387* NE Mozambique
Monaragala *504* SE Sri Lanka
Monastir *543* *var.* Al Munastīr. NE Tunisia
Monastir *see* Bitola
Mönchengladbach *236* *prev.* München-Gladbach. W Germany
Monchy *465* N St Lucia
Monclova *370* N Mexico
Moncton *147* SE Canada
Mondego *442* river of N Portugal
Mondsee *82* lake of N Austria
Money Island *627* island of W Paracel Islands
Monfalcone *295* N Italy
Mongar *110* E Bhutan
Mongo *156* C Chad
Mongolia *380-381* country of NE Asia divided into 21 admin. units (18 provinces, 3 cities)
Mongomo *208* E Río Muni, Equatorial Guinea
Mongora *see* Mingãora
Mongos, Chaîne des *see* Bongo, Massif des
Mongouge *465* SW St Lucia
Mongoumba *154* SW Central African Republic
Mongu *611* W Zambia
Mönh Hayrhan Uul *380* mountain of W Mongolia
Moni *187* S Cyprus
Monkey Bay *353* SE Malawi
Monkey River Town *102* SE Belize
Mono *108, 537* river of Benin and Togo
Monopoi *295* E Italy
Monos *540* island to the NW of Trinidad, Trinidad & Tobago
Mon Repos *465* E St Lucia
Monrovia *336* ❖ of Liberia, W Liberia
Mons *99* *Dut.* Bergen. SW Belgium
Montana *568-569* state of NW USA
Montana *128* *prev.* Mikhaylovgrad, *var.* Mihajlovgrad, Mikhailovgrad, *prev.* Ferdinand. NW Bulgaria
Montauban *225* S France
Montbéliard *225* NE France
Mont Blanc *225, 294* *It.* Monte Bianco. Mountain of France and Italy
Mont-de-Marsan *225* SW France
Monteagudo *112* S Bolivia
Monte-Carlo *378* NE Monaco
Monte Cristi *198* NW Dominican Republic
Monte Croce Carnico, Passo di *see* Plöcken
Montegiardino *468* SE San Marino
Montego Bay *303* NW Jamaica
Montelindo *428* river of C Paraguay
Montenegro *602* *Serb.* Crna Gora. Republic of Yugoslavia
Monte Plata *198* C Dominican Republic
Montepuez *387* N Mozambique
Montería *171* NW Colombia
Montero *112* C Bolivia
Monterrey *370* N Mexico
Montes Claros *121* SE Brazil
Montevideo *577* ❖ of Uruguay, S Uruguay
Montgomery *569* Alabama, SE USA
Montgomery *see* Sāhīwāl
Monthey *516* SW Switzerland
Montijo *442* W Portugal
Montpelier *569* Vermont, NE USA
Montpellier *225* S France
Montréal *147* *Eng.* Montreal. SE Canada
Montreux *516* SW Switzerland
Montserrat *625* British dependent territory of the Caribbean Sea. ❖ Plymouth
Montsinéry *621* NE French Guiana

Mur *82, 486 SCr.* Mura. River of C Europe
Mura *see* Mur
Muragarazi *see* Malagarasi
Murai Reservoir *483* reservoir of NW Singapore
Muramba *138* NE Burundi
Murambi *460* C Rwanda
Muramvya *138* C Burundi
Murang'a *316 prev.* Fort Hall. SW Kenya
Murata *468* S San Marino
Murchison Falls *554 var.* Kabalega Falls. Waterfall of NW Uganda
Murcia *501* autonomous community of SE Spain
Mureş *448 var.* Mureşul, *Hung.* Maros, *Ger.* Muresch. River of Hungary and Romania
Murehwa *612 var.* Murewa. NE Zimbabwe
Muresch *see* Mureş
Murgab *551 var.* Murghab. River of SE Turkmenistan
Murgab *528* E Tajikistan
Murgap *551 prev.* Murgab. SE Turkmenistan
Muri *516 var.* Muri bei Bern. W Switzerland
Murilo *375* atoll of N Micronesia
Mūrītānīyah *see* Mauritania
Müritz 237 *var.* Müritzee. Lake of NE Germany
Murmansk *452* NW Russia
Muroran *304* Hokkaidō, N Japan
Muroto *304* Shikoku, SW Japan
Murray *77* river of SE Australia
Murray, Lake *426* lake in swamp region of W Papua New Guinea
Murrumbidgee *77* river of SE Australia
Murska Sobota *486 Ger.* Olsnitz. NE Slovenia
Murua Island *426 var.* Woodlark I. Island of SE Papua New Guinea
Murupara *401* SE North Island, New Zealand
Mururoa Atoll *622* var. Moruroa. Atoll of French Polynesia
Murzuq *339 var.* Marzūq, Murzuk. W Libya
Murzuq, Ḩammādat *339* plateau of W Libya
Muş *547* E Turkey
Mūša *344* river of N Lithuania
Musaffah *560* C United Arab Emirates
Musā'id *339* NE Libya
Musala *128 prev.* Stalin Peak. Mountain of W Bulgaria
Musan *413* NE North Korea
Musandam Peninsula *418 Ar.* Ra's Musandam, *var.* Ras Masandam. Peninsular of N Oman
Musay'īd *447 var.* Umm Sa'īd. SE Qatar
Muscat *418 Ar.* Masqaţ. ❖ of Oman, N Oman
Muscat and Oman *see* Oman
Musema *138* C Burundi
Musenyi *138* W Burundi
Mushin *408* SW Nigeria
Musi *276 prev.* Moesi. River of Sumatra, W Indonesia
Musoma *530* N Tanzania
Mussau Island *426* island of NE Papua New Guinea
Mustafa-Pasha *see* Svilengrad
Mustique *466* island of C St Vincent & the Grenadines
Mustvee *212 Ger.* Tschorna. E Estonia
Mutalau *626* N Niue
Mutambara *138* SW Burundi
Mu-tan-chiang *see* Mudanjiang
Mutare *612 prev.* Umtali. E Zimbabwe
Mutoko *612 prev.* Mtoko. NE Zimbabwe
Mutorashanga *612 prev.* Mtorashanga. N Zimbabwe
Mutsamudu *174* NW Anjouan, Comoros
Muyaga *138* C Burundi
Muyaga *138* E Burundi
Muyebe *138* C Burundi
Muyinga *138 var.* Muhinga. NE Burundi
Muy Muy *404* C Nicaragua
Muynak *580 var.* Mujnak, *Uzb.* Mŭynoq. NW Uzbekistan
Muyunkum, Peski *312* desert region of S Kazakhstan
Muzaffargarh *421* E Pakistan
Muzarabani *612* N Zimbabwe
Mvuma *612 prev.* Umvuma. C Zimbabwe
Mvurwi *612 prev.* Umvukwes. N Zimbabwe
Mwali *see* Mohéli
Mwanza *530* NW Tanzania
Mwanza *353* SW Malawi
Mweka *607* C Zaire
Mwenda *611* N Zambia
Mwene-Ditu *607* S Zaire
Mwenezi *612* river of S Zimbabwe
Mwenezi *612 prev.* Nuanetsi. S Zimbabwe
Mweru, Lake *607, 611 Fr.* Lac Moero. Lake of Zaire and Zambia
Mweru Wantipa, Lake *611* lake of N Zambia
Mwombezhi *611* river of W Zambia
Myanaung *135* SW Burma
Myanmar *see* Burma
Myaungmya *135* SW Burma
Myingyan *135* C Burma
Myitkyina *135* N Burma
Myitnge *135* river of NE Burma
Mykines *620* island of W Faeroe Islands
Mykolayiv *556 Rus.* Nikolayev. S Ukraine
Mymensingh *93 prev.* Nasirābād. N Bangladesh
Myŏngch'ŏn *413* NE North Korea
Mýrdalsjökull *268* glacier of S Iceland
Mysore *270 var.* Maisur. S India
My Tho *593* S Vietnam
Mytilene *see* Mitilíni
Mývatn *268* lake of C Iceland
Mzimba *353* NW Malawi
Mzuzu *353* N Malawi

N

Naas *288 Ir.* Nás Na Riogh, An Nás. E Ireland
Nabatîyé *332 var.* Nabatiyet et Tahta, An Nabatīyah at Taḩtā. SW Lebanon
Nabavatu *218* Vanua Levu, N Fiji
Naberezhnyye Chelny *452 prev.* Brezhnev. W Russia
Nabeul *543 var.* Nābul. N Tunisia
Nabgha *560* NE United Arab Emirates
Nabīh aş Şalīḩ, Jazīrat an *91 var.* Nabih Saleh, Nabīh Salīh. Island of NE Bahrain
Nabī Shu'ayb, Jabal an *599* mountain of W Yemen
Nablus *291, 292 Heb.* Shekhem. N West Bank
Nabouwalu *218* Vanua Levu, N Fiji
Nacala *387* NE Mozambique
Nacaome *260* S Honduras
Na-Chii *see* Nagqu
Nachingwea *530* SE Tanzania
Na Cruacha Dubha *see* Macgillicuddy's Reeks
Nacula *218 prev.* Nathula. Island of the Yasawa Group, NW Fiji
Nadi *218 prev.* Nandi. Viti Levu, W Fiji
Nador *382 prev.* Villa Nador. NE Morocco
Nadur *363* Gozo, Malta
Naduri *218 prev.* Nanduri. Vanua Levu, N Fiji
Nadym *452* N Russia
Næstved *190* Sjælland, SE Denmark
Nafūsah, Jabal *339* mountain range of NW Libya
Naga *435 prev.* Nueva Caceres. Luzon, N Philippines
Nagano *304* Honshū, C Japan
Nagaoka *304* Honshū, N Japan
Nagarote *404* SW Nicaragua
Nagasaki *304* Kyūshū, SW Japan
Nāgercoil *270* S India
Nagorno-Karabakh *86* former autonomous region of SW Azerbaijan
Nagoya *304* Honshū, C Japan
Nāgpur *270* C India
Nagqu *162 Chin.* Na-Ch'ii, *prev.* Hei-ho. Xizang Zizhiqu, W China
Nagua *198* N Dominican Republic
Nagybánya *see* Baia Mare
Nagybecskerek *see* Zrenjanin
Nagykanizsa *264 Ger.* Grosskanizsa. SW Hungary
Nagykőrös *264* C Hungary
Nagymihály *see* Michalovce
Nagysurány *see* Šurany
Nagyszeben *see* Sibiu
Nagyszombat *see* Trnava
Nagytapolcsány *see* Topoľčany
Nagyvárad *see* Oradea
Naha *304* Nansei-shotō, SW Japan
Naḩal Elisha *292* E West Bank
Nahariyya *291* N Israel
Nahiçevan' *see* Naxçıvan
Furāt *see* Euphrates
Urdunn *see* Jordan
Nairai *218* island to the E of Viti Levu, C Fiji
Nairobi *316* ❖ of Kenya, S Kenya
Naitaba *218 prev.* Naitamba. Island of the Lau Group, E Fiji
Naitamba *see* Naitaba
Naivasha *316* SW Kenya
Naivasha, Lake *316* lake of SW Kenya
Najaf *see* An Najaf
Najafābād *281* W Iran
Najd *472 var.* Nejd. Region of C Saudi Arabia
Najin *413* NE North Korea
Najrān *472* S Saudi Arabia
Naju *see* Kumsong
Nakadōri-jima *304* island of Gotō-rettō, SW Japan
Nakamura *304* Shikoku, SW Japan
Nakasongola *554* W Uganda
Nakatsu *304* Kyūshū, SW Japan
Nakatsugawa *304* Honshū, C Japan
Nakfa *210* N Eritrea
Nakhichevan' *see* Naxcivan
Nakhodka *453* SE Russia
Nakhon Pathom *533* C Thailand
Nakhon Phanom *533* NE Thailand
Nakhon Ratchasima *533 var.* Korat. E Thailand
Nakhon Sawan *533 var.* Muang Nakhon Sawan. W Thailand
Nakhon Si Thammarat *533* S Thailand
Nakskov *190* Lolland, S Denmark
Naktong *496 var.* Nakdong, *Jap.* Rakutō-kō. River of South Korea
Nakuru *316* W Kenya
Nāl *421* river of W Pakistan
Nalayh *380* C Mongolia
Nal'chik *452* SW Russia
Nālūt *339* NW Libya
Nam *413* river of C North Korea
Nam *496* river of S South Korea
Namaacha *387* S Mozambique
Namacurra *387* E Mozambique
Namak, Daryācheh-ye *281* lake of W Iran
Namak, Kavīr-e *281* desert region of NE Iran
Namanga *316* S Kenya
Namangan *580* E Uzbekistan
Namatanai *426* New Ireland, Papua New Guinea
Nam Đinh *593* N Vietnam
Namen *see* Namur
Namhae-do *496 Jap.* Nankai-tō. Island of S South Korea
Namib Desert *391* coastal desert region of W Namibia
Namibe *64 Port.* Moçâmedes, *var.* Mossâmedes. SW Angola
Namibia *390-391* officially Republic of Namibia, *prev.* South-West Africa, German Southwest Africa. Country of Southern Africa divided into 13 admin. units (districts)
Namoluk *375* island of SE Micronesia
Namonuito *375* atoll of NW Micronesia
Namorik *364* island of S Marshall Islands
Nampa *568* Idaho, NW USA
Namp'o *413* SW North Korea
Nampula *387* NE Mozambique
Namsos *414* C Norway
Namu *364* island of C Marshall Islands
Namuka-i-lau *218* island of the Lau Group, E Fiji
Namunukula *504* SE Sri Lanka
Namur *99 Dut.* Namen. SE Belgium
Namutoni *391* N Namibia
Namwŏn *496 Jap.* Nangen. S South Korea
Namyit Island *628* island of S Spratly Islands
Nan *533 var.* Muang Nan. N Thailand
Nanaimo *146* Vancouver Island, SW Canada
Nanao *304* Honshū, C Japan
Nanchang *163* Jianxi, SE China
Nan-ching *see* Nanjing
Nancy *225* NE France
Nanda Devi *270* mountain of N India
Nandaime *404* S Nicaragua
Nandi *see* Nadi
Nanduri *see* Naduri
Nanga Eboko *144* C Cameroon
Nangbéto, Retenue de *537* reservoir of C Togo
Nangen *see* Namwŏn
Nan Hai *see* East China Sea and South China Sea
Nan-hsi *525* SW Taiwan
Nanjing *163 var.* Nanking, Nan-ching. Jiangsu, E China
Nankai-tō *see* Namhae-do
Nanning *163 prev.* Yung-ning. Guangxi, S China
Nanortalik *622* S Greenland
Nansei-shotō *304* island group to the SW of Kyūshū, SW Japan
Nanshan Island *628* island of E Spratly Islands
Nansio *530* NW Tanzania
Nanterre *225* N France
Nantes *224* W France
Nanthi Kadal Lagoon *504* lagoon of N Sri Lanka
Nan-t'ou *525* W Taiwan
Nanuku Passage *218* channel of the Pacific Ocean between the Lau Group and Taveuni, NE Fiji
Nanumaga *553 prev.* Nanumanga. Coral atoll of NW Tuvalu
Nanumea *553* coral atoll of NW Tuvalu
Nan Wan *525* bay of the South China Sea, S Taiwan
Nanyang *163* Henan, C China
Nanyuki *316* C Kenya
Naogaon *93* NW Bangladesh
Napier *401* SE North Island, New Zealand
Naples *see* Napoli
Napo *200, 431* river of Ecuador and Peru
Napoli *295 Eng.* Naples, *Ger.* Neapel. S Italy
Nāra *421* irrigation canal of S Pakistan

Nara *304* Honshū, C Japan
Narathiwat *533* S Thailand
Narayani *395* river of C Nepal
Narbada *see* Narmada
Narbonne *225* S France
Nare's Strait *622* strait of NW Greenland
Narew *439* river of E Poland
Narganá *424* NE Panama
Narikrik *364* *prev.* Knox Atoll. Atoll of SE Marshall Islands
Narmada *270* *var.* Narbada. River of C India
Narok *316* SW Kenya
Närpes *221* *Swe.* Närpiö. SW Finland
Narrows, The *462* channel connecting the Atlantic Ocean and Caribbean Sea, between Nevis and St Kitts
Narsingdi *93* C Bangladesh
Nartës, Gjol i *see* Nartës, Liqeni i
Nartës, Liqeni i *57* *var.* Gjol i Nartës. Lake of SW Albania
Naruto *304* Shikoku, SW Japan
Narva *212* *prev.* Narova. River of Estonia and Russia
Narva *212* NE Estonia
Narva Bay *212* *Est.* Narva Laht, *Rus.* Narviskiy Zaliv. Bay of the Gulf of Finland
Narva Reservoir *212* *Est.* Narva Veehoidla. Reservoir of Estonia and Russia
Narvik *414* NE Norway
Nar'yan-Mar *452* *prev.* Dzerzhinskiy, *prev.* Beloshchel'ye. NW Russia
Naryn *325* E Kyrgyzstan
Naryn *325* river of Kyrgyzstan and Uzbekistan
Nasau *218* Koro, C Fiji
Nāshik *270* *prev.* Nāsik. W India
Nasho, Lac *460* lake of E Rwanda
Nashville *569* Tennessee, SE USA
Näsijärvi *221* lake of SW Finland
Nasirābād *see* Mymensingh
Nâşir, Buḩeiret *202* *var.* Buḩayrat Nāşir, *Eng.* Lake Nasser. Lake of Egypt and Sudan
Nasiriya *see* An Nāşirīyah
Nás Na Ríogh *see* Naas
Nassau *88* ❖ of Bahamas, New Providence, Bahamas
Nassau *620* island of Northern Cook Islands, N Cook Islands
Nasser, Lake *see* Nâsir, Buheiret
Nata *118* NE Botswana
Natal *121* E Brazil
Nathula *see* Nacula
Natitingou *108* NW Benin
Natl *310* *var.* Nitil. NW Jordan
Nator *93* W Bangladesh
Natron, Lake *530* lake of Kenya and Tanzania
Natuna Besar, Pulau *276* island of Kepulauan Natuna, W Indonesia
Natuna, Kepulauan *276* island group to the NW of Borneo, W Indonesia
Nau *528* NW Tajikistan
Naujoji Akmenė *344* NW Lithuania
Nā'ūr *310* NW Jordan
Nauru *392-393* officially Republic of Nauru, *prev.* Pleasant Island. Island country of the Pacific Ocean divided into 14 admin. units (districts)
Naushahra *see* Nowshera
Nausori *218* Viti Levu, Fiji
Navabad *528* W Tajikistan
Navaga *218* W Koro, W Fiji
Navahrudak *104* *Rus.* Novogrudok, *Pol.* Nowogródek. W Belorussia
Navangar *see* Jāmnagar
Navapolatsk *104* *Rus.* Novopolotsk. N Belorussia
Navarra *501* autonomous community of N Spain
Naviti *218* island of the Yasawa Group, NW Fiji
Navoalevu *218* NE Vanua Levu, N Fiji
Navoi *580* *Uzb.* Nawoly. S Uzbekistan
Navua *218* Viti Levu, W Fiji
Nawābganj *93* NW Bangladesh
Nawābshāh *421* S Pakistan
Nawmah, Ra's *91* *var.* Ra's Noma. Cape of SW Bahrain
Nawoly *see* Navoi
Naxçıvan *86* *Rus.* Nakhichevan', *var.* Nahičevan'. SW Azerbaijan
Náxos *245* island of SE Greece
Nayau *218* island of the Lau Group, E Fiji
Nazareth *see* Naẕerat
Nazca *431* S Peru
Naze *304* Nansei-shotō, SW Japan
Naẕerat *291* *Eng.* Nazareth. N Israel
Naẕerat 'Illit *291* N Israel
Nazilli *546* SW Turkey
Nazrēt *215* *var.* Adama, Hadama. C Ethiopia
Nazwá *418* N Oman
Nchelenge *611* N Zambia
Ncheu *see* Ntcheu
Nchisi *see* Ntchisi
Ncue *208* N Río Muni, Equatorial Guinea
Ndaghamcha, Sebkra de *see* Te-n-Dghâmcha, Sebkhet
N'Dalatando *64* *Port.* Vila Salazar. NW Angola
Ndali *108* C Benin
Ndélé *154* N Central African Republic
Ndendé *230* S Gabon
Ndeni *see* Nendö
Ndindi *230* S Gabon
N'Djamena *156* *var.* Njamena, *prev.* Fort-Lamy. ❖ of Chad, W Chad
Ndjolé *230* C Gabon
Ndoki *176* river of N Congo
Ndola *611* C Zambia
Ndora *138* NW Burundi
Ndrhamcha, Sebkha de *see* Te-n-Dghâmcha, Sebkhet
Nduindui *488* S Guadalcanal, Solomon Is
Nduke *see* Kolombangara
Neagh, Lough *563* lake of Northern Ireland, UK
Neapel *see* Napoli
Nébeck *see* An Nabk
Nebitdag *551* W Turkmenistan
Nebk *see* An Nabk
Neblina, Pico da *120* mountain of NW Brazil
Nebraska *569* state of C USA
Neckar *236* river of SW Germany
Necochea *71* E Argentina
Nederland *see* Netherlands
Neder-Rijn *397* *Eng.* Lower Rhine. River of C Netherlands
Nefasit *210* C Eritrea
Nefta *543* *var.* Naftah. W Tunisia
Neftezavodsk *see* Seydi
Negara Brunei Darussalam *see* Brunei
Negēlē *215* *var.* Negelli, *It.* Neghelli. S Ethiopia
Negev *see* HaNegev
Neghelli *see* Negēlē
Negomane *387* *var.* Negomano. N Mozambique
Negombo *504* SW Sri Lanka
Negotino *349* C FYR Macedonia
Negril *303* W Jamaica
Negro, Rio *120, 171* river of N South America
Negro, Río *see* Sico
Negro, Río *577* river of Brazil and Uruguay
Negro, Río *see* Chixoy
Negros *435* island of C Philippines
Neiafu *538* Uta Vava'u, Vava'u Group, Tonga
Neiba *198* SW Dominican Republic
Neiges, Piton des *628* mountain of C Réunion
Neily *178* SE Costa Rica
Nei Mongol Zizhiqu *163* *Eng.* Inner Mongolian Autonomous Region, *prev.* Nei Monggol Zizhiqu. Autonomous region of N China
Neiva *171* W Colombia
Nek'emtē *215* *var.* Nakamti, Lakamti, Lekemti. W Ethiopia
Nelson *146* river of C Canada
Nelson *401* N South Island, New Zealand
Nelson Island *619* island of N British Indian Ocean Territory
Nelspruit *493* Eastern Transvaal, NE South Africa
Néma *366* SE Mauritania
Neman *104, 344* *Bel.* Nyoman, *Lith.* Nemunas, *Ger.* Memel, *Pol.* Niemen. River of NE Europe
Německý Brod *see* Havlíčkův Brod
Nemunas *see* Neman
Nenagh *288* S Ireland
Nendeln *342* C Liechtenstein
Nendö *488* *var.* Ndeni, Santa Cruz Is, Solomon Islands
Nepal *394-395* officially Kingdom of Nepal. Country of Asia divided into 5 admin. units (regions)
Nepalganj *395* W Nepal
Nepean Island *626* island of C Norfolk Island
Neretva *116* river of S Bosnia & Herzegovina
Neris *344* *Bel.* Viliya, *Pol.* Wilja. River of Belorussia and Lithuania
Neskaupstadhur *268* E Iceland
Ness, Loch *563* lake of N Scotland, UK
Néstos *128, 245* *Turk.* Kara Su, *Bul.* Mesta. River of Bulgaria and Greece
Netanya *291* C Israel
Netherlands *396-399* officially Kingdom of the Netherlands, *var.* Holland, *Dut.* Nederland. Country of W Europe divided into 12 admin. units (provinces)
Netherlands Antilles *589, 626* *prev.* Dutch West Indies. Autonomous part of the Netherlands, Caribbean Sea.
Netherlands East Indies *see* Indonesia
Netrakona *93* N Bangladesh
Netze *see* Noteć
Neubrandenburg *237* NE Germany
Neuchâtel *516* *Ger.* Neuenburg. W Switzerland
Neuchâtel, Lac de *516* *Ger.* Neuenburger See. Lake of W Switzerland
Neuenburger See *see* Neuchâtel, Lac de
Neugradiska *see* Nova Gradiška
Neuhäusl *see* Nové Zámky
Neumarkt *see* Târgu Mures
Neumarktl *see* Tržič
Neumünster *237* N Germany
Neunkirchen *82* E Austria
Neuquén *71* SE Argentina
Neusatz *see* Novi Sad
Neusiedler See *82, 264* *Hung.* Fertő-tó. Lake of Austria and Hungary
Neusohl *see* Banská Bystrica
Neustadt *see* Baia Mare
Neustadtl *see* Novo Mesto
Neutra *see* Nitra
Neu-Ulm *237* S Germany
Nevada *568* state of W USA
Nevers *225* C France
Nevis *462* island of the Lesser Antilles which, with St Kitts, forms the independent state of St Kitts & Nevis
Nevis Peak *462* mountain peak of C Nevis, St Kitts & Nevis
Nevşehir *547* C Turkey
Newala *530* SE Tanzania
New Amsterdam *256* E Guyana
New Britain *426* island of E Papua New Guinea
New Brunswick *147* province of SE Canada
New Bussa *408* W Nigeria
New Caledonia *626* French overseas territory of the Pacific Ocean ❖ Nouméa
Newcastle *77* E Australia
Newcastle *462* N Nevis, St Kitts & Nevis
Newcastle upon Tyne *563* NE England, UK
New Delhi *270* ❖ of India, N India
Newfield *68* SE Antigua, Antigua & Barbuda
Newfoundland *147* *Fr.* Terre-Neuve. Island of S E Canada
Newfoundland *147* province of E Canada
New Georgia *488* island of the New Georgia Is, W Solomon Is
New Georgia Islands *488* island group of W Solomon Is
New Guinea *277, 426* *Dut.* Nieuw Guinea, *Ind.* Irian. Large island of W Pacific Ocean, divided administratively into the Indonesian state of Irian Jaya and the independent country of Papua New Guinea
New Halfa *see* Halfa el Gadida
New Hampshire *569* state of NE USA
New Haven *569* Connecticut, NE USA
New Hebrides *see* Vanuatu
New Ireland *426* island of NE Papua New Guinea
New Jersey *569* state of E USA
Newman *76* W Australia
New Mexico *568-569* state of SW USA
New Mīrpur *421* *prev.* Mīrpur. NE Pakistan
New Orleans *569* Louisiana, SC USA
New Plymouth *401* SW North Island, New Zealand
Newport *563* S Wales, UK
Newport News *569* Virginia, E USA
New Providence *88* island of C Bahamas
New River *256* river of SE Guyana
New River *102* river of N Belize
New Ross *288* SE Ireland
Newry *563* Northern Ireland, UK
New Sandy Bay Village *466* N St Vincent, St Vincent & the Grenadines
New Siberian Islands *see* Novosibirskiye Ostrova
New South Wales *77* state of SE Australia
Newton Ground *462* NW St Kitts, St Kitts & Nevis
Newtownabbey *563* Northern Ireland, UK
New Winthorpes *68* N Antigua, Antigua & Barbuda
New York *569* state of NE USA
New York *569, 573* New York, NE USA
New Zealand *400-403* country of the Pacific Ocean, divided into 14 admin. units (regions)
Nezhyn *556* N Ukraine
Ngabé *176* SE Congo
Ngadda *409* river of NE Nigeria
Ngala *409* NE Nigeria
Ngangerabeli Plain *316* plain of SE Kenya
Ngaoundéré *144* *var.* N'Gaoundéré, N'Gaundere. N Cameroon
Ngara *530* NW Tanzania
Ngarama *460* N Rwanda
Ngardmau *627* C Palau
Ngaruangl *627* island of N Palau
Ngatik *375* atoll of E Micronesia
Ngau *see* Gau
N'Gaundere *see* Ngaoundéré

Nggamea *see* Qamea
Nggatokae *488* island of the New Georgia Islands, W Solomon Islands
Nggwavuma *510 var.* Ingwavuma. River of South Africa and Swaziland
N'Giva *64 var.* Ondjiva *Port.* Vila Pereira de Eça. S Angola
Ngo *176* SE Congo
Ngogolo *510* C Swaziland
Ngoko *144, 176* river of Cameroon and Congo
Ngorongoro Crater *530* crater and conservation area of N Tanzania
Ngororero *460* W Rwanda
Ngounié *230* river of Congo and Gabon
Ngouoni *230* E Gabon
Ngourti *407* E Niger
Ngozi *138* N Burundi
N'Guigmi *407* SE Niger
Ngulu *375* atoll of W Micronesia
Ngum *327* river of C Laos
Nguna *585* island of C Vanuatu
Ngundu *612* S Zimbabwe
N'Gunza *see* Sumbe
Nguru *408* NE Nigeria
Ngwempisi *510* river of South Africa and Swaziland
Ngweze *see* Katima Mulilo
Nhacra *254* W Guinea-Bissau
Nhamundá *120 var.* Yamundá, Jamundá. River of NW Brazil
Nha Trang *593* SE Vietnam
Nhlangano *510 prev.* Goedgegun. SW Swaziland
Niagara Falls *147* SE Canada
Niagassola *253 var.* Nyagassola. NE Guinea
Niamey *407* ❖ of Niger, SW Niger
Niamtougou *537* N Togo
Niandan *253* river of E Guinea
Niangay, Lac *360* lake of E Mali
Nianija Bolon *233* river of Gambia and Senegal
Niantanina *253* E Guinea
Niari *176* river of S Congo
Nias, Pulau *276* island to the W of Sumatra, W Indonesia
Niassa, Lago *see* Nyasa, Lake
Nicaragua *404-405* officially Republic of Nicaragua. Country of Central America divided into 16 admin. units (departments)
Nicaragua, Lago de *404 var.* Gran Lago. Lake of S Nicaragua
Nicastro *295* S Italy
Nice *225 It.* Nizza. SE France
Nicholls Town *88* Andros I, Bahamas
Nickerie *508* river of NW Suriname
Nicobar Islands *270* island group to the SE of India
Nicosia *187 var.* Lefkosia, *Turk.* Lefkoşa. ❖ of Cyprus, C Cyprus
Nicoya *178* W Costa Rica
Nicoya, Península de *178* peninsula of W Costa Rica
Nictheroy *see* Niterói
Nidaros *see* Trondheim
Niedere Tauern *82* mountain range of C Austria
Niefang *208 var.* Sevilla de Niefang. NW Río Muni, Equatorial Guinea
Niemen *see* Neman
Niéri Ko *476* river of SE Senegal
Nieuw Amsterdam *508* N Suriname
Nieuwegein *397* C Netherlands
Nieuwkoop *397* W Netherlands
Nieuw Nickerie *508* NW Suriname
Niğde *547* C Turkey
Niger *108, 253, 360, 407, 408,* river of W Africa
Niger *406-407* officially Republic of Niger. Country of West Africa divided into 7 admin. units (departments)
Nigeria *408-411* officially Federal Republic of Nigeria. Country of West Africa divided into 20 admin. units (19 states and 1 federal capital Territory)
Niger, Mouths of the *408* delta of the river Niger, on the S coast of Nigeria
Niigata *304* Honshū, N Japan
Niihama *304* Shikoku, SW Japan
Niihau *568* island of Hawaii, USA, C Pacific
Niimi *304* Honshū, W Japan
Nijmegen *397 Ger.* Nimwegen. SE Netherlands
Nikki *108* E Benin
Nikolainkaupunki *see* Vaasa
Nikolayev *see* Mykolayiv
Nikol'skiy *312* C Kazakhstan
Nikol'sk-Ussuriyskiy *see* Ussuriysk
Nikopol' *556* SE Ukraine
Nikšić *602* W Montenegro, Yugoslavia
Nikumaroro *320 var.* Gardner I. Island of the Phoenix Is, C Kiribati
Nikunau *320* island of the Gilbert Is, W Kiribati
Nile *202, 506 Ar.* Nahr an Nīl. River of N Africa
Nile Delta *202* delta of N Egypt
Nīl, Nahr an *see* Nile
Nilphāmāri *93* NW Bangladesh
Nimba, Monts *253 var.* Nimba Mountains. Mountain range of W Africa
Nimba, Mount *300, 336* mountain of W Africa
Nimba Mountains *see* Nimba, Monts
Nîmes *225* SE France
Nimwegen *see* Nijmegen
Ningbo *163 var.* Ning-po, *prev.* Ninghsien. Zhejiang, E China
Ning-hsia *see* Ningxia
Ninghsien *see* Ningbo
Ning-po *see* Ningbo
Ningxia *163 Chin.* Ningxia Huizu Zizhiqu, *Eng.* Ningsia Hui Autonomous Region, *var.* Ning-hsia. Autonomous region of N China
Ninotsminda *234 prev.* Bogdanovka. S Georgia
Ninove *99* C Belgium
Niokolo Koba *476* river of SE Senegal
Niono *360* C Mali
Nioro *360 var.* Nioro du Sahel. W Mali
Nioro du Rip *476* SW Senegal
Niort *225* W France
Nippon-kai *see* Japan, Sea of
Niquero *182* S Cuba
Nirin *see* Erh-lin
Niš *602 Eng.* Nish. E Serbia, Yugoslavia
Nişāb *599 var.* Anşāb. SW Yemen
Nisporeni *376 Rus.* Nisporeny. W Moldova
Nissan Islands *see* Green Islands
Nissum Bredning *190* inlet of North Sea on the NW coast of Denmark
Nistru *see* Dniester
Niterói *121 prev.* Nictheroy. SE Brazil
Nitil *see* Natl
Nitra *485 Ger.* Neutra, *Hung.* Nyitra. River of SW Slovakia
Nitra *485 Ger.* Neutra, *Hung.* Nyitra. SW Slovakia
Niuafo'ou *538 var.* Niuafoo. Island of NW Tonga
Niuatoputapu *538 var.* Niuatobutabu, *prev.* Keppel Island. Island of N Tonga
Niuatui *553* islet of Nukufetau, Tuvalu
Niue *626* territory in free association with New Zealand, Pacific Ocean
Niulakita *553 var.* Nurakita. Coral atoll of S Tuvalu
Niutao *553* coral atoll of NW Tuvalu
Nizāmābād *270* C India
Nizhnevartovsk *452* C Russia
Nizhniy Novgorod *452 prev.* Gor'kiy. W Russia
Nizhniy Pyandzh *528 var.* Nižnij Pjandž. SW Tajikistan
Nizhnyaya Tunguska *453 Eng.* Lower Tunguska. C Russia
Nizza *see* Nice
Njaba *see* N'ja Kunda
Njaiama *480* E Sierra Leone
N'ja Kunda *233 var.* Njaba. NW Gambia
Njamena *see* N'Djamena
Njardhvík *268* SW Iceland
Njazidja *see* Grande Comore
Njoeng Jacobkondre *508* C Suriname
Njombe *530* S Tanzania
Njoro *316* W Kenya
Nkanini *510* W Swaziland
Nkata Bay *see* Nkhata Bay
Nkayi *176 var.* N'Kayi, *prev.* Jacob. S Congo
Nkhata Bay *353 var.* Nkata Bay. N Malawi
Nkhotakota *353 var.* Kota Kota, Nkota Kota. C Malawi
Nkonfap *408* S Nigeria
Nkongsamba *144 var.* N'Kongsamba. W Cameroon
Nkumekie *208* C Río Muni, Equatorial Guinea
Nkundla *510* W Swaziland
Nkusi *554* river of W Uganda
Nmai Hka *135 var.* Me Hka. River of N Burma forming a headstream of the Irrawaddy river
Noākhāli *93 prev.* Sudharam. S Bangladesh
Noboribetsu *304* Hokkaidō, N Japan
Nogal, Uadi *see* Nugaal
Noire, Rivière *368* river of SW Mauritius
Noire, Rivière *see* Black River
Noirmoutier, Île de *224* island of W France
Nokia *221* SW Finland
Nokou *156* W Chad
Nokoué, Lac *108* lake of S Benin
Nola *154* SW Central African Republic
Nólsoy *620* island of E Faeroe Islands
Noma, Ra's *see* Nawmah, Ra's
Nomuka *538* island of the Nomuka Group, Tonga
Nomuka Group *538* island group of W Tonga
Nomwin *375* atoll of C Micronesia
Nông Hèt *327* E Laos
Nong Khai *533* NE Thailand
Nonouti *320* island of the Gilbert Is, W Kiribati
Nonsan *496 Jap.* Ronzan. W South Korea
Nonsuch Island *619* island of E Bermuda
Noord *618* N Aruba
Noord-Beveland *397* island of SW Netherlands
Noordoewer *391* S Namibia
Noordpunt *626* headland of Curaçao, W Netherlands Antilles
Noordzee *see* North Sea
Nor Achin *see* Nor Hachn
Nor Ačin *see* Nor Hachn
Nord *622* N Greenland
Nordaustlandet *629* island of NE Svalbard
Norddeutsches Tiefland *236-237 Eng.* North German Plain. Plain of N Germany
Nordfriesische Inseln *236 Eng.* North Frisian Islands. Island group of NW Germany
Nordhausen *237* C Germany
Nordishavet *see* Arctic Ocean
Nord, Massif du *258* mountainous region of Haiti
Nord, Mer du *see* North Sea
Nord-Pas de Calais *228* administrative region of N France
Nordsee *see* North Sea
Nordsjøen *see* North Sea
Nordsøen *see* North Sea
Nordtiroler Kalkalpen *82* mountain range of W Austria
Nore *288 Ir.* An Fheoir. River of SE Ireland
Norfolk *569* Virginia, E USA
Norfolk Island *626* Australian external territory of the South Pacific Ocean. ❖ Kingston
Norge *see* Norway
Nor Hachn *74 var.* Nor Hachyn, *Rus.* Nor Achin, *var.* Nor Ačcin. C Armenia
Nor Hachyn *see* Nor Hachn
Noril'sk *453* N Russia
Norman *569* Oklahoma, SC USA
Normanby Island *426* island of SE Papua New Guinea
Normandie *225 Eng.* Normandy. Cultural region of N France
Normandie, Collines de *225* hilly region of NW France
Norman Island *619* island of S British Virgin Islands
Norrköping *513* S Sweden
Norseman *76* SW Australia
Norskehavet *see* Norwegian Sea
Norsup *585* Malekula, Vanuatu
North Albanian Alps *57, 602 SCr.* Prokletije, *Alb.* Bjeshkët e Nemuna. Mountain range of Albania and Yugoslavia
Northam *76* SW Australia
Northampton *563* C England, UK
North Andaman *135, 270* island of the Andaman Is, E India
North Battleford *146* SW Canada
North Bay *147* SE Canada
North Caicos *629* island of NW Turks and Caicos Islands
North Carolina *569* state of SE USA
North Channel *563* strait of Atlantic Ocean, between Northern Ireland and Scotland, UK
North Comino Channel *see* Ghawdex, Il-Fliegu ta'
North Dakota *569* state of NC USA
North Devon Island *see* Devon Island
Northern Territory *77* territory of N Australia
North East China *167*
North East Point *620* headland on the NE coast of Christmas Island
Northeast Providence Channel *88* channel between Eleuthera I and Great Abaco I, Bahamas
Northern Cape *493* province of W South Africa
Northern Cook Islands *620* island group of N Cook Islands
Northern Cyprus, Republic of *see* Cyprus
Northern Dvina *see* Severnaya Dvina
Northern Forest Reserve *196* nature reserve of N Dominica
Northern Ireland *568 var.* the Six Counties. Political division of UK
Northern Karoo *493 var.* High Veld, *Afr.* Hoë Karoo. Plateau region of W South Africa
Northern Mariana Islands *626* Commonwealth territory of the USA, Pacific Ocean. ❖ Garapan.
Northern Rhodesia *see* Zambia
Northern Sporades *see* Vor eioi Sporades
Northern Transvaal *493* province of NE South Africa
North Frisian Islands *see* Nordfriesische Inseln
North German Plain *see* Norddeutsches Tiefland
North Huvadhu Atoll *358 var.* Gaafu Alifu Atoll. Atoll of S Maldives
North Island *401* northernmost of the two main islands that comprise New Zealand
North Keeling Island *620* island of NW Cocos Islands

O

Ogražden *349* mountain range of Bulgaria and FYR Macedonia
Ogre *330 Ger.* Oger. C Latvia
Ogulin *181* N Croatia
Ohau, Lake *401* W South Island, New Zealand
Ohio *569* river of NC USA
Ohio *569* state of NE USA
Ohobela *334* N Lesotho
'Ohonua *538* 'Eua, Tongatapu Group, Tonga
Ohře *188 Ger.* Eger. River of Czech Republic and Germany
Ohrid *349 var.* Ochrida. SW FYR Macedonia
Ohrid, Lake *57, 349 var.* Lake Ochrida, *Alb.* Liqeni i Ohrit, *Maced.* Ohridsko Ezero. Lake of Albania and Macedonia
Oiapoque *121, 621 var.* Oyapok, Oyapock. River of Brazil and French Guiana
Oil Islands *see* Chagos Archipelago
Oise *225* river of N France
Oistins *97* S Barbados
Ōita *304* Kyūshū, SW Japan
Ojos del Salado, Nevado *159* mountain of N Chile
Okahandja *391* C Namibia
Okakarara *391* N Namibia
Ókanizsa *see* Kanjiža
Okāra *421* E Pakistan
Okarem *551 Turkm.* Ekerem. W Turkmenistan
Okavango *see* Cubango
Okavango Delta *118* large wetland area of N Botswana
Okaya *304* Honshū, C Japan
Okayama *304* Honshū, W Japan
Okazaki *304* Honshū, C Japan
Okeechobee, Lake *569* lake of Florida, SE USA
Okhotsk, Sea of *453 Rus.* Okhotskoye More. Sea of Pacific Ocean, bordering E Russia
Oki *304* island to the N of Honshū, W Japan
Okinawa-shotō *304* island group of Nansei-shotō, SW Japan
Oklahoma *569* state of SC USA
Oklahoma City *569* Oklahoma, SC USA
Okondja *230* E Gabon
Okovanggo *see* Cubango
Okoyo *176* W Congo
Okpara *108* river of Benin and Nigeria
Oktemberyan *see* Hoktemberyan
Oktyabr'skoy Revolyutsii, Ostrov *453 Eng.* October Revolution Island. Island of Severnaya Zemlya, N Russia
Okushiri-tō *304* island to the W of Hokkaidō, N Japan
Ólafsfjördhur *268* N Iceland
Ólafsvík *268* W Iceland
Olaine *330* C Latvia
Olanchito *260* C Honduras
Öland *513* island of S Sweden
Olavarría *71* E Argentina
Olbia *294* Sardegna, W Italy
Oldenburg *236* NW Germany
Old Fort Point *625* headland on the S coast of Montserrat
Old Harbour *303* S Jamaica
Old Road *68* SW Antigua, Antigua & Barbuda
Old Road Town *462* W St Kitts, St Kitts & Nevis
Olëkminsk *453* C Russia
Oleksandriya *556 Rus.* Aleksandriya. C Ukraine
Olenëk *453 var.* Olenyok. N Russia
Oléron, Île d' *224* island of W France
Ölgiy *380* W Mongolia
Olhão *442* S Portugal
Olimarao *375* atoll of C Micronesia
Olimar Grande *577 var.* Olimar. River of E Uruguay
Ólimbos *see* Ólympos
Olinda *121* E Brazil
Olita *see* Alytus
Olmaliq *see* Almalyk
Olmütz *see* Olomouc
Olocuilta *207* SW El Salvador
Oloitokitok *316 var.* Laitokitok. S Kenya
Olomouc *188 Ger.* Olmütz. SE Czech Republic
Olongapo *435* Luzon, N Philippines
Olosega *618* island of Manua Islands, E American Samoa
Olsnitz *see* Murska Sobota
Olsztyn *439 Ger.* Allenstein. N Poland
Olt *448 Ger.* Alt. River of S Romania
Olten *516* NW Switzerland
O-luan Pi *525 var.* Cape Olwanpi. Cape on the S coast of Taiwan
O-luan-pi *525* S Taiwan
Olympia *568* Washington, NW USA
Ólympos *245 Eng.* Mount Olympus, *prev.* Ólimbos. Mountain of N Greece
Olympus, Mount *187 var.* Troodos, Olympos. Mountain of C Cyprus
Olympus, Mount *see* Ólympos
Omagh *563* Northern Ireland, UK
Omaha *569* Nebraska, C USA
Oman *418-419* officially Sultanate of Oman, *prev.* Muscat & Oman. Country of SW Asia divided into 3 admin. units (governorates)
Oman, Gulf of *281, 418, 560 Ar.* Khalīj 'Umān. Gulf of the Arabian Sea
Omaruru *391* C Namibia
Omba *see* Aoba
Omboué *230* W Gabon
Omdurman *506 var.* Umm Durmān. C Sudan
Ometepe, Isla de *404* island on Lago de Nicaragua, S Nicaragua
Om Hajer *210* SW Eritrea
Ōmiya *304* Honshū, SE Japan
Omo Wenz *215* river of SW Ethiopia
Omsk *452* C Russia
Ōmuta *304* Kyūshū, SW Japan
Ondangwa *391 var.* Ondangua. N Namibia
Ondava *485* river of NE Slovakia
Ondjiva *see* N'Giva
Ondo *408* SW Nigeria
Öndörhaan *380* E Mongolia
One and Half Degree Channel *358* channel of the Indian Ocean, S Maldives
Oneata *218* island of the Lau Group, E Fiji
Onega, Lake *see* Onezhskoye Ozero
Onezhskoye Ozero *452 Eng.* Lake Onega. Lake of NW Russia
Onga *230* E Gabon
Ongjin *413* SW North Korea
Oni *234* N Georgia
Onilahy *350* river of SW Madagascar
Onitsha *408* S Nigeria
Ono *218* island to the S of Viti Levu, SW Fiji
Ono-i-lau *218* island to the S of the Lau Group, SW Fiji
Onomichi *304* Honshū, W Japan
Ononte *see* Orantes
Onotoa *320* island of the Gilbert Is, W Kiribati
Onslow *76* W Australia
Onsŏng *413* NE North Korea
Ontario *146-147* province of S Canada
Ontario, Lake *147, 569* lake of Canada and USA
Ontong Java Atoll *488 prev.* Lord Howe Island. Atoll of N Solomon Is
Onverwacht *508* N Suriname
Ooma *320* Banaba, W Kiribati
Oos-Londen *see* East London
Oostende *99 Fr.* Ostende, *Eng.* Ostend. NW Belgium
Oosterhout *397* SW Netherlands
Oosterschelde *397 Eng.* Eastern Scheldt. Inlet of the North Sea, on the coast of SW Netherlands
Opava *188 Ger.* Troppau. E Czech Republic
Opole *439 Ger.* Oppeln. SW Poland
Oporto *see* Porto
Oppdal *414* S Norway
Oppeln *see* Opole
Opuwo *391* NW Namibia
Oqtosh *see* Aktash
Oradea *448 prev.* Oradea Mare, *Ger.* Grosswardein, *Hung.* Nagyvárad. NW Romania
Oral *see* Ural'sk
Oran *59 var.* Ouahran, Wahran. NW Algeria
Orange *77* SE Australia
Orange Free State *493* province of C South Africa
Orange Mouth *see* Oranjemund
Orangemund *see* Oranjemund
Orange River *334, 391, 493 Afr.* Oranjerivier. River of southern Africa
Orange Walk *102* N Belize
Orango, Ilha de *254* island of Arquipélago dos Bijagós, SW Guinea-Bissau
Orangozinho, Ilha de *254* island of SW Guinea-Bissau
Oranjemund *391 var.* Orangemund, *Eng.* Orange Mouth. S Namibia
Oranjestad *626* St Eustatius, N Netherlands Antilles
Oranjestad *618* ❖ of Aruba, W Aruba
Orantes *332, 521 var.* Ononte, Orontes, *Ar.* Nahr al 'Aṣī, *var.* Nahr al 'Āsī Oronte, Nahr el Aassi. River of SW Asia
Orany *see* Varėna
Orapa *118* C Botswana
Orcadas *66* Argentinian research station of Greater Antarctica, Antarctica
Orchid Island *see* Lan Yü
Orchila, Isla le *589* island of N Venezuela
Ordino *62* NW Andorra
Ordu *547* N Turkey
Ordubad *86* SW Azerbaijan
Ordzhonikidze *see* Yenakiyeve
Ordzhonikidze *see* Vladikavkaz
Ordzhonikidzeabad *see* Kofarnikhon
Orealla *256* E Guyana
Örebro *513* S Sweden
Oregon *568* state of NW USA
Orem *568* Utah, SW USA
Orenburg *452 prev.* Chkalov. W Russia
Orense *see* Ourense
Orestiáda *245 prev.* Orestiás. NE Greece
Öresund *see* Sound, The
Øresund *see* Sound, The
Oreti *401* river of S South Island, New Zealand
Orgeyev *see* Orhei
Orhei *376 var.* Orheiu, *Rus.* Orgeyev. N Moldova
Orhon Gol *380* river of N Mongolia
Oriental, Cordillera *112* range of the Andes in C Bolivia
Oriental, Cordillera *171* range of the Andes in C Colombia
Oriental, Cordillera *431* range of the Andes of C Peru
Orikum *57 var.* Oriku. SW Albania
Orinoco *171, 589* river of Colombia and Venezuela
Oristano *294* Sardegna, W Italy
Orizaba, Pico de *see* Citlaltépetl
Orkhanie *see* Botevgrad
Orkney *563* islands of NE UK
Orlau *see* Orlová
Orléanais *225* cultural region of N France
Orléans *225* N France
Orléansville *see* Chlef
Orlová *188 Ger.* Orlau, *Pol.* Orlowa. SE Czech Republic
Ormoc *435 var.* MacArthur. Leyte, E Philippines
Ormsö *see* Vormsi
Ormuz, Strait of *see* Hormuz, Strait of
Örnsköldsvik *513* NE Sweden
Oro *413* E North Korea
Orodara *132* SW Burkina
Orol Dengizi *see* Aral Sea
Oroluk *375* atoll of C Micronesia
Oron *408* S Nigeria
Orona *320 var.* Hull I. Island of the Phoenix Is, C Kiribati
Oronoque *256* river of SE Guyana
Orontes *see* Orantes
Orosháza *264* SE Hungary
Orotina *178* W Costa Rica
Orsha *104* NE Belorussia
Orsk *452* C Russia
Ørsta *414* SW Norway
Ortoire *540* river of S Trinidad, Trinidad & Tobago
Orto-Tokoy *325 var.* Orto Tokoj. N Kyrgyzstan
Orūmīyeh *281 prev.* Reẕā'īyeh, Urmia. NW Iran
Orūmīyeh, Daryācheh-ye *281 prev.* Daryācheh-ye Reẕā'īyeh, *Eng.* Lake Urmia. Lake of NW Iran
Oruro *112* W Bolivia
Orvieto *295* C Italy
Oryakhovo *128 var.* Orjahovo. NW Bulgaria
Oryokko *see* Yalu
Ōsaka *304, 309* Honshū, C Japan
Osa, Península de *178* S Costa Rica
Ösel *see* Saaremaa
Osh *324 var.* Oš. SW Kyrgyzstan
Oshakati *391* N Namibia
Oshawa *147* SE Canada
Oshikango *391* N Namibia
Oshogbo *408* W Nigeria
Osijek *181 Hung.* Eszék, *Ger.* Esseg. NE Croatia
Osipenko *see* Berdyans'k
Osipovichi *see* Asipovichy
Öskemen *see* Ust'-Kamenogorsk
Ösling *346* physical region of N Luxembourg
Oslo *414 prev.* Christiania. ❖ of Norway, S Norway
Oslofjorden *414* fjord of S Norway
Osmaniye *547* S Turkey
Osnabrück *236* NW Germany
Osogovski Planini *349 var.* Osogovske Planine. Mountain range of Bulgaria and FYR Macedonia
Oss *397* S Netherlands
Ossa, Serra de *442* mountain range of SE Portugal
Ostee *see* Baltic Sea
Ostend *see* Oostende
Ostende *see* Oostende
Österbotten *see* Pohjanmaa
Östermyra *see* Seinäjoki
Österreich *see* Austria
Östersund *513* C Sweden
Ostfriesische Inseln *236 Eng.* East Frisian Islands. Island group of NW Germany
Ostrava *188 Ger.* Mährisch-Ostrau, *prev.* Moravská Ostrava. E Czech Republic
Ostrobothnia *see* Pohjanmaa
Ostrov *188* NW Czech Republic
Ostrowiec Świętokrzyski *439* E Poland
Ostyako-Voguls'k *see* Khanty-Mansiysk
Ōsumi-shotō *304* island group of Nansei-shotō, SW Japan
Osumit *57 var.* Osum. River of SE Albania
Otago Peninsula *401* peninsula of SE South Island, New Zealand
Otaru *304* Hokkaidō, N Japan
Otavalo *200* N Ecuador
Otavi *391* N Namibia
Otepää *212 Ger.* Odenpäh. SE Estonia
Oti *108, 242, 537* river of W Africa
Otjinene *391* NE Namibia

P

Petite Butte *368* Rodrigues, Mauritius
Petite Côte *476* coastal region of W Senegal
Petite Dominique *248* island to the NE of Carriacou, Grenada
Petite Martinique *248* island to the NE of Carriacou, Grenada
Petite-Rivière-de-l'Artibonite *258* C Haiti
Petite-Rivière Noire, Piton de la *368* mountain range of SW Mauritius
Petite Savane *196* S Dominica
Petite Soufrière *196* E Dominica
Petite-Terre *625* island, E Mayotte
Petit-Goâve *258* S Haiti
Petitjean *see* Sidi Kacem
Petit Mustique *466* island of C St Vincent & the Grenadines
Petit Piton *465* mountain of SW St Lucia
Petit-Popo *see* Aného
Petit St. Vincent Island *248* island to the NE of Carriacou, Grenada
Petra *310* archaeological site of W Jordan
Petra Pervogo, Khrebet *528* *Eng.* Peter I Range. Mountain range of C Tajikistan
Petre Bay *401* bay of the South Pacific Ocean, on the coast of Chatham Island, New Zealand
Petrich *128 var.* Petrič. SW Bulgaria
Petrinja *181* N Croatia
Petroaleksandrovsk *see* Turtkul'
Petropavlovsk *312* N Kazakhstan
Petropavlovsk-Kamchatskiy *453* NE Russia
Petrópolis *121* SE Brazil
Petrosani *448* W Romania
Petrovgrad *see* Zrenjanin
Petrovsk-Port *see* Makhachkala
Petrozavodsk *452 Fin.* Petroskoi. NW Russia
Pettau *see* Ptuj
Pevek *453* NE Russia
Peyia *187 var.* Pegeia. SW Cyprus
Pezinok *485 Ger.* Bösing, *Hung.* Bazin. SW Slovakia
Pforzheim *236* SW Germany
Phalaborwa *493* Northern Transvaal, NE South Africa
Phangan, Ko *533* island of S Thailand
Phan Rang-Thap Cham *593* SE Vietnam
Phan Thiêt *593* S Vietnam
Phet Buri *see* Phetchaburi
Phetchaburi *533 var.* Phet Buri. C Thailand
Philadelphia *569* Pennsylvania, NE USA
Philip Island *626* island of S Norfolk Island
Philippeville *see* Skikda
Philippines *434-437* officially Republic of the Philippines. Country of SE Asia divided into 14 admin. units (regions).
Philippine Sea *375, 435* sea of the Pacific Ocean to the E of the Philippines
Philipsburg *626* St Martin, N Netherlands Antilles
Phillips *462* NE St Kitts, St Kitts & Nevis
Phitsanulok *533 var.* Muang Phitsanulok. N Thailand
Phlórina *see* Flórina
Phnom Penh *141 Cam.* Phnum Pénh. ❖ of Cambodia, S Cambodia
Phnum Aôral *141 prev.* Phnom Aural. Mountain of W Cambodia
Phoenix *568* Arizona, SW USA
Phoenix *368* C Mauritius
Phoenix Island *see* Rawaki
Phoenix Islands *320* island group of C Kiribati
Phôngsali *327 var.* Phong Saly. N Laos
Phong Saly *see* Phôngsali
Phou Bia *327 var.* Pou Bia. Mountain of C Laos
Phrae *533 var.* Muang Phrae. N Thailand
Phra Nakhon Si Ayutthaya *see* Ayutthaya
Phu Cuong *see* Thu Dâu Môt
Phuket *533 Mal.* Ujung Salang. S Thailand
Phuket, Ko *533* island of S Thailand
Phumĭ Chhlong *141* S Cambodia
Phumĭ Chhuk *141* S Cambodia
Phumĭ Chŏâm *141* SW Cambodia
Phumĭ Kâmpóng Trâbék *141 prev.* Phum Kompong Trabek. C Cambodia
Phumĭ Koŭk Kdoŭch *141* NW Cambodia
Phumĭ Krêk *141* SE Cambodia
Phumĭ Labăng Siĕk *141* NE Cambodia
Phumĭ Mlu Prey *141* N Cambodia
Phumĭ Sâmraông *141 var.* Phumĭ Sâmroŭng, *prev.* Phum Samrong. NW Cambodia
Phumĭ Spoe Tbong *141* C Cambodia
Phumĭ Thmâ Pôk *141* NW Cambodia
Phumĭ Véal Rénh *141* SW Cambodia
Phuntsholing *110* SW Bhutan
Phu Quôc, Đao *593* island of SW Vietnam
Piacenza *294 Fr.* Paisance. N Italy
Piatra-Neamţ *448* NE Romania
Piave *295* river of N Italy
Piaye *465* S St Lucia
Pibor *215* river of Ethiopia and Sudan
Picardie *225 Eng.* Picardy. Cultural region of N France
Pichelin *196* S Dominica
Pico *442 var.* Ilha do Pico. Island of the Azores, Portugal
Picton, Isla *159* island of S Chile
Pidjani *174* SE Grande Comore, Comoros
Pidurutalagala *504* mountain of S Sri Lanka
Piedras *431* river of E Peru
Pielinen *221 var.* Pielisjärvi. Lake of E Finland
Pierre *569* South Dakota, NC USA
Piešťany *485 Ger.* Pistyan, *Hung.* Pöstyén. W Slovakia
Pietermaritzburg *493* Kwazulu Natal, E South Africa
Pietersaari *see* Jakobstad
Pietersburg *493* Northern Transvaal, NE South Africa
Piet Retief *493* Eastern Transvaal, E South Africa
Piggs Peak *510* NW Swaziland
Pigs, Bay of *182* bay of the Caribbean Sea, on southern coast of C Cuba
Pihkva Järv *see* Pskov, Lake
Pikelot *375* island of C Micronesia
Pikine *476* W Senegal
Pikounda *176* C Congo
Piła *439 Ger.* Schneidemühl. NW Poland
Pilar *428 var.* Villa del Pilar. S Paraguay
Pilas Group *435* island group of Sulu Archipelago, SW Philippines
Pilcomayo *71, 112, 428* river of C South America
Pilgrimkondre *508* NE Suriname
Pilis *264 var.* Philis. Mountain range of N Hungary
Pillories, The *466* islands of C St Vincent & the Grenadines
Pillsbury Sound *629* strait of the Caribbean Sea, C Virgin Islands
Pilsen *see* Plzeň
Pimpri *270* W India
Pinang *see* George Town
Pinang, Pulau *354 prev.* Prince of Wales Island. Island of NW Peninsular Malaysia
Pinar del Río *182* W Cuba
Píndos *245 prev.* Píndhos, *Eng.* Pindus Mountains, *var.* Píndhos Óros. Mountain range of C Greece
Pine Bluff *569* Arkansas, SC USA
Pineiós *245 prev.* Piniós. River of C Greece
Pines, Isle of *see* Juventud, Isla de la
Pinetown *493* Kwazulu Natal, E South Africa
Ping Chau *262* NE Hong Kong
P'ing-chen *525 Jap.* Heichin. N Taiwan
Pingelap *375* atoll of E Micronesia
P'ing-tung *525 Jap.* Heitō. SW Taiwan
Pinkiang *see* Harbin
Pinos, Isla de *see* Juventud, Isla de la
Pins, Île des *626 var.* Kunyé. Island of S New Caledonia
Pinsk *104 Pol.* Pińsk. SW Belorussia
Pinta, Isla *200* island of N Galapagos Is, Ecuador
Piracicaba *121* S Brazil
Pirada *254* NE Guinea-Bissau
Piran *486 It.* Pirano. SW Slovenia
Piriápolis *577* S Uruguay
Pirita *212* river of N Estonia
Pirna *237* E Germany
Pirojpur *93* SW Bangladesh
Pirot *602* SE Serbia, Yugoslavia
Pisa *294* N Italy
Pisco *431* SW Peru
Písek *188* SW Czech Republic
Pishpek *see* Bishkek
Pissila *132* C Burkina
Pistoia *294* N Italy
Pistyan *see* Piešťany
Pita *253* NW Guinea
Pitalito *171* SW Colombia
Pitcairn Island *627* island of S Pitcairn Islands
Pitcairn Islands *627* British dependent territory of the Pacific Ocean. ❖ Adamstown
Pitche *254* E Guinea-Bissau
Piteå *513* NE Sweden
Piteşti *448* S Romania
Pitseng *334* N Lesotho
Pitt Island *401* island of Chatham Islands, New Zealand
Pittsburgh *569* Pennsylvania, NE USA
Pitt Strait *401* strait of Pacific Ocean, between Chatham Island and Pitt Island, New Zealand
Piura *431* NW Peru
Piva *602 var.* Diva. River of C Montenegro, Yugoslavia
Pivdennyy Bug *556 Rus.* Yuzhnyy Bug. River of W and S Ukraine
Pivsko Jezero *602* lake of NW Montenegro, Yugoslavia
Pjandž *see* Pyandzh
Placetas *182* C Cuba
Plačkovica *349* mountain range of E FYR Macedonia
Plaine Corail *368* Rodrigues, Mauritius
Plaines *368* river of W Mauritius
Plaisance *258* N Haiti
Plakenska Planina *349* mountain range of SW FYR Macedonia
Plana Cays *88* islets of S Bahamas
Planken *342* C Liechtenstein
Plasencia *501* W Spain
Plate, Ile *368 Eng.* Flat Island. Island of N Mauritius
Platte *568-569* river of C USA
Platte, Île *478* Island of E Seychelles
Plattensee *see* Balaton
Plauer See *237* lake of NE Germany
Plây Cu *593 var.* Pleiku. S Vietnam
Pleasant Island *see* Nauru
Pleebo *see* Plibo
Pleiku *see* Plây Cu
Plenty, Bay of *401* inlet of the Pacific Ocean, on the coast of NE North Island, New Zealand
Pleskau *see* Pskov
Pleven *128 prev.* Plevna. N Bulgaria
Plezzo *see* Bovec
Plibo *336 var.* Pleebo. SE Liberia
Pljevlja *602 prev.* Plevlje. W Serbia, Yugoslavia
Płock *439* C Poland
Plöcken *82 It.* Passo di Monte Croce Carnico, *var.* Plöcken Pass, *Ger.* Plöckenpass. Mountain pass of SW Austria
Ploieşti *448 prev.* Ploeşti. SE Romania
Plovdiv *128 Gk* Philippopolisanc, *prev.* Eumolpias. SW Bulgaria
Plover Cove Reservoir *262* reservoir of NE Hong Kong
Plumtree *612* SW Zimbabwe
Plungė *344* NW Lithuania
Plyeshchanitay *104* N Belorussia
Plymouth *625* ❖ of Montserrat, SW Montserrat
Plymouth *563* SW England, UK
Plymouth *540* SW Tobago, Trinidad & Tobago
Plzeň *188 Ger.* Pilsen. W Czech Republic
Po *295* river of N Italy
Pô *132* S Burkina
Poabil *336* E Liberia
Pobè *108 var.* Pobé. S Benin
Pobedy, Pik *325 var.* Pobeda Peak, *Chin.* Tomur Feng. Mountain of China and Kyrgyzstan
Pocatello *568* Idaho, NW USA
Pocrí *424* S Panama
Podgorica *602 prev.* Titograd. S Montenegro, Yugoslavia
Podil's'ka Vysochyna *556* mountain range of SW Ukraine
Podkamennaya Tunguska *453 Eng.* Stony Tunguska. River of C Russia
Podravska Slatina *181 prev.* Slatina, *Hung.* Szlatina. NE Croatia
Poeketi *508* E Suriname
Pogradec *57 var.* Pogradeci. SE Albania
P'ohang *496 Jap.* Hokō. E South Korea
Pohjanlahti *see* Bothnia, Gulf of
Pohjanmaa *221 Swe.* Österbotten, *Eng.* Ostrobothnia. Physical region of W Finland
Pohnpei *375 prev.* Ascension, Ponape. Island of E Micronesia
Pohnpei Islands *375* island group E Micronesia
Poindimié *626* C New Caledonia
Point de Galle *see* Galle
Pointe-à-Pitre *622* C Guadeloupe
Pointe-à-Raquette *258* Île de la Gonâve, Haiti
Pointe Michel *196 var.* La Pointe. SW Dominica
Pointe-Noire *622* W Guadeloupe
Pointe-Noire *176* S Congo
Point Fortin *540* SW Trinidad, Trinidad & Tobago
Poitiers *225* C France
Poitou *224-225* cultural region of W France
Poivre Atoll *478* atoll of the Amirante Islands, C Seychelles
Pokhara *395* C Nepal
Pokigron *508* C Suriname
Pokrovka *325* NE Kyrgyzstan
Pola *see* Pula
Poland *438-441* officially Republic of Poland, *Pol.* Polska. Country of E Europe divided into 49 admin. units (województwo)
Polatli *546* C Turkey
Polatsk *104 Rus.* Polotsk. N Belorussia
Pol-e Khomrī *53 var.* Pul-i-Khumri. NE Afghanistan
Poliçan *57 var.* Poliçani. S Albania
Polillo Islands *435* island group of N Philippines
Polis *187 var.* Poli. W Cyprus
Polochic *250* river of C Guatemala
Polonnaruwa *504* C Sri Lanka
Poltava *556* NE Ukraine
Poltoratsk *see* Ashgabat
Põltsamaa *212 Ger.* Oberpahlen. C Estonia

Põltsamaa *212 var.* Pyltsamaa. River of C Estonia
Põlva *212 Ger.* Pölwe. SE Estonia
Pomeranian Bay *237, 439 Pol.* Zatoka Pomorska, *Ger.* Pommersche Bucht. Bay of the Baltic Sea, on the coasts of Germany and Poland
Pomio *426* New Britain, Papua New Guinea
Pommersche Bucht *see* Pomeranian Bay
Pomona *102* E Belize
Pomorie *128 var.* Pomoriye. E Bulgaria
Pomorska, Zatoka *see* Pomeranian Bay
Ponape *see* Pohnpei
Ponce *627* S Puerto Rico
Pondicherry *270* S India
Ponérihouen *626* C New Caledonia
Ponferrada *501* NW Spain
Pongo *506* river of S Sudan
Ponta Delgada *442* São Miguel, Azores, Portugal
Ponta Grossa *121* S Brazil
Pontevedra *501* NW Spain
Pontianak *276* Borneo, C Indonesia
Pontian Kechil *354 var.* Puntian Kecil, Pontian Kecil. S Peninsular Malaysia
Pontoise *225* N France
Pontypridd *563* S Wales, UK
Ponziane, Isole *295* island of C Italy
Pooh San *620* NE Christmas Island
Poole *563* S England, UK
Poona *see* Pune
Pooneryn *504* N Sri Lanka
Poopó, Lago *112 var.* Lago Pampa Aullagas. Lake of W Bolivia
Popayán *171* SW Colombia
Popomanaseu, Mount *488* mountain of S Guadalcanal, Solomon Islands
Popondetta *426* SE Papua New Guinea
Popovo *128* N Bulgaria
Poprad *485 Ger.* Deutschendorf, *Hung.* Poprád. NE Slovakia
Poprad *485 Ger.* Popper, *Hung.* Poprád. River of Poland and Slovakia
Pori *221 Swe.* Björneborg. SW Finland
Porirua *401* S North Island, New Zealand
Porlamar *589* Isla de Margarita, Venezuela
Porsangen *414* fjord of N Norway
Porsgrunn *414* S Norway
Portachuelo *112* C Bolivia
Portage la Prairie *146* S Canada
Portalegre *442* E Portugal
Port Alfred *493* Eastern Cape, S South Africa
Port Antonio *303* E Jamaica
Port Augusta *77* S Australia
Port-au-Prince *258* ❖ of Haiti, S Haiti
Port Blair *270* S Andaman, SE India
Port-Bouët *300* SE Ivory Coast
Port d'Envalira *62* zigzag pass of E Andorra
Port-de-Paix *258* N Haiti
Port Dickson *354* SW Peninsular Malaysia
Port Elizabeth *466* Bequia, St Vincent & the Grenadines
Port Elizabeth *493* Eastern Cape, S South Africa
Port Erin *623* SW Isle of Man
Port Étienne *see* Nouâdhibou
Port Florence *see* Kisumu
Port Francqui *see* Ilebo
Port-Gentil *230* W Gabon
Port Harcourt *408* S Nigeria
Port Hedland *76* NW Australia
Port Howard *621* West Falkland, C Falkland Islands
Portimão *442 var.* Vila Nova de Portimão. S Portugal
Port Láirge *see* Waterford
Portland *569* Maine, NE USA
Portland *568* Oregon, NW USA
Portland Bight *303* bay of Caribbean Sea
Portland Point *628* headland on the SW coast of Ascension Island
Port Laoise *288 Ir.* Portlaoighise, Portlaoise, *prev.* Maryborough. C Ireland
Port Lincoln *77* S Australia
Port Loko *480* W Sierra Leone
Port-Louis *622* N Guadeloupe
Port Louis *368 var.* Port-Louis. ❖ of Mauritius, NW Mauritius
Port Lyautey *see* Kénitra
Port Macquarie *77* E Australia
Port Maria *303* N Jamaica
Port Mathurin *368* Rodrigues, Mauritius
Port Morant *303* E Jamaica
Portmore *303* SE Jamaica
Port Moresby *426* ❖ of Papua New Guinea, SE Papua New Guinea
Porto *442 Eng.* Oporto. NW Portugal
Porto Alegre *121 prev.* Pôrto Alegre. S Brazil
Porto Alegre *471* S São Tomé, Sao Tome & Principe
Porto Alexandre *see* Tombua
Porto Amélia *see* Pemba
Portobelo *424 var.* Porto Bello, Puerto Bello. N Panama
Porto Edda *see* Sarandë
Porto Exterior *624* harbor of NE Macao
Port-of-Spain *540* ❖ of Trinidad & Tobago, NW Trinidad, Trinidad & Tobago
Porto Gole *254* C Guinea-Bissau
Porto Grande *see* Mindelo
Porto Interior *624* harbor of NW Macao
Porto-Novo *108* ❖ of Benin, S Benin
Porto Santo *442 var.* Ilha do Porto Santo. Island of the Madeira Is, Portugal
Porto Torres *295* Sardegna, W Italy
Porto Velho *120 prev.* Pôrto Velho. W Brazil
Portoviejo *200 var.* Puertoviejo. W Ecuador
Port Pirie *77* S Australia
Port Refuge *620* strait of the Indian Ocean between Horsburgh Island and Direction Island, C Cocos Islands
Port Royal *303* SE Jamaica
Port Said *202 Ar.* Bur Sa'íd. N Egypt
Port St Mary *623* S Isle of Man
Portsmouth *563* S England, UK
Portsmouth *196 var.* Grande-Anse. NW Dominica
Port Stanley *621* ❖ of Falkland Islands, East Falkland, Falkland Islands
Port Stephens *621* West Falkland, W Falkland Islands
Port Sudan *506 var.* Būr Sūdān. NE Sudan
Port Swettenham *see* Kelang
Port Talbot *563* S Wales, UK
Portugal *442-445* officially Republic of Portugal. Country of W Europe divided into 18 admin. units (districts)
Portuguese East Africa *see* Mozambique
Port-Vila *585 var.* Vila. ❖ of Vanuatu, Éfate, Vanuatu
Porvenir *159* Tierra del Fuego, Chile
Porvenir *112* NW Bolivia
Posadas *71* NE Argentina
Posen *see* Poznań
Posŏng *496* river of S South Korea
Poste de Flacq *368* river of E Mauritius
Postojna *486 Ger.* Adelsberg, *It.* Postumia. SW Slovenia
Pöstyén *see* Piešťany
Potaro *256* river of C Guyana
Potchefstroom *493* North West, N South Africa
Potenza *295* S Italy
Potgietersrus *493* Northern Transvaal, NE South Africa
Pot House *97* E Barbados
P'ot'i *234* W Georgia
Potiskum *408* NE Nigeria
Po Toi Island *262* island of S Hong Kong
Potoru *480* S Sierra Leone
Potosí *112* S Bolivia
Potsdam *237* NE Germany
Potters Village *68* C Antigua, Antigua & Barbuda
Pott, Île *626* island of Îles Belep, W New Caledonia
Pottuvil *504* SE Sri Lanka
Potwar Plateau *420* plateau of NE Pakistan
Poudre d'Or *368* NE Mauritius
Pouembout *629* W New Caledonia
Poum *626* W New Caledonia
Pout *476* W Senegal
Poutasi *596* Upolu, Western Samoa
Poŭthĭsăt *141 var.* Pursat. River of W Cambodia
Poŭthĭsăt *141 prev.* Pursat. W Cambodia
Po Valley *294* valley of N Italy
Považská Bystrica *485 Ger.* Waagbistritz, *Hung.* Vágbeszterce. NW Slovakia
Povoaçao de Hác-Sá *624* Coloane, S Macao
Povoaçao de Ká-Hó *624* Coloane, S Macao
Povoaçao de Sai Sa *624* Taipa, C Macao
Povoaçao de Samka *624* Taipa, C Macao
Póvoa de Varzim *442* NW Portugal
Powell, Lake *568* reservoir of SW USA
Poya *626* C New Caledonia
Poyang Hu *163* lake of E China
Poyan Reservoir *483* reservoir of W Singapore
Poza Rica *370 var.* Poza Rica de Hidalgo. C Mexico
Poznań *439 Ger.* Posen. W Poland
Pozo Colorado *428* C Paraguay
Pozsega *see* Slavonska Požega
Pozsony *see* Bratislava
Prábis *254* W Guinea-Bissau
Præstø *190* Sjælland, SE Denmark
Prague *188 Cz.* Praha, *Ger.* Prag. ❖ of Czech Republic, NW Czech Republic
Praia *152* ❖ of Cape Verde, Santiago, S Cape Verde
Praia Grande, Baia da *624* bay of the South China Sea, N Macao
Praslin *478* island of the Inner Islands, NE Seychelles
Praslin *465* E St Lucia
Prato *294* N Italy
Preguiça *152* São Nicolau, N Cape Verde
Prenjas *see* Përrenjas
Preparis Island *135* island of SW Burma
Přerov *188 Ger.* Prerau. SE Czech Republic
Presidente Prudente *121* S Brazil
Prešov *485 Ger.* Eperies, *var.* Preschau, *Hung.* Eperjes. NE Slovakia
Prespa, Lake *57, 245, 349 Alb.* Liqen i Prespës, *Mac.* Prespansko Ezero, *Gk* Límni Megáli Préspa, *var.* Limni Prespa. Lake of SE Europe
Prespës, Liqen i *see* Prespa, Lake
Pressburg *see* Bratislava
Prestea *242* SW Ghana
Preston *563* NW England, UK
Pretoria *493* ❖ of South Africa. Pretoria-Witwatersrand-Vereeniging, NE South Africa
Pretoria-Witwatersrand-Vereeniging *493* province of NE South Africa
Préveza *245* W Greece
Prey Vêng *141* S Cambodia
Priboj *602* W Serbia, Yugoslavia
Příbram *188* W Czech Republic
Prickly Pear Cays *618* island group of NW Anguilla
Prieska *493* Northern Cape, C South Africa
Prievidza *485* C Slovakia
Prijedor *116* NW Bosnia & Herzegovina
Prilep *349 Turk.* Perlepe. S FYR Macedonia
Prince Albert *146* SW Canada
Prince Edward Island *147* province and island of SE Canada
Prince Edward Island *493* island of the Prince Edward Islands, S South Africa
Prince Edward Islands *493* island group of S South Africa
Prince George *146* W Canada
Prince Island *see* Príncipe
Prince of Wales Island *see* Pinang, Pulau
Prince of Wales Island *146* island of N Canada
Prince Patrick Island *146* island of Parry Islands, N Canada
Prince Rupert *146* W Canada
Prince Rupert Bay *196* bay of the Caribbean Sea, to the NW of Dominica
Princes Town *540* SW Trinidad, Trinidad & Tobago
Príncipe *471 var.* Príncipe Island, *Eng.* Prince Island. Island to the N of São Tomé, Sao Tome & Principe
Pripet *104* river of S Belorussia
Pripet Marshes *104, 556* forested and swampy region of Belorussia and Ukraine
Priština *602* S Serbia, Yugoslavia
Privas *225* SE France
Privigye *see* Prievidza
Priwitz *see* Prievidza
Prizren *602 Alb.* Prizreni. S Serbia, Yugoslavia
Probištip *349* N FYR Macedonia
Probolinggo *276* Java, C Indonesia
Progreso *577* S Uruguay
Prome *135 var.* Pyè. SW Burma
Promissão, Represa de *121* reservoir of S Brazil
Proskurov *see* Khmel 'nyts'kyy
Prostějov *188 Ger.* Prossnitz. SE Czech Republic
Provadiya *128 var.* Provadija. E Bulgaria
Provence *225* cultural region of SE France
Providence *569* Rhode Island, NE USA
Providence *97* S Barbados
Providence Atoll *478 var.* Providence. Atoll of the Farquhar Group, S Seychelles
Providenciales *629* island of NW Turks and Caicos Islands
Provo *568* Utah, SW USA
Prudhoe Bay *568* Alaska, USA
Prune Island *466* island of SW St Vincent & the Grenadines
Prut *376, 448, 556 Ger.* Pruth. River of E Europe
Pruth *see* Prut
Pruzhany *104* SW Belorussia
Pryazova'ks Vysochyna *556* mountain range of SE Ukraine
Prychornomors'ka Nyzovyna *556* mountain range of S Ukraine
Prydniprovs'ka Nyzovyna *556* mountain range of NE Ukraine
Prydniprovs'ka Vysochnya *556* mountain range of NW Ukraine
Przemyśl *439* SE Poland
Przheval'sk *see* Karakol
Pskov *452 Ger.* Pleskau. W Russia

Pskov, Lake *212 Est.* Pihkva Järv, *Rus.* Pskovskoye Ozero. Lake of Estonia and Russia
Ptsich *104 Rus.* Ptich'. River of C Belorussia
Ptuj *486 Ger.* Pettau. NE Slovenia
Pua'a, Cape *596* cape on the coast of Savai'i, NW Western Samoa
Pu'apu'a *596* Savali'i, Western Samoa
Pucallpa *431* C Peru
Puch'ŏn *496 prev.* Punwŏn. NW South Korea
Pudasjärvi *221* C Finland
Puebla *370 var.* Puebla de Zaragoza. S Mexico
Pueblo *569* Colorado, SW USA
Pueblo Nuevo Tiquisate *250 var.* Tiquisate. SW Guatemala
Puente Alto *159* C Chile
Puerto Acosta *112* W Bolivia
Puerto Aisén *159* S Chile
Puerto Armuelles *424* W Panama
Puerto Ayacucho *589* SW Venezuela
Puerto Bahía Negra *428* N Paraguay
Puerto Baquerizo Moreno *200* San Cristobal I, Galapagos Is.
Puerto Barrios *250* E Guatemala
Puerto Bello *see* Portobelo
Puerto Berrío *171* N Colombia
Puerto Busch *112 var.* Puerto General Busch. SE Bolivia
Puerto Cabello *589* N Venezuela
Puerto Cabezas *404 var.* Bilwi. NE Nicaragua
Puerto Carreño *171* E Colombia
Puerto Casado *428* C Paraguay
Puerto Cooper *428* C Paraguay
Puerto Cortés *260* NW Honduras
Puerto El Carmen de Putumayo *200 var.* Putumayo. NW Ecuador
Puerto el Triunfo *207* S El Salvador
Puerto Inírida *171 var.* Obando. E Colombia
Puerto Iradier *see* Kogo
Puerto La Cruz *589* NE Venezuela
Puerto Lempira *260* E Honduras
Puertolland *501* SW Spain
Puerto Maldonado *431* E Peru
Puerto México *see* Coatzacoalcos
Puerto Montt *159* C Chile
Puerto Natales *159* S Chile
Puerto Padre *182* SE Cuba
Puerto Pinasco *428* C Paraguay
Puerto Plata *198 var.* San Felipe de Puerto Plata. N Dominican Republic
Puerto Presidente Stroessner *see* Ciudad del Este
Puerto Princesa *435* Palawan, W Philippines
Puerto Príncipe *see* Camagüey
Puerto Rico *627* Commonwealth territory of the USA, Caribbean Sea
Puerto Rico Trench *627* undersea feature of the Caribbean Sea, N Puerto Rico
Puerto San José *250 var.* San José. S Guatemala
Puerto Suárez *112* E Bolivia
Puerto Vallarta *370* W Mexico
Puerto Varas *159* C Chile
Puerto Viejo *178* NE Costa Rica
Puertoviejo *see* Portoviejo
Pujehun *480* S Sierra Leone
Pukaki, Lake *401* lake of C South Island, New Zealand
Pukapuka *620* island of Northern Cook Islands, N Cook Islands
Pukch'ŏng *413* E North Korea
Pukë *57 var.* Puka. N Albania
Pukekohe *401* NW North Island, New Zealand
Pukhan *496* river of North Korea and South Korea
Pula *181 prev.* Pulj, *It.* Pola. W Croatia
Pulangi *435* river of Mindanao, S Philippines
Pulap *375* atoll of C Micronesia
Pulau *277* river of Irian Jaya, E Indonesia
Pulau Tekong Reservoir *483* reservoir of E Singapore
Pul-i-Khumri *see* Pol-e Khomrī
Pully *516* SW Switzerland
Pulusuk *375* island of C Micronesia
Puluwat *375* atoll of C Micronesia
Puna, Isla *200* island to the SW of Ecuador, in the Gulf of Guayaquil
Punakha *110* C Bhutan
Punata *112* C Bolivia
Pune *270 prev.* Poona. W India
Punggol *483* area of NE Singapore
Púngoè *387 var.* Pungue, Pungwe. River of C Mozambique
Punkudutivu *504* island of N Sri Lanka
Puno *431* SE Peru
Punta Arenas *159 prev.* Magallanes. S Chile
Punta Chame *424* C Panama
Punta del Este *577* S Uruguay
Punta Gorda *102* S Belize
Puntarenas *178* W Costa Rica
Punta Santiago *208* S Bioko, Equatorial Guinea
Punto Fijo *589* NW Venezuela
Punwŏn *see* Puch'ŏn
Purari *426* river of C Papua New Guinea
Puri *270* E India
Purmerend *397* NW Netherlands
Pursat *see* Poŭthĭsăt
Purus *120* river of Brazil and Peru
Pusan *496 var.* Busan, *Jap.* Fusan. SE South Korea
Pusat Gayo, Pegunungan *276* mountain range of Sumatra, W Indonesia
Pushkino *see* Biläsuvar
Pu-tai *525* W Taiwan
Putorana, Plato *453* mountain range of N Russia
Puttalam *504* W Sri Lanka
Puttalam Lagoon *504* lagoon of W Sri Lanka
Putumayo *171, 431* river of NW South America
Putumayo *see* Puerto El Carmen de Putumayo
Puyo *200* C Ecuador
Pyandzh *528 var.* Panj. River of Afghanistan and Tajikistan forming a headstream of the Amu Darya
Pyandzh *528 var.* Pjandž. SW Tajikistan
Pyapon *135* S Burma
Pyarnu *see* Pärnu
Pyinmana *135* C Burma
Pyltsamaa *see* Põltsamaa
Pyongyang *413 Kor.* P'yŏngyang. ❖ of North Korea, SW North Korea
Pyramiden *629* Spitsbergen, W Svalbard
Pyramid Rock *627* island of E Paracel Islands
Pyrenees *62, 224-225, 501 Sp.* Pirineos, *Fr.* Pyrénées. Mountain range of SW Europe
Pyu *135* S Burma
Pyuntaza *135* S Burma
Pyuthan *395* W Nepal

Q

Qabatiya *292* N West Bank
Qābis *see* Gabès
Qacentina *see* Constantine
Qafṣah *see* Gafsa
Qahremānshahr *see* Bākhtarān
Qala' en Nahl *506 var.* Qala' an Naḩl. E Sudan
Qalali *91* Jazirat al Muharraq, Bahrain
Qalansīyah *599* NW Suqutra, Yemen
Qalāt *see* Kalāt
Qal 'at Bīshah *472* SW Saudi Arabia
Qal'eh-ye Now *53 var.* Qala Nau. NW Afghanistan
Qalīb ash Shuyūkh *322 var.* Jleeb al Shuyoukh. C Kuwait
Qalīb, Shiqqat al *322 var.* Shagat Al Jleeb. Desert region of NW Kuwait
Qamar, Ghubbat al *599* bay of Arabian Sea, E Yemen
Qamar, Jabal al *418* mountain range of SW Oman
Qambar *see* Kambar
Qamea *218 prev.* Nggamea. Island to the E of Taveuni, N Fiji
Qandahār *see* Kandahār
Qaraghandy *see* Karaganda
Qaraoun, Lac de *332 var.* Buḩayrat al Qir'awn. Lake of S Lebanon
Qara Qum *see* Karakumy
Qarataū *see* Karatau
Qardho *490 It.* Gardo. N Somalia
Qareh Chāy *281* river of NW Iran
Qarkilik *see* Ruoqiang
Qarshi *see* Karshi
Qartaba *332 var.* Qarṭabā. N Lebanon
Qatar *446-447* officially State of Qatar. Country of SW Asia divided into 9 admin. units (municipalities)
Qaṭṭâra, Monkhafad el *202 var.* Munkhafaḍ al Qaṭṭārah, *Eng.* Qattara Depression. Arid desert basin of NW Egypt
Qazaqstan *see* Kazakhstan
Qazax *86 Rus.* Kazakh. W Azerbaijan
Qazbegi *234 Rus.* Kazbegi. NE Georgia
Qazimämmäd *86 Rus.* Kazi-Magomed. SE Azerbaijan
Qazvīn *281 var.* Kazvin. NW Iran
Qena *202 var.* Qina. E Egypt
Qena, Wâdi *202 var.* Wādī Qinā. Seasonal river of E Egypt
Qeshm *281 var.* Jazīreh-ye Qeshm, Qeshm Island. Island of S Iran
Qezel Owzan *281* river of NW Iran
Qibilī *see* Kebili
Qilian Shan *162 var.* Kilien Mountains. Mountain range of W China
Qingdao *163 var.* Tsintao, Ching-Tao, Ch'ing-tao. Shandong, E China
Qinghai *162 var.* Chinghai, Tsinghai. Province of W China
Qinghai Hu *162 var.* Tsing Hai, Ch'ing Hai *Mong.* Koko Nor. Lake of W China
Qing-Zang Gaoyuan *162 Eng.* Plateau of Tibet. Plateau of Xizang Zizhiqu, W China
Qiqihar *163 prev.* Lungkiang, *var.* Tsitsihar, Ch'i-ch'i-ha-erh. Heilongjiang, NE China
Qir'awn, Buḩayrat al *see* Qaraoun, Lac de
Qirba, Khashim Al *see* Girba, Khashm el
Qiryat Ata *291* N Israel
Qiryat Gat *291* C Israel
Qiryat Motzkin *291* N Israel
Qiryat Shemona *291* N Israel
Qishn *599* SE Yemen
Qishon, Naḩal *291* river of N Israel
Qīzān *see* Jīzān
Qizilqum *see* Kyzyl Kum
Qom *281 var.* Qum, Kum. NW Iran
Qomolangma Feng *see* Everest, Mount
Qomul *see* Hami
Qondūz *see* Kunduz
Qondūz, Daryā-ye *53* seasonal river of NE Afghanistan
Qorakŭl *see* Karakul'
Qormi *363* C Malta
Qornet es Saouda *332* mountain of NE Lebanon
Qoryooley *490 It.* Coriole. SW Somalia
Qoubaiyat *332 var.* Al Qubayyāt. NE Lebanon
Qoussantîna *see* Constantine
Quang Ngai *593* E Vietnam
Quan Long *see* Ca Mau
Quanzhou *163 var.* Ch'uan-chou, *prev.* Chin-chiang, *var.* Tsinkiang. Fujian, SE China
Quaraí *see* Cuareim
Quarles, Pegunungan *276* mountain range of Celebes, W Indonesia
Quarnero *see* Kvarner
Quartier Militaire *368* C Mauritius
Quatre Bornes *368* W Mauritius
Quatre Bornes *478* Mahé, Seychelles
Quatre, Isle à *466* island of C St Vincent & the Grenadines
Quba *86 Rus.* Kuba. N Azerbaijan
Queanbeyan *77* SE Australia
Québec *147* SE Canada
Québec *147, 151* province of SE Canada
Quebo *254* S Guinea-Bissau
Queen Charlotte Bay *621* bay of the South Atlantic Ocean, W Falkland Islands
Queen Charlotte Islands *146 Fr.* Îles de la Reine-Charlotte. Island group of SW Canada
Queen Charlotte Sound *146* area of the Pacific Ocean between the Queen Charlotte Islands and Vancouver Island, SW Canada
Queen Elizabeth Islands *146 Fr.* Îles de la Reine-Élisabeth. Island group of N Canada
Queen Mary's Peak *628* mountain of C Tristan da Cunha
Queen Maud Gulf *146* gulf of the Arctic Ocean on the coast of N Canada
Queen Maud Land *66* physical region of Greater Antarctica, Antarctica
Queensland *77, 81* state of N Australia
Queenstown *483* area of S Singapore
Queenstown *493* Eastern Cape, S South Africa
Queguay Grande *577* river of W Uruguay
Quelimane *387* E Mozambique
Quelpart *see* Cheju-do
Queluz *442* W Portugal
Quepos *178* S Costa Rica
Que Que *see* Kwekwe
Querétaro *370* C Mexico
Quesada *178* N Costa Rica
Questelles *466* SW St Vincent, St Vincent & the Grenadines
Quetta *421* NW Pakistan
Quezaltenango *250 var.* Quetzaltenango. W Guatemala
Quezaltepeque *207* C El Salvador
Quibdó *171* W Colombia
Quillacollo *112* C Bolivia
Quilpué *159* C Chile
Quimper *224* W France
Quinhámel *254* W Guinea-Bissau
Quiniluban Group *435* island group of C Philippines
Quissico *387* S Mozambique
Quito *200* ❖ of Ecuador, N Ecuador
Qum *see* Qom
Qŭnghirot *see* Kungrad
Qŭqon *see* Kokand
Qurayn, Ra's al *91* cape of SE Bahrain
Qurayyāt *418 var.* Qurayat, Quraiyat. NE Oman
Qurlurtuuq *see* Coppermine
Qus *202 var.* Qūṣ. E Egypt
Quthing *see* Moyeni
Quy Nhon *593 var.* Quinhon. SE Vietnam
Qvareli *234 Rus.* Kvareli. E Georgia
Qyteti Stalin *see* Kuçovë
Qyzylorda *see* Kzyl-Orda

Raab *see* Rába
Raab *see* Győr
Raahe *221 Swe.* Brahestad. W Finland
Ra'ananna *291* C Israel
Rába *82, 264 Ger.* Raab. River of Austria and Hungary
Rabat *363* W Malta
Rabat *382* ❖ of Morocco, NW Morocco

Rabaul *426* New Britain, NE Papua New Guinea
Rabbit Island *466* island of SE St Vincent & the Grenadines
Rábca *264* river of NW Hungary
Rabi *218* *prev.* Rambi. Island to the E of Vanua Levu, N Fiji
Rābigh *472* W Saudi Arabia
Rabinal *250* C Guatemala
Râbniţa *see* Rîbniţa
Rabyānah, Ramlat *339* *var.* Şaḩrā' Rabyānah. Desert of SE Libya
Rachaïya *332* *var.* Rāshayyā. S Lebanon
Rach Gia *593* SW Vietnam
Rach Gia, Vinh *593* bay of the Gulf of Thailand on the SW coast of Vietnam
Racine *569* Wisconsin, NC USA
Radā *599* *var.* Ridā. W Yemen
Radom *439* C Poland
Radoviš *349* *var.* Radovište. E FYR Macedonia
Radviliškis *344* N Lithuania
Rafaela *71* E Argentina
Rafah *291, 292* *Heb.* Rafiaḩ. SW Gaza Strip
Rafḩā' *472* N Saudi Arabia
Ragged Island Range *88* island group of S Bahamas
Ragusa *295* Sicilia, S Italy
Ragusa *see* Dubrovnik
Rahachow *104* *Rus.* Rogachëv. E Belorussia
Rahaeng *see* Tak
Rahīmyār Khān *421* SE Pakistan
Raiatea *622* island of W French Polynesia
Raipur *270* C India
Rairok District *364* district of Majuro, SE Marshall Islands
Rājahmundry *270* SE India
Rajang *354* river of SW Borneo, Malaysia
Rājbāri *93* C Bangladesh
Rajbiraj *395* E Nepal
Rājkot *270* W India
Rajo, Cabo *627* cape on the SW coast of Puerto Rico
Rājshāhi *93* *prev.* Rampur Boalia. W Bangladesh
Rakahanga *620* island of Northern Cook Islands, N Cook Islands
Rakaia *401* river of C South Island, New Zealand
Rakhshān *420* river of W Pakistan
Rakiraki *218* N Viti Levu, W Fiji
Rakka *see* Ar Raqqah
Rakutō-kō *see* Naktong
Rakvere *212* *Ger.* Wesenberg. N Estonia
Raleigh *569* North Carolina, SE USA
Ralik Chain *364* island group of W Marshall Islands
Rama *404* SE Nicaragua
Ramādah *599* W Yemen
Ramallah *291, 292* C West Bank
Ramat Gan *291* C Israel
Ramatlabama *118* S Botswana
Rambi *see* Rabi
Ramechhap *395* C Nepal
Ramier Island *see* Glover Island
Ramla *291* C Israel
Ramlat, Ahl Wahībah *418* N Oman
Ramm, Jabal *310* mountain of SW Jordan
Râmnicu Sarat *448* E Romania
Râmnicu Vâlcea *448* *prev.* Rîmnicu-Vîlcea. C Romania
Ramotswa *118* S Botswana
Rampur Boalia *see* Rajshahi
Ramree Island *135* island of W Burma
Ramsey *623* NE Isle of Man
Ramsey Bay *623* bay of the Irish Sea on the NE coast of Isle of Man
Ramsgate *563* SE England, UK
Ramu *426* river of NE Papua New Guinea
Rancagua *159* C Chile
Rānchi *270* E India
Randa *194* C Djibouti
Randers *190* Jylland, N Denmark
Rāngāmāti *93* SE Bangladesh
Rangiora *401* E South Island, New Zealand
Rangitaiki *401* river of E North Island, New Zealand
Rangitata *401* river of C South Island, New Zealand
Rangitikei *401* river of S North Island, New Zealand
Rangoon *135* *var.* Yangon. ❖ of Burma, S Burma
Rangpur *93* N Bangladesh
Rankin Inlet *146* C Canada
Rankovićevo *see* Kraljevo
Rann *see* Brežice
Rann of Kachch *270* *var.* Rann of Cutch, Rann of Kutch. Salt marsh of India and Pakistan
Ranongga *488* *var.* Ghanongga. New Georgia Is, Solomon Islands
Rantau, Puala *see* Tebingtinggi, Pulau
Rapallo *294* N Italy
Rapid City *569* South Dakota, NC USA
Räpina *212* *Ger.* Rappin. SE Estonia
Rapla *212* *Ger.* Rappel. NW Estonia
Rapperswil *516* NW Switzerland
Rappin *see* Räpina
Rarotonga *620* island of Southern Cook Islands, S Cook Islands
Ra's al 'Ayn *521* N Syria
Ras al Hadd *see* Al Ḩadd
Ras al Khaimah *560* NE United Arab Emirates
Ra's an Naqb *310* SW Jordan
Ras Dashen Terara *215* mountain of N Ethiopia
Rasdu Atoll *358* atoll of C Maldives
Raseiniai *344* W Lithuania
Rashîd *202* *Eng.* Rosetta. N Egypt
Rasht *281* *var.* Resht. NW Iran
Rashū *see* Kŭmsong
Raso, Ilhéu *152* island of NW Cape Verde
Rass Jebel *543* *var.* Ra's al Jabal. N Tunisia
Rastalt *236* SW Germany
Ras Tannūrah *472* E Saudi Arabia
Ras Xaafuun *490* *It.* Ras Hafun. NE Somalia
Ratak Chain *364* island group of E Marshall Islands
Ratchaburi *533* *var.* Rat Buri. C Thailand
Rathkeale *288* SW Ireland
Rätische Alpen *see* Rhaetian Alps
Ratnapura *504* S Sri Lanka
Ratō *see* Lo-tung
Raub *354* C Peninsular Malaysia
Raufarhöfn *268* NE Iceland
Raukawa *see* Cook Strait
Rauma *221* *Swe.* Raumo. SW Finland
Rauna *330* NE Latvia
Răuţel *376* *var.* Reuţel. River of N Moldova
Ravenna *295* N Italy
Ravensthorpe *76* SW Australia
Rāvi *421* river of India and Pakistan
Ravne na Koroškem *486* *Ger.* Gutenstein. N Slovenia
Rawaki *320* *var.* Phoenix Island. Island of Phoenix Islands, C Kiribati
Rāwalpindi *421* NE Pakistan
Rawson *71* SE Argentina
Rayak *332* *var.* Riyāq. E Lebanon
Rayong *533* C Thailand
Raysūt *418* SW Oman
Razāzah, Buḩayrat ar *284* *var.* Baḩr al Milḩ. Lake of C Iraq
Razdan *see* Hrazdan
Razim, Lacul *448* *prev.* Lacul Rezelm. Lagoon of E Romania
Reading *563* SE England, UK
Reăng Kései *141* W Cambodia
Rebun-tō *304* island to the NW of Hokkaidō, N Japan
Rechytsa *104* *Rus.* Rechitsa. SE Belorussia
Recife *121* *prev.* Pernambuco. E Brazil
Recklinghausen *236* W Germany
Redange *346* W Luxembourg
Redcliff *612* C Zimbabwe
Red Deer *146* SW Canada
Redhead *540* NE Trinidad, Trinidad & Tobago
Redon *224* NW France
Red River *146* river of Canada and USA
Red River *569* river of SC USA
Red River *593* *var.* Sông Coi, *Chin.* Yuan Jiang. River of China and Vietnam
Red Sea *210, 599* sea of Indian Ocean, between the Arabian Peninsula and NE Africa
Red Sea Hills *506* hilly region of NE Sudan
Red Volta *132* *Fr.* Volta Rouge. River of Burkina and Ghana
Ree, Lough *288* *Ir.* Loch Ri. Lake of C Ireland
Reefton *401* N South Island, New Zealand
Regar *see* Tursunzade
Regensburg *237* SE Germany
Reggane *59* C Algeria
Reggio di Calabria *295* *var.* Reggio Calabria. S Italy
Reggio nell' Emilia *294* *var.* Reggio Emilia. N Italy
Reghin *448* N Romania
Regina *146* S Canada
Régina *621* E French Guiana
Rehoboth *391* C Namibia
Reḩovot *291* C Israel
Reichenberg *see* Liberec
Reifnitz *see* Ribnica
Ré, Île de *224* island of W France
Reims *225* *Eng.* Rheims. NE France
Reine-Charlotte, Îles de la *see* Queen Charlotte Islands
Reine-Élisabeth, Îles de la *see* Queen Elizabeth Islands
Reisduoddarhalde *see* Haltiatunturi
Reisui *see* Yŏsu
Reka *see* Rijeka
Relizane *59* *var.* Ghilizane, Ghelîzâne. NW Algeria
Remel el Aboid *543* desert region of S Tunisia
Remich *346* SE Luxembourg
Rempart *368* river of NE Mauritius
Remscheid *236* W Germany
Rendezvous Bay *618* bay of the Caribbean Sea on the S coast of Anguilla
Rendova *488* island of the New Georgia Is, W Solomon Is
Renens *516* SW Switzerland
Rengo *159* C Chile
Rennell *488* *var.* Mu Nggava. Island of S Solomon Islands
Rennes *224* *Bret.* Roazon. NW France
Reno *568* Nevada, W USA
Réo *132* W Burkina
Republiek *508* N Suriname
Rere *488* E Guadalcanal, Solomon Is
Resen *349* SW FYR Macedonia
Reservatório *624* reservoir of Coloane, SW Macao
Resistencia *71* NE Argentina
Reşiţa *448* *Hung.* Resicabánya, *Ger.* Reschiza. W Romania
Resolute *146* Cornwallis Island, N Canada
Resolution Island *401* island to the SW of South Island, New Zealand
Retalhuleu *250* SW Guatemala
Retan Laut, Pulau *483* island SW Singapore
Retiche, Alpi *see* Rhaetian Alps
Réunion *628* French overseas department of the Indian Ocean. ❖ St Denis
Reus *501* E Spain
Reutlingen *236* S Germany
Reval *see* Tallinn
Rewa *256* river of S Guyana
Rey *281* *var.* Shahr Rey. NW Iran
Reyes *112* NW Bolivia
Rey, Isla del *424* island of SE Panama
Reykjahlídh *268* NE Iceland
Reykjavík *268* ❖ of Iceland, W Iceland
Reynosa *370* N Mexico
Reza, Gora *551* *var.* Gora Riza. Mountain of SW Turkmenistan
Reẕā'īyeh *see* Orūmīyeh
Reẕā'īyeh, Daryācheh-ye *see* Orūmīyeh, Daryācheh-ye
Rēzekne *330* *Ger.* Rositten, *Rus.* Rezhitsa. E Latvia
Rezina *376* NE Moldova
Rēznas Ezers *330* lake of SE Latvia
Rhadames *see* Ghadamis
Rhaetian Alps *516* *Ger.* Rätische Alpen, *Fr.* Alpes Rhétiques, *It.* Alpi Retiche. Mountain range of E Switzerland
Rheden *397* SE Netherlands
Rhein *see* Rhine
Rheine *236* NW Germany
Rheinisches Schiefergebirge *236* *Eng.* Rhenish Slate Mountains. Mountains of W Germany
Rhenish Slate Mountains *see* Rheinisches Schiefergebirge
Rhétiques, Alpes *see* Rhaetian Alps
Rhine *225, 236, 342, 516* *Ger.* Rhein, *Fr.* Rhin, *Dut.* Rijn. River of W Europe
Rhino Camp *554* NW Uganda
Rhode Island *569* state of NE USA
Rhodes *see* Rodos
Rhodesia *see* Zimbabwe
Rhodope Mountains *128, 245* *Gk* Orosirá Rodópis, *Bul.* Despoto Planina, *Turk.* Dospad Dagh. Mountain range of Bulgaria and Greece
Rhône *225, 516* river of France and Switzerland
Rhum *563* *var.* Rum. Island of Inner Hebrides, W Scotland, UK
Riaba *208* *prev.* Concepción. S Bioko, Equatorial Guinea
Riau, Kepulauan *276* *var.* Riau Archipelago, *Dut.* Riouw Archipel. Island group to the E of Sumatra, W Indonesia
Riban i Manamby *350* S Madagascar
Ribáuè *387* NE Mozambique
Ribble *563* river of NW England, UK
Ribe *190* Jylland, SW Denmark
Ribeira da Barça *152* Santiago, S Cape Verde
Ribeira Funda *152* São Nicolau, N Cape Verde
Ribeira Grande *152* Santo Antão, N Cape Verde
Ribeirão Preto *121* S Brazil
Riberalta *112* N Bolivia
Ribnica *486* *Ger.* Reifnitz. S Slovenia
Rîbniţa *376* *var.* Râbniţa, *Rus.* Rybnitsa. NE Moldova
Richard's Bay *493* Kwazulu Natal, E South Africa
Richard Toll *476* N Senegal
Riche Fond *465* E St Lucia
Richmond *569* Virginia, E USA
Richmond Vale *466* NW St Vincent, St Vincent & the Grenadines
Ridā *see* Radāa
Ridderkerk *397* SW Netherlands
Rif *382* *var.* Riff, Er Rif. Mountain range of N Morocco
Rift Valley *see* Great Rift Valley
Riga *330* *Latv.* Rīga. ❖ of Latvia, C Latvia
Riga, Gulf of *212, 330* *Est.* Liivi Laht, *prev.* Riia Laht, *Rus.* Rizhskiy Zaliv, *Latv.* Rīgas Jūras Līcis. Gulf of the Baltic Sea, on the coasts of Estonia and Latvia
Rīgestān *53* *var.* Registan. Desert region of S Afghanistan
Riihimäki *221* SW Finland
Rijeka *181* *Slvn.* Reka, *Ger.* Sankt Veit am Flaum, *It.* Fiume. NW Croatia
Rijn *see* Rhine
Rijssel *see* Lille
Ri, Loch *see* Ree, Lough

Ruvironza *138* *var.* Luvironza. River of C Burundi
Ruvubu *138* *var.* Ruvuvu. River of C Burundi
Ruvuma *387, 530* *Port.* Rovuma. River of Mozambique and Tanzania
Ruwais *see* Ar Ru'ays
Ruwaisv *see* Ar Ru'ays
Ruwenzori *554* mountains of Uganda and Zaire
Ruya *612* river of Mozambique and Zimbabwe
Ruyigi *138* C Burundi
Ružomberok *485* *Hung.* Rózsahegy, *Ger.* Rosenberg. N Slovakia
Rwamagana *460* E Rwanda
Rwamatamu *460* W Rwanda
Rwanda *460-461* officially Republic of Rwanda, *prev.* Ruanda. Country of Central Africa divided into 10 admin. units (prefectures)
Rwanyakizinga, Lac *460* lake of NE Rwanda
Rwasanga *138* C Burundi
Rweru *138, 430* *var.* Lac Rugwero. Lake of Burundi and Rwanda
Rwesero *138* C Burundi
Rwesero *460* SW Rwanda
Ryazan' *452* W Russia
Rybinskoye Vodokhranilishche *452* *Eng.* Rybinsk Reservoir. Reservoir of W Russia
Rybnik *439* S Poland
Rybnitsa *see* Rîbniţa
Rykovo *see* Yenakiyeve
Rysy *439* mountain of S Poland
Rzeszów *439* SE Poland

S

Saale *237* river of C Germany
Saarbrücken *236* *Fr.* Sarrebruck. SW Germany
Sääre *212* Saaremaa, Estonia
Saaremaa *212* *var.* Saare, Sarema, *Ger.* Ösel, *var.* Oesel. Island of W Estonia
Saaristomeri *221* strait connecting the Gulf of Bothnia and Gulf of Finland
Saartuz *528* W Tajikistan
Saati *210* E Eritrea
Saatlı *86* *Rus.* Saatly. C Azerbaijan
Saatta *210* NW Eritrea
Sab *141* river of S Cambodia
Saba *626* island of N Netherlands Antilles
Šabac *602* NW Serbia, Yugoslavia
Sabadell *501* E Spain
Sabana, Archipiélago de *182* island group of N Cuba
Sabana de la Mar *198* E Dominican Republic
Sabanalarga *171* N Colombia
Sabaneta *198* NW Dominican Republic
Sab'atayn, Ramlat as *599* desert region of C Yemen
Sabaya *112* S Bolivia
Şāberī, Hāmūn-e *53* *var.* Sīstān, Daryācheh-ye. Lake of Afghanistan and Iran
Sabhā *339* W Libya
Sabi *233* E Gambia
Sabi *see* Save
Sabinal, Cayo *182* island of NE Cuba
Sabirabad *86* C Azerbaijan
Sabkha *see* As Sabkhah
Sabkhat al Mūh *520* river of S Syria
Sabyah *see* Aş Şabīyah
Sabzevār *281* NE Iran
Sacavém *442* W Portugal
Sachs Harbour *146* Banks Island, NW Canada
Sacramento *568* California, W USA
Sada *625* W Mayotte
Sá da Bandeira *see* Lubango
Şa'dah *599* NW Yemen
Sadaï *194* river of NE Djibouti
Sa Đec *593* S Vietnam
Sādiqābād *421* SE Pakistan
Sa'dīyah, Hawr as *284* lake of E Iraq
Sadlers *462* N St Kitts, St Kitts & Nevis
Sado *304* island to the W of Honshū, N Japan
Safāqis *see* Sfax
Safi *382* W Morocco
Safi *see* Aş Şafī
Safīd Khers, Kūh-e *53* mountain range of NE Afghanistan
Safīd Kūh *53* mountain range of NW Afghanistan
Safim *254* W Guinea-Bissau
Saga *304* Kyūshū, SW Japan
Sagaing *135* C Burma
Saganthit Island *135* *var.* Sakanthit, *prev.* Sellore I. Island of S Burma
Sagarmatha *see* Everest, Mount
Sagay *435* Negros, C Philippines
Sagua la Grande *182* C Cuba
Saguia al Hamra *382* river of N Western Sahara
Saḩam *310* *var.* Sahm. N Jordan
Sahara *156, 339, 360, 366, 407* *Ar.* Aş Şaḩrā'. Vast desert area of N Africa
Sahara el Gharqîya *202* *var.* Aş Şaḩrā' al Gharbīyah, *Eng.* Western Desert. Desert of C Egypt
Sahara el Sharqîya *202* *var.* Aş Şaḩrā' ash Sharqīyah, *Eng.* Eastern Desert. Desert of E Egypt
Sāhīwāl *421* *prev.* Montgomery. E Pakistan
Šahrisabz *see* Shakhrisabz
Saïda *332* *var.* Şaydā. W Lebanon
Saïda *59* NW Algeria
Saidpur *93* NW Bangladesh
Saigon *see* Hô Chi Minh
Saiki *304* Kyūshū, SW Japan
Sai Kung *262* E Hong Kong
Sail Rock *466* islet of S St Vincent & the Grenadines
Saimaa *221* lake of SE Finland
Saint Albert *146* SW Canada
St. André *628* NE Réunion
St. Anne *623* Alderney, N Guernsey
St. Ann's Bay *303* N Jamaica
St Aubin *624* S Jersey
St Austell *563* SW England, UK
St. Barthélémy *622* island of N Guadeloupe
St. Benoit *628* E Réunion
Saint-Brieuc *224* NW France
St. Catherine, Mt *248* mountain C Grenada island, Grenada
St. Catherine Point *619* headland of E Bermuda
Saint Catherines *147* SE Canada
Saint-Chamond *225* E France
Saint Croix *629* island of S Virgin Islands
St. David's *248* SE Grenada island, Grenada
St. David's Island *619* island of E Bermuda
St Denis *628* ❖ of Réunion, N Réunion
Ste Anne *625* SE Martinique
Ste. Anne *622* E Guadeloupe
Saint-Élie *621* N French Guiana
Ste. Rose *622* W Guadeloupe
Saintes *225* W France
Saint-Étienne *225* E France
St Eustatius *626* island of C Netherlands Antilles
St. François *622* E Guadeloupe
Saint-Gall *see* Sankt Gallen
St-Georges *621* E French Guiana
St. George *619* St. George's Island, N Bermuda
St. George's *248* ❖ of Grenada, SW Grenada
St. George's Channel *288, 563* *Ir.* Muir Bhreatan. Channel connecting the Celtic Sea and Irish Sea
St. George's Harbour *619* bay of E Bermuda
St. George's Island *619* island of E Bermuda
St. Giles Islands *540* *prev.* Melville Islands. Islands to the NE of Tobago, Trinidad & Tobago
St Helena *628* British dependent territory of the South Atlantic Ocean ❖ Jamestown
St. Helena Bay *493* bay of Atlantic Ocean, of coast of W South Africa
St Helier *624* ❖ of Jersey, S Jersey
St John *624* N Jersey
St John *623* C Isle of Man
Saint John *147* SE Canada
St. John *336* river of Guinea and Liberia
Saint John Island *629* island of NE Virgin Islands
St John's *625* N Montserrat
Saint John's *147* Newfoundland, E Canada
St. John's *68* ❖ of Antigua & Barbuda, NW Antigua
St. John's Island *see* Sakijang Bendera, Pulau
St. Johnston Village *68* C Antigua, Antigua & Barbuda
St. Joseph *628* S Réunion
St Joseph *196* W Dominica
St. Joseph *540* SE Trinidad, Trinidad & Tobago
St Julian's *363* N Malta
St Kilda *563* island of NW Scotland, UK
Saint Kitts *462* island of the Lesser Antilles, which, with Nevis, forms the independent state of St Kitts & Nevis
Saint Kitts and Nevis *462-463* officially Federation of Saint Christopher and Nevis. Country of the West Indies
Saint-Laurent, Golfe du *see* Saint Lawrence, Gulf of
St.-Laurent-du-Maroni *621* NW French Guiana
Saint Lawrence *147* *Fr.* Fleuve Saint-Laurent. River of SE Canada
Saint Lawrence, Gulf of *146* Gulf of of the Atlantic Ocean, SE Canada
Saint-Lo *224* NW France
St. Louis *628* SW Réunion
St Louis *622* Marie-Galante, S Guadeloupe
St Louis *569* Missouri, C USA
Saint-Louis *476* NW Senegal
St-Louis-du-Nord *258* *var.* St-Luis du Nord. N Haiti
Saint Lucia *464-465* independent island state of the Caribbean
Saint Lucia Channel *465* channel connecting the Atlantic Ocean and Caribbean Sea
St. Lucia, Lake *493* lake of Kwazulu Natal, E South Africa
Saint Malo *224* NW France
Saint-Malo, Golfe de *224* gulf of the English Channel to the NW of France
St-Marc *258* W Haiti
St-Marc, Canal de *258* channel of the Caribbean Sea between Île de la Gonâve and W Haiti
Sainte Marie, Nosy *350* *var.* Nosy Boraha. Island of NE Madagascar
Ste Marie *625* NE Martinique
St. Marie *628* NE Réunion
St Martin *626* island of N Netherlands Antilles
St. Martin *622* island of N Guadeloupe
St. Martins *97* SE Barbados
Saint-Nazaire *224* W France
St.-Nicolas *see* Sint-Niklaas
St. Patricks *97* S Barbados
St. Paul *628* NW Réunion
St Paul *569* Minnesota, NC USA
St. Paul *336* river of Guinea and Liberia
St. Paul's *462* NW St Kitts, St Kitts & Nevis
St. Paul's Bay *363* area of the Malta Channel
Saint Paul's Bay *see* San Pawl il Bahar
St Paul's Point *627* headland of Pitcairn Island, S Pitcairn Islands
St Peter Port *623* ❖ of Guernsey, C Guernsey
St Peters *462* SE St Kitts, St Kitts & Nevis
St Petersburg *569* Florida, SE USA
Saint Petersburg *452, 458* *var.* Sankt-Peterburg, *prev.* Leningrad, Petrograd. NW Russia
St. Philips *68* SE Antigua, Antigua & Barbuda
Saint-Pierre *628* ❖ of Saint Pierre and Miquelon, SE Saint Pierre
Saint Pierre *628* island of SE Saint Pierre and Miquelon
St. Pierre *628* SW Réunion
St Pierre *625* NW Martinique
St. Pierre *478* island of the Farquhar Group, Seychelles
Saint Pierre and Miquelon *628* French territorial collectivity of the Atlantic Ocean ❖ Saint-Pierre
St. Sampson *623* S Guernsey
Saint Sauveur *196* E Dominica
Saint Thomas Island *629* island of W Virgin Islands
Saint Thomas Island *see* São Tomé
St.-Trond *see* Sint-Truiden
Saint Vincent *466* island of the Lesser Antilles which, with the Northern Grenadines forms the independent state of St Vincent & the Grenadines
Saint Vincent and the Grenadines *466-467* country of the West Indies
St Willibrordus *626* Curaçao, S Netherlands Antilles
Saipan *626* island of S Northern Mariana Islands
Saishū *see* Cheju
Sajama, Nevado *112* mountain of W Bolivia
Sakaide *304* Shikoku, SW Japan
Sakākah *472* N Saudi Arabia
Sakalua *553* islet of Nukufetau, Tuvalu
Sakanthit *see* Saganthit Island
Sakarya *see* Adapazarı
Sakarya *546* river of NW Turkey
Sakata *304* Honshū, N Japan
Sakchu *413* W North Korea
Sakété *108* S Benin
Sakhalin, Ostrov *453* island of SE Russia
Sakha, Respublika *452* *var.* Respublika Yakutiya. Autonomous republic of E Russia
Şäki *86* *Rus.* Sheki, *var.* Šeki, *prev.* Nukha. NW Azerbaijan
Sakijang Bendera, Pulau *483* *prev.* St. John's Island S Singapore
Sakijang Pelepah, Pulau *483* *prev.* Lazarus Island S Singapore
Sakis-Adasi *see* Chíos
Sakishima-shotō *304* island group of Nansei-shotō, SW Japan
Sakon Nakhon *533* NE Thailand
Sakra, Pulau *483* island of SW Singapore
Sakskøbing *190* Lolland, SE Denmark
Sal *152* island of NE Cape Verde
Šaľa *485* *Hung.* Sellye. SW Slovakia
Sala Ban Thin *327* C Laos
Salacgrīva *330* N Latvia
Salado *182* river of SE Cuba
Salaga *242* C Ghana
Sala'ilua *596* Savai'i, Western Samoa
Salala *336* C Liberia
Şalalah *418* SW Oman
Salamá *250* C Guatemala
Salamanca *370* C Mexico
Salamanca *500* NW Spain
Salamat *156* river of S Chad
Salamīyah *521* *var.* Selemia. W Syria

Shashemenē 215 *var.* Shashemenne, Shashhamana, *It.* Sciasciamana. S Ethiopia
Shashi 163 *var.* Sha-shih, Shasi. Hubei, C China
Sha Tin 262 C Hong Kong
Shāṭi', Wādī ash 339 dry watercourse of W Libya
Shaykh, Jabal ash *see* Hermon, Mount
Shaykh 'Uthmān 599 SW Yemen
Shcheglovsk *see* Kemerovo
Shchuchinsk 312 N Kazakhstan
Shea 256 S Guyana
Shebeli 490 *Som.* Webi Shabeelle, *Amh.* Shebele Wenz, *It.* Scebeli. River of Ethiopia and Somalia
Sheberghān 53 *var.* Shibarghan. N Afghanistan
Shedadi *see* Ash Shadādah
Shefar 'am 291 N Israel
Sheffield 563 N England, UK
Shekhem *see* Nablus
Shekhūpura 421 NE Pakistan
Sheki *see* Şäki
Shek Wu Hui 262 N Hong Kong
Shelikhova, Zaliv 453 *Eng.* Shelekhov Gulf. Gulf of Sea of Okhotsk, bordering NE Russia
Shemakha *see* Şamaxı
Shembe *see* Isembe
Shemgang 110 C Bhutan
Shendi 506 *var.* Shandī. NE Sudan
Shengking *see* Liaoning
Shensi *see* Shaanxi
Shenyang 163 *prev.* Fengtien, *Eng.* Mukden. Liaoning, NE China
Shepherd Islands 585 islands to the C of Vanuatu
Shepparton 77 SE Australia
Sherbro Island 480 island of SW Sierra Leone
Sherbrooke 147 SE Canada
Sheridan 568 Wyoming, NW USA
Sherpur 93 N Bangladesh
's-Hertogenbosch 397 *Ger.* Herzogenbusch, *Fr.* Bois-le-Duc. S Netherlands
Sherwood Ranch 118 SE Botswana
Shetland 563 islands of NE Scotland, UK
Shevchenko *see* Aktau
Shibām 599 C Yemen
Shibarghan *see* Sheberghān
Shibata 304 Honshū, N Japan
Shibh Jazīrat Sīnā' *see* Sinai
Shibîn el Kôm 202 *var.* Shibīn al Kawm. N Egypt
Shihmen *see* Shijiazhuang
Shijak 57 *var.* Shijaku. W Albania
Shijiazhuang 163 *var.* Shihkiachwang, Shih-chia-chuang, *prev.* Shihmen. Hebei, NE China
Shikārpur 421 S Pakistan
Shikoku 304 island of SW Japan
Shiliguri 270 *prev.* Siliguri. NE India
Shimbiris 490 *var.* Shimbir Berris. Mountain of N Somalia
Shimizu 304 Honshū, SE Japan
Shimonoseki 304 Honshū, W Japan
Shimonoseki-kaikyō 304 strait connecting the Sea of Japan and Inland Sea, between Honshū and Kyūshū, W Japan
Shinano 304 river of Honshū, N Japan
Shināş 418 NW Oman
Shīndand 53 W Afghanistan
Shinei *see* Hsin-ying
Shinshō *see* Hsin-chuang
Shinshū *see* Chinju
Shinten *see* Hsin-tien
Shinyanga 530 NW Tanzania
Shiogama 304 Honshū, N Japan
Shīrāz 281 SW Iran
Shire 353 *Port.* Chire. River of Malawi and Mozambique
Shire Highlands 353 hilly region of S Malawi
Shirvanskaya Step' *see* Şirvan Düzü
Shirwa, Lake *see* Chilwa, Lake
Shizuoka 304 Honshū, SE Japan
Shkodër 57 *var.* Shkodra, *It.* Scutari, *SCr.* Skadar. NW Albania
Shkodrës, Liqeni i *see* Scutari, Lake
Shkubinit 57 *var.* Shkumbî, Shkumbin. River of C Albania
Shoe Rock 625 headland on the S coast of Montserrat
Shōka *see* Chang-hua
Sholāpur *see* Solāpur
Shorkot 421 NE Pakistan
Shortland Island 488 *var.* Alu. Island of the Shortland Is, W Solomon Islands
Shortland Islands 488 island group of the W Solomon Islands
Shostka 556 N Ukraine
Shreveport 569 Louisiana, SC USA
Shrewsbury 563 C England, UK
Shū *see* Chu
Shu'aybah 322 *var.* Shuaiba. E Kuwait
Shubrâ el Kheima 202 *var.* Shubrā al Khaymah. N Egypt
Shūlgareh 53 N Afghanistan
Shumen 128 *var.* Šumen. E Bulgaria
Shunsen *see* Ch'unch'ŏn
Shuqrah 599 *var.* Shaqrā. SW Yemen
Shurugwi 612 *prev.* Selukwe. C Zimbabwe
Shwebo 135 N Burma
Shweli 135 river of Burma and China
Shymkent 312 *prev.* Chimkent. S Kazakhstan
Shyashchytsy 104 C Belorussia
Siāhān Range 420 mountain range of W Pakistan
Sīāh Kūh 53 mountain range of W Afghanistan
Siālkot 421 NE Pakistan
Siam *see* Thailand
Siam, Gulf of *see* Thailand, Gulf of
Sian *see* Xi'an
Siangtan *see* Xiangtan
Siargao Island 435 island of E Philippines
Šiauliai 344 *Ger.* Schaulen. NW Lithuania
Siazan' *see* Siyäzän
Šibenik 181 *It.* Sebenico. S Croatia
Siberut, Pulau 276 island of Kepulauan Mentawai, W Indonesia
Sibi 421 C Pakistan
Sibiti 176 S Congo
Sibiu 448 *Ger.* Hermannstadt, *Hung.* Nagyszeben. C Romania
Sibu 354 W Borneo, Malaysia
Sibut 154 *prev.* Fort-Sibut. C Central African Republic
Sibutu Passage 354 passage connecting Celebes Sea and Sulu Sea
Sibuyan Island 435 island of C Philippines
Sibuyan Sea 435 sea of the Pacific Ocean
Sichuan 163 *var.* Szechuan, Ssu-ch'uan. Province of SW China
Sicilia 295 *Eng.* Sicily. Island of S Italy
Sicily *see* Sicilia
Sico 260 *var.* Tinto, Río Negro. River of NE Honduras
Sicunusa 510 SW Swaziland
Siders *see* Sierre
Sidi Bel Abbès 59 NW Algeria
Sidi Bouzid 543 *var.* Sīdī bū Zayd, Gammouda. C Tunisia
Sidi el Hani, Sebkhet de 543 *var.* Sabkhat Sīd' al Hānī'. Salt flat of NE Tunisia
Sidi Kacem 382 *prev.* Petitjean. N Morocco
Sidra *see* Surt
Sidra, Gulf of *see* Surt, Khalīj
Sidvokodvo 510 C Swaziland
Siegen 236 W Germany
Sielo 336 N Liberia
Siĕmréab 141 *prev.* Siem Reap. NW Cambodia
Siena 295 *Fr.* Sienne. C Italy
Sienne *see* Siena
Sierra de Guadarrama 501 mountains of C Spain
Sierra Leone 480-481 officially Republic of Sierra Leone. Country of W Africa divided into 4 admin. units (provinces)
Sierra Madre 435 mountain range of Luzon, N Philippines
Sierra Madre 250, 370 mountain range of Guatemala and Mexico
Sierra Madre del Sur 370 mountain range of S Mexico
Sierra Madre Occidental 370 *var.* Western Sierra Madre. Mountain range of NW Mexico
Sierra Madre Oriental 370 *var.* Eastern Sierra Madre. Mountain range of N Mexico
Sierra Maestra 182 mountain range of SE Cuba
Sierra Morena 500-501 mountain range of SW Spain
Sierra Nevada 568 mountain range of W USA
Sierra Nevada de Mérida *see* Mérida, Cordillera de
Sierre 516 *Ger.* Siders. SW Switzerland
Sigatoka 218 *prev.* Singatoka. Viti Levu, W Fiji
Siġġiewi 363 S Malta
Sighişoara 448 C Romania
Siglufjördhur 268 N Iceland
Signy 66 UK research station of South Orkney Islands, Antarctica
Sigsig 200 S Ecuador
Siguatepeque 260 W Honduras
Siguiri 253 NE Guinea
Sigulda 330 *Ger.* Segewold. NE Latvia
Sihanoukville *see* Kâmpóng Saôm
Siirt 547 SE Turkey
Sikasso 360 S Mali
Sikwane 118 S Botswana
Silay 435 Negros, C Philippines
Silesia 439 region of SW Poland
Silgadhi 395 *var.* Silgarhi. W Nepal
Silhouette 478 island of the Inner Islands, SE Seychelles
Siliana 543 *var.* Silyānah. NW Tunisia
Silicon Valley 572 business region of SW USA
Siliguri *see* Shiliguri
Silil 490 *var.* Silel. Seasonal river of NW Somalia
Silinhot *see* Xilinhot
Silisili, Mount *see* Mauga Silisili
Silistra 128 *var.* Silistria. NE Bulgaria
Silkeborg 190 Jylland, W Denmark
Sillamäe 212 *Ger.* Sillamäggi. NE Estonia
Sillein *see* Žilina
Šilutė 344 *var.* Šilute. W Lithuania
Silva Porto *see* Kuito
Silver City 620 NE Christmas Island
Silverek 547 SE Turkey
Sima 174 W Anjouan, Comoros
Simanggang *see* Bandar Sri Aman
Simbirsk *see* Ul'yanovsk
Simeto 295 river of Sicilia, S Italy
Simeulue, Pulau 276 island to the NW of Sumatra, W Indonesia
Simferopol 556 S Ukraine
Simikot 395 W Nepal
Siminiout 621 S French Guiana
Šimonovany *see* Partizánske
Simony *see* Partizánske
Simplon Pass 516 mountain pass of S Switzerland
Simplon Tunnel 516 tunnel of Italy and Switzerland
Simpson Desert 77 desert region of C Australia
Simunye 510 NE Swaziland
Sinai 202 *Ar.* Shibh Jazīrat Sīnā'. Desert region of NE Egypt
Sinazongwe 611 S Zambia
Sincelejo 171 NW Colombia
Sinchwang *see* Hsin-chuang
Sin Cowe Island 628 island of SW Spratly Islands
Sindh 421 administrative region of SE Pakistan
Sindhulimadi 395 C Nepal
Sindi 212 SW Estonia
Sine 476 river of W Senegal
Sinendé 108 N Benin
Sinfra 300 C Ivory Coast
Singa 506 *var.* Sinjah, Sinja. E Sudan
Singapore 483 river of S Singapore
Singapore 482-483 officially Republic of Singapore. Country of SE Asia divided into 5 admin. units (districts)
Singapore Strait 354, 483 *var.* Strait of Singapore. Strait connecting Strait of Malacca and South China Sea
Singatoka *see* Sigatoka
Sîngerei 376 *var.* Sângerei, *prev.* Lazovsk. N Moldova
Singida 530 C Tanzania
Singora *see* Songkhla
Sining *see* Xining
Sinj 181 SE Croatia
Sinjavina 602 *var.* Sinjajevina. Mountain range of N Montenegro, Yugoslavia
Sinkiang Uighur Autonomous Region *see* Xinjiang Uygur Zizhiqu
Sinnamary 621 N French Guiana
Sinnûris 202 *var.* Sinnūris. N Egypt
Sino *see* Greenville
Sinoe *see* Greenville
Sinoia *see* Chinhoyi
Sinoie, Lacul 448 *prev.* Lacul Sinoe. Lagoon of E Romania
Sinop 547 N Turkey
Sinp'o 413 E North Korea
Sintien *see* Hsin-tien
Sint-Niklaas 99 *Fr.* St.-Nicolas. N Belgium
Sint-Truiden 99 *Fr.* St.-Trond. E Belgium
Sinŭiju 413 W North Korea
Sinyang *see* Xinyang
Sió 264 river of W Hungary
Sion 516 *Ger.* Sitten. SW Switzerland
Siorapaluk 622 NW Greenland
Sioux City 569 Iowa, C USA
Sioux Falls 569 South Dakota, NC USA
Sipalwini 508 river of S Suriname
Siparia 540 SW Trinidad, Trinidad & Tobago
Siphofaneni 510 *var.* Sipofaneni. C Swaziland
Siping 163 *var.* Ssu-p'ing, Szeping, *prev.* Ssu-p'ing-chieh. Jilin, NE China
Siple 66 US research station of South Orkney Islands, Antarctica
Siput 354 *var.* Sungei Siput. NW Peninsular Malaysia
Siquirres 178 E Costa Rica
Siracusa 295 *Eng.* Syracuse. Sicilia, S Italy
Sirājganj 93 N Bangladesh
Şīr Banī Yās 560 island of W United Arab Emirates
Sirdaryo *see* Syr Darya
Sir Edward Pellew Group 77 island group of N Australia
Siret 448 *var.* Siretul, *Ger.* Sereth. River of Romania and Ukraine
Sir Francis Drake Channel 619 channel connecting the Atlantic Ocean and Caribbean Sea, C British Virgin Islands
Sirte *see* Surt
Sirte, Gulf of *see* Surt, Khalij
Şirvan Düzü 86 *Rus.* Shirvanskaya Step'. Mountain range of C Azerbaijan
Sirwan *see* Diyālá
Sisak 181 *Hung.* Sziszek, *Ger.* Sissek. N Croatia
Sisian 74 SE Armenia
Sisŏphŏn 141 NW Cambodia

Sissek *see* Sisak
Sīstān, Daryācheh-ye *281* *var.* Hāmūn-e Şāberī, Daryācheh-ye Hāmūn. Lake of E Iran
Sisters, The *248* islands N of Grenada island, Grenada
Siteki *510* *var.* Stegi. E Swaziland
Sithoniá *245* peninsula of NE Greece
Sitobela *510* S Swaziland
Sitona *210* SW Eritrea
Sitrah *91* *var.* Sitra. Island of NE Bahrain
Sittang *135* *var.* Sittoung. River of C Burma
Sittard *397* S Netherlands
Sitten *see* Sion
Sittwe *135* *prev.* Akyab. W Burma
Siuna *404* NE Nicaragua
Sivas *547* C Turkey
Sivers'kyy Donets' *see* Donets
Six Counties, the *see* Northern Ireland
Siyäzän *86* *Rus.* Siazan'. NE Azerbaijan
Sjælland *190* *Ger.* Seeland, *Eng.* Zealand. Island of E Denmark
Skadar *see* Shkodër
Skadarsko Jezero *see* Scutari, Lake
Skagaströnd *268* *prev.* Höfdhakaupstadhur. N Iceland
Skagen *190* Jylland, N Denmark
Skagerrak *190, 414, 513* *var.* Skagerak. Area of the Baltic Sea
Skalica *485* *Hung.* Sellye. W Slovakia
Skeleton Coast *391* coastal region of NW Namibia
Skellefteå *513* NE Sweden
Skellefteälv *513* river of N Sweden
Skien *414* S Norway
Skikda *59* *prev.* Philippeville. NE Algeria
Skíros *245* island of E Greece
Skive *190* Jylland, NW Denmark
Skjálfandafljót *268* river of C Iceland
Skjern *190* Jylland, W Denmark
Skjern Å *190* river of W Denmark
Skon *141* S Cambodia
Skopje *349* *prev.* Skoplje, *Turk.* Üsküb. ❖ of FYR Macedonia, N FYR Macedonia
Skoplje *see* Skopje
Skövde *513* S Sweden
Skrunda *330* W Latvia
Skúvoy *620* island of C Faeroe Islands
Skye, Isle of *563* island of W Scotland, UK
Slagelse *190* Sjælland, SE Denmark
Slaney *288* *Ir.* An tSláine. River of SE Ireland
Slatina *see* Podravska Slatina
Slatina *448* S Romania
Slave Coast *537* coastal region of W Africa, Atlantic Ocean
Slavonska Požega *181* *prev.* Požega, *Hung.* Pozsega. NE Croatia
Slavonski Brod *181* *prev.* Brod, *Hung.* Bród. E Croatia
Slavyansk *see* Slov"yans'k
Sléibhte Chill Mhantáin *see* Wicklow Mountains
Slēmānī *see* As Sulaymānīyah
Sliema *363* N Malta
Sligo *288* *Ir.* Sligeach. N Ireland
Sliven *128* *var.* Slivno. E Bulgaria
Slobozia *448* SE Romania
Slobozia *376* *Rus.* Slobodzeya. E Moldova
Slonim *104* *Rus.* Slonin. W Belorussia
Slovakia *484-485* officially Slovenská Republika, *prev.* constituent republic of Czecholsovakia. Country of C Europe divided into 4 admin. regions (kraj)
Slovenia *486-487* officially Republic of Slovenia, *Slvn.* Slovenija. Country divided into 62 admin. units (občina)
Slovenské Rudohorie *485* *Ger.* Slowakisches Erzgebirge, *var.* Ungarisches Erzgebirge. Mountain range of C Slovakia
Slov'yans'k *556* *Rus.* Slavyansk. E Ukraine
Słupsk *439* *Ger.* Stolp. N Poland
Slutsk *104* C Belorussia
Smallwood Reservoir *147* lake of S Canada
Smarhon' *104* NW Belorussia
Smederevo *602* *Ger.* Semendria. N Serbia, Yugoslavia
Smila *556* C Ukraine
Smith's Island *619* island of E Bermuda
Smithson Bight *620* bay of the Indian Ocean on the S coast of Christmas Island
Smolensk *452* W Russia
Smolyan *128* *var.* Smoljan, *prev.* Pashmakli. SW Bulgaria
Smyrna *see* İzmir
Snaefell *623* mountain of C Isle of Man
Snake *568* river of NW USA
Sneeuw-gebergte *see* Maoke, Pegunungan
Sněžk *188* *Ger.* Schneekoppe. Mountain of N Czech Republic
Snow Mountains *see* Maoke, Pegunungan
Snug Corner *248* SW Grenada island, Grenada
Snuŏl *141* E Cambodia
Soacha *171* C Colombia
Sobaek-sanmaek *496* mountain range of S South Korea
Sobat *506* river of Ethiopia and Sudan
Sobradinho, Represa de *121* *var.* Barragem de Sobradinho. Reservoir of E Brazil
Soča *295, 486* *It.* Isonzo. River of Italy and Slovenia
Socabaya *431* SE Peru
Sochi *452* SW Russia
Société, Îles de la *622* island group of W French Polynesia
Socotra *see* Suquṭrá
Soc Trăng *593* *var.* Khanh, *Hung.* S Vietnam
Sodankylä *221* N Finland
Södertälje *513* SE Sweden
Sodiri *506* *var.* Sawdirī, Sodari. C Sudan
Sodo *215* *var.* Soddo, Soddu. SW Ethiopia
Soekaboemi *see* Sukabumi
Soela Väin *212* strait of Baltic Sea, between the islands of Hiiumaa and Saaremaa, W Estonia
Soembawa *see* Sumbawa
Soerabaja *see* Surabaya
Soerakarta *see* Surakarta
Sofala, Baía de *387* Bay of Indian Ocean, off Mozambique
Sofia *350* seasonal river of NW Madagascar
Sofia *128* *var.* Sofija, *Bul.* Sofiya. ❖ of Bulgaria, W Bulgaria
Sogamoso *171* C Colombia
Sognefjorden *414* fjord of SW Norway
Sohâg *202* *var.* Sawhaj. C Egypt
Sŏjosŏn-man *413* inlet of Korea Bay , on W coast of N Korea
Sokch'o *496* N South Korea
Söke *547* SW Turkey
Sokhumi *234* *Rus.* Sukhumi. NW Georgia
Sokodé *537* C Togo
Sokoto *408* NW Nigeria
Sokoto *408* river of NW Nigeria
Sola *414* SW Norway
Solapur *270* *var.* Sholapur. SW India
Sol, Costa del *501* coastal region of S Spain
Soldeu *62* NE Andorra
Soledad *589* E Venezuela
Soledad *171* N Colombia
Soleure *see* Solothurn
Soligorsk *see* Salihorsk
Solimões *121* local name for a stretch of the Amazon river, NW Brazil
Solin *181* *It.* Salona. S Croatia
Solingen *236* W Germany
Sollum, Gulf of *202* *Ar.* Khalīj as Sallūm. Gulf of the Mediterranean Sea, NW Egypt
Solokov *188* NW Czech Republic
Sololá *250* W Guatemala
Solomon Islands *488-489* *prev.* British Solomon Islands Protectorate. Country of the South Pacific Ocean divided into 7 admin. units (provinces)
Solomon Sea *426, 488* sea of the Pacific Ocean, to the E of Papua New Guinea
Solothurn *516* *Fr.* Soleure. NW Switzerland
Solway Firth *563* arm of the Irish Sea, W UK
Solwezi *611* NW Zambia
Solyn *see* Thessaloníki
Soma *233* C Gambia
Somalia *490-491* officially Soomaaliya, *prev.* Somaliland Protectorate, Italian Somaliland. Country of E Africa divided into 16 admin. units (regions)
Sombor *602* *Hung.* Zombor. NW Serbia, Yugoslavia
Somerset *619* Somerset Island, W Bermuda
Somerset Island *619* island of W Bermuda
Somerset Island *146* island of N Canada
Somerset Nile *see* Victoria Nile
Someş *264, 448* *Hung.* Szamos, *Ger.* Samosch. River of Hungary and Romania
Sŏmjin *496* *Jap.* Senshin-kō. River of S South Korea
Somme *225* river of N France
Somosomo *218* Taveuni, N Fiji
Somotillo *404* W Nicaragua
Somoto *404* NW Nicaragua
Soná *424* SW Panama
Sonaco *254* NE Guinea-Bissau
Sonda des Vieques *627* bay of the Caribbean Sea, E Puerto Rico
Sønderborg *190* *Ger.* Sonderburg. Als, S Denmark
Søndre Stømfjord *622* *var.* Kangerlussuaq. SW Greenland
Songea *530* S Tanzania
Songhua Jiang *see* Sungari
Sŏngjin *see* Kimch'aek
Songkhla *533* *Mal.* Singora. S Thailand
Sŏngnam *496* *var.* Seongnam. NW South Korea
Songnim *413* SW North Korea
Songo *387* NW Mozambique
Songt'an *496* NW South Korea
Sông Tiên Giang *see* Mekong
Songwe *353* river of Malawi and Tanzania
Sonmiāni Bay *421* bay of the Arabian Sea, on the S coast of Pakistan
Sonsonate *207* W El Salvador
Sonsori Islands *627* island group of Palau
Soochow *see* Suzhou
Soomaaliya *see* Somalia
Soome Laht *see* Finland, Gulf of
Sop Hao *327* NE Laos
Sopron *264* *Ger.* Ödenburg. NW Hungary
Sôp Xai *327* NE Laos
Sórd Choluim Chille *see* Swords
Soria *501* N Spain
Soriano *577* W Uruguay
Soro *see* Ghazal
Sorø *190* Sjælland, SE Denmark
Soroca *376* *Rus.* Soroki. N Moldova
Sorocaba *121* S Brazil
Sorol *375* atoll of W Micronesia
Soroti *554* C Uganda
Sørøya *414* *var.* Sørøy. Island of N Norway
Sŏsan *496* *Jap.* Zuisan. W South Korea
Sosnowiec *439* *Ger.* Sosnowitz. S Poland
Sota *108* river of NE Benin
Sotavento, Ilhas de *152* southernmost of the two main island groups comprising Cape Verde
Sotouboua *537* C Togo
Souanké *176* NW Congo
Soubré *300* S Ivory Coast
Soueida *see* As Suwaydā'
Soufrière *196* S Dominica
Soufrière *465* W St Lucia
Soufrière Hills *625* mountain range, E Montserrat
Souillac *368* S Mauritius
Souk Ahras *59* NE Algeria
Soukhné *see* As Sukhnah
Sŏul *see* Seoul
Sound, The *513* *Swe.* Öresund, *Nor.* Øresund. Strait between Denmark and Sweden, connecting the Baltic Sea and Kattegat
Soûr *332* *var.* Şūr. SW Lebanon
Sousse *543* *var.* Sūsah. N Tunisia
South Africa *492-495* officially Republic of South Africa. Country of southern Africa, divided into 9 admin. units (provinces)
Southampton *563* S England, UK
Southampton Island *147* island of N Canada
South Andaman *270* island of the Andaman Islands, SE India
South Australia *77* state of S Australia
South Bend *569* Indiana, C USA
South Caicos *629* island of C Turks and Caicos Islands
South Carolina *569* state of SE USA
South Carpathians *see* Carpaţii Meridionali
South China Sea *354, 435, 483, 525, 593* *Ind.* Laut Cina Selatan, *Chin.* Nan Hai, *Vtn.* Biên Đông. Sea of the Pacific Ocean
South Comino Channel *see* Malta, Il-Fliegu ta'
South Dakota *569* state of NC USA
South East China *166* region of SE China
South East Head *628* headland on the E coast of Ascension Island
Southeast Island *see* Tagula Island
Southend-on-Sea *563* SE England, UK
Southern Alps *401* mountains of N South Island, New Zealand
Southern Cook Islands *620* island group of S Cook Islands
Southern Uplands *563* mountain range of S Scotland, UK
South Hill Village *618* C Anguilla
South Huvadhu Atoll *358* *var.* Gaafu Dhaalu Atoll. Atoll of S Maldives
South Island *620* *var.* Pulu Atas. Island of SE Cocos Islands
South Island *401* southernmost of the two main islands that comprise New Zealand
South Island *316* NW Kenya
South Korea *496-499* officially Republic of South Korea, *Kor.* Taehan. Country of E Asia divided into 9 admin. units (provinces)
South Maalhosmadulu Atoll *358* *var.* Baa Atoll. Atoll of N Maldives
South Miladummadulu Atoll *358* atoll of N Maldives
South Nilandhe Atoll *358* *var.* Dhaalu Atoll. Atoll of C Maldives
South Orkney Islands *66* island group to the NE of Antarctic Peninsula, Antarctica
South Point *628* headland on the S coast of Ascension Island
South Point *620* headland on the S coast of Christmas Island
South Rukuru *353* river of NW Malawi

South Saskatchewan *146* river of SW Canada
South Shetland Islands *66* island group to the W of Antarctic Peninsula, Antarctica
South Sound *619* Virgin Gorda, E British Virgin Islands
South Taranaki Bight *401* area of the Tasman Sea, SW of North Island, New Zealand
South Town *620* Little Cayman, C Cayman Islands
South Uist *563* island of Outer Hebrides, NW Scotland, UK
South West Bay *628* bay of the South Atlantic Ocean on the SW coast of Ascension Island
Sowa *118 var.* Sua. NE Botswana
Soweto *493* Pretoria-Witwatersrand-Vereeniging, NE South Africa
Soyang-ho *496* reservoir of N South Korea
Sozh *104* river of NE Europe
Spain *500-503* officially Kingdom of Spain, *Sp.* España. Country of SW Europe divided into 18 admin. units (autonomous communities, comprising 50 provinces)
Spalato *see* Split
Spaldings *303* C Jamaica
Spanish Point *68* S Barbuda, Antigua & Barbuda
Spanish Town *619* Virgin Gorda, E British Virgin Islands
Spanish Town *303* SE Jamaica
Spanish Wells *88* Eleuthera I, Bahamas
Spartanburg *569* South Carolina, SE USA
Spárti *245 Eng.* Sparta. S Greece
Speedwell Island *621* island of S Falkland Islands
Speery Island *628* island of SW St Helena
Speightstown *97* N Barbados
Spence Bay *146* N Canada
Spencer Gulf *77* gulf of S Australia
Spey *563* river of NE Scotland, UK
Spice Islands *see* Maluku
Spiez *516* W Switzerland
Spijkenisse *397* SW Netherlands
Spīn Būldak *53* S Afghanistan
Spišská Nová Ves *485 Ger.* Zipser Neudorf, *Hung.* Igló. E Slovakia
Spitak *74* NW Armenia
Spitsbergen *629* island of NW Svalbard
Spittal an der Drau *82 var.* Spittal. S Austria
Split *181 It.* Spalato. S Croatia
Spokane *568* Washington, NW USA
Spot Bay *620* Cayman Brac, NE Cayman Islands
Spratly Island *628* island of Spratly Islands
Spratly Islands *628* Disputed island group of the South China Sea
Spree *237* river of E Germany
Springfield *569* Illinois, C USA
Springfield *569* Massachusetts, NE USA
Springfield *569* Missouri, C USA
Spring Garden *256* NE Guyana
Springs *493* Pretoria-Witwatersrand-Vereeniging, NE South Africa
Springs *248* SW Grenada island, Grenada
Srbija *see* Serbia, Yugoslavia
Srê Âmbĕl *141* SW Cambodia
Srebrenica *116* E Bosnia & Herzegovina
Sredna Gora *128* mountain range of Bulgaria
Srednesibirskoye Ploskogor'ye *453 Eng.* Central Siberian Plateau, *var.* Central Siberian Uplands. Large upland area of C Russia
Sreng *141* river of NW Cambodia
Srêpôk *141* river of Cambodia and Vietnam
Sri Jayawardenapura *504 prev.* Kotte. Suburb of Colombo and admin. ❖ of Sri Lanka, W Sri Lanka
Sri Lanka *504-505* officially Democratic Socialist Republic of Sri Lanka, *prev.* Ceylon. Country of South Asia divided into 25 admin. units (districts)
Srimongal *93* E Bangladesh
Srīnagar *270* N India
Ssu-ch'uan *see* Sichuan
Ssu-p'ing *see* Siping
Ssu-p'ing-chieh *see* Siping
Stacklen *see* Strenči
Stadskanaal *397* NE Netherlands
Stäfa *516* NE Switzerland
Stalin *see* Braşov
Stalin *see* Varna
Stalinabad *see* Dushanbe
Stalingrad *see* Volgograd
Stalino *see* Donets'k
Stalin Peak *see* Kommunizma, Pik
Stalin Peak *see* Musala
Stalinsk *see* Novokuznetsk
Stampriet *391* S Namibia
Stamsund *414* NE Norway
Stange *414* S Norway
Stanislav *see* Ivano-Frankivs'k
Stanke Dimitrov *see* Dupnitsa
Stanley *see* Chek Chue
Stanley Pool *176, 607 var.* Pool Malebo. Expanded section of the Congo river between Congo and Zaire
Stanleyville *see* Kisangani
Stann Creek *see* Dangriga
Stanovoy Khrebet *453* mountain range of E Russia
Stara Kanjiža *see* Kanjiža
Stara Planina *see* Balkan Mountains
Stara Zagora *128* C Bulgaria
Starbuck Island *320* island of the Line Is, E Kiribati
Staten Island *see* Estados, Isla de los
Station Hill *97* SW Barbados
Stavanger *414* SW Norway
Stavropol' *452 prev.* Voroshilovsk. SW Russia
Stavropol' *see* Tol'yatti
Steels Point *626* headland of E Norfolk Island
Stefanie, Lake *see* Ch'ew Bahir
Steffisburg *516* W Switzerland
Stegi *see* Siteki
Stein *see* Kamnik
Steinamanger *see* Szombathely
Steinkjer *414* C Norway
Steirisch *82* mountain range of C Austria
Stendal *237* C Germany
Stende *330* NW Latvia
Stepanakert *see* Xankändi
Step'anavan *74* N Armenia
Sterlitamak *452* W Russia
Stettin *see* Szczecin
Stettiner Haff *see* Oderhaff
Stewart Island *401* island to the S of South Island, New Zealand
Steyr *82* N Austria
Stif *see* Sétif
Štip *349* E FYR Macedonia
Stirling *563* C Scotland, UK
Stjørdal *414* C Norway
Stockerau *82* NE Austria
Stockholm *513* ❖ of Sweden, SE Sweden
Stockton-on-Tees *563* NE England, UK
Stoelmanseiland *508* E Suriname
Stoke-on-Trent *563* C England, UK
Stolp *see* Słupsk
Stonyhill Point *628* headland on the S coast of Tristan da Cunha
Stony Tunguska *see* Podkamennaya Tunguska
Stóra Dimun *620* island of S Faeroe Islands
Storebælt *190 Eng.* Great Belt, *var.* Store Bælt. Channel between Fyn and Sjælland Denmark
Store Heddinge *190* Sjælland, E Denmark
Støren *414* C Norway
Storfjorden *629* area of the Greenland Sea, S Svalbard
Stornoway *563* Isle of Lewis, Outer Hebrides, NW Scotland, UK
Strakonice *188* SW Czech Republic
Stralsund *237* N Germany
Stranraer *563* SW Scotland, UK
Strasbourg *225 Ger.* Strassburg. NE France
Străşeni *376 var.* Strasheny. C Moldova
Strassburg *see* Strasbourg
Stratford-upon-Avon *563* C England, UK
Strenči *330 Ger.* Stacklen. NE Latvia
Streymoy *620 var.* Strømø. Island of N Faeroe Islands
Strickland *426* river of W Papua New Guinea
Strimón *245 var.* Strimon, Strimónas. River of Bulgaria and Greece
Struer *190* Jylland, W Denmark
Struga *349* SW FYR Macedonia
Struma *128 Gk* Strimon, *var.* Strymon. River of Bulgaria and Greece
Strumeshnitsa *see* Strumica
Strumica *349* E FYR Macedonia
Strumica *349 var.* Strumitsa, *Bul.* Strumeshnitsa. River of Bulgaria and FYR Macedonia
Strumitsa *see* Strumica
Strymon *see* Struma
Stuart Peak *493* mountain of Central Marion Island, South Africa
Stubbs *466* SE St Vincent, St Vincent & the Grenadines
Studen Kladenets, Yazovir *128* reservoir of Bulgaria
Stuhlweissenburg *see* Székesfehérvár
Štúrovo *485 prev.* Parkan, *Hung.* Párkány. S Slovakia
Stuttgart *236, 241* SW Germany
Stykkishólmur *268* W Iceland
Sua *see* Sowa
Su-ao *525 Jap.* Suō. NE Taiwan
Subic Bay *434* bay of South China Sea, Luzon, N Philippines
Subotica *602 Hung.* Szabadka, *Ger.* Maria-Theresiopel. N Serbia, Yugoslavia
Suceava *448 Ger.* Suczawa. NE Romania
Suchow *see* Suzhou
Sucre *112* ❖ (judicial & legal) of Bolivia, S Bolivia
Suczawa *see* Suceava
Sud, Canal de *258* channel of the Caribbean Sea between Île de la Gonâve and Haiti
Sudan *506-507* officially Republic of Sudan, *prev.* Anglo-Egyptian Sudan. Country of NE Africa divided into 9 admin. units (states)
Sudan *132* physical region of C Africa, composed of desert region, plains and grassy steppes
Sudbury *147* S Canada
Sudd *506* swamp region of S Sudan
Suddie *256* NE Guyana
Sudeten *188, 439 var.* Sudetenland, Sudetes, Sudetic Mountains, *Cz./Pol.* Sudety. Mountain range of Czech Republic and Poland
Sudharam *see* Noākhāli
Sudhuroy *620 var.* Suderø. Island of S Faeroe Islands
Sudhuroyarfjørdhur *620* strait between Sudhuroy and Sandoy, C Faeroe Islands
Sudong, Pulau *483* island of SW Singapore
Sudostroy *see* Severodvinsk
Sue *506* river of S Sudan
Sue Wood Bay *619* bay of the North Atlantic Ocean, C Bermuda
Suez *202 Ar.* As Suways, *var.* El Suweis. NE Egypt
Suez Canal *202 Ar.* Qanāt as Suways. Canal of NE Egypt
Suez, Gulf of *202 Ar.* Khalīj al 'Aqabah. Gulf of the Red Sea, to the NE of Egypt
Sūf *310* NW Jordan
Sugar Loaf *248 var.* Levera Island. N of Grenada island, Grenada
Şuḩār *418 var.* Sohar. NW Oman
Sühbaatar *380* N Mongolia
Suigen *see* Suwŏn
Suir *288 Ir.* An tSiúir. River of S Ireland
Sukabumi *276 prev.* Soekaboemi. Java, C Indonesia
Sukagawa *304* Honshū, N Japan
Sukarnapura *see* Jayapura
Sukarno, Puntjak *see* Jaya, Puncak
Sukhne *see* As Sukhnah
Sukhumi *see* Sokhumi
Suki *506* E Sudan
Sukkertoppen *622 var.* Maniitsoq. SW Greenland
Sukkur *421* S Pakistan
Sukuta *233* W Gambia
Sulaimaniya *see* As Sulaymānīyah
Sulaimān Range *421* mountain range of C Pakistan
Sula, Kepulauan *276 prev.* Xulla Islands, Soela. Island group to the E of Celebes, E Indonesia
Sulawesi *see* Celebes
Sulawesi, Laut *see* Celebes Sea
Sulby *623* N Isle of Man
Sullana *431* NW Peru
Sullivan Island *see* Lanbi Island
Sultan Alonto, Lake *see* Lanao, Lake
Sulu Archipelago *435* island group of SW Philippines
Sulu Sea *355, 435* sea of the Pacific Ocean, to the NE of Borneo, Malaysia
Sulyukta *325 Kir.* Sülüktü. SW Kyrgyzstan
Sumatera *see* Sumatra
Sumatra *276 var.* Sumatera. Island of W Indonesia
Šumava *see* Bohemian Forest
Sumba *620* Sudhuroy, S Faeroe Islands
Sumba *276 prev.* Soemba, *Eng.* Sandalwood Island. Island of Nusa Tenggara, C Indonesia
Sumba, Selat *276* strait of the Indian Ocean between Sumba and Sumbawa, C Indonesia
Sumbawa *276 prev.* Soembawa. Island of Nusa Tenggara, C Indonesia
Sumbawanga *530* W Tanzania
Sumbe *64 Port.* Novo Redondo. W Angola
Sumbuya *480* S Sierra Leone
Šumen *see* Shumen
Sumisu-jima *304* island to the SE of Honshū, SE Japan
Šumperk *188 Ger.* Mährisch-Schönberg. E Czech Republic
Sumpul *207* river of Honduras and El Salvador
Sumqayıt *86 Rus.* Sumgait. E Azerbaijan
Sumy *556* NE Ukraine
Sunan *413* SW North Korea
Sunch'ŏn *413* SW North Korea
Sunch'ŏn *496 Jap.* Junten. S South Korea
Sunda, Selat *276* strait connecting Indian Ocean and Laut Jawa between Java and Sumatra, W Indonesia
Sunderland *563* NE England, UK
Sundsvall *513* C Sweden
Sungai Seletar Reservoir *483* reservoir of N Singapore

T

Talish Mountains *86* *Az.* Taliş Dagları, *Rus.* Talyshskiye Gory, *Per.* Kūhhā-ye Ţavālesh. Mountain range of S Azerbaijan and Iran
Talladi *504* NW Sri Lanka
Tall 'Afar *284* N Iraq
Tallahassee *569* Florida, SE USA
Tall Fadghāmī *521* *var.* Fadghāmī. NE Syria
Tallinn *212* *prev.* Revel, *Ger.* Reval, *Rus.* Tallin. ❖ of Estonia, NW Estonia
Talofofo *623* SE Guam
Tāloqān *53* NE Afghanistan
Talsi *330* *Ger.* Talsen. NW Latvia
Talyshskiye Gory *see* Talish Mountains
Tama Abu, Banjaran *see* Penambo, Banjaran
Tamabo, Banjaran *355* mountain range of Borneo, E Malaysia
Tamale *242* C Ghana
Tamana *320* island of the Gilbert Is, W Kiribati
Tamanrasset *59* SE Algeria
Tamar *563* river of SW England, UK
Tamarin *368* E Mauritius
Tamatave *see* Toamasina
Tambach *316* W Kenya
Tambacounda *476* SE Senegal
Tambov *452* W Russia
Tâmchekkeţ *366* *var.* Tamchaket. S Mauritania
Tamiš *see* Timiş
Tam Ky *593* E Vietnam
Tammerfors *see* Tampere
Tampa *569* Florida, SE USA
Tampere *221* *Swe.* Tammerfors. SW Finland
Tampico *370* C Mexico
Tamuning *623* NW Guam
Tamworth *77* E Australia
Tana *221, 414* *Fin.* Tenojoki. River of Finland and Norway
Tana *414* NE Norway
Tana *316* river of SE Kenya
Tanabe *304* Honshū, C Japan
T'ana Hāyk' *215* *var.* Lake Tana. Lake of NW Ethiopia
Tanami Desert *77* desert region of N Australia
Tân An *593* S Vietnam
Tananarive *see* Antananarivo
Tanaro *294* river of N Italy
Tanārūt, Wādī *339* dry watercourse of NW Libya
Tanch'ŏn *413* E North Korea
Tandil *71* E Argentina
Tando Ādam *421* *var.* Adam-jo-Tando. S Pakistan
Tane Range *533* *Bur.* Tanen Taunggy. Mountain range of N Thailand
Tanezrouft *59* desert region of Algeria and Mali
Tanga *530* E Tanzania
Tangail *93* C Bangladesh
Tanganyika, Lake *138, 530, 607, 611* lake of E Africa
Tangarare *488* W Guadalcanal, Solomon Is
Tanger *382* *var.* Tangiers, *Sp.* Tánger, *Fr/Ger.* Tanger. NW Morocco
Tanggula Shan *162* *var.* Tanglha Range. Mountain range of Xizang Zizhiqu, W China
Tangiers *see* Tanger
Tangkak *354* S Peninsular Malaysia
Tangshan *163* Hebei, NE China
Tanguiéta *108* NW Benin
Tanimbar, Kepulauan *276* island group of Maluku, E Indonesia
Tanjungkarang *276* *var.* Tanjungkarang-Telukbetung. Sumatra, W Indonesia
Tanna *585* island of S Vanuatu
Tansen *395* C Nepal
Tan-shui *525* *Jap.* Tansui. N Taiwan
Tan-shui Kang *525* river of N Taiwan
Ţanţā *202* N Egypt
Tan-Tan *382* SW Morocco
Tan-tung *see* Dandong
Tanzania *530-531* officially United Republic of Tanzania, *Swa.* Jamhuri ya Muungano wa Tanzania, *prev.* Tanganyika and Zanzibar, earlier German East Africa. Country of E Africa divided into 21 admin. units (districts)
Taoa *629* Île Futuna, N Wallis & Futuna
T'aon-an *see* Baicheng
Taoudenit *360* N Mali
Taourirt *382* NE Morocco
T'ao-yüan *525* *Jap.* Tōen. N Taiwan
Tapa *212* *Ger.* Taps. N Estonia
Tapachula *370* SE Mexico
Tapaga, Cape *596* *var.* Tapaga Point. Cape on the SE coast of Upolu, Western Samoa
Tapajós *121* *var.* Tapajóz. River of NW Brazil
Tapanahony *508* *var.* Tapanahoni. River of E Suriname
Tapeta *336* C Liberia
Tāpi *270* *prev.* Tāpti. River of W India
Tapiantana Group *435* island group of Sulu Archipelago, SW Philippines
Tapiwa *320* Banaba, W Kiribati
Tapoa *132* river of E Burkina
Tapoa *407* SW Niger
Taps *see* Tapa
Tapul Group *435* island group of Sulu Archipelago, SW Philippines
Ţarābulus al-Gharb *see* Tripoli
Taraclia *376* *Rus.* Tarakilya. S Moldova
Taranto *295* S Italy
Taranto, Golfo di *295* *Eng.* Gulf of Taranto. Gulf of the Mediterranean Sea, on the S coast of Italy
Tarapoto *431* N Peru
Tarawa *320* island of the Gilbert Is, W Kiribati
Tarbela Reservoir *421* reservoir of N Pakistan
Tarbes *225* SW France
Tarca *see* Torysa
Taree *77* E Australia
Tărgovište *see* Tŭrgovishte
Târgovişte *448* Tîrgovişte. S Romania
Târgu-Jiu *448* *prev.* Tîrgu Jiu. W Romania
Târgu Mureş *448* *Hung.* Marosvásárhely, *prev.* Tirgu Mures, *Ger.* Neumarkt. C Romania
Tarhūnah *339* NW Libya
Ţarīf *560* W United Arab Emirates
Tarifa, Punta de *500* cape to the SW of Spain
Tarija *112* S Bolivia
Tarīm *599* C Yemen
Tarime *530* N Tanzania
Tarim He *162* river of Xinjiang Uygur Zizhiqu, NW China
Tarīn Kowt *53* C Afghanistan
Tarkwa *242* S Ghana
Tarlac *435* Luzon, N Philippines
Tarma *431* C Peru
Tarn *225* river of S France
Tarnopol *see* Ternopil'
Tarnów *439* S Poland
Tarrafal *152* Santiago, S Cape Verde
Tarrafal *152* Santo Antão, N Cape Verde
Tarragona *501* E Spain
Tarrasa *see* Terrassa
Tarsus *547* S Turkey
Tärtär *86* *Rus.* Terter. River of SW Azerbaijan
Tartu *212* *prev.* Yu'rev, *var.* Yurev, *Ger.* Dorpat. SE Estonia
Ţarţus *521* W Syria
Tarxien *363* E Malta
Tašauz *see* Dashkhovuz
Tasek Kenyir *354* region of NE Peninsular Malaysia
Tashauz *see* Dashkhovuz
Tashigang *110* E Bhutan
Tashir *74* *prev.* Kalinino. N Armenia
Tashi Yangtsi *110* E Bhutan
Tashkent *580* *var.* Taškent, *Uzb.* Toshkent. ❖ of Uzbekistan, E Uzbekistan
Tash-Kumyr *325* *Kir.* Tash-Kömür. W Kyrgyzstan
Tasikmalaya *276* *prev.* Tasikmalaja. Java, C Indonesia
Tasiusaq *622* W Greenland
Tasman Bay *401* inlet of the Tasman Sea, on the N coast of South Island, New Zealand
Tasman Sea *77, 401* sea of the Pacific Ocean, to the of SE Australia
Tassili N'Ajjer *59* *var.* Hamada du Tinghert. Desert plateau of SE Algeria
Tassili ta-n-Ahaggar *59* *var.* Tassili du Hoggar. Desert plateau of S Algeria
Tastrup *190* Sjælland, E Denmark
Tatabánya *264* NW Hungary
Tataouine *543* *var.* Ţātawīn. SE Tunisia
Tatar Pazardzhik *see* Pazardzhik
Tatarskiy Provliv *453* *Eng.* Tatar Strait. Strait connecting Sea of Okhotsk and Sea of Japan, between Ostrov Sakhalin and the coast of SE Russia
Tatarstan, Respublika *452* autonomous republic of W Russia
Tathlīth *472* S Saudi Arabia
Tatlisu *187* *var.* Akanthou. NE Cyprus
Tatra Mountains *439, 485* *var.* High Tatra, *Slvk.* Tatry, *var.* Vysoké Tatry, *Ger.* Tatra, *var.* Hohe Tatra, *Hung.* Magas Tátra, *Pol.* Tatry. Mountains of Poland and Slovakia
Ta-t'ung *see* Datong
Tatvin *547* E Turkey
Tau *see* Amouli
Tau *618* island of Manua Islands, E American Samoa
Taubaté *121* S Brazil
Taumarunui *401* S North Island, New Zealand
Taungdwingyi *135* W Burma
Taunggyi *135* C Burma
Taunton *563* SW England, UK
Taupo *401* S North Island, New Zealand
Taupo, Lake *401* lake of C North Island, New Zealand
Tauragė *344* W Lithuania
Tauranga *401* C North Island, New Zealand
Taurus Mountains *546* *Turk.* Toros Dağları. Mountain range of S Turkey
Tauz *see* Tovuz
Ţavālesh, Kūhhā-ye *see* Talish Mountains
Tavastehus *see* Hämeenlinna
Taveta *316* S Kenya
Taveuni *218* island of N Fiji
Tavoy *135* *var.* Dawei. SE Burma
Tavua *218* Viti Levu, W Fiji
Tavuki *218* Kadavu, SW Fiji
Tawau *355* E Borneo, Malaysia
Tawi-Tawi *435* island of Tawi-Tawi Group, Philippines
Tawi-Tawi Group *435* island group of Sulu Archipelago, SW Philippines
Ţawkar *see* Tokar
Tawzar *see* Tozeur
Tay *563* river of C Scotland, UK
Tay, Firth of *563* estuary of the Tay, E Scotland, UK
Taymā' *472* NW Saudi Arabia
Taymyr, Ozero *453* Lake of N Russia
Taymyr, Poluostrov *453* Peninsula of N Russia
Tây Ninh *593* SW Vietnam
Taza *382* N Morocco
Tbilisi *234* *Geor.* T'bilisi, *prev.* Tiflis. ❖ of Georgia, SE Georgia
Tchad, Lac *see* Chad, Lake
Tchamba *537* E Togo
Tchaourou *108* E Benin
Tchetti *108* SW Benin
Tchibanga *230* S Gabon
Tchibenda, Lac *176* lake of S Congo
Teafatule *553* islet of Nukufetau, Tuvalu
Teafuaniua *553* islet of Nukufetau, Tuvalu
Teafuanonu *553* islet of Nukufetau, Tuvalu
Teafuone *553* islet of Nukufetau, Tuvalu
Te Anau *401* SW South Island, New Zealand
Te Anau, Lake *401* lake of W South Island, New Zealand
Tebaga, Jebel *543* mountain range of C Tunisia
Tébessa *59* NE Algeria
Tebicuary *428* river of S Paraguay
Tebingtinggi *276* NE Sumatra, W Indonesia
Tebingtinggi, Pulau *276* *var.* Pulau Rantau. Island to the E of Sumatra, W Indonesia
Teboe Top *508* SE Suriname
Tecuci *448* E Romania
Tedzhen *551* *Turkm.* Tejen. S Turkmenistan
Tedzhen *551* *Turkm.* Tejen, *Per.* Harīrūd. River of Turkmenistan and Iran
Tees *563* river of NE England, UK
Tegal *276* Java, C Indonesia
Tégua *585* Torres Islands, N Vanuatu
Tegucigalpa *260* ❖ of Honduras, SW Honduras
Tehrān *281* *var.* Teheran. ❖ of Iran, NW Iran
Tehuantepec, Golfo de *370* gulf of the Pacific Ocean
Tehuantepec, Istmo de *370* *var.* Isthmus of Tehuantepec. Narrowest part of Mexico, between the Bahía de Campeche and Golfo de Tehuantepec
Teiga Plateau *506* plateau of W Sudan
Teisen *see* Chech'ŏn
Teixeira Pinto *see* Canchungo
Tejo *see* Tagus
Tekapo, Lake *401* lake of C South Island, New Zealand
Tekeli *312* SE Kazakhstan
Tekeze *210, 215* *var.* Takkaze. River of Eritrea and Ethiopia
Tekirdağ *546* *It.* Rodosto. NW Turkey
Tekong, Pulau *483* island of E Singapore
Tekong Kechil, Pulau *483* island of E Singapore
Tela *260* NW Honduras
Telanaipura *see* Jambi
T'elavi *234* E Georgia
Tel Aviv-Yafo *291* C Israel
Teles Piras *see* São Manuel
Telica *404* W Nicaragua
Télimélé *253* W Guinea
Telire *178* river of E Costa Rica
Tell Abaid *see* At Tall al Abyaḑ
Tell Shedadi *see* Ash Shadādah
Tel'mansk *551* *Turkm.* Tel'man. N Turkmenistan
Telok Blangah *483* area of S Singapore
Telšiai *344* *Ger.* Telschen. NW Lithuania
Teluk Intan *354* *prev.* Teluk Anson. W Peninsular Malaysia
Tema *242* SE Ghana
Tembakul, Pulau *483* *prev.* Kusu Island. S Singapore
Temboni *see* Utamboni
Temburong, Sungai *126* river of NE Brunei
Temelín *188* SW Czech Republic
Temerluh *354* *var.* Temerloh. SE Peninsular Malaysia
Temes *see* Timiş

U

Ulan Bator *380 var.* Ulaanbaatar. ❖ of Mongolia, C Mongolia
Ulan-Ude *453 prev.* Verkhneudinsk. C Russia
Ulawa Island *488* island of E Solomon Is
Uleåborg *see* Oulu
Uleälv *see* Oulujoki
Uleträsk *see* Oulujärvi
Uli *312* NW Kazakhstan
Uliastay *380* W Mongolia
Ulithi *375* atoll of W Micronesia
Ulla *see* Ula
Ullapool *563* N Scotland, UK
Ulm *237* S Germany
Ulonguè *387 var.* Ulongwé. NW Mozambique
Ulsan *496 Jap.* Urusan. SE South Korea
Ulster *563* province of Ireland, mostly included within Northern Ireland, UK
Ulúa *260* river of NW Honduras
Uluru *77 var.* Ayers Rock. Rocky outcrop of C Australia
Ulverstone *77* Tasmania, Australia
Ul'yanovsk *452 prev.* Simbirsk. W Russia
Uman' *556* C Ukraine
Umanak *622* W Greenland
'Umān, Khalīj *see* Gulf of Oman
Umatac *623* SW Guam
Umboi *426 var.* Rooke I. Island of E Papua New Guinea
Umbro-Marchigiano, Appennino *295* mountains of C Italy
Umeå *513* NE Sweden
Umeälv *513* river of NE Sweden
Umm al Ḩayt, Wādī *see* Amilḩayt, Wādī
Umm al Qaiwain *560 Ar.* Umm al Qaywayn. NE United Arab Emirates
Umm an Na'sān *91* island of W Bahrain
Umm aş Şabbān *see* Al Muḩammadīyah
Umm as Samin *418* seasonal desert lake of W Oman
Umm Bāb *447* W Qatar
Umm Durmān *see* Omdurman
Umm Ruwaba *506 var.* Umm Ruwābah, Um Ruwāba. C Sudan
Umm Sa'īd *see* Musay'īd
Umm Şalāl 'Alī *447 var.* Umm Silal Ali. NE Qatar
Umm Şalāl Muḩammad *447 var.* Umm Silal Mohammed. E Qatar
Umtali *see* Mutare
Umtata *493* Eastern Cape, SE South Africa
Umvukwes *see* Mvurwi
Umvuma *see* Mvuma
Umzingwani *612* river of S Zimbabwe
Una *116, 181* river of Bosnia & Herzegovina and Croatia
'Unayzah *472 var.* Anaiza. C Saudi Arabia
Ungama Bay *316 var.* Formosa Bay. Bay of the Indian Ocean to the SE of Kenya
Ungarisches Erzgebirge *see* Slovenské Rudohorie
Ungarisch-Hradisch *see* Uherské Hradiště
Ungava Bay *147* bay of the Labrador Sea, E Canada
Ungava, Péninsule d' *147* peninsula of E Canada
Ungheni *376 Rus.* Ungeny. W Moldova
Ungvár *see* Uzhhorod
Union *248* NW Grenada island, Grenada
Union Island *466* island of SW St Vincent & the Grenadines
United Arab Emirates *560-561 prev.* Trucial States, *abbrev.* U.A.E. Country of SW Asia comprising 7 admin units (states)
United Kingdom *562-567* officially United Kingdom of Great Britain and Northern Ireland, *abbrev.* UK. Country of NW Europe comprising England (86 admin. units -47 counties, 6 metropolitan counties, 32 London boroughs and the City of London), Wales (8 admin. units - counties), Scotland (12 admin. units - 9 regions, 3 island authorities) and Northern Ireland (26 admin. units - districts)
United States of America *568-575* officially United States of America, *abbrev.* USA. Country of North America divided into 51 admin. units (50 states, 1 federal district)
Uno *254* Ilha de Uno, Guinea-Bissau
Uno, Ilha de *254* island of SW Guinea-Bissau
Uoleva *538* island of the Ha'apai Group, Tonga
Uozu *304* Honshū, C Japan
Upaar Lagoon *504* lagoon of E Sri Lanka
Upala *178* NW Costa Rica
Upata *589* E Venezuela
Upernavik *622* W Greenland
Upington *493* Northern Cape, W South Africa
Upolu *596* island of SE Western Samoa
Upper Bann *563* river of Northern Ireland, UK
Upper Conaree *462* E St Kitts, St Kitts & Nevis
Upper Hutt *401* S North Island, New Zealand
Upper Lough Erne *563* lake of Northern Ireland, UK
Upper Mortlocks *375* island group of C Micronesia
Upper Peirce Reservoir *483* reservoir of C Singapore
Upper Volta *see* Burkina
Uppsala *513* SE Sweden
Ural *312, 452 Kaz.* Zayyq. River of Kazakhstan and Russia
Ural Mountains *452 var.* Ural'skiy Khrebet, Ural'skiye Gory. Mountain range of W Russia
Ural'sk *312 Kaz.* Oral. NW Kazakhstan
Ura-Tyube *528* NW Tajikistan
Uréparapara *585* Banks Islands, N Vanuatu
Urfa *see* Şanlıurfa
Urgench *580 var.* Urgenč, *prev.* Novo Urgench, *Uzb.* Urganch. W Uzbekistan
Urgut *580* SE Uzbekistan
Urlings *68* SW Antigua, Antigua & Barbuda
Urmia *see* Orūmīyeh
Urmia, Lake *see* Orūmīyeh, Daryācheh-ye
Urmston Road *262* W Hong Kong
Uroševac *602 Alb.* Ferizaj. S Serbia, Yugoslavia
Uruapan *370 var.* Uruapan del Progreso. SW Mexico
Urubamba *431* river of C Peru
Uruguay *71, 121, 577 Port.* Uruguai. River of S South America
Uruguay *576-579* officially Oriental Republic of Uruguay. Country of South America divided into 19 admin. units (departments)
Urukthapel *627* island of C Palau
Ürümqi *162 var.* Urumchi, Wu-lu-mu-ch'i, *prev.* Ti-hua. Xinjiang Uygur Zizhiqu , NW China
Urusan *see* Ulsan
USA *see* United States of America
Uşak *546 prev.* Ushak. W Turkey
Usakos *391* C Namibia
Usborne, Mount *621* mountain of East Falkland, E Falkland Islands
Ushant *see* Ouessant, Île d'
Ushuaia *71* S Tierra del Fuego, Argentina
Usk *563 Wel.* Wysg. River of S Wales, UK
Üsküb *see* Skopje
Usmas Ezers *330* lake of W Latvia
Usol'ye-Sibirskoye *453* C Russia
Ussuriysk *453 prev.* Voroshilov, Nikol'sk-Ussuriyskiy. SE Russia
Ust'-Abakanskoye *see* Abakan
Uster *516* NE Switzerland
Ustica, Isola de *295* island of S Italy
Ústí nad Labem *188 Ger.* Aussig. NW Czech Republic
Ustinov *see* Izhevsk
Ust'-Kamchatsk *453* NE Russia
Ust'-Kamenogorsk *312 Kaz.* Öskemen. E Kazakhstan
Ust'-Sisol'sk *see* Syktyvkar
Ustyurt Plateau *312, 580 Uzb.* Ustyurt Platosi. Plateau of Kazakhstan and Uzbekistan
Usulután *207* SE El Salvador
Usumacinta *250, 370* river of Guatemala and Mexico
Usumbura *see* Bujumbura
Usutu *see* Lusutfu
Utah *568* state of SW USA
Utamboni *208 var.* Temboni. River of Equatorial Guinea and Gabon
'Uta Vava'u *538* island of the Vava'u Group, Tonga
Utena *344* E Lithuania
Utirik *364* island of N Marshall Islands
Utrecht *397* C Netherlands
Utsunomiya *304* Honshū, SE Japan
Uttaradit *533 var.* Utaradit. N Thailand
Utuado *627* C Puerto Rico
Utupua *488* island of the Santa Cruz Is, E Solomon Is
Uvea, Île *629* island of S Wallis & Futuna
Uvs Nuur *380* lake of NW Mongolia
Uwajima *304* Shikoku, SW Japan
Uyo *408* S Nigeria
Uyuni *112* W Bolivia
Uzbekistan *580-583* officially Republic of Uzbekistan. Country of C Asia divided into 12 admin. units (oblastey)
Uzgen *325 Kir.* Özgön. W Kyrgyzstan
Uzhhorod *556 Rus.* Uzhgorod, *Cz.* Užhorod, *Hung.* Ungvár. W Ukraine
Užice *602 var.* Titovo Užice. W Serbia, Yugoslavia

V

Vaal *493* river of C South Africa
Vaasa *221 prev.* Nikolainkaupunki, *Swe.* Vasa. W Finland
Vác *264 Ger.* Waitzen. N Hungary
Vaches, Île aux *478 var.* Bird Island. Island group of the Inner Islands, N Seychelles
Vacoas *368* W Mauritius
Vadar *245 prev.* Axios. River of Greece and FYR Macedonia
Vadile *see* Vatili
Vadodara *270 prev.* Baroda. W India
Vaduz *342* ❖ of Liechtenstein, W Liechtenstein
Vágar *620 var.* Vågø. Island of W Faeroe Islands
Vágbeszterce *see* Považská Bystrica
Vágújhely *see* Nové Mesto nad Váhom
Vágur *620 var.* Våg. Sudhuroy, S Faeroe Islands
Váh *485 Ger.* Waag, *Hung.* Vág. River of W Slovakia
Väike-Emajõgi *212* river of S Estonia
Väinameri *212 prev.* Muhu Väin. Area of Baltic Sea, off the coast of W Estonia
Vaitogi *618* Tutuila, W American Samoa
Vaitupu *553* coral atoll of C Tuvalu
Vakhah *528 var.* Vahš. SW Tajikistan
Vākhān, Kūh-e *53 Per.* Kowtal-e Khaybar. Mountain range of C Asia
Vakhsh *528 var.* Vahš. River of SW Tajikistan
Valdecañas, Embalse de *501* reservoir of W Spain
Valdez *568* Alaska, USA
Valdia *see* Weldiya
Valdivia *159* C Chile
Valence *225* SE France
Valencia *501 Cat.* València. Autonomous community of NE Spain
Valencia *589* NW Venezuela
Valencia, Golfo de *501* area of the Mediterranean Sea, E of Spain
Valera *589* W Venezuela
Valga *212 Ger.* Walk. S Estonia
Valira *62* river of Andorra and Spain
Valira del Nord *62* river of NW Andorra
Valira d'Orient *62* river of C Andorra
Valkeakoski *221* SW Finland
Valladolid *501* NW Spain
Valle de la Pascua *589* C Venezuela
Valledupar *171* N Colombia
Vallée de Mboun *476* river of C Senegal
Vallée du Ferlo *476 var.* Ferlo. River of N Senegal
Vallegrande *112* C Bolivia
Vallenar *159* N Chile
Valletta *363 prev.* Valetta. ❖ of Malta, E Malta
Valley *97* C Barbados
Valley, The *618* ❖ of Anguilla, E Anguilla
Vallgrund *221* island of W Finland
Valmiera *330 Ger.* Wolmar. NE Latvia
Valona *see* Vlorë
Valona, Bay of *see* Vlorës, Gjiri i
Valparaíso *159* C Chile
Valsayn *540* NW Trinidad, Trinidad & Tobago
Van *547* E Turkey
Vanadzor *74 prev.* Kirovakan. N Armenia
Vanard *465* NW St Lucia
Vana-Vändra *see* Vändra
Vancouver *146* SW Canada
Vancouver Island *146* island of SW Canada
Vanda *see* Vantaa
Vanderbijlpark *493* Pretoria-Witwatersrand-Vereeniging, NE South Africa
Vändra *212 prev.* Vana-Vändra, *Ger.* Fennern. C Estonia
Vaner, Lake *see* Vänern
Vänern *513 Eng.* Lake Vaner, *prev.* Lake Vener. Lake of SW Sweden
Vangaindrano *350* S Madagascar
Van Gölü *546 Eng.* Lake Van. Lake of E Turkey
Vangunu *488* island of the New Georgia Is, Solomon Is
Vanikolo *488 var.* Vanikoro. Island of the Santa Cruz Is, E Solomon Islands
Vanimo *426* NW Papua New Guinea
Van, Lake *see* Van Gölü
Vannes *224* W France
Vantaa *221 Swe.* Vanda. SW Finland
Vanua Balavu *218 prev.* Vanua Mbalavu. Island of the Lau Group, E Fiji
Vanua Lava *585* Banks Islands, N Vanuatu
Vanua Levu *218* island of N Fiji
Vanuatu, Republic of *584-585* officially Republic of Vanuatu, *prev.* New Hebrides. Country of the Pacific Ocean divided into 11 admin. units (districts)

Vanua Vatu *218* island of the Lau Group, E Fiji
Vao *626* Île des Pins, S New Caledonia
Varadero *182* NW Cuba
Vārānasi *270 prev.* Benares. NE India
Varangerfjorden *414* fjord of NE Norway
Varannó *see* Vranov nad Topľou
Varaždin *181 Hung.* Varasd, *Ger.* Warasdin. N Croatia
Vardar *349* river of Greece and FYR Macedonia
Varde *190* Jylland, W Denmark
Vardenis *74* E Armenia
Varėna *344 Pol.* Orany. S Lithuania
Varese *294* N Italy
Vârful Moldoveanu *448 prev.* Vîrful Moldoveanu. Mountain of C Romania
Varkaus *221* SE Finland
Varna *128 prev.* Stalin. E Bulgaria
Varnenski Zaliv *128 prev.* Stalinski Zaliv. Bay of the Black Sea to the E of Bulgaria
Varnensko Ezero *128* lake of E Bulgaria
Vasa *see* Vaasa
Vaslui *448* Romania
Västerås *513* S Sweden
Västervik *513* S Sweden
Vasto *295* C Italy
Vaté *see* Éfaté
Vatganai *585* Banks Islands, N Vanuatu
Vatican City *295, 586-587* officially Vatican City State. City state at the C of Rome, C Italy
Vatili *187 var.* Vadili. C Cyprus
Vatnajökull *268* glacier of SE Iceland
Vatneyri *268* NW Iceland
Vatoa *218* island to the S of the Lau Group, SE Fiji
Vättern *513 Eng.* Lake Vatter, *prev.* Lake Vetter. Lake of S Sweden
Vatukoula *218* Viti Levu, W Fiji
Vatulele *218* island to the S of Viti Levu, SW Fiji
Vatu Vara *218* island of the Lau Group, E Fiji
Vaupés *171* river of Brazil and Colombia
Vava'u Group *538* island group of N Tonga
Vavuniya *504* N Sri Lanka
Vawkavysk *104 Rus.* Volkovysk, *Pol.* Wołkowysk. W Belorussia
Växjö *513* S Sweden
Vaygach, Ostrov *452* island of NW Russia
Vayk' *74 prev.* Azizbekov. SE Armenia
Vedi *74* S Armenia
Vega Baja *627* N Puerto Rico
Veglia *see* Krk
Vejle *190* Jylland, W Denmark
Velasco Ibarra *200* W Ecuador
Velebit *181* mountain range of C Croatia
Velenje *486 Ger.* Wöllan. NE Slovenia
Vele, Pointe *629* headland of Île Futuna, N Wallis & Futuna
Veles *see* Titov Veles
Velika Čvrsnica *116* mountain range of C Bosnia & Herzegovina
Velika Gorica *181* N Croatia
Velika Morava *see* Morava
Velika Plana *602* C Serbia, Yugoslavia
Veliki Bečkerek *see* Zrenjanin
Veliko Tŭrnovo *128 prev.* Tŭrnovo. C Bulgaria
Vélingara *476* S Senegal
Velingrad *128* W Bulgaria
Velké Meziříčí *188* SE Czech Republic
Vella Lavella *488 var.* Mbilua. New Georgia Is, Solomon Islands
Vellore *270* S India
Velsen *397* W Netherlands
Venda Bantustan 'self-governing homeland' comprising 2 non-contiguous territories of NE Transvaal, South Africa; created in 1979, abolished in 1994
Venedig *see* Venezia
Vener, Lake *see* Vänern
Venezia *295 Eng.* Venice, *Ger.* Venedig, *Fr.* Venise. N Italy
Venezuela *588-591* officially Republic of Venezuela, *prev.* United States of Venezuela. Country of South America divided into 24 admin. units (20 states and 4 federal entities)
Venezuela, Cordillera de *see* Costa, Cordillera de la
Venezuela, Gulf of *589* gulf of the Caribbean Sea, on the N coast of Venezuela
Venice *see* Venezia
Venice, Gulf of *181, 295, 486 It.* Golfo di Venezia, *Slvn.* Beneški Zaliv. Gulf of the Adriatic Sea
Venise *see* Venezia
Venlo *397* SE Netherlands
Vennesla *414* SW Norway
Venoste, Alpi *see* Otztaler Alpen
Venta *330, 344 Ger.* Windau. River of Latvia and Lithuania
Ventoso *468* N San Marino
Ventspils *330 Ger.* Windau. NW Latvia
Veracruz *370 var.* Veracruz Llave. SE Mexico
Vercelli *294* N Italy
Verdal *414* C Norway
Verde *112* river of Bolivia and Brazil
Verde, Costa *500-501* coastal region of N Spain
Verdun *147* SE Canada
Vereeniging *493* Pretoria-Witwatersrand-Vereeniging, NE South Africa
Verin T'alin *see* T'alin
Verkhneudinsk *see* Ulan-Ude
Verkhoyanskiy Khrebet *453* Mountain range of E Russia
Vermont *569* state of NE USA
Vernon *146* SW Canada
Verőcze *see* Virovitica
Véroia *245 Turk.* Karaferiye. N Greece
Verona *294* N Italy
Versailles *225* N France
Versecz *see* Vršac
Vert, Cap *476* cape of W Senegal
Verte, Île *628* island of E Saint Pierre and Miquelon
Vértes *264* mountain range of NW Hungary
Vertientes *182* S Cuba
Verviers *99* E Belgium
Vesoul *225* NE France
Vesterålen *414 var.* Vesteraalen. Island group of NW Norway
Vestfjorden *414* fjord of NW Norway
Vestmanna *620 var.* Vestmanhavn. Streymoy, N Faeroe Islands
Vestmannaeyjar *268* Heimaey I, S Iceland
Vesuvio *295* volcano of S Italy
Veszprém *264 Ger.* Veszprim. W Hungary
Vetter, Lake *see* Vättern
Vevey *516 Ger.* Vivis. SW Switzerland
Viacha *112* W Bolivia
Viana *64* NW Angola
Viana do Castelo *442* NW Portugal
Vianden *346* NE Luxembourg
Viangchan *see* Vientiane
Viangphoukha *327 var.* Vieng Pou Kha. NW Laos
Viareggio *294* N Italy
Viborg *190* Jylland, NW Denmark
Vicente Noble *198* SW Dominican Republic
Vicenza *295* N Italy
Vichada *171* river of C and E Colombia
Vichy *225* C France
Victoria *77* state of SE Australia
Victoria *146* Vancouver Island, SW Canada
Victoria *159* C Chile
Victoria *248* NW Grenada island, Grenada
Victoria *355 var.* Labuan. Pulau Labuan, NW Malaysia
Victoria *363* Gozo, NW Malta
Victoria *478* ❖ of Seychelles, Mahé Island, Seychelles
Victoria *see* Limbe
Victoria, Mount *see* Tomanivi
Victoria Falls *612* W Zimbabwe
Victoria Falls *611, 612* falls of the Zambezi river, Zambia and Zimbabwe
Victoria Falls *see* Iguaçu, Salto do
Victoria Harbour *262* harbor of S Hong Kong
Victoria Island *146* island of N Canada
Victoria, Lake *316, 530, 554 var.* Victoria Nyanza. Lake of E Africa
Victoria Land *66* physical region of Greater Antarctica, Antarctica
Victoria Nile *554 var.* Somerset Nile. River of C Uganda
Victoria Peak *102* mountain of C Belize
Victoria Peak *262* S Hong Kong
Videm-Krško *see* Krško
Vidin *128* NW Bulgaria
Vidoy *620* island of N Faeroe Islands
Vidzeme *330 Eng.* Livonia. Cultural region of NE Latvia
Viedma *71* E Argentina
Vieille Case *196 var.* Itassi. N Dominica
Viekšniai *344* NW Lithuania
Vienna *82 Ger.* Wien, *Hung.* Bécs, *Slvn.* Dunaj. ❖ of Austria, NE Austria
Vienne *225* river of C France
Vientiane *327 Lao.* Viangchan. ❖ of Laos, C Laos
Vieques *627* Isla de Vieques, SE Puerto Rico
Vieques, Isla de *627* island of SE Puerto Rico
Vierwaldstätter See *516 Eng.* Lake of Lucerne, Lake of C Switzerland
Vietnam *592-595* officially Socialist Republic of Vietnam, *Vtn.* Công Hoa Xa Hôi Chu Nghia Viêt Nam. Country of SE Asia divided into 53 admin. units (50 provinces, 3 municipalities)
Viêt Tri *593* N Vietnam
Vieux Fort *465* S St Lucia
Vieux-Fort, Pointe du *622* headland of S Guadeloupe
Vigo *500* NW Spain
Vijayawāda *270 prev.* Bezwada. SE India
Vila Artuur de Paiva *see* Cubango
Vila da Ponte *see* Cubango
Vila de Brava *152* São Nicolau, N Cape Verde
Vila de João Belo *see* Xai-Xai
Vila de Macia *see* Macia
Vila de Maio *see* Maio
Vila de Manica *see* Manica
Vila de Mocímboa da Praia *see* Mocímboa da Praia
Vila de Sal Rei *see* Sal Rei
Vila de Sena *387 var.* Sena. C Mozambique
Vila do Conde *442* NW Portugal
Vila Henrique de Carvalho *see* Saurimo
Vila Marechal Carmona *see* Uíge
Vila Maria Pia *152* Santo Antão. N Cape Verde
Vila Nova de Gaia *442* NW Portugal
Vila Nova de Portimão *see* Portimão
Vila Pereira de Eça *see* N'Giva
Vila Real *442* N Portugal
Vila Robert Williams *see* Caála
Vila Salazar *see* N'Dalatando
Vila Teixeira da Silva *see* Bailundo
Vil'cheka, Zemlya *453 Eng.* Wilczek Land. Island of Zemlya Frantsa-Iosifa, N Russia
Viliya *see* Neris
Viljandi *212 Ger.* Fellin. S Estonia
Villa Altagracia *198* C Dominican Republic
Villach *82 Slvn.* Beljak. S Austria
Villa Concepción *see* Concepción
Villa del Pilar *see* Pilar
Villa Dolores *71* C Argentina
Villa Hayes *428* S Paraguay
Villahermosa *370* SE Mexico
Villalcampo, Embalse de *501* reservoir of NW Spain
Villa Martín *112* SW Bolivia
Villa Nador *see* Nador
Villa Nueva *71* W Argentina
Villanueva *260* NW Honduras
Villa Rosario *171* NE Colombia
Villarrica *428* SE Paraguay
Villa Sandino *404* S Nicaragua
Villa Sanjurjo *see* Al Hoceima
Villavicencio *171* C Colombia
Villazón *112* S Bolivia
Villmanstrand *see* Lappeenranta
Vilnius *344 Pol.* Wilno, *Ger.* Wilna, *prev. Rus.* Vilna. ❖ of Lithuania, SE Lithuania
Vilvoorde *99 Fr.* Vilvorde. C Belgium
Vilyeyka *104* NW Belorussia
Vina *144* river of Cameroon and Chad
Viña del Mar *159* C Chile
Vincent, Point *626* headland of N Norfolk Island
Vinces *200* C Ecuador
Vindeby *190* S Denmark
Vindhya Range *270 var.* Vindhya Mountains. Mountains of C India
Vinh *593* NE Vietnam
Vinh Loi *see* Bac Liêu
Vinh Long *593* S Vietnam
Vinica *349* NE FYR Macedonia
Vinkovci *181 Ger.* Winkowitz, *Hung.* Vinkovce. NE Croatia
Vinnitsa *see* Vinnytsya
Vinnytsya *556 Rus.* Vinnitsa. W Ukraine
Viranşehir *547* SE Turkey
Virgin Gorda *619* island of E British Virgin Islands
Virginia *493* Orange Free State, C South Africa
Virginia *569* state of E USA
Virgin Islands (US) *629* Unincorporated territory of the USA, Caribbean Sea. ❖ Charlotte Amalie.
Virgin Passage *627, 629* passage of the Caribbean Sea, between Puerto Rico and the Virgin Islands (US)
Virôchey *141* NE Cambodia
Virovitica *181 Ger.* Virovititz, *prev.* Werowitz, *Hung.* Verőcze. NE Croatia
Virtsu *212 Ger.* Werder. W Estonia
Vis *181 It.* Lissa. Island of S Croatia
Vis *see* Fish
Visākhapatnam *270* SE India
Visale *488* NW Guadalcanal, Solomon Is
Visayan Sea *435* sea of the Pacific Ocean
Visby *513 Ger.* Wisby. SE Sweden
Viscount Melville Sound *146 prev.* Melville Sound. Area of the Arctic Ocean between Melville Island and Victoria Island, N Canada
Viseu *442 prev.* Vizeu. N Portugal
Vistula *see* Wisła
Vistula Lagoon *439 Pol.* Zalew Wiślany, *Rus.* Vislinskiy Zaliv, *Ger.* Frisches Haff. Lagoon of N Poland.
Viterbo *295* C Italy
Vitiaz Strait *426* strait connecting the Bismarck Sea and Solomon Sea
Vitim *453* river of C Russia
Vitória *121* SE Brazil
Vitoria *501 Cast.* Gasteiz, N Spain
Vitória da Conquista *121* E Brazil

W

X

Y

Z

Zhlobin *104* E Belorussia
Zhob *421* river of C Pakistan
Zhodino *see* Zhodzina
Zhodzina *104* *Rus.* Zhodino. N Belorussia
Zhytkavichy *104* SE Belorussia
Zhytomyr *556* *Rus.* Zhitomir. NW Ukraine
Žiar nad Hronom *485* *var.* Sväty Kríž nad Hronom, *Ger.* Heiligenkreuz, *Hung.* Garamszentkereszt. W Slovakia
Zia Town *336* E Liberia
Zībāk *53* NE Afghanistan
Zibo *163* *var.* Zhangdian, Chang-tien. Shandong, E China
Zielona Góra *439* *Ger.* Grünberg in Schlesien. W Poland
Zienzu *336* C Liberia
Zigong *163* Tzekung. Sichuan, SW China
Ziguinchor *476* SW Senegal
Zilah *see* Zalău
Žilina *485* *Hung.* Zsolna, *Ger.* Sillein. NW Slovakia
Zillah *339* C Libya
Zillenmarkt *see* Zalău
Ziller *82* river of W Austria
Zillertaler Alpen *82* *It.* Alpi Aurine, Zillertal Alps. Mountain range of Austria and Italy
Zilupe *330* *Ger.* Rosenhof. E Latvia
Zimbabwe *612-615* officially Republic of Zimbabwe, *prev.* Rhodesia (1964-1979) part of Central African Federation (1953-1963). Country of Africa divided into 8 admin. units (provinces)
Zimmi *480* S Sierra Leone
Zinder *407* S Niger
Ziniaré *132* C Burkina
Zinjibār *599* SW Yemen
Zinov'yevsk *see* Kirovohrad
Zion *462* E Nevis, St Kitts & Nevis
Zipaquirá *171* C Colombia
Zipser Neudorf *see* Spišská Nová Ves
Zitundo *387* S Mozambique
Ziway Hāyk' *215* *var.* Lake Zway. Lake of C Ethiopia
Ziyamet *187* *var.* Leonarisso. NE Cyprus
Zlatarsko Jezero *602* lake of SW Serbia, Yugoslavia
Zlaté Moravce *485* *Hung.* Aranyosmarót. SW Slovakia
Zletovo *349* NE FYR Macedonia
Zlín *188* *prev.* Gottwaldov. SE Czech Republic
Zlīţan *339* *var.* Zliţān. N Libya
Znaim *see* Znojmo
Znojmo *188* *Ger.* Znaim, S Czech Republic
Zóbuè *387* NW Mozambique
Zoetermeer *397* W Netherlands
Zólyom *see* Zvolen
Zomba *353* S Malawi
Zombor *see* Sombor
Zongo *607* N Zaire
Zonguldak *546* NW Turkey
Zorzor *336* N Liberia
Zou *108* river of S Benin
Zouar *156* N Chad
Zouérat *366* *var.* Zouérate, Zouîrât. N Mauritania
Zrenjanin *602* *prev.* Petrovgrad, Veliki Bečkerek, *Ger.* Grossbetschkerek, *Hung.* Nagybecskerek. N Serbia, Yugoslavia
Zsily *see* Jiu
Zsolna *see* Žilina
Zsupanya *see* Županja
Zueila *see* Zuwaylah
Zuénoula *300* C Ivory Coast
Ẓufār *418* *Eng.* Dhofar. Administrative region of SW Oman
Zug *516* C Switzerland
Zugdidi *234* W Georgia
Zugspitze *237* mountain of Austria and Germany
Zuid *508* river of SW Suriname
Zuid-Beveland *397* island of SW Netherlands
Zuider Zee *see* IJsselmeer
Zuisan *see* Sŏsan
Zumbo *387* *var.* Zumbu. NW Mozambique
Županja *181* *Hung.* Zsupanya. NE Croatia
Zürich *516* *Eng.* Zurich. N Switzerland
Zürichsee *516* *Eng.* Lake Zurich. Lake of NE Switzerland
Żurrieq *363* S Malta
Zurūd, Wādī *see* Zeroud, Oued
Zuwārah *339* NW Libya
Zuwaylah *339* *var.* Zawīlah, *It.* Zueila. SW Libya
Zvishavane *612* *prev.* Shabani. S Zimbabwe
Zvolen *485* *Ger.* Altsohl, *Hung.* Zólyom. C Slovakia
Zvornik *116* E Bosnia & Herzegovina
Zway, Lake *see* Ziway Hāyk'
Zwedru *336* E Liberia
Zwickau *237* SE Germany
Zwijndrecht *397* SW Netherlands
Zwolle *397* NE Netherlands
Zyryanovsk *312* E Kazakhstan

ACKNOWLEDGEMENTS

DORLING KINDERSLEY would like to express their thanks to the following individuals, companies and institutions for their help in preparing this atlas:

ADDITIONAL CARTOGRAPHY
Advanced Illustration (Congleton, UK)
Andrew Bright
Cosmographics (Watford, UK)
Malcolm Porter
Swanston Publishing (Derby, UK)
Andrew Thompson

DESIGN
Boyd Annison, Icon Solutions (Chesham, UK) *for Macintosh consultancy and chart templates*
Bruno Maag, Dalton Maag (London, UK) *for font consultancy and production*

RESEARCH AND REFERENCE
Dr D Alkhateeb, Organization of Petroleum Exporting Countries (OPEC, Vienna, Austria)
Amnesty International (London, UK)
Caroline Blunden
CNN International (New York, USA)
Dataquest Europe SA (Paris, France)
CSL Davies
Department of Trade and Industry Export Market Information Centre (London, UK)
The Flag Institute (Chester, UK)
Foreign and Commonwealth Office (London, UK)
Alexander Fyges-Walker
Christel Heideloff, Institute of Shipping Economics and Logistics (Bremen, Germany)
International Bank for Reconstruction and Development (World Bank, Washington, DC, USA)
International Committee of the Red Cross (ICRC, Geneva, Switzerland)
International Civil Aviation Organization (ICAO, Montreal, Canada)
International Criminal Police Organization (INTERPOL, Lyon, France)
International Institute for Strategic Studies, for information from *The Military Balance* (London, UK)
Institute of Latin American Studies, University of London (London, UK)
Intermediate Technology Development Group (Rugby, UK)
Chris Joseph, United States Travel and Tourism Administration (USTTA, London, UK)
Latin American Bureau (London, UK)
Patrick Mahaffey, Ohio European Office (Brussels, Belgium)
Peter Mansfield
Robert Minton-Taylor
National Meteorological Library and Archive (Bracknell, UK)
Oil and Gas Journal (Houston, Texas)
Organization for Economic Cooperation and Development (OECD, Paris, France)
Penal Reform International (London, UK)
Matt Ridley
Screen Digest (London, UK)
William Smith, Chicago Sun-Times (Chicago, USA)
Tourism Concern (London, UK)
United Nations Crime Prevention and Criminal Justice Branch (UNCPC, Vienna, Austria)
United Nations Development Programme (UNDP, New York, USA)
United Nations Environment Programme (UNEP, Nairobi, Kenya)
United Nations Food and Agriculture Organization (UNFAO, Rome, Italy)
United Nations International Labour Organization (UNILO, Geneva, Switzerland)
United Nations Population Fund (UNFPA, New York, USA)
Westminster Reference Library (London, UK)
World Conservation Monitoring Centre (Cambridge, UK)
World Health Organization (WHO, Geneva, Switzerland)
World Tourism Organization (Madrid, Spain)

The many embassies, High Commissions, airports, national information and tourist offices in London and around the world.

PICTURE CREDITS

t=top, b=below, a=above, l=left, r=right, c=center

Adams Picture Library: 482bl. **Ancient Art & Architecture Collection**: 38bcr, 39cra, 39bl, 41tc, 43br; G. Tortoli 39tr. **G. Andrews**: 426ca. **Arcaid**: P. Mauss Esto 568bc. **Aspect Picture Library Ltd.**: D. Bayes 338bl; K. Naylor 606tr; F. Nichols 276tr; B. Seed 386ca. **Associated Press**: 215bcr, 588tr, 603bcl; AFP 383 bcr. **Australian High Commission**: 78br. **Belgian Embassy**: 99bcr. **Bridgeman Art Library**: (artist: J-M Nattier) Hermitage, St. Petersburg 40bcr; ('Bonaparte Crossing The Alps', artist: J.L. David) Lauros-Giraudon, Chateau de Malmaison 42bcr; National Maritime Museum 41br; (artist: G. de Castro) Private Collection 42bcl. **D. Doug Bryant Stock Photos**: 429tc; B. Augustin 404tr. **Camera Press**: 129bcr, 613cr; H. Andrews 599bcr; L. Brook 401tcl; T. Charlier 449cbr, 577bl; F. Goodman 625cbr; A. Pucciano 71cr; S. Smith 215bcl.
J. Allan Cash Ltd.: 49tl, 82ca, 92bc, 122br, 125tl, 144tr, 147tr, 164tr, 211tr, 261tc, 280tr, 292br, 311cra, 316bl, 351tc, 354ca, 406bc, 408tr, 421cb, 422tr, 423bc, 536bc. **Bruce Coleman Ltd.**: 466bl; M. Berge 364tr; B&C Calhoun 150bc; G. Cubitt 64tr, 214bc; P. Davey 186bc; B. Fogden 430ca; J. Fry 477tc; J. Jurka 512bc; Dr. M.P. Kahl 70tr; G. Langesbury 232bc; O. Langrand 338tr; L. Lee Rue 67tl; K. Maj 438ca; L.C. Marigo 251tc; S. Prato 244bc; F. Prenzel 80tc; K. Taylor 481tr. **Colorific!**: J. Howard 305bl; J. Polleross/JB Pictures 54br; M. Rogers 506tr. **Colorific!/Black Star**: M. Kreiner 48cl; S.Tucci 135bl. **Compix**: 320tr, 335tc, 393bc; J. Leach 488ca; B. McGrath 510ca; J. Thomas 552bc. **Comstock Ltd.** : 170bc, 298tl, 505tc; T.Eigeland 367tc; G.L. Scarfiotti 446bc. **Cuban Embassy**: 183bcl. **James Davis Travel Photography**: 62cla, 117bc, 120bl, 121tl, 127tl, 190ca, 220bc, 302bc, 347tl, 358tr, 369ca, 379tl, 396bc, 400bc, 461tc, 462bl, 464bl, 468tr, 520bc, 528tr, 556tr, 571tr, 598bl, 619cr, 636cbl; Prisma 198tr; S. Thingeyjar 269tc; World View/Fotothek 153tc. **ET Archive**: 38bcl; (artist: N.Dance) 43cr; ("Halt of Boer Family" artist: S. Daniel) 43bl; (artist: D. Gregory) 45tcl. **Embassy of the Islamic Republic of Iran**: 281tcl. **Embassy of the People's Democratic Republic of Laos**: 326bcr, 326br. **Embassy of Peru**: 431tl. **Mary Evans Picture Library**: 41cra, 41bcl. **Chris Fairclough Colour Library**: 45cr, 343tl, 542br. **J. Guest**: 140ca, 592bc. **Robert Harding Picture Library**: 52tr, 156ca, 197tl, 243tc, 252bl, 265tr, 284tr, 308bl, 324bc, 419tc, 434tr, 448tr, 452tr, 479tc, 597tc; P. Craven 224tr; F. Dubes 124bl; Explorer 345tc; Explorer/Roy 86tr; R. Frerck/Odyssey 370tr; Gascoine 580bl; R. Harding/C. Martin 241bl, G. Hellier 189tr, 484tr; D. Hughes 229bc; C. Martin 236bc; Photri 194ca; R. Rainford 563tl; C. Rennie 550ca; G. Roli 414tr; Rosehaven Management Ltd. 629cr; J. Ross 333bc; Sassoon 110cb, 234cl; A. Woolfitt 90bc.
Paul Harris Photography: 459bl. **High Commission for India**: 272cb, 272cbr, 272br. **High Commission for The People's Repulic of Bangladesh**: 92cla. **Hulton Deutsch Collection**: 44br, 45br, 47br. **Robert Hunt Library**: 47tc. **Hutchison Library**: 112ca, 337tc, 566bc, 612tr; R. Francis 530tr; J.G. Fuller 626br; B. Gerard 231bc; J. Henderson 256ca; A. Hill 610bc; M. Macintyre 538ca; T. Page 490ca; C. Pemberton 182tr; Penn 635tl; L. Taylor 452bl. **The Image Bank**: M. Beebe 181cl; G. Jung 546tr; T. Madison 163br; M.E. Newman 296tr; C.M. Pasdzior 564br; A. Rippy 162tr; G.A. Rossi 622bl; H. Sund 455tr; P. Trummer 202tr. **Images Colour Library**: 394bl. **Impact Photos Ltd.**: J. Arthur 492tcr; P. Cavendish 435c; B. Edwards 420tr, 422tr; A. le Garsmeur 380ca, 649cra; R. Lubbock 206tr; G-J. Norman 322tr; C. Penn 554tr. **Japan Information & Cultural Centre**: 306tr, 306cb, 306cbr. **David King Collection**: 49cra.
Magnum Photos Ltd.: H. Cartier-Bresson 47cra; H. Gruyaert 639tr; J. Hillelson Agency 649tc; C. Steele-Perkins 641cbl. **Mexican Embassy**: 371bc, 371bcr. **NASA**: 49br. **Network**: M. Goldwater 643tl; J. Jordan 645cr. **New Zealand High Commission**: 401tl. **Novosti Press Agency**: 105cbr. **Office of the Leader of the Opposition, Australia**: P. West 78cbr. **PA News**: 415c; AFP 53tr, 387bcl; AFP/M. Clement 543tr; AFP/M. Shoraf 521br. **Panos Pictures**: N. Cooper 102tr, 635cra; M. French 259tc; R. Giling 508tr; J. Hartley 132bc, 635bc; D. Hulcher 326tr; S. Sprague 112bl, 138tr; B. Tobiasson 301bc. **N. Peck**: 182bl. **Picturepoint Ltd.**: 109tc, 208tr, 470bc, 618c. **Popperfoto**: 45cra, 46br, 49bl, 203bcr; AFP/Armand 48br; EPA 113cr; Official U.S. Air Force Photo 49cr. **Reuters Television**: 105cbl, 122tcl, 272cb, 272bc, 473br, 557tr. **Rex Features Ltd.**: 92cra, 135bcl, 148cbr, 148bc, 164br, 221tr, 226cbr, 238cbr, 245tr, 265bcr, 265bcl, 296cbr, 306bc, 312bcl, 355bcl, 409bcl, 421tr, 423tr, 449cb, 454bcr, 455bcl, 492tr, 497bcl, 501tr, 513tcr, 513tr, 557tcr, 564tr, 564cra, 571bcl, 581bcr, 599bcl, 638bl; Sipa-Press 53tc, 59bl, 59bcl, 71c, 99bcl, 158tr, 164bcl, 164bcr, 183bcr, 245tcr, 277bcr, 285c, 290br, 387cbl, 397tcl, 415cr, 454br, 455bl, 533tcr, 603bcr, 621bl, 639tl, 644cbl. **Ann Ronan At Image Select**: 36bc. **Royal Danish Embassy**: 191tcr, 191tr. **Royal Geographical Society**: R. Mear 646cbl. **Royal Thai Embassy**: 533tr. **Science Photo Library**: J. Baum 642bl; Dr. D. Millar 648cbl; Novosti Press Agency 641tc. **Harry Smith Collection**: 40cbl. **Embassy of The Socialist Republic of Vietnam**: 593tl, 593tcl. **South-American Pictures**: J. Berrange 178br; P. Dixon 424tr; T. Morrison 576tr. **Spanish Embassy**: 501tcr. **Sovfoto/Eastfoto**: 649clb. **Frank Spooner Pictures**: 47cbl, 296bcl, 317tcr, 577bcl; Amin-Camera Pix 317tr; L. Anticoli 296cbl; Arnaud 129bc; W. Christopher 570bcr; A. Denize 339tcr; A. Duclos 158tcr, 281tcr; K.J. Eddy 83cbl; C. Hires 521bcr, 639bcl; P. Perrin 285cr; C. Poulet 623cr; Reglain 141tr; N. Sagansky 607cr; A. Sassaki 122tr, 122cra; Versele-Deville 226bc. **Frank Spooner Pictures/Gamma**: 83cbr, 226cb; K. Al Arab 543tc; C. Angel 171tcr, 588tcr, 590tr; F. Apesteguy 473cb; F. Arthur 443bcr; J.C. Aunos 290bcr; V. Brynner 421tcr, 423tcr; L. Chaperon 238cbl; R. Gaillarde 443bcl; B. Iverson 203bcl; Iliona-Figaro Magazine 89tc; N. Jallot 376tr; Jasmin 645tc; E. de Keerle 439tcr; K. Kuukka 221tcr; Loviny 141trc; A. Movan 277bcl; Najer 355bcr; Photo News 607cl; P. Piel 238bcr; E. Vandeville 171tr; C.H. Vioujard 383bcl; Xinhua 164bl. **Frank Spooner Pictures/Liaison**: Anderson 497bcr; T. Arthur 570br; B. Asoto 435cr; Ferry 431tcl; Halstead 113c; Markel 571bl, 613c; Peterson 409bcr; B. Stern 213tr. **Frank Spooner Pictures/Stills**: Ponopresse 148cb. **Tony Stone Images**: 155bc, 174tr, 414br, 498bl; G. Allison 575bl; D. Armand 148tr; O. Benn 69tc, 249tr; K. Biggs 640cbl; M. Brooke 134tr; J. Callahan 262ca; A. Cassidy 274br; P. Chesley 374ca; J. Cornish 289bc; S. Egan 500tr, 516tr; R. Evans 128tr; R. Everts 383tr; D. Hanson 532bl; A. Kearney 158bc, H. Kurihara 240bc; G. Pease 637tc; J. Pragen 586tr; F. Prenzel 584bc; S. Rothfeld 361tc; D. Schultz 44bl; A. Smith 330ca; R. Smith 78tr; 201tl; D. Stone 316tr; P. Tweedie 352bc; C. Waite 562bc. **Swiss Embassy**: 517c, 517cr. **Sygma**: Baldev 412tc; R. Reuter 468bl. **Taipei Representative's Office in the U.K.**: 525tcr, 525tr. **TASS**: Itar 312bcr. **Telegraph Colour Library**: 76tr; Ford Motor Co. Ltd. 46cbl. **J. Tempest**: 219tc, 561cb. **Texas Medical Center**: 572bl. **Topham**: A. Azakir 339tr. **Travel Photo International**: Fotoworld 362bl. **Trip**: 472bl; M. Barlow 239br, 241tl; T. Goodman 255tc; V. Shuba 104ca; V. Sidoropolev 312tr; G. Spenceley 348tr. **Viva**: M. Franck 74tr. **S. Wheat**: 647cra. **P. Woods**: 271tl, 273br. **World Pictures**: 59cla, 294br, 404ca, 524tr, 633tl. **Zefa**: 56bc, 96bl, 176ca, 492bl, 540bc, 590bl, 647cbl; Damm 637cr; Everts 602ca; F. Lanting 118tr; H. Lutticke 491tc; Smith 624br; Streichan 238bl, 241c; Sunak 588bl.

Key to symbols, icons & abbreviations

All symbols and icons used in the Atlas are illustrated and defined here. A fuller explanation can be found on pages 9, 10 and 11. Other detailed references include: the list of International Organizations (pages 652–655), the Glossary of Geographical Terms (pages 656–657) and the Glossary of Abbreviations used in the Atlas (page 658).

Abbreviations most regularly used throughout the Atlas are listed below.

bbl	billion barrels
b/cd	barrels per calendar day
b/d	barrels per day
bn	billion (one thousand million)
°C	degrees Celsius (Centigrade)
cm	centimeters

SWITCHES

yellow infill = conditions apply;
gray infill = conditions do not apply

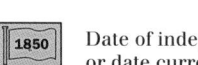

Date of independence or date current borders established

Multiparty democracy

Convertible currency

Net aid receiver

Net aid donor

No significant aid donations or receipts

Net energy importer

Net energy exporter

Compulsory military service

Death penalty currently in use

Full social security provisions

Unemployment benefit only

Free health service only

COMMUNICATIONS

Main international airport

Merchant fleet, total tonnage

Extent of national road network (miles/kilometers)

Extent of expressways or major national highways (miles/kilometers)

Extent of commercial railroad network (miles/kilometers)

Extent of inland waterways navigable by commercial craft (miles/kilometers)

TOURISM

Total number of tourists per year

Trend indicators: increase/no variation/ decrease in tourism over previous year

PEOPLE

Main languages spoken (including official language)

Population density (per sq. mi.)

POLITICS

Date of next election

Head of state

WORLD AFFAIRS

Membership of international organizations

Non-membership of additional international organizations

UN and World Bank membership is assumed

AID

Total aid donations or receipts in US$

Trend indicators: increase/no variation/ decrease in aid over previous year

DEFENSE

Annual defense budget in US$

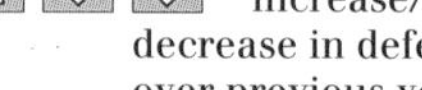
Trend indicators: increase/no variation/ decrease in defense spending over previous year

Army: equipment and personnel

Navy: equipment and personnel

Air force: equipment and personnel

Nuclear capability: armaments

ECONOMICS

Average exchange rate against the US$ over the last year

Gross National Product (GNP) in US$